DICTIONARY
OF AMERICAN BIOGRAPHY

The *Dictionary of American Biography* was published originally in twenty volumes. Supplementary volumes were added in 1944 and 1958. This edition of the work combines all twenty-two volumes.

The present Volume I (Abbe–Brazer) contains Volumes I and II of the original edition, but these are now denominated "Part 1" and "Part 2" of the Volume. Volumes II through XI are arranged similarly, the Second Part in each instance representing a volume of the original series. For ease in reference, although the articles follow one another in strict alphabetical order, each Second Part is preceded by a half-title page which relates that Part to its place in the original numbering of the volumes.

The Errata list at the head of Volume I contains corrections of fact and additional data which have come to the attention of the Editors from the first publication of the work up to the present. Minor typographical corrections have been made in many instances directly on the plates.

DICTIONARY

OF

American Biography

VOLUME VIII
PLATT-SEWARD

―――

Edited by

DUMAS MALONE

Charles Scribner's Sons *New York*

Prompted solely by a desire for public service the New York Times Company and its President, Mr. Adolph S. Ochs, have made possible the preparation of the manuscript of the Dictionary of American Biography through a subvention of more than $500,000 and with the understanding that the entire responsibility for the contents of the volumes rests with the American Council of Learned Societies.

VOLUME VIII, PART 1
PLATT - ROBERDEAU

(VOLUME XV OF THE ORIGINAL EDITION)

CROSS REFERENCES FROM THIS VOL-
UME ARE MADE TO THE VOLUME
NUMBERS OF THE ORIGINAL EDITION.

CONTRIBUTORS
VOLUME VIII, PART 1

Contributors

Stella M. Drumm	S. M. D.	Fred E. Haynes	F. E. H.
Edward A. Duddy	E. A. D.	Henry Hazlitt	H. H.
Raymond S. Dugan	R. S. D.	Earl L. W. Heck	E. L. W. H.
Andrew G. Du Mez	A. G. D—M.	Samuel J. Heidner	S. J. H.
J. Harold Easterby	J. H. E.	Frank Wilson Cheney Hersey	F. W. C. H.
Edward Dwight Eaton	E. D. E.	John Donald Hicks	J. D. H.
Walter Prichard Eaton	W. P. E.	Roger Wolcott Higgins	R. W. H.
Edwin Francis Edgett	E. F. E.	John Haynes Holmes	J. H. H.
Howard A. Edson	H. A. E.	Oliver W. Holmes	O. W. H.
Everett E. Edwards	E. E. E.	Harlan H. Horner	H. H. H.
Frederick C. Eiselen	F. C. E.	Walter Hough	W. H—h.
Edward C. Elliott	E. C. E.	Albert V. House, Jr.	A. V. H., Jr.
Elizabeth Breckenridge Ellis	E. B. E.	Leland Ossian Howard	L. O. H.
Barnett A. Elzas	B. A. E.	M. A. DeWolfe Howe	M. A. DeW. H.
William M. Emery	W. M. E.	Walter Howe	W. H—e.
Daniel Evans	D. E.	Will D. Howe	W. D. H.
Paul D. Evans	P. D. E.	William Jackson Humphreys	W. J. H.
John O. Evjen	J. O. E.	Asher Isaacs	A. I.
Henry Pratt Fairchild	H. P. F.	James Alton James	J. A. J.
Charles Fairman	C. F.	Edward Alden Jewell	E. A. J.
Harold U. Faulkner	H. U. F.	Hope Frances Kane	H. F. K.
Albert B. Faust	A. B. F.	Paul Kaufman	P. K.
Charles J. Finger	C. J. F.	Robert Porter Keep	R. P. K.
John E. Flitcroft	J. E. F.	Katharine Amend Kellock	K. A. K.
King Logan Forsyth	K. L. F.	Louise Phelps Kellogg	L. P. K.
Wilbur G. Foye	W. G. F.	Robert W. Kenny	R. W. K.
John H. Frederick	J. H. F.	Grayson L. Kirk	G. L. K.
John C. French	J. C. F.	Grant C. Knight	G. C. K.
Harry Friedenwald	H. F—d.	Ernst C. Krohn	E. C. K.
Herbert Friedmann	H. F—n.	John A. Krout	J. A. K.
Joseph V. Fuller	J. V. F.	Ernest A. Kubler	E. A. K.
John F. Fulton	J. F. F.	Beverly Waugh Kunkel	B. W. K.
Eilene Marie Galloway	E. M. G.	Ralph S. Kuykendall	R. S. K.
Winfred Ernest Garrison	W. E. G.	Leonard W. Labaree	L. W. L.
George Harvey Genzmer	G. H. G.	William G. Land	W. G. L.
W. J. Ghent	W. J. G.	Fred Landon	F. L.
Armistead Churchill Gordon, Jr.	A. C. G., Jr.	Fred V. Larkin	F. V. L.
Kenneth M. Gould	K. M. G.	Kenneth S. Latourette	K. S. L.
Dorothy Grafly	D. G.	George Lawton	G. L.
Alice Archer Graham	A. A. G.	Ida Reid Leonard	I. R. L.
Frank Graham	F. G.	Charles Lee Lewis	C. L. L.
Stephen V. Grancsay	S. V. G.	George M. Lewis	G. M. L.
Charles Graves	C. G.	Harlow Lindley	H. L.
Virginia Gray	V. G.	Anna Lane Lingelbach	A. L. L.
Edwin L. Green	E. L. G.	Walter Lee Lingle	W. L. L.
Fletcher M. Green	F. M. G.	Charles Sumner Lobingier	C. S. L.
Anne King Gregorie	A. K. G.	Ella Lonn	E. L.
Ivor Griffith	I. G.	Harry Miller Lydenberg	H. M. L.
Gurney C. Gue	G. C. G.	Thomas Ollive Mabbott	T. O. M.
Sidney Gunn	S. G.	Eugene I. McCormac	E. I. McC.
Percival Hall	P. H.	Henry Noble MacCracken	H. N. M.
Marguerite Bartlett Hamer	M. B. H.	Roger P. McCutcheon	R. P. M.
Philip M. Hamer	P. M. H.	Philip B. McDonald	P. B. M.
J. G. deR. Hamilton	J. G. deR. H.	W. J. McGlothlin	W. J. M.
Talbot Faulkner Hamlin	T. F. H.	Warren B. Mack	W. B. M.
Elizabeth Deering Hanscom	E. D. H.	Seth Shepard McKay	S. S. M.
Alvin F. Harlow	A. F. H.	Donald L. McMurry	D. L. M.
		T. F. McNeill	T. F. M.

Contributors

Dumas Malone	D. M.	Julius W. Pratt	J. W. P.
Helen Taft Manning	H. T. M.	Herbert I. Priestley	H. I. P.
Frederick H. Martens	F. H. M.	Richard J. Purcell	R. J. P.
Rudolph Matas	R. M.	James Garfield Randall	J. G. R.
Albert P. Mathews	A. P. M.	Albert G. Rau	A. G. R.
William R. Maxon	W. R. M.	P. O. Ray	P. O. R.
Robert Douthat Meade	R. D. M.	Herbert S. Reichle	H. S. R.
Leila Mechlin	L. M.	Irving B. Richman	I. B. R.
Franklin J. Meine	F. J. M—e.	J. Fred Rippy	J. F. R.
A. Howard Meneely	A. H. M.	Burr Arthur Robinson	B. A. R.
Robert L. Meriwether	R. L. M.	William A. Robinson	W. A. R.
George P. Merrill	G. P. M.	William M. Robinson, Jr.	W. M. R., Jr.
Roger B. Merriman	R. B. M—n.	William Walker Rockwell	W. W. R.
Frank J. Metcalf	F. J. M—f.	Carl B. Roden	C. B. R.
Leo J. Meyer	L. J. M.	A. S. W. Rosenbach	A. S. W. R.
Broadus Mitchell	B. M.	Victor Rosewater	V. R.
Samuel Chiles Mitchell	S. C. M.	W. Carl Rufus	W. C. R.
Carl W. Mitman	C. W. M.	William Sener Rusk	W. S. R.
Frank Monaghan	F. M.	George H. Ryden	G. H. R.
Robert E. Moody	R. E. M.	Joseph Schafer	J. S—r.
Austin L. Moore	A. L. M.	H. A. Schuette	H. A. S.
Charles Moore	C. M.	Robert Francis Seybolt	R. F. S.
John Hill Morgan	J. H. M.	William Bristol Shaw	W. B. S.
Samuel Eliot Morison	S. E. M.	William R. Shepherd	W. R. S—d.
Richard B. Morris	R. B. M—s.	Guy Emery Shipler	G. E. S.
George Fulmer Mull	G. F. M.	Clifford K. Shipton	C. K. S.
H. Edward Nettles	H. E. N.	Francis Butler Simkins	F. B. S.
Allan Nevins	A. N.	Fred M. Smith	F. M. S.
Lyman C. Newell	L. C. N.	Marion Parris Smith	M. P. S.
A. R. Newsome	A. R. N.	William E. Smith	W. E. S.
Jeannette P. Nichols	J. P. N.	William Roy Smith	W. R. S—h.
Robert Hastings Nichols	R. H. N.	Herbert Weir Smyth	H. W. S.
Roy F. Nichols	R. F. N.	James P. C. Southall	J. P. C. S.
Herman C. Nixon	H. C. N.	E. Wilder Spaulding	E. W. S.
W. A. Noyes	W. A. N.	Oliver L. Spaulding, Jr.	O. L. S., Jr.
Grace Lee Nute	G. L. N.	Thomas M. Spaulding	T. M. S.
Francis R. Packard	F. R. P.	Harris Elwood Starr	H. E. S.
Mildred B. Palmer	M. B. P.	Wendell H. Stephenson	W. H. S.
Victor H. Paltsits	V. H. P.	Witmer Stone	W. S.
John I. Parcel	J. I. P.	R. H. Sudds	R. H. S.
Stanley M. Pargellis	S. M. P.	James Sullivan	J. S—n.
Julian Park	J. P.	William W. Sweet	W. W. S.
Charles W. Parker	C. W. P.	William Virgil Sweetland	W. V. S.
Julius H. Parmelee	J. H. P—e.	Charles S. Sydnor	C. S. S.
John Jay Parry	J. J. P.	Marion Talbot	M. T.
Fred Lewis Pattee	F. L. P.	Thomas E. Tallmadge	T. E. T.
Charles O. Paullin	C. O. P.	William S. Taylor	W. S. T.
C. C. Pearson	C. C. P.	David Y. Thomas	D. Y. T.
Theodore C. Pease	T. C. P.	Ernest Trice Thompson	E. T. T.
James H. Peeling	J. H. P—g.	Edward Larocque Tinker	E. L. T.
Charles E. Persons	C. E. P.	Francis A. Tondorf	F. A. T.
Frederick T. Persons	F. T. P.	Harrison A. Trexler	H. A. T.
James M. Phalen	J. M. P.	Alonzo H. Tuttle	A. H. T.
Francis S. Philbrick	F. S. P.	Henry H. Tweedy	H. H. T.
Paul Chrisler Phillips	P. C. P.	George B. Utley	G. B. U.
Charles S. Plumb	C. S. P.	Carl Van Doren	C. V–D.
James K. Pollock	J. K. P.	Henry R. Viets	H. R. V.
David deSola Pool	D. deS. P.	Harold G. Villard	H. G. V.

Contributors

OSWALD GARRISON VILLARD . . O. G. V.
ALBERT T. VOLWILER . . . . . A. T. V.
JAMES ELLIOTT WALMSLEY . . J. E. W.
JAMES J. WALSH . . . . . . J. J. W.
PAUL ALFRED FRANCIS WALTER P. A. F. W.
HARRY F. WARD . . . . H. F. W.
ROBERT A. WARNER . . . . . R. A. W.
THEODORE H. WEISENBURG . . T. H. W.
FRANCIS P. WEISENBURGER . . F. P. W.
F. ESTELLE WELLS . . . . . . F. E. W.
THOMAS JEFFERSON WERTEN-
    BAKER . . . . T. J. W.
ALLAN WESTCOTT . . . . . . A. W.
LAURA A. WHITE . . . . . . L. A. W.
MELVIN J. WHITE . . . . . . M. J. W.
NATHAN WINSLOW . . . . . . N. W.
ROBERT W. WINSTON . . . . . R. W. W.
CARL WITTKE . . . . C. W.

FRANCIS CARTER WOOD . . . . F. C. W.
GEORGE EDWARD WOODBINE . . G. E. W.
HELEN SUMNER WOODBURY . . H. S. W.
MAUDE H. WOODFIN . . . . . M. H. W.
CARL R. WOODWARD . . . . . C. R. W.
THOMAS WOODY . . . . T. W.
HARRY A. WRIGHT . . . . . . H. A. W.
HELEN WRIGHT . . . . H. W.
WALTER L. WRIGHT, JR. . . . W. L. W., Jr.
JAMES INGERSOLL WYER . . . J. I. W.
AVRAHM YARMOLINSKY . . . . A. Y.
DONOVAN YEUELL . . . . . . D. Y.
KIMBALL YOUNG . . . . K. Y.
MAHONRI M. YOUNG . . . . . M. M. Y.
EVERETT I. YOWELL . . . . . E. I. Y.
HAROLD ZINK . . . . H. Z.
ADOLF EDWARD ZUCKER . . . . A. E. Z.

Platt — Roberdeau

PLATT, CHARLES ADAMS (Oct. 16, 1861–Sept. 12, 1933), architect, landscape architect, painter, etcher, was the son of John H. Platt, a prosperous New York lawyer, a man of wit, charm, and cultivation, and of Mary Elizabeth (Cheney), of the family of silk manufacturers of South Manchester, Conn. The Platt and Cheney children grew up together, and among them Charles's wit and ingenuity made him a leader. When about fifteen years old he became absorbed in painting landscapes in Connecticut and about the Platt summer home at Rhinebeck, N. Y. His art training began at the National Academy of Design and the Art Students' League, New York. Stephen Parrish encouraged him to take up etching. In 1882 he was in Julian's atelier in Paris, studying under Boulanger and Lefebvre. He exhibited in the Salon of 1885. In 1887, having married (Apr. 10, 1886) Anne C. Hoe, daughter of Richard March Hoe [q.v.], he returned to America. After the death of his wife in 1888 he joined his friend H. O. Walker at Cornish, N. H., where Saint-Gaudens had established his summer home and workshop, and whither Kenyon Cox, T. W. Dewing, George de Forest Brush, Herbert Adams, Maxfield Parrish, and Norman Hapgood also repaired. Into this group of friends he brought Eleanor, daughter of Alpheus Hardy, Boston merchant and philanthropist, sister of Arthur Sherburne Hardy [q.v.] and widow of Dennis Bunker, painter. They were married July 18, 1893. Adeline Adams has commemorated the death of their first child in *Sylvia,* poems privately printed in 1912. Of their four sons, two carry on their father's work. He received medals for both painting and etching at the World's Columbian Exposition, Chicago, in 1893, and in 1894 the Webb prize for landscape from the Society of American Artists.

With his younger brother, William Barnes Platt, Charles went to Italy in 1892 to study Renaissance gardens. Shortly after their return William died. Charles published the results of their careful studies and measurements, first in *Harper's Magazine* (July–August 1893) and afterwards in his book, *Italian Gardens* (1894). From the Renaissance builders he had learned the lesson that "villa" connotes a house and gardens, devised as a unity for the enjoyment and comfort of the owner. At Cornish he built for himself a "villa" so simple and charming in its architecture and so satisfying in its gardens and landscape setting that friends there and elsewhere besought him to build also for them. Thus he glided into the vocation of architecture, while still finding an avocation in painting and etching.

In association with Charles L. Freer [q.v.] he designed the Freer Gallery in Washington, built after a fashion reminiscent of Florence. As a member of the national Commission of Fine Arts (1916–21) he had large part in shaping the details of Meridian Hill Park, an American approximation of an Italian hillside garden with elaborate water effects. He also prepared plans for a National Gallery of Art, to be built at some future date. A town house on Crescent Place with a broad terrace overlooking the city, the Parmalee suburban estate, the architectural setting for Herbert Adams' McMillan Fountain, and a carefully planned addition to the Corcoran Art Gallery complete the list of his Washington works. Between 1922 and 1930 he made the general plan and designed nine buildings for the University of Illinois; and in 1930 he planned the Deerfield, Mass., Academy. Dartmouth, Johns Hopkins, and the University of Rochester called him into consultation over their plans; the seminary at Northfield, Mass., and the college for women and the Lyman Allyn Museum at New London, Conn., have buildings he designed. The Leader-News building, Cleveland, is his most significant commercial structure.

His most characteristic work, combining architecture and landscaping, was the rebuilding of Phillips Academy, Andover, Mass. With Guy Lowell [*q.v.*], he made a comprehensive plan in 1923, and two years later designed George Washington Hall. After Lowell's death in 1927, Platt became the supervising architect of the school buildings. Unhampered as to expense, he remodeled, moved, or removed old buildings, and built halls, commons, library, art gallery (selecting the paintings), and chapel as one organized composition, all in Colonial Georgian style. These buildings he centered on a broad carpet of grass reaching to the edge of the Academy grounds where they dip into a valley which the eye spans, to be arrested by the New Hampshire hills twenty miles away. For the American World War cemetery at Suresnes, he built a chapel architecturally as much at home in France as it would be in America. By nature and training a traditionalist, Platt transcended tradition by his individuality and charm.

He was a member of the American Academy of Arts and Letters, a fellow of the American Institute of Architects, a member of the Society of American Etchers and of the British Society of Etchers. In 1928 he succeeded Elihu Root as president of the Century Association and W. R. Mead as president of the American Academy in Rome.

[*Monograph of the Work of Charles A. Platt* (1913), with a biographical and critical introduction by Royal Cortissoz; article by Cortissoz in *N. Y. Herald Tribune*, Apr. 15, 1933; editorial and obituary, *Ibid.*, Sept. 13, 14, 1933; *On Andover Hill* (1933), describing and picturing Platt's work at Phillips Academy; R. A. Rice, *A Descriptive Catalogue of the Etched Work of Charles A. Platt* (1889); *The Reminiscences of Augustus Saint-Gaudens* (2 vols., 1913), ed. by Homer Saint-Gaudens; *American Gardens* (1902), ed. by Guy Lowell; G. L. Platt, *The Platt Lineage* (1891); C. H. Pope, *The Cheney Geneal.* (1897); list of Platt's later works and letters of Mrs. H. B. Learned regarding his youth in MSS. Div., Lib. of Cong.]   C. M.

PLATT, ORVILLE HITCHCOCK (July 19, 1827–Apr. 21, 1905), senator from Connecticut, was born in Washington, Conn., the son of Daniel Gould and Almyra (Hitchcock) Platt. The first of his line in America was Richard Platt, an Englishman who settled in New Haven in 1638. Through both parents he was descended from New England farmers, many of whom had impressed themselves upon the communities in which they lived. His parents embraced the anti-slavery cause at a time when such an espousal invited ridicule and social ostracism in conservative northwestern Connecticut. After attending the common school, young Platt, at the age of thirteen, came under the influence of Frederick W. Gunn [*q.v.*], an ardent abolitionist and, later, the founder of "The Gunnery" academy. The friendship that developed between teacher and pupil lasted a lifetime and was a significant influence in moulding the character of Platt. In 1847, after one year of teaching at New Preston, Conn., he followed Gunn to Towanda, Pa., as his assistant. The next year he returned to Litchfield where he took up the study of law under Gideon H. Hollister [*q.v.*]. In 1850, after admission to the bar, he returned to Towanda to marry, on May 15, Annie Bull and begin the practice of law. A few months later saw him back in Connecticut setting up an office in Meriden. Here for twenty-eight years he specialized in patent, real estate, and corporation law.

He served as chairman of the American and Republican state committees, as clerk of the state Senate in 1855 and 1856, and as secretary of state for Connecticut in 1857. In 1864 he was a member, and in 1869 he was speaker, of the state House of Representatives. While serving as state's attorney for New Haven County in 1879, as a "dark horse" he won the nomination to the United States Senate after the Republican caucus had been deadlocked for thirty-six ballots by the struggle between the supporters of Gen. Joseph R. Hawley and Marshall Jewell [*qq.v.*]. Elected by the legislature, he served in the Senate from Mar. 4, 1879, until his death. He was not long in impressing his colleagues with his untiring industry, honesty, and sound judgment. While not an orator, he had the gift of direct, pungent, and virile speech that made him a forceful debater. In 1881 he became chairman of the patents committee, a position that he held intermittently for ten years. His name became associated with practically every patent law passed during his long career. One of his speeches, in which he unsuccessfully advocated the separation of the Patent Office from the Interior Department, has been called "the most comprehensive and authoritative public utterance" on the development of the American patent system (Coolidge, *post*, p. 75). Platt also took up the cudgels for liberal copyright relations with Europe. As a result of his efforts an international copyright bill putting an end to literary piracy finally became law on Mar. 3, 1891 (26 *U. S. Statutes at Large*, 1106–10). For this particular service he was offered the French Legion of Honor, a decoration he was obliged to decline because of his position. From 1887 to 1893 he served as chairman of the committee on territories, and as such his name was linked with the admission of six Far-Western states. It was in fiscal and tariff legislation, however, that he found his main interest. Generally speaking, he can be classed as a "sound-money" man. He believed in silver as a medium of exchange but opposed free coinage at sixteen to one except under international agreement. It was his influence with the West that finally led that section to accept the compromise Silver Purchase Act of 1890. On the tariff question Platt was the typical Connecticut senator, working zealously in behalf of industry with scant sympathy for theories of tariff reform, and glorying in the term "protectionist." As a member of the finance committee, he played a leading rôle in the framing of the Dingley tariff.

In international relations Platt consistently stood with the administration in office. Even Cleveland, whom he suspected and disliked, received his whole-hearted support in the Venezuela dispute with Great Britain. Later, in the troubles with Spain over Cuba, Platt became one of the props of the McKinley administration. Like the President, he feared the growth of the war spirit and labored unceasingly for a peaceful solution. During the crisis following the sinking of the *Maine,* he, more than any one else except possibly "Mark" Hanna, was the administration's spokesman in the Senate and to the press. When war became inevitable he set himself against the enthusiasts who would recognize Cuban independence and thereby hamper the President's program. The close of the war brought new problems to the United States. Upon Platt, now recognized as an elder statesman and the sage among the four—Nelson W. Aldrich, William B. Allison, John C. Spooner [*qq.v.*], and Platt—who ruled the Senate (Stephenson, *post,* p. 134) fell much of the burden of solving them. Almost overnight he became an ardent expansionist. He voted for the annexation of Hawaii and, particularly attracted by the possibilities of the Philippines as a field for the spread of American civilization, strongly urged their retention. That his advice was influential in helping McKinley make up his mind can hardly be doubted in view of the close relations between the two men. When the decision to keep the islands was finally made, it fell upon Platt to voice the opinion of the administration against the able anti-imperialist attacks of Senators George G. Vest, George F. Hoar [*qq.v.*], and others. As chairman of the committee on Cuban relations, Platt, on Feb. 25, 1901, intro-

duced the famous amendment to the army appropriation bill which bears his name (31 *U. S. Statutes at Large,* 897–98). This provided for American intervention in Cuba in certain contingencies and forbade Cuba's entering into any treaty with a foreign power that would infringe upon her independence or her territory. These provisions were also written into the Cuban constitution and incorporated in a special treaty with the new republic. In some sense, the amendment became the foundation of American policy in the Caribbean. The authorship of the articles has usually been ascribed to Secretary of War Elihu Root, whose letter of instructions, containing the main ideas of the amendment, was sent to General Leonard Wood on Feb. 9, 1901 (*Annual Report of the Secretary of War ... 1901,* pp. 43–47). Regarding this, Platt wrote privately in January 1904: "The letter of instructions to General Wood was written by Secretary Root after the Platt amendment had been much considered by the Republican members of the Cuban Committee. The original draft was my own, ... It was changed from time to time, somewhat in language but not in spirit, in consultations both with the Republicans of the Committee, President McKinley and Secretary Root. A final consultation between myself and Senator Spooner put the document in its complete form" (Coolidge, p. 351). With the withdrawal of American troops from Cuba in 1902, Platt threw himself into the struggle for a reciprocity treaty which had been promised as a reward for the acceptance of the amendment. His support of the administration on this issue was a decisive factor in eventually securing ratification. In July 1901 he published an article, "Our Relation to the People of Cuba and Porto Rico" (*Annals of the American Academy of Political and Social Science,* July 1901, pp. 145–59), and in the following year another, "Cuba's claim upon the United States" (*North American Review,* Aug. 1902, pp. 145–51).

Following the death of McKinley, Platt, always regular, became a stanch defender of his successor. Unlike most other conservatives, he considered Roosevelt perfectly safe and not the enemy of "big business" that he was pictured. Roosevelt in turn learned to lean heavily on Platt for support, and before long there developed a mutual affection between the old statesman and the impetuous young President that was not without historic significance. After Platt's death, Roosevelt referred to him as "the grandest and noblest man" he ever knew (Coolidge, p. 512). Platt's last chairmanship was that of the judiciary committee, a distinction he enjoyed but a brief time. The many burdens that he had assumed without protest had sapped his strength and, in the midst of his labors, he was stricken with pneumonia and after a short illness died on Apr. 21, 1905, at Meriden, Conn. His son and his second wife, Jeannie P. (Smith) Hoyt Platt, to whom he had been married on Apr. 29, 1897, survived him.

Nature had endowed Platt with a splendid physique which enabled him in his youth to excel in athletics. Throughout life he was attracted by outdoor activity and nothing pleased him more than to retire to his quiet shack in the Adirondacks after a strenuous session. His interest in New England customs and history is indicated by a list of articles written by him (Coolidge, p. 593). "If I had leisure and means," he wrote, "I should have been thoroughly taken up with archaeological investigations" (*Ibid.*). Although the son of radical abolitionists, Platt was a conservative of the "stand-pat" variety. He had never been able to accumulate riches himself, yet he defended wealth vigorously against attack. His exaggerated fears regarding the radical movements of his day led him to liken J. P. Altgeld, Benjamin R. Tillman, and William Jennings Bryan [*qq.v.*] to Robespierre, Danton, and Marat, and to oppose stubbornly all legislation that threatened to hamper business in any way. Because of his character and unselfish service he was generally viewed as the first citizen of his state. But for geographical considerations he might have received the highest national honors. He was several times mentioned for the vice-presidential nomination, but his own political ambitions never went beyond the senatorship from Connecticut.

[Platt MSS., State Library, Hartford, Conn.; L. A. Coolidge, *An Old Fashioned Senator, Orville H. Platt* (1910); "The Origin and Purpose of the Platt Amendment," editorial comment in *Am. Jour. of International Law*, July 1914, pp. 585–91; E. R. de Leuchsenring, "La Enmienda Platt," *Cuba Contemporánea*, July, Aug. 1922; L. J. Meyer, "The Relations between the U. S. and Cuba 1895–1917," doctoral dissertation, Clark Univ., 1928; A. L. P. Dennis, *Adventures in American Diplomacy* (1928); N. W. Stephenson, *Nelson W. Aldrich* (1930); *Orville Hitchcock Platt Memorial Addresses, Sen. Doc. 534*, 59 Cong., 1 sess.; obituary in *Hartford Times*, Apr. 22, 1905.]   L. J. M.

PLATT, THOMAS COLLIER (July 15, 1833–Mar. 6, 1910), politician, was born in Owego, N. Y., his father being William Platt, a lawyer, and his mother Lesbia Hinchman, of a Long Island family represented in the colonial and Revolutionary wars. He himself stated (*Autobiography*, p. 1) that he was descended from Richard Platt, an English emigrant of 1638, but his connection with the latter's Connecticut descendants cannot be traced. An an-

cestor of his, Benoin Platt, was living in Westchester County, N. Y., in 1730 (G. L. Platt, *The Platt Lineage*, 1891). Reared in a Presbyterian atmosphere and designed by his father for the ministry, he attended Owego Academy and Yale College, leaving the latter because of bad health before his class (1853) was graduated. Entering business in Owego as a druggist, he shortly bought a store and on Dec. 12, 1852, married Ellen Lucy Barstow, who bore him three sons and was an efficient helpmeet and custodian of his political secrets till her death in 1901. In 1859 he was elected county clerk on the Republican ticket, but soon returned to business as president of the Tioga County National Bank and speculator in Michigan timber lands, as well as druggist. Specimens of humorous writings of this period, chiefly advertisements, of which he was still proud when in old age he prepared his autobiography, are appalling in their crudity and lack of taste.

During the sixties he served as chairman of the Tioga County committee and attended Republican state conventions, but his political career really began when in 1870 he became the close friend and lieutenant of Roscoe Conkling [*q.v.*]. He helped organize the "southern tier" counties for Conkling against Horace Greeley and Senator Reuben E. Fenton [*qq.v.*], and in the convention of 1871 aided in the dramatic overthrow of the Fenton faction. Thereafter he was consulted by Conkling "on practically every phase" of New York politics (*Autobiography*, p. 60). When in 1873 President Grant offered Conkling the chief justiceship, the latter promised Platt the leadership of the state machine if he accepted. In 1874 Platt was elected to the federal House of Representatives for the first of two consecutive terms. He made little impression there. But in state politics he became an indispensable behind-the-scenes worker for the "Stalwart" or administration organization, displaying tact, quickness of decision, a businesslike instinct for detail, and complete fidelity to his own group, combined with entire lack of principle in fighting others (Alexander, *Political History of the State of New York*, III, 363, 364). He was seldom in the public view, but in 1877 emerged in the state convention as chairman and as a vitriolic assailant of Hayes, Evarts, George W. Curtis, and "Half-Breed" reformers generally. Meanwhile he remained in business; in 1879 he became secretary and a director of the United States Express Company, and in 1880 was made president, then removing to New York City.

In 1880, Platt was one of the 306 delegates

who supported Grant at the Republican National Convention through thirty-five ballots. Returning to New York deeply distrustful of the presidential nominee, Garfield, he was prominent at the latter's meeting with various "Stalwart" leaders in the Fifth Avenue Hotel, presented an ultimatum that they would do no work unless promised recognition and rewards, and received satisfactory assurances (*Autobiography*, p. 135). As executive chairman of the state committee he did much to conciliate Conkling, to rally other "Stalwarts" behind Garfield, and to plan the New York campaign. His reward was election to the Senate in January 1881. He had paved the way by putting many legislators under obligations to him for campaign funds or offices (Gosnell, *post*, p. 25), but, in order to win, he had to promise Chauncey M. Depew that he would support President Garfield unreservedly (J. D. Champlin, ed., *Orations . . . of Chauncey M. Depew*, 1910, II, 213). He was placed in a fateful dilemma when Garfield appointed the "Half-Breed" William H. Robertson as collector of the port of New York. If he acquiesced, he would face Conkling's fury; if he resisted, Depew's scorn. When Robertson's confirmation became certain, Platt and Conkling resigned, appealing to the legislature for reëlection. Their defeat at Albany closed Conkling's career, and marked the eclipse of Platt's power for half a dozen years. In 1884, resentful at Arthur for failing to undo the "wrongs" committed by Garfield, he supported Blaine for the presidential nomination, but not till 1888 did he again attain prominence.

In that year he led the New York delegation to the Republican National Convention, received from Stephen B. Elkins what he thought a pledge that Benjamin Harrison would appoint him secretary of the treasury if elected, and swung fifty-eight New York delegates to Harrison (*John Sherman's Recollections of Forty Years*, 1895, II, 1029). When Harrison failed to redeem his alleged promise, Platt was implacably angry. "I had for many years," he confesses, "been very ambitious to conduct the government's finances" (*Autobiography*, p. 206). Harrison's offer of the mission to Spain was curtly rejected. Starvation fare in federal patronage increased his discontent. He opposed Harrison's renomination in 1892, was further offended by the nomination of Whitelaw Reid for the vice-presidency, and took such a frigid part in the ensuing campaign that Cleveland easily carried the state. Yet in the years 1889–93 he was by no means without federal offices to dispense. Assistant Postmaster-General Clarkson, in charge of fourth-class post-offices, was his stanch friend, while he succeeded in having his old lieutenant, J. Sloat Fassett, temporarily made collector of the port of New York.

Even during David B. Hill's governorship (1885–91) Platt was perfecting the organization to which he had fallen heir on Conkling's retirement. With the Republican sweep that elected Levi P. Morton [*q.v.*] governor in 1894, his power became almost irresistible. The cementing agency was patronage, local, state, and federal. His lieutenants in New York were numerous and able: B. B. Odell, tireless and aggressive; Lemuel E. Quigg, master of publicity; George W. Aldridge in Rochester, William H. Barnes in Albany, Louis F. Payn east of the Hudson; John Raines in the Senate and S. Fred Nixon in the Assembly. Year after year state conventions carried out his preordained program, and were used chiefly to stimulate party enthusiasm. Legislative programs were likewise planned by an autocratic clique under Platt's dictation, whose fiats were enforced by the caucus. His practice was to obtain large secret contributions from "big business," by promising favors, and to use these funds for the nomination and election of legislators who would obey orders (Roosevelt, *Autobiography*, pp. 301–02; Alexander, *Four Famous New Yorkers*, p. 208). Disloyalty was ruthlessly punished. Though hated by the Union League Club, Platt was cordially regarded by Wall Street and most large corporations. In 1896 he urged Levi P. Morton for the presidential nomination on the ground that he was safer on monetary issues than McKinley, but when outmaneuvered before the convention by Hanna he cordially fell in line behind McKinley. In the next few years he, Hanna, and Quay were stanch allies.

Platt's sun declined as that of Theodore Roosevelt rose. Originally opposed in 1898 to Roosevelt's nomination for governor, urged on him by Odell, he partially and reluctantly acquiesced after Quigg had received a promise at Montauk Point that Roosevelt would not "make war on Mr. Platt or anybody else if war could be avoided" (Roosevelt, *Autobiography*, pp. 294–95). Of Governor Roosevelt's independent first message Platt remarked, "Any one can issue manifestoes" (Alexander, *Four Famous New Yorkers*, p. 326). When Roosevelt insisted on his own appointments, "this produced an explosion" (Roosevelt, *Autobiography*, p. 308), but the governor had his way. Roosevelt consulted Platt often, gave full reasons for his actions, and treated him with the utmost tact; but Platt had to admit that "he frequently did just what he pleased" (Platt, *Autobiography*, p. 374). When he suddenly drove a bill to tax street-railway franchises through the legislature, Platt could only protest feebly against "Populistic" notions. By 1900 Platt was determined to shelve Roosevelt by nominating him for vice-president. He returned to New York from the Republican National Convention jubilant, and he was pleased when his lieutenant Odell was elected governor. Actually two heavy blows had been struck his control. Roosevelt was soon president, while Governor Odell showed such courage and progressiveness that a widening gulf opened between him and Platt. Within two years power rested rather with Odell than with the aging Senator, and when the state convention of 1902 rejected Platt's candidate for lieutenant-governor and took Odell's, Platt passed into the political background.

Thereafter he counted for little in New York or Washington. Though reëlected to the Senate in 1904, his power was so slight that he called a conference to determine whether he possessed any; the result being that "Odell got the goods and Platt the title" (Alexander, *Four Famous New Yorkers*, p. 418). Physically ailing, he shortly disclaimed all voice in state affairs. In the Senate he had almost never spoken, never offered an important bill, never voted except with the party regulars, and never expressed an opinion on national issues which carried any weight. Till his death he remained president of his express company, but gave it slight attention. A second marriage, to Mrs. Lillian Thompson Janeway, on Oct. 11, 1903, had proved unhappy and resulted in a separation in 1906. The failure of his faculties is evident in the autobiography which he partly prepared in his last months, and which is a curious farrago of fact, fiction, naïveté, and denunciation. His death evoked from the press a nation-wide denunciation of the machine politics which he had long personified.

Platt was tall, thin, and cadaverous-looking. His principal traits, industry, tenacity, and patience, were all expended upon politics, which were his passion. His career may be summed up in Roosevelt's statement that he "had the same inborn capacity for the kind of politics which he liked that many big Wall Street men have shown for not wholly dissimilar types of finance" (Roosevelt, *Autobiography*, p. 301). He was kindly and tactful; he was above the grosser forms of corruption, though he saw to it that immediate members of his family profited from politics; but his personal morals were reputed bad.

[*The Autobiography of Thomas Collier Platt* (1910), compiled and ed. by L. J. Lang; H. F. Gosnell, *Boss Platt and His New York Machine* (1924); D. S. Alexander, *A Pol. Hist. of the State of N. Y.*, III (1909); D. S. Alexander, *Four Famous New Yorkers* (1923); A. R. Conkling, *The Life and Letters of Roscoe Conkling* (1889); M. P. Breen, *Thirty Years of New York Politics* (1899), pp. 656 ff.; E. P. Wheeler, *Sixty Years of American Life* (1917); *Theodore Roosevelt, An Autobiography* (1915); Henry Pringle, *Theodore Roosevelt* (1931).]
A. N.

PLEASANTS, JAMES (Oct. 24, 1769–Nov. 9, 1836), governor of Virginia, was born in Goochland County, the son of James and Anne (Randolph) Pleasants. His grandfather, John Pleasants, was a Quaker who had emigrated to Virginia from Norwich, England, in 1665; his mother, who had been married twice before she married his father, was an aunt of Thomas Jefferson. The family was one of substance and the youth was sent to the College of William and Mary. After graduating there, he read law under Judge William Fleming of the court of appeals, and in 1791 commenced practice in Amelia County.

In 1796 he began his political career when elected to the House of Delegates from Goochland. In this body he supported the views of his famous cousin and voted for the resolutions of 1798. In 1803 he was made clerk of the House of Delegates, which office he held until 1811, when he was elected to the federal House of Representatives. Here he supported Madison's policy and the War of 1812. Continuing in the House until 1819, he was elected to the United States Senate in that year, and in 1822 resigned from this body to become governor of Virginia. He held the governorship for three annual terms and then retired to private life, emerging only to sit in the constitutional convention which assembled in Virginia in 1829. A career of such uninterrupted progress during the stormy period that stretched from the rise of Jeffersonian Republicanism to the advent of Jacksonian Democracy is not a little remarkable.

As governor, Pleasants showed great interest in the leading reform movements of his day, the education of the children of the poor and the improvement of the penitentiary system. He objected strenuously to the use of the whipping post in the punishment of free whites and desired fair treatment for free blacks. He was an enthusiastic advocate of the construction of internal improvements by the state, but as a strict-constructionist he opposed improvements by the federal government, and objected to a tariff for protection as adverse to the interests of the South. (Governor's messages, *Journal of the House of Delegates*, 1823, pp. 6–10, 1824, pp. 6–8, 1825, pp. 6–9.) He found himself unable to support Andrew Jackson when that personage became the leader of the forces of the new Democracy. Though his messages to the Assembly avoided the subject, he doubtless favored Crawford for the Presidency in 1824. In the campaign of 1828 he supported Adams against Jackson, and his son, John Hampden Pleasants [q.v.], became the editor of the Richmond *Whig,* the principal organ of the anti-Jackson party in the state (H. H. Simms, *The Rise of the Whigs in Virginia,* 1929, p. 22; C. H. Ambler, *Thomas Ritchie,* 1913, p. 116).

He was tall and slightly corpulent, with red hair. His features were rugged, and his manners distinguished by pleasantness rather than formality. John Randolph of Roanoke said that he never made an enemy nor lost a friend. He was, in other words, a true gentleman of the Virginian democracy of his day. He married Susanna Lawson Rose, who became the mother of eight children, and lived all his life in Goochland County, dying there in his sixty-eighth year (Richmond *Whig,* Nov. 18, 1836). It is said of him that he never solicited an office except the first which he held, and relished no public position except the clerkship of the House of Delegates.

[The best available sketch of Pleasants is in A. C. Gordon, *William Fitzhugh Gordon* (1909), p. 120; see also L. G. Tyler, *Encyc. of Va. Biog.,* vol. II (1915); M. V. Smith, *Va. . . . A Hist. of the Executives* (1893); R. A. Brock, *Va. and Virginians* (1888), vol. I; *Biog. Dir. Am. Cong.* (1928).]   T. P. A.

PLEASANTS, JOHN HAMPDEN (Jan. 4, 1797–Feb. 27, 1846), journalist and politician, was the son of James [q.v.] and Susanna (Rose) Pleasants. He was born at his father's homestead "Contention" in Goochland County, Va., and was educated at the College of William and Mary, where he was graduated in 1817. After completing his study of law, he entered the practice of the profession at Lynchburg, but soon abandoned it to become a journalist. In 1823 he was acting as editor of the Lynchburg *Virginian* (C. H. Ambler, *Thomas Ritchie,* 1913, p. 90). The following year he removed to Richmond and on Jan. 27, 1824, appeared the first number of the Richmond *Whig,* founded by Pleasants and edited by him for more than twenty years. Under his management it became the leading exponent of Whig doctrines in Virginia and the able antagonist of the Democratic *Enquirer,* edited by Thomas Ritchie [q.v.]. In 1824 and 1828 the *Whig* supported John Quincy Adams for the presidency, and in 1832 it was enlisted under the banner of Henry Clay (H. H. Simms, *The Rise of the Whigs in Virginia,* 1929, pp. 16, 58). Up to this time National Republicanism and the "American System" constituted its creed. When the furor over nullification arose in the land, the *Whig* condemned the doctrines of South

Carolina, but also denounced the presidential proclamation. State-rights principles now became its shibboleth as Ritchie and the *Enquirer* swung to the Nationalist side (L. G. Tyler, *The Letters and Times of the Tylers,* 1884, I, 451–52, 525–26, 536–37). In 1836 Hugh Lawson White [q.v.] was the ideal candidate for Southern state-rights Whigs, and the *Whig* supported him as a matter of course. Thereafter it became increasingly hard for leaders like Pleasants to maintain their particular point of view within the Whig fold, and he, in fact, drifted with his Southern partisans in the direction of Nationalism. Thus he completed the circle of political belief and returned to the point whence he had started (A. C. Cole, *The Whig Party in the South,* 1913, pp. 21, 87–88). In this he merely followed the dictates of partisan warfare.

In 1841 Pleasants collaborated with Edward W. Johnston and John Woodson in the establishment of the Washington *Independent,* but, with some interruptions, he continued his editorial activities in connection with the *Whig,* which on July 19, 1841, was transformed into a daily paper. During 1846, while the *Enquirer* was under the management of Thomas Ritchie's sons, an article appeared in that journal accusing Pleasants of abolitionist leanings. This was a serious matter, especially in view of the fact that a duel had only recently been averted between the *Whig* editor and one of the Ritchie brothers. Pleasants now sent word to Thomas Ritchie, Jr., that he would meet him at a designated time and place, equipped with side arms only. It appears that the challenger disapproved of dueling, but had decided that the issue could no longer be averted with honor. Appearing at the appointed place but lightly armed, he advanced to within striking distance of his antagonist, apparently making only a perfunctory attempt to defend himself. He fell with several wounds, but lived for two days. The power of the *Whig* departed with him. He had been twice married: first, to Ann Irving; and second, to Mary Massie. His only son, James, became a prominent lawyer of Richmond, and his only daughter, Ann Eliza, married Douglas H. Gordon.

Unlike so many leaders of his day, Pleasants stuck to his occupation with single-minded devotion. While he was active in matters of civic interest, and took a vigorous part in the attempt to develop internal improvements within his state, the allurements of public office never attracted him. As an editor, he was not only master of the vigorous and vitriolic style of his day, but was an effective political strategist, versed in the art of sowing discord among the enemy while keeping his own forces intact (C. H. Ambler, *op. cit.*, pp. 95–97, 103–04, 192–93, 216–17). Except for Thomas Ritchie, ante-bellum Virginia produced no other newspaper editor of his caliber.

[The only good account of Pleasants' life is in R. W. Hughes, *Editors of the Past* (1897), pp. 14–17; the facts concerning his death are contained in *A Full Report . . . in the Case of the Commonwealth vs. Thomas Ritchie, Jr.* (1846); see also R. A. Brock, *Va. and Virginians* (1888), vol. I; W. A. Christian, *Richmond, Her Past and Present* (1912); J. A. Parker, *What Led to the War . . . With an Appendix Containing Sketches* (1886); *Daily Richmond Enquirer*, Mar. 2, 1846.]

                        T. P. A.

PLEASONTON, ALFRED (June 7, 1824–Feb. 17, 1897), soldier, son of Stephen and Mary (Hopkins) Pleasonton, was born in Washington, D. C. He was educated in the Washington schools until he entered the United States Military Academy in 1840. He graduated in 1844, seventh in a class of twenty-five; was commissioned second lieutenant, 2nd Dragoons, Nov. 3, 1845. He served throughout the Mexican War and for gallant and meritorious conduct at Palo Alto and Resaca de la Palma was brevetted first lieutenant, May 9, 1846. Following the Mexican War, he did frontier duty and was promoted first lieutenant, Sept. 30, 1849. He was Gen. W. S. Harney's acting assistant adjutant-general during the Sioux expedition, receiving his captaincy Mar. 3, 1855. From 1856 to 1860 he served as Harney's adjutant-general in Florida against the Seminoles and in campaigns in Kansas, Oregon, and Washington Territory. He commanded the 2nd Cavalry on its march, September to October 1861, from Utah to Washington, D. C., where he was assigned to the defenses of the capital.

He was commissioned major, 2nd Cavalry, Feb. 15, 1862, served brilliantly throughout the Peninsular campaign, and was promoted brigadier-general of volunteers, July 16, 1862. In the Army of the Potomac, he commanded the cavalry division that pursued Lee's invading army into Maryland, Sept. 8–Nov. 18, 1862. He fought at South Mountain, Antietam, and Fredericksburg, being brevetted lieutenant-colonel Sept. 17, 1862. He was engaged in the Rappahannock campaign from December 1862 to June 1863. At Chancellorsville, May 2, 1863, he helped to check the decisive advance of "Stonewall" Jackson's corps against Hooker's right flank. Pleasonton ordered the 8th Pennsylvania Cavalry to charge and thus checked Jackson long enough for all available Union artillery to get into position. Loading the guns with grape and canister, he depressed their muzzles so that the shot would strike midway between the guns and the woods

and, when the Confederates emerged from the woods, poured death into their ranks. His prompt and energetic action saved the Federals from complete disaster. Later he wrote "The Successes and Failures of Chancellorsville," published in the third volume of *Battles and Leaders of the Civil War* (1888). Pleasonton was promoted major-general of volunteers, June 22, 1863, and participated in all the operations leading up to Gettysburg, where he was in command of all Union cavalry and won the brevet of colonel. He was engaged in battles at Culpeper Courthouse and Brandy Station, Va., and was then transferred to Missouri, Mar. 23, 1864. Campaigning against Gen. Sterling Price, he defended Jefferson City, Oct. 8, 1864, and later routed Price near Marais des Cygnes River, Kan., Oct. 25, 1864. For his services against Price he was brevetted brigadier-general, Mar. 13, 1865, and on the same date brevetted major-general for meritorious services in the field during the war.

Upon the reorganization of the army, Pleasonton was required to serve under officers he had commanded in battle. Embittered, he resigned his commission, Jan. 1, 1868. His petition for a pension was refused, and from April 1869 to March 1870 he served as collector of internal revenue for the fourth district, New York, and from March to December 1870 of the thirty-second district. On Dec. 16, 1870, his appointment as commissioner of internal revenue was confirmed. A conflict over authority arose between Pleasonton and Secretary of the Treasury Boutwell, which resulted in the former's being asked to resign. He declined and was suspended (Rogers, *post*). From 1872 to 1874 he was president of the Cincinnati & Terre Haute Railway. Congress tardily recognized Pleasonton's splendid war service by commissioning him major on the retired list, Oct. 19, 1888. This commission he reluctantly accepted. During the last twenty years of his life he lived in the Greason House, Washington, D. C., where he slept by day and at night, with his old comrades, fought again the battles of the past. He was a most agreeable gentleman and, when not hindered by a chronic throat disorder, a brilliant and entertaining conversationalist. Afflicted with a painful fistula for eight years, he isolated himself in his hotel, never leaving his room and seldom his bed. In accordance with his wish, he was buried without military ceremony, in the Congressional Cemetery, Washington, D. C. He lived and died a bachelor, the last of a family of several children.

[*Twenty-Eighth Ann. Reunion Asso. Grads. U. S. Military Acad.* (1897); F. B. Heitman, *Hist. Reg. and*

Dict. U. S. Army (1903), vol. I; G. W. Cullum, *Biog. Reg. Officers and Grads. U. S. Military Acad.* (1891), vol. II; *Battles and Leaders of the Civil War*, vols. II–IV (1887–88); "Report of the Secretary of War," *Sen. Ex. Doc. 2*, 36 Cong., 1 Sess.; A. C. Rogers, *Sketches of Representative Men, North and South* (1871); *War of the Rebellion: Official Records* (*Army*); *Evening Star* (Washington), Feb. 17, 1897.]

C. C. B.

PLOWMAN, GEORGE TAYLOR (Oct. 19, 1869–Mar. 26, 1932), etcher, was born in Le Sueur, Minn., the son of George and Seline (Taylor) Plowman. He graduated from the University of Minnesota with the class of 1892, being one of the first students to pursue the newly established course in architecture, and soon began work under Daniel H. Burnham [*q.v.*], chief of construction for the World's Columbian Exposition in Chicago, 1893. In that year he went to Paris to continue his architectural studies, and later made a sketching tour through France, England, and Italy. Returning to Paris, he had charge of an exhibit at the international exposition of 1900. After his return to the United States, he became a draftsman in the office of Cass Gilbert in New York. He was connected with the Louisiana Purchase Exposition at St. Louis in 1904, and for five years was superintendent for J. G. Howard, supervising architect for the University of California at Berkeley. In this capacity he supervised the erection of the mining building given to the University by Mrs. Phoebe A. Hearst in memory of her husband, Senator George Hearst. Later he opened an office for himself at Berkeley.

He did not take up etching until he was forty-two years old, but then became so thoroughly interested that he abandoned his architectural work and from 1911 to 1913 studied in the Royal College of Art, London, under Sir Frank Short. After that time he devoted himself almost exclusively to drawing and etching, for which his architectural training had been an excellent preparation. For a period he was a pupil of Douglas Volk and of the Art Institute of Chicago. His etchings were shown in the Paris Salon, the Royal Academy, London, and in many exhibitions in the United States and England. He was a draftsman of high order, and whatever his theme—old houses, cathedrals, towers, streets, or covered bridges—all were seen as by "an architect, painter and poet." He made many picturesque etchings of old covered bridges, in two that are especially interesting—one at Windsor, Vt., and one at Hanover, N. H.,—using both drypoint and etching with most artistic effect. A charming print of the cathedral of Chartres shows the great cathedral beyond a group of old houses and a bridge. In his etching of Mount Hood, Oregon, a mass of pine trees in the foreground are soft and beautiful, while the mountain stands cold and white beyond. Many of his prints are published in sets; there are collections of French, London, Italian, and German views, besides etchings of scenes in Boston, New York, and Princeton. He was the author of two illustrated books, *Etching and Other Graphic Arts* (1914) and *Manual of Etching* (1924), both of which are valuable reference works giving practical and helpful directions for making prints.

Plowman is represented in the Library of Congress, the Boston Museum of Fine Arts, the New York Public Library, the British Museum, the Luxembourg, and elsewhere. He received the bronze medal at the Panama Pacific International Exposition in San Francisco, 1915. He was a member of the leading art associations, the Boston and London authors' clubs, the Brooklyn Society of Etchers, and a fellow of the Royal Society of Arts in London. During the World War he served in 1918 as divisional secretary of the Young Men's Christian Association in France, and the next year he organized and directed its art department at the University of Coblenz. On Dec. 25, 1895, he married Maude Houston Bell, who with three sons survived him. He died at his home in Cambridge, Mass.

[*Am. Art Annual, 1931* (1932); *Who's Who in America*, 1930–31; W. H. Downes, "George T. Plowman's Etchings," *Print Connoisseur*, Sept. 1921; Maude Bell Plowman, "Covered Bridges—A Pictorial Record," *Am. Mag. of Art*, June 1931; *N. Y. Times*, Mar. 27, 1932.]

H. W.

PLUMB, GLENN EDWARD (Sept. 30, 1866–Aug. 1, 1922), railroad lawyer, was born in Clay, Washington County, Iowa, the son of Edward B. and Isabel (Mills) Plumb. He lived most of his early life in Streator, Ill., where he graduated from high school in 1885. His summers were spent at work in a glass factory or as a farm hand, and during at least one winter he taught a district school before entering Oberlin College, from which he received the degree of Ph.B. in 1891. In college he established a record as a runner and gymnast, and he spent part of one winter at Beloit as director of athletics. He studied at the Harvard Law School in 1891 and 1892, but in September of the latter year moved to Chicago, and received the degree of LL.B. at Northwestern University in 1893. During this period he entered the law office of Miller & Starr, and continued with that firm and its successor, Peck, Miller & Starr, until July 1897, spending a large part of his time on railroad cases. He left this office to become attorney for the Chicago General Railway Company. In 1900, this company went into the hands of a receiver, whom Plumb represented; in 1903 he took charge as general manager for the reorganizing bondholders. In 1900 he organized and promoted the Illinois & Rock River Railway Company; he was later vice-president of the Chicago Midland Transit Company and president of the Calumet & South Chicago Railroad, a street railway in the southern part of the city, until its absorption by the Chicago City Railway Company. As a result of these activities he became known as a specialist in railroad law.

In 1905 Edward F. Dunne, who had just been elected mayor, engaged him as special attorney and counsel for the city in an effort to "straighten out the traction tangle" of Chicago. In cooperation with Clarence Darrow and Edgar B. Tolman, corporation counsel, Plumb represented the city before the United States Supreme Court in the case of *Blair* vs. *City of Chicago* (201 *U. S.*, 400), known as the "ninety-nine year case." He was also special counsel for the state's attorney of Cook County and the corporation counsel of the city in negotiations concerning the elevated railways and other public utilities.

During most of this time he was fighting the traction interests, and accordingly the street railway employees turned to him to represent them in the settlement of their strike of 1916. The following year he was retained by the four big railway brotherhoods to represent them in proceedings before the Interstate Commerce Commission under the railroad valuation act. After the World War, when the question arose as to the terms upon which the railroads, which since January 1918 had been operated by the government, should be restored to their former owners, Plumb devised the so-called Plumb plan for government ownership. In accordance with this plan the roads would be operated under the supervision of a board of directors consisting of five representatives of the government, five representatives of the operating officials, and five representatives of the employees. Half the profits would go to the government and the other half be divided between officials and employees. This proposal was indorsed by the organized railroad employees' associations, and was approved in principle by the American Federation of Labor and by radical groups like the National Nonpartisan League. It was fiercely debated for a couple of years, both in Congress and out, but never came to a vote. The plan was described by Plumb in an article in the *Nation* (Aug. 16, 1919), in *Labor's Plan for Government Ownership and Democracy in the Opera-*

tion of the Railroads (1919), and in "An Industrial Program" (MS.) in New York Public Library. A posthumous volume, *Industrial Democracy; a Plan for its Achievement* (1923), which he wrote in conjunction with W. G. Roylance, developed the original Plumb plan into a scheme for the reorganization not only of the railroads but of all industry along the lines of a modified guild socialism.

Plumb began his career as a Republican, but later became a Democrat. He married on Jan. 1, 1895, Grace Edith Clarke of Chicago, who died Feb. 8, 1899, leaving two children; and on June 27, 1907, he married Marie Coyle of Chicago, who survived him. He died in Washington, after an illness of several months.

[*Who's Who in America*, 1922–23; *The Book of Chicagoans* (1905; 1917); *Literary Digest*, Aug. 23, 1919; *Locomotive Engineers Jour.*, Mar. 1920; *Railway Clerk*, Jan. 1922; *Machinists' Monthly Jour.*, Sept. 1922; *Current Opinion*, Mar. 1924, pp. 338–39; *Washington Post*, Aug. 2, 1922.]   E. L. B.

PLUMB, PRESTON B. (Oct. 12, 1837–Dec. 20, 1891), journalist, soldier, United States senator, was born at Berkshire, Delaware County, Ohio, the eldest child of David and Hannah Maria (Bierce) Plumb. Named simply Preston Plumb, he adopted the middle initial to improve the appearance of his signature. An ancestor, John Plume, settled at Wethersfield, Conn., in 1635, and another, Ichabod Plumb, grandfather of Preston, migrated to Ohio in 1804. Preston attended a preparatory school for three years, learned the printer's trade, acquired experience on the *Marysville Tribune,* and in 1854, with a partner, established the *Xenia News.*

In the summer of 1856 he visited Kansas and the following autumn he formed a company and escorted arms and ammunition into the Territory. He soon disposed of his interest in the *Xenia News* and found employment on the Lawrence *Herald of Freedom.* In June 1857 he established the *Kanzas News* at Emporia. Although he was only twenty, his paper immediately became a vigorous advocate of the Free-State cause, and residents of Emporia constantly looked to him for leadership. He attended numerous Free-State meetings and served in the Leavenworth constitutional convention. During the winter of 1858 he acquired his first military experience in southern Kansas as aide-de-camp to Gen. James H. Lane. Near the close of the territorial period he studied law at Cleveland, Ohio, and in 1861 was admitted to the bar. He was the first reporter of the Kansas supreme court, and in 1862 served in the lower house of the second state legislature.

On Sept. 25, 1862, Plumb was mustered into

the Federal service as major of the 11th Kansas Cavalry which operated as part of the Army of the Frontier in northwestern Arkansas. He was appointed chief-of-staff and provost marshal by Gen. Thomas Ewing in 1863, and partially cleared the District of the Border of guerrillas, although he failed to capture Quantrill after the Lawrence massacre. Plumb was promoted lieutenant-colonel, May 17, 1864, and early in 1865 his regiment was assigned the duty of guarding three hundred miles of the Oregon Trail.

He returned to Kansas in September 1865, resumed the practice of law, established the Emporia National Bank, and invested in Texas cattle and Colorado mines. On Mar. 8, 1867, he married Caroline A. Southwick of Ashtabula, Ohio, and to them six children were born. Plumb served in the state House of Representatives in 1867–68, the first year as speaker. Always independent in politics, he supported Greeley for the presidency in 1872. In spite of this defection from the regular Republican party he was elected to the United States Senate in 1877, and reelected in 1883 and 1889, the third time unanimously. In 1880 and again in 1884 he headed the Kansas delegation to the Republican National Convention. In the latter year he placed John A. Logan in nomination for vice-president.

In the Senate, Plumb was assigned to the committee on public lands and became its chairman in 1881. Perhaps his greatest contribution was the land law of 1891 which repealed the timber-culture and preëmption acts and inaugurated reclamation and conservation projects. He favored free coinage of silver, advocated a moderate tariff, and opposed the McKinley bill. In the civil service he preferred rotation to permanency; in foreign affairs he wished to emphasize the consular rather than the diplomatic service. He was a useful member of the Senate and performed more than his share of the routine business. His whole career was marked by strenuous effort, untiring industry, and wholesome enthusiasm. He was so typically western that William H. Crane selected him as a model for make-up and manner in the drama, *The Senator*. He died in Washington during his third senatorial term.

[W. E. Connelley, *The Life of Preston B. Plumb* (1913), is neither critical nor well-organized. For Plumb's military career see *War of the Rebellion: Official Records* (*Army*), 1 ser. XXII, XXXIV, XLI, XLVIII; for his senatorial career, *Cong. Record*, 1877–91. A broken file of the *Kansas News* is available in the Kan. State Hist. Lib. See also: D. W. Wilder, *The Annals of Kan.* (1886); *Biog. Dir. Am. Cong.* (1928); *Memorial Addresses on the Life and Character of Preston B. Plumb* (1892); H. B. Plumb, *The Plumbs 1635–1800* (1893); *Evening Standard* (Leavenworth, Kan.), Dec. 21, 1891.] W. H. S.

PLUMBE, JOHN (July 1809–July 1857), railroadman, publicist, photographer, was born in Wales and came to the United States with his family in 1821. In 1831–32 he was an assistant under Moncure Robinson, of Richmond, Va., in surveying and locating a railway route across the Alleghanies in Huntingdon County, Pa. In 1832, on Robinson's recommendation, he was made superintendent, at its southern terminus, of the railway extending from Richmond to the Roanoke River in North Carolina. He migrated in 1836 to Dubuque, Iowa, which was nominally his home until his death. His brother Richard settled in Dubuque County, and he probably had other relatives in the vicinity.

Though he has been so completely forgotten that even Prof. L. H. Haney fails to mention him in his *Congressional History of Railways* (1908), Plumbe appears to have been the first responsible and effective advocate of a railway to the Pacific. Late in 1836 he was talking of the subject in private conversations, and within the next few months the project had become the ambition of his life. He called meetings at various towns in Iowa, Illinois, and Wisconsin, delivered lectures, and drafted resolutions; he filled the mails with letters to Eastern newspapers; he memorialized Congress, and through his Representative, George Wallace Jones [*q.v.*], he secured in 1838 a $2,000 appropriation for the survey of a route from Milwaukee to Sinipee, Wis., on the Mississippi above Dubuque. He himself worked on the survey and contributed to its expenses. The next year he published the first part of *Sketches of Iowa and Wisconsin, Taken During a Residence of Three Years in Those Territories* (St. Louis, 1839), of which the second part never appeared. It is an enthusiastic description of the country, with much detailed information, and is now a rare book. In 1840 Plumbe went East to work for his railroad scheme in Washington, but he suffered the usual penalty for being in advance of his time. In 1849 he made the trip to California by South Pass and convinced himself that the railroad was feasible. As surveyor and register of the Squatter Association, he published *A Faithful Translation of The Papers Respecting the Grant Made by Governor Alvarado to Mr. J. A. Sutter* (Sacramento City, 1850), in which the "remarks of the committee" are from his pen. This was the first pamphlet printed and published in Sacramento County; only one copy is known. He also published articles on the Pacific railroad and on land titles in the *Placer Times* (San Francisco), for Jan. 26, Feb. 2, 16, 23, Mar. 9, 1850. He returned East that summer. In 1851 he published a *Memorial against Mr. Asa Whitney's Railroad Scheme* (Washington, 1851), which scheme he exposed as a land-grab.

His work as a photographer seems to have begun in Philadelphia in 1840, and by 1845, according to advertisements in the *Scientific American,* he had a main office in New York and branches in Boston, Saratoga Springs, Philadelphia, Baltimore, Washington, Alexandria, D. C., Petersburg, Va., Harrodsburgh Springs, Ky., Louisville, Cincinnati, St. Louis, Dubuque, and Newport, R. I. He also dealt in German-made cameras and photographic goods, and was evidently one of the prominent photographers of the time. His special claim to distinction was the Plumbeotype, which he advertised as "a reproduction on paper of a Daguerreotype." He did not patent the process and its nature can only be surmised. To circulate his Plumbeotypes he started the *Popular Magazine,* issued weekly Oct. 31–Nov. 28, 1846, with Augustine J. H. Duganne [*q.v.*] as editor. In December 1846 it became a monthly, *The Plumbe Popular Magazine,* but it probably suspended within a few months. Stray copies of it are preserved in the Library of Congress and in the libraries of Brown University and the American Antiquarian Society. The final course of Plumbe's fortunes is unknown. He committed suicide at Dubuque about the beginning of July 1857.

[John King, "John Plumbe, Originator of the Pacific Railroad," *Annals of Iowa,* Jan. 1904, with portrait, the fullest and most authoritative account; obituary notice, copied from the *West Urbana Press,* in the *New-Eng. Hist. and Geneal. Reg.,* Oct. 1857, which establishes the connection between Plumbe the railroadman and Plumbe the photographer; L. H. Langworthy, *Dubuque . . . in Two Lectures* (Dubuque, 1855), pp. 54–57; H. H. Bancroft, *Hist. of the Pacific States,* vol. XIX (1890); H. R. Wagner, *Cal. Imprints August 1846–June 1851* (1922), nos. 60 and 96; N. Y. and Phila. city directories; Plumbe's advertisements in *Scientific American,* vol. I, *passim* (1846); notes on Plumbe's magazines by C. S. Brigham; reprint of *Sketches of Iowa and Wis.* in *Annals of Iowa,* Jan., Apr., 1925.]   G. H. G.

PLUMER, WILLIAM (June 25, 1759–Dec. 22, 1850), senator from New Hampshire, was born at Newburyport, Mass., the eldest of the six children of Samuel and Mary (Dole) Plumer and the descendant of Francis Plumer who emigrated from England and settled at Newbury in 1634. His father removed in 1768 to a farm in Epping, N. H., where William's childhood was spent and where he obtained a scanty schooling. When about twenty years old he passed through a period of religious fervor, became a Baptist exhorter, and conducted revival services in the outlying settlements. His own account of his emotional experience, the struggle between faith

and skepticism, is an interesting psychological document that helps to explain in some degree his rejection of Calvinism, his subsequent support of religious freedom, his desertion of Federalism, and his lifelong interest in humanitarian projects (Plumer, *post,* pp. 26–31).

His political career began with his election as selectman in 1783. A year later he began the study of law under Joshua Atherton [*q.v.*], but he soon returned to the farm and, owing to various interruptions, was not admitted to the bar until November 1787. He began practice in Epping and became engaged to Sally Fowler of New Market, to whom he was married on Feb. 12, 1788. They had six children. He took part in the suppression of the insurrectionary disturbances of this troubled era and supported the adoption of the federal Constitution, although defeated for membership in the ratifying convention. He served in the legislature, 1785–86, 1788, 1790, 1791, and from 1797–1800. He was speaker of the House in 1791 and 1797 and was regarded in the state as one of the ablest members of the Federalist party, being largely responsible for its efficient organization and campaign methods. He also was a member of the constitutional convention of 1791–92. He served in the United States Senate from June 17, 1802, to Mar. 3, 1807, and declined to be a candidate for reëlection. His career in the Senate was not conspicuous, and he seldom spoke. He followed the orthodox Federalist course in politics, and his letters show that he had most of the prejudices but not the social intolerance of his party. For Jefferson he appears to have had a certain partiality, which later developed into friendship and admiration. "I wish his French politics were as good as his French wines; but to me, at least, they have by no means so exquisite a flavor," he wrote in 1802 (*Ibid.,* p. 246). During his tenure he kept a diary of the Senate proceedings, which is an important but seldom used historical source (*Wm. Plumer's Memorandum of Proceedings of the United States Senate, 1803–1807,* ed. by E. S. Brown, 1923). He had at this time serious doubts as to the permanence of the Union, and in 1828 he corroborated John Quincy Adams' charge that in 1804 leading Federalists were discussing the possible withdrawal of the northern states. He acknowledged frankly that his own temporary sympathy for the movement was "the most erroneous [opinion] that I ever formed upon political subjects" (*Ibid.,* 292). The foreign difficulties of Jefferson's second administration had changed his attitude, and his statement in 1806 that he was no longer a fervent party man was followed by his repudiation of

Federalism and his support of Madison in 1808.

He was soon active in the Republican party, served as president of the state Senate in 1810 and 1811, and in 1812 was elected governor in a close and acrimonious campaign, when the popular vote was so close that final choice was made by the legislature. As governor he made stirring pleas for support of the Madison administration and the preservation of the Union. His loyal compliance with the president's requisitions for troops was in striking contrast to the opposition of several other New England governors. A candidate for the same office in the three succeeding years, he was defeated by narrow majorities in campaigns of extraordinary bitterness. His voice and pen were used in vigorous support of the federal government and denunciation of the course of the Federalist party. With the restoration of peace he was elected and served as governor from 1816 to 1819. He was instrumental in obtaining several legal and administrative reforms, and his messages to the legislature show his humanitarian interests and his realization of impending economic changes. Of most importance, however, was his recommendation for alterations in the charter of Dartmouth College, which he declared "contained . . . principles congenial to monarchy" (Lord, *post*, p. 85) and prevented its rendering a proper measure of service to the state. His views, which incidentally received Jefferson's cordial indorsement, were followed by appropriate legislative action, and the memorable controversy that followed, contemporaneously, with a protracted struggle over the judicial reorganization of the state, made his administration a stormy one and affected state politics for many years thereafter. He performed his last official service in 1820, when as presidential elector he cast the only vote against the choice of James Monroe.

He wrote for the press for many years following his retirement and began a history of the United States, a project he had discussed with Jefferson while in the Senate (part of manuscript in Library of Congress). His labors were finally concentrated on sketches of American biography, and he wrote more than nineteen hundred articles. The few that have been published show considerable literary and historical ability. The entire collection is in possession of the New Hampshire Historical Society (indexed in *Proceedings*, I, 1874). He retained his faculties to an advanced age, his physical and mental strength declining gradually until his death at his old home in Epping. The constitutional convention then in session at Concord in fitting resolutions noted the fact that his long life had

spanned the entire history of New Hampshire as a state and that he was the last of the men who had taken a prominent part in the laying of the foundations of the commonwealth.

[Plumer Collection in Lib. of Cong. and in Lib. of N. H. Hist. Soc.; material in archives of Dartmouth College; Wm. Plumer, Jr., *Life of Wm. Plumer* (1857); A. H. Hoyt, *Memoir of Wm. Plumer* (1871) reprinted from *New-England Hist. and Geneal. Register*, Jan. 1871; biog. and other material in "Early State Papers of N. H.," ed. by A. S. Batchellor, *N. H. State Papers*, vols. XXI, XXII (1892–93); A. S. Wait, "The Life, Character, and Public Services of Gov. Wm. Plumer," *Proc. N. H. Hist. Soc.*, vol. III (1902); S. C. Bartlett, "Dr. John Wheelock," *Ibid.*, vol. II (1895); J. K. Lord, *A Hist. of Dartmouth College* (1913).]

W. A. R.

PLUMER, WILLIAM SWAN (July 26, 1802–Oct. 22, 1880), Presbyterian clergyman, was born at Griersburg (now Darlington), Beaver County, Pa. His father, William Plumer, was a native of Maryland and a direct descendant of Francis Plumer, who emigrated from England, was made a freeman in Ipswich, Mass., May 14, 1634, and in the fall of that year settled at Newbury. His mother, Catherine (McAllister) Plumer, was a native of Pennsylvania, the daughter of John McAllister, who was of Scotch descent. While William was still an infant his parents migrated to Kentucky, then to Ohio. His father had a floating store, which he moved from place to place on the Ohio River. At the age of seventeen young Plumer was teaching school at Malden, in what is now West Virginia. When he was about nineteen he walked across the mountains to Lewisburg and entered the Academy, conducted by Dr. McElhenney, to prepare for college. He graduated from Washington College (now Washington and Lee University), Lexington, Va., in 1824, and from Princeton Theological Seminary in 1826. On June 14, 1826, he was licensed to preach by the New Brunswick Presbytery, New Jersey, and on May 19, 1827, he was ordained by the Orange Presbytery, North Carolina. For several years he did evangelistic work in North Carolina and in Virginia, founding several well-known churches. In 1829 he was married to a widow, Mrs. Eliza (Garden) Hasell, a native of Charleston, S. C., who was of French Huguenot descent, and about fourteen years his senior.

Plumer was pastor successively of Tabb Street Presbyterian Church, Petersburg, Va. (1831–34); the First Presbyterian Church, Richmond, Va. (1834–47); and the Franklin Street Presbyterian Church, Baltimore, Md. (1847–54). From 1854 to 1862 he was professor of didactic and pastoral theology in the Western Theological Seminary, Allegheny, Pa., and at the same time served as pastor of the Central Presbyterian

Church of that city. He was recalled to the Central Church when he was seventy-six years of age, but declined. He supplied Arch Street Presbyterian Church, Philadelphia (1862–65), and was pastor of the Second Presbyterian Church, Pottsville, Pa. (1865–66). From 1867 to 1880 he was a professor in Columbia Theological Seminary, Columbia, S. C. Moses D. Hoge [q.v.], who, as a young man, was Plumer's assistant in Richmond, describes him in his latter years as follows: "His majestic stature, his slow measured step, his easy and graceful carriage, his dark eyes and heavy eyebrows of still darker shade, contrasting with his white hair falling back in heavy masses from his forehead, his snowy beard waving on his breast like a flowing vestment, reminded the beholder of some majestic patriarch or ancient prophet, a living sculpture of heroic mold." The Rev. W. H. Ruffner, who knew Plumer intimately, wrote regarding him (post, p. 28): "When he was pastor in Richmond, no one could, I think, have hesitated to place him at the head of the Virginia pulpit, and at the head of popular orators. His power of terse, pithy statement was unequalled." In the Old School and New School controversy, which divided the American Presbyterian Church into two nearly equal parts in 1837, he was the outstanding leader and debater on the Old School side. The Old School General Assembly elected him moderator in 1838, when he was only thirty-six years of age. In 1871 he was elected Moderator of the General Assembly of the Presbyterian Church in the United States, thus having the distinction of being the only man in that Church who was ever elected twice to the moderatorship.

Plumer was the author of twenty-five or thirty books and of more than a hundred printed pamphlets. Some of these have been translated into French, German, Greek, and Chinese. As a rule, his writings were of a devotional nature. His *Studies of the Book of Psalms, Being a Critical and Expository Commentary* (1866) is a volume of more than 1200 pages. He also wrote commentaries on Romans and Hebrews, *The Law of God, as Contained in the Ten Commandments* (1864), *Vital Godliness* (1864), *Hints and Helps in Pastoral Theology* (1874), and published many books of sermons. While pastor in Richmond he founded *The Watchman of the South,* a religious paper, and was its sole editor for eight years. This paper still lives in *The Presbyterian of the South.* During the course of his life he was a contributor to numerous papers. In 1846 he delivered a learned legal address before a committee of the Virginia legislature against a proposed law to incorporate churches, and won his case against the ablest lawyers in Virginia.

He retained his vigor even in old age. In 1877 he attended the Pan-Presbyterian Alliance in Edinburgh, and made a profound impression upon that distinguished body. During the summer prior to his death, at the age of seventy-eight, he was in demand as a preacher in the largest churches in Baltimore and other surrounding cities. He died in Baltimore, survived by two daughters, and was buried in Hollywood Cemetery in Richmond.

[Unpublished letters and manuscripts in the Presbyterian Lib., Phila.; scrap book of newspaper clippings kept by Plumer's daughter, Mrs. Kate Plumer Bryan, from 1845 to 1888; an account of Plumer's last days (no title page, apparently printed 1880) by E. D. Bryan and K. P. Bryan; Moses D. Hoge, *Semi-Centennial of Columbia Theological Seminary* (1884); memorial in Minutes of the Synod of Va., 1881; W. H. Ruffner, in *Washington and Lee Univ. . . . Hist. Papers, no. 5* (1895); S. Irenæus Prime, in *N. Y. Observer,* Jan. 13, 1881; Sidney Perley, *The Plumer Geneal.* (1917); H. A. White, *Southern Presbyterian Leaders* (1911); *Sun* (Baltimore), Oct. 22, *Daily Dispatch* (Richmond), Oct. 23, 26, 1880; many of his published volumes and several short biographical sketches by contemporaries in the Hist. Foundation of the Presbyterian and Reformed Churches, at Montreat, N. C.; information as to certain facts, including day of birth, from his grandson, S. S. Bryan, Titusville, Pa.]

W. L. L.

PLUMLEY, FRANK (Dec. 17, 1844–Apr. 30, 1924), Vermont jurist and congressman, was the son of William Plumley, a prosperous Vermont farmer, and Eliza (Little) Plumley. On his father's side, his first American ancestor was Alexander Plumley, who settled in Boston in 1639. Born at Eden, Vt., and educated in the common schools and in the People's Academy at Morrisville, Frank read law at Morrisville before attending the University of Michigan for work in law and literature. At the age of twenty-four he was admitted to the bar in Lamoille County in his native state and commenced his distinguished legal career at Northfield, which became his home. His marriage to Lavinia L. Fletcher of Eden, by whom he had two children took place Aug. 9, 1871.

A partnership with Heman Carpenter was followed in 1876 by four years as state's attorney of Washington County. After a term in the Vermont legislature (1882), and perhaps because of his consistent Republicanism, his gift of oratory, and his earlier connections with Michigan, he was drafted in 1884 to stump that state for Blaine. He performed a similar service to his party in a number of subsequent presidential years. In 1886 he was chairman of the Republican State Convention and two years later attended the Republican National Convention, where as a member of the platform committee he drafted a

Plumley

temperance plank which was adopted by the Convention. President Harrison appointed him United States district attorney (1889–94), in which office he secured a number of important convictions. He served a two-year term in the Vermont Senate in 1894–96.

One of Plumley's principal public services occurred in connection with the British, Dutch, and French claims against Venezuela. The British-Venezuelan Mixed Claims Commission, established under the Protocol of Feb. 13, 1903, was to consist of one British and one Venezuelan appointee. An umpire, nominated by President Roosevelt, was to make the decisions when the commissioners failed to agree. A similar Mixed Claims Commission for the Netherlands and Venezuela was established under the Protocol of Feb. 28, 1903. Plumley, who had been appointed in 1902 a member of the Vermont court of claims and was later (1904–08) to serve as its chief justice, was named umpire for both commissions by President Roosevelt and sat with the commissions at Caracas for about six months in 1903 (*Papers Relating to the Foreign Relations of the United States ... 1904*, p. 865). The refusal of the Spanish Ambassador to France to serve as umpire for the Franco-Venezuelan Mixed Claims Commission led to the selection of Plumley for that work. The sessions of this Commission were continued in 1905 in Northfield, Vt.

Unsuccessful in his first attempt to secure a nomination for Congress (1900), Plumley was elected to the Sixty-first, Sixty-second, and Sixty-third congresses (1909–15). He was one of the four delegates from the United States Congress to the Interparliamentary Union, which met at Geneva in 1912. In 1914 he refused a renomination to Congress in order to devote himself to his law practice. Plumley was of impressive build and substantial character. He was an active member of the Methodist Church, served on the Northfield board of education for twenty years, and was an ardent temperance advocate, attending the anti-saloon conference in New York City in 1888. He was lecturer on constitutional law at Norwich University, Northfield, from 1887 to 1902, and became a trustee of the University in 1888. He died at Northfield.

[J. M. Comstock, *A List of the Principal Civil Officers of Vt.* (1918); J. H. Ralston, *Venezuelan Arbitrations of 1903* (1904) and *Report of French-Venezuelan Mixed Claims Commission of 1902* (1906); Hiram Carleton, *Geneal. and Family Hist. of ... Vt.* (1903); W. R. Cutter, *New England Families*, vol. IV (1914); *Biog. Dir. Am. Cong.* (1928); *Who's Who in America*, 1924–25; *Burlington Free Press*, May 2, 1924; information as to certain facts from a son, President C. A. Plumley of Norwich Univ.]   E. W. S.

Plummer

PLUMMER, HENRY (d. Jan. 10, 1864), bandit, began his public career at Nevada City, Cal., in 1852. Of his early life and antecedents nothing was known, and the etiquette of the time and place, apart from other considerations, forbade inquiry. He was then, probably, about twenty-five years old and was joint proprietor of a bakery. He was above medium height, slender, with mild blue eyes, regular features, and chestnut-brown hair. He was neat, even fastidious, in his dress and person, and his carefully modulated voice, correct English, good manners, and general suggestion of poise and power seemed to indicate a man of breeding. He was elected town marshal in 1856 and in the following year, but was an unsuccessful candidate for state assemblyman on the Democratic ticket. While he was still marshal of Nevada City he murdered a man named Vedder, with whose wife he was carrying on an intrigue. After two trials he was sent to the Yuba County, Cal., penitentiary to serve a ten-year sentence, but Gov. John P. Weller pardoned him on the assumption that he was dying of tuberculosis. In the course of the next year or two Plummer established a reputation for seduction, brawling, murder, banditry, and jail-breaking but managed to escape punishment. In the spring of 1861 he left hurriedly for Washington Territory, stayed long enough in Walla Walla to send back to California newspapers a plausible account of his being lynched, and then proceeded, accompanied by the wife of a citizen of Walla Walla, to Lewiston, Idaho. In Lewiston he posed as a gambler but devoted his main energies to organizing a gang of bandits who, in 1862, commanded the routes from Lewiston to Orofino and other mining camps, and murdered and robbed with impunity.

In the fall of that year he crossed the Continental Divide into what is now Montana; tarried two months at Sun River, where he was the guest of J. A. Vail, superintendent of a government school for Blackfoot Indians; and became engaged to Vail's sister-in-law, Electa Bryan, of Cedar Rapids, Iowa. Shortly before Christmas he arrived at Bannack. On Jan. 14, 1863, he killed his former confederate, Jack Cleveland, the one man in Bannack who knew his history and could have betrayed him. Plummer was tried and acquitted. He then hounded the sheriff, Henry Crawford, into leaving the Territory and on May 24 was elected to the vacant office. On June 20, at Sun River, he married Electa Bryan, who on Sept. 2 quietly departed for the East. Meanwhile Plummer had become the directing genius of a company of desperadoes who soon had all of southern Montana at their mercy. In organizing the gang and maintaining his ascendency over it undisputed he displayed ability of a high order. In the course of a few months 102 men were robbed or murdered, and the decent element of the population was compelled to take drastic measures for its own preservation. A committee of Vigilantes was formed at Bannack and at Virginia City, with Wilbur Fisk Sanders [q.v.], John S. Lott, John X. Biedler, and Capt. James Williams among its leaders, and the work of exterminating the outlaws was pushed vigorously. A complete list of Plummer's gang was obtained, and no halt was called until twenty-four were hanged and eight banished. The discovery of Plummer's leadership was a complete surprise to all but a few of the Vigilantes: almost to the last he had played his double rôle successfully. He was apprehended at Bannack Jan. 10, 1864, and hanged on a gallows that he had erected in his capacity as sheriff.

[T. J. Dimsdale, *The Vigilantes of Mont.* (first pub. in *Mont. Post*, Virginia City, Aug. 26, 1865–Mar. 14, 1866; 3rd ed., with Al Noyes, *Hist. of Southern Mont.*, appended, 1915); N. P. Langford, *Vigilante Days and Ways* (2 vols., 1890); W. J. McConnell, *Early Hist. of Idaho* (1913); H. H. Bancroft, *Popular Tribunals* (1887), I, 675–83, and *Hist. of Wash., Idaho, and Mont., 1845–89* (1890), with numerous references to contemporary newspapers; Hoffman Birney, *Vigilantes* (1929).]

G. H. G.

PLUMMER, JONATHAN (July 13, 1761–Sept. 13, 1819), peddler, ballad-monger, poet laureate to "Lord" Timothy Dexter [q.v.], was a native of Newbury, Mass., the eldest of eight children born to Jonathan and Abigail (Greenleaf) Plummer. His father, a well-to-do cordwainer, was a descendant of Francis Plumer who emigrated to Boston in 1634 and was one of the founders of Newbury. Early given to understand that he was "peculiar," Plummer was permitted but a meager share of school education, and was set to peddling halibut from a wheelbarrow. To a contemporary he appeared as a strange and wayward boy, who had a great fondness for reading, and possessed a remarkable memory. His face was long, with a prominent nose, wide mouth, and thick lips. His voice was deep-toned and solemn (Knapp, *post*, pp. 87, 97).

Unhappy at home, he became a traveling trader, then, successively, country-school teacher, militiaman, and scullion in a tavern. Everywhere he sought the friendship of owners of books, in this way securing opportunity to read Shakespeare, Montaigne, Ovid, Dryden, Swift, Sterne, and Cervantes. But "Allan Ramsay's tuneful works," he says, "ravished my soul with such transporting joys that I soon attempted to write in poetry myself." A brief career as itinerant preacher ended in discouragement. Success attended him as a trader, however, and he soon began to print and peddle his sermons. At the age of twenty-six he decided to marry for money. Decisive rejections by nine "vigorous and antiquated virgins" in two months left him vowing celibacy. A Plummer broadside issued in 1795 bore this colophon: "The author still continues to carry on his various branches of trifling business" and enumerates, among other enterprises, the filling of underbeds with straw, pawnbrokerage, the buying of bottles, the treatment of secret diseases, and the writing of love letters in prose or verse. A fellow citizen's sudden rise from poverty to wealth gave Plummer the material for a broadside called *The Author's Congratulatory Address to Citizen Timothy Dexter on His Attaining an Independent Fortune* (1793). Dexter, craving notoriety, exploited Plummer's peculiar genius. Styling himself "Lord," he employed the ballad-monger as poet laureate, and decked him out in a long black frock coat garnished with silver stars and fringes, an imposing cocked hat, large-buckled shoes, and a goldheaded cane. After Dexter's death (1806), Plummer, reduced again to peddling, at times became objectionably personal in his printed sermons. Characteristic is one entitled *Parson Pidgin, or Holy Kissing ... Occasioned by a Report that Parson Pidgin Had Kissed a Young Woman* (1807).

There are more than thirty Plummer broadsides and several pamphlets extant (mainly in Salem and Boston libraries), while Newburyport newspapers contain a number of his "odes" and other compositions. The broadsides commonly consist of a brief "ode" and a semi-journalistic prose exposition, invariably didactic in tone and often with autobiographical citations, and woodcuts to point the moral. Subjects include "vastly remarkable conversions," "smallpox by inoculation," elegies, private scandals, suicides, executions and dying confessions, Indian massacres, epidemics, shipwrecks and similar "acts of God." He also wrote *Sketch of the History of the Life of Jonathan Plummer*, which was issued (*c.* 1797) in pamphlet form in three parts. For many years Plummer appeared daily in Market Square with his basket of notions and verses. He died in Newburyport, supposedly of self-starvation. In his will he directed that the greater part of his estate, appraised at over fifteen hundred dollars, be used to defray the cost of printing several hundred copies of his memoirs for public distribution. The will was disallowed.

[Part I of Plummer's autobiographical *Sketch* is extant in the collection of R. W. Lull of Newburyport; Parts II and III, in the Essex Institute, Salem, Mass.

See also Sidney Perley, *The Plumer Geneal.* (1917); Alvin Plummer, *The Plummer System of Geneal. Enumeration* (1904); *Vital Records of Newburyport, Mass.* (1911), vol. II; J. J. Currier, *Hist. of Newburyport, Mass.* (1909), vol. II; W. C. Ford, *Broadsides, Ballads, Etc., Printed in Mass., 1639–1800* (1922); S. L. Knapp, *Life of Lord Timothy Dexter* (1848); J. P. Marquand, *Lord Timothy Dexter of Newburyport* (1925).]

R. W. H.

PLUMMER, MARY WRIGHT (Mar. 8, 1856–Sept. 21, 1916), librarian, teacher, poet, was a native of Richmond, Ind., the daughter of Jonathan Wright and Hannah (Ballard) Plummer, and a descendant of Thomas Plummer born in Prince Georges County, Md., in 1723. The characteristics of a long line of Quaker and pioneer ancestors were reflected in her personality; she displayed poise, reserve, high ideals, independence, and fearlessness. She received her education in local, private and public schools, and in her early days was described as a "book hungry" girl. After special study at Wellesley in 1881–82, she spent the following four years with her family in Chicago, reading widely, and teaching. On Jan. 5, 1887, she entered the recently opened library school at Columbia College. Her impressions of that first year are set forth in a paper she read at the meeting of the American Library Association, Sept. 1, 1887, "The Columbia College School of Library Economy from a Student's Standpoint" (*Library Journal*, September-October, 1887). In the following October she entered as student in the senior course and as a teacher for the incoming junior class. The next two years she served as cataloguer in the St. Louis Public Library under Frederick M. Crunden [*q.v.*].

Resigning in 1890, she spent the summer in Europe, and in the autumn went to the library of Pratt Institute established in Brooklyn in 1887. In 1894 she was made librarian and put in charge of the library school, being given a year's leave of absence, which she spent in Europe. In September 1895 she returned to finish the planning of the new library building, which was opened in 1896. This was the first building with a children's room included in the original plan, also the first with an art-reference collection for general use, both of which innovations must be credited to her. In 1900 she served as one of the United States delegates to the International Congress of Libraries in Paris. In 1904 she resigned as librarian of the Institute to give her whole time to the school. She left Pratt Institute in 1911 and became head of the new library school opened in connection with the dedication of the central building of The New York Public Library, and there she spent the rest of her life. She was elected president of various local and state library organizations from time to time, and in June 1915 was chosen president of the American Library Association. Her fatal illness prevented her presiding at the next meeting in 1916, but her presidential address on "The Public Library and the Pursuit of Truth" was read in her absence (printed in *Papers and Proceedings of the Thirty-eighth Annual Meeting of the American Library Association,* 1916; *Library Journal,* August 1916; *Public Libraries,* October 1916). She died at the home of her brother in Dixon, Ill.

Private study, reading, and travel gave her command of French, Italian, and Spanish. A happy facility for expression in verse showed itself early, and her occasional contributions to magazines were collected in a volume entitled *Verses,* privately printed in 1896 and reprinted with additions in 1916 by a sister. Other writings of hers were: *Hints to Small Libraries* (1894; 4th edition, 1911), the third edition of which was translated into Russian by S. Povarnin (St. Petersburg, 1905); *Contemporary Spain as Shown by Her Novelists* (1899); *The Pros and Cons of Training for Librarianship* (1903); *Roy and Ray in Mexico* (1907); *Roy and Ray in Canada* (1908); *Stories from the Chronicle of the Cid* (1910); "Training for Librarianship," issued as chapter xiii of the *Manual of Library Economy,* published by the American Library Association. At the meeting of the New York Library Association at Lake George in 1909 she read a paper on "The Seven Joys of Reading," which was first printed in the *Sewanee Review* of October 1910 and later (1915) appeared as a separate publication, passing through two subsequent editions.

[A biog. by A. C. Moore is in preparation for publication in the series of American Library Pioneers, published by the Am. Lib. Asso.; for published sources see: A. W. Young, *Hist. of Wayne County, Ind.* (1872); *Am. Ancestry,* vol. XII (1899); *Lib. Jour.,* Dec. 1916; *Public Libraries,* Oct. 1916; *Who's Who in America,* 1916–17; *N. Y. Times,* Sept. 22, 1916.]

H. M. L.

PLUNKETT, CHARLES PESHALL (Feb. 15, 1864–Mar. 24, 1931), naval officer, was born in Washington, D. C., son of William H. Plunkett, who came to the United States from England and was a commissioned officer in the Union forces in the Civil War, and of Letitia (Peshall), daughter of Sir Charles Peshall of the British army. Charles entered the Naval Academy at sixteen and graduated in 1884. Made junior lieutenant in 1895, he was in the gunboat *Petrel* at Manila Bay in the War with Spain, receiving advancement to lieutenant in November 1898, on his return home. During the next decade he had the responsible post of executive, or second in command, on four ships—the *Topeka, Texas, Georgia,* and *North Dakota,* with intervening shore duty in the Office of Naval Intelligence (1904–05) and as inspector with the Fore River Shipbuilding Company, Quincy, Mass. (1908–10). He then commanded successively the *Missouri, Culgoa, Wabash, South Dakota* and *North Dakota,* the last named of which went to Vera Cruz in April 1914 and remained there five months during trouble with Mexico.

In September 1915 he was made director of target practice and engineering competitions, and continued in this duty during the preparation and first year's participation by the United States in the World War. His position and special knowledge of ordnance led to his selection for command of the five batteries of 14-inch naval guns on railway mounts sent abroad in June 1918. It was only by his drive and indomitable energy in overcoming practical difficulties and official delays that this powerful artillery reached the front for employment in the Layon-Longuyon sector from Sept. 6 till the armistice, where it did excellent work in destroying enemy communications, dumps, and bases. His temporary promotion to rear admiral, July 1, 1918, was made permanent in 1919, and he received the distinguished service medal from both army and navy, and the rank of commander in the French Legion of Honor. In command of destroyer forces, United States Fleet, January–July 1919, he had full charge of the transatlantic flight of *NC* planes in May and June, during which destroyers were stationed at fifty-mile intervals from New Foundland to the Azores. Thereafter, until December 1920, he commanded the destroyer squadrons of the Atlantic Fleet. After duty as chief of staff at the Naval War College, 1920–21, he was president of the board of inspection and survey, and from December 1922 until his retirement Feb. 15, 1928, in command of the Third Naval District and Brooklyn Navy Yard.

During this period he was frequently in the public eye, first in 1923–24 by his vigorous campaign to drive bootleggers and drug peddlers from the neighborhood of the Brooklyn Yard; in 1924 by his protest at the profanity attributed to officers in uniform in the play "What Price Glory"; and in 1927 by his conflict with the Red Cross over solicitations in the yard. His frankness and force made him a popular public speaker, and he took every opportunity to urge a strong navy and merchant marine. Protests were aroused by his declaration before the National Republican Club, Jan. 21, 1928, that "you are

going to have war . . . if you contest the control of the sea with your goods, not with your guns." His home after retirement was in Washington, where he died of heart trouble. He was survived by his wife Nellie, formerly Mrs. Richard Lee Leary of Washington, whom he married in 1919. By earlier marriages to Ruth, daughter of Judge Tuck of Maryland, and after her death to her sister Julia, he had three children.

[*Who's Who in America,* 1930–31; *N. Y. Times,* Mar. 25, 26 (editorial), 27, 1931; *Army and Navy Jour.,* Mar. 28, 1931; Commander J. W. Bunkley, "The Woozlefinch: The Navy 14-Inch Railway Guns," *U. S. Naval Inst. Proc.,* May 1931; information from family.]

A. W.

POCAHONTAS (*c.* 1595–March 1617), Indian "princess," whose personal name was Matoaka, was the daughter of Powhatan [*q.v.*], head of the Powhatan confederacy, in Virginia. The word *pocahontas* means "playful one," and apparently was applied to several of Powhatan's daughters. This fact may account for William Strachey's statement (*post,* p. 54) that a "Pocahuntas . . . rightly called Amonate . . . married a private captaine called Kocoum."

John Smith's *True Relation* speaks of Pocahontas as being "a child of tenne yeres old" in 1607, when the English first landed in Virginia, "which in feature, countenance, and proportion much exceedeth any of the rest of [her] people" (Arber and Bradley, *post,* I, 38). Strachey (p. 111) describes her (or perhaps another daughter of Powhatan) as "resorting to our fort, of the age then of eleven or twelve years," where she would get the boys "forth with her into the market place," and there vie with them in turning handsprings. In 1608 Capt. John Smith [*q.v.*] was captured by Powhatan, and, according to his statement in the *Generall Historie,* printed in 1624, would have been killed had it not been for Pocahontas. "Two great stones were brought before *Powhatan,*" he says, "then as many as could layd hands on him, dragged him to them, and thereon laid his head, and being ready with their clubs, to beate out his braines, *Pocahontas* the King's dearest daughter, when no intreaty could prevaile, got his head in her armes, and laid her owne upon his to saue him from death" (Arber and Bradley, II, 400). The story of this rescue has caused a protracted dispute among Virginia historians. Charles Deane, Edward D. Neill, and others early doubted the truth of Smith's account, pointing out that he made no mention of the incident in his early *Relation,* and spoke of it only after Pocahontas had aroused widespread interest by her marriage and her visit to England. On the other hand William Wirt Henry, in an address (*post*) delivered before the Virginia Historical Society in 1882, defended Smith's veracity. Henry argued that a part of Smith's original account had been suppressed, and that in the so-called "Oxford Tract" (*The Proceedings of the English Colony in Virginia*) printed in 1612, he had spoken of Pocahontas' affection for him (Arber and Bradley, I, 169). Later historians have also taken sides for or against the story.

In the spring of 1613, Pocahontas fell into the hands of the English. The maid, then about eighteen years of age, was visiting the chief of the Potomacs, when Capt. Samuel Argall [*q.v.*], in the *Treasurer,* came into the Rappahannock River. When Argall heard of her presence in this region he determined to take her as security for the English prisoners and for some stolen arms and tools held by her father. Bringing his vessel around into the Potomac, by alternate threats and persuasions he induced the chief to surrender her. The youthful prisoner was brought to Jamestown, where she was treated with every courtesy. The acting governor, Sir Thomas Dale, was touched by her gentleness and intelligence. "*Powhatans* daughter I caused to be carefully instructed in Christian Religion," he stated, "who, after shee had made some good progresse therein, renounced publickly her countrey Idolatry, . . . and was . . . baptised" (Hamor, *post,* p. 55). She took the Christian name of Rebecca.

While Pocahontas was at Jamestown, John Rolfe, an English gentleman, fell in love with her. After struggling long against a passion so unusual, he wrote to Governor Dale, asking permission to marry her. He was not ignorant, he said, of the inconveniences which might arise from such a marriage, and he recognized the strangeness of being "in love with one whose education hath bin rude, her manners barbarous, her generation accursed, and so discrepant in all nurtriture from myself" (Hamor, p. 64). Nevertheless, he continued, with Pocahontas "my hartie and best thoughts are, and have a long time bin so intangled, and inthralled in so intricate a laborinth, that I was even awearied to unwinde myselfe thereout" (Hamor, p. 63). Dale assented readily to Rolfe's desire, for he saw in this marriage a means of securing the friendship of the Indians. Powhatan, too, expressed his approval, and sent Opachisco, an uncle of the bride, and two of her brothers to represent him at the wedding, which took place in the church at Jamestown in April 1614, with the Rev. Richard Buck officiating. Both English and Indians regarded this union as a bond of friendship between the two races, and it brought a peace which lasted eight years and greatly aided in establish-

ing the colony on a firm footing. "The great blessings of God have followed this peace . . . and it hath bredd our plentie," wrote Rolfe himself (*Southern Literary Messenger,* June 1839).

In 1616 Pocahontas, accompanied by her husband, her brother-in-law Tomocomo, and several Indian maids, sailed for England. She was received with the consideration due a princess, was entertained by the Bishop of London "with festivall, state and pompe," attended a masque, and was presented to the King and Queen by Lady De La Warr. Everywhere she "did not only accustome her selfe to civilitie, but still carried her selfe as the Daughter of a King" (Purchas, *post,* p. 118). Early in 1617 she prepared to return to Virginia with her husband in the *George,* but at Gravesend she became ill and died. "She made not more sorrow for her Vnexpected death, than ioy to the beholders to heare and see her make so religious and godly an end" (Smith, *Generall Historie,* Arber and Bradley, II, 535). She was buried in the chancel of the Gravesend church. Her one son, Thomas Rolfe, who was left at Plymouth in the care of Sir Lewis Stukly, later came to Virginia, where many of his descendants now reside.

[*Travels and Works of Capt. John Smith* (2 vols., 1910), ed. by Edward Arber and A. G. Bradley; Ralph Hamor, *A True Discourse of the Present Estate of Virginia* (1615; facsimile reprint, 1860); W. W. Henry, in *Proc. Va. Hist. Soc.,* 1882; Alexander Brown, *The Genesis of the U. S.* (2 vols., 1890); Wm. Strachey, *The Historie of Travaile into Virginia Britannia* (Hakluyt Society, 1849); Samuel Purchas, *Hakluytus Posthumus, or Purchas His Pilgrimes,* vol. XIX (Glasgow, 1906).]

T. J. W.

POE, EDGAR ALLAN (Jan. 19, 1809–Oct. 7, 1849), poet, critic, and writer of short stories, was born in Boston, Mass., the son of David and Elizabeth (Arnold) Poe. On his father's side his ancestors were of Scotch-Irish descent, having emigrated out of Ireland to Lancaster County, Pa., about 1748. David Poe, the grandfather of the poet, married Elizabeth Cairnes (also spelled Carnes), likewise of an Irish family settled in Pennsylvania, and shortly before the outbreak of the Revolution he moved to Baltimore, Md., where he set up as a furniture maker and also took an active and patriotic part in driving out the British authorities. He was appointed quartermaster at Baltimore, Nov. 19, 1777 (F. B. Heitman, *Historical Register of the Officers of the Continental Army,* 1914, p. 444), and during Lafayette's Virginia campaign is said to have rendered important aid to the American arms. He was afterward referred to as "General" Poe. Lafayette visited his grave in 1824 and the widow of the "General" was long in receipt of a pension. David and Elizabeth (Cairnes) Poe had seven children of whom David Poe was the eldest son. Maria Poe their daughter (afterwards Mrs. William Clemm), the poet's aunt, became his mother-in-law.

Elizabeth Arnold Poe [*q.v.*], the poet's mother, born in London, was the daughter of Henry and Elizabeth (Smith) Arnold, an actor and actress. After the death of Henry Arnold his widow brought Elizabeth to America early in 1796. They landed in Boston. Shortly before this or soon afterward, Mrs. Arnold married a fellow actor, Charles Tubbs, and in company with him she appeared in various cities, along with her daughter, who filled juvenile rôles. In the theatre set up by Tubbs at Portland, Me., Elizabeth Arnold played Biddy Bellair in *Miss in Her Teens,* Nov. 21, 1796. Left an orphan, apparently about 1798, she continued her career as an actress, and in 1802 married C. D. Hopkins, an actor in her company. He died Oct. 26, 1805. There were no children from this union. David Poe, the poet's father, was born July 18, 1784 (Killis Campbell, *Poems of Edgar Allan Poe,* p. xi). He was brought up in Baltimore and put to reading law. Becoming stagestruck from acting in amateur theatricals, he went to Augusta, Ga., and later to Charleston, S. C., where he went on the professional stage. Later, coming north, he found himself in the same company with Elizabeth Arnold Hopkins, whom he soon married. While in Boston, Mrs. Poe gave birth to two sons, William Henry Leonard early in 1807, who was left with his grandparents in Baltimore, and Edgar. The parents were very poor and had only their stage earnings, which were trivial. Mrs. Poe was good looking, with the high forehead and great eyes that characterized Edgar, was popular in a minor way, and possessed of considerable histrionic powers. Her husband's abilities were meager, and he seems to have been a weak character. The date of his death is uncertain; perhaps he died in October 1810; and previously he may have deserted her. Mrs. Poe continued her labors to support herself, taking Edgar with her from place to place. In December 1810, at Norfolk, Va., she gave birth to a daughter, Rosalie. She went to Charleston, S. C., soon afterward. In the summer of 1811 she returned to Richmond where she succumbed, probably to an attack of pneumonia, under circumstances of dire poverty in the house of a Richmond milliner on Dec. 8, 1811. She was buried in St. John's churchyard, Richmond, where a monument was unveiled Apr. 10, 1928. Of the three children who survived, William Henry Leonard remained with his grandparents in Baltimore, Rosalie was taken home by Mrs. William Mackenzie of Richmond, and Edgar was fostered by Mrs. John Allan.

John Allan (1780–1834), in whose household Poe was brought up as a foster son (never legally adopted), was a Scotch merchant in moderate circumstances, the junior partner in the firm of Ellis & Allan, in Richmond, Va. His wife, Frances Keeling Valentine (1784–1829), was childless, and it was largely due to her influence that the child Edgar, despite some attempt on the part of his relations in Baltimore to obtain the care of him, became a fixture in the Allan household. According to trustworthy legend the boy was early put to a dame school kept by an old Scotch woman, and at the age of five or six he attended the school of a Master William Ewing for a short time. Early accounts agree that the young Poe was carefully nurtured, somewhat "spoiled" by his foster mother and her sister Anne Moore Valentine, and rather sternly but none the less carefully corrected by his foster father, who for long took a great pride in Edgar's precocious and pretty ways.

In 1815 John Allan and his family, including Edgar Poe and Miss Valentine, sailed for Great Britain in order to establish an English office of his firm. The boy was sent to Irvine, Scotland, where he was at school a short time. He then went to the boarding school of the Misses Dubourg in Chelsea, remaining until the spring of 1817. In the fall of that year he was entered at the Manor House School of the Rev. Mr. Bransby at Stoke Newington. Here he continued until, Allan's business in London proving unsuccessful, he left England with his foster parents in June 1820, reaching Richmond in August. For a short time they occupied the house of the senior partner, Charles Ellis, at the corner of Franklin and Second streets. Although Poe was young, this trip abroad left a profound impression upon him. In later years he frequently referred to it in his prose and even his verse, and in "William Wilson" he has left a vivid impression of his English schooldays.

In the fall of 1820 Poe was sent to school in Richmond to an Irishman, Master Joseph H. Clarke of Trinity College, Dublin, in company with the sons of many of the best families of the place. Poe now began to write verses, "a volume" of which was shown about 1824 to Master William Burke, Clarke's successor at the academy, by Allan (Woodberry, *post,* p. 24; Allen, *Israfel,* p. 101). Several childish but characteristic verses of about this time still exist (*Israfel,* pp. 93, 124). They are in a tragic or satirical vein. Allan had in the meanwhile involved himself in great financial difficulties. It was while at Burke's academy that Poe was taken home by a younger schoolmate, Rob Stanard, the son of Judge Robert Stanard, and introduced to the boy's mother. Jane Stith Stanard was a beautiful and sympathetic woman who aroused in the young Poe a youthful and romantic worship. In April 1824 the lady died in circumstances of great tragedy and there is a tradition that Poe visited her grave at night. At any rate in "To Helen" his most famous lines are addressed to her: "Helen, thy beauty is to me" (S. H. Whitman, *Edgar Poe and His Critics*, 1860, p. 50).

In 1824 Lafayette visited Richmond, and upon this occasion Poe as the lieutenant of a cadet organization helped to receive him. The boy now first seems to have been really "about town" and to have come across evidences of his foster father's domestic infidelity. From this time on, evidence of great stress in the Allan household is not lacking. In November 1824 John Allan wrote a letter to Poe's elder brother in Baltimore in which, by hinting at possible indiscretions of Mrs. Poe and the illegitimacy of Rosalie, the poet's sister, the older man attempted to seal the mouth of his ward as to his own marital indiscretions. The letter is a decidedly "pious" and cold-blooded affair in which Poe is pictured as ungrateful, with bitter complaints. In 1825 John Allan inherited a fine fortune from his uncle, William Galt ('Galt's will, in *Israfel*, II, 859–64), which made him one of the richest men in Virginia. The family soon moved into a "mansion" long known as the "Allan House" at the corner of Main and Fifth Streets, Richmond, where they lived in considerable style and with lavish hospitality. In this turn for the better young Poe fully participated and he also confidently counted on a future participation as the long-cherished foster child of the house. For some time he had been known as "Edgar Allan," but by 1824 he was signing himself "Edgar A. Poe," thus preserving at least in part the use of his foster father's name. He had done well at school, was rather brilliant at languages, and a remarkably able swimmer. A swim of six miles under a hot sun in the James was long remembered in Richmond. This was accomplished when he was only about fifteen. He seems even then to have had Lord Byron in mind. In the loft of his father's firm, which imported books, music, and periodicals, Poe had early become familiar with much of the current of literary tendencies and criticism. His literary horizon was for a young man in a provincial capital surprising. He had also followed his heart as well as his head and had been paying court to a neighbor's daughter,

Sarah Elmira Royster, to whom he was secretly engaged when his foster father, after a brief period of tutoring, sent him to the University of Virginia early in 1826. The relations between Allan and his "son" it is safe to say were already somewhat strained. Poe had considered his foster mother ill-used and had taken her part in domestic strife.

Poe matriculated on Feb. 14, 1826, in the schools of ancient and modern languages but remained at the University only for one term. He left the following Christmas under a distinct cloud. The causes of this were somewhat complicated. Owing to the apparently calculated stinginess of his foster father (Poe to Allan, Jan. 3, 1831, Stanard, *post*, pp. 253–58), Poe found himself in debt to the institution upon the date of his arrival and with no spending money whatever. He was known to be the "son" of a rich man, the University was new, its students mostly the gay sons of easy-going planters, and the discipline was at that time very lax. Poe attempted to provide himself with funds at cards, lost, plunged heavily, exploited his credit with local merchants in order to pay, and ended about $2,500 in debt. Tales of his heavy drinking as a student can be dismissed as fond recollections of classmates in a moral old age. Poe drank enough, however, to prove that a very little was extraordinarily disastrous to him. "Less than a little was with him too much." Correspondence with his sweetheart Miss Royster had been intercepted by her parents, and Poe had no word from her. Despite these worries, he distinguished himself in both Latin and French and was in excellent standing with the authorities. Bills for his debts being rendered to Allan, however, that gentleman withdrew his "son" from the University in great indignation. Poe wished to return, but his foster father refused to pay his losses at cards. Without that, return was impossible. Allan now wished to have Poe take up the reading of law; Poe on his part was bent on a literary career. With this ambition Allan had no patience. A violent quarrel between the two occurred, Mar. 18, 1827, and the next day Poe left his foster father's house to seek his fortune under an assumed name.

He took ship either from Richmond or Norfolk, Va., and went to Boston where he arrived some time in April 1827 (Stanard, *post*, pp. 51–53). He did not, as some biographers assert, at this time go to England. Arrived in Boston, Poe now entered into an arrangement with an obscure young printer, Calvin F. S. Thomas, to print his first volume, *Tamerlane and Other Poems* (1827), a small pamphlet bound in tea-colored wrappers. The author, who was probably still under an alias, Henri Le Rennét, was content to let his poems appear as "By a Bostonian." The edition must have been small; only a few copies were sent out for review or exposed for sale. What became of the rest is not known. The verse in this volume gives only a hint of the poet's more mature powers but it is not without a peculiar distinction and great promise. The influence of Byron is evident, but the usual note of "blasted hope" is lifted out of the commonplace by lines of genuine emotion rooted in experience, and a delicate mystical touch is achieved here and there. The strange beauty of Poe is already adumbrated. The young poet, probably because of the cost of printing his poems, and his inability to find employment, now found himself in desperate circumstances. On May 26, 1827, he enlisted in the United States Army under the assumed name of Edgar A. Perry, giving his age as twenty-two although he was only eighteen. He is described in army records as having gray eyes, brown hair, a fair complexion, and as being five feet eight inches in height. The new recruit was assigned to Battery H of the 1st United States Artillery at Fort Independence, Boston harbor.

Poe's regiment was ordered south at the end of October. From November 1827 to December 1828 he performed garrison duty at Fort Moultrie, Sullivan's Island, S. C., near Charleston. Here much of the material for his story, "The Gold Bug," written years later, was gathered. He attracted the favorable attention of his officers, was given clerical employment, appointed artificer and finally sergeant, and upon the removal of his unit to Fortress Monroe was made regimental sergeant-major Jan. 1, 1829. In the meantime he had entered into correspondence with John Allan, desiring to be released from the army. Allan was obdurate, but upon Poe's proposal that he should be sent to West Point, backed by the hearty recommendations of his officers, Allan consented to interest himself. The foster father's decision was also brought about by the death of his wife on Feb. 28, 1829 (*Richmond Enquirer*, Mar. 3, 1829). She on her deathbed pleaded for her foster son, and upon the arrival of Poe "the night after the burial" (Poe to Allan, Jan. 3, 1831, Stanard, pp. 253–58), a reconciliation, formal rather than real, took place between him and John Allan. Poe was honorably discharged from the army Apr. 15, 1829, and hastened to Richmond. Here he received letters of warm recommendation from friends and a cold one from his guardian, and set out for Washington where he presented them to the secretary

of war, requesting an appointment to West Point. For this he had long to wait.

He proceeded, in May 1829, to Baltimore, where he lived on a pittance sent him by John Allan. He now first saw his relatives, his grandmother Mrs. David Poe, Mrs. Maria Clemm his aunt, and her daughter Virginia, his future wife, and others. For some time he lived with Mrs. Clemm and his elder brother, William Henry Leonard Poe. On May 11 he called on William Wirt to obtain help in publishing another volume of poems and the next day went to Philadelphia to try to get Carey, Lea & Carey to publish them. Allan refused indignantly to guarantee a small amount and on July 28 Poe withdrew his manuscript. He now secured Hatch & Dunning of Baltimore as his publishers, and, heralded by notices by John Neal [*q.v.*] in the *Yankee; and Boston Literary Gazette* for September and December 1829, his second volume appeared in December as *Al Aaraaf, Tamerlane, and Minor Poems*. Its contents showed a great gain in poetical form over the preceding book. Of the two longer poems, "Al Aaraaf" contained some beautiful passages but was deficient in "architecture." "Tamerlane" was greatly revised and seems to echo Poe's love affair with Miss Royster, now married to A. Barrett Shelton of Richmond at the behest of her parents. In January 1830 Poe returned to Richmond, where he had further quarrels with his foster father. He received his appointment to West Point, passed his examinations, and entered the Military Academy on July 1, 1830.

His presence there was entirely due to his desire to get an education, to escape from the lower ranks of the army, and to reinstate himself in the good graces of John Allan, which he could do only in this way. Allan married a second time in October 1830 and it was soon amply apparent that Poe now had little to expect from him or his family. A letter of Poe's containing an unfortunate remark about Allan now fell into the latter's hands and he wrote forthwith disowning Poe, who now determined to leave the army entirely. He deliberately neglected his roll calls and academic duties and was dismissed for "gross neglect of duty" and "disobedience of orders" on Mar. 6, 1831. Released a few days earlier, he arrived in New York Feb. 20, 1831, sick and penniless. At West Point he had arranged for the publication of a volume of poetry, subscribed to by the cadets, to whom it was dedicated. This appeared, probably in April 1831, as *Poems by Edgar A. Poe* (2nd ed., New York, published by Elam Bliss, 1831); the titlepage contained a line from La Chaussée attributed to Rochefoucault.

This book, Poe's third, contained thirteen poems, notably "To Helen," "Israfel," and "The Doomed City," all later much revised, and "Letter to B" as a preface, in which Poe first developed some of his favorite critical theses, certain of which were taken almost verbatim from Coleridge. The book attracted little attention. From New York Poe went to Baltimore, where he arrived about the end of March 1831 and took up residence with Mrs. Clemm and her daughter Virginia. He continued in Baltimore until the summer of 1835. His early years there are obscure, but there is no genuine evidence of his having gone on foreign voyages as some of his biographers suggest. Letters to John Allan in Richmond show that he still hoped to mollify his guardian's opinion. He now became quite intimate with many of his cousins, paid attention to a neighbor's daughter with evident serious intent, and, it seems all but certain, narrowly escaped going to jail for a debt of his brother W. H. L. Poe, who died Aug. 1, 1831. On this occasion John Allan aided Poe for the last time. Poe now first began to write prose extensively. On Jan. 14, 1832, he published his story, "Metzengerstein" in the *Saturday Courier* of Philadelphia, having entered it for a prize which went to Delia Bacon. He was now experiencing desperate poverty, which spurred him on. In June 1832 he paid a visit to Richmond in order to see his foster father, who was in precarious health. He had an unfortunate encounter with the second Mrs. Allan and was ordered from the house with furious indignation by John Allan, whom he never saw again. All hopes of a legacy were now at an end. Allan died Mar. 27, 1834 (*Richmond Enquirer,* Apr. 1, 1834). He provided for his legitimate and several natural children in his will but did not mention Poe. The latter half of the year 1832 appears to have been spent in Baltimore, but there exists a letter from Dumas the elder which tells of his meeting Poe in Paris "in the summer of 1832."

In October 1833 Poe first attracted considerable notice. He had already published five stories in Philadelphia in 1832 with little or no effect, but in the month mentioned he won a prize of $50 for the best short story submitted to the *Baltimore Saturday Visiter.* This was "A MS. Found in a Bottle," which appeared in the issue of the paper for Oct. 19, 1833. The story had been submitted with several others as one of "The Tales of the Folio Club." The judges would also have awarded the poetry prize to Poe for "The Coliseum" but, not desiring to give two prizes to one person, awarded that for poetry to "Henry Wilton" (J. H. Hewitt) for "Song of

the Winds." The publicity connected with the prize gave Poe something of a reputation. A more important outcome, however, was that it gained for the young writer the friendship of an influential and kindly disposed Baltimorean, John P. Kennedy [*q.v.*]. Kennedy now became Poe's patron, aided him substantially, and in the spring of 1835 introduced him to T. W. White, the editor of the *Southern Literary Messenger* in Richmond, Va. Poe now began to contribute to the *Messenger,* and in June 1835 it was suggested to him that he come to Richmond on the staff of the paper (Woodberry, I, 110 ff.). An attack of illness, which from now on became frequent with Poe, and the death of his grandmother Mrs. David Poe delayed his acceptance of White's offer. It was midsummer when he finally went to Richmond, leaving Mrs. Clemm and his cousin Virginia in Baltimore.

Poe rapidly proved himself an "inspired" editor, and the light of his literary, critical, and poetical genius began to glow brightly in the pages of the *Southern Literary Messenger.* Subscribers increased rapidly. Despite this, White was forced to part with Poe who was now drinking in order to ward off melancholia (Poe to Kennedy, Sept. 11, 1835; Woodberry, I, 138–39). The results were disastrous and Poe returned to Baltimore. On Sept. 22, 1835, he took out a license in that city to be married to his cousin Virginia Clemm. Authorities disagree as to whether or not a secret marriage took place at this time. Virginia was only a child of thirteen while Poe was twenty-six. Upon a promise to abstain from drink, Poe was now reinstated on the *Messenger* staff by White, and he returned to Richmond where he was joined a few weeks later by Virginia and Mrs. Clemm at a boarding-house on Capitol Square. Poe's activities were now threefold: editing the *Messenger,* trying to borrow money from relatives and funds to set up Mrs. Clemm as a boarding-house keeper, and endeavoring to get some of his stories published in book form. Only in the first was he entirely successful. By the end of December 1836 he had published eighty-three reviews, six poems, four essays, and three stories in the *Messenger.* His criticism was trenchant and attracted material notice to his magazine; both favorable comment and indignant replies were forthcoming. During his incumbency as assistant editor the subscription list leaped from 500 to 3,500 and over (Woodberry, I, 184). He was now receiving about $1,000 a year salary. Negotiations for publishing his stories in volume form proved abortive, but "Arthur Gordon Pym," two installments of which were first published as a serial in the *Messenger* (Jan., Feb. 1837), was finally accepted by Harper & Brothers. Poe had soon become discontented with the limited scope of his audience, and, having already formed convictions as to the kind of magazine he desired to edit, he now broke off his connection with the *Southern Literary Messenger* to go to New York. The parting with White was friendly, but there are indications that by the end of 1836 Poe had again been drinking. In Richmond a public marriage had been celebrated with Virginia; this was performed by the Rev. Amasa Converse in May 1836. Taking Mrs. Clemm and his child-wife with him, Poe left for New York in January 1837.

Here they took up residence with William Gowans, a bookseller, and other boarders, at 113½ Carmine St. Poe was soon disappointed in his hopes of obtaining literary work and found himself poverty stricken during a time of financial panic. In June 1837 he published "Von Jung, The Mystific," in the *American Monthly Magazine,* and "Siope—A Fable," somewhat later in the *Baltimore Book* (1838). A review of John Lloyd Stephens' *Incidents of Travel in Egypt, Arabia Petraea, and the Holy Land* (1837) followed in the *New-York Review* for October 1837. In July 1838 was published Poe's fourth book, *The Narrative of Arthur Gordon Pym.* This is a highly imaginative tale of shipwreck and gloomy horrors in the South Seas and antarctic regions, in the genre of Nordhoff and Hall's *Mutiny on the Bounty,* combined with Jules Verne-like adventure and Coleridgian landscape. The narrative purported to be by Pym himself. In this book Poe's interest in cryptograms was first evidenced.

Unable to make a living in New York, Poe moved to Philadelphia in the summer of 1838, where he resided successively in a boarding house on 12th Street near Arch, at 127 Arch St., and at the corner of 16th and Locust streets. Shortly after his arrival, he was engaged by a Prof. Thomas Wyatt to edit for the latter *The Conchologist's First Book: or, A System of Testaceous Malacology, Arranged Expressly for the Use of Schools* (1839). This was a "pirated" textbook typical of the loose publishing of the time. The preface was by Poe, the text by Thomas Brown from whose book the engravings also were copied, the descriptions were translated from Cuvier, and the glossary and index were by Wyatt. To this, Poe, for a small consideration, lent his name, and it is hence reckoned as his fifth published volume. He was later attacked for plagiarism for this book and got into ill odor with Harper & Brothers about it.

Poe now for some time engaged in free-lance publishing. In May 1839 he was offered regular employment by an Englishman, William E. Burton [*q.v.*], and in July became co-editor of *Burton's Gentleman's Magazine,* continuing in this capacity until June 1840. To this sheet Poe contributed many famous stories, notably "The Fall of the House of Usher," "William Wilson," and "Morella" in the fall of 1839, besides book reviews and poems. He now also entered into correspondence with Washington Irving, soliciting criticism for his own (Poe's) work. Another contribution to *Burton's,* in installments, was "The Journal of Julius Rodman" (beginning in Jan. 1840), for some time overlooked as part of Poe's work but undoubtedly his. About the beginning of 1840 he moved to a house on Coates Street. The end of the year 1839 was marked by the publication of his sixth bound work: *Tales of the Grotesque and Arabesque* (copyright 1839, title-page date 1840). The two volumes contained some of the most famous of the author's tales. The sale was nil (Lea & Blanchard to Poe, Aug. 16, 1841, Woodberry, I, 295–96).

Poe quarreled with Burton; became reconciled, and quarreled again. He now set about the establishment of a magazine of his own, and before January 1841 sent out a *Prospectus of The Penn Magazine* in which his theory of magazine publishing, a sound one for the times, was well set forth. "The Penn" was about to become a fact when the plans for it were dropped by its proposed editor to accept a position with George Rex Graham [*q.v.*], a Philalelphia purchaser and editor who had purchased the *Casket* and later *Burton's Gentleman's Magazine,* and now established his own, *Graham's Lady's and Gentleman's Magazine,* on a rather lavish scale. Poe continued as literary editor of *Graham's* from January 1841 until May 1842 (*Poe Census,* II, 33). During that time the magazine increased from 8,000 to 40,000 subscribers and became the most popular in the United States. It was the first magazine in America or Europe on a "huge" modern scale. Graham was kind to Poe but gave him only $800 a year, and a small page rate. As literary editor of *Graham's* he vastly increased his influence and fame, while he entered into correspondence with most of the famous American authors of his time. He had already become a force in American letters. In the spring of 1842, because of precarious health, irregularities owing to lapses into drink, and the revival of his ambition to publish his own magazine, Poe parted from *Graham's.* After a long spree and a visit to an old Baltimore flame, he was found in destitute circumstances and brought back to Philadelphia by Mrs. Clemm.

The remainder of Poe's sojourn in Philadelphia was a period of great poverty, visionary schemes to publish his magazine, now called "The Stylus," which never appeared, and attempts to obtain government employ which were also abortive. Dissipation played its part. His wife was now advanced in tuberculosis, and an incurable poverty kept him wretched. Occasional contributions to *Graham's* and other publications scarcely served to keep the wolf from the door. The benign and provident Mrs. Clemm alone kept the family alive at times. Poe now began to perfect the mystery story, of which "The Murders in the Rue Morgue," "The Mystery of Marie Rogêt," and "The Gold Bug" were outstanding examples. It is debatable whether he was the first to write such stories but it is true that he now conferred upon them a perfection of method and form which has ever since caused them to be recognized as a distinct type of short prose fiction.

In March 1842 Poe had an interview with Charles Dickens at the United States Hotel in Philadelphia at which the state of international copyright law was discussed and Dickens' aid was asked for obtaining Poe's English publication (Woodberry, I, 327). Poe's review of *Barnaby Rudge* had attracted Dickens' attention, and from the story came Poe's idea of the croaking raven in his poem of that name. In Philadelphia, Poe was intimate with various members of the literary and artistic groups. From Washington, F. W. Thomas wrote and came to visit Poe; he once secured him a lecture at the Capital City where Poe went in March 1843, lapsed into drink, and embarrassed his friends greatly. There is also some record of a visit to Saratoga Springs for recovering from illness, and news of the first drafts of "The Raven." Hopes of bringing out "The Stylus" were for a time abandoned. Poe won a $100 cash prize with his story, "The Gold Bug," published in the *Dollar Newspaper*, June 21, 28, 1843. This proved to be one of his most popular efforts. A recorded attempt to sell an early version of "The Raven" to *Graham's* failed, but a collection was taken up for its unfortunate author. Some time during 1843 Poe attempted to publish his prose romances in "a uniform serial edition" of pamphlets at twelve and a half cents each. One octavo pamphlet, containing "The Murders in The Rue Morgue," and "The Man That Was Used Up," is known. Another, containing only the first story, was almost certainly a salesman's dummy. He had now exhausted or

lost his opportunities in Philadelphia, and on Apr. 6, 1844, he took Virginia with him, left Mrs. Clemm to close the house at 234 (now 530) North 7th St., where he had been living for almost two years—and with $4.50 in pocket arrived in New York.

In New York, Poe for a time engaged again in free-lance publishing; the New York *Sun* for Apr. 13, 1844, carried his "Balloon Hoax." In the summer of 1844 he and his family boarded at a farmhouse near 84th Street and Broadway. Here "The Raven" was written into final form. "The Raven" was first published anonymously in a newspaper, the *New York Evening Mirror,* on Jan. 29, 1845, in advance of the *American Review* (Feb. 1845). On Feb. 8 it was published in the weekly *New-York Mirror,* and signed by Poe. The success of this poem was enormous and may be said to have first really rendered him famous. Its author had been retained by N. P. Willis [*q.v.*] for editorial work on the *New-York Mirror,* where Poe now began to attack Longfellow in a series of articles. With replies, signed "Outis," these developed into what has been called "The Little Longfellow War." Much of Poe's criticism of Longfellow was well taken, but his cries of plagiarism, favorite ones with him, were based on specious resemblances and without foundation. An article on Poe by J. R. Lowell which appeared in *Graham's Magazine* for February 1845 also served to concentrate attention upon him. It was accompanied by a ludicrously bad "portrait."

In 1845 Poe found himself editor of the *Broadway Journal* with Charles F. Briggs, who withdrew in June, leaving its conduct entirely to Poe. On Oct. 25, 1845, Poe, who borrowed the money, was announced as proprietor. In this sheet he published and republished a mass of his material and contributed a constant stream of critical, newsy, dramatic, literary, and personal matter, much of it ephemeral, but much of trenchant interest. He was now much about town, famous, and received by the *literati* of the day in various self-important "salons." In June 1845 the eighth of his bound works, *Tales,* was published. Late in that year appeared *The Raven and Other Poems.* The first book was a collection of the more popular of Poe's tales made by a well-known editor, Evert A. Duyckinck [*q.v.*], twelve in all. The second contained all of the best of the author's poems to date, and may be said to have been the finest contribution to poetry that had so far been made by an American. A combination of debt, bad health, poverty, his wife's decline, and his own dissipation forced

Poe to relinquish the *Broadway Journal,* the last number appearing on Jan. 3, 1846.

In the spring of 1846 Poe moved his family to "Turtle Bay" on the East River, and in May to a little cottage at Fordham (now in Poe Park at that place) where the poet's life entered upon its all but final tragic phase. In *Godey's Lady's Book* from May to October 1846 inclusive he published a series of articles known as "The Literati of New York City," in which he discussed with a freedom that sometimes gave offense both the personalities and the work of various literary lights, men and women, then present in and about Manhattan. A considerable dash of genuine literary criticism is to be found in them, but they are too often referred to as if they constituted the main body of his criticism, whereas they were conceived in a popular, journalistic, and ephemeral manner which their subjects for the most part warranted. Out of these papers arose a quarrel with Thomas Dunn English [*q.v.*], who charged Poe with forgery. Poe sued the *New-York Mirror,* which published the charges, for libel, and won the suit on Feb. 17, 1847 (*New York Tribune,* Feb. 18, 1847). English did not appear to defend himself. Poe was now in constant bad health, his wife was dying, and at Fordham he sounded the depths of poverty. He was for almost six months unable to write anything and lived withdrawn from the world (Poe to Chivers, July 22, 1846; Allen, *Israfel,* II, 710). In the winter of 1847 the whole family nearly died of cold and starvation. To all of these miseries and her dread disease, the poet's wife Virginia finally succumbed Jan. 30, 1847 (*New York Tribune,* Feb. 1, 1847). Her remains were buried at Fordham but were later removed to Baltimore beside those of her husband. Mrs. Clemm now remained the sole refuge of the soul-stricken poet who would certainly have long since perished without her.

Poe now sought female sympathy ardently. Apparently, the comfort and devotion of some woman, rather than gratification of passion, was the main desire. Some biographers have supposed him, with considerable show of reason, to have been impotent (Krutch, *post*). Certain proof cannot be deduced, but there can be no doubt whatever that by 1848 Poe was in a depressed, erratic, and thoroughly abnormal condition of body and mind. He attempted to find a "refuge" in Mrs. Mary Louise Shew, a nurse of much experience and the wife of a physician; realizing his condition, she did all she could to alleviate it. The first draft of "The Bells" was composed at her house under peculiar circumstances in the spring of 1848 (Ingram, *post,* who gives a portion of Mrs. Shew's diary). It first appeared in *Sartain's Magazine* a month after its author's death. Poe's demands upon Mrs. Shew became embarrassing, and she was forced to withdraw to avoid gossip. Poe now turned to a widow, Mrs. Sarah Helen Whitman, a minor poet of occasional felicity of Providence, R. I. Correspondence was begun on the basis of admiration for her verses in which Poe claimed to recognize an affinity, and a rather hectic courtship began soon afterwards. In the meantime Poe published *Eureka: A Prose Poem.* An edition with the date 1848 is known. The book, which is marked by a certain grandeur of imagination due partly to Poe's now "exalted" state of ego, contains an ingenious theory of cosmogony and not a few misapplications of contemporary science. Very few people were interested. In July 1848 Poe lectured on the "Poetic Principle" at Lowell, Mass., where he first met a Mrs. Annie Richmond and visited her house, described in part in his "Landor's Cottage." He now "fell in love" with her. He then went to Richmond in hopes of getting subscribers for his darling magazine scheme, "The Stylus," but lapsed again into drink, was rescued by friends, and attempted to fight a duel with John M. Daniel [*q.v.*], editor of the *Richmond Examiner,* over some fancied wrong. The matter was passed off as a joke. After remaining among old friends in Richmond until September he returned north and went to Providence, R. I., where on the first visit he proposed marriage to Mrs. Whitman. She delayed; a romantic correspondence couched in "burning terms" followed. In the meantime Poe was distracted between Mrs. Whitman and Mrs. Richmond. Mrs. Whitman's relatives objected, as property was involved and Poe was known not to be dependable. Poe again visited Mrs. Richmond. Torn between his affection for her and Mrs. Whitman's indecision and attraction, he went to Providence to secure an interview with the latter, but in despair took the train to Boston and attempted to commit suicide by drinking laudanum. An overdose of the drug proved an emetic, and he again went to Providence and secured Mrs. Whitman's promise to marry him on condition that he would never take liquor again. All was arranged for the marriage, when Poe again lapsed and Mrs. Whitman dismissed him finally. He returned alone to Mrs. Clemm at Fordham.

Occasional flashes of intense poetical genius continued to illumine his gloomy existence. "For Annie," addressed to Mrs. Richmond, "Ulalume," "Annabel Lee," and the beautiful "El

Dorado" belong to these latter years. "The Bells" has already been noted. Poe now entered into a correspondence with E. H. N. Patterson of Oquawka, Ill., relative to the publishing of "The Stylus." Money was advanced and on June 29, 1849, the poet took leave of Mrs. Clemm and a befriending poetess, Mrs. S. A. Lewis, and left for Richmond, Va. On the way he stopped off in Philadelphia where he took to drink, had an attack of *mania-a-potu* (Poe to Mrs. Clemm, July 19, 1849, Woodberry, II, 315), wandered the streets in delirium, was arrested, and only finally rescued and sent on to his destination by the kindness of friends.

Arrived in Richmond almost dead, he now attempted to gain control of himself and joined a lodge of teetotalers. For a brief time he succeeded, and during the summer of 1849 was received by his old friends gladly. He renewed many old associations, and lectured with applause. Poe was already famous enough to attract attention on the street when he passed. He began to pay attention to his old flame, Sarah Elmira Royster, now a prosperous widow, Mrs. A. Barrett Shelton, of a rather conventional, pious, and trusting turn of mind. The day of marriage was set and Poe left Richmond Sept. 27, 1849, to go north in order to bring back Mrs. Clemm to his marriage. He proceeded to Baltimore by steamer, where he arrived five days before the election of Oct. 3, 1849. During those five days Poe disappeared. The town was the scene of great political corruption and it is possible that Poe fell into the hands of one of the gangs of "repeaters" and was held while in a drugged or drunken condition, or both, in one of their "notorious coops." On election day he was rescued by Dr. James E. Snodgrass, an old friend, in a semi-conscious and shocking condition at Cooth & Sergeant's tavern. The doctor removed him in a carriage, and in company with Mr. Herring, the poet's cousin, placed him in the care of Dr. J. J. Moran at the Washington Hospital. Poe survived for four days, much of the time in delirium, with few fully conscious intervals. There can be no doubt that his condition was immediately due to alcohol, although there seem to have been other serious complications. Romantic statements as to the edifying nature of the poet's departure made years later by the attendant physician during his subsequent lecture tours cannot be credited. Poe died in great mental agony on the morning of Sunday, Oct. 7, 1849. He was buried two days later in the churchyard of the Westminster Presbyterian Church, Baltimore, where he now rests with Virginia and Mrs. Clemm beside him. Mrs. Clemm after Poe's death lived a hand-to-mouth existence for some years, staying at times with various of his female devotees, and exploiting the growing reputation of her son-in-law in various ways to alleviate her dire poverty. She finally died, Feb. 16, 1871, an inmate of the Church Home and Infirmary in Baltimore. The poet's sister Rosalie lost her home with the Mackenzies in Richmond because of the devastations of the Civil War and also, in July 1874, died in a charitable institution. Poe had no progeny.

A persistent controversy, biographical and literary, has raged about Poe since his death. In this cross fire of attacks and defense the truth has frequently been distorted or overlooked. (The most available account of this controversy is to be found in Ingram, *post*, vol. II.) A treacherous attack by Rufus W. Griswold [*q.v.*], long appended to the only available collected edition of Poe's works, served effectively to malign him for years despite numerous "defenses" published in more ephemeral form. All of this, and there was a vast deal of it, served to build up a legend about Poe's name which will take some determination on the part of any student to penetrate. Only by considerable patience, judgment, and labor can a true estimate of Poe be arrived at even yet. Distorted ones are legion, and the man himself and his work constitute the happy hunting ground for the literary tyro, the "psychologizing" exploiter of pet theories by special pleading, and the maker of snap judgments.

In the practical affairs of everyday life, in many of the common amenities, in the domestic circle, and in the general give and take of earthly existence, Poe was greatly lacking and frequently a complete failure. He could not and did not in any sense of the words "get along" with his fellow men. His relations with women, at least during the latter part of his life, were fantastic and nothing more. He certainly at various times resorted to opiates and he was the victim of alcohol. Combined with all this was an undoubted charm and fascination, a magnetism and a reverse power of antagonism which caused him to be greatly loved by a few, hated by many, and memorable to everybody. He was subjected to devastating influences in youth, practised literature in a time and place when what he had to say and his way of saying it were little appreciated, was constantly ground down by poverty and disappointments and the victim of a succession of tragedies which cannot all be attributed to his own failings. All of this can be summed up by saying that as a man Poe was abnormal, and as a genius unique.

His vogue in the United States from 1845 on,

contrary to the belief of foreign critics, has always been immense. At his death he was already in his native country a famous man. Owing to the fact that his genius was so peculiar and his legend so dark, his effect upon American literature has been less than that of many other writers who bid fair to be forgotten sooner. In England critics such as Saintsbury and Andrew Lang have ranked him among the great minor poets; by too many other critics there, Poe, it is safe to say, has constantly been ignored or belittled. In France, owing largely to the early and brilliant translations of Baudelaire, Poe has exerted in recent years an influence greater than that of any other person writing in English (see chiefly Cambiaire, *post*).

Poe's fame rests on a small bulk of exquisite lyrical poetry, on a few of his stories, and on his contribution to the methods of writing certain types of short prose fiction. His style in prose is essentially a product of his own peculiar genius, unusually effective when used by him, but not to be imitated. His characters are either grotesques or the inhabitants of another world than this. As a critic there is much to be learned from him, but his dicta should be carefully compared with the sources from which he took them, principally Coleridge. Poe's much-quoted pronouncement against long poems is a case in point. Most of his estimates of his contemporaries have been confirmed by time. Owing to the publishing conditions of his day, he was forced frequently into journalistic and fragmentary publication. A much more consistent philosophy, esthetic, critical, and social, emerges from his collected works than might at first blush appear. Much of this must be retrieved from comments upon long-forgotten contemporaries. J. R. Lowell said of Poe in 1845: "As it is, he has squared out blocks enough to build an enduring pyramid, but has left them lying carelessly and unclaimed in many different quarries" (*Graham's Magazine,* Feb. 1845, p. 50). The task of reclaiming them has been a slow one, but as Edgar Allan Poe has one of the most generally admitted claims to the title of "America's Most Famous Man of Letters," it is still going on.

[The *Cambridge Hist. of Am. Literature,* vol. II (1918), contains the best bibliography to the time of its publication. The original sources for the story of Poe's youth are to be found very largely in the Ellis and Allan Papers at the Lib. of Cong., and in *Edgar Allan Poe Letters Till Now Unpublished In The Valentine Museum Richmond, Va.* (1925), ed. by M. N. Stanard. See also Killis Campbell, "Some Unpublished Documents Relating to Poe's Early Years," in *Sewanee Review,* Apr. 1912. For textual references, Killis Campbell, "The Poe Canon," in *The Mind of Poe and Other Studies* (1933), *The Poems of Edgar Allan Poe* (1917), and *Poe's Short Stories* (1927), are to be relied upon. Prof. Campbell has made valuable sugges-

tions in connection with this article. A variorum edition of Poe's complete works is in process of completion by T. O. Mabbott. *The Works of Edgar Allan Poe* (10 vols., 1894–95), ed. by E. C. Stedman and G. E. Woodberry, is generally reliable, but should be checked by Campbell, "The Poe Canon," *ante.* C. F. Heartman and Kenneth Rede, *A Census of First Editions and Source Materials by Edgar Allan Poe in American Collections* (1932), called the *Poe Census,* is extremely useful in running down Poe items. *The Works of the Late Edgar Allan Poe,* with notices by N. P. Willis, J. R. Lowell, and R. W. Griswold (3 vols., 1850; vol. IV, 1856), is now out of date both as to selection and editing. J. H. Ingram, *Edgar Allan Poe, His Life, Letters and Opinions* (2 vols., 1880), contains valuable source material but is frequently mistaken as to facts. J. A. Harrison, *The Life and Letters of Edgar Allan Poe* (2 vols., 1903), and *The Complete Works of Edgar Allan Poe* (17 vols., 1902), though a veritable mine of material, are not to be depended upon for accuracy. G. E. Woodberry, *The Life of Edgar Allan Poe* (revised ed., 2 vols., 1909), is scholarly and accurate but in some places now out of date. M. E. Phillips, *Edgar Allan Poe, The Man* (2 vols., 1926), is valuable for its lavish illustration and its bibliography. Hervey Allen, *Israfel, The Life and Times of Edgar Allan Poe* (2 vols., 1926), embodies the latest discoveries in sources to the date of publication. See also Hervey Allen and T. O. Mabbott, *Poe's Brother* (1926), for the poetry and life of William Henry Leonard Poe. C. P. Cambiaire, *The Influence of Edgar Allan Poe in France* (1927), is exhaustive. See also: Arvède Barine (Cécile Vincens), *Poètes et Névroses* (1898); Charles Baudelaire, *Histoires Extraordinaires* (1856); and Stéphane Mallarmé, *Poèmes d'Edgar Poe* (1888). Among books on Poe in which the various theories of the authors are ingeniously set forth see J. W. Krutch, *Edgar Allan Poe, A Study in Genius* (1926); J. W. Robertson, *Edgar A. Poe, A Psychopathic Study* (1922). R. W. Griswold's famous obituary appeared in *N. Y. Tribune,* Oct. 9, 1849.]   H. A.

POE, ORLANDO METCALFE (Mar. 7, 1832–Oct. 2, 1895), soldier and engineer, was born at Navarre, Stark County, Ohio, the son of Charles and Susanna (Warner) Poe and fifth in descent from George Jacob Poe, who came from Germany before 1742 and settled in western Maryland. One of the sons of the latter, Adam Poe, great-grandfather of Orlando, followed the frontier to Ohio. Orlando entered the United States Military Academy in 1852, was graduated sixth in his class in 1856, and was appointed brevet second lieutenant of Topographical Engineers. He served as assistant topographical engineer on the survey of the northern lakes from 1856 to 1861, attaining the grade of first lieutenant in July 1860. He was married at Detroit, Mich., June 17, 1861, to Eleanor Carroll Brent, daughter of Capt. Thomas Lee Brent, United States Army; she, with one of their four children, survived him.

At the outbreak of the Civil War, Poe assisted in organizing Ohio volunteers. Later he served as topographical engineer in the operations in West Virginia and, as a member of McClellan's staff, assisted in organizing the defenses of Washington. Appointed colonel of the 2nd Michigan Volunteers, Sept. 16, 1861, he commanded that regiment during the Peninsular campaign. At the battles of Williamsburg and Fair Oaks, he was conspicuous for skilful leadership and personal gallantry. He commanded a brigade at Manassas and during the Maryland campaign was commissioned brigadier-general of volunteers, Nov. 29, 1862, and commanded a brigade of the IX Army Corps during the Fredericksburg campaign, and a division of that corps during its subsequent movement to Ohio. His volunteer commission expired Mar. 4, 1863; the senate failed to confirm his reappointment, and he reverted to his regular army rank of captain of engineers. He served as chief engineer of the XXIII Army Corps in the march on Knoxville and after the occupation of that place became chief engineer of the Army of the Ohio. In this capacity he planned and constructed the fortifications of Knoxville, and directed with skill the defensive organization during the siege by Longstreet's army, some months later (July 6, 1864) receiving for his gallant services the brevet rank of major. Years after the war he read before the Michigan Commandery of the Loyal Legion a paper on "Personal Recollections of the Occupation of East Tennessee and the Defenses of Knoxville" which was published in part in *Battles and Leaders of the Civil War* (vol. III, 1889). In December 1863 he was assigned to duty as assistant engineer of the Military Division of the Mississippi. His zeal and versatility soon won the favor of General Sherman who, in April 1864, selected him as his chief engineer. He was brevetted lieutenant-colonel and colonel for gallant services in the capture of Atlanta and Savannah, respectively, and brigadier-general, United States Army, for gallant and meritorious services in the campaign terminating with the surrender of Gen. Joseph E. Johnston.

Brilliant as was his career as a soldier, it was overshadowed by his accomplishments as an engineer. After the war, Poe served as engineer secretary of the Lighthouse Board, 1865–70, being commissioned major, Corps of Engineers, in 1867. In 1870 he became engineer of the Upper Lakes Lighthouse District and superintendent of river and harbor work in the lake region. During this service he built the Spectacle Reef Light, Lake Huron. On Jan. 1, 1873, he was appointed colonel and aide-de-camp to General Sherman, which status he retained until Sherman's retirement in 1884. His duties during this period were concerned with the work of the army in protecting the transcontinental railways under construction at that time, and with varied engineering problems connected with the improvement of communication between the West and the East. He published in 1884, *Ordnance Notes—No. 345 . . . Report on Transcontinental Railways, 1883*. Poe was promoted lieutenant-colonel, Corps of Engineers, in 1882, and colonel in 1888. Becoming, in 1883, superintending engineer of improvement of rivers and harbors on Lakes Superior and Huron and of St. Mary's Falls Canal, he had charge of the improvement of the St. Mary's and Detroit rivers; the ship channel between Chicago, Duluth, and Buffalo; the construction of the dry dock, St. Mary's Falls Canal; and the design and construction of the locks—one of which bears his name—at Sault Sainte Marie. He died in Detroit, of erysipelas contracted as the result of an injury received while inspecting his work at Sault Sainte Marie, and was buried in Arlington National Cemetery.

[Records of the War Dept., 1856–95; G. W. Cullum, *Biog. Reg. Officers and Grads. U. S. Mil. Acad.* (3rd ed., 1891), vol. II; G. O. Seilhamer, in *Kittochtinny Mag.*, Apr. 1905; *Mil. Order of the Loyal Legion of the U. S., Commandery of the State of Mich., Circular No. 14, Ser. of 1895* (1895); *Twenty-seventh Ann. Reunion, Asso. Grads. U. S. Mil. Acad.* (1896); *Battles and Leaders of the Civil War*, vols. III, IV (1888); *War of the Rebellion, Official Records (Army); Detroit Free Press*, Oct. 3, 1895.]   T. F. M.

POINDEXTER, GEORGE (1779–Sept. 5, 1853), delegate, representative, senator from Mississippi, was born in Louisa County, Va., the seventh child of Thomas and Lucy (Jones) Poindexter. His own restless nature and the thinness of the family pocket book made his schooling sporadic, and he read law in several offices before he was admitted to the practice of law, which he began at Milton, Va. In 1802 he removed to Natchez, Miss., taking little with him beyond his own great ability and deep loyalty to Jeffersonian Democracy. Shortly after he reached his destination, W. C. C. Claiborne, the newly chosen governor of the Mississippi Territory, appointed him attorney-general, and, in this capacity, he took part in the efforts to bring Aaron Burr to trial. In 1805 he became a member of the territorial Assembly, which soon sent him as a delegate to Congress. Possibly the most important event of his three terms, from Mar. 4, 1807, to Mar. 3, 1813, was his spirited opposition to the celebrated disunion speech of Josiah Quincy of Massachusetts (*Annals of Congress*, 11 Cong., 3 Sess., col. 525). In 1813 he became a district judge for the territory and though he was bitterly assailed by Andrew Marschalk, an able newspaper editor of the territory, the bar considered him an able and upright judge (Claiborne, *post*, pp. 376–79). In 1815 he published *To the Public*, a pamphlet designed to meet the charges against him. He was a very influential member of the convention that framed the first constitution of Mississippi in 1817, and he founded this document on the philosophy of the Virginia school of democracy. Reëntering Congress as the first representative of the state of Mississippi he served from Dec. 10, 1817, to Mar. 3, 1819. He defended Andrew Jackson's conduct of the Seminole campaign (*Annals of Congress*, 15 Cong., 2 Sess., cols. 936–85), "and the national verdict then was that his arguments were unanswerable" (Claiborne, *post*, p. 391). He was governor of Mississippi from 1820 to 1821. At the request of the legislature while he was governor, he codified the laws of the state and in 1822 was able to present to the legislature his work, the consideration of which was the principal object of the session of 1822. This *Revised Code of the Laws of Mississippi* (1824) was the first real code in Mississippi, and it met with instant and sustained approval. He was defeated for Congress in 1822.

This and other troubles sent him into gloomy retirement. His health was poor, and at times he was unable to walk. The enemies he had made were bitter and unrelenting in exposing the seamy side of his life, particularly by accusing him of unfairness in a duel in which he had killed Abijah Hunt. His family life was also embittered, for with public charges he had divorced Lydia (Carter) Poindexter, his first wife, and disinherited their son; and his second wife, Agatha (Chinn) Poindexter, and their only son died. Though one of the ablest men in Mississippi in his day, he was constantly involved in personal quarrels and newspaper altercations, for he was moody and variable in temper. Because of poor health he refused the commission of chancellor tendered him by Governor Brandon in 1828, and this was also the probable cause of his defeat for the Senate the following year.

His condition improving, he was appointed to the Senate to fill the unexpired term of Robert H. Adams, and later he was elected with negligible opposition to this office. He served from Oct. 15, 1830, to Mar. 3, 1835. In the Senate, he underwent a change that was important in his own career and in national affairs. Beginning with a dispute over the distribution of the patronage in Mississippi he became an unrelenting enemy of Andrew Jackson. The Democratic party in Mississippi detested his course, and hints were dropped that financial transactions with the Bank of the United States explained the change. Yet it seems to be true that he sensed the essential difference between Jacksonian and Jeffersonian Democracy, and he believed his course was more consistent than that of the Democratic party. This party nominated Robert

J. Walker to succeed him; thereupon he campaigned on the Whig ticket in 1835 but was defeated. He did not again serve his state in public office. Broken in body by dissipation and by a severe fall, he removed to Lexington, Ky., but later returned to Jackson, Miss., where he practised law until his death.

[J. F. H. Claiborne, *Mississippi* (1880), able but prejudiced; *Biographical Sketch of the Honorable George Poindexter* (1835), a campaign biography; H. S. Foote, *Casket of Reminiscences* (1874); J. D. Lynch, *The Bench and Bar of Mississippi* (1881); *Woodville* (Miss.) *Republican*, Mar. 11, 1837; *Letters from Jesse Hoyt, Late Collector, to the Sec. of the Treas.* (1842?); W. H. Sparks, *The Memories of Fifty Years* (1870), pp. 335–42; Dunbar Rowland, *Mississippi* (1907), vol. II; M. D. Ackerly and L. E. J. Parker, *"Our Kin"* (1930); *Va. Mag. of Hist. and Biog.*, Apr., Oct. 1912; *Mississippian State Gazette* (Jackson), Sept. 9, 1853; Mack Swearingen, *The Early Life of George Poindexter* (1934).]
C. S. S.

POINSETT, JOEL ROBERTS (Mar. 2, 1779–Dec. 12, 1851), diplomat, statesman, was born in Charlestown (Charleston), S. C., the son of Dr. Elisha Poinsett, a prominent physician, and Ann (Roberts) Poinsett, an English lady and a relative both of the principal of St. Paul's School (London) and of John Dollond, inventor of the achromatic telescope. On the paternal side he was descended from Peter Poinsett, a Huguenot, who emigrated from Soubise, France, near La Rochelle, to Charlestown about 1700. He received his earliest education at the side of his father and under the tuition of the Rev. J. H. Thompson. In 1794 he was sent to the academy of Timothy Dwight [*q.v.*], later president of Yale, which was located at Greenfield Hill, Conn. In 1796 he began his studies abroad, at St. Paul's School, at the medical school in Edinburgh, and under a former teacher in a military academy at Woolwich. His interests centered mainly in the languages, several of which he learned to read and speak fluently, and in natural and military science. Natural inclination led him to prefer the life of a soldier, but his father objected and called him home (1800) to study law under H. W. De Saussure [*q.v.*], who subsequently became chancellor of South Carolina. Law was not suited to his taste. The sojourn in England and a winter spent in Portugal had developed a desire for travel, and late in 1801, after having secured his father's consent, he set out on a long tour of Europe and western Asia. On this he spent the next seven years, with the exception of the brief period (1804–06) required to return to the United States and bury his father and sister, who were the last members of his immediate family. While abroad he met and conversed with many distinguished men, including Necker, Prince de

Ligne, Napoleon, Metternich, and Alexander I.

When war between Great Britain and the United States appeared to be approaching in 1808, he hastened to his native land in the hope of securing a high military appointment. Failing in this, he accepted in 1810 the post of special agent in Rio de la Plata and Chile. Setting sail late in 1810, he proceeded by way of Rio de Janeiro, and early in 1811 reached the mouth of the Plate, in the guise of an Englishman (Rippy, *post*, p. 9). In Buenos Aires he soon began to encourage a movement for independence from Spain. He also negotiated a commercial agreement with the authorities of Rio de la Plata before setting out for Chile, where he was officially received by the provisional government on Feb. 24, 1812. He remained in Chile until April 1814, although he doubtless would have preferred to be employed in the army of his native land, which was at that time engaged in a war with Great Britain. While in Chile, Poinsett became the ardent friend of the Carrera brothers and other patriots who were directing the movement for independence from Spain, following their armies, reconciling their personal differences, and giving them political and military advice. The overthrow of the Carreras, the precarious state of the Chilean insurgents, and the hostile influence of the British, made it necessary for him to leave the country.

He returned to Buenos Aires, where he remained until the middle of September 1814; he then set out for the United States, making his way home via the Madeira Islands. In May 1815, he finally reached Charleston. He did not forget his Chilean friends, however, for during most of the following year he was in correspondence with José Miguel Carrera, who had come to the United States in search of aid for the revolutionary movement. Moreover, in the spring of 1817 President Monroe tendered him an appointment as a special commissioner to southern South America. This appointment Poinsett considered it best to decline.

Poinsett had now become interested in South Carolina politics. Late in 1816 he had been elected as a member of the legislature and in 1818 he was reëlected. His services to his native state during this period were related mainly to the movement for internal improvements—the dredging of rivers and the construction of roads. For two years, 1818–20, he was chairman of the Board of Public Works, under the supervision of which parts of several rivers were improved for navigation and the Saluda Mountain road and the road from Charleston to Columbia were constructed. Moreover, at his own private expense he developed Poinsett Springs, in the heart of the Saluda Mountain. In 1821 he succeeded Charles Pinckney in the federal House of Representatives, taking his seat on Dec. 3, 1821, and continuing his services until Mar. 7, 1825. As a member of Congress Poinsett was not conspicuous. He made only four speeches of any length: in favor of the recognition of the Spanish-American republics; in behalf of a more efficient military organization; in opposition to the recognition of the independence of Greece, not because of lack of sympathy with the Greeks but because he thought the United States might be involved "in a war foreign to its interests" (*Annals of Congress*, 18 Cong., 1 Sess., p. 1105); and in opposition to a protective tariff. The election of 1824 was decided by the House of Representatives, and Poinsett cast his vote for Andrew Jackson.

His career in Congress was interrupted for a brief period, August 1822–January 1823, by a special mission to Mexico. He passed by Cuba on his return and reported to President Monroe on the conditions in that island as well as in Mexico. In 1824 he published *Notes on Mexico*. Probably because he was so well acquainted with Spanish-American affairs, he was appointed (March 1825) as the first American minister to Mexico, although not until this post had been offered to others who possessed greater political influence. His diplomatic services in Mexico extended over a period of nearly four years, which were not altogether happy. Suspected as an intriguer and expansionist, opposed by the British *chargé d'affaires*, allowing himself—unavoidably perhaps—to become involved in the turbulent politics of the young republic, he accomplished little or nothing, became known as a sort of scourge, and finally left Mexico City (January 1830) at the reiterated demand of the Mexican government and the hesitating request of his own.

Returning to Washington, he found his friend President Jackson considerably worried over the threats of South Carolinians to nullify the tariff act of 1828. A few months later he proceeded to Charleston and soon became the leader of the Unionist party of South Carolina. For the next three years he was in the midst of a bitter struggle which required on his part consummate courage and organizing ability of the highest type. He was largely responsible for the organization of militia to defend the Unionist cause, arms and munitions being placed at his disposal by Jackson, though he sought a peaceful settlement (Stillé, *post*, pp. 279–97). After the contest had ended, he married (Oct. 24, 1833)

Mrs. Mary (Izard) Pringle, the widow of his deceased friend John Julius Pringle, and retired to a plantation near Georgetown, where he enjoyed the cultivation of his fields, and the reading of his books.

In 1837 President Van Buren called him from his happy retirement to become secretary of war, and he served as such during the whole of this administration. Of the distinguished ante-bellum war secretaries, it may be doubted whether any surpassed Poinsett in training, industry, or originality. Long a student of military affairs and wholeheartedly devoted to the subject, he took up his duties with energy and fervor. The organization, maintenance, and equipment of the army constituted only a portion of the tasks which devolved upon the secretary of war. They also involved the supervision of internal improvements, the equipment and direction of exploring expeditions, the administration of the mineral lands of the United States, and, indirectly, responsibility for Indian affairs, pensions, and the bounty land offices. During the four years in which he was in charge of the War Department, he improved the status of the regular army, proposed a plan for universal military training and frontier defense, organized a general staff and improved the artillery, added to the equipment and broadened the course of study at the West Point Military Academy, removed more than forty thousand Indians to territory west of the Mississippi River, directed the war against the Seminoles in Florida, and made a sincere, although largely futile, effort to improve the schools devoted to the education of the natives.

In 1841 he again retired to his South Carolina plantation. Although he took no further part in politics, he opposed the Mexican War and the secession movement of 1847–52, refusing to go as a delegate to the Nashville Convention of 1850. He died near Statesburg, Sumter County, S. C., and his remains lie buried in the Cemetery of the Church of the Holy Cross in that village. His devotion to learning was scarcely excelled by his readiness to serve his country. His interest in the Wilkes exploring expedition, the contribution which he made to the founding (1840) of the National Institute for the Promotion of Science and the Useful Arts (whose museum and library were turned over to the Smithsonian Institution in 1862), his gifts of manuscripts and other treasures to the American Philosophical Society and the Pennsylvania Historical Society, the beautiful Poinsettia which he developed from a Mexican flower, all bear testimony to this phase of his interests.

[No adequate biography of Poinsett has been published. The correspondence and Miscellaneous MSS. of Joel R. Poinsett (23 vols.) are in Pa. Hist. Soc., Philadelphia. The chief printed sources are: C. J. Stillé, "The Life and Services of Joel R. Poinsett," in *Pa. Mag. of Hist. and Biography,* July, Oct. 1888; (G. E. Manigault) "A Biog. Sketch of the Hon. Joel R. Poinsett, of S. C.," in *Charleston Year Book* (1887); "Joel R. Poinsett," in *U. S. Mag. and Democratic Review,* Feb., Mar. 1838; W. R. Manning, *Early Diplomatic Relations between the U. S. and Mexico* (1916); W. R. Manning, ed., *Diplomatic Correspondence of the U. S. Concerning the Independence of the Latin-American Nations* (3 vols., 1925); J. F. Rippy, *Rivalry of the U. S. and Great Britain over Latin America* (1929); W. M. Collier and G. F. Cruz, *La Primera Misión de los Estados Unidos de América en Chile* (1926); C. S. Boucher, *The Nullification Controversy in S. C.* (1916); P. M. Hamer, *The Secession Movement in S. C., 1847–52* (1918); obituary in *Charleston Courier,* Dec. 16, 1851.]   J. F. R.

POLAK, JOHN OSBORN (Mar. 12, 1870–June 29, 1931), obstetrician and gynecologist, was born in Brooklyn, N. Y. His father, Karl Theodore Polak, a native of Aix-la-Chapelle, came to the United States in 1856 and in 1868 married Mary Elizabeth Osborn, whose father and maternal grandfather had emigrated from England. John, not very strong in his youth, attended Rutgers Grammar School and was graduated from Rutgers College in 1889. He studied medicine at the Long Island College Hospital and the University of Vermont, receiving the degree of M.D. from both places in 1891. His first appointment was as interne at the Long Island College Hospital, to which he devoted many years of his life. From 1911 to 1931 he was chief obstetrician and gynecologist there and from 1924 to 1929 he was director of the department of obstetrics and gynecology at the Israel-Zion Hospital. As attending or consulting obstetrician or gynecologist, he was connected with a large number of hospitals. His capacity for work seemed unlimited. His teaching positions were numerous, including appointments at the New York Post-Graduate Medical School, the Long Island College Hospital, and Dartmouth Medical School. On Mar. 26, 1931, he was made president of the board of regents of the Long Island College Hospital.

Polak had no hobbies, but devoted his time exclusively to his profession. Seemingly never tired, never diverting his attention from the problem at hand, he directed to each detail an abundance of energy and force that was his most striking characteristic. His tact and diplomacy made him a valuable member of numerous committees on which he served. He was a shrewd business man and organizer; a hard driver but an inspiring teacher, winning the respect and affection of his students. As one of the foremost American obstetricians of the early twentieth century, he was a skilled operator; as one of the best gynecologists, an expert diagnostician. His financial contributions made him a conspicuous benefactor to the medical profession of Brooklyn in general and the Long Island College Hospital in particular. He was president of the American Association of Obstetricians, Gynæcologists and Abdominal Surgeons in 1927; of the New York Obstetrical Society in 1916; of the Medical Society of the County of Kings in 1915; regent of the American College of Surgeons, 1927–30; vice-president of the New York Academy of Medicine, 1931, and of the American Gynæcological Society, 1924; and member of a number of other societies. His writings include: *Manual of Obstetrics* (1913); *Students' Manual of Gynæcology* (1915); *Pelvic Inflammation in Women* (1921); which have all gone through several editions. He served as advisory and contributing editor to the *American Journal of Obstetrics and Gynecology, American Journal of Surgery, and Medical Times and Long Island Medical Journal*. In 1895 he married Bertha Louise Pitkin, to whom he always showed the deepest devotion. One daughter survived him. He died very suddenly of coronary thrombosis —a kind ending of a vigorous, forceful life.

[*Surgery, Gynecology and Obstetrics,* Aug. 1931; *Bull. Medic. Soc. of the County of Kings,* July 1931; *Jour. Am. Medic. Asso.,* July 11, 1931; *Jour. of Obstetrics and Gynæcology of the British Empire,* Autumn 1931; *Who's Who in America,* 1918–19; information from colleagues and daughter.] G. L. A.

POLAND, LUKE POTTER (Nov. 1, 1815– July 2, 1887), jurist, senator, representative, was born in Westford, northwestern Vermont, the eldest son of Luther and Nancy (Potter) Poland. His parents were of good Puritan stock from Massachusetts and he began life with the advantages of a strong body, unusual intellectual power, and inborn qualities of industry, honesty, and faithfulness. These gifts were more than an offset to the handicap of irregular attendance at the public schools. He was obliged by frontier conditions and the straitened circumstances of his family to give a large part of his time in boyhood to labor on the farm and in his father's sawmill, and his formal education ended when he was seventeen with a five months' course at Jericho Academy. After teaching a village school for a brief period he began the study of law and was admitted to the Vermont bar at the age of twenty-one. Beginning his practice at Morrisville, he rose so rapidly in his profession that in 1848 he was elected by a Whig legislature to the supreme court, an unusual tribute to his strong character and professional standing in view of the fact that he was at the time the Free-Soil

candidate for the lieutenant-governorship. Removing his residence to St. Johnsbury in 1850, he served continuously for fifteen years as a member of the highest court of the state, the last five years being its chief justice. In 1865, although apparently assured a life tenure in his high office, he resigned to accept appointment and subsequent election as United States senator to fill the unexpired term caused by the death of Jacob Collamer.

Entering the Senate as a Republican at the beginning of the era of Reconstruction, he served in that body from November 1865 to March 1867. At once assigned to the committee on judiciary, he quickly won respect by his able arguments on constitutional questions, his resistance to extreme partisan demands, and his proposals for constructive legislation—especially for a new bankruptcy law and the compilation and revision of all the statute laws of the United States. Succeeded in the Senate after a term of only sixteen months by Justin S. Morrill [*q.v.*], author of the famous tariff of 1861, Poland was elected to succeed Morrill in the House, an exchange of position which he humorously explained by saying that the Vermont farmers seemed to think that the Senate needed more wool and the House more brains.

He entered the House in March 1867 and served continuously in that body till March 1875. Assigned in the Fortieth Congress to the committee on elections, he was also made chairman of the committee on revision of the laws. The confidence of the House in his judicial-mindedness, independence, and courage led to his being made chairman in succession of three of its select committees whose reports made memorable contributions to Reconstruction history. The first of these committees was that appointed in 1871 to investigate the outrages of the Ku Klux Klan in the South, and its voluminous report greatly influenced Congressional legislation (*House Report No. 22,* 42 Cong., 2 Sess.). The second, appointed in 1872 to investigate the scandalous activities of the Crédit Mobilier Company, submitted a unanimous report which resulted in relegating several high officials to private life and smirched the reputation of others (*House Report No. 77,* 42 Cong., 3 Sess.). The third was appointed in 1874 to investigate affairs in Arkansas and to inquire whether federal interference was advisable in the existing contest in that state between a corrupt and defeated Carpetbag government and the native white government which had supplanted it. The report of this committee (*House Report No. 127,* 43 Cong., 2 Sess.), declaring against any interference by any department of the federal government with the existing government of Arkansas and maintaining that such interference would be unconstitutional, was adopted by the House, 150–81, on Mar. 2, 1875, despite the strenuous opposition of President Grant and his radical followers. The closing speech in the debate by the venerable chairman of the committee was a brief statement of the facts in the case and a strong argument based upon the Constitution and numerous precedents which denied the right of the Executive to interfere in any state government established in an orderly manner, generally supported by its people, and republican in form, as was that of Arkansas. The vote, taken amid great excitement, not only showed the confidence of the House in his wise judgments, but also disclosed the fact that "the tragic era of reconstruction," foisted upon the country mainly by one native of Vermont, Thaddeus Stevens, was soon to end through this patriotic action of another native of that state. Poland's independent course, however, which thwarted the policy of the Administration, cost him what, in his weariness of political strife, had become the goal of his ambition, a federal judgeship.

His most constructive work as a legislator was done as chairman of the House committee on revision of the laws, which position he held from December 1867 to March 1875. The purpose of this committee—which he himself had proposed when in the Senate—was to revise the whole of the statute law of the United States, which already filled seventeen large octavo volumes, and, omitting all obsolete matter, to arrange and consolidate for reënactment by Congress all the statute law which was general and permanent in its nature. The accomplishment of this difficult undertaking within eight years and under extraordinary conditions in both houses in the closing hours of the first session of the Forty-third Congress was universally recognized to be more largely due to Poland than to any of his able colleagues and assistants (*Report . . . of the American Bar Association,* 1887, p. 433). Comprised now in a single volume, *The Revised Statutes of the United States . . . in Force . . . December 1, 1873,* appeared in 1875.

After 1875 Poland resumed the practice of the law in the higher courts except while serving in the Forty-eighth Congress and later for two terms as representative of his fellow townsmen in the Vermont legislature (for St. Johnsbury, 1878; for Waterville, 1886). The interruptions in his political career were due to his conservative character, aristocratic bearing, unwillingness to sacrifice his self-respect in order to win popularity and, more than all, to his complete lack of the small arts of the politician. He married Martha Smith Page of Waterville, Vt., Jan. 12, 1838. She died in 1853, leaving a son and two daughters, and the following year he married her sister, Adelia H. Page. He died of apoplexy at his home in Waterville in his seventy-second year.

[Jonathan Ross, "A Memorial Sketch of Luke Potter Poland," *Proc. Vt. Bar Asso., 1886* (1887) ; *Report . . . of the Am. Bar Asso.,* 1887 ; W. H. Crockett, *Vermont,* vol. V (1923) ; *Biog. Dir. Am. Cong.* (1928) ; C. E. Potter, *Geneals. of the Potter Families and Their Descendants* (1888), pt. ix ; J. F. Rhodes, *Hist. of the U. S.,* vols. VI–VII (1906) ; *Burlington Daily Free Press,* July 4, 1887 ; personal acquaintance.]

J. F. C.

POLK, JAMES KNOX (Nov. 2, 1795–June 15, 1849), eleventh president of the United States, was born in Mecklenburg County, N. C., the eldest of the ten children of Samuel and Jane (Knox) Polk. His ancestry has been traced back to an early time in Scotland. A branch of the family removed to Ireland where their name, Pollok, was contracted into Polk. Late in the seventeenth century Robert Bruce Polk emigrated from Ireland to Maryland, whence his grandson, William Polk, removed to North Carolina. William's son, Ezekiel, colonel in the Revolution, married Mary Wilson, and their fourth child was Samuel Polk, father of the future president. Jane Knox was the daughter of James Knox, of Iredell County, N. C., a captain in the Revolution. She was a rigid Presbyterian, and a woman of intellect and high character. From her James inherited or acquired many of his personal characteristics. Among these were a keen interest in politics and firm religious convictions. Throughout his life James was a strict sabbatarian. His wife was an ardent Presbyterian and he accompanied her regularly to the church of her choice. But his "opinions and predilections" were in favor of the Methodists, with whom he united just before his death. In 1806 Samuel Polk and his family settled in the valley of Duck River, Tenn., where he became a prosperous farmer. Unfitted for manual labor because of his frail body, James was enabled to satisfy his desire for an education. After preparatory studies in academies in Tennessee, he entered the sophomore class at the University of North Carolina in 1815. Then, as in later years, he took life seriously; it is said that he "never missed a recitation nor omitted the punctilious performance of any duty" (*United States Magazine and Democratic Review,* May 1838, p. 200). At his graduation, in 1818, he was awarded first honors in mathematics and the classics, subjects of which he was very fond, as each appealed to his taste for industry and precision.

After his graduation, Polk returned to Tennessee and began the study of law in the office of Felix Grundy [*q.v.*]. Unremitting industry led to quick results, and in 1820 he was admitted to the bar. He began immediately the practice of law at Columbia, in his home county of Maury, where "his thorough academical preparation, his accurate knowledge of the law, his readiness and resources in debate, his unswerving application to business, secured him, at once, full employment, and in less than a year he was already a leading practitioner" (*Ibid.*, p. 201). After three years devoted exclusively to law practice he served two years in the state legislature. Here he quickly established a reputation for business capacity and for superiority in debate. He enjoyed the friendship of Andrew Jackson who had already become an outstanding figure in American politics. On Jan. 1, 1824, Polk married Sarah Childress, whose father was a prosperous farmer near Murfreesboro (Nelson, *post*, page 17). A lady of ability and culture, during the course of her husband's career she was admired by many who despised him, and was one of the most popular mistresses of the White House.

Polk entered Congress in 1825, and among his first messmates were Hugh L. White and John C. Calhoun, both of whom later became his bitter political enemies. His political principles were opposed to the policies advocated by President John Quincy Adams, and loyalty to Jackson also influenced him to aid in putting down the man who was alleged to have cheated the "Old Hero" out of the presidency by a "corrupt bargain" with Henry Clay. He took a leading part in defending Jackson when the latter's execution of the six militiamen was under investigation in Congress. When Jackson became president, Polk was a recognized leader of the administration forces in the House of Representatives. In his first annual message, Jackson displayed hostility to the Bank of the United States; but committees which included several of his friends reported in favor of the institution. Nicholas Biddle, by asking for a new charter, made the bank question the dominant issue in the presidential campaign of 1832. Triumphantly reëlected, Jackson resolved to exterminate the "monster," but he was embarrassed by the fact that many of his supporters had been ardent advocates of the institution. The assault could not be intrusted to the recently converted, but must be conducted by those whose record was unassailable. Polk's orthodoxy could not be questioned, and to him Jackson turned.

When Congress convened in the winter of 1832, Polk was made a member of the committee of ways and means, where he could more effectively train his batteries on the bank. In a confidential letter (Dec. 16, 1832) Jackson furnished him with information to show that "the hydra of corruption is only *scotched, not dead,*" and issued a peremptory order, "Attend to this" (Bassett, *Correspondence of Andrew Jackson,* IV, 501). Polk introduced a bill to sell the bank stock owned by the government and adduced arguments to show that the bank was an unsafe custodian of government money. When, after investigation, the committee of ways and means decided in favor of the bank, Polk submitted a very able minority report in which he said: "Whether the existing facts are sufficient to justify the Executive in taking any steps against the bank . . . is a matter for the decision of the proper officers, acting upon their own views and responsibility" (*House Report No. 121,* 22 Cong., 2 Sess., p. 42). This remark seems to portend the removal of the deposits by which Jackson dealt the bank its mortal blow; in September 1833, the President was ready to take the "executive action" at which Polk had already hinted. In the following December, Polk was made chairman of the committee of ways and means, and he succeeded in having all questions relating to the bank referred to his committee. He was the chief defender of the President, and his speech covered the ground so thoroughly that, although the debate lasted nearly two months longer, there was little for any other administration member to add. Even his most bitter opponent, George McDuffie, gave him credit for debating "with a tact and skill and zeal worthy of a better cause" (*Congressional Globe,* 23 Cong., 1 Sess., p. 286).

During the Jackson administration there arose a controversy involving other Tennesseeans which affected Polk's political future. Jackson had decided to make Van Buren his successor, but Judge Hugh L. White caused dissension in the Democratic ranks by accepting a nomination from the Tennessee legislature. In 1834 Polk and John Bell were rival candidates for the office of speaker of the House. Bell won by soliciting anti-administration votes, and he was also alleged to have instigated White's nomination. White and Bell were added by Jackson to his list of enemies to be denounced, and they soon joined other anti-Jackson elements in forming the new Whig party. Polk was regarded as a martyr who had suffered for his loyalty to the President. He defeated Bell at the next session of Congress, and was later rewarded by being selected by Jackson as the candidate for the presidency. As speaker he was the object of more heckling and abuse than any of his predecessors. On his own account, he had to endure the vituperation of his personal enemies, Bell, Peyton, and Crockett. In addition, enemies of the administration, whether Nullifiers or Whigs, vented their spleen on the Speaker, whom they charged with being the abject slave of the President. Wise and Peyton tried to goad him into fighting a duel, but he suffered their taunts with composure and dignity and set an example of treating such conduct with contempt. His policy was commended by the veteran duelist, General Jackson. As speaker, he was master of the situation. Hard study enabled him to anticipate difficulties before they arose, and he was never caught unprepared. He did not exaggerate when he said in his farewell address: "It has been made my duty to decide more questions of parliamentary law and order, many of them of a complex and difficult character . . . than had been decided . . . by all my predecessors, from the formation of this Government" (*Congressional Globe,* 25 Cong., 3 Sess., p. 252).

Although he would have preferred to remain in Congress, Polk was drafted by his party to be the candidate for governor as the only person who could "redeem" Tennessee from Whig control. Levi Woodbury voiced the party sentiment when he wrote: "I have seldom known the result of any election to be more triumphant & gratifying over the whole Union than that of yours" (Oct. 20, 1839, McCormac, *post,* p. 156). Clay, on the other hand, regarded the outcome as "disastrous" (letter of Oct. 12, 1839, Abernethy, *post,* p. 303 note). The administration of Polk as governor (1839–41) was satisfactory but not eventful. Both he and the legislature were absorbed primarily in national politics. In his campaign for reëlection in 1841, and again in 1843, he was defeated by James C. Jones [*q.v.*], who relied more on buffoonery than on a discussion of political issues.

The Whigs gained control of the federal government in 1840; and, much chagrined, the Democrats began early to lay plans for "redeeming" the country in 1844. Clay would surely be the Whig candidate; and Van Buren's nomination by the Democrats was thought to be inevitable. The main question seemed to be, whether Polk or Richard M. Johnson should be given the nomination for vice-president. Polk had coveted this honor, but not until Van Buren wrote the fatal anti-Texas letter was Polk's name associated with the presidency. By his Texas treaty, Tyler had made annexation the dominant political issue, and candidates for both the presidency and the vice-presidency were sounded as

to their views on the subject. Clay and Van Buren responded in opposition to annexation, but Polk answered: "Let Texas be reannexed, and the authority and laws of the United States be established and maintained within her limits, as also in the Oregon Territory, and let the fixed policy of our government be, not to permit Great Britain or any other foreign power to plant a colony or hold dominion over any portion of the people or territory of either" (Washington, *Daily Globe,* May 6, 1844).

When the news of Van Buren's anti-Texas letter reached Tennessee, Jackson took prompt action. Polk and others were summoned to meet at "The Hermitage" to discuss the situation. The General declared that Van Buren had committed political suicide and could not be elected. The party must have a candidate from the Southwest who stood for annexation, and he pointed to Polk as the logical nominee (McCormac, pp. 231–40). Several of those present were delegates to the national convention and went to Baltimore fully cognizant of Jackson's desires. Van Buren's nomination was prevented by adherence to the two-thirds rule, and Polk was brought forward as a "dark horse." He was nominated on the ninth ballot and thus reaped the reward of his loyalty to the party and its indomitable leader. Although the Whigs asked derisively, "Who is James K. Polk?" he was far from being unknown in the field of politics. Jackson aptly summarized Polk's fitness for the office when he wrote that "his capacity for business [is] great—and to extraordinary powers of labor, both mental and physical, he unites that tact and judgment which are requisite to the successful direction of such an office as that of Chief Magistrate of a free people" (*Nashville Union,* Aug. 13, 1844). He defeated Clay in the election.

As a soldier in the ranks Polk had accepted party commands without a murmur, but he felt that his new position entitled him to dictate the party policies for the next four years. In a letter written to Cave Johnson on Dec. 21, 1844, he said that he desired party harmony, but "in any event I intend to be *myself* President of the U. S." ("Polk-Johnson Letters," *post,* p. 254). In selecting his cabinet and shaping his policies he sought and accepted advice, but in the end he made his own decisions. He was independent enough to reject even the advice of "Old Hickory" on several occasions; he dismissed from office the General's bosom friend, William B. Lewis, and he declined to have Blair's *Globe* as the organ of his administration. When constructing his cabinet, Polk prepared a form letter (Moore, *Works of James Buchanan,* VI, 110–

11), which was to serve as an invitation to those whom he desired to fill the various positions. In it he stated that the "principles and policy" of his administration were to be found in the Democratic platform and his inaugural address. Each member of the cabinet would be expected to devote his time and energy to the Polk administration and not be a candidate "to succeed me in the presidential office." When any member could no longer adhere to these limitations, he was expected to resign. The most important of his heads of departments were: James Buchanan, secretary of state; Robert J. Walker, secretary of the treasury; William L. Marcy, secretary of war; and George Bancroft, secretary of the navy [*qq.v.*].

Not yet fifty years old when inaugurated on Mar. 4, 1845, Polk had reached the highest executive office at an earlier age than any of his predecessors. Few presidents have entered upon their duties with a more definite program, and none has been more successful in carrying his program into execution. His inaugural address exalted the Union, frowned upon sectional discord, opposed tariff "for protection merely," and asserted the American title to Oregon to be "clear and unquestionable." Still more clearly were his plans disclosed in a conversation held with George Bancroft, a few days after his inauguration. "There are," he said, "four great measures which are to be the measures of my administration: one, a reduction of the tariff; another, the independent treasury; a third, the settlement of the Oregon boundary question; and lastly, the acquisition of California" (James Schouler, *History of the United States,* IV, 1889, p. 498). These constituted an ambitious program; but, as Schouler has well remarked, what Polk "went for he fetched" (*Ibid.,* p. 496). Before he left the White House in 1849 each measure had been carried successfully into effect.

The Walker tariff law of 1846 placed import duties substantially on a revenue basis and substituted *ad valorem* for specific duties. Although Webster and others predicted that manufactures would be ruined and the treasury crippled, manufactures continued to flourish and the revenues of the government increased. The independent treasury bill of 1846 reëstablished a financial system which continued, with slight modifications, until supplemented by the Federal Reserve system.

The Oregon question involved a long-standing dispute with Great Britain over the ownership of the region between California and Alaska. In 1818 the two nations had agreed upon what was called "joint occupation"; but Polk was elected on a platform which laid claim to the whole territory, and the Democratic battle cry was "54° 40' or fight." In his inaugural address, Polk asserted bluntly that "our title to the country of the Oregon is 'clear and unquestionable'"; but in the following July he instructed Buchanan to propose a division of the territory by extending to the Pacific coast the boundary of the forty-ninth parallel. Buchanan made the offer to Pakenham, the British minister, and explained that the President felt committed to this compromise by the acts of his predecessors. Without consulting his government, Pakenham rejected the offer (*Works of Buchanan,* VI, 194 ff.), and Polk now reasserted claim to the entire region and refused to make another proposal. Fearing war, Buchanan desired to say that the President would consider an offer if made by Great Britain, but Polk answered, "Let our proposition be absolutely withdrawn & then let the Brittish Minister take his own course" (Polk, *Diary,* I, 3). To a timid member of Congress he remarked that "the only way to treat John Bull was to look him straight in the eye"; and that he "considered a bold & firm course on our part the pacific one" (*Ibid.,* I, 155). His judgment proved to be sound. Pakenham's conduct was not approved by his government, and he was instructed to propose the same boundary line that he had rejected, except that all of Vancouver Island was to remain in possession of the British. Polk submitted the new offer to the Senate and stated that it would be rejected unless a "constitutional majority" should advise him to accept it. The Senate advised acceptance, and the treaty was signed on June 15, 1846. It was a fair adjustment, for neither nation had a valid claim to the entire territory.

When he asserted that the acquisition of California would be one of the measures of his administration, Polk evidently had in mind the purchase of the territory rather than conquest. Mexico had long owed the United States money for damage claims. Polk resolved to collect this debt, and, since Mexico could not pay in cash, he was ready to force her to cede territory. He was willing to pay fifteen or twenty million dollars in money and assume the claims if she would cede both New Mexico and California (*Diary,* I, 33–35). John Slidell was sent to Mexico to make the offer, but he was not received. By May 9, 1846, the President had decided to ask Congress to declare war on account of the unpaid claims (*Ibid.,* pp. 382–85); but on the same evening news arrived that American troops had been killed by the Mexican army. On May 11, Polk notified Congress that "Mexico has passed the boundary of the United States, has invaded our territory, and shed American blood on American soil" (Richardson, *post*, IV, 442). By the treaty which closed the war (1848) the United States acquired both New Mexico and California, and, in turn, paid Mexico fifteen million dollars and assumed the damage claims. Opposing politicians asserted that the President had wantonly forced war upon Mexico in order to extend the institution of slavery, but students of this period have shown these charges to have been unfounded.

When formulating his plans to buy Mexican territory, however, Polk unwittingly precipitated a sectional controversy which later resulted in civil war. Believing that no Mexican government would dare to sell territory unless it should receive, before the publication of the treaty, a sum sufficient to pay the army, Polk asked Congress to appropriate $2,000,000 for diplomatic purposes. To the appropriation bill David Wilmot [*q.v.*] attached his famous proviso that slavery should be excluded from all land to be acquired by the use of this money. Polk regarded this as "a mischievous & foolish amendment," intended to embarrass him in his negotiations, and was prepared to veto it (*Diary*, II, 75–78; IV, 342–45, 364–69). The "Wilmot Proviso" did not pass, but it opened the "irrepressible conflict" which was ended only at Appomattox.

Polk was the first successor of Monroe to change the fundamental character of the original Monroe Doctrine. Monroe opposed forcible interference in American affairs; Polk took a firm stand against interference of any kind, even the acceptance of sovereignty over Yucatan, by Spain or Great Britain, when voluntarily offered by the people of that province (McCormac, ch. xxiv). An inveterate foe to "pork-barrel" legislation, Polk not only applied his veto to specific measures, but felt it to be his patriotic duty to incorporate in his last annual message an indictment of Clay's "American System" which would convince the public of its iniquity (*Diary*, IV, 144, 157–58, 167–68; Richardson, IV, 654–62). It is one of his ablest state papers. Although a consistent party man, he had a supreme contempt for the spoils system. The unscrupulous methods employed by members of Congress to procure offices for their clients led him to "distrust the disinterestedness and honesty of all mankind" (*Diary*, II, 278). Convinced that the greed for spoils would crush any president who desired to do his duty, he resolved: "If God grants me length of days and health, I will, after the expiration of my term, give a history of the selfish and corrupt considerations which influence the course of public men, as a legacy to posterity. I shall never be profited by it, but those who come after me may be" (*Ibid.*, II, 329–30).

Seldom in American history has such an ambitious and so varied a program as that of Polk been consummated in the brief period of four years. It was a program conceived, mainly, by the President himself, and his dogged persistence procured the legislation necessary to put it in operation. At his request wholesome financial and tariff laws were passed. His expansion policy added over 5000 square miles of territory and gave the United States free access to the Pacific, and his "Polk Doctrine" shielded the American continents from European aggression. In normal times the chief executive would have received due credit for such notable achievements, but Polk has usually been either ignored or condemned. He possessed little personal magnetism and he had few intimate friends to sound his praises. His life was serious and laborious. He regarded time as wasted when spent in mere pleasure. Naturally secretive, he often gave offense by his enigmatical silence. But the main reason why his public services were not appreciated was his uncompromising independence in the controversy which resulted from the Wilmot Proviso. He favored the middle course of extending to the Pacific the Missouri Compromise line (Richardson, IV, 641). He opposed extremists on both sides, for he believed that their agitation would destroy the Union. He was called a tool of the slave power, but he resolutely refused to cooperate with its leaders, and he considered Calhoun to be the "most mischievous man in the Senate" (*Diary*, II, 371). Siding with neither faction, he was disliked by both, and he was charged, alternately, with autocracy and weakness. Total exclusion of slavery from the territories was demanded on one side, non-intervention on the other. The people focused their attention on this subject, sought leaders who urged drastic measures, and overlooked the achievements of the retiring President. Nevertheless, he was a sound statesman, an unusually capable executive, and an unwavering patriot. Extremely conscientious, he felt that duty required him to "supervise the whole operations of the Government" (*Diary*, IV, 261). He undermined his health by arduous labor, and lived but a few months after his retirement, dying on June 15, 1849, in the fifty-fourth year of his age. He was buried in the garden of his Nashville residence, "Polk Place," but in 1893 his remains, with those of his wife, were removed to the grounds of the state capitol.

[Polk Papers in Lib. of Cong., and papers of other statesmen, chiefly there; "Polk-Johnson Letters, 1833–

1848," and "Polk-Donelson Letters," in *Tenn. Hist. Mag.*, Sept. 1915, Mar. 1917; M. M. Quaife, ed., *The Diary of James K. Polk* (4 vols., 1910); abridgment by Allan Nevins, *Polk: The Diary of a President* (1929); material on life as planter in J. S. Bassett, *The Southern Plantation Overseer as Revealed in His Letters* (1925); "Letters of Gideon J. Pillow to James K. Polk, 1844," *Am. Hist. Rev.*, July 1906, pp. 832–43; James K. Polk and His Constituents," *Ibid.*, Oct. 1922, pp. 68–77; E. I. McCormac, *James K. Polk, A Political Biography* (1922); sketch of early career in *U. S. Mag. and Democratic Rev.*, May 1838, pp. 197–208; A. V. Goodpasture, "The Boyhood of President Polk," *Tenn. Hist. Mag.*, Apr. 1921; H. B. Learned, "The Sequence of Appointments to Polk's Original Cabinet," *Am. Hist. Rev.*, Oct. 1924; Anson and Fanny Nelson, *Memorials of Sarah Childress Polk* (1892); W. H. Polk, *Polk Family and Kinsmen* (1912); M. W. Garrett, "Pedigree of the Pollok or Polk Family," *Am. Hist. Mag.* (Nashville), Apr. 1896–Apr. 1898; J. D. Richardson, *A Compilation of the Messages and Papers of the Presidents, 1789–1897*, vol. IV (1897); J. S. Bassett, *Correspondence of Andrew Jackson* (6 vols., 1926–33); J. B. Moore, ed., *The Works of James Buchanan* (12 vols., 1908–11); C. F. Adams, ed., *Memoirs of John Quincy Adams* (2 vols., 1874–77); N. M. Scott, *A Memoir of Hugh Lawson White* (1856); T. P. Abernethy, *From Frontier to Plantation in Tenn.* (1932), for local political background; J. H. Smith, *The War with Mexico* (2 vols., 1919), excellent account of war period.]   E. I. McC.

POLK, LEONIDAS (Apr. 10, 1806–June 14, 1864), bishop of the Protestant Episcopal Church and lieutenant-general in the Confederate army, was a kinsman of James K. Polk [*q.v.*] and, therefore, of the same sturdy Scotch-Irish stock. He inherited an interest in military affairs and in education from his father, Col. William Polk [*q.v.*] of North Carolina—son of Thomas [*q.v.*] —who served gallantly in the Revolutionary War and was a founder of the University of North Carolina. William Polk was married twice, the second time to Sarah Hawkins of Raleigh, daughter of Col. Philemon Hawkins and sister of the North Carolina governor, William Hawkins. Leonidas, the second of their twelve children, was born in Raleigh and received his early education there. In 1821 he entered the University of North Carolina, but left in 1823 to go to West Point. Here he received good marks and during the first three years, according to a fellow cadet, was "full of life" and "ready for anything" (W. M. Polk, *post*, I, 74). In his last year, however, the entire course of his life was changed by the appearance at the Military Academy of a new chaplain, Dr. Charles P. McIlvaine [*q.v.*]. This eloquent divine, afterwards bishop of Ohio, quickly made his influence felt among the unholy cadets. "At length the whole corps was aroused as by a thunderbolt at the announcement that Leonidas Polk and others had been 'converted' and that Polk was to lead a 'praying squad'" (*Ibid.*, I, 89). Influenced by Dr. McIlvaine, Polk resigned his army commission six months after his graduation in June

1827 and entered the Virginia Theological Seminary. On Apr. 9, 1830, he was ordained deacon and the following month he married Frances Devereux of Raleigh, a childhood playmate. In May 1831 he was advanced to the priesthood. For a time he was assistant rector of Monumental Church, Richmond, but, his health failing, he resigned and traveled in Europe.

In 1838, he was appointed missionary bishop of the Southwest—a vast thinly settled region including Louisiana, Alabama, Mississippi, Arkansas, and part of Indian Territory. Making his first tour of his diocese, he crossed pathless forests, prairies, swamps, and swollen streams; he journeyed for six months, "travelled 5,000 miles, preached 44 sermons, baptized 14, confirmed 41, consecrated one church and laid the cornerstone of another" (*Ibid.*, I, 159). In 1841 he was made bishop of Louisiana. Polk felt that he would exert the best influence in the state by becoming a planter. His wife having inherited a large number of negroes, he bought a sugar plantation and settled on it with four hundred slaves. These negroes Polk tended as became the most enlightened master; among his innovations was a colored Sunday-school. This plantation enterprise proved a financial failure, however; the duties of sugar planter and bishop were conflicting, and Polk would not sacrifice those of the latter. For many years, he had been contemplating the establishment of a great Episcopal university in the South. Bishop Otey of Tennessee had also suggested such a plan, but it was Polk who enlarged upon it and brought it to fruition. Polk felt that emancipation of the negroes could only be accomplished gradually, and that a Church university would train the Southern aristocracy for its responsibilities as the masters of a subject race; it would also teach them to maintain a salutary conservatism in the America then being changed by industrialism and immigration. In 1856, therefore, he began to enlist aid in obtaining a great "university domain" fit "for a home of all the arts and sciences and of literary culture in the southern States." Assistance was obtained from the Southern Churchmen, especially the scholarly Bishop Stephen Elliott; more than 9,500 acres of land at Sewanee, Tenn., were contributed as a site; and over $500,000 raised. On Oct. 9, 1860, Bishop Polk laid the cornerstone of the University of the South.

When the Civil War broke out the next year, Polk felt that the South was fighting for a sacred cause. Jefferson Davis, his fellow cadet at West Point, offered him a position as major-general in the Confederate army. Urged by numerous persons to accept, he hesitated, but on June 25,

1861, was commissioned, and from then until his death he did not exercise his episcopal authority. Entrusted with the important task of defending the Mississippi River, he set to work to fortify it. On Sept. 4, 1861, his troops occupied the strategic post of Columbus, Ky., thus causing the Confederates to be the first to violate the neutrality of that state. Polk defended his action on the ground of military necessity and of partiality shown by Kentucky to the North. His action, however, harmed the Confederate cause in the state. On Sept. 15 he was succeeded in command by Albert Sidney Johnston, his West Point roommate and intimate friend, whose appointment he had previously urged upon Davis. Johnston assigned Polk the defense of the Mississippi River. In the following campaigns, whoever commanded, "it was upon Polk and Hardee," corps commanders, "that the weight of organization and discipline rested" (Johnston, *post,* p. 325). On Nov. 7, with a superior force, Polk defeated Grant in a small engagement at Belmont, Mo. At Shiloh, he commanded the Confederate right and kept a position near the front, four times personally leading charges. Though he won the admiration of his men, he risked his life unnecessarily. During the invasion of Kentucky, in September 1862, Bragg left Polk in command of his army while he himself inaugurated the Confederate governor. He ordered Polk to move northward and attack Buell in the flank, but Polk, knowing Buell's force to be largely superior, refused and retired toward the southeast. At Perryville, Oct. 8, he was second in command to Bragg, who highly praised him in his official report. On Oct. 10 he was appointed lieutenant-general. At Murfreesboro, Dec. 31, Polk, in command of the center, fought gallantly, but made the mistake of assaulting with only a part of his available force. Two months later, as a result of Bragg's fault-finding and incompetence as a field general, Polk wrote to Jefferson Davis recommending Bragg's transfer and replacement by Joseph E. Johnston, another of his West Point associates. At Chickamauga on Sept. 20, 1863, Polk did not attack at daybreak as ordered by Bragg, but the fault lay partly elsewhere. Although Bragg ordered Polk to be court-martialed and he was removed from command, Davis declared the procedure unjustifiable and soon reinstated him. He was killed at Pine Mountain, near Marietta, Ga., in June 1864.

Polk had had only a limited military training, and his appointment as a Confederate general was made partly for its moral and psychological effect. In view of his lack of military experience, he made a much better corps commander than might have been expected. He was well liked by his men and exerted a good influence over them. His lasting work, however, was the upbuilding of the Episcopal Church in the Southwest, and, especially, the founding of the University of the South. He is described as being of good stature and erect military carriage. "The first glance revealed him as a man to be obeyed"; a closer scrutiny showed him to be "a man whom noble men might love and meaner men might fear" (W. S. Perry, *History of the American Episcopal Church,* 1885, II, 563). He was evangelical in his beliefs, a rather dry preacher, but a good executive and an interesting conversationalist. William M. Polk [*q.v.*] was his son.

[The only biography, *Leonidas Polk, Bishop and General* (2 vols., 1893, rev. ed., 1915), by Polk's son, W. M. Polk, is full and authoritative, though with a natural bias in favor of Polk; see also W. P. Johnston, *The Life of Gen. Albert Sidney Johnston* (1878); W. S. Perry, *The Episcopate in America* (1895); *War of the Rebellion: Official Records (Army)*; C. A. Evans, *Confederate Military Hist.* (1899), vol. I; J. B. Cheshire, *The Church in the Confederate States* (1912); G. R. Fairbanks, *Hist. of the Univ. of the South* (1905); *Funeral Services at the Burial of the Rt. Rev. Leonidas Polk* (1864); W. H. Polk, *Polk Family and Kinsmen* (1912).]
R. D. M.

POLK, LEONIDAS LAFAYETTE (Apr. 24, 1837–June 11, 1892), farmer, editor, president of the National Farmers' Alliance and Industrial Union, was born in Anson County, N. C., the son of Andrew Polk by his second wife, Serena Autry. He was a descendant of Robert Bruce Polk who settled in Maryland some time before 1687. Left an orphan when only fourteen years of age, Leonidas followed his father's example and became a farmer. In 1857 he was married to Sarah P. Gaddy, also of Anson County. They became the parents of seven children, a son who died in infancy, and six daughters. During the Civil War and Reconstruction period Polk attained some prominence. In 1860 and again in 1864–65 he was a member of the state legislature; he saw military service with two North Carolina regiments; and sat in the first state constitutional convention held in North Carolina after the war was over. He was always a farmer, however, and it was as such that he began to advocate in 1870 the establishment of a state department of agriculture. When in 1877 his efforts in this direction were successful, he was chosen the first commissioner, an office which he held until 1880. He became editor of the *Raleigh News* in 1880, which in September of that year was consolidated with the *Observer,* under the name *News and Observer*; this position he relinquished in 1881.

Genuinely desirous of improving agricultural

conditions in his state, Polk began in 1886 the publication of a journal known as the *Progressive Farmer*. The paper sought to teach the Southern farmers better agricultural methods, but it soon came to take an interest in politics as well. Through its columns Polk urged the formation of "farmers' clubs," by means of which, he believed, the legislature could be forced to concede whatever the farmers wanted. Many such clubs were organized and with their support, he succeeded in securing the establishment of a state college of agriculture, to which, instead of to the state university, the landscrip fund obtained under the terms of the Morrill Act should go. His attempt to unite the farmers of the state politically had barely begun when organizers of the "Southern" Alliance, an expanding Texas farm order, entered North Carolina. Polk allied himself with the new movements and turned his paper into an official Alliance publication. In 1887 he became national vice-president of the Alliance, and, two years later, its president. By this time the organization numbered millions of members, and since its constitution centered great authority in the president, Polk became at once a powerful figure in national politics. He sought at first to work towards the adoption of Alliance reforms through the older parties; but this method was attended with such slight success that at length he turned reluctantly, for he was a Southern Democrat, to the new People's party, which promised the Alliance all it asked. In February 1892 he presided at St. Louis over the great Industrial Conference of twenty-two reform organizations, which met in order to agree upon joint political demands. He planned also to attend the Omaha nominating convention in July 1892, and his friends confidently predicted that he would there be given either first or second place on the Populist ticket; but death suddenly terminated his career less than a month before the convention met. In appearance Polk was the typical, heavily whiskered Populist. He excelled in the type of oratory that appealed to farmer audiences, and he presided with dignity over turbulent conventions that would have put a less resourceful chairman to rout. His death was a serious blow to the third party movement, particularly in the South.

[W. S. Morgan, *Hist. of the Wheel and Alliance and the Impending Revolution* (1921); Jerome Dowd, *Sketches of Prominent Living North Carolinians* (1888); W. H. Polk, *Polk Family and Kinsmen* (1912); K. P. Battle, *Hist. of the Univ. of N. C.,* vol. II (1912); J. D. Hicks, "The Farmer's Alliance in N. C.," in *N. C. Hist. Rev.,* Apr. 1925; files of the *Progressive Farmer* (Raleigh); files of the *National Economist* (Washington), especially June 18, 1892; *News and Observer* (Raleigh), June 12, 1892; information as to certain facts (including name of mother) from a grandson, L. P. Denmark of Raleigh, N. C.]   J. D. H

POLK, LUCIUS EUGENE (July 10, 1833–Dec. 1, 1892), Confederate soldier, was a grandson of Col. William Polk [q.v.] of the Revolutionary army and a nephew of Leonidas Polk [q.v.]. He was born in Salisbury, N. C., the fourth son of Dr. William Julius Polk and Mary Rebecca Long, the grand-daughter of Allen Jones [q.v.] of Halifax, N. C., and daughter of Lunsford Long. Two years after Lucius' birth, Dr. Polk moved to Columbia, Tenn., and became a large planter. After attending the University of Virginia (1850–51), young Polk settled in Phillips County, Ark., near Helena, and engaged in planting.

Upon the outbreak of the Civil War he enlisted as a private in the "Yell Rifles," raised by Capt. "Pat" Cleburne [q.v], "the Stonewall Jackson of the West," under whom Polk served throughout almost the entire war. Shortly after his enlistment he was promoted third lieutenant. At Shiloh he commanded the company and was in the thick of the fight, receiving a wound in the face. Several of the higher officers of the regiment having been killed or wounded, he was unanimously elected colonel a few days later. Polk's regiment covered the retreat from Corinth, Miss. Cleburne's brigade, to which it belonged, was already becoming known as one of the bravest in the Confederate western army. During Bragg's invasion of Kentucky, Polk was wounded at Richmond, Aug. 30, 1862, and again at Perryville, Oct. 8. On Dec. 13, 1862, Cleburne was promoted major-general and Polk was made brigadier-general, succeeding to the command of Cleburne's brigade. He was in heavy fighting at Murfreesboro and during the subsequent retreat to Chattanooga and North Georgia. In his official report of Chickamauga, General Cleburne wrote that to the "intrepidity and stern determination" of Polk and his men he was "principally indebted" for the successful charge which won the victory (*Official Records,* I ser., vol. XXX, pt. II, p. 156). Though Polk's brigade did not become engaged at New Hope Church, Ga., Cleburne reported that the fact that he commanded the weakest part of the line gave confidence to the entire division. At Kenesaw Mountain, Ga., in late June 1864, he received his fourth wound, from which he never fully recovered, and he was forced to retire from the army.

After the war, Polk returned on crutches to his home near Columbia, Tenn. There he lived quietly until his death about twenty-five years later. Once he defied some Ku Klux Klansmen when they tried to whip, unjustly, one of his negro hands. He was a delegate to the Democratic Convention at Chicago in 1884, and in 1887 was elected to the Tennessee Senate. He was a distinguished looking man, brave but extremely modest. He married, Aug. 19, 1863, his cousin, Sallie Moore Polk, and they had five children. Two of their sons served in the Spanish-American War, and one of these, Rufus, was also a member of Congress from Pennsylvania.

[*War of the Rebellion: Official Records (Army)*; C. A. Evans, *Confed. Military Hist.* (1899), esp. X, 410–11; M. P. Branch, *Memoirs of a Southern Woman "Within the Lines" and a Geneal. Record* (copr. 1912); W. H. Polk, *Polk Family and Kinsmen* (1912); I. A. Buck, *Cleburne and His Command* (1908); *Daily American* (Nashville), Dec. 2, 1892.]   R. D. M.

POLK, THOMAS (*c.* 1732–Jan. 26, 1794), Revolutionary soldier, great-grandson of the Scotch-Irish immigrant Robert Bruce Polk (or Pollok) who settled in Maryland sometime before 1687, and the son of William and Margaret (Taylor) Polk, was born about 1732 in Cumberland County, Pa., whither his father had moved from Maryland. With two brothers, he migrated southward in 1753 to the frontier piedmont county of Anson, N. C., where two years later he married Susan Spratt and quickly achieved leadership by virtue of his personal qualities and comparatively superior education. In the 1760's, he led the land-hungry settlers in a violent, lawless movement, known locally as the war of Sugar Creek, against Henry Eustace McCulloh, land agent of George Selwyn. He promoted the establishment in 1762 of Mecklenburg County, of which he became a justice of the peace, and in 1768 of the town of Charlotte, of which he was commissioner and first treasurer. He represented Mecklenburg County in the House of Commons in 1766–71 and in 1773–74. As captain of militia, he aided Governor Tryon in his conflict with the Regulators, 1768–71; in 1772 he was employed as a surveyor in running the North Carolina-South Carolina boundary line.

In the conflict with Great Britain, Polk was a zealous patriot—a local leader in firing the public mind, in intimidating Loyalists, and in the drafting and adoption by the Mecklenburg committee of the resolves of May 31, 1775, which declared null and void all commissions granted by the Crown and provided for the reorganization of the county government. In the third Provincial Congress (August–September 1775) he was a member of the committee which formulated a temporary state government. Late in the year, as colonel of militia, he participated in the "Snow Campaign" against the Loyalists in upper South Carolina. In the spring of 1776 he was commissioned colonel of the 4th North Carolina Continental Regiment, which joined General Moore on the lower Cape Fear and marched Northward in the spring of 1777 to reënforce Washington. He was in the battle of Brandywine and at Valley Forge. He went back to North Carolina in February 1778 for supplies and recruits, but disappointed and irritated over not being promoted to succeed Brigadier-General Francis Nash, deceased, and by the loss of his command through consolidation of the North Carolina regiments, he resigned his commission to Washington on June 26 and returned to civil life.

In the critical summer of 1780 Polk accepted two difficult appointments—commissary general of provisions for North Carolina and commissary of purchases for the Continental troops from General Gates, and superintendent commissary for Salisbury district from the provincial board of war. During the invasions of Cornwallis, he was active and alert in resistance and made liberal use of his own credit in purchasing supplies; but responsibility to two masters, and dependence upon county commissioners over whom he had no control, and general confusion, impaired his usefulness and brought an expression of lack of confidence from Gates. Polk offered his resignation, though he continued to serve until after General Greene replaced Gates. Greene, who regarded Polk highly, appointed him brigadier-general of the militia of Salisbury district in the spring of 1781; but the Assembly sent him instead a commission as "colonel commandant," which he returned, though he continued his duties until relieved in May.

In 1783 and 1784 the General Assembly elected Polk councilor of state, and in 1786, delegate to the Continental Congress, but no record of his attendance can be found. He was a promoter and trustee of Queen's College at Charlotte (1771) and of Liberty (1777) and Salisbury (1784) academies. In 1790, he owned forty-seven slaves and much land. He was the host of President Washington at Charlotte in 1791, and died at his home in that town. He had nine children. William [*q.v.*] was his son; Leonidas [*q.v.*], his grandson; and Lucius E. and William M. [*qq.v.*], his great-grandsons. James K. Polk [*q.v.*] was a grandnephew.

[W. L. Saunders, *The Colonial Records of N. C.*, vols. VI–X (1888–90); Walter Clark, *The State Records of N. C.*, vols. XI–XXVI (1895–1905); Gates Papers in the N. Y. Hist. Soc.; Letter Book, 1774–81, Gov. Burke, in N. C. Hist. Commission; *The N. C. Jour.*, Feb. 19, 1794; *Jours. of the Am. Cong. from 1774 to 1788* (4 vols., 1823); *Jours. of the Continental Cong., 1774–1789*, vol. IV (1906); G. W. Greene, *The*

Life of Nathanael Greene (3 vols., 1867–71) ; Wm. M. Polk, *Leonidas Polk, Bishop and General* (rev. ed., 1915), vol. I ; S. A. Ashe, *Biog. Hist. of N. C.*, vol. V (1906) ; W. H. Hoyt, *The Papers of Archibald D. Murphey* (2 vols., 1914) ; W. H. Polk, *Polk Family and Kinsmen* (1912) ; Greene's Letterbooks in the Lib. of Cong. and Greene's Papers in the William L. Clements Lib., Ann Arbor, Mich.]   A. R. N.

POLK, TRUSTEN (May 29, 1811–Apr. 16, 1876), senator, was born on a farm in Sussex County, Del. His mother was Lavenia (Causey) Polk, a sister of Peter Causey who was governor of Delaware from 1855 to 1859, and his father was William Nutter Polk, descended from Robert Bruce Polk (or Pollok), who had settled in Maryland by 1687. Trusten Polk attended a grammar school in Delaware, and an academy at Cambridge, Md., before he entered Yale College, where he graduated with honors in 1831. He wished to enter the ministry, but his father persuaded him to study law, and after about a year in the office of James Rogers, attorney-general of Delaware, he took a two-year law course at Yale. Perceiving that legal practice in Delaware "was monopolized by a few old lawyers" he moved in 1835 to St. Louis, Mo., where he soon rose to a position of recognized leadership at the bar.

Polk was appointed city counselor of St. Louis in 1843, but soon afterwards his health failed, and he traveled (1844–45) through the South, Cuba, and Canada in a successful effort to restore it. While on this tour he made a careful study of the public school systems of several states. During his absence he was elected (1845) one of the two St. Louis delegates to the convention to revise the state constitution. In this body he served as chairman of the committee on education, and, keenly aware that the census of 1840 placed Missouri almost at the "tail end of the Union" in education, devoted himself to the double aim of devising a better state educational system and a scheme of taxation which would render that system practicable. He was largely successful in the realization of both objects. He also took an active part in the framing of a constitutional provision prohibiting the future creation of state banks empowered to issue paper money.

In 1856 he was elected governor on the anti-Benton Democratic ticket, but a few weeks later was elected United States senator, and on Feb. 27, 1857, resigned the governorship. In the Senate he was counted a worthy colleague of the pro-Southern senior senator from Missouri, James S. Green [*q.v.*]. Although his convictions were Southern, he was not a fire-eater. Among the half dozen really able speeches defending the Southern cause in 1860 and 1861, those of Trus-

ten Polk must be accorded a place. In two powerful addresses (Jan. 14 and July 10–11, 1861) he marshaled the arguments for the South in a masterly analysis of the national crisis. Conscientious convictions forced him to absent himself from the Senate in the session beginning Dec. 2, 1861, and upon the basis of a resolution introduced by Charles Sumner Dec. 18, and formally voted upon Jan. 10, 1862, he was expelled from that body. Late in 1861 he went to New Madrid, Mo., and enlisted as a colonel in the Confederate military service. He held, until he was taken prisoner in 1864, the position of presiding military judge of the Department of the Mississippi. At the close of the war he returned to St. Louis, where he continued the practice of law until his death. On Dec. 26, 1837, he married Elizabeth Skinner of St. Louis, who with four daughters survived him, a son having died in infancy. Polk was a man of the purest private character, and a prominent and faithful member of the Methodist Episcopal Church, South.

[*The Messages and Proclamations of the Govs. . . . of Mo.*, vol. III (1922) ; W. B. Stevens, *Mo. the Center State* (1915), vol. II ; *The Commonwealth of Mo.* (1877), ed. by C. R. Barns ; W. B. Davis and D. S. Durrie, *An Illus. Hist. of Mo.* (1876) ; Richard Edwards and M. Hopewell, *Edwards's Great West* (1860) ; H. L. Conard, *Encyc. of the Hist. of Mo.* (1901), vol. V ; W. H. Polk, *Polk Family and Kinsmen* (1912), pp. 691, 694 ; *Obit. Record Grads. Yale Coll.*, 1876 ; contemporary newspapers, especially *Jefferson City Tribune*, Apr. 18, 1876, and *St. Louis Globe-Democrat*, Apr. 17, 1876.]   H. E. N.

POLK, WILLIAM (July 9, 1758–Jan. 14, 1834), Revolutionary soldier, was born near Charlotte, N. C., the son of Thomas Polk [*q.v.*] and Susan (Spratt), the former a great-uncle of James K. Polk [*q.v.*]. In April 1775, while still a student at Queen's College, Charlotte, William was appointed second lieutenant in a South Carolina regiment composed of troops from both of the Carolinas, and saw service against the Loyalists in South Carolina, attracting notice as a daring and resourceful young officer. He was desperately wounded at the battle of Reedy River and confined to bed for nine months. Thereafter it was his proud boast that his was the first American blood spilt south of Lexington.

On Nov. 27, 1776, the provincial congress elected him major of the 9th Regiment of the North Carolina Line, which he commanded when it went to Charleston and when it joined Washington's army in New Jersey in March 1777. He participated in the battles of Brandywine and Germantown, and was severely wounded in the latter. He spent the winter at Valley Forge and when the nine North Carolina regiments were consolidated into four, the officers fell out by lot and he was retired. He returned to North Carolina on recruiting service and presently joined General Caswell's staff and was with him at Camden. He then joined the staff of General Davidson, with whom he served until Davidson was killed at Cowan's Ford. He was a volunteer officer at Guilford Court House, after which he served with General Pickens for a short time until Governor Rutledge commissioned him lieutenant-colonel commandant of the 4th South Carolina Cavalry. Transferred later to the command of the 3rd Regiment, he fought with it in the engagements at Friday's Ferry, Orangeburg, Fort Motte, Eutaw Springs, Watboo Creek, and Quinby.

In 1783 he was appointed a surveyor general of the state land office with headquarters in what is now Davidson County, Tenn., which he represented in the North Carolina House of Commons in 1785 and 1786. The following year he returned to Mecklenburg, which he represented in the House in 1787 and again in 1790. In 1791 he became supervisor of internal revenue for North Carolina, serving until 1808. In 1799 he moved to Raleigh, where he was increasingly prominent in political, business, and social affairs. He was president of the state bank from 1811 to 1819, president of the Neuse River Navigation Company, an active and devoted trustee of the University of North Carolina from 1790 to 1834 and president of the board from 1802 to 1805, and grand master of Masons for North Carolina and Tennessee from 1799 to 1802. He was several times a candidate for governor before the General Assembly, but, a Federalist, he had no chance of election. Opposed to the War of 1812, he refused to consider the command of a regiment, and when President Madison appointed him a brigadier-general, he declined in spite of much embarrassment. Later, he refused to consider an informal tender of a major-general's commission. In 1824 and 1828 he was an enthusiastic supporter of Jackson, his close friend, and managed his campaign in North Carolina.

Polk was widely popular; a county and three towns in North Carolina and a county and town in Tennessee are named for him. In the latter state he owned more than one hundred thousand acres of land. He was twice married: on Oct. 15, 1789, to Grizelda, daughter of Judge Thomas and Martha (Jones) Gilchrist of Suffolk, Va., who died in 1799; on Jan. 1, 1801, to Sarah, daughter of Philemon Hawkins, Jr. By his first marriage he had two children, one of whom, William J., was the father of Lucius Eugene Polk [q.v.]; by the second he had twelve children, one of whom was Leonidas [q.v.]. William Polk died in Raleigh.

[William Polk Papers in Lib. of Cong.; transcripts in N. C. Hist. Commission; W. H. Hoyt, *The Papers of Archibald D. Murphey* (2 vols., 1914), which contains reprint of an autobiog. in the William Polk Papers; Walter Clark, *The State Records of N. C.*, vols. XI (1895), XVI–XXII (1899–1907); H. M. Wagstaff, ed., *The Papers of John Steele* (2 vols., 1924); J. G. deR. Hamilton, ed., *The Papers of Thomas Ruffin* (3 vols., 1918–1920); *Raleigh Reg.*, May 19, 1826, Jan. 21, 1834; S. A. Ashe, *Biog. Hist. of N. C.*, vol. II (1905), pp. 361–68; W. M. Polk, *Leonidas Polk, Bishop and General* (2 vols., 1893, rev. ed., 1915); K. P. Battle, *Hist. of the Univ. of N. C.*, vol. I (1907); W. H. Polk, *Polk Family and Kinsmen* (1912).]

J. G. deR. H.

POLK, WILLIAM MECKLENBURG (Aug. 15, 1844–June 23, 1918), physician, was born in Ashwood, Maury County, Tenn. His father, Leonidas Polk [q.v.], bishop of Louisiana and later lieutenant-general in the Confederate army, was killed at Pine Mountain; his mother was Frances (Devereux) Polk. William started his schooling in Marion, Ala., attended the grammar school of the College of St. James, Washington County, Md. (1858–59), and then entered the Virginia Military Institute at Lexington. Here he was under the personal supervision of "Stonewall" Jackson. Intending to enter West Point, he studied mathematics and the sciences. At the outbreak of the Civil War, though but seventeen years old, he was appointed drill master under Jackson and later transferred to the staff of General Zollicoffer. In April 1861 he entered active field service. It is said that no soldier in the Civil War took part in more battles and skirmishes. At its close he was a captain on the staff of Gen. Joseph E. Johnston.

After the surrender of Johnston, Polk became superintendent of the Brierfield (Alabama) Iron Works. Here he met Dr. E. W. Bailey, who aroused his interest in medicine. He began his medical education at the University of Louisiana (now Tulane University) and in 1868 went to New York City, where he graduated from the College of Physicians and Surgeons in 1869. An internship of eighteen months was spent in Bellevue Hospital, where he worked under Austin Flint [q.v.] and other medical celebrities of the day. He progressed rapidly from curator of the pathological department of Bellevue Hospital Medical College and assistant demonstrator of anatomy to the professorship of materia medica. In 1879 he accepted the position of professor of obstetrics and gynecology at the University of the City of New York. Besides these teaching duties, he acted as visiting physician to Bellevue Hospital, where he helped to create a gynecological service. In 1878 he accepted the position of visiting physician to St. Luke's.

Polk's most important activity followed his appointment in 1898 to the office of dean of the new Cornell University Medical School and head of its gynecological department. Here he had the opportunity to express in a new organization the modern ideals of medical education. To the development of a higher standard of teaching in American medical schools he devoted most of his interest from then on. He wrote a biography of his father, *Leonidas Polk, Bishop and General* (2 vols., 1893; revised edition, 1915), and published many medical articles in the *American Journal of Obstetrics*. These contain only observations of momentary interest and have had no influence upon the fundamental trends of medical thought. His value to American medicine lies rather in the organization of departments of gynecological service in New York City, a work for which he was fitted because of his excellent training and also apparently because of his pleasing personality. It is said that "his understanding of womankind and his diplomatic management of their ailments was almost miraculous" (*Transactions of the Southern Surgical Association,* vol. XXXI, 1919, 376). He was married, Nov. 14, 1866, to Ida Ashe Lyon of Alabama, and after this union was broken by death, to Maria H. Dehon of New York City, May 12, 1914. There were five children by the first wife; three died in infancy, one son died after graduation from medical school, and one son survived the father. Polk died in Atlantic City.

[*Am. Jour. of Obstetrics,* Oct. 1918; "Sketches of Eminent Living Gynæcologists and Obstetricians of America—William Mecklenburg Polk," *N. Y. Jour. of Gynæcology and Obstetrics,* Nov. 1892; H. A. Kelly and W. L. Burrage, *Am. Medic. Biogs.* (1920); *Trans. Am. Gynecological Soc.,* vol. XLIV (1919); W. H. Polk, *Polk Family and Kinsmen* (1912); *Who's Who in America,* 1918–19; *Cornell Alumni News,* July 1918; death notice and obituary in *N. Y. Times,* June 25, 1918.]   H. S. R.

POLK, WILLIS JEFFERSON (Oct. 3, 1867–Sept. 10, 1924), architect, was born on a plantation near Frankfort, Ky., the eldest of five children of Willis W. Polk and his second wife, Endemial Josephine (Drane) Burch. He was a descendant of Robert Bruce Polk who received a grant of land in Maryland in 1687. When Willis was about six years old the family moved to St. Louis, where the mother managed a boarding-house and the father practised as an architect, served as president of the Mechanics' Exchange, and in 1882 ran unsuccessfully for Congress. The boy was tutored at home and in his fourteenth year became an apprentice to J. B. Legge,

a local architect. He is said to have won, at the age of sixteen, a competition for a six-room school-house at Hope, near Hot Springs, Ark., to which place his family had moved. Lured by the desire to see the world, before he was twenty-one he went to San Francisco, where some two years later his father opened an architectural office. The younger Polk still felt the lack of preparation for his profession, and obtained employment in various architectural offices in the East, at one time assisting Stanford White [*q.v.*] in New York City.

On Apr. 24, 1900, in San Francisco, he married Christine (Barreda) Moore, a widow, of Spanish descent, and with her visited Europe. Upon his return he entered the Chicago office of Daniel H. Burnham [*q.v.*], where he designed the First National Bank Building, Chicago, the Merchants Exchange, San Francisco, and the Indianapolis Terminal Building. When Burnham's firm undertook, in 1903, a plan for the adornment of San Francisco, Polk designed the bungalow on a spur of Twin Peaks whence Burnham could see the entire city spread out beneath him. He assisted in the preparation of the San Francisco Plan and for the rest of his life was an untiring enthusiast for the civic development thus initiated. Later, he visited St. Louis with Burnham to urge the value of a city plan. After 1904 Polk practised independently in San Francisco. He was chairman of the architectural commission of the Panama-Pacific International Exposition (1915) during the planning of that successful fair. In a preliminary article in *Sunset* (April 1912), he compared the site selected for the exposition to the orchestra of a Greek theatre, with the blue harbor forming the stage and the Marin hills the background. The "palaces" of the exposition were designed to serve as the "costumed chorus," observing the drama furnished by the ships of the world maneuvering on the surface of the water. By a system of inner courts and by uniform roofs and façades, a colorful individuality was permitted, and yet a general unity was obtained.

Polk's buildings in the new San Francisco, erected after the earthquake and fire of 1906, were mainly of a monumental, conservative style. He himself thought his Water Temple, Sunol, was his masterpiece—a restrained Doric peristyle. Many of his later buildings were marked by freshness of handling as he studied the possibilities of new materials and the requirements of new functions. His Hallidie Building with its glass front and metal trims illustrates the use of new materials; the Central Pumping Station of the Spring Valley Water Company and Station "D" of the Gas and Electric Company, with their adaptations of Spanish motives, the meeting of new requirements. His careful restoration of the Mission Dolores is an example of his erudition. Other notable buildings in San Francisco include the First National Bank Building, the Pacific Union Club, the Mills Building, the Cuyler Lee Building, the Chronicle Building, the Hobart Building, St. Mary's Hospital, the Western Pacific Station, and the Ferry Building, in which he collaborated with C. P. Brown. The Mills Building in Sacramento and many of the finest residences in San Francisco and throughout the peninsula were also of his designing. He is considered one of the creators of the "California style" of domestic architecture. A fine draftsman, a skilful designer in the manner of Bramante or Peruzzi, he infused his compositions with a flavor of individuality, subtle and beautiful. After his death the Willis Polk Company continued, in the McDuffie House, Claremont, and the Metcalf House, Piedmont, the "poetic interpretations of classical architecture" shown in Polk's own designs, but later, modern trends began to be blended with the office traditions.

As a personality, Polk was always vivid. According to some, he was lovable, witty, and sarcastic, an indomitable champion of the beautiful as preferable to the utilitarian; according to others, he was egotistical, combative, a tactless self-advertiser. He was a man of magnetic presence and aristocratic appearance, generous, extravagant, a born "romancer" when autobiographical. He died at his country home, San Mateo, his wife and a stepson surviving him, leaving his plans for the Opera House in the Civic Center, on which he had worked for many years, still unrealized.

[Information from T. E. Tallmadge and W. B. Faville, former colleagues; Pauline Jacobsen, "The Whip of Discontent," *Sunset*, Apr. 1922, an unreliable account of Polk's early days; W. H. Polk, *Polk Family and Kinsmen* (1912); Charles Moore, *Daniel H. Burnham* (2 vols., 1921); *Architectural Record*, Jan., Aug. 1912, Dec. 1913, Feb., Oct. 1918, Mar. 1919, Nov. 1920; *Architect and Engineer*, Sept. 1924; *Pacific Coast Architect*, Oct. 1924; *Western Architect*, Jan. 1919, Dec. 1921, Nov. 1923; *Am. Architect*, Nov. 5, 1924; *San Francisco Chronicle, San Francisco Examiner*, Sept. 12, 1924; obituary of Willis Polk, Sr., in *St. Louis Globe-Democrat*, Dec. 1, 1906; St. Louis and San Francisco directories; letter from R. B. Maybeck; memorandum from Mrs. Willis Polk.]   W. S. R.

POLLAK, GUSTAV (May 4, 1849–Nov. 1, 1919), editor and critic, was born in Vienna, of Austrian Jewish parents, Lazar Pollak, a doctor, and Magdalena (Klein). Gustav was the second of their four children. He was educated in the public schools of Vienna, and emigrated to America at the age of seventeen. Since it had

been the belief of Vienna physicians that he was threatened with consumption and that a warmer climate would be better for him, he went almost immediately to the South. The years he spent there were the chaotic years of the Carpet-bag era, of which he retained vivid memories. During most of the period he was at Tuscaloosa, Ala., working in stores as a clerk and tutoring at the same time. He had gained a sound knowledge of English through study before he came to America; but he was always delicately scrupulous in his use of words and, not content with mere correctness, he aimed at a precise and completely idiomatic style. For years he made it a point to look up in the dictionary every English word concerning which he had any doubt. The result was that in an amazingly short time he was writing English with the same ease as German. Shortly after his arrival in America he established a friendship with Michael Heilprin [*q.v.*], who exercised a profound intellectual influence upon him, and whom he almost idolized. His health having been fully restored, he returned for a year or two to Vienna, and appears for a time to have contemplated remaining there permanently, but in 1874 he was back in America and on May 23, 1875, he married Heilprin's daughter, Celia. She was a woman of extraordinarily fine character, and the marriage, until her death in 1911, appears to have been one of ideal felicity.

Pollak began to contribute to the New York *Nation* in 1874, and joined the New York *Evening Post* as cashier in 1881 when the latter journal acquired the *Nation*. It was not long before the editorial staff of the *Evening Post* recognized his remarkable knowledge of European affairs, and he soon became a regular contributor to the paper, first on foreign politics and later on literary subjects. He remained cashier of the Evening Post Publishing Company until 1893, and continued his literary connections with the *Nation* and the *Evening Post* thereafter. From 1884 to 1909 he edited the magazine *Babyhood* with Dr. L. M. Yale. He contributed an article on Vienna to Appletons' *American Cyclopædia* (vol. XVI, 1876), and was connected with the editorial revision of *The Century Cyclopedia of Names* in 1895, *The New International Encyclopædia* from 1902 to 1904, and *Nelson's Encyclopædia* from 1906 to 1907. He lectured on the Austrian dramatists at Johns Hopkins in 1905. From 1884 to 1901 he resided at Summit, N. J., and took an active part in Democratic politics. He was an ardent admirer of Cleveland. He was one of the founders of the German-American Reform Union during the presidential campaign of

1892, and a candidate of the Gold Democrats for state senator from Union County, N. J., in 1896. He was also interested in local political activities in Summit, and served on the board of health and on the board of education of the town for a number of years.

Pollak was the author of *The Century Book for Mothers* (1901), with Dr. L. M. Yale; *Franz Grillparzer and the Austrian Drama* (1907); *The Hygiene of the Soul* (1910), a memoir of an Austrian physician; *Michael Heilprin and His Sons* (1912); *International Perspective in Criticism* (1914); *Fifty Years of American Idealism: The New York Nation, 1865–1915* (1915); and *The House of Hohenzollern and the Hapsburg Monarchy* (1917). His book on the Austrian dramatist and critic, Grillparzer, is still the standard work in English on the subject. His *International Perspective in Criticism* is an admirable example of his merits as a critic. The three main figures treated in it are Grillparzer, Goethe, and Sainte-Beuve. These essays are gracefully written, balanced, scholarly, and distinguished, and deserve to be better known than they are. The viewpoint throughout is that of a cosmopolitan critic who deplores provincial standards of literary judgment wherever they exist.

Pollak's equal mastery of English and German is an index of his powers as a linguist. He also read French and Italian, and in his later years a great deal of Latin and some Greek. His conversation enjoyed a rather remarkable reputation for its high spirits, its geniality, and its spontaneous wit; he was, in short, an authentic example of the traditional Viennese. He wrote occasional verse, and at the age of fifty began to paint as a diversion. His sympathies in the World War were with America, and during a few months at the end of 1917 and the beginning of 1918 he worked with the "Enquiry" headed by Colonel House at Washington. He was disgusted with the terms of the peace treaty, however, and depressed particularly by the break-up of Austria-Hungary. He died of heart disease at Cambridge, Mass., survived by a daughter and a son. The eldest of his three children, Francis D. Pollak, a New York lawyer, predeceased him.

[*Who's Who in America*, 1918–19; (inaccurate in one or two dates); *Nation*, Nov. 8, 1919; *Evening Post* (N. Y.), Nov. 3, 1919; information from friends and surviving members of the family.]   H. H.

POLLARD, EDWARD ALFRED (Feb. 27, 1831–Dec. 16, 1872), journalist, author, was born at "Alta Vista," Albemarle County, Va., the seventh of nine children of Richard and Paulina Cabell (Rives) Pollard. His name appears in some accounts as Edward Albert; he generally signed it Edward A., but in the preface to *The Lost Cause* (1867) he wrote it Edward Alfred, as it is given in most sources. His father was *chargé d'affaires* in Chile, 1834–41; his mother was the daughter of Robert and Margaret Jordan (Cabell) Rives (Childs, *post*, pp. 593–94; Brown, *post*, pp. 433–34, 438). He was a student at Hampden-Sidney College about 1846, and then entered the University of Virginia, where he remained from 1847 to 1849. He is recorded as having entered the College of William and Mary as a law student, Oct. 14, 1850, at the age of eighteen, but the latter statement is in disagreement with other references to the date of his birth (Wilson, *post*). On Nov. 19, he was "given leave to withdraw," and later, by unanimous vote of the faculty, denied readmission. He then studied law in Baltimore, and afterward spent some years in California. According to his own story he traveled in Mexico, Nicaragua, China, Japan, Siam, and in Europe as a journalist, but it is difficult to reconcile his account with the time then necessary for such an extended journey. During the Buchanan administration he was for a time clerk of the judiciary committee of the House of Representatives.

About this time he married but the name of his wife, who died very soon, is unknown. Under the influence of Bishop Meade he began studying for the Episcopal ministry, but his journalistic bent was too strong; in 1861 he became editor of the *Daily Richmond Examiner,* and held that post until 1867. In 1864 he was captured while running the blockade in the steamer *Grayhound,* with the intention of going to England to promote the sale of his books, and was carried to Fortress Monroe. After an unsuccessful attempt to induce Lord Lyons, the British minister, to demand his release, he was carried to New York and later to Boston, where he was first paroled and then confined in Fort Warren until Aug. 2. Later he was again paroled, sent to Brooklyn and then south, where Grant, under Stanton's orders, placed him in solitary confinement at Fortress Monroe until he was exchanged, Jan. 12, 1865; he then returned to Richmond. At the close of the war he was given a pass to leave the country and went to Europe, but soon returned, and in 1867 established *Southern Opinion*, a weekly newspaper, which ran until 1869. In 1868 he founded *The Political Pamphlet,* which also died early. He spent the last few years of his life in New York, continuing to write for the press and publishing books until the end. He died in Lynchburg, Va., of albuminaria. After the war he married Marie Antoinette Nathalie

Pollard

Granier, who had separated from her first husband, James R. Dowell, during the war because of political differences (*Library of Southern Literature*, XV, n.d., p. 349). She survived Pollard and later acquired some note as a writer and public speaker.

For some years prior to the war, Pollard had been an advocate of secession, and he was a fiery and devoted partisan of the Confederacy. But he quickly became convinced that President Davis was unfit for his office, and the *Examiner* was therefore a merciless and caustic critic and a bitter enemy of him. To the end Pollard insisted that Davis was the prime cause of the South's defeat, and, denying any prejudice towards him, asserted that he attacked him only "through supreme devotion to a great cause." Pollard was the ablest and most prolific Southern writer of his day, though his literary output, on account of constant repetition and republication under different titles, looms larger than its deserts. His chief published works were: *The Southern Spy, or Curiosities of Negro Slavery in the South* (1859), reprinted the same year as *Black Diamonds Gathered in the Darkey Homes of the South; Black Aaron: A Christmas Story* (1859); *Letters of the Southern Spy, in Washington and Elsewhere* (1861), which was reprinted that year, and in 1862, under a slightly different title, and which took the form of letters to Lincoln accusing him of forcing the war; *The Second Battle of Manassas* (1862); *The First Year of the War* (1862); *The Second Year of the War* (1863, 1864); *The Rival Administrations: Richmond and Washington in December 1863* (1864); *The Two Nations: A Key to the History of the American War* (1864); *The War in America, 1863–64* (1865); *The Third Year of the War* (1865); *A Letter on the State of the War* (1865); *Observations in the North: Eight Months in Prison and on Parole* (1865); *The Last Year of the War* (1866); *Southern History of the War* (2 vols., 1866); *The Lost Cause: A New Southern History of the War of the Confederates* (1866); *Lee and His Lieutenants* (1867), reprinted later under a somewhat different title; *The Lost Cause Regained* (1868); *Life of Jefferson Davis; With a Secret History of the Southern Confederacy* (1869); *Memoir of the Assassination of Henry Rives Pollard* (1869); *The Virginia Tourist* (1870); *A Southern Historian's Appeal for Horace Greeley* (1872); *The Political Literature of America* (n.d.); and *The Key to the Ku Klux* (n.d.), a furious attack on Davis and a denunciation of the Klan.

Pollard's works are journalistic, unscientific,

bitterly prejudiced, and often unjust, yet possessed of a certain power and, at times, keen judgment. His literary style is good. Gen. D. H. Hill, criticizing certain of Pollard's books, quoted with approval a characterization of him as "partial, prejudiced, dogmatic, determined" (*The Land We Love*, Feb. 1868, p. 272) and, after Pollard had attacked the review, charged him with falsehood and with "the most stupendous, wholesale plagiarism, ever perpetrated in the literary annals of the world," an estimate with which, Hill said, the Cincinnati *Enquirer* and the Louisville *Courier* substantially agreed (*Ibid.*, July 1868, p. 283). While extreme, this estimate is not without a certain justification.

[*War of the Rebellion: Official Records (Army)*; *Am. Ann. Cyc.*, 1872, p. 676; J. S. Wilson, "Edward Alfred Pollard," in *Lib. of Sou. Literature*, IX (1909), 4147–50; Alexander Brown, *The Cabells and Their Kin* (1895); J. R. Childs, *Reliques of the Rives* (1929); obituaries in *Richmond Enquirer* and *Richmond Dispatch*, Dec. 18, 1872.]
J. G. deR. H.

POLLARD, JOSEPH PERCIVAL (Jan. 29, 1869–Dec. 17, 1911), literary and dramatic critic, author, better known as Percival Pollard, was born at Greifswald, Pomerania, of English-German parentage, the son of Joseph and Marie Pollard. He was educated at Eastbourne College, Sussex, England. He never lost his early interest in German civilization and later became one of the foremost interpreters of German literature in the United States. Coming to New York in 1885, he entered the field of journalism on the *St. Joseph News*, St. Joseph, Mo., in 1891. From 1897 until his death in 1911 he was literary reviewer for *Town Topics*, a position from which he was able to exert a not inconsiderable influence upon contemporary criticism. At the turn of the century, he collaborated with Vance Thompson, Walter Blackburn Harte, Bliss Carman, and others in founding the *Criterion*, a radical and militant literary journal filled with personalities and prejudices, which, after about a year, gradually "succumbed to the increasing cowardice of its business managers" (Pollard, *Their Day in Court*, p. 309). The Criterion Independent Theatre was a brave effort on the part of this same group to emancipate drama from the tyranny of the box-office, but it was equally short-lived.

Between 1892 and 1911 Pollard published ten volumes of fiction and criticism and translated a book on Oscar Wilde from the German. During a year of his career he had worked as a "rewrite man" for the celebrated actor, Richard Mansfield [*q.v.*], whom he satirized as Arthur Wantage in his novel, *The Imitator* (1901). The year 1906 saw the production of *Nocturno*, writ-

48

ten with Leo Ditrichstein. It was not successful. A like fate attended the production of his *The Ambitious Mrs. Alcott,* at the Astor Theatre, New York, the following year. At the same time from his prolific pen there poured forth a stream of reviews and articles, published under a variety of pseudonyms : as many as six appeared the same month, and often several in the same periodical. As a novelist Pollard was not successful and as a dramatist he was frankly a failure, but although his reputation has greatly diminished since his death, his reviews entitle him to an honorable position in the field of American literary criticism. He was one of the pioneers of realistic criticism in the United States and he ranks only below James Gibbons Huneker [*q.v.*] as one of the best interpreters of European literature to the American public in the early years of the twentieth century. He fought, as Huneker did not, to raise the level of American letters; he sought, by his withering criticism, to purge them of all that was false and cheap. His pen was brutal and audacious and his attacks against individuals were frequent, since, as he explained, "denouncing a crime against literature has never seemed to me so efficacious, or so dishonest, as denouncing the criminal" (Pollard, *op. cit.,* p. 13). He was independent and honest in his judgments, but his friendly enthusiasm sometimes led him astray, as in his extravagant eulogies of Ambrose Bierce. His most substantial volume of criticism, *Their Day in Court* (1909), contains many autobiographical passages and reveals the wide variety of his talent, his enthusiasms, and his prejudices.

To his few friends it seemed that Pollard, like Pooh-Bah, must have been born sneering. For every friend he made a score of enemies, and he possessed an extraordinary facility for alienating his friends. His publisher, Walter Neale, described him as: "Taciturn, rather morose, suspicious of his associates; inordinately stingy; apparently without the slightest affection for any human being" (Neale, *post,* p. 251). He was twice married; his second wife, Charlotte T. Rénea, whom he married Jan. 22, 1899, and a child of his first marriage survived him (*Sun,* Baltimore, Dec. 18, 1911). He died in a Baltimore hospital and his body was cremated. His funeral was attended by four friends: H. L. Mencken, Walter Meade, Ambrose Bierce, and his second wife, who shortly afterward remarried.

[*Who's Who in America,* 1910–11; *Evening Post* (N. Y.), Dec. 18, 1911; Los Angeles *Sunday Times,* Dec. 31, 1911; *Current Literature,* Mar. 1912; Walter Neale, *Life of Ambrose Bierce* (1929); private information from H. L. Mencken and Walter Neale.]   F. M.

POLLOCK, JAMES (Sept. 11, 1810–Apr. 19, 1890), governor of Pennsylvania, congressman, was born at Milton, Northumberland County, Pa., the son of William and Sarah (Wilson) Pollock, and a grandson of Samuel Pollock who came to America about 1732. William Pollock was a farmer and merchant. James received his early education at Milton Classical Academy, and graduated with honors from the College of New Jersey, at Princeton, in 1831. He then studied law in the office of Samuel Hepburn at Milton, Pa., in November 1833 was admitted to the county bar, and subsequently to that of the supreme court of Pennsylvania. In 1834 he opened a law office in Milton and in 1835 was appointed deputy attorney-general for Northumberland County, serving for three years. In 1844 he was elected as a Whig representative to the Twenty-eighth Congress, to fill the vacancy caused by the death of Henry Frick. He was twice reëlected, serving in all from Apr. 5, 1844, to Mar. 4, 1849, and retiring of his own accord. While in the House he served as chairman of a special committee appointed to consider the desirability of building a railroad to the Pacific Coast, and on June 23, 1848, presented its report, which constituted the first official recommendation of this project ("Railroad to Oregon," *House Report No. 733,* 30 Cong., 1 Sess.). He was also one of the men who gave encouragement to Samuel F. B. Morse [*q.v.*], inventor of the telegraph, when he went to Washington to secure assistance from the government. While in Congress, Pollock was a friend of both Lincoln and Stephen A. Douglas.

Pollock was appointed president judge of the eighth judicial district in Pennsylvania, Jan. 15, 1850, and served until the adoption of the amendment to the state constitution making such offices elective. Declining nomination for the office, he returned to the practice of law, but the same year was nominated for the governorship of Pennsylvania by the Whig and Native American ("Know-Nothing") parties, and was elected by a majority of 37,007 over his Democratic opponent, William Bigler, for the term extending from Jan. 16, 1855, to Jan. 19, 1858. Among the important accomplishments of his administration was the sale of the state-owned canals and railroads between Philadelphia and Pittsburgh to the Pennsylvania Railroad and other railroad companies. By this and other means he considerably reduced the state debt and thus reduced state taxes. He also obtained the passage of a series of acts laying the foundation for the public school system of the state. On the outbreak of the financial crisis of 1857 he aided in restoring public confidence by calling an extra session of the legislature, which passed a bill permitting the state banks to suspend specie payments.

At the expiration of his term as governor he refused to become a candidate for reëlection and returned to the practice of law. He represented Pennsylvania at the Peace Conference which met in Washington during the winter of 1860–61 to devise a means of averting the impending war. In May 1861 he was appointed director of the United States Mint in Philadelphia, which office he held until his resignation, Oct. 1, 1866. It was during this time that he suggested the placing of the motto "In God We Trust" on all United States gold and silver coins large enough to contain it, which practice continues today (*Annual Report of the Director of the Mint*, 1862, p. 7; 1863, p. 10; 1865, p. 14; 1866, p. 9). In 1869 he was again appointed director of the Mint and retained the position until 1873, when a reorganization took place under the Coinage Act of that year and he was made superintendent under R. H. Linderman [*q.v.*], director of the Bureau of the Mint. He served as naval officer of customs at Philadelphia, 1879–83, and in 1886 was federal chief supervisor of elections. This was his last public office. He was a member of the board of trustees of Lafayette College (1855–76) and one of the founders and president of the board of trustees of the Pennsylvania Military College at Chester (1862–90). He was also a member of various charitable boards and organizations in Philadelphia. He married Sarah Ann Hepburn, Dec. 19, 1837. He died at the home of a son-in-law, in Lock Haven, Pa. Pollock is said to have been extremely Puritanical in his attitude toward cards and liquor. He was a firm believer in the ancient code of "an eye for an eye," and for this reason did not mind signing a death warrant. As a lawyer, he "was not up to date" (McClure, *post*) and enjoyed only moderate success.

[*James Pollock, Gov. of Pa., 1854–57* (n.d.); H. E. Hayden, *Pollock Geneal.: A Biog. Sketch of Oliver Pollock, Esq.* (1883); G. G. Evans, *Hist. of the U. S. Mint at Phila.* (1885); H. M. Jenkins, *Pennsylvania—Colonial and Federal* (1903), II, 348–53; A. K. McClure, *Old Time Notes of Pa.* (1905), I, 212–33; W. C. Armor, *Lives of the Governors of Pa.* (1872); *Biog. Dir. Am. Cong.* (1928); *Princetonian*, May 7, 1890; *Times* (Phila.), Apr. 20, 1890; *Pub. Ledger* (Phila.), Apr. 21, 1890.]   J. H. F.

POLLOCK, OLIVER (c. 1737–Dec. 17, 1823), trader, planter, financier, was born near Coleraine in northern Ireland, the second son of Jaret Pollock. When twenty-three years of age, he emigrated with his father and older brother to Carlisle, Pa. Returning to Philadelphia with-

in two years and securing a vessel and crew, he was entrusted by a group of merchants with a cargo of flour and other merchandise which he sold in the West Indies. As trader and merchant he became connected with an "eminent house" in Havana.

During this period of five years, he acquired the use of Spanish. Through his friend, Father Butler, president of the Jesuit College, he was brought into intimate relations with Don Alexander O'Reilly [*q.v.*], second in command of the Spanish army in Cuba. In 1768, Pollock removed to New Orleans. From this center he extended his trading ventures, speculated in lands, and also became a planter. The following year, Count O'Reilly, commanding a force of 2,600 men, appeared before New Orleans and demanded the cession of Louisiana in conformity with the treaty of 1762. The task of feeding his army proved more difficult than the capture of a town of three thousand inhabitants. Pollock, who had recently come from Baltimore with a boat loaded with flour, proffered it to the General on his own terms. For this generosity Pollock was granted freedom of trade in Louisiana, and a period of marked expansion in his commercial career followed. As he wrote: "For twelve years before the Revolution, I was supply'd with dry-goods from London, negroes from Africa and flour from Philad'a to the River Mississippi (for all which I had no bills protested); and by the correspondence I had with the principal Commercial Houses in Philad'a I became known to the United States" (*Calendar of Virginia State Papers*, vol. V, 1885, p. 251).

At the opening of the Revolution, ammunition was greatly needed by the American army, especially for frontier protection and for winning the friendship of the Indians. In early August 1776, Capt. George Gibson of the Virginia Line, aided by Pollock, procured from Governor Unzaga, O'Reilly's successor, 10,000 pounds of powder. The greater portion was taken to Fort Pitt and the remainder to Philadelphia. In a letter addressed to the Virginia Council of Safety and in another to the Continental Congress, Pollock furnished information regarding the situation at New Orleans, and tendered his "hearty Services."

Upon the arrival of Don Bernardo de Galvez [*q.v.*], governor of Louisiana, Pollock was presented to him by Unzaga as a "faithful and zealous American in whom he might repose implicit confidence." A demand by British officers that he be surrendered was refused. Following his advice, Galvez, by the close of the year 1777, had aided the Americans by sending to the upper

Mississippi posts and to the frontiers of Pennsylvania and Virginia arms, ammunition, and provisions amounting to $70,000. For this sum, Pollock became personally responsible. Early in 1778, he received appointment as commercial agent for the United States. The following year, he accompanied Galvez on an expedition in which Manchac, Baton Rouge and Natchez were captured by the Spaniards.

After the capture of Kaskaskia in 1778, George Rogers Clark [*q.v.*], following the order of Gov. Patrick Henry, turned to Pollock for assistance. With the aid of American friends in New Orleans and funds obtained by contracting for the use of his slaves on the public works, the latter was enabled to meet Clark's appeals for powder, cannon, and other supplies. Bills of credit on Virginia, drawn by Clark, were accepted by the merchants and traders of the Illinois country in payment for their goods as long as they were received and paid at face value in silver by Pollock. "The invoice Mr. Pollock rendered upon all occasions in paying those bills," Clark wrote in 1785, "I considered at the time and now to be one of the happy circumstances that enabled me to keep possession of that country" (Clark MSS., Virginia State Archives).

By July 1779, Pollock's advances had so far exhausted his credit that to meet an order from Governor Henry for $10,000 worth of goods he was compelled to mortgage some of his lands. The promised supplies of flour and meal had not been forwarded to him. During the war, as agent for the United States and, by implication, of Virginia—although that state protested later that his formal appointment had never been confirmed—he made advances of some $300,000. His claim against Virginia, by January 1782, was $139,739, and for some months he vainly prayed the Assembly for relief. The following year he accepted the office of commercial agent for the United States at Havana, with the hope of discharging his debts. Unable to satisfy the claims of former creditors, he was arrested and held in custody eighteen months. Through the influence of Governor Galvez, he returned to Philadelphia, and renewed his petitions to Congress and the Virginia Assembly for relief. From time to time he received small sums, and he was awarded the sum of $90,000 by Congress (December 1785), but this obligation was not finally met for a number of years.

With funds secured on his credit, he fitted out a vessel, loaded it with flour, and returned to the West Indies and New Orleans as a trader. So successful was he, that by 1790 he was able to meet all of his financial obligations in New Or-

leans. His claim against Virginia, to the amount of $108,609, was paid by the federal government, and his other accounts against Virginia were eventually paid by that state. He returned to Cumberland County, Pa., where he purchased an estate. During 1804 he became a candidate for a seat in Congress but was defeated. He took up his residence in Philadelphia for a short time and then in Baltimore. Some years later he went to live with a married daughter at Pinckneyville, Miss., where he died in 1823.

About 1770, he was married to Margaret O'Brien, who died Jan. 10, 1799. Their family consisted of five sons and three daughters. On Nov. 2, 1805, he married Mrs. Winifred Deady of Baltimore, who died in 1814.

[The best brief account of Pollock is found in H. E. Hayden, *Pollock Geneal.: A Biog. Sketch of Oliver Pollock, Esq.* . . . (1883). See also J. A. James, "Oliver Pollock, Financier of the Revolution in the West," *Miss. Valley Hist. Rev.*, June 1929, and *The Life of George Rogers Clark* (1928), pp. 93, 124–26, 292–97; a biography of Pollock is in preparation and a volume of his letters is being edited by the same writer.]

J. A. J.

POLOCK, MOSES (May 14, 1817–Aug. 16, 1903), publisher, rare-book dealer, bibliophile, was born in Philadelphia, the son of Hyman Polock, of Amsterdam, who with his wife, Rebecca (Barnett), emigrated to America in 1811 immediately after their marriage in London and, settling in Philadelphia, became one of the most prominent and active members of the Jewish community in that city. Moses early showed a remarkable interest in books, and his inclinations were encouraged by his father, who determined to allow him to follow his hobby as a career. The leading firm of booksellers and publishers in Philadelphia at that time was McCarty & Davis, successors to Johnson & Warner, whose firm had been established by Jacob Johnson about 1780. On the retirement of William McCarty from the business in 1831, Moses Polock, then fourteen years of age, obtained a clerkship in the store. He made the best use of the opportunities offered by such a position, and also made many notable friends, since the store was at various times a rendezvous for Edgar Allan Poe, James Fenimore Cooper, Noah Webster, Charles Godfrey Leland, Herman Melville, and other men of letters.

On the death of Thomas Davis in 1851, Moses Polock acquired the business, with money bequeathed to him by his former employer for that purpose. From 1853 he carried on the business in his own name. As a publisher he was extremely successful and issued a large number of books, including fiction, drama, school books, and general literature. One of his best-known achievements in this connection was the publication in 1857 of the first collected edition of the works of Charles Brockden Brown [q.v.], America's first novelist. As soon as he had made a sufficient fortune by publishing modern books, Polock retired from that business and established himself as a rare-book dealer, being the first bookseller in the United States to deal exclusively in Americana. At this time many famous American collections were being formed, and among the habitués at Pollock's store were such collectors as James Lenox, Samuel L. M. Barlow, Samuel W. Pennypacker, Henry C. Murphy, and Clarence S. Bement [qq.v.], George Brinley, and J. C. Brevoort, whose libraries, together with those of the Historical Society of Pennsylvania, the John Carter Brown Library in Providence, and other notable institutions, owe much to the knowledge and acumen of the Philadelphia bibliophile and dealer. In the course of time Moses Polock's passion for his book treasures grew to such an extent that money would not buy them from him. On the rare occasions when he could be persuaded very reluctantly to part with one for a price, he invariably made an exact copy in pen and ink. A number of these beautiful and laboriously made copies are still in existence—remarkable specimens of calligraphy.

As a collector, Polock specialized in Frankliniana, Washingtoniana, and in American children's books, becoming one of the leading authorities on these subjects and on Americana in general. His knowledge of the early history of Pennsylvania and particularly of Philadelphia was profound, and both historians and bibliographers have frequently acknowledged their indebtedness to him. His collection of children's books, the first of its kind in the United States, he bequeathed to his nephew and successor in the business, Dr. A. S. W. Rosenbach.

In 1895, having spent sixty-five years in the book trade, he made a *quasi* retirement, and a large portion of his remarkable stock of Americana, including the Franklin imprints and books from the library of George Washington, were sold at public auction by Stan V. Henkels of Philadelphia. He died, unmarried, eight years later, and the remainder of his vast stock, advertised as "the estate of the oldest bookseller in the United States," was sold on Mar. 9 and 10, 1904, by the same firm of Philadelphia auctioneers.

[William Brotherhead, *Forty Years among the Old Booksellers of Phila.* (1891); A. S. W. Rosenbach, *Books and Bidders* (1927), with two portraits of Moses Polock; H. S. Morais, *The Jews of Phila.* (1894); *Public Ledger* (Phila.), Aug. 17, 1903; personal recollections.]
A. S. W. R.

POMEROY, JOHN NORTON (Apr. 12, 1828–Feb. 15, 1885), legal author and educator, was born in Rochester, N. Y., the son of Enos Pomeroy and Sarah Strong Norton and a descendant of the seventh generation from Eltweed Pomeroy who left England and helped to found Dorchester, Mass., in 1630. Enos Pomeroy, born at Buckland, Mass., in 1791, studied law at Ithaca, N. Y., married in 1816 and the same year settled in the then small village of Rochester where he practised for the remainder of his active life. His son John received the usual preparation in the public schools of his native town and in 1843 entered Hamilton College at Clinton, N. Y. After graduating in 1847 he taught school first in Rochester and later near Cincinnati, where he enrolled as a law student under Senator Thomas Corwin [q.v.]. Upon his return to Rochester, he studied further with Judge Henry R. Selden and in 1851 was admitted to the bar and began practice in his native town. It does not appear that much resulted directly from this venture, for one of his eulogists describes him at thirty-five as "a lawyer . . . without practice." It was not until nearly the close of his career, when he appeared in the celebrated Debris case (*Woodruff* vs. *North Bloomfield Gravel Mining Company,* 9 *Sawyer,* 441) and the railroad tax case (*San Mateo County* vs. *Southern Pacific Railroad Company,* 8 *Sawyer,* 238) before the United States circuit court for California, that he had an opportunity to display his real forensic ability. Judge Deady described his argument in the former as "a masterly and exhaustive presentation of the case," and that in the latter Judge Sawyer characterized as "lucid, exhaustive and eminently instructive."

After nine years at Rochester Pomeroy moved to New York City and in the spring of 1861 became the head of an academy at Kingston, N. Y. In 1864 he published his first book, *An Introduction to Municipal Law* (2nd ed., 1883, reprint, 1886). In the same year he received a call to the law faculty of the University of the City of New York (later New York University). The book, which purported to be an elementary text for law students, really marked a departure from the conventional treatises based upon Blackstone. It disclosed Pomeroy's acquaintance with Roman and other legal systems, as well as with the ideas which Bentham and Austin were then spreading in England. In 1868 he published *An Introduction to the Constitutional Law of the United States* in which he displayed the same scholarly and scientific method. After about six years of teaching in the New York institution he returned to Rochester and devoted himself to writing. In 1874 he published a new edition, with ample notes, of Theodore Sedgwick's treatise on statutory and constitutional law, followed two years later by his own work: *Remedies and Remedial Rights . . . According to the Reformed American Procedure* (2nd ed., 1883). This was an outgrowth of the codification movement initiated in New York under David Dudley Field [*q.v.*] and spreading over about two-thirds of the states. It met the need for a text which would interpret the spirit of the new system and was by far the most philosophical treatise of its time on that theme. Republished later under the title of *Code Remedies* (4th ed., 1904), it is still much used in code states. In 1877 he published a pamphlet entitled *The Code of Remedial Justice Reviewed and Criticised,* containing his protest against changes in the Field Code of Practice, and *A Complete Practical Treatise on Criminal Procedure, Pleading and Evidence,* an edition of the work of J. F. Archbold.

Pomeroy's greatest opportunity came after he had passed fifty. On Mar. 26, 1878, the California legislature established the Hastings College of Law as a department of the state university and Pomeroy was called to its faculty. He delivered the inaugural address, on Aug. 9, 1878, and for the first two years he was the principal instructor. As others joined the faculty he found more leisure for his favorite pursuit—writing. His *Treatise on the Specific Performance of Contracts* appeared in 1879 (2nd ed., 1897) and his *Treatise on Equity Jurisprudence,* pronounced by Justice Field his "greatest work," in 1881–83 (3 vols.). He delivered a course of lectures at the college on "International Law in Time of Peace" which were edited and published posthumously in 1886 by Theodore S. Woolsey of Yale. In 1884 he published *A Treatise on the Law of Riparian Rights* (enlarged ed., 1890) and in 1885 he embodied in a pamphlet of sixty-nine pages his objections to the Civil Code in California. Meanwhile he found time to establish and, with his son Carter, to edit, the *West Coast Reporter* in which he published (Nov. 13–Dec. 4, 1884) what appears to have been the first article in English on the "community property" system which he had found in California. Just when he seemed to have reached the zenith of his fame and productivity, he was stricken with pneumonia and after only a week's illness he passed away. While perhaps not entitled to rank as a world jurist, Pomeroy, in his eight major treatises and numerous articles, has exercised a very considerable influence upon the bench and bar of America and the consequent development of its law. He was married on Nov. 21, 1855, to

Anne Rebecca Carter at Savannah, Ga. They had three sons and one daughter.

[Sources include: J. N. Pomeroy, Jr., "John Norton Pomeroy," in W. D. Lewis, *Great Am. Lawyers,* vol. VIII (1909); Chauncey B. Ripley, *Address on the Presentation of the Memorial Portrait of John Norton Pomeroy to . . . the Univ. of N. Y.* (1888), to which is appended a biographical sketch by Carter Pomeroy; A. A. Pomeroy, *Hist. and Geneal. of the Pomeroy Family* (1912); C. W. Slack, "Hastings Coll. of the Law," *Green Bag,* Dec. 1889; *Daily Examiner* (San Francisco), Feb. 16, 1885.]   C. S. L.

POMEROY, MARCUS MILLS (Dec. 25, 1833–May 30, 1896), popularly known as "Brick" Pomeroy, was a journeyman printer, newspaper editor and publisher, propagandist, politician, and at times, humorist. It was during his youthful editorship of the Horicon (Wisconsin) *Argus* in 1857 that a playful skit on the neighboring town of Beaver Dam won for him from George D. Prentice, then editor of the *Louisville Daily Journal,* the sobriquet of perfect "Brick." He was born in Elmira, N. Y., the son of Hunt Pomeroy, a practical watchmaker, and a descendant of Eltweed Pomeroy who settled in Dorchester, Mass., in 1630. His mother, Orlina Rebecca White, daughter of Dr. Amos Gates White of Orange County, a prominent descendant of Revolutionary stock, died when he was but two, and at her request the child was brought up in her brother's family. There in a log cabin, on a small farm, heavily mortgaged, Mark was reared to hard labor and adversity, and was taught rigid economy from the first. In his youth he helped his uncle in the village smithy, did the usual chores about the farm, and lived the pioneer farm life of that day.

In April 1850 he set out from home, and in true journeyman-printer fashion, tramped to Corning, N. Y., where he began his apprenticeship on the Corning *Journal.* After some years of traveling from one printing office to another, he returned to Corning, established his first paper, the *Sun,* and on Jan. 26, 1854, was married to Anna Amelia Wheeler of that city. Soon afterward he moved to Athens, Pa., and in March 1857, with a total cash capital of $20.29, moved family and baggage to Wisconsin, where he started the Horicon *Argus.* After some journeyman's work in Milwaukee, and Washington, D. C. (including some early political experience), he returned to Wisconsin and in 1860 established the paper that was later to make him nationally famous, the La Crosse *Democrat.* From 1860 to 1866 he engineered the *Democrat* through poverty, prejudice, and political bitterness; his closest friend was the sheriff. The circulation of the paper grew from twenty-seven copies in 1866 to 100,000 in 1868. In New York that year for the political convention, with Tweed's encouragement, Pomeroy published the *New-York Democrat,* and later a weekly called *Pomeroy's Democrat,* but the daily languished after Seymour's defeat, and Pomeroy sold it to Tweed (1870), although he continued the adverse struggle with the weekly. Shortly thereafter he was divorced by his first wife and married Mrs. Louise M. Thomas of Cleveland. In 1873 he moved to Chicago, continuing the *Democrat* there; and from 1876 to 1880 he was actively engaged in organization work for the Greenback cause, organizing some four thousand clubs. Later he again returned to La Crosse to meet reverses in his paper there. He then went to Colorado, where he regained even a greater fortune that he had lost through his New York journalistic ventures by organizing and promoting the Atlantic-Pacific Railway Tunnel, of which he became president, with offices in New York, in 1890. Here, too, he published a general news monthly called *Advance Thought,* and from the offices of the Advance Thought Publishing Company issued many pamphlets and books. He died in Brooklyn, May 30, 1896, survived by his third wife, Emma Stimson, whom he had married on Sept. 2, 1876.

Pomeroy's journalism was sensational, intensely personal, and independent. By its vividness, its personal combativeness, and political partisanship, it gained national notoriety. He was essentially a Jeffersonian Democrat at heart, and was ever a belligerent champion for the people, particularly the "under-dog." In his books he collected both the humorous sketches from his various papers and the sentiment and fireside musings, strongly tinged with moral preachments so characteristic of his day. His six most popular books were: *Sense* (1868); *Nonsense* (1868); *Gold-Dust* (1871); *Brick-Dust* (1871); *Our Saturday Nights* (1870); *Home Harmonies* (1876).

[See: *Journey of Life: Reminiscences and Recollections of "Brick" Pomeroy* (1890), written by himself; M. E. Tucker, *Life of Mark M. Pomeroy* (1868); A. A. Pomeroy, *Hist. and Geneal. of the Pomeroy Family* (1912); *Brooklyn Daily Eagle,* May 30, 1896.]

F. J. M—e.

POMEROY, SAMUEL CLARKE (Jan. 3, 1816–Aug. 27, 1891), Kansas Free-State advocate and United States senator, was born at Southampton, Mass., the son of Samuel and Dorcas (Burt) Pomeroy, and a descendant of Eltweed Pomeroy who emigrated from England to Dorchester, Mass., in 1630. Samuel entered Amherst College in 1836 but withdrew shortly afterward. Later he spent four years in Onondaga County, New York, where he taught school and

engaged in business. Returning to Southampton in 1842, he joined the Liberty party, filled several local offices, and served in the General Court in 1852. Appointed financial agent of the New England Emigrant Aid Company in 1854, he accompanied the second party of settlers to Kansas Territory in the fall of that year. During the Wakarusa War of November–December 1855 he started for Boston to secure aid, but was captured and detained until the crisis was over. When Sheriff Jones assembled "border ruffians" before Lawrence in May 1856, Pomeroy was chosen chairman of a committee of public safety, but he failed to prevent the destruction of the town. He was a delegate to the first Republican National Convention and received eight votes for vice-president. In a sensational speech he declared that freedom for Kansas must be accompanied by reparation and atonement by the South for depredations committed and lives destroyed. The following year he settled at Atchison, where he served as mayor, 1858–59. During the drought and famine in Kansas, 1860–61, he headed a relief committee which distributed eight million pounds of provisions and seeds, besides clothing and medicine.

When Kansas was admitted into the Union, Pomeroy was elected to the United States Senate. He joined the radicals in opposition to Lincoln's administration, and in 1864 became chairman of a committee to promote the candidacy of Salmon P. Chase [*q.v.*] for president. The "Pomeroy Circular," a campaign document widely distributed, asserted that the reëlection of Lincoln was neither possible nor desirable, and that Chase was an able administrator who possessed just those qualifications which would be needed by a president during the next four years. In a speech before the Senate he declared that old political alignments were dead and recommended the creation of a new party with a vigorous program (*Congressional Globe,* 38 Cong., 1 Sess., pt. 2, pp. 1025–27). The movement, however, met with little popular response. Pomeroy's unexpected election to the Senate in 1861 was not free from charges of bargain; his reëlection in 1867 was investigated by a committee of the legislature which reported unanimously that he had bribed members of the General Assembly. He was slated for a third term in 1873, but when the legislature convened in joint session Senator A. M. York announced dramatically that Pomeroy had bargained for his vote for $8,000. The belief in Kansas was almost unanimous that he was guilty, and both houses demanded his resignation. Pomeroy asserted before a select committee of the United States Senate that the money was intended to assist in establishing a bank, and the committee concluded after hearing voluminous testimony that the affair was a plot to defeat him for reëlection. Nevertheless, the incident ended his political career, although he was nominated for president in 1884 by the American Prohibition National Convention. After his failure to secure reëlection in 1873, he continued to live in Washington for several years, but eventually returned to Massachusetts, making his home at Whitinsville, where he died. He was married three times. His first wife was Annie Pomeroy, who died in 1843. On Apr. 23, 1846, he married Lucy Ann Gaylord, who died July 30, 1863. His third wife was Mrs. Martha Whitin of Whitinsville.

[Pamphlets relating to Pomeroy in the Kan. State Hist. Lib., Topeka, include *Political Affairs in Kan., a Review of the Official Acts of Our Delegates in Cong.* (1870); E. H. Grant, *Twelve Years in the U. S. Senate: A Brief Sketch of the Senatorial Record of Hon. S. C. Pomeroy of Kan. . . . from Official Records* (1872); S. C. Knight, *The Truth at Last: or What I Know About Pomeroy . . . Thrilling Disclosures Concerning A. H. Horton and S. C. Pomeroy* (1874); several letters of Pomeroy are preserved by the Mass. Hist. Soc.; for bribery testimony see *Sen. Report, No. 523, 42 Cong., 3 Sess.*; consult also D. W. Wilder, *The Annals of Kan.* (1886); *Trans. Kan. State Hist. Soc.,* esp. vols. IV (1890), VIII (1904), IX (1906); *Biog. Dir. Am. Cong.* (1928); A. A. Pomeroy, *Hist. and Geneal. of the Pomeroy Family* (1912); *Springfield Daily Republican,* Aug. 28, 1891.]   W. H. S.

POMEROY, SETH (May 20, 1706–Feb. 19, 1777), gunsmith, soldier, was born in Northampton, Mass., the son of Ebenezer Pomeroy and his second wife, Sarah King. He was the great-grandson of Eltweed Pomeroy who came to America in 1630. As blacksmiths and gunsmiths the Pomeroys achieved considerable prosperity and long played a prominent part in Northampton affairs. Seth Pomeroy's boyhood and youth were spent in his native town where he joined the local military force, and where, on Dec. 14, 1732, he married Mary Hunt. Nine children were born to them, eight of whom lived to maturity. His name first appears on the military rolls in 1743 as an ensign of the local militia. A year later he received a commission as captain, and in 1745 was a major in the 4th Massachusetts Regiment in the expedition against the French fortress of Louisbourg. His principal service at Louisbourg seems to have been the repairing of captured French cannon which could be used to bombard the town. After his return from Cape Breton Island, he spent three years as the major of troops scattered along the Massachusetts frontier where he directed scouting parties and superintended the construction of military roads through the wilderness. When Sir William Johnson led an army

against Crown Point in 1755, Seth Pomeroy was lieutenant-colonel of the troops raised in western Massachusetts. This regiment bore the brunt of the fighting with the French and Indians in the battle of Lake George on Sept. 8, 1755, and the French commander, Baron Jean Hermant de Dieskau, fell into Pomeroy's hands. As Ephraim Williams, the colonel of the Massachusetts regiment, was killed in the opening skirmish, Pomeroy, after some delay, was given the command. Soon afterward he returned home on sick leave, but he continued as the head of the militia of his district and was in command of the forts along the frontier of his province. Apparently politics held little interest for him since he played only a minor rôle in the affairs of Northampton, being more of a supporter than a member of the political machine directed by Major Joseph Hawley [*q.v.*]. During the quarrel which led to the dismissal of Jonathan Edwards from the pastorate of the Northampton Church in 1750, Pomeroy was instrumental in organizing the opposition to the pastor.

With the approach of the Revolution in 1774, Pomeroy was listed among those "very high in Liberty." He sat on the Northampton Committee of Safety and was one of the town's representatives at the First and Second Provincial Congress. With Artemas Ward [*q.v.*], and Jedidiah Preble, he was appointed to the military command of the province (*Journals of Each Provincial Congress of Massachusetts,* p. 35). His greatest contribution to the American cause was the raising and drilling of troops in western Massachusetts in 1775 and 1776. On June 22, 1775, he was appointed the first brigadier-general in the Continental Army, but he never acted under the commission (*Journals of the Continental Congress,* II, 103). Five days earlier he had fought as a volunteer in the ranks at the Battle of Bunker Hill. On Feb. 19, 1777, while on his way to join the American forces in New Jersey, he died of pleurisy at Peekskill, N. Y.

Though apocryphal accounts describe him as a man of great strength and agility, tall, spare and erect, a "hardy intrepid adventurous soldier, a keen and celebrated hunter, an honest, open hearted man" (Swett, *post,* p. 8), he remains a shadowy figure whose qualities can be little more than surmised. He insured immortality for himself by keeping careful journals which have promoted a fuller understanding of portions of eighteenth-century American life.

[Judd MSS. in Forbes Library, Northampton, Mass.; Pomeroy Papers (Forbes Library), published in *The Journals and Papers of Seth Pomeroy,* ed. by L. E. de Forest (1926); *Jour. Cont. Cong.,* vol. II (1905); *Jour. of Each Provincial Cong. of Mass.* in 1774 and 1775

(1838); *Am. Rev.*, May 1848; S. E. Dwight, *The Life of President Edwards* (1830); A. A. Pomeroy, *Hist. and Geneal. of the Pomeroy Family* (1912); Samuel Swett, *Hist. of Bunker Hill Battle* (2nd ed., 1826); J. R. Trumbull, *Hist. of Northampton*, vol. II (1902).]

E. F. B.

PONCE DE LEÓN, JUAN (*c.* 1460–1521), Spanish explorer, discoverer of Florida, came of an ancient though somewhat decadent noble family of Aragon. He was born at San Servos in the province of Campos, Spain; as a lad, was page to Don Pedro Nuñez de Guzman; and as a youth, fought against the Moors of Granada. He is thought to have shipped with Columbus in 1493 on his second voyage to Hispaniola, where in 1502–04 he served with great credit in the conquest of Higuey under Nicolas de Ovando, who appointed him governor of that province. About the year 1508 an Indian of Boriquen (Puerto Rico), which as yet the Spaniards had not explored, crossing to Hispaniola in a canoe, brought Juan Ponce some grains and a nugget of gold, with the report that in San Juan de Puerto Rico the sands were full of gold. Ponce fitted out a caravel and, guided by the Indian, crossed to Puerto Rico, where he found gold in considerable quantities. He returned at once to Hispaniola and was empowered by Ovando to enlist soldiers for the subjugation of the former isle. The conquest was effected, and Ponce was appointed governor in 1509. Diego Columbus, son of the Discoverer, claiming a right to the post, contested the appointment and in 1512 secured it for himself. Meanwhile, however, from the fruit of the island in gold, lands, and slaves, Ponce had derived a fortune.

His success in Puerto Rico caused him to listen eagerly to the tales told by Indians of the Lesser Antilles—Caribs accustomed to long voyages—of an island called Bimini, where there abounded all that man could desire, gold and delicious fruits, and a spring the waters of which had the power of making the aged young again. It became his ambition to find Bimini, and on Feb. 23, 1512, he was commissioned by King Ferdinand of Spain to discover, possess, and colonize this wonderful island; and at the same time he was given the title of *adelantado,* or governor, for life. On Mar. 3, 1513, he set out with three vessels from Puerto Rico. He cast anchor at the island known today as Grand Turk, and from there sailed on to Guanahani, the San Salvador of Columbus. Continuing to Little Bahama Bank, he proceeded westward, and on Apr. 2 struck the coast of Florida, in true latitude 27° 30′, a little north of Rio de Canoas (Indian River Inlet) and about 175 miles south of the site of St. Augustine (Scisco, "The Track of Ponce de

León," *post,* p. 725). The Spaniards named the new land La Florida either because of the beauty of its vegetation or because they discovered it at the time of the Easter feast (Pascua Florida).

Turning southward on Apr. 8, Juan Ponce on Apr. 20 discovered some Indian huts on the shore, and cast anchor opposite them. The Indians signaled to the crew to land, and when they did so, tried to take possession of their boat and arms. A fight ensued, during which two Spaniards were wounded but the Indians suffered little. Hereabouts (Jupiter Inlet), Ponce took water and firewood and seized one Indian for a pilot, from whom he also expected to learn the language. Continuing southward along the Florida coast, he stopped at Lakeworth Inlet, and passed the bay at the modern Miami. His course was next along the Florida Keys to Key West, thence to the Tortugas group, and thence northeast to some islands off the west Florida mainland between Cape Romano and Charlotte Harbor.

From Cape Romano, on June 14 he began to retrace his route (by way of Cuba) to the vicinity of the modern Miami, whence he crossed the Bahama Channel, still in search of Bimini, supposed to lie somewhere in the western part of the Bahama Archipelago, the sole official object of his voyage. His course took him to the island of Eleuthera northwestward of San Salvador. Here he detailed one of his smaller vessels under Juan Pérez de Ortubía, with Anton de Alaminos, who had been at one time with Columbus, as pilot, to continue the search for Bimini while he himself sailed homeward. He went reluctantly, for he had been eager to find the island himself, especially because of "that particular spring, as the Indians said, that restores men from old ones to youths" (Herrera, quoted by Scisco, *op. cit.,* p. 733). Alaminos, working westward, found Habacon, the modern Andros Island, which from its water places and woodlands he identified with Bimini, but which disappointingly offered no fountain of youth.

Having regained Puerto Rico, Juan Ponce found it necessary to pacify the island, a task which he valiantly undertook but accomplished only in part. Thereupon he proceeded to Spain to make known to King Ferdinand conditions in the island and to relate his adventures. The King listened graciously and in September 1514 commissioned Ponce to settle "the isle of Bimini and the isle of Florida which he had discovered under the royal orders." Before settling the new islands, however, he was to lead an expedition against the Caribs of the islands south of Boriquen (Puerto Rico). This expedition, in 1515,

met with fierce resistance, and Ponce returned
to Puerto Rico, where for five years he remained
in a state of "growling repose." Then on a day
in 1521 he fitted out two ships with 200 men, fifty
horses, and other domestic animals and farm implements, and sailed for Florida. "Among my
services," he had written to King Charles I of
Spain (Emperor Charles V) from Puerto Rico
on Feb. 10, 1521, "I discovered at my own cost
and charge the Island Florida and others in its
district . . . and now I return to that island, if
it please God's will, to settle it . . . and I also
intend to explore the coast of said island further,
and see whether it is an island . . ." (translated
in Winsor, *post*, II, 234–35). On this second expedition to Florida, Ponce made land on the west
coast, probably in the neighborhood of Charlotte
Harbor, or possibly of Tampa Bay. Whatever the
point, he and his landing party were met by the
Indians in fierce array. Ponce himself was smitten by an arrow in the body and so severely hurt
that as soon as he had been carried aboard his
flagship it set sail for Cuba. Here, within a few
days, he died. He had married in Hispaniola and
was survived by a son and a daughter. The son
was granted his father's title and rights in Florida but of his fate nothing further is known.
Ponce was given sepulture in Puerto Rico, beneath the high altar of the Dominican Church of
San Juan. The Latin epitaph inscribed above his
grave, translated (Bourne, p. 136), reads: "Beneath this stone repose the bones of the valiant
Lion whose deeds surpassed the greatness of his
name."

[F. A. Ober, *Juan Ponce de León* (1908), a popular
treatment; Justin Winsor, *Narrative and Critical Hist.
of America*, vol. II (1886); Woodbury Lowery, *The
Spanish Settlements within the Present Limits of the
U. S., 1513–1561* (1901); L. D. Scisco, "The Track of
Ponce de León in 1513," *Bull. Am. Geog. Soc.*, Oct.
1913, and "Ponce de León's Patents for Colonization,"
Records Am. Cath. Hist. Soc., Dec. 1912; *Boletín His-
tórico de Puerto Rico*, May–June, July–Aug. 1914; E.
G. Bourne, *Spain in America* (1904); *Colección des
Documentos Inéditos Relativos al Descubrimiento . . .
de América y Oceanía*, I (1864), 260–61, XI (1869),
283–84, 293–98, XXII (1874), 26–32, XXXIV (1880),
336–516; Antonio Herrera y Tordesillas, *Historia General de los Hechos de los Castellanos en las Islas* (8
vols., 1726–27); Andrés Gonzalez de Barcia Carballido
y Zúñiga, *Ensayo Cronologico, para la Historia General de la Florida* (1723); Gonzalo Fernandez de Oviedo
y Valde, *Historia General y Natural de las Indias*, vols.
I (1851), III (1853).]   I. B. R.

POND, ALLEN BARTLIT (Nov. 21, 1858–
Mar. 17, 1929), architect, humanitarian, was
born in Ann Arbor, Mich., and died in Chicago.
He never married. His parents, Elihu Bartlit
and Mary Barlow (Allen) Pond were both born
in New York State of New England stock, the
father being descended from Samuel Pond who
was in Windsor, Conn., as early as 1642. They

were intellectuals imbued with a strong sense of
an individual responsibility in social and civic
relationships. Elihu B. Pond for many years
edited and published a newspaper in Ann Arbor.
Allen was brought up in an atmosphere of high
thinking and straight living. He attended the
University of Michigan where he majored in
civics and received his degree of A.B. in 1880.
After teaching Latin in the Ann Arbor high
school for three years he became assistant to his
father, who had been made warden of the state
prison at Jackson, and helped him reorganize its
methods of administration and of book-keeping.
He then studied contract- and real-estate law at
the University, and in 1886 moved to Chicago
where, after a year in the architectural office of
Solon S. Beman, he joined his brother, Irving K.
Pond, in the practice of architecture under the
firm name of Pond & Pond. He shared the credit
and responsibility of erecting a great many buildings of all kinds, including Hull House, a group
of structures (1895–1915); Chicago Commons
(1899–1901); the City Club (1910–12); the
Hotel Whitcomb (1927), at St. Joseph, Mich.;
the Michigan Union (1916–21) and the Michigan
League (1928–30) at Ann Arbor; and the Memorial Union at Purdue University (1923–25
and 1929). He was a Fellow of the American
Institute of Architects.

At least half of his time and energies, however,
were deliberately dedicated to social and civic
work. He was a close associate of Jane Addams
in Hull House, and from 1895 to the time of his
death was a trustee and secretary of Hull House
Association. He was president and trustee of
Gads Hill Center from 1914, associate superintendent of Armour Mission, and a leader in many
other social and civic organizations. During the
World War he served on the board of the Fuel
Administration, as special distribution agent of
the United States on public information, and as
secretary of the war committee of the Union
League Club.

He made several trips to Europe, on each
taking time to study city planning and zoning
as practised in England and on the Continent.
He loved the landscape of the Tyrol, and the art
and mellowing architecture of the Continent;
and returned to Chicago only because he was
impelled by a sense of duty, which could not be
gainsaid. Perhaps his finest work was done as
chairman of the board of appeals under the zoning law of the city of Chicago, 1923–27. In this
capacity, he exercised keen analytical insight,
absolute fairness, and a predominating share of
human kindness. His great value as the champion of right versus corruption, when the issue

arose, lay in his fearlessness. Though not robust in health and slender in physique, he loved a fight. It almost seemed at times as if he sought out the battle, and perhaps for this reason defeat to him never meant discouragement. His work for civic betterment in Chicago bore fruit in legislative acts relating to architecture, city planning, playgrounds, and parks. He was a thorough student of international relations and a director in the English Speaking Union. Notwithstanding his wide activities, which he pursued with conscientious zeal, he still found time for study and kept alive his interests in scholarship and art.

[D. S. Pond, *A Geneal. Record of Samuel Pond and His Descendants* (1875); *Who's Who in America*, 1928–29; *Am. Architect*, Feb. 1, 1922, Apr. 20, 1929; *Brickbuilder*, July, Aug., Sept. 1902, Oct. 1915; *Octagon*, May 1929; *Western Architect*, Nov. 1918, Mar. 1923, Apr. 1929; *Chicago Daily Tribune*, Mar. 18, 1929; Jane Addams, *Twenty Years at Hull House* (1910); information from brother, Irving K. Pond; personal recollections.]   T. E. T.

POND, ENOCH (July 29, 1791–Jan. 21, 1882), Congregationalist clergyman, professor in Bangor Theological Seminary, author, was born in Wrentham, Mass., the eldest son of Elijah and Mary (Smith) Pond. The first American ancestor of the family was Daniel Pond who settled in Dedham, Mass., about 1652. Enoch's was the usual New England boyhood of the period, spent in a plain home, the district school, and in outdoor work on a farm. He began teaching at sixteen, and after a preparation partly self-acquired and partly at Day's Academy at Wrentham, he entered Brown University as a sophomore. Though he taught for eight weeks each winter, he graduated in 1813 with the valedictory. He then studied theology for a year with Dr. Nathaniel Emmons [*q.v.*] of Franklin, during which time he mastered the latter's "system" and taught a school for ten weeks. In 1814 he was called to a country church at Ward (now Auburn), Mass., where he was ordained on Mar. 1, 1815. He carried on arduous and successful ministerial labors, began writing tracts and articles for the religious press, and conducted a private school in his parsonage. His success as a writer was so marked that he was invited in 1828 to assume the editorship of the *Spirit of the Pilgrims*, a periodical recently founded in Boston for the purpose of controverting Unitarianism. After editing five volumes of this paper, about half of the articles being from his own pen, he received a call to Bangor Theological Seminary and began there in 1832 a service which ended only with his death fifty years later.

When he went to Bangor, the Seminary had one building and seven students. He shared the teaching and administration with one other professor, he himself occupying the chairs of church history and systematic theology and giving instruction also in homiletics and pastoral theology. So successful was his leadership that he has been called the "Second Founder" of the institution. Under him the faculty and student body were augmented, three commodious buildings were erected, and substantial endowment was secured. During his term of service, over 700 students were instructed by him. He resigned the chair of theology in 1856 but continued to teach church history till 1870. In 1856 he was made president of the faculty, which office he held for the remainder of his life.

Pond's literary activities began with his tract, *Divinity of Christ* (1815), and ended with *Conversations on the Bible* (1881), a book of 630 pages. A list of his writings includes some fifty-eight separate publications on biographical, historical, and religious subjects, about forty of which are books. Among his more important volumes are *The Young Pastor's Guide* (1844), *Lectures on Pastoral Theology* (1866), *Lectures on Christian Theology* (1868), *A History of God's Church* (1870), *The Seals Opened* (1871). He also wrote about two hundred articles for various religious and theological reviews, and his contributions to religious weeklies and the secular press are innumerable. He remained an exponent of the New England Theology, which he had learned from Dr. Emmons. He was strongly opposed to German Biblical scholarship and had no part in the rising tide of modernism of his day; but his spirit was always sweet and tolerant and there was nothing of the militant Fundamentalist in him. He was untiring in promoting the cause of the churches of Maine and was an ardent supporter of evangelistic, missionary, and temperance movements. His nature was social, he was charitable in his judgments, and he combined gentleness with tact and dignity. He was married three times: first, Aug. 28, 1814, to Wealthy Ann Hawes of Wrentham, Mass., who died in September 1824; second, May 17, 1825, to Julia Ann Maltby of Northford, Conn., who died Sept. 9, 1838; and third, July 9, 1839, to Mrs. Anne Pearson of Bangor, widow of John S. Pearson, and daughter of Thaddeus Mason. There were seven children by the first marriage and seven by the second.

[*The Autobiography of Enoch Pond* (1883); E. D. Harris, *A Geneal. Record of Daniel Pond and His Descendants* (1873); C. M. Clark, *Hist. of Bangor Theolog. Sem.* (1916); *The Congreg. Year-Book*, 1883; *Congregationalist*, Jan. 25, 1882.]   F. T. P.

POND, FREDERICK EUGENE (Apr. 8, 1856–Nov. 1, 1925), writer on field sports, better known by his pen name of "Will Wildwood," was born at Packwaukee, Marquette County, Wis., the eldest of the four children of Simeon and Flora (Hotchkiss) Pond. His father, descended from Samuel Pond who was living at Windsor, Conn., in 1642, had gone to Wisconsin from Addison, Steuben County, N. Y. He was a lumber merchant and during the Civil War a soldier in the 1st Wisconsin Heavy Artillery. Growing up amid the forests and lakes of his native county, Pond became an enthusiastic hunter and fisherman. He attended school at Montello, sent news items to various sporting papers, and, though only eighteen years old, took a leading part in the organization at Portage in 1874 of the Wisconsin State Sportsmen's Association. For the rest of his life he was a journalist. He was in New York as field editor of *Turf, Field, and Farm,* 1881–86, and then returned to Westfield, Wis., where he started his own periodical, *Wildwood's Magazine.* About a year later he sold it to his former associates in New York and joined their staff again as a corresponding editor. On June 22, 1892, he married Frances Harriet Fox, a grand-daughter of Solomon Laurent Juneau [*q.v.*], who survived him. He was secretary of the National Game, Bird, and Fish Protective Association, 1893–95; editor of the *Sportsmen's Review* in Cincinnati, 1897–1917; editor of the *American Angler* in New York, 1917–18; and editor of the rod and gun column of the *New York Herald* and *Herald Tribune* from 1923 until his death. He was a close student of the literature of sport and was interested especially in the work of "Frank Forester" [Henry William Herbert, *q.v.*], whose *Fugitive Sporting Sketches* (Westfield, Wis., 1879) and *Sporting Scenes and Characters* (2 vols., Philadelphia, 1881) he edited. He also edited Isaac McLellan's *Poems of the Rod and Gun* (1886) and Charles Hallock's *An Angler's Reminiscences* (1913). He was the author of a *Handbook for Young Sportsmen* (1876), *Memoirs of Eminent Sportsmen* (1878), *Life and Adventures of Ned Buntline* (1888; 1919), and several other books. His fresh, informal, good-natured style won him friends, but his practice of listening with flattering attention to the interminable reminiscences of his companions won him even more. Among anglers and hunters with strong autobiographical propensities he was prized as a perfect auditor. For years he suffered from stomach trouble without knowing, or without revealing, the fatal character of his malady. The end came quickly. While packing his books preparatory to moving from Brooklyn to a Long Island suburb, he collapsed and died a few days later. He was buried at Warwick, Orange County, N. Y., near the memorial erected to his favorite writer.

[D. S. Pond, *A Geneal. Record of Samuel Pond* (1875); *Portr. and Biog. Album of Green Lake, Marquette and Waushara Counties, Wis.* (1890), pp. 590–91; *Bibliog. of Wis. Authors* (1893); *Who's Who in America,* 1924–25; *N. Y. Herald Tribune,* Nov. 2, 3, 6, 1925; *Sportsmen's Rev.* and *Am. Field,* Nov. 14, 1925.]
G. H. G.

POND, GEORGE EDWARD (Mar. 11, 1837–Sept. 22, 1899), editor and journalist, was the son of Moses and Nancy (Adams) Pond, and a descendant of Daniel Pond who settled in Dedham, Mass., about 1652. Born in Boston, where his father was well established in business, George later attended the high school and the Latin School of Boston. In 1858 he graduated from Harvard, and two years afterward received the degree of bachelor of laws. While at Harvard, he had the privilege of attending one of the first classes conducted by James Russell Lowell in the study of Dante—an experience which Pond was later to record in "Lowell at Harvard," a paper published in *The First Book of the Authors Club; Liber Scriptorum* (1893). A further reminder of Pond's college days is his sketch of his classmate, Henry Lyman Patten, contributed to *Harvard Memorial Biographies* (1866), edited by Thomas W. Higginson.

Pond was entering upon the practice of law when the Civil War broke out. Giving up his chosen profession, to which he never returned, he served from 1862 to 1864 as first lieutenant of the 45th Regiment, Massachusetts Volunteers. His resignation from the army in 1864 and his acceptance of the associate editorship of the *Army and Navy Journal* marked a turning point in his career, for it was now that his literary and journalistic abilities began rapidly to mature. Of his contributions to the *Journal,* especially noteworthy were the accounts of General Sherman's movements while lost in Georgia during his famous march to the sea. These accounts, ingeniously pieced together from scraps of information received from within the Confederate lines, are said, because of their accuracy, to have amazed General Sherman and his associates when they reached Savannah.

Leaving the *Army and Navy Journal* in 1868, he served for the next two years on the editorial staff of the *New York Times.* In 1870 he removed to Philadelphia, where he became editor-in-chief of the *Record,* a daily newspaper. When in 1877 the *Record* changed proprietors, Pond resumed an editorial connection with the *Army and Navy Journal* which lasted for probably two years. About 1880 he became an editorial writer on the New York *Sun,* and retained this position until his death. In the midst of these journalistic duties he found time to write for the *Galaxy* (May 1868–Jan. 1878) a series of light essays on topics of current interest, which appeared each month under the title "Drift-Wood," and were signed "Philip Quilibet." He wrote for *Appletons' Annual Cyclopædia* for 1883 the article on Gen. Philip H. Sheridan, and published *The Shenandoah Valley in 1864* (1883), the eleventh volume of Scribner's series, Campaigns of the Civil War. Regarding this last-named book, critics have differed in opinion. Although considered by some a most authoritative treatment of the subject, the book at the time it appeared was criticized both by a Southern and by a Northern reviewer as giving but an inadequate idea of the Confederate side of the campaign. In 1866 Pond married Emilie Guerber, who died in 1880. He was for some years prior to his death a member of the Authors Club, and seems to have been much beloved by his associates. "Modest to an extreme that permitted the full revelation of his ability only to those who knew him intimately, conscientious, of the most sensitive honor, faithful to every duty, . . . George Pond [was] one of the best types of an American gentleman" (*The Sun*, New York, Sept. 23, 1899, p. 6). His sudden death at his summer home at Como, N. J., was due to heart disease.

[E. D. Harris, *A Geneal. Record of Daniel Pond and His Descendants* (1873); *Who's Who in America*, 1899; *Appletons' Ann. Cyc. . . . 1899* (1900); *Army and Navy Jour.*, Sept. 30, 1899; *N. Y. Times, Evening Post*, and *Sun*, Sept. 23, 1899; reviews of *The Shenandoah Valley* in *The Southern Hist. Soc. Papers*, June 1883, and in the *Nation* (N. Y.), Mar. 8, 1883.]
N.F.A.

POND, JAMES BURTON (June 11, 1838–June 21, 1903), lecture manager, was born at Cuba, Allegany County, N. Y. Descended from Phineas Pond, who was living in Branford, Conn., in 1735, he was the eldest son of Willard Elmer and Clarissa (Woodford) Pond. His father, a blacksmith and farmer, left New York state in 1844, taking his wife and five children on a journey by the Erie Canal and the Great Lakes to Kenosha (then Southport), Wis., and thence by wagon to Lake County, Ill., where he worked land "on shares" for three unfruitful years. The family then emigrated northward to Alto, Fond du Lac County, Wis., where they preëmpted a quarter-section of government land. Still, however, the father seemed unable to succeed at farming, and eventually he reverted to his trade. When James was fifteen, after a few terms in the country schools of the vicinity, he struck out for himself and became a printer's apprentice at Fond du Lac. In a short time he "learned the case,"

after the fashion of those days, and acquired enough skill to run a local newspaper. He worked at the printer's trade in several Wisconsin towns and for a time in 1856 was employed on the *Herald of Freedom,* at Lawrence, Kan. Although in later life he spoke of carrying a Sharps rifle under the leadership of John Brown during this period, there is no reason to believe that his activity with Brown was more than casual; it was certainly brief. In 1859 he visited Pike's Peak. At the outbreak of the Civil War he was owner and manager of a paper at Markesan, Wis. He abandoned that venture to join the 3rd Wisconsin Cavalry. During most of the Civil War he was engaged in service against guerrilla bands in Kansas and Missouri. In 1863, as lieutenant in command of a small force at Baxter Springs, he repelled an attack of the guerrilla leader William C. Quantrill with a band of desperadoes wearing the Federal uniform and carrying the Union flag. He was commended by his superior officers for gallantry on that occasion. After the close of the war he was commissioned major.

He returned to Wisconsin but, not finding a newspaper opening to his liking, soon left for the West, where he was a rolling stone for several years. Finally bringing up at Salt Lake City, he worked on the *Tribune* and for a time owned a furniture business. He made the acquaintance of Ann Eliza, the nineteenth wife of Brigham Young [*q.v.*], and when she left Young's household and renounced the practices of Mormonism, Pond managed her first lecture tour. Such was his introduction to the calling that he followed for the last thirty years of his life. He went to Boston and joined the staff of the lyceum bureau then directed by James Redpath [*q.v.*], whom he had known in Kansas. In 1875, Pond and George H. Hathaway bought Redpath's interest in the business, which they jointly operated until 1879, when Pond removed to New York City and opened an office of his own.

His work at Boston had been largely the promotion of foreign authors and orators on the American lecture platform, and this he continued in New York, but he also became identified in a remarkable way with the lecture experiences of Henry Ward Beecher [*q.v.*], with whom in twelve years (1875–87) he traveled 300,000 miles. During that period, under Pond's management, Beecher lectured 1,261 times. There had been little in Pond's earlier experience to indicate his success in meeting the delicate requirements of a career in the lyceum field, but within a few years he scored a rather imposing list of achievements for that time. His judgment in the selection of celebrities to present to the

American public rarely failed. Henry M. Stanley, Conan Doyle, Bill Nye, and Mark Twain were among his "stars." It was in Pond's time that the most famous lecturers first received thousand-dollar fees. Several of these men made substantial fortunes under his management. He published accounts of his experiences in *A Summer in England with Henry Ward Beecher* (1887), and *Eccentricities of Genius* (1900), a series of impressions of platform personalities. He also wrote the story of his early life in "A Pioneer Boyhood," contributed to the *Century Magazine* (October 1899). He was married in January 1859 to Ann Frances Lynch, who died in 1871; and on Mar. 10, 1888, to Martha Glass. A daughter was born to the first marriage and a son to the second.

[Pond's publications mentioned above; *N. Y. Tribune*, June 22, 1903; *Ibid.*, June 28, 1903; *War of the Rebellion: Official Records (Army)*, 1 ser., vol. XXII, pt. 1, pp. 688–700; W. E. Connelley, *Quantrill and the Border Wars* (1910); *Who's Who in America*, 1901–02; D. S. Pond, *A Geneal. Record of Samuel Pond and His Descendants* (1875).]   W. B. S.

POND, PETER (Jan. 18, 1740–1807), soldier, fur-trader, and explorer, was a Connecticut Yankee, born at Milford, eldest son of Peter and Mary (Hubbard) Pond, and a descendant of Samuel Pond who settled in Windsor, Conn., not later than 1642. As a soldier he served in the French and Indian War; in 1756 under Capt. David Baldwin of the 7th Connecticut Regiment; two years later with General Abercromby at Ticonderoga; in 1759 as sergeant in the New York regiment from Suffolk County; and, as a commissioned officer (1760) under General Amherst at Montreal. Of his services at Lake George and Niagara he gives a circumstantial account in his journal, which has a crude power and is the evident report of an eye witness. While in Milford, sometime between 1761 and 1765, he married Susanna Newell by whom he had at least two children.

After the close of the war he undertook a trading voyage to the West Indies, but in 1765 entered the western fur trade, which occupied him for the most part for over twenty years. His first venture was at Detroit, whence he traded for five years and bought property at Grosse Point. In 1770 he transferred his headquarters to Mackinac but returned to Milford in 1771 and made another trip to the West Indies the following year. In 1773–74 he made two journeys from Mackinac to the upper Mississippi, trading particularly among the Sioux on St. Peter's, now the Minnesota, River. His journal of his experiences in Wisconsin, ending in 1775, while illiterate and uncouth in form, is vivid and picturesque in description. In 1775 he determined to try his fortune in the Far West and went via Grand Portage on Lake Superior to winter in the interior, overtaking Alexander Henry on the way and accompanying him. After two years on the Saskatchewan River, Pond pooled interest with the Frobishers and Alexander Henry for a push into the farther north. He was one of the first traders to explore the Athabaska and there opened a rich fur-region. In a quarrel at his post in 1782 a rival trader, Jean Étienne Waden, was slain, and in 1784 Pond was summoned to Montreal for trial, where he was acquitted. In the winter of 1783–84 the North West Company was organized, in which Pond had one of the sixteen shares.

Before returning to the Northwest he visited his home and presented to Congress a map of his voyages, which was copied for the archives of Great Britain and of France. Going back to the Athabasca in 1785, he prepared another map for the Empress of Russia. In 1788 he withdrew from the fur-trade company, selling his share for eight hundred pounds, and by 1790 was again at Milford. He visited President Stiles of Yale College, who made a copy of his revised map of the West. Little is known of his last years; he is said to have died in poverty at Boston. Pond had the virtues and defects of his calling. He was bold, enterprising, courageous, and persevering, but ruthless in competition, sacrificing all for success.

[Pond's diary is printed in *Wis. Hist. Soc. Colls.*, vol. XVIII (1908); one copy of his map is in *Report on Canadian Archives, 1890* (1891); see also G. C. Davidson, *The North West Company* (Berkeley, Cal., 1918); H. A. Innis, "Peter Pond," in *Trans. Royal Soc. of Canada*, 3 ser. XXII, Sec. 2 (1928), and *Peter Pond: Fur Trader and Adventurer* (1930); C. M. Gates, *Five Fur Traders of the Northwest* (1933); N. G. Pond, "The Ponds of Conn.," in *Conn. Mag.*, Jan., Feb., Mar. 1906.]   L. P. K.

POND, SAMUEL WILLIAM (Apr. 10, 1808–Dec. 12, 1891), Congregational missionary to the Indians, was born in New Preston, Conn., fifth child of Elnathan J. and Sarah (Hollister) Pond, and a descendant of Samuel Pond who came to Windsor, Conn., not later than 1642. After a brief elementary education he was apprenticed to a clothier, and later taught a local school. As a result of a revival he and his brother, Gideon Hollister (June 30, 1810–Jan. 20, 1878), wholly inexperienced and without help from any mission board or church, entered the hitherto untouched mission field of the Dakota, or Sioux, Indians in May 1834, by way of Fort Snelling. They received assistance from the commandant and from the Indian agent, were assigned to an Indian settlement at Lake Calhoun, and in 1835 helped to establish a mission at Lake Harriet. Over six feet in height, strong, and genial, "they seemed the children of a king." Even before reaching Fort Snelling they had begun the study of the Dakota language, for which there was neither grammar nor dictionary. Throughout much of the remainder of their lives the study of this difficult tongue was a major concern with them. Before the end of the first year they had evolved an alphabet, begun work on a grammar, and collected many words. As other missionaries came during the next few years, the alphabet was generally adopted and the grammar and dictionary accepted and improved. Samuel accompanied the Indians on long hunts, plowed for them, and associated with them on intimate terms in order to gain mastery of the language. In 1836 he published a spelling book. This was the first work ever printed in the Dakota language.

Returning to Connecticut, he studied privately and on Mar. 4, 1837, was ordained missionary to the Sioux Indians by the Litchfield South Association of Congregational Ministers, Connecticut. The following October he received an appointment from the American Board of Commissioners for Foreign Missions. He was married in 1838 to Cordelia Eggleston of the Lake Harriet mission, and in 1839 took charge of that station. The same year he published, with his brother's revision, *The History of Joseph, in the Language of the Dakota or Sioux Indians,* a translation of the story in Genesis. Soon afterwards hostilities reopened between the Sioux and the Chippewa, and the Indians to whom Pond ministered left their home and settled eventually at Oak Grove on the lower Minnesota River. After a brief residence near Fort Snelling, therefore, the brothers joined the Indians at Oak Grove in 1843. Meantime Samuel had published *Wowapi inonpa . . . The Second Dakota Reading Book* (1842), *The Dakota First Reading Book* having been published by his brother and Stephen Return Riggs [*q.v.*] in 1839. In 1844 appeared Samuel's *Dakota Wiwangapi Wowapi: Catechism in the Dakotah or Sioux Language.* In 1847 he established a mission at Shakopee, which place he called Prairieville. This remained his station till the Sioux, having sold their lands in 1851, removed in 1853, and it was his residence from that time until his death. His first wife died in February 1852, and that same year he married a former schoolmate, Rebecca Smith. Meantime, the American Board had published *Dakota Dowanpi Kin: Hymns in the Dakota or Sioux Language* (1842), largely his work, though his name does not appear on the title

page. In 1852 "Grammar and Dictionary of the Dakota Language," edited by S. R. Riggs, was issued (*Smithsonian Contributions to Knowledge,* vol. IV, 1852). Though this publication does not bear Pond's name, its inception and much of its copiousness and accuracy were due to him.

After the Indians left Prairieville, Pond remained as pastor to the incoming white settlers. In 1866 he also relinquished this charge. The remainder of his life was devoted largely to his studies. He wrote "The Dakotas or Sioux in Minnesota as They Were in 1834," published many years after his death in *Collections of the Minnesota Historical Society* (vol. XII, 1908). He was also the author of "Indian Warfare in Minnesota" (*Ibid.,* vol. III, 1880); *Winona's Rock* (n.d.), a poem published in pamphlet form; and other verse collected in *Legends of the Dakotas and Other Selections from the Poetical Works of Rev. Samuel Pond* (1911). He made contributions to *The Dakota Friend,* and a study of the Septuagint by him appeared in the *Herald and Presbyter* (Cincinnati) during the week that he died. His death occurred at Shakopee, Minn. By his first wife he had four children.

[Pond family papers, Minn. Hist. Soc.; letters from the brothers to the Am. Board, and its replies, in the Board's archives in Boston; D. S. Pond, *A Geneal. Record of Samuel Pond* (1875); W. W. Folwell, *A Hist. of Minn.,* vol. I (1921); S. W. Pond, Jr., *Two Volunteer Missionaries among the Dakotas or The Story of the Labors of Samuel W. and Gideon H. Pond* (1893); E. D. Neill, "A Memorial of the Brothers Pond, The First Resident Missionaries among the Dakotas," in *Macalester College Contributions,* 2 ser., no. 8 (St. Paul, 1892).]

G. L. N.

PONTIAC (d. 1769), Ottawa chief, is permanently identified through Francis Parkman's classic account, *The History of the Conspiracy of Pontiac* (1851), with the French and Indian War in the old Northwest. His name has been spelled Ponteach, and always appears as Pondiac in contemporary documents. Accounts of his early life are largely legendary. Parkman had probably only a traditional source for establishing his birth in the year 1720 and on the Maumee River. He claimed that Pontiac's maternal Chippewa blood gave him influence over this tribe as well as his own tribe, the Ottawa, but during the siege of Detroit the chief had great difficulty in retaining the allegiance of the Chippewa. The "Sachem of the Outawawas" encountered by Major Robert Rogers [*q.v.*] on his way to Detroit in 1760 to take over the fort surrendered by the French may have been Pontiac, as asserted in Rogers' *Concise Account of North America* (1765), although Rogers' "Journal" of that year (Paltsits, *post,* pp. 6–9) and George Croghan's journals do not mention him by name. He may have been among those present at the conference between the Detroit Indians and Sir William Johnson [*q.v.*] on Sept. 3, 1761.

His claim to fame, however, lies in his activities during the siege of Detroit in 1763–64, although his importance at this time was probably much less than Parkman thought. He it was who attempted to surprise by treachery the garrison at Detroit commanded by Maj. Henry Gladwin [*q.v.*], and during the long siege which followed, he was the greatest local menace. He was chief of the Ottawa, the strongest band besieging the fort; yet the other local Indians retained their own chiefs and were free to make separate peace negotiations. Pontiac is mentioned in contemporary documents as commandeering the houses and supplies of the French *habitants* and he is said to have issued bills of credit bearing the otter mark in return for these favors (Rogers, *Concise Account*, p. 244). By July 2, 1763, Amherst had ordered him killed if found in arms against the English. The following autumn some bands made offers of peace; at this time it was rumored within the fort that the Ottawa were angry at Pontiac for proposing to go off, and they chose one Manitoo for their chief in his place. This suggests that Pontiac's power was not as great as Parkman believed. When on Oct. 17 a group of Indians sued for peace, Manitoo was mentioned as being an Ottawa chief present, while Pontiac was not named. Pontiac's group seemed bent on breaking the truce made by the other Indians. Yet there are in the Gage and also in the Bouquet Papers copies of a letter dated Oct. 30, 1763, from Pontiac to Gladwin, suing for peace (*Report on Canadian Archives . . . in 1889*, 1890, Bouquet Collection," pp. 242–43; *Michigan Pioneer and Historical Society Collections,* vol. XXVII, 1897, p. 675). Apparently he and his band retired to their winter camp on the Maumee River shortly thereafter.

In the fall of 1764, when Col. John Bradstreet [*q.v.*] proceeded westward with an army, Pontiac was to have met him at Sandusky to treat for peace, but he did not put in an appearance. It was now that he proved very annoying to the English. Probably he did not start the uprising to which Parkman gave the name of Pontiac's conspiracy; this very likely was begun by belts sent by the Shawnee, Delaware, and Seneca nations, while Pontiac merely took up the opposition at Detroit. Most of the nations, however, came to terms with Col. Henry Bouquet [*q.v.*], Col. John Bradstreet, or Sir William Johnson, while Pontiac and his followers, supposedly encouraged by the French, refused to leave their

quarters on the Maumee. Capt. John Montresor records in his journal, under date of Sept. 6: "Arrived this evening . . . Pondiac's own Band of Ottawas . . ." (*Collections of the New York Historical Society, Publication Fund Series,* vol. XIV, 1882, p. 289) ; but Pontiac himself sent a belt and speech which so displeased those present that they hacked the belt to pieces. He declined to appear until his pardon should be granted. During the summer of 1765, however, he accepted belts of peace carried by Lieut. Alexander Fraser. George Croghan, Johnson's deputy, succeeded in settling matters so that, despite rumored French efforts to withdraw his allegiance, Pontiac attended a conference at Fort Ontario in July 1766. Once he had made peace with the English, he abode by it. The circumstances of his death, which occurred in 1769, remain obscure. The account given in Parkman's *Conspiracy* has been shown to be based on a legend which is contradictory in itself and which comes from an unreliable source. A letter from Gage to Johnson cites a rumor attributing his death to a Peorie of the Illinois, excited by the English. Various colonial newspapers for 1769 print letters reporting his death; the earliest is dated Fort Chartres, May 15. These papers say he was killed at the Illinois by Indians of that country; one says this was during a drunken frolic; another says the murderers were two Kaskaskias.

Instead of being a great organizer, Pontiac was more likely only a local villain; at least two people who were in Detroit during the siege call him a noted coward. The reports of his resistance appealed to the popular imagination, however, so that he gained, even during his own lifetime, a reputation more romantic than he deserved. In 1766 Rogers published a tragedy, *Ponteach: or the Savages of America* (reprinted, 1914, with introduction and biographical account by Allan Nevins), which probably did much to foster the legend. Jonathan Carver's *Travels through the Interior Parts of North America,* published in 1778, continued the tradition. These accounts, together with the recollections of old frontier residents casting a rosy glow over past events, form the basis of the dramatic picture Parkman draws of his hero.

[Francis Parkman, *The Hist. of the Conspiracy of Pontiac* (1851) gathers most of the then known sources on Pontiac, but must be read with caution; E. S. Ellis, *Life of Pontiac* (1861) is an uncritical abstract from Parkman; F. W. Hodge, in *Handbook of Am. Indians North of Mexico* (1912), gives some traditional material. Manuscript sources include Thomas Gage MSS. in the possession of William L. Clements and James Sterling Letter Book in the William L. Clements Library ; Jeffery Lord Amherst Papers, now W. O. 34 in Pub. Record Office, London ; Parkman Transcripts, Mass. Hist. Soc.; papers of John Porteous and other

MSS. in Burton Hist. Coll., Detroit, whose publications should be consulted. Printed sources include: *Journals of Maj. Robert Rogers* (London, 1765) and "Journal of Robert Rogers the Ranger," ed. by V. H. Paltsits from the MS., in *Bull. N. Y. Pub. Lib.*, Apr. 1933; Croghan's letters and journals in R. G. Thwaites, *Early Western Travels*, vol. I (1904); E. B. O'Callaghan, *Docs. Rel. to the Col. Hist. of the State of N. Y.*, vols. VII–X (1855–58); C. E. Carter, *The Corr. of Gen. Thos. Gage*, vols. I, II (1931–33); *The Papers of Sir Wm. Johnson*, vols. I–VIII (1921–33); *Diary of the Siege of Detroit* (1860), ed. by F. B. Hough; *Jour. of Pontiac's Conspiracy, 1763* (1912), attributed to Robert Navarre. See also E. O. Randall, "Pontiac's Conspiracy," *Ohio Archeol. and Hist. Quart.*, Oct. 1903; O. W. Collet, "Notes on Parkman," *U. S. Cath. Hist. Mag.*, Jan. 1888; and bibliography appended to sketch of Henry Gladwin.]   R. G. A—s.

POOL, JOHN (June 16, 1826–Aug. 16, 1884), senator, was born in Pasquotank County, N. C., the son of Solomon and Martha (Gaskins) Pool. He was prepared for college at home and was graduated from the University of North Carolina in 1847. He was admitted to the bar in the same year, and while he soon became successful, he never liked his profession. In 1856 and again in 1858 he was a member of the state Senate and made such a reputation for ability that in 1860 he was nominated by the Whigs for governor. He made a brilliant campaign and, in spite of the influence which the national crisis exerted in behalf of the Democratic party, was defeated by only six thousand majority. A strong Union man, he took no part in the secession movement. In 1861 the Confederate commissioner of loans sought his assistance in the work of his office and Pool made public the terms of the loan, but evaded taking subscriptions and sought to discourage them. By this time he had made up his mind not to participate in any way in the war, but in 1864, having moved to Bertie County, he became a peace candidate for the state Senate, stating afterward in justification that he did so only to work for peace and to embarrass the Confederate government. In the legislature he introduced peace resolutions which provided for the appointment of peace commissioners by the state, and which were, of course, defeated.

Pool was a member of the constitutional convention of 1865–66 but took no prominent part in its work. He was also a member of the state Senate in 1865. He supported William W. Holden for governor but he was a close friend of Jonathan Worth who was elected, and, both political groups in the state claiming him as a member, he was elected to the United States Senate. While attempting without success to secure his seat, he made public his reason for his legislative service in 1864 and the next legislature did not reëlect him. He then definitely identified himself with the Radicals but was never so partisan

and proscriptive as most of his associates. He urged Governor Worth to accept the demands of Congress while they were relatively moderate and in December 1866 went to Washington and seeking out Thaddeus Stevens, whom he had never met, urged him to exempt North Carolina from the general plan of reconstruction. In the state Republican convention of 1867 he introduced resolutions demanding universal suffrage, restriction of the taxing power of the legislature in order to avoid the quasi-confiscation which he feared would come, and the immediate removal of all disabilities. These were voted down and he withdrew from the convention. He was strongly opposed to the reckless railroad legislation of the convention of 1868 and went to Raleigh and held a meeting of Republican leaders in the hope of checking it. He could do nothing but continued in the party, and in 1868 was elected to the United States Senate and admitted.

In the Senate, while partisan, he still favored removal of disabilities and introduced bills relieving many persons. He was bitterly aroused by the Ku Klux movement and in Washington furnished newspaper men with cleverly and carefully manufactured accounts of outrages, chiefly mythical, and told them when they should be released. The evidence is very strong, in spite of his vehement denials, that he suggested to Governor Holden the use of an illegal armed force to carry the state election of 1870 and to punish the leaders of the opposition party. Through him some of the leading features of the North Carolina anti-Ku Klux laws were incorporated into the national Ku Klux act. He declined an appointment in January 1871 as one of the committee to investigate disorders in the South, but he spoke constantly on the subject in the Senate and urged strong measures (*Congressional Globe*, 42 Cong., 1 Sess.). He failed of reëlection in 1873 but remained in Washington practising law until 1876 when he went to North Carolina to accept an appointment as superintendent of public instruction to fill a brief vacancy. He then returned to Washington where he spent the rest of his life. He was quite successful, but increasingly he lost interest in his profession and gave more time to the organization of peace propaganda. He joined a labor organization in 1876 and left the Republican party and in 1880 he became a Democrat. He died in his sleep from heart disease. A man of unusual ability, he was at his best in debate, where he was easy and effective. He was handsome with a graceful and suave manner which softened many political asperities. He was twice married: first to Narcissa D. Sawyer of Elizabeth

City, and upon her death to Mollie Mebane of Bertie County.

[Sources include: *Biog. Dir. Am. Cong.* (1928); J. G. deR. Hamilton, *Reconstruction in N. C.* (1914); W. K. Boyd, ed., *Memoirs of W. W. Holden* (1911); *Evening Star* (Washington, D. C.), and *Washington Post*, Aug. 18, 1884; information from members of the Pool family.]   J. G. deR. H.

POOL, MARIA LOUISE (Aug. 20, 1841– May 19, 1898), writer, was born in Rockland, Mass., the daughter of Elias and Lydia (Lane) Pool, and a descendant of Edward Poole who emigrated to Weymouth, Mass., in 1635. She was educated in the public schools of her native town. Reared in the plain and simple home typical of New England villages, she seems to have had no experiences to distinguish her childhood from that of countless others. Her love of books and writing was fostered by her father, and her school "compositions" won sufficient praise to stimulate ambition. Making at first the almost inevitable choice of teaching, she soon abandoned that profession, partly on account of her health, and devoted herself to fiction.

With the exception of the years 1870–77, spent in Brooklyn, she lived always in Massachusetts, for fifteen years on a farm in Wrentham and the remainder of the time in Rockland, where she died. Beginning when the vogue of short stories of local color was somewhat new, she contributed to Boston and New York papers sketches of New England life, later revised and published in book form. She made good use of her limited travels. Two trips to Florida furnished the background of several tales; for example, *A Golden Sorrow* (1898); but the strongest influence was that of a single trip to the North Carolina mountains, which so impressed her that she returned repeatedly to their scenery and people for material, notably in *Dally* (1891), *Against Human Nature* (1895), and *In Buncombe County* (1896). Written by an outsider, these tales are noticeable for their sharpness and vividness, and they played a part in arousing Northern interest in Southern mountain conditions.

Her chief and best work, however, dealt with her native state: *Roweny in Boston* (1892); *In a Dike Shanty* (1896); *Boss and Other Dogs* (1896). Within a limited field she worked well and successfully. From her own door she painted the prospect. The procession of the seasons, the stretches of country, the busy routine of village life, the amusing contrasts of town and country ways, horses, dogs, but above all "folks," interested her. The austerity of New England did not deaden her; the sadness of life did not embitter her; she neither sentimentalized

nor philosophized; people were what they were and she liked them. Consequently, her writing had ease and pleasantness, although it lacked the ultimate grace of style. In plotting she was less successful than in sketching situations. Her chief merit lay in suggesting personality, and she had real ability in the use of homely speech made vibrant by humor. Friendly to many reforms, she seems to have participated actively in none. Death came quickly from pneumonia while she was still writing, and *A Widower & Some Spinsters* (1899) and *The Meloon Farm* (1900) were published posthumously.

[A brief sketch of her life and work by Dr. A. M. Hale forms the introduction to *A Widower and Some Spinsters*; see also, M. E. Poole, *The Hist. of Edward Poole of Weymouth, Mass. and His Descendants* (1893); *N. Y. Tribune,* and *Boston Transcript,* May 20, 1898.]   E. D. H.

POOLE, FITCH (June 13, 1803–Aug. 19, 1873), journalist, humorist, librarian, was born in South Danvers (now Peabody), Mass., the son of Fitch and Elizabeth (Cutler) Poole, and a descendant of John Poole who was an early resident of Cambridge, Lynn, and Reading, Mass. Manasseh Cutler [*q.v.*] was the younger Fitch's grandfather. After a common-school education and six months at Bradford Academy under Benjamin Greenleaf [*q.v.*], he carried on his father's business, that of dressing sheepskins. Following the depression of 1852, he withdrew from business activities. His first poems were addressed to Mary Ann, daughter of Enoch Poor, and he married her July 8, 1824; they had nine children, two of whom died in infancy. For diversion he modeled heads in plaster and commemorative medals. He also devised ingenious games for children. As a member of a committee of the Essex Agricultural Society, his amusing reports in 1844 and 1849 on swine were widely quoted.

As early as 1836 he wrote for the *Salem Register* his "Lament of the Bats Inhabiting the Old South Church in Danvers," and the same year published in the *Salem Observer* a letter alleged to have been written by Lawrence Conant in 1713, describing an ordination in Salem. This fiction deceived historical students, though Poole quickly confessed himself the author. In 1846 he became one of the editors of the *Danvers Courier.* Thirteen years later he began work on the *Wizard* (South Danvers), known after Poole ceased to be connected with it in 1869 as the *Peabody Press.* This paper he made famous by his witty articles and poems on politics, people, and local affairs. His poem, "Giles Corey & Goodwyfe Corey" (1850), in the *Salem Observer,* was followed by "Giles Corey's Dream"

(1852), and by a second "Dream" (1858). He wrote addresses for the carriers of newspapers, anniversary hymns, reminiscences of passing statesmen, and articles in defense of Whig policies. The Mexican War being unpopular with the Whigs, Poole satirized it in "The House that Zack Built"; "Mr. Polk's Bridge of Sighs"; "An Epigram"; and "Trial for Murder: The People vs. James K. Polk." The last work appeared as a pamphlet (Boston, 1847). His articles and poems ridiculing the coalition forces that elected Boutwell governor of Massachusetts in 1852 were reprinted in part in Boston newspapers and were referred to as those of "a writer of rare wit and powers of satire." For the Carrier's Address of the *Salem Register,* 1852, he wrote "The Political John Gilpins" in sixty-six stanzas. Two other Gilpin ballads appeared in the *Wizard.* Indeed, his writings arranged chronologically would be a commentary on his times, ranging from town trifles to national affairs. His "Lines to a Mouse in the Peabody Institute," and "The Librarian's Epitaph," both printed in the *Wizard,* are of special merit.

He was officially connected with the Mechanics Institute Library, founded in 1841, and in 1856 he became librarian of the Peabody Institute established in South Danvers by George Peabody in 1852. Here his knowledge of books, his love of order, and his unfailing industry enabled him to render service of value for the remainder of his life. In February 1872 his eldest surviving son, Francis, died and the shock weakened Poole's health, his own death occurring a year and a half later. He was tall and thin, slightly bent, with massive head, smooth-shaven face, clean-cut features, heavy brows, and deepset eyes. His delicate sense of humor, his scholarly tastes, his knowledge of politics, history, and literature made his writings effective. Had they been issued in book form, his reputation would have been more secure.

[M. E. Poole, "Fitch Poole," in *The Hist. Colls. of the Danvers Hist. Soc.,* vol. XIV (1926), containing extracts from Poole's diary; D. H. Hurd, *Hist. of Essex County, Mass.* (1888), vol. II; *Peabody Press,* Aug. 20, 1873; *New-England Hist. and Geneal. Reg.,* Oct. 1874, which contains titles of poems and articles.]
C. K. B.

POOLE, WILLIAM FREDERICK (Dec. 24, 1821–Mar. 1, 1894), librarian, historian, was born in that part of old Salem, Mass., which is now the town of Peabody. He was the second son of Ward and Eliza (Wilder) Poole and eighth in direct descent from John Poole, one of the founders of Newtowne (Cambridge), Mass. When he was between ten and eleven years old, his school days were interrupted by

family reverses, but after seven years in various occupations, he was enabled, chiefly through his mother's efforts, to resume his education at Leicester Academy, supplementing his resources by intermittent teaching in the district schools. He entered Yale in 1842, but his progress was again delayed by financial straits, which necessitated three years of teaching and postponed his graduation until 1849.

In his junior year he became assistant to John Edmands [*q.v.*], student-librarian of the Brothers in Unity, one of Yale's famous literary societies, whom he soon succeeded as librarian. In this capacity he continued the practice, begun by Edmands, of maintaining an index on slips of paper to material in books and magazines useful for current student exercises and debates and, perceiving the value of a more comprehensive index, expanded the project to cover the entire contents of the periodical collection in the Brothers' library. In 1848, *An Alphabetical Index to Subjects Treated in the Reviews and Other Periodicals, to which No Indexes Have Been Published* was issued by G. P. Putnam—the forerunner of the well-known *Poole's Index to Periodical Literature.* It was promptly recognized as a valuable library aid and brought the name of its compiler to the attention of the literary world on both sides of the Atlantic. The first edition was quickly taken up and Poole went to Boston, after his graduation, to prepare a second and enlarged edition, which was published by C. W. Norton in 1853.

In 1851 Poole became an assistant in the library of the Boston Athenæum, and, eleven months later, librarian of the Boston Mercantile Library Association, where his four years' administration was marked by the introduction of new methods that were widely copied. On Nov. 22, 1854, he was married to Fanny M. Gleason, daughter of Dr. Ezra Gleason of Boston. When Charles Folsom [*q.v.*], librarian of the Boston Athenæum, retired in 1856, Poole was appointed to succeed him, and for the next thirteen years devoted his extensive bibliographical knowledge to the service of that scholarly institution. His sudden resignation, in 1869, from this apparently congenial post mystified his friends and closed his Boston career. For two years he served as a library expert in the organization of new libraries, including that of the United States Naval Academy and, finally, the public library of Cincinnati, where he became librarian, serving from 1871 to 1873. On Jan. 1, 1874, he accepted a call to Chicago as the first librarian of the new public library, which under his progressive management soon took rank as the largest circulating library in the country. In 1887 he was invited to organize a new reference library in Chicago upon a munificent endowment created under the will of Walter Loomis Newberry [*q.v.*]. The Newberry Library, with which he remained connected until his death, bears ample testimony to his sound and spacious scholarship and his preëminent skill as a bibliographer and book buyer.

Poole's pioneer contributions to the theory and principles of library administration still form an important part of the body of doctrine upon which modern librarianship is based, and contributed measurably to the recognition of that calling as one of professional rank. An undisputed leader among his contemporaries, he was also a wise and patient counselor to his younger colleagues. His career exactly coincides with the rise of the American public library, and his advice was frequently sought by communities and officials concerned with the organization of such institutions. The centennial publication of the United States Bureau of Education, entitled, *Public Libraries in the United States, Their History, Condition and Management* (1876), contains several of his papers, which were rightly accepted in their day as those of a high and competent authority. He was one of the promoters of the first conference of American librarians, in New York in 1853, and one of the organizers of the American Library Association in 1876 and its president from 1885 to 1887. He was vice-president of the International Conference of Librarians held in London in 1877. A member of Phi Beta Kappa, he delivered an address before the chapter at Northwestern University in 1893, published under the title, *The University Library and the University Curriculum* (1894).

There is some basis for the surmise that Poole's earliest ambitions lay in the direction of historical writing and, perhaps, teaching, and that his first connection with library work was formed rather from necessity than from choice. Studies and researches in the by-paths of American history, especially of the Colonial period and of the early West, continued as his chief avocation. He was a speaker and writer of high ability and commanded a fluent and pungent style well adapted to the uses of controversy, in which he was frequently engaged and from which he usually emerged as the victor. At Lowell's invitation he wrote for the *North American Review* (April 1869) a notable article, in which he defended Cotton Mather and the contemporary New England clergy from the common assumption of their complicity in the witchcraft persecutions. This was subsequently reprinted under the title, *Cotton Mather and Salem Witchcraft* (1869). He contributed the chapter on "The West, From the Treaty of Peace with France, 1763, to the Treaty of Peace with England, 1783" to Justin's Winsor's *Narrative and Critical History of America* (vol. VI, 1888), and one on "Witchcraft in Boston" to Winsor's *Memorial History of Boston* (vol. II, 1881). Other historical writings, mostly monographs and magazine articles, include *The Ordinance of 1787 and Dr. Manasseh Cutler as an Agent of Its Formation* (1876), reprinted from the *North American Review* of April 1876, discussions of episodes in early colonial history, and numerous critical reviews of historical publications. In 1888 he was elected president of the American Historical Association. He was a man of impressive appearance, tall and vigorous, with a genial personality, though on occasion stern and unbending, and impatient with triflers. He was fond of society and in the cultivated circles of the cities in which he lived he was a popular and welcome figure. He died in Evanston, Ill., survived by his wife and four of their seven children.

[*Obit. Record Grads. Yale Univ.*, 1894; *Memorial Sketch of Dr. Wm. F. Poole* (Newberry Lib., Chicago, 1895), including bibliog. of Poole's writings; *In Memoriam Wm. F. Poole* (Chicago Lit. Club, 1894); *Dial* (Chicago), Mar. 16, 1894; *Bull. of Bibliog.*, Apr. 1914; *Papers and Proc. . . . Am. Lib. Asso.*, 1891; *Ibid.*, 1894; *Lib. Jour.*, Mar., Dec. 1894; Z. S. Holbrook, "Wm. F. Poole and the New England Clergy," *Bibliotheca Sacra*, Apr. 1900; W. E. Foster, "Five Men of '76," *Bull. Am. Lib. Asso.*, Oct. 1926; *Nation* (N. Y.), July 7, 28, 1898; *Chicago Tribune*, Mar. 2, 1894.]

C. B. R.

POOR, CHARLES HENRY (June 9, 1808–Nov. 5, 1882), naval officer, was born at Cambridge, Mass., the son of Moses and Charlotte (White) Poor, and a descendant in the sixth generation of John Poore. He was appointed midshipman on Mar. 1, 1825, made his first cruise in the *John Adams,* and was later in the *Java* in the Mediterranean. After four more years at sea in the *Delaware* of the Mediterranean Squadron and in the *Lexington* and the *Boxer* of the Brazil Squadron, he was made lieutenant on Dec. 31, 1835. Up to the time of his promotion to the rank of commander on Sept. 14, 1855, he was chiefly on shore duty or on leave, making only two long cruises, in the *Independence,* Brazil Squadron, 1840–43, and in the *St. Lawrence,* Pacific Squadron, 1852–55. He was at the Norfolk navy yard, 1856–58, and in 1860–61 commanded the *St. Louis* of the Home Squadron, which, from February 1861 until after the opening of the Civil War, was among the ships stationed off Pensacola for the support of Fort Pickens. He commanded the landing party of soldiers, marines, and sailors sent ashore on Apr. 12 to reinforce the garrison. Shifted on Apr. 18 to command the steam-sloop *Brooklyn,* he was from May 26 through June on blockade duty at the mouth of the Mississippi, where he incurred departmental disfavor by allowing the Confederate cruiser *Sumter* to escape, June 30, after a chase of three and a half hours. He was tried by court martial the following November and exonerated. Subsequently he was assigned to special ordnance work, in which duty he was at Hampton Roads during the *Monitor-Merrimac* action on Mar. 8 and 9, 1862, and in the *Roanoke* when she passed under the fire of the batteries at Sewall's Point to assist the *Congress* and *Cumberland.* In the same month he had command of the *Illinois,* a chartered steamer intended for ramming the *Merrimac,* but had no opportunity to test her powers. Through the summer of 1862 he was stationed at Fort Monroe as ordnance officer for the North Atlantic Blockading Squadron.

He was promoted to the rank of captain on July 16, 1862, and to commodore the following January. This latter advancement, however, was not altogether to Secretary Welles's liking, for he remarked upon it as "the most objectionable" of the promotions made at that time (*Diary of Gideon Welles,* 1911, vol. I, 77). The following summer he was given the not especially desirable command of the *Saranac,* Pacific Squadron, where he remained till the end of the war. His main activities here were to protect commerce. In one instance, he brought pressure to bear on the authorities at Aspinwall to release a mail steamer, and at another time forced a salute to the American flag because of an offense committed by Colombian officials at Rio de la Hache. After the war he commanded the naval station at Mound City, Ill., for two years, was made rear admiral on Sept. 20, 1868, was head of the Washington navy yard, from January to August 1869, and then commanded the North Atlantic Squadron until his retirement in the summer of 1870. Of his character his contemporaries speak in warm terms. Though he was a strict disciplinarian, his even temper and unfailing courtesy won the devotion of his subordinates. After his retirement he made his home in Washington. He was married at Norfolk, Va., on May 13, 1835, to Mattie Lindsay Starke, daughter of Dr. Robert Boling Starke, a former naval surgeon. There were eight children born to them, two sons and six daughters. Poor died in Washington after an illness of seven months, and was buried in Oak Hill Cemetery.

[Alfred Poore, *A Memoir and Geneal. of John Poore* (1881); *The Poor-Poore Family Gathering at Peabody, Mass.* (1893); L. R. Hamersly, *The Records of Living Officers of the U. S. Navy and Marine Corps* (1878); *War of the Rebellion: Official Records (Navy),* 1 ser., vols. I–VI; *Defense of Lieut. Commander C. H. Poor before the General Court Martial assembled at Washington, Nov. 18, 1861* (1861); *Washington Post,* Nov. 6, 1882; two of Poor's letter-books, 1869–70, are preserved in the Henry C. Huntington Library, San Gabriel, Cal.]

A. W.

POOR, DANIEL (June 27, 1789–Feb. 3, 1855), Congregational missionary, was the youngest of the twelve children of Joseph and Mary (Abbott) Poor of Danvers, Mass. His early years were passed in the common school and in labor in his father's tannery. Being of a thoughtful turn of mind and fond of reading, he was sent at the age of seventeen to Phillips Academy at Andover from which he entered the sophomore class at Dartmouth College where he was graduated with high honors in 1811. After a period of theological study with the Rev. Asa Burton [*q.v.*] of Thetford, Vt., he entered Andover Seminary where he graduated in 1814. It was while there that he dedicated himself to foreign missions—a cause in which he had felt an interest from early boyhood. On June 21, 1815, he was ordained with five other candidates in the Presbyterian church at Newburyport, Mass., and on Oct. 23, all but one of the group sailed from that town as the second missionary band of the American Board. They arrived at Colombo, Ceylon, on Mar. 22, 1816, and began work in the northern province of Jaffna. Poor, whose first station was at Tillipally, began to preach at once through an interpreter, but his progress in Tamil was so rapid that he spoke the language freely in less than a year. In 1823 he removed to Batticotta where he founded a boarding school for boys. In 1835 he was transferred to Madura, India, where he remained until 1841 when he returned to his original station at Tillipally. In 1848 he visited the United States where he created a profound impression by his able and eloquent advocacy of the cause of missions. He returned to Ceylon in two years and carried on his labors at Mampy till he fell a victim to the cholera.

In his mission work he combined the educational with the evangelistic method. Boarding schools were established at all the stations and there were numerous day schools. The Missionary Scientific Seminary founded by Poor at Batticotta in 1826 became an important educational center for the entire region, and succeeded in sending out well-trained teachers and preachers to schools and churches. In Madura he followed the same method and by 1840 there were 3316 pupils in schools which he had founded at that place. He attracted the attention and won the respect of the educated classes and was more expert than other missionaries in the use of the native language. He preached constantly and gave daily religious instruction in the schools and to groups of adults and children in their homes. Poor's chief literary work and an important source for his biography, is his journal, generous extracts from which were published in the *Panoplist* and in its successor, the *Missionary Herald,* from 1817 to the time of his death. It is an unusually informing missionary document enlivened by vivid pictures of the manners, customs, and beliefs of the people among whom he labored. In addition to this his published works consist of tracts and letters in English and Tamil. He was a man of eminent ability and learning and an outstanding figure in the history of Protestant missions. In stature he was short, broadshouldered, and somewhat lacking in the physical graces, but he had a gentle spirit, a winning address, and a striking personality. On Oct. 9, 1815, he married Susan Bulfinch of Salem, Mass., who died at Tillipally on May 7, 1821, leaving one son and two daughters. On Jan. 21, 1823, he was again married to Ann Knight of Stroud, England, who survived him.

[W. B. Sprague, *Annals of the Am. Pulpit,* vol. II (1857); G. T. Chapman, *Sketches of the Alumni of Dartmouth Coll.* (1867); Rufus Anderson, *Hist. of the Missions of the Am. Board of Commissioners for For. Missions in India* (1874); W. E. Strong, *The Story of the Am. Board* (1910).]   F. T. P.

POOR, ENOCH (June 21, 1736–Sept. 8, 1780), Revolutionary soldier, was born at Andover, Mass., the son of Thomas Poor, who served under Sir William Pepperrell [*q.v.*], at the siege of Louisbourg in 1745, and Mary (Adams) Poor. Daniel Poor (or Poore), his great-grandfather, had come to America from England in 1636 to join his brothers, John and Samuel, who were already settled at Newbury, Mass. Brought up on a farm with plenty of hard work and little schooling, Enoch served as apprentice to a cabinet maker and then enlisted in the provincial forces at the time of the French and Indian War, participating in the expedition to Nova Scotia under Col. John Winslow in 1755. About 1760 he removed from Andover to Exeter, N. H., returned to his native town long enough to claim for his bride Martha, the daughter of Col. John Osgood, then settled permanently in Exeter to become a trader and ship-builder. In 1765, although disapproving of the Stamp Act, he combined with several other citizens to combat the lawlessness created by its enactment. In 1770 and 1774 he served on committees appointed by the town to restrict the consumption of English goods. He was twice elected a member of the provincial congress of New Hampshire, and

when that body at the outbreak of the Revolution voted to raise three regiments of foot soldiers, he was chosen on May 24, 1775, colonel of the 2nd New Hampshire, the other two being assigned to the command of John Stark [*q.v.*], and James Reed. His men were not present with the other New Hampshire forces at the battle of Bunker Hill, being engaged at that time in building fire-rafts for the protection of Exeter and in strengthening the coast defenses. Later they reported at Cambridge, Mass., and participated in the siege of Boston.

In the spring of 1776 his regiment proceeded to New York whence it was presently dispatched to Canada in order to succor the retiring American forces under Arnold. When it was proposed at a council of war to fall back from Crown Point to Ticonderoga, Poor joined several other regimental officers in earnest protest. His conduct as president of a court martial provoked a controversy with Arnold (Beane, *post,* p. 4). In December 1776 he left Ticonderoga in order to join Washington on the Delaware, taking part in the battles of Trenton and Princeton. Partly in recognition of his services and partly to adjust a factional dispute, Congress voted him the rank of brigadier-general on Feb. 21, 1777. He played a significant rôle in the operations in northern New York in that year. Together with another officer he advocated the relinquishment of Ticonderoga to the British and as a result was ordered by Congress to report to headquarters for investigation. Washington, believing the evacuation inevitable, succeeded in getting the order suspended. In the two battles of Saratoga his men fought with effective courage and suffered heavy losses. He shared the miseries of Valley Forge during the winter of 1777–78, and participated in the battles of Barren Hill and Monmouth.

In 1779 he accompanied Sullivan in his expedition against the Six Nations, and was commended in the dispatches for "intrepidity and soldierly conduct in the battle of Newtown." In 1780 his brigade was incorporated in a division of light infantry under command of Lafayette. He died at Paramus, N. J. The circumstances of his death are shrouded in uncertainty. One theory is that he was killed by a junior officer in a duel; another, more likely, is that he perished of a fever. A portrait of him by Tenney, based upon a sketch made by Tadeusz Kościuszko, with whom Poor shared a warm friendship, adorns the capitol at Concord, N. H. Washington described him as ". . . an officer of distinguished merit, who, as a citizen and a Soldier, had every claim to the esteem of his Country" (W. C. Ford, *The*

Writings of George Washington, vol. VIII, 1890, 442–443).

[Among the Force transcripts at the Library of Congress in a "Journal of the March of General Poor's Brigade from Soldier's Fortune in the Western Expedition," and in The Papers of the Continental Congress, vol. 163, are two of Poor's letters dated Dec. 21, 1777, and Jan. 2, 1778, containing appeals for the right of court martial in the matter of the relinquishment of Ticonderoga. See also, *The Poor-Poore Family Gathering, Andover, Mass., Aug. 1900* (1900) ; Israel Evans, *An Oration . . . at the Interment of . . . Enoch Poor* (1781), in the *Hazard Pamphlets,* vol. 32, no. 12 ; *New Hampshire State Papers,* vols. VII–VIII (1873, 1874), and XIV–XVII (1885–1889) ; *Proc. Mass. Hist. Soc.,* vol. XIX (1882) ; S. C. Beane, *Gen. Enoch Poor* (1899) ; C. H. Bell, *Exeter in 1776* (1876) ; *New Eng. Hist. and Geneal. Reg.,* July 1906.]   E. E. C.

POOR, HENRY VARNUM (Dec. 8, 1812– Jan. 4, 1905), railroad journalist and economist, was born in East Andover (now Andover), Me., a son of Dr. Silvanus and Mary (Merrill) Poor. He was educated at home and at Bowdoin College, from which he graduated in 1835. He subsequently studied law in the office of his uncle, Jacob McGaw, and was admitted to the Maine bar. A member of the Whig party, he campaigned for William Henry Harrison. He practised until 1849, when he went to New York City with his brother John Alfred Poor [*q.v.*], who purchased the *American Railroad Journal,* the first periodical on railroads managed on a commercial basis, and made Henry its editor. Remaining as editor until 1863, he continued and elaborated the collection, compilation, and publication of data on railroad development, both in the United States and abroad. In 1853 he collaborated with Israel D. Andrews in the preparation of material for the chapter on railroads and canals in Andrews' report on the commerce of British North America published as *Senate Executive Document 112* and *House Executive Document 136* (32 Cong., 1 Sess.). Returns for railways in twenty-eight states were made, and this chapter is sometimes referred to as the "first Poor's Manual."

With the assistance of Dr. Richard Swainson Fisher, Poor undertook the preparation of an exhaustive history of internal improvements and in 1860 published Volume I of the *History of the Railroads and Canals of the United States of America, Exhibiting their Progress, Cost, Revenues, Expenditures and Present Condition,* covering the development of transportation in the New England and Middle Atlantic states and Maryland. The outbreak of the Civil War prevented the publication of the other two volumes planned. Poor retired from the editorship of the *American Railroad Journal* in 1862, and for at least two years was an editorial writer on the staff of the *New York Times.* Like his brother,

John Alfred Poor, he was interested in the extension of internal improvements, particularly railways, for the opening up of the West. He was an earnest advocate of a railroad to the coast, and in 1864 was elected the first secretary of the Union Pacific Railroad Company.

In 1867 he formed a partnership with his son Henry William Poor in the firm of H. V. & H. W. Poor, to import rails and railway supplies. The firm also, at first as a "sideline," began to collect, compile, and publish in manual form railway statistics and annual reviews of the progress of railway development in the United States. The first manual in this series, *Manual of the Railroads of the United States,* appeared in 1868 and comprised 442 octavo pages. A "Sketch of the Rise, Progress, Cost, Earnings, Etc., of the Railroads of the United States" preceded the statistical compilations and historical notes for each railway in the country, and was a feature of the annual issues of *Poor's Manual of Railroads* under varying titles down to and including the issue for 1900. These data remain among the most valuable source materials on railroad expansion and development, although after 1888 the publication of the Interstate Commerce Commission's annual reports on statistics of railways took away some of the exclusive value of *Poor's Manual.* The *Manual* was continued as a separate publication until 1924, years after both founders had died. H. V. and H. W. Poor also issued annuals entitled, *Poor's Directory of Railway Officials* (1886–95) and *Poor's Hand-Book of Investment Securities* (1890–92). Henry V. Poor was a recognized authority and a forceful writer on economic questions. In addition to the compilations mentioned above, his publications included: *Money and Its Laws, Embracing a History of Monetary Theories and a History of the Currencies of the United States* (1877) ; *Resumption and the Silver Question* (1878) ; *The Pacific Railroads and the Relations Existing Between Them and the Government of the United States* (pamphlet, 1879) ; *Twenty-two Years of Protection* (1888) and *The Tariff: Its Bearing upon the Industries and Politics of the United States* (1892), two arguments in favor of protection; as well as many articles in periodicals.

Poor married Mary Wild Pierce on Sept. 7, 1841; he died in Brookline, Mass. Of his seven children, three daughters and a son survived him. The son, Henry William Poor (June 16, 1844– Apr. 13, 1915), his father's associate in the business of H. V. & H. W. Poor, made a fortune as a member of the firm of Poor & Greenough, dealers in securities, later H. W. Poor & Company, but lost it when his firm failed in 1908

(New York Times, Apr. 14, 1915). He accumulated a valuable private library, which along with other real and personal property was sold to satisfy his creditors.

[*Am. Railroad Journal,* 1849–1863; *Railway Mechanical Engineer,* Oct. 1932; *Railroad Gazette,* esp. Jan. 13, 1905; *Obit. Record Grads. Bowdoin Coll.,* 1905; *Boston Transcript,* Jan. 5, 1905; information as to certain facts from a grandson, Charles Lyon Chandler, Esq.]
                                                    J. H. P—e.

POOR, JOHN (July 8, 1752–Dec. 5, 1829), educator, born at Plaistow, N. H., was the son of Daniel and Anna (Merrill) Poore, and the great-great-grandson of John Poore of Wiltshire, England, who came to Newbury, Mass., in 1635. On both sides of the family his forebears had been prominent in public life. He received a classical education sufficient to prepare him for Harvard College, from which he was graduated in 1775. On Nov. 2, 1777, he married Sarah Folsom, of Stratham, N. H., to whom four children were born. Soon after her death (Aug. 3, 1784), he removed from his native state to Pennsylvania, where he spent the remainder of his life. On Jan. 7, 1789, he married one of his pupils, Jane Neely. From this union there were six children, three of whom died while young.

After completing his work at Harvard, Poor turned to teaching as a profession. About his earliest labors there was apparently nothing remarkable, but, in Philadelphia, he became head of the justly famous Young Ladies' Academy, June 4, 1787. This institution, though not without predecessors of some consequence, such as the Moravian school at Bethlehem and several others taught by "venture" masters in the greater cities, soon rose above them in importance, and drew pupils from Canada, Nova Scotia, and the West Indies, as well as from the several states. With the aid of a number of prominent citizens of Philadelphia, including Benjamin West, Benjamin Rush, Pelatiah Webster, William Smith, and Benjamin Say, a charter was obtained from the state, Feb. 1, 1792—the first encouragement of the sort given to girls' education in the United States. The institution failed, however, to secure financial aid, such as was given to boys' academies in the state. Sixteen citizens were named visitors, the institution granted diplomas and premiums for merit, as it was authorized to do by charter, and in public commencements the young ladies celebrated their victory over ignorance. The course of study, though it seems slender to modern ears, was elaborate for that day, comprising reading, writing, arithmetic, history, English grammar, composition, rhetoric, geography with globes and maps, and vocal music. Poor continued as principal of the Academy more

than twenty years, removing to Solebury in 1809. After 1815, he conducted for several years a young ladies' school at New Hope, Pa., where he resided till his wife's death in 1827. He then took up residence with his son Charles M. Poore, at York Haven, Pa., where he died. Throughout his life, he was active in the Presbyterian church, serving as elder while living at New Hope.

[Alfred Poore, *A Memoir and Geneal. of John Poore* (1881); W. S. Ely, *Geneal. of the Wilson-Thompson Families* (1916); Thomas Woody, *A Hist. of Women's Education in the U. S.* (2 vols., 1929); J. P. Wickersham, *A Hist. of Education in Pa.* (1886); J. F. Watson, *Annals of Phila. and Pa.* (3 vols., 1881), vol. I; death notice in *York Recorder,* Dec. 15, 1829.]
                                                          T. W.

POOR, JOHN ALFRED (Jan. 8, 1808–Sept. 5, 1871), lawyer, railroad official, was born in East Andover (now Andover), Me., the second son of Dr. Silvanus and Mary (Merrill) Poor. He varied farm work with occasional terms of school and regular study with his brother-in-law, Rev. Thomas T. Stone in Andover. When he was nineteen he entered the law office of his uncle, Jacob McGaw, in Bangor, and at twenty-four was admitted to the bar. After a few months of practice in Oldtown, he returned to Bangor and became his uncle's partner. On July 8, 1833, he married Elizabeth Adams Hill, eldest daughter of Thomas Adams Hill. She died Jan. 14, 1837. Of their three children only the eldest, a daughter, survived her parents. Poor later married Elizabeth, daughter of Benjamin Orr of Brunswick. She died in 1844. Her only child, a son, died before his mother. Poor's third wife, Mrs. Margaret Robinson (Barr) Gwynne of Cincinnati, whom he married July 19, 1860, survived him. He practised law fourteen years in Bangor, earning a reputation as a sound, even brilliant, lawyer and public-spirited citizen. He took part in the town government, was a member of the Whig state committee, and was active in forming the Bangor Lyceum and the Bangor Social Library. Years later, in Portland, he endeavored to establish a free public library with no success, because the idea was far in advance of the time. He himself collected rare books. He was keenly interested in local history, and in 1839 when the dispute over the boundary between Maine and New Brunswick was raging, he prepared three letters for the *Portland Advertiser* discussing the history of attempts at boundary settlements and pressing the claims of Maine.

Railroads gradually became both his avocation and his vocation. On Apr. 16, 1834, he was among those who saw the first train of the Boston & Worcester Railroad pull out of Boston, and after the first railway in Maine was built, from Bangor to Oldtown, in 1836, he devoted much time to the study of the possibilities of railways in the economic and social development of the state. In 1844 he made public a plan for two lines, one with a terminus at Halifax, N. S., the other with a terminus at Montreal, converging upon Portland. This project aroused powerful and determined opposition in Massachusetts from promoters of the Boston, Concord & Montreal Railroad. In the face of a blizzard, in February 1845, utilizing what horses he could engage as he proceeded, Poor journeyed to Montreal, where on Feb. 10 he met the Montreal Board of Trade and prevented the adoption of a resolution in favor of building their line to Boston instead of to Portland. To the end of his life he suffered from the results of the strain and fatigue of that journey and the ensuing struggle against the Boston opposition before the committee on railways of the Canadian Parliament. In securing favorable action on his proposal he was greatly aided by the arrival a week later of Judge William P. Preble [*q.v.*], with the railroad charter granted by the State of Maine.

It was six months after Poor's return to his home before he was physically able to take up his work. He then moved to Portland, in 1846, to devote himself to railway interests. The Atlantic & Saint Lawrence Railroad Company was organized to build the railway from Portland to the Canadian border, with Preble as president and Poor as one of the directors (1845–49). On July 4, 1846, work was begun at Fish Point, at the entrance to Portland Harbor. The Canadian company, the St. Lawrence & Atlantic, began work at the same time, and the entire road between Portland and Montreal was opened on July 18, 1853, having been leased on July 1 to the Grand Trunk Railway of Canada for 999 years.

In 1849, Poor went to New York City and purchased the *American Railroad Journal,* of which his brother, Henry Varnum Poor [*q.v.*], assumed the editorship. Returning to Portland, John A. Poor became president of the Gas-Light Company, but resigned in 1852, having extricated it from its financial troubles. In 1851 he had been elected president of the York & Cumberland (later the Portland & Rochester) Railroad, had won a lawsuit for the company, reorganized it, and provided for the construction of its line from Gorham to the Saco River. From this office also he resigned in 1852, to devote his whole attention to international railway expansion. In 1850 he had been the moving spirit behind a convention at Portland which launched a project for connecting the railroads of Maine with those of lower Canadian provinces in the direction of St. John, N. B. The convention appointed Poor

chairman of the executive committee which it created, and on Aug. 20, 1850, he secured the charter of the European & North American Railway Company. The road had a lively history, whether viewed as a construction feat or as the subject of international negotiations; the last rail was laid Sept. 20, 1871, fifteen days after Poor's death; and in 1882 the line in Maine was leased in perpetuity to the Maine Central Railroad.

In 1853 Poor established the newspaper, *State of Maine,* in Portland, and edited it from 1853 to 1859, when it merged with the *Portland Daily Advertiser,* in which he had purchased an interest. In the columns of these newspapers he published all possible arguments favorable to his railroad project, even though political developments had superseded railways in importance in the public mind in the state. In 1864 he contributed some fourteen pages of material to a report of a committee of the national House of Representatives (*House Report No. 119,* 38 Cong., 1 Sess.) urging federal aid for the European & North American Railway as compensation to the state of Maine for her alleged losses in the Northeastern boundary compromise. He also brought to public attention the fertility of the lands of Aroostook County, Me., now world-famous for potatoes; and in 1857 suggested to the Maine legislature the construction of a railroad to open the county to settlement. In 1858 he urged a geological and water-power survey and the compilation of general statistics of the state, an enterprise toward which he had made a beginning in 1855 with the publication of his *Commercial, Railway, and Shipbuilding Statistics of the City of Portland and the State of Maine.* He had become a member of the Maine Historical Society in 1846, and was something of an authority upon Sir Ferdinando Gorges and English settlement on the North Atlantic Coast. He was the author of *English Colonization in America: A Vindication of the Claims of Sir Ferdinando Gorges* (1862) and *Memoir of Hon. Reuel Williams* (1864). Transcontinental railroad projects occupied his attention from about 1869, although he had corresponded with Asa Whitney on the subject as early as 1845. He became president of the Portland, Rutland, Oswego, & Chicago Railway in 1871. In September of that year he died suddenly of heart-failure. An article entitled "Railroad Improvements," which he had finished the night before, was published in the Portland *Eastern Argus* on the day of his death.

[*The First International Railway and the Colonization of New England: Life and Writings of John Alfred Poor* (1892), ed. by his daughter, Laura E. Poor; C. W. Tuttle, "Hon. John Alfred Poor, of Portland,

Me.," in *New-Eng. Hist. and Geneal. Reg.*, Oct. 1872; *Railroad Gazette*, Sept. 16, 1871; *Bangor Daily Whig & Courier*, Sept. 6, 1871; J. P. Baxter, "Reminiscences of a Great Enterprise," *Colls. and Proc. Me. Hist. Soc.*, 2 ser. III (1892); annual reports of the railroads with which Poor was connected; files of the *Am. Railroad Journal*, 1849–71.]　　　　　　　　　　J. H. P—e.

POORE, BENJAMIN PERLEY (Nov. 2, 1820–May 29, 1887), newspaper correspondent, editor, and author, son of Benjamin and Mary Perley (Dodge) Poore, was born at "Indian Hill Farm" near Newburyport, Mass., an estate which had belonged to the Poore family since the seventeenth century. He was a descendant of Samuel Poore who was living in Newbury, Mass., in 1652. Benjamin Poore the elder was a man of some means, who traveled considerably, and was drowned while returning from Hong Kong in 1853. At the age of seven young Benjamin was taken to Washington, D. C., his mother's birthplace, where he was destined to spend the greater part of his life. Four years later, he accompanied his parents to Europe. On their return he was sent to Dummer Academy, South Byfield, Mass., to prepare for West Point, but chafing under the strict discipline in force there, he ran away and apprenticed himself to a printer in Worcester, Mass. Having learned his trade, he became the editor of the *Southern Whig* in Athens, Ga., a position made for him, a youth still in his teens, by the generosity of his father, who had bought the paper for him.

After two years in this position, Poore became attaché of the American legation in Belgium (1841). Three years later he went to Paris as agent for the Massachusetts legislature to secure copies of documents in French archives relating to American history. The product of his labors was ten large volumes of papers and maps, which were deposited in the State House in Boston and afterward published under the title *Collection de manuscrits contenant lettres, mémoires et autres documents historiques relatifs à la Nouvelle-France* (4 vols., Quebec, 1883–85). During the seven years which he spent abroad he traveled extensively through Asia Minor and Egypt as well as through Europe. He also contributed regularly to the *Boston Atlas*. On his return in 1848 he became editor of the *Boston Daily Bee* and later of the *American Sentinel*, Philadelphia.

With such wide experience crowded into his early years, Poore began his distinctive career in 1854, when he became the Washington correspondent of the *Boston Journal* and other papers. For more than three decades he was the well-known columnist, "Perley." As one of the pioneers in this important type of journalistic service he made a record which in length of time has probably not been surpassed. At the beginning of the Civil War he was commissioned major of the 6th Massachusetts Regiment and served for a few months under Gen. Benjamin F. Butler in Maryland. In December 1861, however, he came back to his duties in Washington. Subsequently these included the editing of the *Journal of Agriculture* (1857–62) for the United States Society of Agriculture, of which he was secretary, and the official editing of the *Congressional Directory*, the first issue of which prepared by him and copyrighted appeared in 1865. He also served as clerk of the Senate committee on printing public records and was responsible for the compilation of lists of public documents, notable among which are *A Descriptive Catalogue of the Government Publications of the United States, September 5, 1774–March 4, 1881* (1885), *The Federal and State Constitutions, Colonial Charters, and Other Organic Laws of the United States* (2 vols., 1877), and *The Political Register and Congressional Directory . . . 1776–1878* (1878).

In his generation Poore was one of the most popular persons in Washington. His buoyant spirits and unfailing fund of stories made him welcome everywhere. In appearance he was of the heavy, rugged Scotch type, with large head, long gray hair, and full scraggly gray beard. Some of his more picturesque characteristics are revealed in his public declaration that he would wheel a barrel of apples from Newburyport to Boston if Fillmore failed to carry Massachusetts in the Presidential election of 1856, a promise which he actually fulfilled in a two-day journey, trundling his apples to the State House amid cheering crowds who lined the streets. Although living at the capital while Congress was in session, he spent considerable time in developing his ancestral home at Newburyport. Here he built up a notably varied collection of rare books, autographs, colonial furniture, Indian relics, and mementoes of the Revolution and the Civil War. His wife was Virginia Dodge of Washington, whom he married on June 12, 1849.

In the midst of his varied undertakings, he found time to write a number of books, the title pages bearing the name "Ben: Perley Poore." They include *The Rise and Fall of Louis Philippe* (1848); *Life of Gen. Zachary Taylor* (1848); *The Early Life and First Campaigns of Napoleon Bonaparte* (1851); *The Life and Public Services of John Sherman* (1880); *The Life and Public Services of Ambrose E. Burnside, Soldier-Citizen-Statesman* (1882); *Life of U. S. Grant* (1885) with O. H. Tiffany; *Sketches of the Life and Public Services of Frederick Smyth, of New Hampshire* (1885); and *Perley's Reminiscences of Sixty Years in the National Metropolis* (2 vols., 1886).

[J. J. Currier, *Hist. of Newburyport, Mass., 1764–1909* (2 vols., 1909) and *"Ould Newbury": Hist. and Biog. Sketches* (1896); D. H. Hurd, *Hist. of Essex County, Mass.* (1888), vol. II; *Boston Transcript, Evening Star* (Washington), *Boston Post,* and *Springfield Republican,* May 30, 1887.] P.K.

POPE, ALBERT AUGUSTUS (May 20, 1843–Aug. 10, 1909), bicycle and automobile manufacturer, was born at Boston, Mass., the son of Charles and Elizabeth (Bogman) Pope. Both his father and mother were of old New England stock, the former tracing his ancestry back to John Pope who was in Dorchester, Mass., by 1634. The financial reverses of Albert's father, who was a merchant and real-estate operator, forced the boy to work after school hours and during vacations, and to leave the Brookline High School at the age of fifteen in order to contribute to the support of the family. He worked in the Quincy Street Market, and later as clerk in a shoe-finding store. At nineteen he enlisted in the Union army, becoming second lieutenant Company I, 35th Massachusetts Regiment. He was promoted to the grades of first lieutenant and captain in 1863. With his regiment, he not only participated in the principal Virginia campaigns, but was with Burnside in Tennessee, Grant at Vicksburg, and Sherman at Jackson, Miss. He commanded at one time "Fort Hell" before Petersburg, and led his regiment in the last attack upon the city. He was brevetted (1865) major "for gallant conduct at Fredericksburg, Va." and lieutenant-colonel "for gallant conduct at the battles of Knoxville, Poplar Spring Church, and in front of Petersburg."

At the conclusion of the war, he went into business for himself in Boston, manufacturing and selling shoe manufacturers' supplies. In this venture he was successful from the start, and in twelve years amassed a small fortune. In 1877 he organized at Hartford, Conn., the Pope Manufacturing Company, for the making and marketing of small patented articles; but the chief business of this concern soon became the manufacture of bicycles. Pope saw his first bicycle at the Philadelphia Centennial Exposition in 1876 and soon afterward made a study of such vehicles in England. Having determined to stake his future upon the manufacture of them, he began to import them in 1877 and to purchase European patents. His first order for bicycles to be manufactured in the United States was placed with the Weed Sewing Machine Company in 1878. In the meantime he was enlarging his plant at Hartford, where later the famous Columbia and Hartford bicycles were manufactured. By 1898 it comprised five large factories, covering seventeen acres, and employed over 3,000 men. Pope's career as "the founder of American bicycle industries" included much more than manufacturing. He found it necessary to overcome public prejudice and to fight municipal ordinances restricting the use of bicycles. In meeting this situation Pope took the lead, becoming responsible for the cost of test cases between wheelmen and various city governments, with the result that bicycles were soon admitted to parks and boulevards on the same footing as carriages or other vehicles. To promote cycling, he founded *The Wheelman* in October 1882 under the editorship of S. S. McClure (McClure, *post,* p. 148), combining it a year later with *Outing.* Pope's business interests also made him one of the most enthusiastic pioneers in the better-roads movement which swept the country in the early nineties. He built a piece of macadam on Columbus Avenue, Boston, to demonstrate what good roads could be like, and kept up an incessant propaganda. Through his influence and financial backing, special instruction in road engineering was introduced into the curriculum of the Massachusetts Institute of Technology and the Lawrence Scientific School. He also seems to have been largely responsible for the establishment of the Massachusetts Highway Commission and a Bureau of Road Engineering in the Department of Agriculture. In behalf of the latter, he secured a petition with 150,000 signatures including those of seventeen governors.

In his later years, Pope entered the field of automobile manufacturing with the same zeal that twenty years earlier he had displayed in connection with bicycles. He began in 1896 the manufacture of electric phaetons and runabouts through the Columbia Electric Vehicle Company. Within a few years, three plants controlled by him were making automobiles: at Toledo the company turned out the Pope-Toledo gasoline cars; at Hartford, the Pope-Hartford cars; and at Indianapolis, the Pope-Waverly electrics. The passing of the bicycle craze and a lull in the development of the automobile forced the overexpanded Pope Manufacturing Company into a receivership. Pope had pioneered in the manufacturing of automobiles just as he had in that of bicycles, but it was left to others to reap the harvest. The strain of reorganizing the finances of his large enterprises hastened his death, which occurred at his summer residence at Cohasset, Mass.

Among his philanthropies are the Pope Memorial Church at Cohasset in memory of his son; the Pope Dispensary at the New England Hospital in honor of the long professional services of his two sisters, who were physicians; and the gift of seventy-four acres and $100,000 to the city of Hartford for a park. Pope was married Sept. 20, 1871, to Abby Linder, daughter of George and Matilda (Smallwood) Linder of Newton. There were six children, of whom four survived their father.

[C. H. Pope, *A Hist. of the Dorchester Pope Family* (1888); *Representative Men of Massachusetts, 1890–1900* (1898); C. W. Burpee, *Hartford County, Conn.* (3 vols., 1929); *Mass. Soldiers, Sailors, and Marines in the Civil War*, vol. III (1932); *Hist. of the Thirty-fifth Reg., Mass. Vols., 1862–1865* (1884); S. S. McClure, *My Autobiography* (1914), pp. 145–59, 214–15; *The Picturesque Parks of Hartford* (Travelers Insurance Company, 1900); *Who's Who in America, 1908–09*; *Hartford Courant, Springfield Republican,* and *Boston Transcript,* Aug. 11, 1909.]   H. U. F.

POPE, FRANKLIN LEONARD (Dec. 2, 1840–Oct. 13, 1895), electrician, inventor, eldest son of Ebenezer and Electa (Wainwright) Pope, was born on his father's farm at Great Barrington, Mass. He was a descendant of Thomas Pope who was living in Plymouth, Mass., as early as 1632. Franklin's education was that of the average New England youth of his day, with the addition of one term at Amherst Academy. He was an ardent student of natural philosophy and geography and possessed a natural bent for drawing, especially of mechanical subjects. While in his early teens he began earning money by selling sketches of the various locomotives that came to Great Barrington, and, in partnership with a chum, he edited and published a small newspaper. In 1857, when a branch of the American Telegraph Company's line was extended from Pittsfield to Great Barrington, Pope, although but seventeen years old, was selected by the company to learn the operation of the telegraph printer, invented by David E. Hughes [q.v.], and upon completing the course was appointed the company's operator in his native town. He had charge of the office for two years and was then transferred to Springfield, Mass., as the circuit manager of the Boston & Albany Railroad telegraph lines.

In 1860 he resigned this position and went to New York in the hope of finding work as an artist. For a time he was employed by the *Scientific American,* but at the outbreak of the Civil War he reëntered the telegraph service as an operator for the American Telegraph Company, and spent a year in the Providence, R. I., office. The following two years he was engaged in New York on the preparation of a series of maps of all the company's telegraph lines from Maine to Virginia. When, during the draft riots of 1863, the lines between New York and Boston were cut, Pope, disguising himself as a farm laborer, made repairs, reëstablishing communication. He also began an investigation for the company with a view to determining standards of telegraph apparatus from the host of equipment then available. Due primarily to Pope's ill health, this work was interrupted in 1864, and he accepted an appointment as assistant to the engineer-in-chief of the Russo-American Telegraph Company, organized to effect telegraphic communication between the United States and Europe by way of Bering Strait. For the next two years he was engaged in making a preliminary exploration and survey in British Columbia and Alaska, preparatory to laying the line; but before this work was fully consummated the successful completion of the Atlantic cable caused the abandonment of the project.

Returning to New York, Pope was editor of *The Telegrapher* from August 1867 to February 1868. He published in 1869 *Modern Practice of the Electric Telegraph* which, between that year and 1892, because of its great value to the electrical world, passed through fifteen editions. Turning his attention to invention, he made valuable improvements in the stock-ticker invented by Samuel S. Laws [q.v.] in 1867. In 1869 he formed a partnership with Thomas A. Edison and James N. Ashley under the firm name of Pope, Edison & Company. Edison and Pope took out a joint patent (No. 103,924) on June 7, 1870, for a single-wire printing telegraph, which they sold to the Gold & Stock Telegraph Company. The partners did not get along well together, and in 1870 the firm dissolved. By devising a system in which the track itself acted as the electric conveyor, Pope also made practicable the original automatic electric block signal for railways invented by Thomas S. Hall [q.v.]. In 1875 he was put in charge of all the patent interests of the Western Union Telegraph Company and for six years the whole patent system of this great company was in his exclusive care. In 1881, however, he gave up this position to engage in private practice as a patent expert and solicitor. This practice he continued until his death.

After 1884 he undertook editorial work for several electrical journals, including *Electrician and Electrical Engineer* and *Engineering Magazine.* About two years before his death he retired to his home at Great Barrington, Mass., where he served as consulting engineer for the Great Barrington Electric Light Company, and converted its works from a steam to a waterpower plant. To facilitate his labors, he had installed in the basement of his house the transformers of the system, and he was accidentally killed when going to the cellar to investigate some trouble. Pope was one of the ablest and most fluent electrical writers of his day. Among his best-known books are *The Telegraphic Instructor* (1871), and *Evolution of The Electric Incandescent Lamp* (1889, 1894). He also published *The Western Boundary of Massachusetts; a Study of Indian and Colonial History* (1886). He was a charter member of the American Institute of Electrical Engineers, one of its original vice-presidents, and its second president (1886–87). On Aug. 6, 1873, he was married in Amherst, Mass., to Sarah Amelia Dickinson; she and three of their five children survived him.

[C. H. Pope, *A Hist. of the Dorchester Pope Family* (1888); D. P. Worden and others, *Geneal. of Thomas Pope and His Descendants* (1917); *Electricity*, Oct. 23, 1895; *Electrical World*, Oct. 19, 1895; *Engineering Mag.*, Nov. 1895; *Electrical Rev.* (London), Oct. 18, Nov. 8, 1895; *Trans. Am. Institute of Electrical Engineers*, vol. XII (1896); Waldemar Kaempffert, *A Popular Hist. of Am. Invention* (1924), vol. I; *N. Y. Times*, Oct. 14, 1895.]   C. W. M.

POPE, JOHN (Mar. 16, 1822–Sept. 23, 1892), soldier, was born in Louisville, Ky., the son of Nathaniel Pope [*q.v.*] and Lucretia (Backus) Pope. He was appointed a cadet at the Military Academy in 1838, and graduated in 1842, No. 17 in his class. Assigned as brevet second lieutenant to the topographical engineers, he was engaged in survey work for the next four years, first in Florida and later on the northeastern boundary line. Promoted second lieutenant May 9, 1846, he was ordered to General Taylor's army in Texas, and served throughout the latter's Mexican campaign. He received the brevet rank of first lieutenant, Sept. 23, 1846, for his services at Monterey, and of captain, Feb. 23, 1847, for Buena Vista. After the war he came north for a short time, on survey duty in Minnesota. Returning to the Southwest in 1851, he served at headquarters of the Department of New Mexico as chief topographical engineer until 1853; then for six years he was in the field, surveying a route for a Pacific railway, and experimenting with artesian wells as a water supply for the Llano Estacado. From 1859 until the opening of the Civil War he was again in the North, on lighthouse duty. He became first lieutenant Mar. 3, 1853, and captain July 1, 1856.

From Apr. 15 to July 29, 1861, he was mustering officer at Chicago. Then, appointed brigadier-general of volunteers, with rank from May 17, he was ordered to General Frémont's force in Missouri. In March and April 1862, he commanded the Army of the Mississippi in Halleck's operations for the opening of that river. While Grant moved up the Tennessee River to break up the Confederate field force, Pope moved directly against the defenses of the Mississippi at New Madrid, Mo., and at Island No. 10. A flotilla of gunboats under Commodore Andrew H. Foote [*q.v.*] cooperated with him. First taking New Madrid by siege, he cut a canal which enabled him to bring transport boats down to that point, avoiding the batteries at Island No. 10. The gunboats ran the batteries, and rejoined him. Under the protection of the gunboats, and of his own shore batteries, he brought his troops across to the east bank, cutting the communications of the defenses of Island No. 10 and forcing their surrender. This opened the river nearly down to Memphis. During these operations he was made major-general of volunteers (Mar. 21, 1862). He now prepared to continue his advance down the river, but in April his army was recalled to join Grant's and Buell's forces (the Armies of the Tennessee and of the Ohio) on the Tennessee River for an advance upon Corinth, Miss., under Halleck's personal command. Throughout the month of May his army formed Halleck's left wing in the advance to and siege of Corinth, and in the subsequent pursuit.

The reputation which he won in this theatre of operations caused his selection for higher independent command. He was handsome, dashing, soldierly, and a fine horseman; his personal appearance and manner combined with his military successes to bring about his advancement. Under orders issued June 26, he organized and concentrated all the separate forces in the region of the Rappahannock and the Shenandoah into the Army of Virginia, which was expected to protect Washington, and to relieve the pressure upon McClellan in the Peninsula. During this concentration, on July 14, he was appointed brigadier-general in the regular service, continuing to serve, however, under his commission as major-general of volunteers. In the middle of July, McClellan's Peninsular Campaign was regarded as having definitely failed. His troops were withdrawn to the vicinity of Washington, and transferred as they arrived to Pope's Army of Virginia. The Confederate army, relieved from anxiety for Richmond, moved toward Pope, whose operations, originally conceived as secondary, now became of primary importance.

He assumed his new command with misgivings. Possibly in an effort to overcome or conceal these, he spoke, wrote, and acted in an unduly optimistic and confident manner. All his new corps commanders were originally his seniors; one, Frémont, had been his immediate commander in Missouri, and resented his arrival so keenly that he asked to be relieved of his command. Many of the reinforcing troops from the Army of the Potomac, intensely loyal to McClellan, deeply regretted his eclipse and their own transfer. Pope showed little appreciation of the delicate situation, and, instead of handling his command tactfully and turning this loyalty to himself, issued orders contrasting the eastern troops unfavorably with the western armies that he had just left.

Jackson's corps was the first to come against him from Richmond, and on Aug. 9 it defeated Banks's corps at Cedar Mountain, but failed to prevent Pope's concentration at Culpeper. The remainder of Lee's army now arrived, and Pope withdrew behind the Rappahannock. Lee now began a wide turning movement, sending Jackson's corps around Pope's right, through Thoroughfare Gap, and following with Longstreet a day later. Pope somewhat tardily appreciated this separation of the Confederate army, and attempted to take advantage of it by concentrating against Jackson. But his movements were groping and ineffective, and Longstreet was nearer than he had supposed, so that the Confederate corps effected their junction in time. In the ensuing Second Battle of Manassas (Aug. 27–30) Pope was decisively defeated, and fell back to the defenses of Washington. On Sept. 5 he was relieved of his command, and the troops were reassigned to McClellan's Army of the Potomac.

Throughout the campaign, Pope was poorly informed of the Confederate movements, and he misjudged the entire situation. As a result, his orders were vague, and his dispositions never appropriate. Pope insisted that his failure was due to the disloyalty and disobedience of subordinate commanders, notably General Fitz-John Porter [q.v.] whose corps (V) remained inactive on Aug. 29. According to Pope's conception of the situation, and under his orders, this corps should have struck Jackson's right flank, cutting him off from Longstreet and insuring his defeat. Porter's contention was that Longstreet had already arrived and prolonged Jackson's line, and that the moves ordered had become impossible. Porter was tried and dismissed from the Army for his conduct, but immediately began a campaign for reinstatement, which he finally won many years after. The controversy lasted throughout the lives of both generals; in fact, it may be said to continue even to this day. Pope was not again employed in field operations. He was sent to the Department of the Northwest, where he served with credit in Indian troubles. In January 1865, he assumed command of the Division (later Department) of the Missouri.

Near the close of the war (Mar. 13, 1865) Pope received the brevet rank of major-general in the regular army, for his conduct of the expedition against Island No. 10. He commanded the 3rd Military District (Georgia, Alabama, and Florida) in 1867; the Department of the Lakes, 1868–70; the Department of the Missouri, 1870–83; and the Department of California and Division of the Pacific, from 1883 to Mar. 16, 1886, when he was retired for age. On Oct. 26, 1882, he was promoted major-general. The Department of the Missouri was a particularly important command at this time, since the region of Kansas City and Leavenworth was the starting point for emigration both to the Northwest and to the Southwest, and the base for military operations in both directions. Pope's name is closely identified with this country, and especially with the post of Fort Leavenworth, where he long maintained his headquarters. After the war, he wrote rather extensively concerning operations in which he took part. His narrative of his explorations in the Southwest is published in *House Executive Document No. 129,* 33 Cong., 1 Sess.

He was married on Sept. 15, 1859, to Clara Pomeroy Horton, a daughter of Valentine B. Horton [q.v.] of Pomeroy, Ohio, who predeceased him. They had two sons and two daughters. He died of nervous prostration at Sandusky, Ohio, at the quarters of his wife's brother-in-law, Gen. Manning F. Force, governor of the Ohio Soldiers' and Sailors' Home.

[G. W. Cullum, *Biog. Register of the Officers and Grads. of the U. S. Mil. Academy . . .* (1891), vol. II; *War of the Rebellion: Official Records (Army)*; J. C. Ropes, *The Army under Pope* (1881); *The Va. Campaign of Gen. Pope in 1862. Papers Read before the Mil. Hist. Soc. of Mass.,* vol. II (1886); sketch by M. F. Force, in *Twenty-fourth Annual Reunion of the Asso. of the Grads. of the U. S. Mil. Academy . . .* 1893 (1893); *Genealogy of Major General John Pope, U. S. Army* (1875?); obituaries in Louisville *Courier-Journal,* Sept. 24, 1892, and *Army and Navy Journal,* Oct. 1, 1892.]   O. L. S., Jr.

POPE, NATHANIEL (Jan. 5, 1784–Jan. 22, 1850), territorial secretary and delegate from Illinois, was born in Louisville, Ky., the son of William and Penelope (Edwards) Pope. He was the descendant of Nathaniel Pope who settled in Westmoreland County, Va., in the middle of the seventeenth century and whose daughter Ann married John Washington, the great-grandfather of George Washington. Most sketches of his life state that he was a graduate of Transylvania University at Lexington, but his name is not on the list of graduates of that institution. However, there is a record showing that he attended in 1802. After leaving Transylvania, he studied law in the office of his brother, John Pope, a federal senator from Kentucky. After admission to the bar he removed to Sainte Genevieve in Upper Louisiana, now in Missouri, and after a brief sojourn moved on to Kaskaskia, Ill. When in 1809 Congress authorized the organization of the Illinois Territory, through the influence of his brother John and of Henry Clay he received the appointment as secretary of the territory. In that year he was married to Lucretia, the daughter of Elijah Backus. Of their six children the most distinguished was John Pope [q.v.]. Since the appointed governor, his cousin Ninian Edwards [q.v.], was detained in Kentucky until June, Pope proceeded to organize the territory, reëstablishing certain counties and appointing necessary officials. In 1812 he served as an officer under Governor Edwards on an expedition to Peoria Lake against the Indians, who became increasingly menacing after the declaration of war against Great Britain. Under the authority of the legislature he revised and digested the *Laws of the Territory of Illinois* (2 vols., 1815).

In the fall of 1816 he was elected territorial delegate to Congress. He resigned his position as secretary to the territory, took his seat in Congress on Dec. 2, 1816, and served until the territory became a state on Dec. 3, 1818. When Illinois applied for admission to the Union, as territorial delegate he was asked to draw up a resolution for admission, which was adopted by Congress. It was largely due to his influence that the northern boundary of Illinois was changed from a line running east and west through the southern bend of Lake Michigan, as provided by the ordinance of 1787, to the present boundary of forty-two degrees and thirty minutes, a change that gave Illinois an outlet on Lake Michigan and control of the site of Chicago. He was also largely responsible for the educational provisions of the enabling act. Ordinarily, new states created from the Northwest Territory were granted five per cent. of the proceeds of the sale of public lands for the building of roads, but because of his plea for education, based on his belief that roads would be built sooner or later anyway, the Illinois act set aside two per cent. of the proceeds of the sale of public lands for roads and gave three per cent. to be used by the legislature of the state for the encouragement of learning. In 1819 he was appointed federal district judge for Illinois, a position which he held until his death. In 1824 he was an unsuccessful candidate to fill a vacancy in the United States Senate, and he spent the winter of 1826 in Washington vainly trying to obtain for himself an appointment to the United States Supreme Court. He was a firm but not an active advocate of the anti-slavery movement. He died at the home of his daughter in St. Louis.

[Newton Bateman and Paul Selby, *Hist. Encyc. of Ill.* (1900); W. A. Meese, "Nathaniel Pope," *Jour. Ill. State Hist. Soc.*, Jan. 1911; S. J. Buck, *Ill. in 1818* (1917); John Moses, *Ill., Hist. and Statistical* (1889), esp. pp. 237, 242, 276–82; *Geneal. of Major General John Pope* (1875?) to be compared with G. W. Beale, "Col. Nathaniel Pope and his Descendants," *Wm. and Mary College Quart.*, Jan. 1904, which has itself certain obvious mistakes; G. H. Edwards, *Hist. Sketches of Edwards and Todd Families* (1895); W. W. Backus, *A Geneal. Memoir of the Backus Family* (1889); death date from *St. Louis Daily Intelligencer*, Jan. 23, 1850. Paul M. Angle, Springfield, Ill., is now (1934) preparing a biography.]
E. B. E.

POPHAM, GEORGE (d. Feb. 5, 1608), colonist, was the second son of Edward and Jane (Norton) Popham of Huntsworth, Somerset. Sir John Popham was his uncle. Few facts relating to his early life are known. From November 1594 to May 1595 he served as captain of one of the vessels in Robert Dudley's expedition to Guiana and the West Indies, returning by way of Bermuda. While thus engaged, he captured from a Spanish vessel documents describing Guiana, which he turned over to Sir Walter Raleigh. He was among those who petitioned King James for a patent for lands in America and was among those named in the Virginia Company Patent of Apr. 10, 1606. In 1607 he was holding the post of collector of customs at the port of Bridgewater. Sir John Popham and Sir Ferdinando Gorges projected a colony for "Northern Virginia." His Majesty's Council for Virginia appears to have approved the scheme, and George Popham was named one of the council of seven to govern on the spot. On May 31, 1607, he and Raleigh Gilbert commanded the two small vessels, *Gift of God* and *Mary and John*, which sailed from Plymouth, England, with the colonists. They reached the coast of Maine late in July, spent some time exploring, and Sunday, Aug. 9, landed on what is probably the island of Monhegan to conduct church services. They chose their place of permanent settlement, Aug. 18, on a point on the western side of the mouth of the Kennebec, and Popham was chosen governor. The two ships were sent home and the colony suffered a hard winter. Gorges describes Popham as "an honest man, but ould, and of an unwildy body, and timerously fearfull to offende, or contest with others that will or do oppose him, but otherwayes a discreete carefull man." He died Feb. 5, 1608, and, owing to troubles both in England and Maine, the colony was abandoned in the following summer. Its historical importance is slight, but a lengthy and somewhat acrimonious controversy arose a generation ago over an effort, due to local pride, to overemphasize it.

[For source material, see H. O. Thayer, *The Saga-dahoc Colony* (1892); J. P. Baxter, *Sir Ferdinando Gorges and His Province of Maine* (3 vols., 1890); William Strachey, *Historie of Travaile into Virginia Britannia* (Hakluyt Soc., 1849), portion relating to the Popham Colony printed in *Colls. Mass. Hist. Soc.*, 4 ser. vol. I (1852) and in *Colls. Me. Hist. Soc.*, vol. III (1853); Alexander Brown, *The Genesis of the U. S.* (2 vols., 1890). For the controversy mentioned above, consult Edward Ballard, *Memorial Vol. of the Popham Celebration, Aug. 29, 1862* (1863); S. F. Haven, *Remarks on the Popham Celebration of the Me. Hist. Soc.* (1865); Justin Winsor, *Narrative and Critical Hist. of America*, vol. III (1885); F. B. Hough, *Pemaquid in Its Relations to Our Colonial Hist. . . . An Address Delivered . . . Aug. 1874* (n.d.). A letter from Popham to King James, with introductory remarks, is in *Colls. Me. Hist. Soc.*, vol. V (1857).]   J. T. A.

PORCHER, FRANCIS PEYRE (Dec. 14, 1825–Nov. 19, 1895), physician, botanist, was born at St. John's, Berkeley County, S. C., the son of Dr. William Porcher and his wife, Isabella Sarah Peyre. His ancestor, Isaac Porcher, was one of the early group of Huguenot immigrants to South Carolina; his mother's grandfather, Thomas Walter, was a famous English botanist. Francis received his preparatory education at Mount Zion Academy, whence he went to the South Carolina College, graduating with the degree of A.B. in 1844. He graduated from the Medical College of the State of South Carolina in 1847, taking first honors in a class of seventy-six. His thesis, which was published by the College, bore the title, *A Medico-Botanical Catalogue of the Plants and Ferns of St. John's, Berkeley*. He completed his medical education with two years' study in Paris followed by some months in Italy. In 1849 he published *A Sketch of the Medical Botany of South Carolina*.

Settling for practice in Charleston, he took an active part until his death in the professional life of the city. He helped establish the Charleston Preparatory Medical School; served for many years on the Board of Health; was surgeon and physician to the marine and city hospitals, and professor of clinical medicine, materia medica, and therapeutics in the Medical College. In 1852 he traveled extensively in Europe, visiting hospitals and clinics, and contributed reports of his trip to a number of issues of the *Charleston Medical Journal and Review*; in his later years he translated and reviewed in the same journal technical books and articles written in French and Italian. Before the American Medical Association, in 1854, he read a paper on "The Medicinal, Poisonous, and Dietetic Properties of the Cryptogamic Plants of the United States." In 1855, with Dr. J. J. Chisholm, he opened a hospital for negroes which was especially designed to care for the slaves from the plantations where suitable accommodations for the sick were lacking. He served through the Civil War, first as surgeon to the Holcombe Legion and then at the naval hospital at Norfolk and the South Carolina Hospital at Petersburg, Va. Under the orders of the surgeon-general of the Confederacy he prepared a medical botany of the Southern states. This large volume of over seven hundred pages, *The Resources of the Southern Fields and Forests*, was published first in 1863 and revised and republished in 1869. Paul Hamilton Hayne, writing in 1873, said that Porcher might "justly claim a national and European reputation, especially for his elaborate work on the botany of the Southern States" (*Courier*, Rome, Ga., May 3, 1873).

Porcher was identified with a number of learned societies, including the South Carolina Medical Association, of which he was president in 1872; the Elliott Society of Natural History; the American Medical Association, of which he was vice-president in 1879; and the College of Physicians of Philadelphia, of which he was an associate fellow. He attended the organization meeting of the Association of American Physicians, an association whose membership was limited to 100 men who had achieved some work of national importance. In 1890 he was named as a member of a committee of ten American physicians to attend the tenth International Medical Congress in Berlin in August. The following year he attended the eleventh Congress, held in Rome, and was the only Southerner on the official American representation. In 1892 he was elected president of the section on general medicine of the Pan-American Congress. He was a prolific contributor to the medical journals of his time: in his own state, where he was for eight years editor of the *Charleston Medical Journal and Review* (old series, 1853–58, new series, 1873–76), hardly an issue of which did not contain some contribution from his pen; and also quite generally over the United States. He was considered an authority on diseases of the heart and chest, and contributed a paper on differential diagnosis of organic valvular diseases to *A Reference Handbook of the Medical Sciences* (vol. III, 1886), edited by A. H. Buck.

Porcher was twice married, first to Virginia Leigh, of Richmond, Va., daughter of Benjamin Watkins Leigh [*q.v.*], and second to Margaret Ward of Georgetown, S. C. He died following a stroke of paralysis in his seventieth year.

[Wilson Gee, *S. C. Botanists: Biog. and Bibliog.* (1918), being Bull. Univ. of S. C., no. 72; Julia Porcher Wickham, "Francis Peyre Porcher," in *Confederate Veteran* (Nashville), Dec. 1925; *Cyc. of Eminent and Representative Men of S. C.* (1892), vol. I; H. A. Kelly and W. L. Burrage, *Am. Medic. Biogs.* (1920); *News and Courier* (Charleston), Nov. 20, 1895; names of parents from Isaac Porcher, Esq., Pinopolis, S. C.]

A. R. C.

PORMORT, PHILEMON (*c.* 1595–*c.* 1656), schoolmaster, was born in Grimsby, Lincolnshire, England, the second son of Thomas and Dorothy (Dawson) Pormort, who were married Nov. 4, 1591. A younger brother, who died in infancy, was buried June 19, 1597. (*The Publications of the Harleian Society,* vol. LII, 1904, p. 790.) It would appear, therefore, that Philemon's birth occurred sometime between 1593 and 1596. Having established himself at Alford, in Lincolnshire, he married there, Oct. 11, 1627, Susanna, daughter of William Bellingham. According to the parish records, three children of this marriage were baptized at Alford: Elizabeth, Feb. 20, 1628/29; Maria, Sept. 28, 1631; Martha, Nov. 24, 1633 (*The Parish Registers of Alford & Rigsby,* 1917, ed. by R. C. Dudding, pp. 38, 39, 41). In 1634 he emigrated to Boston in New England and was admitted to membership in the First Church on Aug. 28; that same year he took the oath of a freeman of the Massachusetts Bay Colony. After the death of Susanna, Dec. 29, 1642, he married one Elizabeth. The entry "Martha of Philemon & Elizabeth Pormott born 16th June" 1653 (*Report of the Record Commissioners . . . of Boston,* IX, 40), supplies the latest date which may with certainty be attached to his lifetime. A Boston record of the marriage of "Samuel Norden & Elizabeth Pormott dau. of Philemon Pormott late of Boston" (*Ibid.,* IX, 57), in 1656, indicates that he died before that date.

On "The 13th of the 2d moneth, 1635 . . . Att a Generall meeting" of the inhabitants of Boston, "it was then generally agreed upon, that our brother, Philemon Pormont, shal be intreated to become scholemaster for the teaching and nourtering of children with us" (*Ibid.,* II, 5). This action established the first public school in Boston, the beginning of the Public Latin School, destined through its many distinguished graduates and its high standards, as well as its long history, to become the most famous in North America. If Pormort accepted the invitation of Apr. 13, 1635, he may have remained until 1638. With the Rev. John Wheelwright [*q.v.*] and other adherents of Ann Hutchinson [*q.v.*], he withdrew from the First Church, Jan. 6, 1638, and, a few months later, left Boston, to assist in founding the town of Exeter, N. H. He seems to have remained there about two years, but was probably in Boston again in 1640, for the birth of his son Pedajah, June 3, 1640, and the death of his wife, Dec. 29, 1642, are entered in the town

records. About 1643 he accompanied Wheelwright to Wells, Me., and his name is signed as witness to an Indian deed of 1649. Because of theological differences, he was excluded from the communion there (Bourne, *post,* pp. 22, 27). Town and church records of 1645–1656 indicate that he made Boston his headquarters until the end of his life.

[Jeremy Belknap, *The Hist. of N. H.* (1792), vol. I; *Reports of the Record Commissioners of the City of Boston,* vols. II (1877), IX (1883), XXXII (1903); Nathaniel Bouton, *Provincial Papers, Documents and Records Relating to the Province of N. H.,* vol. I (1867); E. E. Bourne, *The Hist. of Wells and Kennebunk* (1875); C. H. Bell, *Hist. of the Town of Exeter* (1888); H. F. Jenks, *Cat. of the Boston Pub. Latin School* (1886), and *The Boston Pub. Latin School, 1635–1880* (1881).]

R. F. S.

PORTER, ALBERT GALLATIN (Apr. 20, 1824–May 3, 1897), governor, congressman from Indiana, was born at Lawrenceburg, Ind., the descendant of John Porter, possibly an emigrant from Ireland, who was living in Lancaster County, Pa., in the eighteenth century. He was the son of Thomas and Miranda (Tousey) Porter. The family soon moved to a farm in Kentucky just across the Ohio River, where the boy grew up. He attended Hanover College and Asbury College, now De Pauw University, and was graduated from Asbury in 1843. He read law in Lawrenceburg with the father of John C. Spooner [*q.v.*] and in 1845 began practice in Indianapolis. On Nov. 30, 1846, he was married to Minerva Virginia Brown of Indianapolis, who died in 1875. They had five children. He supplemented his slender income as a lawyer by writing digests of the state supreme court opinions for the *Indianapolis Journal.* So creditably were these written that, when the court's reporter died, the judges unanimously recommended him for the vacancy, and he was appointed by the governor on Jan. 21, 1853. In the next election the Democrats elected him to this office, and he served till 1856 (*3–7 Ind. Reports,* 1853–56). He had been city attorney from 1851 to 1853 and was elected city councilman for the years 1857 to 1859.

Meanwhile, the proslavery attitude of the Democratic party caused him to join the newly formed Republican party. By it he was twice elected to the federal House of Representatives; he served from 1859 to 1863 and declined a third term because of the small salary. In Congress he favored the vigorous prosecution of the war and the abolition of the franking privilege, and he gave much time to judicial matters. Resuming the practice of law in 1863, he became the head of one of the most successful legal firms in Indiana. From 1863 to 1865 his partner was W. P. Fishback; at the close of the Civil War, Benjamin Harrison, later president of the United States, joined the firm. From 1863 to 1877 Porter gave his undivided attention to law. The large clientele that was built up by his firm enabled him to amass a comfortable fortune. In 1878, President Hayes, at the suggestion of John Sherman, appointed him first comptroller of the treasury. As comptroller, he settled numerous claims against the government, many of which grew out of the Civil War. He resigned in 1880, after he had been nominated as governor of Indiana. Nominated against his will in order to carry the important October election in a doubtful state, he brought to bear all his great political skill and charm. The campaign of 1880 was one of the most intense and memorable in the state. The Republicans, well financed by local and eastern contributions and led by Porter and Harrison, won. On Jan. 5, 1881, he was married to his second wife, Cornelia Stone, in New York City. As governor, from 1881 to 1885, he did much to make possible the drainage of 800,000 acres of swamp land in the state, and he improved the administration of state institutions.

In 1888, as delegate-at-large to the Republican National Convention at Chicago, he made the leading speech nominating his former partner, Benjamin Harrison, for president. On Mar. 13, 1889, he was appointed minister to Italy. Residence in Rome appealed to him, for he loved classical literature and art. His natural tact, culture, and geniality enabled him to fill his position successfully. He assisted in the delicate negotiations that followed the killing of several Italians during the Mafia riots in New Orleans in 1891, though the major principles maintained by the United States were determined in Washington by Harrison and Blaine. Fortunately, before this incident occurred he had applied to the department of state for his annual leave, and by granting it and extending it until the question was settled, the department avoided the necessity of recalling him, when the Italian government recalled Baron Fava. After his return home he devoted the remainder of his life to the gathering of material and writing a history of Indiana. He died in Indianapolis.

[Diaries and papers in the Ind. State Lib., Indianapolis, and in the possession of his grand-daughters, Mrs. Frank R. Jelleff, Washington, D. C., and Mrs. Gordon Varney, Bradenton, Fla.; Benjamin Harrison Papers in Lib. of Cong.; C. W. Taylor, *Biog. Sketches . . . of the Bench and Bar of Ind.* (1895); G. I. Reed, *Encyc. of Biog. of Ind.*, vol. II (1899); T. C. Rose, *The Tousey Family in America* (1916); *Indianapolis News*, May 3, 1897; *Indianapolis Jour.*, May 4, 1897.]
A. T. V.

PORTER, ALEXANDER (June 24, 1785– Jan. 13, 1844), jurist, senator, and sugar planter, was born in County Donegal, Ireland. His paternal grandparent, after whom he was named, owned a farm and operated a flax-scutching mill near Ballindrait. James Porter, his father, received a classical education at Glasgow, entered the Presbyterian ministry, and supplemented his professional income by farming. His satire, *Billy Bluff and Squire Firebrand* (Belfast, 1796), popularized his name in Ulster, but his lectures upon chemistry and natural philosophy in that province excited suspicion in England that he had also a political mission. Though not affiliated with the United Irishmen it was believed that he was an emissary of that organization during the rebellion of 1798, and in spite of his advocacy of only constitutional means of redress, he was court-martialed and executed. His widow, Anna Knox, and seven children survived. In 1801 the two sons, Alexander and James, accompanied their uncle, Alexander Porter, to Nashville, Tenn. There the elder Porter established himself as a merchant and young Alexander worked in his store, studied law, was admitted to the bar in 1807, and practised his profession three years. Desiring more rapid progress he emigrated in 1809 to the Attakapas region of the Territory of Orleans where he immediately gained the confidence of the French inhabitants. In the constitutional convention of 1811–12 his Irish ancestry and wit enabled him to reconcile conflicting American and French elements. He served in the lower branch of the state legislature, 1816–18, and as associate justice of the Louisiana supreme court, 1821–33. His research in Spanish law and the establishment of the Law Merchant of England were important contributions to Louisiana jurisprudence; his decisions in private international law were of broader significance (W. W. Howe, "Alexander Porter," in *Columbia Law Review*, April 1906, 237–43).

On Dec. 13, 1833, Porter was elected to fill an unexpired term in the United States Senate. Though an active Whig he was not a rigid partisan and often worked harmoniously with Western Democrats. He championed the United States Bank and ascribed all economic and financial woes to the veto of the recharter bill and the removal of the deposits. His ablest speech in the Senate was a reply to Benton on the Expunging Resolution. Porter also labored for a reorganized circuit court system that would serve the West more efficiently, sought better mail service between New Orleans and the East, and advocated improved frontier defense. Although his term would not expire until Mar. 4, 1837, ill health caused him to resign his senatorship in the previous January. A decade earlier he had purchased land in St. Mary Parish which he organized as "Oak Lawn" plantation. It extended nearly a mile on both sides of the Teche, in the fertile Louisiana prairies. By the end of the thirties he had 2,000 acres under cultivation, worked by 160 slaves. He raised sugar cane, imported short-horn, Devon, and Ayreshire cattle, kept a large flock of Southdowns, maintained a race-course and a stable of fine horses including "Harkforward," an English importation. His manor house, completed in 1840, became a Mecca for visitors from many parts of the world.

Shortly after retiring from the Senate Porter visited Cuba to regain his health, and in 1840 he toured England. He did not lose interest in politics but continued a lively correspondence with Whig leaders. In 1843 without solicitation on his part he was returned to the Senate by a Democratic legislature, a tribute to his liberal attitude and personal popularity. He did not take his seat, however, for he was not in good health and died the following January at Oak Lawn. His wife and two daughters were already deceased and his brother inherited the estate. The owner of one of the handsomest plantations in Louisiana, master of many slaves, a cultivated and refined gentleman, a linguist and a lover of good books, an entertaining conversationalist and an extensive traveler, he was the typical planter in politics. John Quincy Adams wrote soon after Porter's death: "He was a man of fine talents, amiable disposition, pleasant temper, benevolent heart, elegant taste, and classical acquirements" (*Memoirs of John Quincy Adams*, vol. XI, 1876, p. 500).

[There are important Porter letters in the John J. Crittenden Papers and the J. Burton Harrison Collection, both in the Lib. of Cong. Valuable notes are available in W. H. Sparks, *The Memories of Fifty Years* (1870); T. H. Benton, *Thirty Years' View* (2 vols., 1854–56); Chas. G. B. Daubeny, *Jour. of a Tour through the U. S. . . . 1837–38* (Oxford, 1843); *Am. Agriculturist*, July 1847, pp. 213–14. The *New Orleans Bee, New Orleans Commercial Bulletin*, and *La. Advertiser* contain much political comment, and legislative journals record his career in public office. For the creation of his estate the Parish of St. Mary Conveyance Records (Franklin, La.) contain valuable data. There is a brief account of Porter in the *Biog. Dir. Am. Cong.* (1928), and a biography of his father, James Porter, in the *Dict. Nat. Biog.*] W. H. S.

PORTER, ANDREW (Sept. 24, 1743–Nov. 16, 1813), teacher, Revolutionary soldier, surveyor, son of Robert Porter and one of fourteen children, was born on a farm in Montgomery County, Pa. His father emigrated from Londonderry, Ireland, to Londonderry, N. H., about 1720, later moving to Pennsylvania where he became a prosperous farmer near Norristown. He expected his son Andrew to become a carpenter,

but the drudgery of an apprentice held no attractions for the boy. He loved books and figures, his mathematical inclinations once inspiring him to construct a sun dial from a stone which he reduced to the proper size and shape by using his brother's carpenter tools. He was forthwith banished from their shop. Attempts to make him a farmer proving equally futile, his father decided that he should be a schoolmaster. He was sent to Patrick Menan's school where he made rapid strides in mathematics, and, after what was considered adequate preparation, opened a school near his home. On the advice of David Rittenhouse, however, in 1767 he went to Philadelphia to take charge of an English and mathematical school which he conducted until 1776. His school enjoyed a reputation for high standards and enabled him to support his family comfortably.

On June 25, 1776, Porter was commissioned a captain of marines by Congress and assigned to the frigate *Effingham*. Not finding this branch of the service to his liking, he obtained a transfer to the artillery shortly thereafter where he found a better opportunity for his mathematical abilities. He saw action at Trenton, Princeton, the Brandywine, and at Germantown, where nearly all of his company were killed or taken as prisoners, and in 1779 joined Sullivan's expedition against the Indians of central New York. In 1781 he supervised the manufacture of ammunition at Philadelphia for the siege of Yorktown, though remonstrating against his removal from active service to a chemical laboratory. His objections were silenced by Washington's assurance that "there is no officer in the army better qualified than yourself for the station I have assigned you" and that the success of the campaign depended upon the management of the laboratory (W. A. Porter, *post*, p. 265). Proud and quick-tempered, while in the army he wounded a fellow officer fatally in a duel which was provoked by insulting remarks about his being a schoolmaster. He was acquitted by a court martial and curiously was appointed to his opponent's place in the army, becoming a major on Mar. 12, 1782. Subsequently he became a lieutenant-colonel and also colonel of the 4th or Pennsylvania Artillery.

After the war Porter took up farming. He declined the post of professor of mathematics at the University of Pennsylvania, humorously remarking that having commanded men so long he could not go back to flogging boys. In 1784 he was commissary for the commission which surveyed the southwestern boundary of Pennsylvania and during the years 1785–87 was one of the commissioners appointed to run the western and northern boundaries of the state. He was appointed a commissioner to settle land claims in the Wyoming Valley (1800) but resigned before actively assuming the duties of the post. Governor McKean commissioned him brigadier-general of militia (1800) and later major-general. From 1809 until his death at Harrisburg he was surveyor-general of Pennsylvania. President Madison tendered him the posts of brigadier-general and secretary of war respectively (1812–13), but he declined them on account of his age. As a public servant Porter was faithful and exacting. He was married twice: first, on Mar. 10, 1767, to Elizabeth McDowell, by whom he had five children. She died in 1773 and on May 20, 1777, he married Elizabeth Parker, eight children issuing from this marriage. James Madison and David Rittenhouse Porter [*qq.v.*] were his sons.

[A sketch of Porter's life by William A. Porter is printed in the *Pa. Mag. of Hist. and Biog.*, vol. IV, no. 3 (1880), pp. 261–301. See also: *Minutes of the Supreme Executive Council of Pa.*, vols. XII, XIII, XIV, XV (1853) ; *Pa. Archives*, 1 ser. VI, VIII, IX, X, XI (1853–55) and 2 ser. XI (1880) ; *Hist. Sketches: . . . Hist. Soc. of Montgomery County, Pa.*, I (1895), 79 ; *Poulson's Am. Daily Advertiser*, Nov. 20, 1813.]

J. H. P—g.

PORTER, BENJAMIN CURTIS (Aug. 29, 1845–Apr. 2, 1908), portrait and figure painter, was born at Melrose, Mass., the son of Charles and Julia (Curtis) Porter. He began the study of his art under Albion H. Bicknell and Dr. William Rimmer, in Boston, and continued it independently during four sojourns in France and Italy, in 1872, 1875, 1878, and 1881. Soon after opening his first studio in Boston, in the early seventies, he met with great success as a portraitist, and before long he had more commissions than he could fulfil. His early works included a number of crayon heads somewhat in the style of those by S. W. Rowse. From the first he had the knack of making a pleasing counterfeit presentment of the beautiful women and children of the period, the members of those fortunate families which, in Dr. Holmes's phrase, could "afford the expensive luxury of beauty." A discerning critic of 1880 pointed out the fact that he was peculiarly sensitive to the pictorial possibilities of his sitters.

One of the best of his early oil portraits was that of a "Lady with Dog." This canvas was seen at the Centennial Exhibition, Philadelphia, 1876; at the National Academy exhibition of 1877; and became the property of the Corcoran Gallery, Washington. It was followed by a life-size portrait of Mrs. Thomas F. Cushing of Boston, shown at the National Academy in 1878, and a series of similar works which were received with so much favor in New York that

the artist, in 1883, opened a studio in that city, afterward dividing his time between New York and Boston. In the summer he usually went to Newport, R. I., where his services were in constant demand. The list of his sitters resembles a page from the Social Register. He found time to paint a few subject pictures such as "The Hour Glass," and "The Mandolin Player," and essayed at least one historical piece, "Henry V and the Princess Kate." In 1887 he married Mary Louise Clark of Bridgeport, Conn. They had one son. Porter was a member of the National Academy of Design, the Society of American Artists, the National Arts Club, the National Sculpture Society, and the National Institute of Arts and Letters. Medals came to him from the Paris Exposition of 1900, where he exhibited two portraits; from the Buffalo Exposition of 1901, and from the Louisiana Purchase Exposition of 1904. At the time of his death at his New York home, in 1908, he was in his sixty-third year.

[See Maud Howe Elliott, article in *Bull. of Newport Hist. Soc.*, Jan. 1921 ; *Art Jour.* (London), July 1880 ; *Am. Art News*, Apr. 11, 1908 ; *Am. Art Annual*, 1909–10 ; *Who's Who in America*, 1908–09. *Boston Transcript*, Apr. 3, 1908, *Boston Evening Traveller*, May 9, 1878. The date of Porter's birth is given in the *Art Jour.* (*supra*) as Aug. 27, 1843. The date given in this biography is taken from the *Am. Art Annual*, 1909–10.]

W. H. D.

PORTER, DAVID (Feb. 1, 1780–Mar. 3, 1843), naval officer, was born in Boston, Mass., the grandson of Alexander Porter, a merchant sea captain, and the eldest of the six children of David Porter (1754–1808) and Rebecca (Gay) Porter. The elder David, founder of one of the most noted naval families, was bred to the sea and served during the Revolution as commander of several privateersmen and as first lieutenant of the *General Putnam* in the Penobscot expedition. He died at New Orleans a sailing master in the navy, an office to which he had been appointed by President Washington. In 1796 the younger David went to sea with his father, and at Jérémie, Haiti, received his baptism of fire in an encounter with a British man-of-war. After making two subsequent voyages to the West Indies, he entered the navy on Apr. 16, 1798, as a midshipman, and had the good fortune to be on board the *Constellation* when she captured the *Insurgente* in the main frigate action of the naval war with France. Obtaining the rank of a lieutenant on Oct. 8, 1799, he was ordered to the *Experiment* and took part in several small actions, one of which resulted in the capture of the *Deux Amis*, which he brought into port as a prize. He was first employed in the war with Tripoli on board the *Enterprise* as her first lieutenant, and later as her commander. He gallantly led an expedition against the enemy on shore at Tripoli, lost several men, and was twice wounded. He was captured with the unfortunate *Philadelphia* and suffered a long imprisonment.

In 1806 he was promoted master commandant. Now well established in his profession, he married Evelina Anderson of Chester, Pa., on Mar. 10, 1808, and received as a marriage present from her father a handsome residence in Chester overlooking the Delaware and known as "Greenbank." Soon thereafter he took command of the New Orleans naval station, a post that he filled for two years. In 1811 he was made commander of the *Essex,* employed on the Atlantic coast for the protection of merchantmen. His appointment to a captaincy was confirmed by the Senate on July 2, 1812, and on the next day he sailed from New York on a cruise during which he captured nine prizes, including the *Alert,* the first naval ship taken from the enemy in the War of 1812. In November the *Essex* again went to sea and early in 1813 rounded Cape Horn and entered the Pacific, being the first naval vessel to display the American colors in those waters. Her chief object was the protection of American, and the capture of British, whalemen. Her cruise of more than a year in the Pacific, far from home and friendly ports, was at that time unprecedented in the United States navy. She was able to support herself from her prizes, laden with naval stores, ordnance, provisions, and even money, with which Porter paid his officers and crew. For a time he made his headquarters at the Galapagos Islands and within six months had captured twelve British whalers, retaining one as a store ship and converting another into a naval vessel with his first lieutenant, John Downes [*q.v.*], in command.

On receiving news that a small British fleet was expected in the Pacific, Porter became ambitious to signalize his operations with a crowning achievement and sailed for the Marquesas Islands to refit his fleet and make preparations to meet the enemy. One of these islands, Nukahiva, he renamed Madison Island, took possession of it in behalf of the United States, erected thereon Fort Madison and the village of Madison, and admitted its inhabitants into the "great American family" (Porter, *Memoir,* p. 193). By these acts he established his rank as the first imperialist among American naval officers. (As early as 1815, Porter had proposed an expedition to Japan. See *De Bow's Southern and Western Review,* December 1852, p. 560.) After par-

ticipating in some of the tribal wars of the islanders, he sought the enemy on the coast of Chile and came to anchor in the harbor of Valparaiso, where he was shortly blockaded by the British ships *Phoebe* and *Cherub,* of greatly superior force. On Mar. 28, 1813, while attempting to run the blockade, he lost his main topmast in a squall and was forced to fight under great disadvantage and in the end to surrender, losing 155 men out of 225. It was one of the most desperate defenses made by a naval ship in the war. He was later paroled and returned home in time to participate in the operations on the Potomac in September 1814. Commanding a mixed force of sailors, marines, and militia at White House, Va., he harassed the retreating British ships, and suffered a loss of twenty-nine men.

In 1815, after commanding the *Fulton,* an experimental war steamer, he was appointed commissioner of the Navy Board, a new naval administrative body in Washington, composed of officers of the highest rank and reputation. With his prize money, he purchased a farm on the heights directly north of the White House, and erected there a fine, large residence, "Meridian Hill," which became one of the social centers of official Washington. He adopted farming as an avocation and pursued it eagerly with much pecuniary loss. He resigned from the navy board in 1823 to become commander-in-chief of the West India Squadron then employed in suppressing piracy, a tedious, laborious, and dangerous task, which he performed so effectively that when he turned over the squadron to his successor this nefarious practice was nearing its end. His two years in the West Indies changed the whole course of his career and aroused personal animosities that embittered the rest of his life. In his assiduous search for pirates, one of his officers landed at Fajardo, Puerto Rico, and received ill treatment at the hands of the local authorities. Porter landed a considerable force in retaliation, seized a fort, and demanded and received apologies. For these hostile acts against a friendly power, he was recalled by the secretary of the navy and court-martialed. Before his trial in the summer of 1825 he wrote disrespectful letters to his superiors and in other ways aggravated his offense. The court sentenced him to suspension from duty for six months, a rather light punishment, which it softened by adding that it ascribed his conduct to an anxious disposition to maintain the honor of his nation and to advance its interests. Proud and sensitive, convinced that he had been unjustly punished by his enemies, he tendered his resignation from the navy, which was accepted on Aug. 18, 1826.

Earlier in that year he had gone to Mexico, then in revolt against Spain, and had received an offer of employment. He was to be commander-in-chief of the Mexican navy with the rank of general of marine, was to be paid a salary of $12,000 a year, and was to be granted a large tract of land. He accepted the offer and remained in the Mexican service for three years. The first year he spent in organizing and disciplining the navy; the second, in cruising, chiefly near Key West; and the third, in inaction at Vera Cruz. Intrigued against by Mexican officials, his assassination twice attempted, his salary unpaid, a nephew and a son (subalterns under him) dead, he returned to the United States broken in health, his fortune wrecked, but animated by an irrepressible desire to go to Mexico as a United States official and even the score with his enemies. His Democratic friends were now in power and eager to serve him, but fortunately there was no vacancy in the ministry to Mexico. President Jackson offered him various offices, including a captaincy in the navy, which he declined on the ground that he could never associate with officers who had punished him for upholding the honor of the flag. Finally in 1830 he accepted the consul-generalship for Algiers. After Algiers had become a French dependency, he was made chargé d'affaires to Turkey, becoming minister in 1839, when the rank of that office was advanced. For twelve years he creditably filled the not very exacting post at Constantinople. Of small frame and a naturally delicate constitution, he was often ill, suffering from yellow fever and finally from angina pectoris. His remains, which were first buried in the garden of his home at San Stefano, were brought to the United States in December 1843, and eventually interred in Woodlands Cemetery, Philadelphia, Pa.

He was the author of several interesting books, valuable chiefly for their factual information. In 1815 he published a *Journal of a Cruise Made to the Pacific Ocean* (2nd ed., 2 vols., 1822), and in 1835 his friend James Kirke Paulding [q.v.], brought out a two-volume edition of Porter's letters to him under the title *Constantinople and Its Environs*. In 1825 he published several pamphlets relating to his court-martial, and about 1842, a guide-book to Constantinople, now very rare. In natural talents and professional attainments, he was superior to most of his contemporaries in the navy. In his fearlessness, impetuosity, and intense antipathies, he resembled his devoted friend, An-

drew Jackson. He has the remarkable distinction of having given to his country two of its most notable naval officers: David Glasgow Farrugut, by adoption, and David Dixon Porter [qq.v.], by blood. Another son, William D. Porter, saw important service on the Mississippi River during the Civil War and rose to the rank of commodore. Two other sons died in the service and one, an army officer, was killed in the Mexican War. He had ten children.

[In addition to the books mentioned above, see Records of Officers, Bureau of Navigation, 1798–1831; Letters to Officers, Ships of War, 1798–1831, Navy Dept. Arch.; D. D. Porter, *Memoir of Commodore David Porter* (1875); J. R. Soley, *Admiral Porter* (1903); G. W. Allen, *Our Naval War with France* (1909), *Our Navy and the Barbary Corsairs* (1905), and *Our Navy and the West Indian Pirates* (1929); A. T. Mahan, *Sea Power in its Relations to the War of 1812* (2 vols., 1919); Robert Beale, *A Report of the Trial of Commodore David Porter* (1825).]

C. O. P.

PORTER, DAVID DIXON (June 8, 1813– Feb. 13, 1891), naval officer, was born in Chester, Pa., the third of the ten children of David Porter [q.v.], and Evelina (Anderson) Porter. His formal education was limited, not extending beyond the elementary studies. At the age of ten he made a cruise with his father in the West Indies and three years later accompanied him to Mexico city where, after a brief period in school, he entered the Mexican navy as a midshipman. He saw his first active service as an officer on board the *Esmeralda,* commanded by his cousin, David H. Porter, cruising off Key West and the Cuban coast in search of Spanish vessels. Later he participated in the desperate encounter between the Mexican ship *Guerrero* and the Spanish frigate *Lealtad* and was taken prisoner. After suffering confinement at Havana he returned home and on Feb. 2, 1829, was appointed midshipman in the American navy, sailing in the same year on board the *Constellation* for the Mediterranean station. This service of two years was followed by a period of leave, and this by two more years in the Mediterranean, one of the most enjoyable cruises of his life. He was attached to the *United States,* the flagship of Commodore Daniel Todd Patterson [q.v.] who was accompanied by his daughter, George Ann. The companionship between the two young people which began at this time culminated in marriage on Mar. 10, 1839, a happy union that lasted more than half a century.

He was warranted passed midshipman in 1835 and in the following year was sent to the Coast Survey where he was employed for six years, either on the Atlantic Coast making hydrographic surveys or in Washington compiling field notes. Promoted to the rank of lieutenant on Feb. 27, 1841, he was ordered to the *Congress* in 1842, serving first in the Mediterranean and later on the coast of Brazil. His next duties on shore, similar to those of the Coast Survey, were performed at the Hydrographic Office in Washington. In 1846 these were interrupted for four months while he visited the Dominican Republic and acquired information respecting political, social, and economic conditions, then desired by the State Department. In July 1846, he applied for active service in the Mexican War and was given a mediocre appointment at New Orleans as recruiting officer. He arrived at Vera Cruz with a detachment of recruits in February 1847, and was assigned to the steamer *Spitfire* as first lieutenant. In that capacity, he participated in the fruitless attack on the city with the Mosquito Division under the command of Josiah Tattnall [*q.v.*]. Later, at Tabasco, he commanded a landing party of seventy seamen, and in a spirited charge captured the fort. In recognition of this service he was made commander of the *Spitfire,* his first naval command. When he was ordered home in July, Matthew Calbraith Perry [*q.v.*], his commander, commended him as a "brave and zealous officer" (Soley, *post,* p. 76).

After a few months at the Naval Observatory in Washington, he was once more ordered to the Coast Survey and was placed in command of the surveying vessel *Petrel.* As the navy offered little prospect for active service, he obtained command of the merchant steamer *Panama* in 1849 and made a voyage through the Straits of Magellan to the Pacific. On returning home he commanded the privately owned mail steamer *Georgia* and for two years made regular trips between New York and Havana and Chagres. He then entered the service of the Australian Steamship Company as captain of the *Golden Age,* which was one of the fastest steamers of her day and which plied between Melbourne and Sydney. In 1855 he returned to the navy as commander of the steamship *Supply* and made two voyages to the Mediterranean for camels which the army desired to use for pack animals in the Southwest. On his first voyage he found occasion to visit the Crimea and see something of the war in progress there. From 1857 to 1860 he was first lieutenant of the Portsmouth navy yard, having charge of various trivial improvements. Disgusted with his prospects in the navy, he decided to take employment with the Pacific Mail Steamship Company and, as a preliminary step, sought and obtained an assignment to duty

on the Pacific Coast with the Coast Survey. He was in Washington in March 1861, preparing for this service. More than thirty-two years had elapsed since he had entered the navy, and more than twenty years since he had reached the rank of lieutenant. He was now in the forty-eighth year of his age, spare and muscular, a little below the middle height, obviously a man of action, restless, energetic, high-spirited, buoyant, and frank. He was generous to his subordinates, but critical of his superiors. Keenly intelligent in matters relating to a profession in which he was a natural leader, he was an amateur outside of it.

On Apr. 1, a few hours before he planned to leave for California, he was chosen by Secretary of State Seward to command the *Powhatan* in a joint expedition which the Secretary was secretly preparing for the relief of Fort Pickens, Fla. Porter wrote his own orders and also an order to Secretary of the Navy Welles, notifying him that Samuel Barron [*q.v.*] was appointed chief of the Bureau of Detail, an office of great responsibility. Barron was a Virginian and Porter's intimate friend. He entered the Confederate navy five days before the date of Porter's order put him in charge of the personnel of the federal navy. To the suspicious Secretary of the Navy, Porter at this time was wavering in his loyalty to the Union (*Diary, post,* p. 20). It seems that Porter, flattered by the attention of his superiors, and eager to grasp an opportunity for active service, sought to place in power a responsive friend, and at the same time to gratify an itch to assert himself in the management of the navy. When the President learned from Welles the character of the papers that he had signed, he canceled the order respecting Barron and directed Seward to order Porter to give up the *Powhatan.* When Porter received Seward's telegram he was off Staten Island. He at once put to sea, as in his opinion the orders signed by the President took precedence over Seward's telegram. He arrived off Pensacola with the intention of entering the harbor and recovering the city at any cost. Disregarding signals, he proceeded to carry out his intention, when a vessel bearing the orders of the commanding officer of the army to desist therefrom was put across the course of the *Powhatan.* He remained at Pensacola for six weeks performing reconnoissance, guard and blockade duty. He then proceeded to Mobile where he instituted a blockade, and later to similar duties at the southwest pass of the Mississippi. In August he left the pass to cruise in the West Indies and off the South American coast in a fruitless search for the commerce destroyer *Sumter.* In August he was promoted to the rank of commander to date from Apr. 22.

Porter had a prominent part in the preliminary planning of the New Orleans expedition, and if his rank had permitted, he probably would have been chosen to command the expedition. He warmly recommended Farragut for the command and was chosen as the intermediary of the department in sounding out the future admiral. His idea that the main fleet should be accompanied by a mortar flotilla was not favored by Farragut, but since the plan was already well advanced, Farragut offered no further objection and Porter was chosen to command it. From Apr. 18 to Apr. 23, 1862, the flotilla kept up an almost continuous bombardment of the forts, St. Philip and Jackson, below New Orleans, firing with great accuracy and doing much damage, but giving convincing proof that they could not thus be reduced. On the 24th when Farragut ran past the forts, the flotilla effectively supported the movement by engaging the water batteries and Fort Jackson. On the 25th, Porter, who now commanded the fleet below the forts, demanded their surrender and was refused. Fearing that the Confederate fleet might attack his vessels, he moved them to points of safety and assumed the defensive (Porter, *The Naval Hist. of the Civil War*, p. 185). On the 27th he again demanded the surrender of the forts offering very favorable terms, and on the following day they were accepted. The capitulation was drawn up and signed on board his flagship, the *Harriet Lane*. In June when Farragut's fleet ran past the batteries at Vicksburg, the mortar flotilla covered the movement and once more proved its value in such operations. Its commander, after receiving the commendation of Farragut, was detached from the squadron in July.

On Oct. 9, 1862, Porter was chosen to succeed Charles Henry Davis [*q.v.*] as commander of the Mississippi Squadron, with the rank of acting rear admiral. More than eighty officers—commanders, captains, and commodores—had superior claims to the appointment on grounds of seniority. In the selection of Porter, Professor Soley thinks he sees the hand of the President (*Admiral Porter, post,* p. 235). It is not to be overlooked that Porter's intimate friend Gustavus Vasa Fox [*q.v.*] was assistant secretary of the navy (*Diary, post,* II, 147). Secretary Welles credits himself with the appointment, stating that the appointee possessed "stirring and positive qualities," fertility in resources, great energy, bravery, vim, and dash, but noting also that he was boastful, excessively ambitious, and "given to cliquism" (*Diary,* I, 157–58). On

Oct. 15, Porter relieved Davis at Cairo, Ill., where he remained two months organizing his squadron. The principal waters under his command consisted of the upper Mississippi north of the region of Vicksburg and the tributaries thereof, notably the Ohio, Cumberland, Tennessee, and Arkansas rivers. His tasks included keeping these waters open to transports carrying troops and to steamers carrying supplies for the army, and cooperating with the army in the reduction of Vicksburg. In January 1863, he joined with the army in the capture of Arkansas Post, himself receiving the surrender of the fort, and for the bravery and skill displayed in making this capture as well as for his successful operations on the Mississippi, he was thanked by Congress. Several of his vessels passed the defenses at Vicksburg and gave a good account of themselves below that city. In the battle of Grand Gulf, fought in May 1863, they lost seventy-five men.

In the same month Porter cooperated with Grant in his assault upon Vicksburg and during the siege that followed frequently engaged the Confederate batteries. After the surrender both Grant and Sherman expressed their appreciation of his services and he was promoted to the rank of rear admiral from July 4, the date of the surrender. He never held the rank of captain or commodore. On Aug. 1, 1863, he took charge of the lower Mississippi as far down as New Orleans. He now divided his long line of waterways, more than three thousand miles in length, into eight districts and appointed a commander for each district. With a building yard at Cairo, Ill., in addition to a fleet of more than eighty vessels, it is apparent that his administrative tasks were of no mean order. In the spring of 1864 he commanded the naval force that cooperated with the army in the Red River expedition and when the movement failed he made an extraordinarily successful retreat down the river under circumstances that tested his reputation for energy, ingenuity, and courage. While his services were in no way spectacular nor comparable in popular appeal with those of Farragut, they had demanded great energy and unusual organizing and administrative abilities.

He was recalled from the West to take command of the North Atlantic Blockading Squadron and to reduce Fort Fisher, the chief defense of Wilmington, N. C., and the most important still remaining in the hands of the Confederates. He organized his squadron, consisting of 120 vessels, into four divisions, corresponding to the four divisions of the waters under his command, extending northward from the North Carolina-

South Carolina line to the region of the Rappahannock River, and including the sounds of North Carolina and the York and James rivers. Late in December he bombarded Fort Fisher, but failed to capture it, not receiving, as he thought, proper support from the army. In January a second and stronger expedition was sent against the fort. The fleet consisted of more than sixty vessels, then the largest ever assembled under the flag of the United States. The army was commanded by Gen. Alfred Howe Terry [q.v.]. After three days of terrific bombardment the fort was taken by the assaulting troops and within a few days thereafter he captured the remaining defenses guarding Wilmington. He again received a message of appreciation from Congress for his victory, the only naval commander of the war to receive three times the thanks of his government. He passed the last weeks of the war in the James River where he received President Lincoln on board the *Malvern,* his flagship.

During the war Porter had expressed a desire to command the Naval Academy and "get the right set of officers into the Navy" (Thompson and Wainwright, *post,* p. 95). He realized his ambition in August 1865, when he was chosen superintendent. His term of four years was epoch-making. By reason of his national fame he was able to obtain increased appropriations and to enlarge the physical plant of the academy. Determined to make the spirit, government, and instruction of the school predominantly "naval," he substituted line for staff officers and gave himself three votes as a member of the Academic Board. Practical and professional work was emphasized, and new drills, physical exercises, and amusements were introduced. For obedience he depended upon the personal honor of the midshipmen and established friendly relations with them. In 1866–67 his work at the academy was interrupted by an unsuccessful diplomatic mission to Santo Domingo, the object of which was to secure the cession or lease of Samaná Bay. When Farragut was advanced to the grade of admiral in 1866, Porter was made vice-admiral from July 25.

In March 1869, President Grant installed Porter in the navy department as the "adviser" of the secretary, Adolph Edward Borie [q.v.], and for more than a year Porter virtually ran the department. Long dissatisfied with the way in which the navy had been administered, he instituted a policy of reform and issued numerous general orders covering a wide range of subjects, some of which were rather "fanciful," some "ill-timed." and some "distinctly harmful" (Soley,

post, p. 460). He organized boards to inspect the fleets and the navy yards and began the repair of numerous vessels, insisting that the steamers should be equipped with auxiliary sail power, one of his favorite notions. His exercise of authority aroused much opposition, especially among the staff officers who fared badly under him, and on the coming of a new secretary, his power and influence waned rapidly. On the death of Farragut, Porter succeeded him as admiral from Aug. 15, 1870. During the *Virginius* affair of 1873 the government once more sought Porter's active services and chose him to command the fleet assembled at Key West. Fortunately the difficulty was peacefully settled. From 1877 until his death he was the head of the Board of Inspection.

For the last twenty years of his life his chief naval duties, the inspection of ships and navy yards, were relatively unimportant. He made annual reports to the secretary of the navy, in which he discussed freely and fully the lamentable condition of the fleet and vigorously insisted on the construction of a new navy. His position was anomalous and highly unsatisfactory to him. Holding the highest rank, he was subordinate to navy bureau chiefs in the councils of the navy. For years he seldom entered the department. He occupied his leisure with literary efforts which achieved results that he alone greatly admired. His best historical writing is his *Memoir of Commodore David Porter* (1875). *Incidents and Anecdotes of the Civil War* (1885) is a gossipy and amusing book. His *Naval History of the Civil War* (1886) is said by his biographer to be inaccurate in many particulars. His fiction like all his writings is verbose and amateurish. One of his novels, *Allan Dare and Robert le Diable* (2 vols., 1885), was dramatized and presented in a New York City theatre. He never lost his zest for living and for many years his home in Washington, at 1718 H Street, was noted for its generous hospitality. He died in Washington and was buried in Arlington Cemetery. His biography, written at his request by his naval friend, Professor James Russell Soley, is not always judicious (*Nation,* Nov. 5, 1903, 365). Porter had eight children. One of his four sons entered the navy, and another, the marine corps. Gen. Fitz-John Porter [q.v.] was a first cousin.

[Collection of Porter papers, 1851–1891, in the Lib. of Cong.; Record of Offs., Bur. of Navigation, 1825–93; J. R. Soley, *Admiral Porter* (1903); *War of the Rebellion: Official Records* (*Navy*), 1 ser., vols. X–XII, XVII–XVIII, XXV–XXVII; A. T. Mahan, *The Gulf and Inland Waters* (1883); Daniel Ammen, *The Atlantic Coast* (1883); *Diary of Gideon Welles* (3 vols., 1911); R. M. Thompson and R. Wainwright, *Confi-*

dential Corresp. of Gustavus Vasa Fox (1919), vol.
II; B. F. Butler, Statement of Facts in Relation to Ad-
miral D. D. Porter's Claim (1889); D. D. Porter, An
Answer to Misrepresentations (1872); Park Benjamin,
The U. S. Naval Acad. (1900); Gideon Welles, "Ad-
miral Farragut and New Orleans," Gallaxy, Nov. and
Dec. 1871; Washington Post, Feb. 14, 1891.]

C. O. P.

PORTER, DAVID RITTENHOUSE (Oct.
31, 1788–Aug. 6, 1867), statesman and iron manufacturer, father of Horace Porter [q.v.], was
born near Norristown, Pa., the son of Andrew
Porter [q.v.] and Elizabeth (Parker) Porter.
He attended Norristown Academy and after his
father's appointment as surveyor-general of the
state accompanied him to Harrisburg as a clerk
and remained there until 1812. At the same time
he studied law but his health failed and it was
necessary for him to abandon his studies. He
therefore moved to West Township, Huntingdon
County, to learn the business of making iron. He
spent a year as a clerk at Dorsey's Iron Works
on Spruce Creek and then was made manager.
Later, in partnership with Edward Patton, he
purchased in 1814 the Sligo Iron Works in the
same county and operated them until the firm
failed in 1819. He then resumed the study of
law with Edward Shippen at Huntingdon, but
was never admitted to the bar. At this time he
also owned several farms and introduced a fine
breed of horses and cattle into this section. In
1819 he was sent from Huntingdon County as a
member of the House of Representatives of
Pennsylvania and was reëlected in 1820 and
1822. On Dec. 23, 1823, he was appointed prothonotary and clerk of the several courts of Huntingdon County, and on Feb. 16, 1827, was also
appointed to the offices of recorder of deeds and
register of wills. On Jan. 2, 1836, he was elected
to the Senate of Pennsylvania where he made
sufficient reputation as a leader to become the
Democratic candidate for the governorship
against Joseph Ritner in 1838. He was elected
for the term extending from January 1839 to
January 1842 and was reëlected in 1841 over
John Banks, his Whig competitor, for the term
extending from January 1842 to January 1845.

The outstanding accomplishments of Porter's
administrations were the upholding of the state
credit through extraordinary means when a large
faction advocated debt repudiation; the forcing
of the state banks to resume specie payments in
1840; the suppression of the anti-Catholic riots
in Philadelphia in 1844; the attempts to restrict
the spread of corporations, and the abolition of
imprisonment for debt. His administrations
were characterized by constant conflicts with
the legislature as he resisted the encroachments
of that branch of the government on his own

prerogatives. On this account he made political
enemies who, in 1842, went so far as to make an
unsuccessful attempt to impeach him. He retired
from office in 1845, largely estranged from his
party, chiefly because his manufacturing interests were in conflict with the party's views on
the protective tariff question. Recognizing the
possibilities of using anthracite coal in manufacturing iron, he erected at Harrisburg an anthracite iron furnace which was one of the first to be
built in that part of the state and which was
used as a model for numerous other furnaces.
He was a close friend of President Buchanan,
who often visited him, and was also intimate
with Gen. Sam Houston of Texas, with whom
he was associated in an unsuccessful attempt to
finance the construction of a railroad through
Texas to the Pacific Coast just prior to the outbreak of the Civil War. He married Josephine
McDermett in 1820. He died at Harrisburg, Pa.,
in his seventy-ninth year.

[W. A. Porter, Life of David Rittenhouse Porter
(privately printed, n.d.); W. C. Armor, Lives of the
Govs. of Pa. (1872); H. M. Jenkins, ed., Pa., Colonial
and Federal (1903), vol. II; M. S. Lytle, Hist. of Huntingdon County, . . . Pa. (1876); Lives of David R.
Porter and Joseph Ritner (1838); J. M. Swank, Introduction to a Hist. of Ironmaking . . . in Pa. (1878)
and Hist. of the Manufacture of Iron in All Ages
(1884); the Press (Phila.), Aug. 7, 8, 1867.]

J. H. F.

PORTER, EBENEZER (Oct. 5, 1772–Apr. 8,
1834), Congregational clergyman, educator, the
son of Thomas and Abigail (Howe) Porter, was
born in Cornwall, Conn. He was descended from
Thomas Porter who died at Farmington in 1697.
His early life was moulded by the religious atmosphere and the high moral principles of his
home. Prepared for college by private instructors, he entered Dartmouth College in 1788 and
was graduated with distinction in 1792. He then
taught school for several months in Washington,
Conn., where he made a profession of religion
and joined the Congregational church. Feeling
called to the ministry, he prepared therefor under the instruction of Dr. John Smalley of Berlin, Conn., and became pastor of the Congregational church in Washington, Conn., being
ordained Sept. 6, 1796. In May of the following
year he married Lucy Pierce Merwin. His ministry was marked by growth in the membership
of his church and in the intellectual interest and
moral character of the young people of his congregation. Under the strain of his parish work
and a religious revival his health became impaired and he was compelled to rest for nearly a
year. After thirteen years' service, he resigned
his parish, and of the several new opportunities
offered him, accepted the invitation to become

Bartlet Professor of Pulpit Eloquence in Andover Theological Seminary. He was inducted into the professorship in April 1812. In 1827 he was made president of the Seminary, to which he dedicated the rest of his life. He declined to consider a professorship in Yale College and the presidencies of the universities of Vermont and Georgia, Hamilton College, Middlebury College, South Carolina College, and Dartmouth College.

During most of his time at Andover he was an invalid and was obliged to go South for the winters, but in spite of this handicap he performed his tasks as professor and president to the complete satisfaction of the trustees. As professor of the art of preaching he was obliged to break new ground in the field of homiletics. In theology he was in the "Edwardsean succession" and held to these theological views as modified and improved by Bellamy, Smalley, and Dwight. While not a controversialist, he defended the conservative position against the more liberal New Haven theology taught by Prof. Nathaniel W. Taylor [q.v.]. He was instrumental in starting the "Monthly Concert for Prayer," in founding the American Tract Society, and in furthering the interests of home and foreign missions, the American Educational Society, and the temperance movement. In addition to a number of sermons he published *The Young Preacher's Manual* (1819); *An Analysis of the Principles of Rhetorical Delivery* (1827); "Letters on Revivals of Religion" (*Spirit of the Pilgrims,* May 1832–August 1833), reprinted as *Letters on Religious Revivals* (1858); and *Lectures on Homiletics* (1834). Some of these works ran into several editions and were regarded in their day as the best treatises on their subject. Porter was tall of stature and well-proportioned in body, his face thin, his forehead high, his expression kindly, with, however, the suggestion of power of decision and self-control. He was engaging and frank in manner, urbane and friendly. His religious character was distinguished for its profound humility, cheerful resignation, and good common sense. He died at Andover in his sixty-second year.

[Lyman Matthews, *Memoir of the Life and Character of Ebenezer Porter, D.D.* (1837); W. B. Sprague, *Annals Am. Pulpit,* vol. II (1857); *Am. Quart. Reg.,* Aug. 1836; Leonard Woods, "Sermon on the Death of Dr. Porter," *Am. National Preacher,* July 1834; *New-Eng. Hist. and Geneal. Reg.,* Jan. 1855; H. K. Rowe, *Hist. of Andover Theol. Seminary* (1933); *Boston Transcript,* Apr. 8, 1834.] D. E.

PORTER, FITZ-JOHN (Aug. 31, 1822–May 21, 1901), soldier, was born at Portsmouth, N. H. He was a son of Captain John Porter of the Navy, and so a nephew of Commodore David Porter and cousin of Admiral David Dixon Porter [qq.v.]. His early education was at Phillips Exeter Academy. In 1841 he was appointed a cadet at the Military Academy, and graduated in 1845, No. 8 in his class, as brevet second lieutenant in the 4th Artillery with station at Fort Monroe, Va. Promoted second lieutenant June 18, 1846, he joined General Taylor's army in Texas, served under him in his campaign in northern Mexico, and the next year under General Scott in his entire campaign from Vera Cruz to Mexico city. In the capture of the city he was wounded, at Belen Gate. During this campaign (May 29, 1847) he was promoted first lieutenant, and received the brevets of captain (Sept. 8, 1847) and major (Sept. 13, 1847) for gallantry at Molino del Rey and Chapultepec.

After the war he returned to West Point, where he served from 1849 to 1855, as assistant instructor in artillery, as adjutant, and as instructor in artillery and cavalry. On June 27, 1856, while serving at Fort Brady, Mich., he was transferred to the Adjutant General's Department with rank of captain, and took station at Fort Leavenworth. In 1857, while on temporary duty in the East, he was married to Harriet Pierson Cook, daughter of John and Hannah (Sanford) Cook of New York. From 1857 to 1860 he was with Col. A. S. Johnston's Utah expedition as assistant adjutant-general; then came east to headquarters of the Army. During the latter months of 1860 and the early part of 1861 he was charged with various special missions—inspection of the defenses of Charleston harbor, withdrawal of troops from Texas after secession, and restoration and protection of rail communication between Washington and the North.

Upon the increase of the regular army, May 14, 1861, he was made colonel of the newly organized 15th Infantry; on May 17 he became brigadier-general of volunteers, and served under Patterson and Banks in the Shenandoah. In McClellan's Peninsular campaign he commanded first a division in Heintzelman's III Corps; later he was given command of the V Corps. In June 1862, the army stood close to Richmond, astride the Chickahominy; Porter's corps, isolated on the north bank, was heavily attacked at Mechanicsville and Gaines's Mill. Porter's defense was obstinate, and with some reinforcement from the south bank he succeeded in withdrawing his corps. McClellan then began his movement across the Peninsula to the James River; Porter's corps went ahead, protected the wagon trains, and occupied the position at Malvern Hill upon which the rest of the army fell back.

McClellan's troops were withdrawn by water to the region of Washington, and assigned as they arrived to Pope's new Army of Virginia. Porter's corps came by way of the Rappahannock River and Falmouth. After some preliminary operations, Pope took position behind the Rappahannock. Lee made a wide turning movement, sending Jackson's corps around Pope's right, west of the Bull Run Mountains, and out again by Thoroughfare Gap. The rest of the army followed a day behind. Pope somewhat tardily appreciated the situation, and moved to crush Jackson while isolated. Porter's corps was intended to play a leading part in this maneuver, striking Jackson's right flank on Aug. 29, cutting him off from Longstreet and insuring his defeat, but failed to do so. On the 30th it was energetically and usefully engaged. Pope was decisively defeated (Second Manassas or Bull Run), and fell back to Washington, where his army was broken up and his troops transferred again to McClellan's Army of the Potomac. In the ensuing Antietam campaign Porter's corps took part, but was not seriously engaged.

In November Porter was relieved of his command and ordered to trial by court martial on charges growing out of his action on Aug. 29. Pope urged that the failure of his campaign was chiefly due to disobedience, disloyalty, and misconduct in the face of the enemy on the part of Porter. Porter insisted that Pope's orders were vague and conflicting; that Longstreet had already arrived, prolonging Jackson's line, and that the moves ordered had become impossible. The trial continued throughout December and part of January; Porter was found guilty and cashiered on Jan. 21, 1863. He at once began efforts to clear his record. In 1879 he secured a review of his case by a board of general officers, which reported in his favor. In 1882 the President remitted that part of his sentence which forever disqualified him from holding office under the United States; and finally, Aug. 5, 1886, he was reappointed as colonel of infantry in the army, to rank from May 14, 1861, without back pay, and placed on the retired list Aug. 7.

After his trial he went first to Colorado, where he was employed as a mining superintendent. From 1865 to 1871 he was engaged in mercantile business in New York City. In 1869 he declined the Khedive's offer of chief command in the Egyptian army, an appointment later accepted by his friend Gen. C. P. Stone. Later he was superintendent of construction for the New Jersey State Asylum at Morristown; assistant receiver for the Central Railroad of New Jersey; commissioner of public works, police commissioner, and fire commissioner of New York City, and cashier of the New York post-office. He died at Morristown, N. J., leaving a widow and four children, two sons and two daughters.

[There is abundant information about Porter's official career in G. W. Cullum, *Biog. Register of the Officers and Grads. of the U. S. Mil. Academy* . . . (1891), vol. II; *War of the Rebellion: Official Records (Army)*; and in the voluminous controversial literature dealing with his trial and campaign for reinstatement. Official documents are *Proc. of a General Court Martial, for the Trial of Maj. Gen. Fitz John Porter, U. S. Volunteers* (1862); *Proc. and Report of the Board of Army Officers . . . in the Case of Fitz-John Porter* (2 vols., 1879). The best summary of the case in his favor is U. S. Grant, "An Undeserved Stigma," *North Am. Review*, Dec. 1882. J. C. Ropes, *The Army under Pope* (1881), is a good defense. For the case against him, see J. D. Cox, *The Second Battle of Bull Run* (1882), and the speech by J. A. Logan in the Senate, Dec. 29, 1882, Jan. 2, 3, 1883, in *Cong. Record*, 47 Cong., 2 Sess. See also sketch by J. G. Wilson, in *Thirty-Second Ann. Reunion of the Asso. of the Grads. of the U. S. Mil. Academy . . . 1901* (1901); *Who's Who in America*, 1899–1900; obituary in *N.-Y. Daily Tribune*, May 22, 1901. The name is most often written Fitz-John, though Fitz John also appears in signatures.]   O. L. S., Jr.

PORTER, HOLBROOK FITZ-JOHN (Feb. 28, 1858–Jan. 25, 1933), mechanical and industrial engineer, was born in New York City, the son of Gen. Fitz-John Porter [*q.v.*] and Harriet Pierson (Cook). While acquiring his preparatory education at Saint Paul's School, Concord, N. H., Porter manifested an interest in mechanical engineering and, accordingly, entered Lehigh University, one of the few polytechnic colleges of the time. His college career brought him recognition on the athletic teams and second honors at his graduation in 1878.

Following his graduation, Porter moved from job to job and from one industry to another over a period of twenty-seven years, during which he gained the experience and made the acquaintances which formed the foundation for his notable work as consulting engineer. From 1878 to 1882 he was apprentice and draftsman with the Delamater Iron Works, New York City; from 1882 to 1884 he was assistant engineer with the New Jersey Steel & Iron Company at Trenton. Then for six years he was engineer and superintendent of buildings and grounds at Columbia University, and in 1890–91 was superintendent and engineer for the Cary & Moen Company, New York, manufacturers of steel wire and wire springs. From 1891 to 1894 he served as assistant mechanical engineer and assistant chief of the machinery department of the World's Columbian Exposition, Chicago, being in charge of Machinery Hall during the period of the exposition. It was in this connection that he first became a national figure. Subsequently, 1894–1902, he was successively western representative, sales manager, and manager of the eastern office for the Bethlehem Steel Company. It is notable that with the same company, at the same time, Frederick W. Taylor [*q.v.*] was conducting his researches in "Scientific Management."

Unlike Taylor's, Porter's interest seems to have been largely in the social and humanitarian aspects of industry, and during his reorganization work with the Westinghouse Company as vice-president of the Nernst Lamp Company (1902–05) he installed the first shop committee with employee representation to function in the United States. This committee was composed of representatives of the clerical force, the factory operatives, and the foremen with the superintendent of the plant as permanent chairman. In 1905 he retired from active industrial life, and spent thereafter twenty-eight busy and effective years, writing, doing consulting engineering, and personally espousing various social movements relating to the human side of industry. Fire protection, prison reform, safety, efficiency in turn challenged his attention. His activities were instrumental in the organization in 1912 of the Efficiency Society and of the International Congress for Testing Materials held that year, both of which he served as organizing secretary.

During the World War, 1915–18, Porter was adviser on employment management to the Hercules Powder Company, where, building on the pioneer work which he had done at the Westinghouse plant thirteen years before, he gave such impetus and form to the development of industrial relations and employee representation in industry that he became an outstanding authority in that field, and later, under the auspices of the Chamber of Commerce of New Jersey, held many public conferences in the interests of better relations between employer and employee. From 1920 until his death, he was active as founder and secretary of the National Museum of Engineering and Industry, with headquarters at Washington, D. C., an institution created for the purpose of "commemorating the achievements and perpetuating the records of engineering and industrial progress."

Among Porter's best-known writings are: "The Delamater Iron Works, The Cradle of the Modern Navy" (*Transactions of the Society of Naval Architects and Marine Engineers,* vol. XXVI, 1919); *The Realization of Ideals in Industrial Engineering* (1905); *The Rationale of the Industrial Betterment Movement* (1906); *Labor Efficiency Betterment* (1911); *Report on the Fire Hazard* (1912); and an article on

"American Competition" which appeared in *Engineering* (London). He was married on Aug. 27, 1888, to Rose Smith of New York. Only one of their two children survived him.

[*Who's Who in Engineering,* 1925; *Who's Who in America,* 1930–31; *Trans. Am. Soc. Mech. Engineers,* vol. LV (1933); *N. Y. Times,* Jan. 26, 1933; alumni records of Lehigh Univ.; information as to certain facts from Porter's son, Fitz John Porter, New York City.]

F. V. L.

PORTER, HORACE (Apr. 15, 1837–May 29, 1921), soldier, railroad executive, diplomat, son of David Rittenhouse Porter [*q.v.*] and Josephine McDermett, was born at Huntingdon, Pa., and attended the Harrisburg and Lawrenceville academies. After a year at the Lawrence Scientific School of Harvard University, he entered the United States Military Academy in 1855 and graduated third in the class of 1860. Entering the ordnance service, he was assigned to the Watervliet arsenal. His first important active service in the Civil War was as commander of the artillery in the capture of Fort Pulaski, Apr. 11, 1862. He was appointed ordnance officer of the Army of the Potomac in July and of the Army of the Cumberland in January 1863. His gallantry in organizing a temporary check of the retreat at Chickamauga, Sept. 19, was recognized thirty-nine years later by award of the Congressional Medal of Honor. He was recalled in November 1863 for duty at Washington. On Apr. 4, 1864, with the rank of lieutenant-colonel, he was appointed aide-de-camp to General Grant, a position he fulfilled throughout the remainder of the war. He was brevetted brigadier-general on Mar. 13, 1865.

After Lee's surrender, at which he was present, Porter continued with Grant, and with the rank of colonel of staff, he took up residence at Washington with his wife, Sophie McHarg of Albany, whom he had married on Dec. 23, 1863. He made numerous inspection tours in the South and acted as assistant secretary of war during Grant's brief administration of that department. Having become indispensable to his chief by speaking for him on public occasions, when Grant became president Porter was made one of his military secretaries. Though he managed to keep his record clear of the scandals which beset the administration, he resigned his position with relief on Dec. 1, 1872. He then established himself in New York as local representative and vice-president of the Pullman Company. He was also a promoter and president of one of the elevated railway lines, for which he invented the "ticket chopper," and was president of the short-lived New York, West Shore, & Buffalo Railway. A rival of Chauncey Depew as orator and raconteur, he was prominent in civic affairs, acting as president of the Union League Club (1893–97), president-general of the Sons of the American Revolution (1892–97), and president of the Grant Memorial Association, organizing its "drive" for funds. He conducted a similar solicitation for the Republican party in 1896 and organized the "sound money parade" and the inauguration parade.

In March 1897 Porter was appointed ambassador to France. His direct but tactful conduct of affairs, which established cordial relations with Hanotaux, then minister of foreign affairs, was influential in dispelling the hostility toward the United States aroused by the Spanish-American War. His persistent efforts were helpful in breaking down Delcassé's hesitation to accept Secretary Hay's propositions on the "open door" in China. Although Porter's resignation took effect Mar. 4, 1905, he remained in France four months longer to complete his six years' quest for the body of John Paul Jones, which was found, Apr. 7, and, after a careful process of identification, transported for interment at Annapolis. The sum voted by Congress to reimburse Porter for his expenses he contributed to the fund for the memorial. He delivered the oration at its dedication, as he had at the dedication of Grant's tomb. His contact with European politics and his public addresses on international peace rendered him a fitting choice as delegate to the Hague Conference of 1907. His principal contribution to that body's labors was the incorporation into a convention of the Drago Doctrine, sometimes called the "Porter proposition," limiting the employment of force for the collection of contract debts.

In the following years he combined his advocacy of peace with support of the Navy League, of which he became president in 1909. He was a champion of preparedness and a vigorous policy in the World War and an opponent afterward of America's entrance into the League of Nations. Besides articles on railway matters, on the Civil War, and published addresses on various subjects, he was the author of *West Point Life* (1866), in verse, and *Campaigning with Grant* (1897).

[*An Am. Soldier and Diplomat* (1927) is a biography by Porter's daughter, Elsie Porter Mende, and H. G. Pearson. See also: G. W. Cullum, *Biog. Reg. . . . U. S. Mil. Acad.*, vol. II (1891); *Who's Who in America*, 1920–21; *Papers Relating to the Foreign Relations of the U. S.*, 1897–1905; J. B. Scott, *Am. Addresses at the Second Hague Peace Conference* (1910); *N. Y. Times*, May 30, 1921.]   J.V.F.

PORTER, JAMES DAVIS (Dec. 17, 1828–May 18, 1912), governor of Tennessee, educa-

tor, was born at Paris, Tenn., at a time when that part of the state was emerging from the conditions of a frontier community. He was of pioneer stock, a descendant of early settlers in Massachusetts. His father, Thomas Kennedy Porter, a graduate of Transylvania University, had married Geraldine Horton in 1822 and had moved to Paris to begin the practice of medicine. The son was given the best education that could be had in West Tennessee and at the age of sixteen entered the junior class of the University of Nashville, from which institution he graduated in 1846. Although handicapped by poor health for several years after his graduation, he studied law in the office of John H. Dunlap in Paris and later took law courses at Cumberland University. In 1851 he began to practise at Paris and married Susanna Dunlap, the daughter of his preceptor. He was elected to the lower house of the state legislature in 1859 and was an active participant in the proceedings of the special session of 1861, through which Tennessee dissolved its relations with the federal government. He was the author of the resolution which pledged the state to cooperate with the South in case of war, and when hostilities began he became adjutant-general under Gen. Gideon J. Pillow, with the rank of major, and assisted in organizing the Confederate troops in West Tennessee. He was then appointed chief of staff to Gen. Benjamin F. Cheatham and served in that position throughout the war. At the close of the war he resumed his law practice at Paris and in 1870 was elected as delegate from his county to the state constitutional convention. In that convention he served as a member of the judiciary committee, and following its adjournment he was elected judge of the twelfth judicial circuit of Tennessee for a term of eight years, but resigned in 1874 to become a candidate for governor. In the election of that year he defeated Horace Maynard, the Republican candidate, by a large majority and two years later was reëlected, serving from 1875 to 1879.

During his term as governor the most important question to be faced was that of the settlement of the state debt. In his messages to the legislature he urged that the consent of the creditors should be obtained before any scaling of the debt should be accepted, and that no forcible adjustment should be made, but it proved impossible to secure a satisfactory adjustment. Among the constructive measures of his administration were the establishment of the state bureau of agriculture, statistics, and mines, and the creation of the state board of health, while he used the pocket veto to defeat a move to abolish the state board of education and the office of state superintendent of schools. After the close of his term as governor he turned his attention chiefly to business and educational interests, with the exception of the years from 1885 to 1887, when he served as assistant secretary of state of the United States, and in 1893–94, when he was United States minister to Chile. He was president of the Nashville, Chattanooga & St. Louis Railroad Company from 1880 to 1884, and during his later years he was active in the business life of Nashville.

His most important work was centered around his interest in the cause of education. During his term as governor he was informed by an agent of the Peabody Education Fund that it would be necessary to have grounds and buildings before a college for teachers could be established in the South. He at once turned his attention to securing from the trustees of the University of Nashville the loan of their plant for this purpose, and his success assured the beginning of the Peabody Normal College. In 1883 he was appointed a trustee of the Peabody Fund, in which capacity he served until his death. In 1888 he became president of the board of trustees, and in 1901 chancellor, of the University of Nashville, and following his selection in 1902 by the trustees of the Peabody Fund to serve as president of Peabody Normal College the merging of the two institutions was completed through the creation of George Peabody College for Teachers. Under his leadership this college expanded its activities through the addition of a summer school, and was changed from the status of "a mere normal college of the same order and character as the normal colleges which have now been established in every Southern state . . . into . . . a real college for the higher education of teachers" (*Proceedings of the . . . Peabody Education Fund*, vol. VI, p. 265). When the realization of his ambition for an adequate endowment for this institution was assured in 1909, he resigned from the presidency and retired to his country home at Paris where he spent the remainder of his life.

[Brief sketches of Porter's career are in John Allison, *Notable Men of Tenn.* (1905); W. T. Hale and D. L. Merritt, *A Hist. of Tenn. and Tennesseans* (8 vols., 1913); *Who's Who in Tenn.* (1911); G. R. McGee, *A Hist. of Tenn.* (rev. ed., 1930); W. S. Speer, *Sketches of Prominent Tennesseans* (1888). The sketch in *Who's Who in America*, 1910–11, contains numerous errors. Obituary news items appeared in the Nashville *Democrat*, May 19, 20, 1912, and *Nashville Banner*, May 20, 1912. For his educational work see C. E. Little, *George Peabody Coll. for Teachers* (1912) and the *Proc. of the Trustees of the Peabody Educ. Fund*, especially vol. VI (1914).]   W. C. B.

PORTER, JAMES MADISON (Jan. 6, 1793–Nov. 11, 1862), jurist, politician, a founder of Lafayette College, was the son of Andrew Porter [q.v.] and Elizabeth Parker and was born near Norristown, Pa. With two of his brothers he received his early education at home and attended the Norristown Academy. They were preparing to enter college when the college building at Princeton was burned during a student "rebellion" and the boys continued their education in their father's library. In 1809 James Madison Porter took up the study of law, first in an office at Lancaster and then with his brother, Judge Robert Porter, at Reading. He went to Philadelphia in 1812 as a clerk in the prothonotary's office. In March of 1813 there were rumors that the British fleet was coming up to burn the city. The impetuous young Porter, upon hearing some Federalist merchants in a coffee house denouncing President Madison for leaving the city defenseless, lectured them upon their duty and called a meeting of Democratic young men to raise a volunteer company. This company, in which Porter was second lieutenant, garrisoned Fort Mifflin until relieved by regulars. He continued to serve in the militia, soon rising to the rank of colonel. Meanwhile he was admitted to the bar, Apr. 23, 1813, and began to practise law. In 1818 he moved to Easton as deputy attorney-general for Northampton County. He married Eliza Michler of that city, Sept. 18, 1821. Within a few years he stood at the head of the bar of the county, with the largest practice in that vicinity. When the redoubtable Mrs. Anne Royall visited Easton in 1828, she included him in her list of "eminent and scientific men" who resided there (E. A. Weaver, *Local Historical and Biographical Notes . . . from Files of Newspapers Published in Easton, Pa.*, 1906, p. 19). A contemporary described Porter in 1833 as "a shrewd and accomplished lawyer, celebrated for his dexterity as an examiner of witnesses, which, combined with a certain amount of impudence, caused him greatly to be feared" (Samuel D. Gross, *Autobiography*, 1887, vol. I, p. 53). He was noted for his retentive memory and wide reading, his unusual capacity for work, and the vigor of his arguments.

Porter was probably more than any other individual responsible for the founding of Lafayette College, chartered in 1826. He was president of the board of trustees, 1826–52, and professor of jurisprudence and political economy, 1837–52. In the state constitutional convention of 1837–38 he was the Democratic candidate for presiding officer, losing by a single vote. In June 1839 he was appointed to fill a vacancy as president judge of the twelfth judicial district. He soon presided over cases of Democrats persecuted for their participation in the bloodless "Buckshot War" and discharged the accused on technicalities, thereby gaining much abuse from his political opponents. When his nomination was presented to the state Senate, the Whigs tried unsuccessfully to defeat it by preventing a quorum. He resigned in 1840 to resume his legal practice. In 1843 President Tyler appointed him secretary of war, *ad interim,* and he assumed the duties of that office on Mar. 8. In Pennsylvania the cry was raised both by Whigs and by "Loco Foco" Democrats opposed to the conservative Porter faction, that the Porter brothers (Governor David Rittenhouse and James Madison) were trying to sell out their party to Tyler. The Senate rejected his nomination on Jan. 30, 1844, and he went home just in time to miss the explosion on the steam frigate *Princeton* which killed two cabinet members. In 1849 he was elected to the legislature, where he became chairman of the judiciary committee, and in 1853 he was elected president judge of the twenty-second judicial district for ten years. He resigned in 1855 because of ill health, having suffered a stroke of apoplexy which left his mental powers somewhat impaired. Porter's other activities did not prevent his engaging in a series of business enterprises. After an early interest in canals he turned to railroads. He was first president of the Delaware, Lehigh, Schuylkill & Susquehanna Railroad, chartered in 1847, and when its name was changed in 1853 to Lehigh Valley Railroad he became president of the new company. The road was built from Easton to Mauch Chunk during his administration. He declined reëlection when the offices were moved to Philadelphia in 1856. He was also president of the Belvidere Delaware Railroad and of several corporations in Easton.

[See: M. S. Henry, *Hist. of the Lehigh Valley* (1860); Chas. H. Hart, "James Madison Porter," in *Memorial Biogs. of the New-Eng. Hist. Geneal. Soc.,* vol. V (1894); D. B. Skillman, *A Biog. of a Coll. . . . Hist. of . . . Lafayette Coll.* (2 vols., 1932); W. J. Heller, *Hist. of Northampton County, Pa.,* vol. II (1920); and the files of the *Easton Centinel* and the *Easton Whig and Journal.* His only report as secretary of war is in *Executive Document 2,* 28th Cong., 1 Sess., vol. I. Several of his public addresses were printed.]
D. L. M.

PORTER, JERMAIN GILDERSLEEVE (Jan. 8, 1852–Apr. 14, 1933), astronomer, was born in Buffalo, N. Y., the son of the Rev. John Jermain Porter a Presbyterian minister, and Mary (Hall) Porter. His early years were spent in St. Louis, where his father was pastor of a Presbyterian church. Here he studied at home; but when near the close of the Civil War his father returned to Buffalo, he attended the public schools there and later those of Watertown, N. Y. A book by Ormsby M. Mitchel [q.v.], founder of the Cincinnati Observatory, aroused his interest in astronomy; and at Hamilton College he came under the influence of the brilliant astronomer, Christian H. F. Peters [q.v.]. He received the degree of A.B. at Hamilton in 1873, and then for a year pursued astronomical studies at the University of Berlin under Johann Foerster. He returned to Hamilton as Peters' assistant, received his master's degree in 1876, and two years later went to Washington to take a position in the United States Coast and Geodetic Survey. Here he met and married Emily Snowden in 1879; they had the happy privilege of celebrating their golden wedding with their two sons and their families. In 1884 Porter was called to the Cincinnati Observatory and remained its active director for forty-six years, until his retirement in 1930 as director emeritus. Death came to him from a heart attack on Apr. 14, 1933.

Porter's scientific reputation rests mainly on his work at the Cincinnati Observatory. His interest was in those lines of work now called astrometric: although photography and spectroscopy were developing rapidly, their application to astronomy did not appeal to him, and he confined his instrumental work to visual observations with the meridian circle, equatorial and zenith telescopes. His first work at Cincinnati was the compilation of a zone catalogue of some 4,000 stars at −20°, published in 1887; the results indicated that the 3-inch transit was not adequate, and he obtained a 5-inch meridian circle from Fauth & Company. A catalogue of positions of nebulae (published 1891) occupied his time while waiting for the new meridian circle. With the new instrument he began observing stars for their proper motions, and this determination of proper motions became the main work of his life. *A Catalogue of 1340 Proper Motion Stars* (1892) was followed by similar catalogues for the epochs of 1890 and 1895 (published in 1895 and 1898 respectively). He then cooperated with the International Geodetic Association for the determination of the variation of latitude, until the World War disrupted the International Association. The meridian circle was kept busy, and the positions of the northern stars of Piazzi's catalogue were published in 1905. A new equatorial was acquired in 1904 and with it a number of nebulae were charted and their positions measured. Comets were observed at various times, and the prize offered by the *Astronomical Journal* for the best series of comet observations was awarded to him in 1894. Another list of proper motions prepared in collaboration with E. I. Yowell and Elliott Smith was published in four parts 1915–18, and the corresponding positions appeared in 1922. His last work, a list of proper motions greater than 40″ a century, again in collaboration with Yowell and Smith, was published the year he retired.

In addition to his research work at the Observatory, Porter offered introductory courses in astronomy at the University of Cincinnati and advanced courses at the Observatory. One popular book from his pen, *The Stars in Song and Legend*, appeared in 1901; and he wrote the article on Ormsby MacKnight Mitchel for the *Dictionary of American Biography*. Most of his work, however, was published in the astronomical journals and the publications of the Cincinnati Observatory. Rather shy and retiring, he cared nothing for society, and devoted himself to his science. He was a member of Phi Beta Kappa and Sigma Xi, of the American Astronomical Society, and of the Washington Academy of Sciences.

[*Who's Who in America*, 1932–33; *Popular Astronomy*, Aug.–Sept. 1933; *Cincinnati Enquirer*, Apr. 15, 1933; manuscript of publications; consultation with Mrs. J. G. Porter; personal acquaintance extending back to 1884.]   E. I. Y.

PORTER, JOHN ADDISON (Mar. 15, 1822– Aug. 25, 1866), chemist, son of Addison and Ann (Hogeboom) Porter, was born at Catskill, N. Y., and died at New Haven, Conn. His earlier years were spent in Catskill. The family left there in 1831, going first to New York City, and five years later to Philadelphia. Here he completed his preparation for Yale College, which he entered in 1838. He graduated in 1842, and after further study became in May 1844 tutor in Delaware College, Newark, N. J.; in December of the same year he was appointed professor of rhetoric. He was naturally of literary tastes, was particularly interested in poetry, and wrote poetry at intervals throughout his academic life, beginning with his valedictory poem (1842) and ending with *Selections from the Kalevala*, translated from a German version and posthumously published in 1869. He was also interested in science, and this interest became so intense that he resigned his professorship in 1847 and went to Germany, where he studied chemistry, particularly agricultural chemistry, most of the time under Justus von Liebig at Giessen.

Upon his return to the United States in 1850

he was an assistant to Prof. Eben N. Horsford [*q.v.*] of the Lawrence Scientific School, Harvard University, for a few months and in September of that year went to Brown University as professor of chemistry applied to the arts. Two years later, he succeeded Prof. John P. Norton [*q.v.*] as professor of analytical and agricultural chemistry at Yale (later Sheffield) Scientific School. In July 1856 he was appointed professor of organic chemistry and held this position until 1864, when he was forced to resign by declining health.

He was greatly influenced in his methods of work by his stimulating association with Liebig. His first papers were published in Liebig's *Annalen der Chemie und Pharmacie* and he was favorably mentioned by Liebig in the preface of his famous *Chemische Briefe* (3rd ed., 1851). Through Liebig's influence he wrote helpful textbooks and focused his teaching and investigations on chemical problems related to life processes. Many of his papers were published by the *American Journal of Science*. He wrote *Plan of an Agricultural School* (1856), reprinted from Barnard's *American Journal of Education* (March 1856), *Outlines of the First Course of Yale Agricultural Lectures* (1860), *Principles of Chemistry* (1856), and *First Book of Chemistry and Allied Sciences* (1857).

On July 16, 1855, he married Josephine Sheffield, daughter of Joseph E. Sheffield [*q.v.*] of New Haven, by whom he had two sons. Partly through his influence, doubtless, his father-in-law became deeply interested in the aims and needs of the Yale Scientific School, made generous donations, and finally gave adequate funds for a building, equipment, and maintenance of professorships. In 1861 the institution was named the Sheffield Scientific School. As its first dean, Porter shared fully in the work of consolidating the departments of instruction, establishing and extending courses of study which emphasized science, and providing public and private opportunities for disseminating reliable and useful information about agriculture and nutrition. The last activity developed rapidly and its remarkable growth in later years verified the wisdom of Porter and his early associates. Yale conferred the degree of M.D. upon him in 1854. He was one of the founders (1842) of the famous Scroll and Key of Yale, and in 1871 this society established in his memory and as a tribute to his literary and scientific abilities the John A. Porter Prize of $500, awarded annually for the best essay on a subject of general human interest, and the only prize open to all members of the University.

[Biog. Record Class of 1842 of Yale Coll. (1878); Obit. Record Grads. Yale Coll., 1867; In Memoriam, Prof. John Addison Porter (1869); R. H. Chittenden, Hist. of the Sheffield Scientific School of Yale Univ. (1928); First Ann. Report of the Visitors of the Sheffield Scientific School (1866); Am. Chemist, Dec. 1874; Jour. Chemical Education, Apr. 1932; Am. Jour. Science and Arts, Sept. 1866; N. Y. Times, Aug. 29, 1866.] L. C. N.

PORTER, JOHN LUKE (Sept. 19, 1813–Dec. 14, 1893), naval constructor, was born in Portsmouth, Va., the youngest in a family of five sons and two daughters. His mother was Frances (Pritchard) Porter. His father, Joseph Porter, was of English ancestry, the son of William Porter, a captain in the Continental Army. After securing an education in Portsmouth private schools, he learned shipbuilding at his father's shipyard. In 1834 he married Susan Buxton. Eventually, he began to construct naval vessels, designing and building the steamtug, *Water Witch*, in Washington, 1843–1844, and superintending as acting constructor the building of the *Alleghany* at Pittsburgh, 1846–1847. He conceived at this time his idea of an ironclad warship, drew plans and forwarded them to the Navy Department, but received no favorable results. Returning home, he became the first president of the Portsmouth Common Council in 1852. He superintended, at Pensacola, the construction of the naval steam sloops, *Seminole* and *Pensacola*, launched in June and August 1859. Commissioned naval constructor on Oct. 1, 1859, he was attached to the Pensacola navy yard where he remained until it was captured early in 1861. He was then stationed at the Washington navy yard until ordered to Norfolk on Apr. 17, 1861. A few days later, when Virginia seceded, that navy yard was captured, and Porter resigned his commission to enter the service of Virginia. Later he served the Confederacy as naval constructor, though he was not commissioned until June 1862.

In June 1861, the secretary of the Confederate navy, Stephen Russell Mallory [*q.v.*], ordered Porter and Chief Engineer William P. Williamson to Richmond to consult with Lieutenant John Mercer Brooke [*q.v.*] concerning the construction of an ironclad. Brooke had already presented to the secretary rough plans of a warship with inclined iron-plated shield on a deck with submerged ends. Porter brought a model of an ironclad, similar except that the shield covered the entire deck. The committee recommended a reconstruction of the U. S. S. *Merrimac*, which had been scuttled and partially burned at Norfolk, by placing an iron shield on all her decks except the ends, thus combining the ideas of Brooke and Porter. In accordance with the recommendation of the committee Porter submitted drawings, and on July 11, 1861, Mallory issued orders for reconstructing the *Merrimac*, renamed C. S. S. *Virginia*. Williamson was to recondition the engines, Brooke to prepare the iron-plating and guns, and Porter to remodel the hull and construct the shield. It is still a debatable question as to which of the two men deserves the more credit for initiating the plan of the ironclad, but certainly Porter had most to do with the actual construction and equipping of the *Virginia*.

Porter remained at Norfolk until the Confederates evacuated it and then he went to Richmond as Chief Constructor of the Navy. With great energy he produced drawings and specifications for ironclad steam sloops and rams, among them being the *Albemarle, Mississippi, Virginia II, Richmond, Palmetto State, Chicora, North Carolina, Raleigh, Charleston, Columbia,* and *Savannah*. He also designed for Mallory a 2,300-ton, sea-going ironclad, with iron casemate amidships and an ingenious arrangement of gun ports, to be built abroad. He made tours of inspection to supervise construction work, reporting March 3, 1863, "23 gunboats, 20 ironclads, and 3 wooden boats" under construction. A lack of iron for armor and inadequate engines was his chief obstacle. Anticipating this need early in June 1861, he urged Mallory to import immediately steam engines and iron. On Nov. 1, 1864, he regretfully reported that twelve vessels had been completed except for iron armor, of which 4,230 tons were needed. After the war, Porter became manager of the naval department of the Atlantic Works in Norfolk, was later associated with the Baker Shipyards in Berkley, Va., and finally was superintendent of the Norfolk and Portsmouth ferries. He died in Portsmouth, leaving six children.

[Information from Mrs. Frank P. Brent, a daughter of John L. Porter; J. W. H. Porter, *A Record of Events in Norfolk County, Va.* (1892); J. T. Scharf, *Hist. of the Confed. States Navy* (1887); *Battles and Leaders of the Civil War,* vol. I (1887); J. M. Brooke, "The Virginia, or Merrimac: Her Real Projector," *Southern Hist. Soc. Papers,* Jan. 1891; *Norfolk Landmark,* Dec. 16, 1893.] C. L. L.

PORTER, NOAH (Dec. 14, 1811–Mar. 4, 1892), Congregational clergyman, educator, president of Yale College, was born in Farmington, Conn., of which town, in 1640, his ancestor, Robert, had been one of the original proprietors. Noah's father, after whom he was named, was for sixty years pastor of the Congregational church there, and in 1808 married Mehetabel, daughter of Giles Meigs of Middletown, Conn.

Of their seven children, Samuel and Sarah [*qq.v.*], as well as Noah, attained eminence in the educational field. As a boy he was backward physically but keen and acquisitive mentally. Having received his preparation at the Farmington Academy, he entered Yale at the age of sixteen and graduated in 1831. In college he displayed exceptional acumen and ability to express his thoughts with clearness and precision, distinguishing himself particularly in mathematics. Here, too, he formed an intimate acquaintance with the writings of Coleridge, which broadened his outlook and stimulated his mind. After his graduation he was rector of the Hopkins Grammar School, New Haven, for two years, and tutor at Yale for two more, during the latter period also studying in the divinity school. Here he was under Nathaniel W. Taylor [*q.v.*], to whose theological system he thereafter adhered. On Apr. 13, 1836, he married Taylor's daughter, Mary, and on Apr. 27, was ordained at New Milford, Conn., where he assumed charge of an extensive and well-to-do rural parish. The genuineness of his interest in people, his tolerant kindness, and his wise judgment won for him both the respect and the affection of all classes. A good horseman, he rode about the country, faithfully ministering to his scattered flock. In a period of violent controversy, although keenly interested in metaphysics, he had the good sense to keep theological discussion out of the pulpit, because to bring it in, he wrote later, "seemed a sin against the gospel itself . . . when the living truths in which all Christians agree needed to be made more real and the duties to which they are indifferent needed to be enforced upon their lives" (*Noah Porter: A Memorial, post*, p. 50). On Jan. 12, 1843, he was installed as pastor of the Second Congregational Church, Springfield, Mass., which position he occupied until 1846, when he was called to Yale College to be Clark Professor of Moral Philosophy and Metaphysics. From that time on, he remained in the service of the college, but gained through his writings an international reputation as a scholar, the University of Edinburgh conferring the degree of D.D. upon him in 1886. The year 1853–54 he spent in travel and in study at the University of Berlin. In 1871 he succeeded Theodore D. Woolsey [*q.v.*] as president of the college. After fifteen years in this position he resigned because of failing strength, but retained his professorship, the duties of which he had all along performed. President Hayes, in the course of his administration, offered Porter the position of minister to Great Britain, for the reason, among others,

that he represented the best type of American character (*Ibid.*, pp. 140, 141).

His reputation rests wholly upon his character and his achievements as a scholar. He had little aptitude for teaching, though some of his later graduate students professed much indebtedness to him. The undergraduates respected and liked him, but he awakened in them little interest in his subject. He helped them answer his own questions in the class room, and was too kind-hearted to humiliate them or to inflict penalties. As an administrator he was even less successful. Under his headship the college expanded materially, and able men were added to the faculty, but such progress in educational policy as was made, was made in spite of him rather than with his aid. He was a conservative and the champion of conservatism. In *The Christian College: An Address Delivered at Wellesley College* (1880), he contended at length that higher schools of education should be kept "distinctively and earnestly Christian." His objection to the introduction by William Graham Sumner [*q.v.*] of Herbert Spencer's *Study of Sociology* as a textbook at Yale, in 1879–80, created much newspaper comment and almost resulted in Sumner's resignation from the faculty. In *The American Colleges and the American Public* (1870, 1878) he opposed almost all the modern tendencies in education, pleading for the retention of Greek and Latin as the basis for the liberal arts course and the subordination of the sciences, compulsory attendance at all college exercises, and required courses in preference to the elective system. Theologically, he was a champion of Christianity as against positivism and materialism, and of orthodoxy as against Unitarianism, contributing regularly to the *New Englander,* and also to other magazines, vigorous polemics. As in the days of his pastorate at New Milford, however, when he invited the Quaker, Joseph Gurney, into his pulpit, he was fair and generous toward those with whom he differed, the spirit he displayed making even so radical a person as Theodore Parker his warm friend and admirer.

Within the limits of his conservatism, nevertheless, his scholarship was penetrating, sound, and varied. His thirst for knowledge was never satisfied, and he was a tireless seeker. Probably no writer in America in the philosophical field, during Porter's lifetime, was more widely read. His chief work, *The Human Intellect*, reissued many times, was first published in 1868. It was "incomparably superior to any treatise on psychology in English existing at the time when it appeared. . . . It is a thesaurus of its subject, containing in outline the results of the best thinking which had been done in all ages on the human mind" (G. M. Duncan, in *Noah Porter: A Memorial*, pp. 199, 200). Among his other philosophical publications are *The Sciences of Nature versus the Science of Man* (1871), *Science and Sentiment* (1882), *The Elements of Moral Science, Theoretical and Practical* (1885), *Kant's Ethics* (1886), and many articles in periodicals. When Prof. Chauncey A. Goodrich [*q.v.*] died, Porter took over the editorship of the edition of Noah Webster's *American Dictionary of the English Language* which appeared in 1864. He also edited *Webster's International Dictionary of the English Language,* which was issued in 1890. His characteristics as a preacher are disclosed in *Fifteen Years in the Chapel of Yale College, 1871–1886* (1888). His thinking and methods belonged to an era that was fast passing, though his writings contain much that is still of value.

In appearance he was a frail, modest person, without comeliness, grace of bearing, or pride of mien. "He had the rugged, old-time Roundhead face, severe and yet serene"; his keen steadfast blue eyes revealed a fearless but kindly soul (Robert Cameron Rogers, in *Noah Porter: A Memorial,* pp. 74, 75). During summer vacations in the Adirondacks, he proved himself a good woodsman and oarsman, a tireless tramper, and a cheerful, capable associate in times of discomfort and danger.

[*Obit. Record Grads. Yale Univ.,* 1892; F. B. Dexter, *Sketches of the Hist. of Yale Univ.* (1887); Timothy Dwight, *Noah Porter, D.D., LL.D.: Address Delivered at the Funeral Service* (1892), and *Memories of Yale Life and Men, 1845–1899* (1903); *Noah Porter: A Memorial by Friends* (1893), ed. by G. S. Merriam; A. P. Stokes, *Memorials of Yale Men* (1914), vol. I; H. E. Starr, *William Graham Sumner* (1925); *New Haven Register,* Mar. 4, 1892; information from pupils and associates.]   H. E. S.

PORTER, PETER BUELL (Aug. 14, 1773–Mar. 20, 1844), congressman, major-general, and secretary of war, was born at Salisbury, Conn., the son of Col. Joshua Porter and Abigail Buell and a descendant of John Porter who settled in Dorchester, Mass., in 1630, and later moved to Windsor, Conn. After his graduation from Yale in 1791 he studied law at the noted law school of Judge Reeve in Litchfield, Conn. Moving to Canandaigua, N. Y., in 1795, he practised law in that frontier community. In 1797 he was appointed clerk of Ontario County, then embracing all of western New York, and held this position until 1805, when he was removed by Gov. Morgan Lewis because of his identification with the Burr faction of the Republican party (D. S. Alexander, *A Political History of*

the *State of New York,* I, 1906, 138, 147). Meanwhile he had been elected to the state legislature in 1801 and had served one term. In 1810 he removed to Black Rock on the Niagara River within the present limits of Buffalo, and from this time on his name is closely associated with the development of that locality. He became a member of the firm of Porter, Barton & Company, which acquired a monopoly of the transportation business on the portage between Lewiston below the falls and Schlosser above. As a member of Congress from 1809 to 1813 he was an unsuccessful advocate of grants of public land in aid of roads and canals. In the spring of 1810 the New York legislature appointed him a member of a commission on inland navigation for the purpose of surveying a canal route from Lake Erie to the Hudson. The commission reported in favor of a state-owned canal by the inland route, thus proposing the essential features of the policy subsequently adopted (*Buffalo Historical Society Publications,* II, 1880, 281–86). These activities were cut short by the approach of the War of 1812.

In Congress Porter was a leader of the "war hawks" and chairman of the committee which recommended preparation for war with the conquest of Canada as chief objective. He did not seek reëlection in 1812, preferring to enter the military service. As quartermaster-general of New York he served both militia and regulars on the New York frontier from May to October 1812, when he was succeeded by a deputy quartermaster of the United States army (*Public Papers of D. D. Tompkins,* III, 1902, 230). In December 1812 he was serving as a volunteer with the army commanded by Gen. Alexander Smyth, and his harsh criticism of that officer resulted in a bloodless duel. In the summer of 1813 he was authorized by the War Department to raise and command a brigade of militia or volunteers, and in October of the same year, at his request, he was instructed to incorporate with them a "corps" of Six Nations Indians (E. A. Cruikshank, *The Documentary History of the Campaign upon the Niagara Frontier in . . . 1813,* II, 109; III, 119, 190). The Indians responded readily to Porter's persuasions and to a "talk" sent them by Secretary of War Armstrong, and in the campaigns of 1814 Porter commanded about six hundred of these in addition to about the same number of volunteer militia from Pennsylvania and New York (L. L. Babcock, "The War of 1812 on the Niagara Frontier," *Buffalo Historical Society Publications,* XXIX, 1927, 147; Henry Adams, *History of the United States,* VIII, 1891, 37). At the engagements of Chippewa, Lundy's Lane, and Fort Erie his brigade was so well handled that the Council of Appointment of New York made him a major-general of militia and Congress voted him a gold medal. He was on the point of being named to a high command in the United States army when the news of peace arrived (Porter Manuscripts, Buffalo Historical Society).

Porter had been reëlected to Congress in 1814. He resigned in January 1816, served for a year as secretary of state of New York, and in 1817 was defeated for the governorship by De Witt Clinton. In the meantime he had accepted an appointment as commissioner of the United States under the sixth and seventh articles of the Treaty of Ghent to determine the international boundary from the St. Lawrence River to the Lake of the Woods. The commissioners began work in November 1816 and on June 18, 1822, submitted their report on the boundary from the St. Lawrence to the St. Mary's River. On the remaining part of the boundary they were unable to agree (*American State Papers, Foreign Relations*, V, 1858, 242–44; Manuscripts, Buffalo Historical Society). In May 1828, at Clay's suggestion, President Adams appointed Porter secretary of war. He took the oath of office June 21 and served until Mar. 3, 1829. His chief problem as secretary of war was with the Indians of the Eastern states. He advocated removal beyond the Mississippi of all who could be persuaded to emigrate, and subjection of all others to state law (*American State Papers, Military Affairs*, IV, 1860, 1–4). Porter's home in Washington at this time was a center of society, said to have been equally hospitable to Jacksonians and National Republicans, and Mrs. Porter (Letitia Breckenridge of Kentucky, whom Porter had married in 1818) was declared to be "the most popular woman we have ever had here since Mrs. Madison" (Mrs. S. H. Smith, *The First Forty Years of Washington Society*, 1906, pp. 249, 274). The remainder of Porter's life was devoted to his private affairs. He kept up his interest in politics, however, was a close friend and frequent correspondent of Henry Clay, and in 1840 was a Whig presidential elector. He is described by contemporaries as a man of commanding personality, a dashing figure on horseback, a keen thinker and polished speaker, though Van Buren, who testifies to several of these virtues, adds that he had the reputation of being too much devoted to the advancement of his personal fortunes. His later years were spent at Niagara Falls, where he and his brother, Augustus Por-

ter, had visioned something of the water power development of the future, and there he died, Mar. 20, 1844.

[In addition to references cited see: H. P. Andrews, *The Descendants of John Porter of Windsor, Conn.* (2 vols., 1893); and F. B. Dexter, *Biog. Sketches of the Grads. of Yale Coll.*, vol. IV (1907). C. M. Robinson, "The Life of Judge Augustus Porter," *Buffalo Hist. Soc. Pubs.*, vol. VII (1904), and Augustus Porter's own account of his early life in the same volume contain many references to his younger brother, Peter B. Porter. There is some manuscript material in the Buffalo Historical Society.]   J. W. P.

PORTER, ROBERT PERCIVAL (June 30, 1852–Feb. 28, 1917), journalist and author, was born in Norwich, England, the son of James Winearls Porter. His ancestors for many generations were Norfolk gentleman farmers. Because of delicate health Porter was taken in his teens from the King Edward VI School of Norwich and sent to America to join cousins on their farm in California. There his education was continued under private tutors. At the age of twenty he chose journalism as a career and, except when interrupted by political appointments, followed it to the end of his life. His first job, as reporter on the Chicago *Daily Inter Ocean*, gave him a broad basis of acquaintance with the newspaper business and with American life. Besides reporting local news, he occasionally wrote leading articles, and conducted, for another paper, a question and answer column. He acquired also a valuable familiarity with printing technique and by writing advertisements became familiar with the business problems of newspapers. In 1880–81 he worked under Francis A. Walker in the preparation of the Tenth Census. In compiling reports on wealth, debt, and taxation for the census he acquired valuable training in statistical work. Having attracted the attention of President Arthur he was appointed to the Tariff Commission in 1882. From 1884 to 1887 he held positions on the editorial staffs of the *New York Tribune* and the Philadelphia *Press*. During these years he was sent abroad on special assignments to investigate industrial conditions and housing in Europe. Upon his return he founded, with Frank Hatton [*q.v.*], the *New York Press* with which he was connected until 1894.

In 1889 Porter took over the administration of the Eleventh Census. He greatly widened the scope of the census and increased the efficiency of its staff by the introduction of tabulating machines. His interest in mechanical tabulation led later to his becoming one of the founders and directors of the British Tabulating Machine Company. While serving as head of the Census office (1889–1893) he made a report to the Senate recommending the establishment of a permanent organization (*Senate Executive Document 1, 52 Cong., 1 Sess.*). His recommendation was supported by the opinions of prominent foreign and American statisticians. During his residence in Washington, Porter had gained the confidence of William McKinley and when the latter became president he selected Porter for several missions. He was sent to Cuba and Porto Rico in 1898 as special fiscal and tariff commissioner and in 1899 undertook for the President the task of inducing General Maximo Gómez to disband the Cuban army, a mission which he accomplished with great tact and success.

After the assassination of McKinley in 1901 Porter devoted his entire attention to journalism. In 1904 he joined the staff of the London *Times* as the first editor of its engineering supplement and removed his residence to England. Because of his intimate knowledge of American politics he was sent back to Washington in 1906 as principal correspondent of the *Times*. This position he held until 1909 when he returned to London as editor of the special supplements of the paper. Though he had become a naturalized American while living in the United States, he had retained his English sympathies and upon returning to his native land he took steps to regain his British citizenship. For several years thereafter he traveled widely in North and South America, Japan and Russia, preparing supplements dealing principally with economic features of those countries. At the time of his death in 1917 he was in charge of the *Times* "History of the War." He possessed a comprehensive and exact knowledge of the subjects on which he wrote. "Few have had such a genius for friendship as Porter, and the range and variety of his friends and acquaintances . . . in the United States, in Japan, and in this country was extraordinary" (*Times*, London, Mar. 1, 1917). His published works included: *The West: From the Census of 1880* (1882), *Breadwinners Abroad* (1885), *Free Trade Folly* (1886), *Commerce and Industries of Japan* (1896), *Life of William McKinley* (1896), *Industrial Cuba* (1899), *Lectures and Addresses on Municipal Ownership* (1903), *The Dangers of Municipal Ownership* (1907), *The Full Recognition of Japan* (1911), and *The Ten Republics* (1911). A final book, *Japan: The Rise of a Modern Power* (Oxford, 1918), was left uncompleted and was published after his death. He died from injuries received in an automobile accident. He had married in 1884 Alice Russell Hobbins, daughter of Dr. Joseph Hobbins of

Madison, Wis. She with three sons and a daughter survived him.

[*Who's Who in America*, 1908–09; *Who's Who* (London), 1916; Walter Willcox, "The Development of the Am. Census Office since 1890," *Pol. Sci. Quart.*, Sept. 1914; *N. Y. Times*, Mar. 1, 2, 17, 1917; *Times* (London), Mar. 1, 1917.]
P. W. B.

PORTER, RUFUS (May 1, 1792–Aug. 13, 1884), inventor, founder of the *Scientific American*, was born in Boxford, Mass. He was the son of Tyler and Abigail (Johnson) Porter, and was a descendant of John Porter who emigrated from England about 1635 and settled in Hingham, Mass. Other than learning to read and write, he had but six months' schooling in the Fryeburg Academy, Fryeburg, Me., when twelve years old. At the age of fifteen he was apprenticed to a shoemaker, but he was not interested in this work, and taking his fife and fiddle, both of which instruments he could play well, he went to Portland, Me., where for three years he occupied his time playing the fife for military companies and the violin for dancing parties. In 1810 he apprenticed himself to a house painter and soon became accomplished both in house and sign painting. With the outbreak of the War of 1812 he was occupied painting gunboats, and in playing the fife in the Portland Light Infantry. He moved to Denmark, Me., in 1813, where he painted sleighs, played the drum, and taught that art. The following year he enrolled in the militia but after a few months of active service he began his wanderings from place to place, taught school at Baldwin, and at Waterford, Me., made wind-driven gristmills at Portland, and painted in Boston, in New York, in Baltimore, Md., and in Alexandria, Va. In 1820 at Alexandria he invented and made a camera obscura, with which he could make rather good portraits in fifteen minutes. He then secured a hand cart and again took the road, traveling northward through Virginia, painting portraits from village to village, and at odd times inventing mechanisms of various sorts. At one time he devised a revolving almanac, stopping for a moment to make and introduce it, but the process was managed poorly and without success.

He appeared in Hartford, Conn., in 1823, with a project to make a twin boat to be propelled by horse power, but nothing came of this idea and he again took to the road with his camera. The following year he added the painting of mural landscapes for dwellings and public buildings to his repertory and, traveling about as before, made a considerable sum of money. In 1825 at Billerica, Mass., he invented a successful cord-making machine but Porter's total lack of business sense caused the enterprise to fail. During the succeeding fifteen years he is heard of in various places and as the inventor of many devices. These included a clock, a steam carriage, a corn sheller, a fire alarm, and a washing machine. None of his inventions was ever patented and as soon as an idea was developed he would sell the invention for a small sum. While in New York he was offered an interest in a newspaper and at once decided to become an editor. He made it a scientific newspaper, the first of its kind in the country, and gave it the name, *American Mechanic*. The undertaking prospered and the office was moved to Boston, but in a few months Porter's attention was diverted to something else, and publication ceased. During the next three years he learned electro-plating, joined the Millerites, and invented a revolving rifle which he sold to Samuel Colt [*q.v.*] for one hundred dollars. In 1845 Porter was back in New York, working as an electro-plater. In addition he began a new newspaper which he called the *Scientific American,* the first number bearing the date Aug. 28, 1845. The prospectus indicates that the *Scientific American* of today follows substantially the plan outlined by him. Within six months, however, he sold the publication to Orson Desaix Munn and Alfred Ely Beach [*qq.v.*]. In 1849 he published a book entitled *Aerial Navigation . . . New York & California in Three Days*. The latter half of his life was practically a repetition of the first. He finally settled down in Bristol, Conn., and died in his ninety-third year while visiting his son in New Haven. It is not known to whom he was married.

[*Scientific American,* Sept. 6 and Nov. 8, 1884; J. W. Porter, *A Geneal. of the Descendants of Richard Porter and Allied Families, also some account of the Descendants of John Porter who settled at Hingham, Mass., in 1635* (1878); *New Haven Evening Register,* Aug. 14, 1884.]   C. W. M.

PORTER, SAMUEL (Jan. 12, 1810–Sept. 3, 1901), teacher of the deaf, came of a distinguished New England family, marked by vigorous physical as well as mental characteristics. He was the eldest son of the Rev. Noah Porter of Farmington, Conn., and Mehetabel Meigs of Middletown. His first ancestor in America, Robert Porter, was the son of a Puritan minister and was one of eighty proprietors who settled Farmington, Conn., in 1640. His sister, Sarah Porter [*q.v.*], established and managed for many years a famous school for young ladies at Farmington. His brother, Noah Porter [*q.v.*], was the president of Yale College from 1871 to 1886.

Samuel graduated from Yale at the age of nineteen, and was employed for a brief time as a tutor in a Southern family. He then studied for the ministry and was licensed to preach, but before his graduation a partial loss of hearing caused him to change his plans and become a teacher of the deaf. In this occupation he was eminently successful and widely known. From 1832 to 1836 he was an instructor in the American Asylum at Hartford for the Education and Instruction of the Deaf and Dumb, founded by Thomas Hopkins Gallaudet [*q.v.*]. For the next two years he was a student in the Yale Divinity School; later (1840–42), associate editor of the *Congregational Observer*. In 1843 he joined the staff of the New York Institution for the Deaf, remaining with this institution until 1846. He then returned to the American Asylum, Hartford, where he served as instructor until 1866. He was a deep scholar and an able writer on many topics. He contributed numerous articles to the *New Englander,* the *Princeton Review,* the publications of the American Philological Society, and the *American Annals of the Deaf,* of which he was editor from 1854 to 1861. His contributions to the last-named magazine dealt with the teaching of English, the formation of vowel and consonant sounds in the English language, instruction in arithmetic, and the mental processes of the deaf. For several years after leaving the American Asylum at Hartford he studied and wrote, particularly along the line of the pronunciation of the English language, in which he became an expert. His brother, Noah Porter, was the editor of *Webster's Dictionary* (1864), and Samuel Porter was the associate editor, contributing to this volume a valuable essay on vowel sounds and pronunciation. While at Hartford he had become acquainted with Edward Miner Gallaudet [*q.v.*], who later became president of the National Deaf-Mute College (now Gallaudet) in Washington, D. C. On his invitation Porter accepted the professorship of mental science and English philology in that institution. He continued his successful labors here for some seventeen years as an active member of the faculty. In 1894 he was made emeritus professor, assisting with library work and with voluntary classes until a short time before his death. He visited several foreign schools for the deaf in 1873 and reported his impressions in the *American Annals of the Deaf*. He was a man of striking appearance, tall and well built, with a kindly countenance and a friendly manner. He always carried with him a speaking tube and was ready to use it with friends or strangers. In spite of his deafness he studied and understood thoroughly the mechanics of sound. He was greatly interested in music and musical instruments, and was also appreciative of art, having at his death a collection of more than one thousand fine etchings. He returned to his birthplace, Farmington, a few months before he died, to live with his sisters. His life ended quietly and painlessly in the house where he had been born, ninety-one years before. He never married.

[*Obit. Record Grads. Yale Univ.*, 1902; E. A. Fay, in *Am. Annals of the Deaf*, Sept. 1901; E. M. Gallaudet, in *Ibid.*, Nov. 1901; *Noah Porter: A Memorial by Friends* (1893), ed. by G. S. Merriam; *Forty-fourth Ann. Report of the Columbia Institution for the Deaf and Dumb to the Secretary of the Interior* (1901); *Who's Who in America*, 1901–02; *Hartford Courant*, Sept. 4, 1901.]   P. H.

PORTER, SARAH (Aug. 16, 1813–Feb. 17, 1900), teacher, was born in Farmington, Conn., of which town her paternal ancestor, Robert Porter, had been one of the original proprietors in 1640. She was the third of the seven children of Rev. Noah Porter, for more than sixty years pastor of the Farmington Congregational Church, and of Mehetabel, daughter of Giles Meigs of Middletown, Conn. Of the seven children in the Porter household, Noah [*q.v.*], afterwards president of Yale College, and Sarah were nearest in age and were closely united in intellectual sympathy. Her early schooling was obtained at Mr. Hart's Academy in Farmington, where she pursued the same studies in the same way as her three brothers, who all went to Yale. A year (1832) spent in New Haven at the school of Professor Andrews, the Latinist, was the only opportunity afforded her for study away from home and gave her a foundation on which she was able to build the self-directed studies of her later years. It resulted, also, in her becoming acquainted with members of the Yale faculty and acquiring a useful familiarity with the thought and life of a college town.

In the decade following her New Haven experience, she did her first teaching—in Springfield, Mass., Philadelphia, and Buffalo successively—always continuing her studies and in particular devoting herself to German, which was to be of the greatest importance in her intellectual development. Returning to Farmington, in 1843, she opened a day school for the girls of the village. Almost at once she was urged to make provision for a few boarding pupils—and thus began Miss Porter's School. As the number of pupils increased, she gradually acquired additional land and buildings in the center of the town near her father's church, and until her death her personality was the dominant feature of the school and of its life.

Clearness of mind, power of thought, calmness of judgment, strength of constitution, were parts of her inheritance from her father. From her mother came a vivacity and an optimism somewhat lacking in the Porter temperament. Without this Meigs inheritance she would hardly have been able to touch by her understanding sympathy her innumerable pupils. There was a reasonableness and a moderation about her counsel which kept it from seeming impracticable. The greater the responsibility which wealth and social connections were certain to bring to her pupils in after years, the more important she felt it to be that she should awaken them, while in her care, to true intellectual effort, to self-direction, to a sense of responsibility for others; and in so awakening them she was successful. Until the last few years of her life she taught Greek, Latin, French, German, literature, history, "moral philosophy," or mathematics, as the case might be; yet her teaching and the routine business of the school never exhausted all her energy. She always prosecuted her own studies and her own reading and kept in touch with the intellectual movement of the world by contact with distinguished scholars and authors, many of whom (John Fiske, for example) came yearly to visit in the home where she lived with her sisters and to give lectures at her school. Shortly after her death, Prof. George Trumbull Ladd [*q.v.*] of Yale said of her, "I remember Miss Porter as in her mental equipment, mental habits and attainments, the most magnificent example of symmetrical womanhood that I have ever known."

[*Noah Porter: A Memorial by Friends* (1893), ed. by G. S. Merriam; H. B. Meigs, *Record of the Descendants of Vincent Meigs* (1901); A. F. Ferry, *When I Was at Farmington* (1931); *Outlook*, Mar. 3, 1900; *Century*, July 1900; *New Haven Evening Reg.*, Feb. 19, 1900; family records and personal acquaintance.]   R. P. K.

PORTER, STEPHEN GEYER (May 18, 1869–June 27, 1930), representative from Pennsylvania, was born on a farm near Salem, Ohio, the youngest son of David and Maria (Hope) Porter, who had emigrated from Scotland in 1848. When he was eight years old the family removed to Allegheny, Pa., where he attended the public schools and graduated from the high school. He graduated in pharmacy and studied medicine for a short time but abandoned it to read law in the office of his brother L. K. Porter, with whom he formed a partnership after his admission to the bar in 1893. He was married in 1895 to Elizabeth Foster Ramaley of Allegheny. They had two daughters. He served as city solicitor of Allegheny from 1903 to 1906.

In 1910 he was elected as a Republican to the federal House of Representatives and was reelected to every Congress until his death. In 1919 he became chairman of the House committee on foreign affairs. During the World War he had been frequently consulted by President Wilson, and under the subsequent Republican administrations he came to be one of the most influential figures in the determination of American foreign policy. In 1921, as a member of the advisory committee of the Washington conference on limitation of armaments, he was chairman of the subcommittee on the Pacific and Far Eastern questions. He played an active part in the framing of the four-power and nine-power Pacific pacts. He wrote the resolution remitting the remainder of the Chinese Boxer indemnity in 1924, and at one time he was urged by Filipino leaders for appointment as governor-general of the Philippines. He was the colleague of the secretary of state, Charles E. Hughes, on the Pan American economic commission of 1922 and represented the United States at the centennial of Brazilian independence later in the same year.

The two subjects with which his name will be most closely associated are the housing of diplomatic representatives of the United States abroad and the control of narcotic drugs. As chairman of the commission provided for in the act of 1926, he was responsible for the purchase or building of many office and residential structures in Paris and other important capitals ("Report of the Progress on the Purchase of Sites and Construction of Buildings for the Foreign Service," *House Doc. 616,* 70 Cong., 2 Sess., 1929). A close student of the narcotic drugs problem, he was appointed head of the delegation of the United States to the session of the opium advisory committee of the League of Nations at Geneva in 1923. One school of thought on the opium traffic, represented by official American policy and ardently championed by Porter, held that the only effective means of control would be a world agreement limiting the amount of raw opium and coca produced annually to quantities necessary to supply the "legitimate" needs of medicine and science. The other, held generally in opium-producing countries, argued that limitation of production was a political and economic impossibility, and that efforts should be concentrated on limiting the manufacture, distribution, and sale of opium and coca derivatives, such as morphine, heroin, cocaine. The 1923 meeting accepted the American program in principle and called two conferences to be held in November 1924. Porter again headed the American delegation at the second conference and with Bishop Brent protested against the domination of the first conference by the "opium bloc" and the restriction of the second conference to export problems only. A joint committee of both conferences, formed to examine the American program, produced compromise protocols unsatisfactory to the direct limitationists. In an atmosphere of great tension Porter declared that there was evidently no hope of the American principles being adopted, and the American and Chinese delegations withdrew from the conference on Feb. 6, 1925. His critics complained that his intransigent attitude was impractical, and that he treated the opposing powers with discourtesy. On the other hand, he was widely praised in America and China for his vigorous leadership of the abolitionist group. He was also active in internal efforts toward narcotic control. He sponsored bills, enacted during his last illness, to create in the treasury department a bureau of narcotics and to establish two narcotic farms for the treatment and rehabilitation of addicts in federal prisons, one of which bears his name.

[*Memorial Services Held in the House of Representatives of the U. S. . . . in Eulogy of Stephen G. Porter* (1931); R. L. Buell, "The Opium Conferences," *Foreign Affairs,* July 1925; "International Limitation of Dangerous Drugs," *Foreign Policy Reports,* Apr. 1, 1931; R. L. Buell, "The International Opium Conferences," *World Peace Foundation Pamphlets,* vol. VIII, nos. 2, 3 (1925); W. W. Willoughby, *Opium* (1925); C. E. Terry and Mildred Pellens, *The Opium Problem* (1925); *Pittsburgh Press,* June 27, 1930; *Pittsburgh Post-Gazette,* June 27, 28, 1930.]   K. M. G.

PORTER, THOMAS CONRAD (Jan. 22, 1822–Apr. 27, 1901), botanist, was born in the town of Alexandria, Pa., the eldest son of John and Maria (Bucher) Porter. His father emigrated from Ireland and his mother was the grand-daughter of John C. Bucher, a native of Neunkirch, Switzerland. His early life was spent in the small town of his birth. He was fond of study and reading but was not a bookworm. At the age of twelve he was sent to Harrisburg Academy, and two years later he entered Lafayette College, where he graduated in 1840. The next three years he studied at Princeton Theological Seminary, graduating in 1843. The following year he spent at his father's home in Alexandria, during which time he did much reading and began the study of botany, which he continued throughout his life.

Having previously served as stated supply of a church at Monticello, Ga., he was ordained by the German Reformed Classis at Lebanon, Pa., on Nov. 14, 1848, and became pastor of the Second German Church at Reading, Pa. In 1849 he was called to teach chemistry, zoölogy, and botany at Marshall College, which was later combined with Franklin College as Franklin and Marshall College, Lancaster, Pa. He continued in this position until 1866, when he was called to the chair of botany, zoölogy, and geology at Lafayette College, which position he occupied until 1897, when he became emeritus professor and curator of the museum. Between 1877 and 1884 he was also pastor of a church in the city of Easton, Pa. In 1850 he married Susan Kunkel of Harrisburg. He was a member of a number of societies, including the Torrey Botanical Club of New York, the Academy of Natural Sciences of Philadelphia, and the American Philosophical Society. At the time of his death he was the president of the Pennsylvania-German Society.

In 1840 he began a collection of plants from the neighborhood of his birthplace and continued collecting till his death. In company with Joseph LeConte [q.v.] he explored northern Georgia in 1846 and discovered a number of new species of plants. His herbarium became widely known to botanists because of the completeness of the Pennsylvania species which it contained. In 1869–74 he did pioneer botanical work in the Rocky Mountains, giving considerable aid to John M. Coulter [q.v.], botanist of the United States Geological and Geographical Survey of the Territories under F. V. Hayden [q.v.]. In collaboration with Coulter, he published Synopsis of the Flora of Colorado (1874). With Joseph Leidy [q.v.] he also collected plants in Wyoming and Colorado.

He contributed a summary of the flora of Pennsylvania to the New Topographical Atlas of the State of Pennsylvania (1872), edited by H. F. Walling and O. W. Gray, and the section entitled "Botanical Description" to Gray's Atlas of the United States (1873). His most noteworthy papers are The Flora of Pennsylvania (1903), edited by J. K. Small, and his Catalogue of the Bryophyta and Pteridophyta Found in Pennsylvania (1904), also edited by Small. In his scientific work he was primarily a co-operator. So freely did he share his abundant knowledge that his own original work failed sometimes of the degree of recognition which it deserved. His knowledge of plant habitats was almost uncanny. He seldom failed to find the species which he thought should occur in a particular place.

In addition to his botanical writings he also made a number of translations and contributed verses and essays to the reviews of his time. Among his translations were The Life and Labors of St. Augustine (1854), from the German of Philip Schaff; The Life and Times of Ulric Zwingli (1856), from the German of J. J. Hottinger; and Goethe's Hermann and Dorothea (1854). In the field of literature his most sig-

nificant contribution was "Kalewala and Hiawatha," published in the Mercersburg Review, April 1856. In this paper he contended that Longfellow, instead of creating an American epic, simply imitated the Finnish Kalevala, and failed to mention his indebtedness to that work. Porter had an unusual fund of information and a genial wit; he was often testy and impatient, but never dull. He died in Easton, Pa.

[Essays, Verses, and Translations by Thomas Conrad Porter with Biog. Sketch by Samuel A. Martin (Chambersburg, n.d.); Necrological Report, Princeton Theol. Sem., 1902; Biog. Cat. of Lafayette Coll. (1913); Pa. German Soc., Proc. and Addresses, vol. XII (1903); Addresses Delivered at a Celebration in Honor of Thomas Conrad Porter at Lafayette Coll., Oct. 20, 1897 (1898); J. W. Harshberger, The Botanists of Phila. and Their Work (1899); Bull. of the Torrey Botanical Club, July 1901; Plant World, July 1901; Who's Who in America, 1899–1900; Public Ledger (Phila.), Apr. 29, 1901.]
B. W. K.

PORTER, WILLIAM SYDNEY (Sept. 11, 1862–June 5, 1910), story writer, better known by the pseudonym "O. Henry," was born at Greensboro, N. C., the son of Algernon Sidney Porter and Mary Jane Virginia Swaim, his wife. Both the father and the father's father, who had come from Connecticut as a clockpeddler about 1823, had married into families somewhat above them in social standing. The father, a physician, gradually lost interest in his practice and wasted his time in mechanical ingenuities among which was a perpetual motion water-wheel. The mother had a better education and more enterprise, but she died when her son was only three years old. The boy grew up in a community which, easy-going at best, was too busy surviving the process of Reconstruction to have much time for study. He left his only school, which was taught by an aunt, at fifteen, and for five years worked in an uncle's drug store. So far as the facts can be made out through the bright haze of legend which his subsequent fame and the local pride of his native town have thrown about his youth, he appears to have been quick, cheerful, popular, and fairly talented, particularly in drawing. He read eagerly but seldom went outside of the fiction of his century, though he is said to have been attached to the Arabian Nights and the Anatomy of Melancholy. He made, however, no definite plans for any career.

In 1882 he left North Carolina for Texas, partly to regain his health and partly to find his fortune in a larger world. For two years he lived on a ranch managed by friends who had preceded him from Greensboro, and he there became acquainted with phases of life about which he was later to tell many of his most successful stories. Here he learned a little French and

German, and a reasonable amount of Spanish, and he began to try his hand at short stories with which he had the taste to be dissatisfied. From the ranch in La Salle County he went to Austin, again to live in the household of a clannish North Carolinian. Austin was a small town, but it was the capital of the state and seat of the newly established University of Texas, and it offered, after the isolated years on the ranch, exciting opportunities for the varied friendships which Porter had the knack of forming and continuing. As clerk and bookkeeper (1885–87), draftsman in the state land office (1887–91), teller in a bank (1891–94), and member of various groups organized for amusement, he moved about in the community as one of its most familiar figures. On July 5, 1887, he was married to Athol Estes, a girl of seventeen with whom he dashingly eloped. That same year he began to contribute jocular sketches to the *Detroit Free Press* and later to other newspapers elsewhere. In 1894 he resigned his position in the bank to give all his time to editing a humorous weekly, the *Rolling Stone,* which he conducted for a year but which failed to support him, or itself, though it brought encouraging letters from such contemporaries as Edgar Wilson Nye and John Kendrick Bangs [*qq.v.*]. After this failure Porter went in 1895 to Houston where he wrote for the *Houston Daily Post* a daily column, called first "Tales of the Town" and then "Some Postscripts," more or less in the manner of Eugene Field [*q.v.*] and George Ade.

From Houston he was summoned in 1896 to Austin to stand trial for the alleged embezzlement of funds from the First National Bank in which he had been teller. Had he obeyed the summons he would probably have been acquitted, for the bank had been managed very loosely and the loss of not much over a thousand dollars seems to have been due to him only in a technical sense. But instead, unnerved by the prospect, he acted like a guilty man. He fled to New Orleans, and from there by boat to Honduras, where he remained until he learned that his wife was hopelessly ill. Returning to Austin early in 1897, he was arrested and released on bail, suffered the death of his wife that year, and in March 1898 was sentenced to the federal penitentiary at Columbus, Ohio, for a term of five years, which was reduced by his flawless behavior to three years and three months, ending July 1901. Except for the disgrace, which Porter felt intensely then and all the rest of his life, he escaped the customary horrors of a prison. A registered pharmacist, he was given easy work in the prison drug store. He was a favorite of the officials

and saw few of the other prisoners except certain men, most of them from the West, whose stories interested him. One of them, Al Jennings, Porter had met in Honduras and now befriended.

Using various pseudonyms, of which "O. Henry" eventually displaced all the others, he wrote and published several stories while in prison, and on his release, after a short stay in Pittsburgh, went to New York in 1902 on the invitation of Gilman Hall, an editor of *Ainslee's Magazine.* In New York O. Henry at last found himself. He already knew the Old South, Texas, New Orleans, Honduras, and the aspects of the criminal world represented in the penitentiary, but nowhere had he encountered any such range and diversity of human life as the city offered him. He haunted streets, parks, and restaurants, observing men and women, talking with them, and catching at picturesque details of experience or expression. For a year or so he did not begin to use this new material, but confined himself to meeting the demands upon him for stories dealing with his remoter worlds of eccentricity and adventure. Such a raconteur as he was, furnished with such pungent knowledge as he had, had no difficulty in making his way. His fame grew so fast he could hardly keep up with it. In 1904 he wrote sixty-five stories, and in 1905 fifty. Beginning with *Cabbages and Kings* (copyright 1904), a collection of stories concerned with Latin America, he gathered up his work in annual or semi-annual books: *The Four Million* (1906), *Heart of the West* (1907), *The Trimmed Lamp* (1907), *The Gentle Grafter* (1908), *The Voice of the City* (1908), *Options* (1909), *Roads of Destiny* (1909), *Whirligigs* (1910), *Strictly Business* (1910). Toward the end of his life he experimented with other literary forms, but his musical comedy, *Lo,* written with Franklin P. Adams and produced in 1909, was not successful, and the ambitious novel which he planned was hardly more than planned.

There is little reason to think that the fate which limited him to his single mode did him any real injustice. He was essentially a raconteur. He had himself, in his observant forty years, encountered many amusing episodes, and he invented more, with a facility which seems to prove that he saw human life as a tissue of episodes rather than as any broad general process. The episodes which touched his imagination enough to make him write stories about them were, as a rule, instances of the sort of irony which lets unexpected consequences follow familiar causes. For example, in "The Gift of the Magi," perhaps the best known of all his stories, the husband sells his watch to buy combs for his wife's hair, and the wife sells her hair to buy a chain for her husband's watch. In "The Ransom of Red Chief," perhaps the funniest of O. Henry's stories, the kidnappers who have been holding a boy for ransom find him so obnoxious that they pay their own money to get him taken back. And even when the whirligig of fortune is not so simple as in these cases, the stories still concern themselves almost always with sharp turns in human affairs. There is in them, however, little of the long memory of tragedy, which cherishes one fatality after another until the lives of men are made to seem the playthings of blind, malicious forces. As if the shorter memory of comedy were recounting these episodes, each is taken up by itself and laughed at, without tragic generalization. O. Henry's vision was ironic, but not embittered. Nor did his art use any of the methods of bitterness. He evolved his few formulas and introduced minor variations into them with an ingenuity which is an evidence of the delight which he took in his vision and in his art.

His irony and his ingenuity by themselves would not have made him the most popular American writer of his decade. In addition there was that comforting tribute to the populace which is generally called his all-embracing humanity. His stories do not indicate a preference for great virtues or high intelligence or distinguished passions. They do not show him preferring wit to dullness, beauty to plainness, industry to idleness, intensity to casualness. As anybody can be the hero of an O. Henry episode, provided the right events happen to him, nobody reading the stories ever felt shut out from the world in which they happen. Though the plots may be fantastic, they are no more so than the little miracles which most men and women hope or fear will occur to them. The characters are familiar and simple. They live, love, work, play, and die, with nothing demanded of them except to be decent and kind. The rest is accident. Thanks to his geographical range, O. Henry was able to please his readers both by letting many of them recognize the manners of their own communities and by taking all of them into other communities where there was novelty in the manners displayed. In something like the same two ways he pleased with his language, which is ordinarily plain vernacular, diversified with adventurous slang.

Most of the final, busy period of O. Henry's life was spent in New York. He lived at various lodgings in the neighborhood of Madison Square, disliked leaving town summer or winter,

and had few intimates outside of the editors of the magazines which printed his stories. After Nov. 27, 1907, when he was married to Sara Lindsay Coleman, a friend of his boyhood, he lived part of the time in Asheville, N. C., but he returned to New York to die. With his death his fame, which had hitherto only begun to reach beyond his popular audience, grew rapidly. It called forth his posthumous books—*Sixes and Sevens* (1911), *Rolling Stones* (1913), *Waifs and Strays* (1917), *Postscripts* (1923). The Society of Arts and Sciences in 1918 founded an O. Henry Memorial award for the best American short story to be published each year. The town of Greensboro erected a memorial in the O. Henry Hotel. His collected works had an enormous sale. Only gradually did opinion come to realize that the art of O. Henry, though excellent in its kind, was of uneven merit, only occasionally at its amusing, ingenious best, and often trivial and impermanent.

[The authorized life of O. Henry is the *O. Henry Biography* (1916) by C. Alphonso Smith. Information concerning the Honduras and the penitentiary chapters is to be found in *Through the Shadows with O. Henry* (1921) by Al Jennings (Alphonso J. Jennings). *Waifs and Strays* contains a representative selection of critical and biographical comment with a useful index of the short stories. See also R. H. Davis and A. B. Maurice, *The Caliph of Bagdad* (1931); *N. Y. Times*, June 6, 1910.]   C. V–D.

PORTER, WILLIAM TROTTER (Dec. 24, 1809–July 19, 1858), journalist and promoter of sporting literature, was born in Newbury, Vt. He was the third son of Benjamin Porter (a descendant of Samuel Porter who settled in Plymouth in 1622) and Martha (Olcott) Porter. Both his father and his grandfather were gentlemen of the English type, who prided themselves on their extensive lands and horses. Young Porter grew up on his father's estate, where he indulged to the fullest his love of out-door life. His education began at home under private tutors, but on the death of his father and the removal of the family to Hanover, N. H., he attended a college preparatory school. The characteristic New England urge toward a practical life so far modified his inherited gentility that he left school, inspired in part by Franklin's example, to enter a printing office. It was then but a step to journalism.

Porter's editorial career began in 1829 in St. Johnsbury, Vt., where for about a year he was in charge of the *Farmer's Herald*. He then removed to Norwich as the associate editor of the *Enquirer*. In these country villages, however, the ambitious young journalist found no scope for his abilities, and "with a light heart and a lighter purse" he set out for New York. His ambition was to found a sporting journal. After working for some time in a printing office, he established the *Spirit of the Times,* the first number of which appeared on Dec. 10, 1831. Horace Greeley [*q.v.*], then a young compositor from the country, helped Porter for several months in bringing out the paper. Although the initial circulation of the *Spirit* was relatively large, its existence for a time was precarious. A few months after its establishment, it merged with the *Traveller*—an arrangement which lasted until Jan. 3, 1835, when Porter was able to repurchase it and make it once more an independent unit. In the meantime, he had been connected editorially with the *New-Yorker,* the *Constellation,* and the *New-York Atlas Magazine.*

During the next few years, the *Spirit* proved so successful financially that in February 1839 Porter purchased the *American Turf Register and Sporting Magazine,* which had been established ten years earlier by John Stuart Skinner [*q.v.*]. This periodical, which preserved in somewhat more ponderous and serious form than the *Spirit* the records of the turf, ceased publication in December 1844. By this time financial reverses had come to Porter. In 1842 the proprietorship of the *Spirit* had passed into the hands of John Richards, although Porter retained the editor's chair until September 1856. In that year the paper became the property of George Wilkes [*q.v.*], who renamed it *Porter's Spirit of the Times* and made Porter an associate editor, in which capacity he continued until his death.

Of a gay and social temperament, Porter was a favorite wherever good fellowship abounded; and his extreme generosity found him many devoted friends. His appearance was striking, owing in large part to his unusual height, which gave him the sobriquet of "York's Tall Son." For the greater part of his life, he took a personal interest in sports. He was especially devoted to angling, and in 1842 he was one of the founders of the New York Cricket Club. At the beginning of his editorial career he was obliged to combat the deep-seated prejudice against the turf which prevailed in some districts of the United States. For this task he was well fitted, since he was a gentleman of high ideals, and in prosecuting it he displayed much perseverance and tact. He actively studied the problems of stock raising and breeding, and for this purpose made several extended tours of the South and West. The practical results of these investigations, as well as contributions from the most competent sporting authorities of America, gave to his periodicals an enviable prestige. The circu-

lation of the *Spirit* is said to have extended to England, India, and Australia.

In 1846 he published an English sporting manual by Colonel Peter Hawker, *Instructions to Young Sportsmen,* to which he added much new material relative to North American hunting and shooting. This work, he states in his preface, "is the first of a purely sporting character ever published in the United States." Two volumes, *The Big Bear of Arkansas* (1845) and *A Quarter Race in Kentucky* (1847; republished in 1858 as a part of *Colonel Thorpe's Scenes in Arkansaw*), contain sketches of Southern and Western life which Porter gathered from contributions made to his periodicals. The latter collection was of valuable assistance to John Russell Bartlett [*q.v.*] in the compilation of his *Dictionary of Americanisms* (2nd ed., 1859; see p. x). Porter never married, but was bound by a strong affection to his several talented brothers, whose successive deaths toward the close of his life much saddened his remaining years. He himself died in New York City at the age of forty-eight.

[Francis Brinley, *Life of William T. Porter* (1860); Thomas Picton, "Reminiscences of a Sporting Journalist," in *Spirit of the Times,* Apr. 1, 1882; *Life and Writings of Frank Forester* (1882), vol. I, *passim*; obituaries in the *N. Y. Times,* July 20, 1858, and in *Porter's Spirit of the Times,* July 24, 1858; F. L. Mott, *A Hist. of Am. Mags.* (1930); portraits of Porter, in *Ballou's Pictorial,* Aug. 16, 1856, and *Porter's Spirit of the Times,* July 31, 1858.]   N. F. A.

PORTIER, MICHAEL (Sept. 7, 1795–May 14, 1859), Catholic prelate, was born at Montbrison, near Lyons, France. Well schooled by devoted parents, he was in attendance at the seminary of Lyons when he answered the personal appeal of Bishop Louis Guillaume Valentin Du Bourg [*q.v.*], of New Orleans, for missionaries. Along with the Bishop and thirty-five volunteers, he sailed on a French warship from Bordeaux and arrived at Annapolis, Md., Sept. 4, 1817. After stopping for two months as a guest of Charles Carroll of Carrollton, he completed his theological studies at St. Mary's Seminary, Baltimore, and was ordained priest by Du Bourg in the St. Louis cathedral on Michaelmas day, 1818. As a youthful mission priest, he was gaining a character for sound judgment, liberality of sentiment, and generous service among the poor —especially in a yellow-fever epidemic during which he was prostrated by the disease—when he was called to New Orleans by Du Bourg. There he established a collegiate school on the Lancastrian plan and acted as vicar-general. In 1825, he yielded to peremptory orders from Rome and accepted appointment as vicar-apostolic of the Floridas and Alabama, for which purpose he was consecrated titular bishop of Oleno by Bishop Rosati in St. Louis, Nov. 5, 1826.

The vicariate had only three churches—at Mobile, St. Augustine, and Pensacola—and the Bishop himself was the only priest. His poverty was extreme, but he appears to have managed temporarily without mitre or crozier and to have aroused the declining faith of new settlers, of Indians, and of old Spanish colonists whose language he spoke with some fluency. Ordaining his sole deacon, he left him as administrator when he visited France in 1829 in search of priests and financial support from the Society of the Propagation of the Faith. He returned with two priests and four seminarians to find that the vicariate had been erected into the diocese of Mobile. Thirty years of strict attention to his diocese brought results: the frame church gave way to a brick cathedral which was consecrated in 1850; Spring Hill College, founded in 1830 with Jean Mathias Pierre Loras [q.v.] as rector, was put under the direction of the Eudist Fathers and later (1846) assigned to the Jesuits; the Visitation nuns, introduced from Georgetown, erected an academy at Mobile in 1833; the Sisters of Charity from Emmitsburg founded Providence Infirmary and an orphanage at Mobile; the Brothers of the Sacred Heart from France opened a boy's orphanage in 1847; and a dozen churches were erected in the larger towns under twenty-seven priests. Outside of the diocese, Portier was known in ecclesiastical circles as a conspicuous member of the various councils of Baltimore and of New Orleans. He died of dropsy after long suffering.

[R. H. Clarke, *Lives of the Deceased Bishops of the Cath. Church in the U. S.*, vol. I (1888); *Cath. Encyc.*, X (1911), 411; J. G. Shea, *Hist. of the Cath. Church in the U. S.*, vol. IV (1892); Peter Guilday, *The Life and Times of John England* (1927), vol. I; M. Kenny, *Cath. Culture in Ala.* (1931); Mother Austin, *A Cath. Hist. of Ala. and the Floridas* (1908); letters in *Annales de l'Association de la Propagation de la Foi*, vols. I (1825), II (1827), IV (1831), XXIV (1852); *The Metropolitan Cath. Directory*, 1860; *Records of the Am. Cath. Hist. Soc.*, vol. XIV (1903); *N. Y. Freeman's Journal*, May 28, 1859; *Mobile Daily Register*, May 15, 1859.]

R. J. P.

PORTOLÁ, GASPAR de (fl. 1734–1784), first governor of Upper California, founder of San Diego and Monterey, was born about 1723 at Balaguer in Catalonia, of a Spanish noble family. Commissioned ensign in 1734, lieutenant in 1743, and captain in 1764, he saw military service in Italy and Portugal. In 1767 he was sent out as governor of the Californias to take charge of the expulsion of the Jesuits from that territory.

His contribution to the history of what is now the United States consists in his march from Velicatá, Lower California, to Monterey, Upper California, a distance of about one thousand miles, through untrod country, and in his founding of the missions and presidios of San Diego and Monterey. This late northward thrust of Spain was in reaction to fear that the English, recent conquerors of Canada, or the Russians, pressing down from Alaska, would seize a position from which to threaten the rich Manila galleons and menace the northern Mexican silver mines. Dispatches of Jan. 23, 1768, exchanged between the viceroy and the king, laid the administrative foundation for the enterprise. The Visitor General, José de Galvez, in May proceeded to prepare the expedition, consisting of two land and two sea detachments, which Portolá volunteered to command. The two vessels left Lower California early in 1769, the *San Carlos* on Jan. 10, and the *San Antonio* on Feb. 15. The first land party, under Captain Fernando Rivera y Moncada, left the base at Velicatá on Mar. 24, and Portolá led forward the final detachment on May 15. With Rivera was Father Juan Crespi [q.v.], famed as diarist of the whole expedition, and with Portolá was Junípero Serra [q.v.], spiritual father of California. Portolá reached San Diego, Upper California, on June 29, welcomed by Rivera, who had in May established a camp in "Old Town." The *San Antonio* and the *San Carlos* had arrived on Apr. 11 and Apr. 29 respectively. Though his followers were ravaged by scurvy, Portolá chose some forty, with whom and a hundred provision-laden mules, he pressed on, setting forth July 14 for a march of some four hundred miles to an assumedly identifiable harbor near latitude 37°, noted in the reports of earlier explorers. Marching two to four leagues a day, winding from Los Angeles to Santa Monica, then to Saugus, and then north through the Santa Lucias, Portolá's party emerged at the mouth of the Salinas River on Oct. 1. Being at the moment on the bay of their quest, they failed to discern in its open roadstead the port round like an "O" described by Vizcaino and Cabrera Bueno, although twice members of the party marched precisely along its beach. They did, however, see and attempt to reach Drake's (San Francisco) Bay, and explored and named many localities in the region south of the Golden Gate. Disappointed by their failure to find Vizcaino's harbor, they returned to San Diego, subsisting for most of the march on mule meat. Upon their arrival, Jan. 24, 1770, however, Portolá was persuaded by Captain Vicente Vila that he had been exactly on the Bay of Monterey when he placed his second cross at Pacific Grove. He therefore mustered what forces he could and on Apr. 17 set out once more, the *San Antonio* under Juan Perez having sailed on the quest the day before. Arriving at his second cross on May 24, 1770, Portolá saw that on a clear day and from a certain point of view, the round harbor assumed the proportions remarked by its early enthusiastic visitors. After 235 years the quest for a spot upon which to occupy Upper California had been attained. Near the very oak under which Vizcaino's Capuchins had worshiped in 1603 a new mass was said and possession was taken. On June 3, 1770, were laid the beginnings of the mission and the presidio of San Carlos Borromeo at Monterey. With work begun on these foundations the Governor's task in the north was completed, and on June 9, leaving Captain Pedro Fages [*q.v.*] in charge, he sailed away to San Blas, never to return to "The New Establishments." In 1776 he was appointed governor of the city of Puebla, and in 1784, after the appointment of his successor, was advanced money for the expenses of his return to Spain.

[Narratives of the Portolá expedition in *Pubs. Acad. of Pacific Coast Hist.*, vols. I, II (1909–11) ; *Francisco Palóu's Life and Apostolic Labors of the Venerable Father Junípero Serra* (1913), ed. by G. W. James ; Z. S. Eldredge, *The March of Portolá* (1909) ; I. B. Richman, *Cal. under Spain and Mexico* (1911) ; H. H. Bancroft, *Hist. of Cal.* (1890), vol. I ; T. H. Hittell, *Hist. of Cal.*, vol. I (1885) ; H. E. Bolton, *Fray Juan Crespi* (1927) ; Francisco Palóu, *Hist. Memoirs of New Cal.* (4 vols., 1926), ed. by H. E. Bolton.]   H. I. P.

PORY, JOHN (1572–September 1635), geographer, traveler, and secretary to the Virginia council at Jamestown, was born at Thompston, Norfolk, son of William Pory of Butters Hall. After being graduated B.A. (1591/92) and M.A. (1595) at Gonville and Caius College, Cambridge, he studied "cosmographie and forren histories" (*c.* 1597–1600) under Richard Hakluyt, who in the second edition of his *Principal Navigations* (1600, vol. III, Epistle Dedicatorie) eulogized the skill and promise of his "very honnest, industrious, and learned friend." In 1610 he was incorporated M.A. at Oxford. In accordance with Hakluyt's suggestion, he translated and published *A Geographical Historie of Africa, Written in Arabicke and Italian by John Leo, a More* (1600), adding notes and other original matter ; the work was reprinted, somewhat abridged, by Purchas in his *Hakluytus Posthumus, or Purchas His Pilgrimes,* and brought Pory considerable distinction. From 1605 through 1610, during which period he represented Bridgewater in Parliament, he resided in London ; but he had a wandering foot which his earlier studies had doubtless quickened, and in 1611 he obtained license to travel. The next

seven years he spent chiefly abroad, in Ireland, Europe, and the East, as a traveler or as an attaché in several embassies. He was ever a copious correspondent, and his gossipy, graphic, and detailed, if sometimes turgid, letters to various distinguished acquaintances have provided valuable information for subsequent historians.

Although a patentee under the royal charter of 1609, he first landed in Virginia on Apr. 19, 1619, having been appointed secretary of state for the colony by the London Council through the influence of Gov. George Yeardley [*q.v.*], who had married Pory's first cousin. When the first legislative assembly of the new world met at Jamestown, July 30, 1619, Pory, already a member of the governor's council, was elected its speaker. Despite impaired health, he filled this rôle with such industry and skill as to evoke a handsome tribute from Yeardley. During his remaining residence in the colony he not only made himself useful as parliamentarian and scribe but also conducted several important explorations and voyages of discovery. In June 1621, however, the London Company voted not to renew his commission as secretary, doubtless largely because Yeardley and Sandys suspected him of dividing his allegiance between Rich's faction and their own. In the summer of 1622 he left Virginia in the *Discovery* for an exploratory trading voyage along the New England coast, but some time after visiting Plymouth was driven off his course and wrecked on the Azores. Captured by the Spaniards, he was reputedly in danger of hanging, but escaped or was released and returned to England. Late in 1623 the Privy Council chose him to publish in Virginia certain of their recent orders, and likewise appointed him a member of the investigating commission whose report of conditions in the colony immediately preceded the recall of the letters patent of the London Company and the resumption of crown control. He served on the Virginia Commission in July 1624 and continued a member in England of the council for Virginia, but never afterwards returned to America. He died, unmarried, at Sutton St. Edmund, whither he had retired about 1631.

[Posterity has dealt somewhat summarily with Pory's fame : William Stith, for instance, in *The Hist. of the First Discovery and Settlement of Va.* (1747 ; repr. 1865), on incomplete and one-sided evidence, misinterprets his motives and under-values his generally useful career ; while Edward D. Neill, in his *Hist. of the Va. Company of London* (1869), exaggerates Pory's unquestioned shortcomings by speaking of his "reputation of being a chronic tippler, and literary vagabond and sponger" (p. 135). Neither of these positions seems to take into serious account the repetition of Pory's various state and diplomatic trusts or the continued genuine regard of his many prominent friends. See Alexander Brown, *The Genesis of U. S.* (2 vols.,

1890), and *The First Republic in America* (1898); *Mass. Hist. Soc. Colls.*, 4 ser., IX (1871), 11–21 and *passim*; J. H. R. Yardley, *Before the Mayflower* (1931); *Va. Hist. Soc. Colls.*, n.s., vols. VII–VIII (1888–89); John and J. A. Venn, *Alumni Cantabrigienses*, pt. 1, vol. III (1924); John Venn, *Biog. Hist. of Gonville and Caius College*, I (1897), 130; S. M. Kingsbury, *The Records of the Va. Company of London*, vols. I (1906), III (1933); Thomas Birch, *The Court and Times of James the First* (2 vols., 1849); Charlotte Fell-Smith, in *Dict. Nat. Biog.*; Champlin Burrage, *John Pory's Lost Description of Plymouth Colony* (1918); M. A. E. Green, *Calendar of State Papers, Domestic Series . . . 1611–18* (1858).]

A. C. G., Jr.

POSEY, ALEXANDER LAWRENCE (Aug. 3, 1873–May 27, 1908), journalist and poet, was born on a farm eight miles west of Eufaula, Indian Territory, in what is now McIntosh County, Okla. His father, Lewis H. Posey, was a white man of Scotch-Irish ancestry with possibly one-sixteenth Creek blood, and his mother was a full-blooded Creek woman, the daughter of Pohos Harjo, who, however, bore the English name of Nancy Phillips. She was a very intelligent woman and early began teaching her son the mythology and folklore of the Creeks. He spoke little or no English until he was about twelve years old but learned from his mother much of the legendary history of the Creek tribe. He received instruction from a private tutor for a time and also attended public tribal school in Eufaula and in 1890 was sent to Indian University at Bacone near Muskogee. During the five years he stayed there he was librarian on Sundays and set type after school hours for a little magazine published by the faculty, the *Instructor*. In this magazine appeared a number of his poems and prose sketches, one or two of which attracted considerable attention. In 1895 he was elected to the Creek House of Warriors, the lower branch of the Creek national legislature. He was a delegate to virtually every council or convention called in the Indian Territory. In 1896 he became superintendent of the orphans home at Okmulgee. On May 9 of that year he was married to Minnie Harris of Fayetteville, Ark. They had two children. In December 1897 he was appointed superintendent of public instruction of the Creek Nation but resigned after a few months to retire to his farm near Stidham, Okla. He was soon called upon by the Creek national government to take charge of the national high school of Eufaula and later of the national high school at Wetumka. He resigned, probably in 1901, and became editor of the *Indian Journal*, published at Eufaula.

Meanwhile he had been engaged during his spare time in writing poems and prose sketches, which were published in various magazines and

newspapers. In the *Indian Journal* he began to publish the "Fus Fixico Letters," a series of satirical sketches written in Indian vernacular that were intended to call attention to the wrongs heaped upon the Indians by the whites. It is upon these that his claim to distinction as a writer chiefly rests. After two years he became joint editor with Ira L. Reeves of the *Muskogee Times* and soon was appointed Indian agent at Muskogee. He served as secretary of the constitutional convention that met at Muskogee in 1905 to make a constitution for the proposed state of "Sequoyah," and immediately after the Sequoyah convention he began work for the Dawes commission as clerk in charge of the field party that had the task of obtaining the names of so-called "lost Creeks," or those members of the tribe who had refused to come in and be enrolled. When this work was completed he planned to purchase the *Indian Journal* at Eufaula and return to newspaper work. He left Muskogee for Eufaula in order to further his plans for this purchase, but, in attempting to cross the North Canadian River in a light skiff, he was drowned.

He was a handsome man of erect carriage and typically Indian features. He was somewhat shy and reserved in the presence of strangers, but cordial and gracious toward his friends. He was a great lover of nature, as is apparent in much of his writing. In addition to the "Fus Fixico Letters" his best known writings are his poems, which were first signed with the pseudonym Chinnubbie Harjo, the name of one of the chief characters in Creek mythology. These were published by his widow in 1910 in a volume called *Alex Posey, . . . The Poems*.

[Letters, journals, and papers in possession of his widow at Fayetteville, Ark.; copies of the journals in Lib. of Univ. of Okla.; biog. sketch in volume of poems, *ante*; J. B. Thoburn and M. H. Wright, *Oklahoma* (1929), vol. II.]

E. E. D.

POSEY, THOMAS (July 9, 1750–Mar. 19, 1818), soldier, governor of Indiana Territory, was born in Fairfax County, Va., and grew up as a country boy with few educational advantages. At the age of nineteen he removed to the Virginia frontier. A little later, trouble with the Indians opened the way to a military career, and he enlisted in the Virginia militia that Lord Dunmore and Andrew Lewis led against the Indian tribes beyond the western frontier in 1774. With the outbreak of the Revolutionary War he became a member of the Committee of Correspondence. He was a captain and later major in the 7th Virginia Regiment and saw arduous service in various campaigns and engagements, including the battle of Saratoga and the operations against the Indians on the Pennsylvania frontier. At the storming of Stony Point he was one of the first to enter the fort. On Sept. 8, 1782, he was promoted to the rank of lieutenant-colonel. He retired from the service on Mar. 10, 1783.

Ten years after the Revolution, on Feb. 14, 1793, he became a brigadier-general, and he was again with his old commander, Wayne, in the campaign against the Indians of the Northwest but seems to have returned to the East before the battle of Fallen Timbers. He resigned on Feb. 28, 1794. At the close of the Indian war he settled in Kentucky, where he was elected to the state Senate. He was chosen speaker in 1805 and 1806 and, by virtue of that office, lieutenant-governor of the state. In 1809, when there was a call for troops owing to complications with France and Great Britain, he was assigned to the command of volunteers with the rank of major-general. Later he removed to the Attakapas region of Louisiana, where he was living when the War of 1812 broke out, and at once he raised a company of volunteers, though he is not credited with active military service during that conflict. He was appointed United States Senator from Louisiana and served from Oct. 8, 1812, to Feb. 4, 1813, when he was appointed governor of Indiana Territory by President Madison to succeed William Henry Harrison. He served until Indiana became a state in 1816. His health was so impaired that he lived at Jeffersonville, a place more convenient to medical attendance than Corydon, the territorial capital. This caused some legislative inconvenience and some criticism, but at the end of his service the law-making body complimented him highly as having won its "perfect approbation" (Sparks, *post*, p. 401). He was a member of the Presbyterian Church, interested in the promulgation of religion, and a member of the Masonic fraternity. He became a candidate for governor of the new state but was defeated by Jonathan Jennings. In 1817 he lost the election for representative to Congress. He was agent for Indian affairs for Illinois Territory from 1816 until his death at Shawneetown, Ill. He was twice married: first to Martha Matthews of Augusta County, Va., and, second, to Mary (Alexander) Thornton. He left a large family of children.

[Some letters, papers, and brief biog. sketch in "Governors Messages and Letters. Messages and Letters of Wm. H. Harrison," *Ind. Hist. Colls.* (1922), vol. II, ed. by Logan Esarey; *The Lib. of Am. Biog.*, 2 ser., vol. IX (1846), ed. by Jared Sparks; F. B. Heitman, *Hist. Register of Officers of the Continental Army*, new ed. (1914); L. G. Tyler, *Encyc. of Va.*

Biog. (1915), vol. II; Lewis and R. H. Collins, *Hist. of Ky.* (1874), vol. I; W. W. Woolen, *Biog. and Hist. Sketches of Early Ind.* (1883).]   G. S. C.

POST, CHARLES WILLIAM (Oct. 26, 1854–May 9, 1914), food manufacturer, advertising expert, anti-union labor agitator, was born at Springfield, Ill. His parents were Charles Rollin and Caroline (Lathrop) Post who sent him to the common schools and for a time to the University of Illinois, although he did not graduate. He was first married to Ella Merriwether from whom he separated. His second wife was Leila D. Young of Battle Creek, Mich. His first business connection was as traveling salesman in the West for an agricultural implement firm. At twenty-six he returned to Springfield and later became manager of a plow factory. In 1884 his health failed and for seven years he sought relief from his illness. He spent some time in Texas where he rode range and was interested in real estate and in a woolen factory at Fort Worth. In 1891 he went to Battle Creek, Mich., and established La Vita Inn, an institution for healing by the practice of mental suggestion. Three years later he began experimenting with prepared food products, beginning with the production of a coffee substitute, Postum. Later he developed various breakfast foods which he advertised extensively. It is stated that his annual advertising appropriation reached a million dollars. Under this stimulus his business prospered and at the time of his death his estate was estimated at twenty million dollars.

His factories were models of cleanliness and sanitation and the firm spent money freely to encourage home-owning by employees. But Post early became a bitter opponent of trade unions and an advocate of open-shop conditions. Applying his advertising methods and spending money freely in the seven years preceding 1912, he attacked organized labor as the "greatest, most tyrannical and dangerous trust this country has ever seen." His newspaper advertisements in this campaign abounded in charges of violence and gave lurid details of assaults and riots. In 1902 Post launched a plan for an organization known as the Citizens' Industrial Alliance, composed of the elements in the National Association of Manufacturers most opposed to union organizations and tactics. Of this body he served as president from 1905 to 1908. In 1910 it was succeeded by the National Trades' and Workers' Association, designed to become a substitute for trade unions. It is stated that Post offered Theodore Roosevelt $100,000 to serve as its president for a year. To it Post gave a home for aged and dependent members. As a stockholder of the Buck's Stove and Range Company he was a persistent inciter of its officials in their famous case with the American Federation of Labor (219 *U. S.*, 581). In 1910 he was sued by *Collier's* for libel growing out of a controversy over his advertising methods. The journal refused his advertising as dishonest and dangerous in its medical implications. Post retorted by accusing his adversary of methods resembling blackmail. By verdict of a jury in December 1910 Post was assessed $50,000.

Post's business and office were in Battle Creek; his permanent home in Washington, D. C. He had a winter home in Santa Barbara, Cal., and a ranch of 200,000 acres in Garza County, Tex. During the later years of his life he traveled extensively in Europe and acquired a considerable art collection. He carried on rain-making experiments on his ranch which he believed to be successful. At one time he attacked Senator T. C. Platt and attempted to have the Supreme Court restrain him from sitting in the United States Senate on the ground that "he does not fulfill his duties according to his oath of office." For four years he served as president of the National Association of American Advertisers. As a director of the National Association of Manufacturers he was active and influential. His intense activities invited penalties. In 1914 his health failed. He made a sensational trip by special train from California to Rochester, Minn., in March and was operated on for appendicitis. Seemingly he was on the road to recovery but under stress of a highly nervous condition he committed suicide at his Santa Barbara home.

[See *Who's Who in America*, 1912–13; *Chas. Wm. Post, Born Oct. 26, 1854, Died May 9, 1914* (n.d.), a pamphlet; *Collier's*, July 27, Sept. 21, 1907; Dec. 17, 24, 31, 1910, Jan. 7, 14, 21, 28, 1911; the *Square Deal*, especially June 1914; W. G. Merritt, *Hist. of the League for Industrial Rights* (1925); *N.-Y. Daily Tribune*, *N. Y. Times*, Sept. 4, 1907. Post's rain-making experiments are discussed in an article by himself in *Harper's Weekly*, Feb. 24, 1912, and his mental-healing beliefs are discussed in his *Modern Practice: Natural Suggestion, or, Scientia Vitae* (1894). Information as to certain facts was supplied for this sketch by the General Foods Corporation.]   C. E. P.

POST, CHRISTIAN FREDERICK (*c.* 1710–May 1, 1785), lay missionary of the Moravian Church to the Indians, was born in Conitz, East Prussia. He was a cabinet maker by training, but fell under the influence of the Zinzendorf movement and in 1742 came to Bethlehem, Pa. His early work was as an itinerant missionary to the various German groups in Pennsylvania. He tried to bring about the union of those people in a church federation, but his impulsive habits did not fit him for this task, and the next year he went with Christopher Pyrlaeus, Martin Mack, and Joachim Senseman, to take charge of the Indian converts in the "Oblong" between New York and Connecticut, just east of Poughkeepsie. Here his sympathetic insight into Indian character and his rapid acquisition of the Mohican language made him very useful, and the mission prospered remarkably. In 1743 Post married Rachel, a Wampanoag, declaring that such a connection would assist the progress of his work. The Indian wars of 1744, however, made the settlers of New York and Connecticut very suspicious of the Moravian workers and they were arrested, ordered out of the state, and warned not to return. Along with David Zeisberger [*q.v.*], Post was then sent to the Iroquois country to live among the Six Nations and learn their language. Here they were again arrested, taken to New York, and imprisoned for about seven weeks.

Two years after the death of his first wife in 1747, he married Agnes, a Delaware convert, and took up residence in the Wyoming Valley on the banks of the Susquehanna near Wyalusing. As a frontier mission scout here, he maintained a close contact with the Indians for two years. When his second wife died in 1751, he went to London in order to join the first mission to Labrador. Here his party was set upon by the natives, several were murdered, and the survivors were forced to man the vessel in order to escape. He again occupied his cabin in Wyoming in 1754, attempting to counteract the threatened alliance of the Delawares with the French. In the fall of 1755 he hurried to Bethlehem to warn the colony of the impending raids planned by Tedyuskung [*q.v.*] and his Shawnee allies, but the warning came too late, and a band of blood and fire was drawn across the colony in November. In 1758, at the request of the governor and council of Pennsylvania, Post and Charles Thompson met Tedyuskung and two Indian chiefs in the Wyoming district and arranged for a later and more largely attended conference to be held on the Ohio River. At that time the Forbes expedition against the French at Fort Duquesne was in preparation and if the French alliance with the Indians could be broken, the French would lose their hold on western Pennsylvania. Post and Isaac Stille proceeded to the Ohio River, where an important conference with many Indians of the Delaware, Shawnee, and allied tribes was held, the inside story of which was told by Post in a letter sent to Bethlehem, describing vividly the precarious situation of the envoys, for some days, and the clever duplicity of the French commander. Post's patience finally won the Indians over to a British alliance, and the French abandoned Fort Duquesne.

Immediately after his report to the governor had been accepted and the fort occupied by the British, he penetrated into the Ohio country and gathered a group of Indian converts to begin a settlement near the present town of Bolivar. For a time he was assisted by youthful John Gottlieb Ernestus Heckewelder [*q.v.*]. Later he proceeded on his own responsibilty to extend mission work down the Ohio River, and in 1762 left the Moravian service and disappeared into the West. His eccentric and impatient habits of mind gave him no rest even when he was engaged in executing his own plans, and in 1764 he was to be found hard at work among the Mosquito Indians of eastern Nicaragua. On Aug. 27, 1763, he had married Mary Margaret (Miller) Stadelman (or Hadelman) Bolinger, who died in Hagerstown, Md., in 1810. In 1767 he visited Bethlehem once more, but the Moravian authorities refused to accept the offer of his services. He was given a cordial letter of recommendation to the Anglican Church, however, and under the supervision of this body he returned to the Mosquito Shore. In 1784 he retired to Germantown where he died during the following year. He had four half-breed children all of whom died in infancy.

There is no question as to Post's devotion to the cause of civilizing the Indians, but that devotion was often encumbered by his impatience and his inability to cooperate. Three of the fields in which he was a pioneer later became fruitful areas of Moravian effort, and his successful parley with the Indians in 1758, leading to the abandonment of Fort Duquesne, was of great significance in opening the West to British occupation.

[Numerous reports and letters written by Post are in the archives of the Moravian Church at Bethlehem, Pa.; his journals are published in Charles Thompson, *Causes of the Alienation of the Delaware and Shawanese Indians from the British Interests* (London, 1759, Phila., 1867), and in *Pa. Archives*, vol. III (1853); see also, *Pa. Colonial Records*, vol. VIII (1852); J. M. Levering, *A Hist. of Bethlehem, Pa.* (1903), H. H. Humrichouse, *Rev. Christian Frederick Post and Peter Humrickhouse* (1913), and E. W. Hocker, *Germantown, 1683–1933* (1933).] A. G. R.

POST, GEORGE ADAMS (Sept. 1, 1854–Oct. 31, 1925), manufacturer, was born in Cuba, Allegany County, N. Y., the son of Ira Allen and Harriet Newell (Curtis) Post. His father was a conductor and station agent on the Erie Railway. He was educated in the public schools of Tioga County, N. Y., the Oswego Academy, and at the Normal School of Oswego, N. Y. On Apr. 1, 1873, he became a clerk in the freight office of the Erie Railway at Susquehanna, Pa., remaining in the employ of this company in various minor capacities until November 1883. He took an active part in local politics and was elected mayor of Susquehanna in February 1877, serving one year. During this time he studied law in the evenings and in August 1881 was admitted to the bar of Susquehanna County and commenced practice in Montrose, Pa. In 1883 he bought a half interest in the *Montrose Democrat* and edited the paper until Mar. 1, 1889. He was elected as a Democrat to the House of Representatives of the Forty-eighth Congress (Mar. 4, 1883–Mar. 3, 1885), and although he was the youngest member of the House at the time, he served on various committees. He was chosen secretary of the Democratic Congressional Committee of Pennsylvania for the campaign of 1884, and was a delegate to the national convention of his party for that year. The following year he was chairman of the Pennsylvania Democratic State Convention. In March 1889 he abandoned his political activities and moved to New York City where he joined the staff of the New York *World*, remaining there until 1891 when he became interested in the Standard Coupler Company. He was vice-president of this company from 1892 to 1894 and its president from 1894 until 1921, when he resigned to establish the George A. Post Company of New York, a firm dealing in railway materials and supplies, of which he was president until his death. As chairman of the executive committee of a temporary association of railway supply manufacturers in 1904, he helped organize the permanent Railway Supply Manufacturers' Association and was chairman of the committee on general arrangements for the American Railway Appliance Exhibition held in connection with the convention of the International Railway Congress at Washington, D. C., in 1905. As a result of this experience he believed that there was a need for an association of the suppliers of railroad equipment to protect the purchasing power of the railroads against government regulation and public opinion and to promote constructive railroad legislation. In 1909, therefore, he was one of the founders of the Railway Business Association composed of manufacturers of railway materials and equipment, contractors in railway construction, and dealers in railway supplies. He was elected the first president of this association, serving until 1918, when he declined reëlection and became chairman of the Railroad Committee of the Chamber of Commerce of the United States. He performed very valuable services in this position in helping to develop the Transportation

Act of 1920 and in upholding it after its passage. For a time he served as president of the Hudson River Bridge & Terminal Association and as a trustee of the New Jersey State Chamber of Commerce. He married Minnie C. Munson on June 22, 1881, by whom he had one son. He died in Somerville, N. J.

[*Biog. Dir. Am. Cong.* (1928); *Who's Who in America*, 1924–25; Chas. Dillon, "What the Railway Business Asso. Means," *Railway Rev.*, Nov. 14, 1925; *Railway Age*, Nov. 7, 1925; *N. Y. Times*, Nov. 2, 1925.]
J. H. F.

POST, GEORGE BROWNE (Dec. 15, 1837–Nov. 28, 1913), architect, the son of Joel Browne Post and Abby Mauran (Church), was born in New York City. His immigrant ancestor on his father's side was Lieut. Richard Post, who came to Southampton, Long Island, from Lynn, Mass., in 1640; on his mother's side, he was descended from Col. Benjamin Church [*q.v.*], a leader in King Philip's War, who was born at Duxbury, Mass., in 1639 and later settled in Rhode Island. George Post was educated at Churchill's Military School, Ossining, N. Y., and later at New York University, where he graduated with the degree of B.S. in civil engineering in 1858. Being interested chiefly in architecture, he then entered the office of Richard Morris Hunt [*q.v.*] as a student draftsman, remaining until 1860, when he formed an architectural partnership with Charles D. Gambrill. The Civil War put an end to their thoughts of architecture, however, and Post, who had previously been a captain in the "Union Greys," was on Sept. 24, 1861, commissioned a captain of Company C, 22nd Regiment, New York National Guard. He was volunteer aide to General Burnside at the battle of Fredericksburg. On Nov. 3, 1863, he was elected major, and after the war he became lieutenant-colonel in 1866, and colonel in 1867; but in 1868 press of business forced him to resign his commission. The war had effectually stopped what work the partnership of Gambrill & Post had enjoyed; it was therefore dissolved, and Post opened his own office.

His first important work, the Williamsburgh Savings Bank, New York City, came in 1874. It was one of the early banks in the country to be built in Renaissance style, with a dome. Chickering Hall, a *néo-Grec* building, now destroyed, followed, and from that time Post's practice grew rapidly. His interest had always been in the engineering side of architecture, and the field of high buildings, then beginning to open up, furnished him with many rich opportunities. In 1869, he had served as consulting architect for the New York Equitable Building, of which Arthur Delevan Gilman [*q.v.*] was the designer, and had been

instrumental in making it a pioneer in the use of elevators—it was the earliest New York business building equipped with them—and also in the extensive use of iron floor beams. He was one of the first to introduce steam heating into commercial buildings. A capable business man, he soon had an enormous practice. Among his most important business buildings were the original New York Western Union Building, another early use of the elevator; the New York Produce Exchange (1881–85); the New York Cotton Exchange (1883–86); the original New York Times Building (1889); Pulitzer Building (1889–92); Havemeyer Building (1891–93); the Mutual Benefit and Prudential Life Insurance buildings in Newark; Bank of Pittsburgh (1895–96); Commercial Trust Company, Jersey City (1903); Cleveland Trust Company with its branches (1906–08); and the 22-story St. Paul Building in New York which, when it was built (1897–99), was the highest in the city. In the nineties he published a project for a 500-foot tower which, like a somewhat similar project published about the same time by Bruce Price [*q.v.*], shows many elements later given expression in Le Brun's Metropolitan Tower.

In addition to his commercial buildings, Post designed many of the largest residences of the time. The Cornelius Vanderbilt House at Fifty-seventh Street and Fifth Avenue (1889), in 1895 much enlarged and carried through to Fifty-eighth Street, and the Huntington residence on the southeast corner of Fifty-seventh Street and Fifth Avenue are early and remarkable examples of his work, much admired in their day, and extraordinarily lavish both outside and in. His earliest monumental structure was the great Manufactures and Liberal Arts Building at the World's Columbian Exposition, Chicago, 1893. The largest building in the group, it was a vast hall or shed surrounded by a rich Roman classic screen. Later he won the competition for the College of the City of New York, and the earlier buildings of this group, in native stone and white terra cotta (built 1902–11) are by him. He designed the Wisconsin State Capitol, which was begun in 1904 although its construction spread over many years. The New York Stock Exchange (1904) was also his design. Towards the end of his life, Post became much interested in hotels, and he is one of those responsible for the development of the typical modern hotel plan, with its hundreds of rooms, each with bath, and a monumental suite of public rooms below—all arranged to give the maximum income through the leasing of shops and concessions. The Oswego Hotel, and the Hotel Pontiac, Detroit

(1911–12), began this development; in the Stat-
ler Hotel, Cleveland (1911–12), the type found
its first complete expression.

Post's interest was chiefly structural; there is
little artistic unity in his buildings. All are excellent machines, dressed in any decorative clothing that seemed expedient. Thus the St. Paul
Building used applied classic orders, the Times
Building was Romanesque, the old Cotton Exchange was a romantic pile with curved towers
like a French château. This complete and uncritical eclecticism was undoubtedly characteristic of the time; but there were architects who
fought it, or, at least, transcended it. Yet as a
planner Post was original and masterly. The
original conception of the City College group was
superb, however unfortunate the material in
which it was carried out; and the cross-shaped
plan of the Wisconsin State Capitol was one of
the few creative variations of the typical state
capitol scheme. Post was a tireless worker, and
a driver with the capacity of arousing the enthusiasm of those he drove. He traveled abroad
nearly every year, returning laden with sketches.
He was an accomplished water colorist and made
many of his firm's renderings. He was president
of the New York Architectural League (1893–
97); president of the National Arts Club (1898–
1905); a member of the American Institute of
Architects from 1860, president, 1896–99, and
president of the New York chapter in 1905. He
became an Associate of the National Academy
of Design in 1906, and an Academician in 1908;
he was also a member of the American Academy
of Arts and Letters. In 1907 he was made an
honorary member of the Royal Institute of British Architects. In 1900 he received a silver medal
from the Paris Exposition.

Post married Oct. 14, 1863, Alice Matilda
Stone, daughter of William W. Stone; they had
four sons and a daughter. In 1905 he took two
of his sons into partnership, organizing the firm
of George B. Post & Sons, which still continues
architectural practice. He died suddenly at his
country home, Bernardsville, N. J.

[Russell Sturgis, "A Review of the Work of George
B. Post," *Architectural Record,* June 1898; Montgomery
Schuyler, "George Browne Post," *Ibid.,* Jan. 1914; *Am.
Art Annual,* vol. XI (1914); tribute by Thomas Hastings (with many inaccuracies), in *Proc. Am. Acad.
Arts and Letters,* vol. X (1922); *Jour. Am. Inst. of
Architects,* Jan. 1914; M. C. de T. Post, *The Post Family* (1905), copy in N. Y. Pub. Lib., with additions to
1913; *Who's Who in America,* 1912–13; *N. Y. Times*
and *Evening Post* (N. Y.), Nov. 29, 1913; personal
reminiscences supplied by Post's son, James Otis Post,
and by Robert R. Houston, a member of the Post organization since 1887.]   T. F. H.

POST, GEORGE EDWARD (Dec. 17, 1838–
Sept. 29, 1909), physician and missionary, was
born in New York City, the son of Harriet
(Beers) and Alfred Charles Post and a descendant of Richard Post who moved from Lynn,
Mass., and settled in Southampton, L. I., in 1640.
After graduating in 1854 from the New York
Free Academy (now the College of the City of
New York), he began preparation for the work
of a medical missionary and studied simultaneously at the medical school of New York University, where his father was professor of surgery, and at Union Theological Seminary.
Receiving degrees in medicine (1860) and theology (1861), he was appointed chaplain of the
15th Regiment of New York Volunteers, and
during two years of Civil War service was able
to study at the Baltimore College of Dentistry,
which graduated him in 1863 as a doctor of dental surgery. On Sept. 17 of the same year he
married Sarah, daughter of Robert and Frances
Read of Georgetown, D. C., and shortly afterward sailed for Syria, where he was stationed
at Tripoli as a missionary of the American Board
of Commissioners for Foreign Missions. There
he served until 1867, when his health necessitated
a visit to the United States. Returning the following year, he became professor of surgery and
diseases of the eye and ear in the recently established Syrian Protestant College (now the American University of Beirut), where he later
became dean of the medical department and continued to teach until shortly before his death.
During his first twenty years there instruction
was given in Arabic and for his classes Post
translated into that language a number of English texts on anatomy, physiology, hygiene, surgery, materia medica, botany, and zoölogy, all
published in Beirut.

Both as teacher and as surgeon Post gained an
enviable reputation throughout the Near East
and is said to have performed more major operations than any other missionary physician. His
clinics at the German Johanniter Hospital were
always crowded and in recognition of his services and ability he was decorated by the Saxon
and Ottoman governments. At the hospital and
in the college chapel he preached regularly. In
great demand as a speaker whenever on furlough,
he assisted materially in raising money in the
United States for extending and endowing the
work of the medical department. For five years
he edited the Arabic medical journal *Al-Tabib.*
As fruits of a lifelong study of botany he published *Plantae Postianae* (10 fascicules, Lausanne and Geneva, 1890–1900) and the *Flora of
Syria, Palestine, and Egypt* (Beirut, n.d.), as
well as articles in scientific journals, having himself collected and arranged the herbarium on

which these are based. In cooperation with Eli Smith and C. V. A. Van Dyck he composed a concordance to the Arabic version of the Bible. For Hastings' *Dictionary of the Bible* he wrote voluminously on botanical, zoölogical, and archeological subjects, and for many years he contributed regularly to the *Sunday School Times*. A man of wide interests, vast energy, and notable professional skill, Post was somewhat autocratic in nature and disconcertingly direct in manner. Throughout Syria and the neighboring lands he was celebrated as an almost infallible surgeon, while in Europe and the United States he received honorary degrees and memberships in numerous learned societies.

[M. C. de T. Post, *The Post Family* (1905); *Gen. Alumni Cat. of N. Y. Univ., 1833–1907: Medic. Alumni* (1908); H. H. Jessup, *Fifty-three Years in Syria* (2 vols., 1910); *Boston Medic. and Surgic. Jour.*, Oct. 7, 1909; *Missionary Rev. of the World*, Dec. 1909; N. Y. *Evening Post*, Sept. 30, 1909; information as to certain facts furnished by Post's son, Dr. Wilfred M. Post of Williston Park, L. I., N. Y.]   W. L. W., Jr.

POST, ISAAC (Feb. 26, 1798–May 9, 1872), abolitionist and spiritualist, was born in Westbury, Long Island, N. Y., the son of Edmund and Catherine (Willets) Post and the descendant of Richard Post who removed to Southampton on Long Island from Lynn, Mass., about the middle of the seventeenth century. He removed in 1823 to the town of Scipio, Cayuga County, N. Y., and about this time married Hannah Kirby. She died in 1827, leaving two children who survived her only a few years. On Sept. 18, 1828, he married Amy Kirby, a sister of his first wife. He removed in 1836 from Cayuga County to Rochester, N. Y., where he lived until his death. Besides his widow he left four children. At first a successful farmer, he later went into the drug business, in which he remained for thirty years. He was a pioneer in antislavery reform, taking a leading part in all the efforts to aid the colored race. He was a friend of Frederick Douglass and William Lloyd Garrison. When the Fugitive-slave Law was passed, his house became a well-known station on the "Underground Railroad." Hundreds of negroes owed their liberation to him and to his wife, who in this, as in all his other reforms, supported him valiantly. She herself was a friend of Susan B. Anthony and an ardent supporter of the woman's suffrage and the friends of human progress movements. Their "house . . . has ever been the hottest place in our reputed 'hot-house for isms'—so many reforms, agitations, and new questions have been furthered in its parlors" (Parker, *post*, p. 258). He was born and educated in the Hicksite branch of the Society of Friends, but in 1845 he and his wife, also a Quaker, felt that membership in the society interfered with their activity as abolitionists, and they resigned. Both always maintained the dignified and plain simplicity of language and life characteristic of the Friends.

In 1848 he was converted to spiritualism by Margaret Fox [*q.v.*] and her sister. He and his wife and three others were among the earliest converts and the first to meet regularly at the Fox home. These five, and especially Post, did more, perhaps, than any other single group toward furthering the spiritualist movement, giving the sisters advice and encouragement and even protecting them from bodily harm, when the first public investigations were held. A spirit message from his mother is supposed to have played some part in directing the course of the movement: "Isaac, my son, thy feeling is not exactly right towards low spirits, as thee calls them. A reformation is going on in the spirit world, and these spirits seek the company of honest men like you. It will do them great good and thee no harm" (Parker, *post*, pp. 268–69). He became noted as a writing medium and in 1852 published a volume entitled *Voices from the Spirit World, being Communications from Many Spirits, by the hand of Isaac Post, Medium*. This contained an introduction purporting to be from the spirit of Benjamin Franklin and about forty "communications" from spirits of distinguished people including Washington, Jefferson, Elias Hicks, Calhoun, Margaret Fuller, Swedenborg, Daniel O'Connell, Voltaire, William Penn, and George Fox, a group that indicates the type and range of Post's interests. He had a mind quick and vigorous in the perception and acceptance of new ideas and ready to acknowledge them regardless of consequences. That he was widely known in his community and was respected for his convictions, even by his enemies, is a tribute to his personal qualities in view of the unpopular ideas and reforms for which he stood. Frederick Douglass in a letter read at the funeral (*Democrat and Chronicle*, *post*, May 13) said of him that he never knew a man more just, simple-hearted, charitable, unselfish, and full of good works.

[J. M. Parker, *Rochester: A Story Historical* (1884); Emma Hardinge, *Modern American Spiritualism* (1870); Adelbert Cronise, "The Beginnings of Modern Spiritualism," *Rochester Hist. Soc. Pubs.*, vol. V (1926); *William Lloyd Garrison: The Story of His Life Told by His Children* (1885), vol. III; M. C. de T. Post, *The Post Family* (1905); *Democrat and Chronicle* (Rochester), May 9, 10, 13, 1872; *Rochester Evening Express*, May 9, 1872; "Memorandum on Isaac Post" submitted by Edward R. Foreman, Rochester, and other material deposited by writer in Lib. of Columbia Univ.]   G. L.

POST, LOUIS FREELAND (Nov. 15, 1849–Jan. 10, 1928), writer, reformer, government official, was born on a farm in northwestern New Jersey between Danville and Vienna, the first child of Eugene J. and Elizabeth (Freeland) Post. His paternal grandparents were Dr. Lewis Post (descended from Stephen Post who came from England to Cambridge, Mass., in 1633 and afterward settled at Saybrook, Conn.), and Theodosia Steele; his maternal grandparents were David Freeland and Sarah Vliet. His childhood, colored by a charming companionship with his grandfather Freeland, was sturdy and imaginative, and these qualities remained with him always. He attended two country schools and left another in New York City at the age of fourteen for a brief clerkship in a Seventh Avenue pawnshop. He joined the Presbyterian church, of which the Rev. Howard Crosby was pastor, but fell away from it promptly on reading Paine's *Age of Reason*. For eighteen months he was printer's apprentice in the antique office of the Hackettstown (N. J.) *Gazette,* transferring then to a job in New York, and again to the *Brooklyn Union,* which last he left in 1866 because he was refused full "space" wages. He entered the New York law office of Thomas, Glassey & Blake and after three years (1870) was admitted to the bar. Next came a complete change of scene. Through a family connection he was offered the position of clerk to Maj. David T. Corbin, United States attorney at Charleston, S. C., and state senator in the Reconstruction legislature. Post got an intimate view of Reconstruction by acting as secretary of three legislative committees, assisting Corbin in the codification of the South Carolina laws, and particularly in taking the confessions of accused Ku-Kluxers at Yorkville and later, with Benn Pitman, making stenographic reports of the Ku-Klux trials in November 1871. During this South Carolina period he married Anna Johnson, July 6, 1871, whom he had known in his apprentice days in Hackettstown.

Returning to New York and law practice, he served for a year and a half (1874–75) as assistant United States attorney for the southern district, quitting the work in disgust at the demands of Republican political bosses and forming the law partnership of Lockwood & Post in which he remained in practice, mostly in the federal courts, until 1880. He then became, for two years, an editorial writer for the new morning penny paper, *Truth,* which soon attained the fourth largest circulation in New York, and which, through his advocacy, was chiefly responsible for the first observance of Labor Day (1882). With others of the staff he was indicted for libel in connection with the publication, in the last days of the presidential campaign of 1880, of the "Morey" letter, which undercut Garfield's pro-labor professions, and which later, to the dismay of *Truth,* was shown to be a clever forgery. Post published in *Truth* a hasty criticism of the writings of Henry George which ended in a fast friendship between the two; he became a leading protagonist of the Georgist "Single Tax" philosophy, and this was really his distinctive service for the rest of his life. He edited the campaign daily, the *Leader,* when George ran for mayor in 1886, and during the succeeding six years was successively editorial writer, news editor, and editor of the *Standard,* the weekly of the Single-Tax movement. His wife died in 1891 and on Dec. 2, 1893, he married Alice Thacher, who was at the time an editor on two Swedenborgian papers. From 1892 to 1897 he lectured widely on the Single Tax and became an editorial writer on the Cleveland *Recorder.* In 1898 he and his wife established and thereafter edited the *Public* (Chicago) which was a journal of liberal opinion with the Single-Tax point of view, and which grew in fifteen years to a circulation of 10,000 copies weekly. The paper had the financial backing, among others, of Tom L. Johnson [*q.v.*] and later of Joseph Fels [*q.v.*]. His work on the *Public* was the most important of Post's life.

Post was appointed to the Chicago school board by a reform mayor, Edward F. Dunne. Here he fought against the looting of school funds, and stood for academic freedom and the right of teachers to organize. In 1908 and 1910 he made trips to Great Britain, the first to attend the International Free Trade Conference, the second to observe, and, as it turned out, to participate as a speaker in Lloyd George's "land for the people" campaign of the Liberals. He received appointment (June 1913) as assistant secretary of labor, continuing in office through President Woodrow Wilson's two administrations. He performed his uncongenial work with personal and official fortitude. Impeachment proceedings, urged against him in 1920 because he sought to temper deportation of "radical" aliens with humanity and liberalism, collapsed when he made a brilliant defense which shamed his inquisitors. He tried, unsuccessfully, to have returned soldiers colonized on public lands on a lease-hold basis, allowing economic rent to go to the community, rather than permitting private ownership which, he felt, through entrance of speculation, would deprive the settlers of their opportunities and earnings. His official position was unsatisfactory to him—he found himself offending both liberals and conservatives. After his retirement he continued to live in Washington, giving himself, despite declining health, to industrious writing, much of it in recapitulation of his long and varied life experience. Typical of his more theoretical writings are *The Ethics of Democracy* (1903), *Ethical Principles of Marriage and Divorce* (1906), *What Is the Single Tax?* (1926), and *The Basic Facts of Economics* (1927). In personal appearance Post was short but square-shouldered, erect, and vigorous; his manner spoke directness and sincerity. He was a Swedenborgian, and he believed in and practised the religion of social service.

[Post left with his widow a manuscript autobiography, "Living a Long Life Over Again." His *Deportations Delirium of Nineteen Twenty* (1923) is largely autobiographical and his *Prophet of San Francisco* (1930) details his connection with Henry George. See also his *Account of the George-Hewitt Campaign* (1886). Other sources include: E. N. Vallandigham, "Louis F. Post . . . A Personal Tribute," *New-Church Rev.*, Jan. 1929; Belle C. La Follette, "Louis F. Post," *La Follette's Mag.*, Feb. 1928; *Land and Liberty*, Mar. 1928, pp. 41, 49–50; W. M. Reedy, "A Cabinet Photograph," the *Mirror* (St. Louis), Jan. 24, 1913; the *New-Church Messenger*, Nov. 5, 1930; *Washington Post*, Jan. 11, 1928.]   B. M.

POST, MELVILLE DAVISSON (Apr. 19, 1871–June 23, 1930), short-story writer, novelist, lawyer, was born at Romines Mills, near Clarksburg, W. Va., the son of Ira Carper Post and Florence May (Davisson) Post. He was reared on his father's farm and educated first in rural schools and then at an academy at Buckhannon, W. Va. After receiving the degree of A.B. and LL.B. at West Virginia University in 1891 and 1892, he formed a law partnership with John A. Howard at Wheeling, W. Va., and practised six years in the criminal courts. He turned then to corporate law and formed a partnership with John T. McGraw of Grafton, W. Va., one of the leading Democrats of the state. Post very early took an active part in politics. In 1892 he was chosen presidential elector-at-large by the Democratic party and was made secretary of the electoral college, the youngest member ever to sit in that body. In 1898 he was made chairman of the Democratic Congressional Committee in West Virginia. As a member of the firm of McGraw & Post, one of the strongest in the state, he practised in the state supreme court, the circuit court of appeals, and the federal courts. After five years, however, the firm was dissolved and he thereafter devoted most of his time to literature.

While practising law in Wheeling in 1896, he published his first volume of detective stories, *The Strange Schemes of Randolph Mason*, introducing a new treatment growing out of his knowledge and practice of criminal law. It had occurred to him that instead of dealing with the ferreting power of the state, as all other writers of the detective stories had done, an entirely new type could be created by treating the punishing power, showing how it might be baffled by one knowing the loop-holes of the law. He invented the character of Randolph Mason, an unscrupulous lawyer who used his knowledge of the law to defeat the ends of justice. When readers objected to the book on the ground that it gave too much advice to criminals, he met these criticisms in the preface to his sequel, *The Man of Last Resort* (1897), by saying that the friends of law and order should be warned of its weaknesses. His third book, *Dwellers in the Hills* (1901), his first long story, dealt with cattle buyers in West Virginia. He returned to Randolph Mason in his *Corrector of Destinies* (1909), but this time, at the request of *Pearson's Magazine*, let Mason use his shrewd wit on the side of justice. In 1910 he published *The Gilded Chair*, a story of love and adventure, but came back to mystery in *The Nameless Thing* (1912). In 1918 appeared another treatment of the detective story in *Uncle Abner; Master of Mysteries*, in which a rural Sherlock Holmes solves mysteries in the mountains of western Virginia. His travels in Europe were reflected in *The Mystery at the Blue Villa* (1919), with various settings in London, Paris, Ostend, the Riviera, and Cairo. Except for *The Mountain School Teacher* (1922), an allegory of the life of Christ translated into a modern background, he wrote in the 1920's only detective and mystery stories. *The Sleuth of St. James's Square* was published in 1920, *Monsieur Jonquelle* in 1923, *Walker of the Secret Service* in 1924, and *The Man Hunters* in 1926. A textbook on the detection of crime, *The Revolt of the Birds*, followed in 1927, and *The Bradmoor Murder* in 1929. *The Silent Witness* (1930) was published posthumously. Most of his stories before publication in book form appeared in magazines.

As to his place in American literature criticism ranges from the statement of Blanche C. Williams (*post*, p. 306) who gives him a rank second only to Poe and judges that ". . . before the age of fifty he had established himself in narrative one of the immortals," to that of Edward J. H. O'Brien who denies, in his *Advance of the American Short Story* (1931, p. 230), that he has any "relation to literature." O'Brien says, however, that in his ability to construct a plot he surpassed many of the great masters. Fred Pattee, in his *Development of the American Short Story* (1923), states that Post is typical of the O. Henry school of writers,—able to catch the attention of the public, but whose stories lack repose and are quickly forgotten. Post's own theory was that the short story must have popular appeal, that if it also ennobles, well and good, but that at any cost it must be entertaining (see essays in the *Saturday Evening Post*, Dec. 26, 1914, and Feb. 27, 1915). Plot to him was more important than character. The development of the mystery and its solution had to go side by side, and the climax must occur at the end of the story instead of at the middle, as in Poe's detective stories. During the last years of his life he lived at "The Hill of the Painted Men," Lost Creek, Harrison County, W. Va. He married Ann Bloomfield Gamble of Roanoke, Va., on June 29, 1903. In 1914 and 1915 he served on the Advisory Committee of the National Economic League to consider questions of efficiency in the administration of justice. In 1924 he headed a group of writers supporting John W. Davis for president. He died at Clarksburg, W. Va., after an illness of two weeks.

[*Who's Who in America*, 1930–31; B. C. Williams, *Our Short Story Writers* (1920); M. M. Atkeson, *A Study of the Literature of W. Va.* (1923); E. M. Turner, *Stories and Verse of W. Va.* (1923); G. M. Overton, *Cargoes for Crusoes* (1924); Warren Wood, *Representative Authors of W. Va.* (1926); obit. in *N. Y. Times*, June 24, 1930.] F. M. S.

POST, TRUMAN MARCELLUS (June 3, 1810–Dec. 31, 1886), educator, Congregational clergyman, was born in Middlebury, Vt., third son of Martin and Sarah (Hulburd) Post. His father, a lawyer of ability and high character, died when Truman was eight months old. When ten years old the boy saved the life of a ship captain who had fallen through the ice into Lake Champlain. He was a leader in boyish sports, a local champion in wrestling, and an eager student of history and poetry. At fifteen he entered Middlebury College, where he supported himself by teaching country schools and graduated in 1829, valedictorian of his class.

For a year he was principal of Castleton (Vt.) Seminary and for two years tutor in Middlebury College. After a few months at Andover Theological Seminary, he reverted to his purpose of studying law and spent the winter of 1832–33 in Washington, listening to arguments before the Supreme Court, where Marshall was still presiding, and to debates in Congress led by Clay, Webster, Calhoun, Benton, and John Quincy Adams. These months he regarded as among the most important of his life. Gen. Joseph Duncan of Illinois, then in Congress, urged him to come to the developing West, and the following spring he went to St. Louis, then a French vil-

lage of some 6,000 inhabitants. Before entering there the profession of law he visited his friend Duncan at Jacksonville, Ill., which he found "a huddle of log cabins clustered around a public square." Here he was asked by President Edward Beecher [*q.v.*] of Illinois College to assist temporarily in its classical department. He was soon appointed professor of ancient languages and shortly afterwards of ancient history; he held both chairs for fourteen years. His teaching was interrupted by the cholera epidemic of 1833, when the college was closed for a time and he devoted himself to nursing stricken victims. Later he suffered a persistent disorder of the eyes, necessitating for two years dependence upon others in reading, which resulted in the strengthening of his memory and power of analytic thought. At Middlebury, Vt., Oct. 5, 1835, he married Frances A. Henshaw. Two daughters and three sons survived them.

Post's reputation as a stimulating teacher and brilliant lecturer grew rapidly. In 1840 he was urged to become pastor of the Congregational Church in Jacksonville and on Oct. 8 was ordained. Since this responsibility had been assumed in addition to his full college work, it was impossible for him to prepare written sermons, and he accustomed himself to consecutive thinking while taking exercise in the open air. His disciplined mind, wide historical and philosophical outlook, intense spiritual conviction, poetic imagination, and passionate love of mountain, prairie, and sea gave power and interest to his preaching. After repeated and urgent invitations in 1847 to the pastorate of the Third Presbyterian Church, St. Louis, he wrote that he must be guaranteed liberty of opinion and speech on the subject of slavery; otherwise he did not believe he was called to add himself "to the number of slaves already in Missouri." The church replied that they wished more than ever to have him come, and he accepted their call. In the years immediately following he did much literary work and gave historical lectures which were attended by large audiences.

Some of the residents of St. Louis had been Congregationalists, and discussion arose as to organizing a Congregational church, but Post refrained from commenting upon the project until his church in 1851 voted by a large majority to become Congregational, one of the first west of the Mississippi. He now felt free to be a leader in a church order in which he strongly believed, and soon became a potent factor in advancing Congregationalism in the city and state and beyond. For years he was non-resident lecturer on ecclesiastical history in Chicago Theological Seminary. The election of Lincoln in November 1860 threw St. Louis into a turmoil of dissension and foreboding. Post was outspoken and eloquent in advocacy of the Union cause and his church was a tower of strength to that cause throughout the war. After thirty-five years of continuous service in St. Louis he insisted upon closing his pastorate, Jan. 1, 1882, but remained among his people with still widening influence, local and national, until his death.

In 1856 was published his *Skeptical Era in Modern History.* Of his many published addresses and articles, the following are characteristic: *Voices of History* (1851), *Religion and Education* (Iowa College, 1856), *Palingenesy: National Regeneration* (Middlebury College, 1864), "Free Missouri" (*North American Review*, April 1865), *History as a Teacher of Social and Political Science,* address delivered before the governor and constitutional convention of Illinois in 1870; address at the Pilgrim Memorial Convention, Chicago, published in the *Congregational Review* (July 1870) ; "The Things Which Cannot be Shaken" (*Andover Review,* December 1886).

[T. A. Post, *Truman Marcellus Post, D.D.: A Biog.* (1891) ; C. H. Rammelkamp, *Illinois College* (1928); *The Advance,* Jan. 6, 1887 ; *Congregationalist,* Jan. 6, 1887 ; J. G. Merrill, in *Andover Rev.,* July 1887 ; Williston Walker, *A Hist. of the Congregational Churches in the U. S.* (1894) ; *St. Louis Globe-Democrat,* Jan. 1, 1887.]   E. D. E.

POST, WRIGHT (Feb. 19, 1766–June 14, 1828), New York surgeon, was born at North Hempstead, L. I., the son of Jotham Post and Winifred Wright, and a descendant of Richard Post, an early settler in Southampton, L. I. He was baptized Philip Wright but dropped his first name. He went to a local school for his early education and was also tutored privately by David Beatty. At fourteen he was placed under the guidance of Dr. Richard Bayley [*q.v.*], chief of staff of New York Hospital, whose daughter, Mary Magdalen, he married in 1790. He spent four years apprenticed to Dr. Bayley and then went to London, where in the spring of 1784 he served as house pupil of John Sheldon, the well-known surgeon of Westminster Hospital, with whom he came to be on intimate terms; he also studied at the London Hospital. He returned to New York in September 1786 and the following year was encouraged by Dr. Bayley to give anatomical lectures at the New York Hospital. He played a prominent and creditable part in the anatomical riots known as the "Doctors' Mob" which occurred in New York, Apr. 13, 1788. In 1791 he entered into partnership with his father-in-law. After his ap-

pointment to the professorship of surgery in the medical department of Columbia College in 1792 he made a second journey abroad to visit foreign medical schools and to collect specimens for his remarkable anatomical museum at Columbia, which for half a century was the largest of its kind in the United States. While in London he studied under Matthew Baillie, and under William Cumberland Cruikshank, who was at that time at work on the structure of the lymphatic vessels; he was also on friendly terms with Astley Cooper, Everard Home, William Blizard, and other contemporary English surgeons. In 1814 he made another trip to Europe collecting further specimens for his museum. After the union of the medical faculty of Columbia with the College of Physicians and Surgeons in 1813 Post, resigning from the chair of surgery, was appointed professor of anatomy and physiology in the new faculty, and from 1821 to 1826 he served as its president. From 1792 to 1821 he was attending surgeon at New York Hospital, and from 1821 until his death he served as consulting surgeon.

Post's reputation as a surgeon became established in 1813 (*American Medical and Philosophical Register,* April 1814) when he successfully tied the external iliac artery for aneurism (this had first been done, 1811, by John Syng Dorsey of Philadelphia) and in 1817 he ligated the subclavian outside the scaleni muscles. Throughout his life he kept close contact with foreign schools of surgery and he did much to introduce the Hunterian principles of surgical thought and procedure in America. As a teacher he was successful, even though not an animated lecturer. Mott says of him: "As a man he was tall, handsome, dressed stylishly and wore his hair powdered and in a queue. . . . He read little, was averse to writing, and was not brilliant in speaking."

[See: J. Augustin Smith, "An Eulogium on the late Wright Post," *N. Y. Medic. and Physical Jour.,* July, Aug., Sept. 1828 ; Valentine Mott, *A Biog. Memoir of Wright Post, M.D.* (1829) ; S. W. Williams, *Am. Medic. Biog.* (1845) ; J. C. Dalton, *Hist. of the Coll. of Physicians and Surgeons* (1888). The most recent biography of Post is that of Alfred Stillman in *Surgery, Gynecol. and Obstetrics,* Aug. 1925. See also E. H. Pool and F. J. McGowan, *Surgery at the N. Y. Hospital One Hundred Years Ago* (1929). Certain information was supplied for this sketch from the records of Columbia University.]   J. F. F.

POSTL, CARL [See SEALSFIELD, CHARLES, 1793–1864].

POSTON, CHARLES DEBRILL (Apr. 20, 1825–June 24, 1902), explorer and author, delegate from Arizona Territory to Congress, was born in Hardin County, Ky., the son of Temple and Judith (Dubrill) Poston. He went to the public schools and at twelve started an apprenticeship of seven years in the county clerk's office to learn the rudiments of law. He was later clerk of the state supreme court at Nashville, Tenn. Admitted to the bar he practised in Tennessee and later in Washington, D. C. In 1848 he married Margaret John Haycraft of Elizabethtown, Ky., who died in 1884 and left one daughter. In 1850 he went to San Francisco, where he served as clerk in the custom house for two years. Even before the Gadsden Purchase was officially recognized, he led a party to explore along the east coast of the Gulf of California for harbors and in the region that is now southern Arizona for reputed mineral deposits. Enthusiastic over the prospects he went to New York, where the Sonora Exploring and Mining Company was organized. In 1856, with a group of engineers, he went to Arizona and, from Tubac as a center, opened several properties, among which was the Cerro Colorado. On a second eastern trip the capitalization was raised to about a million dollars, modern machinery was ordered, the Arivaca property was purchased, and steps taken politically to obtain a port on the Gulf of California. However, all was abandoned in 1861 because the devastations of the Apache Indians swept Arizona unchecked during the Civil War. With Raphael Pumpelly he escaped to California, and returning to the East he joined the union forces in Washington.

In Washington he directed his attention to gaining a territorial organization for Arizona, and when the Territory of Arizona was created, he returned to the Southwest late in 1863 as superintendent of Indian affairs. Accompanied by J. Ross Browne [q.v.] he traveled through the Apache country, visiting the different tribes and at the same time gaining the support that elected him first delegate to Congress from Arizona. He served from Dec. 5, 1864, to Mar. 3, 1865, and advocated the building of irrigation works on the ground that they would aid the reservation tribes to become self-supporting (*The Speech of Charles D. Poston . . . on Indian Affairs in the House of Representatives . . . Mar. 2, 1865*, 1865). He obtained a congressional appropriation for the promotion of irrigation. By his defeat for reëlection in 1864, his political career was closed.

Returning in 1868, however, from a visit to the Paris exhibition he received from Seward, then secretary of state, an honorary commission to study immigration and irrigation in Asia. He accompanied his friend, J. Ross Browne, the newly appointed minister to China under the Burlingame Treaty. As commissioner he traveled in Asia and Egypt. Arriving in Europe in 1870, he served as foreign correspondent for the *New York Tribune,* and he returned to America in 1876 to attend the centennial in Philadelphia. A ready writer, he gave expression to his varied experiences in many forms, a volume of verse, *Apache Land* (1878), and books of travel, *Europe in the Summer-Time* (1868) and *The Parsees* (1870?), as well as articles in Western periodicals, among which was a series "Building a State in Apache Land," in *Overland Monthly* (July to Oct. 1894) and "C. D. Poston" in *Arizona Graphic,* Oct. 14, 1899. Of his articles those dealing with the pioneer days are of most value.

Well informed on irrigation, he received several government appointments, where this training would be useful. He served as register of the Federal Land office at Florence, Ariz. Returning to Washington in 1882, he was soon taken back to the territory by official work. In 1885 he was again in government service in Washington. In 1890 he returned to the Southwest, where he held for short periods such minor offices as consular agent at Nogales, Mexico, and military agent in El Paso, Tex. In 1899 a tardy recognition of his services, a small pension, was granted to him by the territorial legislature. He died in Phoenix. In 1925 his remains were transferred to the top of Poston's Butte near Florence, and, in the place where he had hoped to erect a temple to the sun, there now stands a shaft erected to his memory by the state of Arizona and the local chapter of the Daughters of the American Revolution.

[F. C. Lockwood, *Ariz. Characters* (1928); H. H. Bancroft, *Hist. of Ariz. and N. Mex.* (1889); *A Hist. and Biog. Record of . . . Ariz.* (1896); J. H. McClintock, *Arizona* (1916), vol. II; *Biog. Directory Am. Cong.* (1928); J. R. Browne, *Adventures in the Apache Country* (1869), pp. 19, 235–54, 269–70, 287; Raphael Pumpelly, *My Reminiscences* (2 vols, 1918); *Arizona Republican* (Phoenix), June 25, 1902, Apr. 26, 1925; brief autobiog. sketch and other information from his nephew, James C. Poston, Louisville, Ky.; authority for the varied spellings of his middle name and his mother's name from his grandson, Gustavus Debrille Pope, Detroit, Mich.]

I. R. L.

POTAMIAN, BROTHER (Sept. 29, 1847–Jan. 20, 1917), Catholic educator and scientist, was born in County Cavan, Ireland, the son of James and Julia (Finnegan) O'Reilly, and was christened Michael Francis. His parents brought him to New York in the post-famine exodus of 1850. Trained in the public and Christian Brothers' schools of that city, he joined the congregation of the Brothers of the Christian Schools as Brother Potamian and in 1859 entered its noviate in Montreal. Within the following decade, he completed a normal course, acquired a thorough knowledge of French, the classics, and the natural sciences, and taught in the elementary schools of Montreal and the Christian Brothers' academy in Quebec. In 1870 he was ordered to St. Joseph's College in London, where he taught the sciences and read for degrees at the University of London (B.Sc., 1878; D.Sc., 1883), being the first Catholic to win its doctorate in science. During a score of years, he gained reputation as a master whose boys passed the matriculation examinations for Universities; as a scientist who associated with Huxley, Tyndall, and Kelvin; and as a religious who enjoyed the friendship of prelates like Newman and Manning. As president of St. Joseph's College, he erected a new building in 1880 at a cost of £100,-000—no small undertaking for a school-master. As a representative of the British government, he was a delegate to the world's fairs at Vienna (1873), Philadelphia (1876), Paris (1889), and Chicago (1893), and at the last named was a member of the jury of awards. In 1893, he was transferred to the De La Salle Normal School, Waterford, Ireland, where he remained until 1896. His final assignment (1896–1917) was as professor of physics in Manhattan College in New York, which, after the withdrawal from the Christian Brothers of their privilege of teaching Latin, laid special stress upon the natural sciences.

Potamian was not merely an administrator, an instructor, and a laboratory investigator; he was also a writer who, in addition to semi-popular articles in *Engineering* (London), *Electrical World* (New York), *Manhattan Quarterly, Catholic World,* and the *Catholic Encyclopedia,* published a number of volumes. These included *The Theory of Electrical Measurements* (1885); *The Makers of Electricity* (1909), with James J. Walsh; and an annotated *Bibliography of the Latimer Clark Collection of Books and Pamphlets Relating to Electricity and Magnetism* (1909). The preparation of this last work was assigned to him by the American Institute of Electrical Engineers at the suggestion of Sylvanus P. Thompson, the English scientist, who declared that in America only Potamian and Park Benjamin were capable of such an undertaking.

[*Records of the Am. Cath. Hist. Soc.,* Sept. 1917; *Cath. World,* Apr. 1917; *Am. Cath. Who's Who* (1911); *The Cath. Encyc. and Its Makers* (1917); *Sun* (N. Y.), Jan. 21, 1917; *Tablet* (London), Nov. 26, 1932; information from members of his congregation.]

R. J. P.

POTT, JOHN (?–*c.* 1642), colonial physician and governor of Virginia, was born in England, presumably the son of Henry and Grace Pott of

"Harrop," Cheshire. A master of arts, acquainted with Latin, Greek, and Hebrew, he came to Virginia as physician-general with Governor Wyatt in 1621, upon the recommendation of Theodore Gulston who pronounced him "well practised in Chirurgerie and Phisique, and expert allso in distillinge of waters" (*Records of Virginia Company,* I, 516). The Company provided free transportation for Pott, his wife, and a man and a maid, making an appropriation also for a "chest of phisique" and "Books of phisique." Pott appears to have lived up to his excellent professional testimonials, although from his arrival in the colony he was likewise busied with politics and affairs: besides finding time for considerable litigation and some conviviality—George Sandys observed that Pott was fond of the company of his inferiors "who hung upon him while his good liquor lasted"—he enjoyed the confidence of the settlers for his skill in treating epidemic diseases. In 1624, rumor having reached England that he was chiefly responsible for poisoning a number of Indians following a peace treaty with them, he was dropped from the Council at the instigation of Warwick. Charles I reinstated him as councilor in March 1626, however, and when Francis West returned to England, Pott was elected deputy-governor. He held this office from Mar. 5, 1629, until Mar. 24, 1630, during which period he twice convened the Assembly, furthered regulations for the colony's defense, and sought to forestall the possibility of a Catholic settlement in Virginia by proffering a deliberately left-handed welcome to Lord Baltimore and tendering him the oath of supremacy. Shortly after Sir John Harvey succeeded him as governor, Pott was arrested and tried on charges of "pardoninge willful murther, markinge other men's cattell for his own, and killinge up their hoggs" (*Virginia Magazine of History and Biography,* Apr. 1900, p. 378). Convicted on two counts, he was removed from the Council and confined to his plantation, besides having his estate ordered confiscated (Hening, *Statutes,* I, 145–46). Undoubtedly politics, Harvey's courting of Baltimore's favor, and the machinations of an anti-Pott faction underlay the trial and conviction: Harvey inconsistently suspended execution of sentence in deference "to his quality and practice" and petitioned the King for clemency (*Calendar of State Papers, Colonial, 1574–1660,* p. 118), while all the Council (three of whom had been among his jurors) became Pott's security. Mrs. Elizabeth Pott, although in poor health, proceeded to England to appeal in her husband's behalf. The commission there which sat on the case reported that the condemning of Pott for felony, "upon this superficial hearing" (*Ibid.*, p. 133) was very rigorous if not erroneous; and on July 25, 1631, the King pardoned him.

He resumed his medical practice, settling near the present site of Williamsburg, and kept an eye upon the arbitrary and arrogant Harvey. When the latter's misgovernment eventually became intolerable, Pott and his brother Francis were among the leaders agitating revolt, and both participated in the actual deposing of the Crown's deputy in 1635. Two years later, after Harvey was reëstablished as governor, Pott and other principals in this early American assertion of popular rights were summoned before the Star Chambers on charges of treason, but their case was never brought to trial. Pott seemingly returned to Virginia and died without issue before 1642, a court record of that year referring to Francis Pott as his "brother and heir."

[H. R. McIlwaine, ed., *Minutes of the Council and General Court of Colonial Va.* (1924); W. N. Sainsbury, *Calendar of State Papers, Colonial, 1574–1660* (1860); *Va. Mag. of Hist. and Biog.*, July 1893, pp. 88–89; Apr. 1900, pp. 368–86; *William and Mary College Quart. Hist. Mag.*, Oct. 1905, pp. 97–100; T. J. Wertenbaker, *Va. Under the Stuarts* (1914), ch. III; W. B. Blanton, *Medicine in Va. in the Seventeenth Century* (1930). S. M. Kingsbury, ed., *The Records of the Va. Co. of London*, vol. I (1906), III (1933).]

A. C. G., Jr.

POTTER, ALONZO (July 6, 1800–July 4, 1865), Protestant Episcopal bishop, was born at Beekman, later known as La Grange, Dutchess County, N. Y., a descendant of Robert Potter of Coventry, England, who came to America in 1634. His parents, Joseph and Anne (Knight) Potter, were of the Society of Friends and had moved from Rhode Island and settled on a farm in Beekman. The elder Potter prospered in his business and became a member of the state legislature. After attending the common school in Beekman, Alonzo was sent to an academy at Poughkeepsie, ten miles away. Thence he passed to Union College, Schenectady, an institution which, under President Eliphalet Nott [*q.v.*], was being transformed into one of the best colleges in the country. Here young Potter greatly distinguished himself.

Graduating in 1818, he went to Philadelphia, where he was employed for a time by his elder brother, Sheldon, a book-seller. Alonzo soon became interested in the Protestant Episcopal Church, was baptized by Bishop William White at St. Peter's, and began studies for the ministry under the Rev. Samuel H. Turner. In 1819 he returned to Union College as a tutor and in 1822 was made professor of mathematics and natural philosophy. The following year he published a brief treatise on logarithms. In the meanwhile he continued his studies in preparation for Holy Orders. He was made deacon May 1, 1822, by Bishop John Henry Hobart of the diocese of New York, and ordained priest Sept. 16, 1824, by Bishop Thomas G. Brownell. In 1824 he married Sarah Maria, the daughter of President Nott. The newly founded Geneva College, later known as Hobart College, called him to be its first president, but he declined this offer and in 1826 removed to Boston, Mass., to serve for five years as the rector of St. Paul's. Recalled to Union College as professor of moral and intellectual philosophy and political economy, he remained nearly fifteen years. He declined an election as assistant bishop of what then was known as the Eastern Diocese, comprising all New England except Connecticut, and became in the same year, 1838, vice-president of the college.

In 1845 he was elected bishop of Pennsylvania in succession to Henry U. Onderdonk [*q.v.*], and was consecrated Sept. 23, 1845. As a bishop, Potter did his best work. His years of experience at Union College were an aid to him in the administrative work of his office. Under his direction this work was not mere routine, but a development of the work of his Church in the community. In 1846 he revived the Protestant Episcopal Academy, which had long been closed. With a view to developing cooperation among the clergy and preparing for the creation of new dioceses, he instituted the system of convocations. For nine years he devoted himself to his greatest achievement, the establishment of the Episcopal Hospital in Philadelphia, and in 1860 he laid the corner stone of its first building. He founded the Divinity School of the Protestant Episcopal Church in Philadelphia in 1863. Potter was broad-minded and tolerant toward those of differing opinions, but he held that the Church of which he was a bishop had a definite position to maintain. This he found not so much in ancient definitions as in the progressive proposals which had first been set forth in the famous Muhlenberg Memorial of 1853. His important essay, "Church Comprehension and Church Unity," in *Memorial Papers* (1857) lies at the base of much of the work since done by his Church in the direction of church unity.

Bishop Potter became favorably and widely known by his *Political Economy* (1840), and his educational publication, *The School and the Schoolmaster* (1842), prepared in collaboration with G. B. Emerson. His last literary work was his four series of Lowell Lectures, delivered in Boston, upon natural theology and Christian evidences. Begun in the winter of 1845, and continued in the two following winters and in 1853, they were published after his death under the title *Religious Philosophy; or Nature, Man and the Bible Witnessing to God and to Religious Truth* (1872). His public interests were very wide. He was active in founding clubs and societies for young men, and often lectured before them. He was an advocate of temperance reform. He opposed slavery and wrote in confutation of the claim that it was justified by the Bible. During the last years of his life he suffered from physical ailments, which European travel did not relieve. Early in 1865 he started on a voyage to California by the Strait of Magellan. He reached San Francisco Bay, but died aboard ship on July 4. In 1841 he married Sarah Benedict, the cousin of his first wife. She died in 1864, and a few months before his death he married Frances Seaton. Robert Brown, Henry Codman, and Eliphalet Nott Potter [*qq.v.*] were his sons, and Horatio Potter [*q.v.*], a brother.

[M. A. DeWolfe Howe, *Memoirs of the Life and Services of the Rt. Rev. Alonzo Potter* (1871); *A Record of the Commemoration of the One Hundredth Anniversary of the Founding of Union Coll.* (1897); Journals of the Convention of the Diocese of Pa.; W. S. Perry, *The Episcopate in America* (1895).]

J. C. A.

POTTER, EDWARD CLARK (Nov. 26, 1857–June 21, 1923), sculptor, was born in New London, Conn., the son of Nathan Day and Mary (Clark) Potter and a descendant of Anthony Potter who was in Ipswich, Mass., before 1648. His mother hoped to see him enter the ministry, but after a year at Amherst College, in the class of 1882, he made up his mind to follow art. He studied drawing at the Boston Museum School of Fine Arts under Frederic Crowninshield and Otto Grundmann and in 1883 was received as assistant in the studio of Daniel Chester French, with whom he formed a lifelong friendship. For two years he worked under French; he also made many studies of animals, particularly of horses. He next went to Senator Redfield Proctor's marble quarry in Proctor, Vt., where he superintended the cutting of French's figures for the Boston Post-Office, acted as assistant foreman, and even took a brief turn at salesmanship. After this interval of not wholly congenial endeavor, he used his savings to go to Paris in 1887, where he spent two years of intensive study, working under Mercié in the human figure, and Frémiet in animal form, meanwhile familiarizing himself with the art of the museums. In 1889 he exhibited in the Salon a delightful "Sleeping Faun," with a vine-wreath nibbled by a rabbit, a genre work now in the Art Institute of Chicago. Of a somewhat later period is his marble bust of Vice-

President William A. Wheeler in the Senate chamber of the National Capitol; for this portrait he was chosen by Wheeler himself. On Dec. 31, 1890, he married May Dumont, daughter of Gen. James Allen Dumont of Washington, D. C.

Potter first became widely known through his collaborations with French in important sculptures for the World's Columbian Exposition at Chicago in 1893. These included not only the colossal Quadriga of Columbus (for which Potter made the horses and outriders), but also four admirable groups of great draft oxen and horses with their attendant figures. It was often a matter of regret to Daniel French that in these and in later collaborations, Potter, largely because of his retiring disposition, failed to receive due appreciation from the public. Equestrian monuments in which the two sculptors collaborated are the General Grant, Fairmount Park, Philadelphia (1899), the General Washington, in Paris and Chicago (1900), the General Hooker, Boston (1903), and the General Devens, Worcester, Mass. (1905).

After his marriage, Potter had a home and studio in Enfield, Mass., and there, in the ample space country life afforded, he created many of his distinguished animal groups, including those shown at the Buffalo Exposition of 1901. Later, finding himself too far from art circles, he took up his permanent residence in Greenwich, Conn., where he was near New York and yet could have the large open-air outlook his equestrian work demanded. In 1912 he was chosen president of the newly founded Greenwich Society of Artists. He did not limit himself to animal sculpture. He had an unusually just conception of the architectural fitness of a figure or group. Among the sixteen bronze heroes installed in the rotunda of the Library of Congress at Washington, his Robert Fulton fills all requirements; the same is true of his "Indian Philosophy" and "Indian Religion" for the façade of Brooklyn Institute, and his Zoroaster for the roof of the Appellate Court Building, New York. In front of the Capitol at Lansing, Mich., is his dignified portrait statue of Gov. Austin Blair; his monument to Col. Raynal C. Bolling, the first high officer of the American Expeditionary Forces to fall in the World War, stands before Havemeyer School, in Greenwich.

Potter's true eminence as a sculptor is seen in equestrian works of his own design and execution. These excel not only through his vivid and masterly representations of horse and rider, but also through the artistic unity of his compositions. He received a gold medal at the St. Louis Exposition of 1904, for which he made several animal groups such as his Bull and Lynx, as well as a memorably gallant equestrian statue of De Soto. Equally spirited is his Civil War Bugler, the soldiers' monument at Brookline, Mass. Other equestrian works are the General McClellan in Fairmount Park, Philadelphia, the General Kearny in Washington, D. C., the General Custer in Monroe, Mich., and the General Slocum in Gettysburg, of which Lorado Taft wrote, "There is no more impressive sculpture on the famous battlefield."

Reverence for nature was part of Potter's religion; falsity of construction in sculpture he abhorred as a kind of unjustified lying. His fame suffered temporarily from journalistic jibes at his great lions in front of the New York Public Library. The lower the jibes fell, the swifter their circulation. Potter's fellow sculptors deeply resented the outrage, but only time could make the proper answer to it. An animated letter of protest from French, describing these would-be witticisms as "not only useless and silly, but cruel and unjust," was printed in the *American Art News,* Feb. 5, 1916. Other New York lions by Potter were those executed for the residences of Collis Potter Huntington [*q.v.*] and for the J. P. Morgan Library. Potter was a member of the National Academy of Design, the Architectural League of New York, the National Institute of Arts and Letters, and a charter member of the National Sculpture Society. He never seemed aware that wherever he went he was a striking figure. With his thick black hair, his large melancholy dark eyes, his aquiline features, his moustache and imperial, he looked more like a Confederate colonel facing disaster than a Yankee sculptor reasonably fond of a joke. Beloved and respected, he died in New London, Conn., leaving a widow, two daughters, and a son, Nathan, a sculptor.

[See: *Amherst Coll.: The Class of Eighteen Hundred Eighty-Two: Record 1882–1907* (1907) ; Lorado Taft, *The Hist. of Am. Sculpture* (1903) ; M. F. French, *Memories of a Sculptor's Wife* (1928) ; C. E. Potter, *Geneals. of the Potter Families and Their Descendants in America* (1888) ; H. W. Lanier, "The Sculpture of E. C. Potter," *World's Work,* Sept. 1906 ; *Fairmount Park Art Asso.: An Account of Its Origin and Activities* (1922) ; *Springfield* (Mass.) *Sunday Republican,* Oct. 17, 1915 ; *N. Y. Times,* June 23, 1923.]
A—e. A.

POTTER, ELIPHALET NOTT (Sept. 20, 1836–Feb. 6, 1901), Episcopal clergyman, college president, was born at Schenectady, N. Y., and died in the City of Mexico. He was the son of Alonzo Potter [*q.v.*] by his first wife Sarah Maria (Nott) Potter. On his father's elevation to the episcopate and removal to Philadelphia, the boy entered the Protestant Episcopal Academy there, from which he passed to St. James College,

Md. In 1861 he graduated from Union College, Schenectady. After a year spent at the Berkeley Divinity School, Middletown, Conn., he was ordained deacon by his father, June 22, 1862. For a short time during the Civil War he served as a chaplain in the army, but soon became rector of the Church of the Nativity, South Bethlehem, being ordained priest by his father on Mar. 19, 1865. In Lehigh University, Bethlehem, which was chartered in 1866, he became the first professor of ethics and secretary of the board of trustees, retaining these two offices until after his removal in March 1869 to Troy, N. Y., where he became assistant minister of St. Paul's Church.

Two years later he was chosen the seventh president of Union College, of which his maternal grandfather, Eliphalet Nott [*q.v.*], had been the fourth. Here Potter's organizing ability found full employment. Under his administration the faculty was augmented, new buildings erected, and the equipment and endowment increased. He also brought the college into affiliation with the Albany Law School, the Albany Medical College, and the Dudley Observatory. He declined an election as bishop of Nebraska in 1884, but this same year resigned his position at Union to become president of Hobart College, Geneva, N. Y., where he displayed like energy and enthusiasm in developing the resources of the institution. Resigning in 1897, he became president of a newly founded institution of more problematical character—Cosmopolitan University, located at Irvington on the Hudson. The courses of this institution were conducted on the correspondence plan, which was just then being put into operation on a large scale. It soon got into difficulties with the regents of the University of the State of New York and its life was short. Before it collapsed, however, Potter had died. His publications were of slight importance, the most ambitious being, *Washington a Model in His Library and Life* (1895), the Hoffman Library lecture of that year. He also edited memoirs of Tayler Lewis and Isaac W. Jackson. A man of great energy and zeal, Potter was an organizer rather than an educator; he contributed little to educational methods or improvements in instruction. On Apr. 28, 1870, he married Helen Fuller, daughter of Joseph W. Fuller, of Troy, N. Y.

[F. H. Potter, *The Alonzo Potter Family* (1923) ; *A Record of the Commemoration of the One Hundredth Anniversary of the Founding of Union Coll.* (1897) ; *The Twenty Year Book of the Lehigh Univ.* (1886) ; C. E. Potter, *Geneals. of the Potter Families* (1888) ; *Troy Daily Times,* Apr. 28, 1870 ; *Albany Jour.,* Feb. 8, 1901.]
J. C. A.

POTTER, ELISHA REYNOLDS (June 20, 1811–Apr. 10, 1882), congressman, jurist, writer, was born in the family homestead on Little Rest Hill, South Kingston, R. I. Through his father, for whom he was named, he was descended from Nathaniel Potter who was in Portsmouth, R. I., as early as 1638; through his mother, Mary (Mawney) Potter, he was the descendant of a French Huguenot named Le Moine, who with others of his faith settled in East Greenwich, R. I., in 1686. Elisha Reynolds Potter, Sr. (Nov. 5, 1764–Sept. 26, 1835), who had been in turn blacksmith, farmer, and practising lawyer, served for some thirty years in the Rhode Island legislature, was four times elected to the federal Congress, and in 1818 was unsuccessful candidate for governor of this state. Wherever he went he was a conspicuous figure, by reason of his gigantic stature, vigorous personality, and keen wit.

The son, eldest of five children, inherited neither his father's physique nor his temperament. He was slight of build, with clear-cut, sensitive features, quiet in manner, and scholarly in his tastes. A portrait of him in the Rhode Island Historical Society suggests the poet rather than the politician. He fitted for Harvard at the Kingston Academy, entered college in 1826, and graduated in 1830. The winter following, he returned to the Academy to teach the classics, but left in the spring to study law in the office of Nathaniel Searle of Providence. On Oct. 9, 1832, he was admitted to the bar and began to practise his profession. The father's reputation made the son's entrance into public life a natural expectation. He was adjutant-general of the state from 1835 to 1837, in 1839 became a representative in the General Assembly, serving a year, and in 1841–42 sat in the state constitutional conventions. When in the latter year the uprising known as the Dorr War was precipitated, he took his stand with those who were opposed to violent action and military force and was one of three commissioners sent to consult with President Tyler. In 1842 he was elected as a Whig to the Twenty-eighth Congress, and served Mar. 4, 1843, to Mar. 3, 1845. On his return to Rhode Island he became intimately concerned with the reorganization of the educational system of the state. In 1849 he was appointed commissioner of public schools, which office he held until 1854. Earnest in his effort to promote efficient administration of the schools he was also zealous in endeavoring to keep public education free from sectarian influences. To create an interest in his work he undertook in 1852 the publication of the *Rhode Island Educational Magazine,* of which he was editor and chief contributor until August 1853. In 1861 he was elected a member of the

upper house of the state legislature, serving until 1863. Five years later he became an associate justice of the supreme court of Rhode Island, and was still holding this office at the time of his death. To the bench he brought distinction by his exceptional knowledge of the law, and his natural courtesy and patience.

Although devoted to his profession, he was also an eager student of history and a prolific writer. His best-known work, published in 1835, is *The Early History of Narragansett,* a collection of documents gathered at the cost of laborious search and reproduced with great accuracy. Among his other works are *A Brief Account of Emissions of Paper Money, Made by the Colony of Rhode-Island* (1837), *Considerations on the Questions of the Adoption of a Constitution and Extension of Suffrage in Rhode Island* (1842), and *Memoir Concerning the French Settlements and French Settlers in the Colony of Rhode Island* (1879). Potter never married, and he lived all his life in the house where he was born. He never became a very rich man, but was always possessed of ample means and was known to the poor and distressed of a wide community as a generous benefactor and a kind counsellor.

[Henry Barnard, in C. E. Potter, *Geneals. of the Potter Families* (1888); S. S. Rider, *Hist. Research and Educational Labor Illustrated in the Work of Elisha Reynolds Potter* (1901); *Biog. Dir. Am. Cong.* (1928); *Providence Daily Jour., Providence Press,* and *Evening Telegram* (Providence), Apr. 11, 1882; *Evening Bulletin* (Providence), Apr. 14, 1882.] E. R. B.

POTTER, HENRY CODMAN (May 25, 1835–July 21, 1908), Protestant Episcopal bishop, was born in Schenectady, N. Y., the son of Alonzo [*q.v.*] and Sarah Maria (Nott) Potter. He received his early education in Philadelphia and in his nineteenth year was an employee in a dry-goods house. In August 1854, however, he passed through a religious experience which awakened in him a desire to enter the ministry. Enrolling at once as a student in the Theological Seminary in Virginia, at Alexandria, he graduated from that institution in 1857, and in May of that year was ordained deacon by his father, who placed him in charge of the parish of Greensburg in western Pennsylvania. While here, Oct. 8, 1857, he married Eliza Rogers Jacobs, of Spring Grove, Lancaster County, Pa. On Oct. 15, 1858, he was advanced to the priesthood by Bishop Samuel Bowman, in Pittsburgh.

The next year he removed to Troy, N. Y., to become rector of St. John's Church. In his work here he was notably successful. Interested in the welfare of young people, he vigorously supported the Young Men's Christian Association and other means of promoting their interests. In

April 1866 he became the assistant minister of Trinity Church, Boston, of which Manton Eastburn, bishop of Massachusetts, was rector. In the same year he was appointed secretary of the House of Bishops of the General Convention, holding this office until his elevation to the episcopate. In 1868 he became rector of Grace Church, New York. Following the lead of Dr. W. A. Muhlenberg [q.v.], and holding with him that organized religion should minister to the whole man, he made his conventional, fashionable family parish a center of Christian work of every sort. Society after society was organized and set to work with constantly extending usefulness. Annual reports of the parish, then a novelty, roused interest and won support. Grace Chapel, Grace House, and other buildings were erected.

On Sept. 27, 1883, Potter was elected assistant bishop of New York, and was consecrated the 20th of the following October. The bishop, Horatio Potter [q.v.], Henry's uncle, was retired from all active work and left the diocese entirely to the charge of his assistant. His first duty was to deal with serious problems arising out of the development of parties in the Church. By training Potter was Evangelical, but had moved toward a moderate Broad Church position; as bishop, however, he was the representative of no party. First of all, he had to deal with the dispute over the teaching of R. Heber Newton [q.v.] as to the authority and integrity of the Bible. The new bishop persuaded Dr. Newton to discontinue his very popular lectures on the Pentateuch, which were causing an unreasonable commotion; but twice, in 1884 and again in 1891, he refused to allow presentments of Dr. Newton for trial for heresy. In the matter of the profession of the Rev. J. O. S. Huntington as a member of the Order of the Holy Cross, Nov. 25, 1884, Potter was sharply criticized by bishops and clergy of the Evangelical party. Although not in sympathy with the theology of the new order, Potter believed in its work. Attempts were made to embroil the bishop with the ritualists: on account of ritual irregularities, he declined to "visit" the Church of St. Ignatius in New York; but the rector soon complied with the bishop's directions. His last serious trouble with partisans was in the case of Prof. Charles A. Briggs [q.v.] who had been found guilty of heresy by the General Assembly of the Presbyterian Church. Briggs applied for orders to Bishop Potter and was ordained by him to the Episcopal ministry on May 14, 1899. This action raised a storm which raged around the head of the bishop for a time, but it passed and Briggs became a dis-

tinguished presbyter of the Church and remained professor in Union Theological Seminary. Potter was more than a diplomat in adjusting party difficulties, however; he was intensely interested in the spiritual welfare of his diocese. The Advent Mission inaugurated by him in 1885 was an Episcopalian form of revival, which has since been frequently imitated. Retreats for clergy and ordinands were instituted. In 1887 Potter put forth an appeal for the erection of a great cathedral. The matter had been broached by his predecessor in 1871, but nothing had been done. An excellent site was now secured and soon work began on the Cathedral of St. John the Divine, the corner stone being laid in 1892.

Potter broke fearlessly with the conventions that hampered the clergy, and spoke with no uncertain voice on matters affecting the moral and social well-being of the community. During the Washington Centennial commemorating the inauguration of the first President, a great public service was held, Apr. 30, 1889, at St. Paul's Chapel, New York, where Washington had worshipped immediately after taking the oath of office and where the Bishop of New York had read the prayers. Potter took advantage of this occasion to speak in behalf of civic righteousness and honesty in public administration. His words caused little less than a sensation, and from every part of the country came commendations of his timely utterance. Determined to know the darker side of New York life at first hand, he spent the summer of 1895 in a little mission in Stanton Street, regarded as the worst and most criminal neighborhood in the city. In 1899 the priest in charge of this mission was insulted by the police authorities when he protested to them against the police protection of vice. The matter was brought up in the Diocesan Convention; the bishop wrote directly to Mayor Van Wyck; the public conscience was stirred and an uprising against the corrupt system in vogue drove the party in power out of office. He became widely known, also, as the impartial friend of every class, and was constantly called upon to act as arbitrator in labor disputes.

He was well read and thoughtful rather than learned. Of his many publications the most notable are *The Scholar and the State* (1897); *The Citizen in His Relation to the Industrial Situation* (1902); and *The Modern Man and His Fellow Man* (1903). His bearing was that of an aristocrat, and the English often spoke of his resemblance to the mid-Victorian bishops. His first wife died suddenly, June 29, 1901, leaving a son and five daughters; on Oct. 4, 1902, he married Elizabeth (Scriven) Clark, the widow of

Alfred Corning Clark. He died in Cooperstown, N. Y., in his seventy-fourth year.

[F. H. Potter, *The Alonzo Potter Family* (1923); H. A. Keyser, *Bishop Potter, the People's Friend* (1910); *Memorial to Henry Codman Potter by the People's Institute, Cooper Union, Sunday Dec. 20, 1908* (1909); George Hodges, *Henry Codman Potter, Seventh Bishop of N. Y.* (1915), inaccurate in regard to certain important dates; *Henry Codman Potter Memorial Addresses Delivered Before the Century Asso., Dec. 12, 1908* (1908); *The Centennial Hist. of the Protestant Episcopal Church in the Diocese of N. Y.* (1886), ed. by J. G. Wilson; James Sheerin, *Henry Codman Potter* (1933); W. S. Perry, *The Episcopate in America* (1895); Journals of the Convention of the Diocese of New York; *Who's Who in America*, 1908–09; *N. Y. Times*, July 22, 1908.]   J. C. A.

POTTER, HORATIO (Feb. 9, 1802–Jan. 2, 1887), Protestant Episcopal bishop, was born at Beekman, now known as La Grange, Dutchess County, N. Y., the son of Joseph and Anne (Knight) Potter, and a brother of Alonzo Potter [*q.v.*]. Horatio was educated in the local schools and at Union College, where he received the degree of A.B. in 1826. After his graduation he began preparation for the ministry and was made deacon July 15, 1827, by Bishop John Henry Hobart. His diaconate was spent in Saco, Me. Ordained priest Dec. 14, 1828, by Bishop Hobart, he became professor of mathematics and natural philosophy in the recently founded Washington College, now Trinity College, Hartford, Conn. He resigned in 1833 to accept the rectorship of St. Peter's Church, Albany, N. Y., where he remained twenty-one years, declining the election to the presidency of Trinity College in 1837.

In 1854 he was elected bishop of New York. The diocese of that time was in a troubled condition. Bishop Benjamin T. Onderdonk [*q.v.*] had been suspended from his office, and Jonathan M. Wainwright [*q.v.*], "provisional bishop," had died Sept. 21, 1854, within two years of his consecration. Potter was a man admirably qualified for the intricate and delicate task of soothing the excited party feelings which had been roused by the Onderdonk episode. He was consecrated Nov. 22, 1854, and served as "provisional bishop" until Onderdonk's death in 1861, when he became automatically bishop of the diocese in the fullest sense. He was distinctly a man of the older ecclesiastical type, not only in his conception of his office, but in his theological position. As was stated at his death by his nephew and successor, Henry Codman Potter [*q.v.*], there was "a singular wisdom and meekness in his episcopate and his habitual reserve was one of its largest elements of strength, founded upon a sounder conception of the Church as a church and not as a sect, than was understood by those who misjudged his patience and forbearance." In obedi-

ence to his convictions, he had little to do with public matters, entering into none of the controversies arising in the nation, but confining himself to the strictly ecclesiastical side of his office. At times he was so cautious as almost to seem timid; yet it was in part due to him that it was possible for the bishops from the South to return to their places in the General Convention and for the breach in the Church to be immediately healed. He was recognized as an eminently just man, unaffected by partisan feelings, and he commanded whole-hearted respect. Under him the diocese prospered exceedingly, and in 1868 from a part of it were created the new dioceses of Albany, Central New York, and Long Island. Bishop Potter contributed to the short-lived *New York Review* of 1837, and during his rectorship in Albany published various sermons and pamphlets, but the exacting labors of his diocese left him little time for literary work. He lived to be a dignified old man—every inch a gentleman in manners and bearing—his conservatism manifesting itself in his dress, which was that of thirty years past. He was twice married: first, Sept. 22, 1827, to Mary Jane Tomlinson of Schenectady; second, to Margaret Atcheson Pollock, niece of the Scotch poet Robert Pollock. Of his six children three survived him. During the last three years of his life he withdrew from active work, surrendering all duties of the episcopate to his nephew, Henry C. Potter, who in 1883 had become his coadjutor.

[*A Record of the Commemoration of the One Hundredth Anniversary of the Founding of Union Coll.* (1897); W. S. Perry, *The Hist. of the Am. Episcopal Church* (1885), and *The Episcopate in America* (1895); Morgan Dix, in *The Centennial Hist. of the Protestant Episcopal Church in the Diocese of N. Y.* (1886), ed. by J. G. Wilson; C. E. Potter, *The Geneals. of the Potter Families* (1888); *Churchman*, Jan. 8, 15, 1887; Journals of the Convention of the Diocese of N. Y.; *N. Y. Tribune*, Jan. 3, 1887.]   J. C. A.

POTTER, JAMES (1729–November 1789), farmer, Revolutionary soldier, son of John Potter, was born in County Tyrone, Ireland. His family landed at New Castle, Del. (1741), and settled on a farm in western Pennsylvania, his father becoming the first sheriff of Cumberland County (1750). James was educated in the hard experiences of the frontier. At twenty-five he was a lieutenant in the border militia and in 1756 he participated in the Kittanning campaign under Lieutenant-Colonel Armstrong. He was promoted to captain in 1759. During 1763–64 he was major and lieutenant-colonel respectively against the French and Indians on the northern frontier and when not engaged with the militia devoted his time to farming. The provincial government appointed him one of the commissioners to induce settlers in western Pennsylvania to withdraw from Indian lands in accordance with the treaty of 1768. One of the first settlers to penetrate the beautiful Penn's Valley in central Pennsylvania, he took up a large tract of land and established his home there about 1774.

A leader in early Revolutionary meetings, Potter was chosen colonel of a battalion of associators early in 1776. He was a member of the constitutional convention at Philadelphia (1776), but was in the field during most of its sessions. He commanded his Northumberland militia at Trenton and Princeton and was appointed brigadier-general Apr. 5, 1777. At Brandywine and Germantown, as well as during the remainder of 1777, he performed valiantly on the outposts of Washington's army in obstructing British raiding and foraging expeditions. His stout opposition to Cornwallis (Dec. 11, 1777) while the American army was on its way to Valley Forge elicited the personal commendation of the Commander-in-Chief. Pressure of business and the illness of his wife compelled him to leave the army early in 1778. Eager for his return the following spring, Washington declared that "his activity and vigilance have been much wanted during the winter" (Hamilton, *post*, p. 348). Indian invasions in Penn's Valley engaged his attention during the years 1778–1780 and in 1779 obliged him to remove his family to more thickly settled areas. In 1780 he was elected to the supreme executive council of Pennsylvania on the Constitutionalist ticket, the following year was elected vice-president of council, and in 1782 was his party's unsuccessful choice for council president against John Dickinson. He was commissioned major-general of militia May 23, 1782, and in 1784 was on the council of censors. From 1785 until his death he was deputy surveyor for Pennsylvania in Northumberland County and also superintended the development of land schemes in Penn's Valley for a company of land speculators. While assisting in a building project on one of his properties in September 1789 he suffered serious internal injuries which caused his death two months later. Enterprising and accustomed to hard work, possessing sound judgment and a penetrating mind, he accumulated a large and valuable estate consisting principally of choice lands in central Pennsylvania. His first wife was Elizabeth Cathcart of Philadelphia, by whom he had two children. His second wife was Mary (Patterson) Chambers, daughter of James Patterson of Mifflin County, from which marriage he had five children.

[*Commemorative Biog. Record of Central Pa.* (1898); *Hist. Sketches . . . Hist. Soc. of Montgomery County,* *Pa.*, vol. IV (1910); J. B. Linn, *Annals of Buffalo Valley, Pa., 1755–1855* (1877); *Pa. Archives*, 1 ser., VI–XI (1853–55), 2 ser., XIV (1888); *Minutes of the Provincial Council of Pa.*, vols. IX, XI (1852), XII–XIV, XVI (1853); A. B. Hamilton, "Gen. James Potter," *Pa. Mag. of Hist. and Biog.*, vol. I, no. 3 (1877), and incidental references, *Ibid.*, vol. I, no. 1 (1877), vol. IV, no. 2 (1880), and Jan. 1894.]   J. H. P—g.

POTTER, LOUIS McCLELLAN (Nov. 14, 1873–Aug. 29, 1912), sculptor, son of Louis and Mary Elizabeth (McClellan) Potter, was born in Troy, N. Y. He received his early education in art from Charles Noel Flagg. After leaving Trinity College, Hartford, Conn., he went in 1896 to Paris, where he studied painting under Luc-Olivier Merson and sculpture under Jean Dampt. A friend of the Boutet de Monvel family, he carved a bust of Bernard Boutet de Monvel and exhibited it in the Champs de Mars. Having spent three years in Paris, he went to Tunis to model North-African types. He was greatly interested in the universal brotherhood of man and in his later development of his beliefs, often stressed the ethnological side of a subject. The Bey of Tunis commissioned him as the sole artist to represent Tunisian types at the Paris Exposition of 1900 and conferred upon him the decoration of Officier du Nichan Iftikhar (Order of Renown). Potter's work at this period was vividly realistic; good examples are his "Bedouin Mother and Child," "A Tunisian Jewess," and "The Snake Charmer." Returning to the United States, he exhibited "The Snake Charmer" in the Pan-American Exposition at Buffalo, N. Y. (1901), where it "attracted favorable comment," while busts later shown, especially the "Tunisian Jewess" and "The Young Bedouin," were said to be "worthy of high praise" (Taft, *post*, p. 448). After some years spent in civilized surroundings, he felt a desire to portray primitive American man and to that end traveled among the Indians. In Southern Alaska he made numerous studies of the Tlingit Indians at their various tasks and rites. Their squat bodies doubtless induced the heavy archaic quality found in such pieces as "The Hunter with his Dogs," "The Shaman," and "The Spirit of the Night"; the interest is ethnological rather than artistic.

In the spring of 1909 Potter held an exhibition at the Modern Athenian Club in New York City. He showed "bronzes, marbles, studies, finished pieces, groups, portrait busts, statuettes." His ideal of man's brotherhood inspired some of his more important works. "Earth Bound" (shown a second time in the Child's Welfare Exhibit of 1911) depicts three generations: a child as yet untouched by sorrow stands between its parents and its grandsire, who are struggling under heavy loads. In the marble group called "The Molding of Man," a male and a female figure arise from the hands of God. In "The Call of the Spirit," a nude Indian gazes upward in spiritual exaltation. Other Indian pieces were "Arrow Dance," "Herald of the Storm," "Dance of the Wind Gods," and "Fire Dance." A bronze copy of the "Fire Dance" is in the National Gallery at Washington. To this period belong his Horace Wells Memorial at Hartford and his bust of Mark Twain, made without the subject for a model, but commended for realism. His final works included two symbolic figures, one male, the other female, exhibited in the Paris Salon of 1912 under the titles "The Earth Man" and "The Earth's Unfoldment," the former typifying struggle upward, the latter spiritual awakening. Potter's ideals led him to researches in occultism, but these he later abandoned as useless in reaching a "deeper spiritual insight." Often his work was overweighted with some messages of mysticism or symbolism but was lacking in technical competence. Though that delicate craftsman Jean Dampt was his early master, his output shows rather the influence of Constantin Meunier, sculptor of labor, and also, to some extent, a leaning toward Rodin's methods. He died suddenly at Seattle, Wash., from a treatment administered by a Chinese herb doctor.

[M. I. MacDonald, "Louis Potter: A Sculptor Who Draws his Symbolism from Intimate Understanding of Primitive Human Nature," the *Craftsman*, June 1909; *Who's Who in America*, 1912–13; Lorado Taft, *The Hist. of Am. Sculpture* (1924); W. H. Holmes, *Cat. of Colls.* (1926), pub. by the Nat. Gallery of Art; *Am. Art Annual*, vol. X (1913); *Internat. Studio*, Oct. 1912; *Seattle Post-Intelligencer*, Aug. 30, 31, 1912.]

A—e. A.

POTTER, NATHANIEL (1770–Jan. 2, 1843), physician, great-grandson of Dr. Nathaniel Potter, of Rhode Island, and son of Dr. Zabdiel Potter, of Caroline County, Maryland, a surgeon in the Continental forces during the Revolution, and Lucy (Bruff) Potter, was born at Easton, Md. He was educated at a college in New Jersey and received his medical degree from the University of Pennsylvania in 1796. During his medical course he was a favorite pupil of Benjamin Rush and after graduation was an intimate friend of the great physican. In 1797 he went to Baltimore and by his energy, ability, and erudition, he attained an eminent position in the community. Upon the organization of the Medical College of Maryland (the present School of Medicine of the University of Maryland) in 1807, he was elected professor of the theory and practice of medicine and continued in the occupancy of this chair with distinction until he died. His fame as a teacher extended far and wide. He was an im-

pressive lecturer and his diagnoses and prognoses were considered infallible by his pupils. He relied largely upon calomel and the lancet and held the *vis medicatrix naturae* in supreme contempt.

Potter was a liberal contributor to medical literature and also wrote on other subjects. Among the more important of his many articles are: *An Essay on the Medicinal and Deleterious Qualities of Arsenic* (1796), his graduation thesis; *Memoir on Contagion* (1818); *Some Account of the Rise and Progress of the University of Maryland* (1838), and *Notes on the Locusta Septentrionalis Americanae Decem Septima* (1839). He published an annotated edition of the work of John Armstrong entitled *Practical Illustrations of Typhus Fever* (1821), and in association with Samuel Colhoun (or Calhoun), published George Gregory's *Practice* (1826, 1829). He was editor of the *Baltimore Medical and Philosophical Lycaeum*, 1811; and co-editor of the *Maryland Medical and Surgical Journal*, 1840–43. He held positions as secretary of the Medical and Chirurgical Faculty of Maryland, 1801–09; attending physician of the Baltimore General Dispensary, 1802–05; dean of the faculty of physic, University of Maryland, 1812, 1814; president of the Baltimore Medical Society, 1812; president of the Medical Society of Maryland, 1817; attending physician of the Baltimore Almshouse, and member of the Board of Medical Examiners of Maryland.

Potter was of medium height, full figure, and ruddy complexion. A fine portrait of him by St. Mémin hangs in the library of the Medical School. His reputation as a teacher, author, and clinician is richly deserved, but his extraordinary service as an epidemiologist, in which he exhibited not only great courage but also scientific attainments of the highest order, has never been adequately appreciated or heralded. His most significant work in this field was done on the epidemiology of yellow fever. By courageously lending himself to experimentation he established the non-contagiousness of the disease. He accomplished this feat by tying a piece of muslin dipped in the perspiration of a patient dying with yellow fever around his head (1797) and by keeping it on all night, breathing the fetid odor. Moreover, he inoculated himself (1798) with the perspiration of a yellow-fever patient in the last stages of the disease. He also inoculated himself with the pus from such patients. Potter's latter days were clouded by adverse pecuniary circumstances and when at last he died the charity of his friends had to be invoked to secure for him a final resting place in Greenmount Cemetery, Baltimore, where his remains still repose in an unmarked grave. He had married a Miss Ford and was survived by two daughters.

[Sources include: *Md. Medic. and Surgic Jour.*, Mar. 1843; J. R. Quinan, *Medic. Annals of Baltimore* (1884); E. F. Cordell, *Medic Annals of Md.* (1903), *Hist. Sketch of the Univ. of Md.* (1891), and article on Potter in *Md. Medic. Jour.*, Apr. 6, 1889; H. A. Kelly and W. L. Burrage, *Am. Medic. Biogs.* (1920); the *Sun* (Baltimore), Jan. 3, 1843; information as to certain facts from Miss Mary W. Holland, a collateral descendant.]   N. W.

POTTER, PAUL MEREDITH (June 3, 1853–Mar. 7, 1921), dramatist, was one of the many writers for the stage who began their professional work in journalism. He was a native of Brighton, England, the son of a teacher who was at one time head master of King Edward's School at Bath and editor of the *Bibliotheca Classica*. Although as a dramatist in America he was known by the name given above, the *New York Herald* stated, at the time of his death, that "his friends were well aware that he was in reality Walter A. Maclean" (*New York Herald*, Mar. 8, 1921). If this statement is true, he was doubtless the son of Arthur John Macleane, an editor of *Bibliotheca Classica* and sometime head master at Bath, who was in Brighton at the time of Potter's birth (English Clergy Lists). As early as 1876 Potter was foreign editor of the *New York Herald,* filling that position until 1883, when he became the London correspondent and later the dramatic critic of the same paper. In 1888 he was a member of the editorial staff of the *Chicago Tribune,* and while thus engaged began his career as a dramatist. His first successful effort at the making of plays was the writing of a hodge-podge entertainment entitled *The City Directory,* produced by the Russell Comedians in May 1889, but his first real play was a drama, *The Ugly Duckling,* acted by Mrs. Leslie Carter in 1890 during her first days on the stage. He soon advanced to the position of a dramatist whose work was constantly sought for, being especially ingenious in the adapting of plots, scenes, and characters to the capabilities of stars.

Play followed play from his pen in rapid succession, many of them being acted under the auspices of Charles Frohman [*q.v.*], then at the outset of his career. For William H. Crane he wrote *The American Minister* (1892); for E. H. Sothern, *Sheridan or the Maid of Bath* (1893) and *The Victoria Cross* (1894). He was a facile and competent workman at the making over of popular novels for the stage, his most notable achievement in this direction being the dramatization of George Du Maurier's *Trilby,* first acted on any stage at the Park Theatre in Boston on Mar. 11, 1895, with Wilton Lackaye as Svengali and Virginia Harned as Trilby, and in England on Oct. 30, 1895, at the Haymarket Theatre, London, with Beerbohm Tree and Dorothea Baird in the leading rôles. In 1898 *The Conquerors* was acted by Charles Frohman's Empire Theatre Company, and not long afterward there arose a furious controversy over the claim that in it Potter had utilized incidents and scenes from Sardou's *La Haine* and Guy de Maupassant's *Mademoiselle Fifi.* In 1901, *Under Two Flags,* Potter's stage version of Ouida's novel, offered Blanche Bates the opportunity to make a name for herself as a star in the character of Cigarette, and in 1909, upon his return from Switzerland, where he had been living for some time, his dramatization of *Arsène Lupin* gave further evidence of his skill and brought to the stage a popular hero of mystery stories. Other plays of his at this time were *Nancy Stair,* based on the novel of the same name by Elinor Macartney Lane, and *The Honor of the Family,* from a French source, for Otis Skinner. Later he wrote a musical play, *The Queen of the Moulin Rouge,* and another of the same type, *The Girl from Rectors,* both of which brought him more money than artistic reputation. Potter contributed nothing that was new or lasting to dramatic literature, but he was a student of the drama, thoroughly acquainted with the French modes of Scribe and Sardou, and he knew how to write plays filled with action that would satisfy the demands of sensation-craving audiences.

[*Who's Who in America*, 1916–17; Dixie Hines and H. P. Hanaford, *Who's Who in Music and Drama*, 1914; *Era* (London), Jan. 11, 1896; *Sun* (N. Y.), June 17, 1911; I. F. Marcosson and Daniel Frohman, *Charles Frohman* (1916); T. A. Brown, *Hist. of the N. Y. Stage* (1903); obituaries in *The Times* (London), Mar. 18, 1921; *Boston Transcript*, Mar. 7, 1921; *N. Y. Herald*, and *N. Y. Times*, Mar. 8, 1921.]   E. F. E.

POTTER, PLATT (Apr. 6, 1800–Aug. 11, 1891), jurist, was born in Galway, Saratoga County, N. Y., the son of Restcome Potter who was born in Massachusetts in 1762 and removed to Galway in 1794, and there engaged in business until 1806, when he moved to Schenectady. His mother was Lucinda Strong of Litchfield, Conn., a woman of distinguished New-England lineage. Platt was the sixth of fifteen children and outlived all the others. He attended the Academy of Schenectady, from which he graduated in 1820, then studied law in the office of Alonzo C. Paige. He was admitted to practice in Schenectady in 1824 and to the supreme court in 1825, and in 1826 opened a law office in the village of Minaville. After seven years' experience there he returned in 1833 to Schenectady to enter into a law partnership with Paige. Upon the dissolution of the partnership in 1847, after Paige's election to the supreme bench, Potter continued the firm with the addition of other partners for another decade. In 1831, when he was in Minaville, he represented his district in the legislature, served on several committees, and was responsible for legislation providing for the erection of an asylum for the insane at Utica, the first state asylum in New York. On June 15, 1836, he married Antoinette (Paige) Smith, the sister of his partner and the daughter of the Rev. Winslow Paige. From 1828 to 1847 he was a master and examiner in Chancery, and in addition held the office of district attorney for Schenectady County from 1835 to 1847. In 1856 he became a candidate for the position of justice of the supreme court of New York and defeated his former law partner, Judge Paige, by a small majority. He also served as a judge of the court of appeals, and in 1865, after a successful term of eight years, he was reelected to the supreme bench without opposition. In the same year he was made a trustee of Union College. His second judicial term expired Dec. 31, 1873, and he retired from active service.

Potter had a jealous regard for the independence of the judiciary. In 1870 his court issued a subpoena requiring Henry Ray, a member of the New York Assembly, to appear as a witness in criminal proceedings before the grand jury of Saratoga County. Ray ignored the summons and was arrested, whereupon the Assembly ordered Potter to appear before the bar of the House to be censured for violation of the privileges of the House. Potter appeared and made such a masterly defense of his action that he was exonerated. In politics he was a Republican and a party leader. He was a man of broad sympathies and mental alertness. Eminent as a jurist, he left behind him a record of many carefully drawn opinions. He was for many years an elder of the First Presbyterian Church in Schenectady. He was six feet four inches in height, of a spare frame, and robust in health. His home was a frequent gathering place for men of distinction in law, statesmanship, and public life, whose friendship he cherished and whose association he sought. He held many offices, including the vice-presidency of the New York Bar Association and the presidency of the Mohawk National Bank of Schenectady. He died in Schenectady, leaving no descendants. In 1871 he published *A General Treatise on Statutes,* a work upon the construction and interpretation of American statutes and constitutions, and including the law of England applicable in accordance with the interpretation of the English law writer, Sir F. W. L. Dwarris. It had a large sale the first year. It was followed

in 1875 by *A Treatise on Equity Jurisprudence,* an expansion and revision of John Willard's earlier work, and in 1879 by Potter's two-volume *Treatise on the Law of Corporations,* which was used as a law-school text.

[See: G. R. Howell and J. H. Munsell, *Hist. of the County of Schenectady, N. Y.* (1886); A. A. Yates, *Schenectady County, N. Y.: Its Hist. to the Close of the Nineteenth Century* (1902); David McAdam and others, *Hist. of the Bench and Bar of N. Y.,* vol. I (1897); *N. Y. Times,* Aug. 13, 1891. For his conflict with the New York legislature see O. L. Barbour, *Reports of Cases in Law and Equity Determined in the Supreme Court of the State of N. Y.,* LV (1870), 625–80. Potter left autobiographical notes.]   J. W. B.

POTTER, ROBERT (*c.* 1800–Mar. 2, 1842), representative from North Carolina, Texas pioneer, was born of humble parentage in Granville County, N. C. He was warranted a midshipman in the United States Navy on Mar. 2, 1815, and served until 1821. He became a lawyer at Halifax, N. C., and in 1824 was involved in a series of brawls. He engaged in fisticuffs, near-duels, and riots, in which he was run through with a sword and one man was killed (*A Statement of the Circumstances Connected with the Affair between Jesse A. Bynum and Himself,* 1825, and Jesse A. Bynum, *An Exposition of the Misrepresentations Contained in a Publication . . . by Robert Potter,* 1825). In spite of this he was elected in 1826, after two defeats, to the House of Commons, where he introduced a political college bill to organize a state institution to train poor boys for public service. In 1827 he published a mock-heroic poem, *The Head of Medusa,* ridiculing Bynum and the town of Halifax. He returned to Granville County and was again elected to the state legislature in 1828. He introduced a bill to annul the charters of banks that demanded specie payment and sponsored a bill to limit attorney's fees to ten dollars. The same year on a wave of popular resentment against the financial system, caused by the depression, he won a seat in Congress as a Jackson Democrat. He offered a bill to destroy banks and another to sell the public lands and divide the proceeds among the states. Reëlected in 1830, he resigned in November 1831 as the result of a scandal involving his charges against his wife's character and his mutilation of two reputable citizens whom he accused without proof. He was tried for the offense and at the trial acted as his own lawyer. He served two years in the Orange County jail, from which he is said to have harangued mobs, and he issued *An Address to the People of Granville County* (1832) to announce his candidacy for the legislature. In the election of 1834 he was successful, but in 1835 he was expelled for overpowering a fellow-legislator and recapturing money won at a game called "Thirteen the Odd."

Shortly afterward he removed to Texas. He was elected to the convention, signed the declaration of independence on Mar. 2, 1836, was on the committee to draft a constitution, and was secretary of the navy. He advocated disbanding the civil government to go to relieve the Alamo, and he also urged the execution of Santa Anna. Less turbulent at forty, he was a hunter and fisherman, with some property and a home on Ferry Lake near the northeastern border of Texas. Divorced from his first wife, who had been a Miss Pelham, he is said to have entered into a marriage by bond with Mrs. Harriet A. Page (*Lewis & McGinnis* vs. *Harriet A. Ames, 44 Texas Reports,* 319–51). Strikingly handsome, he was also fluent, quick at repartee, and a fine actor. A portrait in the possession of Sarah Frances Knott, Stovall, N. C., suggests the elegance and the cynicism of a Byron. As a member of the Texas Senate of 1842 he put through a resolution of outlawry against William P. Rose, a leader of the Moderators, and with his supporters sought the "outlaw" but failed to find him. The next night he was surprised in bed by Rose and his followers. He fled, plunged into Lake Caddo, and was shot by Rose's son-in-law.

[R. W. Winston, "Robert Potter: Tar Heel and Texan Daredevil," *South Atlantic Quart.,* Apr. 1930; J. B. Cheshire, *Nonnulla* (1930); *Biog. Directory Am. Cong.* (1928); J. H. Wheeler, *Hist. Sketches of N. C.* (1851), vol. II; *Register of the Commission and Warrant Officers of the Navy* (1821); C. L. Coon, *The Beginnings of Public Education in N. C.* (1908), vol. I; Charles Dickens, *Am. Notes* (1842), vol. II, p. 271.]

R. W. W.

POTTER, ROBERT BROWN (July 16, 1829–Feb. 19, 1887), Union soldier, was the son of Bishop Alonzo Potter [*q.v.*] and his wife, Sarah Maria Nott, daughter of Eliphalet Nott [*q.v.*]. He was a descendant of Robert Potter of Coventry, England, who came to America in 1634. He was born in Schenectady, N. Y., and entered Union College in that city but did not graduate. He studied law, was admitted to the bar, and practised in New York City. On Apr. 14, 1857, he married Frances Paine Tileston who died a year later, leaving an infant daughter. When the Civil War broke out, he enlisted as a private in the New York Rifles. He was promoted to the rank of lieutenant and was commissioned major on Oct. 14, 1861, in the Scott Rifles, a unit which later became part of the 51st New York Volunteers. Potter became a lieutenant-colonel on Nov. 1, 1861. His command was attached to Reno's Brigade in Burnside's North Carolina expedition which sailed from

Annapolis, Md., on Jan. 9, 1862. In the victorious assault at Roanoke Island, Feb. 8, he was the first field officer over the enemy's works. At New Bern, Mar. 14, he was severely wounded but continued in battle until victory had been won. His command moved north with Burnside's army, and fought at Slaughter or Cedar Mountain, Manassas Junction, Greenville, and at Chantilly (Ox Hill). On Sept. 10, 1862, he was promoted colonel. At South Mountain on Sept. 14, 1862, his regiment fought gallantly, and at Antietam, Sept. 17, made the brilliant and valiant charge across the bridge which saved the day for the Union army. Potter crossed in advance of his troops and incited them to heroic action by his own personal courage. He also commanded the 51st Regiment in the fighting at Fredericksburg, Dec. 11–15, 1862.

Potter was made brigadier-general of volunteers on Mar. 3, 1863, several weeks before he joined Burnside at Cincinnati. On June 3, the 2nd Division under his command accompanied Burnside's IX Corps to Nicholasville, Ky. He participated in the capture of Vicksburg on July 4, 1863, and two of his brigades were first to enter into Jackson, Miss., on July 16, 1863. In the siege of Knoxville, Tenn., in the autumn of 1863, Potter prevented Longstreet from getting supplies through to the besieged. During 1864, his division fought at Spotswood Tavern, Spotsylvania, Ox Ford on the North Anna River, Bethesda Church on the Totopotomy, and at Petersburg. It was a unit of his command that mined the Confederate position at Petersburg and he was the only division commander present in the crater or connecting lines when the mine was exploded on July 30, 1864. He was severely wounded, Apr. 2, 1865, in the final assault on Petersburg. Upon recovery, he was given command of the Connecticut and Rhode Island District of the Department of the East. He was brevetted major-general of volunteers in August 1864, and was promoted major-general on Sept. 29, 1865, on which date he married Abby Austin Stevens. He was mustered out of the volunteer service on Jan. 15, 1866, and from 1866 to 1869, was receiver for the Atlantic and Great Western Railroad. He then went to England to recuperate his health. While abroad he lived the life of a country gentleman; entertaining frequently, and riding to hounds with his English friends. He returned to the United States in 1873 and settled down to a life of leisure on his estate, "The Rocks," at Newport, R. I. During his later years, he was harassed by serious physical ailments which he suffered until his death.

[C. E. Potter, ed., *Geneal. of the Potter Families and Their Descendants in America* (1888); *Seldon Ancestry* (1931); F. B. Heitman, *Hist. Reg. and Dict. of the U. S. Army* (1903); Frederick Phisterer, *N. Y. in the War of the Rebellion* (5 vols., 3rd ed., 1912); *Lloyds Battle Hist. of the Great Rebellion* (1865); G. J. Fiebeger, *Campaigns of the Am. Civil War* (1914); Augustus Woodbury, *Maj. Gen. A. E. Burnside and the Ninth Army Corps* (1867); *N. Y. Tribune*, Feb. 22, 1887.]   C. C. B.

POTTER, WILLIAM JAMES (Feb. 1, 1829–Dec. 21, 1893), clergyman, editor, son of William and Anna (Aiken) Potter, was born in North Dartmouth, Mass. He was a descendant of Nathaniel Potter who died in Rhode Island some time before 1644. William was educated in the public schools of Dartmouth, the Friends' School, Providence, R. I., and the State Normal School, Bridgewater, Mass. After teaching for a short time in the public schools of Kingston and Taunton, Mass., he became a student in the Harvard Divinity School, where he remained for a year, going thence to the University of Berlin, Germany (1857–58). Although of a long Quaker ancestry, he entered the Unitarian fellowship, unmindful of his father's sarcastic protest, and was ordained minister of the First Congregational Society of New Bedford, Mass., on Dec. 28, 1859. In this capacity he served for almost thirty-four years. He was drafted into the Union army in 1863 and detailed as inspector of military hospitals, being later appointed chaplain to the convalescent camp at Alexandria, Va. Naturally shy and retiring, he lacked those social gifts which make for popularity. Though preferring the companionship of his own thoughts to the everyday company of men, he was genuinely interested in all human affairs and played an effective and constructive part in the social, religious, and charitable activities of the community. He won and kept the confidence of the people because he was so plainly honest and unselfish. When, after seven years of service, he informed his New Bedford parish that he could no longer conscientiously administer the sacrament of holy communion and would henceforth refrain from doing so, he received a unanimous vote of confidence.

He was averse to wearing a label of any sort. He soon refused to call himself a Christian, because to do so, he felt, would deny the universal religious fellowship he cherished as an ideal. For this reason his name was dropped from the list of Unitarian ministers published in the Unitarian Year Book. When in 1867 the Unitarian National Conference voted to limit its fellowship to "followers of Christ," Potter, with several others, felt the time had come to organize a religious fellowship as nearly universal in its ideas and plan as was humanly possible. Accordingly, he joined with Ralph Waldo Emerson, Col. T. W. Higginson, Rev. O. B. Frothingham [*qq.v.*], and other notable persons in calling a meeting which resulted in the organization of the Free Religious Association. Its purpose was "to promote the interests of pure religion, to encourage the scientific study of theology, and to increase fellowship in the spirit" (*Proceedings of the First Annual Meeting of the Free Religious Association*, 1868). Potter was the life of the Association. It was his unwavering faith that sustained it; it was his hand and mind that guided it for the fifteen years he served as its secretary and for the ten years he served as its president. When the editor of the *Index*, the official journal of the Association, resigned, Potter assumed its editorship rather than let it pass out of existence. For a few issues it was called the *Free Religious Index*, but quickly resumed its old name. Even Potter's enthusiasm could not keep the journal alive, however, and it was discontinued in 1886. His devotion to the Association sprang from his belief that it would bring about the realization of his ideal of an all-inclusive religious fellowship based on "the various ethical principles which constitute the only saving virtue in any religion." He welcomed the World's Parliament of Religions (1893) as a partial fulfillment of his hopes. Undisillusioned, he died in Boston that same year. On Nov. 26, 1863, he married Elizabeth Claghorn Babcock, who bore him two children before her death in 1879. He published *Twenty-five Sermons of Twenty-five Years* (1885), and in 1895 *Lectures and Sermons, With a Biographical Sketch by F. E. Abbot*, was issued.

[C. E. Potter, *Geneals. of the Potter Families and Their Descendants in America* (1888), pt. 8, p. 44; S. A. Eliot, *Heralds of a Liberal Faith* (1910), vol. III; E. S. Hodgin, *One Hundred Years of Unitarianism in New Bedford, Mass.* (1924); *Vital Records of Dartmouth, Mass.*, vol. I (1929); *Christian Register*, Dec. 28, 1893, Jan. 4, 1894; *Boston Transcript*, Dec. 22, 1893.]   C. G.

POTTS, BENJAMIN FRANKLIN (Jan. 29, 1836–June 17, 1887), Union soldier, territorial governor of Montana, was born in Carroll County, Ohio, the son of James and Jane (Maple) Potts. He grew up on a farm and attended a neighboring public school. He worked in a store for a year and in 1854 entered Westminster College at New Wilmington, Pa., but his finances were so limited that he could stay there only a year. For the next two years he taught school in Ohio and studied law. From 1857 to 1859 he read law with E. R. Eckley in Carrollton, Ohio, and was admitted to the bar. He began practice in Carroll County, soon became active in politics, and in 1860 was a delegate to the Democratic conventions at Charlestown and at Baltimore, where he vigorously supported Douglas. On May 28, 1861, he was married to Angeline Jackson of Carrollton. In August 1861 he became captain of Company F of the 32nd Ohio Volunteers in the Union Army. He became lieutenant-colonel in 1862 and was promoted to the rank of colonel later in the same year. He served with his regiment under Grant at Memphis and at the siege of Vicksburg. In 1864 he was given command of a brigade in Sherman's army. He distinguished himself in battles around Atlanta and Savannah, but, not until January 1865 was he officially promoted to the rank of brigadier-general. When the war was ended Sherman recommended him for a colonelcy in the regular army, but the appointment was not made.

Potts resumed the practice of law in Ohio and reëntered politics as a Republican. He was elected to the state Senate, and in 1870 Grant appointed him governor of Montana to succeed James M. Ashley [q.v.]. He went to Montana still young, and his appearance impressed the people of the territory. He was more than six feet tall, with a huge body and great energy. Although he did not have the national reputation that distinguished his predecessors in Montana, his tact and good judgment won him respect. His reports (*Report of the Governor of Montana...to the Secretary of the Interior...1878–1889*, 10 vols. in 1, 1878–89) were sympathetic with the problems of the territory. He was tolerant of opposing views, and he generally managed to work in harmony with the Democratic majority in the legislature. He favored economy, and during the twelve years of his administration the territorial debt was almost paid off. He was eager to bring railways to Montana but was cautious about granting them subsidies. Largely through his recommendations the legislature modernized the civil and criminal laws and procedure. Throughout his administration he advocated more appropriations for public education. He gave much attention to Indian affairs and urged upon the government more stringent control of the Indian tribes. When the flight of Joseph [q.v.] across Montana aroused alarm throughout the territory, he took prompt measures to protect the people. His administration was ushered in by hard times, and the panic of 1873 hurt Montana severely. The people were demanding free silver and cheap transportation. He interpreted their demands without offense to Grant and Hayes, both of whom disliked western radicalism. Arthur finally came to distrust him

and in January 1883 removed him from office. Potts had long since identified himself with Montana, and at the next election he was elected to the territorial legislature. Soon after this he and Russell B. Harrison established a large stock farm near Helena, in which for the remaining years of his life he was chiefly interested.

[*Progressive Men of the State of Mont.* (1900); Whitelaw Reid, *Ohio in the War* (1868), vol. I; *Hist. of the Thirty-Second Regiment,* ed. by E. Z. Hays (1896); *Hist. Colls. Relating to the Potts Family,* comp. by T. M. Potts (1901); *War of the Rebellion: Official Records (Army),* 1 ser., XII, pt. 2, XIX, pt. 1, XXIV, pts. 1–3, XXXII, pts. 1–3, XXXVIII, pts. 3, 5, XLIV; "The Nez Percé War ... Letters to Gov. B. F. Potts," *Frontier,* Nov. 1929; *Daily Rocky Mountain Gazette* (Helena), Sept. 10, 1870, *Helena Daily Herald,* July 15, Sept. 26, 1870, Nov. 25, 1871, May 7, 9, 29, 1873; *Helena Weekly Herald,* June 23, 1887.]
P. C. P.

POTTS, CHARLES SOWER (Jan. 30, 1864– Feb. 16, 1930), physician, neurologist, was born in Philadelphia, Pa., the son of Francis Cresson Potts and Emma (Bilger) Potts. He was a direct descendant of David Potts who settled in Pennsylvania before the arrival of William Penn. He was graduated from Central High School, Philadelphia, in 1882, and received the degree of M.D. from the University of Pennsylvania in 1885. Following his internship in the Philadelphia General Hospital, he began to practise medicine in the coal-mining communities near Hazleton, Pa., but after several years he returned to Philadelphia to assist Dr. Horatio C. Wood in the neurological department of the University of Pennsylvania. He became professor of nervous diseases in the Medico-Chirurgical College in 1907, and held the same position in the Graduate Medical School of the University of Pennsylvania when it absorbed the former institution. He was attending neurologist to the Graduate Hospital of the University, the Lankenau, and the Philadelphia General Hospital, and was consulting neurologist to the Eastern Penitentiary and the Atlantic County Hospital for the insane.

He was widely known as a good teacher, an excellent clinician and consultant, his scientific work being done largely in the clinical field. He was the author of *Nervous and Mental Diseases, A Manual for Students and Practitioners* (1900, 1908, 1913), and *Electricity; Its Medical and Surgical Applications* (1911). He made many contributions to neurology, most of them in the organic field which claimed his interest rather than the study of functional disease. Among the most important are the following: "A Case of Progressive Muscular Atrophy Occurring in a Man Who Had Had Acute Anterior Poliomyelitis Nineteen Years Previously," in the *University of Pennsylvania Medical Bulletin,* March

1903; "Pseudo-Sclerosis, ... with a Report of a Case with Necropsy" in the *Journal of the American Medical Association,* Nov. 11, 1905; an article on tumors and the relation of the Babinski reflex to motor lesions in the *Review of Neurology and Psychiatry,* October 1910; and "What Neurologists Should Know about Electro-therapeutics," in the *Therapeutic Gazette,* May 15, 1917. He also wrote an account of the witch craze in Salem for the *Archives of Neurology and Psychiatry,* May 1920.

His interests outside his profession were many and varied. He enjoyed doing historical research in the colonial history of Pennsylvania and the New England states, he was a student of literature and possessed a very extensive general library, and he was deeply interested in music. Collecting phonograph records was a particular hobby and it was his custom for many years to give concerts every few days for the nervous patients of the hospitals with which he was associated. He was a member of the varsity crew of the University of Pennsylvania in 1884–85, and during good weather, it was a familiar sight to see his racing shell on the Schuylkill River in Fairmount Park. His robust good health suddenly failed him after he reached the age of sixty-six, and in the fall of 1929 he was confined to a hospital where he died of a cerebral condition in the following February.

[*Who's Who in America,* 1928–29; T. M. Potts, *Hist. Coll. Relating to the Potts Family in Great Britain and America* (1901); *Semi-Centennial Vol. of the Am. Neurolog. Asso., 1875–1924* (1924); *Arch. of Neurol. and Psychiat.,* May 1930; *Public Ledger* (Phila., Pa.), Feb. 17, 1930.]   T. H. W.

POTTS, JONATHAN (Apr. 11, 1745–Oct. 1781), physician, was born at "Popodickon," Colebrookdale, Berks County, Pa., the son of John and Ruth (Savage) Potts, the eleventh in a family of thirteen children. He was a descendant of Thomas Potts who came to America about 1684 to settle in Pennsylvania. He attended school in Ephrata and Philadelphia, and at the age of nineteen sailed for England in company with his friend and relative, Benjamin Rush [*q.v.*], with the intention of studying medicine in Edinburgh. Scarcely had he reached Edinburgh when he received word that his fiancée, Grace Richardson, was seriously ill and he returned home at once. He found the lady recovered and married her on May 5, 1767. They had seven children, five sons and two daughters. After his marriage he studied at the medical school of the College of Philadelphia, now the University of Pennsylvania, and received the degree of Bachelor of Medicine in the class of 1768, the first to be graduated from the school. His graduating thesis, published in 1771 by John Dunlap [*q.v.*] of Philadelphia, was entitled *Dissertatio Medica Inauguralis de febribus intermittentibus potentissimum tertianis.* In 1768 he received his doctorate from the same school and commenced to practise in Reading, Pa. The Potts family took an active interest in the discussions leading up to the Revolution, but they were not of one mind. Two brothers were Loyalists, but Jonathan and the four others espoused the cause of the colonists from the first. He was a delegate from Berks County to the provincial meeting of deputies in Philadelphia on July 15, 1774, and a member of the Provincial Congress meeting in Philadelphia on Jan. 23, 1775.

In the early part of 1776 Jonathan was providing medical care for battalions of Pennsylvania troops and for prisoners of war at Reading. In May of that year Congress resolved that he be taken into the pay of the Continental Army and be employed in Canada or at Lake George. On June 26 he started north with General Gates. On arriving at Crown Point he was assigned by Dr. Samuel Stringer to duty at Fort George. The assignment was made by the following letter, which reveals the conditions confronting the new medical officer: "As the whole of the sick will be removed from this post to Fort George as quick as possible, and are very numerous, beg you will, with all dispatch, have the sheds on the lake shore fitted up with cribs or berths for their reception; and hurry those that are to be built where the old fort stood, as fast as possible. ... A quantity of hemlock tops, if procured, will be no bad bedding, and immediately wanted. They may be gathered along the lake shore and brought in battoes" (Neill, *post,* p. 7). In January 1777, Dr. Stringer was dismissed, and Potts succeeded him in April as deputy director general of the hospitals of the Northern Department, a most trying position because of the large amount of sickness and almost complete lack of medical supplies. He held this position at the time of Burgoyne's surrender. On Nov. 6, 1777, Congress thanked him for his work in the Northern Department, and on Feb. 6, 1778, appointed him deputy director-general of the Middle Department. He retired from the service on Oct. 6, 1780, and died one year later in Reading.

[Potts papers in the archives of the Pa. Hist. Soc.; Mrs. T. P. James, *Memorial of Thomas Potts, Jr.* (1874); E. D. Neill, *Biog. Sketch of Doctor Jonathan Potts* (1863); H. A. Kelly and W. L. Burrage, *Am. Medic. Biogs.* (1920); L. C. Duncan, *Med. Men in the Am. Rev.* (1931); W. O. Owen, *The Med. Dept. of the U. S. Army During the Period of the Rev.* (1920); J. M. Toner, *The Med. Men of the Rev.* (1876); *Gen. Alumni Cat. of the Univ. of Pa.* (1922).]   P. M. A.

POTTS, RICHARD (July 19, 1753–Nov. 25, 1808), jurist, United States senator, was born in Upper Marlborough, Prince George's County, Md., the seventh child of William and Sarah (Lee) Potts. His father had emigrated from Barbados and settled in Maryland about 1740; when he returned to Barbados in 1757 he took with him his Maryland wife—the daughter of Philip Lee—and his numerous children. After his death in 1761 the surviving children returned to Maryland. Richard lived in Annapolis until he became of age; he received the requisite legal preparatory education there and entered the office of Judge Samuel Chase with whom he read law. About 1775 he moved to Frederick, where he lived until his death. His first public service was in 1776 as a member of the County Committee of Observation. He also served as an aide to Brig.-Gen. Thomas Johnson, the commander of the Maryland militia which went to the relief of General Washington during the gloomy winter of that year. On May 20, 1777, he became clerk of the Frederick county court, an office which he held until the winter of 1778. During the remainder of his life, when he was not in public office, he devoted himself to his profession. For two terms (1779–80; 1787–88) he served as a member of the Maryland House of Delegates; between these two terms he was sent on June 12, 1781, as a delegate to the Continental Congress where he remained until 1782. Two years later, on Nov. 1, he was appointed by Luther Martin, then attorney-general of Maryland, state's attorney for Frederick, Montgomery, and Washington counties. He declined a nomination to the state Senate in the winter of 1787; in the following year he was elected a member of the state convention which met in Annapolis to consider the proposed Federal Constitution to which it gave its approval on Apr. 28, 1788.

Potts received from President Washington a commission, dated Sept. 26, 1789, appointing him United States attorney for the Maryland district. This office he held until he was appointed in January 1791 chief judge of the fifth judicial district, a jurisdiction embracing the three counties he had previously served as prosecuting attorney. In 1792 he was one of the Maryland electors at the second election of President Washington. When Charles Carroll of Carrollton vacated his seat in the United States Senate, Potts was elected to fill the vacancy (Dec. 6, 1792). He took his seat the following month and resigned in October 1796. Edmund Randolph wrote to him on July 24, 1794, to convey the wish of President Washington that he accept, in the event of his resignation from the Senate, an appointment as

one of the commissioners for the federal city. Potts declined this offer but accepted a reappointment as chief judge of the fifth judicial circuit (Oct. 15, 1796). He held this office until Oct. 10, 1801, when he was named an associate judge of the court of appeals of Maryland. This last encumbency he held until the judiciary was revised in 1804, when he resumed the practice of law. Potts was married twice: on Apr. 15, 1779, to Elizabeth Hughes of Hagerstown, by whom he had nine children, and on Dec. 19, 1799, to Eleanor Murdoch of Frederick, by whom he had four children. He died at his home in Frederick in his fifty-sixth year. He was first buried in the old graveyard in All Saints Episcopal Parish; later his body was moved to Mt. Olivet Cemetery, Baltimore.

[Sources include: L. H. Steiner, "A Memoir of Hon. Richard Potts," *Md. Hist. Mag.*, Mar. 1910; T. J. C. Williams, *Hist. of Frederick County, Md.* (1910); J. M. Potts, *Hist. Colls. Relating to the Potts Family* (1901); Frederick Town *Herald*, Dec. 3, 1808. Potts's opinions as judge of the court of appeals are reported in 1 *Harris* and in *Johnson*.]

H. Ca—s.

POULSON, NIELS (Feb. 27, 1843–May 3, 1911), iron-master, architect, and philanthropist, was born in Horsens, Denmark, the son of a day-laborer named Poulsen. (The son's name was Anglicized after he came to America.) He spent his boyhood stripping tobacco leaves and attending school every other working day; at fourteen he was apprenticed to a mason, and at sixteen transferred his apprenticeship to Copenhagen, where he received his theoretical mechanical training in the evening sessions of the local technical school. Here he also learned model drawing from the sculptor Herman Vilhelm Bissen. A journeyman at eighteen, he continued his studies in the technical institution until he was twenty-one, when he left for America.

In New York Poulson immediately secured employment as a bricklayer, but since the contractor wanted quantity rather than quality, he was soon discharged for lack of speed. He then accepted a job as a hod-carrier, but thought, observation, and self-education soon brought him consciousness of greater ability, and after two years in New York as an architectural draftsman he received an appointment in the government office of the supervising architect in Washington. While here he visualized the possibilities for iron and steel construction in the United States. He returned to New York after two years and was employed by the Architectural Iron Works until 1876, when the plant was closed. This marked the turning point in Poulson's career. With great confidence and determination he built up within eight years, in partnership with Charles Michael Eger, a Norwegian of training and experience like his own, the firm known at first as Poulson & Eger, after 1897 as the Hecla Architectural Iron Works, which in its Brooklyn plant employed a thousand men. Emphasis was placed on original design and modeling, and among the employees were many artists and scientific metallurgists. The construction and ornamental details of the Grand Central and Pennsylvania railroad stations in New York were made in the Hecla Works, and models of designs were demanded in technical schools from Berlin to Tokio. Poulson's own house in Brooklyn, once a showplace, was constructed almost entirely of steel and copper.

The plans for this house had been drawn by his wife, Lizzie (Brown) Clausen, of English extraction, the widow of a Danish consul in Washington. She died soon after the house she had planned was finished, leaving her husband without an heir. Eventually he began to wonder how he should dispose of his fortune. An ardent believer in popular education, he had established in his factory a technical evening school where employees might obtain free training. Gradually a greater idea developed in his mind and, guided by a movement which had already started, he left the bulk of his estate, about half a million dollars, to endow the American-Scandinavian Foundation for the purpose of fostering closer understanding between the United States and the Scandinavian countries. Its subsequent work through publications and exchange fellowships and lectureships has proved the value of Poulson's dreams. For such gifts as he made for the same purpose while living he was honored by the King of Denmark with the Order of Dannebrog. He died in Brooklyn, at the age of sixty-eight.

Poulson was a public-spirited pioneer in American iron construction. His improvements of method were seldom patented. The Congressional Library received from him gratuitously plans of construction which were widely copied in large institutions. He was the inventor of several mechanical devices, such as fireproof stairs and library bookstacks; he labored zealously to relieve the traffic congestion in New York; he exhibited exceptional fairness and honesty in business; and he proved a model employer of men. Because of his forceful personality, his services were often enlisted as an arbitrator of labor troubles, and he struck terror to the hearts of unscrupulous agitators. It was he who put the "extorting delegate," Sam Parks,

in prison. During his later years Poulson traveled extensively abroad. To posterity his most lasting work was that connected directly or indirectly with public betterment through the spread of knowledge. He believed thoroughly that nobody with a real education could ever fail.

[Articles by Joost Dahlerup, Catherine D. Groth, and the editor in the "Niels Poulson Number" of the *Am.-Scandinavian Rev.*, Sept.-Oct. 1915; G. G. Wheat, "The Home of Niels Poulson," *Ibid.*, Feb. 1931; *N. Y. Times*, *N. Y. Tribune*, May 4, 1911.]   A. B. B.

POULSON, ZACHARIAH (Sept. 5, 1761–July 31, 1844), publisher and philanthropist, was born and died in Philadelphia. His mother, Anna Barbara Stollenberger, had come to America from Germany with her parents eight years before her marriage to Zachariah Poulson, Sr. The latter, born in Copenhagen, Denmark, had been brought by his father to Philadelphia, where he learned printing in the office of the second Christopher Sower [*q.v.*]. Later he became one of the leaders among the Moravian Brethren.

The younger Poulson spent his formative years in the atmosphere of the printing house at a time when the press of Philadelphia was reflecting every phase of the struggle of the colonies for independence. He wrote later, "James Humphreys [*q.v.*] was to have taught me printing. Before I was bound he was necessitated to fly on account of the troubles which then agitated our country. After his materials were packed up and secreted, I went with my Father to Hall and Seller's office, where we remained until the first rumor of the approach of the British army. We then worked with Joseph Crukshank until they [the British] took possession of the city, when we returned to James Humphreys and remained with him until it was evacuated. After its evacuation, we went again to Joseph Crukshank. While here we experienced all the hardships which malicious neighbors and unfeeling fine-collectors could occasion. As my father could not, from religious motives, pay militia fines, his property was sacrificed in the most wanton manner." (Letter to William Rawle, 1791, *American-Scandinavian Review*, July 1920, p. 513.) Among the conscientious objectors who suffered most was Sower, whose wife's sister, Susanna Knorr, Poulson married Apr. 23, 1780.

Not until 1785 did the young printer meet with even a modicum of success. Then began his connection with the Philadelphia Library Company which was to continue for nearly fifty-nine years. For twenty-one years he was its librarian, for six years its treasurer, and for thirty-two years a director. Meanwhile he began to prosper in the printing business. Among the many valuable works he published were *Poulson's Town and Country Almanac,* 1788–1801 (continued by J. Bioren); Robert Proud's *History of Pennsylvania* (2 vols., 1797–98); *The American Tutor's Assistant* (1797); the curious mystical works of John Gerar William De Brahm; and the *Journals of the General Conventions of Delegates from the Abolition Societies of the United States,* from 1794 to 1801. He printed in folio the *Minutes* of the convention which was appointed to revise and amend the constitution of the state in 1789, and was for many years printer to the Senate of Pennsylvania.

In 1800 he purchased *Claypoole's American Daily Advertiser,* successor of the *Pennsylvania Packet,* the first daily newspaper in the United States. For some time it had been the official organ of the government. Poulson moved its office to his residence, No. 106 Chestnut St., opposite the Bank of North America, changed its name to *Poulson's American Daily Advertiser,* and continued its editor and publisher until Dec. 28, 1839, when it was sold to the owners of the *North American* and passed out of existence. During all these years it remained essentially an "Advertiser," with about twenty-two columns of advertisements to six of reading matter. It seemed, however, "to suit the family hearth and fireside comforts of good and sober citizens" and like the good old times from which it descended carried with it "something grave, discriminative, useful, and considerate" (Watson, *post,* II, 397–98). It was a Whig journal and the last number proclaimed support for Harrison and Tyler as "Candidates of the People and of the Whig National Convention."

Throughout his long life Poulson gave earnest and untiring support to many philanthropic organizations. He was a founder and president of the Philadelphia Society for Ameliorating the Miseries of Public Prisons, was a manager of the Pennsylvania Hospital, and was interested in the Society for Promoting the Abolition of Slavery. For thirty-five years he served as a director of the Philadelphia Contributionship for the Insurance of Homes from Loss by Fire, the first fire-insurance company in America. Unassuming and unostentatious, he had to a rare degree the gift of inspiring affection and veneration in those who knew him. The year before his death the Library Company had a portrait of him painted by Thomas Sully that still hangs on its walls and impresses the passerby with the beauty and serenity of his expression.

[J. T. Scharf and Thompson Westcott, *Hist. of Phila.* (1884), vols. II, III; J. F. Watson, *Annals of Phila.* (1844), vol. II; Minutes (MSS.) of the proceedings of the Directors of the Library Company of Phila.,

vol. III; Henry Simpson, *The Lives of Eminent Philadelphians Now Deceased* (1859); Isaiah Thomas, *The Hist. of Printing in America* (2nd ed., 1874), vol. II; M. A. Leach, in *Am. Scandinavian Rev.,* July 1920; *Public Ledger* (Phila.), Aug. 2, 1844; further information furnished by Agnes Poulson Opie.]   A. L. L.

POUND, THOMAS (*c.* 1650–1703), pirate, cartographer, captain in the Royal Navy, was born probably in England. In 1687 he was in New England and on May 27 of that year was ordered by Governor Andros to serve as pilot on the frigate *Rose.* On Apr. 4, 1688, he was again ordered to the *Rose,* but the order was cancelled, and three months later, July 11, Andros gave him command of the sloop *Mary.* In August 1689, Pound, Thomas Hawkins, and six or eight others left Boston in a boat belonging to Hawkins, planning to capture the first suitable vessel they encountered and go to the West Indies to prepare for an expedition against the French. Near Nantucket they captured a fishing ketch which they took to Casco Bay. Here they recruited more men and took on supplies, then sailed for Cape Cod. On Aug. 16 they captured the sloop *Goodspeed* under Race Point, and on Aug. 27, the brigantine *Merrimack,* out of Newburyport, near Martha's Vineyard. From this vessel, according to Pound's statement ("Deposition," *post,* pp. 216–17), they took, "eighteen halfe barels of Flower, two hogsheads of Sugar and one hogshead of Rhum, and three small Armes, and so dismist the Briganteen." Going south, and driven by winds to the Virginia shore, they entered York River and captured a negro whom they subsequently sold to a Salem shipmaster. Returning to the New England coast, they continued to stop vessels, taking foodstuffs chiefly, until Oct. 4, when they were captured by the *Mary* under Capt. Samuel Pease, after a fight in which four of Pound's men were slain and nine wounded. The pirates were examined on Oct. 19 and on Jan. 3, 1690, all were condemned to be hanged. Only one was executed, however; the others, "except Tom Pounds," being reprieved Feb. 20. Four days later, "at the Instance of Mr. Epaphras Shrimpton and sundry women of quality" Pound also was reprieved (*Proceedings of the Massachusetts Historical Society,* vol. XVI, 1879, p. 104). While in prison they had been visited by Judge Samuel Sewall and the Rev. Cotton Mather, who prayed with them. Hawkins' sisters were the wives of eminent citizens—two of his brothers-in-law were members of the Court of Assistants—and undoubtedly it was family influence that saved the culprits. The following year Pound and Hawkins were on their way to England in the *Rose* when the frigate was attacked by a French privateer and the captain and Hawkins were killed. Pound assumed command and took the ship to England, where he reported the incident to Andros in July. On Aug. 5, 1691, he became captain of the frigate *Sally Rose* of the Royal Navy.

To Pound belongs the credit of producing the first map of Boston Harbor to be engraved. Made, probably, about 1691 or 1692 and entitled *A New Mapp of New England from Cape Codd to Cape Sables, Describiing all the Sands, Shoals, Rocks and Difficultyes together with a Sand Draft of the Mattathusetts Bay,* it was engraved at Cheapside, London, by John Harris and sold by Phillip Lea. Pound dedicated it to his friend the Earl of Macclesfield. From 1692 to 1695 Pound served in the British navy in European waters. On Feb. 2 of the latter year he was transferred to the *Dover Prize* and assigned to the Irish station. Two years later, Apr. 17, 1697, he was sent to America in the same vessel to serve on the Virginia station. On Mar. 22, 1698, he sailed again for England. Losing his command in the following year, he quit the sea forever and settled down as a country gentleman near Isleworth, Middlesex. There he died in 1703, survived by his wife, Elizabeth.

[In 1912 F. L. Gay issued a photolithographic facsimile of Pound's map from the unique copy at the Lib. of Cong. See J. H. Edmonds, *Captain Thomas Pound* (1918), also pub. in *Col. Soc. Mass. Pubs.,* vol. XX (1920); *Proc. Mass. Hist. Soc.,* 2 ser. II (1886), 479; "Deposition of Thomas Pound, the Pirate," *New-Eng. Hist. and Geneal. Reg.,* July 1891; Justin Winsor, *The Memorial Hist. of Boston,* II (1881), 448; *Records of the Court of Assistants of the Colony of the Mass. Bay,* I (1901), 307–08, 320–21; G. F. Dow and J. H. Edmonds, *The Pirates of the New England Coast* (1923).]
E. L. W. H.

POURTALÈS, LOUIS FRANCOIS DE (Mar. 4, 1823–July 18, 1880), marine zoölogist, was born at Neuchâtel, Switzerland, where he received his early education. He belonged to an old and titled family, widely scattered in France, Prussia, Bohemia, and Switzerland. While still a lad, he came under the magnetic influence of Jean Louis Rodolphe Agassiz [q.v.] and in 1840 accompanied him on one of his first expeditions to study the glaciers of the Alps. He was trained for the profession of an engineer, but his natural tastes were biological and Agassiz's influence proved the determining factor in his life. When the great teacher came to the United States in the fall of 1846, Pourtalès came with him and was a member of his household until 1848, when he became associated with the United States Coast Survey. In 1864 he was put in charge of the tidal division, and remained in that position until 1873. In the late sixties, the death of his father gave him the title of Count and made him financially independent. He became connected

with the Museum of Comparative Zoology at Harvard University, under Agassiz, in 1870, but did not sever his connection with the Coast Survey and take up his residence in Cambridge until 1873. In the reorganization of affairs at the Museum after the death of Agassiz, he was made "keeper," sharing the administrative duties with the "curator," his life-long friend and colleague, Alexander Agassiz [q.v.].

Pourtalès' scientific work was exclusively in the field of oceanography and his fame rests upon the large amount and high quality of the work he did in collecting and studying animal life at great depths. This work began in the intensive study of material brought up on sounding leads and other apparatus by the vessels of the Coast Survey. He devised improved methods for collecting such material and for dredging and trawling in deep water. In 1866–68, he was in charge of extensive dredging explorations carried on by the Coast Survey steamer *Bibb* in the waters of southern Florida, northern Cuba, and the western Bahamas. Among the most important discoveries of this period was the locating of an extensive area off southeastern Florida, teeming with animal life, to which the name of "Pourtalès Plateau" has been given. In December 1871 Pourtalès accompanied Agassiz on his famous voyage in the *Hassler* around Cape Horn to San Francisco, being in charge of the dredging and other deep-sea work. After his return from that expedition, his duties at the Museum, including the preparation of special reports on various collections of deep-sea material accumulated there, occupied his time until his death.

Pourtalès' publications are neither numerous nor extensive but they are notable for their high quality. His most important work was with corals from deep water and the best known of these reports is the one published in 1871 under the title *Deep Sea Corals.* He was also the author of several memoirs based on collections made by the *Hassler* expedition. His name is indissolubly connected with the fauna of the deep sea by means of a very remarkable sea-urchin first collected by him off southern Florida and named by Alexander Agassiz *Pourtalesia*; it has since been found in the great depths of the sea in all parts of the world.

In his personal characteristics Pourtalès was reserved and quiet, modest to a fault, most industrious and painstaking. He proved a model administrative officer. So wide was his learning and so good his memory, it was said among his colleagues at the Museum—"if Count Pourtalès does not know, it's useless to ask anyone else." He married Elise Bachmann of Boston, who with one daughter survived him. His death occurred at Beverly Farms.

[Alexander Agassiz, in *Nature*, Aug. 19, 1880, *Am. Jour. Sci.*, Sept. 1880, *Proc. Am. Acad. Arts and Sci.*, vol. XVI (1881), and *Nat. Acad. Sci. Biog. Memoirs*, vol. V (1905); H. N. Moseley, in *Nature*, Aug. 5, 1880; Theodore Lyman, in *Proc. Boston Soc. of Nat. Hist.*, vol. XXI (1883); *Pop. Sci. Mo.*, Feb. 1881, with portrait; *Boston Transcript*, July 20, 1880; personal items given orally by J. Henry Blake, 1931.]   H. L. C.

POWDERLY, TERENCE VINCENT (Jan. 22, 1849–June 24, 1924), labor leader and government official, was born in Carbondale, Pa., one of twelve children of Terence Powderly and Margery Walsh. His father and mother came from County Meath, Ireland, in 1827, and after two years on a farm at Ogdensburg, N. Y., settled at Carbondale where his father was employed as teamster by a coal-mining company. He attended school from seven to thirteen at Carbondale and then went to work on the railroad, first as switch-tender and later as car-repairer and brakeman. At seventeen he was apprenticed to the machinists' trade and after the expiration of his apprenticeship in 1869 worked at that trade until March 1877. On Nov. 21, 1871, he joined the Machinists' and Blacksmiths' Union in which he soon became prominent. While living at Oil City in April 1874 he was appointed organizer for western Pennsylvania for the Industrial Brotherhood, and the liberal principles but ineffective methods of that organization influenced his entire career as a labor leader. In the same year he was initiated at Philadelphia into the secret order of the Knights of Labor, and on Sept. 6, 1876, joined Assembly No. 88 at Scranton, on Oct. 14 was elected Master Workman of Assembly No. 222, and on Feb. 24, 1877, was chosen corresponding secretary of the newly organized district assembly. As a member of the committee on constitution of the First General Assembly of the Knights in January 1878, he assisted in securing the adoption of a preamble based on that of the Industrial brotherhood. A year later he was chosen Grand Worthy Foreman of the order, and in September 1879, Grand Master Workman (General Master Workman after 1883). This office he held until November 1893, throughout the entire period of the rise and fall of the Knights of Labor as a powerful labor organization. Meanwhile, in 1878, he was elected mayor of Scranton on a Greenback-Labor ticket, and was reëlected in 1880 and again in 1882, serving in all six years.

As head of the largest and most powerful labor organizations which up to that time had ever existed in the United States, Powderly showed himself an idealist and reformer, but not an aggressive leader. To him the Knights of Labor was a great educational organization, destined to reform the world by converting the working people to demand government ownership of public utilities, regulation of trusts and monopolies, reform of the currency and of the land system, and such measures as the abolition of child labor. Personally sober he denounced drink as one of the great evils under which working men suffered. He opposed the trade form of organization because he believed skilled workers should assist the unskilled. He laid little stress on immediate demands, such as higher wages and shorter hours, and opposed strikes as an outmoded industrial weapon which should be superseded by arbitration. His ultimate ideal was the abolition of the wage system, not through revolution but through producers' cooperatives in which every man would be his own employer. As General Master Workman of the Knights he was instrumental in securing the alien contract labor law of 1885 and the establishment of labor bureaus and public arbitration systems in a number of states. An energetic, handsome man of medium height and somewhat stocky build, with keen blue eyes under heavy brows, a ruddy complexion, a strong, indented chin, long mustaches with curling ends, and a smooth yet alert manner, he was a fluent and nimble-witted orator, and his unpretentious, kindly, and good-humored bearing gave him a strong hold on the affections of his followers. At the same time he was feared and reviled by employers and the press. When, in 1884, he endeavored to secure the newly created post of United States commissioner of labor he was vigorously and successfully opposed by a group of employers who asserted that he was in sympathy with communists.

In 1886 Powderly spoke at a mass meeting in New York for the Labor party which had nominated Henry George for mayor and in 1891 he was present at the political convention, originally called by the Citizens' Alliance and the Knights of Labor, which organized the People's party, but he was always opposed to the formation of a labor party on the ground that such a party was not in accord with the genius of American institutions. Instinctively he turned to the paths of diplomacy, which fitted his natural bent and abilities, endeavoring to smooth over differences between local units of the Knights and those of the rapidly growing American Federation of Labor and attempting to secure arbitration of disputes with employers. In the Congressional investigation of the Missouri Pacific strike of 1886, perhaps the first opportunity offered in the United States to the leader of a large labor organization to confront under official auspices a powerful industrial magnate, Powderly showed himself fully a match for his opponent, Jay Gould. A lifelong student during his leisure hours, even before his retirement from the Knights of Labor he had begun to study law, and on Sept. 24, 1894, he was admitted to the bar in Lackawanna County, Pa. In 1897 he was admitted to practice before the supreme court of Pennsylvania and in 1901 before the Supreme Court of the United States. In 1894 he stumped his state for the Republican ticket and two years later worked in half a dozen states for McKinley, who rewarded him in March 1897 by an appointment as United States commissioner-general of immigration. His administration of that office was distinguished by the first order excluding persons suffering from contagious eye diseases and by his advocacy of the examination of immigrants before their emigration to prevent hardships in such cases, but in 1902 he was removed by Roosevelt for having attempted to exercise political pressure on the commissioner of immigration in New York. In 1906 he was appointed special representative of the Department of Commerce and Labor to study the causes of emigration from Europe, and on July 1, 1907, became chief of the Division of Information of the Bureau of Immigration. He held this office until 1921, attempting unsuccessfully to make his division the nucleus for a federal employment exchange, and then became a member of the Board of Review of the Immigration Department. He served on this board, and also at times as a commissioner of conciliation of the Labor Department, until the long illness which preceded his death.

Powderly married, at Scranton, Pa., on Sept. 19, 1872, Hannah Dever, and after her death took as his second wife Emma Fickenscher in Washington on Mar. 31, 1919. He was a Mason and an honorary member of G.A.R. posts in seventeen states. During his years in the Knights of Labor he was a frequent contributor to the *Journal of United Labor,* and later he wrote occasional articles for magazines and gave speeches before labor and other organizations which were printed in their proceedings. In 1892 his debate with Samuel C. T. Dodd on *Trusts* was published. He contributed a chapter on "The Army of Unemployed" to *The Labor Movement: The Problem of Today* (1887), edited by George E. McNeill, and wrote several pamphlets, including *The History of Labor Day* and *A Little Journey to the Home of Elbert Hubbard,* published by the Roycrofters in 1905. But his most important written work was his *Thirty Years of Labor, 1859 to 1889,* first published in the latter year,

which is primarily not an autobiography but a history of the national labor organizations with which he was connected. He died in Washington, D. C., at the age of seventy-five.

[*Who's Who in America,* 1916–17; W. D. P. Bliss, *The Encyc. of Social Reform* (1897); J. R. Commons and others, *Hist. of Labour in the U. S.* (1918), vol. II, *passim*; the *Nation,* Sept. 28, 1916; obituary notices in the *Outlook,* July 9, 1924, and in the *N. Y. Times,* June 25, 1924, and June 26, 1924 (editorial); and information furnished by his widow, Mrs. T. V. Powderly, of Washington, D. C.]   H. S. W.

POWEL, JOHN HARE (Apr. 22, 1786–June 14, 1856), soldier, statesman, agriculturist, and author, was born in Philadelphia, Pa., the fifth son and sixth child of Robert and Margaret (Willing) Hare. His father, a well educated Englishman of good family, had come to America in 1773. Robert Hare [*q.v.*], the distinguished chemist, was his brother. John Hare was adopted by his maternal aunt, Mrs. Elizabeth Powel, whose husband, Samuel Powel, was mayor of Philadelphia in 1775. When he became of age he changed his name by act of the legislature to John Hare Powel. He was given a good education first under his father and subsequently in the College of Philadelphia where he registered as a student in 1800. After leaving college in 1803 he entered the counting-house of his relatives, Willing and Francis. He was successful in business, having made $20,000 on one voyage to Calcutta before he was twenty-one years old. He made a pleasure trip abroad soon after he reached his majority, and while in England, 1809–11, was the secretary of the United States legation in London, under William Pinkney. He made occasional trips to France, and became acquainted with distinguished men in that country as well as in England. He was noted for his pleasing personal appearance, portrayed in a painting by Sir Thomas Lawrence in 1810.

After his return to America in December 1811, he entered military service as brigade-major of volunteers under his old friend, Thomas Cadwalader [*q.v.*]. Near the close of the War of 1812, he entered the regular army of the United States, received a commission as inspector-general with the rank of colonel, and served under General Scott until the end of the war. On Oct. 20, 1817, he married Julia De Veaux, a daughter of Colonel Andrew De Veaux, a Huguenot of South Carolina. He turned from military to agricultural pursuits, and having settled on his estate at Powelton (now in West Philadelphia), he directed his attention to the improvement of livestock breeds. From England he introduced improved Durham Short Horn cattle which were better in dairy quality than the larger Durham

Short Horns then being raised, and also the Southdown breed of sheep which were excellent for producing meat. His efforts to popularize improved Durham Short Horn cattle led him into a controversy with Timothy Pickering [*q.v.*] of Massachusetts, in the course of which his *Reply to Colonel Pickering's Attack upon a Pennsylvania Farmer* (1825) was published. He was one of the organizers of the Pennsylvania Agricultural Society in 1823, and served that organization as secretary. He wrote numerous papers for agricultural periodicals, among which were the *American Farmer,* and the *Memoirs of the Pennsylvania Agricultural Society.* His book, *Hints for American Husbandmen,* was published in Philadelphia in 1827.

He served in the Pennsylvania state senate from 1827 to 1830, but retired in the latter year and went to Europe a second time. On this visit he appeared as a patron of the fine arts and purchased many works of noted masters. He was fond of outdoor sports which he pursued in later life until he was forced to abandon them because of an injury resulting from a fall on the ice. After this accident his health failed rapidly, and he died at his summer home in Newport, R. I., leaving three sons and two daughters, the survivors of nine children.

[T. F. DeVoe, *Geneal. of the De Veaux Family* (1885); Henry Simpson, *The Lives of Eminent Philadelphians* (1859); Charles Morris, *Makers of Phila.* (1894); J. L. Chamberlain, ed., *Univ. of Pa., Its Hist., Influence, Equip., and Character,* vol. II (1902); C. K. Gardiner, *A Dict. of All Officers . . . Army of the U. S.* (1860); *Ann. Report of the Trans. Pa. State Agricultural Soc.,* vol. II (1855); *Pa. Mag. of Hist. and Biog.,* June 1884, Oct. 1925; *Newport Mercury,* June 21, 1856.]   W. B. M.

POWELL [See OSCEOLA, *c.* 1800–1838].

POWELL, ALMA WEBSTER (Nov. 20, 1874–Mar. 11, 1930), singer, teacher of singing, was the daughter of William Henry and Alma (Webster) Hall and was born in Elgin, Ill. She studied at the Girls' High School of Chicago and with private tutors in that city, and while she was still a young girl she went to New York to develop her vocal gifts, which were considerable. She secured a position as soprano in a leading church choir and in time came to the notice of A. Judson Powell, an organist and piano manufacturer, who devoted himself to the development of her voice and ultimately married her (Apr. 16, 1891). In 1894 she went to Europe where, after studying with various masters, she made her début in opera at Frankfurt-am-Main in the difficult coloratura rôle of Queen of the Night, in Mozart's *Magic Flute,* May 16, 1895. She sang abroad until 1897, when she was engaged by the Damrosch-Ellis Opera Company. In that

year she made a successful American début in the Mozart rôle in Philadelphia, Pa., and in 1898 she joined the Savage Opera Company, scoring successes in *Martha.* Forced by a nervous breakdown to abandon singing for a time, she took a course in law at New York University and was granted the degree of LL.B. in 1900. She then reëntered the operatic field in Germany, singing at the Breslau *Stadt-Theater,* the royal opera houses of Berlin (Rosina, in *Il Barbiere di Siviglia,* 1901), in Munich, Dresden, and Prague, and at the Vienna *Hofoper,* appearing in *Martha, Lakme, Faust, Don Giovanni, Traviata,* and *Lucia* with notable success.

In Prague, on Apr. 6, 1902, she created the rôle of Renata in Eugenio Pirani's *Das Hexenlied.* After three years of singing in concert and opera throughout Europe, she returned to the United States in 1904 and sang at the Metropolitan Opera House in New York. She then toured the United States and Canada with success, established the Powell Musical Institute (1905) in Brooklyn, and founded the Webster-Powell Opera Company, which gave opera until 1912. In 1910 she had secured the degree of Mus. B. at Columbia University, to which she added the degree of M.A. in 1911, and of Ph.D., in the department of political science, in 1914. In 1913 she became co-director with Eugenio Pirani of the Powell & Pirani Musical Institute in Brooklyn and after concertizing in the United States from 1914 to 1918, in 1920 assumed the directorship of the Powell Vocal Academy in Brooklyn. She was the author of *Advanced School of Vocal Art* (1901), a text-book for singers and students; *Black Blood,* the libretto of a manuscript opera by Pirani, and *Music as a Human Need* (1914), her doctoral thesis. During the war she served in the motor corps of the National League for Women's Service. She died in Mahwah, N. J., of a heart attack following a fracture of the hip.

[*Who's Who in America,* 1928–29; *Musical Courier,* Mar. 22, 1930; *Grove's Dict. of Music and Musicians; Am. Supp.* (1920); *Brooklyn Daily Eagle,* Mar. 13, 1930; *N. Y. Times,* Mar. 14, 1930.]   F. H. M.

POWELL, EDWARD PAYSON (May 9, 1833–May 14, 1915), teacher, clergyman, author, was born in Clinton, N. Y., the son of John and Mary (Johnson) Powell. He was educated in the public schools and in 1853 graduated from Hamilton College. After a year as head teacher in the Clinton Academy, he entered Union Theological Seminary, graduated in 1858, and served the Congregational church in Deansville, N. Y., as stated supply. In 1861 he received a call to the Congregational church in Adrian, Mich., where he was ordained, Oct. 29, 1861, by the Detroit Association. His pastorate of ten years here was notably successful. Under his leadership there was built one of the largest Congregational churches in the state. He became widely known for his influence among young men, and was affectionately styled "friend of boys" and "pastor of the city." His unusual influence was due in part to the fact that he preached the new vision of life, nature, and history which was just being introduced to the world through Darwin's *On the Origin of Species.* From 1871 to 1874 he was pastor of the Mayflower Congregational Church in St. Louis, Mo. He was then called upon to decide whether he would continue along the old religious paths or accept the invitation which had come to him from the Third Unitarian Church in Chicago. The Chicago call seemed to offer him a free pulpit in which he could express and develop his changing religious views. A further attraction was the fact that in that city was the Rev. Jenkin Lloyd Jones [*q.v.*], a kindred spirit, with whom he was to become associated (1894–96) in the editing of *Unity,* a Unitarian weekly. At this time he was much occupied trying to adjust his religious views to the theory of evolution, the truth of which seemed to him so compelling. He embodied the results of these efforts at readjustment in a series of popular lectures published in 1887 under the title *Our Heredity from God.* The book went through several editions and served as a textbook in many study clubs of the period. He dedicated the volume to "all those who, like the author, have lost faith in authoritative Revelation, in hopes that they, like himself, may find satisfaction in that revelation of Eternal Life and Truth which is steadily unfolded to us by Science." His kindliness of manner coupled with simplicity of speech and clarity of thought made his exposition of evolution and the new religious point of view helpful and acceptable at a time when this matter was regarded with great fear. A second volume, *Liberty and Life* (1889), was of much the same character as the first, and would perhaps have had greater influence had it not been overshadowed by the popularity of the former work. His historical studies resulted in the publication of *Nullification and Secession in the United States* (1897).

In 1877 ill health forced him to retire from his Chicago pulpit to the ten-acre family homestead near Clinton. Although horticultural interests soon became dominant in his life he never ceased to be a preacher with voice and pen. For six years he preached to the Independent Religious Society in Utica, composed of like-minded friends who gathered about him. He continued to be a regular contributor to the *St. Louis Globe-Democrat* and the New York *Independent.* He was associate editor of the *Arena,* and contributed to many other periodicals. In his later years he became widely known for his delightful series of books on gardening and other outdoor subjects: *Hedges, Windbreaks, Shelters and Live Fences* (1900), *The Country Home* (1904), *The Orchard and Fruit Garden* (1905), *How to Live in the Country* (1911). He loved "to plant and prune and build," increasing the loveliness and the fruitfulness of the world and inspiring others to a like enthusiasm. On Aug. 4, 1874, he married Lucy Maltbie of Sedalia, Mo. He died at Sorrento, Fla., survived by four children.

[*Who's Who in America,* 1912–13; *Alumni Cat. Union Theol. Sem.* (1926) ; *Christian Register,* May 27, 1915; *Unity,* May 27, 1915; *N. Y. Times,* May 15, 1915.]
C. G.

POWELL, GEORGE HAROLD (Feb. 8, 1872–Feb. 18, 1922), horticulturist, was born at Ghent, Columbia County, New York, son of George Townsend and Marcia Rebecca (Chace) Powell, both Quakers, and grandson of Townsend and Catherine (Macy) Powell. His father owned a large fruit farm at Ghent and was well known as a lecturer and writer on horticulture, floriculture, and agriculture. As a boy, George Harold Powell assisted in the duties of the farm and orchard and early developed a fondness for fruit growing.

He attended the public schools, the Union Free High School in Chatham, N. Y., and Cornell University, where he took the agricultural course, working under Prof. L. H. Bailey. He received from Cornell in 1895 and 1896 respectively the degrees of B.S. and M.S. in agriculture. On July 1, 1896, at Collings, N. Y., he married Gertrude E. Clark, daughter of William H. Clark, a lawyer of Buffalo. In this same year he was appointed horticulturist at the Experiment Station of the Delaware Agricultural College, Dover. His work here attracted the attention of the United States Department of Agriculture, and in September 1901 he was called to the Bureau of Plant Industry as assistant pomologist to study the problems of the apple industry connected with cold storage. In 1904 he was appointed pomologist in charge of fruit storage and transportation investigations. In this same year a request came to the Department from California orange growers for an investigation of the rotting of citrus fruits in transit. Powell soon proved that most of the rot was due to outward mechanical injuries, and following his recommendations a campaign for better handling was instituted, producing important improvements. The results of his principal investigations while in the Department of Agriculture were published under the titles: *Cold Storage with Special Reference to the Pear and Peach* (1903), *The Apple in Cold Storage* (1903), *The Decay of Oranges While in Transit from California* (1908), all Bulletins of the Bureau of Plant Industry; "The Handling of Fruit for Transportation" (*Yearbook, 1905*, 1906, of the Department of Agriculture); *Italian Lemons and Their By-Products* (1909), another Bulletin of the Bureau of Plant Industry. The last-named paper was written after his visit to Europe in 1908 to study conditions and practices in the fruit industry.

In 1909 he was appointed assistant chief of the Bureau of Plant Industry and in 1911 was made acting chief, but resigned the same year to accept the position of secretary and manager of the California Citrus Protective League. After further investigations in Europe, he became general manager (September 1912) of the California Fruit Growers' Exchange, a corporation with headquarters in Los Angeles, representing 62 per cent. of the California Citrus Industry. Even before leaving the Department of Agriculture he had written on "Cooperation in the Handling and Marketing of Fruit" (*Yearbook, 1910*, 1911, pp. 491–596). In his later work he came to see still more clearly that some of the most difficult problems were essentially sociological and humanistic and in consequence there developed in him an intense and practical interest in human cooperation which was akin almost to a religion. His book, *Cooperation in Agriculture,* published in 1913, became the standard work on this subject and has had a wide influence. In 1913 he was offered but declined the position of dean of the College of Agriculture of the University of California.

When the United States entered the World War he was called to Washington, July 9, 1917, to take charge of the perishable foods division of the Food Administration, one of its most responsible positions. In recognition of his outstanding service in this capacity, he was awarded the Cross of the Chevalier of the Order of the Crown by King Albert of Belgium. He returned in January 1919 to his former position. The month before his death he served as chairman of the committee on marketing of farm products of the National Agricultural Conference called by President Harding and he also took a prominent part in the general proceedings, delivering a notable address on "Fundamentals of Cooperative Marketing" (*Report of the National Agricultural Conference, 1922*). He died suddenly of a heart attack while attending a dinner at the Hotel Maryland, Pasadena, in February 1922. A public memorial service was held at the Morosco Theatre, Los Angeles, Monday, Mar. 20, at which Herbert Hoover, then secretary of commerce, delivered the principal address.

Powell was a member of numerous horticultural and agricultural societies and associations. With his broad knowledge of the fruit industry and his ability as an educational leader, he combined geniality of character, a keen sense of humor, and an appreciation of psychology which made him markedly successful in handling troublesome and controversial problems.

[*G. Harold Powell Memorial, Los Angeles, Cal., Mar. 20, 1922* (1922); *Presentation of Memorial Tablet of the Late George Harold Powell to the U. S. Dept. of Agric.* (1923); *California Citrograph*, Mar., May 1922, Sept. 1923; *California Countryman*, Apr. 1922; *Am. Fruit Grower Mag.*, Apr. 1922; *Los Angeles Times*, Feb. 19, 1922.]
                                    C. R. B.

POWELL, JOHN WESLEY (Mar. 24, 1834– Sept. 23, 1902), geologist, philosopher, and administrator, brother of William Bramwell Powell [*q.v.*], was born at Mount Morris, in the Genesee Valley of western New York. His parents, Joseph and Mary (Dean) Powell, were both of English birth and well educated. The father, a licensed exhorter in the Methodist Episcopal Church, had come to America as late as 1830, settling first in New York City, and later moving to Mount Morris. After John was born the family lived for short periods in Jackson, Ohio; South Grove, Wis.; and Bonus Prairie, Ill.; finally settling in Wheaton, Ill. Because of this frequent moving, the boy's early training was somewhat fragmentary, but after his parents had settled in Wheaton, he entered a Methodist preparatory school which was later absorbed by Wheaton College, and here, with intervals of teaching and work on the farm, he continued until 1855, when he was enabled to enter the preparatory department of Illinois College, Jacksonville. In the next few years he studied also at Oberlin and Wheaton colleges, but took no degree.

Up to this time he had anticipated following his father's calling, for which his ability as a public speaker well fitted him. He became interested in the local botany, however, and joined the State Natural History Society in 1854, and during his spare hours roamed far and near over the state making observations and collections. He was a youth of independent thought and action and at an early age made long trips alone in his boat on the Mississippi and Ohio rivers. Through his collections, which he generously distributed, he came into touch with scientific men, and ultimately was elected secretary of the Illinois Society of Natural History. With the outbreak of the Civil War, he enlisted, and was soon commissioned second lieutenant. In 1861–62 he recruited a company of artillery of which he was commissioned captain. At the battle of Shiloh he received a wound which resulted in the loss of his right arm at the elbow. Returning to active service as soon as his wound would permit, he rose to the rank of major of artillery.

After being honorably discharged, Jan. 14, 1865, he accepted the position of professor of geology in the Illinois Wesleyan College at Bloomington, and later that of lecturer and curator of the museum of the Illinois Normal University. In 1867 and again in 1868, while holding this position, he organized and conducted parties of students and amateur naturalists across the plains to the mountains of Colorado, being furnished by General Grant with troops for protection from the Indians. It was while on the second of these trips that Powell first saw the gorges of the Green and Colorado rivers and conceived the daring scheme of exploring them by means of boats. On May 24, 1869, financed by the Smithsonian Institution and an appropriation from Congress, his party of eleven men and four boats embarked near the place where the Union Pacific Railroad crossed the Green River. They emerged safely from the mouth of the Grand Canyon Aug. 29 following, having made a journey of nearly nine hundred miles.

With the aid of small Congressional appropriations, Powell continued his western explorations in 1871, 1874, and 1875, entering in the last year upon his career as director of the second division of the United States Geological and Geographical Survey of the Territories, renamed in 1877 Survey of the Rocky Mountain Region. This position he continued to hold until the consolidation in 1879 of all the western surveys as the United States Geological Survey, under the temporary directorship of Clarence King [q.v.]. To Powell was given charge of continuing under the Smithsonian Institution the anthropological investigations that had been conducted in connection with his surveys. With King's resignation in 1880, Powell succeeded him as director of the Geological Survey and held the office with marked success until 1894.

The immediate geological results of Powell's Grand Canyon trip were slight. The results of his explorations of the adjacent regions were published in a quarto volume of 300 pages under the caption, *Explorations of the Colorado River of the West and Its Tributaries* (1875), revised and enlarged twenty years later as *Canyons of the Colorado* (1895). It was in this report that he made his one bold appeal for immortality as a geologist by calling attention to the fact that the Uinta canyons were gorges of corrosion and due to the action of rivers upon rocks which were undergoing gradual elevation. As he expressed it, the rivers preserved their level, but the mountains were lifted up, as the saw revolves on a fixed pivot while the log it cuts is moved along. The idea was not wholly new, but it had remained for Powell to bring it forward in all its effectiveness. In this same report he first made use of the expressions "antecedent" and "consequent" rivers, "superimposed valleys" and "baselevel of erosion," terms now forming a part of every geologist's vocabulary. With this report, his geological work practically ceased, though in 1874 and 1875 he gave much attention to the land laws of the Western states and in 1878 published a monograph entitled, *Report on the Lands of the Arid Region of the United States.*

It is upon his success as an administrator rather than a geologist that his reputation rests, though the impetus given to the study of physiographic geology by his Grand Canyon and Uinta Mountain reports can scarcely be overestimated. Through affiliation with the state surveys and professors of geology in the various universities and institutions of learning, he succeeded in overcoming whatever jealousies may have threatened, and under his enthusiastic guidance the federal Geological Survey became the largest and most powerful organization of its kind the world had ever known. Recognizing the need of prompt publication to meet the demands of the public, he inaugurated in 1883 the series of Bulletins which have been continued down to the present day. For presentation of the results of detailed studies of larger or more abstruse problems, there was inaugurated in 1890 the striking series of quarto Monographs which were continued by his successors Walcott and Smith down to 1915, when they were superseded by the Professional Papers. The greatest innovation in form of publication was, however, the series of folio atlases, established in 1894, with geologic and topographic maps on a scale of four miles to the inch and contour intervals of 200 feet. These maps and atlases, which undoubtedly brought the work of the Survey home to the public more than either of the other series mentioned, have been continued, with some changes, under the successive administrations down to the present time, though appearing only at intervals of gradually increasing length.

Powell's interests were not wholly geological. He early took an interest in the native tribes with which he came in contact in his western explorations and conceived of the establishment of a government bureau to carry on investigations relative to them and their predecessors on the American continent. Under the Rocky Mountain survey, while he was its director, were inaugurated (1877) the *Contributions to North American Ethnology*. With the establishment of the United States Geological Survey as a permanent organization, in 1879, the anthropological work was given to Powell, with the new title of director of the Bureau of Ethnology, under the Smithsonian Institution. This position he held until his death, though he was relieved of much of the administrative work by W J McGee [*q.v.*].

Powell was in appearance a somewhat rough and striking figure, with tumultuous hair and beard. He was hearty and eminently magnetic, at times given to enforcing his views with military arbitrariness. He had a remarkable faculty for leadership and was likable in the extreme. In his administration he gave every man a chance to demonstrate his capacity, and was thus instrumental in launching the careers of a number of younger men who later attained distinction. He was always accessible to the least of his subordinates and interested in their welfare. His retirement from the leadership of the Survey was brought about in part by antagonism to his forest preservation and irrigation projects and in part by ill health, his amputated arm being a periodic source of great suffering. After his retirement he devoted himself principally to administrative duties in connection with the Bureau of Ethnology and to abstruse psychological problems. In 1898 he published *Truth and Error, or the Science of Intellection*. Though not a college graduate, he was honored with the degree of Ph.D. from the University of Heidelberg and that of LL.D. from Harvard University. In March 1862 he married a cousin, Emma Dean of Detroit. They had one child, a daughter. He died at his summer home, Haven, Me., from a cerebral hemorrhage, in his sixty-ninth year.

[A short bibliography in smaller type:] ["John Wesley Powell: Proceedings of a Meeting Commemorative of His Distinguished Services, . . . Feb. 6, 1903," with full bibliog., in *Proc. Wash. Acad. Sci.*, vol. V (1903–04), reprinted separately; W. M. Davis, in *Nat. Acad. Sci. Biog. Memoirs*, vol. VIII (1919), also issued separately (1915); F. S. Dellenbaugh, *John Wesley Powell* (1903), repr. from last chapter of Dellenbaugh's *The Romance of the Colorado River* (1902); G. K. Gilbert, *John Wesley Powell* (1903), reprinted, with some revision, from the *Open Court*, Dec. 1902–June 1903; *Evening Star* (Washington), Sept. 24, 1902.]

G. P. M.

POWELL, LAZARUS WHITEHEAD (Oct. 6, 1812–July 3, 1867), governor of Kentucky, senator, was born in Henderson County, Ky., the third son of Lazarus and Ann (Mc-

Mahon) Powell. His formal schooling was begun in his home county, and he graduated from St. Joseph's College in Bardstown, Ky., in 1833. He immediately began to study law under John Rowan at Bardstown, and continued his course in law at Transylvania University in Lexington, where he enjoyed the excellent lectures of George Robertson [*q.v.*]. On his admission to the bar in 1835 he formed at Henderson a partnership with Archibald Dixon, which lasted for four years. He also became interested in agriculture, and as a planter he added to his fortune.

Attracted by the opportunity for a political career, he ran as a Democrat for the lower branch of the state legislature in 1836 and was elected. He failed to be reëlected and resumed the practice of law. On Nov. 8, 1837, he married Harriet Ann Jennings who bore him three sons and died in 1846. By 1848 he had attained a prominence that got for him the nomination for the governorship, but he found it impossible to defeat a Whig of the strength of John J. Crittenden. In 1851, running against his former law partner, Archibald Dixon, he obtained the election and became the first Democratic governor since the days of Andrew Jackson. Failing to capture the legislature, he found it necessary to veto many bills during his four years of office. In January 1858 he was elected to the federal Senate for the term to begin on Mar. 4, 1859, and in April following his election he was appointed by President Buchanan to be one of the two commissioners to go to Utah to seek to compromise the difficulties there. Though of strong Southern sympathies, he did not favor the secession of Kentucky; yet he rejected the idea of the coercion of the South. In line with the mass sentiment of Kentuckians, he stood for the neutrality of his state, and he worked feverishly in the Senate to bring about a compromise between the sections. He was the author of the resolution providing for the committee of thirteen, of which he became chairman; and in the committee and on the floor of the Senate he fought resolutely for the Crittenden propositions. He looked with many misgivings on the war waged by the Union against the Confederacy, and throughout the struggle he opposed the Government's policy of political arrests and military interference with elections. The Kentucky legislature in October 1861 requested his resignation; and shortly thereafter his colleague, Garret Davis [*q.v.*], introduced resolutions for his expulsion. The Senate refused to expel him; and before the end of the war both his state and his colleague admitted that they had been wrong, and he had been right.

After the expiration of his term on Mar. 3,

1865, he returned to his home in Kentucky, where he continued the practice of law. In 1866 he attended the Johnson convention in Philadelphia, and the next year he was a strong contender before the Kentucky legislature for the Senate. On the first ballot he received a higher vote than any other person, but finally he lost to Garret Davis. Six months later he died of apoplexy at his home near Henderson. The next year, a state thoroughly chastened by its war experiences voted to erect a monument over his grave and to have prepared at the expense of the state 3,800 copies of his biography. Previously, in 1852, the state had created a new county and named it for him.

[*Biog. Sketch of the Hon. Lazarus W. Powell*, pub. by direction of the General Assembly of Ky. (1868); Lewis and R. H. Collins, *Hist. of Ky.* (2 vols., 1874); *Biog. Encyc. of Ky.* (1878); *The Am. Ann. Cyc.* . . . *1867* (1868); *Kentucky Statesman* (Lexington), July 9, 1867; *Cincinnati Daily Gazette*, July 6, 1867.]

E. M. C.

POWELL, LUCIEN WHITING (Dec. 13, 1846–Sept. 27, 1930), painter, the son of John Levin and Maria Louise (Grady) Powell, was born at "Levinworth Manor," near Upperville, Va., an estate granted in 1770 by the British Crown to Powell's ancestors who emigrated to America from Wales. At seventeen, in spite of a slight lameness occasioned by an accident in boyhood, he entered the Confederate army. At the conclusion of the Civil War he went to Philadelphia to study art and became a pupil of Thomas Moran [q.v.]. When he was about thirty years of age, he made a trip to Europe, visited the great galleries, studied especially the works of Turner, but did not enroll in any school or study under any individual master. It was fifteen years before he visited Europe again, by which time his reputation was established. The dominant influences in the development of his art were the teaching of Moran and the works of Turner. Although he did not visit the West until he was fifty-five, he will be longest remembered by his paintings of the Grand Canyon, rendered somewhat in the style of Moran, but with less accuracy. He was equally well known during his life time, however, for his paintings of Venice—dream pictures full of light and color —reminiscent of Turner. Powell painted both in oil and in water color, producing in the former many large and imposing canvases, but in the latter medium, his works, fresh and spirited, more truly reflected his inherent gift.

In 1910 he and his wife (Nan Fitzhugh, whom he had married on Oct. 20, 1880) made a trip to the Holy Land, stopping in Egypt and Italy on the way. From this trip Powell brought back an interesting series of water colors; picturesque, colorful, and spontaneous. His career was powerfully influenced by the friendship and patronage of Mrs. John B. Henderson, wife of Senator Henderson of Missouri—a woman of wealth and public spirit—who, admiring his work and believing him to be a great genius, fitted a studio for him in her palatial home in Washington and subsidized him for years. She is said to have owned, at the time of his death, more than two hundred examples of Powell's paintings. During the last twenty or more years of his life he maintained his own studio independently, and divided his time between his homes in Washington and in Loudoun County, Virginia. He was a member of the Society of Washington Artists and the Washington Water Color Club, and his works were exhibited from time to time in the Corcoran Gallery of Art and at the National Gallery of Art. Two of his large canvases, one of the Canyon of the Colorado and the other a marine, "Mid-Ocean," long hung on the walls of the Carnegie Public Library of Washington. He was one of the first to hold an exhibition on an ocean steamer. Although he cannot be considered a great artist, his paintings were exceedingly popular and found their way through purchase into private collections in all parts of the world.

Powell lived to be eighty-four years of age, but he never had robust health and was inclined to pessimism, apparently finding less pleasure than others in the practice of his profession. He was proud of his successes, however, and was generous to a fault, giving away many of his paintings to his friends, and contributing money with a free hand to those less fortunate than himself. He was survived by his wife, a son, and two daughters. His death occurred in Washington, D. C., after an illness of less than a month. He was buried at Arlington.

[*Who's Who in America*, 1930–31; *Am. Art Annual*, 1930; *Cat. of the Paintings in the Corcoran Gallery of Art* (1911); catalogues of the annual exhibitions of the Washington Water Color Club; *Art News*, Oct. 4, 1930; *Evening Star* (Washington), Sept. 27, 1930; information as to certain facts from Powell's son; personal acquaintance.]

L. M.

POWELL, MAUD (Aug. 22, 1868–Jan. 8, 1920), violinist, was the daughter of William Bramwell Powell [q.v.] and Minnie Paul, of Peru, Ill., where she was born. Her father was an author and school superintendent; her uncle, Maj. John Wesley Powell [q.v.], was the distinguished ethnologist and pioneer explorer of the Grand Canyon. Her mother was of German-Hungarian ancestry and was an amateur composer, and the daughter showed musical talent at an early age. In 1870 the family moved to Aurora, Ill. Maud Powell began the study of the violin while attending school in Aurora and continued for four years with William Lewis in Chicago, where she also studied piano with Agnes Ingersoll. At this time she often appeared in concert as an infant prodigy, and also made a six weeks' tour with the Chicago Ladies' Quartet through Illinois, Wisconsin, and Michigan. Her unusual gifts justified sending her abroad to study with the best teachers, and in 1881 she took a course with Charles Dancla, at the Paris Conservatory. She also studied with Henry Schradieck in Leipzig. She later said of these masters that Dancla "was unquestionably the greatest," but that while the French method made her an artist, in Germany she learned to become a musician. At Léonard's suggestion she toured for a year in England, playing before Queen Victoria. Joseph Joachim, who had heard her play in London, invited her to the *Hochschule für Musik,* where she studied with him until her début with the Berlin Philharmonic in 1885 when she played Bruch's G-minor Concerto.

Returning to New York she appeared the same year with the New York Philharmonic under Theodore Thomas and during the following seven years made annual concert tours of America, in 1892 accompanying the New York Arion Society under Frank van der Stucken on its tour of Germany and Austria as "a representative American violinist." In 1893 she played in the same capacity at the World's Columbian Exhibition in Chicago and read a paper on "Women and Music" at the Women's Musical Congress. In 1894 she organized the Maud Powell String Quartet with which she appeared in leading American cities until 1898, when the group disbanded. By this time she was generally acknowledged to be one of the most notable violin virtuosi America had produced, and her masterly breadth of style, absolute technical command, and deep interpretative insight were placed at the service of the best in violin literature. Aside from giving American composers a first hearing, she was the first to introduce to American audiences such well-known works as Bruch's D-minor Concerto and his *Konzertstück,* the Tschaikovsky, Tor Aulin, Dvořák, Arensky, Sibelius, and Saint-Saëns concertos, Lalo's F-minor Concerto and "Concerto Russe," Coleridge Taylor's D-minor Concerto, and the Rimsky-Korsakoff "Fantaisie."

Maud Powell's favorite instrument, after 1903, was a fine Joseph Guarnerius. Among the conductors with whom she had played were Leopold Damrosch, Emil Paur, Horatio Parker, Wilhelm Gericke, Anton Seidl, and Sir Henry Joseph Wood. A proof of her attainment was her great popularity in Europe, where violinists of eminence were common and audiences critical. In 1898 she revisited London and toured the British Isles and Continental Europe. In the season 1900–01, after appearing in America, she made a second successful English and Continental tour, during which she played for King Edward VII, the Duke of Cambridge and Edinburgh, and the Princess Royal of England. She repeated the tour in 1903 with John Philip Sousa and his band, in Russia playing "by command" for the Czar Nicholas II. In 1904 she organized a second string quartet but her uninterrupted solo engagements gave her no time for rehearsal or performance, and after a few concerts she was reluctantly obliged to disband the group. On Sept. 21, 1904, she married H. Godfrey Turner, of London, who thereafter acted as her manager. During 1905–06 she toured South Africa with a concert party of her own.

In 1907 she substituted for the Guarnerius she had used a large Giovanni Battista Guadagnini of admirable tone quality. With this instrument she continued her alternate European and American concert tours until 1910. Thereafter she played in the United States, contributed to various musical journals, made records for the Victor Talking Machine Company, and wrote a number of excellent transcriptions for violin and piano. The vogue of the Russian violinists of the Auer tradition did not lessen Maud Powell's established popularity and she remained a favorite until her death. She died on tour, in Uniontown, Pa., after more than thirty years of triumph on the concert platform. No one contested her reputation as the greatest woman violinist of the United States. She had been successful as a performer from the beginning of her career. The brilliancy, power, and finish of her playing were combined with an unusual interpretative gift. She was a woman with a cultural background rare among virtuosi, kind and generous, especially toward aspirants in her own field, and she won by her charm and native humor many devoted friends.

[See: H. C. Lahee, *Famous Violinists of Today and Yesterday* (1899); F. H. Martens, *Violin Mastery* (1919); the *Metronome,* Dec. 1904; *Musical Observer,* Feb. 1908; *Musical America,* Jan. 17, 1920; *Who's Who in America,* 1918–19; *N. Y. Times,* Jan. 9, 1920.]

F. H. M.

POWELL, SNELLING (1758–Apr. 8, 1821), actor, manager, was closely affiliated, frequently in association with his brother, Charles Stuart Powell, with the theatre in Boston from its beginnings in the nineties of the eighteenth century. He was a native of Carmarthen, Wales, the son of S. Powell, a theatre manager. He began his connection with the stage in early life by acting children's parts. He later learned the printer's trade and when he came to the United States with his brother in 1793, he brought with him a printing outfit which he put to good use in the preparation of announcements for their theatrical undertakings. His American début as an actor was made on Feb. 3, 1794, at the opening performance of the Boston Theatre in Federal Street, of which his brother was manager, the play being Henry Brooke's tragedy, *Gustavus Vasa, the Deliverer of His Country*. With the exception of brief excursions to several cities not far from Boston, including Providence and New York, he was almost uninterruptedly identified with the stage of the city of his adoption. He married in 1794 Elizabeth Harrison, a native of Cornwall, and an actress of great ability and no little distinction. She was born in 1774 and had acted in London and on tour with Mrs. Siddons before coming to the United States.

Snelling Powell joined the company at the new Haymarket Theatre, Boston, on the occasion of its opening on Dec. 26, 1796, under the management of his brother, playing Doricourt in *The Belle's Stratagem*, with his wife as Letitia Hardy. With John Bernard and J. H. Dickson (who was his brother-in-law) he took over the joint lesseeship of the Boston Theatre in 1806, and under their auspices the theatre did a "most flourishing business" (Clapp, *post*, p. 47). Powell is described by Clapp as "the first successful manager of a theatre in Boston," although his brother Charles is certainly as prominent in the Boston theatrical annals of that epoch. As an actor, Snelling Powell appears to have been more skilful in the technique of the stage than gifted as an artist, for the contemporary references to him are more emphatic in their praise of him as a gentleman, a friend, and an honest and highly esteemed citizen than they are as an actor. John Hodgkinson, with whom he was closely associated at one time, is quoted as saying that his Romeo, George Barnwell, and similar characters "were respectable and often excellent," which is certainly very moderate commendation. He was seen in many characters in the repertory of tragedy, comedy, farce, and melodrama prevalent in his day, but during his last years he acted seldom, though his business connections with the theatre continued until the end of his life. He died in Boston, after a long illness. His wife remained on the stage for many years after his death, dying in 1843, and

their daughter Elizabeth, who was one of their eight children, became the wife of Henry James William Finn [*q.v.*], a distinguished American actor of the middle of the nineteenth century.

[Wm. Dunlap, *Hist. of the Am. Theatre* (1833); W. W. Clapp, Jr., *A Record of the Boston Stage* (1853); T. Allston Brown, *Hist. of the Am. Stage* (1870); John Bernard, *Retrospections of America* (1887); George O. Seilhamer, *Hist. of the Am. Theatre* (3 vols., 1888–91); George O. Willard, *Hist. of the Providence Stage* (1891); Arthur Hornblow, *A Hist. of the Theatre in America* (1919); G. C. D. Odell, *Annals of the N.Y. Stage*, vols. I and II (1927); newspaper clippings in the Harvard Library Theatre Collection; and personal information from Powell's great-grand-daughter.]   E. F. E.

POWELL, THOMAS (Sept. 3, 1809–Jan. 14, 1887), poet, dramatist, journalist, was active in literary work of many kinds in England before he came to the United States in 1849. He was an industrious worker, and both as author and editor, he published more than a dozen books before his emigration. These included dramas, tragedies, comedies and poems. His first book of poetry appeared in 1833, and in 1841 in collaboration with Wordsworth, Leigh Hunt, Richard Hengist Horne, and others he edited *The Poems of Geoffrey Chaucer Modernized* (1841). Among his plays during these years were *The Wife's Revenge* and *The Blind Wife* (1842), *Marguerite* (1846), *True at Last* (1848), and *Love's Rescue* (1848), none of which appears ever to have been acted in America. In addition to his other writing, he was also a frequent contributor to London periodicals.

Immediately upon his arrival in the United States he joined the editorial staff of the Frank Leslie publishing house and remained active in its work during the rest of his life. He was the first editor of *Frank Leslie's Illustrated Newspaper*, established in 1855, and of *Frank Leslie's New Family Magazine*. He was also associated from time to time in the editorship of the *Lantern, Figaro*, the *New York Reveille*, and several other short-lived publications. He found time from his work, however, for hours of congenial companionship, and for conversation upon many subjects to which his friends never wearied of listening. In personal appearance he was the conventional bluff, hearty, and bulky Englishman of the John Bull type, and he retained his national characteristics through all the years of his association with Americans, living in the memories of his friends and associates as one of the liveliest and best-liked of the coterie of New York journalists and literary men that assembled regularly at the famous Pfaff's. Among his books published in the United States were *The Living Authors of England* (1849), *The Living Authors of America* (1850), *Pictures of Living*

Authors of Great Britain (1851), and *Chit Chat by Pierce Pungent* (1857). His last piece of writing was *Leaves from My Life,* in which he tells about the literary life of the London of the thirties, of his meeting with Weber in 1826, and of dining with Spohr and Mendelssohn. He also wrote a number of burlesques for performance by Buckley's Minstrels in New York, and a great deal of his journalistic work was signed with the pseudonyms: Diogenes, Pierce Pungent, Ernest Trevor, and other pen names. He died in Newark, N. J., about a year after his retirement from regular professional duties.

[S. A. Allibone, *A Critical Dict. of English Lit. and British and Am. Authors,* vol. II (1870) ; *Frank Leslie's Illustrated Newspaper,* Jan. 22, 1887 ; *Appleton's Ann. Cyc.,* 1887 ; *N. Y. Mirror,* Jan. 29, 1887 ; *Boston Morning Jour.,* Jan. 15, 1887 ; *N. Y. Herald,* Jan. 15, 1887.]　　　　　　　　　　　　　　E. F. E.

POWELL, WILLIAM BRAMWELL (Dec. 22, 1836–Feb. 6, 1904), educator, son of Joseph and Mary (Dean) Powell and brother of John Wesley Powell [*q.v.*], was born at Castile, N. Y. The father, of English descent, was a farmer and Methodist circuit preacher, and during his frequent absences from home, William did much of the farm work and assumed family responsibilities. Later the Powells moved to Illinois, where he attended the public schools. He also studied in the preparatory department of Oberlin and at Wheaton (Ill.) College. In 1860 he became principal of the Hennepin, Ill., schools and in 1862, superintendent of schools at Peru, Ill. There in May 1865 he married Minnie Paul. Their daughter, Maud Powell [*q.v.*], became a distinguished violinist. From 1870 to 1885 Powell was in charge of the schools in Aurora, Ill., and then for the next fifteen years he was superintendent in Washington, D. C., retiring from this position in 1900, as the result of a Congressional investigation which severely criticized his educational methods. In 1901, as representative of D. Appleton & Company he visited the Philippines to study educational and textbook needs there. His health was impaired by this trip and two years later he died suddenly at his home in Mount Vernon, N. Y., while reading his morning paper.

Powell was a man of vigorous personality and pronounced educational views. At Aurora, Ill., he founded a training school for teachers and adopted the practice of placing promising high-school graduates as assistants in the various grades. He was active in state and national education associations and in 1874 was nominated as superintendent of public instruction in Illinois, but failed of election because of the defeat of his party. His career in Washington was a stormy one. According to an Illinois colleague, the District of Columbia schools, when Powell took charge of them, were twenty-five years behind the times and given over to mechanical routine. Powell reformed the teaching body by employing trained supervisors and requiring better education and training for teachers, enlarged the scope of the city normal school, and modernized both school buildings and teaching methods. The business high school, the first in the country, was the result of his initiative (J. W. Cook, *post*). On the other hand, an editorial in a Washington newspaper at the time of Powell's retirement said: "The school system of late in vogue in the District has been convicted of insufficiency in the public mind. It has been shown to lack harmony, to be devoid of the essentials of education, to run to extremes, to produce bad results. The lack of examinations and text-books is but an index of the course of the whole process. Fads have replaced fundamentals, a theory has supplanted the experience of generations of educators" (*Evening Star,* June 27, 1900). Powell was doubtless a man in advance of his time, who sought to release the school system from traditional bonds; but he lacked tact, carried theories to extremes, and antagonized conservatives.

Though an organizer rather than a writer, he produced several textbooks embodying his pedagogic ideas. Among them were *How to Talk; or Primary Lessons in the English Language* (1882) ; *How to Write; or, Secondary Lessons in the English Language* (1882) ; *How to See; or, First Steps in the Expression of Thought* (1886) ; *Normal Course in Reading* (1889), and *How to Teach Reading* (1889), with Emma J. Todd ; *A Rational Grammar of the English Language* (1899), with Louise Connolly; and *History of the United States for Beginners* (1900). He was a founder of the National Geographic Society and a member of several learned societies.

[J. W. Cook, *Jour. of Proc. and Addresses of the 43rd Ann. Meeting of the National Educ. Asso.,* vol. XLIII (1904) ; reports of the board of trustees of public schools of the D. C., 1885–1900; *Who's Who in America,* 1903–05 ; *Evening Star* (Washington), July 1, 1885, June 27, 1900, Feb. 9, 11, 1904.]　　S. G. B.

POWELL, WILLIAM BYRD (Jan. 8, 1799–May 13, 1866), eclectic physician, was born in Bourbon County, Ky. His parents were of English stock, having removed to Kentucky from Orange County, Va. In 1808 the family moved to Kenton County and settled near Covington where the father prospered ; he was able to send his son to Transylvania University for his general and medical education. Powell began the study of medicine with Charles Caldwell [*q.v.*], a member of the faculty, and received his medical degree in 1826. Probably through the influence of his preceptor he early became interested in physiology, with special reference to the brain. In 1825 he attended lectures at the University of Pennsylvania and about this time took up the study of phrenology. He began an investigation into the relations between temperament and cranial conformation and in 1836 announced his discovery that human temperament could be read from an examination of the cranium alone. In the pursuit of his studies he began a tour of the western Indian tribes in 1843 and for three years was lost to his family and friends among these people, whose dress and manner of living he adopted. On this trip he was able to add considerably to a collection of human crania which he had previously begun.

His teaching experience began in 1835 when he was appointed professor of chemistry at the Medical College of Louisiana, a position which he held for three years. Somewhere in his career he was converted to eclectic medicine, and, in 1847, he obtained from the Tennessee legislature a university charter for the Memphis Institute which opened in 1849 with departments of law, and commerce, and a school of eclectic medicine in which Powell was professor of cerebral physiology and medical geology. In 1851 he moved to Covington, Ky., where he resided for the remainder of his life. He was appointed to the chair of cerebral physiology in the Eclectic Medical Institute of Cincinnati in 1856, a post which he held for two years. In 1866 he was made emeritus professor of cerebral physiology in the Eclectic Medical College of New York, but his death prevented any service under this appointment. Powell was a prolific writer. In addition to numerous contributions to periodicals he published in 1856 his *Natural History of the Human Temperaments,* a second edition of which appeared in 1869. He collaborated with Robert Safford Newton [*q.v.*] in publishing *The Eclectic Practice of Medicine* (1854), and *The Eclectic Practice of Medicine* (*Diseases of Children*) (1858). For one year, 1860, he was co-editor of the *Journal of Human Science.*

In his discussions of human temperaments he modified the Hippocratic classification by dividing them into bilious, sanguine, encephalic and lymphatic. He viewed the former two as the primitive temperaments, the latter two as acquired or subjunctive. Brain work produced the encephalic type while wealth and luxurious ease developed the lymphatic type. He insisted

that marriages between individuals of the same primitive temperament or individuals into whose constitutions adjunctive temperaments entered were in effect incestuous and were attended by all the ill-effects inherent in such unions. He tabulated the physical and mental defects which might be expected from the mating of persons with different combinations of these temperamental classes. His views were subjects of intense controversy which lasted long after his death. His preceptor, Dr. Caldwell, was one of his earliest and strongest opponents, but his views had sturdy support as well as bitter opposition. Powell's exceedingly eccentric manners led to some question of his mental soundness. A portrait made late in life shows long, unkempt hair and beard, and deep-set, piercing eyes, the whole suggestive of a psychopathic taint. His remarkable collection of human crania, of more than five hundred specimens, was given to Dr. A. T. Keckeler, his literary executive, by his will, which further provided that his own head should be added to the collection. This was done over the protest of his relatives after his death in Covington following a paralytic stroke.

[R. S. Newton, biog. sketch in *Trans. Eclectic Med. Soc., State of N. Y., 1866* (1867); E. B. Foote, *Powell and His Critics* (1888); H. W. Felter, *Hist. of the Eclectic Med. Inst. of Cincinnati* (1902); H. A. Kelly, W. L. Burrage, *Am. Med. Biog.* (1920); *Cincinnati Daily Gazette,* May 14, 1866.]   J. M. P.

POWELL, WILLIAM HENRY (Feb. 14, 1823–Oct. 6, 1879), historical and portrait painter, was born in New York City, the son of William Henry and Mary (Cowing) Powell. While he was still an infant the family moved to Cincinnati, Ohio. In his boyhood he devoted many of his leisure moments to drawing, and his youthful ambition to adopt the profession of a painter was encouraged by the elder Nicholas Longworth [*q.v.*]. His first instructor was James H. Beard [*q.v.*]. In his seventeenth year he went back to New York, where he became a pupil of Henry Inman [*q.v.*]. He made rapid progress, and soon received gratifying recognition as a painter of portraits. His chief desire, however, was to win success as an historical painter, and his earliest essays in this field were "Salvator Rosa with the Brigands" and "Columbus and the Egg." This latter work aroused considerable interest and discussion. In 1847, when Congress undertook to obtain a suitable picture to fill the vacant panel in the rotunda of the Capitol at Washington, the twenty-four-year-old Powell entered the lists, and after a lively contest in which several of his seniors in the profession took part (including S. F. B. Morse, Henry Inman, and Daniel Huntington), the coveted commission fell to him. Tuckerman (*post*, p. 458) intimated that he owed this unexpected honor to the fact that he came from Ohio, and made some dry comments upon the system of applying to art commissions the principle of state rights. Washington Irving wrote a letter, Jan. 7, 1847, to the library committee of the Senate strongly urging that the commission be given to Powell (manuscript letter in possession of the family). The subject chosen was "The Discovery of the Mississippi River by De Soto"; the canvas was to measure 18 x 12 feet, and the price was $12,000. In order to carry out this important commission to the best advantage, Powell deemed it desirable to do the work in Paris; accordingly, he went thither in 1848 and took a studio, where he toiled at the task for about five years, only relaxing long enough to paint an occasional portrait. He took his work seriously and had the advantage of the friendship of Horace Vernet, Thomas Couture, Alexandre Dumas, A. M. L. Lamartine, Eugene Sue, and other literary and artistic personages. Of several of these he painted portraits; he also made one of Abd-el-Kader, famous Arab chief, who had been taken prisoner by the French forces in Algeria after an heroic defense of his nation's independence. When Powell returned to America in 1853 he brought back with him the "De Soto," which was exhibited in several cities before being installed in the Capitol. It met with severe criticism; but in an artistic sense it is no worse than the general run of historical pictures painted to order for public buildings. After it was put in place, Powell remained in Washington several years, painting portraits of statesmen and government officials.

The state of Ohio then gave him another opportunity to win fame, commissioning him to paint for the state capitol a picture of Commodore Oliver Hazard Perry at the naval battle of Lake Erie as he transferred himself and his flag from the sinking *Lawrence* to the *Niagara*. This work, completed in 1863, led to an order for an enlarged replica for the Capitol in Washington, for which, in 1873, the painter received $25,000. The replica hangs above the landing of the Senate stairway. In style it is distinctly reminiscent of the dramatic battle pieces by Vernet in the Palace of Versailles. Among other historical pictures by Powell are "Washington's Last Interview with His Mother," "The Siege of Vera Cruz," "The Battle of Buena Vista," "The Landing of the Pilgrims," "Scott's Entry into the City of Mexico," "Washington at Valley Forge." His portraits include those of Albert Gallatin, Peter Cooper, Washington Irving,

Peter Stuyvesant, Gen. George B. McClellan, Major Robert Anderson, and Gen. Robert Schenck. Powell was married in 1842, and had two sons and three daughters. He died in New York in his fifty-seventh year.

[H. T. Tuckerman, *Book of the Artists. Am. Artist Life* (1867); H. L. Earle, *Biog Sketches of Am. Artists* (1924); C. E. Fairman, *Art and Artists of the Capitol of the U. S. A.* (1927); *Am. Art Rev.*, Nov. 1879; *N. Y. Tribune*, Oct. 7, 1879; Rand-McNally *Washington Guide*, 1921; information from family.]   W. H. D.

POWER, FREDERICK BELDING (Mar. 4, 1853–Mar. 26, 1927), chemist, son of Thomas and Caroline (Belding) Power, was born at Hudson, N. Y., and died at Washington, D. C. His early education was obtained at a private school and at an academy in his native town. Compelled at the age of thirteen to earn a living, he worked for five years in the local drug store. Here he not only became familiar with drugs and chemicals, but also acquired some knowledge of elementary chemistry by reading and experimenting. In 1871 he accepted a similar position in Chicago, but soon after the disastrous fire of that year he went to Philadelphia, where he obtained a part-time position in the pharmaceutical establishment of Dr. Edward Parrish [*q.v.*] and also, through the help of friends at the Philadelphia College of Pharmacy, began to study in that institution. He graduated in 1874, remained two years in the Parrish establishment, and then went to Germany, where he continued his studies in pharmacy and related fields. Among his teachers were Fittig and F. Rose in chemistry, Flückiger in pharmacognosy, and Schmiedeberg in pharmacology. He was Flückiger's private assistant for a year.

Upon receiving the degree of Ph.D. at Strassburg in 1880, he returned to the United States to accept the professorship of analytical chemistry at the Philadelphia College of Pharmacy, where he stayed three years. During this period, in addition to teaching and investigating, he wrote in collaboration with Dr. Frederick Hoffmann *A Manual of Chemical Analysis* (1883). This same year, Dec. 27, he married Mary Van Loan Meigs, by whom he had two children. In 1883 he went to the University of Wisconsin, where he organized the school of pharmacy and became its dean and professor of pharmacy and materia medica. During the ten years he was at Wisconsin he published many articles on essential oils and alkaloids, and translations of two of Flückiger's works—*The Cinchona Barks* (1884) and *The Principles of Pharmacognosy* (1887). He also served as a member of the committee on the 1890 revision of the *United States Phar-*

macopeia and made valuable contributions to other revisions.

Resigning in 1892, he spent the next two years as the scientific director of the technical laboratories of Fritzsche Brothers, Passaic, N. J. During this connection he continued his publication of articles on essential oils, and in 1894 issued, through his employers, *Descriptive Catalogue of Essential Oils and Organic Chemical Preparations*. In 1896 he went to London, England, as director of the Wellcome Chemical Research Laboratories, which had been established by Henry S. Wellcome, his classmate at the Philadelphia College of Pharmacy. Here he stayed about eighteen years. It was a productive period almost without parallel in the fields of pharmaceutical and plant chemistry. Power made exhaustive investigations of the constituents of over fifty different plant products, thereby extending greatly knowledge of the distribution of various organic compounds in plants. His papers describing this work number about seventy-five. A conspicuous example of his studies in this field was his long investigation of the constituents of chaulmoogra seeds which led to the publication, with F. H. Gornall, of "The Constituents of Chaulmoogra Seeds," and "The Constitution of Chaulmoogric Acid," and, with Marmaduke Barrowcliff, of "The Constitution of Chaulmoogric and Hydnocarpic Acids," in *Journal of the Chemical Society: Transactions* (London, vol. LXXXV, pt. 1, 1904, vol. XCI, pt. 1, 1907). The fundamental significance of this investigation may be appreciated when it is realized that derivatives of chaulmoogra oil are used in the treatment of leprosy.

The World War disrupted his work in England and he returned to the United States to become in 1916 the head of the newly established phytochemical laboratory of the bureau of chemistry in the United States Department of Agriculture. Here he worked about eleven years and as co-author with V. K. Chestnut published some twelve papers on plant constituents. His work while in London was recognized by the awarding of numerous honors—prizes, medals, and honorary degrees. The medals included one from his life-long friend Wellcome (1921) and the Flückiger Gold Medal (1922). He was a member of many learned societies, including the National Academy of Sciences. Throughout his life he held firmly to his religious convictions.

[Memorial pamphlet by C. A. Browne, U. S. Department of Agriculture (privately printed, no date); *Jour. Am. Pharmaceutical Asso.*, Apr., May 1927; *Am. Jour. of Pharmacy*, Apr. 1927; *Pharmaceutical Era*, May 1927; *Pharmaceutical Jour. and Pharmacist* (London), Apr. 9, 1927; *Druggists Circular*, May 1927; bibliog. in *Collective Index to Vols. Fifty-one to Fifty-nine of the Proc. and to Vols. One to Fourteen of the Year Books of the Am. Pharmaceutical Asso.* (1930); Ivor Griffith, *A Half Century of Research in Plant Chemistry; a Chronological Record of the Scientific Contributions of Frederick Belding Power* (1924), reprinted from *Am. Jour. of Pharmacy*, Aug. 1924; *The First Century of the Phila. Coll. of Pharmacy, 1821–1921* (1922); *Who's Who in America, 1926–27*; *Evening Star* (Washington), Mar. 28, 1927.]   L. C. N.

POWER, FREDERICK DUNGLISON (Jan. 23, 1851–June 14, 1911), minister of the Disciples of Christ, son of Robert and Abigail M. (Jencks) Power, was born in Yorktown, Va. His father was a physician with an extensive practice in the surrounding country. Frederick received his early education at the old-field school, near his home, and graduated from Bethany College in 1871, remaining there for a short time as an instructor. While in college he supplied small churches on Sundays, frequently riding twenty miles on horseback over the mountains to his appointments. On Aug. 13, 1871, he was ordained at Mathews Court House, Va. Invited to take charge of a city church, he chose rather to minister for several years to three country churches in eastern Virginia at a salary of $500. In 1874 he was called to the Disciples church in Charlottesville, Va., and on Mar. 17 of that year married Emily Browne Alsop of Fredericksburg, Va. In September he went to Bethany College to become adjunct professor of ancient languages, and in 1875 he became pastor of the Vermont Avenue Christian Church, Washington, D. C., where he remained for the rest of his life.

During this period of more than thirty-five years he became one of the most prominent clergymen of the Capital and a leader in his own denomination. He was a man of scholarly tastes, a preacher of more than ordinary gifts, and a writer of ability. The work of the Disciples in the vicinity of Washington took on new life with his coming. His own church increased in size and influence, and some eight other churches were more or less its direct offshoots. He was also the founder of the Maryland, Delaware and District of Columbia Christian Missionary Society. President Garfield was his parishioner and intimate friend, and Power was the preacher of the former's funeral sermon. From 1881 to 1883 he was chaplain of the House of Representatives. Early in the history of the Christian Endeavor Society he became interested in this interdenominational organization and was one of its trustees at the time of his death. He was also a trustee of Bethany College and served as president of the General Christian Missionary Society. He was on the staff of the *Christian Evangelist*, St. Louis, and contributed to the literature of his denomination minor works on its doctrine and progress, including *Sketches of Our Pioneers* (1898). His most substantial book was his *Life of William Kimbrough Pendleton, LL.D.* (1902), which contains much information regarding the history of the Disciples and Bethany College, of which Pendleton [*q.v.*] was for many years president. In 1905 selections from Power's writings, entitled *Thoughts of Thirty Years,* was published with an introduction by Francis E. Clark [*q.v.*]. He died in Washington, survived by his wife and an adopted daughter.

[In addition to *Thoughts,* see *Who's Who in America,* 1910–11; J. T. Brown, *Churches of Christ* (1904); *Christian Evangelist* (St. Louis), June 22, 1911; *Evening Star* (Washington), June 14, 1911; *Washington Herald,* June 15, 1911.]　　　　　　H. E. S.

POWER, FREDERICK TYRONE (May 2, 1869–Dec. 30, 1931), actor, was born in London, England, the son of Harold Power and Ethel Laveneu, and grandson of Tyrone Power, the well-known Irish actor. When a boy he was sent to Florida to learn to grow citrus fruit, but at seventeen he slipped away and made a stage appearance in St. Augustine and then secured a small part in the company of Madame Janauschek, with whom he toured for two or three seasons. Through Ellen Terry he secured a letter to Augustin Daly and was then engaged by that famous manager, remaining in the Daly company for nearly a decade, and in 1894 making, with the company, his first appearance in London. On Sept. 12, 1899, in New York, he appeared as Lord Steyne in Mrs. Fiske's production of *Becky Sharp,* acting with "grizly eccentric force" (Winter, *post,* II, p. 285). The play was a huge success, and Power's playing attracted country-wide attention. A tour of Australia followed, and another London appearance, in support of Irving. In the autumn of 1902 he joined Mrs. Fiske once more, acting Judas in her production of *Mary of Magdala,* and once more winning much praise. In 1903, at the Garden Theatre, New York, he assumed the title rôle in Stephen Phillips' poetic drama, *Ulysses,* but the play was not successful. In 1905 he was engaged by Belasco to support Mrs. Leslie Carter in *Adrea,* a romantic tragedy, which opened at the Belasco Theatre, New York, on Jan. 11, 1905. His next performance to attract wide attention was that of the Drain Man in Charles Rann Kennedy's play, *The Servant in the House,* produced in New York on Mar. 23, 1908. Here his playing was notable for rugged strength and pathos, and he remained with the drama during its long and prosperous career. In 1912 William Faversham revived *Julius Cæsar,* and Power played Brutus to his Antony. By that time

Power had became identified with wnat are sometimes called "heroic" or "poetic" rôles, or we might better say with the romantic or rhetorical rather than the realistic drama. His training had been in these parts, and his methods were adapted to them. But the realistic drama was coming rapidly to dominate the stage, and as a result after the War Power's opportunities for conspicuous employment grew fewer, and he ceased to occupy a prominent place on the American stage. In 1927, however, he once more played Brutus, in the Players' Club revival of *Julius Cæsar,* and was cheered by friendly audiences in New York. Shortly after he went to Hollywood and was working into a new career in the "talking pictures" when he died in California on Dec. 30, 1931.

Power was a striking figure, with a large, powerful frame, a handsome face from which dark eyes shone, and what somebody once described as "nobility of bearing." He was, certainly, always acutely conscious that he was an actor upholding certain eminent traditions, and it gave to him, both on and off the stage, an old-school dignity. He was jealous of this dignity, too, and his temper was quickly roused by any slight to his profession. His voice was as powerful as his frame and was one of his effective weapons. In fact, it was too sonorous an organ for the naturalistic drama. He excelled in serious, not comic, rôles. The "gaunt grim strength" of his Lord Steyne, in *Becky Sharp,* the terrific remorse of his Judas in *Mary of Magdala,* and the rough pathos of his Drain Man in *The Servant in the House* were remembered by all who witnessed them. He was a picturesque and effective force in the older theatre, whose method and personality could not be toned down to the humdrum level of naturalistic drama. He was several times married and was survived by a divorced wife, Mrs. Patia Power.

[Wm. Winter, *The Wallet of Time* (2 vols., 1913); John Parker, *Who's Who in the Theatre* (1925); *N. Y. Times, N. Y. Herald Tribune,* Dec. 31, 1931.]
　　　　　　　　　　　　　　　　　　W. P. E.

POWER, JOHN (June 19, 1792–Apr. 14, 1849), Roman Catholic priest, was born in Roscarberry, County Cork, Ireland, and received his classical training in Cork. Subsequently, he pursued the courses in philosophy and theology at Maynooth, where he was associated with two future Irish leaders, Theobald Mathew and John McHale of Tuam. After his ordination, Father Power taught at the diocesan seminary at Cork and served as a curate at Youghal. In 1819 he came to New York as pastor of St. Peter's Church on the invitation of the trustees—with whom he managed to keep on friendly terms, for he was not only an eloquent preacher of imposing appearance but a clever politician and a man of liberal tendencies. He soon became the idol of the Irish element, and was invariably called upon as its spokesman. As preacher on such occasions as ordinations and the laying of cornerstones for churches within a considerable range of New York, his name appeared continually in the Catholic press. He was extremely active as Bishop Connolly's vicar general and as administrator on the bishop's death in 1825. Intimate friends like Bishop John England [q.v.] sought his appointment to the see of New York; but Rome named John Dubois [q.v.].

Power loyally supported Dubois, whom he represented at the First Provincial Council of Baltimore (1829) and whom he served as vicar general along with Felix Varela [q.v.]. In 1825, he was instrumental in establishing the Truth Teller under William Denman and George Pardow, though the former believed that Power was too active in furthering the circulation of England's United States Catholic Miscellany. As a consulting theologian, he attended the Second Provincial Council of Baltimore (1833), where he was recognized as the translator of part of the Bible de Royaumont, the editor of a pioneer Laity's Directory (1822), the compiler of the New Testament by Way of Question and Answer (1824) and of a manual of prayers, True Piety (1832), and as an opponent of Parson William Craig Brownlee [q.v.] of The Protestant in a heated religious controversy. He founded an orphan asylum, aiding the Sisters of Charity in New York, constructed the new St. Peter's Church, purchased a Presbyterian edifice for the parish of St. Mary's, and preached along the canals of New York and Connecticut to Irish laborers, in whose problems he interested himself. With his brother, William Power, M.D., he was a promoter of the Irish Emigrant Society and a friend of every movement in America or Ireland for the social or political advancement of the Irish cause, which was championed in the British Parliament by his brother Maurice Power.

Again, in 1837, when Dubois required a coadjutor, Power's friends sent his name to Rome. Bishop Purcell [q.v.] believed that his merits were not "sufficiently appreciated," and England with usual exaggeration feared a schism if Power were not named. Nevertheless, despite the rather general desire of the priests and people to see him elevated, Bishop Kenrick and Bishop Dubois obtained the appointment of their candidate, Father John Hughes [q.v.] of Philadelphia.

Once more Power fell in line and aided in silencing considerable dissatisfaction. Hughes appreciated his strength and ability, and named him vicar general in 1839. Bishop McCloskey in gratitude selected him as preacher at his consecration, declaring: "From my boyhood upward, Dr. Power was ever to me a kind and affectionate father, and in my mature years a trusted counsellor and friend" (John Farley, The Life of John Cardinal McCloskey, 1918, p. 16). Despite all his notable services, however, he was allowed to complete his days as pastor of St. Peter's Church.

[Archbishop Corrigan, in U. S. Cath. Hist. Soc., Records and Studies, Oct. 1900; J. T. Smith, The Cath. Church in N. Y. (2 vols., 1905); J. G. Shea, Hist. of the Cath. Church in the U. S., vol. III (1890); A. J. Thébaud, Forty Years in the U. S. A. (1904); Peter Guilday, The Life and Times of John England (2 vols., 1927); Jeremiah O'Callaghan, Usury (ed. of 1834); J. R. G. Hassard, Life of the Most Reverend John Hughes, D.D. (1866); The Metropolitan Cath. Almanac and Laity's Directory for . . . 1850 (1849); Sun (N. Y.), Apr. 16, 1849; N. Y. Freeman's Jour. and Cath. Reg., Apr. 21, 1849.]   R. J. P.

POWER, TYRONE [See Power, Frederick Tyrone, 1869–1931].

POWERS, DANIEL WILLIAM (June 14, 1818–Dec. 11, 1897), banker, was born near Batavia, N. Y., the son of Asahel and Elizabeth (Powell) Powers, who had emigrated in 1812 from Vermont to Genesee County, N. Y. After his father's death about 1821 he was given a home and an opportunity to attend school by Webster Powers, an uncle. Later he went to Rochester, where he became a clerk in a hardware store, of which he in time became the directing head. He remained in the hardware trade until Mar. 1, 1850, when he started in business for himself as a banker and broker. To this vocation he devoted himself until the time of his death.

He met with great success in his new undertaking and in time came to be known as a leading financier of western New York. His private bank was deemed safer than many state-chartered financial institutions, and its deposits were correspondingly large. It weathered the panic of 1857 successfully, and, when in 1866 a run on the bank seemed imminent, he raised a million dollars in currency within twenty-four hours. In 1890 his bank was incorporated with a capital of $100,000 and was subsequently merged with another institution. During the Civil War he supported the financial policies of the federal government. He fought and won a suit in the state courts to establish the legality of payment for debt in treasury notes made legal tender by the act of Congress on Feb. 25, 1862 (Paul A. Hague agt. *Daniel W. Powers, 25 Howard's Practice Reports,* 17–58). He bought heavily of the United States bonds, whenever they were depressed. When these obligations of the federal government rose later to a premium he found himself in possession of a handsome fortune. This enabled him to complete in 1870, on the site of the first dwelling house erected within the city limits of Rochester, one of the earliest large fireproof office buildings constructed west of New York City. Equipped with five elevators this structure of iron and stone was originally seven stories in height but was later surmounted by a tower two stories high, in which the federal signal-service station was housed. Still standing today (1934) it contains three hundred rooms including stores, halls for public entertainments, studios, and offices for business and professional men. For his lawyer tenants he acquired Roscoe Conkling's law library of 6,000 volumes. The building proved a good advertisement for Rochester and doubly so on account of the art gallery, which he started and made its chief feature in 1875, and which drew thousands of visitors annually. In the course of several trips to Europe he acquired one of the most extensive and valuable art collections owned at that time by a single individual in the United States. It made his name known throughout the country and, before its dispersal after his death, contained over a thousand art objects, including statuary, oil paintings, and water colors. In it were fine copies of the old masters and original paintings of some of the best-known modern artists (C. C. Merriman, *A Catalogue of the Paintings in the Art Gallery of D. W. Powers,* 1880). In 1883 he erected a fireproof hotel named for himself, which is still one of Rochester's leading hostelries.

In civic affairs he helped establish the Rochester park system, represented the city's interest in the Genesee Valley Railway directorate, served twice as alderman, and was on the committee that supervised the construction of the city hall and directed the elevation of the New York Central tracks. He gave freely and unostentatiously to charities, was president of the board of trustees of the city hospital and of the home for the friendless, and was trustee of the industrial school and the house of refuge. He was twice married. His first wife was Lucinda Young, who died in early womanhood leaving a son who did not live long. In 1856 he married Helen M. Craig, by whom he had three sons and two daughters.

[Information from his grand-daughter, Mrs. Robert L. Paddock; W. F. Peck, *Hist. of Rochester and Monroe County* (1908), vol. I; John Devoy, *Rochester and the Post Express* (1895); J. N. Larned, *A Hist of Buffalo* with a sketch of . . . Rochester by C. E. Fitch, (1911), vol. II; *Sun* (N. Y.), and *N. Y. Times,* Dec. 12, 1897.]   H. G. V.

POWERS, HIRAM (July 29, 1805–June 27, 1873), sculptor, was descended from Walter Powers who settled near Concord, Mass., about 1661. Eighth of the nine children of Stephen and Sarah (Perry) Powers, he was born on a hillside farm near Woodstock, Vt. The natural beauty of his native region he never forgot. His father was poor and is said to have become still poorer through making himself surety for a friend. The family moved westward, first to New York, then to Ohio, where the father died of malaria. Hiram of necessity did whatever work he could. He was library attendant, tavern boy, bill collector. In Cincinnati, at the age of seventeen, he found regular employment in a clock and organ factory. Here he remained some six years, developing an extraordinary ingenuity. From 1829 to 1834 he was engaged in the waxworks department of Dorfeuille's Western Museum, Cincinnati. In 1832 he married Elizabeth Gibson of that city. She assisted him in devising the ingenious clockwork mechanisms by which the "Satan" and other monsters were set in motion in the "Chamber of Horrors," which under his vivifying touch became the most profitable feature of the museum. Aside from these grotesque creations, there were wax figures of celebrities to mend and to make. In this work Powers discovered that he had the gift, even more prized then than now, of "seizing the likeness," and to his delight, he began to receive orders for portrait busts. Always skilful with tools, he learned how to take casts from the human face, a process which he later forswore. For a short time in Cincinnati, the young sculptors Henry Kirke Brown and Shobal Vail Clevenger [*qq.v.*] worked together with Powers, all aiding each other, and receiving some instruction from Eckstein, a German modeler.

Late in 1834, with an eye to better opportunities, Powers moved to Washington, D. C., where for two years he found employment in portraiture. He made busts from life of Chief Justice Marshall, Andrew Jackson, John C. Calhoun, Daniel Webster, and others. Powers was always an able talker, and thereby won the alert attention of men who would otherwise have proved but laggard sitters and indifferent patrons of his art. He next turned eager eyes toward Italy, the promised land for sculptors of the time. Aided by Nicholas Longworth [*q.v.*] and the Prestons, W. C. and John S. [*qq.v.*], of South Carolina, with loans gratefully accepted and afterward conscientiously repaid, he packed up numerous plaster busts for reproduction in marble, and sailed on a thirty days' voyage to Europe, accompanied by his wife, by a babe in arms, and a child of four. A case of smallpox broke out in the next cabin, Mrs. Powers contracted the disease, and the family were obliged to stay in Paris during her convalescence, but Powers thus found opportunity to study the art treasures of that city. In the autumn of 1837, they reached Florence. There Powers was to spend the rest of his life, at first not without adversity and poverty, but afterward with increasing fame, fortune, and influence. There other children were born. Two sons were named Longworth and Preston, for their father's benefactors. The sculptor Horatio Greenough [q.v.], six weeks younger than Powers, had reached Italy twelve years earlier, and on his *confrère's* arrival, showed him great kindness.

While working on the marble busts which gave him ready money for his family's needs, Powers set up in clay a life-size figure called "Eve Before the Fall," later carved in marble, and highly praised by Thorwaldsen. This was a precursor of the "Greek Slave," a nude female figure, finished in marble in 1843, and thereafter reproduced in at least six marble copies, one of which is now owned by the Corcoran Gallery, Washington. This was without doubt the most celebrated single statue of the day. Its fame gathered a momentum checked only by the coming of the French neo-Renaissance in sculpture. The hour of its appearance was propitious. Its subject, a beautiful Greek captured by the Turks, had a strong appeal to a generation to whom the Greek struggle for independence was still a vivid memory. Mrs. Browning wrote a sonnet (not a very good sonnet) concluding with a widely quoted apostrophe to the "fair stone," calling upon her to

> "strike and shame the strong,
> By thunders of white silence overthrown."

The critic Tuckerman also expressed his emotion in verse. The eloquent prose of Edward Everett and of Nathaniel Hawthorne took up the tale. At the Crystal Palace, London, 1851, the "Greek Slave" was the cynosure of all eyes. In the United States interest in it was enhanced by discussions of its morality; in Cincinnati the matter was solemnly referred to a committee of clergymen who after due consideration gave the statue their approval. The original was sold in England for a sum variously reported as $4,000, $6,000, and $7,000. Other ideal feminine figures in marble were "Eve Before the Fall" (a second version), 1850; "America," partly draped in classic fashion, modeled in 1854, and destroyed

by fire in a Brooklyn warehouse; "Il Penseroso," 1856, fully costumed according to the specifications furnished by Milton in the lines beginning "Come, pensive Nun," and ending "Forget thyself to marble"; "California," 1858, a nude which modern criticism considers superior to the "Greek Slave"; "Eve Disconsolate," 1871; and "The Last of the Tribe," an Indian maiden, 1872. A lone little masculine figure of 1846 is the "Fisher Boy," a slender lad, standing, a shell held to his ear. Powers used models freely—to refer to, so he said, rather than to copy.

In 1853, Capt. Montgomery C. Meigs [q.v.], then superintendent of construction at the United States Capitol, wrote: "The immense popularity of the Greek Slave is probably due to its meaning being within the comprehension of all. Its eminent beauty alone would not have gained it such success" (Fairman, *post*, p. 143). The same year, in answer to inquiries as to the American sculptors best fitted to produce works for the adornment of the Capitol, Edward Everett wrote to Captain Meigs recommending Thomas Crawford [q.v.] and Powers, and adding, "I consider Mr. Powers in some respects the first living artist" (*Ibid.*, p. 144). Powers, however, promptly declined to submit designs in competition for the important decoration of the Senate pediment, which was later assigned to Crawford. His refusal was written with dignity not untinged with resentment; he felt that the creator of the "Greek Slave" should be given a free hand. He had strong partisans in Congress, and his name was often brought forward in resolutions "to embellish the Capitol." Nevertheless, the building has but three works from his hand. One is the bust of John Marshall mentioned above. The others are statues of Franklin and of Jefferson, placed in 1863, the former in a corridor of the Senate, the latter in the House wing. Carefully costumed, these works seem feeble and characterless; even the heads are less good than those of most of his portrait busts.

His famous statue of Webster, erected in 1859 on the terrace in front of the Boston State House, did not escape condemnation from some of the colder critics; James Jackson Jarves, in *The Art Idea* (1864), was especially caustic. "The face," wrote Hawthorne in 1858 (*op. cit.*, p. 428), "is very grand, very Webster." That year, Hawthorne found Powers at work on his statue of George Washington as a Freemason. The statue of Edward Everett came in 1870. Powers made about one hundred and fifty portrait busts. Nearly all were men, and issued in marble from the studio in Florence. These are now considered his strongest works. There is mention also of a bust of the Grand Duchess of Tuscany, a work so pleasing to the lady's husband that he accorded to the sculptor many privileges in the matter of museum research. His ideal busts of various heroines of song and story—Ginevra, Proserpine, Psyche, Diana, Clytie, Faith, Hope, and Charity—differ more in name than in nature. Smooth and on the whole insipid, they lack the individuality seen in his portraits of men.

At the height of his success, he built himself a fine house in the newer, more healthful part of Florence, and his home, with its gardens, workrooms, and household apartments, became a center of hospitality and artistic activity. Thither came famous personages from America, England, and Italy—Longfellow, Bryant, Browning, Dickens, Dom Pedro, and an occasional prince or duke. Powers' striking personality won men's attention, his honest strength of character, their esteem. He was honorable, diligent, genial; respected by his large corps of workmen; especially tender toward children and animals; and frankly happy in being the center of a circle. Believing in his own merit and accepting his fame with boyish delight, he kept always a great zest in life. He was tall, well-made, bearded, with strongly modeled features and large, observant eyes. Both Hawthorne and Edward Everett were fascinated by him. The sculptor Thomas Ball [q.v.] was his dear friend.

As oracle and autocrat of sculpture in Florence, he was dogmatic and opinionated. He could change another's mind more easily than his own. His comments on the work of other artists were often scathing beyond necessity. There was naïveté in his makeup: he prided himself on his patriotism, yet never recrossed the Atlantic; he professed supreme devotion to art, yet never made groups because these were less remunerative than single pieces. His religion was Swedenborgian. At one time, he had felt an interest in spiritualism, but he gave up allowing séances in his home, because he concluded that their influence was morbid. He was in full possession of his artistic endowments when "a violent fall brought upon him infirmity and death." His grave is in the Protestant Cemetery in Florence.

With the exception of his friend the English artist Fuller, his sons Longworth and Preston were his only pupils. Preston Powers, in whose home Daniel Chester French resided during his studies in Florence, was born in 1843 and lived chiefly in Florence. At times during his varied life, he practised his art in the United States, his chief public works being the "Closing Era," a group on the grounds of the Capitol in Denver,

Colo., and the statue of Jacob Collamer of Vermont in the national Capitol, Washington, D. C.

Though the art of Hiram Powers has long been outmoded, no thoughtful person can consider it valueless. Many of his portrait busts of virile characters are admirable evocations, worthy of close study. At present, the "Greek Slave" is viewed not as a masterpiece, but as a milestone. It is historically important in the artistic development of the United States because, far more than any other work of its time, it spurred the public to think about and to discuss, however lamely, a piece of sculpture by an American.

[Nathaniel Hawthorne, Passages from the French and Italian Note-Books (Complete Works, Riverside Ed., vol. X, 1888); H. T. Tuckerman, Book of the Artists (1867); Wm. J. Clark, Jr., Great Am. Sculptures (1878); Lorado Taft, The Hist. of Am. Sculpture (1903); C. E. Fairman, Art and Artists of the Capitol (1927); Edward Everett, in Littell's Living Age, Oct. 16, 1847; S. Y. Atlee, Ibid., Sept. 16, 1854; Samuel Osgood, in Harper's Mag., Aug. 1870; Henry Boynton, in New Eng. Mag., July 1899; E. L. Powers, "Recollections of my Father," Vermonter, Feb., Mar. 1907; J. J. Jarves, The Art Idea (1864); "Letters of Hiram Powers to Nicholas Longworth," Hist. and Phil. Soc. of Ohio, Quart. Pub., Apr.-June 1906; A. H. Powers, The Powers Family (1884); N. Y. Tribune, June 28, 1873; manuscript letter from Longworth Powers (N. Y. Pub. Lib.), giving a fairly complete list of works and dates.]
                                                    A—e. A.

POWHATAN (d. 1618), Indian chief, whose personal name was Wa-hun-sen-a-cawh or Wa-hun-son-a-cock, was the chief or "emperor" of the Powhatan federation which at the beginning of the seventeenth century extended over tidewater Virginia. His father was of a southern tribe, said to have been driven north by the Spaniards, possibly from Florida or even from the West Indies (Hamor, post, p. 13). Upon his arrival in Virginia, he conquered five of the local tribes, while his son, known to the settlers of Jamestown as Powhatan, extended his sway over many more. At the time of the Jamestown settlement (1607), according to Capt. John Smith [q.v.], Powhatan was "of personage a tall, well proportioned man, with a sower looke; his head somewhat gray, his beard so thinne that it seemeth none at al. His age neare 60, of a very able and hardy body" (Smith, Map of Virginia, 1612, Arber and Bradley, post, I, 80). He ruled with an iron hand, being excessively cruel to prisoners and malefactors. In 1609 he was crowned more or less formally under orders from Christopher Newport [q.v.]. According to Smith, Powhatan seemed more appreciative of the gifts he received than of the honor of the ceremony ("he neither knowing the majesty nor meaning of a Crowne") and was with difficulty persuaded to stoop sufficiently for the crown to be set upon his head (Generall Historie, Arber and Bradley, post, II, 437). Despite frequent protestations of good will, he annoyed the English by ambushing small parties, murdering workers in the field, and refusing to sell them corn when their provisions fell low, but with the marriage of his daughter Pocahontas [*q.v.*] to John Rolfe, he concluded a peace to which he steadily adhered thereafter. Powhatan died in April 1618, and was succeeded by his brother, Itopatin or Opitchapam.

[Capt. John Smith, *Map of Virginia* (1612), and *Generall Historie of Virginia* (1624), best available in *Travels and Works of Capt. John Smith* (2 vols., 1910), ed. by Edward Arber and A. G. Bradley; Ralph Hamor, *A True Discourse of the Present Estate of Virginia* (1615; facsimile reprint, 1860); William Strachey, *The Historie of Travaile into Virginia Britannia* (Hakluyt Society, 1849); Samuel Purchas, *Hakluytus Posthumus, or Purchas His Pilgrimes,* vol. XIX (Glasgow, 1906); Alexander Brown, *The Genesis of the U. S.* (2 vols., 1890); C. W. Sams, *The Conquest of Virginia: The Forest Primeval* (1916).]   T. J. W.

POWNALL, THOMAS (1722–Feb. 25, 1805), colonial governor, deserves more than any other Englishman of his time to be called a student of colonial administration. He was the second son of William Pownall of Saltfleetby, Lincolnshire, descendant of an old Cheshire family, and his wife Sarah, whose father John Burniston was deputy governor of Bombay. Educated at Lincoln and at Trinity College, Cambridge, Thomas received the bachelor's degree in 1743 and soon afterward entered the office of the Board of Trade, of which his brother John was secretary. In 1753 the president of the board, Lord Halifax, secured for his own brother-in-law, Sir Danvers Osborn, the governorship of New York and sent Pownall along as the governor's secretary. They reached the colony in October 1753, but Osborn, melancholy over the recent death of his wife, committed suicide two days after taking office. Had Pownall been less ambitious and independent his American career might have ended then and there. But instead of turning back at once he seized the opportunity to become a sort of free-lance observer for Halifax and the Board of Trade. He came into intimate contact with such men as William Shirley, James De Lancey (1703–1760), and Sir William Johnson [*qq.v.*], and formed with Benjamin Franklin what was to prove a lifelong friendship. At the Albany Congress in June and July 1754, Pownall, though not a delegate, presented a memorandum pointing out the importance of British control of the Great Lakes (*Administration,* 1774, II, 234–44). He assisted Shirley in the following spring in gaining the cooperation of New York and Pennsylvania for the coming campaign, and in April 1755 he attended General Braddock's council of governors at Alexandria, Va. The governor of New Jersey, Jonathan Belcher [*q.v.*],

was aged and infirm and in May 1755 Pownall was appointed lieutenant-governor. But as long as the Governor lived Pownall's office was purely nominal and he was free to move about studying closely the problems of defense and administration in which he was most interested.

His observations bore fruit, when he returned to England early in 1756, in a scheme of operations presented to the Duke of Cumberland, captain-general of the army. In this paper Pownall stressed the need of a unified command and a common plan of campaign for all the colonies; he laid emphasis upon control of the inland waterways of America and urged that an immediate beginning be made by securing command of Lake Ontario (*Administration,* 1774, II, 174–233). Shortly after reaching England, Pownall was offered the governorship of Pennsylvania, but decided instead to accompany to America the new commander-in-chief, Lord Loudoun [*q.v.*], as secretary extraordinary. This time Pownall remained in the colonies for a few months only, returning to England in October 1756 to present Loudoun's case against Shirley. He arrived just as the Newcastle ministry was falling and William Pitt was assuming control. The situation was ideal for the furthering of Pownall's career: young, ambitious, full of ideas and of first-hand information about America, he was easily able to bring himself to the favorable attention of the energetic Pitt. He strongly advocated the familiar plan for a two-fold attack upon Quebec—by water up the St. Lawrence and by land from New York—the plan which ultimately proved successful. Apparently Pownall made a striking impression, for Pitt soon appointed him to the important office of governor of Massachusetts in succession to Shirley. It is not necessary to assume, as Shirley's supporters believed, that Pownall, De Lancey, and Johnson had plotted Shirley's downfall. Doubtless Pownall wanted the office and had strong backing, but Shirley, in disfavor with the military and civilian officials in England, had already been recalled. Pownall's appointment was primarily a recognition of the young man's zeal, knowledge, and attainments.

Pownall reached Boston Aug. 3, 1757, and had hardly assumed office when he received an urgent message from General Webb on the Hudson begging for reënforcements at Fort William Henry, which was threatened by Montcalm. He acted promptly and vigorously. Consulting only the Council and without calling the Assembly which alone could legally send the militia out of the province, he dispatched troops to Webb's assistance. But it was too late; the fort had already fallen. At the end of the month Governor Belcher died. Pownall, still lieutenant-governor of New Jersey, hurried to that province, put the administration in the senior councilor's hands, and rushed back to Boston where he was more urgently needed. The rest of his three years in office was largely devoted to problems raised by the war. In his efforts to get the maximum of participation from the province he cultivated the popular "anti-prerogative" party, thereby alienating the friends of Shirley and gaining the distrust of such stanch supporters of the Crown as Thomas Hutchinson. He stoutly upheld the constitutional authority of the civil government against the war-powers claimed by the military, an attitude which led to a quarrel with his good friend Loudoun over the quartering of troops (Pargellis, *post*, pp. 268–78). Like many other governors, Pownall wanted a military command of his own and frequently though vainly offered his services to the Commander-in-Chief. His only military exploit was the leading of an expedition to build a fort on the Penobscot in May 1759, the desirability of which he had often pointed out (*Collections of the Maine Historical Society*, V, 1857, pp. 363–87; Sawtelle, *post*, pp. 255–81). Pownall was an able governor—too able and too independent from the point of view of a military commander like Loudoun, who sought unified leadership of all the governors in prosecuting the war and who called Pownall "the greatest Man I have yet met, and from whom I foresee more trouble to whoever commands in this Country than from all the People on the Continent" (Pargellis, *post*, p. 270). The Board of Trade believed, quite correctly, that in gaining popular support for the war the Governor was conceding to the House of Representatives powers legally belonging to the executive. The conservatives disliked him. Not only did he ignore them politically but he offended them socially by his carelessness of dress and ceremony and by his gaiety of manner. Yet he kept his popularity with most of the assemblymen and years later was described by John Adams as "the most constitutional and national Governor, in my opinion, who ever represented the crown in this province" (C. F. Adams, ed., *Works of John Adams*, X, 1856, p. 243). By the end of 1759 the Board of Trade felt that he had outlived his usefulness in Massachusetts. They wrote in November announcing his transfer to the more profitable though less important governorship of South Carolina, with leave to visit England first. At his embarkation in the following June both houses of the General Court escorted him to his barge.

On reaching England he was offered the lucrative governorship of Jamaica but declined the post, it was currently reported, because of a courtship which ultimately failed of success. He also resigned the South Carolina governorship without assuming office, and although he often expressed in later life a desire to visit America and kept in correspondence with many colonial friends, he never crossed the Atlantic again. His hopes of military service met with partial fulfilment, however, in his appointment as first commissary-general to the British-Hanoverian army operating on the Rhine. Pownall held this post with its accompanying rank of colonel from the summer of 1761 to the end of the war. Though charged with misconduct of his office, he was easily cleared and his accuser dismissed from service.

The year after the peace Pownall published the work which constitutes his chief claim to lasting remembrance, *The Administration of the Colonies*, which first appeared anonymously in 1764 and was republished over Pownall's name in five subsequent editions (1765, 1766, 1768, 1774, 1777), each considerably revised and enlarged in the light of recent developments in the colonial situation. Based upon the author's long experience with colonial affairs in England and America, the work is essentially a discussion of the reorganization in administration, in law, and in the status of the colonies that was necessary to form permanently "all those Atlantic and American possessions into one Empire of which Great Britain should be the commercial and political center" (*Administration*, 1774, II, 10). He argued for a centralization of British colonial administration and for a more precise definition of the powers of the various branches of government at home and in the colonies; he discussed the problems of revenue and taxation, currency, Indian affairs, and commerce—all matters which needed careful handling at the time. While he had no pronounced constitutional objections to parliamentary taxation, he believed that the colonies should first be allowed to send representatives to the House of Commons, thus making Parliament truly imperial. In retrospect it is possible to detect many errors of judgment in the analysis, but the work as a whole places Pownall ahead of almost all his contemporaries in his understanding of the colonial attitude, of the constitutional issues at stake, and of the adjustments necessary if Great Britain were to retain the loyalty of her maturing colonies. It is too much to say that the acceptance of Pownall's advice would in itself have averted the American Revolution; but the adoption of his policies might have led men of good will on both sides of the ocean to seek a less violent settlement of the approaching crisis—a settlement which might even have anticipated by three-quarters of a century the recommendations of Lord Durham and the accomplishments of Lord Elgin.

In August 1765 he married Harriet, natural daughter of Gen. Charles Churchill. She was the widow of Sir Everard Fawkener, former ambassador at Constantinople and secretary to the Duke of Cumberland, and even after her marriage to Pownall she continued to be known as Lady Fawkener. She died in 1777. Pownall entered the House of Commons in 1767, and sat as a member for Tregony until defeated for reelection in 1774. Although independent of party affiliation, he fought strenuously against the ministerial policies of colonial taxation and coercion. A poor speaker, he always revised his speeches for publication. In 1774, tired perhaps of his hopeless opposition and sanguine of good results from Lord North's plan of conciliation, he came to terms with the Prime Minister and accepted a seat at the latter's disposal as member for Minehead. Pownall had no sympathy with the colonists' final methods of resistance and supported the prosecution of the war during its first years. But by 1777 he was convinced that independence was inevitable and sought to end hostilities on the basis of alliance with America before the French should intervene. On May 24, 1780, he introduced a bill to enable the king to negotiate peace with America but was defeated 113 to 50. After the dissolution in the following summer Pownall avoided reëlection and withdrew to private life.

On Aug. 2, 1784, he married Hannah (Kennett), widow of Richard Astell, and he passed his remaining years in writing and reflection at her country place in Bedfordshire or at his own London residence. Even in his more strenuous period his interests were varied. The complete list of his writings includes books and pamphlets not only upon political and constitutional problems, but also upon international relations, economics, philosophy, topography, and archeology. His chief biographer, almost alone among investigators of the subject, has also claimed for him authorship of the *Letters of Junius*. He was a fellow of the Royal Society and of the Society of Antiquaries and had some ability at sketching. Personally, he was a man of middle height inclined to stoutness. Extremely vain and ambitious as he was, his failure to gain higher office or the wider acceptance of his views was a source of bitter disappointment. He had no chil-

dren. He died at Bath, survived only by his second wife and two nephews, and was buried in Walcot Church.

[The only full-length biography is C. A. W. Pownall, *Thomas Pownall, M.P., F.R.S., Governor of Massachusetts Bay Author of the Letters of Junius* (1908), which is detailed but uncritical and too laudatory. Shorter accounts are in *Dictionary of Nat. Biography* (1896), and by W. O. Sawtelle in *Mass. Hist. Soc. Proceedings*, LXIII (1931), pp. 233–84. The first two of these three contain lists of Pownall's writings. The Junius claim was first advanced in Frederick Griffin, *Junius Discovered* (1854) and was developed by C. A. W. Pownall, *supra*. Pownall's relations with Loudoun are covered in S. M. Pargellis, *Lord Loudoun in North America* (1933). A hostile contemporary account of his early American career is the anonymous *Review of the Military Operations in North-America, from the commencement of the French Hostilities on the Frontiers of Virginia in 1753, to the Surrender of Oswego, on the 14th of August, 1756; in a Letter to a Nobleman* (1757) reprinted in *Mass. Hist. Soc. Coll.*, 1 ser., VII (1801), 67–163. Thomas Hutchinson's account of his governorship in *The Hist. of the Province of Mass. Bay*, III (1828) is more fair. Pownall's parliamentary speeches, listed in C. A. W. Pownall, are given in T. C. Hansard, *The Parliamentary Hist. of England*, XVI-XXI (1813–14); and J. Almon, *The Parliamentary Register*, I–XVII (1775–81). Manuscript correspondence and papers are in Colonial Office Papers, Public Record Office; King's MSS. 202, British Museum; and Loudoun Papers, Huntington Lib., San Marino, Cal. Many letters are in print, especially in G. S. Kimball, ed., *Correspondence of William Pitt . . . with Colonial Governors and Military and Naval Commissioners in America* (2 vols., 1906); Jared Sparks, ed., *The Works of Benjamin Franklin* (10 vols., 1836–40); and *The Papers of Sir William Johnson*, vols. I–VIII (1921–33). There are good obituaries in *Gentleman's Mag.*, Mar. 1805, pp. 288–89; Apr. 1805, pp. 380–82.]

L. W. L.

POYDRAS, JULIEN DE LALANDE (Apr. 3, 1746–June 23, 1824), poet, public servant, philanthropist, the son of François Poydras and his wife, Magdeleine Simon, was born in the parish of Rezé, a mile south of Nantes, Brittany. While serving in the French navy, he was captured by the British in 1760, but managed to escape to Santo Domingo. He reached New Orleans about 1768. A year or so later he became a pedler, and, pack on back, traveled widely over the lower Mississippi Valley. He was soon able to buy a plantation in Pointe Coupée Parish, La. This proved to be an excellent location for a trading post, and he rapidly extended his interests, building a store at False River, and later erecting a cotton gin. His trading interests extended even to Texas. In 1779 the English fort at Baton Rouge was captured by Louisiana forces commanded by Galvez. Poydras celebrated this event in *La Prise du Morne du Baton Rouge* (1779), the earliest attempt at epic poetry in Louisiana literature. The poem (reprinted by Alcée Fortier in *Comptes-Rendus de l'Athénée Louisianais*, January 1892) shows indebtedness to the classics and to Boileau. Two recently discovered four-page leaflets, *Épitre à*

Don Bernard de Galvez (1777) and *Le Dieu et les Nayades du Fleuve St. Louis* (1777) have also, on the basis of internal evidence, been attributed to Poydras (Tinker, 1933, *post*). These poems are "dull and grandiloquent" pieces of flattery, with a "hard-worked pony ballet of nymphs" (*Ibid.*).

It is said that Poydras had intended to return to France, but was prevented by the French Revolution. After the Revolution he decided to remain in Louisiana. His reputation for shrewd and honest dealing grew, he continued to prosper, and became widely known for his philanthropy, his piety, and morality. He visited New Orleans two or three times a year, traveling in a lavishly equipped boat with six oarsmen. He kept open house at his plantation, and is said to have entertained Louis Philippe and the Duke of Orleans in 1798. After the Louisiana Purchase, he became a close friend of Governor Claiborne, and entered upon a career of public service. He became civil commandant at Pointe Coupée in January 1804, was president of the first Legislative Council of the territory of Orleans later in the year, and delegate to the Eleventh Congress, 1809–11. He was president of the constitutional convention of Louisiana in 1812, and a presidential elector in this same year. In 1812–13, and again in 1820–21, he was president of the state Senate. During the argument of the famous "batture case" Poydras published five pamphlets supporting the right of the public to the batture. The first of these, *Adresse au Conseil Législatif du Territoire d'Orléans* (1808), was published in New Orleans, and the other four, in Washington.

Poydras is described as tall, well built, with regular and pleasing features, somewhat inclined to melancholy. There are three portraits of him in the Poydras Asylum and a bronze bust is in the Cabildo, New Orleans. He died at his home in Pointe Coupée Parish and, though a Protestant, was buried in the cemetery of St. Francis Church, in that parish, but was reinterred in the grounds of Poydras High School at New Roads when the crumbling of the river bank threatened his first burial place. At the time of his death he owned six large plantations, considerable real estate in New Orleans, and more than five hundred slaves. He had never married, and his closest relative was a nephew. By his will, dated Apr. 16, 1822, he made careful provision for the freeing of all his slaves, to be accomplished within twenty-five years after his death, and for pensions for all his slaves over sixty years old, but according to Fortier (*post*) the plan to free his slaves was not carried out.

He also left large sums to Charity Hospital and the Poydras Female Orphan Asylum, New Orleans; $30,000 to Pointe Coupée Parish for the founding of an academy or college; and $30,000 each to the parishes of Pointe Coupée and West Baton Rouge, the income from which was to be used to provide dowries for the poor girls of those parishes. In Pointe Coupée this bequest has been diverted into a school fund, but in West Baton Rouge eleven young women shared the annual income for 1930.

[Alcée Fortier, *Louisiana Studies* (1894); *Le Courrier* (New Orleans), June 30, 1824; *La. Gazette* (New Orleans), June 30, 1824; *Times Picayune* (New Orleans), Feb. 15, 1931; E. L. Tinker, *Les Écrits de Langue Française en Louisiane au XIXe Siècle* (1932); and *Louisana's Earliest Poet: Julien Poydras and the Paeans to Galvez* (1933), repr. from *Bull. N. Y. Pub. Lib.*, Oct. 1933; *N. Y. Times Book Review*, Jan. 14, 1934; *Official Letter Books of W. C. C. Claiborne* (6 vols., 1917); Poydras' will, a copy of which is in the Howard Memorial Library, New Orleans; copy of certificate of his baptism, furnished by the archivist of the Dept. de Loire Intérieure, Nantes.]   R. P. M.

POZNANSKI, GUSTAVUS (1804–Jan. 7, 1879), Jewish religious leader and reformer, was born at Storchnest, Poland, the son of Joseph and Sarah Poznanski. He received his early education in Hamburg, at that time the center of the Jewish reform movement in Europe. He came to America in 1831 and for five years occupied a minor position in the Shearith Israel Congregation of New York City. In 1836 he was elected minister of the Congregation Beth Elohim of Charleston, S. C., then the wealthiest and most cultured Jewish community in America, where he served with distinction for thirteen years. Reform Judaism in America was born in Charleston. The first reform movement lasted only eight years, from 1824 to 1833, but it had sowed the seeds of progress which germinated soon thereafter. When the Reformed Society of Israelites came to an end, many of its members re-affiliated with the old orthodox Congregation and formed the nucleus of a progressive party. Being without a minister in 1835, the Congregation had no small difficulty in finding a suitable occupant for its pulpit, for it had literally been rent in twain by the long struggle between the fundamentalists and liberals. Isaac Leeser [*q.v.*], the influential protagonist of orthodox Judaism in America, thought that he had found the right man in Poznanski and recommended him for the position which he afterwards regretted. Poznanski was elected for a probationary period of two years but his ministrations met with such signal success that he was elected for life before the expiration of his term. Meanwhile, on Dec. 5, 1838, he had married Hetty Barrett, of Charleston, daughter of the wealthy

Isaac Barrett. His religious views now underwent a great change. Strictly orthodox when he arrived in Charleston, he developed into an extreme radical.

In the great fire of 1838, the synagogue was burnt to the ground and before the new building was completed, a petition was presented to the trustees, with the approval of Poznanski, praying "that an organ be erected in the Synagogue, to assist in the vocal parts of the service" (Elzas, *post*, p. 209). The petition was granted and the first organ ever used in a synagogue in America was installed, but the introduction of instrumental music led to a division in the congregation and nearly forty members withdrew. In 1843 the case was carried to the courts by the seceders, the most brilliant lawyers of the day being employed by both sides. The dominant party won the case, *State* vs. *Ancker* (2 *Richardson, S. C. Reports*, 245). During the same year, when Poznanski recommended the abolition of the second day of the festivals, changing the creed of the congregation in essential particulars, and suggesting other alterations in the ritual and observances, many more members withdrew. Beth Elohim was now a house divided against itself.

From now on Poznanski was incessantly persecuted, and in 1843, with a view to restoring peace, he resigned and ceased to officiate for four months, but, persuaded that it would be disastrous for him to withdraw, he continued in office until 1847 when he decided to retire. A successor was not appointed until 1850. Among those who applied for the position was Isaac Mayer Wise [*q.v.*], who later became the great organizer of American Judaism. Some years after his retirement, Poznanski removed to New York City where he lived for the rest of his life. At his funeral, Gustav Gottheil and Samuel Adler [*qq.v.*], of Temple Emanu-El, made addresses.

[Minute Books of the Congregation Beth Elohim, 1838–43, 1846–1852; B. A. Elzas, *The Jews of S. C.* (1905); David Philipson, *The Reform Movement in Judaism* (rev. ed., 1931); *Jewish Marriage Notices . . . Charleston, S. C.* (1917); *Occident and Am. Jewish Advocate*, vols. I–IV, VIII, IX; *Sinai* (Balt., Md., 1856); *Jewish Messenger*, Jan. 17, 1879.]   B. A. E.

PRANG, LOUIS (Mar. 12, 1824–June 14, 1909), publisher, lithographer, was born in Breslau, Prussian Silesia. His father, Jonas Louis Prang, was a French Huguenot, and his mother, Rosina (Scherman) Prang, was German. In his father's factory for dyeing and printing calico Louis Prang served an apprenticeship from the time he was thirteen till he was eighteen; he then went to Hagen in Westphalia to study further the technique of printing and dyeing.

Through favoritism, according to his own account (autobiography, *post*), he escaped military service, and instead of entering the army he helped his sister's husband manage a paper-mill for about a year. He then went to Bohemia in search of work, and was engaged by one Peter Walzel, but had to agree to spend a further five years as a journeyman, acquiring a wider knowledge of printing and dyeing. He spent a year in Vienna, and visited Switzerland, Alsace, Rouen, and Great Britain. Returning to Germany, he found himself under the ban of the Prussian government, but his offense seems to have been holding liberal opinions rather than active participation in the Revolution of 1848. He fled to Bohemia, however, and from there sought greater security in Switzerland, finally deciding to emigrate to America.

Landing in New York Apr. 5, 1850, he went to Boston, where with his small amount of capital he formed a partnership with an American of German descent, planning to publish architectural works, but the venture was short-lived. He next engaged in the manufacture of leather goods, but found this enterprise unsatisfactory and decided to learn wood engraving. He worked for a time under Frank Leslie, then head of the art department of *Gleason's Pictorial*, and continued as a journeyman till 1856, when he started in business as a lithographer, first in partnership with Julius Mayer as Prang & Mayer, and after 1860 as L. Prang & Company. His industry and enterprise soon secured him a profitable return from the printing of business cards, announcements, and various forms of small advertising. He was constantly devising novelties. During the Civil War he took advantage of the public interest in the territory being fought over to publish maps and plans of battles, which were sold in large numbers. In 1864 he visited Europe with his family, and on his return he began the reproduction of famous works of art. It was not believed that the American public would appreciate these works or pay the six dollars it was necessary to charge for them, but they proved very popular. "Mr. Prang was the first to apply ... the designation of 'chromos'" to this type of colored lithograph (*Oxford English Dictionary*, quoting *Printing Times*, London, Jan. 15, 1875). In 1867 he established a model printing establishment in Roxbury, where, in addition to reproducing his "chromos," he employed the printing craft as a subsidiary to art in various other ways. He devised appropriately decorated Christmas cards which he first sold in England and then in 1875 put on the American market.

In 1882 he established the Prang Educational

Company, Boston, for the publication of drawing books that came to be widely used in schools; characteristic titles were *Teacher's Manual for Prang's Shorter Course in Form Study and Drawing* (copyright 1888), *A Course in Water Color* (copyright 1900), *Art Education for High Schools* (copyright 1908). Meanwhile, L. Prang & Company continued to publish lithographs and to deal in artist supplies. Prang's water colors were a standard make for many years. In his lifetime, Prang was credited with having increased the popular appreciation of art, or at least the popular knowledge of the great masterpieces, much as the perfection of mechanical sound-reproducing devices has increased the popular knowledge of classical music, while the textbooks he published influenced methods of teaching drawing in its elementary stages. He retired from active business in 1899 and died ten years later in a California sanitarium. Four months after his death, on Oct. 10, 1909, a memorial meeting was held in Boston at which high tribute was paid to him as a public benefactor. On Nov. 1, 1851, he married Rosa Gerber, who died in 1898. His second wife, Mary Amelia (Dana) Hicks Prang [*q.v.*], whom he married on Apr. 15, 1900, with one daughter by his first marriage, survived him.

[*Who's Who in America*, 1908–09; Frank Weitenkampf, *Am. Graphic Art* (1924); *Printing Times* (London), Jan. 15, 1875; *Los Angeles Times, Evening Post* (N. Y.), *Springfield Union* (Springfield, Mass.), June 16, 1909; *Pacific Outlook* (Los Angeles), June 26, 1909; *Boston Transcript*, Oct. 11, 1909, *Syracuse Journal* (Syracuse, N. Y.), Nov. 30, 1909; certain details from an unpublished autobiography in the possession of Prang's daughter.]   S. G.

PRANG, MARY AMELIA DANA HICKS (Oct. 7, 1836–Nov. 7, 1927), art teacher, author, was born in Syracuse, N. Y., the only daughter of Major and Agnes Amelia Livingston (Johnson) Dana. Her father, whose name was conferred by his parents and was not a military title, was of the sixth generation in descent from Richard Dana, who settled in Cambridge, Mass., in 1640; and her mother was also of Massachusetts birth and ancestry. Mary Dana was educated at the Allen Female Seminary of Rochester, N. Y., graduating there in 1852, and she supplemented her work at the Seminary by taking courses at the University of Rochester from 1850 to 1852. On Oct. 7, 1856, she married Charles S. Hicks, who died in 1858. Left with a daughter to support, she took up the teaching of art as a profession. In 1868 she became director of art education in the Syracuse public schools, and in 1875 she was elected president of the Social Art Club of the same city. She left Syracuse to be-

come identified with the rapidly expanding activities of the Prang Educational Company, founded in Boston in 1882 by Louis Prang [*q.v.*], but she still retained her connection with many of her interests in Syracuse, and she also undertook further study, first at the Massachusetts Normal Art School and afterwards at the School of the Boston Museum of Fine Arts. In 1884 she was made director of the Prang Normal Art Classes, and between that year and 1900 she prepared for the Prang press, either alone or in collaboration with others, a number of books presenting material or methods for art instruction. These included *The Use of Models* (1887), *Color Instruction* (1893), *Notes on Egyptian Architecture and Ornament* (1899). In her capacity as an editor for the Prang Company as well as through her teaching she did much to extend the teaching of drawing and allied subjects in the public schools, and her manuals and other works, which were widely used, had some effect on the development of methods of instruction.

On Apr. 15, 1900, she married Louis Prang, and in the next nine years traveled much with her husband. After his death, she took up her residence with her step-daughter in Boston, her own daughter having died. Although she was now seventy-three years old, she continued and even extended her connection with a great many organizations of an intellectual, political, or philanthropic nature; and she also took courses at Radcliffe College and Harvard University, receiving the degree of associate in arts from the former institution in 1916, and that of master of education from the latter in 1921, when she was in her eighty-fifth year. She died in Melrose, Mass.

[*New Eng. Hist. and Geneal. Reg.*, Oct. 1928; *Who's Who in America*, 1926–27, containing a list of publications; *Boston Transcript*, Nov. 8, *Boston Herald*, Nov. 9, and *N. Y. Times*, Nov. 10, 1927.]   S. G.

PRATT, BELA LYON (Dec. 11, 1867–May 18, 1917), sculptor, son of George and Sarah Victoria (Whittlesey) Pratt, and a descendant of Mathew Pratt, an early settler of Weymouth, Mass., was born in Norwich, Conn. His father, a Yale graduate, was an able lawyer. His mother was deeply religious, and reared her children strictly; her nobility of character is revealed in the marble portrait bust made by her son when she was eighty-two. Her father was the once famous Orramel Whittlesey, proprietor of Music Vale Seminary, Salem, Conn. From him the grandson may have derived his musical taste. At the age of sixteen, the boy was sent to the Yale School of Fine Arts, where he studied under two excellent masters, John Ferguson Weir and John

Henry Niemeyer [*qq.v.*]. In 1887, he entered the Art Students' League of New York, where his instructors were F. E. Elwell and Augustus Saint-Gaudens [*qq.v.*] in modeling, and Kenyon Cox and William M. Chase [*qq.v.*] in drawing and painting. Saint-Gaudens, always a vivid and inspiring teacher, thoroughly interested in youthful talent, received him as assistant in his private studio. It was an invaluable privilege, and this early contact with Saint-Gaudens at work influenced Pratt's whole career.

In 1890, advised by Saint-Gaudens, Pratt went to Paris, to study under the solid Chapu and the brilliant Falguière. He entered the École des Beaux-Arts at the head of his class, captured prizes, and after two years abroad returned to America in time to take part in the joyous interlude of preparation for the World's Columbian Exposition at Chicago in 1893. His pair of colossal groups for the Water Gate received praise for sculptural fitness. In 1893, he was chosen instructor in modeling at the Boston Museum School of Fine Arts, a position which he filled until his death. He was a representative of the Boston tradition in sculpture, begun by Greenough and continued by Ball, Milmore, and French. Influential members of the intellectual circles sought his work. On Aug. 11, 1897, he married Helen Lugada Pray. Their home was in Jamaica Plain; Pratt's studio was in Boston. Later, a summer home at North Haven, Me., gave the family the outdoor life which Pratt's frail physique especially needed.

Among his earlier works in Boston was a series of intimate portrait bas-reliefs in the manner of Saint-Gaudens, and hence in full contrast with his groups for the World's Columbian Exposition. These reliefs included portraits of the two daughters of Dr. Frederick C. Shattuck (1893), the Slater children (1894), and Mrs. Shattuck and daughter (1894). At this time he modeled also the medal presented by Harvard University alumni to President Eliot. All these efforts showed refined technical skill as well as that power in characterization which was afterward to give him success in portrait busts. The likeness in the Eliot medal was considered the best yet obtained of its subject; a bust of Dr. Eliot followed. Later came the Yale-Bi-Centennial medal, relief portraits of the Sears children, an angel figure for the Sears monument in Cambridge, Mass., and designs for the five-dollar gold piece.

The years 1895 and 1896 Pratt devoted chiefly to sculptures for the Library of Congress, Washington, D. C. He made six large spandrel figures for the main entrance; a well-composed statue of "Philosophy," one of eight colossal figures surmounting columns in the rotunda; and most successful of all, four circular high reliefs representing the four seasons, placed in the southwest pavilion. In 1896 came a bronze "Victory" for the battleship *Massachusetts*; of later date were the bronzes for the *Kearsarge* and the *Alabama*. The recumbent marble figure of Dr. Coit for St. Paul's School, Concord, N. H., an evocation of a Renaissance motive, won honorable mention at the Paris Salon of 1897, and led to two subsequent works of similar design, the "Dr. John Cotton" in the First Church, Boston, and the "Bishop Neely," Portland, Me. At the opposite pole in theme and treatment was his figure exhibited at the Salon of 1898, an "Orpheus" showing the direct influence of Falguière.

Pratt's truer vein appeared in the next works issuing from his busy studio. The bust of Phillips Brooks for Brooks House, Harvard University (1899) is a solid achievement in the delineation of a great personality. Other thoughtful portraits varying in merit are the bust of Dr. Shattuck, St. Paul's School (1900); the Avery memorial bust, Groton, Conn.; the bust of John E. Hudson of the Bell Telephone Company, and that of Henry Lee Higginson, for Symphony Hall, Boston. With these may be cited the high-relief portrait of Dr. E. Winchester Donald for Trinity Church, and medallions of John C. Ropes for Trinity Church and for Memorial Hall. Side by side with these realistic representations of virile character Pratt was developing idealistic themes of feminine beauty, as in the classically draped relief figures of "Peace" and "War" in the admirable General Butler Memorial, Lowell, Mass. An enchanting nude marble statuette of a young girl received a silver medal at the Pan-American Exposition, Buffalo, 1901. In his "Fountain of Youth," the central feature is a slender ideal nude. Many similar creations are in private ownership. His nude marble figure of a "Young Mother" is in the Art Museum, Worcester, Mass.

A work which today holds its own as among his best in feeling and in treatment is the bronze statue of a young Spanish War soldier in undress uniform, placed on the grounds of St. Paul's School in honor of 120 St. Paul's boys. The dignity of this figure led to his selection as sculptor of the "Nathan Hale" for Yale University (1914), a copy of which has been placed at Hale's birthplace, Coventry, Conn. Less fine as a work of art than the famous "Hale" by MacMonnies, it is probably truer to the nature and appearance of the young patriot in homespun. Another Puritan statue is that of the younger John Winthrop, New London, Conn. Akin to Pratt's "Hale" is his "Andersonville Prisoner Boy," in the National Cemetery, Andersonville, Ga. (1907).

Within the decade following his return from Paris, Pratt had already won success in five branches of his art: decorative groups, portrait bas-reliefs, busts of men, ideal nudes of women and children, and youthful soldierly figures. In these last three fields he was thereafter to gain his chief distinction. His divination of character gave a fine authenticity to such portrait busts as that of Gen. Charles J. Paine (1905). His sensitive perception of the grace in adolescent bodies is apparent in the three architectural panels in pastoral vein entitled "Music," "Drama," and "The Dance," executed in blue and white terra cotta for the façade of the Boston Opera House. Vigorous American manhood is portrayed in the soldier, the marine, and the standard-bearer in the bronze group surmounting the four-square rough-hewn base of the Soldiers' and Sailors' Monument in Malden, Mass., dedicated in 1910. Similar in vigor is the whaleman, harpoon in hand, standing firm in the bow of his boat, and forming the chief feature of the Whalemen's Monument, presented in 1913 by Hon. W. W. Crapo to New Bedford, Mass. The bronze group of man, boat, and decorative wave is placed near the Library, and against a granite background on which sculptured gulls fly high above an inscription from Melville's *Moby Dick*.

At the Panama-Pacific International Exposition in San Francisco, 1915, Pratt received a gold medal for a collection of seventeen pieces indicating his remarkable range of power. The Boston State House has two of his works in bronze, the Gen. Thos. G. Stevenson Memorial (1905), in which the General is shown in high relief against a background of orderly and horse in low relief, and the Memorial to the Army Nurses of the Civil War (1914). Two bronze portraits of Pratt's later period are the "Nathaniel Hawthorne," seated in contemplation as tutelary genius of Salem, Mass., and the "Edward Everett Hale," familiarly shown with hat, cane, and overcoat, and standing on a low pedestal in Boston's Public Garden. Pratt was not at his best in the important bronze figures of seated and draped women personifying Art and Science in front of the Boston Public Library, nor was he unfailingly happy in his solutions of what Saint-Gaudens called "the always complicated and terrible" problem of handling drapery. He sometimes fell into the snare of the pictorial, as in his "Barefoot Boy," on a boulder at Ashburnham, Mass.

His output was too ample for his physical strength. His sympathies were both ready and profound; he loved other arts besides his own; he enjoyed music and painting; he collected pictures. In repose, his sober, clean-shaven countenance gave little hint of his abundant humor; as Dr. Eliot wrote of the architect Bulfinch, he was "a grave, modest, just, and cheerful man." He was a member of the Guild of Boston Artists, the National Sculpture Society, the National Institute of Arts and Letters, the Architectural League of New York, the Connecticut Academy of Fine Arts, and an associate member of the National Academy of Design. At the time of his death in Boston from heart disease, he had in his studio a colossal figure of Alexander Hamilton, for Chicago, and a heroic statue of Bishop Brooks in academic gown, for Boston.

[Lorado Taft, *The Hist. of Am. Sculpture* (1924, 1930); C. R. Post, *A Hist. of European and Am. Sculpture* (1921), vol. II; C. H. Caffin, *Am. Masters of Sculpture* (1903); *Mich. State Lib., Biog. Sketches Am. Artists* (1924); *Who's Who in America,* 1916–17; F. G. Pratt, *The Pratt Family* (1889); C. B. Whittelsey, *Geneal. of the Whittelsey-Whittlesey Family* (1898); Wm. H. Downes, in *New Eng. Mag.,* Feb. 1903 and *Internat. Studio,* July 1909; F. W. Coburn, in *Palette and Bench,* Feb.–Mar. 1910, and in *Art and Progress,* Sept. 1910; C. H. Dorr, in *Architectural Record,* June 1914; L. M. Bryant, *Internat. Studio,* Feb. 1916, supp.; *Art and Progress,* Aug. 1911; E. M. Burrill, *The State House* (1927); Chas. B. Reynolds, *Washington Standard Guide,* 1924; *Am. Art Annual,* vol. XIV (1918); *Boston Transcript,* May 18, 1917; *N. Y. Times,* May 19, 1917.]   A–e. A.

PRATT, CHARLES (Oct. 2, 1830–May 4, 1891), oil merchant, philanthropist, was born in Watertown, Mass. He came of New England ancestry and was the son of Asa and Elizabeth (Stone) Pratt. His father, a cabinet maker by trade, was a descendant of Richard Pratt, said to have been a son of John Pratt of Malden, Essex County, England, who settled in Malden, Mass., about 1630 (D. P. Corey, *The History of Malden, Mass.,* 1899, pp. 7, 12). Charles was one of eleven children, his mother was in poor health, and the care of his younger brothers devolved upon him. The sense of responsibility for others was thus early impressed upon him, while the straitened circumstances of the family taught him to be frugal and economical. When ten years of age he went to work on a neighboring farm and attended a country school. At thirteen he obtained the position of clerk in a grocery store in Boston, which he held for one year. He then became an apprentice to a machinist at Newton, Mass. As soon as he had saved a little money he entered Wesleyan Academy, Wilbraham, Mass., where he was a student for three winters living for a time, it is said, on a dollar a week. In 1849 he became a clerk with a Boston firm dealing in paints and oils.

Two years later, at the age of twenty-one, he moved to New York City and worked for the firm of Schenck & Downing, a firm specializing in paints and oils. In 1854 he became a partner in the firm of Raynolds, Devoe & Pratt, which engaged in the same line of business. Foreseeing the great growth of the petroleum industry, which came into existence with the discovery of oil in Pennsylvania, Pratt withdrew from this concern in 1867, and in conjunction with Henry H. Rogers [q.v.] established the firm of Charles Pratt & Company. It began the refining of crude oil on a large scale at Greenpoint, Long Island, as well as the manufacture of many valuable by-products, which had theretofore been unknown. Under the trade mark "Pratt's Astral Oil" the firm produced a high quality of illuminating oil, the fame of which spread all over the world. On Oct. 15, 1874, the Pratt works, which had then a capacity of 1500 barrels a day and were regarded as the most successful of all refineries, were acquired by John D. Rockefeller. Pratt joined the Standard Oil combination with considerable reluctance, since he was afraid that the product of his refinery, for which he felt a personal responsibility, might suffer in quality once it was swallowed up in a larger organization. This fear proved to be unfounded. On account of his shrewdness and business acumen Pratt came to rank high in the councils of the Standard Oil Company and was one of its principal guiding spirits. With the rise in its resources, his own personal fortune increased correspondingly, so that he died the richest man in Brooklyn, where he had made his home.

Frugal in disposition and averse to all flaunting or squandering of wealth, he felt that he should devote part of his rapidly growing fortune to furthering projects that would be of benefit to the community. Near his oil refinery in Greenpoint, he erected a model tenement for workingmen, "The Astral," with clean, convenient, and sanitary accommodations, which was the first of its kind. Mindful of his own limited scholastic opportunities, he was especially interested in the subject of education. He sent his children to Adelphi Academy, Brooklyn, and, having been made president of its board of trustees, presented it in 1886 with a building that had accommodations for 1000 pupils. He also gave large sums to Amherst College and the University of Rochester.

Manual training, however, appealed to him most of all. In the belief that the best way to help others was to teach them how to help themselves, he determined to endow an institution where the pupils could learn trades that would enable them to be self-supporting through the skilful use of their hands. At this period the United States could boast of numerous engineering schools, but possessed no educational establishment covering the field of secondary technical education. In search of needed information he visited England, France, Germany, Switzerland, and Austria gathering data on technical schools, and at length founded Pratt Institute in Brooklyn for the training of skilled artisans, foremen, designers, and draftsmen. It opened on Oct. 17, 1887, with a class of twelve students, and its total annual enrollment in both day and evening classes has since grown to over 5,000; more than 170,000 men and women have been taught within its walls. Through his interest in the New York Mercantile Library he was led to establish the Pratt Institute Free Library open to all citizens. This was the first free public library in either Brooklyn or New York City. A firm believer in inculcating habits of saving, he organized in 1888 "The Thrift," a Savings and Loan Association patterned after the Birkbeck Building Society in London.

Below the medium height and inclined to stoutness, Pratt had a sharp, pointed face, keen searching eyes, a firm mouth, and wore a goatee. He was modest and reserved in manner, but his jovial disposition, unselfishness, and generous spirit made him deeply beloved. By temperament he was irresolute and slow in making up his mind, although possessed of great nervous energy. In business he was shrewd and far-seeing and his success as a merchant was in no small measure due to careful attention to details and an avoidance of waste. He was twice married: in December 1854, to Lydia Ann, daughter of Thomas Richardson of Belmont, Mass., by whom he had a son and a daughter; she died in August 1861, and in September 1863 he married her sister, Mary Helen Richardson, by whom he had five sons and a daughter. He was wrapped up in his family and cared little for clubs or places of amusement. In order to keep his descendants together he purchased as a summer residence Dosoris, an 800-acre tract at Glen Cove, Long Island, where he built a manor house for himself and homes for his children as they married. He was very religious, a devout Baptist, and strict in his church attendance. To his generosity was due the erection of the beautiful Emanuel Baptist Church in Brooklyn.

[*In Memoriam: Charles Pratt, 1830–1891* (n.d.); *Charles Pratt, An Interpretation, 1830–1930* (1930). containing tributes by F. B. Pratt, Henry C. Folger. Jr., and others; W. S. Perry, *Pratt Institute, Its Be-*

ginnings and Development (1926); Encyc. of Biog. of
N. Y., vol. II (1916); N. Y. Times, Sun (N. Y.), and
Brooklyn Daily Eagle, May 5, 1891.]   H. G. V.

PRATT, DANIEL (July 20, 1799–May 13, 1873), industrialist, was a New Englander who went South and became the first great manufacturer of Alabama. He was born in Temple, N. H., the fourth son of Edward Pratt, a typical Yankee farmer, and Asenath (Flint) Pratt. After attending school for a short time, Daniel served an apprenticeship as a carpenter, and at the age of twenty sailed for Savannah, Ga. Leaving there in 1821, he went to Milledgeville, then the capital of the state, where for ten years he worked at his trade. He then moved to Clinton, Ga., and took charge of a cotton-gin factory belonging to Samuel Griswold, a year later becoming a partner. About this time he married Esther Ticknor, also of New England, by whom he had three daughters.

In 1833 he moved to Elmore County, Ala. After looking about for a site for a plant, and feeling that the residents were endeavoring to exploit his needs, he went to Autauga County, where in 1838 he established himself twelve miles north of Montgomery, the settlement being named Prattville. He first erected a grist mill and a lumber and shingle mill; to these he soon added a cotton-gin plant, which gained such a reputation that its product was exhibited in England. The business shortly increased to such an extent as to warrant a warehouse in New Orleans. Subsequently Pratt built a cotton mill of 2,800 spindles and a hundred looms, a woolen mill, a foundry, a carriage factory, a tinshop, and a mercantile establishment. In 1858 these properties were capitalized at more than $519,000. The following year he advertised that he was annually running 1,200 bales of cotton and 120,000 pounds of wool through his mills. The University of Alabama in 1846 conferred on him the degree of master of mechanic and useful arts. He was elected to the state House of Representatives in 1860 and he served throughout the Civil War. Although a New Englander and opposed to secession he was an ardent Southerner in sympathies, organizing and equipping the "Prattville Dragoons" for the Confederate service. He took a great interest in railroads and became a director of the North & South railway, now a portion of the Louisville & Nashville system. Through Henry F. De Bardeleben [q.v.], who married his second daughter, Ellen, Pratt, the year before his death, invested in the Red Mountain Iron & Coal Company and controlled the Oxmoor iron furnaces in the new Birmingham industrial district. He furnished most of the money for the enterprise and De

Bardeleben became its superintendent. In his honor the great vein of coal west of the new town of Birmingham was named the Pratt Seam.

For many years he was the greatest industrialist and capitalist of Alabama, and Prattville, the industrial center of the state. His plants were the pride and admiration of all. He lived on a large scale; his plantations were noted for their blooded stock; and contemporary accounts reveal that his opulence made a great impression on his place and time. He died just as the Birmingham district was developing and left his son-in-law the capital which made him the most imposing figure in Alabama's iron and coal history.

[H. A. Blood, The Hist. of Temple, N. H. (1860); S. F. H. Tarrant, Hon. Daniel Pratt: a Biog. with Eulogies on His Life and Character (1904); Ethel Armes, The Story of Coal and Iron in Ala. (1910); William Garrett, Reminiscences of Public Men in Ala. (1872); A. B. Moore, Hist. of Ala. and Her People (1927), vol. I; B. F. Riley, Makers and Romance of Alabama Hist. (n.d.); Willis Brewer, Ala.: Her Hist., Resources, War Record, and Public Men (1872); DeBow's Rev., Feb. 1851; Am. Cotton Planter, May 1857; Ala. State Jour. (Montgomery), May 14, 1873.]
H. A. T.

PRATT, DANIEL (Apr. 11, 1809–June 20, 1887), vagrant, was born in the Prattville district of Chelsea, Mass., the son of Daniel and Mary (Hall) Pratt, and belonged to a humble branch of the ancient and numerous family that gave its name to his birthplace. In his youth he became a carpenter's helper, but disappeared, and was not seen for twelve years. When he did return he was incurably demented. His relatives showed him more tenderness than may be expected in such cases, but he was able to take care of himself, and for a half a century he roamed the land. His wanderings extended from the backwoods of Maine and New Brunswick to remote army posts in the Dakotas. In 1874 he wrote in an autograph album that he had traveled 200,000 miles, been in twenty-seven states and among sixteen tribes of Indians, visited Washington seventeen times, and seen five presidents inaugurated. He styled himself the Great American Traveler and insisted on his title of General. His chief delusion was that he had been elected to the presidency and was being kept out of office by a coalition of unscrupulous rivals. He was the most widely known and affectionately remembered man of his class, the subject of innumerable anecdotes, reminiscences, rhymes, and allusions. This fame he owed in large measure to his devotion to the New England colleges, where among the students he was greatly admired as an orator. For many years he descended on his favorite institutions in spring and fall almost with the regularity of a scheduled holiday.

Arriving in town, he would put up at a cheap hotel and then sally forth unannounced to greet his constituents. He seemed quite in place under the campus elms. He had the formal, slightly awkward manners of a retired scholar and a dignity that only the most untoward accidents could ruffle, and he dressed appropriately in a worn frock coat and dingy stovepipe hat. Thus arrayed, his tall, spare frame, craggy, massive head, and shrewd features had a counterfeit distinction, like a battered simulacrum of William Maxwell Evarts. The disciplinary officers of the college usually frowned upon him and sometimes used coercive tactics to accelerate his departure, but by the students he was received with an enthusiasm that quickly permeated the community and mounted to a height of ebullient demonstration scarcely distinguishable from a riot. As the climax to a reception the General would deliver an address, which was followed by a collection. Among his topics were "The Four Kingdoms," "The Harmony of the Human Mind," "The Solar System," "The Vocabulaboratory of the World's History," and his own life and troubles. His platform style was characterized by a dazzling faculty for word-creation, a complete mastery of the non-sequitur, and a lambent humor. An impressive but quite unofficial convocation at Dartmouth College conferred on him the degree of C.O.D. In his last years he endured the miseries of the homeless derelict. In his seventy-ninth year he suffered a paralytic stroke while wandering about Boston. He died a few weeks later in the City Hospital.

[*Vital Records of Chelsea, Mass., to the Year 1850* (1916); W. M. Pratt, *Seven Generations: A Story of Prattville and Chelsea* (privately printed, 1930); R. P. Brown and others, *Memories of Brown* (1909); W. D. Quint, *The Story of Dartmouth* (1914); Clarence Deming, *Yale Yesterdays* (1915); *Boston Transcript,* June 21, 1887; *N. Y. Tribune,* June 22, 1887.]   G. H. G.

PRATT, ELIZA ANNA FARMAN (Nov. 1, 1837–May 22, 1907), editor and writer of juvenile stories, was born at Augusta, N. Y. Her father, Rev. Tural Tufts Farman, was a Methodist clergyman, also justice of the peace and town clerk at Augusta; her mother was Hannah (Burleson) Farman. On her father's side she was a descendant of William Foreman who settled in Maryland in 1675. His grandson, John, served in the French and Indian War on the Canada-New York frontier, settling in New Hampshire after the war. Several of his sons moved into New York.

Eliza attended a private school, and early began to write for her own pleasure. Not until about 1870, however, did her work, under the name "Ella Farman," appear in magazines. When *Wide Awake* was started for children, she became its editor and held that position from July 1875 to August 1893, when it was merged with *St. Nicholas.* In her work on this magazine she became acquainted with Charles Stuart Pratt, a native of South Weymouth, Mass., to whom she was married in that town on Nov. 11, 1877. He joined her in the editorship of *Wide Awake*; they also edited *Babyland* from 1877, and *Little Men and Women* from 1895 until it was absorbed by *Babyland* in 1899. In 1897 they became editors of *Little Folks,* which was merged with *Babyland* in 1900. Mrs. Pratt published many books, among which are: *A Little Woman: A Story for Other Little Women* (1873); *A White Hand: A Story of Noblesse Oblige* (1875); *The Cooking Club of Tu-Whit Hollow* (1876); *Sugar Plums: Poems* (1877); *Christmas Snowflakes: Illustrated Poems by Favorite American Authors* (1879); *Mrs. White's Party, and Other Stories* (1879). She also collaborated with other American authors in the writing or compiling of numerous books of a similar nature. Her best work was in simple stories for young children. After 1886 her home was in Warner, N. H., where, in the summertime, she used to write under the big maples of the Pratt home, in sight of the Mink Hills and Kearsarge Mountain. Many of her stories were based on the play and adventures of her son and his companions. Typical of these is *The Little Cave-Dwellers* (1901), which has for its setting the caves of the Mink Hills. Aside from her writing, her chief pleasures were work in her garden and cooking, for which she was famous among her friends. At the time of her death she had planned and partly written a nature series. She died at Warner after suffering from heart and nervous troubles, and was buried at South Weymouth. She was survived by her husband and her son.

[E. E. Farman, *Foreman-Farman-Forman Genealogy* (1911); *Who's Who in America,* 1906–07; *Daily Patriot* (Concord, N. H.), May 24, 1907; *Concord Evening Monitor,* May 23, 1907; *Manchester Union,* May 24, 1907; information from the son, Ralph Farman Pratt.]   S. G. B.

PRATT, ENOCH (Sept. 10, 1808–Sept. 17, 1896), capitalist, philanthropist, was a shrewd, honest, quick-witted, and public-spirited man who took New England qualities to the predominantly Southern city of Baltimore and made a fortune which he devoted to promoting education and health. He was born in North Middleborough, Mass., the son of Isaac and Naomi (Keith) Pratt. His first ancestor in America on his father's side was Mathew Pratt, who was in Weymouth,

Mass., as early as 1628; the first in the maternal line is said to have been Rev. James Keith, who came from Scotland in 1662 and settled at Bridgewater, Mass. Enoch Pratt early learned of the iron industry from the crude nail-making carried on in the homes of the farmers in his neighborhood. At fifteen he left the Bridgewater Academy for a seven-year clerkship in Boston, for, he said, "I suspect I am old enough to do considerable business."

In 1831 he went to Baltimore, where he had relatives; despite the possession of only $150, he was soon established as an iron commission merchant, nails and mule shoes being his staples. The story is told that at first he made deliveries in a wheelbarrow. Success came quickly and he began to sell on his own account; he later took in a succession of partners, but the firm was longest known as E. Pratt & Brothers, at 23–25 South Charles Street. The development of iron furnaces in Maryland assisted the business. Pratt branched out to wider enterprise—transportation, banking, and fire insurance. In 1872 he obtained the controlling interest in the Maryland Steamboat Company, and during the next twenty years greatly improved the service to Chesapeake Bay and river wharves, constantly adding new steamers. He was a director in the Susquehanna Canal Company, was for twenty-seven years vice-president of the Philadelphia, Wilmington, & Baltimore Railroad, and was a director in three smaller railways in the South. For almost sixty years he was a director of the National Farmers' & Planters' Bank of Baltimore, and at his death had been its president for thirty-six years. He was president of the Baltimore Clearing House and of the Maryland Bankers' Association, and was heavily interested in two fire-insurance companies. Though a Republican, he was made a finance commissioner of Baltimore under a Democratic administration (1877). Braving popular disfavor, he was a leading supporter of the Union cause in Baltimore during the Civil War, and personally contributed to the comfort of the troops passing through the city.

Pratt is most widely known, however, through his public benefactions, which stood out in some contrast to the rigor of his business dealings and the parsimony of his private life. The most important of his gifts was that of the Enoch Pratt Free Library to Baltimore. Uncertain of the fidelity of trustees to the precise intent of a testator after his death, he carried out the project himself, having the central building well along toward completion before its purpose was made public. It was formally opened in January 1886, with 32,000 books and four branches. In addi-

tion to the buildings and books, he gave the city as an endowment $833,333.33, the provision being that this sum was to accumulate until it reached $1,000,000, the city from the first paying interest at 5 per cent. Acceptance of the gift on these terms was confirmed at the polls; Pratt prided himself on the arrangement, for at the time the city was paying only 4 per cent. on its bonds. Andrew Carnegie was influenced by his friend Pratt's library, saying "Pratt was my pioneer." Pratt made himself a student of the library problem, and was the first to embody the idea of branches to facilitate lending. Twenty years earlier he had endowed the academy in his native town and later gave it a library. He donated a building for the Maryland Academy of Sciences, which had been largely an institution for popular education, and assisted the Maryland Institute for the Promotion of the Mechanic Arts. Improvement of the condition of the black race always had Pratt's solicitude. He opposed slavery, was a member of the American Colonization Society, donated a farm of over 700 acres in Prince Georges County for a reform school for colored boys and girls ("Cheltenham"), and was eager to have both races use the public library. Childless himself, he was especially fond of children, and gave much time to the Nursery and Child's Hospital in Baltimore and the Maryland School for the Deaf at Frederick. Impressed by the faithfulness of the trustees of Moses Sheppard, a Quaker merchant of Baltimore, in carrying out the plans for an asylum for the treatment of nervous and mental diseases, Pratt made this institution his residuary legatee on the condition that his name be incorporated into the designation of the hospital. He was a generous patron of Edward S. Bartholomew [q.v.], the sculptor. He gave substantially to the Unitarian Church in Baltimore, where he was a regular attendant, and to the Meadville Theological School, Meadville, Pa. He was survived by his widow, Maria Louisa Hyde, whom he married Aug. 1, 1837. He was small in stature, with a square jaw, thin, straight lips, and piercing, very blue, eyes. He was, to say the least, unostentatious in dress.

[F. G. Pratt, *The Pratt Family. A Geneal. Record of Mathew Pratt of Weymouth, Mass.* (1889); *Lib. Jour.*, Oct. 1896; *Baltimore American* and *Sun* (Baltimore), Sept. 18, 1896; unpublished MS. by Dr. A. K. Bond and other manuscript material in Pratt Library, Baltimore; private information.]   B. M.

PRATT, FRANCIS ASHBURY (Feb. 15, 1827–Feb. 10, 1902), pioneer toolmaker, inventor, the son of Nathaniel M. and Euphemia (Nutting) Pratt, was born in Woodstock, Vt. He was descended from the John Pratt who came from the southern part of England and settled in Dorchester, Mass., where he was made a free-man on May 4, 1632. When Francis was eight years old, his father, who was a leather merchant, moved to Lowell, Mass., and here the boy obtained a common-school education. While still in his teens he was apprenticed to a machinist and upon completing his apprenticeship in 1848, he entered the employ of the Gloucester (N. J.) Machine Works, where he continued for four years, first as a journeyman machinist and afterwards as a contractor. In 1852 he entered the Colt armory at Hartford, Conn., and worked there two years. It was here he met his future partner, Amos Whitney, and after accepting the superintendency of the Phoenix Iron Works, Hartford, in 1854, he soon secured the transfer of Whitney to the same establishment, where they worked together until 1864.

Meanwhile, in 1860, Pratt and Whitney began doing machine work on their own account in their spare time, and in 1862 took a third person, Monroe Stannard, into partnership and enlarged their shop. By 1864 their business had grown to such extent that the two men gave up their positions at the Phoenix Iron Works, and in 1865 constructed the first building of the Pratt & Whitney firm. Pratt was a pioneer and leading spirit in improvements in manufacture of machine tools, and tools for making guns and sewing machines. He was active in promoting the manufacture of interchangeable parts, a system now in universal use, inaugurating it in his own factory during the Civil War in the making of firearms. After the war Pratt introduced this system abroad, and his company manufactured practically all of the machinery for many of the armories of western Europe, the company's orders from abroad in the period between 1865 and 1875 exceeding $2,000,000 in value. One great hindrance to the general adoption of the system of interchangeable parts was the irregularity in the standards of measure, particularly of length; and it was due largely to Pratt's efforts that there came about the establishment of a standard system of gages for both the United States and Europe. The standards so obtained became the basis of the gages which Pratt & Whitney subsequently produced. In 1888 the company began the manufacture of the Hotchkiss revolving cannon for the United States Navy, as well as three- and six-pound rapid-fire guns, and in subsequent years, until the Hotchkiss gun was discontinued, turned out over four hundred of them. Pratt patented a number of machine tools, the most important being a machine for planing metal, Aug. 17, 1869; a gear-cutting machine, July 1, 1884; and a milling

machine, July 28, 1885. The second of these, which permitted the production of correctly shaped teeth of gears, was the first to permit the production of fine gear work. Pratt remained as president of his company until 1898. Thereafter, he served as consulting engineer to the organization until his retirement about two years prior to his death. He was an alderman of Hartford for several years and a director of a number of industrial corporations in New England. He was a charter member of the American Society of Mechanical Engineers and a vice-president in 1881. On Oct. 31, 1850, he married Harriet E. Cole of Lowell, and at his death was survived by his widow and two children.

[*Trans. Am. Soc. Mech. Engineers*, vol. XXIII (1902); *Men of Progress . . . in and of the State of Conn.* (1898); J. A. Spalding, *Illustrated Popular Biog. of Conn.* (1891); J. W. Roe, *English and Am. Tool Builders* (1926); *Accuracy for Seventy Years, 1860–1930* (Pratt & Whitney Company, 1930); *Hartford Courant*, Feb. 11, 1902; Patent Office records.]

C. W. M.

PRATT, JOHN (Apr. 14, 1831–*c.* 1900), journalist, inventor, was born in Unionville, S. C., the son of John J. and Dorcas E. (Moore) Pratt. After attending the local public schools, he entered Cokesbury College, a church school in the village of that name in his native state, and was graduated in 1849, receiving the degree of B.A. He immediately began newspaper work and at the same time studied law, working in various small towns both in South Carolina and Alabama. Presumably journalism was the more appealing occupation and in the course of fifteen years he obtained some reputation in this field. In 1852 he married Julia R. Porter, daughter of Benjamin F. Porter of Alabama. Accompanied by his wife Pratt went abroad in 1864 and lived in England for a number of years. This was just at a time when the press had become greatly interested in the efforts of a few inventors to produce a writing machine, realizing the great advantages in the way of legibility, compactness, and neatness of print as well as increased speed over against long-hand writing. Pratt had no mechanical training but a writing machine was particularly appealing to him as a journalist and it seems that, shortly after reaching England, he began experiments, employing an English model-maker to assist him. He received from the British Patent Office provisional protection of his idea in 1864, and on Dec. 1, 1866, was granted a British patent, No. 3,163, for a writing mechanism which he called a "ptereotype." A month or two later he was invited to exhibit his device before the Society of Arts, the Society of Engineers in London, and before the Royal Society of Great Britain. George C. Mares, in his *His-*

tory of the Typewriter (1909, p. 40), writes: "Pratt's machine was by far the most complete and practicable machine which had appeared up to that date, and it is owing to its appearance, and the newspaper articles and discussions which it provoked, that we owe the typewriter of to-day."

It was a description of Pratt's machine that caused Christopher Latham Sholes [*q.v.*] to take up the subject. Writing machines had been made prior to Pratt's, but most of these were of the type in which the printing character was mounted on a type bar, whereas the printing characters in Pratt's machine were arranged on a single revolving wheel. This class immediately gained considerable prominence and Pratt was able to sell several machines in London in 1867. Encouraged by the reception of his machine, he returned to the United States in 1868, settled at Center, Ala., and in August of that year received a patent for his typewriter. It comprised a wheel and selecting devices actuated by key levers, the impression being effected by a hammer. This invention was the forerunner of the well known Hammond typewriter. In 1882 he obtained a second typewriter patent which he immediately sold to the Hammond Company, and shortly thereafter he moved to Brooklyn, N. Y., where the typewriters were being made and where he continued to make inventions in this field until his death. While his contribution to the early development of the typewriter was an important one, the particular model invented by Pratt did not meet the manifold requirements of commercial users and soon fell by the wayside.

[C. V. Oden, *Evolution of the Typewriter* (1917); sketch of A. M. Pratt in T. M. Owen, *Hist. of Ala. and Dict. of Ala. Biog.* (1921), vol. IV; sketch of B. F. Porter in William Garrett, *Reminiscences of Public Men in Ala.* (1872); *Annual Report of the Comm. of Patents, 1868, 1882*; *Cat. of the Mech. Engineering Collection in the Science Division of the Victoria and Albert Museum, South Kensington, London, Eng.* (1908); *Scientific American*, July 6, 1867.]   C. W. M.

PRATT, MATTHEW (Sept. 23, 1734–Jan. 9, 1805), portrait painter, was of a family of artist artizans of Philadelphia, Pa., where he was born at a house in Taylor's Alley. His father, Henry Pratt, goldsmith, was a friend of Benjamin Franklin and a charter member of the Library Company. His mother was Rebecca (Claypoole) Pratt. Matthew, one of ten children, went to Stephen Vidal's school and at fifteen, after his father's death, was apprenticed to his uncle James Claypoole, a painter. From him Matthew learned the painter's craft, artistic and commercial. After nearly seven years' apprenticeship he joined with Francis Foster in opening their

own shop. On Dec. 11, 1756, he was married to Elizabeth Moore, the daughter of Charles Moore, a merchant. The next year Pratt made a trading voyage to Jamaica, incidents of which he later related entertainingly, but the venture was unsuccessful. He resumed his painting and in 1764 he accompanied Betsy Shewell, a relative, and John West to London where the romantic wedding of Benjamin West and his Pennsylvania sweetheart took place. Pratt remained in England four years, receiving instruction from West, exhibiting "A Fruit Piece" at the Society of Artists in 1765, and spending some months at Bristol "where," he wrote, "I practised to much advantage in my professional line" (Lee, *post*, p. 252).

In 1768 Pratt reopened his Philadelphia shop at Front and Pine streets. He was socially agreeable and his clientèle included the Penns, Dickinsons, Willings, and other prominent families. Quest of a legacy due his wife took him in 1770 to Ireland, where he looked up the scenes of Cromwell's campaigning. At Dublin he painted Archdeacon Mann in canonical robes, a work exhibited at the Dublin Society of Artists and specially commended. Crossing to England he executed several orders at Liverpool and returned thence home. In the depressed years of the Revolution and thereafter he resorted to sign-painting to support a growing family. His signs for taverns and shops were described by John Neagle as "of a higher character than signs generally, well colored and well composed." Of historical consequence was a sign titled "The Representation of the Constitution," containing accurate portraits of thirty-eight members of the Constitutional Convention. When first displayed at Fourth and Chestnut streets it attracted great crowds, "occupied in identifying likenesses." Several Philadelphia tavern signs carried verses of Pratt's own composition. None of these works of pictorial and literary art, unfortunately, has been preserved.

Pratt at all times maintained his standing as "a gentleman of pleasing manners, and a great favorite with the first citizens in point of wealth and intelligence" (Dunlap, *post*, p. 114). He died in 1805 from a gout attack and was buried in Christ Church Cemetery, Philadelphia. As an artistic technician he deserves to be ranked with his English contemporaries, Allan Ramsay and Richard Wilson, and with the American-born West and Copley. His color was refined and delicate; his knowledge of values beyond that of most eighteenth-century painters. His most familiar work is "The American School," at the Metropolitan Museum of Art, New York. It depicts West among his pupils in 1765. The Pennsylvania Academy of the Fine Arts, Philadelphia, has Pratt's admirable portraits of West and his wife. A full-length likeness of Cadwallader Colden was painted by Pratt in 1772 for the Chamber of Commerce of the state of New York. A portrait of Benjamin Franklin, erroneously said to be the earliest ever painted, is privately owned.

[Autobiographical notes which Pratt wrote for his son Thomas were edited by C. H. Hart and published in the *Pa. Mag. of Hist. and Biog.*, vol. XIX (1895). See also: Wm. Dunlap, *A Hist. of the Rise and Progress of the Arts of Design in the U. S.* (ed. 1918), vol. I; Cuthbert Lee, *Early Am. Portrait Painters* (1929); R. I. Graff, *Geneal. of the Claypoole Family* (1893); Helen W. Henderson, *The Pa. Acad. of the Fine Arts* (1911); C. H. Hart, "A Limner of Colonial Days," *Harper's Weekly*, July 4, 1896.]   F. W. C.

PRATT, PARLEY PARKER (Apr. 12, 1807– May 13, 1857), apostle of the Latter-day Saints, was born in Burlington, N. Y., the son of Jared Pratt and Charity Dickinson (or Dickison) and a descendant of William Pratt who was one of the first settlers of Hartford, Conn. He spent his boyhood on his father's and neighboring farms and as a youth went with an elder brother to buy some uncultivated land in western New York. When their failure to meet the payments lost them the property, Parley moved farther west and settled in Ohio. In the summer of 1827 he returned to New York and in September he was married to Thankful Halsey of Canaan, whom he took to his Ohio farm. About 1829 he joined the religious group headed by Sidney Rigdon [*q.v.*]. Occasionally he expounded the Scriptures himself and in time he became convinced that his mission in life was to devote himself to religious teaching. Settling his affairs in Ohio, he went to New York in August 1830 and was shortly won over to the fledgling Mormon Church. He was baptized in Seneca Lake, was ordained an elder, and joined the main body of Mormons. After his first mission, which took him as far as Independence, Mo., he returned to Kirtland, Ohio, and on June 6, 1831, at the general conference of the church, was ordained a high priest. On Feb. 21, 1835, after further evidences of his faith, he was ordained one of the twelve apostles. In 1836 he was preaching in Canada; the next year he was in New York City. There he was married, a brief interval after the death of his first wife, to Mary Ann (Frost) Stearns, who later divorced him. In 1838 he settled in Caldwell County, Mo. For his part in the hostilities between the Mormons and Missourians he was committed to jail on charges of murder. He escaped from prison some eight months later (July 4, 1839) and made his way to Quincy, Ill., where his wife had found refuge. In August he was again on the road, and in Washington memorialized Congress for a redress of Mormon grievances in Missouri. The next year he was in England. He began the publication of the *Latter-Day Saints' Millennial Star* at Manchester and helped compile a hymnbook which contained "near fifty" of his original hymns and songs. He returned to tour, preach, and write, but in 1846 he was again in England. That excursion ended, he accompanied the Mormon migration to Great Salt Lake in the spring of 1847. In the far-western community of the Mormons he helped to frame the constitution of the State of Deseret and at times engaged in legislative service. His most spectacular but least fruitful mission was that which took him to Chile, South America, in the winter of 1851– 52. During his lifetime he published a few miscellaneous works and contributed articles to Mormon periodicals. His account of his life and travels was edited and posthumously published by his son.

Pratt emerges from his autobiography as a pious and self-sacrificing servant of Truth, suffering hardships in the name of the Saints, preaching to large and enthusiastic audiences, and performing miraculous cures by the laying on of hands. He appears less heroic in non-Mormon accounts, in which he is portrayed as attempting to give one of his wives to an Indian chief in exchange for ten horses, and as sacrificing his obligations to his family or creditors for his religion. His last days were dramatic. A convert to Mormonism in whom he took a special interest left her husband and with two children went to meet the missionary near Fort Gibson in the Cherokee Indian reservation. She was followed by her husband, who overtook them and brought Pratt to trial on charges of larceny. He was acquitted of the charges but was followed by his accuser and was killed a few miles from the scene of his trial. Though to the church it was martyrdom, local public opinion was so strongly in sympathy with the murderer that he was not held for his action.

[Sources include: *The Autobiog. of Parley Parker Pratt* (1874), ed. by his son, Parley P. Pratt; *Latter-Day Saint Biog. Encyc.*, vol. I (1901); *Latter-Day Saints' Millennial Star*, issue of July 4, 1857; F. W. Chapman, *The Pratt Family* (1864); *Arkansas Intelligencer* (Van Buren), May 15, 22, June 5, 1857; *True Democrat* (Little Rock), June 2, 1857.]   M. B. P.

PRATT, RICHARD HENRY (Dec. 6, 1840– Mar. 15, 1924), soldier and Indian educator, was born at Rushford, N. Y., the son of Richard Smalley and Mary (Herrick) Pratt, both of English ancestry. His education in the village school at Logansport, Ind., to which his parents removed in 1846, ended when he was thirteen. After his father was robbed and murdered while returning from the California gold fields, the lad became an apprentice tinsmith. At the outbreak of the Civil War he joined Company A of the 9th Indiana Infantry, in which he became corporal, saw service in skirmishes in West Virginia, and was mustered out in July 1861. He became sergeant in the 2nd Indiana Cavalry, was commissioned first lieutenant, and assigned to the 11th Indiana Cavalry, with which he served until the end of the war. He became a captain on Sept. 1, 1864, and left the service on May 29, 1865. Though he had two horses shot under him, he was never wounded. He was married on Apr. 12, 1864, while on leave from the front, to Anna Laura Mason, the daughter of B. B. Mason. They had four children. During the difficult financial days that followed the Civil War he entered the hardware business, but in 1867 he returned to the army as second lieutenant of cavalry. He was assigned to the 10th Cavalry, a colored regiment then newly organized, and was promoted to first lieutenant in the regular establishment the same year. He participated in the winter campaigns against the Cheyenne, Comanche, and Kiowa in 1868–69 and again in 1874–75.

At the close of the latter campaign he took a detail of about seventy Indian prisoners in irons to Fort Marion at St. Augustine, Fla. While in charge of these prisoners during the next three years he carried on his first experiments in the methods of Indian education that were to be his lifework. Owing to his remarkable success, he was transferred in 1878 to Hampton Normal and Agricultural Institute in Virginia, where he remained for a year organizing its Indian branch. Becoming doubtful of the wisdom of educating Indians and negroes together, he requested the use of Carlisle Barracks at Carlisle, Pa., in which to begin the first non-reservation federal Indian school. The first party of students arrived on Oct. 6, 1879, under his personal care. It consisted of eighty-two Sioux, still wearing tribal costume. The school was formally authorized by Congress in 1882. At first no effort was made to give instruction of more than grammar-school grade, and it was frequently necessary to begin by teaching the young Indians English. The course was ultimately extended to include the first two years of high school and some teacher-training. The first class was graduated in 1889. After the Spanish-American War, Porto-Rican students were added. In his years of service five thousand Indian boys and girls of more than seventy tribes passed under his tutelage. It was never necessary to diverge greatly from the founder's original plan. The school divided its work between ordinary academic instruction and vocational training. Government funds were supplemented by private contributions. Students were paid for much of their work, encouraged to save, and paid interest on their savings. Under the "outing" system, Indian boys and girls were placed in carefully selected white homes, mostly in Pennsylvania, and they attended public schools, with some supervision by visiting members of the Carlisle staff. The Indian School encouraged athletics and recreation, and the school football team and the school band were for many years among the most famous in the East. He believed that the solution of the Indian problem did not lie in any attempt to preserve and develop a distinctively Indian culture but lay rather in teaching the individual Indian to make a place for himself in the white man's world. To achieve this, he endeavored to separate young Indians from tribal influences, give them sound elementary educations, and bring them into contact with the better elements in white society. He was naturally a severe critic of many aspects of the official Indian policy and had many conflicts with bureaucrats. Such a course aroused the opposition of those who disagreed with his underlying philosophy, of certain western communities that disliked having Indian appropriations spent in the East, and of those who resented his methods and his criticism. He was made colonel on Jan. 24, 1903, was retired on Feb. 17, 1903, and was advanced to rank of brigadier-general on the retired list by act of Congress on Apr. 23, 1904. On July 1, 1904, he was relieved of the superintendency of the school of which he had been an integral part for twenty-five years. After his retirement, he devoted himself to discussions of Indian policy and advocacy of citizenship for Indians. In 1908 he published a pamphlet, *The Indian Industrial School,* that told a good deal of the history of the school at Carlisle and of his own attitude toward his work. He died in the army hospital at San Francisco.

[MSS. in possession of the family; newspaper clippings in Lib. of Columbia Univ.; *Ann. Report, U. S. Indian School, Carlisle, Pa.* (6 vols., 1897–1913); Jere Zeamer, *Biog. Annals of Cumberland County, Pa.* (1905); *Who's Who in America,* 1924–25; *Sun* (N. Y.), Nov. 1, 1896; *Indian School Jour.,* Mar. 1924; *N. Y. Times,* Mar. 16, 1924.]   J. B.

PRATT, SERENO STANSBURY (Mar. 12, 1858–Sept. 14, 1915), journalist, editor, author, was born at Westmoreland, Herkimer County, N. Y. His father was Enfield Loring Pratt, a

Vermonter, and his mother, Mary E. Jessup of Honesdale, Pa. Pratt grew to manhood in Burlington, Vt., where he graduated from high school and at sixteen matriculated at the University of Vermont. Here he remained two years gaining honors in English but left in 1876 to enter newspaper work. He joined the staff of the St. Albans (Vermont) *Advertiser*, was soon made its editor, and then became political reporter of the Montpelier *Argus and Patriot*. In 1878 he obtained a position with the New York *Daily Commercial Bulletin* and also wrote articles for the *New York Journal of Commerce*. From this time dated his interest in financial and economic questions. In 1882 he became the Wall Street reporter for the New York *World*; in 1885 New York correspondent of the Baltimore *Sun*; from 1887 to 1902 manager of the New York office of the Philadelphia *Public Ledger*; and in 1903 financial editor of the *New York Times*. Later in 1903 he was made associate editor of the *Wall Street Journal* and from 1905 to 1908 he was its editor-in-chief. In December 1908 he was elected to the secretaryship of the Chamber of Commerce of the state of New York. This position, which he filled until the time of his death, he regarded as the culminating point in his career. He worked unceasingly to enlarge the scope of the Chamber's activities, started the publication of its monthly *Bulletin* in May 1909, brought about the appointment of its Committee on Arbitration, and proved an engaging host to all its foreign visitors.

Pratt was an Episcopalian and a member of the Masonic order. On Oct. 19, 1882, he married Ada Stuart Bryden of Wellsboro, Pa., who bore him a son and two daughters. He was a tall, lean man with black hair and a serious scholarly face. Genial in disposition, he had great tact and courtly manners. His conspicuous fairness made him popular with the leading financiers of the day and Henry Clews termed him "the most honest man in Wall Street." His fame as a writer rests upon his book, *The Work of Wall Street*, which appeared in January 1903. It was immediately acclaimed in economic circles as the best description of the functioning of the New York stock and money market and with the publication of later editions continued to be regarded as the most authoritative treatise of its kind. In his work Pratt did not attempt to defend or criticize the Wall-Street system but confined himself to an impartial statement of fact concerning its *modus operandi*. He also wrote several magazine articles chiefly on banking and financial topics, which appeared in the *World's Work* (1903–07) and in the *Independent* (1904–

05). He died in 1915 at Troy, N. Y., survived by his wife and three children.

[There is a sketch of Pratt's life prefacing the 1910 edition of his *Chamber of Commerce*. See also: *Fifty-eighth Ann. Report . . . of the Chamber of Commerce . . . of N. Y.* (1916); C. E. Fitch, *Encyc. of Biog. of N. Y.*, vol. V (1916); *Who's Who in America*, 1914–15; the *Sun* (N. Y.), *Wall Street Jour.* and *N. Y. Tribune*, Sept. 15, 1915.]   H. G. V.

PRATT, SILAS GAMALIEL (Aug. 4, 1846– Oct. 30, 1916), pianist, composer, conductor, was born in Addison, Vt., the son of Jeremiah and Esther (Derby) Pratt. When he was quite young the family moved to Illinois and he attended the common schools of Plainfield and Chicago. While he showed very early a decided taste for music, he had little opportunity to study, for his father's failure in business compelled him to go to work at the age of twelve. His first position was in the music house of H. M. Higgins in Chicago. From there he went to the music store of Root & Cady, and later became a clerk at Lyon & Healy's, where he had better opportunities and more time for his own study. By 1868 he had developed sufficiently to appear in a series of concerts in Chicago, and he had saved enough money to go abroad for three years of study (1868–71). He went first to Berlin where he studied piano with Franz Bendel and Theodor Kullak and theory and composition with Richard Wüerst and Friedrich Kiel. He made rapid progress, but in his eagerness to succeed he practised too strenuously and impaired the free use of his right wrist, thereby being compelled to give up the plan of becoming a concert pianist. He immediately turned his attention to composition. His first orchestral work was "Magdalene's Lament," a single symphonic movement. This was followed by his lyric opera, *Antonio*, begun in Munich and completed in Berlin. In 1871 he returned to Chicago where his first symphony was performed and he became organist of the Church of the Messiah. He made his first public appearance in April 1872 at a concert featuring his own compositions. In the same year, 1872, with George P. Upton, he organized the Apollo Musical Club, which is still (1934) an important choral organization.

In 1874 Pratt gave selections of his opera, *Antonio*, at Farwell Hall under the direction of Hans Balatka. Encouraged by the reception of this performance, he returned to Germany in 1875 and studied piano with Franz Liszt and score-reading with Heinrich Dorn. Besides some short orchestral pieces he wrote at this time the "Prodigal Son" symphony and the "Centennial Overture." The latter was performed under his own direction in Berlin on July

4, 1876, and scored a great triumph. He returned to America by way of London. General Grant, to whom the "Overture" was dedicated, was there at the time and the work was performed at the Crystal Palace with a huge demonstration. In 1877 Pratt returned to Chicago and in 1878 gave a series of symphony concerts. In 1882 his opera, *Zenobia,* had its première in Chicago with Annie Louise Cary in the cast, and two years later he was general director of the Chicago Grand Opera Festival. Meantime he had revised his first opera, *Antonio,* and it was given in Chicago in 1887 under the name of *Lucille.* From 1888 to 1902 he taught piano in the Metropolitan College of Music in New York and in 1906 he founded the Pratt Institute of Music and Art in Pittsburgh which he served as president until his death. Throughout his life he had been industrious and persevering and had succeeded in bringing his name before the public as a composer of rank. In this he was greatly aided by his exaggerated opinion of the worth of his own compositions. Pratt was married in 1886 to Flora Spencer Colby of Chicago. He died in Pittsburgh but was buried in Chicago, survived by his wife, a son, and a daughter. Among his other works are an opera, *Ollanta,* for which he wrote the libretto; "Lincoln" Symphony; a symphonic poem, "Sandalphon," and "A Tragedy of the Deep" (written on the *Titanic* disaster); an "Ode to Peace"; about fifty piano pieces and many songs; two cantatas, "The Last Inca" and "The Triumph of Columbus," and many shorter choruses. He also wrote two books: *Lincoln in Story* (1901) and *The Pianist's Mental Velocity* (1905). His novel entertainment, *The Musical Metempsychosis,* was composed and performed in 1888.

[J. T. Howard, *Our Am. Music* (1931); W. S. B. Mathews, *A Hundred Years of Music in America* (1889); L. C. Elson, *A Hist. of Am. Music* (1904); A. T. Andreas, *Hist. of Chicago,* vol. III (1886); *Musical Courier,* Nov. 23, 1916; *Pittsburg Dispatch,* Oct. 31, 1916.]   F. L. G. C.

PRATT, THOMAS GEORGE (Feb. 18, 1804–Nov. 9, 1869), governor of Maryland, was born in Georgetown, D. C., now a part of Washington, the son of John Wilkes and Rachel (Belt) Pratt. It is probable that he went to the College of New Jersey (Princeton), although he did not graduate and the college records of the period are too incomplete to prove his attendance. He read law in the office of Richard S. Coxe [*q.v.*] in Washington and settled in Upper Marlboro, Prince George's County, Md. Shortly afterward he embarked upon a career of public service, which, with brief intermissions, lasted

through his entire life. In 1832 he entered the lower house of the state legislature, where he sat until 1835. On Sept. 1, 1835, he was married to Adeline McCubbin Kent, with whom he was thrown by his intimacy with her father, Joseph Kent [*q.v.*]. They had six children. In 1836 he was a member of the Maryland electoral college for the selection of a Senate at a critical period, when nineteen Democratic members revolted against an inequitable system of representation. His candidacy for presidential elector on the Whig ticket in 1836 met with success, although the Whig candidate was defeated. From 1838 to 1842 he served as a member of the state Senate. He was responsible for making payment of the state debt the crucial issue in the gubernatorial campaign of 1844, when as the Whig nominee he advocated, unequivocally, the discharge of the state's obligations. After one of the bitterest campaigns of Maryland's history he carried the election by a narrow majority. During his three years of office he was untiring in his efforts to devise means whereby Maryland could resume interest payments, and he saw his purpose achieved just before the close of his term. He could not escape the disputes and inflamed feeling that the passage of the Fugitive-slave Law had created. Hence, his correspondence is marked by an acrimonious exchange with the authorities of Pennsylvania, who refused to honor his demands for the rendition of escaped slaves. When the Mexican War imposed unusual demands upon the state executives, he was so untiring in his support of the federal war measures that Maryland offered more men than could be accepted.

Though he settled down at Annapolis after his gubernatorial term to resume his law practice, he was not allowed to remain in private life, for in 1850 he became a federal senator in the place of Reverdy Johnson, who had resigned to become attorney-general. At the close of that term he received election in his own right for a full term. He was a friend of Webster and Clay, who were often entertained at his Annapolis home. After his term in Washington he returned to Annapolis but remained only until 1864, when he removed to Baltimore. About this period came his transfer of allegiance to the Democratic party, a natural alignment for a proslavery man. During the Civil War he was so bold a supporter of the Confederacy that he was brought into conflict with the federal power and was imprisoned for several weeks in Fortress Monroe. The last bits of public service were his appearance at the Democratic convention in Chicago in 1864, at the Union convention in Philadelphia in 1866, and his unsuccessful candidacy for senator in 1867.

[Some letters in Lib. of Md. Hist. Soc. and in Lib. of Cong.; C. C. Magruder, *Thomas George Pratt* (1913) extracted from *Year Book of American Clan Gregor Soc.*, 1913; M. P. Andrews, *A Tercentary Hist. of Md.* (1925), vol. IV; H. E. Buchholz, *Governors of Md.* (1908); J. T. Scharf, *Hist. of Md.* (1879), vol. III; *Am. and Commercial Advertiser* (Baltimore), Nov. 10, 1869; *Sun* (Baltimore), Nov. 10, 1869.]   E. L.

PRATT, THOMAS WILLIS (July 4, 1812–July 10, 1875), civil engineer and inventor, son of Caleb and Sally (Willes or Willis) Pratt (*A Volume of Records . . . Containing Boston Marriages*, 1903, p. 503), was born in Boston, where his father was a noted architect. He obtained his elementary education in the Boston public schools, later attending the Rensselaer School (afterward Rensselaer Polytechnic Institute) at Troy, N. Y. During his school years, he spent all his spare time assisting his father in his work as architect and builder, and he is said to have made complete plans and working drawings for a large residence when only twelve years old. While at Rensselaer, he showed such unusual aptitude for mathematics and the natural sciences that, despite his youth, he was offered a permanent position on the teaching staff of the school. He had, however, upon the advice of his father, already determined upon an engineering career, and refused the proffered instructorship to become an engineering assistant with the United States government on the construction of dry docks at Charleston, S. C., and Norfolk, Va.

After a few years' experience on government work, Pratt turned to the field of railroad construction which, chiefly, was to occupy the remainder of his professional career. His first engagements were with the Boston & Lowell and Boston & Maine railways. In 1835 he became division engineer on the construction of the Norwich & Worcester, and subsequently superintendent of the road. He was successively engineer and superintendent of the Providence & Worcester (1845–47) and the Hartford & New Haven (1847–50) railways. Following these engagements, he became chief engineer of the Middletown Branch railroad, then chief engineer and superintendent of the New York & Boston, and finally, from 1871 to his death, chief engineer and superintendent of the Conway & Great Falls branch of the Eastern (later Boston & Maine) railway. In his work as engineer for these roads, he became especially interested in bridge construction, which field presented the most difficult technical problems confronting the railroad builder in Pratt's day. He built a number of important bridges, of which the largest and best known was one over the Merrimac at Newburyport, Mass. This structure consisted of six long timber truss spans and a metal draw span. Many original features were embodied in the design and construction of both the substructure and superstructure. Pratt undertook this work as consulting engineer in 1865, before he became chief engineer of the road.

As a railroad and bridge builder, Pratt ranked among the foremost of his time, but his greatest fame in engineering circles derives from his "invention" of the bridge and roof truss which bears his name. Prior to about 1850, the mechanical action of trusses was imperfectly understood, and patented forms, laying claim to many real and fancied advantages, were common. Pratt's invention, patented Apr. 4, 1844, claimed certain advantages in regard to detail, but the truss achieved no especial distinction until the advent of all-metal truss construction, for which the internal bracing of the Pratt truss is particularly well adapted. Though these advantages do not appear to have been fully realized when the truss was patented, they led to its very wide adoption in bridge construction when the use of iron and steel became general. The popularity of the invention was so long deferred, however, that Pratt received little or no financial return from it.

His inventive genius was evinced by numerous other patents taken out by him; among these were patents for a new type of steam boiler, Sept. 26, 1865; for an equalizer for drawbridge supports, Feb. 22, 1870; for an improved type of combined timber and steel truss, Apr. 1, 1873; for a new method of hull construction for ships, May 4, 1875, and for a new method of propulsion, June 1, 1875. Pratt was married between 1835 and 1840 to Sarah Bradford of Plainfield, Conn., by whom he had one son and one daughter. Though one of the most gifted and highly esteemed engineers of his day, he was modest and reticent very nearly to the point of eccentricity. He almost never wrote technical papers or took part in technical discussions, either orally or in print; his occasional contributions to newspaper discussions invariably appeared under the *nom de plume* "Bruno." From 1849 until his death he lived in Boston.

[*Proc. Am. Soc. Civil Engineers*, vol. I (1876); J. B. Johnson, C. W. Bryan and F. E. Turneaure, *The Theory and Practise of Modern Framed Structures* (8th ed., 1904); J. A. L. Waddell, *Bridge Engineering* (1916), vol. I; *Boston Transcript*, July 10, 1875; *Boston Morning Jour.*, July 12, 16, 1875.]   J. I. P.

PRATT, ZADOCK (Oct. 30, 1790–Apr. 6, 1871), manufacturer and congressman, was the son of Zadock and Hannah (Pickett) Pratt and a descendant of William Pratt who settled in

Hartford, Conn., in 1636. He was born at Stephentown, Rensselaer County, N. Y., but removed with his parents to Middleburg, Schoharie County, and then to Windham (now Jewett), Greene County. From the age of twelve until his majority, with scant opportunity for schooling, he worked at the tanner's trade with his father, whose health was impaired by service in the Revolution. When of age he took up the business of a saddler at Lexington and the following year opened a general store. In the War of 1812 he was a soldier in New York City, occupied on the fortifications of the city. From 1819 to 1823 he was active in the militia, first as a cavalry sergeant, later as captain of the 5th Artillery, afterward as colonel of the 116th Infantry, displaying at each post enthusiasm and initiative. At the age of thirty-four he removed from Lexington to the Schoharie-kill, where he built an extensive tannery and founded a village to be known as Prattsville. There from the first to last were employed many thousands of workers and large capital. To create a community and attract home-seekers, Pratt built more than a hundred houses and furnished aid in establishing an academy and a newspaper.

It is easier for men like Zadock Pratt to get into politics than to keep out. With or without political ambition, he was the natural representative of his people. Justice of the peace at Lexington; supervisor of the town of Windham; state senator; a democratic presidential elector in 1836–37; occupying a seat in Congress from 1837 to 1839 and from 1843 to 1845; a delegate to the national convention which nominated Franklin Pierce for president, and also a presidential elector: that is the record of his public life. At Washington he was forceful and influential. He gave particular attention to the care and improvement of public buildings and to the erection and preservation of national memorials. Agriculture and cheap postage had his support. He was instrumental in establishing a bureau of statistics and commerce at Washington (*Congressional Globe,* 28 Cong., 1 Sess., p. 204), and in 1845 he offered an amendment to an appropriation bill to permit a survey for a railroad to the Stony (Rocky) Mountains (*Ibid.,* 28 Cong., 2 Sess., p. 363). It proposed that the survey be extended from Michigan to the South Pass of the Rocky Mountains, but the design was to prepare the way for a railway to the Pacific.

In 1851 Pratt was appointed by the Mechanics' Institute in New York City a delegate to the World's Fair in London; on two occasions he received a medal from the American Institute for excellence in the tanning of leather. Retiring

from business at about the age of seventy, he continued the benevolent activities in which he found satisfaction, preferring forms of aid that called forth self-help. At seventy-five he won a diploma at the county agricultural exhibition for equestrianship. He left a unique memorial in causing a mountain-side at Prattsville to be adorned with carvings, exhibiting various figures and presenting a likeness of himself and of his son, who fell in the Civil War. By travel he enriched his mind; and in his hemlocks, the foundation of his industry, there was beauty that appealed keenly to his sensibilities. Pratt died at Bergen, N. J., where he was visiting his daughter. He married four times and was a widower four times. Beda Dickerman and her sister Esther, and Abigail Watson and her sister Mary were successively his wives.

[*Biog. Dir. Am. Cong.* (1928); Stuart Clos, "Zadock Pratt—A Personality," *Quart. Jour. N. Y. State Hist. Asso.,* Apr. 1931; *Biog. of Zadock Pratt, of Prattsville, N. Y.* (1852); *Hist. of Greene County, N. Y.* (1884); F. W. Chapman, *The Pratt Family* (1864); F. E. Pratt, *Supp. to a Hist. Entitled "The Pratt Family . . ."* (1916); *N. Y. Times,* Apr. 7, 1871.]
R. E. D.

PRATTE, BERNARD (June 11, 1771–Apr. 1, 1836), merchant, fur-trader, was born at Ste. Genevieve, Mo., the son of Jean Baptiste and Marie Anne (Lalumandiere) Pratte. His father emigrated from France to Fort Chartres but later moved across the Mississippi to Ste. Genevieve. The son received a good education for that time, completing his studies in Canada. In 1793 he began trading on the Mississippi between St. Louis and New Orleans, later establishing stores at St. Louis and Ste. Genevieve, and regularly traveling to the East for supplies. He entered the fur trade in 1816 as one of the partners of Cabanne & Company, the firm name later becoming Berthold, Chouteau & Pratte. In 1823 the company was reorganized as Bernard Pratte & Company, when they made a contract with the American Fur Company for exclusive rights to purchase their furs. In 1827 the firm secured an interest in the Western Department of the American Fur Company. Three years later Pratte retired from active connection with the fur trade.

Pratte was a man of ability and enjoyed the confidence of the people of his community to a marked degree. He held positions of trust as member of the first St. Louis grand jury, 1804; one of the territorial judges, 1807; treasurer of the District of St. Louis; one of the trustees of the town, 1808–20; incorporator of the Bank of St. Louis; member of the constitutional convention, 1820; and United States receiver of public monies, 1825. He was one of three citizens who in 1833 financed the movement to save the harbor of St. Louis from sand bars, ultimately leading to the assignment of Robert E. Lee to this task by the war department. He was also conspicuous in military affairs of the community and was captain of a militia company called out in 1807 to resist anticipated attack by Osage Indians. In May 1809 he was sent with reinforcements to Fort Madison to repel an attack on the northern frontier. In some published sketches, supported by family tradition, it is said that Pratte got the title of "General" in the War of 1812, but the records do not seem to bear out these statements. When citizens of St. Louis were called upon to fortify and defend the town during the war, Pratte was appointed a member of the Committee of Safety. From this time on he was referred to in letters and newspapers as General Pratte, and his family and intimates spoke of him as *"Mon Général."* On Mar. 14, 1822, his friends proposed him as a candidate for the office of major-general of the Missouri militia, but his name was publicly withdrawn soon after. Pratte was married at St. Louis on May 13, 1794, to Emilie Sauveur Labbadie, daughter of Sylvestre Labbadie and Pelagie Chouteau. They had seven children—one of whom married Ramsay Crooks [*q.v.*]. The others married into prominent families. A son, Bernard, also attained prominence in St. Louis history. He was twice elected mayor and held many other positions of trust.

[Registre de la Paroisse de Notre Dame des Kaskaskias (Bernard Pratte's baptismal record) ; *Missouri Gazette*, June 7, 1809 ; Minutes of the Trustees of the Town of St. Louis ; Pratte Collection and Pierre Chouteau Collection, *Mo. Hist. Soc.* ; St. Louis Cathedral (old) church registers ; Richard Edwards and M. Hopewell, *Edwards's Great West* (1860) ; Louis Houck, *A Hist. of Mo.* (1908), vol. III ; F. L. Billon, *Annals of St. Louis* (1886) ; J. F. Darby, *Personal Recollections* (1880).]   S. M. D.

PRAY, ISAAC CLARK (May 15, 1813–Nov. 28, 1869), journalist, dramatist, actor, manager, had so varied a career in the allied professions of journalism and the stage that it is difficult to follow him through the chronicles and records of a lifetime of constant work as he shifted back and forth between the editorial chair, the author's desk, and the theatre. At times he seemed to be following all these professions at once, and even they were not sufficient to satisfy his versatility and energy, for he was often engaged in the training of pupils for the stage, some of whom became famous, and at the same time he would be writing prose and verse for publication in periodicals and books. There seems to have been no logical sequence in his work, which was the obvious result of a diversified skill at the doing of many things. He was born in Boston, the son of Isaac and Martha (Haggens) Pray. In 1829 he entered Harvard College but soon afterward he transferred to Amherst College and was graduated in 1833. While at Amherst he edited a monthly magazine called the *Shrine*. Before he was twenty he had written a play entitled *The Prisoners*, which was produced in Albany. His first book, *Prose and Verse from the Portfolio of an Editor*, published in Boston in 1836, has been described as showing "sensibility of temperament and a graceful fancy" (Winter, *post*, p. 247). During the thirties he edited the *Boston Pearl* and other papers. In 1836 he went to New York and assumed the management of the National Theatre where his tragedy, *Giuletta Gordoni*, was acted. At about the same time, there was produced at the Park Theatre in New York a farce he had written, *The Old Clock*, dramatized from a story he had contributed to the *Sunday Morning News*, of which he was editor. He also edited the *Dramatic Guardian*, the *Ladies Companion*, and wrote dramatic criticism for the *Express* and other New York papers.

In England in 1846 and 1847 Pray suddenly blossomed forth as an actor, playing such leading characters as Hamlet, Romeo, Othello, Macbeth, Claude Melnotte, and Sir Giles Overreach. He appeared in London and other cities. After starring tours, and management of the Theatre Royal in Cork, he returned to New York and along with his other diverse activities served as manager for Gustavus Vaughan Brooke, with whom he had acted in Ireland. In 1849 he was back in Boston as manager of the Beach Street Museum, going again to New York for the next year to become musical and dramatic critic of the *Herald*. Off and on he was tutoring aspirants for the stage. Among his many pupils were Charlotte Cushman and Agnes Ethel, who at the age of eighteen toured under his management, and others of lesser note. His numerous dramas included *Medea, Orestes, Virginius*, and *The Hermit of Malta*, and the range of his work extended through comedies, tragedies, dramas, farces, librettos, and burlesques, among the last being a popular piece called *The Female Forty Thieves*. He was editor of the *Philadelphia Inquirer* in 1859–60, and his *Memoirs of James Gordon Bennett and His Times, by a Journalist*, described by W. A. Croffut as "a friendly biography of an unfriendly man," was published in New York in 1855. He was, again says William Winter, "an amiable man, gentle in character and serene in life." He was survived by a widow, Sarah (Henry) Pray, and by two children.

[S. A. Allibone, *A Critical Dict. of English Lit. and British and Am. Authors,* vol. II (1870) ; Wm. Winter, *Brief Chronicles,* pt. 2 (1890) ; T. A. Brown, *A Hist. of the Am. Stage* (1870) ; J. B. Clapp and E. F. Edgett, *Players of the Present,* pt. 3 (1901) ; Wm. A. Croffut, *An Am. Procession* (1931) ; *Amherst Coll. Biog. Record of the Grads. and Non-Grads.* (1927) ; *N. Y. Tribune,* Nov. 29, 1869 ; *Boston Transcript,* Nov. 30, 1869.]

E. F. E.

PREBER, CHRISTIAN [See PRIBER, CHRISTIAN, fl. 1734–1744].

PREBLE, EDWARD (Aug. 15, 1761–Aug. 25, 1807), naval officer, was born at Falmouth, now Portland, Me. He was the fourth child and third son of Gen. Jedidiah Preble, an officer of the Revolution, his great-grandfather, Abraham Preble, having settled in Scituate, Mass., about 1636. His mother, Mehitable (Bangs) Roberts, was the second wife of General Preble. Edward was educated at Dummer Academy, Newbury, Mass. He married Mary Deering, daughter of Nathaniel Deering of Portland, on Mar. 17, 1801, and they had one son. At the age of sixteen he ran away to sea on a privateer of Newburyport, and in 1779 was appointed a midshipman on the frigate *Protector* of the Massachusetts navy. This ship fought two severe actions with the British ships *Admiral Duff* and *Thames.* In 1781 she was captured and Preble was confined for a time on the prison-ship *Jersey.* In 1782 he was a lieutenant under Captain George Little [*q.v.*] on the Massachusetts cruiser *Winthrop,* which succeeded in taking five prizes during a short cruise. After the Revolution he spent fifteen years in the merchant service and visited many parts of the world, being once captured by pirates.

Upon the opening of hostilities with France in 1798, he was appointed a lieutenant in the newly reorganized navy and was given command of the brig *Pickering* in the squadron of Commodore John Barry [*q.v.*] in the West Indies. He received a commission as captain on May 15, 1799, and was ordered to the new frigate *Essex.* The frigate *Congress* and the *Essex* set sail with a convoy of merchantmen for the East Indies in January 1800, but six days out the *Congress* was dismasted in a gale and the *Essex* proceeded alone. She was the first American warship to show the flag beyond the Cape of Good Hope. After cruising for two months about the Straits of Sunda, rendering important service in protecting American trade from French privateers, the *Essex* sailed for home with a convoy of fourteen vessels, arriving at New York in November.

The naval war with France was scarcely brought to a close before the war with Tripoli began and in 1803 Preble was put in command of the third squadron to be sent to the Mediterranean. His flagship was the *Constitution* and

the squadron included six other vessels: the frigate *Philadelphia,* the brigs *Siren* and *Argus,* and the schooners *Vixen, Nautilus,* and *Enterprise.* Each vessel sailed when ready and the *Constitution* was the fourth to get away on Aug. 14, 1803, arriving at Gibraltar on Sept. 12. After adjusting a difficulty with Morocco in November, Preble sailed east, but before reaching Syracuse, the rendezvous of the squadron, he learned of the capture of the *Philadelphia* by the Tripolitans and the captivity of Captain William Bainbridge [*q.v.*] with more than 300 members of the crew. The *Philadelphia,* lying in the harbor of Tripoli, was later destroyed by a prize ketch called the *Intrepid,* commanded by Stephen Decatur, 1779–1820 [*q.v.*]. Meanwhile, the blockade of Tripoli had been proclaimed by the commodore and was maintained, as well as circumstances permitted, by the squadron, which was also employed in cruising and in preparing for an attack upon the town. Preble borrowed two mortar-boats and six gunboats from the king of the Two Sicilies. Aside from these auxiliaries the squadron comprised the six American vessels and two prizes taken into the service, the *Intrepid* and the brig *Scourge.* The squadron carried forty-two heavy guns, one on each gunboat and the others on the *Constitution,* all the other vessels' guns being too light for assaulting the enemy's batteries.

The commodore had under his command 1060 officers and men. Tripoli was defended by strong forts and batteries, many gunboats, several larger vessels, and 25,000 men. After much delay because of bad weather, the first assault on Tripoli was made on Aug. 3, 1804. Most of the fighting was done by the gunboats, which closed with the enemy's gunboats and necessitated many desperate hand-to-hand contests. The squadron bombarded the town, inflicting considerable but not vital damage. The Americans were victorious at sea, three of the enemy's gunboats being captured and three sunk. Four subsequent attacks were made, two of them at night, with great loss to the enemy, but Tripoli was not captured. On the night of Sept. 4, the *Intrepid,* with 15,000 pounds of powder on board and commanded by Richard Somers [*q.v.*], was sent into the harbor to be exploded in the midst of the Tripolitan fleet, but for some reason never explained, the explosion was premature and all hands perished. Preble's total loss during the summer, including the crew of the *Intrepid,* was thirty killed and twenty-four wounded.

Soon after this a larger and more powerful squadron appeared under the command of Commodore Samuel Barron and Preble was superseded. This was a most unfortunate and seemingly avoidable circumstance and Preble was bitterly disappointed in not being able to carry through his plans for the capture of Tripoli, which he could probably have accomplished with a heavier force. Very little was accomplished by Barron's squadron and the next year peace was concluded with Tripoli on terms far from satisfactory. After his return home Preble was employed in building gunboats for the navy. His health, which had long been declining, broke completely and he died at Portland at the early age of forty-six. He was a tall man and of distinguished appearance. A hot temper and ill health increased a natural irascibility. His discipline was severe but was imposed upon himself as well as others. He was impartial in his judgments and free from prejudice, and justly earned the respect and admiration of his officers in spite of his rough exterior. He in turn acquired a real affection for them and during his command in the Mediterranean there was neither a court martial nor a duel. His squadron was a training school for many of the young officers who later distinguished themselves in the struggle with the British navy during the War of 1812. William Bainbridge, Stephen Decatur, Charles Stewart, Issac Hull, David Porter [qq.v.], and many of the still younger officers, were worthy pupils of a great teacher.

[Twenty-five vols. of Edward Preble papers in the Lib. of Cong., including nautical journals, correspondence, and family papers; G. H. Preble, Geneal. Sketch of the First Three Generations of Prebles in America (1868); Jared Sparks, ed., The Lib. of Am. Biog., ser. 2, vol. XII (1847); J. T. Kirkland, Life of Commodore Preble (n.d.); S. P. Waldo, Biog. Sketches of Distinguished Naval Heroes (1823); G. W. Allen, Our Navy and the Barbary Corsairs (1905); G. H. Preble, The First Cruise of the U. S. Frigate Essex (1870); Mag. of Am. Hist., Mar. 1879.]   G. W. A.

PREBLE, GEORGE HENRY (Feb. 25, 1816–Mar. 1, 1885), naval officer, author, was born in Portland, Me., the son of Enoch and Sally (Cross) Preble. His father was a sea captain, and Commodore Edward Preble [q.v.] was his uncle. He attended public schools until he was thirteen years of age, becoming a clerk first in a Portland bookshop, then in a grocery business started by his father, and subsequently in a Boston publishing house, where he worked until he was appointed midshipman in October 1835. After cruises in the Mediterranean and Caribbean, he studied at the Philadelphia naval school and was made passed midshipman in June 1841. A year's strenuous service in Florida during the Indian wars was followed by an oriental cruise in the St. Louis. At Canton in 1844, he commanded the first American armed landing force

in China. Upon his return he was married on Nov. 18, 1845, to Susan Zabiah, daughter of John Cox of Portland. They had four children, two daughters, one of whom died in infancy, and two sons. During the Mexican War he had a year's active blockade service as executive of the schooner Petrel, 1846–47. This was followed by another Gulf cruise in the Saratoga and then by coast survey duty, 1849–52. In the Macedonian, 1853–56, he accompanied Perry's mission to Japan, commanded a steamer operating against Chinese pirates, and, in 1855, prepared surveys and sailing directions for the Wu-sung River leading to Shanghai. After a year as lighthouse inspector stationed at Portland, and two years at the Boston navy yard, he was executive of the Narragansett in the Pacific until December 1861.

With the Civil War came his first regular command, the steam gunboat Katahdin, which joined Farragut in the Gulf, was the fourth ship to pass the forts below New Orleans, and was actively engaged in operations up to Vicksburg. Preble was made commander on July 16, 1862, and in August he took over the steam sloop Oneida, which joined the Mobile blockade. Here, on Sept. 4, while temporarily senior officer of the blockading force, he suffered the most serious misfortune of his career when he allowed the Confederate cruiser Oreto (Florida) to break through into the bay. The Oreto boldly approached the Oneida and Winona, the only vessels barring her passage, at full speed by daylight. Unwarned of the raider's being at large, and taking her for a British cruiser, Preble allowed her to get almost opposite, but then, after three quick warning shots, opened fire with all guns. The Oreto escaped by superior speed and lighter draft, though her commander, John Newland Maffitt [q.v.], later reported her badly injured with four shots in her hull and twelve casualties among her crew. On the basis of Preble's hasty report, forwarded the same night by Farragut from Pensacola, Secretary Welles dismissed him from the service. Even as wartime punishment this action was hasty and unjust. Preble's only fault, as decided by a court of inquiry in 1872, was the "venial" one of delay in halting the Oreto because of his supposition that she was British. He protested energetically and in February 1863 was restored to his former rank, but was again chagrined on being assigned to the old sail-sloop St. Louis off Lisbon. Soon after, at Funchal, Madeira, he once more encountered the Florida, but, through perhaps an over-scrupulous regard for the neutrality of the port, let her steam away (see C. H. Davis, Life of Charles Henry Davis, 1899, p. 302). At last, in September 1864, he was ordered to the southeast coast blockade, and found opportunity for distinction as the commander of the fleet brigade, 500 strong, which in November and December operated with the army preparing for Sherman's approach to the sea. The brigade was sharply engaged at Grahamville, De Vaux's Neck, and elsewhere, lost fifty-one men, and won warm commendation from army officers and from Admiral Dahlgren in general orders. From March to August 1865 Preble commanded the *State of Georgia,* protecting commercial interests at Panama, and in June rescued more than 600 passengers of the steamship *Golden Rule* wrecked on Roncador reef. Owing to the *Oreto* affair he was passed over in the special promotions of July 1866, but he finally secured a court of inquiry, his name was fully cleared, and in 1874 he was made commodore with a commission dating from 1871. In the meantime he had served at the Boston navy yard, 1865–68, and in the Pacific as chief-of-staff for Admiral Thomas Tingey Craven [*q.v.*]. He was made rear admiral in 1876 and commanded the South Pacific Squadron until his retirement in 1878, after which he made his home in Boston.

In later years he was an indefatigable student, writer, and collector of material on historical subjects, chiefly naval. His excellent book, *Our Flag: Origin and Progress of the Flag of the United States of America* . . . (1872) appeared in revised form in 1880 and again in 1917. He also wrote a genealogy of the Preble family, published in 1868, *The First Cruise of the United States Frigate Essex* (1870), a *Chronological History of . . . Steam Navigation* (1883), and many memoirs and historical sketches for the *New England Historical and Genealogical Register* and other magazines. His collection of children's sayings was published by his descendants under the title *Did Your Child Say This?* (1909). For many years he contributed each week to the *Army and Navy Journal.* These scholarly interests doubtless detracted somewhat from his reputation as a practical officer, as is evidenced by Secretary Welles' comment "not distinguished for vigor" (*War of the Rebellion: Official Records, post,* p. 459), but by naval men his courage and abilities were generally recognized. Admiral Craven indorsed him as second to no one of his rank.

[Twelve vols. of Preble's manuscripts and letters in the Mass. Hist. Soc. archives; G. H. Preble, *Geneal. Sketch of the First Three Generations of Prebles in America* (1868); *War of the Rebellion: Official Records (Navy),* ser. 1, vol. I, pp. 431–467; *The Chase of the Rebel Steamer of War Oreto . . . into the Bay of Mobile* (1862); *Memorial of Capt. G. H. Preble to the ıst Sess. of the 43rd Cong.* (1874); *Army and Navy*

Jour., Mar. 7, 1885; *Daily Eastern Argus* (Portland, Me.), Mar. 2, 1885.]

A. W.

PREBLE, WILLIAM PITT (Nov. 27, 1783–Oct. 11, 1857), jurist, diplomat, railroad president, was the eleventh child of Esaias and Lydia (Ingraham) Preble of York, in the district of Maine, and a descendant of Abraham Preble who emigrated from England in 1636 and by 1642 was in York. He prepared for college under the blind clergyman, Rosewell Messinger, and graduated from Harvard in 1806. His mathematical talents procured for him appointment as tutor at the college in 1809. This position he held for two years, when, having studied law with Benjamin Hasey of Topsham and with Benjamin Orr of Brunswick, he opened a law office in York, removing the same year to Alfred upon his appointment as county attorney. From 1813 to 1818 he resided in Saco. Thereafter he made his home in Portland. His political conversion from Federalism influenced President Madison to appoint him United States district attorney in 1814. A particularly active advocate of the separation of Maine from Massachusetts, he wrote many of the articles appearing in the newspapers on that subject from 1816 to 1820. As a member of the Brunswick Convention, he was responsible for the casuistical calculations of the votes for separation in 1816 which came to be known as "Holmes' arithmetic" [see biography of John Holmes]. At the organization of the new state in 1820 he was selected one of the three justices of the supreme judicial court. "He paid little deference to the authority of decided cases, when conflicting with his own views of the law, and his mannerism on such occasions was more supercilious than gracious. . . . His power of invective was almost fearful" (Emery, *post,* p. 115). He won respect for his ability but never popular favor or a large practice. Indeed he was never popular in the general sense, and never held an elective political office.

Preble left the bench in 1828 to aid Albert Gallatin in the preparation of the Northeastern boundary case in which the King of the Netherlands had been agreed upon as arbitrator. President Jackson appointed him minister at the court of the King of the Netherlands in 1830 in order that American interests might be fully cared for. When the King made a decision in January 1831 which was a compromise between the American and British claims, Preble immediately protested and returned home to fight ratification. A wearisome dispute, in which Preble played an active part, began and was ended only by the Webster-Ashburton Treaty of 1842 in the negotiation of which he served as one of Maine's four commissioners. The remainder of his life was devoted to the building of the Atlantic & St. Lawrence Railroad in close association with John Alfred Poor [*q.v.*]. Money for the enterprise had to be raised and considerable political opposition had to be met. The American company was incorporated on Feb. 10, 1845, and the Canadian company on Mar. 18, 1845. Upon the completion of the organization, Sept. 25, Preble was elected president and two months later sailed to England for financial support, in which he was only partly successful owing to the acrimonious opposition from those hoping to make Boston the railway's terminal. Terms of union with the Canadian company were settled upon and on July 4, 1846, the first ground was broken at Portland, Me. Preble was forced to retire on July 22, 1848, worn out by his unceasing efforts. His estate at his death was estimated at forty thousand dollars. He was twice married, in September 1810 to Nancy Gale Tucker, who died in 1849, and in 1852 to Sarah Forsaith, who survived him.

[Wm. Willis, *A Hist. of the Law, the Courts, and the Lawyers of Me.* (1863), pp. 597–614; G. H. Preble, *Geneal. Sketch of the . . . Prebles in America* (1868), pp. 20–22; G. F. Emery, "Reminiscences of Bench and Bar," *Me. Hist. Soc. Colls.*, 2 ser. VIII (1897); H. S. Burrage, *Me. in the Northeastern Boundary Controversy* (1919); the *Eastern Argus* (Portland), Oct. 12, 1857.]   R. E. M.

PREETORIUS, EMIL (Mar. 15, 1827–Nov. 19, 1905), journalist, publicist, was born in Alzey, Rhenish Hesse, Germany, the son of William and Louise Preetorius, a leading family of the community. Educated first by private tutors he prepared for college at Mainz and in 1848 was awarded the degree of doctor of laws at the University of Giessen, after which he continued the study of law at Heidelberg. At the threshold of a promising legal career he espoused with enthusiasm the movement for constitutionalism in Germany; the repressive politics of the existing government repelled him. His participation in the revolutionary activities forced his withdrawal from the country, and in 1853 he joined the large German colony at St. Louis. The year following he married Magdalena Schmidt of Frankfort. He entered the mercantile business but public affairs were his chief interest, and he shortly assumed a prominent position among the Germans in Missouri. Strongly opposed to the extension of slavery he joined the Republican party in 1856 and labored unceasingly with voice and pen for the election of Lincoln. During the early and critical months of the war he and other German leaders joined with F. B. Blair, Jr., in the successful effort to prevent the secession of Missouri. He raised funds for German regiments, and, as a humanitarian, supported hospitals for soldiers of both armies. In the years 1862–64, as a member of the legislature, he advocated immediate and uncompensated emancipation of Missouri slaves.

His ability and inclination brought him actively into journalism in 1862 when he founded *Die Neue Zeit*, which two years later was merged with the *Westliche Post* with Preetorius as editor-in-chief. He opposed Johnson but was singularly free from the bitter and proscriptive spirit of the Radicals. In 1867 his intimate friend, Carl Schurz, became his partner, and the *Post* entered upon a long era of prosperity and of power. It supported effectively the Liberal Republicans in Missouri in 1870 and reluctantly indorsed the Greeley ticket in 1872 (*Westliche Post*, May 6, 1872). He was one of the notable group of scholarly editors who were keenly aware of the economic and political ills of the nation, and, although Republican, always opposed party abuses and sought reforms, particularly tariff and civil-service reform and the elimination of corruption in government. During his editorship of forty years, the journal was an important political and cultural force in the city and state, reflecting accurately the opinions and personality of its chief. In national politics he remained a mildly partisan Republican, although not seeking political preferment himself. In state and in local affairs he was independent and courageous. He believed whole-heartedly in democracy but was inclined occasionally to mistake the form for the substance, and to place too great emphasis upon mere mechanical change. He was in the best sense a public-spirited citizen, sharing his prosperity with worthy civic enterprises and dispensing charity lavishly. His range of scholarship and breadth of view were unusual; he was an eloquent speaker, with a remarkable memory and a deep interest in politics, history, and philosophy. It was his policy both to assist his readers in understanding American institutions and to uphold the German language, culture, and civilization. At times impractical and intolerant, he lacked the spirit of compromise, but he never lost his early enthusiasm for progress and for personal liberty. As the Nestor of the German-American journalists, with great and pervasive influence, he passed into the best tradition of the foreign-language press in America.

[J. T. Scharf, *Hist. of St. Louis* (2 vols., 1883); A. B. Faust, *The German Element in the U. S.* (2 vols., 1909); *The Reminiscences of Carl Schurz* (3 vols., 1907–08); *Intimate Letters of Carl Schurz* (1928), ed. by Joseph Schafer; W. B. Stevens, *St. Louis, the Fourth City* (2 vols., 1911); William Hyde and H. L. Conard, *Encyc. of the Hist. of St. Louis*, vol. III (1899); *Who's Who in America*, 1903–05; *St. Louis Republic* and *St. Louis Globe-Democrat*, Nov. 20, 21, 1905; *Westliche Post*, Nov. 20, 21, 22, 1905.]   T. S. B.

PRENDERGAST, MAURICE BRAZIL
(Oct. 27, 1861–Feb. 1, 1924), genre painter, born
in Roxbury, Mass., was the son of Maurice Prendergast, a wholesale grocer, and Malvina (Ger-
maine) Prendergast. He was graduated from
the Rice grammar school, Boston, and studied
drawing from the cast at the Starr King school
in the evening classes. He made occasional excursions into the country for the purpose of
sketching from nature. With his elder brother,
Charles, who made artistic picture frames and
was a talented wood-carver, Maurice embarked
for Europe on board a cattle ship in 1887. Arrived in Paris, he first studied painting in the
Colorossi Academy, then at the Julian Academy,
under Joseph Blanc, Gustave Courtois, J. L.
Gérôme, and J. P. Laurens. Returning to Boston in 1889, he practised painting during the daylight hours and in the evening assisted his brother
in carving frames whenever there was need of
help. The brothers presently moved from Boston
to Winchester, Mass. It was at this period that
Maurice's sketchy but animated street scenes in
Boston and bright water colors of Revere Beach
with its throngs of pleasure-seekers began to attract the attention of the public to his work. Mrs.
J. Montgomery Sears, herself an accomplished
artist, was one of his first patrons. He made his
second trip to Europe in 1898–99. He went to
Venice, Rome, and Naples, and brought back a
group of vivacious and sparkling impressions,
some of which were shown at Chase's Gallery,
Boston, in 1900. Five years later, in company
with Charles Hopkinson and Charles Hovey Pepper, he held an exhibition at the Kimball Gallery,
Boston, and the same year he opened an exhibition at the Macbeth Gallery, New York. Then
came an exhibition at the Art Institute of Chicago, which brought to view not only gay water
colors of holiday scenes in Italy but also a score
of color prints of children at play in Franklin
Park, Boston, and several diverting circus motives. Still another exhibition was held at the
Macbeth Gallery, New York, in 1908.

In 1914 the Prendergast brothers moved to
New York, where they took a studio in Washington Square and remained until Maurice's
death in 1924. During this decade Maurice's
style underwent a radical change in the direction
of a more abstract and purely decorative art. The
light touch, the joy in life, and the beautiful color
of his early period were replaced by a more con-
ventionalized and less realistic manner, in which
the appeal was doubtless more esthetic but with
less of human interest. Nevertheless, though the
pictures of this late period may have been "caviar
to the general," they met with a considerable

degree of enthusiastic approval from the cogno-
scenti. At the Corcoran Gallery exhibition of
1923 he was awarded the third W. A. Clark
prize of $2000 and the Corcoran bronze medal
for his "Landscape with Figures." In 1926 a
memorial exhibtion of his oil paintings, water
colors, and pastels was held at the Cleveland Art
Museum; three years later another memorial exhibition was held at Cambridge, Mass., under the
auspices of the Harvard Society for Contemporary Art. Another exhibition was opened at the
Kraushaar Gallery, New York, in 1930. Prendergast's pictures are to be seen in the Phillips
Memorial Gallery, Washington, the Cleveland
Art Museum, the John Herron Art Institute,
Indianapolis, the Art Institute of Chicago, the
Newark (New Jersey) Museum, the Detroit Art
Museum, the art gallery of Yale University, the
Whitney Museum, New York, and at Andover
Academy, Andover, Mass.

[Margaret Breuning, *Maurice Prendergast* (1931);
Bull. Detroit Inst. of Arts, Oct. 1924; the *Arts*, Mar.
1924, Apr. 1926, Nov. 1930; Walter Pach, Foreword
in the catalogue of the memorial exhibition of the Harvard Soc. for Contemporary Art, 1929; *Boston Transcript*, Feb. 14, 1924.]   W. H. D.

PRENTICE, GEORGE DENNISON (Dec.
18, 1802–Jan. 22, 1870), journalist, the younger
of two children of Rufus and Sarah Stanton
Prentice, and a descendant of Thomas Prentice
who became a freeman of Cambridge, Mass., in
1652, was born in New London County, Conn.
A precocious child, he was taught by his mother
to read at three and a half and was then sent to
the district school. Between the years of nine
and fourteen he was obliged to work on his father's farm but that did not deaden his ambition
for a professional career. By studying he prepared himself and by teaching he earned money
to pay his expenses at college and in 1820 he
entered the sophomore class of Brown University. He graduated in 1823 and after another
period of teaching he began to study law and
gained admission to the bar, although his practice was brief and small. In 1827 he had his first
newspaper experience in the editorship of a New
London paper; in 1828 he became first editor of
the *New England Review*, a Hartford weekly.
Because he displayed an unusual aptitude for
political leadership he was sent in 1830 to visit
Henry Clay in Kentucky in order to compile a
biography of the candidate. Published in 1831,
the *Biography of Henry Clay* was hastily written
and over-eulogistic but its author's personality
made upon Kentucky politicians so favorable an
impression that he was invited to take charge of
a projected newspaper to combat the spread of
Jacksonian Democracy throughout the state.

186

Prentice

This paper was the *Louisville Daily Journal*, first issued on Nov. 24, 1830. In a short time it brought to its editor a reputation for fearlessness and ability. Prentice had need of those qualities, for with political feeling at high pitch only a courageous and capable man could have controlled the policies of the *Daily Journal* and made it, as he did, the most influential Whig paper in the South and West. One authority has been willing to call him "one of the greatest editors of the middle nineteenth century" (J. M. Lee, *A History of American Journalism*, 1917, p. 340). The honesty and intelligence of his editorials and paragraphs could not be denied even by those who dreaded the sharpness of his wit or who disagreed with him. Courage and honesty were tested by personal and national crises : more than once he was forced to physical encounter in self-defense, and at the opening of the Civil War he was offered great inducements to support the cause of the South. Prentice's own family was divided on the question of loyalty ; his wife, Henrietta Benham, whom he had married on Aug. 18, 1835, was from Ohio ; his two sons entered the Confederate army, and one of them was killed. He himself was not an abolitionist, but he was a Unionist and upheld Lincoln's administration so vigorously as to be largely responsible for Kentucky's refusal to secede. The Emancipation Proclamation cooled him toward the President but did not alter his belief in the principle of union. Left somewhat morbid by his experiences, he withdrew from the management of his paper which, as a result of a merger, appeared on Nov. 8, 1868, as the Louisville *Courier-Journal*, under Henry Watterson's editorship.

Prentice is described as having been slightly above medium height, with a pleasing face of irregular features. His nature was generous and impulsive. His verse, which does not rise above the sentimental mediocrity of many writers of the period, is represented in *The Poems of George D. Prentice* (1876, 1883). *Prenticeana*, a collection of his wittiest editorial paragraphs, had two editions (1860, 1870). Selections from his poetry are to be found in four anthologies of Kentucky and Western literature.

[There is a biographical sketch of Prentice by J. J. Piatt, in *The Poems of Geo. D. Prentice* (1876). See also : C. J. F. Binney, *The Hist. and Geneal. of the Prentice, or Prentiss, Family in New England* (2nd ed., 1883) ; Mary Scrugham, "Geo. D. Prentice," *Reg. of the Ky. State Hist. Soc.*, Sept. 1915, concerning his political opinions ; Henry Watterson, *Marse Henry* (1919), pp. 169–76, and *Geo. Dennison Prentice : A Memorial Address* (1870) ; C. G. Shanks, "Geo. D. Prentice," *Lippincott's Mag.*, Nov. 1869 ; E. M. Coulter, *The Civil War and Readjustment in Ky.* (1926) ; Bayard Taylor, *Critical Essays* (1880), pp. 314–18.]

G. C. K.

Prentice

PRENTICE, SAMUEL OSCAR (Aug. 8, 1850–Nov. 2, 1924), jurist, was born at North Stonington, Conn., the son of Chester Smith and Lucy (Crary) Prentice and a descendant of early New England colonists, among whom were Thomas Prentice who emigrated from England to Boston before 1649 and was made a freeman of Cambridge in 1652 and Elder William Brewster of the *Mayflower*. His education was obtained in the schools of North Stonington and at the Norwich Free Academy and finally at Yale College (A.B., 1873) and at the Yale School of Law. Upon his graduation from the law school in 1875 he received a Townsend prize for the best oration at Commencement. He was admitted to the bar in June 1875 and for a year was law clerk in a Hartford office. In 1876 he formed a partnership with Elisha Johnson which lasted until his appointment to the bench. He was prominent and active in the political and legal life of his community, serving from 1882 to 1889 as city attorney of Hartford and from 1875 to 1889 as clerk of the Hartford County bar. He was also chairman of the Republican committees of the town and state and delegate of the state conventions. In 1889 he was executive secretary to Gov. Morgan G. Bulkeley, and that same year was appointed to the superior court of the state. His judicial career thus begun was long and distinguished. For twelve years he acted as trial court judge. In 1901 he became associate justice of the supreme court of errors, and in 1913 he was appointed chief justice by Gov. Simeon E. Baldwin, his former colleague and chief on that court. In 1920, then in active vigor, he was retired in accordance with the provision of the Connecticut constitution requiring the retirement of all judges at the age of seventy.

In 1896 Prentice was appointed instructor in pleading in the Yale School of Law and he served as professor of that subject from 1901 to 1915. He was a member of the bar examining committee of the state bar from its formation in 1890 and was chairman from 1898 to 1913. For many years he was associated with various civic interests, serving on two Hartford library boards, on the Hartford Park Board, and on the board of directors of the Connecticut Humane Society, of which he was president for several years. He was married on Apr. 24, 1901, to Anne Combe Post of Jersey City. Her death in 1924, after a happy married life, probably hastened his own death which occurred the same year. Prentice's outstanding service to his state was as supreme court judge. His opinions were carefully reasoned, were clear and convincing, and felicitously expressed. Of striking and imposing physique, he was in appearance and action the ideal judge. For the most part, especially while he was chief justice, his court was unanimously in accord with his views. Occasionally, however, he would disagree and then he would express himself in dissent with a fire and a spirit which showed his force. As professor at Yale he showed the same clarity of thought and facility of expression which distinguished his judicial utterances. His subject was difficult, but even the intricacies of common law pleading became clear under his logical analysis and presentation.

[Sources include: F. J. Shepard, compiler, *Hist. of the Yale Class of 1873* (1901) and *Fifth Supplement to the Hist. of the Yale Class of 1873* (1926); *Obit. Record of Yale Grads.*, 1923–24; J. P. Andrews, "Obit. Sketch of Samuel O. Prentice," 104 *Conn. Reports*, 750; C. J. F. Binney, *The Hist. and Geneal. of the Prentice, or Prentiss, Family in New England* (2nd. ed., 1883); *Who's Who in America*, 1922–23; *Hartford Courant*, Nov. 3, 1924. Prentice's opinions appear in Volumes 74 to 95 of the *Conn. Reports.*]   C. E. C.

PRENTISS, BENJAMIN MAYBERRY (Nov. 23, 1819–Feb. 8, 1901), soldier, the son of Henry Leonidas and Rebecca (Mayberry) Prentiss, was born at Belleville, Va. He was directly descended from Valentine Prentice who became a member of the First Church in Roxbury, Mass., in 1632, and from William Brewster, 1567–1644 [*q.v.*], of the *Mayflower* colony. He spent his early childhood in Virginia, where he was educated in the country schools and at a private military school. He accompanied his parents to Missouri and settled in Marion County in 1836, where he manufactured cordage. In the spring of 1841 he removed to Quincy, Ill., and engaged in business with his father. In 1844–45 he served as a lieutenant of militia against the Mormons in Hancock County, Ill., and during the Mexican War he served as a captain in the 1st Illinois Volunteers, which distinguished itself at the battle of Buena Vista in February 1847. He was discharged at Camargo, Mexico, on June 17, 1847, by reason of expiration of service, and returned home, where he studied law. In 1860 he was an unsuccessful Republican candidate for Congress.

At the outbreak of the Civil War, he was a colonel of Illinois militia, and in April 1861, was placed in command of seven companies of Illinois troops sent to Cairo, Ill. On Apr. 24–25, two river steamers, the *C. E. Hillman* and the *John D. Perry*, carrying contraband, were seized by Prentiss' men. This was probably the first seizure of munitions on the Mississippi River and was made four days before orders were received from the War Department authorizing the suspension of the shipments of munitions to ports under rebel control. Later the same month Prentiss was mustered into the service of the United States, in command of the 10th Infantry, Illinois Volunteers. In May 1861 he was promoted to brigadier-general and in August was detailed to command all of north and central Missouri. He took part in the battle of Mount Zion and other minor engagements in the state. Being ordered to the field by General Halleck, he proceeded to Pittsburg Landing, Tenn., where he arrived on Apr. 1, to organize and take command of the 6th Division, Army of the Tennessee. On the first day of the battle of Shiloh, he distinguished himself by holding a difficult position against great odds, but he finally was captured along with most of his command and held in Talladega, Selma, Madison and Libby prisons until October 1862, when he was exchanged. After his release, he was appointed a member of the general court martial in the case of Fitz-John Porter [*q.v.*]. He was made a major-general in November 1862, and ordered to report at Milliken's Bend, to General Grant, who assigned him to command the eastern district of Arkansas. On July 4, 1863, he commanded the Union forces in the battle of Helena and gained a decided victory over a numerically superior force. He resigned his commission in October 1863, and returned to Quincy, where he resumed the practice of law.

During his residence at Quincy, he was appointed a federal pension agent by General Grant, an office which he held for eight years. In 1878 he moved to Missouri, spent a short time in Sullivan County, and then engaged in the practice of law at Kirksville. In 1881, he moved to Bethany, Mo., and was a special agent for the general land office with station at Denver, Col. In 1888, after the election of President Harrison, he was appointed postmaster at Bethany and received the same appointment later from President McKinley. He held this position until his death at Bethany. He was married in Marion County, Mo., in March 1839, to Margaret Sowdowsky, who died at Quincy in 1860. He subsequently married Mary Worthington Whitney who died in 1894. There were six children by the first marriage, and four by the second.

[Pension Bureau records; C. J. F. Binney, *The Hist. and Geneal. of the Prentice or Prentiss Family* (1883); Walter Williams, *A Hist. of Northwest Missouri* (1905), vols. I, III; *Official Army Reg. of the Vol. Force, U. S. Army*, Part VI (1865); *St. Louis Globe-Democrat*, Feb. 9, 1901.]   R. C. C.—n.

PRENTISS, ELIZABETH PAYSON (Oct. 26, 1818–Aug. 13, 1878), writer of religious and juvenile fiction, was born in Portland, Me., fifth of the eight children of the Rev. Edward [*q.v.*] and Ann (Shipman) Payson. Her mother was a forceful woman, intellectually vigorous, and punctilious in religious duties, whose character was the model from which the mother in Elizabeth's *Stepping Heavenward* was drawn. Her father died when she was nine years old and she received her education at schools in New York (1830) and in Portland (1833–34), where her older sister, Louisa, was a teacher. Louisa was the mainstay of the family after her father's death, and greatly influenced Elizabeth during her girlhood.

Her literary work began in 1834 with a contribution to *Youth's Companion,* to which she later sent many short didactic tales and sketches over the signature "E." When a young woman she began a career of teaching, opening a school for small children in her mother's house in Portland (1838); two years later she taught in a girl's school in Richmond, Va., but her delicate health soon compelled her to return to Portland. After recuperating, she again taught in the Richmond school until its failure in 1843, when she went back home and eventually became engaged to the Rev. George Lewis Prentiss [q.v.], whom she married in April 1845. They moved to New Bedford, Mass., where Prentiss began his ministry, and where the first of their children was born. After a visit to her friends, Susan and Anna Warner [qq.v.], who probably encouraged her in her literary aspirations, in 1853 she returned to her writing and, despite growing domestic responsibilities, produced volumes, stories, and articles with surprising regularity. Her editorials, religious dialogues, and sketches were printed chiefly in the *Youth's Companion,* the *New York Observer,* and the *Advance* (Chicago). Many of these were collected in a posthumous volume, *Avis Benson* (1879). A novel, *The Flower of the Family* (1854), exalting filial piety in young ladies, was her first great success, and was translated into French and German. A story for young children, *Little Susy's Six Birthdays* (1853), was the first of a series of "Little Susy" books, which were popular in America and in England, where they were republished. Her most popular book, *Stepping Heavenward* (1869), sold over one hundred thousand copies in America alone and appeared in more than a dozen editions in Europe. For several decades it was widely used in Sunday-school libraries and was considered ideal as a prize award for school children. She placed her pen at the disposal of various societies; *The Old Brown Pitcher* (1868), for instance, was written at the request of the National Temperance Society and was published by its press. Two of her works were translations from the German: *Peterchen and Gretchen* (1860), and

Griselda (1876), the latter a dramatic poem by Friedrich Halm, printed for the Young Women's Christian Association. A volume of religious verse which appeared in two editions, best known as *Golden Hours* (1873), is described by her husband as her spiritual autobiography. It contains simple, emotional lyrics, which show her constant reliance upon religion to assist her through the sorrows and trivialities of earthly life. Many of them have found their way into church hymnals.

In 1858 she went to Europe with her family and, because of her husband's poor health, spent more than two years abroad, chiefly in Switzerland. During the first half of 1860 they lived at Paris where Dr. Prentiss was in charge of the American chapel. They returned in the fall to New York, where he became pastor of the Church of the Covenant. They were both popular and happy in this new and prosperous parish. In 1868 they built a summer home in Dorset, Vt., which served as an annual retreat for the family. Here, after a short illness, Elizabeth Prentiss died in her sixtieth year.

[*Geneal. of the Descendants of John Eliot* (1905); G. L. Prentiss, *The Life and Letters of Elizabeth Prentiss* (1882, 1898); *N. Y. Tribune,* Aug. 14, 1878.]
R. W. B.
A. A. G.

PRENTISS, GEORGE LEWIS (May 12, 1816–Mar. 18, 1903), clergyman, teacher, and author, was born at West Gorham, Me., the son of William Prentiss, a sea-captain, and Abigail (Lewis) Prentiss. He attended Gorham Academy and Bowdoin College, graduating from the latter with the degree of A.B. in 1835. Never robust, for four years after graduation he was a semi-invalid. He studied Hebrew and German privately in New York under Isaac Nordheimer [q.v.], then one of the ablest Orientalists in the United States. Financed by his elder brother, Seargent Smith Prentiss [q.v.], he spent two years in Europe, studied philosophy and theology under Prof. August Tholuck and others at Halle, made numerous visits to St. Peter's at Rome, had an audience with Gregory XVI, and met a number of celebrated people including Archdeacon Hare, Carlyle, Wordsworth, and Mrs. Gillman, patroness of Samuel Taylor Coleridge, whose writings had influenced Prentiss profoundly.

Returning to the United States, he was ordained, Apr. 9, 1845, to the Congregational ministry and installed as pastor of the South Trinitarian Church, New Bedford, Mass. A week later he married Elizabeth [see Elizabeth Payson Prentiss], daughter of Rev. Edward Payson [q.v.]. On Nov. 6, 1850, he became associated with Dr. Jonathan B. Condit in the pastorate of the Second Presbyterian Church of Newark, N. J., but in April of the following year was called to the Mercer Street Presbyterian Church, near Washington Square, New York. Worn down by city life, he resigned and resided with his family in Switzerland and France from 1858 to 1860. Early in 1862 he organized for the New School Presbyterians the Church of the Covenant in the growing Murray Hill section of New York, which erected a church building at Park Avenue and 35th Street, dedicated Apr. 30, 1865. Here was held the General Assembly which voted to unite the Old and New Schools, thus healing the schism of 1837.

Prentiss became part-time instructor in pastoral theology at Union Theological Seminary in 1871, and two years later resigned his parish to give his full time to a professorship of pastoral theology, church polity, and mission work, later transferring to the chair of catechetics, apologetics, and Christian ethics. In the controversy which arose out of the heresy trial of Dr. Charles Augustus Briggs [q.v.], Prentiss urged the Seminary to rescind the agreement of 1870 with the Presbyterian Church in the United States of America, which action was taken on Oct. 13, 1892. He retired in 1897. At his death, some six years later, he was buried at Dorset, Vt., near his summer home. His tastes were literary; his theology Biblical and Christocentric; his preaching and his teaching rarely elicited enthusiasm.

Besides numerous addresses, sermons, and articles, he published *A Memoir of S. S. Prentiss* (2 vols., 1855; reprinted, 1879 and 1886); *Our National Bane: or, the Dry-rot in American Politics* (1877); *The Life and Letters of Elizabeth Prentiss* (copr. 1882); *The Union Theological Seminary in the City of New York: Historical and Biographical Sketches of Its First Fifty Years* (1889); *The Agreement Between Union Seminary and the General Assembly* (1891); *The Union Theological Seminary in the City of New York; Its Design and Another Decade of Its History* (1899); *The Bright Side of Life: Glimpses of It Through Fourscore Years: A Family Story* (2 vols., 1901).

[In addition to the last named work, see *Union Theolog. Sem.; In Memoriam George Lewis Prentiss* (1903); Shepherd Knapp, *A Hist. of the Brick Presbyt. Church, New York* (1909); C. R. Gillett, *Alumni Cat. of the Union Theolog. Sem.* (1926); *N. Y. Observer*, Mar. 26, 1903; *N. Y. Times*, Mar. 19, 1903.]

W. W. R.

PRENTISS, SAMUEL (Mar. 31, 1782–Jan. 15, 1857), jurist, United States senator from Vermont, was born at Stonington, Conn., the son of Samuel and Lucretia (Holmes) Prentiss.

His paternal ancestor, Capt. Thomas Prentice, came from England to Massachusetts, where he was made a freeman of Cambridge in 1652. His grandfather, Samuel, served in the Revolution as a colonel; his father, as a doctor. At Northfield, Mass., where his father settled in 1786, the boy was educated in part under the direction of Rev. Samuel Allen, who seems to have encouraged in him a taste for literature which he never lost. At the age of nineteen he began the study of law in an office at Northfield, continuing later at Brattleboro, Vt. Admitted to the bar in 1802, he opened an office the following year at Montpelier. Here, except for absences while in political or judicial offices, he lived the rest of his long life.

At first, as a young lawyer in a small village, his practice was slight, leaving him ample leisure for that scholarly and unremitting study of the fundamentals of legal science which he pursued throughout his life. Excessively modest and unassertive, he but slowly built up a reputation as the most learned lawyer in the state. Though his scruples prevented his accepting any client whose cause he distrusted, his learning and honesty eventually gave him a wide practice which included most of the important cases in the state. In spite of his success, he was so lacking in self-confidence that he refused in 1822 the offer of a place upon the state supreme bench. Three years later he did accept such a position, however; but for some time he rarely wrote the court's decisions, though his counsel seems to have determined the character of the most important of them. In 1829 he became chief justice of his tribunal.

When, in 1830, a United States senator was to be elected from Vermont, Prentiss was proposed for the place. Except for two years in the state legislature (1824–25), he had held no political office nor was he known as a politician. So outstanding, however, was his ability that, though calling himself a Federalist and later becoming a Whig, he was elected on the first ballot by a legislature with a Democratic majority. For eleven years he sat in the Senate, an unassuming, unaggressive figure, speaking rarely, and making no effort to win popularity or publicity. Though counted as one of the ablest men in a body which contained the greatest political figures of the day, he exercised no outward leadership. What influence he possessed came neither from eloquence nor skill as a political manager, but rather from the respect which his intellect and character inspired among his colleagues. His name is therefore not connected with any of the great legislative acts of his pe-

riod. He sponsored the law which forbade dueling in the District of Columbia and in opposition
to his party resisted unsuccessfully the bankruptcy act of 1841.

A vacancy occurring in the federal court for
the Vermont district, in 1842 Prentiss resigned
his senatorship to accept it. For the rest of his
life he presided over this court with simple, kindly dignity, a gracious, conservative judge of
great learning and perfect honesty, scrupulous
in his care for justice. His tall spare figure,
neatly clothed in the fashion of an older day,
and his formal but kindly courtesy gave him
even among his contemporaries the name of a
gentleman of the old school. On Oct. 3, 1804,
he married Lucretia Houghton of Northfield,
Mass. They had twelve children of whom nine
of the sons who reached maturity followed their
father's profession of the law.

[C. J. F. Binney, *The Hist. and Geneal. of the Prentice or Prentiss Family* (2nd ed., 1883) and *Memoirs of
Judge Samuel Prentiss of Montpelier, Vt., and His Wife,
Lucretia (Houghton) Prentiss* (n.d.) ; E. J. Phelps,
*Address on . . . Samuel Prentiss . . . with the Proc. of
the Vt. Hist. Soc. Oct. 17, 1882* (1883) ; D. P. Thompson, *Hist. of the Town of Montpelier* (1860) ; *Records
of the Governor and Council of the State of Vermont*,
vol. VII (1879) ; *Biog. Dir. Am. Cong.* (1928).]

P. D. E.

PRENTISS, SEARGENT SMITH (Sept.
30, 1808–July 1, 1850), orator, congressman
from Mississippi, was born in Portland, Me., a
descendant of Henry Prentice who emigrated
from England and settled in Cambridge, Mass.,
before 1640. He was the third child of Abigail
(Lewis) and William Prentiss, a shipmaster,
and he was the brother of George Lewis Prentiss [*q.v.*]. When the War of 1812 ruined commerce, the family moved inland to Gorham, and
there the boy attended school. A fever in early
childhood, which sent him through life limping,
turned him to books, and the straitened finances
of the family warned him to make the best of his
opportunities. He graduated from Bowdoin College in 1826; before attaining his majority he
had read law in Maine and in Natchez, taught
school near the latter and passed the Mississippi bar examination. He embarked on his
profession at Natchez as junior partner of Felix
Huston and rapidly attained prominence, being
particularly successful in criminal law. Early in
1832 he removed to Vicksburg and formed a
partnership with John I. Guion that became "one
of the most celebrated in the Union" (Lynch,
post, p. 218). In 1836 he entered the lower
house of the state legislature and next year was
elected to Congress, but he was not seated for
this was the time of the noted Mississippi contested election. He was allowed to address Con-

gress on this issue, and his great speech, continued on three consecutive days, established his
reputation as an orator of the first rank. As Congress declared the seats vacant, Mississippi held
another election in which he was again successful, and he served from May 30, 1838, to Mar. 3,
1839. In 1839 he was defeated for the Senate by
Robert J. Walker [*q.v.*], in whose office he had
earlier read law. Except for his ability as a
speaker, he was not a good practical politician.
He had little desire for public office and took no
great interest in political news. In statecraft he
was conservative rather than original. He distrusted the trend toward democracy in the Mississippi constitution of 1832 and opposed the repudiation of the Union Bank bonds. He was a
consistent Whig, being led thereto by his admiration for Henry Clay and by his own career,
which gave him a non-sectional point of view.

While his opinions were generally sound, his
fame rested chiefly on his ability to express these
in a compelling form. Though he spoke with a
very slight lisp, his voice "had a clear silvery
ring, which, in spite of his rapid enunciation,
permeated distinctly every part of the" (Shields,
post, p. 144) old chamber of the House of Representatives; and his gestures and appearance
harmonized with his voice. A second foundation for his success as an orator was his ability
to speak with little preparation, an art that he
had cultivated in debating societies. He read
widely and rapidly, but years later he could use
precise quotations and illustrations to adorn an
extempore address. Further, he could arrange
his material in orderly form as he spoke. It is
small wonder that with these abilities he said he
had rather make ten speeches than write one.
In cold, lifeless print the fragments of his
speeches are yet interesting, but his personality,
on which his magnetic appeal largely rested, can
be apprehended better through his letters. He
spoke in many places and on many occasions, for
example, in 1840 he campaigned for Harrison
from New Orleans to Portland and from Newark to Chicago.

In 1845, by a decision of the Supreme Court of
the United States, he lost extensive property in
Vicksburg and was plunged deeply into debt. A
few months later he removed to New Orleans,
seeking a more lucrative practice. In spite of
the change to a different system of law he met
with success, but his health was already giving
way, partly because of his heavy drinking, to
which, with gambling, he had early become addicted. His eloquence was undimmed when he
defended Lopez, the Cuban Revolutionist, in
New Orleans, but returning to his room he col-

lapsed. He was taken by steamer to Natchez to the girlhood home of his wife, Mary Jane (Williams) Prentiss, whom he had married in 1842, but her care could not arrest the inroads of disease. He died there at "Longwood" and was buried at "Gloucester," survived by his widow and four children.

[G. L. Prentiss, *A Memoir of S. S. Prentiss* (2 vols., 1855); J. D. Shields, *The Life and Times of Seargent Smith Prentiss* (1884); C. J. F. Binney, *The Hist. and Geneal. of the Prentice, or Prentiss Family in New England* (2nd ed., 1883); H. H. Hagan, *Eight Am. Lawyers* (1923); H. S. Foote, *Bench and Bar of the South* (1876); J. D. Lynch, *The Bench and Bar of Miss.* (1881); Reuben Davis, *Recollections* (1889); W. H. Sparks, *The Memories of Fifty Years* (1870).]

C. S. S.

PRESBREY, EUGENE WILEY (Mar. 13, 1853–Sept. 9, 1931), stage manager and dramatist, was associated in various capacities with the American theatre through his entire active life. He was born in Williamsburg, a small country town in western Massachusetts, the son of Luther Clarke Presbrey, a cloth finisher who had come from Willington, Conn., and Julia (Hillman) Presbrey, a native of Williamsburg. Going to Boston before he had reached the age of twenty, Presbrey became first an art student, and then dabbled in art in his own studio for several years after he had begun to make the stage his profession. He was taken into the company at the Boston Theatre and acted minor utility parts there from 1874 to 1879, appearing under the name of E. Wiley, and sometimes as Gene Wiley, in *The Two Orphans, The Exiles, Sardanapalus,* and other melodramas and spectacles that were then popular. "Drifting to New York," as he himself expressed it, he acted first at the Madison Square Theatre, then under the direction of Daniel Frohman, in *The Professor* and *Esmeralda,* and when the latter play was taken on the road he filled the position of stage director and manager. When the Madison Square Theatre came under the direction of A. M. Palmer, he was retained by him, and remained in his employ and at Palmer's Theatre from 1884 to 1896, taking an active part in the stage production of *Jim the Penman, Captain Swift, Aunt Jack, Sealed Instructions, Alabama, Trilby,* and many other plays. During this period he also lectured on dramatic subjects before the students of the American Academy of Dramatic Arts.

In an interview Presbrey declared as his professional objective and as the result of his personal experience that "the ideal stage manager should be the epitome of versatility, and should be familiar with art, science, literature, music, for these are his tools." He wrote, rearranged, adapted, and dramatized many plays, drawing

his material mainly from novels and the work of other dramatists. He was primarily a play constructor with all the tricks of his trade in his head and at his fingers' ends, and it is doubtful if he ever contributed anything original to the stage. One of his earliest plays was *The Squirrel Inn* (1893) made from Frank R. Stockton's story of that title with the aid of its author, and this was followed by *A Virginia Courtship* (1901), its theme being that of *The Rivals* with its scene changed to colonial America; *Raffles* (1904), from E. W. Hornung's stories of the exploits of a gentleman burglar; *The Right of Way* (1907), from Sir Gilbert Parker's novel; *The Adventures of Gerard* (1905), from Arthur Conan Doyle's romantic story, and *The Barrier* (1908), from Rex Beach's romance. He went to California in 1919, and during his later years he was associated in an advisory capacity in the motion pictures at the studios in Hollywood. Aside from his stage interests he was a designer and builder of yachts and an expert in marine and land shells, of which he had a large collection. He was married in June 1877 to Carrie Paine, later to Annie Russell, the actress, and on June 16, 1897, to Alice L. Fifield, who with a son survived him.

[Eugene Tompkins and Quincy Kilby, *The Hist. of the Boston Theatre* (1908); Dixie Hines and H. P. Hanaford, *Who's Who in Music and Drama* (1914); John Parker, *Who's Who in the Theatre* (1925); *Who's Who in America,* 1930–31; J. W. Presby, *Wm. Presbrey of London, England, . . . and His Descendants* (1918); H. W. Hillman, *Ancestral Chronological Record of the Hillman Family* (1905); article in the Chicago *Inter Ocean,* May 8, 1892; interview in the *N. Y. Dramatic Mirror,* Oct. 10, 1896, and the *Indianapolis News,* Feb. 23, 1905; obituaries in the *N. Y. Times, Boston Transcript,* and *Los Angeles Times,* Sept. 10, 1931.]

E. F. E.

PRESCOTT, ALBERT BENJAMIN (Dec. 12, 1832–Feb. 25, 1905), chemist, son of Benjamin and Experience (Huntley) Prescott, was born at Hastings, N. Y., and died at Ann Arbor, Mich. He was descended from John Prescott who settled in Watertown, Mass., in 1640, and in 1643 was one of the first settlers of Lancaster, Mass. His early years were spent on a farm. An accident at an early age partially crippled him for life and his enforced leisure he spent in studying language, literature, and science. Stirred by current topics, he espoused the cause of antislavery and wrote articles for the *Liberator.* Later he acted as a general reporter for the *New York Tribune.* About 1854 he decided to study medicine, and during the next six years he reviewed chemistry and zoölogy and also spent some time in the office of a physician. Entering the department of medicine of the University of Michigan in 1860, he soon attained a high rank and served for two years as an assistant in the department of chemistry. He received the degree of M.D. in 1864. Soon afterward he enlisted in the United States Army and served as assistant surgeon until his honorable discharge, with the brevet rank of captain, in August 1865. He then went to the University of Michigan where he spent the remainder of his life.

Beginning as assistant professor of chemistry and lecturer in organic chemistry, he subsequently held all important positions in the department, taught most branches of chemistry, organized and directed certain sub-departments, and in addition wrote several textbooks and upwards of two hundred technical articles. With others he took a major part in establishing the school of pharmacy of the university and was its dean for thirty years (1874–1905). Through this administrative work and his fifty or more articles on pharmacy he exerted a wholesome influence in this field. For many years he served as an active or advisory member of the committee on the revision of the *Pharmacopœia,* and many of the methods of analysis in this official publication, particularly those dealing with alkaloids, are due to investigations carried out in his laboratory. As director of the chemical laboratory for twenty years (1884–1905) he stimulated his colleagues and students to maintain high standards of technique. He also aroused dynamic interest in the teaching of chemistry and other sciences by numerous papers and addresses. His work in pharmacy led him into the allied field of toxicology where he won distinction by the precision of his investigations. He also did considerable work in sanitary and food chemistry, and rendered notable service by improving the drinking water of Michigan, formulating laws dealing with the sale of foods and drugs, and devising methods for detecting adulterations and preservatives in food. He was intensely and continuously interested in organic and analytical chemistry. Beginning in 1874 as the joint author, with S. H. Douglas, of *Qualitative Chemical Analysis* and as sole author of *Outlines of Proximate Organic Analyses* (1875), he continued to write books and revisions in these branches of chemistry for practically the rest of his life, usually as the sole author, though later editions bear also the name of a colleague. These books were widely used and contributed vitally to the progress of chemistry in the United States.

In 1866 Prescott married Abigail Freeburn of Ann Arbor, Mich. For many years their peaceful, scholarly home gave inspiration and pleasure to thousands of students. They had no children, but they adopted a son. Prescott was a member of many scientific societies and served several in an official capacity; in 1886 he was president of the American Chemical Society. He was so methodical in his work, that despite the onerous duties performed for his university through nearly half a century, he found time to travel in Europe, discharge obligations in religious and benevolent organizations, give wise and unprejudiced service to his colleagues, and maintain loving companionship with a wide circle of friends.

[The fullest account of Prescott is given in the privately printed memorial booklet entitled *Albert Benjamin Prescott, Dec. 12, 1832–Feb. 25, 1905* (1906). Other sources are: *Cat. of Grads., Non-Grads., Officers, and Members of Faculties, 1837–1921, Univ. of Mich., Ann Arbor* (1923); *Jour. Am. Chem. Soc.,* Sept. 1905; *Science,* Apr. 21, 1905; *Am. Jour. Pharm.,* June 1905; *Pharmaceut. Era,* Mar. 2, 1905; Wm. Prescott, *The Prescott Memorial* (1870), and the *Detroit Jour.,* Feb. 25, 1905. For a bibliography of Prescott's works see the memorial booklet cited above; the *Gen. Index to Vols. One to Fifty of Proc. Am. Pharmaceut. Asso.* (1902), and *Collective Index to Vols. Fifty-one to Fifty-nine of the Proc. and to Vols. One to Fourteen of the Year Books of the Am. Pharmaceut. Asso.* (1930).]
L. C. N.

PRESCOTT, GEORGE BARTLETT (Sept. 16, 1830–Jan. 18, 1894), telegraph engineer, author, the third child of Mark Hollis and Priscilla (Bartlett) Prescott, was born in Kingston, N. H., of which town his earliest American ancestor, James Prescott, was an incorporator in 1694. He received his primary education there, and later attended private schools in Portland, Me., until he was sixteen years old. From his youth he had shown a keen interest in electrical science, and had followed very closely the introduction of the electro-magnetic telegraph by Samuel F. B. Morse. While still in school he learned the Morse code and the methods of sending messages and maintaining telegraphic equipment.

Upon completing school, he made his way to New York, where he acquired additional knowledge and on Mar. 6, 1847, entered the service of the New York & Boston Magnetic Telegraph Company as telegraph operator and assistant at New York. Three months later he was transferred to the Boston office of the company and made assistant manager. After another three months, he was placed in charge of the newly opened office at New Haven, Conn. He continued here until 1850, when he left the company to join the New York & New England Telegraph Company, which organization had just become the owner of the Bain Chemical telegraph system. For two years Prescott was chief operator for this company in Boston, but on Nov. 1, 1852, resigned to take the managership of the New York & Boston, or "Commercial," Telegraph

Company at Springfield, Mass. In the course of the following three years a number of individual submarine telegraph companies were established along the Eastern seaboard. These were united in 1855 and Prescott was made manager of the group with headquarters in Boston. While he was serving in this capacity, the American Telegraph Company was established, which became the chief telegraph organization in the eastern part of the United States, controlling all of the separately organized companies established in the preceding twelve years, including those operating the marine lines. In 1859 Prescott was appointed general manager of this company at Boston. Two years later he became superintendent of all of the American Telegraph Company's lines in eastern New York, Connecticut, and Vermont. In 1866 the American and the Western Union telegraph companies were consolidated and Prescott was appointed electrician of the new organization, which was thereafter called the Western Union Telegraph Company. In this position he had to act as barrier to a flood of inventions brought to the company for attention, and all of the telegraph innovations of the time, such as the duplex and quadruplex systems, were put into practical operative shape under his immediate direction; subject to his supervision, also, was all the construction and reconstruction work of the company. Meanwhile, the question of private or government ownership of the telegraph began to be seriously discussed both in Congress and in the country generally. Because of his great experience and his keen analytical mind, Prescott was called to New York in 1869, given the title of statistician, and assigned the work of studying the relative merits of the two systems. As a result, he became the expert witness of his company before various congressional committees in the succeeding ten years, and probably did more than any other single individual to prevent the proposed acquisition of the telegraph by the government.

In 1877 the Western Union Telegraph Company obtained control of the telephone patents of Elisha Gray and Thomas A. Edison, and organized the American Speaking Telephone Company as a rival to the Bell Telephone Company. Prescott, who had made a thorough study of the telephone, was active in the organization of this subsidiary, and was an original member of the board of directors. He became, too, in 1878, vice-president and a member of the board of the Gold & Stock Telegraph Company, which was the largest of the organizations maintaining private telegraph lines throughout the country.

He was also one of the incorporators of the Metropolitan Telephone & Telegraph Company in New York, but in 1882 he resigned all active connections with his many communication interests and devoted the remainder of his life to literary work.

He began his writing about 1852 when he published in Boston an account of his discovery that the aurora borealis is of electrical origin. The printed descriptions of his many experiments in connection with this subject attracted much attention throughout the world, being reproduced in all the leading scientific journals of Europe and America. Chief among his works on electrical subjects are *History, Theory and Practice of the Electric Telegraph* (1860); *Electricity and the Electric Telegraph* (1877); *The Speaking Telephone* (1878); *Dynamo Electricity* (1884); *Bell's Electric Speaking Telephone, Its Invention, Construction, Application, Modification and History* (1884); and *The Electric Telephone* (1890). Prescott was married at Springfield, Mass., on Dec. 9, 1857, to Eliza C. Parsons, and at the time of his sudden death in New York was survived by his widow and one daughter.

[William Prescott, *The Prescott Memorial, or a Geneal. Memoir of the Prescott Families in America* (1870); J. D. Reid, *The Telegraph in America* (1879); *Electrical Rev.*, Jan. 24, 1894; *N. Y. Tribune*, and *N. Y. Times*, Jan. 19, 1894.]   C. W. M.

PRESCOTT, OLIVER (Apr. 27, 1731–Nov. 17, 1804), physician and soldier, was born at Groton, Mass., the son of Benjamin and Abigail (Oliver) Prescott and a brother of William Prescott [*q.v.*]. He was graduated from Harvard in 1750, and after studying medicine under Dr. Ebenezer Robie of Sudbury, settled in Groton where he built up a successful practice. Military as well as medical matters early claimed his interest. Prior to the Revolution, he held various regimental commissions under the King in the provincial militia. At the outbreak of hostilities between England and the colonies, he received appointment from the revolutionary government of Massachusetts as brigadier-general of the militia of Middlesex County, and later (1778) as major-general of militia throughout the commonwealth. During the British occupation of Boston, he was employed in detailing guards at bridges and other places to prevent Loyalist sympathizers from holding intercourse with the garrison. On Apr. 17, 1775, by direction of the committees of safety and supplies, four pieces of rebel artillery at Concord were transferred to his custody at Groton, and thus escaped capture by the redcoats during their memorable expedition of Apr. 19. On Oct. 30 he was elected a member of the board of war but declined to serve. After the Revolution his martial ardor found outlet in the suppression of Shays's Rebellion, during the course of which he was busily engaged in recruiting troops, arresting law-breakers, and dispatching intelligence of the movements of the insurgents to the state authorities.

His civilian services were no less notable and varied than his military. He was town clerk of Groton for thirteen years and selectman for over thirty. He served on many important town committees, including a committee (of which he was chairman) to protest against the Stamp Act, the Committee of Correspondence, and a committee charged with the duty of enforcing the Association of 1774. He was a member of the supreme executive council from 1777 to 1780, justice of the peace and of the quorum, and judge of probate for Middlesex County from 1779 until his death. Keenly interested in education, he was one of the original trustees of Groton Academy and the first president of the board. His high professional standing is attested by the fact that he was awarded an honorary degree of M.D. by Harvard in 1791. He was one of the original incorporators of the Massachusetts Medical Society, a member of the New Hampshire Medical Society, president for many years of the Middlesex Medical Society, and of the Western Society of Middlesex Husbandmen. In 1780 he was incorporated a fellow of the American Academy of Arts and Sciences. On Feb. 19, 1756, he married Lydia, daughter of David Baldwin, of Watertown. He was over six feet tall and inclined to corpulence. His courtly manners, engaging conversation, and considerate kindliness, especially to the needy and distressed, made him, despite his deafness in later years, a welcome figure to sick and well alike. His medical practice embraced an extensive area, and in covering it he was frequently obliged to take exhausting trips. Hence it is said that he acquired the habit of sleeping on horseback. He died at Groton of pectoral dropsy.

[*Columbian Centinel*, Nov. 21, 1804; James Thatcher, *Am. Medic. Biog.* (1828), vol. I; Caleb Butler, *Hist. of the Town of Groton* (1848); Wm. Prescott, *The Prescott Memorial* (1870); S. A. Green, *Groton Hist. Series* (4 vols., 1887–99) and *Groton during the Revolution* (1900); Timothy Alden, *A Collection of Am. Epitaphs and Inscriptions*, vol. II (1814).] E. E. C.

PRESCOTT, SAMUEL (Aug. 19, 1751–*c.* 1777), physician, one of the "warners" of Apr. 18, 1775, was born in Concord, Mass., the son of Dr. Abel and Abigail (Brigham) Prescott and a descendant of John Prescott who settled in

New England in 1640. Both his father and his grandfather, Dr. Jonathan Prescott, were physicians. His fame in American history lies in the fact that he successfully completed the midnight ride of warning after Paul Revere was captured. The evening of Apr. 18, 1775, he had spent in Lexington, and after one o'clock he started on his journey home by horseback. He overtook Revere and William Dawes, who had just aroused John Hancock and Samuel Adams at the parsonage with the news that the British troops were marching from Boston to destroy the military stores of the provincials at Concord. Revere found Prescott to be "a high Son of Liberty," and they all proceeded together on the road to Concord which ran through the northern part of Lincoln. As they approached a pasture on the right (now marked by a tablet), Revere, who was riding ahead, saw two mounted British officers in the moonlight waiting under a tree. Two more officers came through the bars from the pasture and all four spurred up to Revere with pistols in their hands. At sight of the officers Dawes turned rein and escaped down the road. Prescott galloped up to Revere, used the butt end of his whip as a weapon, and they both attempted to push through. But the officers, armed with pistols and swords, forced them into the pasture. "Put on!" cried Prescott to Revere; and turning suddenly to the left, he jumped his horse over a stone wall, and made off down a rough farmway into a ravine near a swamp. Revere took to the right in the direction of a wood and was captured there by six other officers. Prescott, being familiar with the country, circled westward until he came out into the fields behind the house of Samuel Hartwell of the Lincoln Minute Men. Here he awakened the household and then sped on to Concord where he gave the alarm. Prescott's exploit enabled the Minute Men to assemble and to conceal most of the stores before the British arrived. Prescott was in service at Ticonderoga in 1776. "He was taken prisoner on board a privateer afterwards, and carried to Halifax, where he died in jail" (Shattuck, *post*, p. 114).

[Wm. Prescott, *The Prescott Memorial* (1870); Lemuel Shattuck, *A Hist. of the Town of Concord* (1835); Frank W. C. Hersey, *Heroes of the Battle Road . . . 1775* (1930); Paul Revere's narratives of his ride, printed in E. H. Goss, *The Life of Col. Paul Revere* (2 vols., 1891); *Mass. Soldiers and Sailors of the Revolutionary War*, Vol. XII (1904).] F. W. C. H.

PRESCOTT, WILLIAM (Feb. 20, 1726–Oct. 13, 1795), Revolutionary soldier, brother of Oliver Prescott [*q.v.*], was born in Groton, Mass. His father, Benjamin Prescott, was a man of property and position, a descendant of John

Prescott who arrived in New England in 1640 and in 1643 was one of the first settlers of Lancaster, Mass. His mother was Abigail, daughter of Thomas Oliver of Cambridge, a member of the governor's council. Of his boyhood little is known. He saw service with the provincial forces during King George's War and the French and Indian War. For about twenty years prior to the Revolution he lived quietly as a farmer in Pepperell, Mass., marrying Abigail Hale, of Sutton, on Apr. 13, 1758, and occasionally serving as a town officer. When the port of Boston was closed by act of Parliament in 1774, he was instrumental in sending supplies of food to the distressed inhabitants. He was presently chosen colonel of a regiment of minute-men. On Apr. 19, 1775, he led a detachment to Concord, but arrived too late to participate in the fighting. Proceeding to Cambridge, the headquarters of the provincial army, he became a member of the council of war. Ordered by Gen. Artemas Ward, the commander of the American troops, to fortify Bunker Hill, he left Cambridge on the night of June 16 with a detachment of about a thousand men. On arriving at Charlestown peninsula, he consented, after consultation with the officers, to fortify Breed's Hill instead of Bunker Hill, since the former commanded Boston more effectively. The task was partially accomplished by starlight. When the astonished British observed the American works in the morning, they opened fire. Despite the fact that his tall form offered an easy target, Prescott strolled nonchalantly along the top of the entrenchments, directing and encouraging his men. The day being warm, he discarded his heavy uniform and donned a broad-brimmed hat and banyan coat, which are depicted in Story's spirited statue of him on Bunker Hill. In this attire, characteristic of the man in its simplicity and unconventionality, he mingled in the thick of the combat. His clothing was pierced in several places and he narrowly escaped being bayonetted. Whether he or Israel Putnam was in general command of the patriot forces on the field of battle has been warmly debated. Whatever the merits of the controversy, it is certain that Prescott was in direct charge of operations at a vital point in the American lines, namely, the redoubt. After the engagement he offered, if supplied with three fresh regiments, to retake the hill lost to the British. While he took part in the operations connected with the evacuation of New York in 1776 and the surrender of Burgoyne in 1777, age and an injury sustained in agricultural work prevented him from winning further laurels as a soldier. Retiring to his farm, he served the community in various civil capacities, including those of selectman and representative in the general court. On the occasion of Shays's Rebellion, he buckled on his sword and prepared to aid in the suppression of the uprising. He died at Pepperell and was buried with military honors. William Hickling Prescott [q.v.] was his grandson.

[The Boston Athenæum possesses a manuscript paper on Prescott written by S. L. Guild for the Abigail Adams Chapter, D. A. R. Consult also: Caleb Butler, *Hist. of the Town of Groton* (1848); G. E. Ellis, *Hist. of the Battle of Bunker's [Breed's] Hill* (1875); R. C. Winthrop, *Addresses and Speeches*, vol. IV (1886); S. A. Green, *Groton Hist. Ser.* (4 vols., 1887–99); Wm. Everett, *Oration in Honor of Col. Wm. Prescott* (1896); Richard Frothingham, *Hist. of the Siege of Boston* (6th ed., 1903); Harold Murdock, *Bunker Hill* (1927).]

E. E. C.

PRESCOTT, WILLIAM HICKLING (May 4, 1796–Jan. 28, 1859), historian, was born in Salem, Mass., the eldest of the seven children of Judge William Prescott and Catherine Greene (Hickling). A descendant of John Prescott, who settled in New England in 1640, he was the grandson of Col. William Prescott [q.v.] of Bunker Hill. His wife, Susan Amory, whom he married on May 4, 1820, was the grand-daughter of that Capt. John Linzee who commanded the British sloop of war *Falcon* in June 1775, and cannonaded the besieged from the waters of the Charles during the progress of the battle. The crossed swords of the two heroes of the American Revolution adorned the walls of the historian's library at 55 Beacon St., Boston, for many years, and are now among the most treasured possessions of the Massachusetts Historical Society (Ticknor, *post*, pp. 461–63).

The boyhood and youth of Prescott were singularly carefree and happy. His vivacity and wit made him universally popular, and his parents were able to afford him ample means to satisfy his individual tastes. Even before he went to college there is evidence that he was fond of reading; but his record at Harvard—where he entered as a sophomore in the class of 1814, and lived in the room that his father had occupied before him and his son was to have afterward—was not particularly distinguished; certainly *joie de vivre*, rather than scholastic eminence, was at the outset the dominant note. It was in the course of his junior year that he met with the accident which was to determine his career; leaving the Commons one day after dinner, he turned his head to observe the course of a frolic which had broken out behind his back, and was struck by a hard crust of bread in the left eye, whose sight was thereby immediately and permanently destroyed. Two years later he was attacked with an acute inflammation of his right eye as well, and the trouble grew steadily worse until the day of his death. Never again was he able to use his eye, save with extreme caution, for short periods, and at the cost of much pain; at intervals he was to all intents and purposes totally blind.

He had intended, after leaving college, to follow his father's profession and enter the law, but a little reflection soon convinced him that the results of his accident had rendered this impossible. The notion, on the other hand, of a mere life of leisure repelled him; and though he was assured by his physicians that it would involve the most rigorous self-denial he decided to attempt a literary career. The conviction that he had chosen wisely was strengthened during a trip to Europe in the years 1815–17. Most of his time was spent, convalescing, on his grandfather's estates in the Azores, but he also visited Italy, France, and England, and in London he bought his first noctograph. This was an implement consisting of a frame crossed by a number of brass wires, and holding a sheet of thin, carbonated paper to be written on with a short, pointed stylus instead of a pen; it thus went far to obviate what he characterized as "the two great difficulties in the way of a blind man's writing . . . his not knowing when the ink is exhausted in his pen, and when his lines run into one another" (Ogden, *post*, p. 34). On his return to Boston he began a thorough and extensive course of preparation in the history and literature of the principal countries of western Europe. Most of the books had to be read aloud to him by paid secretaries, though he always insisted on having at least a look at them himself; and it is not improbable that his enforced abandonment of German, because the script was impossible for his eyes, was a contributory cause of his turning his attention to Spain. In 1821 the first fruits of his patient, arduous labors began to appear—first in the form of reviews and articles on literary and historical subjects in the *North American Review*. During the next fifteen years a whole series of essays followed, the most important of which were collected and published in 1845 in a volume entitled *Biographical and Critical Miscellanies*. Of these the first and, in some respects, the most interesting is his "Life of Charles Brockden Brown," which he undertook for *The Library of American Biography* (vol. I, 1834), edited by Jared Sparks. In a letter (Aug. 9, 1833) in which Sparks accepted it and congratulated him on it, the following significant sentence occurs: "All your dates are 1493, etc. This shows your mind was running on the age of Ferdinand and Isabella" (Ogden, p. 71).

At the time that letter was written Prescott had been at work for over seven years on the first of his masterpieces. The choice of the theme had cost him much anxious deliberation. Works on the revolution which converted the Roman republic into a monarchy and on the critical periods of Italian literature were attractive alternatives. The advice of his friend and contemporary, George Ticknor [*q.v.*], doubtless counted for much in the making of the final decision. He apparently knew nothing of Washington Irving until 1829, when *A Chronicle of the Conquest of Granada* first appeared and was reviewed by Prescott in the *North American Review* (October 1829); indeed, it was not until 1838–39 that the two men began to correspond (Ticknor, pp. 166–72). The labor of teaching his readers to pronounce Spanish so that he could understand it was profoundly discouraging; more than once he was on the verge of abandoning the enterprise. Only a few persons apparently were even aware of the fact that he was at work on it. When at last the manuscript was completed—after ten years' labor—in October 1836, he hesitated long before sending it to the press. However, a remark of his father's to the effect that "the man who writes a book which he is afraid to publish is a coward" (*Ibid.*, p. 102) was a challenge to his pride which he refused to leave unanswered; in April 1837 the manuscript was turned over to the American Stationers Company in Boston. The *History of the Reign of Ferdinand and Isabella the Catholic* appeared, in three volumes, on the following Christmas Day, with the year 1838 on the title-page. Any doubts which the author may have entertained in regard to its sale were speedily dispelled. Three-fifths of the first edition were sold in Boston before a copy could be sent to New York, and the whole edition was exhausted in five weeks. In view of the position and popularity of the author in the literary society of the Boston of that day this triumph was perhaps inevitable, but evidences of a more convincing sort were not slow to arrive from abroad. In London both Murray and Longmans refused it, and only with difficulty was Bentley induced to accept it, but the moment that it appeared there was a chorus of applause. The reviews were unanimously favorable. A host of laudatory letters—from Henry Hallam at one end to Maria Edgeworth at the other—poured in upon the author, and there followed a stream of honorary and corresponding memberships in learned and literary societies on both sides of the Atlantic.

The year after the publication of *Ferdinand and Isabella* was largely one of enforced idleness for Prescott, owing to severe attacks of the inflammation in his eye; but neither the pain of his malady nor the increased restrictions which its progress entailed could induce him permanently to desist from his labors, or to rest on the laurels he had already won. Nor was he in the least puffed up with success; never were his private memoranda so full of self-criticism and of expressions of desire to perfect his matter and his style, as in the years 1839–41. He decided that he would next devote himself to the history of the conquests of Mexico and Peru—themes which formed natural sequels to the work which he had already done and "which had the superior advantages of relating to his own quarter of the globe" (Ogden, p. 131). He began reading for the *History of the Conquest of Mexico* first, in April 1839, the last difficulty having been cleared away by Washington Irving's renunciation in his favor of a topic on which he had already himself begun to write. So well established by this time was Prescott's reputation in Europe that archivists and librarians were eager to send him manuscripts; but he had now learned to handle his materials so much more easily than before that he published the three volumes in 1843. The Introduction, on the civilization of the Aztecs, occupied him about as long as the remaining two and a half volumes of "dashing narrative" which he vastly preferred (Ticknor, p. 202, note). The two volumes of the *History of the Conquest of Peru* were written at an even more rapid rate; two years apparently were sufficient for the actual composition, though the work was not published until March 1847. Of the two books, the latter probably ranks slightly higher today, principally because less fresh material has been discovered in the field with which it deals than in that of the former; but both have nobly stood the test of time, and remain the standard authorities on the two greatest achievements of the Spanish *conquistadores* in the New World. The work on Mexico won him the admiration and friendship of Alexander von Humboldt, and election (1845) as corresponding member of the Royal Academy of Berlin. In the same year he was chosen to fill the vacancy caused by the death of the Spanish historian Martín Fernández de Navarrete, in the Institut de France; and constant invitations from his many European admirers and correspondents persuaded him at last to visit England for a few months in the summer of 1850. He was given the degree of D.C.L. at Oxford, and was received by the Queen; he was entertained by the world of fashion as well as by the world of scholars. Ticknor, writing in 1864, described his visit

with but slight exaggeration as "the most brilliant visit ever made to England by an American citizen not clothed with the *prestige* of official station" (Ticknor, p. 339).

As far back as 1838 there are evidences that Prescott contemplated writing a history of the reign of Philip the Second. In 1842 he had begun to collect materials for it. In February 1849 he drew up a sort of preliminary outline of the work in four volumes; on July 26 of the same year he began the composition of it. There can be no question that he would have greatly preferred to deal with every phase of the period with a thoroughness comparable to that which he had shown in writing his *Ferdinand and Isabella*. On the other hand, his fears for the state of his eyesight, and a dawning, though quite incomplete, realization of the fact that the materials for a history of the Prudent King were many times more abundant than those for the age of his great-grandparents, made him question his ability to carry through such an ambitious program. Yet the thought of slurring over any portion of the reign, of departing from his habits of careful and elaborate research, was so abhorrent to him, that he started to write at a rate which would have carried his work—had he lived to complete it—to ten volumes instead of the four he had originally planned. The constitutional and economic sides of the history he relegated indeed to the background. The three volumes of the *History of the Reign of Philip the Second* which were published (the first two in 1855, the last in 1858) deal principally with the rebellion of the Moriscos, the battle of Lepanto, the beginnings of the Escorial, the Don Carlos episode, and the troubles in the Low Countries. In 1856, moreover, he interrupted his researches into the reign of Philip to prepare a new edition of William Robertson's *The History of the Reign of the Emperor Charles the Fifth* (1857), with a continuation, "The Life of Charles the Fifth after His Abdication." No fewer than four well-known European scholars had investigated the final chapter of Charles's career with the utmost care during the preceding five years, and had published the results of their researches, so that there was little left for Prescott to do save to compare and comment on them. This labor he performed with his accustomed thoroughness; but his thoughts kept reverting to the reign of the Prudent King; and he continued to work on it as unremittingly as his health would permit, until the day of his death. As a piece of historical writing the book is not worthy of comparison with Prescott's other works; one feels instinctively that the author is constantly oppressed by his failure accurately to gauge the amount of his material, and by his consciousness that he had undertaken more than he could possibly hope to perform. But as a tribute to Prescott's high courage, patience, and splendid historical conscientiousness it stands unrivaled.

History for Prescott was primarily a form of polite literature, written quite as much for the entertainment as for the instruction of his readers; it was, therefore, in the recounting of stirring events and thrilling scenes that he took pleasure and excelled. He was too scrupulous to omit all consideration of social, constitutional, and economic problems, but it is only too obvious that they did not really interest him, and that he seldom inquired into the significance of the facts he set down. "The book lacks philosophy," wrote Theodore Parker of the *Conquest of Mexico,* "to a degree exceeding belief. The author seems to know nothing of the philosophy of history, and little, even, of political economy" (Parker, *Collected Works,* X, 116). But it is unfair to criticise an historian for the absence of qualities which he makes no pretense of possessing. Prescott was primarily, like his models, William Robertson and Sir Walter Scott, a narrator of events; it is, therefore, as a political, not as a constitutional historian that he should be judged, and in this rôle he has seldom been surpassed. He is better, indeed, on the battle-field than in the council chamber; and his New England inheritance and upbringing, though they did not color his verdicts to the extent that they did those of his younger friend, John Lothrop Motley, were still sufficiently dominant to prevent him from putting himself wholeheartedly back into the atmosphere of the sixteenth century. The style, too, though always elegant and refined, is often prolix; there are occasional touches of pedantry; and he not seldom, as Theodore Parker rather maliciously observes, "refers events to Providence which other men would be content with ascribing to human agency" (*Ibid.,* X, 153). All these characteristics, however, were inherent in the historiography of the early Victorian period; and they pale into insignificance in comparison with Prescott's outstanding merit —a merit the more remarkable because of his physical infirmity—namely, the scrupulous care and integrity with which he used his materials, and the pains that he took to find the exact truth. All his statements are supported by abundant and accurate references; if there is any possible doubt as to the interpretation of his authorities, it is fairly expressed in the footnotes; in short, one may be certain of the source for every fact that Prescott gives, though one may differ with

him over the significance of it. So it comes about, by the irony of fate, that it is today the professional historical student and investigator, rather than the casual reader of polite literature for whom Prescott's books were primarily intended, who can most fully appreciate how truly great, within their limits, they are.

Tall, erect, and handsome, Prescott succeeded to an unusual degree in retaining his youthful appearance until after he had passed fifty. The gayety and charm which had been his most prominent traits in his boyhood never deserted him; in spite of his increasing blindness, he was from first to last a universal social favorite. "If I were asked," said Theophilus Parsons, "to name the man whom I have known whose coming was most sure to be hailed as a pleasant event by all whom he approached, I should not only place Prescott at the head of the list, but I could not place any other man near him" (Ticknor, p. 139). His charity and generosity to the poor were almost proverbial in the Boston of his day. One of his secretaries tells us that he regularly gave away one-tenth of his income, most of it, no doubt, to deserving institutions, of which his favorite was the Perkins Institution for the Blind, but a goodly portion of it also to private pensioners. With all these popular and lovable qualities there was united an abundance of sterner stuff. The rigorous self-discipline to which Prescott had been obliged to submit himself in order to carry out his chosen work is ample proof of it. He had his share of Yankee shrewdness too, and the accounts that he has left us of the arrangements he made for the publication of his successive volumes make it evident that "if he had not been a famous historian, he could have been a successful business man" (Ogden, p. 90). Politically, his sympathies were those of a conservative Whig, but there is no evidence until the very close of his life that he was vitally interested in any of the great issues of his time. It is characteristic of him that when in 1848 he was offered an opportunity to write a history of "The Second Conquest of Mexico," achieved by General Winfield Scott in the preceding year, he promptly refused, on the ground that he would "rather not meddle with heroes who had not been under the ground for two centuries, at least" (Ticknor, p. 292). In 1856, however, he voted for John C. Frémont, an act which, in view of the political tenets of his most intimate friends, demanded high courage and independence.

In addition to his house in Boston he had a comfortable cottage at Nahant and afterwards at Lynn; but the place which he loved most was the old family homestead in Pepperell, where his grandfather had established himself before the middle of the eighteenth century. Many accounts of the simple, happy life there have come down to us—the early morning ride or walk, the hours of work, the afternoon drive, the gay dinners with his family and friends, and the joyous romps with the children. On the morning of Jan. 28, 1859, after a happy chat with his wife, he withdrew to the library in his Beacon Street home, where he was stricken with apoplexy and died within a few hours. His wife, two sons, and a daughter survived him. "All who knew him," declared his friend, George Bancroft (*post*, pp. 10–11), in a tribute delivered before the New York Historical Society two weeks after Prescott's death, "will say, that he was himself greater and better than his writings. . . . Standing as it were by his grave, we cannot recall anything in his manner, his character, his endowments, or his conduct, we could wish changed."

[Some nine feet of the bookshelves of the Mass. Hist. Soc. are filled with the original manuscripts of Prescott's notes, correspondence, and diaries from his college days to the end of his life. They have been left there on deposit by their owner, the historian's great-grandson, Roger Wolcott, who edited a selection from them in 1925, under the title, *The Correspondence of William Hickling Prescott, 1833–1847.* A small volume, *Prescott, Unpublished Letters to Gayangos in the Lib. of the Hispanic Soc. of America,* was published by Clara L. Penney in 1927. The standard biography is George Ticknor, *Life of William Hickling Prescott* (1864) ; it contains numerous valuable letters and documents. Briefer biographies are Rollo Ogden, *William Hickling Prescott* (1904) ; and H. T. Peck, *William Hickling Prescott* (1905). Tributes and memoirs are available in *Proc. of the Mass. Hist. Soc.*, vol. IV (1860). Bancroft's tribute appeared in *Proc. of the N. Y. Hist. Soc. on the Announcement of the Death of William Hickling Prescott, February 1859* (n.d.). Of the various estimates of Prescott as an historian, one of the earliest and most valuable is that of Theodore Parker, in *The Collected Works of Theodore Parker,* ed. by F. P. Cobbe, vol. X (1865), pp. 81–153 ; one of the latest is that of Eduard Fueter, in *Histoire de L'Historiographie Moderne* (1914), pp. 648–651. The *Works of William H. Prescott* (22 vols., 1904) is the last complete edition.]   R. B. M—n.

PRESSER, THEODORE (July 3, 1848–Oct. 28, 1925), music publisher, philanthropist, editor, was born in Pittsburgh, Pa., the son of Christian Presser, a German emigrant from the Saar Valley in Rhenish Prussia, who came to the United States in 1820, and his wife, Caroline Dietz of Gettysburg, Pa. In the last years of the Civil War the boy worked in a foundry where cannonballs were cast for the Union armies, but the hard manual labor proved too much for his youthful strength, and in 1864 he entered the retail music and piano store of Charles C. Mellor of Pittsburgh as a clerk. He rented a piano and took lessons, later continuing them at Mount Union College, Alliance, Ohio, and established himself as a teacher of piano. He taught piano at the Ohio Northern University, Ada, Ohio, from 1869 to 1871 ; at Smith College and at Xenia Conservatory, in Xenia, Ohio, 1872–75, and at the Ohio Wesleyan University, Delaware, Ohio. In the meantime he took courses in the New England Conservatory of Music, in Boston, where he studied with Stephen Albert Emery, Benjamin Johnson Lang [*qq.v.*], and George Elbridge Whiting. In 1878, like many other American students and teachers, he went to Leipzig to complete his musical education. There he studied from 1878 to 1880, under Salomon Jadassohn, Karl H. C. Reinecke, and Bruno Zwintscher. On his return to the United States, Presser went to Hollins College, Hollins, Va., as professor of music, a position he held from 1880 to 1883.

In 1883 with a capital of two hundred and fifty dollars he founded the *Étude,* a monthly musical journal, in Lynchburg, Va. His own wide experience as a private and conservatory teacher had made him realize the possibilities of a magazine of a very popular educational type, one that would appeal especially to the average piano teacher, whose objectives were strictly practical, rather than purely cultural or esthetic. The magazine and its owner removed to Philadelphia in 1884. Beginning as a teachers' journal, with simple articles on applied pedagogy and a supplement of studies and "pieces," it rose from a circulation of 5,000 copies a few years after its launching to one of over 250,000 copies at the time of Presser's death. Not long after the foundation of the *Étude,* Presser established in Philadelphia The Theodore Presser Company, a publishing house for music and books about music. In 1891 Presser resigned the editorship of the *Étude* in order to devote more time to his publishing and philanthropic activities. As a publisher, with the substantial aid of the *Étude,* he showed that strange combination of commercial shrewdness and altruism which was one of his outstanding characteristics. He interested his employees and safeguarded his own interests by the allotment to them of stock in the business. In the formation of his policies he was an independent, who dealt with prices and terms as suited him best—a trait which did not tend to make him popular with his competitors. His commercial gains, however, were devoted to the alleviation of distress and the furtherance of appreciation in the field of music.

In 1907 he established the Presser Home for Retired Music Teachers, which was later permanently located in Germantown in a handsome building with accommodations for sixty-five inmates. In 1916 the Presser Foundation was established for the consolidation and administration of various private philanthropies which the founder was conducting at the time. It included a department for the relief of deserving musicians and a department for assigning to colleges scholarships for music students. A third department was instrumental in assisting colleges to erect music buildings. In the year of its founder's death the Foundation was providing 137 scholarships in music in the United States. Presser wrote *First Steps in Pianoforte Study* (1900), *School for the Pianoforte* (3 vols., 1916), and *Polyphonic Piano Playing* (1921), and a number of piano studies and pieces of a routine nature. He was a founder of the National Music Teacher's Association in 1876, and a founder and honorary member of the Philadelphia Music Teacher's Association. He married, in 1890, Helen Louise, daughter of John Curran of Philadelphia, and three years after her death in 1905, married Elise, the daughter of Russell Houston of that city. He died of heart failure, following an operation in the Samaritan Hospital, Philadelphia, Pa.

[*Who's Who in America*, 1924–25; W. R. Tilford, "A Character Study of Theodore Presser the Man," *Étude*, Jan. 1926, contains also tributes by Owen Wister, William Arms Fisher, John Philip Sousa, O. G. Sonneck, and Charles Wakefield Cadman; sketch by W. S. Smith, *Grove's Dictionary of Music and Musicians*, vol. IV (1928); *Public Ledger* (Phila.), Oct. 29, 1925.]   F. H. M.

PRESTON, ANN (Dec. 1, 1813–Apr. 18, 1872), physician, was born of Quaker parents, Amos and Margaret (Smith) Preston, in Westgrove, Chester County, Pa., where she spent the greater part of her life and received her early education. When she was still a young girl her mother fell ill and Ann was faced with the responsibility of managing the home for the invalid, the father, and six active brothers. This duty she performed capably and cheerfully and found time and enthusiasm also to take part in various community activities. She was a member of the Clarkson Anti-Slavery Society and as secretary wrote reports for that society which were models of clearness, strength, and simplicity. On one occasion she aided a slave in escaping along the Underground Railway. She was also secretary of a temperance convention of women in Chester County in 1848, and was one of three delegates sent to Harrisburg to present to the legislature a memorial urging the prohibition of the sale of intoxicating liquors. Her literary ability in another direction was demonstrated by her poems and a volume of stories published in 1848 under the title of *Cousin Ann's Stories for Children*.

Feeling keenly her lack of higher education she studied Latin at home for its rigid mental discipline, and also read physiology and hygiene with the hope of fitting herself to be a popular lecturer. When she learned in 1850 that the Female Medical College of Pennsylvania was being opened in Philadelphia (the first of its kind in the world to be chartered for the education of women in medicine), it seemed the perfect answer to her desire for a career that would combine scholarship and service. She was one of the first applicants for entrance and was graduated at its first Commencement in 1852. Desiring further training she continued to attend lectures all the following winter, and in the spring of 1853, accepted the chair of physiology and hygiene in the College. About this time she began giving lectures in Baltimore, New York, Philadelphia, and neighboring towns, and these served to introduce her to the public and aided her in securing a practice. She realized the need for clinical instruction for her students, and since at this time women physicians were forbidden the use of hospitals, she turned her energies to establishing an institution primarily for them. She interviewed and importuned everyone she thought could give her money or influence. So great was her success that the Woman's Hospital of Philadelphia was opened in 1861 and she was appointed a member of the board of managers, consulting physician, and corresponding secretary. In 1866 she was chosen the first dean of the college in addition to her professorship, and in 1867 was elected to the board of corporators.

One of her most memorable works was the article she wrote in reply to a resolution adopted by the Philadelphia County Medical Society in 1867 expressing its disapproval of women in the medical profession (see the *Medical and Surgical Reporter*, Philadelphia, Mar. 30, May 4, 1864). So aptly and thoroughly did she answer their objections that no rebuttal could be made and the matter was dropped. She was a small, frail person. For years she suffered from articular rheumatism and was forced to limit her private practice to office consultations, and in 1871 she suffered an acute attack from which she never wholly recovered. The exertion of writing the annual announcement for the college session overtaxed her strength and brought on complete nervous exhaustion which caused her death. Her published writings, other than those mentioned above, consist of addresses to the students of the Woman's Medical College.

[E. E. Judson, *Address in Memory of Ann Preston, M.D.* (1873); sketch by Frances Preston in H. A. Kelly, W. L. Burrage, *Am. Med. Biog.* (1920); F. E. Willard, M. A. Livermore, *A Woman of the Century*

(1893); *Eminent Women of the Age* (1869); Clara Marshall, *The Woman's Med. Coll. of Pa.* (1897); J. S. Futhey and Gilbert Cope, *Hist. of Chester County, Pa.* (1881); *Press* (Phila., Pa.), Apr. 19, 1872.]

F. E. W.

PRESTON, HARRIET WATERS (Aug. 6, 1836–May 14, 1911), author, translator, daughter of Samuel and Lydia (Proctor) Preston, was born at Danvers, Mass. She was a descendant of Roger Preston who came to America in 1635, lived in Ipswich, Mass., and in 1660 moved to Salem. She was educated at home. For many years she lived abroad, chiefly in England, France, and Italy, and acquired a thorough knowledge of Latin, French, and Italian. She was in England during the later life of Cardinal Newman and became much interested in the history of the Oxford movement and his conversion to Roman Catholicism. In America Harriet Prescott Spofford was her intimate friend. She began to write when young and contributed reviews and critical articles to magazines, among them the *Atlantic Monthly*. Her first important volume was *Portraits of Celebrated Women* (1868), translated from the French of C. A. Sainte-Beuve. Other translations, which she published later, were: *The Writings of Madame Swetchine* (1870); *Memoirs of Madame Desbordes-Valmore by the late C. A. Sainte-Beuve, with a selection from Her Poems* (1873); *The Biography of Alfred de Musset* (1877), from the French of Paul de Musset; *The Georgics of Vergil* (1881). She contributed "Roman Poets of the Later Empire," with translations from Annus Florius, Hadrian, the "Pervigilium Veneris," Calpurnius, Siculus, Ausonius, Claudianus, Rutilius, and Boëthius, to C. D. Warner's *Library of the World's Best Literature* (vol. XXI, 1897). With Martha Le Baron Goddard, she compiled *Sea and Shore: A Collection of Poems* (1874) and edited *The Complete Poetical Works of Elizabeth Barrett Browning* (Cambridge Edition, 1900). Her especial field was Provençal literature, in which, from the time of her translation (1872) of *Mirèio*, by Frédèric Mistral, she was recognized as an authority. In this field she published *Troubadours and Trouvères, New and Old* (1876), and contributed "The Troubadours 1090–1290, with Illustrative Translations," to Warner's *Library of the World's Best Literature* (vol. XX, 1897). Her original writings include *Aspendale* (1871); *Love in the Nineteenth Century, A Fragment* (1873); *Is That All?* (1876); *A Year in Eden* (1887), a novel of New England village life; *The Guardians* (1888), with her niece, Louise Preston Dodge; *The Private Life of the Romans* (1893), with Louise Dodge. Her scholarship was genuine and

thorough; her reviews and criticisms were fair and stressed salient points; her style was a smooth essay style, without striking characteristics. Her work in fiction is negligible. During her later years she lived with a friend at Keene, N. H. Her friends there admired her scholarship and linguistic accomplishments and were amused by certain superstitious practices of hers which seemed surprising in a woman of her intelligence. Her death occurred from a stroke of apoplexy at Cambridge, Mass., at the home of James F. Muirhead, editor of Baedeker's *United States,* where she had been spending the winter.

[*Who's Who in America,* 1910–11; *Boston Transcript,* May 15, 1911; *New Hampshire Sentinel,* May 17, 1911; *Vital Records of Danvers, Mass.* (1909), vol. I; C. H. Preston, *Descendants of Roger Preston of Ipswich and Salem Village* (1931); information received from friends.]

S. G. B.

PRESTON, JOHN SMITH (Apr. 20, 1809–May 1, 1881), orator and soldier, was born near Abingdon, Va., the son of Francis Smith and Sarah Buchanan (Campbell) Preston, and the brother of William Campbell Preston [*q.v.*]. Contemporary accounts state that he received the degree of A.B. from Hampden-Sydney College, but the college records indicate only that he was in attendance from 1823 to 1825. He was a student at the University of Virginia from 1825 to 1827 and afterward studied law at Harvard for a short time. After a trip to Europe he married, Apr. 28, 1830, Caroline Martha, the daughter of Gen. Wade Hampton, Sr. [*q.v.*], and settled at Abingdon to practise law. But his wife's family lived near Columbia, S. C., and his brother William had attained prominence there, and in 1840 he moved there. Not long afterward he went to Louisiana where he owned a large sugar plantation, "The Homus," which he operated so successfully that in a few years he amassed a fortune. He became an enthusiastic collector of paintings and statuary, and, recognizing ability in Hiram Powers [*q.v.*], who was called to his attention by his brother William, furnished him money with which to go to Europe. Preston was back in South Carolina in 1848, and made the first of his better-known speeches in welcoming the "Palmetto regiment" on its return from Mexico. In the same year he was elected to the state Senate and served continuously until 1856. During this time he became increasingly known for his genuine power as a public speaker and as a radical champion of state rights. From 1856 to 1860 he lived in Europe where his children were educated. In 1860, upon his return, he was chairman of the state delegation in the Charleston convention, and in February 1861 he was appointed commissioner to visit Virginia and urge secession upon the convention then in session.

At the outbreak of the war Preston became a volunteer aide to Beauregard and was with him in Charleston and in the Manassas campaign. Beauregard entrusted him with important duties and after the battle officially commended his services. On Aug. 13, 1861, he was commissioned assistant adjutant-general with the rank of lieutenant-colonel. In October he was relieved of duty with the Army of the Potomac and expected to join General Lovell's staff, but instead he was sent to Charleston to muster troops into the Confederate service. In December Beauregard recommended that he be commissioned brigadier and placed in command of the second brigade of Kentucky troops. On Jan. 28, 1862, he was assigned to command of the prison camp at Columbia, and in April to command of the conscript camp there. He disliked the task, but he carried out its duties cheerfully and so effectively that in July 1863 Secretary Seddon, in a most complimentary letter, requested him to become superintendent of the Bureau of Conscription in Richmond. In the meantime, on Apr. 23, he had been promoted colonel. Accepting, he was assigned to the post and held it until the bureau was discontinued in March 1865.

As superintendent Preston made an excellent record. He established an effective administrative system and so improved the service that in December he was given control of conscription in the West where it had been separately administered. He acted with a vigor, initiative, and independence that at times involved him in controversies from which he regularly emerged victor. One of these was with Beauregard over the assignment of conscripts; another with General Kemper, who, like all the reserve commanders, was irritated by Preston's activity and close supervision; and still another was with a group of lukewarm North Carolina members of Congress who resented the apparent discrimination against their state in the execution of the conscript laws. Late in 1864 he prepared an elaborate and able discussion of the administration of the law, with numerous suggestions for improvement (*War of the Rebellion: Official Records, Army,* 4 ser. III, p. 883). On June 10, 1864, he was promoted brigadier-general. After the discontinuance of the bureau he returned to South Carolina. After the war he spent some time in England. Upon his return in 1868 he made an address at the University of Virginia which attracted attention and criticism in the North. Then and thereafter he was completely unreconstructed, and his speech was a passionate defense of secession and an

argument against reconciliation. His last speech was delivered at the unveiling of the Confederate monument in Columbia in 1880. He was a speaker of real force and had the power of sweeping his audiences to a high pitch of enthusiasm. He died in Columbia, S. C.

[*War of the Rebellion: Official Records (Army);* *Confed. Mil. Hist.* (1899), vol. V; *Appletons' Ann. Cyc.,* 1881; G. R. Fairbanks, *Hist. of the Univ. of the South* (1905); *Celebration of the Battle of King's Mountain . . . and the Address of the Hon. John S. Preston* (1855); *Addresses Delivered before the Va. State Convention* (1861); *Virginia: Address before the Washington and Jefferson Socs., of the Univ. of Va.* (1868); W. B. Preston, *The Preston Geneal.* (1900); T. L. Preston, *Hist. Sketches and Reminiscences of an Octogenarian* (1900); *News and Courier* (Charleston), May 2, 1881; information from the family.]   J. G. deR. H.

PRESTON, JONAS (Jan. 25, 1764–Apr. 4, 1836), physician, was born at Chester, Pa., the son of his father's fourth marriage and of his mother's third. His parents were Jonas Preston, a physician who had come to America from Yorkshire, England, some time before 1732, and Mary Pennell Lea Preston, *née* Yarnall. His boyhood was spent chiefly in Chester until the outbreak of the Revolution, when, his father having died some time previously, his mother settled in Wilmington, Del. Here he studied medicine with a Dr. Way and in 1783 and 1784 attended lectures at the medical school of the University of Pennsylvania, being graduated there in the latter year. He then went to Europe and attended hospital lectures in Edinburgh, London, and Paris. Upon returning to America he bought a farm near Chester, but soon sold it and spent some time in Georgia with General Wayne. He finally returned to Chester and built up a large medical practice being particularly noted as an obstetrician. In 1794 he married Orpah (?) Reese, a woman with a considerable fortune, and moved to Newtown, Delaware County. Here he took an active interest in public affairs. At the time of the Whiskey Insurrection he volunteered his medical services and served in the field. For so doing he was disowned by the Society of Friends, of which he was a member, but he was later taken back into Meeting. From 1794 to 1800 he was a member of the lower house of the Pennsylvania legislature and from 1808 to 1811 sat in the state Senate where, as chairman of the committee on education, he prepared the bill which provided for the free education of the poor children of the state.

After the death of his first wife, he married Jane Thomas, Aug. 19, 1812, and four years later moved to Philadelphia. Here he was soon elected to the City Council and heartily supported the building of the municipal water works. In his later years he gave but little attention to his profession, devoting considerable time to the management of the fortune left him by his first wife. He was a director of the Bank of Pennsylvania and of the Schuylkill Navigation Company and took an active interest in the affairs of a number of benevolent institutions. At his death, which occurred in Philadelphia, he bequeathed a large portion of his estate for the support of "a lying-in hospital for indigent married women of good character." By the act of June 16, 1836, the Pennsylvania legislature incorporated The Preston Retreat, but financial difficulties resulting from the panic of 1837 delayed its opening for nearly thirty years, and not till Jan. 1, 1866, was it opened according to his wishes.

[Henry Simpson, *The Lives of Eminent Philadelphians Now Deceased* (1859); J. T. Scharf and Thompson Westcott, *Hist. of Phila.* (1884), vols. I, II; H. A. Kelly and W. L. Burrage, *Am. Medic. Biogs.* (1920); J. S. Futhey and Gilbert Cope, *Hist. of Chester County, Pa.* (1881); *Founders' Week Memorial Vol.* (1909), ed. by F. P. Henry; J. H. and G. H. Lea, *The Ancestry and Posterity of John Lea* (1906); *Poulson's Am. Daily Advertiser*, Aug. 21, 1812, Apr. 5, 1836.]

J.H.F.

PRESTON, MARGARET JUNKIN (May 19, 1820–Mar. 28, 1897), poet and prose writer, was born at Milton, Pa., the eldest child of the Rev. George Junkin [*q.v.*] and Julia Rush (Miller) Junkin. Her paternal great-grandfather, Joseph Junkin, of Scotch ancestry, had come to America from Ireland. Her grandfather, also named Joseph, a soldier in the American Revolution, married Eleanor Cochran, and the sixth of their fourteen children was Margaret's father. At the time of his marriage, June 1, 1819, George Junkin was a minister of the Associate Reformed Church, and soon thereafter went with his bride, a native of Philadelphia of Scotch parentage, to Milton, where he assumed charge of a parish. Margaret was educated at home, chiefly by her father, who taught her Greek and Latin and encouraged her taste for reading. When she was ten years old, the family moved to Germantown, where for two years Junkin was head of a manual labor school. In 1832 he went to Easton, Pa., to be president of the newly founded Lafayette College. He resigned in 1841 to become president of Miami University at Oxford, Ohio; and in 1844 was recalled to Lafayette. He left Easton in 1848 to accept a call to the presidency of Washington College (now Washington and Lee University) at Lexington, Va.

By the time she was twenty-one, Margaret had so taxed her eyes by reading and sewing that her sight was seriously impaired. Nevertheless, she continued her interest in literature, and after removal to Lexington, began to write prose narratives, some of which took prizes. She spent nine happy years in her father's house at Lexington. Her sister Eleanor married Maj. Thomas Jonathan Jackson [*q.v.*], professor of mathematics in Virginia Military Institute, later to be famous as "Stonewall" Jackson; and in 1857 Margaret herself became the wife of another member of the same faculty, Maj. John T. L. Preston. Major Preston, a widower with several young children, was professor of Latin in the Institute. Two sons were born of this marriage. The Civil War divided the family. Margaret's father and a sister sympathized with the North and felt constrained to leave Lexington. Her husband and her brother-in-law became officers in the Confederate army. Major Preston was commissioned lieutenant-colonel and later became adjutant-general on the staff of General Jackson. Margaret maintained the home in his absence and endured many of the hardships of the war. Her first published book, a prose tale entitled *Silverwood, a Book of Memories* (1856; reviewed in *Southern Literary Messenger,* January 1857), had appeared anonymously shortly before the conflict began. As the struggle drew toward its end she wrote a verse narrative of those trying times under the title *Beechenbrook, a Rhyme of the War.* This was printed, necessarily on poor paper, in Richmond in 1865 and nearly the whole edition was burned when the city was evacuated. It was reprinted in Baltimore in 1866. In 1870 J. B. Lippincott published her *Old Song and New,* and in 1875 a volume of verse entitled *Cartoons,* containing her most successful poetry, was issued in Boston.

At the close of hostilities Preston returned to his professorship, which he held until 1882, when, having reached seventy, he retired. From 1874 to 1888 the Prestons were accustomed to spend their summers at the home of Col. William Allan, principal of the McDonogh School near Baltimore and husband of Mrs. Preston's step-daughter. In 1884, in company with her husband and other members of the family, Mrs. Preston made an extensive trip abroad. She is described by relatives as short in stature, having dark auburn hair and small refined features. She was noted for an unusually attractive personality and gracious and winning manners. Her husband died in 1890, and from 1892 until her death she lived in Baltimore at the home of her son, Dr. George J. Preston. She was buried in Lexington, Va.

[See E. P. Allan's *Life and Letters of Margaret Junkin Preston* (1903); W. B. Preston, *The Preston Geneal.* (1900); W. H. Hayne, in *The American* (Philadelphia), June 3, 1882; *Sun* (Baltimore), Mar. 29, 1897.]

J. C. F.

PRESTON, THOMAS SCOTT (July 23, 1824–Nov. 4, 1891), Catholic priest and writer, was the son of Zephaniah and Ann (Canfield) Preston. His father was vice-president of the Connecticut Mutual Life Insurance Company, and Thomas was born in Hartford, Conn. While of Puritan stock—a descendant of Roger Preston who came from England to Ipswich, Mass., in 1635—he was reared an Episcopalian and graduated from Washington (now Trinity) College, Hartford, in 1843 and from the General Theological Seminary in New York in 1846. That same year he was ordained deacon in the Episcopal Church. Deeply spiritual and idealistic, he served as an assistant rector at Trinity and the Church of the Annunciation in New York, and at Holy Innocents, West Point. In 1847 he was ordained priest by Bishop William H. De Lancey [*q.v.*] of the diocese of Western New York. Assigned to fashionable St. Luke's Church, New York City, he was in full harmony with the High Church practices of its rector, John M. Forbes.

Convinced that his position as an Episcopalian was not logically tenable, on Nov. 14, 1849, Preston entered the Roman Catholic Church, thus resigning assured preferment and causing a rift in his family circle, although later three of his four brothers followed his example. After a year at St. Joseph's Seminary, Fordham, he was ordained a Catholic priest by Bishop John McCloskey [*q.v.*] on Nov. 16, 1850. He was first stationed as a curate at the Cathedral and later as pastor at St. Mary's Church, Yonkers. In 1853 he was appointed secretary to Archbishop John J. Hughes [*q.v.*], who also promoted him to the chancellorship of the diocese (1855), an office which he administered with businesslike ability until his death. From 1862 he was pastor of St. Ann's parish, where he built a costly church and school. As a vicar-general (1873–91) he is accredited in large part with the successful conduct of the archdiocese under Archbishops McCloskey and Corrigan. During the latter's absence in 1890, Preston as the sole vicar-general administered the diocese. Intensely loyal to the three archbishops whom he served, unduly zealous and uncompromising in enforcing ecclesiastical discipline, and extremely conservative, he was nevertheless generally respected by the priesthood, who were largely of Irish stock. As a convert, he was rather more Catholic than the Pope, yet somewhat Puritan in his views and in his formal but courteous dignity. He could not tolerate the economic views of Dr. Edward McGlynn [*q.v.*] or his liberal attitude on the parochial school question; and as vicar-general, he was partly responsible for McGlynn's excommunication. Interested in social relief work, he organized the House of the Holy Family as a refuge for children and young girls and founded the Sisterhood of the Divine Compassion (1873). In recognition of his versatility as a confessor, preacher, and writer, he was appointed a domestic prelate to His Holiness (Dec. 13, 1881) and later a prothonotary-apostolic (Aug. 21, 1888) by Pope Leo XIII.

A popular controversial preacher, Monsignor Preston published a number of brochures and books of a controversial, doctrinal, or devotional nature. Among these are *The Ark of the Covenant* (1860); *Life of St. Mary Magdalene* (1860); *The Purgatorial Manual* (1866); *Life of St. Vincent de Paul* (1866); *Lectures on Christian Unity* (1867); *Lectures on Reason and Revelation* (1868); *The Triumph of the Faith* (1869); *Christ and the Church* (1870); *The Catholic View of the Public School Question* (1870); *The Vicar of Christ* (1871); *Lectures upon the Devotions to the Most Sacred Heart of Jesus Christ* (1874); *Ritualism* (1878); *The Divine Sanctuary* (1878); *Vicar of Christ* (1878); *The Protestant Reformation* (1878); *The Divine Paraclete* (1879); *Protestantism and the Church* (1882); *God and Reason* (1884); *The Watch on Calvary* (1885); *The Sacred Year* (1885); and *Gethsemane* (1887).

[C. H. Preston, *Descendants of Roger Preston of Ipswich and Salem Village* (1931); *Cath. Encyc.*, vol. XII; T. C. Cornell, *The Beginnings of the Roman Catholic Church in Yonkers* (1883); *Golden Jubilee of St. Ann's Parish* (1902); H. A. Brann, in *The Illustrated Cath. Family Annual for 1893* (1892); and manuscript eulogy in the files of the Sisters of the Divine Compassion, White Plains, N. Y.; a manuscript copy of William Preston's "Remembrances of my Brother Thomas" also in files of the Sisters of the Divine Compassion; *Sadliers' Cath. Directory*, 1892; *Sun* (N. Y.) and *N. Y. Times*, Nov. 4, 1891.]

R. J. P.

PRESTON, WILLIAM (Oct. 16, 1816–Sept. 21, 1887), soldier, congressman from Kentucky, diplomat, was born near Louisville, Ky., the great-grandson of John Preston who emigrated from County Derry, Ireland, to Augusta County, Va., about 1740 and became there a large landowner. He was the grandson of William and Susannah (Smith) Preston and the son of William Preston, a major in the regular army under Gen. Anthony Wayne, and of Caroline (Hancock) Preston, the daughter of George Hancock, a colonel in the Revolution and a member of the Third and Fourth congresses. His parents removed to Kentucky in 1815 and settled near Louisville on a large estate his father had inherited. The boy attended Augusta College, in Bracken County, Ky., and then St. Joseph's College at Bardstown. He entered Harvard University in 1836 and received the LL.B. degree in 1838. He was admitted to the bar in Louisville, where much of his time was taken up with legal business concerning the family estate. He married in 1840 Margaret Wickliffe, the daughter of Robert Wickliffe of Lexington, who bore him one son and five daughters. At the outbreak of the Mexican War, he obtained in Louisville loans to the state for $50,000. Soon he was appointed lieutenant-colonel of the 4th Kentucky Infantry under Gen. William O. Butler. On his return from the war he was elected one of three delegates from Louisville to the constitutional convention of 1849. In 1850 he became a member of the lower house of the state legislature. The next year he was elected to the state Senate. In 1852 he was elected to Congress as a Whig to fill the vacancy left by the resignation of Humphrey Marshall, 1812–1872 [q.v.]. Reëlected, he served from Dec. 6, 1852, to Mar. 3, 1855. He was defeated in 1854 by Marshall. On the break-up of the Whig party he joined the Democrats and was strenuously opposing his former associates. In 1856, as a delegate to the National Democratic Convention at Cincinnati, he supported the candidacy of James Buchanan and in 1858 was appointed minister to Spain. In Madrid he opposed the designs of the Spaniards at Samaná Bay and actively promoted the interests of the United States in other respects.

At the outbreak of the Civil War he resigned and returned to Kentucky to aid in inducing that state to join the Confederacy. In September 1861, in company with John C. Breckinridge, he joined the command of Albert Sidney Johnston at Bowling Green and served on his staff as colonel until Johnston's death at Shiloh. He was soon made brigadier-general, was engaged in the battles of Corinth, Vicksburg, Murfreesboro, and Chickamauga, and for a short time was in command of troops in southwestern Virginia. On Jan. 7, 1864, President Davis appointed him minister to Maximilian's government in Mexico with the hope that a treaty of friendship and commerce might be effected. He left for Havana with many misgivings as to the success of his mission. In his efforts to reach Maximilian, he found it convenient to go to Europe. Then, unsuccessful in his mission and unable to run the blockade either at Wilmington or Charleston, he landed in Mat-

amoras and crossed the Rio Grande into Texas. He soon joined E. Kirby-Smith's command and was elevated to a major-generalship.

With the war over he recrossed the Rio Grande into Mexico, but conditions there soon forced him and many others from the Confederacy to leave. He then went to the West Indies and on to England. He soon turned up in Canada to join his family, which had been exiled there by the federal government. In 1866 he returned to Kentucky with his family and settled in Lexington, now impoverished by the confiscation of his property by the federal government. He had hoped to avoid politics, but Kentucky was in no mood to let her ex-Confederate leaders go unhonored and talked much of making him her governor. In 1868 and 1869 Fayette County made him a representative in the state legislature. His only other political activities were recorded in his attendance as a delegate at the Democratic national conventions in 1868 and in 1880.

["Journ. in Mexico" and a few letters in Lib. of Cong.; E. P. Thompson, *Hist. of the First Ky. Brigade* (1868); *Biog. Cyc. of . . . Ky.* (1896); *Biog. Encyc. of Ky.* (1878); Lewis and R. H. Collins, *Hist. of Ky.* (2 vols., 1874); *War of the Rebellion: Official Records* (*Navy*), 2 ser. III; F. B. Heitman, *Hist. Register . . . of the U. S. Army* (1903); F. L. Owsley, *King Cotton Diplomacy* (1931); *Lexington Morning Transcript*, Sept. 22, 1887.]   E. M. C.

PRESTON, WILLIAM BALLARD (Nov. 29, 1805–Nov. 16, 1862), representative from Virginia, secretary of the navy, was born at "Smithfield" in Montgomery County, Va., the eldest son of James Patton and Ann (Taylor) Preston, a grandson of William and Susannah (Smith) Preston, and a great-grandson of John Preston, first of the family in America, who came to Virginia from Ireland about 1740. He entered Hampden-Sydney College in 1821, took an active part in literary and forensic activities, and was graduated in 1824. In 1825 he studied law at the University of Virginia, which had been chartered during his father's governorship, and was admitted to the bar in 1826. He soon rose to prominence in the legal profession and served in the House of Delegates, 1830–32 and 1844–45, and in the state Senate, 1840–44. In the session 1831–32 he took an active part in the opposition to slavery, supporting the "post natal plan of abolition" enunciated by Thomas Jefferson, and in this he had the support of his uncle, John Floyd [q.v.], who was then governor. On Nov. 21, 1839, he was married to Lucinda (Lucy) Staples Redd, of Patrick Court House, Va. In 1846 he was elected as a Whig to Congress, where on Feb. 7, 1849, he made a speech in support of the Whig policy of admitting California as a free state, *California and New Mexico* (1849). In March 1849 he was appointed secretary of the navy by President Taylor and served until the reorganization of the cabinet by President Fillmore in July 1850. Resuming his law practice, he acquired a state-wide reputation as a defense lawyer. In 1858 he was sent on a mission to France to negotiate for the establishment of a line of steamers from Norfolk to Havre, but this plan, apparently on the way to success, became impossible with the opening of the Civil War a few years later.

After the secession of the states of the Lower South, he opposed the secession of Virginia, though believing in the abstract right of secession. He was elected from Montgomery County to the secession convention of Virginia that met in February 1861. On Apr. 8, this convention appointed him, who was known as a conservative middle man, Alexander H. H. Stuart of Augusta County, known as an extreme Union man, and George W. Randolph of Richmond City, known as an ultra Southern man, to act as a committee to wait on Lincoln to ask for a statement of the policy which he "intends to pursue in regard to the Confederate States" (*Journal, post*, p. 141). With his committee he met Lincoln informally on Apr. 12, the next morning heard him read a statement of policy, and reported to the convention on Apr. 15 (*Documents, post*, no. XVII). Since on the same day came the call for 75,000 volunteers, the report was not discussed except in one speech by Stuart of the committee. Preston was chosen to present the ordinance of secession, probably because his well-known previous opposition to secession would emphasize the supposed necessity of the step; and on Apr. 17, Virginia seceded. He was elected senator from Virginia to the Confederate States Congress and served till his death. He was buried at "Smithfield."

[Material from MS. of "Life of James Patton Preston" by Preston Davie; A. J. Morrison, *College of Hampden Sidney: Dict. of Biog.* (1921); *The Preston Geneal.* (1900), ed. by L. A. Wilson under the direction of W. B. Preston; *Jour. of the Acts and Proceedings of a General Convention of . . . Va.* (1861); *Va. Convention . . . 1861. Documents* (1861); A. F. Robertson, *Alexander Hugh Holmes Stuart* (copr. 1925), p. 188; date of birth from grave-stone; date of marriage from Staples records in Roanoke.]

J. E. W.

PRESTON, WILLIAM CAMPBELL (Dec. 27, 1794–May 22, 1860), United States senator, brother of John Smith Preston [*q.v.*], was a grandson of William Preston, who with his father, John, came to Virginia from Ireland about 1740. William Campbell Preston was born in Philadelphia, where his father, Francis Smith

Preston, of Abingdon, Va., a member of Congress, was attending a session of that body. His mother, Sarah Buchanan (Campbell), was the only daughter of Col. William Campbell [*q.v.*] of King's Mountain fame. Preston entered Washington College (now Washington and Lee University), Lexington, Va., at the age of fourteen, but after a year, his health requiring a milder climate, he was sent to South Carolina College, where he received the degree of A.B. in 1812. He at once began the study of law in Richmond under William Wirt, but his health continued poor and after traveling on horseback in Tennessee, Kentucky, Ohio, Indiana, Illinois, and Missouri for some months, in 1817 he went to Europe. He continued his legal studies at Edinburgh, rooming with Hugh S. Legaré [*q.v.*], and formed a close intimacy with Washington Irving, whom he accompanied on several walking tours. Returning to Virginia in 1820, he was licensed and began practice. In 1822 he married in Missouri Maria, daughter of David Coalter of Columbia, S. C., by whom he had a daughter. Two years later he moved to Columbia and formed a partnership with William Harper [*q.v.*], who had married Mrs. Preston's sister. Mrs. Preston died in 1829, and in 1831 he married Louise Penelope, the daughter of Dr. James Davis of Columbia.

Preston's political career began with his election in 1828 to the lower house of the South Carolina legislature, to which he was twice reelected. In this body he was an intense advocate of free trade and state rights, and an eloquent champion of nullification. In 1833 he broke with some of the more radical nullificationists on the question of the test oath and was influential in preventing the taking of any action against the judges who pronounced it unconstitutional. This same year he was elected to the United States Senate to fill the vacancy caused by the resignation of Stephen D. Miller [*q.v.*], and was reëlected in 1837. Here he was a stanch defender of slavery, of the "gag law," and of closing the mails to abolition literature. He advocated in 1836 the annexation of Texas, which he regarded as merely reannexation, and introduced a resolution favoring it. An intense opponent of Jackson, he voted to censure him and opposed the expunging resolution. By his opposition to Van Buren's financial policy he broke with Calhoun and alienated many of his constituents. The legislature of 1842 instructed him as to his action in the Senate and he resigned rather than obey, returning to his profession. So great was his personal popularity that although he had been elected as a Democratic nullifier and returned a Whig, the dinner given in his honor was attended chiefly by Democrats. In 1845 Preston was elected president of South Carolina College, taking office Jan. 1, 1846. In this position he remained until 1851, when he suffered a stroke of paralysis and retired. He was a gifted classical scholar and his brief career as a college president was successful. He founded Columbia Lyceum with his own library of 3000 volumes.

Preston won fame at the bar as a brilliant and learned lawyer, chiefly in the realm of criminal practice; his legislative career was also highly creditable; but it is chiefly as an orator that he is remembered. A great-nephew of Patrick Henry, he cultivated the arts of the orator from youth as a matter of course and became, according to the taste of the day, a brilliant speaker. He had an imposing figure, was endowed with a superb voice—deep, rich, and mellow—and he developed a fervid style, which many people thought too ornate to be natural. Magoon characterized him as "The Inspired Declaimer" (*post*, p. 274), but he had real force and his speeches show clear analysis. He possessed a brilliant mind and was unexcelled in quick and graceful repartee. On occasion, however, he could be very caustic. He spoke frequently in Congress and delivered many formal addresses, that on Hugh S. Legaré (*Eulogy on Hugh Swinton Legare,* 1843) probably being the best known. He was much interested in the arts, and was instrumental in enabling Hiram Powers [*q.v.*] to go to Italy, introducing him to his brother John, who gave him considerable financial aid. Preston died in Columbia, S. C., in his sixty-sixth year.

[E. L. Magoon, *Living Orators in America* (1849); B. F. Perry, *Reminiscences of Public Men* (1883); J. B. O'Neall, *Biog. Sketches of the Bench and Bar of S. C.* (1889), vol. II; Linda Rhea, *Hugh Swinton Legaré, a Charleston Intellectual* (1934); A. W. Weddell, *A Memorial Vol. of Va. Hist. Portraiture 1585–1830* (1930); W. B. Preston, *The Preston Geneal.* (1900); T. L. Preston, *Hist. Sketches and Reminiscences of an Octogenarian* (1900); M. C. Yarborough, *The Reminiscences of William C. Preston* (1933); Maximilian La Borde, *Hist. of the S. C. Coll.* (1859); E. L. Green, *A Hist. of the Univ. of S. C.* (1916); *Charleston Mercury,* May 24, 1860.] J. G. deR. H.

PREUS, CHRISTIAN KEYSER (Oct. 13, 1852–May 28, 1921), Lutheran clergyman, college president, was born at Spring Prairie, Wis., the son of Herman Amberg Preus and Caroline Dorothea Margrethe (Keyser) Preus. His father, a graduate of theology from the University of Oslo, emigrated from Norway in 1851, and was one of the six founders of the Synod of the Evangelical Lutheran Church in America (Norwegian Synod). He received his early educa-

tion from tutors, entered Luther College, Decorah, Iowa, in 1868, and graduated with the B.A. degree in 1873. He then studied theology for three years at Concordia Seminary, St. Louis, Mo., graduating in 1876. He was ordained the same year and accepted, temporarily, a charge at Our Saviour's Church in Chicago. He was assistant pastor to his father in the large Spring Prairie charge with adjacent territories from 1876 to 1897. The long pastoral journeys in these pioneer regions tested the physical endurance of both, especially the father, who was president of the Norwegian Synod from 1862 until his death in 1894. A close association with his father gave him first-hand information about many an ecclesiastical controversy in and about the Synod, which had been committed to the defense of Lutheran dogmatics of the seventeenth century. In "Minder fra Spring Prairie prestegaard," in *Symra,* 1906, a periodical published in Decorah, Preus has recorded interesting reminiscences from his earlier field of work twenty miles north of Madison. In 1897 he resigned because of ill health.

In 1898 he was appointed a teacher in Luther College at Decorah, and in 1902 was elected president of the institution, a position which he held until his death. His teaching experience was limited, but he possessed qualities which were highly prized by the rank and file of the Norwegian Synod, and had had twenty-one years of experience in the ministry. He was uncompromisingly orthodox, a champion of the claim that his alma mater must teach the classics and train young men for the study of theology. He was a man of even temper, of attractive presence, kindly manners, and unusual eloquence. His administration was one of expansion for the college, witnessing the creation of several new buildings and a creditable development of the physics, chemistry, and biology buildings. There was a hundred per-cent increase in the faculty, the endowment fund was doubled, and the number of volumes in the library was tripled. The conservative changes which Preus had effected in the curriculum were forced to give way, however, when the S. A. T. C. was established at the college in 1918. With bitter disappointment, he saw the classical, theological, and linguistic *requireds* supplanted by elective courses and requirements in "war aims," "military English," and only one hour in "religion." This curricular disintegration was made all the more acute by the drastic governmental edict that no language of instruction save the English was to be used in Iowa. Preus was vice-president of the Norwegian

Synod from 1911 to 1917, when it merged to form the Norwegian Lutheran Church of America, and from 1917 until his death, he was vice-president of the Iowa District of the new body. In 1911 while attending a theological conference in Norway, he lectured at the University of Oslo and was decorated with the Order of St. Olav by King Haakon VII. He was not inclined to write books, although articles of his appeared from time to time in the church papers of his synod or in Norwegian newspapers published in the West. He preached in Norwegian, English, and German. His subjects of instruction in college were chiefly religion and Norwegian. He had a large family, eleven children being born to him and his wife, Louisa Augusta Hjort, whom he had married on May 24, 1877.

[*Who's Who in America,* 1912–13; *Stamtavler over Familien Breder og De Med den Beslaegtede Familier Preus og Arctander* (1876); *Luther College Through Sixty Years* (1922); A. K. Bergh, *Den Norsk Lutherske Kirkes Historie i Amerika* (1914); C. K. Preus, "I hvilken retning og mot hvilket maal bör Luther College utvikles for bedst at tjene Synoden?" Decorah, Iowa (1903).]   J. O. E.

PREVOST, FRANÇOIS MARIE (c. 1764–May 18, 1842), surgeon, pioneer in the use of the Cæsarean section, born in the South of France at Pont-de-Cé, was the eldest son of Marie Anne Kenotaire and Jean Pierre Prevost, natives of the Eastern Department of Marbelleau. He graduated in medicine at Paris, and settled in the "Isle et Cote Saint Dominique" (Haiti), where he served as health officer at Port de Paix. Here, on Dec. 13, 1799, he married Marie Thérèse, the widowed daughter of Marie Thérèse Giroud and Joseph Burruchon (marriage certificate registered in the Court House of Ascension Parish, La., as C. A. B., "R," p. 132). Taking his bride to Louisiana, he settled in Donaldsonville, Ascension Parish, a government post surrounded by plantations on which lived a few white planters who controlled a large population of negro slaves. Here he practised for nearly half a century.

Prevost's claim to distinction rests upon his daring and successful performance of the Cæsarean section at a time when even in the great medical centers of the world that operation was regarded as almost necessarily fatal. Only one American physician, so far as is known, had successfully performed it previously (Dr. Jessee Bennett of Rockingham County, Va., on his own wife, Jan. 14, 1794, saving both mother and child), and he had published no report of the case (J. L. Miller, in *Virginia Medical Monthly,* January 1929, reprinted in *West Virginia Medical Journal,* July 1929; Louis Frank, "Lest We Forget," *Transactions of the Southern Surgical Association,* vol. XLV, 1933). In Prevost's experience the most common cause of dystocia apparently was rickets, with resulting pelvic deformity. His first two operations, probably between 1822 and 1825, were performed upon the same woman, a slave, in two successive pregnancies complicated by rachitic pelvic deformity, and resulted in recovery for both mother and child. He made his third Cæsarean section about 1825 on a slave woman, the property of a German blacksmith, Krolin, the child alone surviving. His fourth operation was performed in 1831 on a twenty-eight year old negress, Caroline Bellau or Bellak, the property of Madame Maurous. A laparotomy by left lateral incision saved both mother and child. Prevost named the girl, a mulatto, Cesarine, and she was freed upon his stipulation, married, and lived in New Orleans. A plantation rumor sprang up about the mother, Caroline, shortly after the operation, to the effect that she had had six or seven similar operations, but investigation has shown this rumor to be fictitious.

Prevost's courage and his success are amazing in view of the difficulties under which he labored. Alone, in a negro cabin dimly lit by a candle or an oil lamp, assisted only by a slave woman, without anesthesia, without asepsis, without modern instruments to control hemorrhage, probably without even common cleanliness, he saved seven out of eight lives by an operation which had been condemned in the greatest hospitals of the world—in Paris, London, Vienna—because it had proved almost invariably fatal even in the hands of the greatest masters. He was not prompted in his daring by any craving for fame or glory—he never published a line to record or proclaim his achievements; he expected no material reward, and only made it a condition that if his patients should recover they should be freed from slavery. After the death of his first wife, he married, May 29, 1838, Victorine Castellain, of Donaldsonville. Prevost had apparently retired from practice when he died in Donaldsonville, at the age of seventy-eight. He left a son, Jean Louis Prevost, living in Brittany, who inherited his estate. Of the fate of an adopted son, John Robertson, nothing is known.

He left his books and instruments to Dr. Thomas E. Cottman, a graduate of the University of Maryland, who settled in Donaldsonville about 1831 and subsequently became closely associated with Prevost, learning from him the history of his Cæsarean operations and his methods of performing them. Cottman performed the Cæsarean section in 1831 and again in 1849, saving the mother but losing the child in each instance. From Cottman, in 1877, Dr. Robert P. Harris obtained the story of Prevost's operations. Up to this time, Dr. John L. Richmond [*q.v.*] of Newton, Ohio, had been generally credited with the first performance of the Cæsarean operation in the United States; but from the first publication of Harris' researches until 1891, when Dr. A. L. Knight, in his history of medicine in the Great Kanawha Valley of Virginia (see Miller, *op. cit.*), brought to light the claim of Dr. Bennett, Prevost held the claim to priority.

[R. P. Harris, in *New Orleans Medic. and Surgic. Jour.*, June, Oct. 1879, Apr. 1880, and in *Am. Jour. Med. Sci.*, Apr. 1878, Jan. 1879; J. G. Nancrede, in *Am. Jour. Medic. Sci.*, Aug. 1835; Edmond Souchon, in *Trans. Am. Surgic. Asso.*, vol. XXXV (1917).]

R. M.
V. G.

PRIBER, CHRISTIAN (fl. 1734–1744), Utopian, whose surname appears also as Pryber and Preber, is said to have been a Saxon of good family and education, an army officer, and an accomplished linguist, whose subversive ideas compelled him to flee to England. About 1734 he emigrated to South Carolina, but in 1736 he retired from Charlestown to the mountains to live among the Cherokee Indians, the "noble savages" of the generous tradition to which he subscribed. His attempt to found an ideal commonwealth among the southern Indians made that frontier for a few years the first frontier of eighteenth-century radicalism. "Being a great Scholar," one Carolina trader averred, "he soon made himself master of their Tongue, and by his insinuating manner Indeavoured to gain their hearts, he trimm'd his hair in the indian manner & painted as they did going generally almost naked except a shirt & a Flap" (Grant, *post*, p. 59). These methods, and his warnings to the Indians of English encroachments, convinced the colonists that he was a French agent, some declared a Jesuit. It is true that he promoted a trade between these old friends of the English and the French at New Orleans, but he did so "only to preserve their liberties" until they could "throw off the yoke of their European allies, of all nations" (*Annual Register, post*, p. 24). Meanwhile he labored to form all the southern Indians into a great independent confederation. James Adair [*q.v.*] asserted that his "red empire" at the moment of his arrest threatened to embrace the Creeks, Choctaw, and the Mississippi River tribes, as well as the Cherokee.

Under the protection of this Indian league Priber further sought to found a communistic "Town and Society" which might in time serve as a model for a republic to be set up in France. Ancient Cusawatee at the foot of the mountains was the chosen site. To this city of refuge, reported Oglethorpe, he "expected a great resort for the benefit of the Asylum from the numbers of Debtors, Transport Felons, Servants, and negroe Slaves in the two Carolina's and Virginia" (*post*). Liberty and equality were the foundation principles of the new "Paradise," with such corollaries as community of goods and of women, and the rearing of children by the state; there, indeed, "the law of nature should be established as the sole law." He anticipated the axiom of the Saint-Simonists: that each would find what he needed for subsistence or for other needs and that each should contribute his share toward the good of society. It was Priber's misfortune that his scheme—an epitome of eighteenth-century "socialism"—ran right athwart the imperial purposes of the English in America. When in 1739 a commission from South Carolina was sent to arrest him, he was shielded by the Cherokee. However, in the spring of 1743 the traders among the Upper Creeks incited those Indians to seize him; he was sent down, with his bundle of mysterious manuscripts, to Georgia to be treated by Oglethorpe and his officers as a political prisoner. A few years later he died in the fort at Frederica.

[V. W. Crane, "A Lost Utopia of the First American Frontier," *Sewanee Review*, Jan. 1919; "Jour. of Antoine Bonnefoy," *Travels in the Am. Colonies*, 1916, ed. by N. D. Mereness, pp. 246–250; Ludovick Grant's deposition in *S. C. Hist. and Geneal. Mag.*, Jan. 1909; a letter signed "Americus" in *Annual Register . . . of the Year 1760*, "Characters," pp. 22–25; James Adair, *The Hist. of the Am. Indians* (1775), pp. 240–43; Oglethorpe's memorandum in the Public Record Office, London, C. O. 5: 655, p. 112.]

V. W. C.

PRICE, BRUCE (Dec. 12, 1845–May 29, 1903), architect, the son of William and Marion (Bruce) Price, was born in Cumberland, Md. On his father's side he was descended from Peter Reese Price (the name sometimes appears as Ap Rhys and Ap Rice), an early Welsh settler of Western Maryland, and from William Williams, a religious fanatic, said to have been a descendant of Owen Glendower, who settled in what was later Washington County, Md. On his mother's side, he was descended from Norman Bruce, who settled in Western Maryland in 1762. Bruce Price was educated in the public schools of Cumberland and had just entered the College of New Jersey (Princeton) when the death of his father, a lawyer and judge, compelled him to undertake the partial support of the family. Accordingly, he went to Baltimore and worked for some time as a shipping clerk, meanwhile giving his evenings to the study of architecture under the well-known Baltimore firm of Niernsee & Neilson. In 1864 he entered the office of this firm as a draftsman, remaining four years. He studied abroad in 1868–69, and upon his return opened his own office in Baltimore. His first work of significance was Saint Paul's Church. In April 1871, he married Josephine Lee, the daughter of Washington Lee, of Wilkes-Barre, Pa. They spent most of the following year in Europe, especially in Paris. In 1873, he opened an office in Wilkes-Barre. While here, his most important designs were those for the Methodist Church, Wilkes-Barre, and the Lee Memorial Church, Lexington, Va.

In 1877 he moved his family to New York, which was his home for the rest of his life. His first important New York work was the Long Beach Hotel (since burned), nearly a quarter of a mile long. In the early eighties, he designed the West End Hotel at Bar Harbor, and a series of cottages there, culminating in the enormous cottage called "The Turrets." By this time his reputation was wide and his practice grew rapidly. His earlier work included the layout of Tuxedo Park (1885–86) for Pierre Lorillard [q.v.] and many of the individual houses there, the Scott and Lorillard houses at Newport, R. I., Osborn Hall and the Welch Dormitory at Yale (1888), and a large amount of work in Canada, extending over many years, including the Château Frontenac at Quebec, the Windsor Street and Place Viger railroad stations and the Royal Victoria College for Women at Montreal, and the Banff Springs Hotel, Alberta. The largest and most lavish of his domestic work was the great group called "Georgian Court" (1898–1900), for George Jay Gould [q.v.], at Lakewood, N. J. During the nineties, his practice grew to include more and more commercial work. In 1891 he had prepared a project—widely published and commented on—for a tower building for the New York *Sun,* which in general composition was a forerunner of the type developed later in Le Brun's Metropolitan Tower. His St. James Building and the building of the International Bank, both in New York, were merely characteristic of the taste of the time, but in the American Surety Building, New York (1895), still standing, though much altered, he set a new standard of clarity of composition, lavishness of classic detail, and careful refinement. In this building he made noteworthy use of a series of dignified free-standing figures (by J. Massey Rhind) as important features of the exterior. He was also the designer of the exquisite memorial to Richard Morris Hunt [q.v.] in the Central Park wall at Fifth Avenue and 70th–71st streets, New York.

Price was the choice of a committee of Japanese architects who had made an extended world tour for the purpose of selecting the architect for a palace in Tokio for the Crown Prince of Japan; the drawings for the palace were completed when he fell fatally ill. He had also at that time just completed a rough preliminary sketch for a tower building for the *New York American* on The Circle, New York City, but this was never built. In his last year, when he left on a trip to Europe for his health, he took into partnership Henri de Sibour. He died in Paris, after two months' illness.

As a whole, the work of Bruce Price is extremely personal, always carefully studied, and full more of the artist's devotion to beauty than of engineering significance. Although his early work is expressive of the Victorian spirit, all of it is instinct with refinement and a sort of modest inventiveness. In a different field, this inventiveness was shown in his patented parlor-car bay windows, used for some time on the Pennsylvania and Boston & Albany railroads. He was the author of *Modern Architectural Practice, No. 1, A Large Country House, N. Y.* (1887), containing the plans of a house at San Mateo, Cal., for Col. W. H. Howard. He was awarded a bronze medal at the Paris Exposition of 1900.

Price was immensely popular with all kinds of people; the St. James Club of Montreal created for him the post of permanent visitor, with himself as the sole incumbent. He was a member of the Architectural League of New York (president, 1897–99), a fellow (1890) of the American Institute of Architects, and at one time president of the Municipal Art Society. He had two children, a son who died in infancy, and a daughter, Emily (Price) Post. His grandson, Bruce Price Post (1895–1927), was an architect of extraordinary promise and brilliance.

[Genealogical data and personal reminiscences from Price's daughter, Mrs. Post; Russell Sturgis, "The Works of Bruce Price," and Barr Ferree, "A Talk with Bruce Price," *Architectural Record,* June 1899; *Am. Art Annual,* vols. I (1898), III (1900); *Who's Who in America,* 1901–02; *Evening Post* (N. Y.), May 30, 1903; *N. Y. Times,* May 31, 1903.]   T. F. H.

PRICE, ELI KIRK (July 20, 1797–Nov. 15, 1884), lawyer and law reformer, was born at East Bradford, Chester County, Pa., the son of Philip and Rachel (Kirk) Price. He was a descendant of Philip Price, a Welsh coreligionist of William Penn, who came to the new colony on the Delaware in 1682, and finally settled at Haverford, Montgomery County. His maternal ancestors were from northern Ireland, and all were Friends. Eli attended the Friends' boarding school at Westtown, served as clerk in a store at West Chester, and, at the age of eighteen, joined the staff of Thomas P. Cope [q.v.], leading Philadelphia shipping merchant. After about four years of business experience, during which he used his leisure time for the study of law, especially that relating to commerce and shipping, he entered the law office of John Sergeant, and in 1822 was admitted to the bar. Six years later he married Anna Embree, also a Friend. They had three children, of whom the eldest, Rebecca, predeceased her father and was the subject of his *Memorial of Our Daughter, for Her Child* (1862).

While a young practitioner, surrounded by many of much greater experience, "he appeared to advantage." His preference, however, was for a line of professional work which, if it brought less immediate publicity, insured eventually a more permanent reputation and income. Specializing in equity and real property law, he became, ultimately, the leading Philadelphia exponent of these branches. While he sometimes diverted his activities from strictly professional channels, he did so usually in the line of public benefaction. In 1833 he published his *Digest of the Acts of Assembly and of the Ordinances of the Inhabitants and Commissioners of the District of Spring Garden* and in 1838, his *Institutes of Morality for the Instruction of Youth*. In 1845, and again in 1848, he was a member of the newly created board of Revenue Commissioners and contributed materially to the performance of its duties and the preparation of its report. He soon became conscious of the evils resulting from the municipal situation in which the *de jure* City of Philadelphia proper, comprising about 1200 acres, was surrounded by a group of districts, legally distinct but actually a part of it. As a representative of the inhabitants, he urged reform upon the legislature at Harrisburg. No results appearing, he consented, reluctantly, and at the sacrifice of his private interests, to stand for election to the state Senate and served there from 1854 to 1856 inclusive. In the first named year he secured the passage of a new charter—the "Consolidation Act"—which is believed to have laid the foundation of the city's growth and importance. His interest in municipal improvement never flagged and his efforts led to the establishment in 1867 of Fairmount Park, on the governing commission of which he served as chairman from the first. In 1873 he published *The History of the Consolidation of the City of Philadelphia.*

Meanwhile, he had undertaken reform in another field—the antiquated and complicated law of real property. At the request of Gov. William Bigler [q.v.] he prepared and secured the passage in 1853 of "An Act Relating to the Sale and Conveyance of Real Estate"; in 1855 of another act, broadening the law of descent; in 1856 of "An Act for the Greater Security of Title"; and in 1859, of a supplementary one relative to the statute of limitations. Largely growing out of these labors and supplementing them was his book, entitled, *Of the Limitation of Actions, and of Liens, against Real Estate, in Pennsylvania,* which appeared in 1857. A commentary on the "Price Act" of 1853, *The Act for the Sale of Real Estate in Philadelphia,* was published in 1874. Reform of the law of domestic relations also claimed his attention, and the act of 1855 protecting the wife's property from the improvident husband and providing for adoption, and that of 1856 in aid of the deserted or neglected wife were the results of his activities. Except David Dudley Field [q.v.], few if any American lawyers devoted so much of their time and experience to the improvement of the law; yet he managed to keep abreast of the increasing business of "a pressing and urgent clientage." More important estates are said to have been handled by him than by any other Philadelphia lawyer, but this work did not prevent him from taking an active part in various organizations for intellectual and philanthropic ends. His fees were moderate, but his professional career of sixty years enabled him to accumulate a large fortune; yet he never lost his simple tastes nor his interest in the faith of his fathers.

[E. K. Price, *Centennial Meeting of the Descendants of Philip and Rachel Price* (1864); B. H. Brewster, *Address on the Late Eli K. Price* (1896); J. T. Rothrock, *Biog. Memoir of the Late Eli K. Price* (1886); J. S. Futhey and Gilbert Cope, *Hist. of Chester County, Pa.* (1881); *Phila. Inquirer*, Nov. 17, 1884.]
C. S. L.

PRICE, HIRAM (Jan. 10, 1814–May 30, 1901), congressman from Iowa, banker, was born in Washington County, Pa., the son of a farmer of English, Welsh, and Irish descent. When he was five he was taken to Mifflin County and later to Huntingdon County, Pa. He was educated in local schools taught by old-fashioned traveling country school teachers and developed a love of reading that gave him most of his limited education. In April 1834 he married Susan Betts, the daughter of prosperous Quaker parents. Of their five children, the eldest became the wife of John F. Dillon [q.v.]. In 1844 the family removed to Davenport, Iowa, where he opened a small store which he conducted successfully. In 1847 he was elected school fund commissioner and the following year recorder and treasurer of Scott County. Early in the fifties he was active in the building of a railroad from Davenport to Council Bluffs, a pioneer railroad in Iowa. He also had an important part in the construction of other railroad enterprises of local and state importance. A determined opponent of the use and sale of intoxicating liquors, he helped to draft the Iowa prohibitory liquor law passed in 1855 and was active in its enforcement. He was a Democrat until the formation of the Republican party in Iowa in 1856. He had become known as a financier, and, when in 1858 the state bank of Iowa was established, he represented the Davenport branch. In 1860 he became president and retained the office until the end of 1865, when the state system was superseded by the federal banking system. Many of the features of that system were suggested by the Iowa law and were successfully tested during its existence. His admirable management of the state bank of Iowa in times when the West was flooded with worthless paper money is deserving of great praise. His part in furnishing funds for the raising, arming, and equipment of volunteers in 1861, before they were mustered into the service of the United States, was another noteworthy example of public service.

He represented Iowa in Congress from 1863 to 1869 and from 1877 to 1881. During his second term he advocated the resumption of specie payments and also favored the remonetization of silver. From 1881 to 1885 he was commissioner of Indian affairs. After his retirement he resided in Washington. He was a life-long Methodist and was both an active supporter and a liberal contributor. He never compromised with any opposition, and he was aggressive in sustaining and disseminating his radical views. He contributed to the *Annals of Iowa* two articles that are perhaps more valuable for what they tell of their author rather than for the historical information they contain, "Recollections of Iowa Men and Affairs" (Apr. 1893) and "The State Bank of Iowa" (Jan. 1894).

[B. F. Gue, "The Public Services of Hiram Price," *Annals of Iowa*, Jan. 1895; S. S. Howe, "Biog. Sketch of Hiram Price," *Ibid.*, Jan. 1864; John F. Dillon, *Anna Price Dillon: Memoirs and Memorials* (1900); E. H. Stiles, *Recollections and Sketches of Notable Lawyers and Public Men of Early Iowa* (1916); H. H. Preston, *Hist. of Banking in Iowa* (1922).]
F. E. H.

PRICE, JOSEPH (Jan. 1, 1853–June 6, 1911), physician and surgeon, the son of Joshua and Feby (Moore) Price, was born in Rockingham County, Va. He was educated at the Fort Edward Collegiate Institute, Fort Edward, N.

Y., and Union College, Schenectady, N. Y., but left college to join the engineering corps of the New York Central Railroad. He subsequently entered the University of Pennsylvania as a medical student and was graduated in 1877. His first professional post was that of surgeon on a transatlantic passenger ship on which he made three trips between Antwerp, Liverpool, and Philadelphia. He then began his work at the old Philadelphia Dispensary where he became head of the obstetrical division and organized the gynecological department. Under his leadership the clinic for women became one of the most conspicuous and largest in the country. It was here, working among the poor of the slums, under unsanitary conditions, that he laid the foundation of his brilliant career in abdominal surgery.

The year 1887 was an important one in his life. He went abroad and while in England he met Lawson Tait, England's pioneer surgical genius, whose work was a great inspiration to him. The same year he was married to Louise Troth of Philadelphia, and immediately after his marriage accepted the position of director and resident physician of the Preston Retreat, a philanthropic maternity hospital in Philadelphia. He held this post for seven years during which time there was not one death from sepsis. In 1888 he and Dr. C. B. Penrose founded the Gynecean Hospital. In 1891 he withdrew from the Gynecean to open, with Dr. J. W. Kennedy, his own hospital, now known as the Joseph Price Memorial Hospital, the largest private institution in the United States for abdominal surgery. He was a member of the American Association of Obstetricians and Gynecologists, president in 1895, and was also a member of the American Medical Association and the Mississippi Valley Medical Association. In June 1911, suffering from a retroperitoneal infection which had existed as a metastatic condition from a prior septicemia, he left his sick room and successfully performed an operation for appendicitis. Shortly afterwards he was seized with violent pains, recognized the symptoms, conferred with his fellow surgeons, and made all the arrangements for his own operation. He died the same night without recovering from the shock of the operation. He was survived by his wife, three daughters, and four sons.

By his clinical teaching Price influenced the activities of nearly every surgeon in the United States, yet he never wrote a book nor held a teaching position in any institution. He taught constantly by and through his operations. To form a just estimate of his work it is necessary to remember that he came into the field of abdominal and pelvic surgery in the early eighties when the principles of aseptic and antiseptic surgery were on trial. He tirelessly preached asepsis and radical cleansing of the operative field. Dr. Howard A Kelly writes of him "... he found gynecology and abdominal surgery twin babes in swaddling clothes and left them, after a life of extraordinary activity, full-grown specialties" (Kelly and Burrage, *post,* p. 940). His surgical genius consisted in his ability to grasp essentials and to eliminate all unnecessary moves in operation, and having perfected a technique, simple but effective, he taught and demonstrated it to all members of his profession who desired to learn. He was a clear and forceful speaker and his apt and epigrammatic remarks, made while demonstrating, did more to impress his teachings than pages of manuscript or hours of formal lectures. He made common the radical operation for the treatment of pelvic suppurations, and taught how to operate with clamp, serre noeud, and external treatment of the stump, so as to make hysterectomy a safe operation instead of an almost inevitably fatal one. He never wore gloves when operating, believing that they lessened his dexterity and were unnecessary if the hands were surgically clean. Surgery was his profession, his hobby, and his life, and to it he devoted his keen mind, piercing vision, deft fingers, and unbounded enthusiasm. He was fiercely intolerant of quackery, commercialism or slovenly work. His professional charity made his hospital accessible to the poorest patients. Although he never published a lengthy volume he was a frequent contributor of short papers to the proceedings of the societies of which he was a member. Some of the titles are: "Cleanliness in Maternities," *Medical and Surgical Reporter,* (Phila.), July 26, 1890; "A Retrospect of Abdominal Surgery," *Medical News,* June 14, 1890; and "Surgical Conception of Peritonitis," *Transactions of the American Association of Obstetricians and Gynecologists, 1890* (1891).

[H. A. Kelly, W. L. Burrage, *Am. Medic. Biog.* (1920); J. W. Kennedy, *Practical Surgery of the Joseph Price Hospital* (1926); *Am. Medic. Jour.,* July 1911; *Public Ledger* (Phila., Pa.), June 8, 1911.]

F. E. W.

PRICE, RODMAN McCAMLEY (May 5, 1816–June 7, 1894), naval officer, governor of New Jersey, was born in Sussex County, N. J., the son of Francis and Ann (McCamley) Price. His grandfathers, Zachariah Price and David McCamley, were both extensive land-owners in the northern region of the state. The boy attended the Lawrenceville School and entered the College of New Jersey (Princeton) but was forced to leave because of lack of health. He studied law and married Matilda Trenchard, the daughter of a naval captain and the sister of Steven Decatur Trenchard [*q.v.*]. The combined political and naval influence obtained him an appointment as naval purser in 1840. After serving on the *Fulton* he was assigned to the new *Missouri,* which was sent on an exhibition cruise to Europe, one of the first steam warships to cross the Atlantic. She was burned at Gibraltar, and he spent some time touring Europe with Capt. John T. Newton, being received by Queen Victoria and Wellington, learning Spanish, and helping Irving to copy the Columbus records in the Spanish archives. He played an active part in the American occupation of California. Early in 1846, after what he described as a confidential interview with Polk and Secretary Bancroft, he was ordered to the *Cyane* in Sloat's Pacific Squadron. He claimed that he gave the irresolute commodore the necessary prodding to occupy Monterey. He related that, being rowed to the flagship at midnight on July 6, he strongly urged Sloat to occupy California before Sir George Seymour's British squadron should do so. The commodore, still in his nightshirt, paced the cabin for an hour and finally exclaimed "Mr. Price, you have convinced me. I will hesitate no longer." In the morning Price read the proclamation of annexation from the Monterey custom house (*True American,* June 9, 1894, but see Bancroft, *post,* p. 229 note). He was appointed alcalde and was said to be the first American to exercise judicial authority in California. He was later sent with dispatches to Scott and thence to Polk, who asked him to draw up a report on California. While he was in Washington, news came of the gold discovery, and he was sent back to San Francisco with added fiscal powers as naval agent to facilitate transmission of funds and prevent gold shipments to England. He made heavy profits in real estate, furnished money for San Francisco's first wharf, sat in its first municipal council, and was a member of the California constitutional convention. In December 1849 he was relieved from duty as naval agent. He settled his accounts and advanced $75,000 to his successor for government use, but while traveling on the Alabama River on his way to Washington the steamer was burned, and he lost all his receipts and vouchers. This created an embarrassing tangle resulting in litigation that stretched over more than forty years and resulted in his imprisonment just before his death.

Returning to New Jersey, he plunged into Democratic politics and was elected in 1850 to the House of Representatives, where he spoke and worked in the interest of the Paterson silk industry. He was defeated for reëlection, but in 1853 he was elected governor. In January 1854 he began his three-year term. In spite of his youth, he made an excellent record of constructive legislation. Supported by a Democratic legislature, he was instrumental in establishing the state geological survey, a life-saving apparatus on the Jersey coast, and an improved system of road construction. He appointed judges from both parties, took preliminary steps to modify the railroad monopoly, helped to improve the militia, and assisted the rebuilding of Nassau Hall at Princeton. His crowning work was his support of the movement for educational reform, led by Richard S. Field [q.v.], Christopher C. Hoagland, and David Cole. Not eligible for reelection, he retired to private life. After serving as one of New Jersey's nine delegates to the unsuccessful "peace conference" at Washington in 1861, he startled the state on Apr. 4, 1861, by a public letter in the *Newark Evening Journal* declaring that slavery was no evil and that New Jersey would serve its interests best by siding with the South (see Knapp, *post*, pp. 53–54). He remained a Copperhead throughout the war. He lived for some time at Weehawken but in 1862 settled for the remainder of his life in northern New Jersey on the Ramapo near Oakland. He urged the development of the New Jersey shore as the logical center of the activity of the port of New York, owing to its rail connections, and he started the successful ferry from Weehawken to 42nd Street, later acquired by the West Shore Railroad. He also reclaimed some of the marsh lands of the Hackensack River, converting them into farm lands and orchards, and he was active in quarrying paving blocks. The litigation over his missing naval papers clouded his last years.

[Obituary by F. G. DeFontaine in *Daily True American* (Trenton), June 9, 1894; *Biog. Directory Am. Cong.* (1928); C. M. Knapp, *N. J. Politics during the . . . Civil War* (1924); J. Whitehead, *Judicial and Civil Hist. of N. J.* (2 vols., 1897); H. H. Bancroft, *Hist. of Cal.*, vol. V (1886); David Murray, *Hist. of Education in N. J.* (1899), p. 177; financial trouble reviewed in *House Report 3315*, 51 Cong., 2 Sess. (1891) and *House Exec. Doc. 45*, 52 Cong., 1 Sess. (1892).]
R. G. A—n.

PRICE, STEPHEN (Sept. 25, 1782–Jan. 20, 1840), theatrical manager, was the son of Michael Price, a New York merchant, and of his wife Helena Cornell (or Cornwell). In 1799 he graduated from Columbia College. Apparently in 1805 he began practising law in New York and continued that profession for five or six years (*Longworth's American Almanac, New York Register, and City Directory*, 1805–10). In 1808 he entered upon the major activity of his life when he purchased from Thomas Abthorpe Cooper [q.v.], manager of the Park Theatre, New York, a share in that establishment. Being an astute business man, Price made the Park pay as no American theatre had ever paid before. He and Cooper shortly became men of wealth and fashion. Occupying adjoining houses at the corner of Broadway and Leonard Street, they lived in extravagant luxury, and their homes were among the social centers of the town. Upon Cooper's withdrawal from the management of the Park about 1815, Price became sole lessee and manager. After two or three years, however, he took the actor Edmund Simpson into a partnership that continued until Price's death. On May 24, 1820, the Park Theatre was destroyed by fire, but the managers promptly shifted their company to the Anthony Street Theatre and went on with the season. The Park was rebuilt as rapidly as possible and was opened Sept. 1, 1821. About 1823 the enterprising partners added to their affairs the proprietorship of a dramatic and equestrian company, which they stationed for several weeks each year at the Broadway Circus, sending it on tour the remainder of the time.

For the season of 1826–27 Price was lessee of Drury Lane Theatre, London (John Genest, *Some Account of the English Stage*, 1832, vol. IX, p. 377), but a single season is said to have proved ruinous (Wemyss, *post*, pp. 85 ff.), and he returned to New York. This foreign contact, however, cemented his ties with the British managers and aided him in carrying out the plan that was his contribution to the American theatre. Realizing that American audiences were more impressed by foreign reputations than by native, he hit upon the scheme of importing British stars for brief and intensive campaigns in the United States. With keen business acumen he saw in the idea greater possibilities than could be realized in the Park Theatre alone; consequently he entered into an agreement with managers in Philadelphia, Boston, and other cities to "farm out" his visiting artists for a sufficient consideration. Thus Price became the first American theatrical magnate, as he was the first manager to enter the field, not from the ranks of the actors or the playwrights, as did Hallam, Wignell, Cooper, and Dunlap, but solely with a business man's interest in the theatre as a moneymaking concern. The first international star to tour the Eastern cities under his ægis was George Frederick Cooke, for whose coming to America in 1810 Cooper probably deserves chief credit. Subsequently Price imported and managed such celebrities as Edmund Kean, Charles Mathews, William Macready, Tyrone Power, Fanny Kemble, and Ellen Tree. Small wonder that he was known in England as "Star Giver General to the United States" (Wemyss, p. 86). Much as this system gratified American audiences, it exerted a harmful influence on American actors, who, playing subordinate rôles to support foreign notables, found that the dignity of their work had departed.

During his later years Price spent much time abroad and relaxed his efforts to keep the Park in a position of leadership; hence it was outdistanced by more energetic rivals, and at the time of his death was in serious financial straits. By his associates (Wemyss, p. 86) he was regarded as an excellent friend, a good manager, and, although a strict disciplinarian, in all his business dealings a man of honor.

[J. N. Ireland, *Records of the N. Y. Stage*, vols. I and II (1866–67); G. C. D. Odell, *Annals of the N. Y. Stage*, vols. II, III, IV (1927–28); F. C. Wemyss, *Twenty-six Years of the Life of an Actor and Manager* (1847); *Morning Herald* (N. Y.), Jan. 21, 1840; John Cornell, *Geneal. of the Cornell Family* (1902); records of Columbia College; records of Trinity Ch., N. Y.]   O. S. C.

PRICE, STERLING (Sept. 20, 1809–Sept. 29, 1867), governor of Missouri, representative, Confederate soldier, was born in Prince Edward County, Va., the son of Pugh Williamson and Elizabeth (Williamson) Price and the descendant of John Price who emigrated from Wales to Henrico County, Va., about 1620. He attended Hampden-Sydney College in 1826–27. He then studied law under Creed Taylor of Virginia. About 1831 with his parents he removed to Fayette, Mo., and later he purchased a farm near Keytesville in Chariton County, which was his home for practically the rest of his life. On May 14, 1833, he was married to Martha Head in Randolph County. From 1836 to 1838 and from 1840 to 1844 he was Chariton County's representative in the state legislature, and he was speaker of the House during the last four years of this period. In 1844 he was elected to Congress, but, largely because he was disinclined to play the game of politics, he failed to receive the nomination for reëlection. He resigned on Aug. 12, 1846, to enter the Mexican War as colonel of the 2nd Missouri Infantry. He was made military governor of Chihuahua and also promoted to the rank of brigadier-general. He was nominated as an anti-Benton Democrat and was easily elected governor of Missouri in 1852. During his four-year term the public school system was reorganized, much new land was opened to settlement, and railroad construction grew apace.

On one notable occasion he displayed rare courage, however, by vetoing a bill that provided for over-generous state aid to railroads. Because of his general popularity and because he was a conditional Union man he was chosen president of the state convention of 1860. He thought that this convention was wise in voting down all proposals looking toward secession, but, when the convention adjourned, the pro-Southern governor, Claiborne Fox Jackson [q.v.], placed him in command of the state troops. It was the subsequent irritatingly aggressive policies and activities of such Unionists as Frank P. Blair and Nathaniel Lyon [qq.v.] that drove him into the arms of the Southerners.

After the famous Planters' Hotel conference in June 1861 with Blair and Lyon, he hastened to Jefferson City and soon retreated with a small force to the southwestern corner of the state. He collected and trained some 5,000 troops, moved them eastward, and early in August temporarily united his forces with the smaller Confederate army of Gen. Ben McCulloch [q.v.] twelve miles south of Springfield. There at the battle of Wilson's Creek the combined armies, nominally under the command of McCulloch but principally led by Price, defeated the Union army and killed the commander, Nathaniel Lyon. This victory not only revealed Price's military ability but also placed him upon a high pinnacle of popularity among Southerners. He marched northward and besieged and captured 3,000 Federal troops at Lexington, Sept. 17–20, 1861. However, the forces of John C. Frémont were hot on his trail, and he retreated into Arkansas, where he and his troops officially joined the Confederate army in April 1862. That summer he was defeated in the campaign around Iuka and Corinth, Miss. In the early part of 1864 he again suffered reverses at Helena, Ark., but was in turn able to inflict a severe defeat on General Steele, when the latter attempted to gain the Red River. The raid through Missouri, his last important military effort, was a failure. Finally retreating to the plains of Texas, 1864–65, he decided to take up his abode in Mexico. He was perhaps the leading secession figure west of the Mississippi. His critics charged, however, that he harbored unwarranted if not illegitimate ambitions for high office in the Confederacy, that he was disrespectful toward the president, and that he was not properly obedient to his superior officers. Jefferson Davis, after a conference and no doubt a quarrel with Price, pronounced him the "vainest man he ever met" (Stevens, *post*, p. 850) but those who knew him best placed no such estimate on his character. His friends, on the contrary, insisted that the charge that he deliberately sought to become generalissimo of the armies or president of the Confederacy was unfounded. They asserted, moreover, that he not only failed to receive at Richmond the recognition his character, influence, and military genius deserved, but that he was deliberately placed under the command of men who were distinctly inferior to him in military ability. Following the collapse of Maximilian's empire he returned in 1866 to Missouri a broken man.

[Manuscript dissertation by Lucy Simmons, State Teachers College, Kirksville, Mo.; J. T. Scharf, *Hist. of St. Louis* (1883), vol. I; W. B. Stevens, *Centennial Hist. of Mo.* (1921), vol. I; B. L. Price, *John Price . . . with Some of his Descendants* (1910); John McElroy, *The Struggle for Mo.* (1909); E. A. Pollard, *The Lost Cause: A New Southern Hist. of the War* (1866), vol. I; *War of the Rebellion: Official Records (Army)*, esp. I ser. XLI, pts. 1–4; *Messages and Proclamations of the Governors of . . . Mo.*, vol. I (1922), ed. by Buel Leopard and F. C. Shoemaker; *Jefferson City People's Tribune*, Jan. 24, 1866, Jan. 9, Oct. 2, 1867, Sept. 13, 1871.]   H. E. N.

PRICE, THOMAS FREDERICK (Aug. 19, 1860–Sept. 12, 1919), Roman Catholic priest, editor, and missionary, son of Alfred Lanier and Clarissa (Bond) Price, was born in Wilmington, N. C., where his father published the *Wilmington Journal* (1848–72). The Prices were of old Carolinian stock, proud of their ancestors' service in the War of Independence. The father, until shortly before his death when he joined the Catholic Church, was an Episcopalian; but his wife, converted from Methodism and disinherited by her family, was a devout Catholic and reared her ten children accordingly. Trained in Catholic schools, Thomas, intending to continue his education, took passage (Sept. 16, 1876) from Wilmington to Baltimore, but the ship he was on sank and he was almost miraculously rescued. This escape and the long fever which followed intensified his religious fervor. A few months later, he enrolled at St. Charles' College, Ellicott City, Md., where he was graduated in 1881. He studied theology at St. Mary's Seminary, Baltimore, and received the deaconate at the hands of Cardinal Gibbons, whose Mass he had served as a boy when Gibbons was in North Carolina. On June 30, 1886, he was ordained in Wilmington by Bishop H. P. Northrop—the first North Carolinian to become a priest—and assigned to missionary work in the eastern section of his native state.

For a number of years, Father Price as pastor of St. Paul's Church in New Bern and of the Sacred Heart Church in Raleigh preached missions throughout the state, talked religion on the street corners and to men in the fields, built churches or chapels at Goldsboro (with the aid

cf Jewish admirers), Chinquapin, Halifax, Newton Grove, and Nazareth. He understood the Southern people, won the respect of the backwoodsmen, and was held in warm regard by the negroes, in whose conversion he was especially interested. As a preacher, he was grave and sincere; and as a man, he led a life of simple, devoted sacrifice and of mortification. About 1896 he founded *Truth,* an apologetic magazine, which in the beginning he printed in the kitchen of his Raleigh rectory. This publication remained under his editorship until 1911. In 1897 he established, near Nazareth, an orphanage for boys under the direction of the Sisters of Charity, and in connection therewith founded an Apostolate, where with a few clerical associates he lived a community life and undertook to train neophytes for the domestic missions. While this undertaking was only partially successful because of the lack of men and money, the idea was later developed by the Paulists, and Price's own name became a household word among American priests.

At the Eucharistic Congress, in 1910, Price met the Rev. James Anthony Walsh, director of the Propagation of the Faith in Boston and editor of *The Field Afar* (1907), and determined to join forces with him in the establishment of the first American Catholic foreign missionary society. The project was approved by the archbishops (1911), and Price went to Rome and obtained Papal sanction. While on this journey he spent some time in Lourdes with the brother of Bernadette Soubirous, a life of whom he later translated from the French and published (1915), under the *nom de plume* J. H. Gregory. This work and *The Lily of Mary* (1918), a translation of a shorter life of Bernadette of Lourdes, comprised his literary output. Soon the Catholic Foreign Mission Society of America was established temporarily at Hawthorne, N. Y. A site was acquired at Pocantico Hills, but an agent of John D. Rockefeller outbid the society and the owner denied the sale. In the resulting civil action, the society obtained damages and purchased a site (Maryknoll) near Ossining, N. Y. Associated with the missionary priests in this Maryknoll movement were a fraternity of brothers and the Maryknoll Sisters. Growth was rapid and donations soon transformed the primitive but practical seminary into an elaborate institution, which was awarded the Decree of Praise from Rome in 1915. Price assisted in establishing a preparatory seminary near Scranton, Pa. (1916), and a Maryknoll Procure in San Francisco (1917). In 1918, when a band of young priests were prepared for

Yeungkong mission in China, Price begged to go as a stabilizing leader, and his petition was granted. Although rather old for this rigorous life and unable to learn Chinese, he contributed the inspired zeal of a visionary to the cause. Stricken with acute appendicitis while alone, he managed to reach St. Paul's Hospital in Hongkong, where he died and was buried by Bishop Pozzoni in the Happy Valley Cemetery.

[P. J. Byrne, *Father Price of Maryknoll* (1923); G. C. Powers, *The Maryknoll Movement* (1926); *The Missionary,* Nov. 1919; *The Field Afar,* Oct., Dec. 1919; *Truth,* Nov.–Dec., 1919; *N. Y. Times,* Sept. 24, 1919; information from P. W. Browne, an associate.]

R. J. P.

PRICE, THOMAS LAWSON (Jan. 19, 1809–July 16, 1870), railroad builder, congressman, was born near Danville, Va., the son of Major Price and a Miss Lawson, both descendants of English families which had early settled in the state. Although his father was a prosperous and influential tobacco-planter and land-owner, Price received only a meager common-school education. After inheriting in 1829 an ample fortune, he moved to Missouri, where economic conditions seemed favorable. Deterred by a cholera epidemic from settling in St. Louis, he pushed westward in 1831 to the new capital, Jefferson City, then a mere village. His inheritance gave him a favored status in a community of little wealth. He organized a mercantile and trading business which achieved immediate success, and became a speculator in lands in central Missouri. He was a pioneer and explorer of new fields of economic enterprise, confident in the future and eager to assume great risks in his quest for success. He established in 1838 the first stage line between St. Louis and Jefferson City; subsequently, he founded other lines and controlled the entire stage business in the state. He organized the Capital City Bank; he operated a building and loan association, the Jefferson Land Company; he leased convict labor. Early recognizing the vast significance of railroads, he was a leader in their development, employing his financial and political influence in securing state aid in 1850 for the Missouri Pacific Railroad, and similar assistance during the early fifties for the Kansas Pacific and other railroad projects. To all these enterprises, he made liberal donations of time and of money, and his construction company built a substantial portion of the railroads in the state prior to the Civil War.

During the early forties he entered politics, but retained full control of his numerous business interests. When Austin A. King [*q.v.*] was elected governor in 1848, Price was elected lieu-

tenant-governor, both representing the Thomas H. Benton [*q.v.*] element of the Democratic party. As presiding officer of the state Senate, Price was deeply involved in the factional politics of a time when the Missouri Democracy was torn with internal dissension. Devoted personally and politically to Benton, he opposed the proslavery Jackson Resolutions of 1849, yet presided with firmness and decorum over two turbulent legislative sessions. In 1852 he was the choice of the Benton group for governor, but Colonel Benton forbade his followers to participate in the deliberations of the state convention. Unsuccessful in his quest for a congressional nomination in 1854, he nevertheless continued a prominent leader of the Benton wing during a period in the middle fifties when the question of slavery in the territories seriously threatened the integrity of the party organization. In 1860 he was elected to the legislature. With other Benton Democrats, Price, a slave owner, became an unconditional Unionist, opposing the abortive secession efforts of the state administration. Frémont designated him a general in charge of state troops; he was subsequently recommissioned by Lincoln. Following the expulsion of John W. Reid, he was elected as a War Democrat to the Thirty-seventh Congress and took his seat in January 1862. During two significant sessions he opposed certain administration measures, including the confiscation bill and all emancipation proposals. He was instrumental in the defeat of compensated emancipation for Missouri slaves by a federal appropriation, which he characterized as "only one part of the grand scheme of the abolition radicals" (*Congressional Globe,* 37 Cong., 3 Sess., Appendix, p. 138). He persisted in his moderate, border-state opinion that the war was waged to save the Union (*Ibid.,* 2 Sess., Appendix, pp. 213–14). He was defeated for reëlection in 1862; the interference with the election by the militia and the conduct of certain polling officials caused him unsuccessfully to contest the result (*House Miscellaneous Document, No. 16,* 38 Cong., 1 Sess., pp. 482, 520). In 1864, under demoralized conditions of intimidation, disfranchisement, and violence, he was defeated as the Democratic nominee for governor. A relentless opponent of the triumphant Radical party, he became a Conservative Unionist, but later was prominent in the reorganization of the Democratic party and its unsuccessful candidate for Congress. He died, after a lingering illness, during the campaign which witnessed the return of his party to power. Standing well over six feet, he was a man of demonstrated physical courage, impetuous and imprudent on occasion, but generous, friendly, and loyal. He was essentially the business man in politics. His first wife, Lydia Bolton, of North Carolina, whom he married in 1828, died in 1849; on Apr. 20, 1854, he married Caroline V. Long, of Virginia. A son and daughter by his first wife survived him.

[W. F. Switzler, *Switzler's Illustrated Hist. of Mo.* (1879); P. O. Ray, *The Repeal of the Mo. Compromise* (1909); H. C. McDougal, "A Decade of Missouri Politics—1860 to 1870," *Mo. Hist. Rev.*, Jan. 1909; H. L. Conard, *Encyc. of the Hist. of Mo.* (1901), vol. V; *The U. S. Biog. Dict. and Portrait Gallery . . . Mo. Vol.* (1878); *Biog. Dir. Am. Cong.* (1928); *Mo. Republican* (St. Louis), July 17, 1870.] T. S. B.

PRICE, THOMAS RANDOLPH (Mar. 18, 1839–May 7, 1903), philologist, born in Richmond, Va., was named for his father; his mother, Christian Elizabeth (Hall), was the granddaughter of the second bishop of Virginia, Richard Channing Moore [*q.v.*]. In 1858 Price received the degree of A.M. from the University of Virginia, where he had formed what was to be a lifelong friendship with Basil Lanneau Gildersleeve [*q.v.*]. After dutifully pursuing the study of law for a year more in the University, he received from his father the freedom and the means to follow his bent toward the study of literature. At Berlin from 1859 he studied Latin with Benary and Haupt, Greek with Boeckh, Sanskrit and comparative grammar with Bopp and Steinthal; at Kiel he attended lectures of Curtius. In Greece in the spring of 1861 he was occupied less at the university than with topography, archeology, and the modern language. The succeeding six months in Paris gave him lasting interest in French literary criticism. Then, when he was about to receive his doctorate, he sacrificed his studies to Virginia, ran the blockade on Christmas Eve, 1862, became a member of J. E. B. Stuart's staff, was transferred later to the bureau of engineers, and was about to be commissioned major when the war ended. On Dec. 26, 1867, he married Lizzie Triplett in Richmond, where he was teaching at the University School. He was professor of Greek and Latin in Randolph-Macon College, 1869–70, having previously collaborated on the first part of Gildersleeve's *Latin Grammar* (1867); in 1870 he became professor of Greek and English and from 1876 to 1882 was professor of Greek in the University of Virginia, where his last task was an essay, at once scientific and charming, on "The Color-System of Vergil" (*American Journal of Philology*, April 1883). He was professor of English in Columbia University from 1882 until his death.

This unusual academic history indicates neither diffusion nor uncertainty. His consistent purpose was to realize for American youth the educational values of philology. Philology, as Germany had taught him to conceive it, comprehended the whole field of expression in words; and each of its aspects depended on all the others. His rebuttal of J. Churton Collins' "Language versus Literature at Oxford" (*Nineteenth Century*, February 1895) as fostering "the most deadly danger of our time to the successful teaching of either" urges that "the true study of literature is the study, not of theories about relations of history and philosophy and aesthetics, but of the meaning and significance of the great works of literature themselves" (*Educational Review*, January 1896; see also "The New Function of Modern Language Teaching," *Publications of the Modern Language Association of America*, vol. XVI, 1901, no. 1). His lectures in 1885 on the technique of the English paragraph were sounder, larger, and more practical than anything published up to that time. He was equally suggestive and more minute in his studies of English verse (*e.g.*, "The Construction and Types of Shakespeare's Verse as seen in the Othello," *Papers of the New York Shakespeare Society*, no. 8, 1888). All such studies were parts. Complete in themselves, they were contributory. Scrutinizing the detail, he comprehended the whole. He ranged from small variations of syntax to the full scope of artistic movement. In 1895 and again in 1898 he studied Frisian in Frisia; in 1891, a year in Denmark had made him a penetrative critic of Ibsen (see "Ibsen's Dramatic Construction Compared with Shakespeare's," *Shakespeariana*, January 1892; "Solness: a Study of Ibsen's Dramatic Method," *Sewanee Review*, May 1894). Perhaps his keenest interest was in dramaturgy. His study of *King Lear* (*Publications of the Modern Language Association of America*, vol. IX, no. 2, 1894) shows both this interest and the character of his teaching: its enthusiasm, its wideness of outlook, its scientific method, its artistic presentation, its focus on form.

The form itself, its capacity, its adaptation, its significance as a stage in linguistic consciousness or in artistic development; the form as personal achievement—these were all aspects of one preoccupation. His own writing was so firm and finished that students readily appreciated its lucid order. In a wider sense form controlled all his teaching of literature. It determined his point of view and his method of approach, as in his study of Chaucer's *Troilus and Criseyde* (*Publications of the Modern Language Association of America*, vol. XI, 1896, no. 3) and of Shakespeare's sonnets (*Studies in Honor* of *Basil L. Gildersleeve*, 1902). He carefully studied biography and history but always held them subordinate. Steadily rejecting all concession to anecdotage and sociology, he read and taught the poet through the poem. He interrogated the art, not the artist. His method was to kindred minds keenly suggestive. Even the trifling, the impatient, the doubters, were often moved as the patiently detailed evidence was capped by the insight of his feeling and by his certitude that art is its own sufficient and final revelation.

After his death, his library was given by his widow and his daughter to the University of Virginia.

[For further details of biography see the memoir in *Jour. of English and Germanic Philology*, Dec. 1903. See also the brief appreciation by B. L. Gildersleeve in *Am. Jour. of Philology*, Apr., May, June 1903; and Woodberry's poem, "Requiem," in *Bulletins of the Univ. of Va.*, Oct. 1903, which also contains a memoir. An obituary appeared in the *N. Y. Times*, May 9, 1903.]

C. S. B.

PRICE, WILLIAM CECIL (Apr. 1, 1818–Aug. 6, 1907), proslavery leader in Missouri, was born probably in Russell County, Va., the son of Crabtree and Linny (Cecil) Price. He was educated at Knoxville, Tenn. In his youth his parents removed to Greene County, Mo. He began the study of law at the age of twenty and was admitted to the bar at Springfield, Mo. In June 1842 he was married to Sarah J. Kimbrough of Kentucky, who died in 1859 leaving seven children. He served as county judge from 1842 to 1845, when he was appointed deputy federal surveyor of lands. He served as state senator from 1854 to 1857 and resigned in March to accept appointment to a vacancy on the circuit bench. Defeated in the August election for this position, he returned to his law practice. In 1859 Governor Stewart appointed him to represent the state in the general land office at Washington, where he helped to prevent land frauds in the states of Missouri, Illinois, and Iowa. In February 1860 he was appointed treasurer of the United States by President Buchanan. In August of that year he was married to Lydia C. Dow of Hardwick, Vt., who bore him three children.

He held a conspicuous and influential place in the counsels of the Democratic party in Missouri between 1845 and 1860, and he was in close and constant communication with John C. Calhoun, Jefferson Davis, and other leading proslavery Democrats throughout the South. He always maintained that the idea of the repeal of the Missouri Compromise, effected by the Kansas-Nebraska Act of 1854, originated with him. For twenty years before the Civil War he preached the doctrine that Missouri, in order to remain a slave state with free states on her northern and eastern borders, must accomplish the repeal of the compromise restriction upon slavery. With the zeal of an evangelist tempered by sound political discretion, he agitated for the repeal in all parts of the state. In 1844 he went so far as to suggest the repeal to Thomas H. Benton, who instantly and vehemently spurned the suggestion. Up to this time he and Benton had been warm friends; but they never spoke afterward, and Price publicly registered a vow to drive Benton from public life because of his antislavery sympathies. During the next six years he visited every part of the state to organize the groups against Benton and in favor of slavery. He claimed that he selected Henry S. Geyer [*q.v.*] as the man to defeat Benton for election to the United States Senate in 1851. Later he claimed he selected the governor elected in 1860, Claiborne F. Jackson [*q.v.*]. Intellectually, Price was a man of more than average ability along some lines; in others his vision of events was narrow. He was a man of intensely religious nature, exceedingly familiar with the Scriptures and a member of the Methodist Church, though he later stopped attending its services. He believed whole-heartedly in the righteousness of slavery, was fanatically devoted to the Southern cause, and became an uncompromising advocate of secession. He had a great command of language and was a plausible, though not logical, speaker. Joining the Confederate army at the beginning of the war, he was taken prisoner and was confined in the military prison at Alton, Ill., until September 1862. He removed to Arkansas, near Mt. Olive, then to St. Louis, and later lived in Springfield, Mo., where he was engaged in the business of loaning money for eastern people. He died in Chicago, at the home of his son-in-law, William S. Newberry. He was tall and slender, of commanding presence and imperious manner. His face was classic in outline and features with clear eyes "as dark as steel and penetrating as daggers." He was a man of great courage, moral and physical, and a dead shot with the rifle. When challenged to duels, he invariably selected this weapon, a fact that always led to an accommodation without a tragedy.

[*The U. S. Biog. Dict. . . . of Eminent and Self-Made Men*, Mo. vol. (1878); B. L. Price, *John Price . . . with Some of his Descendants* (1910), pp. 56–67; *Hist. of Greene County, Mo.* (1883), pp. 220, 227, 244, 249, 270, 279; *War of the Rebellion: Official Records (Army)*, 1 ser., XXII, pt. 1, L, pt. 1; *Jour. of the Executive Proceedings of the Senate*, vol. XI (1887); *Nebr. State Hist. Soc. Trans.*, 2 ser., vol. III (1889); P. O. Ray, *The Repeal of the Mo. Compromise* (1909), App. B.]

P. O. R.

PRICE, WILLIAM THOMPSON (Dec. 17, 1846–May 3, 1920), critic, author, playwright, teacher, was born in Jefferson County, Ky., and was the son of Joseph Crocket and Susan (Meade) Price. His education in the public schools was interrupted by the Civil War, for he ran away and joined the Confederate army, serving with the cavalry raiders of Morgan, Forrest, and Wheeler. He was captured, imprisoned at Rock Island, Ill., and escaped. In 1867 he was sent by his parents to the University of Leipzig, Germany, and there and at Berlin he studied for three years. Returning, he prepared to enter the profession of law, according to his father's wish, but his bent was toward letters instead, and he at length found work on the Louisville *Courier-Journal,* where he contracted a friendship with the great editor, Henry Watterson [*q.v.*], which continued until the latter's death. From 1875 to 1880 Price was dramatic critic of the *Courier-Journal.* It was during these earlier years that he wrote his only play, *The Old Kentucky Home* (which was not given a professional production), and a remarkable little book called *Without Scrip or Purse* (1883), a psychological study of the life and work of a locally famous mountain evangelist. He also wrote *A Life of William Charles Macready* (1894), which in his latter years he did not think worthy of mention. In 1881 he sought a wider field in New York. He was dramatic critic of the New York *Star* in 1885–86, then was employed by A. M. Palmer, whose stock companies at the Union Square and Madison Square theatres were in their day the finest in America. For nearly twenty years he read plays for Palmer. From 1901 almost until his death he likewise did play-reading for Harrison Grey Fiske. Meanwhile, he was writing an occasional book, such as *The Technique of the Drama* (1892), and *A Life of Charlotte Cushman* (1894). The former work, together with many shorter essays, established him as an authority on dramatic construction. In 1901 he founded in New York the American School of Playwriting, the first such school in history, the faculty consisting of himself alone. He would not attempt to teach anybody who did not appear to be endowed with genius or talent, arguing that no human agency could impart such gifts. Many writers, some of them eminent ones, brought plays to him to be "doctored." His name did not appear on programs, and audiences never knew that many plays owed their success to his finishing touch. His quiet methods and unconquerable modesty kept him unknown to the public, but within the dramatic

profession he was looked upon as the highest of authority, although after his one youthful venture, he had never himself written a play. From 1912 to 1915 he conducted a magazine of scientific discussion of the drama and dramatic writing, entitled *The American Playwright.* He produced three more books—*The Analysis of Play Construction and Dramatic Principle* (1908), *Why Plays Fail,* a collection of first-night reviews written for the *Theatre Magazine,* to which he was a (usually anonymous) contributor for the last twenty years and more of his life, and *The Philosophy of Dramatic Principle and Method.* The last two were printed and used as textbooks but not generally circulated. Price never married. When he died in May 1920 he was at first buried in Greenwood Cemetery, Brooklyn; but in October 1921 his remains were removed to Frankfort, Ky., attended by a remarkable cortège of famous playwrights, producers, and actors.

[*Who's Who in America,* 1920–21; obituaries in all New York and Louisville, Ky., papers of May 4, 1920; article in *N. Y. Times,* May 9, 1920; articles and editorials in *Louisville Herald, Courier-Journal* (Louisville), *Ketucky State Journal,* Oct. 28–29, 1921; "William Thompson Price," *Ky. State Hist. Soc. Reg.,* Jan. 1922.]   A.F.H.

PRIEST, EDWARD DWIGHT (Nov. 9, 1861–Mar. 26, 1931), electrical engineer, was the son of Dwight Solomon and Susan M. (Caldwell) Priest and a descendant of John Priest who was in Woburn, Mass., as early as 1675. He was born at Northfield, Franklin County, Mass. Until he was nineteen years old he lived with his parents, first in Northfield, then, after 1872, in South Vernon, Vt. He attended school at the Vermont Academy and assisted his father in his various undertakings, which included at the same time the successful operation of a farm, a sash and blind factory, a store, a hotel, and a real-estate business. When his parents moved to Iowa in 1880, Priest remained in the east and entered the Worcester County Free Institute of Industrial Science, later Worcester Polytechnic Institute, from which he was graduated in 1884 with the degree of B.S. in mechanical engineering. After taking some postgraduate work there in electrical engineering he obtained employment in Chicago, Ill., with Charles J. Van Depoele, a successful inventor and manufacturer of electric-arc lamps and street-railway trolleys. When the Van Depoele interests were merged, in 1887, with the Thomson-Houston Electric Company of Lynn, Mass., Priest became associated with the latter company as designer and draftsman, and devoted his time from then until his retirement in 1926 principally to railway electrification problems. One of his first contributions was the perfection in 1888 of a box-frame motor. This was cast in one piece and was so capably designed that it remains generally in use at the present time. In 1892 the Thomson-Houston Company became one of the group of manufactories composing the General Electric Company, and Priest was transferred to Schenectady, N. Y., where he maintained his residence until his death. Three years later he was appointed designing engineer in charge of railway motors, and one of his first achievements in this field was the conception of a special type of railway motor, light in weight, for use on elevated railroads. The first real opportunity to put this new motor to the test occurred about 1901, when the Manhattan Elevated Railway in New York City was electrified, the Priest motors being used for motive power. As a matter of fact, it was under Priest's leadership that the electrification of this railway was carried out. Even before this time his expert knowledge had been called into play in the design of special electric locomotives for the Baltimore & Ohio Railroad, and in the succeeding years of his active career he did much original work to advance his company's interests in the electric transportation field. Following his retirement from the General Electric Company in 1926, he became actively engaged as chairman of the board of the Parker Wire Goods Company, Worcester, Mass., of which he was an organizer. He was serving in this office at the time of his death. On Feb. 27, 1894, at Lynn, Mass., Priest married Alenia Videtto of Middleton, Nova Scotia. He was survived by his widow and four children.

[G. E. Foster, *The Priest Family* (1900); biographical records of Worcester Polytechnic Inst. Alumni Asso.; *Schenectady Union-Star*, Mar. 26, 1931; *N. Y. Times*, Mar. 27, 1931; *Electrical Engineering*, May 1931.]　　　　　　　　　　　　　　　　C. W. M.

PRIESTLEY, JAMES (d. Feb. 6, 1821), educator, was the son of a devout Presbyterian who may have been the William Pressley, Sr., who was living in Rockbridge County, Va., at the close of the eighteenth century. There seems to be no authority for the tradition that he was closely related to Joseph Priestley [q.v.]. James owed the beginning of his career to his faithful study of the Westminster Catechism. As a young boy he attracted the attention of his pastor, the Rev. William Graham, first rector of Liberty Hall Academy, who took the lad into his family and gave him the foundation of a liberal schooling. He was for a while a student at Liberty Hall (forerunner of Washington and Lee University), and for two years (1782–84)

an instructor in mathematics and the classics there. His favorite subject was Greek literature, and "he sometimes entertained his pupils by spouting, with astonishing vehemence, the orations of Demosthenes, in Greek" (Archibald Alexander, *post*, p. 136). He was a classical tutor for a time at Annapolis and at Georgetown, Md., and in December 1788 became principal of Salem Academy in Bardstown, Ky., which under his direction became one of the foremost institutions of learning in that region. During his four years here he had as pupils two who became United States senators (Felix Grundy [q.v.] and John Pope), and five for whom counties were later named. For some three years, beginning in 1792, he was principal of a classical school in Georgetown, D. C. On Feb. 25, 1796, he became principal of the "male department" of Baltimore Academy, a development from the ill-fated Cokesbury College. Presently, the Academy burned and Priestley organized and conducted an academy in Paul's Lane, Baltimore, from 1798 to 1803. In 1800, he joined with Bishop John Carroll [q.v.] in forming the Maryland Society for the Promotion of Useful Knowledge. In 1803, he became principal of the newly founded Baltimore College, but it is uncertain how long he continued in this position. In 1809, he became principal of Cumberland College, Nashville, Tenn., the forerunner of the University of Nashville which, in turn, became Peabody Normal College, now George Peabody College for Teachers. He was recommended for this place by his former pupil, Felix Grundy. Priestley was a firm disciplinarian and an outstanding scholar in mathematics and the classics, and under him Cumberland became one of the important institutions of learning in the West, but he was not a successful administrator, and the college was forced to suspend in 1816 for lack of funds. In the meantime, Priestley had bought a farm of 226 acres from Andrew Jackson and to this tract, six miles above Nashville, he retired and opened an academy for girls. When Cumberland College reopened in December 1820 he again became its principal, but died some two months later. Years afterward, one of his former pupils at Liberty Hall (Archibald Alexander, pp. 136–37) said of him: "He was indeed a very eccentric, though a very amiable man, and married a woman as eccentric as himself." They had a daughter and three sons, one of whom was killed at the battle of New Orleans.

[Address by Archibald Alexander in *Washington and Lee Univ. . . . Hist. Papers*, no. 2 (1890); J. W. Alexander, *The Life of Archibald Alexander* (1854); *Cat. of the Officers and Alumni of Washington and Lee*

Univ. (1888); O. F. Morton, *A Hist. of Rockbridge County, Va.* (1920); J. T. Scharf, *The Chronicles of Baltimore* (1874) and *Hist. of Baltimore City and County* (1881); L. P. Little, *Ben Hardin: His Times and Contemporaries* (1887); L. S. Merriam, *Higher Educ. in Tenn.* (1893); *Cat. of the Officers . . . of the Univ. of Nashville, with . . . Hist. Notices* (1850); manuscript minutes of Cumberland College.]

A. L. C.

PRIESTLEY, JOSEPH (Mar. 13, 1733–Feb. 6, 1804), scientist, educator, and voluminous writer on politics and Unitarian theology, came to America from England in June 1794 seeking political and religious freedom, and remained (without becoming naturalized) until his death. The eldest son of Jonas Priestley, a dyer and dresser of woollen cloth, by his wife Mary, only daughter of Joseph Swift, a Yorkshire farmer, Joseph Priestley was born at "Fieldhead," a wayside farmhouse in Birstall parish, six miles from Leeds, Yorkshire. His mother, before her death in 1740, taught her son the Westminster Catechism, but his education after 1742 was entrusted to his father's Calvinistic sister, Sarah Keighley, a talented woman, who about 1745 sent him to a local grammar school, evidently Batley (N. L. Frazer in *Transactions of the Unitarian Historical Society,* London, vol. V, 1932–33). Here he learned Latin and Greek, mastered and improved upon Peter Annet's shorthand, and wrote verses on shorthand which Annet later printed. Under John Kirkby, a Congregational minister, he learned Hebrew, but ill health then caused him to leave school for three years, during which time he taught himself French, Italian, and Dutch, the rudiments of Chaldee, Syriac, and Arabic, and also studied natural history, observing among other things how long spiders would live sealed in a bottle (Timothy Priestley, *A Funeral Sermon Occasioned by the Death of . . . Rev, Joseph Priestley,* 1804). In 1751 Priestley entered Daventry, a dissenting academy, where he remained three years under Caleb Ashworth (Herbert McLachlan, *English Education under the Test Acts,* 1931, p. 153), and in this liberal atmosphere his nonconformist tendencies ("Arianism") took firm root.

In September 1755 he took his first parish in the village of Needham Market, Surrey, although he was not ordained until May 18, 1762. His stammering (*Memoirs,* p. 23), heterodoxy, and bachelorhood detracted from his popularity and he ultimately went as minister to Nantwich, Cheshire, a parish of "travelling scotchmen" (*Memoirs,* p. 42), where he subsisted by establishing a private school. From there he was called as tutor in belles-lettres to Warrington, the chief of the dissenting academies of England

(V. D. Davis, *A History of Manchester College,* 1932, pp. 41–44). Here amongst a cultivated and liberal-minded group of tutors (John Seddon, John Aikin, Gilbert Wakefield, John Holt) and an intelligent local printer (William Eyres) Priestley found adequate channels of expression for his multifarious interests. He preached (*Memoirs,* p. 56) and published *The Rudiments of English Grammar* (1761), *An Essay on a Course of Liberal Education for Civil and Active Life* (1765), *A Chart of Biography* (1765), for which he received the degree of LL.D. from Edinburgh, *A New Chart of History* (1769), wrote his *Lectures on History and General Policy* (published in 1788), delivered discourses on anatomy and astronomy, and took his students out onto the surrounding hills to collect fossils and botanical specimens. Priestley was the first to give formal instruction in modern history (Irene Parker, *Dissenting Academies in England,* 1914, p. 116), and his teaching of the sciences was entirely new in secondary education.

On June 23, 1762, Priestley had married Mary, eighteen-year-old daughter of Isaac Wilkinson of Wrexham, and in September 1767 her failing health and his slender salary caused him to go to Leeds, where he remained in charge of the Mill Hill congregation until December 1772. He then became librarian to Lord Shelburne (William Petty, later Marquis of Lansdowne), a post which he held until 1780. At the end of that year he removed to Birmingham and became minister there of the New Meeting until the riots of 1791, when on account of his sympathies with the French Revolution his house, his books, and all his private effects were burned. He remained for a time in seclusion, but later became pastor of Hackney. The French Assembly made him a citizen of France in September 1792; and as Burke was bitterly opposed to him his position was highly insecure. Accordingly, with his longing for greater freedom, he determined to emigrate to America, sailing with his wife in April 1794.

They reached the Old Battery, New York, the evening of June 4, 1794, and were met by their son Joseph. Priestley's arrival in America aroused much public comment. A notice that he was expected appeared in *Dunlap and Claypole's American Daily Advertiser* (Philadelphia), on June 5, and was followed on June 9 by an editorial. The first morning he was visited by Governor Clinton and the Bishop of New York (Samuel Provoost); and he received wordy testimonials from the Medical, Democratic, and Tammany societies, the Republican

Natives of Great Britain and Ireland, and the Associated Teachers of the City of New York, to each of which Priestley made formal and courteous reply (E. F. Smith, *post*, pp. 22–34). To his grief, however, he was not invited to preach. On June 18 he left New York for Philadelphia and again received public welcome (*Daily Advertiser*, June 23, 1794) and a testimonial from David Rittenhouse as president of the American Philosophical Society. But Priestley did not like the distractions of Philadelphia, especially its banqueting habits (Smith, pp. 55–56), and he decided in July to join his son at Northumberland, Pa. There he settled for the remainder of his life, ultimately building himself a house and laboratory which still stand (1934) as a museum, Priestley's chief memorial in the United States.

In November 1794 he was invited to become professor of chemistry at Philadelphia, but declined. He made frequent trips to Philadelphia, however, and read a number of papers, chiefly on chemistry, before the American Philosophical Society (see its *Transactions*, vols. IV–VI, 1799–1809). He sent many other scientific papers to the *Medical Repository*, New York (for complete bibliography of scientific contributions from America see T. L. Davis, in *Journal of Chemical Education*, February 1927). A few of his many theological writings composed in Northumberland are listed below. Priestley's health began to fail in 1801 (he suffered from pleurisy) and from then on he had to live carefully, but he was able to continue his writing until an hour before his death, which occurred at Northumberland Feb. 6, 1804. He was buried there (W. H. Walker, *post*) on Feb. 9, and William Christie preached his funeral sermon. His books were sold in Philadelphia in 1816 by Thomas Dobson, who issued an auction catalogue of his library.

In science Priestley made important discoveries both in physics and chemistry. His scientific interests had manifested themselves early; at Nantwich he had collected an air-pump, globes, and other physical instruments, but he did not begin active experimentation until 1766. Following a trip to London in December 1765 where he met John Canton, Richard Price, and Benjamin Franklin, he was made a Fellow of the Royal Society, and later (W. C. Walker, *post*) made his first excursion into science by writing *The History and Present State of Electricity* (published February 1767), to which he appended an account of the well-known experiments (made between June 1766 and January 1767) in which he enunciated, but did not fully prove, the inverse-square law of electrostatics, explained the formation of the ("Priestley") rings occurring as a result of electrical discharges on metallic surfaces, attempted to measure electrical resistance and impedance, and proposed an explanation of the oscillatory nature of the discharge from a Leyden jar.

As a result of these studies Priestley believed that "mephitic air" (air which passed over burning charcoal or through the lungs of animals, *i.e.*, air containing carbon dioxide) would, unlike normal air, conduct electricity. On his removal to Leeds in September 1767 he was able to obtain "mephitic" air from a neighboring brewery and, though unable to confirm his impression concerning the electrical conductivity of this gas, he was led through his experiments in this connection to discover oxygen. He first proved that "mephitic air" was absorbed by water and fancying that the "soda water" so produced prevented scurvy, he recommended it to the navy. In March 1772 came his "Observations on Different Kinds of Air" (*Philosophical Transactions*, vol. LXII, 1773), in which he recorded the isolation of nitrous oxide ("nitric air") and hydrochloric acid ("marine acid air"). Priestley had isolated oxygen before November 1771 (Sir Philip Hartog, "Date and Place of Priestley's Discovery of Oxygen," *Nature*, July 1, 1933, p. 25), but had not recognized its peculiar properties; now, while in the house of his patron, Lord Shelburne, at Bowood near Calne, on Aug. 1, 1774, he caused a gas to be evolved by heating red "calx of mercury" with a burning glass. A candle "burned in this air with a remarkably vigorous flame" (*Experiments . . . on Different Kinds of Air*, II, 1775, p. 34), and the gas supported respiration better than ordinary air. He had thus again isolated oxygen and had now described its fundamental properties, but, as a follower of the phlogistic doctrine, he designated the new gas "dephlogisticated air." He met Lavoisier in Paris in October 1774 and told him of the discovery. Lavoisier immediately appreciated its significance, repeated and confirmed the experiment, and established in 1775 the elemental nature of the gas. Priestley continued to carry out "pneumatic" experiments of great importance in the history of chemistry, which were published in the successive volumes of his *Experiments and Observations on Different Kinds of Air* (3 vols., 1774, 1775, 1777), but until his death he adhered to the phlogistic theory of combustion (Priestley, *The Doctrine of Phlogiston Established*, 2nd ed., with additions, 1803).

In addition to oxygen and nitrous oxide,

Priestley isolated and described the chief properties of the following gases: nitric oxide, nitrogen peroxide, ammonia, silicon fluoride, sulphur dioxide, hydrogen sulphide, and (after coming to America) carbon monoxide; and he made other contributions to science, such as the decomposition of ammonia by electricity (1781), and a notable study upon optics: *The History and Present State of Discoveries Relating to Vision,.Light and Colours* (1772). As an investigator he worked rapidly and resourcefully, observing clearly and describing accurately the things he saw. He was able to generalize and to see the practical applications of many of his studies (Hartley, *post*), but his faculties of correlation and interpretation were slender, much as in the case of Robert Boyle a century earlier.

Priestley's versatility and his peculiar qualities of mind were more clearly manifested in his theological and political writings than in his science. Brought up as a Calvinist, he early became allied with liberal theology and he left Daventry Academy an "Arian." By the time he went to Warrington his Unitarian ("Socinian") beliefs were well developed, *i.e.*, he rejected the Atonement and the inspiration of the sacred text. In 1775 he put forward the doctrine of the homogeneity of man, which brought upon him the accusation of atheism (see his *Disquisition Relating to Matter and Spirit*, 1777; also *A Free Discussion of the Doctrines of Materialism*, 1778, a correspondence with Richard Price; and *An History of the Corruptions of Christianity*, 1782, which was burned by the hangman of Dort). His chief theological treatises were written in America: *A General History of the Christian Church* (4 vols., 1790–1802); *Unitarianism Explained and Defended* (1796); *A Comparison of the Institutions of Moses with Those of the Hindoos and Other Ancient Nations* (1799); *Socrates and Jesus Compared* (1803); *Notes on All the Books of Scripture* (4 vols., 1803–04); *The Doctrines of Heathen Philosophy Compared with Those of Revelation* (1804), written at the instance of his friend Jefferson (Rutt, *Life, post,* II, 508–09, 511, 519, 525); *A General View of the Arguments for the Unity of God; and against the Divinity and Pre-existence of Christ* (1793, new ed., corrected, 1812). Full details concerning the later development of Priestley's Unitarian doctrines are given by Gordon, Holt, and Rossington (*post*).

In politics Priestley was a utilitarian and a republican, but he prided himself on never having joined a political party. His *Essay on the First Principles of Government* (1768) suggested to Jeremy Bentham the doctrine that the object of all law is "the greatest happiness of the greatest number." In two anonymous pamphlets (against war), *The Present State of Liberty in Great Britain and Her Colonies* (1769) and *An Address to Protestant Dissenters . . . with Respect to the State of Public Liberty in General and of American Affairs in Particular* (1774), he rebuked the government for their treatment of the Colonies. Prior to 1783 he was intimate with Burke, but Priestley's republican leanings estranged them and their differences were brought dramatically to a climax by the French Revolution; Priestley's *Letters to the Right Honourable Edmund Burke* (January 1791) led more or less directly to the Birmingham riots on Bastille Day (July 14, 1791), in which Priestley's house was destroyed. Priestley was also opposed to slavery (see *A Sermon on the Subject of the Slave Trade,* 1788). In American politics he sided with the Democrats against the Federalists and on arriving in America he was accordingly attacked by William Cobbett [*q.v.*] in a pamphlet, *Observations on the Emigration of Dr. Joseph Priestley* (1794), and later in the columns of his *Porcupine's Gazette.*

Entertaining some fear of being deported under the Alien Act, Priestley defended himself in *Letters to the Inhabitants of Northumberland* (1799, 2nd ed., 1801; see Rutt, *Life,* II, 454–55). By 1797, or earlier, he had become acquainted with Jefferson, and the two men, who had so many common intellectual interests, cemented their growing friendship by correspondence. It was to Priestley that Jefferson turned for counsel about the University of Virginia, then germinating in his mind; and, after Priestley's death, writing to the latter's disciple, Thomas Cooper [*q.v.*], who inherited the friendship, he spoke of his "affectionate respect" for Priestley and of his high appreciation of Priestley's service in religion, in politics, in science (P. L. Ford, *Writings of Thomas Jefferson,* IX, 1898, p. 102; see also Dumas Malone, *The Public Life of Thomas Cooper,* 1926, esp. ch. iii).

Priestley's contributions in the fields that he particularly cultivated were fundamental: in chemistry he isolated nine new gases, in education he introduced the teaching of modern history and practical instruction in the sciences, and in theology he was the chief early protagonist of the Unitarian movement in the United States. In personal appearance he was slender, erect, of middle height, with gray "kindly" eyes which were extraordinarily active and alert as he himself was in all his movements. He generally carried a cane, and wore a black coat, a well-powdered wig (abandoned after coming to America), cocked hat, and shoes with buckles. His habits were methodical and throughout his life he kept a diary in Annet's shorthand. He was a rigid economist of time, retiring and arising early, devoting two to three hours daily to games and exercise, and the rest to reading and writing; he worked very rapidly and had an exceptional capacity for concentrated application upon a single subject, which undoubtedly accounts for his most unusual sustained productivity. Much of his writing was done in the evening, "in the parlour before the fire," with his wife and children conversing about him; and he could chat and write without experiencing any inconvenience from interruption. His children were: Sarah, who married William Finch; Joseph, who returned to England in 1812 and died at Exeter; William, who was naturalized as a French citizen, admitted to the bar in Paris, and died a planter in Louisiana; and Henry, who died at Northumberland, Pa., aged eighteen. Many of Priestley's descendants are still living in Northumberland and elsewhere in America.

[In addition to *Memoirs of Dr. Joseph Priestley to the Year 1765, Written by Himself, with a Continuation to the Time of His Decease by His Son* (1806), J. T. Rutt, *Life and Correspondence of Joseph Priestley* (2 vols., 1831–32), the works cited above, and the other valuable sources listed by Sir Philip Hartog and the Rev. Alexander Gordon in their detailed articles in the *Dict. Nat. Biog.*, new and important material is to be found in the following more recent studies of Priestley: Alice Holt, *A Life of Joseph Priestley* (1931); T. E. Thorpe, *Joseph Priestley* (1906); H. J. Holmyard, *Makers of Chemistry* (1931); A. N. Meldrum, *The Eighteenth Century Revolution in Science —the First Phase* (1930); E. F. Smith, *Priestley in America* (1920); C. F. Himes, *Apparatus Owned and Used by Dr. Joseph Priestley, the Discoverer of Oxygen, Now in the Collection of Dickinson College, Carlisle, Pa.* (privately printed, 1917); articles by R. A. M. Dixon and H. S. Rossington in *Trans. Unitarian Hist. Soc.* (London), vol. V (1932–33); Herbert McLachlan, *The Story of a Nonconformist Library* (1923), giving key to signatures to articles in the *Theological Repository*; articles by L. C. Newell, C. A. Browne, W. H. Walker, S. A. Goldschmidt, and T. L. Davis, in *Jour. Chem. Educ.*, Feb. 1927; R. A. M. Dixon, *Ibid.*, May 1933, May 1934; L. C. Newell, "Peter Porcupine's Persecution of Priestley," Mar. 1933; J. F. Fulton, "The Warrington Academy (1757– 1786) and Its Influence upon Medicine and Science," pub. in Supp. to *Bull. Johns Hopkins Hosp.*, Feb. 1933; W. C. Walker, "The Beginnings of the Scientific Career of Joseph Priestley," *Isis*, Apr. 1934, and "A Portrait of Joseph Priestley and Some of its Associations," *Proc. Leeds Phil. Soc.*, May 1934; G. C. Chandlee, in *Scientific Monthly*, June 1933; Douglas McKie, in *Science Progress*, July 1933; J. R. Partington, in *Nature*, Mar. 11, 1933; Philip Hartog, A. N. Meldrum, and Harold Hartley, "The Bicentenary of Joseph Priestley," *Jour. Chem. Soc.* (London), Nov. 1933; Philip Hartog, "Joseph Priestley and His Place in the History of Science," *Royal Inst. of Grt. Brit., Weekly Evening Meeting, Friday, Apr. 24, 1931*; William Foster, *Considerations on the Doctrine of Phlogiston, and the Decomposition of Water by Joseph Priestley,*

LL.D., F.R.S., and *Two Lectures on Combustion and an Examination of Dr. Priestley's Considerations on the Doctrine of Phlogiston by John Maclean, M.D.* (1929). *The Theological and Miscellaneous Works of Joseph Priestley* (25 vols. in 26, 1817–32) edited by J. T. Rutt, does not contain the scientific papers. A complete bibliography of Priestley's numerous writings has never been attempted; lists of Priestleiana issued between 1928 and 1934 by Messrs. Grafton & Co., Booksellers, London, supplement the lists in the *Dict. Nat. Biog.*; see also Winnifred Reid and J. F. Fulton, "The Bicentenary Exhibition of Joseph Priestley," *Yale Univ. Lib. Gazette*, Oct. 1933. Unpublished MSS. are in the Royal Soc., London.]   J.F.F.

PRIME, BENJAMIN YOUNGS (Dec. 9, 1733, o.s.–Oct. 31, 1791), physician and balladist, was born at Huntington, Long Island, son of the Rev. Ebenezer Prime, and a descendant of James Prime who settled in Milford, Conn., in 1644; his mother, Experience (Youngs), was a grand-daughter of the Rev. John Youngs, first minister of Southold, Long Island. The mother died when Benjamin was but three weeks old. As an only child he was the object of special care and received his early education from his father. He was prepared for the College of New Jersey, at Newark, then under the presidency of the Rev. Aaron Burr, and graduated in 1751, sharing first honors with his friend Nathaniel Scudder [*q.v.*]. He then studied medicine under Dr. Jacob Ogden of Jamaica, Long Island, and began practice at Easthampton. In 1756 he was called to serve as a tutor in the College of New Jersey, which had by that time been moved to Princeton. While here he devoted his leisure to literary pursuits. Resigning in 1757, he returned to practice. In 1760 Yale conferred on him the honorary degree of A.M. The honor was well deserved, for he had made himself an accomplished general scholar, and was master of several languages including the Hebrew.

On June 16, 1762, he embarked for England for travel and study abroad. On the journey his ship was unsuccessfully attacked by a French privateer and Prime was wounded in the encounter. After some months in London, spent in visiting the hospitals and in attendance on anatomical lectures, he went to Scotland and then to the Continent. At Leyden he received the degree of M.D. on July 7, 1764, and published his dissertation, *De Fluxu Muliebri Menstruo*. While he was abroad he also published, in London, an octavo pamphlet of ninety-four pages, entitled *The Patriot Muse, or Poems on Some of the Principal Events of the Late War ... by an American Gentleman* (1764). Among the poems in this volume was one on the capture of Quebec, 1759, entitled "Britain's Glory or Gallic Pride Humbled."

Returning to America in November 1764, he resumed the practice of surgery in New York

City. As the issues that produced the Revolution became acute, he took a keen interest in politics. Upon the passage of the Stamp Act he wrote "A Song for the Sons of Liberty in New York" (printed in *Muscipula, post*). Before the beginning of the War he had been induced by his father's failing health to give up his practice and retire to Huntington, where he devoted himself to literary and scientific pursuits. On Dec. 18, 1774, he married Mary (Wheelwright) Greaton, widow of the Rev. James Greaton, rector of the Episcopal Church of Huntington, and a direct descendant of the Rev. John Wheelwright [*q.v.*]. A son, Ebenezer, was born to them in October 1775. Upon the British occupation of Long Island, Prime, whose arrest was sought because of his patriotic writings, was compelled to abandon his belongings and flee with his family to Connecticut. Three daughters were born while he was in exile, and after his return, a son, Nathaniel Scudder, who was the father of Samuel Irenæus, Edward Dorr Griffin, and William Cowper Prime [*qq.v.*]. In 1791 Prime wrote a parody of his earlier poem on the capture of Quebec, using the title *Columbia's Glory or British Pride Humbled . . . a Poem on the American Revolution*. It consisted of 1,441 lines reviewing the events of the war, praising Washington and other friends of the Cause, and denouncing the enemies of America. In 1840 there was published in New York *Muscipula sive Cambromyomachia: The Mousetrap; or, Battle of the Welsh and the Mice, in Latin and English, with Other Poems in Different Languages by an American*, containing a translation of Edward Holdsworth's poem and original verses by Prime. He died suddenly of apoplexy at Huntington, leaving a reputation for humble piety as well as for scholarship and patriotism. His widow, inheriting an estate depreciated by the war, successfully provided for the education of the five children and survived her husband till 1835.

[Edward D. G. Prime, *Notes, Geneal. Biog. and Bibliog. of the Prime Family* (1888); introduction and notes to *Muscipula*; E. A. and G. L. Duyckinck, *Cyc. of Am. Literature* (1875), I, 450; E. I. Stevens, "Four Primes," in *N. Y. Geneal. and Biog. Record*, July 1886.]   J. C. F.

PRIME, EDWARD DORR GRIFFIN (Nov. 2, 1814–Apr. 7, 1891), Presbyterian clergyman, author, was born at Cambridge, Washington County, N. Y., the fourth child and third son of the Rev. Nathaniel Scudder and Julia Ann (Jermain) Prime. He was the grandson of Benjamin Youngs Prime [*q.v.*] and a lineal descendant of James Prime, who emigrated from England to Milford, Conn., in 1644. Graduating from

Washington Academy at Cambridge, of which his father was principal, he entered Union College at the age of fourteen and received his degree with high honors in 1832. The next three years he spent at Sing Sing on the Hudson (now Ossining) as assistant to his father, then head of the Mount Pleasant Academy. He began the study of medicine in 1834, but soon decided to enter Princeton Theological Seminary. Completing the three-year course there in 1838, he was called to the Presbyterian Church of Scotchtown, N. Y., as assistant, and was ordained on June 12 of the following year. On Sept. 26, 1839, he married Maria Darlington, daughter of John S. Wilson of Princeton. In 1847 he became pastor of the Scotchtown church, and held the position until 1851, though during the preceding winter tuberculosis forced him to seek the warmer climate of New Orleans, where he supplied the Lafayette Square Church. During the return journey his wife died of cholera on a Mississippi steamer. The next winter Prime spent in Augusta, Ga., but in the spring returned to New York and took charge of the Eighty-sixth Street Presbyterian Church for a year. While his brother, Samuel Irenæus [*q.v.*], was traveling abroad in 1853, Edward took his place as editor of the *New York Observer*. He had long been a contributor under the signature "Eusebius," and after his brother's return continued as associate editor. The winter of 1854–55 he spent as chaplain of the United States diplomatic mission in Rome and in European travel.

On June 14, 1860, he married Abbie Davis Goodell, daughter of the pioneer American missionary in Constantinople. A few years later he published a life of his father-in-law, which is based largely on the latter's diaries and letters, *Forty Years in the Turkish Empire: or Memoirs of Rev. William Goodell, D.D., Late Missionary of the A. B. C. F. M. at Constantinople* (1876). In 1869 recurring ill health again made imperative a year of vacation, which he and his wife spent on the journey commemorated in his book *Around the World: Sketches of Travel Through Many Lands and Over Many Seas* (1872), and in numerous articles printed in the *Observer*. After crossing the United States to San Francisco, he visited Japan, China, India, and the Mediterranean lands, studying as he went religious conditions and the problems of evangelical missionary work, of which he had become an ardent supporter. After the death of Samuel Irenæus in 1885, he assumed the chief editorship of the *Observer*, but his ebbing strength was unequal to the task, from which he finally retired in the following year. Long a leading though unobtrusive Presbyterian minister and religious journalist, he was a man of sound judgment and information who wrote with ease and force. Besides the works already mentioned, he published "Calvinism and Missions: an Address Before the Synod of New York" (*Foreign Missionary*, January 1853); "Civil and Religious Liberty in Turkey" (*Presbyterian Quarterly and Princeton Review*, October 1875); and *Notes, Genealogical, Biographical, and Bibliographical, of the Prime Family* (1888). He died at his home in New York City, leaving no children. William Cowper Prime [*q.v.*] was a brother.

[Brief biog. by Wm. C. Prime in the work last mentioned above; *Necrological Reports and Ann. Proc. of the Alumni Asso. of Princeton Theological Sem.* (1899); *N. Y. Observer*, Apr. 9, 1891; *N. Y. Tribune*, Apr. 8, 1891.]   W. L. W., Jr.

PRIME, SAMUEL IRENÆUS (Nov. 4, 1812–July 18, 1885), Presbyterian clergyman, editor, and author, was born at Ballston, N. Y., but grew up at Cambridge, N. Y., where in 1813 his father, Nathaniel Scudder, son of Benjamin Youngs Prime [*q.v.*], became pastor of the Presbyterian church. His mother was Julia Ann Jermain, of Sag Harbor, Long Island. The Prime family had been prominent in Long Island since the days of Samuel's great-grandfather, Ebenezer, minister of the Presbyterian church at Huntington from 1723 to 1779. Samuel graduated from Williams College at the age of seventeen, and after some teaching studied in Princeton Theological Seminary (1832–33). In 1834 he took charge of the Presbyterian church at Ballston Spa, N. Y., where he was ordained on June 4, 1835. Soon forced by illness to leave his church, he taught for a while at Newburgh, and then became pastor at Matteawan, N. Y., only to meet failure of health again after two years. In 1840 he became assistant editor of the *New York Observer*, and went to live at Newark, N. J. His connection with this paper was interrupted in 1849, but in 1851 he returned, to be its editor for thirty-four years. He lived in Brooklyn from 1850 to 1858, and thenceforth in New York City.

To the *Observer*, a religious weekly of Presbyterian affiliations, Prime gave broad scope and unfailing interest. It commented on important events of all kinds, though emphasizing church affairs, religious activities, and social reforms. Contributions were gathered from men of leadership and able writers. Prime himself wrote enough to make a hundred volumes, all in capital editorial style. He took sides emphatically and in good temper on numerous subjects, religious, educational, literary, political. His

"Irenæus" letters, weekly essays of varied contents, many reporting his travels, were a great attraction. They were later published in two series, *Irenæus Letters* (1882, 1885). Read by many influential people and guiding the thought of many families, the *Observer* was a force in American life in the third quarter of the nineteenth century.

Prime conducted from 1853 the "Editor's Drawer" in *Harper's Magazine*. This repository of anecdotes and bits of wit and humor, gathered far and wide, he made a popular institution. He was a favorite preacher and lecturer, an energetic worker in religious and philanthropic organizations, and a great diner-out. Through a very large correspondence he helped many people with counsel and money. He was always busy; he radiated good cheer, and was full of jokes and stories. The list of his publications contains nearly forty titles. All of the following books except the last went through several editions: *The Old White Meeting House* (1845); *Thoughts on the Death of Little Children* (1850); *Travels in Europe and the East* (1855); *The Power of Prayer* (1859), of which 100,000 copies were issued in five years; *Life of Samuel F. B. Morse* (1875). On Oct. 15, 1833, he was married to Elizabeth Thornton Kemeys, who lived less than a year thereafter; and on Aug. 17, 1835, to Eloisa L. Williams of Ballston Spa. Edward Dorr Griffin and William Cowper Prime [*qq.v.*] were his brothers.

[Biog. sketch in *Irenæus Letters*, 2 ser. (1885); *Harper's Weekly*, July 25, 1885; *Samuel Irenæus Prime: Autobiog. and Memorials* (1888), ed. by Wendell Prime; *Princeton Theol. Sem. Biog. Cat.* (1909); W. B. Sprague, *Annals Am. Pulpit*, vol. III (1858); E. D. G. Prime, *Notes, Geneal., Biog., and Bibliog. of the Prime Family* (1888); S. A. Allibone, *A Critical Dict. of English Literature and British and Am. Authors*, vol. II (1870); *N. Y. Tribune*, July 19, 1885.]
                                              R. H. N.

PRIME, WILLIAM COWPER (Oct. 31, 1825–Feb. 13, 1905), journalist, author, professor of the history of art, the youngest son of Nathaniel Scudder Prime and his wife, Julia Ann Jermain, was a grandson of Benjamin Youngs Prime [*q.v.*] and a brother of Samuel Irenæus and Edward Dorr Griffin Prime [*qq.v.*]. He was born in Cambridge, N. Y., where his father, a Presbyterian minister, was headmaster of Washington Academy. When the boy was five years of age the family moved to Sing Sing (now Ossining), where the father took charge of Mount Pleasant Academy. William graduated from the College of New Jersey (Princeton) in 1843, studied law, was admitted to the bar in 1846, and entered practice in New York City. In 1851 he married Mary Trumbull, of Stonington, Conn.

Ten years later Prime exchanged law for journalism under peculiar circumstances. The *New York Journal of Commerce,* then controlled by Gerard Hallock [*q.v.*], was summarily suppressed in 1861 for alleged disloyal conduct, and resumption of publication was conditioned by the authorities upon the installation of another responsible editor. Hallock, in disgust, withdrew altogether in favor of David Marvin Stone [*q.v.*], who persuaded Prime to join him in purchasing Hallock's interest. For the next eight years, Prime held the editorship of the paper and also the presidency of the Associated Press which went with it. He was editor when in 1864 a second order of suspension fell upon the *Journal of Commerce* because it had published, over the name of President Lincoln, a spurious proclamation fixing a day of fasting and calling for more troops. The order of suspension was speedily rescinded, however, when the innocence of the paper and the stock-jobbing origin of the fabrication became apparent. Prime likewise figured in the forefront of the news association war of 1866, when the western publishers openly rebelled against New York domination of their news service, and his signature is attached to the terms of settlement which restored harmonious relations. In 1869, he was succeeded by Stone both as editor of the *Journal of Commerce* and as president of the Associated Press, though he retained his proprietary holdings in the newspaper.

Convinced at the very outset of his career that every man should possess an avocation, Prime had begun collecting works of art of all kinds. He specialized at first in numismatics, but, progressing from die-cutting to steel engraving, eventually developed a deep interest in the history of illustration and accumulated a notable library of early illustrated books and medieval wood cuts. Both Prime and his wife were also interested in old porcelain, and they formed a fine collection illustrating the history of pottery. Two authoritative books, *Coins, Medals and Seals* (1861) and *Pottery and Porcelain* (1878) embodied some of his studies in these fields. Traveling widely in pursuit of his hobby he found material for other books of a different character: *Owl Creek Letters* (1848), *The Old House by the River* (1853), *Later Years* (1854). After a visit to the Near East in 1855, he published *Boat Life in Egypt and Nubia* (1857) and *Tent Life in the Holy Land* (1857). His interest in Biblical background was reflected later in his analytical study, *The Holy Cross* (1877). Other vacation books were: *I Go A-fishing* (1873), *Along New England Roads* (1892),

and *Among the Northern Hills* (1895). As literary executor of Gen. George B. McClellan he edited *McClellan's Own Story* (1886) and wrote the biographical introduction.

Prime was one of the principal promoters of the Metropolitan Museum of Art, holding for years the positions of trustee and vice-president. His efforts and contributions induced the governing board of the College of New Jersey to establish an art department, to which in 1884 he was summoned as professor of the history of art. After retiring from active duties, he ended his days in New York City.

[E. D. G. Prime, *Notes, Geneal., Biog., and Bibliog. of the Prime Family* (1888); C. D. Warner, *Lib. of the World's Best Lit.,* vol. XX (1897); *Samuel Irenæus Prime: Autobiog. and Memorials* (1888), ed. by Wendell Prime; Victor Rosewater, *Hist. of Coöperative News-Gathering* (1930); *Harper's Encyc. of U. S. Hist.,* vol. VII (1902); Alfred Nevin, *Encyc. of the Presbyt. Ch. in the U. S. A.* (1884); *Gen. Cat. Princeton Univ.* (1908); *Who's Who in America,* 1903–05; *N. Y. Tribune,* Feb. 15, 1905.]   V. R.

PRINCE, LEBARON BRADFORD (July 3, 1840–Dec. 8, 1922), jurist, author, territorial governor of New Mexico, was born and died in Flushing, Long Island, the home of his family for five generations. The son of William Robert Prince [*q.v.*] and Charlotte Goodwin (Collins) Prince, he traced his descent, through his mother, from Governor Bradford of Plymouth Colony. His father, grandfather, and great-grandfather had been leading citizens of the community and at eighteen the boy began his public career, founding the Flushing Library. At thirty he organized the Flushing St. George Brotherhood, at forty-six he instituted the Flushing Civic Association. As a youth he worked in the nurseries run by his father and brother, but after the sale of this property at the close of the Civil War he studied law at Columbia, receiving the degree of LL.B. in 1866. In the following year he published *E Pluribus Unum: The Articles of Confederation vs. the Constitution* (1867), which by its conservative tone gave him some prestige among Republican leaders, and for twelve years thereafter he was regularly elected delegate to the party's state conventions. He was also a delegate to the Republican National Convention which nominated Grant to the presidency in 1868. From 1871 to 1875 he served in the New York Assembly and in 1876–77 sat in the state Senate. As chairman of the judiciary committee of the Assembly he took a leading part in the impeachment of two judges. In the Republican National Convention of 1876, he was among those who broke with Roscoe Conkling, and as a result was offered by President Hayes the governorship of the territory of Idaho. This he declined, but in 1879 he accepted the chief justiceship of the territory of New Mexico.

Thrust into a Spanish-speaking frontier commonwealth, compelled to cover by primitive conveyance a circuit as large as the state of New York, he adjusted himself readily to unaccustomed hardships. Often presiding in court from eight in the morning to eleven at night, he still found time to compile and publish *The General Laws of New Mexico; Including All the Unrepealed General Laws from the Promulgation of the "Kearney Code" in 1846 to . . . 1880* (1880). In 1882 Prince resigned from the bench and two years later was the unsuccessful Republican candidate for delegate to Congress. In the five years that followed he devoted himself to the practice of law, historical research, civic development, church government, public speaking, writing for the press, fruit raising, mining, and financial operations. He directed the Tertio-Millennial pageant at Santa Fé in 1883 and the same year was elected president of the New Mexico Historical Society, in which office he continued until his death.

In the spring of 1889, President Harrison appointed Prince governor of New Mexico, in which capacity he served until 1893. Soon after his inauguration, he initiated a call for a constitutional convention which formulated a fundamental law, but the people of New Mexico failed to ratify the constitution when submitted to them. The legislative assembly upon Prince's recommendation adopted the first public-school code on the statute books and created the University of New Mexico and other state institutions. Politically his administration was stormy, although socially it was brilliant. His advocacy of bimetallism for a time split the Republican party in New Mexico, and brought him temporary political eclipse. Nevertheless, he presided repeatedly over the Trans-Mississippi Congress, the International Mining Congress, the National Irrigation Congress, and the American Apple Congress. He represented New Mexico at the Chicago, the Omaha, and the St. Louis expositions. He founded and was president of the New Mexico Horticultural Society and the Society for the Preservation of Spanish Antiquities, and held membership in the New Mexico Archaeological Society. In 1909 he was elected to the territorial council. He was an incessant agitator for statehood, and when it had been granted presided over the first Republican state convention and published *New Mexico's Struggle for Statehood* (1910), the authoritative volume on the subject. For a number of

years he was president of the board of regents of the New Mexico College of Agriculture and Mechanic Arts and from 1909 to 1912 was president of the Spanish American Normal School. He was active in the affairs of the Protestant Episcopal Church, in which he was a lay reader, served as chancellor of his diocese and was president of the Association of Church Chancellors. He delivered the oration in the First Church, Plymouth, Mass., on Nov. 20, 1920, in connection with the celebration of the *Mayflower* Tercentenary. Besides his numerous contributions to the periodical press, he was the author of the following books: *A Nation or a League* (1880), *Historical Sketches of New Mexico* (1883), *The American Church and Its Name* (1887), *The Money Problem* (1896), *The Stone Lions of Cochiti* (1903), *Old Fort Marcy* (1911), *A Concise History of New Mexico* (1912), *The Student's History of New Mexico* (1913), *Spanish Mission Churches of New Mexico* (1915), *Abraham Lincoln, the Man* (1917).

On Dec. 1, 1879, Prince married Hattie E. Childs, who died less than three months later. On Nov. 17, 1881, Mary C. Beardsley of Oswego, N. Y., like himself of *Mayflower* and Revolutionary descent, became his wife. They had one son.

[R. E. Twitchell, *The Leading Facts of New Mexican Hist.*, vol. II (1912); *Who's Who in America*, 1922–23; F. W. Clancy, "In Memory of L. Bradford Prince," *Hist. Soc. of N. Mex.*, no. 25 (1923); M. L. Stockwell, *Descendants of Francis LeBaron of Plymouth, Mass.* (1904); G. M. Fessenden, "A Geneal. of the Bradford Family," *New-Eng. Hist. and Geneal. Reg.*, Jan. 1850; *Living Church*, Dec. 30, 1922; *Santa Fe New Mexican*, Dec. 9, 1922; newspaper files in Lib. of the Hist. Soc. of N. Mex.; personal acquaintance.]
                                                    P. A. F. W.

PRINCE, MORTON (Dec. 21, 1854–Aug. 31, 1929), physician, psychologist, was the son of Frederick Octavus and Helen Susan (Henry) Prince. His father, four times mayor of Boston, was active in state and national politics; his mother was a member of a Philadelphia family. Morton Prince was graduated from Harvard College in 1875, and from Harvard Medical School in 1879. His interest in abnormal psychology developed naturally from various sources. One of these was a sermon, in which the preacher pointed to a chandelier swinging in the breeze and remarked that our bodies are affected by our spirits in the same way. This explanation puzzled young Prince greatly, and he resolved to find out some time, if he could, the relation between body and mind. After an internship at the Boston City Hospital (1878 to 1879), he studied abroad, especially in Vienna and Strassburg, also in Paris and Nancy, where he derived much from the work of Charcot, Janet, Liébeault, and Bernheim. Upon his return to the United States he entered upon the practice of general medicine. In 1885, he married Fanny Lithgow Payson, of Salem, Mass. To this union two children were born.

Specializing in neurology, psychotherapy, and abnormal psychology, Prince was encouraged by Dr. S. Weir Mitchell, who predicted for him a brilliant future. From 1882 to 1886, he was physician for diseases of the nervous system at the Boston Dispensary, and from 1885 to 1913, at the Boston City Hospital. He was instructor in neurology at Harvard Medical School from 1895 to 1898; professor of neurology at Tufts College Medical School from 1902 to 1912, and professor emeritus thereafter; associate professor of abnormal and dynamic psychology at Harvard University from 1926 to 1928. He lectured at various times at the University of California, Clark University, and the universities of London, Oxford, Cambridge, and Edinburgh; and he read papers before numerous medical, neurological, psychiatric, and psychological congresses. At different times he was president of the American Neurological Association and of the American Psychopathological Association. He published six books: *The Nature of Mind and Human Automatism* (1885), *The Dissociation of a Personality* (1906), *The Unconscious* (1913), *The Psychology of the Kaiser* (1915), *The Creed of Deutschtum* (1918), and *Clinical and Experimental Studies in Personality* (1929, edited by Dr. A. A. Roback), in addition to several collaborations and over a hundred articles and monographs on various political, philosophical, medical, and psychological subjects, especially on phases of neurology and abnormal psychology. In 1906, he founded the *Journal of Abnormal Psychology,* which he edited up to the time of his death.

From a rather delicate childhood, Prince had developed into a vigorous, even robustious, personality, whose love of activity and contest was tempered by a fine sportsmanship and personal detachment. Becoming keenly interested in mental dissociation, he was able, in the early years of the century, to draw much attention to this important subject and to its significance in determining the treatment of certain types of nervous disorder at a time when the "rest cure" was much in vogue. The "Beauchamp" case in particular, which he described in *The Dissociation of a Personality,* soon became, as it remains, famous. He established a great many significant facts, particularly in the field of psychoneurotic and hypnotic phenomena; he was judicious in

his inferences; he put forward useful and stimulating conceptions; he continued to investigate and to learn from other investigators (including Freud), while disclaiming finality for his own system; and he saw the importance of allied subjects, and the economy of formulating his own results in scientifically acceptable language. He developed a psychology of the abnormal which integrates neurology, general psychology, and allied subjects very effectively, with great benefit to them all, including psychiatry and mental hygiene.

He showed how the most striking functional abnormalities could be conceived neuro-psychologically, sometimes as simple habits, sometimes as conflicting patterns in the personality, and sometimes as dissociated systems, but always as resultants of varied motivation in a complex environment. Conflict and dissociation are the destructive factors in any such situation, he maintained, while opposed to them as tendencies, yet aiding them at times, are the processes of association and integration, which come out particularly in the meanings things have for us. Meanings, for Prince, are the product of experience; and when they became so untoward as to favor disruption of personality, the psychotherapist must see that these meanings become changed, by analytic reëducation, to the end of dissolving the conflicts and reintegrating the personality as a dynamic whole. Hence while his panpsychism, his answer to the early mind-body problem, failed to impress scholars, he developed abnormal psychology fundamentally.

At the same time, he influenced his fellows in other ways. In college he was prominent as an athlete, was active in introducing Rugby football; throughout his life he was an active yachtsman. He organized the Public Franchise League, which did much for his city's position in relation to the public-utility corporations; he was instrumental in securing the passage and adoption of the present Boston Charter. During the World War, on his own account he organized extensive propaganda for the Allies; his *Psychology of the Kaiser* influenced the type of propaganda put over the German lines by the British government; he lectured in various countries on the War; in 1915, he was chairman of the Serbian Distress Fund; in 1918, as a representative of the State of Massachusetts, he directed the Soldiers' and Sailors' Information Bureau in Paris; he was chairman of various Boston and Massachusetts reception committees for missions from abroad; and for his services during the War he received decorations from the Serbian, Japanese, and French governments.

[G. H. Monks, "Morton Prince," *Harvard Grads'. Mag.*, Dec. 1929; *N. Y. Herald Tribune*, Sept. 1, 1929; *Harvard College, Class of 1875, Fiftieth Anniversary Report, 1875–1925* (n.d.); *The H Book of Harvard Athletics, 1852–1922* (1923), ed. by J. A. Blanchard; *Problems of Personality: Studies Presented to Dr. Morton Prince, Pioneer in American Psychopathology* (1925), ed. by A. A. Roback; W. S. Taylor, *Morton Prince and Abnormal Psychology* (1928); certain important particulars from Dr. Lydiard H. Horton, Dr. Henry A. Murray, Jr., Miss Minny H. Moran, and Mrs. Morton Prince.]   W. S. T.

PRINCE, THOMAS (May 15, 1687–Oct. 22, 1758), theologian, scholar, bibliophile, was born at Sandwich, Mass., the son of Samuel Prince by his second wife, Mercy, daughter of Gov. Thomas Hinckley of New Plymouth. He was the grandson of John Prince, a native of East Shefford, Berkshire, who was in Watertown, Mass., as early as 1633 and in 1644 settled at Hull. Thomas graduated in 1709, from Harvard, where he had been styled a "praying student" by Increase Mather. After two years of travel in the West Indies and Europe, he settled in England, holding a partial ministry at Coombs in Suffolk. He was invited to remain in England, but rejected the proposal in favor of his native Massachusetts, and in May 1717 embarked for Boston. On his arrival he was promptly offered the parish at Hingham, but a subsequent invitation to join Joseph Sewall at the "Old South" drew him to Boston. He was inducted into office as Sewall's colleague on Oct. 1, 1718, and remained in this connection until his death. On Oct. 30, 1719, he married Deborah Denny, who had been a member of his congregation at Coombs. They had four daughters and a son, the last affectionately referred to as "my Tommy" in the intimate pages of his diary. The family lived in Governor Winthrop's house and took an active part in social and political life. Prince Street, Boston, and the town of Princeton, Mass., bear Prince's name.

During the early years of his ministry he preached and subsequently printed a considerable number of funeral sermons, marked with the conventional Congregationalist attitude towards death, as shown in the titles of two of them: *The Faithful Servant Approv'd at Death and Entring into the Joy of His Lord* (1732) on the one hand, and *Morning Health No Security against the Sudden Arrest of Death before Night* (1727) on the other. He also shared the general pulpit interest in Indian conversions, writing addenda for Experience Mayhew's *Indian Converts* (1727); preached on *Earthquakes the Works of God and Tokens of His Just Displeasure* (1727); and published in 1719 *An Account of a Strange Appearance in the Heavens . . . March 16, 1716, as It was Seen over Stow-Mar-*

ket in Suffolk in England, describing an aurora borealis. His association with the Mathers was close: he not only prefaced Samuel Mather's *Life of the Very Reverend and Learned Cotton Mather* (1729) but began early to collect and preserve the Mather papers, an invaluable storehouse of Colonial information. These were published, with Prince's notes, in the *Collections of the Massachusetts Historical Society* (4 ser., vol. VIII, 1868).

Of greater significance was his accomplishment as a historian. Although the first volume of his major work, *A Chronological History of New England in the Form of Annals,* was not published until 1736, he appears to have begun it as early as 1730. His sources were varied: Increase Mather, the manuscript of Bradford's history of Plymouth Plantation, the notebooks of William Brinsmead and John Marshall, and the like. The history is lively and discursive, free from the marks of pedantry and propaganda that many of its contemporaries bore. Despite the fact that it achieved a tremendous subscription list, it ended its course with the year 1633, because of the magnitude of the task and the difficulty of finding adequate material—Prince had the scholar's love for accuracy.

When the coming of George Whitefield [*q.v.*] divided the Boston ministry into two factions, Prince became a leading champion of the evangelist. The cool and deliberate Charles Chauncy [*q.v.*] said that Prince gave "too much credit to surprising stories" (*Collections of the Massachusetts Historical Society,* 1 ser., X, p. 164), and it may be that Prince, like many others, was hypnotized by Whitefield's theatrical conversions. Whatever the cause, Prince's enthusiasm was great, and his support was a vital factor in sustaining Whitefield's popularity. His accounts of some of the revivals of 1743–44 were published in *The Christian History* (1744–45), edited by his son, Thomas Prince, Jr. Outwardly a zealous patriot, ardent in his advocacy of civil and religious liberty, he was privately devoted to his library. It is undoubtedly as bibliophile and student that he will be longest remembered. "I do not know of any one that had more learning among us, except Doct. Cotton Mather," wrote Charles Chauncy (*Ibid.*), and if the extent of Prince's library is evidence of his scholarship, there can be no quarrel with the statement. He had acquired a number of books during his European sojourn, but his bookplate bears the statement that the volumes of "The New-England-Library [were] Begun to be collected by Thomas Prince, upon his entring Harvard-College, July 6, 1703." The only libraries of the time comparable to his were those of the Mather family and Governor Hutchinson. Of the fifteen hundred books and tracts, the majority related to the civil and religious history of New England. As an indication of colonial literary taste and as a testimony to the love of learning, the collection is significant. At his death the books were left in the tower of the Old South Church; some were destroyed during the British occupation of Boston, but many of them were preserved and are now in the Boston Public Library.

On the eve of his death, there appeared his edition of *The Psalms, Hymns, & Spiritual Songs of the Old and New Testaments Faithfully Translated into English Metre: Being the New England Psalm Book Revised and Improved* (1758), in which he showed his acquaintance with Oriental languages and his knowledge of religious prosody. Joseph Sewall, in a memorial sermon, declared that he had an additional taste for "logic, natural philosophy, and mathematics."

[S. G. Drake, *Some Memoirs of the Life and Writings of the Rev. Thomas Prince, Together with a Pedigree of His Family* (1851), pub. also in *New-Eng. Hist. and Geneal. Reg.*, Oct. 1851 and as the introduction to Drake's edition of Prince's *Chronological Hist.* (1852); Joseph Sewall, *The Duty, Character, and Reward of Christ's Faithful Servants; a Sermon Preached after the Funeral of Thomas Prince* (1758); H. A. Hill, *Hist. of the Old South Church* (2 vols., 1890), containing excellent bibliog.; *Mass. Hist. Soc. Colls.*, vols. I (1792), X (1809); W. H. Whitmore, *Catalogue of the American Portion of the Library of the Rev. Thomas Prince* (1868); *The Prince Library, A Catalogue . . .* (1870), with preface by Justin Winsor; "Life and Labors of Thomas Prince," *North Am. Rev.*, Oct. 1860; Victoria Reed, "The New England Library and Its Founder," *New Eng. Mag.*, Apr. 1886; W. B. Sprague, *Annals Am. Pulpit*, vol. I (1857).]

E. H. D.

PRINCE, WILLIAM (c. 1725–1802), nurseryman, was one of six children born to Robert and Mary (Burgess) Prince, probably at Flushing, Long Island, where he spent his active life and where he died. Fruit culture, which became an important industry on Long Island, was apparently given its original impetus by the French Huguenot settlers, who brought with them varieties of fruit not native to America. Robert Prince propagated trees and shrubs to grow on his own grounds; his son William found it profitable to raise seedlings for sale. As early as 1771 he issued a broadside, printed by Hugh Gaine [q.v.] in New York, advertising a number of different varieties of cherries, plums, apricots, nectarines, peaches, and apples, as well as English and American mulberries, currants, gooseberries, strawberries, and ornamental trees and shrubs. During the Revolution several thousand of his young cherry trees were cut down and sold for barrel hoops. While the British oc-

cupied New York, General Howe stationed a guard at Prince's nursery for its protection. Prince was one of the first nurserymen in America to sell budded or grafted stock and perhaps the first to attempt to breed new varieties (U. P. Hedrick, *A History of Agriculture in the State of New York*, 1933, p. 381). From the pits of twenty-five quarts of Green Gage plums planted in 1790 he obtained "trees yielding fruit of every color; and the White Gage, Red Gage, and Prince's Gage, now so well known, form part of the progeny of these plums; and there seems strong presumptive evidences . . . that the Washington plum was one of the same collection" (William Prince, Jr., *A Short Treatise on Horticulture*, 1828, pp. 24–25). William Prince married Ann Thorne and had thirteen children. About 1793 he retired from business and left the conduct of his affairs to his sons William [q.v.] and Benjamin. The latter maintained the original nursery for several years, calling it "The Old American Nursery," but it eventually passed into the younger William's hands and was merged with the Linnæan Botanic Garden and Nurseries which he had established on an adjacent tract.

[L. B. Prince, in L. H. Bailey, *The Standard Cyc. of Horticulture*, vol. III (1915); B. F. Thompson, *Hist. of Long Island* (3rd ed., 1918), vol. III; G. H. Mandeville, *Flushing Past and Present* (1860); *Hist. of Queen's County, N. Y.* (1882).]

R. H. S.

PRINCE, WILLIAM (Nov. 10, 1766–Apr. 9, 1842), nurseryman, was one of thirteen children born to William Prince [q.v.] and Ann Thorne, his wife, at Flushing, Long Island. In 1793, before the death of his father, he bought a tract of land adjoining his father's nurseries and on part of this new ground established the Linnæan Botanic Garden and Nurseries. At about the same time his brother Benjamin took over the original small nursery, which he continued as The Old American Nursery. Some years later, when The Old American Nursery was no longer in production and a considerable portion of the land had been sold for building lots, William bought what remained of the original establishment (*Magazine of Horticulture*, March 1842). He continued to import and introduce many varieties of fruits and ornamentals and in return exported many plants and trees from the United States to Europe. In 1816, he named and shortly afterward introduced the Isabella grape, which, though now of little more than historical interest, was, with the Catawba, for half a century after its introduction, one of the mainstays of American viticulture (U. P. Hedrick, *Grapes of New York*, 1908, p. 308). He is also supposed to have standardized the name of the

Bartlett pear. In 1827, his Linnæan Botanic Garden and Nurseries contained more than a hundred species of Australian plants, among which were two Eucalyptus and several Banksias. In 1828, the nurseries covered an extent of thirty acres, the collection of roses occupying an acre and including more than 600 different kinds (*Gardener's Magazine*, London, January 1827; *New England Farmer*, Apr. 6, 1827, Aug. 15, 1828; Robert Manning, *History of the Massachusetts Horticultural Society, 1829–1878*, 1880, pp. 28–29). In 1828, he published *A Short Treatise on Horticulture*, giving a few brief remarks on the culture of fruit trees and describing many fruit varieties; it was designed primarily as an advertisement of his nursery, to accompany the catalogues. Two years later, with the aid of his son, William Robert Prince [*q.v.*], he published *A Treatise on the Vine* (1830), and in 1831 he collaborated with his son in the production of *The Pomological Manual*. Prince was a member or honorary member of many horticultural societies in America and Europe, including the New York Horticultural Society, the Massachusetts Horticultural Society, the Linnæan Society of Paris, the Horticultural Society of London and Paris, which named an apple in his honor, the Imperial Society of the Georgofili at Florence, Italy.

William Prince married Mary Stratton and had four children. He was a friendly man, well liked by his neighbors. About 1835, he turned his nursery business over to his sons, but before his death the Linnæan Botanic Garden and Nurseries had passed, through mortgage and foreclosure, into the hands of his brother-in-law, Gabriel Winter. The situation provoked a bitter controversy, in the course of which an attack by Winter was published in Hovey's *Magazine of Horticulture* (April 1842). To this attack one of Prince's sons attributed the stroke of apoplexy that caused his father's death.

[Memorandum by Prince's son, attached to several letters and clippings regarding the Winter affair now in the U. S. Dept. of Agric. Lib., Washington, D. C.; L. B. Prince, in L. H. Bailey, *The Standard Cyc. of Horticulture*, vol. III (1915).]   R. H. S.

PRINCE, WILLIAM ROBERT (Nov. 6, 1795–Mar. 28, 1869), nurseryman, writer on horticultural subjects, was one of four children born to the second William Prince [*q.v.*] and his wife Mary Stratton at Flushing, L. I. He was educated, it is said, at Jamaica Academy and at Boucherville, Canada. While a young man, he botanized the entire range of Atlantic states in company with John Torrey or Thomas Nuttall [*qq.v.*]. Following in his father's footsteps, he became associated with him in the Linnæan Bo-

tanic Garden and Nurseries at Flushing. He collaborated with his father in writing *A Treatise on the Vine* (1830), which embraced the history of the grape "from the earliest ages to the present day with descriptions of above two hundred foreign, and eighty American varieties; together with a complete dissertation on the establishment, culture, and management of vineyards." With this volume, magnificent compared with similar books of the time, native grapes were introduced to the fruit growers of America and viticulture took its place in the literature of American pomology. In 1831 father and son published *The Pomological Manual* in two volumes; a second edition appeared in 1832. This work was a cyclopedia of varieties which included practically all of the fruits then cultivated in the United States, except apples. About 1835, Prince and his brother took over from their father the management of the nursery. In 1837 William Robert Prince became enthusiastic over the introduction of silk culture; from Tarascon, near Marseilles, he imported the mulberry *Morus multicaulis* which during the "mulberry craze" everybody planted. He even built a cocoonery for accommodating the silk worms. The chief result of the episode to him, however, was the loss of a large fortune and the mortgaged Linnæan Botanic Garden and Nurseries.

In 1846, William Robert Prince published *Prince's Manual of Roses,* an admirable enlargement, with additional directions and comments, of *The Rose Amateur's Guide* (1837) of Thomas Rivers, an English nurseryman. During the gold fever of 1849, he went to California, where he broadened his knowledge of the western trees and plants. He traveled through Mexico in 1851 and upon his return endeavored with indifferent success to retrieve the horticultural fame of the Linnæan Botanic Garden and Nurseries of which he had regained control. He introduced the culture of osiers and sorghum in 1854–55 and when it seemed as if the diseases of the Irish potato would cause its eventual replacement by some other vegetable, he imported in 1854 the Chinese yam (*Dioscorea batatas*), paying $600 for the tubers. At some time in the late 1850's, he resigned the nursery business into the hands of his sons, who continued it under the name of Prince & Company Nurseries until the outbreak of the Civil War, when the head of the new firm entered the Union army. After the war, since he chose to accept a commission in the regular army, the nurseries were offered for sale and passed out of the family's hands (*Gardener's Monthly*, June 1865). In his declining years, William Robert Prince devoted much of his time to spiritualism and the preparation of patent medicines (*Gardener's Monthly,* May 1869, p. 142), although he still found time to carry on some horticultural correspondence. His last published article, on the Chinese yam, appeared in the same issue of the *Gardener's Monthly* that contained his obituary notice.

Prince was a prolific writer; besides the three books referred to above, he wrote many short articles and arguments for the *Gardener's Monthly,* edited by Thomas Meehan, and others for the *Rural New-Yorker.* The annual reports of the Massachusetts Horticultural Society, of which he became a corresponding member in 1829, and the *Proceedings* of the American Pomological Society show that he took an active part in all the meetings he attended. His style in controversy was frequently acrimonious and he made numerous enemies; nevertheless, most of his assertions were essentially sound—his memory was remarkable—and he emerged from battle the victor more often than not. One of his greatest contributions to American horticulture was the advancement of viticulture. After nearly half a century of experimentation, he gave up the culture of the European wine grape (*Vitis vinifera*), which was not adapted to the eastern United States, and largely devoted the last years of his life to the growing and dissemination of native varieties.

On Oct. 2, 1826, he married Charlotte Goodwin Collins, daughter of Charles Collins of Newport, lieutenant-governor of Rhode Island from 1824 to 1832. Prince and his wife had four children, one of whom was LeBaron Bradford Prince [*q.v.*]. The night before his death he was in perfect health, engaged, as usual, in writing, at his Flushing home. He died as the result of a stroke of apoplexy in his seventy-fourth year.

[Most of the famous Prince library, gathered by three generations of horticulturists, is in the hands of a book dealer in Flushing, the New Mexico State Library, and the United States Dept. of Agric. Library, Washington, D. C. For published material see: L. B. Prince, in L. H. Bailey, *The Standard Cyc. of Horticulture,* vol. III (1915); *Gardener's Monthly,* May 1869; B. F. Thompson, *Hist. of L. I.* (3rd ed., 1918), vol. III; *Hist. of Queen's County, N. Y.* (1882); U. P. Hedrick, *Grapes of N. Y.* (1908); *N. Y. Times,* Mar. 29, 1869.]   R. H. S.

PRING, MARTIN (*c.* 1580–1626), explorer and naval commander, was the son of John Pring of Awliscombe, Devonshire. The details of his early life are obscure but at the age of twenty-three he was considered "sufficient Mariner for Captaine" of an expedition to northern Virginia. This voyage was planned by Richard Hakluyt and "sundry of the chiefest Merchants of Bristoll," who profited by Gosnold's experience and before proceeding secured a trading patent from Sir Walter Raleigh. Pring sailed from Milford Haven on Apr. 10, 1603, in command of the *Speedwell* and the *Discoverer,* vessels of fifty and twenty-six tons, laden with trucking goods. He made land at Penobscot Bay, coasted westward into Cape Cod Bay, and landed at Plymouth Harbor, to which he gave the name of Whitson Bay. Here he built a barricado, planted test seeds, collected sassafras and cedar, and escaped an Indian attack only because of the awe which two great mastiffs inspired. On Oct. 2 he landed again at Bristol and reported a successful voyage.

In 1604 one Martin Prinx (*sic*) sailed as master of the *Olive Branch* on Charles Leigh's unfortunate expedition to colonize Guiana. Leigh accused him of inciting the crew to mutiny, but another member of the expedition reported only that Prinx became discontented and returned by a Dutch ship (Purchas, *post,* IV, 1253, 1260). If this was Martin Pring, as seems probable, the occurrence did not prejudice his reputation, for in 1606 he was appointed by Sir John Popham to serve as master under Captain Hanham on an expedition sent to join Challons on the coast of Virginia. Failing to find Challons, who had fallen into the hands of the Spanish, they explored the coast, of which Pring made a chart and a report which Gorges called the most perfect and exact discovery that had come into his hands (*Advancement of Plantations, post,* p. 6). In 1621 Pring made a contribution of ten marks to a fund to be used for "some good worke to be begun in Virginia," in return for which he was made a freeman of the Virginia Company and given two hundred acres of Virginia land (J. H. Pring, *Captaine Martin Pringe,* 1888).

In 1610 Pring was employed to survey Bristol Channel (Latimer, *post,* p. 206). In 1613 he appears as master in the service of the East India Company, where in 1619 he attained the rank of commander of naval forces. He served with distinction and launched a policy of friendship with the Dutch in order to secure a joint monopoly against the Spanish and Portuguese. While in the East, he was responsible for the seizure of two semi-piratical ships belonging to Lord Rich (later Earl of Warwick), who appealed the matter to the Privy Council. Sir Thomas Smythe, governor of the East India Company and treasurer of the Virginia Company, supported Pring. This was one of the chief causes of the quarrel which resulted in the capture of the Virginia Company by the Rich-Sandys faction.

In 1621 Pring returned to England where he narrowly escaped a Privy-Council trial in consequence of his private trading and his pro-Dutch policy. Under this cloud he quitted the service of the Company in 1623. In the same year he was elected a member of the Merchant Venturers Society of Bristol, and in 1625 one of the wardens. In the following year, when the government began to issue letters of marque and reprisal on France and Spain, Pring took command of the 300-ton privateer *Charles*. He was notably successful in bringing in prizes, one of which was a Spanish man-of-war of about 30 guns (Latimer, p. 152). In 1626 Pring died and was buried in St. Stephen's Church, Bristol, where his monument remains. His will mentions his wife Elizabeth and six children.

[For Samuel Purchas, *Hakluytus Posthumus, or Purchas His Pilgrims*, see index in vol. XX (1907). *A Briefe Relation of the Discovery and Plantation of New England* (1622) and *A Briefe Narration of the Originall Undertakings of the Advancement of Plantations into the Parts of America* (1658) are reprinted in J. P. Baxter, *Sir Ferdinando Gorges and His Province of Me.* (3 vols., 1890). John Latimer, *The Hist. of the Soc. of Merchant Venturers of the City of Bristol* (1903), includes several important extracts from the unprinted minutes of the Privy Council. The article on Pring in the *Dict. Nat. Biog.* is inaccurate and unjustly disparaging. The best secondary account is that of A. L. P. Dennis, "Capt. Martin Pring, Last of the Elizabethan Seamen," in the *Me. Hist. Soc. Colls.*, 3 ser., II (1906). This contains a full and critical bibliography.]   C.K.S.

PRINGLE, CYRUS GUERNSEY (May 6, 1838–May 25, 1911), plant breeder and collector, was born at East Charlotte, Vt., the grandson of Gideon Prindle, who had settled in Charlotte in 1792, and the son of George Prindle (or Pringle), whose wife was Louisa Harris. His paternal ancestors were Scotch Presbyterians, his mother's family of English Puritan stock. From the latter came his unusual physical strength and endurance. Reared in the country he was educated at the village school in Hinesburg and was finishing his preparation for college at Stanbridge, Quebec, when the death of his elder brother, following that of his father, called him back to the farm. Here in his leisure hours he completed his education, perfecting his knowledge of French and Spanish while waiting for the blacksmith and the miller. Here too he joined the Society of Friends whose tenets harmonized with his religious temperament and his pacific disposition. Perhaps the step was facilitated by the encouragement of a gifted school teacher of the vicinity, Almira L. Greene, whom he married in February 1863. The sincerity of his belief in Quaker teachings was amply demonstrated in the next few months. Drafted for service in the Union army he refused on principle an uncle's offer to purchase his exemption but, when mustered into the ranks, he refused with equal determination to do military service or even service in the hospitals. Though treated with great severity and threatened with death, he persisted in his course until he was at last released by the intervention of President Lincoln.

Back on his farm in Vermont he devoted much of his time during the next fifteen years to the breeding of plants. What he lacked in formal training he made up in infinite patience and care. He found the basis of his method in foreign technical journals; the rest he worked out by experience. After much crossing and careful selection he developed several "improved varieties of wheat, oats, grapes, and potatoes." If many of these proved of little value and others have been superseded by better varieties, Pringle nevertheless merits recognition as one of America's pioneer plant breeders. In the meantime he was developing his interests and talents as a botanical collector. He began with the flora of Vermont and later extended his search into other regions of northern New England and of eastern Canada. Encouraged and aided by Professor Asa Gray of Harvard he was soon supplying carefully mounted specimens to numerous collectors in America and Europe. Domestic troubles shortly led to a change in his field of activity. His wife had found life difficult with her mother-in-law and, failing to persuade her husband to join her in evangelistic work, she separated from him and eventually secured a divorce in 1877. Deeply affected and eager for a change of environment Pringle in 1880 began his important botanical explorations in the Pacific states. Five years later he crossed the frontier on the first of many expeditions into Mexico which continued until he had made a systematic study of Mexican flora and had placed specimens in most of the important herbaria at home and abroad. Botanically Mexico was largely an undiscovered country at the time; he revealed its riches to the botanists of the world. Having completed his task he spent the later years of his life at the University of Vermont where his own extensive herbarium was housed. By exchanges with collectors everywhere he continued to add to it until his death in 1911.

His powerful physique, deep chest, and broad shoulders were combined with a sturdy constitution maintained by the most frugal living. Throughout his later life he prepared his own simple meals even when living in the university science hall. He was extremely sensitive, almost painfully shy, and so modest that though he wrote well he published little out of his rich experience. Despite his small income he was generous to a fault. Wanting little for himself he was the more ready to give to others. His wife after their divorce attained some reputation as a social worker in New York City. They had one daughter.

[Part of Pringle's wartime diary appears in "The U. S. versus Pringle," *Atlantic Monthly*, Feb. 1913. It was separately republished, with an introduction by R. M. Jones, as *The Record of a Quaker Conscience* (1918). See also: *Rhodora, Jour. New Eng. Botanical Club*, Nov. 1911; *Science*, Aug. 11, Dec. 1, 1911; *Bull. Friends' Hist. Soc. of Phila.*, Fifth month, 1918; *Proc. Am. Acad. Arts and Sci.*, vol. LI (1916); W. S. Rann, *Hist. of Chittenden County, Vt.* (1886); *F. C. Prindle, The Prindle Geneal.* (1906); *Who's Who in America*, 1910–11.]   P. D. E.

PRINGLE, JOEL ROBERTS POINSETT (Feb. 4, 1873–Sept. 25, 1932), naval officer, was born on his father's plantation, "Greenfield," Georgetown County, S. C., of distinguished ancestry, the son of Dominick Lynch and Caroline (Lowndes) Pringle, a descendant in the fourth generation of John Julius Pringle [q.v.], and in the fifth, of Robert Pringle, South Carolina jurist, who came to Charleston from County Edinburgh, Scotland, about 1725. His father was educated at Heidelberg and had been United States minister to Turkey. His mother was a daughter of Richard Henry Lowndes, a retired naval officer. Joel Roberts Poinsett [q.v.], for whom he was named, was his great-grandmother's second husband. After studying at the Porter Military Academy in Charleston, he entered the United States Naval Academy, graduating in 1892. During the Spanish-American War he served in the *Columbia*, and thereafter continued in routine sea and shore duty, the latter chiefly at the Naval Academy. His first command was the destroyer *Perkins*, Atlantic Torpedo Flotilla. He was executive of the battleship *Nebraska*, 1911–13, being promoted to commander in 1912. In June 1916, he was ordered to command the destroyer tender *Dixie* and Divisions 3 and 4, Torpedo Flotilla, and in November was given command of Flotilla 2, Destroyer Force. The *Dixie* joined the destroyers operating at Queenstown, Ireland, in the World War in June 1917, and shortly thereafter Pringle was shifted from her to the destroyer tender *Melville*. He received the temporary rank of captain on Aug. 31, 1917 (made permanent July 1, 1918), and on Oct. 9 became Admiral Sims's chief of staff and the senior American officer at Queenstown. He was also the United States chief of staff to Admiral Sir Lewis Bayly of the Royal Navy, commander-in-chief on the coast of Ireland. His administrative work in charge of the American forces and the base at Queenstown was a model of its kind and has been generally pronounced the best ever seen in the American navy. Repairs were made wholly by the *Melville* and *Dixie* according to definite schedules announced to destroyers upon their arrival in port and rarely modified. Admiral Bayly wrote after Pringle's death (London *Times*, Sept. 29, 1932). "He was a man of perfect tact and exceptional ability. . . . He was as universally liked as he was implicitly obeyed. He never once failed me during the War, and was just as ready to help British ships as American, his one idea being to do his duty; and no man ever did it better."

He left Queenstown in March 1919. Following a year's study at the Naval War College in Newport, R. I., he served a year on the staff of Admiral Sims, president of the college, and after commanding the *Idaho*, was again at the college as chief of staff, from 1923 to 1925. He became the chief of staff to the commander, Battleship Divisions, Battle Fleet, in July 1925, and after September 1926, was the chief of staff to the commander, Battle Fleet. Made rear admiral on Dec. 6, 1926, he served as president of the War College from 1927 to 1930. He was an adviser at the London Naval Conference in 1930, and from May 1930, to May 1932, commanded Battleship Division Three of the United States Fleet. Thereafter he was commander, Battleships, United States Fleet, with the rank of vice admiral. At his death, which occurred at San Diego, Cal., he was definitely in line for Chief of Naval Operations, the highest post in the navy. His burial was in the Naval Academy Cemetery in Annapolis. He was survived by his wife Cordelia, daughter of Commodore R. L. Phythian, whom he married on Jan. 25, 1899, and by a daughter.

[Information from the family; *Who's Who in America*, 1932–33; Service Record, *Bur. of Navigation Files*, Navy Dept.; *Hearings Before the Committee on Naval Affairs*, U. S. Senate, 71 Cong., 2 Sess., on the *London Naval Treaty of 1930* (1930); W. S. Sims, *The Victory at Sea* (1920); *N. Y. Times*, Sept. 22, 26, 27, 28, 1932.]   A. W.

PRINGLE, JOHN JULIUS (July 22, 1753–Mar. 17, 1843), speaker of the South Carolina House of Representatives, attorney-general of South Carolina, was born in Charleston, S. C., the eldest child of Robert Pringle by his second wife, Judith (Mayrant) Bull Pringle. The father, the second son of Robert Pringle of Symington, Parish of Stow, Edinburgh County, Scotland, emigrated to America about 1725, became one of a group of prosperous Charleston merchants in the southern Indian trade, in later life served as one of the assistant lay judges of the court of common pleas, and as such concurred in the famous order in which the court expressed its intention to function without the use of the stamps required by the law of 1765 (McCrady, *post*, pp. 572–73). The son was christened John but later added a middle name and was known as John Julius Pringle. He commenced the study of law in the office of John Rutledge in 1772 and the next year was admitted to the Middle Temple in London, where he was still enrolled when the Revolution began. He went to France and there acted for a time, 1778–79, as secretary to Ralph Izard, commissioner to the court of Tuscany. In the difficulties that arose between Izard and Benjamin Franklin he served the former faithfully without forfeiting the regard of the latter (*The Revolutionary Diplomatic Correspondence*, 1889, II, 562–64, ed. by Francis Wharton; O'Neall, *post*, pp. 3–4). He returned to Charleston and in 1781 was admitted to the bar. On Jan. 1, 1784, he married Susannah, the youngest daughter of James Reid of St. Bartholomew's Parish. They had ten children.

Much against his tastes he was almost immediately drawn into a public career that lasted twenty-five years. Certain appointments to office he successfully declined, notably that to the attorney-generalship of the United States in 1805, but others he was impelled by a sense of duty to accept. He entered the state house of representatives for the parishes of St. Philip and St. Michael, the city of Charleston, in 1785, was returned in 1786 and 1788, and was speaker during the sessions of 1787 and 1788. He was a member of the convention in 1788 that ratified the constitution of the United States and of the convention that drew up the state constitution of 1790, in both of which he supported the policies of the low-country (*Journal of the Convention of S. C. which Ratified the Constitution of the U. S.*, 1928, indexed by A. S. Salley; Jonathan Elliot, *The Debates in the Several State Conventions*, vol. IV, 1836, 262–63; Charleston *City Gazette*, May 18–June 9, 1790). From 1789 to 1792 he was federal district attorney and from 1792 to 1808 attorney-general of South Carolina. Thereafter he devoted himself wholly to private practice. As a careful student of the law, as a practitioner who appeared in many of the leading cases that came before the courts in the critical period following the Revolution, and as a teacher of young men who later occupied positions on the bench of the state, he made an important contribution to the principles of South Carolina jurisprudence. In spite of a defect of speech he was an able advocate (see his address to the jury in the Simons-Snipes duel case, *Charleston Morning Post and Daily Advertiser*, Feb. 25 and 27, 1786). In the intellectual and religious activities of Charleston he had an active part. He was a trustee of the College of Charleston from 1796 to 1824 and from 1811 to 1815 president of the board, from 1812 to 1816 president of the Charleston Library Society, and for several years chairman of the vestry of St. Michael's Church. In 1795 he purchased "Runnymede" on the Ashley River, which he made his country residence, and at the time of his death he was possessed of two additional plantations, one on the Pedee and another on the Black River, with upwards of 400 slaves (Charleston County Probate Court, *Will Book I and J*, 284–288; *Inventories, Appraisements, and Sales A*, 436–437, 497).

[J. B. O'Neall, *Biog. Sketches of the Bench and Bar of S. C.* (1859), vol. II; Edward McCrady, *The Hist. of S. C. under the Royal Government* (1899); *S. C. Hist. and Geneal. Mag.*, Apr. 1919, Jan. 1921, Jan., Apr. 1925, Apr., Oct. 1926; E. A. Jones, *Am. Members of the Inns of Court* (1924); *Charleston Daily Courier*, Mar. 20, 1843.]   J. H. E.

PRINTZ, JOHAN BJÖRNSSON (July 20, 1592–May 3, 1663), Swedish colonial governor, was born in the parsonage at Bottnaryd, Småland, Sweden, the son of the Rev. Björn Hansson and his wife, Gunilla Svensdotter. According to ordinary Swedish usage he would have been known as Johan Björnsson; the name Printz he adopted from his maternal grandfather, the Rev. Sven Benedictus Putt (d. 1587), who had assumed it on being raised to the nobility by King Johan III. His father, who died about 1616, was pastor at Bottnaryd for over seventy years. Printz attended schools at Jönköping and Skara, entered the Linköping Gymnasium in 1608, and went to Germany in 1618 to study theology at the universities of Rostock and Greifswald. The next year, as a candidate for ordination, he delivered some sermons from his father's old pulpit. Granted a stipend by King Gustavus Adolphus, he returned to Germany in 1620 and is said to have visited the universities of Leipzig, Wittenberg, Helmstedt, and Jena. While on a journey he was seized by a band of roving soldiers and forced to enlist in a regiment marching toward Italy. This sudden, apparently ruinous, change of fortune suited his temperament exactly. For the next few years he was a mercenary in the service of Archduke Leopold of Austria, Duke Christian of Brunswick, and King Christian IV of Denmark. Between campaigns in 1622 he married Elizabeth von Boche, daughter of the Ducal Privy Councilor Lydeche von Boche of Brunswick. In 1625 he received an appointment in the Swedish army. In 1638 he attained the grade of lieutenant-colonel, and in 1639 Gen. Johan Banér placed him in command of Chemnitz. The next year, after a short but spirited resistance, he surrendered to a superior Saxon force and returned to Stockholm without asking leave. A court martial exonerated him for the loss of Chemnitz, but for absenting himself without leave the Council of State removed him from his command. His wife died about this time, and in 1642 he married Maria von Linnestau, widow of Colonel Von Stralendorff. In April 1642 he was appointed director (governor) of New Sweden to succeed Peter Hollender Ridder; he received his commission and instructions in August and was knighted by Queen Christina; and on Feb. 15, 1643, his ships, the *Fama* and *Swan*, dropped anchor at Fort Christina (Wilmington, Del.).

Printz was governor of New Sweden for ten years and six months. He was handicapped from the outset by a shortage of men and supplies, and during the last five years of his administration the Swedish government left him to shift for himself. He was amply qualified for his job. His Latin had grown rusty in the wars, making diplomatic correspondence a nuisance to him, but otherwise he complained of no infirmities. He was a giant in height and girth, was reputed to weigh four hundred pounds, and ate and drank like a hero out of Rabelais. The Indians called him "Big Guts," but respectfully. His profanity was famous from Massachusetts Bay to Old Point Comfort. An alumnus of the Thirty Years' War, he has been suspected of being a past master of the arts of pillage and rapine and is sometimes represented, accordingly, as a primordial Hans Breitmann, but he was more than that. He was a gentleman born and bred, an intrepid soldier, an intelligent, versatile, energetic administrator, and a wily diplomat. Though determined that he should be well paid for his services to his Queen, he was also determined that his Queen should not be ill served. Every pound of him was of the stuff that builds empires.

Within two weeks of his arrival he had inspected his domain from Cape Henlopen to Sankikan (Trenton, N. J.) and on Mar. 1 he began the construction of Fort Elfsborg at Varkens Kill. For his residence he chose Tinicum Island, naming it New Gothenborg, and erected a commodious house. This house, with its comfortable furnishings, was burned in 1645, with a loss estimated at 5,520 rix-dollars, and was re-built. Printz assigned land to settlers for farming, maintained peaceful relations with the Indians, sent an agent to trade at New Amsterdam, conducted diplomatic correspondence with the English to the South and North of him, and built a blockhouse, a church, a wharf, a gristmill, and other works, among them a brewery that probably entitles him to rank as the Gambrinus of America. His pleasure yacht makes him the first American yachtsman. The chief exports from the colony were tobacco and beaver skins. He was undoubtedly a harsh ruler. Disputes between him and his subjects came to a head on July 27, 1653, when a group of them petitioned for the right to send two men to Sweden to present their grievances to the government. Printz treated this move as rebellion and promptly hanged the leader of the good-government movement, Anders Jönsson. But with the Dutch and English encroaching on him, the Indians restless, and his own subjects dissatisfied, Printz felt the game no longer worth the candle. In September 1653, having turned the government over to his deputy and son-in-law, Johan Papegoja, he departed, sailing in October from New Amsterdam. In 1657 he was made commander of Jönköping Castle and the next year he was appointed governor of his native district, Jönköping Län. A few miles from his native place he built a manor, "Gunillaberg." He died as a result of a fall from his horse. His son Gustaf had predeceased him, but his widow and five daughters survived.

[Amandus Johnson, *The Swedish Settlements on the Delaware 1638–64* (2 vols., 1911) and *The Instruction for Johan Printz* (1930); A. C. Myers, ed., *Narratives of Early Pa., West N. J., and Del. 1630–1707* (1912); Peter Lindeström, *Geographia Americae* (1925), ed. and tr. by Amandus Johnson; H. D. Paxson, *Sketch and Map of a Trip from Phila. to Tinicum Island* (1926).]

                                      G. H. G.

PRITCHARD, FREDERICK JOHN (Dec. 24, 1874–Jan. 13, 1931), plant-breeder, the son of a veterinarian, Dr. James Pritchard, was born at Camanche, Iowa. His mother, Ella Sage Pritchard, early gave to her children ambition for education and a desire for advancement. On the grain and stock farm where the family made its home the boy acquired habits of thrift, industry, and self-reliance, along with a practical knowledge of plant production and applied animal genetics. After completing the common-school courses, he worked his way. A business course at Nebraska Commercial College, Omaha, high-school attendance at Woodbine, Iowa, and Lincoln, Nebr., and a period of teaching in the Woodbine schools, preceded his matriculation in general agriculture at the University of Nebraska, from which he graduated in 1904 with the degree of B.S. His summers, during the years he was in college, were occupied in various grades of clerical work in a railroad office in South Omaha. During his senior year he served as laboratory assistant in farm crops. Upon graduation he became instructor in botany at the University of North Dakota Agricultural College. One year later he was promoted to the rank of assistant professor, but he resigned in 1907 to do graduate work under a fellowship for two years at Cornell University and for one year at the University of Wisconsin. In 1910 he joined the staff of the Bureau of Plant Industry of the Department of Agriculture, Washington, D. C., where he remained until his death.

His position at North Dakota College involved teaching in the University and research at the Agricultural Experiment Station upon plant diseases, particularly the grain rust, *Puccinia Graminis Tritici E. & H.* His early work in the Department of Agriculture was centered on sugar-beet breeding and the production of sugar-beet seed. In 1915 he began his study of tomato disease control and the breeding of disease-resistant varieties, upon which he was occupied, with signal success, during the remainder of his career. By crossing and selection, he originated seven valuable commercial varieties of disease-resistant tomatoes, namely, Marvel, Norton, Columbia, Norduk, Marvana, Marvelosa, and Marglobe. The Marglobe in particular has proved to be an exceedingly valuable and popular variety, grown both as a trucking and as a canning crop. He contributed to professional and trade journals and publications of the United States Department of Agriculture and the North Dakota Agricultural Experiment Station some thirty articles dealing with problems in plant physiology, plant pathology, agronomy, plant breeding and selection. (A full bibliography appears in *Phytopathology*, March 1932.)

Pritchard was as faithful in the follow-up work of introducing his productions and establishing adequate commercial supplies of seed stock of authentic character as he was in the original and, to him, more fascinating work of crossing and selection. He was critical and exacting in his standards and tenacious in the pursuit of an objective. As a friend and companion he was genial and approachable. Commercial tomato growers and seed men throughout the country sought his counsel and esteemed him as a fellow worker. He married Selma Irene Kantz, and they had two children. The

death of his infant son in 1926 deeply affected Pritchard and continued to exercise an influence on his personality, perceptible to his intimate associates during the remainder of his life. He died suddenly at his office on Jan. 13, 1931. He had mentioned trivial symptoms of indigestion during the morning, but so far as is known neither he nor his friends had any knowledge of a predisposing weakness or any intimation of danger.

[The foregoing sketch is based on information from Mrs. Selma I. Pritchard, Washington, D. C., and Dr. William T. Pritchard, North Platt, Nebr.; Government personnel records and records of Bureau of Plant Industry, Dept. of Agric.; personal and official contact for seventeen years. An article on Pritchard by W. S. Porte, with full bibliography, appeared in *Phytopathology*, Mar. 1932, and an obituary was published in the *Evening Star* (Washington), Jan. 15, 1931.]   H. A. E.

PRITCHARD, JETER CONNELLY (July 12, 1857–Apr. 10, 1921), United States senator, federal judge, was born in Jonesboro, Tenn., of Irish and Welsh ancestry. His father was William H. Pritchard, a carpenter and builder, who died during service in the Confederate army; his mother was Elizabeth Brown. Brought up in poverty, he was apprenticed to a printer and at the end of his term of service became foreman of the Jonesboro *Tribune-Herald*. In 1874 he walked to Bakersville, N. C., to take a similar position on the *Roan Mountain Republican,* of which he later became joint owner and editor. Here he attended first the Odd Fellows Institute and later Martin's Creek Academy in Tennessee where he received the whole of his formal education. He then read law, and, admitted to the bar in 1889, began practice at Marshall, N. C.

Ambitious and actively interested in politics, and a Republican from tradition, environment, and conviction, he was a candidate for elector in 1880 and was elected a member of the lower house of the General Assembly from Madison County in 1884 and in 1886. There he won attention and respect by his vigorous expression of his decided and progressive views, his fighting spirit, and his straight-forward dealings with men and measures. He was the candidate of his party for lieutenant-governor in 1888, and so greatly added to his reputation by his extended campaign that in the legislature of 1891, of which he was a member, he was the party nominee for the United States Senate. The next year he was a delegate at large to the Republican National Convention. He was also nominated for Congress but was defeated after a brilliant campaign which made him the undisputed leader of his party. In 1894, as a result of a fusion of the Republicans and Populists, the

Democrats lost control of the state and the legislature elected him to the Senate to fill out the unexpired term of Zebulon B. Vance, and in 1897 he was reëlected for a full term. During this period he was state chairman of his party and a member of its national committee.

The fact that he was the only Republican senator from the South gave Pritchard prominence from the beginning, and that fact combined with his character and ability to give him a unique place in Washington. Consulted at first on all Southern matters, he presently, by his personality and power in debate, won larger influence in the Senate. He became also the intimate friend and adviser of Presidents McKinley and Roosevelt. Defeated in 1903 he accepted a place as division council of the Southern Railway, but in November President Roosevelt appointed him associate justice of the supreme court of the District of Columbia. In April of the next year Roosevelt made him circuit judge of the fourth circuit, and in 1913 he was appointed presiding judge of the fourth circuit of the circuit court of appeals and held the position until his death. On the bench, though not a learned or profound man, he gained reputation for his sound, practical judgment, and in the course of time for legal learning which he acquired by close study. On appeal he was usually sustained by the Supreme Court. His opinions on cases involving the relations of capital and labor and of employers and employees were particularly able. During this period his attention was not completely absorbed by his judicial duties. Always interested in labor questions, he served in 1914 as president of a board of arbitration to settle the wages of employees of ninety-eight railroads. In 1907 he was a leader in advocating state prohibition. He also took a lively interest in education and in movements for the uplift of the negroes. Pritchard was married three times: in 1877 to Augusta Ray, who died in 1885; on Oct. 18, 1892, to Melissa Bowman; and on Nov. 14, 1903, to Lillian E. Saum of Washington, D. C.

[See: *Who's Who in America*, 1920–21; S. A. Ashe, ed., *Biog. Hist. of N. C.*, vol. I (1905); *Biog. Dir. Am. Cong.* (1928); *News and Observer* (Raleigh), Jan. 21, 1897; *Charlotte Observer, Asheville Times* and *Greensboro Daily News*, Apr. 11, 1921. Pritchard's decisions are to be found in 128–271 *Federal Reporter*.]

J. G. deR. H.

PROCTER, JOHN ROBERT (Mar. 16, 1844–Dec. 12, 1903), director of the Kentucky geological survey, United States civil-service commissioner, was born in Mason County, Ky. His parents were George Morton and Anna Maria (Young) Procter. His mother having died soon after his birth, he was taken by an aunt and brought up by her and prepared for college in her home. Though only seventeen years old when the Civil War broke out, he developed a strong desire to fight for the Southern Confederacy. His aunt opposed his wishes, and to get him out of the way of war contagions, she sent him to the University of Pennsylvania in 1863 to take a scientific course. Having finished the work of the freshman class he returned to Kentucky the next year and enlisted in the Confederate army. He fought to the end, rising to the rank of lieutenant of artillery. Unreconciled to the hard fate that he saw awaiting the South, he sought service in Mexico, but failing to secure a place he settled down upon a farm in Kentucky. Farming still had some appeal to a gentleman but when he came into contact with Nathaniel S. Shaler [*q.v.*], who taught geology in Harvard University and at the same time acted as the Kentucky state geologist, he became interested in geology and in 1874 joined the Harvard camp in Kentucky. The next year he took work in geology at Harvard University, and now definitely became a part of the Kentucky survey as an assistant to Shaler.

Though Shaler was a native Kentuckian and a great geologist, the state legislature thought that he should not continue as state geologist unless he were willing to live in Frankfort. Preferring Cambridge to Frankfort, Shaler resigned and Governor Blackburn immediately appointed Procter to the directorship of the geological survey and the state unwisely added to his duties those of the commissioner of immigration. Owing to the division of effort, interest, and funds that this combination required, Procter did not make an outstanding contribution in either field. Outside of a few county and regional surveys, he carried on little more work of a scientific nature. His geological reports and separate studies appear in the *Geological Survey of Kentucky* (1880–92). Though his work as a geologist did not place his name high among the scientists, his administration of his two departments led him into a national reputation in a field that was related neither to geology nor to immigration. He scrupulously held to fitness in making his appointments and refused to be moved by the expediency of political considerations. When Gov. John Young Brown demanded a place in the survey for a son, Procter resolutely held out against the exploitation of his activities by politicians, and thereby lost his position through the abolition of the survey in 1893.

This political assault upon an honest civil-service reformer attracted national attention and led President Cleveland, through the recommendation of Theodore Roosevelt, to appoint Procter to the United States Civil Service Commission (December 1893). Soon thereafter he became president of the Commission and remained so until his death ten years later. In Washington he won the universal praise and support of all friends of civil-service reform, for with all of his zeal he had a sense of humor as well as a knack of good-natured ridicule for the political transparencies of the spoils system, and was even able to make some of his worst enemies like him. He embraced the best qualities of those which went into the make-up of the traditional Southern gentleman. During his term of office the positions in the classified service rose from 43,000 to 120,000. Procter wrote during his lifetime many articles for scientific and general magazines. In addition to geology and civil-service reform, he was interested in the international aspects of America's expanding possessions, especially following the Spanish-American War. On Dec. 2, 1903, at a White House luncheon, he was presented by President Roosevelt with a loving cup to commemorate a decade of public service. Ten days later, he died suddenly in Washington, survived by his wife, Julia Leslie Dobyns, and two sons.

[See: *Reg. Ky. State Hist. Soc.*, Sept. 1921, Jan. 1927; *Who's Who in America*, 1903–05; *Outlook*, Dec. 19, 1903; M. F. Halloran, *The Romance of the Merit System* (1928); W. D. Foulke, *Fighting the Spoilsmen* (1919); *Evening Star* (Wash., D. C.), Dec. 12, 14, 1903.]

E. M. C.

PROCTER, WILLIAM (May 3, 1817–Feb. 9, 1874), pharmacist, teacher, and writer, was born in Baltimore, Md., the ninth child of Isaac Procter, who died three years after William's birth, and Rebecca (Farquhar) Procter. From the ages of six to ten the boy attended Friends' School in Baltimore and then went to work in his sister's cooper shop. Induced by a friend to take up pharmacy as his life's work, he apprenticed himself in 1831 to Henry M. Zollickoffer, who conducted a drug store in Philadelphia. Here he remained for nearly fourteen years serving his employer and studying. During this time he also attended the Philadelphia College of Pharmacy and was awarded the diploma of the institution in 1837. On May 12, 1844, he opened a drug store on the southwest corner of Lombard and Ninth streets which proved to be a successful venture and which he continued to conduct during the remainder of his life. In 1846 he was elected to the professorship of the theory and practice of pharmacy in the Philadelphia College of Pharmacy and four years later he became the editor of the *American Jour-*

nal of Pharmacy, published by the institution. He retained his professorship until 1866. In addition to his other studies he published the American edition of Mohr and Redwood's *Practical Pharmacy*, which appeared in 1849, and assisted Wood and Bache in the revision of several editions of the United States *Dispensatory*. During his editorship of the *American Journal of Pharmacy* (1850–71), he contributed more than five hundred articles to the journal under his name.

In 1840 Procter was elected a member of the Philadelphia College of Pharmacy and a year later was made a member of the board of trustees, which office he held during his life. In 1855 he was made corresponding secretary of the college and in 1867 he was elected first vice-president. He served as a member of the revision committee of the United States *Pharmacopœia* for three revisions (1851, 1863, 1873). In October 1851 he was a delegate to the convention of pharmaceutists which met in New York to fix standards for the use of the customs officials in the inspection of drugs. He was one of the founders of the American Pharmaceutical Association, which was organized in 1852, and took an active part in its development. From 1852 to 1857 he served as corresponding secretary, was elected first vice-president in 1859, and president in 1862. In recognition of the service which he rendered pharmacy, this association raised a fund for the erection of a memorial monument to his memory in Washington, D. C. He was twice married: in October 1849 to Margaretta Bullock, who died in 1859, and in 1864 to Catherine Parry.

[*Proc. Am. Pharmaceut. Asso. at the Forty-eighth Ann. Meeting* (1900); *Am. Jour. Pharmacy*, Nov. 1, 1874; the *Press* (Phila.), Feb. 11, 1874.]

A. G. D–M.

PROCTOR, FREDERICK FRANCIS (c. 1851–Sept. 4, 1929), vaudeville theatre owner and manager, was a son of Dr. Alpheus Proctor, a practising physician of Dexter, Me., who was probably descended from Robert Proctor of Concord and Chelmsford, Mass. His father's death, during the Civil War period, left his mother with a family of five to support on a limited income. Frederick then gave up schooling and went to Boston, where he got work as an errand boy in a dry-goods store. Becoming a leader among his mates in athletic sports, he finally attracted the notice of a veteran circus man and was induced to leave the store for a career as a professional acrobat. As "Fred Levantine" he repeatedly toured the United States and as a climax "made" the European circuit of music halls. Entering the show business on his own account in 1886, he bought an interest in a popular-price theatre at Albany, N. Y. He remained there three years, at first in partnership and later as sole proprietor. Believing that the city of New York held better prospects for him, he opened a legitimate theatre on Twenty-third Street in 1889. That enterprise prospered and an alliance with Charles Frohman for two seasons was a later development. In the early nineties, however, Proctor was giving increasing attention to vaudeville. By 1895 he was turning all his energies to that form of entertainment. The "continuous performance" from noon to midnight for every element of the population had not yet captured New York. The Proctor Pleasure Palace on East Fifty-eighth Street, with its program of fifteen acts, and a "sacred concert" on Sundays, appealed to women and children quite as much as to men. The next step was the opening of the "Ladies' Club Theatre" on Twenty-third Street, with a daily list of twenty acts, in progress from 11 A.M. to 11 P.M. The operatic tenor Campanini was engaged to sing mornings and New Yorkers, accustomed to enjoy most of their musical entertainment after dark, were exhorted to hear the Italian singer immediately after breakfast!

In the effort to make the Proctor theatres "family" resorts, coarseness and vulgarity were largely eliminated from the stage performances. There was soon evolved a form of entertainment that differed both from the London music hall of the period and from the ordinary American variety show, which before that time had been patronized almost exclusively by men. A "10, 20, 30" circuit was organized, and Proctor at one time controlled twenty-five houses and road shows operated in New York, Albany, Troy, and other eastern cities. In course of time the moving picture demanded a place on his programs, which Proctor was quick to concede, but most of the original features of his bills were retained, including acrobatic "stunts," in which Proctor himself had excelled in his youth. In the spring of 1929 the Proctor theatrical holdings were taken over by the Radio-Keith-Orpheum circuit. Proctor was then suffering from congestion of the lungs and four months later he died at Larchmont, N. Y., survived by his wife, Georgena Mills, and two daughters.

[*N. Y. Times,* Sept. 5, 1929; *Variety* (N. Y.), Sept. 11, 1929, p. 67; N. Y. *Star,* Sept. 14, 1929; W. L. Proctor, *A Geneal. of Descendants of Robert Proctor* (1898.).]   W. B. S.

PROCTOR, HENRY HUGH (Dec. 8, 1868–May 12, 1933), Congregational clergyman, was born near Fayetteville, Tenn., and grew up on a farm with his parents, Richard and Hannah (Wetherley) Proctor, who had formerly been slaves. After studying in the public schools he worked his way for seven years through the preparatory and college courses at Fisk University in Nashville, winning the degree of A.B. in 1891. He then entered the Yale Divinity School, from which he was graduated in 1894.

On July 1, 1894, he was ordained to the Christian ministry at Atlanta, Ga., and at once began work as pastor of the First Congregational Church of that city. There he remained for twenty-five years, becoming one of the most prominent and effective ministers of the negro race. He soon won the confidence and esteem of his fellow citizens, white as well as black; and as the church edifice was utterly inadequate both for the congregation and for the social work of which it came to be the center, he built —largely by means of generous contributions from the white people—the first institutional church for negroes in the South. Through its various agencies it served some ten thousand persons; it was visited by many social workers and notables, among them President Theodore Roosevelt and President Taft. Throughout his ministry Proctor was always active in the civic, moral, and religious life of the city. During the race riots he was instrumental in helping to organize the Inter-racial Commission, which did much to check further outbreaks and to ameliorate the unhappy conditions. From Mar. 10 to Aug. 1, 1919, he served under the War Work Council of the Young Men's Christian Association as special lecturer to negro soldiers in France. It was estimated that he spoke to more than 275,000. Born with oratorical gifts, he had become one of the noted speakers in America; and this ability coupled with a fine physique, a magnetic personality, and great vigor and courage made him a power for good.

In 1920 he was called to the pastorate of the Nazarene Congregational Church in Brooklyn, N. Y. When he came, there were one hundred and sixty members; when he died, there were more than a thousand. Furthermore, he had succeeded in purchasing church property in the very heart of the city, and from that center he once more interested himself in a multitude of good causes. He was the first to propose a definite program for aid to Fisk University by the alumni, so that he has been called "the father of organized alumni work at Fisk." When the University was in need, he launched a campaign among negroes which brought in $100,000, much of it in dimes and nickels and even pennies. He was a pioneer in all inter-racial movements, an ardent prohibitionist, and a warm friend of missions. His challenging appeal at a meeting of the American Board of Commissioners for Foreign Missions, of which he was a corporate member from 1923 to 1930, led to the establishment of the de Galanquo Angola Mission, which has proved to be one of the notable stations in Portuguese West Africa. As an author he wrote a terse, readable style. Of his publications, his autobiography, *Between Black and White* (1925), is best known. He also published *Sermons in Melody* (1916), and contributed various articles to some of the leading newspapers and magazines. In 1904–06 he served as assistant moderator of the National Council of Congregational Churches, and in 1926 the New York City Congregational Church Association elected him as its moderator—the first negro to hold the office in an organization composed of sixty-nine churches, only five of which were churches of his own race. He was vice-president of the American Missionary Association, 1906–09, of the Negro Urban League of Brooklyn, and of the Brooklyn Lincoln Settlement; from 1906 to 1908 he was president of the National Convention of Congregational Workers Among the Colored People, and from 1908 to 1933 its corresponding secretary. His death was due to septicemia, and he was buried in South View Cemetery, Atlanta, Ga. He was survived by his wife, Adeline Davis, whom he married Aug. 16, 1893, in Chattanooga, Tenn., and by two sons and three daughters.

[Proctor's autobiography, *Between Black and White* (1925); *Obit. Record Grads. Yale Univ.*, 1933; *Who's Who in America*, 1932–33; *Brooklyn Daily Eagle*, Mar. 12, 1933; clippings and letters in files of Yale Univ.; personal acquaintance.]   H. H. T.

PROCTOR, JOSEPH (May 7, 1816–Oct. 2, 1897), actor and manager, was born in Marlboro, Mass., the son of Nicholson Broughton and Lucy (Bond) Proctor. He was educated in the schools of his native town, and after the venture into amateur theatricals customary in those times, he began to play leading rôles from the outset of his professional career. His first appearance was made in Boston at the Warren (afterward the National) Theatre, on Nov. 29, 1833, as Damon to the Pythias of Edmon S. Conner. Other performances in Boston and elsewhere followed quickly, and they gave him the necessary experience and training essential to the acting of the robustious characters that he made his specialty during more than sixty years of active life on the stage. In 1837 he was acting leading rôles in Philadelphia, and as early as May 6, 1839, he is recorded as play-

ing, at the Bowery Theatre in New York, the principal character in *Nick of the Woods, or the Renegade's Daughter,* a play with which his name was so continuously associated as to create the impression that he never acted any other characters of any consequence. This play, later known as *Nick of the Woods, or the Jibbenainosay,* and frequently as *The Jibbenainosay,* was at that time only a year old, and was a dramatization by Louisa Medina of a story by Robert Montgomery Bird which is described by Arthur Hobson Quinn as the best of all his romantic novels. Six of the characters were played by one actor.

To follow Proctor through the years would be to visit with him every important city and multitudes of small towns throughout the United States, to see him in all the great Shakespearean characters, and in the leading rôles of many melodramatic and tragic plays now long forgotten. From time to time he acted in association with Edwin Forrest, Junius Brutus Booth, Edward L. Davenport and other stars. In 1859 he went to Europe, traveling and remaining there for about two years. He acted for one hundred nights in London, and he gave many performances in other cities of the United Kingdom, including Glasgow, where he played Macbeth to the Macduff, Othello to the Cassio, and Richelieu to the De Mauprat of Henry Irving, who was then serving his novitiate as a secondary member of a stock company. Now and then Proctor ventured into the management of various theatres, and in the fall of 1861, soon after his return from Europe, he made a starring tour of the country under the direction of Edward L. Davenport. At the Boston Theatre, on Nov. 30, 1883, a testimonial performance of scenes from various plays was given in honor of his completion of fifty years on the stage, he himself appearing as Damon, the part he had acted at the Warren Theatre on Nov. 29, 1833. About nine years before his death, advancing age compelled his retirement, although he acted at occasional benefits, perhaps the most notable being a performance in April 1890, at the Globe Theatre in Boston, where he acted Macbeth to the Lady Macbeth of Mrs. Edward L. Davenport, this being their last professional appearance. For several years he found both pleasure and profit in serving as professional instructor to ambitious young aspirants for the stage, maintaining a school in Boston for that purpose.

In appearance, Proctor was tall and of imposing figure, with a sonorous voice. He could assume a stern and forbidding aspect that served him well in the interpretation of the passions of hate and revenge that dominated many of his most successful and popular characters. He was distinctly an actor of the Forrest school. His first wife, to whom he was married in 1835, was Hester Warren, daughter of William Warren the elder, and sister of William Warren of Boston Museum fame. At the time of her marriage to Proctor she was a widow, Mrs. Willis, and when she died in Boston, Dec. 7, 1841, at the early age of thirty-one, she had gained considerable distinction on the stage. For his second wife he married, in February 1851, Elizabeth Wakeman, a young actress who remained on the stage in his support for many years, and who died in 1911. Their daughter, Anna E. Proctor, also accompanied her father on his tours and after his death continued to act until failing health compelled her retirement.

[J. N. Ireland, *Records of the N. Y. Stage* (1867), vol. II; T. Allston Brown, *A Hist. of the N. Y. Stage* (1903), vol. I; E. F. Edgett, *Biog. of Edward L. Davenport* (1901); Eugene Tompkins and Quincy Kilby, *The Hist. of the Boston Theatre* (1908); G. C. D. Odell, *Annals of the N. Y. Stage*, vols. IV (1928), VI and VII (1931); *Vital Records of Marlborough, Mass.* (1908); articles in *N. Y. Clipper*, Dec. 1, 1883, and July 30, 1910; *N. Y. Dramatic Mirror*, Oct. 9, 1897; *N. Y. Sun*, Oct. 17, 1897; *Boston Daily Globe, Boston Herald* and *Boston Transcript*, Oct. 2, 1897; newspaper clippings on the Harvard Lib. Theatre Collection.]   E. F. E.

PROCTOR, LUCIEN BROCK (Mar. 6, 1823–Apr. 1, 1900), writer of legal history and biography of New York, the son of Jonathan and Ruth (Carter) Proctor, was born at Hanover, N. H. His English forefather, Robert Proctor, had become a freeman of Concord, Mass., in 1643, and his grandfathers fought at Bunker Hill and Bennington. When Lucien was yet a child his father, a cutlery manufacturer, moved to Oneida, then to Chenango County, N. Y., and finally to the town of Auburn, where Lucien attended the academy. Young Proctor was early attracted to the law, spending much of his time in the office of William H. Seward. He studied with Angel and Grover at Angelica, N. Y., and with I. L. Endress at Dansville. Admitted to the bar in 1852, he began practice at Port Byron but later returned to practise in Dansville. He was successful in criminal and civil cases, but he gained a more enduring reputation in his writings on legal history and on New York state biography, an occupation to which he turned when ill health required him to give up the practice of law. In *The Civil, Political, Professional and Ecclesiastical History ... of the County of Kings and the City of Brooklyn, N. Y., from 1683 to 1884* (1884), which he assisted Henry R. Stiles in compiling, he recounted interesting details of court-houses, judges, judicial procedure, and cases in the early courts.

His biographies of the Kings County bar are full of personal flavor, written with ease and grace and a fund of knowledge of the social and professional characteristics of the early lawyers. His painstaking accounts of lawyers and legal practices contributed to the comprehensive survey which Stiles undertook. A number of articles by Proctor appeared in the *Albany Law Journal*. His other published works include: *The Bench and Bar of New York* (1870); *Lawyer and Client* (1882); and *William H. Seward as a Lawyer* (1887), the latter written as a result of the intimate friendship between Proctor and Seward. At the time of his death he had almost completed a revision of Hammond's *History of Political Parties in the State of New York*.

The Bench and Bar of New York was made up of biographical sketches dedicated to the junior bar of New York in the hope that it would serve as an inspiration to young men in the profession. The title is not suggestive of the readable, often exciting, accounts of human incidents and experiences which made up the lives of early New York lawyers. Proctor was not concerned with legal red tape, nor merely with lawyers, but with justice and right, and all the circumstances of a man's life which combined to assure him success in the law. In 1884 Proctor moved to Albany. He contributed "The Bench and Bar; or Legal History" to Howell and Tenney's *History of the County of Albany*, published in 1886. For thirteen years he was secretary of the state bar association and helped to found the Livingston County Historical Society. He died in Albany having fulfilled his hope of rendering service to the law profession in his day and generation. He was twice married. His first wife was Araminta D. Whitney of Auburn, N. Y., whom he married in January 1843 and by whom he had two children. His second wife was Margaret Scott Wylie of Albany, N. Y.

[See C. J. Hailes, "Lucien Brock Proctor," *Albany Law Jour.*, Jan. 6, 13, 20, 1900; J. H. Smith, *Hist. of Livingston County, N. Y.* (1881); W. L. Proctor, *A Geneal. of Descendants of Robert Proctor* (1898); *Proc. N. Y. State Bar Asso., Twenty-fourth Ann. Meeting* (1901); *Livingston County Hist. Soc., Twenty-sixth Ann. Meeting* (1902); *Albany Eve. Jour.*, Apr. 2, 1900.]   E. M. G.

PROCTOR, REDFIELD (June 1, 1831–Mar. 4, 1908), governor of Vermont, secretary of war, was the descendant of Robert Proctor, who became a freeman of Concord, Mass., in 1643, and the grandson of Leonard Proctor, who founded the town of Proctorsville on the frontier in Vermont, where Redfield was born. The early death of his father, Jabez Proctor, left the training of the five children in the hands of their mother,

Betsey (Parker) Proctor, a woman of rare ability and character. Redfield graduated from Dartmouth College in 1851, and on May 26, 1858, he married Emily J. Dutton, by whom he had five children. After spending some years in business in Proctorsville he studied law at Albany, N. Y., and had practised for a time with his cousin, Isaac F. Redfield [*q.v.*], in Boston, when the Civil War broke out. He at once enlisted and became major in the 5th Vermont Regiment. In 1862 an army surgeon ordered him home from Virginia because of tuberculosis. Outdoor life, especially fishing and hunting, restored his health, and he returned as colonel of the 15th Vermont Regiment and participated in the battle of Gettysburg. After his return home he formed a law partnership in Rutland with Wheelock G. Veazey. Since indoor life and the searching for authorities in law books did not attract him, he gradually drifted into business. His appointment in 1869 as the receiver of a small marble company at Sutherland Falls proved to be a turning point in his life. With keen business sense he organized a company to utilize available natural resources, to consolidate all activities, and to develop them under one management. His success was phenomenal; by 1880 he was the able president of the Vermont Marble Company, which became the largest producer of marble in the world. He always took a personal interest in his employees and built up a loyal organization. Good houses at low rentals, accident insurance, a library, a Y. M. C. A., and a free hospital were among the things he provided for them. He moved his family into a house in the village of Sutherland Falls, within sound of the mills, and participated in all phases of community activity. This contributed largely to his business success and to the moral tone and civic pride of the community.

Meanwhile, he had risen in politics from selectman to governor and had had service in the Vermont legislature. As governor from 1878 to 1880, he had a businesslike and progressive administration. In 1888 as leader of the Vermont delegation to the Republican National Convention at Chicago, he was the only chairman who on each ballot announced the solid vote of his state for the successful presidential nominee, Benjamin Harrison. After the election he was appointed secretary of war. His interest in human beings, along with his business and political ability, enabled him to gain the cooperation of Congress and to achieve excellent results in his department. By removing causes for desertion, its rate was reduced materially. The system of courts martial was revised in the interests of a larger degree of justice to the common soldier. For officers, a system of efficiency records and examinations for promotion were instituted. He organized the record and pension division and, with no increase in the number of clerks, introduced a card index system so efficient that ninety-eight per cent. of all pension cases were answered within twenty-four hours of their receipt. His letter to the mayor of New Orleans, explaining the failure to order the flag at half mast on the death of Jefferson Davis, a former secretary of war, was written with appreciation of the fitness of things and with respect for the South (New Orleans *Daily Picayune*, Dec. 9, 1889).

After almost three years of service, he resigned to enter the United States Senate as the successor of George F. Edmunds. He was reelected three times and served in the Senate from 1891 till his death. On Mar. 17, 1898, he delivered an important speech—one of those rare utterances that seem to shape public policies. Desiring first-hand information about conditions in Cuba he had gone to the island and made his own investigation. Upon his return, at the request of his colleagues, without prearrangement or realization of the remarkable effect, he told in simple, clear language what he had seen and believed (*The Condition of Cuba. It is not Peace, nor is it War*, 1898, and in *Congressional Record*, 55 Cong., 2 Sess., pp. 2916–19). Harrison wrote that this speech "aroused the nation, and yet there was not a lurid adjective in it" (Partridge, *post*, p. 91). The war with Spain soon followed. While senator, he was particularly interested in his work on the committees on agriculture and military affairs. He was not an orator, but he usually spoke convincingly and upon a solid basis of fact that he had previously mastered. In the Republican National Convention in 1896 he played a prominent rôle, particularly in framing the important "gold" plank in the platform. In the great campaign that followed he also played a leading part. His charitable gifts included many small churches in his state. He established the Vermont sanatorium to lead the fight against tuberculosis in his state. In 1904 he edited from the original manuscripts in the Library of Congress the *Records of Conventions in the New Hampshire Grants for the Independence of Vermont, 1776–1777*. He died of pneumonia in Washington.

[F. C. Partridge, "Redfield Proctor," *Vt. Hist. Soc. Proc., 1913–14* (1915); *Redfield Proctor . . . Memorial Addresses, Sixtieth Cong. . . . Jan. 9, 1909* (1909); W. L. and A. P. Proctor, *A Geneal. of Descendants of Robert Proctor* (1898); *Men of Vt.* (1894), comp. by J. G. Ullery.]   A.T.V.

PROPHET [See TENSKWATAWA, 1768–1837].

PROSSER, CHARLES SMITH (Mar. 24, 1860–Sept. 11, 1916), educator, geologist, was born at Columbus, Chenango County, N. Y. His father, Smith Prosser, a farmer, was the son of William H. Prosser, one of the pioneers of the Unadilla Valley in New York. His mother, Emeline A. Tuttle, was descended from William and Elizabeth Tuttle who came to America from England in 1635, settling first in Massachusetts and then in Connecticut. Prosser attended the district school and Union School at Brookfield, from which he graduated in 1879. In the fall of that year he entered Cornell University, where his chief interest was about equally divided between botany and geology. He graduated with the degree of B.S. in 1883, but remained at Cornell as a graduate student. In 1884–85 he held the Cornell Fellowship in natural history. From 1885 to 1888 he was instructor in paleontology and assistant to Prof. Henry Shaler Williams [q.v.], who was engaged in a study of the Devonian faunas for the United States Geological Survey. As a boy on the farm in the Unadilla Valley he had collected and preserved plants and fossils; as an undergraduate at Cornell he was interested in research, and as a graduate student he at once undertook research of his own in addition to the work in which he assisted Professor Williams. He received the degree of M.S. from Cornell University in 1886 and that of Ph.D. in 1907.

In 1888 Prosser became assistant paleontologist on the United States Geological Survey in the division of paleobotany, under Lester F. Ward [q.v.], a position which he held for four years. In 1892 he was elected professor of natural history at Washburn College, Topeka, Kan., and in 1894 he was called to Union College, Schenectady, N. Y., to organize a department of geology. At Union as previously at Washburn, he was a successful teacher and very active in geological research based upon field studies carried on during the summer vacations. In 1893, 1894, and 1896 he studied the Carboniferous and Permian formations of Kansas, publishing about ten papers on related subjects. From 1895 to 1899 he was assistant geologist on the New York Geological Survey and his work in this connection, together with his earlier studies in that state, resulted in some twenty-five articles, published in the reports of the state geologist, in the *Journal of Geology,* or in the *Bulletin of the Geological Society of America.* In 1898 he became chief of the Appalachian Division of the Maryland Geological Survey, and

contributed to the detailed reports on the Devonian of Maryland. In 1899 he was appointed associate professor of historical geology at Ohio State University and in 1901 was made head of the department, which position he held until his death. From 1900 to 1916 he was a member of the Geological Survey of Ohio and he wrote over a score of papers dealing with the geology of that state.

Prosser's field studies were thorough, his reports were detailed, and his conclusions well founded. His period of scientific productivity extended from 1887 to 1916, and during these thirty years he produced about seventy-five articles and reports dealing with the stratigraphy and paleontology of the Paleozoic formations of New York, Kansas, Maryland, and Ohio. Almost coordinate with his zeal for research was his interest and success in teaching. The thoroughness and honesty of his work, his quiet modesty and reserve, his willingness to give freely of his time and counsel attracted the serious student, and he always had around him a small group of advanced students who counted it a privilege to be permitted to work with him and who were in turn stimulated to take up and carry on research work of their own. He was an original fellow of the Geological Society of America, a fellow of the American Association for the Advancement of Science (vice-president, Section E, 1916), and one of the first initiates of the Society of Sigma Xi. Prosser was drowned at Columbus, Ohio, in September 1916, at the age of fifty-six. On Aug. 28, 1893, he married Mary Frances Wilson of Albany, N. Y., who survived him some ten years.

[G. F. Tuttle, *The Descendants of William and Elizabeth Tuttle* (1883); *A Centennial Biog. Hist. of the City of Columbus and Franklin County* (1901); E. R. Cumings, in *Bull. Geol. Soc. of America,* Mar. 1917, with full bibliography; J. M. Clarke, in *Science,* Oct. 20, 1916; Clara G. Mark, in *Sigma Xi Quarterly,* Dec. 1916; *Who's Who in America,* 1916–17.]   J. E. C.

PROUD, ROBERT (May 10, 1728–July 5, 1813), educator and historian, son of William and Ann Proud, was born in Yorkshire, England, at a farm house called "Low Foxton," about a mile from the small market town of Yarm. Later he moved with his family to a farm called "Wood End," some twenty miles north of York. Even as a boy he showed the love of learning that characterized his long life. When nearly grown, he left home to attend a boarding school kept in a distant part of Yorkshire by David Hall, a preacher in the Society of Friends and a writer of some repute. A friendship developed that was continued during the remain-

der of the master's life by means of "a correspondence in the Latin tongue." In 1750 Proud
went to London, where a distinguished relative,
Dr. John Fothergill, introduced him to Sylvanus
and Timothy Bevan, eminent scientists and
leaders among the Friends. He soon became preceptor to the sons of the last named, a position
which gave him a pleasant home, leisure to improve himself in literature and science, and opportunity for association with men of distinction.
Under the influence of Dr. Fothergill, he even
studied medicine with success.

His future seemed assured, when for some
obscure reason he decided to go to Philadelphia,
where he arrived Jan. 3, 1759. With the kindly
cooperation of James Pemberton [q.v.], he
opened a school for boys; on Sept. 11, 1761, he
became master of the Friends Public School. In
1770 he resigned his position and engaged in an
unsuccessful mercantile venture. During the
Revolution his sympathies were ardently Loyalist; this fact, together with his financial losses,
somewhat soured his disposition toward his
adopted country. Under the circumstances, it is
rather remarkable that he should have undertaken to write a history of Pennsylvania. As
preliminary to this task, he brought together
the finest private collection of source material
ever made for the early history of the state. The
work naturally involved much time and labor.
In 1780 he resumed his former position as master in the Friends School and retained it until
May 31, 1790. Here, at a salary of £250 per
annum, he instructed thirty or forty boys in
mathematics and in ancient languages. He
seems to have held the affection as well as the
respect of his boys, many of whom became men
of standing. When he relinquished his teaching
in order to prepare his history for publication,
he received financial aid for the project from
several former pupils. Though he failed to secure the support he had expected from some of
the Friends, twelve of the most public-spirited
men in Philadelphia each loaned him £50 to meet
the expense of the enterprise. The work appeared in two volumes, 1797–98, under the title
*The History of Pennsylvania, in North America,
from the Original Institution and Settlement of
that Province . . . in 1681, till after the Year
1742.* It included, also, a chapter covering 1760–
1770, and by way of introduction, a life of William Penn. Although lacking in literary style,
the work is valuable, and remained for years the
only history of Pennsylvania. Among its subscribers were Adams, Jefferson, and Cobbett,
but it was a financial failure. Proud's later years
were spent in poverty and seclusion. Occasion-

ally, he made translations from the Latin; more
often he wrote poetry, some of which is good.

In personal appearance "Dominie" Proud was
a striking figure, tall, with a Roman nose and
"most impending brows." Thomson (*post,* 407–
08) says: "I well remember the imposing effect,
which the curled, gray wig, the half-cocked,
patriarchal-looking hat and the long, ivory-
headed cane, had on my boyish imagination. . . .
He was a zealous advocate for useful learning,
a man of regular habits and great temperance,
and in his manners the model of a gentleman."
His portrait, cane, and chair are preserved in
the Historical Society of Pennsylvania. He died
in Philadelphia.

[Proud MSS. and Pemberton MSS. in Hist. Soc. of
Pa.; S. V. Henkels, *Catalogue: The Proud Papers
(Robert Proud, Historian of Pennsylvania) . . . to be
sold . . . May 8, '03* (1903); C. W. Thomson, "Notices
of the Life and Character of Robert Proud," in *Memoirs of the Hist. Soc. of Pa.,* vol. I (1826); J. F. Watson, *Annals of Phila. and Pa.* (2nd ed., 1844); Thomas
Woody, *Early Quaker Education in Pa.* (1920); Robert Proud, *Hist. of Pa., 1681–1770* (2 vols., 1797–98);
Poulson's Am. Daily Advertiser, July 6, 1813, for date
of death.]   A. L. L.

PROUTY, CHARLES AZRO (Oct. 9, 1853–
July 8, 1921), lawyer, member of the Interstate
Commerce Commission, was born at Newport,
Vt., the son of John Azro and Hannah (Lamb)
Prouty, and a descendant of Richard Prouty
who was in Scituate, Mass., as early as 1676.
He was graduated at Dartmouth College with
distinction in 1875. After serving as assistant
to Prof. S. P. Langley [q.v.] at Allegheny Ob-
servatory from 1875 to 1876, he returned to
Newport and became principal of the Newport
Academy. On Mar. 26, 1879, he married Abbie
Davis. He entered the law office of Theophilus
Grout in Newport, and was admitted to the bar
in 1882. He practised in Newport f om 1882 to
1896, serving in the lower house of the state
legislature in 1888. From 1888 to 1896 he was
reporter of the decisions of the supreme court of
Vermont. He acquired a wide reputation as a
pungent and pithy speaker, and as a notably successful practitioner in court and jury cases. An
important part of his practice was representing
railroad interests. In addition to his law work,
he served as president of a trust company in
Newport and as managing head of the local electric works. He had great powers of concentration and mastered the technique of several applied sciences.

In politics he was originally a Republican.
Though unsuccessful in an early attempt (1900)
to become United States senator, he was so outstanding a figure in the public life of his state
that on the resignation of Wheelock G. Veazey

[*q.v.*], of Vermont, from the Interstate Commerce Commission in 1896, he was appointed to that body on Dec. 17 of the same year. By virtue of reappointment in 1901 and 1907, he served continuously until he resigned, Feb. 2, 1914, to take the newly created post of Director of Valuation, which he held until his death, at Newport, seven years later. During American participation in the World War, when the activities of the Valuation Bureau were somewhat in abeyance, he was appointed, February 1918, Director of Public Service and Accounting, in the United States Railroad Administration, a post which he occupied until the return of the railroads to corporate operation, Mar. 1, 1920. He was nominated for the United States Senate in 1914, as coalition candidate of the Progressive and Democratic parties, but failed of election.

While a member of the Commission he strongly supported President Roosevelt's railroad policy, particularly the Hepburn Act of 1906. He energetically organized the Commission's Bureau of Valuation, and was the dominant spirit in determining its activities and shaping its early valuation reports. It is this achievement by which he was most influential in public life. In his *Memorandum upon Final Value* (1920) he gave concise expression to the views he had advocated ever since the submission of the original valuation report on the Texas Midland Railroad (1917). He contended that the "value" required to be found by the Valuation Act was not exchange or condemnation value; that it must primarily proceed from the estimated cost of reproduction less depreciation; and that while neither the franchise, nor the business, nor the strategic position, nor the operating advantage of the carrier was property devoted to the public service and hence could not be included in "value," there must be appropriate additions for appreciation extant on valuation date (provided it had not been previously paid for out of operating expenses), and for "structural going value" inherent in the property itself by reason of its organization and reputation. His views have not been without substantial influence upon the Commission's decisions in valuation matters.

Prouty's individuality was sharply etched on all who came in contact with him. He was frequently testy in manner, peppery in speech, often short tempered, and at times more than caustic. He was witty, a shrewd judge of human nature, charitably disposed to the unfortunate, personally ambitious, but public spirited. Alert of eye, lithe in build, quick in rejoinder, he was a dangerous antagonist in debate. His opinions in the Interstate Commerce Reports are terse and clear. His occasional addresses in public are more casual and less firmly knit. Among them may be mentioned "The Dependence of Agriculture on Transportation," in *Publications of the Michigan Political Science Association* (July 1902); *President Roosevelt's Railroad Policy* (1905), address before the Economic Club of Boston; *A Fundamental Defect in the Act to Regulate Commerce* (1907), American Bar Association, Portland, Me.; "Transportation," in *Every-Day Ethics: Addresses . . . before the . . . Sheffield Scientific School, Yale University* (1910); *Railway Accounting under Federal Control* (1919). At his death he was survived by his widow and two sons.

[Interstate Commerce Commission, office memorandum, entitled "Interstate Commerce Commissioners"; C. H. Pope, *Prouty Geneal.* (1910); W. H. Crockett, *Vermont*, vol. V (1923); *Who's Who in America, 1920–21*; *Burlington Daily Free Press*, July 9, 1921; information from former associates.] W. M. D.

PROVOOST, SAMUEL (Feb. 26, 1742 O.S.– Sept. 6, 1815), first Protestant Episcopal bishop of New York, was born in New York City, the son of John and Eve (Rutgers) Provost. A distant ancestor, William (or Guillaume) Prévost, fled from France to Holland in 1572; his grandson David emigrated to New Netherland in 1624, returned to Holland, married, and came again to New Amsterdam in 1634. Samuel was his great-great-grandson. In Holland the name became Provost; after the Revolution the Bishop adopted the spelling Provoost. A member of the first class graduated by King's College (Columbia) in 1758, Samuel went to England in 1761, entering Peterhouse (St. Peter's College), Cambridge, as a fellow-commoner. While there he determined to take holy orders and was ordained deacon, Feb. 3, 1766, at the Chapel Royal, St. James Palace, Westminster, by the Rt. Rev. Richard Terrick, Bishop of London. On Mar. 25 of the same year he was advanced to the priesthood at King's Chapel, Whitehall, by the Rt. Rev. Edmund Keene, Bishop of Chester, acting for the Bishop of London. Before leaving England he was married in St. Mary's Church, Cambridge, June 8, 1766, to Maria, daughter of Thomas Bousfield of Lakelands, Cork, member of the Irish House of Commons.

Returning to New York, he was appointed an assistant minister of Trinity Church, but as an ardent Whig his sympathy for the cause of the colonists was so marked that it brought him under condemnation by the Loyalist members of the parish, who charged him with "endeavoring to sap the foundations of Christianity." Provoost ascribed this charge to his sermons against evangelical enthusiasm, but politics were at the bottom of it. As a result of the opposition, he resigned, Mar. 21, 1771, retiring to East Camp, Dutchess County, N. Y., where he remained in straitened circumstances until 1784. During this period he was elected chaplain of the New York state convention which drafted the first constitution of the state, but did not accept. He also refused a call to the rectorship of St. Michael's Church, Charleston, S. C., and another to King's Chapel, Boston. In 1784 he accepted an invitation to officiate at St. Paul's and St. George's chapels, of Trinity Parish, New York, Trinity Church having been burned by the British. This invitation was extended by the patriotic vestry of Trinity, following the evacuation of the city by the British, in recognition of Provoost's loyalty to the American cause. In the same year he was appointed regent of the University of the State of New York, and in the following year, chaplain of the Continental Congress.

Having been elected first bishop of New York, he sailed for England with William White (who had been elected first bishop of Pennsylvania) for consecration. His election and the signing of the testimonials at the convention in Wilmington, Del., Oct. 10, 1786, followed assurance by the Archbishops of Canterbury and York that such consecration could be undertaken under a special act of Parliament, passed in 1786, authorizing the consecration of American bishops without their taking the oath of allegiance to Great Britain. The negotiations leading to the passage of this act had been carried on by John Adams, American minister at the Court of St. James's. Provoost and White were consecrated in the chapel of Lambeth Palace, Feb. 4, 1787, by the Most Rev. John Moore, Archbishop of Canterbury, assisted by the Most Rev. William Markham, Archbishop of York, the Rt. Rev. Charles Moss, Bishop of Bath and Wells, and the Rt. Rev. John Hinchcliffe, Bishop of Peterborough. The return passage to New York occupied a period of seven weeks. Provoost was formally received as Bishop of New York at a convention at St. Paul's Chapel in June 1787. His first ordination and confirmation service was held at St. Paul's in September of the same year, when over 300 people were confirmed. He officiated at the first confirmation service ever held in New Jersey, at St. Peter's Church, Perth Amboy, July 9, 1788. Provoost conducted the service held at St. Paul's Chapel, Apr. 30, 1789, following Washington's inauguration, which was attended by the President, his staff, and all the leading officials of the new government. On this occasion he read prayers from the "Proposed Book," no prayer book having yet been officially

adopted by the Episcopal Church. In the same year he became chaplain of the United States Senate. He officiated also at the memorial service for Washington held at St. Paul's, Dec. 31, 1799. Provoost was chairman of the committee which drafted the constitution of the Church and was responsible for the necessary changes in the Prayer Book, following the establishment of the Church as an American entity. In 1801 he offered his resignation as bishop, his health having become impaired by grief over the death of his wife (1799) and the suicide of his youngest son. The House of Bishops refused to accept it, but consented to the consecration of a bishop coadjutor. Thereafter, Provoost appeared in public only once, at the consecration of Bishop Griswold and Bishop Hobart, May 29, 1811. He died in his seventy-fourth year, survived by two daughters and a son, and was buried in the family vault in Trinity churchyard. He was proficient in the German, French, Hebrew, and Latin languages; while at Cambridge he made a poetical version of Tasso. He was also a gifted botanist and made an elaborate index of Johann Bauhin's *Historia Plantarum Universalis* (3 vols., 1650–51). He published nothing.

[A. J. Provost, *Biog. and Geneal. Notes of the Provost Family from 1545 to 1895* (1895); E. R. Purple, *Geneal. Notes of the Provoost Family of N. Y.* (1875); J. G. Wilson, "Samuel Provoost, First Bishop of New York," in *N. Y. Geneal. and Biog. Record*, Jan. 1887; H. G. Batterson, *A Sketch-Book of Am. Episcopate* (1878); W. S. Perry, *The Bishops of the Am. Church* (1897); J. N. Norton, *Life of Bishop Provoost of N. Y.* (1859); Morgan Dix, *A Hist. of the Parish of Trinity Church in the City of N. Y.* (4 vols., 1898–1906); W. B. Sprague, *Annals Am. Pulpit*, vol. V (1859); *Jour. of the Convention of the Diocese of N. Y.* (1844); E. C. Chorley, "Samuel Provoost, First Bishop of New York," in *Hist. Mag. of the Protestant Episcopal Church*, June, Sept. 1933; *N. Y. Evening Post*, Sept. 6, 11, 1815.]   G. E. S.

PROVOST, ETIENNE (c. 1782–July 3, 1850), hunter, boatman, guide, was born in Canada, the son of Albert and Marianne (Menard) Provost. There appears to be no trace of his early life. While generally known as a "free trapper," he was at times connected with William Ashley and the Western Department of the American Fur Company. In 1823 he journeyed from St. Louis to the Green (Colorado) River. He is supposed to have been the first white man to visit the Great Salt Lake. It is also possible that in the same year he discovered the South Pass in the Rocky Mountains, supposing that the Astorians missed the pass proper on their return in 1813. In 1825 he had a trading post in the Rocky Mountains with Sublette. He was in the service of Ashley from 1822 until 1826, when the latter sold out to Smith, Jackson, and Sublette, and at that time the two men had some disagreement.

Provost tried to organize a rival expedition through negotiations with Bernard Pratte & Company. Ashley followed him to St. Louis, arriving Sept. 9, 1826, and offered Bernard Pratte & Company a share in his 1827 expedition. They accepted and abandoned the Provost project.

In the fall of 1828, Provost was sent by Kenneth Mackenzie to search for trappers of the American Fur Company. If there was ever a difficult job to be done, Provost was usually chosen to carry it through. In 1830 he was one of the hunters at Fort Union, and in 1831 was listed as a boatman on the roll of the American Fur Company. In 1834 he guided Fontenelle and Drips to Bayou Salado (South Park, Colo.). In the spring of that year he led a party for the American Fur Company and was at Ham's Fork on the Colorado in July 1834. In 1843 Provost served as guide for Audubon in his expedition into the upper Western country and is frequently mentioned in the latter's journals. Provost was married in St. Louis, on Aug. 14, 1829, to Marie Rose Sallé *dit* Lajoie, daughter of Lambert and Madeleine (Delor) Sallé *dit* Lajoie; one child, Marie, lived to majority. His last trip to the mountains was probably in 1847, after which he settled down in St. Louis. His will, probated on July 24, 1850, gave all his property to his wife, including lands in Iowa Territory and St. Louis. A city, river, and valley in Utah have been named for Provost, the name being abbreviated to Provo. South Dakota also has a town of that name. Etienne Provost is not to be confused with Jean Baptist Provost, also conspicuous in the fur trade.

[Wm. R. Harris, *The Cath. Ch. in Utah* (1909); H. M. Chittenden, *The Am. Fur Trade of the Far West* (1902), vol. I; H. C. Dale, *The Ashley-Smith Explorations* (1918); Maria R. Audubon, *Audubon and His Journals* (2 vols., 1897); St. Louis Cathedral (old) church registers; St. Louis Probate Court records; Pierre Chouteau, Jr., and Company account books, Mo. Hist. Soc.; *Mo. Republican*, Aug. 26, 1834; *Daily Mo. Republican*, July 4, 1850.]
                S. M. D.

PROVOSTY, OLIVIER OTIS (Aug. 3, 1852–Aug. 3, 1924), Louisiana jurist, was born in Pointe Coupée Parish. He was the son of Auguste and Eliska (Labry) Provosty, members of prominent Creole families. His paternal grandfather, also named Auguste, emigrated from Nantes, France, in 1815, and settled in New Orleans; his father served in the Louisiana legislature and was one of the original signers of the secession ordinance adopted by the state at the opening of the Civil War. The son spent his youth in his native parish, receiving his early education at home from private tutors, and at Poydras Academy, New Roads, Pointe Coupée

Parish. After graduating from the academy he attended Georgetown University, Washington, D. C., for a time, but the death of his father compelled him to leave before graduation. Returning to Louisiana, he studied law in the offices of two New Orleans attorneys and attended for a time the law department of the University of Louisiana (now Tulane University). On Jan. 14, 1873, he was admitted to the Louisiana bar. From 1873 to 1876 he was district attorney for the parishes of Pointe Coupée, Avoyelles, and West Feliciana. In December 1876 he was married to Euphemie Labatut, of Pointe Coupée Parish.

In 1888 Provosty was elected to the state Senate. He served through 1890 and as senator drafted and procured the adoption of the statute creating the Atchafalaya Basin Levee District, said to have been the model for the organic law of the numerous levee districts subsequently created. He also drafted and unsuccessfully advocated the adoption of a bill to put an end to the convict lease system in the state, later adopted with very little change, and he was conspicuous in the fight to prevent the recharter of the Louisiana Lottery. He was an active member of the Louisiana constitutional convention of 1898. From 1898 to 1901 he was referee in bankruptcy for the Baton Rouge division of the eastern district of Louisiana, and in 1904 he was appointed chairman of the Torrens Land Law Commission. For a number of years he was legal advisor to the Pointe Coupée police jury. In April 1901 he was appointed an associate justice of the Louisiana supreme court by Gov. W. W. Heard, and seven years later, in 1908, he was elected to succeed himself. In 1912 he was made a member of the Louisiana Tax Commission. In January 1922 he was elevated to the office of chief justice of the supreme court of Louisiana, but after holding the position for one year he voluntarily retired from public life. His decisions as a judge, while uneven, maintained a high average. Provosty was studious by nature, and extremely well read in both English and French literature. He delighted in social life and was a member of several clubs and fraternal organizations. He was also very fond of golf and other outdoor sports. In religion he was a Roman Catholic. He died in New Orleans upon the seventy-second anniversary of his birth.

[Sources include: "In Memoriam: Olivier O. Provosty," 156 *La. Reports*; H. E. Chambers, *A Hist. of La.*, vol. III (1925); "Olivier O. Provosty," *La. Hist. Quart.*, Apr. 1923; *New Orleans States, Times-Picayune* (New Orleans), Aug. 4, 1924; *New Orleans Item*, Aug. 4, 6, 1924. Information as to certain facts was supplied for this sketch by Provosty's son, Mr. Michel Provosty.]
                M. J. W.

PRUDDEN, THEOPHIL MITCHELL (July 7, 1849–Apr. 10, 1924), pathologist, bacteriologist, was born in Middlebury, Conn., the son of George Peter and Eliza Anne (Johnson) Prudden. His father was a Congregational clergyman, graduate of Yale College in 1835, and a direct descendant of the Rev. Peter Prudden, one of the founders of the New Haven colony in 1638. The boy's early days were spent between the three Connecticut parsonages of Middleton, Southbury, and Watertown. Books were always available and he made the most of his opportunities, but he was a rather frail child and his early schooling was somewhat desultory. He prepared for Yale College at the Wilbraham (Mass.) Academy and entered the Sheffield Scientific School under a state fellowship with free tuition. He was graduated in 1872 with honors. A course in drawing attracted his interest, and the results are evident in the numerous admirable sketches which adorn his publications. His work in zoölogy under Professors Addison Emery Verrill [q.v.] and Sidney Smith laid the foundation of that broad point of view which was revealed later in his work on human pathology. He was an instructor in the Sheffield Scientific School at Yale from 1872 to 1874 and, in the meantime, studied in the Medical School. In 1873 he accompanied Prof. Othniel Charles Marsh [q.v.] on one of his expeditions, searching for fossils among the sand mounds of Nebraska. Prudden wrote an account of this for the *New York Tribune,* the first of many contributions to the newspaper press. In 1875 he came to New York and there met Prof. Francis Delafield [q.v.] and worked in the latter's laboratory. Thus began a scientific partnership which was to last until Delafield's retirement.

After graduating from the Yale Medical School in 1875, he was an intern in a New Haven hospital for a year and then went abroad to study in Heidelberg, Vienna, and Berlin, particularly under Julius Arnold and Rudolf Virchow. Upon his return he taught histology and pathology at the College of Physicians and Surgeons in New York, attracting to his wretched laboratory of those days a group of men who have since become famous. The time was one of important scientific development. Robert Koch had just published his monograph on the tubercle bacillus. Von Behring and Roux had discovered diphtheria antitoxin. Prudden's knowledge of bacteriology enabled him to comprehend the importance of these discoveries and he was the first to make diphtheria antitoxin in the United States, the serum being used to check an epidemic of diphtheria in the city of New York.

For years he was confidential advisor to Hermann Michael Biggs [q.v.], the director of the diagnostic laboratory of the health department of New York City. In order to familiarize himself first-hand with Koch's work he went to Germany in 1885 and there worked under Koch and F. A. T. Hueppe. During this period he made a number of studies of the changes produced in animal tissues by the injection of dead tubercle bacilli, of the organisms which cause malignant heart disease, and of those which cause pneumonia and pleurisy. More than eighty papers of his own and eleven substantial volumes of reprints represent the work of himself and his associates during these active years. Some of his more important works are: "Beobachtungen am lebenden Knorpel," *Archiv für Pathologische Anatomie und Physiologie,* vol. LXXV (1879); "On the Occurrence of the Bacillus Tuberculosis in Tuberculosis Lesions," *Medical Record,* N. Y., Apr. 14, 1883; "On Bacteria on Ice," *Ibid.,* Mar. 26, Apr. 2, 1887; "On the Etiology of Diphtheria," *American Journal of Medical Sciences,* April and May 1889 (also a second series on the same subject in the *Medical Record,* Apr. 18, 1891); "Studies on the Action of Dead Bacteria in the Living Body" (with Eugene Hodenpyl), *New York Medical Journal,* June 6, 1891.

Prudden was a splendid teacher, a lucid speaker, for a long time the central figure in the scientific medical life of New York City. He joined Francis Delafield in the writing of the great standard textbook of pathology, *Hand-book of Pathological Anatomy and Histology,* which was published in 1885 as a revised edition of Delafield's *Handbook of Post Mortem Examinations and of Morbid Anatomy* (1872), and which, after many revisions, is still widely used in medical schools and affectionately known in student vernacular as "D. & P." In 1901 he became a member of the Board of Scientific Directors of the Rockefeller Institute, and in 1921, a member of the International Health Board of the Rockefeller Foundation. He was consulting pathologist to the Board of Health of New York City, and a member of the Public Health Council of the State of New York. In 1901, he was elected to membership in the National Academy of Sciences. About 1895 he began to spend his summer holidays in the desert region of the southwest where he studied the remains of the prehistoric inhabitants, and prepared a succession of articles on the cliff-dwellers. The results of his explorations were finally compressed into a book *"On The Great American Plateau,"* published in 1906. His wide knowledge of geology made him very competent to study the country topography of the West. He excavated ruins, corrected government maps, and made a remarkable collection of materials from the cliff-dwellings which he bequeathed to the Yale museum. As his strength failed he gave up the long and difficult exploring trips and spent his summer holidays on the rim of the Grand Canyon.

[*Who's Who in America,* 1922–23 ; Ludvig Hektoen, "Biog. Memoir of T. M. Prudden," *Natl. Acad. of Sci., Biog. Memoirs,* vol. XII (1928) ; L. E. Prudden, *Biog. Sketches and Letters of T. M. Prudden, M.D.* (1927), and *Peter Prudden, . . . with The Geneal. of Some of His Descendants* (1901) ; *N. Y. Times,* Apr. 11, 1924.]

F. C. W.

PRUD'HOMME, JOHN FRANCIS EUGENE (Oct. 4, 1800–June 27, 1892), engraver, was born on the island of St. Thomas, West Indies, of French parents. The family came to the United States in 1807 and settled in New York City. About 1814 the boy John Francis was apprenticed to his brother-in-law, Thomas Gimbrede, to learn the art of engraving. Gimbrede was later a teacher of drawing at West Point and was considered an art connoisseur. By the time he was twenty-one, Prud'homme was signing engravings of his own. His first work was as a portrait engraver, in the stipple manner, but to extend his market he was soon doing general illustrative engravings. In 1831 when James Herring started *The National Portrait Gallery of Distinguished Americans,* Prud'homme engraved a number of plates for the work. Some of his best engravings were done for annuals and other books during the period 1839–52. Catalogues of engravings of his period list numerous plates by him, among them portraits of Philander Chase, Fisher Ames, Fredrika Bremer, Henry Clay, DeWitt Clinton, Oliver Cromwell, Stephen Decatur, Alexander Hamilton, Andrew Jackson, John Paul Jones, from a miniature in the possession of the Naval Lyceum, Brooklyn, N. Y., Dolly Madison, Horatio Nelson, and George Washington. He also engraved the title-page and frontispiece for Maria Edgeworth's *Novels and Tales* (2 vols., 1832) ; "New York City Hall," from a work by Richard Wilcox, representing the celebration of the Grand Canal, Nov. 4, 1825; "St. Patrick's Cathedral," New York, designed also by Prud'homme, as an advertisement for the Douai Bible; "The Declaration of Independence," from the work of John Trumbull, engraved for the *New York Mirror*; and "Trinity Church" and "Christ Church," New York.

From 1834 to 1853 Prud'homme was curator of the National Academy of Design and was for a time instructor in a life class there. From 1852 to 1869 he was employed by a banknote engraving firm in New York as designer and engraver of decorative work. In 1869 he went to the bureau of engraving and printing in Washington as a designer of the ornamentation of bank notes and securities and remained there until he resigned in 1885. He was considered excellent both as a draftsman and as an engraver. After some years of failing health, he died at his home in Georgetown, D. C., survived by one daughter

[Mantle Fielding, *Am. Engravers upon Copper and Steel* (1917) ; D. McN. Stauffer, *Am. Engravers upon Copper and Steel* (1907), vol. I, p. 215, vol. II, pp. 423–33; W. S. Baker, *Am. Engravers and their Works* (1875) ; Wm. Dunlap, *A Hist. of the Rise and Progress of the Arts of Design in the U. S.* (revised ed., 1918), vol. III ; *Evening Star* (Washington), June 28, 1892.]

S. G. B.

PRUYN, JOHN VAN SCHAICK LANSING (June 22, 1811–Nov. 21, 1877), lawyer, was born at Albany, N. Y., the son of David and Hybertje (Lansing) Pruyn, and a descendant of Francis Pruyn, called Frans Jansen, who settled in Albany as early as 1665. Educated in private schools and graduated from the Albany Academy in 1826, he studied law in the office of James King. He was admitted to the bar in 1831, appointed an examiner in chancery in 1833, and a master in 1836. For the next ten years his practice of law was principally in the court of chancery, and it is said that Chancellor Reuben H. Walworth [*q.v.*] never overruled any of his reports. In 1848 he was admitted to practice as an attorney and counselor in the United States Supreme Court. From 1835 to 1838 and from 1843 to 1845 he was a director of the Mohawk & Hudson Railroad Company; in 1843 he was appointed attorney and counsel. He was also connected with other railroads. When in 1853 ten companies united to form a new corporation called the New York Central Railroad, Pruyn drew up the consolidation agreement, which was considered a remarkable instrument, and withdrew from the practice of the law to become secretary, treasurer, and general counsel of the company. He was counsel for the Hudson River Bridge Company, and in its behalf made the final argument before the United States Supreme Court of a case decided (1864) in its favor, which ended long controversies in different parts of the country as to the right to bridge navigable streams (66 *U. S.,* 582; 69 *U. S.,* 403). Directly or indirectly Pruyn was connected with many of the leading financial and railroad enterprises in the United States. He was a trustee of the Mutual Life Insurance Company from its foundation and a director in the Union Trust Company of New York.

In 1861 he was elected a state senator, accepting the nomination on condition that no money should be used for the election. At the end of his term (1862–63), he distributed his salary among the poor of Albany. He represented the Albany district in Congress from Dec. 7, 1863, to Mar. 3, 1865, and from Mar. 4, 1867, to Mar. 3, 1869. Here he served on a number of important committees and in the Thirty-eighth Congress was unanimously elected by the Democratic members from New York to present on their behalf to the House of Representatives a resolution of censure of the executive authority for closing the offices and suspending publication of the New York *World* and *Journal of Commerce*. When Grant was first elected president of the United States, Pruyn was one of the tellers of the House of Representatives and made suggestions as to laws that would remedy the difficulties then existing in counting the presidential vote, but the House refused to entertain them.

In May 1844 Pruyn was appointed a regent of the University of the State of New York, and in 1862 he was elected chancellor. This office he held until his death. He was a member of the executive committee of the state normal school in Albany, and was president of the board of trustees of St. Stephen's College, Annandale, N. Y., a training school of the Protestant Episcopal church. It was upon the recommendation of Pruyn that in 1866 Governor Fenton established the state commission of charities. From its organization until the time of his death Pruyn was president of the commission. He was a member of many historical and scientific societies, a member of the Association for the Codification of the Law of Nations, and at his death, president of the board of the state survey. At one time he was a regent of the Smithsonian Institution. He was always actively interested in church affairs and was a vestryman of St. Peter's Protestant Episcopal Church, Albany. On Oct. 22, 1840, he married Harriet Corning, daughter of Thomas and Mary Ruggles (Weld) Turner; she died on Mar. 22, 1859, and on Sept. 7, 1865, he married Anna Fenn, daughter of Hon. Amasa Junius and Harriet Langdon (Roberts) Parker of Albany. Pruyn's death occurred at Clifton Springs, N. Y.

[*N. Y. Geneal. and Biog. Record*, Apr. 1883; P. A. Chadbourne, *Public Service of the State of N. Y.*, vol. III (1882); C. E. Fitch, *Memorial Encyc. of the State of N. Y.*, vol. II (1916); F. W. Stevens, *The Beginning of the N. Y. Central Railroad* (1926); *Biog. Dir. Am. Cong.* (1928); W. H. Barnes, *The Fortieth Cong. of the U. S.*, vol. II (1870); Univ. of the State of N. Y., *Ninety-first Ann. Report of the Regents of the Univ.* (1878); *Daily Press and Albany Knickerbocker*, Nov. 22, 1877.]   J. S—n.

PRUYN, ROBERT HEWSON (Feb. 14, 1815–Feb. 26, 1882), lawyer, legislator, diplomat, the son of Casparus F. and Anne (Hewson) Pruyn, was born at Albany, N. Y. His father traced descent from a Flemish immigrant, Frans Jansen Pruyn (or Pruen), who was in Albany as early as 1665. Robert attended Albany Academy and Rutgers College (A.B. 1833, A.M. 1836), and studied law in the office of Abraham van Vechten of Albany. Upon admission to the bar in 1836, he was appointed attorney and counsel to the city corporation. He became a member of the municipal council in 1839 and, two years later, judge advocate-general of the state forces, which office he held for five years. On Nov. 9, 1841, he married Jane Anne, daughter of Gerrit Y. and Helen (Ten Eyck) Lansing of Albany, by whom he had two sons. He was a member of the state assembly, 1848–50, failing narrowly of election in the last year as Whig candidate for the speakership. In 1851 he was reappointed judge advocate-general; in 1854 he was returned to the assembly and elected speaker. For the next two years (1855–57) he was adjutant general. Having followed Seward into the Republican party, he ran, as candidate for the assembly in 1860, well ahead of Lincoln in his district, but was defeated by a small margin.

He was commissioned, Oct. 12, 1861, minister resident in Japan as successor to Townsend Harris [*q.v.*]. On his arrival at Yedo (Tokio), Apr. 25, 1862, he stepped into a delicate situation. The international position of his government and its power to afford him armed support were diminished by the Civil War, the anti-foreign element in Japan was prevailing over the efforts of the Shogunate to carry out the terms of the treaties, and murders of foreigners were of frequent occurrence. Pruyn's good offices at a critical moment in the spring of 1862 were instrumental in restraining the European ministers from hasty action in enforcing indemnity claims, which would have weakened the Shogun's position, and in persuading the Japanese to assume payment (*Papers Relating to Foreign Affairs*, 1863, pp. 993–1032). When the indemnity settlement, on June 24, 1863, was accompanied by communication of the Mikado's orders for expulsion of foreigners, Pruyn advised a joint naval demonstration (*Ibid.*, 1863, pp. 1032–36); and when an American ship was fired on near the Straits of Shimonoseki, he authorized the destruction, by the warship *Wyoming*, of the offending vessels belonging to the local prince (*Ibid.*, 1863, pp. 1040–45). His firm stand, together with that of the European representatives, for maintenance of the treaties strengthened the Shogunate and brought about the recall of the expulsion orders Nov. 11, 1863, (*Ibid.*, 1864, pt. III, p. 457). He concluded, Jan. 28, 1864, a convention reducing the tariff on American manufactured goods from twenty per cent. to five, consenting in return to a postponement of the opening of new ports (*Ibid.*, 1864, pt. III, pp. 479–84). He had the American flag carried by an armed chartered steamer in a joint attack on the Straits of Shimonoseki in September 1864, which broke the power of one of the leading opponents of foreign penetration (*Ibid.*, 1864, pt. III, pp. 543–57).

Following his return home on leave, in the spring of 1865, Pruyn resigned his post. Illness forced him to withdraw his candidacy for the lieutenant-governorship of New York in the next year. He presided, in 1872, over the commission to draft amendments to the state constitution for submission to popular vote. In his last years he was president of the Albany National Commercial Bank and served on the boards of several financial and educational institutions.

[J. V. L. Pruyn, "The Pruyn Family," in *N. Y. Geneal. and Biog. Record*, Jan., Apr., Oct. 1882; F. A. Virkus, *The Abridged Compendium of American Geneal.*, vol. I (1925); *Papers Relating to Foreign Affairs, 1862–65*; P. J. Treat, *Japan and the U. S. 1853–1921* (1928); Tyler Dennett, *Americans in Eastern Asia* (1922); F. E. Ross, *The Am. Naval Attack on Shimonoseki in 1863*, reprinted from *Chinese Social and Pol. Sci. Rev.*, Apr. 1934; *Albany Argus* and *Albany Evening Jour.*, Feb. 27, 1882.]   J. V. F.

PRYBER, CHRISTIAN [See PRIBER, CHRISTIAN, fl. 1734–1744].

PRYOR, NATHANIEL (c. 1775–June 10, 1831), sergeant in the Lewis and Clark expedition, soldier, trader and Indian agent, was born probably in Amherst County, Va. Through his mother, a daughter of William Floyd and Abadiah Davis, he traced his descent from Nicketti, a sister of Pocahontas, but his Pryor ancestry is untraceable. As a youth he moved to Kentucky, probably with the family of Charles Floyd, his uncle. At Louisville, Oct. 20, 1803, he enlisted with the Lewis and Clark expedition, and on Apr. 1 following, at the Wood River camp, was made a sergeant. His faithful services during the expedition are copiously recorded in the journals of Lewis and Clark.

He entered the regular army, Feb. 27, 1807, as an ensign in the 1st Infantry. In the same year he led an expedition to return the Mandan chief, Shehaka, but was attacked by the Arikaras, Sept. 9, and though maintaining a brave and skilful defense was driven back with loss. On Apr. 1, 1810, he resigned from the army and

later started a trading post near the present Galena, Ill. The Winnebagos attacked him on New Year's day, 1812, and he lost all his property and barely escaped with his life. On Aug. 30, 1813, as a first lieutenant of the 44th Infantry, he reëntered the army; on Oct. 1, 1814, he became a captain, and later served with distinction in the battle of New Orleans. "A braver man," wrote Gen. Sam Houston to President Jackson some years afterward, "never fought under the wings of your eagles" (*American Historical Review*, January 1919, p. 262). On June 15, 1815, he was honorably discharged. With a partner he started a trading house at Arkansas Post, Ark., but in 1819 moved upstream to the Verdigris, where he established another post. He married an Osage woman and after 1820 lived with the tribe. In ill health, poor, and unable to collect a claim against the Government, he had a hard struggle for a livelihood. On May 7, 1831, he was formally appointed a sub-agent of the Osages, a place he had temporarily held twice before, but died at the agency about a month later.

Pryor, though widely noted in the life and records of his time, had passed into almost complete oblivion within two generations of his death. When Elliott Coues [*q.v.*], in 1893, published his edition of the journals of Lewis and Clark, he was unable to add a single fact regarding Pryor's career. Two years later, however, he was himself to discover the records of the Shehaka expedition, and since then much biographical material has come to light. Pryor was in many respects unfortunate, and he seems to have been fated to experience the constant "impact of disaster." He won and retained, however, the high regard of all who knew him, and perhaps no character of the early frontier has drawn so many warm tributes to his worth as a soldier and a man. A number of writers have confused him with the Nathaniel Pryor (possibly a nephew) of Fowler's and Pattie's expeditions.

[Thomas James, *Three Years Among the Indians and Mexicans* (1916), ed. by W. B. Douglas; Grant Foreman, *Pioneer Days in the Early Southwest* (1926); "Old Fort Madison," *Iowa Journal of Hist. and Politics*, Oct. 1913; documents relating to Pryor in *Am. Hist. Rev.*, Jan. 1919; Pryor's account of Shehaka expedition in *Annals of Iowa*, Jan. 1895; manuscript notes from Miss Stella M. Drumm, of the Mo. Hist. Soc.]   W. J. G.

PRYOR, ROGER ATKINSON (July 19, 1828–Mar. 14, 1919), congressman, Confederate soldier, jurist, was the son of Theodorick Bland Pryor, a descendant of the Blands and Randolphs of Virginia, and of Lucy Eppes (Atkinson). He was born near Petersburg, in Dinwiddie County, Va., but after his mother's death before he was two years old, he spent his early years at the "Old Place" in Nottoway County, where his father, earlier a distinguished lawyer, was now pastor of the Presbyterian church. He attended the old-field schools of the county and later the Classical Academy at Petersburg. In 1843 he entered Hampden-Sidney College with advanced standing and was graduated in 1845 as valedictorian of his class and with a reputation for wide reading and convincing oratory. He studied law at the University of Virginia (1846–47) and married, on Nov. 8, 1848, Sara A. Rice, later the author of *Reminiscences of Peace and War* (1904) and other works.

Admitted to the bar in 1849, he practised law for a short time at Charlottesville, Va., and at Petersburg, and that year founded and edited for a time the *Southside Democrat* at Petersburg. In 1851–52 he was associated with John W. Forney [*q.v.*] on the Washington *Union*. In July 1855 he was sent to Athens as a special commissioner to investigate the claims of an American citizen against Greece and secured a satisfactory indemnity (H. M. Wriston, *Executive Agents in American Foreign Relations,* 1929, p. 663). In 1853 he had become associated with Thomas Ritchie [*q.v.*] in editing the *Richmond Enquirer,* and his courageous and combative editorials involved him in several duels from which he came unhurt. In the campaign against the Know-Nothing party in 1855, Pryor spoke ably, and he deserves considerable credit for the victory of Gov. Henry A. Wise. He founded *The South* in 1857 as an ultra-Southern newspaper published in Washington and was also associated during the same period with the staff of the Washington *States.*

He attended the Montgomery commercial convention of 1858 and delivered the reply of the border states and the conservative element in the South which led to the defeat of William L. Yancey's resolution demanding the reopening of the slave trade (Herbert Wender, *Southern Commercial Conventions, 1837–1859,* 1930, pp. 214–23). He was elected in 1859 to the Thirty-sixth Congress to succeed William O. Goode, deceased, and reëlected in 1860, serving till he resigned Mar. 3, 1861, to join the Confederacy. In the presidential campaign of 1860 he was a strong supporter of Breckinridge, and was considered the most effective secessionist speaker in Virginia. Incidents are told of his having changed the sentiments of whole communities by one speech.

He was one of the visiting Virginians who urged the attack on Fort Sumter and is said to have used as an argument: "Strike one blow and Virginia will secede in an hour by Shrewsbury clock" (*New York Times,* Mar. 15, 1919). He was offered the honor of firing the first shot but declined in favor of Edmund Ruffin. He was elected to the Confederate Provisional Congress and served a short time, but soon resigned to enter military service as colonel of the 3rd Virginia Regiment. On Apr. 16, 1862, he was promoted brigadier-general by Joseph E. Johnston for gallantry on the battlefield, but, impatient with the Confederate War Department, which he thought was leaving him a brigadier without a brigade, he resigned his rank and fought as a private in Fitzhugh Lee's cavalry. While serving as a special courier around Petersburg he was captured during an informal truce, Nov. 27, 1864, and was confined in Fort Lafayette. He was released for exchange by Lincoln's personal order a short time before the surrender at Appomattox.

In September 1865, with borrowed money and clothing bought by pawning his wife's jewelry, he went to New York and became associated with the New York *Daily News.* Writing *incognito* for political reasons and studying New York state law in spare moments, he was admitted to the New York bar in 1866 and was successful in both fields. In 1890 he was appointed by Gov. David B. Hill judge of the court of common pleas, largely through the influence of his old war enemy and congressional associate, Gen. Daniel E. Sickles. In 1896 he became for the remainder of an unexpired term a justice of the supreme court of New York (*Manual of the State of New York, 1898,* p. 529), and was later elected at the head of the ticket. In 1899 he resigned from the court on reaching the age limit and resumed his private practice. Appointed official referee by the appellate division of the supreme court, Apr. 10, 1912, he served till his death in New York City, March 14, 1919. He was buried in Princeton, N. J. He had seven children.

Pryor was tall and straight, with the elastic step of an Indian. As an orator he was fiery, impassioned, and convincing; as a judge he was clear and searching and had a reputation for unusual chivalry toward litigants. He published *Essays and Addresses* in 1912.

[In addition to the brief sketches in the *Biog. Directory of the Am. Congress, 1774–1927* (1928), and *Who's Who in Am.,* 1918–19, there is a factual summary in C. A. Evans, ed., *Confed. Mil. Hist.,* III (1899). A fuller sketch, frankly laudatory but accurate, is by T. T. Epes in the Hampden-Sidney *Kaleidoscope,* vol. XI (1903). Genealogical sources are T. D. Suplée, *The Life of Theodorick Bland Pryor* (1879); J. H. Claiborne, *Seventy-five Years in Old Virginia* (1904). His capture is described in R. A. Pryor, Jr.,

The Capture of Gen. Roger A. Pryor (1889). A character sketch on his eightieth birthday was published in the N. Y. Times, July 19, 1908. The N. Y. Times, and Richmond Times-Dispatch, of Mar. 15, 1919, and other papers, contained obituary sketches. See also Sara A. R. Pryor, Reminiscences of Peace and War (1904), and My Day (1909).]
                      J. E. W.

PUGET, PETER RICHINGS [See RICHINGS, PETER, 1797–1871].

PUGH, ELLIS (June 1656–Oct. 3, 1718), Quaker preacher and writer, was born in the parish of Dolgelley, Merionethshire, North Wales. His father died before his birth and his mother a few days after it. When he was eighteen, he was "reached through the testimony of John ap John," who, before his convincement by George Fox, had been one of the congregation of Morgan Lloyd at Wrexham. Six years later Pugh began to preach, although he continued to follow his trade of stone-mason. By 1686 the persecution of the Quakers had become so severe in the neighborhood that he and his family resolved to emigrate in the party of Rowland Ellis of Bryn Mawr. While waiting for a ship he fell ill and at this time the Lord revealed to him that there was yet work for him to do in Wales and that he must return there again. The party was on the sea all the winter; in January 1687 they arrived in Barbados, and the following summer in Philadelphia. Here Pugh continued to preach and to work at his trade; in 1706 he went back to Wales in obedience to the vision he had had before he sailed, but after two years he returned to his family in America.

During his last illness when he was not well able to follow his calling, he wrote *Annerch ir Cymru* addressed to "poor, unlearned, people such as artisans, laborers, and shepherds, men of low degree like myself," in order "to call them from the many things to the one thing needful for the saving of their souls." This he left to the Gwynedd (Pa.) Meeting with the request that it be printed and circulated in Wales. A committee having examined and approved the book, it was printed in 1721 by Andrew Bradford of Philadelphia. This is the first book in Welsh known to have been printed in America. An English translation by Rowland Ellis, corrected by David Lloyd [q.v.], was published in Philadelphia in 1727 under the title *A Salutation to the Britains*. The work enjoyed sufficient popularity to call for two more editions of each version, all printed in London. According to the testimony of those who knew him best, Pugh was honest and careful in his calling, of a meek and quiet spirit, considerate and solid in his judgment, of few words, and his inclina-tion was to support love and unity amongst all. Notwithstanding he was not one of the wise in this world nor had human learning, he was made a profitable instrument to turn divers from vanity and to exhort and strengthen many in their spiritual journey in his native land and in this country where he finished his course.

[Memoir prefixed to Annerch ir Cymru; James Jones, "Dolgellau, Ellis Pugh, y Crynwr, a rhai o'u Syniadau," in Y Beirniad (Llanelly, Wales) for Jan. 1864; T. M. Rees, A Hist. of the Quakers in Wales and Their Emigration to North America (1925); C. H. Browning, Welsh Settlement of Pa. (1912); William Rowlands, Llyfryddiaeth y Cymry (1869), enlarged and ed. by D. S. Evans; A Coll. of Memorials Concerning Divers Deceased Ministers and Others of the People Called Quakers (1787).]
                     J. J. P.

PUGH, EVAN (Feb. 29, 1828–Apr. 29, 1864), chemist, college president, was of Welsh Quaker stock, five generations removed from one of the earliest settlers of Chester County, Pa., John Pugh (d. 1760), ancestor of both Lewis Pugh and Mary (Hutton), Evan's parents. Born at Jordan Bank, East Nottingham township, he was reared on his father's farm with all the usual accompaniments of hard work and scanty educational facilities. At sixteen he was apprenticed to a blacksmith, but at nineteen, ambitious for an education, he was released from his obligations and allowed his time. After a year of study in the manual training school at Whitestown, N. Y., and two years of teaching in a private school for boys at Oxford, Pa., he was off, with what seems the meagerest of preparation, for advanced study in Europe. So thoroughly had he applied himself in every leisure moment, however, that in the fall of 1853 he was able to matriculate in the University of Leipzig for the advanced course in chemistry and mathematics. After a year and a half here he went to the University of Göttingen for study under the direction of the celebrated scholar Friedrich Wöhler, and in March 1856, was awarded after examination the degree of Ph.D. in chemistry, a distinction which at that time had been won by few American scholars. His dissertation, *Miscellaneous Chemical Analyses,* was published that same year. After six months in the laboratories of Heidelberg University, where he was engaged in experimentation to determine whether or not plants assimilate free nitrogen, he was invited to transfer his investigation to the richly endowed laboratories of Sir John Bennett Lawes and Sir Joseph Henry Gilbert at Rothamsted, England. Here in 1859, after two years of brilliant work, he was able to lay down principles of plant growth that placed him at once among the foremost investigators in

Europe. Two of his distinctive publications belong to this period: "On a New Method for the Quantitative Estimation of Nitric Acid" (*Quarterly Journal of the Chemical Society of London*, vol. XII, 1860); and "On the Sources of the Nitrogen of Vegetation" (*Philosophical Transactions of the Royal Society of London*, vol. CLI, 1862, in collaboration with J. B. Lawes and J. H. Gilbert). The laboratory at Rothamsted was anxious to retain him with adequate compensation, but what to him seemed like an imperative call to service had come from his native land, and in the autumn of 1859, after six years abroad, he returned to assume the presidency of the newly chartered institution to be known as the Agricultural College of Pennsylvania.

In accepting this position Pugh became a pioneer in a rich and unexplored field, and no pioneer ever plunged into his work with more of enthusiasm, energy, and vision. During the next five years he gave himself unreservedly to laying broadly and deeply the foundations of what today is the Pennsylvania State College. In Pennsylvania, as elsewhere, the idea of a college education based upon agriculture and the mechanic arts met from the first with violent opposition, but after a severe struggle Pugh induced the state legislature to grant funds to complete the college building. He then enlarged his area of battle by helping push through Congress the Land-Grant College Act; after this had been passed in 1862, he was able, against the opposition of many of the strong colleges of the state, to secure the funds it provided for his own institution. In connection with this work he published in 1864 *A Report upon a Plan for the Organization of Colleges for Agriculture and the Mechanic Arts, with Especial Reference to the . . . Agricultural College of Pennsylvania . . . in View of the Endowment of this Institution by the Land Scrip Fund*. In addition to his outside activities and the details of executive administration, he insisted on carrying on laboratory and lecture work in chemistry and mineralogy, and on continuing so far as he was able his own research work. The strain was too severe and the penalty came in his sudden death when he was but thirty-six, less than three months after his marriage, Feb. 4, 1864, at Bellefonte, Pa., to Rebecca Valentine.

[D. S. Maynard, *Industries and Institutions of Center County, with Hist. Sketches* (1877); J. S. Futhey and Gilbert Cope, *Hist. of Chester County, Pa.* (1881); *Evan Pugh* (1903), reprinted from *Contemporary Am. Biog.*, vol. III, (1902); *Press* (Phila.), May 3, 1864.]

F. L. P.

PUGH, GEORGE ELLIS (Nov. 28, 1822–July 19, 1876), senator from Ohio, was born in Cincinnati, the son of Rachel (Anthony) and Lot Pugh, a bank cashier and successful merchant. After attending various schools, including St. Xavier and Cincinnati colleges, in his home city, he was graduated from Miami University in 1840. Admitted to the bar in 1843, his legal practice in Cincinnati was interrupted by the Mexican War, in which he became a captain in the 4th Ohio Infantry. Serving under Taylor and on the staff of Joseph Lane, he "gained," as he said, "no other laurels than those which belonged to the soldier who had gallanted mules up the Rio Grande" (S. S. Cox, *Three Decades of Federal Legislation*, 1885, p. 60). Upon his return home he formed a law partnership with George H. Pendleton [q.v.] and in 1848 was elected as a Democrat to the state legislature. He was returned to the same body the next year, participated in the movement for a new Ohio constitution, became city solicitor of Cincinnati, and in 1851 was attorney-general. Noteworthy services in the organization of this office and Democratic factional difficulties involving the Kansas question aided his election to the federal Senate in 1854. Realizing that disturbed political relations with the South might ruin the commercial importance of Cincinnati he consistently advocated congressional nonintervention in the slavery question in the territories. Acting upon instructions from the Ohio legislature he joined three other Democratic senators, including Douglas, in opposing the acceptance of the proslavery Lecompton constitution in 1858 (*Speech . . . on the Kansas Lecompton Constitution . . . in the Senate . . . Mar. 16, 1858*, 1858), though he parted company with them in voting for the English bill.

As head of the Ohio delegation to the Democratic convention at Charleston in 1860 he opposed the demand of Yancey that the northern wing accept the extreme southern position as to the protection of slavery, his splendid oratorical effort ringing with the refusal: "Gentlemen of the South, you mistake us . . . we will not do it" (Murat Halstead, *Caucuses of 1860*, 1860, pp. 49–50). A few weeks later, when Jefferson Davis' famous resolutions reiterating the southern position were passed in the Senate, he alone among the Democrats, Douglas being absent, cast a vote in the negative. Although defeated for reëlection, with the development of the secession movement he was extremely active in urging the acceptance of the Crittenden Compromise. In May 1863 when C. L. Vallandigham was tried by a military tribunal for sedition,

Pugh advised him and ultimately sought unsuccessfully to have the case reviewed by the Supreme Court of the United States (1 *Wallace*, 243–54). When Vallandigham, then an exile from Union territory, was nominated for governor by the Ohio Democrats in 1863, Pugh reluctantly accepted the second place upon the ticket. Stressing the issue of free speech, he assumed the active leadership of the campaign, which he carried zealously but ineffectually into every corner of the state. The next year he was defeated for Congress. Later he assisted Charles O'Conor as counsel for the defendant in the case of Jefferson Davis. Although elected to the state constitutional convention of 1873, he declined to serve. Illness gradually overcame him, and paralysis brought the end at his residence in Cincinnati. Brusque on occasion and of scant courtesy when preoccupied, he was a man of deep learning and broad culture. Descended from Quaker stock and for a short time an exhorter at Baptist meetings, after the death in 1868 of his wife, Theresa (Chalfant) Pugh, he entered the Roman Catholic Church of which she had been a member. An extraordinarily retentive memory, a lively imagination, and laborious application made him an eminent lawyer, sought by corporations in important railroad and insurance cases. "Small in person, keen of eye, with a voice full of music, over which he had rare command, he conquered as much by his logical persuasion and defiant manner as by his fervent eloquence" (Cox, *ante*, pp. 59–60), but his independent convictions and a noticeable deafness were handicaps to political leadership. He was survived by three of his four children.

[*Bench and Bar of Ohio* (1897), vol. II, ed. by G. I. Reed; R. C. McGrane, *William Allen* (copr. 1925); James L. Vallandigham, *A Life of Clement L. Vallandigham* (1872); *Cincinnati Commercial*, July 16, 1876, *Cincinnati Enquirer*, July 20, 1876, *Cincinnati Daily Gazette*, July 25, 1876.]   F. P. W.

PULASKI, CASIMIR (*c.* 1748–October 1779), Polish patriot and Revolutionary soldier, the eldest son of Count Joseph Pulaski, was born at Podolia, Poland. After serving in the guard of Duke Charles of Courland he returned to Poland and, in 1768, joined in active rebellion with his father, who had founded the Confederation of Bar, to combat the foreign domination of Poland through Stanislaus II. His military exploits were heroic and temporarily successful, but his forces were finally crushed and scattered, his estates confiscated, and he fled to Turkey in 1772. He spent several years trying to incite Turkey to attack Russia and, late in 1775, he arrived in Paris, penniless

and without employment. It was suggested that he be sent to the aid of the American insurgents; Rulhière, an agent of Vergennes, put him in touch with Franklin and Deane. On May 29, 1777, Franklin wrote a letter to Washington introducing Pulaski and on June 5 Deane advanced him the necessary money for the voyage.

Pulaski arrived in Boston in July, met Washington the following month, and received from him a letter to the Continental Congress. During the first eighteen months of the war there had been no regular cavalry, but in the reorganization of the army four regiments had been included. On Aug. 27 Washington wrote John Hancock suggesting that Pulaski be placed in command of all the cavalry; two days before this Pulaski had given Hancock plans for the organization of a corps of volunteers. In September he joined Washington as a volunteer and participated in the battle of Brandywine with distinction. During the battle of Germantown (Oct. 4) Pulaski was in charge of a small patrol. The later charge that he was responsible for that defeat because he fell asleep in a farmhouse seems without foundation. In November and December he sent Washington two memorials concerning the increase of the cavalry and the formation of a squadron of Bosniques (light cavalry). He commanded the cavalry during the winter of 1777 at Trenton, and later at Flemington, and acted in unison with Gen. Anthony Wayne in scouting for supplies for the famishing troops at Valley Forge. But he refused to continue to serve under Wayne and often incurred the open hostility of his own subordinates. In order to end this unhappy situation he resigned his command in March 1778. His enemy Stephen Moylan [*q.v.*] was advanced to the command which he had vacated.

Congress gave Pulaski, supported by Washington, permission to organize an independent corps of cavalry in March and Pulaski established headquarters at Baltimore. On Sept. 17 he appeared before Congress and stated that he blushed to find himself "languishing in a state of inactivity." He was sent to protect American supplies at Egg Harbor, N. J., and on Oct. 15, through information given by a deserter, the British surprised and cut up the legion. The Indian massacres in the Cherry Valley caused Pulaski to be sent to Minisink on the Delaware River, but here he was restless and wished to return to Poland. He complained to Congress (Nov. 26) that there was "nothing but bears to fight." After three months he was ordered (Feb. 2, 1779) to the support of General Lincoln in South Carolina. He arrived at Charlestown on May 8. Learning of the approach of General Provost northward from Savannah he rushed to the attack of the British advance guard and suffered a decisive defeat. He later contemplated an attack against Wappo, but this expedition was countermanded and another disaster averted.

Pulaski now joined forces with General Lincoln, who, assisted by the French fleet, was preparing to attack Savannah. On Aug. 19 he wrote Congress a long letter in which he detailed the disappointments that he had encountered in a service "which ill treatment makes me begin to abhor" and expressed the hope that he might still find the opportunity of proving his devotion to the American cause (Griffin, *post,* p. 101). On Oct. 9, at the siege of Savannah, he bravely but impatiently charged the enemy lines at the head of his cavalry and fell with a grapeshot in the loin. He was removed to the *Wasp,* where surgeons were unable to remove the bullet, and he died on board, probably on Oct. 11. Whether he was buried at sea, or beneath the oaks of St. Helena's Island, or in Greenwich, Ga., has never been established. His American career was tragic, for it was a chronicle of disaster and embittered disappointment. He was fortunate in his last days, for his gallant death served to ennoble even his mistakes in the eyes of posterity.

[There is no adequate biography of Pulaski. Most satisfactory is Wladyslaw Wayda's *Kazimierz Pulaski w Ameryce* (Warsaw, 1930) which publishes a number of documents. See also: M. I. J. Griffin, "Gen. Count Casimir Pulaski . . .," in *Am. Cath. Hist. Researches,* Jan. 1910; Jared Sparks, "Life of Count Pulaski," in *The Lib. of Am. Biog.,* 2 ser. IV (1845); L. H. Girardin, *Pulaski Vindicated* (Baltimore, 1824); C. C. Jones in *Ga. Hist. Soc. Colls.,* vol. III (1873); W. W. Gordon in *Ga. Hist. Quart.,* XIII (1929), 169–227; and Thomas Gamble, "Story of Gen. Casimir Pulaski and the Siege of Savannah in 1779," *Savannah Morning News,* July 14–Oct. 9, 1929. C. H. Thompson's *Hist. Facts in the Lives of Count Pulaski and Baron de Lovzinski* (Plattsburg, Mo., 1928) curiously supposes that Louvet de Couvrai's fiction is a genuine historical narrative.]   F. M.

PULITZER, JOSEPH (Apr. 10, 1847–Oct. 29, 1911), journalist, the second son of Philip Pulitzer (or Politzer), a Jew of Magyar descent, and of Louise (Berger), a Catholic, was born in Mako, Hungary, and grew up in Budapest where his father, a retired grain merchant, died. At seventeen he left his home in search of military adventure. Successively rejected, because of defective sight and a poor physique, by the Austrian army, the French Foreign Legion, and the British military, he encountered at Hamburg a recruiting agent for the Union forces in the United States, and obtained passage to Boston where he arrived in August or September

1864, "the irregularity of his arrival" obscuring the exact date of his landing. It is said that he jumped overboard at Boston and swam ashore to collect his own bounty (Seitz, *post,* p. 42). He promptly enlisted for a year and on Nov. 12, 1864, joined the 1st New York (Lincoln) Cavalry, a regiment originally organized by Maj.-Gen. Carl Schurz and largely composed of Germans; his active service was limited to participation in four skirmishes. Mustered out on July 7, 1865, he did not succeed in obtaining work until he reached St. Louis in the following October. There, like many other emigrants, he found no job too menial to keep body and soul together; he went from one employer to another until, after being secretary of the Deutsche Gesellschaft, he became in 1868 a reporter on the German daily, the *Westliche Post,* then owned and directed by Carl Schurz and Emil Preetorius [*qq.v.*], and began thus a career which in time profoundly affected the journalism of America. He had received his certificate of naturalization on Mar. 6, 1867.

At first the butt of many jokes because of his rather eccentric appearance, Pulitzer speedily became a foremost figure in local journalism because of his unbounded energy, extraordinary resourcefulness, pertinacity and success in the search for news, vivid picturing of the political life of Missouri, and personal fearlessness. Because of this record he was elected and seated as a representative in the lower House of Missouri on Dec. 21, 1869, although not eligible because of his youth, thus becoming an illegal legislator as well as the legislative correspondent of the *Westliche Post.* Soon thereafter (Jan. 27, 1870) he shot and slightly wounded a prominent lobbyist, Edward Augustine. His fine of $105 and his legal expenses were contributed by friends and admirers. Later, Pulitzer became one of the three police commissioners in St. Louis, an ardent partisan of the Liberal Republican movement, and a secretary of the Cincinnati convention which nominated Horace Greeley for president in 1872. In the ensuing campaign he made sixty vigorous and able speeches in German in behalf of Greeley. Bitterly disappointed by the failure of that movement, Pulitzer joined the Democratic party, his loyalty to which never wavered.

Pulitzer became a part proprietor of the *Westliche Post* in 1871, but in 1873 disposed of his interest. After travel abroad, on Jan. 6, 1874, he bought the bankrupt St. Louis *Staats-Zeitung* for a song and immediately made a handsome profit by selling its membership in the Associated Press to the *St. Louis Daily Globe* for the sum of $20,000, which enabled him to study law and devote some of his time to politics and public service. He had by 1874 so mastered English as to write it with complete accuracy, force, vigor, and clearness, supported by a remarkable knowledge of American history and a most loyal appreciation of the spirit of the American democracy. In 1875, a delegate to the Missouri constitutional convention, he contributed much to the debates by his carefully prepared addresses. Throwing himself with complete enthusiasm into the Tilden campaign, he was able to indulge to the full his great passion for public speaking, in which he was aided by his excellent voice, his ability to reason rapidly, and his skill in handling his audiences. His first appearance in New York was in the historic Cooper Union on Oct. 31, 1876.

In the fall of that year he was admitted to the bar in the District of Columbia. Not until after his marriage to Kate Davis, a distant connection of Jefferson Davis, June 19, 1878, did he decide between the two callings which lured him so strongly. Finally, his purchase of the *St. Louis Dispatch* in that year settled his career. This completely wrecked daily he bought for $2,-500, subject to a lien of $30,000, which left him only $2,700 as his sole remaining resource. As the *Dispatch* possessed an Associated Press membership, and the *Post* had none, John A. Dillon, the proprietor of the latter, immediately offered to join the two papers. Before Pulitzer's $2,700 was exhausted, the new daily, the *St. Louis Post-Dispatch,* had begun to pay; it has paid ever since, and is today (1934) the only newspaper remaining in the hands of his heirs. Becoming the sole owner, within a year Pulitzer had doubled the circulation of the combined dailies, and by the end of 1881 his profits were fully $45,000 a year. He was now in his element with the weapon forged to his hand, and at once assailed the political and municipal corruption in St. Louis, at the price of being twice personally assaulted. He was a delegate to the National Democratic Convention in June 1880, and became an unsuccessful candidate for Congress in the same year. His final personal plunge into politics occurred in 1885, when he was elected to Congress from New York. He found the position so distasteful that he resigned on Apr. 10, 1886.

Unfortunately for Pulitzer, his chief editorial writer, John A. Cockerill [*q.v.*], on Oct. 5, 1882, shot and killed Col. Alonzo W. Slayback, a prominent lawyer, in an altercation growing out of criticism of his firm in the *Post-Dispatch.* There was no prosecution of the murderer, who claimed that he acted in self-defense. The resultant popular ill-will was vented upon the paper, its owner, and editor. Always extremely sensitive to criticism, Pulitzer speedily felt that he was *persona non grata* in St. Louis, and looked for other fields of activity. His constant bad health growing worse, he left for New York en route to Europe, only to be induced in the metropolis to buy (May 10, 1883) the *World* from Jay Gould for the sum of $346,000, payable in instalments; the first of these were contributed by the profits of the *Post-Dispatch,* the others being earned by the *World.* With his Midas touch, Pulitzer converted his new daily into a money-maker almost from the hour of his taking hold. Thus began an ownership which lasted twenty-eight years, during which the *World* became a great national force, the leading exponent of the Democratic party in New York—although retaining its political independence. Gradually it evolved under Pulitzer's control from a sensationalized daily into the clean, non-sensational, editorially distinguished daily which it was at his death under the brilliant editorial leadership of Frank I. Cobb [*q.v.*].

The program which Pulitzer announced on acquiring control made him immediately popular with the workers. The *World* declared that it opposed the aristocracy of money (whose sins of omission and commission it sensationally exploited at great length) but that it wished to become the organ of the true American aristocracy, "the aristocracy of labor." The ten planks in its program were the following: the taxation of luxuries, of inheritances, of large incomes, of monopolies, of the large and privileged corporations; the enactment of a tariff for revenue only; the reform of the civil service; the punishment of corrupt officials and of the purchasers of votes at elections; and, finally, the punishment of employers who coerced their employees at election times—a mild program, indeed, to be considered dangerously radical. So successful was this appeal to the workers, plus the extraordinary ability, courage, and enterprise of Pulitzer's management, that within three years the *World* earned a profit of $500,000. The journalism of that day—even the formerly "yellow journalism" of the James Gordon Bennetts —was scandalized by Pulitzer's methods. He resorted to "features," to "stunts," to long stories, increasing headlines, cartoons, sketches, pictures, sensational exploitation of crime. On Oct. 10, 1887, he founded the *Evening World,* which was a great money-earner for years after the decline of its morning ally.

Early in 1896 the elder daily cut its price to

one cent and entered upon a phase of extreme "yellowness," the least creditable part of its career, owing to the boundless rivalry between it and the dailies of William Randolph Hearst, then a newcomer in metropolitan journalism. The irresponsible sensationalism of both groups was by many held largely responsible for the whipping up of public opinion for the war with Spain. Its decadence led to a veritable uprising against the *World* and its banning from clubs and libraries, until Pulitzer, who like Hearst had found this journalistic warfare exhausting financially, again took personal charge, and brought the paper back to its former standards. He had dropped the personal management of the daily in 1887 because of lung trouble, increasing nervousness, and failing eyesight, which led to his suddenly becoming almost totally blind, and thereafter an invalid tortured by every noise. In the six and one-half years of his ownership up to his formal withdrawal from the editorship, Oct. 16, 1890, the *World* had repaid its purchase price, made its owner a very rich man, and equipped and built the World Building at a cost of $2,500,000.

Despite his formal retirement Pulitzer never relaxed his complete control of the policies of his New York dailies, which he could no longer see. He bombarded their offices with suggestions, advice, complaints, reprimands, orders, and the most detailed criticisms as to reporting, editing, tone and composition of articles, the headlines, and pictures. Most of his suggestions were brilliant and were eagerly carried out. One of his memoranda of instructions reads as follows: "Concentrate your brain upon these objectives: 1st. What is original, distinctive, dramatic, romantic, . . . odd, apt to be talked about, without shocking good taste or lowering the general tone, good tone, and above all without impairing the confidence of the people in the truth of the stories or the character of the paper for reliability and scrupulous cleanness. . . . 4th. Accuracy, accuracy, accuracy. Also terseness, intelligent, not stupid, condensation. No picture or illustration unless it is first class, both in ideas and execution (quoted in Seitz, pp. 416–17).

Pulitzer in later years himself impressed upon the *World* its high character as an internationally minded, extremely well-informed daily, with a remarkably able editorial page, no longer an organ of the working classes, but of all those who favored democratic policies and such objectives as "sound money," government by constitutionalism, liberalism, the upholding of free speech, and personal liberty. It especially op-posed prohibition, a large army and navy, all jingo movements, the annexation of Hawaii, the Philippines, and the Virgin Islands. No daily spoke out more emphatically against government by and for the privileged classes and the "money power." It bolted the party in 1896 when Bryan was the presidential candidate, and it refused to follow the party on various other occasions. It was a never-failing opponent of Tammany Hall, and always a fearless scourge of all political corruption. Its courage was boundless, especially in its complete freedom from advertising domination. Indeed, it would be impossible to measure the great influence of the *World* upon the political life and the press of the country after it abandoned its career of sensationalism and vulgarity. Shortly before Pulitzer's death the circulation of the morning *World* was around 300,000, that of the evening paper 400,000, and of the Sunday edition 600,000 copies.

For a series of bitter attacks in 1908 upon the actions of the American government in fomenting a revolution in Colombia and setting up the Republic of Panama, and upon the American and French personalities involved, the *World* incurred the anger of President Theodore Roosevelt. Roosevelt replied in a letter to William Dudley Foulke of Indianapolis, attacking Delavan Smith, the owner of the *Indianapolis News*, for an editorial based upon the *World's* charges that only $3,500,000 of $40,000,000 had reached the original Panama Canal owners, the rest of the purchase money going to brokers, lawyers, promoters, and others. The *World* then declared that Roosevelt's letter contained scandalous falsehoods, and contrasted his assertion that the $40,000,000 was paid to the French Government and distributed by it, with the previous sworn testimony of William N. Cromwell, attorney for the French interests, that the money was paid to J. P. Morgan & Company and distributed by Cromwell himself, in a way that Cromwell described in detail. On Dec. 15, 1908, Roosevelt sent a special mesage to Congress, denouncing Pulitzer (*Congressional Record*, 60 Cong., 2 Sess., pp. 249–52); and on Feb. 17, 1909, the government procured in the District of Columbia the indictment on five counts of Pulitzer and two of his editors, for criminally libelling Roosevelt, J. P. Morgan, Charles P. Taft, Douglas Robinson, Elihu Root, and William N. Cromwell. The case was dropped, so, unfortunately, the facts were never definitely established. Another indictment, of the Press Publishing Company, in New York, Mar. 4, 1909, was quashed in the federal district court, and this decision was upheld by the Supreme Court of the United

States, Jan. 3, 1911 (219, *U. S. Reports,* 1).

Pulitzer died aboard his yacht in Charleston harbor, S. C., on Oct. 29, 1911. Of his seven children, three sons and two daughters survived him. In 1903 he had announced his intention to found a school of journalism in connection with Columbia University. This was established by his will, which provided two millions of dollars for the purpose. Of this, $500,000 supplied a building, while the income of half of the second million was applied to "prizes or scholarships for the encouragement of public service, public morals, American Literature, and the advancement of education"—the Pulitzer prizes, which have attracted great attention and caused sharp discussions. The school of journalism led to the establishment of numerous others throughout the country. In Pulitzer's will (which disposed of $18,645,000) it was also decreed that his three dailies could not be sold and should be carried on in his spirit as great, liberal, politically fearless, and independent journals. The management of his sons failed, however, to keep the *World* and *Evening World* profitable. The will was therefore broken by a judicial decree in 1931, and both dailies were sold to the Scripps-Howard newspaper group, the former being extinguished, the latter merged with the *New York Telegram* as the *New York World-Telegram.*

[D. C. Seitz, *Joseph Pulitzer, His Life and Letters* (1924); Alleyne Ireland, *Joseph Pulitzer, Reminiscences of a Secretary* (1914); G. S. Johns, "Joseph Pulitzer," *Mo. Hist. Rev.,* Jan.–Oct. 1931, Jan.–Apr. 1932; J. L. Heaton, *The Story of a Page* (1913); J. W. Barrett, *The World, the Flesh and Messrs. Pulitzer* (1931); obituaries in *N. Y. Times, N. Y. World,* Oct. 30, 1911.]   O. G. V.

PULLMAN, GEORGE MORTIMER (Mar. 3, 1831–Oct. 19, 1897), inventor, industrialist, one of the ten children of James Lewis and Emily Caroline (Minton) Pullman, was born in Brocton, Chautauqua County, N. Y., where his father worked as a general mechanic. He attended school until he was fourteen years old and then took a position in a small store in Westfield, N. Y. Three years later, 1848, he joined his brother, a cabinet-maker in Albion, N. Y., and remained there seven years, learning the trade and undertaking independently a number of contracting jobs. These he found profitable and much to his liking, so when work around Albion slackened he gave up cabinet-making and, in 1855, removed to Chicago, Ill. Here he quickly found contracting work, which included the raising of the level of several streets and the buildings flanking them. His success in this and in similar jobs soon gained for him a substantial reputation.

Meanwhile, he began giving serious attention to the development of his idea, formulated some years earlier, of providing better sleeping accommodations on railway trains. By 1858 his plans had materialized to such a point that he boldly contracted with the Chicago & Alton Railroad to remodel two day coaches into sleeping cars. In these he incorporated his basic idea of an upper berth hinged to the side of the car and supported by two jointed arms. With the experience gained in this first venture, Pullman constructed a third car in 1859. Although the three cars were put into service on the Chicago & Alton Railroad and were extremely popular, the railroad companies generally were reluctant to adopt them. Pullman thereupon left Chicago for the Colorado mining fields, where from 1859 to 1863 he ran a general store and in his spare time worked out plans for his first real Pullman car. Upon returning to Chicago, he and his intimate friend, Ben Field, of Albion, N. Y., together consummated these plans. They also applied for a patent on the folding upper berth, which was granted them jointly on Apr. 5, 1864 (No. 42,182). They then began the construction of their first car, *Pioneer,* which required a year to complete. In addition to the upper berth they incorporated a lower berth, made by hinging the back and seat cushion so that the former could be placed on the seat and the seat cushion extended to meet that of the opposite seat. A joint patent for this was granted Field and Pullman on Sept. 19, 1865 (No. 49,992). The upper and lower berth inventions, in principle, have remained unchanged to the present day. The *Pioneer* was even more enthusiastically received by the traveling public than its predecessors, and in spite of its size, which prevented its passage under many bridges and by many station platforms, one railroad company after another made the necessary structural changes to accommodate it. Thus encouraged, the partners constructed a number of other cars modeled after the *Pioneer,* and in 1867 organized the Pullman Palace Car Company which, through Pullman's business ability, grew to be the greatest car building organization in the world. He established his first manufacturing plant at Palmyra, N. Y., but removed it in a short time to Detroit, Mich. As the business developed, additional plants were established in St. Louis, Mo., Elmira, N. Y., Wilmington, Del., San Francisco, Cal., and Pullman, Ill., now part of the city of Chicago. In connection with the last-named plant, Pullman built the entire town which bears his name, for the accommodation of his employees. It was completed in 1881 and during the sixteen years of its independent existence it was judged the most healthful industrial city in the world. In addition to the sleeping car, Pullman brought into being the combined sleeping and restaurant car in 1867; the dining car in 1868; the chair car in 1875; and the vestibule car in 1887. From the initial agreement which he effected in 1859 with the Chicago & Alton Railroad to insure the constant use of his cars, Pullman developed the vast system of Pullman car operation which today embraces the entire country.

Outside of his own business he was financially interested in other car manufactories and was the owner of the Eagleton Wire Works, New York. He was, also, president of the Metropolitan Elevated Railroad in New York City. His philanthropies were many and included a bequest of $1,200,000 for the establishment of a free manual training school at Pullman. On June 13, 1867, he married Hattie Sanger of Chicago, and at the time of his death was survived by his widow and four children.

[John McLean, *One Hundred Years in Ill.* (1919); Joseph Husband, *The Story of the Pullman Car* (1917); Waldemar Kaempffert, *A Popular Hist. of Am. Invention* (1924), vol. I; *Railroad Gazette*, Oct. 22, 1897; *Chicago Daily Tribune*, Oct. 20, 1897.]   C. W. M.

PULTE, JOSEPH HIPPOLYT (Oct. 6, 1811–Feb. 25, 1884), homeopathic physician, and author, was born at Meschede in the Prussian province of Westphalia. His father, Dr. Herman Joseph Pulte, was the medical director of one of the government institutions for the education of midwives. His education was obtained at the gymnasium of Soest and at the University of Marburg where he received the M.D. degree in 1833. An invitation from his eldest brother to come to St. Louis, Mo., brought him to the United States in 1834. On his journey through Pennsylvania, he stopped at Cherryville, where he formed the acquaintance of Dr. William Wesselhoeft and through him became converted to homeopathy. He joined the Northampton County Homeopathic Medical Society, the first one of the kind in America, and practised in Allentown, Pa., where he remained for six years. He then proceeded on his western trip to St. Louis in company with an Englishman, Edward Giles, who induced him to stop off at Cincinnati. Pulte opened a private dispensary in this city and soon was engaged in such a lucrative and successful practice that he decided to stay permanently. In the autumn of the same year, he married Mary Jane Rollins of Pittsburgh, Pa. In 1844 Pulte, Constantine Hering, Charles Neidhard [*qq.v.*], and others met in New York City and founded the American Institute of Homeopathy. In 1852

he lectured on obstetrics and clinical medicine in the institution now known as the Cleveland Homeopathic Medical College. In 1872 was founded the Pulte Medical College, named in his honor, at which he delivered a series of lectures on clinical medicine. His health began to fail in 1873, and he died at his home in Cincinnati at the age of seventy-three.

His writings were numerous: in 1846, he published *Organon der Weltgeschichte;* and in 1850, the *Homeopathic Domestic Physician,* which went through thirteen editions before 1872 and 58,000 copies of which were sold. The seventh edition was translated into Spanish and published in Spain in 1859, and a London reprint sold in England and in the colonies to the extent of 50,000 copies. In 1853 he published the *Woman's Medical Guide;* in 1866 a treatise, *Asiatic Cholera,* and the following year, a book on the spectroscope. He was co-editor of the *American Magazine Devoted to Homeopathy and Hydropathy* from 1851 to 1854.

[H. A. Kelly, W. L. Burrage, *Am. Medic. Biog.* (1920); T. S. Bradford, *Biog. of Homeopathic Physicians* (1916), vol. XXV; Otto Juettner, *Daniel Drake and His Followers* (1909); W. H. King, ed., *Hist. of Homeopathy* (1905), vols. I, III; *Cincinnati Enquirer*, Feb. 26, 1884.]   C. B.

PUMPELLY, RAPHAEL (Sept. 8, 1837– Aug. 10, 1923), geologist, explorer, was descended from Jean Pompilie, a French Huguenot emigrant to Canada, through his son John who moved to Massachusetts about 1700. Later descendants migrated to Owego, Tioga County, N. Y., where Raphael, son of William Pumpelly and his second wife, Mary H. (Welles), was born. He acquired his preliminary education in private schools and the Owego Academy, and early developed a spirit of adventure that thrice nearly cost him his life. Entering William Russell's Collegiate and Commercial Institute in New Haven, to prepare for Yale, he abruptly changed his mind and in June 1854 sailed with his mother for Europe, where he spent the next two years in travel, learning the languages and a little science through absorption rather than through serious study. Seized one beautiful morning in 1856 with an attack of wanderlust, he left his mother in Florence and sailed for Corsica, returning four months later to find that she had received none of his brief notes and had given him up for dead. Soon afterward, however, he entered the Royal School of Mines in Freiberg, Saxony, and settled down to the first serious work of his life.

Upon his return to America, a mining engineer, in 1859, he took charge of the development of silver mines in southern Arizona, a country at that time infested by murderous Apaches and renegade whites, "a land of hell and sudden death" (Willis, *post*, p. 56). Here he remained for more than a year, accomplishing the purpose he had undertaken and finally emerging with a whole skin at Los Angeles, Cal., in the fall of 1861. Proceeding thence to San Francisco, he found awaiting him an appointment as geologist for the Japanese government, to explore the resources of the empire. In company with William Phipps Blake [*q.v.*], who held a similar appointment, he sailed on Nov. 23, 1861, reaching Japan Feb. 18, following. When his duties were brought to a close in 1863 by internal political disturbances of the empire, he was seized again by the spirit of wanderlust, and made an expedition up the Yangtze-kiang to study coal deposits, upon his return sailing for Tien-tsin and Pekin, whence, in 1865, he journeyed overland through Tartary and Siberia to St. Petersburg. These travels bore fruit in his "Geological Researches in China, Mongolia, and Japan," published in the *Smithsonian Contributions to Knowledge* (vol. XV, 1867), and in *Across America and Asia* (1870).

The period following his home-coming was one of speculation in natural resources, and Pumpelly was soon engaged in an exploration of the copper and iron districts of Michigan and the Lake Superior district, becoming associated with Maj. Thomas Benton Brooks [*q.v.*] in the work upon which his reputation as a mining geologist chiefly rests. He contributed a report on "Copper-bearing Rocks" to Part II of *Geological Survey of Michigan; Upper Peninsula, 1869–73* (vol. I, 1873). In 1869 he settled in Cambridge, Mass., where on Oct. 20 of that year he married Eliza Frances Shepard. During the winter he lectured at Harvard on ore deposits. In 1870 he was again in Michigan in quest of iron, copper, and timber lands; in the autumn of 1871 he accepted the position of state geologist of Missouri, but in the winter of 1872–73 resigned on account of ill health, and settled in Balmville, near Newburgh, N. Y., where he busied himself in the preparation and study of thin sections of rocks in an effort to solve the problem of ore genesis.

In the autumn of 1875 he moved his family to Boston and accepted an appointment for the investigation of the mineral resources of the United States in connection with the Tenth Census. Becoming interested about this time in water pollution, he made important, though then not fully appreciated, investigations in connection with the Board of Health. In 1881, under the patronage of Henry Villard [*q.v.*], he under-

took a geological survey along the lines of a projected northwestern railway, a work brought to an untimely end through Villard's financial and nervous collapse. Three years later, in 1884, Pumpelly was placed in charge of the New England division of the United States Geological Survey under John Wesley Powell [*q.v.*], where, to quote his own words, "for five years we struggled with the obscure structural problems of the Green Mountains" (*My Reminiscences,* II, 647). His "Geology of the Green Mountains in Massachusetts" was published in *United States Geological Survey Monographs,* vol. XXIII (1894). With this task his work as a geologist practically ceased, although from 1895 to 1902 he was engaged from time to time in an advisory capacity in the Lake Superior region.

In 1903 and 1904, still restlessly active, although he had reached seventy, under the auspices of the Carnegie Institution of Washington he organized and conducted expeditions into Central Asia, seeking traces of prehistoric civilization and evidences of geological and climatic changes. On these expeditions he studied especially the effects of the desiccation of Central Asia on the development of civilization, studies later carried further by Ellsworth Huntington. Pumpelly contributed "Archaeological and Physico-Geographical Reconnaissance in Turkestan" to *Explorations in Turkestan . . . Expedition of 1903,* published by the Carnegie Institution in 1905, and "Ancient Anau and the Oasis World" to *Explorations in Turkestan; Expedition of 1904* (2 vols., 1908).

His first claim to immortality in geological history is based upon his studies of the loess of China and his "Relation of Secular Rock-Disintegration to Loess, Glacial Drift, and Rock Basins," in the *American Journal of Science,* February 1879. His next most important work was in connection with the copper and iron ores of Michigan. He was the first to set forth clearly the secondary nature of the iron ores and establish their age. Equally important and suggestive was his work on the paragenesis of the copper deposits, as expounded in his "Metasomatic Development of the Copper-bearing Rocks of Lake Superior" (*Proceedings of the American Academy of Arts and Sciences,* vol. XIII, 1878).

The character of the man, his picturesque career—so well described in *My Reminiscences* (2 vols., 1918)—and finally the results of his last Asiatic expedition have made him one of the most fascinating figures in American geology. He has been described by one of his biographers as "a great, blue-eyed giant, with long, flowing beard" (Keyes, *post,* p. 250). He was a man of taste and culture, thoroughly humane, and to the end of his life fond of the society of young people. His associates were of the best and his fortunate investments enabled him to live the life of an aristocrat in a truly democratic manner. His wife died in 1915, leaving one son and two daughters. The later years of Pumpelly's life were spent at his home in Dublin, N. H., and Newport, R. I., and at Roseland, Ga., where, beginning about 1883, his family and that of his friend Major Brooks lived for a time a delightful communistic life. He also traveled much, both in America and in Europe. He died at Newport, in his eighty-eighth year.

[An abridged edition of Pumpelly's *My Reminiscences* was published in 1920 as *Travels and Adventures of Raphael Pumpelly*, ed. by O. S. Rice. See also Bailey Willis, "Memorial of Raphael Pumpelly," *Bull. Geol. Soc. of America*, Mar. 1925 (with bibliography); Charles Keyes, "Raphael Pumpelly: Premier Explorer," *Pan-American Geologist*, Nov. 1923; *Am. Jour. Sci.*, Oct. 1923; *Who's Who in America*, 1922–23; *N. Y. Times*, Aug. 11, 1923.]　　　　　　G. P. M.

PURCELL, JOHN BAPTIST (Feb. 26, 1800–July 4, 1883), Roman Catholic prelate, son of Edmond and Johanna (O'Keefe) Purcell, was born in Mallow, Ireland. Though of a conspicuous family, his parents were in poor circumstances. They sent John to the local St. Patrick's College, however, and here he obtained sufficient classical lore to enable him on his arrival in Baltimore (1818) to pass an examination at Asbury College for a teacher's certificate. Thus equipped, he obtained a private tutorship in Queen Anne's County, where his ability challenged the attention of the authorities of Mount St. Mary's College, Emmitsburg, Md., who arranged for him to enter the institution as a seminarian (1820). His scholarship won the favor of Simon Bruté and John Dubois [*qq.v.*], who in 1823 sent him to complete his theological studies under the Sulpicians in Paris. Ordained at the Cathedral of Notre Dame by Archbishop Quelen on May 21, 1826, Purcell spent some months in travel before returning to America.

He was assigned the chair of moral philosophy at Mount St. Mary's, of which college he became president in 1829. During a short tenure of office, he made a permanent impression on the college, among other services obtaining for it a charter of incorporation. On the death of Bishop Edward D. Fenwick [*q.v.*], Rome appointed Purcell to the see of Cincinnati on the recommendation of Bishop P. R. Kenrick [*q.v.*] of St. Louis, despite the opposition of Archbishop Whitfield [*q.v.*] of Baltimore, who feared that the "Mount" would suffer in losing a progressive rector. Consecrated in the cathedral at Baltimore, Purcell remained to attend the Second

Provincial Council (*New York Weekly Register,* Oct. 19, Dec. 21). Then, with a loan of $300, he went to Cincinnati, where he was formerly installed by two old friends, Bishop David and Bishop Flaget [*qq.v.*].

He ruled his diocese, but did so with tact. Above racial bias, he won the Germans, who soon outnumbered English-speaking Catholics in the Ohio region. He did not hesitate to advance German priests or to nominate them for bishoprics, and hence he had no more loyal supporter than John Martin Henni [*q.v.*], who edited *Der Wahrheits Freund*. In 1835 and again in 1838–39, he visited Europe in quest of missionaries and financial aid from the Society of the Propagation of the Faith, of Paris, and from the Leopoldine Society of Austria (see *Catholic Herald*, Dec. 6, 1838, Aug. 22, 1839). His interest in education was intense. He brought the Sisters of Notre Dame de Namur to Cincinnati, where they founded their first American convent. He invited the Ursulines and Sisters of Charity into the diocese, who took charge of parochial schools and aided in founding academies. In 1841 he assisted the Jesuits in establishing St. Francis Xavier College as the successor of the Athenaeum, which he had personally directed for a time. Two years later, while in Europe, he encouraged the Fathers of the Precious Blood to enter the American mission field and establish their seminary and college at Carthagena (1844); he also gave similar encouragement to the Passionists. With the assistance of a wealthy convert, Mrs. Sarah Worthington King Peter [*q.v.*], he brought into the diocese the Sisters of Mercy of Kinsale, the Sisters of Francis of Cologne, the Sisters of the Good Shepherd, and the Little Sisters of the Poor. Hence there was no shortage of teaching sisters for the thirty parochial schools which he urged his pastors to build, or nuns for the orphanages, hospitals, and asylums which were erected as the diocese grew during the flood decades of Irish and German immigration. In 1847 he commenced the erection of the new Mount St. Mary's Seminary at Price Hill, Cincinnati, and a year later laid the cornerstone for the new Cathedral of St. Peter.

A loyal American, Purcell answered anti-Catholic criticism and doubts on the eve of the war with Mexico by declaring editorially, through his brother (Father Edward), who was editor of the diocesan *Catholic Telegraph,* that: "Catholics well understand their duty on this point, for it is certain that if war should be proclaimed by the United States against the Sovereign Pontiff as a temporal prince, it would be the duty of every Catholic . . . to carry the war into the Roman states." Though an ardent supporter of the Mexican War, he was opposed to slavery and its extension. He was on intimate terms with Ewing, Harrison, and lesser political figures in the Mid-West, but he took no active partisan interest, not even voting for twenty years, until he supported Lincoln in both campaigns. During the Civil War, he encouraged enlistments, made provisions for prisoners, sent Sisters of Charity as war nurses under Sister Anthony [q.v.], flew the flag from his cathedral, and maintained the *Catholic Telegraph* as a Unionist organ. In Rome for the canonization of the Japanese martyrs (1862), he took occasion to correct European impressions of the American conflict. Incidentally, he had hopes of retiring to a monastery, but Pius IX refused permission to the prelate whom he had so recently made a papal count.

In the meantime, Purcell had become known as a controversialist. Alexander Campbell [q.v.], a minister with a national reputation as an orator, made charges against the Catholic Church at a convention of the Ohio College of Teachers (1836). The bishop accepted the challenge and there resulted a debate of two days' duration in a Campbellite church. In general the bishop had the best of the controversy; at least he succeeded in moderating nativist hostility aroused by Campbell and by Lyman Beecher's *Plea for the West* (1835). In book form (1837) the debate attracted attention. He had some vogue, also, as a lecturer on current European subjects, with which he was familiar because of frequent tours of Europe and intimate associations with foreign leaders in state and church.

Aside from John Hughes [q.v.], Purcell had now become the most influential figure in the American hierarchy, and probably no bishop was better known in Rome. He was styled a bishopmaker, for his nominees soon occupied the western bishoprics. It was not surprising, therefore, that when Cincinnati was erected into an archepiscopal see, Purcell should be named archbishop (July 19, 1850). Going to Rome the following year, he received the pallium at the hands of Pius IX. On his return to Cincinnati, he became a more ardent temperance advocate as a result of Father Mathew's visit. In 1853 he displayed both physical and moral courage in acting as host and escort to the papal legate, Archbishop Bedini, who was threatened with assassination and attacked by a Cincinnati mob on Christmas Eve. Other than this outbreak, Purcell suffered little annoyance from the Know-Nothings. In 1855 he held the first of a series of provincial councils the acts and decrees of

which did much for the ecclesiastical organization of the archdiocese. He was a leading preacher in the Second Council of Baltimore, 1866, and a year later took part in the centennial celebration of St. Peter's martyrdom in Rome.

At the Vatican Council, Purcell believed that the time was not propitious for a definition of infallibility and voted *non placet* (July 13, 1870). Leaving the Council before the final ballot, he returned to his diocese, but on the publication of the decree conformed thereto. To an audience at the Catholic Institute, which included representatives of the New York press who had leased direct telegraph lines, he explained the subject, and declared: "I am here to proclaim my belief in the infallibility of the Pope in the words of the Holy Father defining the doctrine." Six years later, the archbishop celebrated his golden jubilee, an epochal date in Catholic circles of the Mid-West. For fifty-three years he had been a power in the church. Then came the collapse.

Alarmed by bank failures during the panic of 1837, many Catholics deposited their savings with the bishop in the apparent belief that piety insured financial acumen. Father Edward Purcell, who, incidentally, refused the appointment of coadjutor bishop of Pittsburgh (1858), took charge of administering this trust. During the panic of 1857 and the Civil War, deposits increased; millions of dollars were handled; and the funds were invested in church properties the revenues of which permitted the payment of six per cent. interest. The early years of the panic of 1873 were weathered; but about 1877, with money still tight, fear caused a run on the "Purcell bank." Investments were in properties which could not be liquidated. Business men to whom loans had been made were in bankruptcy. The resultant failure in 1879 was for about four million dollars. It was learned that the books were so poorly kept that accounts were confused and that there was no accurate record of the amount involved. Edward died a broken man; the bishop's resignation was refused by Rome, but William Henry Elder [q.v.] was named coadjutor with right of administration; and Purcell retired to the convent of the Brown County Ursulines. He bore the failure with a sorrow which made death a welcome release.

[The chief collection of Archbishop Purcell's letters is in the archives of Notre Dame University. M. A. McCann, *Archbishop Purcell and the Archdiocese of Cincinnati* (1918), is an uncritical study of some merit; see also *Cath. Hist. Rev.*, July 1920; J. H. Lamott, *Hist. of the Archdiocese of Cincinnati* (1921); *Die katholischen Kirchen Klöster, Institute und Wohlthätigkeits, Anstaeten von Cincinnati* (1889); R. H. Clarke, *Lives of the Deceased Bishops of the Cath. Church in the U. S.*, vol. III (1888); J. G. Shea, *Hist. of the Cath.*

Church in the U. S., vols. III, IV (1890, 1892); *John B. Mannix, Assignee, vs. John B. Purcell et al., District Court, Hamilton County, Ohio* (1882); C. F. X. Mc-Sweeny, *The Story of the Mountain* (1911); M. J. Kelly and J. M. Kirwin, *Hist. of Mt. St. Mary's Sem. of the West* (1894); Cuthbert Butler, *The Vatican Council* (1930); *Banker's Mag.* (N. Y.), Apr. 1879; *Nation* (N. Y.), Mar. 13, 1879; *Enquirer* (Cincinnati), July 4, 1883.]   R. J. P.

PURDUE, JOHN (Oct. 31, 1802–Sept. 12, 1876), merchant, philanthropist, was the son of Charles and Mary (Short) Purdue. He was born in Huntingdon County, Pa., in the little village called Germany, where his father had settled on coming from Scotland. John was the only son in a family of nine children. During his boyhood the family migrated to Ohio, set-tling first in Adelphi, Ross County, and later at Worthington, near Columbus. Having had the advantages of such community schools as were to be found on the frontier, at an early age he became a wage earner. While in his twenties he taught for four years in the district schools of Pickaway County, Ohio. Some time about 1830 he acquired land holdings in Marion County and began operations as a commission merchant. On one occasion he made a journey to New York, where he served with marked suc-cess as the representative of his neighbors in the marketing of hogs.

Moving westward in search of new oppor-tunities Purdue, in 1837, visited Lafayette, Ind., then a flourishing and promising trade center. Two years later he settled there. With charac-teristic energy and enterprise he soon became one of the commercial leaders of the region, con-ducting, with changing partners, a wholesale and retail dry-goods and grocery business for more than twenty-five years. He possessed to a marked degree those qualities requisite for material success in the rapidly developing In-diana region, and, measured by the times, he was very prosperous. In the fifties he estab-lished, with a partner, a commission house in New York City. This branch of his business flourished, particularly during the Civil War, and yielded a large share of his wealth. Like many other men of his type in his day, Purdue dabbled in politics and journalism. Unsuccess-fully he sought in 1866 an independent nomina-tion for Congress. To further his campaign he purchased a local newspaper—the *Lafayette Journal*. These ventures made serious inroads on his fortune, which was further diminished by heavy and unprofitable investments in local manufacturing and railway enterprises.

He was more than a successful merchant, however. From the beginning he displayed a practical, broadminded, and far-sighted citizen-ship, participating in all movements for civic development. The public schools of the com-munity were special objects of his assistance. As a stockholder, trustee, or benefactor—sometimes as all three—he promoted numerous educational enterprises and institutions of the city and the nearby region. In consequence of the land-grant college act, passed by Congress in 1862, the In-diana legislature in 1865 gave legal existence to the "Indiana Agricultural College." To secure the location of this institution in Tippecanoe County, Purdue made a proposition to the legis-lature in 1869, in which he offered to donate $150,000 to supplement the $50,000 and certain lands and buildings already proffered by the citizens of the county, specifying that the in-stitution should bear his name. This proposal was accepted by the state. By the terms of the founding legislation, Purdue was a life member of the trustees of the new institution. As such he was a dominating influence in its organiza-tion and in the erection of its first buildings. He never married. His death occurred quite sud-denly in Lafayette, and he was buried, as he had requested, on the campus of the university, with an unmarked stone at the head of his grave.

[W. M. Hepburn and L. M. Sears, *Purdue Univ.: Fifty Years of Progress* (1925); H. W. Wiley, *An Autobiog.* (1930), especially pp. 123–25; J. P. Dunn, *Ind. and Indianans* (1919), vol. III; *Indianapolis Jour.*, Sept. 13, 1876.]   E. C. E.

PURNELL, WILLIAM HENRY (Feb. 3, 1826–Mar. 30, 1902), lawyer, college president, eldest of six children of Moses and Maria (Bow-en) Purnell, was born on a farm in Worcester County, Md., which had been owned by five generations of ancestors. After preparatory training in Buckingham Academy, Berlin, Md., he entered Delaware College (now the Univer-sity of Delaware), where he was graduated in the class of 1846. He then read law with Judge John R. Franklin in Snow Hill, and was admit-ted to the bar in 1848. The following year, June 13, 1849, he married Margaret Neill Martin. In 1850 he was appointed prosecuting attorney of Worcester County and upon the death of Judge Franklin, was chosen to succeed him in 1853 as deputy attorney-general of Maryland. He held this office until 1855, when he was elected comptroller of the state treasury. Dur-ing the early part of his career, he was a Whig, but later joined the American or Know-Nothing party, and in its state convention, 1857, received thirty-four votes on the first ballot in the con-test for nomination for governor. When Thomas Holliday Hicks [q.v.] was finally nominated for the office, Purnell was nominated to succeed him-self as state comptroller. He was elected and reëlected in 1859. In 1861 he was appointed deputy postmaster of Baltimore by President Lincoln.

Following the battle of Bull Run, Purnell hurried to Washington and secured permission to organize a military force. The "Purnell Legion," as it later was called, was composed of one regiment of infantry, two companies of cavalry, and two batteries of artillery. With a commission as colonel, he had succeeded in recruiting 700 men when he was ordered by General McClellan to join the troops under General Lockwood at Salisbury, Md., for the purpose of opposing a Confederate force which was reported forming on the Eastern Shore of Virginia. When later the Legion was ordered back to Baltimore it numbered 1,240 men. In 1862, Purnell resigned his command, devoting himself during the remainder of the war to his duties in the post office and to political affairs. From 1864 to 1866 he was chairman of the Union Party state central committee. President Johnson reappointed him deputy postmaster of Baltimore in 1866, but the Senate rejected the appointment. Johnson then gave him a recess appointment to the post of assessor of internal revenue at Baltimore, which he held until the rejection of his name by the Senate in February 1867.

After his retirement from politics he practised law in Baltimore until 1870, when he was elected president of Delaware College. During his presidency (1870–85), he was also professor of English literature and language and of mental, moral, and political science, and for a time taught Latin. He proved very successful as a college executive and teacher. According to a colleague: "His scholarship was certainly not that of a modern specialist but he was a somewhat widely read lover of good letters, and a public speaker of more than common charm and force" (E. N. Vallandigham, *Fifty Years of Delaware College, 1870–1920*, n.d., p. 18). He favored coeducation and was mainly responsible for securing favorable action by the Board for the admission of women in 1872, although coeducation was abolished shortly after his resignation. By the Delaware public-school law of 1875, which he had earnestly advocated, he was made *ex-officio* president of the Delaware board of education. He continued as a trustee of Delaware College for the remainder of his life. In 1885 he became principal of the Frederick Female Seminary, now Hood College, Frederick, Md., and later became president of New Windsor College in Carroll County, Md. In 1897, he returned to Delaware College as instructor in elocution and oratory, which post he held until his death. He

was buried at Annapolis, Md., beside his wife, who died Sept. 3, 1895. Five of their ten children died in childhood; a daughter, Caroline Martin Purnell, became a fellow of the American College of Surgeons.

[MSS. in possession of Joseph Brown Turner, Newark, Del., and of Purnell's daughter, Mrs. Walter E. Smith, Wilmington, Del.; E. G. Handy and J. L. Vallandigham, *Newark, Del., Past and Present* (1882); minutes of board of trustees, Delaware College; annual catalogues of Delaware College; H. C. Conrad, *Hist. of the State of Del.* (1908), vol. III; L. P. Powell, *The Hist. of Educ. in Del.* (1893); *The Sun* (Baltimore), Apr. 1, 1902; *Jour. of the Exec. Proc. of the Senate of the U. S.*, vols. XI, XIV, XV.]

G. H. R.

PURPLE, SAMUEL SMITH (June 24, 1822–Sept. 29, 1900), physician, editor, was born in Lebanon, Madison County, N. Y. His father, Lyman Smith Purple, shoemaker and tanner, came from pioneer, farming stock, his ancestors having left England in the seventeenth century to settle in Haddam, Conn. His mother, Minerva Sheffield, also of English descent, was the daughter of Dr. James Sheffield of Earlville, N. Y. The Purple family moved to Earlville in 1836, where three years later the father died, leaving Samuel, a lad of seventeen, the burden of maintaining a small trade encumbered with debts and of supporting his mother and two brothers. About this time he came under the influence of Dr. David Ransom, who kindly loaned the eager boy books on medicine, thus paving the way for the obscure young shoemaker to travel towards a hard-earned and successful career. The boy studied after working long hours to earn enough for his family's needs, and by carefully hoarding each spare penny, he was enabled in 1842 to take a free course at Geneva Medical College. The following year he went to New York, worked under Valentine Mott [q.v.] and others at the University Medical College, and was graduated from that institution in 1844.

He started practising in New York City, and entered upon service at the Marion Street Maternity. Patients were slow in coming to his door, but he was aided somewhat by his appointments. He was physician to the New York Lying-in Asylum (1844–46), physician to the New York Dispensary (1846–49), ward physician during the cholera epidemic of 1849, and later, examining surgeon for the state drafts. Although he made no great contribution to medical science, he became an enthusiastic leader of his profession in New York. He never lost his early love of books, and spent much of his leisure in the interests of bibliography and genealogy. Through his tireless efforts in preserving early medical publications, the New York

Academy of Medicine, of which he was one of the founders, received a remarkable collection of 5,000 volumes of American medical journals. He assisted Charles G. Lee in editing the *New York Journal of Medicine* (1845–48) and published therein several medical papers. From 1848 to 1858 he was editor of the *New York Journal of Medicine*. He also edited the *New York Genealogical and Biographical Record* (1874–86), making valuable contributions to the genealogy of early New York families. He accumulated one of the largest private libraries in New York City, which ultimately formed the nucleus of the library of the New York Academy of Medicine. His unpublished manuscript material indicates his painstaking diligence and rare patience in the compiling of important information, biographical and bibliographical. He was far ahead of his generation in the realization of the future value of old books and letters, and his library contains more than one valuable book which he saved from an ignominious ending 'in the maw of a paper mill.' He was a member of the New York Pathological Society; a trustee of the New York Veterinary College; from 1893 until his death, first vice-president of the New York Genealogical Society; and from 1875 to 1879, president of the New York Academy of Medicine, which in 1887 named him a benefactor. The oil painting which hangs there portrays a kindly, bewhiskered gentleman, dignified but genial. In 1899 he had a hemorrhage into the posterior chamber of the eye, and his sight was destroyed. The following year he succumbed to Bright's disease. He never married, his devotion being lavished upon his immediate relatives and their children.

[*N. Y. Geneal. and Biog. Record*, Jan. 1901; *Medic. Lib. and Hist. Jour.*, Apr. 1903; H. A. Kelly and W. L. Burrage, *Am. Medic. Biogs.* (1920); *N. Y. Tribune*, Oct. 2, 1900.]   G. L. A.

PURRY, JEAN PIERRE (1675–*c.* July 1736), colony promoter, the son of Henry de Purry and Marie Ersel, was born at Neuchâtel, Switzerland. A wine merchant in his earlier years, about 1713 he went out as a planter to Batavia. In 1717 he proposed to the Dutch East India Company to settle a colony in South Australia. The next year he returned to Amsterdam to promote this scheme, and another for a settlement in the same latitude in South Africa. In two pamphlets, *Mémoire sur le Pais des Cafres, et la Terre de Nuyts*, and *Second Mémoire* (Amsterdam, 1718), he expounded a pseudo-scientific theory which he later employed to support his American projects: that the ideal climate in both hemispheres exists at or near the latitude of 33.°

Failing as a promoter in Holland, he turned without any better success to France, where he suffered losses in the Mississippi Bubble. Once more he revamped his proposals, this time to fit the English colonies. In London he now published *A Memorial Presented to . . . the Duke of Newcastle* (1724). The English, he urged, should draw distressed Protestants from the Continent, especially from Switzerland, to plant their own ideal climate zone south and west of South Carolina, to be called "Georgia" or "Georgina." Thus a wedge of settlement would ultimately be driven between the French colonies of Canada and Louisiana. As a beginning he proposed to plant a military colony of six hundred Swiss. The Board of Trade was friendly, and in 1725–26 much excitement was aroused in Switzerland by the advertisements of Purry *et Cie.* The Carolina Proprietors withdrew their offers of transport, however, and in 1726 this scheme also collapsed. In 1730, after the soil of Carolina had passed to the crown, Purry came forward once more with an offer to settle one of the eleven new border townships, a scheme which was closely interwoven with the origins of Georgia. Late in that year, with a party of pioneers, he went to South Carolina to select the town site, Yamasee Bluff on the north bank of the Savannah River, some twenty miles above the later site of Savannah. The South Carolina assembly made a grant of money and supplies, and Purry was commissioned a colonel. On his return to London he secured the promise of a larger grant, of 48,000 acres, in lieu of an exemption from quit-rents which was now withdrawn. In Switzerland, in 1731–32, Purry with his new promotion tracts was reviving the Carolina fever. By December 1732, he had brought some hundred and fifty Swiss to South Carolina, and Purrysburgh was begun. In 1734 he conducted another group of 260 Swiss Protestants to Purrysburgh. The town attracted some other colonists, but it was not destined to endure. The site was poorly chosen; there were difficulties over intruding grants within the six-mile square; and after Purry's death in Carolina, Georgia, gradually drew off most of his followers. Yet Purry's influence was not negligible. Aside from his leadership of the emigrating Swiss, his advertisements and activities aided notably in creating a wider interest in the southern frontier, in its defense and settlement.

Purry married Lucrèce de Chaillet, by whom he had two sons and a daughter. One of the sons, Charles, accompanied his father to America; the other, David, became a prominent banker in Lisbon and a benefactor of Neuchâtel.

[An anonymous memoir of Purry was printed in the "Advertisement" to John Peter Purry, *A Method for Determining the Best Climate of the Earth* (London, 1744). See also H. A. M. Smith, "Purrysburgh," *S. C. Hist. and Geneal. Mag.*, Oct. 1909; and V. W. Crane, *The Southern Frontier, 1670–1732* (1928), index and bibliography. For other Purry tracts see *Gentleman's Mag.*, Aug. 1732, pp. 886, 894 ff., Sept. 1732, pp. 969 f., Oct. 1732, pp. 1017 f.; and L. L. Mackall, in *Ga. Hist. Quart.*, June 1918. For family, see F. A. M. Jeanneret, *Biographie Neuchateloise* (1863), II, 250–54; and for note of death, *The Colonial Records of . . . Ga.*, XXV (1910), 180.]   V. W. C.

PURSH, FREDERICK (Feb. 4, 1774–July 11, 1820), botanist, horticulturist, and explorer, is one of the least known of early writers on American botany. Even the main facts of his life have been grossly misstated. His name was originally Friedrich Traugott Pursch, and according to a letter published in 1827 by his brother, Carl August Pursch, he was born in Saxony, at Grossenhain. After there obtaining a public-school education he joined his brother in Dresden, where the latter was secretary of the Royal Saxon Cabinet-Council. In Dresden Pursh proved an apt student of the natural sciences, and shortly obtained a position in the local Royal Botanic Gardens. Here he pursued his studies of botany and horticulture, until, in January 1799, he sailed for America to assume management of a botanical garden near Baltimore—the realization of a long-cherished dream of foreign travel. From 1802 to 1805 he was in charge of the famous botanical garden of William Hamilton, near Philadelphia, and met the botanists G. H. E. Mühlenberg, William Bartram, Humphry Marshall, and Benjamin Smith Barton [*qq.v.*]. During this period, as ever after, he was engaged in assembling plants "from all parts of North America."

Barton, as Pursh's patron, now provided funds for two memorable journeys of botanical exploration. The first (1806) was through the mountains from western Maryland to the border of North Carolina, and back along the coast. The second, the following year, was across the Pocono region of Pennsylvania to Central New York, thence east to the Green Mountains of Vermont. Inclement weather, illness, and scant funds proved too great a handicap, however, and Pursh returned from Rutland directly to Philadelphia. He was now in charge of the Hosack garden, New York, until 1810, when illness necessitated a trip to the Lesser Antilles. Returning in the fall of 1811, restored in health, he landed at Wiscasset, Me., and revisited New York, but shortly embarked for England with his collections. Here, under the patronage of A. B. Lambert, a wealthy amateur botanist, and with access to many historic early American collections, he completed in two years his *Flora Americae Septentrionalis,* published early in 1814. This was the first complete flora of America north of Mexico, and for a generation remained the standard work. It included many new species brought back by the Lewis and Clark transcontinental expedition to the Columbia River, these the first to be described from the western interior.

Little is known of Pursh's later years. Instead of revisiting Saxony, as planned, he returned to America, settled in Montreal, and gathered extensive materials (mainly in the province of Quebec) for a flora of Canada. These were destroyed by fire, however, and he died shortly afterward at Montreal, destitute. His body now lies in Mount Royal Cemetery, of that city. Aside from his *Flora,* Pursh is known chiefly from his *Journal of a Botanical Excursion in the Northeastern Parts of the States of Pennsylvania and New York* (1869), a quaint and absorbing document which in itself reveals the simple, kindly nature and botanical acumen of the man, and his remarkable perseverance under adverse circumstances. Dying at forty-five, he left, nevertheless, a deep and permanent impress on North American descriptive botany.

[Errors in the scant sketches of Pursh are numerous, varied, and persistent; *e.g.* his birth in Tobolsk, Siberia, his death Sept. 22, 1825, the dates of his two excursions, which he himself erroneously gives as 1805 and 1806. The circumstances of his death, burial, and reinterment are authentically stated by D. P. Penhallow, in *Proc. and Trans. of the Royal Soc. of Canada,* 2 ser., vol. III, pt. 4 (1897). See also, *Flora* (Ratisbon), X, 491–96 (Aug. 21, 1827); *Am. Jour. Sci. and Arts,* IX, 269–74 (1825); C. S. Sargent, *Scientific Papers of Asa Gray,* II (1889), 32–33, 245–51; *Memoirs of the Torrey Bot. Club,* XVI, 298 (1921); *Jour. of the N. Y. Botanical Garden,* XXIV, 109 (June 1923); *Jour. Washington Acad. Sci.,* XVII, 351 (1927).]
                              W. R. M.

PURVIANCE, DAVID (Nov. 14, 1766–Aug. 19, 1847), frontier preacher and legislator, one of the founders of what came to be known as the Christian denomination, was born in Iredell County, N. C., the son of John and Jane (Wasson) Purviance, and the second of their eleven children. John, a native of Pennsylvania, had moved to North Carolina soon after his marriage in 1764. David attended the neighborhood schools, was grounded in the doctrines of the Presbyterian Church at home, and studied the classics at the seminary of Rev. James Hall [*q.v.*], pastor of the Fourth Creek (Statesville) Church. During the Revolution, in which his father served as an officer, his studies were more or less interrupted by demands upon him at home. Subsequently, he taught and was for a time employed in the town clerk's office at Salisbury,

N. C. After his marriage in 1789 to Mary, daughter of John and Martha Ireland, his father established him on a farm on the south fork of the Yadkin River; later he moved to the vicinity of Nashville, Tenn., where the Indians killed and scalped a younger brother; and about 1792 he settled at Cane Ridge, Bourbon County, Ky., clearing from the wilds land sufficient to yield a livelihood for his family.

Soon, both in religious and political affairs, he became one of the prominent persons of that section. In 1797 he was elected to the legislature by those opposed to the reëstablishment of the oyer and terminer court. A speech in reply to John Breckinridge [q.v.], who sought to carry through a reëstablishment bill, won Purviance high regard and was instrumental in defeating the measure. During the several sessions he was in the legislature he was the leader of the farmer members, who would follow him blindly because of their faith in his honesty and independence. His opposition to slavery and advocacy of gradual emancipation prevented his election to the constitutional convention of 1799.

Purviance was a ruling elder in the Cane Ridge Presbyterian Church and in 1801 was licensed by the presbytery as an exhorter. He had been profoundly stirred by the Great Revival and imbued with its New Light doctrines. When Barton W. Stone [q.v.] and others withdrew from the Kentucky Synod and formed the Springfield Presbytery, Purviance cast in his lot with them and was ordained to the ministry. Stone made him co-pastor with himself of the congregations at Cane Ridge and Concord. With the other members of the Springfield Presbytery, in 1804 he renounced all man-made creeds, agreed to acknowledge no name but Christian and no creed but the Bible, and signed "The Last Will and Testament" of that presbytery. He was the first of the seceders to repudiate infant baptism and insist on immersion as the form required by the New Testament. He made preaching tours into North Carolina, Tennessee, and Ohio, and in 1807 removed to the Ohio frontier, whither a company of Cane Ridge families had migrated, settling at what is now New Paris, Preble County. Here he established a church, the first in that section, which grew rapidly and of which he remained in charge till toward the close of his life. The first school, also, in that neighborhood he taught in his own kitchen. Again he entered politics, was elected representative in 1809, and served three terms in the state Senate (1810–16). He was once more elected to the legislature in 1826. As in Kentucky, he took an active part in legislation

and was respected for his fearlessness and integrity. A friend of the negro, he opposed the "black laws"; he was instrumental in having Miami University located at Oxford, and was appointed one of its trustees. The records of the college show that on occasion he acted as president *pro tempore* (*Laws Relating to the Miami University,* 1833). He died in Preble County at the residence of a son.

[Levi Purviance, *The Biog. of Elder David Purviance* (1848); *The Biog. of Eld. Barton Warren Stone, Written by Himself* (1847); Robert Davidson, *Hist. of the Presbyt. Ch. in the State of Ky.* (1847); J. R. Rogers, *The Cane Ridge Meeting-house* (1910); M. T. Morrill, *A Hist. of the Christian Denomination in America* (1912).]   H. E. S.

PURYEAR, BENNET (July 23, 1826–Mar. 30, 1914), educator, publicist, was born on a plantation in Mecklenburg County, Va., the youngest son of Thomas and Elizabeth (Marshall) Puryear. His great-grandmother was a first cousin of Thomas Jefferson, and his mother a cousin of Chief-Justice John Marshall. Prepared for college by a neighborhood tutor, he was graduated A.B. at Randolph-Macon College (then at Boydton, Va.), in 1847, and received the degree of A.M. three years later. In his time the college had about sixty students. After teaching school for a year in Alabama, he spent the session of 1848–49 at the University of Virginia, studying medicine, though balancing in his mind various careers. In 1849 he went to Richmond College as tutor in chemistry, and was made professor in 1850. In 1858 he returned to Randolph-Macon as professor of chemistry, where he remained until February 1863, when the Civil War put an end for a time to academic life.

When Richmond College reopened after the Civil War, Puryear was called back to his former chair of chemistry, which he held until his retirement in 1895. During most of this time he was also chairman of the faculty, the chief academic officer of the college. His strong personality, gift for teaching, and administrative ability made a lasting impression on Richmond College (now the University of Richmond). His interest in rural life was notable, and his influence among farmers was wide. He was a pioneer in applying chemistry to agriculture in Virginia. While of a practical turn of mind and a teacher of science, he had also great taste for literature. As a writer he contributed to the *Religious Herald,* Richmond *Dispatch,* and *New York Times* forceful articles, generally signed "Civis," dealing with the educational, racial, and political problems growing out of the Reconstruction era in Virginia. His attitude toward the public-school system was reactionary and provoked violent discussion. In *The Public School in Its Relations to the Negro,* a pamphlet printed in 1877, he summarized his views: "The political principles which are invoked in the support of the public school are foreign to free institutions and fatal to liberty; . . . the theory upon which the system is based is well calculated to emasculate the energies of a people, and to debauch public and private morality; . . . the education of children is not the business of government, but the sacred and imperative duty of parents."

In personal appearance Puryear was tall and striking. His first wife was Virginia Catherine Ragland, of Richmond; his second, Ella Marian Wyles, of Mecklenburg County. After his retirement he made his home at "Edgewood," Madison County, Va., until his death in 1914. He was buried in Hollywood Cemetery, Richmond. His second wife survived him, with their six children and five children of his first marriage.

[MSS. in possession of Puryear's daughter, Mrs. Allan Hill, Richmond, Va.; Richard Irby, *Hist. of Randolph-Macon College* (n.d.); Wm. Cathcart, *The Bapt. Encyc.* (1881); *Religious Herald,* Apr. 2, 1914; *Times-Dispatch* (Richmond), Mar. 31, 1914.]

S. C. M.

PUSEY, CALEB (*c.* 1650–Feb. 25, 1727 o.s.), builder and manager of Chester Mills, Pa., political leader and Quaker controversial writer, was the son of William Pusey. He was born in Berkshire, England, but in early life moved to London, where he married Ann Worley in 1681. He was a last-maker by trade. Although educated as a Baptist, he joined the Society of Friends and was keenly interested in William Penn's Holy Experiment. He was associated with Penn and eight other proprietors in a scheme for the "setting up" of mills in Pennsylvania and was selected as resident manager of the enterprise. In 1682 he and his wife emigrated to Pennsylvania and settled on Chester Creek near Upland in Chester (now Delaware) County. The corn mill which he erected on this site in 1683 attained wide fame as the Chester Mills. It was not the oldest mill in the province —the Swedes had built one a few years earlier on Cobb's Creek—but it was the first erected under Penn's proprietorship and Penn himself laid the corner-stone. Seven of the partners soon disposed of their interests and for several years the mill belonged to Penn, Pusey, and Samuel Carpenter. Pusey continued to serve as manager until about 1717, when he and his family removed to Marlborough township in Chester County, where he spent the last years of his life.

His wife died in 1726. He died the following year, survived by two daughters.

Pusey was for many years a justice of the peace of Chester County. He was also sheriff in 1692–93 and county treasurer for a short time in 1704. He was offered an appointment as judge of the supreme court in 1701 but refused to accept it. He served in the provincial assembly for several terms between 1686 and 1713 and was a member of the governor's council in 1695, 1697, and from 1699 to 1715. He was a prominent member of the Society of Friends and played a leading part in three important movements: the settlement of private disputes by arbitration, the collection of historical records, and the writing of pamphlets in defense of the orthodox Quaker point of view. He founded and for several years presided over an informal court, called "the Peacemakers," which settled controversies between Quakers. He also made a large collection of historical manuscripts which was preserved and increased by Samuel Smith [*q.v.*], the historian of West Jersey, and was later used by Robert Proud [*q.v.*] in his *History of Pennsylvania* (2 vols., 1797–98). His controversial writings were mainly directed against George Keith, Daniel Leeds, Francis Bugg, and other Quaker apostates. The following is a list of these works, though the titles are somewhat abbreviated: *A Serious and Seasonable Warning unto all People occasioned by two most dangerous Epistles to a late Book of John Falldoe's* (1675); *A Modest Account from Pennsylvania of the Principal Differences in Point of Doctrine, between George Keith and those of the People called Quakers* (1696); *Satan's Harbinger Encountered* (1700); *Daniel Leeds, Justly Rebuked for abusing William Penn, and his Foly and Fals-Hoods Contained in his two Printed Chalenges to Caleb Pusey, made Manifest* (1702); *Proteus Ecclesiasticus, or George Keith varied in Fundamentalls . . . and Prov'd an Apostate* (1703?); *George Keith once more brought to the Test and proved a Prevaricator* (1704?); *The Bomb Search'd and found stuff'd with False Ingredients, being a Just Confutation of an abusive Printed Half-Sheet . . . originally published against the Quakers, by Francis Bugg* (1705); *Some Remarks upon a late Pamphlet signed part by John Talbot and part by Daniel Leeds, called The Great Mystery of Fox-craft* (1705?). These pamphlets are rarely found in good condition, but there is an almost complete set in the library of the Historical Society of Pennsylvania. The first two were printed in London; the others bear the imprint of Reinier Jansen of Philadelphia.

[See: "A Testimony from New-Garden Monthly-Meeting . . . Concerning Caleb Pusey," in *A Collection of Memorials Concerning . . . the People called Quakers, in Pa.* (1787), pp. 68–70; Mrs. R. P. Leys, "Caleb Pusey and his Times," *Proc. Del. County Hist. Soc.*, vol. I (1902); J. S. Futhey and Gilbert Cope, *Hist. of Chester County, Pa.* (1881); Pennock Pusey, *The Pusey Family* (1883); Dillwyn Parrish and S. P. Wharton, *The Parrish Family* (1925). There is also some material, including a view of Pusey's residence at Chester Mills, in George Smith, *Hist. of Delaware County, Pa.* (1862). A list of Pusey's writings is given in Joseph Smith, *A Descriptive Cat. of Friends' Books* (1867), II, 438–40.]   W. R. S–h.

PUSHMATAHA (c. 1765–Dec. 24, 1824), Choctaw chief, was born probably in what is now Noxubee County, Miss. His origins, early history, and rise to prominence were subjects of speculation and curiosity in his own generation. Aware of the dramatic value of mystery, he is said to have accounted for himself by the statement: "I had no father. I had no mother. The lightning rent the living oak, and Pushmataha sprang forth" (but see Halbert, *post,* pp. 115–17). Having attained distinction by his exploits in tribal warfare on both sides of the Mississippi River, in 1805 he was the elected chief of his tribe and was living near what is now Meridian, Miss. (*American State Papers, post,* I, 749; Gaines, *post,* June 27). In that year he signed the treaty at Mount Dexter. This provided for the cession of a large tract of land in Alabama and Mississippi, for the payment to him of a lump sum of $500, and for an annuity of $150 while he should continue to be a chief. He opposed the efforts of Tecumseh [*q.v.*] to form an Indian confederacy against the westward thrust of white settlement, and his prestige and eloquence were important in the failure of Tecumseh's visit south in 1811. In the wars that followed he, with John Pitchlynn, persuaded the Choctaw to join the United States, led a band of some 500 warriors in the forces of Andrew Jackson, and fought brilliantly at Holy Ground against the Creeks under William Weatherford [*q.v.*]. After the peace, he signed the treaties of cession in 1816 and 1820. In 1824 he visited the city of Washington, where he and his party met Lafayette and enjoyed the hospitality of the federal capital. Exposed to inclement weather, he fell ill and died there. He was buried in the Congressional Cemetery, according to the rites of white civilization, with a great procession and booming guns. A stone monument marks his grave.

[Gideon Lincecum, "Life of Apushimataha," *Miss. Hist. Soc. Pubs.*, vol. IX (1906); H. S. Halbert, "Creek War Incidents," *Trans. Ala. Hist. Soc.*, vol. II (1898); reminiscences of G. S. Gaines, *Mobile Daily Register*, June 19, 27, July 3, 10, 17, 1872; J. F. H. Claiborne, *Life and Times of Gen. Sam. Dale* (1860); *Am. State Papers: Indian Affairs*, vols. I, II (1932–34); *Niles' Weekly Register*, Dec. 4, 1824, Jan. 1, 1825; authority for date of death a few minutes after midnight from *Washington Gazette,* Dec. 24, 1824.]   K. E. C.

PUTNAM, ARTHUR (Sept. 6, 1873–May 27, 1930), sculptor, was the second of three children of Oramel Hinckley Putnam, a civil engineer, and Mary (Gibson) Putnam, both of New England stock. He was born in Waveland, Miss., from which place his parents soon moved to Omaha and later, in 1880, to San Francisco, where the father died. The family then returned to Omaha, where Arthur spent his boyhood. Although an attractive and affectionate boy, he was hard to control, and after trying for some months to keep him in Kemper Hall, a military academy at Davenport, Iowa, his mother put him to work. For a time he had a job in a photo-engraving establishment, where he may have learned the rudiments of drawing; then he worked in an iron foundry at New Orleans; at eighteen he rejoined his mother on a ranch near San Diego, Cal. When he was twenty, over six feet tall and very strong, he applied for drawing lessons at the Art Students' League in San Francisco. His genius was soon evident, and he was permitted to work for a few months in the studio of Rupert Schmidt, a sculptor. For the next six years he studied chiefly by himself, with criticism and encouragement from his San Francisco friends, supporting himself by working in a slaughter-house, surveying, trapping pumas for the San Francisco zoo. In 1897–98, he worked under the sculptor Edward Kemeys in Chicago. In July 1899, at Sacramento, he married Grace Storey, a teacher of water color. Two children were born to them.

Soon after his marriage, Putnam won the enduring friendship of the architect Willis Polk [*q.v.*], through whom he thereafter received numerous commissions for architectural decorations. In 1903, E. W. Scripps ordered from him a series of large figures illustrating the history of California. Three of these, Indian, Priest, and Plowman, were completed and ultimately cast in bronze. In December 1905, aided by Scripps and Mrs. W. H. Crocker, Putnam and his wife went to Europe. In Rome he studied bronze casting and exhibited several animal groups at the Spring Salon of 1906; in Paris, he had several groups accepted for the Salon of 1907, but he became homesick and returned early in that year to California. The rebuilding of San Francisco after the earthquake kept him busy with architectural commissions, but, driving himself constantly, he continued to experiment with bronze casting and in 1909 started a foundry of his own where he produced a number of fine bronzes by the *cire-perdue* process. He was steadily winning recognition when, in 1911, he submitted to an operation for a brain tumor which permanently impaired his brain, leaving his left side paralyzed and destroying his sense of proportion and his self-control. He never again could draw; he had seizures of furious rage and became estranged from his wife, who at length reluctantly permitted him to divorce her. Through the ensuing years he was enabled to exist largely by the help of his friends, who saw to the marketing of his accumulated bronzes and even took some of his plaster models to Paris to be cast. On Mar. 19, 1917, he married Marion Pearson, who cared for him during the rest of his life. After 1921 they lived abroad; he regained a measure of serenity; and in 1927 his former wife took her children to see their father. Death came to him suddenly at his home near Paris in his fifty-seventh year.

In 1915, fourteen of Putnam's bronzes ("Indian and Puma," "Skunked Wildcat," "Sneaking Coyote," "Leopard and Gnu," "Combat," "Tiger Love," "Resting Puma," "Little Cub Bear," "Buffalo Hunt," "Coyote Head," "Crouching Wildcat," "Two Pumas," "Puma and Snake," "Snarling Jaguar") were exhibited at the Panama-Pacific International Exposition in San Francisco, and he was honored by a gold medal. His "Mermaid Fountain" on the Exposition grounds was commended by critics as opposite in standpoint as Christian Brinton (*Impressions of the Art at the Panama-Pacific Exposition*, 1916) and Lorado Taft (*Modern Tendencies in Sculpture*, 1921). A good collection of his bronzes is on view at the California Palace of the Legion of Honor, San Francisco. He is represented also in the Fine Arts Society of San Diego, Cal., the Boston Museum of Fine Arts, and the Metropolitan Museum, New York. His larger works include the Sloat Monument at Monterey, Cal., and the bronze figures for E. W. Scripps. Thoroughly familiar with the animals of the West, he "drew less well from a model than from his imagination. 'The damn thing' (the model) he once said . . . 'disturbs me by thrusting his individual peculiarities between my conception and the work I am doing' " (Heyneman, *post*, p. 41). Perhaps because he never received any academic instruction, and (save for the undoubted influence of works by Barye and Frémiet seen abroad) depended wholly on his own intensity of observation, his sculpture, though not revolutionary, has won high praise from those modernists who oppose academic ideals.

[Julie Helen Heyneman, *Arthur Putnam, Sculptor* (1932); R. V. S. Berry, in *Am. Mag. of Art*, May 1929; Bruce Porter, in *Sunset Mag.*, Nov. 1904; Su-

zanne La Follette, *Art in America* (1929); J. M. Baltimore, in *Craftsman*, Nov. 1905; Phyllis Ackerman, in *Arts and Decoration*, Sept. 1923; *Monumental News*, May, Aug., Sept. 1905; *Art Digest*, June 1930; *N. Y. Times*, May 29, 1930; *Am. Art Annual*, vol. XXVII (1931); comment from Mrs. Herbert Adams.]

E. R. D.

PUTNAM, CHARLES PICKERING (Sept. 15, 1844–Apr. 22, 1914), physician, was born in Boston, Mass., the son of Charles Gideon and Elizabeth Cabot (Jackson) Putnam and brother of James Jackson Putnam [q.v.]. His father was a physician and his ancestors had long been distinguished in Massachusetts as jurists or physicians, his maternal grandfather being James Jackson [q.v.]. He was graduated by Harvard College in 1865 and by the Harvard Medical School in 1869, after which time he continued his medical studies at the Massachusetts General Hospital, Boston, and, later, in Germany. Beginning in 1871 he carried on a general practice in Boston, later specializing, partially, in pediatrics and orthopedics. He also lectured at the Harvard Medical School from 1873 to 1879 and served at the Boston Dispensary as a physician from 1871 to 1873 and as orthopedic surgeon from 1873 to 1876. In 1898 he was elected president of the American Pediatric Society.

Putnam's chief contributions, however, were outside of his strictly professional activities. He was the most important leader in charitable and social work in Boston in his day. In 1873 he founded, with others, the Boston Society for the Relief of Destitute Mothers and Infants, a pioneer establishment which fostered the idea of keeping mother and child together, and he served as president of the society from 1904 until his death. He became physician to the Massachusetts Infants Asylum in 1875 and under his direction the death-rate in this institution was greatly reduced. In 1879, when the Associated Charities of Boston was founded, he was made president and served as chairman of many committees up to the time of his death. In addition, he took an active part in almost every social and charitable project in Boston from 1875 to 1914. He reorganized the Boston institutions for the care of prisoners, the poor, and delinquent children, serving under two mayors from 1892 to 1897, and was appointed chairman of the unpaid board of trustees of the Children's Institutions of Boston, serving from 1902 to 1911. He helped to organize the Directory of Nurses, the Boston Medical Library, with James R. Chadwick [q.v.], the Mental Hygiene Association, the Massachusetts Civic League, the State Board of Insanity, and many other projects which had to do with the schools of Massachusetts, playgrounds, juvenile courts, and the probation service for prisoners. "In short, Dr. Putnam was for a generation the backbone of social work in Boston" (Lee, *post*, p. 742).

In 1889 he was married to Lucy Washburn, daughter of William and Susan Tucker Washburn; there were three children, one son being a physician. He was a member of numerous medical societies and of the American Academy of Arts and Sciences. As a practitioner, especially in pediatrics, he was greatly loved; his work in the field of social medicine made him one of the outstanding medical figures of his generation. Completely unselfish and endowed with great sympathy and a fertile mind, he helped to establish a new era in social medicine in America.

[The best account of Putnam is the notice by Joseph Lee in the *Boston Medic. and Surgic. Jour.*, May 7, 1914. Other sources include: *Boston Transcript*, Apr. 22, 23, 1914; *Proc. Am. Acad. Arts and Sci.*, vol. LI (1916); information from the family.]   H. R. V.

PUTNAM, EBEN (Oct. 10, 1868–Jan. 22, 1933), historian, genealogist, editor, publisher, and soldier, was born in Salem, Mass., son of Frederic Ward [*q.v.*] and Adelaide Martha (Edmands) Putnam. His father was an eminent anthropologist. Although the son assisted his father in scientific investigation, he began his career in 1885 in a Boston banking and brokerage house. From 1890 to 1894 he managed the historic Salem Press with which he remained connected until 1907. He became widely known as an editor and publisher, and as a writer on historic and genealogical topics. For many years he carried on extensive researches in the United States and England, being recognized as one of the leading authorities in genealogy. He served for a time as treasurer and a director of a Boston investment house of which his son, Frederic L. Putnam, was the head, likewise holding directorships in various public utility corporations. Early becoming a member of the Salem Light Infantry Veteran Corps, he was subsequently one of the petitioners for the establishment of the Massachusetts Naval Brigade, the first state naval militia to be organized. At the outbreak of the World War he attended camp at Plattsburg, N. Y., was commissioned a captain in the Quartermaster Corps, and served overseas in that branch of the army, with headquarters at Nantes. After the war he was commissioned major in the Quartermaster Reserve Corps, and in 1927 he was made a lieutenant-colonel. On the organization of the American Legion he entered actively into its affairs. He became historian of his local post (Wellesley, Mass.) and of the Department of Massachusetts, and from 1920 to his death he was national his-

torian. He was interested in the erection of the national archives building in Washington, serving on the commission on national archives of the American Historical Association (1919–29), and received in 1932 the thanks of the national convention of the American Legion for his endeavors.

Putnam's published contributions to history and genealogy were notable. He was author of *A History of the Putnam Family in England and America* (2 vols., 1891–1908); *The Putnam Lineage* (1907); *Lieutenant Joshua Hewes, A New England Pioneer* (1913); *Military and Naval Annals of Danvers* (1914); and *The Holden Genealogy* (1923). He assisted in the preparation of genealogies of the Osgood, Converse, and Bixby families. At different times he edited periodicals of genealogical and antiquarian interest, most important among them being the *Genealogical Magazine* (originally the *Salem Press Historical and Genealogical Record* and issued by Putnam under a succession of titles), which he conducted from 1890 to 1917. As compiler and editor of the *Report of the Commission on Massachusetts' Part in the World War* (2 vols., 1929–31), he accomplished an important task with distinction. His lesser works included articles descriptive of British and American archives, and various reports. He was a member and officer of many military, historic, and patriotic organizations, some of which he founded. His death occurred at his home in Wellesley Farms, Mass., from the effects of influenza and pneumonia contracted shortly after the armistice. In 1890 he had married Florence Tucker, daughter of Frank and Elizabeth (Joyce) Tucker of Bath, Me., by whom he had three children. To the American Legion "he not only proved to be a wise counsellor, but also protested courageously against proposals which he believed to be detrimental to the best interests of the organization," wrote Professor Claude M. Fuess. "It might be said of him . . . that he rounded out a life of useful work, sacrificing his own interests for those of Commonwealth and country, and retaining the affection and respect of those who knew him."

[*Who's Who in America*, 1932–33; Putnam's *The Putnam Lineage* (1907); obituary articles in *Boston Herald* and *Boston Transcript*, Jan. 23, 1933; and an appreciation by C. M. Fuess in the *Boston Transcript*, Jan. 25, 1933.]   W. M. E.

PUTNAM, FREDERIC WARD (Apr. 16, 1839–Aug. 14, 1915), archeologist, naturalist, museum administrator, and university professor, was born in Salem, Mass. His father, Ebenezer Putnam, as well as his grandfather and great-grandfather of that name, were all graduates of

Harvard College and descended from John Putnam who came from England and settled in Salem before 1641. His mother, Elizabeth Appleton, was the daughter of Nathaniel Appleton, a descendant of Samuel Appleton who settled in Ipswich. Educated at home and in local private schools, Putnam early began to aid his father, a horticulturist, and rapidly developed a keen interest in the study of nature. In 1856 he entered Harvard College, where his ability and enthusiasm attracted the attention of Louis Agassiz, who made him his assistant the following year. Until 1864 he carried on his studies in close association with Agassiz, whose influence in emphasizing the importance of collecting and studying concrete data dominated Putnam's whole after life. His work at Harvard was pursued without reference to the formal requirements for the degree, but in 1898 he was awarded an S.B. "as of" the class of 1862. He also received the honorary degrees of A.M. (Williams, 1868) and S.D. (University of Pennsylvania, 1894).

From Cambridge Putnam returned to Salem to be curator of vertebrata and later superintendent of the Museum of the Essex Institute, thus beginning the long series of administrative positions which he held throughout his life. From 1859 to 1868 he served as curator of ichthyology at the Boston Society of Natural History, and was its president from 1887 to 1891. From 1867 to 1869 he was superintendent of the Museum of the East India Marine Society of Salem. Acting in concert with A. S. Packard, Alpheus Hyatt, and E. S. Morse, fellow students under Agassiz, he was influential in inducing the philanthropist George Peabody to found the Peabody Academy of Science in Salem, and from 1869 to 1873 served as its director. With the same three young scientists he founded the scientific journal known as the *American Naturalist* and was one of its first editors. The Peabody Museum of American Archæology and Ethnology had been established by George Peabody at Harvard College in 1866. With Jeffries Wyman, its first curator, Putnam later carried on excavations in the shell-heaps along the New England coast, and after Wyman's death in 1874, he was selected as his successor. His interests were now turned from the study of animals to that of man, and to the gathering of great collections illustrative of man's development and culture he devoted all his energies and enthusiasm. Despite his preoccupation with anthropological and archeological work, however, he found time to carry on other activities as well. In 1874 he served as assistant on the Geological Survey of Kentucky,

from 1876 to 1878 as assistant in ichthyology at the Museum of Comparative Zoölogy in Harvard, from 1876 to 1879 as assistant to the United States Engineers survey west of the 100" meridian, and from 1882 to 1889 as state commissioner of inland fisheries in Massachusetts. From 1873 to 1898 he fulfilled the arduous and important duties of permanent secretary of the American Association for the Advancement of Science, becoming its president in 1898.

As Curator of the Peabody Museum, Putnam revolutionized the methods of museum administration, for instead of merely purchasing collections, he organized and sent out numerous expeditions which were the pioneers in the scientific exploration of Southwestern and Central American archeology. Chosen as director of the anthropological section of the World's Columbian Exposition in Chicago, he instituted important field studies and gathered together an impressive exhibit which served for the first time to awaken a wide-spread interest in the subject. The materials thus brought together formed the nucleus of the great collections of the Field Museum in Chicago. In 1894, while retaining his position in Cambridge, Putnam was made curator of anthropology in the American Museum of Natural History in New York City, spending half his time in his new position. He reorganized and greatly strengthened this department of the museum, gathering about him an able group of investigators, and was instrumental in sending out the Jessup Expedition, whose researches in Northeastern Asia and Northwestern America were productive of most important results. In 1901, when a department of anthropology was organized at the University of California, he gave much of his time to its planning and early administration. To all of these activities, Putnam added that of teaching, having been appointed Peabody Professor of American Archæology and Ethnology at Harvard in 1887. Under his leadership a strong department of anthropology grew up, whose influence was far-reaching in introducing the comparatively young science as a subject of university instruction.

Putnam's activities were, however, not confined to administration and teaching, for he took active part for many years in archeological field-work, chiefly along the Atlantic Coast, in the Ohio Valley, and in the Southwest. The results of his studies were published in a large number of short papers. His exacting duties, however, as editor of museum and other publications and for twenty-five years as permanent secretary of the American Association for the Advancement of Science left him little opportunity for the preparation of larger and more comprehensive works. Recognition of the value of his services led to his election to numerous scientific societies and academies both in this country and abroad, and to his being made chevalier of the Legion of Honor by the French government. In recognition of his seventieth birthday, a large volume of special papers was published by his associates and former students. Putnam was married on June 1, 1864, to Adelaide M. Edmands, a descendant of Walter Edmands who came from England to Concord in 1635. She died in 1879 and on Apr. 29, 1882, he was married to Esther Orne Clark of Chicago. He died in Cambridge, survived by three children of the first marriage, one of whom was Eben Putnam [q.v.].

In the rise and development of anthropology in America, Putnam played a leading, perhaps the foremost part. Directly or indirectly he was largely responsible for the growth of most of the anthropological museums, for the acceptance of anthropology as a university study, and for the spread and popularization of an interest in the subject. His students and associates held important positions in practically every institution in the United States where anthropological work was carried on. Much of his influence and success lay in his personality. His enthusiasm, energy, and tact enabled him to enlist interest and cooperation in whatever he undertook, his patience and tenacity of purpose made it possible to carry through projects against serious difficulties and in spite of aggravating delays. His kindliness and generosity endeared him to all his students and associates, who felt for him a very warm and personal affection.

[For a bibliography of Putnam's publications, which up to 1909 numbered over four hundred titles, see *Putnam Anniversary Vol.: Anthropol. Essays presented to Frederic Ward Putnam in Honor of his Seventieth Birthday* (1909), pp. 601–27. For notices of his life and work see: *Science*, Sept. 10, 1915; *Jour. Am. Folk-Lore*, July-Sept. 1915; *Am. Anthropologist*, Oct.-Dec. 1915; *Essex Inst. Hist. Colls.*, July 1916; Eben Putnam, *The Putnam Lineage* (1907); *Who's Who in America*, 1914–15; *Boston Transcript*, Aug. 16, 1915.]

R. B. D.

PUTNAM, GEORGE HAVEN (Apr. 2, 1844–Feb. 27, 1930), soldier, publisher, and author, continued in a remarkable way the life work of his father, George Palmer Putnam [q.v.]. He carried on his father's publishing business, brought to successful completion the fight for international copyright which his father had begun, and was, like his father, interested in authorship and public service. He even continued his father's professional relationships. The elder Putnam dealt with the second and third John Murray of the famous line of British publishers.

The younger Putnam dealt with the fourth and fifth.

He was born in London, while his father and mother, Victorine (Haven) Putnam, were living in England, the former as representative of his publishing firm, and was brought to the United States when he was three years old. Having been born on British soil of American parents, he had a legal claim to either citizenship. Under the treaties in force at the time, he was required to make a definite choice at twenty-one, but having, when he reached that age, been an American officer on active service he took his citizenship for granted. As a property-holder in London, however, he voted in British parish elections for half a century and once took the stump for Gladstone during a Parliamentary election. His first American ballot was cast in an unofficial poll of officer-prisoners at Libby Prison, and was cast for Abraham Lincoln.

Putnam's education, like his father's, was much interrupted. From 1857 to 1859 he earned his way as assistant and tutor in a grammar school at the corner of Broadway and Twentieth Street. In 1859 he entered the Columbia Grammar School under Charles Anthon [q.v.], working in the summer and earning enough money to help send him later to Göttingen. He had, at this period, a small share in the landscaping of Central Park. He passed the examination for entrance to Columbia College with the class of 1864, but owing to eye trouble had to be sent abroad for treatment, and after some months of study at the Sorbonne, in Paris, and at the University of Berlin, he undertook scientific work at Göttingen in preparation for a career in forestry. When it became apparent that the Civil War would be of long duration, he returned to the United States, and joined Company E, 176th New York Volunteers, with which regiment he served throughout the war, except while a prisoner. During an emergency he acted as regimental chaplain, his preaching leading to such broadening of his religious views that he later insisted on leaving the Baptist Church. He was soon made a commissioned officer, and attained the rank of major. He was captured, Oct. 19, 1864, at the battle of Cedar Creek, made an unsuccessful attempt to escape, and was then sent to Libby Prison. Later, he was transferred to the prison at Danville, from which he was released by exchange in 1865. He again saw active service in the closing months of the war and during the occupation of the Confederacy. In the latter years of his life he recorded his war experiences in *A Prisoner of War in Virginia 1864-5* (1912) and in *Some Memo-*

278

ries of the Civil War (1924). After his resignation from the army in September 1864, as deputy collector he assisted his father, who was then collector of Internal Revenue for the Eighth District, New York. In 1866 he became a partner in the firm of G. P. Putnam & Son, succeeding his father as head of the firm at the latter's death in 1872 and remaining the active head until his own death. He was twice married: on July 7, 1889, to Rebecca Kettell Shepard, who died in July 1895; on Apr. 27, 1899, to Emily James Smith, first dean of Barnard College. By his first wife he had four daughters, and by his second, one son.

Putnam's achievement of most enduring value was probably the copyright act of 1909, which—though not all that he desired, since it did not bring the United States into the international copyright union—was the most equitable copyright law the United States had ever had. Early interested in the copyright movement, in which his father was prominent, Putnam made himself a copyright expert. As such he was called to England to testify before a royal commission in 1879, and a few years later he electrified a hearing in America by supplying the lawyer who was cross-examining him with correct references to leading cases which the lawyer had forgotten. He organized in 1886 the American Publishers' Copyright League, which was largely responsible for the copyright acts of 1891 and 1909. For these services he received the Légion d'Honneur and a memorial signed by leading British authors.

His notable publishing successes were Anna Katharine Greene's first novel, *The Leavenworth Case* (1878), one of the earlier American detective stories, which had an immense popular success; and writings of American statesmen, including the *Complete Works of Benjamin Franklin* (10 vols., 1887–88). Among the authors whose works he published were Myrtle Reed, Florence L. Barclay, Guglielmo Ferrero, Norman Angell, James M. Beck, and J. J. Jusserand. Putnam's own writings dealt mainly with the question of copyright and with publishing, though they also include biography, and a story for children, *The Little Gingerbread Man* (1910), which was still selling well at the time of his death. His most important works were *The Questions of Copyright* (1891); *Authors and Their Public in Ancient Times* (1894); *Books and Their Makers During the Middle Ages* (2 vols., 1896–97); *A Memoir of George Palmer Putnam . . .* (2 vols., 1903), republished in 1912 as *George Palmer Putnam; a Memoir; Abraham Lincoln; the People's Leader*

in the Struggle for National Existence (1909); and *The Censorship of the Church of Rome and Its Influence upon the Production and Distribution of Literature . . . with Some Consideration of Protestant Censorship and of Censorship by the State* (2 vols., 1906–07). Putnam himself vigorously opposed all literary censorship. In addition to the books on his war experiences, he also wrote two other autobiographical works—*Memories of my Youth, 1844–1865* (1914) and *Memories of a Publisher, 1865–1915* (1915).

Putnam was essentially an independent in politics. As an officer of the Union army, he had been a Republican, but he opposed the third presidential term sought for General Grant in 1880; thereafter he usually classed himself as a Democrat. He helped elect Cleveland and was active in securing the nomination of Woodrow Wilson in 1912, though he supported Hughes in 1916. He was interested in the work of numerous organizations, including the City Club, the Citizens' Union, the Bureau of Municipal Research, the American Rights League, the American Free Trade League, and the Peace Society. He founded the American branch of the English-Speaking Union. In 1903 he was a member of the Committee of Fifteen which undertook to improve vice conditions in New York, in 1905 of the Committee of Fourteen, which endeavored to suppress "Raines Law" hotels. He served on the grand jury from 1879 to 1914 and on one occasion, as foreman, secured a court decision to the effect that the grand jury had a right to control its own proceedings independently of the district attorney. He was of slight stature but of immense vitality and energy. Even in his old age, he habitually walked to work through the worst New York winter weather, and he remained an ardent tennis player and surf bather. He died in New York City.

[The chief sources for Putnam's life are the autobiog. works; see also *Who's Who in America*, 1928–29; *N. Y. Times* and *N. Y. Herald Tribune*, Feb. 28, 1930.]

J.B.

PUTNAM, GEORGE PALMER (Feb. 7, 1814–Dec. 20, 1872), publisher, was born in Brunswick, Me., the fourth child of Henry and Catherine Hunt (Palmer) Putnam and the descendant of John Putnam, originally probably Puttenham, who before 1641 emigrated from Buckinghamshire, England, to Salem, Mass. Owing to his father's lack of health, a large part of the family income was derived from a coeducational school managed by his mother. His own formal education ceased, however, when at the age of eleven he was apprenticed to John

Gulliver, a Boston carpet merchant who had married his father's sister. In after life he referred to this period—when all reading other than devotional was considered "frivolity"—as one of "literary starvation." In 1829 he removed to New York, where he worked as errand boy and sweeper in a book store at $25 a year and board. Leaving the store at nine or ten o'clock at night, he read regularly in the Mercantile Library until closing time and took books home to read until one or two in the morning. While he was thus educating himself, he began his historical manual, *Chronology, or an Introduction and Index to Universal History* (1833), which sold out an edition of a thousand copies, was revised, and went through many editions as *The World's Progress,* and part of which was printed as *Putnam's Handbook of Universal History* as late as 1927.

In 1833 he became an employee of the firm of Wiley & Long, which in 1840 became Wiley & Putnam. On Mar. 13, 1841, he was married to Victorine Haven, then sixteen, whom he had met while she was a pupil in his mother's school. Among their eleven children were Mary Corinna (Putnam) Jacobi, Ruth and George Haven Putnam [*qq.v.*]. After his marriage he settled in London and opened in Paternoster Row an agency for the sale of American books in England, thus laying the foundation for a relation to the British book trade that was to prove important in the family publishing business for three generations. The Putnam home became a gathering place for publishers and for revolutionary refugees from the Continent, whose number included Mazzini and Louis Napoleon, later Napoleon III. Impressed by the British misunderstanding of American problems he compiled a volume of *American Facts* (1845), designed to improve Anglo-American relations. During this period he also served as correspondent for the New York newspapers, the *New World, Commercial Advertiser,* and *Evening Post,* endeavoring especially to make the Americans of that day understand the ignominy of their wholesale repudiation of state bonds. In 1853 he began publication of *Putnam's Monthly Magazine,* which broke away from the customary use of foreign reprint and depended on American material. The panic of 1857, coupled with the revelation that an associate had played fast and loose with the firm's financial affairs, very nearly ruined him. He was compelled to suspend his magazine and to assign his business. He was able, however, to begin business again, partly at least by the generosity of his life-long friend, Washington Irving, who bought the

plates of his own works and returned them to Putnam. This action led Bayard Taylor and other authors to stand by Putnam in his difficulties. His unsigned "Recollections of Irving" in the *Atlantic Monthly* (November 1860) reflected his pleasure in Irving's companionship and his gratitude for Irving's friendship.

The Civil War, however, made publishing so difficult that he turned over his books to Hurd & Houghton, who printed and sold them on commission from 1862 to 1866. During the early part of the war, he planned with Frank Moore [*q.v.*] a series called *The Rebellion Record* (11 vols. and 1 supp., 1861–68). He had been made collector of internal revenue for the eighth district of New York and was thus under no financial strain, in spite of business difficulties. In 1866 he was removed from office by President Johnson after he had indignantly refused to pay a political assessment on office-holders, but on removal he was officially commended by the secretary of the treasury.

He returned to publishing, established the firm of G. P. Putnam & Son in 1866, and in 1871 adopted the name of G. P. Putnam & Sons. *Putnam's Magazine* was reëstablished in 1868, ran for six more volumes, and in 1870 was merged into *Scribner's Monthly.* He was a singularly scrupulous publisher of high personal and professional standards, suffering at times from his tendency to estimate public taste too highly. At a time when American publishers made a practice of pirating the work of English authors then unprotected by copyright, he refused to publish contemporary work except by arrangement with the authors and in 1837, as secretary of an international copyright association, began the fight for copyright that he continued until his death (see sketch of George Haven Putnam). He also helped to improve the mechanical standards of American book making. He died suddenly in his office.

[G. H. Putnam, *A Memoir of George Palmer Putnam* (2 vols., 1903), and in condensed form as *George Palmer Putnam* (1912); some details in G. H. Putnam, *Memories of my Youth* (1914) and *Memories of a Publisher* (1915); Eben Putnam, *The Putnam Lineage* (1907); *Scribner's Monthly,* Mar. 1873; *N. Y. Tribune,* Dec. 21, 1872.]
J. B.

PUTNAM, GIDEON (Apr. 17, 1763–Dec. 1, 1812), founder of Saratoga Springs, N. Y., was born in Sutton, Mass., the son of Stephen and Mary (Gibbs) Putnam and the descendant of John Putnam, an emigrant from Buckinghamshire, England, to Salem, Mass. He was the nephew of Rufus Putnam [*q.v.*]. At Hartford, Conn., he was married to Doana Risley, the daughter of Benjamin Risley. The young couple pioneered for a time on the Vermont frontier, building their cabin on land that later became the site of Middlebury College, then removed to Rutland, and later to Bemis Flats. They settled at the site of Saratoga Springs, N. Y., in 1789. He at once began making staves and shingles which he rafted down the Hudson River to the city of New York, where much building was in progress after the Revolutionary War. Leasing 300 acres of land, he built a sawmill, the product of which soon paid for the land. The medicinal value of the springs, where he settled, had been known to the Indians and to the earliest white explorers, and a few sporadic attempts had been made to capitalize that value, but he was the first white settler to grasp the possibilities of the springs as a permanent attraction to visitors and to plan accordingly. In 1802 he began building a section, seventy feet long, of a great hotel to be known as Union Hall and, years later, as the Grand Union Hotel. He then laid out a village, tubed several of the springs, and began the erection of Congress Hall. At his death, which resulted in the following year from inflammation of the lungs, Saratoga Springs was well started on its century-long career as an American watering place.

[R. L. Allen, *Hand-book of Saratoga* (1859); W. L. Stone, *Reminiscences of Saratoga* (1875); Eben Putnam, *The Putnam Lineage* (1907).]   W. B. S.

PUTNAM, ISRAEL (Jan. 7, 1718–May 29, 1790), Revolutionary soldier, was born in Salem Village, now Danvers, Mass., the son of Joseph and Elizabeth (Porter) Putnam and the great-grandson of John Putnam who in the seventeenth century emigrated from Aston Abbotts, Buckinghamshire, England, and was in Salem, Mass., in 1640/41. His education seems to have been practically negligible, and his writing remained illiterate to a degree unusual even in his time. Many stories, such as the one about his capture of the wolf in its den, have been told to illustrate his undoubted self-reliance and courage in youth and early manhood, and they have become a part of American legendary history. In 1738 he built a house on land bequeathed him by his father and the following year, on July 19, 1739, married Hannah Pope, who bore him ten children and died in 1765. Not long after his marriage he removed to a new home in that part of Pomfret, Conn., which later became Brooklyn. There he prospered and had become one of the substantial men of the locality by the outbreak of the French and Indian War. Joining the Connecticut forces as a volunteer, he was commissioned second-lieutenant by the colony in August and was in the expedition that

went to Albany. He soon became connected with Robert Rogers as one of his rangers and continued to see active service throughout the war. He was commissioned captain in the autumn of 1755 and did much work on scouting expeditions to the north, examining the situation at Ticonderoga. In 1758 the colony advanced him to the rank of major, and in that year he was captured by the Indians. He was rescued at the last moment after he had been tied to a tree and all preparations made to burn him alive. The following year, with the rank of lieutenant-colonel, he was again in the expedition that was operating to the north by way of Albany. In the expedition of 1762 to capture Havana, the ship on which he sailed was wrecked by a hurricane on the Cuban coast, but his company escaped to be later almost annihilated by sickness and privation. In 1764, as major of the Connecticut forces in March and as lieutenant-colonel in May, he campaigned in Bradstreet's expedition in Pontiac's War. On his return he settled down to a peaceful life on his farm.

At the time of the Stamp Act agitation he became active in the organization of the Sons of Liberty and was one of the three delegates chosen by them to warn Governor Fitch that he could not enforce the law. In 1766 and 1767 he was a representative to the General Assembly. On June 3, 1767, he was married to Deborah (Lothrop) Avery Gardiner, the widow of John Gardiner, proprietor of Gardiner's Island, a marriage by which he greatly improved his social position and to some extent his fortune. He opened a tavern that became a noted rendezvous of ex-soldiers and patriots, and he was elected to various local offices, such as selectman. False hopes having been raised by Gen. Phineas Lyman [*q.v.*] that Great Britain was about to make large grants of land in West Florida to the veterans of the war, Putnam was chosen a member of an exploring expedition to discover what value the lands might have, and in 1773 he cruised for that purpose through the West Indies, Gulf of Mexico, and up the Mississippi River. Part of the journal he kept on this expedition has been printed in *The Two Putnams . . . in the Havana Expedition 1762 and in the Mississippi River Exploration 1772–73* (1931). In 1774 the town of Brooklyn made him chairman of the local committee of correspondence, and that year he went to Boston driving a flock of sheep, the gift of the village to those distressed in that town, and while there he stayed with Joseph Warren. In October he was made lieutenant-colonel of the 11th Regiment of the Connecticut militia, and in April 1775, on news of

Lexington, came the famous episode of his leaving the plow and hastening to the scene of operations without changing his clothes.

He was soon summoned back to Connecticut as a brigadier-general, and the more noted and less successful part of his career began. Within a week he set out for Boston again and joined the forces about that city. He was appointed major-general in the Continental Army. His popularity at this time was great and his energy unbounded. He was a leading spirit in planning for the battle of Bunker Hill, and during the whole of the fight itself he was everywhere; but he seems not to have been in supreme command (controversial literature about the command at Bunker Hill listed in Justin Winsor, *Narrative and Critical Hist. of America,* vol. VI, 1888, pp. 190–91; later reviewed in Charles Martyn, *Life of Artemas Ward,* 1921). The scale on which the war was henceforth conducted put general officers to much severer tests than any he had passed. Washington recognized his peculiar value but hesitated as to his fitness for separate command (Livingston, *post,* p. 267). However, after the siege of Boston was ended, he was ordered to New York and was in chief command there for about ten days before Washington himself arrived. There has been much controversy over the part played by Putnam in the battle of Long Island, but he can hardly be held responsible, as he has by some, for the disaster. He was given charge of the removal of all troops and stores from New York, and after the retreat he was assigned command of Philadelphia and was one of the two officers summoned by Congress to consult as to the advisability of leaving the city. In January 1777 Washington ordered him to Princeton, but, to Washington's intense annoyance, Putnam used his own judgment and delayed obeying the order. In May Washington gave him command in the Highlands, on the Hudson, although by this time he had made up his mind as to the weakness of Putnam. In his new post Putnam again refused to obey Washington's peremptory orders and called down a sharp rebuke. His dilatoriness and apparent unfitness for high command resulted in a court of inquiry, which, however, exonerated him, and after some delay he was put in charge of the recruiting service in Connecticut. Owing to his importunity he was subsequently ordered to rejoin the main army; but his new posts were not important, and in December 1779 a paralytic stroke ended his military career. His activity, disinterestedness, and personal bravery were always beyond question. Unfortunately his self-confidence, his be-

lief in his own ability, and his great popularity necessitated appointing him to a position beyond his powers.

[W. F. Livingston, *Israel Putnam* (1901); David Humphreys, *Life of . . . Israel Putnam* (1810); John Fellows, *The Veil Removed; or, Reflections on David Humphrey's . . . Life of Israel Putnam* (1843); Eben Putnam, *The Putnam Lineage* (1907); *The Public Records of the Colony of Conn.,* vols. X–XV (1877–90); death date from gravestone and Livingston, *ante,* pp. 416–17.]   J. T. A.

PUTNAM, JAMES JACKSON (Oct. 3, 1846–Nov. 4, 1918), neurologist, brother of Charles Pickering Putnam [*q.v.*], was born in Boston, Mass., the son of Charles Gideon, a physician, and Elizabeth Cabot (Jackson) Putnam, and a descendant of John Putnam who emigrated to Salem, Mass., before 1641. He was graduated by Harvard College in 1866 and the Harvard Medical School in 1870. After completing an internship at the Massachusetts General Hospital, he began his neurological studies in Leipzig, Vienna, and London. Returning to Boston, he at once identified himself with the field of nervous diseases, first receiving an appointment at the Harvard Medical School as a lecturer on that subject (1874) and subsequently serving as professor of diseases of the nervous system (1893–1912). In 1872 he started one of the first neurological clinics in the United States, at the Massachusetts General Hospital, and also established in his own house a neuropathological laboratory. In his early studies he was closely allied with Henry P. Bowditch [*q.v.*], professor of physiology at the Harvard Medical School.

Putnam's interests were wide, his capacity for work insatiable, and for nearly fifty years he contributed papers to local and national neurological societies. His first important contribution was published in 1880 on paresthesia (*Archives of Medicine,* October 1880) and has been described as "probably the earliest adequate description of a condition which has since become generally recognized" (Taylor, *post,* p. 309). Other papers followed in rapid succession on organic diseases of the nervous system. In 1895 he published his first paper on the psychoneuroses, a branch of neurology in which he took special interest throughout the rest of his life. He wrote two important published addresses. The first, a Shattuck lecture before the Massachusetts Medical Society, *Not the Disease Only, But also the Man* (1899), treated the obligations of the physician "as a healer of the mind as well as of the body." His other address was a contribution to the broader aspects of neurology, read at the International Congress at St. Louis, entitled *The Value of the*

Physiological Principle in the Study of Neurology (1904).

Putnam's mind was naturally analytical and philosophical and he was greatly influenced in his views by his friends, William James and Josiah P. Royce [*qq.v.*], and by the German school of philosophy. When the work of Sigmund Freud came to his attention in 1909, it made an important and instant appeal and for the last ten years of his life his papers were devoted to the task of reconciling the views of Freud "with his own unquenchable optimism and with the moral purpose of the world, in which he so thoroughly believed" (Taylor, *post*, p. 311). His ethical standard, which was of the highest order, was set forth in a book, *Human Motives* (1915). He was one of the founders of the American Neurological Association in 1875 and served as president in 1888. He was a member of the American Academy of Arts and Sciences and of the Association of American Physicians, and he had the friendship of most of the leading physicians of his time. Besides his strictly professional activities, he found time for recreations of a simple sort. For many years he maintained a camp in the Adirondacks with Henry P. Bowditch, where he entertained his friends. In 1905 he published *A Memoir of James Jackson*. He was married, on Feb. 15, 1886, to Marion Cabot, daughter of Francis and Louisa Higgison Cabot. His wife, two daughters, and a son survived him. Putnam is chiefly remembered for his pioneer work in neurology. He contributed many important papers to the fields of both structural and functional neurology, many of which contained ideas well in advance of his time. He was characterized at the time of his death by President Lowell of Harvard University as "a man of science, eminent in his field, a philosopher and a saint."

[The chief reference is the biographical note by E. W. Taylor in *Archives of Neurol. and Psychiatry*, Mar. 1920. Other sources include: *Proc. Am. Acad. Arts and Sci.*, vol. LXI (1926); *Boston Transcript*, Nov. 4, 7, 1918; *Boston Medic. and Surgic. Jour.*, Dec. 26, 1918; a biographical sketch by Ernest Jones in the posthumously published *Addresses on Psychoanalysis* (1921), by Putnam, and family notes.]

H. R. V.

PUTNAM, JAMES OSBORNE (July 4, 1818–Apr. 24, 1903), lawyer, diplomat, was the son of Harvey and Myra (Osborne) Putnam, and a descendant of John Putnam who emigrated to Salem, Mass., before 1641. James was born in the village of Attica, N. Y., a few miles east of Buffalo, with the interests of which city he was connected almost all his long life. Entering Hamilton College in 1836, he transferred to Yale two years later, but was compelled by ill health to leave college at the end of his junior year, Yale awarding him the honorary degree of M.A. in 1865. On Jan. 5, 1842, he married Harriet Palmer, who died in 1853; and on Mar. 15, 1855, he married Kate Wright, who died in 1895. By his first wife he had three children, and by his second, four. He was admitted to the bar in 1842, and nine years later, at the age of thirty-three, was appointed by President Fillmore, his fellow townsman, postmaster at Buffalo, in which office he served until May 1853. In that year he was elected to the state Senate, where he served 1854–55 and became noted as an orator. "As a speaker he was polished, smooth, and refined, and even when impassioned kept his passion well within conventional bounds" (Alexander, *post*, II, 156). A volume of his utterances, entitled *Addresses, Speeches and Miscellanies* appeared in 1880. He was a consistent Whig and sorrowed so intensely over the dissolution of the party that for a time he was attracted to the new American party; but it did not take him long to realize its ephemeral character, and he was influential in bringing many who had joined it into union with the Republicans. In 1860 he was one of the two Republican presidential electors-at-large, and was active in the campaign. In 1861 President Lincoln appointed him consul at Havre, France, where he remained until 1866. Returning to Buffalo, he resumed the practice of law, but was again for a brief time drawn into the public service as minister to Belgium, which position he held from 1880 to 1882.

His chief influence, however, was in his community. He loved Buffalo with almost a fanatic devotion and chose to remain in that city. At the beginning of his career it was sadly lacking in educational and cultural institutions, and Putnam exerted a considerable influence in changing this condition. He took an essential part in establishing, in the early sixties, the Buffalo Historical Society and the Buffalo Fine Arts Academy, with both of which he was officially connected. Especially noteworthy was his service to education. He was one of the group which in 1846 founded the University of Buffalo, and he served for thirty-two years on its board of trustees. In 1895 he accepted the chancellorship, which was then an unpaid office. Old age and weakened physique were upon him, yet during his term the university saw considerable enlargement. In 1902, a few months before his death, he resigned the chancellorship.

[Eben Putnam, *The Putnam Lineage* (1907); *Obit. Records Grads. Yale Univ.* (1910); J. N. Larned and L. G. Sellstedt, in *Buffalo Hist. Soc. Pub.*, vol. VI, (1903); D. S. Alexander, *A Pol. Hist. of the State of N. Y.*, vol. II (1906); H. W. Hill, *Municipality of*

Buffalo, N. Y., A Hist. (1923); Who's Who in America, 1901–02; N. Y. Tribune, Apr. 25, 1903; information supplied by the family.]
J.P.

PUTNAM, RUFUS (Apr. 9, 1738–May 4, 1824), soldier and pioneer, was born at Sutton, Mass., the descendant of John Putnam who emigrated from England to Salem, Mass., before 1641, and the son of Elisha and Susanna (Fuller) Putnam. His father, who, like his cousin Israel Putnam [q.v.], represented the fourth generation in New England, died when Rufus was barely seven, and his mother soon married John Sadler, an inn-keeper. The boy was cared for by different relatives, and in 1754 he was apprenticed to a millwright. The greater part of his education he obtained unaided, studying geography, history, and especially mathematics. Enlisting during the French and Indian War in 1757, he saw service in the region of Lake Champlain, and his practical training came into play in the construction of defensive works (*Journal of Gen. Rufus Putnam Kept . . . 1757–1760*, 1886, ed. by E. C. Dawes). In December 1760 he arrived home in New Braintree and Apr. 6, the following year, he was married to Elizabeth Ayres of Brookfield, who died in November leaving an infant son to survive her only a year. On Jan. 10, 1765, he was married to Persis Rice of Westborough, who died Sept. 6, 1820. They had nine children. He worked his farm, practised surveying, and built mills. In 1773 he served upon a committee to explore and survey lands on the Mississippi that were claimed as bounties for the veterans of the French and Indian War. Although this project failed, it aroused his interest in the possibilities of western lands for colonization and for military bounties.

Entering the Revolutionary army as a lieutenant-colonel, he soon took charge of the defensive works around Boston. During the winter of 1775–76, when the ground was frozen so deeply that ordinary breastworks could not be constructed, he proposed the use of chandeliers —really movable wooden parapets—to screen the batteries on Dorchester Heights and force the British evacuation of Boston. Next he reconnoitered around New York, constructing defensive works in this same region. On Aug. 5, 1776, Congress appointed him engineer with the rank of colonel, but he insisted upon a distinct and properly organized engineering corps. As Congress took no definite action, he resigned his commission and accepted the command of a Massachusetts regiment. After serving under Gates in the campaign against Burgoyne, he was stationed in the Hudson Valley, where he rebuilt the fortifications at West Point and was in numerous engagements, notably at Stonypoint and Verplanck Point. In January 1783 Congress gave him the rank of a brigadier-general. Meanwhile on several occasions he had acted as spokesman to present the grievances of the troops and had obtained some relief from the Massachusetts General Assembly. As chairman of the officers' organization he framed the Newburgh Petition in June 1783 for some definite provision in the Ohio country for the land bounties that had been promised the Revolutionary veterans. As Congress failed to act upon this petition, he undertook the survey and sale of lands in Maine that belonged to Massachusetts. When Congress in 1785 appointed him a surveyor of western lands, he sent Gen. Benjamin Tupper [q.v.] as a substitute. After Tupper's return with a favorable report of the western country, Putnam issued with him a joint call for a meeting at Boston on Mar. 1, 1786, in order to consider a settlement in the Ohio country. The outcome was the organization of the Ohio Company, composed largely of Revolutionary veterans, which soon contracted for some 1,500,000 acres on the north bank of the Ohio. Putnam, who became superintendent of the new colony, left his home at Rutland and reached Marietta with the first party of settlers on Apr. 7, 1788. His practical sense was all-important to the new settlement, especially in the matter of protection from the Indians.

As settlement increased, his influence was felt in the Western country beyond the limits of the colony he had had such a large part in founding. In March 1790 Washington appointed him a judge of the Northwest Territory and in May 1792 commissioned him also a brigadier-general in the regular army. In this latter capacity his first task was to treat with the hostile Indians on the Maumee. Induced by Indian hostility to alter the original plan of this mission, he finally made a treaty at Vincennes on Sept. 27, 1792, with the lower Wabash tribes. Resigning soon from the army, he took charge of important surveys in the neighborhood of Marietta, and on Oct. 1, 1796, Washington appointed him surveyor-general of the United States. His first important task, the survey of the military tract, was inaccurately done, chiefly because of his deficiencies in mathematics, and it was necessary to adjust these errors in the Land Act of 1800. In 1803 Jefferson, in rather summary fashion, replaced him as surveyor-general with Jared Mansfield [q.v.], an eminent mathematician. Putnam was also a delegate to the Ohio constitutional convention in 1802, exerting a strong influence there for moderation and against the admission of slavery. In his declining years he continued his interest in the colony he had in so large a measure founded. Indeed it is upon this accomplishment that his chief claim to fame rests. As a soldier he was brave and resourceful, but he was neither a great strategist nor an eminent military engineer. Washington aptly characterized him as possessed of a strong mind, discreet and firm, with nothing "conspicuous" in his character (*The Writings of George Washington*, XII, 1891, ed. by W. C. Ford, p. 510). In person he was almost six feet tall, with a sturdy figure and a face that had strong lines, clearcut features, and a peculiar oblique expression that was due to an injury to an eye in childhood. *The Memoirs of Rufus Putnam,* with much of his official correspondence were edited by Rowena Buell and published in 1903.

[Buell, *ante* ; S. P. Hildreth, *Biog. and Hist. Memoirs of . . . Ohio* (1852) ; *The Records of the Original Proceedings of the Ohio Company* (2 vols., 1917) and *Ohio in the Time of the Confederation* (1918), ed. by A. B. Hulbert ; Eben Putnam, *The Putnam Lineage* (1907).]
B. W. B., Jr.

PUTNAM, RUTH (July 18, 1856–Feb. 12, 1931), author, daughter of George Palmer Putnam [*q.v.*] and Victorine (Haven) Putnam, was born in Yonkers, N. Y., but spent her early years in Morrisania, to which place the family removed in 1857. Her home surroundings offered unusual stimulus to mind and character, for her father was the founder of the publishing house which bears his name; her eldest brother was George Haven Putnam [*q.v.*], who was to succeed his father as head of the firm; and her eldest sister, Mary Corinna Putnam Jacobi [*q.v.*], a pioneer in the medical education of women. The influence of her early environment is well described in her *Life and Letters of Mary Putnam Jacobi* (1925).

Ruth Putnam was graduated in 1878 from Cornell University, of which institution she served as alumni trustee from 1899 to 1909. In her undergraduate days her choice of studies indicated a strong interest in language and literature, especially Latin and Italian. The same interest was shown in her first publication, the Pearl Series (1886), six volumes of poetical selections. She also collaborated with Alfred J. Church in an historical novel entitled *The Count of the Saxon Shore* (1887). Soon, however, her interest became concentrated on the history of the Dutch, partly as settlers of New York. She was one of the joint editors of *Historic New York* (1897–99), and contributed to the collection a paper on Annetje Jans' Farm. The particular problem of Dutch history to which she

first addressed herself was the life of William the Silent. When, in 1890, Putnam's announced the Heroes of the Nations Series, Ruth Putnam's name appeared as prospective author of a volume on William of Orange. This did not appear, however, until 1911, when it was published under the title, *William the Silent, Prince of Orange, and the Revolt of the Netherlands.* In the meantime she published *William the Silent, Prince of Orange: the Moderate Man of the Sixteenth Century* (2 vols., 1895). It was something of a venture to walk in the footsteps of Motley, but her equipment was equal to the undertaking. She examined the documents in the British Museum, the Royal libraries at The Hague and at Brussels, and in various local archives in the Netherlands. Because of her abilities as an investigator and a writer she soon came to be regarded as the principal American scholar interested in Netherlands studies. Her next work in the field was *A Mediæval Princess; . . . Jacqueline, Countess of Holland* (1904). Its purpose was to show how the Burgundian power in the Netherlands was built up. A second contribution to this phase of European history was a biography in the Heroes Series of *Charles the Bold* (1908). This was based upon material much of which had become available since the volumes of John Foster Kirk [*q.v.*] were published. Miss Putnam's historical interests were also characterized by a literary sense of what the reading public desired to know. When the World War broke out she wrote a small volume entitled *Alsace and Lorraine from Cæsar to Kaiser* (1915). In 1918 appeared her companion volume on *Luxemburg and Her Neighbors,* written when the fate of the duchy was still uncertain. One of her most practical contributions to the knowledge of the Netherlands in the United States was her part in the translation and adaptation of P. J. Blok's general history of the Netherlands. She reduced the amount of political detail, especially in the early volumes, in order that cultural history might receive greater emphasis. During the last six years of her life she resided in Geneva, Switzerland, where she died. She was an honorary member of the Maatschappij van Nederlandsche Letterkunde at Leyden and of the Institut G. D. de Luxembourg. King Albert of Belgium decorated her with the Order of the Crown.

[Information from members of the family; records of G. P. Putnam's Sons; records of Cornell University; *Who's Who in America*, 1928–29.]   H. E. B.

PUTNAM, WILLIAM LE BARON (May 26, 1835–Feb. 5, 1918), diplomat, jurist, son of Dr. Israel and Sarah Emery (Frost) Putnam, and a descendant of John Putnam who settled at Salem, Mass., before 1641, was born in Bath, Me. He was educated in the public schools and at Bowdoin College, graduating in 1855. In the office of Bronson & Sewall of Bath he studied law, serving at the same time as editor of the *Bath Daily Times* and as assistant clerk (1856) of the state House of Representatives. In 1858 he was admitted to the bar and moved to Portland to become the law partner of George Evans [*q.v.*]. This association, which lasted until Evans' death in 1867, was of great value to Putnam, introducing him to a desirable clientele and training him in mercantile and corporation law. During his active practice he was prominent as a counsel for railroads and for railroad men. He defended the will of Abner Coburn [*q.v.*], and, as the executor of Israel Washburn's estate, held the controlling interest in the Rumford Falls & Buckfield Railroad, which he served as president, 1884–92. Though a Democrat by inheritance and conviction, he was mayor of Portland in 1869.

He became known in Washington through his appearances before the Supreme Court in *Alabama* Claims cases and in the Peleg Chandler $200,000 bond case. He was also retained for the Portland owners of the *Ella M. Doughty,* one of the fishing schooners seized and held at Halifax by the Canadian government. His skill and knowledge in this case induced Secretary of State Bayard to ask him to be a member of the commission appointed to negotiate with Great Britain over the rights of American fishermen in Canadian waters. A treaty was concluded by this commission Feb. 15, 1888, only to be defeated in Congress. The same year Putnam was the defeated Democratic candidate for the governorship of Maine. He was also the American member of the Bering Sea Claims Commission, 1896–97, under the treaty of Feb. 8, 1896. An award in favor of Great Britain brought to an end the difficult seal-fisheries question.

By appointment of President Harrison he became, Mar. 17, 1892, judge of the circuit court of appeals for the first circuit, a position which he occupied until his resignation in September 1917. Neither unusually ready of speech nor quickwitted, he gained his place in the legal world not as a jury lawyer, but as a consultant and judge with a wide knowledge of legal principles and details achieved by long study. He had a great and perhaps undue respect for English and eastern United States precedents; he was very proud of his library of English chancery reports. In questions of equity he was much more at home than in the technical details of the patent cases with which he often had to deal. Of patent law

he had complete command (see for example his decision in *American Bell Telephone Company* vs. *United States, 68 Fed. Reporter, 542*) but, perhaps because of his near-sightedness, he was not quick in comprehending the workings of machines. He sometimes irritated lawyers who argued cases before him by ignoring their elaborately prepared pleas and basing his decision on points not even brought up in the litigation. His decision of which he was most proud was that in the Reece Button-Hole case (61 *Fed. Reporter,* 958). Perhaps the best-known case with which he was connected was that of the German steamship *Kronprinzessin Cecilie.* His vigorous dissenting opinion in that case (238 *Fed. Reporter,* 668) though upheld when the Supreme Court reversed the decision of the circuit court of appeals (244 *U. S.,* 12), has not won universal acceptance among admiralty lawyers. It was held by Putnam and by the Supreme Court that the commander of the German vessel was justified in returning to the United States instead of proceeding to English or French ports on the eve of the World War, since in a port of either belligerent his ship would have been seized and his crew detained, and that the libelants had no cause for action in the failure to deliver their shipments of gold.

From his father, Putnam inherited a rugged strength, both physical and mental, and a brusque, booming voice, not unfamiliar with sarcasm. Underneath his gruff exterior he was sympathetic and warm-hearted, with a keen appreciation of a good story, and many a young lawyer was aided by his friendly interest and advice. He married, May 29, 1862, Octavia Bowman Robinson of Augusta, Me. There were no children.

[*In Memory of the Hon. William Le Baron Putnam, Proc. of the Cumberland Bar, Me., and of the U. S. Circuit Court of Appeals for the First Circuit* (1919), with portrait; *Portland Daily Press,* Feb. 6, 1918; *Portland Evening Express,* Apr. 5, 1919; P. M. Reed, *Hist. of Bath* (1894); G. T. Little, *Geneal. and Family Hist. of the State of Me.* (1909), vol. I; M. L. Stockwell, *Descendants of Francis LeBaron* (1904), with portrait; *Who's Who in America,* 1916–17; Eben Putnam, *The Putnam Lineage* (1907); *Daily Eastern Argus* (Portland), Feb. 6, 1918.]   R. E. M.

PYE, WATTS ORSON (Oct. 20, 1878–Jan. 9, 1926), Congregational missionary to China, was born on a farm near Faribault, Minn., the son of Caleb G. and Florence (Cook) Pye. His home was a preparation both for his earnest religious purpose and for his pioneer life as a missionary. His father was the son of one of the early settlers of Minnesota, and the younger Pye himself was inured to the hard manual labor of a farm. The father, also, was a deacon in a

Congregational church, and his mother, descended from one of the old Dutch families of New York which had given many of its sons to the Christian ministry, was active in the church and especially interested in missions. One who knew Pye in adolescence described him as a tall youth, rather slow in maturing, but singularly high-minded, devout, and earnest. His education was obtained in a district school near his home, in the Central High School of Faribault (from which he graduated in June 1898), then, after a year of work on his father's farm, at Carleton College (B.A. 1903). He spent the next two years in Texas caring for an invalid sister, and during this time studied theology at the seminary of the Southern Presbyterian Church in Austin, and for a year taught Biblical literature in Tillotson College, a mission school for negroes. Entering Oberlin Theological Seminary in the autumn of 1905, he graduated in 1907. He was above the average as a student, but rather because of hard work than of native brilliance. It was during his first year in Carleton College that he decided to be a missionary, a step taken because of the influence of fellow students and members of the faculty. At Carleton he was very active in creating an interest in foreign missions and in leading others to enter that calling.

Pye was ordained May 7, 1907, and in September of that year sailed for China as a missionary of the American Board of Commissioners for Foreign Missions. He had hoped to go to Kalgan, but instead was appointed to Fenchow, in the province of Shansi. Here the mission was still suffering from the effects of the Boxer persecution of 1900. On Oct. 5, 1915, he was married, at Peking, to Gertrude Chaney. Much of his time was first given to educational work, but in the course of the years, from Fenchow as headquarters, he developed one of the most noteworthy pioneer missionary enterprises in the history of China. He regarded as his parish an area of about 30,000 square miles in west central Shansi and northern Shensi, where, with the exception of four points, no Protestant mission work had so far been begun. He made a thorough survey of the region, to determine its main physical features, its roads, and its towns and villages. On the basis of this survey, and almost entirely through the agency of Chinese associates, he directed the introduction of Protestant Christianity. He dreamed of planting Christianity in each of the thousands of towns and villages of the region and of making the churches centers for improving their religious, intellectual, social, and economic environment. Pye was a man of charm, of singularly radiant

religious life, of complete integrity, of rare humility, with a great capacity for remembering faces and names, for leading without arousing antagonism, and for winning, inspiring, and holding friends. Possessed of these gifts, he made rapid strides toward accomplishing the task to which he had set his hand. Through correspondence, travel, and annual conferences held near Fenchow, he directed the large staff of Chinese through whom most of the work was done. He was even extending his activities north of the Great Wall. An enterprise which had grown so rapidly could not fail to have weaknesses, but Pye was cognizant of these and would probably have remedied at least part of them had it not been for his untimely death.

[Archives of the American Board of Commissioners for Foreign Missions, 1907–27; annual reports of the same; *China Mission Year Book*, 1919; *Student Volunteer Movement Bull.*, May 1925; *Chinese Recorder*, Apr. 1926; *Missionary Herald*, Mar., Dec. 1926; *N. Y. Herald-Tribune*, Jan. 12, 1926.]   K. S. L.

PYLE, HOWARD (Mar. 5, 1853–Nov. 9, 1911), artist, author, teacher, was born in Wilmington, Del. Both his father, William Pyle, and his mother, Margaret Churchman (Painter) Pyle, were of Quaker origin, descendants of Pennsylvania's first settlers. Both, like the majority of Friends, were possessed of varied intellectual interests, but it was particularly from his mother that Howard Pyle inherited his artistic and literary ambitions. Thwarted in her desires by the demands of a large family, she passed on to her son the aims which had enlivened her own youth. Pyle's childhood, like the most productive years of his later life, was spent in Wilmington or the surrounding country. His early education he received first at the old Friends' School, and finally at the private establishment headed by Thomas Clarkson Taylor, a Virginia Hicksite and excellent schoolmaster. Here, though generally popular, he did not distinguish himself; the more valuable training was that which he gathered in the family circle. His mother's enthusiasm was infectious; from her he learned to know and to love the best in literature, and, what was more important, to understand the art of the great English illustrators, Leech, Doyle, and Tenniel. From his mother, whose intellectual adventurousness had led her on from Quakerism to Swedenborgianism, he received also a firm and permanent conviction of the truth and beauty of the Scandinavian mystic's doctrines. A distaste for the routine of academic study prevented him from entering college, though both his parents were intent upon his doing so. He had, however, even in early boyhood begun to exercise his talent for drawing and writing, and when with continual practice his skill began to increase, his mother determined that he should seriously study art. Consequently, he was sent regularly, though he continued to live at home, to the studio of Van der Weilen in Philadelphia. Here for three years he received a rigorous training. The class was small and Van der Weilen, a native of Antwerp, was able to give him a great deal of personal attention. These years provided, with the exception of a few sporadic lessons later at the Art League in New York, the whole of his supervised training. He found his own style and his own technique in later years without instruction.

After the "Van der Weilian course of sprouts," as he called his years of study, he nearly allowed his artistic interests to perish. Steady work in his father's leather business was not conducive to art and had it not been for a fortunate and almost accidental recrudescence of ambition, he would probably have developed into a respectable business man. A visit to the little known Virginia island Chincoteague, however, inspired him to write and illustrate an article on its people and their customs. This article was sent to *Scribner's Monthly* and attracted the attention of Roswell Smith, one of the magazine's owners, who encouraged him to come to New York and to devote himself to illustration. Urged by Smith's enthusiasm, and with the approval of his parents, he went to New York in the fall of 1876. There he found that life was considerably more difficult than he had imagined. Smith's encouragement proved to be more verbal than actual. Neither *Scribner's* nor the other magazines were so hospitable as to receive many of his productions. He was discouraged, but discouragement only made him more obstinately determined to conquer. He was handicapped by an ignorance of the proper technique; he had ideas, but he could not work them up in a way suitable to the magazines. He labored however, patiently and endlessly; he studied, when he had time, at the Art Students' League; and he made the acquaintance of other artists who gave him valuable advice. It was just at this period that American magazines were becoming more and more notable for their illustrations, and they were, therefore, offering every opportunity to artists. New York was full of capable men, and the whole atmosphere was one of experiment and improvement. Pyle fell in with Abbey, who had just risen into prominence, with A. B. Frost, with F. S. Church, and with others, all of whom gave him aid and encouragement. His sketches began to find favor, even though they had to be

redrawn before they could be reproduced. He bent every effort to acquire a new proficiency, and finally, after more than a year's struggle, Charles Parsons, art editor for Harper & Brothers, permitted him to work up one of his own ideas. The picture was successful, was accepted, and was reproduced as a double-page cut, "The Wreck in the Offing," in *Harper's Weekly,* Mar. 9, 1878. From this time his advance was rapid, and by 1880, when he had returned to Wilmington, he was well established in his profession.

At home the intensity of his work did not diminish. His ties with the magazines were now strong, and he was kept supplied with plenty to do. In April 1881 he married Anne Poole and settled comfortably and securely under his own rooftree. There was nothing Bohemian or extravagant in his habits. Never was there artist who took his art more seriously, but his seriousness never interfered with his domestic life. He was devoted to his family, which became a large one, and he enjoyed the social life of the community. He had an enormous capacity for work, but he had also the ability to finish all that lay before him and to lead, at the same time, a normal life. His jovial manner, his high spirits, and his unfailing kindliness made him everywhere popular, so that his large form and benevolent face were well known in Wilmington circles. The thirty remaining years of his life were packed with one accomplishment after another. He continued, of course, to make illustrations for all the important magazines, though the major portion of this kind of work was done for the Harper publications. He was particularly successful in delineating the characters and events of early American history, concerning which his knowledge, gained by omnivorous reading, was amazing. His pictures for Woodrow Wilson's *Washington* (1897) and *History of the American People* (1902), as well as for Henry Cabot Lodge's *Story of the Revolution* (1898), all of which appeared first in periodicals, are his masterpieces in this line. They portray with accuracy and spirit, but with a distinct romantic air, the life of colonial days. In the same vein, but more delicate and certainly more esthetically pleasing, were the decorations for Holmes's *One Hoss Shay* (1892) and *Dorothy Q* (1893). These were pen-and-inks, and show his consummate mastery of that technique. In black and white, oils, or in colors, he was always competent and often admirable, but in pen-and-inks he showed his real supremacy. When the new process for reproducing pictures in color came into being, Pyle was one of the first in the field. Notable among his productions after this new fashion were illustrations for stories by James Branch Cabell and Brian Hooker, and for tales of his own. They combine a real illustrative value with a feeling for harmonious, though often startling, color. Another interesting series of pictures, done originally as pen-and-inks and finished with water-colors, is "The Travels of the Soul" (*Century,* December 1902). They show another side of his genius, his ability to present, with reserve and yet with a poetic fervor, subjects of a mystical and allegorical nature.

Important as are these illustrations for the works of other men, Pyle's reputation really rests upon his own tales and their pictures. From his earliest days he had been fascinated by books for children and he felt himself to possess a talent for writing them. He recognized rightly his peculiar ability. Nothing that he did is so sure of a permanent place in the world of art and letters as the long series of books which began in 1883 with *The Merry Adventures of Robin Hood.* The text was only a retelling of the old stories, familiar in Percy and Ritson, but to them he had added a new reality, a definiteness, which so completely revivified their whole spirit that they could not fail to gain the ear of any normal child. No small part of the strength of the volume lay in the carefully executed illustrations, which were pen-and-inks of a strictly medieval character, modeled very closely after the engravings of Dürer. In artistic circles the book attracted much attention, especially in England, where even William Morris, "who thought up to that time . . . nothing good artistically could come out of America" (says Joseph Pennell), praised it. The *Robin Hood* has been the most popular of his productions, yet its somewhat similar successors are not at all less prepossessing: *Pepper and Salt* (1886), *The Wonder Clock* (1888), *Otto of the Silver Hand* (1888), *Twilight Land* (1895), and four volumes of Arthurian legend (1903, 1905, 1907, 1910). In addition to these he produced in other veins, but also for children, *Men of Iron* (1892), a stirring account of chivalric adventure in medieval England; *The Story of Jack Ballister's Fortunes* (1895), a vigorous yarn of piracy in Virginia and Carolina waters; and *The Garden Behind the Moon* (1895), an exquisite, but perhaps too subtle, fairy-tale, treating allegorically of death and immortality, and growing out of his own meditations over the loss of a son. His intense and bibliomaniacal passion for pirates also gave birth to a variety of books, appealing as much to adults as to children. Most important among these are *Within the Capes* (1885), *The Rose of Paradise* (1888), *The Ghost of Captain Brand* (1896),

The Price of Blood (1899), *Stolen Treasure* (1907), and *The Ruby of Kishmoor* (1908). Some of these, with their pictures, were collected in *Howard Pyle's Book of Pirates* (1921). Two other books, both extravaganzas, but of entirely different natures, require mention: *A Modern Aladdin* (1892), which Stevenson called "a boguey tale, and a good one at that"; and *Rejected of Men* (1903), a serious but never popular novel, built around the story of Christ (as if He had lived in nineteenth-century New York), and embodying many of Pyle's religious reflections.

From 1894 to 1900 he conducted a class in illustration at the Drexel Institute in Philadelphia, practising there his personal and somewhat unorthodox methods of instruction. He was violently criticised, but he succeeded in developing such workers as Maxfield Parrish, Violet Oakley, and Jessie Willcox Smith. In 1900 he established his own school in Wilmington, admitting only a limited number of carefully selected pupils, giving them the full benefit of his personal advice and of his experience, and accepting no pecuniary return for his teaching. Here he trained, among others, N. C. Wyeth, Stanley Arthurs, and Frank Schoonover. As a teacher he was extraordinarily able, but he left, perhaps, too much of himself, of his own manner and style, with his pupils. Toward the end of his career, influenced probably by the example of Abbey, he decided that he would gradually give up illustration and devote himself wholly to mural decoration. His first important work was "The Battle of Nashville" in the state capitol of Minnesota (1906); this was followed by two commissions in New Jersey court houses. These productions, all of them historical subjects, show the same manner, the same skill, which had marked his early colonial pictures. They are in every way illustrations rather than decorations. He realized his own lack of knowledge, his need for a familiarity with the great tradition of painting. Before this, he had felt that for the production of an American Art a knowledge of America was enough; now for his new venture he needed a more universal background. With this in view, he went with his family in 1910 to Italy, there to study for the first time the work of the old masters. But his health had grown feeble, his enthusiasm and his ability to absorb were waning, and he was mentally depressed. When he had been abroad only one year, he was stricken by a severe attack of renal colic, and died in Florence.

[There exists one autobiographical fragment, "When I was a Little Boy," *Woman's Home Companion,* Apr. 1912, but the indispensable sources are W. S. Morse and Gertrude Brincklé, *Howard Pyle, A Record of his Illustrations and Writings* (1921), and C. D. Abbott, *Howard Pyle: A Chronicle* (1925). Critical estimates may be found in Joseph Pennell's *Pen Drawing and Pen Draughtsmen* (1889) and *Modern Illustration* (1895).]

C. D. A.

PYLE, WALTER LYTLE (Dec. 20, 1871– Oct. 8, 1921), ophthalmologist, was born in Philadelphia, Pa., the son of William J. and Sarah Lane (Thomas) Pyle. His early education was obtained in the public schools, and he received from the Central High School of Philadelphia the degree of A.B. in 1888, and that of A.M. in 1893. In the latter year he graduated from the medical department of the University of Pennsylvania with the degree of M.D. After serving as resident physician in the Emergency Hospital, Washington, D. C. (1893–94), he did graduate work in London and Paris. Upon returning to Philadelphia, he became affiliated with the Polyclinic and Wills hospitals, securing in 1898 the appointment as assistant surgeon in the service of Dr. Conrad Berens at the latter institution. This position he held until his retirement in 1905. From 1908 to 1912 he was ophthalmic surgeon to Mount Sinai Hospital. He was married, Apr. 11, 1898, to Adelaide Besson, by whom he had a son and a daughter.

Pyle was an editorial writer of considerable prominence in the field of medical literature. In 1897, in collaboration with Dr. George M. Gould [*q.v.*], he published *A Compend of Diseases of the Eye,* a second edition of which appeared in 1899; in further collaboration with the same author, he brought out *Anomalies and Curiosities of Medicine* (1897), and *Cyclopedia of Practical Medicine and Surgery* (1900). He was editor of the *International Medical Magazine* in 1898. In collaboration with Dr. Samuel Horton Brown, he edited the section on ophthalmology in the *American Year Book of Medicine and Surgery* for 1903 and 1904. From 1902 to 1907 he edited the section on ophthalmology in *American Medicine.* He also had editorial supervision of *An International System of Ophthalmic Practice,* begun in 1910, of which four volumes had appeared up to 1918. This work was planned to cover every phase of ophthalmic practice, each volume being assigned to some authority of international prominence. The untimely death of the editor terminated this commendable undertaking.

He practised ophthalmology exclusively and by reason of the exceptional care and kindly consideration he gave to his patients, he built up an extremely large practice in Philadelphia and vicinity. A man of indefatigable industry and inexhaustible patience, he was consulted by many persons with reputed irremediable ocular affections, and by reason of the personal qualities mentioned he was frequently able to attain success where others had obtained but mediocre results. Coupled with his talent for close application was a good memory and a brilliant mind, making the pursuit of knowledge for him a simple task. As a result of his pronounced familiarity with medical literature he was in constant demand in a consultant capacity by the various medical book publishers. Ill health prevented the full exercise of his remarkable ability during the last decade of his life, although he remained extremely active until the last, stoically continuing in his daily work where others less courageous would have sought rest and retirement.

[J. L. Chamberlain, ed., *Universities and Their Sons, Univ. of Pa.,* vol. II (1902); *Trans. Am. Ophthalmological Soc.,* vol. XX (1922); *Jour. Am. Medic. Asso.,* Oct. 22, 1921; *Who's Who in America,* 1920–21; *Public Ledger* (Phila.), Oct. 10, 1921; records of the institutions with which Pyle was connected.]

S. H. B.

PYNCHON, JOHN (*c.* 1626–Jan. 17, 1702/03), colonial industrialist, public servant, son of William [*q.v.*] and Anna (Andrew) Pynchon, was born at Springfield, a parish of Chelmsford, Essex, England, and came to New England with his father on the *Arbella,* of Governor Winthrop's fleet. The family settled first at Dorchester, but shortly removed to Roxbury. In 1636, William Pynchon founded Springfield, Mass., the most northerly of the four Connecticut River towns settled at that time as a part of the plan to oust the Dutch from the territory east of the Hudson River. Here the boy grew up under the tutelage of his father. There is evidence that he acquired more than a common-school education, together with an unusual knowledge of business and finance, under this most able master.

In 1652 the elder Pynchon permanently retired to England, leaving John with a profitable colonial business which provided for the parent a life of leisure in England and gave to the son a controlling interest in the community. Thus at twenty-six years of age he was a leader in financial life, destined to become one of the wealthiest and most influential men in contemporary New England. He continued and extended the family fur monopoly, establishing posts and factors at Westfield, Northampton, Hadley, and in the Housatonic Valley. As a merchant, his activities extended not only over western and southern New England, but to Boston. He had extensive interests in Barbados, all of these enterprises being served by his own ships, in which he also sent his furs direct to England. His ability was early recognized, and his associates chose him for a succession of public offices. He was selectman in 1650, town clerk in 1652, magistrate to try small causes in 1653, deputy to the General Court in 1662, and soon afterward assistant in the Council, or upper house, which position he held until 1701, almost to the close of his life. He was confirmed by the General Court in 1653 as lieutenant of the Train Band; became captain of the company in 1657, and later was made major of the Troop, with command of the military forces of the region. In 1662 he built the first brick house in the valley (later known as the Old Fort) which became the refuge of the town's people when the settlement was practically destroyed by the Indians in King Philip's War. On Oct. 5, 1675, the day of the assault on the town, Pynchon was in command of the troops at Hadley, some twenty miles away. Being hastily summoned, he made a forced night march which enabled him to relieve the inhabitants with the loss of but three men and one woman. In 1680 he was sent to Albany to confer with Sir Edmund Andros concerning the depredations of the Mohawks, and succeeded in establishing friendly relations with the natives, for which service the General Court awarded him £12. The same year he was appointed with Joseph Dudley to establish the boundary line between Massachusetts and Connecticut.

Pynchon was able and astute, honest and just in his dealings, his life largely controlled by his deep religious convictions. His knowledge of the language and characteristics of the Indians enabled him to build up a successful business with them. Peculiarly fitted by training and mentality, he was eminently successful in acquiring large land holdings for himself and his community without hazarding the confidence of the natives. On Oct. 20, 1645, he married Amy, daughter of George Willys of Hartford. She died Jan. 9, 1699, aged seventy-four. Their children were: Joseph (1646–1682), unmarried; John (1647–1721), who married Margaret, daughter of Rev. William Hubbard [q.v.] of Ipswich; Mary (b. 1650), who married Joseph Whiting of Hartford; William and Mehitable, who died in infancy.

[Records in possession of the Conn. Valley Hist. Soc., Springfield, including seven account books (1651–94) which illustrate dealings over a large territory at a time when Pynchon was the principal merchant serving western New England; Winthrop Papers, Mass. Hist. Soc.; Mass. Archives; town and county records, Springfield; court records, Northampton; material in Conn. State Lib. and Conn. Hist. Soc., Hartford; Solomon Stoddard, God's Frown in the Death of Usefull Men . . . a Sermon Preached at the Funeral of the Hon. Col. John Pynchon, Esq. (1703); N. B. Shurtleff, Records of the Governor and Company of the Mass. Bay, vols. III–V (1854); E. B. O'Callaghan, Docs. Rel. to the Col. Hist. of the State of N. Y., vols. III–IV (1853–54); J. H. Trumbull, The Public Records of the

Colony of Conn., vols. II–IV (1852–68); Henry Morris, "The Old Pynchon Fort and Its Builders," Papers and Proc. of the Conn. Valley Hist. Soc., 1876–81 (1881), pp. 123–33; summary of account books in S. E. Morison, "William Pynchon," Proc. Mass. Hist. Soc., vol. LXIV (1932); M. A. Green, Springfield (1888); H. M. Burt, The First Century of the Hist. of Springfield (2 vols., 1898–99).]   H. A. W.

PYNCHON, THOMAS RUGGLES (Jan. 19, 1823–Oct. 6, 1904), Protestant Episcopal clergyman, college president, descended from William Pynchon [q.v.], chief founder of Springfield, Mass., was born in New Haven, Conn., the son of William Henry Ruggles Pynchon, a banker, and his wife, Mary Murdock. Because of the death of his father during his boyhood, Thomas went to Boston to live with his mother's sister. He attended the Boston Latin School and planned to enter Harvard, but was persuaded to go to Washington College (now Trinity), Hartford, by Professor John Smyth Rogers, a friend of the family, who promised to take him under his care. He entered a preliminary class at Hartford when he was thirteen, matriculated in the college in 1837, and was graduated as salutatorian of his class in 1841.

From 1843 to 1847 he was a tutor in the college. Meanwhile, probably under the influence of his friend John Williams, subsequently Bishop of Connecticut, he had decided to enter the ministry of the Episcopal Church. He studied theology and on June 14, 1848, was made a deacon by Bishop Thomas Church Brownell in Trinity Church, New Haven. He took charge of St. Paul's Church, Stockbridge, and Trinity Church, Lenox, in Massachusetts, and was ordained priest in Trinity Church, Boston, June 25, 1849, by Bishop Manton Eastburn. Six years later, having been elected Scovill Professor of Chemistry and Natural Science at his alma mater, he resigned his church at Stockbridge and went abroad for a year to prepare for his new duties. He studied in Paris and at Cambridge, and took a geological trip through southern France and Italy.

From 1855 to 1877 he taught science as it was understood in his day, giving instruction in chemistry, geology, and zoölogy. During this period he published The Chemical Forces—Heat, Light, Electricity (1870), the second edition of which, issued in 1873, bore the title, Introduction to Chemical Physics. From 1857 to 1882 he was college librarian, and from 1860 to 1864 and during the year 1866–67 he served as chaplain, also. In 1874, he was elected president of the college, serving till 1883. The nine years of his presidency were a critical period in the history of Trinity College. The site and buildings had been sold to the state for the new Capitol, and a new site for the college had been purchased. The heavy burden of superintending the erection of new buildings and of planning for the removal devolved upon President Pynchon. He carried through the task with good judgment, and the college entered upon its work in the new buildings in the fall of 1878. With the assumption of executive duties, however, he did not relinquish his teaching; he was professor of moral philosophy from 1877 until his retirement in 1902 (Hobart Professor, 1877–83; Brownell Professor, 1888–1902). In 1889 he published a volume entitled *Bishop Butler, a Religious Philosopher for All Time.* He was a member of the standing committee of the Diocese of Connecticut from 1871 to 1882, served from 1872 to his death as an examining chaplain, and from 1875 to his death as a trustee of the Episcopal Academy at Cheshire. He was also a trustee of the General Theological Seminary in New York.

Pynchon was a dignified gentleman, precise in his habits of thought and of expression, who seemed to belong to an earlier generation. He did not marry. He died in New Haven, in his eighty-second year, and was buried in the Grove Street Cemetery there. Trinity College has a portrait in oil, and a bust of him in bronze by Louis Potter.

[Records of Trinity College, Hartford (MSS.), authority for date of birth and parents' names; J. C. Pynchon, *Record of the Pynchon Family in England and America* (1898); *Who's Who in America,* 1903–05; *Churchman,* Oct. 15, 1904; *New Haven Evening Reg.,* Oct. 7, 1904.]   A—r. A.

PYNCHON, WILLIAM (*c.* 1590–Oct. 29, 1662), magistrate and trader, son of John Pynchon and Frances (Brett), was one of the original patentees and assistants of the Massachusetts Bay Company. With his wife and children he emigrated in the Winthrop fleet of 1630, settling first at Dorchester. Here his wife, Anna Andrew, died, and he married the widow Frances Sanford. A gentleman of distinguished connections (great-grandson of Sir Richard Empson and uncle of the Countess of Portland), himself the squire of Springfield in Essex, he brought considerable capital to the colony and started fur-trading operations at Roxbury, where he was the first signer of the church covenant. From 1630 to 1636, inclusive, he was annually reëlected assistant of the colony, and for two years (1632–34), served as treasurer, retiring from this position just as Thomas Hooker [*q.v.*] and the people of Newtown were seeking permission to emigrate to the Connecticut. Pynchon was appointed one of the commissioners to govern the new settlement on Mar. 3, 1635/36, and had probably made some beginning of the plan-

tation "over against Agawam" (later named Springfield after his English home) the previous summer. He was certainly at Springfield in May 1636, when with seven men he signed an agreement concerning land allotments and settling a minister.

Pynchon was elected a magistrate of Connecticut in March 1636/37 and again the following year. In consequence of his falling out with Thomas Hooker and the River authorities over a matter of supplying corn during the Pequot War, and being, as he felt, unjustly censured and fined by them, Pynchon washed his hands of the River Colony and supported the claim of the Bay Colony to Springfield, which took no further part in the Connecticut government after 1638.

Springfield was admirably situated for obtaining the peltry of the Connecticut and its tributaries. All kinds of furs, but principally beaver skins, were packed in hogsheads, teamed or boated to Pynchon's warehouse at the head of deepwater navigation on the Connecticut—still called Warehouse Point—and shipped to London. Separated by a hundred miles of wilderness from Boston, this frontier community was practically independent; and although the forms of town-meeting democracy were followed, Pynchon, who paid over half the taxes at first and was the largest landowner, virtually ruled the community with a cabinet consisting of his son, John, his two sons-in-law, Elizur Holyoke and Henry Smith, and the minister, George Moxon. He was chosen magistrate of the community by the inhabitants on Feb. 14, 1638/39. The records of his court of petty sessions, kept in his own hand, show that he was acquainted with the forms of English procedure, but aimed at doing justice rather than following the rules. Most of the causes were for petty thieving, breach of contract, and slander; but one, the witchcraft case of Hugh and Mary Parsons, was sent up to be tried at Boston.

Pynchon was reëlected to his former chair on the Massachusetts Board of Assistants in 1642, and annually thereafter until 1651. The previous year, he had had printed in London a theological tract called *The Meritorious Price of Our Redemption,* in which he attacked the current orthodox view of the atonement. It was a valid and constructive criticism, anticipating later conclusions of more liberal theologians. When the first copy reached Boston, the General Court took cognizance of it, and upon the report of a committee of clergy headed by Rev. John Norton [*q.v.*], denounced both book and author as heretical. The clerical committee drew up a counter pamphlet on behalf of the General Court, and reasoned with Pynchon, who made a partial recantation of his "errors"; but he was not re-elected an assistant, his book was publicly burnt, and he was twice ordered to appear before the Court and retract the rest of his heresies. It is likely that Pynchon, having accumulated a small fortune in the fur trade, would in any case have returned to England to enjoy it, but no doubt this incident hastened his departure to the more tolerant country. On Sept. 28, 1651, he deeded his property at Springfield to his son John [q.v.] and his sons-in-law. Accompanied by his wife and the Rev. George Moxon, who apparently shared his views, he sailed for England, probably in the spring of 1652. There he purchased an estate at Wraysbury, near Windsor, where he lived quietly, wrote several theological tracts, and died on Oct. 29, 1662.

[Consult S. E. Morison, "William Pynchon," *Proc. Mass. Hist. Soc.*, vol. LXIV (1932); S. E. Baldwin, "The Secession of Springfield from Connecticut," *Pubs. Col. Soc. Mass.*, vol. XII (1911), containing the best reproduction of the only known portrait of Pynchon, painted in England in 1657 (original in the Essex Institute, Salem); H. M. Burt, *The First Century of the History of Springfield*, vol. I (1898); M. A. Green, *Springfield* (1888). Pynchon's manuscript records of the Springfield court are in the Harvard Law Library; the most important single collection of his letters and other documents, in the Mass. Hist. Soc., is printed in *Proc. Mass. Hist. Soc.*, vols. XLVIII (1915), LVIII (1925), and *Mass. Hist. Soc. Colls.*, 2 ser. VIII (1819), 4 ser. VI (1863). H. F. Waters, *Geneal. Gleanings in England* (1901), vol. I, contains the fullest account of the Pynchon family. For a bibliography of writings, see Joseph Sabin, *Bibliotheca Americana*, XVI (1886), 151–54. A part of the rare pamphlet of 1650 is reprinted in Burt (*op. cit.*), I, 89–121; its theological significance is described in F. H. Foster, *A Genetic Hist. of the New England Theology* (1907), pp. 16–20.]

S. E. M.

QUACKENBUSH, STEPHEN PLATT (Jan. 23, 1823–Feb. 4, 1890), naval officer, was born in the old Quackenbush mansion, Albany, N. Y., the son of John N. and Nancy (Smith) Quackenbush, and a descendant of Pieter Quackenbosh who emigrated from Leyden, Holland, about 1660. He was appointed midshipman from New York on Feb. 15, 1840, and after cruises in the *Boston* to the East Indies and around the world, 1841–42, and in the *Raritan* to Brazil, 1843–45, he studied for a short time at the naval academy and was made passed midshipman on July 11, 1846. He was in the sloop *Albany* on blockade duty and in operations against Vera Cruz during the Mexican War; then in the *Supply*, Mediterranean Squadron; and after two years in the Coast Survey, an officer of the mail steamers *Pacific* and *Illinois*, 1850–52. His promotion to the rank of lieutenant came in 1855, after two years in the *Perry* on the African coast. He served in the *Wabash*, Home Squad-

ron, from 1857 to 1858; at the Philadelphia navy yard; and in the *Congress* on a Brazilian cruise, 1859–61. In the Civil War his first command was the gunboat *Delaware*, which participated in the capture of Roanoke Island on Feb. 7 and 8, 1862, and was the flagship of the division commanded by Stephen Clegg Rowan [q.v.] in the destruction of the Confederate "mosquito" flotilla on Feb. 10, the capture of New Bern, N. C., and subsequent operations in the Carolina sounds. Later in February the *Delaware* underwent heavy fire from shore batteries and infantry near Winter, N. C., after the enemy had supposedly displayed a white flag, whereupon Rowan destroyed the town. Ordered in May 1862 to the James River, and made lieutenant commander in July, Quackenbush was in action during the summer with shore defenses at Sewall's Point, Wilcox Landing, Malvern Hill, and elsewhere, supporting McClellan's army. Still in the *Delaware*, he covered Burnside's evacuation of Aquia Creek in August and afterward operated in the Potomac patrol. On Sept. 8 he was transferred to the *Unadilla*, in which he served a year on the southeast coast blockade, his most notable capture being the *Princess Royal* with ordnance machinery, medicines, etc., valued at nearly $250,000.

After a month's leave late in 1863 he again took up blockade duty off Wilmington, N. C., in the *Pequot*, a speedy propeller designed for pursuing blockade runners, and on Mar. 4, 1864, he captured the *Don*, a new British steamer worth $200,000. During the summer of 1864 while on patrol duty in the James River, he received a shot that took off his right leg. In December he took command of the monitor *Patapsco* off Charleston. While dragging for torpedoes in Charleston harbor on Jan. 15, 1865, the ship struck one and sank in twenty seconds with a loss of sixty-eight of her crew of 116. His last war command was the *Mingoe* off Georgetown, S. C. His post-war duty included command of the *Conemaugh, Tuscarora,* and *Terror* of the Atlantic Squadron in the period 1866–72, of the receiving ship *New Hampshire*, 1873–75, and of the Pensacola naval station, 1880–82. He was made commander in 1866, commodore in 1880, and rear admiral in 1884. After his retirement in 1885 he made his home in Washington. He was married on Jan. 18, 1849, to Cynthia Herrick Wright, daughter of Judge Deodatus Wright of Albany, and had two sons and a daughter. He died of heart trouble in Washington and was buried in Oak Hill Cemetery. At the time of his death a fellow officer, Rear Admiral Thomas Holdup Stevens, 1819–1896 [*q.v.*] (*Army and Navy Register,* Feb. 8, 1890), paid him high tribute as a gallant, resolute and just man, typical of the old Knickerbocker stock, "loyal to his friends and charitable to the erring."

[Letters and papers in *Personnel Files,* Navy Dept. Lib.; A. S. Quackenbush, *The Quackenbush Family* (1909); L. R. Hamersly, *The Records of Living Officers of the U. S. Navy and Marine Corps* (1890); *Army and Navy Jour.,* Feb. 8, 1890; *Washington Post,* Feb. 5, 1890.]   A. W.

QUANAH (*c.* 1845–Feb. 23, 1911), chief of the Comanche Indians, was born probably in northern Texas. His father was Peta Nocone, a chief of the Kwahadi, the most turbulent and hostile of the Comanches. His mother was Cynthia Ann Parker, who as a child had been a survivor of a massacre of whites on the Navasota River, Tex., nine years before he was born. In a battle with Texas Rangers, in 1860, the mother, with an infant daughter, was taken and returned to her people. About 1866 he organized a band of his own. His boldness, skill, and energy brought him many recruits, and by 1867 he was made chief. He refused to accept the Medicine Lodge treaty of 1867, requiring the Comanches, Kiowas, Kiowa Apaches, Southern Cheyennes, and Arapahos to settle on a reservation in the Indian Territory, and by a series of daring raids during the next seven years he terrorized the frontier settlements. In June 1874, as chief of the Comanches and war leader of the other hostiles, he led an attack of about 700 warriors against a party of twenty-eight white buffalo hunters at Adobe Walls, in the present Hutchinson County, Tex., but after an all-day fight was badly defeated. A vigorous campaign by Ranald S. Mackenzie and Nelson A. Miles brought hostilities to a close by the middle of 1875, and, after some delay Quanah surrendered.

After his surrender his conversion to the white man's way was immediate, and, except for the retention of many of his Indian beliefs and observances, it was thorough. He had been all savage, but he quickly adapted himself to the new conditions. Learning the facts about his mother, he took the name of Quanah Parker. To the memory of his mother, who, with her infant daughter, had died among her kinfolk, probably in 1864, he was devoted, and in the year before his death he had their remains exhumed and reburied near his home. Among his people and the confederated tribes he fostered building and agriculture, popularized education, and discouraged extravagance and dissipation. By leasing the surplus pasture lands to stockmen he added greatly to the tribal income. He became a shrewd business man, and at one time was said to be the richest Indian in the nation. Some twelve miles

west of Fort Sill, Okla., he built a large house and cultivated a good farm. He traveled extensively, usually accompanied by the youngest of his three wives, known as Too-nicey; and he rode, as did Geronimo, in the inaugural procession of President Theodore Roosevelt. He was tall, straight, and powerfully built. Despite his white blood, his complexion was darker than that of most of his tribesmen. Those who had chanced to see him in his savage days said that his expression was ferocious. In his days of peace, however, he became widely known as a genial and at times jovial companion, with a fondness for racy stories and a practice of using forthright and not too choice speech. He spoke a broken English and a fairly good Spanish. He died at his home.

[James Mooney in *Handbook of Am. Indians,* ed. by F. W. Hodge, pt. 2 (1910); *Seventeenth Ann. Report of the Bureau of Am. Ethnology,* pt. 1 (1898); N. B. Wood, *Lives of Famous Indian Chiefs* (copr. 1906); R. G. Carter, *Tragedies of the Cañon Blanco* (1919); J. T. De Shields, *Cynthia Ann Parker* (1886); F. R. Bechdolt, *Tales of the Old Timers* (1924); *Daily Oklahoman* and *Okla. State Capital,* Feb. 24, 1911.]   W. J. G.

QUANTRILL, WILLIAM CLARKE (July 31, 1837–June 6, 1865), guerrilla chieftain, was born at Canal Dover, Ohio, and was the eldest of the eight children of Thomas Henry and Caroline Cornelia (Clarke) Quantrill. After teaching school for brief periods in Ohio and Illinois, in 1857 he went to Kansas with a party of settlers, where he filed claim to a tract of land; but he was too restless, too fond of adventure, to be satisfied with a farmer's life. In 1858 he traveled with an army provision train bound for Utah, and at Fort Bridger, Salt Lake City, and other places he seems to have been a gambler under the name of Charley Hart. Returning to Kansas, he taught school in the winter of 1859–60. During the rest of 1860 he lived near Lawrence, either with Indians or with whites of questionable character, again going by the name of Charley Hart. Several murders and thefts were attributed to him; finally, a warrant was issued for him on a charge of horse-stealing, but he fled before he could be arrested. In December 1860 he attached himself to five young abolitionists who intended to seize the three slaves of Morgan Walker, a Missouri farmer, and free them. Quantrill, whose sympathies were now proslavery, betrayed his companions to Walker, and three of them were killed. Returning to Kansas, he was arrested on the horse-stealing charge but was aided in escaping to Missouri.

When the Civil War began, he was for a time irregularly connected with the Confederate army and fought at Lexington, Mo. He next appeared as the chief of a band of guerrillas, a scourge to Missouri and Kansas, robbing mail coaches, raiding and sacking communities and farms supposed to be Union in sympathy, frequently slaying Northern partisans, and having occasional brushes with Federal troops. In 1862 the Union authorities formally declared him and his men outlaws. They were part of a Confederate force that captured Independence, Mo., in August 1862. The troop was then regularly mustered into the Confederate service, and he was given the rank of captain. At dawn on Aug. 21, 1863, he rode into Lawrence with a band of about 450 men. Stores, hotels, and homes were pillaged; men, women, and children were butchered (estimates of the dead vary from 150 to 182); and a considerable portion of the town was burned. Two months later he defeated a small body of Federal cavalry at Baxter Springs, Kan., capturing seventeen musicians and noncombatants, who were put to death. Dissension finally arose among his troop, and it broke up into smaller bands. Early in 1865 he with thirty-three men entered Kentucky, robbing, foraging, and occasionally killing. In May of that year, probably May 10, a small, irregular Federal force surprised the guerrillas near Taylorsville, Spencer County; Quantrill was fatally wounded; and he died nearly a month later at Louisville.

[W. E. Connelley, *Quantrill and the Border Wars* (1910); J. N. Edwards, *Noted Guerrillas* (1877); John McCorkle, *Three Years with Quantrell* (copr. 1914); Kit Dalton, *Under the Black Flag* (copr. 1914); Wiley Britton, *The Civil War on the Border* (2 vols., 1890–99); *Kan. Hist. Soc. Colls.*, vol. VII (1902); *War of the Rebellion: Official Records (Army)*, I ser. VIII, XXII, pt. 1, XLIX, pt. 1.]   A. F. H.

QUARTER, WILLIAM (Jan. 21, 1806–Apr. 10, 1848), Catholic prelate, son of Michael and Ann (Bennet) Quarter, was born in King's County, Ireland. Drilled in his first lessons by a pious, educated mother, he was trained soundly in the classics by a Presbyterian minister and the Fitzgerald brothers, typical Irish schoolmasters, who enforced application and exemplary conduct. In his sixteenth year, he entered the seminary at Maynooth as a protégé of Bishop Doyle. Through an association with Father McAuley (a brother of Count McAuley) who had traveled in the United States, he learned of the scarcity of priests in America and of the deplorable religious status of scattered Irish immigrants. Thereupon, he asked for an *exeat* from his ordinary and in 1822 took an emigrant's farewell from parents and friends as he sailed for Quebec. Denied admission to Quebec and Montreal seminaries because of his youth, he ap-

pealed successfully to Dr. John Dubois [*q.v.*] of Mount St. Marys, Emmitsburg, Md., where he was permitted to teach mathematics and the classics in the preparatory school while studying theology. Ordained priest Sept. 19, 1829, by Dubois, now bishop of New York, he was assigned to St. Peter's Church, from which he was promoted in 1833 to the pastorate of St. Mary's Church. As a prudent, self-sacrificing priest, he challenged popular attention by heroic service during the cholera epidemic, and gained episcopal notice by the establishment of two parochial schools under the Sisters of Charity whom he enlisted in Emmitsburg, by the conversion of John Oertel, a Lutheran minister, who became editor of an influential German Catholic journal in Baltimore, and by his social work among immigrants. When Chicago was created a diocese, Quarter was named its first bishop, much to the satisfaction of the Irish element in Illinois. In an unusual triple ceremony, Mar. 10, 1844, he was consecrated, along with Andrew Byrne and John McCloskey [*qq.v.*], by Bishop Hughes, who was no doubt responsible for all three nominations.

Quarter's episcopal tenure in Chicago was brief, but he laid permanent foundations. Imbued with Hughes's views, he was deeply concerned with Catholic education. With this purpose in mind, he established the University of St. Mary's of the Lake, and introduced the Sisters of Mercy of Pittsburgh under Sister Mary Francis Ward for parochial schools and orphanages. He built a number of churches—including Saint Peter's **and Saint Joseph's—for the rapidly** increasing German population, introduced some forty priests, sponsored devotional confraternities, inaugurated the first diocesan theological conferences in the United States, and obtained a legislative enactment which incorporated the bishops of Chicago as a corporation sole to hold diocesan properties. This enactment prevented the rise of trusteeism with its usual difficulties. In his constructive program Quarter was aided materially by his brother, Rev. Walter Quarter (1812–1863), and by such builders of Chicago as Walter Newberry, W. B. Ogden, and J. Y. Scammon, whose confidence he won by an approved policy of attracting immigrants westward.

[*U. S. Cath. Mag.*, May 1848; J. E. McGirr, *Life of the Rt. Rev. William Quarter* (1850, repr. 1920); R. H. Clarke, *Lives of the Deceased Bishops of the Cath. Church in the U. S.*, vol. II (1888); *Cath. Encyc.*, III (1908), 653; J. G. Shea, *Hist. of the Cath. Church in the U. S.*, vol. IV (1892); official Cath. directories; G. J. Garraghan, *The Cath. Church in Chicago* (1921); *Chicago Journal*, Apr. 11, 1848; *N. Y. Freeman's Journal*, Dec. 26, 1863.]   R. J. P.

QUARTLEY, ARTHUR (May 24, 1839–May 19, 1886), painter of seascapes, was born at Paris, France. His father, Frederick William Quartley, was an English engraver; his mother, Ann (Falkard) Quartley, the daughter of William and Mary (Duncan) Falkard. The family spent seven years in France and then returned to England where Arthur as a young boy was soprano soloist in the royal chapel, Windsor Castle. Upon the death of his wife in 1851, Frederick Quartley emigrated and settled at Peekskill, N. Y. Arthur, in the new environment, became an enthusiastic angler and huntsman but the father continued a rule begun in England that the boy must show him each Saturday evening two carefully finished drawings. While the senior Quartley was establishing himself as an American engraver, some of his best work appearing in the publications *Picturesque America* and *Picturesque Europe,* the son thus laid the foundations of his clever and highly competent draftsmanship. His youthful desire, however, was to have a lucrative business of his own, and he accordingly apprenticed himself to a New York sign-painter.

Having learned his trade Quartley in 1862 set up for himself in Baltimore where he had relatives. His firm, Emmart & Quartley, "did only high grade work and were regarded as the best decorators in the city" (C. G. Quartley, *post*). Arthur at this time began to make pictures, mostly marines, of which he had a successful exhibition and sale at the photographic studio of Norval H. Busey. His health, meantime, had suffered from overwork and he sold his business in order to devote himself exclusively to his art. Returning to New York about 1875, he opened a studio and soon won distinction. He painted summers at the Isle of Shoals, off the New Hampshire coast, where he was associated with Celia Thaxter [*q.v.*] and her group of literary and artistic workers. He early discovered the beauty of New York harbor and his "From a North River Pier Head," now in the permanent collection of the National Academy of Design, was described as "an excellent example of what may be done with the picturesque material that lies right at our own doors" (*Academy Sketches, post,* p. 33). Other important canvases of Quartley's, shown at the Academy, were: "Morning Effect, North River" (1877); "Trinity from the River" (1880); "Queen's Birthday" (1883); and "Dignity and Impudence" (1884). In 1879 the artist was elected an associate of the National Academy; in 1886, an academician. He was also one of the early members of the Society of American Artists.

A strikingly handsome man, of agreeable personality, Quartley was achieving a reputation as the foremost American painter of seascapes when, after a protracted illness, he succumbed to a disease of the liver at his home, 52 South Washington Square, New York. He left a wife, Laura (Delamater) Quartley, and three children. Quartley's technical method, which he seems to have acquired as a decorator, was based upon careful delineation of the principal objects of his picture, prior to laying in the background and accessories. How his very promising art might have developed had he lived longer can only be conjectured. He was represented in the National Academy's centennial exhibition by "North River Pier Head."

[See: *Acad. Sketches, with Descriptive Notes by "Nemo"* (1877); S. G. W. Benjamin, *Our Am. Artists,* 2 ser. (1881); C. E. Clement and Laurence Hutton, *Artists of the Nineteenth Century* (1884); *Cat. of Commemorative Exhibition by Members of the Nat. Acad. of Design, 1825–1925* (1925); *Twentieth Century Biog. Dict. of Notable Americans* (1904); *Art World,* Sept. 1918; and *N. Y. Tribune,* May 21, 1886. Manuscript letters from Charles G. Quartley, Baltimore, Md., a nephew, and Mrs. Arthur Van Winkle, Scarsdale, N. Y., a niece of the artist, to the author of this sketch, contain previously unpublished information and correct several errors in existing accounts of Quartley.]

F. W. C.

QUAY, MATTHEW STANLEY (Sept. 30, 1833–May 28, 1904), politician, was born at Dillsburg, York County, Pa. The son of Anderson Beaton and Catherine (McCain) Quay, he was of Scotch-Irish ancestry, his forebears having settled in Chester County in 1713. His father was a Presbyterian minister. In 1840 the family moved to Beaver County. At the age of seventeen, Matthew was graduated from Jefferson College at Canonsburg, Pa., after which he traveled, taught school, lectured, and studied law with the firm of Penney & Sterrett, Pittsburgh; he was admitted to the bar in 1854. He was married, on Oct. 10, 1855, to Agnes Barclay of Beaver and they had two sons and three daughters.

His first public office was that of prothonotary of Beaver County, to which position he was elected in 1856 and reëlected in 1859. In 1860, by his success in securing delegates for Andrew G. Curtin [*q.v.*], elected governor that year, he attracted the attention of western Pennsylvania leaders. When the Civil War broke out, he was called to positions of great responsibility as assistant commissary-general of the state, **private** secretary to Governor Curtin, colonel of the 134th Pennsylvania Infantry (August–December 1862), military state agent in Washington, major and chief of transportation and telegraphs of Pennsylvania, and military secretary to Governor Curtin (1863–65). For his distinguished war services, especially at the battle of Fredericksburg, he was awarded the Congressional Medal of Honor. Whatever may be said of his later political career, his war record was unsullied.

Before the war was over he was elected to the state House of Representatives, where he served from 1865 to 1867. As chairman of the committee on ways and means, he was responsible for the enactment of legislation which freed real estate from state taxation, and transferred a share of the burden to corporations. From 1867 to 1872 he owned and edited the *Beaver Radical,* to strengthen his political position at home. In 1872 he was made secretary of the commonwealth and served in this position until 1878, when the legislature created for him the position of recorder of Philadelphia, the most lucrative public office in the state. At the same time, he was chairman of the Republican state committee. Being unable to gain control of the Philadelphia political machine, he resigned the position of recorder, and was again appointed secretary of the commonwealth in 1879; this position he held until 1882. Then for the brief period of about three years he was out of office. Following a scandal in the state treasurer's office in which Quay was charged with being implicated, he ran for state treasurer by way of vindication, and was elected by a large vote in 1885. From this time until his death, the political control of Pennsylvania rested in his hands. In 1887 he was elected to the United States Senate, serving in that body until Mar. 3, 1889. Owing to the failure of the Pennsylvania legislature to elect his successor, he was appointed to fill the vacancy. But the United States Senate by resolution of Apr. 24, 1900, decided that he was not entitled to the seat. He was re-elected, however, on Jan. 15, 1901, and he served as senator from Pennsylvania until his death in Beaver, Pa., on May 28, 1904.

Quay was not one of the great leaders of the Senate and in his fifteen years in that body did not hold a major committee chairmanship. Nevertheless, his influence was decisive in several important matters, notably in connection with tariff legislation. He is chiefly to be remembered for his brilliant and consummate genius as a politician. Never in the history of Pennsylvania, with all of its great politicians, has there been a man with such great powers of leadership in political organization. His whole career was a constant fight. He was rarely able to rest on his laurels and then only for brief periods. This strenuous life which he led was partly due to his peculiar methods of manipulating political forces. He always had a machine, but he would build up a new alignment for each major contest. Despite the opposition of the Philadelphia and Pittsburgh machines, and usually the corporate influence as well, Quay was able to hold sway over the affairs of Pennsylvania. In the memorable fight for the treasureship in 1885, and in the more difficult struggle in 1895 for the state chairmanship against Christopher L. Magee [*q.v.*], William Flinn, Boss David Martin of Philadelphia, Governor Daniel H. Hastings, and B. Frank Gilkeson, he displayed a coolness under fire, a cunning, a determination, a resourcefulness, which have been rarely equaled. He was verily a Napoleon in politics.

His management of the Harrison campaign of 1888, as chairman of the Republican National Committee, was notable. Scarcely ever has a national campaign depended so completely on the sagacity and cunning of one man. His break with Harrison and his failure to take an active part in the campaign of 1892 was one of the prime factors in the Democratic victory of that year. In 1896 he was a member of the executive committee of the Republican National Committee, and in 1900 he was in charge of the New York headquarters during that year's presidential campaign. He elected Harrison, and together with Platt secured Roosevelt's nomination as vice-president. He brought "Mark" Hanna into national politics by making him a member of the Republican executive committee in 1888. He attended every Republican National Convention from 1872 until his death, except that of 1884. He was never strong physically, and when he had finished a political battle he would slip away to recuperate. He went as often as possible to his winter home at Saint Lucie, Fla., on the Indian River, to fish for tarpon. He went to Maine occasionally, and to Brigantine Beach, near Atlantic City, where he enjoyed yachting as well as fishing.

Quay could read and speak several languages, being particularly fond of reading Horace in the original, and he had a great love for military and religious history. The only subject on which he would talk freely was literature, and he possessed one of the finest private libraries in America. Yet at the same time he displayed an utter contempt for ordinary ideals. Many of his contemporaries believed him to be an utterly corrupt man and yet his methods were no worse than those of his adversaries. He was certainly one of the best-hated men in politics. His strong interest in protecting the Indians and his many kindnesses to persons in distress are well known;

yet he would occasionally act in a political maneuver without any sentiment or mercy. He may be ranked as one of the greatest tacticians and managers in the whole realm of American politics.

[Letters, papers, and clippings in possession of the family; S. W. Pennypacker, *The Autobiography of a Pennsylvanian* (1918), and *Pennsylvania in Am. History* (1910); *Pennsylvania Politics; The Campaign of 1900 as Set Forth in the Speeches of Hon. Matthew S. Quay* (1901); E. J. Stackpole, *Behind the Scenes with a Newspaper Man* (1927); A. K. McClure, *Old Time Notes of Pennsylvania* (1905), vol. II; *Smull's Legislative Handbook*, 1885–1904; *Congressional Directory*, 50–58 Cong.; *Who's Who in America*, 1903–05; "Matthew Stanley Quay: Memorial Addresses," *Sen. Doc. 202*, 58 Cong., 3 Sess.; *Biog. and Hist. Cat. of Washington and Jefferson College* (1902); *Biog. Dir. Am. Cong.* (1928); *Press* (Phila.), May 29, 1904.] J.K.P.

QUAYLE, WILLIAM ALFRED (June 25, 1860–Mar. 9, 1925), Methodist bishop, was the only son of two Manx emigrants, Thomas and Elizabeth (Gale or Gell) Quayle, who were cousins. He was born in Parkville, Mo., probably while his parents were on their way to the mining fields of Colorado. His mother died soon after his birth and was buried in an unknown grave. His father took him to Kansas and placed him in the home of Edward Gill, a brother-in-law and a Methodist minister. For many years, until sometime in his college course, the boy was known as William Gill. When he was thirteen, at the death of Mrs. Gill, he went to live in the home of another Methodist minister, James Boicourt. Meanwhile his father settled near the town of Auburn, Kan., where William did the work of a farmer boy and attended country school. After a brief period in the state agricultural school at Manhattan, he entered Baker University at Baldwin, Kan., where he acted as tutor during the last two years of his college course. On graduation in 1885 he was retained by the college to teach the ancient languages. On Jan. 28, 1886, he was married to the daughter of the first president of the college, Allie (Davis) Perry Robbins. They had two children. In 1888 he was elected president. He left the presidency of the college at the end of four years to become the pastor of Independence Avenue Methodist Episcopal Church in Kansas City, Mo. Three years later he was called to the pastorate of Meridian Street Methodist Church at Indianapolis only to be called back to Kansas City to the pastorate of the Grand Avenue Church in 1900. His last pastorate was St. James Methodist Episcopal Church at Chicago, where he served four years, until his election to the episcopacy at the General Conference of the church in 1908. His three episcopal residences were Oklahoma City from 1908 to 1912,

St. Paul, Minn., from 1912 to 1916, and St. Louis from 1916 to 1924.

As a boy he had a love of nature, to which he soon added "an unsuppressable appetite for literature." He early achieved a reputation as a preacher of unusual gifts, and commanding pulpits were open to him. His preaching was characterized by new phrases, apt and unexpected words, imagination, and feeling. His unusual preaching drew crowds to hear him, and he was soon in great demand as a popular lecturer. In this respect few in his generation excelled him. The plays of Shakespeare and the romances of Victor Hugo gave scope to his talent, and so remarkable was his histrionic gift that he did for the hearer almost all that the actor could do with the accessories of costume and scenery. He was the author of many books. His essays on literary subjects were always revealing; his poetry was seldom great but always characteristic; his books of sermons and addresses were filled with new phrases and new insights, though perhaps his best writing was on nature subjects; *In God's Out-of-doors* (1902) and *With Earth and Sky* (copr. 1922) are two of his best-known books. His first book was a volume of literary essays called *The Poet's Poet and Other Essays*, which appeared in 1897. From that time until his death he published about one book a year. The volume *The Pastor-Preacher* (copr. 1910) is drawn largely out of his own experience as a minister. He loved people and was never content simply to preach to them; he got in close personal touch with them, especially those who most needed pastoral care. He was a collector of rare books; the royalties he received from his own books he put into others. He liked rare bindings and first editions, and he gathered about him an interesting library. His most valuable collection consisted of 210 early Bibles, which on his death were given to the library of Baker University. He was a man of more than medium height and heavy build. His large head was covered with long tousled tawny red hair, while his dress was inelegant, though never shabby. He had a remarkably winsome personality, and he never permitted his elevation to put him out of touch with the heart of everyday humanity. Paralysis rendered him helpless in 1924. He died at his home in Baldwin, Kan.

[M. S. Rice, *Wm. Alfred Quayle* (copr. 1928); *Northwestern Christian Advocate*, Mar. 19, 1925; C. C. Alexander, "Wm. Alfred Quayle as a Man of Letters," *Methodist Review*, Sept. 1925; *N. Y. Times*, Mar. 10, 1925.] W.W.S.

QUEEN, WALTER W. (Oct. 6, 1824–Oct. 24, 1893), naval officer, the son of John William and Mary G. (Wells) Queen, was born in Washington, D. C. Appointed a midshipman on Oct. 7, 1841, he served in the *Macedonian* and *Marion,* of the West India Squadron, and in the *Perry,* of the East India Squadron, from 1843 to 1845. Attached to the *Cumberland* and the *Ohio* during the Mexican War, he landed at Fort Point Isabel with a detachment of midshipmen and marines to cooperate in the battles of Palo Alto and Resaca de la Palma. Later, he participated in the attacks on Tampico and Alvarado, and in the capture of Vera Cruz and Tuspan. He was made a passed midshipman on Aug. 10, 1847, and was ordered, after the war, to the naval school at Annapolis, where he engaged in a duel with Midshipman Byrd W. Stevenson and was severely wounded. Both principals were dismissed from the service, but were reinstated in 1853. Made lieutenant on Sept. 16, 1855, he served successively on the storeship *Relief,* Brazilian Squadron; the steamer *Michigan* on the Great Lakes; the *San Jacinto,* East India Squadron; the receiving ship *Alleghany* at Baltimore; and the steamer *Powhatan* in the West Indies. At the outbreak of the Civil War, the *Powhatan,* Capt. David Dixon Porter [*q.v.*], reënforced Fort Pickens, where Queen had charge of the squadron's boats for nineteen days. In April 1862, he commanded the seven vessels comprising the second division of Porter's mortar flotilla, which bombarded Forts Jackson and St. Philip, and assisted Farragut to force the passage and capture New Orleans. He participated later in a similar bombardment at Vicksburg, while Farragut ran past the batteries.

Promoted for gallantry to the rank of lieutenant commander on July 16, 1862, he commanded the *Florida* and the gunboat *Wyalusing* of the North Atlantic Blockading Squadron from 1863 to 1864. On May 5, 1864, Queen's gunboat, accompanied by six others of the "pasteboard fleet" under Capt. Melancton Smith [*q.v.*], gallantly engaged the Confederate ram *Albemarle* and two wooden vessels off the mouth of the Roanoke River. Though the Federal vessels were badly damaged, the *Bombshell* was captured, and the ram retired with her tiller disabled and smokestack riddled, unable to cooperate in an attack on New Bern. From 1865 to 1867 Queen was ordnance inspector at the Scott Foundry, Reading, Pa., and on a board to examine volunteer officers for the navy at Hartford, Conn., and at Washington, D. C. He was made a commander on July 25, 1866, commanded the *Tuscarora,* South Pacific and North Atlantic Stations, the receiving ship *Potomac,* and was on duty at the Washington navy yard. Pro-

moted to the rank of captain on June 4, 1874, he was in command of the *Saranac,* North Pacific Station, when she was lost on an uncharted sunken rock off the coast of Alaska. His important later commands were: the receiving ships, *Worcester* and *Franklin,* Norfolk; the flagship *Trenton,* European Station; and the Washington navy yard. He became a commodore on Feb. 9, 1884, and a rear admiral on Aug. 28, 1886. After his retirement in October of the same year, he joined Admiral John Jay Almy [*q.v.*] in profitable real estate investments in northwest Washington. He died of heart disease and was buried in Arlington Cemetery. His wife, Christiana Crosby, a sister of Admiral Peirce Crosby [*q.v.*], survived him.

[Official papers and records, Navy Dept.; Minutes of Proceedings of a Naval Court of Inquiry Convened at the Naval School, Annapolis, Md., May 29, 1848; M. S. Hawley and J. C. Hawley, "Some of the Queen Family of Md." (1933, manuscript at Lib. of Cong.); W. H. Parker, *Recollections of a Naval Officer* (1883); J. R. Soley, *Admiral Porter* (1903); *Washington Post,* Oct. 25, 1893.]   C. L. L.

QUELCH, JOHN (c. 1665–June 30, 1704), pirate, was born in London about 1665 and first claimed public notice in the summer of 1703. In July of that year the brigantine *Charles,* owned by a number of respectable Boston merchants, was commissioned by Governor Dudley as a privateer to sail against the French in Acadia and Newfoundland. On Aug. 1 the ship lay off Marblehead, fully manned, but the sailing was delayed by the illness of Capt. Daniel Plowman. The crew showing signs of disorder, Plowman wrote the owners to come and safeguard their interests, but before anything could be accomplished, the crew took possession of the ship and locked Plowman in his cabin. John Quelch, the lieutenant-commander, then came aboard, and acquiescing in the arrangement, was chosen captain—probably because of his knowledge of navigation—over one Anthony Holding, who was the ringleader of the plot. The vessel sailed immediately and shortly after it had gained the open sea, Plowman was thrown overboard. Instead of heading north, the *Charles* was turned south to the coast of Brazil, where between Nov. 15, 1703, and Feb. 17, 1704, nine vessels were captured and looted by the crew. All these vessels were Portuguese, and as Portugal was at peace with England, the acts constituted flagrant piracy—specifically covered by Article XVIII of the Treaty of May 16, 1703, between England and Portugal. While the captures were small, the booty included valuable quantities of provisions, cloth, silks, sugar, rum, and slaves.

together with gold dust and coin to the value of £1,000.

Following a notice in the *Boston News-Letter* of May 22, 1704, that the *Charles* had arrived at Marblehead, the owners filed charges with the authorities that led the attorney-general to set out to capture Quelch and his crew, who in the meantime had deserted the vessel and had begun to scatter. By May 25 the attorney-general had safely lodged in Boston jail Quelch and six of his companions, and several more of the malefactors were later captured. On June 13, 1704, a court of Admiralty was held under the presidency of Governor Dudley. Most of the prisoners were arraigned on this day, several pleading guilty and turning Crown witnesses. On June 19, Quelch was brought to trial. Under the Statute of King William, "for the more effectual suppression of piracy," a court of Admiralty was competent to try principals in piracy cases without a jury. From the first, it was evident that the court was determined upon a conviction, and although Quelch was ably defended by his counsel and the Crown's case rested on the evidence of accomplices—at that time not admissible under the civil law—Quelch and six of the principal leaders among the crew were sentenced to death. On June 30, 1704, the culprits were brought to the gallows. The efforts of several Boston ministers, led by Cotton Mather, to bring the prisoners to repentance continued to the very foot of the gallows, but in the case of Quelch, at least, were unavailing. His only remarks were to warn the people to "take care how they brought money into New England, to be hanged for it" (Dow and Edmonds, *post,* p. 113), and to complain of conviction on purely circumstantial evidence. The gallows were erected on a point of land in the Charles River below Copp's Hill, and Samuel Sewall records that when the scaffold was dropped beneath Quelch, such a screech went up from the crowd as to be heard by his wife over a mile away.

While Quelch was clearly involved in the acts of piracy, no evidence appeared that he was directly responsible for the death of Plowman or any of the Portuguese captives. The speed and questionable procedure of the trial, together with the evident eagerness of the authorities to confiscate and divide the treasure between themselves and the Crown, led a later official report to characterize it as "one of the clearest cases of judicial murder in our American annals" (*Acts and Resolves,* post, p. 397). The interest the trial aroused at the time is evidenced by the issue of a broadsheet by the *Boston News-Let-ter,* probably the first "Extra" in American newspaper history, and the republication of the same broadside in London.

[*Acts and Resolves of the Province of Mass. Bay,* vol. VIII (1895), pp. 386–98; *Boston News-Letter,* issues for May and June 1704; *Diary of Samuel Sewall,* vol. II (1879); G. F. Dow and J. H. Edmonds, *The Pirates of the New-Eng. Coast, 1630–1730* (1923); D. C. Seitz, *Under the Black Flag* (1925).]   W. H—e.

QUESNAY, ALEXANDRE-MARIE, Chevalier de Beaurepaire (Nov. 23, 1755–Feb. 8, 1820), French soldier in the American Revolution, projector of an academy of arts and sciences at Richmond, Va., was born at Saint-Germain-en-Viry (Nièvre), the son of Blaise Guillaume Quesnay and Catherine Deguillon. His grandfather, François Quesnay, court physician and economist, was the first prominent member of the family. Besides the ordinary secondary education, Quesnay received special training in music, drawing, painting, and in the gentlemanly arts of dancing and fencing. Before coming to America he was a member of the *Gendarmes de la Garde du Roi.* He arrived in Virginia during April 1777, and after serving as a captain in the Revolutionary army until the autumn of 1778, he retired on account of poor health and the loss of his baggage and letters of recommendation. The following two years he spent in Gloucester County, Va., at the home of Col. John Peyton. He engaged in some unsuccessful shipping ventures there with James Nuttall and was induced by John Page of "Rosewell" to establish an Academy in Virginia. Early in 1780 he set out to see what the prospects for such an institution in America were. He spent four years in Philadelphia, where he conducted a school and interested himself in dramatics, presenting Beaumarchais's *Eugénie,* the first French play to be produced in America. From Philadelphia he went to New York and there also organized a school. Returning to Virginia in the autumn of 1785, he opened a school in Richmond. After great discouragement he raised enough money to erect a building for the Academy. The following March he went to France. In the spring of 1787 he presented his plan of an Academy of the United States of America to the royal academies of science and of painting and sculpture, and to Thomas Jefferson, then American minister to France. The plan was that of an extensive system of schools and universities in the cities of Richmond, Baltimore, New York, and Philadelphia—all being centered around an establishment at Richmond. Besides a system of schools the Academy was to have been a learned society for the advancement of art and science. Quesnay received the approval of the French academies, but Jefferson, while not actively opposing it, claimed that America was too poor to support such undertakings. The project failed. The French Revolution and the objections of his family kept Quesnay from returning to America or advancing his project in Europe.

At the beginning of the Revolution Quesnay was mildly radical, as the issues of his *Avis Impartial aux Citoyens* show. He was later obliged to leave France, but he returned to become a government official during the Napoleonic régime. He died at Saint-Maurice (Seine). From his marriage with Catherine Cadier he had one son who became a lawyer. His grandson, Jules Quesnay de Beaurepaire, also a lawyer, prosecuted Boulanger and Dreyfus.

[H. B. Adams, *Thos. Jefferson and the Univ. of Va.* (1888); Bernard Faÿ, *The Revolutionary Spirit in France and America* (1927); R. H. Gaines, "Richmond's First Acad., Projected by M. Quesnay de Beaurepaire in 1786," *Va. Hist. Soc. Colls.*, new ser. XI (1892); T. C. Pollock, *The Phila. Theatre in the Eighteenth Century* (1933); Quesnay's *Mémoire, Statuts et Prospectus Concernant L'Académie des Sciences et Beaux Arts des États-Unis* (1788); Jefferson's letters to Quesnay in the Lib. of Cong.; Registres des Actes de décès, Mairie de Saint-Maurice (Seine); Va. House Lib. Colls., Richmond, Va.]
K. L. F.

QUICK, JOHN HERBERT (Oct. 23, 1861–May 10, 1925), lawyer, politician, editor, author, was born on a farm in Grundy County, Iowa, near Steamboat Rock, the son of Martin and Margaret (Coleman) Quick. He was of New York Dutch stock, with an admixture of Irish and probably of other strains. Besides three sisters he had a half-sister on his mother's side, another half-sister and four half-brothers on his father's. They were a sober, industrious, dutiful family, held together by strong though undemonstrative affection, but with little schooling, no money, and neither time nor opportunity for self-improvement. When twenty months old Herbert was stricken with infantile paralysis, which left him with feet and ankles permanently deformed. Though sickly and awkward, he labored manfully on the farm, assimilated everything that the district school could give him, and early developed an insatiable craving for books and for the life of the mind. Books, however, were scarce in that region, and good books almost unobtainable. In his early, impressionable years he knew the English classics only through the selections in the McGuffey readers; he was nineteen years old before he chanced upon a single novel of Dickens or the poems of Tennyson. In 1877 he attended a teachers' institute at Grundy Center and received a certificate of competence; from then till 1890 he

taught in various schools in the state, finally becoming principal of a ward school at Mason City. He meanwhile studied law for several years in the office of John Cliggitt, who put him through a thorough course of Blackstone, Kent, and J. F. Stephen before allowing him to take up the *Code of Iowa* and the *Iowa Reports*. More important to him than any law book was *Progress and Poverty*, which he read with intense excitement and growing conviction, and which became his economic and social Bible. He was admitted to the Iowa bar in 1889, and on Apr. 9, 1890, he married Ella Corey of Syracuse, N. Y., whom he had met in 1887.

He was now twenty-nine years old and on the threshold of a busy, varied career. From 1890 until 1908 he practised law in Sioux City, Iowa. He gained prominence by his successful prosecution of some municipal grafters, became a member of the Democratic state committee, was mayor of the city from 1898 to 1900 but failed of reëlection, and was a nominee for the state supreme court in 1902. Despite his Single Tax principles he was guilty of certain aberrations: at one time he was a publicity agent for O. P. and M. J. Van Sweringen, and at another time he was involved in a flamboyant scheme to develop Palmetto Beach, Ala., as a rival to Mobile. He also wrote much in behalf of dry-farming. All the while his real ambition was literary. In 1901 he sent a short poem entitled "A Whiff of Smoke" to the *Century Magazine*. The editor, Robert Underwood Johnson, published it in the February 1902 issue and urged Quick to keep on with his writing. His first book was a volume of Indian folklore, *In the Fairyland of America* (1901), and was followed by several novels in which honest realism, an irresistible impulse to preach, and melodrama derived from his early reading of the *New York Ledger*, were strangely mixed: *Aladdin & Co.* (1904); *Double Trouble* (1906); *The Broken Lance* (1907); *Virginia of the Air Lanes* (1909); *Yellowstone Nights* (1911); *The Brown Mouse* (1915); and *The Fairview Idea* (1919). During this period he also published three volumes of non-fiction: *American Inland Waterways* (1909); *On Board the Good Ship Earth* (1913); and *From War to Peace* (1919). He was associate editor of *La Follette's Weekly Magazine* from December 1908 to July 1909; editor of *Farm and Fireside*, 1909–16; a member of the Federal Farm Loan Bureau, on President Wilson's appointment, 1916–19; and chairman of a commission to wind up the business of the American Red Cross at Vladivostok in 1920.

He returned from Siberia with his mission

accomplished but his health irreparably injured. During the short five years remaining to him he did, along with much else, the work by which he is remembered: a trilogy of Iowa novels— *Vandemark's Folly* (1921), *The Hawkeye* (1923), *The Invisible Woman* (1924)—and his autobiography, *One Man's Life* (1925). Of the novels, *The Invisible Woman* is distinctly inferior to the others, but the trilogy as a whole was a distinguished achievement, and the autobiography belongs with it as an indispensable commentary. Quick never mastered fully the craft of the novelist, but in *Vandemark's Folly* and *The Hawkeye* he forgot about what he called technique and wrote sincerely out of his love of the soil, his pride in the character and achievements of the humble folk from whom he sprung, his passionate belief in democratic idealism. No one else has written so vividly and truthfully of the life of pioneer Iowa. A pamphlet, *The Real Trouble with the Farmers* (1924), is his best essay in economic analysis. His other publications, aside from numerous magazine articles on a variety of subjects, were: *There Came Two Women* (1924), a drama in verse, revelatory chiefly of Quick's defective literary sense; *We Have Changed All That* (1928), an anti-Bolshevik novel, done, apparently out of pure kindness, in collaboration with a Russian woman, Elena Stepanoff MacMahon; and *Mississippi Steamboatin'* (1926), which was completed by his son Edward. He was during these years a national figure and widely beloved. His home was a farm, "Coolfont," near Berkeley Springs, W. Va. He died of a heart attack at Columbia, Mo., after filling a speaking engagement. His wife, a son, and a daughter survived him.

[*Who's Who in America*, 1906–25; Herbert Quick, "I Picked My Goal at Ten—Reached It at Sixty," *Am. Mag.*, Oct. 1922; Wm. E. Ogilvie, *Pioneer Agricultural Journalists* (1927); Donald Murphy, in *A Book of Iowa Authors* (1930), ed. by Johnson Brigham; A. G. Kennedy, review of the Midland Trilogy and *One Man's Life* in *Am. Speech*, Dec. 1926; *Sioux City Journal*, May 11, 1925; *N. Y. Times*, May 11, 12 (editorial), 1925.]   G. H. G.

QUIDOR, JOHN (Jan. 26, 1801–Dec. 13, 1881), portrait and figure painter, was born at Tappan, N. Y., the son of Peter and Maria (Smith) Quidor. In 1826 he moved to New York City and was for a short time a pupil of John Wesley Jarvis [q.v.] and a friend of Henry Inman. He began his professional life, as did many other artists at that period, as a coach painter, earning a precarious livelihood by decorating stage coaches and fire engines. Then he took up portrait work, but few examples have been identified, and it is probable that he did not meet with much encouragement. One of his sit-

ters was Col. Benjamin Tallmadge (1754–1838), an officer in the Revolutionary army, who had custody of Major André until his execution. Quidor is mentioned in the New York directories from 1828 to 1833 as a portrait painter, and from 1828 to 1839 he exhibited pictures in the National Academy of Design. For a time he lived on a farm near Quincy, Ill., but in 1851 he returned to New York.

He is best known for his paintings illustrative of scenes from the books of Washington Irving. He was a personal friend of the author, whose *History of New York by Diedrich Knickerbocker* furnished him with subjects for a series of large pictures, several of which became the property of Col. Henry T. Chapman of New York. Four of these works were shown in the first exhibition of the Brooklyn Museum, in 1897, and remained there for fourteen years: "Peter Stuyvesant Watching the Festivities on the Battery," "The Vigilant Stuyvesant's Wall Street Gate," "Peter Stuyvesant's Journey up the Hudson," and "The Voyage to Hell Gate from Communipaw." Chapman also owned "Ichabod Crane Pursued by the Headless Horseman." The Chapman collection was sold in New York in 1913, but Quidor's pictures fetched insignificant prices. A number of his works were also in the collection of Joseph Harrison, Jr., of Philadelphia. These represented episodes in tales by Irving, such as "The Return of Rip Van Winkle," "Scene at the Village Tavern," "The Revellers," and "The Fright." Perhaps the most typical example is "The Return of Rip Van Winkle," which was first seen at the National Academy of Design in 1839 and was later acquired by Thomas B. Clarke. It hung in the Pennsylvania Museum of Art at Philadelphia from 1928 to 1931. It depicts in a Hogarthian spirit the bewilderment of Rip as to his own identity after his long nap in the Catskill Mountains: "I'm changed, and I can't tell what's my name nor who I am." Quidor died in Jersey City, N. J., in 1881. He cannot be called a first-rate painter, but the animation and humor of his works make them interesting in spite of their technical inadequacy.

[David Cole, ed., *Hist. of Rockland County, N. Y.* (1884); *Am. Art Annual*, vol. XI (1914); Wm. Dunlap, *Hist. of the Rise and Progress of the Arts of Design in the U. S.* (rev. ed., 3 vols., 1918); Mantle Fielding, *Dict. of Am. Painters, Sculptors, and Engravers* (1926); catalogues of the Thos. B. Clarke (1928) and Jos. Harrison, Jr. (1912), collections; *N. Y. Herald*, Dec. 14, 1881.]   W. H. D.

QUIGG, LEMUEL ELY (Feb. 12, 1863–July 1, 1919), journalist, congressman from New York, was one of three sons of an itinerant Methodist clergyman, John B. Quigg and Jane

Holland (Townsend). He was born near Chestertown, Md. Most of his formal education was obtained in the public schools of Wilmington, Del. After a brief apprenticeship at newspaper work in Montana Territory, he appeared in New York City at the age of seventeen and got work as a reporter for the *New York Times*. Before he reached his majority he was editor of the Flushing, L. I., *Times*, 1883–84, and in 1884 he became connected with the *New York Tribune*, then owned and edited by Whitelaw Reid. He wrote special articles, largely on political subjects, and remained on the *Tribune* staff ten years. He published a series of stories and sketches of the city called *Tin-types Taken in the Streets of New York* (copr. 1890). In the national campaign of 1892, in which Reid figured as vice-presidential candidate on the defeated Harrison ticket, Quigg served as press agent for the Republican National Committee. A year later, to the surprise of nearly every one he was sent to Congress by one of the strong Tammany districts of the city.

In his campaign he had been materially aided by Thomas C. Platt, then the recognized head of the Republican organization in state and city. From that time on he seemingly had no higher ambition than to be Platt's lieutenant. In an article in the *North American Review* of May 1910 he expressed his admiration and abiding loyalty to Platt. He entered Congress on Jan. 30, 1894, and reëlected twice he served until Mar. 3, 1899. At the same time, having left the *Tribune,* he served for one year as editor and publisher of the *New York Press*, an organization Republican newspaper. In 1896 he was chosen president of the Republican county committee and during his four years' incumbency of that position he consistently carried out the Platt policies, notably in preventing a fusion of the Republicans and the Citizens' Union in the New York mayoralty election of 1897, thus insuring Tammany's success. He was a delegate to the Republican National Convention of 1896 and had some part in the fight for the gold-standard plank in the platform (memorandum by C. W. Hackett, quoted in *Autobiography of Thomas Collier Platt,* pp. 324–25). In Congress he was an attractive speaker and an early and persistent advocate of American intervention in Cuba. In 1898 he was sent by Platt to ask Theodore Roosevelt to run for governor (*Ibid.,* pp. 368–69; C. G. Washburn, *Theodore Roosevelt,* 1916, pp. 25–29). In 1900 he was ousted from political leadership by Gov. Benjamin B. Odell [*q.v.*]. He was admitted to the bar in 1903, and his later years were largely devoted to the promotion of

the traction interests of Thomas Fortune Ryan. He told an investigating commission in 1907 that he had spent $200,000 in "accelerating sentiment" in behalf of those interests (*N. Y. Times,* Oct. 3, 4, 1907; *Nation,* Oct. 10, 1907). Not much of this could have stuck to his fingers. At the age of fifty-six he died of Bright's disease, leaving a modest estate. He was survived by his widow Ethel G. (Murray) Quigg and by one son.

[Information from his son, Murray T. Quigg, New York City; *N. Y. Times,* July 3, 1919; D. S. Alexander, *Four Famous New Yorkers* (1923); H. F. Gosnell, *Boss Platt and his New York Machine* (1924); *The Autobiog. of Thomas Collier Platt* (1910), ed. by L. J. Lang.]

W. B. S.

QUIGLEY, JAMES EDWARD (Oct. 15, 1854–July 10, 1915), Catholic prelate, son of James and Mary (Lacey) Quigley, immigrants to Canada from Ireland in 1847, was born in Oshawa, Ontario, from which place his parents soon removed to Lima, and then to Rochester, N. Y. Here his father prospered as a building contractor. The boy attended the local parochial schools and St. Joseph's College, Buffalo, where he was graduated at the head of his class in 1872. Following a religious bent, he entered the Vincentian Seminary of Our Lady of Angels in Buffalo, from which he was transferred to the University of Innsbruck in the Austrian Tyrol. On completion of the course of studies there in 1874, he was sent to the college of the Propaganda in Rome, from which he received the doctorate in sacred theology in 1879. After his ordination to the priesthood (Apr. 12, 1879) by the cardinal-vicar of Rome, Father Quigley served as pastor of St. Vincent's Church, Attica (1879–84); as rector of St. Joseph's Church, Buffalo (1884–86), and then became irremoveable pastor of St. Bridget's Church, Buffalo. Named by Pope Leo XIII as successor of Bishop Stephen Vincent Ryan [*q.v.*], Quigley was consecrated bishop of Buffalo by Archbishop Corrigan on Feb. 24, 1897.

As ruler of the see of Buffalo, he proved a generous, approachable man, who divorced himself from confidants and favorites, and labored unselfishly for the best interests of his people. A believer in trade unionism, he sponsored this movement but fought socialist propaganda in the ranks of labor. As mediator, he settled the Buffalo dockers' strike (1899) through personal influence, since a majority of the men were members of his old parish—St. Bridget's. On Jan. 8, 1903, he was promoted to the metropolitan see of Chicago, to which rumor had assigned Bishop Spalding [*q.v.*] of Peoria. Again, he proved an able but not an autocratic administrator, winning the love of a priesthood which increased during his régime from 566 to about eight hundred. His responsibilities were heavy, for the Catholic population increased by 500,000, because of the heavy immigration of Poles, Bohemians, and Italians. This growth necessitated a large building program and the establishment of racial churches. Aside from parochial education and charitable institutions such as St. Mary's Training School and the Chicago Industrial School for Girls, his chief concerns were the establishment of the Catholic Church Extension Society through Rev. Francis C. Kelley, the promotion of the first Catholic Missionary Congress in Chicago (1908), the settlement of the Mexican religious question, and efforts to prevent the growth of socialism, the establishment of Cathedral College for the preparatory training of priests, and the sponsorship of Loyola and De Paul universities. In 1911 his friends had vain hopes of his elevation to the cardinalate. In the spring of 1915 he was stricken with paralysis while in Washington. He died at the home of a brother, Joseph M. Quigley, chief of police in Rochester, N. Y. His remains were buried in a mausoleum at Mount Carmel cemetery near Chicago.

[F. C. Kelley, *Archbishop Quigley, a Tribute* (1915); *Am. Cath. Who's Who*, 1911; *Who's Who in America*, 1914–15; files of the diocesan paper, *The New World*, especially for July 1915; *Diamond Jubilee of the Archdiocese of Chicago* (1920); G. J. Garraghan, *The Catholic Church in Chicago, 1673–1871* (1921); *Chicago Tribune*, July 11–16, 1915.]   R. J. P.

QUIMBY, PHINEAS PARKHURST (Feb. 16, 1802–Jan. 16, 1866), founder of mental healing in America, was the son of a blacksmith named Jonathan Quimby and of his wife, Susannah (White) Quimby. He was born in Lebanon, N. H., but when he was two years old his family moved to Belfast, Me., where he was brought up. He was put to work at an early age, receiving no more than six weeks of schooling in his whole life. Apprenticed to a clockmaker, he learned his trade thoroughly and practised it successfully for many years. On the side he amused himself by making daguerreotypes and by inventing a bandsaw similar to those in use today. He married Susannah B. Haraden and had four children. In 1838 he became interested in mesmerism through the lectures and experiments of Charles Poyen, who visited Belfast in the course of his American tour. The exhibitions of another mesmerist, named Collyer, increased this interest. Studying the subject with great energy, Quimby discovered that he himself possessed remarkable mesmeric powers, and he be-

gan to give private exhibitions. These were followed by appearances in public which were so successful that he abandoned clock-making and gave all his time to his new art. In 1843 he made a trip through New England, accompanied by his "subject," Lucius Burkmar, a very suggestible lad, who exhibited what were considered to be clairvoyant and telepathic faculties. Mesmerists were then frequently called upon to heal the sick, and Quimby found that Burkmar, when in the hypnotic state, could apparently diagnose diseases correctly and prescribe the proper medicines. Further experiments, however, gradually convinced him that Burkmar's prescriptions had nothing to do with the cures that were usually effected. These, Quimby came to believe, were solely due to the faith of the patients in the healer. Hence in 1847 he gave up mesmerism, devoting himself thenceforward entirely to mental healing. In this he was very successful. In 1859 he established himself in Portland, Me., where he conducted a large practice.

By this time he had begun to work out a kind of philosophy to explain the facts of his experience. All disease, he held, was of mental origin, due to erroneous belief in physical causation. Thus he reached an idealistic interpretation of the universe, which placed all reality in God, an impersonal principle of Wisdom acting through the human mind when the latter functions properly. The knowledge of the relation between the divine and the human Quimby called "Science," or, occasionally, "Christian Science." He developed an elaborate christology in which, without knowing it, he trod in the footsteps of the early Gnostics, reviving their distinction between the divine Christ and the human, phantasmal Jesus. In his psychological views he foreshadowed later theories of the subconscious, mingled with a belief in various occult powers of the mind. In his metaphysics he hesitated between subjective and objective idealism, usually considering matter an illusion but sometimes, more consistently, regarding it as an idea or manifestation of God. While his whole outlook was essentially religious, he distrusted church organizations and looked upon orthodox Christianity as a mass of superstition.

Beginning to write out his theories merely for the guidance of patients, he was led on to produce a number of manuscripts, which remained unpublished until long after his death. In 1862 and again in 1864 he had as a patient Mary M. Baker Eddy [*q.v.*], who was then Mrs. Daniel Patterson; she held long discussions with him, studied and copied some of his manuscripts, and became temporarily his most enthusiastic follower; there can be no doubt that she derived from him the basic ideas of her own subsequent system of Christian Science, although she gave to them a much stronger subjective bias. Quimby himself, who was generous to a fault, utterly lacking in personal ambition, and wholly concentrated on the work of healing, made no effort to advertise his doctrines or to capitalize them in any way. For years he suffered from an abdominal tumor but consistently refused medical treatment for it. At last his condition became so serious that he was obliged to give up his practice. He returned to Belfast in the summer of 1865 and devoted his few remaining months to putting his manuscripts into better shape. Among all the early American healers and eccentric philosophers his reputation stands the highest for beauty of character and honesty of purpose. After his death, his doctrines were zealously promulgated by two of his patients, Warren Felt Evans [*q.v.*] and Julius Dresser. From the long-continued efforts of Dresser, especially, came the New Thought movement, which thus unquestionably stems from Quimby.

[*The Quimby Manuscripts* (1921), ed. by H. W. Dresser; A. G. Dresser, *The Philosophy of P. P. Quimby* (1895); Julius A. Dresser, *The True Hist. of Mental Science* (1887); George Quimby, "Phineas Parkhurst Quimby," *New England Mag.*, Mar. 1888; Georgine Milmine, *Mary Baker Eddy and the History of Christian Science* (1909); F. C. Springer, *According to the Flesh* (1930); E. F. Dakin, *Mrs. Eddy, the Biography of a Virginal Mind* (1929); H. C. Quinby, *Geneal. Hist. of the Quinby (Quimby) Family*, II (1923), 57–60; E. S. Bates and J. V. Dittemore, *Mary Baker Eddy, the Truth and the Tradition* (1932); for relations with Mrs. Eddy, controversy in the *Boston Post*, Feb. 8, 19, 24, Mar. 9, 1883.]   E. S. B.

QUINAN, JOHN RUSSELL (Aug. 7, 1822–Nov. 11, 1890), medical historical writer, was the son of the Rev. Thomas Henry Quinan of Balbriggan, County Dublin, Ireland, and his wife, Eliza Hamilton, a native of Enniskillen, County of Fermanagh. His father emigrated to the United States and opened a seminary for women in Philadelphia but made a series of removals that carried him to Reading and Lancaster, Pa., to Louisville, Ky., and to Cincinnati, Ohio. John Russell, one of five generations of physicians, was born at Lancaster, Pa., the fifth of six children, and received his education at Woodward High School, Cincinnati, and at Marietta College, Marietta, Ohio. He began the study of medicine under John Kearsley Mitchell [*q.v.*], of the well known medical family of Philadelphia, and received the degree of M.D. at Jefferson Medical College in Philadelphia in 1844. He took up the practice of medicine in Calvert County, Md., and soon became the leading physician of the district. In 1860 he gave up his

practice to become superintendent of schools and turned his house practically into a teachers' institute, greatly improving the quality of the teaching. He was an ardent Union sympathizer but continued to have the confidence of his Southern neighbors. At the end of the war he took up the practice of medicine again and in 1869 moved to Baltimore where he attracted attention for his scholarship as well as for his ability as a physician. He became a member of the Medical and Chirurgical Faculty of Maryland about 1884 and served both as vice-president and as president of that organization.

His most important work is *Medical Annals of Baltimore from 1608 to 1880.* He began the work at the invitation of the committee in charge of the celebration of the sesquicentennial of the founding of the city of Baltimore. He was unable to finish it for the anniversary, but on its appearance in 1884, it was hailed as a landmark in the history of Baltimore and a noteworthy contribution to the history of Maryland. His historical work was entirely without compensation, and in his enthusiasm, he would have issued a second and enlarged edition of his history, which was to have included the story of medicine in the rest of Maryland under the title "Medical Annals of Maryland." The extent of his practice, his professional charity (for which he was widely noted), and his editorial work, however, prevented him from accomplishing this purpose. The later years of his life were devoted largely to writing articles for *An Illustrated Encyclopædic Medical Dictionary* (4 vols., 1888–94), edited by Frank Pierce Foster [*q.v.*], a work for which Quinan was peculiarly fitted because of his knowledge of ancient and modern languages. His articles were chiefly on botany and materia medica but the whole work benefited from his scholarship. A favorite expression of his was that he was doubtful of the skill of any doctor who knew nothing but medicine. His only teaching position was that of lecturer on medical jurisprudence in the Woman's Medical College in Baltimore from 1883 to 1885. A list of his writings appears in the *Maryland Medical Journal*, Mar. 7, 1891. He died suddenly on Nov. 11, 1890, and was survived by his wife, Elizabeth Lydia Billingsley of Calvert County, Md., whom he had married on Aug. 31, 1845, and five of their ten children.

[E. F. Cordell, biog. sketch in H. A. Kelly and W. L. Burrage, *Am. Medic. Biogs.* (1920), and in *The Medic. Annals of Md. 1799–1899* (1903); W. S. Forwood, biog. sketch with bibliog. in *Trans. Medic. and Chirurgic. Faculty of the State of Md.*, 1891 (1891); G. W. Archer, "A Tribute to the Memory of Dr. John Russell Quinan," *Md. Medic. Jour.*, Mar. 7, 1891; obituary in *Sun* (Baltimore), Nov. 12, 1890.]   J. J. W.

QUINBY, ISAAC FERDINAND (Jan. 29, 1821–Sept. 18, 1891), soldier and educator, was born in Morris County, N. J., the son of Isaac and Sarah (DeHart) Quinby. He was a descendant of William Quinby who came from England about 1638 and settled in Connecticut. He entered the United States Military Academy in 1839 and was graduated sixth in his class in 1843, standing first in engineering. Ulysses S. Grant was a classmate and lifelong friend. After brief service as brevet second-lieutenant, 2nd Artillery, he returned to West Point in 1845 as instructor in mathematics, later becoming assistant professor of natural philosophy. He left the Academy in June 1847 for service in the Mexican War and participated in several skirmishes during the last months of that conflict. He married Elizabeth Greenbury Gardner, daughter of John Lane Gardner [q.v.], on Oct. 6, 1848, and they had thirteen children, eight boys and five girls. In September 1851 he became professor of mathematics and natural and experimental philosophy in the University of Rochester, in Rochester, N. Y. He resigned his commission in the army on Mar. 16, 1852, and remained actively associated with the growth and development of the university for thirty-three years.

After the evacuation of Fort Sumter he raised a volunteer regiment, which, as the 13th New York, was the first Federal force to enter Baltimore after the attack on the 6th Massachusetts in April. Quinby's firm and skilful measures forestalled a repetition of hostile action by the mob. He led the regiment well at Bull Run, but it shared the demoralization that attended the retreat from that field. On Aug. 4, 1861, he resigned from the service and resumed his chair in the university, but the following March, he reëntered military service as brigadier-general of volunteers and was assigned to command the District of the Mississippi, and later, the 7th Division, Army of the Tennessee. In March 1863, he was in command of the Yazoo Pass expedition, one of Grant's abortive efforts to reach Vicksburg from the north. He pushed the project with characteristic initiative and persistence, but Grant, unaware of Quinby's progress and disturbed by reports that filtered back from disaffected sources, recalled the expedition. Hardship and exposure in a malarial region brought on a severe illness and made it necessary for General Quinby to go north to recover. On learning of the progress of Grant's movement in the rear of Vicksburg, he hastened back and rejoined his division during the battle of Champion's Hill. He participated in the crossing of Big Black River in the assaults of May 19 and 22 against Vicksburg. Illness again rendered him unfit for field service, and on June 3, 1863, he relinquished his command and went north under orders. Failing to recover his health, he resigned his commission in December 1863, but continued to serve as provost-marshal of the 28th Congressional District in New York until Oct. 15, 1865. He was appointed United States Marshal for the Northern District of New York in April 1869, and held that office along with his professorship during both terms of Grant's administration. He was city surveyor of Rochester from 1885 to 1889 and was frequently employed as a consulting engineer. He died in Rochester after an illness of six months.

[H. C. Quinby, *Geneal. Hist. of the Quinby (Quimby) Family in Eng. and Am.*, vol. I (1915); *Ann. Reunion, Asso. Grads. U. S. Mil. Acad.*, 1892; W. F. Peck, *Hist. of Rochester and Monroe County, N. Y.* (1908); J. L. Rosenberger, *Rochester, The Making of a University* (1927); *N. Y. Times*, Sept. 19, 1891.]

             T. F. M.

QUINCY, EDMUND (Feb. 1, 1808–May 17, 1877), reformer and author, was born in Boston, Mass., the second son of Josiah Quincy, 1772–1864 [q.v.], member of Congress, mayor of Boston (1823–28), and president of Harvard, and of Eliza Susan (Morton) Quincy. After preparation for college at Phillips Academy, Andover, Mass., 1817–23, he entered Harvard College, graduating with high honors in 1827 and receiving a master's degree in 1830. On Oct. 14, 1833, he married Lucilla P. Parker.

Stirred by the murder of the abolitionist Elijah P. Lovejoy [q.v.], by a proslavery mob in Alton, Ill., in 1837, Quincy shocked the aristocratic, lettered class to which he belonged by becoming an active Garrisonian abolitionist. In 1837 he became a member of the Massachusetts Anti-Slavery Society, of which he was corresponding secretary from 1844 to 1853; and in 1838 he joined the American Anti-Slavery Society, of which he was vice-president in 1853 and 1856–59. A prominent member of the Non-Resistance Society, formed in 1839, he abjured all recourse to force in resisting evil, renounced all allegiance to human government, and, in the interests of abolition, agitated disunion between the North and the South. He was associated with William Lloyd Garrison and Maria Weston Chapman [qq.v.] in conducting the *Non-Resistant,* a paper which gave expression to these doctrines from 1839 to 1842. In 1839 he also became an editor of the *Abolitionist,* an organ of the Massachusetts Anti-Slavery Society, and from 1839 to 1856 was a chief contributor to the *Liberty Bell,* edited by Mrs. Chapman for the annual

Boston anti-slavery fairs. In 1844 he became an editor of the *Anti-Slavery Standard,* the journal of the American Anti-Slavery Society. He also frequently conducted the *Liberator,* as in 1843, 1846, and 1847, when its editor, Garrison, was absent. In addition to his work for these journals he contributed to the *New York Tribune,* the *Albany Transcript,* the *Independent,* and others, and his trenchant writings on slavery, called by Lowell "gems of Flemish art" (J. P. Quincy, *post,* p. 414), if collected, would make many volumes and furnish a valuable contribution to the history of the anti-slavery struggle.

Apart from his activities as an abolitionist, Quincy was also well known among literary people as a writer of fiction and biography. His *Wensley, a Story without a Moral* (1854; reprinted in *Wensley and Other Stories,* 1885), a sympathetic study of early American society, reveals a cultivated mind, a genial humor, and a graceful style, and was called by Whittier "the most readable book of the kind since Hawthorne's Blithedale Romance" (*Proceedings of the Massachusetts Historical Society,* 1 ser. XV, 283). In *The Haunted Adjutant and Other Stories* (1885) are collected some of his best short stories. With the help of his sister, Eliza Susan Quincy, he wrote an excellent biography of his father, *Life of Josiah Quincy* (1867), and edited *Speeches Delivered in the Congress of the United States: by Josiah Quincy* (1874). He was also a fellow of the American Academy of Arts and Sciences, recording secretary of the Massachusetts Historical Society, a member of the American Philosophical Society, and a member of the Board of Overseers of Harvard College. In spite of the strenuous participation in active life which his devotion to the abolitionist cause entailed, he remained to the end the old-fashioned scholar and gentleman, his exalted and uncompromising idealism being tempered by wit and humor, friendliness and simplicity, cultivation and refinement.

[Henry Wilson, *Hist. of the Rise and Fall of the Slave Power in America* (3 vols., 1872–77); J. P. Quincy, "Edmund Quincy," *Proc. Mass. Hist. Soc.,* 2 ser. XVIII (1905); W. P. and F. J. Garrison, *William Lloyd Garrison* (4 vols., 1885–89); *Later Years of the Saturday Club* (1927), ed. by M. A. DeWolfe Howe; J. L. Chamberlain, *Universities and Their Sons: Harvard Univ.* (1900); *Proc. Mass. Hist. Soc.,* 1 ser. XV (1878); *New-Eng. Hist. and Geneal. Reg.,* Jan. 1857; *Nation* (N. Y.), May 24, 31, 1877; E. E. Salisbury, *Family Memorials* (1885), vol. I; *Boston Transcript,* May 18, 1877.]   A. R. B.

QUINCY, JOSIAH (Feb. 23, 1744–Apr. 26, 1775), lawyer, patriot, was fifth in descent from Edmund and Judith Quincy who came to Massachusetts with the Rev. John Cotton in 1633.

He was the youngest of the three sons of Josiah Quincy, a prosperous Boston merchant, and his wife, Hannah Sturgis of Yarmouth, Mass. Since he died at the age of thirty-one and during the lifetime of his father, his contemporaries usually referred to him as Josiah Quincy, Jr. He was always frail and extremely sensitive. Born in Boston, he received his early schooling at Braintree, under Joseph Marsh. In 1759 he entered Harvard, taking his bachelor's degree in 1763 and his master's three years later. On the latter occasion he delivered the English oration, which was considered the highest academic honor. Immediately upon his graduation he began the study of law in the office of Oxenbridge Thacher, one of the leading lawyers of Boston. Thacher died in July 1765 and Quincy took charge of the office, continuing his law studies. In spite of his youth, his ability and character enabled him to retain a large part of Thacher's lucrative practice. It was during these early years that he wrote *Reports of Cases . . . in the Superior Court of Judicature of the Province of Massachusetts Bay between 1761 and 1772,* which, edited by S. M. Quincy, was printed from the original manuscript in 1865.

Quincy took an active interest in the political crisis of the times and published two articles, signed "Hyperion," in the *Boston Gazette* of Sept. 28 and Oct. 5, 1767. Two years later, Oct. 26, 1769, he married Abigail, the eldest daughter of William Phillips, a rich and prominent merchant. In 1770 Quincy wrote a number of essays on the non-importation agreement and other questions, taking strongly the Patriot side. Among these may be mentioned: "An Address of the Merchants, Traders, and Freeholders of the Town of Boston," denouncing violators of the non-importation agreement, published as a broadside with the caption *At a Meeting of the Merchants & Traders at Faneuil Hall, on the 23rd of January, 1770;* two essays signed "An Independent," in the *Boston Gazette,* Feb. 12 and 26, 1770; another, signed "An Old Man," in the same journal, Aug. 6, 1770; and the report of the committee appointed to draft instructions for the representatives of the Town of Boston, May 15, 1770 (printed in *A Report of the Record Commissioners . . . Containing the Boston Town Records, 1770–1777,* 1887). After the attack by a Boston mob on the British soldiers had resulted in the "Boston Massacre" of Mar. 5, 1770, Quincy and John Adams undertook, from a stern sense of duty, the task of defending the soldiers in court, although Quincy's elder brother, Samuel, solicitor-general of Massachusetts, assisted by Robert Treat Paine [*q.v.*], conducted the prosecution. Quincy's father expressed horror at this action of his youngest son, not comprehending the fact that it was the finest act in his career and saved the good name of Massachusetts. During the next two years Quincy continued actively to practise law and wrote a number of articles for the press, including one signed "Mentor" urging the annual commemoration of the "Massacre" (*Boston Gazette*, Feb. 11, 1771).

He now began to develop symptoms of tuberculosis, and decided to make a trip to a warmer climate. On Feb. 8, 1773, he sailed for Charleston, S. C., whence he returned by land to Boston, reaching home in May. He met many of the prominent men in all the chief coast cities and thus had an unusual opportunity to study the political tendencies of the various colonies. His "Journal" of this trip, printed in the *Memoir* by his son (*post*) is an interesting and useful record of the sentiment of that time in the Carolinas, Virginia, and Maryland. It is probable that the two series of articles in the *Boston Gazette* beginning June 7, 1772, and Dec. 20, 1773, the first signed "Marchmont Nedham," the second called "Nedham's Remembrancer" were from his pen (Buckingham, *post*, I, 186–92). In May 1774 he published his chief political work, *Observations of the Act of Parliament Commonly Called the Boston Port-Bill; with Thoughts on Civil Society and Standing Armies,* in which he presented the case against the bill with great ability and set forth the theories that were the basis of his criticism. As a result he received an anonymous letter warning him that his life would be in danger if he should continue his course. To this he replied in the *Massachusetts Gazette,* no. 3685 (*Memoir,* pp. 156–58).

Although only thirty years old, he had now become one of the leaders of the Patriot cause, not only in Massachusetts but throughout the colonies, and was in correspondence with such men as John Dickinson. He was, of course, in the inner councils of the Boston group. His gift for oratory had also made him a power with the people. It was thought that he might be of use at the English court by presenting the case of the colonies in the proper light, and it was arranged that he should go to England, but the plan was kept secret as long as possible so that no misrepresentation might be made before his arrival. For that reason he went on board ship quietly at Salem, Sept. 28, 1774. His father wrote him that when the news leaked out all of the Tories and some of the Whigs resented his sudden departure. Quincy kept a journal of this trip which is of considerable historical interest.

He landed Nov. 8, and proceeded to London. There he had interviews with Lord North, Lord Dartmouth, and other leading men, but without result. Events were moving rapidly and his friends in Boston wished him to return. His health was failing, but in spite of the warnings of his physician he started for home Mar. 16, 1775. He was most anxious to communicate by word of mouth information which he had gleaned from interviews in London and which he did not feel at liberty to put in writing. What this information was has never been learned. Quincy grew steadily worse on the voyage and died with his message undelivered, a week after the battle of Lexington, a few hours before the ship entered Gloucester harbor. Probably it was already too late for any information he possessed to change the course of events. Quincy left one son, Josiah [*q.v.*], his only daughter having died Apr. 13, 1775. By his will he bequeathed to his son, when he should have reached the age of fifteen, the works of Algernon Sidney, John Locke, Bacon, Gordon's Tacitus, and Cato's Letters.

[The main source is the *Memoir of the Life of Josiah Quincy, Jun.* (1825), by his son Josiah Quincy, containing extracts from the two journals and the full text of the *Observations on the . . . Boston Port-Bill*; the second edition (1874) contains some additions by the editor, Eliza Susan Quincy. See also J. T. Buckingham, *Specimens of Newspaper Literature* (1850), I, 186–92; and references in the writings of contemporaries, esp. *The Works of John Adams* (10 vols., 1850–56), ed. by C. F. Adams.]   J. T. A.

QUINCY, JOSIAH (Feb. 4, 1772–July 1, 1864), politician, municipal reformer, and college president, was the only son of the young patriot leader known as Josiah Quincy, Jr., 1744–1775 [*q.v.*], and his wife Abigail Phillips, sister of Lieut.-Gov. William Phillips [*q.v.*]. The Quincy family (pronounced Quinzy), after whom that part of Braintree where he was born was named (1792), had been merchants, councillors, and judges since the seventeenth century. His father died on the eve of the Revolution, leaving him, with property of more substantial nature, a set of Sidney and Locke, by whose precepts he was brought up, even to winter plunges in cold water at the age of three. When six years old, he was sent to Phillips Academy, Andover, the boarding school founded by his mother's cousin, Samuel Phillips [*q.v.*]. There he spent eight years under a severe classical discipline. Entering Harvard, he graduated first in the class of 1790. After three years' study in a law office, Quincy was admitted to the Boston bar; but having a sufficient fortune, he never practised law seriously. He was tall and handsome, sociable and convivial, albeit an abstainer for medical reasons. The first of the many impetuous actions that marked his life was proposing to Eliza Susan Morton, a famous young beauty of New York, a week after he first met her, in 1794. They were married, on June 6, 1797, by the lady's tutor, President Samuel Smith of Princeton, who had conferred a master's degree on Quincy in 1796. Two sons, Josiah and Edmund [q.v.], and five daughters were born to them. With the ancestral fortune he was able to support the family estate at Quincy, and a mansion in Pearl St., Boston, while still a young man.

Like most members of his class in eastern Massachusetts, Quincy accepted the Federalist party without question. An oration at Boston, July 4, 1798, gave notice of political ambition, and in 1800 he ran for Congress unsuccessfully. Shortly afterward he began contributing political satire, over the signature "Climenole," to Dennie's *Port Folio,* and to the *Monthly Anthology.* Elected to the state Senate in 1804, he supported the "Ely Amendment" to abolish slave representation as provided for in the federal Constitution, striking the sectional keynote that his party followed during the next ten years; and that fall he was elected to Congress from the Boston district. At Washington he found a congenial friend in John Randolph of Roanoke [q.v.]. The two understood each other perfectly. They had in common a distaste for the new West, for nationalism, and for democracy; a love of good conversation, good books, classical letters, and English culture. Each was passionately devoted to his native soil, and a liberal in religion; a colonial whig, born too late.

Quincy believed that it was far more important not to hamper Great Britain in her struggle against Napoleon, than to defend American rights on the high seas. Reëlected for three successive terms, he became the minority leader in Congress, opposing the Embargo and non-intercourse system as cowardly, futile, and unconstitutional. On Jan. 14, 1811, he startled the country by a speech on the bill to admit Orleans Territory to the Union as the state of Louisiana. If a territory from outside the original Union is admitted by majority vote, without the consent of the original partners, "I am compelled," he said, "to declare it *as my deliberate opinion that, . . . the bonds of this Union are virtually dissolved; that the States which compose it are free from their moral obligations; and that as it will be the right of all, so it will be the duty of some to prepare definitely for a separation—amicably, if they can; violently, if they must*" (Edmund Quincy, *Speeches, post,* p. 196). Two years later,

in the Massachusetts legislature, he got this doctrine adopted in a set of resolutions (H. V. Ames, *State Documents on Federal Relations,* 1900, pp. 65–68).

In the war Congress that convened in November 1811, Quincy made a grave tactical error. Assuming that the "war hawks" were insincere, that Madison was a pacifist, and that Congress "could not be kicked" into hostilities, he outdid the westerners in shouting for preparedness. Undoubtedly he was one of the Federalists who advised the British minister that his government maintain the anti-neutral system, in order to force war on the United States, when Republican incompetency would return the Federalists to power (S. E. Morison, *The Life and Letters of Harrison Gray Otis,* 1913, II, pp. 33–35). Early in 1812, seeing the true drift, he changed face completely, voting against the declaration of war, opposing war legislation, and advising "the monied interest" to lend no money to the government (Washburn MSS., *post,* XVIII, 11). This ended his usefulness in Congress; and after denouncing the invasion of Canada as "cruel, wanton, senseless, and wicked," and describing military glory as "the glory of the tiger, which lifts his jaws, all foul and bloody, from the bowels of his victim, and roars for his companions of the wood to come and witness his prowess and his spoils" (Jan. 5, 1813, Edmund Quincy, *Speeches,* pp. 366, 372), he resigned, and returned happily home.

As a "solid man of Boston" Quincy now engaged busily in the affairs of the Massachusetts Historical Society, the American Academy of Arts and Sciences, Phillips Academy, the Boston Athenaeum, and the Massachusetts General Hospital. Attempting to make his Quincy estate a model farm, he set out hedges of imported English hawthorn, through which the hardy New England cows cheerfully ate their way; but his published lecture to New England farmers on the sins of wasting manure and subdividing land, was much needed (*An Address Delivered before the Massachusetts Agricultural Society, . . . Oct. 12, 1819,* 1819). In 1813 Quincy was elected to the state Senate, where he continued his campaign against the war, slave representation, and Southern dominance. When the General Court voted to thank Captain Lawrence for his naval victory, he proposed and carried a resolution that such a war, "waged without justifiable cause, and prosecuted in a manner indicating that conquest and ambition" were its purpose, should not be supported by "a moral and religious people" (Edmund Quincy, *Life,* p. 324). Quincy was always stronger with the people than with Federalist leaders; they found him too undisciplined and indiscreet. That is why he never received the nomination for governor, and was not sent to the Hartford Convention. After the war was over, Quincy continued in the state Senate until 1820, when he was dropped from the Federalist slate for insurgency, but got elected to the lower house. When speaker in 1821, he resigned in order to accept a place on the Boston municipal bench. There he addressed the Suffolk grand jury on the condition of Massachusetts jails, where little children were confined with hardened criminals (*Remarks on Some of the Provisions of the Laws of Massachusetts, Affecting Poverty, Vice, and Crime,* 1822).

That year Boston adopted the city form of government. Quincy, after losing the Federalist nomination for mayor, "bolted" and lost again; but his popular strength was great, and in 1823 he won. He found his city being run like a colonial New England town, and vigorously applied the besom of reform. He gave Boston its first thorough street cleaning in two centuries. First steps were taken to introduce municipal water and sewer systems, and to forbid burials in crowded districts. It was the Mayor's boast that during his administration the death rate fell from one in forty-two to one in sixty-three (*An Address to the Board of Aldermen, Jan. 1, 1828,* 1828). He segregated paupers from criminals, built a House of Reformation for Juvenile Offenders that won the admiration of Tocqueville (*Life,* p. 395), and attacked breeding-places of crime by revoking liquor licenses and vigorously enforcing the laws against gambling and prostitution. When a mob swept the feeble police force from the streets, Quincy summoned the draymen, and, putting himself at their head, dispersed the rioters by muscular force. He tore down a nest of tenements on the water front, put through six wide streets, filled pestilential tidal flats, and built the Quincy or New Faneuil Hall Market, the last providing substantial income to the city to this day. The volunteer fire companies were reorganized as a fire department, hose was substituted for buckets, and insurance rates were reduced twenty per cent. Like a Harun al-Rashid on horseback, Quincy galloped around Boston at daybreak to see for himself how his subjects did; and on one of these jaunts was arrested for riding so as to endanger the public. Although he was five times reëlected mayor (1823–27), his reforms accumulated such opposition that in December 1828 he was defeated; but "his administration . . . has formed a standard to which the

efforts of his successors are continually referred" (Winsor, *post,* III, 226). Largely on the strength of his name, his son Josiah and great-grandson Josiah were elected mayors of Boston.

Now that the popular but unbusinesslike president of Harvard, John T. Kirkland [*q.v.*] had resigned, the Corporation seized the opportunity to obtain a president of proved practical ability. Elected on Jan. 29, 1829, Quincy was the first layman to occupy the office since John Leverett [*q.v.*]. This, coupled with the fact that he was a Unitarian, infuriated the Trinitarian Congregationalists, who redoubled their efforts to prove that the University was a centre of atheism, aristocracy, and dissipation. Quincy struck back vigorously in *The History of Harvard University* (2 vols., 1840), belaboring the Mathers and emphasizing the liberal traditions of the University. In spite of the haste with which it was composed, and the few printed sources then available, this work has lasted almost a century as the standard history of Harvard. After studying conditions and asking advice, Quincy inaugurated changes calculated to reform the spirit of disorder then prevalent among Harvard students. He improved the food and service in commons, trusting that if the students were served like gentlemen, they would behave as such; he broke an ancient tradition by addressing them as "Mr."; instituted a system of mathematical grading; and retained in his own hands all petty details of parietal administration, hoping to remove every source of misunderstanding and discontent. But he did not go to the root of the trouble by providing athletic and other outlets for ebullient youthful spirits. Student riots continued, and Quincy destroyed what spirit of confidence he had established when, unable to get to the bottom of one outbreak, he violated a college tradition older than Harvard in announcing his intention of turning over to the grand jury, like common criminals, those suspected of destroying college property. On this occasion the students burned the President in effigy in the college yard; and in 1841 there was a terrific explosion in the chapel, where, after the smoke cleared away, "A bone for old Quin to pick" was found written on the wall (M. T. Higginson, *Thomas Wentworth Higginson,* 1914, p. 30). His successor, Edward Everett, thought that Quincy had been too lenient.

In his inaugural address (MS., University Archives), Quincy had urged the necessity of adjusting education to the age, but he seems to have had no clear ideas on undergraduate studies; he was not an educator, but an administrator, with a *flair* for choosing the right man. Among his appointees were Jared Sparks, Henry Wadsworth Longfellow, and Benjamin Peirce [*qq.v.*]. It was the faculty rather than the President that initiated an extension of the voluntary or elective system; but Quincy was warmly interested in the Law School, then functioning most feebly. He became an ardent advocate of academic law teaching over the prevailing Anglo-American practice of apprenticeship; and with the bequest of Nathan Dane [*q.v.*] and the appointment of Justice Joseph Story [*q.v.*], as Dane Professor in 1829, made that department into an academic professional school. After vain efforts to obtain a state appropriation for a new library building, on the ground that the college library of some 40,000 volumes, "unrivalled in this country," was in constant danger from fire (*Seventh Annual Report of the President of Harvard University*, 1833, pp. 4–6), Quincy turned the Christopher Gore bequest to that purpose, and in 1841 Gore Hall, the most sumptuous American college library yet built, was opened. He launched the public subscription which provided the Astronomical Observatory. During his sixteen years as president, the faculty, the endowment, and the student body of the University greatly increased.

Advancing age and the opportunity to secure Edward Everett [*q.v.*] as a successor led Quincy to resign on Aug. 27, 1845. He resumed residence in Boston, humorously complaining that the unearthly quiet of city streets, in contrast to the turbulent college yard, kept him awake o' nights. Literary labors engrossed much of his time; works such as *The Journals of Mayor Samuel Shaw, . . . With a Life of the Author* (1847), *The History of the Boston Athenæum* (1851), *A Municipal History of the Town and City of Boston* (1852), a *Memoir of the Life of John Quincy Adams* (1858); and as a result of experiments at his Quincy estate, an *Essay on the Soiling of Cattle* (1852). Earlier he had published a *Memoir of the Life of Josiah Quincy, Jun., of Massachusetts* (1825).

For twenty-three years Quincy had said nothing on politics in public; and to his dying day he refused to call himself anything but a Federalist. Whig protective tariffs revolted him. As the century entered its second half, he felt more and more that his early stand against the "slave power" had been correct; and at the age of eighty-two, political pamphlets began to flow once more from his pen, denouncing the Fugitive-slave Law and Daniel Webster, supporting Frémont, but opposing the abolitionists as disunionists. Unlike many Boston conservatives,

he heartily supported Lincoln and the war, notably in his last public address, to the members of the Union Club, delivered in his ninety-second year. He died in Boston on July 1, 1864, happily confident that the Union which he had once so vigorously attacked, would be preserved.

Josiah Quincy was a fine example of a cultured and aristocratic public servant, with the faults and virtues of his class, and a pungency and impetuosity all his own. These individual qualities unsuited him for party politics; but in a position of responsibility and quasi-autocratic power, like the Boston mayoralty and the Harvard presidency, he was really great.

[A portrait of Quincy as mayor, by Gilbert Stuart, is in the Boston Museum of Fine Arts. The Quincy family papers have disappeared (except for a few MSS. in the possession of M. A. DeWolfe Howe, and one volume of letters, the Washburn MSS., vol. XVIII, at the Mass. Hist. Soc.) since they were used in the filial biography, Edmund Quincy, *Life of Josiah Quincy* (1867, and later editions). There are shorter memoirs by C. M. Fuess, in *Men of Andover* (1928); by James Walker, "Memoir of Josiah Quincy," in *Proc. Mass. Hist. Soc.*, IX (1867), pp. 83–156, and separately printed (1867). About fifty of Quincy's speeches were printed in pamphlet form, and his son Edmund published *Speeches Delivered in the Congress of the U. S.: by Josiah Quincy . . . 1805–1813* (1874). His annual addresses to the Board of Aldermen throw much light upon municipal affairs, but his annual reports as president of Harvard are disappointing; perhaps the best comment on college studies during his administration is found in *Annual Report of the President and Treasurer of Harvard College, 1883–84* (1885). But there is much pamphlet and archival material on his Harvard career. For portraits and statues, see Justin Winsor, *The Memorial Hist. of Boston*, III (1881), p. 227 *n.* A drawing by his daughter Eliza Susan of his house at Wollaston in Quincy is reproduced in his son Josiah Quincy's *Figures of the Past*, ed. by M. A. DeW. Howe (1926), p. 134.]

S. E. M.

QUINCY, JOSIAH PHILLIPS (Nov. 28, 1829–Oct. 31, 1910), author and historian, was the son of Josiah Quincy, mayor of Boston (1845–49), and Mary Jane (Miller) Quincy, and the grandson of Josiah Quincy, 1772–1864 [*q.v.*], member of Congress, mayor of Boston (1823–28), and president of Harvard. Characterized by Emerson as "a youthful prophet" at the age of six (Howe, *post*, p. 339), he received his early education at the school of A. Bronson Alcott, the Boston Latin School, and the academy of Stephen Weld. He then attended Harvard College, graduating in 1850 and receiving his master's degree in 1853. After a few months' travel in Europe, he took up the study of law at the Harvard Law School and was admitted to the bar in 1854; but because of the lack of necessity of earning a living and the fact that his interests lay in things of the mind and the spirit rather than in business, he gave up his practice and became a writer.

Commencing as a poet, he published the dramatic poems *Lyteria* (1854) and *Charicles* (1856) ; but although both were warmly received by the critics, he relinquished the publishing of poetry and became a diligent writer of stories for the magazines, mainly *Putnam's* and the *Atlantic Monthly*. His most ambitious piece of fiction, *The Peckster Professorship*, a satirical study of academic and intellectual society, appeared serially in the *Atlantic Monthly*, then as a book in 1888. In the field of politics, through the Civil War period he was a frequent contributor to the *Anti-Slavery Standard*, being assistant and successor to his uncle, Edmund Quincy [*q.v.*], as Boston correspondent; contributed unsigned articles on passing political topics to the Boston press; wrote two articles on taxation : *Tax-Exemption No Excuse for Spoliation* (1874) and *Double Taxation in Massachusetts* (1889) ; and published *The Protection of Majorities* (1876), a collection of educational and political essays. As a historian, he contributed a great variety of historical and biographical material to the *Proceedings* of the Massachusetts Historical Society, of which he was a member from 1865 to 1910; wrote a chapter on the social life of Boston for Justin Winsor's *Memorial History of Boston* (vol. IV, 1881) ; and through his inspiration and aid made possible his father's valuable book of historical reminiscences, *Figures of the Past* (1883).

On Dec. 23, 1858, he married Helen Fanny Huntington and established himself in Quincy, Mass., where he lived for the greater part of thirty-five years. Of his five children, the eldest, Josiah, was mayor of Boston from 1895 to 1899. Of an intellectual and highly speculative type of mind, Quincy had wide interests, his reading embracing spiritualism, psychic research, biography, science, sociology, and government. He was also a keen Shakespearian student. His writing was marked by its nicety of phrase, felicity of epithet, and polish. He was a representative of pre-Civil War society, distinguished "of mien and carriage," democratic and friendly, and modest and unworldly to a rare degree.

[Memoir by M. A. DeWolfe Howe in *Proc. Mass. Hist. Soc.*, vol. XLV (1912) ; *Harvard Graduates' Mag.*, Dec. 1910; *Boston Herald*, Nov. 1, 1910; *Boston Transcript*, Nov. 1, 1910.]   A. R. B.

QUINN, EDMOND THOMAS (Dec. 20, 1868–Sept. 9, 1929), sculptor and painter, eldest son of John and Rosina (McLaughlin) Quinn, was born at Philadelphia, Pa., of Irish ancestry and in humble circumstances. Thomas, his confirmation name, is often omitted by writers. His early studies in art were made at the Pennsylvania Academy of the Fine Arts, and especially under Thomas Eakins. Since he had a gift for color and an aptitude for seizing a likeness, he seemed destined for the career of a portrait painter. After undergoing the usual privations of the young artist with more talent than money, he was able in his twenty-fifth year to spend some months in Spain, where he came under the influence of Velazquez. He next went to Paris. Delighting in form as well as in color, he studied modeling under the French sculptor J. A. Injalbert. During one of his later sojourns in Paris he made some excellent oil portraits, including one of Anatole France (1906). This likeness, fine in color and in drawing, discloses that psychological penetration which was one of his many gifts. His sensitive temperament was ill-adapted to the difficult contacts often the lot of a portrait painter; he therefore chose sculpture as a means of livelihood and as his chief mode of expression. Quality, not quantity, was his aim, and no work left his studio until after he had devoted to it his best efforts. In time he attained distinction in three branches of the sculptor's art : the portrait bust, the portrait statue, and the ideal figure.

Notable among Quinn's earlier works are the statue of John Howard at Williamsport, Pa. (1905), and the reliefs for the battle monument at King's Mountain, S. C. (1908). In 1909 he completed a series of decorative figures in relief for the Athletic Club, Pittsburgh, Pa., as well as a sensitively imaginative bust of Edgar Allan Poe for the cottage at Fordham, N. Y., and a colossal limestone figure, "Persian Philosophy" (often listed as Zoroaster), for the façade of the Brooklyn Institute of Arts and Sciences. In 1917 his statue of Gen. John C. Pemberton was erected in the National Cemetery, Vicksburg, Miss. His most significant work is the strikingly beautiful bronze statue of Edwin Booth as Hamlet, gift of the Players' Club to Gramercy Park, New York City. The commission was awarded to him out of a number of competing sculptors of note. Dedicated in 1918, the figure is not only a true portrait of Booth, but also a noble conception of Hamlet. A decade later, Quinn completed the model for another admirable statue, the portrait of Henry Clay in an attitude of impassioned eloquence. This work, the gift of the United States government to Venezuela in return for Venezuela's gift of a statue of Bolivar, was erected at Caracas in 1930, a year after the sculptor's death in New York City.

Among the sitters for his many masterly busts

(or heads) were Father Sylvester Malone, Prof. Franklin Hooper, Cass Gilbert, Brander Matthews, Clayton Hamilton, Albert Sterner, Felix Salmond, Victor Herbert, Vincente Blasco Ibáñez, Edwin Markham, Francis Wilson, Eugene O'Neill, James Stephens, Leon Kroll, Miss Clare Eames, and Mrs. H. K. Murphy. In New York University are his busts of Chancellor Kent, Edwin Booth, James McNeill Whistler, and Dr. Oliver Wendell Holmes. Besides his dignified female figure of "Victory" for the war memorial at New Rochelle, N. Y. (1921), he created ideal figures of "Eve," "Grief," and "Aspiration," as well as vigorous realistic statuettes. His "Nymph" is owned by the Metropolitan Museum. He received a silver medal at the Panama-Pacific Exposition, San Francisco, Cal. (1915). He was a member of the Players and of the Century Club, an associate member of the National Academy of Design and a member of the Architectural League of New York, the National Sculpture Society, the Newport Art Society, and the National Institute of Arts and Letters. He served on the Municipal Art Commission of New York, 1918–19, and was treasurer of the New Society of Artists.

In 1917 Quinn married Emily Bradley, of Newport, R. I. Soon afterward the couple moved from Brooklyn to Manhattan, where their home became an intellectual center frequented by leaders in all the arts. Quinn had a keen sense of humor, though in his make-up Celtic melancholy predominated over Celtic mirth. The closing months of his life were clouded with melancholy, no trace of which appears in his final work. He ended his life by drowning. A memorial exhibition at the Century Club in 1933 showed his technical competence, his grasp of character, and his feeling for beauty.

[*Contemporary Am. Sculpture* (1929), issued for the exhibition held by the National Sculpture Society in cooperation with the Trustees of the California Palace of the Legion of Honor; Lorado Taft, *Modern Tendencies in Sculpture* (1921) and *The Hist. of Am. Sculpture* (1924, 1930); *Arts and Decoration*, Jan. 1919; Royal Cortissoz, article in the *N. Y. Tribune*, Dec. 7, 1918; Albert Sterner, article in the *Players Bull.*, Nov. 1929; obituaries, *N. Y. Times, N. Y. Herald Tribune*, Sept. 13, 1929.]   A-e. A.

QUINTARD, CHARLES TODD (Dec. 22, 1824–Feb. 15, 1898), physician, Episcopal bishop of Tennessee, was born in Stamford, Conn., the son of Isaac and Clarissa (Hoyt) Shaw Quintard and the brother of George William Quintard [*q.v.*]. He was a descendant of Isaac Quintard who was born in Bristol, England, and died in Stamford in 1738. He went to Trinity School in New York City, studied medicine with Dr. James R. Wood and Dr. Valentine Mott

[*q.v.*], and in 1847 received the degree of M.D. from University Medical College (New York University). After a year at Bellevue Hospital he settled in Athens, Ga., and began practice, but in 1851 he became professor of physiology and pathological anatomy in the Memphis (Tenn.) Medical College and also one of the editors of the *Memphis Medical Recorder*.

A devoted member of the Episcopal Church, he came into close personal relations with Bishop James H. Otey and in 1854 began to study for the ministry. In 1855 he was ordered deacon, and in 1856 he was ordained priest and soon became rector of Calvary Church at Memphis. A little later he went to the Church of the Advent in Nashville. A man of deep and wide learning, a man's man of intense human feeling and sympathy, a powerful and eloquent preacher, he quickly acquired great influence in his community. At the outbreak of the Civil War he was chaplain of a Nashville military company that joined the 1st Tennessee Regiment, of which he was elected chaplain. He served the Confederacy as chaplain, as surgeon, and, for a brief period, as an aide to Gen. W. W. Loring. His first service was under Lee in western Virginia. He was with Bragg's army during the invasion of Kentucky. He was present at the battles of Cheat Mountain, Munfordville, Perryville, Murfreesboro, Chickamauga, and Franklin. His unfinished reminiscences of the war were later published by Noll (*Doctor Quintard, post*). "Quick in movement, in apprehension, in sympathy; affectionate, generous; a skilled physician and surgeon, as well as a devout and ardent Christian Priest, he made for himself a place in the hearts and minds of the soldiers of the Army of Tennessee, and by a natural, and all but necessary, transition became their Bishop when he could no longer be their chaplain" (J. B. Cheshire, *The Church in the Confederate States*, 1912, p. 84).

In 1865 he was elected bishop of Tennessee and was consecrated at Philadelphia during the General Convention that accomplished the reunion of the Northern and Southern branches of the Episcopal Church. For thirty-three years thereafter he performed miracles of labor, in what was virtually a missionary field. An adherent of the Oxford movement, he was never an extremist, and increasingly he endeared himself not only to his own flock but to the whole state. He became well known in the North and in England, which he visited frequently, attending every Pan-Anglican Conference from 1867 to 1897. The University of Cambridge conferred on him the degree of LL.D. in 1868. One

of the first Americans to preach in the royal
chapel at Windsor, he was made a chaplain of
the order of the Knights of Saint John of Jerusalem and in 1888 assisted at the installation of
the Prince of Wales as grand prior. During the
whole of his bishopric he was vitally interested
in education, which he believed a fundamental
function of the Church as well as an urgent
need of Southern youth. He aided in the establishment of a number of preparatory schools,
but his most important work in aid of the cause
was his second founding of the University of the
South at Sewanee, the dream of Leonidas Polk
and James H. Otey [qq.v.] that had been close
to fulfillment at the outbreak of the war. The
war had swept away its endowments and blasted
all hope of new ones, and the ten thousand acres
granted by the state of Tennessee in 1858 would
lapse in 1868 unless the institution were then
in operation. In March 1866 he climbed the
mountain, selected locations for the buildings,
and planted a cross on the site. He brought
about a meeting of the trustees and obtained
the modest funds with which temporary buildings were erected. Elected vice-chancellor, he
went to England, obtained generous aid there,
and in 1868 opened the institution to students
with a small but able faculty. In 1872 he retired
from the direct oversight of the institution, but
his labors for it ceased only with his death. His
was a unique personality. His French inheritance was marked in manner and gesture, in
sprightly and ready wit, and in mental process.
Highly gifted socially, full of anecdote, of original ideas, and of elemental intellectual force,
he was, however, above all things a spiritual
leader and, in the better sense of the term, an
inspired evangelist. He was survived by his
widow Katharine (Hand) Quintard and by
three children.

[A. H. Noll, *Doctor Quintard* (1905) and *Hist. of
the Church in the Diocese of Tenn.* (1900); G. R.
Fairbanks, *Hist. of the Univ. of the South* (1905);
E. B. Huntington, *Hist. of Stamford, Conn.* (1868);
Nashville American and *Knoxville Jour.*, Feb. 16,
1898; *Churchman* (N. Y.), Feb. 26, 1898; personal
acquaintance; name of mother's first husband as William Shaw from D. W. Hoyt, *A Geneal. Hist. of . . .
Hoyt* (1871), p. 397.]   J. G. deR. H.

QUINTARD, GEORGE WILLIAM (Apr.
22, 1822–Apr. 2, 1913), manufacturer of marine
engines, born at Stamford, Conn., was the son
of Isaac and Clarissa (Hoyt) Shaw Quintard.
His younger brothers, Charles Todd [q.v.] and
Edward, became bishop and bank president respectively. At fifteen, after attending the public schools, George went to New York, which
was thereafter his home. After working for
grocery and ship-chandlery firms, he became a

ship-chandler on his own account. On Feb. 15,
1844, he married Frances Eliza, daughter of
Charles Morgan [q.v.]. Some three years later,
at twenty-five, he entered the iron works of
T. F. Secor & Company on the East River at
Ninth Street. In 1850, his father-in-law got
control of this plant, which he called the Morgan
Iron Works, and by 1852, since Morgan was
busy with his shipping operations in the Gulf,
Quintard was in full charge. The latter seems
to have been more of a business executive than
a technical innovator like his rivals Cornelius
H. Delamater and John Roach [qq.v.]. The
firm made iron pipe for the Chicago water
works in 1853, but its specialty was marine machinery. The recent mail subsidies had centered
the building of ocean liners in New York, and
although Hogg & Delamater, Allaire's Works,
and Stillman, Allen & Company's Novelty Iron
Works had already equipped most of the first
crack liners, the Morgan works by 1867 had built
engines for some forty ocean, coastwise, and
lake steamships. Most of these were paddle-
wheel, walking-beam affairs, for the New York
works were notorious for conservative prejudice against the screw propeller.

During the Civil War, in addition to the *Seminole,* which they had equipped in 1859, the
Morgan works supplied machinery for thirteen
naval vessels, including the large screw cruisers
Ammonoosuc, Idaho, Ticonderoga, and *Wachu-
sett*; the side-wheel "double-enders" *Algonquin,
Ascutney, Chenango, Mahaska,* and *Tioga,* for
river work; and the small screw gunboats *Chippewa, Kineo,* and *Katahdin.* Quintard himself
contracted for the twin-screw, double-turret
monitor *Onondaga,* having T. F. Rowland construct the hull in Brooklyn. Analysis of the records shows that of some thirty-five concerns on
the coast engaged in building engines for the
navy, Quintard's easily stood first in point of
numbers, although his numerical primacy
might be offset by the size and importance of
the engines Delamater built for the *Monitor,
Dictator, Puritan,* and other Ericsson ships. In
1863, Quintard also built engines for the Italian
frigate *Re d'Italia,* sunk in 1866 by the Aus-
trians at Lissa.

In 1867, he sold the Morgan Iron Works to
Roach, and inaugurated a line of four steamships to Charleston. He later established a line
from Portland to Halifax. By 1869, however,
he had returned to his marine engines, founding,
with James Murphy of the Fulton Foundry, the
Quintard Iron Works, two blocks above the
Morgan plant. He was active in this concern
for more than thirty years, although in 1882, fol-

lowing the family custom, he made his son-in-law president. N. F. Palmer, Jr., & Company, as the firm was called, was gradually over-shadowed by the Cramps [qq.v.] and Roach, who were building hulls as well as engines and gaining most of the contracts for the "New Navy" and the largest liners. Quintard's firm contracted for the gunboats *Bennington* and *Concord,* having the hulls built by Roach at Chester, and also made the engines for the ill-fated *Maine.*

Prominent in New York financial circles, Quintard was a director of numerous corporations and head of a company which for a while mined nearly a million dollars worth of silver a year in southern Chihuahua. In 1873, he was appointed a commissioner of immigration and he also served as a park commissioner during a period of active park expansion. He was an Episcopalian, a yachtsman, and a member of many clubs. Just before his wife's death, he built a mansion at 922 Fifth Avenue where he himself died twenty years later. His daughter Fannie had died when about to christen the *Onondaga;* he had a son and another daughter. His estate, appraised at $2,220,285, was left entirely to relatives.

[*Who's Who in America,* 1912–13 ; James Parton and others, *Sketches of Men of Progress* (1870–71) ; D. W. Hoyt, *A Geneal. Hist. of the Hoyt, Haight, and Hight Families* (1871) ; N. H. Morgan, *Morgan Geneal.* (1869) ; E. B. Huntington, *Hist. of Stamford, Conn.* (1868) ; *Official Records of the Union and Confederate Navies during the Civil War,* 2 ser. I (1921) ; *Trans. Soc. of Naval Architects and Marine Engineers,* I (1893), 128–39 ; *Jour. Franklin Inst.,* see Index (2 vols., 1826–85, and 1886–1905) ; J. H. Morrison, *Hist. of Am. Steam Navigation* (1903) and *Hist. of N. Y. Ship Yards* (1909) ; Daniel Van Pelt, *Leslie's Hist. of the Greater N. Y.* (1898), vol. III ; *N. Y. Herald,* July 29, 30, 1863, Apr. 3, 1913 ; *N. Y. Times,* Apr. 3, Sept. 18, 1913.]
R. G. A—n.

QUITMAN, JOHN ANTHONY (Sept. 1, 1798–July 17, 1858), lawyer, soldier, champion of state rights, was born at Rhinebeck, N. Y., the third son of the Rev. Frederick Henry Quitman and Anna Elizabeth (Hueck) Quitman, the former a licentiate of the University of Halle and for twelve years a Lutheran pastor in Curaçao, W. I., where he married. The son was educated by his father, who intended him for the ministry, by private tutors, and at Hartwick Academy, Otsego County, N. Y., where he was also a tutor. In 1818 he became adjunct professor of English at Mount Airy College, Germantown, Pa., where he utilized an opportunity to study Spanish under a native teacher. Finding that he had no vocation for the ministry, he resolved to study law and proceeded westward, stopping first at Chillicothe and later at

Delaware, Ohio, where he began his legal studies, at the same time holding a clerkship in the government land office. In 1821 he was admitted to the bar. For some time his eye had been on the South, and by the end of that year he had settled at Natchez, Miss., and begun practice. On Dec. 24, 1824, he married Eliza Turner, daughter of a highly respected and well-to-do citizen; they had four children, two of whom died in childhood.

Quitman was active in Masonry and his connection therewith doubtless contributed not a little to his professional and political progress. From 1826 to 1838 and again in 1840 and 1845 he was Grand Master of the Mississippi Masons. Meanwhile, in 1827 he was elected to the lower house of the state legislature (session of 1828), where he served on the judiciary committee. From 1827 until 1835 he held the office of chancellor (1 *Miss. Chancery Reports*) and during that period he was also chairman of the judiciary committee of the constitutional convention of 1832. He earnestly advocated submitting the convention's work to the people for ratification, managed to secure nineteen votes for his proposal as against twenty-six to the contrary, and succeeded in providing for popular approval of subsequent amendments (C. S. Lobingier, *The People's Law,* 1909, p. 212).

In 1834 he became identified with the political group known as "Nullifiers" who held the views expressed by the Nullification leaders in South Carolina. He prepared an address in their behalf, which was adopted May 21, 1834, by a convention of "Nullifiers" at Jackson. While the sentiments therein set forth were not then popular in Mississippi (Claiborne, *post,* I, 135) he was nevertheless elected to the state Senate in 1835, became its president on Dec. 3, and until Jan. 7, 1836, was acting governor. When he was a candidate for Congress in 1836, however, he was defeated. About this time he was offered and declined the position of judge of the high court of errors and appeals (*Ibid.,* I, 135).

Turning aside for the time from the political arena, he recruited and led a company called the "Fencibles" to the relief of the Texans in their struggle with Mexico, but took part in no actual fighting. Returning from this expedition, he was appointed brigadier-general of the Mississippi militia. His interest in military affairs continued until practically the end of his life. In 1839 he visited Europe and was particularly interested in "Old Bailey" and the Inns of Court at London. Returning to Mississippi, he devoted himself to his law practice, which had become highly lucrative. In the controversy over the bonds issued by the state in aid of the Union Bank, which in 1843 agitated the electors, he took his stand against repudiation. Three years later, when the Mexican War began, he was given a commission as a brigadier-general of volunteers and served under General Taylor. He took part in the battle of Monterey and the investment of the Mexican capital, and his command was the first to enter the city upon its surrender. General Scott thereupon appointed him governor of the city, with high civil and military powers, and on Apr. 14, 1847, he was promoted major-general. Returning to the United States, he visited Washington and submitted to President Polk a carefully wrought plan for the permanent occupation of Mexico (Claiborne, II, 8). He also visited Charleston, S. C., where he was accorded signal honors by the Grand Lodge of Masons and was elected an active member of the Scottish Rite Supreme Council.

In 1848 his name was placed before the National Democratic Convention at Baltimore for the vice-presidential nomination, but although he is said to have had "more personal strength and popularity in that body than any other" candidate (Claiborne, II, 14), he was not nominated. He was later chosen as a presidential elector, however, and in the following year, governor of Mississippi. His term, beginning Jan. 10, 1850, was a stormy one, with the slavery question growing daily more acute. He opposed the compromise measures of 1850 and after their adoption by Congress called a session of the legislature to take measures of protest. In his message, he declared "that the only effectual remedy," in case amendments could not be secured, would be "prompt and peaceable secession" (*Ibid.*, II, 50). Meanwhile Quitman had become interested in the liberation of Cuba, and Lopez, a leader of the movement for independence, visited him at Jackson and offered him command of the revolutionary forces. This he declined, on the ground that to accept it would be desertion of the pro-slavery cause; but it was evident that the Cuban *junta* had his moral support, and he with others was indicted by a federal grand jury at New Orleans for violating the neutrality laws. He thereupon resigned the office of governor, deeming it incompatible with the sovereignty of Mississippi for the governor "to be detained as a prisoner by another authority" (*Ibid.*, II, 77); but the case against him was dismissed after a third failure to convict a codefendant. He continued, however, his correspondence with the *junta*. In 1851 he was

again a candidate for governor, on an anti-compromise platform, but he withdrew after the election of delegates to the convention had resulted in a large "Union" majority. Jefferson Davis was named as the state-rights candidate and defeated.

Elected to Congress, Quitman began to serve Mar. 4, 1855. On Apr. 29, 1856, he delivered an extended speech advocating repeal of the neutrality laws, contending that Congress had no "right to brand as criminal, acts clearly permitted by the law of nations" (*Congressional Globe*, 34 Cong., 1 Sess., App. p. 671). He was reëlected to Congress, and was a member thereof when he died, at his home, "Monmouth Plantation," near Natchez, after several months of illness. The decline of his health was ascribed by some of his friends to poisoned food which he had eaten at the National Hotel in Washington. His death was the occasion of numerous tributes, not the least of which was the "Lodge of Sorrow" held at the Unitarian Church in Washington, Mar. 30, 1860, in connection with the session of the Scottish Rite Supreme Council.

[The chief source is J. F. H. Claiborne, *Life and Correspondence of John A. Quitman* (2 vols., 1860). See also Rosalie Quitman Duncan (Quitman's daughter), "Life of Gen. John A. Quitman," *Miss. Hist. Soc. Pubs.*, vol. IV (1901), and C. C. Hearon, "Mississippi and the Compromise of 1850," *Ibid.*, vol. XIV (1913), reprinted separately, both of which rely mainly on Claiborne for their material; Dunbar Rowland, *Hist. of Miss.* (1925), vol. I; G. W. Baird, "Great Men Who Were Masons: John Anthony Quitman," *The Builder*, June 1925; *The New Age*, XIII, 337; *Freemasons' Monthly Mag.*, Oct. 1858; *Daily National Intelligencer* (Washington, D. C.), July 20, 1858; a small collection of Quitman's papers, not used by Claiborne in his biography, is in the Harvard Univ. Lib. (*Harvard Alumni Bulletin*, Nov. 11, 1932); year of birth is that given by Claiborne, and H. H. Morse, *Historic Old Rhinebeck* (1908); Duncan and *Biog. Dir. Am. Cong.* (1928) give 1799.]   C. S. L.

RABY, JAMES JOSEPH (Sept. 17, 1874– Jan. 15, 1934), naval officer, was born at Bay City, Mich., the son of Cyril and Mary (Billiard) Raby, and a descendant of French forebears who came to Michigan from Quebec. He attended the United States Naval Academy from 1891 to 1895, and played on the Academy football team. In the Spanish-American War he was an ensign in the monitor *Marietta*, which joined the *Oregon* on the west coast of South America and accompanied her to the east coast to operate on the Cuban blockade. Thereafter until the World War his naval career followed routine lines, with two assignments as an instructor at the Naval Academy, and promotions to the rank of lieutenant on Sept. 24, 1902, lieutenant commander, July 1, 1908, and command-

er, July 1, 1914. While he was in command of
the *Supply* base at Guam, 1912–13, his ship took
the deepest sea soundings then recorded—5269
fathoms. After duty as executive of the battle-
ship *Maryland,* 1914–15, and two years as head
of the department of English at the Naval Academy, he took command of the cruiser *Albany,*
June 18, 1917, which operated out of New York
in the wartime transport service. The *Albany*
escorted 142 ships to Europe, and, according to
her commander's statement (*Who's Who in
America,* 1932–33), not only took out the first
merchant convoy under American naval protection but also escorted a larger number of ships
to Europe than any other American naval vessel. From April 1918 to April 1919, he commanded successively the battleships *Missouri*
and *Georgia* in the Atlantic Fleet, his temporary appointment as captain, Oct. 15, 1917, being made permanent on Nov. 23, 1919.

After a year in the Bureau of Navigation and
in the Office of Operations, Navy Department,
Washington, and another year at the Washington navy yard, he commanded the 9th Destroyer
Squadron, Scouting Fleet, during the spring of
1922, and then the cruiser *Rochester* until June
1923. While commandant of the Naval Air
Station at Pensacola, 1823–26, he qualified as
naval airplane operator, Aug. 16, 1926, being
the second captain so to qualify, and after his
promotion to rear admiral on Nov. 1, 1927, he
was for some time the only commissioned aviator in this grade. He commanded the Aircraft
Squadrons, Scouting Fleet, from September
1926 to May 1928, returned for a year to command the Pensacola Air Station, and after taking the War College course at Newport, R. I.,
commanded Training Squadron 1, Fleet Base
Force. In June 1931 he was made commandant
of the 6th Naval District and of the navy yard
at Charleston, S. C., an assignment which was
extended, in July 1933, to include the 7th and 8th
Districts and all naval activities in the South.
He met his death in an automobile accident near
Midway, Ga., en route from Florida to Charleston, suffering a fractured skull from which he
died within fifteen minutes. His funeral was
held in the Catholic Cathedral of St. John at
Charleston, and he was buried with military
honors at Arlington. He was married on Oct.
12, 1897, to Jane, daughter of Daniel Callaghan
of San Francisco, Cal., and had two daughters
and one son. He was earnest and unassuming
in his religious faith, and, as an officer, was
distinguished for his unfailing tact and friendliness, combined with firmness of character and
a constant devotion to duty.

[Service Record, Files of Bureau of Navigation,
U. S. Navy Department; *Who's Who in America,*
1932–33; Albert Gleaves, *A Hist. of the Transport
Service* (1921); *Army and Navy Jour.,* Jan. 20,
1934; *N. Y. Times,* Jan. 16, 1934.]   A. W.

RACHFORD, BENJAMIN KNOX (Nov.
28, 1857–May 5, 1929), physiologist, pediatrician, philanthropist, was born in Alexandria,
Ky., the son of Hugh Knox Rachford and Elizabeth Jane (Beall). Both his father and his
grandfather were physicians. After attending
grammar school at Alexandria and Hughes High
School in Cincinnati, he entered the Medical College of Ohio, Cincinnati, and received the doctorate of medicine in 1882, together with the
Joseph Ransohoff gold medal for excellence in
descriptive anatomy. After a year as interne
in the Cincinnati General Hospital, he began
practice with his father. In 1888, however, he
moved to Newport, Ky., across the river from
Cincinnati, and entered practice for himself. A
year later he went abroad to study and spent
some time in the laboratory of Professor Gad
in Berlin. While there he began his work on
the digestive action of the bile and pancreatic
gland. In April 1891, in the *Journal of Physiology,* he published a paper, since become a classic, entitled "The Influence of Bile on the Fat-
Splitting Properties of the Pancreatic Juice." In
subsequent years he published papers on the influence of bile on the proteolytic action of the
pancreatic juice and also on its influence on the
starch-splitting action of that secretion. These
papers, together with other contributions along
the same line, established for him an international reputation in physiology.

In 1894 he removed to Cincinnati and became
professor of bacteriology in the Medical College
of Ohio. He had published in 1888 a paper on
the cause of the epidemic of typhoid fever in
Cincinnati, and had succeeded in isolating the
typhoid bacillus from the reservoir of the public
water supply. About 1894 he became greatly interested in auto-intoxication and published several experimental investigations into the cause
of migraine, which he attributed to toxic products of xanthine nature formed from the bac-
terial decomposition of proteins. His practical
experience as a physician also caused him to experiment on the absorption of drugs from the
skin, and he showed that guaiacol when combined
into a salve with lanolin and fat and rubbed on
the skin appeared in the urine in one and a half
hours. In 1895 he became professor of physiology in the Medical College of Ohio, but retained
this professorship only until 1898. He published
a series of articles in 1895 in the *Archives of
Pediatrics* (New York) which were collected

and published as a book under the title, *Some Physiological Factors in the Neuroses of Childhood* (1895). His investigations into the activity of various toxins related to uric acid in producing symptoms, and the appearance of these substances in more than normal amount in the urine of patients in these states, led him to recognize a distinct disease which he named "Lithemia." Besides various papers on this subject published in medical journals, he contributed a chapter on it to the *American Text Book of the Diseases of Children* (1894), edited by Louis Starr.

In 1897 he was elected director of pediatrics in the Cincinnati General Hospital and at once reorganized the handling of the children patients by establishing a children's ward. He also established in this hospital one of the first outdoor wards in America for the treatment of tuberculosis and pneumonia of children. In 1898 he became professor of materia medica and therapeutics and three years later, professor of pediatrics, in the Ohio Medical College, which by that time had become a part of the University of Cincinnati. The latter professorship he held until 1920. In 1909 he initiated the enterprise which became his greatest philanthropy, the Babies Milk Fund, a charity which has grown in Cincinnati into a great, beneficent, and widely diversified philanthropic work. Its success led Mrs. Mary M. Emery to donate money to endow the chair of pathology in the medical school, to give liberally to its building fund, and to establish in the University of Cincinnati the Benjamin Knox Rachford department of pediatrics.

Rachford published *Neurotic Disorders of Children* in 1905, and seven years later, his well-known textbook, *Diseases of Children* (1912). In the later years of his life he had a great influence in formulating the plans for the medical department of the University of Cincinnati (see his article, "The Medical Department of a Municipal University," *Cincinnati Journal of Medicine*, January 1925). He brought to the medical center there the Children's Hospital, and was instrumental in arousing the interest of William Cooper Procter, who endowed the magnificent Institute for Research in Children's Diseases now attached to that hospital. He took a prominent part also in founding the School of Nursing and Public Health under the auspices of the medical department of the University. He was a member of various medical societies and was president of the American Pediatric Association. In 1897 he married Gretchen Louise Wherry, daughter of William Wherry, United States

Army; they had no children. He died at Cincinnati from septic poisoning.

[Articles by Max Dreyfoos and R. A. Lyon, with bibliog. of Rachford's writings, seventy-five in number, in *Jour. of Medicine* (Cincinnati), July 1929; *Am. Jour. Diseases of Children*, July 1929; *Who's Who in America*, 1928–29; *Cincinnati Enquirer*, May 6, 1929.]
A. P. M.

RADCLIFF, JACOB (Apr. 20, 1764–May 6, 1844), lawyer, mayor of New York, one of the founders of Jersey City, N. J., was born in Rhinebeck, N. Y., the eldest of four sons of William Radcliff and his wife, Sarah Kip. The father was a commissioned officer in the Revolutionary war. Jacob attended the College of New Jersey at Princeton, was a member of the Cliosophic Society (1781), and graduated Sept. 24, 1783, debating with Joseph Venable before an audience which included George Washington, President Boudinot of the Continental Congress, James Madison, and the French Minister, the question: "Can any measure that is morally evil be politically good?" He studied law with Egbert Benson, attorney-general of New York, was admitted to the bar in 1786, and engaged in practice, first in Poughkeepsie and later in New York City. Although he possessed little inclination for politics or the bench, he served two terms in the New York Assembly (1794–95), was for two years assistant attorney-general (1796–98), and for six years (1798–1804) a justice of the supreme court of New York. To the latter office Gov. John Jay had appointed him along with James Kent [*q.v.*] to succeed J. S. Hobart and Robert Yates. Pursuant to an act of the legislature in 1801, Kent and Radcliff codified the laws of the state by omitting the laws or parts of laws abrogated. Their revision (*Laws of the State of New York*, 2 vols., 1802) was standard until 1813.

On Apr. 20, 1804, Radcliff, Anthony Dey, and Richard Varick obtained a lease on Paulus Hook from the Van Vorst family for the annual sum of $6,000 and became the founders of Jersey City. Planning to lay out a city in accordance with a map completed by Joseph F. Mangin [*q.v.*], they secured by act of the legislature the incorporation of the "Associates of the Jersey Company," Nov. 10, 1804, to which part of Paulus Hook was conveyed on Feb. 1, 1805.

Radcliff was a member of the New York Committee of Correspondence of the Federalist party in 1808, when Charles Cotesworth Pinckney was nominated for president, and again in 1812. When in 1809 the Federalists carried New York state, the Council of Appointment chose Radcliff as mayor of New York City (1810) to succeed DeWitt Clinton. As mayor, he was automatically a commissioner to decide the question of land for the Brooklyn Navy Yard. Removed from office in 1811 by a combination of Clinton and Livingston factions, he was again chosen in 1815. During his term he granted certificates of freedom to many negroes who appeared before him and exhibited proof of their free status. He was a delegate from New York City to the state constitutional convention of 1821 which abolished the councils of appointment and revision and liberalized the suffrage. When not holding office he practised law and gained a great reputation as a chancery lawyer. He was a trustee of Columbia College, 1805–17. He married Juliana, daughter of the Rev. Cotton Mather Smith of Sharon, Conn., and they had two daughters. At the home of one of them, in Troy, N. Y., he died.

[W. B. Aitken, *Distinguished Families in America Descended from Wilhelmus Beekman and Jan Thomasse Van Dyke* (1912); V. L. Collins, *The Continental Cong. at Princeton* (1908); M. J. Lamb, *Hist. of the City of N. Y.*, vol. II (1881); J. G. Wilson, *The Memorial Hist. of the City of N. Y.*, vol. III (1893); D. S. Alexander, *A Pol. Hist. of the State of N. Y.*, vol. I (1906); W. H. Shaw, *Hist. of Essex and Hudson Counties, N. J.* (1884), II, 1141; Charles Warren, *A Hist. of the Am. Bar* (1911); S. E. Morison, *The Life and Letters of Harrison Gray Otis* (1913), vol. I; *N. Y. Spectator,* May 11, 1844; *N. Y. Daily Tribune,* May 8, 1844.]

A. L. M.

RADFORD, WILLIAM (Sept. 9, 1809–Jan. 8, 1890), naval officer, was born at Fincastle, Va., of English ancestry, the son of John and Harriet (Kennerly) Radford. The family soon moved to Maysville, Ky., and, upon the father's death in 1816, the widow with her three children went to St. Louis, Mo., to join her cousin, the wife of William Clark [q.v.]. In 1821, after the death of his first wife, Clark married Mrs. Radford. During the next four years William attended boarding school at Perth Amboy, N. J. In these early days he acquired an interest in the sea which led him to obtain through his stepfather an appointment as midshipman on Mar. 1, 1825. The following September he sailed in the *Brandywine*, which carried Lafayette to France. A two-year Mediterranean cruise in the *Constitution* ensued, and then a year's furlough in St. Louis. This alternation of sea and shore billets continued through the next fifteen years, his cruises including two to the Mediterranean in the *John Adams* and the *Preble*, and two to the West Indies in the *Erie* and the *Constellation,* the latter involving participation in an Indian campaign in Florida in the spring of 1838. He was made passed midshipman on Mar. 3, 1831, and lieutenant on Feb. 9, 1837. After a year or more commanding the receiving ship *Ontario* at New Orleans he sailed for the Pacific in October 1843, and subsequently, as executive

of the *Warren,* shared in the early west-coast operations of the Mexican War, leading the force which captured the Mexican war-brig *Malek Adhel* on Sept. 7, 1846, at Mazatlan, and was frequently in charge of boarding and landing parties there and on the California coast. In June 1847, he returned home overland with his brother-in-law, Stephen Watts Kearny [q.v.], his shotgun, the only one in the party, providing game supply during the arduous sixty-six-day journey.

During leave in the East he married Mary Elizabeth, daughter of Joseph Lovell of Morristown, N. J., on Nov. 21, 1848. The family, which included two daughters and four sons, subsequently made their home at Morristown. Save for a Pacific cruise in 1851–52 in the storeship *Lexington,* Radford was at home for the next ten years. He was made commander in 1855 and served as lighthouse inspector at New York from 1858 to 1859. In June 1860, he sailed in command of the steam-sloop *Dacotah,* which joined Commodore Stribling's China Squadron and was in the first American naval expedition up the Yangtse River to Hankow. At the outbreak of the Civil War, Radford, like other officers of Southern antecedents, was removed from his command and ordered home. Though chagrined, he accepted the action, in the words of his friend Samuel Francis Du Pont [q.v.], with the ". . . good sense and calm judgment, for which he had always been noted" (De Meissner, *post,* p. 241). He served again as lighthouse inspector until February 1862, when he was restored to active duty as commander of the *Cumberland* at Hampton Roads. When the *Merrimac* attacked the *Congress* and *Cumberland* on Mar. 8, he had left his ship for court-martial duty, and though the horse on which he hastened back dropped dead as he dismounted, he arrived only in time to see his ship sink with colors flying. The following May he became executive of the New York navy yard, an arduous post which, with small opportunity for glory, demanded full measure of administrative ability and skill in handling personnel, and which he filled with conspicuous success until May 1864. He was made captain in July 1862, and commodore in April 1863, and was then given the *New Ironsides,* which he commanded as flagship and in which he led the ironclads in the attacks on Fort Fisher in December 1864 and January 1865. The heavy broadsides of his ship were most effective, especially during the almost constant two days' firing of the second attack. Admiral Porter wrote: "To your vessel more than to any other in the squadron is the country indebted for the capture . . . you have, in my opinion, shown the highest qualities an officer can possess" (*War of the Rebellion: Official Records, Navy,* 1 ser. XI, 608). Returning to the Chesapeake, he was ordered in the *Ironsides* up the James River to protect Grant's base at Citypoint from threatened attack by the Confederate flotilla, and remained in command there until the war ended. From April to October 1865, he commanded the Atlantic Squadron, then the Washington navy yard, and the European Squadron from February 1869 to August 1870. He was made rear admiral on July 25, 1866. After retirement he lived in Washington, with a summer home at Barnstable, Mass. In later years as in youth he was a strikingly handsome man, dark-complexioned, of middle stature, cordial but never demonstrative in manner, and highly esteemed by naval and civil personnel under his command.

[Letters and other Radford papers of the Civil War period in Navy Dept. Lib., *Misc. Files* (personal papers), 8120–8151; Sophie Radford De Meissner, *Old Naval Days: Sketches from the Life of Rear Admiral William Radford* (1920); L. R. Hamersly, *The Records of Living Officers of the U. S. Navy and Marine Corps* (1890); *War of the Rebellion: Official Records* (*Navy*), 1 ser. vols. X–XII; *Army and Navy Jour.,* Jan. 11, 1890; *Washington Post,* Jan. 9, 1890.] A.W.

RADISSON, PIERRE ESPRIT (1636–*c.* 1710), explorer, was born in France; his parents were probably Pierre Esprit Radisson, of a family identified with Lyons and its vicinity, and his wife, Madeleine Hainault, who seem to have been living in Paris at the time of young Pierre's birth. About 1651 he arrived in Canada, and the following year, while hunting near Three Rivers, he was captured and adopted by some wandering Iroquois. He accompanied his captors on a journey to the trading post at Fort Orange (Albany), where he might have escaped, but, "being that it was my destiny to discover many wild nations," as he said, "I would not strive against destinie" (*Voyages, post,* p. 80), and he returned with the Indians to their village. Before long, however, he made his escape, went back to Fort Orange, was sent by the commander to New Amsterdam, and sailed for Europe, reaching La Rochelle early in 1654.

Later in the spring of that year he returned to Three Rivers. In 1653 his widowed half-sister, Marguerite (Hayet), who had been living for some time at Three Rivers, married Médard Chouart, known as Sieur des Groseilliers [*q.v.*], and during the next two years Radisson may have made a trip to the West with his brother-in-law. In 1657 he joined an expedition to plant a French colony in the Onondaga country, and in 1659, made another western journey with Groseilliers, in the course of which he may have

reached the upper Mississippi. During these years in the forest Radisson and his brother-in-law became aware of the significance of the beaver trade of inland North America and recognized the importance of controlling either or both of the main exits for that trade—New York and Hudson Bay. The governor of Canada had desired them to take two of his men with them on their western trip in 1659, to share the profits, but Radisson and Groseilliers indignantly refused, and departed in defiance of the governor. Hence, upon their return in 1660, their furs were confiscated and they were heavily fined.

In anger, after a futile visit by Groseilliers to France, the two entered the service of the English at Port Royal and Boston. At least one contemporary attributed the English conquest of New Amsterdam to Radisson and his knowledge of how the fur trade might be controlled through the Iroquois. In the employ of New Englanders, Radisson and Groseilliers made a journey to the entrance of Hudson's Straits. In 1665 they were sent by the King's commissioners to England, where their enthusiastic reports of the new region led to the founding, under the patronage of King Charles II, of the Hudson's Bay Company, chartered in 1670. Radisson visited Hudson Bay in 1670 and 1672, but in 1674, with his brother-in-law, resumed his French connections. He served in the French fleet in campaigns against Guinea and Tobago. In 1681 he was residing in Quebec, according to census records. While in England (1672), he had married a daughter of Sir John Kirke, and in 1683 he returned to France, thence, as he said, "passing over to England for good." Reengaged by the Hudson's Bay Company, he made at least three more voyages to Hudson Bay in their employ. During his last years he received a pension from the company.

Presumably for his employers, Radisson wrote accounts of his voyages, most of them in vigorous, picturesque, though extremely faulty, English. They are valuable for their vivid portrayal of the life of the northern country in the early days of the *coureur de bois* rather than for dates or accurate information regarding the routes of the explorers. The manuscript narratives of the voyages of 1652, 1654, 1657, and 1659 are now in the Bodleian Library, Oxford; that of 1682–83, in French, is in Hudson's Bay House; a translation of the last named and the narrative of 1684 are in the British Museum. In 1885 the English accounts and a translation of the French manuscript were edited by Gideon D. Scull for the Prince Society and published under the title, *Voyages of Peter Esprit Radisson,* while *Report* on *Canadian Archives . . . 1895* (1896) contains the French account, with an English translation.

[In addition to the primary sources mentioned above, see: H. C. Campbell, "Radisson and Groseilliers," *Parkman Club Papers*, no. 2 (1896); George Bryce, "The Further History of Pierre Esprit Radisson," *Proc. and Trans. Royal Soc. of Canada*, 2 ser. IV (1898), and *The Remarkable Hist. of the Hudson's Bay Company* (1900); Benjamin Sulte, "Découverte du Mississipi en 1659," *Proc. and Trans. Royal Soc. of Canada*, 2 ser. IX (1903), and article in J. V. Brower, *Memoirs of Explorations in the Basin of the Mississippi*, vol. VI (1903); Warren Upham, "Groseilliers and Radisson," *Minn. Hist. Soc. Colls.*, vol. X, pt. 2 (1905); L. P. Kellogg, *The French Régime in Wis. and the Northwest* (1925); A. T. Adams, "A New Interpretation of the Voyages of Radisson," *Minn. Hist.*, Dec. 1925; articles by A. M. Goodrich and G. L. Nute, "The Radisson Problem," *Ibid.*, Sept. 1932; Donatien Frémont, *Pierre Radisson* (Montreal, 1933); J. B. Brebner, *The Explorers of North America* (1933). A book on Radisson and Groseilliers is in preparation by Dr. Grace Lee Nute, of the Minn. Hist. Soc., who has kindly supplied certain information for this sketch.]

H. C. B.
E. R. D.

RAE, JOHN (June 1, 1796–July 14, 1872), economist, man of letters and science, was born at Footdee, at that time a suburb of Aberdeen, Scotland. His father, who bore the same name, was a ship-builder or ship-broker, who rose from a peasant background to comfortable circumstances; he was known for his honorable dealings, and his son speaks of his strong common sense. The mother, Margaret Cuthbert, came of prosperous farmers; though fifteen years younger than her husband, she died early, before her son John was grown. John Rae entered the University of Aberdeen when fourteen; it is known that he attended Marischal College for the sessions 1810–11, 1811–12, and 1814–15, receiving the degree of M.A. in the latter year. He studied medicine in the University of Edinburgh, and, though he was afterward known as Dr. Rae, he took no medical degree because he was discouraged from presenting his "inaugural dissertation," which embodied a revolutionary view of physiology. He had "come to the conclusion that the physiological medical theories of the day were opposed to all true philosophy," and had reached "a conclusion concerning the origin of man very different from the orthodox one" (Mixter, *post*, p. xxi). His father, believing in his precocious son, recommended further study in Paris. He probably went thither, and in 1818 made a tour through Norway. In these post-Edinburgh years he began to study the history of society on a most ambitious plan, believing that "by gathering together all that consciousness makes known to us of what is within, and all that observation informs us of what lies without . . . might be . . . discovered . . . the materials

for a true *Natural History* of man" (*New Principles*, p. iv).

The prospect of leisure on which he had counted for carrying out these designs was dispelled by his disappointment in an inheritance; at about the same time his chance of study was further lessened by a hasty marriage to the daughter of a Scotch shepherd. He emigrated in the spring of 1821 to Canada; "I exchanged," he said, "the literary leisure of Europe for the solitude and labors of the Canadian backwoods. I found, notwithstanding, that this accident could not altogether put a stop to my inquiries, though it retarded them and altered their form" (Mixter, *post*, p. xlvii). For study in libraries he now perforce substituted observation of the developing new country of his settlement. Adam Smith's *Wealth of Nations* was one of the few books to which he now had access, and further intensive study in this revealed the inapplicability of its principles to the changed environment in which he found himself. Invited to teach the children of the fur traders of the Hudson's Bay Company, he set up a private school at Williamstown, fifty miles from Montreal. A decade later he gave up this school and lived in Quebec, Montreal, and Boston, where he worked on the manuscript which was published at Boston in 1834 with the title: *Statement of Some New Principles on the Subject of Political Economy, Exposing the Fallacies of the System of Free Trade, and of Some other Doctrines Maintained in the "Wealth of Nations."* He at first intended to publish his views in England, but was moved to bring them out in America instead because the latter country, with a strong protectionist sentiment, was much less predisposed toward classical economic doctrines. This situation, however, brought his book a more languid, not a more eager reception, because, as said by a commentator in the *North American Review* (January 1835), it seemed mainly to reiterate received opinion and practice. There is good reason for believing that Rae was influenced by the writings of Mathew Carey, Daniel Raymond, and Georg Friedrich List [*qq.v.*] who were the chief figures at this period in opposing nationalist views to the system of Smith. Particularly Raymond, List, and Rae correspond at many points, and are significantly near together at others.

Soon after his book appeared, Rae became head-master of the Gore District Grammar School at Hamilton, Ontario. Here he gained the affection and respect of his pupils, more by his scholarship and friendliness than by talent as a teacher. His service was interrupted in December 1837 when he went with the Hamilton Volunteers to Toronto and the Niagara frontier to fight those in rebellion against the British government in Canada. In 1848 the trustees of the school ousted him, apparently on the ground that he was a free-thinker, or at least opposed the privileges of the Church of England. On top of this misfortune, his wife died the next year. He went to Boston and New York, taught for a short time in the latter city, then sailed to the Isthmus of Panama, whence, as ship's doctor, he sailed on the *Brutus* for California, just then experiencing the gold rush. He taught school near Sutter's Creek and made cradles for washing and balances for weighing gold. In 1851 he went on to the Sandwich Islands, where he became medical agent and later district justice of the island of Maui. During twenty years here he carried on desultory philological and sociological studies, the results of some of which appeared in obscure newspapers. He reverted to invention, which had interested him in youth, projecting nautical and aeronautical devices. He spent the last year of his life on Staten Island, New York, as the guest of a former pupil, Sir Roderick Cameron.

Essentially, Rae made a study of economic capacities rather than of mere wealth. An optimist, he was led on by the thought of man's social potentialities. He clearly perceived the differences in behavior and the possibilities of economic growth, between a society or nation and a mere aggregate of individuals. In the broad sense he was thus a collectivist; in the narrow sense a nationalist and protectionist. "The effective desire of accumulation," which implies the willingness to amass capital for a distant result, measures the maturity and progressiveness of a people. He worked out the time discount theory of interest a half-century in advance of more recent and better-known expositors.

[Chas. W. Mixter edited Rae's *New Principles* under the title *The Sociological Theory of Capital* (New York, 1905), and supplied valuable notes and a biographical sketch which is the chief source of information on his life. See also Sidney Sherwood, "Tendencies in Am. Econ. Thought," in *Johns Hopkins Univ. Studies in Hist. and Pol. Sci.*, ser. XV, no. 12 (1897), and the *N. Y. Tribune*, July 19, 1872. References to Rae will be found in J. S. Mill's *Principles of Pol. Economy* (2 vols., 1848) and Eugen von Böhm-Bawerk's *Geschichte und Kritik der Capitalzins-Theorien* (2nd ed., 1900).]
B. M.

RAFFEINER, JOHN STEPHEN (Dec. 26, 1785–July 16, 1861), Roman Catholic missionary, was born in Walls in the Austrian Tyrol and was educated by the Benedictine Fathers in Innsbruck and in a Roman medical college. In Milan, while in charge of a military hospital, he experienced a religious calling. He studied theology in Rome, was ordained a priest in May

1825, and served as assistant and pastor in his native diocese of Brixen. Learning of the dire need of missionary priests among the German emigrants to America, he volunteered for this service with the consent of his ordinary, who supplied his traveling expenses. On his arrival in New York (1833), he was authorized by Bishop John Dubois [*q.v.*] to visit his compatriots in all parts of the diocese and urge them to establish churches and mission centers.

In 1836, he erected St. Nicholas Church in New York, over which he presided for several years. He became vicar general for the Germans under Bishop Hughes [*q.v.*], who relied wholly upon his judgment in handling all matters touching the German groups. A spiritual man, ready as a preacher in German, French, and Italian, tactful in settling racial differences and the problems of trusteeism, Raffeiner was everywhere. He visited the Germans of Boston twice a year, organized parishes in Roxbury (1835) and in Boston. He was instrumental in building St. John's Church in New York (Bayley, *post*), Holy Trinity in Williamsburg on Long Island, St. John's Church in Newark, and a church at Macopin, N. J. He assisted in organizing the first German congregations in Rochester, Utica, Inama, and Buffalo, as well as a score of scattered missions throughout New York and New Jersey which became thriving parishes. Though beloved of his own people and honored by Hughes, Raffeiner as a German was not advanced to the see of Brooklyn on its creation in 1853 but continued as a vicar general of that diocese under Bishop John Loughlin and as the father and apostle of the Germans of the archdiocese until his death.

[Scattered references in *Berichte der Leopoldinen Stiftung* (1829 *et seq.*); J. R. Bayley, *A Brief Sketch of the Hist. of the Cath. Ch. on the Island of New York* (1853); Bernard Vogt, *The Cradle of the Cath. Ch. in Northern N.J.* (1930); O. W. Moosmüller, *St. Vincenz in Pennsylvanien* (1873); J. T. Smith, *A Hist. of the Diocese of Ogdensburg* (n.d.); *Records Am. Cath. Hist. Soc.*, June 1900; J. M. Flynn, *The Cath. Ch. in N. J.* (1904); *Der Apologet*, July 24, 1862; *N. Y. Freeman's Journal*, July 27, 1861; *N. Y. Tribune*, July 18, 1861.]
R. J. P.

RAFINESQUE, CONSTANTINE SAMUEL (Oct. 22, 1783–Sept. 18, 1840), naturalist, was born at Galata, a suburb of Constantinople. His father was G. F. Rafinesque, a prosperous French merchant of Marseilles; his mother, whose maiden name seems to have been Schmaltz, was born in Greece of German parents. Until 1814 Rafinesque called himself Rafinesque-Schmaltz. His father died at Philadelphia in 1793, while on a voyage to the United States, leaving the boy, with his brother and sister, to be reared by their mother, who was a woman of culture and independence. The children were educated under private tutors at Marseilles and Leghorn. A precocious boy, Rafinesque read widely in books of travel, learned several languages, and conceived a boundless enthusiasm for the study of nature. When eleven years old he began the systematic collection of a herbarium. In 1802, intending to collect birds, he shot a titmouse and was so conscience-struck that thereafter he killed only for food. His private education and separation from his fellows allowed both his talents and his peculiarities to develop unhindered: he never grew accustomed to the behavior and ideas of ordinary men, and never acquired the orderly methods and mental attitude of the trained scientist. Much of his personal suffering and of the ineffectiveness of his work can be traced to this unconquerable innocence.

In 1802 he and his brother made a voyage to Philadelphia. During part of his three years' sojourn in the United States he was employed in the counting-house of the Clifford Brothers of Philadelphia, but he found time also for considerable travel. The plants, animals, and minerals of the New World filled him with indescribable delight. He received benevolent attention from Benjamin Rush, became acquainted with the whole company of Philadelphia scientists, journeyed to Lancaster to meet G. H. E. Mühlenberg, visited President Jefferson at Washington, talked through an interpreter with a delegation of Osage Indians at the Capital, and collected a vocabulary of their language. He botanized in southern New Jersey and the Dismal Swamp of Virginia. At the end of December 1804 he and his brother returned to Leghorn, taking with them a great store of botanical specimens.

For the next ten years Rafinesque lived at Palermo in Sicily, where for a while he was secretary and chancellor to the American consul. In 1808 he took a house and became an exporter of squills and medicinal plants. He had sound business instincts—in later life he devised the coupon bond—and, whenever he abandoned his mind to it, made money. But the natural sciences, especially botany and ichthyology, were what he lived for. He was already publishing, in various pamphlets and periodicals, the results of his investigations and was studying carefully the ichthyology of Sicilian waters. One of his closest friends in these years was the English scientist, William Swainson. In 1809 he married Josephine Vaccaro, by whom he had a daughter, Emily, who became an actress, and a

son, who died in infancy. His married life was unhappy; his wife was indifferent to his work and perhaps unfaithful; to the harassed naturalist Sicily became a land of "fruitful soil, delightful climate, excellent productions, perfidious men, deceitful women"; and in 1815, with a quantity of drugs and other merchandise and fifty boxes of personal belongings he sailed for the United States. There he was destined to live out the remaining twenty-five years of his life.

He arrived naked and penniless, for his ship was wrecked off Fisher's Island, at the entrance to Long Island Sound, and he narrowly escaped drowning. His wife, hearing of his disaster, promptly married a comic actor, and news of her duplicity soon reached him. He kept the whole humiliating story of his marriage to himself, disclosing it only in his will. Meanwhile he was befriended in his distress by Samuel Latham Mitchill and found a place as tutor for some months in the Livingston household at Clermont. He explored the Hudson Valley, Lake George, Long Island, and other regions, and in Philadelphia enjoyed the companionship and hospitality of Zaccheus Collins, the Quaker naturalist. In the spring of 1818 he went to Lexington, Ky., to visit his old friend, John D. Clifford. Through Clifford's influence he was appointed professor of botany, natural history, and modern languages at Transylvania University. To Rafinesque's lasting grief his friend died in 1820, but despite friction between himself and President Holley he continued in his professorship until 1826. He was a brilliant teacher. He traveled extensively in Kentucky and Tennessee, visited many points in Ohio, Indiana, and Illinois, and in 1825 made a journey through Washington, Baltimore, and Philadelphia.

From 1826 until his death he lived in Philadelphia but continued to travel and to make various field trips whenever opportunity offered. No other American naturalist traveled so widely. He met, at one time or another, most of the scientists of note in the United States and was on friendly terms with them. He wrote and published incessantly, as he had done ever since his residence in Sicily (see bibliographical note). Many of his publications are excessively rare, for his method of publishing was as eccentric and irregular as his other habits. Botany and ichthyology continued to be his chief interests, but he wrote also on banking, economics, the Bible, and other topics, and even produced a few volumes of verse. His descriptions of plants and fishes are often vague or inaccurate, and he had a passion for announcing new species. Behind this passion lay the conviction, expressed more than once in his writings, that "every variety is a deviation which becomes a species as soon as it is permanent by reproduction. Deviations in essential organs may then gradually become new genera" (*Atlantic Journal*, Spring, 1833, p. 164). He thus had a glimpse, if no more than a glimpse, of the later development of biological thought. He was ahead of his generation in the United States, also, in advocating Jussieu's method of classification. His contemporary fame was injured, in fact, quite as much by his superior intelligence as by his shortcomings.

During his last years he suffered from dire poverty, neglect, and ill health, and some of his later schemes and activities indicate that he was not entirely sane. He died in a miserable garret in Philadelphia, of cancer of the stomach. His landlord intended to sell the corpse to a medical school, but some friends smuggled it out of the house and gave it decent burial. In 1924 his remains were reinterred on the campus of Transylvania University at Lexington, with honors appropriate to the memory of one of the great pioneers of natural science in America.

[The chief source of information is Rafinesque's autobiography, *A Life of Travels and Researches in North America and South Europe* (1836). R. E. Call, *The Life and Writings of Rafinesque* (Filson Club Pubs. No. 10, Louisville, Ky., 1895) and T. J. Fitzpatrick, *Rafinesque: A Sketch of his Life with Bibliog.* (Historical Dept. of Iowa, Des Moines, 1911) are indispensable; the latter lists 939 items (books, pamphlets, periodicals, articles, notes, circulars, etc.) by Rafinesque and 134 referring to him and locates his manuscripts and portraits. Audubon's highly colored version of his meeting with him is most accessible in *Delineations of Am. Scenery and Character* (1926), ed. by F. H. Herrick. See also: James Whaler, *Green River: A Poem for Rafinesque* (1931).]   G. H. G.

RAFTER, GEORGE W. (Dec. 9, 1851–Dec. 29, 1907), civil engineer, son of John and Eleanor (Willson) Rafter, was born in Orleans, N. Y. On his father's side he was descended from a Scotch-Irish settler of Northumberland County, Pa.; on his mother's, from James Willson, a pioneer settler of Cherry Valley, N. Y. After the death of John Rafter, when his son was seven years old, his widow sold the water-power at Orleans which had been the main source of the family's income, but the purchasers had difficulties because of the irregularity of the water flow, and several times the property reverted to Mrs. Rafter. This experience of his boyhood may have influenced George's later bent.

He received his education in the public schools of Phelps, N. Y., in the old Canandaigua Academy, and at Cornell University, where he was enrolled for a short time. In 1872 he married Alyda Kirk, of Phelps, who died in May 1907.

He began his engineering career in 1873 by part-time work in the City Surveyor's office at Rochester, N. Y. Simultaneously he studied architecture and in addition taught mathematics in a private school. In 1876 he became assistant engineer of the Rochester water works, and then for two years practised as a consulting civil engineer. In this capacity he served the Rochester & Lake Ontario Railway Company. From 1880 to 1882 he was employed by the Texas & Pacific and Missouri Pacific railways, for the former road supervising the water supply piped across the Staked Plains. Then followed a year in the construction of water works at Fort Worth, Tex. Back in New York State (1883–90), he served as assistant engineer of the Rochester water works and engineer of the Fredonia water works. In 1883, he surveyed Honeoye Lake for use as a storage reservoir for water power for Rochester mills. In 1890, while acting chief engineer of the Rochester water works, he inaugurated an original scheme for throttling down certain districts when a water famine threatened, distributing the insufficient supply so as to preserve public health and minimize discomfort. He designed sewage disposal plants at Albion, Holley, Lawrenceville, and Geneva, N. Y., and the West Virginia State Hospital for the Insane; and water works at Berwick and Nescopeck, Pa.; and served as consulting engineer for the Warsaw (N. Y.) Water Company. In collaboration with M. N. Baker, he published *Sewage Disposal in the United States* (1894), which became a standard textbook in the field. For a time he was sanitary expert to the Boston water works, and during this period collaborated with Prof. William T. Sedgwick [*q.v.*] in developing the Sedgwick-Rafter method of water analysis. He was one of the first engineers to use the microscope in the study of the biology of water supplies, writing several papers in connection with this subject.

In 1893, he entered the employ of the State of New York to study especially the problems of river control; he devised a system of storage reservoirs to regulate the flow of the Genesee and Hudson rivers, notably the reservoir at Schroon Lake, and superintended the construction of the dam which formed Indian Lake in a tributary of the upper Hudson. In 1902 he was made a member of the newly founded state Water Storage Commission. Sent abroad in 1894 to study movable bridges and to investigate high masonry dams, he made reports to the state engineer of New York on these subjects.

In charge of water-supply investigation for the federal board of engineers on deep waterways (1898–99), he made surveys and estimates for a ship canal from Lake Ontario through Oneida Lake down the Mohawk to the Hudson River (see his *Water Resources of the State of New York,* 2 parts, 1899). This elaborate undertaking included a plan for great reservoirs and a ninety-mile water-supply canal or an alternate twenty-eight-mile tunnel, also pioneer study of the application of hydraulic formulas to heavy flows over weirs. Rafter himself considered his investigation of the hydraulics of the Hemlock Lake reservoir in the Rochester water-supply system his most important work, because of the reforms it brought about (see *Transactions of the American Society of Civil Engineers,* vol. XXVI, pp. 13, 23, January 1892). After 1900, he engaged in private consulting practice. His report on *Hydrology of the State of New York* (1905) is recognized as authoritative on matters relating to stream flow. In all, he was sole or joint author of some 175 books and papers in addition to innumerable professional reports. He died of pleurisy, in Karlsbad, Austria, less than a year after the death of his wife. They were survived by two daughters.

[The "W." in Rafter's signature stands for no name, according to a letter from Rafter himself in the Cat. Div., Lib. of Cong. A good biog. sketch is that by J. Y. McClintock, in *Trans. Am. Soc. Civil Engineers,* vol. LXII (1909); see also *Democrat and Chronicle* (Rochester, N. Y.), Dec. 30, 1907. Information as to certain facts has been supplied by Rafter's daughter, Myra Rafter Taylor.]   B. A. R.

RAGUET, CONDY (Jan. 28, 1784–Mar. 21, 1842), editor and economist, son of Paul Claudius Raguet, probably of Burgundy, was born in Philadelphia and received his education in that city. After some training in a Philadelphia mercantile house, he was sent as supercargo to Santo Domingo in 1804 and 1805. From these two voyages he derived material for his first published works: *A Short Account of the Present State of Affairs in St. Domingo* and *A Circumstantial Account of a Massacre in St. Domingo.* Not long after his return from the second of these journeys he established himself in an independent business which he pursued until the outbreak of the War of 1812. During this war he raised and commanded a company stationed not far from Wilmington, Del. At its close he abandoned commercial life for law, was admitted to the bar, published *An Inquiry into the Causes of the Present State of the Circulating Medium of the United States* (1815), and served one term in the Pennsylvania Senate. Here, as chairman of a committee appointed to inquire into the extent and causes of the general distress, he made comprehensive reports, much of the material of which later appeared in pamphlet form as *The Currency* (Albany, 1830) and *Of the Principles of Banking* (Albany, 1830).

In 1822 the direction of his endeavors once more shifted and he accepted an appointment as consul to Rio de Janeiro, where in March 1825 he was made chargé d'affaires. Disputes between the United States and Brazil were rife, many of them were extremely troublesome, and Raguet felt himself entirely unsupported by the State Department. In 1827 he abruptly called for his passports and returned to the United States to find that his conduct had failed to gain the approbation of his superiors and that further diplomatic posts were closed to him. His request for a committee of investigation failed of a hearing (Official Letters from Rio de Janeiro, 1825, to J. Q. Adams and Henry Clay, in the possession of the Pennsylvania Historical Society), but his defense against the charges of weakness and want of judgment and his own view of his services to his country he set forth at considerable length in the *Banner of the Constitution* (Feb. 13, 17, 1830).

The remainder of his life Raguet devoted to what he described as the "cause of constitutional liberty." He spared no effort to enlighten his countrymen concerning problems of currency and the tariff, in both of which subjects he was distinctively in advance of his time and thoroughly conversant with the work of the English classical economists. (See his letters to Ricardo in *Minor Papers on the Currency Question,* 1932, ed. by J. H. Hollander.) His work of education was first undertaken in the pages of the *Free Trade Advocate, and Journal of Political Economy,* established in 1829 in "the camp of the enemy," Philadelphia. Raguet had the most cordial personal relations with Henry C. Carey, who was the leader of the rising protectionists, and whose theories may well owe some of their elaboration to arguments of Raguet. In a few months the scope of Raguet's paper was enlarged and it was transferred for a time from Philadelphia to Washington in order that he might be at hand during the pending tariff struggle. It became the *Banner of the Constitution,* and during its brief existence it contained summaries of domestic and foreign news, statistical material relating to industry, and original articles on issues before Congress and on political economy. The closing number of this venture heralded the appearance of its successor, *The Examiner, and Journal of Political Economy,* "devoted to the advancement of the cause of state rights and free trade." This first appeared in August 1833. In 1835 it was transferred from

Philadelphia to Washington, under the editorship of Duff Green, Raguet becoming proprietor of the Philadelphia *Gazette*. In any study of the early history of the tariff these three periodicals are invaluable. Not only is Raguet's own writing informed and ingenious but many of the important state papers of the period appeared in these publications. In 1835 he published a selection of his editorial articles as *The Principles of Free Trade, Illustrated in a Series of Short and Familiar Essays.*

His last venture into the periodical field was the *Financial Register of the United States,* which appeared from July 1837 to December 1838 and was intended to be a documentary history of the commercial crisis of the period. Here appeared the Bullion Report of 1810, and extracts from Torrens and Ricardo. *A Treatise on Currency and Banking* appeared in the United States and in England in 1839 (2nd ed., 1840). His last work was "Impolicy of Countervailing Duties," published in *Hunt's Merchants' Magazine* (January 1842), but a few months before his death. He was a member of the American Philosophical Society of Philadelphia, and in the year of his death was president of the Chamber of Commerce of Philadelphia. By one of his contemporaries he was described as a "man of fine figure and imposing presence; affable, well educated, fluent in conversation." He should be remembered not only for his work for free trade but for his acute analyses of currency questions which give him a place among early students of the business cycle.

[Sources, in addition to those cited above, include: a manuscript biography of Raguet by Samuel Breck in the possession of the American Philosophical Society of Philadelphia; H. M. Lippincott, *Early Phila.: Its People, Life and Progress* (1917); *Niles' Nat. Reg.,* Mar. 26, 1842; Philadelphia newspapers, Mar. 23, 1842.]   E. D—n.

RAHT, AUGUST WILHELM (Feb. 25, 1843–Dec. 25, 1916), metallurgist, was born at Dillenburg, Nassau, Germany. His father, Adolf Raht, was a prominent jurist; his mother was Wilhelmine Marie von Goedecke.

Raht was educated at the Polytechnic Institute, Hesse-Cassel, and the Royal School of Mines, Freiberg, Saxony. In 1867 he came to the United States, where most of his professional life was spent. His first engagement was at a copper-smelting plant at Ducktown, Tenn. Subsequently, in Utah, Colorado, New Mexico, and Montana, he became a prominent figure among the pioneer metallurgists who established American lead-silver smelting practice. The Mingo and the Horn Silver plants, as well as the plant of the Helena & Livingston Reduction Company, afterwards combined with the Great Falls plant built by Anton Eilers [*q.v.*] under the ownership of the United Smelting and Refining Company, were among his earlier Western operations. His reputation was such that in 1891, when the "Philadelphia" smelter at Pueblo, Col., was experiencing disastrous metallurgical results, he was engaged at a startling salary by Meyer Guggenheim [*q.v.*] to remedy the situation. He thus became the metallurgical authority of the Guggenheims. With the extension of their interests his sphere of operation was extended from Colorado into Mexico, and after the combination with the American Smelting & Refining Company, into a wider field. He remained with the last-named company, except for some two years of professional work in Australia, until his retirement in 1910.

Raht was one of the first to recognize the benefit of a reduced fuel in the lead blast-furnace and was insistent upon this reduction at the plants under his management. He was always willing to discuss metallurgical problems, but was not noted as a contributor to technical literature. It is therefore difficult to point to the improvements for which he was responsible. For example, he was an early investigator of the bessemerizing of copper matte, but the patent for the process is in his brother's name. This work and his later work at the "Philadelphia" smelter upon the bessemerization of leady mattes is of permanent value. Of more temporary value, yet important in its day, was his share in developing the "gum-drop" method of sampling silver-lead bullion. Raht's modesty was such that only upon intimate acquaintance did one become aware of his great fund of knowledge of all the branches of natural history, upon which he could discourse most interestingly, his facts gained from his own observations. He was a true sportsman, enjoying hunting and fishing, but never wantonly destructive of wild life. Raht's first wife, Marie Katherine Schulz, whom he married at Cassel, Germany, on July 15, 1869, died Dec. 24, 1874, at Ducktown, Tenn., leaving two daughters. He was married a second time, in September 1886, to Julia F. Brown of New York City, who died in 1915. There were no children by this marriage. Raht died at San Francisco in his seventy-fourth year, survived by his two daughters.

[Obituary in *Engineering and Mining Jour.,* Mar. 10, 1917, repr. in *Monthly Bull., Am. Inst. of Mining Engineers,* Apr. 1917; information concerning family from Raht's son-in-law, L. G. Eakins, Berkeley, Cal.]
R. C. C—y.

RAINES, JOHN (May 6, 1840–Dec. 16, 1909), lawyer and legislator, was born at Canandaigua,

N. Y., the son of John and Mary (Remington) Raines. His father and grandfather were Methodist clergymen, the latter having emigrated to the United States from Yorkshire, England, in 1817. Young Raines was educated in the public schools of Canandaigua and was graduated from the Albany (N. Y.) Law School. After spending a brief term teaching school he began the practice of law in Geneva, N. Y., early in 1861. Within a few months he was commissioned captain of Company G, 85th Regiment, New York Volunteer Infantry, and served in the Army of the Potomac and in North Carolina until July 1863. Having married Catherine A. Wheeler on Sept. 18, 1862, he established his family, as soon as his military service ended, in Geneva where he continued to practise law until 1867, when he moved to Canandaigua. The next ten years he devoted to legal matters, an expanding insurance business, and his first tentative ventures into politics. Entering the state Assembly in 1881 as an organization Republican, he served for three sessions and then was defeated for reelection, but he regained his seat in the session of 1885. The following year he began a term of service in the state Senate which lasted until 1889. As a reward for party service he received the nomination for Congress in his district and was elected to the Fifty-first and Fifty-second congresses (1889–93). In 1892, at the time of a redistricting of the state, he withdrew in favor of Serene E. Payne. But he was not long out of public office. A special election held in December 1894 resulted in his return to the upper house of the state legislature, where he remained a prominent Republican leader until his death.

Raines was a worthy representative of the older school of political orators, but his most effective legislative work was done in committee rooms rather than on the floor of the Senate. His zeal as a reformer manifested itself chiefly in efforts to curb the fraudulent elections engineered by the Democrats in New York City and to combat the sinister influence of the liquor interests in state affairs. Concerning most economic questions he strongly supported the conservative viewpoint and he frequently conferred with Thomas C. Platt, the Republican "boss" of the state, in formulating his party's legislative program. He achieved national prominence as a result of his vigorous fight for the liquor excise bill of 1896, which placed the retail trade in intoxicants under a system of high license fees and prohibited Sunday sales. The law contained a section granting exemption from the Sunday closing regulation to inns and hotels, a provision which resulted in a rapid increase in the number of hotels in the larger cities of the state. At best the "Raines law" hotels were subterfuges which permitted liquor dealers to sell on Sunday and after closing hours on weekdays; many of them became houses of assignation. Despite the popular clamor against this feature of the law, Raines long defended it and demanded its scrupulous enforcement. In 1906, however, he cooperated with leaders of the Anti-saloon League and representatives of the Committee of Fifteen, which had been investigating the social evil in New York City, to modify those features of the excise system which had proved to be unenforceable.

Although his public career was concerned mainly with state and national affairs, Raines never lost contact with the life of his native village. For twenty-two years he served as president of the local board of education, a service terminated by his death which occurred at Canandaigua in December 1909.

[There is a laudatory account of Raines's career in C. F. Milliken, *A Hist. of Ontario County, N. Y.* (1911), vol. II. Some of his contacts with Platt may be traced in *The Autobiog. of Thos. Collier Platt* (1910) and in *McClure's Mag.*, Aug. 1910. On the liquor excise law see *The Speech made by Senator Raines— Convincing and Logical* (1896) and J. P. Peters, "Suppression of the 'Raines Law Hotels,'" *Annals of the Am. Acad. of Pol. and Social Sci.*, Nov. 1908. For obituary notices see the *Rochester Democrat and Chronicle*, Dec. 16, 17, 1909.]   J. A. K.

RAINEY, JOSEPH HAYNE (June 21, 1832– Aug. 1, 1887), negro congressman from South Carolina, was born at Georgetown, S. C., the son of mulatto parents. His father was a barber who had bought the freedom of his family. The son secured a limited education through private instruction and at the outbreak of the Civil War was practising the trade of his father in Charleston. For a time he served as a steward on a blockade runner, and in 1862, when the Confederate authorities drafted him to work on the fortifications of Charleston, he escaped to the West Indies. At the close of the war he returned to South Carolina where he emerged into political prominence in 1867 as a member of the executive committee of the newly formed Republican party in that state. In the following year he was elected as a delegate from Georgetown to the state constitutional convention. Although he did not play a prominent part in this convention, shortly after its adjournment he was elected to a seat in the state Senate. In 1870 he resigned from this body to take a seat in the national House of Representatives made vacant by the refusal of the house to accept the credentials of B. F. Whittemore. He thereby won the distinction of being the first negro to be a member of that body. He served in Congress until Mar. 3, 1879, when he was replaced by a Democrat. Because of his color he attracted far more attention than is usually accorded a congressman of his limited experience, and he demonstrated considerable ability as the expounder of the political aspirations of his race. In debate he was courteous and suave rather than aggressive, but he possessed the ability to defend himself well when necessary. Although a regular Republican he did not attempt to humiliate the Southern whites whom he had replaced. He made impressive speeches in favor of legislation to enforce the Fourteenth Amendment, the Ku Klux Act, and the Civil Rights Bill. Although he did not advocate legislation designed to enforce social equality between the races he demanded that the negro be given all civil rights and be admitted to all public places. In order to show that he was in earnest in this respect he entered the dining room of a white hotel in Suffolk, Va., and refused to leave until he was forcibly ejected. His most notable speech was a eulogy of Charles Sumner at the time of the death of the Massachusetts senator. Upon his retirement from Congress he was appointed a special agent of the treasury department for South Carolina, serving in this capacity until July 15, 1881, when he resigned. He subsequently engaged in the banking and brokerage business in Washington, D. C., but broken in health and fortune he retired in 1886 and returned to Georgetown, S. C., where he died the following year.

[The fullest sketch of Rainey is that in S. D. Smith, "The Negro in Congress," a manuscript in the library of the Univ. of N. C. Other sources include: *Jour. of Negro Hist.*, Jan. 1920; W. W. Brown, *The Rising Son* (1874); J. S. Reynolds, *Reconstruction in S. C.* (1905); *Charleston Daily News*, Nov. 10, 1870; *News and Courier* (Charleston), Aug. 4, 1887.]   F. B. S.

RAINS, GABRIEL JAMES (June 4, 1803– Aug. 6, 1881), soldier, superintendent of the Torpedo Bureau, C. S. A., was born in Craven County, N. C., the son of Gabriel M. and Hester (Ambrose) Rains. He was a brother of George Washington Rains [*q.v.*] who built and operated the Confederate powder works at Augusta, Ga. Gabriel, after receiving a common-school education, graduated from West Point in 1827 and was appointed a second lieutenant, 7th Infantry. He saw service in the West until 1839 and rose to the rank of captain. From 1839 to 1842 he took active part in the Seminole War, being severely wounded and receiving brevet rank of major for gallantry. About this time, according to statements made later, he began to experiment with explosives. He served with dis-

tinction in the Mexican War, after which he engaged in recruiting, garrison, and frontier duties, taking part in another Seminole War in 1849–50 and reaching the grade of lieutenant-colonel, June 5, 1860. In the summer of 1861 he resigned from the Army of the United States and on Sept. 23 was appointed brigadier-general, C. S. A. He was assigned a brigade under Gen. D. H. Hill in the Department of the Peninsula. During the winter of 1861–62 he commanded at Yorktown and mined the nearby waters. In May 1862, when McClellan moved through the Peninsula in overwhelming force, Rains withdrew from Yorktown but arranged shells with percussion fuses in the road so that the pursuing Union cavalry detonated them and suffered casualties. He employed the same devices at the battle of Williamsburg and was accused by the Northern inspectors of mining the streets and outer defenses of Yorktown and of leaving booby-traps similar to those accredited the Germans in the World War. He himself denied leaving the booby-traps but claimed credit for the detonating devices. Considerable outcry was raised in the northern papers at these methods of making war, and his corps commander, Longstreet, forbade the use of land mines. The exploits, however, were reported to Richmond, and the whole matter of use of explosives became a question of policy for the Confederate government. The secretary of war, Randolph, ordered Rains to obey Longstreet but further declared the use of explosives in mines an approved method to be used by the Confederacy. Rains's last field service occurred a few days later at Seven Pines, where Hill commended him highly for a flank attack which was credited with saving the battle. He was then removed from Longstreet's corps and thereafter acted under the War Department.

Rains forwarded a memorial to Jefferson Davis on the subject of explosives and convinced Davis of the ethics and effectiveness of his methods. For a short time, while a policy was being formulated, he was placed in charge of the Bureau of Conscription in Richmond, but beginning May 25, 1863, he was given a series of defense missions, finally being assigned as superintendent of the Torpedo Bureau in June 1864. From them until the end of the war he arranged demolitions and mines and torpedo protection for threatened points, notably Richmond, Mobile, Charleston, and the James River. He evolved a new technique and focussed military attention upon the future possibilities of explosives. His opponents in the Confederacy, who opposed him upon ethical grounds, notably Joseph Johnston, were finally converted to his ideas. Sketches of his land mines show them to have been very ingenious devices of the percussion type, with little tin shields to protect them from rain. Perhaps his chief single exploit was in August 1864, when two of his operatives blew up two federal barges and an ammunition warehouse at City Point, Va., causing heavy casualties and a four-million-dollar loss. Following the Civil War, he lived for some years in Atlanta, then served as clerk in the United States Quartermaster Department at Charleston, S. C., from 1877 to 1880. He died in Aiken, S. C. His wife was Mary Jane McClellan, a grand-daughter of Gov. John Sevier of North Carolina, by whom he had six children.

[See: G. W. Cullum, *Biog. Reg. of the U. S. Army* (ed. 1891), vol. I; F. B. Heitman, *Hist. Reg. U. S. Army* (1890), vol. I; *War of the Rebellion: Official Records (Army)*; Zella Armstrong, "The Sevier Family," *Notable Southern Families*, vol. IV (1926); *Thirteenth Ann. Reunion, Asso. Grads. U. S. Mil. Acad.* (1882); *News and Observer* (Raleigh, N. C.), Aug. 14, 1881; *News and Courier* (Charleston, S. C.), Aug. 12, 1881.]

D. Y.

RAINS, GEORGE WASHINGTON (1817–Mar. 21, 1898), Confederate soldier, inventor, and author, was born in Craven County, N. C., the eighth child of Gabriel M. and Hester (Ambrose) Rains, and a brother of Gabriel James Rains [*q.v.*]. He attended New Bern Academy, near his home, before entering the United States Military Academy at West Point in 1838, from which institution he was graduated first in scientific studies in 1842. He was assigned to duty as a second lieutenant, Corps of Engineers, at Boston, but he transferred to the artillery and was ordered to the 4th Artillery stationed at Fort Monroe, Va. In 1844 he was detached to West Point as assistant professor of chemistry, geology, and mineralogy. At the outbreak of the Mexican War in 1846, he was ordered back to his regiment, which proceeded to Point Isabel, Tex. He was promoted first lieutenant in March 1847, was brevetted captain for gallant conduct at Contreras and Churubusco, and major for gallantry at Chapultepec. After the termination of hostilities he returned to the United States and was stationed successively at New Orleans, at Pascagoula, Miss., and in lower Florida. In 1850 he was returned to the North and was stationed in turn at Forts Hamilton, Mackinaw and Columbus, and on Governors Island. While at the last post, on Apr. 23, 1856, he was married to Frances Josephine Ramsdell. In October 1856 he resigned and went to Newburgh, N. Y., where he became president of the Washington Iron Works and of the Highland Iron Works. During 1860 and 1861 he obtained patents on several inventions he had made relating to steam engines and boilers.

In the Civil War Rains went with the Confederacy. He was commissioned major in the Corps of Artillery of the regular army on July 10, 1861, and was assigned to ordnance duties. He was promoted lieutenant-colonel on the emergency staff officers' list as of May 22, 1862, and colonel as of July 12, 1863. Immediately upon his entrance to duty in 1861 he was assigned to the procurement of gunpowder. He made a rapid tour of the South to find a suitable site for the establishment of a government manufactory and selected Augusta, Ga. He initiated the wholesale collection of nitre from limestone caves in Tennessee, Alabama, Georgia, and North Carolina, publishing a pamphlet: *Notes on Making Saltpetre from the Earth of the Caves*. From his efforts grew the Nitre and Mining Bureau of the War Department. Rains followed the manufacturing processes of the Waltham Abbey Government Gunpowder Works of England, but experience dictated sundry improvements greatly promoting the efficiency of the plant, and these improvements he patented in the Confederate States Patent Office (Patent No. 259, Oct. 25, 1864). When operations were discontinued on Apr. 18, 1865, the mills had produced two and three quarter million pounds of gunpowder.

Rains was placed in charge of all munitions operations in Augusta on Apr. 7, 1862. These included the old United States arsenal, which had been converted from a storage depot into a manufacturing armory, and three private foundries and machine works which had been taken over and enlarged for the manufacture of pistols, field artillery, ammunition, and ordnance equipment. He was also commanding officer of troops at Augusta until a general officer was sent there to defend the place against Sherman in the fall of 1864. After the collapse of the Confederate government he remained for some time in Augusta as the guest of Governor Jenkins. Here in August 1866 he was elected professor of chemistry in the Medical College of Georgia, and in the following year he was also made regent of the Academy of Richmond County (an old military school). In 1867 the Medical College conferred upon him the degree of M.D. He attained the deanship of the Medical College and served on the city board of health. In 1883 he resigned as dean but continued on the faculty of the Medical College until 1894. Retiring as professor emeritus, he returned to his wife's home near Newburgh, where he died. In addition to the pamphlet already mentioned he published *Steam Portable Engines* (1860); *Rudimentary Course of Analytical and Applied Chemistry* (1872); *Interesting Chemical Exercises in Qualitative Analysis for Ordinary Schools* (1880), and *History of the Confederate Powder Works* (1882).

[G. W. Cullum, *Biog. Reg. . . . U. S. Mil. Acad.* (ed. 1891), vol. II; *Twenty-ninth Ann. Reunion, Asso. Grads. U. S. Mil. Acad.* (1898); *War of the Rebellion, Official Records* (*Army* and *Navy*); C. S. A., *Ann. Report of the Commissioner of Patents, Jan. 26, 1865* (1865); *Army and Navy Jour.*, Apr. 2, 1898; *Chronicle and Sentinel* (Augusta, Ga.), Aug. 19, 1866; *Daily Constitutionalist* (Augusta), Dec. 19, 1867, *Daily Register* (Newburgh, N. Y.), Mar. 22, 23, 1898; official records at the U. S. arsenal, Augusta, Ga.; War Dept. records.]   W. M. R., Jr.

RÂLE, SÉBASTIEN (d. Aug. 23, 1724), Jesuit missionary, was born on Jan. 4, 1657, or Jan. 20, 1654, at Pontarlier in the former province of Franche Comté. In early life he entered the Jesuit order, his novitiate dating from 1675. From 1677 to 1684 he was an instructor at Carpentras and Nimes, and finished his studies in theology at Lyons. From the latter place he volunteered for the Canadian mission. He sailed, July 23, 1689, from La Rochelle on the same ship with the Count de Frontenac, who was returning to Canada for his second term as governor.

Râle's first experiences in New France were among the settled Indian villages near Quebec, especially those of the Abnaki and Hurons. He devoted himself to the acquisition of the Indian languages, in which he soon became adept. In 1691 he was transferred to the Illinois mission to succeed Marquette and Allouez. He made the long journey to the upper country by way of the Ottawa River, arrived too late to proceed that season to Illinois, and passed the winter at Michilimackinac. In a letter to his brother (*Jesuit Relations, post,* vol. LXVII) he gave a very good account of the customs and beliefs of the Ottawa Indians. The next spring he continued his journey to the Indian villages on the Illinois River, but in 1693 was recalled to Canada and sent to the Abnaki mission in what is now the state of Maine. The Abnaki had early come under Christian influences and the branch of the tribe that lived on the Kennebec River received Râle with joy, helped him to build a chapel, and devoutly attended services and performed the offices of the faith. The missionary was the most popular man in the village. When a kindred tribe of the Malecites visited Narantsouac (Norridgewock), his village on the Kennebec, he had the happiness of converting the whole tribe (*Jesuit Relations,* LXVII, 183–95). All the while, however, the Abnaki Indians

were sending out parties to ravage the Massachusetts frontier, killing pioneer women and children, in the war then existing between the French and British colonies.

In the interval between the Treaty of Ryswick (1697) and the outbreak of Queen Anne's War (1702), Râle endeavored to keep the Indians quiet and made a brief visit to France (1700) to collect funds for his mission. He beautified the chapel, trained a choir of boys as choristers, and made candles of the wax of the bayberry for the altar. But with the outbreak of war again, trouble began. The governor of Massachusetts came to the mouth of the Kennebec and had a council with the Abnaki, urging them to send the French Missionary away. They refused, whereupon in 1705 an English expedition made its way up the Kennebec and burned the Abnaki village and its chapel, while the missionary fled to the woods. After the Treaty of Utrecht (1713) the trouble was intensified. The British claimed sovereignty over all the region, while the governor of New France attempted to retain the allegiance of the Indians and employed the missionaries as secret political agents. Vaudreuil ordered Râle to encourage the Indians in acts of hostility against the English frontier (*Report on Canadian Archives . . . 1883,* 1884, p. 36).

In 1717 Governor Shute of Massachusetts held a council with the Abnaki, offering them an English missionary in place of the French priest. Again they refused and a state of *petite guerre* ensued, in time of peace. The English were highly incensed against Râle and, according to his own report, placed a price upon his head. In 1721 Norridgewock was again raided by the British, the missionary's Abnaki dictionary and other treasures carried off, and the chapel once more burned, but Râle was warned and escaped. In August 1724, however, he was shot down at the door of his house by a British party, and his scalp taken and carried to Boston, to "the great joy and exultation of the people of Massachusetts" (*Collections of the Massachusetts Historical Society,* 1 ser. IX, 1804, p. 209).

Râle perished, not as a martyr to the faith but as a victim of the political policy of Canada's officials, who used the missionaries as agents to maintain their hold on the Indian tribes in the district that had been ceded to the British by treaty. Râle was a very able missionary, a fine linguist, and a bold, courageous champion of the policy of the French. Had he been less successful he would have been less dangerous to the New England colonists and less hated by them. His Abnaki dictionary is in the Harvard library; it was published in 1833 in the *Memoirs of the American Academy of Arts and Sciences* (n.s., vol. I). His prayers are yet in use among the Indians of Maine. The bell of his chapel and other relics are in the Maine Historical Society. A monument to his memory was erected at Norridgewock in 1833 by Bishop Fenwick of Boston.

[R. G. Thwaites, editor, *The Jesuit Relations,* vols. LXVI and LXVII (1900), contain Râle's own letters on his mission. J. P. Baxter, *Pioneers of New France in New England* (1894) deals at length with Râle's activities and adds documents. E. B. O'Callaghan, *Docs. Rel. to the Col. Hist. of the State of N. Y.,* vols. IX, X (1855–58), contain the translations of the letters of the governor of Canada. See also *Report on Canadian Archives ... 1883* (1884), p. 36; *Mass. Hist. Soc. Colls.,* 2 ser. VIII (1819), 245–49; *Me. Hist. Soc. Colls.,* 1 ser. I (1831), 2 ser. IX (1898); *New-Eng. Hist. and Geneal. Reg.,* Apr. 1894, pp. 186–88; J. G. Shea, *The Cath. Church in Colonial Days* (1886), *passim*; T. J. Campbell, *Pioneer Priests of North America,* III (1911), 265–308; Convers Francis, "Life of Sebastien Râle," in Jared Sparks, *The Lib. of Am. Biog.,* 2 ser. VII (1845).]
                                                    L. P. K.

RALPH, JAMES (*c.* 1695–Jan. 24, 1762), literary and political writer, was born, probably in the present New Jersey, and died in Chiswick, England. He married Rebekah Ogden of Elizabethtown and by her had one daughter, Mary, born in March 1724. While living in Philadelphia, he became acquainted with Benjamin Franklin, whom he accompanied to London in December 1724, deserting his family because of a quarrel with his wife's parents. Unable for some months to secure literary work in London, Ralph lived upon Franklin's generosity until he secured employment as a teacher in Berkshire, where he assumed Franklin's name. Franklin held himself responsible for unsettling Ralph's religious beliefs, and to him he dedicated his sceptical *Dissertation Upon Liberty and Necessity, Pleasure and Pain,* in 1725. In his *Autobiography* Franklin blames himself for disrupting their friendship, by unwelcome attentions to Ralph's mistress, which were "repulsed with a proper degree of resentment." Turning to poetry in 1727, Ralph wrote *The Tempest* and *Night,* blank-verse poems, imitative of Thomson's *Winter,* which had just appeared. The poems have occasional American references. *Sawney,* an attack on Pope, inspired by the first edition of *The Dunciad,* ended Ralph's poetic career, for in the next edition Pope inserted the fatal couplet:

Silence, ye Wolves! while Ralph to Cynthia howls,
And makes Night hideous—Answer him ye Owls.

Ralph next tried revising old plays, which, however, had but short runs. His original ballad-opera, *The Fashionable Lady* (1730), had a fair success, and is further noteworthy as the first play by an American to be produced on the London stage; John Crowne, Harvard's first playwright, had been English-born. In 1728 Ralph had written *The Touchstone,* a burlesque guide to the city's amusements; it contained suggestions for plays based upon British folk-lore, which Henry Fielding utilized in *Tom Thumb. A Tragedy* (1730). The two men were friends, and in 1735 Ralph was Fielding's assistant in the management of the Little Theatre in Haymarket, a position he filled until the Licensing Act of 1737 ended Fielding's dramatic career. Ralph now became a contributor to the *Prompter* and the *Universal Spectator,* but in 1739 joined Fielding as assistant editor of the *Champion* and devoted his talents to scathing attacks upon Sir Robert Walpole.

Probably after Walpole's fall in 1742, Ralph entered the employ of George Bubb Dodington, writing several long political pamphlets of considerable effectiveness, as well as editing *Old England* and *The Remembrancer,* in the interests of Frederick, the Prince of Wales, Dodington's leader of the moment. The only one of these politically inspired works of interest now is *The History of England* (2 vols., 1744–46), from the Restoration through the reign of William III. It was written, in part, to refute Burnet and Oldmixon, but despite its partisan purpose is today a valuable compilation for the student of Restoration and Revolutionary England. Ralph had planned the history to cover the reigns of Anne and George I, but did not finish it. He was also employed by both Frederick and Dodington as a sort of political liaison officer. With the death of Frederick in 1751, Ralph could not, like his patron Dodington, make peace with the ministry, and in 1753 launched a new opposition weekly, the *Protester,* in the service of the Duke of Bedford. The paper ran less than half a year, for, through the good offices of David Garrick, Ralph was granted a pension of £300 per year by the Pelham administration for renouncing political writing. Ralph's active career was ended, but his letters to the Duke of Newcastle, always written when a pension payment was due, show keen political interest; one in particular, Jan. 31, 1756, urged the extension of the stamp tax to the American colonies, to lessen the burden on the mother country. In 1756 Ralph joined the staff of the *Monthly Review* as political and historical critic but carefully avoided discussing anything which might be unpleasing to the ministry. In 1759 Franklin, now on good terms with Ralph, secured his assistance in preparing for the press *An Historical Review of the Constitution and*

Government of Pennsylvania. Franklin, as agent of the Assembly, was seeking relief from the abuses of the colonial proprietors. It is highly probable that Ralph, an old hand at the business, actually did considerable work on the text.

Ralph had experienced all the hardships of Grub Street in a period of declining private patronage; unsuccessful as poet and dramatist, for a time a bookseller's hack, he finally found his metier as a political writer and attained a state of comparative ease. In *The Case of Authors by Profession* (1758) he ably surveyed the unhappy lot of the hack writer and showed him to be entirely at the mercy of the bookseller, theatre manager, or party minister. *The Case* is an acute defense of the professional writer written when such defense was sorely needed, for the era of patronage of writers by the public was still many years in the future. Ralph has been represented as being completely venal; it is undeniable that he wrote for the side which paid the most. There is no evidence, however, that once the bargain was struck, he was false to his employer; once bought, he stayed bought. Judged by the standards of his own day, he was an able political writer; and was certainly the first American to succeed in eighteenth-century Grub Street.

[References include: W. O. Wheeler, *The Ogden Family in America* (1907); Benjamin Franklin, *Autobiography* (1793); W. L. Cross, *Hist. of Henry Fielding* (3 vols., 1908); Walter Graham, *English Literary Periodicals* (1930); Newcastle additional MSS., Nos. 32,737 to 32,923, in the British Museum; Thos. Davies, *Life of Garrick* (2 vols., 1780); and *The Diary of the Late Geo. Bubb Dodington* (1784), ed. by H. P. Wyndham. The *Dict. Nat. Biog.* contains a full account of Ralph's English career, which it is now possible to supplement.]

R. W. K.

RALPH, JULIAN (May 27, 1853–Jan. 20, 1903), journalist, was born in New York City, the son of Dr. Joseph Edward and Salina (Mahoney) Ralph. At the age of fifteen he became a printer's apprentice in the office of the Red Bank, N. J., *Standard.* After serving as a reporter on that paper, he attempted to publish a rival newspaper in Red Bank, but the venture failed after a short trial. He then went to Webster, Mass., as editor of the *Times.* On returning to New York in 1872 he was a reporter on the *World* and later on the *Daily Graphic,* the first illustrated daily paper in the United States, established in 1873. His reports of the trial of Henry Ward Beecher in 1875 attracted the attention of Charles A. Dana of the New York *Sun,* who offered him a position as reporter after the trial was over. For the next twenty years Ralph was one of Dana's staff of brilliant writers who helped to make the *Sun* "the newspaper

man's newspaper." Because of his vivid and picturesque style as a descriptive writer, it was said of him that he "could write five thousand words about a cobblestone." On the occasion of the funeral of General Grant in 1885, he wrote with a pencil in seven hours an eleven-thousand-word account of the obsequies that filled the front page of the *Sun.* He was also credited with an uncanny sixth sense that enabled him to anticipate the breaking of an unexpected piece of important news. His skill as a humorist was shown in his "German Barber" dialect sketches which were a weekly feature of the *Sun,* and which were published in book form as *The Sun's German Barber* (1883). While still a member of the *Sun* staff, he was commissioned by *Harper's Magazine* to travel through the United States and Canada in the years 1891–93 and to write articles for that publication. These articles were brought together in book form under the titles *On Canada's Frontier* (1892), *Our Great West* (1893), and *Chicago and the World's Fair* (1893). During the years 1894–97 he traveled through the Far East and Russia and wrote magazine articles based on his observations and experiences. During the Chinese-Japanese War he served as a newspaper correspondent.

When in 1895 William Randolph Hearst bought the *New York Journal* and built up a staff of outstanding newspaper men taken from New York newspapers, he engaged Ralph as his London correspondent. After war broke out between Greece and Turkey in the spring of 1897, Ralph went to the front for the *Journal* and followed Osman Pasha in the campaign in Thessaly. He reported the Diamond Jubilee of Queen Victoria and the coronation of the Czar of Russia for the same paper. Later he became London correspondent for the *New York Herald* and *Brooklyn Eagle.* During the Boer War he represented the London *Daily Mail,* accompanying Lord Roberts in the victorious march to Blomfontein. In the spring of 1900, Ralph with several English war correspondents issued a daily paper at Blomfontein for the British Army, called the *Friend,* to which Rudyard Kipling and Dr. A. Conan Doyle, both of whom were in South Africa, contributed poems and articles. Ralph on his return to the United States published an account of this novel undertaking, together with the best contributions, under the title, *War's Brighter Side; The Story of "The Friend" Newspaper* (1901). In 1902 he was appointed Eastern representative of the St. Louis World's Fair. He had been elected a member of the Royal Geographical Society in 1898.

Ralph was married, in 1876, to Isabella Mount of New Jersey. In addition to the books mentioned, his published works include: *Along the Bowstring* (1891), *Dixie, or Southern Scenes and Sketches* (1895), *People We Pass; Stories of Life among the Masses of New York City* (1896), *Alone in China* (1897), *An Angel in a Web* (1899), *A Prince of Georgia and Other Tales* (1899), *Towards Pretoria* (1900), *At Pretoria,* the American edition of which was called *An American with Lord Roberts* (1901), *The Millionairess* (1902), and *The Making of a Journalist* (1903).

[Sources include: Frank M. O'Brien, *The Story of the Sun* (1918); *Who's Who in America,* 1901–02; files of the N. Y. *Sun,* and of the *N. Y. Jour.*]

W. G. B.

RALSTON, SAMUEL MOFFETT (Dec. 1, 1857–Oct. 14, 1925), United States senator, governor of Indiana, lawyer, one of eight children of Sarah (Scott) Ralston and John Ralston, was born on a farm near New Cumberland, Tuscarawas County, Ohio. A Scotch paternal great-grandfather, Andrew R. Ralston, fought in the American Revolution. His son, David Ralston, moved westward to Ohio and engaged in farming. The third American Ralston, John, father of Samuel, sold his ancestral acres in Ohio, moved to Owen County, Ind., where he purchased a four-hundred-acre stock farm, lost the property in the panic of 1873, and thereafter mined coal. On the maternal side, Ralston descended from Alexander Scott, an eighteenth-century Irish immigrant. Endowed with extraordinary vitality and ambition young Ralston farmed, mined, assisted a butcher, and helped support his parents and in addition managed to complete common school, attend Valparaiso Normal School, and finally at the age of twenty-six receive a diploma from the Central Indiana Normal School. He later collected a varied library and spent much time in general reading. After seven years of teaching he decided to practise law. Poverty limited his preparation to a single year's reading in a law office. After admission to the bar in 1886 he entered practice in Lebanon, Ind., where for more than a quarter of a century he became increasingly prominent as a vigorous member of the bar, a Presbyterian, and a Democrat. On Dec. 26, 1881, he married Mary Josephine Backous. She died within a year, and on Dec. 30, 1889, he was married to Jennie Craven, the mother of his two sons and one daughter.

In 1888 Ralston was defeated for the state Senate and in 1896 and 1898 he was unsuccessful Democratic nominee for secretary of state.

In 1908 he sought the Democratic nomination for governor of Indiana but, after a convention deadlock, withdrew and supported Thomas R. Marshall [*q.v.*] who received the nomination and election. Upon the nomination of Marshall as vice-president in 1912 the Democrats nominated Ralston for governor by acclamation and elected him by the largest plurality ever given a governor of Indiana up to that time. As governor from 1913 to 1917 he labored quite effectively for economical government, the regulation of lobbying, good roads, conservation, adequate state institutions, banking, labor, and utilities legislation, and greater centralization. He resumed the practice of law in Indianapolis in 1917. In 1922 he easily won the Democratic nomination for the United States Senate and defeated Albert J. Beveridge [*q.v.*] by approximately thirty thousand votes. A Democratic senator during a Republican administration, handicapped by illness, and with committee assignments of only fair importance, he spoke at length only once in the Senate—on federal taxation (*Congressional Record,* 68th Cong., 1 Sess., pp. 2355–61). He exerted himself, however, for farm relief, a soldiers' bonus, tax reduction, and the printing of territorial papers in the national archives, and against the cession of the Isle of Pines to Cuba. When the Democratic national convention in 1924 gave him 196½ votes for president on the ninety-third ballot, Thomas Taggart, who had left no stone unturned in an attempt to make him the nominee, telegraphed Ralston that he would be nominated. To the keen disappointment of Taggart, Ralston replied with a telegram ordering his name withdrawn. More than six feet in height and approximately three hundred pounds in weight, Ralston was thought to resemble Presidents Cleveland and Taft. He was an earnest, modest man, conservative yet courageous, who regarded public office seriously and made few enemies.

[Sources include: J. B. Stoll, *Hist. of the Ind. Democracy, 1816–1916* (1917); J. P. Dunn, *Ind. and Indianans* (1919), vol. III; Logan Esarey, *A Hist. of Ind.,* vol. II (1918); Chas. Roll, *Indiana* (1931), vol. III; *Who's Who in America,* 1924–25; *Indianapolis News, Indianapolis Times, Indianapolis Star,* Oct. 15, 1925; information as to certain facts from Ralston's son, Julian C. Ralston.]   H. Z.

RALSTON, WILLIAM CHAPMAN (June 12, 1826–Aug. 27, 1875), banker, steamship owner, capitalist, was born in Wellsville, Ohio, the son of Robert and Mary (Chapman) Ralston. His formal education did not extend beyond the common schools. Dissatisfied with economic conditions in Ohio in his father's sawmill, he became a clerk on a Mississippi River steamboat in 1842. His efficiency and industry attracted favorable attention, and in 1850 he was appointed agent at Panama City of the steamship company of Garrison and Morgan. In 1854 he removed to San Francisco, his demonstrated ability having won him a partnership in the enterprise. He quickly realized the importance of San Francisco as a financial and trading center and was instrumental in the establishment in 1856 of the banking firm of Garrison, Morgan, Fretz, and Ralston, of which he was the directing force. During the panic of 1857 his courage and decision won him the complete confidence of the business and commercial interests of the city. The institution was successfully managed and was regarded as reliable and conservative in policy. In 1864 Ralston and D. O. Mills organized the Bank of California, which soon became the leading financial institution of the Far West. Ralston brought to the bank his extensive business connections and the philosophy of the speculative capitalist. His quick and often sagacious decisions, his audacity, and his impetuosity were frequently mistaken for financial genius. As cashier, however, he was checked and guided by his directors. The bank symbolized to the public mind the wise and beneficent use of its resources to advance the progress of the city and state, and "the farmer, the mechanic, the miner, and the capitalist found in the Bank of California a friend in need" (Lloyd, *post,* p. 73). In 1872 he became president of the institution, a position easily demanding his exclusive attention, but only an item in the multiplicity of his affairs. Included in his vast plans of imperial expansion and control were railroads, steamship lines, woolen and silk mills, irrigation projects, hotels, theatres, and important mining interests. He used the resources of the bank to aid these enterprises, some of an extremely dubious character, in which he was personally interested.

By 1874 Ralston was completely enmeshed in a complicated net-work of financial and political interests. The officers of the bank and the public seemed to have unbounded faith in him. He lived in almost oriental splendor and extravagance, spending more than he earned, dispensing lavish hospitality in a lavish period, and donating generous amounts of money to civic and charitable causes of every sort. He liked to regard himself as a benevolent despot, the leader in the development of California. It seems probable that he promoted unwarranted speculative schemes with the bank's funds, and he doubtless made many injudicious and unauthorized loans on inflated values. It is alleged that by false statements he withheld both from direc-

tors and from examiners the true condition of affairs. In many of his projects political assistance was essential, and he was active for years in California and in Nevada politics, seeking franchises, concessions, and favors. Accusations were frequently made that he had attempted corruptly to influence public officials. During the middle seventies he became increasingly secretive and dogmatic while his speculations in real estate and in mines were conducted on a colossal scale. The bank was the exclusive agent of all business relating to the Comstock Lode and to the milling of the ores, while his personal holdings in this mine gave him a profit of four million dollars. His mills and railroads also yielded large dividends, but the enormous profits were absorbed by recurring losses sustained in new speculations in San Francisco. He endeavored to regain financial security by the purchase in 1875, with associates, of additional Nevada mines, imagined bonanzas. The market broke, however, with a loss of millions. Meanwhile, the bank, which had survived the panic of 1873, was in a desperate struggle for existence. Dividends were paid with depositors' funds, the directors being deceived by Ralston. In August 1875 the two leading newspapers of the city attacked him and made grave charges concerning the management and condition of the bank. The collapse soon came when it suspended payment to depositors. The bewildered directors closed its doors and requested his resignation on Aug. 27. He was drowned that day under painful and peculiar circumstances. Investigations revealed that he owed the bank several million dollars. His wife, Elizabeth Fry, whom he married on May 20, 1858, and four children survived him.

[*Memorial of Wm. C. Ralston* (1875) ; C. G. Tilton, "Life of Wm. C. Ralston" (1925), in manuscript ; J. S. Hittell, *A Hist. of the City of San Francisco* (1878) ; H. H. Bancroft, *Hist. of Cal.,* vol. VII (1890) ; B. E. Lloyd, *Lights and Shades in San Francisco* (1876) ; B. C. Wright, *Banking in Cal.* (1910) ; I. B. Cross, *Financing an Empire: Hist. of Banking in Cal.* (1927), vols. I and III ; Herbert Asbury, "The Great Diamond Swindle," *Am. Mercury,* May 1932; San Francisco *Daily Morning Call* and *Daily Evening Bull.* for August 1875.]

T. S. B.

RAMAGE, JOHN (*c.* 1748–Oct. 24, 1802), miniature painter, is believed to have been born in Dublin and to have entered the school of the Dublin Society of Art in 1763. He is first heard of in America as in Halifax in 1772, through the fact that in the court records there are listed two suits brought against him for trifling amounts. He apparently moved from one place to another, and as early as 1775 is mentioned as a practising goldsmith and miniature painter in Boston. At the outbreak of the Revolution, an ardent Loyalist, he received a commission as second lieutenant in "The Loyal Irish Volunteers," a regiment formed among the "Irish merchants residing in town and their adherents" for its defense. On Mar. 8, 1776, he married Maria Victoria Ball, who did not accompany him when he embarked nine days later for Halifax upon the evacuation of Boston by the British. According to a letter from the Rev. Mather Byles, Jr., shortly after his arrival in Halifax, Ramage married a Mrs. Taylor, and Maria Ball Ramage, following him, obtained a divorce. Ramage and his second wife settled in New York, then occupied by the British, probably sometime in 1777.

Dunlap records that in 1777, established in William Street, Ramage "continued to paint all the military heroes or beaux of the Garrison, and all the belles of the place," a statement that is borne out by his existing miniatures. In 1780 he was commissioned a lieutenant in Company 7 of the city militia by Gen. James Pattison, and after the final evacuation of that city he remained in New York and became an influential and respected citizen. Dunlap also gives a word picture of the man himself, saying: "Ramage was a handsome man of the middle size. . . . He dressed fashionably, and according to the time, beauishly" (post, I, p. 268). On Oct. 3, 1789, Washington wrote in his diary: "Sat for Mr. Rammage [sic] near two hours today, who was drawing a miniature Picture of me for Mrs. Washington." This miniature depicts the President in uniform, three-quarters to left, with the Order of the Cincinnati hanging from the left lapel of his coat. Ramage also painted memorial and allegorical miniatures, did "hair work," and drew in pastel, "the size of life." C. H. Hart states that he also made the beautiful cases which hold his miniatures, and this is probably so in part, as his work desk, with the tools in place, is still in the possession of his kin; but the *Royal Gazette* of Oct. 18, 1780, carries his advertisement to the effect that he had received "by the last vessels from England a large assortment of Ivory Chrystals and Cases, with every other thing necessary in his branch of business." On Jan. 29, 1787, Ramage married Catharine Collins, a daughter of John Collins, a New York merchant.

In 1794, having become involved in debt which, according to the family tradition, arose through indorsing the notes of a friend, he left New York and settled in Montreal, where he spent the remainder of his life. Unable to extricate himself from his difficulties, and borne down by persistent ill health, he died and was buried in the cemetery of Christ Church. The list of his sitters—including such well-known names as that of the President, Mrs. Washington, and at least one of her children, members of the Van Cortlandt, Gerry, Pintard, Ludlow, McComb, Rutgers, and Van Rensselaer families—tends to prove that he was the leading miniature painter in New York from 1777 to 1794. His miniatures are small in size, carefully and accurately painted in the line manner, delicate in color, and executed with scrupulous care. The gold cases are exquisitely fashioned and the ivory itself is held in place usually by a gold scalloped edge. The recent discovery and publication (*A Sketch of the Life of John Ramage, post*) of eleven letters written by John Ramage to his wife during his residence in Montreal after 1794, together with his commissions and other papers relative to his career, have added much to contemporary knowledge of the painter.

[Wm. Dunlap, *A Hist. of the Rise and Progress of the Arts of Design in the U. S.* (ed. 1918), vol. I; J. H. Morgan, *A Sketch of the Life of John Ramage, Miniature Painter* (1930) and "Memento Mori, Mourning Rings, Memorial Miniatures and Hair Devices," *Antiques*, Mar. 1930; F. F. Sherman, *John Ramage* (1929); W. G. Strickland, *Dict. of Irish Artists* (1913); H. S. Stabler, "Two Unpublished Portraits of Washington," *Century*, Feb. 1894; C. H. Hart, "Original Portraits of Washington," *Century*, May 1890.]   J. H. M.

RAMBAUT, MARY LUCINDA BONNEY (June 8, 1816–July 24, 1900), educator and reformer, was born at Hamilton, N. Y., the daughter of Benjamin and Lucinda (Wilder) Bonney and the descendant of Thomas Bonney who emigrated from Sandwich, England, in 1634 and settled in Duxbury, Mass. Her grandfathers, Benjamin Bonney and Abel Wilder, both of Chesterfield, Mass., fought in the Revolutionary War. Her father took part in the War of 1812 and later became a colonel of the 165th Regiment of the New York state militia. After graduating in 1835 from the Troy Female Seminary, she taught in Jersey City, New York City, De Ruyter, N. Y., Troy Female Seminary, Beaufort and Robertville, S. C., Providence, R. I., and Miss Phelps's school in Philadelphia. In 1850 she established the Chestnut Street Female Seminary of Philadelphia and in 1883 moved the school to Ogontz, Pa., and changed its name to the Ogontz School for Young Ladies. In 1887 she retired from active management of the school.

Her energies were not confined to the classroom but extended to problems of the day. When the growing consciousness of the facts of white invasion of Indian lands, the severity with which the army quelled the Indians in such cases as

Chivington's massacre, and the entire disregard of Indian rights on the Black Hills' reservation aroused in the eastern states a reform movement in behalf of the Indians, she bore an active part. Indignant over the government's injustice to the Indians, she instigated a protest in a petition which she took to the White House on Feb. 14, 1880. With Mrs. Amelia Stone Quinton she helped form the Women's National Indian Association with the purpose of stirring public opinion and legislative action in favor of the Indians. She was the first president of the organization and contributed liberally to its cause. The measures sought were partly realized in the Dawes Act of 1887, which provided for Indian ownership of land in severalty and for Indian attainment of citizenship with full personal, property, and political rights. The association also had an educational program for Indians that consisted of missions, libraries, schools, and loan funds. Interested in missionary work, she helped to found the Women's Union Missionary Society. In June 1888 she went to the world's missionary convention in London. She was married to a fellow-delegate, Thomas Rambaut, a Baptist minister and reformer, formerly president of William Jewell College at Liberty, Mo. They went to live in Hamilton, N. Y., but their companionship was of short duration as he died in October 1890. She continued to live in Hamilton with her brother, Benjamin Franklin Bonney, until her death ten years later.

[*Public Ledger* (Philadelphia), July 25, 1900; *Ogontz Mosaic*, Oct. 1900; *Emma Willard and her Pupils* (copr. 1898); C. L. Bonney, *The Bonney Family*, 2nd ed. (1898); *The Women's Indian Assoc. Report*, Oct. 27, 1883, Dec. 1900.]   E. M. G.

RAMÉE, JOSEPH JACQUES (Apr. 18, 1764–May 18, 1842), architect and landscape architect, was born at Charlemont (Ardennes), France. Precociously interested in architecture, he was made inspector of buildings at the court of the Count of Artois when he was only sixteen. Indicted as a suspect by a Revolutionary court in 1792, he fled to the army of Dumouriez, where he served as a major. In 1794 he went to northeast Germany, and spent the years 1794–1811 there and in Denmark as an architect and landscape designer. A plan for an estate at Friedrichstal, Copenhagen, dated 1804, is published in his book, *Parcs et jardins*; he was the architect of the Hamburg Bourse, and in Denmark designed the château of Sophienholm, and with his compatriot, P. Lesueur, directed the decoration of the Eriksen Palace (Reau, *post*).

In 1811 he came to America, probably first to New York; in 1813 and 1814 Philadelphia directories show that he was resident there. The papers of Benjamin Henry Latrobe [*q.v.*] indicate that in 1816 Ramée was in Baltimore, the guest of Dennis A. Smith, whose great estate, "Calverton," he designed. In that year he was unsuccessful in the attempt to be architect of the Baltimore Exchange, despite Smith's enthusiastic backing, and in the same year he returned to Europe. He worked in Belgium and Germany, settled in Paris in 1823, and died nineteen years later at Beaurains, near Noyon. He was married, and his son Daniel, later a well-known writer on Gothic architecture, was with his father in America. Some time after Ramée returned to France he published a collection of his designs. This book is called by the French biographers *Jardins irréguliers et maisons de campagne*, but a volume in the possession of C. W. Leavitt & Company, New York, bears the title *Parcs et jardins, composées et executées dans differens countrées de l'Europe et des États Unis d'Amérique, par Joseph Ramée, architecte* (Paris, no date).

Ramée's most important American work was the layout and the first buildings for Union College, Schenectady, N. Y. The original plan is in the college library. The scheme is truly monumental: two long buildings flanking a great semicircular court of honor, with a rotunda in the center. Unfortunately this central portion was not built until the late nineteenth century, when it was carried out in an inharmonious style, but the two flanking buildings, built 1813–20, are from Ramée's designs. They are distinguished by delicacy, simplicity, and classic dignity. Union thus became the first college in the country to be built from an architect's carefully studied and composed plan. At about the same time (1812–13) Ramée designed the estate of Miss Catherine Duane at Duanesburgh, and possibly designed the house (erected 1812) as well. His original plan in water color for the Duane place is in the possession of Mr. George W. Featherstonhaugh, of Duanesburgh; it is dated 1813. Part at least of the ambitious scheme was carried out. The triumphal arch scheme which Ramée submitted for the competition for the Washington Monument in Baltimore is in the historical museum (Peale's Museum) of that city. Besides these projects, his *Parcs et jardins* shows a plan of an estate on "Rapide Long Island" in the St. Lawrence, now known as Ogden Island, opposite Waddington, N. Y. It has been stated (*e.g.*, Hough, *post*, p. 13), that Ramée was employed by the federal government in planning "fortifications and public works," and, by French writers, that he laid out the plan of several cities in the state of New York, but no further evidence of either of these activities has come to light. In all his gardens Ramée followed the naturalistic style that was then supplanting the earlier formality. As an architect, he seems to have been unusually adaptable; the Union buildings are surprisingly "American" in spirit, and the central rotunda shown on the early drawings is a remarkable precursor of the Jefferson rotunda at the University of Virginia.

[*Nouvelle Biographie Générale* (Paris, 1866); P. Larouse, *Grand Dictionnaire Universel du XIXe Siècle Français* (Paris, 1864–76); Montgomery Schuyler, "The Architecture of American Colleges," *Arch. Record*, Dec. 1911; Richard Schermerhorn, Jr., "Early American Landscape Architecture," *Arch. Rev.* (N. Y.), Apr. 1921; *Union College Alumni Monthly*, Mar. 1929, containing a reproduction of an old birdseye view showing Ramée's original scheme complete, and an editorial note; *Ibid.*, Dec. 1932, listing some thirty drawings recently discovered and reproducing an elevation of the proposed chapel; F. B. Hough, *Hist. Sketch of Union College* (1876); Louis Reau, *L'Art Français aux États-Unis* (1926); material kindly furnished by Fiske Kimball, by Charles Fickus, Acting Librarian, Md. Hist. Soc., by D. Richard Weeks, Asst. Librarian of the Graduate Council of Union College, by Richard Schermerhorn, Jr., and by F. C. Latrobe; H. A. Larrabee, *Joseph Jacques Ramée and America's First Unified College Plan* (Franco-Am. Pamphlet Ser., no. 1, 1934.]   T. F. H.

RAMSAY, ALEXANDER (1754?–Nov. 24, 1824), anatomist, was born "to ease and competence" in, or near, Edinburgh, Scotland (Bradley, *post*, p. 164). From an early age he devoted himself to the sciences, especially anatomy, and in due time, after studying under the masters of the day, William Cumberland Cruikshank and his pupil, Matthew Baillie, of the Hunterian school in London, and under Alexander Monro, the second, in Edinburgh, he returned to his native city about 1790, where he began independent teaching and founded an anatomical society. He had considerable success and established a museum, lecture theatre, and a dissecting-room, where he stated that "fifty subjects a year were dissected in the highest style" (*Ibid.*, p. 166). Although popular as a teacher, he was constantly at odds with his contemporaries. "I acknowledge only two superiors as anatomists—God Almighty and John Hunter," he once said, a remark which could not have endeared him to the all-powerful Monro. For many years, it was his dream to emigrate to America, and in 1801, after disposing of his property, and with only a letter to a clergyman in his pocket, he sailed,—a solitary, embittered, but highly learned man.

He found his way to Fryeburg, Me., "the American wilderness" he had contemplated, and there built an institute of anatomy in accord with his own ideas. The school, as might be expected, was never a success, and, although Ramsay was received in the United States with a certain amount of cordiality in academic circles, his uncivil temper soon alienated his new friends. Nathan Smith [*q.v.*], recognizing his ability as an anatomist and considering him the best in the United States, secured him for a course of lectures at the Dartmouth Medical School in 1808. For about eight years Ramsay lectured in neighboring states, practised medicine, unsuccessfully sought funds from state legislatures for his "institute," and worked on his atlas of anatomy. His lectures were ill-attended and, after a period in New York, he went back to Europe, where he remained from 1810 to 1816. There, too, he was a failure as a popular lecturer, in spite of his powerful friends and patrons, Matthew Baillie, Sir Joseph Banks, then the president of the Royal Society, and the Duke of Sussex. At this time he published the first part of his book, *Anatomy of the Heart, Cranium, and Brain*, the plates of which he had drawn and engraved himself at Fryeburg. Although it was projected in five volumes, only the sections on the brain and heart were ever issued, the first edition in 1812 and a second in 1813. The work is one of considerable beauty and accuracy. On his return to America he became an itinerant lecturer on anatomy and natural philosophy, traveling throughout eastern Canada, New England, New York, and even to Charleston, S. C.

Bradley describes Ramsay as "a sort of monstrous compound of personal deformity, immense learning, . . . ferocious insolence and ill-temper, and inordinate vanity" (*Transactions Maine Medical Association, post*, p. 161). He quarreled with his colleagues, one after another, both in Scotland and America. His work, although admired by his contemporaries, was, necessarily, done alone. He was granted an honorary M.D. degree by the University of St. Andrews in 1805, and his few carefully written papers were accepted by the leading medical journals. His book was reasonably well received, but no one, with the possible exception of Nathan Smith, could tolerate the man for more than a short time. His best work, aside from his teaching of anatomy, was accomplished during the yellow-fever epidemic in New York in 1803, when he abolished blood-letting and furnished a liberal diet in opposition to the usual practice of the day. He died at Parsonsfield, Me., while giving a course of lectures, and was buried in Fryeburg.

[Original drawings and notes, Boston Medic. Lib.; G. P. Bradley, biog. sketch in *Trans. Me. Medic. Asso.*,

1883–1885, vol. VIII (1885); J. A. Spalding, biog. sketch in H. A. Kelly and W. L. Burrage, *Am. Medic. Biog.* (1920), and *Dr. Lyman Spalding* (1916); Emily A. Smith, *The Life and Letters of Nathan Smith* (1914); *Records N. H. Medic. Soc., 1791–1854* (1911); *Eastern Argus* (Portland, Me.), Dec. 7, 1824.]

H. R. V.

RAMSAY, DAVID (Apr. 2, 1749–May 8, 1815), physician, historian, the son of James and Jane (Montgomery) Ramsay, was born in Drumore Township, Lancaster County, Pa. Nathaniel Ramsay [*q.v.*] was his brother. David graduated from the College of New Jersey in 1765, tutored in a Maryland family for two years, then began the study of medicine. After receiving his degree from the College of Pennsylvania in 1772, he practised a year in Maryland and in 1773 went to Charleston. He bore a letter from his preceptor and friend, Dr. Benjamin Rush, who declared that he was "far superior to any person we ever graduated at our college." He appears to have been successful in his practice from the start, but politics immediately began to absorb much of his abundant energy. From 1776 to the end of the war he represented Charleston in the legislature. In August 1780 he was, with thirty-two other leaders, exiled to St. Augustine. On his release a year later he was returned to the House of Representatives. During most of 1782 and 1785, however, he was a delegate in the Continental Congress. He was regular in attendance and supported the moves for strengthening the powers of the central government. From 1784 to 1790 he served in the state House of Representatives. In 1792, 1794, and 1796 he was elected to the state Senate, and for the three terms was president of that body. He then retired from political life. In the legislature he opposed the issuing of paper money, the easing of the obligations of debtors, the importation of slaves, and the weakening of the tidewater control of the legislature. Throughout this period he appears as a moderate Federalist, representative of the coast country group, a man of ability, integrity, and influence.

Meanwhile he was busy in speculation and investment, which, he fondly hoped, would be of great advantage to the public and to himself, but "want of judgment in the affairs of the world was the weak point of his character." Sales of lands, complicated mortgages and agreements came in bewildering confusion, both before and after his bankruptcy in 1798, and he who a few years before had steadily opposed leniency to debtors was now fain to compound a debt by pledging his professional services for a period of years to sundry tradesmen of Charleston. How faithfully he followed Dr. Rush in his abuse of the human body by incessant bleeding and administering of calomel and jalap are fairly indicated by his *Eulogium upon Benjamin Rush, M.D.* (1813). But his permanent contribution to medicine was not inconsiderable. His *Review of the Improvements, Progress and State of Medicine in the XVIIIth Century,* a scholarly treatise, was one of several medical studies (see Carnes Weeks, "David Ramsay," in *Annals of Medical History,* September 1929).

It is as historian, however, that Ramsay is best known. A ready writer and a careful observer, of encyclopedic memory and intense patriotism, he early set himself to the work for which his gifts and position fitted him. His *History of the Revolution of South Carolina* (2 vols., 1785) was in considerable part copied from the *Annual Register,* and in such manner as to justify the charge of plagiarism, but a great part consisted of the conclusions of a patriotic but judicious eye-witness, and of South Carolina papers published then for the first time. He proceeded next to write a *History of the American Revolution* (2 vols., 1789), but as he moved farther from South Carolina he leaned more heavily upon the *Register.* The first volume of his *History of South Carolina* (2 vols., 1809) was in part taken from Alexander Hewat [*q.v.*], and in part from his own preceding work, but the second, comprising a survey of South Carolina life, is still of great value. His *Life of George Washington* (1807) was a mere political and military narrative, but was very popular. The *History of the United States* (3 vols., 1816–17) was part of a far more ambitious project which was to contain the "quintessence" of other histories. The larger work, *Universal History Americanized,* was published in nine volumes in 1819, with the *History of the United States* forming Volumes X to XII. The author did not live to see his grand design in print, for on May 6, 1815, he was shot by a maniac and died two days later. Ramsay was three times married: in February 1775 to Sabina Ellis, daughter of a Charleston merchant, who died the next year; in 1783 to Frances Witherspoon, a daughter of John Witherspoon [*q.v.*], who died in 1784, and on Jan. 23, 1787, to Martha, daughter of Henry Laurens [*q.v.*], who died June 10, 1811. The following year he published *Memoirs of the Life of Martha Laurens Ramsay.* Ramsay himself, saddened but not soured by affliction and reverses, remained to the end the pious, benevolent, and unwearied public servant.

[A sketch by R. Y. Hayne was published in the *Analectic Magazine* for Sept. 1815, and prefixed to the *Hist. of the U. S.* and *Universal Hist.* See also for Ramsay's birth and early training articles by W. U.

Hensel and H. F. Eshleman, in *Papers read before the Lancaster County Hist. Soc.*, Nov. 2, 1906, and Sept. 17, 1921. For his finances see Inventory Book E, 1809–19, pp. 283–84, Charleston Court House; Register Mesne Conveyances, Charleston, especially R5, 300, R6, 372, S6, 202, 208, T6, 252; Miscellaneous Records (Hist. Commission, Columbia), 3K, 20, 3O, 48–49, 161–64, 196, 213, 4H, 310–12. Other sources include: O. G. Libby, "Ramsay as a Plagiarist," *Am. Hist. Rev.*, July 1902; A. S. Salley, Jr., *Marriage Notices in the S. C. Gazette and Its Successors (1732–1801)* (1902); V. L. Collins, *President Witherspoon: A Biog.* (2 vols., 1925); the *Courier*, May 9, 1815.]   R. L. M.

RAMSAY, FRANCIS MUNROE (Apr. 5, 1835–July 19, 1914), naval officer, was born in Washington, D. C., the only son of Frances Whetcroft (Munroe) Ramsay and George Douglas Ramsay [*q.v.*]. Appointed a midshipman on Oct. 5, 1850, he spent one year at the United States Naval Academy and then went to sea on the practise-ship *Preble* and on the *St. Lawrence*, Pacific Station. Returning to the Naval Academy, he was graduated on June 20, 1856, with a promotion the same month to passed midshipman. During the next six years, he served on the *Falmouth*, Brazil Squadron; the *Merrimac*, Pacific Squadron; at the Washington navy yard, ordnance duty; and on the *Saratoga*, African Squadron. He was made a lieutenant on Jan. 23, 1858, and lieutenant commander on July 16, 1862. In the Civil War, he commanded the ironclad *Choctaw*, Mississippi Squadron, 1863–64, under David Dixon Porter [*q.v.*]. At Drumgould's Bluff, Yazoo River, Apr. 30, 1863, the *Choctaw* was under very heavy fire, and Kidder Randolph Breese [*q.v.*], writing Porter on May 1, said, "Ramsay is worthy of all you old commanders; fought his ship very handsomely and on deck all the time" (*War of the Rebellion: Official Records (Navy)*, 1 ser., XXIV, 589). From May 18 to May 23, the *Choctaw*, the *DeKalb*, and four light draught vessels ascended the Yazoo River, attacking a strong position at Haynes' Bluff, and at Yazoo City where the well-equipped Confederate navy yard and three formidable war vessels, in process of construction, were destroyed. Later, at Milliken's Bend, Mississippi River, the *Choctaw*, at a critical time on June 7, repulsed a Confederate attack on the garrison.

During the siege of Vicksburg, Ramsay commanded a battery of three heavy guns, mounted on scows in an exposed position and gained Porter's warm official commendation. From July 1863 to September 1864, he commanded the Mississippi River Third District, leading an expedition of six gunboats of the "tin clad" fleet up the Red River and thence up the Black River to Trinity, La., where an engagement was fought. He then proceeded up the Ouachita River to Harrisonburg, La., where he had a second engagement. Porter recommended Ramsay for promotion to Secretary Welles on May 19, 1864, and, in a letter to the Secretary, he called him "one of my best officers" (*Official Rec., post*, XXVI, 444). Commanding the gunboat *Unadilla*, North Atlantic Blockading Squadron, also under Porter, he participated in the attacks on Fort Fisher in December 1864 and in January 1865, and later in several engagements with Fort Anderson and other forts on the Cape Fear River. In April he was with the flotilla which removed torpedoes from the James River, and was present at the capture of Richmond. He was assistant to the commandant, Stephen Bleecker Luce [*q.v.*], and senior instructor in gunnery at the Naval Academy while Admiral Porter was superintendent. Made commander on July 25, 1866, he was, in turn, on navigation duty at the Washington navy yard; fleet captain and chief of staff, South Atlantic Squadron, flagship *Guerriere*; commander of the *Guerriere*; on ordnance duty, Washington navy yard; in the Bureau of Ordnance; naval attaché in London, 1872–73; commander of the *Ossipee*, North Atlantic Station, and of the *Lancaster*; at the Naval Asylum, Philadelphia; and inspector of ordnance, New York navy yard. He was promoted to the rank of captain on Dec. 1, 1877, commanded the Torpedo Station, Newport, R. I., from 1878 to 1881, and the *Trenton*, European Station, 1881. As superintendent of the Naval Academy from 1881 to 1886, the first graduate to have this honor, he systematized the practical instruction and improved the discipline, arousing great discontent and insubordination among the midshipmen, who were dealt with severely. After promotion to commodore in March 1889, he commanded the *Boston*, and the New York navy yard, and was Chief of the Bureau of Navigation, 1889–97. He became a rear admiral on Apr. 11, 1894, and retired on Apr. 5, 1897. He was a member of the Schley Court of Inquiry with Admiral Dewey and Rear Admiral Benham. He died in Washington and was buried in Arlington Cemetery. On June 9, 1869, he married, in the United States Legation at Buenos Aires, Anna Josephine, the daughter of Patrick and Mary (Powers) McMahon of Ireland. They had three children, two boys and one girl.

[Letter from Miss Mary Ramsay, Apr. 17, 1931; *Who's Who in America*, 1912–13; L. R. Hamersly, *The Records of Living Officers of the U. S. Navy and Marine Corps* (4th ed., 1890); *Battles and Leaders of the Civil War*, vol. III (1884); *War of the Rebellion: Official Records (Navy)*, 1 ser., XXIV, XXV, XXVI; J. R. Soley, *Admiral Porter* (1903); *Army and Navy Jour.*, and *Army and Navy Register*, July 25, 1914; *N. Y. Times*, July 21, 1914.]   C. L. L.

RAMSAY, GEORGE DOUGLAS (Feb. 21,

1802–May 23, 1882), soldier, the son of Andrew and Catherine (Graham) Ramsay, was born in Dumfries, Va. His father, a Scottish-born merchant of Alexandria, Va., moved to Washington, D. C., and it was from there that his son, at the age of twelve, received his appointment as a cadet to the United States Military Academy. Graduating on July 1, 1820, he was commissioned second lieutenant in the corps of light artillery. The next year, when the artillery was reorganized into regiments, he was assigned to the 1st Artillery. He was promoted to first lieutenant of the 1st Artillery in 1826 and in 1833 he became adjutant of that regiment, having previously served in garrisons in the New England states and at Fortress Monroe, Va., and on topographical duty. In 1835 he was promoted to captain of ordnance, which grade he held for over twenty-six years. From 1835 to 1845 he commanded arsenals in Washington, D. C., New York, Pennsylvania, New Jersey, and Georgia. During the military occupation of Texas in 1845 and 1846, Ramsay served as ordnance officer at Corpus Christi and at Point Isabel. He was with General Taylor's army in the Mexican War, was brevetted major for gallant and meritorious conduct in the several conflicts at Monterey, and was chief of ordnance of that army from June 1847 to May 1848. After the Mexican War he commanded, successively, the Frankford Arsenal in Pennsylvania, the arsenals at Fortress Monroe, Va., at St. Louis, Mo., and at Washington, D. C., where he was on duty at the outbreak of the Civil War.

On Apr. 22, 1861, he was promoted to the rank of major; on Aug. 3 of the same year to lieutenant-colonel; and on June 1, 1863, to colonel of ordnance, continuing all the while in command of the Washington Arsenal which had become an important munitions supply depot for the Union armies. On Sept. 15, 1863, he was appointed brigadier-general and chief of ordnance of the army, which post he held until Sept. 12, 1864, when he was retired from active service for age. He continued to serve, however, by special assignment as inspector of arsenals until June 8, 1866, and in command of the Washington Arsenal until Feb. 21, 1870, when he retired from all public duty. In 1865 he was brevetted major-general for long and faithful service in the army. After his retirement, he continued to make his home in Washington, D. C., where he was active in the vestry of St. John's Episcopal Church. On Sept. 23, 1830, he married Frances Whetcroft Munroe of Washington, D. C., who died in 1835 leaving one child, Francis Munroe Ramsay

[q.v.], who became a rear admiral in the navy. He was married a second time on June 28, 1838, to Eliza Hennen Gales of Louisiana, the niece and adopted daughter of Joseph Gales, 1786–1860 [q.v.]. They had three daughters and two sons, both of whom became army officers.

[J. V. Hagner, biog. sketch in *Ann. Reunion, Asso. Grads. U. S. Mil. Acad.* (1882); G. W. Cullum, *Biog. Reg. . . . U. S. Mil. Acad.* (1891); *War of the Rebellion: Official Records (Army)*, 1 ser., vols. V, XI, XIX, XXV, XXVII, XXIX, XXXV, XXXVII, XL, XLI, XLII, LI, 3 ser., vols. II, IV; *Army and Navy Register*, May 27, 1882; *Daily Natl. Intelligencer* (Wash., D. C.), Sept. 25, 1830, June 30, 1838; *Washington Post*, May 24, 1882.]

S. J. H.

RAMSAY, NATHANIEL (May 1, 1741–Oct.

24, 1817), Revolutionary officer and politician, was the son of James and Jane (Montgomery) Ramsay and a brother of David Ramsay [q.v.]. His father had emigrated from the North of Ireland and settled in Lancaster County, Pa. Nathaniel graduated at the College of New Jersey in 1767, studied law, and practised in Cecil County, Md., where he acquired an estate. He was a delegate to the Maryland Convention in 1775, to the Continental Congress the same year, and on Jan. 14, 1776, he was chosen captain of Smallwood's Maryland regiment. In July 1776 that unit became a part of the Continental Army and on Dec. 10, 1776, Ramsay was commissioned lieutenant-colonel of the 3rd Maryland. He served throughout the war. In the battle of Long Island the Maryland troops of Smallwood's regiment were especially noted, but Ramsay's chief distinction came at the battle of Monmouth in 1778. In the course of the unexplained retreat in that struggle, so disgracefully started by Gen. Charles Lee, Washington encountered Colonel Stewart and Ramsay—who led a regiment—and ordered them to form and check the retreat. Tradition adds that the commander-in-chief reinforced the order by a solemn appeal to Ramsay. The latter fulfilled his part, often considered as a decisive one, in the battle, showed in addition great personal gallantry, was wounded and left for dead on the field, and taken captive. He was paroled and exchanged in December 1780. The following month he retired. From 1785 to 1787 he was again a member of the Continental Congress. In 1790 he was appointed by Washington United States marshal of the district of Maryland. Four years later he was made naval officer of the Baltimore district, and this latter position he held until his death. In person he was unusually tall. His first wife was Margaret Jane Peale, sister of Charles Willson Peale [q.v.], who is said to have been a widow when he married her in 1771. She died in 1788 and in 1792 he was married to Charlotte Hall. A son and two daughters of the second marriage survived him. Ramsay's portrait hangs in Independence Hall, Philadelphia, and he is commemorated on the monument erected upon the battle-ground of Monmouth.

[See: W. F. Brand, "A Sketch of the Life and Character of Nathaniel Ramsay," *Md. Hist. Soc. Fund-Publication*, no. 24 (1887) ; sketch by Isaac R. Pennypacker in Geo. Johnston, *Hist. of Cecil County, Md.* (1881), pp. 537–48 ; *Papers Read before the Lancaster County Hist. Soc.*, Nov. 2, 1906 ; W. S. Stryker, *The Battle of Monmouth* (1927) ; "Muster Rolls . . . of Md. Troops in the Am. Revolution," *Archives of Md.*, vol. XVIII (1900) ; Esmeralda Boyle, *Biog. Sketches of Distinguished Marylanders* (1877), pp. 140ff.; *U. S. Gazette* (Phila.), Oct. 29, 1817.]   E. K. A.

RAMSEUR, STEPHEN DODSON (May 31, 1837–Oct. 20, 1864), Confederate soldier, the son of Jacob A. and Lucy M. (Wilfong) Ramseur and a descendant of John Wilfong who fought in the Revolution, was born in Lincolnton, N. C. He attended the schools of Lincolnton and Milton and at sixteen matriculated as a freshman at Davidson College, Davidson, N. C. Deciding upon a military career, he left Davidson in April 1855, to accept an appointment to the United States Military Academy from which he was graduated on July 1, 1860, standing fourteenth in a class of forty-one. He was appointed brevet second lieutenant, 3rd Artillery with station at Fortress Monroe, Va., and was for a short time at Washington, D. C. He was promoted to the rank of second lieutenant of the 4th Artillery on Feb. 1, 1861, but, the Civil War having begun, he resigned on Apr. 6, 1861, without having joined his new regiment, and offered his services to the Confederacy. By this government he was commissioned first lieutenant of artillery and shortly thereafter was appointed captain of a North Carolina battery. In the spring of 1862 he reported with his battery at Yorktown, Va., to Gen. John Bankhead Magruder [*q.v.*], who was opposing the advance of General McClellan up the Peninsula, was detached from his battery to be placed in command of the artillery of the right wing, and was promoted to the rank of major. In April 1862, he was elected colonel of the 49th North Carolina Infantry. He rapidly trained his new regiment, led it with distinction in the Seven Days' Battle in front of Richmond, and though severely wounded at Malvern Hill, refused to leave the field until the engagement was over.

Upon the recommendation of General Lee he was promoted to brigadier-general on Nov. 1, 1862, and assigned to command a brigade of four North Carolina regiments in D. H. Hill's division of Stonewall Jackson's corps in the Army of Northern Virginia. He fought gallantly with his brigade at Chancellorsville where he was

again wounded, participated in the battles at Gettysburg, in the Wilderness, and at Spotsylvania, where he received another wound and where his brigade won fame by its charge which drove General Hancock's men from the "bloody angle." On June 1, 1864, he was promoted to the rank of major-general. He commanded a division at Cold Harbor and in the force of Gen. Jubal A. Early [*q.v.*], which invaded Maryland in June and July 1864. Returning to the Shenandoah Valley his division bore the brunt of General Sheridan's attack at Winchester, Va., and fell back in good order. At Cedar Creek, Va., on Oct. 19, 1864, after assisting in the initial defeat of the Union forces, he fell mortally wounded while rallying his men to stop Sheridan's counter-attack. He was taken prisoner and died the next day at Sheridan's headquarters in Winchester. Just a year previous, on Oct. 22, he had married Ellen E. Richmond of Milton, N. C., and only the day before receiving his fatal wound he learned of the birth of a daughter. General Early ably depicted the spirit of Ramseur in the following words: "He was a most gallant and energetic officer whom no disaster appalled, but his courage and energy seemed to gain new strength in the midst of confusion and disorder" (*Battles and Leaders of the Civil War*, vol. IV, 1888, p. 529).

[William R. Cox, *Address on the Life and Character of Maj. Gen. S. D. Ramseur before the Ladies Memorial Asso. of Raleigh, N. C., May 10, 1891* (1891), also in W. J. Peele, *Lives of Distinguished North Carolinians* (1898) ; *Conf. Mil. Hist.* (1899), vol. IV ; F. B. Heitman, *Hist. Register and Dict. of the U. S. Army* (1903) ; *Address by Col. DuPont at the Unveiling of the Monument . . . to Maj. Gen. S. D. Ramseur* (1920) ; C. R. Shaw, *Davidson College* (1923) ; *Richmond Whig*, Oct. 24, 1864.]   S. J. H.

RAMSEY, ALEXANDER (Sept. 8, 1815–Apr. 22, 1903), governor of Minnesota, United States senator, secretary of war, was born near Harrisburg, Pa., the son of Elizabeth Kelker and Thomas Ramsey. His ancestry was Scotch and German. As a youth Ramsey, who was orphaned at the age of ten, was employed in the store of a grand-uncle, was clerk in the office of register of deeds, and worked for a time as a carpenter, meanwhile pursuing his studies as best he could. At the age of eighteen he entered Lafayette College, but he left before completing his course to study law. After his admission to the bar in 1839 he practised law at Harrisburg and became a zealous worker in the interests of the Whig party. In 1840 he was secretary of the Pennsylvania electoral college, and the year following, chief clerk of the House of Representatives. From 1843 to 1847 he represented his district in Congress. In 1848, as chairman of the Whig central committee of Pennsylvania, he labored diligently for the election of Zachary Taylor, who, after his inauguration, rewarded Ramsey with a commission as governor of the newly organized territory of Minnesota.

When Ramsey assumed his new duties, on June 1, 1849, he found himself governor of a large territory, of which only a small portion, containing a few thousand white inhabitants, was open to settlement, the remainder being Indian country. After declaring the territorial government established, he ordered an election and when the first legislature assembled in September he read a message abounding in practical suggestions for the benefit of the territory, many of which were later adopted. The outstanding event of his territorial administration was the negotiation in 1851 of treaties of cession with the Sioux, with Ramsey as one of the two government commissioners, which opened an immense area in southern Minnesota to settlement. He was later charged with fraud in the conduct of the negotiations; but the United States Senate, after an investigation, completely exonerated him (*Senate Executive Document 61, 33* Cong., 1 Sess.). His territorial governorship ended in 1853, with the appointment of a Democratic governor under President Pierce, and he retired to private life in St. Paul, devoting much of his attention to judicious investments in real estate. He was mayor of St. Paul in 1855. In 1857 he was defeated by only a few votes as Republican candidate for governor of Minnesota, soon to be admitted as a state. Two years later, however, he was elected to that office by a decisive majority, and he was reëlected in 1861. During his administration the legislature, following his recommendations, materially reduced state expenses, simplified county government, and took effective measures to safeguard the state's school lands against premature sale at low prices. Ramsey's official duties were greatly complicated by the responsibilities connected with the Sioux outbreak of 1862 and the Indian war following it and with providing troops for the Civil War. He was in Washington when Fort Sumter was fired on, and made the first offer of armed troops to Lincoln.

Ramsey retired from the governorship in July 1863 to take his place in the United States Senate, to which he had been elected the preceding January. His senatorial career, which was extended by a reëlection in 1869 to twelve years, was marked by the industry and practical ability that had characterized his administrations as governor. He served on several important committees, and as chairman of the committee on

post offices and post roads he made important contributions to postal reform. From 1879 to 1881 he was secretary of war under President Hayes, and in 1882 he was made chairman of the commission to carry out the provisions of the Edmunds bill to suppress polygamy in Utah. Upon his resignation from the commission in 1886 he retired permanently to private life. He was president of the Minnesota Historical Society from 1849 to 1863 and from 1891 to 1903 and was the author of several papers in the *Minnesota Historical Collections.* On Sept. 10, 1845, he married Anna Earl Jenks. They had three children, two of whom died in childhood. Ramsey is described by a contemporary as "the finest specimen of a physical man in the Northwest" (T. M. Newson, *Pen Pictures of St. Paul.* 1886, p. 123). He was clear-headed, cautious, and judicious, above all a man of practical sense. He was a shrewd politician and an excellent judge of human nature, with a gift for making friends. Although he was not an orator, his public addresses were forceful and direct. One of the first counties established in Minnesota bears his name.

[Sources include: J. H. Baker, *Lives of the Govs. of Minn.* (1908); E. D. Neill, *The Hist. of Minn.* (4th ed., 1882); J. F. Williams, *A Hist. of the City of St. Paul* (1876); C. C. Andrews, *Hist. of St. Paul* (1890), pt. 2; W. W. Folwell, *A Hist. of Minn.,* vols. I and II (1921–24); "Memorial Addresses in Honor of Gov. Alexander Ramsey," *Minn. Hist. Soc. Colls.,* vol. X, pt. 2 (1905); *Minneapolis Jour.,* Apr. 23, 1903. The Minn. Hist. Soc. has a collection of Ramsey's papers.]

S. J. B.

RAMSEY, JAMES GETTYS McGREADY (Mar. 25, 1797–Apr. 11, 1884), physician, author, was the fourth of the seven children of Peggy Alexander, daughter of John McKnitt Alexander of North Carolina, and Francis Alexander Ramsey, a native of Pennsylvania who had moved to the future Tennessee at the close of the Revolution. James was born near Knoxville, where his father was a man of considerable local importance, and he was educated by tutors, at Ebenezer Academy, and at Washington College, in Tennessee, where he received the degree of B.A. at the age of nineteen. He read medicine in the office of a local physician, spent one year in professional study at the University of Pennsylvania, and began practice at Knoxville in 1820. The honorary degree of M.D. was awarded him by the Medical College of South Carolina in 1831 (*Knoxville Register,* Apr. 13, 1831). In 1821 he married Margaret Barton Crozier, by whom he was the father of eleven children. Like many contemporaries in his profession he had many interests and his activities were broadly diversified. He gave support locally to the early movement for public schools. He was probably the first East Tennessean to advocate (in 1828) the establishment of connection by rail between the Tennessee River and the South Atlantic Seaboard. He was prominently associated in the promotion of the Louisville, Cincinnati, & Charleston Railroad, and served as one of its directors. Later he gave support to other railroads, and acted as agent for the state in financing the completion of the East Tennessee & Georgia Railroad. Ramsey also, like his father, was a banker, serving as president of the Knoxville branches of the short-lived South Western Railroad Bank and the Bank of Tennessee. An accomplishment in which he took particular pride was the writing of *The Annals of Tennessee to the End of the Eighteenth Century* (1853), which was reprinted with a critical index by J. T. Fain in 1926. This substantial volume on the pioneer period of the history of this state was the first in which an attempt was made to give a detailed narrative on the basis of a careful collection and examination of public and private papers. The manuscript of a second volume and many records which Ramsey had collected were destroyed by fire during the Civil War. In this war Ramsey was an ardent supporter of the Confederacy. He had been a Democrat and a champion of slavery and of the reopening of the African slave trade. He served the Confederacy in minor civil office and was compelled to flee from Knoxville when Federal troops occupied the city. For some years after the war he remained "in exile" in North Carolina, but ultimately (1872) returned to Knoxville. Two years later he was chosen president of the reorganized Tennessee Historical Society and held this office until his death.

[Ramsey's manuscript autobiography is in the Univ. of Tenn. Lib. Other sources include: P. M. Hamer, *Tennessee: A Hist.* (1933), vol. I; Mary M. Hoskins, "Jas. Gettys McGready Ramsey" (1929), Master's thesis, *Univ. of Tenn.; Knoxville Jour.* and *Daily Chronicle* (Knoxville), Apr. 12, 1884.]   P. M. H.

RAND, ADDISON CRITTENDEN (Sept. 17, 1841–Mar. 9, 1900), manufacturer of rock drills, was the son of Jasper Raymond and Lucy (Whipple) Rand, and a descendant of Robert Rand who settled in Charlestown, Mass., about 1635. He was born in Westfield, Mass., where he received his education. In 1865, with his brother Jasper, he succeeded to his father's business of manufacturing whips. His connection with this enterprise gave him the mechanical training which later was to prove so useful to him.

In 1871 he moved to New York City, where his brother Alfred T. Rand had helped to found the Laflin & Rand Powder Company. After studying the numerous designs for rock-drilling machinery which had been offered to the powder company, Addison Rand organized the Rand Drill Company, of which he became president and Jasper treasurer. At this time (1871) the manufacture of rock drills was in its pioneer stage, with an uncertain future before it. Aided by the inventive genius of Joseph C. Githens and Frederick A. Halsey, Rand developed rock drills and air-compressing machinery, widening their field of usefulness. He was the leading factor in inducing mining companies to substitute rock drills for hammer and chisel, and was instrumental in making rock drills and air compressors standard equipment in tunnels and aqueducts and in mining and quarrying operations throughout the world.

Rand established a plant at Tarrytown, N. Y., to take advantage of the cheap river transportation, but found that in the winter, when navigation ceased and shipments had to be made by rail, rates on the local line were raised to exorbitant figures. Rather than submit to what he considered extortion, Rand hauled his goods across country to an independent railroad, until it was absorbed by the first company. He was as careful in selecting his employees as he would have been in adopting a person into his own family, and to his choice of associates may be attributed much of his success. While he was not given to praising his employees, his appreciation was expressed in practical ways. One man with but meager schooling was urged to take a correspondence course and was given time off in which to complete it, and upon Rand's death, eight employees found themselves recipients of substantial bequests. When, about 1886, a strike occurred at his Tarrytown plant, it was a great shock to him. Considering the demands unjust, he stubbornly fought the strike, and a settlement was not reached until after nearly a year's shutdown.

Rand was one of the incorporators and the first treasurer of the Engineers' Club of New York City, for which he labored at a time when success seemed doubtful. In addition to the Rand Drill Company, he was associated as officer or director with the Rendrock Powder Company, the Pneumatic Engineering Company, the Davis Calyx Drill Company, and the Laflin & Rand Powder Company. His favorite recreation was horseback riding or driving. He died, unmarried, in New York City.

[Interview with Herbert T. Abrams, employee and associate of A. C. Rand; F. O. Rand, *A Geneal. of the Rand Family in the U. S.* (1898); *Trans. Am. Inst. Mining Engineers*, vol. XXXI (1902); *Am. Machinist,*

Mar. 22, 1900; obituary of J. C. Githens, *Ibid.*, Jan. 11, 1900; *N. Y. Times*, Mar. 11, 1900.]　　　　B. A. R.

RAND, EDWARD SPRAGUE (June 23, 1782–Oct. 22, 1863), merchant, manufacturer, was born in Newburyport, Mass. He was the son of Edward and Ruth (Sprague) Rand and a grandson of Dr. Isaac Rand of Charlestown and of Dr. John Sprague, a prominent physician of Newburyport. His father established himself in Newburyport as a merchant dealing in imported English goods, and Edward Sprague Rand went to work in this store after receiving his education at Dummer Academy. When he was eighteen he went to sea as a supercargo, and before he was twenty-one he had taken up his residence at Amsterdam as a merchant, remaining there several years, and returning home by way of the Canary Islands. He then made a voyage to Russia, but the ship on which he was returning in 1810 was wrecked on the coast of Norway. This necessitated his spending the winter there and led to his being given up as lost. On returning from Norway he was forced by commercial conditions to restrict his activities, but with the coming of peace and the economic revival it brought he became prominent in commerce and finance. He started business as an East India merchant and general freighter, but he apparently saw the opportunities afforded by the application of machinery to manufacturing and by the growing practice of financing business ventures by selling shares to the public, for he took a leading part in promoting enterprises involving these things. In 1816 he was identified with a project for building a canal, in 1825 he was connected with a hosiery manufactory, and from 1825 to 1827 he was president of the Mechanics' Bank of Newburyport.

Rand's greatest prominence came as a woolen manufacturer. In 1821, in association with several others, he purchased a woolen mill, and for many years he was the president and chief figure in its management. Under his direction the factory developed into the Salisbury Mills, one of the conspicuous industrial plants in New England in the middle decades of the nineteenth century, and he became a recognized leader in industry and finance. He was also active in public affairs. From 1813 to 1815 he was selectman of Newburyport. In 1815, 1816, and 1819 he was elected to the lower branch of the Massachusetts legislature, and in 1822 he was a member of its Senate. After this his increasing responsibilities apparently prevented his holding political office, but he was still prominent in exerting his personal influence in the support of policies in which he believed, as is shown by a letter to Daniel Webster dated Apr. 8, 1850, in which Rand and several others congratulate Webster on his stand on the Union. The letter, together with Webster's reply, was printed for public circulation. Rand was married on Apr. 6, 1807, to Hannah Pettingill, by whom he had two daughters and a son. The house in which they lived, which his wife inherited from her father, became the property of the city, and because of its age and prominence in Colonial days, was preserved as a historical exhibit.

[See: D. H. Hurd, compiler, *Hist. of Essex County, Mass.* (1888), vol. II; J. J. Currier, *Hist. of Newburyport, Mass.*, vol. II (1909); Florence O. Rand, *A Geneal. of the Rand Family in the U. S.* (1898); *Boston Transcript*, Oct. 23, 1863; *Daily Herald* (Newburyport), Oct. 24, 1863.]　　　　S. G.

RANDALL, ALEXANDER WILLIAMS (Oct. 31, 1819–July 26, 1872), lawyer, governor of Wisconsin, politician, administrator, was born at Ames, Montgomery County, N. Y., a son of Phineas Randall, a lawyer, native of Massachusetts, and Sarah (Beach) Randall, a native of New York state. Alexander received a thorough academic education at Cherry Valley Academy. After a period of legal study under his father, he removed in 1840 to the new village of Prairieville (afterward Waukesha), in Wisconsin Territory. There he practised law successfully but soon became absorbed in public affairs. At first, like his father, he bore the Whig label. Soon he showed Democratic leanings and in 1845 President Polk appointed him postmaster in his village, an office that paid a very low salary but offered important political advantages. The next year he was chosen a delegate to the state constitutional convention where he gained prominence through his successful championship of a resolution submitting separately the question of negro suffrage. This action, highly unpopular, kept him out of politics long enough to make him a seasoned lawyer and a sagacious leader. Acting in 1848 with the Van Buren free-soil Democrats, and a little later with the "Barnburner" faction which in 1854 generally went "Free-soil," he was elected to the state Assembly where he quickly gained a remarkable ascendancy. For a few months, under appointment by the first Republican governor, he filled an unexpired term as judge of the Milwaukee circuit. In 1857 he was elected governor, although Carl Schurz, Republican candidate for lieutenant-governor, was defeated. Reëlected in 1859, he was in office when the Civil War broke.

Randall proved one of the noted "war governors." In his message of Jan. 10, 1861, he predicted a conflict and urged preparedness. After Lincoln's proclamation of Apr. 15, he instantly enlisted a regiment of militia, which was ready to go forward in six days. The executive office became the army headquarters for the state, the governor's fiery zeal and exceptional organizing ability serving to unite all loyal elements in enthusiastic support of the nation. Randall also contributed notably, along with the other leading governors, to Lincoln's plans for the prompt mobilization of the national resources. So energetically did he proceed in Wisconsin that when he left the executive office, nine months later, the state had already supplied nearly 25,000 troops. Like many other political leaders, Randall, having missed a senatorship, desired a military appointment, but Lincoln sent him as minister to Rome. The next year he was back, still intent upon a military appointment. Again he missed that objective, but being made first assistant postmaster-general in 1863, he gave full sway to his genius for political organization in preparing the ground for Lincoln's triumphant reëlection. Andrew Johnson received him into his cabinet as head of the Post-Office Department, where he remained till the close of that stormy administration, to the last one of Johnson's most ardent defenders. His friendship for the widely hated President sufficed to send him back to the practice of law. He preferred, however, not to return to Wisconsin, but settled in Elmira, N. Y. There he remained active in his profession for a time, but his death from cancer ended his career at the early age of fifty-two. He had married in 1842 Mary C. Van Vechten of New York state, who died in 1858. Five years later he married Helen M. Thomas of Elmira, N. Y., who survived him.

Randall was endowed with a sound, keen, and quick, though not profound, intelligence, and was handsome of face and figure. He was effective and even eloquent in address, and he always gave the impression of perfect adequacy in any situation. A consistent and orderly worker, he rose very early and performed the day's drudgery before office hours. That method provided leisure for conferences, visits, and the joviality of which he was exceptionally fond. He was a formidable opponent in the court room and on the hustings, yet kindly in disposition, rarely making personal enemies. From a party viewpoint he was extraordinarily "mobile," but although he was often charged with political opportunism, his party shiftings were determined more on principle than on expediency. He performed much useful work at Washington, but he

will be longest remembered as Wisconsin's dynamic war governor.

[The best biographical sketch of Randall, albeit somewhat too laudatory, is that by Tenney, in H. A. Tenney and David Atwood's *Memorial Record of the Fathers of Wis.* (1880). See also: C. S. Matteson, *The Hist. of Wis.* (1893); C. R. Tuttle, *An Illustrated Hist. of the State of Wis.* (1875); "Reminiscences of Alex. W. Randall," *Milwaukee Sentinel*, Nov. 14, 1897; and R. G. Thwaites, *Civil War Messages and Proclamations of Wis. War Governors* (1912). U. S. *Ministers to the Papal States* (1933), ed. by Leo F. Stock, contains Randall's correspondence as minister to Rome. Randall's manuscripts, letter copy books, and other papers, during the governorship, are in the State Hist. Lib.]   J. S—r.

RANDALL, BENJAMIN (Feb. 7, 1749–Oct. 22, 1808), founder and organizer of the Free-will Baptists, was a descendant in the fourth generation from William Randall, who came from England to Rhode Island in 1636, removing soon to Marshfield, and by 1640 to Scituate in the Old Colony. Benjamin, the eldest of nine children, was the third of that name in succession; his mother was Margaret Mordantt. For some reason of his own, he alone of the family usually wrote his name Randal. Born in New Castle, N. H., the son of a sea-captain, the lad accompanied his father to sea rather constantly. Despite a lack of formal schooling, he was later considered an educated man. For three years before attaining his majority, he was apprentice to a sailmaker at Portsmouth, from whom he also learned the tailor's trade, knowledge which he subsequently used as a means of income and to repay hospitality received during his travels.

Interested in religion, he heard Whitefield preach on Sept. 24, 25, and 28, 1770; on his way to hear him again two days later, he learned of the preacher's sudden death. He considered his conversion, which he dated from Oct. 15, 1770, as in part a fruit of Whitefield's preaching. On Nov. 28, 1771, he married Joanna Oram of Kittery, Me., by whom he had four sons and five daughters. In 1772 he united with the Congregational church at New Castle, but soon became dissatisfied with its spiritual condition and in May 1775 separated from that body, associating himself with a small group of similarly minded persons who were essentially New Lights. The following year he and others of the group adopted believer's immersion, and with three companions all of whom later became ministers, he was baptized by William Hooper of Medbury. Although feeling called to preach and occasionally doing so, he hesitated to enter the ministry. Stopping to preach at New Durham when passing through the place, he was called there and on Mar. 26, 1778, settled in what was to be his future home. He revolted not only against the cold formality of much of the conventional religious life around him, but also against the current doctrine of election, asserting categorically, "I do not believe in it." On Apr. 5, 1780, he was publicly ordained at New Durham "to the work of an evangelist." His supporters there signed a covenant which at their request he drew up, and what became known as the Freewill Baptist, later the Free Baptist, denomination thus had its beginning.

The whole movement, in its general character, emphases, and methods, may be viewed as a renewal of the Great Awakening. For over twenty-five years Randall traveled eastward and westward, confining his journeys primarily to Maine, New Hampshire, and Vermont, preaching, baptizing (in winter through holes cut in the ice), and establishing churches. Some of these became the most influential in their communities, while many were in villages or rural regions where previously there had been no church. Against much opposition he continued his endeavors, averaging probably over a thousand miles of itinerary each year, at the same time retaining his pastorate at New Durham. As the number of churches increased he devised a system of quarterly meetings (1783) and a yearly meeting (June 1792), with a type of polity blending the Meetings of the Friends and the Association of the Baptists. In the local church, the polity was definitely congregational. Without formal ecclesiastical distinction, Randall moved among the Free Will Baptists as their actual leader, persisting in his active labors even after his health had been broken. His deep religious conviction often led him into controversy, yet he was of well-balanced judgment, of irenic temperament, and of recognized honesty. The permanency of his influence is to be tested, not by the gradual return of the Free Baptists to the main group of Northern Baptists, but by the modification of the latter's Calvinism, from which Randall's moral sense had revolted.

[F. L. Wiley, *Life and Influence of the Rev. Benjamin Randall, Founder of the Free Baptist Denomination* (copr. 1915) adds little to what is contained in the more authoritative work, *The Life of Elder Benjamin Randal: Principally Taken from Documents Written by Himself* (1827), by John Buzzell, who accompanied Randall on many of his journeys; see also I. D. Stewart, *The Hist. of the Freewill Baptists* (1862); G. A. Burgess and J. T. Ward, *Free Baptist Cyc.* (1889); *Vital Records of Newburyport, Mass.* (1911).]

W. H. A.

RANDALL, BURTON ALEXANDER (Sept. 21, 1858–Jan. 4, 1932), ophthalmologist and otologist, son of Alexander Randall, a lawyer and banker, and his wife, Elizabeth Philpot

Blanchard, was born at Annapolis, Md. Wyatt William Randall [*q.v.*] was his brother. After graduating from St. John's College, Annapolis, he entered the medical department of the University of Pennsylvania from which he graduated with honor in 1880. From 1880 to 1882 he was assistant demonstrator of histology in the University of Pennsylvania and throughout his life he continued his interest in the study of microscopic anatomy and histology, although two years after graduation he began his work in ophthalmology and otology. He devoted an immense amount of time to hospital work and was noted for the conscientious manner in which he attended the clinics and wards. For many years he was surgeon to the eye and ear department of the Episcopal, the Children's, and the Methodist Episcopal hospitals. From 1888 to 1912 he was professor of diseases of the ear in the Philadelphia Polyclinic and College for Graduates in Medicine. He was elected clinical professor of diseases of the ear in the University of Pennsylvania in 1891 and served in that capacity until 1912 wnen he was appointed professor of otology, which position he held until his retirement in 1924.

Randall took the keenest interest in his teaching. He had a large collection of gross and microscopic preparations, the greater part made by himself, and he was most generous in lending them to students for purposes of study. In 1887 he published in collaboration with Dr. H. L. Morse of Boston a beautifully illustrated work entitled *Photographic Illustrations of the Anatomy of the Human Ear,* which embodied excellent reproductions of anatomic preparations suitable for teaching purposes. He was co-editor with Dr. George E. de Schweinitz of the *American Text-Book of Diseases of the Eye, Ear, Nose and Throat* (1899), a standard work which has gone through many editions. Randall's bibliography shows no less than 144 contributions to periodic medical literature. He wrote with ease and his articles are distinguished by accuracy of statement and clarity. As a practitioner he was a bold, dexterous, and most successful operator, particularly upon the mastoid. A large part of his success was due to the scrupulous care with which he attended to the postoperative dressing and care of his patients. He was a regular attendant at the annual meetings of the national societies concerned with his specialties and a frequent contributor to their publications. He was a member of the College of Physicians of Philadelphia, of which he was a member of the Council many years; the Philadelphia Pathological Society;

the American Medical Association; the American Ophthalmological Society; the American Laryngological Association, and the American Otological Society, of which he was president in the years 1903–05. He was a member of the Protestant Episcopal Church and took a deep interest in its affairs. He died at his home in Philadelphia early in 1932. He had married, in 1893, Emma F. Leavitt, who with two sons and a daughter survived him.

[James A. Babbit, memoir in the *Laryngoscope*, Feb. 1932, with complete bibliography; *Trans. Am. Otological Soc.*, vol. XXII (1932); *Annals of Otology, Rhinology, and Laryngology*, Mar. 1932; *Evening Pub. Ledger* (Phila.), Jan. 4, 1932; information as to certain facts from Randall's widow, and personal acquaintance.]   F. R. P.

RANDALL, HENRY STEPHENS (May 3, 1811–Aug. 14, 1876), agriculturist, educator, author, was born at Brookfield, Madison County, N. Y., and died at Cortland, in the same state. The eldest child of Roswell and Harriet (Stephens) Randall, he was sixth in direct descent from John Randall, the Puritan ancestor, who died at Westerly, R. I.. about 1685. The family lived at Westerly and at Stonington, Conn., until its removal to central New York about 1800. Randall attended the Cortland and Geneva (N. Y.) academies and graduated from Union College in 1830, where he was a marked favorite of President Eliphalet Nott. From 1830 to 1834 he practised politics and studied law in the offices of his uncle, Henry Stephens, first judge of Cortland County, and supreme court justice William H. Shankland. He was admitted to the bar in 1834, but never practised law, nor intended to. On Feb. 4, 1834, at Auburn, N. Y., he married Jane Rebecca Polhemus, who with two daughters and a son survived him.

During his legal and literary studies, Randall gave particular attention to the constitutional and political history of the United States, and as a result, became an ardent convert to the Jeffersonian theory of government, a predilection which accounts for his later *Life of Thomas Jefferson*. He was a delegate in political conventions before he was of age, wrote articles for Democratic papers which were widely reprinted, and was the youngest regular delegate to the National Democratic Convention of 1835. In 1839 he became paid school visitor for his county, holding the position until the office of county superintendent of schools was legally established. In this new position he served from 1843 to 1847. His vigorous work and his writings on educational subjects during these years brought him offers to become state superintendent of schools in several states. In 1844 he contrib-

uted a sixty-page account of "Common School Libraries" to *Mental and Moral Culture and Popular Education*, edited by his cousin, Samuel S. Randall [*q.v.*]. When, in 1851, he was elected secretary of state of New York, after being defeated in 1849, his strongest reason for serving was that the post carried with it, *ex officio*, the superintendency of public instruction. During his two years' service he was author of the bill creating the separate state department of public instruction. He was a member of the National Democratic Committee at Charleston in 1860, and in 1871 was elected to the New York legislature, where he served as chairman of the committee on public education.

Meanwhile, he called himself "a practical farmer" and throughout most of his active life was engaged to some degree in agriculture, being especially interested in sheep. As early as 1838, *The Cultivator* for March carried a "Report on Sheep" by him. His earliest considerable work, *Sheep Husbandry in the South* (1848), a series of letters to R. F. W. Allston of South Carolina, at once established its author as a leading authority in this field. It was reprinted in 1852 under the title, *Sheep Husbandry,* and had five other printings, without substantial change, between that date and 1880. He contributed "Sheep Husbandry and Wool-growing in the United States" to the section on agriculture of the *Report of the Commissioner of Patents, for the Year 1850* (1851) and "Sheep" to the *Report of the Commissioner of Agriculture* for 1863. His "Fine Wool Sheep Husbandry," first submitted as a prize-winning article to the New York State Agricultural Society in 1861 (*Transactions,* vol. XXI, 1862), was reprinted separately with a considerable appendix in 1863 and 1865, while his *The Practical Shepherd* (1863) went through thirty printings. These books had an extraordinary total circulation, and produced important results in the domestic wool-growing industry. Their author had read widely, and repeatedly cited the important British and American literature on the subject. For years he was corresponding secretary of the New York State Agricultural Society, and as a member of its executive committee he is said to have proposed the New York state fair, first among such projects. From 1864 to 1867 he was editor of the sheep-husbandry department of *Moore's Rural New-Yorker*.

Although Randall published some nine volumes and a dozen minor articles, mostly dealing with agricultural subjects, he will be judged as an author by his most pretentious work, *The Life of Thomas Jefferson* (3 vols., 1858). This shows ability, scholarship, a strong if sometimes ungraceful style, and effective use of abundant materials. The family manuscripts that were made available to Randall were subsequently scattered, as he predicted; to no later biographer have they been accessible as a whole. His book is unjudicial, always partisan, often unfair (especially in the estimates of Hamilton and Josiah Quincy), yet it remains the most detailed and useful life of Jefferson.

[*Geneal. of a Branch of the Randall Family* (1879); H. P. Smith, *Hist. of Cortland County* (1885); contemporary reviews of *The Life of Thomas Jefferson*, reprinted in *Littell's Living Age*, Aug. 1861; *Moore's Rural New-Yorker*, Aug. 26, 1876; *N. Y. Times*, *N. Y. Tribune*, Aug. 17, 1876; Randall MSS. in N. Y. State Lib., Albany.]   J. I. W.

RANDALL, JAMES RYDER (Jan. 1, 1839–Jan. 14, 1908), poet and journalist, author of "Maryland, My Maryland," was born in Baltimore, the son of John K. Randall, a merchant, and Ruth M. (Hooper) Randall. Through his father he was descended from Randalls of English and Irish stock who came to Maryland in the seventeenth century and later gave their name to Randallstown, Md. On his mother's side he was a descendant of the Acadian exiles who found a home in Baltimore in 1755, for he was a great-great-grandson of René Leblanc, the notary in Longfellow's poem *Evangeline*. Taught in Baltimore by Joseph H. Clarke, who had been Poe's schoolmaster in Richmond, he was prepared for Georgetown College, which he entered when he was ten years of age. There he was recognized as having exceptional ability in English courses and was the author of lyrics dealing with college affairs. While in his final year at Georgetown he was so severely ill of pneumonia that he left without graduating and sailed to Brazil and thence to the West Indies to regain his health. Returning to Baltimore he was for a short time in the employ of Lucas Brothers, printers and type-founders, and then went to Florida. From there he moved in 1859 to New Orleans, where he was a clerk in the office of a shipbroker, using his leisure time for writing. The next year he was invited to become tutor in English and Latin in Poydras College, a Creole school in Pointe Coupée Parish, and accepted the appointment. Here in April 1861 he read the news of the attack on the 6th Massachusetts as it marched through Baltimore and the wounding of one of his classmates when the troops fired on the crowd. Deeply stirred, he was unable to sleep, and rose at midnight to jot down the lines beginning

The despot's heel is on thy shore.

Next morning he read them to his pupils and was urged to send the poem to the New Orleans *Delta*. It appeared in the Sunday edition, Apr. 26, and was immediately reprinted all over the South. The Misses Jennie and Hetty Cary of Baltimore adapted the words to the music of an old German song and sang it with such effect that it became the battle song of the South.

Randall sought to enlist in the Confederate army, but he was prevented by his health from giving active service in the field. After the War he became associate editor of the *Constitutionalist* in Augusta, Ga., and continued in some form of newspaper work for the rest of his life. For a number of years he lived in Washington, serving as secretary to Representative W. H. Fleming and later to Senator Joseph E. Brown, both of Georgia, and acting at the same time as Washington correspondent for the Augusta *Chronicle*. He also wrote for various periodicals, including the *Catholic Mirror* in Baltimore and the New Orleans Morning *Star*. He was married in 1866 to Katherine Hammond, daughter of Marcus C. M. Hammond, of South Carolina. They had eight children. Recognition of the poet as the author of the best known of state songs was accorded to Randall in 1907, when he was made an official guest of the state of Maryland at the Jamestown Exposition and received the same year a similar invitation from the City of Baltimore for its Homecoming Week. His collected poems were not published during his lifetime but arrangements for a volume of verse were just being completed when he died. Death came to him in August from congestion of the lungs following an attack of grippe. He was survived by his wife, a son, and three daughters.

[M. P. Andrews, *The Poems of James Ryder Randall* (1910); G. C. Perine, *The Poets and Verse-Writers of Md.* (1898); the *Sun* (Baltimore), Jan. 15, 1908; *Lib. of Southern Lit.*, vol. X (1909); *Who's Who in America*, 1906–07.]   J. C. F.

RANDALL, ROBERT RICHARD (*c.* 1750–June 1801), privateer, merchant, philanthropist, son of Thomas and Gertrude (Crooke) Randall, is supposed to have been born in New Jersey about 1750. He followed his father, a prosperous privateer, on the sea and became a shipmaster at an early age. On Apr. 8, 1771, he became a member of the Marine Society in New York which his father had helped to found for the relief of indigent and distressed seamen and seamen's widows and orphans. During the Revolution Randall volunteered his services to the Provincial Congress of New York. His offer was not accepted, possibly because of his greater value to the cause as an experienced privateer. Near the close of the war he became his father's partner and they carried on their business under the firm name of Randall, Son & Stewart. On Apr. 1, 1788, he became a member of the New York Chamber of Commerce of which his father had been one of the founders twenty years before. In the years following the war, the Randalls bought several pieces of land in different parts of New York City, the most famous being the Minto farm which Robert Randall purchased in 1790 from Frederick Charles Hans Bruno Poelnitz, a German baron with horticultural interests (New York County *Conveyances,* Lib. 46, p. 212). This purchase included a part of the old Peter Stuyvesant farm and extended from "the Bouwerie" west to "Minite Water" and approximately from what is now East Tenth Street south to Waverly Place. In his father's will, however, the property was treated as a bequest to Robert who resided on the farm from the time of the purchase until he died.

On June 1, 1801, Randall made his will, and sometime between that date and July 10, when the will was probated, he died, probably on June 5. Tradition has it that the will was drawn up by Alexander Hamilton who was undoubtedly a friend of the Randall family. In it, after bequeathing certain small sums to relatives and friends and quaintly disposing of his watch, shoe buckles, and silver buttons to friends and retainers, he left the rest of his property, which consisted of the farm, four lots in the first ward of the city, and certain stocks, bonds, and cash, in trust to provide an asylum and hospital for aged, decrepit, and worn-out seamen which should be called the Sailors' Snug Harbor. The property was put in the hands of an automatically self-perpetuating group of trustees who were to take charge of the property until the income from it warranted the establishment of an asylum which could accommodate fifty seamen. In spite of efforts to break the will on the part of certain of Randall's relatives on his mother's side, the courts allowed it to stand, and the Randall fortune acquired at sea became the foundation of the seamen's charity. In 1884, a statue by Augustus Saint-Gaudens, representing Randall, was placed on the grounds of the Sailors' Snug Harbor on Staten Island.

[Sources include: I. N. Phelps Stokes, *The Iconography of Manhattan Island* (6 vols., 1915–28); J. A. Stevens, *Colonial Records of the N. Y. Chamber of Commerce* (1867); *The Marine Soc. of the City of N. Y.* (1925); *Copy of the Last Will . . . of the Late Robert Richard Randall, Esq. . . . Respecting the Sailors' Snug Harbor* (1876); John Inglis vs. The Trustees of the Sailors' Snug Harbor, 3 Peters, 99; records of the N. Y. Chamber of Commerce, the Marine Society, the Sailors' Snug Harbor, and N. Y. County *Wills* and *Conveyances.*]   M. L. B.

RANDALL, SAMUEL (Feb. 10, 1778–Mar. 5, 1864), playwright, journalist, judge, son of Joseph and Esther (Fisher) Randall, was a descendant of one of the earliest settlers of the town of Sharon, Mass., where he himself was born. His father was a well-to-do farmer. After receiving his primary education in the public schools of Sharon, Samuel attended the Latin Grammar school of the Rev. William Williams of Wrentham. In the year 1800 he entered Rhode Island College, now Brown University, and graduated in 1804. While in college he gained considerable recognition as an orator and writer of plays. *The Miser* and *The Sophomore,* both printed as pamphlets in Warren, R. I., in 1812, were probably written by him while in college and were performed there between 1800 and 1804. The plays are genuine American primitives, springing from the college emphasis on oratory and declamation, instead of from the English plays acted at the local theatres. *The Miser* is "A comedy in 4 acts, written and designed to be performed in schools and academies." *The Sophomore, a Dialogue in One Act,* has no authorship given, but all the internal evidence goes to prove it was by Randall. Both plays are farces contrived to persuade doubting parents of the advantages of a college education for their sons. The characterizations are shrewd and the action lively.

After his graduation, Randall studied law with Judge Howell of Providence. In 1805 he went to Warren, R. I., to become "a preceptor" in the Warren Academy. In 1809 he married Patty Maxwell, daughter of James Maxwell of Warren, and established his home in that town. Six children were born of this marriage. One of them, the Rev. George M. Randall, became an Episcopalian clergyman and the first missionary bishop of Colorado. As a leading citizen of Warren, Randall held numerous offices in the town. At various times he was postmaster, town clerk, justice of the peace, and clerk of the town council. Between 1813 and 1826 he published three local newspapers, the *Telescope,* the *Clarion,* and the *Telegraph,* all rather short-lived. Though a stanch Republican he was singularly restrained as an editor in a period characterized by fierce party rancor. In 1822 he was appointed judge of the court of common pleas for Bristol County, R. I., and served in that capacity until 1824, when he was made justice of the supreme court of the state. He held this office until 1833, when he was displaced through a change of parties. His active life terminated about 1858 when ill health forced him to resign many of his duties. He died in 1864 at the age of eighty-six.

[The material for this biography was gathered mainly from the town records in the Town Hall at Warren, R. I.; the records of the Baptist Church and of various benevolent, Masonic, and military organizations stored in the Warren Branch of the Industrial Trust Company; from the manuscript records and scrapbook compilations at the Sharon Historical Society; and from the archives of Brown University. Printed references include: Brown necrology, *Providence Jour.*, Sept. 6, 1864; *Brown Hist. Cat.*, 1764–1904; *Sharon Hist. Soc. Pubs.*, no. 5, Apr. 1908. There is a sketch of Randall in *Biog. Cyc. of Representative Men of R. I.* (1881), but it is inaccurate in some details.]
W. V. S.

RANDALL, SAMUEL JACKSON (Oct. 10, 1828–Apr. 13, 1890), congressman from Pennsylvania, speaker of the House of Representatives, was born in Philadelphia. His father, Josiah Randall, a leading lawyer of the city, was a personal friend and political adviser of President Buchanan. His mother, Ann Worrell, was a daughter of Joseph Worrell, one of Thomas Jefferson's local political lieutenants. Before entering public life, Randall had attended University Academy in Philadelphia, gained initial business experience in a mercantile establishment, and later launched an iron and coal company of his own in Philadelphia.

His first public service was on the Common Council of the city, 1852–56, during which period he called himself an "American Whig." In 1858 he was elected to the state Senate, where he served on the committee on retrenchment and reform, but acted also as a franchise broker for street railway companies, joining with them in berating the iniquities of all banks. His military activity during the Civil War was confined to routine reconnoitering and patrol duty in his home state, during two short enlistments. In 1862 he was elected to Congress as a Democrat. His district, the old first, was the only Democratic one in Philadelphia and might have been gerrymandered out of existence by Republican legislatures if Randall had not reflected the protectionist desires of his state and city. He never lost contact with the residents of this waterfront district, made up of mechanics, factory and dock workers, and small tradesmen, who rewarded him by continually returning him to Congress until his death.

During Reconstruction, Randall tried to protect the South by supporting the policies of President Johnson. Later, he gained national prominence through his brilliant filibusters against the Civil Rights and Force bills in January and February 1875. During the Grant era, by questioning thousands of items in Republican appropriation bills and by helping to institute the investigation of the Crédit Mobilier, the Sanborn contracts, and the Pacific mail subsidy, he supplied his party with the battle cry of "Retrenchment and Reform," which was to lead it out of the wilderness of post-war wanderings. However, he unblushingly supported the "salary grab," in the belief that congressmen were underpaid and on the excuse that all previous salary raises had been retroactive.

The summer of 1875 found Randall capturing the Democratic organization of his home state, in the first of a series of rough-and-tumble political battles with William A. Wallace. Thus fortified by local and national support, Randall expected to be elected speaker of the House in December 1875 (Black Manuscripts), but rumors of support by questionable railroad and other subsidy-seeking interests, and an uncertain record on "soft money" discredited him. When Michael C. Kerr, his successful rival for the speakership, appointed him chairman of the committee on appropriations, Randall made good his economy claims by reducing total appropriations $30,000,000, even in the face of the opposition of the Republican Senate. His election to the speakership in December 1876 was a foregone conclusion after the death of Kerr in August. During the electoral count of 1876–77, Randall often conferred with Tilden, did much loud talking in caucus, and otherwise cooperated with the filibusterers in his own party, until the so-called "bargain" to withdraw the troops from the South was secured from Hayes. Thereupon he accepted the duties imposed on him by the electoral act and forced a completion of the count. (W. E. Chandler Manuscripts, Feb. 27, 28, 1877; *New York Times* and New York *World*, Feb. 18–28, 1877.)

As speaker of the Forty-fifth and Forty-sixth congresses, he played the rôle of party wheelhorse in such partisan activities as the Potter investigation and Senator Thurman's attempts to repeal the test-oath and election laws. He sidetracked all major tariff revisions and subsidy grants by his rulings and committee appointments. Randall's rulings added much to the power of the rules committee, and in 1880, under his guidance, the accumulation of nearly a century of tangled growth was condensed into forty-five compact rules. The subsequent problem of Speaker Thomas B. Reed [*q.v.*], of felling the tall timber of obstruction would have been much more difficult if Randall had not cleared out the underbrush before him.

With the temporary return of the Republicans to power in 1881, Randall was succeeded by J.

Warren Keifer as speaker. The debates over the tariff commission of 1882 and the Kelley tariff of 1883 presented him with the dilemma of choosing either the path which led to national leadership of his party or that which loyalty to his state demanded. His decision to support protection led to his defeat for the speakership by John G. Carlisle [q.v.], in caucus, in 1883. However, this did not mean oblivion, for as chairman of the appropriations committee he now entered the period of his greatest power. The aid of a faithful minority of his party and the powers given him by the rules of 1880 and the Holman amendment, enabled him practically to dictate both appropriations and general legislation. He held such complete sway during the Forty-eighth Congress that his committee was stripped of a portion of its power by the Forty-ninth. Even so, he was able to cut down extravagances in the various departments and continued to prevent tariff legislation, despite the desires of a majority of his party. At the National Democratic Convention of 1884 he successfully fought for a non-committal tariff plank, and afterward conducted a vigorous speaking campaign in the industrial states, where his word carried weight with the factory workers.

During 1885–86, Randall worked in real harmony with President Cleveland, especially in the attempts to repeal the silver-coinage laws. Randall was then at the height of his power in his home state, since he had been given control of most of the federal patronage, largely because of his friendship with Tilden and Manning, and also because of his aid in nominating and electing Cleveland. But early in 1888 he suddenly lost control of the Democratic organization in Pennsylvania. Because of Randall's unwillingness to acquiesce in Cleveland's tariff message of December 1887, the President gave the power of patronage to W. L. Scott and W. M. Singerly (Cleveland Manuscripts). Though Randall still kept his closest personal friends, his political friends at home and in Congress now left him, one by one. His physical energy, greatly reduced by cancer, was unequal to the task of holding his forces in line. None the less, he kept at his amazing schedule of long hours of work. His high-pitched voice was still heard in attack on the Republicans. He was still considered the best informed man in Congress on the details of governmental business, but his attachment to his own manufacturing state had left him alone when his party made "tariff for revenue only" a fundamental tenet of its political faith.

Randall died in Washington on Apr. 13, 1890, and was buried in Philadelphia. On June 24,

1851, he had married Fannie Agnes Ward, daughter of Aaron Ward of Sing Sing, N. Y., a Democratic congressman of the Jackson era. She, with their two daughters and son, survived him.

[Some references to Randall are to be found in J. A. Barnes, *John G. Carlisle* (1931); Allan Nevins, *Grover Cleveland* (1932); W. A. Robinson, *Thomas B. Reed* (1930). The following works dealing with congressional procedure contain sketches and references: D. S. Alexander, *Hist. and Procedure of the House of Representatives* (1916); M. P. Follett, *The Speaker of the House of Representatives* (1896); H. B. Fuller, *The Speakers of the House* (1909); A. C. Hinds, *Hinds' Precedents of the House of Representatives of the U. S.* (8 vols., 1907–08). The following collections contain considerable Randall correspondence: Jeremiah Black MSS., and Grover Cleveland MSS., Lib. of Cong.; James Buchanan MSS., Pa. Hist. Soc.; Samuel J. Tilden MSS., N. Y. Pub. Lib. For genealogy, see G. K. Ward, *Andrew Warde and His Descendants, 1597–1910* (1910). See also *Memorial Addresses on the Life and Character of Samuel J. Randall*, 51 Cong., 1 sess., *House Miscellaneous Doc. No. 265* (1891); obituary in *Public Ledger* (Philadelphia), Apr. 14, 1890.]
A. V. H., Jr.

RANDALL, SAMUEL SIDWELL (May 27, 1809–June 3, 1881), educator, was born at Norwich, Chenango County, N. Y., the son of Perez and Betsey (Edmunds) Randall. Henry Stephens Randall [q.v.] was his cousin. He was prepared for college at the Oxford Academy and entered Hamilton College in 1824, but he withdrew at the end of his sophomore year to take up the study of law in a law office at Norwich. Upon his admission to the bar in 1830 he established himself in practice in his native town. In May 1837 he was appointed by the secretary of state, then *ex officio* state superintendent of common schools, as a clerk in the department of common schools. In 1841 he became general deputy superintendent and held this office until 1846, serving for a time within this period as acting superintendent when the office of secretary of state was vacant. He was a frequent contributor to the *District School Journal* and for a time its editor. He wielded a strong influence upon the administration of the common-school system. His retirement from the department in 1846 was due to ill health. He spent some time in the South lecturing upon the subject of education but he was recalled to his former position in 1849 and continued in it until Jan. 1, 1852, when he left to take an appointment in the War Department at Washington. In 1851 the New York legislature had authorized the governor to appoint a commissioner to embody in a single act and to report to the legislature a common-school code for the state. Randall received this appointment and made his report on Jan. 1, 1852, urging that the office of state superintendent be separated from that of secretary of state; that a permanent tax be substituted for the fixed sum appropriated for the support of common schools, and that the office of county superintendent be restored. The first recommendation was adopted in 1854, the third in 1856, and the second in 1867.

Randall held the Washington appointment until November 1853, when he became superintendent of the public schools of Brooklyn. He remained as superintendent for a few weeks and in January 1854 returned to the state service for a third time. Shortly thereafter the supervision of common schools was separated from the office of secretary of state and Randall became a candidate for the new office of state superintendent of public instruction. He was defeated by Victor M. Rice [q.v.]. He aided the new superintendent in organizing his department and withdrew in the summer of 1854 to become superintendent of the public schools in the city of New York. He held this position until June 1, 1870, when he resigned on account of failing health. He died on June 3, 1881. His first wife was Lucy Ann Breed, whom he married on Oct. 29, 1829. His second wife was Sarah Hubbell, by whom he had four children. The range of his intellectual interests may be understood from the following partial list of his published works: *A Digest of the Common School System of the State of New York* (1844); *Mental and Moral Culture and Popular Education* (1844); *The Common School System of the State of New York* (1851); *History of the State of New York* (1870); *History of the Common School System of the State of New York* (1871).

[*Am. Jour. of Educ.*, June 1863; *School Bull.*, June 1881; P. K. Randall, *Geneal. of a Branch of the Randall Family* (1879); *Fiftieth Ann. Report of State Supt. of Pub. Instruction: State of N. Y.* (1904); *N. Y. Herald*, June 4, 1881.]   H. H. H.

RANDALL, WYATT WILLIAM (Jan. 10, 1867–July 22, 1930), chemist, son of Alexander and Elizabeth Philpot (Blanchard) Randall, and brother of Burton Alexander Randall [q.v.], was born at Annapolis, Md. Upon graduating from St. John's College, Annapolis, in 1884, he entered the graduate department of the Johns Hopkins University, specialized in chemistry, and received the degree of Ph.D. in 1890. He was retained by the University and served as an instructor in chemistry for two years and then as associate professor for five. A part of the year 1895 he spent in Ramsay's laboratory at University College, London, on an investigation on the expansion of argon and helium as compared with that of air and hydrogen. During the next twelve years he taught chemistry in preparatory schools, first (1898–1900) at the Lawrenceville School, N. J., then (1900–01) at the Tome Institute,

Port Deposit, Md., and finally (1901–10) at the Mackenzie School, Dobbs Ferry, N. Y., where he was also headmaster. In 1911 he became associated with the bureau of chemistry of the Maryland State Department of Health where he remained until his death. He rose rapidly from the position of assistant through assistant chief to chief of the bureau, and held the last grade for fourteen years (1916–30). From 1921 to 1930 he was also associate professor of biochemistry at the School of Hygiene and Public Health of Johns Hopkins. His interest in the varied problems of the department of health led to his official connection with agricultural associations. He joined the Association of Official Agricultural Chemists in November 1913, attended its meetings regularly, and held various offices. In 1925 he was elected president of the Association and at the time of his death he was a member of the important committee on editing methods of analysis.

In February 1918 Randall was appointed a member of the joint committee on definitions and standards of the United States Department of Agriculture and served in this capacity for eight years. He was one of the founders of the Central Atlantic States Dairy, Food, and Drug Officials and was president of the organization in 1922. His writings were varied. With Ira Remsen [q.v.] he wrote *Chemical Experiments* (1895 and subsequent editions), and in 1902 he published *The Expansion of Gases by Heat*. In the *American Chemical Journal*, which Remsen founded and edited, he published between 1891 and 1897 about forty articles which included reports on his own investigations, reviews of the progress of chemistry, short papers on scientific subjects, obituary notices, and book reviews. He also contributed about thirty articles on chemical subjects to non-technical magazines and nearly an equal number on agricultural and health topics to both technical and non-technical publications. Randall died in Baltimore at the age of sixty-three. He had married, on June 23, 1898, Eliza P. Colston. There were no children. His professional career was characterized by precision in experimenting and in recording results, and by decisions based upon mature judgment. He was enthusiastic in his research, and he performed his official duties without regard for the allurements of commercial rewards.

[Sources include: *Jour. Asso. Official Agric. Chemists*, Nov. 15, 1930; *Science*, Aug. 8, 1930; *Who's Who in America*, 1930–31; the *Sun* (Baltimore), July 23, 1930.]   L. C. N.

RANDOLPH, ALFRED MAGILL (Aug. 31, 1836–Apr. 6, 1918), Protestant Episcopal bishop, was fifth in descent from William Randolph [q.v.], founder of a famous Virginia family, and fourth in descent from his son William. He was born near Winchester, Va., the son of Robert Lee Randolph, a first cousin of Robert E. Lee [q.v.], and Mary Buckner Thruston (Magill), daughter of Col. Charles Magill, a Revolutionary officer. Since he was by breeding and association an Eastern Virginian, it was fitting that he should be educated at the College of William and Mary. Here he studied diligently (he is said to have learned a Greek grammar by heart) and was graduated in 1855 as final orator. For the deeply religious youth it was another natural step to the Theological Seminary in Virginia, at Alexandria, where he was ordered deacon in 1858 by Bishop Meade. Among his fellow students and intimate friends on Seminary Hill were Phillips Brooks and Henry Codman Potter [qq.v.]. In 1859 he married Sallie Griffith Hoxton of Alexandria, great-grand-daughter of Rev. David Griffith, George Washington's chaplain and personal friend; the following year he was ordained priest.

From the beginning Randolph's ministry was notably successful. He first served St. George's, Fredericksburg, until in December 1862 the congregation was scattered and the church partly destroyed by Federal guns. After seeking shelter for his wife and day-old baby, he became a Confederate chaplain, ministering on battlefield and in hospital until 1864. He was rector of churches in Halifax County and at Alexandria until 1867, when he went to Emmanuel Church, Baltimore; of Emmanuel he remained the beloved pastor until 1883, retaining on it "a lifelong hold." While in Baltimore he became a prominent opponent of tractarianism and ritualism and a leader in the resistance to what he believed the unwarranted assumption of powers by the bishops. In his opposition to tractarianism and ritualism he was carrying on the Low-Church tradition of the Virginia Seminary and the Church in Virginia. At the height of his vigor, in 1883, he was elected coadjutor bishop of Virginia, and served most creditably for nine years. In 1892, the diocese being divided, he chose to become bishop of the new Diocese of Southern Virginia, where he labored until his death.

A stranger would find it difficult to appreciate the depth of the love and reverence in which Bishop Randolph was held by his contemporaries. Inheriting a tradition of gentlemanliness and of devotion to the Virginia Church, and having a broad human sympathy, he was ideally suited to his aristocratic and old-fashioned, yet zealous, diocese. No doubt many bishops have been more efficient in administration, though it is not to be inferred that he was inefficient; his well-known absent-mindedness was in regard to trivial matters. His outstanding abilities were those of the preacher and pastor. Possessing a remarkably sweet and controlled voice, a scholarly mind, and a cultured background, he was called "the silver-tongued orator of the House of Bishops." Twice he received, and on account of his duties felt it necessary to decline, invitations to deliver the opening address at the decennial Pan-Anglican Conference at Lambeth Palace, London. Though not illiberal, he did not seek doctrinal controversy: "Cling to faith beyond the forms of Faith," he was wont to quote from Tennyson's poem, "The Ancient Sage." His sermons were, like himself, unostentatious but impressive. Despite his deep consecration, he was not puritanical and was a genial, witty, social companion. He was elected to full membership in the Shakespearian Club in England, and received numerous honorary degrees. His only published volume was *Reason, Faith, and Authority in Christianity* (1902), a reprint of his Paddock Lectures, delivered in 1901–02 at the General Theological Seminary, New York.

[*Bull. Fauquier Hist. Soc.*, June 1923; W. A. R. Goodwin, *Hist. of the Theol. Sem. in Va., and Its Hist. Background* (1924), vol. II; *Diocesan Record of Southern Va.*, June 1918; *Virginian Pilot* (Norfolk) and *Richmond Times-Dispatch* (Richmond), Apr. 7, 1918; *Who's Who in America*, 1916–17; information from kinsmen and associates.]					R. D. M.

RANDOLPH, EDMUND (Aug. 10, 1753–Sept. 12, 1813), attorney general, secretary of state, originally had the middle name Jenings (sometimes given as Jennings), but did not use it in public life. He was born at "Tazewell Hall," near Williamsburg, Va. His father, John Randolph, his uncle, Peyton Randolph, and his grandfather, Sir John Randolph [qq.v.], had been King's attorneys, and for generations members of the family had been prominent in the province. His mother was Ariana Jenings (*William and Mary Quarterly*, Apr. 1900, p. 265), daughter of Edmund Jenings, at one time King's attorney of Maryland. In boyhood he had the fortunate opportunity of meeting in his home, at the family table, many of the most distinguished men of his time. He naturally attended the College of William and Mary, and he studied law under his father. The latter was a Loyalist and followed Lord Dunmore to England. Edmund was thereupon taken into the family of his distinguished uncle, Peyton Randolph. Bearing letters from prominent Virginians, he presented himself in August 1775 at

Cambridge and received from Washington an appointment as aide-de-camp. His uncle having died, he returned to Williamsburg and at the age of twenty-three became the youngest member of the Virginia convention that adopted the first constitution for the state. Under the new state government he became attorney general. He was also mayor of Williamsburg. On Aug. 29, 1776, he was married to Elizabeth Nicholas, daughter of Robert Carter Nicholas [q.v.], the state treasurer.

In the spring of 1779 he was elected to the Continental Congress, retaining however his position as attorney general of Virginia. He threw his influence in the state in favor of the import duty of five per cent. that was asked by Congress. On Nov. 7, 1786, he was elected governor against Richard Henry Lee and Theodorick Bland. He was a delegate to the Annapolis Convention and to the Federal Convention of 1787. He probably had considerable influence in securing Washington's acceptance of membership in the latter body. Randolph was put forward in the Federal Convention to propose the famous Virginia Plan (Farrand, *post*, I, 20–22; III, 593–94), and also drew a draft, perhaps the first, of the work of the committee of detail, to which he was appointed on July 24, 1787 (*Ibid.*, I, xxii; II, 137–51). In company with George Mason, he declined to sign the completed Constitution because he thought it insufficiently republican. He had stated that he regarded "a unity in the Executive magistracy" as "the foetus of monarchy" and had favored an executive department of three men (Speech of June 1, 1787, *Ibid.*, I, 66). The single executive being accepted, he had advocated his being made ineligible for reëlection (*Ibid.*, II, 54, 145). Since the committee of detail worked from Randolph's draft, many of the features of the completed Constitution are similar to it. A second convention, after sufficient time for discussion, Randolph thought eminently desirable (*Ibid.*, II, 479). He wrote a *Letter . . . on the Federal Constitution* (1787), in criticism of the document. However, when the time came for Virginia to act upon it, in the state convention of 1788, despite bitter criticism of him for inconsistency, he stood with Madison and Marshall in advocating ratification, his reason being that "the accession of eight states reduced our *deliberations* to the single question of *Union or no Union*" (Jonathan Elliot, *The Debates in the Several States, on the Adoption of the Federal Constitution,* 1836, III, 652; see also, III, 62–86).

Under the new government, Washington, who had every reason to be familiar with the abilities and character of Randolph, appointed him attorney general. This position he filled with credit, but with embarrassment on account of the effort he made to be non-partisan in the conflict between Jefferson and Hamilton. When Jefferson retired as secretary of state, Randolph filled the office from Jan. 2, 1794, to Aug. 19, 1795. The position was extremely difficult. While Randolph endeavored to continue an independent rôle, Hamilton regarded himself as a kind of premier and took a keen interest and an active part in foreign affairs. These were in tangled condition and the people of the United States were divided in their opinions and affections as respected France and Great Britain. Randolph got rid of the offensive French minister, Edmond Charles Genet [q.v.], but protected him from arrest as requested by the French government. He approved of the recall of Gouverneur Morris [q.v.], minister to France, and the appointment of James Monroe [q.v.] as his successor. He ably upheld the interest of the United States in his correspondence with Fauchet, Genet's successor, and advised Monroe with reference to his negotiations with the French government, at times finding that Monroe went too far in his manifestations of affection for France.

In addition to infringing upon the rights of the United States as a neutral, Great Britain had failed to fulfil the terms of the treaty of 1783, retaining the western posts and failing to surrender negroes that had been carried off. The situation became so acute that, under the influence of Hamilton and his friends and with the approval of Randolph, Washington decided to send a special envoy to England. Randolph was opposed to the selection of Hamilton, the first choice of the group that were engineering the special mission, and though personally friendly to John Jay [q.v.], was opposed to him for this appointment. In addition to other grounds of opposition, Randolph personally objected to the appointment of a justice of the Supreme Court as a diplomatic agent and thought Jay should resign his judicial position. Randolph, with advice from Hamilton and others, drew the instructions to Jay. They covered the ground of the protection of American rights and authorized the negotiation of a commercial treaty. To this latter grant of power Randolph was opposed. His efforts to keep Jay in line with his own thinking were attended by great difficulty. The time required for communication, the lack of complete sympathy between the envoy and the Secretary of State, and the persistent interference by Hamilton in foreign affairs, both in his dealings with Jay and with the British minister in America,

Hammond, created a complicated and embarrassing situation for Randolph. Jay treated him with formal courtesy, but did not refrain from lecturing him. The treaty as negotiated by Jay came far short of carrying out the detailed instructions given him, and the Senate refused to accept the twelfth article, which pledged the United States not to export molasses, sugar, coffee, cocoa, or cotton. Randolph was favorable to the ratification of the treaty without this article, provided an Order in Council authorizing the seizure of ships laden with provisions should be withdrawn. Washington apparently supported Randolph's position up to the time when the Secretary of State came under serious criticism for his relations with the French minister, Fauchet.

While Randolph was having difficulty enough dealing with Jay, he was finding it hard to satisfy Monroe and France. Monroe was kept purposely in semi-darkness about the full purpose of Jay's mission. The French were naturally suspicious and, when the contents of Jay's Treaty were known, protested that it violated the treaty obligations of the United States to France. Randolph was compelled to maintain that it did not. Negotiations with Spain during his period of service resulted, soon after his retirement, in the Treaty of San Lorenzo, according to which the free navigation of the Mississippi from its source to its mouth was assured American citizens and the southern boundary was established according to the terms of the treaty of peace between the United States and Great Britain.

Randolph's retirement was brought about by revelations through the British minister of intercepted communications of the French minister, Fauchet, to his government. Fauchet had written a rambling account in which he seemed to imply that Randolph made improper revelations to him and indicated that French money would be welcome (*Annual Report of the American Historical Association for the Year 1903*, 1904, II, 414–15, 451). When called in question by Washington, under humiliating circumstances, Randolph resigned. Fauchet denied that he meant any reflections on his honor, and Randolph himself wrote an elaborate vindication (*A Vindication of Mr. Randolph's Resignation*, 1795; for Jefferson's comment, see P. L. Ford, *The Writings of Thomas Jefferson*, VII, 1896, pp. 41–42). Withdrawing to Richmond, Randolph entered again upon the practice of law and became a leading legal figure. His accounts with the government were called in question and settled, but were allowed to encumber the books of the Treasury Department and embarrass the friends

of Randolph until 1889, when the criminal carelessness that had gone on for nearly a century was revealed in a report called for under a resolution offered by Senator Daniel of Virginia (*Senate Executive Document No. 58*, 50 Cong., 2 sess.).

His greatest prominence in later years was as senior counsel for Aaron Burr in the famous treason trial. He spent his leisure time in writing a history of Virginia, most of which was destroyed by fire, the rest being preserved in manuscript for posterity in the archives of the Virginia Historical Society. His devoted wife died in 1810. He succumbed to the family disease of paralysis, which some years before had overtaken him, on Sept. 12, 1813. Among their four children, a son and three daughters, were Peyton (d. 1828), who married Maria Ward, once engaged to John Randólph of Roanoke, and Lucy, who married Peter V. Daniel [*q.v.*]. Peyton's son Edmund [*q.v.*] became a distinguished lawyer in California.

[The most recent account is D. R. Anderson, "Edmund Randolph," in S. F. Bemis, ed., *The Am. Secretaries of State and Their Diplomacy*, II (1927). M. D. Conway, *Omitted Chapters of History, Disclosed in the Life and Papers of Edmund Randolph* (1888), contains many personal papers elsewhere inaccessible. There are a few Randolph MSS. in the Lib. of Cong., and letters and other materials are in the published and unpublished writings of Washington, Jefferson, and Hamilton. A portion of his diplomatic correspondence is in *Am. State Papers. Foreign Relations*, I (1832); much unpublished material is in the archives of the Dept. of State. *Am. Hist. Review*, Apr. 1907, contains some Randolph material with reference to Jay's Treaty. See also W. P. Palmer, ed., *Calendar of Va. State Papers*, IV (1884), for his governorship; Max Farrand, *The Records of The Fed. Convention of 1787* (3 vols., 1911); obituary in *Enquirer* (Richmond), Sept. 17, 1813.]

D. R. A.

RANDOLPH, EDMUND (June 9, 1819– Sept. 8, 1861), California lawyer, grandson of Edmund Randolph [*q.v.*], Washington's attorney-general, was born in Richmond, Va., the son of Peyton Randolph and his wife Maria Ward. The son was graduated from the College of William and Mary in 1836 and then studied law for a year at the University of Virginia. Moving to New Orleans shortly thereafter, he entered upon the practice of law and soon became clerk of the United States circuit court for Louisiana. He married Thomassa Meaux, the daughter of Dr. Meaux of that city; she and two daughters survived him. In 1849 he moved to San Francisco and the same year was elected to represent that town in the lower branch of the first California legislature, meeting at San Jose, Dec. 15, 1849. After the close of his term he never held public office but frequently appeared in political conventions, on the stump, or as a candidate. Early in 1851 he formed a law partnership in

San Francisco with R. A. Lockwood and Frank Tilford, and the firm became prominent and highly successful. The greatest case in which Randolph was engaged was the Alameden quicksilver mine case. He was leading counsel for the government along with Edwin M. Stanton, and the opposing counsel included Reverdy Johnson and Judah P. Benjamin. The trial of the case was described as the "acme of his fame, the flower of his power," and his "most enduring monument." The decision was appealed to the United States Supreme Court (*United States* vs. *Castillero*, 23 *Howard*, 464) where the elaborate brief prepared by Randolph was the basis upon which the government won its case. His prolonged and exhausting labors in this litigation led to his untimely death before the case came on for argument before the Court. Although the suit involved millions, Randolph's fee, paid to his widow, was a paltry $17,000. With John Nugent and William Walker, Randolph was associated in the editorship of the San Francisco *Herald* when it was established in 1850. He publicly and defiantly opposed the Vigilance Committees of 1851 and 1856. He took an active part in Walker's scheme for the conquest of Nicaragua and in the winter of 1855–56 went to Nicaragua to counsel with Walker and help him organize a government there.

In the Kansas controversy of 1857–58, Randolph warmly espoused the Anti-Lecompton position of Stephen A. Douglas, and in 1859 was the Anti-Lecompton-Republican fusion candidate for attorney-general of California. In 1861 he was a candidate for the United States Senate. Although a stanch defender of slavery, he openly opposed secession and upheld the Union. But he was untroubled by considerations of consistency and was soon denouncing the early measures of the Lincoln administration. In his last public speech, before the Breckinridge Democratic convention held at Sacramento, in the summer of 1861, "his whole soul," says a contemporary who was present, "seemed to have become one vast volcano of molten rage," and he spoke with "the fury of an inflamed patriot and the frenzy of an inspired prophet," fervently praying for the slaying of Lincoln, the "despot usurper." The same contemporary declares that Randolph was "more powerful in invective than any other lawyer among his contemporaries." He had little wit, never told a joke, and was sarcastic to a superlative degree. He was gifted, excitable, and impetuous in temper, full of poetry and enthusiasm, but he was not a powerful, or even a logical, reasoner. He won wide public admiration, but he had few intimate friends

and was not companionable. Some of these traits may be attributable to the dyspepsia from which he suffered throughout his life.

[The best printed sketches of Randolph appear in three books by O. T. Shuck: *Representative and Leading Men of the Pacific* (1870); *Bench and Bar in Cal.* (1889); and *Hist. of the Bench and Bar of Cal.* (1901). See also: H. H. Bancroft, *Hist. of Cal.*, vol. VI (1888), note p. 679; W. G. Stanard, "The Randolph Family," *Wm. and Mary Coll. Quart. Hist. Mag.*, Oct. 1898, Apr. 1900; and editorial in the *Daily Alta Cal.*, Sept. 9, 1861. The Sacramento speech is quoted in W. J. Davis, *Hist. of Pol. Conventions in Cal., 1849–92* (1893), p. 173.]   P. O. R.

RANDOLPH, EDWARD (c. July 9, 1632–April 1703), British agent, was one of fifteen children born to Dr. Edmund and Deborah (Master) Randolph of Canterbury, England. The exact date of Edward's birth is unknown, but he was baptized July 9, 1632. He entered Gray's Inn as a law student, Nov. 12, 1650, and was admitted pensioner at Queens' College, Cambridge, in 1651. He did not take a degree and there is no record of his being called to the bar. Before 1660 he had married Jane Gibbon of West Cliffe, Kent, whose father was a progenitor of Edward Gibbon, the historian. For some years after his marriage he was employed by the Commissioners of the Navy in buying timber. By 1666 he was in sore financial straits, sold part of his estate, and feared he would have to flee the country to avoid his creditors. He again secured employment, however, this time as agent for the Duke of Richmond in Scotland, in connection with timber speculations which, apparently, were not successful. For a time he was commissary of the Cinque Ports, living near Dover. In 1672 he had lost much property by fire. During all these years he was in correspondence with influential persons in the Court circle.

In March 1675/76 he was appointed to carry the royal instructions to Massachusetts requiring the colonial government to send agents to England to answer complaints of the Mason and Gorges heirs. His orders also called for a complete report on the colony. Landing in Boston, June 10, 1676, he received scant courtesy from the government, which ignored the king's command that he carry back their answer. He remonstrated with the Council over certain flagrant violations of the laws of trade, and was told that the laws of England did not apply to Massachusetts. Receiving only curt replies to his complaints to the government, he next proceeded to investigate conditions on the spot in New Hampshire, Maine, and Plymouth, and left for England on July 30.

In his report to the king, Sept. 20, 1676 (Toppan, *post*, II, 216–25), he denounced the colonists in plain language. A fuller report was made to the Committee for Trade and Plantations on Oct. 12 (*Ibid.*, 225–59). Except that he exaggerated the amount of local disaffection toward the colonial government, there was much truth in what he wrote, though it was tinged with the dislike he had conceived for the extreme Puritan party, a dislike they heartily reciprocated. On May 6, 1677, he wrote a paper, "Representation of Ye Affaires of N :England" (*Ibid.*, 265–68), which was a direct attack on the legality of the Massachusetts charter. Meanwhile, the colony had sent agents to England, with very limited powers, and the heirs of Gorges and Mason were pressing their claims to Maine and New Hampshire. As a result of many hearings, the administration of these two provinces was withdrawn from Massachusetts and that colony was instructed to enforce the navigation acts, to repeal all laws which were repugnant to those of England, and to make no discrimination against non-church-members in public life. Randolph naturally became a hated figure.

One of the drastic measures taken by the Crown to discipline the unruly colony was Randolph's appointment in 1678 to take charge of all the customs throughout New England. He landed in New York on Dec. 7, 1679, and proceeded to New Hampshire, where he inaugurated the new government. He then settled at Boston to carry out his duties as collector of customs. Although nominally the colonial government voted him assistance, he never received it. The colonists were determined not to obey the laws of trade, to maintain as great independence of England as possible, and to hamper her efforts and agents in every way they could. On the other hand, Randolph had always been prejudiced against them, and the history of his relations with the people is a long story of bitter and ignoble bickering. He made every effort to have the Massachusetts charter annulled, journeying to England several times to accomplish his purpose. He presented prejudiced accounts, but they always had a sound basis of fact when they dealt with colonial law breaking. In 1684 the charter was declared forfeit, Randolph was commissioned secretary and register for the Dominion of New England, Sept. 21, 1685, and became a councilor in the new royal government set up six days later with Joseph Dudley [*q.v.*] as president. Under this government Randolph returned to New England, arriving in May 1686. He soon had a disagreement with Dudley and urged the speedy sending of a permanent royal governor from England. Under Sir Edmund Andros [*q.v.*] he retained his councillorship and collectorship, but in May 1687 leased his office of secretary to John West for four years, although, with the addition in 1688 of New York and the Jerseys to the Dominion of New England, he was commissioned secretary of the enlarged jurisdiction.

He fell with the rest of the government in the revolution of April 1689, was held prisoner in the common jail for a number of months, and sent to England only when the king ordered it. Arrived in London, he was at once set at liberty, and in 1691 he was made surveyor general of customs for all North America, including the Bahama and other islands. He reached Virginia in 1692 and traveled through all the colonies to Boston. Everywhere he found violations of the laws of trade and the same difficulty in enforcing them, and came constantly into conflict with the authorities. He returned to England in 1695 to push his plans for reorganizing colonial administration, but was in Maryland by the end of 1697. He continued to pursue his stormy career and on an official visit to Bermuda was imprisoned from May 16, 1699, to Jan. 3, 1700. He sent constant memorials to England describing conditions and filled with bitterness against the colonials. He had one more trip home, later in 1700, and took part in an attack in Parliament on the charter and proprietary colonies, but returned to America in 1702 and died in April of the following year.

Randolph was married three times; his first wife, Jane Gibbon, died in 1679, having borne him four daughters; Grace Grenville, his second, died in 1682; and his third wife, Sarah (Backhouse) Platt, by whom he had one child, in 1684. He was temperamentally unfitted for his post. His judgment became less balanced and his temper steadily worse at the constant thwarting he received from judges, juries, and governments in the attempt to carry out his duty. To expect one man to enforce the laws of trade in America was an absurdity and the career of Randolph in all its aspects illustrates the reason why, in time, imperial administration broke down.

[*Edward Randolph* (7 vols., 1898–1909), ed. for the Prince Soc. by R. N. Toppan (vols. I–V) and A. T. S. Goodrick (vols. VI–VII), contains a long memoir and documents. See also *The Hutchinson Papers*, vol. II (Prince Soc., 1865) ; *Cal. of State Papers, Col. Ser., America and West Indies*, covering 1675–1703 (1893–1913) ; R. N. Toppan, "Andros Records," *Proc. Am. Antiq. Soc.*, n.s. XIII (1901) ; V. F. Barnes, *The Dominion of New England* (1923) ; Everett Kimball, *The Public Life of Joseph Dudley* (1911) ; K. B. Murdock, *Increase Mather* (1925).]   J. T. A.

RANDOLPH, EPES (Aug. 16, 1856–Aug. 22, 1921), railroad president, was born in Lunenberg, Lunenberg County, Va., the son of William Eston and Sarah Lavinia (Epes) Randolph. At the age of twenty he entered railroad service which he was to make his life work. His primary interest was in the pioneering and constructive aspects of the industry. He early associated himself with Collis P. Huntington [q.v.] while the latter was engaged in building the Southern Pacific, and among other surveys ran the location west from San Antonio, Tex., toward California. In the eighties and early nineties Randolph was Huntington's representative in Kentucky where he acted as chief engineer of the Kentucky Central. At the same time he served in similar capacity for the Cincinnati Elevated Railway, Transfer, and Bridge Company for which he built a double-track railway, highway and foot bridge over the Ohio River from Cincinnati to Covington. Until 1894 he was associated with other Huntington projects. In that year he was obliged to give up active service because of an attack of tuberculosis and went to reside in Arizona. He entered the service of the Southern Pacific, and although handicapped by his poor health, accomplished extraordinary results in his chosen field for twenty-five years. His two chiefs, Huntington and his successor, Harriman, found in him a man after their own hearts, and came to rely upon his judgment in critical emergencies and concerning problems of construction and reconstruction.

In 1901 Huntington took Randolph to Los Angeles to build and operate the Pacific Electric Railway. After two years as vice-president and general manager he was forced by the condition of his health to return to Arizona. By establishing headquarters in Tucson, he was enabled to continue in active service in spite of his disabilities. He was constantly on the frontier of new problems and became well known throughout the Southwest and Mexico for his accomplishments. In 1904 he became president of a group of small railroads in Arizona and vicinity and following their merger (1910) into the Arizona Eastern became its president and general manager. Not an unimportant feature of Randolph's service was the protection of these small lines against the inroads of the Santa Fé. With a vision of the future which would have carried him far had his health permitted he built nearly a thousand miles of line in Mexico and became president in 1911 of the Southern Pacific of Mexico. This position, together with a similar position in the Arizona Eastern, he held until his death in Tucson in 1921.

The achievement most closely associated with Randolph's name was that which concerned the rescue of the Imperial Valley from destruction.

The problem of the control of the Colorado River, which the California Development Company had been unable to cope with, and the permanent protection of the Valley became acute in 1905. The vital interest of the Southern Pacific led Harriman to place Randolph in charge of the situation, and from this time until February 1907, when the turbulent and lawless stream was finally forced back into its bed and the Valley was made safe once more, Randolph was more or less continuously occupied with the problem. Failure after failure did not daunt him, and it became at the end a question of dumping rock into the stream faster than the River could carry it away. Randolph was a man of the pioneer type, a devoted follower of Huntington and Harriman, daring, courageous, tackling difficult problems with zest, and conquering them by the force of his drive and efficiency. He was impatient of restraint, and looked with misgiving upon the growing tendency toward federal and state interference with railway building and operation. He had little sympathy with attempts to check the activities of men of the Harriman type whom he whole-heartedly regarded as public benefactors. Randolph was married in January 1886 to Eleanor Taylor of Winchester, Va., who survived him. He had no children.

[See George Kennan, *The Salton Sea* (1917) and *E. H. Harriman: A Biog.* (1922), vol. II; obituary notice, *Railway Age*, Aug. 27, 1921; "Epes Randolph: An Appreciation," by a former staff officer, *Ibid.*, Sept. 3, 1921; "Honored Career of Epes Randolph Closes," *Southern Pacific Bull.*, Sept. 1921; *Who's Who in America*, 1920–21. Randolph's attitude toward political interference is expressed in a letter in the Los Angeles *Times*, Aug. 23, 1921, reprinted in the *Railway Age*, Sept. 17, 1921, with the title "For Politics Only."]

F. H. D.

RANDOLPH, GEORGE WYTHE (Mar. 10, 1818–Apr. 3, 1867), lawyer, Confederate secretary of war, was born at "Monticello," Virginia, the home of his maternal grandfather, Thomas Jefferson. The son of Gov. Thomas Mann Randolph [q.v.] and Martha Jefferson, and a brother of Thomas Jefferson Randolph [q.v.], he was named for his distinguished grandfather's law teacher. After Jefferson's death in 1826, Randolph was sent to his brother-in-law, Joseph Coolidge of Boston, to be educated; he attended school at Cambridge, but, when thirteen years old, was appointed a midshipman in the navy, and for the next six years served almost constantly at sea. At the age of nineteen he entered the University of Virginia where he continued for two years. He then resigned from the navy and studied law.

After practising his profession for a brief period in Albemarle County, he moved, shortly before 1850, to Richmond, where he won considerable success. A conscientious and hard-working lawyer, he resembled, in industry, his grandfather, Jefferson. He is said to have read a Latin or Greek author in the original every morning before breakfast. Before the Richmond voters he courageously advocated the white basis of representation in the General Assembly. About 1852 he was married to a young widow, Mary E. (Adams) Pope.

After the John Brown raid, Randolph used his military knowledge in organizing an artillery company, the Richmond Howitzers, which is still in existence. He served as one of the peace commissioners from Virginia to the United States government early in 1861. He was elected as a secessionist to the state convention of that year and made "the most practical and sensible speech in favor of secession" delivered before that body (*Richmond Dispatch,* Apr. 5, 1867). As a member of the military committee of the convention, he also rendered valuable service. He was one of the first advocates of a stringent conscription law and did more, perhaps, than any other man to influence the Virginia legislature in favor of such a measure, which was later adopted by the Confederate government. During the Peninsula campaign of early 1861, Randolph served in command of the Howitzers. He was promoted colonel, and became chief of artillery under Magruder, who attributed to him its high state of efficiency. At Big Bethel, in June, he was cited for "skill and gallantry." He was promoted brigadier-general and was opposed to Butler in southeastern Virginia.

On Mar. 22, 1862, he was appointed secretary of war, the first Confederate military official to hold this difficult position. His predecessor, Judah P. Benjamin [*q.v.*], had introduced order and efficiency into the chaotic War Department; Randolph profited from his work, and secured better coördination with the Confederate generals. After his death, the *Richmond Dispatch* (Apr. 5, 1867) called him the best secretary of war the Confederacy ever had. He was in office during nearly all the difficult campaigns of 1862. On Oct. 21 of that year J. B. Jones (*post,* I, 174) wrote that he was "thin, frail"; his face was "pale and will soon be a mass of wrinkles." Because Jefferson Davis dominated the Cabinet even in the matter of detail appointments, as early as April, the blunt General Wise had asserted, "There is no Secretary of War," adding that Randolph "is merely a *clerk*, an underling, and cannot hold up his head in his humiliating position" (*Ibid.,* I, 120). Finally, on Nov. 15,

he resigned and was replaced by James H. Seddon, a civilian who was sufficiently subservient to Davis. Randolph applied for a command in the field, but soon resigned. He was found to have pulmonary tuberculosis and went to France for his health. After the war he returned to Virginia, but did not recover, and died in his fiftieth year, at "Edgehill," a family estate.

[*War of the Rebellion: Official Records (Army)*; C. A. Evans, *Confed. Mil. Hist.* (1899), esp. I, 607; *Battles and Leaders of the Civil War* (4 vols., 1887–88); J. B. Jones, *A Rebel War Clerk's Diary* (2 vols., 1866); *Richmond Dispatch* and *Richmond Times,* Apr. 5, 1867; sketch and other data from Randolph's greatnephew, Gen. Jefferson Randolph Kean.]   R. D. M.

RANDOLPH, ISHAM (Mar. 25, 1848–Aug. 2, 1920), civil engineer, was the son of Robert Carter Randolph, a physician, and his wife, Lucy Nelson (Wellford). He was a descendant of William Randolph [*q.v.*], founder of the family in Virginia, tracing his ancestry through the paternal line to William's son Isham. He was born on his father's farm at New Market, Clarke County, Va. The Civil War, during which his family suffered greatly, deprived him of educational advantages. Apart from what his mother taught him, his schooling under masters was limited to twenty-one months in private schools near his home. In 1868, deciding to become a civil engineer, he took up railroad work, rising by persistent effort and hard, independent study, coupled with native resourcefulness, through the grades of axman, rodman, levelman, and transitman, to that of resident engineer. In this capacity, in 1873, he built twenty-seven miles of the Baltimore & Ohio Railroad, and the roundhouse and shops at South Chicago, Ill. Later (1880), as chief engineer of the Chicago & Western Indiana Belt Railway, he built terminals and freight houses. After seventeen years in the employ of different railroad companies, he opened an office in Chicago and was engaged in general engineering practice from 1885 to 1893. During this period he served the Illinois Central Railroad as chief engineer in locating and building the Chicago, Madison & Northern Railroad and the Freeport & Dolgeville line. He also acted as consulting engineer for the Union Stock Yards and the Baltimore & Ohio Railroad.

In June 1893 he was appointed chief engineer of the Sanitary District of Chicago, a position he held for fourteen years, during the entire construction period of the Chicago Drainage Canal. This notable enterprise, which changed the direction of the Chicago River so that its waters flow into the Mississippi instead of into Lake Michigan, was the largest artificial canal in the world until the completion of the Panama Canal.

In recognition of the achievement, Randolph was awarded a gold medal by the Paris Exposition in 1900, and he was retained as consulting engineer for five years after the completion of the project.

In 1905, he was appointed by President Theodore Roosevelt as a member of a board of consulting engineers to determine the type of the Panama Canal. He was one of the minority of five whose recommendation of the lock type, as opposed to the sea-level canal, was ultimately adopted. Subsequent experience with the Culebra Cut proved the wisdom of the minority report. In 1908, he was a member of the advisory board of six engineers which accompanied President-Elect Taft to Panama to consider whether there was necessity for any fundamental change in the plans upon which construction had begun. This board unanimously approved the lock canal across the Isthmus.

Randolph designed and constructed for the Queen Victoria Niagara Falls Park Commission the obelisk dam above the Horseshoe Falls, building it on end, on the river bank, like an obelisk, and then tilting it over into the rapids. He was consulting engineer for the city of Toronto in connection with track elevation and the construction of a new water supply system and works. As chairman of the Internal Improvement Commission of Illinois he assisted in plans for a canal from Lockport, Ill., to Utica, Ill., including five hydro-electric power plants for developing 140,000 horsepower. He was a member of the Illinois State Conservation Commission, of the state River and Lakes Commission, and of the Chicago Harbor Commission. In later years he was engaged in land reclamation work, serving as consulting engineer for the Little River Drainage District of Southeast Missouri and as chairman of the Florida Everglades Commission to consider the drainage of the Everglades. In February 1913, the Franklin Institute of Philadelphia awarded him the Elliott Cresson Medal in recognition of "distinguished achievement in the field of civil engineering." During the World War, he was instrumental in the organization of the Citizens' Unit of the 108th Engineers, of which he was elected president.

Randolph married, June 15, 1882, Mary Henry Taylor, daughter of Capt. George Edmund Taylor. She, with three sons, survived him. His was a long, active, and useful life. He ranked high in his profession and enjoyed the unlimited confidence of the public. "The name of Isham Randolph attached to any enterprise was a guarantee of honesty, integrity and technical ef-

ficiency" (Modjeski, *post*, p. 580). He died in Chicago at the age of seventy-two.

[*International Who's Who, 1912* (1911); *Who's Who in America,* 1920–21; Ralph Modjeski, in *Jour. Franklin Inst.,* Oct. 1920; C. G. Elliott, in *Trans. Am. Soc. Civil Engineers,* vol. LXXXIV (1921); *Chicago Daily Tribune,* Aug. 3, 1920.]   B. A. R.

RANDOLPH, JACOB (Nov. 25, 1796–Feb. 29, 1848), surgeon, was born in Philadelphia, Pa., the son of Edward Fitz-Randolph (who later changed his name to Randolph) and his wife Anna Julianna Steel. He was descended from Edward Fitz-Randolph who was in Scituate, Mass., in 1634 and later moved to Perth Amboy, N. J. His father served during the whole period of the Revolution as an officer in a Pennsylvania regiment; after the war he took up his residence in Philadelphia, entered into business, and became an influential member of the Society of Friends. Jacob was educated in a Quaker School, studied medicine under a local physician, Joseph Woollens, and in 1817 received the degree of M.D. from the University of Pennsylvania. He then visited England, Scotland, and France. Returning to Philadelphia he established himself in practice and in 1822 married Sarah Emlen Physick, the eldest daughter of Philip Syng Physick [*q.v.*]. Randolph's career in medicine was soon assured, partly because of his connection with Physick and partly on account of his own distinct ability as a surgeon. During his early years of practice he lectured on surgery in a summer school and served as assistant in the Almshouse Infirmary, Philadelphia. In 1835, his reputation as a surgeon being established, he was elected one of the surgeons of the Pennsylvania Hospital, a position he retained until the time of his death. In 1840 he again visited Europe where he spent two years, largely in hospitals in Paris. During his absence he was elected professor of operative surgery at the Jefferson Medical College, Philadelphia, a post he declined. On his return he devoted himself to surgery, especially to the treatment of stone in the bladder. He later became professor of surgery in the University of Pennsylvania (1847).

Randolph was a conservative surgeon, basing his treatment upon careful diagnosis and using simple methods. As a clinical teacher he was clear and precise and his best lectures were those on traumatic surgery. He made no great discoveries in medicine but he advanced surgery through his innovation of an operation for removing stones from the bladder, lithotripsy. A few reports of this operation had been published before Randolph's time but he was the first to demonstrate the technique publicly at the Pennsylvania Hospital and to him is "chiefly due the credit of introducing it in our country" (Norris, *post*, p. 287). His first paper on the subject was published in the *American Journal of the Medical Sciences* (November 1834). Six cases of stone in the bladder were reported successfully operated upon. Randolph also should receive credit for performing some early radical operations, such as the amputation of the lower jaw for osteosarcoma (*Ibid.*, November 1829); ligation of an external iliac aneurism (*North American Medical and Surgical Journal,* January 1829) and, in addition, for his description of Physick's method of treating tuberculosis of the hip by conserving splinting (*American Journal of the Medical Sciences,* February 1831). He also wrote an excellent biography of his father-in-law: *A Memoir of the Life and Character of Philip Syng Physick* (1839).

Randolph was an exceedingly handsome man and "at all times he exhibited a remarkably commanding appearance. His face was oval, regular in its features, and expressive of the frankness, independence, and energy of his character. In stature he was somewhat above the middle height, and his whole person displayed the signs of an unusual amount of health and vigor" (Gross, *post*, p. 520). He died rather suddenly of "intermittent fever" at the age of fifty-one.

[The best contemporary account of Randolph is by a colleague, G. W. Norris, in *Summary of the Trans. of the Coll. of Physicians of Phila.*, vol. II (1849). Another memoir, written a few years later by J. A. Meigs, a Philadelphia physician, was published in S. D. Gross, *Lives of Eminent Am. Physicians and Surgeons* (1861). Other sources include: H. A. Kelly and W. L. Burrage, *Am. Medic. Biogs.* (1920); J. W. Jordan, *Colonial Families of Phila.* (1911), vol. I; *Pa. Inquirer and Nat. Gazette,* Mar. 1, 1848.]   H. R. V.

RANDOLPH, Sir JOHN (*c.* 1693–Mar. 2, 1736/37), King's attorney of Virginia, diplomat, speaker of the House of Burgesses, was born at "Turkey Island" plantation, Henrico County, Va., the son of William [*q.v.*] and Mary (Isham) Randolph. With the favor of the fortune and position inherited from his father, and through his own unusual mental powers and varied gifts, he became the lawyer most distinguished in the first half of the eighteenth century in Virginia for his talents and learning. To a private tutor's early discipline he added the general knowledge to be gained as a student at the College of William and Mary. He entered Gray's Inn, May 17, 1715, and was called to the bar on Nov. 25, 1717. Through his brief span of mature years, for he died in his prime, he held offices of political preferment but always those in which his keen intellect and legal knowledge would have outlet. When less than twenty years

old he was appointed by Governor Spotswood in 1712 to represent the Crown in the county courts of Charles City, Henrico, and Prince George counties in the absence of the attorney-general. He substituted for Attorney-General John Clayton for a year during the latter's absence in England in 1727 and at the same time served as clerk of the Council. Before 1721 he was married to Susanna Beverly. He was King's attorney just long enough to continue the precedent set by his father and carried on by his sons, Peyton and John Randolph, 1727–1784 [*qq.v.*]. He became clerk of the House of Burgesses in 1718 and served in that remunerative and influential office until 1734.

In 1728 Randolph went to England on a threefold mission. The sea voyage was expected to better his health. He was instructed by the College of William and Mary to ask either for the better collection of the penny-a-pound export tax on tobacco or the substitution for it of a certain valuable yearly consideration out of the quit rents of Virginia. He was also to ask the Archbishop of Canterbury to sanction the use by the College of part of the Boyle fund for the education of the Indians for the purchase of books and was to select the books. By the Virginia Assembly he was authorized to present their address to the King and their petition to Parliament asking repeal of the act of Parliament prohibiting the shipping of stripped tobacco. The obnoxious act was repealed and a grateful Assembly voted Randolph a thousand pounds for his diplomatic efforts. Again, in 1732, the Assembly sent Randolph to England to urge their plan for an excise collected through a bonded warehouse system in substitution for the import duties on tobacco. While not gaining the concession, he was rewarded by the Burgesses with double his previous remuneration for his efforts. Randolph was knighted, presumably in 1732, in recognition of his legal abilities and diplomatic skill (W. A. Shaw, *The Knights of England,* 1906, II, 284); he was the only Virginian to be given such rank in the colonial period.

In 1734, when it was clear that the speakership of the House of Burgesses would be vacant through the resignation of John Holloway, Randolph gave up his clerkship, was chosen by the faculty of the College of William and Mary as their representative, was seated, and was elected speaker within the record span of three days. Later in the session he was also made treasurer of the colony. He was reëlected speaker in 1736, though with some opposition, and filled that position until his death the following year. The newly chartered borough of Norfolk honored him in 1736 by naming him recorder and gave him a warm demonstration of their esteem on the occasion of his visit to be sworn into that office (*Virginia Historical Register*, IV, 1851, p. 137).

As a lawyer, Randolph's preëminence was attested by his contemporaries, among whom he was known as a man of distinguished bearing, wide learning, fidelity in office, impartiality, justice, and high character. In sketches he wrote of his colleagues at the Williamsburg bar he revealed the high standards of learning and charactor that he deemed desirable in members of his profession (*Ibid.*, I, 1848, pp. 119–23). He left reports of cases in the General Court of Virginia between 1728 and 1732 that show something of his legal talents (Barton, *post*). His speeches as presiding officer of the House of Burgesses revealed his understanding of and faith in representative government, though he was a conservative in his interpretation of the rights of the burgesses and of the people. In his will, neither his other property nor the disposition of his own body was so carefully provided for as the care of his remarkable library which he left to his son Peyton. In his cultural interests Sir John Randolph was one of the first self-conscious Virginians, and his engraved armorial book plate is one of the earliest preserved of a native Virginian. At one time he gathered together documentary material with a view to writing the history of the political development of Virginia as a preface to an edition of the laws. Though he did not fulfil his purpose, his nephew, William Stith [*q.v.*], later used these collected sources for his history of the colony. Randolph did aid in the publication of the laws of Virginia in 1733. He was among the first of the eighteenth-century Virginia scholars in public life to be suspect by the clergy as a deist and heretic. He was a vestryman of Bruton Parish Church in Williamsburg and in his will declared his faith in God and Christ, though expressing greater concern for virtue than theological wrangles. While he owned lands and even speculated in them on a large scale, he was unique in the first half of the eighteenth century in the province as being, in his interests and attainments, a scholar rather than a planter.

[R. T. Barton, ed., *Va. Colonial Decisions. The Reports by Sir John Randolph and by Edward Barradall of Decisions of the Gen. Court of Va., 1728–1741* (2 vols., 1909); *The Case of the Planters of Tobacco in Va., as Represented by Themselves: . . . To Which is Added, A Vindication of the Said Representation* (London, 1733), the latter probably written by Randolph (see William Clayton-Torrence, *A Trial Bibliography of Colonial Va.*, 1908, pp. 109–10); *A Reply to the Vindication . . . In a Letter to Sir J. R.* (John Randolph) from the Merchants or Factors of London

(London, 1773); William Maxwell, *Va. Hist. Register and Lit. Companion*, vol. I (1848), 119–23; IV (1851), 137–41; *Va. Mag. of Hist. and Biography*, Jan. 1902, pp. 239–41; Apr. 1924, pp. 136–41; Oct. 1928, pp. 276–81 (will); *William and Mary Coll. Quart.*, Jan.–Apr. 1893; Apr. 1900, p. 264; July 1903, pp. 66–69; *Va. Law Jour.*, Apr. 1877, pp. 193–96; *Va. Gazette*, Mar. 4, 1736/37, Apr. 1, 29, 1737; bibliography of sketch of William Randolph.]   M. H. W.

RANDOLPH, JOHN (1727 or 1728–Jan. 31, 1784), clerk of the Virginia House of Burgesses, King's attorney, Loyalist, was born at "Tazewell Hall," Williamsburg, Va. Though but a lad of ten at the death of his father, Sir John Randolph [*q.v.*], he had in his youth the continued guidance of his mother Susanna (Beverly) Randolph. He grew up in the midst of the official and aristocratic group in the colonial capital. After his college work at William and Mary, like his brother Peyton [*q.v.*], he went to London for his training in the law. He was enrolled in the Middle Temple Apr. 8, 1745, and called to the bar, Feb. 9, 1750, N.S. Returning to Williamsburg, he practised law. Several years later he married Ariana Jenings, daughter of Edmund Jenings, attorney-general of Maryland, and his wife Ariana Vanderhuyden. His home was a literary and social center and he numbered among his intimate friends George Washington and his kinsman Thomas Jefferson, with whom he had many congenial tastes.

With his excellent training and the asset of inherited position, John Randolph soon entered on a career of political preferment, but, like his father, he held for a considerable time only such offices as, while remunerative, were vehicles for his legal learning and talents. He did not scorn, however, to serve in local government for in 1751 he was elected a member of the Common Council of Williamsburg. Like his father, he served long as clerk of the House of Burgesses (1752–56), and then in the established tradition of his family became attorney-general for the Crown, succeeding his brother Peyton. Governor Dunmore counted on his loyalty and influence in dealing with the recalcitrant burgesses and secured his election as burgess for the College of William and Mary in 1774 and 1775. With the approach of the Revolution, Randolph found himself embarrassed by a thousand considerations acting, he later testified, in direct opposition to one another. After reading everything available on both sides he determined to remain loyal to the Crown, following, he said, the dictates of his reason. In the heated differences between Dunmore and the revolutionary party he aided the Governor and sought to reconcile the differences between the King's government and the people. He fled to England with his wife and two lovely young daughters, Susanna and Ariana, in the late summer or early autumn of 1775. His only son, Edmund [*q.v.*], recently arrived at his legal majority, was left behind in Virginia, in sympathy with the patriot cause.

For a time Randolph had a refuge at the Scotch home of Lord Dunmore, whence his daughter Ariana was married to a fellow Virginian in exile, James Wormley. He then took residence at Brompton and lived on a meager pension from the Crown. In 1779 he drew up a plan of conciliation with America that he proposed to the English ministry and sought to influence the colonies to seek reconciliation with the Mother Country by writing his friend Jefferson and counseling him that independence would never be granted. In an hour of apparent peril he headed a movement of the Loyalist refugees offering their military services to the King to defend England against a feared invasion by the French (*William and Mary College Quarterly*, Jan. 1921, p. 70). He died at Brompton three years after Yorktown. When his daughter Ariana returned to Virginia after the Revolution she brought her father's remains. As he had requested, they were laid to rest in the chapel of the College of William and Mary, where his father and elder brother Peyton were buried.

To an engrossing interest in books John Randolph added knowledge of music, playing the violin in his youth. When he left Virginia in 1775 the violin he had brought from London became the property of Thomas Jefferson. He took great pride and experimental interest in his garden in Williamsburg and wrote, for the aid of his friends, the first book on gardening in the colonies (*A Treatise on Gardening*, 1924, edited by M. F. Warner; first published 1793, or earlier). Such of his writings and letters as have survived reveal him as a man of keen intellect and rational point of view. In religion a free thinker, in friendship divorcing personal affection from political alliance, in political philosophy an aristocrat and following reason more than emotion, he came to adverse days though not to mental defeat.

[L. L. Mackall, ed., "A Letter from the Virginia Loyalist John Randolph to Thomas Jefferson Written in London in 1779," *Proc. of the Am. Antiquarian Soc.*, n.s., Vol. XXX (1921), covering his career; *Considerations on the Present State of Virginia, attributed to John Randolph Attorney General and Considerations on the Present State of Virginia Examined by Robert Carter Nicholas* (1919), ed. by E. G. Swem; Letter of Thomas Jefferson, supposedly to John Randolph, Philadelphia, May–Sept. 1776, Mass. Hist. Soc.; P. L. Ford, ed., *The Writings of Thomas Jefferson*, I (1892); K. P. Wormeley and others, *Recollections of Ralph Randolph Wormeley* (1879); obituary in *Gentleman's Magazine*, Feb. 1784, p. 152; *Va. Mag. of Hist.*

and Biography, Apr. 1908, p. 149; *William and Mary Coll. Quart.*, Oct. 1916, pp. 138–39; Apr. 1900, pp. 264–65 (genealogy); Jan. 1921, p. 70; *The Spurious Letters Attributed to Washington* (1889), with a bibliographical note by W. C. Ford; H. J. Eckenrode, *The Revolution in Va.* (1916); H. S. Randall, *The Life of Thomas Jefferson* (1858), I, 121–23, 131; William Wirt, *Sketches of the Life and Character of Patrick Henry* (1817).]
                                                    M. H. W.

RANDOLPH, JOHN (June 2, 1773–May 24, 1833), best known as "John Randolph of Roanoke," statesman, orator, was born at "Cawsons," Prince George County, Va., the home of his mother's father, Theodorick Bland, Sr. He was the third son of John Randolph (1742–1775) and a great-grandson of William Randolph of "Turkey Island" [*q.v.*], the progenitor of the most noted of Virginia families. His mother, Frances Bland (1752–1788), a sister of Theodorick Bland, 1742–1790, and a niece of Richard Bland [*qq.v.*], was also a descendant of William Randolph and was her husband's second cousin. John's father left him the land on the Staunton River in Charlotte County where "Roanoke" was located, but he did not make this his permanent residence until 1810. About the same time he added "of Roanoke" to his name, in order to distinguish himself from a detested distant kinsman (Bruce, *post*, II, 737). The home of his parents, "Bizarre," on the Appomattox River, Cumberland County, near Farmville, was bequeathed in 1775 to his eldest brother, Richard. To his mother was left "Matoax," in Chesterfield County, near Petersburg. In September 1778, the widow married St. George Tucker and she became in due course the mother of Henry St. George and Nathaniel Beverley Tucker. John Randolph idolized his stepfather at first, but ultimately became estranged from that amiable man. He himself later said that he was always thin-skinned and passionate, and, he might have added, capricious. He had in him also much of the poet and delighted in the "groves and solitudes" of "Matoax," whence the family were forced to flee to "Bizarre" in 1781 during Arnold's invasion.

His education until this time had been under the direction of St. George Tucker. Shortly afterward, with his brothers Richard and Theodorick, he was sent to the school of Walker Maury in Orange County, where, according to his later statement, he "was tyrannized over and tortured by the most peevish and ill-tempered of pedagogues" (Bruce, I, 56). In the winter of 1783–84, the school was moved to Williamsburg. Disciplinary measures were continued, but the spirit of John Randolph was not humbled. He had plenty of exercise in the classics, and by voracious independent reading gained an intimate acquaintance with English literature. Soon sent for his health to Bermuda, the birthplace of his stepfather, he continued his reading there. On his return he was back at Maury's for a time, then at home, and in March 1787, with pleasure-loving Theodorick, was sent to Princeton, where he was in the grammar school that spring and in the college the following fall. His stay was terminated by his return to the bedside of his dying mother. For a time he was with Theodorick in New York and gained great intellectual stimulus, during a brief period, from his private studies with Professor Cochrane of Columbia, with whom he read Demosthenes. In September 1790 he went to Philadelphia to study law with Edmund Randolph [q.v.], but the Attorney-General was too engrossed to pay much attention to him. John Randolph had almost got through the first book of Blackstone when he abandoned the law for gaiety. In 1792–93 he was at William and Mary, where he had a duel with Robert Barraud Taylor; and in 1793–94 he was again in Philadelphia. His education had been desultory, and most of his teachers, he thought, were inferior; there is no reason to suppose that he ever accepted any serious discipline, but his reading was extensive and there could be no question of the brilliance of his talents. After the attainment of his majority, he made "Bizarre" his headquarters. Theodorick had died in 1792 and Richard, whom John idolized, died in 1796. Without doubt the iron had already entered John's soul, but his contemporaries were most impressed by his restlessness and extreme impudence. He rode from race course to race course, and made a horseback trip of 1800 miles to Charleston and Savannah which proved fatal to his steed. Several years before he entered public life, he was described as "a tall, gawky-looking, flaxen-haired stripling, . . . with a complexion of a good parchment color, beardless chin, and as much assumed self-consequence as any two footed animal I ever saw" (Garland, *post*, I, 65).

Previous to his candidacy for Congress in 1799, at the instance of Creed Taylor, there is little evidence that Randolph was much interested in public affairs. He used the jargon of the French Revolution in letters, but if egalitarian philosophy made any impression on him he showed no signs of it afterward. From the outset, however, he was a Jeffersonian, or at least an opponent of the Federalists. As a candidate for Congress, he made his début in March 1799 by audaciously speaking at Charlotte Court House in opposition to Patrick Henry, who was a Federalist candidate for the state Senate, and

apparently acquitted himself with credit. Both candidates were successful, as Randolph continued to be in successive elections until 1813. In the Sixth Congress the stripling attracted considerable attention, while advocating the reduction of the regular army, by characterizing the regular soldiers as "mercenaries" and "ragamuffins." After a couple of officers of the Marine Corps had tried to insult him, he wrote President John Adams, demanding that notice be taken of this attack on the independence of the legislature. The letter was transmitted to the House and led to a heated debate which served no purpose beyond the advertisement of the fiery young representative from Virginia.

Following the victory of the Jeffersonians in 1800, Randolph, in the next Congress, though only twenty-eight years of age, was appointed chairman of the standing committee on ways and means and became in effect administration leader. Whatever may have been the reasons for his appointment, he soon demonstrated his extraordinary powers of expression, and, until 1805, retained his position. According to William Plumer, this "pale, meagre, ghostly man" showed greater talents than any other member of his party in Congress, but many of the northern Democrats were reluctant to acknowledge the leadership of one who had "the appearance of a beardless boy more than a full grown man" (William Plumer, Jr., *Life of William Plumer*, 1857, pp. 248–49). Booted and spurred, he swaggered about the House, whip in hand, but in labors he was indefatigable and in parliamentary matters a master. His support of the Louisiana Purchase was hardly consistent with his philosophy of state rights and strict construction. In the attack on the federal judiciary he was entirely in character, but as manager of the impeachment of Justice Samuel Chase [q.v.] he was miscast, for he was not a lawyer and could help his cause little by intemperate eloquence. The failure of the trial, for which he bore the chief blame, was a bitter disappointment to him and a blow to his reputation. The beginnings of a breach with the administration had already appeared in his violent opposition to all compromise in connection with the Yazoo claims. This "Virginian Saint Michael—almost terrible in his contempt for whatever seemed to him base or untrue" (Henry Adams, *History*, III, 157), stigmatizing all that favored compromise, alienated not only less scrupulous leaders but Gallatin and Madison as well. Though restive under the commanding leadership of the President, and averse to the compromises incident to party leadership, he had hitherto played an important part in the administration, and he afterward looked back upon Jefferson's first term with rare satisfaction.

Though he retained the chairmanship of the ways and means committee throughout the Ninth Congress, he soon lost his formal leadership. His open breach with the administration grew out of the rather secretive efforts of Jefferson to acquire Florida and the violent opposition of Randolph to an appropriation of two million dollars, which, he felt, was intended as a bribe to France. Objecting to halfway measures as well as to secretive policies, he characterized the non-importation bill as "A milk-and-water bill, a dose of chicken broth to be taken nine months hence" (Mar. 26, 1806, *Annals of Congress*, 9 Cong., 1 Sess., col. 851). If, during the rest of this session, he "controlled the House by audacity and energy of will" (Henry Adams, *History*, III, 173), terrifying and silencing his opponents, it was as a vexatious critic of the administration. With the "Decius" letters (beginning in the Richmond *Enquirer*, Aug. 15, 1806), he ranged himself in open opposition. Later, he dubbed Jefferson, "St. Thomas of Cantingbury" (Bruce, II, 775; Garland, II, 346). There is no reason to suppose that he had ever been sympathetic with Jefferson's democratic ideas, but at the outset he had whole-heartedly supported him in his opposition to tyranny. Until a considerably later time, Randolph's animus was not so much against the leader of the party, but against Madison, Robert Smith, secretary of the navy, and Senator Samuel Smith of Maryland, together with the northern Democrats as a group. This scrupulous precisian, unwilling to make any concession to the exigencies of politics, hectored Jefferson's northern allies in a way that they found intolerable. Against the despised Madison, he favored Monroe as Jefferson's successor in the presidency, but he had little use for Monroe after the latter again became an orthodox party man and a member of Madison's cabinet.

Randolph, a free lance, a *"tertium quid"* (Mar. 13, 1806, *Annals of Congress*, 9 Cong., 1 Sess., col. 775), remained in Congress without interruption until 1813. As he had opposed the Embargo, he opposed the War of 1812, but was overborne by the new group of powerful young leaders. From 1799 to 1811 he had shone against a background of congressional mediocrity, but with the appearance of Clay, Calhoun, and Lowndes, soon to be followed by that of Webster, he ceased to be preëminent as an orator. Chiefly because of his hostility to the war, he suffered in 1813 at the hands of John W. Eppes [*q.v.*] his only defeat as a candidate for the House. Re-

turned to his old seat in 1815, in the Fourteenth Congress he bitterly opposed the chartering of the second Bank of the United States, the tariff, and other nationalistic measures. Because of his poor health, he refused to stand for reëlection in 1817, but he was returned in 1819 and served continuously until 1825. With the rise of the Missouri question he became a sectional leader, and during the next few years was probably at the height of his popularity in Virginia. Suspicious of Clay and bitterly hostile to John Quincy Adams, he described the alliance of these two leaders as "the coalition of Blifil and Black George," the combination "of the puritan with the blackleg" (Mar. 30, 1826, *Register of Debates*, II, pt. 1, 1825–26, 19 Cong. 1 Sess., col. 401). The result was the famous duel between him and Clay on the Virginia side of the Potomac, on Apr. 8, 1826. Clay's second shot pierced the skirt of Randolph's coat, but he himself fired in the air.

In the Nineteenth Congress, Randolph, elected to serve the unexpired term of James Barbour, was in the Senate (1825–27). During the first session his mind was disordered and his speeches, while still brilliant, were more than ever extravagant, irrelevant, eccentric. In the second session, after John Tyler had been brought forward against him as a candidate, he refrained from speaking until the result of the action of the Virginia legislature was known. He was defeated by Tyler, but, almost by acclamation, was returned to the House, where in his last term (1827–29) he was in effect the leader of the opposition to Adams. After the victory of Jackson in 1828, he announced that he would not be a candidate for reëlection. A delegate to the Virginia convention of 1829–30, he was perhaps the most conspicuous member of that assembly of notables. Defending eastern interests against western, he opposed any significant change in the constitution of the state and shares a large measure of credit, or of blame, for the victory of the conservatives. Then, unwisely accepting Jackson's appointment as minister to Russia, he sailed on June 28, 1830, arriving at St. Petersburg on Aug. 10. Endeavoring to attain the special object of his mission, he began negotiations for a treaty of commerce, but his health broke down and he remained in Russia less than a month. After weeks of anguish in England, on Apr. 6, 1831, he resigned and in October was back in America.

During the winter of 1831–32 he was unquestionably demented, though in May 1832 his mind cleared. Meanwhile, he drank excessively, used opium, and though ordinarily a kind master was harsh and abusive to his hapless slaves, who, he was convinced, had been faithless in his absence. His last public activity was a successful campaign, in his district, for the adoption of resolutions condemning Jackson's proclamation against South Carolina, though he did not accept the doctrines of nullification. Purposing to go to England, where on past visits he had been relatively happy, he went to Philadelphia to take a packet and there, on May 24, 1833, he died. He was buried at "Roanoke" with his face to the West, in order, it is said, that he might keep his eye on Henry Clay. In 1879 his remains were removed to Richmond. The long litigation about his will ended only in 1845, when the will of 1832, in which he had ordered his slaves to be sold, was declared null and void because of his mental condition at the time, and the will of 1821, in which he had ordered that they be freed, was declared valid (Bruce, II, ch. iii).

After 1810 he had lived, in considerable solitude, at "Roanoke," his retreat in the wilderness. The two modest houses there, one of logs, seemed hardly fitting for a man of his means and cultivation, but he retained the place, he said, because it had never belonged to any one except the Indians and his ancestors. He had added considerably to his inheritance and, though often lacking in cash, owned more than 8,000 acres of land, nearly 400 slaves, and a valuable stud of blooded horses. His personality, about which countless legends have gathered, can be explained to a considerable degree in physical terms. Always highstrung, he suffered most of his life from bad health, his feats of tireless oratory and horsemanship to the contrary notwithstanding. To his contemporaries it seemed incredible that he suffered as much as he said he did; but at the age of thirty he looked, when closely viewed, like an old man. His insomnia was well known to his friends; after 1811 he suffered from chronic diarrhoea; he was cursed with rheumatism; he died, probably, of tuberculosis. It would appear that most of the stories of his excesses are attributable to his last years; ordinarily he used spirits little. The universal contemporary opinion that he was impotent was verified after his death, but opinions still differ about the time and the cause of his loss of virility. He seems to have shaved when a student in Philadelphia, but during most of his life he was practically beardless. His voice was a rich soprano. In early manhood he became engaged to Maria Ward, but the engagement was broken off for reasons not known and she afterward married Peyton Randolph, son of Edmund. That John Randolph, naturally a social though always

a fastidious being, was embittered by his physical limitations needs no arguing. Apparently he was never really demented before 1818, but on several conspicuous occasions thereafter he was out of his mind, and during most of his public life his genius was dangerously near the dim border line of insanity. It is inconceivable that his abnormalities should not have accentuated his irritability and tinctured his political philosophy.

Except during Jefferson's first term, Randolph as a public man was always a member of the opposition, a constitutional purist, an unsparing critic, a merciless castigator of iniquity, which sometimes he imagined. He will go down in history as the champion of lost causes, unless perchance a tithe of the personal liberty which above all things he cherished should be preserved. "I am an aristocrat"; he said, "I love liberty, I hate equality" (Bruce, II, 203). In his hierarchy of values, Virginia came first, followed by England, and the rest of the "old thirteen states." He boasted that he had never voted for the admission of a new commonwealth to the Union. His philosophy of state rights is nowhere better summarized than in his vivid but specious epigram: "Asking one of the States to surrender part of her sovereignty is like asking a lady to surrender part of her chastity" (Ibid.). Toward slavery he was most nearly humanitarian; he deplored the institution while passionately insisting on its constitutional safeguards. His particularistic doctrines, instead of being regarded as merely corrective, in the course of events became in his state and section a body of political dogma. He thus marked the transition from the relatively flexible philosophy and the enlightened opportunism of Jefferson to the rigid Virginia orthodoxy of the ante-bellum era. The old order in his beloved state produced no successor that equaled him; orthodox doctrines could be repeated, but by no one else could they be expressed half so well.

Since there never was another like him, he must be described as an incomparable orator. For hours on end his shrill but flute-like voice irritated and fascinated, pouring upon his audience shafts of biting wit, literary allusions, epigrams, parables, and figures of speech redolent of the countryside. In the Gilbert Stuart portrait of him, there is rare poetic beauty, but in later years the man himself must have seemed a living caricature. Few dared ridicule so vitriolic an adversary; perhaps no one had the temerity openly to pity him. Dauntless in spirit though he was, he now seems one of the most pathetic as well as one of the most brilliant figures that ever strutted and fretted his hour upon the American public stage.

[Few readers are likely to exhaust the monumental work of W. C. Bruce, *John Randolph of Roanoke, 1773–1833* (2 vols., 1922), which contains extensive references to printed sources and MSS. in private hands, and reproduces important portraits. The materials used in the preparation of this, chiefly in the form of typewritten copies and photostats, were given by Mr. Bruce to the Va. State Lib., Richmond. A good sample of MS. sources is in the Lib. of Cong. G. W. Johnson, *Randolph of Roanoke, A Political Fantastic* (1929), is a readable biography, based chiefly on Bruce but less sympathetic. Henry Adams, in *John Randolph* (1882), and *Hist. of the U. S. of America* (9 vols., 1889–91), *passim*, is unforgiving. H. A. Garland, *The Life of John Randolph of Roanoke* (2 vols., 1850), is laudatory but contains valuable personal materials. Powhatan Bouldin, *Home Reminiscences of John Randolph of Roanoke* (1878), by drawing on the last years gives an unfair impression. See also W. G. Stanard, "The Randolph Family," *William and Mary Coll. Quart. Hist. Mag.*, Oct. 1898, Jan. 1901; Edmund Quincy, *Life of Josiah Quincy* (1867); Gamaliel Bradford, *Damaged Souls* (1923), pp. 123–56.]   D. M.

RANDOLPH, PEYTON (*c.* 1721–Oct. 22, 1775), King's attorney, speaker of the House of Burgesses, chairman of the Virginia committee of correspondence, first president of the Continental Congress, was born in Virginia, presumably at "Tazewell Hall," Williamsburg, the home of his father, Sir John Randolph [*q.v.*]. His mother was Susanna (Beverly) Randolph. In accordance with the wish of his father, expressed in his will, he entered the law as his profession. After a general education at the College of William and Mary he was admitted to the Middle Temple, Oct. 13, 1739, and called to the bar on Feb. 10, 1744, N.S. In the group of lawyers at Williamsburg he soon won distinction and in 1748 was appointed King's attorney for the province. He won favor while he held this office through the qualities of his personality and his policy of regarding himself as the spokesman of the rights of the Colony as well as those of the Crown. He was constantly a member of the House of Burgesses, representing Williamsburg in 1748–49, the College of William and Mary, 1752–58, and Williamsburg from 1758 to 1775. After the death of John Robinson [*q.v.*], Randolph resigned as King's attorney and was elected speaker in his place in November 1766 (*Journals of the House of Burgesses,* 1766–69, pp. xiii–xv, 11). In successive Assemblies until the Revolution he was reëlected.

Conservative in temperament and representative of the point of view of the colonial aristocracy, Randolph, while serving the King, was on several occasions brought into sharp conflict with the royal governor. When Governor Dinwiddie sought to correct certain abuses of the Crown's interests in land grants in Virginia and to augment the revenues by charging a fee of a pistole on every land patent, Randolph was sent by the Burgesses to England to oppose the Governor's policy and secure the withdrawal of the fee. Randolph, who prosecuted the mission with vigor, was suspended from his office by the irate Dinwiddie, but was voted a reward of £2500 by the grateful House of Burgesses who placed the item as a rider on the supply bill in an effort to force the reluctant Governor to sign the appropriation. Dinwiddie reinstated Randolph as attorney-general on the suggestion of the Lords of Trade and Randolph, with his customary urbanity, acknowledged to the uncomfortable Governor his error in having left his office without His Majesty's leave. When English and Scotch merchants protested against the use of paper money in Virginia he replied in 1759 in a pamphlet defending the action of the Assembly. His patriotism was challenged by the news of Braddock's defeat and he led in the formation of a company of a hundred lawyers and other gentlemen in Williamsburg who went at their own expense to the assistance of the regular force and militia. He served from 1759 to 1767 on the Virginia committee of correspondence, a group officially keeping in touch with the Virginia agent in London.

When Patrick Henry carried through his challenging resolutions against the Stamp Act after a bitter fight in the House of Burgesses, Randolph declared as he left the House that he would have given one hundred guineas for a single vote, so deeply did he deplore the radical expressions passed that day (P. L. Ford, *The Writings of Thomas Jefferson,* IX, 1898, p. 468). Yet Randolph himself had written a moderate protest the year before to the King for the House of Burgesses against the Act. Between 1765 and 1774 Randolph moved steadily with the current of revolutionary sentiment in Virginia, though he was moderating in his influence and cautious in his leadership. His judgment and sagacity were extolled by his contemporaries and attested by his fellows. He was made the presiding officer of every important revolutionary assemblage in Virginia. In 1773 he was named chairman of the committee of correspondence. In 1774 and again in 1775 he presided over the revolutionary conventions. He was named first in the list of seven delegates appointed by the Virginia convention to the first session of the Continental Congress and in turn was elected president of that body in 1774 and again in 1775.

Without doubt Peyton Randolph was the most

popular leader in Virginia in the decade before the Revolution. His sense of justice, his kindly and moderate tone, his legal knowledge, and steady tact made him trusted. When the volunteers of Fredericksburg were ready to march against Dunmore at the news of his removal of the powder, it was Randolph's voice that restrained them. And it was Randolph who persuaded Dunmore it was well to pay for the powder. Jefferson gave this estimate of him: "He was indeed a most excellent man; and none was ever more beloved and respected by his friends. Somewhat cold and coy towards strangers, but of the sweetest affability when ripened into acquaintance. Of attic pleasantry in conversation, always good humored and conciliatory. With a sound and logical head, he was well read in the law; and his opinions when consulted, were highly regarded, presenting always a learned and sound view of the subject but generally, too, a listlessness to go into its thorough development; for being heavy and inert in body, he was rather too indolent and careless for business, which occasioned him to get a smaller proportion of it at the bar than his abilities would otherwise have commanded" (Ford, X, 1899, p. 59). In his social relations Randolph consorted with the leading gentlemen of the colony, Governor Fauquier and George Washington being among his intimates.

As King's attorney he opposed the right of the persuasive dissenter Samuel Davies [q.v.] to preach in Virginia, though the latter proved Randolph's equal in the legal encounter. Randolph was a member of the vestry of Bruton Parish Church and of the board of visitors of the College of William and Mary. He was often called on to serve as executor of the estates of friends, was generous in charitable endeavors, was one of the directors in William Byrd's lottery for the sale of lands in Richmond, and was president of the Williamsburg textile factory, organized about 1770. In 1774 he was made provincial grand master in the Masonic Order in Williamsburg. His sudden death in Philadelphia in October 1775 from a stroke of apoplexy brought great distress in Virginia for he was widely beloved. His wife, Elizabeth (generally known as Bettie) Harrison, daughter of Col. Benjamin Harrison of "Berkeley" in Charles City County and sister of Benjamin Harrison [q.v.], signer of the Declaration of Independence, whom he had married on Mar. 8, 1745/46, survived him. There were no children and his large estate, including 105 slaves, was left to his wife in life tenure and at her death to his nephew Edmund Randolph [q.v.]. He was buried in the chapel of the College of William and Mary.

[*A Letter to a Gentleman in London from Va.* (1759), attributed to Peyton Randolph; *Jours. of the House of Burgesses of Va.*, ed. by H. R. McIlwaine and J. P. Kennedy, vols. for period 1752–76 (1905–09); *Va. Hist. Register and Lit. Companion*, vol. VI (1853), ed. by William Maxwell; *Va. Mag. of Hist. and Biography*, Apr. 1908; Jan. 1911, p. 87; Oct. 1911, pp. 415–16; Jan. 1924, pp. 102–06; *William and Mary Coll. Quart.*, July 1892, pp. 5–8; Apr. 1900, pp. 264–65; July 1901, p. 34; July 1907, pp. 36–41; July 1911, p. 18; July 1913, pp. 2–3, 18; Jan. 1917, pp. 144–50; Apr. 1919, p. 239; R. A. Brock, ed., *The Official Records of Robert Dinwiddie* (2 vols., 1883–84); A. W. Weddell, ed., *A Memorial Volume of Va. Hist. Portraiture, 1585–1830* (1930); Charles Campbell, *Hist. of the Colony and Ancient Dominion of Va.* (1860); H. B. Grigsby, *Hist. of the Va. Convention of 1776* (1855), pp. 9–12; H. J. Eckenrode, *The Revolution in Va.* (1916); J. M. Leake, *The Va. Committee System and The Am. Revolution* (1917).]

M. H. W.

RANDOLPH, SARAH NICHOLAS (Oct. 12, 1839–Apr. 25, 1892), teacher, author, was the daughter of Thomas Jefferson Randolph [q.v.] and his wife, Jane (Nicholas). Both of her grandfathers had been governor of Virginia, and Thomas Jefferson was her great-grandfather. She was born at "Edgehill" in Albemarle County, an estate which had been in the Randolph family for four generations. Martha Jefferson Randolph was a member of the household, and since she had the advantage of education in France, and was otherwise highly accomplished, she doubtless took an active part in the training of her granddaughters. We have her testimony that four of them were good French and Italian scholars, and that few girls of their age had read so widely (Martha Jefferson Randolph to Ellen Coolidge, June 20, 1834, Jefferson Manuscripts, University of Virginia). This was before Sarah's birth, but it indicates the intellectual influences under which she grew up. Her father was a man of considerable property and business ability, but he used a large part of his wealth to pay off the debts of Jefferson's insolvent estate, of which he was trustee, and this so impoverished the family that they opened a school for girls at "Edgehill," in which for some years Sarah taught. In 1879 she went to Patapsco, near Baltimore, and established a school. Being dissatisfied with conditions there, she left after five years and opened a school in Baltimore where she remained until her death.

This Virginia gentlewoman was tall with dark hair and gray eyes. She was fond of reading history and serious literature but took little interest in fiction. As an author, her most important work was *The Domestic Life of Thomas Jefferson* (1871) for the writing of which her qualifications were unique. It contains many intimate personal letters and is still an invaluable source-book. She also wrote *The Life of Gen. Thomas J. Jackson* (1876), and an article on her paternal grandmother which was published in Sarah B. Wister and Agnes Irwin's *Worthy Women of Our First Century* (1877). In addition to writing history, she took an active interest in its preservation in stone and marble. She had a leading part in the movement for the erection of the Robert E. Lee monument in Richmond and was consulted by the designers of the Grant monument in New York. She died in Baltimore and lies buried at "Monticello."

[The only published sketch is a meager one in E. A. Alderman and J. C. Harris, eds., *Lib. of So. Literature*, XV (1910), 359. There are brief notices of her death in the *Sun* (Baltimore), Apr. 26, 1892, and in the Richmond *Dispatch*, Apr. 27, 1892; and there is scant information in R. C. M. Page, *Genealogy of the Page Family in Virginia* (1883), p. 263. E. C. Mead, *Historic Homes of the Southwest Mountains of Virginia* (1899), has something on the school at "Edgehill." Mrs. William Randolph of Charlottesville, a niece, furnished most of the facts stated above.]   T. P. A.

RANDOLPH, THEODORE FITZ (June 24, 1826–Nov. 7, 1883), governor of New Jersey, United States senator, was descended from Edward Fitz-Randolph, an early emigrant from England to Scituate, Mass. (Leonard, *post*). Theodore was born at New Brunswick, N. J., the son of James Fitz Randolph, member of Congress from New Jersey (1827–33) and publisher of the New Brunswick *Fredonian*. He attended the Rutgers Grammar School and at sixteen began to work. At twenty he went to Vicksburg, Miss., but in 1850 returned to his native state to enter his father's extensive coal and iron business, which involved both mining and transportation. For the next fifteen years he resided in Jersey City, then moved to Morristown, where he had a large property which he set about developing. Meanwhile he had become increasingly wealthy. In 1867, when he was elected president of the Morris & Essex Railroad, he was already known as "Mr. Moneybags of Morristown." Elected by a union of "Americans" and Democrats, he served as assemblyman from Hudson County in 1861; the following year he took a seat in the state Senate to fill a vacancy and in 1863 was returned for the full three-year term. By this time he had become a recognized leader of the conservative Democrats and in the legislature was chief spokesman for the reconciliation policy of Gov. Joel Parker [*q.v.*]. Like the Governor, Randolph was a Union Democrat, and, though a stanch defender of state rights, he accepted the necessity of war after the failure of the peace attempt and was influential in moderating the extreme tendencies of some of the "Copperheads" in the legislature.

In 1868 Randolph was elected governor of New Jersey by a majority of nearly five thousand over his Republican opponent. As governor he secured the repeal of the so-called Camden & Amboy Railroad "monopoly tax," which was a transit duty levied on that company for the persons and goods transported across the state, recommending in its place a uniform tax upon all rail and canal companies, a measure which was adopted much later (Sackett, *post*, I, 226). Other accomplishments for which he claimed credit were the adoption of laws against bribery at elections and of a policy designed to make the prison self-supporting, and the inception of a plan for establishing at Morristown one of the largest insane aslyums in the world.

After the expiration of his term as governor, Randolph was elected to the United States Senate and served from 1875 to 1881. He had been a delegate to the National Democratic Conventions of 1864 and 1872, in the latter year being chairman of the executive committee. In national politics, however, he was undistinguished. Representing vested interests, he stood for conservative policies, always opposing his party's agitation for monetary inflation and supporting "hard money" and early redemption of paper issues. For two years he was chairman of the Senate committee on military affairs. He was not brilliant, nor a persuasive speaker, but he was an agreeable man, whose sound business reputation, evident sincerity, and carefully prepared knowledge of the subject in hand won him support. He appears to have had considerable mechanical ability, and invented a ditching machine and a steam typewriter. He married, in 1852, Fannie Coleman, daughter of Congressman Nicholas Coleman of Kentucky.

[*The Biog. Encyc. of N. J.* (1877); *Biog. Dir. Am. Cong.* (1928); *Docs. of the Legislature of the State of N. J.*, 1869–72; W. E. Sackett, *Modern Battles of Trenton*, vol. I (1895); C. M. Knapp, *N. J. Politics during the Period of the Civil War and Reconstruction* (1924); O. B. Leonard, "The Fitz Randolphs of Massachusetts" (clippings, in Lib. of Cong.); *Daily True American* (Trenton), Nov. 8, 1883.]   H. M. C.

RANDOLPH, THOMAS JEFFERSON (Sept. 11, 1792–Oct. 7, 1875), author and financier, was the eldest son of Thomas Mann Randolph [*q.v.*] and Martha (Jefferson) Randolph. He was born at "Monticello" and became the favorite grandson of Thomas Jefferson. His early education was acquired locally, but at the age of fifteen he was sent to Philadelphia to pursue studies in botany, natural history, and anatomy. Jefferson took a keen interest in his plans and advised him to cultivate, above all things, good humor and good manners, and to abstain from arguments (A. A. Lipscomb and A. E. Bergh, ed., *The Writings of Thomas Jefferson*, 1904, XI, 242-43; XII, 196-202). There can be no question but that he followed this advice and added careful industry to his list of virtues. So good a disciple did he become that in 1814 Jefferson, whose financial affairs were somewhat tangled, began turning over the management of his estate to his grandson. By 1816 young Randolph had assumed the whole financial burden and from that time forward carried it upon his shoulders (H. S. Randall, *The Life of Thomas Jefferson*, 1858, III, pp. 334, 433, 531). While most of his time was devoted to these private matters, he was developing other qualities, as is indicated by the fact that he made the welcoming address when Lafayette visited Charlottesville in 1824 (A. C. Gordon, *William Fitzhugh Gordon*, 1909, p. 142).

When Jefferson died in 1826, Randolph became the chief executor of his estate. He sold "Monticello" and the library to liquidate the indebtedness, but the assets were not equal to the liabilities, and he finally paid the balance with $40,000 from his own funds. Meanwhile, after considering removal to Louisiana, he with his mother and sisters quitted "Monticello" and took up their abode at "Edgehill," the old Randolph estate nearby (Virginia R. Trist to Ellen Coolidge, Mar. 23, 1827, Jefferson Manuscripts, University of Virginia). Jane Nicholas, daughter of Gov. Wilson Cary Nicholas [*q.v.*], became his wife (1815) and the large family lived here for the remainder of their lives. On taking up his permanent residence at "Edgehill" in 1828, Randolph moved the old frame house which had been built by his father, and erected the present brick structure on the original site. He was a good farmer and a careful manager, and we have his mother's testimony that they all lived comfortably and happily together (Martha J. Randolph to Ellen Coolidge, June 20, 1834, Jefferson Manuscripts).

In 1829 Randolph published his *Memoir, Correspondence, and Miscellanies from the papers of Thomas Jefferson* in four volumes, the first published collection of his grandfather's writings, and during the same year became a member of the Board of Visitors of the University of Virginia (Minutes of the Board, University of Virginia, II, 1). In this capacity he served for thirty-one years, and for seven years was rector of the University. In 1831 he was elected to the House of Delegates and served in that body for several years. He took a special interest in banking and finance, and in 1832 made a memorable

speech in the Assembly favoring the gradual emancipation of slaves. This was published that year as a pamphlet. After several years, however, he dropped out of public life and held no further civil post except for membership in the Virginia constitutional convention of 1850-51 and the general convention of 1861. From the days of Andrew Jackson he was a Democrat in politics (H. H. Simms, *The Rise of the Whigs in Virginia*, 1929, pp. 94, 111). During the Civil War he held a colonel's commission in the Confederate army, but was too old to take the field. In 1872 he was chairman of the National Democratic Convention. He died at "Edgehill" in 1875 and lies buried at "Monticello."

Most of his time had been devoted to the affairs of his family, of his community, and of the University of Virginia. He served as a magistrate, a member of the Albemarle Agricultural Society, before which he delivered *An Essay* (1842), and was president of the Farmers' Bank of Charlottesville (Edgar Woods, *Albemarle County*, 1901, p. 302). More successful in a financial way than either his famous grandfather or brilliant and erratic father, he apparently lacked their keen interest in matters of the intellect. An aversion to music would seem to mark him as having had that deficiency of imagination so common among practical men (Martha J. Randolph to Ellen Coolidge, Nov. 26, 1826, Jefferson Manuscripts).

[Important facts are given in P. A. Bruce, *Hist. of the Univ. of Va.*, III (1921), pp. 22-23, 183-84, 196-97. There is a brief sketch in L. G. Tyler, *Encyc. of Va. Biography* (1915), II, 210. See also W. B. Giles, *To the Public* (1828); *A Memorial to Col. Thomas J. Randolph* (1875), from Charlottesville *Chronicle*, Oct. 22, 1875; Richmond *Dispatch, Richmond Enquirer*, Oct. 9, 1875.]　　　　　　　　　　　　　　　　T. P. A.

RANDOLPH, THOMAS MANN (Oct. 1, 1768–June 20, 1828), member of Congress, governor of Virginia, was the son of Thomas Mann and Anne (Cary) Randolph of "Tuckahoe" in Goochland County, Va. His great-grandfather, Thomas, was the son of William Randolph [*q.v.*] of "Turkey Island," founder of the noted clan. He was educated first at the College of William and Mary, and then at the University of Edinburgh, where he resided from 1785 to 1788. During the summer of 1788 he visited in Paris his kinsman, Thomas Jefferson [*q.v.*], the American minister to France. The ties between the two families were close, for they owned adjoining estates in Albemarle County, and Jefferson's father had acted as guardian for Randolph's father at "Tuckahoe." The connection became still closer when, on Feb. 23, 1790, at "Monticello," young Randolph married Jefferson's daughter Martha, who was his third cousin. Randolph now built a home on the Albemarle estate and called it "Edgehill" (R. A. Lancaster, *Historic Virginia Homes and Churches,* 1915, pp. 395–96). Here he maintained a residence for a time, but Jefferson did not like to be separated from his daughter and it was not long before the Randolphs became permanent residents of "Monticello." There were in the course of time ten children, of whom the eldest was Thomas Jefferson Randolph, and the youngest George Wythe Randolph [*qq.v.*].

In many ways Randolph and the master of "Monticello" were congenial. They were both scholars and thinkers. Randolph once said that he considered theology a "department of the imagination" (Randolph to Cabell, Aug. 5, 1820, Cabell Manuscripts). He was versed in the classics, botany, agriculture, and in military science. Some of Jefferson's scientific friends looked upon Randolph with great respect, particularly as a botanist (Correa da Serra to F. W. Gilmer, Dec. 28, 1818, Gilmer Manuscripts), and he claimed to have been the originator of the practice of transverse, rather than horizontal, ploughing on hillsides (Randolph to Cabell, July 20, 1820, Cabell Manuscripts). He also took an interest in politics and was a member of the Virginia Senate in 1793–94. From 1803 until 1807 he represented the state in Congress. In 1806 he nearly involved himself in a duel with John Randolph of "Roanoke," over a supposed insult in the House (W. C. Bruce, *John Randolph of Roanoke,* 1922, I, 262–64). When the War of 1812 came on, he was commander of the 1st light corps of Virginia militia, but in 1813 was made colonel of the 20th United States Infantry and took part in the Canadian campaign of that year. Resigning at the end of this service, he sought appointment as brigadier-general of Virginia militia with the hope that the defense of Norfolk would fall to his lot. He wrote to Senator Joseph Cabell that his wife had secured for him appointment as collector of internal revenue for his district and that the income was necessary in order to save his estate, but that he would give up the post if he could get the military command (Dec. 29, 1813, Jan. 3, 1814, Cabell Manuscripts). It turned out that he got neither place and that his estate became much involved, owing partly to the loss of large shipments of flour on account of the blockade.

In 1819 he was elected to the House of Delegates and was chosen governor of the state in the same year. Serving until 1822, he took a keen interest in educational and other progressive measures. In 1823 he was sent back to the legislature and served until 1825. By this time his financial affairs were hopelessly involved and some of his property had to be sold (Randolph to F. W. Gilmer, June 21; July 9, 1825, Gilmer Manuscripts). Out of this situation there developed some bitterness between him and his family, particularly in the case of his son Thomas Jefferson Randolph, who had been handling Jefferson's financial affairs since 1814. It appears that the elder Randolph began to live apart from his family at this time, and they, in turn, quitted "Monticello" shortly after the death of Jefferson in 1826. In 1828 they returned for a brief time, and Randolph rejoined them under his express stipulation that he have no relations with them. He desired only the north pavilion and the right to do his own cooking on a charcoal fire (Randolph to Nicholas P. Trist, Mar. 10, 11, 1828; Trist to Randolph, same date, Jefferson Manuscripts, University of Virginia). He died during the year but was reconciled to his family before the end. He was buried near Jefferson at "Monticello."

A man of brilliant intellectual parts, a daring horseman and a brave soldier, recklessly generous and extremely proud, Thomas Mann Randolph had no mind for practical affairs, and he was possessed of a rash temper which made him many enemies. Except for these characteristics, he would doubtless have risen to great position (A. C. Gordon, *William Fitzhugh Gordon,* 1909, pp. 69–70). As it was, he died amid the ashes of his life from exposure on a cold night ride after having given his cloak to a suffering wayfarer.

[Letters of Thomas Mann Randolph are scattered through the Jefferson, Cabell, and Gilmer MSS. of the Univ. of Va., the collection of Harold J. Coolidge, of Boston, and the Jefferson MSS. in the Lib. of Cong. The best personal sketches are in H. S. Randall, *The Life of Thomas Jefferson* (1858), II, 224–25; III, 327–28, 564. There are brief notices in L. G. Tyler, *Encyc. of Va. Biography* (1915), II, 49; M. V. Smith, *Virginia . . . with a Hist. of the Executives* (1893), 330–33; *Biog. Directory of the Am. Congress* (1928). An obituary appeared in the *Richmond Enquirer,* June 27, 1828.]   T. P. A.

RANDOLPH, WILLIAM (*c.* 1651–Apr. 11, 1711), planter, merchant, colonial official, came to Virginia from Warwickshire, England, about 1673. He was the son of Richard Randolph of Morton Hall, Warwickshire, half-nephew of the poet Thomas Randolph, grandson of William Randolph of Little Haughton, Northamptonshire, and great-grandson of Richard Randolph, of Hams, Sussex, Gentleman. His mother was Elizabeth, daughter of Richard Ryland. Below the site of the later Richmond on the James River he acquired by purchase in 1684 lands known from the days of John Smith and Newport as "Turkey Island." He married Mary, daughter of Henry and Katherine Royall Isham of "Bermuda Hundred," a neighboring plantation. By headright, purchase, grant, legacies, and other means he acquired vast tracts of land, owning 10,000 acres in Henrico County alone, by the year 1705. His fortunes linked him with the conservative political group and he was despoiled of many of his fine linens, broadcloths, and other luxuries by his less-endowed neighbors in Bacon's Rebellion. The land at Curles on the James belonging to Nathaniel Bacon, escheated to His Majesty, was granted by patent by Governor Nicholson to Randolph for a modest consideration. He imported slaves in large number and became one of the leading planters in the colony. He established on estates of their own his seven sons, William of "Turkey Island," Thomas of "Tuckahoe," Isham of "Dungeness," Sir John of "Tazewell Hall," Williamsburg, with lands in York County, Richard of "Curles," Henry of "Chatsworth," and Edward of "Bremo," though the last forsook the land for the sea. In time these sons and his two daughters were allied by marriage to the outstanding families in Virginia and among their long line of notable descendants are included not only a host of Randolphs but also Thomas Jefferson, John Marshall, and Robert E. Lee.

As a privileged gentleman of his period in colonial Virginia, Randolph held lucrative official appointments. When his uncle, Henry Randolph, who had preceded him in Virginia by several decades, died in 1673, William Randolph succeeded him as clerk of Henrico County. He held the clerk's office until 1683, and then became sheriff, coroner, justice of the peace, and justice of the county court of chancery in Henrico. He held successive military appointments in the county until in 1699 he was appointed lieutenant-colonel of militia. Often he represented the county in the House of Burgesses and he served in repeated sessions on important committees. He was speaker of that House in 1696 and 1698 and served as clerk of the Burgesses in 1699-1701 and in 1702. He was escheator-general for lands on the south side of James River, where more desirable tracts were yet to be taken up than on the already well-exploited north side. In 1694 Randolph was named attorney-general for the Crown in Virginia and, while a fight was made on his tenure because of his ignorance of the law, he held the office for four years, establishing the well nigh inviolable tradition that a Randolph in Virginia could best serve the King's legal interests. The office was subsequently held by his son and two grandsons, Sir John, Peyton, and John Randolph, 1727-1784 [qq.v.]. Though repeatedly included by the royal governors in lists of Virginians proposed as suitable persons for appointment to the Council, William Randolph was never added to that privileged group.

In neighborly relations he was active in a rôle akin to that of lord of the manor. He had a determining voice in the settlement of his neighbors' affairs, both in their life spans and after their demise, frequently serving in legal matters for them. He liked the sport of horse racing and for close companionship consorted with the equally successful William Byrd and the prominent families of Eppes and Cocke, though sometimes at odds with these neighbors over land boundaries and disputed elections. He was among the founders and first trustees of the College of William and Mary, later sending six sons to test the value of that institution. On his death in 1711 he was buried at "Turkey Island," potent in death through the lands and prestige he willed his sons and daughters as fortresses for the later fame and fortune of his line.

[H. R. McIlwaine, ed., *Jours. of the House of Burgesses of Va.*, vols. for period 1659/60–1712 (1912–14); *Executive Jours. of the Council of Colonial Va.*, vols. I–II (1925–27); and *Legislative Jours. of the Council of Colonial Va.*, vol. I (1918); *The Edward Pleasants Valentine Papers* (n.d.), vol. III, 1317–1478, containing will of Randolph, pp. 1368–72; William Maxwell, ed., *Va. Hist. Register and Lit. Companion*, vol. VI (1853), pp. 103–05, description of Turkey Island; *Va. Mag. of Hist. and Biography*, Jan. 1895, p. 296; Oct. 1896, p. 123; July 1929, pp. 206–07, portrait; W. G. Stanard, "The Randolph Family," *William and Mary Coll. Quart.*, Oct. 1898 and later numbers; L. W. Burton, *Annals of Henrico Parish* (1904), ed. by J. S. Moore; R. C. M. Page, *Genealogy of the Page Family in Va.* (2nd ed., 1893); *A Collection and Report on the Old Randolph Epitaphs at Turkey Island, Curls, Mattoax, Tuckahoe* (1913), compiled by W. Miles Cary.]   M. H. W.

RANEY, GEORGE PETTUS (Oct. 11, 1845–Jan. 8, 1911), Florida legislator and jurist, was born at Apalachicola, Franklin County, Fla., the son of David G. and Frances (Jordan) Raney. His parents were from Petersburg, Va., but they had removed to Florida in 1826 and had settled at Apalachicola in 1834. The son attended the local schools for his elementary education and then entered the University of Virginia. Before completing his academic work he enrolled in the Confederate army, seeing considerable service in Florida and Georgia until the end of the war. He reëntered the University in the Law School and after a year's study returned to Apalachicola, was admitted to the bar, and began the practice of law.

In 1868 Raney began his long public career with his election as a Democrat from Franklin County to the lower house of the Florida legislature. After two years in this office, during which time he served as chairman of the judiciary committee, he returned to private life and spent the next seven years practising law at Tallahassee, where he had established his residence in 1869. His increasing influence in the Democratic party led to his selection as a member of the Democratic State Executive Committee in 1876 in which capacity he took part in the redemption of the state from Carpet-bag rule. He was one of the counsel for Governor Drew before the Florida supreme court in the gubernatorial contest and in January 1877 he was appointed by Drew attorney-general of the state. The appointment was renewed by Governor Bloxham in 1881. While in this position Raney was ex-officio reporter of the state supreme court. He held the office of attorney-general until 1885 in which year he was appointed associate justice of the court and in 1888 was continued in office by election. In 1889 he was made chief justice by his colleagues and in that capacity he remained on the bench until 1894. In this latter year he resigned as chief justice and resumed the practice of law at Tallahassee. He remained in private life for five years, holding no public office except that of presidential elector in 1896. In 1897 he was a candidate for United States senator but withdrew from the contest before the election. In 1899 he was elected from Leon County to the Florida House of Representatives and served until 1902. He was a member of the Florida Senate from 1902 until 1906. Upon his retirement from the Senate he was appointed counsel for the Seaboard Airline Railway and continued in this employment until his death.

Raney was married on Nov. 4, 1873, to Mary Elizabeth Lamar of Athens, Ga., by whom he had four children. She died in 1899 and in 1901 he was married to Evelyn Byrd Cameron, who died in 1902. He was a member of the Episcopal Church. His greatest achievements were as a jurist. His most important decision as chief justice was in the case of *The Pensacola and Atlantic Railroad Company* vs. *Florida* (25 *Fla.*, 310) in which he laid down the principle that a railway was not subject to such regulation as would deprive it of a reasonable profit. He was for thirty years a controlling influence in the Democratic party in Florida as a member not only of the state committee but from 1900 to 1904 as a member of the national committee. His service as a legislator was creditable but was overshadowed by his juristic career.

[Sources include: *Who's Who in America*, 1910–11; R. H. Rerick, *Memoirs of Fla.* (2 vols., 1902), ed. by F. P. Fleming; *Fla. Times Union* (Jacksonville), Jan. 9, 1911; information as to certain facts from Judge W. J. Oven, Tallahassee.]   R. S. C.

RANGER, HENRY WARD (Jan. 29, 1858– Nov. 7, 1916), landscape painter, was born in Syracuse, N. Y., the son of Ward Valencourt and Martha Marie (Ranger) Ranger. The father was for many years a commercial photographer at Syracuse, and from 1873 to 1888, instructor in photography in the College of Fine Arts of Syracuse University; in his studio the son early learned to make photographic pictures. He attended the Syracuse public schools and Syracuse University, 1873–75 (date supplied by the Syracuse Art Museum), but did not graduate. Of his aspiration to become an artist he later wrote: "As a boy I took to art naturally as a duck takes to water. My father rather encouraged the idea at the start as he thought it would keep me out of mischief. Later, when he learned that I thought of taking it up as a profession he manifested the usual opposition that comes from a sensible, strong-headed parent" (letter from M. Frances Ferris, of the staff of the Syracuse Public Library, which has a collection of newspaper clippings concerning the Rangers). Having had relatively little academic training in art, he opened a studio in New York about 1884, and pleasantly disappointed his father's expectation of his failure. His quite salable water colors, based on the practices of the Barbizon and modern Dutch painters, brought the young artist a modest income which he so managed as to become a well-to-do man. He was also a clever musician and for some years had frequent employment as a music critic. In 1884 he married Helen E. Jennings.

Ranger spent much time abroad and became an intimate friend of Josef Israels and Anton Mauve. He did considerable painting in Holland, and described his impressions of that country in "Artist Life by the North Sea," contributed to the *Century Magazine*, March 1893. Although "he never became a master technician, for his touch was at times heavy" (Daingerfield, *post*, p. 86), he chose his subjects cleverly and his experiments with pigments and varnishes were of fascinating interest. About 1900 he discovered the picturesqueness of the Connecticut shore and Fisher's Island. At his studio on the water front at Noank, he painted the pictures, usually in oil color over damp varnish, by which he is best known. They reflect the personality of a rugged, vigorous man who reproduced from nature much of its poetry and tenderness.

Ranger's year followed a definite pattern: the late autumn and early winter he spent in New York; in mid-January he left for Puerto Rico, whose landscape and people he loved; for six or seven months he was at Noank. He was not only socially agreeable but was also a good business man; he sold his paintings well and successfully projected studio buildings in New York. He was elected to the National Academy of Design in 1906. The Syracuse Museum acquired his "Long Pond," "Noank Harbor," and several water colors; the Metropolitan Museum, "Spring Woods" and "High Bridge"; the National Gallery of Art, "Groton Long Point Dunes" and several others. In 1916 heart trouble sent him to a sanitarium at Watkins Glen, N. Y., from which he returned to his New York home apparently improved in health, but in November of that year he died, in his sleep. His residuary estate, amounting to about $250,000, was bequeathed to the National Academy of Design, the income to be used for purchase of paintings by Americans, these to be administered by the National Gallery of Art, Washington, which under stipulated conditions, places them among American art museums.

[*Who's Who in America*, 1916–17; *Alumni Record and Gen. Cat. of Syracuse Univ.* (1899); Elliott Daingerfield, in *Century*, Nov. 1918; Arthur Hoeber, *Ibid.*, Aug. 1905; R. H. Bell, *Art Talks with Ranger* (1914); *Am. Art News*, Nov. 11, 1916, Mar. 1, 15, 1919; *Am. Mag. of Art*, Jan. 1917; *Outlook*, Nov. 22, 1916; *Boston Transcript*, *N. Y. Times*, Nov. 8, 1916; *Ann. Report . . . of the Smithsonian Inst. . . . 1917* (1919); date and place of birth from records of Nat. Acad. of Design.]   F. W. C.

RANKIN, JEREMIAH EAMES (Jan. 2, 1828–Nov. 28, 1904), Congregational clergyman, poet, university president, was born in Thornton, N. H., of Scottish-English ancestry, son of Rev. Andrew and Lois (Eames) Rankin. His mother's father, Jeremiah Eames, served in the Revolutionary War; her grandfather, Col. William Williams, having been a captain in the French and Indian War, commanded a troop of militia from the east side of the Green Mountains at the battle of Bennington.

Rankin prepared for college in academies at Berwick, Me., Concord, N. H., and Chester, Vt., and graduated at Middlebury College in 1848. After teaching in New London, Conn., and Warren County, Ky., and serving, 1850–51, as tutor in Middlebury College, he studied theology at Andover Seminary, graduating in 1854. He married Mary Howell Birge, Nov. 28, 1854, in Washington, D. C. The following year, Feb. 27, 1855, he was ordained by a Congregational council at Potsdam, N. Y. After serving the church there for more than a year he became pastor of the Congregational Church, St. Albans, Vt., in 1857. In 1862 he accepted a call to the Appleton Street Church, Lowell, Mass., and in 1864 to the Winthrop Church, Charlestown. In 1869 he was called to the pastorate of the First Congregational Church, Washington, D. C.,

where he rendered distinguished service for nearly fifteen years. Large audiences filled the auditorium of the church, including many public men, judges, officials of the government, and members of Congress.

Rankin preached with prophet-like intensity, with rapid utterance in a rich, musical voice. His thought was keenly logical, his style forcible and epigrammatic, illuminated by a poetic imagination. He often closed his sermon with an original poem. His heavy dark eyebrows and hair gave him an austere appearance, but the depth of his sympathies was unmistakable. His influence was widely felt in the city and his relations with ministers of other religious bodies were intimate and stimulating. He was a steadfast friend of the colored race and served as trustee and member of the executive committee of Howard University for colored students. During his pastorate the burdensome debt of his church was virtually extinguished and its membership increased more than fourfold.

In 1884 he accepted the pastorate of the Valley Congregational Church, Orange, N. J., but after five years was recalled to Washington to the presidency of Howard University. During his administration of more than thirteen years, closing in 1903, the institution made constant and substantial growth in number of students and in the character of its work, and its life was unified and enriched. Rankin died in Cleveland, Ohio, on the fiftieth anniversary of his marriage.

He was the author of *The Auld Scotch Mither and Other Poems* (1873); *Ingleside Rhaims* (1887); *Subduing Kingdoms* (1881); *Hotel of God* (1882); *Atheism of the Heart* (1886); *Christ his Own Interpreter* (1886); and *The Law of Elective Affinity* (1899), discourses preached at Howard University. Three volumes—*Broken Cadences* (1889), *Hymns Pro Patria* (1889), and *German-English Lyrics* (translations; 2nd ed., 1898)—were collections of verse privately printed. His religious fervor found expression in hymns, several of which were given place in hymnals. His "God be with you till we meet again" has been widely sung and is still in use.

[*Who's Who in America*, 1903–05; *Congreg. Year Book*, 1905; *Gen. Cat. of the Theol. Sem., Andover, Mass., 1808–1908* (n.d.); *In Memoriam, Jeremiah Eames Rankin* (1905); John Julian, *Dict. of Hymnology* (1915), which contains minor inaccuracies; "A Ministry at the Capital," *Congregationalist*, May 16, 1903; *Fiftieth Anniversary of the First Congreg. Church, Washington* (1915); D. S. Lamb, *Howard Univ. Medic. Dept., a Biog. and Hist. Souvenir* (1900); *Cleveland Plain Dealer*, Nov. 29, 1904.]   E. D. E.

RANKIN, McKEE (Feb. 6, 1844–Apr. 17, 1914), actor, theatrical manager, was born in Sandwich, Ontario, Canada. He was named

Arthur McKee, but he dropped his first name soon after going on the stage. He began his connection with the theatre in amateur performances and the next fifty years he ran the gamut of the entire range of stage characters. At the age of twenty-one he was on the professional stage and acting important rôles in Mrs. John Drew's stock company at the Arch Street Theatre in Philadelphia, and in 1865 he even attempted a starring tour. In 1869 he was married to Kitty Blanchard, a popular young actress and dancer whose repute was no less than his. In 1874-75 they were leading players in the Union Square Theatre stock company in New York, taking part in the first production of *The Two Orphans* as the villain Jacques Frochard and as the youthful Henriette, whose pathetic blind sister was at the same time acted by Kate Claxton. Soon afterward they began a long career as joint stars which continued about twenty years, being always billed as Mr. and Mrs. McKee Rankin. The principal play in their repertory for several seasons was *The Danites,* a dramatization by P. A. Fitzgerald of Joaquin Miller's sketch, *The First Families of the Sierras,* in which Rankin played Sandy McGee and his wife appeared as Nancy Williams and as Billy Piper. Their tours in this play, which was a melodrama of crude quality and wholly popular appeal, included an engagement in London. "Its reception was most flattering," wrote Rankin, but they remained in England scarcely long enough to justify that remark. Another melodrama of the same type, *The Golden Giant Mine,* by Clay M. Greene, did not duplicate the success of *The Danites* in the United States, and his later career, during his association with his wife, and after their separation in the nineties, was one of extreme diversity. He traveled far and wide from the Atlantic to the Pacific, he went to England and Australia, and he acted in many plays and vaudeville sketches, and in stock and touring companies. He was Nance O'Neil's manager and leading actor when she suddenly rose to fame as an emotional actress in the early years of the twentieth century, his most important character while in her support being the father Schwartze in *Magda* (known as *Heimath* in the original), a German play which for some time was in vogue and was a leading feature in the repertories of Duse, Bernhardt, Modjeska, and Mrs. Patrick Campbell. In his early days he is said to have been handsome and dashing, the perfect representative of the *jeune premier* on the stage; in his later years his long experience in melodrama made him hard and labored, with an astonishingly artificial technique. Rankin had two daughters, both of whom were on the stage: Phyllis, who married Harry Davenport, son of Edward L. Davenport; and Gladys, who married Sidney Drew, son of Mrs. John Drew.

[H. P. Phelps, *Players of a Century* (1880); J. B. Clapp and E. F. Edgett, *Players of the Present,* pt. 3 (1901); T. Allston Brown, *A History of the N. Y. Stage* (1902); Interview with Kitty Blanchard, in *N. Y. Dramatic Mirror,* Dec. 11, 1897; *Brooklyn Eagle,* Apr. 29, 1900; obituary notices in the *Boston Transcript,* Apr. 17, 1914, and *N. Y. World,* Apr. 18, 1914.]
E. F. E.

RANKINE, WILLIAM BIRCH (Jan. 4, 1858–Sept. 30, 1905), lawyer, promoter, and officer of the Niagara Falls Power Company, was born at Owego, Tioga County, N. Y., where his father, the Rev. James Rankine, was rector of the local Episcopal church. His mother, Fanny (Meek), was an Englishwoman, but on his paternal side Rankine was of Scotch ancestry. He entered Canandaigua Academy in 1868 and in 1873 was admitted to the freshman class of Hobart College, Geneva, which his father had served as president from 1869 to 1871. At the end of his junior year he enrolled in Union College, Schenectady, from which institution he graduated in 1877 with the degree of A.B., *summa cum laude*. He then studied law for three years in the office of A. Augustus Porter in Niagara Falls. During this legal apprenticeship his attention was first drawn to the century-old plan of harnessing the tremendous volume of water going to waste over the great cataract for the generation of useful power. In 1880 he was admitted to the bar and moved to New York City, where he became associated with the legal firm of Vanderpoel, Green & Cuming. A few years later he formed a partnership with Robert W. Hawkesworth, which lasted until 1890, when Rankine retired from active practice in order to devote himself to the Niagara power project.

In 1886 a corporation, ultimately known as the Niagara Falls Power Company, had been formed under an enabling act of the New York legislature by residents of the western part of the state, who retained Rankine to interest leading capitalists in the contemplated enterprise. After several years of effort, in 1889 he prevailed upon Francis Lynde Stetson, one of the leaders of the New York City bar, to further actively the new power project. The cooperation of the prominent banking house of Winslow, Lanier & Company was secured and the Cataract Construction Company formed to build the world's pioneer hydro-electric plant for transmitting power over long distances. In February 1890 Rankine was made secretary (later also treasurer) of this concern, and he was subsequently appointed vice-president and treasurer of the Niagara Falls

Power Company itself. As one of an executive committee of four he for nine years supervised the work of construction and more than any one else helped solve the financial and mechanical difficulties that confronted the enterprise. In recognition of this service to the community a bronze bust has been erected in the city hall grounds at Niagara Falls, to his memory as the "Father of Niagara Power."

In 1897 Rankine moved to Niagara Falls, where until his death he was head executive of the Power Company's operating department. A severe illness that befell him in 1886 left his health permanently impaired. Shortly before his demise he married, on Feb. 23, 1905, Annette Kittredge Norton. He was a life trustee of Union College and a member of the bar associations of both New York City and New York State, and of many clubs. A devoted churchman, he was elected in 1904 chancellor of the Episcopal Diocese of Western New York.

[*Memorabilia of William Birch Rankine* (1926), comp. by DeLancey Rankine, containing tributes by Francis Lynde Stetson, Frederick L. Lovelace and others; E. D. Adams, *Niagara Power: Hist. of the Niagara Falls Power Company, 1886–1918* (2 vols., 1927); E. T. Williams, *Niagara County, N. Y.* (1921), II, 456; *Sun* (N. Y.) and *N. Y. Times,* Oct. 1, 1905.]

H. G. V.

RANNEY, AMBROSE LOOMIS (June 10, 1848–Dec. 1, 1905), physician, was born at Hardwick, Mass., the son of Lafayette and Adeline Eliza (Loomis) Ranney. He had twelve brothers, six of whom became physicians. His grandfather was Waitstill Ranney, a physician, at one time lieutenant-governor of Vermont. His father, a police surgeon for many years, was one of three brothers, all of whom were physicians.

Ranney graduated (A.B.) from Dartmouth College in 1868, having previously begun the study of medicine with his uncle, Prof. Alfred L. Loomis, in New York City. Upon the completion of three courses of lectures in the medical department of the University of the City of New York, he received the degree of M.D. in 1871, having won the Mott gold and silver medals during his course. He then served for a time as resident surgeon in Bellevue Hospital. From 1872 to 1885 he was adjunct professor of anatomy in the medical department of the University of the City of New York and then, 1885–90, professor of applied anatomy at the New York Post-Graduate Medical School and Hospital. During a part of this time, 1886–88, he also held the professorship of nervous diseases in the medical department of the University of Vermont.

In the earlier part of his career his major interest seems to have been in surgery and anatomy. He published *A Practical Treatise on Surgical Diagnosis* in 1879, which was followed at short intervals by *Essentials of Anatomy* (1880), *Applied Anatomy of the Nervous System* (1881), *Practical Medical Anatomy* (1882), *Static Electricity in Medicine* (1887), and *Lectures on Nervous Diseases* (1888). These books went through several editions and some were translated into German and French. Becoming increasingly interested in neurology, and recognizing eye-strain as a cause of functional nervous disease, he became a proficient ophthalmologist and published a number of authoritative works on the subject of eye-strain and the treatment of anomalous conditions of the ocular muscles. Among these papers were: "The Eye as a Factor in the Causation of Some Common Nervous Symptoms" (*New York Medical Journal,* Feb. 27, Mar. 13, 1886); "Eye-Strain in Its Relation to Neurology" (*Ibid.,* Apr. 16, 1887); "Eye-strain: Its Bearing Upon the Duration of Human Life" (*Medical Examiner,* New York, May 1889); "Can Eye-strain Cause Epilepsy?" (*Boston Medical and Surgical Journal,* Jan. 2, 1890); "Some Prevalent Errors Relating to Eye-strain as a Cause of Nervous Derangements" (*New York Medical Journal,* June 11, 18, 1892); "The Eye Treatment of Epileptics" (*Ibid.,* Jan. 13, 20, 27, Feb. 17, 1894).

For many years Ranney was a railroad surgeon, and this work frequently brought him to court in the capacity of expert witness. His reputation in this connection was such that Chief Justice Van Brunt once said, "Any lawyer who attempts to cross-examine Dr. Ranney is a fool" (F. L. Wellman, *The Art of Cross Examination,* 1908, p. 66). Ranney was well known for his geniality. He was an owner and driver of fast horses, an expert billiard player, and a yachtsman. His death, from heart disease, was sudden and cut short a career which promised many further years of usefulness. He had married Marie Celle of New York City, on July 25, 1876. They had two children, a son and a daughter.

[*Jour. Am. Medic. Asso.,* Dec. 9, 1905; *N. Y. Medic. Jour.,* Dec. 9, 1905; H. A. Kelly and W. L. Burrage, *Am. Medic. Biogs.* (1920); *N. Y. Tribune,* Dec. 2, 1905.]

G. M. L.

RANNEY, RUFUS PERCIVAL (Oct. 30, 1813–Dec. 6, 1891), jurist, politician, was the third of the eight children of Rufus and Dolly (Blair) Ranney, both natives of Blandford, Mass., where he was born. He was descended from Thomas Ranney (Rany or Ranny) who became a landowner in Middletown, Conn., in 1658. In 1824 the family made the pilgrimage to northeastern Ohio and settled at Freedom.

The annals of pioneers are usually meager, and this is particularly true of the Ranney family for the next decade, but in that time the younger Rufus acquired some schooling, taught school, and enjoyed the luxury for a western farm boy of a brief residence at a near-by academy. In 1833 he entered Western Reserve College at Hudson, but his resources held out for one year only. Denied a college training, he studied law in the office of Joshua R. Giddings and Benjamin F. Wade at Jefferson, Ohio, and in 1836 he was admitted to the bar. His rise in the legal profession was rapid. When Giddings entered Congress in 1838 Ranney was taken into partnership with Wade. In 1845, when Wade became a judge of the court of common pleas, the firm dissolved and Ranney moved to Warren, Ohio. He was a candidate for Congress in 1846 and again in 1848, but the Democratic party was usually a hopeless minority in the Western Reserve counties. Two years later (1850) he was chosen to represent Trumbull County in the second Ohio constitutional convention, where he took a leading part. He shared the Jeffersonian faith in democracy, the Jacksonian confidence in direct popular rule; his chief concern in the framing of the constitution was to increase the share of the masses in government. He submitted a minority report in the committee on judiciary, of which he was a member, which provided for a supreme court with judges chosen by the people and holding sessions in circuits from county to county, in order to keep the court close to the people. He favored extreme separation of powers of legislature, executive, and judiciary, to the extent of opposing the governor's veto in legislation, and short terms and popular election for all public officials.

Ranney's record in the convention won him prompt recognition, for in March 1851 the legislature chose him for a short-term vacancy in the state supreme court, and in October at the first election under the new constitution he was continued in office by popular vote. Five years later on the expiration of his term he retired from public life in order to resume the practice of law, this time in Cleveland. In 1859 he was the unsuccessful Democratic candidate for governor of Ohio. In 1862 he was again elected to the state supreme court, but he resigned at the end of two years. On the bench Ranney was distinguished for the clearness and force of his opinions and his influence on the side of expeditious court procedure. After the Civil War he devoted himself to his law practice in Cleveland, a practice very wide and very remunerative. On the establishment in 1881 of the Ohio State Bar

Association he became the first president. While living in Jefferson, Ranney was married on May 1, 1839, to Adaline Warner, the daughter of Jonathan Warner, a lawyer and associate judge of the court of common pleas. They had six children, three of whom died young.

[See: E. J. Blandin, "Rufus Percival Ranney," in *Great Am. Lawyers*, vol. VI (1909), ed. by W. D. Lewis; C. C. Adams, *Middletown Upper Houses* (1908); memoir in 49 *Ohio State Reports*, v–ix; *Report of the Debates and Proc. of the Convention for the Revision of the Const. of . . . Ohio, 1850–51* (2 vols., 1851); *Cleveland Plain Dealer*, Dec. 7, 1891.]   E. J. B.

RANNEY, WILLIAM TYLEE (May 9, 1813–Nov. 18, 1857), historical and genre painter, was born at Middletown, Conn., the son of William and Clarissa (Gaylord) Ranney. The middle name given him at baptism he never used. At the age of thirteen he was taken to Fayetteville, N. C., by his uncle, and there he was apprenticed to a tinsmith. Seven years later (1833) he was studying drawing in Brooklyn, N. Y. Beginning in 1843 he is listed in the New York City directories as a portrait painter. At the outbreak of the war with Mexico he enlisted in the army commanded by General Taylor and proceeded to Texas, where he fell in with many hardy adventurers and picturesque types of Southwestern character—trappers, hunters, explorers, and pioneers—who interested him intensely as novel subjects for pictorial treatment. After his return to New York he devoted himself to portraying their life and habits. In 1850 he was elected an associate of the National Academy of Design, and thereafter he was a frequent exhibitor at the annual exhibitions. Among his best known paintings may be mentioned "Duck Shooters" (1849), which was engraved by Charles Burt, the print being issued as one of the premiums offered by the American Art Union. He also painted "On the Wing," "Wild Horses," "The Muleteer," and "The Old Oaken Bucket." His essays in historical painting were somewhat crude but interesting for their dramatic vigor of expression and action. In this line of work his more important pieces were "Daniel Boone and his Companions discovering Kentucky," "The Sale of Manhattan by the Indians," "Washington on his Mission to the Indians" (1847), "Marion Crossing the Pedee" (1851), engraved by Charles Burt, and "The Burial of De Soto."

Ranney was married in 1848 to Margaret Agnes O'Sullivan of New York City. After his marriage he moved to West Hoboken, N. J., where he built a home and studio. There Tuckerman found him busily at work, with cutlasses, guns, and pistols hanging on the walls of the studio, curious saddles and primitive riding gear, and other properties suggestive of his Southwestern experience and taste for border adventure. His pictures, "albeit not remarkable for finish in detail or maturity of execution," were not wanting in dramatic truth, natural and local interest, or picturesque effect. They were therefore quite popular. Ranney's closing years, however, were darkened by failing health and poverty, and when he died in 1857 his family was left nearly destitute. His fellow-artists in New York came to the aid of his widow and children. The members of the National Academy freely contributed their own pictures and organized a large exhibition of some two hundred works, including all the pictures and studies left in Ranney's studio. The public sale that followed was so successful that the mortgage on the house in West Hoboken was paid and $5000 was left in the hands of trustees for the support of the bereaved family. The consensus of opinion among contemporary critics and artists was that, while Ranney was not skilful, owing to his lack of thorough training, the freshness and immediacy of his impressions, together with the interest attaching to his subjects, lent his pictures a distinct historical and graphic worth.

[H. T. Tuckerman, *Book of the Artists* (1867); T. S. Cummings, *Hist. Annals of the Nat. Acad. of Design* (1865); S. G. W. Benjamin, *Art in America* (1880); F. Weitenkampf, *Am. Graphic Art* (1912); C. C. Adams, *Middletown Upper Houses* (1908); *Cat. of the Corcoran Gallery of Art* (1897); *N. Y. Times*, Nov. 21, 1857.]   W. H. D.

RANSOHOFF, JOSEPH (May 26, 1853–Mar. 10, 1921), surgeon, was born in Cincinnati, Ohio, and died in the same city. He was the only son and youngest child of Nathan and Esther Ransohoff from Westphalia, who settled in Cincinnati about 1830. Since Joseph's father and mother were pious and orthodox Jews, the boy was brought up strictly in the faith. He was at first destined for the rabbinate and was trained in Hebrew lore and tradition. This training had a great effect on his character. He attended the public schools and Woodward High School, graduating in 1870. Having decided to be a physician rather than a rabbi, he then entered the Medical College of Ohio at Cincinnati. After receiving his doctorate in medicine from that school in 1874 and winning a gold prize for his essay on puerperal eclampsia, he proceeded to Europe to study, attending lectures and clinics during the next three years in London, Germany, Austria, and France. He came under the influence of Billroth, Kölliker, Virchow, Langenbeck, and other great teachers and in London passed the examinations for membership in the Royal

College of Surgeons. A few months later, at the instigation of Sir James Paget, he came up for the fellowship examination, which he passed successfully in June 1877. On his return from Europe he was made demonstrator in anatomy in the Medical College of Ohio and began also to teach surgery; in 1879 he was made professor of descriptive anatomy and in 1902, professor of surgery in the same college, which in 1896 had become a part of the University of Cincinnati. He continued actively engaged in the practice of his profession and in teaching until his death.

Ransohoff was an inspiring teacher, with a clear mind, good insight in diagnosis, and great manual dexterity as a surgeon. He was one of the earliest to operate on the gall bladder and kidney. Much respected in the community, he was revered and loved by his students. His many publications included 145 papers on surgical subjects, chiefly case reports, contributed to the *Cincinnati Lancet-Clinic*, the *Journal of the American Medical Association*, *Archives of Clinical Surgery*, *Annals of Surgery*, *American Journal of Medical Science*, and *Klinische Wochenschrift* of Berlin. His longer papers were "Injuries and Disease of the Neck," published in *The International Encyclopædia of Surgery*, edited by John Ashhurst (vol. VII, 1895); and "Intra Thoracic Surgery (Heart and Œsophagus Excluded)," written in collaboration with his son, Dr. J. Louis Ransohoff, in *American Practice of Surgery*, edited by J. D. Bryant and A. H. Buck (vol. VIII, 1911). For several years he was a member of the Literary Club of Cincinnati, and to it he contributed a number of short stories which were collected and published after his death in a volume entitled *Under the Northern Lights and Other Stories* (1921). He was a great admirer of Daniel Drake [q.v.], and at the hundredth anniversary of the founding of the Medical College of Ohio, in 1920, he delivered an address on "Drake and Holmes" which was published in the *Medical Bulletin* of the University of Cincinnati. He married in 1879 Minnie Workum Freiberg, who with two sons and three daughters survived him. Ransohoff was remarkable as a man, physician, and teacher rather than as a scientist. His whole philosophy, as well as his sense of humor, might have been considered Talmudic. A portrait of him by J. E. Weis hangs in the College of Medicine of the University of Cincinnati.

[Life of Ransohoff by Dr. Albert Freiberg, in *The Ransohoff Memorial Volume* (Cincinnati, 1921); *Who's Who in America*, 1920–21; C. E. Caldwell, in *Medic. Bull.* (Univ. of Cincinnati), vol. I (1921); *Jour. Am. Medic Asso.*, Mar. 19, 1921; *Medic. Record*, Mar. 26, 1921; *Ohio State Medic. Jour.*, Apr. 1921; *Cincinnati Enquirer*, Mar. 11, 1921.]   A. P. M.

RANSOM, MATT WHITAKER (Oct. 8, 1826–Oct. 8, 1904), soldier, United States senator, was born in Warren County, N. C. He was the son of Robert and Priscilla (Whitaker) Ransom, the latter a native of Halifax County. Prepared for college at the Warrenton Academy, he entered the University of North Carolina in 1844, was graduated in 1847, and, having studied law during his senior year, was at once admitted to the bar. He began practice in Warrenton and, proving to be a highly magnetic jury lawyer, soon achieved success. A Whig in politics, he was a candidate for elector on the Scott ticket in 1852 and became so widely and favorably known from this campaign that the succeeding legislature, although Democratic, elected him attorney general of the state. Three years later, when the Know-Nothing party absorbed the Whigs in North Carolina, he refused to support the move, resigned his office, and was thereafter identified with the Democratic party.

On Jan. 19, 1853, Ransom had married Martha Anne, the daughter of Joseph Exum of Northampton County, and he now moved to "Verona," her fine plantation on Roanoke River, which was his home thereafter. Of the eight children born to them, six survived their father. He represented Northampton in the House of Commons from 1858 to 1861, and in 1861 was chosen by the legislature as one of a commission of three to represent the state near the Confederate government in Montgomery, Ala. At this time a strong Union man, he opposed secession, but with Lincoln's call for troops he at once volunteered as a private in the Confederate army, and was almost immediately commissioned lieutenant-colonel of the 1st North Carolina Regiment. He became colonel of the 35th Regiment in 1862, and in June 1863 brigadier-general, succeeding his brother Robert in command of the brigade of which his old regiment formed a part. During the war he participated in the battles of Seven Pines, Malvern Hill, Sharpsburg, Plymouth, Drewry's Bluff, Fort Stedman, and Five Forks, as well as in numerous skirmishes, and surrendered his brigade at Appomattox. He was twice wounded at Malvern Hill, and once at Drewry's Bluff. He was not a trained soldier and never became a tactician, but he was a born leader of men, and the officers and soldiers of his brigade idolized him and continued to do so as long as he lived.

At the close of the war Ransom returned to farming and the practice of law, taking no part in the bitter politics of the day. But when the Kirk-Holden war came in 1870, and the writ of *habeas corpus* was suspended by Gov. William Woods Holden [*q.v.*], Ransom, much disturbed at the invasion of fundamental civil rights, persuaded Judge George W. Brooks [*q.v.*] of the United States district court to issue the writ; when the United States government supported the judge the movement to overawe the state collapsed. In 1872 Ransom was elected to the federal Senate to succeed Zebulon B. Vance, who had been elected in 1870 but denied his seat because of disabilities. Ransom was returned repeatedly and served until 1895.

In Washington he acquired considerable influence, though he seldom spoke, his speech "The South Faithful to Her Duties," delivered in 1875 (*Congressional Record,* 43 Cong., 2 Sess., App., pp. 61–82), being his only formal speech during his senatorial career. But he was a leader in securing the compromise of 1876–77 by which the disputed presidential election was peacefully settled, and to him belongs much of the credit for the defeat of the Federal Election Bill, popularly known as the Lodge "Force Bill," of 1890. As chairman of the committee on the Potomac River fronts, which was appointed upon his motion, he developed the plans which resulted in the transformation of the Potomac Flats into Potomac Park. As a result of a fusion of Populists and Republicans in North Carolina, he was defeated in 1895, and President Cleveland at once appointed him minister to Mexico, where he remained for two years. During this time he acted as arbitrator in finally settling the dispute between Mexico and Guatemala. He then retired permanently to private life.

While he was in the Senate, Ransom was active in politics in North Carolina, being a member of the Democratic national committee from 1876 to 1895, and canvassing a large part of the state in every campaign. In spite of the fact that he cared little for people, he was a most magnetic and effective public speaker and he exerted a wide influence. Tall and of impressive figure, possessed of a rich and resonant voice, he was always deeply serious; and his faultless diction, rounded periods, and powerful arguments could hold a popular audience spellbound for hours.

[Ransom's first name is sometimes incorrectly given as "Matthew," but "Matt" appears in the Univ. of N. C. catalogue for the year of his graduation. See W. H. S. Burgwyn, *An Address on . . . Gen. Matt W. Ransom* (1906); "Addresses at the Unveiling of the Bust of Matt W. Ransom," *Pubs. N. C. Hist. Commission, Bull. No. 10* (1911); S. A. Ashe, *Biog. Hist. of N. C.,* vol. I (1905); *War of the Rebellion: Official Records (Army); Who's Who in America,* 1903–05; *News and Observer* (Raleigh, N. C.) and *Charlotte Daily Observer,* Oct. 9, 1904.] J. G. deR. H.

RANSOM, THOMAS EDWARD GREENFIELD (Nov. 29, 1834–Oct. 29, 1864), soldier, was born at Norwich, Vt., the son of Truman Bishop and Margaret Morrison (Greenfield) Ransom. His father, a distinguished educator and soldier, was killed at the storming of Chapultepec. He was a descendant of Joseph Ransom who settled at Lynn, Conn., about 1715. Thomas entered the preparatory course at Norwich University, a military college of which his father was then president. During the Mexican War he studied practical engineering on the Rutland and Burlington Railroad, under the tutelage of an older relative. He reëntered Norwich in 1848 and completed the civil engineering course in 1851. After graduation, he went to Illinois to practise engineering and later he embarked in the real-estate business.

When the Civil War began, he was living in Fayette County. He raised a company which was incorporated in the 11th Illinois Infantry. He became major, and, on reorganization three months later, lieutenant-colonel. The command and instruction of the regiment soon devolved upon him, and he brought it to a high state of discipline and training. He served as a volunteer aide in the surprise of a Confederate force at Charleston, Mo., on Aug. 19, 1861, and was wounded in personal combat with a Confederate officer, whom he killed. At Fort Donelson his regiment bore the shock of the Confederate sortie with veteran steadiness. Surrounded on the retreat of supporting forces, it cut its way out, losing more than half its strength. Ransom, though severely wounded, refused to leave the field and retained command throughout the day. For his skill and bravery in this action, he was promoted to the rank of colonel. At Shiloh, his regiment surpassed its previous brilliant record. He was seriously wounded early in the action, but again refused to leave the battlefield and continued in command with conspicuous valor and success until late in the afternoon, when he was carried to the rear. He served on the staff of Gen. John Alexander McClernand [*q.v.*] in the Corinth campaign and subsequently he commanded a brigade. Appointed brigadier-general, he led his brigade in the Vicksburg campaign with such ability that Grant rated him equal to the command of a corps. After the surrender of Vicksburg he was put in charge of an expedition against Natchez. This mission was executed with such energy and initiative that Grant wrote of him, "He has always proved himself the best man I have ever had to send on expeditions. He is a live man and of good judgment" (*War of the Rebellion: Official Records, Army*, ser. 1, XXXII, part 2, 141).

In October 1863, Ransom joined the Texas expedition, and during the next three months conducted successful operations along the Gulf coast from Aransas Pass to Matagorda Peninsula. In March 1864, he took command of the XIII Corps, a part of the army concentrated for the Red River expedition. He commanded the advance guard at Sabine Cross-Roads, and with one tired division met the attack of three Confederate divisions. Due to faulty dispositions and to interference by his superiors, he was overwhelmed. Though badly wounded while rallying his troops, he retained command until the attack had been checked. When only partially recovered from his wound, he reported to Sherman on Aug. 2, 1864, and was assigned to command the 4th Division, XVI Army Corps. He took part in the siege of Atlanta; and after General Dodge was wounded on Aug. 19, commanded the corps in the turning movement south of Atlanta which terminated in a victory at Jonesboro, Ga. He was brevetted major-general of volunteers on Sept. 1, 1864, for gallant and meritorious service in the Atlanta campaign. He was next assigned to command the XVII Corps, pursuing Hood's army in north Georgia during the month of October. He was ill at the beginning of the campaign, but refused to quit the field and accompanied his command in an ambulance until the pursuit ended at Gaylesville, Ala., on Oct. 21. Here his illness became critical, and an escort started to carry him to Rome, Ga., on a litter. He died while resting at a house six miles west of Rome. His body was sent to Chicago and interred in Rosehill Cemetery.

One of the most capable volunteer soldiers developed by the Civil War, Ransom was a man of irreproachable character and Cromwellian religious faith. Besides exceptional personal courage, power of physical endurance, and coolness in action, he displayed qualities of leadership of high order.

[W. C. Ransom, *Hist. Outline of the Ransom Family of America* (1903); G. M. Dodge, W. A. Ellis, *Norwich University, 1819–1911* (1911), vol. II; M. E. Goddard, H. V. Partridge, *A Hist. of Norwich, Vt.* (1905); James Barnet, ed., *The Martyrs and Heroes of Ill.* (1865); J. G. Wilson, *Biog. Sketches of Ill. Officers* (1862); T. M. Eddy, *The Patriotism of Ill.*, vol. I (1865); F. B. Heitman, *Hist. Reg. and Dict. of the U. S. Army* (1903); *Proc. First Reunion of the Eleventh Regiment, Ill. Infantry, Oct. 27, 1875, Civil War Pamphlets*, p. 260, Lib. of Army War College.]
T. F. M.

RANTOUL, ROBERT (Nov. 23, 1778–Oct. 24, 1858), reformer, was the son of Robert and Mary (Preston) Rantoul. His father emigrated from Scotland to Salem, Mass., in 1769, became a ship captain, and was lost at sea in 1783. Although born in Salem, the son spent most of his life in Beverly, where he established himself as an apothecary in 1796. On June 4, 1801, he married Joanna Lovett of Beverly. Of their seven children, Robert Rantoul, 1805–1852 [*q.v.*], was to forward many of the reforms in which his father was a pioneer. Chosen overseer of the poor in 1804, he devoted thereafter a large part of his time to the affairs of the town. For fifty years he acted as justice of the peace, and he was also actively interested in school affairs. Elected as a Federalist to the legislature in 1809, he served, in one or the other house, for almost a quarter of a century. It was only when John Quincy Adams began to advocate the "American System" that Rantoul became a supporter of Jackson. As a friend of liberty and equality, he watched jealously the rapid growth of corporations, favored the right of the legislature to build a free bridge in 1826, and won the displeasure of men of wealth who were peculiarly sensitive in regard to vested rights and who insisted on immunity of private corporations from legislative interference. He was also a member of the constitutional conventions of 1820 and 1853, being temporary chairman of the latter.

His significance lies in the part he played in promoting reform and humanitarian movements. A pioneer in the liberal religious revolt, he corresponded with Rammohun Roy of Calcutta on Unitarianism and helped to found in 1810 at Beverly what was probably the first Sunday school in America. Long before he became a life member of the Massachusetts state temperance society when it was organized in 1813, he had been advocating temperance. Although the greater part of the community jeered him in 1816 for dispensing with liquor at funerals, he consistently advocated temperance until 1833, when he became converted to the cause of total abstinence. A participator in the War of 1812 by the services he rendered to the militia, he became one of the earliest members of the Massachusetts peace society, when it was founded shortly after the war came to a close. As early as 1809 he had opposed capital punishment, but it was not until 1831 that, as a member of the legislative committee appointed to consider the subject, he definitely contributed to the movement for its abolition. In all these reform activities he was typical of a new spirit that aimed definitely to improve social conditions. In the decade before his death he wrote his reminiscences, parts of which were published later by R. S. Rantoul in *Essex Institute Historical Collections* (vols. V, VI, 1863–64).

[Reminiscences, *ante*; R. S. Rantoul, *Personal Recollections* (1916).]
                 M. E. C.

RANTOUL, ROBERT (Aug. 13, 1805–Aug. 7, 1852), reformer, was born in Beverly, Mass., and in his brief life did much to further the political and moral convictions of his parents, Joanna (Lovett) and Robert Rantoul, 1778–1858 [*q.v.*]. He was graduated from Phillips Academy at Andover in 1822 and from Harvard College in 1826. Members of the class at Harvard remembered him for his facility and rapidity of mental action, for his frankness and independence, and for his modest, scholarly tastes. To the practice of law, which he began in Salem in 1829, he brought erudition, skill in debate, and, above all, moral conviction. On Aug. 3, 1831, he married Jane Elizabeth Woodbury. They had two children. After 1838 he practised in Boston, but he never identified himself with the wealth, power, and society of that city. Without directing the policy of the Democratic party in Massachusetts, he played an important part in it. Jackson's bank veto, the removal of the deposits, the independent treasury, and free trade found in him a vigorous and intelligent champion. He was given a recess appointment as collector of the customs for Boston in 1843, was rejected by the Senate in 1844, but on Feb. 3, 1846, was confirmed in another recess appointment, as district attorney for Massachusetts.

He began his humanitarian struggles when, as a member of the judiciary committee of the state legislature, 1835–39, he advocated in a comprehensive and widely cited report the abolition of the death penalty on the grounds of expediency and humanitarianism (*Memoirs, Speeches, and Writings of Robert Rantoul, Jr.,* ed. by Luther Hamilton, 1854, pp. 425–515). After a notable legal contest, the Massachusetts supreme court upheld in 1842 his reasoning in the defense of the journeymen boot-makers, who had been charged with unlawfully conspiring to compel their employers to recognize collective bargaining (*Commonwealth* vs. *Hunt and Others, 45 Mass. Reports,* 137). That same year he also defended some of the Rhode Islanders indicted for revolutionary attempts in connection with the Dorr rebellion. A liberal Unitarian, he was a thorough-going advocate of religious tolerance and spoke in the legislature in support of a bill for the indemnification of the Ursuline convent in Charlestown, after it had been destroyed by a mob. He was also one of the earliest advocates of the lyceum and tax-supported public schools. From 1837, when the Massachusetts state board of education was established, until 1842 he was one of its most effective members. By speeches and articles (for example see *North American Review,* Oct. 1838, pp. 273–

318) he did much to popularize this cause, which he thought would elevate the people and insure them against unjust exploitation by aristocracy and wealth. Against the will of party leaders he supported the fifteen-gallon liquor law and advocated the furtherance of temperance by education and moral suasion. He also favored the punishment of the retailer who sold liquor to persons known to make an improper use of it. In lectures and speeches, in newspaper articles, and on the floor of the legislature this reformer attacked special privileges for corporations. He insisted on the necessity of careful inquiries into charters and specific limitations on the powers they granted to their incorporators. Indeed, he never tired, during his entire career in the legislature, of denouncing corporations for stimulating over-speculation and the creation of fictitious wealth. His influence was largely responsible for defeating, in 1836, the petition of Boston bankers and merchants for the chartering of a ten-million-dollar bank. He also attacked the claims of Harvard College to an exclusive control of transportation over the Charles River bridge and insisted on the rights of the people to build and use freely their own bridges and highways.

He became interested, about 1845, in business enterprises in the Mississippi Valley. Although his project for a timber and mining corporation in Minnesota involved him in financial ruin (*Personal Recollections, post,* pp. 25–26) he successfully carried through the Illinois legislature a liberal charter, which he himself had drawn up, for the Illinois Central Railroad. If he was inconsistent in his attitude towards corporations, it was partly due to his enthusiastic belief that the welfare of the different sections of the country depended on the maximum free interchange of commerce, which would be accelerated by liberal favors to railroads (*Letter to Robert Schuyler . . ., on the value of the Public Lands of Illinois,* 1851).

Although his political career was sometimes hindered by his espousal of unpopular causes, it was his opposition to the extension of slavery that led to his election to the Senate in 1851 to fill Webster's unexpired term. In 1851 the coalition between the Free-Soilers and Democrats sent him to the federal House of Representatives. For his political independence and especially for his opposition, on constitutional grounds, to the Fugitive-slave Law he was unseated from the National Democratic Convention in 1852. His early death was a great loss to the anti-slavery Democrats and to the humanitarian causes in which he had interested himself. He achieved

some notable victories for human rights and endeavored, without avail, to check the social irresponsibility of corporate wealth, the character and evils of which he only partly understood.

[*Memoirs, ante; United States Mag., and Democratic Review,* Oct. 1850; R. S. Rantoul, *Personal Recollections* (1916); *North Am. Review,* Jan. 1854; *Jour. of the Executive Proc. of the Senate . . . 1841 . . . 1845* (1887), *Ibid. . . . 1845 . . . 1848* (1887); C. L. Woodbury, "Some Personal Recollections of Robert Rantoul," *Essex Institute Hist. Coll.,* vol. XXXIV (1898); G. S. Boutwell, *Reminiscences* (1902), vol. I; *Charles Sumner: his Complete Works* (1900), vol. III, ed. by G. F. Hoar; "Rantoul," *The Complete Poetical Works of J. G. Whittier* (1900), p. 188; *Jour. of Ralph Waldo Emerson,* vol. VIII (1912), p. 113, ed. by E. W. Emerson and W. E. Forbes; A. B. Darling, *Political Changes in Mass.* (1925); a portrait by Joseph Ames in state house at Boston.]   M. E. C.

RAPHALL, MORRIS JACOB (Oct. 3, 1798–June 23, 1868), rabbi, was born in Stockholm, Sweden, the son of Jacob Raphall. In gratitude for the boy's recovery from a dangerous illness, his father, a banker, dedicated him at the age of five years to the rabbinate, and sent him to a Hebrew grammar school in Copenhagen (1807–12). In 1812 the family moved to England, and later Raphall traveled in France, Belgium, and Germany. He attended the universities of Giessen and Erlangen, receiving from the latter the degree of Ph.D. In 1825 he returned to England and married. His wife, Rachel Goldstein, bore him six children, of whom four survived.

He began his career in 1832 as a professional lecturer. His ability to make his discourses at once scholarly and popular drew large audiences, both Jewish and Christian, throughout the United Kingdom. In 1840 he became secretary to Chief Rabbi Solomon Hirschell, and supported him particularly in the refutation of the blood accusation brought that year in Damascus. In 1841 he accepted the post of rabbi and preacher and master of the Hebrew school of the Birmingham Hebrew Congregation. Here he built up a national reputation as orator and scholar, his addresses helping to remove prejudices and misunderstanding and contributing towards the subsequent success of the Jewish battle for equal rights in England. On his departure for America eight years later, the entire citizenry of Birmingham, Jewish and non-Jewish, united in honoring him.

He came to New York at the end of 1849 on a life contract to be lecturer and preacher to the Congregation B'nai Jeshurun at a salary of $2,000, then said to be the highest paid to any clergyman in the country. He served that congregation until he was made rabbi emeritus in December 1865. He was the first rabbi in New York to preach regular weekly English sermons, his addresses attracting large congregations. He was also the first Jew to be invited to open a session of the House of Representatives with prayer (Feb. 1, 1860). He lectured in various cities in the United States, and before such bodies as the New York Historical Society and the University of Pennsylvania. He showed deep interest in Jewish communal life and endeavored, though without lasting success, to establish a more satisfactory system of Jewish religious instruction. He stimulated charitable activities and was active in gathering funds for the relief of distressed Jews in the Holy Land and elsewhere. Moses Montefiore, prince of Jewish philanthropy, found in him an ever ready and able American ally. An outstanding episode in his American career was the publication of his discourse, *The Bible View of Slavery* (1861), in which he maintained that slave-holding was not a sin according to Biblical law. When the wide publicity and editorial comments on his address threatened to give an impression that American Jews as a class were pro-slavery, rabbis and Jewish laymen alike emphatically contraverted his views. His loyalty to the Union remained beyond question, however, and one of his sons served as a commissioned officer in the Union army.

Raphall's literary activity was important in its day. While in England he founded and edited the *Hebrew Review, or Magazine of Rabbinical Literature* (1834–36), the first Jewish weekly in Great Britain; he was one of the editors of the Book of Genesis for *The Sacred Scriptures in Hebrew and English; a New Translation with Notes* (vol. I—the only volume published—1844); and a co-translator of *Eighteen Treatises from the Mishnah* (1845). In addition, he wrote *Judaism Defended* (pamphlet, 1840); *The Unity of God* (sermon, published in 1845 by Unitarians "for the sake of civilization and the benefit of mankind"); *Post-Biblical History of the Jews* (2 vols., 1855), an ambitious and useful work; and *The Path to Immortality* (1859), besides other devotional books and pamphlets. He is remembered as a talented and scholarly orator rather than as a great leader; but his permanent importance rests in his championship of the Jewish people and their time-honored traditions. Side by side with Isaac Leeser, Sabato Morais, and Samuel M. Isaacs [*qq.v.*], he defended orthodox Judaism in America from the growing encroachments of reform, and improved the standards of the orthodox synagogue.

[Israel Goldstein, *A Century of Judaism in New York* (1930), *passim*, esp. pp. 111–15, 148–53 and references there given: H. S. Morais, *Eminent Israelites of the Nineteenth Century* (1880); *Jewish Messenger*, June 26, July 3, 1868, Aug. 10, 1888: *Occident and Am.*

Jewish Advocate (Phila.), Apr. 1850; E. M. F. Mielziner, *Moses Mielziner* (1931), pp. 212–50; F. S. Drake, *Dict. of Am. Biog.* (1872); *N. Y. Times,* June 24, 1868.]   D. de S. P.

RAPP, GEORGE (Nov. 1, 1757–Aug. 7, 1847), religious leader, founder of the Harmony Society, was born at Iptingen, Oberamt Maulbronn, Württemberg, the son of Hans Adam Rapp, a farmer and grape-grower in moderate circumstances, and his wife, Rosine (Berger). Named Johann Georg (Bole, *post*, p. 176), Rapp was always known as George Rapp in America. He received a good elementary schooling, added weaving to the crafts learned from his father, and in 1783 married a farmer's daughter, Christine Benzinger, who bore him a son and a daughter. Endowed with a sturdy mind and a strongly religious temper, he was a devout student of the Bible and knew the works of Arndt, Spener, Francke, Böhme, Swedenborg, and his contemporary, Jung-Stilling. Preaching in his house to a growing number of like-minded followers, he became the leader of a group of separatists numbering about two hundred families.

For a number of years his adherents endured fines, imprisonment, and much petty persecution. In 1803, accompanied by his son John and a few friends, Rapp came to the United States to make a permanent settlement. From Detmar Basse, grandfather of William Alfred Passavant [*q.v.*], he bought 5,000 acres of unimproved land in Butler County, Pa., and sent for his people, who crossed the Atlantic in three shiploads early in the spring of 1804. Rapp and a band of his followers, acting as pioneers, built the town of Harmony, and early in 1805 the greater part of the original company joined them. On Feb. 15, 1805, they organized themselves as the Harmony Society and adopted a written constitution. In form the Society was a communistic theocracy, with Rapp the actual dictator. His religious teachings were those of Lutheran pietism heavily overlaid with a millenarianism derived from Bengal and Jung-Stilling, a fantastic interpretation of Genesis out of Swedenborg, various minor features from Böhme and other mystics, and the practice of celibacy, adopted in 1807, which seemed to follow logically from his millenarian views. This doctrine doomed the Society to declining power and ultimate extinction.

Of the more than two hundred communistic societies that have sprung up in the United States, the Harmony Society was one of the most successful. This success was achieved in the face of two expensive changes of location, two serious defections, and various lawsuits. It was due in part to the intelligence, industry, and sincerity of its members but chiefly to Rapp's extraordinary energy, intellect, and moral power. From 1814 to 1824 the community was established in the Wabash Valley at Harmony, Posey County, Ind., but between fever-and-ague and barbarous neighbors the Harmonists found themselves neither safe nor comfortable, and in 1825 they sold their lands, through Richard Flower [q.v.] as their agent, to Robert Owen [see *Dictionary of National Biography*]. Meanwhile, they had established their third and last settlement at Economy, Pa., on a 3,000-acre tract on the Ohio River eighteen miles below Pittsburgh. Through its manufactures and its use of labor-saving machinery the Society grew wealthy, gave generously to many charities and philanthropic enterprises, and was long famous for its wines, whiskey, woolens, and other products. The communal life was far from ascetic: members lived in family groups, ate five appetizing meals a day, and cultivated music, painting, and even poetry. Rapp ruled them with the kindness and, when necessary, the severity, of a father, and was revered and obeyed unquestioningly. On the Sunday before his death, unable to go to the church, he preached to his people from a window in the house, and later each one came to his bedside for a personal farewell. He was buried, like the humblest member of the sect, in an unmarked grave.

[Theodor Schott, article in *Allgemeine Deutsche Biographie*, vol. XXVII (1888), with bibliog.; Aaron Williams, *The Harmony Society, at Economy, Pa.* (1866); J. A. Bole, *The Harmony Society: A Chapter in Ger.-Am. Culture Hist.* (1904), with bibliog.; J. S. Duss, *George Rapp and His Associates* (privately printed, 1914).]   G. H. G.

RAPP, WILHELM (July 14, 1828–Mar. 1, 1907), German revolutionist, journalist, was born in Leonberg, Württemberg, Germany, the son of a Protestant minister, Georg Rapp, and his wife, Augusta Rapp. While a student at the University of Tübingen, he became an ardent supporter of the revolutionary movement of 1848, and was sent by the "Demokratischer Verein" of Tübingen as their delegate to the convention at Reutlingen in May 1849. There he advocated the union of the revolutionists of Württemberg and Baden in the cause of a politically free and united German nation. Joining the Tübingen volunteers, he took part in the Baden insurrection, and after the collapse sought refuge in Switzerland. At Ilanz in the Canton of Graubünden he taught in a private school, but while on a secret visit to his home in the Swabian highlands in January 1851 he was taken captive and transported to the prison of Hohenasperg, where he awaited trial for over a year. He was acquitted of the charge of high treason at Ludwigsburg and was set at liberty, but his refusal to recant deprived him of any chance of a career in his native land. He emigrated to the United States in 1852 and first attempted to support himself in Philadelphia at various odd jobs. In the following year he received an offer from the Turners, convening at Cleveland, Ohio, to edit their journal. As editor of the *Turner-Zeitung*, in Cincinnati from 1855 to 1856, and at the same time as president of the Turnerbund, the organized union of German-American athletic clubs in the North and West, he cast his political influence with the newly founded Republican party. He traveled extensively in the West and East and became widely known as a political speaker.

In 1857 he accepted the editorship of the German daily newspaper, *Der Wecker*, at that time the only newspaper in Baltimore supporting the Republican party. The *Wecker* had been founded a few years before by the Baden refugee Carl Heinrich Schnauffer [q.v.]. Rapp was attracted by the opportunity of carrying the fight against slavery and Know-Nothingism into the danger zone, and he waged his war with native vigor and characteristic courage. In the turbulent month of April 1861, a Baltimore mob invaded the office of the *Wecker* and drove the editor out of that city. He returned to his newspaper before the occupation of Baltimore by General Butler, but soon accepted an invitation to join the editorial staff of the *Illinois Staats-Zeitung* in Chicago, where he became one of the most effective supporters of the government and Union among the large German population of the Northwest. After the war he returned to Baltimore as editor and part owner of the *Wecker* from 1866 to 1872. He was married in that city in 1869 to Gesine Budelmann. The lure of a larger field of labor sent him again to Chicago, as editor and part owner of the *Illinois Staats-Zeitung*, on the invitation of the principal owner, A. C. Hesing, and his brilliant editor-in-chief, Hermann Raster. When Raster died in 1891, Rapp assumed sole charge and for seventeen years led the German press of Chicago through local and national issues and events. When he died "in the saddle," as he wished, having absented himself from his office only a few days before, he could well claim to be the Nestor among journalists of the German language press in the United States.

A number of his best speeches are contained in his *Erinnerungen eines Deutsch-Amerikaners,* which he published in 1890. His newspaper articles were written in plain and forceful language, and had great popular appeal. His style and personality were as one, sincere, virile, and scornful of polish. His writing was not confined to editorials on political questions or topics of the day. He was a conscientious book reviewer and a discriminating critic on literary and scholarly subjects. In his youth it had been his ambition to follow in the footsteps of the great Swabian poets, especially Schiller, Uhland, and Justinus Kerner, and while a student at Tübingen he had sent to the revered, aged poet, Kerner, a volume of his first lyrics. His youthful aspirations, however, were forgotten in his life-long daily struggle for united action for freedom and humanity both in his native and his adopted country.

[*Who's Who in America*, 1906–07; *The Book of Chicagoans* (1905); W. Rapp, *Erinnerungen eines Deutsch-Amerikaners an das alte Vaterland* (1890); W. Lang, biog. sketch in *Biog. Jahrbuch und Deutscher Nekrolog*, 1907 (1909); E. Mannhardt, in *Deutsch-Amerikanische Geschichtsblatter*, Apr. 1907; W. Vocke, "Erinnerungen an Wilhelm Rapp," *Die Glocke*, May 1907; *Ill. Staats-Zeitung*, Apr. 21, 1898; *Chicago Daily Tribune*, Mar. 2, 1907.]   A. B. F.

RAREY, JOHN SOLOMON (Dec. 6, 1827–Oct. 4, 1866), horse tamer, was born at Groveport, Ohio, the son of Adam and Mary Catherine (Pontius) Rarey. His father, at one time an innkeeper, reared horses, and the son in early youth began to study humane methods of breaking and training them, apparently based on the traditional methods of the Arabs, of whose horsemanship he was a lifelong admirer. "The horse," he once said, "must be convinced by humane treatment and undeviating firmness that man is his natural master," and upon this principle he acted. The stubborn or vicious subject he first rendered powerless by means of leg straps and hobbles, then brought him gently to his knees, and finally to a prostrate position, where the animal was allowed to remain until he gave the signal of surrender. He was then liberated by degrees and encouraged by a pat of the hand or an approving word, but again rendered helpless at the first sign of disobedience. Rarey's methods were for the most part merely an improvement upon those of earlier horse tamers, but more than his methods, it was his indomitable courage, iron nerve, rare patience and self-control, and seemingly intuitive knowledge of the character of every horse coming before him that enabled him to achieve results which astonished the world and which none of his thousands of pupils could approach.

Before he was twelve years old Rarey had shown that he could coax wild colts in pasture to come up and let him put halters on them. This gift of horsemanship gave him more than a neighborhood reputation in boyhood, but it was not until he was past twenty-five that he began giving lessons for a fee and, later, selling at Ohio fairs *The Modern Art of Taming Wild Horses* (1856), a little book of instructions he had written explaining his system. In the meantime he had studied with Denton Offutt, a noted horse tamer of Georgetown, Ky., who practised the methods of the Arabs and advocated them in his book, *The Educated Horse*, published in 1854. With R. A. Goodenough, of Toronto, Canada, as his manager, Rarey went to England late in 1857. When arrangements were made for an exhibition before Queen Victoria and the royal family at Windsor Castle fame and fortune came to him almost overnight. The Queen and Prince Consort headed a class of more than a thousand men and women who paid ten guineas each for instruction. From his London triumphs Rarey went to France, Sweden, Germany, Russia, Norway, Egypt, Turkey, and Arabia, everywhere receiving the same marked attention and achieving the same uninterrupted success. P. T. Barnum, then in Europe, had an interest in his earnings, and, it is believed, planned the Rarey tour along the same lines that a few years before had reaped a fortune for Jenny Lind and for himself in America. Rarey returned to the United States in 1860, bringing with him the English thoroughbred stallion Cruiser, notorious as an equine maniac before the American horseman, in response to a public challenge in London, broke his spirit by leaving him all night alone in a stable with his forelegs tied up and his hind legs drawn up and tied to a collar which had been put over his head (*Turf, Field and Farm*, July 13, 1883). Rarey's exhibitions were continued in America until his health began to decline in 1862. Never having married, he lived with his mother at Groveport after he retired, building a mansion for her on the site of the modest farm house in which he had been born.

In appearance Rarey resembled a clergyman rather than a typical professional horseman. He was of medium height and weight, wiry and active rather than muscular, with complexion almost effeminately fair, and frank, unaffected manners. He had little schooling, his whole life having been devoted to horses, yet reading and association had given him the presence of an educated and cultivated man.

[Sara Lowe Brown, *Rarey, the Horse's Master and Friend* (1916), and *The Horse Cruiser and the Rarey Method of Training Horses* (1925); J. H. Walsh, *The Horse in the Stable and the Field* (1861, new ed., 1869); obituary in *Turf, Field and Farm*, Oct. 13, 1866; *N. Y. Times*, Oct. 8, 1866.]   G. C. G.

RASLE, SÉBASTIEN [See RÂLE, SÉBASTIEN, d. 1724].

RATHBONE, JUSTUS HENRY (Oct. 29, 1839–Dec. 9, 1889), founder of the Order of

Knights of Pythias, was born in the town of Deerfield, Oneida County, N. Y. He was descended from John Rathbone, one of the purchasers of Block Island in 1660, who became a freeman of Rhode Island in 1664. The son of Justus Hull Rathbone, a Utica lawyer, and his wife, Sarah Elizabeth (Dwight), the boy was named Henry Edwin Dwight, but at the age of ten changed his name to Justus Henry. After a schooling received in academies in New York State and perhaps a brief period at Madison (now Colgate) University, he went west at the age of nineteen, and during the winter of 1858–59 taught school at Eagle Harbor in the Michigan copper region.

On Aug. 11, 1862, Rathbone married Emma Louisa Sanger of Utica, who bore him five children, of whom only two daughters lived to maturity. From January to July 1863 he was in the Federal hospital service as a citizen nurse, stationed at Cuyler General Hospital, Germantown, Pa.; from July 1863 until nearly the end of the war he served as a hospital steward in Washington, D. C. He was subsequently employed as a clerk in the Treasury Department, 1865–69; by the Independent News Company of Boston and New York, 1869–73; and as a clerk in the War Department from 1874 until his death.

In 1863, while at the hospital in Germantown, Rathbone first disclosed the fact that he had drawn up a ritual for a fraternal order which should include the three ranks of page, esquire, and knight. It had been suggested to him by John Banim's play, *Damon and Pythias,* with its lesson of friendship even in the face of death. The chief steward of the hospital, Robert Allen Champion, indorsed Rathbone's idea and advised that when a favorable opportunity arrived an attempt should be made to establish the order. Shortly afterward both were transferred to Washington and, with three other government clerks, on Feb. 19, 1864, they organized Washington Lodge, No. 1, the mother lodge of the Order of Knights of Pythias. Its declared purpose was "to disseminate the great principles of friendship, charity, and benevolence"; its cardinal principles, "Toleration in religion, obedience to law, and loyalty to government." Although it was originally planned as an order of Government clerks, "nothing of a political or sectarian character" was to be "permitted within its portals." At the time, when the guns of war were still echoing, Rathbone's project was received as an effort to allay the feelings engendered by sectional strife, and to help restore peace, harmony, and mutual prosperity.

He was elected "worthy chancellor" of Wash-

ington Lodge which, by the end of 1864, had fifty-two members, but he was not honored with the position of grand chancellor of the Grand Lodge of the District of Columbia, which was formed during the same year. The idea had soon gone beyond the conception of the founder, who was innocent of unworthy ambition or scheming and always ready to step aside for what he deemed best for the Order. Others seized the opportunities presented by the organization, and, for a time, personal aims nearly wrecked the fraternal structure, which, however, eventually took its place with other benevolent institutions. In May 1868 a supreme lodge was formed, with representatives from five grand lodges; in 1877 the endowment rank, an insurance branch, was incorporated, and the next year, the Uniform Rank, a semi-military branch, was added. By 1932 the fraternity had a membership of 501,104.

In 1877 Rathbone was made Supreme Lecturer of the Order—a position created for him. The Silver Anniversary celebration in 1889 found him broken in health. The death of his wife, in 1887, and other sorrows and disappointments, had overwhelmed him, and he asked the editor of *The Pythian Knight* to write for him the Anniversary Address, which he managed to deliver on Feb. 19, 1889. He died at Lima, Ohio, honored and beloved, and officially designated as the founder of the Order, on Dec. 9 of the same year. He was buried at Utica, N. Y., where in 1892 a monument was erected to his memory.

[J. R. Carnahan, *Pythian Knighthood: Its History and Literature* (1888; 2nd ed., 1889); John Van Valkenburg, *Jewels of Pythian Knighthood* (1889), and *The Knights of Pythias Complete Manual and Text Book* (1877); W. D. Kennedy, *Pythian Hist.* (1904); J. C. Cooley, *Rathbone Geneal.* (1898); *The Rathbone Family Historian* (Oberlin, Kan.), Feb. 1892, Feb. 1893; *Evening Star* (Washington), Dec. 10, 1889; information from Rathbone's daughters; personal acquaintance.]   W. M. B.

RATHBUN, RICHARD (Jan. 25, 1852–July 16, 1918), zoologist and museum official, was born in Buffalo, N. Y., the son of Charles Howland Rathbun and Jane (Furey) Rathbun. He was a descendant of Richard Rathbun who settled at Ipswich, Mass., before 1616. He was educated in the public schools of Buffalo, and at the age of fifteen entered the service of his grandfather's firm with which he continued for four years, acquiring a thorough knowledge of business methods. Meanwhile, he became interested in fossils and made the collection in the museum of the Buffalo Society of Natural Sciences, and was made curator of paleontology in that institution. In 1871 he entered Cornell University and came under the influence of Prof. Charles F. Hartt, who in 1875 secured for him an appointment as assistant geologist on the Geological Commission of Brazil. During that year Rathbun investigated the geological formations of Brazil for the purpose of determining the mineral, especially coal, resources of that country. He had also acquired knowledge of marine life during the summers from 1873 to 1875, while serving as a voluntary assistant to Spencer Fullerton Baird [q.v.] of the United States Fish Commission in the marine explorations along the New England coast, and in 1874–75, he was an assistant in zoology in the Boston Society of Natural History. On his return from Brazil in 1878, Baird promptly appointed him scientific assistant to the Fish Commission, whose collections were then in New Haven, Conn. In 1880 he was transferred from New Haven to Washington, where he also became curator of marine invertebrates in the National Museum, a position which he continued to fill until 1914. In 1896 he was called to the Smithsonian Institution, and on July 1, 1898, was made assistant secretary in charge of the National Museum, in which capacity he remained until his death. He served frequently as acting secretary, especially after the death of Samuel Pierpont Langley [q.v.], when for more than a year the important duties of full secretaryship devolved upon him.

His publications, numbering nearly one hundred, are characterized by careful study and clear presentation. Those dealing with Brazil treat of geological conditions and include an extended description of the coral reefs along the coast, but later he specialized on marine invertebrates. His works on echinoids and parasitic copepods are particularly well known. He devoted much attention to the economic aspects of marine biology and his account of the natural history of crustaceans, worms, radiates, and sponges is considered a work of highest excellence. His papers published by the Tenth Census on the various fishery grounds of North America and a survey of ocean temperatures are said to form one of the most important of all contributions to marine economic zoology. As he rose to administrative duties, his advice was sought on many important questions pertaining to marine biology. He was called upon to prepare the material for the case of the United States at the Paris fur seal tribunal in 1891. He cooperated with the international commission sent to the Fur Seal Islands in 1896, and in 1892 President Harrison appointed him as the American representative on the Joint Commission with Great Britain to study the condition of the fisheries in the boundary waters between the United States and Canada.

When he passed to the service of the Smithsonian Institution his acumen was quick to appreciate the value of a gallery of art in connection with that Institution, and the magnificent collection now deposited in the National Gallery of Art is very largely the result of his efforts. The new natural history building of the National Museum was begun during his administration and he supervised its construction with painstaking care. His name will always be preserved in the literature of science by a genus of fishes, *Rathbunella,* and by a genus of starfish, *Rathbunaster,* as well as by many species of plants, batrachians, fishes, and mollusks. He was president of the Philosophical Society of Washington in 1902. In 1892 he was made a fellow of the American Association of Museums, and was elected a corresponding member of the Zoological Society of London in 1917. On Oct. 6, 1880, he married Lena Augusta Hume of Eastport, Me., who, with one son, survived him.

[For a bibliog. of Rathbun's works, see: *Report on the Progress and Condition of the U. S. Nat. Museum, 1919* (1920); for biog. data, see: *Who's Who in America,* 1918–19; J. C. Cooley, *Rathbone Geneal.* (1898); Marcus Benjamin, "Richard Rathbun," *Science,* Sept. 6, 1918, also in *Ann. Report of the Board of Regents of the Smithsonian Institution, 1919* (1921); W. R. Coe, "Richard Rathbun and his Contributions to Zoology," *Am. Jour. of Sci.,* Dec. 1918; *Wash.* (D. C.) *Post,* July 17, 1918.]
M.B.

RATTERMANN, HEINRICH ARMIN (Oct. 14, 1832–Jan. 6, 1923), historian, man of letters, was born in the Hanoverian town of Ankum, near Osnabrück, Germany, the son of a cabinet maker, Hermann Rat(h)ermann, and his wife, Katharine Helmsing. The education of the precocious boy was brought to a close at the age of thirteen, when he emigrated with his parents to the United States. Arriving in 1846 in Cincinnati, where a brother had settled before him, the father found immediate though not very remunerative employment at his trade. The son toiled at various occupations, in a brickyard, slaughter-house, restaurant, decorator's and carpenter's shop. The situation was aggravated when his father died in 1850, leaving to him the main support of his mother and two younger children. His uncle took him into his lumber business, but economic success did not come to the young man until, at the age of twenty-six, he established the German Mutual Fire Insurance Company, of Cincinnati and Hamilton County, Ohio. At the fiftieth anniversary of the founding in 1908, the company possessed a capital of one and one-third millions of dollars and a surplus of $500,000. While his self-made position did not bring him great wealth, it enabled him to support a large family, gather a valuable private library, and make frequent trips in the interests of his historical investigations.

Though he was a faithful servant of his clients, business and statistics never completely satisfied him. Between 1862 and 1870 he wrote and published, in English and in German, several librettos for operas performed in Cincinnati: D. F. E. Auber's *La Muette de Portici*; G. A. Lortzing's *Undine*, and *Der Wildschütz*; Carl M. von Weber's *Oberon*; *The Interrupted Sacrifice*, an American opera, the scene of which was laid in Peru; and *Die Fehme im Froschreiche*, a satirical farce with music by a local composer, Theodore Wilmes, which was performed with acclaim at a Cincinnati carnival in 1869. Rattermann was also one of the founders in his city of German singing societies such as the Sängerbund, the Männerchor, and the Orpheus, and for twelve years he directed the choir of the Catholic Church of St. John. His very active participation in the promotion of vocal and instrumental music became less in the early seventies, when his interest in historical investigations grew. In 1874 Rattermann accepted the editorship of the monthly historical journal *Der Deutsche Pionier*, founded a few years previously. In his hands it became a mine of information on the German pioneers and a most valuable source for the history of the German element in the United States. He continued the work through the eighteenth volume and then published a continuation in 1886–87 called *Deutsch-Amerikanisches Magazin*. He spared neither pains nor expense in getting access to family documents, to court and land records, and to hidden archive materials. His work shows the inevitable faults of pioneer production, but he is at his best in biographical sketches, the material being well sifted and drawn from his own recollections.

Rattermann never aspired to political office, though his political speeches sometimes furnished material for campaign documents. He was influential in the nomination of Tilden at the convention in St. Louis, and subsequently stumped the state of Ohio for Tilden. Late in life he began to publish a selection of his works, *Gesammelte Ausgewählte Werke*. He was his own publisher, even his own type-setter, and with the aid of his daughter, he would have accomplished the task had not bad health and the delays of the printers thwarted him. Twelve volumes of the eighteen he had originally planned were published between 1906 and 1914. When he wrote verse Rattermann assumed the suggestive pseudonym, Hugo Reimmund, for very skilful rhymer he was, and from his inexhaustible mine he

occasionally brought forth a nugget of gold. A volume of poems, *Nord-Amerikanische Vögel in Liedern* (1904), is dedicated to his friend, the ornithologist, Henry Nehrling [*q.v.*], and is a tribute to American birds.

His private library was that of a self-educated scholar and very wide reader. It comprised more than 7,000 volumes and a large number of pamphlets, also files of newspapers, and was particularly rich in travel literature concerning colonial North and South America, and in works on the history of German settlers and pioneers from the earliest times to the nineteenth century. A group of friends bought the Rattermann library and presented it to the University of Illinois in 1916, when the collector could no longer enjoy the use of it himself. Rattermann lived to the age of ninety-one. He was quite deaf and totally blind during his last years, but never lost his cheerful and serene spirit. He was twice married, his first wife dying within a year after her marriage. His second wife, Dorothea Müller, died in 1896. He was survived by four sons, two daughters, and thirteen grandchildren.

[Julius Goebel, biog. sketch in *Deutsches Biog. Jahrbuch, 1923* (1930); "Aus H. A. Rattermann's Leben," *Deutsch-Amerik. Geschichtsblätter, 1918–19,* vols. XVIII, XIX (1920); *Monatshefte für deutsche Sprache und Pädagogik,* vols. XVI (1905); *Deutscher Pioneer Verein von Cincinnati, Ohio. Vorstandsbericht 1922–23* (1924); *Cincinnati Enquirer,* Jan. 7, 1923.]
A.B.F.

RAU, CHARLES (1826–July 25, 1887), archeologist, museum curator, was born at Verviers, Belgium. The details of his family and his early life are lacking. His attainments show, however, that he had the advantages of basic training of the finest sort in languages and other lines thought essential in the European curriculum of the period. Attendance at the University of Heidelberg is the sole clew to his advanced education. It may be deduced from his subsequent development that he first became interested in European archeology and thus formed the basis of his work in the American field. In 1848 he sailed for America, arriving in New Orleans. He subsequently secured a position as teacher of languages at Belleville, Ill., and later in New York City. The study of American archeology, which he had evidently begun under the stimulus of his instruction at Heidelberg, was continued in the United States. In 1863 he published *An Account of the aboriginal inhabitants of the California peninsula*, a translation of the investigations of Jacob Baegert. *North American Stone Implements and Ancient Aboriginal Trade in North America* followed, being published in 1873 as part of the annual report of The Smithsonian Institution for 1872. In 1875 he was appointed resident collaborator in ethnology, in the United States National Museum, a branch now comprising anthropology. His talent was enlisted in preparing for the Centennial Exposition of 1876. In cooperation with Frank Hamilton Cushing and Otis Tufton Mason [qq.v.], his contributions to the process of classification were invaluable.

Rau's work, *The Archeological collection of the United States National Museum,* was published by the Institution in 1876 and also appears in the *Smithsonian Contributions to Knowledge,* vol. XXII (1880). *Early man in Europe* appeared also in 1876. *The Palenque tablet in the United States National Museum* was first published in 1879 and one year later appeared in the *Smithsonian Contributions to Knowledge,* vol. XXII. "Observations on Cupshaped and other lapidarian sculptures in the Old World and in America" appeared in *Contributions to North American Ethnology,* vol. V (1881). An extensive work, *Prehistoric fishing in Europe and North America,* was his last important contribution to science, appearing in the *Smithsonian Contributions to Knowledge,* vol. XXV (1885). A list of his writings from 1859 to 1882 was published in the *Proceedings of the United States National Museum,* vol. IV (1882). Established in reputation as the foremost American archeologist, he was the recipient of many honors from the archeological and anthropological societies of Europe and America. The University of Freiburg, Baden, conferred the degree of Ph.D. upon him in 1882. In 1881 he was made curator of the department of archeology in the National Museum, holding the position till his death. He was a painstaking and methodical scholar, reaching conclusions from which he could not be shaken. His analytical and orderly mind grasped readily and completely the subject of classification. The first in America to recognize the importance of the study of aboriginal technology, he had great and beneficial influence on pioneer anthropology. He was of medium height, spare and ascetic, with gray eyes and beard, and concealed great kindness and benevolence under a gruff exterior. He was never married.

[Personal knowledge of the author; *Annual Report of the Board of Regents of The Smithsonian Institution, 1888* (1890); *Washington Post,* July 27, 1887.]
W. H—h.

RAUCH, FREDERICK AUGUSTUS (July 27, 1806–Mar. 2, 1841), educator, philosopher, was born in Kirchbracht, Prussia, the second son of Friederike (Haderman) and Heinrich Rauch, a minister of the Reformed Church. He was fond of music and became an accomplished pianist. His formal education took him to three universities, Marburg, where he received the Ph.D. degree in 1827, Giessen, where he became *Privat Docent* and later *Professor Extraordinarius,* and Heidelberg, where in 1831 he was on the eve of being appointed as *Professor Ordinarius* in the department of metaphysics. His range of studies included philology, philosophy, and theology. At Heidelberg he came under the powerful influence of Karl Daub, who was then at the height of his brilliant career, the acknowledged head of a school that undertook to reconcile theology and philosophy. The *Zeitgeist* of a tumultuous period in Prussian history also influenced him as a youth. After a public expression of sympathy for the political fraternities the government was trying to suppress, professional advancement became impossible for him.

Coming to America as a political refugee in 1831 he first settled in Easton, Pa., where he gained a livelihood by giving music lessons and by teaching German in Lafayette College. In June 1832 he became principal of the Hochschule connected with the theological seminary of the German Reformed Church at York, Pa. In the autumn of the same year he was ordained to the ministry and elected professor of Biblical literature in the seminary. His salary for both positions was six hundred dollars; he refused a larger amount because, as he said, he had yet to prove his fitness. As credentials of qualification for this professorship he submitted a list of his publications in Europe consisting of nine titles, two of which were written in Latin. One worthy of special mention was *Vorlesungen über Göthe's Faust* (1830). In 1833 he was married to Phebe Bathiah Moore of Morristown, N. J. On the removal, 1835–37, of the literary institutions from York to Mercersburg, Pa., he became organizer and first president of Marshall College in 1836. The groundwork was laid for the doctrinal system known as "Mercersburg theology," which in the following years profoundly affected the trend of religious belief and worship in the United States. There he, a German Zwinglian, ably abetted by his colleague and successor, John W. Nevin [q.v.], developed his dream of an Anglo-American type of philosophy as an essentially complete system, whose keynote was the spiritual interpretation of the universe. In 1840 he published his *Psychology or a View of the Human Soul, including Anthropology.* One of his reasons for writing it was "to give the science of man a direct bearing upon other sciences, and especially upon religion and theology" (preface, p. 2). As far as he knew, this was the first attempt to unite German and American mental philosophy. The book met with instant approval. Orestes A. Brownson hailed it as a work of genius. Its extensive and continued popularity as a textbook in the schools and colleges is evidence of its merit. His untimely death prevented the publication of his teachings in ethics and esthetics as he had planned. They were, however, left in the form of lectures copied by his students. A volume of his sermons appeared posthumously under the title of *The Inner Life of the Christian,* edited by E. V. Gerhart, 1856. He also made numerous contributions to the periodicals of the time, notably an article on "Ecclesiastical Historiography in Germany," in the *American Biblical Repository* (Oct. 1837); and a series of articles on "German Characteristics," in the *Home Missionary* (1835–36). Probably the best concrete expression of his intelligent purpose was Marshall College merged since 1853 in Franklin and Marshall College at Lancaster, Pa., which after the lapse of nearly a century continues to cherish his principles of cultural discipline. He died at Mercersburg and was buried there. Later his remains were transferred to Lancaster and with fitting ceremonial buried in the college burial plot.

[R. C. Schiedt, "Dr. Rauch as Man and Philosopher," *Reformed Church Review,* Oct. 1906; J. W. Nevin, *Life and Character of Frederick Augustus Rauch* (1859); J. H. Dubbs, *Hist. of Franklin and Marshall College* (1903); Theodore Appel, *Recollections of College Life* (1886) and *The Life and Work of John Williamson Nevin* (1889); *Weekly Messenger of the German Reformed Church,* Mar. 10, 1841.]   G. F. M.

RAUCH, JOHN HENRY (Sept. 4, 1828–Mar. 24, 1894), physician, publicist, was born at Lebanon, Pa., the son of Bernard Rauch, who was of German ancestry, and his wife, Jane Brown, of Scotch-Irish descent. He attended Lebanon Academy, commenced the study of medicine under the preceptorship of Dr. John W. Gloninger, and graduated from the medical school of the University of Pennsylvania in 1849. He wrote his graduation thesis upon *Convalaria polygonatum,* thus early showing his love for botany and materia medica.

In 1850 he moved to Iowa, where he joined the newly organized state medical society and the next year published in its *Proceedings* a "Report on the Medical and Economical Botany of Iowa." In 1852 he was the society's first delegate to the American Medical Association. From his young manhood he was both public spirited and scientific. He interested himself in the condition of river boatmen and secured the establishment of marine hospitals at Galena and Burlington. He was a member of the Horticultural, Historical, and Geological societies of Iowa. In 1855–56 he worked with Louis Agassiz and made a natural history collection, consisting mainly of fish, from the upper Mississippi and Missouri rivers. In 1856 he aided in securing the passage of a bill providing for a geological survey of Iowa. He was professor of materia medica in Rush Medical College, Chicago, 1857–58; and was a founder (1859) of the Chicago College of Pharmacy, and its first professor of materia medica. He served as a surgeon throughout the Civil War, being mustered out of service in 1865. He and his work are mentioned several times in the *Medical and Surgical History of the War of the Rebellion.*

After the war he returned to Chicago and in 1867 helped to reorganize the Board of Health, upon which he served until 1873. During this period he cared for the sanitation of the burned city and the welfare of the 112,000 persons rendered homeless by the great fire of 1871, and effected a notable diminution in the city's mortality. He also wrote much on sanitary matters, including eight volumes of Board of Health Reports, and special reports on the Chicago River, public parks, drainage, and the sanitary history of Chicago. In 1870 he visited Venezuela in the interest of mine sanitation and there made valuable collections, which, with several of his unpublished writings, were destroyed in the great fire the following year. He helped found the American Public Health Association and was its treasurer in 1872 and its president in 1876.

His most notable contribution to medicine in the United States was his share in the promotion of higher medical education. When the Illinois State Board of Health was organized, in 1877, Rauch was made its first president and, as such, he had to superintend the administration of the Medical Practice Act, passed at the same session of the legislature. He rapidly reduced the number of non-graduate practitioners in the state, and by setting a requirement for pre-medical education and a four-year course in medical college as qualifications for licensure in Illinois, he was influential in forcing medical colleges all over the country to raise their standards and amplify their courses. (See his *Report on Medical Education, Medical Colleges, and the Regulation of the Practice of Medicine in the United States and Canada,* 1889.) He continued on the State Board of Health until 1891, taking a great interest in all public health matters and writing upon many, including quarantine against yellow fever. In 1892 he assisted in the establishment of a quarantine station for cholera cases and suspects, in view of a threatened invasion of the country by that disease. In

1893, broken in health, he returned to his boyhood home in Pennsylvania, but he served actively in connection with the board of awards of the World's Columbian Exposition at Chicago. The following year he undertook the editorship of the public health department of the *Journal of the American Medical Association,* and made a nation-wide study of the prevalence and control of smallpox, published as "The Smallpox Situation in the United States," in the *Journal* the week after his death. He was found dead in his bed, at Lebanon, on Mar. 24, 1894.

Rauch never married. His interest in everything relating to the American Medical Association was intense. He was a member of its board of trustees and a leader in the organization. His earlier writings on medicine and hygiene, though not of great present worth, show the workings of a keen and active mind applied in a scientific manner. The last twenty years of his life saw the rise of antiseptic surgery, bacteriology, and modern hygiene. He accepted and applied them, helped to secure their recognition in medicine, and did much to guide and accelerate the revolution which their acceptance made inevitable.

[*Hist. of Medicine and Surgery and Physicians and Surgeons of Chicago* (1922); F. M. Sperry, *A Group of Distinguished Physicians and Surgeons of Chicago* (1904); H. A. Kelly and W. L. Burrage, *Am. Medic. Biogs.* (1920); *Trans. Ill. State Medic. Soc.,* 1894; J. F. Percy, "Dr. John H. Rauch—A Pioneer in the Fight against Quackery," *Jour. Am. Medic. Asso.,* Dec. 12, 1908; editorial, *Ibid.,* Mar. 31, 1894; *Sanitarian,* May 1894; *Chicago Tribune,* Mar. 25, 1894.]   P. M. A.

RAUE, CHARLES GOTTLIEB (May 11, 1820–Aug. 21, 1896), homeopathic physician, was born in Nieder Cunnersdorf, a village near Loebau, Saxony, the son of Hans Gottlieb Raue and Christine Julienne Frederick Seiler. His collegiate education was gained at the Teacher's College at Bantzen, 1837–41. Early in life he became strongly impressed with the teachings of Prof. F. E. Beneke of Berlin. He taught school for several years at Berkau, at which place he wrote his first work on psychology—*Die Neuz Seelen Lehre Beneckes* (1847). This work went through five editions and was translated into English, French, and Flemish. At Bantzen, where he was organist in a church, he became acquainted with Carl Hering, brother of the eminent Dr. Constantine Hering [*q.v.*], and through him first heard of homeopathy. In 1848, with letters of introduction to Dr. Hering from his brother, Raue emigrated to America, settling in Philadelphia, and became a member of Dr. Hering's household. He at once began the study of medicine and graduated from the Philadelphia College of Medicine in 1850.

Immediately after graduation he associated himself in practice with a Dr. Gosewich of Wilmington, Del., but in 1852 removed to Trenton, N. J., where he remained until 1859, when he transferred his professional activities to Philadelphia. The old intimacy with Dr. Hering was renewed, and from that time until the latter's death in 1880, Raue paid a visit each day to Dr. Hering's office. In 1864 he was made professor of pathology and diagnosis in the Homœopathic Medical College of Pennsylvania, and in 1867 became professor of practice of medicine, special pathology, and therapeutics in the Hahnemann Medical College of Philadelphia, founded that year by Dr. Hering. He resigned this position in 1871.

Throughout his life, Raue was a deep student and an active contributor to homeopathic literature. In 1867 the first edition of his *Special Pathology and Diagnostics* appeared; this work went through four editions. From 1870 to 1875 inclusive he published *Annual Record of Homeopathic Literature,* but notwithstanding its great value, this publication was discontinued at the end of the sixth year for lack of adequate support. In 1889 Raue published *Psychology as a Natural Science as Applied to the Solution of Occult Psychic Phenomena.* He was twice married. His first wife was Philippina Welfling who died in 1867, and his second, Mathilde Hermine Jungerich, daughter of Johannis and Maria (Kley) Jungerich, of Westphalia, Germany, who survived her husband, dying in 1920. He had two sons. Small of stature but possessing a powerful physique, he was a tireless worker. He was very systematic in his habits, was fond of the society of his intimate friends, whom he frequently entertained and visited, but was diffident among strangers. He enjoyed his lectures and did not refuse to read an occasional paper before a medical society but dreaded making extemporaneous addresses, although he spoke excellent English. His therapeutic optimism augmented his natural cheerfulness in the sick room and no doubt many times turned the scale from disaster to success. He was a member of the Church of the New Jerusalem. He died in Philadelphia of debility of old age.

[*Hahnemannian Inst.,* Nov. 1895; T. L. Bradford, "Biographies of Homœopathic Physicians," vol. XXVI, in library of Hahnemann Medic. Coll., Phila.; T. L. Bradford, *Hist. of the Homœopathic Medic. Coll. of Pa.* . . . (1898); *Press* (Phila.), Aug. 22, 1896; letters in Hahnemann Medic. Coll., Phila., personal letters of Raue's son, Dr. C. Sigmund Raue.]   C. B.

RAUM, GREEN BERRY (Dec. 3, 1829–Dec. 18, 1909), soldier, politician, was born at Golconda, Ill., the son of John and Juliet Cogswell

(Field) Raum, and a descendant of Konradt Rahm, an Alsatian who emigrated to Pennsylvania in 1742. John Raum, who had served as an officer in the War of 1812, went to Illinois in 1823, was a brigade major in the Black Hawk War, member of the state Senate, and a clerk of the county and circuit courts. As a boy, Green Berry Raum studied in the public schools and with a tutor, worked on a farm and in a store, and made three trips to New Orleans on a flatboat. In 1853 he was admitted to the bar. He went to Kansas in 1856, but returned in two years to settle in Harrisburg. In 1860 he was alternate delegate to the National Democratic Convention which nominated Douglas and like his leader he supported the administration on the outbreak of war. He was commissioned a major of the 56th Infantry, Illinois Volunteers, which he had helped organize, on Sept. 28, 1861. He was promoted to the rank of lieutenant-colonel on June 26, 1862, colonel on Aug. 31, 1862, and brigadier-general of volunteers on Feb. 24, 1865. He participated in the siege of Corinth, the attack on Vicksburg, and the attack on Missionary Ridge, where he was seriously wounded in the thigh. Returning to the service on Feb. 15, 1864, he took part in the Atlanta campaign, and was responsible for forestalling an attack by General Hood upon Resaca. The 56th Infantry proceeded on Sherman's march to the sea and the capture of Savannah, Ga. Raum resigned from the service on May 6, 1865.

After the war he practised law in Harrisburg, Ill. In 1866 he aided in securing the charter for the Cairo and Vincennes Railroad, and served as its first president. In 1867, now an ardent Republican, he was elected to the Fortieth Congress where he spoke chiefly on railroad measures and others concerning the commercial development of southern Illinois. He opposed Johnson's reconstruction program and voted for all the articles of impeachment. He was defeated for Congress in the next election, but remained active in the party. From 1876 to 1883 he was commissioner of internal revenue and did much to suppress illicit distilling and violence to revenue agents, partly by aiding in the establishment of legalized distilleries. From 1883 to 1889 he practised law in Washington, D. C., and was engaged in various business enterprises.

In 1889 he became commissioner of pensions. His efficiency was attested by the secretary of the interior, but Raum himself, his son, Green Jr., chief clerk of a newly created division of appointments and the operations of the bureau, were investigated by two committees from the House of Representatives. The first committee, by a vote of three to two, exonerated Raum of the charge of using his office to further business interests; the second, by a vote of three to two, upheld similar charges, the minority laying the vote to the impending political campaign. After his retirement from office in 1893 he moved to Chicago, where he began to practise law. He wrote the following books, *The Existing Conflict between Republican Government and Southern Oligarchy* (1884), and the *History of Illinois Republicanism* (1900). He was married on Oct. 16, 1851, to Maria Field. They had ten children, eight of which survived their father. Raum died in Chicago and was buried at Arlington National Cemetery.

[An autobiog. sketch is to be found in Raum's *Hist. of Illinois Republicanism* (1900); see also, *Who's Who in America*, 1908–09; F. C. Pierce, *Field Geneal.* (1901), vol. II; *Biog. Directory of the Am. Cong., 1774–1927* (1928); *Report of the Adj. Gen. of the State of Ill.*, vol. IV (1901); *House Document No. 3732*, 51 Cong., 1 Sess.; *House Document No. 1868*, 52 Cong., 1 Sess.; *Chicago Daily Tribune*, Dec. 19, 1909.]

T.C.P.

RAUSCHENBUSCH, WALTER (Oct. 4, 1861–July 25, 1918), Baptist clergyman, professor of church history, and writer on the social aspects of Christianity, was born in Rochester, N. Y. His father, Rev. Augustus Rauschenbusch, and his mother, Caroline (Rhomp), were of the company of immigrants whom the abortive revolution of 1848 in Germany contributed to the making of the United States. Walter received his early education in Rochester and was then sent to Germany, where he graduated *primus omnium* at the Gymnasium of Gütersloh, Westphalia, in 1883. Returning to the United States, he received the degree of A.B. from the University of Rochester the following year, and in 1886 graduated from the Rochester Theological Seminary. He was immediately ordained to the Baptist ministry—the seventh in a direct line of ministers—and, declining a more comfortable pastorate, took charge, at a meager salary, of the Second German Baptist Church, New York. In this position he engaged in religious work among German immigrants until 1897. During this period he became acquainted with Henry George and his writings, and read Tolstoi, Mazzini, Marx, Ruskin, Bellamy, and others. Most of all, in the eleven years of this, his only pastorate, he became acquainted with the common people, whose champion he became, his first book being written, he declared, to discharge a debt to them. In 1891–92 he spent some time abroad studying economics and theology at the University of Berlin, and industrial conditions in England. There, through Sidney and Beatrice Webb, he became interested in the Fabian socialist movement, and also was much influenced by the work of the Salvation Army and the Consumers' Cooperatives. He was profoundly influenced by what he saw the industrial depression of 1893 in the United States do to human lives. "One could hear human virtue cracking and crumbling all around," he says. He found he had to revise his religious ideas—"they didn't fit"—and he was impelled to discover the relation between religious and social questions.

In 1897 he was called to Rochester Theological Seminary to take the chair of New Testament interpretation in the German department, a position his father had held before him. From 1902 until his death he was professor of church history, in the seminary, visiting Germany again in 1907 to do research work in the universities of Kiel and Marburg. In the meantime he had become the most influential figure in the development in the United States of what is colloquially called the "social gospel." This position of leadership came to him immediately upon the publication of his *Christianity and the Social Crisis* (1907). This book made him a national figure, in constant demand for addresses and, as a writer, for magazine articles. It revealed the fact that he knew both books and people; that he possessed critical insight and dynamic passion; and that he combined the historical point of view with a rare capacity to analyze and ethically to evaluate current situations and the social order as a whole. His leadership in demonstrating the social aspects of Christianity was increased by his later books: *Prayers of the Social Awakening* (1910); *Christianizing the Social Order* (1912); *The Social Principles of Jesus* (1916); *A Theology for the Social Gospel* (1917). Some of his writings have been translated into French, German, Norwegian, Swedish, Finnish, Russian, Chinese, and Japanese. His *Prayers* constituted a new and imperishable landmark in the history of devotional literature. In addition to his teaching, writing, and lecturing he found time for other activities. He served for some years as secretary of the Northern Baptist Convention. In 1892, with some friends, he founded a religious organization called "The Brotherhood of the Kingdom" which published a quarterly periodical and in modified form still survives. In the city of Rochester he was active in improving the public school system, in civic reform, and in founding a Sunday evening forum.

Rauschenbusch's personality was dynamic; he had power to kindle others to action as well as to give them vision and direction. Few of his opponents could resist the graciousness of his spirit, and an unfailing sense of humor gave ad-

ditional power to his passion for justice and his search for fellowship. His winter avocation was wood-carving, which he had learned from German artists. In summer he engaged with enthusiasm in gardening, canoeing, and camping. In youth he was a lover of music, but for over thirty years he carried the handicap of deafness. It came as a result of going out in the great blizzard of 1888 in New York to minister to sick and needy parishioners before he was fully recovered from epidemic influenza. His wife, Pauline Rother, whom he married in Apr. 12, 1893, was the medium through which much of the world came to him. The family circle, with two daughters and three sons, was one of strong mutuality and in its atmosphere devotion to worthwhile causes was added to the old-fashioned ideal of plain living and high thinking.

The keynote to his personality is to be found in some instructions given when death was in sight. "I leave my love to those of my friends whose souls have never grown dark against me. I forgive the others and hate no man. . . . Since 1914 the world is full of hate, and I cannot expect to be happy again in my lifetime." These words were written in March 1918, when to have a German name, no matter how distinguished one's citizenship, was to be suspect by the mob, and when to be a lover of mankind was to be classed with the enemy and to feel the full force of the atavistic fury that had been artificially awakened for his destruction. Before the United States entered the World War Rauschenbusch had published a small book, *Dare We be Christians* (1914), a companion volume to his *"Unto Me"* (1912). He had also joined in circulating a statement against the export of munitions from the United States, entitled "Private Profit and the Nation's Honor, a Protest and a Plea." With blood kin on both sides of the battle line, his spirit desolated by the destruction of the ideals by which he had lived and for which he had labored, he died, knowing how true was his foreboding that the new chapter in the story of Christendom he had seen beginning was too splendid, "too contradictory of all historical precedent," then to be completed.

[Personal contacts and notes furnished by members of the family; *The Record* (Rochester Theological Seminary) "Rauschenbusch Number," Nov. 1918; R. S. Baker, "The Spiritual Unrest, A Vision of the New Christianity, Conversations with Professor Walter Rauschenbusch," *Am. Mag.*, Dec. 1909; *Who's Who in America*, 1918–19; *Rochester Democrat and Chronicle*, July 26, 1918.]   H. F. W.

RAVALLI, ANTONIO (May 16, 1811–Oct. 2, 1884), Jesuit missionary among the Indians, was born of an aristocratic family in Ferrara,

Italy, and entered the Society of Jesus on Nov. 12, 1827. His noviceship was followed by several years in the study of belles-lettres, philosophy, and the sciences in various Jesuit colleges and in Rome. Thereafter, he taught in the Society's schools in Turin and Piedmont, completed his theological studies, and was ordained priest in 1843. Joining a party of missionaries which included John Nobili [q.v.], Michael Accoloti, and a number of nuns of Notre Dame de Namur who were answering an appeal of Father Pierre-Jean De Smet [q.v.], Ravalli arrived in Vancouver on Aug. 5, 1844, after a tedious voyage of eight months. He remained a few months at St. Paul's Mission on the Willamette before becoming an assistant to Father Adrian Hoecken at St. Ignatius among the Kalispel Indians of the region that is now Montana. Here he learned to get along with only the bare necessities of life, as he braved the northern climate and learned the Selish dialects. After a brief service among the Colvilles, he was ordered to St. Mary's Mission where Gregory Mengarini [q.v.] was in charge. Here life was still harder; for in the isolation of the mission, there was little intercourse with white men and letters were years apart. Nevertheless, he grieved when Indian disturbances forced the temporary abandonment of this center in 1850. Assigned to work among the Cœur d'Alènes of northern Idaho, he built a small flour mill with mill-stones brought from Italy, improvised a saw-mill, and built a church for which he himself carved the altar and statues. He was not only handy with tools but an artist skilled in the use of chisel and brush. In medicine, too, he had some training and attained a greater reputation among the natives by restoring a half-strangled squaw who had attempted suicide. He was accepted as a leader, and, heeding his counsel, the northern tribes remained quiet in the days of the Yakima outbreak of 1856-57. In 1857 he commenced a three-year term with the Colvilles, who welcomed him as an old friend.

In 1860, Ravalli was called to Santa Clara College as a master of novices; but since he preferred the open county, he was allowed to return to Montana in 1863. Life was changing, the wilderness had been invaded by the miner and even the farmer and stockman. Accordingly, Ravalli now served as priest and physician to tribesmen and to the isolated whites who were placer mining in Alder Gulch (Virginia City), Last Chance (Helena), Silver City, French Bar, Crook Creek, Montana Bar, Bear, and other gulches in the hills, or who were raising cattle in the Deer Lodge, Bitter Root, or Flint Creek val-

leys. From St. Peter's Mission, Hell Gate, and St. Mary's, which was reëstablished in 1866, he made many journeys to aid the sick or ease the departure of a soul. Laboring to the last despite the feebleness of years, Ravalli was the ideal missionary—patient under suffering, simple, affectionate, and physically robust. His reputation, in the Rockies, won through forty years of hardship, was second only to that of De Smet.

[L. B. Palladino, *Indian and White in the Northwest* (1894); *Cath. Encyc.* XII (1911), 662; J. G. Shea, *Hist. of the Catholic Missions among the Indian Tribes of the U. S.* (1854); H. M. Chittenden and A. T. Richardson, *Life, Letters, and Travels of Father Pierre Jean DeSmet, S. J.* (1905); tributes of senators H. L. Dawes and G. G. Vest (1884), *Cong. Record*, 48 Cong., 1 Sess., p. 4067; *Ann. Report of the Commissioner of Indian Affairs, 1856* (1857).]   R. J. P.

RAVENEL, EDMUND (Dec. 8, 1797–July 27, 1871), physician, professor, and planter, holds place among pioneer American naturalists by his work in conchology. Born and educated in Charleston, S. C., he was the sixth child of Daniel and Catherine (Prioleau) Ravenel of "Wantoot Plantation," and a descendant of René Ravenel, a French Huguenot, who emigrated to South Carolina in 1685. In 1819 he received the degree of M.D. from the University of Pennsylvania. In 1823 he began summering on Sullivan's Island, where he collected most of his marine shells, but he also visited Rhode Island and exchanged specimens with naturalists of Europe and America. In 1824 he was elected by the state medical society professor of chemistry in the first faculty of the Medical College of South Carolina. The faculty had to provide quarters and equipment at their own expense, and Ravenel, after borrowing apparatus from friends, spent $1,200 in equipping his laboratory. In April 1832 he was elected corresponding member of the Academy of Natural Sciences of Philadelphia. His collection numbered 735 species in 1834 when he published his catalogue, said to have been the first in the United States. The next year, when the Medical Society and the college faculty were at odds, his connection with the college was severed, to the regret of the students. He then bought "The Grove," on Cooper River, a plantation of 3,364 acres and 104 slaves. Here it is said he entertained Agassiz, Audubon, Bachman, Holbrook, and others, and even drained his rice reserves that they might study animal remains at the bottom. He also collected here terrestrial and fluviatile shells, Eocene fossils, and, from Cainhoy, post-Pliocene specimens. His drawings and paintings of shells are said to have been beautiful. In 1848 he published *Echinidae, recent and fossil of South Carolina*. He became vice-president of the Elliott Society of Natural

History when it was organized in 1853, and contributed to its *Proceedings* "Description of Three New Species of Univalves Recent and Fossil" (I, 1859, p. 280); "The Limestone Springs of St. John's Berkeley" (II, p. 28); and "Tellinidae of South Carolina" (II, p. 33). In 1859, when his collection numbered about 3,500 species, he began arranging it by Woodward's plan, but he had only completed univalves when he was halted by cataract of the eyes.

Always progressive, Ravenel was interested in machinery and purchased in 1836 patent rights for South Carolina in Sawyer's brick-making machine, and in 1838 similar rights in Brown's machine. He experimented with fruit growing, purchasing 1,000 apple trees in 1852. His planting interests were then so extensive that he acquired "Brabant," "Moreland," and "Pagett's Landing," adjoining plantations, which consolidated 7,615 acres. His letters on the dredging of Maffitt Channel were printed in the Charleston *Mercury* and *Courier*, 1857–59. Several times he was in charge of the Ft. Moultrie hospital. When yellow-fever in 1858 caused a general migration to Sullivan's Island, as intendant of Moultrieville and as physician he did valiant service among the refugees. He was chairman of the political meeting in St. Thomas's Parish, Nov. 10, 1860, which indorsed secession, but he evinced far greater interest in resolutions concerning oyster boats in the Wando. In the ruin that followed the Civil War he deeded his plantations to his son in trust for the payment of debts, and, almost totally blind, retired to Charleston. In the summer of 1871 he succumbed to typhoid fever and was buried on "Summerton Plantation," Berkeley County, where no stone yet marks his grave. He was married twice: first to Charlotte, daughter of Timothy Ford, and after her death, to Louisa, her half-sister. He is described as slim, and small, with a singularly pure and lovable character. The remains of his collection, *in memoriam,* are in the Charleston Museum.

[H. E. Ravenel, *Ravenel Records* (1898); manuscript memoir by Catherine P. Ravenel, 1914, in Huguenot Church; notes and recollections of Ravenel's pupil in conchology, Wm. G. Mazyck; Ravenel's manuscript papers in the possession of the S. C. Hist. Soc.; records of Mesne Conveyance and Health offices, Charleston, S. C.; obituary in the *Charleston Daily News,* July 29, 1871.]   A. K. G.

RAVENEL, HARRIOTT HORRY RUTLEDGE (Aug. 12, 1832–July 2, 1912), author, was born in Charleston, S. C., the daughter of Edward Cotesworth Rutledge, of "Hampton Plantation," and his wife Rebecca Motte Lowndes, daughter of William Lowndes [*q.v.*].

She grew up in her birthplace and was educated by private teachers and at Madame Talvande's school for girls. On Mar. 20, 1851, she married Dr. St. Julien Ravenel [*q.v.*] and lived an uneventful life in Charleston until during the Civil War, when she went with her husband to Columbia. At the time of the invasion of Sherman's army, with her servants she courageously fought fire all night, saving her home and some of her possessions. Her account of this experience, "When Columbia Burned," was published in *South Carolina Women in the Confederacy* (1903). After the war she returned to Charleston, where she devoted herself to the interests of her husband, who was in frail health, and did much for the education of her children. In 1879, under the pseudonym of "Mrs. H. Hilton Broom," she won the *News and Courier* prize for "Ashurst" (*Weekly News,* Charleston, Apr. 30–June 18), a novel of Southern life which created tremendous local interest and which some consider her best work. After her husband's death she went to live in the country at Acton, near Stateburg, where, since her Charleston home on East Battery was seriously damaged by the earthquake of 1886, she remained eleven years, with only occasional visits to Charleston.

Preserved in her family were many letters and documents of interesting forebears, and during the nineties she busied herself with the surviving letters of a paternal ancestress, in whom Alice Morse Earle also was then interested. In the spring of 1896 she published *Eliza Pinckney,* a small volume containing extracts from a precious old letter-book and a narrative of such charm that few realize its shortcomings in research. Next she turned to *The Life and Times of William Lowndes of South Carolina, 1782–1822* (1901), an uncritical study of her grandfather which is not without value, but which proved to be the least popular of her writings. Although interrupted by serious illness, during the next five years she completed a work for which she possessed every qualification, *Charleston, the Place and the People* (1906), a blend of antebellum history, legend, and discreet reminiscence. Mrs. Ravenel has been aptly described as a great lady of the Old South. Tall, fair, and slender, combining simplicity with distinction, she possessed unusual dignity and charm of manner and voice. A good raconteur, with a sensitive appreciation for words and a knack for clever verses, she enjoyed social intercourse, and it was considered a compliment to procure for a distinguished visitor an introduction to her. Although she was not a club woman, she was active in the Ladies' Memorial Society and the Daughters of the Confederacy, and for three years, 1896, 1897, and 1898, she was president of the South Carolina Society of the Colonial Dames. After many years of poor health and a brief illness, she died in Charleston and was buried at Magnolia Cemetery. Her portrait by Charles Van Dyke, completed a few days before her death, is full of character, and shows her as a stately figure in white cap, seated in her favorite chair.

[H. E. Ravenel, *Ravenel Records* (1898) ; *S. C. Hist. and Geneal. Mag.,* Jan., Apr. 1930 ; *News and Courier* (Charleston), July 3, 1912 ; personal recollections.]

            A. K. G.

RAVENEL, HENRY WILLIAM (May 19, 1814–July 17, 1887), South Carolina botanist and agricultural writer, the son of Henry and Catherine (Stevens) Ravenel, was of a distinguished Huguenot family long prominent in St. Johns, Berkeley. He was born on his father's plantation, "Pooshee." His mother died in his early childhood. He lived with his grandmother until his father's third marriage, when he returned to "Pooshee." At the age of fifteen he was sent to a private school in Columbia, from which he entered the South Carolina College in 1829, graduating in 1832. In college he was especially interested in chemistry and natural philosophy. He wished to study medicine but was dissuaded by his father, himself a retired physician, who felt that his son's constitution was too frail to endure an arduous profession. The elder Ravenel gave his son a plantation, and slaves, thus starting him on his career as a planter which he continued until after the war. Ravenel thus describes his turn to botany as an avocation: "I lived in the country and took up a fondness for plants and fossils. I had a visit from a travelling naturalist, a Mr. Olmstead who was collecting plants. He initiated me fairly into the mode of making collections, and so interested me in the subject that I commenced then to collect and study . . . and with the aid of Dr. Bachman at first, and then afterwards of Dr. Curtis, Prof. Grey and others continued the recreation. About 1846 I commenced the investigation of Cryptogamia botany" (Private Diary of H. W. Ravenel, July 22, 1866). Between 1853 and 1860 he published the best known of his botanical works, *The Fungi Caroliniani Exsiccati,* in five volumes. This was the first published series of named specimens of American fungi. The original edition of thirty copies was purchased by scientists and for museums in Europe and America. Further demand for the work led to the issue of additional volumes after the war (Diary, Mar. 26, 1868, specifies exact disposition of

thirty-nine copies). In collaboration with the English botanist, Prof. M. C. Cooke, Ravenel later published a second series, *Fungi Americani Exsiccati* (in 8 parts, 1878–82). These publications established Ravenel as the leading authority in this country on American fungus and led to extensive scientific correspondence.

From 1861 to 1865, although prevented by physical disability from active participation in the Civil War, Ravenel was so engrossed in its progress as to set aside his scientific pursuits entirely. The close of the war found his previously comfortable fortune swept away. He made various attempts to earn a living for a large family by a nursery and seed business, by publication of a newspaper, and by writing for agricultural journals. In 1869 he was sent by the United States government to Texas to aid in the investigation of a cattle disease then prevalent. This investigation disproved the theory that the disease was due to the eating of a poisonous fungus. (See *Report of the Commissioner of Agriculture on the Diseases of Cattle in the United States, 1871.*) He received the offer of professorships of botany from the University of California and from Washington College at Lexington, Va., in 1869, but he was obliged to decline because of deafness (Diary, July 3, 1869). For a number of years he derived a variable income by collecting and classifying botanical specimens for various scientists and societies. In 1882 he became the agricultural editor of the *Weekly News and Courier,* continuing this work until his death.

Ravenel's name is perpetuated in the names of many plants. He was elected to membership in a number of learned societies, including the Royal Zoölogical and Botanical Society of Vienna (Diary, Apr. 18, 1883). He collected and classified an extensive herbarium of fungi, mosses, and lichens, and in 1881 his summary of his specimens indicated a total of 11,105 species (Diary, Oct. 10, 1881). The cryptogamic section of the herbarium was sold in 1893 to the British Museum, the phænogamic was later sold to Converse College, Spartanburg, S. C. (Gee, *post,* p. 39). Ravenel was twice married: his first wife, whom he married in 1835, was Elizabeth Gilliard Snowden, who died in 1855; his second wife was Mary Huger Dawson, whom he married in 1858. In 1853 he moved to Aiken, S. C., where he died. He was survived by four children of the first marriage and by five children of the second marriage.

[The main source for this sketch is the "Private Diary of H. W. Ravenel," in nine volumes, in the library of the Univ. of S. C. Printed sources include: Wilson Gee, *S. C. Botanists: Biog. and Bibliog.* (1918) ;

Botanical Gazette, Aug. 1887; *Bull. of the Torrey Botanical Club*, Aug. 1893; H. E. Ravenel, *Ravenel Records* (1898).]
         A. R. C.

RAVENEL, ST. JULIEN (Dec. 19, 1819–Mar. 17, 1882), South Carolina physician and agricultural chemist, was born in Charleston, S. C., the son of John Ravenel, of a prominent Huguenot family, and Anna Elizabeth Ford, of Morristown, N. J. Edmund Ravenel [*q.v.*] was his uncle. He received his elementary education in the Charleston schools and then went to New Jersey for further study. He returned to Charleston where he read medicine in the office of a prominent physician, subsequently graduating from the Charleston Medical College in 1840. He continued the study of medicine in Philadelphia and in Paris. Upon his return to Charleston he was for a short time demonstrator of anatomy at the Medical College. Although he early developed great skill as a diagnostician, he disliked the general practice of his profession and turned from it to pursue his studies in science. He was interested in natural history, but chemistry claimed his chief interest, and in the field of agricultural chemistry lay his life work. In 1857 he established at Stoney Landing on the Cooper River the first stone lime works in the state. He served through the war, first in the "Phœnix Rifles," later as surgeon in charge of the Confederate hospital in Columbia, and, finally, in charge of the Confederate laboratory in Columbia where much of the medicine used for the Confederate army was made. He designed the torpedo cigar-boat, *Little David*, which had an encounter with *Old Ironsides*.

After the war Ravenel returned to Charleston and began to experiment with the phosphate deposits along the Ashley and Cooper rivers with the object of manufacturing commercial fertilizer. He originated a process which rendered the phosphate rocks readily soluble, and with the addition of ammonia to animal matter, he produced an ammoniated fertilizer. In 1868 the Wando Fertilizer Company began the production of ammoniated fertilizer by Ravenel's process. He next turned his attention to the production of phosphate fertilizer without the use of ammonia. This he succeeded in doing, and the new fertilizer was known as acid fertilizer. It was soon found, however, that the free acid in this fertilizer destroyed the bags in which the fertilizer was packed for shipping. In working on this problem, Ravenel found that the addition of marl overcame the free acid and, at the same time, increased the fertilizing properties of the product. While working as chemist for the Charleston Agricultural Lime Company, he found that the lime made from the marl mined on the property of this company contained a percentage of phosphate of lime, with enough silica to prevent caustic action on plants. The process which he developed for this company was also used by the Stono-Phosphate Company and the Atlantic Phosphate Company.

Another of Ravenel's contributions to the agriculture of the South Carolina low country lay in his discovery that the planting and plowing of leguminous plants restored to the worn-out soil properties which made it produce larger crops. At the time of his death he was working on plans for irrigating the abandoned rice fields of the low country and for using these rich lands for the cultivation of grasses for hay. He proposed the artesian well system by which the city of Charleston is supplied with drinking water, and was especially interested in the boring of artesian wells to supply the needs of the mills and factories near the city. Although he avoided all public recognition, he freely gave the results of his scientific study for the benefit of the state. The wide newspaper comment on his death, together with the numerous and varied resolutions of respect, indicated that his services to the people of the state were well known and appreciated. Ravenel married on Mar. 20, 1851, Harriott Horry Rutledge [see Ravenel, Harriott Horry Rutledge], who with nine children survived him.

[*Proc. Am. Acad. Arts and Sci.*, vol. XVII (1882); H. E. Ravenel, *Ravenel Records* (1898); *Year Book 1882: City of Charleston, S. C.* (1882); *News and Courier* (Charleston), Mar. 18, May 9, 10, 18, 1882.]
         A. R. C.

RAVENSCROFT, JOHN STARK (May 17, 1772–Mar. 5, 1830), first Episcopal bishop of North Carolina, was born near Petersburg, Va., of a prosperous and genteel family of English descent. Samuel Ravenscroft had come to Boston, Mass., about 1679, but in 1692 settled in Virginia. John Stark's father was John Ravenscroft, a physician, his mother was Lillias Miller, the daughter of Hugh Miller, a Virginia gentleman of Scotch descent. Less than a year after John Stark's birth, the family moved to England and shortly thereafter to Scotland. Having been educated there and in North England, he returned to Virginia when sixteen years of age in order to look after the remains of his father's large property. In this effort he was so successful as to be placed in comfortable, even luxurious circumstances. He then studied law at the College of William and Mary. Here the youth was under little restraint, and he soon became known to his college-mates as "Mad Jack." He was vehement in "temper, speech, and manner" and "not an infrequent attendant at horse races" (Haywood, *post,* pp. 44–45).

On September. 29, 1792, the course of his life was changed by his marriage to Anne Spotswood Burwell, the daughter of an old Virginia family, and a woman of beauty, tact, and high character. At his wife's solicitation, Ravenscroft purchased an estate of 2,500 acres in Lunenburg County, near the home of her father, and became a country gentleman, highly respected in the community. But for eighteen years he did not once read the Bible and only occasionally attended church. About 1810, however, Ravenscroft began to ponder over his spiritual condition and to seek to overcome his "besetting sins—passionate temper" and a "hateful habit of profane swearing" (Haywood, *post,* p. 47). There was a congregation of Republican Methodists near his plantation. He began to attend their services and then to serve as their lay reader, but he came to doubt the authority of the sect's ministers, and decided to join the Episcopal Church and to become one of its clergymen. He was ordained by Bishop Richard Channing Moore [*q.v.*] on May 6, 1817. After ministering successfully for a few years in Mecklenburg County, he was made the assistant of Bishop Moore at Monumental Church, Richmond, Va. Before he had moved there, however, he accepted the position of bishop of North Carolina, being consecrated in Philadelphia on May 22, 1823. Efforts at organization of this very weak diocese had been made in 1790, in 1791, and in 1794, when the Rev. Charles Pettigrew [*q.v.*] was elected bishop. But he died in 1807, without having been consecrated. In 1817 a successful effort at revival had been made, but when Ravenscroft was chosen as the first bishop of the diocese there were still only a handful of ministers and a few hundred parishioners, mostly in the eastern part of the state. The diocese was unable to pay a sufficient salary for his support, so an arrangement was made whereby he should serve half of his time as rector of Christ Church, Raleigh, N. C.

The North Carolinians were little acquainted with the doctrines of the Episcopal Church and Ravenscroft sought to impress his interpretation of these doctrines upon the people. He endeavored to convert first the more intellectual and influential class and "with the aid of their example to build up congregations and parishes as opportunity might offer" (Green, *post,* p. 10). A large proportion of the prominent men of the state became members or friends of the Episcopal Church. Ravenscroft also exerted an abiding influence upon a number of his clergy and laity

who later became bishops. Regardless of the weather and bad roads, he traveled each year from one end of his diocese to the other, a distance of more than five hundred miles, and once journeyed via Tennessee and Kentucky to a General Convention of the Church in Philadelphia. His strenuous activity wore down his vigorous constitution and in 1828 he gave up his charge at Raleigh and became rector of the small church at Williamsboro, N. C. He died in Raleigh. In 1814 his first wife died and four years later he married Sarah Buford of Lunenburg County, Va. She preceded him in death one year. Ravenscroft had no children of his own but had adopted two. He was a tall and powerful man, of commanding presence and manner. His fearless and uncompromising advocacy of his opinions was, however, often carried to the point of tactlessness. But his strong personal conviction and power made a deep impression upon his diocese. He set for North Carolina a standard of conservative churchmanship which has endured to the present day.

[Walker Anderson, memoir including extracts from Ravenscroft's own pen published in first vol. of *The Works of the Rt. Rev. J. S. Ravenscroft* (3 vols., 1830), and also in W. B. Sprague, *Annals of the Am. Pulpit,* vol. V (1859); M. B. Buford, *Hist. and Geneal. of the Buford Family in America* (1924); M. D. Haywood, *Lives of the Bishops of N. C.* (1910); W. M. Green, "Bishop Ravenscroft," *N. C. Biog.* (3 vols., 1858); *Am. Quarterly Church Rev.,* Jan. 1871; *Journals of the Proc. of the Protestant Episc. Ch. in the U. S., 1817–1830; Raleigh Register,* Mar. 8, 1830.]
R. D. M.

RAVOUX, AUGUSTIN (Jan. 11, 1815–Jan. 17, 1906), missionary priest, was born at Langeac, France. He was educated at the Petit Seminaire and the Grand Seminaire in Le Puy and was ordained a sub-deacon there. When, in the spring of 1838, Bishop Jean Mathias Loras [*q.v.*] visited the seminary to get recruits for his large diocese on the upper Mississippi, Ravoux was one who offered himself and in September of that year journeyed with others to Dubuque. There he was ordained deacon in November 1839 and priest in January 1840. After some months' ministry at Prairie du Chien, he was sent in September 1841 to determine whether a mission could be started among the Sioux Indians of the upper Mississippi and to select the best place for a station. He was thus the first Roman Catholic missionary among these Indians since the abortive attempts of the Jesuits nearly a century earlier. The years from 1841 to 1844 were spent among the Indians and half-breeds of the St. Peter's, now the Minnesota River, with intervals of service and rest at the residence of Father Lucian Galtier, the missionary priest at Mendota, and at St.

Paul across the Mississippi. In 1843 he commenced a mission station at Little Prairie, now Chaska, on the St. Peter's River. There he built a chapel and remained till obliged to take over Father Galtier's work among whites and half-breeds in the spring of 1844. During these years from 1841 to 1844 he was intent on learning the Dakota language, and he mastered it sufficiently to prepare a devotional volume entitled, *Wakantanka Ti Ki Chanku, or The Path to the House of God,* printed at Prairie du Chien in 1843 and in a second edition in 1863. Later it was reprinted several times with additions as *Katolik Wocekiye Wowapi Kin* (copies in library of St. Paul Seminary), which had been prepared some thirty years earlier.

With Father Galtier's departure in 1844 ended formal Roman Catholic mission work among the eastern Sioux for many years. The necessity of traveling among the white settlements up and down the Mississippi, St. Peter's, and St. Croix rivers left Ravoux no time for other tasks. He did find opportunity, however, to make two extensive missionary trips in 1845 and 1847 among the Roman Catholics and the Indians on the Missouri. An account of the second trip appears over his name in the *United States Catholic Magazine* (Jan., Feb. 1848). After the uprising of the Minnesota Sioux in 1862 he did valiant work among the Indian prisoners and their families, converting many, and relieving the distress of others. From 1844 to 1851 he was the pastor for all the vast area on the headwaters of the Mississippi. Though outside the diocese of Dubuque the rapidly increasing population of St. Paul claimed his attention more and more. Finally, in 1850, and largely through his influence, a new diocese was erected, and the Right Reverend Joseph Crétin [*q.v.*] came as the first bishop of St. Paul in 1851. Ravoux, while serving as parish priest for Mendota, proved the bishop's right-hand man in the organization of the diocese and the founding and building of churches and schools, and in 1853 he journeyed to Europe to obtain seminarians for the extensive diocese, now rapidly filling with emigrants from the East and from Europe. When Bishop Crétin died in 1857, Ravoux was appointed administrator of the diocese and was in charge of the furtherance of the work already begun until the arrival of Bishop Thomas Grace in 1859. Thereafter his health did not permit of regular parish duties, but he was made the vicar-general of both Bishop Grace and his successor, Bishop John Ireland [*q.v.*]. He also preached occasionally and served in the confessional. His special care for the remainder of

his life was the sisterhood of the city. In 1868 he was named titular bishop of Limyra and vicar apostolic of Montana, but lack of health caused him to beg to be relieved of the honor and of a charge that he felt he could not sustain. In 1887 Pope Leo XIII made him a domestic prelate, *antistes urbanus,* with the title of Monsignor. The last years of his life were spent in retirement. In 1890 he published *Reminiscences, Memoirs, and Lectures of Monsignor A. Ravoux* (published in French as *Mémoires, Reminiscences, et Conférences* in 1892), and in 1897 *The Labors of Mgr. A. Ravoux Among the Sioux or Dakota Indians . . . 1841 . . . 1844.* He died in St. Paul.

[Manuscript register of baptisms, deaths, and marriages kept by Father Ravoux, 1841–47, and other miscellaneous manuscripts at the St. Paul Seminary; information from Father Busch, St. Paul Seminary; letters by Ravoux and his confrères, archiepiscopal archives, Dubuque; Sister Mary Aquinas Norton, *Catholic Missionary Activities in the Northwest, 1818–1864* (1930); J. C. Pilling, *Bibliog. of the Siouan Languages* (1887); *The Official Catholic Directory . . . 1907; Daily Pioneer Press* (St. Paul), Jan. 21, 1906.]

G. L. N.

RAWLE, FRANCIS (*c.*1662–Mar.5,1726/27), merchant, political economist, member of the provincial assembly of Pennsylvania, was the son of Francis Rawle (d. 1697) of the parish of St. Juliot in Cornwall and Jane Rawle (d. 1696), who is believed to have been a native of Devonshire. He was born probably at Plymouth, where his father was living in 1660 (Joseph Besse, *An Abstract of the sufferings of the People Called Quakers,* vol. I, 1733, p. 152). The elder Rawle, who was a devout Quaker, was frequently imprisoned for conscience's sake and in 1683 he and his son were both sent to gaol at Exeter (*Ibid.,* 163). To escape persecution, they emigrated to Pennsylvania in 1686, bringing with them a deed from William Penn for a tract of 2500 acres of land, which was subsequently located in Plymouth township, Philadelphia (now Montgomery) County. The younger Rawle settled in Philadelphia and became a prosperous merchant. He was made a justice of the peace and judge of the county court in January 1689, an alderman of the city of Philadelphia in 1691, and deputy register of wills in 1692. He was also a member of the assembly from 1704 to 1709 and again from 1719 until 1727. As a leader of the anti-proprietary party he came into frequent conflict with James Logan (*Correspondence between William Penn and James Logan,* vol. II, 1872, p. 171), which fact may account for his refusal to accept an appointment on the provincial council offered to him in 1724 (*Minutes of the Provincial Council of Pennsylvania,* vol. III, 1852, p. 232; J. W.

Jordan, *Colonial Families of Philadelphia*, 1911, I, 149). He died in Philadelphia.

Rawle is said to have been the first person in America to write on political economy and its application to local conditions. A pamphlet entitled *Some Remedies Proposed for the Restoring the Sunk Credit of the Province of Pennsylvania* was published anonymously in Philadelphia in 1721. The chief remedy proposed was the issue of a moderate amount of legal tender paper currency based on landed security. Rawle was probably the author of this pamphlet and he was certainly the most active member of the committee that drafted the Paper Money Act of 1723. He also wrote *Ways and Means for the Inhabitants of Delaware to Become Rich* (1725). Logan published a facetious attack upon this pamphlet in the form of a dialogue, to which Rawle replied in *A Just Rebuke to a Dialogue betwixt Simon and Timothy . . .* (1726). His arguments are based on the mercantile theory. Exports were to be stimulated by bounties and imports discouraged by high tariffs. Foreign liquors in particular were to be excluded in order to protect the farmers who produced the raw materials for beer and cider. Molasses was to be on the free list so that rum could be manufactured locally for those who demanded strong drink.

Rawle married Martha Turner, the daughter of a wealthy Irish merchant of Philadelphia, on Oct. 18, 1689. They had six sons and four daughters.

[Biographical sketches appear in E. J. Rawle, *Records of the Rawle Family* (1898) ; T. A. Glenn, *Some Colonial Mansions and Those Who Lived in Them*, 2 ser. (1900) ; *Memoirs of the Hist. Soc. of Pa.*, vol. IV, pt. I (1840). The Society also has a few Rawle manuscripts and copies of the three pamphlets, which are excessively rare. For a discussion of the authorship of *Some Remedies*, see *Pa. Mag. of Hist. and Biog.*, vol. III, no. 1 (1879).]   W. R. S—h.

RAWLE, FRANCIS (Aug. 7, 1846–Jan. 28, 1930), lawyer, author, was born at Freedom Forge, Mifflin County, Pa., the son of Francis William Rawle, iron master and lay judge, and Louisa Hall, and grandson of William Rawle [*q.v.*]. He was educated at Phillips Exeter Academy and at Harvard College, where he received the degree of A.B. in 1869. He played on the Harvard baseball team and always maintained an interest in the college, serving from 1890 to 1902, when he was ineligible for reëlection, on the Board of Overseers. After a year in the law office of his cousin, William Henry Rawle [*q.v.*], he attended the Harvard Law School and graduated with the degree of LL.B. in 1871. In November of the same year he was admitted to the Philadelphia bar, of which he was a mem-

ber for nearly sixty years. But in him, as in others who bore his name, the literary bent was manifest early in his career and his work was accordingly diversified. On Nov. 25, 1873, he married Margaretta C. Aertsen. They had five sons, three of whom died young. In 1878 Rawle participated in organizing the American Bar Association at Saratoga Springs, N. Y., and for over a half-century it provided a field for his extraforensic activities. He was its first treasurer and served until 1902, nearly a quarter-century. In the latter year he was elected president and served the usual annual term. He was present at each of its first twenty-six meetings and was but rarely absent thereafter. He attended the convention of 1924 in London and often presided by invitation over sessions of the Association's meetings. In 1926, at the Denver meeting, he was one of three founders to be honored with life membership and at his death he was the last surviving founder.

Rawle's literary output included a life of Edward Livingston, for S. F. Bemis' *American Secretaries of State and Their Diplomacy* (vol. IV, 1928), and numerous magazine articles, legal and historical. He published three revisions (1883, 1897, 1914) of Bouvier's *Law Dictionary*, and at the time of his death he had an extensive accumulation of notes for a fourth revision. The appearance of his first revision of Bouvier marked the centenary of his grandfather William's admission to the bar, and the office which the latter established continued uninterruptedly under a member of the family until 1930. From the arrival of the first Francis in Philadelphia (1686) to the death of the last, nearly a quarter millennium had elapsed with no generation failing to include a Rawle among those prominent in the civic life of Philadelphia. It is a record equaled by few American families.

[See: E. A. Armstrong, "Francis Rawle, Gentleman," *Am. Bar Asso. Jour.*, June 1930 ; *Tenth Report of the Class of 1869 of Harvard Coll.* (1908) ; *Who's Who in America*, 1928–29 ; T. A. Glenn, *Some Colonial Mansions and Those Who Lived in Them*, 2nd ser. (1900) ; J. W. Jordan, *Colonial Families of Phila.* (1911), vol. I ; *N. Y. Times*, Jan. 29, 1930.] C. S. L.

RAWLE, WILLIAM (Apr. 28, 1759–Apr. 12, 1836), lawyer and philanthropist, was born at Philadelphia, Pa., the son of Francis Rawle II (1729–1761) and Rebecca (Warner) Rawle, and great-grandson of Francis Rawle [*q.v.*]. William attended the Friends' Academy at Philadelphia until the British evacuation in 1778. As the family were Loyalists, he followed his step-father, Samuel Shoemaker, who had been mayor of the city under the British military government, to New York City and there entered upon the study of law with John Tabor Kempe, a former attorney-general of the province. In 1781 he sailed for England, arriving in August, and enrolled as a student in the Middle Temple. While his primary purpose was to complete his legal studies under the most favorable auspices, it is probable that he intended, should the Revolution succeed, to remain there, and his letters afford a valuable source as to contemporary conditions, especially respecting Loyalists. After the Revolution he decided to return to his native city, though he admitted that the step was "in some degree humiliating." On a passport granted by Franklin on May 8, 1782, he returned to Philadelphia and was there admitted to the bar on Sept. 15, 1783. On Nov. 13 he married Sarah Coates Burge. They had twelve children, several of whom predeceased their parents. In 1786 he became a member of the American Philosophical Society and three years later he was elected to the state legislative assembly. When Benjamin Franklin organized the Society for Political Inquiries, Rawle was invited to join the group. President Washington, then having his official residence in Philadelphia, was one of the members, and probably in this way Rawle came to know him quite well. In 1791 the President appointed him United States attorney for Pennsylvania. He held the office for more than eight years, during which time the Whiskey Insurrections of 1794 and 1799 occurred, and it fell to him to prosecute the authors, for which purpose the court followed the military to the western part of the state.

Rawle's early professional progress was slow and he found time for many other activities, taking, to some extent, the place of the lamented Franklin. In 1792 he accepted honorary membership in the Maryland Society for "promoting the abolition of slavery," and from 1818 to the close of his life he was the Society's president. In 1805 he argued against the constitutionality of slavery in the highest court of the state. He was elected a trustee of the University of Pennsylvania in 1795 and held the position nearly forty years. In 1805 he joined the Philadelphia Society for Promoting Agriculture and in 1819 delivered the annual address before it. Also in 1805 he helped to found the Pennsylvania Academy of the Fine Arts and addressed it in 1807. The same year he was elected an honorary member of the Linnæan Society and on several occasions he served as a director of the Library Company of Philadelphia. He was a founder in 1820 of the "Society for the Promotion of Legal Knowledge and Forensic Eloquence," which included the Law Academy, and before the latter

in 1832 he delivered his "Discourse on the Nature and Study of the Law." In 1822 he became Chancellor of the Society of Associated Members of the Bar, before whom, within the next couple of years, he delivered two notable addresses which were published in 1824. His *View of the Constitution of the United States* appeared in the following year and was one of the earliest works on that much-discussed theme. Coming from one who had been a Loyalist at least in sympathy it soon attracted wide attention and was used as a textbook in various institutions, including the United States Military Academy. It passed through two editions and, shortly before the author's death, there was a demand for a third which he was unable to meet. Rawle was the first president of the Historical Society of Pennsylvania, founded in 1825, and he contributed to it, besides his inaugural discourse, "A Vindication of the Rev. Mr. Heckewelder's History of the Indian Nations" (*Memoirs of the Historical Society of Pennsylvania*, vol. I, 1826); a "Biographical Sketch of Sir William Keith" (*Ibid.*); and "Sketch of the Life of Thomas Mifflin" (*Ibid.*, vol. II, pt. 2, 1830), the first commonwealth governor. He also ventured into the field of religion and left several manuscripts upon theological subjects. He retained until the last his connection with the Society of Friends, and he was known as one who lived his religion. Literature also claimed much of his attention. He wrote some poetry and made a partial translation of Plato's *Phaedo*. In 1830 he was appointed one of three commissioners "to revise, collate, and digest" the statutes of Pennsylvania, a task which consumed four years. His last decade was one of steadily failing health, culminating in death at his home in Philadelphia.

[The best account of Rawle is by his friend and associate on the code commission, Thos. I. Wharton. There are several editions of it, one appearing in the *Memoirs of the Hist. Soc. of Pa.*, vol. IV, pt. 1 (1840). D. P. Brown delivered a "Eulogium" on Dec. 31, 1836, which was published in book form in 1837, and the same author contributed a sketch of Rawle to Henry Simpson's *Lives of Eminent Philadelphians* (1859). Other sources include, E. A. Jones, *Am. Members of the Inns of Court* (1924); John Hutchinson, *A Cat. of Notable Middle Templars, with Brief Biog. Sketches* (1902); T. A. Glenn, *Some Colonial Mansions and Those who Lived in Them*, 2 ser. (1900); J. W. Jordan, *Colonial Families of Phila.* (1911), vol. I.]
C. S. L.

RAWLE, WILLIAM HENRY (Aug. 31, 1823–Apr. 19, 1889), lawyer and legal author, was born at Philadelphia, Pa., the son of William and Mary Anna (Tilghman) Rawle, and grandson of William Rawle [*q.v.*]. He received his academic training at the University of Pennsylvania, graduating in 1841. Entering his father's office upon graduation, he read law for three years and was admitted to the bar in October 1844. He appeared professionally before the Pennsylvania supreme court in 1848, and again in 1850, and thenceforth was a conspicuous figure in the courts for nearly forty years. True to the characteristics of the family, he pursued his literary work along with his practice and in 1852 published *A Practical Treatise on the Law of Covenants for Title,* which was several times republished, "each time improved by alterations and additions." In 1853 he published the third American edition of Smith on *Contracts,* and in 1857 the second American edition of Williams on *Real Property,* "which elevated both those treatises into recognized American textbooks." Although of Quaker descent, he did not hesitate to fight for a cause in which he believed and in the second year of the Civil War he enlisted, serving first as a private in the artillery and later in the quartermaster's corps. After the close of the war he resumed his place in the professional life of Philadelphia, serving from 1865 to 1873 as a vice-provost of the Law Academy and for several years as vice-chancellor of the Law Association, holding that office at the time of his death.

He also resumed his literary work following the war but it was generally of a less serious character than before. In 1868 he published a lecture, *Equity in Pennsylvania,* appending thereto "The Registrar's Book of Governor Keith's Court of Chancery." His grandfather, William Rawle, had written a sketch of the Governor which may have suggested a search for the "Registrar's Book" which was thus recovered. In 1881 he published *Some Contrasts in the Growth of Pennsylvania and English Law.* Two notable addresses marked his last years: one on Chief Justice Marshall, delivered in 1884 on the occasion of the unveiling of the statue in front of the Capitol at Washington; the other, "The Case of the Educated Unemployed," delivered before the Phi Beta Kappa Society at Harvard University on June 25, 1885. At the time of his death it was said of him: "He was born and bred and lived in the law. For one hundred and six consecutive years has the honorable office of counsellor at this Bar been continuously and uninterruptedly filled by grandfather, father and son. He commenced his career with a compliment from the Bench of the Circuit Court of the United States for the marked ability which he displayed in his first cause, and he continued that career amidst the plaudits of both Bar and Bench" (A. T. Freedley, in *Legal Intelligencer, post,* p. 178). Rawle

was married, on Sept. 13, 1849, to Mary Binney Cadwalader, who bore him three children. She died in 1861 and on Oct. 7, 1869, he was married to Emily Cadwalader, who survived him. Although he was of slight build, he was active and energetic and "had a large fund of physical force and power."

[W. W. Wiltbank, memoir in *Current Comment and Legal Miscellany,* May 15, 1889; *Legal Intelligencer* (Phila.), May 3, 1889; *Report of the Twelfth Ann. Meeting of the Am. Bar Asso.* (1889); T. A. Glenn, *Some Colonial Mansions and Those Who Lived in Them,* 2nd ser. (1900); J. W. Jordan, *Colonial Families of Phila.* (1911), vol. I; *Am. Law Rev.,* July–Aug. 1889; the *Press* (Phila.), Apr. 20, 1889.]

C. S. L.

RAWLINS, JOHN AARON (Feb. 13, 1831–Sept. 6, 1869), soldier, was born at Galena, Ill., the son of James Dawson and Lovisa (Collier) Rawlins. The family was Scotch-Irish, having settled originally in Culpeper County, Va. His father was born in Kentucky, and lived as a farmer in Missouri and later in Illinois. In 1849 he joined the gold rush to California, and was absent three years, during which time the conduct of affairs at home devolved chiefly upon the son. The farm was largely in timber, and its principal income was from the sale of charcoal to the lead mines in the vicinity. John's early education was scanty. He attended local schools, and had a year and a half at the Rock River Seminary at Mount Morris, Ill. He then studied law in the office of Isaac P. Stevens of Galena, was admitted to the bar in 1854, and practised in partnership with his instructor and later with a pupil of his own, David Sheean. He was married on June 5, 1856, to Emily, daughter of Hiram Smith of Goshen, N. Y. He rapidly gained prominence locally; was city attorney in 1857, and in 1860 was nominated for presidential elector on the Douglas ticket. After the fall of Fort Sumter, he came out unqualifiedly for armed defense of the Union. He took an active part in the organization of the 45th Illinois Infantry, and was designated to become a major in that regiment. Meanwhile, Grant, then a resident of Galena, had reëntered the army as colonel of the 21st Illinois Infantry, and had been appointed brigadier-general of volunteers. Early in August 1861, he asked Rawlins to take a commission as lieutenant, and to become his aide-de-camp. He accepted, and soon after, on Aug. 30, was appointed captain and assistant adjutant-general of volunteers on Grant's staff.

Just at this time his wife died of tuberculosis, after a long illness. He arranged for the care of his three children, reported to Grant at Cairo, Ill., on Sept. 14, and remained constantly with him from this time on as his principal staff officer and most intimate and influential adviser. Like most officers of the new army, he was without military training, but in other respects he was admirably fitted for his position. He possessed a keen, penetrating mind, a remarkably retentive memory, a good practical knowledge of business methods, high moral standards, a strict sense of justice, tireless energy, and a great enthusiasm for his cause. In personal appearance he was not striking; his voice was low and quiet, but on occasion his manner could be most impressive, his language forcible and even violent, and he spoke his mind earnestly and convincingly, to his chief as well as to subordinates. Grant fully appreciated him and his work, and once, in asking a promotion for him, called him "the most nearly indispensable" officer of his staff (Wilson, *post*, p. 140).

It was Grant's custom personally to prepare outline drafts of important papers. These Rawlins verified, edited, and put in final form. This was no easy task, since Grant was often inclined to insist upon the original form, and to reject essential changes; but Rawlins showed both tact and persistence, and was generally able to prove his point. His influence upon Grant in the matter of temperance was freely exercised, strong, and salutary, but the necessity for it has sometimes been greatly exaggerated.

As Grant rose in rank and responsibility, Rawlins was promoted accordingly. He became major on May 14, 1862; lieutenant-colonel, Nov. 1, 1862; brigadier-general of volunteers, Aug. 11, 1863; and brigadier-general and chief of staff of the army—a new permanent position created by act of Congress, Mar. 3, 1865. He received the brevet ranks of major-general of volunteers on Feb. 24, 1865, and major-general in the regular army on Apr. 9, 1865. Throughout the latter part of the war Rawlins had been suffering from an affection of the lungs, which finally proved to be tuberculosis, and, at the close of hostilities, he was unable to continue heavy work. In the hope that the dry air of the western plains might benefit him, he accompanied General Dodge, chief engineer of the Union Pacific Railroad, on a trip over the proposed route, traveling with a military escort as far as Salt Lake City, Utah. The name Rawlins was later given by General Dodge to the town which grew up at one of their camp sites in Wyoming. He returned to Washington in the fall of 1867, having been absent four months, without material improvement in his health.

Upon Grant's election to the presidency, he at first considered giving Rawlins a military command in the Southwest, for the benefit of his health, but later tendered him an appointment as secretary of war, which he accepted on Mar. 11, 1869, resigning his commission in the army. His service in this office was brief, however, for he died in Washington five months later. On Dec. 23, 1863, he had married Mary Hurlburt of Danbury, Conn., who, with two children of his first marriage, survived him.

[J. H. Wilson, *The Life of John A. Rawlins* (1916); J. R. Rollins, *Records of Families of the Name Rawlins or Rollins in the U. S.* (1874); F. B. Heitman, *Hist. Register and Dict. of the U. S. Army* (1903); *Army and Navy Jour.*, Sept. 11, 1869; *Evening Star* (Wash., D. C.), Sept. 6, 7, 1869.]   O. L. S., Jr.

RAY, CHARLES BENNETT (Dec. 25, 1807–Aug. 15, 1886), negro journalist and clergyman, was born at Falmouth, Mass. It was his boast that the blood of the aboriginal Indians, of the English white settlers, and of the first negroes brought to New England mingled in his veins. His parents were Joseph Aspinwall and Annis (Harrington) Ray. His mother was a great reader and very religious, while his father was for twenty-eight years mail carrier between Falmouth and Martha's Vineyard. The eldest of seven children, Ray was educated at the schools and academies of his native town.

His schooling completed, he worked for the next five years on his grandfather's farm at Westerly, R. I. He next learned the shoemaker's trade at Vineyard Haven but in a short while made up his mind to prepare himself for the ministry. He studied at Wesleyan Seminary, Wilbraham, Mass., and later attended Wesleyan University, Middletown, Conn. After leaving there in 1832, he went to New York and opened a boot and shoe store. In 1833 he joined the American Anti-Slavery Society and through his connection with the Underground Railroad actively furthered the escape of runaway slaves with means furnished by Lewis Tappan [*q.v.*] and others. In 1843, after the formation of the committee of vigilance for the protection of those fleeing from bondage, he became its corresponding secretary; in 1850 he was made a member of the executive committee of the New York state vigilance committee.

In the meantime, 1837, he had been ordained as a Methodist minister. The same year he was appointed general agent of the *Colored American,* a recently established negro weekly and the second one of its kind to be published in the United States. He traveled extensively in the interest of this journal, lectured on its behalf in Eastern and Western cities, and contributed to its columns. In 1838 he became part, and subsequently sole, owner of this paper, and was its only editor from 1839 on. Although he conducted the publication ably and proved himself a terse and vigorous writer, it suspended publication in April 1842 after a checkered career. It served, however, as a prototype for later negro journals. In 1846 he was installed as pastor of the Bethesda Congregational Church, New York, and continued as such until 1868. From 1846 until his death he held the position of city missionary. He was also keenly interested in educational subjects, and in 1847–48 helped organize a number of temperance societies. He was married in 1834 to Henrietta, the daughter of Green Regulus; she died in 1836 as did the infant girl born of this union. In 1840 he married Charlotte Augusta, the daughter of Gustavus J. and Pacella (Cuthbert) Burroughs of Savannah, Ga.; she bore him seven children, of whom only three daughters were living at the time of his death. He was light in color, of small stature and wiry frame, and polished in manners. He had a gentle disposition, was modest in demeanor, and fair-minded and effective as a speaker.

[F. T. Ray, *Sketch of the Life of Charles B. Ray* (1887); I. G. Penn, *The Afro-Am. Press* (1891); *Congregational Year Book*, 1887.]   H. G. V.

RAY, ISAAC (Jan. 16, 1807–Mar. 31, 1881), psychiatrist, was born in Beverly, Mass., the son of Isaac Rea, a shipmaster, and Lydia (Simonds) Rea. The family later changed the spelling of the name. The younger Isaac was educated at Phillips Academy, Andover, and at Bowdoin College, taking high rank in scholarship. He studied medicine under Dr. George Shattuck of Boston and received the degree of M.D. from the medical department of Bowdoin (Medical School of Maine) in 1827. He opened an office in Portland, Me., two years later removing to Eastport, where he remained till 1841. In 1838 he published *A Treatise on the Medical Jurisprudence of Insanity*, still an accepted authority in courts of law. In 1841 he became superintendent of the Maine Insane Hospital, Augusta, which institution he left in 1845 to assume medical charge of Butler Hospital, Providence, R. I., a recently established private, incorporated hospital for mental diseases. Its trustees commissioned Ray and Dr. Luther Bell [*q.v.*] of McLean Asylum (now McLean Hospital, Waverley, Mass.) to visit hospitals and asylums in Europe with a view to devising plans which should embody the best known construction of that period. Ray's "Observations on the Principal Hospitals for the Insane in Great Britain, France, and Germany" (*American Journal of Insanity*, April 1846) was a result of that visit,

and the hospital when completed (1847) bore witness in its arrangements and architecture to the fruitfulness of the foreign experience.

Returning to Providence in 1846, he remained at Butler Hospital as physician-in-chief and superintendent till the close of 1866, when he resigned on account of impaired health. He had been during those two decades not only a laborious administrator, but, as physician, keenly interested in the scientific aspects of mental medicine and a prolific contributor to the literature of his specialty. Going from Providence to Philadelphia, he made the latter city his residence till his death. There he acquired an extensive and lucrative consultation practice and was often in the courts as an expert. He was an accomplished psychiatrist and in those days a giant among men of his specialty. He also possessed an intellect which he had cultivated not only in pursuit of the sciences but in that of the humanities. Proof of his literary ability may be found in his annual reports, his many contributions to the *American Journal of Insanity*, and indeed in all that came from his active pen. The bibliography of his writings for the fifty-three years of his authorship includes over a hundred titles. Worthy of special mention are his *Mental Hygiene* (1863); *Contributions to Mental Pathology* (1873), a collection of twenty-two essays, among which are "Insanity of King George the Third," "Shakespeare's Illustrations of Insanity," and "Illustrations of Insanity by Distinguished English Writers"; and "Recoveries from Mental Disease" read before the College of Physicians of Philadelphia and published in its *Transactions* (3 ser., vol. IV, 1879). His versatility is best shown in *Ideal Characters of the Officers of a Hospital for the Insane* (1873), sketches conceived in the vein of Thomas Fuller, in one of which "The Good Superintendent," he unconsciously delineated his own life and character.

Ray was president of the Rhode Island Medical Society, 1856–58; and president, 1855–59, of the Association of Medical Superintendents of American Institutions for the Insane (now American Psychiatric Association), of which in 1844 he was one of the founders. Ray Hall, Butler Hospital, was built as a memorial to him by two of his friends at a cost of $38,000. He married, in 1831, Abigail May Frothingham. There were two children, a daughter, who died young, and Dr. B. Lincoln Ray who died in 1879. Ray left his fortune ($75,000) to Butler Hospital.

[*Gen. Cat. of Bowdoin Coll. and the Medic. School of Maine, 1794–1912* (1912); *Am. Jour. of Insanity*, Apr. 1881; *Trans. R. I. Medic. Soc.*, vol. II, pt. 5

(1882), containing bibliog.; *Butler Hospital: Reports of the Trustees and Supt.*, Jan. 25, 1882; T. S. Kirkbride, in *Transactions of the Coll. of Physicians of Phila.*, 3 ser., vol. V (1881); H. M. Hurd, *The Institutional Care of the Insane in the U. S. and Canada* (1917, vol. IV.]
G. A. B.

RAYMOND, BENJAMIN WRIGHT (Oct. 23, 1801–Apr. 5, 1883), Chicago merchant and capitalist, was born in Rome, N. Y. His father, Benjamin, a descendant of William Raymond who emigrated to America about 1652, was a civil engineer. A native of Richmond, Berkshire County, Mass., he moved to Rome in 1796, where he married Hannah, daughter of Thomas Wright, one of the first settlers of that place. Benjamin Wright Raymond was her eldest son. At her death, five years after his birth, he went to live with an aunt. At the age of ten he was sent to a school in Potsdam, N. Y., established by his father. After four years here and two years in Montreal, where he studied practical mathematics, he began work as a surveyor. Soon he bought a stock of goods and went into business as a merchant at Norfolk, St. Lawrence County, N. Y. The income from this venture proved insufficient for his needs—his father had died and the care of several younger children now devolved upon him—and he returned to Rome, where he became first a clerk in the store of William Wright, a leading merchant of the town, and later his partner. About this time he came under the influence of Rev. Charles G. Finney [*q.v.*], who awakened in him a lasting interest in religion and temperance. In 1831 he formed an acquaintance with S. Newton Dexter, agent of the Oriskany Manufacturing Company of Oriskany, N. Y., who now became his financial backer. This same year, with Dexter's assistance, he made two prospecting trips into the West, one to Ohio, the other to Michigan. The outlook for establishing a merchandising business was not bright, however, and he returned to conduct a wool buying enterprise for four years at East Bloomfield, N. Y. While here, Jan. 12, 1834, he married Amelia Porter. They had two sons, one of whom, George Lansing Raymond [*q.v.*], became a professor in Princeton University. In 1836, with a considerable stock of merchandise, Raymond went to Chicago with the intention of establishing himself in business. He found the field so well occupied, however, that he had great difficulty in disposing of his stock, and was compelled to open a branch store in Milwaukee, one at Geneva, Ill., and another at Des Plaines, Ill. The business depression which continued through 1837–39 left the firm of B. W. Raymond & Company heavily in debt, but his friend and partner, Dexter, again came to his assistance with additional credit and he was able to weather the storm.

He had so well established himself in the good will of the people of the pioneer city that in 1839 he was elected mayor on the Whig ticket, serving for one year. Much against his will, he was again elected, as a compromise candidate, on the Democratic ticket in 1842. Through good management he brought the city through the after effects of the depression. Typical of his character was the donation of his salary as mayor to unemployed workers. He was instrumental in having State Street widened, and in bringing an important addition within the city boundaries. When the Fort Dearborn reservation was ordered sold, he induced the government to grant part of the reservation and all of the lake front east of Michigan Avenue to the city for a park. Thus the city's park system may be said to have had its start under him.

In 1843 he sold out his mercantile business and invested his money largely in city real estate. He was active in 1846 in promoting the Galena & Chicago Union Railroad, the first railroad built west of Chicago, and was on the first board of directors. He laid out the town of Lake Forest and was president of the board of trustees of Lake Forest University for twelve years. He was also a trustee of Beloit College, Beloit, Wis., and of the Rockford Female Seminary, Rockford, Ill. With part of the proceeds from the sale of his mercantile business, he bought a half interest in the town of Elgin from its founder, James T. Gifford. He established a store there, and in 1844 built for his partner, Dexter, the first woolen mill in Illinois. He acted as agent for various eastern insurance companies and gave much time to promoting the building of railroad lines into the country west of Chicago. In 1864 he organized the National Watch Company (later the Elgin National Watch Company), was its first president, and continued active as a director until 1878. In 1842 he helped to organize the Second Presbyterian Church of Chicago, of which he was long a ruling elder. In qualities of character and capacity, Raymond belongs with those other early merchants, John V. Farwell and Marshall Field [*qq.v.*], whose faith in the future of their city contributed so largely to the successful growth of Chicago as a commercial metropolis.

[Samuel Raymond, *Genealogies of the Raymond Families in New England* (1886); A. T. Andreas, *Hist. of Chicago*, vol. I (1884); Joseph Kirkland, *The Story of Chicago*, vol. I (1892); W. H. Bushnell, *Biog. Sketches of Some of the Early Settlers of the City of Chicago* (1876), pt. II; *Chicago Daily Tribune*, Apr.

6, 1883; unpublished memoranda from the Elgin National Watch Company of Elgin, Ill.]   E. A. D.

RAYMOND, CHARLES WALKER (Jan. 14, 1842–May 3, 1913), military engineer, was born at Hartford, Conn., the son of Robert Raikes and Mary Anna (Pratt) Raymond, and a younger brother of Rossiter Worthington Raymond [q.v.]. The Raymonds were descended from Richard who was made a freeman of Salem, Mass., in 1634. Charles's father was a professional man of unusual versatility, and his home life was one of culture and literary interest. In 1861 he was graduated from Brooklyn Polytechnic Institute, of which his uncle, John H. Raymond [q.v.], was president and in which his father was for a time professor of English. He then went to West Point and became a student at the United States Military Academy. While still a cadet he was commissioned lieutenant of artillery and served on the staff of Gen. D. N. Couch in the Gettysburg campaign. He then returned to West Point and was graduated at the head of his class in 1865, being made a first lieutenant of engineers in June of that year. His personality marked him as one of the outstanding members of the corps of engineers, and he was promoted to captain in 1867, to major in 1883, to lieutenant-colonel in 1898, to colonel in January 1904, and to brigadier-general upon his retirement at his own request in June of the last-named year.

In 1869, two years after Alaska was bought by the United States, he was ordered to accompany an expedition of American fur-traders on the first steam vessel that went up the Yukon River. He made one of the first maps of this river, determined by astronomical observation that Fort Yukon was on American soil, and ejected the British fur-traders from that post. His "Report of a Reconnaissance of the Yukon River, Alaska Territory, July to September 1869" (*Senate Executive Document 12, 42* Cong., I Sess.) is well written and interesting. Throughout most of the seventies he was an instructor at West Point and he designed new buildings and a water-supply system for the Academy. In 1874–75 he was on special service in command of the United States expedition to Tasmania to observe a transit of Venus. He published in 1881 *Contributions to the Theory of Blasting, or Military Mining*, a translation of the work of Hans Höfer von Heimhalt. During the mid-eighties he was in charge of river and harbor improvements in Massachusetts, notably at Boston, Newburyport, and Sandy Bay. Later he was in charge of harbor improvements at Philadelphia and in Delaware River and Bay, including the

construction of the Delaware breakwater, a design which he courageously advocated despite hostile criticism. The extensive dredging operations at Philadelphia involved the removal of several islands and gave that city a deep-sea harbor. Other important technical work included fortifications, bridge designs, and observations of terrestrial magnetism. As a military and civil engineer, he was versatile and ingenious, and he was skilled in expressing his ideas in clear English. In 1888–89 he served as engineer commissioner of the District of Columbia. Among the numerous chairmanships that he held were those of the Board of Engineers on Deep Waterways (1897) to report on routes to connect the Great Lakes with the Atlantic Ocean (for report see *House Document 149, 56* Cong., *2* Sess.), and the American Section of the Permanent International Commission of Navigation Congresses (1903). As chairman of the board of engineers that advised on the driving of the Hudson tunnels of the Pennsylvania Railroad, he was active, despite failing eyesight, in adapting the design to the serious obstacles encountered, sometimes against the opposition of his colleagues. He published his report to the railroad company in 1911, and his name heads the list of engineers on the memorial tablet in the entrance of the Pennsylvania station in New York. General Goethals held his advice in high esteem in connection with the digging of the Panama Canal, and only Raymond's failing health prevented his taking a much more important part therein. On Nov. 8, 1866, he married Clara Wise of Brooklyn, who died in 1901. His second wife was Alice D. Krause, widow of Capt. William Krause, United States Army, whom he married in 1904 and who survived him. Two of his sons became officers in the army.

[Samuel Raymond, *Geneals. of the Raymond Families of New England* (1886); G. W. Cullum, *Biog. Reg. Officers and Grads. U. S. Military Acad.* (1891), vol. III; R. W. Raymond and Alfred Noble, *Memoir of Charles Walker Raymond*, reprinted from *Proc. Am. Soc. Civil Engineers*, vol. XL (1914); William Couper, ed., *Hist. of the Engineering Construction and Equipment of the Pa. Railroad Company's N. Y. Terminal and Approaches* (1912); *Forty-fourth Ann. Reunion, Asso. Grads. U. S. Mil. Acad.* (1913); *Who's Who in America*, 1912–13; *Who's Who in New York City and State*, 1909; *N. Y. Times*, May 4, 1913.]   P. B. M.

RAYMOND, DANIEL (1786–1849?), lawyer, known today exclusively on account of his highly original economic writings, was born at or near New Haven, Conn., a descendant of a settler of the same name at Lyme, who died in 1696. Daniel was a law pupil of the celebrated Tapping Reeve [q.v.] at Litchfield, from whom he may have learned his Federalism. In 1814, having settled in Baltimore, he was admitted to the bar of that city. Sometime after 1840 he appears to have moved to Cincinnati. He was married, first, to Eliza Amos of Baltimore, who died about 1835, leaving a son and a daughter; second, in 1837, to Delia Matlock of Virginia, by whom he had five sons and a daughter.

Raymond's distinction rests upon his *Thoughts on Political Economy,* which appeared in 1820, and in other editions, characterized by unimportant amendments and omissions, in 1823, 1836, and 1840. Being briefless, he read critically, though not widely, in political economy, and deprecating the fact that no systematic treatise had been produced on this subject in America, he undertook to prepare one, working at first merely for self-amusement. The chief influence upon his thought, as earlier upon that of Hamilton and Mathew Carey, and later on that of John Rae and Georg Friedrich List [*qq.v.*], was the American economic environment. Raymond based his system upon principles fundamentally opposed to those of the English and French classical schools. He made a distinction at the outset between individual wealth, or the sum of individual riches, and national wealth. The latter was not an accumulation of commodities, but the development of economic capacities; he insisted that political economy, as the science of public prosperity, was concerned far less with property than with productive power. He declared that the problems of individual economy, as embraced chiefly in the division of labor, were not extensible to the universe of individuals, as Smith and his school contended, because the nation as an economic unit interposed itself. National prosperity required, in Raymond's view, a liberal measure of deliberate economic control, as opposed to the *laissez faire* policy which had been impressed upon Europe. He made a successful "effort to break loose from the fetters of foreign authority—from foreign theories and systems of political economy, which from the dissimilarity in the nature of the governments, renders them altogether unsuited to our country" (*Thoughts on Political Economy,* 1820, pt. 1, pp. v, vi). He came out so boldly for protection to American industry that Mathew Carey, then the chief protagonist of this view, offered the University of Maryland substantial financial support for a chair of political economy if Raymond were invited to occupy it, but the offer was not accepted. Raymond dissented sentimentally though not logically from the Malthusian principle of population. In his *Elements of Constitutional Law,* published in the volume containing the fourth edition of his *Political Economy,* 1840, and separately in a first stereotype edition in Cincinnati

in 1845, he showed his same intolerance of traditional authority, and also his perfect conviction that social principles are always relative to place and time. His detestation of slavery, first evident in his pamphlet on *The Missouri Question* (1819), rendered his work unacceptable to the South, and his opposition to a central bank, and indeed all banks of issue, was calculated to dilute the enthusiasm of the nationalist economic thinkers and propagandists for whose cause he did so much to supply a theoretical basis. His pamphlet on *The American System* appeared one year later (1828) than List's *Outlines of American Political Economy,* but there is room to believe that List drew upon Raymond's earlier work, and it is even more probable that Rae was influenced by Raymond. In his lively appreciation of the importance of excellent social administration, as compared with mere legislative fiat, Raymond anticipated later development. He was an early pleader for formal instruction in political economy in schools and colleges in the United States.

[C. P. Neill, *Daniel Raymond* (1897), in Johns Hopkins Univ. Studies in Hist. and Pol. Sci., 15 ser., no. 6; Ernest Teilhac, *Histoire de la pensée économique aux États-Unis au dix-neuvième siècle* (1928); Jas. Savage, *A Geneal. Hist. of the First Settlers of New England,* vol. III (1861); Samuel Raymond, *Geneals. of the Raymond Families of New England* (1886); *Federal Gazette and Baltimore Daily Advertiser,* Dec. 26, 1823; Mathew Carey, *Autobiog. Sketches* (1829); *North Am. Rev.,* Apr. 1821; *Blackwood's Edinburgh Mag.,* Feb. 1825. Raymond's authorship of *The American System* (37 pp., Baltimore, 1828) has been determined from his autograph letter, Jan. 26, 1829, Madison papers, vol. LXX, folio 9, in Lib. of Cong.; see also *Argument of D. Raymond, Esq., before the Court of Appeals of Md. at the Dec. Term, 1821,* in Misc. Pamphlets, Lib. of Cong., vol. DCXXXIV. Elaborate hostile reviews of Raymond's economic opinions appeared in a dozen numbers of the *Richmond Enquirer,* reprinted in William B. Giles's *Political Miscellanies* (1829).]
B. M.

RAYMOND, GEORGE LANSING (Sept. 3, 1839–July 11, 1929), educator, author, was born in Chicago, the son of Benjamin Wright Raymond [*q.v.*], a prosperous merchant, and Amelia (Porter) Raymond. On both sides, the family background was thoroughly New England. George, an only son, was sent East to school, attending Phillips Academy, Andover, Mass., and Williams College, from which he received the degree of A.B. in 1862. Inclined toward the ministry, he pursued the requisite studies at the Princeton Theological Seminary, graduating in 1865. He spent the next three years in Europe studying art, but returning to the United States, was ordained a Presbyterian minister in 1870. For four years he held a small pastorate at Darby, Pa., and in 1872 was married to Elizabeth Blake of Philadelphia, by whom he had two daughters, only one of whom survived him.

Although religion maintained an important place in Professor Raymond's thought throughout his long life, it gradually became an interest secondary to his passion for æsthetics and oratory. Quitting the pulpit, he returned to Williams as professor of English literature, æsthetics, rhetoric, and elocution. That he was successful as an instructor is attested by the fact that year after year his pupils won prizes in intercollegiate contests. In teaching oratory he always strove to estimate the true temperament of a pupil, and to shape his instruction accordingly. His *Orator's Manual* (1879) remains a standard textbook.

It was as a student of æsthetics, however, that Raymond did his most enduring work. In 1880, leaving Williams College, he accepted a chair of oratory and æsthetic criticism at Princeton; but since his health was not good, he gave up this dual responsibility in 1893, devoting his attention thereafter to æsthetics. He continued at Princeton until 1905, from which year until 1912 he was professor of æsthetics at George Washington University. As in the realm of religion his creed resolved itself into recognition simply of the fatherhood of God and the brotherhood of man, so in his study of æsthetics he concerned himself with fundamentals. He perceived the profound inter-relation of the arts, which he drew into an illuminating synthesis, accompanied at every step by comparison and by careful, specific analysis. His series of sound and penetrating studies, brought out in a uniform edition in 1909 under the general title "Comparative Aesthetics," now stands as his most valuable and enduring contribution to culture. This monumental series includes the following volumes: *Poetry as a Representative Art* (1886), *The Genesis of Art Form* (1893), *Art in Theory* (1894), *Painting, Sculpture, and Architecture as Representative Arts* (1895), *Rhythm and Harmony in Poetry and Music, Together With Music as a Representative Art* (1895), *Proportion and Harmony of Line and Color in Painting, Sculpture, and Architecture* (1899), *The Representative Significance of Form* (1900). A related volume is *The Essentials of Aesthetics: Being a Compendium of the System, Designed as a Text-book* (1906). Two other volumes, *A Poet's Cabinet* (1914) and *An Art Philosopher's Cabinet* (1915), composed of classified extracts from Raymond's writings, prepared by Dr. Marion Mills Miller, are convenient compilations giving in condensed form the substance of this æsthetic philosophy. Besides the books of criti-

cism he published a novel, *Modern Fishers of Men* (1879), several volumes of verse, and a few plays.

[M. M. Miller, preface to *An Art Philosopher's Cabinet*; *Who's Who in America*, 1928–29; *N. Y. Times*, July 12, 1929; information from Dr. M. M. Miller and from Raymond's daughter, Mrs. Tyler Dennett.]

E. A. J.

RAYMOND, HENRY JARVIS (Jan. 24, 1820–June 18, 1869), editor, politician, was born at Lima, N. Y., the son of Jarvis and Lavinia (Brockway) Raymond. His father, whose ancestors had migrated in the previous century from Connecticut, where the family had long been settled (Samuel Raymond, *Genealogies of the Raymond Families of New England*, 1886), was a farmer, comfortably off; the son was educated at the Genesee Wesleyan Seminary and at the University of Vermont, where he graduated with high honors in 1840. Like most of his honors, they cost more than they were worth; he contracted at college the habit of overwork that contributed to his early death. He had taught a country school and had some idea of teaching in the South, but his real interest was already journalism. He went to New York, supported himself by free-lance writing, and presently got a regular job from Horace Greeley [*q.v.*], to whose weekly, the *New Yorker*, he had contributed while still in college.

Raymond's first employer was to be his bitterest rival throughout most of his life. The temperamental difference between the two is illustrated by their later judgment of the *New Yorker*: Greeley despised it as weak and ineffective; Raymond admired its "fair examination of both sides"—an exception in the journalism of the time, which was passionately partisan and was to become more so as the slavery question sharpened animosities. In the spring of 1841 Greeley founded the *New York Tribune* and took Raymond with him as his chief assistant. Here Raymond was thoroughly indoctrinated in the new journalism which the elder James Gordon Bennett [*q.v.*] had invented and Greeley adapted to the taste of the "moral element"; he became brilliantly successful, and a close friendship which he formed with George Jones, 1811–1891 [*q.v.*], then in Greeley's business office, led the two to project a paper of their own.

They had no capital then, however; so Jones moved to Albany and Raymond went over in 1843 to James Watson Webb's *Morning Courier and New-York Enquirer*. His reputation grew, not only as a newspaperman but also as an orator and Whig politician; in 1849 he was elected to the state assembly and "leaped into prominence in the week he took his seat" (Alexander, *post*, 11, 159). He was reëlected the next year and became speaker in January 1851. His alignment with the Free-soil group in the party led by William H. Seward and Thurlow Weed led to a break with his employer, General Webb, in the spring of that year. He was already managing editor of *Harper's New Monthly Magazine*, which had appeared in the previous June, but though he held this position till 1856 he never had much time to give to it. In 1848 he and Jones had almost succeeded in buying the *Albany Evening Journal* from Weed; now they prepared to establish the *New York Daily Times* (so-called until 1857) with Raymond as editor and Jones in charge of the business office.

The first issue of the *Times* (Sept. 18, 1851) declared that "we do not mean to write as if we were in a passion,—unless that shall really be the case; and we shall make it a point to get into a passion as rarely as possible." This and similar statements were interpreted as a bid for the support of conservative Whigs, alienated from the *Tribune* by Greeley's political and social radicalism; but they also reflected Raymond's innate moderation of opinion and expression. In a period when the American press was given to intemperate personal controversy and usually to partisan distortion of the news, he longed for the time when men should be governed by cool reason and judgment instead of prejudice and passion. From this habit of mind sprang what his biographer Maverick calls "his unfortunate tendency to temporize, in all circumstances except those of pressing emergency" (Maverick, *post*, p. 170), which ultimately ruined him as a politician. But the same quality made his paper, as E. L. Godkin wrote in the *Nation* after his death (June 24, 1869, p. 490), "nearer the newspaper of the good time coming than any other in existence" in its impartiality of reporting and temperance of discussion.

The *Times* was immediately successful; it appealed not only to those who disliked violence and personalities, but also to the many who were repelled by the *Herald's* lack of "principle" and the *Tribune's* excess of it. Greeley fought the new competitor hard, calling Raymond a "little villain" when he got a state advertising contract that Greeley wanted; but within four years he confessed privately that the *Times* had more than twice the *Tribune's* city circulation. Raymond's moderation, however, debarred him from any such influence as Greeley wielded, especially among the farmers, in an age when prejudice and passion were steadily getting the better of cool reason and judgment.

At the Whig national convention of 1852

Raymond won renown by a spectacular defiance of the Southern oligarchy, but the party's failure in the campaign of that year disgusted him and he wrote to Seward that he meant "to navigate the *Times* into a position of independent thought and speech" (F. W. Seward, *post*, II, 196). But he could not bring himself to leave the organization; and two years later, when the Kansas-Nebraska Bill upset political alignments, he argued that the Free Soilers should bore from within the Whig machine instead of founding a new party. They did this successfully in New York, where Raymond played a considerable part in the Anti-Nebraska movement that imposed its views on the Whig convention. But the paramount state issue that year was prohibition; Greeley had made it and expected the nomination for governor but Weed, who controlled the convention, passed him over in favor of an up-state nonentity. Greeley then begged for second place on the ticket but Weed, arguing that an up-state dry should be balanced by a city wet, gave Raymond the nomination for lieutenant-governor.

The strategy was sound as far as it went, but Weed elected his state ticket at the price of mortal offense to the most powerful editor of the time. "No other name," said Greeley, "could have been ... so bitterly humbling to me" (Weed and Barnes, *Life of Thurlow Weed*, II, 280); and the consequence was the break with Seward and Weed which ultimately brought Greeley to the Republican National Convention of 1860 ready to support any presidential candidate who might beat Seward. Raymond's lieutenant-governorship was accordingly an important factor in making Abraham Lincoln president; but in itself it was of small value to him or the paper, and it meant the breaking of a promise which Jones had prudently exacted when the *Times* was founded, that he would no longer seek office. He never had Greeley's ludicrous and pathetic lust for any office, however small; but, less fortunate than Greeley, when he tried for office he usually got it, in the end with disastrous consequences.

The Whig party was breaking up; in February 1856 Raymond attended the Pittsburgh meeting that founded the national Republican party, and wrote its statement of principles. Thereafter the *Times* was steadily Republican (though never abolitionist till war had begun) and Raymond's activity in the new party was interrupted only in 1859, when he went to Italy to report the Franco-Austrian War. In 1860 he worked hard for Seward at the Chicago convention but gave energetic support to Lincoln in the campaign. When the cotton states began to secede he supported the compromise proposals of the winter; at the same time, in a series of open letters to W. L. Yancey of Alabama (published as *Disunion and Slavery,* 1860), he attacked secession and subjected the issues of the time to an analysis that is still cogent.

The war once begun, the *Times* was Lincoln's most steadfast supporter in New York. Raymond could have been a general, but knew he had no military talent; twice drafted, he offered substitutes, but was often at the front as a newspaperman. He was again speaker of the Assembly in 1862 and unsuccessfully tried for the United States senatorship in the following year. The year 1864 saw him one of the Republican leaders in the nation; he wrote most of the platform of the Republican convention at Baltimore and played the chief part in Andrew Johnson's nomination for vice-president, apparently as Lincoln's agent (A. K. McClure, *Abraham Lincoln and Men of War-Times,* 1892, pp. 425 ff.). His skilful management in the convention earned him the chairmanship of the national committee, but the prospect was not bright. On Aug. 22 he wrote to Lincoln that "the tide is setting strongly against us" on account of military reverses and a conviction that Lincoln would continue the war till slavery was abolished. Never in favor of abolition till July 1861, Raymond had always regarded it as subsidiary to the preservation of the Union; so he now proposed a peace offer "on the sole condition of acknowledging the supremacy of the Constitution,—all other questions to be settled in a convention of the people of all the states" (Nicolay and Hay, *post,* IX, 218–19). The purpose, unlike that of Greeley's contemporaneous peace efforts, was purely political; Raymond thought the offer would be rejected and Lincoln's position strengthened accordingly. But Lincoln saw that it would not do and talked him out of it. The victories of Sherman and Sheridan reëlected Lincoln; and Raymond was elected to the House of Representatives.

"He entered Congress with a prestige rarely if ever equalled by a new member" (Alexander, *post,* III, p. 137); and his career there was the one great failure of his life. He had been close to Lincoln and was closer still to Johnson; when Congress reconvened in December 1865, with its Radical leaders bitterly hostile to Johnson's reconstruction policy, Raymond became the administration leader in the House. But a man who could see both sides and preferred accommodation to violence had no more chance against Thaddeus Stevens than Kerensky against Lenin. Blaine's comments (*Twenty Years of Congress,*

1886, II, 139) suggest that Raymond was further handicapped by overconfidence, and by the jealousy of veteran members for so highly advertised a newcomer. At any rate, he completely missed the significance of Stevens' proposal of the joint committee on reconstruction and offered no objection, either in the caucus or in the House; thereby losing "the only real opportunity he ever had of administering a severe blow, if not a defeat," to Stevens (B. B. Kendrick, *The Journal of the Joint Committee of Fifteen on Reconstruction,* 1914, p. 141). Even the exclusion of the Southern members on Dec. 4 failed to rouse him, and the *Times* of the following day betrayed a complete lack of realization that Stevens was master of the reconstruction committee. Awakening too late, Raymond spoke in the House on Dec. 21, attacking Stevens' secessionist doctrine as ably as he had once attacked Yancey's, and as ineffectually. When the test came (Jan. 9) on the Voorhees resolution declaring secession an impossibility, only one other Republican (and that a personal friend) stood by Raymond. It may be that the stars in their courses had fought against him, but he had not given them much of a tussle. Thereafter he could not agree even with Johnson; he voted for the Freedman's Bureau Bill and had trouble explaining his support of the President's veto; he opposed the Civil Rights Bill, but voted for its substance in the Fourteenth Amendment. It was this course chiefly that made men call him a "trimmer"; and led Stevens to remark, when Raymond wanted a pair for some division in the House, that he would have no difficulty in pairing with himself.

Beaten in Congress, Johnson tried to organize against the Radicals a Union party of Conservative Republicans and War Democrats. Raymond, when he first heard of the projected National Union Convention, was afraid it would fall into the hands of "former Rebels and Copperheads"; but Weed, Seward, and the President talked him into attending it, and supporting it in the *Times.* As in 1854, he opposed the formation of a new party and called for support of all congressional candidates committed to the immediate admission of loyal Southerners. Unfortunately, most of the Republican nominations had already been captured by the Radicals, and many of the Democratic nominations by Copperheads.

At the Philadelphia convention (August 1866), which he reluctantly attended, the chairman of the Republican National Committee could not help being the most prominent figure; especially as he wrote the declaration of principles which the convention set before the country. It was a sound piece of constitutional reasoning, but prejudice and passion had got the upper hand. Raymond's program was too much for some, too little for others; it needed all his skill to keep harmony in the convention. "Let us set aside feeling and go to business," he begged a wrangling committee; but the country chose to set aside business and go to feeling. After Johnson's disastrous "swing around the circle" the Radical reaction set in, and Raymond was the first victim.

He was expelled (Sept. 3) from the national committee; and two weeks later, declining renomination for Congress, admitted his "evident and signal failure" in rallying the Unionists (Maverick, *post*, p. 189). The gleeful Greeley called him a Judas and a Copperhead, and profited by his unpopularity. Raymond had never used the *Times* as an organ of personal advancement, an abnegation almost unparalleled in his day; but it suffered with him, losing (though only temporarily) thousands of readers to the *Tribune*. He and Weed still hoped to form a Union bloc in the state; but at the Albany convention of Conservatives and Democrats in September the Tammany delegation outgeneraled them, nominating John T. Hoffman for governor. The Conservatives were left out on a limb; Weed clung to it, supporting Hoffman, but Raymond soon dropped off. The first intimation that he would bolt the Albany ticket provoked the Democratic press to violent attacks, which Greeley reprinted under the heading, "Shocking Cruelty to a Fugitive Slave" (*New-York Tribune*, Sept. 19, 1866). He bolted it none the less, and presently was complaining that the "President's party" had generally fallen into the hands of Copperheads. The country shared his view, and the fall election put an end to Raymond's dream of a moderate and Unionist Congress. A *Times* editorial from another hand, about that time, observed that, "Great changes in the fate of nations are never achieved by men of the *juste milieu* order" (Sept. 16, 1866, p. 4). The reference was to the rise of Bismarck, but the man who wrote it must have had his mind on the fall of Raymond.

Raymond recognized a *fait accompli* and did little more kicking against the pricks. The *Times* finally broke with Johnson on financial issues and the campaign of 1868 saw the paper back in the party, but with an independence of spirit that commended it to such young men of the new generation as Henry Adams and John Hay. Raymond began to devote himself to less partisan issues; he commenced the attacks on the "Tweed ring" which his partner Jones later finished so brilliantly, and by his advocacy of tariff reduction, sound money, and civil-service

reform set his paper in courses which it followed long after his death. Still young, and cured of his political ambitions, he seemed only on the threshold of greater achievement. His personal affairs, too, were going better; in 1869 he was reunited with his wife, Juliette Weaver of Winooski, Vt., whom he had married on Oct. 24, 1843, and who had been living in Europe for some years. But he had weakened himself by habitual overwork, and an emotional crisis brought on the cerebral hemorrhage that killed him. Of his seven children, two sons and two daughters survived him.

"Nobody has done more, we doubt if anybody has done as much, for the elevation of the profession," wrote Godkin after his death (*Nation*, June 24, 1869, p. 490). Raymond's contribution to journalism was the substitution of decency for personal invective and fairness for black-and-white partisanship. He had not Bennett's originality or Greeley's force, but he was a technical newspaperman of the first rank. He was one of the earliest and greatest of the great local reporters, with a prodigious speed and accuracy that became legendary; his eye-witness battle pictures of Solferino and Bull Run are models of clarity and vividness; his editorials were lucid and persuasive, but they usually lacked the smashing force that some of his contemporaries derived from conviction of their own utter rightness and the wickedness of those who held divergent views. He once said that when he wrote a sentence he could not help seeing before he got to the end how only partially true it was. This trait, and lack of a realistic appraisal of public opinion, were his fatal weaknesses as a politician. His misfortune was not only that he was a temperamental non-partisan in an age of bitter partisanship, but that he was a temperamental non-partisan incurably addicted to party politics.

The charm of his urbane, accomplished, and affable personality was felt by every one—except Gideon Welles, who calls Raymond a "whiffler" and "unscrupulous soldier of fortune," and the *Times* a "profligate and stipendiary sheet" (*Diary of Gideon Welles*, 1911, vol. II, 87, 104, 523). This abuse, echoed by no other memoirs of the period, may be a reflection of Raymond's demand in 1861 for Welles's removal on the ground of "indolence, indifference, and inadequacy." The obituaries in the New York papers reflect a deep feeling of personal loss among the men who had worked with him and against him. This is noteworthy in Greeley's editorial (*Tribune*, June 19, 1869). For all their political and professional rivalry, Greeley seems to have felt a real affection for Raymond; and no doubt this, as well as a natural impulse to speak well of the dead, informed his comment. But it is a singularly just and accurate appraisal of Raymond's character and political position, and a flat contradiction of almost everything Greeley had written about him for twenty-five years past.

Of Raymond's separately published writings only the letters to Yancey (*Disunion and Slavery*, 1860) show him at anything like his best. His *History of the Administration of President Lincoln* (1864) was a hastily compiled campaign document, expanded after Lincoln's death into *The Life and Public Services of Abraham Lincoln* (1865). He always intended to rewrite this into a thorough and solid study; but as commonly happens with newspapermen, he never got around to it. Other publications, in pamphlet form, include various legislative and patriotic speeches; and *Association Discussed; or, the Socialism of the Tribune Examined* (1847), originally a newspaper controversy with Greeley.

[For his early life and professional career, Augustus Maverick, *Henry J. Raymond and the N. Y. Press* (1870), which incorporates many valuable documents, is still the best authority. On his political activity, see D. S. Alexander, *A Pol. Hist. of the State of N. Y.*, vols. II (1906), III (1909); H. A. Weed and T. W. Barnes, *Life of Thurlow Weed* (2 vols., 1883–84); F. W. Seward, *William H. Seward* (3 vols., 1891); and "Extracts from the Journal of Henry J. Raymond," ed. by his son, Henry W. Raymond, in *Scribner's Monthly*, Nov. 1879, Jan., Mar., June 1880, which seem to be all of the journal that is extant. The last installment gives his version of the Philadelphia convention and its antecedents. The history of the peace suggestions of 1864 is in J. G. Nicolay and John Hay, *Abraham Lincoln: A History*, 1890, vol. IX, 218 ff. The official *Hist. of the N. Y. Times, 1851–1921* (1921), by Elmer Davis, contains a useful summary, and a digest of his editorial opinion on the principal issues of the period. Unpublished correspondence in the possession of the Raymond family contains some items of personal interest but little bearing on his public life. The newspaper obituaries, *N. Y. Times, N. Y. Tribune*, June 19, 1869, give one version of the circumstances of his death; another, related by Henry Ward Beecher and more generally credited, may be found in John Bigelow, *Retrospections of an Active Life*, IV (1913), pp. 289–90.]   E. D—s.

RAYMOND, JOHN HOWARD (Mar. 7, 1814–Aug. 14, 1878), college president, was born in New York City, the son of Eliakim and Mary (Carrington) Raymond and the descendant of Richard Raymond who emigrated from England to Salem, Mass., before 1634. He was a pupil in the classical school of Goold Brown [*q.v.*], and, though he left the school at the age of ten, he always spoke of Brown and his then well-known English grammar as the origin of his life-long enthusiasm for the study of language. At the age of fourteen he entered Columbia College, now Columbia University, New York City. Because of his immaturity and self-satisfaction at being

ranked at the head of the class, he became indolent and insubordinate and in his junior year was expelled from the college. Admitted to Union College, Schenectady, N. Y., he was graduated from there in the class of 1832. After his graduation he studied law, first in New York and then in New Haven. A sermon by Leonard Bacon [*q.v.*] containing one searching question, "Is religion a delusion or is it not?" changed the whole course of his life. Giving up his purpose of becoming a lawyer, he entered the Baptist theological seminary in Madison University, now Colgate University, at Hamilton, N. Y., where he graduated in 1838 and remained as professor until 1850. On May 12, 1840, he married Cornelia Morse who bore him nine children and survived him twenty-seven years. In 1850 with a group of professors and students known as the Removal party he left Madison University to organize a university in Rochester, N. Y. At that time Madison was a struggling college with no endowment, but those left behind, indignant at the seeming disloyalty of the others, immediately raised a large amount of money and from one small college came two well-endowed institutions, Colgate and Rochester universities. During the five years he was in Rochester, 1850–55, antislavery was the burning question of the day, and his natural interest in the cause was increased by his friendship with such men as Henry Ward Beecher, William Henry Channing, and Frederick Douglass. In the summer of 1863 he was Beecher's companion in his European lecture tour and made one speech. Beecher afterward described it as a tropical tornado which electrified his lukewarm English audience (letter in *Life and Letters, post*, p. 179).

In 1855 he became the first president of the Brooklyn Collegiate and Polytechnic Institute, assuming responsibility for the plan of organization and policy of government. Because of his tact and understanding, the Polytechnic was one of the first large schools to rely wholly on a boy's sense of honor, and corporal punishment was not used. In 1861 he was appointed a member of the first board of trustees of Vassar College. When Milo P. Jewett [*q.v.*] resigned from the presidency in 1864, a year before the opening of the college, Raymond was invited to become his successor. This offer he accepted, though with some hesitation, as he had just resigned from the presidency of the Polytechnic because of lack of health. During the short administration of Jewett buildings had been erected, but on Raymond fell the entire responsibility of internal organization, including the selection of a faculty and making of a curriculum. To him in large measure is due the success of what was then felt to be a very doubtful experiment in the higher education of women. He defended vigorously the cultural aims of college education and was insistent upon high standards. His curriculum was notable for its natural science and modern language as well as for the classics and mathematics. His work continued through the first thirteen years of Vassar, ending with his death at the college. He was a man of strong convictions without a trace of bigotry. Possessing a keen sense of humor, he never lost his dignity. Because of his broad scholarship and culture on the one hand and his genuine love of all that was human on the other, he easily gained the friendship of men and women in all classes of society.

[*Life and Letters of John Howard Raymond* (1881), ed. by H. R. Lloyd; *The Autobiog. and Letters of Matthew Vassar* (1916), ed. by E. H. Haight; J. M. Taylor and E. H. Haight, *Vassar* (1915); J. M. Taylor, *Before Vassar Opened* (1914); *The First Half Century of Madison Univ.* (1872); Samuel Raymond, *Geneal. of the Raymond Families of New England* (1886); date of death and other information from his daughter, Miss Cornelia M. Raymond, Poughkeepsie, N. Y.]

H. N. M.

RAYMOND, JOHN T. (Apr. 5, 1836–Apr. 10, 1887), actor, will be remembered chiefly in American theatrical annals for his acting of Colonel Mulberry Sellers in *The Gilded Age,* with his famous catch phrase of "there's millions in it." He was born in Buffalo, N. Y. His real name, John O'Brien, he abandoned early in life for the professional name by which he became universally known. It was not until 1881, however, that he made it his legal name by authorization of the courts. From June 27, 1853, the day of his first appearance on the professional stage in the small part of Lopez in John Tobin's old comedy, *The Honeymoon,* he lacked no opportunity to appear before the public, and it was not long after his début before he was receiving the reward of incessant laughter for acting that was as uniquely comic as was his own personality. He was one of the type of actors who rely upon facial and physical eccentricities to obtain their effects. Among his early engagements were appearances in stock companies in Philadelphia, Baltimore, and other cities, and tours in support of Julia Dean Hayne and Anna Cora Mowatt. In 1861 he became a member of Laura Keene's company at her theatre in New York and succeeded Joseph Jefferson in the rôle of Asa Trenchard in a revival of *Our American Cousin,* appearing also while there in a number of diverse characters, including Tony Lumpkin in *She Stoops to Conquer* and Crabtree in *The School for Scandal.* Jefferson, who subsequently acted with Raymond in Washington, describes him at this period as "a creator of American characters." Later in the same season he was taking part in operatic performances in a company of which Caroline Richings was the leading member. In 1867 he rejoined Sothern, with whom he had acted in New York, playing Asa Trenchard to that actor's Lord Dundreary in London. It was not until after a season in California that in 1873 he first acted and became permanently identified with the character of Colonel Sellers, which he acted no less than one thousand times. When he took that play to London in 1880, it disappointed his expectations by receiving little applause from English theatre-goers. Other rôles followed in which he struck a similar note of comedy, *Wolfert's Roost, Fresh, the American, For Congress, In Paradise, Risks,* and *The Woman Hater.* He rarely appeared, after he had become a star and could select his own plays, in anything but comedies of American authorship and atmosphere, the most notable exception being his acting of Mr. Posket in Pinero's farce, *The Magistrate.* His comedy methods were limited in range, but his long face, his nimble manner, his imperturbability and his artificial seriousness, held him in high favor with multitudes to whom he seemed to be a genius of comedy acting. For a long time he was in poor health, but he remained on the stage to the end, dying suddenly in a hotel at Evansville, Ind., during one of his mid-western tours. His popularity both with members of his profession and with the public was attested by the fact that his funeral services at the Church of the Transfiguration ("the little Church Around the Corner") were attended by an immense crowd of mourners. His first wife was Marie E. Gordon, an actress whom he married in 1868, and from whom he was divorced. His second wife, to whom he was married Apr. 11, 1881, was Rose Courtney Barnes, daughter of Rose Eytinge [*q.v.*] and of David Barnes.

[T. Allston Brown, *Hist. of the Am. Stage* (1870); *The Autobiog. of Jos. Jefferson* (1890); G. C. D. Odell, *Annals of the N. Y. Stage,* vol. VII (1931); Franklin Fyles, in *Famous Am. Actors of Today* (1896), ed. by F. E. McKay and C. E. L. Wingate; Wm. Winter, *Brief Chronicles,* pt. 3 (1890); obituary notices in *N. Y. Herald, N. Y. Times,* and *Boston Transcript,* Apr. 11, 1887.]

E. F. E.

RAYMOND, MINER (Aug. 29, 1811–Nov. 25, 1897), theologian, educator, was born in New York City, the son of Nobles and Hannah (Wood) Raymond and the eldest of nine children. He was descended from Huguenot ancestors who had been driven from France, some of them settling in England, and subsequently emigrating to New England. Soon after Miner's birth the family moved to Rensselaerville,

N. Y., where the boy acquired his early education, exhausting the local schooling facilities by the time he was twelve. He yearned for more schooling but for this the family was too poor, so the father—to quote the sufferer's own words, "set me on a shoe-bench drawing the cords of affliction on the stool of repentance for six years and I wanting to go to school all the time" (Terry, *post*, p. 17). At the age of seventeen he joined the Methodist Church and soon afterward entered Wesleyan Academy, Wilbraham, Mass., to study for the ministry. He had to earn his own way, but made a splendid scholastic record and was graduated in 1831. He was later given a place on the faculty, first as a teacher of English, then of mathematics. In 1838, while still teaching, he entered the New England Conference of the Methodist Episcopal Church. Two years later he relinquished his teaching position and for the next eight years served churches in Worcester, Westfield, and Boston, Mass. In 1848 he was elected principal of Wesleyan Academy and served in this capacity for sixteen years, a period which has been characterized as "probably the most brilliant" of his career (*Ibid.*). In 1864 he was called to the chair of systematic theology in the Garrett Biblical Institute at Evanston, Ill. He continued to be active in this position until 1895 when ill health compelled him to resign. On Aug. 20, 1837, he married Elizabeth Henderson of Worcester, Mass. Four of their five children survived the father. Mrs. Raymond having died in 1877, he married, on July 28, 1879, Mrs. Isabella (Hill) Binney, who also survived him.

Though his formal schooling was limited, Raymond was truly an educated man; Wesleyan University, Middletown, Conn., recognized his scholarly interests and achievements when it honored him with the degree of Master of Arts in 1840 and with the degree of Doctor of Divinity in 1854; thirty years later Northwestern University, Evanston, Ill., conferred on him the degree of Doctor of Laws. He occupied a prominent place in the councils of the church, and was frequently called upon to represent the church on special occasions. During the years preceding the Civil War he was an untiring leader in the anti-slavery movement. It was as a theologian, however, that he was most widely known and exerted his greatest influence. As teacher in a theological school he profoundly impressed a whole generation of ministers and missionaries in all parts of the world. The three volumes of his *Systematic Theology*, published in 1877, attracted wide attention, and for many years was accepted as the standard exposition

of Arminian theology, being translated even into Japanese. The third volume of the work, dealing with ethics and ecclesiology, is of less significance than the first two.

One of his biographers enumerates seven qualities which in his judgment explain in large part Raymond's power and achievements: a well-balanced mind, a philosophical habit of mind, superior clearness of apprehension, clearness and force of expression, practical sagacity, an imperious will, and a constitutional optimism. In every position in which he served ". . . the combination of these superior qualities made him a great power among men, and largely explain the successes of his long and varied life" (Terry, *post*).

[M. S. Terry, "Address . . . at the Funeral of the Distinguished Theologian," *Northwestern Christian Advocate*, Dec. 8, 1897, also pub. in pamphlet form; *Ibid.*, Dec. 1, 1897; C. J. Little, memoir in *Minutes of the Fifty-ninth Sess. of the Rock River Conf., of the Meth. Episc. Ch.*, 1898 (1898); Minute adopted by the faculty of Garrett Biblical Institute; *Daily Inter Ocean* (Chicago, Ill.), Nov. 27, 1897.]　　　　F. C. E.

RAYMOND, ROSSITER WORTHINGTON (Apr. 27, 1840–Dec. 31, 1918), mining engineer, editor, exerted a unique influence among American engineers during the formative period of his profession. He was born in Cincinnati of English stock, the eldest of seven children. Charles Walker Raymond [*q.v.*] was his brother. His father, Robert Raikes Raymond, was successively newspaper editor, professor of English at the Brooklyn Polytechnic Institute, and principal of the Boston School of oratory. He had studied law, and had spent some time preparing for the Baptist ministry; he was a man of great charm and talent. Raymond's mother, Mary Anna (Pratt) Raymond, came from Providence, was highly educated, and possessed qualities of quiet steadfastness. The son spent an imaginative boyhood in the cultivated atmosphere of their home in the several cities to which they moved. In 1858 he was graduated at the head of his class from the Brooklyn Polytechnic Institute, in which his father was teaching and of which his uncle, John H. Raymond [*q.v.*], was president. In Brooklyn he joined Plymouth Church (Congregational), of which Henry Ward Beecher was pastor. The three years following his graduation were spent in Germany, as a student at the universities of Heidelberg and Munich and at the Royal Mining Academy of Freiberg, Saxony.

Returning home in 1861, he served as aide-de-camp on the staff of Maj.-Gen. John C. Frémont, attaining the rank of captain. On Mar. 3, 1863, he married Sarah Mellen Dwight of Brooklyn; the following year he resigned from the army and was taken into partnership by Dr. Justus Adelberg, a consulting mining engineer of New York. In 1867 he became editor of the *American Journal of Mining,* the name of which was later changed to *Engineering & Mining Journal.* He was joint editor with Richard P. Rothwell [*q.v.*] from 1874 until 1890, when they had a friendly disagreement over the coinage of silver, Raymond being for a gold standard; he then became a special contributor. Some of the early articles which he wrote for the *American Journal of Mining* on the relation of government to mining attracted attention in Washington, and in 1868 he was appointed United States commissioner of mining statistics, a position which he held until 1876. The work required long trips in the Far West and voluminous annual reports, which his ability at writing made models of clarity and technical excellence (*Statistics of Mines and Mining in the States and Territories West of the Rocky Mountains,* eight reports, 1869–77). Along with these two engagements, he served as lecturer on mining geology at Lafayette College from 1870 until 1882, and from 1875 to 1895 he was consulting engineer for Cooper, Hewitt & Company, operators of iron works and of iron and coal mines. This connection brought him into contact with labor problems which produced in him an antagonism against the tyranny of labor unions and brought him an occasional threatening letter when he wrote editorially about such savage strikes as that of Homestead, Pa. While attached to Cooper, Hewitt & Company, he assisted Abram S. Hewitt [*q.v.*] in the management of Cooper Union, where he often lectured. He served from 1885 to 1889 as one of the three state commissioners of electric subways for Brooklyn; his report on municipal engineering problems attracted deserved attention. Later he was consulting engineer for the New York & New Jersey Telephone Company. In his late fifties he studied law and in 1898 was admitted to the bar for the practice of mining and patent law. His writings on mining law were lucidly phrased, and his expert testimony at suits over mining rights helped to clarify a tangled subject; he lectured on mining law at Columbia University and elsewhere.

The rôle in which he achieved his greatest eminence and rendered his chief service was that of secretary of the American Institute of Mining Engineers. He held this post from 1884 to 1911; he had been one of the founders of the Institute in 1871, and had been president from

1872 to 1875. During his long service as secretary he elevated ideals for technical and professional societies in America. His influence as editor of the Institute's publications was marked throughout the engineering profession, and he helped many struggling young men to express their ideas. In temperament he combined enthusiasm with dignity; possibly his only fault was dislike of opposition and criticism. which he usually overwhelmed with arguments. He introduced European writings on geology to American readers; translated several of them, and conducted discussion and continuation studies which his encyclopedic grasp and editorial skill made of particular value.

Among his writings were a notable address on Alexander L. Holley, published in *Memorial of Alexander Lyman Holley* (1884); *Peter Cooper* (1901); almost innumerable obituary appreciations of his associates, compilations of technical terms and statistics, imaginative sketches, children's stories, poems, and a novel. For fifty consecutive years he composed Christmas stories for Plymouth Sunday school. He taught a Bible class for years and for nearly a generation served as superintendent. At Beecher's death in 1887 he was asked to accept the pastorate of Plymouth Church—a remarkable compliment to a mining engineer—but declined the offer (Hillis, *post*). In 1910, at a dinner in honor of his seventieth birthday, attended by many members of his profession, he was presented with a handsome silver service and awarded the gold medal of the Institution of Mining and Metallurgy of London. When he was in Japan a year later, he was given by the Mikado the Order of the Rising Sun, fourth class; previously he had received several honorary doctor's degrees. He died suddenly, of heart disease, at his home in Brooklyn. His wife, and, of his five children, one daughter survived him; a son, Alfred, an architect and engineer of great promise, had died in 1901 at the age of thirty-six.

[*Rossiter Worthington Raymond, a Memorial* (1920), ed. by T. A. Rickard and pub. by the Am. Inst. of Mining Engineers; *Dinner Given to Rossiter Worthington Raymond by His Friends, in Commemoration of His Seventieth Birthday* (1910); *Who's Who in America,* 1918–19; Samuel Raymond, *Geneals. of the Raymond Families of New England* (1886); N. D. Hillis, "In Memory of Rossiter W. Raymond," sermon reported in *Brooklyn Daily Eagle,* Jan. 6, 1919; *Engineering and Mining Jour.,* Jan. 18, 1919; *Mining and Scientific Press,* Jan. 11, 1919; *Iron Age,* Jan. 9, 1919; *Brooklyn Daily Eagle, N. Y. Times,* Jan. 2, 1919.]   P. B. M.

RAYNER, ISIDOR (Apr. 11, 1850–Nov. 25, 1912), lawyer, senator, was born in Baltimore, Md. His father, William Solomon Rayner, was a Bavarian Jew and a school teacher with liberal ideas who had left his home in Oberelsbach and emigrated to the United States about 1840. He changed his name from Roehner to Rayner and established himself at Fell's Point, Baltimore, as a dry-goods dealer. He was soon able to send to Bavaria for his boyhood sweetheart and first cousin, Amalie Jacobson, and they were married in Baltimore. Their children were reared in an environment in which traditional culture was reinforced by a rapidly acquired fortune. Isidor was first sent to Frederick Knapp's private school in Baltimore, later to the University of Maryland, and in 1865 to the University of Virginia. After three years of academic work and one of law, he returned to Baltimore where he continued his law studies in the office of Brown & Brune. The following year, 1871, he passed the bar examination and on Dec. 5 was married to Frances Jane Bevan, the daughter of William Francis Bevan of Baltimore.

During the seven years preceding his first public office as delegate to the Maryland Assembly in 1878, Rayner built up a large trial practice which he maintained, in spite of the heavy demands of political office, until he went to the United States Senate in 1905. In 1885 he was elected to the state Senate, but he resigned to become the Democratic candidate for Congress where he served three terms (1887–89; 1891–95). In Congress he was an active advocate of the repeal of the Sherman silver-purchase bill. When in 1895, without explanation, he withdrew his name as candidate for governor of Maryland, he was criticized for lack of political courage—a stigma he never lived down. He practised law for the next few years, then in 1899 he was elected attorney-general of Maryland. During this incumbency he offered his services without fee to Admiral Schley who had requested an inquiry of his conduct at the naval battle off Santiago during the Spanish-American War. Rayner's dramatic handling of the Schley defense before the Naval Court of Inquiry made him a national figure and prepared the way for his election to the United States Senate in 1905.

His seven years in the Senate were his most active. He arrayed himself as a defender of the Constitution against Roosevelt, whom he accused of arrogating the right to make treaties under the guise of executive agreements without the consent of the Senate, of centralizing power in the federal government in derogation of state rights, and of interfering with the functioning of the judiciary at the expense of constitutional government. He fought Senators Aldrich and Allison; he fought imperialism, and he fought tariff for protection instead of revenue. He was informed on domestic and international issues

and although a member of the minority party, exerted an influence on the foreign policy of the government. He was twice asked to run for vice-president but he preferred the floor to the chair. Rayner by temperament was nervous and excitable. He was brilliant but not profound, and as a writer he had none of the effectiveness which distinguished him as a speaker. After a month's illness, he died in Washington and was buried in Rock Creek Cemetery.

[J. F. Essary, *Md. in Nat. Politics* (1915); *Addresses of Hon. Isidor Rayner* (1914); *Essays of Isidor Rayner* (1914); *Isidor Rayner: Memorial Addresses Delivered in the Senate and House of Representatives* (1914); *Argument of Hon. Isidor Rayner Before the Court of Inquiry on behalf of Admiral Winfield Scott Schley* (1901); the *Sun* (Baltimore), Nov. 26, 28, 1912; information as to certain facts from Rayner's widow and from Mr. George A. Foos.]   H. Ca—s.

RAYNER, KENNETH (*c.* 1810–Mar. 5, 1884), member of Congress, was born in Bertie County, N. C. He was the son of Amos Rayner, a Baptist minister and Revolutionary soldier. His mother, whose maiden name was Williams, was wealthy, and the boy grew up in comfort unusual in the home of a rural minister. He was educated at Tarboro Academy and then read law under Chief Justice Thomas Ruffin, with whom he formed a devoted friendship. He never practised, but became a planter in Hertford County and soon entered public life. He was the youngest member of the constitutional convention of 1835 and won instant reputation by his ability. He opposed the disfranchisement of free negroes and favored complete religious toleration, but in other respects he was conservative and voted against all the amendments adopted by the convention. In 1836 and 1838 he was elected to the House of Commons and in 1846 he returned for three more terms. He was state senator in 1854 and a member of Congress from 1839 to 1845.

Rayner entered politics as a supporter of Jackson but he idolized Calhoun, favored the Bank, was a strong state-rights man, and, according to the somewhat doubtful evidence of John Quincy Adams (*Memoirs of John Quincy Adams*, X, 1876, p. 168), who did not like him, a nullifier. So by the time he entered Congress he was an intense Whig and speedily won a place of influence. He was an opponent of the policies of Van Buren, but he also consistently opposed the policy of protection. He joined in the Whig quarrel with Tyler, who he thought should be impeached, and opposed the annexation of Texas as likely to cause war. He spoke but seldom, declaring "silence a great virtue," but when he did speak, he was eloquent and effective though inclined to be fiery. He had rather a stormy congressional career, engaging

416

in a number of quarrels, and coming to blows on the floor of the House with one of his colleagues from North Carolina. One of his quarrels was with Adams, whom he accused of "playing the mountebank and harlequin before the Grand Inquest of the Nation."

In 1848 Rayner came near receiving the nomination for vice-president instead of Fillmore. In 1852 he repudiated the nomination of Scott and a little later was an enthusiastic Know-Nothing and a member of the Grand Council of the American party. In 1855 he wrote and secured the adoption of the third, or Union, degree, the obligation of which was to protect, maintain, and defend the Union under all circumstances. On June 17, 1856, the bolting wing of the party nominated him for vice-president, but he declined in a scathing letter. He broke with the North Carolina Whigs in 1860 on their advocacy of *ad valorem* taxation of slaves, and he began to waver in his Unionism so rapidly that Lincoln's call for troops found him whole-heartedly in favor of secession for which, as a member of the convention of 1861, he voted with enthusiasm. He did not like Davis, and, refusing to vote for him in 1861, became increasingly bitter toward the administration. In 1863, lacking the courage to come out in the open, he secretly joined the peace movement led by William J. Holden (Amnesty Papers, War Department). In 1865 he advocated Johnson's policy and in 1866 wrote anonymously *Life and Times of Andrew Johnson*. In 1869 he moved to Tennessee and for a time ran a sawmill on a tract of forest land belonging to his wife, who was Susan Spratt Polk, daughter of Col. William Polk of North Carolina and Tennessee. Rayner owned cotton plantations in Arkansas and Mississippi and he soon moved to Mississippi to operate them, which he did with little success. In spite of his opposition to Reconstruction he had voted for Grant in 1868 and in 1873 he was nominated for the supreme court of Mississippi by the Alcorn wing of the Republican party. In 1874 Grant appointed him a judge of the *Alabama* claims commission and he served for three years, resigning in 1877 to become solicitor of the treasury, a post which he held until his death. Rayner was a warm-hearted, affectionate man of fiery and impulsive nature, whose character had a considerable element of instability. His natural abilities were great, but they were too often obscured by indolence.

[Sources include: J. H. Wheeler, *Reminiscences and Memoirs of N. C.* (1884); *Proc. and Debates of the Convention of N. C. . . . 1835* (1836); *Jour. of the Convention of the People of N. C. . . . 1861* (1862); *The Papers of Thos. Ruffin* (4 vols., 1918–20), ed. by J. G.

deR. Hamilton; *Biog. Dir. Am. Cong.* (1928); the *Washington Post* and *Nat. Republican* (Washington), Mar. 6, 1884; *Raleigh Register*, Mar. 12, 1884. The date of Rayner's birth is given in the *Biog. Dir. Am. Cong.* as June 20, 1808. It is given in the *Nat. Republican, supra*, as May 2, 1810.]   J. G. deR. H.

REA, SAMUEL (Sept. 21, 1855–Mar. 24, 1929), civil engineer, railroad president, was born in Hollidaysburg, Pa., the son of James D. and Ruth (Moore) Rea. Because of the death of his father in 1868 he left school and began work as a clerk in a general store. In 1871 he entered upon his railroad career as chainman or rodman on the Morrison's Cove Branch of the Pennsylvania Railroad, then under construction, but the panic of 1873 put a stop to this work, and he entered the office of the Hollidaysburg Iron & Steel Company. In the spring of 1875 he returned to the service of the Pennsylvania in the engineering corps stationed at Connellsville, Pa. As assistant engineer, he had a share in the construction of a suspension bridge over the Monongahela River at Pittsburgh, completed in 1877, and was then assigned to the location of the Pittsburgh & Lake Erie Railroad. Upon its completion, he became cashier in the freight office at Pittsburgh. In 1879 he was appointed assistant engineer in charge of the construction of the extension of the Pittsburgh, Virginia & Charleston Railroad, south of Monongahela, Pa. (part of the Pennsylvania System). He directed surveys in the rebuilding of the Western Pennsylvania for use as a low-grade freight line, 1879–83. After a period of executive experience in Philadelphia, as assistant to Vice-President J. N. DuBarry, 1883–88, and assistant to the second vice-president, 1888–89, he resigned from the Pennsylvania to accept the offices of vice-president of the Maryland Central Railway Company and chief engineer of the Baltimore & Ohio Railroad Company.

In 1892, after a year of inactivity because of ill health, he once more returned to the Pennsylvania, becoming assistant to the president. Sent to England to study the London underground railways he published his observations in a book entitled *The Railways Terminating in London, with a Description of the Terminal Stations, and the Underground Railways* (1888). He also investigated an underground railway in Paris. In 1892 he was placed in charge of all general construction work then in progress on the Pennsylvania System, the acquisition of right of way and the real estate in that connection, the promotion of all new lines or branches, and the financial and corporate work incident thereto. Becoming first assistant to the president Feb. 10, 1897, he was elected fourth vice-president of the company in 1899. From this post he advanced through all the grades until on Mar. 3, 1911, he was elected first vice-president, being designated the next year as vice-president in charge of all the companies of the Pennsylvania System east of Pittsburgh and of the promotion and construction of new lines.

In this capacity he had charge of the construction of the tunnels under the Hudson and East rivers at New York, and of the building of the Pennsylvania Station in that city, and directly supervised the building of the New York Connecting Railroad and the Hell Gate bridge, which contained the longest metal arch span in the world. In recognition of these achievements and their value to the public, the University of Pennsylvania conferred on him the degree of doctor of science.

On Nov. 13, 1912, he was elected president of the Pennsylvania Railroad Company, effective Jan. 1, 1913. He was elected a director of the company on this same date and later became a director and president of the other principal railroad corporations constituting the Pennsylvania Railroad System. An authority on problems of accounting and corporate organization, possessed of clear vision and sound judgment on financial matters, he was recognized as among the ablest men in the railroad industry. In 1899 he was offered and declined the presidency of the Southern Pacific Railroad, and in 1903 that of the New Haven System. Soon after the United States entered the World War he became a member of the committee of the American Railway Association which supervised the operation of the railroads until they were taken over by the government. He also served as general chairman of the Railway Presidents' Conference Committee on Federal Valuation. On Oct. 1, 1925, having attained the age of seventy years, he retired from the presidency of the Pennsylvania Railroad Company under its pension regulations. He had a number of civic interests: he was chairman of the regional planning federation of Philadelphia Tri-State District; he was a trustee, and took the lead in raising a large building fund for Bryn Mawr Hospital; he was president of the board of trustees of the Bryn Mawr Presbyterian Church. His professional standing was recognized by honorary membership in the American Society of Civil Engineers and the Institution of Civil Engineers (London). In 1926 he received the Franklin medal of the Franklin Institute for his outstanding engineering accomplishments. For a time he was a member of the New York Stock Exchange and a partner in the firm of Rea Brothers & Company,

bankers and brokers of Pittsburgh, Pa. He was married on Sept. 11, 1879, to Mary M. Black of Pittsburgh and they had two children: a son who predeceased the father and a daughter who survived. He died in Gladwyne, a suburb of Philadelphia.

[W. W. Atterbury, in *Proc. Am. Soc. Civil Engineers*, vol. LV (1929); *Who's Who in America*, 1928–29; W. B. Wilson, *Hist. of the Pa. Railroad Company* (1899), vol. II; H. W. Schotter, *The Growth and Development of the Pa. Railroad Company* (1927); *Railway Age*, Sept. 26, 1925, Mar. 30, 1929; *Public Ledger* (Phila.), *N. Y. Times*, Mar. 25, 1929; *Biog. Sketch of Samuel Rea, Mar. 24, 1929,* and *Minute Adopted by the Board of Directors of the Pa. Railroad Company upon the Death of Samuel Rea* (both pub. by Pa. Railroad Company, 1929).]   J. H. F.

REACH, ALFRED JAMES (May 25, 1840–Jan. 14, 1928), early professional baseball player and popular idol of his day, later a well-known manufacturer of sporting goods, was born in London, England, the son of Benjamin and Elizabeth (Dyball) Reach. In his infancy his parents emigrated to the United States and settled in Brooklyn, N. Y. On the sand lots of this city he gained his first reputation as a ball player. The ability which he displayed won him a position on the Eckford team, organized in 1855, which had its grounds at Greenpoint, an outlying community of Brooklyn. In 1865 Col. Thomas Fitzgerald, owner of the old Philadelphia Athletics, induced him to join that nine at a salary of twenty-five dollars a week "for expenses." Baseball was still, nominally at least, an amateur sport, and Reach was the first player in Philadelphia to receive a stated sum for his services. With this organization he remained more than ten years. It traveled about the country and became a member of the National Association of Base Ball Players when that body was formed in 1871, and of the National League which succeeded it in 1876. In the meantime Reach became one of the greatest players of that period. He was a good second baseman, a hard left-hand hitter, and a clever base runner. When in 1876 the *New York Clipper* picked the first All-American team he was given a place on it; and of the second basemen between the years 1870 and 1880 his name is coupled with that of Ross Barnes as the most notable (Richter, *post,* p. 297). After he stopped playing he continued his interest in the game and was one of the original backers of the present Philadelphia National League Club. For many years, beginning in 1883, he published the *Reach Official . . . Base Ball Guide.*

He was not the type of athlete that squanders his earnings and dies young. On the contrary, he became a millionaire and lived to be eighty-seven. His parents were in humble circumstances and his first money was earned as a newsboy. When he became a professional ball player, he was an iron moulder. After going to Philadelphia he opened a cigar store, which became a gathering place for sporting men. Later, he started a sporting-goods store, in which venture Benjamin F. Shibe, also noted as a baseball promoter, soon joined him. It developed into one of the leading establishments of its kind in the country, under the name of A. J. Reach Company. One of its specialties was the manufacture of baseballs, which were wound on a machine said to have been invented by Reach. He was married, Dec. 25, 1866, to Louise Betts of Brooklyn, who with four children survived him. His death occurred in Atlantic City, N. J.

[A. G. Spalding, *America's National Game* (1911); E. A. Roff, *Base Ball and Base Ball Players* (1912); F. C. Richter, *Richter's Hist. and Records of Base Ball* (1914); *Public Ledger* (Phila.), *N. Y. Times*, Jan. 15, 1928; information from the A. J. Reach Company.]

H. E. S.

READ, CHARLES (*c.* 1713–Dec. 27, 1774), lawyer, landowner, and ironmaster, who attained prominence as a jurist and statesman in colonial New Jersey, was born in Philadelphia, the grandson of Charles Read, Philadelphia merchant, who came from England and settled at Burlington, N. J., in 1678, and the son of Charles Read, also a merchant, who served as mayor of Philadelphia, 1726–27. His mother was Anne Bond. About 1736, after a liberal education under private tutors, he was sent to London, and subsequently was appointed midshipman in the British navy. On one of his cruises to the West Indies he fell in love with Alice Thibou, daughter of a wealthy Creole planter on the isle of Antigua. Resigning from the navy, he married her and returned to America. About 1739 he became clerk of the city of Burlington and shortly after was made collector of the port of Burlington. Thus he began an active public career that embraced the following offices: surrogate; clerk of the circuits (appointed 1739); secretary of the province (appointed 1744); member of the assembly for Burlington City (1751–60, speaker 1751–54); member of the Council (1758–74); Indian commissioner (1755, 1758); associate justice of the supreme court of New Jersey (appointed 1749). For a brief period in 1764 he held the office of chief justice on appointment by Governor Franklin, having been strongly indorsed by Lord Stirling.

In addition to affairs of state, he was engaged in many enterprises. His law practice was one of the best in the province. A land speculator on a large scale, he was party to more than one hundred recorded land transfers, involving many thousands of acres in western New Jersey. He was interested in agriculture, and carried on experiments to improve farm practices. About 1765 he took up the manufacture of iron from bog ore, setting in motion an important industry. In the next few years he established iron furnaces at Taunton, Etna, Atsion and Batsto, in Burlington County, which were a source of munitions during the Revolutionary War. There is record also that he had a fishery on the Delaware River below Trenton. As Indian Commissioner he advocated a liberal policy in dealing with the natives, and was instrumental in having a reservation set aside for them in southern Burlington County. During the French and Indian War he served as colonel of the Burlington County militia. Ill in body and worried by financial troubles, he removed in 1773 to the isle of St. Croix. The following year, according to report, he kept a small shop at Martinburg, on the Tar River, North Carolina, where he died. He left two sons, Jacob and Charles. The latter, who in some published sketches has been confused with his father, served at the beginning of the Revolutionary War as colonel in the Burlington County militia, but subsequently turned Loyalist.

Though not a member of any religious body, Read favored the Quaker faith. His qualities of character are described in the diary of Aaron Leaming, who pictured a dynamic personality, pursuing an extraordinary career that rose to the heights of power and success but came to a tragic end. His whims "to the borders of insanity" were matched by unremitting industry and forceful leadership, and his pursuit of private interests paralleled a zeal for the public welfare. "From 1747 to about 1771," wrote Leaming, "he had the almost absolute rule of Governor, Council and Assembly in New Jersey, except during the short ministration of Mr. Boone, who was Governor without a Prime Minister." Read's rural interests resulted in a unique contribution to the history of American agriculture. An extensive manuscript which contains notes on his observations in the various phases of farming came to light in 1928 and is now in the Rutgers University library. It ranks among the most fruitful of the known sources of information on agriculture in the American Colonies, and has been edited by C. R. Woodward for publication under the title "Charles Read's Notes on Colonial Agriculture."

[C. S. Boyer, *Early Forges and Furnaces in N. J.* (1931); William Nelson, *Members of the N. J. Assembly, 1754. Biog. Sketches* (1895); *Manual of the Legislature of N. J.*, 1927; letters and papers in Harvard

Univ. Lib., N. J. State Lib., Rutgers Univ. Lib., and the libraries of the Pa. Hist. Soc. and the Am. Antiquarian Soc.; *Archives of the State of N. J.*, especially 1 ser., vols. VII–X (1883–1886), XXIV–XXIX (1902–1907); *Pa. Mag. of Hist. and Biog.*, July 1893, pp. 190–94; diary of Aaron Leaming, in lib. of Pa. Hist. Soc., Phila.]   **C. R. W.**

READ, CHARLES WILLIAM (May 12, 1840–Jan. 25, 1890), Confederate naval officer, was born in Yazoo County, Miss. Nothing is known of his parents or his childhood. He entered the United States Naval Academy in September 1856, and was graduated in June 1860. He served as midshipman aboard the *Pawnee* and the *Powhatan*. When he received news of the secession of Mississippi he forwarded his resignation from Vera Cruz, Mexico, and returned to the United States in March 1861. He reported to the Confederate secretary of the navy, who appointed him an acting midshipman on Apr. 13. He was assigned to duty as sailing master on the cruiser *McRae*, which was shortly converted into a river gunboat with Read as executive officer. In February 1862 he was promoted to be lieutenant-for-the-war. He participated in the Ship Island expedition in July, in the successful night attack on the blockading squadron at the Head of the Passes in October, in the unsuccessful defense of Island No. 10, Tenn.; and New Madrid, Mo., and in the unfortunate operations below New Orleans in March and April of the following year. Shortly after the attack began on Apr. 24, the captain was mortally wounded, and the command devolved on Read, who fought the *McRae* with gallantry. After the débâcle at New Orleans he was ordered to the squadron stationed below Fort Pillow, Tenn., being assigned first to a shore battery, then to the C.S.S. *Arkansas*. He commanded the stern gun division of this ram in her five brilliant engagements during July and August. He was next assigned to a shore battery at Port Hudson, La., and was promoted in October to the rank of second lieutenant in the Regular Navy.

On account of his reputation for "gunnery, coolness and determination," he was assigned to the cruiser *Florida,* then in Mobile harbor (E. M. Maffitt, *post*, p. 259). He remained with her from November 1862 until early the following May when Capt. John Newland Maffitt [*q.v.*] placed him in command of the prize brig *Clarence* (off Brazil), and ordered him to raid the coast of the United States. His crew consisted of one officer and twenty men, and his armament of one boat howitzer, which he supplemented by an imposing battery of dummy guns made from spars. He took twenty-one prizes in as many days between the latitude of Charleston, S. C., and Portland, Me. Thirteen of them were burned, six bonded, and two recaptured. He transferred his flag, successively, to his fourth prize, the *Tacony*, and his twentieth, the schooner *Archer*. In the last he sailed boldly into Portland harbor and captured the revenue cutter, *Caleb Cushing,* which was retaken a few hours later. During his consequent imprisonment at Fort Warren, on Jan. 6, 1864, he was promoted to the rank of first lieutenant of the Provisional Navy. He was exchanged in Virginia on Oct. 18, 1864, assigned to the command of Battery Wood below Richmond, and was detached to the command of the torpedo boat division of the James River Squadron in January 1865. Shortly before the evacuation of Richmond, he was ordered to Shreveport, La., to command the seagoing ram *William H. Webb*. Disguised as a Union cotton transport, he ran the gauntlet of the Federal fleet in the Mississippi River but just before gaining the sea he was blocked by the U.S.S. *Richmond,* Apr. 24, 1865. Read beached and fired his ship and escaped with his crew into the swamp where they were subsequently captured. He was again imprisoned at Fort Warren, being released the following July.

After the war he went into the merchant service as an owner-captain and in the rôle of ship broker supplied the Republic of Colombia with a gunboat. He later became a Mississippi River bar pilot and one of the harbor masters of the port of New Orleans. He died at Meridian, Miss., after a painful illness which he bore with an unflinching courage characteristic of the mild-mannered young naval officer whose brilliant record was unsurpassed by any other officer of his rank in either the Union or Confederate Navies.

[C. W. Read, "Reminiscences of the Confed. States Navy," *South. Hist. Soc. Papers,* May 1876; *Register of the Officers of the Confed. States Navy* (1931); *War of the Rebellion:Official Records* (*Navy*), 1 ser., vols. I, II; J. T. Scharf, *Hist. of the Confed. States Navy* (1887); E. M. Maffitt, *The Life and Services of John Newland Maffitt* (1906); Clarence Hale, "The Capture of the 'Caleb Cushing,' " *Me. Hist. Soc. Colls.,* 3 ser., vol. I (1904); J. D. Hill, "Charles W. Read, Confederate von Lückner," *South Atlantic Quart.,* Oct. 1929; E. H. Browne, "The Cruise of the Clarence—Tacony—Archer," *Md. Hist. Mag.,* Mar. 1915.] **W. M. R., Jr.**

READ, DANIEL (Nov. 16, 1757–Dec. 4, 1836), musician, the son of Daniel and Mary (White) Read, was born in Rehoboth, later called Attleboro, Mass., and died in New Haven, Conn. He was a descendant in the fourth generation from John Read, who emigrated from Europe about 1630. During the Revolutionary War he served for short periods in Sullivan's expedition to Rhode Island in 1777 and 1778. Before the close of the war he moved to New Haven, Conn., where he began business as a maker of ivory combs. He also entered into a partnership with Amos Doolittle [q.v.], an engraver, and engaged in the business of publishing and selling books. About 1785 he married Jerusha Sherman in New Haven where they and their four children made their home and where Read entered into many of the activities of civil life. He was one of the stockholders of the bank of the city and a director in the library. He became a member of the Governor's Guards, a famous military organization which, on learning of the attack of the British on the provincials at Lexington in 1775, had marched to Boston under the command of Benedict Arnold.

The composition, editing, and publication of music occupied most of his time, and is the work for which his name is now chiefly known. His first music book was *The American Singing Book* published in 1785 and signed "By Daniel Read, Philo Musico," and contained forty-seven tunes of his own composition. A supplement was added later and a fourth edition was issued in 1793. It had an extensive circulation in New England, and he even arranged for introducing it into singing schools in Alexandria, Va. Oliver Holden [q.v.] became interested in his music and subscribed to all that he might publish. About 1786 he began *The American Musical Magazine,* the first periodical of its kind in this country. It appeared monthly and was made up of music selected from both American and foreign masters. The first volume, the only one issued, bears no date, but is thought to have been printed during the year 1786-1787, and contained music by William Billings [q.v.] as well as some by Daniel Read and others. *An Introduction to Psalmody* appeared in 1790, being a book of instruction for children in vocal music, and was made up of a series of dialogues in which the different musical symbols were explained. The first number of *The Columbian Harmonist* was published in 1793, and numbers two and three soon followed, a fourth edition being printed in Boston in 1810. These were small, oblong books, engraved by Doolittle and selling for forty-five cents.

In 1817 he compiled and arranged a collection of music for the use of the United Society in New Haven. It was printed the following year under the title *The New Haven Collection of Sacred Music* and was his last published work. His last manuscript was completed in 1832, when he was seventy-five years of age, and although it was offered to the American Home

Missionary Society with the request that the proceeds that might arise from its publication be applied to the cause of missions in the United States, the Board did not feel that it was authorized to assume such responsibility and it was never published. His best-known tunes are "Lisbon," "Sherburne" and "Windham."

[Diaries and papers of Daniel Read in New Haven Colony Hist. Soc.; *Vital Records of New Haven,* Parts I and II (1917-24); J. H. Trumbull, *List of Books Printed in Conn., 1709-1800* (1904); biog. sketch by George Hood, in *Musical Herald,* Oct. 1882; J. W. Moore, *Complete Encyc. of Music* (1854); John Daggett, *A Sketch of the Hist. of Attleborough* (1894); F. J. Metcalf, *Am. Writers and Compilers of Sacred Music* (1925), "Daniel Read and His Tune," *Choir Herald,* Apr. 1914; date of birth taken from tombstone.]   F. J. M—f.

READ, DANIEL (June 24, 1805–Oct. 3, 1878), educator, was born on a farm near Marietta, Ohio. Both his parents, before their marriage, had come to this region from Massachusetts. His father, Ezra Read, was of old New England stock. Daniel attended the Cincinnati, Xenia, and Ohio University academies, and in 1820 entered Ohio University, where he was graduated in 1824 with first honors, although the youngest of his class. He then began the study of law, but within a few months became preceptor of the academy of Ohio University. Although by incidental study he acquired a thorough knowledge of law and was admitted to the Ohio bar, his life work was devoted without interruption to education.

In 1836 he was promoted to a professorship in Ohio University. where he taught ancient languages, political economy, and constitutional and public law, and also, having declined the presidency, served as vice-president. Secretary of the board of visitors of West Point in 1840, he wrote a report which was favorably reviewed in the *North American Review* (January 1841). He left Ohio University in 1843 to accept the chair of languages at Indiana State University, and in 1853–54 performed the duties of the presidency. As a member of the constitutional convention of Indiana in 1850, he helped to make provision for a large school fund. He also presented to the legislature a plan of education for the state, and, in addition to his regular university work, organized and instructed a class for the training of teachers. Leaving Indiana in 1856, he served for eleven years as professor of mental and moral philosophy in the University of Wsconsin.

In 1866 the presidency of the University of Missouri was offered to him. Inadequate financial support, the effects of the Civil War, and a wide-spread indifference toward higher education had left this university in a deplorable condition. Read made his acceptance contingent upon financial support of the institution by the state. He presented his views on the matter to the board of curators and made a forceful appeal to the legislature. On Mar. 11, 1867, that body voted its first grant to the university, adding to its income more than $16,000 annually. The next month, Read accepted the presidency, becoming also professor of mental, moral, and political philosophy. His administration marked a new era in the development of the institution; the old-fashioned liberal arts college with a preparatory department gave way to a real university with professional divisions, including a normal college, agricultural and mechanical colleges, the school of mines (at Rolla), the college of law, the medical college, and the department of analytical and applied chemistry. Upon his retirement, July 4, 1876, he was made president emeritus. A little more than two years after his work at the university had ended, he died at Keokuk, Iowa. He was married, when barely twenty-one, to Alice Brice, the daughter of an Ohio merchant, and was survived by four daughters. A son, Gen. Theodore Read, was killed in the closing days of the Civil War.

[W. B. Davis and D. S. Durrie, *An Illustrated Hist. of Mo.* (1876); L. U. Reavis, *St. Louis, the Future Great City of the World* (1875), pp. 247–51; Walter Williams and F. C. Shoemaker, *Missouri: Mother of the West* (1930), vol. II; *In Memoriam. Public Testimony to the Memory of Daniel Read, Late President of the State Univ. of Mo.* (Columbia, Mo., 1878); unpublished history of the Univ. of Mo. by W. F. Switzler, in archives of the University; *Hist. of Boone County, Mo.* (1882).]   J. H. C.

READ, GEORGE (Sept. 18, 1733–Sept. 21, 1798), lawyer, signer of the Declaration of Independence, senator, and chief justice of Delaware, was born near North East, Cecil County, Md. His father, John Read, born in Dublin, Ireland, sixth in descent from Sir Thomas Read of Berkshire, was a landholder of means, and helped to found Charlestown at the head of the Chesapeake as a trade rival to Baltimore. George's mother was Mary Howell, a Welsh lady, whose father also was a planter. Soon after George's birth his father moved to New Castle, Del. The lad attended school at Chester, Pa., and the academy of Rev. Francis Alison [q.v.] at New London, Pa., where he had as fellow students not a few of his later political contemporaries. He remained at Alison's school until his fifteenth year and then studied law in the office of John Moland, Philadelphia lawyer. In 1753 Read was admitted to the bar in Philadelphia and began to practise there, but feeling inadequately rewarded he removed to New Cas-

tle the following year. His profound legal learning, clear reasoning, and calm deliberation soon won him the title of the "honest lawyer" and a practice carrying him through the Lower Counties and Maryland. Although a believer in the maxim that men of ambition should never wed, on Jan. 11, 1763, he married Gertrude (Ross) Till, daughter of Rev. George Ross, rector of Immanuel Episcopal Church, New Castle, and widow of Thomas Till, whom she had married June 18, 1752. A daughter and four sons—one of them being John Read, 1769–1854 [q.v.]— were born to them.

On Apr. 30, 1763, he received his first political appointment, that of attorney general for the Lower Counties. He held this post until his resignation, Oct. 15, 1774, and in this capacity protested against the Stamp Act, declaring in July 1765 that if this or any similar law imposing an internal tax for revenue were enforced, the colonists "will entertain an opinion that they are to become the slaves" of Great Britain and will endeavor "to live as independent of Great Britain as possible . . ." (H. C. Conrad, *post*, I, 89). His rôle during the early Revolutionary period was that of the moderate Whig, a patriot of the same stamp as his close friend, John Dickinson [q.v.]—ready to uphold colonial rights but careful to avoid extreme measures. In October 1765 New Castle County elected him to the provincial assembly, of which he continued a member for the next twelve years. He played a prominent part in bringing about the adoption of a non-importation agreement in his county in 1769, in securing relief for Boston in 1774, and in the proceedings leading up to the First Continental Congress, of which he was a member. In the Second Continental Congress, in which he served until 1777, though irregular in attendance, he was inclined to be cautious and moderate but found himself frequently being carried with the radical tide. He refused to vote for the resolution of independence, July 2, 1776, whether because he believed reconciliation was still possible or because he judged such a step premature on account of the preponderance of Tory sentiment in Delaware is not clear. Following its adoption, however, he not only signed the Declaration but zealously upheld it.

In the Delaware constitutional convention of 1776 Read probably exerted more influence than any other member. "Timoleon," a pamphleteer and political enemy, declared that his influence was paramount (W. T. Read, *post*, p. 468). As the presiding officer of the convention he represented its moderate tendencies, and as a member of the drafting committee his opinions carried much weight. That he was the sole author of the constitution, as his biographer states, has never been substantiated. Under the new frame of government state politics revolved very largely about him. In 1776 he was elected to the legislative council; he became its speaker, and thereby vice-president of the state. The first legislature, controlled by the moderates, returned him to Congress, but at the same time recalled the radical delegates. When the British captured Wilmington in September 1777 and took President John McKinly [q.v.] prisoner, the presidential duties devolved upon Read. Hurrying from Philadelphia by a circuitous route, he barely escaped capture at the hands of the enemy in crossing the Delaware, and after seeing his family safely across the Susquehanna, assumed active charge of the state's affairs in November 1777. Unremitting in his efforts to raise troops, clothing, and provisions, and in removing the general disaffection of the people, he gradually succeeded in injecting a new spirit into the state. Nevertheless, he wrote to Washington, Jan. 9, 1778, "My situation is rather an unlucky one, in a government very deficient in its laws, and those greatly relaxed in their execution, and a Legislature as yet incomplete, and not disposed to unite and give aid to the executive authority" (*Ibid.*, p. 292). At his own request he was relieved of the presidential duties, Mar. 31, 1778, but continued as a member of the Council.

On the Articles of Confederation Read's views were those of the small-state group. He believed taxes should be levied according to population rather than based on the value of lands and improvements, and that title to the western lands should be held jointly with specific limits on each state. Despite these objections, however, he yielded in 1779, and as a member of the assembly drafted the act authorizing Delaware's delegates in Congress to sign the Articles. Later in the year, ill health compelled him to resign his seat in the assembly and also to decline an election to Congress. On Dec. 5, 1782, Congress elected him a judge of the court of appeals in admiralty cases. He accepted only upon assurance that the post would be continued after the war and that he might practise law while holding it. He felt greatly discouraged when Congress in 1786 ordered the salaries of the judges to cease, yet retained the court for such cases as might arise for it. In 1784 New York and Massachusetts appointed him one of nine commissioners to adjust their conflicting land claims. From 1782 to 1788 he again sat in the legislative council of Delaware, his influence

manifesting itself particularly in behalf of measures to improve commerce and the state's finances. In 1785 he vigorously opposed an act redeeming bills of credit previously issued at a ratio of one to seventy-five, on the ground that it would seriously impair the state's credit.

Read was a representative to the Annapolis convention in 1786 and heartily indorsed the movement for a general convention at Philadelphia in 1787. Convinced that revision of the Articles was necessary, he demanded, however, adequate safeguards for the small states. Delaware, he contended, "would become at once a cypher in the union" if the principle of equal representation were not retained and the method of amendment provided for in the Articles (*Ibid.*, p. 439). He would trust nothing to the candor, generosity, or ideas of public justice of the larger states, and on May 21, 1787, urged John Dickinson to hurry to the convention to assist in keeping a strict watch on the stronger states "who will probably combine to swallow up the smaller ones by addition, division, or impoverishment" (*Ibid.*, p. 444). In the convention he was one of the most outspoken advocates for the rights of the smaller states, threatening on one occasion to lead the Delaware delegates from the floor of the convention if there were any change in representation, though he finally accepted the compromise adopted. Read's greatest fears were that the large states would get too much power, and not that the general government would be too strong. He favored a new government; to patch up the old was like "putting new cloth upon an old garment." "If we do not establish a new government," he said, "we must either go to ruin or have the work to do over again" (*Ibid.*, p. 451). Distinctly Hamiltonian in his ideas, he would have given the national legislature the negative on all state laws adjudged improper, would have had senators hold their office during good behavior or at least for a nine-year term, and desired to clothe the chief executive with the broadest possible appointive powers. Largely through his efforts Delaware was the first state to ratify the Constitution. One of the first senators from his state, he was allotted to the class retiring at the end of the first two years, but was reëlected in 1790. A loyal Federalist, though irregular in his attendance as in the Continental Congress, he earnestly supported party measures such as assumption, the national bank, and the excise law. He recommended giving the president broad powers over the removal of his appointees, declaring that the Senate was only a check to prevent impositions by the executive. On Sept. 18,

1793, he resigned his seat to become chief justice of Delaware, which post he held until his death.

Read was tall, slight of frame, had fine features, and was punctilious in his dress. Agreeable and dignified in manner, though somewhat austere, he was a strict and consistent moralist. His mansion with its gardens and stables commanded an extensive view of the Delaware at New Castle. There he lived during the many years of his public service in the style of the colonial gentry, though he never enjoyed more than a moderate income.

[The principal source for Read's life is W. T. Read, *Life and Correspondence of George Read* (1870). See also H. C. Conrad, *Hist. of the State of Del.* (3 vols., 1908), and *The Three Signers: an Address Before the Sons of Del. of Phila.* (1897); E. C. Burnett, ed., *Letters of Members of the Continental Cong.*, vols. I–IV (1921–28); *Minutes of the Legislative Council of Del., 1776–1792* (1886); I. C. Grubb, "The Colonial and State Judiciary of Del." in *Papers of the Hist. Soc. of Del.*, no. XVII (1897); *Proc. of the Convention of the Del. State Held at New-Castle ... August 1776* (1927); J. T. Scharf, *Hist. of Del., 1609–1888* (1888), vol. I; *North American* (Phila.), Feb. 9, 1908, Magazine Section; H. P. Read, *Rossiana* (1908).]   J. H. P—g.

READ, GEORGE CAMPBELL (1787–Aug. 22, 1862), naval officer, was born in Ireland, according to naval records undoubtedly supplied by Read himself. This may perhaps be reconciled with the statement in J. W. Reed's *History of the Reed Family in Europe and America* published in Read's lifetime (1861), that he was the grandson of John Read of London and Virginia and the son of Benjamin Read who came from the Ohio country to Philadelphia in 1787. Read's Irish background is confirmed by the attendance of the Philadelphia Hibernian Society at his funeral. He entered the navy as a midshipman from Pennsylvania on Apr. 2, 1804, served in the merchant marine during furlough, and was made lieutenant in 1810. At the opening of the War of 1812 he was in the *Constitution* and participated in her celebrated escape from Sir Philip Broke's squadron, July 17–20, 1812, and her victory over the *Guerrière* on Aug. 19 following. As third lieutenant, Read boarded the *Guerrière* to receive the surrender. He was also in the *United States* in her action with the *Macedonian* on Oct. 25, 1812, the second famous frigate victory of the war. In 1814 he went to Lake Ontario, but in letters to the Secretary of the Navy, William Jones, 1760–1831 [*q.v.*], a friend and patron, he complains of assignment there to a small schooner. He commanded the *Chippewa* in Bainbridge's squadron against Algiers, 1815, and the *Hornet* in the West Indies, 1818–21, and on two voyages to Spain during treaty negotiations in 1819.

Made captain in 1825, he commanded the *Constitution* in 1826, and the *Constellation* from 1832 to 1834, both in the Mediterranean. In the *Constellation* he had difficulties with refractory younger officers, one of whom he caused to be hoisted forcibly to the masthead when he refused orders to go there. These troubles later received considerable publicity and led Read to request a court martial which was held at Baltimore in June 1835. He was sentenced to a year's suspension, though the court's feelings were obviously not unfavorable (*Court Martial Records No. 622*, Navy Library). His best-remembered service was in the small squadron—flagship *Columbia and John Adams*—which sailed in May 1838, for the Orient. At Bombay news reached Read of the capture and plundering of the Salem pepper schooner *Eclipse* by piratical natives of Quallah Battoo, Sumatra. Sailing thither, he bombarded the town on Dec. 25, 1838, and on Jan. 1 landed 350 men at the neighboring town of Muckie, razing the village and securing finally a pledge of restitution and friendship from the local rajah (printed in Paullin, *post*, p. 348). On the China coast the following April the squadron afforded assurance to foreigners restricted to their factories at Canton during the first efforts of the Chinese government to curb the opium traffic. He sailed for home in August, via Hawaii, and reached Boston in June 1840. Thereafter he commanded the Philadelphia navy yard, and acted in 1845 as president of the midshipmen's examining board which approved the establishment of a naval academy at Annapolis and outlined its organization. He commanded the African Squadron, 1846–49, and was again at the Philadelphia yard until 1853. Placed on the reserved list in 1855, his last service was as governor of the Philadelphia Naval Asylum from May 1861 until his death. His burial was at the Asylum, but his body was subsequently removed to an unknown location. Though Read was married at the time of the China cruise (Taylor, *post*, p. 17), no further information has been found regarding his family.

[Material on Read's earlier career of the 1812–15 period and later appears in *Commandants'* and *Captains' Letters*, Navy Library, and also in the *Personnel Files*. It includes a letter of recommendation from former Secretary of the Navy, William Jones, recording his previous service. On the China cruise, see J. H. Belcher, *Around the World; a Narrative of a Voyage in the East Indies Squadron ...* (1840); F. W. Taylor *The Flagship ...* (2 vols., 1840); W. M. Murrell, *Cruise of the Frigate Columbia* (1840); C. O. Paullin, *Diplomatic Negotiations of Am. Naval Officers* (1912); order book and letter book of the *Columbia*, in Pa. Hist. Soc. Archives. An obituary is in the *Philadelphia Inquirer*, Aug. 23, 1862.]   A. W.

READ, JACOB (1752–July 16, 1816), Revolutionary soldier, delegate to the Continental Congress, and United States senator, was born in Christ Church Parish, S. C., at "Hobcaw," the plantation of his maternal grandfather, for whom he was named. He was the eldest son of Rebecca (Bond) and the Hon. James Read of Charleston, who settled in Savannah, Ga., about the year 1759 as partner in the firm of Read & Mossman, and became one of his Majesty's Council for Georgia. Jacob received his early education, probably with his younger brother William, at the boarding school of Joseph and William Gibbons in Savannah. Soon after his admission to the bar on Mar. 23, 1773, he went to England. Here he was admitted to Gray's Inn, Nov. 3, 1773 (E. A. Jones, *American Members of the Inns of Court*, 1924, p. 182, where he is listed as James Read), and in 1774 he was one of the signers of the petition of the Americans in London against the Massachusetts Government Acts. Upon his return to South Carolina in 1776, he became a captain in the Charleston militia. In 1778, his father, when about to die, conveyed to him in trust his entire estate in South Carolina and Georgia; but because of uncertainty in regard to the value of money and debts due in Great Britain he was unable to settle the estate until the close of his life, and supported his father's family from professional earnings. After the surrender of General Lincoln in 1780, he was among the Americans exiled to St. Augustine, where he remained until transferred to Philadelphia in 1781. When civil government was restored in South Carolina, as representative of Charleston he took his seat in the assembly that met in January 1782, in Jacksonborough, where he was on the committee to amerce Loyalists, and actively opposed the bill for arming the blacks. The next year he became a member of the Privy Council. On Feb. 12, 1783, he was elected to the Continental Congress, and continued an active and important member until 1786, serving on many committees and carrying on correspondence with Jay, Washington, and other prominent men of the day. During the session in New York, he married, Oct. 13, 1785, Catharine, daughter of David Van Horne, merchant, deceased, of that city; two sons and two daughters were born of the union. In 1786 his mother died, leaving him sole executor of her will and guardian of two minors. As one of the counsel of defense that year in the case growing out of the Snipes-Simons duel, he was carrying on his profession, but the contagion of schemes for ending the hard times carried him in 1787 as charter member into a company to build a canal from the Ashley to the Edisto, designed to improve communication with the northwestern portion of the state. Elected speaker of the South Carolina House of Representatives, Jan. 8, 1787, he continued to serve until the close of 1794. In July of that year, as attorney for two Dutch merchants whose vessel had been seized by Americans flying the colors of the French Republic, he experienced a disagreeable encounter and unwelcome publicity, which perhaps hurt him politically. The affair resulted in his challenging the editor of the *South Carolina State-Gazette*, but an officer of the law prevented the duel (see *State-Gazette*, July 26–30, 1794).

As a member of the South Carolina Convention of 1788, he showed Federalist trends in opposing the motions that consideration of the federal constitution be postponed and that re-eligibility of the president be deemed dangerous to liberty. Having voted for ratification, he moved the thanks of the convention to the South Carolina framers of the constitution. As a Federalist he served the term 1795–1801 in the United States Senate, and by a close vote was defeated for reëlection, Dec. 8, 1800, by John Ewing Colhoun. The Judiciary Act of Feb. 13, 1801, provided for sixteen new judgeships. On Feb. 23, 1801, President Adams appointed Read judge of the South Carolina district, to take the place of Thomas Bee, who was advanced to chief judge of the new circuit. The act was repealed in March 1802, however, and a different arrangement of circuits created, so that Read never served (*Journal of the Executive Proceedings of the Senate of the United States*, vol. I, 1828, pp. 383, 385). He became brigadier-general of South Carolina militia and was commanding officer of the Seventh Brigade, 1808–16. Fifteen years after writing his will at his summer home in Newport, R. I., he died at his residence on Montagu Street, Charleston, and was buried in the family cemetery at "Hobcaw."

["Reminiscences of Dr. William Read" in R. W. Gibbes, *Documentary Hist. of the Am. Revolution . . . 1776–1782* (1857); *S. C. Hist. and Geneal. Mag.*, Jan. 1924, pp. 9, 16–17, 22, Jan.–Apr., 1932 to Jan.–Apr. 1933; Robert Wells, *Reg. of the Southern British Am. Colonies for the Year 1774* (1773); John Hoff, publisher, *Hoff's Agricultural and Commercial Almanac* (1808); *The Palladium of Knowledge* (1796–1816); Records of the Probate Court, Charleston, S. C.; *Charleston Courier*, Aug. 1, 1816.]   A. K. G.

READ, JOHN (Jan. 29, 1679/80–Feb. 7, 1749), New England lawyer, was a native of Fairfield, Conn., the son of William and Deborah (Baldwin) Read and a descendant of early settlers in that colony. He matriculated at Harvard College in 1692, graduated five years later, and at once entered the ministry, preaching at Waterbury, East Hartford, and Stratford during the years from 1698 to 1706. It was at this time that he was drawn into protracted litigation over valuable lands on the Housatonic River in New Milford, appearing as attorney in his own defense against suits for ejectment. In a petition to the General Court in 1710, he stated: "Sixteen times have I been to Court about it, ever gaining till ye last Courts Assistants wherein I finally lost; and am utterly discouraged and broken—finding two things, 1st that I am not able to maintain suits forever, and that Indian titles are grown into utter contempt, which things make me weary of the world" (Reed, *post,* p. 6 ff.). This rather expensive legal education appears to have sufficed to lure him professionally from the pulpit into the law courts. Although he was admitted to the Connecticut bar in 1708 (*The Public Records of the Colony of Connecticut,* V, 1870, p. 48 n.), his famous career was begun inauspiciously, for at the very next term he was admonished by the court for contempt and forbidden to plead until he should make acceptable acknowledgment, which he did in the course of the year (*Ibid.,* p. 104).

In 1712 he was appointed attorney for the Crown and appeared in this capacity in numerous lawsuits for several years thereafter, but his principal interest at this time appears to have been centered in real-estate activities directed from his manor-house in Lonetown. He was one of the purchasers of the "Equivalent Lands" given by Massachusetts to Connecticut in settlement of a boundary question, and he served in 1719–20 as commissioner in boundary disputes with New York and with Massachusetts, New Hampshire, and Rhode Island. In 1721 he moved to Boston, and in the same year he was elected attorney-general, a selection which was promptly vetoed by Governor Shute. Owing to the governor's contention that appointment to this office belonged to his prerogative, Read, though repeatedly elected by the legislature, was not permitted to serve except in the years 1723, 1726, and 1734. During this period he took an active part in the political life of Boston. Before his time the political rôle of the professional lawyer had been negligible, and, according to Thomas Hutchinson, Read's election to the General Court in 1738 as a representative of Boston was the first occasion under the second charter that that town was represented by a lawyer (*The History of the Province of Massachusetts Bay,* III, 1828, 104 n.). Read was in great public demand thereafter, serving in 1741 and 1742 on the Governor's Council,

where, through his influence, the custom of renewing the commission of judges upon the appointment of a new governor was suspended (*Ibid.,* II, 1767, 376 n.), and a fiscal pool to turn the tide of specie was adopted.

Read was one of the outstanding colonial lawyers of the first half of the eighteenth century, and he actively participated as counsel in some of the leading cases of his generation. Notable among these were *Banister* vs. *Cunningham,* in which, in a learned opinion, Read buttressed his arguments in behalf of divisible descent by citing the analogies of the English customs of gavelkind and borough English (see R. B. Morris, *Studies in the History of American Law,* 1930, pp. 98, 99), and *Rex* vs. *Checkley,* the famous prosecution for libel upon the Congregational Church (E. F. Slafter, *John Checkley,* 1897, II, pp. 38–44), in the course of which Read argued that the libelous character of the publication should be determined by the jury and not by the court. He also appeared in 1727 in behalf of the Anglican ministers in Boston in urging their claim to membership on the Board of Overseers of Harvard College, and on frequent occasions appeared in behalf of the city of Boston (Reed, *post,* pp. 17, 18) and of the province of Massachusetts in boundary disputes. No other single individual seems to have had as great an influence on the development of legal practices in New England in the first half of the eighteenth Century. To him has been attributed, in conjunction with Paul Dudley [*q.v.*], the introduction of special pleading. He reduced the obscure and redundant phraseology of English deeds to their modern simplified forms. He is also generally credited with the revolutionary legal innovation of conveying the property of a married woman by the simple procedure of a joint deed executed by husband and wife. His legal forms have served as models of pleading for such eminent leaders of the bar as Story, Parsons, and Stearns (Morris, *op. cit.,* p. 147).

Read always maintained extensive real-estate interests, among the most notable in his later life being the purchase at auction of the township, now known as Charlemont, then called Boston Plantation No. I. In the midst of his manifold activities, he found time to write a small Latin grammar which was published in 1736. Brilliant, witty, and benevolent, he was an eccentric genius, to whom tradition has often assigned the rôle of a colonial Haroun-Al-Raschid, who, traveling incognito, would often volunteer his legal services for the defenseless. His wife was Ruth Talcott, daughter of Col. John

Talcott of Hartford and half-sister of Gov. Joseph Talcott. They had several children.

[Printed sources, in addition to those mentioned in the text, include: C. J. McIntire, *Sketch of the Life of the Hon. John Read, 1680–1749* (1898) ; G. B. Reed, *Sketch of the Life of the Hon. John Read, of Boston, 1722–1749* (1903) ; S. L. Knapp, *Biog. Sketches of Eminent Lawyers, Statesmen, and Men of Letters* (1821), pp. 153–161 ; Emory Washburn, *Sketches of the Judicial Hist. of Mass.* (1840), pp. 207–09 ; D. C. Kilbourn, *The Bench and Bar of Litchfield County, Conn., 1709–1909* (1909), pp. 276–77 ; and J. L. Sibley, *Biog. Sketches of Those Who Attended Harvard Coll.*, vol. IV (1933). Read's legal papers, pleas, depositions, and briefs are found in "Early Court Files of Suffolk, 1629–1800," in the office of the clerk of the Supreme Judicial Court for the County of Suffolk, Boston, Mass.]   R.B.M—s.

READ, JOHN (July 17, 1769–July 13, 1854), lawyer, was born at New Castle, Del., the son of George [*q.v.*] and Gertrude (Ross) Read. His father was a prominent lawyer, a signer of the Declaration of Independence, and one of the framers of the Constitution of the United States. He was educated in the public schools and at the College of New Jersey from which he graduated in 1787 with the degree of A.B. He then studied law under his father and was admitted to the bar of New Castle in 1791. Not long afterward he moved to Philadelphia, Pa., where he was admitted to the bar on Apr. 24, 1792. In 1797 he was appointed by President John Adams agent general of the United States to act upon any claims which might be made under the sixth article of Jay's Treaty. He filled this office with marked ability until its termination in 1809. Following this appointment he served as a member of the Philadelphia City Council from 1809 to 1815; as a member of the Assembly of Pennsylvania in the years 1815–16; and as a member of the state Senate in 1817–18. In the latter year he was elected by the Senate to represent the state as a director of the Philadelphia Bank. In the same year he was appointed city solicitor of Philadelphia, serving until 1820. In 1819 he was elected president of the Philadelphia Bank, which office he held until his resignation in 1841. He then retired and moved to Trenton, N. J., where he spent his remaining days. He was active in the national councils of the Episcopal Church and served as senior warden of Christ Church, 1801–17, and of St. James Church, 1817–41. He contributed largely to philanthropic causes and during the outbreak of yellow fever in 1793 was one of the few prominent citizens to remain in Philadelphia, exposing his life throughout the entire course of the epidemic in behalf of his suffering fellow citizens. He also took a prominent part in the defense of the Delaware during the War of 1812. While he did not occupy as important

a position in the country's affairs as did either his father or his son, John Meredith Read [*q.v.*], he nevertheless had the friendship and respect of all who came into contact with him because of his great industry, in spite of a naturally weak constitution, and his personal qualities. He married Martha Meredith on June 25, 1796, and they had three sons and two daughters.

[Henry Simpson, *The Lives of Eminent Philadelphians* (1859) ; C. P. Keith, *The Provincial Councillors of Pa.* (1883) ; H. P. Read, *Rossiana* (1908) ; J. H. Martin, *Martin's Bench and Bar of Phila.* (1883) ; *Daily True American* (Trenton), July 14, 1854.]   J.H.F.

READ, JOHN MEREDITH (July 21, 1797–Nov. 29, 1874), jurist, was born in Philadelphia, Pa., the grandson of George Read [*q.v.*] of Delaware, and son of John [*q.v.*] and Martha (Meredith) Read. Graduated from the University of Pennsylvania in 1812, he was admitted to the bar on Sept. 7, 1818, served as city-solicitor (1830–31) and member of the select-council (1827–28) of Philadelphia, and represented the city in the state legislature (1823–25). Endowed with talents of a high order and with exceptional family connections, punctual and methodical, and indefatigable in labor, he attained before he was forty a place high among the leaders of the city bar, when that bar was in its golden age. After serving as United States district attorney for eastern Pennsylvania from 1837 to 1841 (*Journal of the Executive Proceedings of the Senate*, vol. V, 1887), he was nominated by President Tyler an associate justice of the Supreme Court of the United States (*Ibid.*, vol. VI, 1887), but his opinions on slavery prevented confirmation by the Senate. As a result, at least partly, of the recommendations of James Buchanan (*The Works of James Buchanan*, ed. by J. B. Moore, VI, 1909, p. 77), he was next appointed attorney-general of Pennsylvania, but occupied the position only a few months (June 23–Dec. 18, 1846, 3 *Pa.*, 5). Private practice claimed him thereafter until his election in October 1858 for fifteen years to the supreme court of the state, of which he became chief justice by seniority on Dec. 2, 1872. His failing health increased the labors of his colleagues at the end of his term, and for this reason he retired upon its expiration. His judicial opinions were mines of information when they involved historical research; otherwise they were habitually terse and vigorous, characterized perhaps more by a strong sense of justice than by power of legal reasoning. He was known to call bedroom consultations in earliest morning hours and even to open court in mid-winter before daylight. According to a friendly and very competent contemporary, he was a faithful adherent to precedents and defender of vested rights, even to the point of undoing some innovations of his predecessors.

To Philadelphia Read gave on many occasions unstinted service. Ardent in friendships, zealous in advocacy of causes he espoused, a speaker of earnestness and power, he wielded an influence which counted heavily in the state. Despite early anti-slavery tendencies he approved the annexation of Texas and the Mexican War, but he opposed in the state convention of 1849 any extension of slave territory, joined in the creation of the Free-Soil party, and was an early adherent of the Republican party. His *Speech . . . on the Power of Congress over the Territories, and in Favor of Free Kansas, Free White Labor, and of Fremont and Dayton, Delivered . . . Sept. 30, 1856, at Philadelphia* (1856) was widely used in the national campaign. The first Republican victory in Pennsylvania sent him to the state supreme court. Pennsylvania was indispensable to Republican success in 1860, and Read received mention in the state convention as a presidential candidate (Philadelphia *North American and United States Gazette,* Feb. 23, 1860, p. 2), but Simon Cameron's ambitions stood in the way. Rhode Island gave him one vote in the first ballot of the convention. During the war he was one of the bare majority of his court who steadily sustained the legislation of Congress; and several of his opinions, separately printed, received wide circulation. His *Views, sustained by Facts and Authorities, on the Suspension of the Privilege of the Writ of Habeas Corpus,* published in January 1863, probably had some influence upon the passage by Congress of the Act of Mar. 3, 1863.

Read was a man of dignity, kindness, courtesy, remarkable energy, and strong opinions, and very persistent in his purposes. The standards he set for himself as a lawyer and a citizen were exceedingly high, and he observed them. He was married on Mar. 20, 1828, to Priscilla Marshall of Boston, by whom he had five children. She died in 1841 and on July 26, 1855, he married Amelia Thompson of Philadelphia, the daughter of Edward Thompson and widow of Theodore Thompson. She, with a son by his first wife, John Meredith Read [*q.v.*], survived him. His judicial opinions are in volumes 32 to 73 of the *Pennsylvania State Reports.* His other publications included, aside from unofficial prints of judicial opinions, various pamphlets. His most important reprinted opinions supported the constitutionality of the national draft act of Mar. 3, 1863 (45 *Pa.,* 238, at 284 and 300) and of the

legal tender act (52 *Pa.,* 9, at 71), and the operation of street cars on Sunday, as "the poor man's carriage" and therefore within the state constitutional exception of necessity and charity (54 *Pa.,* 401, at 432).

[See: F. M. Eastman, *Courts and Lawyers of Pa.* (1922), vol. II; J. H. Martin, *Martin's Bench and Bar of Phila.* (1883); E. K. Price, "An Obit. Notice of Chief Justice John Meredith Read," *Proc. Am. Phil. Soc.,* vol. XIV (1876), which notes his influence in various fields of Pennsylvania law; *Proc. of the R. W. Grand Lodge of Pa. . . . Dec. 28th, A.D., 1874 . . . in Reference to the Death of . . . John Meredith Read* (1875); obituary proceedings of the bar of Philadelphia and Pittsburgh, *Legal Intelligencer* (Phila.), Dec. 4 and 11, 1874; H. P. Read, *Rossiana* (1908); F. W. Leach, "Old Phila. Families," *North American* (Phila.), Mag. Section, Feb. 9, 1908.]   F. S. P.

READ, JOHN MEREDITH (Feb. 21, 1837–Dec. 27, 1896), diplomat, son of John Meredith Read [*q.v.*] and Priscilla (Marshall) Read, was born at Philadelphia. He attended a military school and Brown University (1854–57). Upon graduation from the Albany Law School in 1859, he was admitted to the bar at Philadelphia. In the same year, Apr. 7, he married Delphine Marie, daughter of Harmon Pumpelly of Albany, where he took up his residence after a year of travel and study in Europe. Assuming an active rôle in the Republican party, he helped organize the "Wide Awakes" in the campaign of 1860. As adjutant-general (January–August 1861), with the rank of brigadier-general, he directed the military efforts of the state of New York in the opening months of the Civil War. During the following years he acquired some reputation as a scholar and writer, his chief production being *A Historical Inquiry Concerning Henry Hudson* (1866). His support of Grant for the presidency was rewarded by an appointment, Apr. 16, 1869, as consul general at Paris. The most notable duty which there devolved upon him was that of protecting the interests of German subjects during the Franco-Prussian War, his share of which duty was prolonged several months after Elihu B. Washburne, minister to France, ceased to be official representative of the German government, June 1871.

Recognition of Read's services was marked by his appointment, Nov. 7, 1873, as minister resident in Greece. A member of the Archæological Society of Athens, he reported on discoveries and forwarded to the Department of State casts of ancient treaties. An achievement of personal diplomacy was his securing, through informal representations, in 1876, revocation of an order against the sale of translations of the Bible and other religious works circulated by the British and American Bible societies (*Papers Relating to the Foreign Relations of the United States,*

1876, pp. 309–11). In the interference with Russia's grain trade by her war with Turkey, Read saw a commercial opportunity for the United States. In a dispatch of July 23, 1877, he urged that prompt action by American shippers might result in securing the grain markets of Europe (Department of State, Dispatches, Greece, vol. VII, no. 305). His appeal was published and widely commented on in the American press (*Ibid.*, no. 317). The effect of this dispatch as a single factor in so vast and complex a movement as the growth of the grain trade is difficult to assess, especially since Russian exports, as well as American, increased in the very year of the war. Whatever part it played is to the credit of its sender's zeal for his country's interests; but his own estimate of its consequences, as reflected in later dispatches and in biographical statements, was undoubtedly exaggerated.

From motives of economy, Congress reduced Read's rank, in 1876, to that of chargé d'affaires and, in 1878, cut off all appropriations for the legation. His interest in the unsettled fortunes of Greece after the Congress of Berlin prompted him to remain at his post without compensation until September 1879, when his resignation was tendered and accepted. Thereafter he toured Europe as an unofficial advocate of the Greek territorial claims, for which services, after the settlement in 1881, he received the highest Greek decoration. Occupying himself with the collection of manuscripts and with projects of publication, he lived thenceforth in Paris until his death. His *Historic Studies in Vaud, Berne, and Savoy; from Roman Times to Voltaire, Rousseau and Gibbon* (1897) appeared after his death. He was survived by two sons and two daughters.

[H. P. Read, *Rossiana* (1908); *N. Y. Tribune* and *Albany Evening Jour.*, Dec. 28, 1896; *Papers Relating to the Foreign Relations of the U. S.*, 1874–78; archives of the Department of State.]   J. V. F.

READ, NATHAN (July 2, 1759–Jan. 20, 1849), iron manufacturer, inventor, member of Congress, was the son of Reuben and Tamsin (Meacham) Read and was born on the Read estate established by his grandfather at Warren, Worcester County, Mass. He was of English ancestry, the first of the family in America having settled near Boston, Mass., about 1632. He lived at home with his parents until he was fifteen years old, then spent three years in a preparatory school and entered Harvard in 1777. With the intention of entering the ministry, he specialized in Hebrew and became such an apt scholar that, although an undergraduate, he was engaged as instructor of the class during the interval be-

tween the death of the professor and the appointment of his successor. Following his graduation in 1781 he taught school for two years in Beverly and Salem, Mass., and was then elected a tutor at Harvard. Here he remained for more than four years but resigned early in 1787 to study medicine in Salem, Mass. After eighteen months, however, he quit his studies and opened an apothecary shop in Salem. About this time, too, he became interested in the application of the steam engine to land and water transportation, and with constantly increasing zeal applied himself, through study and experimentation for a number of years, to the problem particularly of steam navigation. He first designed a new, light, steam boiler—a multitubular boiler having seventy-eight vertical tubes. He then devised an improved double-acting steam engine, and finally evolved a form of paddle wheel, the design being based upon his experiments with a manually operated paddle-wheel propelled boat which he constructed in 1789.

Early in 1790, after demonstrating his steam navigation plans before a special committee of the American Academy of Arts and Sciences in Salem, he personally presented a petition to Congress in New York for a patent on his inventions on Feb. 8, 1790. This included not only the above plans for a steamboat but also for a steam road carriage as well. Several months later Congress passed the "Act to Promote the Progress of the Useful Arts," and Read's petition in due time came before the commissioners appointed to carry out that act. Meanwhile, however, Read learned that the use of paddle wheels was not original with him as he had supposed, so he presented a new petition to Congress on Jan. 1, 1791, in which he described a chain wheel method of propulsion in lieu of the paddle-wheel method. He also eliminated his plans for a steam road carriage simply because Congress had so ridiculed the idea when his original petition was presented. Seven months later, on Aug. 26, 1791, he was granted letters patent for his three inventions, a portable multitubular boiler, an improved double-acting steam engine, and a chain wheel method of propelling boats. For a time Read made a number of unsuccessful attempts to secure financial aid to build a full-size steamboat and then turned his attention to other matters. In 1795 he settled on a farm in Danvers, Mass., and the following year organized the Salem Iron Factory and for eleven years engaged in the manufacture of iron cables, anchors and other iron materials for ships. During this time he perfected and patented on Jan. 8, 1798, a nail cutting and heading machine.

In 1807 he moved to a larger farm in Belfast, Me., and there lived for the remainder of his life, giving most of his attention to farming but occasionally indulging in invention. Beside his several businesses and his inventive work he was appointed to Congress for Essex County, Mass., in October 1800, to fill an unexpired term, and the following month was elected a member of the succeeding Congress for two years. In 1802 he was appointed a special justice of the court of common pleas for Essex County and after his removal to Belfast he presided as chief justice of the court in Hancock County, Me., for many successive years. Read was a member of the American Academy of Arts and Sciences from 1791, and an honorary member of the Linnaean Society of New England from 1815. He was married on Oct. 20, 1790, to Elizabeth Jeffrey of Salem, Mass., and died in his ninetieth year in Belfast, Me.

["Autobiography of Hon. Nathan Read," *New-Eng. Hist. and Geneal. Reg.*, Oct. 1896; David Read, *Nathan Read, His Invention of the Multi-Tubular Boiler* (1870); G. H. Preble, *A Chronological Hist. of the Origin and Develop. of Steam Navigation* (1883); R. H. Thurston, *A Hist. of the Growth of the Steam-Engine* (1902); Patent Off. records; *Vital Records of Warren, Mass.* (1910); *Vital Records of Salem, Mass.*, vol. III (1924); *Bangor* (Me.) *Daily Whig and Courier*, Jan. 30, 1849.]   C. W. M.

READ, THOMAS (1740?–Oct. 26, 1788), naval officer, was born on his father's estate at the headwaters of the Christiana River, Newcastle County, Del., the fourth son of John and Mary (Howell) Read and brother of George Read [*q.v.*]. Having a brother William in business in Havana, he early took up seafaring and became master of vessels in the West Indies and transatlantic trade. In 1761 he commanded the *Tartar* ("Ship Registers of Phila.," *Pennsylvania Magazine of History and Biography*, No. 3, 1903, p. 348) and family letters show he was still in her in 1765, bound from London to Newfoundland, thence to Lisbon and Port Royal, and in frequent "ill luck" (*Life ... of George Read, post*, pp. 28, 41). He commanded the ship *Fame* in 1769. He was commissioned captain on Oct. 23, 1775, in the Pennsylvania state navy and commodore of the thirteen row galleys constituting the Delaware River defense flotilla during the Revolution. In January 1776, Thomas Caldwell became commodore, and the following March Read was assigned to second rank with command of the newly purchased ship *Montgomery*, in which, during the fight between the galleys and the frigates *Roebuck* and *Liverpool* in May, he was stationed at Fort Island and in charge of the *chevaux-de-frise*. Though he was placed in chief command again from May 29 to

June 5, he then resigned for a captaincy in the Continental navy, standing eighth in the order of precedence. In the Trenton campaign, his ship *George Washington* being still unfinished, he marched on Dec. 5 to join Washington's forces with a naval battery (*Ibid.*, p. 219), with which he raked the bridge over Assanpink Creek, Jan. 2. Upon the British occupation of Philadelphia, Read and his senior, Commodore John Barry [*q.v.*], moved their frigates *Washington* and *Effingham* up the Delaware to Fieldsboro, N. J., just below Bordentown, and in December dismantled and partly sank them. They were destroyed on May 7, 1778, by the British.

In the meantime Read was assigned to the fast brigantine *Baltimore* (*Letters of Members of Continental Congress*, III, 1926, p. 55), intended for carrying dispatches abroad. In April 1778 he was in Baltimore, Md., fitting out the vessel and he appears to have made a voyage in her in that year. In February 1779, he was ordered to protect the Chesapeake, and in June his ship was reported as expected in Philadelphia (*Out-Letters of the Marine Committee*, Naval History Society, vol. I, 1914). On Sept. 30, 1779, he was appointed to the frigate *Bourbon*, building in Connecticut but never completed. On July 22, 1780, he took out letters of marque for the brig *Patty* of Philadelphia, and family letters indicate that he was at sea in 1782 (*Life ... of George Read*, p. 375). Not later than this year, and probably earlier, he married Mary (Peele) Field, widow of Robert Field, and made his home thereafter at "White Hill," Fieldsboro, N. J. (*Ibid.*, p. 372). He joined Barry on Sept. 24, 1785, in presenting to Congress a memorial of naval officers for equal treatment with army officers (Griffin, *post*, p. 105). In the frigate *Alliance*, purchased by his friend and employer Robert Morris, Read subsequently made a remarkably quick voyage to China at an unusual season and by a new route east of the Dutch Indies and through the Solomon Islands, discovering or rediscovering two islands, probably Ponape and another of the Carolines, which he named "Morris" and "Alliance." He left Philadelphia in June 1787, reached Canton on Dec. 22, and returned Sept. 17, 1788, with a cargo of tea worth about £100,000. His death occurred at Fieldsboro, N. J., very shortly thereafter. From his portrait (H. C. Conrad, *History of the State of Del.*, 1908, vol. III) and other evidence, he seems to have resembled his brother George in appearance, intelligence, and amiability of character.

[*Pa. Archives*, 1 ser., IV (1853), 5 ser., I (1906); Peter Force, *Am. Archives*, 4 ser., V (1844) VI (1846); *Jour. of the Continental Cong.*, vol. XX (1912); *Jour.*

and Coresp. of the Council of Md., 1778–1779, Archives of Md., vol. XXI (1901) ; M. I. J. Griffin, The Hist. of Comm. John Barry (1897) ; W. T. Read, Life and Coresp. of George Read (1870) ; J. W. Reed, Hist. of the Reed Family in England and America (1861), pp. 431–463 ; "Letters of Phineas Bond," Ann. Report of the Am. Hist. Asso. for the Year 1896 (1897), vol. I ; information from the Field family.] A. W.

READ, THOMAS BUCHANAN (Mar. 12, 1822–May 11, 1872), painter, poet, was born on a farm at Corner Ketch, near Guthriesville, Chester County, Pa. He was of Scotch-Irish and English descent; his great-grandfather, Thomas Read (1746–1823), son of John and Eleanor Read, Irish immigrants, was a Presbyterian minister and president for a time of the Classical Academy of Newark, Del. As a schoolboy Read evinced an aptitude for drawing and versifying, but on his father's death, in 1832 or shortly thereafter, the family dispersed and the boy was apprenticed to a tailor. Harshly treated, he ran away, became a grocer's helper and learned cigar making in Philadelphia ; journeyed on foot to Pittsburgh in 1837 and thence by flatboat to Cincinnati, where he found shelter in the household of a married sister ; earned a livelihood by rolling cigars, painting canal boats, and doing odd jobs; was hired by Shobal Vail Clevenger [*q.v.*] to chisel figures and inscriptions on tombstones and received some lessons from him in sculpture; opened a sign-painter's shop, practising drawing in his spare hours and writing verse for the *Times* and the *Chronicle* ; wandered through Ohio as an itinerant portrait painter; played female parts in a theatrical troupe at Dayton; and finally, with the generous patronage of Nicholas Longworth [*q.v.*], fitted up a studio in Cincinnati and was commissioned to make a portrait of Gen. William Henry Harrison, then a candidate for the presidency. "A sad daub," Read called it afterwards, but at the time it afforded useful publicity. In 1841 he painted his way eastward to New York and then to Boston, where he opened a studio in the basement of the Park Street Church, made sincere, helpful friends of Longfellow and Washington Allston, and was soon thriving at his profession. Leonard Woods and Moses Stuart were among his first sitters. Read was about five feet tall, slenderly built, and sometimes weighed less than one hundred pounds. He had delicate features, a good voice, engaging manners, was devoutly religious and incapable of deceit. Though modest in his demeanor, he was confident of his powers. It was impossible not to like him; wherever he went he made lasting friends. Then, as later, he would work as long as eight hours at his easel without intermission, and was seldom idle. His recreation was fishing. In 1843 he married Mary

J. Pratt of Gambier, Ohio. In 1845 he published a novelette, *Paul Redding: A Tale of the Brandywine*, a juvenile ragout of Irvingesque idyll, dialect humor, and ten-cent melodrama. Except for a few articles in *Graham's Magazine* and the *Atlantic Monthly* he published no other prose. During this period he contributed several poems to the Boston *Courier*.

His removal to Philadelphia in 1846 marked a turning point in his career. For the rest of his life that city was, in a sense, his home, although he resided for short periods in Cincinnati, New York, and Boston, and for rather longer periods in Europe, where he became well known in London, Liverpool, Manchester, Düsseldorf, Florence, and Rome. In Philadelphia, however, he found his closest friends and most constant patrons, and its newspapers, magazines, and publishing houses printed most of his verse. He compiled an anthology, *The Female Poets of America* (1849), with short biographical notices cribbed from Rufus W. Griswold, who trounced him for the theft and then forgave him. The principal volumes of Read's own verse were: *Poems* (1847) ; *Lays and Ballads* (1849) ; *Poems* (1854, 1856) ; *The New Pastoral* (1855) ; *The House by the Sea* (1855) ; *Rural Poems* (1857) ; *Sylvia, or The Last Shepherd* (1857) ; *The Wagoner of the Alleghanies* (1862) ; *A Summer Story, Sheridan's Ride, and Other Poems* (1865) ; *Poetical Works* (1866), in three volumes. His poetry was praised extravagantly both in the United States and England, and from 1855 until his death he was regarded as one of the foremost American poets. He was, however, an artificer in verse rather than a poet; his work lacks concentration and polish and is plainly imitative of Milton, Cowper, Wordsworth, Scott, and Longfellow. His longer poems are practically unknown today, and of the shorter pieces "Drifting" and "Sheridan's Ride" are alone remembered. His reputation as a painter has also declined to the vanishing point. Few of his pictures are in public collections. He was a competent, but not a brilliant, portrait painter, and was inclined to prettify his feminine sitters; he painted no landscapes; and his figure studies are in a style no longer admired. Perhaps his best-known pictures are "Sheridan's Ride" and the portrait of Longfellow's daughters.

In 1853 Read established himself in Florence, expecting to spend the rest of his life there, but in 1855 his wife and a daughter died of cholera, and he was distraught with grief. He returned to the United States and in the summer of 1856 married Harriet Denison Butler of Northampton, Mass., who outlived him. During the Civil

War he was a major on the staff of Gen. Lew Wallace, but his chief service was on the lecture platform. He and James Edward Murdoch [*q.v.*] frequently appeared together, Murdoch reading a number of Read's patriotic poems. After the war Read made his home in Rome. In 1868 his health began to fail. With a premonition of his approaching death he sailed for New York in April 1872, contracted pneumonia aboard ship, and died at the Astor House, New York, a few days after his arrival. His three children by his first marriage had died before him. He was buried in Central Laurel Hill Cemetery, Philadelphia.

[H. C. Townsend and others, *A Memoir of T. Buchanan Read* (privately printed, Phila., 1889) ; J. R. Tait, "Reminiscences of a Poet-Painter," *Lippincott's Mag.*, Mar. 1877 ; R. H. Stoddard, "T. B. Read," *National Mag.*, Apr. 1855, and *Recollections Personal and Literary* (1903), the account in the latter reprinted from *Lippincott's Mag.*, Feb. 1891 ; *Mary Howitt: An Autobiog.* (1889) ; H. T. Tuckerman, *Book of the Artists* (1867) ; E. P. Oberholtzer, *The Lit. Hist. of Phila.* (1906) ; J. S. Futhey and Gilbert Cope, *Hist. of Chester County, Pa.* (1881) ; L. R. Harley, "Life Experiences of a Painter-Poet," in *Confessions of a Schoolmaster* (1914) ; C. L. Moore, "A Neglected Am. Poet," *Dial*, Jan. 1, 1914 ; I. C. Keller, "Thomas Buchanan Read," *Univ. of Pittsburgh Bull.*, Jan. 10, 1933 ; *N. Y. Daily Tribune*, May 13, 1872 ; *Phila. Press*, May 13, 15, 1872.]
                                                        G. H. G.

READE, EDWIN GODWIN (Nov. 13, 1812– Oct. 18, 1894), jurist, was born at Mount Tirzah, Person County, N. C., the second son of Robert R. and Judith A. (Gooch) Reade. His father died soon after his birth and from early childhood the boy worked—on the farm, in a carriage-shop, and in a tannery—meanwhile studying under his mother. Later he attended two academies. He read law at home, was admitted to the bar in 1835, practising at Roxboro, and became one of the most notable advocates in the history of the state. He was a superb speaker, given to austere simplicity of style and limpid clarity of thought. He was a fighter and thus described his policy: "My practice was to allow a brother to . . . do almost anything he desired to do in fixing up his case before trial, but when the trial commenced and swords were drawn, I threw away the scabbard and fought for a funeral" (*Green Bag, post*, p. 570). Tall and handsome, with a fine voice, he concealed a rather cold nature under a dignified affability. He was a Whig in politics until 1855 when, taking seriously their anti-Catholic and anti-foreign arguments, he joined the American party and was elected to Congress, but served only one term. He was a witness of the assault on Sumner, and, while he voted against expelling Brooks, he alone of Southern members voted to censure Representative Lawrence M. Keitt [*q.v.*].

In 1861 John A. Gilmer [*q.v.*], at Seward's request, sounded Reade as to becoming a member of Lincoln's cabinet. He declined, urging Gilmer to accept. He was elected as a Union candidate to the convention which the people rejected in February 1861, but declined to go to the secession convention. In 1863, he was elected judge of the superior court, but before his term began, he accepted, at Vance's urgent request, an appointment of a month in the Confederate Senate (January-February 1864). He was the candidate of the peace party for election by the legislature, but was defeated.

In 1865, he was president of the "Johnson" or Reconstruction, Convention and was later the same year elected associate justice of the supreme court. In 1868, when reconstruction was completed, although he had definitely aligned himself with the Republican party, he was the choice of both parties for the same position and served until 1879, when he declined to be a candidate. On the bench, he wrote many important opinions, among which were: *Jacobs* vs. *Smallwood* and *Hill* vs. *Kessler* (63 N. C., 112, 437), holding that the homestead exemption was valid against debts contracted before the law was adopted; *People* vs. *McKee* (68 N. C., 429), holding that the governor and not the legislature has the power of appointment to office; and *State* vs. *Parrott* (71 N. C., 311), holding that any one has the right to tear down an obstruction to free navigation of a river. Caustically and trenchantly written, his opinions are short and luminously clear. He was an excellent business man and upon his retirement from the bench became president of a national bank in Raleigh which was in difficulties. He soon rehabilitated it, and remained its head until his death. During these years, he took no part whatever in politics and, after 1874, never cast a vote.

Reade was married twice: first, to Emily A. L. Moore of Person County, who died in 1871 ; and, second, late in that same year, to Mrs. Mary Parmele of Washington, N. C., who survived him. He had no children.

[Reade's opinions, in 61–79 N. C.; "Proceedings in Memory of Hon. Edwin Godwin Reade," 115 N. C., 607–10 ; *Green Bag*, Dec. 1892 ; S. A. Ashe, *Hist. of N. C.*, vol. II (1925) ; Jerome Dowd, *Sketches of Prominent Living North Carolinians* (1888) ; *News and Observer* (Raleigh, N. C.), Oct. 19, 1894.] J. G. deR. H.

REAGAN, JOHN HENNINGER (Oct. 8, 1818–Mar. 6, 1905), representative and senator of the United States, Confederate postmaster-general, chairman of the Texas railroad commission, was born in Sevier County, Tenn., the son of Timothy R. and Elizabeth (Lusk) Reagan. Although hampered by the necessary assistance given his father in the tanyard and on the farm, he went to the schools of the community and to the academy at Maryville, Tenn. He then worked as a clerk for several months and in 1838 served as overseer of a plantation near Natchez, Miss. In 1839 he went to Texas, joined the army of the Republic for the Cherokee campaign, and after participation in two battles was offered a commission as second lieutenant in the Texas army but, believing that promotion would be slow, declined it. While recovering from an attack of fever he studied surveying, became deputy surveyor, and during the next three years made surveys from Nacogdoches to Dallas. In 1842 he was elected justice of the peace and captain of the militia in Nacogdoches County but two years later removed to a farm in what is now Kaufman County, where he also studied law and received in 1846 a temporary license to practise. He was made county judge and lieutenant-colonel of the militia of Henderson County, which he had helped to organize and name. In 1847 he became a member of the state legislature, where he was a very active member, completed his law study, and in 1848 was admitted to the bar with a regular license. He was soon one of Texas' leading lawyers. In 1851 he removed to Palestine, Tex. The next year he was elected to a six-year term as district judge. In 1856, after a change in the area comprising his district and an increase in salaries, he resigned on the ground that the voters in the new part of the district had the right of choice and that, since the higher salary had been advocated in order to obtain better judges, all the voters had the right to decide whether they could get a better man for the money. He was reëlected to another six-year term. Over his own protest and in spite of the opposition of Sam Houston [q.v.], he was nominated and elected by a large majority to the federal Congress, and he served from Mar. 4, 1857, to Mar. 3, 1861. When the leaders of the Southern wing of the Democratic party advocated the reopening of the African slave trade and the acquisition of territory in Cuba, Mexico, and Central America, Reagan, in announcing for reelection in 1859, denounced these extreme views as morally and politically wrong and was elected by a vote of approximately three to one.

Nevertheless, at the outbreak of the Civil War he was elected to the secession convention of Texas in 1861 and by that convention to the provisional Congress of the Confederacy. In March 1861 he was appointed by President Davis to be postmaster-general of the Confederacy and served in that position until the close of the war. During the last few weeks of the Civil War he served also as secretary of the treasury. An efficient cabinet officer, he made the post office department self-sustaining in spite of the obstacles incident to the war. He was loyal to President Davis and maintained a high regard for his ability and judgment. After the war he was imprisoned at Fort Warren in Boston Harbor for several months. On May 28, 1865, he addressed a letter to President Johnson urging the wisdom and justice of a lenient attitude toward the people of the South (for letter see *Southern Historical Association Publications,* vol. VI, 1902, or Appendix B of *Memoirs, post*). He appealed as one descendant of poor East Tennesseeans to another and warned the President against the evil consequences of the policies being urged by Northern partisans. There is reason to believe that the change in the attitude of President Johnson was caused partly, if not largely, by the Reagan letter (See B. H. Good, unpublished manuscripts, *post*). A second Fort Warren letter dated Aug. 11, 1865 (See Appendix C of *Memoirs, post*), was an open one to the Texas people advising that the state should accept the results of the war, acknowledge the extinction of slavery, admit the negro to civil rights, and permit him to vote with educational and property qualifications. He urged this policy in order to avoid for Texas the evils of military government and unqualified negro suffrage. In this letter he had the support and approval of President Johnson, Secretary Seward, and Senator Henry Wilson of Massachusetts, all of whom urged him to go to Texas and try to persuade the people to take the lead in the movement; but his foresight was not shared by other Texans, his plans were emphatically condemned, and he suffered a loss of standing among his Texas constituents (see *Reagan Papers*).

Returning to Palestine in December 1865 he found his home wrecked and his neighbors in poverty, so he went to his farm to live. During a period of comparative inactivity in politics he, with James W. Throckmorton, directed the formation and adoption of the short-lived Texas constitution of 1866, and he influenced the Texas Democrats to support Greeley and the Liberal Republican movement in 1872. He saw the importance of railway transportation and was active in bringing a railroad to Palestine. His foresight and his skill in drawing a contract is shown in the litigation over the provision he made with the railroad for permanent shops at Palestine (*International & Great Northern Railway Co.* vs. *Anderson County,* 106 *Texas* 60 and 246 *U. S.,* 424; Title 1 of Emergency Transportation Act). Having had his disabilities removed, he was elected to Congress and took his seat in December 1875. He served as a delegate to the Texas constitutional convention of 1875, which wrote the present (1934) constitution of that state. He was chairman of the judiciary committee and advocated enlarged jurisdiction of the lower courts, also fewer officials, longer terms, and higher salaries. While he was recognized by the other delegates as their ablest member he was defeated in all of these policies. He was continually reëlected to the lower house of Congress until his selection for the Senate in 1887. As a congressman he advocated economy in governmental expenditures, low tariff, state rights, bimetallism, and the improvement of commercial facilities. He was for ten years chairman of the House committee on commerce and was a member of the Senate commerce committee. His greatest service in Congress was the joint authorship and advocacy of the bill to establish the Interstate Commerce Commission. His long study of railroad transportation caused Gov. James Stephen Hogg [q.v.] to urge him to strengthen the newly authorized Texas railroad commission by accepting appointment to it. Believing in state rights and in the necessity of the states' assuming the responsibility to regulate railroads, then mainly intrastate in operation, he accepted in 1891, became chairman, and served three terms by appointment and one term of six years by election at a salary of $4,000 a year. Within a few years the commission was firmly intrenched in constitutional and legal security within the state; but its efforts at control were largely thwarted by the development and consolidation of railroads that after the panic of 1893 made the problem interstate and national in administration. His personal sacrifice had resulted in losing him a place in the national forum from which to urge his ideas on the changing problems of railroad control. In 1903 he retired to private life. He was married three times: in 1842 to Mrs. Martha Music who died about 1845, in 1852 to Edwina Moss Nelms who bore him six children and died in 1863, and in 1865 to Molly Ford Taylor who with three of their five children survived him. He died from pneumonia and was buried near Palestine. His funeral was attended by the state legislature in a body, and the whole state showed every evidence of a keen realization of its loss of a man of great personal charm and long devotion to the public good.

[Reagan Papers in University of Texas Archives; J. H. Reagan, *Memoirs,* ed. by W. F. McCaleb (1906); manuscript biography by B. H. Good, Austin, Tex.; C. W. Ramsdell, *Reconstruction in Tex.* (1910); S. S. McKay, *Making the Tex. Constitution of 1876* (1924);

C. S. Potts, *Railroad Transportation in Tex.* (1909); *Galveston Daily News* and *Dallas Morning News,* Mar. 7, 1905; information from William M. W. Splawn, Interstate Commerce Commissioner.]   S. S. M.

REALF, RICHARD (June 14, 1834–Oct. 28, 1878), poet, abolitionist, was born at Framfield, Sussex, England. His father was a rural constable, probably Richard Realf (or Relfe); his mother was Martha (Highland). A precocious child, writing lines in verse before he was nine years of age, he early attracted the attention of people in higher grades of society, among them Lady Byron, and through such connections obtained greater educational advantages than might otherwise have come to him. At the age of seventeen he published some immature but promising poems under the title *Guesses at the Beautiful* (1852).

Following an unfortunate love affair he emigrated to America in 1854 and for the next two years was connected with the Five Points House of Industry in New York City. In the fall of 1856, stirred by the events in Kansas, he went west, where he acted as a newspaper correspondent. He met John Brown, 1800–1859 [q.v.], was a prominent member of Brown's convention at Chatham, Canada, in May 1858, and was chosen secretary of state in Brown's mysterious scheme of government for the new era of freedom he aimed to bring about. Realf did not remain to see the actual working out of Brown's plans, but sailed for England in the summer of 1858 and did not return until the following year. When he did return it was to a Southern port and he seems at this time to have joined the Roman Catholic Church and even to have considered studying for the priesthood. He was still in the South when, in October 1859, John Brown led the attack on Harpers Ferry; nevertheless he was arrested, and before the Senate committee of investigation was questioned at length regarding his association with Brown.

In 1862 he enlisted in the 88th Illinois Regiment, in which he later received a commission and served to the end of the war. Afterwards he was for a time on reconstruction duty with a negro regiment in the South. In 1872 he entered upon newspaper work in Pittsburgh and remained there for about five years, achieving considerable reputation also as a public lecturer on temperance and on literary and patriotic subjects. An illness in the fall of 1877 caused almost complete blindness, and when he was able to leave the hospital friends provided the means for him to go to the Pacific Coast. He arrived in San Francisco, badly broken in health, in the early part of July 1878. He sought a position in the United States mint but had to be content for the time with a laborer's job. Ill health and accumulation of domestic troubles, which pursued him even to the Pacific Coast, drove him to contemplate suicide, and in an Oakland hotel, on Oct. 28, 1878, he ended his struggle by poison. A poem written in sonnet form which was found by his bedside contained in its last two lines his farewell and his apologia:

"He loved his fellows, and their love was sweet—
Plant daisies at his head and at his feet."

His friend, Richard J. Hinton, describes Realf as slight and graceful in figure, about five feet five inches in height, with a well-shaped head and fine features. His poems, scattered through many magazines and newspapers, were collected and published in 1898 as *Poems by Richard Realf, Poet, Soldier, Workman*. His verse is marked by fine rhythm and melody, and at times, particularly in his patriotic poems, has a passion akin to the recorded passion of his oratory. Through all his life, tragedy seemed to pursue him and his melancholy reflects itself in many lines of his verses. His domestic relations were most unhappy and entangled his career. He was married three times: in 1865 to Sophia Emery Graves, to whom he never returned after his military service in Mississippi, apparently believing her dead; in 1867, to Catherine Cassidy, whom he divorced in 1873, only to have the divorce set aside on a technicality after he had married his third wife, who bore him one child, then triplets. His search for consolation in religion seems to have been unavailing. In the end he gave up the struggle. His grave is in Lone Mountain Cemetery, overlooking San Francisco Bay.

[Sources include: R. J. Hinton, memoir, in *Poems by Richard Realf* (1898); *Lippincott's Mag.*, Mar. 1879; *Midland Monthly*, Aug. 1895, repr. in *The Agora* (Lawrence, Kan.), Nov. 1895; Realf's testimony before the Senate committee, *Sen. Report No. 278*, 36 Cong., 1 Sess., pp. 90–113; information affording clues to Realf's parentage from Rev. Arthur Haire, Framfield, Sussex, and Rev. Clarence Gee, Delaware, Ohio; obituary in *San Francisco Chronicle*, Oct. 30, 1878. In Mary E. Jackson's novel, *The Spy of Osawotamie* (1881), the character of Hayden Douglas is said by the author to impersonate Richard Realf.]   F. L.

REAM, NORMAN BRUCE (Nov. 5, 1844–Feb. 9, 1915), capitalist, was the son of Levi and Highly (King) Ream. His father, a lifelong resident of Somerset County, Pa., where Norman was born, was of German descent; his mother was of Scotch and English ancestry. The family lived on a farm, but farm life was not to the young boy's taste, and at fourteen he was earning money by teaching in the country school. He began, also, to take photographs with the ambrotype and was getting on in a small way

with this venture when the Civil War broke out. Enlisting with the 85th Pennsylvania Volunteers in 1861, he was commissioned first lieutenant, Dec. 14, 1862, and served until forced to resign because of numerous wounds in 1864. After the war, he spent a year in a commercial college and then opened a general store at Harnedsville, Pa. At the end of one year he sold out his interest to his partner, and in 1866 went to Princeton, Ill., where he conducted a general store until he suffered heavy loss from fire. Pushing on to Osceola, Iowa, he engaged in the business of buying and selling grain, livestock, and agricultural implements. Two years of short crops put him out of business and in 1871 he was in Chicago, heavily in debt.

His courage and tenacity were invincible, however. He began buying and selling hogs in a small way in the Chicago Union Stock Yards, and finally was able to go into the livestock commission business. The business succeeded and in four years he had made enough money to pay off his debts and buy a membership on the Board of Trade. He was a successful speculator from the start. He acted as broker for Philip Danforth Armour [*q.v.*] in the big pork deal of 1879, and this venture was the beginning of his fortune. He was successively a partner in several grain commission houses, and from 1883 to 1886, with John Cudahy, Charles Singer, and Nathaniel C. Jones, he was a power in the speculative markets for grain and provisions. He invested large amounts of money in Chicago real estate and enjoyed the confidence of the elder Marshall Field [*q.v.*], who was pursuing a like policy. He acquired extensive holdings in ranch properties in several of the western states, in Kentucky, and in Illinois. By 1888 this first phase of his business career may be said to have been completed. He retired from the Board of Trade, having discovered a new and more attractive field for his business genius.

As early as 1883 he had reorganized the Western Fire Insurance Company. He now became interested in railroad organization and was a heavy investor in railroad stocks. He became a member of the New York Stock Exchange, and in 1895 moved to New York City. Here he enjoyed the confidence of J. P. Morgan the elder and worked in close cooperation with him in organizing the railroad and steel industries. He served on the executive committee of several railroads and carried through a successful financial reorganization of the Baltimore & Ohio. In 1898 he organized the National Biscuit Company, of which he continued as a director, and the Federal Steel Company, one of the companies which later became a part of the United States Steel Corporation. With the Federal Company, Ream consolidated the Minnesota Iron Company, which included railroad and steamship lines and 150,000 acres of mineral lands, the Illinois Steel Company, and the Elgin, Joliet & Eastern Railway. By 1904 he was rated as one of the leading capitalists of the country. A financial editor writing of him at that time says, "He is probably the only greatly successful man in the United States who has no enemies" (Lefevre, *post*, p. 87). He was genial and pleasant socially, always approachable. The key to his character and one of the chief causes of his success was his absolute confidence in the rightness of his judgments. He was married, Feb. 17, 1876, to Caroline Putnam, daughter of Dr. John Putnam of Madison, N. Y., who with three of their seven children survived him.

[L. S. Dickey, *Hist. of the Eighty-fifth Regiment of Pa. Volunteer Infantry, 1861–1865* (1915); *Am. Elevator and Grain Trade*, June 15 and Oct. 15, 1886, Feb. 15, 1915; *The Biog. Dict. and Portrait Gallery of Representative Men of Chicago* (1892); A. T. Andreas, *Hist. of Chicago*, vol. III (1886); *N. Y. Tribune*, Feb. 10, 1915; Edwin Lefevre, "Interesting Personalities in the Business World," *Cosmopolitan*, May 1904; C. H. Taylor, *Hist. of the Board of Trade of the City of Chicago* (1917), II, 752–58; *Industrial Chicago*, IV (1894), 366–73.]   E. A. D.

RECTOR, HENRY MASSEY (May 1, 1816– Aug. 12, 1899), planter, lawyer, governor of Arkansas, was born in Louisville, Ky., the son of Elias and Fannie Bardella (Thruston) Rector. He was a descendant of John Jacob Rechtor who emigrated from Saxony and settled in Fauquier County, Va., in 1714. Elias moved to St. Louis and died when Henry was a boy of six. At the age of nineteen he went to Arkansas to look after the extensive land claims his father had held in and around Hot Springs. Several individuals and the United States claimed these lands and Rector spent many years and thousands of dollars in litigation. In 1875 the claim of the United States was sustained by the Supreme Court, but Congress later created a commission with authority to sell lots at a nominal price to the claimants who had made improvements thereon. Rector had thirty-two houses occupied by renters, but the commission awarded them to the occupants. Although the decision of the commission was to be final he appealed, in most of the cases successfully. For years afterwards, when a shot was heard in town, some one would exclaim, "Look out, old Governor Rector is collecting his rent."

In 1842 Rector was appointed marshal by President Tyler. From 1848 to 1852 he served in the state Senate. In 1854 he began to practise law in Little Rock and the next year was elected to the House of Representatives. The "Johnson Dynasty," desiring to shelve him, elected him a judge of the supreme court in 1859 and the following year, by clever manipulation of the state convention, nominated Richard H. Johnson for governor. In order to break the hold of the "dynasty," Rector resigned from the supreme court and made a successful contest for the governorship. Two years later, however, the "dynasty" had its revenge when the secession convention so altered the constitution as to terminate Rector's term of office at the end of two years, although the four-year term for other officials was not shortened. Rector unsuccessfully fought this action in the courts (24 *Arkansas*, 1–6). He ran for reëlection, but was defeated. A secessionist from the beginning, he persuaded a reluctant legislature to call a secession convention. To Secretary Cameron's request for Arkansas troops, he replied: "None will be furnished. The demand is only adding insult to injury" (Hempstead, *post*, I, 212–13), and he was delighted when the convention reassembled and voted secession with only one negative vote. The Johnson faction was ready to embarrass him at every turn, however. Gen. T. C. Hindman [*q.v.*], who had supported him in 1860, turned against him, largely because of differences over martial law and conscription. Rector differed with the Richmond government over taking Arkansas troops out of the state, even threatening to secede from the Confederacy, but at heart he was loyal. That he had no confidence in the success of the Union army and the emancipation proclamation is shown by the fact that he bought a negro boy in December 1862.

Following the war, he looked after his plantation in Pulaski County and his claims in Hot Springs. He was a member of the constitutional convention of 1874. In October 1838 he married Jane Elizabeth Field, a niece of Gov. John Pope. She died in 1857, and in February 1860 he married Ernestine Flora Linde, of Memphis. By his first wife he was the father of four sons and two daughters; by his second of one daughter.

[*Jour. of Both Sessions of the Convention of the State of Ark.* (1861); John Hallum, *Biog. and Pictorial Hist. of Ark.* (1887); Fay Hempstead, *Hist Rev. of Ark.* (1911), vol. I; D. T. Herndon, *Centennial Hist. of Ark.* (1922), I, 275–76; D. Y. Thomas *Ark. in War and Reconstruction, 1861–1874* (1926); J. H. Shinn, *Pioneers and Makers of Ark.* (copr 1908); *Ark. Gazette* (Little Rock), Aug. 13, 1899 papers in the possession of Henry M. Rector, a grandson.]   D. Y. T.

RED CLOUD (1822–Dec. 10, 1909), chief of the Oglalas, the largest tribe of the Teton Sioux, was born on Blue Creek, two days' travel by pony above the site of North Platte, Nebr. His father, Lone Man, belonged to the Brulé tribe of Teton Sioux and his mother, Walks as She Thinks, was perhaps a cousin, recognized as a sister, of Old Smoke, described by Parkman in *The California and Oregon Trail* (1849). He early became noted as a warrior and, before he left the warpath, had made a record of eighty individual feats of courage. By the early sixties he led an independent band of his own. In June 1866, as head of the Oglalas and accepted leader of all the Sioux and Cheyenne hostiles, he attended the council at Fort Laramie, but, on learning that the government intended to proceed with the opening of the Bozeman trail and the building of three forts, he defiantly stalked from the meeting and began war. For two years he kept the trail and the forts, which were built with great difficulty, closely besieged. He commanded the hostilities at the Fetterman massacre in December 1866 and at the Wagon Box fight in August 1867. Another part of his command attacked the Hayfield party near Fort C. F. Smith. His resolute campaign induced the government to yield, and by the treaty of 1868 the trail was closed and the three forts were abandoned. Thereafter he was an advocate of peace. In 1870 he visited Washington and New York (*Report of Board of Indian Commissioners, post,* pp. 47–49). Though a persistent critic of the government and of its Indian agents, whom he charged with graft and fraud, he openly opposed the agitation for war in 1876. He remained at loggerheads with the government's representatives. In 1881, on his sending to President Garfield a letter threatening that unless the President removed the agent, V. T. McGillycuddy, he would do so himself, McGillycuddy deposed him from the chieftainship of the Oglalas. From that time, shorn of his power and much of his influence, he lived quietly. After the removal of the tribe to the Pine Ridge agency in South Dakota, he aged rapidly and became blind and decrepit. He died at his Pine Ridge home.

Red Cloud is described by Cook as "a magnificent specimen of physical manhood" who in his prime was "as full of action as a tiger" (*post,* p. 234). He had great dignity of manner and has been spoken of as a natural-born gentleman. His character has been variously appraised. He was charged with duplicity, both in 1876 and in 1890, in secretly encouraging the hostiles while professing peace. Cook, who knew him more intimately than any other white man, asserts that he was sincere and that his efforts for peace caused him great loss of prestige. Among the whites he had many admirers. One of the important associations of his life was his friendship with Othniel C. Marsh, the geologist [*q.v.*]. Though counseling loyalty to the government, he was unfriendly to the ways of civilization. He accepted, however, some Christian ideas, and in later life he was inclined to Roman Catholicism.

[Doane Robinson, "The Education of Red Cloud," *S. D. Hist. Colls.,* vol. XII (1924); J. H. Cook, *Fifty Years on the Old Frontier* (1923); G. R. Hebard and E. A. Brininstool, *The Bozeman Trail* (2 vols., 1922); W. K. Moorehead, *The American Indian* (1914); *Second Ann. Report of the Board of Indian Commissioners . . . 1870* (1871); *Report of the Special Commission Appointed to Investigate the Affairs of the Red Cloud Indian Agency, July 1875* (1875); *Daily Argus-Leader* (Sioux Falls, S. D.), Dec. 21, 1909; place and date of birth from James H. Cook, Agate, Nebr.]

W. J. G.

RED EAGLE [See WEATHERFORD, WILLIAM, 1765–1824].

RED JACKET (*c.* 1758–Jan. 20, 1830), Seneca chief, was probably born at Canoga in what is now Seneca County, N. Y. His English name was derived from his wearing a succession of red jackets, the first of which was given him by a British officer. His Indian name, Sagoyewatha, awarded him on election to chiefship, was an honorable name in his, the Wolf, clan, signifying, in allusion to a wolf's nocturnal howling, "he keeps them awake." In active fighting he was accused of being cowardly and was ridiculed by both Brant and Cornplanter; but skill in oratory and political trickery served his ambitions for leadership. In 1779 during Sullivan's destructive campaign against the Iroquois, he curried favor by attacking the leaders and their unsuccessful policy. At the Indian council at the mouth of the Detroit River in 1786 he echoed popular passions by haranguing against the whites and peace, while other chiefs bowed to what seemed to be inevitable. Successively, in 1787, 1788, and 1790 he played for popularity by opposing land sales, though, fearful for his prestige with the whites, he signed secretly when the agreements were once completed. He advanced in influence while his powerful rival, Cornplanter, declined. In 1791 he was able to halt Col. Thomas Proctor's mission to the Miami, which Cornplanter favored. Then, with his position as a great chief among the Iroquois assured, he matured more statesmanlike policies. Peace with the United States became his aim and avoidance of the toils of British diplomacy. Vainly, he fought to maintain the independence and authority of his people. In 1801 he protested at Washington against the Pennsylvania frontiersmen and in 1821, in the case of Tommy Jemmy, valiantly but unsuccessfully strove to preserve the right of separate Iroquois customs and jurisdiction. He vainly sought in the council on the Sandusky River in 1816 to arouse the tribes to united but peaceful resistance to land sales and encroachments.

He combined an active intelligence and an extraordinary memory with real talent for oratory. Translations of his speeches, now extant, exhibit dramatic organization and effective argument, while contemporaries testified to the skill of their presentation (see *A Long-Lost Speech of Red Jacket*, ed. by J. W. Sanborn, 1912, for example). He is best known for his opposition to white civilization, although in 1792 while on a mission to President Washington he sanctioned moves toward bringing white culture to the Iroquois. Soon, however, he was depressed by the degeneration and decline of his people and reverted to his basic belief that the two races were fated by the creating god to different customs. By 1805 he set his face inflexibly against all change in language, creed, or blood. Most of all he eloquently opposed the establishment of missions and the activities of missionaries. After 1815, when the death of Farmer's brother, the decline of Cornplanter, and the Canadian residence of Brant put Red Jacket at the height of his power, his policy was to drive all white men from the reservations. The appeal of the pagan party under his leadership to Governor Clinton and the New York state legislature obtained the law of 1821 protecting the reservations, and in 1824 he insisted upon its enforcement for the removal of the missionaries. Only gradually, as the growth of the Christian party among the Senecas diminished his influence, were they permitted to return. By 1827 increased dissipation had robbed him of ability and prestige, and his rancorous doctrines had estranged his people. In council assembled they deposed him as chief. Shaking off his habits, he roused himself to a last stand, appealed to Washington, defended himself successfully in a general Iroquois council, and was restored to his chieftainship. Then he fell back into sodden intemperance. Meanwhile, his second wife and his beloved stepchildren had become Christians. He died, childless, in an alien, Christian world and was buried, contrary to his wishes, with Christian funeral in the Christian cemetery of the mission on the reservation.

[W. L. Stone, *Life and Times of Red Jacket* (1841); J. N. Hubbard, *An Account of Sa-go-ye-wat-he* or

Red Jacket (1886); T. L. McKenney and James Hall, *Hist. of the Indian Tribes*, vol. I (1836); *Buffalo Hist. Soc. Pubs.*, vols. I–IV (1879–96); W. M. Beauchamp, *A Hist. of the N. Y. Iroquois* (1905); L. H. Morgan, *League of the Iroquois* (1851); E. H. Brush, *Iroquois Past and Present* (1901).]   R. A. W.

RED WING (*c.* 1750–*c.* 1825), chief of the Khemnichan band of Mdewakanton Sioux, was born probably in the vicinity of the present Red Wing, Minn. Though the name was hereditary, each of the chiefs who bore it appears to have had also an alternative name. Pike mentions this chief both as Talangamane (probably a misprint) and Tantangamini, translating the word into *Aile Rouge* and Red Wing (*post*, I, 69, 342, 347; for a discussion of the variants of the name see Kearny, *post*, pp. 100–01). He was not a chief's son but rising to command by his deeds as a warrior became, perhaps next to Wabasha [*q.v.*], the most powerful leader among the Mdewakanton Sioux. He also gained the reputation of being a seer, able to foretell events. In the War of 1812 he aided the British. He was in the attack on Fort Sandusky in 1813; he was probably in the battle on Mackinac Island, where Major Holmes, the American commander, was killed; and he certainly participated in the capture of Fort Shelby at Prairie du Chien on July 20, 1814. After the last-named engagement he represented himself as having a dream that the British would soon be driven away, leaving his people to the mercy of the Americans. He accordingly returned to the British commander his Royal George medal and announced a policy of peace with both red men and white (for a transcript of his speech in explanation see Anderson, *post*, pp. 197–98). By 1820, according to Kearny who twice met him in that year, he was distinguished for "his friendship & attachment to the Americans" (*post*, p. 101).

He is mentioned in most of the early travels of the region and almost always in terms of respect. The fame of his military record, which was an exceptional one since he is said never to have suffered a defeat, clung to him long after he had given up the warpath, and he was said by Beltrami who saw him in 1823 to have been regarded by his people with something akin to fear. The same writer described him as of hideous aspect, old, bent, and covered with scars but yet of a majestic bearing and deportment. Doty, who accompanied Governor Cass's expedition to the upper Mississippi in 1820, told of his pacific policy and related the incident of his asking Cass what he should do in the case of a band of Sauks and Foxes who a short time previously had waylaid a party of Sioux and killed them.

After listening to Cass's advice he promised that the matter would be settled without further bloodshed (*post,* pp. 218–19). His grand-daughter married Colonel Crawford, a man of wide business interests in Prairie du Chien and the Mackinac region, and through her a number of descendants trace their lineage to the chieftain. The place and date of his death are unknown.

["Jour. of S. W. Kearny," ed. by V. M. Porter, *Mo. Hist. Soc. Colls.,* vol. III (1908); "Papers of James Duane Doty," *Wis. Hist. Soc. Colls.,* vol. XIII (1895); "Personal Narrative of T. G. Anderson," *Ibid.,* vol. IX (1882); "Seventy-two Years' Recollections," *Ibid.,* vol. III (1857); W. H. Keating, *Narrative of an Expedition* (1824), I, 260; J. C. Beltrami, *A Pilgrimage in Europe and America* (1828), vol. II; H. R. Schoolcraft, *Summary Narrative of an Exploratory Expedition . . . in 1820* (1855); *The Expeditions of Zebulon Montgomery Pike* (1895), vol. I, ed. by Elliott Coues.]
W. J. G.

REDFIELD, AMASA ANGELL (May 19, 1837–Oct. 19, 1902), lawyer, legal author, was born at Clyde, Wayne County, N. Y., the son of Luther and Eliza (Angell) Redfield and a lineal descendant of William Redfin who was in Massachusetts as early as 1639 and later settled near New London, Conn. On his mother's side he claimed descent from Roger Williams. He was educated at a school in Bloomfield, N. J., and at the University of the City of New York (now New York University), from which he graduated in 1860. After graduation he entered at once upon the study of the law and was admitted to the New York bar in 1862. The following year he published *A Handbook of United States Tax Law.* When he began practice, which he did independently, he found that the decisions of the important surrogates' courts, which had original jurisdiction in all matters of wills and succession, had not been reported separately for some seven years. He undertook the task of reporting them and, with the assistance of Judge Bradford, who had edited reports of earlier surrogates' decisions, published in 1864 the first volume of *Reports of Cases Argued and Determined in the Surrogates' Courts of the State of New York.* Four other volumes followed, the last in 1882, and the whole series covered more than a score of years, "constituting a most valuable collection of decisions upon wills, trusts and administration of estates" (Lydecker, *post,* p. 108). A fitting sequel to the series was the author's *Law and Practice of Surrogates' Courts* (1875) which by 1903 had passed through six editions. Redfield, however, was far more than a writer of books, for this early specialization in a highly litigious field brought him clients and led to his employment in important cases. Among them was that involving the will of Maria Forman, who, while insane, had de-

stroyed two wills which she had executed almost simultaneously. Redfield's handling of the case, which was complicated, greatly enhanced his reputation.

Meanwhile he had ventured into another field of the law for his researches. With his friend Thomas G. Shearman, he prepared and published *A Treatise on the Law of Negligence* (1869). Like his other textbooks, this was a marked success. It passed through five editions under his editorship and was long recognized as the leading work on the subject. His achievements at the bar enabled him to form desirable connections with various legal firms, and from 1885 to 1897 he lectured at his Alma Mater on testamentary subjects. He also became interested in the history of the law. Before the state bar association in 1899 he described "A Case of *Laesae Majestatis* in New Amsterdam in 1647," and he accumulated a large amount of material for a projected juridical history of New York. In the last decade of the nineteenth century he retired from active practice and took up his residence in Farmington, Conn., where he became successively senior burgess, park commissioner, and finally a delegate to the Connecticut constitutional convention of 1902, in which he took an influential part. Stricken with illness in March of that year, he lingered until autumn when he passed away. His wife was Sarah Louise Cooke, whom he had married on May 6, 1863. They had two children.

[See: C. E. Lydecker, memorial in *Asso. of the Bar of the City of N. Y., Ann. Reports,* 1903; *Who's Who in America,* 1901–02; J. H. Redfield, *Geneal. Hist. of the Redfield Family* (1860); *N. Y. Times,* Oct. 20, 1902.]
C. S. L.

REDFIELD, ISAAC FLETCHER (Apr. 10, 1804–Mar. 23, 1876), judge, author, was born in Weathersfield, Windsor County, Vt., the son of Dr. Peleg and Hannah (Parker) Redfield. He was descended from William Redfin who was an early emigrant to Massachusetts and later settled in New London, Conn. After graduating from Dartmouth College in 1825 he studied law and was admitted to the bar of Orleans County, Vt., in 1827. He began practice at Derby and from 1832 to 1835 he was state's attorney for the county. In the latter year, although he was but thirty-one and of a different political faith from the majority of the legislature, he was elected by that body to the state supreme court. By annual reëlections he served there until 1860, longer than any other member up to his time, and for the last eight years he was chief justice. After his elevation to the bench he took up his residence in Montpelier, but in 1846 he purchased the former

439

homestead of Judge Chase at Randolph Center and lived there for a few years. He then made his home in Windsor until 1861. As a jurist he studied widely the general field of jurisprudence as well as current decisions in the United States and England. It has been said of his opinions that they are "more distinguished in the line of equity and railway law than any other department. He did much towards tempering the rules of the common law by an infusion of equity principles . . . and while he followed the cases, he questioned the authority of those which controverted sound principles or led to unjust judgments. He looked upon the law as a broad and noble science, not a mass of arbitrary rules," and "he probably did as much in determining the great questions that arose during the development of the railroad system in America as any other judge" (Taft, *post*, pp. 128–29).

Toward the close of his judicial career Redfield took on other tasks, publishing in 1858 his *Practical Treatise upon the Law of Railways,* which appeared in various later editions. From 1858 to 1861 he was professor of medical jurisprudence at Dartmouth College, but after his retirement from the bench he removed to Boston and devoted himself more exclusively to legal authorship. In 1864 he published the first part of his *Law of Wills* to which he added two succeeding volumes (3rd ed., 3 vols., 1869–70). His *Law of Carriers . . . and the Law of Bailments* appeared in 1869 and in 1870 his *Leading American Railway Cases,* to which a second volume was added in the edition of 1872. Besides these original works he prepared editions of Story's *Conflict of Laws* and *Equity Pleading,* published in 1865 and 1870, and Greenleaf's *Evidence,* published in 1866. For the last fourteen years of his life he was the New England editor of the *American Law Register.* In 1867 he was appointed special counsel for the United States, in conjunction with Caleb Cushing, to prosecute claims in the British courts for property held by Confederates and for losses caused by privateers fitted out in England. His duties took him to that country and kept him there for some two years, affording an experience which he thoroughly enjoyed. His death occurred at Charlestown, Mass., as a result of pneumonia, and he was interred at his old home in Windsor. He was twice married: on Sept. 28, 1836, to Mary Ward Smith of Stanstead, Quebec, and on May 4, 1842, to Catharine Blanchard Clark, of St. Johnsbury. No children of either marriage survived him.

[See: W. B. C. Stickney, "Isaac Fletcher Redfield," in *Great Am. Lawyers,* vol. V (1908), ed. by W. D.

Lewis; R. S. Taft, "The Supreme Court of Vt.," *Green Bag,* Mar. 1894; 36 *Vt.,* 762–68; J. G. Ullery, *Men of Vt.* (1894), pt. 1, pp. 181–82; J. H. Redfield, *Geneal. Hist. of the Redfield Family* (1860); *Albany Law Jour.,* Apr. 1, 1876; *Burlington Free Press and Times,* Mar. 25, 1876.]   C. S. L.

REDFIELD, JUSTUS STARR (Jan. 2, 1810–Mar. 24, 1888), publisher, was born at Wallingford, Conn., the eldest son of William Redfield and Sarah Dejean, his wife. He was descended from William Redfin who came from England to Massachusetts as early as 1639 and later settled near New London, Conn. The year of Justus' birth his parents moved to Weathersfield, Vt., and in 1812 to Charleston, N. H. There Redfield attended school. About 1827 he went to Boston, and then to New York, where he became a printer. In 1834 he took over the *Family Magazine* founded the year before by Origen Bacheler in imitation of the London *Penny Magazine* of Charles Knight and the Society for the Diffusion of Useful Knowledge. It offered, at $1.50 a year, "systematic courses of general knowledge," and was one of the earliest American periodicals to be well illustrated. Many of the cuts were by Redfield's brother, W. D. Redfield, who died early, and by the celebrated engraver, Benson J. Lossing [*q.v.*], whom Redfield brought to New York to edit the magazine from June 1839 until its suspension in May 1841. Earlier editors were Thomas Allen (1834–36) and an "association of gentlemen" headed by Dr. Augustus Sidney Doane. Frequency of publication varied, and the work was reprinted in Cincinnati, and in part in Philadelphia.

Upon the cessation of the magazine, Redfield opened a bookstore, and during the period 1841 to 1860 was identified with successful printing and general publishing. In addition to a large miscellaneous list, he prided himself on publishing an edition (1854) of John Wilson's *Noctes Ambrosianæ* from *Blackwood's*; works of William Maginn, John Doran, Cornelius Mathews (whose friend George L. Duyckinck [*q.v.*] was a special partner of Redfield from 1855 to 1860); Fitz-Greene Halleck; and Robert Montgomery Bird's *Nick of the Woods* (1853). Impressed by reading *The Yemassee* in youth, Redfield produced an edition of Simms; and through Rufus W. Griswold [*q.v.*] he became the publisher of Alice Carey. Through Griswold, too, came Redfield's greatest opportunity, for despite their unfriendly relations in life, Edgar Allan Poe had appointed Griswold his literary executor, and Mrs. Clemm, Poe's mother-in-law and heir, had commissioned him to collect Poe's works. These he offered vainly to several publishers before Redfield decided to risk an edition. Two volumes, dated 1850, were brought out as an experiment; a third, with Griswold's unfriendly memoir, later the same year; and a fourth, completing the set, in 1856. The work was done, according to Redfield, without financial remuneration to Griswold; editorially the work was fair for the time, and the set was a great success financially. Royalties were at first paid to Mrs. Clemm, but when she wished to enter the Church Home in Baltimore, she needed $250, and for this sum, advanced after hesitation, Redfield became the owner of the copyrights and plates. His firm also published in 1853 the writings of William H. Seward, and a life of him by George E. Baker.

When the Nassau Bank was founded in New York by a former associate of Redfield, named McElrath, the publisher became a director. In 1860 his firm was succeeded by that of W. J. Widdleton, and the next year Redfield became consul at Otranto. He was transferred in 1864 to Brindisi whence, upon resigning, he returned home in 1866. In Europe he seems to have associated with liberals. He "edited" Jean Macé's *Histoire d'une Bouchée de Pain* (Paris, 1861) and controlled the American translation of this physiology and natural history for children; he also translated Henrietta Caracciolo's *The Mysteries of Neapolitan Convents* (1867) and had a hand in a *Traveler's Guide to the City of New York* (1871). He lived at last in retirement, at Florence, Burlington County, N. J. There, on Mar. 24, 1888, he took laudanum and slashed his wrists, asking to be buried without ceremony under an apple tree. He had married, in 1835, Elizabeth C. Hall, who died in 1842 soon after bearing a son. He had another son, born to his second wife, Elizabeth Eaton Jones, and three daughters. At the time of his death, according to the *New York Times* (Mar. 26, 1888), his wife was in an asylum at Trenton.

[J. H. Redfield, *Geneal. Hist. of the Redfield Family* (1860); J. C. Derby, *Fifty Years among Authors, Books, and Publishers* (1884), whose account of the circumstances of the publishing of the Poe edition, obtained from Redfield himself, seems to agree with all known facts; *Appletons' Ann. Cyc. for 1888* (1889); F. L. Mott, *Hist. of Am. Magazines, 1741–1850* (1930).]
T. O. M.

REDFIELD, WILLIAM C. (Mar. 26, 1789– Feb. 12, 1857), saddler and harness maker, meteorologist, transportation promoter, was born at Middletown, Conn., the eldest of the six children of Peleg and Elizabeth (Pratt) Redfield. The middle initial, C, was not in his name when he was christened, but was added by him later to avoid confusion, since there were two other William Redfields in his vicinity. The C, he was

accustomed to say, stood for "Convenience." On his father's side he was of the sixth generation from one William Redfin, Redfen, Redfyn, or Redfyne, who was living in Massachusetts as early as 1639 and about 1653 settled near New London, Conn. Peleg Redfield died Sept. 10, 1802, leaving his family in straitened circumstances. William, thirteen years of age, was apprenticed the next year to a saddle and harness maker at Upper Middletown (now Cromwell), Conn. What spare time he had evenings he spent in studying science by the light of a wood-fire. During the latter part of his apprenticeship he and certain other young men of the village formed a debating society, the "Friendly Association," in which he took great interest. His chief inspiration, though, came from Dr. William Tully, a well-informed local physician, to whose excellent library young Redfield had free access.

In 1804, the year his apprenticeship began, William's widowed mother married Nathan Sears and in 1806, with an ox team, moved with him, his nine children, and her four youngest, to Portage County, Ohio. As soon as his apprenticeship was over William set out afoot to visit her. This seven-hundred-mile trip, much of it along mere trails and through forests, he accomplished in twenty-seven days, of which four were given to resting. During the journey he kept an excellent and interesting diary of his experiences and observations. The next year, 1811, he tramped back along a more southern route to Middletown. Here he worked at his trade and also ran a small store. All the time, however, he gave every possible moment to the study of science. On Sept. 3, 1821, came the "great September gale." Shortly after its occurrence he went on a trip to western Massachusetts and from the lay of the trees felled by the wind and the times of the storm's occurrence at various places he concluded that it had been a progressive whirlwind. It was not until April 1831, however, that, in the *American Journal of Science and Arts,* he brought this correct and fundamental concept of the nature of such storms to the attention of the public, in an article entitled "Remarks on the Prevailing Storms of the Atlantic Coast of the North American States." In October 1833 he set forth in the same journal the facts he had noted and described the behavior of this storm so fully and so accurately as to make his paper, the first of importance on this subject, a meteorological classic ("Observations on the Hurricanes and Storms of the West Indies and the Coast of the United States"). This knowledge of the hurricane he immediately put to use by devising a set of practical rules by which the mariner could know where he was, in such a storm, and what to do to avoid its greatest danger.

His interests were varied. As early as 1820 his attention was directed towards steamboat navigation. Soon after this, when travel by boat had fallen off owing to a number of disastrous explosions, he devised and put into successful operation between New York and Albany a line of "safety barges." The barge, or passenger boat, was towed by the steamboat at a sufficient distance to be safe in case of a boiler explosion. The public soon went back to the cheaper and faster, if less safe, mode of travel, however, and the barges were then used to carry freight. Thus was begun a method of river shipment that still is in force after the lapse of more than a hundred years. He also was interested in railroads, and as early as 1829 published a pamphlet of great foresight on a proposed railroad to connect the Hudson and the Mississippi rivers (*Sketch of the Geographical Rout* [*sic*] *of a Great Railway* . . ., 1829). A second and enlarged edition was issued in 1830. He likewise advocated the construction of other railroads, among them one from New York to Albany, which he urged despite the fact that he was then financially interested in travel and shipment between these points by boat and barge. In 1848 he was elected the first president of the American Association for the Advancement of Science, an organization he had materially helped to found, and presided at its meetings in September of that year in Philadelphia.

On Oct. 15, 1814, he married Abigail Wilcox, daughter of Eliphalet and Abigail (Shephard) Wilcox of Upper Middletown, Conn.; she died May 12, 1819. By this marriage he had three sons, the youngest of whom, Charles Bailey, became the father of William Cox Redfield [*q.v.*]. On Nov. 23, 1820, he married Lucy Wilcox, daughter of Seth and Hannah Wilcox, of Stockbridge, Mass., and cousin of his first wife; she died Sept. 14, 1821. They had one son, who survived but a few days. His third wife, whom he married Dec. 9, 1828, was Jane Wallace, daughter of William Wallace, a New York merchant. They had no children. He died in New York City.

[Denison Olmsted, "Biog. Memoir of William C. Redfield," *Am. Jour. of Sci. and Arts,* Nov. 1857, containing bibliog. of writings; J. H. Redfield, *Geneal. Hist. of the Redfield Family* (1860); *N. Y. Tribune,* Feb. 13, 1857.]   W. J. H.

REDFIELD, WILLIAM COX (June 18, 1858–June 13, 1932), manufacturer, secretary of commerce, was born in Albany, N. Y., the son of Charles Bailey and Mary Ann (Wallace) Redfield, and the grandson of William C. Redfield [*q.v.*]. The family moved to Pittsfield, Mass., in 1867 and there William received his elementary and secondary school education. Obliged by financial adversity at an early age to earn a livelihood, he worked for a time in the Pittsfield post-office and as a salesman for a local paper company, and then sought employment in New York City in 1877. For a few years he was connected with R. Hoe & Company, manufacturers of printing presses, but withdrew in 1883. Soon afterward he associated himself with J. H. Williams & Company of Brooklyn, who made drop forgings; for the next thirty years he was engaged chiefly in the manufacture and exporting of machinery and other iron and steel products. He became treasurer and later president of the Williams Company and had an important part in the direction of several other companies. In 1905, through the influence of Grover Cleveland, Redfield was elected to the board of the Equitable Life Assurance Society and served as a director until 1913.

His participation in politics began in 1896 when he was chosen a delegate to the convention of the Gold Democrats at Indianapolis. In the autumn of that year he unsuccessfully sought election to Congress as a Gold Democrat. In 1902 he was appointed commissioner of public works of Brooklyn in the administration of Seth Low [*q.v.*], and for two years waged a vigorous campaign to enforce compliance with the law by the public utility corporations within the borough. Also he was able to terminate the "reign of the cobblestones" in Brooklyn and to institute the use of modern paving. One hundred miles of new paving were laid in the two years of his commissionership. In 1910 he accepted a Democratic nomination for Congress and won by a substantial majority in the normally Republican fifth district. His outstanding contribution during his term was a powerful speech in behalf of a bill for tariff reduction (June 12, 1911, *Congressional Record,* 62 Cong., 1 Sess., pp. 1939–47); over a million copies of his speech were printed and circulated in 1912 by the Democratic National Committee. That same year he formally announced his candidacy for the vice-presidential nomination of his party; failing to receive it and not wishing to accept a renomination for Congress, he devoted his efforts to the success of the national ticket. Woodrow Wilson cheerfully acknowledged his indebtedness to Redfield's cogent tariff arguments (R. S. Baker and W. E. Dodd, *The Pub-*

lic Papers of Woodrow Wilson, II, 1925, pp. 330, 335, 339), and in recognition of Redfield's practical knowledge of business affairs appointed him secretary of commerce in March 1913.

Redfield entered upon his work with great enthusiasm and in the next six years reorganized and enlarged the Bureau of Foreign and Domestic Commerce, instituted the commercial attaché service, strengthened the Bureau of Standards as a valuable adjunct of war work, and actively associated himself with the Council of National Defense and War Trade Board. A resourceful and progressive administrator and a keen student of economic tendencies, Redfield proved a serviceable cabinet officer. It was with much reluctance that the President accepted his resignation on Nov. 1, 1919. After his retirement Redfield engaged in banking and insurance business in New York City and Brooklyn, but he was also connected with numerous civic organizations and shared in various philanthropic enterprises in his community. He was the author of *The New Industrial Day* (1912), *With Congress and Cabinet* (1924), *Dependent America* (1926), *We and the World* (1927); he also published an extended series of articles, "Glimpses of Our Government," in the *Saturday Evening Post*, May 1924–January 1925. He died in New York City. His wife, Elise Mercein Fuller, to whom he was married on Apr. 8, 1885, and a son and a daughter survived him.

[Redfield's *With Congress and Cabinet* (1924) is partly autobiographical. See also *Official Cong. Directory*, July 1919; J. H. Redfield, *Geneal. Hist. of the Redfield Family* (1860); *Who's Who in Am.*, 1930–31; *N. Y. Times*, Mar. 4, 1913; June 14, 1932; *N. Y. Herald Tribune*, June 14, 1932.]   A. H. M.

REDMAN, JOHN (Feb. 27, 1722–Mar. 19, 1808), physician, the son of Joseph and Sarah Redman, was born in Philadelphia, Pa. After a preliminary classical education he was apprenticed to the morose and churlish-tempered John Kearsley [*q.v.*], a physician of Philadelphia. He later practised medicine in Bermuda, and, after saving some money and acquiring a small amount from his father's estate, went to Europe to complete his education. A year in Edinburgh (1746), where he took notes on the lectures of Alexander Monro *primus* and Charles Alston (now preserved in the College of Physicians, Philadelphia), was followed by study at the University of Leyden, where he was graduated M.D., July 15, 1748, his thesis being entitled, "De Abortu." After obtaining his degree he continued to study in Paris and London, in the latter city at Guy's Hospital. Returning to Philadelphia, he soon established

himself in practice, first in surgery and obstetrics, but later, owing to the delicacy of his health, he confined his work to medicine. He was an ardent disciple of Boerhaave and Sydenham, regulating his treatment of fevers by extreme depletion through purgation. In the yellow-fever epidemics of 1762 and 1793 in Philadelphia, he was the most strenuous advocate of saline purgatives as opposed to emetics and bleeding (*An Account of Yellow Fever as it Prevailed in Philadelphia in . . . 1762*, 1865). He also defended direct inoculation for smallpox (*A Defence of Inoculation*, 1759). He was a good physician for his time; well trained and well read, he exerted considerable influence by the use of Sydenham's principles of practice, by his assistance in establishing the College of Physicians of Philadelphia (1786), and by his education of young physicians, particularly John Morgan, Benjamin Rush, and Caspar Wistar [*qq.v.*].

Redman was one of the consulting physicians to the Pennsylvania Hospital (1751–80) and served as the first president of the College of Physicians of Philadelphia (1786–1804). Aside from his professional duties he served as a trustee of the College of New Jersey, an elder in the Presbyterian Church, trustee of the College of Philadelphia, and as a member of the Philadelphia Common Council (1751). He was also a member of the American Philosophical Society. His wife was Mary Sobers. Two sons died in infancy; a daughter married Daniel Coxe, one of the King's counsel of New Jersey, father of John Redman Coxe [*q.v.*]. Redman's position in American medicine is an unusual one. He lived just before the period of medical schools and therefore taught medicine by the apprentice system, but his pupils, Morgan and Rush, founded medical education in this country. His superior training and high ideals served well the succeeding generation.

[The principal biographical notice is in the *Philadelphia Medic. Museum (Medic. and Philosoph. Register)*, vol. V (1808). It is unsigned but was probably written by Redman's grandson, John Redman Coxe. See also: *Univ. of Pa. Medic. Bull.*, Feb. 1908; *Annals of Medic. Hist.*, Sept. 1926; *Trans. Coll. of Physicians of Phila.*, 3 ser. IX (1887); *Poulson's Am. Daily Advertiser*, Mar. 23, 1808.]   H. R. V.

REDPATH, JAMES (1833–Feb. 10, 1891), journalist, editor, lecture promoter, was born in Berwick-on-Tweed, Scotland, the son of James Redpath, who was Scotch, and Marie Ninian Davidson Redpath, who was English. The father, a man of some education, wished James to become a clergyman, and (though the boy had a fancy for the printing business) began his education with that in view. At sixteen James collaborated with his father in the writing of a little volume, *Tales and Traditions of the Border*. About 1850 the Redpath family emigrated to Michigan and settled on a farm. James soon found work in a printing office at Kalamazoo, twenty miles distant. A few months later he went to Detroit, where his writing attracted the attention of Horace Greeley, who offered him a position on the staff of the *New York Tribune*. Thus at nineteen, young Redpath formed a connection which continued intermittently during thirty years thereafter. The political troubles in Kansas attracted his attention, and he made several visits to that disturbed territory between 1854 and 1859, each time writing a series of newspaper articles which attracted wide attention. He had by this time become a fiery abolitionist. For the better part of his life he was an energetic reformer—always seething with ardor in some cause or other, scornful of compromise, his enthusiasm giving interest and often brilliancy to his writing. Between 1854 and 1860 he traveled through the Southern states, studying slavery and writing articles, some of which were published in 1859 under the title, *The Roving Editor, or Talks with Slaves in the Southern States*. Several more of his books came from the press in those two years— *A Handbook to Kansas Territory* (1859) ; *Echoes of Harper's Ferry* (1860) ; *The Public Life of Captain John Brown* (1860) ; and also *A Guide to Hayti* (1860), for he had pushed his research to that island and had decided that it would be a good asylum for Southern negroes.

In 1859 Redpath had been appointed commissioner of emigration in the United States by the Haitian president. He founded the Haitian Emigrant Bureau in Boston and New York, established a newspaper on the subject, and in the course of years sent several thousand ex-slaves to the negro republic. Later he became Haitian consul at Philadelphia and was instrumental in procuring recognition of Haitian independence by the government of the United States. During the Civil War he was a correspondent with the Union armies. At the close of the war he was made superintendent of education at Charleston, S. C., where he had much to do with reorganizing the school system of the state, especially colored schools. He likewise founded a colored orphan asylum, and in a little cemetery near Charleston established what was probably the first regular decoration of soldiers' graves in May of each year. Observing the need of an organized agency for the booking of lectures (which were important and popular functions

in those days), Redpath established such a business in 1868, at first calling it the Boston Lyceum Bureau, later substituting his own name for "Boston." Among his early clients were Emerson, Greeley, Beecher, Thoreau, Sumner, Bayard Taylor, Wendell Phillips, Mary A. Livermore, and Julia Ward Howe. A little later he began booking humorists, such as Mark Twain, Josh Billings, and Petroleum V. Nasby, and poets, who read their own writings. When he added magicians such as Kellar and Herrmann, there was some criticism, but he insisted that they had a legitimate place in platform entertainment. Next he took on musical soloists and quartettes, and finally organized small opera companies, or groups which gave a varied entertainment. By 1879 Redpath had become much interested in Ireland, and during the next two years he made two journeys to that country, writing journalistic letters which vigorously denounced English rule and landlordism. A volume of these letters was published as *Talks about Ireland* in 1881. In 1886 Redpath became an editor of the *North American Review* but relinquished the place in the following year when he suffered a slight stroke of paralysis. On Feb. 5, 1891, he was run over by a street car in New York City and died five days later. He had married, in 1888, Mrs. Caroline Chorpenning.

[C. F. Horner, *Life of James Redpath and the Development of the Modern Lyceum* (1926) ; *Proc. at a Farewell Dinner given by the Land League of N. Y. to Jas. Redpath, prior to his Departure for Ireland, Delmonico's, June 1, 1881*; obituaries in the New York newspapers, Feb. 11, 1891. Redpath's own writings give a good picture of his crusading years.] A. F. H.

REDWOOD, ABRAHAM (Apr. 15, 1709– Mar. 8, 1788), merchant, philanthropist, was born on the Island of Antigua. His father was Abraham Redwood, an Englishman, who, as a young man, commanded a ship which plied between London and the West Indies. In Jamaica, Captain Redwood met and married Mehetable Langford, the daughter of a wealthy planter, and through this connection became the owner of a valuable sugar plantation in Antigua and a large number of slaves. After his marriage he abandoned the sea, devoting himself to his business interests. He moved to America when his son, Abraham, was two years old, and the boy was educated in Philadelphia.

While still very young he began to assume a man's responsibilities. Early in his eighteenth year, Mar. 6, 1726, he married Martha, daughter of Abraham Coggeshall of Newport, R. I., and established a home in that city. Two years before, owing to the sudden death by accident of an elder brother, the family estate in Antigua, "Cassada Garden," had become his property. Abraham managed the plantation chiefly through the medium of overseers, sending its products to market in English, West Indian, and New England ports. Thus young Redwood was a shipowner and merchant as well as a planter. Though storms and blights at times interfered seriously with his crops, he was in the main highly successful. By the time he was forty he had established an ample fortune and was one of the group of merchant princes whose prosperity, educated tastes, and cosmopolitan sympathies made the Newport of that day a notable center of wealth and culture. Besides his home in the city, he owned an estate of 145 acres in nearby Portsmouth. Here he developed one of the first really pretentious botanical gardens in America. Not only did he cultivate plants native to the soil, but by means of hot-houses introduced all kinds of tropical fruits and flowers.

In Newport he became a member of the Philosophical Society, a Rhode Island institution which doubtless owed its existence to the influence of Bishop Berkeley. Its purpose was to conduct weekly debates on varied subjects—theological, political and literary. As time passed, it undertook the task of founding a public library. With a generosity which was characteristic, Abraham Redwood promptly announced his readiness to contribute five hundred pounds to the project. The gift was a munificent one for that period, and in recognition of it the new library was called by the donor's name. From its founding in 1747 a source of pride and distinction to the city, the Redwood Library in its early days attracted to Newport a cultivated group who were eager to avail themselves of its unusual opportunities for reading and study. Ezra Stiles [q.v.] was one of its librarians, taking the position apparently in order to have constant access to its books.

Redwood's memory owes its perpetuation to this gift, but his benevolence was not confined to it. He found special delight in assisting young men just starting in the business world. He had become a Quaker on his marriage, for his wife belonged to that sect, and in his will he left five hundred pounds to establish a Friends' school in Newport. His will also stipulated that five hundred pounds be given to the founding of a college in Rhode Island, provided that Newport be chosen as its site, a bequest which recalls the controversy between Newport and Providence, when what is now Brown University was in its infancy. He had six children, of whom three sons and a daughter reached maturity.

["Geneal. of the Redwood Family," in *Newport Hist. Mag.*, July 1880; C. P. and T. R. Coggeshall, *The Coggeshalls in America* (1930); J. N. Arnold, *Vital Record of R. I.*, vol. IV (1893), pt. 2, pp. 57, 111, and vol. XV (1906), p. 544; B. M. Bigelow, "Commerce of Rhode Island with the West Indies Before the American Revolution" (doctoral thesis, Brown Univ.); G. C. Mason, *Annals of the Redwood Lib. and Athenæum, Newport, R. I.* (1891); *Colls. Mass. Hist. Soc.*, 7 ser., vol. IX (1914); *A Short Sketch of the Redwood Lib. of Newport, R. I.* (1917); F. B. Dexter, *The Literary Diary of Ezra Stiles* (3 vols., 1901).]   E. R. B.

REED, DAVID (Feb. 6, 1790–June 7, 1870), Unitarian clergyman, editor, son of Rev. William and Olive (Pool) Reed, was born in Easton, Mass., in which town his father was for twenty-five years the Congregational minister. He was a descendant of William Reade who came from England to Boston in 1635 and was one of the early settlers of Weymouth. David graduated from Brown University in 1810. For two years thereafter he was principal of Plymouth Academy, Bridgewater, Mass., at the same time studying theology under Rev. Dr. Sanger of South Bridgewater. In 1813 he went to Cambridge and continued his theological studies at Harvard; the following year he was licensed to preach. From 1814 to 1821 he served churches in Maine, New Hampshire, Connecticut, and elsewhere, but declined to be permanently settled.

His contribution to his denomination and to the religious history of his time consisted in the establishment and publishing of a weekly periodical, and in the influence he exerted through this medium. Traveling about and coming into contact with conditions in different states, he became convinced that the liberal movement needed a weekly paper to disseminate information and to further the purification and greater effectiveness of the Christian faith. Accordingly, with the indorsement of William Ellery Channing and others, he founded the *Christian Register,* the first number of which appeared on Apr. 20, 1821. The venture succeeded and in the issue of Apr. 28, 1921, the paper commemorated the one hundredth anniversary of its first appearance. For some forty-five years Reed was its proprietor and for a considerable portion of this time, its editor, securing for its columns contributions from the leading Unitarians of the day. The period was marked by dissension in the Unitarian body, and also by extension in its organization and work, while the anti-slavery and other reforms were agitating the country at large. Living until after the Civil War, Reed exerted an influence which touched all these matters. He thought clearly, wrote with vigor, and was courageous in the support of the beliefs and measures of which he approved, thereby render-in-- service of value both to Unitarianism and to the cause of moral and civic welfare in general. On May 2, 1836, he was married at Providence, R. I., to Mary Ann, daughter of Capt. Howell Williams, by whom he had three children.

[J. L. Reed, *The Reed Geneal.* (copr. 1901); *Hist. Cat. of Brown Univ., 1764–1904* (1905); S. A. Eliot, *Heralds of a Liberal Faith* (1910), vol. II; G. W. Cooke, *Unitarianism in America* (1902); F. L. Mott, *A Hist. of Am. Magazines* (1930); *Christian Register,* June 11, 1870; *Boston Evening Transcript,* June 7, 1870.]   H. E. S.

REED, EARL HOWELL (July 5, 1863–July 9, 1931), author, etcher, was born in Geneva, Ill., son of Hiram V. and Elizabeth (Armstrong) Reed [*q.v.*], and brother of Myrtle Reed [*q.v.*]. Until middle life he followed a business career, but he also studied at the Art Institute of Chicago, taking up etching as a pastime, which in his later years became an absorbing vocation. He built a country home in the dune-country on the eastern shore of Lake Michigan, where the picturesque surroundings—miles of billowy, wind-blown wastes of sand—appealed to the artist in him, and their historic associations, to his love of romance. He wrote and illustrated with his etchings a number of books which sought to interpret the spirit of the region. Among them are *The Voices of the Dunes* (1912), *The Dune Country* (1916), *Sketches in Duneland* (1918), *Tales of a Vanishing River* (1920), *The Ghost in the Tower* (1921), and *The Silver Arrow* (1926). The frontispiece of *The Dune Country* is one of his most exquisite etchings of the dunes—gnarled trees, wind-blown clouds, and the hills in the distance. In "The Tryst," a black bird perched upon a bough is waiting expectant, and in "The Homing Call" a flock of ducks are flying over the marshes, while a heavy storm broods in the background. A feeling for design is felt in all his work. His etched portraits of some old Indians are also noteworthy. Of "Waukena" (in *The Silver Arrow*), a rugged Indian woman's face, with a grim and lofty reserve, he said: "The features were those of a mother of warriors." He made a set of etchings of the Field Museum and Jackson Park, Chicago, which are of historic value. In 1914 he published *Etching, A Practical Treatise,* a valuable work on the subject. He was mainly responsible for the existence of the Chicago Society of Etchers, established in 1910, and was its first president. His etching "The Edge of the Forest" was exhibited at the Paris Salon in 1912, with several of the Dune series; he exhibited in the principal cities of the United States, and his work is represented in the permanent collections of the Library of Congress, the New York Public Library, the Toledo Museum of Art, the Detroit Museum of Art, the Art Institute, Chicago, the St. Louis Museum of Art, and many private galleries. He was married twice: first to Carrie Collins of Norwood Park, Ill., June 12, 1882, by whom he had two children, and second, Oct. 14, 1922, to Emy Kummer of Chicago.

[W. H. de B. Nelson, "A Front Rank Man in American Etching," *International Studio,* Nov. 1913; Lena Macauley, "Earl Reed—Etcher," *Art and Progress,* June 1915; *Who's Who in America,* 1930–31; *Chicago Daily Tribune,* July 10, 1931.]   H. W.

REED, ELIZABETH ARMSTRONG (May 16, 1842–June 16, 1915), writer on Oriental literature, was born in Winthrop, Me., the daughter of Alvin and Sylvia (Morrell) Armstrong. She was educated in public schools in Maine and in Georgia, where her father taught for a while, and by private tutors. In 1860 she married Hiram V. Reed, of Harvard, Ill., a Campbellite preacher and editor. Most of the rest of her life was spent in Harvard and Chicago. She was the mother of three children, Charles B., who became a surgeon; Earl Howell [*q.v.*], an etcher and painter, and Myrtle Reed [*q.v.*], a novelist.

Always an ardent Christian, Elizabeth Reed learned Greek and Hebrew after her marriage in order to promote her study of the Scriptures, and in 1866 published her first book, *The Bible Triumphant.* Gradually she became more and more interested in the study of comparative religion and although she never learned the Oriental languages or traveled in the East, gave much time to the study of Oriental literatures in translation, and of scholarly writing in the field of Indic philology. In 1891 she published *Hindu Literature: or, the Ancient Books of India*; in 1893, *Persian Literature, Ancient and Modern*; and in 1896, *Primitive Buddhism, Its Origin and Teachings.* These three books were written in a clear and thoughtful style and they won her the praise of Max Müller and of Sir Monier Monier-Williams. She was also a contributor to *The Biblical Encyclopedia* (15 vols. in 8, 1900–01) and *The Encyclopedia Americana.* She became an associate (1885) and a member (1889) of the Victoria Institute or Philosophical Society of Great Britain, one of the first women admitted to membership, and in 1897 was elected a member of the Royal Asiatic Society. She was a leader in the Congress of Religions held in connection with the World's Columbian Exposition, Chicago, 1893, and was chairman of the Woman's Congress of Philology in that same year. She was president of the Illinois Woman's Press Association for four terms. In 1899 she published a short book: *Daniel Webster: A Character Sketch,* containing reminiscences of Webster's personal friendship with her mother and father. The year before her death she wrote *Hinduism in Europe and America* (1914), in which she violently attacked the corruptions of modern Hinduism, and especially the practices of the unscrupulous Hindu "gurus" or priests who had been making fools of many rich American and European women of the time. In this last work she became rather the Christian partisan than the scholar.

[*Who's Who in America,* 1914–15; E. S. Stackpole, *Hist. of Winthrop, Me.* (preface dated 1925); *Chicago Tribune,* June 18, 1915; information as to certain facts from Dr. Charles B. Reed.]　　　　　F. I. C.

REED, HENRY HOPE (July 11, 1808–Sept. 27, 1854), man of letters, was born in Philadelphia, the son of Joseph and Maria Ellis (Watmaugh) Reed. His father was state attorney-general in 1810 and later city recorder. Reed attended the classical school conducted by James Ross, graduated with honors from the University of Pennsylvania in 1825, read law in the office of his uncle John Sergeant [*q.v.*], and was admitted to practice in 1829. Finding the family profession distasteful, he accepted in 1831 an assistant professorship of English literature in the University of Pennsylvania, where after two months he was transferred to the department of moral philosophy. In 1834 he married Elizabeth White Bronson, daughter of Enos Bronson and grand-daughter of Bishop William White [*q.v.*], who with two daughters and a son survived him. Three other children died in infancy.

From 1835 until his death he was professor of rhetoric and English literature in the University. In 1838 he was elected to membership in the American Philosophical Society. Reed prepared an American edition of Wordsworth's *Complete Works* (1837), exceptionally well printed and notable for its successful attempt to anticipate the poet's own classification of his later work; a selection of fifty-one *Poems from the Poetical Works of William Wordsworth* (1841); Alexander Reid's *Dictionary of the English Language* (1845); Thomas Arnold's *Introductory Lectures on Modern History* (1845); George Frederick Graham's *English Synonymes* (1847), for which he supplied quotations from Shakespeare, Milton, and Wordsworth; Philip Henry Stanhope's *History of England from the Peace of Utrecht* (1849); Gray's *Poetical Works* (1851), a handsome edition, based on Mitford's, with illustrations by C. W. Radclyffe; Christopher Wordsworth's

Memoirs of William Wordsworth (1851), with some notes by the editor; and Wordsworth's *Complete Poetical Works* (1851), issued like the edition of 1837 in one double-column volume; but of his own work, except contributions to magazines, he published only a *Lecture on the Literary Opportunities of Men of Business* (1838) and a life of his grandfather Joseph Reed [*q.v.*] in Jared Sparks's *Library of American Biography* (2 ser., vol. VIII, 1846). After Reed's death, his brother, William Bradford Reed [*q.v.*], edited his *Lectures on English Literature from Chaucer to Tennyson* (1855); *Lectures on English History and Tragic Poetry as Illustrated by Shakespeare* (1855); *Two Lectures on the History of the American Union* (1856); and *Lectures on the British Poets* (2 vols., 1857). Engagingly written, the volumes on literature are expository and appreciative rather than analytical, and bear comparison with similar work by Robert Southey. They were much read in the United States for some twenty years and were republished in England.

Although Wordsworth had readers and even admirers in the United States from the time of the republication of the *Lyrical Ballads* at Philadelphia in 1802, Reed was his first American exponent. His admiration for the poet stopped just short of idolatry; his friends were half amused and half incensed by his skill in maneuvering a conversation around to his inexhaustible, beloved topic. By his editorial work, lectures, and articles he did more than any one else to secure Wordsworth's fame in America. His critique in the *New York Review* for January 1839 was especially notable. He corresponded with Wordsworth; with Bishop George Washington Doane [*q.v.*] he persuaded him to insert .. reference to the American Episcopal Church in the *Ecclesiastical Sonnets*; in 1844 he sent Henry Inman [*q.v.*] to Rydal Mount to paint the portrait that now hangs in the Library of the University of Pennsylvania. Reed's admiration for Wordsworth was not wholly undiscriminating, but as a devout Episcopalian he was as much edified by the later as by the earlier poetry. In the spring of 1854 Reed made his only visit to Europe, accompanied by his sister-in-law, Miss Bronson. In England he was cordially received, and his charm and scholarship left a deep impression on his hosts. After a tour on the Continent, he returned to England, and on Sept. 20, 1854, he and his sister-in-law sailed for home in the steamer *Arctic.* A week later the *Arctic* struck a French vessel in a fog and sank with the loss of the captain and three hundred passengers. When last seen, Reed and Miss Bronson were sitting in a passage abaft the dining saloon, waiting calmly but with evident anxiety for the end.

[W. B. Reed, memoir prefixed to *Lectures on English Literature* (1855); *Littell's Living Age*, Dec. 1854; J. F. Frazer, obituary in *Proc. Am. Phil. Soc.*, vol. VI (1859); J. L. Chamberlain, *Universities and Their Sons: Univ. of Pa.*, vol. II (1902); J. T. Coleridge, *Memoir of the Rev. John Keble* (1870); *Trans. Wordsworth Soc.*, no. 5 (1883); *Letters of the Wordsworth Family, 1787–1855*, vol. III (1907); L. N. Broughton, *Wordsworth and Reed* (1933); Esther Cloudman Dunn, "Inman's Portrait of Wordsworth" and "A Retrospect of Rydal Mount," *Scribner's Mag.*, Feb. 1920, May 1921; *The Ecclesiastical Sonnets of Wm. Wordsworth* (1922), ed. by A. F. Potts; Annabel Newton, *Wordsworth in Early American Criticism* (1928).]

G. H. G.

REED, JAMES (Jan. 8, 1722 o.s.–Feb. 13, 1807), Revolutionary officer, was born in Woburn, Mass., the son of Thomas and Sarah (Sawyer) Reed and the grandson of George Reed who emigrated from England in 1635 with his father, William, and settled in Woburn several years later. James acquired an elementary education and learned the tailor's trade. About 1745 he was married to Abigail Hinds of New Salem, Mass. He lived in Lunenburg, Mass., and for a time in Brookfield, where his second child was born. By 1748 he was again living in Lunenburg. There he kept an inn, was a church member, and a selectman. During the French and Indian War he served almost continuously with the rank of captain; he went with the expedition of 1755 to Crown Point, served under General Abercromby in 1758, and was with the British army in the closing campaign. About 1765 he removed to Monadnock no. 4, after 1773 known as Fitzwilliam, N. H., of which he was one of the original proprietors and for many years proprietors' clerk. There he also had a tavern, served in the militia, owned a large tract of land, and was an influential townsman.

Upon hearing the news of the battle of Lexington he raised troops and on Apr. 28, 1775, became colonel of the 3rd New Hampshire Regiment. On June 14 he was stationed on the Medford road near Charlestown Neck to watch the Neck, the ferry, and Bunker Hill. Three days later, at the battle of Bunker Hill, he was able to hold this regiment as a unit throughout the critical fighting at the rail fence. On Jan. 1, 1776, he became colonel of the 2nd Regiment in the Continental Army. After service through the siege of Boston he was sent with the forces to relieve Arnold, met the American army in retreat, and reached Ticonderoga in July 1776. Soon, however, he was stricken with an illness that destroyed his sight and impaired his hearing. Although, as the senior colonel from his state, he was made brigadier-general of the Continental

Army by act of the Congress on Aug. 9, 1776, he was no longer able to serve in the army and was retired in September. His wife died in 1791, and he married Mary Farrar, the daughter of John Farrar of Fitzwilliam. During the three decades of his blindness he lived at Keene, N. H., at Fitzwilliam, and at Fitchburg, Mass., where he died.

[J. F. D. Garfield, *General James Reed* (1908), also printed in *Proc. Fitchburg Hist. Soc.*, vol. IV (1908); A. J. Blake, "Gen. James Reed," *Proc. N. H. Hist. Soc.*, vol. I, pt. 3 (1885); J. F. Norton, *The Hist. of Fitzwilliam, N. H.* (1888); *N. H. Provincial and State Papers*, vols. XI, XV, XVI (1882–87), ed. by I. W. Hammond: *The Early Records . . . of Lunenburg, Mass.* (1896), comp. by W. A. Davis; *Vital Records of Brookfield, Mass.* (1909); Samuel Sewall, *The Hist. of Woburn* (1868); F. B. Heitman, *Hist. Reg. of Officers of the Continental Army* (1893); Harold Murdock, *Bunker Hill* (1927); *Proc. Mass. Hist. Soc.*, 1 ser., XIV (1876); J. W. Reed, *Hist. of the Reed Family* (1861), inaccurate; names of parents and date of birth from *Woburn Records of Births, Deaths, and Marriages*, pt. 3 (1891) and pt. 1 (1890), with correction in accord with statement on p. 7 of preface.]

K. E. C.

REED, JAMES (Dec. 8, 1834–May 21, 1921), minister of the Church of the New Jerusalem, was born in Boston, Mass., the son of Sampson Reed [*q.v.*] and Catharine (Clark) Reed. His father, a classmate of Thomas Worcester [*q.v.*] at Harvard, was one of the leading laymen of the church and his mother, a sister of Mrs. Thomas Worcester, was an early member of the church in an age when membership in it usually meant ostracism. Reed was educated in the school conducted by the Boston New-Church Society, in the Boston Latin School, and at Harvard College, from which he graduated in 1855. In the Boston Latin School and in college he was a classmate of Phillips Brooks [*q.v.*], and after graduation from Harvard they served together on the Latin School faculty.

On Dec. 19, 1858, Reed married Emily E. Ripley of Brookline. He was ordained to the ministry of the Church of the New Jerusalem in 1860 and served the Boston society for nearly sixty years: as assistant pastor from 1860 to 1868 and as pastor from 1868 to 1919, when he became pastor emeritus. He also served as general pastor of the Massachusetts Association from 1900 to 1921, and was general pastor emeritus from 1919 until his death. In addition, he was president of the New-Church Theological School from 1894 to 1908, one of the editors of the *New-Jerusalem Magazine* from 1865 till its suspension in 1872, associate editor of the *New-Church Review* (1894–99) and member of its advisory board (1899–1921), and chairman of the Council of Ministers of the General Convention of the New Jerusalem in the United

States of America from 1894 to 1908. He was the author of many books and pamphlets, of which the following are representative: *Man and Woman, Equal but Unlike* (1870); *Swedenborg and the New Church* (1880); and, with the Rev. H. Clinton Hay, three volumes: *Earthly Problems in Heavenly Light* (1905), *Death and the Life Beyond* (1906), and *The Essential Needs of the Soul* (1909). He was also a regular contributor to New-Church periodicals. In addition to his services to his church, he served on the school board of the City of Boston from 1871 to 1875, and was president of the Massachusetts Home for Intemperate Women.

Although Reed's thinking was clear and careful, the qualities which seem to have made the deepest impression on his associates were singleness of purpose, fidelity to his church, and consecration to the work of the ministry. Steadfast in the faith that in the doctrines of Swedenborg was to be found the truth by which humanity was to be guided into a new era, patient in their exposition throughout a long lifetime, he nevertheless could look beyond the organization to which he gave such whole-hearted allegiance and find everywhere around him signs that the new day was dawning. Never domineering, he yet exercised throughout the church as author, pastor of the largest society, and member of many important committees of the Convention, a strongly stabilizing influence. He died in Boston in the eighty-seventh year of his age, survived by his widow, a son, and two daughters.

[*Journal of the One Hundredth Ann. Sess. of the General Convention of the New Jerusalem in the U. S. A.* (1921); *New-Church Messenger*, June 8, 29, 1921; *New-Church Rev.*, July 1921; *Commemorative Exercises on the Twenty-fifth Anniversary of the Installation of the Rev. James Reed* (1893); *Commemorative Exercises on the Fiftieth Anniversary of the Ordination of the Rev. James Reed* (1910); John Clark, *Records of the Descendants of Hugh Clark, of Watertown, Mass.* (1866); J. L. Reed, *The Reed Geneal.* (1901); *Boston Transcript*, May 23, 1921.]

F. R. C.

REED, JAMES HAY (Sept. 10, 1853–June 17, 1927), lawyer, organizer of corporate enterprises, was born in Allegheny, Pa. (now part of Pittsburgh), the son of Dr. Joseph A. and Eliza (Hay) Reed. After attending the public schools, he entered Western University of Pennsylvania (now the University of Pittsburgh) and graduated in 1872. Thereupon he began the study of law in the office of his uncle, David Reed, the United States district attorney at Pittsburgh. He was admitted to the bar in 1875 and practised with his uncle until the latter's death two years later. He next opened offices for the practice of corporation law with Phil-

ander C. Knox [*q.v.*] under the firm name of Knox & Reed. This firm, which proved phenomenally successful and numbered among its clients the largest manufacturing and commercial concerns of the district, lasted until 1901 with both partners acting in high political capacities—Reed serving as President Benjamin Harrison's appointee to the federal district judgeship for Western Pennsylvania (1891–92) and Knox, as attorney-general in the cabinets of Presidents McKinley and Theodore Roosevelt. After 1901 Reed became the senior partner in the firm of Reed, Smith, Shaw & Beal, later Reed, Smith, Shaw & McClay.

As counselor of Andrew Carnegie, he helped in the organization of the United States Steel Corporation and became a member of the first board of directors, continuing in this capacity for twenty years. He also organized the Union Railroad Company (Pittsburgh) in 1896, and the Pittsburgh, Bessemer & Lake Erie Railroad Company in 1897, acting as president and director of both until the time of his death. Besides representing the Vanderbilt interests in the Pittsburgh district, he served as the vice-president of the Pittsburgh & Lake Erie Railroad Company from 1891 to 1896. He was interested in the public utilities of Pittsburgh, which later were grouped in the Philadelphia Company, of which he was the president from 1898 to 1919, and first vice-president during the remainder of his life. He was also president of the Reliance Life Insurance Company of Pittsburgh from the date of its formation in 1903 until 1927, and a director in several banks and trust companies.

Many honors symbolic of his diversified human interests as well as his great capacities came to Reed during his long life. He served as the federal government's delegate to the Universal Congress of Lawyers and Jurists which was held in St. Louis in 1904; was a member of the important Pennsylvania Commission on Constitutional Revision and Amendment, 1919 and 1920; and a member of the Pennsylvania Tax Commission, 1923–27. He established the Pittsburgh Skin and Cancer Foundation, was a director of the Western Pennsylvania Hospital, treasurer and member of the board of trustees of the Carnegie Institute of Technology and the Carnegie Hero Fund Commission, and vice-president and director of the United States Steel and Carnegie Pension Fund. He was married, June 6, 1878, to Kate J. Aiken, by whom he had three children. He died in Pittsburgh.

[*Pittsburgh Sun*, June 18, 1927; *Pittsburgh Post*, June 18, 1927; *Memoirs of Allegheny County, Pa.* (1904), vol. I; G. T. Fleming, *Hist. of Pittsburgh and Environs* (1922), vol. IV; J. W. Jordan, *Encyc. of Pa.*

Biog., vol. VIII (1917); Who's Who in America, 1926–27.]   A. I.

REED, JOHN (Jan. 6, 1757–May 28, 1845), soldier, farmer, and gold miner, was born in Hesse-Cassel, Germany, and died in Cabarrus County, N. C. Nothing is known of his parents or of his youth. He was among the mercenaries sent by Frederick II to aid the forces of George III in the American Revolution. After serving in the northern campaigns, he was transferred to the South and seems to have been among the "number of Hessian soldiers (who) deserted the British Army, after the siege of Savannah, and found their way to the German settlement on Dutch Buffalo Creek" in Mecklenburg, now Cabarrus County, N. C. (pamphlet on St. John's Evangelical Church of Cabarrus County). He purchased a tract of land in 1784, increased later by grants from the state, and began farming. He married Sarah Kisor, daughter of a refugee from Charleston, S. C., and reared a family of eight children.

While fishing in Meadow Creek in 1799, Conrad Reed, twelve-year-old son of John, found a lump of yellow metal which was used as a doorstop in the Reed home until 1802. At his wife's suggestion, Reed took the metal to a silversmith in Fayetteville, N. C., who pronounced it gold and paid Reed three dollars and fifty cents for it. Reed began to search for the precious metal and in 1803 discovered a nugget which weighed twenty-eight pounds and for which he received $8,000. Other large nuggets were discovered and Reed became comparatively wealthy. He feared that his neighbors, suspicious of him as a former British soldier and envious of his suddenly acquired wealth, might persecute him for illicit practices. Therefore, he associated with Frederick Kisor, his brother-in-law, the Rev. James Love, and Martin Pfifer, one of the leading citizens of the state, and began mining operations. Reed supplied the land and his associates provided the capital and labor, the profits being divided equally. The enterprise was successful and others began to search for gold. By 1830 some 30,000 miners were at work in North Carolina and activities had spread to Virginia, South Carolina, and Georgia. Gold mining became second in economic importance to agriculture in North Carolina, and in 1836 a branch mint was opened at Charlotte. The Reed mine was the most noted in the entire region. At first the placers were worked with pick and pan and with little scientific management. Later, Reed built a machine for washing the gold from the sand and gravel. In 1831, he opened a vein mine, and shafts were sunk several hundred feet

into the ground. Steam power was applied and the mine worked on an extensive scale until 1835 when he secured an injunction against his partners for alleged fraudulent returns, and operations were temporarily suspended. Yielding nuggets remarkable both in size and in number, the total production of the mine from 1803 to 1845 was estimated at $10,000,000.

Reed took little interest in politics and while he exercised citizenship rights, such as voting, jury service, and membership on local government boards, he did not become naturalized until shortly before his death. Reticent about his military career and his ancestry, unable to read and write, he was nevertheless able to win the confidence and respect of his associates, and to manage successfully a large slave plantation and mining establishment.

[There are few available sources for John Reed. The Cabarrus County Court Records contain some personal material as do local newspapers, especially the Charlotte Miners' and Farmers' Jour., the Salisbury Carolina Watchman and the Salisbury Western Carolinian. Accounts of Reed's mining activities are found in The Southern Review, vol. I, the Medical Repository, 2 ser. vols. I (1804), p. 307, and IV (1805), pp. 149–150, Silliman's Journal and W. R. Johnson, Gold and Silver Produced by the Mines of America from 1492 to 1848, reprinted from the Mining Magazine for 1853.]
F. M. G.

REED, JOHN (Oct. 22, 1887–Oct. 19, 1920), journalist, poet, revolutionist, was born in Portland, Ore., the son of Charles Jerome and Margaret (Green) Reed. He belonged to a wealthy family of high social standing, and after completing his secondary education in the Portland schools he entered Harvard College. Tall, handsome, and light-hearted, he threw himself into all manner of student activities. He was a member of the swimming team and the dramatic club; he served on the editorial boards of the Lampoon and the Harvard Monthly; he wrote a play produced by the Hasty Pudding Club, and was made ivy orator and poet. Graduating in 1910, he joined the staff of the American Magazine in 1911, and in 1912 published "Sangar," probably his finest poem (Poetry, December 1912; also privately printed), besides producing the first of the Dutch Treat Club shows, "Everymagazine." The following year he issued privately The Day in Bohemia.

His serious interest in social problems was first aroused, at about this time, by Lincoln Steffens and Ida Tarbell, and once aroused it quickly led him to a far more radical position than theirs. In 1913 he joined the staff of The Masses, edited by Max Eastman. The first of Reed's many arrests came in Paterson, N. J., in 1914, for attempting to speak on behalf of the strikers in the silk mills. During the same year he put on

"The Pageant of the Paterson Strike" in Madison Square Garden for the benefit of the strikers. Sent to Mexico by the *Metropolitan Magazine* to report the Mexican revolution, he participated for four months in the perils of Pancho Villa's army, while his brilliant if biased articles brought him national reputation as a war correspondent. They were republished in book form as *Insurgent Mexico* (1914). When the World War broke out, he was at once sent to Germany by the same magazine and was successively with the armies of Germany, Serbia, Bulgaria, Rumania, and Russia—his reports being republished as *The War in Eastern Europe* (1916). He returned to America for an operation at Johns Hopkins Hospital resulting in the removal of one kidney, and was thus rendered ineligible for conscription and saved from the fate of a conscientious objector. During 1916 appeared *Tamburlaine and Other Poems* (privately printed).

In January 1917 he was married to Louise Bryant, a journalist, who retained her own name, and in August of the same year they sailed for Russia in time to be enthusiastic observers of the October revolution in Petrograd. Reed won the close friendship of Lenin and wrote much of the Bolshevist propaganda dropped over the German lines. In January 1918 he spoke at the All-Russian Soviet convention to correct the impression of the likelihood of an immediate revolution in America. Meanwhile, his articles in *The Masses* and particularly a headline, "Knit a straight-jacket for your soldier boy," had been largely instrumental in bringing an indictment against that magazine for sedition. Absent at the first trial, Reed returned to America for the second, which, like the first, resulted in a divided jury. He was also indicted at this time for an "incendiary speech" in the Bronx, but the indictment was later quashed. In February 1919 he and his wife appeared before a Senate investigating committee, and a few days later he was arrested for an "incendiary speech" in Philadelphia, but was released without trial. During the year he published *Red Russia* and *Ten Days that Shook the World,* reprinted in 1926 with an introduction by Lenin. Both works were translated into practically every important language in the world.

Affiliated with the left wing of the Socialist party, Reed with the other radicals was expelled from the National Socialist Convention on Aug. 30, 1919. The radicals then split into two bitterly hostile groups, forming the Communist Party and the Communist Labor Party. Reed headed the latter, wrote its manifesto and platform, edited its paper, *The Voice of Labor,* and was denounced as "Jack the Liar" in the Communist Party organ, *The Communist.* Indicted for sedition, he escaped from America by means of a forged passport, worked his way to Finland as a stoker, and after being kept for twelve weeks in a Finnish prison was released to Russia on an exchange of prisoners. He was making speeches in Moscow while the American government was still conducting a nation-wide search for him. At the height of his career he was stricken with typhus and died after a brief illness. His body was buried in the Kremlin. John Reed Clubs, affiliated with the Communist Party, now exist in his honor in nearly all the large cities of the United States.

[*Who's Who in America,* 1918–19; Max Eastman, "John Reed," *The Liberator,* Dec. 1920; Julian Street, "A Soviet Saint," *Saturday Evening Post,* Sept. 13, 1930; *N. Y. Herald Tribune,* Oct. 19, 1920; Harriet Monroe and Alice C. Henderson, *The New Poetry* (rev. ed., 1932), p. 746; *N. Y. Times* "morgue"; personal information from Louise Bryant.] E. S. B.

REED, JOSEPH (Aug. 27, 1741–Mar. 5, 1785), lawyer, Revolutionary statesman and soldier, was a native of Trenton, N. J., the son of Andrew and Theodosia (Bowes) Reed. His paternal grandfather, Joseph, emigrated from northern Ireland and his father was a local merchant of substantial wealth. He received his elementary education in the Academy of Philadelphia and obtained the degree of B.A. at the College of New Jersey in 1757. On leaving college he began the study of law under Richard Stockton, the celebrated New Jersey lawyer, and was admitted to practice in May 1763. His colonial education was supplemented by a two-year sojourn in London, where he studied at the Middle Temple. He devoted these years to close attendance, not only at the principal courts of law, but at Parliamentary debates concerning colonial affairs (Reed MSS., vol. I). On his return he followed his profession in Trenton, and in 1767 was appointed deputy secretary of New Jersey. His rather extensive colonial business interests, including the iron trade and real-estate tracts in upper New York, brought him into contact with important leaders in other colonies, such as Otis and Cushing. In 1770 he made another visit to England, where on May 22 he married Esther De Berdt, daughter of Dennys De Berdt [*q.v.*], agent for Massachusetts in England, and on his return he established his law practice in Philadelphia. Through a brother-in-law he was prevailed upon to take up in 1773 a correspondence with Lord Dartmouth, the newly appointed secretary of state for the colonies, in order to provide the ministry with correct information on the colonial attitude. He warned Dartmouth on Dec. 27 of that year that any further attempt to enforce the Tea Act "must end in blood" (W. B. Reed, *Life and Correspondence,* I, p. 56). But Dartmouth continued to give more credence to the letters of General Gage, which indicated that the colonists were not united upon measures of resistance, and Reed, realizing the futility of this correspondence, eventually discontinued it. In November 1774 he was appointed a member of the committee of correspondence for Philadelphia; in January 1775 he served as president of the second Provincial Congress; and he gradually shifted his allegiance from the cause of moderation to that of independence.

After the battle of Lexington Reed was appointed lieutenant-colonel of the Pennsylvania Associated Militia, and on the appointment of his friend, George Washington, as commander-in-chief, he became his military secretary. In the same year he was elected a member of the Continental Congress and of the Committee of Safety. On June 5th he was made adjutant-general of the Continental Army with the rank of colonel and was active in the Long Island campaign. In the negotiations with Admiral Howe conducted in July 1776, Reed represented Washington and declined to receive the communication in his behalf as it was addressed to "George Washington, Esquire." He urgently advocated that New York be evacuated and burned to prevent its affording winter quarters to the enemy, but other counsels prevailed, and Fort Washington and its garrison, the special target of his criticism, fell into the hands of the enemy. When the retreat into Jersey had begun, Reed addressed a letter to Gen. Charles Lee, criticizing the policy in regard to Fort Washington. Lee replied, denouncing "that fatal indecision of mind" (Washington Irving, *Life of Washington,* II, 1855, p. 442). Lee's letter fell into the hands of Washington, who assumed that it had been provoked by derogatory statements on the part of Reed. In this affair, however, Washington acted with characteristic forbearance, and Reed remained his favorite aide and intimate friend. Both desired an offensive campaign in New Jersey. Because of his perfect acquaintance with that territory, Reed was able to be of inestimable service in the surprise attack on Trenton, the second passage of the Delaware, and the night march upon Princeton ("General Joseph Reed's 'Narrative of the Movements of the American Army in the Neighborhood of Trenton in the Winter of 1776–77,'" *Pennsylvania Magazine of History and Biog-*

raphy, December 1884, pp. 391–402), and he served with credit at the battles of Brandywine, Germantown, and Monmouth.

Though tendered command of the Continental cavalry in 1777 and appointed first chief justice of Pennsylvania under the new constitution the same year, Reed declined both offices. He was elected a delegate to the Continental Congress from Pennsylvania in 1777 and served during the following year on many important committees. In 1778 Governor George Johnstone, one of the three British peace commissioners, through Elizabeth Graeme Ferguson [*q.v.*] of Philadelphia, acting as intermediary, sought to win Reed over to the cause of conciliation with an alleged bribe of £10,000 and a high government post, but his reply was scornful. Reed recorded this episode in his *Remarks on Governor Johnstone's Speech in Parliament* (1779). In December 1778 he was chosen president of the Supreme Executive Council of Pennsylvania, in which office he served until 1781, when he resumed the practice of law. His administration is distinguished for the abolition of slavery in the state, for measures placing Pennsylvania soldiers on half pay for life, and for the prosecution, personally directed by Reed, of Benedict Arnold for corrupt practices in office during his command in Philadelphia (Reed to Washington, Apr. 24, 1779, in Jared Sparks, *Correspondence of the American Revolution,* 1853, II, pp. 275–78). On his return from a vacation in England in 1784, Reed was elected to Congress, but poor health prevented him from serving. He died on Mar. 5, 1785, in his forty-fourth year, five years after the premature death of his wife, who had overtaxed her health in the performance of notable war relief work in Philadelphia (E. F. Ellet, *The Women of the American Revolution,* I, 1848, pp. 36–56).

By nature courteous and conciliatory, and possessed of influential connections in England, Reed was frequently attacked as lacking in patriotic zeal and for evincing, in the early part of the war, a discouragement with the course of military affairs which he shared with Washington. In 1778 he was accused by Arthur Lee of treacherous correspondence with the enemy, but he treated the accusation with magnanimity. (See letter to wife, Reed MSS., vol. IV.) His military record was assailed in an article in the *Independent Gazetteer,* Sept. 7, 1782, signed "Brutus." The author was generally supposed to have been Dr. Benjamin Rush, but Reed thought his former comrade, Gen. John Cadwalader [*q.v.*], was the author, and spirited communications passed between them during the course of the next few years. The attack was once more renewed in 1856 in a pamphlet, entitled *Nuts for Future Historians to Crack,* by Horace W. Smith. Ten years later George Bancroft reopened the controversy in his *History of the United States* (vol. IX, 1866), to which William B. Reed, Joseph Reed's grandson, replied, and rather vitriolic polemics ensued (W. B. Reed, *President Reed of Pennsylvania: A Reply to Mr. George Bancroft and Others,* 1867; Bancroft, *Joseph Reed, a Historical Essay,* 1867; Reed, *A Rejoinder to Mr. Bancroft's Historical Essay,* 1867). It was conclusively shown, however, by William S. Stryker nine years later (*The Reed Controversy,* 1876) that Bancroft had confused him with Col. Charles Read, who had gone over to the British in December 1776, and the historian graciously acknowledged the error in the Centenary Edition of his *History* (1876, vol. V, p. 479).

[See: W. B. Reed, *Life and Correspondence of Jos. Reed* (2 vols., 1847); Henry Reed, "Life of Jos. Reed" in *The Lib. of Am. Biog.,* ed. by Jared Sparks, 2 ser., VIII (1846); John Hutchinson, *A Cat. of Notable Middle Templars* (1902), p. 203; E. A. Jones, *Am. Members of the Inns of Court* (1924); *Reprint of the Original Letters from Washington to Jos. Reed* (1853), ed. by W. B. Reed; *Independent Gazetteer,* Mar. 12, 1785. The Reed papers, consisting of nine folio volumes relating to legal, business, military, and public affairs, are in the possession of the N. Y. Hist. Soc.]
R. B. M—s.

REED, LUMAN (June 4, 1787–June 7, 1836), merchant, art patron, was a son of Eliakim and Rebecca (Fitch) Reed, both of whom were natives of Norwalk, Conn. His earliest American ancestor was John Reed, or Read, who emigrated to New England in 1660. At the time of Luman's birth his father was a farmer in Austerlitz, Columbia County, N. Y., but within a few years the family removed to Coxsackie, on the west bank of the Hudson, where Eliakim engaged in store-keeping. The son received some schooling, partly at the expense of a second cousin, Roswell Reed, who was in business in New York City, but soon Luman was at work in his father's store. His first venture into the outer world was in the form of a lumber speculation at Oswego. Within a year, however, he was back on the Hudson, serving as supercargo on a sloop carrying farm produce from Coxsackie to New York City and returning with goods to stock the Coxsackie store. Prospering in this river trade, he won the favorable notice of Roswell Reed, who gave him a clerkship in his New York grocery business. In 1815 he was made a partner and within fifteen years had acquired a substantial fortune and become one of New York's leading merchants.

A man of severely limited cultural opportunities, Reed was somehow inspired to devote his money to the encouragement of a native American art, in a period when the fine arts were receiving scant recognition in the United States. His first commission was to Asher B. Durand [*q.v.*], the engraver and landscape painter, for a portrait of President Andrew Jackson, a commission which soon extended to include Jackson's six predecessors in the presidency. The entire series Reed presented to the museum and library of the Brooklyn Navy Yard. He also encouraged other artists, notably George W. Flagg, Thomas Cole, and William Sidney Mount [*qq.v.*], not only by purchasing their works, but by paying their expenses in extended periods of European study. His own private residence on Greenwich Street, accounted one of the finest dwellings in the city, had an entire floor given over to a gallery of paintings, which was thrown open to the public one day in every week. His example stimulated and broadened the public interest in art, and within a decade important private collections were begun by business associates and friends of Reed. Contemporary estimates credit him with "a natural pictorial perception and good taste." Most of his friends among the artists found that his judgments coincided generally with their own. They made him a member of the Sketch Club, theretofore a strictly professional group. William Dunlap, the historian of American art beginnings, writing in Reed's lifetime, ranked him among the greatest benefactors to the fine arts, and "the most purely disinterested" that the country had produced. But for his untimely death, there can be no doubt that the American public, as well as art in general, would have profited still further from Reed's wisely directed generosity. He was survived by his wife, Mary (Baker), two daughters, and a son. His collection of paintings finally went to the New York Historical Society.

[John Durand, *Life and Times of A. B. Durand* (1894); William Dunlap, *Hist. of the Rise and Progress of the Arts of Design in the U. S.* (3 vols., 1918), ed. by F. W. Bayley and C. E. Goodspeed; B. J. Lossing, *Hist. of N. Y. City* (1884); Ella Reed-Wright, *Reed-Read Lineage* (1909).]
W. B. S.

REED, MYRTLE (Sept. 27, 1874–Aug. 17, 1911), author, was born in Norwood Park, Ill., now part of Chicago, and spent practically her entire life in that city. She was the only daughter and the youngest of the three children of Hiram and Elizabeth (Armstrong) Reed [*q.v.*]. Her father, at the time of her birth, edited a periodical called *The Millenarian* and eked out a livelihood by lecturing on religious topics.

Her mother was a student of Oriental literature and religions. One of her brothers, Earl Howell Reed [q.v.], became an etcher of note. Both parents were resolved that Myrtle should be a writer and reared her with that purpose steadily in view. She received, however, only a superficial education and never moved in literary society. After graduating in 1893 from the West Division High School in Chicago, where she was editor of the school paper, she became a free-lance journalist and magazine writer in her native city and in New York, but for six years she published nothing over her own name. Her *Love Letters of a Musician* (1899), which she wrote with characteristic speed in the course of five hectic days, hit the popular taste, and was followed by *Later Love Letters of a Musician* (1900) and *The Spinster Book* (1901). Adding a thin strain of narrative to her meditations on romantic love, she produced a short novel, *Lavender and Old Lace* (1902), which belongs to publishing, if not to literary, history. It was an instantaneous success and went through forty printings during the nine years of her career. Her popularity, thus established, suffered no diminution: her faculty for turning romantic day-dreams into deftly written novels of sentiment made her the most widely read and well remunerated authoress of her decade. Her subsequent volumes, issued by her publisher in a dainty format with lavender casing and profuse rubrication, were: *Pickaback Songs* (1903); *The Shadow of Victory: A Romance of Fort Dearborn* (1903); *The Master's Violin* (1904); *The Book of Clever Beasts* (1904); *At the Sign of the Jack o'Lantern* (1905); *A Spinner in the Sun* (1906); *Love Affairs of Literary Men* (1907); *Flower of the Dusk* (1908); *Old Rose and Silver* (1909); *Sonnets of a Lover* (1910); and *Master of the Vineyard* (1910). In 1905, under the pen-name of Olive Green, she published *What to Have for Breakfast,* which was so successful that it became the first of ten cookbooks. Two volumes, *A Weaver of Dreams* (1911) and *The Myrtle Reed Year Book* (1911) were in the press when she died, and four others were issued afterward.

Myrtle Reed was of medium height, with dark hair and eyes, physically robust, and more than a little corpulent. She took a craftsman's pride in her writing and left several accounts of her habits of composition (*e.g.,* "How Myrtle Reed Writes Books," *Chicago Record-Herald,* Feb. 24, 1907). When ready to write a novel, she would isolate herself from her friends and family, often going to a hotel in a distant city, and work at high nervous tension for four, five, or

six weeks, completing her manuscript in that time. She had a rollicking sense of humor, was a loyal friend and daughter, and, though a free spender, managed her business affairs well. Her longing for affection was as apparent in her life as in her writings. On Oct. 22, 1906, she married James Sydney McCullough, an Irish-Canadian real-estate salesman then resident in Chicago. They were hopelessly incompatible, but she tried to conceal her misery from herself and her intimates until her mind collapsed under the strain and she ended her life with an over-dose of a sleeping powder.

[M. B. Powell, biog. intro. to *The Myrtle Reed Year Book* (1911) and foreword to *Happy Women* (1913); *The Books of Myrtle Reed: Prize Review Competition* (G. P. Putnam's Sons, 1909); E. S. Colson and N. B. Carson, *Myrtle Reed* (1911); *Who's Who in America,* 1910–11; *Publishers' Weekly,* Aug. 26, Sept. 23, 1911; *Chicago Daily Tribune,* Aug. 19, 21, 1911; *Chicago Daily News,* Aug. 18, 19, 20, 1911; information from personal acquaintances.]   G. H. G.

REED, RICHARD CLARK (Jan. 24, 1851–July 9, 1925), Presbyterian clergyman, professor of theology, and author, was born near Soddy, Hamilton County, Tenn., the son of James Landrum Reed, also a Presbyterian minister and a contributor to religious papers. His mother, Elizabeth Jane, was the daughter of Maj. Robert Clark McRee, a native of Mecklenburg County, N. C., grandson of Rev. Alexander Craighead, and a ruling elder in the Presbyterian Church. Upon her death Richard, at the age of two years, was taken to live in the home of Major McRee, whose wife had previously died. Thus his grandfather became a large factor in the molding of the boy's life. During his early days he worked on his grandfather's farm and attended a local school. In 1873 he graduated from King College, Bristol, Tenn., with distinction, and in 1876, from Union Theological Seminary in Virginia. Shortly afterwards he was licensed to preach by the Presbytery of Knoxville, and in September 1876 he was ordained by the Presbytery of Memphis. On Oct. 17 of the same year he was married to Mary Cantey Venable of Farmville, Va.; two daughters and three sons were born of this marriage.

For twenty years after his ordination he was a pastor, serving the following Presbyterian churches: Charlotte Court House, Va. (1877–85); Franklin, Tenn. (1885–89); Second Church, Charlotte, N. C. (1889–92); and Woodland Street Church, Nashville, Tenn. (1892–98). In 1898 he became professor of church history and polity in Columbia Theological Seminary, Columbia, S. C., and held that position until his death. He took a leading part in the removal of the institution to Atlanta, but died before the transfer was actually made. He was a prolific writer. A frequent contributor to religious papers, in his early ministry, under a pen-name, he replied to some of his father's articles, taking the opposite views. For two years (1902–04) he was associate editor of the *Presbyterian Quarterly,* and for twenty years (1905–25), associate editor of the *Presbyterian Standard,* Charlotte, N. C., contributing regularly to its editorial pages. He was also the author of a number of useful books. His *History of the Presbyterian Churches of the World* (1905), a work of more than four hundred pages, is still one of the best authorities on that subject. Later in life he published *What is the Kingdom of God?* (1922), an able discussion of this question from the post-millennial point of view. He was also the author of several smaller works: *The Gospel as Taught by Calvin* (1896), "Presbyterian Church in the United States," in *The New Schaff-Herzog Encyclopedia of Religious Knowledge* (vol. IX, 1911), and *A Sketch of the Religious History of the Negroes in the South* (1914). His literary style was lucid and forceful. He had a keen sense of humor and the articles which he contributed to the papers were often lighted up by unexpected flashes of humor. He had the gift of making dry subjects live. In his thinking, speaking, and writing he was strongly conservative.

He was appointed on many important denominational and inter-denominational committees. His presbytery frequently elected him as a commissioner to the General Assembly, where he was always a leader and strong debater. In 1922 he was elected Moderator of the General Assembly of the Presbyterian Church in the United States. For many years he was a leading spirit in the Pan-Presbyterian Alliance, and thus became known to the Presbyterian churches throughout the world. Few men have rendered a larger service or had a larger influence in the Presbyterian Church. He died while asleep and was buried in Elmwood Cemetery, Columbia, S. C.

[Memorial addresses in *Bull. Columbia Theological Sem.,* Jan. 1926; *Who's Who in America,* 1924–25; *Centennial Gen. Cat. . . . Union Theological Sem. in Va.,* 1807–1907 (1908); *Presbyterian Standard,* July 15, 1925; *The State* (Columbia, S. C.), July 10, 1925; church records and family letters.]   W. L. L.

REED, SAMPSON (June 10, 1800–July 8, 1880), Swedenborgian writer, a descendant of William Reade who settled in Weymouth, Mass., in 1635, was born in West Bridgewater, Mass., the youngest of the eight children of John Reed by his first wife, Hannah (Sampson). His father, a graduate of Yale College in the class of 1772, was pastor for over fifty years of the First Church in West Bridgewater. He held his Arminian opinions quietly but firmly, was a naval chaplain in the Revolution and a member of Congress from 1795 to 1801, and in his old age married his deceased wife's sister. For the last eleven years of his life he was blind. In temper and constitution Sampson was like his father. On graduating in 1818 from Harvard College, he continued his studies in the Divinity School, but, having been converted to Swedenborg's teachings by his room-mate and life-long friend, Thomas Worcester [*q.v.*], he soon realized that a career in the ministry was closed to him and left the Divinity School without completing the course. He became a clerk in the Boston apothecary shop of William B. White, dedicating a tenth of his wages to the support of the New Church in Boston, and later opened a retail shop of his own. He remained in business for many years, with different partners, and slowly built up his establishment into one of the largest wholesale drug houses in New England. On Dec. 25, 1832, he married Catharine, daughter of John and Lydia (Sanderson) Clark of Waltham, who with three sons and a daughter survived him. One of the sons, James Reed [*q.v.*], became a Swedenborgian minister.

The main concern of Sampson Reed's life was his religion. He was one of the chief supports of the *New Jerusalem Magazine,* of which his brother Caleb was editor, regularly contributing articles and notices to its first forty-eight volumes (1828–82). In 1854 he became one of its editors. In 1843 he founded the *New Church Magazine for Children* (after 1863 the *Children's New-Church Magazine*), and in all the work of the Church he was constantly and intelligently active. He is still remembered for two productions of his early manhood, or rather, for the extraordinary and lasting influence that they exerted on Ralph Waldo Emerson. In 1821, when he received his master's degree at Harvard, Reed delivered an oration on "Genius" which Emerson remembered ever after for its eloquence and truth. Five years later he published a small volume of less than a hundred pages, *Observations on the Growth of the Mind* (1826), which was republished in its eighth edition in 1886 and again reprinted in 1910. It is an essay in Swedenborgian thought, although Swedenborg himself is unnamed in its pages, and contains many acute psychological observations. What appealed to Emerson was the exposition of the doctrine of correspondences and its application to poetic imagery, and the hopeful, prophetic note in which the essay is pitched. He pressed the book upon

Thomas Carlyle, James Freeman Clarke, his aunt, Mary Moody Emerson (who did not like it at all), Dr. Samuel Brown of Edinburgh, and other friends; and on his own thinking and writing it left an indelible mark. Emerson's knowledge of Swedenborg seems to have derived almost entirely from Reed, but he admired Reed, both as man and thinker, more than he did Swedenborg, and praised him nobly in his Journals. Reed's only other publications of any importance were *The Correspondence of the Sun, Heat, and Light* (1862) and *A Biographical Sketch of Thomas Worcester, D.D.* (1880). He was blind for some years before his death, which occurred in Boston at the beginning of his eighty-first year.

[J. L. Reed, *The Reed Geneal.* (1901); John Clark, *Records of the Descendants of Hugh Clark, of Watertown, Mass.* (1866); F. B. Dexter, *Biog. Sketches Grads. Yale Coll.*, vol. III (1903); memoir by Warren Goddard, funeral discourse by John Worcester, and editorial tribute, *New Jerusalem Mag.*, Sept. 1880; *Boston Transcript*, July 9, 1880; biog. preface by James Reed in 8th ed. (1886) of *Observations*; E. G. Sutcliffe, *Emerson's Theories of Literary Expression* (1923); C. P. Hotson, "Sampson Reed, a Teacher of Emerson," *New England Quarterly*, Apr. 1929; M. B. Block, *The New Church in the New World* (1932).]

G. H. G.

REED, SIMEON GANNETT (Apr. 23, 1830–Nov. 7, 1895), merchant, steamboat operator, capitalist, was born in East Abington, Mass., the son of Simeon Gannet [*sic*] and Rachel (Burgess) Reed, and a descendant of William Reade who was in Weymouth, Mass., as early as 1635. Simeon was educated in the public schools and a private academy of his native town. As a young man he worked in an Abington shoe factory; later he became a grain dealer in Quincy, Mass., where, Oct. 17, 1850, he married Amanda Wood. In 1852 they moved to California, traveling by way of Panama; and shortly, to Portland, Ore., at that time a village of a few hundred inhabitants. Here Reed worked in a general store, soon becoming a partner in the business. In 1858 he invested in three steamers on the Columbia River, thus entering upon an enterprise which was to bring him a fortune. In 1860 he joined with J. C. Ainsworth and Robert Thompson in organizing the Oregon Steam Navigation Company, with a capital of $172,500. Two years later the company was reorganized with a capital of $2,000,000. At this time mines were being opened in the interior and the natural passage for men and goods was through the gorge of the Columbia. The Navigation Company had the steamers; it now purchased right of way and built portage railways around the rapids at Cascades and the Dalles. Later it bought a railway from the Columbia to Walla Walla. In seven years it paid dividends of nearly two and three quarters mil-

lions and made investments of over two millions. It was sold in 1879 to the Villard Syndicate for five millions. The fortune accumulated through steamboat transportation Reed augmented by successful mining ventures. He developed valuable mines in eastern Oregon and in 1887 was owner of the Bunker Hill and Sullivan, one of the richest mining properties in northern Idaho.

He now had the means to gratify his personal tastes. Possessing a genuine, though uncultivated, liking for music and art, he made an interesting collection of paintings. He was one of the first to raise the standard of live-stock breeding in the Northwest. In Oregon and afterward in California he bought and bred fine horses and took great pleasure and pride in them. Though childless, he was especially fond of children and youth, and was interested in their education. In his will he left his whole fortune to his wife with the suggestion that she devote some portion of his estate "to the cultivation, illustration or development of the fine arts of said city of Portland, or to some other suitable purpose, which shall be of permanent value and contribute to the beauty of the city and to the intelligence, prosperity and happiness of its inhabitants" (*Reed College Record*, May 1911, no. 2, p. 6). Accordingly, when Amanda Reed died in 1904, she directed in her will that the bulk of her estate should be used to establish and maintain, in memory of her husband, "an institution of learning, having for its object the increase and diffusion of practical knowledge among the citizens of said City of Portland, and for the promotion of literature, science, and art" (*Ibid.*). Thus Reed College, opened in 1911, came into being as a lasting and significant memorial to Simeon G. Reed.

[J. L. Reed, *The Reed Geneal.* (1901); *Vital Records of Abington, Mass.* (1912), I, 192, II, 180, which gives date of birth Apr. 24, though all other sources give Apr. 23; *Reed College Record*, Mar. 1911 (no. 1); *Hist. of Portland, Ore.* (1890); C. H. Carey, *Hist. of Oregon* (1922); Joseph Gaston, *Portland, Ore., Its Hist. and Builders* (1911), vol. I, and *The Centennial Hist. of Ore.* (1912), vol. I; *Morning Oregonian*, Nov. 8, 1895.]

N. F. C.

REED, THOMAS BRACKETT (Oct. 18, 1839–Dec. 7, 1902), lawyer, speaker of the House of Representatives, parliamentarian, was born in Portland, Me., the elder of the two children of Thomas Brackett and Mathilda (Mitchell) Reed. His father was a sailor and water-front watchman of limited means. He had the advantage of good heredity, however, tracing descent on the one hand from Thomas Reade, one of Winthrop's settlers of 1630, and on the other from Experience Mitchell and Jane Cook, a passenger on the *Mayflower*. His mother was a woman of great intelligence and strength of character. Reed attended the public schools of his native city and graduated from Bowdoin College in 1860, ranking high in his class despite a somewhat erratic record in the first years of attendance. He was obliged to support himself in part during his course by doing odd jobs; he also taught school. While he had intended entering the ministry, he became a free-thinker on religious topics and decided on a different profession. He resumed teaching on graduation and began the study of law in Portland, whence he proceeded to California late in 1861. He taught school in the new state and secured admission to the bar at San Jose, Sept. 8, 1863. He returned to Portland soon afterward, and resumed his legal studies, but in April 1864 secured a commission as acting assistant paymaster in the navy. He served until honorably discharged about eighteen months later.

He was admitted to the Maine bar in October 1865 and began practice in Portland. Elected to the Maine legislature two years later, he was re-elected in 1868, and in 1869 became senator from Cumberland County. Throughout his three years' service he was a member of the joint standing committee on the judiciary, and he made a reputation as one of the ablest debaters and floor leaders in the state. In 1870 he was elected attorney-general of Maine and served for three years in that office. On Feb. 5, 1870, he married Mrs. Susan P. Jones, daughter of the Rev. S. H. Merrill, a prominent Congregationalist clergyman of Portland. His domestic life was singularly happy and his wife made an important contribution to his subsequent political and professional successes. Reed was beaten for renomination as attorney-general in 1873, owing to a precedent which had set three years as the maximum term. He had made a reputation as a fearless and vigorous prosecuting officer. His reports indicate, furthermore, a grasp of law and a realization of its shortcomings in protecting the interests of the state against the "rights" of the law-breaker. After retirement he engaged in private practice, serving also as city solicitor for Portland and taking an active part in the activities of the Republican party. He was rewarded for the latter in 1876 by a nomination for the national House of Representatives and in spite of some dissension in the party carried the district. In 1880 he barely escaped defeat by a fusion of Greenback and Democratic opponents. With this exception, he continued to carry the first congressional district by strong majorities until 1898.

In Congress Reed spoke infrequently but soon acquired a reputation as a formidable opponent in running debate. His speech in opposition to a bill indemnifying the College of William and Mary for losses suffered during the Civil War was a fine forensic effort, heavily charged with the sarcasm and invective for which he soon became famous (*Congressional Record,* 45 Cong., 2 Sess., pp. 2488–90). On May 20, 1878, he was appointed a minority member of the select committee headed by Clarkson N. Potter, directed to investigate alleged frauds in the presidential election of 1876. Reed unearthed important evidence regarding fraud and violence in Louisiana, discredited several Democratic witnesses by his skilful and merciless cross-examination, and brought clearly to light the connection of William T. Pelton, nephew of Samuel J. Tilden, with the notorious "cipher telegrams." The partisan clamor which followed the disclosures enabled the Republicans to becloud the original issues and fight the campaign of 1880 on more advantageous ground than would have otherwise been the case. While not a persistent waver of the "bloody shirt," Reed supported federal election laws which would have secured the negro's right to vote. He supported the tariff, rehabilitation of the navy, and liberal national expenditures. Unlike some of his party colleagues, however, he stood firm against inflation, voting against the Bland-Allison Act and denouncing both Greenbackism and Free Silver. He was promoted to the judiciary committee in the Forty-sixth Congress and became its chairman when the Republicans won control of the House in the Forty-seventh.

On Jan. 9, 1882, he was appointed to a vacancy in the committee on rules and soon acquired a dominant place in its deliberations. Early in March he presented amendments to the rules which would have enabled the majority to secure prompt consideration of business regardless of its place on the calendars, but Republican strength was insufficient to secure action on such a highly controversial topic. On May 29, however, after spirited opposition, he secured the adoption of an amendment to the rules, putting an end to filibustering in election cases, and at the next session used the same weapon, a special rule reported by this committee, to drive through the tariff bill of 1883, whose passage the minority had hitherto obstructed by dilatory tactics. The Democrats held control of the House from 1883 to 1889. Reed held his place on the committee on rules and also represented the minority on the committee on ways and means from 1884 to 1889. In the latter capacity he became a noted exponent of protectionist doctrine, his most distinguished effort being a speech, May 19, 1888, against the Mills Bill, one of the greatest speeches on the subject in congressional annals (*Congressional Record,* 50 Cong., 1 Sess., pp. 4440–46). After 1882 Reed was the unquestioned leader of the House Republicans, although formal recognition of the fact was withheld, due to sundry party exigencies, until 1885 when he was first nominated for the speakership.

Throughout the Forty-eighth, Forty-ninth, and Fiftieth congresses he continued to fight for reform of the rules of the House, proposing that procedural checks be removed in order that the majority might actually govern, but the Democratic majority would have none of it. The only change accomplished in this period was the scattering of the power of the committee on appropriations among additional committees, an unfortunate consummation which plagued congressional finance for the next forty years. Reed, as he afterwards regretted, supported the change. The House was attempting, Reed declared, "to run Niagara through a quill." Conditions reached a climax in the Fiftieth Congress, where a series of filibusters reduced the Democratic majority to utter helplessness and led to a widespread demand for reform.

The Republicans carried the country in 1888 and Reed was elected speaker of the House on Dec. 2, 1889. His success was taken to mean that reform of the rules was imminent. This brought up the question of the quorum, the precedents of the House requiring that a member actually vote in order to be recorded present. In the Fifty-first Congress the Republicans had only three votes more than the necessary quorum of 165. Routine absences and a body of silent Democrats could therefore put a stop to every transaction. Reed cut the Gordian knot on Jan. 29, 1890, by counting enough Democrats to make a quorum. For three days the House was in a tumult. Reed delivered a series of rulings which showed his intention to use every power of the speakership in the interest of majority rule and the efficient transaction of public business. His counting of the quorum prepared the way for the adoption of the famous "Reed Rules" on Feb. 14. Obstruction was ended by empowering the speaker to refuse dilatory motions, the "counted" quorum was substituted for the "voting" quorum, the committee of the whole was reduced and its procedure simplified, and the order of business was completely revised.

Under the new rules the majority of the Fifty-first Congress forced through the greatest legislative program since the Civil War. The McKinley tariff, however, and the remarkable increase in expenditures which led this Congress to be dubbed "the billion dollar Congress" produced a strong reaction and led to the sweeping Democratic victory of 1890. Reed defended his code when the Fifty-second Congress reverted to the old system, and bided his time until 1894, when by use of the silent quorums he forced the Democratic majority to adopt the system which they had bitterly denounced four years earlier. In the meantime he gave generous support to the sound-money policy of President Cleveland, delivering one of his greatest speeches on behalf of repeal of the Sherman Silver Purchase Act, Aug. 26, 1893 (*Congressional Record,* 53 Cong., 1 Sess., pp. 950–55). He continued his efforts for protection and spoke at length against the Wilson Bill, Feb. 1, 1894, his speech on this occasion being considered almost on a par with that against the Mills Bill six years before (*Ibid.,* 53 Cong., 2 Sess., pp. 1781–88).

Reed's leadership did much to rehabilitate the Republican party after its defeats of 1890 and 1892. After sweeping Republican victories in 1894, followed by his election to the speakership and the re-enactment of the Reed rules, there was a strong feeling that he had earned a presidential nomination. Active efforts were made on his behalf but he declined to make commitments on matters of patronage, refused to accept funds where future obligations might be involved, and made the tactical error of remaining silent on the currency question. At the Republican National Convention of 1896 he received only 84½ votes.

He took his defeat much to heart and entertained a lively resentment toward various leaders who he believed had betrayed his cause, but was reëlected speaker of the Fifty-fifth Congress. Reed, although he had scant respect for President McKinley, whom he had started on the road to the White House in 1889 by appointment to the chairmanship of the ways and means committee, supported the administration until 1898. He was bitterly opposed to intervention in Cuba and to Hawaiian annexation, feeling that colonial expansion and the governing of subject peoples were contrary to American tradition and entirely impracticable. The continental United States, he argued, already had too many unassimilated elements and, thanks to the equality of states in the Senate, was actually being governed by a minority. Following the war with Spain and the annexation of Hawaii, Reed, disgusted with the situation, resigned on Sept. 4, 1899. He took up the practice of law in New York City and achieved notable professional success, in spite of the fact that his career had been largely political since his earlier practice before the courts of Maine. He had given as the chief reason for retirement the need of making provision for his family, and succeeded in the next three years in accumulating a comfortable estate. He died while visiting Washington on legal business Dec. 7, 1902.

Reed's work in establishing the principle of party responsibility in the House was a notable contribution to American government. While the speakership was subsequently shorn of much of the autocratic power which had been bestowed on Reed, many of the rules which he devised remained in operation and in some particulars are unlikely to be replaced. He believed in the traditional methods of American democracy and had a cynical attitude toward reform and reformers. He defended his parliamentary reforms as merely a restoration of democratic control in the House, the speaker being the chosen instrument of a popular majority. He failed to realize that the changed conditions due to nineteenth-century industrialism rendered his *laissez-faire* doctrines obsolete in the relations of government and private business.

Reed was a great debater. He seldom spoke for more than ten minutes but his brief comments on pending bills frequently determined the entire line of argument and sometimes settled the fate of important measures. He was a master of sarcasm and his use of this weapon often worked to his political hurt. James G. Blaine he once described as a burden to the Republican party like unto "the gentleman Sinbad carried." He was fond of Theodore Roosevelt but once remarked: "Theodore, if there is one thing for which I admire you, it is your original discovery of the ten commandments." His epigrams and aphorisms have become part of American political tradition. "A statesman," he said, "is a successful politician who is **dead**" (Lodge, *post*, p. 191).

Reed read French with facility and was fond of the literary masterpieces of that language. He accumulated a valuable library and enjoyed discussing books and authors. He wrote distinguished prose and made notable contributions to the *North American Review* and other periodicals. But he was above all a great personality, self-reliant, courageous, honest, and inflexible, and gifted with keen insight and pungent wit. He was a giant in stature, standing over six feet three and weighing from 250 to 275 pounds. His size was an asset, conveying a sense of physical mastery over the House. His face was round and bland, almost cherubic. As a result, his drawling comments, his incisive rulings, his rasping sarcasm and pointed wit were startlingly in contrast to his appearance. With his friends he was

affable, fond of joking and good-natured raillery, and extremely sympathetic and kind hearted. He had a most unusual combination of qualities and as one of his colleagues wrote (Powers, *post*, p. 264) "there never was and there never will be another Tom Reed."

[*Orations and Addresses delivered by Thomas Brackett Reed* (1911) containing many addresses not available elsewhere; S. W. McCall, *The Life of Thomas Brackett Reed* (1914), particularly good for its treatment of Reed's personality; W. A. Robinson, *Thomas B. Reed, Parliamentarian* (1930), dealing more fully with Reed's procedural reforms and his significance in the history of the period; D. S. Alexander, *Hist. and Procedure of the House of Representatives* (1916); H. B. Fuller, *The Speakers of the House* (1909); S. L. Powers, *Portraits of A Half Century* (1925); H. C. Lodge, *The Democracy of the Constitution* (1915); O. O. Stealey, *Twenty Years in the Press Gallery* (1906); F. E. Leupp, "Personal Recollections of Thomas B. Reed," *Outlook*, Sept. 3, 1910; R. R. Porter, "Thomas B. Reed of Maine," *McClure's Mag.*, Oct. 1893; F. E. Clark, "Thomas B. Reed as a Neighbor," *Independent*, Jan. 8, 1903; Theodore Roosevelt, "Thomas Brackett Reed and the Fifty-first Congress," *Forum*, Dec. 1895; biographies and memoirs of the period; obituaries in *Daily Eastern Argus* (Portland), Dec. 8, 1902, and other papers, of which the Cumberland Club, of Portland, Me., has preserved a large number.]

W. A. R.

REED, WALTER (Sept. 13, 1851–Nov. 22, 1902), physician, head of the United States Army Yellow Fever Commission, traced his ancestry to a sturdy county family of Northumberland, England. His father, Lemuel Sutton Reed, a North Carolinian by birth, spent forty years of his life in the ministry of the Methodist Church in Virginia. His first wife, Walter's mother, was Pharaba White, daughter of a North Carolina planter, also of English descent. Walter, youngest of a family of six, was born at Belroi, Gloucester County, Va. In 1852 the father was moved to a pastorate at Farmville, Prince Edward County, and there Walter spent the first years of his life and began his education in a private school. His schooling, although somewhat interrupted by the Civil War, was well advanced when the family moved to Charlottesville in 1866. Here he attended a private school for one year and the following year entered the University of Virginia at the age of sixteen. After a year in the academic department and one in the medical school, he was given his medical degree in 1869, before he was eighteen. Proceeding to New York, he matriculated at the Bellevue Hospital Medical College, where he received a second degree of M.D. in 1870. Following an interneship at the Kings County Hospital in Brooklyn, he was employed by the board of health of New York and then by that of Brooklyn.

In 1874, while in Brooklyn, Reed decided to try for an appointment in the Medical Corps of the United States Army. Having passed the prescribed examination, he was commissioned as assistant surgeon with the rank of first lieutenant in June 1875. After a year's duty at Willet's Point, New York, he was ordered to Fort Lowell, Ariz., where began eleven years of frontier garrison life. It was in these surroundings, unfavorable in opportunities for study and intellectual contacts but rich in experiences calling for initiative and ingenuity, that he laid the foundation for his career as a scientist. In 1890, feeling the need of post-graduate study, he asked for leave of absence for that purpose, but was instead ordered to Baltimore as attending surgeon and examiner of recruits, with authority to pursue study at the Johns Hopkins Hospital. After completing a brief course in clinical medicine he was attached to the pathological laboratory, where he specialized in the comparatively new science of bacteriology. This course was directed by Professor William H. Welch and his assistants, Councilman, Abbott, Nuttall, and Flexner, with all of whom Reed formed lasting ties of friendship. In 1893 he was promoted to the grade of major and in this same year was detailed as curator of the Army Medical Museum at Washington and as professor of bacteriology and clinical microscopy at the newly organized Army Medical School. About the same time, Dr. James Carroll [q.v.], then a hospital steward, was assigned to duty as Reed's assistant at the School.

In the years preceding the Spanish-American War, Reed interested himself especially in the bacteriology of erysipelas and diphtheria. He was an early champion of the treatment of diphtheria by antitoxin and of governmental control of the preparation of such biologic remedies. In 1898, he was appointed chairman of a committee charged with the investigation of the causes and mode of transmission of typhoid fever, then epidemic in the camps of the United States volunteers. The other members were Dr. Victor C. Vaughan [q.v.], of Ann Arbor, Mich., and Dr. Edward O. Shakespeare of Philadelphia. The report of this committee showed the relative unimportance of water transmission in this epidemic and the hitherto little suspected importance of transmission by flies and dust and of contact infections. Published in 1904 under the title *Report on the Origin and Spread of Typhoid Fever in U. S. Military Camps during the Spanish War of 1898*, this exhaustive work will always be of value in future studies of the epidemiology of this disease.

Reed's practical interest in yellow fever began with the somewhat premature announcement, in July 1897, of the *Bacillus icteroides* as an alleged specific causative agent, by the Italian scientist, Dr. Giuseppe Sanarelli. Reed and Dr. James Carroll were designated by Surgeon-General George Miller Sternberg [q.v.] to investigate the status of the Sanarelli bacillus in relation to Sternberg's hypothetical *Bacillus X*. In an article entitled "*Bacillus icteroides* and *Bacillus cholerae suis*," published in *Medical News,* Apr. 29, 1899, they demonstrated that the *Bacillus icteroides* had no causal relationship whatever. When, in 1900, the disease made its appearance among American troops in Havana, a commission of medical officers of the United States Army was appointed to investigate its cause and mode of transmission. Reed was placed at its head, the other members being Dr. Carroll, then acting assistant surgeon, Dr. Jesse W. Lazear [q.v.], and Dr. Aristides Agramonte. Reed was the planning head of the commission and exercised general superintendence, Carroll was the bacteriologist, Lazear the entomologist, and Agramonte the pathologist. From observation of an outbreak at Pinar del Rio, soon after his arrival in Cuba, Reed was practically convinced that fomites were insignificant as agencies in the transmission of the disease. Further work upon the *Bacillus icteroides* confirmed his convictions that it was at most a secondary invader, and he decided to turn from the search of the specific cause and pursue the method of transmission.

The theory of mosquito transmission of yellow fever was put forward as early as 1854, by Beauperthuy, who even attributed it to the "striped variety," that is, to the *Stegomyia*. In 1881, Dr. Carlos J. Finlay [q.v.] of Havana advanced the same theory. Then followed the work of Ronald Ross and of Grassi and his associates on mosquito transmission of malaria. In May 1900 Dr. Henry Rose Carter [q.v.] had published an article calling attention to the so-called "extrinsic incubation" of yellow fever, the period of time necessary for the "infection of the environment." Whatever weight these several factors may have had, the commission decided to investigate the possibility of transmission by the *Stegomyia* mosquito. It was at once realized that experimentation with human subjects would be necessary, but that the results, if positive, would fully justify the procedure. In the first uncontrolled experiments, Lazear applied mosquitoes which had fed upon yellow-fever blood to himself, to Carroll, and to some others. From one of these bites Carroll developed the first experimental case of the disease. He was seriously ill for a time, but recovered, although with a damaged heart. Then followed the case of XY, the first soldier volunteer (Private William H.

Dean). In these early experiments, Lazear had direct charge of the handling of mosquitoes. He was accidentally bitten by an infected mosquito and died of yellow fever nine days later, on Sept. 26, 1900. Reed had meanwhile been called to the United States and was there at the time of Carroll's illness and of Lazear's death. Upon his return to Cuba, on Oct. 1, Reed took up the work on controlled experiments, with Dr. Agramonte in charge of the care and handling of the mosquitoes. In all, twenty-two cases of experimental yellow fever were thus produced, happily without fatal result. Of these, fourteen were infected by mosquito bites, six by injections of blood, and two by injections of filtered blood serum.

Coincident with the mosquito experimentation Reed had constructed a detached building where for twenty nights Dr. Robert P. Cook and a group of soldiers slept in close contact with the clothing and bedding of yellow-fever patients from the Camp Lazear hospital. No case of illness resulted from any of these contacts. Thus was demolished the deeply rooted belief in the danger of fomites in this disease.

The work of the commission covered the seven months from June 25, 1900, to Feb. 4, 1901. In that time it was conclusively proved that yellow fever is transmitted by the mosquito then called *Stegomyia fasciata*, but later definitely classified as *Aëdes ægypti*. It was further shown that the case infecting the mosquito must be of less than four days' duration, and that there must elapse a period of at least twelve days for incubation of the virus in the mosquito. The mosquito, once infected, was shown to remain so for at least fifty-seven days. It was proved that the disease could be produced by injections of blood from a fresh case, and that the serum remaining after filtration of this blood was equally infective. The fruits of the commission's labors were quickly made evident. In 1900, there were 1,400 cases of yellow fever in Havana. The attack upon the mosquito began in February 1901 and during that year there were but thirty-seven cases of the disease in the whole of Cuba. In 1902, there was not a single case. With its method of transmission known, there is no longer a yellow-fever hazard in the United States, and New Orleans, formerly harassed by the disease, knows it only as a memory.

Reed returned to Washington in February 1901 and resumed his work at the Army Medical School and as professor of pathology and bacteriology in the Columbian University Medical School. In his preoccupation with his teaching, he neglected the warning pains of a chronic appendicitis until Nov. 17, 1902, when his friend,

Maj. William C. Borden, found an irreparable condition which caused his death five days later.

Reed's name will always be associated with the work of the Yellow Fever Commission and with the consequent control of the disease. His was the planning and supervising mind, although the detailed work was largely done by his colleagues, to whom he always gave generous credit for the commission's achievements. His writings began with *The Contagiousness of Erysipelas* in 1892. During the next ten years he contributed, either alone or in collaboration, thirty articles to periodical literature. His earlier writings covered a variety of medical subjects, while the later ones were largely on the subject of yellow fever. In the summer of 1902, Harvard University conferred upon him the honorary degree of A.M. and shortly afterward the University of Michigan gave him the degree of LL.D. Only a few days before his death, he was appointed librarian of the Army Medical Library. He was buried in Arlington National Cemetery. The great general hospital of the Army Medical Center at Washington, D. C., has been named in his honor.

Reed was of a lively, happy disposition, enthusiastic and optimistic in everything to which he turned his hand. He was sociable and companionable, with a special gift for conversation and for medical teaching. To this attractive personality was added an attractive exterior. He was a little above medium height, with a spare, graceful figure well suited to a military uniform. He was married, in 1876, to Amelia Lawrence, daughter of John Vaughan Lawrence, a planter of Murfreesboro, N. C. They had two children: a daughter and a son who became an officer of infantry in the United States Army.

[H. A. Kelly, *Walter Reed and Yellow Fever* (3rd ed., 1923) contains an exhaustive biography, portraits, and a bibliography of Reed's writings; W. D. McCaw, "Walter Reed, A Memoir," in *Ann. Report . . . of the Smithsonian Inst. for . . . 1905* (1906), is a concise account by a personal friend; "Yellow Fever . . . Results of the Work of Major Walter Reed . . . and the Yellow Fever Commission" (1911), *Sen. Doc. No. 822, 61 Cong., 3 Sess.*, contains detailed information which is either of an official character or of first hand authenticity; for additional bibliography concerning Reed, see the *Index Catalogue of the Library of the Surgeon General's Office, U. S. Army*. A popular account by Paul De Kruif in his *Microbe Hunters* (1926) formed the basis of a play by S. C. Howard and Paul De Kruif, *Yellow Jack: A History* (1934), produced in New York City.]   J. M. P.

REED, WILLIAM BRADFORD (June 30, 1806–Feb. 18, 1876), lawyer, diplomat, author, was born in Philadelphia, son of Joseph and Maria Ellis (Watmaugh) Reed, grandson of Joseph Reed [*q.v.*], and a descendant of Joseph Reed who emigrated from Ireland in 1671 and settled in Lynn, Mass. William graduated from the University of Pennsylvania in 1822 and then studied law with his uncle, John Sergeant [q.v.]. Admitted to the bar in November 1826, he immediately set out as his uncle's private secretary upon the abortive mission to the Panama Congress. While waiting in vain for the congress to reconvene, uncle and nephew stayed six months with Joel R. Poinsett [q.v.], American minister to Mexico, at Mexico city. Returning to Philadelphia, Reed began the active practice of law and also contributed an article upon Mexico to the *American Quarterly Review* (December 1827). He supported the anti-Masonic movement and later became a Whig, serving in the Pennsylvania Assembly in 1834 and 1835. Governor Ritner appointed him attorney-general of the state in 1838 and his service of one year was followed by a term in the state Senate (1841–42). In 1850 he was elected district attorney for Philadelphia, which office he held for two terms (1850–56), making a reputation for himself in criminal prosecution.

During these years his interest was by no means confined to politics. He gratified his scholarly tastes by writing upon historical subjects, and in 1850 he was appointed part-time professor of American history at the University of Pennsylvania, where his brother, Henry Hope Reed [q.v.], was professor of English; here he served six years. In the meantime he had been twice married: first to Louisa Whelan and then to Mary Love Ralston.

With the growth of the Know-Nothing party and the increasingly chaotic condition of the Whig, Reed became discontented with his political affiliation and in 1856 joined the Democratic party, writing to Buchanan (Feb. 7) that it was now the "conservative party of the nation." He earnestly supported Buchanan in the campaign of 1856 and was useful in urging old line Whigs to cast their votes for the Democratic candidate. After Buchanan's election, Reed was rewarded for his services by being appointed to the Chinese Mission. The treaties which the United States and European powers had made with China in the forties had proved unsatisfactory, and England and France had lately joined in requesting the United States to participate in an attempt to force further commercial concessions from the Celestial Empire. Buchanan refused to unite with them, but agreed to send a minister plenipotentiary to seek a new treaty and in doing so to communicate freely with the British and French ministers, meanwhile assuring the Chinese that the United States were not at war with them. Reed arrived in China in November

1857. Following in the wake of the more aggressive allies, he finally concluded, June 18, 1858, the treaty of Tientsin, which permitted the United States advantages similar to those secured for the other powers. By this treaty and two supplementary agreements signed at Shanghai Nov. 8, two additional ports were to be opened to American and European commerce; access was given to the rivers of China; tonnage dues were reduced so that foreign ships would have great advantage in the coasting trade; religious toleration was granted; the tariff was revised, legalizing the opium trade; and arrangements were made to satisfy American claims. Reed returned to the United States in May 1859.

When the Civil War broke out he bitterly and openly opposed it, with the result that he lost caste socially and his law practice dwindled. He spent the remainder of his life unhappily, trying to support himself by writing for Democratic papers. In 1870 he moved to Orange, N. J., and devoted himself to contributing to the New York *World*. He died in New York City, survived by two sons and a daughter. He was a man of austere manner who possessed a great deal of ability and cultivated intellectual taste, but he had an unfortunate temperament which was frequently manifest in foolish impulses. His more important writings include *Life and Correspondence of Joseph Reed* (1847), *President Reed of Pennsylvania, a Reply to Mr. George Bancroft and Others* (1867), and *The Life of Esther De Berdt, Afterwards Esther Reed of Pennsylvania* (1853).

[A number of his letters are in the Buchanan MSS. in the Hist. Soc. of Pa., and his diary as minister to China is in the Lib. of Congress. See also J. W. Reed, *Hist. of the Reed Family* (1861); Manton Marble, introduction to Reed's *Memories of Familiar Books* (1876); J. L. Chamberlain, *Universities and Their Sons: Univ. of Pa.*, vol. II (1902); Tyler Dennett, *Americans in Eastern Asia* (1922); State Dept. Archives, China, Instructions, vol. I, and China, Despatches, vols. XV–XVII; N. Y. *World*, Feb. 24, 1876; *Phila. Inquirer* and *Public Ledger*, Feb. 21, 1776.]

R. F. N.

REEDER, ANDREW HORATIO (July 12, 1807–July 5, 1864), governor of Kansas Territory, was born at Easton, Pa. His ancestor, John Reeder, emigrated from England to Long Island before 1656. Four generations later a lineal descendant, Absalom Reeder, the father of Andrew, served in the Revolution, became a merchant at Easton, acquired a competence, and in 1788 married Christiana Smith. The son attended the classical school of the Rev. Mr. Bishop at Easton for several years and was then sent to Lawrenceville, N. J., for further training. In 1825 he entered the law office of Peter Ihrie and three years later was admitted to the bar.

He was married in 1831 to Amelia Hutter of Easton, who with five of their eight children survived him. In appearance he was corpulent and erect, in manner generous and sincere, in business methodical and industrious.

He had neither sought nor held office before his appointment as governor of Kansas Territory on June 29, 1854. He was a successful lawyer and a reliable popular-sovereignty Democrat. He was, however, little fitted by experience or temperament to govern a frontier community in which bitter factions were struggling for mastery. Not until Oct. 7 did he arrive at Fort Leavenworth, where he established temporary executive quarters. The proslavery Democracy of Missouri expected his cooperation, but he assumed an attitude of independence. In his first speech on Kansas soil he pledged himself to preserve law and order and to protect the ballot box. Accompanied by other officials he made a tour of inspection to acquaint himself with the territory and, incidentally, to invest in land. In November he called an election for delegate to Congress, and the proslavery candidate, John W. Whitfield, easily won a three-cornered contest. A census was taken the following winter, and a legislature was chosen on Mar. 30, 1855. There was illegal voting on both sides, but the proximity of Missouri aided proslavery candidates. At Shawnee, whither the executive office had been removed, Reeder rejected returns of six districts from which protests had been received and ordered special elections. In April he went east to confer with party leaders and found the administration unsympathetic. Pierce suggested another appointment but Reeder declined. He returned to the territory and convened the first legislature on July 2 at Pawnee, in whose "town company" he was financially interested. After unseating antislavery members chosen at special elections, the general assembly passed a bill, over the governor's veto, reëstablishing the seat of government at Shawnee and adopted a memorial requesting Reeder's removal. The president had already determined upon dismissal, and among other reasons cited his belated arrival in the territory and his speculation in land. He attended the Big Springs convention in September and wrote the report of the resolutions committee. This embodied a violent attack upon the legislature, which had passed a stringent slave code since his removal. The radical tone of the resolutions brought him the unanimous nomination as delegate to Congress. At separate elections in October he and Whitfield were chosen by their respective parties, but Congress eventually rejected both. In March 1856 the Free State "legisla-

ture" elected Reeder and James H. Lane [q.v.] to the federal Senate. The ex-governor was soon indicted for treason but, disguised as an Irish laborer, he escaped by way of the Missouri river and arrived in Illinois on May 27. His diary from May 5 to May 31 was later printed in the *Transactions of the Kansas State Historical Society* (vol. III, 1886). He was enthusiastically welcomed at Chicago, and on May 29 he addressed the Republican state convention at Bloomington. A month later he presided at the Cleveland convention for Kansas aid and throughout the summer and fall took an active part in the Frémont campaign. As a spokesman of the Free State party he exerted considerable influence in molding public opinion in the North.

At the close of the presidential contest he resumed the practice of law at Easton. In 1860 he headed the Pennsylvania delegation to the Chicago convention, and on the first ballot for vice-president he received fifty-one votes. There is some evidence that Lincoln tendered him a brigadiership in the regular army (*War of the Rebellion: Official Records, Army,* 1 ser., LI, pt. 2, p. 98), but if so it was declined. He was chairman of the Pennsylvania delegation to the Baltimore convention in 1864.

[*Kan. Hist. Colls.,* vol. III (1886) with his executive minutes and sketch of life; U. W. Condit, *The Hist. of Easton* (copr. 1885); the *Address of Gen. W. E. Doster on . . . Hon. A. H. Reeder* (1901); D. W. Wilder, *The Annals of Kansas* (1886); *Kan. Weekly Herald* (Leavenworth), Sept. 15, 1854; *N. Y. Times,* July 8, 1864.]   W. H. S.

REEDY, WILLIAM MARION (Dec. 11, 1862–July 28, 1920), journalist, was born in St. Louis, Mo., one of three sons of Patrick Reedy, a police captain, and his wife, Ann (Marion). After passing through public school, Reedy entered Christian Brothers' College, and thence went to St. Louis University, where he graduated, at the age of eighteen, with the degree of master of accounts. Being minded to devote himself to literature, he became a reporter on the *Missouri Republican,* where his style, picturesque and unfailingly interesting, marked him for promotion at an early date. He found the newspaper field too narrow, however, and accordingly took to free-lance work, contributing frequently to *Brann's Iconoclast,* of Waco, Tex., and to the *Sunday Mirror* of St. Louis. The owner of this journal, James Campbell, watched the progress of young Reedy with interest, in 1893 put him into the editorial chair of his weekly, and in 1896 made him a present of the *Mirror.* At that time Reedy combined the genial improvidence of a Richard Steele with the polish of an Addison and the humor of a Charles Lamb.

Later, he achieved an incisiveness akin to Hazlitt's and the historical sweep of a Landor.

He published in book form a novel, *The Imitator* (1901), and three short essays. The latter, which show him as a master of prose style, comprise *The Law of Love* (1905), which originally appeared in *Brann's Iconoclast*, and *A Golden Book and The Literature of Childhood* (1910), written for the *Mirror*. Otherwise, his best work is contained in the thirty volumes of *Reedy's Mirror*, as it came to be called. He gave all he had to the readers of his weekly—articles, essays, and editorials dealing with matters political, religious, social, ethical, artistic, cultural, much that was quietly humorous. All his writing was marked by grace and distinction, and his historical trustworthiness was usually beyond question. Fired by Henry George's *Progress and Poverty,* he emphasized on every occasion the evils of land monopoly. Raised in the Catholic faith, he severed his connections with the church but always held aloof from religious controversy and disputes. Politically he was a liberal full of sympathy for humanity, though when labor troubles were to the fore his sympathy was always tempered by a logical sense of justice. Thus there were times when he seemed to reverse his own judgments, in both economic and literary matters, but such change of opinion was the result of honest conviction based on fresh viewpoints, and a passion for justice.

The files of *Reedy's Mirror* reveal the gradual growth of the editor. Beginning as a society journal, the paper became under Reedy's management a link between the cultures of East and West. As a literary and critical journal it came to be known over the English-speaking world, and during the last ten years of its existence it was a theater in which many writers who have since won fame found their first audience. Reedy was impresario for many—Zoe Akins, Babette Deutsch, Fannie Hurst, Edgar Lee Masters, Julia Peterkin, John Gould Fletcher, Sara Teasdale, Orrick Johns, John Hall Wheelock, Yone Noguchi—and was one of the first to introduce to American readers such literary lights as Lord Dunsany, Cunninghame Graham, Conrad, Galsworthy, and the Sitwells. Also, quite early in his career, he exhibited the enthusiasm for art which characterized his life, and thenceforth gave publicity to many young artists. High-spirited, frank and generous, he was a favorite in St. Louis society, and perhaps his reputation as a wit somewhat interfered with his literary aims and aspirations. He was married three times. His first wife he divorced; his second wife, Lalitte Bauduy, died in 1901; in 1909, he married Mrs. Margaret Helen Chambers, who survived him. He died suddenly in San Francisco, where he had gone to attend the Democratic National Convention of 1920.

[Files of *Reedy's Mirror,* esp. Memorial Number, Aug. 5, 1920; *Who's Who in America,* 1920–21; *Poetry,* Sept. 1920; *Nation* (N. Y.), Aug. 7, 1920; *St. Louis Globe-Democrat, San Francisco Chronicle,* July 29, 1920; personal acquaintance.]   C. J. F.

REES, JAMES (Dec. 25, 1821–Sept. 12, 1889), builder of steamboats, inventor, was born in Wales. At the age of seven, with eight brothers and sisters, he was brought to America by his parents, Thomas and Mary (Bowen) Rees. They settled in a small town near what is now Wheeling, W. Va., where one week afterward, the father died. Consequently, James was compelled to work at odd jobs and unable to enjoy even the rudimentary schooling of the time and place. He first tried to learn the trade of shoemaker but soon gave it up for farm work. Later, part of the family moved to Pittsburgh, where for six months the boy was employed in a coal mine, pushing loaded cars out of the pit. He then obtained a job at $1.50 a week in one of the earliest glass establishments and from this place went to earning three dollars a week in the machine shops of Smith & Irwin. During his fifteen months here he acquired a practical knowledge of steamboat engines. Meanwhile, he also worked at night, collecting travelers' trunks at the canal depots for twenty-five cents each and paying a drayman fifty cents to deliver a cartload. He was very frugal during his youth; a friend once said: "I don't think James Rees spent a ten-cent piece for three years needlessly." After some time as foreman for Snowden & Company at Brownsville, Pa., he became foreman for Stackhouse & Thompson and for them, in 1843, supervised the construction of the engines for the revenue cutter, *Lake Michigan,* built for service on the Great Lakes. Later he was in charge of the shop of Rowe & Davis, which he subsequently leased and operated with marked success. When his lease expired, he bought the establishment of Robert Whiteman.

In the early fifties, Rees started a line of passenger and freight steamers on the Allegheny River. His vessels were important factors in the oil-carrying trade until river transportation was superseded by the railroads. He then turned his attention to engine and steamboat-building. Although he did not invent the "stern-wheeler" (an English invention) which displaced the older vessels with their paddle wheels on the side, he popularized them in the United States. The fame of his vessels resulted in orders from

South American countries, and he also built boats for the carrying trade on the Volga and Dnieper rivers.

Rees was the inventor of a hot die press for making nuts for bolts, and also made improvements in steamboat construction, particularly for the protection of working parts. He was a far-seeing employer and must be credited with one of the early steps toward reducing the length of the American working day. While a foreman in Brownsville he was impressed by the exhausting effects of the long hours and accordingly introduced the ten-hour day, which led to an increase in production at a lower money cost. He married Mary Morris, daughter of Robert and Mary (Perry) Morris, and became the father of five sons and five daughters. He was for many years a leading member of the Pittsburgh City Council. Some years after his death the business he had founded was incorporated as James Rees & Sons Company, Pittsburgh.

[*Am. Shipbuilder*, Apr. 18, 1901; J. W. Jordan in J. N. Boucher, ed., *A Century and a Half of Pittsburg and Her People* (1908), vol. IV; Erasmus Wilson, *Standard Hist. of Pittsburg, Pa.* (1898); *Pittsburgh Post, Pittsburg Press*, Sept. 12, 1889; *Pittsburg Dispatch*, Sept. 13, 1889; family names from a son, D. A. Rees.]   A. I.

REES, JOHN KROM (Oct. 27, 1851–Mar. 9, 1907), geodesist and astronomer, was born in New York City. He was the son of Hans and Lucinda (Krom) Rees, a grandson of Iver Jensen and Lena Maria Rees and of Reuben and Mary (Dubois) Krom, and a descendant of Louis DuBois. He graduated from Columbia College in 1872, and from the Columbia School of Mines in 1875, acting as assistant in mathematics in the School of Mines from 1873 to 1876. In the latter year he married Louise, daughter of Nathaniel and Emma (Chambers) Sands of New York. From 1876 to 1881 he was professor of mathematics and astronomy in Washington University, St. Louis, then returned to Columbia as director of the observatory and instructor in the newly formed department of geodesy and practical astronomy. He remained at Columbia for the rest of his life, was promoted to a professorship in 1884, and made head of an independent department of astronomy in 1892. In 1895 he received the degree of Ph.D. from Columbia. He acted as judge of instruments of precision at the Paris exposition in 1900, receiving the decoration of Chevalier of the Legion of Honor in recognition of his services. He was president of the New York Academy of Sciences, 1894–96; secretary of the American Metrological Society, 1882–96, and secretary of the Columbia University Council, 1892–98.

The Columbia Observatory to which Rees went in 1881 was a small wooden structure housing a small telescope and a transit. It served well enough for the instruction of college students and the instructive entertainment of city school children, but it was far from satisfying to the demands of the director's ambition to do real scientific work. Conditions were much improved by the removal in 1883 to a new building on Forty-ninth Street, although difficulties from smoke and railroad vibrations still set embarrassing limits to the kinds of research that could be undertaken. Rees's principal observational research was a study of the variation of terrestrial latitudes and the constant of aberration. This was carried out at Columbia by Rees, Harold Jacoby, and H. S. Davis, in cooperation with the Royal Observatory at Naples, from 1893 to 1900, and the results published as *Contributions from the Observatory of Columbia College*, nos. 8 and 9 (1895–1906). The value of simultaneous observations at two or more stations in approximately the same latitude but in widely different longitudes has since been recognized in the establishment of several international latitude stations.

It was also under Rees's direction that the reduction of Lewis Morris Rutherfurd's measures of his star plates was carried out at the Columbia Observatory and this great mass of valuable material made generally available by publication. As secretary of the American Metrological Society he did the nation a great service by his enthusiastic advocacy of the introduction of standard time. His most important contribution to educational development was his insistence on the importance of practical field work for students of civil engineering which resulted in the establishment of the Columbia summer school of geodesy, first at Cooperstown, N. Y., and later at Osterville, Mass.

[Harold Jacoby, in *School of Mines Quart.*, July 1907; *Who's Who in America*, 1906–07; *Pop. Astron.*, Dec. 1908; *Nature (London)*, Apr. 4, 1907; *Naturwissenschaftliche Rundschau*, Apr. 11, 1907; *Am. Jour. Sci.*, Apr. 1907; *Athenæum*, May 11, 1907; *Bibliotheca Mathematica*, June 27, 1907; *Astronomische Rundschau*, IX, 173 (1907); *Pubs. Astron. Soc. of the Pacific*, XIX (1907), 173; *Observatory*, May 1907; *N. Y. Tribune*, Mar. 11, 1907.]   R. S. D.

REESE, ABRAM (Apr. 21, 1829–Apr. 25, 1908), inventor, manufacturer, was the sixth child of William and Elizabeth (Joseph) Reese and was born in Llanelly, Southern Wales. He came with his parents to the United States in 1832. Some years later, in Pittsburgh, Pa., the family name was changed from Rees to Reese. William Reese was a skilled iron-worker and for five years engaged in his trade in various sections of Pennsylvania, then finally settled in Pittsburgh. Here Abram, after a few years' schooling, began working in the iron mills. When he was about twenty-five years old he left Pittsburgh to become labor boss of the Cambria Iron Works, Johnstown, Pa., where his older brother, Jacob [*q.v.*], was employed as construction engineer and superintendent. At this mill Abram had the honor of puddling the first "heat" produced. About 1857 he gave up steel work temporarily to engage in coal mining with another brother, Isaac [*q.v.*], but this undertaking was soon abandoned because of the meager financial returns.

In 1860 Reese returned to Pittsburgh to become manager of the Petrolite Oil Works, built by his brother Jacob, one of the first refineries in the state; but upon the completion of the Reese & Graff Iron Works (later known as the Fort Pitt Iron Works), erected by Jacob in Pittsburgh in 1862, Abram became manager there. During the Civil War he was engaged at this plant making iron armor plates for the federal government. Following the war, be became general manager of the Excelsior Iron Works in Pittsburgh and early in 1870 was made superintendent of the Vulcan Iron Works at St. Louis, Mo. While here, in June 1871, he rolled the first rails to be made west of the Mississippi River. His last active connection with the steel industry was in Louisville, Ky., where he equipped and operated a mill for rerolling metal rails. After managing this plant for some time he retired and lived in Pittsburgh until his death.

Reese's inventive work began early in his career and was concerned almost wholly with the perfection and improvement of machinery for rolling iron and steel products. His first United States patent, granted Dec. 20, 1859, was for a machine to roll street-railroad rails, and on Feb. 21, 1860, he received Patent No. 27,238 for a rivet- and bolt-making machine. With the additional improvements which he devised and patented in 1861, this machine, which made the head and stem of a bolt or rivet in one operation, was widely used for many years. During the four-year period 1867–70, he confined his attention to horseshoe-making machinery. In this field he acquired eight patents, covering the only machine then known which rolled shaped metal in one operation. It was adapted in the course of time to the making of some fifty other shaped articles. Between 1870 and 1890, more than twenty patents were granted Reese for a variety of inventions, including a railroad-car stove, an air brake, a machine for making corrugated iron, and machinery for manufacturing garden hoes.

On Aug. 16, 1892, he obtained Patent No. 481,058 for his universal rolling mill. The most extensive and valuable application of this invention has been to the manufacture of steel beams; in 1929 the modern form of the Reese universal mill was the subject of a lawsuit brought by the Bethlehem Steel Company against the Carnegie Steel Company. Reese married Mary Godwin of Pittsburgh, Pa., on Dec. 14, 1854, and at the time of his death in Pittsburgh he was survived by his widow and five children.

[J. W. Jordan, *Encyc. of Pa. Biog.*, vol. VII (1916); *Pittsburg Dispatch*, Apr. 26, 1908; Patent Office records; correspondence with family.]   C. W. M.

REESE, ISAAC (Apr. 29, 1821–Jan. 1, 1908), brick manufacturer, inventor, eldest son of William and Elizabeth (Joseph) Reese, brother of Jacob and Abram Reese [*qq.v.*], was born in Llanelly, Southern Wales. When he was ten years old he began working in the iron works in Wales where his father was likewise employed, and at the age of eleven emigrated with his parents to the United States. For the next sixteen years he worked in iron mills with his father in Phoenixville, Bellefonte, and after 1837 in Pittsburgh, Pa., becoming an expert hammerer by the time he was seventeen. Then, in 1848, he began a blast-furnace operation of his own in Clarion County, Pa., but the depression of 1849 put a stop to the enterprise and he returned to his trade in Pittsburgh. Eight years later, with the money he had saved, he engaged in coal mining in western Pennsylvania in association with his brother Abram, but this venture was soon given up as unprofitable. Reese again returned to Pittsburgh and this time, because of his large acquaintance and experience in iron manufacturing, became a salesman for Johnston, Taylor & Company, manufacturers of firebrick. He took up this new work vigorously and at the same time directed his attention toward perfecting a better brick, for his experience in the iron industry had shown him that the available firebrick was hardly satisfactory. In due time, therefore, Reese invented a new process of manufacturing firebrick, and, using a new clay which he had discovered, made and placed on the market the "Woodland" brick. This was far superior, especially for crucible furnaces, to any brick then made. It found a waiting market and for years Reese controlled its sale in the Pittsburgh area. In 1860, three years after entering the brick industry, he bought out his employers' business, which he operated until, in the panic of 1873, he lost every cent he had made.

Just prior to this disaster he had begun experimenting in an effort to perfect a firebrick capable of withstanding the higher furnace temperatures occasioned by the new processes then coming into use. Although he had not completed this work at the time he failed in business, the results attained were so encouraging that he was able to borrow sufficient capital in 1878 to resume his experiments at his brick plant in Manorville, Pa. Four years later, with the help of his eldest son, he produced the "Reese Silica Brick," capable of withstanding a temperature of 5000 degrees Fahrenheit with practically no shrinkage or expansion. It was thus suitable for glass, open-hearth steel, copper, and other metallurgical furnaces, and soon found a market in practically every manufacturing state of the Union. To meet the demand for his product Reese enlarged his plant at Manorville and later erected another at Cowanshannock, Pa. These plants were called the Phoenix Firebrick Works, of which Reese was the sole owner. Still later two other plants were built at Retort, Pa., and continued under the sole ownership of Reese until 1896, when he took his three sons into the business, the firm name being changed to Isaac Reese & Sons. In 1900 the business was incorporated and two years later it was sold in its entirety to the Harbison Walker Refractories Company. Reese then retired and lived in Pittsburgh for the rest of his life. He married Elizabeth Bebb Jones in Pittsburgh on May 24, 1844, three years after she had come to America from Wales, and at the time of his death he was survived by four of his eleven children.

[J. W. Jordan, *Encyc. of Pa. Biog.*, vol. VII (1916); *Iron Age,* Jan. 9, 1908; *Pittsburg Dispatch,* Jan. 2, 1908; correspondence with family; Patent Office records.]   C. W. M.

REESE, JACOB (July 14, 1825–Mar. 25, 1907), inventor, metallurgist, was born in Llanelly, Southern Wales. He was a son of William and Elizabeth (Joseph) Reese, and a brother of Isaac and Abram Reese [*qq.v.*]. He emigrated to America with his parents when he was seven years old. Both his father and brother Isaac were iron workers, and as early as 1836 Jacob helped in making the first iron "bloom" under the boiling process at the iron works in Bellefonte, Pa. The following year the family moved to Pittsburgh where Jacob, then twelve years old, began working in the iron mills with his father and brother. Here he continued for the next thirteen years, except for one year spent in Wilkes-Barre, not only becoming a skilled iron worker but also gaining, through study at night, a thorough knowledge of the chemistry and metallurgy of iron and steel. In 1850 he hap-

pened to see an advertisement offering $1,000 for the best plan of a nail factory. He submitted complete working drawings of a design of his own and won the prize as well as the job of building the plant in Sharon, Pa. From that time on, for the next sixteen years, Reese's services were much in demand by the iron and steel industry.

During this period he began the inventive work which he continued throughout his life. In 1852 he built a rail mill for English, Bennett Company in Pittsburgh, the first of its kind in this region; in 1854–55 he was engineer of construction and management for the Cambria Iron Company, Johnstown, Pa.; and from 1856 to 1859 he was engaged in Pittsburgh in the sale of rolling-mill supplies. From 1860 to 1862 he was in the petroleum business in Pittsburgh, where he built the Petrolite Oil Works, containing both tanks and stills of his own invention. In 1862, in order to make hoop iron for the oil barrels, he designed and built the Fort Pitt Iron Works. He enlarged these mills in 1864 and in 1865 built the Southside Rolling Mill and Tube Works. The following year at a cost of $50,000, he built a metallurgical plant of his own in Pittsburgh, and there for twenty-five years engaged in extensive experimentation which yielded him over 175 United States patents and some five hundred inventions and discoveries. Many of these were for iron-mill machinery— rolls, presses, and hammers for the manufacture of iron and steel products—but, in addition, he made many valuable discoveries in the metallurgy of iron and steel. Probably the greatest of these and the one which brought him the greatest renown was that of the basic open-hearth steel process. He perfected it about 1877 but because of interference proceedings in the Patent Office, his claim as prior inventor was not favorably decided until 1881. Meanwhile he had sold some of the involved patents to Andrew Carnegie. The latter transferred the agreement to the Bessemer Steel Company which, in turn, transferred it to the Steel Patents Company, and for seventeen years Reese was engaged in expensive litigation to obtain payment. The last patent involved in the agreement was granted him just a year before his death.

Reese resided in Pittsburgh until 1892, when he moved to Sharon Hill, Pa., near Philadelphia, which was his home for the remainder of his life. He was interested in many large manufacturing enterprises and was identified with most of the leading philanthropic, civic, and industrial movements in Pennsylvania. He was married twice: first, to Eliza Matthews of Pittsburgh; and, second, about 1901, to Jessie Mc-Elroy of Philadelphia, who with six children by his first wife survived him.

[J. W. Jordan, *Encyc. of Pa. Biog.*, vol. VII (1916); J. M. Swank, *Hist. of the Manufacture of Iron in All Ages* (2nd ed., 1892); *Iron Age*, Mar. 28, 1907; *Public Ledger* (Phila.), Mar. 27, 1907; Patent Office records; correspondence with family.]   C. W. M.

REESE, JOHN JAMES (June 16, 1818–Sept. 4, 1892), toxicologist, was born in Philadelphia, the son of Jacob Reese, a prosperous merchant, and Leah (James) Reese. He was graduated by the University of Pennsylvania, A.B., in 1836 (valedictorian of his class), and A.M. and M.D., in 1839. Settling in Philadelphia, he soon limited his practice to medical chemistry and to the teaching of it and allied subjects. His first appointment was that of lecturer on materia medica and therapeutics in the Philadelphia Medical Institute; later, he served as professor of medical chemistry in the medical department of Pennsylvania College (1852–59) and, finally, as professor of medical jurisprudence and toxicology in the University of Pennsylvania from 1865 until he retired in 1891. For many years he was a member of the firm of Booth, Reese & Camac, analytic chemists of Philadelphia. During the Civil War he was head of the Christian Street Hospital, Philadelphia, with the rank of assistant surgeon, United States Army. He also had numerous connections with Philadelphia hospitals and became a member of local as well as national medical and scientific societies. He served as treasurer of the Philadelphia County Medical Society and as president of the Medical Jurisprudence Society of Philadelphia (1886–87).

Reese's contribution to medical literature was important, especially in the field of toxicology. During his early days as a lecturer on therapeutics he published *The American Medical Formulary* (1850); his *Syllabus of a Course of Lectures on Medical Chemistry* (1857) was a useful students' textbook, as was his *Manual of Toxicology* (1874). His scientific work culminated, however, in a *Text Book of Medical Jurisprudence and Toxicology* (1884), the best book on the subject in its time. It passed through many editions and won for itself a place of deserving distinction in medico-legal literature. As an authority on toxicology, Reese often gave expert testimony in court; his most important case was the trial of Mrs. Wharton (J. T. Morse, Jr., in *American Law Review*, July 1872).

Reese is described as tall and slim with dark complexion and black hair and eyes. Quick and animated, he was greatly admired as a lecturer.

He married Sallie, daughter of William Gibson [*q.v.*], professor of surgery in the University of Pennsylvania. He died at Atlantic City, N. J., leaving his wife and several children.

[J. L. Chamberlain, *Universities and Their Sons: Univ. of Pa.*, vol. I (1901); *Phila. Press, Phila. Record, Boston Transcript*, and *N. Y. Tribune*, Sept. 6, 1892; *Boston Medic. and Surgic. Jour.*, Sept. 8, 1892; *Jour. Am. Medic. Asso.*, Oct. 29, 1892.]   H. R. V.

REEVE, TAPPING (October 1744–Dec. 13, 1823), jurist, teacher of law, author of legal works, the son of Abner Reeve, a Presbyterian minister, was born at Brookhaven, Long Island, N. Y. Graduated from the College of New Jersey (Princeton) in 1763, he spent the next seven years of his life in teaching, finally (1769–70) as a tutor in the college itself. In 1771 he moved to Connecticut and took up the study of law in the office of Judge Root at Hartford. Admitted to the bar in the following year, he moved to Litchfield and began at once the practice of his profession. Though a newcomer in a locality noted for the number and excellence of its lawyers, Reeve in a short time, and apparently without difficulty, won for himself a place of prominence among them. In December 1776 the Connecticut Assembly appointed him a member of a committee formed for the purpose of going through the state and arousing an interest in the Revolution. He accepted an officer's commission, and actually set out to join the Continental Army, but returned home on hearing of Washington's victories in the Jersey campaign of 1776–77. He was state's attorney for 1788. He became a member of the legislature and served once on the Council.

Like most of his contemporaries he was intensely interested in politics. On the development of parties following the adoption of the Constitution he aligned himself with the Federalists, of which group he was an ardent, not to say violent, partisan and local leader. He was a frequent contributor of political articles to the Litchfield *Monitor*, a Federalist newspaper published by Thomas Collier. His usual *nom de plume* was "Phocion" or "Asdrubal," but a number of communications signed "Marcellus" are said likewise to have been his. Engendered in the heat of party conflict, these articles are characterized by a straightforwardness of expression which at times savors of lack of restraint. As a result of one of them, in the *Monitor* for Dec. 2, 1801, he was indicted by a federal grand jury (April 1806) for having libeled President Jefferson, Collier also being indicted for having published the article (U. S. Circuit Court Records, New Haven, vol. III, 271–78). The indictment was later dismissed, according to tradition at the request of Jefferson himself.

Reeve's most notable claim to distinction was the founding of the Litchfield Law School, the first—if we except the "school," or department, of law at the College of William and Mary, of which George Wythe [q.v.] was the professor —and for a long time quite the most important school of its kind in the country. This school, possibly the result of some survival of the teaching instinct which had kept Reeve at Princeton after his graduation, but more probably an expedient devised to supplement the income derived from his law practice which had been curtailed during the Revolutionary War, was formally opened in 1784. For some time before that date Reeve had been giving in his office regular instruction in law in a methodical way, seemingly along much the same lines as those later followed in the school. For fourteen years, during which time some two hundred students attended the school, Reeve alone was the teacher. In 1798 his appointment as a judge of the superior court made it necessary for him to choose someone to help him in teaching. Accordingly he selected as an associate a former pupil and a recent graduate of the school, James Gould [q.v.], who, until his own appointment to the bench in 1816, devoted practically his whole time to the work of the school. To Gould, a far abler administrator and executive than Reeve, unquestionably belongs the major share of the credit for developing an institution that in the early years of the nineteenth century brought to Litchfield hundreds of young men from almost every state in the Union, and numbered among its graduates some of the most prominent men in the public life of the next generation.

In addition to being very active in political and civic affairs, Reeve was a leading figure in the religious life of his community, a matter of far more comparative importance and prestige then than now. He read a printed sermon by Lyman Beecher [q.v.] and brought him to Litchfield. Beecher found Reeve a kindred spirit, "an eminently pious man" (Autobiography, p. 225). Seemingly Reeve's piety was of a mildly militant sort. He was one of thirty-six to sign a temperance pledge in 1789, during a burst of local enthusiasm to curb the drink evil. He was agent in Litchfield for the Connecticut Bible Society, in which capacity he was praised by Beecher for his zeal and success. In 1812 a number of leading men from all parts of the state held a meeting in New Haven to found a society for the suppression of vice and the promotion of good morals; Reeve was appointed chairman of the committee of twenty-six to whom was entrusted the task of organizing the society.

For some sixteen years he was a judge of the superior court. In 1814 he was made chief justice of the supreme court of errors. Within a year he had reached the age of seventy years, the compulsory age of retirement from the bench; actually he retired in 1816. This, together with the fact that the arrangement which he had made with Gould resulted in his receiving only a small share in the proceeds of the law school, led him to turn to the publishing of legal works to augment his income. His principal law book was, The Law of Baron and Femme; of Parent and Child; of Guardian and Ward; of Master and Servant; and of the Powers of Courts of Chancery. With an Essay on the Terms Heir, Heirs, and Heirs of the Body (1816), of which there were four editions. He was the author also of, A Treatise on the Law of Descents in the Several United States of America (1825).

All accounts agree in ascribing to Reeve an unusually attractive personality. Of his appearance, clearly when he was well along in years, Beecher's Autobiography (I, 224) says: "He had a pair of soft dark eyes of rare beauty, a beaming expression of intelligence and benevolence, while his soft gray hair fell in silver tresses to his shoulders. . . . His figure was large and portly, and his manners gentle and dignified. His voice was singular, having failed for some unknown cause, so that he always spoke in a whisper, and yet so distinctly that a hundred students at once could take notes as he delivered his law lectures." This characteristic weakness of voice was made a matter of ridicule by Reeve's political enemies. Thus the Litchfield Witness (Apr. 2, 1806) in reporting a caucus at which Reeve spoke says, "It is certain that Judge Reeve opened his mouth . . . and some say that they heard him speak." Reeve was twice married. His first wife, a former pupil of his early teaching days, was Sally Burr, daughter of President Burr of Princeton, and sister of Aaron Burr, who was one of Reeve's first law students. The result of this union was a son, Aaron Burr Reeve, who died in 1809 leaving an only son, Tapping Burr Reeve, who died unmarried in 1829. There were no children by the second marriage (1799), to his housekeeper, "a most respectable woman" (White, post, p. 98). He died at Litchfield.

[The Autobiography, Correspondence, etc., of Lyman Beecher (2 vols., 1864–65) gives many intimate personal touches. So also does Beecher's funeral sermon, which is printed in the Christian Spectator, Feb. 1827, pp. 62–71. A sketch of Reeve by one who joined his school in 1793 will be found in D. S. Boardman, Sketches of the Early Lights of the Litchfield Bar

(1860), pp. 7–10. Practically complete files of the *Monitor* and the *Witness* are in the library of the Litchfield Hist. Soc. A picture of the law school building, together with a portrait of Reeve and much information on both him and the school, will be found in *Presentation of the Reeve Law School Building to the Litchfield Hist. Soc.* (1911). For the pedagogical side of the Litchfield Law School see, W. D. Lewis, ed., *Great American Lawyers*, II (1907), 469–71; A. C. White, ed., *The Bi-Centennial Celebration of the Settlement of Litchfield* (1920), pp. 49–58; T. D. Woolsey, *Hist. Discourse . . . Pronounced before the Alumni of the Law Dept. of Yale Coll. at the Fiftieth Anniversary of the Foundation of the Dept.* (1874). A considerable number of the typical Reeve-Gould Law School students' note-books are now in the library of the Yale Law School. Quite the best and most extensive single collection of materials having to do with Reeve and the law school is in the possession of Samuel H. Fisher of Litchfield, whose book, *The Litchfield Law School, 1775–1833* (1933), is the latest treatment. A number of letters written by Reeve are included in the collection. Of general value are: A. C. White, *The Hist. of the Town of Litchfield* (1920), pp. 98–109; D. C. Kilbourn, *The Bench and Bar of Litchfield County, Conn.: 1709–1909* (1909), pp. 181–214. Written opinions by Reeve will be found in I *Connecticut Reports* (Day). There is an obituary in *Connecticut Courant* (Hartford), Dec. 23, 1823.]

G. E. W.

REEVES, ARTHUR MIDDLETON (Oct. 7, 1856–Feb. 25, 1891), philologist and historian, was born in Cincinnati, Ohio, the youngest son of Mark Ewen and Caroline (Middleton) Reeves. His father, a native of New Jersey who had first removed to a Quaker community at Richmond, Ind., later to Cincinnati, and again to Richmond in 1865, had from humble surroundings become a prosperous merchant. During the Civil War the boy attended school at Cincinnati but prepared for college at the Friends' academy in Richmond. When he was fifteen he had the opportunity to travel extensively in the United States, Europe, and the Near East, and he kept a journal of everything he saw abroad. Returning in 1872 he resumed his studies, learned the printer's trade, and established a thriving business, which later became consolidated with the *Palladium,* a leading newspaper of the county. In September 1873 he entered Cornell University but after a few months was obliged to leave because of lack of health. He returned, however, and graduated in 1878. His college record was brilliant. Owing to his retiring disposition he made friends slowly, but those he made were permanent. He wrote college songs and edited various college publications with unusual skill and enthusiasm. He early displayed a decided bent for languages and through the encouragement of his professors, Daniel Willard Fiske and Thomas Frederick Crane [*qq.v.*], became familiar with German, Swedish, Icelandic, French, and Italian. "In these tongues, as well as in Danish and Spanish, he later acquired excellent conversational ability, while in Icelandic he became a philological authority. It was the influence of Professor Fiske that first directed his attention to the Norse languages, and developed in him an enthusiasm for what presently became his life work" (Foulke, *post,* p. xii). During his senior year his interest in the Swedish poet Tegnér led to the choice of *Frithiofs Saga* as the subject for his graduation thesis and to the publication of metrical translations from that poem in the *Cornell Era* (Feb. 8, Mar. 22, 1878).

After graduation he went abroad again, to France, Germany, and Spain, and met such Americans as Andrew D. White and Bayard Taylor. In 1879 he traveled in Iceland with Professor Fiske. He studied Icelandic culture with unflagging industry, and the descriptions of Iceland in his private letters are charming. Later he spent considerable time in Copenhagen, where he examined Old Norse manuscripts, in the British Isles, and in Berlin, where he attended lectures on philological subjects. In America his studies were frequently interrupted by the necessity of managing "Grasmere," a large farm in Indiana left to his care by his father's death in 1883. He never married and was deeply attached to his parental family. He was killed in a railroad accident near Hagerstown, Ind. Returning whenever possible to his first interest, Old Norse, he translated various minor sagas and modern stories, of which Thoroddsen's *Lad and Lass* was published in 1890. The completion of a translation of the *Laxdaela Saga* was prevented by his early death. His greatest achievement was the preparation and publication of *The Finding of Wineland the Good* in 1890 (2nd ed., 1895), a large quarto volume with translations and phototypes of the vellum manuscripts of the saga dealing with the Norse discoveries of America. This was a pioneer historical work of excellent scholarship. The English portion of it was posthumously reproduced in 1906 in *The Norse Discovery of America*, a compilation of investigations by himself, North L. Beamish, and Rasmus B. Anderson. The latter also reprinted Reeves's version of the *Hauksbok* in his edition of *The Flatey Book* (1906).

[W. D. Foulke, "Biog. and Correspondence of Arthur M. Reeves," *The Finding of Wineland, the Good, ante* (2nd ed. 1895); T. F. Crane, "In Memoriam Arthur Middleton Reeves," *Cornell Era,* Mar. 7, 1891; alumni records of Cornell Univ.]

A. B. B.

REHAN, ADA (Apr. 22, 1860–Jan. 8, 1916), actress, was born at Limerick, Ireland, the daughter of Thomas and Harriett Crehan. Five years later the family emigrated to the United States and settled in Brooklyn, N. Y., where Ada lived as a child. Her elder sisters went on the stage, and in 1873, at Newark, N. J., she played a small part in *Across the Continent*, by her brother-in-law, Oliver Doud Byron, who was her first coach. Her sister, Mrs. Byron, soon secured her a place in Mrs. Drew's famous company at the Arch Street Theatre, Philadelphia. By a printer's error, she was billed as Ada C. Rehan for her début, much to her distress. But as the début was highly successful, Mrs. Drew finally persuaded her to keep the name Rehan under which it was made. After a season in Philadelphia she played in stock in Louisville, two seasons in Albaugh's company at Albany and Baltimore, and in the supporting companies of Fanny Davenport, Booth, Lawrence Barrett, John T. Raymond, and other stars. Both in the stock companies and with the stars, she was frequently called upon for Shakespearian rôles, and it was while she was playing Bianca in *The Taming of the Shrew* in Albany, in 1877, that Augustin Daly first saw her. He saw her again in 1879, supporting Fanny Davenport in his own play, *Pique*. He thereupon engaged her for his New York company, and in May 1879, at the Olympic Theatre, New York, she began the association that was to last as long as Daly lived, appearing in his version of *L'Assommoir*. On Sept. 17, 1879, Daly opened his own theatre, on Broadway at Thirtieth, and Ada Rehan then played Nelly Beers in *Love's Young Dream*. Almost immediately *Divorce* was revived, and she took the leading part. From that date until the Daly company was disbanded more than twenty years later, she was its leading woman, one of the group of players there who came to be known as the "Big Four," and a popular idol of the New York and London play-going public.

Miss Rehan's training was secured in a large number and variety of rôles. She probably played, in twenty-six years, over two hundred parts, ranging from Rosalind to Tilburina, from Meg Merrilies to Miranda. But under the Daly régime the style of the plays in which she appeared had less variety than the number of her parts might indicate, and the style of her acting was conditioned both by her own personality and the demands of the Daly repertory. When she joined Daly, a girl in her teens, the poetic drama (especially Shakespeare) and the "old comedies" were still the dignified base of most ambitious players' repertories. They remained the base of Daly's to the end. For his more popular bills, he turned most often to foreign farce, which he freely adapted to the needs of his company, especially Mrs. Gilbert, Miss Rehan, James Lewis, and John Drew—the "Big Four." His aim was theatrical effect. Miss Rehan's art accordingly developed along different lines from the main

current of evolution in the theatre during her prime. Nearly all the parts she played (the best of them comedy rôles, for by nature she was most gifted as a comedienne) came to be considered "artificial" before the new century was under way. Some, of course, were artificial because they belonged to the poetic drama; some because they belonged to the older Comedy of Manners; some, and these chiefly the Daly adaptations of German farces, because they had little relation to life in the original, and less in the adaptations. Naturally poetic drama requires its rhetorical technique, and the old Comedy of Manners demands a style of precision and sparkle and unselfconscious artificiality. Translated into terms of over-emphasis and comic artificiality, this style fitted the Daly farces of the eighties and nineties. In it Ada Rehan was reared and became its complete mistress: and on the death of Daly and the passing of his company, it meant the end of her career when she was still in her prime. In that fact, much more than in the list of parts she played or triumphs she enjoyed, lies the real interest of her story to a later day. Unlike John Drew, who escaped from the Daly company in the early nineties and adapted his style (always much more instinctively naturalistic than hers) to the new drama, she remained devoted to her manager till it was too late. This was expanded prophetically by G. B. Shaw, in his *Dramatic Opinions and Essays* (1906, vol. I, p. 174 ff.), when he reviewed her acting in London during the nineties. There is no better or more vivid appreciation of her merits, and no keener analysis of her weakness, to be found in print than this passage.

Outside of the theatre, her life was uneventful. She was unmarried, and she devoted herself ardently to her professional work. As early as 1884 Daly took his company to London, where in July she acted at Toole's Theatre. In May 1886 the Daly company again visited London, playing at the Strand for nine weeks, and then made a tour to Paris, Hamburg, Berlin, as well as the English provincial cities. On Jan. 18, 1887, in New York, Miss Rehan first acted her most famous part, Katherine in *The Taming of the Shrew*. The Induction was played for the first time in America. In June 1888 she was playing Katherine in London, and in August she played it at the Memorial Theatre in Stratford. She also acted again in Paris. On Dec. 17, 1889, in New York, she first appeared as Rosalind, and in June 1890 she played that rôle in London. In September 1891 the Daly troupe again invaded Paris, acting at the Vaudeville, where Miss Rehan played Lady Teazle, Katherine, and Rosalind.

The company then went to the Lyceum in London. The actress visited Tennyson at this time, to hear him read *The Foresters,* and in October laid the cornerstone of Daly's Theatre, Leicester Square, in which she was a partner. *The Foresters* was first produced in New York the next March, with Miss Rehan as Marian. On June 27, 1893, Daly's London theatre was opened, and Miss Rehan acted therein till the following May, giving 111 performances of *Twelfth Night* and more than fifty of *The School for Scandal.* In 1896 she and the Daly company toured America to San Francisco and in July 1896 again played in London. She first played Miranda on Apr. 20, 1897, in New York, but in August she was in England, giving a benefit performance at Stratford, and touring the provinces. In 1898 she was the Roxane in Daly's rather ineffective production of *Cyrano de Bergerac,* and early in 1899 played in *The Great Ruby.* She went to England with Daly in the late spring of 1899, and in June he died, in Paris. In 1900–01 she acted in a play of Paul Kester, *Sweet Nell of Old Drury,* and in 1903–04, in association with Otis Skinner, revived *The Taming of the Shrew* and other plays of her repertory. The next season she continued to present these plays, on tour, with Charles Richman, but the glamor of the Daly company was lacking, taste had changed, and public response was not great. Her last public appearance was at a benefit in New York, May 2, 1905, given at the Metropolitan Opera House for Madame Modjeska. Thereafter she lived in retirement, in New York and at her summer home on the Cumberland coast of England. She died at Roosevelt Hospital, New York, after a long arterial illness, in January 1916. She left an estate of about $200,000, partly derived from her partnership with Daly in his London Theatre.

Ada Rehan was an Irish-eyed, brown-haired, tall, ample, and vivacious woman, not conventionally beautiful but arch, piquant, incessantly alive, with great feminine charm, sensitive perception, and a fine voice under perfect control. Otis Skinner has told of her "abounding joy and vitality." "She gave her audiences no opportunity for indifference of mood," he says. She was at her best in rôles which called for arch or even tempestuous comedy, touched with sincerity of feminine feeling or with poetry, as in "The Shrew," where her absolutely regal whirlwinds of temper never quite hid the woman beneath. Writing of her revival of Lady Teazle in 1904, James Huneker said, "It is still adorably artificial, artlessly artificial. . . . She executes passages of old comedy in the right key, with *bravura*

in the grand manner. There are few surviving on the stage who are to the grand manner born as is Miss Rehan. Miss Terry is more intimate, more contemporary. But the Rehan is still the goddess in the cloud." The term applied not at all to her private character. She was simple, studious, full of fun. But her acting style was set to the music of blank verse, to the artificial glitter of "old comedy," to the romantic elevation of the stage above the range of the all-conquering naturalism which by 1900 ruled in drama.

[See: Wm. Winter, *The Wallet of Time* (1913), vol. II, and *Ada Rehan* (privately printed, N. Y. and London, 1898), containing a list of her rôles and excerpts from foreign criticisms; J. B. Clapp and E. F. Edgett, *Players of the Present* (2 vols., 1899) ; L. C. Strang, *Famous Actresses of the Day in America* (1899) ; *N. Y. Times,* Jan. 9, 1916. Information as to certain facts was supplied for this sketch by Miss Rehan's nephew, Arthur Byron.]   W. P. E.

REHN, FRANK KNOX MORTON (Apr. 12, 1848–July 6, 1914), artist, was born in Philadelphia, Pa., the son of Isaac and Abigail Frances (Zelly) Rehn. His forebears came to America from Holland. His father was an inventor who is credited with some of the first telescopic photographs of the sun and moon. Painting was his hobby. Until Rehn was eighteen, he gave no thought to art. At that time he was taken seriously ill, and during convalescence his father brought him some paints. As a result, he decided to become an artist but met instant opposition from his father who had himself led a precarious life as an inventor. A friendly disagreement developed. The family removed to Washington, but young Rehn remained in Philadelphia to live on his own resources and devote himself to painting. He found instruction at the Pennsylvania Academy of the Fine Arts, and his many friends kept him busy with portrait commissions. But lean years followed. After a struggle with poverty he sold quite successfully some terra cotta placques which he had painted with still-life, heads, landscape, and marines. With the money earned from them he went to the Jersey coast, discovering in the sea a motif that marked the turning point in his art career, and that caused him to specialize in marines. In 1881 the young painter was married to Margaret Selby, daughter of George C. Bower of Philadelphia. They went to New York and established themselves at the Hotel Chelsea, which had studios on the top floor. Rehn was thrown with other artists and soon his reputation was made. He also became a member of the Lotos and Salmagundi clubs.

As early as 1882 Rehn received first prize for marine painting at the St. Louis exhibition, and three years later a water-color prize from the

American Art Association in New York, followed by the gold medal of honor of the Prize Fund exhibition of the next year. In 1896 he built his summer home in Magnolia, Mass., where he was associated with such men as Twachtman, Hassam, and Chase. Although he exhibited frequently in America, he did not travel abroad and sent only one picture to the Paris Exposition of 1900, a small harbor scene of Gloucester on which he won honorable mention. He was elected an associate of the National Academy of Design in 1899 and academician in 1908. At the Pan-American Exposition at Buffalo in 1901 he won a bronze medal, and at the St. Louis Exposition of 1904 a silver medal. He is represented in various American collections. His "Missing Vessel" is owned by the Detroit Institute of Arts; "Close of a Summer Day" by the Buffalo Fine Arts Academy; and "In the Glittering Moonlight" by the Corcoran Gallery in Washington. On July 6, 1914, he was stricken with heart failure and died several hours later without regaining consciousness. He was survived by his wife and by a son.

[J. D. Champlin and C. C. Perkins, *Cyc. of Painters and Paintings* (1887); E. Benezit, *Dict. des Peintres, Sculpteurs, Dessinateurs, et Graveurs*; *Am. Art News*, July 18, 1920; *Am. Art Ann.*, 1914; *N. Y. Times*, July 8, 1914; information as to certain facts from Rehn's son, F. K. M. Rehn, New York City.]   D. G.

REICHEL, CHARLES GOTTHOLD (July 14, 1751–Apr. 18, 1825), educator, bishop of the Moravian Church, was born at Hermsdorff, Silesia, the son of Carl Rudolph and Eleonore Sophia (Müller) Reichel. His father was a Lutheran clergyman and on both sides of his family he was descended from a line of Lutheran churchmen that went back to the Thirty Years' War. He was educated in the Moravian schools at Gross-Hennersdorf and Niesky, because of his father's friendship for Zinzendorf and some of his co-workers. Later, with other members of the Reichel family, he joined the Moravian Church and received his theological degree at Barby, Saxony. He was a teacher at Niesky in 1774 and from 1778 to 1780, the years 1775–77 being spent in educational work at Barby. From 1780 to 1784 he was secretary to the governing board of the Church. In the latter year he was sent to America to be the first principal, or inspector, of the academy at Nazareth, Pa., and Oct. 3, 1785, in cooperation with George Mueller and Louis Huebner, he became the teacher of eleven boys, who constituted the first class in that institution. The rather imposing building of the Silesian type in which this work started had been erected some years before as a manor house for Count Zinzendorf when he should visit the American world. Zinzendorf never returned to America after his first visit, and there had been sporadic attempts to start a school in the building ever since 1750, all of them failing by reason of lack of skilled leadership. The school begun by Reichel in 1785 was looked upon as a final attempt, and his experience and talent enabled him to carry through the enterprise successfully. One of the early students was John Konkaput, a Housatonic Indian from Stockbridge, Mass., who was placed there by Congress. In a few years the institution became popular, not only with families in Pennsylvania and the neighboring states, but also with those of the West Indies and the Southern states. In 1791 there were forty pupils, and by 1795 the number had increased to 163. Special attention was paid to the acquisition of English, German, and French, and the pupils were required on certain days to use one of these languages exclusively. Reichel himself was the author of the geography textbook used in the institution, *Geographie zum Gebrauch der Schulen in den evangelischen Brüdergemeinen* (2 vols., Barby, 1785), a book that was later adopted in schools throughout the country, and he edited for American use *Lesebuch für Deutsche Schulkinder* (1795), by G. G. Otterbein.

On Dec. 6, 1801, he was consecrated bishop at Bethlehem and undertook, at Salem, N. C., supervision of the southern province, since this extension of Moravian work in America, begun in 1763, seemed in need of a far-seeing administrator. In the nine years Reichel reorganized the activities of the province, opening new centers of effort in the state and creating a social mechanism that has operated to the present day (1934). In 1811 he removed to Bethlehem and became head of the northern province. He was sent to the General Synod at Herrnhut, Saxony, in 1818, and after the adjournment of the synod, his health being uncertain, he went to Niesky, where he died. He was genial in habit, searching of mind, mild in speech, but apt to be tempestuous of disposition if aroused. His only published work was the geography, but he left a large number of manuscripts on education and administration. He was married at Gnadenfrei, Oct. 2, 1780, to Anna Dorothea Maass, who died at Salem, N. C., on Aug. 15, 1806. They had six sons and a daughter. On July 31, 1809, at Lititz, Pa., he married Catharina Fetter of Lancaster, who died in Silesia May 20, 1820. By her he had three sons. William C. Reichel [*q.v.*] was a grandson.

[Manuscript autobiog.; archives of the Moravian Church at Bethlehem, Pa.; W. C. Reichel, *Hist. Sketch* of Nazareth Hall (1869); H. H. Hacker, *Nazareth Hall: An Hist. Sketch and Roster of Principals, Teachers, and Pupils* (1910); O. J. Reichel, *Reichel Pedigree* (1872).]   A. G. R.

REICHEL, WILLIAM CORNELIUS (May 9, 1824–Oct. 25, 1876), Moravian clergyman, educator, and historian, was born in Salem, N. C., the son of the Rev. Gotthold Benjamin and Henrietta Frederica (Vierling) Reichel. His ancestors were distinguished clergymen of the Lutheran Church until his grandfather, the Rev. Charles Gotthold Reichel [q.v.], joined the Moravians at Herrnhut, Saxony. William received his early education at Nazareth Hall, of which his grandfather was the first principal, and then studied for the ministry in the Moravian College and Theological Seminary at Bethlehem, Pa., receiving his bachelor's degree in theology in 1844. He taught drawing and Latin at Nazareth Hall from 1844 to 1852, and was then transferred for like duty to the Boy's School at Bethlehem. Four years later, 1858, he was made professor of classical languages at the Moravian College, serving until 1862, when he was put in charge of Linden Hall School for Girls at Lititz, Pa. In 1870 he retired to Bethlehem to engage in historical research, though he continued to devote a few hours of each week to teaching drawing and water-color painting in the Bethlehem Seminary for Young Ladies. His first wife, Mary Jane Gray of Camden Valley, N. Y., whom he married in 1852, died at Lititz in May 1863, leaving two daughters; on Oct. 27, 1867, he married Addie Harkins, who survived him.

In personal contacts he was timid and reserved, and to the casual acquaintance he seemed to lack force of character. To those who knew him, however, he was revealed as persistent and determined, with a wealth of sentiment and of scholarly attainments. He wrote in a graceful and picturesque style, and the historical work of the last years of his life derives much of its appeal from the vividness of its presentation. Among his publications were *A History of the Rise, Progress, and Present Condition of the Bethlehem Female Seminary* (1858); *A Memorial of the Dedication of Monuments . . . to Mark the Sites of Ancient Missionary Stations in New York and Connecticut* (1860); *Historical Sketch of Nazareth Hall, from 1755 to 1869* (1869); *Memorials of the Moravian Church* (1870); *A Red Rose from the Olden Time* (1872); *The Crown Inn near Bethlehem* (1872); *The Old Sun Inn at Bethlehem* (1873); and an edition (1876), for the Historical Society of Pennsylvania, of J. G. E. Heckewelder's *History, Manners, and Customs of the Indian Nations.*

[Archives of the Bethlehem Church; *Trans. of the Moravian Hist. Soc.*, vol. I (1876); O. J. Reichel, *Reichel Pedigree* (1872); *Bethlehem Daily Times*, Oct. 26, 1876; *The Moravian*, Nov. 11, 1876.]   A. G. R.

REICK, WILLIAM CHARLES (Sept. 29, 1864–Dec. 7, 1924), journalist, was born in Philadelphia, Pa., and was the son of Charles William and Margaret (Turner) Reick. He received a high-school education with the idea of entering Harvard but instead joined the reportorial staff of the Philadelphia *North American* at nineteen. For five years he labored as reporter and correspondent; then his great opportunity came when a dog believed to be mad bit two children in Newark, N. J. Reick was then Newark correspondent for the *New York Herald,* and his story of the incident led James Gordon Bennett, owner of the paper and always alert for *coups,* to order that the two children be sent to Paris at the *Herald's* expense and under the care of the correspondent, to be given the newly discovered Pasteur antitoxin for rabies. Reick escorted the children to Paris and there met Bennett, who was so impressed with him that he first put him in charge of the London and Paris offices of the paper, and a year later sent him to New York as city editor, which in this case meant managing editor as well—an unusual advance for a man of twenty-five. Perhaps youth gave him confidence, for he assumed a firm and commanding attitude which previous editors had not ventured upon, because of the absentee owner's imperious character. Reick was city editor of the *Herald* for fourteen years, and there became known as one of America's great journalists. He had an uncanny scent for news in advance, and ability to trace it to its sources. When the Spanish-American War began in 1898, the *Herald* had a fleet of dispatch boats provisioned and ready for service in the Gulf of Mexico, and its own correspondent aboard Dewey's flagship to send in the first full account of the battle of Manila Bay.

In 1903 Bennett made Reick president of the New York Herald Company, publishers of the *Herald* and the *Evening Telegram.* But he was unhappy away from the editor's desk, and early in 1907 he resigned and entered the service of the Ochs interests, which controlled the *New York Times* and Philadelphia *Public Ledger.* He spent some time with each paper, serving as president of the Public Ledger Company from 1907 to 1912. In 1911, presumably with the backing of wealthy friends, he bought a controlling interest in the New York *Sun,* where he remained for ten years and, as other journalists declared, greatly improved the paper. Frank A. Munsey purchased the *Sun* in 1916, and in 1921 combined it with the *Herald*. Reick then became president of the company publishing the *New York Journal of Commerce* and *Commercial Bulletin,* and so continued until 1923. He was decorated by the German Emperor in 1908 with the Order of the Crown of Prussia, second class. At his death in 1924 he was survived by his wife, Carrie L. Ridgway of Burlington, N. J., whom he married on Dec. 4, 1894, and by three daughters.

[See: *N. Y. Times* and other New York newspapers of Dec. 8, 1924; *Evening Post* (N. Y.), Dec. 16 and 23, 1911; *Sun* (N. Y.), July 14, 1918; *N. Y. Times,* June 14, 1921; E. W. Gearing, article in *Human Life,* Aug. 1909; *Who's Who in America,* 1924–25; Don C. Seitz, *The James Gordon Bennetts* (1928).]   A. F. H.

REID, CHRISTIAN [See TIERNAN, FRANCES CHRISTINE FISHER, 1846–1920].

REID, DAVID BOSWELL (June 1805–Apr. 5, 1863), chemist, educator, and ventilation engineer, was born in Edinburgh, the second son of Peter Reid (1777–1838), a physician distinguished for his scholarship and literary attainments and noted as an education reformer, and of his wife, Christian, eldest daughter of Hugo Arnot of Balcormo, advocate and antiquarian. David was educated in the Edinburgh high school and at the University of Edinburgh. His introduction to chemistry came through a short period of employment in the plant of a manufacturing chemist, and he commenced the study of it in 1820 under Dr. John Murray. In 1825, after spending some time abroad, he began a series of private classes in chemistry, in which he correlated the study of theory with laboratory experimentation by the pupil himself. The following year found him a medical student at the University and a member of the Royal Medical Society, an organization of talented students who sought to improve themselves by writing, debating, and discussing papers on medical subjects. Of this society he was senior president in 1826–27.

He received the degree of M.D. in July 1830. The success of his venture as an independent lecturer on "practical" chemistry had led to his appointment, two years earlier, as assistant to Prof. Thomas Charles Hope in the University. Differences arose between them after Reid had become a "privileged" teacher, and in 1833 he proposed to the governing board the establishment of a professorship of practical chemistry. His request denied, Reid resigned his position and became a private lecturer on chemistry and sanitation in a well-equipped and efficiently ventilated laboratory and lecture room of his own design. Theoretical and applied chemistry as well as reforms in the sanitation of private dwellings as a means of preventing disease, and observations based upon his own medical practice, comprised the curricula of his school. His venture proved to be popular and successful. It led to an opportunity for performing a public service for which, however, adequate reward and recognition was not to be accorded him.

Destruction of the Houses of Parliament in 1834 brought him a commission the following year to put to a practical test in the temporary Houses his principles of ventilation and acoustics. The success of this "first systematic plan of ventilation ever carried out in any public building" led to his removal to London in 1840 to arrange and superintend the ventilation and the lighting of the new Houses. Differences arose between him and the architect relating to the installation of his system, with the result that Reid was relieved from duty in 1852, although his plans in their main features were carried on. That his system was sound was demonstrated in the successful ventilation of St. George's Hall, Liverpool, and numerous other public buildings, jails, and ships.

In 1855 he removed to the United States. Here his lectures on the progress of architecture in relation to ventilation and the general preservation of health brought him in 1859 appointment to the faculty of the infant University of Wisconsin as professor of physiology and hygiene and director of the museum of practical sciences. A Polytechnic School was then contemplated, but the condition of the University's finances made the project impossible, with the result that Reid found himself without a chair early in the fall of 1860. His next place of residence was St. Paul, Minn., where he attempted unsuccessfully to arouse interest in the plan which miscarried in Wisconsin. America apparently had few opportunities to offer a man of his peculiar training and experience; but one finally came early in 1863 in the form of an inspectorship of the military hospitals erected throughout the country. He died in Washington, D. C., however, while about to leave on a tour of inspection. His wife, Elizabeth Brown, to whom he was married in 1834, and five children survived him.

In addition to pamphlets and scientific articles Reid published the following textbooks on chemistry: *Academical Examinations in the Principles of Chemistry* (1825); *Elements of Practical Chemistry* (1829); *Text-Book for Students of Chemistry* (1834); *Rudiments of Chemistry* (1836); *Study of Chemistry* (1836); *Elements of Chemistry, Theoretical and Practical* (1837); *Elements of Chemistry and Electricity* (1850). He was also the author of two treatises on ventilation: *Illustrations of the Theory and Practice of Ventilation* (1844) and *Ventilation in American Dwellings* (1858).

[*Illustrated London News*, Mar. 20, 1852; Hugo Reid, *Memoir of the Late David Boswell Reid* (1863); *Proc. Royal Soc. of Edinburgh*, vol. V (1866); *Dict. Nat. Biog.*; the *Times* (London), May 14, 1863; information from the University of Edinburgh.]

H. A. S.

REID, DAVID SETTLE (Apr. 19, 1813–June 19, 1891), governor of North Carolina, was born in Rockingham County, N. C., the son of Reuben and Elizabeth (Settle) Reid. He went to the local schools and to the academy at Middletown, Conn., and later read law. He settled at Wentworth, N. C., about 1834 and soon afterward married his cousin, Henrietta Settle, the sister of Thomas Settle [*q.v.*]. He was a stanch Democrat, and in 1835 he was sent to the state Senate and, three times reëlected, served until 1842. He was elected to Congress and served from Mar. 4, 1843, to Mar. 3, 1847, but he was "gerrymandered" out of office. In 1848 he was nominated by his party for governor. The Whigs were so strongly fixed in power that it was a forlorn hope offered him, and he at first declined but finally yielded to pressure and accepted, after he had made clear to the party leaders his intention of advocating "free suffrage" or, in other words, the abolition of the requirement that a voter for a state senator must possess a freehold of fifty acres of land. He made a spirited campaign, cut the Whig majority to the bone, and was defeated, only to be renominated in 1850 on the same issue and to win the election. He was reëlected in 1852. He made an excellent governor, and, just before the expiration of his term, resigned to accept election for the federal Senate. He served from Dec. 6, 1854, to Mar. 3, 1859. He was active and became quite influential. He spoke seldom but was a good debater, and his speeches were notable for brevity, common sense, and point. He was a supporter of the Buchanan administration, and even his strong friend and connection, Stephen A. Douglas, could not detach him. He was never a fire-eater but, a strong defender of slavery, was one of those who quietly warned the North that secession would be the result of antislavery agitation. He was defeated for reëlection and retired to his farm, but in 1861 he was chosen by the legislature one of the delegates to the peace conference at Washington, where he acted with the conservatively pro-Southern group. Soon after his return to the state, he was elected to the secession convention, where he was numbered among the secessionist group. Upon the final adjournment of the convention in 1862 he once more retired but

emerged in 1875 as a delegate to the constitutional convention of that year. There, in association with Thomas J. Jarvis, he obtained the organization of the convention after a deadlock and was largely responsible for the success achieved. He was a little man of delicate frame but of tireless spirit. As a political leader he had excellent ability with intuitive and almost unerring judgment, and he was characterized by the most frank sincerity. In him the Democratic party in North Carolina found perhaps their wisest and most resourceful leader between the day of Nathaniel Macon and 1861. He was paralyzed in 1881 and died ten years later.

[Reid Collection in possession of N. C. Hist. Commission; *The Papers of Thomas Ruffin*, ed. by J. G. deR. Hamilton, vols. II, III (1918); L. E. Chittenden, *A Report of the Debates and Proceedings of the . . . Conference . . . at Washington . . . Feb. . . . 1861* (1864); J. G. deR. Hamilton, "Party Politics in N. C., 1835–1860," in *The James Sprunt Hist. Pubs.*, vol. XV (1916); "Memoirs of W. W. Holden," *The John Lawson Monographs of the Trinity College Hist. Soc.*, vol. II (1911); *News and Observer* (Raleigh), June 21, 1891.]

J. G. deR. H.

REID, GILBERT (Nov. 29, 1857–Sept. 30, 1927), missionary to China, editor, author, was born in Laurel, Long Island, N. Y., the son of John and Ann Elizabeth (Lawrence) Reid. His father was a Scotch Presbyterian minister whose rigid orthodoxy was tempered by appreciation of honest quest for truth. Gilbert received his early education in nearby schools and at Whitestone Academy. He graduated from Hamilton College in 1879, and from Union Theological Seminary in 1882. During his seminary course he supplied various churches, and on May 7, 1882, he was ordained by the Presbytery of New York. In the fall of that year, a tall, angular youth, self reliant and intellectually eager, he sailed as a missionary to China. On the mission field the independence of his methods was soon evident. Three years at Chefoo and seven years at Tsinan revealed the direction of his interests. Chinese scholar-officials and the Chinese religious background fascinated him. Differences of opinion arising between Reid and the leaders of his mission, he returned to the United States in 1892 and advocated before the missionary board an intellectual approach to the Chinese *literati*. The board feared that emphasis on such a method would compromise the uniqueness of the Christian claim, and after two years Reid presented his resignation and started back to China as an independent missionary. He continued to have cordial relations with the board's representatives, however; and though later some of his acts were criticized as "wrong-headed," there was never question of his Christian spirit and his outstanding ability. Meanwhile, he had written two books —*Glances at China* (1890), and *Sources of Anti-Foreign Disturbances in China* (1893)—which, though rather slight and journalistic in style, were significant because of their appreciation of the Chinese and their occasional censure of foreigners.

Until the Boxer uprising in 1900, Reid knew the exhilaration of a rising tide of success. During the war between Japan and China he became correspondent of the London *Times,* a connection which gave him access to the highest officials, and opened the way for his launching of the International Institute of China. The purpose of the Institute was to promote the welfare of China by enlightenment of the influential classes, by cultivation of harmony among nations, and by fostering a spirit of mutual appreciation in adherents of different religions. The Chinese government gave it official sanction in 1897, in 1909, and in 1914. Reid, who had matured into a man of striking personality, became director-in-chief. During 1897 and 1898 he traveled in the United States and Europe and awakened substantial interest in the enterprise. In 1897 he was married, in Columbia, S. C., to Sallie B. Reynolds, who had been a Methodist missionary in Shanghai.

As resources increased, property was acquired for the Institute, a library and a museum were opened, publications were issued, and an open forum was maintained. The Institute was essentially an instrument for the promotion of peace; wars wellnigh wrecked it. Reid and his wife were confined in Peking during the Boxer siege, and Reid himself was wounded. Again he undertook newspaper correspondence, this time for the London *Morning Post.* He was also appointed interpreter for the British legation. In 1903 the Institute was moved to Shanghai, and for several years was in a thriving condition; but the Director's fear of the devastations of revolution brought him into disfavor with the Chinese revolutionary party of 1911. Severe reverses occurred during the World War. Reid engaged in public discussion by contributions to various newspapers, and in 1917 became proprietor and editor of the *Peking Post.* By June he had been summoned before the consular authorities because of criticisms of the American government. He apologized, and the matter was dropped; but since he was stoutly opposed to China's entering the war, his daily editorials exposed him to attack by the Allies generally. The paper was suppressed by the Chinese police, and on his attempt to use other channels for publicity, the Chinese government requested his deportation for the duration of the war. This action was taken by the United States consular court on Dec. 19, 1917.

After several months in the Philippines, he returned to the United States and used his enforced leisure to prepare two books, both of which were published in 1921. The first—*China, Captive or Free?*—was a brief for the position he had held in 1917, and revealed his fundamental desire for the good of China; the second—*A Christian's Appreciation of Other Faiths*—contained an effective presentation of his religious position and of his attitude toward missions. In 1921 he courageously returned to China, and, aided by his wife and son and daughter, strove to rehabilitate the discredited Institute. There were glimmerings of encouragement. China was plunged in warfare, however, and Reid's health had become enfeebled. He died in Shanghai, shortly after the thirty-third anniversary of the founding of the Institute.

[*Who's Who in America,* 1926–27; *China Weekly Rev.,* Oct. 8, 1927; *Christian Century,* Nov. 3, 1927; *Hamilton Coll. Bull., Necrology No.,* 1928; *Anniversary No. . . . Reports . . . of the International Institute of China . . .* (1927); *International Journal* (Shanghai), Dec. 1927; *Millard's Rev. of the Far East,* Dec. 1917–Jan. 1918; *N. Y. Times,* Oct. 1, 1927; J. G. Reid, in *Open Court* (Chicago), Dec. 1929; unpublished material supplied by the Board of Foreign Missions of the Presbyterian Church in the U. S. A., and by Union Theological Sem., New York City.]   H. Cl—s.

REID, JAMES L. (Dec. 26, 1844–June 1, 1910), corn breeder, son of Robert and Anne (Moore) Drake Reid, was born in the Red Oak settlement, near Russellville, Ohio. No middle name was given him, but early in life he adopted the letter "L" to distinguish himself from other James Reids among his relatives. In the spring of 1846 the family moved to a rented farm in the vicinity of Delavan, Ill.; four years later they bought a farm nearer the town, which remained the family homestead for over half a century. Because of Robert Reid's ill health, the son early assumed responsibilities, and his father's exacting guidance was a potent factor in the formation of his character. He attended the district school and James Kellogg's academy at Tremont. During 1865, while recovering from typhoid fever, he taught school, and later began farming for himself near Boynton Center. In April 1870 he married Marietta, daughter of George and Henrietta Jenks of Tremont, by whom he had three children.

For his first corn planting in Illinois, Robert Reid used a late-maturing Ohio variety, the Gordon Hopkins. The crop, although good, ripened imperfectly, probably because of non-acclimatization, the rawness of the soil, and the slightly shorter growing season. Although only the best ears were selected as seed for the following year, their immaturity caused a poor stand and the missing hills were replanted with Little Yellow, an early flint corn then widely used locally and held to be a direct legacy from the Indians. The purely accidental cross of the two varieties resulted in a corn with wide diversity of type, which was the foundation of the variety known as Reid's Yellow Dent. To the development of this corn James Reid gave special attention, raising it exclusively and endeavoring to induce his neighbors to do likewise. In 1880, because of low prices, he moved to Osage County, Kan., where he tried farming by Illinois methods, but failed because of the hot winds. Returning to the family homestead in Illinois in 1888, he continued corn breeding. His main objective was a hardy, large-yielding corn with a high protein content. He was not a scientific corn breeder from the standpoint of plant pathology, but he noted the results that followed natural conditions and was guided by his observations. Every step of corn growing received his thought and attention. As a show corn, Reid's Yellow Dent began its career in the seventies and eighties at local fairs. The Illinois State Fair at Peoria in 1891 introduced it to growers in neighboring states, but it remained for the World's Columbian Exposition to bring it the wide recognition that resulted in its becoming the leading variety in the Corn Belt. To meet the demands for seed corn, Reid established a retail mail-order trade, which, after 1902, was conducted from a larger farm near East Lynn in Vermillion County. In 1908 he attended the National Corn Exposition at Omaha, where he was rightfully heralded as the man who had put more millions of dollars into the pockets of corn-belt farmers than had any other. He was quiet and reserved in manner, and had somewhat the temperament of an artist and mystic.

[Forrest Crissey, "James Reid, Master of Corn," *Country Gentleman*, Sept. 18, 1920; W. R. Curran, "Indian Corn; Genesis of Reid's Yellow Dent," *Jour. Ill. State Hist. Soc.*, Jan. 1919; P. H. DeKruif, *Hunger Fighters* (1928); P. G. Holden, "James Reid and His Yellow Dent," *Wallace's Farmer*, Dec. 24, 1920; O. G. Reid, "One Great Accomplishment in Corn Breeding," *Breeder's Gazette*, Feb. 25, 1915; *Journal of Heredity*, Sept. 1930; "The Story of Reid's Yellow Dent Corn," *Prairie Farmer*, Jan. 20, 1923; "Who Put King Corn on the Throne?" *Breeder's Gazette*, Jan. 18, 1923; H. A. Wallace, "The Civilization of Corn," *Palimpsest*, July 1930; correspondence with Olive G. Reid, Delavan, Ill.]

E. E. E.

REID, JOHN MORRISON (May 30, 1820–May 16, 1896), Methodist clergyman, college president, editor, and missionary secretary, was born in New York City, the son of John and Jane (Morrison) Reid, natives of Ireland. His parents were poor, but by hard work and borrowed money he secured an education, gradu-

ating from the University of the City of New York at nineteen, and then, 1839–41, pursuing a course in Union Theological Seminary, New York. For the next three years he taught in the Mechanics' Institute School of that city. He had been licensed to preach when he was eighteen, and had carried on religious work in prisons, asylums, and on the docks; now, in 1844, his debts paid, he entered the New York East Conference, in which he was ordained May 15, 1846.

Though not brilliantly endowed, he was a person of diverse gifts and excellent training, a good administrator, a preacher of more than average ability, an effective writer. He had the unselfish devotion, the sound judgment, and the capacity for persevering labor which enabled him to carry forward to greater usefulness what had already been begun. His church employed him in various important offices and he became one of the eminent men of the day in his denomination. For fourteen years he was engaged in the work of the pastorate, serving churches in Connecticut and New York, among them that in Middletown, Conn., the seat of Wesleyan University (1851–53), one in New York City (1853–55), and one in Brooklyn (1855–57). He was a strong abolitionist, and as such was elected to the General Conference of 1856. For the next thirty-two years he was a member of all its quadrennial sessions. From the pastorate he was called into the educational field, and for the period 1858 to 1864 was president of Genesee College, Lima, N. Y., the faculty and students of which, six years later, became the nucleus of Syracuse University. At the completion of his administration at Genesee he was intrusted with the management of denominational papers, the General Conference in 1864 electing him editor of the *Western Christian Advocate*, and in 1868, editor of the *Northwestern Christian Advocate*. The crowning service of his career, however, and in some ways the most valuable, was his work as a corresponding secretary of the Methodist Missionary Society. He was put into this office by the General Conference of 1872, and, declining an election as bishop of the Methodist Church in Canada in 1874, continued in it for sixteen years. Relieved of its duties at his own request in 1888, he was made honorary secretary. His labors in behalf of the foreign field were untiring and fruitful. He traveled widely in Europe and the East and in 1879 published a valuable two-volume work setting forth in detail Methodist missionary enterprises, entitled *Missions and Missionary Society of the Methodist Episcopal Church*, a revised and enlarged edition of which, edited by J. T. Gracey, appeared in 1895. Another volume, *Doomed Religions; A Series of Essays on Great Religions of the World,* edited by Reid, was published in 1884. Possessing ample means in his later life, he contributed liberally to the endowment of Syracuse University, and purchased for it the Leopold Von Ranke Library; he came to the rescue of the Methodist missionary interests in India with a gift of fifteen thousand dollars; established a fund at Clifton Springs Sanitarium that returned missionaries might recuperate there; and educated several young men at his own expense.

After his retirement he resided in New York, where he died in his seventy-sixth year. He was twice married: first, Nov. 14, 1844, to Anna Mason; and second, May 10, 1848, to Caroline S. Fanton, daughter of Thomas B. Fanton, a prominent citizen of Redding, Conn.

[*Gen. Alumni Cat. of N. Y. Univ. 1833–1905* (1906); *Gen. Cat. of the Union Theolog. Sem. in the City of N. Y.* (1919); *Minutes of the Mich. Ann. Conf. of the Meth. Episc. Ch.* (1896); *The Gospel in All Lands,* June 1896; *Northwestern Christian Advocate,* May 6, 20, 1896; *N. Y. Times,* May 17, 1896.]   H. E. S.

REID, MAYNE [See REID, THOMAS MAYNE, 1818–1883].

REID, ROBERT (July 29, 1862–Dec. 2, 1929), portrait, figure, and mural painter, was born at Stockbridge, Mass. His father was Jared Reid, Jr., a schoolmaster, and his mother was Louisa (Dwight) Reid. After several years at his father's school and at Phillips Academy, Andover, Mass., he entered the School of the Museum of Fine Arts, Boston, at the age of eighteen, remaining there four years, and for a part of this time acting as assistant instructor. In 1885 he went to New York and studied for a short time at the Art Students' League. Then he went to Paris, where he continued his studies under Boulanger and Lefebvre. He stayed four years; made his début at the Salon of 1886, and did much summer work outdoors in Normandy. There he found the subject for his first picture shown in America, "The First Born," upon which he was elected a member of the Society of American Artists. Returning to New York in 1889, from the start he was successful in portraiture and figure painting. He conducted classes in painting at the Art Students' League and the Cooper Union; became a member of the Ten American Painters; won his share of medals and prizes; and in 1906 became an Academician. He was popular in society as well as among his fellow artists. In 1907 he married Elizabeth Reeves, who had sat to him twice for her portrait and posed for the figure in his "Open Fire," for which he re-

ceived the third Clark prize of $1000 at the Corcoran Gallery exhibition of 1908. They were divorced in 1916.

In 1892–93 Reid was one of the eight men commissioned to embellish the domes of the main building at the World's Columbian Exhibition at Chicago, and he later devoted a large part of his time and thought to mural painting. His work in the Library of Congress in Washington may be seen in the north corridor. The Five Senses, typified by figures of young women, occupy octagonal spaces in the ceiling; and on the north wall are four circular panels with as many figures symbolizing Wisdom, Understanding, Knowledge, and Philosophy. In the Appellate Courthouse, New York, the frieze on one side of the entrance hall is devoted to the subject of Justice, and in a panel on another wall Poetry, Painting, Sculpture, Architecture, and Fame are symbolized. The paintings in Washington and New York, graceful and engaging as they are, show no remarkable invention, and narrowly escape the banality which characterizes so many of the ready-made allegorical devices that are the common property of the modern American decorator. The most elaborate scheme of interior decoration confided to Reid was that in the H. H. Rogers Memorial Church, Fairhaven, Mass., where he designed and executed some twenty stained-glass windows, and painted an important "Adoration of the Magi." To this work he devoted nearly five years.

The three mural paintings in the Massachusetts State House, Boston, dating from 1901, relate to three events in the early history of the colony, and are not only true to the spirit of the episodes depicted, but of special interest for their essentially decorative character. All three panels deal with the effects of reflected firelight, which forms the keynote to an original color scheme of reds, blues, and grays. In the chief painting, that describing Otis arguing his case, the rosy glow of an unseen fire on the hearth, with the scarlet robes of the five bewigged judges, contrasted with the shadows of bluish cast on the gray wall behind them, produces an unusual and interesting chromatic scheme. The picturesque effect of illumination coming from an unseen source is consistently carried out in the "Boston Tea Party" and "Paul Revere's Ride," to which the painter has given the same historic authenticity in a personal and spirited style. Other noteworthy murals of Reid's are in the church of the Paulist Fathers, New York, and the Central High School, Springfield, Mass. In his easel paintings he constantly shows his strong natural bent for the decorative aspect of his art. Beautiful young women and splendid flowers appear and reappear; color, now bold and brilliant, now delicate, adds its sensuous appeal.

Reid's last years were overclouded by physical infirmity, bravely borne. He went to Colorado Springs to teach in the Broadmoor Art Academy, incidentally to make sketches in the Rocky Mountains and the Garden of the Gods; but a few years before his death he suffered a stroke which paralyzed his right side. He was taken to a sanatorium at Clifton Springs, N. Y., where he taught himself to draw and paint with his left hand, and so successfully that his pictures were shown at the National Academy in 1928 and a group of them were hung in the Grand Central Galleries, New York. His death occurred at Clifton Springs and he was buried at his native town of Stockbridge, Mass. Good examples of his work are "The Open Fire" and "The Japanese Screen" in the Corcoran Gallery, Washington; "The White Parasol" in the National Gallery, Washington; "Fleur de Lys" in the Metropolitan Museum, New York; "Sunset Glow" in the Brooklyn Museum; "Yellow Flower" in the Minneapolis Institute of Art; "The Miniature" in the Detroit Museum; "The Pink Carnation" in the Albright Art Gallery, Buffalo; with other canvases in the museums of Cincinnati, Denver, Omaha, San Antonio, Lincoln, Nebr., Richmond, Ind., and Colorado Springs.

[Royal Cortissoz, article in *Appleton's Booklovers Mag.*, Dec. 1905; C. H. Caffin, article in the *Artist*, Apr. 1899; Christian Brinton, article in *Arts and Decoration*, Nov. 1911; Irene Sargent, article in *Craftsman*, Mar. 1905; H. W. Goodrich, article in *Internat. Studio*, Feb. 1909; Pauline King, *Am. Mural Painting* (1902); *Am. Art Ann.*, 1911; H. Small, *Handbook of the Lib. of Cong.* (1897); *N. Y. Times*, Dec. 3, 1929; catalogues of exhibitions at the St. Botolph Club, Boston, 1912, 1917; Albright Art Gallery, Buffalo, 1913; Milch Gallery, N. Y., 1922; Brooklyn Museum, 1929; Grand Central Galleries, N. Y., 1929.]   W. H. D.

REID, SAMUEL CHESTER (Aug. 25, 1783– Jan. 28, 1861), sea captain, designer of the present form of the American flag, was born at Norwich, Conn., the son of Lieut. John Reid, a former British naval officer, of distinguished Glasgow family, who resigned his commission and joined the cause of the American Revolution after having been captured, and later married Rebecca Chester of Norwich. Samuel went to sea at the age of eleven, was captured by a French privateer and imprisoned for six months at Basse-Terre, Guadaloupe, served as acting midshipman in the U. S. S. *Baltimore* in the West Indies for a year, and at twenty was master of the brig *Merchant* of New York. Com-

manding the privateer *General Armstrong* (246 tons, 90 men, 9 guns) in the War of 1812, he left New York on September 9, 1814, and put in at Fayal in the Azores on Sept. 26 following. That same day the British warships *Carnation* (18), *Rota* (38), and *Plantagenet* (74), under Commodore Edward Lloyd, entered Fayal, en route to join the forces concentrating at Jamaica against New Orleans. About seven o'clock in the evening, as Reid was moving closer under the Portuguese fort, four armed boats approached from the *Carnation,* with the evident purpose of making a surprise capture. Reid challenged and then fired into them. In this first attack the Americans lost one killed and the first lieutenant wounded, the British about twenty killed and wounded. Despite a warning from the Portuguese governor, the British again attacked about midnight with twelve or fourteen boats and about 400 men, but were repulsed with terrible slaughter, estimated at from 175 to 250 casualties, while the Americans lost but two killed and seven wounded. At daylight the *Carnation* engaged with her broadsides, but was temporarily driven off by the *Armstrong's* 42-pounder "Long Tom." Anticipating attack by the whole force, Reid now scuttled and abandoned his ship, which the enemy soon afterward burned. Remaining for repairs and to bury their dead, the British insisted on examining the American crew for deserters, but left them further unmolested. The week or ten days' delay thus caused to the expedition against New Orleans greatly aided Jackson's defense of that city.

On returning to America the *Armstrong's* indomitable defenders were accorded high honors, Reid receiving a sword from the New York legislature and a silver service from New York merchants. Upon vigorous protests from the Portuguese government England apologized and paid £319 indemnity for injuries to shore structures, but denied responsibility for starting the battle, and was instrumental in preventing Portugal's acknowledgment of the American claim against her for $131,000. This was repeatedly rejected, until in Taylor's administration diplomatic relations were severed and an American squadron took off Clay, the American minister. But upon Taylor's death in July 1850 when Webster became secretary of state, the claim was submitted to arbitration and decided favorably to Portugal. Reid and his son, Samuel Chester, junior, thereupon sued the United States in the Court of Claims, but the case, which enjoyed great publicity for many years, was not settled until April 1882, when Congress voted a payment of $70,739. The son, whose name was first known to the public in connection with the publication of an account of his experiences during the Mexican War under the title *The Scouting Expeditions of McCulloch's Texas Rangers* (1847), had prosecuted the claim with remarkable persistence and during his last years supplemented his efforts by writing a history of his father's career, but at the time of his death in 1897, a considerable balance was still unpaid.

Reid was for many years harbor master at New York, where he did notable work in improving pilot-boat service, publishing a signal code for American vessels, and securing a lightship off Sandy Hook. He also devised a system of rapid signaling on land, and in 1826 demonstrated that a message could be sent from New York to New Orleans in two hours, but a bill for its adoption was killed by the advent of electric telegraphy. As definitely recognized by a Congressional committee (*House Report 160,* 35 Cong., 1 Sess., Feb. 5, 1859), Reid must further be given credit for the present design of the American flag. When the admission of new states raised the question of alterations in 1818, Representative Peter Wendover of New York consulted Reid, who proposed thirteen stripes and a star for each state, with the stars in parallel rows for military use and arranged in one great star for other purposes. This, without specification as to arrangement of stars, was adopted by Congress on Apr. 4, 1818, and a flag made by Mrs. Reid was hoisted on the Capitol eight days later. Reid was given the equivalent of a pension by appointment as sailing master in the navy on July 3, 1843. He married Mary, daughter of Capt. Nathan Jennings of Fairfield, Conn., on June 8, 1813. They had eight children, among whom were Samuel Chester, already mentioned, Mary Isabel, the wife of Luigi Palma di Cesnola [*q.v.*], and Louise Gouvernour, the wife of John Savage, a prominent New York journalist. The elder Reid died at his home near Franklin Square in New York City.

[S. C. Reid, Jr., *The Hist. of the Wonderful Battle of the Brig-of-War General Armstrong . . .* (1893) including a biog. sketch of her commander; *A Coll. of Sundry Publications, and Other Docs. . . . upon the Private Armed Brig General Armstrong* (1833); *The Case of the Private Armed Brig of War General Armstrong . . . with the Decision of the Court* (1857); *Reasons for Asking a Reconsideration . . . of the Claim of the Brig General Armstrong* (1882); J. H. Brown, *Am. Naval Heroes* (1899); G. H. Preble, *Hist. of the Flag of the U. S. of America* (1880).] A. W.

REID, THOMAS MAYNE (Apr. 4, 1818–Oct. 22, 1883), novelist and writer of juvenile fiction, was born at Ballyroney, County Down,

Ireland. His father, Thomas Mayne Reid, was a Presbyterian clergyman; his mother was the daughter of the Rev. Samuel Rutherford. His studies were directed toward the ministry, but about his twentieth year a desire for travel and adventure overcame him and he set out for America, eventually arriving at New Orleans. From there he worked north, explored the Platte and Missouri rivers, and lived in the forests, hunting, trapping, and trading with Indians. He afterward tried a variety of jobs and served for a time as tutor in the family of Peyton Robertson of Tennessee. His literary work seems to have begun with some early verse which appeared in the *Pittsburgh Morning Chronicle* in 1842 under the pen-name, The Poor Scholar. Early in 1843 he went to Philadelphia, where he lived for about three years and established a friendship with Edgar Allan Poe. In the fall of 1843 two of Reid's poems appeared in *Godey's Lady's Book,* and during this period he also wrote a few short stories and a five-act tragedy in blank verse, *Love's Martyr,* which was produced at the Walnut Street Theatre, Oct. 23, 1848. In the summer of 1846 he joined the staff of the *New York Herald* as society correspondent at Newport, R. I. In the fall he wrote for the *Spirit of the Times,* but his taste for excitement soon urged him into the Mexican War. He was commissioned second lieutenant in the 1st New York Volunteers and was mustered in on Dec. 3. In March 1847 his regiment was at Vera Cruz and participated in several engagements, culminating in the battle of Chapultepec, where he was severely wounded in the thigh (Sept. 13, 1847). Three days later he was promoted first lieutenant. He remained in Mexico, convalescing until the spring. After a furlough, he resigned from service, May 5, 1848. He then visited a friend, Donn Piatt, in Ohio, where he lived through the fall and winter, writing the greater part of *The Rifle Rangers* (London, 1850) for which he used his experiences in Mexico.

In the spring of 1849 he went to New York, associating himself with adventurer-volunteers to aid in revolutionary movements in Germany and Hungary. He sailed with Friedrich Hecker, but by the time of his arrival in Paris in June, the revolutions in Germany and Hungary had collapsed. He went to England and threw himself into literary work, rapidly turning out novels, serials, and magazine articles. About 1853 he married Elizabeth Hyde, daughter of George William Hyde (who claimed lineal descent from the first Earl of Clarendon), and removed from London to Gerrard's Cross, Buckinghamshire.

Because of financial reverses in 1866, he moved to London to publish a new evening daily, the *Little Times*. This failed and with his wife he returned to America in 1867. He went to Newport, R. I., where he wrote a novel, *The Child Wife* (1868), which fictionalized his romance with Elizabeth Hyde. In 1869 he moved to New York to publish a magazine, *Onward,* which lasted little more than a year. His health was not good and in the summer of 1870 he was confined in St. Luke's Hospital, New York, with an infection in the leg which was injured during the Mexican War. In October 1870 he and his wife returned to England. He bravely maintained his literary productivity. He bought up copyrights to earlier novels which he revised, and contributed new stories and articles to periodicals. After further trouble with his leg in October 1874, he was never able again to walk without crutches. Moving to Ross, Herefordshire, he took up farming. This agricultural interest yielded several articles to English and American journals. His health was increasingly poor, and just before his short final illness he moved to London, where he died on Oct. 22, 1883. One child is mentioned with his widow who survived him.

There are more than ninety items in the list of titles representing Reid's literary work. Nearly seventy of these are novels; romance and adventure stories predominate. Although the majority of his books appeared first in London, there were numerous American editions as well as foreign translations. *The Quadroon* (1856) was dramatized in London and was later the basis of Boucicault's sensational play, *The Octoroon.* His books for boys generally narrated exciting adventures. He was picturesque and dashing in his dress and, even late in life, in visiting London from his country retreat, was a well-known figure hobbling on crutches along Fleet Street.

[The best source of information is Elizabeth Reid, *Mayne Reid; a Memoir of his Life* (1890), although occasionally vague and inaccurate. Also see: M. Q. Holyoake, "Captain Mayne Reid," *Strand Mag.,* July 1891; E. P. Oberholtzer, *The Lit. Hist. of Phila.* (1906); R. R. Wilson, "Foreign Authors in America," *Bookman,* Mar. 1901; *N. Y. Herald,* Oct. 23, 1883; *N. Y. Daily Tribune,* Oct. 23, 1883; *Times* (London), Oct. 24, 1883; *Newport Mercury,* Oct. 27, 1883; *Saturday Rev.* (London), Nov. 3, 1883, *Spectator* (London), Oct. 27, 1883.]

R. W. B.
C. W. C.

REID, WHITELAW (Oct. 27, 1837–Dec. 15, 1912), journalist, diplomat, was born near Xenia, Ohio. His paternal grandfather, James Reid, had come to America from County Tyrone, Ireland, but was of Scotch blood; his fa-

ther, Robert Charlton Reid, was a farmer in modest circumstances. His mother, Marion Whitelaw Ronalds, also of Scotch descent, had been born at Ryegate, Vt., removing to Ohio shortly before her marriage. The family, which was devoutly Presbyterian, had traditions of culture on both sides, enjoyed music, and possessed a small library. Reid, who was delicate in health, was given to reading. From the district school he went to Xenia Academy and Miami University, where he was thoroughly grounded in Latin and studied Greek, French, and German. He showed a distinct literary bent and before graduation with honors from Miami in 1856 had begun to write for country newspapers. After a year as superintendent of schools in South Charleston, Ohio, he acquired an interest in the *Xenia News,* a weekly which he edited with much spirit for almost two years. He had spoken for Frémont in 1856, and ardently supported Republican principles. Following the Lincoln-Douglas debates he became an admirer of Lincoln, in 1860 advocated his nomination by the Republican party, and was influential in securing support for him among the Ohio delegates, though the state convention had indorsed Salmon P. Chase. After Lincoln's nomination he left the *News,* but served during the campaign as secretary of the Republican committee for Greene County.

At the beginning of 1861, eager for a broader field of activity, Reid secured an assignment from the Cincinnati *Times* to report the legislative session at Columbus. He wrote political correspondence also for the *Cleveland Herald* and the *Cincinnati Gazette*; and his dispatches to the latter paper, signed "Agate," at once attracted attention by their energy, vividness, and independence. His real career now began. During the spring he became city editor of the *Gazette,* but almost immediately went into the field as its war correspondent, making his headquarters in Washington and covering political as well as military affairs. His spurs were first won as correspondent and also aide-de-camp with Rosecrans in the West Virginia campaign. His reports from this front showed a shrewd appraisal of military events and the work of the military leaders, including McClellan, whose lack of aggressiveness he quickly recognized. Later he was at Shiloh and Gettysburg, his descriptions of these battles being regarded by officers who participated as remarkable for comprehensiveness, clarity, and accuracy as well as color and vigor. Edmund Clarence Stedman subsequently used Reid's account of Gettysburg as the basis for his poem on the battle. In the intervals of his field excursions he was in Washington ably interpreting the political background of the war. He became well acquainted with such civil leaders as Chase, Sumner, Henry Winter Davis, Garfield, Hay, and Greeley. He also served for three years, 1863–66, as librarian for the House, and for a shorter period as clerk of its military committee. His work as war correspondent closed with an account of a visit to Richmond immediately after its fall—he was one of the first three newspapermen to reach the city—and a description of the funeral of Lincoln. Few journalists attracted more attention during the conflict. A passionate Union man, he was at the same time independent in thought and statement, while he saw not only the immediate drama but its larger implications (Cortissoz, *post*, I, 57–117). His combination of invincible reserve with unusual ambition, self-confidence, and self-assertiveness led some to regard him as a selfish careerist.

Immediately after the close of hostilities, Reid made two extended tours of the South, the first in company with Chief Justice Chase, recording his observations in graphic newspaper letters later republished, with additions, under the title *After the War* (1866). This volume still possesses value for students of the period. In 1865 he invested in cotton land in Louisiana, hoping for quick and extensive profits. But he lacked the tastes and experience required for a successful planter. Crop and labor conditions were bad, and the venture proved unfortunate. After removal to Alabama, where his luck was somewhat better, he was glad in 1867 to withdraw his capital, return to the North, and re-enter journalism. While busy as a planter he had begun an elaborate two-volume history called *Ohio in the War,* covering both the civil and military record of the state, 1860–65, which was published in 1868. He had never completely severed his connection with the *Gazette,* to which he now returned as stockholder as well as writer. He wrote editorials, helped otherwise in shaping its policy, and ably reported such important events as the trial of Andrew Johnson and the national conventions of both parties in 1868. Finally, in the fall of 1868 he joined the *New York Tribune.*

Horace Greeley [*q.v.*], who had followed Reid's work with approval, had made previous advances to him on behalf of the *Tribune*: he at once became second in command in editorial matters, and in 1869 succeeded John Russell Young [*q.v.*] as managing editor. He improved the foreign news service, giving the *Tribune* a special eminence in treating the Franco-Prus-

sian War, and he enlarged the list of American contributors by such names as Mark Twain, Richard Henry Stoddard, and Bret Harte. At his invitation John Hay joined the editorial staff in 1870. The *Tribune* in 1870–72 grew more and more bitterly opposed to the Grant administration, and lent early and vigorous support to the Liberal Republican movement. When demands arose, chiefly in the West, for Greeley's nomination, Reid at first opposed the suggestion. He tried to dissuade Greeley from considering it; but when the editor proved ambitious to run, he attended the Cincinnati convention as a loyal supporter, and played an important part in the strategic moves which gave Greeley a majority of the delegates (E. D. Ross, *The Liberal Republican Movement,* 1919, pp. 94 ff.). On Greeley's temporary retirement from the *Tribune* Reid took charge, writing that the campaign policy would be "aggressive," and making the paper an effective Greeley organ. He also helped raise campaign funds. After the defeat of the Liberal Republican party he stepped aside and Greeley resumed the editorship, but not for long. When a combination of circumstances resulted in Greeley's collapse and withdrawal, swiftly followed by death, Reid played as disinterested a part as could have been expected. Charles A. Dana's allegations to the contrary apparently have no foundation though stated with great explicitness (Cortissoz, I, 237–53; John Bigelow, *Retrospections of an Active Life,* V, 1913, pp. 88, 89; J. B. Bishop, *Notes and Anecdotes of Many Years,* 1925, pp. 30–32). A brief struggle for the vacant editorship, with Reid and Schuyler Colfax as chief contenders, resulted (partly through financial support furnished by William Walter Phelps and others) in Reid's victory. At thirty-five he was head of the most powerful newspaper in America.

The following years were so busy that Reid often worked eighteen hours a day, and had a bedroom fitted up in the *Tribune* tower (Cortissoz, I, 230). The circulation of the weekly *Tribune* steadily declined, but he increased that of the daily to more than 50,000 in 1875, more than 60,000 in 1876. Reporting was kept at a high level: the *Tribune* covered the Whiskey Ring scandal, the Pacific Mail investigation, the overthrow of the Canal Ring, and other events with unrivalled comprehensiveness, while its verbatim reports of testimony at the Beecher-Tilton trial were made authoritative by the court. While still devoted to Republican principles, Reid and the *Tribune* maintained their fight against the Grant administration, vigorously aided in exposing its corruption, attacked the third-term movement, and demanded a reorganization of the party. However, he defended the admirable foreign policy of Hamilton Fish, who sent him a special word of commendation for the *Tribune's* position in the Cuban difficulties of 1873. The editorial page remained forcible and influential, and was more scholarly than in Greeley's day. The paper supported Samuel J. Tilden as a reform candidate for governor of New York in 1874, and did much to effect his election, but it frankly expressed distrust of the Democratic party as a whole, and in 1876 threw its influence behind Hayes. In the dispute over the election Reid took a moderate stand, and demanded an impartial investigation of the vote in Louisiana, South Carolina, and Florida; a fact which emphasized the brilliant stroke of the *Tribune* when under his direction it unravelled the famous "cipher dispatches," and thereby estopped the Democrats from using the cry of fraud. The *Tribune* gave general support to the Hayes administration, and tried to compose the quarrel between the "Stalwarts" and "Half-Breeds"; for this reason, while applauding specie resumption and the Southern policy, it deplored Hayes's civil service reform measures as extreme and certain to estrange the Grant-Conkling faction. But after the election in 1880 of Garfield, an old and close friend, Reid urged a defiant attitude toward the "Stalwarts," and encouraged Garfield in the measures which resulted in the resignation and discomfiture of Senator Roscoe Conkling [q.v.]. Both Hayes and Garfield offered Reid the ministership to Germany, but in the hope of greater honors he declined.

In 1872 the *Tribune* had shown a deficit and was close to financial disaster; fifteen years later Reid, with the assistance of John Hay, John R. G. Hassard, Isaac Bromley, George Ripley, Ralph Keeler, George W. Smalley, and others of a brilliant staff, had made it secure and strong. In 1875 it removed to a handsome Nassau Street building, equipped with the most recent Hoe presses, and taller than any other business structure in the city. Reid believed in innovations, and was the first to install the Mergenthaler linotype, which was largely developed in the *Tribune* composing rooms. He believed also in spending money liberally for talent, and wrote: "In making a newspaper, the heaviest item of expense used to be the white paper. Now it is in the news. By and by, let us hope, it will be the brains." In the middle seventies the *Tribune* began publishing an annual index; in 1879 a Sunday edition was introduced. For twenty years at the close of the century Reid kept the *Tribune* circulation relatively stable, at an average of 50,000 to 60,000 for the daily and 100,000 for the weekly. It was moderately prosperous, incorruptible, well written, well printed, totally devoid of sensationalism, and by the nineties particularly distinguished by its critical staff, which included William Winter, Royal Cortissoz, and Henry E. Krehbiel. In journalism Reid performed, along with E. L. Godkin, a valuable service in maintaining an important newspaper based on brains and character at a time when Dana, Pulitzer, and Hearst were in varying degrees depending upon sensationalism. Like Godkin, he believed in the open shop, and his protracted quarrel with the typographical union, beginning in 1877, resulted in a sensational boycott of the paper by union labor, affecting even the Republican party. In 1892 Reid yielded and the *Tribune* became a union office again.

Reid's marriage, on Apr. 26, 1881, to Elizabeth Mills, daughter of Darius Ogden Mills [q.v.] and Jane Templeton (Cunningham), took him to Europe for a protracted wedding trip. During this absence the *Tribune* was left in charge of John Hay, who steered a careful course amid the political difficulties caused by the assassination of Garfield and accession of Arthur. Reid on his return vigorously combated the efforts of Arthur to restore "Stalwart" supremacy in New York state, and in 1882 the *Tribune's* bolt of the "Stalwart" state ticket contributed to the election of Grover Cleveland [q.v.] as governor. Two years later the nomination of Blaine, a political favorite of Reid's since 1876, aroused the *Tribune* to enthusiasm, and he thought Cleveland's election an "appalling calamity" (Cortissoz, II, 98). From his town house at Madison Avenue and Fiftieth Street, or his country estate "Ophir Farm" near White Plains, Reid now directed the *Tribune* in more leisurely fashion than before, while he gave greater time to society and general political activity. During the four years 1885–1889 he and the *Tribune* played the rôle of critic. He went on the stump for Harrison in the tariff campaign of 1888, and immediately afterward accepted the ministry to France.

Leaving his former secretary and managing editor, Donald Nicholson, in charge of the *Tribune,* Reid spent three years in Paris, where he negotiated a favorable commercial treaty and an extradition treaty, watched European politics intently, and made important French friends. He returned in 1892 to assist Harrison's campaign and particularly to work for harmony within the Republican party, threatened by the rising power of Thomas C. Platt [q.v.]. Actually Reid's nomination for vice-president, which took place at

Minneapolis in June, made the ticket more repugnant than ever to Platt and accentuated the schism. Reid felt bitter disappointment over his and Harrison's defeat that autumn. The following year an open feud broke out between Platt and the *Tribune* over the reorganization of the New York County Committee, and was maintained until Platt was shelved by the emergence of Theodore Roosevelt to full power. In national affairs Reid and the *Tribune* (upon which his sufferings from asthma, with frequent absences from the office, henceforth loosened his grasp) supported Cleveland's chief policies: his Venezuela message, course in the Chicago strike, defence of the gold standard, and pacific Cuban policy. In 1894–95 Reid was in North Africa and Asia Minor, and early in 1896 in Arizona. He gave early and ardent support to McKinley for the Republican nomination, lent the *Tribune* to vehement denunciation of Bryan, and advised McKinley immediately after the election on both his cabinet and policies. Already committed to expansion, he wrote the President-elect: "Some day we will have Cuba as well as the Sandwich Islands. To that extent I believe in Manifest Destiny" (Cortissoz, II, 214).

Reid was now receptive to office. With Ambassador John Hay's somewhat grudging consent, McKinley sent him to England in June 1897, as special ambassador at the Queen's jubilee. On this trip Reid informally sounded the Spanish government on its attitude toward the sale of Cuba. The *Tribune* supported the administration so long as it opposed a conflict with Spain, but when McKinley yielded to circumstances and the public demand it upheld the decision for war. From the outset, as Reid had already indicated, he and the paper advocated territorial acquisitions. It was with full comprehension of this fact that McKinley appointed him a member of the American commission to negotiate peace with Spain in the summer of 1898. When differences of opinion developed among the commissioners, Reid on Oct. 25 drew up a memorandum favoring retention of the entire Philippine archipelago (A. L. P. Dennis, *Adventures in American Diplomacy*, 1928, pp. 83, 84); he paid scant attention to Spanish protests, though he believed in liberality in the financial clauses of the treaty (Cortissoz, II, 251). On his return to the United States he made various speeches for a frank acceptance of wider overseas responsibilities. His writings on this subject were collected in a series of volumes: *Some Consequences of the Last Treaty of Paris* (1899); *Our New Duties* (1899); and *Problems of Expansion* (1900).

At first somewhat distrustful of Roosevelt, Reid soon warmed to his acts as president and gave cordial adherence to him on every important issue. He was particularly pleased by the Panama coup, writing that it would prove overwhelmingly successful: "It is obviously the right thing for the country, which, according to my notion as you know, has the right to assert its paramount authority at any rate in any great emergency, anywhere in the region of the Caribbean Sea or the Gulf of Mexico" (Cortissoz, II, 292). He was sent in 1902 as special ambassador to the coronation of King Edward VII, and three years later, in Roosevelt's general reorganization of the diplomatic service following his reëlection, was made ambassador to Great Britain. Before sailing, in May 1905, he relinquished active editorship of the *Tribune*, though retaining his financial control. His ambassadorship was uneventful but quietly useful. Taking Dorchester House, he entertained on an unexampled scale; he made a number of well-received addresses, collected posthumously in *American and English Studies* (1913); and he was on cordial terms with the Foreign Office. After a brief illness he died in London. His body was returned to the United States on a British cruiser. As a wielder of the editorial pen he had made no such mark as Greeley or Godkin, and he had failed to stamp his personality upon his newspaper as sharply and indelibly as Dana or Pulitzer did. But he nevertheless attained a place of high distinction in the journalism of his time; for he was easily the leader among the Republican editors of the country, while for more than thirty years he had maintained the vigor and extended the usefulness of one of the great American newspapers.

He was survived by his widow and two children. His son, Ogden Mills Reid, became editor of the *Tribune*. Elizabeth Mills Reid (Jan. 6, 1858–Apr. 29, 1931) had shared in her husband's public activities and played an important part in New York society, but her bent was primarily philanthropic. A lifelong interest in hospitals found many expressions on both sides of the Atlantic, but particularly in her labors on the board of the Nurses' Training School at Bellevue in New York City and for the hospital which she erected at San Mateo, near San Francisco, in honor of her parents. She was a member of the New York chapter of the American Red Cross established in 1881; during the Spanish-American War she became acting head of the nursing division of the Red Cross; and in the World War she was chairman of the American Red Cross in London and a deputy commissioner of the

British Red Cross. She assisted Dr. E. L. Trudeau in founding his sanatorium at Saranac Lake, N. Y., and in 1912 helped establish there the D. O. Mills Training School for Nurses. In 1914 she founded in her husband's name an institute for workingmen in the Islington district in London, while she also established a club and home for boys and girls in northwest London.

[Royal Cortissoz, *The Life of Whitelaw Reid* (2 vols., 1921), an exceptionally full and careful work; D. C. Seitz, *Horace Greeley* (c. 1926); C. S. Olcott, *The Life of William McKinley* (2 vols., 1916); W. R. Thayer, *The Life and Letters of John Hay* (2 vols., 1915); Tyler Dennett, *John Hay* (1933); John Hay, *Letters of and Extracts from Diary* (printed but not published 1908); files of the *N. Y. Tribune*; obituary, *Ibid.*, Dec. 16, 1912; H. F. Keenan, *The Money-Makers, a Social Parable*, published anonymously in 1885, containing a fictional picture of Reid which scathingly emphasizes certain self-seeking characteristics. For Mrs. Reid, see obituaries in *N. Y. Herald Tribune*, *N. Y. Times*, Apr. 30, 1931.]
                        A. N.

REID, WILLIAM SHIELDS (Apr. 21, 1778–June 23, 1853), clergyman and educator, was born in West Nottingham township, Chester County, Pa. He was the second son of Adam Reid, a farmer of moderate means, and Martha (Shields), whose fathers had emigrated about 1740 from the North of Ireland. Deciding to enter the ministry, William studied Latin grammar during intervals of labor on his father's farm, and later by teaching a small school secured the means for a college education. He graduated from the College of New Jersey with honors in 1802, and for the next two years was instructor in an academy at Georgetown, D. C., pursuing theological studies under the direction of Dr. S. B. Balch, organizer of Presbyterianism in that community. Subsequently, he continued these studies under Dr. Moses Hoge [*q.v.*] at Shepherdstown, in what is now West Virginia. In 1804 he became a tutor in Hampden-Sydney College, and in 1806 he was licensed to preach by the Winchester Presbytery. About this time Dr. Archibald Alexander [*q.v.*] resigned as president of Hampden-Sydney, and Reid was put in charge of the college for the coming year. On Dec. 12, 1807, he married Clementina, daughter of Col. Samuel W. Venable, one of the wealthiest and most prominent citizens of Prince Edward County.

In 1808 he took up his residence in Lynchburg, Va., then a town of about 3,000 inhabitants, where he spent the remainder of his life. Here he took over a school for boys, previously conducted by the Rev. James Tompkins, and also devoted himself to the work of building up a Presbyterian church. His efforts were successful; in 1815 the church was organized, and a two-story brick building erected on land adjoin-

ing the school, donated by Reid. After preaching for some time with little or no salary, he was formally installed as pastor in 1822. Eight years later the congregation divided as a result of the strife between the Old and New School parties, Reid continuing as pastor of the Old School majority.

The most of his energies, however, were devoted to his school, which was his chief means of support. After a time it was transformed into a boarding school for young ladies. Its average attendance for many years was above sixty, and it ranked high among similar institutions in Virginia. Declining health finally forced him to abandon teaching and in 1848 he resigned his church. His death occurred five years later. He is described as "a handsome blue-eyed man of charming countenance," and was considered a finished scholar and an eloquent preacher. He educated more young ladies around Lynchburg than any other man of his time. Dr. C. R. Vaughan, his successor, wrote shortly after Reid's death: "I am not aware that any man has ever lived in this community, for whom a veneration so profound was mingled with an affection so strong" (Sprague, *post*, p. 390). He was the father of twelve children, three sons, and nine daughters, five of whom died in early life.

[W. B. Sprague, *Annals of the Am. Pulpit*, vol. IV (1858); M. C. Cabell, *Sketches and Recollections of Lynchburg* (1858); W. A. Christian, *Lynchburg and Its People* (1900); E. M. Venable, *Venables of Va.* (1925) and Alice Read, *The Reads and Their Relations* (1930), both giving father's name as Abram; *Daily Richmond Enquirer*, June 28, 1853.]
                        E. T. T.

REID, WILLIAM WHARRY (1799–Dec. 9, 1866), surgeon, was born in Argyle, Washington County, N. Y., entered Union College, Schenectady, Apr. 26, 1823, and was graduated A.B., with high scholastic standing, July 27, 1825. He began the study of medicine as a pupil of Dr. A. G. Smith of Rochester, N. Y., and was in that city in the years 1826, 1827, and 1828. He may have attended a medical college in the East, but it is more than likely that his degree of M.D. (he signed "M.D." to his writings) was conferred on him by the Monroe County Medical Society, of which he was president in 1836 and 1849. The records of this society were burned and further data have been lost. Reid practised in Rochester from 1828 until about 1864 when he moved to the vicinity of New York City. On Oct. 4, 1830, he married Elizabeth Manson, of Framingham, Mass. He was drowned in December 1866 while crossing from Jersey City to New York, and was buried at Framingham.

During his student days in Rochester he saw several cases of dislocation of the hip and was impressed with the futility of the unscientific method, then in vogue, by which they were treated—a method which inflicted great suffering upon the patients. From that time he made a special study of this type of injury. The English plan of treatment, sponsored by Sir Astley Cooper, was to pull down the thigh by force. Reid showed by experiments on isolated muscles of a sheep's leg that, after the first stretching, a muscle cannot be lengthened without rupture, that traction is incompatible with mechanical and physiological action of the muscles, thus impeding reduction. With Dr. Edward Mott Moore [*q.v.*], professor of surgery in the Woodstock medical school and in the Berkshire Medical Institution, he dissected a cadaver, dislocated the hip, and practised reduction by first flexing the leg on the thigh and the thigh on the abdomen. Then, moving the limb to the sound side, he abducted and rotated it outward, and the head of the bone slipped back into place. Reid did not publish his discovery until he had had the opportunity of treating three cases of dislocation by his method—the first in 1844 and the third in 1849—all painless and quick reductions. His paper, "Dislocation of the Femur on the Dorsum Ilii Reducible without Pulleys or Any Other Mechanical Means," a well-written exposition with a diagram explaining the process, was read before the Monroe County Medical Society, May 8, 1850, and published in the *Buffalo Medical Journal* of August 1851 and in the *Boston Medical and Surgical Journal* of Aug. 13 of the same year.

There was criticism of Reid's views and of his claims to originality. In the four and a half months between the appearance of his article and the issue of the weekly *Boston Medical and Surgical Journal* of Dec. 31, 1851, in which he answered criticisms most effectively, five different writers opposed his claims to originality in this journal alone. For instance, it was alleged by two of the sons of the great Nathan Smith, that their father had advocated in his lectures previous to 1831 the use of the flexion method in reducing hip dislocations. There was no written proof, however; and since no one else had reported a case treated by this method, which has since been generally adopted, credit for perfecting and publishing it must go to Reid.

[*Buffalo Medic. Jour.*, Aug. 1851; *Trans. Medic. Soc. of the State of N. Y.*, 1852; *Boston Medic. and Surgic. Jour.*, Aug. 13, 27, Sept. 17, Oct. 8, Nov. 12, Dec. 3, 31, 1851; W. F. Peck, *Hist. of Rochester and Monroe County, N. Y.* (1908); *N. Y. Tribune*, Dec. 13, 1866; personal communications from Charles W. Henningston, M.D., of Rochester, N. Y., and D. Richard Weeks, Asst. Secretary, Graduate Council, Union College.]
W. L. B—e.

REIERSEN, JOHAN REINERT (Apr. 17, 1810–Sept. 6, 1864), immigrant leader, editor, and author, was born at Vestre Moland, Norway, the son of Ole and Kirsten Gjerulfsdatter Reiersen. He studied at the Arendal *Middelskole* and was about to enter the university at Christiania when he suddenly broke off his schooling to embark upon a literary career in Copenhagen. There in the thirties he edited several ephemeral Danish magazines and published nearly twenty volumes of translations, chiefly of English, French, and Swedish works, including George Sand's *Valentine* and a half dozen of Bulwer-Lytton's novels. In 1839, having returned to Norway, he established *Christianssandsposten*, through which he soon provoked a nation-wide newspaper controversy on America, emigration, the status of the Norwegian farmer, and the need of reform. Unlike most Norwegian editors of the time, Reiersen pictured America in a favorable light and argued for emigration. It was his belief that those who were departing for the western world were the most energetic and progressive of Norway's working people; that they were seeking, not gold and luxury, but bread and freedom; that over-population made planned colonization a desideratum. Egged on by journalistic and official criticism of his theories, Reiersen determined to put them into practice. In the summer of 1843 he emerged from his editorial sanctum and set out for the United States on a trip of investigation in behalf of a group of prospective emigrants. The man proved a tireless investigator. He landed at New Orleans, journeyed north to St. Louis, visited Illinois, Wisconsin, and Iowa, then went to Austin, where Sam Houston expressed warm interest in the prospect of a Norwegian settlement in Texas, and finally, after pushing his way north to Cincinnati and New York, he returned to Norway. There, in 1844, he published his *Pathfinder for Norwegian Emigrants to the United North American States and Texas*.

The *Pathfinder* was the most comprehensive book about America published in Norway up to that time. In ten detailed chapters, Reiersen discussed natural conditions in America, agriculture, how to start a farm, trade and industry, minerals and mining, the public lands, conditions in the Middle West, government, the republic of Texas, and the Norwegian pioneer settlements. He praised the enterprising nature, versatile culture, and practical knowledge of the Americans, and asserted that the new-world environment awakened a new spirit of tolerance, independence, and self-respect among the immigrants. His book was widely read and exercised a marked influence upon Norwegian emigration, though his advocacy of the New Orleans route and of the South as the most promising area for immigrant settlement failed to win any wide popular ratification.

In the spring of 1845 Reiersen led a small group of emigrants to Texas and established, at Brownsboro, the first Norwegian settlement in that state. Before he left Norway he founded, with characteristic zeal, a monthly magazine, *Norway and America,* through which he could place before the Norwegian public his own and other reports from America. It was issued for two years, he himself editing it during the first year from far-distant Texas. In its pages appeared a series of valuable "Sketches from Western America," several interesting reports from Texas, immigrant letters, and a number of polemical articles on emigration. In 1848 Reiersen founded the second Norwegian settlement in Texas, with Prairieville as its nucleus. In 1852, in a letter published in Norway, he wrote, "I am free and independent, among a free people who are not bound by the chains of old class and caste conditions, and I feel proud to belong to a mighty nation, the institutions of which must necessarily conquer eventually the entire civilized world. . . ." (*Arbeider-foreningernes Blad,* Jan. 11, 1853). Reiersen died at Prairieville, Texas. His first wife, Henriette Christiane Waldt, whom he had married on Aug. 5, 1836, at Copenhagen and who bore him six sons and two daughters, died in Texas in 1851. His second wife, who was the widow of his brother Christian, survived him; her maiden name was Ouline Jacobine Orbek.

[Chapter x of Reiersen's *Veiviser for Norske Emigranter til De forenede nordamerikanske Stater og Texas* (Christiania, 1844) is translated by T. C. Blegen in *The Norwegian-American Hist. Asso., Studies and Records,* vol. I (1926). A small collection of Reiersen papers is in the possession of Mr. C. L. Reiersen, of N. Y. City, and Mr. R. R. Reiersen, of Houston, Tex., grandsons of the subject of the sketch. Letters written by Reiersen at Iowa City and at Cincinnati, Ohio, respectively on Jan. 24 and Mar. 19, 1844, were published in the *Christianssandsposten,* July 1 and 5, 1844; transcripts are in the possession of the undersigned. A file of this newspaper is in the University library at Oslo, which also has a copy of the first volume of the rare and valuable *Norge og Amerika;* a copy of the second volume is owned by Luther College, Decorah, Iowa. For further information see R. B. Anderson, *The First Chapter of Norwegian Immigration, 1821–1840* (1895), ch. xxv; T. C. Blegen, *Norwegian Migration to America, 1825–1860* (1931); J. B. Halvorsen, *Norsk Forfatter-Lexikon, 1814–1880,* vol. IV (1896); Elise A. Wærenskjold, "Beretning om de norske Setlementer i Texas," in *Billed-Magazin,* Feb. 19 and 26, Mar. 5, 1870; and Emil Olsen, ed., "Elsie Wærenskjolds breve," in *Tønsbergs Blad,* May 11–26, 1925.]
T. C. B.

REILLY, MARION (July 16, 1879–Jan. 27, 1928), educator, suffrage leader, and philan-

thropist, was born at Altoona, Pa., and died in Philadelphia. She was the youngest child and only daughter of John and Anna E. (Lloyd) Reilly. Her father, long associated with the Pennsylvania Railroad, represented the seventeenth Pennsylvania district in Congress from 1875 to 1877. Marion Reilly received her early education at the Agnes Irwin School in Philadelphia, was awarded the degree of A.B. at Bryn Mawr College in 1901, and carried on advanced studies in mathematics and physics at Bryn Mawr College (1902–07), the University of Göttingen and Newnham College, Cambridge (1907–08), and at the University of Rome (1910–1911). She was appointed dean of Bryn Mawr in 1907 to succeed in that office President M. Carey Thomas, who for many years had served as both president and dean. Upon her resignation in 1916, she was made a director of the college and remained an active member of the board until her death. During the World War, she organized and headed the Bryn Mawr Service Corps, which financed and sent overseas a small army of experts in various lines of social and educational work. Though she was essentially a student, with the tastes of a humanist and a passion for scholarship, her executive ability was so marked and her knowledge of educational problems so extensive, that demands, often overtaxing her physical strength, were made on her for academic administration. She was a director of the Agnes Irwin School of Philadelphia, of the Bryn Mawr School of Baltimore, and of the School of Horticulture at Ambler, Pa. From 1907 to 1927 she was closely associated with the American Association of University Women, serving on its board of directors, and as chairman of some of its most responsible committees; she was also one of the first to promote its relations with European university women.

Academic duties absorbed only a part of her interest, which embraced civic, social, and national affairs. Before 1920, she worked in college, state, and national suffrage organizations. She served on the Committee of Seventy of Philadelphia, on the committee that awards the Bok Prize, and until 1927 she was the chairman of the Philadelphia branch of the League of Women Voters. The learned societies, and the civic and social associations to which she gave time, money, and intelligent cooperation, were numerous. Her generosity, which was anonymous and without assignable limits, was chiefly devoted toward helping deserving people get the education they needed. In the midst of her varied activities she found time to become a connoisseur in two fields. With her mother, she formed a distinguished collection of Japanese prints, and independently she assembled one of the finest collections in America of Napoleon prints and cartoons. These she bequeathed to the Brooklyn Museum of Fine Arts. She was an enthusiastic traveler and an accomplished linguist, with a specialist's knowledge of Italian.

No bare enumeration of her activities and accomplishments, however, can give an adequate idea of the personal qualities that brought to her the devotion and respect of those who came to know her. Her outstanding qualities were spiritual—sympathy, faith in the fundamentals of character, and a willingness to serve others. These perfections were balanced by a rapier-like wit, a perfectly human impatience at meanness, and a charm of manner which made her in every society a distinguished member.

[*Bryn Mawr Alumnae Bull.*, May 1928, memorial number; *N. Y. Times, Public Ledger* (Phila.), *Evening Bulletin* (Phila.), Jan. 28, 1928; personal acquaintance and letters.]   M. P. S.

REINAGLE, ALEXANDER (1756–Sept. 21, 1809), musician, composer, was born at Portsmouth, England, and was baptised in the Parish of Portsea, Apr. 23, 1756. His father was Joseph Reinagle, an Austrian musician. Alexander's childhood was spent in Portsmouth. Before his eighteenth year, the family moved to Edinburgh, where he apparently studied with Raynor Taylor. His early development as a composer is indicated by the publications of this period: *Twenty-four Short and Easy Pieces for the Pianoforte* (*opus* 1, London, copy in Library of Congress); *A Second Set of Twenty-four Short and Easy Lessons* (*opus* 2, London, copy in Library of Congress); *A Select Collection of the most Favourite Scots Tunes with Variations for the Harpsichord* (London, republished at Philadelphia, 1787, copy in Boston Public Library), and *Six Sonatas for the Pianoforte: With an Accompaniment for a Violin* (London, copy in British Museum). In the orchestra assembled for the Händel Commemoration Festival at London, May–June, 1784, a "Mr. Reinegale," who may have been either Alexander or his younger brother Joseph, sat among the second violins. At some time prior to February 1785, Alexander visited the celebrated composer, C. P. E. Bach, at Hamburg. On Oct. 23, 1784, he arrived in Lisbon with his consumptive brother Hugh, the 'cellist. Alexander gave a concert there, Jan. 8, 1785, and a week later, performed for the royal family. After the death of his brother he returned to Portsmouth, May 17, 1785, and the next year journeyed to America, arriving in New York

before June 9, 1786. He gave a concert July 20, appearing as pianist, 'cellist, and vocalist. Within a few months he visited Philadelphia, participating in the benefit concert of Henri Capron, Sept. 21, 1786. His reception in Philadelphia was encouraging; his talent as a teacher and his genius as a pianist and composer found ready recognition. Cooperating with other musicians, he revived the series of "city concerts," and gave seasons of excellent concerts from 1786 to 1794. He sponsored similar subscription concerts in New York and Baltimore. Reinagle participated in the majority of these concerts, occasionally playing a piano sonata by some contemporary, often one of his own compositions. To this period belong the four delightful piano sonatas preserved in manuscript at the Library of Congress. These sonatas may prove to be his chief claim to fame. They have a melodic freshness and a rhythmic piquancy that must have endeared them to their post-Revolutionary auditors. They are the finest surviving American instrumental productions of the eighteenth century.

In 1791 Thomas Wignell, the actor, left the Old American Company and induced a group of Philadelphians to finance a new theatrical company. An organization was effected and Wignell and Reinagle were appointed managers. Wignell went abroad to recruit a company, while Reinagle remained in Philadelphia to superintend the construction of the New Theatre. It was opened first for a series of concerts in February 1793. After being closed for a year it was reopened on Feb. 17, 1794, with Arnold's opera, *The Castle of Andalusia*. The new company gave regular seasons thereafter in Philadelphia and Baltimore, Reinagle remaining in charge of the musical department until his death at Baltimore in 1809. From the very outset an exceedingly high musical standard was attained; the singers were of unusual excellence and the orchestra of twenty contained the best instrumental talent available. In the first six seasons over seventy-five operas were produced. Reinagle developed an extraordinary facility in adapting the current English ballad operas to the American stage, often rewriting the accompaniments, composing new overtures, or contriving additional music. He wrote original incidental music for the plays *Slaves in Algiers* (1794), *Columbus* (1797), *The Savoyard* (1797), *The Italian Monk* (1798), *The Gentle Shepherd* (1798), *Pizarro* (1800), and *The Castle Spectre* (1800), and composed the entire score of the operas *The Sicilian Romance* (1795), and *The Volunteers* (1795, copy in Library of Congress). He wrote a fine "Federal March," the patriotic

489

songs "America, Commerce and Freedom" and "The Tars of Columbia," a choral setting of the words sung before Washington at Trenton, and, with Raynor Taylor, a Monody on the death of Washington. Toward the end of his life he was engaged in the composition of an oratorio based upon Milton's *Paradise Lost*. Reinagle was elected honorary member of the St. Andrew's Society of Pennsylvania, Nov. 30, 1794. He was married twice. By his first wife he had two sons, Thomas and Hugh. On Sept. 20, 1803, he married Anna Duport at Baltimore. A daughter, Georgianna, was born after Reinagle's death.

[Sources include: personal data from Reinagle's great-grand-daughter, Mrs. Philip J. Ryan of Washington, D. C.; autograph memorandum book of Lisbon trip in the Lib. of Cong.; J. R. Parker, article in the *Euterpeiad*, Jan. 19, 1822; Wm. B. Wood, *Personal Recollections of the Stage* (1855); O. G. Sonneck, *Bibliog. of Early Secular Am. Music* (1905), *Early Concert-Life in America* (1907), *Early Opera in America* (1915), "Early American Operas," in *Sammelbände der Internat. Musikgesellschaft*, Apr.–June 1905, and "Zwei Briefe C. P. E. Bach's an Alexander Reinagle," *Ibid.*, Oct.–Dec. 1906; R. R. Drummond, *Early German Music in Phila.* (1910), and article in *German-Am. Annals*, Sept.–Oct. 1907; E. C. Krohn, "Alexander Reinagle as Sonatist," *Musical Quart.*, Jan. 1932; *Fed. Gazette and Baltimore Daily Advertiser*, Sept. 22, 1809; American theatrical histories of Dunlap, Seilhammer, Hornblow, and Odell. "Jerry's Song" and "I have a silent Sorrow" have been reprinted in *Pioneer Am. Composers*, vols. I, II (1921–23), ed. by H. V. Milligan. An abridged version of the "Sonata in E" was published in *A Program of Early Am. Piano Music* (1931), ed. by J. T. Howard. An edition of Reinagle's piano works is in preparation.]   E. C. K.

REINHART, BENJAMIN FRANKLIN

(Aug. 29, 1829–May 3, 1885), historical, genre, and portrait painter, was born near Waynesburg, Pa., the youngest of the nine children of Joseph and Sarah (Smith) Reinhart. His first paternal ancestor in America came from Lorraine to Pennsylvania in 1704. Charles Stanley Reinhart [q.v.] was his nephew. As a child he manifested a precocious talent for drawing and an early determination to adopt the profession of a painter. He went to Pittsburgh to take his first lessons in painting in 1844 and began to paint portraits when he was but sixteen years old. In 1847 he went to New York, where he entered the schools of the National Academy of Design. After three years he went to Europe and spent another three years in study at Düsseldorf, Paris, and Rome. He paid especial attention to what was then called "grand composition," for it was his ambition to qualify as a historical painter. On his return to New York in 1853, however, he found that portrait painting was the readiest means of support. Several times he traveled to the Middle West and the South to paint the likenesses of notable men.

When the Civil War began in 1861 he went to

England and for seven years lived in London, where he was very successful. He made many portraits of the nobility and gentry, among others the Princess of Wales, the Duchess of Newcastle, the Countess of Portsmouth, Lady Vane-Tempest, and Lord Brougham, and of several literary lions, including Carlyle and Tennyson. He also found time to paint a few genre pictures. Among his important works of this English period was "Cleopatra" (1865), the studies for which were made in Egypt. It is in an English collection. In 1868 he returned to America, and the rest of his professional life was passed in New York. He was made an associate of the National Academy in 1871. Many of his portraits and genre pieces have been engraved. One of the most popular examples was "Evangeline" (1877); another which had almost as great an appeal was his "Pride of the Village" (1884). He had among his sitters a number of eminent Americans, including James Buchanan, Edwin M. Stanton, Salmon P. Chase, Winfield Scott, Stephen A. Douglas, John C. Breckinridge, Samuel Houston, George M. Dallas, Bishop Leonidas Polk, and Charles O'Conor. Of his historical paintings the more important are "Washington Receiving the News of Arnold's Treason," "Young Franklin and Sir William Keith," and "Captain Kidd and the Governor."

[Wm. Hanna, *Hist. of Greene County, Pa.* (1882); G. W. Sheldon, *Am. Painters* (1879); C. E. Clement and Laurence Hutton, *Artists of the Nineteenth Century* (1893).]   W. H. D.

REINHART, CHARLES STANLEY (May

16, 1844–Aug. 30, 1896), genre painter and illustrator, born at Pittsburgh, Pa., was the son of Aaron Grantley and Catherine (McHenry) Reinhart, and a nephew of Benjamin Franklin Reinhart [q.v.]. His father died in 1853. Charles attended Sewickley Academy, near Pittsburgh, until 1861, when he became a telegraph operator in the United States railroad corps, a branch of the quartermaster's department of the Army of the Potomac. After three years in the service he returned to Pittsburgh and secured employment as a clerk in the steel works of Hussey, Wells & Company. In 1867 he went to Paris and studied for a year in the Atelier Suisse, then he moved on to Munich and entered the Royal Academy, where his masters were Streyhüber and Otto. After he had worked there for two years he returned to America in 1870 and settled in New York. He accepted an offer from Harper & Brothers by the terms of which he was to make drawings for that firm exclusively. When his contract expired in 1877 he worked independently for a time. In 1880 he went to Paris and made it his headquarters for a decade, or until 1891, traveling extensively in France, Spain, Italy, England, and Germany in search of local color for his illustrations.

In the meantime he had made a new contract with the Harpers, which expired in 1890, after which he worked for several other publishers, including Scribner, Appleton, and Osgood. He made drawings for G. P. Lathrop's *Spanish Vistas* (1883), which Henry James described as "delightful notes of an artist's quest of the sketchable." James was also enthusiastic over his large painting, "Washed Ashore," in the Salon of 1887, now belonging to the Corcoran Gallery, Washington. For C. D. Warner's *Their Pilgrimage* (1887), he furnished an admirable series of drawings of the noteworthy watering-places of America. At the time of his death in 1896 he was engaged on a set of Civil-War illustrations. His picture called "Rising Tide" was bought by the French government in 1890. In 1891 an exhibition of 153 of his drawings was held in the Art Institute of Chicago and at the Paris Exposition of 1900 he was represented by "High Tide at Gettysburg." He was married in 1873 to Emilie Varet of New York who died in 1887. A son and two daughters survived him. Reinhart stands high among the best American illustrators of the nineteenth century. An excellent draftsman, he had a marked talent for depicting the most characteristic types of all classes.

[Henry James, *Picture and Text* (1893); *N. Y. Times* and *Boston Transcript*, Aug. 31, 1896; S. G. W. Benjamin, *Art in America* (1880); H. L. Earle, *Biog. Sketches of Am. Artists* (1924); C. S. Reinhart, *Collector*, Sept. 15, 1896; Frank Weitenkampf, *Am. Graphic Art* (1912); *Cat. of Oil Paintings, Water Colors, and . . . Drawings by . . . Chas. Stanley Reinhart* (1897); and catalogue of the exhibition of Reinhart's paintings at the Art Inst., Chicago, 1891.]

W. H. D.

REINSCH, PAUL SAMUEL (June 10, 1869– Jan. 24, 1923), educator, political scientist, diplomat, was born at Milwaukee, Wis., the son of George and Clara (Witte) Reinsch. His father was a Lutheran clergyman. At the age of ten he entered Concordia College, a Milwaukee preparatory school, then he attended the University of Wisconsin, receiving the B.A. degree in 1892 and the LL.B. in 1894. After practising law for one year, he returned to the University to continue graduate study. He completed work for the Ph.D. degree in 1898 and was thereafter appointed assistant professor of political science. In 1901 he was promoted to a full professorship, a post which he retained until 1913. He was one of the organizers, in 1904, of the American Political Science Association, serving as vice-president for the first year, and from 1906 to 1917 he was a member of the board of editors of the *American Political Science Review*. He was a member of the United States delegation to the third and fourth Pan-American Conferences in 1906 and 1910, and to the first Pan-American Scientific Congress at Santiago in 1909.

Despite his other activities, Reinsch's chief interests were centered at this time in his writing and university teaching. A pioneer in the study of modern international organization, he was among the first to develop systematic courses in world politics. In 1900 he published *World Politics at the End of the Nineteenth Century*, in which he presented a brilliant analysis of the dangers inherent in the excessive nationalism and imperialism then characteristic of the great powers. Always humanitarian in his point of view, he developed a keen and sustained interest in the economic, social, and political problems of the so-called "backward peoples," an interest which first resulted in books on *Colonial Government* (1902) and *Colonial Administration* (1905). Among other published studies during this period were, *American Legislatures and Legislative Methods* (1907), *Readings on American Federal Government* (1909), *Readings on American State Government* (1911), *Public International Unions* (1911), and *Intellectual and Political Currents in the Far East* (1911). He also contributed numerous articles both to learned journals and popular periodicals.

By this time he had achieved a national reputation as a vigorous productive scholar who had declared himself a foe of the imperialist aggressor and a champion of the subject peoples. He had devoted much time and attention to the problems of the Far East, and especially to those of China, and in 1913 he was asked by President Wilson to become the American minister to China. He remained at Peking through six difficult years. Unfailing in his sympathy for the Chinese people, he brought his specialized training as a political scientist to bear upon the many difficulties that beset the republican experiment and, in private and semi-official capacities, he advised freely with the harassed native officials. It was his conviction, emphasized in audiences with President Yuan Shih-kai, that a sound growth of Chinese representative government must be accompanied by constructive policies in public administration, the whole operated, for some time to come, under the guidance of able foreign experts. He endeavored to enlist American Red Cross support for the badly needed Huai river conservation program, and he exerted all possible pressure to prevent the powers from presenting the Chinese government with excessive claims for damages arising out of the destruction of property incident to the revolution. Following the death of Yuan Shih-kai Reinsch urged the American government to use its influence to help bring some order from the chaos that appeared imminent. It seemed to him that this end might be furthered by a definite Chinese policy toward the World War. This, he hoped, would have a unifying effect at home and might aid China to secure in the war settlements the abrogation of some of the unequal treaties.

Early in February 1917 he learned from the Chinese government that, while there was much official sympathy with President Wilson's policy toward Germany, the government did not feel able to associate itself with The United States "unless assured that it could obtain from American sources such financial and other assistance as would enable it to take the measures appropriate to the situation which would thus be created" (*An American Diplomat in China*, p. 249). Cable contacts with the State Department were temporarily disrupted and Reinsch, fearing that delay might be fatal, announced on his own initiative that he had recommended to Washington the desired grant of financial assistance. He also pressed his suggestion that, as a *quid pro quo* for China's entrance into the war, the Allied governments should adopt a common declaration of policy toward China, pledging themselves to fortify her sovereignty and to prevent the further growth of special privileges and spheres of influence. But all of these attempts were in vain. China's participation in the war did not secure for her the allied support that Reinsch had endeavored to obtain. When the Shantung award was announced, a death blow seemed to have been dealt to Chinese aspirations, and Reinsch resigned his post shortly thereafter (August 1919). His departure from China was the occasion of a great popular demonstration, and he was immediately appointed a legal advisor to the Chinese government, a position which he retained for the remainder of his life. Returning to the United States, he resumed tentatively the practice of law but continued to devote the major portion of his time to writing, lecturing, and the duties involved in the Chinese advisory work. In the latter connection he participated actively in the Washington Arms Conference of 1921–22 and made frequent trips to the Orient. His writings of this period include many short articles and two books: *Secret Diplomacy: How Far Can it be Eliminated?*, and *An American Diplomat in China*

(1922). While in China in the autumn of 1922 he became ill and the malady was eventually diagnosed as encephalitis. Bronchial pneumonia developed and he died at Shanghai, Jan. 24, 1923. He had been married on Aug. 1, 1900, to Alma Marie Moser, of Ashland, Wis., who with three children survived him.

[For an early estimate of Reinsch's work, see L. G. McConachie, "Paul Reinsch," *World To-Day*, Aug. 1906. Further material may be found in the *Am. Pol. Sci. Rev.*, May 1923; *Who's Who in America*, 1922–23; the *N. Y. Times*, Aug. 28, 1919, Jan. 26, 1923; and *China Review*, Feb. 1923. R. T. Pollard, *China's Foreign Relations, 1917–31* (1933) contains a good account of the World-War negotiations. For the official texts, see the annual volumes of *Papers Relating to the Foreign Relations of the U. S.*]
                                              G. L. K.

REISINGER, HUGO (Jan. 29, 1856–Sept. 27, 1914), merchant, art-collector, philanthropist, was born at Wiesbaden, Germany, the son of Franz and Apollonia (Busch) Reisinger. His father was a university graduate and as secretary of Kossuth had taken an active part in the Hungarian revolution of 1848. He was also the owner and editor of the *Mittelrheinische Zeitung*, one of the oldest German newspapers. From him Hugo seems to have derived his interest in things pertaining to culture as well as the gift of handling practical affairs successfully. He graduated from the Gymnasium of his native city in 1875, but the prospect of peaceful activity in an academic career was not to his liking. After an apprenticeship in a business firm he became a salesman and sales-manager for the Siemens Glass works at Dresden. Sent to the United States in 1882, he succeeded so well in winning confidence and trade that he was sent again the following year and in 1884 became the firm's permanent agent in America. In 1886 he established himself as an importer and exporter. Because of his stern but fair methods and his agreeable personality, his business in this field was soon one of the largest in the country. On Feb. 10, 1890, he married Edmée, daughter of Adolphus Busch of St. Louis, by whom he had two sons.

A director in several enterprises, among them the Linde Air Products Corporation of New York City and Buffalo and the Owens European Bottle Machine Company of Toledo, Ohio, he accumulated through his various activities a large fortune, and resided in a hospitable home on Fifth Avenue, New York. "Possession had value for him only as an incentive," however; and "although he was primarily a man of affairs he was not the kind of man who became absorbed in affairs" (Francke, *post*). He conceived as his main interest the cultivation of a better understanding between the nation of his birth and that of his adoption. As a means to this end he used his great love and knowledge of German and American art. To own the best collection of modern German paintings in the United States, including pictures by Menzel, Böcklin, and Lenbach, and to collect works from the brushes of Whistler, Gari Melchers, and others would not have meant very much to Reisinger had he not found a way to acquaint his American fellow citizens and his German countrymen with them. Accordingly, under the auspices of the German government and aided by his own collection and those of the leading art galleries of Germany, he arranged the first exhibition of modern German art. It was displayed in the new wing of the Metropolitan Museum of Art, New York, and later, in Boston and Chicago. He also arranged an exhibition of American paintings in Germany and England, "to prove to German artists and art lovers that the modern American school of painting is the peer of any of its European contemporaries" (Faust, *post*). Reisinger not only took upon himself the burden of choosing pictures to be exhibited, but also paid the costs of transportation to Europe and the setting up of the collection. Reisinger was also instrumental in making possible the publication of *The German Classics of the Nineteenth and Twentieth Centuries* (20 vols., 1913–14), edited by Kuno Francke and W. G. Howard, a collection of the translations into English of the gems of German literature. He took an active interest in the foundation of the Germanic Museum, and probably persuaded his father-in-law, Adolphus Busch, to make a gift of $250,000 for the construction of the Museum building in Cambridge, Mass.; Reisinger himself contributed $50,000 to the project. His patronage of art brought him recognition on both sides of the Atlantic. The Order of the Prussian Crown was bestowed upon him, the Deutsches Museum at Munich invited him to membership on its board of trustees, and the Metropolitan Museum of Arts and the National Arts Club elected him to honorary membership. He died at Langenschwalbach, Germany, where he had been delayed by the war when on the point of returning to the United States.

[Otto Spengler, *Das Deutsche Element der Stadt N. Y.* (1913); *Germanistic Soc. Quart.*, Mar., Dec. 1914; A. B. Faust, *The German Element in the U. S.* (ed. of 1927); Kuno Francke and Hugo Münsterberg, addresses at the bier of Hugo Reisinger, Oct. 28, 1914, privately printed; *N. Y. Times*, Sept. 29 and Oct. 29, 1914; *Who's Who in America*, 1914–15.]   E. A. K.

REITZEL, ROBERT (Jan. 27, 1849–Mar. 31, 1898), German-American poet, editor, and critic, was born at Weitenau, Amt Schopfheim, Ba-

den, Germany, the son of the village schoolmaster, Reinhard Reitzel, and his wife Katharina, *née* Uehline. He was named Robert in memory of Robert Blum, a victim of the Revolution of 1848, and the ideals held by the revolutionists made a profound impression upon his childhood. In the Gymnasium he devoted more time to the reading of literature than to his studies, and just before he was ready to enter the university he was dishonorably dismissed because of offenses against school discipline in the course of a tour which extended a considerable time beyond the vacation period. With the university and the professions closed to him, he emigrated to the United States in 1870.

After some months of wandering he won the interest of a pastor of the Reformed Church in Baltimore who urged him to prepare himself for the ministry, and in April 1871, having passed an examination, he was elected pastor of the First German Reformed Church in Washington, D. C. As he began to prepare sermons regularly he moved consistently to a more liberal position than that held by the church; he says that his position as pastor was difficult also because of his marriage in 1872 to Anna Martin, one of the numerous young ladies of the congregation. Eleven months after he had been inducted as pastor he was tried by a committee of clergymen and asked to resign. He now started a "free church" in which there were no dogmatic restraints on "the speaker," but after a short time this venture failed, and he became an itinerant lecturer before German "free congregations" and "Turner" societies. In 1884, during a visit to Detroit, some friends helped him to launch a weekly, *Der arme Teufel*, in which he found his life work. It came to be the most popular German-American publication outside the church circles and was read from coast to coast. In a number of cities Arme Teufel Klubs were organized; kindred spirits among literary journals in Germany frequently quoted from its columns, and on occasion certain numbers were forbidden the mails by the German postal authorities.

The essential feature of the journal was the personality of the editor. A short stocky man with curly black hair and a powerful moustache (in profile his features recall Nietzsche), he was an enthusiastic and inspiring orator, but his gifts were displayed at their best in his editorial causeries. In these, he combined drollery, satire, romantic reminiscences from two continents, a wealth of poetic allusion, and an unabashed truth-telling that reveled in exposing sham and bigotry wherever they existed. Cherishing above all things liberty—freedom from kings and tyrants, from dogma and superstition, from moral laws and hypocritical conventions, he stood for the education of the masses, general enlightenment, and the call of beauty in the arts; while he opposed marriage, prohibition, nationalism, militarism, and oppressive capitalism. As literary critic, he had a catholic taste. Shakespeare, Lessing, Goethe, and Schiller received a great deal of his attention, but frequently he brought obscure writers out of their niches for the delight of his readers. Among American authors Thoreau, Hawthorne, and Whitman were his favorites. Though he wrote only in German he felt himself distinctly an American, and frequently expressed gratitude for the freedom of expression which he had found in the United States. In his verse he resembled perhaps most closely Heine, who insisted that the social note has a place in poetry. Among his poems there are also some in an Anacreontic strain, as well as purely personal lyrics filled with a manly, but melancholy resignation. His verses appeared in the columns of *Der arme Teufel,* and his only work published separately was a reprint of his droll account of his adventures during his first year in the United States, *Die Abenteuer eines Grünen* (2nd ed., 1902). Like Heine, Reitzel spent the last years of his life confined to bed, but he continued to send out his paper with exuberant joy in life until the end. He died in Detroit. Of his eight children, two daughters and a son survived him.

[Reitzel's collected works, verse and prose, were published in Detroit by the Reitzel Club, *Des armen Teufel gesammelte Schriften* (3 vols., 1913). For biography see A. E. Zucker, *Robert Reitzel* (1917); *Biographisches Jahrbuch und Deutscher Nekrolog—1898* (1900). An unpublished doctoral dissertation by R. T. Rieder, "Ein Bild Robert Reitzels und des 'armen Teufels' aus seinem Verhältnis zur Litteratur" (1918), is in the Univ. of Wis. library.]   A. E. Z.

RELLSTAB, JOHN (Sept. 19, 1858–Sept. 22, 1930), journeyman potter, lawyer, judge, was a picturesque and outstanding personality in the civil, religious, and professional life of New Jersey and particularly of Trenton, where he was born and spent his life. He was emphatically a son of the people, his parents being of the laboring class. His father, John Rellstab, was an emigrant from Switzerland and his mother, Theresa Schaidnagel, was a Bavarian. He spent his early years acquiring a common-school education, mainly at the Lutheran parish school attached to the church which his parents attended, but by the time he was fourteen he was at work in one of the Trenton potteries. As a mere youth he led a movement among the potters for higher pay, which resulted in a lockout by the employers, and Rellstab, like many others, was compelled to make a scanty living as best he could. In 1877 he was again in a pottery in a clerical capacity, and there he utilized his spare time in carrying out his resolution to become a lawyer in order to protect the legal rights of the laboring classes. After four or five years of preparation he was admitted as an attorney at law in November 1882, immediately took up his practice, and about the same time entered politics. His ability was almost immediately recognized by appointment to public office, and save for one short interval, he was an official for the rest of his life. From 1884 to 1888 he was borough attorney of Chambersburg, a suburb of Trenton; from 1889 to 1892, and again from 1894 to 1896, city counsel of Trenton. In 1896 his judicial career began with appointment to the judgeship of the Trenton district court. In 1900 he was promoted to be judge of the Mercer court of common pleas, a position carrying with it the administration of the probate and criminal courts of the county. Here he served nine years, being reappointed in 1905, and in 1909 he was appointed by President Taft as judge of the United States district court for New Jersey. In this capacity he showed to the larger public his personal qualities and a strong grasp of the law which he had always possessed but which had previously been confined to a limited sphere of operation. The son of two immigrants, he never faltered in his allegiance to the country of his birth, and his charges to federal grand juries during and after the World War rang with patriotism, and stressed the necessity for a firm administration of the law. In a rate case involving the fare to be charged on certain street railways, he concurred with Judge Woolley in an opinion in which the rate fixed by the state utilities board was held to be confiscatory, and the board was enjoined from interfering (276 *Fed. Reporter,* 979). In 1928 he was eligible for retirement but preferred to continue working on part time, heedless of the warning given by a serious throat affection. In the summer of 1930 he was stricken with appendicitis and other complications developed, leading to his death in September at Lake Placid. Rellstab was an active member of the Presbyterian Church, and a trustee of Princeton Theological Seminary and of several charitable institutions in Trenton. He was married twice: on Aug. 1, 1880, to Mary L. Francis, who died in 1899, and on May 4, 1905, to Mary J. Whittaker, who died in 1921.

[Sources include: F. B. Lee, *Geneal. and Personal Memoirs of Mercer County, N. J.* (1907), vol. I; E. R.

Walker and others, *A Hist. of Trenton* (1929), vol. II; T. F. Fitzgerald, *Manual of the Legislature of N. J.*, 1929; *N. J. Law Jour.*, Oct. 1930; *Who's Who in America*, 1928–29; *Trenton State Gazette* and *Newark Evening News*, Sept. 23, 1930; information from Rellstab's friends and personal acquaintance.]

C. W. P.

REMEY, GEORGE COLLIER (Aug. 10, 1841–Feb. 10, 1928), naval officer, was born in Burlington, Iowa, the second son of William Butler and Eliza Smith (Howland) Remey. He was a descendant of Abram Remy, a Huguenot who came to Virginia in 1700, and of John Howland, a pilgrim who came in the *Mayflower*. He entered the United States Naval Academy on Sept. 20, 1855, the youngest and also the smallest of his class, and was graduated fourth among the twenty members of the class of 1859. A cruise in the *Hartford* to China and Japan preceded active Civil War service. He was in the gunboat *Marblehead*, operating in Virginia waters during the Peninsular Campaign from March to July, 1862, and afterward on the Charleston blockade. In April 1863, he became executive of the *Canandaigua*; commanded for ten days the *Marblehead* during attacks on Fort Wagner; and had charge of a battery of heavy naval guns on Morris Island from Aug. 23 to Sept. 7. On the night of Sept. 7–8 he commanded the second division in an ill-fated boat attack on Fort Sumter. His boat, the only one of his divisions to make shore, was smashed by gunfire on landing, and about an hour and a half later Remey and his party were compelled to surrender under the walls of the fort. Of the total force of about 450 only 104 got ashore, and all these were captured. With other officers taken in the attack he was imprisoned during the next thirteen months in the jail at Columbia, S. C., making one almost successful attempt at escape by a tunnel under the prison walls.

After his exchange he was executive in the *De Soto*, fitting out at Baltimore, till the close of the war. He was one of six officers assigned to the White House for two days after Lincoln's assassination, and acted as aide to Farragut at the President's funeral. From then until the Spanish-American War his service followed routine lines, including duty off Chile during the Spanish bombardment of Valparaiso in 1866, as second in command of a surveying expedition in Tehuantepec in 1870–71, and in the Mediterranean during the bombardment of Alexandria in 1882. His first command in the grade of captain (1885) was the flagship *Charleston*, Pacific Squadron, 1889–92. At the outbreak of the War with Spain he was called from the command of the Portsmouth navy yard to take charge of

the naval base at Key West, Fla. This duty carried heavy responsibilities, including the supply and repair of all naval forces in Cuban waters, the command of vessels within the administration of the base, which included the Dry Tortugas, and the organization of the convoy for Shafter's army to Cuba. Shortly after peace was concluded he resumed command of the Portsmouth yard. He was made rear admiral in November 1898, and assumed command of the Asiatic station in April 1900, a highly important assignment in view of the Philippine warfare and the Boxer uprising in China. In his flagship *Brooklyn* he was off Taku from July to October 1900, during the march on Peking, and in 1901 he visited Australia at the opening of its first parliament. After a year as chairman of the Lighthouse Board, he retired Aug. 10, 1903, and lived subsequently in Washington, D. C., and Newport, R. I. He died in Washington and was buried at Burlington, Iowa. He was married on July 8, 1873, to Mary Josephine, daughter of Charles Mason [*q.v.*], and had two daughters and four sons. Though not selected for the highest command in the war with Spain, his assignment to Key West and later to the Asiatic was—to quote the Secretary of the Navy's notice at his death—a recognition of the "good judgment and unflagging close attention to duty" which marked his whole career (Johnson, *post*, p. 7).

[Sixteen vols. of the Remey papers and a manuscript and typed copy of Rear Admiral and Mrs. Remey's reminiscences are preserved in the Manuscripts Division of the Lib. of Cong. There are typed copies of the reminiscences also in the N. Y. Public Lib., the Navy Dept. Lib., and the Naval Acad. Lib. For family data see B. F. Johnson, *A Brief Hist. Sketch of the Remey Family* (typewritten, 1923), at Lib. of Cong., and *Who's Who in America*, 1926–27. See also L. R. Hamersly, *The Records of Living Officers of the U. S. Navy and Marine Corps* (5th ed., 1894); *Annual Reports of the Navy Dept.*, 1901, part I, pp. 607–16, and 1902, pp. 439–50; obit. in *Wash.* (D. C.) *Post*, Feb. 12, 1928.]

A. W.

REMINGTON, ELIPHALET (Oct. 27, 1793–Aug. 12, 1861), manufacturer, the eldest son of Eliphalet Remington, a carpenter and mechanic, was born at Suffield, Conn. He was among the descendants of Thomas Remington, a resident of Windsor, Conn., as early as 1672. His mother is said to have been Elizabeth, *née* Kilbourn. When Eliphalet was about six years old, his father bought a large tract of virgin land in Herkimer County, N. Y., near Litchfield, and in the following year moved there with his family. Here the boy grew to manhood, obtained an elementary education, and helped his father clear and operate the farm, continuing in this work even after his marriage in 1814. About 1816 his father purchased a farm along Steele's Creek in Herkimer County, several miles south of the present town of Ilion, to which place both father and son removed with their families in 1816. In addition to farming, the elder Remington established a mechanical shop there, which included a forge powered by a water wheel. Here he carried on the manufacture of the simple agricultural implements used by the farmers of that time. He also did blacksmithing and general mechanical repair work.

The younger Remington inherited much of his father's mechanical genius and became particularly skilful in forging. In the course of his work he undertook to forge a gun barrel out of scrap iron, so that he might have a rifle of his own, and took it to a gunsmith at Utica, N. Y., to be rifled and stocked. The gunsmith complimented young Remington so highly upon his skill that he was encouraged to forge more barrels, which he took from time to time to Utica for rifling. All of the rifles were quickly sold and proved so excellent that Eliphalet's reputation was quickly established and orders for gun barrels came to the Remingtons in constantly increasing numbers. For upwards of twenty-two years the two continued this work, adding equipment gradually, so that by 1828 they were not only forging barrels but were rifling, stocking, and lock fitting guns as well. After the death of the elder Remington in 1828, Eliphalet, realizing the advantages of having a factory on the Erie Canal, which had been opened three years before, purchased a tract of land along that waterway and erected a new gunshop. A settlement soon sprang up around the shop, which came to be known locally as Remington's Corners. At the request and insistence of Remington, however, this name was changed in 1843 to Ilion. In its new location his gun business increased in magnitude year by year and in 1845 he purchased the entire gun-finishing machinery of Ames & Company, Springfield, Mass., assuming, in addition, an unfinished contract with the United States government for several thousand carbines. To accommodate the additional equipment Remington enlarged his works, and before the completion of the new buildings he secured a contract in his own right from the federal government for 5,000 Harper's Ferry rifles. This was followed almost immediately by a second contract of equal magnitude. By this time three sons were taking an active part in the growing business, which now included not only rifle manufacture but also experimental work looking toward the manufacture of other products. In 1847 the Remington pistol was put on the market, which, because of its efficiency and simplicity, became popular in a short time and yielded business of enormous proportions. Again, in 1856, the manufacture of agricultural implements was begun, starting with a cultivator tooth. To this department were quickly added plows, mowing machines, wheeled rakes, horse hoes, and a large variety of smaller tools. This increased output required the addition of three buildings and the employment of some 375 men. At the outbreak of the Civil War, Remington again received large contracts for rifles, carbines, and pistols from the federal government, but the strain attendant on filling these orders, involving as they did the construction of additional manufacturing units, completely undermined his health and caused his death within a few months.

He was greatly interested in the development of Ilion and took an active part in civic affairs. He was one of the first directors and the first president of the Ilion Bank, which position he held until his death. He was survived by three sons, one of whom was Philo [q.v.], and two daughters.

[L. M. Dewey, *Thomas Remington of Suffield, Conn.* (1909); J. L. Bishop, *A Hist. of Am. Manufactures from 1608 to 1860*, vol. II (1864); F. W. Beers & Company, *Hist. of Herkimer County, N. Y.* (1879); G. A. Hardin, *Hist. of Herkimer County, N. Y.* (1893); Remington Arms–Union Metallic Cartridge Company, *A New Chapter in an Old Story* (1912).] C. W. M.

REMINGTON, FREDERIC (Oct. 4, 1861–Dec. 26, 1909), illustrator, painter, author, and sculptor, was born at Canton, N. Y. A descendant of John Remington, who was living in Newbury, Mass., in 1639, he was the son of Seth Pierre and Clara (Sackrider) Remington. After the Civil War his father settled in Ogdensburg, N. Y., where he edited the *Ogdensburg Journal* and became an influence in politics. Remington was educated at the Vermont Episcopal Institute, Burlington, and the Yale School of the Fine Arts (1878–80), playing on the football eleven with Walter Camp [q.v.]. After his father's death when Frederic was nineteen he made a trip to the West, and upon his return studied at the Art Student's League, New York. In the West he was cowboy and scout, ran a sheep and mule ranch, made some money, lost it, and was helped East by Emerson Hough [q.v.]. With him he brought a number of drawings, determined to be an illustrator.

On Oct. 10, 1883, he married Eva Adele Caten of Gloversville, N. Y. For a time he was in financial difficulties, and Mrs. Remington had to go back to her parents temporarily, but he was aided by his father's friends, who got him a job in Albany. At twenty-three he looked "very much like some Greek god in modern clothes" (Nellie Hough, *post*). He was over six feet tall, blond, and sometimes wore a small mustache. Later in life he became very heavy.

At nineteen he had determined upon his career, and thereafter all the time he could afford was spent in traveling and working on his illustrations and paintings. With Poultney Bigelow he visited Germany and Russia. From the latter country they were expelled. He visited North Africa. During the Spanish-American War he was artist and correspondent in Cuba. His travels took him over all of North America. Everywhere it was life in the raw he sought—men near nature—often men of war, preferably with horses. He was famous for his horses in action; at the time he began his work Eadweard Muybridge [*q.v.*] had just published his book of photographs, *The Horse in Motion,* and shortly afterward the snap-shot camera was invented. Remington took advantage of these devices, sometimes to the detriment of his drawings; malformations are recorded, owing to the distortions of the lens, and often truth of movement is defeated because of the stoppage of the action.

His work with the human figure is notable for its swift action and rendering of character. His Indians are Indians: his Apache is an Apache, his Sioux is a Sioux. His cowboys and frontiersmen are better than his Indians because they interested him more. His American soldiers in the field are splendid. His landscape settings at first lacked the sense of light; later he got more brightness into his Western sunshine, and his ability to suggest the character of the land, the time of day, the season of the year, and the state of the weather greatly improved. In his approach to nature he resembles Winslow Homer —the thing as it existed suited him. He was an illustrator, a reporter, a recorder. In all the branches of the arts he essayed, his aim was to fix the image of the thing seen, or imagined as seen. Scattered through his vast output, however, are pictures which are not illustrations, but are self-contained works of art, and in his later years he painted pictures more and illustrated less. His pictures were most often done in oil and in full color on subjects selected by himself. His last exhibition was of pictures, not illustrations. His sculpture was essentially illustration in bronze with the accent on character and action, and it had the same excellence as his two-dimension illustrations. Since his "Bronco Buster," which was exhibited at the Pan-American Exposition in Buffalo in 1901, many sculptures of bucking horses have been done, but none, so

far, have approached his except as imitations. He wrote fresh, vigorous, journalistic prose, and published his books and articles so that he might illustrate them and introduce the subjects he was drawing, painting, and modeling. His published volumes include *Pony Tracks* (1895) ; *Drawings* (1897) ; *Crooked Trails* (1898) ; *Sundown Leflare* (1899) ; *Stories of Peace and War* (1899) ; *Men with the Bark On* (1900) ; *Done in the Open* (1902) ; *John Ermine of Yellowstone* (1902) ; *The Way of an Indian* (1906). He was a stickler for accuracy of detail and his home at New Rochelle, N. Y., was filled with canvases, bronzes, and sketches and an accumulation of Indian trappings, cowboy outfits, and army equipment. His collection of his own work, with his trappings and equipment, is now in the Remington Art Memorial at Ogdensburg; his library of western history is in the Ogdensburg public library; and a large collection of his work is in the New York Public Library. In 1891 he was elected an Associate of the National Academy of Design. Though there were delineators of the West and frontier before Frederic Remington— notably Karl Bodmer, F. O. C. Darley, George Catlin, and the makers of the Currier and Ives lithographs—and there have been many since, none have surpassed him. He remains the outstanding artist in his field. In 1909 he sold his home in New Rochelle and built a house and studio in Ridgefield, Conn. He had lived in his new home but six months when he was stricken with appendicitis and died. He is buried in Canton, N. Y.

[R. W. G. Vail, *Frederic Remington, Chronicler of the Vanished West* (1929), repr. from *Bull. N. Y. Pub. Lib.,* Feb. 1929; Giles Edgerton, in *Craftsman,* Mar. 1909; Nellie Hough, "Remington at Twenty-three," *Internat. Studio,* Feb. 1923; Royal Cortissoz, in *Scribner's Mag.,* Feb. 1910, repr. in his *Am. Artists* (1923); *Pearson's Mag.,* Oct. 1907; *Outlook,* Jan. 8, 1910; *Collier's Weekly,* Mar. 18, 1905; F. H. Smith, *Am. Illustrators* (1892); Joseph Pennell, *Pen Drawing and Pen Draughtsmen* (1889); Poultney Bigelow, *Seventy Summers* (1925) and *The Borderland of Czar and Kaiser* (1895); *Obit. Record Grads. Yale Univ.,* 1910; *Am. Art News,* Jan. 1, 1910; *Am. Art Annual,* 1910–11; information from a sister-in-law, Miss E. L. Caten, Ogdensburg.]   M. M. Y.

REMINGTON, JOSEPH PRICE (Mar. 26, 1847–Jan. 1, 1918), pharmacist, was born in Philadelphia, where for three generations his ancestors had been residents and members of the Society of Friends. His father was Dr. Isaac Remington, a well-known Philadelphia physician; his mother, Lydia, daughter of John Hart, who was a descendant of Townsend Speakman, an apothecary in Philadelphia early in the eighteenth century. After a preliminary training in the private and public schools of the city, he was graduated from the Philadelphia College of Pharmacy in 1866. He received his early training at the hands of Charles Ellis, Dr. E. R. Squibb [*q.v.*], Edward Parrish [*q.v.*], and William Procter [*q.v.*], the greatest American pharmacists of the nineteenth century. After a few years of service with Dr. Squibb, and in the employ of the Powers, Weightman & Rosengarten Company, he successfully engaged in the retail drug business, also acting as assistant in pharmacy (1871–74) at the Philadelphia College. In 1874 he succeeded Professor Procter in the chair of theory and practice of pharmacy; later he became also professor of operative pharmacy and director of the pharmaceutical laboratory, which he had been instrumental in establishing, equipping it in part at his own expense. In 1893 he was made dean of the college. He was married in 1874 to Elizabeth Baily Collins, also of Quaker ancestry, and in the early eighties established a summer home on the then almost unpopulated beach below Atlantic City known as Longport, where he did most of his writing.

In 1878 he became one of the organizers and charter members of the Pennsylvania Pharmaceutical Association, and, in 1879, one of the associate editors of the *United States Dispensatory,* a position which he held until his death. He gave up his retail business in 1885, and in that year published his great work, *Practice of Pharmacy,* which is probably the most widely known textbook on the subject in the world, having passed through six editions.

Having joined the American Pharmaceutical Association in 1867, he served it in many capacities. In 1887 he elaborated and secured the adoption of a plan for its reorganization by which the scientific work was divided into sections. That same year the Association appointed him as a delegate to visit the American Medical Association, and he induced that organization to establish a section of materia medica and pharmacy, which has since become the section of pharmacology and therapeutics. He served the Pharmaceutical Association as president (1892–93) and as secretary (1893–94). He was president of the Seventh International Pharmaceutical Congress (1893), a delegate to the Pan-American Medical Congress (1893), and to the Second Congress in Mexico (1896); represented the United States in the Eighth International Pharmaceutical Congress at Brussels (1896) and was president of the pharmaceutical section of the Eighth International Congress of Applied Chemistry (1912).

Probably his greatest service, however, was that performed as chairman of the committee to revise the *Pharmacopoeia of the United States of America,* a work which has become of vast importance by reason of its legal standing under the federal and state food and drug acts. His connection with the *Pharmacopoeia* began in 1877, when he served on an auxiliary committee of revision. Upon the death of Dr. Charles Rice [*q.v.*], chairman of the revision committee, in 1901, Remington was made chairman, and was again elected in 1910, holding the position until his death. The ninth revision, issued in 1916, might be truly called his monument.

[*The First Century of the Phila. Coll. of Pharmacy, 1821–1921* (1922), ed. by J. W. England; *Jour. Am. Pharmaceutical Asso.,* Jan., Feb. 1918; *Who's Who in America,* 1916–17; *Public Ledger* (Phila.), Jan. 2, 1918.]
I. G.

REMINGTON, PHILO (Oct. 31, 1816–Apr. 4, 1889), manufacturer, was born at Litchfield, Herkimer County, N. Y., the eldest son of Eliphalet Remington [*q.v.*]. His mother is said to have been Abigail, *née* Paddock, of Litchfield. When he was two years old his parents moved to his grandfather's farm on Steele's Creek, near Ilion, N. Y., and here Philo spent his youth working and playing on the farm and in the shops and foundry. He received his education in local schools and at Cazenovia Seminary, Cazenovia, N. Y. Having a bent for mechanics and having veritably grown up in a gun factory, he naturally entered his father's armory at Ilion. By the time he was twenty-four years old he was in charge of the manufacturing department, in which capacity he was serving in 1861 when his father died. Assuming charge of the entire establishment, with the admirable assistance of his two brothers he carried on its affairs throughout the period of the Civil War.

Early in 1865 he reorganized the manufactory, separating the agricultural implement business from the armory and bringing about the organization of the latter as a corporation under the name of E. Remington & Sons. He served as president of this corporation until his death, and conducted the agricultural machine business in partnership with his brother Eliphalet until 1887. The reorganization having been effected, Remington proceeded vigorously to make good the great financial loss incurred by the cessation of the war. Since pistol making was much more profitable than that of other small arms, he concentrated on this branch of the industry. In the course of ten years he was marketing eighteen different sizes and patterns of holster and other pistols, from the very effective single shot 50-calibre arm to the "vest pocket companion" weighing three and one-half ounces. He also instituted intensive experimental work looking toward the perfection of a breech-loading military arm, and in due time the Remington breech-loader, simple in design, its working parts few, and its strength extraordinary, was officially adopted not only by the American government but by many European governments as well.

During the early part of this reconstruction period much of the corporation's gun-making machinery was not used, and to correct this unprofitable condition Remington undertook to utilize the idle machinery to manufacture other products than guns. Among these products were sewing machines, first marketed in 1870. They were well made and in time the sales increased to about 35,000 machines a year. Again, in 1873, within a month after seeing a working model of the Sholes and Glidden typewriter, brought to him by James Densmore, Remington had contracted to manufacture the machine and soon acquired complete ownership of it. It was crude and imperfect, but so great was Remington's confidence in the future use of the typewriter that he immediately brought into service the ample resources and the skilful workmen available in his establishment to perfect it. Actual manufacture of the Remington typewriter began in September 1873, but it was not introduced to the public until 1876, at the Centennial Exhibition in Philadelphia, Pa. The delay was due chiefly to the financial conditions prevailing throughout the country at that time, from the effects of which the Remington company never recovered. For six years Remington tried both to make and to market the typewriter, but in 1882 he was obliged to dispose of the merchandising end of the business, and finally, in 1886, to sell the entire typewriter plant. Similarly, in 1882, in an effort to provide further relief for his corporation and thereby obtain quicker returns on the remaining business, he brought into being the Remington Sewing Machine Company, to which firm he sold the sewing machine branch of his concern. Even this move was not sufficient, however, and in 1887 the agricultural business went on the auction block. Two years later Remington died in Silver Springs, Fla., where he had gone to regain his health. He was married on Dec. 28, 1841, at Syracuse, N. Y., to Caroline A. Lathrop, and was survived by his wife and two daughters. He was buried in Ilion.

[J. L. Bishop, *A Hist. of Am. Manufactures from 1608 to 1860* (1864), vol. II ; *Hist. of Herkimer County, N. Y.* (1879) ; G. A. Hardin, *Hist. of Herkimer County, N. Y.* (1893) ; Herkimer County Hist. Soc., *The Story of the Typewriter* (1923) ; Remington Arms–Union Metallic Cartridge Company, *A New Chapter in an Old Story* (1912) ; *N. Y. Tribune*, Apr. 5, 1889.]

C. W. M.

REMOND, CHARLES LENOX (Feb. 1, 1810–Dec. 22, 1873), negro leader, was born free in Salem, Mass. His parents were John and Nancy Remond. His father was born in Curacao, became a hairdresser in Salem, Mass., and was admitted to citizenship in the Essex County court on May 2, 1811 (for copy of certificate see W. C. Nell, *The Colored Patriots of the American Revolution,* 1855, p. 319). The boy attended the local schools and had the advantage of an excellent education. Possessing the gift of eloquence, when quite a young man he spoke frequently and effectively at antislavery meetings and was the first negro to address public gatherings on behalf of abolition. In 1838 he was appointed an agent of the Massachusetts Anti-Slavery Society and with the Rev. Ichabod Codding canvassed Massachusetts, Rhode Island, and Maine on behalf of the cause. In May 1840 he was named one of the delegates to represent the American Anti-Slavery Society at the World's Anti-Slavery Convention in London. Sailing on a packet he was obliged to travel in the steerage on account of his color. On the following June 24 he delivered a terse and telling speech in Exeter Hall at the anniversary celebration of the British and Foreign Anti-Slavery Society. A mulatto and distinguished in appearance, he became a great favorite and was invited to all functions to which the other American white delegates were asked. After these returned to the United States he remained behind for almost a year and a half lecturing against slavery to large audiences in many important places in Great Britain and Ireland. He was commended for the pertinency of his facts, the cogency of his arguments, and the fire of his eloquence (for an example see speech to a Dublin audience in the *Liberator,* Nov. 19, 1841).

Landing at Boston in December 1841, he brought with him an address of Irish people to their countrymen in America exhorting them to unite everywhere with the abolitionists. This document bore 60,000 signatures, the first being that of Daniel O'Connell. He returned to find himself outshone as a negro antislavery orator by Frederick Douglass [*q.v.*], who had just accepted a place as lecturer for the Massachusetts Anti-Slavery Society. Although his star as a speaker was in eclipse and illness at times curtailed his lecturing activities, he continued in the employ of the same organization until slavery was abolished. He also wrote some for the press. During the Civil War he became a recruiting officer for the 54th Massachusetts Infantry, the first regiment of colored troops to be sent into action from any Northern state. In

1865 he was appointed light inspector. Several years later he became a clerk in the custom house at Boston and served there until his death. He was a small spare man of wiry build. He had a long and deeply furrowed face with bushy eyebrows and an aquiline nose, and he wore his hair brushed up in a curious fashion. He was extremely sensitive and felt keenly the prejudice against colored people. He died a widower.

[*W. L. Garrison . . . the Story of his Life Told by his Children* (4 vols., 1885–89) ; W. W. Brown, *The Rising Son* (1874) ; John Daniels, *In Freedom's Birthplace* (1914) ; S. J. May, *Some Recollections of our Antislavery Conflict* (1869) ; *Boston Evening Transcript*, Dec. 23, 1873.]　　　　　H. G. V.

REMSEN, IRA (Feb. 10, 1846–Mar. 4, 1927), chemist, educator, was born in New York City. His father, James Vanderbilt Remsen, came from a long line of Dutch ancestors, early settlers in Long Island. His mother, Rosanna (Secor) Remsen, was of Dutch and Huguenot descent. When Remsen was eight, he was sent with his mother, who was in frail health, to a farm in Rockland County, N. Y., and he spent two years in rural surroundings, attending country schools. It does not at all follow, as has been intimated (Harrow, *post*), that the instruction he received was inferior in quality. Often intimate contact with the teacher and the freedom and initiative permitted to the pupils more than compensated for the less formal character of the studies. After two years, and the death of his mother, he returned to New York. There he attended New York schools and the Free Academy, which later developed into the College of the City of New York. He did not graduate from the Academy, however, but after he had become one of the most distinguished chemists in America he was given a bachelor's degree by the College as of the class of 1865.

His father wished him to become a physician, and he therefore attended a homeopathic medical school for some time. He had previously made an excellent record in Latin and Greek but had received very little instruction in science. In the medical school he was directed to read a book on chemistry and he later told, in one of his public lectures, of an amusing and disastrous incident when on his own initiative he attempted to try out the action of nitric acid on copper. He was dissatisfied with the instruction given at the homeopathic college and in later life had little patience with homeopathic doctrines. After some time he induced his father to send him to the College of Physicians and Surgeons, where he graduated in 1867, receiving a prize for his thesis, "The Fatty Degeneration of the Liver,"

although it had been written on the basis of what he could find in available medical books, with no observations of the disease in hospital clinics. The award was doubtless due to the facility in writing English which characterized him throughout his life, making his lectures a delight to those who listened and his textbooks extremely useful.

With his doctor's degree at the age of twenty-one, he was supposed to be ready to enter upon medical practice and was offered a desirable partnership with a prominent physician in New York City. Having reached his majority, however, he felt justified in disregarding his father's wish, and went to Germany to study chemistry. Not knowing that Liebig was devoting his time to writing and no longer worked with students in the laboratory, he went to Munich, where, instead of working with the great master, he studied with a talented *Privatdocent,* Jacob Volhard, who gave him, for a year, thorough instruction in analytical chemistry. He doubtless attended Liebig's lectures and read chemical books, which he could now do to advantage with the background of his intensive work in the laboratory. In the spring of the following year Volhard obtained for him an interview with Wöhler, who had come from Göttingen for one of his friendly visits with Liebig, and it was arranged that Remsen should go to Göttingen. There, in the fall, he began research work in organic chemistry under the direction of Rudolph Fittig. Two years later (1870) he received the degree of Ph.D. from Göttingen. During this time he had met and begun a life-long friendship with the young Scotchman who later became Sir William Ramsay.

In 1870 Professor Fittig was called to Tübingen, and he asked Remsen to go with him as his assistant. Nearly all the leading chemists in Germany were then engaged in developing the science of organic chemistry with the aid of a correct system of atomic weights, based on Avogadro's Law and the theories of valence and of the structure of carbon compounds given by Frankland, Couper, and Kekulé. Thus since first going to Germany Remsen had lived in the atmosphere of intense devotion to research characteristic of German laboratories, and he returned home in 1872 imbued with an earnest desire to devote his life to research. After some delay, during which time he published *Wöhler's Outlines of Organic Chemistry* (1873), translated from Fittig's eighth German edition, and wrote *Principles of Theoretical Chemistry* (published in 1877), he was appointed professor of chemistry and physics at Williams College. The atmosphere of the college was not conducive to research and many Americans returning from Germany to similar conditions at this period fell into lives of routine teaching. Remsen succeeded, however, in obtaining a small laboratory and continued to work much as he had in Germany. The excellent quality of his *Theoretical Chemistry* received immediate recognition, and it was soon translated into German and Italian.

A few years later Daniel Coit Gilman [*q.v.*] was called upon to organize the first institution in America designed primarily not to impart information but to develop men of initiative and ability to add to the knowledge of the world. Seeking suitable professors for the new institution, he was impressed by Remsen's persistence in productive research under discouraging conditions, and chose him as the first professor of chemistry at the Johns Hopkins University. Here he lectured on inorganic chemistry during the first semester and on organic chemistry, the second. Both graduates and undergraduates attended these lectures, which they found to be excellent preparation for teaching the science. To those students who were well prepared in general chemistry and in analysis, Remsen gave work in both inorganic and organic preparations, and then assigned problems requiring experimental work in the laboratory. This work he watched from day to day as it progressed. Both in his lectures and in his conduct of research he followed the methods of the German laboratories, and the work became the joint product of professor and student as it had been in Liebig's laboratory at Giessen. With the aid of the fellowship system instituted at Johns Hopkins, Remsen soon surrounded himself with a group of brilliant, eager students, who were training themselves for academic positions. It would be hard to over-estimate the effect of this group on the development of chemistry in America. Some of the men entered industrial work and a few of these rose to positions of commanding importance.

The chemical investigations which Remsen had continued during his stay at Williams College and which he conducted with his students in Baltimore mostly grew directly or indirectly from problems which he had studied under the direction of Fittig at Göttingen and Tübingen. He discovered that a group in the ortho position with reference to a methyl group in a derivative of benzene protects the methyl from oxidation by the usual oxidizing mixture of sulfuric and chromic acids. It might easily have been supposed that the ortho group interferes with the action of the neighboring methyl by a relation known as steric hindrance, but Remsen carefully refrained from a statement of this sort. When it was discovered that ortho methyl groups are oxidized by potassium permanganate and by other alkaline agents, it became evident that the neighborhood of the groups is not a sufficient explanation for the phenomena. This protection of methyl and other groups from oxidation was thoroughly established by a series of studies and is still known as "Remsen's Law."

During the early years of his work in Baltimore, a young man named Fahlberg, who had already taken his doctor's degree in Germany, was given an opportunity to work in the laboratory and undertook, at Remsen's suggestion, a study of the oxidation of the sulfamide of toluene by means of potassium permanganate. Instead of the sulfamide of benzoic acid, which was expected, he obtained the anhydride of that compound and this was named benzoic sulfinide. By a happy accident, Fahlberg discovered that the compound is intensely sweet, and some years later it became an article of commerce under the name of *saccharin*. Remsen's discovery of the sulfone phthaleins was intimately connected with his previous work on the oxidation of sulfamide derivatives of benzene, as was the case with his study of conditions under which the diazo group is replaced by the ethoxy or methoxy group instead of by hydrogen.

While studying the literature of chemistry in writing his textbook *Inorganic Chemistry* (1889), he formulated the following generalization: "When the halide of any element combines with the halide of an alkali metal to form a double salt, the number of molecules of the alkali salt which are added to one molecule of the other halide is never greater and is generally less than the number of halogen atoms in the latter" (*American Chemical Journal*, May 1889, p. 296). Very few exceptions to this rule have been found, but Remsen's theoretical explanation for the rule has not been accepted, and has been replaced by Werner's theories explaining complex inorganic salts and by recent electronic interpretations.

In 1879 Remsen established the *American Chemical Journal* to make American researches in chemistry available for American readers. Although supported in part by the Johns Hopkins University, it soon became representative of American chemists and was quickly recognized, both at home and abroad, as a worthy medium of publication for important work. The *Journal* had a very important influence on the development of chemical research. It was continued through fifty volumes, and then incorporated with the *Journal of the American Chemical Society*. By a series of textbooks both of organic and of inorganic chemistry, he extended his influence to thousands of students at home and abroad. These included: *An Introduction to the Study of the Compounds of Carbon; or, Organic Chemistry* (1885), *An Introduction to the Study of Chemistry* (1886), *The Elements of Chemistry* (1887), *Inorganic Chemistry* (1889), *A College Text-book of Chemistry* (1901), and two laboratory manuals; several of his books were translated into German, Russian, and other languages.

Up to the time of his retirement from teaching, Remsen consistently refused to undertake chemical work for private parties or for corporations. On several occasions, however, he undertook work for municipalities and for the United States government. In the fall of 1881 the water supply of Boston was contaminated with something which gave to the water a disagreeable taste and odor; he was fortunate enough to discover the cause of the trouble, which proved to be temporary and soon passed away, but he did not discover a method of preventing its return. As a member of the National Academy of Sciences, he was called on to direct certain investigations for the federal government, and by President Roosevelt he was asked to act as chairman of a commission which carried out important investigations of subjects connected with the administration of the Pure Food Law. The publicity and some unfortunate personal enmities which arose in this connection were most distasteful to him. After the Baltimore fire of 1904 he acted as chairman of a board which supervised the installation of a modern system of sewage disposal for the city. The financial trust involved in this undertaking was probably more economically administered than any trust of similar magnitude in the country.

In 1901 Remsen was appointed president of Johns Hopkins University, to succeed President Gilman. While the University was in difficult circumstances because of the depreciation of some of its invested funds, he was able, with the help of certain public-spirited citizens of Baltimore, to secure a magnificent new site in the northern part of the city; and during his administration, with the aid of an appropriation made by the State of Maryland, a school of engineering was established. Otherwise, no very noticeable change was made in the organization or conduct of the institution. The emphasis on research and on the instruction of graduate students continued to be the most distinctive characteristic of the work done by the faculty, and in

spite of the burdens of the presidential office, Remsen continued his active direction of the department of chemistry. He received distinguished honors in many ways. He was president at different times of the American Chemical Society, the American Association for the Advancement of Science, the Society for Chemical Industry (English), and the National Academy of Sciences. He received the Willard Gibbs medal, and was medalist of the Society for Chemical Industry. He retired from the presidency of the Johns Hopkins University in 1913, and in the years that followed was employed for some time as expert by a large industrial corporation.

On Apr. 5, 1875, he married Elizabeth H. Mallory of New York City, whose acquaintance he had made in Williamstown. Two sons were born to them. He died at Carmel, Cal., at the age of eighty-one, and his ashes were placed in a new laboratory at Johns Hopkins University, dedicated to his memory and called Remsen Hall.

Remsen was, like most men of his education and experience, very reticent about his religious life, but he evidently retained a simple religious faith. In his address, "The Life History of a Doctrine," delivered in 1903 when he was president of the American Chemical Society, he said: "Faith is called for at every turn in scientific matters as well as spiritual. It would be as illogical to give them [atoms] up as it is, in my opinion, to deny the existence of a power in the universe infinitely greater than any of the manifestations familiar to us; infinitely greater than man; a power that 'passeth all understanding.'"

[W. A. Noyes and J. F. Norris, *Biog. Memoir of Ira Remsen* (1931), also pub. in *Nat. Acad. Sci. Biog. Memoirs*, vol. XIV (1932), containing bibliog. of Remsen's writings and reminiscent articles repr. from *Johns Hopkins Alumni Mag.*, Mar., Nov. 1928; W. A. Noyes, in *Science*, Sept. 16, 1927, and *Jour. Chem. Soc.* (London), Dec. 1927; J. F. Norris, in "Proc. Am. Chem. Soc.," 1928, issued with *Jour. Am. Chem. Soc.*, Nov. 1928; Benjamin Harrow, *Eminent Chemists of Our Time* (2nd ed., 1927), pp. 197 ff., 428 ff.; *N. Y. Times*, Mar. 6, 1927.]

W. A. N.

RÉMY, HENRI (*c.* 1811–Feb. 21, 1867), Louisiana editor and author, was born in Agen, Department of Lot-en-Garonne, France. His full name was Charles Henri Rémy Carrete, but after his arrival in Louisiana he was known simply as Henri Rémy. He received a thorough classical education, and as a young man became a fervent Republican. This affiliation probably embroiled him in the political upheavals of 1830 and caused him to be exiled from France. He took refuge in London and then wandered through Italy, learning to speak fluently the language of that country. Sailing for America about 1836, he landed in New Orleans, where he supported himself by teaching French and Italian. Soon he entered the office of Pierre Soulé to study law and on May 19, 1840, was admitted to the Louisiana bar. In a short time he received an appointment as a notary and later married Louise Chapdu, a New Orleans Creole.

In 1843 he published, anonymously, in the *Louisiana Courier,* five excellent essays on the early history of his adopted state. Encouraged by their favorable reception, he submitted two additional ones over his signature. The next year he issued a prospectus of a complete history of Louisiana, to be sold for ten dollars a copy. Although he got 160 subscriptions, the book never appeared. Rémy continued to practise law until Senator Auguste Thériot, wishing to increase his political influence, offered to finance a paper in St. James Parish, if Rémy would edit it. Rémy accepted the proposition, because writing was far closer to his heart than the law. Going to Saint Michel (now Convent), a village sixty miles up the river from New Orleans, on Feb. 18, 1854, he brought out the initial issue of a tiny French newspaper with the imposing title, *Saint Michel: Journal Hebdomadaire, Littéraire et Politique.* In almost every number he published an installment of his state history until he had carried it down to 1750; then he again announced that he would publish a complete history of Louisiana, printed under his own supervision in his own plant. He even went so far as to copyright the title; but this plan proved as abortive as the other. The paper continued with moderate success until Senator Thériot died, and in 1854 it was forced to cease publication for lack of financial support.

There must have been, in this quiet, scholarly lawyer and editor, an adventurous streak, for the next thing he did was to join William Walker [*q.v.*], the filibuster, in Nicaragua, to help him seize that little republic by force of arms. Although Walker made himself president, he was finally defeated in 1857 and Rémy escaped to Santo Domingo. After a long trip over the island, including the Haitian end, he crossed to Mexico and finally returned to New Orleans. He published his impressions of Mexico in French in a small volume called *Tierra Caliente* (1859), after they had appeared serially in *Le Messager* of St. James Parish. The book presents a most interesting study of sociological conditions, recorded by a man who observed with the analytical powers of an historian and the humanity of a poet. His sympathies were entirely with the oppressed and exploited Indians, and he pictured the Catholic clergy as selfish, avaricious, and debauched, predicting that they would soon lose their despotic power in Mexico. Although *Tierra Caliente* was Rémy's only published book, he left several interesting manuscripts, among them his much-heralded *Histoire de la Louisiane,* a partial autobiography, a long account of Santo Domingo, another of Haiti, and a history of the Walker Expedition. He died in New Orleans.

[E. L. Tinker, *Les Écrits de Langue Française en Louisiane au XIXe Siècle* (Paris, 1932); H. P. Dart, "Rémy's Lost History of Louisiana," *La. Hist. Quart.,* Jan. 1922; Charles Testut, *Portraits Littéraires de la Nouvelle-Orléans* (New Orleans, 1850), p. 157; *Avant-Coureur,* Mar. 9, 1867; information from Rémy's son, Dr. P. A. Rémy, Bogalusa, La.]   E. L. T.

RENICK, FELIX (Nov. 5, 1770–Jan. 27, 1848), Ohio pioneer, cattleman, was born in Hardy County, Va., a son of William Renick who emigrated from Ireland to America and who became a deputy under Lord Fairfax in the survey of counties in southern Virginia. His ancestors, according to family tradition, were German. As a youth Renick with two friends made a trip of exploration into Ohio and investigated the region lying between the Scioto and Licking rivers. In 1801 he returned to Ohio to settle, purchasing of the government at Chillicothe a large tract of land in Ross County at $2.50 an acre. About 1795 he had married Hannah See of Virginia; they were the parents of nine children. He was interested in children and erected at his own expense on his farm by the turnpike what was long known as the Felix Renick school house. He was also one of the founders and the first president of the Logan Historical Society and contributed several articles to its magazine, the *American Pioneer.*

Felix and his brother George Renick became the outstanding agricultural leaders in south central Ohio. They fed superior cattle for their day and were the first persons to make long overland drives of fat cattle to market. In 1802 they visited Kentucky and bought a herd of longhorns. In 1833 forty-six men in Ohio and two in Kentucky organized "the Ohio Company for importing English Cattle." This company employed Felix Renick to go to England to import some of the best improved cattle of that country. He sailed in January 1834, made a careful inspection of notable herds, and returned to America with nineteen head of shorthorns. This included several animals that later became famous progenitors. In 1835 a second, and again in 1836 a third consignment was brought from England to the Renick farm. On Oct. 29, 1836, an auction sale of these cattle was held on the farm south of Chillicothe. Forty-three animals brought $35,-540. This was the most epoch-making cattle sale held in America up to that time. On Jan. 27, 1848, when in his seventy-eighth year, Renick was killed by a timber falling upon him at the Paint Creek ferry near Chillicothe. His remains lie in a little family cemetery overlooking the farm.

[Sources include: C. S. Plumb, "Felix Renick, Pioneer," *Ohio Archæol. and Hist. Quart.*, Jan. 1924; *Memoirs, Correspondence and Reminiscences of Wm. Renick* (1880); *Am. Pioneer*, Feb., Sept. 1842; Henry Howe, *Hist. Colls. of Ohio*, vol. III (1891); *A Cat. of the Improved Short-Horned Cattle, Imported from England in the Years 1834, '5 and '6 by the Ohio Importing Company* (1836), compiled by Felix Renick; *Ohio State Jour.* (Columbus), Feb. 4, 1848; family papers.]

C. S. P.

RENO, JESSE LEE (June 20, 1823–Sept. 14, 1862), soldier, was born at Wheeling, Va. (now W. Va.), the son of Louis and Rebecca (Quinby) Reno. He was of French descent, the family name having been originally Renault. His parents moved to Pennsylvania and he was appointed to the United States Military Academy from that state, graduating as a brevet second lieutenant of ordnance in 1846. He served in the Mexican War, being brevetted for gallant and meritorious conduct at Cerro Gordo, and captain for actions at Chapultepec. Following the war he served as assistant professor of mathematics at West Point in 1849, secretary of a board on heavy artillery technique in 1849–50, assistant to the ordnance board at the Washington arsenal in 1851–52, was on border and coast surveys in 1853–54, and in command of the arsenal at Mount Vernon, Ala., from 1859 until its seizure by the Confederates in January 1861. He then commanded the arsenal at Leavenworth, Kan., until the fall of 1861. He became permanent first lieutenant in 1853 and captain in 1860. Already of ripe experience when the Civil War commenced, he was commissioned a brigadier-general of volunteers in November 1861. He was given a brigade in Burnside's expedition into North Carolina the winter of 1861 and the spring of 1862, and from April to August commanded a division in the Department of North Carolina, taking part in the movement to Newport News, Va., and the Rappahannock in August. He was commissioned major-general on July 18, 1862. In the August campaign in northern Virginia Reno commanded the IX Corps of Burnside's right wing and took part in the battle of Manassas, Aug. 29–30, and Chantilly on the first of September. In the Maryland campaign, still commanding the IX Corps, he entered Frederick, Md., with his troops in pursuit of Jackson and stayed in that city until the morning of Sept. 13.

Stories of a certain Barbara Fritchie, who had, it was said, kept a Union flag waving from her dormer window while Frederick was occupied by the Confederates, interested Colonel Reno and he stopped at her house while his troops were marching out, talked with the aged widow and offered to buy the flag she had kept waving. She refused to sell or give away the flag made famous later by Whittier's poem, but presented a home-made bunting flag to Reno which he placed in his saddle pocket. The following day he was killed "while gallantly leading his men" at South Mountain. In an order published on Sept. 20, Burnside eulogized him as "one of the country's best defenders" (*War of the Rebellion: Official Records, Army*, 1 ser., vol. XIX, pt. 1, p. 423). His body was taken to Baltimore by his brother and sent to Boston, where Mrs. Reno was then living. He was buried at Trinity Church, Boston, on Sept. 20. The "Barbara Fritchie" flag, which had covered his casket, was given to his wife and was kept by her in his military chest for several years, and was then presented to the Boston Commandery of the Military Order of the Loyal Legion of the United States. On Nov. 1, 1853, he had married Mary Blanes Cross of Washington, D. C. The city of Reno, Nev., was named in his honor.

[G. W. Cullum, *Biog. Reg. . . . U. S. Mil. Acad.* (1891); H. C. Quinby, *Geneal. Hist. of the Quinby (Quimby) Family*, vol. I (1915); E. D. Abbott, *A Sketch of Barbara Fritchie* (1928); Henry Gannett, *Origin of Certain Place Names in the U. S.*, Dept. of the Interior, *Bull. of the U. S. Geol. Survey*, no. 197 (1902); H. H. Bancroft, *Nevada, Colorado, and Wyoming*, in *Hist. of the Pacific States of N. America*, vol. XX (1890); *Daily Nat. Intelligencer* (Wash., D. C.), Nov. 4, 1853; *Daily Intelligencer* (Wheeling, Va.), *Boston Daily Advertiser*, Sept. 16, 1862.]   D. Y.

RENWICK, EDWARD SABINE (Jan. 3, 1823–Mar. 19, 1912), inventor, patent expert, was born in New York City, son of the elder James Renwick [q.v.] and Margaret Anne (Brevoort); the younger James and Henry Brevoort [qq.v.] were his brothers. Edward attended New York schools and when he was thirteen years of age entered Columbia College, the youngest member of his class. After receiving the degree of A.B. in 1839 he did graduate work at Columbia, receiving the degree of A.M. in 1842. His first employment was as assistant and bookkeeper to the superintendent of the New Jersey Iron Company at Boonton, N. J. (1842–44). Next, he was privately employed to examine and report on some mining properties in Maryland, and then went to England to attend to matters pertaining to this report. Although abroad only a short time, he visited the best iron works in both England and Wales, and upon his return to America late in 1845 accepted the superintendency of the

Wyoming Iron Works at Wilkes-Barre, Pa. He was successful in operating this plant, to which he added a small blast furnace for the manufacture of pig-iron.

Resigning this position in 1849, he went to Washington, D. C., where with Peter H. Watson, subsequently assistant secretary of war in the Lincoln administration, he established himself as patent expert. After six years, this association was dissolved and Renwick removed to New York. Here he opened his own office as patent expert and consulting engineer. Although most of his time was occupied with patent cases he engaged in varied engineering work as well. He was consultant to Harrison Gray Dyer while the latter was acting as president of the New York & New Haven Railroad. In 1862 he accomplished the remarkable engineering feat of repairing the steamer *Great Eastern* while it was afloat. The operation consisted in covering with iron plating a fracture in the bilge, eighty feet long and more than ten feet wide, twenty-seven feet beneath the water. In this work he was assisted by his brother Henry. As a witness in patent cases he was "probably . . . subjected to the longest cross-examinations of any expert" (*Transactions of the American Society of Mechanical Engineers, post,* p. 1439). One of his early cases lasted twenty-one days, with the result that the United States circuit court and afterward the United States Supreme Court adopted the construction of the patent given by him.

Renwick himself possessed marked inventive talent and in the course of his life secured in the neighborhood of twenty-five patents, the first in 1850 for an iron railroad rail chair. He also invented a steam valve, a tumbler lock, a domestic furnace grate, and a breech-loading firearm. One of his most important inventions, however, was a grain harvester and binder, patented and improved in 1851 and 1853 respectively. Although he never profited personally from this invention, being ahead of his time, his ideas were widely used by many manufacturers of harvesting machinery after his patents expired. Of far greater value was his series of ten inventions on incubators and chicken brooders, perfected between 1877 and 1886, and it is said that it was largely owing to his efforts that the raising of young chickens was made a paying industry. He was the originator, also, of the system, patented by him in England in 1868, by which that portion of the shaft of a twin-propeller steamboat which extends beyond the vessel may be surrounded with a casing of sufficient size to permit this portion of the shaft to be inspected to the stern

bearing. Although busy with so many and varied concerns, Renwick found time to write two books: *The Thermostatic Incubator. Its Construction and Management* (1883); and *Patentable Invention* (1893). He married Elizabeth Alice Brevoort on June 4, 1862, and at the time of his death in Short Hills, N. J., he was survived by three children.

[H. H. McIver, *Geneal. of the Renwick Family* (1924); R. H. Greene, *The Todd Geneal.* (1867); *Trans. Am. Soc. Mech. Engrs.,* vol. XXXIV (1912); *Who's Who in America,* 1912–13; *N. Y. Times,* Mar. 21, 1912; Patent Office records.]   C. W. M.

RENWICK, HENRY BREVOORT (Sept. 4, 1817–Jan. 27, 1895), engineer, patent expert, was the son of the elder James [*q.v.*] and Margaret Anne (Brevoort) Renwick, and a brother of the younger James and Edward [*qq.v.*]. He graduated from Columbia College in 1833, at the age of sixteen, and for the succeeding two years was a dry-goods clerk in New York. Being interested in mechanics, however, he devoted the years from 1835 to 1837 to the study of engineering and then entered the government service as an assistant engineer. Here he had the opportunity to take part in a number of federal construction jobs, including the building of the breakwaters at Sandy Hook and Egg Harbor, N. J. In 1840 he became associated with the United States Boundary Commission. After seven years' service, which included the survey of the boundary line between Maine and New Brunswick, Canada, he entered the United States patent office as examiner in charge of the divisions of metallurgy, steam engines, navigation, civil engineering, and ordnance. Five years later, in 1853, he was made United States inspector of steam vessels at the port of New York, being the first incumbent of that office. He held this position for a number of years, and thereafter devoted his whole time to work as a patent expert. Soon, because of his great technical knowledge, he was constantly employed by the best patent lawyers of the period and took part in nearly all the great patent litigations between 1870 and the time of his death. Among these were cases having to do with the sewing machine, the McCormick reaper, and the Bell telephone. He was co-author with his father of *The Lives of John Jay and Alexander Hamilton* (1840). On June 22, 1852, he married Margaret Janney of Alexandria, Va., and at the time of his death in New York City he was survived by his widow and two children.

[H. H. McIver, *Geneal. of the Renwick Family* (1924); R. H. Greene, *The Todd Geneal.* (1867); *N. Y. Times* and *N. Y. Tribune,* Jan. 28, 1895; Patent Office reports.]   C. W. M.

RENWICK, JAMES (May 30, 1792–Jan. 12, 1863), teacher, engineer, writer, was born in Liverpool, England, the son of William and Jane (Jeffrey) Renwick. On both his father's and his mother's side he was of Scotch descent. The Rev. James Renwick, last of the Scotch Covenanters to go to the scaffold (1688), was one of his progenitors; his grandfather, also named James, was a Scotch manufacturer, who emigrated to New York in 1783 and organized the mercantile house of Renwick, Son & Hudswell; and his mother was the daughter of the Rev. Andrew Jeffrey of Lochmaben, Scotland. William Renwick, having previously been the Liverpool agent for his father's firm, came to the United States with his family when James was but a few years old. The latter graduated from Columbia College in 1807 at the head of his class. He continued his education by travel, making a tour of Europe with Washington Irving. In 1810 he received the degree of A.M. from Columbia. During the illness of Prof. John Kemp [*q.v.*] in 1812, Renwick lectured on natural philosophy at Columbia. Washington Irving, writing to Henry Brevoort (*post*, I, 78), remarks that the professors speak highly of Renwick "& are pleased because he asks no compensation." In 1814 he was serving as a topographical engineer in the government service. In 1816 he married Margaret Anne Brevoort, daughter of Henry Brevoort who owned the great Brevoort farm, north of Washington Square, New York. In 1817 he was commissioned colonel of engineers in the state militia; and in this same year, though only twenty-five, was made a trustee of Columbia College.

In the meantime, he had succeeded to his father's business, which he carried on until the failure of the English correspondents of the firm. Resigning as trustee of Columbia in 1820, he accepted an appointment there as professor of natural philosophy and experimental chemistry, a post which he filled with distinction for thirty-three years. Until his death, he was a recognized authority in every branch of engineering of that day. Hardly any project of importance, public or private, was undertaken without first securing his expert advice. He investigated the feasibility of uniting the Delaware and Hudson rivers by a canal, a project which was successfully executed according to his plans in the Morris canal. These involved the novel use, at certain places along the route, of a system of inclined planes or railways for transporting the canal boat in a cradle up or down the incline—an invention for which he received a medal from the Franklin Institute in 1826. His report on the subject of weights and measures made to the commissioners for revising the laws of the state of New York was published in the *Quarterly Journal of Science, Literature, and Art* (January to June 1827, pp. 101–16). He was appointed by the President of the United States in 1838 on a commission for testing "the usefulness of inventions to improve and render safe the boilers of steam-engines against explosions." In 1840 he was one of the three commissioners appointed by the government to make a survey of the northeast boundary of the disputed territory between the United States and New Brunswick (*House Executive Document No. 93, and No. 102, 26* Cong., 2 Sess.); and it was partly through his services in connection with this work that the Webster-Ashburton treaty was concluded in Washington in 1842.

Besides his many other activities, Renwick was a prolific writer. He contributed to the first *New York Review*, the *American Whig Review*, and the *American Quarterly Review* and was the author of a number of valuable books, essays, and reports. The more important of his original scientific works were: *Outlines of Natural Philosophy* (2 vols., 1822–23), the first extensive treatise on this subject from the pen of an American writer; *Treatise on the Steam-Engine* (1830), which was translated into several European languages; and *Applications of the Science of Mechanics to Practical Purposes* (1840). To Sparks's *Library of American Biography* he contributed lives of David Rittenhouse, Robert Fulton, and Benjamin Thompson, Count Rumford, and also published the biographies of several American statesmen. In addition to these works, he edited, with notes, the American editions of Parkes's *Rudiments of Chemistry* (1824), Lardner's *Popular Lectures on the Steam-Engine* (1828), Daniell's *Chemical Philosophy* (2 vols., 1840), and Moseley's *Illustrations of Practical Mechanics* (1840).

With evident reluctance the trustees of Columbia College accepted Renwick's resignation Nov. 21, 1853, putting on record their just appreciation of his "long-tried, eminent, and faithful services in the cause of science and sound instruction," and at the same time as a testimonial of their high esteem they made him first emeritus-professor of Columbia College and invited him to sit for his portrait, to be made at their expense and to be hung in the library. He continued to lead an active life for ten years after his retirement and died in New York City. His eldest and youngest sons, Henry Brevoort and Edward Sabine [*qq.v.*], were both capable and eminent engineers; his other son, James [*q.v.*], was a noted architect. He had also one daughter.

[For list of Renwick's writings consult Joseph Sabin, *Dict. of Books Relating to America* (1888); for general information see H. H. McIver, *Geneal. of the Renwick Family* (1924); *Letters of Washington Irving to Henry Brevoort* (2 vois., 1915), ed. by G. S. Hellman; *A Hist. of Columbia Univ.* (1904); J. K. Finch, *Early Columbia Engineers* (1929); *The Franklin Jour. and Am. Mechanics' Mag.*, Nov., Dec. 1826; *Proc. Am. Acad. of Arts and Sciences*, vol. VI (1866); *N. Y. Times*, Jan. 14, 1863. The date of birth, May 30, 1792, is that inscribed on a silver mug which belonged to Renwick when he was a child and is now in the possession of his descendants.]   J. P. C. S.

RENWICK, JAMES (Nov. 1, 1818–June 23, 1895), architect, was born in the Bloomingdale section of New York City, the second son of James Renwick [*q.v.*], engineer and professor at Columbia College, and of Margaret Anne (Brevoort) Renwick. Henry Brevoort and Edward Sabine Renwick [*qq.v.*] were his brothers. James evidently inherited some of his artistic talent and interest in architecture from his father, whose water colors Washington Irving commended highly. With the usual precocity of his brilliant family, he graduated from Columbia College in 1836, before his eighteenth birthday, and immediately joined the engineering staff of the Erie Railroad. He was later one of the engineering staff of the Croton Aqueduct, and it was here he received his first actual construction experience as superintendent of the building of the distributing reservoir that stood for many years on Fifth Avenue between Fortieth and Forty-second streets.

His entrance into architecture was meteoric. In the spring of 1843 a competition was held for designs for the new Grace Church to be built at Broadway and Tenth Street, and on Aug. 29 the building committee reported to the vestry that it had adopted Renwick's plans. The corner stone was laid Oct. 30, and the building, complete except for the stone spire (added later to replace a temporary wooden one), was consecrated on Mar. 7, 1846. Thus the young man, not yet twenty-five at the time of the competition and entirely self-trained in architecture, became noted at once as the architect of New York's wealthiest and most fashionable church. His earlier practice was mainly the designing of churches. Calvary, at Fourth Avenue and Twenty-first Street, and the Romanesque Church of the Puritans on Union Square, both in 1846, were followed by the Church of the Covenant, Saint Stephen's, and many others in and out of the city, the last being Saint Bartholomew's, at Madison Avenue and Forty-fourth Street, in 1872. The climax of Renwick's career as an ecclesiastical architect came with Saint Patrick's

Cathedral. Chosen architect by Archbishop John Hughes [*q.v.*] in 1853, he was able, because of the slow progress of the whole scheme, to give the project careful study, but at last, on Aug. 15, 1858, the corner stone was laid. The building took more than twenty years; it was not dedicated until 1879, under Cardinal McCloskey, and the spires were finally added in 1887.

Renwick's practice was by no means limited to churches, however. As early as 1843 he had designed the fountain for the Bowling Green, and in 1846 he was appointed architect of the New Smithsonian Institution in Washington. This remarkable example of so-called "Norman" architecture was seriously damaged by fire in 1865, and reconditioned and made fireproof by A. Cluss of Washington, but the plan of the building and its exterior are still much as Renwick desiged them. About contemporary with the Smithsonian was the Free Academy— the parent of the College of the City of New York—which long stood on the corner of Twenty-third Street and Lexington Avenue. He designed three New York hotels, the Clarendon, the Albemarle, and the St. Denis; the last building still stands (1934), somewhat altered, at Eleventh Street and Broadway, its detail a melancholy comment on the taste of 1852 when the St. Denis was opened. Renwick designed many commercial buildings as well, including the Fulton Bank and the Bank of the State of New York, both in New York City, and a new façade for the Stock Exchange, long since destroyed. Because of his connections with the first families of the city, he also developed a large practice in opulent and luxurious houses. Among these were residences in New York for Charles Morgan and Courtlandt Palmer and many "cottages" and "villas" in Staten Island, Dobbs Ferry, Lenox, Newport, and similar fashionable suburban and summer localities. During the sixties, he was for several years architect for the Board of Governors of Charities and Correction of New York City and added many units to the group on Blackwell's, Ward's, and Randall's islands. His buildings include a Work House, the City Hospital, and the Smallpox Hospital on Blackwell's Island; the Inebriate and Lunatic asylums on Ward's Island; and the main building of the Children's Hospital on Randall's Island. Much of this work, though out of date in style and to modern eyes outlandish, was basically well planned, and many of the buildings are still in use.

The greater part of Renwick's work thus far mentioned was either Gothic or Romanesque in inspiration, but his eager and experimental mind was not satisfied to confine itself to one style. The trend towards eclecticism heralded earlier in the writing of Arthur Gilman [q.v.] found in Renwick an early acceptance. As early as 1852, in the St. Denis, this interest in non-Gothic forms had appeared, and it grew rapidly. Thus the ungainly building he designed in 1865 for Vassar College in Poughkeepsie was supposedly Renaissance, with its awkward superposed orders and its mansard roof; and Booth's Theatre, opened in 1869 on the corner of Sixth Avenue and Twenty-third Street, was a more advanced, but still incoherent, example of the same bastard classic. The Corcoran Gallery in Washington, a little later, was much more polished; its brick and stone and mansard roof formed a whole much acclaimed at the time as a beautiful example of French Renaissance. During the seventies his practice grew so large that he took Joseph Sands into partnership, the firm becoming Renwick & Sands. When Sands died, in 1880, Renwick took into the firm one of his wife's cousins, James Lawrence Aspinwall, and later included his nephew, William W. Renwick (1864–1934), the firm name becoming Renwick, Aspinwall & Renwick. The last work it completed prior to the founder's death was the house for Frederick Gallatin at Fifty-third Street and Fifth Avenue.

Like his contemporaries, Richard Hunt [q.v.] and Detlef Lienau, Renwick was an inspiring teacher of the apprentices and draftsmen in his office, many of whom later became architects themselves. Among those he trained were William W. Root [q.v.], William Russell of Clinton & Russell, and Bertram Grosvenor Goodhue [q.v.], who entered the office as a lad in his teens. Renwick was eager and experimental, and, like many self-trained men, lacking in the power of rigid self-criticism. Unusually alert to the artistic fashions of his time, he often mistook fashionableness for excellence. This was true even in his early Gothic days, and he was severely criticized by some of his contemporaries. The six towers of the Smithsonian Institution, all so painstakingly different, show to what extremes the desire for romantic picturesqueness could lead, and the Vassar building and Booth's Theatre are in a most unfortunate type of caricatured classic. Nevertheless, his planning was often sound, as in the case of the Smithsonian, and technically his work was not only careful, but advanced. A writer in the *Architectural Record* (October-December 1892) credits him with much of the improvement evident in the manufacture and use of architectural terra cotta, citing especially his terra-cotta altar for St. Mark's Chapel, at Avenue B and Tenth Street. In design as well, his talents were often brilliant and he was full of imagination. Much of the Smithsonian is pleasing. Grace Church still holds its own as one of the best examples of early Gothic Revival in the United States, despite occasional heaviness of detail. His original conception of St. Patrick's was masterly —to combine the triple influences of English, French, and German Gothic into a unified fusion. The original design was much harmed in execution; the stone vault gave way to obvious plaster, and the flying buttresses which would so have strengthened the silhouette were omitted. The stained glass was garish, and the chancel remained long unfinished. Nevertheless, the west front with its portals is commanding, the spires as successful as they are daring, and through it all, outside and in, there is really great scale. Much of his domestic work is good in its quiet and restrained dignity, and in the house built in the seventies on the southwest corner of Park Avenue and Thirty-ninth Street for D. Willis James, he produced what was, until its destruction in 1933, one of the best pieces of polychromatic Victorian Gothic in New York.

Renwick married Anna Lloyd Aspinwall, a daughter of William H. Aspinwall [q.v.], on Dec. 16, 1861; she died childless in 1880, and he never remarried. He was over six feet tall, and commanding in appearance. Though impetuous and hot-tempered, he was popular with men; in the office he was always affectionately referred to as "the old gentleman." He was abroad many times, in 1869–70 spending almost two years in Italy and Egypt. He collected everything—paintings, rugs, furniture, china, but especially Chinese and Japanese *objets d'art*, and his house at Tenth Street and University Place has been compared to a museum. He owned two steam yachts, the *Victory*, used for fishing in Florida, where Renwick was a licensed pilot in four districts, and a larger vessel called the *Jean*, used in the north. He was a member of both the New York and Larchmont Yacht clubs, and an early member of the Century Association and the Union Club. At the time of his death he was senior warden of Grace Church. He was buried in Greenwood Cemetery.

[Personal information supplied by Col. W. W. Renwick and by James Lawrence Aspinwall; *N. Y. Times* and *N. Y. Tribune*, June 25, 1895; Robert Dale Owen, *Hints on Public Architecture* (1849); "Our Streets," department published irregularly in *N. Y. Weekly Rev.*, during the first half of 1865; appreciation by B. G. Goodhue, *Churchman*, July 20, 1895; *Grace Church Year Book*, 1896; M. A. Hamm, *Famous Families of N. Y.* (1902), vol. II; I. N. P. Stokes, *Iconography of*

Manhattan Island (6 vols., 1915–28); Letters from Washington Irving to Mrs. William Renwick and to Her Son James Renwick (privately printed, 1918); W. R. Stewart, Grace Church and Old N. Y. (1924); J. K. Finch, Early Columbia Engineers (1929); Jefferson Williamson, The American Hotel (1930); A. Cluss, "Architecture and Architects of the Capital of the United States from its Foundation to 1875," Proc. Tenth Ann. Convention Am. Inst. of Architects, Phila., Oct. 11 and 12, 1876.]   T. F. H.

REQUIER, AUGUSTUS JULIAN (May 27, 1825–Mar. 19, 1887), poet and jurist, was born in Charleston, S. C., of French parents. His father was a native of Marseilles and his mother was the daughter of a Haitian planter who had fled to the United States at the time of the slave insurrection of 1791. He was educated in Charleston and very early showed evidences of literary talent. His first published work was a blank-verse drama, entitled The Spanish Exile, composed in his seventeenth year, which was performed on the stage and printed in 1842. After the usual classical education, he studied law and was admitted to the bar in Charleston in 1844. He practised law in that city for a few years and then moved to Marion, S. C. While building up a law practice there he served for a time as editor of the Marion Star. In 1850 he settled in Mobile, Ala., where he soon won distinction in his profession. In 1853 President Pierce appointed him United States district attorney for Alabama, and the appointment was renewed by President Buchanan. By the beginning of the Civil War he had become a judge of the superior court. After the secession of Alabama he was appointed by President Davis to serve as district attorney for the Confederacy. In 1866 he left Alabama to make his home in New York City, where he served for a time as assistant district attorney and practised law with success, particularly as counsel for corporations, receiving frequent appointments as referee in important cases. From the first he was identified with the Democratic party and took an active interest in the affairs of Tammany Hall. Shortly before his death he was a member of the Democratic General Committee for the city. He died suddenly of heart disease on Mar. 19, 1887. He was twice married. His first wife was Mary Elizabeth Evans, the daughter of William Evans, whom he married in Marion, S. C. His second wife, who survived him, is said to have been born in Charleston. He left no children. He is described by a contemporary as a small man, nervous and quick-moving—with black eyes and beard, who was "French in general style."

Besides the juvenile drama already mentioned, Requier wrote soon after his admission to the bar a prose narrative of South Carolina in colonial days, entitled, The Old Sanctuary: A Romance of the Ashley, which was published in Boston in 1846. His chief interest, however, was in lyric and narrative verse. In 1859 he wrote a blank-verse tragedy on the theme of Marco Bozzaris and prepared for the press a small volume of verse which Lippincott published in Philadelphia in 1860 under the title Poems. He followed this in 1862 with an Ode to Shakespeare and some two years later published in England a romantic poem with the title The Legend of Tremaine. "Crystalline," his longest and most ambitious poem, is Swedenborgian in its philosophy. It is the story of a young Italian nobleman, an artist who is converted from atheism to Christianity. During and just after the war Requier produced a number of martial lyrics which gave him a sure place among the war poets of the South. His best known poem of this sort is his "Ashes of Glory," written in reply to Father Ryan's "The Conquered Banner."

[J. W. Davidson, The Living Writers of the South (1869); Lib. of Southern Lit., vol. X (1909); E. A. and G. L. Duyckinck, Cyc. of Am. Lit. (ed. 1875), vol. II; N. Y. Daily Tribune, Mar. 21, 1887.]   J. C. F.

RESE, FREDERICK (Feb. 6, 1791–Dec. 30, 1871), Roman Catholic prelate, was born in Weinenburg, Hanover, of impoverished parents, John Gotfried Reese and Caroline (Alrutz). The German pronunciation of his father's name was ray-zay, and for some reason, in after life, Frederick, wishing to preserve the original sound, changed the spelling to Rese. He always wrote it with two grave accents, though contemporary documents from the Roman authorities omit them. He was left an orphan at an early age and was apprenticed to a tailor. Later he traveled from town to town, working at his trade. In 1813 he joined a cavalry regiment and fought throughout the War of Liberation until Waterloo, where he served under Blücher. As a journeyman tailor he worked his way to Rome and here entered the Propaganda as a theological student. Among his intimate friends was count Mastai Ferretti, later Pius IX. Ordained a priest on Trinity Sunday 1822, he volunteered for the African missions. The climate proved detrimental to his health, and about 1824 he returned to Germany and soon answered the appeal of E. D. Fenwick [q.v.], bishop of Cincinnati, for German priests. Accompanying the bishop to the United States, he became the first German priest in the Northwest. He lived laborious days, ministering to the German Catholics in Cincinnati, attending German missions throughout the diocese, and engaging in controversies with bitter Lutheran divines.

Going abroad in 1829 to enlist German priests for the Middle West, he aroused the interest of distinguished leaders of the Church and of the Austrian empire in the American missions and was instrumental in founding the famous Leopoldine Society of Vienna (named for Archduchess Leopoldine, later empress of Brazil), which contributed generously to the support of German parishes and schools in the United States. His appeal for aid at the Redemptorist monastery at Maria Stiegen encouraged the Redemptorist Fathers to extend their activities to the United States (1833), where the society grew rapidly and established German parishes and institutions in a score of dioceses. As Fenwick's vicar-general for Michigan-Wisconsin, Rese attended the scattered Indian missions and white settlements as superior of such missionaries as Stephen Badin, Frederic Baraga, and Samuel Charles Mazzuchelli [qq.v.]. Because of his administrative experience and command of languages, he was named first bishop of Detroit and was consecrated by Bishop Joseph Rosati on Oct. 6, 1833.

During the next four years he established St. Philip's College at Hamtramck; introduced the Sisters of St. Clare, who temporarily maintained academies at Detroit and Green Bay; completed Gabriel Richard's Church of St. Anne, Green Bay; provided several Indian schools; built Holy Trinity Church in Detroit for English speaking Catholics; and bravely struggled with the growing racial rivalries and trusteeism. A broken man with a failing mind, he offered to resign or accept a coadjutor in 1837, but the Third Provincial Council of Baltimore referred the matter to Rome. Not until 1841 was a bishop-administrator, Peter Paul Lefevere [q.v.], appointed. Rese retained his title, however, although the remainder of his life was spent in the seclusion of a Roman monastery and in hospitals at Lappenburg and Hildesheim, Germany. In the latter town he died.

[F. K. Reuss, *Biog. Cyc. of the Catholic Hierarchy of the U. S.* (1898); R. H. Clarke, *Lives of the Deceased Bishops of the Catholic Church in the U. S.*, vol. III (1888); *Cath. Encyc.*, vol. IV (1908); J. H. Lamott, *Hist. of the Archdiocese of Cincinnati* (1921); official Catholic directories; J. G. Shea, *Hist. of the Cath. Church in the U. S.*, vol. III (1890); *U. S. Cath. Hist. Soc. Hist. Records and Studies*, vol. III, pt. 1 (1903); *Katholische Volkzeitung* (Baltimore), Nov. 13, 1869; information regarding Reese's name from the Rev. George W. Paré, Detroit.]   R.J.P.

REULING, GEORGE (Nov. 11, 1839–Nov. 25, 1915), ophthalmologist, was born in Romrod, Germany, the son of Dr. Robert Reuling and Amalie (Vogler). He received his early education in Darmstadt; then attended the University of Giessen, where he was a pupil of von Liebig. Later, he became assistant to Professor Phoebus in materia medica and pharmacology at this University. He was awarded the degree of M.D. there in 1865. His early ophthalmological training was obtained during vacations at the renowned clinic of Prof. Alexander Pagenstecher in Wiesbaden, where, since he was a cousin of the director, he enjoyed special advantages. Here he also came under the influence of Hirschfeld, subsequently professor of ophthalmology at the University of Charkow, and of Iwanoff, later of the University of Kiev. During the Austro-Prussian War of 1866, he served as military surgeon. After a period of study of ophthalmology and of otology at the University of Vienna under Arlt, von Jaeger, Mauthner, Politzer, and others, he was called to be first assistant at the Pagenstecher clinic. While serving in this capacity he was invited by a prominent layman of Baltimore to take up his residence and professional work in that city. Before leaving Europe, however, he spent some time with von Graefe in Berlin, and de Wecker and Liebreich in Paris.

He arrived in Baltimore in 1868, and established, Oct. 1, 1869, the Maryland Eye and Ear Infirmary, equipped with fifteen beds and a dispensary department, which he conducted for a number of years. In 1871 he was appointed professor of ophthalmology and otology at Washington University, Baltimore, and served as such until 1873. Elected professor of ophthalmology and otology at the Baltimore Medical College in 1887, he taught there until his resignation in 1908, when he was made professor emeritus. His reputation was chiefly based upon his skill as an operator, but he was also the author of a number of contributions to medical literature, the most important of which were "Extraction of Cataract within the Lenticular Capsule" (*New York Medical Journal*, January 1879) and "On the Extraction of Cataract within the Capsule, Based on 200 Operations" (*Transactions of the Medical and Chirurgical Faculty of the State of Maryland*, 1880). He enjoyed a large practice and many persons prominent in American life were among his patients. Joseph Jefferson the actor, in writing of his "threatened blindness" says that ". . . the operation, under the skillful hands of Doctor Reuling, was entirely successful" (*Autobiography of Joseph Jefferson*, 1889, p. 388). He was a member of many learned societies, including the Ophthalmological Society of Heidelberg, and a number of prominent clubs, and was known as an excellent art critic and the possessor of a large and valuable art collection. He was married in 1871 to Elisa Külp of Darmstadt, by whom he had two children—a son, who followed his father in the profession of medicine, but died at an early age, and a daughter, who survived him.

[Biog. sketch in *Va. Medic. Monthly*, Oct. 1885, containing an extensive bibliog. of his early medic. contributions; G. W. Howard, *The Monumental City, Its Past Hist. and Present Resources* (1873); W. B. Atkinson, *The Physicians and Surgeons of the U. S.* (1878); *Baltimore, Its Hist. and Its People* (1912), vol. III; E. F. Cordell, *Medic. Annals of Md.* (1903); Julius Hirschberg, *Geschichte der Augenheilkunde* (Leipzig, 1915), Vol. III, p. 117; *Who's Who in America*, 1914–15; *Sun* (Baltimore), and *N. Y. Times*, Nov. 26, 1915.]

H. F—d.

REUTER, DOMINIC (Dec. 5, 1856–May 4, 1933), Catholic priest and educator, was born at Coblenz in the Rhineland, the son of John and Mary Margaret (Shaefer) Reuter. His parents emigrated to New York in 1859 and later settled in Albany. With the completion of his elementary and preparatory schooling, he entered the novitiate of the Friars Minor Conventual (Black Franciscans) at Syracuse, where he made his religious profession a year later, May 7, 1876. He pursued his philosophical studies at St. Francis College, Trenton, N. J., and his course in theology at the University of Innsbruck in the Tyrol, where he was ordained a priest, July 26, 1881, by Bishop Fidelis Dehm. For four years he remained at Innsbruck as lector of philosophy and master of clerics and was then assigned as confessor for English-speaking pilgrims at the Holy House in Loretto, Italy. During his Italian residence he won doctorates in philosophy and in theology at the College of St. Bonaventure (1886, 1889) and was given the degree of master of sacred theology by Bonaventure Soldatich, minister general of the Order (Aug. 1, 1889).

In 1890 Father Dominic returned to America to become master of clerics and regent of studies at St. Francis College, Trenton, of which, in 1899, he became rector, serving as such until 1903. At the provincial chapter (1902), he was named secretary of the Province of the Immaculate Conception, but had held the position only a year when he was called to Rome as procurator general of the Order. On Oct. 12, 1904, he was chosen minister general, the one hundred and seventh successor of St. Francis and the only American up to the present time (1934) to attain that rank in any Franciscan branch. During his generalate he initiated far-reaching movements, such as the return of the Friars Conventual to England and to Spain, the revision of

the constitutions of the Order (1907), the reopening of the College of St. Bonaventure in Rome, the publication of an international periodical for the whole Order, and negotiations with the Italian government for the restoration of the Basilica and Convent of St. Francis at Assisi. He visited every province and convent of the Order, as no general had been able to do for decades. At the conclusion of his term (1910), Pope Pius X urged that he remain in Rome with greater honors in store. He declined to do so, however, and later refused the offer of an American bishopric.

A simple religious, he taught in Mount St. Francis Pro-Seminary at Floyd Knobs, Ind., and at St. Anthony-on-the-Hudson, Rensselaer, until he was appointed consultor of the Sacred Congregation of the Index and of Religious (1913–19) by Pope Benedict XV, who also named him chairman of the papal commission for locating war prisoners and missing soldiers of the warring nations. In 1919 he was again at Syracuse, teaching at St. Francis Convent and Novitiate, from which place he was transferred in 1923 to the newly established Postgraduate House of St. Bonaventure, Washington, D. C., of which he became the head. In ill health, he acted as chaplain for two years at St. Elizabeth's Hospital, Utica; when almost blind, he retired to the motherhouse at Syracuse (1926), where he celebrated the golden jubilee of his profession as a friar and of his ordination to the priesthood. An able man, a sound theologian, a linguist, and a laborious and tactful administrator, Father Dominic left his impress on the Order and upon almost every priest of the American province, who at some time or other had studied under him.

[Notes supplied by Clement M. O'Donnell, O.M.C., based upon records in the archives of the motherhouse in Syracuse; *The Minorite*, June 1926, June 1933; *Am. Catholic Who's Who*, 1934–35; *Commentorium Ordinis Fratrum Minorum S. Francisci Conventualium*, An. XXIII, num. IV, VI, An. XXX, num. V, VI; *N. Y. Times*, Oct. 13, 1904, May 5, 1933; *Catholic News* (N. Y.), Oct. 15, 1904; *Syracuse Post Standard*, Oct. 13, 14, 1904, May 4, 1933; *Catholic Sun* (Syracuse), May 4, 1933.]

R. J. P.

REUTERDAHL, HENRY (Aug. 12, 1871–Dec. 22, 1925), naval painter, illustrator, author, was born at Malmö, Sweden, the son of Frederic and Augusta (Drake) Reuterdahl. His early education was received in the schools of Stockholm. He learned to draw without a master and did some work in scene painting and illustration. In 1893, commissioned to go to Chicago to make a series of illustrations of the World's Fair, he came to America and decided to stay. During the Spanish-American War he served as a newspaper correspondent and wrote about the naval operations in the Caribbean for several periodicals. He married Pauline Stephenson of Chicago in 1899 and shortly afterward moved to New York, establishing his home in Weehawken, N. J. From this time he specialized in naval pictures and soon became a semi-official naval artist. He designed trophies for target practice and made decorations for the wardrooms of battleships. He illustrated John D. Long's *History of the New American Navy* (1903). By *Collier's Weekly* he was commissioned to make a tour of the European navies, the outcome of which was a series of pictures of the "Navies of the World." Scores of his illustrations appeared in *Collier's,* the *Scientific American, Scribner's,* and other periodicals. He was attached to the battleship *Minnesota* during the fleet's cruise around South America and during the cruise to the Mediterranean in 1913; and he was present at the Vera Cruz campaign of 1914. He made himself an advocate of the Navy, urging the duty of sustaining the sea forces, of understanding the work of naval men, and of becoming familiar with naval problems. Of the many papers he contributed to magazines, the most significant was his "Needs of the Navy," published in *McClure's,* January 1908, in which he attacked the bureau system in the Navy Department with so much cogency that his argument led to an investigation by the United States Senate.

He also found time to teach at the Art Students' League, New York, and to send pictures to many exhibitions. He painted panels for the steam yachts *Noma, Viking,* and *Vagrant,* owned respectively by Vincent Astor, George F. Baker, Jr., and Harold S. Vanderbilt. In the permanent collection of the Naval Academy, Annapolis, he is represented by a group of ten paintings donated by George von L. Meyer, secretary of the navy in the cabinet of President Taft. His "Combat between the Monitor and the Merrimac" is in the National Gallery of Art, Washington; his "Blast Furnaces" belongs to the Toledo Art Museum; and other works are in the possession of the Naval War College, Newport, R. I., the Missouri State Capitol at Jefferson City, Culver Military Academy, and the Kalamazoo Art Association. In 1914 the Cincinnati Museum held an exhibition of his works. During the World War he was made a lieutenant-commander in the Naval Reserve; his death occurred in St. Elizabeth's Hospital, Washington, D. C., where he had been a patient for several months, and he was buried in Arlington Cemetery with full military honors.

[*Outlook,* Jan. 6, 1926; F. T. Jane, in *Book Buyer,* June 1902; "Who's Who in Art," in *Am. Art Annual,* 1923; H. L. Earle, *Biog. Sketches of Am. Artists* (1924); catalogue of exhibition, Cincinnati Museum, Mar. 1914; *Who's Who in America,* 1918–19; *Am. Art News,* Jan. 2, 1926; *N. Y. Times,* Dec. 24, 1925.]
W. H. D.

REVELL, FLEMING HEWITT (Dec. 11, 1849–Oct. 11, 1931), publisher, was born in Chicago, Ill., the son of Fleming Hewitt Revell and Emma (Manning) Revell. The father, a descendant of French Huguenots who fled to the north of Ireland, was a shipbuilder in London until, meeting with reverses, he brought his family to America, and in 1849 to Chicago, where he built boats for the Lake Michigan traffic. Success did not attend him in Chicago either, and the only son had to leave school at nine years of age to help support his mother and three sisters. One of these sisters, Emma, married the evangelist, Dwight L. Moody [*q.v.*], and it was under Moody's inspiration that Revell, not yet twenty, began in 1869 to publish *Everybody's Paper,* a little religious monthly. A pocket account book, in the possession of his son, shows that he traveled through the Middle West securing subscriptions, five in one town and ten in the next. When the Chicago fire of 1871 burned his entire establishment, he started again. Doubtless the publishing of Moody's sermons, tracts, and other writings helped him to place his business on a firm basis, for these in cloth and paper bindings sold in time by the hundred thousands. To these were added the books of other evangelists suitable for the Moody audience, and by 1880 his list numbered about one hundred titles, besides booklets, gospel tracts, revival hymnals, and Sunday-school periodicals. A branch of the firm was opened in New York in 1887, and ultimately branches in Toronto, London, and Edinburgh were added. By 1890 he was one of the largest publishers of religious books in America, having gradually widened his scope from strictly evangelical literature. He had a flourishing juvenile department, sold standard Sunday-school libraries of fifty volumes for $25.75, and distributed all the Sunday-school paraphernalia of the period, including picture cards and colored floral mottoes. He moved to New York about 1906 and some years afterward transferred the headquarters of his company to that city. His sixty years of religious publishing not only gave him a remarkable knowledge of the market possibilities of religious books of all kinds but permitted him to accumulate a comfortable fortune, which he invested wisely. Several years before his death he turned the presidency of his firm over to his son,

Fleming Hewitt Revell, Jr., and became chairman of the board. He had married in 1872 Josephine Barbour of Romeo, Mich., who died in 1924.

For years he was active in religious, educational, and financial affairs. Through his earlier association with Moody he developed a strong interest in the Northfield (Mass.) schools and contributed liberally to them. He was a trustee of the Northfield Seminary and of Wheaton College. He was long treasurer of the American Mission to Lepers and at different times a member of educational and mission boards of the Presbyterian Church. He was also a director of the New York Life Insurance Company. His extensive travels in Europe and the Near East during his yearly vacations gave him, in addition, a wide acquaintance with world problems.

[*Who's Who in America*, 1930–31; W. R. Moody, *D. L. Moody* (1930); *Publishers' Trade List Ann.*, 1880 ff.; information from Fleming H. Revell, Jr.; *N. Y. Times*, Oct. 12, 1931.]   O. W. H.

REVELS, HIRAM RHOADES (September 1822–Jan. 16, 1901), Methodist clergyman, United States senator, educator, born of free parents in Fayetteville, N. C., was of mixed African and Croatan Indian descent. For some years he was a barber in Lincolnton, N. C., but in 1844 he went to Indiana and attended a Friends' school at Liberty. Soon afterward, he was at school in Drake County, Ohio, and later attended Knox College. In 1845 he was ordained minister in the African Methodist Church and subsequently carried on religious work among the negroes in Ohio, Illinois, Indiana, Missouri, Kansas, Kentucky, and Tennessee. Settling in Baltimore, he served as pastor of a church there and also as principal of a school for negroes.

During the Civil War he assisted in organizing two negro regiments in Maryland; in 1863 he went to St. Louis to establish a school for freedmen, and there he aided in recruiting another regiment. The following year he became chaplain of a Mississippi regiment, served for a short time as provost marshal of Vicksburg, organized several negro churches in Jackson, and then engaged for two years in pastoral work in Kentucky and Kansas. In 1866 he settled at Natchez and in 1868 joined the Methodist Episcopal Church. That same year he was elected alderman. He entered politics reluctantly, fearing race friction and the possibility of a conflict with his religious activities, but he won the liking and respect of the white people of the state, and he was successful in divorcing his church work from politics. He was elected to the state Senate from Adams County, and in

January 1870 he was elected to the United States Senate, succeeding Jefferson Davis, and served until Mar. 4, 1871. Revels was a Republican, but he was not a Radical, and in the Senate adopted a conservative attitude. His service was dignified and, apart from the fact that he was a negro, unimportant.

After his retirement in 1871 he was elected president of Alcorn University, at Oakland, near Rodney, a recently opened institution for negroes, which position he filled with credit. In 1873 he was secretary of state *ad interim* of Mississippi. In 1874 Governor Ames dismissed him from the presidency of Alcorn and he returned to ministerial work, joining the Mississippi Conference of the Methodist Episcopal Church the following year. In 1875, he was active in behalf of the Democrats in the state campaign which led to the overthrow of the Carpet-bag government, and defended his course in a strong letter to President Grant, printed in the Jackson *Daily Times*, Nov. 10, in which he said that all good men had combined to defeat the Republicans. In 1876 he again became president of Alcorn and did much to restore the confidence of the negroes in it. In June of the same year he became editor of the *Southwestern Christian Advocate*. After his retirement he lived at Holly Springs and was actively engaged in religious work until his death, which occurred while he was attending a Church conference at Aberdeen. His wife, Phoebe A. (Bass), and two daughters survived him.

[*Biog. Dir. Am. Cong.* (1928); J. W. Garner, *Reconstruction in Miss.* (1901); W. H. Barnes, *Hist. of Cong.; The Forty-first Cong. of the U. S., 1869–1871* (1872); *Abbott's Monthly*, Jan. 1931; S. D. Smith, "The Negro in Congress," unpublished doctoral dissertation, Univ. of N. C.; *Official Minutes . . . Upper Miss. Ann. Conference of the M. E. Church*, 1901; *Southwestern Christian Advocate*, Jan. 31, 1901; *Daily Democrat* (Natchez), Jan. 18, 1901.]   J. G. deR. H.

REVERE, JOSEPH WARREN (May 17, 1812–Apr. 20, 1880), naval officer, writer, adventurer, and general in the Civil War, was born in Boston, the grandson of Paul Revere [*q.v.*] and the son of John Revere, who married Lydia LeBaron Goodwin and was a physician in Boston and later professor of medicine in the University of the City of New York. Love of travel led Joseph to enter the navy as a midshipman in 1828, and his taste was abundantly gratified by a three-year Pacific cruise in the *Guerrière*, a year of pirate hunting in the Caribbean, service on the African coast, and, after promotion to passed midshipman in 1832, an enjoyable cruise in the Mediterranean and northward to Russia. In the autumn of 1836 he made an overland journey as dispatch bearer from

Lisbon to Paris and back to Gibraltar. A China cruise, 1838–40, was followed by his promotion to lieutenant in 1841. In 1845 he was assigned to the California coast, where, in command of a landing party from the *Portsmouth*, he raised the flag at Sonoma on July 9, 1846, fought in Stockton's force at the San Gabriel River, and participated in subsequent naval activities on the Mexican west coast. He returned home in 1848 but was soon back in California in the midst of the gold rush as agent for naval timber land. He resigned from the navy in 1850 because of slow promotion and busied himself in developing a ranch he had purchased near Sonoma, and in 1851 made two profitable trading voyages down the Mexican coast. On his second voyage he rescued the crew of a shipwrecked Spanish vessel from hostile Indians, receiving in reward a medal from the city of Cadiz and an order of merit from Queen Isabella. While visiting Mexico city at the close of 1851 he accepted an offer to organize the artillery of the Mexican army, and served as colonel till the following spring, being badly wounded in February during an insurrection in Morelia, Mexico.

From 1852 until the outbreak of the Civil War, he divided his time between his home in Morristown, N. J., and extensive European travel. He first volunteered for the navy, but finding his services not immediately needed, entered the army on Aug. 31, 1861, as colonel of the 7th New Jersey Volunteers. After fighting through the Peninsular Campaign and at Seven Pines and Antietam, he was made brigadier-general on Oct. 25, 1862, and led the 2nd Brigade, 2nd Division, III Corps, at Fredericksburg, and the Excelsior Brigade, same division, at Chancellorsville. In the latter battle, May 3, 1863, after a severe action from daybreak till eight o'clock that morning, he found himself senior officer of the division, and, his forces being short of ammunition and without rations, he moved them without orders about three miles to the rear, where they remained until ordered back about three o'clock in the afternoon. For this action General Sickles sharply censured him and relieved him of the command. He was court-martialed and dismissed, but the sentence—severe in view of his previous record for ability and gallantry—was revoked on Sept. 10, 1864, by President Lincoln, and his resignation accepted.

In later years he suffered from declining health and spent considerable periods in foreign travel. His death from heart trouble occurred suddenly at Busche's Hotel, Hoboken, N. J. His wife, Rosanna Duncan, whom he had married on Oct. 4, 1842, and three of their five children survived

him. He was author of *A Tour of Duty in California* (1849) and *Keel and Saddle: A Retrospect of Forty Years of Military and Naval Service* (1872). The latter is largely autobiographical but contains also a number of romantic stories, both of fact and fiction, entertainingly written and reflecting the author's restless, adventure-loving spirit.

[J. W. Revere, *A Statement of the Case of Brigadier-General J. W. Revere* (1863); E. H. Goss, *The Life of Col. Paul Revere* (2 vols., 1891); *War of the Rebellion: Official Records*, 1 ser., vol. XXV; *Army and Navy Reg.*, Apr. 24, 1880.]
A. W.

REVERE, PAUL (Jan. 1, 1735–May 10, 1818), patriot, craftsman, was the son of Paul and Deborah (Hichborn) Revere. His father, christened Apollos De Revoire, was of French Huguenot descent and came to Boston, Mass., from the isle of Guernsey at the age of thirteen to serve an apprenticeship of three years in the shop of the silversmith, John Coney [*q.v.*]. Once established in his own business, he anglicized his name "merely on account that the Bumpkins should pronounce it easier" (Taylor, *post*, p. 14). Young Paul Revere, the third of twelve children, attended the North Grammar School and under his father's tutelage learned the trade which he was to follow. His pursuits were interrupted in 1756 when he joined the expedition against Crown Point, but after six months he returned to Boston and on Aug. 17, 1757, married Sarah Orne who bore him eight children.

The abundant vitality of the Boston silversmith soon caused him to expand his activities beyond the strict limits of his trade. As early as 1765 he began experimenting with his graver on copper plate and executed a few portraits and a songbook. His intense interest in the developing difficulties between Great Britain and the Colonies and his vigorous patriotism soon became evident in political cartoons, pointed if crude, which provided exceedingly effective propaganda for rebellion. Many of the engravings of the *Royal American Magazine* were his. A constant demand for seals, bookplates, certificates, and coats-of-arms soon caused him to exercise no mean degree of skill in this craft, but he still found time to carve frames for Copley's portraits and to manufacture dental devices which he advertised as not only ornamental but also "of real Use in Speaking and Eating" (*Boston Gazette and Country Journal*, July 30, 1770).

Revere's ability to furnish willing political workers from the mechanic class of Boston, of which he was the acknowledged leader, brought him into close contact with John Hancock, Samuel Adams, and Joseph Warren, to whom he rendered a yeoman's service. When the North

End Caucus, probably the most influential of all the political clubs, voted to oppose the vending of tea by the East India Company, he was one of three special committeemen chosen to suggest the course of action, and along with fifty other sober-minded Boston working men, donned war-paint and feathers for the famous Tea Party. He made a long trip on horseback in the winter of 1773, to apprise the associates of the Sons of Liberty in New York of the Boston Tea Party. When the Boston Port Bill brought distress to the town in the following spring, he carried the protest and appeal for help to New York and Philadelphia. He rode to Philadelphia with the "Suffolk Resolves," made in defiance of the "Intolerable Acts" of Sept. 9, 1774. He then was made the official courier for the Massachusetts Provincial Assembly to Congress and became so familiar a sight to the countryside in general and to the British in particular that his name found its way into London newspapers long before he made the ride which Longfellow's poem put in every textbook of American history. When General Gage planned to carry off to a safer place the valuable store of munitions in the arsenal of Fort William and Mary, Paul Revere galloped off to Durham to warn General Sullivan and then rode on to Portsmouth to stir the New Hampshire Lads into action. He did not have time to share in the raid on the Fort, but the hard-riding silversmith must be given credit for precipitating this first aggressive act of the colonists and for making it possible to seize powder and shot which six months later was used in covering the retreat of the hard-pressed Continental soldiers at Bunker Hill.

Two days before he made his famous ride to Lexington, he rode with the equally important purpose of warning the patriots to move their military stores from Concord, and it was on this journey that he arranged with "a Colonel Conant and some other gentleman that, if the British went by water, we would show two lanthorns in the North Church steeple; and, if by land, one as a signal . . ." (Goss, *post*, vol. I, p. 187). His second ride to Lexington "on the 18th of April, '75," was made to warn Hancock and Adams that the British were out to capture them and to rouse the countryside to the fact that the crown troops were on the march. He crossed the Charles River under the very prows of the British guard-ships, the oars of his boat muffled with a woman's petticoat. It was not the lithe figure of a young man which mounted a fiery steed on the opposite shore, but a figure of forty years who climbed upon a stoutish work-horse to carry the "fate of a nation" that night. He

eluded British patrolmen, reached Lexington, saw his two chiefs on their way and then set out with William Dawes and Samuel Prescott [*q.v.*] to warn Concord. They were stopped, however, by scouting troopers, and Revere was detained and released to make his way back to Lexington without his horse in the confusion of a rising countryside. While history was being made by the minute-men a few hundred yards away, he set himself to the homely task of carrying away to safety a trunk of papers and documents forgotten by Hancock in his haste to leave.

Although he was anxious for action, Revere received no military command in the Continental Army. He was set to work at designing and printing the first issue of Continental money; he made the first official seal for the colonies and the state seal which Massachusetts still uses. He was sent to Philadelphia to learn to manufacture gunpowder and for a time directed the process at a rebuilt mill at Canton, Mass. He became a member of the Committee of Correspondence on Mar. 29, 1776, and helped to draw up the lists of outlawed Boston Loyalists, and to stir up laggard patriots to action. In 1778 and 1779 he was in command at Castle William, the only relief from the dull routine of garrison duty coming in the latter year when he participated in the ill-fated Penobscot expedition that ended in recriminations and failure. He was accused of cowardice, and insubordination, but after many appeals was finally cleared of the charges by a court martial on Feb. 19, 1782.

He returned once more to his business while still under the cloud of his second military adventure. A jack of many trades, he was a master silversmith and many of the gracious and most beautiful specimens of his craft that now survive belong to this period of his work. His silver is marked with the family name in a rectangle, or "P. R." in crude capitals or script in a rectangle, or Roman capitals incised. At the age of fifty-five, he had made his reputation at his trade; he and his second wife, Rachel Walker, whom he had married on Oct. 10, 1773, shortly after the death of his first wife, had eight children; and he was deeply engrossed in numerous civic duties, especially in agitating for the ratification of the federal Constitution. But he still had time and energy to begin casting bells and making cannon. From his foundry he supplied the bolts, spikes, pumps, and copper accessories for *Old Ironsides*. He discovered a process for rolling sheet copper and in 1808–09 made copper plates for the boilers of a steam ferry-boat for Robert Fulton. The quaint figure of the aged silversmith, who persisted in wearing the costumes of Revolutionary days throughout his life, was long a familiar one on the streets of Boston. The loss of his wife and his eldest son were the great sorrows of his old age and he died three years thereafter at the age of eighty-three.

[E. H. Goss, *The Life of Colonel Paul Revere* (2 vols., 1891) ; C. F. Gettemy, *The True Story of Paul Revere* (1905) ; Emerson Taylor, *Paul Revere* (1930) ; A. H. Nichols, *Bells of Paul and Joseph W. Revere* (1911) ; Richard Frothingham, *Life and Times of Joseph Warren* (1865) ; F. H. Bigelow, *Historic Silver of the Colonies and Its Makers* (1917) ; C. L. Avery, *Am. Silver of the XVII and XVIII Centuries* (1920) ; Hollis French, *The Walpole Soc., A List of Early Am. Silversmiths and Their Marks* (1917) ; obit. in the *Columbian Centinel* (Boston, Mass.), May 13, 1818.]

K. A. K.

REYNOLDS, ALEXANDER WELCH (August 1817–May 26, 1876), Confederate soldier, was born in Clarke County, Va. He graduated from the United States Military Academy at West Point in 1838 and served in the Seminole War until 1840. From 1841 until 1846 he was on frontier duty in Iowa, Wisconsin, and Missouri. On Aug. 5, 1847, he was appointed assistant quartermaster, with staff rank of captain, and served in Florida for two years. In 1848 he was ordered to Mexico and until 1852 convoyed trains to Forts Washita and Towson, Indian Territory, and to Santa Fé, N. Mex. Some question as to his accounts came up, and he was ordered to Washington to explain alleged discrepancies, was dismissed from the service on Oct. 8, 1855, but was reinstated with his staff rank of captain in 1858. In February and March 1861 he was on duty at San Antonio, Tex., as assistant quartermaster when state troops took from him the federal funds in his charge in the name of the state of Texas, and took over the city of San Antonio. He was then ordered to Washington, but for failing to report to army authorities, he was dropped again from the service on Oct. 4, 1861. Meanwhile, he had sent his wife to Philadelphia and had joined the cause of the Confederacy, being commissioned colonel of the 50th Virginia Infantry in July 1861. His regiment saw service in West Virginia under Gen. John Buchanan Floyd [*q.v.*] during the winter of 1861–62. After the Fort Donelson campaign, in 1862 he was ordered to support Kirby-Smith in Knoxville and was given a brigade in Stevenson's division. He took part in the defense of Vicksburg and was captured when it fell. Being soon exchanged, he was made a brigadier-general in September 1863, for services at Vicksburg. He took part in the Atlanta campaign, in campaigns in northern Alabama and middle Tennessee, and was highly commended for repelling Federal raids.

Following the war he rejoined his wife in Philadelphia, and in 1869, she and their only son, Frank, who had also served in the Confederacy, accompanied him to Egypt where he joined the forces of Ismail Pasha, with the rank of colonel. He became one of that small but almost unsung band of gentlemen-adventurers, mostly ex-Confederates, who tried to bring order out of chaos in Egypt. Reynolds served in various staff capacities, helping to build up the Egyptian army for its ill-fated campaign in Abyssinia in 1875. Early in that year he was chief of staff for William Wing Loring [*q.v.*], who commanded an infantry division at Alexandria, but Reynolds did not accompany him in the disastrous campaign which followed. Broken in health, and mourning the death of his son, also a colonel under Ismail, he died in Alexandria, Egypt, the following spring.

[Data as to Gen. Reynolds' own family and his wife are not available. No full account of his life is written, and considerable confusion exists in the accounts of his service in Egypt. The present account of his Egyptian service is taken from W. W. Loring, *A Confed. Soldier in Egypt* (1884) and that of W. M. Dye, *Moslem Egypt and Modern Abyssinia* (1880). Other data are taken from the following: G. W. Cullum, *Biog. Reg. ... U. S. Mil. Acad.* (1891) ; F. B. Heitman, *Hist. Reg. and Dict. of the U. S. Army* (1903) ; L. G. Tyler, ed., *Encyc. of Va. Biog.* (1915), vol. III ; *Confed. Military Hist.* (1899), vol. III.]

D. Y.

REYNOLDS, CHARLES ALEXANDER (Mar. 20, 1842?–June 25, 1876), hunter, scout, and guide, was the son of Joseph Boyer and Phoebe (Buah) Reynolds. Both the place and the date of his birth are in dispute. To a recruiting officer, in the summer of 1861, he stated that he was nineteen years old and that he was a native of Illinois, but it seems probable that he was born on a farm near Stephensburg, Hardin County, Ky. His paternal grandfather, Nathaniel Reynolds, of Scotch ancestry, brought his family from Virginia to Kentucky about 1811, served in the War of 1812, and was wounded at the battle of New Orleans. His father, born in Virginia, was reared in Kentucky, where he became a farmer and a practising physician. He later removed with his family to Illinois, and, early in 1859, to Atchison County, Kan. Young Reynolds attended various schools and seems to have acquired a fair education. In 1860 he made a journey into the West. Returning home, he enlisted as a soldier in July 1861, and after three years' service was honorably discharged.

In the spring of 1867, following several hunting and trapping ventures, he left home for the last time. He is next heard of in the Dakota country, where he became a hunter, furnishing game to various military posts. In May 1873, at Yankton, he joined George A. Custer [*q.v.*] as a scout for the Yellowstone expedition under David S. Stanley [*q.v.*]. He was the guide of Custer's Black Hills expedition of 1874, and in August won distinction by the exceptionally hazardous exploit of carrying dispatches through the heart of the hostile country to Fort Laramie. In the following year he was the hunter and chief scout of Forsyth's expedition up the Yellowstone, later of William Ludlow [*q.v.*] in his reconnaissance from Fort Abraham Lincoln; in the following winter he was instrumental in causing the capture of Rain-in-the-Face for the murder of two civilians. On Mar. 3, 1876, he was employed by Custer as a scout for the Big Horn expedition which left Fort Abraham Lincoln on May 17. In the battle of the Little Big Horn he was assigned to Reno's battalion. At the beginning of the retreat from the valley he was shot and instantly killed. The body was recovered and buried in grave No. 260 on Custer Field.

Reynolds was unmarried. He was about five feet eight inches in height, of sturdy build and somewhat round-shouldered. His manner was simple and straightforward, and his voice was gentle. Though friendly in disposition, and though on his hunting trips he usually had one or more companions, his reserve and his reticence of speech caused him to be dubbed "Lonesome Charley," a nickname by which he became widely known. Nothing could induce him to talk about himself or his deeds, and he carefully avoided the stage trappings of the professional scout. His reputation has grown brighter with the years, while that of many of his widely heralded contemporaries has dimmed, and he is now generally ranked as the greatest of the Western scouts. His skill as a hunter was regarded by the Indians with superstitious awe, and his service with the army was marked by the highest degree of courage, endurance, and resourcefulness. He won and retained the unbounded confidence of Custer; and Elizabeth Custer, in an affecting characterization of him (*"Boots and Saddles,"* 1885, pp. 240–42), has left an enduring tribute to his memory.

[J. H. Taylor, *Sketches of Frontier and Indian Life* (2nd ed., 1895); J. E. Remsburg, in the *Weekly Kan-·an* (Potter, Kan.), Dec. 3, 1914–Apr. 15, 1915; J. M. Hanson, *The Conquest of the Missouri* (1909); *Report of the Adjutant General of the State of Kan.*, I (1867), 906; D. S. Stanley, *Report of the Yellowstone Expedition of 1873* (1874); E. A. Brininstool, *A Trooper with Custer* (1925); information from Inspector General H. A. Drum and Adjutant General C. H. Bridges, U. S. A., and from Reynolds' nephew, Charles Edwin Reynolds, Polson, Mont.] W. J. G.

REYNOLDS, EDWIN (Mar. 23, 1831–Feb. 19, 1909), inventor, engineer, son of Christopher

and Charissa (Huntington) Reynolds, was born on his father's farm at Mansfield, Conn. He was a descendant of James Reynolds who was in Rhode Island in 1665. After obtaining a common-school education in his birthplace and working for a while on the farm, at the age of sixteen Edwin entered a local machine shop as an apprentice. Three years later he started on a journeyman's tour of various shops in lower New England. In 1857 he went to Aurora, Ind., where he became superintendent of the shops of Stedman & Company, builders of engines, sawmill machinery, and drainage boilers for Mississippi plantations. This business practically ceased in 1861, and Reynolds then returned East and secured a position with the Corliss Steam Engine Company at Providence, R. I. In ten years he rose to be plant superintendent, a position he held until 1877. His last notable work with this company was the construction of the great Corliss engine for the Centennial Exhibition in 1876, and the designing and building of a rolling-mill engine to run at a speed double that of previous designs.

In 1877 he accepted the position of general superintendent of the Edward P. Allis Company of Milwaukee, Wis., and undertook the development of the Reynolds-Corliss engine. Early in the 1880's his own inventions began to appear in the varied line of machinery manufactured by his company, which included large Corliss engines for pumping service, mining machinery, air compressors, blowing engines, and machinery for street-railway work. One of the greatest of his achievements during this period was the building in 1888 of the first triple expansion pumping engine for waterworks service in the United States. This engine is described as "doing continuously so high a duty as to place it among the most remarkable constructions of its class and time" (*Transactions, post*, p. 1052). On Dec. 4, 1888, he perfected and patented a blowing engine for blast furnaces, the design of which embodied a radical departure from accepted practice. It was selected by the Joliet Steel Company from competitive designs submitted by engineers in the United States and Europe, and after twenty-five years of continuous experimenting no improvements on the essential features of Reynolds' design had been made (*Ibid.*, p. 1053). That it was a valuable product for the Allis Company is evidenced by the fact that it yielded from a single steel concern over five million dollars' worth of business. Another notable accomplishment of Reynolds was the designing and building in 1893 of a horizontal-vertical, four-cylinder, compound steam engine of 12,000 horsepower for the power house of the Manhattan Railway, New York City. It is said that he sketched the design while he was traveling by train from Milwaukee to New York, so marvelously quick was his inventive genius. In the course of time he rose to be second vice-president and director of the Allis Company. About 1902, at his suggestion, the movement was started which resulted in the establishment of the Allis-Chalmers Company, Milwaukee, with a capital of forty million dollars. Reynolds became the consulting engineer of the organization and continued to serve in this capacity until his death. He was the designer of the great machine shops of the company at West Allis, Wis., and of much of the machinery. Between 1880 and 1906 he patented over forty improvements in steam engines, boilers, valve gears, feedwater heaters, air compressors, stamp mills, and ore crushers, and designed the first cross compound hoisting engine for mining work. In addition to his duties in connection with the Allis Company, he organized and was president of the Milwaukee Boiler Company, and served as president of the Daisy Roller Mills Company and the German American Bank, both of Milwaukee. He was the first president of the National Metal Trades Association, vice-president of the American Society of Mechanical Engineers from 1892 to 1894, and president for the year 1902. He was twice married: first, on Sept. 28, 1853, in Mansfield, to Mary Spencer; and, second, in Milwaukee, on May 30, 1904, to Nellie Maria Nettleton. At the time of his death in Milwaukee he was survived by his widow and an adopted daughter; two children died in infancy.

[J. A. Wight, *A Partial Record of the Ancestors . . . of Christopher and Charissa . . . Reynolds of Mansfield, Conn.* (1905); *Who's Who in America*, 1908–09; *Trans. Am. Soc. of Mechanical Engineers*, vol. XXXI (1910); *Milwaukee Sentinel*, Feb. 20, 1909; Patent Office records.]   C. W. M.

REYNOLDS, JOHN (1713–Feb. 3, 1788), first royal governor of Georgia, entered the British navy at fifteen and was gazetted lieutenant at twenty-three. After service in the West Indies and at home, he was given command, on Oct. 30, 1746, of the *Arundel*. From 1748 to 1751 she was detached on the southern American station, and Reynolds was later called to account for spending so much of his time at Charlestown. Because promotion seemed slow, in August 1754 he welcomed the appointment, apparently influenced by the Earl of Hardwicke, as governor of Georgia. On Oct. 30, at Savannah, he took over the government from the old Board representing the proprietary trustees.

Difficulties at once confronted him. To set up the standardized machinery of royal government among a people accustomed to the paternalism of the trustees demanded high abilities, sympathy, energy, and firmness. Reynolds did not possess them, but for some months his administration seemed successful; courts were organized, new settlements encouraged, local defenses strengthened. His relations with the Council and the first Assembly were amicable; both supported him in suppressing Edmund Grey's conspiracy for the protection of "liberties" endangered by royal government. In the Assembly's claim to control finance, however, and in the governor's closing accusations against men who preferred anarchy to order, lay possibilities of conflict, and by September 1755, Reynolds and his Council were at odds. He regarded the Georgians as a "lawless, anti-monarchal people" who required government by military force (Flippin, *post*, p. 28). The Council, and later the Assembly, accused him of incompetence, partiality, and tyranny. The center of their attack was his private secretary, William Little, a former surgeon in the navy whom the governor had appointed to no less than seven offices. Petitions for the removal of this man, "unconversant in business and of most despotic principles" (*Ibid.*, p. 27), were urged upon Reynolds in vain, and he even dissolved the Assembly, during the famous session (February 1756) when the speaker was held in the chair, to prevent inquiry into Little's conduct. While some of the specific charges against the Governor could be duplicated in any royal colony, the telling argument that the widespread dissatisfaction caused by his administration affected the colony's prosperity led in August 1756 to his recall. In February 1757 he surrendered the government to Henry Ellis [*q.v.*]. On his return voyage he was taken by a French privateer into Bayonne and stripped of all his papers.

In 1759, as captain of the *Firm*, he acted as commodore of a cruising squadron in Hawke's fleet, but failed to participate in any major engagement. During the next fifteen years he held short commands in seven ships, and when on shore lived at Newington Butts with his wife and children. In 1768 he proposed to the Admiralty that windmill sails, worked by hand from the deck, could be utilized to move vessels in a calm. He became rear admiral of the Blue in 1775, and though incapacitated by a paralytic stroke which affected both mind and body, following the regular course of preferment was promoted admiral in 1787.

[J. K. Laughton, in *Dict. Nat. Biog.*; P. S. Flippin, "The Royal Government in Georgia," *Ga. Hist. Quart.*,

Mar., June, Dec. 1924; George White, *Hist. Colls. of Ga.* (1855); C. C. Jones, *The Hist. of Ga.* (1883), vol. I; W. B. Stevens, *A Hist. of Ga.*, vol. I (1847); W. L. Clowes, *The Royal Navy*, vol. III (1898); A. D. Candler, *The Colonial Records of the State of Ga.*, vols. VII, XIII (1906–07); *Jour. of the Commissioners for Trade and Plantations from Jan. 1754 to Dec. 1758* (1933); *Gentleman's Mag.* (London), Feb. 1788.]
S. M. P.

REYNOLDS, JOHN (Feb. 26, 1788–May 8, 1865), governor of Illinois, was born in Montgomery County, Pa., the son of Robert and Margaret (Moore) Reynolds who were Irish Protestant emigrants from County Monaghan to Philadelphia in 1785. Six months after the boy's birth his parents removed to a place fourteen miles northeast of Knoxville, Tenn. In 1800 Robert Reynolds with his family, including six children of whom John was the eldest, set out across the wilderness for "New Spain," his destination being the Mississippi shore opposite Kaskaskia. The desire to avoid Catholicism, however, together with the persuasion of some men from Kaskaskia, including Pierre Menard, induced him to settle in Illinois a few miles east of Kaskaskia, where the Reynolds party became the seventh family in the settlement. Later they lived near Edwardsville. In 1809 the boy was given a new homespun suit and rode his horse to Knoxville, Tenn., where he attended the school conducted by the Rev. Isaac Anderson. He also read law with John McCampbell there. In the winter of 1812 he began the study of French, a language he afterward used habitually with his French wife and preferred for domestic use (*My Own Times*, pp. 169, 206). In the War of 1812 he served in Capt. William B. Whiteside's company that "ranged" the Illinois border to awe the Indians, and thus he acquired the sobriquet "Old Ranger." In 1814 he set up a law practice at Cahokia. By what he himself called "a savage self-will to succeed" (*Ibid.*, p. 173) he rose to an associate justiceship of the Illinois supreme court from 1818 to 1825, was chosen to the General Assembly of the state in 1826 and again in 1828, and was elected governor of Illinois in 1830. In his gubernatorial canvass he toured the state on horseback, courted the farmers with his Irish blarney, and made hundreds of speeches. The chief event of his governorship was the Black Hawk War, in which the state militia under his call cooperated with the federal army. Though not directing military operations, he marched with "the boys" accompanied by an impressive staff of colonels.

In 1817 he was married to Madame Catherine (Dubuque) LaCroix Manegle, a beautiful French Creole whose father was honored in the naming of Dubuque, Iowa. She died in 1834, and in 1836 he was married at Georgetown, D. C., to Sarah Wilson of Maryland. He had no children. He was tall and looked the part of a statesman. Though undistinguished in the legal profession, he succeeded as a politician by his knack of electioneering, his frontier lingo, and his readiness to donate legal services to the poor. His anecdotes were sometimes unprintable. To improve a superficial Latinity he read English translations of Cæsar and Virgil; but in the presence of rural folk who disliked "book larnin" he deliberately concealed such culture as he had. Even Snyder (*post*, p. 327) records that "in all business affairs he was honest, and in all social relations . . . honorable." As a regular Democrat he profited by the prestige of a party that dominated the state until 1860. He favored slavery, which he sought to establish even in Illinois, supported Jackson first and last, shifted from upholding a protective tariff to free trade in keeping with the interests of his agrarian constituents, urged that West Point cadets should have no preference in army appointments, contended for state rights, opposed the bank, and joined the expansionist chorus as to Oregon, Mexico, and Cuba. He served in Congress from 1834 to 1837 and from 1839 to 1843; but the historian finds less interest in his mediocre congressional career than in such incidental matters as his traveling with David Crockett on the way to Washington, his vivid description of Clay, and his introduction of the Mormon leader, Joseph Smith, to President Van Buren (*My Own Times, post*, pp. 448, 458, 575). As state financial commissioner he visited Europe to market bonds for the Illinois and Michigan canal, a tour described by an opponent as a "junketing trip at public expense" (Snyder, *post*, p. 278); and he recorded quaint impressions of the "meriods of people," the antiquity of the cities, and the English lack of America's "unbounded ambition" (*My Own Times, post*, pp. 522, 526).

In later life he served further terms from 1846 to 1848 and from 1852 to 1854 in the Illinois legislature. In the slavery crisis of the late fifties he supported the Southern wing of the Democratic party in opposition to Douglas; in 1860 he was selected as an anti-Douglas delegate to the Democratic convention at Charleston but was denied a seat. He detested the Republican party, showed strong sympathy for the Confederate cause, and opposed Lincoln's policies, especially emancipation. His writings are of great interest, especially his colorful life story, *My Own Times* (1855), told at length with a wealth of social comment but with the faults of self-interpretation. His other works include *The Life* and *Adventures of John Kelly* (1853), a romance used as a vehicle for unappreciated scientific lectures he had delivered; *The Pioneer History of Illinois* (1852); *Sketches of the Country on the Northern Route from Belleville, Ill., to New York* (1854); and political tracts such as *The Balm of Gilead* (1860). From the time of his governorship he lived prosperously at Belleville, Ill., where he died.

[Autobiography, *ante*; a full but uncomplimentary characterization in J. F. Snyder, *Adam W. Snyder* (2nd ed., 1906), esp. pp. 297–329; Thomas Ford, *A Hist. of Ill.* (1854); *Memories of Gustave Koerner* (2 vols., 1909); J. M. Scott, *Supreme Court of Ill.* (1896); Randall Parrish, *Historic Illinois* (1905); T. C. Pease, *The Frontier State* (1918); date of birth from autobiography.]   J.G.R.

REYNOLDS, JOHN FULTON (Sept. 20, 1820–July 1, 1863), Union soldier, was born in Lancaster, Pa., the son of John and Lydia (Moore) Reynolds. He was of Irish and French Huguenot ancestry, his grandfather, William Reynolds, having come to America from Ireland in 1762. He received his early education in John Beck's school in the Moravian village of Lititz, Pa., and a school at Longgreen, Md., and later returned to enroll in the Lancaster County Academy. In 1837 he entered the United States Military Academy from which he was graduated in 1841, twenty-sixth in a class of fifty-two. He was brevetted second lieutenant, 3rd Artillery, and Oct. 23, 1841, received his regular commission. In 1843 he served in Florida; in 1844, at Fort Moultrie, S. C.; in 1845, at Corpus Christi; and later at Fort Brown, Tex. The following year he was promoted to the rank of first lieutenant and accompanied General Taylor to Mexico. For bravery at Monterey, he was brevetted captain, and on Feb. 23, 1847, was brevetted major for especial gallantry in action at Buena Vista. For several years after the Mexican War, he did garrison duty in various New England forts, at New Orleans, and Fort Lafayette, N. Y. He accompanied an expedition overland to Salt Lake City in the summer of 1854; was promoted captain, Mar. 3, 1855, and was commended for his service against the Rogue River Indians in Oregon. In December 1856, he arrived at Fortress Monroe, Va., remaining there until 1858, when he crossed the plains again in the campaign against the Mormons. He was stationed at Fort Vancouver, Wash., 1859–60, and in September 1860, he was appointed commandant of cadets at West Point, where he also served as instructor in artillery, cavalry, and infantry tactics.

With the beginning of the Civil War, he was promoted to the rank of lieutenant-colonel, as-

signed to the 14th Infantry and ordered to New London to recruit his regiment. He was made brigadier-general of volunteers on Aug. 20, 1861, and was assigned to the Pennsylvania Reserves. In May 1862, he was made military governor of Fredericksburg. He participated in the fighting at Mechanicsville and later at Gaines's Mill where, on June 28, 1862, he was taken prisoner and sent to Richmond. After spending six weeks in Libby Prison, he was exchanged for Gen. William Barksdale [*q.v.*] through the efforts of the civil authorities of Fredericksburg. He rejoined the army on Aug. 8, and was assigned command of the 3rd Division, Pennsylvania Reserves. He joined Pope on his march to Warrenton on Aug. 21, 1862, and engaged in fighting on Aug. 29 and 30. When Pope's forces retired to Washington, Gov. Andrew Gregg Curtin [*q.v.*] requested Reynolds' assignment in command of the Pennsylvania militia to withstand the expected invasion. He later returned to the Army of the Potomac in command of the I Army Corps. On Nov. 29, 1862, he was appointed major-general of volunteers. He participated in the Rappahannock campaign, and at Fredericksburg his corps and Meade's division broke the enemy line, but, receiving no support, could not hold the gain. At Chancellorsville on May 2 and 3, 1863, he urged Hooker to attack the enemy's left flank, and, had his plan been executed, the Union forces might well have triumphed. On June 1, 1863, he was promoted to the rank of colonel in the regular army.

When it was apparent that the Confederates would force a decisive battle on Northern soil, Reynolds was assigned the left wing of the army and ordered to prevent Longstreet from striking Washington. Sharp engagements at Thoroughfare Gap and Aldie, Va., accomplished this goal. On June 28, 1863, Meade succeeded Hooker in command and immediately ordered Reynolds to occupy Gettysburg. Reynolds set his three corps, I, III, and XI, in motion. Assigning command of the I Corps to Abner Doubleday [*q.v.*], Reynolds set out from Red Tavern on the morning of July 1, 1863, starting Wadsworth's division along with him. At Gettysburg about nine o'clock in the morning, he found the cavalry under Buford sorely pressed and therefore hurried back to speed up Wadsworth's Division. Returning to the battlefield at the head of the 2nd Wisconsin Regiment, Reynolds turned to them as they reached a woods and called out, ". . . push forward men and drive those fellows out of the woods" (Huidekoper, *post*, p. 9). A moment later a sharpshooter's bullet killed him. His body was carried from the battlefield in a blanket swung between soldiers' muskets, and on July 4, 1863, he was buried in Lancaster, Pa.

He had never married and was survived only by his three brothers, of whom one was William Reynolds [*q.v.*]. Fully six feet in height, with dark hair and eyes, very erect in carriage, he was a commanding figure. He was a superb horseman, an exceptionally courageous, self-reliant officer who executed his orders with a personal force that inspired his troops to heights of valor. His advice was frequently sought by his brother officers, who recognized his military genius and appreciated his charity of thought and freedom from personal bias. A monument erected to his memory stands on the spot where he fell on the battlefield of Gettysburg.

[G. W. Cullum, *Biog. Reg. . . . U. S. Mil. Acad.* (1891); F. B. Heitman, *Hist. Reg. and Dictionary of the U. S. Army* (1903); H. S. Huidekoper, *Address at Unveiling of the . . . Statue of Major-General J. F. Reynolds at Gettysburg* (n.d.); J. H. Brown, *Oration on Maj.-Gen. J. F. Reynolds* (1888); J. G. Rosengarten, in *Reynolds Memorial, Addresses Delivered Before the Hist. Soc. of Pa.* (1880); *Daily Evening Express* (Lancaster, Pa.), July 2, 3, 6, 1863.]

C. C. B.

REYNOLDS, JOSEPH JONES (Jan. 4, 1822–Feb. 25, 1899), soldier, sixth son and seventh child of Edward and Sarah (Longley) Reynolds, was born in Flemingsburg, Ky. His father, a hatter, moved with his family to Lafayette, Ind., in 1837. Joseph attended the common schools of Flemingsburg, and in 1838 matriculated at Wabash College, Crawfordsville, Ind. While there, he received an appointment as a cadet to the United States Military Academy, entering in 1839, and graduating in 1843, standing tenth in a class of thirty-nine. Among his classmates was U. S. Grant, with whom he formed a lasting friendship. Upon graduation he was appointed brevet second lieutenant, 4th Artillery, with station at Fortress Monroe, Va., and later at Carlisle, Pa. In 1845 he was assigned to General Taylor's force engaged in the military occupation of Texas. He was promoted to the rank of second lieutenant on May 11, 1846, and in the fall of the same year was assigned to the teaching staff of the United States Military Academy where he remained until 1855. He next served, as first lieutenant, 3rd Artillery, on frontier duty at Fort Washita, Indian Territory, until 1857, when he resigned from the army to become professor of mechanics and engineering in Washington University at St. Louis, Mo. In 1860 he returned to Lafayette to enter a grocery business with one of his brothers.

Upon the outbreak of the Civil War, he was appointed colonel of the 10th Indiana Volunteers and applied his military knowledge very ably in the organizing and training of the new troops. He was appointed brigadier-general of Indiana Volunteers and, on May 17, 1861, was made brigadier-general of United States Volunteers and assigned to command a brigade and later the Cheat Mountain district in the Department of Western Virginia under General Rosecrans. At Cheat Mountain in September he successfully repelled a Confederate advance and thereby secured that portion of western Virginia for the Union. Owing to the death of the brother with whom he was in partnership, he was obliged to resign in January 1862, and look after the business. While thus employed, he unofficially assisted the state authorities in organizing new regiments. In August 1862, he again entered the service as colonel of the 75th Indiana Volunteers and in September was recommissioned brigadier-general of United States Volunteers. He was promoted to the rank of major-general in November and assigned to command a division in the Army of the Cumberland. He was in the engagement at Hoover's Gap, Tenn., on June 24, 1863, and in the battle of Chickamauga, Ga., on Sept. 19 and 20, 1863. In October 1863, he became chief of staff of the army of the Cumberland and took a prominent part in the battle of Chattanooga, Tenn., the following month. In January 1864, he was transferred to the command of the defenses of New Orleans and in the following July he assumed command of the XIX Army Corps and organized the forces for the capture of the coast defenses and city of Mobile, Ala. In the fall of 1864 he commanded a district on the Mississippi from Memphis to its mouth. For the next two years he commanded the Department of Arkansas. He was mustered out of the volunteer service in September 1866 and reverted to the rank of colonel of the 26th Infantry, to which grade in the regular army he had in the meantime been appointed.

During the troublesome days of reconstruction he commanded with admirable tact and judgment, successively, the subdistrict of the Rio Grande, the district of Texas, the fifth military district comprising Texas and Louisiana, and the Department of Texas. In 1867 he was brevetted brigadier-general for gallant and meritorious service at Chickamauga, and major-general for similar services at the battle of Missionary Ridge. He was transferred to the cavalry and from 1872 to 1876 commanded in turn Fort McPherson, Nebr., Fort D. A. Russell, Wyo., and the district of South Platte. He was retired from active service on June 25, 1877, for disability contracted in line of duty, and thus ended his long and varied career of public service which both in peace and war was characterized by ability and devotion to duty. He was elected United States senator by the Texas legislature in 1871, but his election was contested in the Senate and the seat awarded to Morgan C. Hamilton. After his retirement, Reynolds settled in Washington, D. C., where he died. His wife, Mary Elizabeth Bainbridge, whom he had married on Dec. 3, 1846, two daughters and two sons survived him.

[*Who's Who in America*, 1899–1901; G. W. Cullum, *Biog. Reg. . . . U. S. Mil. Acad.* (1891); *Annual Reunion, Asso. of Grads., U. S. Mil. Acad.,* 1899 (1899); G. I. Reed, *Encyc. of Biog. of Ind.,* vol. I (1895); *Cat. and Direct. of Officers* (Wabash College) (1923); C. W. Ramsdell, *Reconstruction in Tex., Studies in Hist., Econ. and Public Law, Columbia Univ.,* vol. XXVI (1910); *Jour. of the House of Rep. (Texas), 12th Legislature* (1871); *Wash.* (D. C.) *Post,* Feb. 27, 1899; *N. Y. Times,* Feb. 27, 1899.]   S. J. H.

REYNOLDS, SAMUEL GODFREY (Mar. 9, 1801–Mar. 1, 1881), inventor, was born in Bristol, R. I., the son of Greenwood and Mary (Caldwell) Reynolds, and a descendant of Robert Reynolds who was in Boston as early as 1634. Samuel was reared on his father's farm and obtained an elementary education, but being of a mechanical turn of mind, became interested in other things than farming. He tried his hand at the tannery business for a number of years and devised some minor improvements in the process then employed; soon he was devoting more time to work on inventions than to his tanning. One of his early contrivances was an improved waterwheel of iron, which he sold to a New Hampshire manufacturer for a nominal sum.

When he was twenty-seven or twenty-eight years old he began considering improvements in nail-making machinery. At that time there had been invented and patented in the United States approximately 125 machines for turning out nails and tacks, and the factories using these were numerous in the larger cities of the East. Reynolds worked upon a machine for making wrought-iron nails and rivets and was granted a patent for his improvements on Apr. 13, 1829. England at that time was very much interested in the American nail-making machines, and in the hope of profiting by the sale of his patent to English interests, Reynolds employed an agent to introduce his invention there. Unfortunately, however, the agent obtained the patents in his own name and sold them. To make good this loss, Reynolds added improvements to his original machine, which he patented Mar. 18, 1835. Nine years later, he patented a spike-making machine and went directly to England, where he

succeeded in interesting the firm of Coats & Company, bankers, in furnishing financial backing for the manufacture of his several machines. He was aided, too, in obtaining patents in England, Holland, Belgium, and France. In the meantime, he turned his attention to pin-making machinery, and on Dec. 31, 1845, obtained United States patent No. 4346 for the machinery for heading and pointing pins. He devised, also, a machine to stick the pins into paper, thus dispensing with manual labor for this work. Coats & Company were much interested in adding the manufacture of this to that of his nail and spike machines, but about the time that the necessary arrangements were made the company failed with large liabilities. As a consequence, Reynolds also failed.

Returning to the United States in 1850, in an effort to recoup his losses he began to devise improvements in horse-nail machinery, and on Jan. 20, 1852, secured patent No. 8677 for a machine he had made. This was manufactured and sold in Providence by William Tollman. In 1866 and 1867 he received patents for improvements thereon, and from these three inventions he derived a considerable income. Turning now to agricultural machinery, he perfected a steam plow designed for use on prairie lands, and a rotary plow; at the time of his death he had nearly completed a cut-nail machine with automatic feed. He was twice married: first, in 1823, to Elizabeth Anthony of Pomfret, Conn., who died in 1834; and second, on Nov. 18, 1845, to Catherine Ann Hamlin of Syracuse, N. Y. Reynolds died in Bristol, R. I., and was survived by five children.

[*Representative Men and Old Families of R. I.* (1908), vol. I; *Providence Daily Jour.,* Mar. 2, 1881; Patent Office records.]   C. W. M.

REYNOLDS, WILLIAM (Dec. 18, 1815–Nov. 5, 1879), naval officer, the son of John and Lydia (Moore) Reynolds, and brother of John Fulton Reynolds [*q.v.*], was born in Lancaster, Pa. His father, publisher of the *Lancaster Journal* and a member of the state legislature, sent William and his brothers to the Lancaster County Academy and to other private schools. On Nov. 17, 1831, he was appointed an acting midshipman in the navy, and after five years at sea, was sent in 1836 to the naval school at Norfolk, Va. The following year he was promoted to passed midshipman, and on the 120-gun *Pennsylvania* made the first and only cruise the ship was destined to make, from Philadelphia to Norfolk. He was sent with the Wilkes exploring expedition to the South Seas in 1838, and was credited by Wilkes with the first discovery of a mountain peak in the antarctic which was named in his honor (Charles Wilkes, *Narrative of United States Exploring Expedition*, 1844, vol. II, pp. 309–10). On this expedition he was promoted to the grade of lieutenant and during the next decade saw active and varied duty. In 1850 impaired health forced him to apply for a furlough and five years later he was retired. In 1857 he was sent to Honolulu as naval storekeeper and while there became strongly impressed with the strategic importance of the Hawaiian Islands to the United States. At the outbreak of the Civil War he returned home, hoping to be restored to active service. He was obliged, however, to undergo surgical treatment and was not able to undertake active duty until 1862. He was then commissioned as commander on the reserved list and given command of the naval depot at Port Royal, S. C., with the sailing-ship *Vermont* as his headquarters, which served as well as a hospital- store- and receiving-ship for the South Atlantic Blockading Squadron. He retained this command throughout the war, an arduous duty filled with monotonous routine, but vital to the success of the fleet. In 1864 his personnel and stores were transferred to the *New Hampshire*.

In 1866 he was restored to the active list and rose successively through the grades of captain and commodore to the rank of rear admiral in 1873. From 1870 to 1875 he was chief of the bureau of equipment and recruiting, and in the latter year was given command of the Asiatic Station. On this duty he did much to promote friendly relations between the United States and the Far East, notably with the Kingdom of Siam. Failing health forced him to relinquish this command in 1877, and he was permanently retired in December of that year. He died in Washington, D. C., and was buried in Lancaster, Pa. His wife, Rebecca Krug, daughter of G. H. Krug of Lancaster, survived him. He was a capable, intelligent officer, zealous for his country's interests and the honor of his service, but his uncertain health prevented him from rising to a position of greater distinction in the navy. He heartily seconded the government's action in negotiating the Hawaiian treaty of reciprocity in 1875. As chief of the bureau of equipment and recruiting he had condensers for distilling fresh water and ovens for baking fresh bread installed for the first time on all navy vessels. He also strenuously advocated and finally succeeded in establishing a system of apprenticeship for training young seamen for the navy.

[L. R. Hamersly, *Records of Living Officers of the U. S. Navy and Marine Corps* (4th ed., 1890); *War of the Rebellion: Official Records* (*Navy*), 1 ser., vols. XII–XVI, XXVII, 2 ser., vol. I; J. G. Rosengarten, in *Reynolds Memorial Addresses Delivered Before the Hist. Soc. of Pa.* (1880); *Army and Navy Jour.*, Nov. 8, 15, 1879; *Daily New Era*, and *Daily Examiner and Express* (Lancaster, Pa.), Nov. 6, 1879.]   L. H. B.

REZANOV, NIKOLAI PETROVICH (Apr. 8, 1764–Mar. 13, 1807), a founder of the Russian-American Company, was born in St. Petersburg. After serving in the army, he entered the civil service in his early twenties, making a brilliant career as an administrator. In 1793 or 1794 Catherine II sent him to Siberia on a special mission relating to the expansion of the Empire in northwestern America, and as a result he became interested in the colonization of Alaska. It was largely owing to his enterprise and connections that the Russian-American Company was formed and granted the exclusive right to exploit that vast dominion. In the summer of 1803 he sailed from Kronstadt at the head of an expedition, organized jointly by the government and the Company, which took him all but around the globe. One of the objects of the trip was to test the possibility of sending supplies to the colonies in Russian America by an all-sea route instead of by the more expensive land route across Siberia that had been followed hitherto. He was to visit the new territory to investigate resources and needs and to set it on the road to civilization. He was also to inspect the offices of the Company and revise its business methods and policies. Prior to undertaking these tasks, however, he was instructed to go to Japan, in the capacity of minister plenipotentiary to that country, and by means of diplomacy and rich gifts, to open the gates of the forbidden empire to Russian trade.

He set out with a heavy heart, having just buried his wife, a daughter of Grigorii Ivanovich Shelekov [q.v.], after a happy married life of eight years. He had been not many weeks at sea when serious friction arose between him and the captain of the frigate which was carrying him. Having rounded the Horn and visited the Sandwich Islands, among other places, he reached Kamtchatka after a year's sail, battered in body and spirit. From there he went to Japan, where he failed dismally, being held a virtual prisoner at Nagasaki through the winter of 1804–05 and being dismissed without so much as a hearing. Returning to Kamtchatka, he set sail for Alaska. He touched at several points and in August 1805 made a landing at New Archangel (Sitka) on Baranov Island, the seat of the governor of the territory. Here he distributed medals, reprimanded, pleaded, advised, gave instructions, and covered reams of paper with memoranda and reports. Amidst all these occupations, to which should be added ship-building, he found time to compile a dictionary of the local Indian tongue.

A terrible winter ensued, starvation and scurvy ravaging New Archangel, and Rezanov set out on a foraging expedition, taking the opportunity to try out his theory that the colonies should obtain their food-stuffs from the Philippines or California. On board an American vessel which he had recently bought for the Company and which was manned by a stricken crew, the envoy sailed south, reaching the port of San Francisco early in April 1806. He achieved his end with difficulty and only by dint of diplomacy. A frequent guest at the home of the commander of the local *presidio,* Don José Darío Argüello, he turned the head of his host's lovely young daughter, Doña Concepción, and, indeed, became affianced to her. The widower of forty-two may well have been smitten by her beauty, but, if we are to credit his own words, he entered into the alliance for reasons of state. When he sailed away in May, his ship held a cargo of provisions which he had exchanged for the goods he had brought with him. The understanding was that as soon as he had made the necessary arrangements, he would return for his bride. He unloaded the provisions at New Archangel, and early in August was again on the high seas in command of two vessels bound for Japan, with the intention of wresting by force what diplomacy had failed to win. He planned to raid the coast, in the hope that the terrorized people would impel their government to open commerce with Russia. He abandoned the military adventure, however, and on reaching Okhotsk, set out for home, inspecting the Company's offices as he went. Being in poor health, he was unable to stand the rigors of a winter journey across the Siberian wastes, and died at Krasnoyarsk.

[The dates are New Style. The papers of the Russian-American Company in the manuscript division of the Lib. of Cong. which were not available to the writer of this sketch, include valuable data on the life and career of Rezanov. Rezanov's reports for 1804–06 are in the supplement to vol. II of P. Tikhmenev, *Istoricheskoye obozreniye obrazovaniye Rossiisko-amerikanskoi kompanii* (St. Petersburg, 2 vols., 1861–63). Thos. C. Russell, *The Rezanov Voyage to Nueva California in 1806* (1926), is an English translation of one of these documents. An extensive excerpt from his description of his trip around the world was published in *Otechestvennyia zapiski* (St. Petersburg), 1822–25. The literature on Rezanov is listed in an article on him in *Russki biograficheski slovar* (St. Petersburg, 1910). See also G. H. Langsdorff, *Bemerkungen auf eine Reise um die Welt* (3 vols., 1812), T. C. Russell, *Langsdorff's Narrative of the Rezanov Voyage* (1927), and A. Yarmolinsky, A Rambling Note on the "Russian Columbus," *Bull. N. Y. Pub. Lib.,* Sept., 1927.]   A. Y.

RHEA, JOHN (1753–May 27, 1832), congressman, was born in County Donegal, Ireland, the eldest of eight children of Joseph and Elizabeth (McIlwaine) Rhea. His father, the third son of Matthew Rhea or Reah or Creah and a descendant of the house of Campbell, was a Presbyterian clergyman who in 1769 emigrated with his family to Pennsylvania, then to Maryland. In 1775 he bought lands in what is now eastern Tennessee, on which the family settled in February 1778. The son served as a soldier in the Revolution, and in 1780 he graduated from the College of New Jersey (Princeton). He was incorporator or trustee of three colleges across the Alleghanies, Washington College, Greeneville College, now Tusculum, and Blount College, now the University of Tennessee. As a clerk of the court of Sullivan County under North Carolina's jurisdiction, he opposed the rebellious state of Franklin movement and recorded the articles of agreement drawn up in March 1787 between North Carolina and the almost defunct state of Franklin. In 1789 he sat in the House of Commons of North Carolina as well as in a special convention of that state, in which he voted for the ratification of the federal Constitution. When Tennessee became a territory, he was licensed to practise law in the several territorial courts. In the convention that framed the first state constitution in 1796 and in the first two sessions of the legislature of the infant state he sat for Sullivan County.

From 1803 until 1823, excepting for the Fourteenth Congress 1815–17, he served in the federal House of Representatives. He was a typical Democrat, hostile to Great Britain, antagonistic to the renewal of the bank charter in 1811, and friendly to agricultural as against commercial interests. He favored a strict interpretation of the Constitution, and he "would not torture and twist it out of its proper shape" (*Annals of Congress,* 9 Cong., 1 Sess., col. 928). Like Jefferson he decried "a consolidated government" (*Knoxville Register, post*). He advocated in 1814 annexation of the Canadas, destruction of naval armaments, and peace at home as well as abroad. On Oct. 24, 1816, as one of three federal commissioners, he signed a treaty with the Choctaw Indians. His friendship for Andrew Jackson involved him in a tortuous correspondence; on Jan. 6, 1818, Jackson wrote to President Monroe offering to conquer the Floridas if the President would signify his approval "through any channel (say Mr. J. Rhea)" (Bassett, *post,* p. 346). Rhea wrote to Jackson vaguely, possibly alluding to another matter, "I am gratified indeed that the plan of the President is satisfactory to you" (*Ibid.*, p. 348) ; and on the floor of the House in January 1819, he defended Jackson as "authorized by the supreme law of nature and nations the law of self-defence . . . to enter the Spanish territory of Florida" (*Annals of Congress*, 15 Cong., 2 Sess., pt. 1, col. 867). As a lover of freedom and as a humanitarian, he opposed the use of drafted labor on roads as a restraint on the liberty of free men. In January 1815 he supported the re-cession of the District of Columbia to Maryland and Virginia inasmuch as the constitutions of neither of these states provided for the cession of any citizens or for depriving them of their right to vote. He opposed slavery and expressed sympathy for the "unfortunate" slave states. Devoutly religious, as chairman of the committee on post office and post roads he opposed the delivery of mails on Sunday; he believed in a "Mighty Being who raises and depresses nations" (see however Ramsey, *post*, p. 663). He died a bachelor, leaving a large estate. He was buried at Blountville near his old home. His name is perpetuated in Rhea County and in Rheatown in Greene County, Tenn.

[Manuscript genealogical notes by C. M. McClung in Lawson McGhee Library, Knoxville; family papers in and near Blountville, Tenn.; information from the secretary of Princeton University; *Journal of the Convention of 1796 and of the first two sessions of the legislature of Tennessee* (1852); *The State Records of N. C.*, XX, 647, XXI, 193, 198, 209, 432, XXII, 36–53 (1902–07); *American State Papers: Military Affairs*, vol. I (1832), 688–762; *American State Papers: Indian Affairs*, vol. II (1834), 95; J. S. Bassett, *Correspondence of Andrew Jackson*, vol. II (1927); M. B. Hamer, "John Rhea of Tenn.," *East Tenn. Hist. Soc. Pubs.*, Jan. 1932; J. G. M. Ramsey, *Annals of Tenn.* (1853); *Knoxville Gazette*, May 6, 1809; *Knoxville Register*, June 18, 1822.]   M. B. H.

RHEES, WILLIAM JONES (Mar. 13, 1830–Mar. 18, 1907), bibliographer, was born in Philadelphia, Pa., the son of Benjamin Rush Rhees and Margaret Grace (Evans). His father was a practising physician in Philadelphia, one of the founders of Jefferson Medical College, and a member of the original faculty; his grandfather was the Rev. Morgan John Rhees, a Baptist clergyman who came from Wales and settled in Somerset, Pa. On his mother's side, he was descended from Evan Evans who organized the 2nd Battalion of militia from Chester County, Pa., and was its colonel, and also from John Lukens, surveyor general for Pennsylvania, and a commissioner in 1781 for extending Mason and Dixon's line.

William Rhees was graduated from the Central High School, Philadelphia, in 1847, and soon after settled in Washington, D. C. Here he had charge of social statistics for the Sev-enth United States Census, and served as secretary of the central executive committee in Washington of the World's Fair held at London in 1851. On July 1 of the following year he was made chief clerk of the Smithsonian Institution, and was thereafter chief executive officer, under the secretary, of the affairs of the Institution and in charge of its publications. This position he held during the lives of Secretary Henry and Secretary Baird and for a time under Secretary Langley. During their absence he frequently served as acting secretary. As he grew older and the duties of his office became more onerous he was made keeper of the archives. At the time of his death it was said of him that "his knowledge of the affairs of the Institution was wide, and with him there passed away the principal human repository of its history for he had been connected with it almost since its inception" (*Annual Report . . . Smithsonian Institution, 1907*, 1908, p. 39).

He was public spirited and during his younger days was active in civic affairs, serving as trustee of the public schools of Washington during 1862–68, 1873–74. He was a founder and at one time president of the Washington Young Men's Christian Association, and during the Civil War was active in its philanthropic work. In 1856 he organized a lecture bureau which secured the services of eminent speakers for lectures throughout the United States, and he had charge of Prof. John Tyndall's lectures during his visit to America in 1872. In later life he became interested in patriotic organizations and was one of the founders of the Sons of the American Revolution in the District of Columbia, of which he served as registrar.

His numerous writings included the annual reports of the Smithsonian Institution and a number of contributions to its Miscellaneous Collections. Among these publications were *The Scientific Writings of James Smithson* (1879) and *James Smithson and His Bequest* (1880). He also made many compilations, among which were *Manual of Public Libraries, Institutions and Societies in the United States and British Provinces of North America* (1859), *Catalogue of Publications of the Smithsonian Institution* (1882), and periodic lists of publications of the Smithsonian Institution (1862–1906). His last work of importance was *The Smithsonian Institution; Documents Relative to Its Origin and History 1835–1899* (2 vols., 1901). He died in Washington, and was buried in Rock Creek Cemetery. To the Smithsonian Institution he bequeathed a fund which bears his name. He was twice married: first, to

Laura O. Clarke; and after her death, to Romenia Fontanette Ellis. His second wife, a son, and three daughters survived him.

[S. M. Ely, "District of Columbia Soc. of the Sons of the Am. Revolution: Report of the Historian . . . 1908" (typed MS. in Lib. of Cong.); W. J. Rhees, *Reg. of the D. C. Soc., Sons of the Am. Rev., 1896* (n.d.); *Who's Who in America*, 1906–07; *Evening Star* (Washington), Mar. 18, 19, 1907; information from family; personal acquaintance.]   M. B.

RHETT, ROBERT BARNWELL (Dec. 21, 1800–Sept. 14, 1876), statesman, was born in Beaufort, an aristocratic community in tidewater South Carolina, the fourth son of James Smith and Marianna Gough. The family on both sides had been eminent in the annals of the state and province, including Sir John Yeamans, Gov. Landgrave Smith, and many other notables. In 1837, at the instance of Robert Barnwell's brothers, the family name was changed from Smith to the less common one of a distinguished ancestor, Col. William Rhett. James Smith did not prosper and the son's schooling ended when he was seventeen. At nineteen he began to study law and at twenty-one was admitted to practice. These meager advantages he supplemented thereafter by long-continued and systematic study and reading. In 1827 he married Elizabeth Washington Burnet, a gentle woman whose influence over her nervous, fiery husband was very great; its absence was noticeable in his later career. She died in 1852 and about a year later he married Catharine Herbert Dent. There was a large family and an attractive home life. Rhett's devotion to his brothers and children was returned by them to a remarkable degree, and their political activity in his behalf was a striking feature of his career. About 1836 he made an advantageous purchase of a plantation, and in the 1850's secured another, having some 190 slaves on the two estates. He had also a town residence, first in Walterboro and later in Charleston, as well as one in Georgetown during his years in Congress. He lived in the manner of the Carolina aristocrat and was accounted well-to-do, although for many years he was heavily indebted to the Bank of the State of South Carolina.

The political career of Rhett (then Smith) began in 1826 with his election to the legislature, where he quickly became prominent. The agitation over the protective tariff in 1827, in which Robert J. Turnbull [*q.v.*] in *The Crisis* summoned men passionately to resistance, made a powerful impression upon him, and fixed in his mind the fundamental ideas for which he was to become the banner-bearer. In those days most men responded with fervor to the shibboleths of the American Revolution and Rhett, deeply religious, accepted as a convert the gospel of liberty and self-government, and of revolution to achieve these ends, and dedicated his life to this great crusade. For him convictions once formed became as logical syllogisms capable of demonstration, so clear that he never thereafter doubted their correctness and so inevitable that they must be translated forthwith into action. His passionate earnestness and fiery eloquence soon won the fervent loyalty of his constituents—South Carolina was later to be dubbed "Rhettsylvania"—and, when the tariff act of 1828 was passed, they supported him, on June 12, 1828, in the "Colleton Address" (*Charleston Mercury*, June 18, 1828). This was his first exhibition of the initiative and incorrigible independence that were to make him the *enfant terrible* of South Carolina politics. He finally accepted the Calhoun theory of peaceful, constitutional nullification, and became a valued leader in the party, but his readjustment from Turnbull to Calhoun was achieved only with difficulty and never with complete success.

In December 1832, he became attorney-general of the state, his term being marked by the test-oath controversy. From 1837 to 1849 he represented Beaufort and Colleton in Congress, where at the very beginning he was advanced to the forefront of the Calhoun "party" and to intimate relations with Calhoun. The failure in 1837–38 of efforts to meet the menace of abolitionism by a Southern convention to demand "new guarantees" in the Constitution made a lasting impression upon Rhett, but for the time he accepted Calhoun's belief that the Constitution, rightly interpreted, would protect the South, and threw himself into Calhoun's plans to secure control of the Democratic party and, as president, to "right the government." But when Calhoun failed of the presidential nomination and Northern Democrats abandoned the South on the tariff, Rhett's faith in the party was shattered, and, in 1844, in defiance of Calhoun, he led the Bluffton movement for separate state action on the tariff. He denied that his purpose was to destroy the Union but declared that the government could not now be "reformed by its central action, and that we will have probably to risk the Union itself to save it, in its integrity" (Letter to R. M. T. Hunter, *Annual Report of the American Historical Association for the Year 1916*, II, 70).

The Bluffton movement was suppressed and Rhett became one of the chief supporters of Polk's administration. He differed frequently with Calhoun during these years, though both fought in defense of slavery in the territorial conflict following the Mexican War. He attended the Nashville convention in 1850 and wrote its address. Returning home he announced that South Carolina would not submit to the compromise measures and began his campaign, not now for the reformation of the Union, but for secession. His people responded zealously, but when it appeared that there was little hope of action by any other Southern state, a conflict developed between the group led by Rhett and the cooperationists under R. W. Barnwell. Rhett, as Calhoun's successor, secured the long-coveted seat in the United States Senate, where during two sessions he had a stormy experience. At home, meantime, he waged the fiercest battle of his life. He called on South Carolina to secede at once and alone. Though confident that she could sustain herself as an independent nation, he always gave the assurance that her action would lead, sooner or later, to a Southern Confederacy. Cooperation, he said, could be secured only after some one state took the initiative and forced the issue. Later (Oct. 16, 1860) he wrote to Barnwell, "I never have, and do not now desire, South Carolina to be a Sovereignty separated from the other Southern States. I have aimed at nothing but a Southern Confederacy" (White, *post*, p. 176, note 41).

The secessionists were defeated in 1851, but the conflict continued confusedly till a state convention met in 1852 and passed an ordinance merely declaratory of the right of secession. Rhett regarded this as "submission" and resigned his seat in the Senate, withdrawing entirely from politics. His party was demoralized and shattered, and the people of the state, bewildered and exhausted, relapsed into apathy. The situation was capitalized by J. L. Orr [*q.v.*], leader of the new National Democrats who stood for the democratization and nationalization of the state. Alarmed by this new menace, Rhett decided that secession must be secured quickly or it would never be secured, and he resolutely refused to be diverted even by projects with which he was fundamentally in sympathy, such as annexation movements and the revival of the African slave trade. In 1857 his son, R. B. Rhett, Jr., became editor of the *Charleston Mercury*, Rhett's organ during most of his career, but he was soon forced to announce that the paper repudiated any extreme measures. In 1858 Rhett met William L. Yancey [*q.v.*] and other Southern radicals in Montgomery; through their utterances they gave public notice of their purposes and methods, but they soon decided that the only possibility of secession lay in a Republican victory in 1860. Through the confusion and difficulties of these years, the Rhetts steered a devious and wary course. The *Mercury*, forced nominally to abandon its advocacy of a purely sectional party, affirmed its adherence to the Democratic party but worked to undermine Southern confidence in it. The paper eagerly hailed the factional fight in the party, though regarding Jefferson Davis as no less national than Orr; and Rhett and Yancey again took counsel together. The "*Mercury* program" failed completely in South Carolina, in spite of the excitement over John Brown's raid, but, to Rhett's surprise, Yancey succeeded in breaking the National Democratic Convention at Charleston. Rhett attended the new Democratic state convention, where, after the sharpest conflict South Carolina had ever witnessed, he was elected a delegate to the Richmond convention.

When Republican victory became probable, Rhett never lost sight of the lesson of 1850–51. There must be no conflict between separate state action and cooperation; the resistance spirit must be aroused but all discussion of method suppressed; and secession must be accomplished immediately after the election before popular feeling had a chance to cool off. Carefully the *Mercury* advanced from one position to another. In the legislature the younger Rhett led the successful fight against postponement of the state convention until January 1861. Secessionists believed that had postponement won, the secession movement would have ended in failure. It did not fail, and Rhett enjoyed a brief triumph as "the father of secession." The convention voted the ordinance of secession and Rhett wrote the "Address to the Slaveholding States." But already evidences of reaction had appeared and Rhett soon suspected that the secession of the other states was merely a political scheme for forcing concessions from the North. He went to the Southern Congress at Montgomery determined to defeat the schemes for reconstruction of the Union. He failed to secure the presidency of the new Confederacy and he was ignored in the appointments. Almost all the provisions which he thought vital to the new Constitution to give permanent significance to the "Revolution" were defeated by what he considered reconstruction influences, which President Davis was suspected of favoring. Rhett's cherished scheme of commercial concessions to England in return for recognition was rejected repeatedly as was his next one, the opposite policy of an embargo on cotton.

He had not anticipated war but he welcomed it, because at first it stopped the talk of reconstruction, and he at once decided that the Confederacy must take the offensive. On July 12 the *Mercury* charged Davis with personal responsibility for the delay, and after Manassas it blazed with criticisms, finally declaring outright that Davis was keeping the army inactive in order to further the policy of reconstruction. "Commercial reconstruction," a commercial alliance with the North, was now advocated by some, and the *Mercury* charged upon this new foe. When Congress denounced violations of its rule of secrecy, the *Mercury* added secret sessions to its indictment of the government. It now began to point out Davis' "usurpations," to oppose centralization, and to emphasize state rights. South Carolina somewhat reluctantly rallied to the administration and ignored Rhett in the elections for the permanent government. He then joined his son on the *Mercury,* where he continued the attack, not now upon reconstruction but upon incompetence and arrogance. His opposition to the Confederate administration was not that of the doctrinaire. He supported the Conscription Act as necessary though unconstitutional. His concern was the achieving of independence; his grievance against Davis was the failure to attain it. The election of a new Congress in 1863 offered a last chance of "invigorating the government." Rhett offered himself as representative to his faithful old district, only to be repudiated by a disillusioned and war-weary people. His last energies were spent in defense of "Southern civilization" against Davis' proposal to arm—and free—the slaves. After the war Rhett wrote a history of the Confederacy, his apologia, which was not published, and helped his son in various newspaper ventures. He died in Louisiana at the home of his son-in-law, Alfred Roman, still serenely confident in his own statesmanship and in the faith that the South must yet be "separate and free."

Rhett's character and the motivation of his career, as well as his statesmanship, are subjects upon which historians are as little likely to reach agreement as were his contemporaries. Noted particularly for his independence and unexampled consistency, he yet presents in many respects a curious mixture—of the revolutionary and the constitutionalist, the doctrinaire and the politician, the aristocrat and the democrat, the state-rights devotee and the Southern nationalist and imperialist. He was generally accused of self-seeking and vaulting ambition, but after struggling for years to reach the United States Senate, he attained the office only to resign when his term had scarcely begun. He won the respect and warm affection of his most un-

compromising political opponents, notably J. L. Petigru and B. F. Perry [*qq.v.*], the stanchest Unionists in South Carolina, who admired and praised his honesty, his warm-hearted and impulsive frankness, his integrity and honor, his high standards of public and private conduct. To his supporters he was the far-seeing statesman whose counsel, if followed, in 1837 or 1844 would have reformed the Union, in 1850 would have achieved peaceable secession, in 1861–62 would have saved the Confederacy. These claims may not be lightly dismissed. But most of his Southern colleagues, even those who shared his views, thought him conceited, intolerant and contemptuous of others, rash and unstable, an altogether untrustworthy guide for the South. Amazed at his disconcerting honesty, appalled by his ruthless logic and his constant insistence upon action, jealous of his consistency, and irritated by his air of eternal rightness, they regarded him as a mixture of doctrinaire and demagogue. But they could never ignore him with impunity. He was the only man in South Carolina who ever defied Calhoun without sacrificing his political career. Repeatedly repudiated by Southern leaders, repeatedly defeated and pronounced politically dead only to seem justified by the event, he was all his life a storm center in Southern politics.

[There are Rhett papers in the family, most of them, including portions of the History, in the possession of A. B. Rhett of Charleston. The J. H. Hammond and F. H. Elmore Papers, and Edmund Ruffin's Diary, in the MSS. Division, Lib. of Cong., are of value, as are published collections, such as J. F. Jameson, ed., "Correspondence of John C. Calhoun," *Annual Report of the Am. Hist. Asso. for the Year 1899,* vol. II (1900); and C. S. Boucher and R. P. Brooks, eds., "Correspondence addressed to John C. Calhoun, 1837–1849," *Ann. Report of the Am. Hist. Asso. for the Year 1929* (1930). The *Charleston Mercury* is essential. Contemporary sketches are Daniel Wallace, *Pol. Life and Services of the Hon. R. Barnwell Rhett* (1859), reprinted from the *Mercury* of Aug. 10, 1857, and based obviously on materials furnished by Rhett; and *Frank Leslie's Illustrated Newspaper,* Feb. 9, 1861. R. B. Rhett, Jr., "The Confed. Government at Montgomery," in *Battles and Leaders of the Civil War,* vol. I (1887); Alfred Roman, *The Mil. Operations of Gen. Beauregard* (2 vols., 1884); and J. W. Du Bose, *The Life and Times of William Lowndes Yancey* (1892), are written from the Rhett point of view. The only biography is Laura A. White, *Robert Barnwell Rhett, Father of Secession* (1931). Studies of nullification and secession in South Carolina by Frederic Bancroft, P. M. Hamer, C. S. Boucher, and others have much on Rhett. The interpretation of him by N. W. Stephenson in *The Day of the Confederacy* (1920); *Texas and the Mexican War* (1921); articles and reviews in *Am. Hist. Rev.,* and elsewhere, should be compared with that given above.]
L. A. W.

RHIND, ALEXANDER COLDEN (Oct. 31, 1821–Nov. 8, 1897), naval officer, son of Charles [*q.v.*] and Susan (Fell) Rhind, was born in New York City. He entered the United

States navy as a midshipman on Sept. 3, 1838, and by 1854 rose to the rank of lieutenant. During the years 1844–45, he attended the naval school at Philadelphia. In the Mexican War he served in the Home Squadron off the coast of Mexico under Commodores Conner and Perry, and participated in the actions at Alvarado and Tabasco. In 1855, while on the *John Adams* in the Pacific Squadron, because of a disagreement with his commander, he was court-martialed, sent home, and then placed on furlough. In September 1855, he was dropped from the service by the Naval Retiring Board, but was reinstated in 1860.

At the beginning of the Civil War he commanded the *Crusader* in the South Atlantic Blockading Squadron, and conducted a series of operations in Edisto Sound, S. C., for which he was commended by the Navy Department. Commissioned lieutenant commander on July 16, 1862, he commanded the *Seneca* in that year, and the iron-clad *Keokuk* in 1862–63. Previous to the attack on the forts at Charleston he buoyed the channels, and in the attack on Apr. 7, 1863, he ran the *Keokuk* within 550 yards of Fort Sumter, where his vessel was hit ninety times in thirty minutes, nineteen of the shots penetrating below the water-line. Obliged to withdraw from action, he kept her afloat until the next morning, and was able to save his entire crew. As commander of the *Paul Jones,* and later, in command of the flagship *Wabash,* he took part in the attacks on Fort Wagner and other Charleston defenses. During Grant's "hammering campaign" he commanded the gunboat *Agawam* in the James River, cooperating with the army. For gallant conduct in the bombardment of three Confederate batteries at Deep Bottom, Va., in August 1864, he was again commended by the Department. In the first attack on Fort Fisher he was assigned to the *Louisiana* which was loaded with 215 tons of explosives and which he anchored within 250 to 300 yards of the fort. The ship was then blown up by a clockwork device, Rhind escaping with his men before the explosion. The fort, however, remained unscathed. For this action Admiral Porter recommended him for promotion, characterizing it "the most perilous adventure that was perhaps ever undertaken..." (*War of the Rebellion...Records, post,* 1 ser., XI, 259). After the war Rhind differed sharply over his management of this affair with Gen. Benjamin Butler [*q.v.*], who had originated the scheme.

Though assigned to relatively unimportant duties after the war, he rose successively through the grades of captain and commodore to the rank of rear admiral in 1883, when he was permanently retired. During his early service he acquired a reputation for insubordination, due to frequent unguarded criticisms of his superiors. His war record, however, was brilliant. Gideon Welles described him as "impulsive but brave and rash" (*Diary of Gideon Welles,* 1911, vol. I, p. 268). He was of a retiring nature, reticent particularly on the subject of his adventurous career. He was unmarried. He died in New York City and was buried at Coldenham, N. Y.

[L. R. Hamersly, *The Records of Living Officers of the U. S. Navy and Marine Corps* (4th ed., 1890); *War of the Rebellion: Official Records* (Navy), 1 ser., vols. II, XI–XIV, 2 ser., vol. I; *The Defence of A. C. Rhind* (1857); *A Reply to the Attacks of Mr. A. C. Rhind* (1857); *N. Y. Herald*, Sept. 18, 1855; *Army and Navy Jour.*, Nov. 13, 1897; *N. Y. Times*, Nov. 10, 1897.]
          L. H. B.

RHIND, CHARLES (fl. 1810–1845), merchant and diplomatic agent, first appears in New York directories in 1810 as a ship-chandler. He was born in Aberdeen, Scotland, probably the son of Alexander Rhind, who conveyed real estate to him in 1812. Between 1804 and 1808 he married Susan, daughter of Peter Renaudet and Margaret (Colden) Fell, by whom he had ten children, one of them being Alexander Colden Rhind [*q.v.*]. Charles early engaged in trade with Smyrna and by 1822 had also become agent for the North River Steam Boat Company. Public spirit and political ambition led him to take a prominent part in municipal activities, and on Oct. 11, 1824, he was thanked by the common council of the city for his "constant, unremitted, and efficient efforts" in connection with the welcoming of Lafayette (*Minutes,* XIV, 98). A year later he again received the council's thanks for serving as admiral of the city fleet during the festivities which accompanied the opening of the Erie Canal.

In August 1829 he was in Washington, "strongly recommended" to Van Buren, and was first made consul at Odessa, then appointed on a commission with David Offley and Commodore James Biddle [*qq.v.*] to renew with the Ottoman Porte the negotiations for a treaty of commerce and navigation which had been begun by Offley in 1828. Leaving New York in October, he joined Biddle at Port Mahon, whence the two proceeded on the frigate *Java* to Smyrna, where the presence of Offley completed the commission. Following President Jackson's instructions, Rhind went to Constantinople alone, arriving on Feb. 8, 1830. Negotiations with the Reis Effendi lasted until May 7, when a treaty was signed. The other commissioners were now

summoned from Smyrna, but were not informed
until four days after their arrival of a secret article authorizing the Porte to obtain materials
for naval construction in the United States.
Rhind's exchange of treaties during their absence, his admission of the secret article and
delay in informing his colleagues regarding it,
and his assumption of complete credit for the
negotiation led to an unseemly wrangle with
Offley and Biddle, who signed only through fear
that refusal would lead to reprisals on American
commerce.

After a hurried excursion to Odessa, Rhind
returned to Constantinople, received from Sultan Mahmud a gift of four Arabian horses, and
late in September left Smyrna for New York.
On Dec. 15 President Jackson transmitted the
treaty to the Senate, which ratified it on Feb. 2,
1831, but excepted the secret article. Difficulties soon arose over the Sultan's present of
horses. Rhind had shipped them "as a commercial adventure, in the name and for the account
of the owners of the vessel" and had stated to
the President his readiness to transfer his personal claims to the government. Jackson sent a
statement of the facts, without recommendation,
to Congress, which took no action. Rhind felt
unfairly treated, claimed the horses as his own,
and emitted vague threats of making embarrassing disclosures; but, under pressure from Jackson and James A. Hamilton, he executed a release of his interests to Howland and Aspinwall,
the owners of the vessel, who sold the horses at
auction for $1990. This sum did not cover the
expenses of shipment and Rhind had to pay a
balance of $585.20. Although he petitioned the
House for this amount in 1842, as did his heirs
in 1860, no action was ever taken.

In November 1831 he sailed for Constantinople with Henry Eckford [q.v.] on a war vessel
which was eventually sold to the Ottoman government, and stayed long enough to embarrass
David Porter [q.v.], American chargé d'affaires. He then returned to New York and resumed his business activities. In 1846 his name
disappears from city directories. He was something of an artist, and painted a panorama of
Constantinople which William Dunlap [q.v.]
regarded as "very interesting" (Diary, 1930,
III, 803). His prejudices and temper were violent and unbridled, his egotism unlimited, and
his regard for the truth questionable, but these
qualities do not obscure his obvious ability and
energy.

[H. M. Wriston, Executive Agents in Am. Foreign
Relations (1929); C. O. Paullin, Diplomatic Negotia-
tions of Am. Naval Officers (1912); Reminiscences of
James A. Hamilton (1869), pp. 143–48, 201–34, J. B.
Moore, A Digest of International Law (1906), IV,
580; J. A. Hamilton to Van Buren, Aug. 23, 1829,
Van Buren Papers, Lib. of Cong., vol. X; State Dept.
Archives, "Negotiations with Turkey" (partly pub.
in House Doc. 250, 22 Cong., 1 Sess.); House Jour.,
27 Cong., 2 Sess., p. 237; Senate Jour., 36 Cong., 1
Sess., p. 272; N. Y. Geneal. and Biog. Record, Oct.
1873; Colls. N. J. Hist. Soc., vol. IX (1916); Minutes
of the Common Council of the City of N. Y. (1917),
vols. XII, XIV, passim; B. J. Lossing, Hist. of N. Y.
City (copr. 1884); birthplace from death certificate of
Alexander Colden Rhind in N. Y. City Health Dept.]
                                                    W. L. W., Jr.

RHOADS, JAMES E. (Jan. 21, 1828–Jan. 2,
1895), philanthropist, editor, first president of
Bryn Mawr College, was born in Marple, Delaware County, Pa. He was named simply
James Rhoads, and assumed the middle initial
"E" rather reluctantly in order to avoid confusion with others of his name. The farm where
he and his six brothers and sisters grew up had
been in the possession of the Rhoads family
since the time of their settlement in America
about 1690. His father, Joseph Rhoads, and
his mother, Hannah (Evans), both belonged to
families which had joined the Society of
Friends in the seventeenth century in England, and had furnished leaders to the Society
in Pennsylvania. Rhoads attended Westtown
School, the leading Quaker school in the neighborhood of Marple, and studied medicine at the
University of Pennsylvania, where he received
his degree in 1851. A few years later, after
serving 1852–54 as resident physician at Pennsylvania Hospital, he became a general practitioner in Germantown. On Mar. 21, 1860, he
married Margaret Wilson Ely, of New Hope,
Pa., and the eldest of their three children was
born in 1863.

It was said by those who knew him that
Rhoads had too sympathetic and too selfless a
nature to be able to endure for very long the
demands of a large medical practice. In 1862
he suffered a slight paralytic stroke and after
his return from six months' recuperation in Europe he did not attempt to resume his practice
but devoted himself to philanthropic and educational work. The first cause which enlisted his
efforts was the work among the freedmen,
whose education and guidance at the close of
the Civil War was one of the greatest problems facing the nation. Within a few years he
also became deeply interested in the American
Indians. With the inauguration of a new Indian
policy by President Grant, the Society of Friends
took a leading part in the educational and missionary work on the Indian reservations, and
Rhoads was made secretary of the executive
committee of the central organization. He was

also for several years president of the Indian Rights Association which had its headquarters in Philadelphia.

From 1876 to 1884 he was editor of the *Friends' Review,* a weekly periodical published in Philadelphia. As a leader among the orthodox Friends it was natural that he should be named by Dr. Joseph Taylor, whom he had known for many years, as one of the original trustees of Bryn Mawr College, the institution for higher learning for women which Dr. Taylor proposed to found and to which he left the greater part of his fortune on his death in 1880. The site for the college, ten miles from Philadelphia, had been selected, and the buildings begun by Taylor himself, but after his death it remained for the trustees to choose the officers and settle the policy for the new institution. In 1883 Rhoads was appointed the first president and Miss M. Carey Thomas the first dean, and in 1885 Bryn Mawr College was opened.

The distinctive features of the new college, which was the first institution of the kind outside of New England and New York, were the high standard of its entrance requirements, the inclusion in its plan of study of the "group system" which had just been introduced into Johns Hopkins University and which was designed to give to each student an opportunity for a certain degree of concentration in a selected field, and the graduate work, which was not offered at any of the other women's colleges. Rhoads was successful from the first in gathering a faculty distinguished in scholarship and active in research. Before retiring from the presidency in 1894 he saw the new college, well out of the experimental stage, recognized as one of the leading institutions of learning in the United States. He died very suddenly, at Bryn Mawr, in 1895.

[Henry Hartshorne, "Memoir of James E. Rhoads," *Proc. Am. Phil. Soc.,* vol. XXXIV (1895); *Addresses Delivered at a Memorial Meeting Held in Honor of James E. Rhoads, LL.D.* (Bryn Mawr College, 1895); *Memorial Minute Respecting Our Late Friend, James E. Rhoads, Adopted by the Monthly Meeting of Friends of Philadelphia for the Western District* (privately printed, 1895); *Addresses at the Inauguration of Bryn Mawr College by President Rhoads and President D. C. Gilman of the Johns Hopkins University* (1886); *Friends' Intelligencer,* Jan. 12, 1895; *Press, Public Ledger* (both of Phila.), Jan. 3, 1895; information as to certain facts from members of the family.]

H. T. M.

RHODES, JAMES FORD (May 1, 1848–Jan. 22, 1927), historian, was born in Cleveland, Ohio. His father, Daniel Pomeroy Rhodes, a native of Sudbury, Vt., had removed to the vicinity soon after he attained his maturity. He named his second son for James M. Ford, one of his early partners in his successful coal-mining business. "Dan" Rhodes was a kinsman, friend, and loyal supporter of Stephen A. Douglas. For James Ford Rhodes the difficult task of mediating between the political views of his father and the predominant Republicanism he met at school doubtless served as an invaluable apprenticeship in historical judgment and tolerance. His mother, Sophia Lord (Russell) Rhodes, came of a family that had been longer identified with the Western Reserve, though she herself was a native of Connecticut. Her husband was a deist, but she was an Episcopalian and her son, who was serious-minded and devout, gained before he was twelve, he said, a familiarity with the Bible and the Book of Common Prayer that he never lost. After a couple of years of private school, the boy attended the public schools, of which he retained a favorable opinion, graduating from high school in 1865. The only college training he had was as a special student: in 1865–66 at the University of the City of New York (now New York University), where he did most of his work in history and became in his mind a disciple of Buckle; and the following year at the University of Chicago, where he showed an impermanent interest in metaphysics and began his lifelong reading of the New York *Nation.* While abroad for more than a year in 1867–68, when for a time he thought of becoming a journalist and literary man, he gained valuable if informal political education and a knowledge of French. He attended lectures on Montesquieu in Paris then, with more practical intent but without enthusiasm, studied metallurgy in Berlin, and visited iron and steel works in Germany and Great Britain. Shortly after his return to America, he was sent by his father to investigate coal and iron deposits in North Carolina, Georgia, and Tennessee; he found the Carpet-baggers more interesting.

To a business career, however, he was now resigned. After a few years' service in another firm, in 1874 he became associated with Rhodes & Company, with his brother Robert and Marcus A. Hanna [*q.v.*], who had married his sister. On Jan. 4, 1872, he had married Ann Card, daughter of Jonathan F. Card, former partner of his father. Rhodes & Company, producers and commission merchants, were highly successful in the coal and iron business. To James Ford Rhodes, however, wealth was a means only, and in 1885, feeling that his fortune was now sufficient, he retired from business "to pursue another line of occupation." Six years later Harper & Brothers accepted the manuscript of the first two volumes of the *History of the United States from the Compromise of 1850,* which was to give him fame. Earlier in the same year (September 1891), he removed to Cambridge, Mass., and within a surprisingly short time this successful man of affairs who, without academic prerogatives, had set out to woo the Muse of history, had penetrated the innermost citadels of the Boston literati. By 1898, when he was elected president of the American Historical Association, he had become a notable national figure in the field of his choice.

The success of his daring venture, while it may be termed a triumph of irregularity, was no more accidental than ephemeral, for the self-education of the historian was thorough and arduous. In Cleveland, Rhodes had kept up his French, and was an enthusiastic member of the Vampire Club, instituted by John Hay. In 1877, while reading Hildreth, he had asked himself why he should not write a history of the United States; henceforth he read with this end in view and started making careful notes. In 1881 he began writing monthly circulars on the condition of the pig-iron trade, in which he tried to apply some philosophy to business affairs; these circulars, which attracted attention, gave him practical experience in composition and revived his purpose to write history. Following his retirement from business, he embarked on a wide course of reading, studying the masters of historical literature with discrimination and assiduity. Few recent "professional" historians in America have pursued such a course in historiography. During 1885-86 he marked his apprenticeship by publishing several articles and reviews in the *Magazine of Western History*; and in the spring of 1886 he went abroad, remaining thirteen months. As a by-product of this trip, a translation, *The Abbess of Jouarre* of Renan, by Rhodes and Georges Delon, a teacher of French in Cleveland, appeared in 1888. For four years, 1887-91, Rhodes devoted his entire time to the first two volumes of his history.

Published in 1893, these were greeted by competent critics with immediate and practically unanimous approval, and five subsequent volumes (III, 1895; IV, 1899; V, 1904; VI, VII, 1906), to which also he gave single-minded devotion, served to enhance the author's fame. Rhodes had originally intended to carry his *History* to 1885, but wisely decided to end it with the restoration of home rule at the South in 1877. The first five volumes, covering the years 1850-66, are on essentially the same scale, but the two last (1866-77) are less comprehensive and betray some eagerness for the completion of an arduous task.

Two subsequent volumes, *History of the United States from Hayes to McKinley, 1877-1896* (1919), and *The McKinley and Roosevelt Administrations, 1897-1909* (1922), were in no real sense a continuation of the original work, either in scale or character, and added nothing to his reputation. Because of his intimate association with political and economic leaders, Rhodes was enabled to impart to these last volumes a flavor of reminiscence, but he appears to have been more circumscribed than aided by his personal success and his identification with the conservative East. *The History of the Civil War, 1861-1865* (1917) was a fresh treatment, valuable to the general reader. Of Rhodes's other published writings his collection of *Historical Essays* (1909), in which with characteristic candor he revealed the secrets of his craft, and gave sage counsel to the prospective historian, is most important.

His fame rests upon his major work, and especially on the first five volumes. Writing while the memory of fratricidal strife was still green, Rhodes brought to his gigantic task great industry, good judgment, and, for his day, notable fair-mindedness. His thoroughness and his skill in handling vast materials were immediately recognized, and, in particular, his extensive but discriminating use of newspapers was favorably commented upon. His contemporaries, however, were most impressed by his candor and relative freedom from partisanship. Indeed, the spirit of his work, more than anything else, made it epochal. Rhodes viewed the South with a sympathy that was not yet common in the North, though at the present time one detects in his attitude more than a trace of condescension toward an "erring" section. Admittedly a narrative historian, ordinarily he indulged in no philosophy beyond that of elevated common sense, but in discussing the causes of the Civil War he was more moralistic than the generality of later scholars have dared to be. As he saw it, the controversy was over slavery, not land; the clash was between ideas, essentially abstract, not between divergent civilizations, each a mixture of good and evil, contending for dominance or for survival. On the actualities of Southern life, he was inadequately informed; the West, as an arena in which economic forces were battling, he largely ignored. He was no legalist, but he was primarily a political historian. In dealing with the war itself, he showed marked ability in military affairs, but confessed to a degree of weakness on the naval side; in diplomatic matters he suffered from lack of technical training. Of the internal history of the Confederacy he knew relatively little; and he was naturally unable to take advantage of the vast literature of Reconstruction that has been created since his volumes on that period were prepared. Most of his major portraits are excellent. That his comments on Andrew Johnson now seem unjudicial, and uncharacteristic of Rhodes himself, may doubtless be attributed to his lack of information. Historical scholars have supplemented his investigations in a score of places, and have modified many of his judgments, but his work still stands as a landmark in American historiography. His style is never brilliant, and at times is clumsy, but it reflects his own mind and personality in its dignity, clarity, and strength.

Happily ensconced in Boston, whither he moved from Cambridge in 1895, Rhodes consorted with the political and literary leaders of his generation and in due course received all the important academic and literary honors his generation could bestow. Large and bearded, cheerful and companionable, he became a notable personage, but never lost his native modesty. He retained a degree of political independence while consorting with the powerful, but viewed the economic scene as a conservative. Full of years and honors, he died in Brookline on Jan. 22, 1927, survived by his wife and his son, Daniel Pomeroy Rhodes. His ashes were buried in Cleveland.

[M. A. DeW. Howe, *James Ford Rhodes, American Historian* (1929), contains the important biographical details, an autobiographical fragment, photographs, personal letters, and a list of Rhodes's writings. See also "Memoir" by J. T. Morse, Jr., *Mass. Hist. Soc. Proc.,* vol. LX (1927), 178–92; obituary in *Boston Evening Transcript,* Jan. 22, 1927. For reviews of his chief works, see A. C. McLaughlin, in *Am. Hist. Review,* Jan. 1896, pp. 366–70; W. A. Dunning, *Ibid.,* Jan. 1900, pp. 371–74; W. G. Brown, *Ibid.,* Oct. 1905, pp. 181–86; Apr. 1907, pp. 680–84; W. R. Livermore, *Ibid.,* Apr. 1919, pp. 520–21; F. L. Paxson, *Ibid.,* Apr. 1920, pp. 525–27; Apr. 1923, pp. 565–66; C. F. Adams, *Mass. Hist. Soc. Proc.,* 2 ser., XIX (1906), pp. 311–56 (also published separately), commented on by Rhodes in letter to Adams, Mar. 1907, Howe, pp. 148–52; L. B. Shippee, *Miss. Valley Hist. Rev.,* June–Sept. 1921, pp. 132–48; N. W. Stephenson, *Yale Review,* July 1921, pp. 860–65.]   D. M.

RIBAUT, JEAN (*c.* 1520–Oct. 12, 1565), French mariner and colonizer, born at Dieppe, was either a son of members of the Reformed faith or a convert thereto. He became a skilful sailor and one of Admiral Coligny's most trusted naval captains. He had many English friends and spent the winter of 1546–47 in London, but when the French took Calais from the English in 1558, Ribaut commanded during the action one of the transports of supplies. The next year he was sent to Scotland to handle the French interests there, and was successful in his mission.

In 1562 Coligny determined to plant a colony in the New World, which Verrazzano, sailing under a French flag in 1524, and Jacques Cartier in 1534–45, had explored for France. The new colony was not only to be an extension of French power but an asylum for the Huguenots, who were regarded with increasing disfavor by the royal family. Ribaut was chosen to lead the expedition to found a New France on the coast of Florida. With a fleet of three vessels and 150 colonists, provisions, artillery, and René de Laudonnière [*q.v.*] as his lieutenant, he set sail, in the spring of 1562. He sighted land on Apr. 30, and on the next day entered St. John's River, which he named Rivière de May, setting up a column bearing the French arms in token of occupation. On the first of May 1924 another column was erected on this spot in commemoration of Ribaut's discovery. Thence he sailed north and settled his colony at the present Port Royal, S. C., which he called Charlesfort, in honor of the king. Here a second column was erected which has recently been replaced by the United States government "in honor of the first Stronghold of France in North America." After laying the foundations of Charlesfort, Ribaut returned to France, reaching Dieppe July 20, 1562.

During his absence civil war had broken out in France between the Huguenots and the Catholics, and Ribaut was unable to keep his promise to return with aid for the new colony. Finding themselves without succor, the colonists at Charlesfort sailed for home. Ribaut, meanwhile, had been drawn into the war; he fought in defense of his native town and upon its capture fled to England, in October 1562. He was cordially received and an English version of his report to Coligny was published in London, under the title, *The VVhole And True Discouerye of Terra Florida* (1563). The subject of Florida was much discussed, and Queen Elizabeth suggested to Ribaut that he join an enterprise being promoted by one of her subjects, Thomas Stukeley, to settle an English colony in that region. Ribaut, however, had no desire to aid an English settlement in New France; furthermore, he learned that Stukeley was a Catholic and in league with Spain. He thereupon attempted to flee from England, but was arrested and imprisoned in the Tower.

Coligny meanwhile had sent Laudonnière to continue the Huguenot colony, and the latter, finding Charlesfort abandoned, had built Fort Caroline on the Rivière de May. In 1565 Ribaut, released from captivity, took out a large reinforcement for the colony in a fleet of seven ships. Spain had, however, taken alarm at the founding of a "heretic" colony on land she claimed as her own, and Pedro Menéndez de Avilés [*q.v.*] had been sent to drive off the French, although there was nominal peace between the two nations. Menéndez, after building St. Augustine, sailed for the St. John's River, had a skirmish with Ribaut's fleet, and was beaten off. Ribaut then sailed to attack the Spaniards, leaving Fort Caroline practically defenseless. Menéndez, during Ribaut's absence, marched overland, attacked and captured the fort, and massacred most of its inhabitants. A few, including Laudonnière, escaped to France. Meanwhile Ribaut ran into a violent storm, his fleet was scattered, and his flagship wrecked on the coast south of St. Augustine. Starvation drove the French into the power of the Spaniards. Menéndez disarmed them, inquired if they were "Lutherans," and on receiving an affirmative answer, "put them to the knife." Ribaut was stabbed to death, and it was reported that his body was treated with indignity. His ability was recognized by his enemy, Menéndez, who said of him (Connor, *post,* pp. 35–36): "He could do more in one year than another in ten, for he was the most experienced seaman and corsair known and very skilful in this navigation of the Indies and the coasts of Florida."

[Ribaut's *VVhole And True Discouerye* was reprinted by Richard Hakluyt, in *Divers Voyages* (London, 1582) and has been reproduced in facsimile together with a manuscript version found in the British Museum and a biography, in Jeannette T. Connor, *Jean Ribaut* (Fla. State Hist. Soc., 1927). See also René Goulaine de Laudonnière, *L'Histoire notable de Floride Française* (Paris, 1586) ; the narrative of a survivor, Nicolas le Challeux, *Discovrs de l'Histoire de la Floride* (Dieppe, 1566), translated as *A True and Perfect Description of the Last Voyage or Nauigation, Attempted by Capitaine Iohn Rybaud* (1566), reproduced in facsimile in Mass. Hist. Soc. Photostatic Reproductions, no. 13 (1920) ; *Requeste au Roy* (1566), the petition of the widows and children of the victims, reproduced in the same series (1929) ; Francis Parkman, *Pioneers of France in the New World* (1865) ; Paul Gafferel, *Histoire de la Floride Française* (Paris, 1875) ; Woodbury Lowery, *The Spanish Settlements within the Limits of the U. S.: Florida* (1905) ; material on the English expedition of Stukeley in *Calendar of State Papers: Spanish, 1558–1567* (1892).]　　　L. P. K.

RICE, ALEXANDER HAMILTON (Aug. 30, 1818–July 22, 1895), manufacturer, congressman, governor of Massachusetts, was the son of Thomas and Lydia (Smith) Rice. Born at Newton Lower Falls, Mass., where his father was proprietor of a paper mill, he attended public and private schools in and near Newton, obtaining at the same time considerable training in his father's business. At seventeen he entered a dry-goods store in Boston as a clerk, but was forced to return home shortly on account of illness. Two years later he was employed in Boston by Wil-

kins & Carter, wholesale dealers in paper and publishers of music books and dictionaries. He joined the Mercantile Library Association, where he found books to study and, at its meetings, stimulating friends. His ambition was stirred, and with the encouragement of J. H. Wilkins, one of his employers, he entered Union College in 1840. A disfigurement of his upper lip, the result of being thrown from a horse, not only delayed his entrance into college but also prevented him from going into law as he had intended. In time, however, the scar on his lip became practically unnoticeable, while he completely overcame the impediment in his speech which had been caused by the injury. He graduated from Union in 1844 with highest honors, and the following year returned to Boston as a member of the firm by which he had previously been employed. He later headed the concern, which in 1889 came to be the Rice-Kendall Company, manufacturing paper in Newton with warehouses and offices in Boston. At the time of his death he was also president of the Keith Paper Company at Turner's Falls, and of the American Sulphate Pulp Company, and a director of the Montague Paper Company. His other business interests included the Massachusetts National Bank, the American Loan and Trust Company (Boston), and the Mutual Life Insurance Company (New York).

Rice entered politics in 1853 as a Whig member of the Common Council of Boston. Reëlected in 1854, he was made its president. He was one of the organizers of the Republican party in Massachusetts, and he was that party's first mayor of Boston (1856 and 1857), though elected on the "Citizen's" ticket over the "Know-Nothing" candidate. During his terms as mayor, improvements in the Back Bay section were inaugurated, the City Hospital was established, and the city's public institutions were organized under a single board. He returned to politics as a Republican congressman (1859–67), being assigned to the Committee on Naval Affairs, of which he was chairman in 1866. From 1876 to 1878 he was governor of Massachusetts. During his three terms he was much interested in social legislation, but a plan for the reorganization of the state charities presented during this period by a special commission was rejected by the legislature. The hospitals for the insane at Danvers and Worcester were completed while he was in office. He commuted, on the grounds of youth, the death sentence of Jesse Pomeroy, the notorious murderer. His stand against change in the new local-option law on the grounds that there were no evidences of flagrant evils resulting from it and that it should be tested further before the passage of other legislation brought upon him unjust criticism from many prohibitionists, but his geniality, combined with thoughtfulness, discernment, and sound judgment, won for him quite general favor. He was a member of many learned societies and a trustee of many important public institutions, while his broad interests and commanding oratory made him much in demand as a speaker on public occasions. He was twice married: first, Aug. 19, 1845, to Augusta E. McKim of Lowell, who died in 1868, having borne two sons and two daughters; and, second, to Angie Erickson Powell of Rochester, N. Y. He died after a long illness at the Langwood Hotel in Melrose.

[*Bostonian,* Nov., Dec. 1895; *Bay State Monthly,* Feb. 1884; *New-Eng. Hist. and Geneal. Reg.,* Jan. 1896; S. F. Smith, *Hist. of Newton, Mass.* (1880); J. C. Rand, *One of a Thousand* (1890); D. P. Toomey, *Mass. of Today* (1892); *Boston Morning Journal,* Jan. 2, 1878, July 23, 1895; *Boston Transcript,* July 22, 1895.]   R. E. M.

RICE, CHARLES (Oct. 4, 1841–May 13, 1901), pharmacist, chemist, philologist, was born in Munich, Bavaria, of Austrian parents. He was educated in private schools and seminaries in Munich, Passau, and Vienna, and spent some time in a Jesuit college in Paris. He was well schooled in the natural sciences, but received an exceptional grounding in the classics, and at Passau, at the age of twelve, began the study of Sanskrit under an enthusiastic teacher. The death of his parents threw him entirely on his own resources, and in 1862, with the aid of an uncle residing in America, he emigrated to the United States. Obtaining almost immediately an appointment as surgeon's steward on the sloop-of-war *Jamestown,* he gained his first experiences in the compounding of medicines. Discharged from the navy, in 1865, he contracted malarial fever and was sent to Bellevue Hospital, New York. After his recovery, he was assigned in a minor capacity to the drug department of this hospital. Because of his unusual qualifications, he was soon advanced to the position of chief chemist of the department of public charities and correction of the City of New York and later became superintendent of the general drug department of Bellevue and its subsidiary hospitals, a position of wide responsibilities in which he served for the rest of his life.

Owing to the nature of his work at Bellevue, Rice devoted much of his time to chemical and pharmaceutical subjects, and associated himself with various pharmaceutical organizations. In 1870 he was appointed trustee and librarian of the College of Pharmacy of the City of New York

and in 1880 was unanimously elected to the post in which he rendered his most distinguished service—the chairmanship of the committee of revision of the *United States Pharmacopœia,* which he held until his death. His unusual talents as an organizer and executive, coupled with his scholarly attainments, enabled him to be instrumental in placing the *United States Pharmacopœia* in the front rank of the pharmacopœias of the world. He also rendered valuable services in the proof-reading of *The Index Catalogue of the Library of the Surgeon General's Office.* Between 1871 and 1901 he contributed many original articles to pharmaceutical journals, in addition to the almost innumerable papers he wrote in connection with the revisions of the *Pharmacopœia.*

As a philologist, Rice was honored by scholars both in the United States and abroad. He was conversant with French, Spanish, Portuguese, German, Dutch and Hebrew, while Latin and Greek were as familiar to him as his classic English. Among the Oriental languages, he had a command of Arabic, Chinese, and Japanese, with Sanskrit as his favorite; indeed, he was at one time classed among the foremost Sanskrit scholars of the United States (see Wimmer, *post,* p. 156). He was an indefatigable worker, modest to a fault, broadminded and charitable, ever ready to advise or assist either a student or a colleague. He died, unmarried, in his sixtieth year, of an aneurism of the aorta complicated with chronic nephritis.

[*Charles Rice* (printed for private circulation, by J. B. Lippincott Company, Phila., 1904), containing biog. sketch, memorial tributes, and bibliog. of Rice's writings; *Am. Druggist and Pharmaceutical Record,* June 15, 1891 (autobiography), May 27, 1901, Oct. 26, 1903; C. P. Wimmer, *The Coll. of Pharmacy of the City of N. Y. . . . A Hist.* (1929); *The First Century of the Phila. Coll. of Pharmacy* (1922); *Jour. Am. Pharmaceutical Asso.,* Aug. 1919; *N. Y. Times,* May 14, 1901; personal acquaintance.]   V. C.

RICE, CHARLES ALLEN THORNDIKE (June 18, 1851–May 16, 1889), journalist, was born in Boston, the son of Henry Gardner and Elizabeth Francis (Thorndike) Rice. His father was derived from an ancient family of Brookfield, Mass.; his mother was seventh in descent from John Thorndike of Ipswich, Mass., who arrived in America in 1633, and a granddaughter of Israel Thorndike [*q.v.*] of Beverly and Boston. When Rice was still very young, his parents separated, the mother obtaining a divorce in Indiana and the father another in Maryland. In 1860, the father having come north with the son for the summer, the mother sought to obtain his custody. When the Massachusetts supreme judicial court denied her right, she caused the boy to be seized while in school at Nahant and after some perilous adventures made her way to Europe with him. The "kidnapping" became a celebrated case, and in the trial of the actual abductors Henry Cabot Lodge, then a lad of eleven and one of "Charley" Rice's playmates, was the principal witness. Mrs. Rice later settled in Germany and there married one of her son's tutors, Dr. Frederick Koffler, an excellent scholar, of Darmstadt. In 1870 Rice matriculated at Christ Church, Oxford, receiving the degree of B.A. in 1874 and the degree of M.A. in 1878. His close friend and college roommate, Lloyd Bryce, said that "he took the highest possible degrees in the shortest possible time." After Oxford he spent some part of a year at the Columbia Law School in New York.

Possessed of ample means, he decided upon the profession of journalism, and almost immediately, taking what has been called "the most distinctive step in his career" (Bryce, *post*), he purchased in 1876 the *North American Review* at that time a stodgy quarterly, profitable to neither publishers, editors, nor contributors. He at once announced his intention to make the magazine "an arena wherein any man having something valuable to say could be heard." He removed the *Review* from Boston to New York, made it a monthly, and filled it with timely articles on public questions by leaders of world opinion. John Sherman and Hugh McCulloch wrote for him on specie payments; James G. Blaine, James A. Garfield, and Wade Hampton on negro franchise; Robert G. Ingersoll and William E. Gladstone on the Christian religion. He himself went afield in quest of material, as when he interviewed President Thomas A. Scott of the Pennsylvania Railroad amidst the rioting of the Pittsburgh strike in 1877. In a few years the periodical became world famous, returning an annual profit of $50,000 from an original investment of a tenth of that sum. The editor meantime multiplied his interests. In 1879 he induced Pierre Lorillard and the French government to finance the Charnay expedition for study of the Mayan ruins in Central America and Mexico. In 1884 he acquired an interest in *Le Matin* in Paris. The next year he edited a well-known volume of *Reminiscences of Abraham Lincoln* (1886), and in 1886 he came within 527 votes of election to Congress as a Republican from a strongly Democratic district. Treachery defeated him and brought him forward as an advocate of ballot reform. In 1889 President Harrison appointed him minister to Russia, perhaps the youngest American since John Quincy Adams to receive a diplomatic mission of such rank, but on the eve of his departure for this post Rice died very suddenly in New York City.

He was handsome and of fascinating personality, enterprising and versatile, a good linguist, admirably equipped for journalism. His friendships, of extraordinary range in both America and Europe, included such men as Laurence Oliphant, William Waldorf Astor, Henry George, Prince Napoleon, Robert Browning, and Victor Hugo.

[Records of St. Paul's Church, Boston, for correct date of birth; records of the Mass. superior and supreme courts for facts as to the kidnapping, and probate court records for family and financial details; Joseph Foster, *Alumni Oxonienses, 1715–1886* (1888), Columbia University records, and the archives of the State Dept.; the files of the *North American Review* (esp. "Tributes to Allen Thorndike Rice by W. W. Astor, Edwards Pierrepont, Gen. W. T. Sherman, and Lloyd Bryce," July 1889); H. C. Lodge, *Early Memories* (1913); Algernon Tassin, *The Magazine in America* (1916); *N. Y. Times*, May 17, 1889; and personal correspondence.]   F. L. B.

RICE, DAN (Jan. 25, 1823–Feb. 22, 1900), circus clown, showman, was born on Mulberry Street, New York City, the son of Daniel McLaren, a grocer and henchman to Aaron Burr, by his wife, Elizabeth Crum, daughter of a Methodist preacher living in Ocean Township, Monmouth County, N. J. His parents' marriage was subsequently annulled. At an early age Dan ran away from home, made his way to Pittsburgh, and for several years was a stable-boy, racerider, and hack-driver. There are at least three versions of how he acquired the name Rice.

His career as a showman covered the period 1841–85. He began at Pittsburgh by buying a half interest in Lord Byron, an educated pig. He and his partner took some of the responsibility off the pig by entertaining their patrons with songs and jigs, but Lord Byron was the real attraction, and with his death the show closed. Rice then became a strong man in Nathan Howes' Philadelphia winter circus and in Barnum's New York Museum and toured Europe in the same capacity. For a few months he was an agent for Joseph Smith, the Mormon prophet. Joining a circus, he made his first appearance as a clown at Galena, Ill., in 1844. During the next thirty years he was associated with Dr. G. R. Spaulding, Seth B. Howes, John O'Brien, Adam Forepaugh, and other circus owners. He himself was the proprietor of several wagon and river-boat circuses. In his day the circus was still a one-ring show, and a clown could command the entire audience. Rice sang and danced, delivered speeches, bantered the audience and the ringmaster, performed all the feats of the strong man and the equestrian, and exhibited various animals that he had trained. His horses, Excelsior and

Excelsior, Jr., were great favorites. Pursuing the American humorous tradition, he disported himself, also, as a crackerbox philosopher and commentator on public affairs. In the late sixties, when he was at the height of his popularity, he drew a salary of $1,000 a week and was as well known as P. T. Barnum. Circus-folk still think of him as the greatest of American clowns and remember him as an honest and kindly man, and a born wag.

He was married three times and made his home, from 1853 to 1875, in Girard, Pa., where he wintered his circus and erected a Civil War monument at his own expense. He gave away his money lavishly and was particularly addicted to building churches for negroes. He made and lost three fortunes. His title of Colonel was conferred on him, *honoris causa*, by Zachary Taylor. In 1868 he convinced himself that the Presidency was within his grasp and began a campaign for the Republican nomination. More than one small-town editor took him seriously, but the boom did not go far. A few years later his heavy drinking began to tell on him; he could not be depended upon to keep his engagements, and he lost the respect of his associates. In 1878 he "reformed" and became a Temperance lecturer, but the water pitcher before him on the lecturer's desk frequently held gin. He made his last circus tour in 1885. For the rest of his life he lived with relatives at Long Branch, N. J., where he died after fifteen years of complete obscurity.

[M. W. Brown, *The Life of Dan Rice* (Long Branch, N. J., 1901) is a large, inchoate collection of materials, some of it purporting to be written by Rice himself. See also: *Appletons' Ann. Cyc.*, 1900; John Miller, *Hist. of Erie County, Pa.* (1909), I, 470–72; H. W. Root, *The Ways of the Circus, Being the Memories and Adventures of George Conklin* (1921); E. C. May, *The Circus from Rome to Ringling* (1932).]　　　G. H. G.

RICE, DAVID (Dec. 29, 1733–June 18, 1816), clergyman, father of Presbyterianism in Kentucky, was born in Hanover County, Va., the son of David Rice, a poor but highly respected farmer; and the grandson of Thomas Rice, an Englishman of Welsh extraction, who emigrated to Virginia at an early date. Upon a return trip to England, to inherit an estate, he was either murdered or lost at sea and was never heard of again. Both the younger David's parents were members of the Established Church, and both were opposed to slavery, the father for economical and the mother for moral purposes. While still very young, David came under Presbyterian influences, including the preaching of Dr. Samuel Davies [*q.v.*], and at about the age of twenty united with the Presbyterian Church. Deciding to study for the ministry, he began his classical

studies under Rev. John Todd, a Presbyterian minister. When, in 1759, Davies became president of the College of New Jersey, Rice entered the junior class there and graduated in 1761. Returning to Virginia, he studied theology under Todd, and was licensed to preach by the Hanover Presbytery in 1762. He at once entered upon evangelistic work in Virginia and North Carolina, but late in 1763 settled in Hanover, Va., where he was ordained in December of that year. In the meantime he had married Mary Blair, daughter of Rev. Samuel Blair [*q.v.*] of Pennsylvania, by whom he had six sons and five daughters.

For four or five years he served the group of churches in Hanover County which had formerly been cared for by Samuel Davies, and also did a notable work among the slaves. He was a pioneer by nature and was always seeking work of the pioneer type. In 1769 he moved from Hanover to Bedford County, near the Peaks of Otter, and did mission work in that vicinity for a dozen or more years. In 1783 he moved to Kentucky, settled in Mercer County, and preached at Danville, Cane Run, Forks of Dick's River, and other points. Fifteen years later he went to Green County in southern Kentucky, where he continued his missionary labors. Later on he visited many parts of Kentucky and Ohio, wherever he went organizing churches until he came to be known as the father of Presbyterianism in Kentucky. He was always interested in education. Before he left Virginia he helped to found Hampden-Sydney College. Soon after he reached Kentucky he began to establish schools, and he was one of the promoters of Transylvania University at Lexington, Ky. Always busy with his pen, he was the author of many newspaper articles, pamphlets, and printed sermons. Among his publications were *An Essay on Baptism* (1789), *Slavery Inconsistent with Justice and Good Policy* (1792), *Sermon* (1802) preached at the erection of the Synod of Kentucky, *An Epistle to the Citizens of Kentucky, Professing Christianity; Especially . . . Presbyterians* (1805), and *A Second Epistle . . .* (1808).

Rice was elected a member of the convention (1792) which framed the constitution of Kentucky, and took an active part in its proceedings. He endeavored to write into the article into the constitution providing for the gradual emancipation of slaves, but it was defeated. In this connection he said: "Holding men in Slavery is the National vice of Virginia; and while a part of that State we were partakers of the guilt. As a separate State we are just now come to birth, and it depends upon our free choice whether we shall be born in this sin or innocent of it" (Bishop, *post,* pp. 417–18). In person Rice is said to have been tall and slender. He was quiet in his manner and by some of his contemporaries considered austere. He was not a great scholar or a great preacher, but was noted for his piety, common sense, sound judgment, executive ability, and indefatigable industry. He died at the ripe age of eighty-two.

[R. H. Bishop, *An Outline of the Hist. of the Church in Ky. . . . Containing the Memoirs of the Rev. David Rice . . .* (1824), which is the authority for most of the titles given above; Robert Davidson, *Hist. of the Presbyterian Church in the State of Ky.* (1847); Minutes of Hanover Presbytery, 1755–1785; W. B. Sprague, *Annals of the Am. Pulpit,* vol. III (1858); W. H. Foote, *Sketches of Va., Hist. and Biog.,* 2 ser. (1855).]

W. L. L.

RICE, EDMUND (Feb. 14, 1819–July 11, 1889), railroad president, congressman, has been called the father of the Minnesota railroad system. He was born in Waitsfield, Vt., the son of Edmund and Ellen (Durkee) Rice, and a descendant of Edmund Rice who settled at Sudbury, Mass., in 1638. He received a limited common-school education and worked as a farm hand and as a clerk in a country store. In 1838 he went to Kalamazoo, Mich., where he studied law and, in 1842, was admitted to the bar. In 1841 he was register of the court of chancery, and subsequently he was master in chancery and clerk of the state supreme court. During the Mexican War he served as first lieutenant in a Michigan regiment. In July 1849, he settled in St. Paul, Minn., where he became senior member of Rice, Hollinshead & Becker, a law firm which during its existence was the most prominent in the territory. During the fifties there was great agitation in Minnesota for railroads. Rice was a leader in the movement, and in 1856 he abandoned his law practice to devote more time to railroad projects. He was a director of the Minnesota & Northwestern Railroad Company, chartered by the legislature of 1854 to receive the lands that Congress was expected to grant to the territory. The importunity of persons interested in the company, who went so far as to tamper with the phraseology of the bill in Congress, deprived the territory of the grant (Folwell, *post,* vol. I). When Congress made a generous grant of lands for Minnesota railroads in 1857, Rice took the lead in working out a plan for railroad lines, which became the basis of the state's present railroad system. As president of the Minnesota & Pacific, one of the companies sharing in the grant, and of its successors, the St. Paul & Pacific and the St. Paul & Chicago, Rice labored, in the face of the many disasters that marked the history of early Minnesota railroads, to build the roads in advance of settlement, relying upon future development to pay for them. In spite of his success in interesting eastern and foreign capital and in obtaining additional grants of lands, the St. Paul & Pacific, after completing some three hundred miles of road, was unable to survive the panic of 1873. The St. Paul & Chicago, after completing its line from St. Paul south to Winona, was sold in 1872 to the Milwaukee & St. Paul Railroad. Rice later shared in the prosperity that came in the wake of the railroads, but his financial gain was due, not to his railroad activities, but to fortunate investments in real estate. He was a member of the legislature at intervals from 1851 to 1878, served two terms as mayor of St. Paul, was defeated for the governorship by John S. Pillsbury [*q.v.*] in 1879, and was a member of Congress from 1887 to 1889. In politics he was an uncompromising Democrat.

Rice married Anna M. Acker of Kalamazoo, Mich., Nov. 28, 1848, and they had eleven children. He was an able executive, tactful and discerning in his business dealings, and had a large amount of practical knowledge. Tall, well-formed, dignified in bearing, and courtly in manner, he was spoken of in the legislature as "the Chesterfield of the House" (Hall, *post,* p. 49). He died at White Bear Lake, Minn., in his seventy-first year. Henry Mower Rice [*q.v.*] was his brother.

[M. B. Jones, *Hist. of the Town of Waitsfield, Vt.* (1909); C. C. Andrews, *Hist. of St. Paul, Minn.* (1890), pt. 2, pp. 86–89; C. L. Hall, *Biog. Sketches of the State Govt. and of the 19th Minn. Legislature* (1877); T. M. Newson, *Pen Pictures of St. Paul* (1886), pp. 153–55; C. E. Flandrau, "The Bench and Bar of Ramsey County, Minn.," in *Mag. of Western Hist.,* Jan. 1888; W. H. C. Folsom, *Fifty Years in the Northwest* (1888), p. 560; W. W. Folwell, *A Hist. of Minn.* (1921–30), I, 327–50, II, 37–58, III, 32–57; *Daily Pioneer Press* (St. Paul), July 12, 1889.]

S. J. B.

RICE, EDWIN WILBUR (July 24, 1831–Dec. 3, 1929), Congregational clergyman, editor, and publisher, was born in Kingsborough (now a part of Gloversville), N. Y., the son of Ebenezer and Eliza Ann (Port) Rice and a grandson of Ebenezer Rice who moved from Connecticut to New York after the Revolution. Like most country boys of his day, Edwin spent his early years in a plain farm home. The district school which he attended was of a high order, and the town had one of the earliest circulating libraries in the state as well as an unusual system of public religious instruction. He began his collegiate preparation at the local academy, completed it at the academy in Little Falls, and entered Union College as a sophomore. While in college he taught two winter schools and spent a third winter in Canada as a missionary of the American Sunday School Union, an undenominational agency founded in 1817 for the promotion of Sunday-school work and the publication of Sunday-school literature. After his graduation in 1854, he studied law for a time, but soon turned to theology and spent two years at Union Theological Seminary, during which period he also did city mission work for the Sunday School Union. Following a year of teaching in Brooklyn, he took up permanent work with this society and remained connected with it for the rest of his life. He did a remarkable work as Sunday school missionary in Wisconsin and Minnesota under difficult frontier conditions, and on Sept. 20, 1860, was ordained at La Crosse by the Presbyterian and Congregational Convention of Wisconsin. After a brief service as assistant secretary at St. Louis, which was terminated by the outbreak of the Civil War, he resumed work as superintendent in Wisconsin and Minnesota, where he held institutes, founded new schools, organized a system of teacher training, and promoted the cause by much editorial writing. In 1870 he was called by the Union to its headquarters in Philadelphia, where he was associate secretary and editor till 1877, editor of periodicals for a year, and thereafter editor of publications till 1915, from which date he was honorary editor until his death.

Rice's entire active life was devoted to the improvement and extension of the Sunday school. He is said to have been the author of more than fifty volumes and the editor of nearly 400 books and pamphlets, mostly on religious subjects. In addition he contributed numerous articles to various papers and periodicals. The following are among his more important publications: *A Pictorial Commentary on the Gospel According to Mark* (1881), and similar commentaries on Matthew (1887), Luke (1889), John (1891), and Acts (1896); *Stories of Great Painters* (copyright 1887); *Our Sixty-Six Sacred Books* (1891, 1902); *People's Dictionary of the Bible* (1893); *Orientalisms in Bible Lands* (copyright 1910); *The Sunday-School Movement, 1780–1917, and the American Sunday School Union, 1817–1917* (1917); *Story of a Nonagenarian and Educators He has Known* (1922). He was an able executive and it was due to his skill as a financier that the American Sunday School Union was relieved of a burden of debt of many years' standing and provided with an endowment that amounted at his death to $3,000,000. He remained abreast of the times and continued his activities till his last months, dying in his ninety-ninth year. He was twice married: first, in

January 1861 to Margaret Eliza Williams, who died in 1864; and second, in 1866, to Mary Gardner, who assisted her husband as a writer on religious subjects. One son by the first marriage and two by the second survived their parents.

[Rice's *After Ninety Years* (1924) contains much biographical material. See also *The Year-Book of the Congregational and Christian Churches ... 1929* (n.d.); *Who's Who in America*, 1928–29; *Alumni Bull. of Union Theological Sem.*, Dec. 1929–Jan. 1930; *Union (College) Alumni Monthly*, Jan. 1930; *Public Ledger* (Phila.), Dec. 6, 1929.]   F.T.P.

RICE, FENELON BIRD (Jan. 2, 1841–Oct. 26, 1901), music teacher, was born in the village of Greensburg, Trumbull County, Ohio. He was the son of a minister in the "Free Will" Baptist denomination, David Lyman Rice, who, with his wife, Emily Johnson, was deeply interested in church music. His grandfather was David Rice [*q.v.*], a well-known Presbyterian pioneer in Virginia and Kentucky. He began the study of music quite early in life, but with the limited opportunities of a small town. In 1856 his father became a member of the board of trustees of the newly established Baptist College at Hillsdale, Mich., in which capacity he served until 1886, part of the time as financial agent of the college and for one year (1857) as chairman of the board. This change enabled Fenelon to enter Hillsdale College in 1858 where he was in attendance three years, but there is no record of his graduation. By this time he had decided on music as a profession, for he had gained some experience as a teacher of voice while in college. Going to Boston in 1861, he studied there under J. W. Tufts, B. F. Baker, and Edwin Bruce at the Boston Music School, from which he was graduated in 1863. During this time he held various organ positions. Soon after his graduation he became an instructor in music at Hillsdale College, where he remained until 1867. On Sept. 26, 1863, he married Helen Maria Libby, a graduate of Maine State Seminary and an accomplished singer. In 1867 they went to Leipzig, at that time the musical center of Germany. Here Rice studied piano with Papperitz, Moscheles, and Plaidy, and harmony with Richter, while his wife devoted herself to voice study and French. Upon their return to America in 1869 Rice was appointed instructor in music at Oberlin College where he became associated with George W. Steele, who was then in charge of a private school of music affiliated with Oberlin College. In 1871 he became director of this school (which from that time was known as the Oberlin Conservatory of Music), a position which he held until his death.

At first he taught theory and history, but the

institution grew so rapidly that he was soon compelled to give up all teaching and devote his entire time to administration. In January 1885 the Conservatory was made a definite department of Oberlin College, and Rice became professor of music, as well as director of the Conservatory. That the school developed into one of the leading schools of music in America was due largely to his artistic ideals and his powers of organization. Soon after taking charge there he interested his teachers in raising the standards and outlined the features essential to the development of a superior school. He took as his model the best European conservatories, especially Leipzig, in demanding a broad, thorough musical culture, and stressed especially the study of the classical literature of music. He saw very early that the Conservatory must have a permanent home with all necessary facilities and he succeeded in interesting his lifelong friend, Dr. Lucien Warner of New York City, an alumnus of Oberlin, who, with Mrs. Warner, contributed funds for the well-equipped building, Warner Hall, the complete construction of which took many years. In 1900 Rice Memorial Hall was added. Rice's plan was not only to educate students, but to encourage the development of teachers for his own school by persuading graduate students to go abroad for further study. In addition to his work, he built up and for thirty years directed Oberlin's musical organization, the Musical Union. In 1880–81 he was president of the Music Teachers National Association. He died in Oberlin, survived by his widow and one son.

[Printed sources include: W. S. B. Mathews, *A Hundred Years of Music in America* (1889); D. L. Leonard, *The Story of Oberlin* (1898); W. B. Allen, *A Hist. of Ky.* (1872); *Music*, Dec. 1901; and the *Cleveland Plain Dealer*, Oct. 27, 1901. Information as to certain facts was supplied for this sketch by Rice's associates, by Clarence S. Brigham of the Am. Antiquarian Soc., by Dr. W. G. Spencer, president of Hillsdale Coll., and by Rice's son, Louis M. Rice.]

F. L. G. C.

RICE, HENRY MOWER (Nov. 29, 1816–Jan. 15, 1894), Minnesota pioneer, United States senator, Indian commissioner, was born in Waitsfield, Vt., the son of Edmund and Ellen (Durkee) Rice, both descendants of early New England ancestors. He was an elder brother of Edmund Rice [*q.v.*]. At the age of nineteen, with an academy education supplemented by two years of law study, he went to Michigan, where he was employed on a survey for the Sault Ste. Marie canal and in a mercantile house in Kalamazoo. In 1839 he went to Fort Snelling, in what is now Minnesota, where he was engaged to manage a sutler's business, and the following summer he became post sutler at Fort Atkinson, Iowa. In 1842 he went to Prairie du Chien to engage in trade with the Winnebago, and in 1847, after those Indians had accepted a reservation in Minnesota in exchange for their Iowa lands, he moved to Mendota, Minn., and conducted the trade with the Winnebago and the Mississippi Chippewa. The remarkable influence that Rice acquired with the Indians is evidenced by the fact that the Winnebago intrusted him with the selection of their new home. He was probably more influential than any other person in procuring the large Chippewa cessions in Minnesota. On Mar. 29, 1849, Rice married Matilda Whitall of Richmond, Va., and established his residence in St. Paul.

By this time he had become one of the most prominent and influential men in the region. That winter he spent some time in Washington lobbying for the bill to establish Minnesota Territory, and it was due largely to his efforts that the bill was passed. He was elected territorial delegate to Congress in 1853 and was reëlected in 1855. His service was marked by extraordinary activity and efficiency in furthering the interests of the territory and of his constituents. He procured the extension of the preëmption right over unsurveyed lands in Minnesota, the establishment of post offices and land offices, and the extension of territorial roads; and his influence was a large factor in obtaining the congressional land grant of 1857 in aid of Minnesota railroads and in procuring the passage of the Minnesota enabling act. With the admission of Minnesota as a state in 1858 he became a member of the Senate. Rice was a Democrat and while the Southern states were seceding he strongly advocated compromise and opposed coercion. Once convinced, however, that his constituents approved of the war, he gave it his hearty support and, as a member of the committee on military affairs, rendered valuable service in connection with the mobilization of troops. His term in the Senate ended in 1863 and in 1865 he was defeated as candidate for governor of Minnesota. His last important public service was performed as a member of the United States Chippewa Commission to carry out the provisions of the act of 1889 for the relief and civilization of the Chippewa Indians in Minnesota. He served on the board of regents of the University of Minnesota and as president of the Minnesota Historical Society. During many years he conducted successful operations in connection with Indian contracts, railroads, and town sites; and he was active in promoting the development of St. Paul, where he owned considerable property.

Rice was ambitious, talented, and shrewd. "He divined with an unerring instinct the motives of men and parties, and knew when and how by appropriate suggestion to let them apparently move themselves towards his desired ends" (W. W. Folwell, *Minnesota, the North Star State,* 1908, p. 103). His gracious manners, tact and address, and engaging personal presence won him popularity among Indians as well as among white men of all sorts and conditions. A Minnesota county bears his name and his effigy has been placed in Statuary Hall in the national capitol. He died in San Antonio, Tex. Of his nine children, four survived him.

[W. W. Folwell, *A Hist. of Minn.* (1921–30), esp. vols. I and II; *Minn. Hist. Soc. Colls.,* IX (1901), pp. 180, 625, 654–58; T. M. Newson, *Pen Pictures of St. Paul* (1886), pp. 128–38; J. F. Williams, *A Hist. of the City of Saint Paul* (1876), pp. 185–90; E. D. Neill, *The Hist. of Minn.* (1882), pp. 498–500; M. B. Jones, *Hist. of the Town of Waitsfield, Vt.* (1909); *Daily Pioneer Press* (St. Paul), Jan. 16, 1894.]   S. J. B.

RICE, ISAAC LEOPOLD (Feb. 22, 1850–Nov. 2, 1915), lawyer, financier, chess expert, was born at Wachenheim, Bavaria, a son of Mayer and Fanny (Sohn) Rice. When he was six years old the family emigrated to America, settling at Philadelphia, where Isaac attended the public grade schools and the Central High School and was instructed by private tutors. At sixteen he was studying literature and music in Paris. Returning after three years to the United States, he wrote for the press and taught in order to support himself while continuing his studies. In 1875 he published an original treatise entitled *What Is Music?* Later his interests turned to jurisprudence and he completed the courses then offered at the Columbia Law School in New York City (LL.B. 1880), remaining six years after graduation as a teacher and advanced student. At that time Prof. John W. Burgess was laying the foundations of the Columbia School of Political Science. Rice was keenly interested in that work and served as librarian for the embryo school (Burgess, in *Columbia University Quarterly,* December 1930).

Thus far an academic career had been indicated for Rice, but in 1886 his thoughts were turned to the practice of the law and his success in several important corporation cases confirmed his attraction to that field. After winning a suit for the bondholders of a Brooklyn traction system, he acted as counsel for various railroad companies in a period of reorganization. In that capacity he served the St. Louis Southwestern and the Texas & Pacific. In the consolidation of the Richmond & West Point Terminal Railway Company and other carriers which

finally resulted in the Southern Railway, he was counsel and director. Still more conspicuous was his part in the formation of the "Reading Company," to settle the difficulties of the Philadelphia & Reading, and his subsequent connection with the affairs of that railroad. He was an early promoter of electrical inventions, and was especially interested in the storage-battery and electric-vehicle industries in their early days, but his holdings in those industries and practically all his possessions, save his stock in the Electric Boat Company, which held submarine patents then non-productive, were swept away in the money panic of 1907. Early in the World War, however, Great Britain placed large contracts with the Electric Boat Company, whose shares quickly rose on the market from $10 to $125, and in July 1915 Rice sold 16,000 shares at a profit of more than $2,000,000; if he had retained them three months longer he might have realized $16,000,000.

During the last twenty years of his life, it is probably not too much to say that Rice had a wider reputation as inventor of the Rice gambit in chess than as a lawyer. He had been a devotee of chess from his early youth and it is related that his first client came to him as the result of a chess game in which Rice made an impressive display of skill. He was also known as the founder (in 1886) and chief proprietor of the *Forum,* a magazine patterned after the English reviews. This publication, always maintained on a high literary level, was for many years run at a financial loss. In 1885 Rice married Julia Hyneman Barnett of New Orleans. After his death she and a daughter succeeded in keeping the *Forum* alive during a difficult period of readjustment. Mrs. Rice was also active in the anti-noise movement in New York. There were four daughters and two sons from the marriage, all of whom survived their father.

[*Who's Who in America,* 1914–15; *N. Y. Times,* Nov. 3, 1915; *Am. Chess Bull.,* Dec. 1915; J. H. Duckworth, "A War-Made Millionaire," in *Am. Magazine,* Jan. 1916; *The Rice Gambit* (1898), ed. by S. Lipschutz, and *The Rice Gambit* (5th ed., privately printed, 1910), ed. by Emanuel Lasker.]   W. B. S.

RICE, JOHN HOLT (Nov. 28, 1777–Sept. 3, 1831), Presbyterian clergyman, educator, was born in Bedford County, Va., the son of Benjaman Rice, an impecunious lawyer, and Catherine Holt, his wife, and a nephew of the Rev. David Rice [*q.v.*]. He was educated under various masters, spent a year and a half at Liberty Hall Academy, and a period of equal length at an academy for boys in New London. In his eighteenth year he took charge of a family school at Malvern Hills, below Richmond; the next year

(1796) he became a tutor at Hampden-Sydney College; in 1799 he conducted a family school in the house of Major Morton at "Willington," and the following year, a similar school in the home of Josiah Smith in Powhatan; in 1800 he returned to teach at Hampden-Sydney. On July 9, 1802, he married Anne Smith Morton, the daughter of Major Morton of "Willington"; there were no children.

While at Hampden-Sydney he determined to study for the ministry, and followed, though unsystematically, a course mapped out for him by Archibald Alexander [q.v.], then president of the college. He was licensed by Hanover Presbytery in 1803, and ordained on Sept. 29, 1804. From 1804 to 1812 he was pastor of the Presbyterian Church on Cub Creek. During this period he cultivated a small farm, with the aid of a few slaves; conducted a school for boys to supplement his inadequate salary; and for a part of the time (1806–08) acted as an agent for the Presbytery of Hanover in raising funds for a theological school to be established at Hampden-Sydney. In 1812, at the invitation of a few Presbyterians, he went to Richmond, and established the first Presbyterian Church of that city, of which he was pastor until 1823. He organized the Virginia Bible Society in 1813 and aided in the formation of the American Bible Society in 1816; edited a weekly (later a bi-weekly) religious newspaper, the *Christian Monitor,* from July 8, 1815, to Aug. 30, 1817, and the *Virginia Evangelical and Literary Magazine,* a monthly, from January 1818 to December 1828. In this periodical he offered strong protest, on religious grounds, to the appointment of Thomas Cooper [q.v.] as professor in the University of Virginia (Dumas Malone, *The Public Life of Thomas Cooper,* 1926, pp. 239–41). Rice also formed a company for the publication of Christian literature; organized the Young Men's Missionary Society of Richmond; and took the lead in promoting home missionary activity throughout Virginia. In 1819 he was elected Moderator of the General Assembly of the Presbyterian Church, and in 1822, president of the College of New Jersey, which call he declined.

On Jan. 1, 1824, he became professor of theology in the Theological Seminary at Hampden-Sydney (later Union Theological Seminary), the activities of which had been suspended since the death of Dr. Moses Hoge [q.v.] in 1820. The organization, equipment, and development of this institution, the first of its kind in the South, was the great work of his life. In 1830 he commenced in the *Southern Religious Telegraph* a series of letters addressed to James Mad-

ison, which aroused keen interest throughout the state. They were published in 1832 under the title *Historical and Philosophical Considerations on Religion: Addressed to James Madison Esq., Late President of the United States.* In 1831 he wrote "Project of an Overture to be Submitted to the Next General Assembly," in which he declared that "the Presbyterian Church . . . is a Missionary Society." This overture stimulated the organization of the Presbyterian Board of Foreign Missions. Rice died in his fifty-fourth year after a prolonged illness.

Rice was fully six feet tall, habitually slow in his physical motions, hesitating in his public speech, but a brilliant writer. A thorough Calvinist, he was nevertheless a man of irenic temper and catholic spirit. In addition to numerous sermons and the letters mentioned above, he published *An Illustration of the Character & Conduct of the Presbyterian Church in Virginia* (1816); *The Pamphleteer, No. 1, Essay on Baptism* (1819), *No. 2, Irenicum or the Peacemaker* (1820); *A Review of 'The Doctrines of the Church, Vindicated from the Misrepresentations of Dr. John Rice, &'* (1827); and *Memoir of James Brainerd Taylor* (1833), in collaboration with B. H. Rice.

[William Maxwell, *A Memoir of the Rev. John H. Rice, D.D.* (1835); W. H. Foote, *Sketches of Va.: Hist. and Biog.,* 2 ser. (1855); W. B. Sprague, *Annals of the Am. Pulpit,* vol. IV (1858); *Union Sem. Mag.,* vol. IX (1898); H. A. White, *Southern Presbyterian Leaders* (1911); *Richmond Enquirer,* Sept. 16, 1831.]
E. T. T.

RICE, LUTHER (Mar. 25, 1783–Sept. 25, 1836), Baptist clergyman, promoter of missionary and educational organizations, was born in Northboro, Mass., a descendant of Edmund Rice who settled in Sudbury, Mass., before 1639, and the ninth child of Capt. Amos Rice, who served in the Revolutionary army and had married Sarah Graves of Shrewsbury. Luther's meager public-school education was interrupted at sixteen, when, under circumstances showing initiative on his part, he secured employment that involved a voyage to Georgia. The reading of books which decades earlier had influenced the Great Awakening largely shaped his religious experience and incited him to prepare for the Congregationalist ministry. After three years at Leicester Academy, he entered Williams College in the sophomore class, graduating in 1810. From 1810 to 1812 he was a student in the recently opened Andover Theological Seminary. Both at Williamstown and at Andover he actively connected with the Society of Inquiry on the Subject of Missions and associated with those whose address to the Massachusetts General Association of Ministers led to the organization of the American Board of Commissioners for Foreign Missions. His request to join the four men appointed by that body for missionary service was granted on condition that he provide the funds for outfit and passage; in this task, after strenuous efforts, he was successful, and was ordained with the others in the famous service at Salem, Feb. 6, 1812. Sailing from Philadelphia, on Aug. 10, 1812, he arrived in Calcutta.

During the voyage Rice made some study of the question of baptism, two of his fellow-voyagers being English Baptist missionaries. On the arrival of Adoniram Judson [q.v.] Rice found that he too was concerned with the same question. Judson was immersed Sept. 6 and Rice on Nov. 1, following. Having thus severed their Congregational affiliation, Judson and Rice agreed that the circumstances required the return of Rice to America to adjust matters there and to secure support from the Baptists. Reaching New York on Sept. 7, 1813, Rice went to Boston to obtain a discharge from further obligations to the American Board. Thereafter, for more than twenty years, he devoted himself to organizing the Baptists of America for missionary and educational work. According to Prof. William H. Whitsitt (Pollard, *post*, p. 125), "The coming of Luther Rice was the most important event in Baptist history in the nineteenth century." Far more clearly than any other up to his time, he sensed the religious task of the American Baptists as a whole. He at once turned his attention to the establishment of a national denominational organization for foreign missionary endeavor, visiting Boston, New York, Philadelphia, Baltimore, Washington, Richmond, and Charleston, attending meetings of associations, and consulting with eminent leaders. Largely as a result of his activities, at a meeting held in Philadelphia in May 1814 there was organized what became popularly known as the Triennial Convention—for years the chief active symbol of American Baptist unity. Throughout the remainder of his life, in journeys covering thousands of miles yearly, he presented the missionary cause to the Baptists of the United States. Very early he recognized the necessity for an educated ministry and saw the strategic importance of a Baptist college and theological seminary at the national capital. While he became most directly concerned with the founding and development of Columbian College at Washington (later George Washington University), he was also instrumental in the establishment of numerous Baptist educational institutions throughout the area of his travels.

He saw the need of supplementing his personal efforts by the use of the printing-press, and as a result a religious weekly, *The Columbian Star*, was established. Later developments of his ideas led to the organization of the American Baptist Home Mission Society and the American Baptist Publication Society. Rice became so much involved in the financial problems of Columbian College that Baron Stow [q.v.] published insinuations reflecting on his character and his reputation became temporarily clouded. It is now evident, however, that he was absolutely honest and that the questionable situations arose from his attempting to carry along, with inadequate assistance, several separate but somewhat inter-related enterprises. With only his own personal requirements to care for—the only woman with whom he fell in love having refused to go with him to the foreign field—he gave unstinted and self-sacrificial devotion to the causes which he promoted. By Baptists he is regarded as the most potent statesman of their denomination in his generation.

[The manuscript journal of Luther Rice, in so far as it is known to be extant, consists of eight parts, five of which are at Hamilton, N. Y., in the Samuel Colgate Baptist Hist. Coll., the other three (Nos. 3, 5 and 8) being at George Washington University; J. B. Taylor's *Memoir of Rev. Luther Rice, One of the First American Missionaries to the East* (1840) contains numerous letters from and to Rice; E. B. Pollard's *Luther Rice, Pioneer in Missions and Education* (1928), completed by D. G. Stevens, is based largely upon Taylor; see also A. H. Ward, *A Geneal. Hist. of the Rice Family* (1858), J. C. Kent, *Northborough Hist.* (1921), pp. 288–89, and J. L. Hill, *The Immortal Seven, Judson and His Associates* (1913).]

W. H. A.

RICE, NATHAN LEWIS (Dec. 29, 1807–June 11, 1877), Presbyterian clergyman, teacher, and writer, was born on a farm in Garrard County, Ky., the son of Gabriel and Phebe (Harrett) Rice. During the first sixteen years of his life he lived on his father's farm and attended local schools. He then began teaching to earn money to attend college, and in the fall of 1826 entered Centre College at Danville, remaining there but two years. While in college he studied theology under the president, Dr. Gideon Blackburn [q.v.], and was licensed to preach by Transylvania Presbytery on Oct. 4, 1828. He immediately received a call to Harmony, his home church, but, declining it, entered Princeton Theological Seminary, where he spent two years. On Oct. 3, 1832, he married Catherine P. Burch, daughter of Rev. James K. Burch. He was ordained on June 8, 1833, and during his ministry served the following Presbyterian churches: Bardstown, Ky. (1833–41); Woodford and Paris, Ky. (1841–44); Central, Cincinnati

(1845–53); Second, St. Louis (1853–58); North, Chicago (1858–61); and Fifth Avenue, New York (1861–67). In all these places he made a distinguished success as preacher and pastor.

He was also actively interested in education. While pastor at Bardstown he founded a school for boys and another for girls. During his ministry in Chicago he served as professor of theology in the Theological Seminary of the Northwest, and helped to influence Cyrus H. McCormick [q.v.], one of his parishioners, to make large contributions to that institution, which later came to be known as McCormick Theological Seminary. After he retired from the pastorate, he was president of Westminster College, Fulton, Mo. (1869–74), and professor of theology in the Danville Theological Seminary, Ky. (1874–77). In addition to his work as minister and professor he successively served as editor of the *Western Protestant* (Bardstown), the *St. Louis Presbyterian,* and the *Presbyterian Expositor* (Chicago). He was distinguished as a controversial debater on religious subjects. The most famous of his debates was with Alexander Campbell [q.v.] in Lexington, Ky., in 1843 on the meaning and mode of baptism. Campbell, the founder of the Disciples of Christ, contended for immersion as the prescribed mode. The debate continued from Nov. 15 to Dec. 2, and Henry Clay presided over some of its sessions. The printed report, *A Debate Between Rev. A. Campbell and Rev. N. L. Rice on . . . Christian Baptism* (1844), is a volume of 912 pages. In 1845 he held a prolonged debate with Dr. Jonathan Blanchard, a Presbyterian minister of Cincinnati, on the subject of slavery, which was published the following year. Rice took the ground that the institution of slavery is not necessarily sinful in itself. He also had a public debate in 1850 with Archbishop John B. Purcell [q.v.] on the doctrines of the Roman Catholic Church. Among his publications were *Romanism the Enemy of Free Institutions and Christianity* (1851); *Baptism, the Design, Mode, and Subjects* (1855); *The Signs of the Times* (1855); *Lectures on Slavery* (1860); *The Pulpit: Its Relations to Our National Crisis* (1862); *Immortality* (1871). Rice was a man of extraordinary energy and industry; usually he carried the work of about three men. He was an effective preacher, a keen debater, a pungent writer, and an inspiring teacher. Many honors were bestowed upon him, among them, election in 1855 as Moderator of the General Assembly of the Presbyterian Church. He died at Chatham, Ky., and was buried at Fulton, Mo.

[*Necrological Report Presented to the Alumni Asso. of Princeton Theol. Sem.* (1878); L. J. Halsey, *A Hist. of the McCormick Theol. Sem.* (1893); M. M. Fisher and J. J. Rice, *Hist. of Westminster Coll.* (1903); Alfred Nevin, *Encyc. of the Presbyt. Church* (1884).]

W. L. L.

RICE, RICHARD HENRY (Jan. 9, 1863– Feb. 10, 1922), engineer, inventor, was born in Rockland, Me., the son of Albert Smith and Frances W. (Baker) Rice and a descendant of Deacon Edmund Rice, who settled in Sudbury, Mass., before 1639. His grandfather was a prominent railway executive, and his father served as a representative in the Maine legislature. Rice received his early education in his native town, and in 1881, being particularly interested in engineering, he entered Stevens Institute of Technology, Hoboken, N. J. After his graduation in 1885 with the degree of mechanical engineer, he spent a year in Dennison, Ohio, as a special apprentice with the Pittsburgh, Cincinnati, and St. Louis Railway; then he entered the employ of the Bath Iron Works, Bath, Me., as a draftsman. In 1887 he accepted the position of designer and chief draftsman with E. D. Leavitt [q.v.], engineer of the Calumet and Hecla Mining Company in Cambridgeport, Mass., and in the course of the succeeding four years gained a reputation as an able engineer and machine designer. This brought him the position (1891–94) of general superintendent of the William A. Harris Steam Engine Company at Providence, R. I., an office he resigned when he organized the Rice and Sargent Engine Company in Providence to manufacture steam engines invented jointly by himself and his partner. He held the office of secretary and treasurer of the company until it was merged with the Providence Engineering Company in 1899; he was treasurer of the latter until 1903, when he resigned to enter the General Electric Company at Lynn, Mass. Here for fifteen years he directed work on the development of the steam turbine; in 1918 he was made general manager of the works. He was serving in this capacity at the time of his sudden death. From the very beginning of his engineering career Rice demonstrated a marked inventive talent and in the course of his life was the recipient of some fifty patents. "Chief among his original creations was the design of the first turbo-blower for blast furnaces to be installed in America, though of equal value were the Rice and Sargent steam engines designed jointly with John W. Sargent. These were recognized as among the best slow and medium speed steam engines in the country and were produced by the Rice and Sargent Engine Company between 1894 and 1903. In his early work at Lynn, Mr. Rice designed the smaller ratings of Curtis turbines up to 5,000 horse-power" (*Steam*, March 1922, p. 90). For the first two years of its existence he was president of the Associated Industries of Massachusetts; he served as president of the National Conference of State Manufacturers' Associations and was a member of the Lynn Fuel Commission during the World War. He also found time to write a number of technical papers dealing with the steam turbine. Rice was both a skilled engineer and an able executive and was widely recognized for fairness, justice, and honesty of purpose, as well as a thorough understanding of industrial problems. In 1924 the General Electric Company established and endowed in his memory the Richard H. Rice Scholarship at Stevens Institute. Rice was married first in 1887 to Mary Sue Durgin of Concord, N. H., who died in 1891, and on Mar. 26, 1898, to Alice Woodman Kimball, who with two daughters by his first wife survived him.

[*Who's Who in America*, 1916–17; F. D. Furman, *Morton Memorial*; *A Hist. of the Stevens Inst. of Tech.* (1905); *Stevens Indicator*, May 15, 1922; *General Electric Rev.*, Mar. 1922; *Trans. Am. Soc. Mech. Engineers*, vol. XLIV (1923); G. T. Little, *Geneal. and Family Hist. of the State of Me.* (1909), vol. IV; *Boston Post*, Feb. 12, 1922.]   C. W. M.

RICE, THOMAS DARTMOUTH (May 20, 1808–Sept. 19, 1860), "the father of American minstrelsy," was born of poor parents in New York City. Although trained as a wood carver, he early became a supernumerary at the Park Theatre. Abandoning his work as an artisan, he took to the open road as an itinerant player, and made his way to the Ohio Valley frontier, where he was employed, under the management of Noah Miller Ludlow [*q.v.*] in Ludlow and Smith's Southern Theatre in Louisville, Ky., as property man, lamp lighter and stage carpenter. In 1828, he played minor stock parts, and between acts, presented negro imitations. It was as an interpolation between the acts of Solon Robinson's *The Rifle* that Rice first sang and jumped "Jim Crow." He found the pattern for his stage success in the performance of a negro whom he encountered in Louisville, cleaning the horses in the stable-yard near the theatre where Rice was employed, crooning an odd melody, doing a curious shuffling step whenever he reached the chorus of his song, and ending with a little jump which set his "heel-a-rickin." Rice apparently concluded that an imitation of the walk and dress of this negro would be welcomed by American audiences as a variation from the stage Irishman with his shillalah. He memorized the old stanzas, improvised many new ones

to fit local situations, and his song and dance became a minstrel sensation. He was equally successful in his mimicry of the plantation hand and in his later creation of "the dandy negro." Though the stanzas multiplied by the hundreds, the chorus of "Jim Crow" remained the same:

"First on de heel tap, den on de toe,
  Ebery time I wheel about I jump Jim Crow.
  Wheel about and turn about and do jis so,
  And ebery time I wheel about I jump Jim Crow."

In 1828–29, Rice appeared at the Columbia Theatre in Cincinnati, Ohio. In Pittsburgh, Pa., where he repeated his success as the impersonator of the shiftless "Jim Crow," William Cumming Peters [*q.v.*] prepared the song for publication. It became the "song hit" of America and England. Nov. 12, 1832, marked his first New York appearance in the rôle of "Jim Crow." In turn, he visited Philadelphia, Boston, and Washington. In the national capital, he used as a partner the four-year-old Joseph Jefferson, 1829–1905 [*q.v.*], dressed as a miniature "Jim Crow." In 1836, he played with phenomenal success at the Surrey Theatre in London, and negro minstrelsy became so popular there, that for the next generation American minstrel troupes made extended tours through the British Isles.

He wrote numerous negro extravaganzas and thus helped to create what was known as "Ethiopian Opera." In these "operas," he introduced old negro songs into his own libretto. His most popular pieces were a negro burlesque of *Othello*, *Bone Squash Diavolo*—a travesty on *Fra Diavolo*, *Long Island Juba* (first produced on Jan. 9, 1833), *Jumbo Jum*, *Ginger Blue*, and *Jim Crow in London* (first produced on Sept. 4, 1837). These burlesques were the patterns for the skits which became fixed parts of minstrel-show programs in later years. Although he was not the first burnt-cork performer, it was Rice's phenomenal success that brought in the vogue for "negro specialists." In the 1840's, the standard American minstrel show evolved from these specialties, and became a unique American contribution to the history of the stage. Negro minstrelsy remained the most popular American form of entertainment from 1840 to 1880. Rice himself played in few minstrel companies. He preferred to act alone, or between the acts of other plays. Charley White's Serenaders and Wood's Minstrels were among the few minstrel troupes to enlist his talents.

Although one of the greatest drawing cards of his day at the box office, Rice indulged in so many extravagances and eccentricities that he was in real financial distress when he died in

New York City, the victim of paralysis. On June 18, 1837, he had married Charlotte B. Gladstone of London, England. He was buried beside his wife and their infant children in Greenwood Cemetery, Brooklyn, N. Y.

[Carl Wittke, *Tambo and Bones: A Hist. of the Am. Minstrel Stage* (1930); Arthur Hornblow, *A Hist. of the Theatre in America* (1919), vol. II; T. Allston Brown, *Hist. of the Am. Stage* (1870); Dailey Paskman and Sigmund Spaeth, *Gentlemen, Be Seated* (1928); Ed. LeRoy Rice, *Monarchs of Minstrelsy* (1911); *Frank Leslie's Illustrated Newspaper*, Oct. 6, 1860; *Literary Digest*, Mar. 11, 1916; *N. Y. Times*, Sept. 20, 21, 1860.]   C. W.

RICE, VICTOR MOREAU (Apr. 5, 1818– Oct. 18, 1869), educator, was born at Mayville, in Chautauqua County, N. Y., the son of William and Rachel (Waldo) Rice. His early education was obtained in the schools of his native town, and in 1841 he graduated from Allegheny College, Meadville, Pa. Moving from Mayville to Buffalo in 1843, he secured employment as a teacher of Latin, language, penmanship, and bookkeeping in a private school, which subsequently became the Buffalo high school. After graduating from college he had begun the study of law privately and in 1845 was admitted to the bar. That same year he opened an evening commercial school for young people with daily occupations. From 1846 to 1848 he was the editor of the *Cataract*, afterward the *Western Temperance Standard*. He was elected city superintendent of schools in Buffalo in 1852 and in 1853 was chosen president of the New York State Teachers' Association, with which he had been prominently identified for several years.

On Apr. 4, 1854, a legislative act established a new department of the state government to administer the common-school system, known as the State Department of Public Instruction, with a state superintendent of public instruction to be chosen by the legislature, at its head. To this office Rice was elected. He at once organized the new department, vigorously enforced the provisions of the common-school law, secured the establishment of the office of local school commissioner, and effected a revision of the state tax laws, thereby largely increasing the subsidy for public schools. He recommended the establishment of more normal schools, a more liberal appropriation for teachers' institutes, and a uniform day for the holding of annual district school meetings. Returning to Buffalo after the completion of his term, he was elected a Republican member of the state assembly and served as chairman of the committee on colleges, academies, and common schools. On Feb. 1, 1862, he was returned to the office of superintendent of public instruction, was reëlected in 1865, and served

until Apr. 7, 1868. During his second incumbency many progressive steps were taken. A training school for primary teachers was established at Oswego, which later became a state normal school. Provision was also made for other normal schools at Cortland, Fredonia, Potsdam, Geneseo, Brockport, and Buffalo. Teachers' institutes were strengthened and attendance upon them greatly increased. The most conspicuous accomplishment of Rice's superintendency, however, was the abolition of the odious rate bill and the final establishment of free schools throughout the state. The principle that the property of the state should educate the children of the state was one that many public-spirited citizens had fought vigorously to establish, but it remained for Rice to incorporate it into the basic education law, and thereby to erect a memorable milestone in the state's history of education.

Upon his retirement from the superintendency in 1868, he became president of the American Popular Life Insurance Company. He was afterward president of the Metropolitan Bank of New York City. On Nov. 26, 1846, he married Maria L. Winter.

[Annual reports of the superintendent of public instruction, N. Y., 1854–57, 1862–68, and 1903; A. W. Young, *Hist. of Chautauqua County* (1875); *N. Y. Times*, Oct. 20, 1869.]   H. H. H.

RICE, WILLIAM MARSH (Mar. 14, 1816– Sept. 23, 1900), merchant and founder of the William Marsh Rice Institute, a university of liberal and technical learning in the city of Houston, Tex., was born in Springfield, Mass. He was the third in a family of ten children, his parents being David and Patty (Hall) Rice. At the age of fifteen he left school to become a clerk in a village store. On his twenty-first birthday he had saved enough money to buy a store from its proprietor. After the panic of 1837, however, times were hard and he decided to move to Houston, Tex., where with a small stock of goods he arrived in the autumn of 1838.

Houston was then only a straggling village, but it was connected with the port of Galveston by a navigable bayou, and was accordingly the natural rendezvous for farmers who sometimes drove their wagons called "schooners" two or even three hundred miles to find a market for their produce. The wagons returned loaded with imported goods to serve until the next visit. To these visitors the merchant was importer, exporter, and banker. In this situation, by a remarkable combination of energy, thrift, and Yankee shrewdness, Rice soon rose from a clerkship in a mercantile establishment to be senior partner in the firm of Rice & Nichols, "Exporters, Importers and Wholesale Grocers, of Houston," which was favorably known from the Gulf to the Red River. As his business increased, he became interested in other enterprises—a stage line to Austin, a railroad to Dallas—and, though he preferred other investments, was frequently compelled to accept land in payment for debts. At the time of his death he was the owner of many thousands of acres in Texas and Louisiana, and his whole estate was estimated to be worth eight million dollars.

In his prosperity, the rising merchant did not forget his family. He was joined first by his elder brother, David, who did not prove successful, and later, in 1850, by a younger brother, Frederick A. Rice, a genial person who became a prosperous banker and left a large family, most of whom later became prominent in the affairs of Houston. Though Rice was twice married—first in 1850 to Margaret Bremond, the daughter of an early railroad builder, who died in 1863, and on June 26, 1867, to a widow, Mrs. Elizabeth (Baldwin) Brown, whose sister had married his brother—he had no children by either marriage. His reputation for eccentricity was increased by the humorous skepticism with which he tended to regard the theological view of his neighbors. He was a Unionist, and at the outbreak of the Civil War withdrew to Matamoras, Mexico, where he continued, in spite of the blockade, to do business as an exporter and importer. At the end of the war he moved to New York where he acted for some years as the financial and purchasing agent for the Houston & Texas Central Railroad, of which he had been one of the builders. During this period he lived on his farm at Dunellen, N. J., removing after the death of his wife in 1896 to an apartment on Madison Avenue. In his last years, his only companion was his valet, Charles F. Jones.

In the meantime he had been considering a suitable memorial, and in 1891, on the occasion of a visit to Houston, he had made definite plans for an educational institution to be opened after his death. In his will, executed in 1896, he made the foundation, to which he had already contributed preliminary gifts, the chief beneficiary of his estate. His death in 1900 was followed by sensational disclosures. The valet, Jones, confessed that he had entered into a plot including extensive forgeries, among them a new will, for the benefit of a lawyer named Albert T. Patrick. From forgery the conspirators had finally gone the length of murder. Patrick, as the principal in this plot, was convicted

and sentenced to death, but supported by large means, secured a series of reprieves and, finally, in 1912, a full pardon. In the same year the Rice Institute, with an endowment conservatively estimated at ten million dollars, had opened its doors to its first students.

[See J. A. Baker, "Reminiscences of the Founder," *The Rice Institute Pamphlets*, vol. XVIII, no. 3, July 1931; E. O. Lovett, "The Foundation, Its History," *Ibid.*, vol. I, no. 1 (Apr. 1915); S. O. Young, *A Thumb Nail Hist. of the City of Houston, Tex.* (1912); B. H. Carroll, *Standard Hist. of Houston, Tex.* (1912); Arthur Train, "The Patrick Case, Complete," *Am. Magazine*, May 1907; E. L. Pearson, *Five Murders* (1928); O. P. Allen, in *Springfield Weekly Republican*, May 21, 1901; *N. Y. Times*, Sept. 25–28, Oct. 5–10, 13, 1900. Important information has been supplied by members of the Rice family. The best likeness is a statue on the campus of the Rice Institute by the sculptor, John Angel, based on a painting in the possession of W. M. Rice, Jr.]   R.G.C.

RICE, WILLIAM NORTH (Nov. 21, 1845–Nov. 13, 1928), geologist, educator, was born at Marblehead, Mass., the son of William Rice, a Methodist minister, and Caroline (North) Rice, a native of Lowell, Mass. He was descended from Edmund Rice who settled in Sudbury, Mass., in 1638. He received most of his preparation for college at Springfield High School; his life was influenced, however, by a geologist, Oliver Marcy, then instructor at Wilbraham Academy. At Wesleyan University he took the regular classical course, which allowed little freedom, but he profited much from the teaching of John M. Van Vleck, professor of mathematics and astronomy. Graduating from Wesleyan in 1865, he entered Yale College, and in 1867 received the first doctorate of philosophy in geology granted by that institution. The subject of his thesis was "The Darwinian Theory of the Origin of Species." He was immediately appointed professor of natural history and geology at Wesleyan, and after studying for a year at the University of Berlin under Röse and von Beyrich, entered upon his duties in the fall of 1868. Caleb Thomas Winchester was then an undergraduate; later Professor Van Vleck with Rice and Winchester became potent influences in the college. In sympathy with the progressive leadership of President Eliot of Harvard, they liberalized the curriculum at Wesleyan in 1873, and were largely responsible for the combined emphasis on teaching and research which has since characterized the institution.

In 1919 Rice published *The Poet of Science and Other Addresses*, in which appears his own key to his life: "The study of the relations of science and religion, which has seemed to me probably the most important part of my lifework, has required the division of my time and interest between the two great territories of thought whose relations to each other I have sought in some degree to interpret. In a certain sense, therefore, I have lived a double life, functioning sometimes, so to speak, as the Reverend Doctor Jekyll, and sometimes as Professor Hyde" (p. 75). Until 1884 he taught botany, zoölogy, physiology, and mineralogy. Thereafter he taught but one class outside the field of geology. The lectures of that course were published in 1903 under the title *Christian Faith in an Age of Science*. The spirit of the book, which is his best-known work, may be gathered from words in its closing paragraph: "The scientific questions of our age and of all ages touch not the central truth of Christianity 'that God was in Christ, reconciling the world unto himself'" (pp. 411–12). Within the field of geology, he was most interested in the paleontological evidence for evolution. He assisted Prof. William Morris Davis in his study of the Connecticut Triassic deposits and was congratulated by Davis on his brilliant solution of the structural problems concerning Cedar Mountain. His greatest service to the science was rendered as first superintendent of the Connecticut State Geological and Natural History Survey, 1903–16. With Prof. H. E. Gregory of Yale, he wrote a *Manual of the Geology of Connecticut* (1906), while the other publications of the survey (vols. I–XXV) profited by his careful editorial work.

Rice was president of the American Society of Naturalists (1891), vice-president of the Geological Society of America (1911), and vice-president and chairman of Section E of the American Association for the Advancement of Science (1905–06). He was most gratified by an engrossed testimonial presented to him by the Geological Society of America at its annual meeting at Washington, Dec. 28, 1923, recognizing his services in the reconciliation of science and religion. Many stories have implied that he was tried for heresy by the Methodist Church. It is sufficient to say that from 1896 to 1924 he was chairman of the board of examiners which passed upon the orthodoxy of ministers entering the New York East Conference. Favorable to church consolidation, he was a leading member of the council of the Connecticut Federation of Churches and a trustee of the West China University. He married Elizabeth W. Crowell in 1870. He died in his eighty-third year, in Delaware, Ohio, at the home of his surviving son, Edward L. Rice, professor of zoölogy at Ohio Wesleyan University.

[L. G. Westgate, "Memorial of William North Rice," with bibliography, *Bull. Geol. Soc. of America*,

Mar. 1929; Dexter North, *John North of Farmington, Conn., and His Descendants* (1921); *Ohio State Journal* (Columbus), Nov. 14, 1928; C. E. Rice, *By the Name of Rice* (1911); *Hist. of the Wesleyan Acad. at Wilbraham* (1893), pp. 163–64; information as to certain facts from Prof. E. L. Rice.]   W.G.F.

RICH, ISAAC (Oct. 24, 1801–Jan. 13, 1872), merchant, philanthropist, the eldest of the eleven children of Robert and Eunice (Harding) Rich, was born at Wellfleet, Mass. He was a descendant of Richard Rich who was in Dover, N. H., before 1673, and in 1680 moved to Eastham, Mass. Isaac received little formal education, but his business training began early. At fourteen he was in Boston, helping to support the family by selling fish on the streets and in his father's fish stall. Untiring and energetic in his salesmanship, he later delighted to tell how he was the first man who ever blew a fish-horn on the streets of Boston. When he was nineteen, his father's death forced him to be increasingly active. He opened an oyster stall in Faneuil Hall Market, and a customer loaned him $600 in order that he might increase his profits by buying in cargo lots. His first profit was $100. On this small beginning he built one of the largest fish businesses in Boston. Accumulated profits he invested in ships, some of which were built in partnership with David Snow. The Civil War caused him to turn from shipping to real estate, in which a considerable portion of his fortune was made.

As a boy selling fish, Rich had been stirred, through the kindly interest of Wilbur Fisk [*q.v.*], then a Methodist pastor in Charlestown and subsequently president of Wesleyan University, by a desire to enter the ministry. "God didn't give me a call," he said later; "I prayed for one but it didn't come." As a member of the Bromfield Street Church, however, he became one of the most prominent Methodist laymen, and his philanthropies were chiefly in connection with educational institutions of the Methodist Episcopal Church. During his lifetime, he gave to Wesleyan Academy at Wilbraham, Mass., over $50,000, and to Wesleyan University, Middletown, Conn., of which he was a trustee (1849–72), $150,000 in addition to Rich Hall. Many of his gifts were conditioned upon an equal amount being donated by others. Thus he persuaded Daniel Drew [*q.v.*] to give $100,000 to Wesleyan in 1868. Rich died in 1872, reputedly one of Boston's wealthiest men. His wife, Sarah Andrews, whom he married in 1822, and four children had predeceased him. To Boston University, a new institution which had been chartered in 1869 with Rich as one of the petitioners, he left practically his whole estate, appraised at $1,500,000. It was to be held in trust for ten years and then turned over to the University. Much of it consisted of Boston real estate holdings and, owing to inflated values, broken by the panic of 1873, and the destruction of buildings in the Boston fire of 1872, the total amount received by the University at the completion of the trust was less than $700,000.

[See *New England Hist. and Geneal. Reg.*, July, Oct. 1929, Jan. 1930; *Harper's Weekly*, Feb. 17, 1872; *Bostonia*, Oct. 1901, Mar. 1932; Geo. Prentice, *Wilbur Fisk* (1890), pp. 171, 173; Geo. Prentice, *The Life of Gilbert Haven* (1883), pp. 464–66; Wesleyan *College Argus*, Jan. 31, Feb. 14, 28, 1872; C. F. Price, *Wesleyan's First Century* (1932); *Zion's Herald*, Jan. 18, 25, Feb. 1, 1872; Suffolk County Probate Records (Boston, Mass.); *Boston Transcript*, Jan. 15, 16, 1872. A portrait and a bust by Milmore are in the custody of Boston Univ.]   R. E. M.

RICH, OBADIAH (1783–January 20, 1850), bibliographer, was born at Truro, Mass., probably in 1783; according to Truro church records, he was baptized there July 13 of that year. His parents were Obadiah Rich (1758–1805) and Salome (Lombard) Rich (1761–1807). Scion of a long line of Cape Cod sea-faring folk, he was born to the tradition of the sea rather than to familiarity with rare books and manuscripts. His father was a master mariner and commander during the Revolution of the brig *Intrepid*, a well-known privateer. About 1790 the family moved to Boston, and there Rich lived until in 1816 he was appointed American consul at Valencia, Spain, a post he held until about 1829. In 1823 he took charge of the archives of the legation in Madrid in the absence of the chargé d'affaires and continued to live there until about 1829, when he moved to London and established himself as a bookseller, later taking several of his sons into partnership. From 1834 to 1845 he held the post of American consul at Port Mahon in the Balearic Islands but spent more time in London during these years than at his official station. Soon after going abroad he married, at Gibraltar, Ann Montgomery, said to have come from the north of Ireland, by whom he had four sons and two daughters.

Rich was apparently interested in books and historical matters in his early years in Boston, for he joined the Massachusetts Historical Society in 1805 and two years later became one of the charter members of the Boston Athenæum; he was for many years a member of the American Antiquarian Society (elected 1834) and of several state historical societies. In Madrid he found opportunity to give free rein to his bibliographical instincts and became one of the most eminent book-collectors of his day. Adopting as his chief province the manuscripts and early printed books relating to America, he entered a collecting field then occupied by few and hence had the unparalleled opportunity to gather for the proverbial song the most remarkable collection of rare Americana which had been made up to that time. He so generously opened this library of source material to American historical scholars working in Spain that his invaluable assistance was acknowledged in print by such historians as Washington Irving, William H. Prescott, George Ticknor, George Bancroft and others (Allibone, *post*). Rich was instrumental in prevailing upon Irving to write the life of Columbus, and that distinguished author lived in Rich's house during a part of his stay in Madrid while engaged upon it. As a bookseller in London, Rich specialized in early Americana, turning to financial advantage the rarities procured during his years of residence in Spain. For years he acted as agent for American libraries and collectors, and many choice books and manuscripts now possessed by American institutions were gathered and furnished by him. He is now chiefly remembered by his bibliographies of books and manuscripts relating to America. Though they are in a sense only glorified booksellers' catalogues, their bibliographical information is in the main reliable and they still hold a respected place in scholarly libraries. The more important are: *A Catalogue of Books, Relating Principally to America, Arranged under the Years in Which They Were Printed* (1832); *Bibliotheca Americana Nova; or, A Catalogue of Books in Various Languages Relating to America, Printed Since the Year 1700* (2 vols., 1835–46); and *Catalogue of a Collection of Manuscripts, Principally in Spanish, Relating to America, in the Possession of O. Rich* (c. 184–). All of these are now extremely rare. Rich also wrote a little gazetteer, *A General View of the United States of America,* published in London in 1833, of which a second edition appeared three years later. He died in London January 20, 1850, in his sixty-seventh year.

[See article by Evelyn Rich, *New Eng. Hist. and Geneal. Reg.*, Apr. 1930; Archives of State Dept., Washington; S. A. Allibone, *A Crit. Dict. of Eng. Lit. and Brit. and Am. Authors* (1870), vol. II; Nicholas Trübner, *A Bibliographical Guide to Am. Lit.* (1859); W. P. Trent and G. S. Hellman, eds., *The Journals of Washington Irving* (1919), vol. III; P. M. Irving, *The Life and Letters of Washington Irving,* vol. II (1862); G. P. Winship, *The John Carter Brown Library: A History* (1914); *The Ann. Reg., 1850* (1851).]
G. B. U.

RICHARD, GABRIEL (Oct. 15, 1767–Sept. 13, 1832), Catholic missionary and educator, born at Saintes, was the son of Francis Richard, a civil servant of Rochefort, France, and Geneviève Bossuet, who was of the same general family as the famed pulpit orator. Educated at the College of Saintes and the Sulpician seminaries at Angers and Issy, he was ordained a Sulpician priest, Oct. 15, 1791, and remained to teach mathematics at Issy where he was associated with Benedict Joseph Flaget [*q.v.*] and Louis G. V. Du Bourg [*q.v.*], later bishops in the United States. Without an opportunity of visiting his family, he fled France of the Revolution (Apr. 2, 1792) with Ambrose Maréchal [*q.v.*], François Cicquard, and Francis Anthony Matignon [*q.v.*] and arrived in Baltimore, June 24, 1792. As his services were not required at the infant seminary, he was assigned by Bishop John Carroll [*q.v.*] to work among the French, half-breeds, and Indians with missionary centers at Prairie du Rocher, Kaskaskia, and Cahokia. Here his zeal and courage were equally tested by the hardships of the frontier, lack of companionship, the impiety of the settlers and furmen, and the danger of roving tribesmen. In June 1798 he arrived in Detroit with John Dilhet, S. S., as an assistant to the aged missionary, Michael Levadoux, who had labored painfully in this primitive trading center. On the latter's retirement to France, Richard succeeded as pastor of St. Anne's Church and became vicar-general of the whole region. As vicar-general he became an institution in the territory, a man of austere life, an eloquent preacher even in English, a reformer of common sense, and a picturesque figure of sepulchral bearing marked by a livid scar received in escaping a Revolutionary mob. He ministered to the Indians of the whole area at Sault Ste. Marie, Mackinac, Arbre Croche, Georgian Bay, and other fur posts; he compromised their difficulties, held French traders in check, and fought the evils of liquor. In 1802 he opened a primary school and two years later an academy for young ladies, in which he himself sought to train teachers. In 1801 he had about 520 parishioners prepared for confirmation which was performed by Bishop Denault of Quebec. In 1805, when Detroit was burned out, he led in relief work and conducted services in a tent until his church was rebuilt. Within a few years he was instrumental in establishing six primary schools, two academies, and a chapel at Côte du Nord Est, despite some difficulties with trustees over the holding of church properties. In 1809 Richard obtained from Baltimore a printing-press and a printer. On Aug. 31, 1809, there appeared the first and possibly the only issue of the *Essai du Michigan ou Observateur Impartial*, the first paper printed in Detroit.

Before the War of 1812 silenced his publishing venture, he edited a child's spelling book, several devotional books, a volume of selections from the French poets, a Bible for Indians, and the laws of Michigan. In addition to books and an organ from France, he imported carding machines, spinning wheels, and looms in an effort to stimulate local industry. A thorough American, a former official chaplain on invitation of the governor, Richard refused an oath to the king and was held by General Brock as a prisoner of war at Fort Malden near Sandwich until his release was demanded by Tecumseh. He is reputed to have prevented a massacre of prisoners through his influence with the Indians. On his return to Detroit, he engaged in relief work among the destitute who had been impoverished by military and Indian raids. Long interested in higher education, he was one of the founders of the Catholepistemiad or University of Michigania (1817), which he served as vice-president under President John Monteith, a minister, who had been graduated from Princeton. He also served as a trustee of the incipient university (1821) and became a charter member of the Michigan Historical Society (1832).

In 1821, on an order of Bishop Flaget, Richard had excommunicated a divorced parishioner who had remarried, and, on suit in the superior court, he had been assessed $1,116 as damages. Refusing to pay, he was sent to jail but released when he was elected a delegate to Congress (1822)—the only priest to serve in that body—over John Biddle, a brother of Nicholas [*q.v.*]. Biddle contested the seat, but the committee on elections upheld Richard. He was later advised by such lawyers as Woodward, Clay, Webster, Tyler, and Sampson that the libel suit was unconstitutional. As he donated his salary to St. Anne's Church, even his austere friend Demetrius Augustine Gallitzin [*q.v.*] was somewhat reconciled to a priest in politics. In Congress he presented petitions relative to school grants, streets in Detroit, and western roads, and on Speaker Clay's request he gave his views upon the desirability of a road connecting Detroit and Chicago. In 1824, when he was defeated for reëlection by Austin E. Wing, he returned to Detroit to give full attention to his extensive missions, the building of a larger Saint Anne's Church, and to civic affairs. He died of the cholera contracted during his ministrations among victims of the plague.

[N. E. Dionne *Gabriel Richard, Sulpicien, Curé et Second Fondateur de la Ville de Détroit* (1911); E. O. Brown, *Two Missionary Priests at Mackinac* (1889); F. A. O'Brien, *The Diocese of Detroit* (1886); A. C. McLaughlin, *Hist. of Higher Education in Mich.*

Richard

Richards

(1891) ; C. G. Herbermann, *The Sulpicians in the U. S.* (1916) ; *Metropolitan Cath. Almanac, 1855* (1854) ; U. S. Cath. Hist. Soc., *Hist. Records and Studies,* vol. V (1907) ; R. R. Elliot in *Am. Cath. Quart. Rev.,* Jan. 1893 ; *Pioneer Colls. . . . Pioneer Soc. of State of Mich.,* vol. I (1877) ; *Am. Cath. Hist. Researches,* Oct. 1886, July 1889, Oct. 1899 ; *Records Am. Cath. Hist. Soc.,* Sept. 1926, Dec. 1926 ; *America,* Mar. 7, 1931 ; Silas Farmer, *The Hist. of Detroit and Mich.* (1884) ; *Democratic Free Press and Mich. Intelligencer* (Detroit), Sept. 27, 1832.]
R. J. P.

RICHARD, JAMES WILLIAM (Feb. 14, 1843–Mar. 7, 1909), clergyman, theologian, educator, was born near Winchester, Va. He was the son of Henry P. Richard, frontier farmer, and his wife Marget Rosenberger, his German forebears having settled in the eighteenth century in the Shenandoah Valley. He attended Roanoke College, Salem, Va., from 1861 to 1862, John Marvin's private school near Winchester in 1863, and taught in Hagerstown, Md., the following year. He was graduated from Gettysburg College, Gettysburg, Pa., in 1868, and from the Gettysburg Theological Seminary in 1871. He was ordained by the Northern Illinois Synod and was pastor in Empire, Ill., from 1871 to 1873. He taught Latin and history in Carthage College, Carthage, Ill., 1873–83; was secretary of the Board of Church Extension of the Lutheran General Synod, 1883–85; taught theology in Wittenberg College, Springfield, Ohio, 1885–88, and in Gettysburg Theological Seminary, from January 1889 until his death.

At the time he went as professor to Gettysburg, there was a tendency in his own synod to regard its nearest rival, the General Council, with a strong faculty at Mount Airy, Pa., as possessor of a more consistent and historic Lutheranism than that which the General Synod represented. As time went on, changes were advocated in liturgy and confessional basis for the sake of immediate comity and a possible future merger. Richard, well at home in ecclesiastical Latin and German, the languages of the period of the Reformation, accepted the challenge as an historian. Prior to coming to the Gettysburg seminary he had written twelve articles for the *Lutheran Quarterly* published in that city ; he now wrote about fifty more—a total of 1800 pages, besides numerous book reviews. Contributions from his pen also found their way to the *Andover Review, Methodist Review, Bibliotheca Sacra, Christian Literature Magazine, American Journal of Theology,* and especially the *Lutheran Observer.* They bore mainly on historical ecclesiastical theology, the weightier ones championing in a nonsectarian spirit the theology of the early Reformation and dealing with questions of liturgy, creeds, and confessional subscription. His opposition to the common service movement and a presentation of his own views on liturgy are found in the *Quarterly,* January and July 1890, and January 1891, and later were summarized in the book *Christian Worship: Its Principles and Forms* (1892, 2nd ed., 1908), written jointly by himself and F. V. N. Painter. His views concerning the history of the Augsburg Confession and other creedal documents accepted in various parts of the Lutheran Church, found expression from time to time in the *Quarterly* and were later embodied in his book, *Philip Melanchthon* (1898), and his monumental work, *The Confessional History of the Lutheran Church* (1909), the most original and scholarly work up to that time penned by a Lutheran theologian in America. Death overtook him, however, before he could read the final proofs of the book.

To him history was not an arsenal in polemics, but he nevertheless frequently reaped hostility instead of gratitude for his work. He was devoted to German scholarship, often visiting Europe, particularly Germany, and was influential in sending several of his best students to continue graduate work in German universities. He was an indefatigable worker, an excellent lecturer, kind and courteous, militant against all insincerity, and feared by the church politicians who made three unsuccessful attempts to deprive him of his chair at the college. At his death his valuable library was given to the institution which he had faithfully served, not without periods of profound sadness, for twenty years. He was twice married, first, on June 19, 1872, to Matilda Emeline Tressler, who died in 1889, and second, on Mar. 31, 1891, to Marie E. Coffinberry, who survived him.

[Private journal, 1873–84, written by M. E. Tressler, owned by a relative in Carthage, Ill. ; S. G. Hefelbower, "James William Richard," in *Luth. Quart.,* Oct. 1909 ; A. R. Wentz, *Hist. of the Gettysburg Theological Seminary* (1927) ; *Public Ledger* (Phila., Pa.), Mar. 8, 1909.]
J. O. E.

RICHARDS, CHARLES BRINCKERHOFF (Dec. 23, 1833–Apr. 20, 1919), mechanical engineer, the son of Thomas Fanning and Harriet Howland (Brinckerhoff) Richards, was born in Brooklyn, N. Y. He received his preliminary education in private schools in the vicinity of his birthplace and gained his theoretical engineering education by broad reading and diligent study while he was engaged in practical daily work at Colt's Armory, Hartford, Conn. Here his mechanical genius was soon recognized. In 1860, he opened an office in New York as consulting engineer. In this capacity he helped Charles T. Porter develop the design of the first high-speed engine, and under Porter's urging, in order to study its action, devised the steam-engine indicator "which has made high-speed engineering possible" (Porter, *post*, p. 58). "Indicators more or less crude had been in use from the time of Watt, but the Richards' indicator was the first one accurate enough and delicate enough to meet the demands of modern engine practice; and its influence has been far-reaching" (Roe, *post*, p. 173). For this achievement he was made a Chevalier of the Legion of Honor of France and received medals from the London Exposition in 1862, the American Institute of the City of New York in 1869, and the French Exposition in 1878.

After the beginning of the Civil War, he returned to the Colt Armory as assistant superintendent and consulting engineer, and retained that position for nearly two decades. During this period he devised the platform-scale testing machine for testing the strength of metals, became a recognized authority on heating and ventilation and was consulting engineer for the Connecticut state capitol at Hartford and several buildings for Yale University, and was responsible for several improvements in the microscope. In 1880 he left Colt's to become superintendent of the Southwark Foundry & Machine Company of Philadelphia and while there patented an exhaust valve and two cut-off governors for steam engines. He was a charter member (1880) of the American Society of Mechanical Engineers, a member of the Connecticut Academy of Sciences, Société Industrielle de Mulhouse, and Society of Naval Architects and Marine Engineers, and a fellow of the American Academy of Arts and Sciences.

In 1884 he accepted an invitation to become Higgin Professor of Dynamic Engineering (later Mechanical Engineering) at the Sheffield Scientific School of Yale University, thus entering upon an entirely new phase of his career. He was fitted for the position not only because of his native talent and his experience as an engineer but also because of his scholarly tastes and point of view, and he continued as head of his department until his retirement in 1909, when he became professor emeritus. As a teacher, he set a high standard for the work of his students. Shy and modest by nature, he considered lecturing an ordeal, but thoroughly enjoyed his contact with individuals in the drafting room. He gained the respect and affection of his colleagues and of a generation of students, who, upon his retirement, presented a portrait of him to the Sheffield Scientific School.

In addition to his teaching, he served as United States commissioner at the Paris Exposition of 1889 and edited the report on machinery and apparatus adapted for general use in mechanical engineering published in Vols. III and IV of the *Reports of the United States Commissioners to the Universal Exposition of 1889 at Paris* (1891). He was an associate editor for technical words and terms in two editions of *Webster's International Dictionary* (1890, 1900). Richards married Agnes Edwards Goodwin at Hartford, Conn., on Sept. 15, 1858, and they had four daughters and a son, all of whom survived their father. He died at New Haven after a long illness, in his eighty-sixth year.

[*Who's Who in America*, 1918–19; *Trans. Am. Soc. Mech. Engineers*, vol. XLI (1920); R. H. Chittenden, *Hist. of the Sheffield Scientific School of Yale Univ.* (1928), vol. I; J. W. Roe, *Eng. and Am. Tool Builders* (1916); C. T. Porter, *Engineering Reminiscences* (1908); Irving Fisher, *Bibliogs. of the Present Officers of Yale Univ.* (1893); *New Haven Journal-Courier*, Apr. 21, 1919.]

B. A. R.

RICHARDS, CHARLES HERBERT (Mar. 18, 1839–Feb. 16, 1925), Congregational clergyman, author, a native of Meriden, N. H., was a son of the Rev. Cyrus Smith Richards and his wife Helen Dorothy (Whiton). His paternal line sprang from William Richards, who was in Plymouth, Mass., in 1633; his first Colonial maternal ancestor was Thomas Whiton, who came to Plymouth in 1635. After preparing for college at Kimball Union Academy in Meriden, of which his father was principal for thirty-five years, he spent two years at Amherst and then transferred to Yale, graduating with high scholastic honors in 1860. His theological course at Union Seminary, begun after a year of teaching at Kimball Union, was interrupted by another year of teaching and by a term at the front in the service of the Christian Commission. He completed his studies at Andover in 1865 and was ordained July 16, 1866, at Kokomo, Ind., where he was pastor from 1865 to 1867. Between 1867 and 1890, when he held a pastorate at the First Congregational Church in Madison, Wis., he became prominently identified with civic and educational affairs and lectured widely throughout the northwest; he also took a deep interest in the state university, upon whose students as well as those of the normal school he exerted a marked influence. Tolerant, hopeful, sympathetic, he was modern in his thinking but not controversial. He was president of the New England Society, chaplain of the state legislature, and from 1885 to 1890 president of the Congregational Home Missionary Society of

Wisconsin. In 1890 he assumed the pastorate of the Central Congregational Church of Philadelphia, where he remained for the next thirteen years. At the end of that time he became corresponding secretary of the Congregational Church Building Society with offices in New York and from 1915 until his death served as educational secretary of the society. On Nov. 18, 1868, he was married to Marie Miner of Charles City, Ia., who died in 1915. Of their six children, three daughters survived their parents.

As a result of his work for the Congregational Church Building Society, Richards became nationally known in his own communion and beyond its borders. Deeply impressed with the need of improving the architecture of the churches of his denomination, he lectured extensively on the subject and contributed many articles to the *Church Building Quarterly* and to the *Congregational Church Building Society Annual,* with both of which he was editorially connected. He was a trustee of the Congregational National Council from 1901 to 1907 and an editor of the *American Missionary* from its foundation. From 1909 to 1919 he served with great ability as chairman of the Commission on Public Worship of the Congregational National Council, for he was an accomplished musician, an authority on hymnology, and deeply interested in improving the services in the Congregational churches. In the course of his career he compiled as aids to worship *Songs of Christian Praise* (1880); *Scripture Selections for Responsive Reading* (1880); *Songs of Prayer and Praise* (1883); *Songs of the Christian Life* (1912); *Book of Church Services* (1922). In addition, he published pamphlets on a variety of subjects, contributed many articles to the religious press, and left in manuscript a book, *Make Your Church Attractive* (1925), which appeared posthumously.

[*Yale Univ. Obit. Record,* 1925, contains much biographical and genealogical information, with an extensive bibliography of Richards' works. Further material is to be found in *Who's Who in America,* 1924–25; *The American Missionary,* Apr. 1925, which contains a portrait; *The Congreg. Ch. Building Soc. Ann.,* 1925; *Congreg. Year Bk.,* 1925.]   F. T. P.

RICHARDS, ELLEN HENRIETTA SWALLOW (Dec. 3, 1842–Mar. 30, 1911), chemist, sanitarian, home economist, the daughter of Peter Swallow and Fanny Gould Taylor, was born at Dunstable, Mass. She was descended on both sides from early settlers in New England. Her early life was spent on her father's farm. After she was sixteen she assisted him in his store in Westford and thus acquired business training which was later of great help to her in her educational and philanthropic undertakings. She studied at Westford Academy but she found difficulty in going on with her education because no proper schools were within reach. In 1868, however, she made her way to Vassar College which had been recently opened. She was classified as a special student and was graduated with the degree of A.B. in 1870. In December of that year she was given special permission to enter the Massachusetts Institute of Technology as a student in chemistry, and in 1873 she received the degree of B.S., the first and for many years the only woman to be so honored. This experience, which led in 1878 to the opening of the doors of the Institute freely to women, marks an epoch in the history of the education of women. As student, student-assistant, and in 1884 as instructor in sanitary chemistry, she continued to work at the Institute until her death. On June 4, 1875, she was married to Prof. Robert Hallowell Richards, head of the department of mining engineering at the Institute. They chose a home at 32 Eliot Street, Jamaica Plain, Mass. Here hosts of students and friends enjoyed a hospitality as distinguished for its kindness and simplicity as it was for its generosity. Her housekeeping, orderly but not rigid or enslaving, left her free to give even more than full working time to her steadily growing number of interests.

Her chief activities followed three general lines: the application of chemistry to living conditions and especially to sanitary science, the broadening of the field of science for women, and the development of the home economics movement. Under the first head may be named, in addition to her work as a teacher, her assistance in the sanitary survey of the waters of Massachusetts, as chemist for the Manufacturer's Mutual Life Insurance Company, her studies in the application of heat to food materials, her share in the directing of the New England Kitchen, the Rumford Kitchen at the World's Columbian Exposition, school lunch projects, the Sunshine Laundry, the Laboratory Kitchen, and the Women's Commons at the University of Chicago, and the publication of many books on different aspects of sanitary science. Her work for women was equally broad. With the help of the Woman's Education Association she established in November 1876 a Woman's Laboratory in space offered by the Institute. It was discontinued in 1883 when the Institute opened a separate laboratory for sanitary chemistry and Mrs. Richards as assistant under Professor W. R. Nichols took possession of the office in the new Walker Building. She was one of the two women who in November 1881 issued the call to women college graduates which led to the organization of the Association of Collegiate Alumnæ, later known as the American Association of University Women. She became head of the science section of the Society to Encourage Studies at Home in 1876, a director of the Woman's Education Association for several terms, a charter member in 1898 of the Naples Table Association for Promoting Laboratory Research by Women, and a trustee of Vassar College.

Her leadership in the home economics movement was her great achievement. She progressed from her early interest in the chemistry of foods to what she called "euthenics," or the science of the controlled environment for right living. In 1899 she organized the Lake Placid Conference which, in 1908, became the American Home Economics Association of which she was the first president and later honorary president. She received the degree of M.S. from Vassar College in 1873 and that of Sc.D. from Smith College in 1910. In 1879 she was elected a member of the American Institute of Mining Engineers and in 1907 was made an honorary life member of the Association of Collegiate Alumnæ. In 1911 the Naples Table Association gave the name "Ellen H. Richards Research Prize" to its prize of one thousand dollars. She died at her home in Jamaica Plain, on Mar. 30, 1911. Her published works include *The Cost of Living* (1899); *The Cost of Food* (1901); *The Cost of Shelter* (1905); *Sanitation in Daily Life* (1907); *The Cost of Cleanness* (1908); *Laboratory Notes on Industrial Water Analysis* (1908); *Euthenics* (1910); and *Conservation by Sanitation* (1911). The pioneer strain which she inherited characterized her entire life. She was not content with going where others had gone but, as she once said, "was eager to do what never had been done before."

[Caroline L. Hunt, *The Life of Ellen H. Richards* (1912); *Jour. of Home Economics*, June, Oct. 1911; *Technology Rev.*, July 1911; *Vassar Coll. Bull.*, Mar. 1912; *Vassar Miscellany*, May 1911; *Who's Who in America*, 1910–11; *Boston Transcript*, Mar. 31, 1911; personal recollections and letters.] M. T.

RICHARDS, JOHN KELVEY (Mar. 15, 1856–Mar. 1, 1909), jurist, son of Samuel and Sarah (Kelvey) Richards, was born in Ironton, Lawrence County, Ohio. His father, of Welsh Quaker ancestry, was one of the pioneers of Ironton. Having received his early education in the schools of his native town, John Richards graduated from Swarthmore College with the degree of A.B. in 1875, and two years later re-

ceived the same degree from Harvard University. Returning to Ironton, he began the study of law in the office of Judge W. W. Johnson, later chief justice of the supreme court of Ohio. In 1879 he was admitted to the bar and soon after (1880) was elected prosecuting attorney of Lawrence County, serving until 1882. From 1885 to 1889 he was city solicitor of Ironton. In the latter year he was elected a member of the Ohio Senate, where on account of his recognized legal ability he was appointed chairman of the judiciary committee. At the close of his two-year term he was elected attorney general of Ohio and reëlected for 1894–96, his terms of office being concurrent with those of William McKinley as governor. In 1895 McKinley appointed him member of a commission to codify the insurance laws of the state, and in 1896 he was counsel for a committee authorized by the General Assembly to revise the tax laws of Ohio. In the same year he was general counsel for the state board of medical registration and examiners and also counsel for the board of appraisers and assessors. In 1897 President McKinley, who had been impressed with the legal ability Richards had shown as attorney general of Ohio, appointed him solicitor general of the United States. He remained in this office until 1903, when President Roosevelt appointed him a member of the United States circuit court for the sixth circuit, to take the place of Judge William R. Day [q.v.], who was elevated to the Supreme Court. Richards remained a member of the circuit court until his death.

The annual report of the attorney general of Ohio for the year 1895 is a small volume of only sixty-eight pages. Comparatively small as was the amount of work done while Richards was attorney general, it was, however, of an unusually important character. The railroads, by grant from the cities of Cincinnati and Akron, had for years occupied the state canal beds within the limits of these cities. He successfully fought through the courts the claim of the state that though it had granted the canal beds to these cities for street and sewage purposes, the cities had no right to turn them over to the railroads and that the railroads must surrender their use to the state. The tax bills which he as counsel for the legislative committee helped to draft, he was called upon to uphold in state courts and in the United States Supreme Court. His successful defense of these bills, which taxed the franchises of foreign corporations, the property of inter-state express companies by the "unit" rule, and the proportionate share of cars of sleeping car companies, gave rise to decisions which have become the basis for much important excise and property-tax law today.

As solicitor general, he was called upon to handle the difficult legal questions arising out of the Spanish-American War, particularly in reference to the territory acquired by the United States. A number of the "Insular cases" were argued by him in the Supreme Court (182 *U. S.*, 222 and 244), as were also the Joint Traffic Association and the Addyston Pipe & Steel Company cases (171 *U. S.*, 505; 175 *U. S.*, 211). He prepared the briefs and handled the Northern Securities case (193 *U. S.*, 197) until his appointment to the bench in 1903. His work as a judge did not add materially to the high reputation he had already gained as solicitor general. He sat upon the bench for nine years and wrote during that time over 140 opinions. They are all short, few being over three pages long, and many only one or two. He did not discuss at length the legal principles involved but based his decisions largely on the authority of decided cases. He seldom wrote a dissenting opinion. A good many of his opinions dealt with master and servant cases involving the interpretation of Ohio statutes. On June 12, 1890, he married Anna Willard Steece of Ironton, Ohio, who with one daughter and two sons survived him.

[*Green Bag*, Apr. 1909; *Proc. Ohio State Bar Asso.*, vol. XXX (1909); *Report of the Attorney General of . . . Ohio . . . 1895* (1896); *Who's Who in America*, 1908–09; *Semi-Weekly Irontonian* (Ironton, Ohio), Mar. 2, 1909; *Cincinnati Enquirer*, Mar. 2, 1909.]

A. H. T.

RICHARDS, JOSEPH WILLIAM (July 28, 1864–Oct. 12, 1921), metallurgist and teacher, was born in Oldbury, Worcestershire, England, of English-Scotch parents, Joseph and Bridget (Harvey) Richards, who brought him to the United States when he was about seven years old. He was not the first of his line to follow the engineering and metallurgical profession, for his grandfather, William Richards, was a locomotive and bridge builder in England, and his father, a manufacturing metallurgical chemist in Philadelphia, was awarded the John Scott medal of the Franklin Institute for the first successful solder for aluminum. Joseph received his early education in the public schools of Philadelphia and entered Lehigh University in 1882, receiving the degree of analytical chemist in 1886. After serving one year as superintendent of the Delaware Metal Refinery in Philadelphia (1886–87), he returned to the university for a period of graduate work, during which he was also successively assistant instructor and instructor in metallurgy, mineralogy, and blow-

piping. In 1891 he received the degree of master of science, and in 1893, that of doctor of philosophy, the first to be granted by Lehigh. He also studied in Heidelberg and Freiberg, Germany. In 1897 he was made assistant professor and in 1903, professor of metallurgy. Richards loved to teach and would spend any amount of time on those who wished to learn. It is not surprising, therefore, that he was rated as an efficient and inspiring instructor with singular success in stimulating the interest of his students in even the drier aspects of the subjects he taught.

Always a student and investigator, he lost no opportunity to add to his knowledge of a wide range of subjects. Travel, which he greatly enjoyed, he used as a means of getting first-hand information on metallurgical practice, not only in the United States but also abroad. He became recognized as an authority in metallurgy, especially the metallurgy of aluminum, electrometallurgy, and metallurgical-chemical calculations, and was widely employed as legal expert and adviser. In 1893 he received a medal at the Columbian Exposition for an exhibit showing the metallurgy of aluminum.

As an author, his principal works include a treatise on *Aluminium*, first published in 1887 and revised and reissued in 1890 and 1896, a recognized authority on the subject in English and the most complete in any language; and *Metallurgical Calculations* (3 vols., 1906, 1907, 1908) which has been translated into German, French, Italian, Spanish, and Russian. He published the following monographs, all translations from the German: *The Electrolysis of Water* (1904), by Viktor Engelhardt; *The Production of Chromium and Its Compounds by the Aid of the Electric Current* (1904), by Max J. L. Le Blanc; *Arrangement of Electrolytic Laboratories* (1905), by Herman Nissenson; and *The Manufacture of Metallic Articles Electrolytically* (1906), by Wilhelm Pfanhauser. From the Italian he translated *The Cementation of Iron and Steel* (1915), by Frederico Giolitti.

He was a member of the naval consulting board from its formation in 1915. For two summers he took no vacation and as Washington representative, on a dollar-a-year basis, gave freely and cheerfully of his time, talents, and energy, at risk to health, performing with dogged persistence the task he had accepted as his patriotic duty. This devotion was characteristic of Richards, as was demonstrated again and again by his whole-hearted service as officer or committeeman in numerous professional societies. "I always have a time for each task and I stick religiously to my schedule" (Stoughton, *post*, p. 29) was his explanation of his ability to accomplish so much outside work. In addition to his activities in the various technical organizations to which he belonged, he also served as member of the United States assay commission (1897); representative of the Franklin Institute to the International Geological Congress in Russia (1897); member of the jury of awards, Department of Chemistry, at the National Export Exhibition, Philadelphia (1899); and member of the jury of awards and chairman of the sub-jury on metallurgy, at the Panama-Pacific International Exposition, San Francisco (1915).

He was a lover of music and sang as a first bass in the Bach Choir of Bethlehem at intervals from 1900 to his death in 1921. He was something of an art connoisseur and collected a number of excellent canvases. Throughout his life he gave much thought to religious and philosophic subjects; he was a member of the Unitarian Church. On Mar. 12, 1887, he married his second cousin, Arnamarie Gadd. Two daughters and one son survived them.

[Bradley Stoughton, "Joseph W. Richards," in *Mining and Metallurgy*, Dec. 1921; *Trans. Am. Electrochemical Soc.*, vol. XL (1922); *Who's Who in America*, 1920–21; *Public Ledger* (Phila.), Oct. 13, 1921.]
B.A.R.

RICHARDS, THEODORE WILLIAM (Jan. 31, 1868–Apr. 2, 1928), chemist, the son of William Trost [*q.v.*] and Anna (Matlack) Richards, was born in Germantown, Pa., and died in Cambridge, Mass. Both his father, a well-known marine artist, and his mother, a writer of both prose and poetry, were intensely interested in the intellectual development of their children. While Richards was still a boy the family lived for two years in England where lifelong friendships were begun. Most of his early education was obtained at home from his mother, and because of his quick intelligence he made such rapid progress that at the age of thirteen he was prepared to enter Haverford College. The next year, however, he spent at home, where, still under the guidance of his mother, he completed the studies of the freshman year at Haverford. In the fall of 1882 he entered the sophomore class at Haverford and graduated (S.B.) with high honors in 1885. His interest in science became evident at an early age when he independently carried on simple chemical experiments at home. Later, in Haverford College, he received a thorough grounding in chemistry under Professor Lyman B. Hall and at the same time became so much interested in astronomy that at one time he considered choosing this

field for his life work. Intimate acquaintance with Prof. Josiah P. Cooke [*q.v.*] of Harvard, who was a summer neighbor at Newport, R. I., probably played a large part in his final decision to follow the career of a chemist.

In the fall of 1885 he entered Harvard College as a senior and devoted the whole of his time for the next three years to the study of chemistry. He received the bachelor's degree with highest honors in chemistry in 1886 and the doctor's degree in 1888. As a graduate student he came largely under the influence of Professor Cooke. At that time Cooke was particularly interested in the numerical relations of the atomic weights and, because of lack of confidence in the reliability of current values of these constants, had undertaken the revision of some of them. Cooke's high estimate of Richards' promise as an investigator led him to intrust to him the experimental determination of the relation of the atomic weights of hydrogen and oxygen, by finding the weight of water obtained in burning a weighed amount of hydrogen with copper oxide. (See *Proceedings of the American Academy of Arts and Sciences*, vol. XXIII, 1888.) In this extremely exacting problem Richards showed at once the qualities which made him the foremost experimental chemist of his time. "An infinite capacity for taking pains, an uncompromising attitude toward the possibilities of hidden errors, a determination to be certain that no precaution had been overlooked, an extraordinary persistence in the patient repetition of exacting and laborious experiments were combined with unusual manual dexterity and ingenuity" (Baxter, *post*, p. 334). The result of this investigation has stood the test of time as one of the most accurate determinations of this ratio.

After completion of his graduate work Richards spent one year as a traveling fellow of Harvard University in Europe. There he studied for short periods under such masters as Jannasch, Victor Meyer, and Hempel. On his return he was appointed assistant in quantitative analysis at Harvard, to become instructor in 1891 and assistant professor in 1894. Seven years later, in 1901, he declined a call to a permanent research professorship in the University of Göttingen when Harvard promoted him to a full professorship with a reduction in the duties expected by the University. In 1912 he was appointed to the Erving Professorship of Chemistry, a title which he held till his death.

The interest which Richards always showed in measurements of precision was founded upon the deep-rooted belief, now universally held, that only through a precise knowledge of the properties of matter was progress in chemical science to be made. As an independent investigator he naturally followed the lines on which he had begun. At that time he was inclined to believe that some concealed relationship existed between the properties of the elements and the atomic weights and therefore undertook the revision of some of these constants. Even as late as 1910 he writes: "But some may contend that the very exact determination of these quantities is after all an abstract and academic question, not of great practical significance. . . . When mankind discovers the fundamental laws underlying any set of phenomena, these phenomena come in much larger measure than before under his control and are applicable for his service. Until we understand the laws, all depends upon chance. Hence, merely from the practical point of view of the progress of humanity, the exact understanding of the laws of nature is one of the most important of all the problems presented to man; and the unknown laws underlying the nature of the elements are obviously among the most fundamental of these laws of nature. In brief, that is the reason why more than twenty years ago the systematic study of the atomic weights was begun at Harvard University by the author" (*Determinations of Atomic Weights,* 1910, p. 98).

Beginning with copper he redetermined with his own hands the atomic weights of barium, strontium, and zinc and later largely with the aid of graduate students as laboratory assistants, he investigated twenty additional elements. While in the course of this work many new analytical processes were devised and perfected, he was early forced to the conclusion realized by Marignac, Dumas, and Stas that the comparison of the chlorides and bromides of the elements with silver and the silver halides provides an analytical operation capable of greater precision than any other. He brought the experimental details of this comparison to a far higher degree of perfection than it had previously reached so that it has been possible for others to follow in his footsteps with comparatively little effort. In all this work especial attention was paid to methods of purification and to the possibility of variability in the composition of an element, long before the suspicion of isotopy arose. He recognized the difficulty of freeing any substance from traces of moisture and devised the "bottling apparatus" for protecting a substance once dried from contact with moisture before it could be weighed. The procedure which he found necessary for determining the end point in the comparison of halides with silver by means of "nephelometer" has suffered little or no modification in the course of years, while his investigations on the contamination of precipitates through occlusion have been largely the basis of modern work on the subject. These determinations of the atomic weights brought to light many inaccuracies in older work, not excepting the classical work of Stas, who was shown, first in the case of chlorine, later in many other instances, to have been appreciably in error. Up to the present time (1934) Richards' redeterminations of the atomic weights have stood practically unchallenged.

Although Richards was best known for his revisions of the atomic weights, during the last half of his scientific career this subject assumed a subordinate part in his work. His interest in physical chemistry, already keen, was considerably stimulated by a period spent in study in Germany under Ostwald and Nernst in 1895, and for twenty-five years before his death a large part of his interest and effort was directed in various fields of physical chemistry. Thermochemistry and thermodynamics in particular engaged his attention. His first published paper (*Proceedings of the American Academy of Arts and Sciences,* vol. XXII, 1887) concerned the constant heat of precipitation of silver chloride. Later he devoted much energy to the perfecting of thermochemical measurements and devised the "adiabatic calorimeter" in order to avoid the troublesome and uncertain corrections due to gain or loss of heat of the calorimeter from its surroundings and to lag of the thermometer. An automatic design of this calorimeter was ultimately devised. New and highly accurate data were obtained in this way, covering heats of solution of metals in acids, heats of combustion of organic substances, heats of neutralization, specific heats of liquids, specific heats of solids at low temperatures, and heats of evaporation of liquids. The study of the data thus obtained led him to the discovery that the magnitude of the difference between "total energy change" and "free energy change" depends upon change in heat capacity of a system during chemical change and that this difference gradually disappears as the absolute zero is approached. The discovery antedated Nernst's third law of thermodynamics.

Richards' work in thermochemistry led him into the field of thermometry and to the exact determination for the first time of the inversion temperatures of hydrated compounds for use as fixed points. As a check upon the determination of the atomic weight of copper by ordinary methods, Richards undertook the comparison of the silver and copper coulometers. The vagaries of these were investigated intimately and after due corrections had been made, Faraday's Law was found to hold within the limits of modern experimental accuracy. This conclusion was later substantiated in the case of silver by comparisons between the deposits formed from aqueous solutions and from solutions in fused salts. Another field of electrochemistry was attacked by the determination of various single potential differences of metals and the electromotive forces between amalgams of different concentration. The latter data showed beyond question that amalgams could not be considered, except at low concentrations, to behave like ideal solutions.

Richards' chief interest during the latter part of his life lay in the consideration of the relation between the physical properties of the various elements, and their compounds, especially those connected with atomic volumes and compressibilities (*The Compressibilities of the Elements and their Periodic Relations,* 1907). He devised new forms of apparatus for determining exactly the compressibilities of the elements and their compounds, as well as certain related properties such as surface tension and heat of evaporation. This work led to the discovery of the periodicity of atomic volume and compressibility and the close parallelism between these properties, as well as to the fact that increase or decrease in volume during a chemical change depends on the one hand upon the compressibilities of the substances involved and on the other upon their chemical affinities. The improbability that an element possesses constant atomic volume in different states of chemical combination was another conclusion drawn from this work as well as very definite and interesting ideas as to the effect of chemical affinity and cohesion upon the configuration of an atom and their relation to such properties as surface tension, vapor pressure, and heat of evaporation. The latest aspect of this work was the attempt to compute from compressibilities and other data the actual internal pressures which hold matter together. (See *Journal of the American Chemical Society,* March 1925, and *Chemical Reviews,* October 1925). He believed this to be the resultant of the compression due to external pressure and intrinsic compressing effects, and the distension due to thermal pressure and intrinsic distending pressure. The cohesive pressures of certain elements calculated by him are in accord with the known physical properties of these substances.

In all, Richards published nearly three hundred papers covering a far wider field than that indicated in the foregoing paragraphs. While many of the theoretical results which he reached have been and will be of the greatest importance, his contribution to the technique of precise physico-chemical investigation will undoubtedly always stand out as being equally important. Indeed he may well be said to have inaugurated a new era in the accuracy of analytical and physico-chemical experimentation. He combined with an uncanny ability to divine previously unsuspected sources of inaccuracy, a determination to leave nothing undone in his effort to eliminate every source of uncertainty. In particular he felt strongly the necessity of making certain that the materials with which he was working conformed in quality to the precision with which the experiments were to be made, and he deplored the unfortunate fact that so much of the earlier precision measurements in chemistry had been made with material of unknown or doubtful purity or definiteness. There can be no question that his attitude has had a profound and salutary effect upon modern precise research.

He taught practically without a break from 1889 until almost the moment of his death. At first he gave instruction only in quantitative analysis but in 1896 he gave for the first time the course in physical chemistry for advanced students, with which he never severed his connection. During the same period he taught elementary physical chemistry from a historical standpoint to undergraduates. In 1907 he was exchange professor from Harvard University to the University of Berlin. He was greatly interested in the work of his research students. His daily visits to each in the laboratory never failed to bring encouragement and to stimulate enthusiasm. The prodigious amount of experimental research of the first quality accomplished by these students bears tribute to his ability to stir up in his associates the same qualities which he possessed himself to such a high degree. Honors came to him in rapid succession. He was chosen a member of the American Academy of Arts and Sciences in 1891 and of the National Academy of Sciences in 1899. The Davy, Faraday, and Gibbs medals were awarded in 1910, 1911, and 1912 respectively. He received the Nobel prize of 1914 for his work on atomic weights. The Franklin medal followed in 1916 and the LeBlanc and Lavoisier medals in 1922 and 1923. In 1925 he was made an officer of the French Legion of Honor. He received numerous honorary degrees. He held office in many American scientific societies and was an honorary member of the most important European societies and academies. In 1925 an endowed professorship was established in Harvard University by Thomas W. Lamont, in memory of his brother Hammond Lamont, to be called the Theodore William Richards professorship of chemistry.

Richards was married on May 28, 1896, to Miriam Stuart Thayer, daughter of Prof. Joseph Henry Thayer, of the Harvard Divinity School. Three children survived him, a daughter and two sons. His personality was delightful, and his interests were very wide, especially in literature, art, and music. As a boy he received a very considerable training from his father in sketching and painting and he never lost the capacity to transfer his impressions to paper with brush and pencil. Always fond of the out-doors, he enjoyed in his early years yachting and tennis, but later these were replaced by golf and motoring. The health and welfare of his wife and children were always in his thoughts. At the same time his wife's sympathetic appreciation of his aims and ideals was a constant source of encouragement, and the promise of his children a great satisfaction. He never failed to give the University his best efforts as a teacher and administrator, even after official release from routine had largely freed him from responsibility.

[G. P. Baxter, "Theodore William Richards," in *Harvard Grads.' Mag.*, Sept. 1928, in *Science*, Oct. 12, 1928 and in *Ann. Report of the Board of Regents of the Smithsonian Institution . . . for the Year Ending June 30, 1928* (1929); Sir Harold Hartley, "Theodore William Richards Memorial Lecture," *Jour. of the Chemical Soc.* (London), Aug. 1930; *Who's Who in America, 1926–27*; *Harvard Univ. Gazette*, Nov. 1928; *Boston Transcript*, Apr. 2, 1928.]   G. P. B.

RICHARDS, THOMAS ADDISON (Dec. 3, 1820–June 28, 1900), author and illustrator of travel books, landscape painter, art teacher, was the son of William Richards, a Baptist minister, and his wife Anne Gardener Richards. He was born in London, England, lived for a short time in Hook Norton, near Oxford, and with his family sailed for America, arriving in New York in September 1831. After brief residence in Hudson, N. Y., the family went to South Carolina (1835) and thence to Georgia, settling in Penfield. At twelve Richards wrote an account of his voyage from England, a manuscript volume of 150 pages, which he illustrated with water-color pictures. His first published book was an illustrated holiday volume on flower painting entitled *The American Artist* (1838). This was followed shortly by *Georgia Illustrated* (1842), a series of steel engravings with ac-

companying text by various authors. Before he left Georgia, to seek his fortune in New York, he apparently enjoyed a local reputation for portrait painting, for while on his way he stopped in Augusta during the presidential campaign in 1844 and was employed to paint pictures of Clay and Polk on a pretentious canvas which stretched across the wide Broad Street in that city. In New York in 1845, he studied at the National Academy of Design for two years, becoming an associate of the Academy in 1848, an Academician in 1851, and in the following year corresponding secretary, a position he held for forty years. He spent many summers traveling about the United States and Europe, sketching and painting. His work belongs with the Hudson River school, which aimed at a faithful and literal transcription of nature. He twice held large auction sales of his work in New York (1863, 1871).

In the fifties he was contributing to *Harper's Magazine* and the *Knickerbocker* illustrated articles descriptive of scenes in the United States. Some of his novelettes and tales appeared in book form in *Tallulah and Jocassee* (1852), which was republished in 1853 as *Summer Stories of the South*. In these and similar stories published a year later under the title of *American Scenery*, he endeavored "so to relieve the gravity of fact with the grace of fiction, as to present at the same time an instructive topography and an entertaining romance" (Preface). *Appletons' Illustrated Hand-book of American Travel*, however, which he published in 1857 (2nd ed., 1860), remains closer to fact and could rival the later Baedeker in accuracy as to modes of travel and historical information. His text and drawings for the work formed the first complete guide of its kind for the United States and Canada. Richardson's scholarly tastes and enthusiasm for natural scenery may be considered the keynote of his artistic and literary career. Doubtless inspired by the reigning taste for Romanticism, he endeavored to reproduce by word and brush the "varying characteristics of the beautiful natural scenery of our country" and of Europe. As a painter of landscape he was considered among the best of his time. Much of his life was spent in New York, where he was constantly represented in the annual exhibitions of the National Academy of Design. In 1858 he organized and for two years directed the first class in the Cooper Union School of Design for Women, an early step in the art education of women. In 1867 he was appointed professor of art in the University of the City of New York (now New York University). After twenty years of service he was made professor emeritus in 1887. In 1857 he was married to Mary Anthony, daughter of Lorenzo Dow Anthony, of Providence, R. I., who wrote numerous juvenile stories. He died without issue in his eightieth year in Annapolis, Md., and was buried at Providence.

[Printed sources include: T. S. Cummings, *Hist. Annals of the Nat. Acad. of Design* (1865); H. T. Tuckerman, *Book of the Artists* (1867); S. A. Allibone, *A Critical Dict. of Eng. Lit. and British and Am. Authors* (1870); T. F. Jones, *N. Y. Univ.: 1832–1932* (1933); *Am. Art Annual*, 1900–01; *Baltimore Sun*, June 28, 1900. Information as to certain facts was supplied by a nephew and grand-niece of Richardson.]   K. L. A.

RICHARDS, WILLIAM (Aug. 22, 1793–Nov. 7, 1847), missionary, diplomatic agent and cabinet minister of the Hawaiian kingdom, was born at Plainfield, Mass., the son of James and Lydia (Shaw) Richards, and a descendant of William Richards who was in Plymouth, Mass., in 1633. In his early youth he was surrounded by missionary influences; his elder brother, James, was one of the Williams College students who held the famous "haystack meeting" and whose zeal led to the formation of the American Board of Commissioners for Foreign Missions. The younger Richards made a public profession of religion in 1811 and was even then looking forward to a missionary career. He graduated from Williams College in 1819 and from Andover Theological Seminary in 1822. Within a few weeks after graduation, he was ordained as a missionary (Sept. 12), married to Clarissa Lyman (Oct. 30), and on Nov. 19, sailed for the Hawaiian Islands. On his arrival there he was stationed at the important town of Lahaina on the island of Maui, where he resided for thirteen years engaged in the varied duties of preacher, teacher, physician, artisan, and translator of part of the Bible. He was thoroughly devoted and very successful in his work, exhibited great courage in the face of danger, and won, to an unusual degree, the love of the Hawaiian people and the confidence of the king and chiefs. In 1837 he visited the United States —partly to provide for the education of his children, six of whom he brought with him, partly, as an agent of the Sandwich Islands Mission, to awaken Christian people to a greater personal participation in the evangelization of the world, and partly to seek some means of hastening the progress of the Hawaiian people in the arts of civilization.

Upon his return to the Islands in 1838, the king and chiefs invited him to become their chaplain, teacher, and interpreter. Their need of an adviser was great, for the rulers were much troubled by the demands of foreigners and too inexperienced to know either the extent or the limits of their rights and authority. With the approval of his associates, Richards accepted the invitation, was released from missionary work, and spent the remainder of his life in government service. He had a great though unobtrusive part in transforming the Hawaiian economic and political system—an oppressive feudalism being superseded by a modern constitutional state—and in giving it the republican bent which it retained as a permanent characteristic. The influence of his teaching is seen in the bill of rights (1839), the constitution of 1840, and the laws enacted from 1838 to 1842, though he did not himself write any of these documents.

In 1842 he was sent on a diplomatic mission having two main objects: first, to obtain an explicit recognition of the independence of Hawaii by the United States, Great Britain, and France; second, to negotiate new and more favorable treaties. In this work he had several associates but the principal responsibility rested on him. The mission was successful in the matter of recognition of independence but failed to get new treaties. Richards had a measure of Yankee shrewdness which aided him in his negotiations, but the success obtained was due more to independent circumstances than to his ability as a diplomat. While in Europe he allowed himself and the Hawaiian government to be drawn into a highly speculative project for developing the agricultural resources of the islands with foreign capital. In this matter he made a serious mistake of judgment, due largely to his natural disposition to repose full confidence in his friends. The project failed to materialize but the episode caused much dissension and ill feeling in Hawaii. He returned to the Islands in 1845 and for some months was without official employment. Upon the organization of the board of commissioners to quiet land titles (1846) he was made president of the board, and later in the same year was appointed minister of public instruction—the first to hold that position in Hawaii. To the work of these two offices he applied himself with great diligence, devoting to the service of the nation his extensive and accurate knowledge of Hawaiian customs and character. It is believed that overwork hastened his death.

Little that Richards wrote was printed under his own name. He was the author of *Memoir of Keopuolani, Late Queen of the Sandwich Islands* (Boston, 1825), published anonymously, and was translator and editor of the *Translation of the Constitution and Laws of the Hawaiian*

Islands (Lahainaluna, 1842). He translated into Hawaiian thirteen books of the Bible and assisted with seven others, and prepared two or three Hawaiian school books which were in part translations and in part original composition.

[Maiden name of mother was supplied by the Am. Antiquarian Soc., Worcester, Mass.; Richards' letters to the Am. Board are in archives of the Board, Boston; his journals covering his trips abroad, 1836–38 and 1842–45, and his official correspondence are in Archives of Hawaii. See also Honolulu *Polynesian*, Nov. 13, 1847, and Dec. 4, 1847; *The Friend* (Honolulu), Dec. 2, 1847; *Heroes and Martyrs of the Modern Missionary Enterprise* (1853), ed. by L. E. Smith; *A Hist. of the Hawaiian Islands* (1907), ed. by Daniel Logan; Abner Morse, *A Geneal. Reg. of the Descendants of Several Ancient Puritans*, vol. III (1861).]

R. S. K.

RICHARDS, WILLIAM TROST (Nov. 14, 1833–Nov. 8, 1905), painter, was born in Philadelphia, the son of Benjamin M. and Annie (Trost) Richards. His middle name was that of his maternal grandfather, a Dutch goldsmith. Educated in the Philadelphia grammar and high schools, the future depictor of the sea became a designer for Archer & Warner, makers of gas fixtures, doubtless confirming at this period the precision of draftsmanship which was later characteristic of his art and the businesslike habits which enabled him to prosper. To perfect himself as designer, he studied wood engraving in his evening hours and presently began to paint pictures, several of which were shown at the Philadelphia Art Union. Having had instruction from Paul Weber, a local artist, he gave up his $1500 salary in 1853, and soon after, with his scanty savings, went abroad. He studied at Florence, Rome, and Paris, though without continuing long under any one master.

Before leaving Philadelphia he had become engaged to Anna Matlack, of a Quaker family, who had already written poems and dramas. On his return they were married, June 30, 1856. They settled at Germantown, experiencing at first vicissitudes of fortune due to the depression of 1857 and the devastating effects of the Civil War. Richards, however, still did some designing and as an artist he found a Maecenas in George Whitney, who bought many of his paintings. He was preoccupied with landscape and still life until 1867, when a storm at sea caught his interest and led to intensive studies of waves and their aspects on the New Jersey coast. Richards' mode of making these marine paintings was original with him, though on account of his literal fidelity to the facts of nature he was sometimes called an American Pre-Raphaelite. He observed so closely and recorded so accurately as to win commendation from

John Ruskin (Downes, *post*). Critics favorable to French impressionism and other later phases of modern art found Richards' manner hard, photographic, and not too colorful. Regardless of fashions in art, however, he painted throughout a long and busy life his luminous and realistic sea pictures. These won him several medals and other similar honors. He was represented in his life time in the permanent collections of the Metropolitan Museum of Art, New York; the Pennsylvania Academy, Philadelphia; the Corcoran Art Gallery, Washington. At the commemorative exhibition by members of the National Academy of Design, 1825–1925, Richards' "After the Storm," owned by William Macbeth, was shown.

In 1874 he began spending his summers at Newport, R. I., which from 1890 on was his permanent residence. He owned for a time "Gray Cliff" on Conanicut Island, but this was taken over by the United States government in 1899. In his later years he painted much abroad —on the Irish west coast, in the Orkneys, and among the Channel Islands. He was an indefatigable worker, a quiet, dignified gentleman, inconspicuous in attire and manners, a prudent manager of his finances. His wife, who died at Newport in 1900, was of gracious personality and notable literary ability. Among their seven children were Prof. Theodore William Richards [*q.v.*], chemist, of Harvard University, and Prof. Herbert Maule Richards (1871–1928), botanist, of Columbia University. After his wife's death Richards aged rapidly. He spent a summer painting in Norway and thereafter worked quietly at Newport until his death. He was buried at Laurel Hill Cemetery, Philadelphia.

[H. S. Morris, *Masterpieces of the Sea; William T. Richards, a Brief Outline of His Life and Art* (1912); H. T. Tuckerman, *Book of the Artists* (1867); W. H. Downes, in *Boston Transcript*, Mar. 11, 1918; "Am. Art," in *N. Y. Times*, Apr. 8, 1877; "The Acad. Exhibition," *Art Jour.*, May 1877; *Who's Who in America*, 1903–05; *Public Ledger* (Phila.), Nov. 9, 1905.]

F. W. C.

RICHARDS, ZALMON (Aug. 11, 1811– Nov. 1, 1899), educator, son of Nehemiah and Betsey Richards, was born at Cummington, Mass. His father, a farmer, was a descendant of William Richards, an emigrant from England, who was in Plymouth in 1633 and moved later to Scituate and in 1693 to Weymouth. Between the ages of three and ten, when not needed on the farm, Zalmon attended the country school, and his first teacher, Sybil Bates, stirred in him a lifelong interest in education and religion. For short periods he studied in a private school at Cummington and in its successor, the Cummington Academy. At fifteen he joined the local Baptist Church, of which his father was a founder. He had already taken a pledge of total abstinence, which he kept throughout his life. At seventeen he was teaching a country school for eight dollars a month and board, and he now resolved to make teaching his profession. Supplementing his early schooling by courses at the Southampton Academy and private instruction, he entered Williams College, where he came under the influence of Mark Hopkins.

Graduating in 1836, he became principal of the Cummington Academy and soon married Minerva Todd, his assistant teacher. In 1839 they took charge of the academy at Stillwater, N. Y. While there he organized teachers' institutes, then an innovation, in Saratoga County, N. Y., and in Vermont. In 1849 he went to Washington, D. C., as principal of the preparatory department of Columbian College. Always an educational organizer, he soon formed the Columbian Teachers' Association. In 1852 he established a private school, the Union Academy, which was fairly prosperous until its career was ended by the departure of the Southern students at the opening of the Civil War. He was an organizer of the Washington Young Men's Christian Association (1852), and was its first president; during the Civil War he was one of the three District of Columbia members of the Christian Commission. In 1861 he was appointed to a clerical position in the United States Treasury Department, but was soon transferred to the bureau of statistics, where he remained until 1867. Here he collected school statistics which he unsuccessfully attempted to have tabulated and published. In 1867 he was elected a member and president of the common council of Washington; for two years he conducted a public-school teachers' institute. He was largely responsible for the passage by Congress of the bill establishing a national department of education (1867), and held a position therein until it was made a bureau of the Interior Department in 1869. As a member of the city common council he secured the creation (1869) of the office of superintendent of public schools and was himself the first incumbent, serving for one year. From 1871 to 1874 he was auditor for the District of Columbia government. He was one of the organizers and the first president of the National Teachers' Association (1857), which, in 1870, became the National Education Association. He was a regular attendant at its meetings until 1896, when his health failed, and numerous papers and reports by him appear in its *Proceedings*. At the Toronto meeting, 1891, he presented a historical sketch of the Association, which later appeared in pamphlet form. He also published a *Teachers' Manual* (1880), for primary schools, and *The Natural Arithmetic* (1885). Although he accumulated considerable property, he lost the most of it through the indorsement of notes for friends and in his old age maintained himself by teaching a small private school in his own home. He outlived his second wife, Mary F. Mather of Darien, Conn., whom he married on Aug. 19, 1874, and at his death in Washington was survived by one son.

[J. O. Wilson, in *Nat. Educ. Asso.: Jour. of Proc. and Addresses*, vol. XXXIX (1900); Abner Morse, *A Geneal. Reg. of the Descendants of Several Ancient Puritans*, vol. III (1861); *Hist. of the Conn. Valley in Mass.*, vol. I (1879); town records of Cummington, Mass.; *Washington Post*, Nov. 2, 1899; *Evening Star* (Washington), Nov. 1, 1899.]   S. G. B.

RICHARDSON, ALBERT DEANE (Oct. 6, 1833–Dec. 2, 1869), journalist, was born in Franklin, Mass., the younger of the two sons of Elisha Richardson by his second wife, Harriet Blake. The Richardsons had lived in Norfolk County, Mass., for five or six generations. Albert's father, a farmer, had been a schoolmate of Horace Mann, was a friend and parishioner of Nathaniel Emmons, and lived his entire life within a few miles of the farm that he had inherited from his father. Albert's brother, Charles Addison Richardson, was for many years editor of the Boston *Congregationalist*. Albert attended the public schools and the Holliston Academy, felt no liking for farm work, and for a few terms taught schools in Medway and other nearby towns. Although he is represented as having been somewhat of a Horatio Alger hero, he did not breathe freely in the atmosphere of the old homestead, and when eighteen years old he set out for the West and got as far as Pittsburgh. There he taught school, worked on a newspaper, studied shorthand, wrote farces for Barney Williams, the actor, and—with some qualms of conscience—appeared a few times on the stage. In 1852 he went on to Cincinnati, where he remained for five years, writing for various newspapers and acquiring local renown as an able, alert, energetic writer. In April 1855 he married Mary Louise Pease of Cincinnati, by whom he had five children. His longing for Western adventure still unsatisfied, he took his family in 1857 to Sumner, Kan., near Atchison, but spent much of his time at Leavenworth, Lawrence, and Topeka as correspondent for the Boston *Journal*.

He served for short periods as adjutant-general of the Territory and secretary of the legislature and campaigned in behalf of free soil. In 1859 he accompanied Horace Greeley and Henry Villard to Pike's Peak and returned by himself through the Southwest, which was then little-known territory. Thereafter, until his death, he was connected with the *New York Daily Tribune*.

He gained great acclaim a year later by going to New Orleans as secret correspondent of his paper. It was a dangerous assignment, but Richardson acquitted himself well and returned safely after more than one close escape from lynching. He then became the chief correspondent for the *Tribune* in the theatre of war. On May 3, 1863, while attempting, with Junius Henri Browne of the *Tribune* and Richard T. Colburn of the New York *World,* to run past the Confederate batteries at Vicksburg in a tugboat, he was captured and spent the next eighteen months in various Confederate prisons. On Dec. 18, 1864, he and Browne made their escape from Salisbury and four weeks later arrived at the Union lines near Knoxville, Tenn. Meanwhile his wife and an infant daughter, whom he had never seen, died at his parents' home in Massachusetts. In the spring of 1865 he went to California with Schuyler Colfax, Samuel Bowles, and Lieut.-Gov. William Bross of Illinois. From his newspaper correspondence he compiled two books, *The Secret Service, the Field, the Dungeon, and the Escape* (1865) and *Beyond the Mississippi* (1866), which were sold by subscription and were enormously popular. His style was clear, concrete, and popular in tone. His *Personal History of Ulysses S. Grant* (1868) was written on Partonian lines and was much superior to the ordinary campaign biography. After his death his widow collected his fugitive writings as *Garnered Sheaves* (1871). His end came with tragic suddenness. In 1869 he became engaged to marry Abby Sage McFarland, who had recently been divorced from her husband, Daniel McFarland, a confirmed drunkard with pronounced paranoiac tendencies. On Nov. 25, 1869, McFarland shot Richardson at his desk in the *Tribune* office. Richardson died a week later at the Astor House. On his deathbed he was married to Mrs. McFarland, the ceremony being performed by Henry Ward Beecher and Octavius Brooks Frothingham. At the trial McFarland, a Fenian and a Tammany henchman, was acquitted amid a great demonstration of popular approval. Mrs. Richardson published several books and translated and adapted plays for Daniel Frohman, whom she

had met in the *Tribune* office. She died in Rome Dec. 5, 1900.

[J. A. Vinton, *The Richardson Memorial* (1876); biog. sketch by his widow in *Garnered Sheaves* (1871); *The Trial of Daniel McFarland* (1870), compiled by A. R. Cazauran; *The Richardson-McFarland Tragedy* (1870); *N. Y. Daily Tribune,* Nov. 26–Dec. 6, 1869, and Apr. 5–May 13, 1870.]   G. H. G.

RICHARDSON, ANNA EURETTA (Sept. 5, 1883–Feb. 3, 1931), home economist, was born in Charleston, S. C., the fourth child of William Henry and Euretta (Miller) Richardson, descendants of English, Scotch, and Huguenot stock. In 1887 the family moved to Summerville, where her father served many terms as mayor. Named for an unmarried, school-teaching aunt, she early announced that she would be an old maid and teach school because all Anna Richardsons did that. After a few years in a little school kept by Summerville women, she entered the Memminger High and Normal School at Charleston and at nineteen received the degree of B.S. from the Peabody College for Teachers at Nashville, Tenn. For the next few years she alternated study at the University of Chicago and Columbia University with teaching in the high schools of Summerville, S. C., and Ocala, Fla., at Agnes Scott College, Decatur, Ga., and at the University of Texas. When she received the degree of M.A. from Columbia in 1911, she expected to devote herself to the study of nutrition. Her ability as a teacher and administrator militated against this, however, and in 1917 she definitely entered the field of home economics education as one of three women employed by the new Federal Board for Vocational Education to develop its home economics service. Of this she later became chief, a position which brought her into close personal association with the home economics departments of schools and colleges throughout the country. The essence of her philosophy regarding "vocational home economics" perhaps lay in her recognition of the fact that "homemaking and wage-earning were not two mutually exclusive fields of work for a woman, but that increasingly, in every social level, her life cycle included both experiences."

In 1922 she left the Federal Board for Iowa State College, where as dean of the home economics division for four years she helped to build the department into one of the largest and most influential in the country. In developing the college work in child care and family relationships she was impressed with the close connection between home economics and the new movement for parental education. When, in 1926, funds were granted to the American

Home Economics Association to promote child development and parental education through home economics, she considered the work sufficiently significant to devote her full effort to it. During her four and a half years as field worker for the Association, she studied the courses already found in schools and colleges, held conferences with home economics teachers and administrators, served on many national committees, and generally acted as interpreter between home economics and the other phases of the movement. At the time of her sudden death in Washington she was working on the White House Conference report on education for home and family life. Always more inclined to direct personal contact than to putting words on paper, she influenced most the institutions and individuals with whom she was associated. Her forceful and gracious presence combined with her liberal spirit and exceptional knowledge of the educational needs of girls and women made her a recognized leader in education for homemaking in the United States.

[Sources include: articles by Mary E. Sweeny, Adelaide S. Baylor, R. A. Pearson, and L. K. Frank in *Jour. of Home Economics,* June 1931; *Who's Who in America*, 1930–31; *Evening Star* (Washington, D. C.), Feb. 4, 1931; *N. Y. Times,* Feb. 5, 1931; information as to certain facts from Miss Richardson's family.]

H. W. A.

RICHARDSON, CHARLES FRANCIS (May 29, 1851–Oct. 8, 1913), teacher, author, was born at Hallowell, Me., the elder of the two sons of Moses Charles Richardson by his second wife, Mary Savary Wingate. He was of English descent, belonging on his father's side to the seventh, on his mother's to the sixth, generation of native stock. His father, a graduate of Dartmouth College, was a physician. Richardson had an early liking for journalism and as a boy of fourteen was a correspondent for a country weekly. After his graduation from Dartmouth in 1871, he had to teach for a year in the South Berkshire Institute at New Marlborough, Mass., where his father was then located, before an opening appeared for him on the New York *Independent*. His zeal for books excited the wonder of his colleagues; thirty years later William Hayes Ward still remembered with awe that the boyish literary editor "could repeat the title and price of every book that had been published by the firm of Ticknor & Fields" (*Independent,* Dec. 10, 1908, p. 1362). On Apr. 12, 1878, he married Elizabeth Miner Thomas of Wilkes-Barre, Pa., who survived him without issue. He was editor of the Philadelphia *Sunday School Times* 1878–80 and of *Good Literature* in New York 1880–82. As by-products of these years of journalism he published: *The College Book* (1878), which he edited in collaboration with Henry A. Clark; *A Primer of American Literature* (1878), of which 70,000 copies were sold eventually; *The Cross* (1879), a sequence of thirty-three short religious poems; and *The Choice of Books* (1881), an inspirational volume somewhat in the manner of Philip Gilbert Hamerton, whom Richardson greatly admired. For the twenty-nine years from 1882 to 1911 he was Winkley professor of Anglo-Saxon and English language and literature at Dartmouth. Till 1894 he was the sole member of his department. With the passage of the years he grew in esteem with undergraduates and alumni and came to be regarded as an exceptionally able teacher of literature. Outside Dartmouth he was known almost exclusively by his *American Literature 1607–1885* (Vol. I, *The Development of American Thought,* 1887; Vol. II, *American Poetry and Fiction,* 1888). Contemporary criticism noted its inadequacy to the subject, its mediocrity as criticism, and occasional aberrations of taste (see the reviews in the *Nation,* Feb. 24, 1887, and Feb. 14, 1889), and later critics have been shocked at a historian who could disparage Melville as a popularity-seeker, dismiss Mark Twain altogether, and then devote two pages to the praise of Josh Billings. Yet with all its shortcomings Richardson's was the one continuously readable account of American literature as a whole before the appearance of Barrett Wendell's *Literary History of America* (1900) and exerted in consequence a considerable influence. His only other works were an anonymously published novel, *The End of the Beginning* (1896)—a namby-pamby imitation of Hawthorne—and *A Study of English Rhyme* (1909). He retired as professor emeritus in 1911 and died two years later at his summer home at Sugar Hill, N. H., of pneumonia.

[J. A. Vinton, *The Richardson Memorial* (1876), esp. pp. 853–54; C. E. L. Wingate, *Hist. of the Wingate Family* (1886); E. F. Nichols, E. J. Bartlett, F. P. Emery, commemorative addresses, *Dartmouth Alumni Mag.,* Nov. 1913, Apr. 1914; *Boston Transcript,* Oct. 8, 1913.]

G. H. G.

RICHARDSON, CHARLES WILLIAMSON (Aug. 22, 1861–Aug. 25, 1929), physician, was the son of Charles E. F. and Charlotte Ann (Williamson) Richardson. The Richardsons traced their ancestry to the family of Daniel Boone in America and in England to Sir John Richardson, surgeon and naturalist of the first two polar expeditions of Sir John Franklin. Born in Washington, D. C., Richardson studied at Columbian College (now the George

Washington University). There, and also at the University of Pennsylvania, he became doctor of medicine in 1884. After study in London, Göttingen, and Vienna, he began practice in Washington in 1886, making a specialty of diseases of throat, nose, and ear. To him medicine was an art. Ever seeking the cause of disease, he published the results of his researches in upwards of one hundred papers, for the most part first read at medical society meetings in America and Europe. Professor in the George Washington University Medical School from 1891 to 1924 (emeritus 1924–29), he served on the staff of various Washington hospitals and was one of the founders of the Episcopal Eye, Ear, and Throat Hospital. He was president of the Medical Society of the District of Columbia (1904), the American Laryngological, Rhinological and Otological Society (1902), the American Otological Society (1914), the American Climatological and Clinical Society (1921), and of the American Laryngological Association (1929). He was a trustee of the American Medical Association (1921–29); fellow of the American Academy of Sciences, the American College of Surgeons, and the Royal Society of Medicine, London.

In 1886, Richardson was one of the first to master and utilize Dr. John P. O'Dwyer's invention of intubation in cases of diphtheria, and was equally quick to champion diphtheria antitoxin. In 1912 he first called attention to abscess of the lungs as a complication following tonsilectomy (*Washington Medical Annals,* May 1912) and published his researches in a series of papers widely circulated at home and abroad. In an address to the American Laryngological Association (1911) he gave results of his investigations into the effects of diet in vasomotor disturbances in the upper air tract, thus leading to the study of biochemistry in connection with diseases of the nose and ear.

When the United States entered the World War, Richardson gave up private practice to devote himself to organizing the work of the Army Medical Reserve Corps, of which he was an original member, rising to colonel's rank. He secured legislation by Congress to retain disabled soldiers under medical authority, and under the surgeon-general's office, established as a branch of Hospital No. 11, at Cape May, a school for reëducation and for the reconstruction of defects of hearing and speech as a means of restoring deaf men to careers of usefulness. (See Richardson's article in the *Transactions of the Twenty-fifth Annual Meeting of the American Laryngological, Rhinological and Otological*

Society, 1919.) In 1924 he obtained from the National Research Council a grant to make a general inquiry into the physical causes of deafness and prepared a comprehensive report based upon the examination of 3,734 pupils in nineteen schools and institutions scattered throughout the country—the first survey ever conducted in this subject (*Archives of Otolaryngology,* May 1928). Richardson was married on May 27, 1889, to Amy Elizabeth Small, of Washington. They had one daughter. He died in Boston and was buried in Arlington National Cemetery.

[Sources include: Medic. Soc. of the District of Columbia, *Memorial Addresses in Memory of Dr. Chas. W. Richardson,* Dec. 8, 1929, containing a bibliography of 105 of Richardson's medical papers; *Laryngoscope,* Sept. 1929; *Jour. Am. Medic. Asso.,* Aug. 31, 1929; *Archives of Otolaryngology,* Sept. 1929; *Jour. of Laryngology and Otology* (London), Feb. 1930; *Evening Star* (Washington, D. C.), Aug. 26, 1929. Information as to certain facts was supplied by Prof. Lee Wallace Dean, Washington Univ. School of Medicine, St. Louis.]
C. M.

RICHARDSON, EDMUND (June 28, 1818–Jan. 11, 1886), cotton planter, factor, and manufacturer, was born in Caswell County, N. C., a few miles from Danville, Va. He was one of seven children born to James Richardson, planter and country merchant, and Nancy Payne Ware. At the age of ten he entered an old-field school where he continued four years, supplementing his study by Saturday work on his widowed mother's farm. After serving as a clerk in a dry-goods store at Danville during 1832, he removed the following year to Brandon, Miss., where he found similar employment at $40 per annum. The settlement of his father' estate in 1840 left him $2,800 and a few slaves which, together with his savings, soon enabled him to form a mercantile partnership at Jackson with branch stores in neighboring communities. While buying goods in New York in 1847 he met Margaret Elizabeth Patton of Huntsville, Ala., a sister of former Governor Robert Patton. They were married in May 1848, and to them were born seven children.

Richardson invested his mercantile profits in land and slaves, and by 1861 he owned five plantations and several hundred negroes. In 1852 he entered the factorage business in New Orleans as junior member in Thornhill & Company, and although the firm prospered, outstanding acceptances amounting to a half-million dollars caused it to suspend business at the beginning of the Civil War. By 1865 he was heavily in debt, but his energy and business acumen enabled him to rebuild his fortune. His cotton commission firm reopened and within a year he was solvent. The dissolution of his partnership with Thornhill in 1867 was soon followed by the establishment of another factorage firm in New Orleans, Richardson & May, which received annually 100,000 bales. Having succeeded as planter and factor, Richardson decided to manufacture cotton, believing that factories should be situated near the source of the raw product. For this purpose he leased in 1868 the Mississippi penitentiary for a three-year period at $18,000 per annum, and was later persuaded to keep it another year. To employ all the convicts he purchased more plantations and leased others. Eventually he acquired about fifty, located in Mississippi, Louisiana, and Arkansas, and on each of them he kept a store and sold merchandise to his employees. He was the largest cotton planter in the world: the 25,000 acres which he cultivated produced in good years some 12,000 bales, worth more than a half-million dollars (New Orleans *Daily Picayune,* Jan. 13, 1886). In 1873 he bought a controlling interest in the cotton mills at Wesson, Miss., and served as president until his death in 1886. His business was expanded to include the Refuge Oil Mill at Vicksburg and the Vicksburg, Shreveport & Pacific Railroad. In his varied activities he enjoyed an enviable reputation for business integrity and sound judgment, industry and enterprise, thrift and perseverance.

Because of his extensive cotton interests Richardson was known as the "Cotton King," and his appointment as commissioner from the cotton states at the Philadelphia Centennial of 1876, and his election as vice-president of the Atlanta Cotton Exposition of 1881, came in recognition of his ability as a cotton magnate. The crowning honor of his career came in 1884 when President Arthur appointed him commissioner of the World's Industrial and Cotton Centennial Exposition, held in New Orleans. Richardson was made president of the board of management, delivered the opening speech, and contributed liberally to the expense of the Exposition. He died in Jackson, Miss., in his sixty-eighth year.

[Much of the information about Richardson was furnished by his grandson, Edmund Richardson of New Orleans, and his niece, Susie Blue Buchanan of Brandon. Obituaries are available in the New Orleans *Daily Picayune,* and New Orleans *Times-Democrat,* Jan. 13, 1886. The files of these papers for 1884–85 contain extensive accounts of the New Orleans Exposition. See also *Biog. and Hist. Memoirs of Miss.* (1891), vol. II.]   W. H. S.

RICHARDSON, HENRY HOBSON (Sept. 29, 1838–Apr. 27, 1886), architect, was born on the Priestley plantation, St. James Parish, La., the son of Henry Dickenson and Catherine Caroline (Priestley) Richardson. His father had come from St. George, Bermuda, of which James Richardson, his great-great-grandfather, was one of the early settlers. Henry Dickenson Richardson became, in New Orleans, a partner in the cotton business of Henry Hobson & Company and named his son for the senior member of the firm. Henry Hobson Richardson's mother was a grand-daughter of the noted chemist and radical, Joseph Priestley [*q.v.*], whose second son, William, moved with his family to Louisiana in 1801 and in a short time amassed a sizable fortune with his sugar-cane plantation.

Richardson was the eldest of four children. He was educated in New Orleans—first at a public school, and then at the private school of George Blackman, where he distinguished himself in mathematics. He had early displayed a marked interest in drawing, and at ten was entered in a drawing class with much older pupils. His family hoped, through the friendship of Judah P. Benjamin, to obtain for him an appointment to West Point, but Henry stuttered, and was accordingly ineligible. It is said that he attended the University of Louisiana (Van Rensselaer, *post,* p. 4), where he again distinguished himself in mathematics. He then went to Cambridge, Mass., to study with a tutor for the Harvard entrance examinations, and entered with the class of 1859. Little is known definitely of his college career. He was slim, handsome, popular, and something of a beau, and was renowned as a chess player. Before his graduation he became engaged to Julia Gorham Hayden, a daughter of Dr. John Cole Hayden of Boston.

Richardson had planned, when he entered Harvard, to become a civil engineer; when he graduated it was with the intention of being an architect, and he was delighted that his father offered to send him abroad to study. To the École des Beaux Arts in Paris he went in the summer of 1859, at once trying, and failing, the entrance examinations. He worked hard during the year, and in the fall of 1860 tried again and was accepted, eighteenth out of sixty. Once in the École, he entered the atelier of Louis Jules André, whose work he admired. Again, as at Harvard, he was popular; he had a large circle of friends both French and American, and he had plenty of money. To this prosperous era the Civil War brought a gradual close. Remittances became spasmodic, and in perplexity he returned to Boston early in 1862, uncertain whether to settle there at once, to return south if he could, or to go back to Paris. But architecture in Boston was languishing and the trip to New Orleans impossible, so in March he returned to Paris, determined to be dependent no longer, but to earn his way (Van Rensselaer, *post*, pp. 10 ff.).

Through the influence of André he got his first job in the office of Theodore Labrouste, brother of Henri Labrouste. Later he worked also for J. I. Hittorff, superintending some of his famous railroad-station work. Richardson's first actual practical experience thus came in the employ of French architects who were thoroughly imbued with the doctrines of Néo-Grec rationalism. Richardson's days were devoted to office work, his evenings to study at the École. He also entered the painting atelier of Leperre (possibly Lepère) for a time. It seems as though in this continuous grind he was attempting to drown the misery of the war and his poverty, and the long, painful separation from his fiancée. Naturally, the school work suffered; he was never awarded his diploma. Those years were also a contributing cause to the invalidism that dogged his working life.

When the war ended, many French friends urged him to become naturalized and to attempt to win the Prix de Rome, for his architectural brilliance was widely recognized. His family wrote him to return to New Orleans, but he finally decided to go back to the North, and settled in New York as the place that offered the best opportunities. For a short time he lived in Brooklyn, in partnership with a builder named Roberts, but the work was oppressive to him and he resigned. Meanwhile, his Boston friends were seeking ways to help him; and in November 1866 one of them arranged to have him invited to submit plans in a competition for the First Unitarian Church in Springfield, a competition that he promptly won. Later, he won another competition for an Episcopal Church in West Medford, and his reputation began to grow swiftly. On Jan. 3, 1867, he married, and the bride and groom set up housekeeping in Clifton, Staten Island; his office was with Emlen T. Littell, a noted architect of the time. In October 1867, he formed a partnership with Charles D. Gambrill (1832–81), who had been a partner of George B. Post [*q.v.*]. The partnership lasted till 1878.

From 1870 on, Richardson's practice grew with extraordinary rapidity. The amount of building to be done in those years was enormous, trained architects were few, and architects of Richardson's brilliance and originality were rare indeed. The winning of the Brattle Street Church competition in Boston, in July 1870, brought him an invitation to the Trinity Church competition, which he won two years later, and that building made his reputation nation-wide.

In 1876, he was appointed with Leopold Eidlitz and Frederick Law Olmstead to complete the building and grounds of the New York State Capitol, begun years before by Arthur D. Gilman [*q.v.*] and Thomas Fuller. The change from the stupid Victorian classic of the lower floors to the Romanesque of the top was undoubtedly due to Richardson's influence; and many of the interiors are entirely his.

Richardson was so frequently in Boston that in 1874 his family settled in Brookline, Mass., and in October 1878 he moved his office to the same place, gradually enlarging it as necessary, but always in such a way that the connection of the house and office—typical of his personal delight in his work—was preserved. In 1882, accompanied by Phillips Brooks and others, Richardson made his only long travel tour of Europe, partly to consult specialists with regard to his health, which was growing more and more uncertain. But, whatever the reason for the trip, it became in reality a strenuous tour of architectural study and recreation—both sampled with that superb gusto that distinguished Richardson's approach to life. Now, for the first time, he saw the Romanesque buildings of Auvergne and northern Spain, which he had so long admired and whose style he had so brilliantly adapted. In Paris he was warmly greeted by his old friends and schoolmates, to whom he urged the necessity of forgetting the old "cut-and-dried" type of traditional architecture and creating anew. But his urging fell on deaf ears; even the rationalism of the Néo-Grec designers was gone.

The list of Richardson's work is too long to give in full. It includes buildings in Boston, Chicago, Pittsburgh, and Cincinnati. In it, however, certain classes stand out as most revealing the ideals that he sought. Beginning chiefly as an ecclesiastical architect, he turned increasingly to more modern problems. He was once heard to say: "The things I want most to design are a grain elevator and the interior of a great river steamboat" (Van Rensselaer, p. 22). The earlier churches are in a simplified Victorian Gothic style, but in the Brattle Street Church tower (1870), with its rich band of sculptured figures, Richardson achieved a result that was new and personal. In Trinity he first employed that modified French and Spanish Romanesque usually termed "Richardsonian." His fully developed ideas of ecclesiastical architecture are seen only in his unsuccessful design for the Albany Cathedral—a competition he lost by a complete disregard of the program, which he found too limiting. It is a design worthy of careful study, remarkable alike for its scale, its subtle rationalism, and its fresh interpretation of his favorite Romanesque style.

In his larger houses he seems to be struggling between fashion and his own desire to be daringly new, and achieves a sort of gay heaviness. By far the best of his domestic work is the shingled, unassuming summer cottage, of which the Rev. P. Browne's at Marion, Mass. (1881), is an example. In this he created a type essentially American, true alike to its function, its site, and its materials. His libraries, despite their "Romanesque" style, are important as showing the development of a rationalism not unlike that of the French Néo-Grec school. The Woburn Library (1877) is least successful, that at North Easton (1877) much clearer in its composition, that at Quincy (1880) best of all in its quiet simplicity; yet all are unforced expressions of their plans, and in all there is a free handling of windows, dictated by the actual need of interior light rather than the mere requirements of exterior design. Of the two Harvard buildings, Sever Hall (1878) is an attempt to be simple and creative, but nevertheless to use forms not too much out of harmony with those of the Colonial "yard." Its grouped classroom windows are typical of Richardson's clear analysis of a problem, but there is in the whole not a little of the current "Queen Anne" influence. Austin Hall (1881), with its massive arched porch and its beautiful lecture-hall wing, is more characteristic in its delightful ornament and its magnificent use of materials.

The monumental public buildings are, in spirit, somewhat similar. Richardson should not be judged by the exterior of the New York State Capitol; the problem set by the earlier building was insoluble. Some of the interiors are superb —rich, yet controlled—and the effect with the Hunt mural paintings (long since destroyed by dampness) must have been magnificent. The Cincinnati Chamber of Commerce (1885) is grand in scale, but its enormous roof shows the dangers of exaggeration to which his own gusto occasionally led him. The Pittsburgh Jail and Court House, like Richardson's Albany City Hall (1880), suffer from the necessity he felt to achieve picturesqueness even in monumental work, but both are superbly composed and show his usual facility in handling materials and bringing out their especial beauties; the Pittsburgh group, moreover, particularly in the jail portion and the bridge leading to it, achieves a power, a grim magnificence that was new in American architecture.

It was in the commercial buildings that Rich-ardson saw truest and created outstanding innovations. The wholesale store buildings in Boston for Pray (c. 1886) and for Ames (1882) show an extraordinary sense of the realities of the problem, and (especially in the former) a marked desire to achieve with those realities a logical and beautiful architectural effect. In the Marshall Field Building in Chicago (1885) perhaps modern commercial architecture was born. During his last days it was his often expressed desire—unfortunately unfulfilled—to live until the completion of the Marshall Field Building and the Pittsburgh group. They were his favorite works. Almost equally revolutionary was the series of railroad stations he designed for the Boston & Albany Railroad, from Auburndale, Mass. (1881), to Wellesley Hills (1885). Here was a problem whose realities delighted him, and here for the first time the possibilities of beauty in long, low platform roofs and spreading waiting rooms were realized. These Richardson stations created a type beautiful in itself and still valid, because so soundly designed. They were widely imitated until very recently.

Among his other important works are: Agawam National Bank, Springfield, Mass. (1869); County Court House, Springfield, Mass. (1871); American Express Company Building, Chicago (1872); Billings Library, University of Vermont, Burlington, Vt. (1883); Converse Library, Malden, Mass. (1883); Baptist Church, Newton, Mass. (1884); Bagley Memorial Fountain, Detroit, Mich. (1888); Railroad stations at Palmer (1881), North Easton (1881), Chestnut Hill (1883), South Framingham (1883), Holyoke (1883), Mass., and at New London, Conn. (1885); and houses for J. J. Glessner and Franklin MacVeagh, Chicago, 1885, both remarkable for their beautiful stone work and subtle fenestration. The work from 1868 to 1878 is under the name of Gambrill & Richardson; that from 1878 on is under Richardson's own name. Beyond designing a few houses, Gambrill's part in the organization seems to have been mainly that of organizer and business executive.

Richardson, during his Boston years, was famous, sought after, and prosperous. He knew most of his great contemporaries; built homes in Washington for Henry Adams and John Hay; was an intimate friend of John La Farge and Saint-Gaudens, for whom he helped procure the commission for the Shaw Memorial in Boston (Saint-Gaudens, post, p. 332). He thoroughly enjoyed his success and the means it brought. He lived well, and he liked the intimate connection of his house and his office. He was noted for his capacity for champagne, for his love of laughter, for his extraordinary gusto. H. H. Townsend, the English architect, who had known him, spoke of him as "one who took delight in life for the sheer pleasure of living." Expressive of this gayety were the bright yellow vests he loved to wear. Saint-Gaudens says that seldom was there a dinner in the Brookline home without some welcome guest.

Meanwhile, the slim figure of college days had become heavy with a sort of jolly, yet powerful, monk-like corpulence; but the illness which dogged him—and which demanded of him an ascetic regimen he could not, or would not, keep —grew upon him. In his office one day he remarked, "There is lots of work to do, isn't there? And such work! And to think I may die here in this office at any moment!"—then, in a moment, "Well, there is no man in the whole world that enjoys life while it lasts as I do" (Van Rensselaer, p. 26). He had had a bad attack in the autumn of 1885; another came in March 1886, and from this he did not recover. He had six children, two daughters and four sons. He was fellow of the American Institute of Architects, of the American Academy of Arts and Sciences, and of the Archeological Institute of America, and just before his death was elected an honorary and corresponding member of the Royal Institute of British Architects.

Richardson's influence was enormous; he set an architectural fashion that dominated the eastern states from 1880 to the Chicago World's Fair. But his imitators rarely realized the deep foundations of his art, copying the mannerisms only. Richardson, where floor heights were low, had often used wide, squat arches, with low spring lines, in order to give the maximum sense of broad welcome (as in the Ames Memorial Hall, North Easton, Mass., and the Harvard Law School); his imitators spread ugly and meaningless squat arches over everything. Richardson had used quarry-faced stone, laid with consummate artistry and an unfailing sense of texture; his imitators used stone as rough as they could make it, without taste or texture. Certain of his followers like Buffington, Emerson, and Halsey Wood achieved something of his spontaneity and his sense of materials, but the greater number copied only his eccentricities. The result was inevitable; after his death the "Richardsonian" style soon fell into disrepute, and it died before the conquering renaissance of classicism that followed the Chicago World's Fair of 1893.

Yet a deeper influence lasted. Both Charles F. McKim and Stanford White [qq.v.] were for several years in Richardson's office, and the influence of his care in handling materials, the brilliance of his planning, and his rationalism was marked in the early work of the firm of McKim, Mead & White. Richardson's demand for interior richness and his love of the decorative arts also had wide effects. In Trinity Church he had insisted on rich mural decoration, and had seen that it was handled by John La Farge (who employed Saint-Gaudens upon some of the painted figures); in the Albany Capitol he had used William M. Hunt. This ideal of architecture and the sister arts as one unity persisted long after Richardson's death, and influenced much of the work of Louis C. Tiffany, and many of the early interiors of McKim, Mead & White. Even the Byzantine-Romanesque ornament of Richardson had results more important than its superficial copies, for its freshness and spontaneity profoundly impressed not only John Wellborn Root [q.v.], but also Louis H. Sullivan [q.v.], and so were not without influence in the birth of advanced twentieth-century architecture.

Richardson's reputation has undergone a strange metamorphosis. During his lifetime he was acclaimed a genius, and yet his contemporaries had but a slight idea of his real importance or the reasons for his greatness. Consequently, after his death, there came a violent reaction. Richardson's own work was considered inappropriate, not suited to America, too expensive, too personal. It was described as "remarkable for its absence of proportion and sense of real beauty; in the hands of his followers lawless and now happily extinct" (Charles Moore, ed., *The Promise of American Architecture*, 1905, p. 23). "Richardson's style," it was said, "was unsuited to the modern requirements in respect to light and air" (Charles Moore, *Daniel H. Burnham*, 1921, p. 28). Later, a change came. At first it was the sheer exuberance of his creative power that impressed the critics. He appeared to them as the typical great romanticist, the poet in building (Lewis Mumford, *Sticks and Stones*, 1924; Fiske Kimball, *American Architecture*, 1928). Later still, his extraordinary inventiveness—his refusal to be bound by any historical or archeological requirements—attracted attention, as earlier it had fired the imagination of Root and Sullivan. Last of all, the sound rationalism of Richardson's basic architectural approach and his amazingly sensitive feeling for the true qualities of building materials have seemed the reason for his greatness (Lewis Mumford, *The Brown Decades*, 1931). To a generation interested in romance, he was the great Romanticist; to war-time America, interested primarily in individual revolt and individual creation, he was the first American architectural rebel; to the present critics who seek for rationalism and functional honesty he is the first American functionalist. Perhaps this is the greatest and truest criterion of the depth and power of his genius—that to successive groups, with varying demands, he has seemed to be the first great American example of the qualities that they seek.

[Mariana G. Van Rensselaer, *Henry Hobson Richardson and His Works* (1888); Horace Townsend, in *Magazine of Art* (London), Feb. 1894, pp. 133–38; obituaries in *Am. Architect and Building News*, May 1, 1886, and *Boston Daily Advertiser*, Apr. 29, 1886; Montgomery Schuyler, *American Architecture* (1892); Talcott Williams, lecture on Springfield architecture, reprinted in *Am. Architect and Building News*, Nov. 12, 1881; Homer St. Gaudens, ed., *The Reminiscences of Augustus St. Gaudens* (2 vols., 1913); Charles Moore, *Daniel H. Burnham* (2 vols., 1921); Lewis Mumford, *Sticks and Stones* (1924), and *The Brown Decades* (1931); C. C. Baldwin, *Stanford White* (1931).]   T.F.H.

RICHARDSON, ISRAEL BUSH (Dec. 26, 1815–Nov. 3, 1862), Union soldier, the son of Israel Putnam and Susan (Holmes) Richardson, and a descendant of Israel Putnam [*q.v.*], was born in Fairfax, Vt. He was appointed a cadet to the United States Military Academy from Vermont in 1836. Upon graduation, July 1, 1841, he was commissioned brevet second lieutenant, 3rd Infantry, and at once saw active service against the Seminole Indians in Florida. He was promoted to second lieutenant on Sept. 30, 1841. After the campaign against the Seminoles, he served in various garrisons from 1842 to 1845, when he joined the army of military occupation in Texas. In the Mexican War he served in General Taylor's army at Palo Alto, Resaca-de-la-Palma, and Monterey during 1846 and was promoted to first lieutenant on Sept. 21 of that year. From February 1847 to the end of the war he served in General Scott's army, being actively engaged in every important battle from the siege of Vera Cruz to the capture of Mexico city. For gallant and meritorious services during this campaign he was twice brevetted, first as captain and later as major. For the calm intrepidity with which he led his company at Cerro Gordo, his comrades dubbed him "Fighting Dick," a name he bore until his death. For seven years following the war he served in various garrisons in the Southwest. He was promoted to the rank of captain on Mar. 5, 1851. In 1855 he resigned from the army and took up farming at Pontiac, Mich.

At the outbreak of the Civil war he organized the 2nd Michigan Volunteer Regiment of which he became colonel on May 25, 1861. Near the end of June he reported with his regiment in the defenses of Washington, D. C., and shortly thereafter was assigned to the command of a brigade. At the Battle of Bull Run, July 21, 1861, his brigade, guarding Blackburn's Ford on the flank of McDowell's army, was able to cover the retreat of the Union forces in an orderly manner. After the battle of Bull Run he was promoted brigadier-general of United States Volunteers with rank from May 17, 1861. The following March he was given command of a division in Sumner's corps, with which he served throughout the Peninsular campaign. His prudence and skill in the command of his division won for him the promotion to major-general of Volunteers on July 4, 1862. After the withdrawal of the Union army from the Peninsula Richardson's division was assigned to Hooker's I Corps. At Antietam, on Sept. 17, 1862, his division won glory in the sanguinary struggle which drove the Confederates from the "Bloody Lane," but its brave commander fell mortally wounded while directing the fire of a battery. He died at Sharpsburg, Md., on Nov. 3, 1862. With his massive frame and iron expression, his unpretentious manners and absolute fearlessness, he had been a real leader of men and his untimely death was an inestimable loss to the Union. He was twice married: first on Aug. 3, 1850, to Rita Stevenson of El Paso, Tex., who died the following year, and again on May 29, 1861, to Frances A. Traver of Kalamazoo, Mich., who with their infant son survived him.

[J. A. Vinton, *The Richardson Memorial* (1876); G. W. Cullum, *Biog. Reg. . . . U. S. Mil. Acad.* (1891); Records of the Adjutant-General, and of the Pension Bureau, Wash, D. C.; *War of the Rebellion: Official Records (Army)*; A. M. Hemenway, ed., *The Vt. Hist. Gazeteer*, vol. II (1871); Charles Lanman, *The Red Book of Mich.* (1871); *Detroit Advertiser and Tribune*, Nov. 5, 8, 12, 1862; *N. Y. Times*, Nov. 6, 1862.]   S.J.H.

RICHARDSON, JAMES DANIEL (Mar. 10, 1843–July 24, 1914), statesman and Masonic leader, was born in Rutherford County, Tenn., the son of John Watkins and Augusta Mary (Starnes) Richardson. He attended the rural schools of his native county and Franklin College near Nashville, but he left before graduation to enlist in the Confederate army. Serving through the war, he retired as adjutant of the 45th Tennessee Volunteer Infantry. On Jan. 18, 1865, he was married to Alabama Pippin, of Greene County, Ala., and soon afterward began to study law. He was admitted to the bar in 1867 and began practice at Murfreesboro, Tenn., which continued to be his legal residence, although for more than half of his active life he actually lived in Washington. Elected to the lower house of the Tennessee legislature in 1871, he was chosen speaker at the opening of the session. In 1873 he was sent to the state Senate, and in 1876 was a delegate to the National Democratic Convention at St. Louis. The year 1884 witnessed his election to the lower house of Congress where he served for a full score of years, becoming eventually the Democratic nominee for speaker of the Fifty-sixth and Fifty-seventh congresses, and chairman of the Democratic congressional committee. Meanwhile he was also a delegate to the party national conventions of 1896 at Chicago and of 1900 at Kansas City, and of the latter he was the permanent chairman. About 1893, pursuant to a resolution of the Fifty-third Congress, he began the preparation of a work published first in ten volumes under the title of *A Compilation of the Messages and Papers of the Presidents* (1896–99). It has since been republished with additions. In 1900 he was authorized by another resolution "to compile, edit, and publish, without expense to the Government, the State papers and diplomatic correspondence of the late Confederate States." This work, in two volumes, was entitled *A Compilation of the Messages and Papers of the Confederacy* (1905).

In 1881 the degrees of Scottish Rite Masonry were conferred upon Richardson by Grand Commander Albert Pike and two years later Richardson was elected Grand High Priest of Tennessee Royal Arch Masons. In the same year he published his *Tennessee Templars* (1883), a biographical account of the Commandery and its membership in that state. In 1884 he was elected to active membership in the Scottish Rite Supreme Council, Southern Jurisdiction, and during the remainder of his life missed but three of its regular sessions. In 1901 at its centenary observance, he delivered an address which was published separately and also in the *Transactions* of that year. At the same session of the Supreme Council Richardson was elected Grand Commander and served until his death. Two years after his election he announced his intention to retire from Congress and devote his entire time to Masonic office. His commandership, which lasted nearly thirteen years (longer than any other save two), was notable for its promotion of internationalism and the construction of the imposing Scottish Rite Temple in Washington, generally regarded as the finest extant specimen of Masonic architecture. His various contacts and experiences had by this time changed him from a local politician to an internationalist with decidedly pacific leanings. He promoted

and attended as a delegate the International Conference of Supreme Councils at Brussels in 1907 and was largely responsible for that of Washington in 1911. Honorary membership was conferred upon him by the Supreme Councils of northern United States, Canada, France, Belgium, Italy, and Greece. He died and is buried at Murfreesboro, but a tablet on the inner wall of the Temple describes that building as his monument.

[See: *The Supreme Council, 33°* (1931), written by C. S. Lobinger; P. M. Hamer, *Tennessee: A Hist.* (1933), vol. IV; *Biog. Dir. Am. Cong.* (1928); *Who's Who in America*, 1912–13; *New Age Mag.*, Aug. 1914; *Washington Post*, July 25, 1914. Richardson's allocutions as Grand Commander, together with other papers, are printed in the *Transactions* of the mother Supreme Council.]   C. S. L.

RICHARDSON, JOSEPH (Sept. 17, 1711–Dec. 3, 1784), silversmith, was born in Philadelphia, Pa., the son of Francis and Elizabeth (Growdon) Richardson and the grandson of Francis Richardson, a member of the Society of Friends, who emigrated to America in 1681. His father was trained as a silversmith and although not a large quantity of his work has been discovered, what remains shows fine workmanship. In a shop at the Corner of Letitia Court in Market Street, Joseph was trained by his father in what was then advertised by masters seeking apprentices as "the Mystery or Art" of silver-smithing. Later the Richardsons moved their shop to Front street, near Walnut, and Joseph inherited this shop and business at the death of his father in 1729. That the young man had a well-established concern is witnessed by his day-books for the years 1733–40 which are now in the possession of the Pennsylvania Historical Society. They reveal the custom of the colonists of conserving extra money in the form of plate. Many citizens preferred to have a part of their hoardings turned into some form that was easily identifiable if stolen, and thus the reputation of a silversmith rested not only upon his technical and artistic ability but upon his integrity.

Joseph Richardson was married on Aug. 13, 1741, to Hannah Worrell, who died in 1747, leaving him with an infant daughter. On Apr. 14, 1748, he married Mary Allen and she bore him two sons and three daughters. The sons, Joseph, born in 1752, and Nathaniel, born in 1754, were trained by the father in his craft and worked with him till his death; Nathaniel gave up his share in the business after the settling of his father's estate. Joseph the younger was associated more closely with his father in the shop and at least one piece of plate has been found that bears the marks of both father and son. Many of the clients of the Richardsons were members of the Society of Friends, who prized fine workmanship while demanding simplicity in their possessions. This demanded simplicity put greater tax on the skill of craftsmen than ornateness would have done. It made fineness of line and correctness of balance imperative. The elder Joseph Richardson became a man of public standing. With fellow members of the Society of Friends he helped to organize in 1756 the Friendly Association for Regaining and Preserving Peace with the Indians. As part of their program of friendship they presented silver medals and neck-ornaments to a number of leading Indians and Richardson was commissioned to cast the dies for the medals and to make the gorgets. His civic interest is further evidenced in the part he played in the foundation of the Pennsylvania Hospital, which he served from 1756 to 1770 as a member of the board. His silver is marked with I. R. in Roman capitals in an oval, rectangle, or square.

[C. L. Avery in *Early Am. Silver* (1930) discusses the work of the Richardsons at some length and shows pictures of the work of Jos. Richardson the elder. M. T. Seaman in *Thos. Richardson of South Shields, Durham County, England, and his Descendants in . . . America* (1929) covers the family history somewhat more thoroughly and gives a number of pictures of the work of Jos. Richardson the elder. Both authors quote from H. F. Jayne and S. W. Woodhouse, "Early Phila. Silversmiths," *Art in America,* Oct. 1921.]

K. A. K.

RICHARDSON, MAURICE HOWE (Dec. 31, 1851–July 30, 1912), surgeon, was born in Athol, Mass., the son of Nathan Henry and Martha Ann (Barber) Richardson, of New England descent. He was graduated by Harvard College in 1873. While teaching the next year in the Salem (Mass.) High School, he came into contact with Edward B. Peirson, M.D., who first turned his thoughts towards medicine. After a year of apprenticeship with Peirson he entered the second-year class at the Harvard Medical School and was graduated in 1877. A brief surgical training at the Massachusetts General Hospital followed. In 1877 he began practice in Boston, at the same time entering upon his work as a teacher at the Harvard Medical School. He gradually worked through the department of anatomy into surgery, finally holding the highest position in that branch of medicine in the Harvard Medical School as Moseley Professor of Surgery from 1907 until the time of his death. During the same period he was actively associated with the Massachusetts General Hospital, acting as visiting surgeon from 1886 to 1910 and subsequently as surgeon-in-chief.

Richardson was well equipped, both physically and mentally, for the strenuous life of a surgeon of his day. Athletic in type, he thoroughly enjoyed long walks, swimming in the open sea, arduous trips to scattered operations over a wide range of country and, when the day proved too short for his numerous undertakings, early morning writing. At home he was delightfully hospitable, played the piano, as well as a number of other musical instruments, and entertained a host of friends. In 1879 he married Margaret White Peirson, daughter of his old preceptor. Three sons became physicians.

His surgical career was marked by his great skill as a teacher and lecturer. Based upon a fundamental knowledge of anatomy and augmented by remarkable skill in drawing on the blackboard, his demonstrations were masterpieces of clear presentation. In later years his work was confined to abdominal surgery and his knowledge of this region of the body, both anatomically and pathologically, was not surpassed by any of his contemporaries. "The surgical problems that lurked in the depths of the body, that could only be uncovered and unraveled by difficult dissection guided by great anatomical knowledge, were the ones that he sought and enjoyed" (A. T. Cabot, in *Harvard Graduates' Magazine, post,* p. 32). No operative surgeon in America had a finer or more deserved reputation than Richardson at the height of his career. Numerous medical societies, both national and international, enjoyed his membership. He wrote many papers on surgical subjects and lectured widely. The most notable of his writings concerned themselves with the development of the operation for appendicitis (1892–98), first clearly outlined by one of his teachers, Reginald Heber Fitz [*q.v.*], and with the diseases of the gall passages, the pancreas, and other organs lying closely in the upper abdominal cavity. The elucidation of diagnostic criteria of abdominal disease and the demonstration of the technique of regional surgery in a cavity of the body which had, previous to his time, been only partially and inadequately explored, were his major contributions to medicine. As a practitioner he was kindly, friendly, and devoted to his patients.

[See especially the *Boston Medic. and Surgic. Jour.,* Dec. 26, 1912. For other references see: *Ibid.,* Aug. 8, 22, 1912, Nov. 21, 1918; *Who's Who in America,* 1910–11; Class of 1873, Harvard Coll., *Ninth Report* (1913); *Harvard Grads.' Mag.,* Sept. 1912; *Boston Herald,* Aug. 1, 1912; *Boston Transcript,* July 31, Aug. 2, 1912.]

H. R. V.

RICHARDSON, ROBERT (Sept. 25, 1806–Oct. 22, 1876), physician, college professor, author, was born at Pittsburgh, Pa. His parents, Nathaniel and Julia (Logan) Richardson, were both born in Ireland. Nathaniel Richardson, an Episcopalian and one of the first vestrymen of Trinity Church, Pittsburgh, was also, in 1815, the first contributor to a fund which Alexander Campbell raised to build a Baptist church in Charleston, Va. (now Wellsburg, W. Va.), and the next year he placed his son in a school conducted by Thomas Campbell in Pittsburgh. Two years later the boy became a pupil of Walter Scott, who after a few months spent in studying the Haldanean and Scotch Baptist churches in New York, Baltimore, and Washington, came to live and conduct a school in the Richardson home. Robert was confirmed in the Episcopal church about 1824 and became a member of Trinity Church. After further study with private tutors he was enrolled in the School of Medicine of the University of Pennsylvania for one year, 1826-27. He also studied medicine under Dr. P. Morey of Pittsburgh. Later he received an A.M. degree from Jefferson College. By 1829 he had begun practice thirteen miles west of Pittsburgh. He was, in his own words, "still a member of the Episcopal church, though at the time in communion with the Presbyterian church in the neighborhood." Scott, who meanwhile had come under the influence of Alexander Campbell and had adopted the views of the "Reformers," soon to be called the Disciples of Christ, and had been evangelizing in the Western Reserve, visited Richardson and expounded to him "baptism for the remission of sins" and the program of the Reformers for the restoration of primitive Christianity. A few days later Richardson followed Scott to Shalersville, Ohio, a three-day journey on horseback, and was immersed in June 1829.

After his immersion, Richardson received a letter of protest from his former rector at Trinity Church, John Henry Hopkins [q.v.], to which he replied in two open letters in Campbell's magazine, the Christian Baptist, signed "Discipulus." His devotion to the new cause was prompt and zealous. Continuing to practise medicine, he preached, evangelized, and made several converts. Early in 1830 he moved to Wellsburg where for four years he divided his time between medicine and the care of the church and visits to neighboring churches. To the first volume of Campbell's new magazine, the Millennial Harbinger, he contributed seven essays on Regeneration, defining it as "a begetting by the Spirit through the Gospel, and a subsequent birth of water in baptism." From Wellsburg, Richardson moved to Carthage,

Ohio, where Scott was publishing the Evangelist, to which he contributed articles distinguishing between the Kingdom of Heaven and the Church. Early in 1836 Campbell invited Richardson to move to Bethany "to assist him in the editorial duties of the Harbinger." Although he is announced as co-editor only for the years 1848-52, he had close relations with the magazine and bore heavy responsibilities on it for many years both before and after those dates. When Bethany College was opened in 1841 under the presidency of Campbell, Richardson was one of the four elected to constitute its first faculty. He remained on the faculty until 1859, first as professor of chemistry and geology, later teaching also physiology, botany, and rhetoric, and taking Campbell's classes during his many absences. From 1859 to 1865 he was vice-president of Kentucky University, Harrodsburg, Ky., after which he returned to Bethany and served as lecturer on the Bible, 1865-67. In the latter year he retired to his farm-home, "Bethphage," on a hillside two and a half miles from Bethany to write, at the subject's request, the memoirs of Alexander Campbell, who had died in 1866.

Throughout his life he continued the practice of medicine so far as permitted by the pressure of other duties—teaching, preaching, writing, and conducting a model farm. He lived on his farm during all his years at Bethany, riding back and forth on horseback daily without, it is said, a single tardiness in twenty-five years—even at early chapel. He was a pioneer in agricultural experiment and made regular reports to the government on crops and weather conditions long before there was a Department of Agriculture or a Weather Bureau. An accomplished linguist, he had a good command of French and a reading knowledge of Latin, Greek, and Hebrew. He played the violin and flute, composed music for both instruments, and painted pictures and wrote poetry for his own entertainment. His wife was Rebecca Encell, to whom he was married at Wheeling, Va., Apr. 10, 1831. They had five sons and five daughters. He died at Bethany, W. Va., in his seventy-first year. Although untrained in theology, he was a bold and original thinker. He exercised a strong influence on Campbell and made an important contribution to the early doctrinal development of the Disciples of Christ. His devotional writings were for many years their most important works in that field. Most of his articles in periodicals were signed "R.R.," "Discipulus," "Alumnus," "D.A.," or by the separate letters of the name "LUKE." His published volumes were: *The Principles and Objects of the Religious Reformation* (1853); *Memoirs of Alexander Campbell* (2 vols., 1868–70); *Communings in the Sanctuary* (1872); and *A Scriptural View of the Office of the Holy Spirit* (1873).

[Sources include: M. C. Tiers, *The Christian Portrait Gallery* (1864); W. T. Moore, *A Comprehensive Hist. of the Disciples of Christ* (1909); B. L. Smith, *Alexander Campbell* (1930); *Christian Standard*, Nov. 4, 11, 1876; files of the *Christian Baptist*, *Millennial Harbinger*, and *Evangelist*; matriculation lists, Univ. of Pa.; and manuscript records of Bethany Coll. Information as to certain facts was supplied by Richardson's daughter, Mrs. Fanny R. Thomson, Battle Creek, Mich.] W. E. G.

RICHARDSON, RUFUS BYAM (Apr. 18, 1845–Mar. 10, 1914), Greek scholar and archæologist, was born in Westford, Mass., the son of Joseph and Lucy M. (Byam) Richardson. He was seventh in direct line of descent from Ezekiel Richardson, who came in the fleet with Winthrop and landed by July 6, 1630, probably the earliest colonist named Richardson in New England. Ezekiel and his wife Susanna were among the first members of the church, gathered in Charlestown, August 27, 1630, which afterwards became the First Church in Boston. He was one of the founders of Woburn, Mass., where he died in 1647. Rufus Richardson served as a boy-soldier in the Civil War in 1862–63, 6th Massachusetts, was prepared for college at Lawrence Academy, Groton, Mass., studied at Yale (A.B. 1869, Ph.D. 1878, B.D. 1883) and in Europe, chiefly at the University of Berlin, 1872–74. He was tutor in Greek at Yale, 1874–78, principal of the high school in Chicopee, Mass., 1878–80, professor of Greek at Indiana University, 1880–82, and Lawrence Professor of Greek at Dartmouth College, 1882–93. In 1890–91 he was granted leave of absence from Dartmouth to hold the annual directorship of the American School of Classical Studies at Athens. Resigning his professorship in June 1893, he became director of the school, a position he held until 1903, after which he made his home in Woodstock, Conn. He was married in 1877 to Alice Linden Bowen, daughter of Henry C. Bowen [*q.v.*].

During the period of his continuous residence in Greece (1893–1903) he had official charge of the excavations conducted by the School at Eretria in Euboea (1894–95), where an important ancient theatre and a gymnasium were laid bare; and on the site of ancient Corinth where in successive campaigns (1896–1902) a substantial part of the ruins of the city was uncovered, the

position of numerous buildings located, and works of sculpture discovered. The exacting requirements of his official position at Athens—the management of the School and of the excavations and excursions conducted by it—absorbed his energies to so great a degree as to prevent him from producing a work of great constructive scholarship. His publications include an edition of Æschines' *Oration against Ctesiphon* (*On the Crown*) (1889), *Vacation Days in Greece* (1903), *Greece Through the Stereoscope* (1907), *History of Greek Sculpture* (1911); contributions to archæological and philological journals (such as "The Appeal to the Sense of Sight in Greek Tragedy," *Transactions of the American Philological Association*, vol. XVI, 1886, and yearly reports on the progress and results of the Greek excavations, published chiefly in the *American Journal of Archæology*), to the *New Englander*, the *Nation*, the New York *Independent*, and *Scribner's*. Richardson's contributions to Greek archæology were recognized, however, by his election to membership in many learned societies: the British Society for the Promotion of Hellenic Studies, the Archæological Society in Athens, the Imperial and Royal Archæological Society of Germany, the Imperial and Royal Archæological Institute of Austria, and the American Academy of Arts and Sciences.

For Greece, in which he lived for eleven years, he had a deep-rooted and abiding love; and of the most varied parts of that classic land where the splendor of mountain and sea are so closely neighbored he had a peculiarly intimate knowledge. Even in his later years his vigorous physical powers enabled him to take protracted walks and to climb high mountains; when he was well over fifty years of age, he rode his bicycle in many rugged parts of Greece. His ready command of modern Greek brought him, too, an understanding of the life of the Greek peasant, in whose speech he sought to hear the echoes of the ancient tongue. To his students, his delight in nature everywhere, in man, and in the visible remains of man's artistic genius communicated itself vividly. Kindly, hearty, without the slightest trace of affectation or of pedantry, buoyant through the unaging youthfulness of his spirit, he created capacities for enduring enjoyment by vivifying and vitalizing his learning and by his conception of the dignity of human nature.

[J. A. Vinton, *The Richardson Memorial* (1882); P. S. Marden in *Lowell Courier-Citizen*, Mar. 13, 1914; G. D. Lord, in *Dartmouth Alumni Magazine*, Sept. 6, 1914; *Yale Alumni Weekly*, Apr. 3, 1914; *Who's Who*

in America, 1912–13; *N. Y. Times*, Mar. 11, 1914; date of marriage from Mrs. R. B. Richardson.]
                                          H. W. S.

RICHARDSON, TOBIAS GIBSON (Jan. 3, 1827–May 26, 1892), surgeon, educator, was the son of William A. and Synia (Higgins) Richardson. Although he was born in Lexington, Ky., and died in New Orleans, he was of New England ancestry, being descended from Samuel Richardson who was in Charlestown, Mass., as early as 1636. Most fortunate in his home life, he received a good English education in Lexington, although he completed no classical or collegiate studies. In 1837 he removed to Louisville, and in 1845 enrolled as a medical student in the University of Louisville, becoming the private pupil of Dr. S. D. Gross [*q.v.*], professor of surgery, whose friendship inspired him throughout his whole professional life. He graduated (M.D.) in 1848, having spent the previous year as a resident student of the Louisville Marine Hospital. For the next eight years he served as demonstrator of anatomy in the University, publishing in 1854 his *Elements of Human Anatomy,* a textbook which long remained standard in Southern medical schools, and from May to October 1856 acting as co-editor of the *Louisville Medical Review.* In 1856 he was offered the chair of surgery at the Kentucky School of Medicine and the chairs of anatomy at the New York Medical College and the Medical Department of Pennsylvania College, Philadelphia. The third of these he accepted, but two years later left Philadelphia to become professor of anatomy at the University of Louisiana (now Tulane) in New Orleans.

When war closed the doors of this institution in 1862, he entered the Confederate army, serving first as assistant medical director of the Army of Tennessee; then, after July 24, 1863, as medical inspector; and finally, in 1865, as General Bragg's medical director until his staff was disbanded. Returning to New Orleans, he resumed his teaching and private practice, continuing in the chair of anatomy until 1872, when he was elected to succeed Dr. Warren Stone [*q.v.*] in the chair of surgery. For twenty years, 1865–85, he was also dean of the College, piloting it through the critical period of Reconstruction. He continued in the chair of surgery until May 18, 1889, when broken health compelled him to resign. As a part of his professional duties, he gave twenty-eight years of free service as a visiting surgeon to the Charity Hospital of New Orleans, in addition to his early years of service as an associate in Dr. Stone's infirmary.

Among the many honors conferred by his professional brethren, perhaps the one he most prized was his election to the presidency of the American Medical Association (1877), the first physician from Louisiana to hold that office. In his presidential address at Buffalo, N. Y., in 1878, besides making a strong plea for a better preliminary education of medical students, he urged the appointment of a national secretary of health, pleaded for appropriations from the federal government to promote research for the investigation and prevention of disease, and insisted that questions of quarantine involving national or interstate relations should be under the supervision of the federal government (*Transactions,* 1878). This was a bold position for a Southerner and Confederate veteran to take at a time when state rights were jealously guarded by the health authorities of the South Atlantic and Gulf states. He was one of the founders of the Orleans Parish Medical Society in 1877, of the Louisiana State Medical Association in 1878, and of the American Surgical Association in 1880. One of the original members of the New Orleans Auxiliary Sanitary Association, organized in 1878 to aid the city health authorities, he was also a member of the American Public Health Association and a fellow of the College of Pharmacy and of the Academy of Physical Sciences of Philadelphia.

As an administrator of the fund established by Paul Tulane in 1884 for the benefit of the University of Louisiana, he was zealous in promoting the educational interests of the medical department and secured for it important benefits. His personal benefactions to the medical college were continued by his wife, who, inspired by him, donated the sum of $50,000 for the erection of a much needed laboratory building. This sum was later increased by an additional $100,000 (May 9, 1891), with which the Richardson Memorial was built on a site provided by the administrators. It housed the whole medical school for fifteen years, until May 19, 1908, when the New Richardson Memorial for preclinical studies was erected on the campus out of the funds provided by the sale of the old property.

Richardson's consummate knowledge of anatomy made him an exceptionally able operator—skilful, quick, and bold "in all those things that are safe; deliberate and cautious in those that are dangerous." He was a man of tall, commanding presence, but while seemingly distant and self contained, was in fact simple, unostentatious, direct, and deeply affectionate. His recreations were botany and travel. From Dec. 23, 1860, to his death he served as a ruling elder of the First Presbyterian Church of New Orleans. The loss of his first wife, Sarah Short Richardson, and their three children, in the boiler explosion of the Mississippi packet *W. R. Carter,* saddened his life. On Nov. 12, 1868, he married Ida Ann Slocum of New Orleans, who survived him eight years; the union was childless, but very congenial and happy.

[*In Memory of Prof. T. G. Richardson, M.D.* (1893); *New Orleans Medic. and Surgic. Jour.,* May 1893, June 1896, June 1908; S. D. Gross, *Autobiography* (2 vols., 1887); Rudolph Matas, "The Surgeon, His Science and His Art," *Boston Medic. and Surgic. Jour.,* Oct. 27, 1927; H. A. Kelly and W. L. Burrage, *Am. Medic. Biogs.* (1920); J. A. Vinton, *The Richardson Memorial* (1876); C. E. Slocum, *Hist. of the Slocums . . . of America,* vol. II (1908); *Times-Democrat* (New Orleans), May 27, 1892.]
R. M.
V. G.

RICHARDSON, WILDS PRESTON (Mar. 20, 1861–May 20, 1929), army officer, was born in Hunt County, Tex., the son of Oliver Preston and Hester Foster (Wingo) Richardson. After some years of schooling he entered the United States Military Academy at West Point in the summer of 1880 and was graduated, a second lieutenant of the 8th Infantry, on June 15, 1884. His early service was in garrison in California and in frontier duty in the Apache country and in western Nebraska. He became a first lieutenant on Dec. 16, 1889, and for six years (1892–97) was an instructor in tactics at West Point. In August 1897, he was ordered to Alaska, where, except for a few brief details elsewhere, he was to remain for twenty years. He became a captain on Apr. 26, 1898, and a major on Apr. 7, 1904. In March 1905, he was made president of the newly authorized United States Alaska Roads Commission and put in charge of the government's extensive construction project for that Territory. His chief work was the building of the Richardson Highway, from Valdez, on the southern coast, to Fairbanks, at the head of navigation on the Tanana River, a distance of 380 miles. He had become a lieutenant-colonel in 1911 and a colonel in 1914. On Aug. 5, 1917, he was made a brigadier-general in the National Army, and in March 1918, he was assigned to the command of the 78th Infantry Brigade, 39th Division, then at Camp Beauregard, La. With his division he arrived at Brest on Sept. 3, in time to take part in some of the closing movements of the war. He was next assigned to the command of the American forces at Murmansk, in northern Russia, where he arrived early in April 1919. For his part in this difficult and trying situation he was awarded, on Apr. 14, 1922, the Distinguished Service Medal. On Aug. 24 he left Murmansk and in October was again

in the United States. With the mustering out of the National Army he was returned to the rank of colonel, and on Oct. 31, 1920, was retired at his own request. Thereafter he made his home at the Army and Navy Club, Washington, D. C.

In January 1928, he published in the *Atlantic Monthly,* an article on Alaska which aroused some controversy. In April 1929, he was taken ill and conveyed to the Walter Reed Hospital, where, a month later, he died. The body was interred at West Point. Two sisters survived him. He was unmarried. He was a man of exceptional height and bulk, with noticeably large hands and feet. His manner was friendly, and it has been said of him that he was "one of the best-loved men in the United States Army" (*Annual Reunion, post,* p. 281). He was a strict disciplinarian, though a kindly one, and he was noted for his sympathy and generosity. In his conduct of affairs in Alaska he displayed great engineering skill, tremendous energy, and an unflinching regard for the government's interests against the efforts of self-seekers. An oil portrait of him, the gift of his fellow-officers, hangs in the Army and Navy Club.

[G. W. Cullum, *Biog. Reg. . . . U. S. Mil. Acad.* (1891); *Who's Who in America,* 1920–21; E. B. Clark, memoir in *Ann. Reunion, Asso. Grads. U. S. Mil. Acad.,* 1929; *Washington* (D. C.) *Post,* May 21, 1929.]
W. J. G.

RICHARDSON, WILLARD (June 24, 1802–July 26, 1875), journalist, was born in Massachusetts of English and Irish stock. An adventurous youth, he traveled at sixteen to South Carolina where he settled at Sumter. He entered South Carolina College, Columbia, as a junior in 1827 and received the degree of B.A. the next year. As an undergraduate and ever afterwards he was an unswerving disciple of John C. Calhoun and other spokesmen of the State Rights school.

After teaching for several years in Tuscaloosa, Ala., he emigrated to Texas in 1837. At Houston, capital of the Republic, he opened a school for young men. One of his most enduring friendships was formed there with Mirabeau B. Lamar [*q.v.*], then serving as the second president of Texas. The political interests of the two were thereafter largely identical, particularly in their opposition to Gen. Sam Houston [*q.v.*], who was far too Jacksonian to win the approval of a disciple of Calhoun. In the summer of 1842 Richardson was invited to conduct the *Houston Telegraph* during an absence of the editor. The clarity, vigor, and charm of his writing attracted wide attention and led to an offer in 1843 of the editorship of the *Galves-*

ton News, a journal started by practical printers only the year before. His first efforts were directed toward the annexation of Texas to the United States. He believed that he was combatting a scheme on the part of Sam Houston to keep Texas an independent nation under an implied British protectorate; since Great Britain was opposed to negro slavery, this scheme must be defeated. In fact, as Richardson later wrote, "it was mainly for the purpose of using our efforts to prevent the success of this abolition policy of England," in so far as Texas was concerned, that he accepted the editorship of the *News* (*Galveston News,* Apr. 13, 1858). He was elated, therefore, when annexation was accomplished in 1845.

Becoming owner as well as editor in that year, Richardson built up his newspaper so that during the fifties it became the most widely circulated and influential as well as the wealthiest journal in Texas. Despite his intense concern over questions that at bottom were political, he early subordinated political issues to commercial, agricultural, and civic development. Thus he was a pioneer in the South in the field of non-political, independent journalism. Through his annual *Texas Almanac,* first published and widely circulated in 1857, he was an important factor in the immigration movement which more than doubled the population of Texas during the decade ending in 1860. He remorselessly campaigned against Sam Houston when that personage became identified with the American or Know-Nothing party. He was influential in bringing about Houston's first and only defeat in Texas, that for the governorship in 1857. The enmity continued until death, Houston's farewell address in the United States Senate being in large part a denunciation of Willard Richardson. The bitterness was intensified by events leading up to the firing upon Fort Sumter, with Richardson urging secession as the only protection left to the South and with Houston stoutly standing by the Union.

Only against the greatest odds was Richardson able to maintain continuous publication during the Civil War. A Federal blockade forced his removal to Houston, where he shortly afterwards suffered the destruction of his printing plant by fire. Under these handicaps the *News* lost first place in enterprise and circulation to its old rival, the *Houston Telegraph.* It was not until the return of the *News* to Galveston in 1866 that Richardson, assisted by two new and younger partners, Alfred Horatio Belo [*q.v.*] and John J. Hand, was able to regain the old primacy of his journal in Texas.

In 1849 Richardson married Louisa Blanche Murrell of Sumter, S. C., by whom he had one child, a daughter. Tall, spare of build, with a mop of hair that early turned gray, "Old Whitey" was the physical embodiment for many of his contemporaries of the gentleman of the old school. His grave, gentle, courteous manner belied the steel in his temperament, however, as his achievements in a new country proved. "Prudent, persevering, cool and indomitable," it was written by an associate at the time of his death, "he was never caught by surprise or unnerved by adversity."

[Files of the *Galveston News,* notably autobiographical references in the issues of Mar. 18, 1856, Mar. 24, 1857, Apr. 13, 1858, Sept. 17, 1862, and July 11 and 18, 1873, and obituary, July 27, 1875; A. C. Gray, "History of the Texas Press," in D. G. Wooten, *A Comprehensive Hist. of Texas* (2 vols., 1898); *N. Y. Times,* July 27, 1875; information from Bess Glenn, librarian of the S. C. Collection, Univ. of S. C., and from Dr. Willard Richardson Cooke of Galveston, a grandson.]   S. H. A.

RICHARDSON, WILLIAM ADAMS (Nov. 2, 1821–Oct. 19, 1896), jurist, secretary of the treasury, was a descendant of Ezekiel Richardson who came to Massachusetts Bay in 1630. He was born in the village of Tyngsborough, Mass., where his father, Daniel, practised law and kept the post-office. His mother was Mary Adams, of Chelmsford. She died in 1825, and the next year her sister became the boy's step-mother. He prepared at Pinkerton Academy in Derry, N. H., and at what is now called Lawrence Academy in Groton, Mass., and graduated from Harvard in 1843. He then read law and completed the law-school course. Admitted to the bar in July 1846, he entered partnership with his elder brother, Daniel Samuel, who had a large practice in Lowell. The junior member was painstaking and methodical, an office lawyer. He was interested in local banks, served on the common council, and held commissions in the militia. In politics he was a Whig, then a Republican. When in 1855 he was appointed with Joel Parker to consolidate and rearrange the statute law of Massachusetts the way was open for him to exercise his faculty for compilation and indexing. He shared in a similar codification in 1873, and from 1874 to 1895 he prepared Richardson's *Supplements* to congressional legislation. In this minute labor he was a master. In 1856 he had been made judge of probate for Middlesex County and two years later was appointed to the combined office of judge of probate and insolvency. He handled this sort of judicial business with general approval.

When Grant became president he appointed Gov. G. S. Boutwell [*q.v.*] secretary of the treasury. He and Richardson had been friends for many years and on Boutwell's urgent solicitation Richardson accepted the post of assistant secretary (appointment confirmed Mar. 20, 1869). At this time he declined a commission to the Massachusetts superior court, but for a long time he held his probate judgeship concurrently with his federal commission. He was sent to London in 1871–72, where he managed the Treasury's funding operations. When Boutwell went to the Senate in 1873, Richardson was promoted to the cabinet. He arranged for the receipt of the $15,500,000 Geneva Award through the simultaneous retirement of United States bonds held in Europe, so that no gold movement was entailed. In the panic of 1873 Richardson for a time resisted inflation, but presently weakened and reissued twenty-six of the forty-four million dollars in greenbacks which were held, uncanceled, in what Boutwell and Richardson were pleased to call a "reserve." The legality of this action was exceedingly doubtful, though Boutwell pointed out that it had been done before on a small scale, and Congress had passed no act to forbid (*Congressional Record,* 43 Cong., 1 Sess., p. 704).

While this was being debated Richardson fell into greater difficulties over the "Sanborn contracts." Through the efforts of Benjamin F. Butler Congress had empowered the secretary of the treasury to retain three persons to assist in recovering unpaid taxes. Richardson conferred one of these monopolies upon John D. Sanborn, a friend of Butler's, granted him a moiety of all he could recover, and allowed him to include in his list of evaders practically all the railroad companies in the country. When the district attorney in New York tried to get an indictment against Sanborn, the Secretary showed no interest in supplying evidence, remarking that the papers sought "affect the interests of private parties" (*House Executive Document 132,* 43 Cong., 1 Sess., pt. 2, p. 8). On May 4, 1874, the House ways and means committee brought in a report of its investigation of the matter, finding that the Secretary deserved "severe condemnation," though they found nothing impeaching his integrity (*House Report 559,* 43 Cong., 1 Sess.). Privately the committee demanded that Grant remove Richardson (G. F. Hoar, *Autobiography of Seventy Years,* 1903, I, p. 328) and in June he was appointed to the Court of Claims—"one other illustration of what General Grant means by the purification of the civil service" said the *Nation* (June 4, 1874), which for months had scoffed at Richardson's ineptitude.

Richardson was well fitted for his work on the court, dealing as it does with statute law. He was courteous, terse, unassuming; he seldom filed a dissent. In January 1885 he became the chief justice. He also taught in the Georgetown law school (1879–94), was a Harvard overseer (1863–75), and was active in Masonry and in the Unitarian church. He took an interest in various genealogical and historical societies, contributing little articles and compilations of data. He had been married to Anna M. Marston, of Machiasport, Me., on Oct. 29, 1849. She died in Paris, in March 1876, after she and her husband had made a trip through the Orient. They had one daughter. Besides the compilations of statutes already named Richardson published: *Banking Laws of Massachusetts* (1855); *Practical Information Concerning the Public Debt of the United States* (1872); and *History, Jurisdiction and Practice of the Court of Claims* (1882, 1885).

[See especially: F. W. Hackett, *A Sketch of the Life and Pub. Services of Wm. Adams Richardson* (privately printed, 1898); J. A. Vinton, *The Richardson Memorial* (1876); *Quinquennial Cat. of . . . Harvard Univ.,* 1636–1925; *Harvard Grads.' Mag.,* Dec. 1896; and the *Springfield* (Mass.) *Republican,* Oct. 20, 1896. General historical works and biograpries of Richardson's contemporaries throw light on his service in the cabinet.]   C. F.

RICHARDSON, WILLIAM LAMBERT (Sept. 6, 1842–Oct. 20, 1932), obstetrician, was born in Boston, the son of Jeffrey and Julia Lambert (Brackett) Richardson. After his graduation in 1864 from Harvard College, for which he had been prepared at the Boston Latin School, he entered the Harvard Medical School and received the degrees of A.M. and M.D. in 1867, after serving for a year as house pupil at the Massachusetts General Hospital. According to the custom of the time, he spent the next two years in study and travel in Europe, first in Dublin, where he was graduated from the Rotunda Lying-in Hospital in 1868 with the degree of L.M. and a special diploma for excellence in obstetrics, then in Berlin and Vienna. He returned to Boston in October 1869 and began his practice of obstetrics early the next year, one of the first to specialize in the subject. After serving for a time on the staff of the Boston Dispensary (1870–74) and the Children's Hospital (1872–74), he became interested in reviving the Boston Lying-in Hospital, which had been founded in 1832 but had not been in operation since 1857. Reopened in 1873 and successfully reestablished through Richardson's efforts, it grew so rapidly that within a comparatively short time it became one of the outstanding hospitals of its type in the United States. Later it came to have a world-wide reputation as a center for teaching physicians and nurses; and when Richardson resigned from the staff, fifty years later, he could look back upon a project, started almost single-handed, that had become a meritorious contribution to medicine. The period of his activity at the Massachusetts General Hospital was also a long one (1871–1903). Closely connected with his work in developing the Lying-in Hospital was his long service to the Harvard Medical School. Entering the obstetrical department in 1871, he moved steadily through successive grades to the professorship, a position he held from 1886 until his resignation in 1907. In 1893 he was appointed dean of the medical faculty; when in 1899 the medical, dental, and veterinary schools were placed under one head, he was reappointed as dean of the combined faculty. He was an overseer of Harvard College from 1909 to 1915.

Richardson's professional interests included the Massachusetts Medical Society, the Massachusetts Medical Benevolent Society, the *New England Journal of Medicine,* and the Boston Medical Library, an institution he had helped found in 1875. Apart from these were his connections with the Boston Y. M. C. A., of which he was treasurer for more than thirty years, and with the First Corps Cadets, Massachusetts volunteer Militia, dating from his days as a student at Harvard. He became surgeon in 1875, and, although he retired with the rank of lieutenant-colonel in 1899, for many years afterward he served as treasurer and as a member of the board of trustees. He was widely known, also, for his philanthropy and gave very substantial sums to the Harvard Medical School and the Lying-in Hospital.

His writings consist largely of papers on obstetrics and gynecology. While serving as its secretary he wrote *A Summary of Seven Years' Work of the State Board of Health of Massachusetts* (1876); and one small book, *Address on the Duties and Conduct of Nurses in Private Nursing,* first published in 1886, was widely read during its time both in the United States and in England. The great accuracy of detail with which he worked is well exemplified in his long series of secretarial reports of the Class of 1864, Harvard College, models of what such reports should be.

Richardson had an unusual personality. Swift and accurate in observation and judgment, he possessed unerring sagacity; though he was laconic and abrupt and often seemed brusque and austere, he had an underlying kindliness that was soon evident. A man with multiple interests

and with an immense capacity for work, he seems to have been able to recreate or enliven any project which he undertook. He married Olivia Lane Aitchison of Portland, Maine, July 24, 1867. She died in 1890; there were no children.

[*New England Jour. of Medicine,* Oct. 27, Dec. 8, 1932; *Harvard College, Class of 1864, Secretary's Report No. 9* (1919); T. F. Harrington, *The Harvard Medical School* (1905), vol. III; *Boston Transcript,* Oct. 21, 1932; *Who's Who in America,* 1930–31.]

H. R. V.

RICHARDSON, WILLIAM MERCHANT (Jan. 4, 1774–Mar. 23, 1838), judge, was born at Pelham, Hillsboro County, N. H., the son of Capt. Daniel and Sarah (Merchant) Richardson and a descendant of Ezekiel Richardson who settled in Charlestown, Mass., in 1630. An accident in early life impaired his efficiency for manual labor on his father's farm and led him to prepare himself for Harvard College, from which he graduated in 1797. After leaving college he taught in an academy at Leicester, Mass., and later was principal of the academy at Groton. In the latter place he became acquainted with Judge Samuel Dana who invited the young man to become a student in his law office. After the usual course of study he was admitted to the bar and began practice at Groton. Meanwhile, on Oct. 7, 1799, he had married Betsy Smith of his native town. They had seven children, one of whom married Henry Flagg French and was the mother of William Merchant Richardson French [*q.v.*].

In 1811 Richardson was elected to fill the vacancy in Congress caused by the resignation of Joseph B. Varnum. He was reëlected to the following Congress, serving from Nov. 4, 1811, to Apr. 18, 1814, when he resigned to become United States attorney for New Hampshire. He took up his residence first at Portsmouth, Rockingham County, but in 1819 he removed to Chester where he resided for the remainder of his life. In 1816 he was nominated by Governor Plumer and confirmed unanimously by the Council, though it was politically divided, as chief justice of the New Hampshire superior court (as the tribunal of last resort was called). There he served for twenty-two years, becoming distinguished for his industry and learning. "With the exception of Judge Jeremiah Smith," says one biographer, "perhaps no occupant of the judicial bench has done so much to shape the jurisprudence of New Hampshire. . . . When he came into office, no printed reports of cases previously adjudicated in the State were in existence, there was little uniformity of practice, and great uncertainty about many branches of the law, more especially in regard to the construction of statutes. At the close of his long, diligent, and efficient service, the rules of practice had become well established, and the decisions of his court had been published to the profession and were recognized as of value and authority in this state and elsewhere" (Bell, *post*, p. 72).

Richardson took part in several notable cases. In his second year on the bench he wrote an opinion of nearly thirty printed pages in the case of *Trustees of Dartmouth College* vs. *Wm. H. Woodward* (1 *N. H.*, 111), holding that the charter of the college was not a contract and that the legislature might add new members without consulting the old corporation. Taken on error to the United States Supreme Court, the judgment was reversed in a famous opinion (4 *Wheaton*, 518) by Chief Justice Marshall; but there have always been prominent members of the American bar who agreed with Richardson and not with Marshall on that point, though the question has become entirely academic. Another famous case in which Richardson participated, though he did not write the opinion, was *Britton* vs. *Turner* (6 *N. H.*, 481), adjudicated in 1834, in which it was held that an employee under a definite term of service might recover wages actually earned though he left the employment without just cause. The doctrine was considered a radical departure from the earlier common-law rule. In addition to his judicial labors, Richardson published some legal works. These included *The New Hampshire Justice of the Peace* (1824), and *The New Hampshire Town Officer* (1829). In 1826 he was made chairman of a commission to revise the statutes. "He kept up his knowledge of the classics, and read the best Italian, French, and Spanish authors in their original tongues. He acquired a thorough knowledge of botany, and more or less familiarity with every branch of natural science" (Bell, *post*, p. 75).

[Sources include: C. H. Bell, *The Bench and Bar of N. H.* (1894); J. A. Vinton, *The Richardson Memorial* (1876); *Biog. Dir. Am. Cong.* (1928); and the *Farmer's Cabinet* (Amherst, N. H.), Mar. 30, 1838. Richardson's opinions appear in 1–9 *N. H. Reports*.]

C. S. L.

RICHINGS, PETER (May 19, 1798–Jan. 18, 1871), actor, opera singer, manager, was of English birth and rearing, although his entire professional career was spent on the American stage. His real name is said to have been Puget, and it seems certain that he was born in London, the son of Peter Puget, a captain in the Royal Navy, and his wife Hannah. The father, who became a rear admiral in 1821, had accompanied Vancouver on his trip around the world,

and it was for him, then a lieutenant, that Puget Sound was named in 1791. After studying at the Charterhouse School and at Pembroke College, Oxford, young Puget abandoned his original intention of entering the ministry and went to India, where for a short time he is said to have been a government clerk at Madras. Returning to England, he began the study of law, but a desire for the stage, opposed by his parents, led him in the absence of opportunities in England to sail for New York, which he reached early in September 1821 with his wife, whom he had married in 1818 (*New York Clipper, post*). Upon his arrival, he immediately sought the acquaintance of Edmund Simpson, manager of the Park Theatre, and on Sept. 25, under the name of Peter Richings, made his debut there as Henry Bertram in *Guy Mannering*. Some seasons elapsed before he was able to emerge from the acting of inconspicuous parts; but so successful was he eventually, and so popular did he become with New York audiences that he remained at that theatre for the greater part of thirteen years. During that period he acted many and varied characters, among them Marcus in *The Green Eyed Monster*, Frank Hardy in *Paul Pry*, Robert Lester in *Captain Kyd*, Sir Benjamin Backbite in *The School for Scandal*, Dick Trifle in *Tom and Jerry*, and Bill Sikes in *Oliver Twist* to the Nancy of Charlotte Cushman. In a series of "Portraits" published in the *New York Mirror* he is described as "a useful performer and evidently strives to please. From a very miserable actor he has already become quite a respectable one. . . . We should be sorry to miss his good-humored, good-looking face, and his unique manner of doing some things" (*New York Mirror*, Aug. 29, 1829, quoted by Odell, *post*, III, 438). He appeared frequently and prominently in musical plays, in which, according to the same judge, "as a vocalist he was rather distinguished by force than sweetness," a close search of the records leading Odell (III, 7) to declare that "his vocal equipment was inadequate." In 1840 he went to Philadelphia, and with occasional absences filled a number of positions as actor and manager in the theatres of that city, including an engagement with W. E. Burton at the National Theatre and service as stage manager at the Walnut Street and Chestnut Street theatres. In the season of 1858–59 he was back at Burton's Theatre in New York. His last important connection with the stage was as manager of an English opera company, organized in 1866, which toured for several seasons in *The Enchantress*, *The Bohemian Girl* and other popular pieces, the principal attraction being his adopted daughter, Caroline Richings, in soprano rôles. He had been appearing with her for several seasons in this type of theatrical entertainment, and she is pronounced by J. N. Ireland (*post*, II, 605) to be "one of the most admired stars in the country." Her real name was Mary Caroline Reynoldson; she died in 1882 after a distinguished career of some thirty years on the operatic stage (*Daily Dispatch*, Richmond, Va., Jan. 15, 1882). Upon her marriage to Pierre Bernard in 1867 Richings gave up his profession and retired to his farm in Media, Pa., where his death occurred as the result of an accident.

[See Bowen Marsh and F. A. Crisp, *Alumni Carthusiani* (1913); Joseph Foster, *Alumni Oxonienses, 1715–1886* (1888); J. N. Ireland, *Records of the N. Y. Stage* (2 vols., 1867); T. Allston Brown, *Hist. of the Am. Stage* (1870) and *A Hist. of the N. Y. Stage* (3 vols., 1903); G. C. D. Odell, *Annals of the N. Y. Stage*, vols. III–VII (1928–31); *Phila. Evening Bull.*, Jan. 19, 1871; *New York Clipper*, Nov. 5, 1910; *N. Y. Daily Tribune*, Jan. 20, 1871. For information on the father, see W. L. Clowes, *The Royal Navy, A Hist.*, vol. III (1899), and E. S. Meany, *Vancouver's Discovery of Puget Sound* (1907).]   E. F. E.

RICHMOND, CHARLES WALLACE (Dec. 31, 1868–May 19, 1932), ornithologist, was born in Kenosha, Wis., and died in Washington, D. C. A descendant of John Richmond, one of the proprietors of Taunton, Mass., in 1637, he was the eldest son of Edward Leslie and Josephine Ellen (Henry) Richmond, and had one brother and two sisters as well as five half-brothers, a step-brother, and a step-sister by his father's second marriage. His mother died when he was twelve and the family moved to Washington, where, at the age of thirteen, Charles became a page in the House of Representatives in the Forty-seventh Congress. When he was advanced to the position of mail page, he was given access to the books in the Library of Congress, and from that time dates his interest in the bibliographic aspects of ornithology. As a boy he had begun to form a collection of birds' eggs, but after seeing the extensive collections of the Smithsonian Institution he presented his material to its museum. He thereby came in contact with Robert Ridgeway [*q.v.*], the curator of birds and the first professional ornithologist he ever knew. He was a student at the Corcoran Scientific School in Washington, 1886–87.

In 1888 he was a member of a Geological Survey expedition to Montana and there gained some first-hand knowledge of western birds, previously known to him only as names in books. The following year he received an appointment in the division of economic ornithology and mammalogy (forerunner of the Biological Survey), in the Department of Agriculture, where he remained until January 1892. Then, in company with his brother and three friends, he went to Central America with the idea of engaging in horticultural work there, especially in Nicaragua. Disaster, illness, and discouragement were the lot of the venture, and after a year Richmond returned to Washington. During his sojourn in Costa Rica and Nicaragua he made extensive collections of birds and became familiar with tropical bird life. After his return, he entered the Georgetown University Medical School, where he was graduated with the degree of M.D. in 1897. He never practised medicine, however, his interests being wholly in ornithology. On Aug. 31, 1897, relieved for the first time from contributing to the support of his large family, he married Louise H. Seville; they had no children.

While a medical student, he had joined the staff of the United States National Museum as a night watchman in the telephone room; the following year he was appointed "assistant to the scientific staff" and was assigned to the bird department. Here he remained until his death, advancing to the position of assistant curator in 1894, and to that of associate curator in 1918. In 1929 he was made curator, but at his own suggestion was reappointed associate curator in the same year to make room for a new chief. His last field work was done in 1900, in Puerto Rico, in company with Dr. Leonhard Stejneger, on behalf of the United States National Museum. His scientific work dealt largely with problems of avian nomenclature and bibliography, in which fields he was a recognized international authority. He published approximately 150 papers, chiefly on these topics. "Through his self-sacrifice in cataloguing all bird names" he furnished "the backbone of recent systematic work" (Mathews, *post*, p. 115). His greatest single contribution to ornithology was his card catalogue of the published names of birds, which came to be consulted by ornithologists all over the world. He was a member of ornithological societies both at home and abroad, including the American Ornithologists' Union, of which he was a fellow and a member of the council; the British Ornithologists' Union, of which he was one of the ten honorary members; and the Cooper Ornithological Club, of which he was made an honorary member only a year before his death. For the last ten years of his life he was in constant ill health.

[G. M. Mathews, *The Birds of Australia*, supp. no. 4 (1925), pp. iv-viii; Witmer Stone, "In Memoriam:

Charles Wallace Richmond," *Auk*, Jan. 1933; *Who's Who in America*, 1930–31; J. B. Richmond, *The Richmond Family* (1897), p. 258; *Evening Star* (Washington), May 19, 1932.]   H. F—n.

RICHMOND, DEAN (Mar. 31, 1804–Aug. 27, 1866), business man, political leader, was born in Barnard, Vt., the son of Hathaway and Rachel (Dean) Richmond and a descendant of John Richmond, one of the original purchasers of Taunton, Mass., in 1637. He was named Elkanah Dean, but apparently never used his first name. His parents, married in Taunton, soon afterward moved to Barnard, and in 1816 to Salina (now Syracuse), N. Y. There his father and three uncles engaged in the manufacture of salt, and upon the death of both his parents when he was seventeen Dean carried on in his father's place. He had little education and no cultural opportunities. All his life he swore to excess; he could not make a speech or even converse in grammatical language, and his handwriting was practically illegible. These things greatly handicapped him later when high offices were offered him which he did not feel qualified to accept. He was energetic, practical, friendly, and honest, however; quickly made a place for himself in the community, and by extending his markets built up a large and successful business.

In 1842 he moved to Buffalo, engaged in the grain forwarding business, and shared in the prosperity of the port after the completion in 1843 of the chain of railroads across the state from Albany. His fleet of steam and sailing vessels on the Lakes made him widely known in the West; and to his Buffalo elevator properties he added property in Chicago and other ports. He was an originator and leading director of the Buffalo & Rochester Railroad, the westernmost of the seven separate corporations which, uniting in 1853, formed the New York Central. Richmond was a member of the committee which drafted the plans for this consolidation and his political influence forced through the legislature the bill incorporating the New York Central despite determined opposition. He was at once made vice-president of the road and in 1864 succeeded Erastus Corning [*q.v.*] as president. He was also an organizer, director, and, in the year of his death, president of the Buffalo & State Line Railroad, which in 1852 met a line extended east from Toledo and closed the gap between Buffalo and Chicago.

In politics he was a leader of the "Barnburner" movement, a conspicuous member of the Utica convention of 1848, and a delegate to the Buffalo Free-Soil convention the same year. Afterwards he became a leader of the "Softs," the Democratic faction which favored a compromise on the slavery issue. From 1850 until his death he served as chairman of the state Democratic committee and won a place among the famous political managers of New York. At the crucial Democratic national conventions at Charleston and Baltimore in 1860 he headed the New York delegation, which at both conventions held the controlling vote. He was one of the firmest of Douglas men, yet at Charleston, after the secession of the extreme Southerners, he dictated the vote which decided that a candidate must receive two-thirds of the votes of the original delegates to be nominated, and thus killed Douglas' chances and deadlocked the convention (Alexander, *post*, II, 277). Seemingly, he had hoped by this evidence of New York's desire for harmony to keep the Border Democrats in the convention and with their help still secure Douglas' nomination by a vote which would be impressive enough to command national support (Milton, *post*, 444). At Baltimore, however, he aligned the decisive New York vote with the majority committee report in favor of excluding the seceded delegates. When on the fifth day Douglas sent Richmond a telegram offering to withdraw if the party could unite on another man, Richmond suppressed it, being by this time convinced that Douglas' supporters would not support a compromise candidate (J. F. Rhodes, *History of the United States*, II, 1892, pp. 474–75; Allen Johnson, *Stephen A. Douglas*, 1908, pp. 426–27; Milton, *post*, pp. 473–75).

In 1862 Richmond secured the nomination and election of Seymour as governor of New York (Alexander, III, 38–39). He refused to support Seymour for president in 1864, however, feeling that McClellan would more vigorously prosecute the war. His last political services were in fostering a National Union Party which should unite Democrats and Conservative Republicans behind Andrew Johnson in opposition to the Radical Reconstructionists. With Thurlow Weed [*q.v.*] he helped to arrange the picturesque National Union Convention at Philadelphia in 1866. Afterwards he expected to control a state convention which should cement the union in New York and unite on a ticket headed by John A. Dix [*q.v.*] for governor. His death at the home of Samuel J. Tilden [*q.v.*] in New York City on the eve of the convention allowed the Tammany Democrats to seize control and nominate John T. Hoffman [*q.v.*], thus dealing a death blow to the National Union movement.

Richmond was a heavy-faced man with a large

frame and uncommon muscular strength. He married, Feb. 19, 1833, Mary Elizabeth Mead, an alert, sagacious woman, who in managing her husband's estate after his death increased it from an estimated value of $1,500,000 to $6,000,-000. Of his eight children, six survived their father.

[J. B. Richmond, *The Richmond Family* (1897); D. S. Alexander, *A Pol. Hist. of the State of N. Y.* (3 vols., 1906–09); F. W. Stevens, *The Beginnings of the N. Y. Central Railroad* (1926); F. E. Cary, *Lake Shore & Michigan Southern Railway System* (1900); *Mag. of Western Hist.*, Oct. 1888; *Am. Ann. Cyc., 1866* (1867); J. N. Larned, *A Hist. of Buffalo* (2 vols., 1911); F. W. Beers, *Gazetteer and Biog. Record of Genesee County, N. Y.* (1890); Murat Halstead, *Caucuses of 1860: A Hist. of the National Pol. Conventions of the Current Presidential Campaign* (1860); G. F. Milton, *The Eve of Conflict* (1934); H. A. Minor, *The Story of the Democratic Party* (1928); *Albany Evening Journal*, Aug. 27, 1866; *N. Y. Herald*, Aug. 28, 1866.]   O. W. H.

RICHMOND, JOHN LAMBERT (Apr. 5, 1785–Oct. 12, 1855), Baptist clergyman, physician, was born on a farm near Chesterfield, Mass., the eldest of the twelve children of Nathaniel and Susannah (Lambert) Richmond, and sixth in descent from John Richmond of Ashton Keynes, Wiltshire, who emigrated to Massachusetts and settled in Taunton about 1837. Nathaniel Richmond was a veteran of the Revolution and held several military commissions subsequently in Herkimer, N. Y., to which place he moved with his family in 1787. Extreme poverty precluded any systematic schooling for the son. Hence his entire education, which came to embrace even the classical languages, was obtained at odd moments between periods of hard labor in coal mines, fields, and forests. On Nov. 23, 1806, he married Lorana Sprague Patchin of Milton, N. Y., who bore him ten children and predeceased him by a year. She was a woman of character and ability who shared her husband's ambitions and aided him in his studies.

In 1816 Richmond was ordained a Baptist minister. He performed his clerical duties on Sundays and on week days continued to work as a laborer. In 1817 he removed to Cincinnati. Here he was employed by Dr. Daniel Drake [*q.v.*] as a janitor for the Medical College of Ohio, the second institution of its kind in the Middle West. He induced Drake to accept him as a student and despite great financial difficulties received the medical diploma on Apr. 4, 1822, and started practice in Newton, Ohio, continuing to preach on Sundays in the Cluff Road Church. It was during such a service, on Apr. 22, 1827, that he was called to a patient on whom he performed the first successful Cæsarean oper-

ation to be reported in the medical press of the United States. The patient was a young colored woman, bearing her first child. She had been unsuccessfully in labor for thirty hours because of a deformity of the genital passages. Convulsions had set in; a heavy rain prevented the transport of the patient to a hospital or even the calling of consulting surgeons. Richmond "feeling a deep and solemn sense of ... responsibility, with only a case of common pocket instruments, about one o'clock at night, ... commenced the Cæsarean section." The operation was performed in a new log cabin without flooring and without chimney. The wind came through the unchinked crevices, making it necessary for assistants to hold blankets to protect the candle flame. The position of the child was so unfavorable that Richmond was compelled to sacrifice it, but he saved the life of the mother. He published a brief preliminary report of the case in the *Western Medical and Physical Journal*, November 1827, and a full history in the same periodical, whose title had been changed to *Western Journal of the Medical and Physical Sciences*, in the issue for January–March 1830. (For notices of earlier performances of the Cæsarean section in America see sketch of François Marie Prevost.)

A cholera epidemic in Cincinnati in 1831 again proved Richmond's mettle. He was among the first to volunteer for service, contracted the disease during his labors, and, though he recovered, never again regained his health. He moved further west, to Pendleton, Ind., and thence to Indianapolis, where he again practised and preached. An attack of apoplexy put an end to his activity and he turned to the home of some of his children in Covington, Fountain County, Ind., where he died. A monument was erected in his honor at Newton, Ohio, in 1912. Richmond's success in his famous operation was apparently not due solely to good fortune. He was skilful in such difficult surgical procedures as plastic surgery, indeed had considerable mechanical skill. He was a fluent and impressive speaker, and devoted to the ministry, in which he continued until as late as 1842.

["Richmond Memorial Celebration," *Indianapolis Medic. Jour.*, May 15, 1912; Otto Juettner, in *Lancet-Clinic*, Jan. 27, 1912; H. A. Kelly and W. L. Burrage, *Am. Medic. Biogs.* (1920); *Trans. Ind. State Medic. Soc.*, 1893, p. 24; J. B. Richmond, *The Richmond Family, 1594–1896* (1897).]   H. S. R.

RICHMOND, JOHN WILKES (Sept. 25, 1775–Mar. 4, 1857), Rhode Island physician and publicist, was born in Little Compton, R. I., son of Dr Benjamin and Sarah (Church) Richmond, and a descendant of John Richmond who settled in Taunton, Mass., in 1637. John Wilkes Richmond graduated from Brown University, then Rhode Island College, in 1794 and, after studying medicine with his father, began its practice in Portsmouth, R. I. He was married, first, in November 1804, to Mary Nichols, daughter of Aaron and Mary (Nichols) Sheffield, who died in 1812; second, in April 1815, to Henrietta (Shaw) Bours, widow of John Bours and daughter of William Shaw of Newport. Soon after the latter marriage, he removed to Providence, where for the ensuing forty years he occupied a prominent place in the professional and public life of the city.

Richmond is chiefly remembered for his conspicuous endeavor, during the later part of his life, to secure the payment of the Revolutionary debt of Rhode Island. The state had issued to individuals notes estimated at more than £153,047 and, although partial payment had been made in the state's unstable currency, and $200,000 of the whole debt had been assumed by the United States, additional notes had been issued on the balance. When in 1844 it became apparent that the state no longer acknowledged the debt, the feeling among the note-holders against this act of repudiation became intense. Himself a holder of original and purchased notes—there had been much speculation in them—Richmond became the most ardent spokesman of these "creditors of the State." The general assembly, however, refused to grant petitions presented by him in 1845, 1846, 1847, and 1848, and frustrated every attempt to secure a judicial investigation of the case. Failing to procure legislative or judicial action, Richmond appealed to public opinion through the press. In addition to pamphlets and many newspaper articles, he published in 1848 a book entitled *The History of the Registered State Debt of Rhode Island,* and in 1855, a revised edition of the same work, entitled *Rhode Island Repudiation or the History of the Revolutionary Debt of Rhode Island.* Sorely disappointed at the failure of an ingenious stratagem devised to bring the case into the courts, ashamed and disgusted with the state's "abandonment of a Just and Acknowledged demand," Richmond determined to withdraw from the community. In 1851 he removed himself and his family to Stonington, Conn.

On his way home from the inauguration ceremonies of James Buchanan, he died in Philadelphia. He is buried in Stonington, and his monument, erected by himself, bears the following inscription: "When Rhode Island, by her legislature from 1844 to 1850 Repudiated her Revolutionary Debt, Dr. Richmond removed from that State to this Borough and selected this as his family burying place, unwilling that the remains of himself and family should be disgraced by being a part of the common earth of a Repudiating State."

[All the known publications of Richmond and the writings of his chief opponent, Wilkins Updike, are in the Lib. of the R. I. Hist. Soc., Providence, the Rider Collection of R. I. Hist., John Hay Lib., Brown Univ., and the Updike Collection, Providence Pub. Lib.; see also J. B. Richmond, *The Richmond Family* (1877); Edward Field, *State of R. I., and Providence Plantations* (1902), vol. II; R. M. Bayles, *Hist. of Newport County, R. I.* (1888); *R. I. Hist. Soc. Scrap Book,* XVIII, 100, XXX, 80, 81; *Report of George Turner, Amherst Everett, and J. Russell Bullock . . . on the Registered State Debt of R. I. . . . Reported at the Oct. Session 1849* (1849); *Appendix to the Report on State Certificates of the Registered State Debt Made Oct. 1849* (1852); *Providence Daily Transcript,* Mar. 16, 1857; *Providence Daily Post,* Mar. 7, 1857.]

H. F. K.

RICHMOND, MARY ELLEN (Aug. 5, 1861–Sept. 12, 1928), pioneer social worker, administrator, and author, was born at Belleville, Ill., the daughter of Henry and Lavinia (Harris) Richmond. Her parents had come from Baltimore, and shortly after her birth they returned to that city, where they remained during the Civil War. Both died in comparative youth of tuberculosis, and Mary was reared by relatives in moderate circumstances. The early years of her life were full of limitations and hardships, but a strong tendency to liberalism which was apparently inherent in her character was encouraged, especially by her grandmother and an aunt, and she heard many discussions of such current subjects as woman's suffrage, vivisection, and spiritualism. Although she was not sent to school until she was eleven years of age, she learned to read very early, and found in literature a channel of escape and enrichment which remained one of her great mainstays all her life. She graduated from the Baltimore Eastern High School in 1878 and went to live in New York with an aunt who was proof-reader for a firm publishing books chiefly of a radical tendency. Mary secured a clerical position with the same firm and worked twelve hours a day, teaching herself stenography at night. Within two or three months her aunt broke down and returned to Baltimore, where she was supported chiefly by Mary's earnings. There followed for the girl a period of poverty and loneliness. She had practically no diversions aside from attending lectures at Cooper Union; she was haunted by the fear of tuberculosis, and in time she contracted malaria. Returning then to Baltimore, she acted as bookkeeper in a stationery store, from about 1881 to 1888, and then as bookkeeper and office assistant in the Altamont Hotel. At about this time she became a member of the Unitarian Church, through which she made congenial acquaintances and was introduced to the realm of music, which was thereafter a second great source of refreshment to her.

In 1889 she happened to read an advertisement for an assistant treasurer of the Charity Organization Society of Baltimore, an organization of which she knew literally nothing. An initial interview allured her, and she accepted the position. Here she came into contact with certain persons who affected her life deeply, particularly Daniel Coit Gilman, Amos G. Warner, and John Glenn. From this time on her life was a steady progression upward to success in the new profession of social work, during which she gained the respect, admiration, and affection of her fellows in that field.

Her position with the Baltimore Society—in 1891 she became its general secretary—was basically one of promotion. Money had to be raised, standards and technic of social work developed, and manifold duties attended to, including the publication of many papers. She recognized the need for professional training of social workers and earnestly advocated it. In 1900 she went to Philadelphia to accept the general secretaryship of the Society for Organizing Charity. Here her task was essentially that of reorganization and introduction of new methods. She became a power in the city and a true community leader, helped to secure important social legislation, and took part actively in reform politics, but usually behind the scenes. At the same time she was continuing to develop the case method, both in her own work and in her teaching at the Summer School of Applied Philanthropy, New York, and in 1906 at the University of Pennsylvania.

In 1909 she accepted the position, which she held to her death, of director of the Charity Organization Department of the Russell Sage Foundation, and took up her residence in New York. In addition to the immediate duties of this office, she continued to teach for a time in the New York School of Philanthropy (now New York School of Social Work), and did editorial work in connection with the bulletin of the Field Department of Charities. She also conducted with great enthusiasm a Charity Organization Institute as a department activity from 1910 to 1922, which attracted promising young case workers from all over the country, and in 1915 she established a supervisor's conference. During the World War she was active in social work.

The closing years of her life were a race between failing health and the completion, in collaboration with F. S. Hall, of *Marriage and the State* (1929), upon which she had set her heart. The book was victorious by a narrow margin, though it was not published until after her death. Throughout her career she wrote voluminously, publishing numerous magazine articles and several notable books, among them *Friendly Visiting Among the Poor* (1899); *The Good Neighbor in the Modern City* (1907); *Social Diagnosis* (1917), perhaps her most important volume; *What Is Social Case Work?* (1922); and *Child Marriages* (1925), with F. S. Hall. In 1921 Smith College conferred upon her the honorary degree of master of arts, in recognition of her work in "establishing the scientific basis of a new profession."

[*The Long View* (Russell Sage Foundation, 1930), ed. by Joanna C. Colcord and Ruth Z. S. Mann; *The Family*, Feb. 1929; *Who's Who in America*, 1928–29; *Woman's Who's Who of America*, 1914–15; *N. Y. Times*, Sept. 12, 1928.]   H. P. F.

RICKARD, GEORGE LEWIS (Jan. 2, 1871–Jan. 6, 1929), prize-fight promoter, better known as "Tex" Rickard, was born in Kansas City, Mo. During his picturesque career he was at one time or another, a cowboy, a rancher, a town marshal, a gambler, and a beef baron, but preëminently he was a showman. When he was four years old his family moved from Kansas City to Sherman, Tex., and subsequently took up a cattle range. When he was ten years old his father died and he became the main support of his family. He grew up in the saddle and at twenty-three was elected town marshal of Henrietta, Tex.

Gaming was his favorite pastime and in the late nineties he was lured to Alaska by a report that flour was selling at a dollar a barrel along the Yukon, his reasoning being that money must be plentiful there and a good gambler might get some. He operated gambling houses in the Klondike for four years, quit with $500,000, and lost it buying up claims that proved to be valueless. He went to San Francisco but the gleanings there were lean and the roar of the mining towns of Tonopah and Goldfield drew him to Nevada. In Goldfield he learned that money could be made in the promotion of prize fights. Purely as an advertising device, the town offered a purse of $30,000 to secure the Gans-Nelson fight (Sept. 3, 1906) for the lightweight title, but Rickard, selected to handle the actual promotion, succeeded so well that the receipts went beyond $62,000. In 1910, venturing into fight promotion on his own responsibility, he paid Jeffries and Johnson $101,000 to fight for him at Reno, Nev., and made money.

Putting aside prize fighting for the time being, he went to Central and South America as a prospector in beef, making and losing a couple of small fortunes. Returning to the United States in 1916, he got a new stake out of the Willard-Moran bout which he sponsored in New York and which brought in $156,000. Now his way was clear and he concentrated on fight promotion. He recognized the possibilities of a good future match even in its embryonic state, and none excelled him in developing them. He lost money on the Willard-Dempsey fight at Toledo, Ohio, on July 4, 1919, but, operating strictly on his nerve, he took in $1,626,580 when, on July 2, 1921, some 90,000 paid to see Dempsey and Carpentier in the arena he had constructed at Boyle's Thirty Acres, Jersey City, with money taken from the advance sale of seats. Having acquired the old Madison Square Garden in 1920, he built the new one and opened it in 1925 with, as he proudly pointed out, "six hundred millionaires" in the crowd. Meanwhile, he had developed Luis Angel Firpo as a rival for Dempsey through the medium of several spectacular and profitable fights, and at the Polo Grounds in New York on Sept. 14, 1923, Dempsey and Firpo had drawn $1,082,590. The "gate" went to $1,-895,723 when Dempsey and Gene Tunney met in the Sesquicentennial stadium in Philadelphia on Sept. 24, 1926. Dempsey and Jack Sharkey drew $1,083,529 at the Yankee Stadium in New York, July 21, 1927, and Dempsey and Tunney, in a return match at Soldier Field, Chicago, Sept. 22 of the same year, drew $2,650,000. It was the last of the golden gates that Rickard, with the aid of Dempsey, had made possible. He was engaged in the promotion of a fight in Florida when he died at Miami Beach. Among his few and simple rules as a promoter was: "See that every purchaser of a ticket gets the seat for which the ticket calls." Other promoters before him had arranged attractive fights but he was the first to guarantee that a patron would find his seat vacant no matter how late he arrived. This bred a confidence in Rickard that was the basis of his success. He was married twice: his first wife was Edith Mae Rickard, whom he married at Sacramento, Cal., in 1902, and who died in 1925; on Oct. 8, 1926, he married Maxine Hodges at Lewisburg, W. Va. His second wife and a daughter survived him.

[*N. Y. Tribune,* May 29, 1921; *Evening Telegram* (N. Y.), Jan. 1, 1922; Jack Dempsey, "The Golden Gates," *Saturday Evening Post,* Oct. 20, 1934; *N. Y. Times,* Jan. 7, 1929; the *Sun* (N. Y.), Jan. 7, 1929.]

F. G.

RICKETSON, DANIEL (July 30, 1813–July 16, 1898), historian and poet, was born in New Bedford, Mass., where his entire life was spent. A descendant of William Ricketson, Quaker, who moved from Portsmouth, R. I., to Dartmouth, Mass., about 1684, he was the son of Joseph and Anna (Thornton) Ricketson. Following his preliminary education he studied law, but abandoned its practice as uncongenial. Possessed of adequate means, he devoted himself to literary pursuits and friendships, the study of nature, and the promotion of humanitarian ideals. As an ardent Abolitionist he was credited with aiding in the escape and concealment of numerous slaves. He was twice married: on June 27, 1834, to Maria Louisa Sampson, who died in 1877, and on Nov. 10, 1880, to Angeline Standish Gidley who died in 1921. Two sons and two daughters were born of the first marriage.

The New Bedford Lyceum, before which were heard many eminent lecturers and writers, afforded Ricketson a medium for forming the personal acquaintance of some of the leading figures in American literature of his time. Others he came to know through correspondence. At his pleasant country seat, "Brooklawn," on the outskirts of New Bedford, he dispensed generous hospitality to Thoreau, Emerson, A. Bronson Alcott, George William Curtis, and others. He was the "Member for Woods and Forests" of the fanciful "Sassafras Club," created by Curtis and chronicled in the "Editor's Easy Chair" of *Harper's Magazine* from 1863 to 1869; his friendship with the Alcotts extended to the second generation.

"Ricketson's tastes are pastoral and simple, even to wildness," wrote Alcott (Salt, *post,* p. 163). Near his house he built a rude shanty to which he often retired for reading, writing, and meditation. In Henry D. Thoreau [*q.v.*] he found a kindred spirit, and for eight years prior to Thoreau's death they were on terms of intimacy, exchanging visits annually and letters frequently; the last letter penned by Thoreau's own hand was addressed to Ricketson. Most of their correspondence has been published, and Thoreau biographers found a store of information in Ricketson, whose insistence that his friend sit for an ambrotype has given posterity perhaps the best of the Thoreau portraits. Subsequently Ricketson's son Walton, a sculptor, executed a bust and a bas-relief medallion of the Concord philosopher. Of Ricketson Thoreau wrote: "He is a man of very simple tastes, notwithstanding his wealth; a lover of nature; but above all, singularly frank and plain-spoken" (*Ibid.,* p. 156). Ricketson published *The History of New Bedford* (1858), still regarded as a standard work in its field, which was supplemented by

New Bedford of the Past (1903), published posthumously. His first book of verse, *The Autumn Sheaf, a Collection of Miscellaneous Poems* (1869), was followed in 1873 by *The Factory Bell and Other Poems*, inspired by sympathy for working people. Two posthumous volumes, *Daniel Ricketson and His Friends* (1902), and *Daniel Ricketson, Autobiographic and Miscellaneous* (1910), edited by his daughter and son, Anna and Walton Ricketson, contain many of his letters, poems, sketches, and other writings.

[In addition to the two volumes prepared by Ricketson's son and daughter, see: F. B. Sanborn, *Henry D. Thoreau* (1882) and *The Life of Henry David Thoreau* (1917); H. S. Salt, *The Life of Henry David Thoreau* (1890); *Familiar Letters of Henry David Thoreau* (1894), ed. by F. B. Sanborn; *The Writings of Henry David Thoreau* (20 vols., 1906), vols. VI, VIII–XIV; Grace Williamson Edes, *William Ricketson and His Descendants*, vol. II (1932); *Boston Transcript*, July 18, 1898.]
W. M. E.

RICKETTS, JAMES BREWERTON (June 21, 1817–Sept. 22, 1887), Union soldier, the son of George R. A. and Mary (Brewerton) Ricketts, was born in New York City. An ancestor, William Ricketts, member of an old English family, settled in the Jerseys in early colonial days. James was appointed a cadet to the United States Military Academy from New York on Sept. 1, 1835, and was graduated on July 1, 1839, commissioned second lieutenant, 1st Artillery, and assigned to duty on the Canadian frontier. He served at various stations in New York and Maine until the outbreak of the Mexican War in 1846, when he was transferred with his regiment to General Taylor's army in Mexico; he took part in the battles of Monterey and Buena Vista. From 1847 to 1861 he served at different stations throughout the United States and participated in hostilities against the Seminole Indians in Florida in 1852. He was promoted to the rank of first lieutenant on Apr. 21, 1846, and to captain on Aug. 3, 1852. At the beginning of the Civil War he commanded a battery in General McDowell's army. At Bull Run, on July 21, 1861, he was dangerously wounded and taken prisoner, being exchanged after six months for a Confederate officer. For his distinguished service at Bull Run he was appointed brigadier-general of volunteers. He recovered sufficiently from his wounds to return to duty on May 8, 1862, and was assigned to command a division in General McDowell's corps with which he fought at Cedar Mountain and Manassas.

In September 1862, his division became part of General Hooker's corps and participated in the battles of South Mountain and Antietam where he was again seriously wounded. He remained with his division until October when his injuries compelled him to leave the field, and he served on court martial duty until March 1864. He now took command of a division in General Sedgwick's corps and fought in the battle of the Wilderness, at Spotsylvania, North Anna, Cold Harbor, and Petersburg until July 6, 1864, when his corps was hurried towards Washington to intercept General Early's advance on that city. In the battle of Monocacy which followed, Ricketts was conspicuous for his gallantry. Gen. Lew Wallace, the Union commander said: ". . . the splendid behavior of Ricketts and his men inspired me with confidence" (*War of the Rebellion: Official Records, Army*, 1 ser., XXXVII, pt. 1, 197). With his division Ricketts now joined General Sheridan's army in the Shenandoah Valley. At the decisive battle of Cedar Creek on Oct. 19, 1864, he was temporarily in command of the VI Corps, which he was ably conducting when he was wounded for the sixth time by a bullet that passed through his chest. Even this wound did not dispirit the heroic general. By April 1865, he was again able to command his division.

After the war he commanded a district in Virginia until he was discharged as a brigadier-general of volunteers on Apr. 30, 1866, reverting to the grade of major in the regular army. In January 1867 he was retired as a major-general for wounds received while in command of a corps. He was brevetted five times for gallant and meritorious services. After his retirement he made his home in Washington, D. C., where he died after much suffering from his old wounds. He was twice married, first, in 1840, to Harriet Josephine Pierce, daughter of Col. B. K. Pierce, who died, leaving one child, and in 1856, to Frances Lawrence, daughter of J. T. Lawrence, of Jamaica, of which union two of five children survived.

[Information from the family; G. W. Cullum, *Biog. Reg. . . . U. S. Mil. Acad.* (1891); Henry J. Hunt, memorial in *Annual Reunion, Asso. Grads., U. S. Mil. Acad.*, 1888; *Harper's Weekly*, Nov. 12, 1864; *Frank Leslie's Illustrated Newspaper*, Jan. 11, 1862; *Army and Navy Reg.*, Sept. 24, 1887; *N. Y. Times*, Sept. 23, 1887.]
S. J. H.

RICORD, FREDERICK WILLIAM (Oct. 7, 1819–Aug. 12, 1897), man of letters, public official, was born on the island of Guadeloupe, the son of Jean Baptiste and Elizabeth (Stryker) Ricord. On his mother's side he was seventh in descent from Jan Strÿcker of Ruinen, province of Drenthe, United Netherlands, who settled with his family at New Amsterdam in 1652 and later founded the village of Midwout (Flatbush) on Long Island. His father was a physician and a brother of the famous Philippe Ricord [*q.v.*].

After the death of the elder Ricord in 1827, the family returned to the United States, living first at Woodbridge, N. J., and later at Geneva, N. Y., where for many years Mrs. Ricord conducted a successful school for girls. She was the author of a textbook, *Elements of the Philosophy of Mind* (1840), and *Zamba, or The Insurrection: A Dramatic Poem in Five Acts* (1842), which was based on her experiences in the West Indies and her prejudices against Roman Catholicism. Ludicrous as poetry, it is of more than a little interest as a social document.

At the age of fourteen her son entered Geneva (now Hobart) College as a member of the class of 1838. He transferred a year later to Rutgers College, but for some unknown reason did not complete the course. He read law for a short time in Geneva and then settled in Newark, N. J., not far from his maternal grandparents, as a teacher and private scholar. In 1843 he married Sophia Bradley, who with a son and three daughters outlived him. From 1849 to 1869 he was the librarian of the Newark Library Association. He was a member of the Newark board of education, 1853–69, serving several terms as its secretary and its president, and for four years was state superintendent of schools. During these years he published *The Youth's Grammar* (1853) and three textbooks of Roman history. The latter were written in a pleasing style and were widely used.

Meanwhile his reputation as a public-spirited citizen had been growing, and although in no sense a politician he became something of a political figure. He was elected sheriff of Essex County in 1865 and was twice reëlected; so well thought of was he that on one occasion he was the nominee of both parties. From 1870 to 1874 he was mayor of Newark, N. J. He antagonized his own party in the city council by opposing a plan to have the streets paved with a patent wood block, but after a long, stubborn fight he succeeded in defeating the measure, thereby saving the city from what turned out to be a barefaced fraud. From 1881 until his death he was treasurer and librarian of the New Jersey Historical Society. He was also for five years a judge of the court of common pleas of Essex County and for another five-year term a judge of the city court. As the first regular librarian of the Historical Society, he did important work in rounding out and cataloguing its collections and in editing various of its publications. He read some fourteen languages and had a genuine gift for translation. His *English Songs from Foreign Tongues* (1879), *The Self-Tormentor from the Latin of Publius Terentius Afer, with More*

English Songs from Foreign Tongues (1885), and several minor publications show his command of the English language. By the diversity of his activities rather than by eminence in any one he was a strong influence on the educational and cultural life of his state. He died at his home in Newark and was buried in the Mount Pleasant Cemetery.

[W. S. Stryker, *Geneal. Record of the Strÿcker Family* (1887), p. 55; *Hobart Coll. Gen. Cat. 1825–97* (1897); *Cat. Officers and Alumni Rutgers Coll. 1766–1916* (1916); *Biog. Notices Grads. Rutgers Coll. Deceased during the Academical Year Ending in June 1898* (1898); *Biog. and Geneal. Hist. of the City of Newark* (1898); Wm. Nelson, *Fifty Years of Hist. Work in N. J.* (1898); *Proc. N. J. Hist. Soc.*, II, 194–95 (Jan. 1902); *Newark Daily Advertiser*, Aug. 12, 1897.]   G. H. G.

RICORD, PHILIPPE (Dec. 10, 1800–Oct. 22, 1889), physician, specialist on venereal diseases, was born of French parents in Baltimore, Md. He was a younger brother of Alexander Ricord, naturalist, and Jean Baptiste Ricord, physician and naturalist, who became the father of Frederick William Ricord [*q.v.*]. At the age of twenty Philippe was sent to Paris for his medical studies. His talents attracted attention and he received the coveted appointment of interne in the service of the distinguished French surgeon, Dupuytren, but his penchant for practical jokes cost him his position. After receiving his degree in 1826, he practised for two years in country towns in France in order to make his living, but in 1828 returned to Paris and on competitive examination received the appointment of surgeon to the Central Bureau. To eke out his living expenses he gave courses in operative surgery at the hospital of La Pitié.

In 1831 he received the appointment of surgeon-in-chief for syphilis at the Hôpital du Midi and continued to hold that position until 1861 when he reached the age limit and retired. His clinics, always practical and thorough, were followed by physicians from all over the civilized world. He was one of the first to show that venereal diseases are more serious than they had been thought, being not merely local affections but often generalized and even fatal pathological conditions. He established a rational therapy of syphilis and in 1834 announced in precise terms the laws of the transmission of that disease. He demonstrated that gonorrhea is entirely distinct from syphilis and that constitutional syphilis always begins as an indurated, localized skin lesion (the hard chancre). Surgery is indebted to him for a new method of curing varicocele as well as for a special technique in urethroplasty, for which he received the Monthyon Prize.

Ricord's reputation deservedly became world

wide. Crowds of students flocked to him, many of them distinguished practitioners of medicine from distant countries. He consistently refused to accept an official teaching position but created for himself a teaching career above that of any professorship that he could have accepted, and other distinctions came unbidden. He was chosen a member of the Academy of Medicine in Paris in 1850 and was accorded the high honor of election as its president in 1868. In 1852 he became official surgeon to Prince Napoleon, afterwards the Emperor Napoleon III. On the establishment of the Empire he received the appointment of consulting surgeon to the imperial troops. As director of the Lazaretto, the institution for the care of the needy and ailing poor during the siege of Paris, he achieved popular and professional prestige. After Napoleon's dethronement he was his medical attendant during the disease of the bladder which proved fatal to the former Emperor. Characterized by Dr. Oliver Wendell Holmes as "the Voltaire of pelvic literature, a sceptic as to the morality of the race in general, who would have submitted Diana to treatment with his mineral specifics, and ordered a course of blue pills for the Vestal Virgins" (*Medical Essays*, 1883, p. 437), he received many decorations from foreign monarchs, most of whom had benefited either in their own persons or in those of members of their families from his professional ministrations. For his services in the Franco-Prussian War, President Thiers made him an officer of the Legion of Honor.

Ricord wrote very simply and directly but effectively. His treatise on venereal disease (*Traité pratique des maladies vénériennes,* Paris, 1838) marks an epoch in the history of medicine because it overthrew John Hunter's erroneous conclusions as to the identity of gonorrhea and syphilis, the autonomy of which Ricord definitely established. Most important among his other works were: *De la Blennorrhagie de la Femme* (1834); *Monographie du Chancre* (1837), the first complete account of his teaching; *Lettres sur la Syphilis* (1851), which went through a number of editions; and *Leçons sur le Chancre* (1857), edited by his pupil and successor, Alfred Fournier, which also went through several editions. He contributed a large number of memoirs, shorter papers, and communications to the *Memoires* and *Bulletins* of the Academy of Medicine of Paris. He continued in good health of mind and body until he was over eighty and practised until almost the end of his life. On Oct. 6, 1889, while waiting for a train, he caught a cold of which he died, at two in the morning of Oct. 22.

[H. A. Kelly and W. L. Burrage, *Am. Medic. Biogs.* (1920), inaccurate in various details; *Svenska Läkaresällskapets Handlinger,* XLVII (1921), 97–105; *Lancet* (London), Oct. 26, 1889; *Edinburgh Medic. Journal,* Dec. 1889; *Progrès Médical,* Oct. 26, 1889; *Annales de dermatologie et syphilographie* (Paris), Oct. 25, Nov. 25, 1889; *La France Médicale* (Paris), Oct. 26, 1889; *Revue de Littérature Médicale* (Paris), June 1, 1876; *N. Y. Medic. Jour.,* Oct. 26, 1889; *Times* (London), Oct. 23, 1889; *Journal des Débats* (Paris), Oct. 23, 1889; *N. Y. Tribune,* Oct. 23, 1889.]
J. J. W.

RIDDELL, JOHN LEONARD (Feb. 20, 1807–Oct. 7, 1865), physician, botanist, inventor, was born in Leyden, Mass., the son of John Riddell of Preston, N. Y., and of Lephe (Gates). He graduated in 1829 from the Rensselaer School, Troy, N. Y., and began his career lecturing on scientific subjects. In 1835 he was appointed adjunct professor of chemistry and professor of botany at Cincinnati Medical College, and in the same year he published his *Synopsis of the Flora of the Western States,* the pioneer botany text of that section. He secured the degree of M.D. in 1836 from Cincinnati Medical College, and went at once to New Orleans as professor of chemistry in the newly founded Medical College of Louisiana (later the Medical Department, Tulane University of Louisiana), a position which he retained until his death. He compiled a catalogue of Louisiana plants (published in abridged form as "Catalogus Florae Ludovicianae," in the *New Orleans Medical and Surgical Journal,* May 1852) which included several new species.

Riddell entered vigorously into the unfolding municipal life of New Orleans. In 1838 he was engaged in a governmental scientific exploration of the state of Texas; and upon his return became, by appointment of the president, melter and refiner in the branch United States Mint. This position he held until 1849. In 1844 he became a member of the commission appointed by the governor and legislature of Louisiana to devise a means of protection for New Orleans against inundations of the Mississippi River. About this time he began to give much time to the study of microscopy, and later discovered the microscopical characteristics of the blood and black vomit in yellow fever. He also became a member of the commission appointed to inquire into the origin, causes, and character of the yellow fever epidemic of 1853.

According to his own account, it was in 1851 that he devised the binocular microscope, dividing light from a single objective. He put the instrument into form in 1852, arranging a combination of four glass prisms just above the objective so as to divide the light equally and pass it on to the two eyes through two parallel tubes, each with its own ocular. He demonstrated the principle involved before the New Orleans Physico-Medico Society on Oct. 2, 1852, and, after eliminating a pseudoscopic effect produced by his first arrangement, demonstrated a new objective before the same society on Apr. 12, 1853. On July 30 he displayed his binocular before the American Association for the Advancement of Science, and in August of that year commissioned Grunow Brothers of New Haven, Conn., to construct a microscope incorporating his innovation. This instrument, finished and sent to him in March 1854, was presented by his widow to the Army Medical Museum in Washington in April 1879. It was cumbersome, had no very high powers, and was not used in serious investigations. Nevertheless, Riddell's contribution to the development of the microscope, although disputed by one or two scientists, has been widely recognized.

Riddell was an active member of the first Louisiana State Medical Society, founded in 1849, and of the New Orleans Physico-Medico Society. He was a prolific writer on a wide variety of scientific subjects. His death, which occurred in his fifty-ninth year, was not unexpected, for his mind, greatly agitated by the stirring political situation at the end of the Civil War, had given signs of failure.

[For Riddell's microscopes, see *New Orleans Mo. Medic. Reg.*, Oct. 1852, Apr. 1853; *New Orleans Medic. and Surgic. Jour.*, Nov. 1853, May 1854; *Am. Jour. Sci.*, Jan. 1853; *Quart. Jour. Microscopical Sci.*, Apr. 1853, Jan. 1854; *Proc. Am. Asso. for the Advancement of Sci.*, vol. VII (1856); Heinrich Frey, *Das Mikröskop* (1863); Pieter Harting, *Das Mikroskop* (1866); Samuel Holmes, "The Isophotal Binocular Microscope," *English Mechanic and World of Science*, July 23, 1880; J. J. Woodward, "Riddell's Binocular Microscopes," *New Orleans Medic. and Surgic. Jour.*, Apr. 1881. For biography, see *New Orleans Medic. and Surgic. Jour.*, Sept. 1866, Apr. 1902; *Am. Jour. Sci. and Arts*, Jan. 1866; L. H. Bailey, Jr., "Some North American Botanists," *Bot. Gazette*, Aug. 1883; H. A. Kelly and W. L. Burrage, *Am. Medic. Biogs.* (1920); *Biog. Record Officers and Grads. Rensselaer Polytechnic Inst.* (1887).]
R. M.
V. G.

RIDDER, HERMAN (Mar. 5, 1851–Nov. 1, 1915), newspaper publisher, was born in New York City, the son of Herman and Gertrude Maria (Tiemann) Ridder, who emigrated to the United States from Westphalia. His schooldays ended at the age of eleven when he was forced to go to work as an errand and office boy. At thirteen he entered the service of the Tradesmen's Fire Insurance Company, resigning after fourteen years, when a successful agent, to found the *Katholisches Volksblatt*, a weekly publication devoted to the interests of the German Catholics in the United States. This paper he discontinued in 1886, feeling the need of carrying on the same

work in the English language, for which purpose he established the *Catholic News*. The success of this weekly made him one of the most influential laymen in his church, to which he was always ardently devoted.

This field of activity proving too narrow for his abilities, Ridder in 1890 became the manager of the *New-Yorker Staats-Zeitung,* the foremost German language daily in the country, and in the course of time purchased the paper from its owner, Oswald Ottendorfer. He directed and managed the *Staats-Zeitung* until his death. From the time that he became associated with it he played an important part in the journalistic, civic, and political life of the metropolis. Politically an independent Democrat, he was especially prominent in the Cleveland campaigns for the presidency as a leader of the German-American group, and in 1895 he organized the German-American Reform Union as part of the anti-Tammany campaign. His opposition to Tammany never flagged. In 1908 he became the treasurer of the national democratic committee, serving as such during the last Bryan campaign for the presidency. In the campaign of 1912 he was an elector on the Democratic ticket and received the highest number of votes cast for the Democratic electors. From 1900 to 1915 Ridder was one of the ablest and most useful directors of the Associated Press, of which he was one of the first members. For two years, from 1907 to 1909 he was its treasurer. From 1907 to 1911 he was president of the American Newspaper Publishers' Association, the most responsible position in the gift of the publishers of the United States, his service being especially valuable because of his aggressive leadership. In an investigation of the print paper situation in the United States and Canada in 1911, which even at that time menaced the welfare of the press, he displayed great determination and courage.

His civic interests were wide and he gave freely of his time and strength to philanthropic and public undertakings. He was the active head of the celebration in 1909 of the three hundredth anniversary of the discovery of New York and the Hudson River by Henry Hudson, and of the centennial of Fulton's putting the steamer *Clermont* in service. According to Mayor George B. McClellan, but for Ridder this celebration "would never have been undertaken" and "never could have been carried to a triumphant conclusion." He deserves especially to be remembered for his advocacy of tariff reform, as well as his fight for good government in New York City, and for the wise stand taken by the *Staats-Zeitung* toward the World War and Germany's part in it; no journalist could have been put into a more difficult position than was he by this struggle and the character that it assumed. Essentially a self-made man, he owed his success to untiring labor, marked executive ability, and unusual powers of persuasion, which usually made him the successful advocate of any cause that he pleaded. On Apr. 6, 1880, he was married in New York to Mary Amend, who bore him five sons.

[C. W. Schlegel, *German-Am. Families in the U. S.,* vol. I (1916); *The Hudson-Fulton Celebration, 1909. Report . . . to the Legis. of the State of N. Y.,* prepared by E. H. Hall (2 vols., 1910); *Proc. of the Electoral College of the State of N. Y.* (1913); *Who's Who in N. Y.,* ed. by W. F. Mohr (1914); *Who's Who in Am.,* 1914–15; *New-Yorker Staats-Zeitung, N. Y. Times,* Nov. 2, 1915; information from his son, Victor F. Ridder.]   O. G. V.

RIDDLE, ALBERT GALLATIN (May 28, 1816–May 16, 1902), lawyer, congressman, author, was the son of Thomas and Minerva (Merrick) Riddle and the grandson of Thomas Ridel or Riddell who emigrated from Ireland as a child and died in Monson, Mass. The grandson was born there, and the next year the family removed to Geauga County, Ohio. When Albert was only seven years old his father died. When he was twelve he was apprenticed to a well-to-do farmer; but he was not inclined toward farming and in 1831 worked with his two elder brothers as a carpenter. His ambition, though, was for something else, and during the following two years he spent part of his time in study. In 1835 he went to Hudson, where he entered school, and later he attended for a year the academy in Painesville. There he became interested in oratory and debating. He began the study of law under the direction of Seabury Ford in the spring of 1838, and after a period of intensive application to his work he was admitted to practice in 1840. He proved himself a successful political speaker in the Harrison campaign of 1840, and three weeks after his admission to the bar he was nominated for the office of prosecuting attorney, was elected, settled at Chardon, and served six years. He was an ardent Whig and very bitter against slavery. Upon the nomination of Zachary Taylor, he issued the call for a mass meeting at Chardon that inaugurated the Free-Soil party of Ohio. Soon afterward, he was nominated by the Whigs and Free-Soilers of his district for the state House of Representatives, was elected, and became at once the recognized leader of these two groups in the House from 1848 to 1850. In January 1845 he married Caroline Avery of Chardon. They had seven children. He removed to Cleveland in 1850. In 1859 he acted as counsel for the defense in the Oberlin-Wellington

Rescue case (for argument see *History of the Oberlin-Wellington Rescue,* 1859, comp. by J. R. Shiperd). He won the respect and confidence of his fellows and was very attentive to business. He distinguished himself in many arguments in Congress, among them on the bill to abolish slavery in the District of Columbia. The first battle of Bull Run was fatal to his congressional career, for in connection with it he made certain confidential critical statements that gained publicity and were used against him. He did not seek reëlection in 1862. He again devoted himself to the law, but in the autumn of 1864 he accepted a consulate in Cuba as a convenient pretext for making an examination into the plans and workings of the blockade runners. This service he performed in a satisfactory manner. He then established himself in the practice of law in Washington. He claimed that, by a just construction of the Fourteenth and Fifteenth Amendments of the Constitution, women were entitled to vote. He was law officer for the District of Columbia from 1877 to 1889.

He was a successful writer as well as orator. His first publication was a series of eight lectures delivered before the law department of Howard University, *Law Students and Lawyers* (1873). His first novel, *Bart Ridgeley* (1873), was commented on as the best American novel of the year. The ensuing year appeared *The Portrait* and in 1875 *Alice Brand,* a story of Washington after the war. He prepared many of the biographical sketches in a *History of Geauga and Lake Counties* (1878). In 1880 he published *The Life, Character, and Public Services of J. A. Garfield. Old Newbury and the Pioneers* was published in 1885 with some family and local history, his *Life of Benjamin F. Wade* in 1886, and *Recollections of War Times* in 1895. He did much newspaper work and wrote many short stories. He died in Washington, D. C., and was buried in Rock Creek Cemetery.

[*Hist. of Geauga and Lake Counties, ante,* but sketch not signed by self; *Pioneer and General Hist. of Geauga County* (1880); *Who's Who in America,* 1901–02; *Biog. Directory Am. Cong.* (1928); G. T. Ridlon, *Hist. of the Ancient Ryedales* (1884); *Cleveland Leader,* May 16, 1902.]   H. L.

RIDDLE, GEORGE PEABODY (Sept. 22, 1851–Nov. 26, 1910), actor and reader, was born in Charlestown, Mass., the son of Edward and Charlotte (Cutter) Riddle. His father, a carriage dealer and auctioneer, had no connection with the stage, but his grandfather, William H. Riddle, was an actor. His grandmother, Mary (Lapsley) Riddle, who came of an old Philadelphia Quaker family, also was on the stage, and their two daughters, Eliza, who married Joseph

M. Field [*q.v.*], and Sarah, who married William Henry Smith [*q.v.*], were of considerable prominence in the theatrical activities of their era. Kate Field [*q.v.*] was his cousin. George Riddle attended the Chauncy Hall School in Boston, and graduated from Harvard in 1874, being odist at the class-day ceremonies, and having in his sophomore year won the Boylston prize for proficiency in public speaking. During his undergraduate days he had dabbled extensively in amateur stage performances and public readings, and immediately after his graduation he set out in earnest to obtain for himself a conspicuous position as an actor on the professional stage.

He made his first professional appearance as a reader in Boston in October 1874, and immediately went to New York, where he secured an engagement as a member of a traveling company. His début as an actor was in a miscellaneous program given at Norwich, Conn., Dec. 24, 1874, in which he appeared as Romeo in the balcony scene of *Romeo and Juliet*; on Jan. 30, 1875, at the Boston Theatre, he acted the same part in the entire play, with Mrs. Thomas Barry as Juliet. On the following Mar. 25, he acted with Edwin Booth, appearing as Titus in John Howard Payne's *Brutus or the Fall of Tarquin*. His first continuous engagement, beginning Aug. 24, 1875, was with the Boston Museum stock company as Captain Dudley Smooth in Bulwer's *Money*. He remained at that theatre for thirty-four weeks, acting thirty secondary characters. He then went to Canada and in Montreal, Toronto, and other cities appeared in a large number of characters varying from Romeo to Willie Hammond in *Ten Nights in a Bar Room*. These engagements were practically the end of his continuous professional acting. From 1878 to 1881 he taught elocution at Harvard College.

He made occasional appearances of note, however—with Mary Anderson at the Boston Theatre, Feb. 21, 1880, as Claude Melnotte to her Pauline in Bulwer's *The Lady of Lyons,* and at the same theatre Feb. 24, 1883, as Romeo to her Juliet. He took the part of Œdipus Tyrannus in a university production of Sophocles' play in Greek at Sanders Theatre, Cambridge, May 17, 1881, and also, with Riddle alone acting his rôle in Greek, at the Globe Theatre, Boston, during the week of Jan. 23, 1882, and during the following week at Booth's Theatre, New York, on both occasions Georgia Cayvan [*q.v.*] appearing as Jocasta. On Apr. 11, 1887, at the Hollis Street Theatre, Boston, came his disastrous experiment with *The Earl*, a blank-verse tragedy written by Edgar Fawcett [*q.v.*]. This play was acted for one week only, and in a letter (*Boston Transcript,* Apr. 15, 1887) he rashly stated that he was "very hopeful of being able to exist without the suffrages of Boston, whose damnation is purely local." Later, in another letter (May 7, 1887), he acknowledged that he had been "injudicious and unreasonable." He was of medium stature, and his mild manner, with an inability to rise to the heights of passion in the type of characters to which he aspired, was doubtless responsible for his abandonment of the profession he had hoped to make his life work. He was recognized as an exceptionally able director of Greek plays, however, supervising the performance of *Agamemnon* in the Cambridge stadium in 1906; *Medea* in Boston, New York, and Philadelphia, in 1910; and Margaret Anglin's production of *Antigone* in the Greek theatre, Berkeley, Cal., in 1910. His home was for many years in Cambridge, Mass., where he lived with his sister, and death came to him in a Boston hospital a few hours after he had been found unconscious on Boston Common as the result of a cerebral hemorrhage. He was the editor of two books, *George Riddle's Readings* (1888) and *A Modern Reader and Speaker* (1900).

[*Harvard Coll. Class of 1874 . . . Report* (1924); Lilian Whiting, *Kate Field, a Record* (1899); J. B. Clapp and E. F. Edgett, *Players of the Present* (1901); Eugene Tompkins and Quincy Kilby, *The History of the Boston Theatre, 1854–1901* (1908); *Who's Who in America,* 1910–11; Benj. Cutter, *A Hist. of the Cutter Family* (1871); *Boston Transcript,* Apr. 15, 1887, Nov. 26, 1910, and May 17, 1919; *New York Sun,* Sept. 29, 1901; Riddle's diary, printed in the *Boston Jour.* in twelve instalments beginning with a biog. sketch, July 10, 1893.]   E. F. E.

RIDDLE, MATTHEW BROWN (Oct. 17, 1836–Aug. 30, 1916), clergyman, Biblical student, teacher, was born in Pittsburgh, Pa., the son of David H. Riddle and Elizabeth Blaine (Brown), daughter of Matthew Brown, president of Jefferson College. Endowed with a superior mind, under the favorable influences of his home he developed rapidly and in 1852, at the age of sixteen, graduated from Jefferson College. From 1853 to 1855 he was a student in Western Theological Seminary, Pittsburgh. Later, for a brief period, he was adjunct professor of Greek at Jefferson. He then enrolled for the senior year's work at the theological seminary of the Reformed Dutch Church, New Brunswick, N. J., graduated from that institution in 1859, and in May of that year was licensed to preach by the Classis of Bergen. In 1860–61 he studied abroad, and on his return became chaplain of the 2nd New Jersey Volunteers, but ill health soon terminated his service.

On Apr. 15, 1862, he was ordained to the ministry by the Classis of Bergen and assumed the pastorate of the First Reformed Church, Hoboken, N. J. On Aug. 21 of that year he married Anna M. Walther of Heidelberg, Germany. From 1865 to 1869 he was pastor of the Second Reformed Church, Newark, N. J., resigning in the latter year to go abroad for further study.

In 1871 he was elected professor of New Testament exegesis at Hartford (Conn.) Theological Seminary, serving in that capacity until 1887, when he accepted a similar position in in Western Theological Seminary, where he later became president of the faculty. In 1911 he was made professor emeritus with the privilege of continuing his lectures in New Testament criticism. An untiring and fearless student, he attained high rank among the scholars and teachers of his day. In the classroom he was alert, vigorous, and stimulating—a vivacious manner, wit, and some eccentricities adding spice to his teaching. He was a member of the American committee on the revision of the New Testament, and was one of the editors of the American version. A prolific writer, he constantly contributed articles to religious periodicals and encyclopedias. He edited several of the New Testament books for Philip Schaff's *A Commentary on the Holy Scriptures*, the American edition of John P. Lange's work, and contributed to other of Schaff's publications; he also edited the gospels of Mark and Luke for the American edition of H. A. W. Meyer's commentary on the New Testament; his editorial services in connection with other standard works were extensive. For many years he contributed notes on the New Testament lessons of the International Sunday School series. He died at Edgeworth, Pa., and was survived by a son and two daughters.

[*Western Theological Sem. Gen. Biog. Cat.* (1927); *In Memoriam, Matthew Brown Riddle* (Western Theological Sem., 1917); E. T. Corwin, *A Manual of the Reformed Church in America* (1902); *Presbyterian Banner*, Sept. 7, 1916; *The Pittsburgh Post*, Sept. 1, 1916.]
W. H. S. D.

RIDEING, WILLIAM HENRY (Feb. 17, 1853–Aug. 22, 1918), writer and editor, was born at Liverpool, England, and died at Brookline, Mass. The sea was in his blood. His father, William Watkins Rideing, was an early official of the Cunard Line; an uncle of his mother, Emily Richards Rideing, was Rear-Admiral Edward Walpole Browne, of the Royal Navy. In boyhood he developed, besides a life-long interest in ships and sailors, a strong desire to express himself in writing, which was nourished by the printing in a Liverpool news-paper of fiction which he wrote as a boy. When he reached sixteen, in 1869, both of his parents were dead, and he came to the United States.

Here he found his first employment in Springfield, Mass., as private secretary to Samuel Bowles [*q.v.*], of the *Springfield Republican*. His engagement by this admirable mentor for a young journalist resulted from a letter which Rideing wrote applying for a place; so did his next engagement, by Whitelaw Reid [*q.v.*], of the *New York Tribune*. Typewriting had not yet superseded manuscript, and Rideing's distinctive "English-man-of-letters" handwriting must have pleaded, as it always did, in his favor. On the *Tribune* he received the valuable journalistic training of a space writer on all manner of subjects, and cultivated the acquaintance of the New York Bohemians of the seventies, literary, artistic, theatrical. Newspaper work led naturally to that of the "handy man of literature," to use his own term for his function as a prolific contributor to the magazines of the day. In this work he shared assignments with such illustrators as Edwin A. Abbey [*q.v.*], on a canal-boat trip, and Howard Pyle [*q.v.*], on the "national pike." He also served as special correspondent of the *New York Times* with a government exploring expedition in the Southwest. The fruits of this experience are preserved in *A-Saddle in the Wild West* (1879). This was the second of fifteen books of his writing. They included travel, biography, reminiscence, and fiction.

It was, however, as an editor that Rideing made his most notable record. In 1881 he joined the staff of the *Youth's Companion* in Boston, under the direction of its shrewd editor, Daniel S. Ford [*q.v.*], and a few years later associated himself also with the *North American Review*, maintaining the first of these connections until his death. The period of magazine history to which he belonged was that in which glittering names were used successfully as bait for subscribers, and the annual "announcement numbers" of the *Youth's Companion* fairly sparkled with such names as those of Tennyson and Gladstone in England of the surviving "Augustans" in America, brought together by Rideing's skilful enticements. Typical of his work for the *North American Review* was the discussion he "arranged between Mr. Gladstone, Cardinal Manning, and Robert Ingersoll on the subject of Faith" (*Many Celebrities, post*, p. 90). His well-formed head and features, his carefully "turned out" figure, gave to his appearance a dignity and distinction unimpaired by his smallness of stature. He married, June 14, 1887, Margaret Elinor Bockus, of Boston, who for the more than thirty remaining years of his life steadied his changeful temperament and played an important part in the social relationships essential to his work. His entertaining volumes of reminiscence provide many side-lights upon the memorable figures of his time. Among these volumes are *Many Celebrities and a Few Others* (1912), *In the Land of Lorna Doone and Other Pleasurable Excursions in England* (1895), and *At Hawarden with Mr. Gladstone and Other Transatlantic Experiences* (1896).

[Personal acquaintance; information from Mrs. Rideing; *Who's Who in America*, 1918–19; *Boston Transcript*, Aug. 23, 1918; autobiog. material in books mentioned above.]   M. A. DeW. H.

RIDEOUT, HENRY MILNER (Apr. 25, 1877–Sept. 17, 1927), author, was born at Calais, Me., the youngest of eight children of Samuel Macomber and Ellen Jane (Greely) Rideout, both of old New England families. His father, a miller, ship chandler, and petty contractor in Calais, died when Henry was twelve, leaving his family with few resources. The lad's education thus might have ended with graduation from the local Academy had not friends helped him to borrow money for a year at Harvard College. With financial assistance from the Price Greenleaf Aid and sums earned by tutoring he was able to continue his course, and received the degree of A.B., *magna cum laude*, in 1899. He had been editor-in-chief of the *Harvard Monthly*, a member of Signet and Hasty Pudding, and class odist. For five years after his graduation he taught English at Harvard, meanwhile publishing *Letters of Thomas Gray* (1899), *Tennyson's "The Princess"* (1899), and *Freshman English and Theme-Correcting at Harvard College* (1901), the last two in collaboration with Charles T. Copeland. During this period he also had stories accepted by various magazines, "Wild Justice" (*Atlantic Monthly*, September-October 1903), receiving especially favorable notice. Having paid his debts and saved some money, and being without dependents since his mother had died, he resigned his Harvard position in 1904 and departed on a year's trip around the world. He returned from the Far East with a rich mine of experiences and a completed novel, *The Siamese Cat*, which was published in 1907. His *Beached Keels* (1906), containing "Wild Justice," and *Admiral's Light* (1907), were volumes dealing with New Brunswick and Maine fisherfolk and mariners. In 1907–09 and again in 1912 he supplemented his income by teaching in the Harvard Summer School.

During 1909 he published *Dragon's Blood*, a story of China; *Selections from Byron, Wordsworth, Shelley, Keats, and Browning* in collaboration with Copeland; and "The Twisted Foot" in the *Saturday Evening Post*. For this serial of the East Indies, published in book form in 1910, the *Post* paid so liberally that Rideout was able to go to California to marry, on June 8, 1909, Frances Cecilia Reed, daughter of the Rev. Frederick Wilcox Reed of Sausalito. Here he planned to settle down to literary work, but during the next five years published only a biography, *William Jones, Indian, Cowboy, American Scholar, and Anthropologist in the Field* (1912). Then appeared six stories of the Far East, *White Tiger* (1915), *The Far Cry* (1916), *Tin Cowrie Dass* (1918), *The Footpath Way* (1920), *Man Eater* (1924), and *Dulcarnon* (1925). Two books, *The Key of the Fields and Boldero* (1918) and *Fern Seed* (1921), were inspired by a European visit just before the World War; two serials in the *Saturday Evening Post* were also issued in book form—*The Winter Bell* (1922), with an American setting, and *Barbry* (1923), a sea story; *Tao Tales* (1927), was based on stories from the author's Chinese cook. A juvenile, *Lola the Bear* (1928), was published posthumously.

In 1927, after a summer in New Brunswick, Rideout and his family sailed from Quebec on the *Montnairn*, for Europe, but he was stricken with virulent influenza pneumonia and died as the ship entered the river Scheldt. His body was cremated and his ashes interred in Mount Tamalpais Cemetery, San Rafael, Cal. Besides his wife, two daughters and a son survived him.

[*San Francisco Chronicle*, Sept. 18, 1927; *Harvard Alumni Bull.*, Oct. 13, 1927; *Who's Who in America*, 1926–27; notes from Mrs. Rideout; and various reviews.]   C. L. L.

RIDGAWAY, HENRY BASCOM (Sept. 7, 1830–Mar. 30, 1895), Methodist clergyman, theologian, was born in Talbot County, Md., the son of James and Mary (Jump) Ridgaway. Carefully nurtured in the Methodist faith, he was dedicated from early childhood to the ministry. He graduated from high school in 1846, and from Dickinson College, Carlisle, Pa., in 1849. The following year, at the age of twenty, he was admitted on trial to the Baltimore Conference of the Methodist Episcopal Church; he was ordained deacon in 1853 and elder in 1855, and for the next five years served various churches in Maryland. In 1855 he married Rosamund Caldwell, daughter of a professor at Dickinson College. After a year at the Chestnut Street Church in Portland, Me. (1861–62), he was assigned successively to a number of churches in New York City and on the Hudson, and from 1876 to 1881 was stationed in Cincinnati. In 1882 he accepted election to the chair of historical theology in Garrett Biblical Institute, Evanston, Ill.; two years later, when Dr. W. X. Ninde, professor of practical theology and president of the Institute, was elected bishop, Ridgaway was transferred to the chair of practical theology, and in the following year was elected president of the school; he continued in both positions until his death.

Two articles contributed by Ridgaway to the *Methodist Quarterly Review* deserve special mention: "Vicarious Atonement" (October 1871), and "Bishop Simpson" (January 1885). Among his published volumes the largest, an octavo of 744 pages, is *The Lord's Land* (1876), which gives a narrative of his travels during 1873–74 in Sinai, Arabia Petrea, and Palestine. Other volumes included *The Life of the Rev. Alfred Cookman* (1873); *The Life of Edmond S. James* (1882), and *Outlines of Theological Encyclopedia* (1889). Ridgaway was the recipient of numerous honors. In 1870 he visited the English Wesleyan Conference; he was a delegate to the General Conference of the Methodist Episcopal Church in 1872 and again in 1892, represented his own church as fraternal delegate to the General Conference of the Methodist Episcopal Church South in 1882, and was in attendance on the Centennial Conference held in Baltimore in 1884. The combination of teaching, administration, and outside activities finally proved too much for his physical endurance, and by 1892 the danger of a complete breakdown became apparent. Accompanied by his wife, he sought renewal of health in a trip around the world, but in the summer of 1894 he suffered a general collapse, and in March of the following year he died.

[*Minutes of the . . . Rock River Conference of the Meth. Episc. Ch.*, 1895; *Methodist Rev.*, Mar. 1905; *Northwestern Christian Advocate*, Apr. 3, 10, 1895; *Chicago Tribune*, Mar. 31, 1895.]   F. C. E.

RIDGE, MAJOR (*c.* 1771–June 22, 1839), leader of the treaty party among the Cherokee, was born probably at Hiwassee, a Cherokee settlement on the north side of Hiwassee River in what is now Polk County, Tenn. He is sometimes confused with his son, John Ridge (1803–1839), who was likewise a leader of the treaty party. He is said to have enjoyed the rank of major in the Cherokee forces allied with the Americans in the Creek War of 1814, and to have derived his English name from that military rank. He learned to speak English, en-

couraged his wife in the practice of Christianity, and sent his son to be educated in the Indian School at Cornwall, Conn. He became speaker of the council, had a comfortable home and farm where Rome, Ga., now stands, maintained a profitable ferry, and was a partner in the lucrative trading ventures of George Lavender. He acquired the manner and appearance of a prosperous Southern planter of the period.

In the earlier struggles with the United States he supported John Ross [*q.v.*] in opposition to further cession of land, but later he advocated cession and removal to the West. On Dec. 29, 1835, at New Echota, Ga., he signed a treaty to cede all Cherokee lands east of the Mississippi and to remove to the other side of the river. This was a grave step in the face of an old Cherokee law (committed to writing in 1829), prescribing the death penalty for ceding lands without tribal authority (*Niles' Weekly Register,* Dec. 5, 1829, p. 235). He and his supporters have maintained that he was actuated by a realization of the futility of resistance to white settlement; his enemies have accused him of acting from thwarted political ambition, greed, and inability to withstand the influence of the agents of the state and federal governments (for his arrangement to realize financial profit from the Creek treaty of 1825 see *American State Papers, post,* II, 667). In one of the most tragic of all the westward migrations of the Indians, he removed with his tribe across the Mississippi. Shortly after their arrival in the Indian Territory the vengeance of the non-treaty party overtook him. On the same day that his son and his nephew, Elias Boudinot, *c.* 1803–1839 [*q.v.*], were also killed, he was waylaid near Van Buren, Okla., and shot down from his horse.

[*"Cherokee Emigration Papers"* and other material in the Indian Office, Department of Interior; "Indian Removal," *Sen. Doc. 512,* 23 Cong., 1 Sess., vol. IV (1835), esp. p. 413; T. L. McKenney and James Hall, *Hist. of the Indian Tribes,* vol. I (1836); M. W. Anderson, *The Life of Gen. Stand Watie* (2nd ed., 1931); G. M. Battey, *A Hist. of Rome and Floyd County,* vol. I (1922); James Mooney, "Myths of the Cherokee," *19th Ann. Report of the Bureau of Am. Ethnology,* pt. I (1900); Jedidiah Morse, *Report to the Sec. of War . . . on Indian Affairs* (1822); *Am. State Papers: Indian Affairs,* II (1834), 469; *Niles' Weekly Register,* Mar. 2, 1816; *Niles' National Register,* July 27, Aug. 3, 1839; *Ann. Report of the Commissioner of Indian Affairs 1839–1840* (1839), esp. p. 38.]   K. E. C.

RIDGELY, CHARLES GOODWIN (July 2, 1784–Feb. 4, 1848), naval officer, the fourth of thirteen children of Dr. Lyde Goodwin and Abigail Levy, was born in Baltimore, Md. He was a descendant of Austin Goodwin of Bristol, England, who settled in Baltimore County, Md., about 1730. As a condition of receiving a legacy under the will of his uncle, Charles Ridgely, he assumed the latter's surname (also spelled Ridgeley, Ridgley). In 1822 he married Cornelia L. Livingston, the daughter of Robert L. Livingston, and had three daughters, one of whom married William Henry Hunt [q.v.]. Ridgely entered the United States navy as a midshipman on Oct. 19, 1799, during the naval hostilities with France, but there appears to be no record of his services at that time. In 1803 and early in 1804 he was attached to the frigate *Constitution,* flagship of Commodore Preble, in the war with Tripoli, and was later transferred to the schooner *Nautilus.* During the bombardment of that city and the naval battle of Aug. 3, 1804, he served on gunboat No. 1, with Richard Somers [q.v.], and took part in the hard fighting in the harbor of Tripoli on that memorable day. On Sept. 4, when Somers took the ketch *Intrepid* into the harbor as a fire-ship, Ridgely, on board the *Nautilus,* was able to follow her movements with a night-glass up to the last moment before she blew up. Many years later he gave an account of this episode in the *Naval Magazine,* March 1836.

He was promoted to the rank of lieutenant on Feb. 2, 1807, and to commander on July 24, 1813. During the war of 1812 he commanded the sloop-of-war *Erie,* but was blockaded in the harbor of Baltimore and unable to get to sea. In 1814 he was transferred with his crew to Lake Ontario where he took command of the 22-gun brig *Jefferson,* in the squadron of Commodore Chauncey. There he took part in the relatively unimportant movements of the squadron. He was promoted to the rank of captain on Feb. 28, 1815, and again commanded the *Erie,* which sailed in July for the Mediterranean in the powerful squadron of nine vessels under Commodore Bainbridge. He remained about three years in the Mediterranean where he took part in the activities incident to the subduing of the Barbary powers. He was in command of the naval station at Baltimore for a few years beginning in 1820 and in 1827, after a short leave of absence, he was given command of the West India Squadron. His flagship was the sloop-of-war *Natchez* and his force consisted of six vessels. Piracy had recently been suppressed in the West Indies after several years of hard struggle but sporadic cases continued to arise from time to time, requiring the presence of a strong naval force in these waters for a prolonged period. He remained on this station about two years and during this time at least one case of piracy and the brutal murder of the crew of an American merchantman took place.

At the end of this tour of duty Ridgely enjoyed a four years' leave of absence. From 1834 to 1839 he was commandant of the New York navy yard. In 1840 and 1841 he served his last sea duty in command of the Brazil Squadron of five vessels with the frigate *Potomac* as his flagship. After a year on waiting orders he again took command of the naval station at Baltimore where he ended his service on the active list. His few remaining years were passed in retirement, among his family and friends in Baltimore.

[Genealogical chart of the Ridgely family, Cary papers, Md. Hist. Soc. Library; T. H. S. Hamersly, *Gen. Reg. of the U. S. Navy* (1882); E. S. Maclay, *A Hist. of the U. S. Navy* (1894), vol. I; G. W. Allen, *Our Navy and the Barbary Corsairs* (1905); *The Goodwins of Hartford, Conn.* (1891); *Md. Hist. Mag.,* Sept. 1917.]　　　　　　　　　　　　　　G. W. A.

RIDGELY, DANIEL BOWLY (Aug. 1, 1813–May 5, 1868), naval officer, was born near Lexington, Ky., where his father, also Daniel Bowly Ridgely, descended from a prominent Maryland family, had moved in 1810. His mother was Jane (Price) Ridgely, the daughter of Col. John Price. Young Daniel and his brother, Richard Henry, were orphaned by their father's early death, and the former was placed in school for eighteen months among relatives at Rock Hill Academy, Ellicott City, near Baltimore, Md. He was appointed a midshipman on Apr. 1, 1828, and saw his first service on the sloop *St. Louis* in the Pacific. This was followed by duty on the receiving ship at Norfolk, the sloop *Warren* in the West Indies, the ship of the line *Columbus* in the Mediterranean and on the coast of Brazil, the brig *Lawrence* of the Home Squadron, the receiving ship *Ontario,* Baltimore, the *Warren* again, and the receiving ship *Pioneer* at Baltimore. Meanwhile he was promoted to passed midshipman on June 14, 1834, and to the rank of lieutenant on Sept. 10, 1840. During the Mexican War, as first lieutenant on the *Albany,* of Commodore Matthew Calbraith Perry's squadron, he participated in the bombardment and capture of Vera Cruz and the taking of Tuspan, Alvarado, and Tampico. He was then attached to the Naval Observatory, Washington, D. C., 1850–52, under Matthew Fontaine Maury [q.v.], to the receiving ship *Ontario,* Baltimore, and to the sloop *Germantown* in the West Indies. Promoted to the rank of commander on Sept. 14, 1855, he was given his first command, the steamer *Atalanta,* 1857–58, of the Paraguayan Expedition, and dispatched to demand satisfaction from the government of Paraguay for an insult to the flag of the United States and injuries to American citizens.

When the Civil War broke out, he was in command of the receiving ship *Alleghany* in Baltimore, which was moved to Annapolis on May 3, 1861, to assist in the protection of the Naval Academy. He received command of the steamer *Santiago de Cuba* on Oct. 5, 1861, and cruised in the Gulf of Mexico and West Indian waters, capturing several blockade runners by August of the following year. On Nov. 16, 1862, he was advanced to the rank of captain. He took command of the steam sloop *Shenandoah*, North Atlantic Blockading Squadron, in June 1863, and cruised independently in West Indian waters, later participating in the blockade off Wilmington and New Inlet. He took part in the attack on Fort Fisher on Dec. 24 and 25, 1864, and in the capture on Jan. 13 and 14, 1865, for which he was recommended for promotion by David Dixon Porter [*q.v.*] in his report to Welles, as one who also "has been very energetic during the war against blockade runners" (*War of the Rebellion, post,* 1 ser., XI, 454). Ridgely was then ordered to Charleston where the *Shenandoah* assisted in the operations at Bull's Bay, and was present at the evacuation of that city. He commanded the *Powhatan* of Admiral Rodgers's squadron in the Pacific, and returned home in 1867 in command of the steamer *Lancaster*. He had been promoted meanwhile to the rank of commodore on July 25, 1866, and was made a member of the examining board in Philadelphia in 1868. He died of heart disease in this city on May 5 of the same year, and he was interred in Greenmount Cemetery in Baltimore. He married Johanna M. Clemm of Baltimore on Oct. 11, 1837, and they had one son, Dr. Nicholas Ridgely. His second wife, Elizabeth Dulany Rogers, whom he married on Feb. 8, 1858, survived him, dying in 1907. Their only child died in infancy.

[Letters from Mrs. J. M. Dennis, Apr. 26, 1931, and Mrs. Margaret R. Leidy, Apr. 17, 1931; records of the city of Baltimore, Md., and the Md. Hist. Soc.; *War of the Rebellion: Official Records (Navy),* 1 ser., vols. II, IX, and XVII; T. H. S. Hamersly, *Gen. Reg. of the U. S. Navy* (1882); J. D. Warfield, *The Founders of Anne Arundel and Howard Counties* (1905); *Army and Navy Jour.,* May 16, 1868; obit. in the *Sun* (Baltimore, Md.), May 7, 1868.]   C. L. L.

RIDGELY, NICHOLAS (Sept. 30, 1762–Apr. 1, 1830), legislator, jurist, was born in Dover, Del., the eldest son of Dr. Charles Greenberry Ridgely by his first wife. His mother, Mary, according to her husband's note in the Ridgely family Bible (*post*), was the daughter of Abraham Wynkoop of Sussex County, Del.; but in Richard Wynkoop's *Wynkoop Genealogy* (1904, p. 35), it is made to appear that she was the daughter of Wynkoop's wife, Mary Dyer, by a former marriage, to Nicholas Hammond.

Ridgely's paternal grandfather, Nicholas Ridgely, who moved to Dover from Maryland and served Kent County for over a decade as prothonotary and clerk of the peace, was the grandson of Col. Henry Ridgeley (*sic*) who settled in Anne Arundel County, Md., in 1659 (Warfield, *post,* pp. 77–81). The younger Nicholas, after securing a liberal education, studied law under Robert Goldsborough of Cambridge, Md., and having taken up the practice of his profession in his native town, soon assumed a leading position at the Delaware bar. He early participated in politics of his state and before he reached the age of twenty-five was elected a delegate from Kent County to the state convention of 1787 which ratified the Federal Constitution. In 1788, 1789, and 1790 he was elected a member of the Legislative Council from Kent County, and thus participated in the election of the first United States senators from Delaware and the first presidential electors. In 1791 his superior legal talents brought him appointment as state attorney-general, which position he held for a decade, and in the same year he was elected a delegate for Kent County to the second state constitutional convention, which was held in Dover in November 1791 and continued into the following year. Under the second constitution, which went into effect in 1792, Ridgely was elected a member of the first state House of Representatives, and was later reëlected to that body five times, in 1796, 1797, 1799, 1800, and 1801. At the first session of the legislature in January 1802, he resigned his seat because he had been appointed chancellor of Delaware to succeed the first chancellor, William Killen. He served his state with great distinction in this office until his death, twenty-eight years later.

Ridgely was married, May 20, 1806, to Mary Brereton, daughter of Henry and Elizabeth Brereton of Sussex County, Del. She survived him twenty-two years, dying in Dover, July 28, 1852. There were no children. Ridgely was a communicant of Christ Episcopal Church in Dover for many years, was elected senior warden in 1786, and in June of that year was a deputy to the second session (Philadelphia) of the convention which organized the Protestant Episcopal Church in the United States of America. He was buried in Christ Churchyard.

[Ridgely Bible in the possession of Henry Ridgely, Esq., Dover, Del.; minutes of Christ Episcopal Church, Dover; minutes of the Legislative Council (MS.), in Public Archives, Dover; "Minutes of the Council of the Del. State, 1776–1792," *Papers of the Hist. Soc. of Del.,* vol. VI (1887); biog. sketch in *Del. Reg. and Farmer's Mag.,* Feb. 1838, repr. in 1 *Del. Chancery Reports,* 484–90; J. M. McCarter and B. F. Jackson, *Hist. and Biog. Encyc. of Del.* (1882); *Biog. and Geneal.*

Hist. of the State of Del. (1899), I, 85–86, II, 788; J. T. Scharf, Hist. of Del. (1888), I, 548–49; H. C. Conrad, Hist. of the State of Del. (1908), III, 924–26; J. D. Warfield, The Founders of Anne Arundel and Howard Counties, Md. (1905); Delaware Gazette (Wilmington), Apr. 6, 1830.]

G. H. R.

RIDGWAY, ROBERT (July 2, 1850–Mar. 25, 1929), ornithologist, was born in Mount Carmel, Ill., the eldest child of David Ridgway, a druggist, and Henrietta James (Reed) Ridgway. His family, on his father's side, was of Philadelphia Quaker stock; his mother's family came originally from Maryland. Robert's education consisted of the course in the local school, supplemented by what he derived from his parents and through his own exertions. Both parents were lovers of nature and in his ninth year Robert was busy making colored drawings of the birds he shot as well as of other objects of interest. He mixed his own colors in his father's drug shop and even manufactured his own gunpowder. In 1864 the mother of one of his boy companions (Lucien Turner, later explorer of Alaska and Ungava) suggested that he write to the Patent Office in Washington for information about certain birds which puzzled him. The resulting correspondence with Prof. Spencer F. Baird, which lasted over several years, determined him more than ever to continue with his study of ornithology.

At the age of seventeen, having received through Baird an appointment as zoölogist on an exploring party to study a possible railway route along the Fortieth Parallel, he went to Washington, where he made the personal acquaintance of Baird, who ever remained his ideal. The party went by sea to San Francisco by way of Panama and spent the next two years (1867–69) in the wilds of Utah, Nevada, and Wyoming. Ridgway's report appeared in Professional Papers of the Engineer Department, U. S. Army: Report of the Geological Exploration of the Fortieth Parallel (vol. IV, pt. 3, 1877). Returning to Washington, he became a member of the staff of the Smithsonian Institution, relieving Baird of the care of the bird collections. In 1880 he was designated curator of birds in the United States National Museum, in which post he continued until his death. In 1883 he was one of the founders of the American Ornithologists' Union, of which he was president in 1898–1900. He was a member of several of its committees, most important being the committee on nomenclature and classification of North American birds which drew up the standard "Check-List." In spite of his exacting duties at the Museum he managed to do important field work, visiting Florida in 1895, 1896, and 1897, and Alaska, as a member of the Harriman Expedition, in 1899; while in 1904 and 1908 he visited his friend José Zeledon at his home in Costa Rica.

In 1915 he arranged to spend his remaining years at Olney, not far from his old home at Mount Carmel, Ill. He had purchased a property which was in fact a natural wild life sanctuary, and here he continued his work on his monumental Birds of North and Middle America, which had for some years occupied all his time in Washington. He later acquired a much larger tract, close by, which was particularly rich in native flora. This tract, named "Bird Haven," has been purchased by the ornithologists of the country and Ridgway's friends and is maintained as a memorial to him. He was a botanist as well as an ornithologist and possessed an intimate knowledge of the plant life of his native state, while he took great delight in horticulture.

His discrimination of colors was remarkable and his interest in the accuracy of color terms in scientific descriptions, especially of birds, led him to publish his Color Standards and Nomenclature (1886, 1912), which has been a boon to systematists throughout America. Besides the volumes mentioned and some five hundred papers in various magazines and proceedings of scientific societies, his important publications are as follows: A History of North American Birds: Land Birds (3 vols., 1874), and The Water Birds of North America (2 vols., 1884), both in collaboration with Spencer F. Baird and Thomas M. Brewer [qq.v.]; A Manual of North American Birds (1887, 1896); The Hummingbirds (1892), from the Report of the United States National Museum for 1890; The Birds of Illinois (2 vols., 1887–95); and The Birds of North and Middle America, of which eight volumes were published (1901–19) and two left in manuscript, nearly completed, at the time of his death. This last, one of the greatest works on systematic ornithology ever written, won the Brewster Medal of the American Ornithologists' Union.

Ridgway at the height of his career was the leading American ornithologist; his systematic knowledge of the birds of the Americas was unsurpassed, and his knowledge brought him honorary membership in the principal foreign ornithological societies. He was a delightful companion to his intimates but was of a shrinking disposition with an extreme aversion to any sort of publicity, never making communications before scientific gatherings and rarely appearing in public. While he did permit his election to the presidency of the American Ornithologists' Union it was with the distinct understanding that he would never be called upon to preside at a meeting. Personally, he was of medium stature, rather quick in action and in speech. His scientific writings were models of accuracy and correct terminology, but he could also write delightfully in a more popular vein, and no matter how deeply interested he might be in technical ornithology, there was always present in him a deep underlying love of the beauties of nature. He married, on Oct. 12, 1875, Julia Evelyn Perkins of Washington. They had one child, Audubon Whelock Ridgway, who died in his twenty-fourth year, soon after being appointed an assistant in ornithology in the Field Museum, Chicago.

["Robert Ridgway: Ornithologist," *Audubon Bulletin,* Winter, 1917–18, pub. by the Illinois Audubon Soc.; Harry Harris, "Robert Ridgway," with bibliog., *Condor,* Jan.–Feb. 1928; *Ann. Report . . . of the Smithsonian Inst.,* 1929 (1930); *Auk,* Apr. 1929; *Bird Lore,* May 8, 1929; *Who's Who in America,* 1928–29; *N. Y. Times,* Mar. 26, 1929; personal acquaintance.]

W. S.

RIDPATH, JOHN CLARK (Apr. 26, 1840–July 31, 1900), educator, writer of popular historical works, was born on a farm in Putnam County, Ind., to which his parents, Abraham and Sally (Matthews) Ridpath, had moved from Virginia. In this frontier community he received such education as was available but his parents were of more than average culture, gave him much instruction themselves, and encouraged him to seek a higher education. At nineteen he entered Indiana Asbury University at Greencastle, Ind., a college founded by the Methodist Episcopal Church. He was a good student and graduated in 1863. His first employment was as teacher, then as principal, of the academy at Thorntown. In 1866 he was called to Lawrenceburg as superintendent of schools and served there until 1869. He then accepted a call to his alma mater as professor of English literature and normal instruction. Here he quickly achieved recognition as a gifted and inspiring teacher. In 1871 his title was changed to professor of belles-lettres and history and in 1879 he became vice-president of the university. His intellectual interests during these years turned increasingly to history, and in 1882 he became professor of history and political philosophy. He retained this chair until his resignation from the university in 1885. He was most influential in persuading Washington C. De Pauw, one of the wealthiest citizens of Indiana at that time, to become the patron of Indiana Asbury and in recognition of De Pauw's large bequest Ridpath advocated and secured the change of name of Indiana Asbury to De Pauw University in 1884. He retired from active teaching to devote himself exclusively to writing and publishing. On

Dec. 21, 1862, he had married Hannah R. Smythe of Greencastle, by whom he had five children. He died in New York City and was buried in Forest Hill Cemetery at Greencastle.

Ridpath was an impressive and forceful personality. Although he was successful as a teacher, it is as a writer of popular history that he is best known. He was a man of great vitality and was capable of long periods of sustained intellectual labor. An omnivorous reader with an exceptional memory, he accumulated and could call up at will an immense store of information. His first book, *History of the United States, Prepared Especially for Schools,* appeared in 1875, and thereafter until his death he published a long series of works. He wrote with ease in a style that was direct and clear, and sufficiently dramatic to intrigue the interest of his readers. His books sold in such numbers that he may certainly be regarded as one of the most popular writers of historical works of his time. The enormous quantity and scope of his work, however, precluded that scrupulous regard for fact and reliance on authority that characterizes the more scholarly historian. His best-known works are: *A Popular History of the United States of America* (1876); *Cyclopedia of Universal History* (4 vols., 1880–85); and *Great Races of Mankind* (4 vols., 1884–94). As editor-in-chief he published *The Ridpath Library of Universal Literature* (25 vols., 1898).

[Sources include: *A Biog. Hist. of Eminent and Self-Made Men of . . . Ind.* (1880), vol. I; A. L. Mason, "John Clark Ridpath, LL.D.," in *DePauw Univ. Alumnal Reg., 1837–1900* (1900); *Alumnal Record: DePauw Univ.* (1920); *Who's Who in America,* 1899–1900; *N. Y. Times,* Aug. 1, 1900. Information as to certain facts was supplied by friends and associates of Ridpath.]

W. W. C.

RIEGER, JOHANN GEORG JOSEPH ANTON (Apr. 23, 1811–Aug. 20, 1869), pioneer Evangelical clergyman, was born in Aurach, Bavaria, Germany. He was left an orphan before he reached the age of eleven, and for a time lived with an aunt in Épinal, France. From earliest childhood he had been destined for priesthood in the Catholic Church, but absorbed some Lutheran doctrine as a boy while helping a classmate with his catechism lessons. An open avowal of his Protestant leaning brought such strenuous opposition on the part of his aunt that he fled in 1832 to Basel, Switzerland, where he found refuge in the home of a Reformed minister and was brought in contact with the mission house of that place. Four years later when a group of American Christians applied to the Basel headquarters for German missionaries for the West, Rieger was chosen to go. He was among the first of the German missionaries who had the vision to introduce the use of English into the evangelical service.

His first mission field was at Alton, Ill., where he arrived on Nov. 28, 1836. During his ministry at this place, he lived at the home of Elijah Parish Lovejoy [q.v.], and assisted in the latter's abolitionist activities, but his most strenuous efforts in the direction of a spiritual revival were so meagerly rewarded that he left in August of the following year for Beardstown, Ill., where he stayed until the spring of 1839. In this year he returned to Germany where he made the acquaintance of Minette Schemel, who returned to the United States with him in 1840 as his bride. They settled first at Highland, Ill., where their two children were born and died. In 1840, when the *Deutsche Evangelische Kirchen-Verein des Westen,* later called the *Evangelische Synode von Nord-Amerika,* was formed, Rieger was recognized as one of the dominating figures in the movement. In October 1843, two months after he had moved from Highland to Burlington, Iowa, his wife died. He made a second trip to Germany in 1844 and married Henrietta Wilkins at Bremen on Apr. 15, 1845. For two years after his return to the United States he sold literature for the Bible and Tract Society of New York and then moved to Holstein, Mo., where his two small daughters fell ill of cholera and died.

His principal work during these years was done in connection with the establishing of the Evangelical Seminary, at Marthasville, Mo., in 1850, after it had been housed in his own home for two years. His ministry of thirteen years at Holstein ended when he moved to Jefferson City in 1860. He became one of the trustees of the Lincoln Institute, a college for negroes, and did admirable work among the prisoners at the state penitentiary. He was universally beloved: Southerners left their valuables in the safe-keeping of this abolitionist preacher when Federal soldiers approached; rich and poor, black and white, Catholic and Protestant sought out the humble clergyman for advice. When he died the whole city went into mourning. His widow and seven children survived him.

[Manuscript diary of Joseph Rieger in the possession of relatives; Edward Huber, "Pastor Joseph Rieger . . .," *Eighth Ann. Report of the . . . Soc. for the Hist. of the Germans in Md.* (1894); Joseph Rieger, *Ein Lebensbild aus der Evangelischen Kirche Nord-Amerikas* (1871); Hugo Kamphausen, *Gesch. des Religiösen Lebens in der Deutschen Evangel. Synode von Nord-Amerika* (1924); Albert Mücke, *Gesch. der Deutschen Evangel. Synode von Nord-Amerika* (1915); J. W. Flucke, *Evangelical Pioneers* (1931); W. G. Bek, "The Followers of Duden, Joseph Rieger—Colporteur," *Mo.*

Hist. Rev., Jan. 1924; *Mo. Democrat* (St. Louis), Aug. 31, 1869.]
                   W. L. B—r.

RIGDON, SIDNEY (Feb. 19, 1793–July 14, 1876), early Mormon leader, was born at Piny Fork, Allegheny County, Pa. He was the third and youngest son of William and Nancy (Gallaher) Rigdon who were descended from English, Scotch, and Irish stock. His schooling was meager and irregular. After twenty-six years on the family farmstead, he left home to reside with a Baptist preacher who influenced him to enter the ministry. In May 1819, with a license to preach in his pocket, he moved to Warren, Trumbull County, Ohio, where he became closely associated with Adamson Bentley, another Baptist minister who introduced to him the views of Alexander Campbell. In June 1820 he married Bentley's sister-in-law Phebe Brook, a native of Bridgeton, N. J. Largely at Campbell's suggestion, he took charge of a small Baptist congregation in Pittsburgh, but in August 1824 he returned to Ohio to enter the tanning business with his brother-in-law, Richard Brook. Within two years he was preaching again, but unattached to any sect. He went about the Western Reserve contending that the only true gospel lay in a return to the Scriptures, foretelling the "restoration of the ancient order of things," described in the Bible, and the imminence of the millennium. He had much to do in converting large numbers of Baptists to the doctrines of Thomas and Alexander Campbell who were then in Ohio. Later he accepted an invitation to take the congregation at Mentor, Ohio, and by 1828 he was definitely allied with the Campbellite movement.

Some writers maintain that Rigdon rewrote and expanded a novel written by Solomon Spaulding and that Joseph Smith, with Rigdon's connivance, palmed it off as the Book of Mormon. Other historians, including, of course, the official chroniclers, take a different view. Rigdon, to the end, denied authorship of the Book of Mormon. It is certain that his public conversion to Mormonism came through his friend, Parley P. Pratt [q.v.], in November 1830. From this time on until the death of Smith, Rigdon played an important rôle in the new movement. He entered enthusiastically into Smith's plan for an "inspired" "re-translation" of the Bible, although neither of them knew Hebrew, Greek, or Latin. He engaged in extensive preaching and writing, helped effect and complete the organization of the church hierarchy, became first counselor to the Prophet, and by "divine" revelation he was appointed "Spokesman" for Smith and the entire church. He accompanied Smith and others to western Missouri in the summer of 1831. Upon the return to Kirtland, Rigdon like his colleagues became deeply involved financially in the craze of land speculation. The debacle of the curious "Kirtland Safety Society Anti-BANKing Company," which had unloaded illegal bank notes on creditors and the general public, brought on such a storm of protest that many followers apostatized and Smith and Rigdon in January 1838 fled to Missouri to escape mob violence and judicial action. The Mormons who had settled in Missouri under Smith's edict soon fell into conflict with the non-Mormons. Following the clash of arms in the late summer and early autumn of 1838, Smith and Rigdon were imprisoned and escaped the death penalty only by Gen. A. W. Doniphan's refusal to execute the orders of the court martial. After some months of imprisonment and subsequent illness Rigdon got to Quincy, Ill., in February 1839, discouraged in spirit and broken in health. Somewhat reluctantly he followed Smith's advice and settled in Nauvoo, where he became city councilman, postmaster, trustee and professor of church history in the newly established "University of the City of Nauvoo," and still later city attorney, although there is no evidence that he was ever admitted to the Illinois bar.

Both in Kirtland and in Missouri Smith and Rigdon had had several serious differences of opinion. In Nauvoo these divergences were even more evident. From 1842 on, Smith was increasingly convinced that Rigdon was aiding and abetting his enemies. Rigdon did not accept the secret practice of polygamy which Smith introduced to his close advisers. The intense reaction of his daughter Nancy to Smith's proposal to make her one of his "spiritual wives" may well have influenced Rigdon's attitude. In 1844 when Smith staged his campaign for no less an office than the presidency of the United States, Rigdon, in spite of an almost open breach between the two, was selected to be his running mate. Rigdon left Nauvoo in June ostensibly to participate in the campaign but there is considerable evidence that he had no intention of returning. When he learned of the assassination of Joseph and Hyrum Smith, however, he hastened back hoping to be selected as "Guardian" of the church. He based his claim upon a "vision" which he had had at Pittsburgh. But he was outmaneuvered by Brigham Young and the other apostles who as a body were chosen to head the church. Rigdon remained at Nauvoo for several weeks until excommunicated on Sept. 8, 1844. He retraced his steps to Pittsburgh where he rounded up a small number of Mormons who like himself were convinced that the successors to

Smith in Nauvoo had misled the "Saints." In April 1845 at a conference his followers voted him First President, Prophet, Seer, Revelator, Translator, Trustee and Trust of their new organization, the Church of Christ. They disowned any connection with the Western Mormons. Rigdon produced revelations and prophecies, including one predicting the destruction of Nauvoo which was fulfilled. He carried on various rituals and appointed new officials, but as the years passed by the new sect practically disappeared. His last days were spent at Friendship, Allegany County, N. Y.

Without doubt Rigdon was a neurotic. He was petty, extremely stubborn, and given to unreasonable bursts of anger. He experienced fantastic visions, especially during his intense emotional states, which in connection with references to his frothing at the mouth suggest a certain tendency to epilepsy. In spite of these handicaps, he was a talented orator although inclined, as Smith himself once remarked, "to dress up the truth." He was essentially an emotional agitator rather than an effective administrator. His chief influence on Mormonism was his contribution to Mormon theology. He doubtless wrote the "Lectures on Faith"—a basic Mormon document —although many Mormons still imagine them the work of Smith, who published them as his own. He carried into Mormonism many ideas of Campbellite origin, particularly those concerned with faith, repentance, baptism for the remission of sins, the gift of the Holy Ghost, and the belief in a restoration of the true gospel and of the millennium. He stimulated the practice of healing, speaking in tongues, and visions, and at one time was enthusiastic in support of a communistic order, which the Mormons attempted but gave up.

[G. B. Arbaugh, *Revelation in Mormonism* (1932); Daryl Chase, "Sidney Rigdon, Early Mormon" (1931), an unpublished manuscript in the Univ. of Chicago Lib.; W. A. Linn, *The Story of the Mormons* (1902); C. A. Shook, *The True Origin of the Book of Mormon* (1914); Jos. Smith, Jr., *Hist. of the Church . . . of Latter-Day Saints*, vols. I–V (1902–09); M. R. Werner, *Brigham Young* (1925); John Jacques, "The Life and Labors of Sidney Rigdon," *Improvement Era*, Dec. 1899–June 1900; *Latter-Day Saint Biog. Encyc.*, vol. I (1901).]
K. Y.

RIGGE, WILLIAM FRANCIS (Sept. 9, 1857–Mar. 31, 1927), Roman Catholic priest, astronomer, was born in Cincinnati, Ohio, the youngest member of a family of eight children. His father, Frederick, and his mother, Elizabeth (Zeppenfeld), natives of Germany, were very poor and Rigge delighted in recalling how he had to run the sewing machine in his father's tailor shop to help the family in their struggle for a livelihood. He pursued his elementary studies at the parochial school of St. Joseph and at St. Xavier's College, Cincinnati. On July 14, 1875, he entered the Society of Jesus at Florissant, Mo. From 1878 to 1881 he was on the faculty of Creighton University, Omaha, Nebr. His studies in philosophy were begun in 1881 at St. Louis University, St. Louis, Mo., and were completed in 1884 at Woodstock College, Woodstock, Md. While at the latter seminary he met Father John T. Hedrick, who for four years had been assistant astronomer at the observatory of the Argentine Republic, and through him Rigge's interest in problems of the heavens was awakened. From 1884 to 1887 he taught at St. Ignatius College, Chicago, Ill. Returning to Woodstock in 1887 to follow his theological studies, he was there ordained to the priesthood by the late Cardinal Gibbons on Aug. 24, 1890. From 1891 to 1895 he taught at St. Louis University, and in the latter year became professional astronomer at the Georgetown College observatory, Washington, D. C. His researches here, conducted under the supervision of Father John G. Hagen, were interrupted by reason of serious eye trouble and he returned, in 1896, to Creighton University, where he remained as director of the Creighton Observatory until his death.

Rigge contributed liberally to the literature of mathematics and astronomy. For more than twenty years he furnished to *Popular Astronomy* the eclipse maps, of planets and bright stars. These maps materially assist amateur astronomers in observing these phenomena while they eliminate the drudgery of long and, at times, intricate computations. He was also a frequent contributor to the *American Mathematical Monthly, School Science and Mathematics,* the *Scientific American,* the *Astronomische Nachrichten,* and the *Astrophysical Journal.* A sensational achievement to his credit was in connection with a notable criminal case at Omaha, during which, by a study of the sun's shadows in a snapshot, he established an alibi for a defendant, arraigned on a charge of placing dynamite with malicious intent, by fixing the time at which the snapshot, produced as evidence at the trial, was taken. Rigge constructed a compound harmonic machine, which was a decided improvement on all preceding machines of its kind. Its functionings prompted him to publish a volume, entitled *Harmonic Curves* (1926), a pioneer work with the avowed purpose of encouraging study of this type of mathematical tracings. Another publication of his, *The Graphic Construction of Eclipses and Occultations* (1924), was

of special interest to the professional astronomer. Rigge held a fellowship in the Royal Astronomical Society of England, and membership in the American Association for the Advancement of Science, the American Astronomical Society, the Société Astronomique de France, and the Nebraska Academy of Science.

[Woodstock Letters, vol. CXLII; *Popular Astronomy,* May 1927; Georgetown Observatory Archives; J. McK. Cattell and D. R. Brimhall, *Am. Men of Sci.* (3rd ed., 1921); *Who's Who in America, 1926–27; Am. Catholic Who's Who,* 1911; *Morning World-Herald* (Omaha), Apr. 1, 1927; *Evening Star* (Washington), Apr. 2, 1927.]   F. A. T.

RIGGS, ELIAS (Nov. 19, 1810–Jan. 17, 1901), missionary and linguist, son of Elias and Margaret (Congar) Hudson Riggs, was born at New Providence, N. J., where his father was pastor of the Presbyterian church. He was a descendant of Edward Riggs who came to New England in 1633, settling in Roxbury, Mass. Possessing remarkable linguistic ability, Elias was learning Greek at the age of nine and at thirteen he began the study of Hebrew. He prepared for college at his birthplace and at Amherst Academy. Entering Amherst College in 1825, he carried on simultaneously with the required courses private studies in Hebrew, Syriac, Chaldee (Aramaic), Arabic, and modern Greek. Graduating in 1829, he entered Andover Theological Seminary. The year he graduated from this institution, 1832, he published *A Manual of the Chaldee Language; Containing a Chaldee Grammar, . . . a Chrestomathy, . . . a Vocabulary.* Subsequent editions appeared in 1842 and 1856. On Sept. 18, 1832, he married Martha Jane, daughter of Johnston Dalzel of Mendham, N. J.

Soon afterward he set sail for Greece as a missionary of the American Board of Commissioners for Foreign Missions. Until August 1834 he was associated with Jonas King at Athens and partly occupied with translating the Aramaic parts of the Bible into modern Greek. In 1834 he was sent to Argos, where he and his wife established a school for girls which flourished until governmental interference led to its abandonment four years later and Riggs's transfer to Smyrna. There he worked among the large Greek population until instructed in 1844 to turn his attention to the Armenians. From 1845 to 1852 he was engaged on a translation of the Scriptures into modern Armenian, published in 1853. By-products of this work were his *Brief Grammar of the Modern Armenian Language, as Spoken in Constantinople and Asia Minor* and *A Vocabulary of Words Used in Modern Armenian but not Found in the Ancient*

Armenian Lexicons, both published at Smyrna in 1847. When the publishing activities of the American Board were transferred to Constantinople in 1853, Riggs removed to that city. There he translated into Armenian, books, tracts, and hymns, at the same time teaching in the Bebek Theological Seminary until 1856, when a complete breakdown necessitated two years' furlough in the United States. During this period he was far from idle, however, supervising in New York the electrotyping of his Armenian Bible, and teaching in Union Theological Seminary. He declined the chair of Hebrew in that institution in favor of return to Turkey and the translation of the Scriptures into Bulgarian, a language which he had quietly acquired. This task he began in 1859 and the publication of the translation was completed in 1871. The added burdens of teaching in the mission girls' school at Hass Köy, of frequent preaching, and of editing vernacular magazines, brought on pulmonary trouble and he spent the winter of 1862–63 in Egypt, whence he returned by way of the mission stations in Anatolia.

Already he had published *Outline of a Grammar of the Turkish Language as Written in the Armenian Character* (Constantinople, 1856), and in 1873 the American Bible Society appointed him to a committee working on a standard Turkish text of the Bible. On this project he was occupied until 1878, when the work was published in both Arabic and Armenian characters. In 1884 he published a Bulgarian Bible dictionary. From 1885 to 1888 he lived at Aintab in Southern Anatolia, but returned to Constantinople to work on a commentary on the New Testament in the same language (3 vols., 1894–98). These works were closely related to his English publications *Suggested Emendations of the Authorized Version of the Old Testament* (Andover, 1873), *Suggested Modifications of the Revised Version of the New Testament* (Boston, 1883), and *Notes on Difficult Passages of the New Testament* (Boston. 1889). Though never robust in health, Riggs completed an amazing amount of painstaking work during his missionary career of sixty-eight years. His translations of the Scriptures were made with the aid of native assistants, but he was personally responsible for their scrupulous accuracy and idiomatic phraseology, and they influenced profoundly the rapidly developing literatures of the Near East. The many hymns which he wrote himself or translated—478 in Bulgarian alone—give evidence of poetical gifts. While "in the Greek, the Armenian, and the Bulgarian . . . he . . . could easily hold his own with the pro-

foundest of native scholars" (*Missionary Review of the World, post,* p. 268), he knew and could make effective use of seven ancient and fourteen modern languages. Quiet and retiring though not taciturn, he was a scholar of vast learning and keen critical ability, one of the great pioneer missionaries. Of his eight children, four of whom survived him, three sons became ministers, and two sons and a daughter missionaries; ten grandchildren also became missionaries.

[J. H. Wallace, *Geneal. of the Riggs Family* (1901); *Missionary Herald,* Mar., May 1901; J. K. Greene, *Leavening the Levant* (1916); *Missionary Rev. of the World,* Apr. 1901; S. M. Jackson, ed., *The New Schaff-Herzog Encyc. of Religious Knowledge,* vol. X (1911); *Obit. Record of Grads of Amherst Coll.,* 1901; diary and other papers in the possession of a grandson, Charles T. Riggs, Constantinople.]   W. L. W., Jr.

RIGGS, GEORGE WASHINGTON (July 4, 1813–Aug. 24, 1881), banker, was born in Georgetown, now a part of Washington, D. C., the son of Elisha and Alice (Lawrason) Riggs and the great-grandson of John Riggs who was mentioned in a will in Anne Arundel County, Md., as early as 1716. The boy was brought up in Baltimore, to which his father removed after he took George Peabody [*q.v.*] into partnership and established the firm of Riggs & Peabody there. He went to the Round Hill School kept by George Bancroft and Joseph Green Cogswell [*qq.v.*] at Northampton, Mass., and entered Yale College in 1829 but left some time in his junior year. He went abroad, and, returning to America, worked for his father in the mercantile firm of Riggs, Taylor & Company in New York City. On June 23, 1840, he was married to Janet Madeleine Cecilia Shedden, the daughter of Thomas Shedden of Glasgow, Scotland. They had nine children. The same year William W. Corcoran [*q.v.*] took him into partnership in the banking firm of Corcoran & Riggs at Washington, D. C. The firm was immediately successful; it was able to obtain a major share of the loans required by the federal government, acquired a reputation in financing the Mexican War, and made large profits. In 1848 he gave up his connection with the firm, to which, however, his younger half-brother Elisha succeeded so that the firm name remained the same. When Corcoran retired in 1854 Riggs bought his interest and, under the firm name of Riggs & Company (since 1896 The Riggs National Bank), directed the business until his death.

He was a member of the board of aldermen of the District of Columbia, in 1873 was chairman of a committee to present to Congress a petition asking for an investigation into the conduct of the board of public works, helped to obtain a committee report favorable to the abolition of the existing territorial form of government, and was active in the establishment of the present (1934) form of government that vests all authority in Congress. He built and owned the Riggs House, a famous hotel of his time, and was one of the organizers of the Washington & Georgetown Railroad Company. He was a trustee of the Corcoran Gallery of Art and of the Peabody Education Fund. He was for many years the treasurer of the Mt. Vernon Ladies' Association of the Union. In 1864 he advanced the money to maintain Mount Vernon until the return of peace should make it possible for the society again to raise funds. He died at his home "Green Hill" in Prince George's County, Md. Although a Protestant in early life he received the last rites of the Roman Catholic Church and was buried from St. Aloysius Church in Washington.

[A few letters in the Lib. of Cong.; information from his son, the Rev. T. Lawrason Riggs, New Haven, Conn., and from the Riggs National Bank, Washington; *Third Record of the Class of 1833 in Yale College* (1870); *Report of the Mount Vernon Ladies' Association, 1866, 1882*; Grace King, *Mount Vernon* (1929); *A Hist. of . . . Washington . . . by the Washington Post* (1903), ed. by A. B. Slauson; W. B. Bryan, *A Hist. of the National Capital*, vol. II (1916); H. W. Crew, *Centennial Hist. of . . . Washington, D. C.* (1892); J. H. Wallace, *Geneal. of the Riggs Family*, vol. II (1901); *Evening Star* (Washington), Aug. 24, 1881.]   K. E. C.

RIGGS, JOHN MANKEY (Oct. 25, 1810–Nov. 11, 1885), dentist, was born in Seymour, Conn., the seventh child of John and Mary (Beecher) Riggs, both of English ancestry and Revolutionary stock. His baptismal name was John, but while a student at college he assumed the middle initial M, and said that it stood for Mankey. He spent his boyhood on his father's farm, attended the district school, and worked for a time as a blacksmith. Deciding to become an Episcopal clergyman, he entered Washington (now Trinity) College at Hartford in 1835, and received the degree of A.B. in 1837. Always an independent thinker, with the courage of his convictions, he rejected the doctrine of the Trinity while at college and therefore abandoned the idea of entering the ministry. Shortly after his graduation he served for two years as principal of the Brown (previously the Stone) School, now the First District School of Hartford. He then took a partial course at the Jefferson Medical College of Philadelphia, but becoming interested in dentistry, studied for that profession with Dr. Horace Wells [*q.v.*], of Hartford, where he began practice as a dentist about 1840. He was associated with Dr. C. Kirkland for a

short time, and with Dr. Daniel Dwyer from 1865 to 1877. Thereafter he practised independently at Hartford. He was also interested in scientific agriculture and often spoke at meetings of agricultural societies.

Throughout his dental career he was a strong advocate of hygienic care of the mouth, which he considered the only preventive of caries of the teeth and disease of the gums and alveolar process. He gained such wide repute as a specialist in the treatment of the dental malady now generally known as pyorrhea alveolaris that in his time it was often called Riggs' Disease. His method of treatment consisted of removing from the teeth, with scalers of his own design, the salivary and serumnal deposits and any necrosed bone, applying tincture of myrrh, and then polishing the teeth. He first demonstrated this method to the dental profession in 1865 at the convention of the American Dental Association, of which he was a member. In the same year he joined the Connecticut Valley Dental Association, and at the meeting of this organization in 1867, he demonstrated his treatment and was credited by a formal resolution with the origination of his method. He was president of the Connecticut State Dental Association in 1867, and of the Connecticut Valley Dental Association in 1871 and 1872. In 1881 he attended the Seventh International Medical Congress at London, demonstrating and lecturing on his treatment of pyorrhea alveolaris before the Dental Section of that congress. He was active as a speaker and clinician at many professional gatherings, but apparently wrote nothing, the three addresses which are published under his name probably having been delivered impromptu (*Pennsylvania Journal of Dental Science*, March 1876; *Dental Cosmos*, October 1882; *Southern Dental Journal*, February 1885).

On Dec. 11, 1844, at Hartford, he performed an operation which is outstanding in the history of modern anesthesia, extracting a tooth from the mouth of Horace Wells while the latter was under the influence of nitrous oxide gas. The anesthetic property of this gas had been discovered by Wells on the previous evening at a public entertainment given by Gardner Q. Colton [*q.v.*], who exhibited the amusing effect of small doses of nitrous oxide, then popularly known as laughing gas. Since one of Wells's teeth needed to be extracted, he had Colton administer the gas the next day, and his former pupil Riggs removed the tooth without pain (John M. Riggs, "On the Discoveries of Morton and Wells," *Southern Dental Journal*, July 1883, August 1885; G. Q. Colton, *Boyhood and Manhood Rec-*

ollections, 1897, pp. 7–8). Riggs was a member of the committee of the Connecticut State Dental Association that succeeded in having a statue of Wells erected at Hartford in 1874.

Riggs was a man of impressive appearance, marked individuality of character, and decided opinions. Originally a Whig in politics, he took part with other Hartford men in the formation of the Republican party, and was a vigorous Abolitionist. In religion he was a Naturalist and a Unitarian. While parading as a veteran of the Foot Guards of the Governor of Connecticut he caught a severe cold which developed into pneumonia and caused his death in his seventy-sixth year. He was a bachelor.

[B. L. Thorpe, in C. R. E. Koch, *Hist. of Dental Surgery*, vol. III (1910); *Am. Jour. Dental Sci.*, Dec. 1885; *Dental Cosmos*, Dec. 1885; *Independent Practitioner*, Dec. 1885; *Hartford Courant*, Nov. 12, 1885.]

L. P. B.

RIGGS, STEPHEN RETURN (Mar. 23, 1812–Aug. 24, 1883), missionary, was the son of Stephen and Anna (Baird) Riggs of Steubenville, Ohio, and a descendant of Edward Riggs of Roxbury, Mass., whose son Edward moved to Connecticut and later settled in Newark, N. J. Stephen was educated at the Latin school of Ripley, Ohio, and at Jefferson College. After a year at Western Theological Seminary, he was licensed by the Chillicothe Presbytery in 1836, and then spent a year preaching in Hawley, Mass. There, on Feb. 16, 1837, he was married to Mary A. C. Longley, the daughter of Gen. Thomas and Martha A. Longley.

An acquaintance of Riggs's, Dr. Thomas S. Williamson, with others, had established a station for the American Board of Commissioners for Foreign Missions at Lac qui Parle on the upper Minnesota River in 1835. Riggs's aptitude for languages caused the physician to recommend to the Board that the young man be added to the mission with the special object of learning the native language and of preparing translations for school and devotional purposes. As a result, in 1837 Riggs and his wife journeyed to Lac qui Parle and began their life work among the Sioux. In 1843 he opened a new station farther down the river at Traverse des Sioux, at which he remained until 1846. He then returned to Lac qui Parle to take the place of Dr. Williamson, who had begun a new mission at the mouth of the river, continuing there until the mission buildings burned in 1854. Thereafter, until 1862, he was at a new station nearby, which bore the name of Hazelwood. A striking feature of this establishment was its adoption of a constitution and the name of the Hazelwood

Republic. As time went on, Riggs became the recognized authority on the Siouan languages. By 1863 he had published either alone or in cooperation with others the following works in Dakota: *The Dakota First Reading Book* (1839), *Wowapi Mitawa: Tamakoce Kaga* (1842), a primer; the book of Genesis and a part of the Psalms (1842); the Acts of the Apostles, the epistles of Paul, and the book of Revelation (1843); *Dakota Tawoonspe* (1850), comprising two books of Dakota lessons; *Grammar and Dictionary of the Dakota Language* (1852), published for the Smithsonian Institution; *Dakota Odowan* (1853, 1855, 1863, 1869), a hymn book; *The Pilgrim's Progress* (1857); *The Constitution of Minnesota* (1858); and a primer prepared for the natives taken prisoners after the Sioux uprising of 1862.

In this uprising, which resulted in the massacre of hundreds of settlers, the missionaries, with one exception, were saved by the help of the Indians they had instructed. After his own narrow escape from death, Riggs returned at once to his flock, now captives, and for the devastating years of their detention in prison and their transfer to the banks of the Missouri he was either with them, teaching and counseling, or at Washington, lobbying in their behalf. A larger part of his time than heretofore was now devoted to preparing books. Young men and women, who had been trained by the two veteran missionaries, now entered the active field, and the two older men superintended their work. Riggs's home for several years was Beloit, Wis. There his wife died in 1869 and thither three years later he brought his second wife, Mrs. Annie Baker Ackley, formerly of the Hazelwood mission. There, too, he did much of his translating. In 1864 he brought out a catechism, *Dakota Wiwicawangapi Kin*; in 1865 he published the entire New Testament in Dakota from the Greek; in 1866, 1867, and 1868 he issued primers. He translated the book of Psalms from the Hebrew and published it in 1869. In 1875 and 1876 respectively he brought out a model first reader and a Dakota version of Guyot's *Elementary Geography*; in 1877 a large part of the Bible, and in 1880, *Dakota Wowapi Wakan: The Holy Bible in the Language of the Dakotas* appeared, a great portion of the translation in each case being his work. Besides these Dakota books he also published: *The Gospel among the Dakotas* (1869); *Mary and I: Forty Years with the Sioux* (1880); "The Dakota Mission" (vol. III, 1880), "Protestant Missions in the Northwest" (*Ibid.*, in *Collections of the Minnesota Historical Society*, vol. VI, 1894); and many articles in newspapers and religious periodicals. Some time after his death his "Dakota-English Dictionary" appeared in the *Contributions to North American Ethnology* (vol. VII, 1890), and his "Dakota Grammar Texts and Ethnography," edited by James Owen Dorsey, in the same series (vol. IX, 1893). Of his nine children at least five entered the mission field, four of whom labored among the Dakota Indians. Though of small stature Riggs was a man of uncommon powers of endurance and physical vigor, as his strenuous life on the frontier for almost half a century bears evidence. He died in Beloit.

[Papers of Stephen R. Riggs, of Samuel W. and Gideon H. Pond, and of Henry H. Sibley, in Minn. Hist. Soc.; several hundred letters by Riggs, his family, and his mission associates in the archives of the Am. Board of Commissioners for Foreign Missions, Boston; archives of the Bureau of Indian Affairs, Washington; the annual reports of the American Board, and its organ, the *Missionary Herald* for the years 1837–83; J. C. Pilling, "Bibliog. of the Siouan Languages," *U. S. Bur. of Am. Ethnol. Bull.*, no. 5 (1887); J. H. Wallace, *Geneal. of the Riggs Family* (1901); *Minn. Hist. Soc. Colls.*, vol. I (1872), III (1880), VI (1894).]

G. L. N.

RIGGS, WILLIAM HENRY (Mar. 22, 1837–Aug. 31, 1924), collector, was born at Bowling Green, New York City, the son of Elisha Riggs, merchant and banker, sometime partner of George Peabody [*q.v.*], by his second wife, Mary Ann Karrick, was educated at the Bacon School in New York, and continued his training abroad at Sillig's Institute, Vevey, Switzerland, at the Technische Hochschule, Dresden, where he studied mining to enable him to take charge of his father's coal and iron property in the Alleghanies, and at the University of Heidelberg. At Sillig's school he was a fellow student of J. Pierpont Morgan [*q.v.*], and they became devoted and lifelong friends. Both became ardent collectors, pursuing the hobbies begun during their student years. Having inherited ample means, Riggs as a young man found it unnecessary to give much attention to mining matters, and for most of his life devoted himself to actively collecting medieval arms, armor, and art. He never married, and from about 1857, he made his home in Paris, where he was one of a group of enthusiastic armor collectors chief among whom was the Emperor Napoleon III. In 1870, during the Franco-Prussian War, Riggs moved his collection to a new home, in the rue Murillo near the Parc Monceau, which he had bought from Count de Nieuwerkerke, commissioner of fine arts under Napoleon III. Many of the finest pieces from his collection were exhibited at the Trocadero in 1878 at the Exposition Universelle Internationale at Paris

in 1889, and at the Exposition Universelle in Paris in 1900.

In 1913 he made his first visit in forty-three years to his native city, to supervise the installation of his armor and art collection in the Metropolitan Museum of Art. In choosing the New York museum as the permanent home for his collection he had been influenced by his friend, J. Pierpont Morgan, who was then president of the Museum, of which Riggs himself, who was, like Morgan, one of the first great American collectors of objects of art, had served as vice-president from 1870 to 1874. When he announced his great gift to the Museum he pointed out that his purpose in forming the collection had been "the education of the American public in a branch of European art which was little known or appreciated in our country" (*Bulletin, post*, January 1915). In addition to his main collection, he had assembled a notable collection of portraits of men in armor, wall hangings, stained glass, and furniture of the Middle Ages and the Renaissance. In 1917 he sent to the Museum the armor of regal splendor ascribed to Jacques Gourdon de Genouillac, called Galiot, master of artillery of Louis XII and Francis I.

Riggs's reminiscences of early collecting and of great collectors were an inspiration to all students who had the opportunity of knowing him. The armor sections of Violett-le-Duc's classic *Dictionnaire Raisonné du Mobilier Français de l'Époque Carlovingienne à la Renaissance* (1854–75) and of Victor Gay's *Glossaire Archéologique du Moyen Âge et de la Renaissance* (1882–1928) were written in part in Riggs's gallery. He was the preceptor in armor matters of Bashford Dean [*q.v.*], founder and curator of the department of arms and armor at the Metropolitan Museum, and was thus indirectly responsible for the formation of Dean's great private collection, which is now exhibited as a memorial in a gallery adjacent to the Riggs Armor Hall. A portrait of Riggs at the age of thirty-three, by Ferdinand Humbert, hangs in the armor gallery of the Metropolitan.

[*Bull. of the Metropolitan Museum of Art*, Mar. 1914, Jan. 1915, Oct. 1919, Dec. 1924, Sept., Dec. 1925; Bashford Dean, *Metropolitan Museum of Art: Handbook of Arms and Armor, European and Oriental* (1915; 4th ed., 1930); *N. Y. Times*, Sept. 2, 1924; Riggs correspondence in the archives of the Armor Dept., Metropolitan Museum, N. Y.]   S. V. G.

RIIS, JACOB AUGUST (May 3, 1849–May 26, 1914), journalist, author, reformer, was born in Ribe, Denmark, the son of Niels Edward and Caroline B. (Lundholm) Riis. He received his education from his father, a teacher in a Latin school, and learned something of journalism from assisting the elder Riis to prepare copy for a weekly paper. His later career was impressively forecast in an incident of his boyhood. As a lad of thirteen years he discovered in his native town a tenement, built over a sewer, which was infested with rats. Horrified by the conditions under which the inhabitants of this loathsome house were living, the boy began a systematic extermination of the rats; and with whitewash and soap, purchased with a bit of Christmas money, undertook to clean away the dirt, and thus to bring some cleanliness and decency to the homes of the poor.

In Copenhagen, young Riis served for four years as apprentice to a carpenter. Having learned his trade, he came to America to seek his fortune. He landed in New York on Whitsunday, 1870. The usual experience of the immigrant, employed at any kind of job that would keep him alive, carried him into farming, coal-mining, brick-making, peddling. More than once he spent the night in the noisome horror of the police lodging-houses of the day. At a critical moment, his early journalistic experience won him a job on a weekly newspaper published at Hunter's Point, Long Island. When no pay appeared after the second week, he left. But a road had been opened which took him, after several years' wandering, to the *New York Tribune* (1877–88) and later to the *Evening Sun* (1888–99), as a police reporter. Afterward he supported himself by articles, books, and lectures.

His activities at police headquarters led Riis to his life's work, the cleansing of the New York slums. Again and again, in pursuit of stories of accident and crime, the young reporter invaded the tenement districts. Day and night his keen eyes and sensitive heart were gathering evidence of the physical wretchedness, the moral and spiritual degradation, of these downtown ghettos of the poor; and he declared war upon them. In vivid newspaper and magazine articles, in countless lectures, in widely read books, he pictured the life of the poor, especially of their children, and rallied and organized support for their relief. His energy was tremendous, his achievements were spectacular. He exposed the contaminated state of the city's water supply, and caused the purchase of the Croton watershed; he abolished police station lodging-houses; he worked for child-labor laws, and for their enforcement; he secured playgrounds for schools and the opening of classrooms to boys' and girls' clubs; he secured a truant school; he forced the destruction of rear-tenements; he demanded light for dark tenement hallways, and revealed

to a horrified country long-hidden dens of vice, crime, and filth; he drove bake-shops, with their fatal fires, from tenement basements (Steffens, *post*, I, 203–04). Perhaps nothing in all his victorious career so overjoyed him as the wiping out of Mulberry Bend, the worst tenement block in the city, and the building in its place of Mulberry Bend Park and his own Jacob A. Riis Neighborhood House (1888, though not called by his name until 1889).

Riis's enemies were numerous and powerful, the allied hordes of politicians on the one hand and of landlords on the other. He fought them single-handed for years, till friends and supporters came. Chief among these was Theodore Roosevelt. The two men might well have been taken for brothers in flesh as well as in spirit. Both as governor and president, Roosevelt offered his friend high office; but Riis insisted he was too busy to enter politics. In his later years Riis enjoyed a fame which overwhelmed him with invitations to write, lecture, lead public movements of reform. Suddenly, in 1904, he was stricken with heart disease which in succeeding years was aggravated by much travel and persistent overwork. In 1913 he was ordered by his physician to seek rest in a sanitarium at Battle Creek. Here his condition improved, but could not be healed. He died in his country home, at Barre, Mass., on May 26, 1914. On Mar. 5, 1876, Riis had married Elizabeth Nielsen, of Ribe, a sweetheart of his boyhood. She died in 1905, but their five children, three sons and two daughters, survived him. On July 29, 1907, he married Mary A. Phillips, who had for some time been his secretary.

Riis was throughout his life natural, spontaneous, unspoiled, always the gayest and most exciting of companions. His unrestrained exuberance was on occasion mistaken for roughness or crudity, but at heart was a tenderness as of a woman, and a sensitiveness as of a child. What moved him was the spectacle of helpless human beings robbed of that sheer joy of living which was his own richest treasure. Called a reformer, he disliked the word, as it seemed to imply the improving of people. He was certain that the poor he knew needed not a change but a chance. So he sought to free them, and thus became the "great emancipator" of the slums. Chief among his writings are: *How the Other Half Lives* (1890); *The Children of the Poor* (1892); *Out of Mulberry Street* (1898); *The Making of an American* (1901); *The Battle with the Slum* (1902); *Children of the Tenements* (1903); *Theodore Roosevelt the Citizen* (1904); *Is*

There a Santa Claus? (1904); *The Old Town* (1909).

[Riis's own writings in content and spirit are autobiographical. See also *Who's Who in America*, 1914–15; *N. Y. Times*, May 27, 28, June 1, 21, 1914; *Jour. of Education*, June 12, 1913, June 4, 1914; *Jacob A. Riis. A Sketch of his Life and Work* (1903); Mary H. Wade, *Pilgrims of Today* (1916); Joseph Husband, *Americans by Adoption* (1920); J. T. Faris, *Men Who Conquered* (1922); H. M. Cary, "A Knight in the Slums," in *Homiletical Review*, Jan. 1917; Margaret E. Benton, *Comrades in Service* (1915); Theodore Roosevelt. *An Autobiography* (1913); *The Autobiography of Lincoln Steffens* (1931), vol. I.]   J. H. H.

RILEY, BENJAMIN FRANKLIN (July 16, 1849–Dec. 14, 1925), Baptist clergyman, educator, author, son of Enoch and Sophronia (Autrey) Riley, was born near Pineville, and died at Birmingham, Ala. His parents were poor but pious and ambitious for their son. After receiving a preliminary education in the schools of his community, he entered Erskine College, Due West, S. C., in 1868, and graduated with the degree of A.B. in 1871. He was converted while in Erskine and although he had intended to study law, was ordained to the Baptist ministry at Pineville in July 1872, and at once entered the Southern Baptist Theological Seminary, then located at Greenville, S. C. His studies were soon interrupted by failing health and he returned home to recuperate. In 1874 he entered Crozer Theological Seminary, where he continued until 1876. Leaving the seminary, he married Emma Shaw of Belleville, Ala., June 21, 1876, and soon afterward accepted the pastorate of Carlowville and Snow Hill churches in his native state. He was called to the church at Albany, Ga., in 1878, but after a brief pastorate interrupted by ill health, he returned to Alabama and became pastor at Opelika (1879–82). In 1888 he was made president of Howard College near Birmingham, Ala., remaining there until 1893, a period of great difficulty in the history of this institution. Resigning the presidency, he accepted the chair of English and oratory in the University of Georgia, which he held with distinction until 1900. He was pastor of the First Baptist Church of Houston, Tex., 1900–07, and from 1907 to 1909 was superintendent of the Anti-Saloon League of Texas. His work with this society led him to see the deadly effects of the saloon upon the negro and inspired in him a deep sympathy for the colored man.

Throughout his life, he constantly alternated between the practical and the scholarly. While he was pastor he was also studying and writing, and while he was in educational work he continued to preach. His most important work,

however, was in the field of education and authorship. He was a diligent writer, contributing constantly to the religious press of his denomination and to other similar periodicals. In 1881 he published *The History of Conecuh County, Alabama*. This was followed in 1888 by *Alabama As It Is*. Other historical writings of his include: *History of the Baptists of Alabama* (1893); *History of the Baptists in the Southern States East of the Mississippi* (1898), *History of the Baptists of Texas* (1907), *Makers and Romance of Alabama History* (1914), *The Baptists in the Building of the Nation* (1922), and *Memorial History of the Baptists of Alabama* (1923). During his work as secretary of the Anti-Saloon League he wrote *The White Man's Burden* (1910). He was also the author of *The Life and Times of Booker T. Washington* (1916). His works show diligence in research, care in statement, and vigor of style; they are, however, the works of a cultured but busy man rather than those of the finished scholar. He will probably be best known for his contributions to the history of the Baptist denomination in Texas, Alabama, and the southeastern part of the United States. His later years were spent at Birmingham, Ala., in quiet study, continuous writing, and frequent preaching and lecturing.

[A. B. Moore, *Hist. of Ala. and Her People* (1927), vol. II; *Alphabetical Biog. Cat. of the Crozer Theological Sem.* (1933); J. E. Dillard, in *Annual of the Southern Baptist Convention*, 1926; *Ala. Baptist*, Dec. 17, 1925; *Who's Who in America*, 1924–25; *Birmingham Age-Herald*, Dec. 15, 1925.]   W. J. M.

RILEY, BENNET (Nov. 27, 1787–June 9, 1853), soldier, was born in St. Mary's County, Md. In the Catholic parish records of St. Mary's County preserved at Georgetown University is registered the marriage of one Bennet Reily to Susanna Drury on Aug. 16, 1784. It is reasonable to suppose that these persons are Riley's parents especially since his widow signs her name "Riley" and "Reily" in the pension office records, but no other evidence has appeared to warrant a more definite statement. He entered the military service of the United States on Jan. 19, 1813, as an ensign of riflemen and at once saw active campaigning at Sacketts Harbor, N. Y., in the War of 1812, after which he accompanied his regiment to the Mississippi frontier. From December 1816 to July 1817, he was adjutant of his regiment. On Aug. 6, 1818, he was promoted to the rank of captain, having previously passed through the grades of third, second, and first lieutenant. Upon the disbandment of the rifle regiment in 1821, he was transferred to the infantry and for the next twenty-five years spent much of his time fighting Indians. He was brevetted major in 1823 for distinguished service in a battle with the Arikara Indians in Dakota Territory. In 1829 he convoyed a large merchant caravan from St. Louis, Mo., to Santa Fé, N. Mex., and back again and received a sword from the legislature of Missouri in recognition of his services. During 1831 and 1832 he fought in the Black Hawk War. He was promoted to the rank of major on Sept. 26, 1837, and to lieutenant-colonel on Dec. 1, 1839. From 1839 to 1842 he participated in the Seminole wars in Florida, where his energy and courage won for him the brevet of colonel.

At the beginning of the Mexican War he commanded the 2nd Infantry, but was quickly advanced to the command of a brigade. He participated in the siege of Vera Cruz and distinguished himself at Cerro Gordo where he was brevetted brigadier-general. It was at Contreras on Aug. 20, 1847, however, that he won lasting fame. His brigade formed part of a force under Persifor Frazer Smith [q.v.], which was sent around to the rear of the Mexican position, and Riley was designated to lead the assault. In his official report of the battle General Smith says: "The opporunity afforded to Colonel Riley by his position was seized by that gallant veteran with all the skill and energy for which he is distinguished. The charge of his noble brigade down the slope, in full view of friend and foe, unchecked even for a moment, until he had planted all his colours upon their farthest works, was a spectacle that animated the army to the boldest deeds" (*Scott and His Staff, post*, p. 160). For his gallant conduct on this occasion he was brevetted major-general. He continued in command of his brigade to the end of the Mexican War. After the war he served in Louisiana and Missouri until the fall of 1848 when he was transferred with his regiment to California and assigned to the important command of the military department on the Pacific and became ex-officio provisional governor of California. In September 1849, he convened the constituent assembly at Monterey which drew up the first constitution for California and applied for admission into the Union. His able direction of affairs at this critical time greatly hastened the formation of the new state government to which he relinquished his authority in November 1849, when the first elected civil governor took office. On Jan. 31, 1850, he was promoted to colonel of the 1st Infantry and ordered to join that regiment on the Rio Grande River, but owing to disability from cancer he was unable to comply with the order. He settled in Buffalo, N. Y.,

where he died leaving a widow, Arbella Riley, and five children.

[Records of the Pension Office, the Adjutant General and the Senate Committee on Pensions, Wash., D. C.; F. B. Heitman, *Hist. Reg. and Dict., U. S. Army* (1903); C. K. Gardner, *A Dict. of All Officers . . . of the Army* (1860); *Official Army Registers*, 1850–53; C. J. Peterson, *The Mil. Heroes of the War with Mex.* (10th ed., 1858); *Gen. Scott and His Staff* (1848); J. H. Smith, *The War with Mex.* (1919), vol. II; Z. S. Eldredge, *Hist. of Cal.*, vol. III (n.d.); *Md. Hist. Mag.*, Sept. 1917; *Buffalo Commercial Advertiser*, June 10, 1853; *N. Y. Times*, June 11, 1853.]   S. J. H.

RILEY, CHARLES VALENTINE (Sept. 18, 1843–Sept. 14, 1895), entomologist, the son of Charles and Mary Valentine Cannon Riley, was born in Chelsea, London, England. His father, a clergyman of the Church of England, died during his childhood; his mother married a second time; and the boy was sent to boarding school at Dieppe in France and later to Bonn in Germany. He was passionately fond of natural history and of drawing and painting. He collected and studied insects and sketched them in pencil and in color. At both Dieppe and Bonn, he carried off first prizes in drawing and he was urged by his drawing master in France to devote himself to art studies in Paris. Financial trouble at home caused him to leave school at the age of seventeen, and he came to the United States. Eventually he reached Illinois and settled upon a farm about fifty miles from Chicago, of which George H. Edwards was the owner. Here his attention was drawn to insect injuries to crops, and he sent accounts of his observations to the *Prairie Farmer*.

At the age of twenty-one he moved to Chicago and became connected with this leading agricultural journal as a reporter and artist and as editor of its entomological department. He enlisted in the Union army toward the close of the Civil War and served until his regiment (the 134th Illinois Volunteers) was disbanded in November 1865. His writings attracted the attention of B. D. Walsh, the state entomologist, with whom he collaborated, and partly through Walsh's influence he was appointed in the spring of 1868 to the newly created office of entomologist to the State of Missouri. From that time until 1877 he was engaged in his Missouri investigations, which thoroughly established his reputation. He published nine annual reports, which have become famous. His careful work on life histories, his very beautiful drawings on wood, which were engraved and used as illustrations to his text, and his knowledge of agriculture made an admirable combination. Many authorities date the modern science of economic entomology from the time of the publication of these reports. During the years 1873 to 1877 many of the Western states and territories were invaded by armies of grasshoppers from the Northwest. Riley studied this plague with the originality and vigor which characterized his work, and in his last three reports he published a mass of important results. In the meantime he worked vigorously to bring the grasshopper scourge to the attention of Congress and succeeded in March 1877 in securing the passage of a bill creating the United States Entomological Commission, of which he was appointed chief, with A. S. Packard, Jr., and Cyrus Thomas [*qq.v.*] as his associates.

In the spring of 1878, while the first report of the Commission was going through the press, Townend Glover [*q.v.*] was retired as entomologist to the United States Department of Agriculture, and Riley was appointed his successor. He held this position for nearly a year, and then resigned, owing to a disagreement with the commissioner of agriculture. Two years later he was reinstated, and remained the chief of the federal entomological service until June 1894. The service was made a division of the Department of Agriculture under his administration, and grew in size and importance. His annual reports were practical and of high scientific value. He began the publication of the journal known as *Insect Life,* which was continued from 1889 to 1894 and received very general praise. Years before, in 1868, he had begun with Walsh the publication of a journal known as the *American Entomologist.* Their association was interrupted by Walsh's death, but Riley continued the publication during its second volume. Then, after years of silence, a third volume was published under his editorship in 1880. He was married while in St. Louis to Emilie Conzelman of that city. Riley received many honors during his life and was decorated by the French government for his work upon the grapevine Phylloxera. He was an honorary member of the Entomological Society of London and founder and first president of the Entomological Society of Washington. His published work shows an unusual sense of economic proportion combined with scientific accuracy and a keen insight into biological matters. His extraordinary observations on the relations between the Yucca moths and the fertilization of the plants of the genus Yucca attracted great attention; and his observations on the hypermetamorphoses of the blister beetles drew to his work widespread attention among scientific men. Very many other problems were illuminated by his investigations.

He was a man of means, and resigned from office in June 1894, intending to spend the rest of his life in research work in the National Museum, where he held an honorary position; but he was killed in September 1895 by a fall from his bicycle. He had the degree of Ph.D. from Washington University in St. Louis, but, although he had never held a university position, he was generally known as "Professor Riley." His bibliography was very large; in 1889 it had reached 1657 individual titles and 479 in co-authorship with B. D. Walsh; additional papers to the number of 364 were published in co-authorship with L. O. Howard, and he continued to publish down to the time of his death.

[G. B. Goode, in *Science,* Feb. 14, 1896; A. S. Packard, in *Ibid.,* Dec. 6, 1895; L. O. Howard, in *Farmer's Magazine* (London), I (1890), 237–41, and *Bull. Philosophical Soc. of Washington,* vol. XIII (1900); *Proc. Entomological Soc. of Washington,* vol. III (1896); R. McLachlan, in *Entomologist's Monthly Mag.* (London), Nov. 1895; W. F. H. Blandford and R. Meldola, in *Trans. Entomological Soc. of London,* 1895; James Fletcher, in *Canadian Entomologist,* Oct. 1895; *Entomological News,* Oct. 1895; *Evening Star* (Washington), Sept. 16, 1895; names of parents from Mrs. Riley; personal acquaintance.]   L. O. H.

RILEY, ISAAC WOODBRIDGE (May 20, 1869–Sept. 2, 1933), philosopher, was the son of the Rev. Isaac Riley and Katherine Antoinette Southmayd (Parker) Riley. He was born in the City of New York where his father was pastor of the Thirty-fourth Street Reformed Church, but in 1875 the family moved to Buffalo when Isaac Riley became pastor of the Westminster Presbyterian Church in that city. During a residence in Italy, Woodbridge attended the English School in Florence, and in 1888 he entered Yale University, receiving the degree of A.B. in 1892. Two years later, he visited Salt Lake City to gather material for a post-graduate study, first presented as a master's thesis at Yale, "The Metaphysics of Mormonism," in 1898 and then greatly expanded into his Ph.D. dissertation in 1902. It was published that year in book form as *The Founder of Mormonism: A Psychological Study of Joseph Smith, Junior,* with a preface by Prof. George Trumbull Ladd, head of the philosophy department—an unusual tribute to be paid a graduate student, indicative of the thoroughness of Riley's work. Meanwhile, he had taken an *ad interim* position as instructor in English in New York University, 1897–98, and subsequently he became professor of philosophy in the University of New Brunswick, 1902–04. He then resigned in order to carry on his own studies as Johnston Research Scholar, under the direction of James Mark Baldwin, at the Johns Hopkins University, 1904–07. The product of these three years of intensive application was his most notable volume, *American Philosophy: The Early Schools,* in five books: "Puritanism," "Idealism," "Deism," "Materialism," "Realism." It was a pioneer work in its field and directed attention to several important phases of American thought that had hitherto been almost entirely neglected. In 1908 Riley became professor of philosophy at Vassar College, a position which he held until his death. He was married on Dec. 18, 1909, to Laura Brooks Troth of Germantown, Pa., who, with their two sons and three daughters, survived him.

His later writings include *American Thought from Puritanism to Pragmatism* (1915, enlarged 1923); three articles under the general heading "La Philosophie Française en Amérique," contributed to *La Revue Philosophique* (Nov. 1917, May–June 1919, Jan.–Feb. 1921); *Le Génie Américain* (1921), lectures delivered at the Sorbonne in 1920; *From Myth to Reason* (1926); *Men and Morals* (1929); *The Meaning of Mysticism* (1930). None of these quite fulfilled the promise of his earlier work. A man of broad culture, a fervent political liberal, and a trenchant writer, Riley was nevertheless essentially an expositor rather than an original thinker; and his own philosophy was largely a restatement of the pragmatism of William James with a decided tendency toward a vague religious mysticism. He drew a sharp line of distinction, however, between the mystical and the occult, this leading him to a caustic criticism of Christian Science and similar American sects. His too witty contribution on Christian Science to *The Cambridge History of American Literature* (1917) caused the publishers to withdraw the edition from circulation until a more sympathetic article could be procured elsewhere (*New York Times,* Apr. 19, 1921). His essay, which was a far from adequate study of Mrs. Eddy's sources, was later republished in *The Faith, the Falsity, and the Failure of Christian Science* (1925), by Riley, Frederick W. Peabody, and Dr. Charles E. Humiston.

[*Who's Who in America,* 1932–33; Isaac Riley, *Westminster Church* (1876); obituary in *N. Y. Times,* Sept. 4, 1933.]   E. S. B.

RILEY, JAMES WHITCOMB (Oct. 7, 1849–July 22, 1916), poet, was born in the little town of Greenfield, Ind., the third of the six children of Reuben A. and Elizabeth (Marine) Riley. His father, of Dutch ancestry, was a native of Pennsylvania, a captain of Union cavalry in the Civil War, a lawyer of ability, and an orator of more than local distinction; his mother belonged to a family in which skill at rhymes was characteristic and was a woman of charac-

ter, sympathy, and understanding. Her death, when James Whitcomb was twenty, made an impression upon him that influenced both his verse and his subsequent life. "My first teacher," Riley wrote in his later years, "was a little old woman, rosy and roly-poly, who looked as though she might have just come tumbling out of a fairy story, so lovable was she and so jolly and so amiable. She kept school in her little Dame-Trot kind of dwelling of three rooms, with a porch in the rear, like a bracket on the wall, which was part of the play-ground of her 'scholars,'—for in those days pupils were called 'scholars' by their affectionate teachers" (*Complete Works,* I, 368). There was but one book in the school in which he found any interest, *McGuffey's Reader.* Fortunately, a later teacher, Lee O. Harris, gave up any hope of teaching him mathematics and encouraged him to read the best literature. The first book which he remembered buying, at an auctioneer's shop, was a copy of Quarles's *Divine Emblems.* School was a mere incident in Riley's life, however. No unimportant part of his education was his visits to the court house with his father, where he became known as "Judge Wick." In those days a Western county seat was a fascinating place for such a boy. Here he became familiar with the manners and speech of the Indiana country folk, acquiring some of the material which he used to such good advantage later. At the age of sixteen he left the schoolroom forever and turned to the field of art. Taking up painting, he finally "graduated as a house, sign, and ornamental painter" and for two summers traveled about in the pursuit of his calling with a small company of other youths. They dubbed themselves "the Graphics," and, according to Riley, "covered all the barns and fences in the state with advertisements" (*Ibid.,* I, 373).

Returning to Greenfield from an unprofitable tour, he became editor of the town paper and, as he afterward said, "in a few months strangled the little thing into a change of ownership" (*Complete Works,* I, 376). Although some of his verses were accepted by various newspapers, his first lasting connection was with the *Anderson Democrat.* It was while he was writing for this paper that an incident occurred which brought Riley into more than local prominence. Stung by the jeers of a rival paper, and to demonstrate his theory that to make a poem successful and popular it is only necessary to prove its author "a genius known to fame," he wrote some verse in the style of Poe, and entitled it "Leonainie." It was published in the *Kokomo Dispatch,* and the hoax was so successful that the editor was pressed by scholars and book collectors for evidence of the original manuscript. (See *Bookman,* September 1904; September 1916.) Throughout his life this incident was a cause of embarrassment to him. Riley's popularity may be said to date from his employment on the *Indianapolis Journal* (1877-85). His verses were widely copied, especially after the beginning of the series signed "Benj. F. Johnson, of Boone." This series included one of his most characteristic and most popular poems, "When the Frost is on the Punkin," the success of which lay in its portrayal of a whimsical and altogether lovable character who became recognized immediately as a real person. In 1883 the series was published in a paper-covered little book of fifty pages, with the title *"The Old Swimmin' Hole" and 'Leven More Poems.* Efforts to secure a publisher had been fruitless until George C. Hitt of the *Journal* issued in his own name one thousand copies, on which the total profit was $166.40. An original copy today would bring many times that amount. A second edition was brought out by Merrill, Meigs & Company, and they and their successors, the Bowen-Merrill Company, and then the Bobbs-Merrill Company became his regular publishers. Among a long list of his books, the most popular are *Afterwhiles* (1887), *Pipes o' Pan at Zekesbury* (1888), *Old-Fashioned Roses* (London, 1888), *Rhymes of Childhood* (1890), *Green Fields and Running Brooks* (1892), *Poems Here at Home* (1893), *Riley Child Rhymes* (1899), *Book of Joyous Children* (1902).

In his youth, Riley had aspired to be an actor but, though his youthful efforts met with local approbation, he never got far in that profession; however, he was all his life an actor and acquired a national reputation as a public reader of his own verse. In his active years he was one of the most sought-after entertainers in the country. His readings in conjunction with "Bill" Nye were perhaps the best-known of any performances on the public platform, and his renditions of such universal favorites as "The Object Lesson," "Out to Old Aunt Mary's," and "The Soldier's Story"—which Mark Twain said was "about the funniest thing I ever listened to" (Dickey, *The Maturity . . ., post,* p. 247)—were as enthusiastically received in Boston and New York as in the smallest village of his native state. In 1887 he was invited with other distinguished American writers, Curtis, Clemens, Cable, Howells, Stockton, Warner, Eggleston, to appear at Chickering Hall. The presiding officer of the evening was James Russell Lowell, who admitted that on the preceding afternoon he had not known

of Riley's work, but since then had read his poems: "Today," he concluded, "in presenting him, I can say to you of my own knowledge that you are to have the pleasure of listening to the voice of a true poet" (*Ibid.,* p. 221). Several universities conferred degrees upon him, but the honor which he appreciated most was on the occasion of his birthday, Oct. 7, 1911, when the schools of Indiana and New York City celebrated the anniversary by special exercises. A year later the school children of practically every section of the country arranged similar commemorative programs. He was never married, and lived for many years with devoted friends in quiet little Lockerbie Street, Indianapolis, his home becoming almost a shrine for his admirers —children and friends from all parts of the world. On his birthday in 1915, a dinner was given in his honor and tributes were read from President Wilson and other eminent Americans.

Although Riley wrote a considerable amount of prose, it was his verse that brought him distinction, and of this, his poems in dialect were his original contributions to American literature. He was veritably the Hoosier poet. The literature of the past, the classics, mythology, gave him little. He wrote always with his eye on the character; The Raggedy Man, Doc Sifers, Little Orphant Annie, Old Aunt Mary, Squire Hawkins, Tradin' Joe, Uncle Sidney, were real people whose own talk and philosophy were set down by a trained observer and artist. Riley was especially interested in characters with marked eccentricities rather than in the usual normal type of the farm or the country town. The dialect was fuller than the usual rustic speech, and although an occasional phrase may not be recognized as accurate, it is likely that Riley had heard every such phrase in his varied mingling with the people that he so well delineated. It was the Hoosier scene that he pictured, the little town of Greenfield on the National Road, or any little town in Indiana, fondly christened "Griggsby's Station." The pervasive characteristics of his poetry are kindliness, sentiment, sympathy, a sense of justice, and a pure blending of humor and pathos. Perhaps if a kinship is to be discovered with any of the great English writers, it is with Dickens, whose works were among the first he read and which he loved throughout his life. So long as his poetry is liked, it will be in large measure for his children and their drolleries, not the proper and refined children but "the rough-and-tumble little fellows 'in hodden grey,' with frowzly heads, begrimed but laughing faces, . . . awful vulgarities of naturalness, and crimes of simplicity, and brazen faith and trust, and love of life and everybody in it" (Nicholson, *post*, p. 168). He knew what they liked and, as one of them, set down their legend, and guesses, and the things they wanted to hear about. In personal appearance he is described as being extraordinarily neat, with clothes always immaculate. He was **impractical in** small ways, and if he traveled alone was almost certain to take the wrong train or get off at the wrong station. In 1913, *The Complete Works of James Whitcomb Riley,* in six volumes, a biographical edition prepared by E. H. Eitel, appeared; in 1930, *Letters of James Whitcomb Riley,* edited by W. L. Phelps.

[The above mentioned works; Meredith Nicholson, *The Hoosiers* (1900); Marcus Dickey, *The Youth of James Whitcomb Riley* (1919) and *The Maturity of James Whitcomb Riley* (1922); *Who's Who in America,* 1914–15; personal acquaintance.]   W. D. H.

RIMMER, WILLIAM (Feb. 20, 1816–Aug. 20, 1879), sculptor, was born in Liverpool, England, eldest of seven children. His mother, Mary, was of Irish birth; his father, known as Thomas Rimmer, belonged to a branch of one of the royal families of France. Born during the Terror, he was sent to England to be reared in seclusion. In early manhood, informed of his origin, he had expectations of a princely inheritance, but his hopes failed, and in despair he sailed for Nova Scotia, where he landed in 1818, soon sending for his wife and child. Although he was a man of talent and education, he supported his growing family by shoemaking. In 1824 he was working in Hopkinton, Mass., and in 1826, he moved to Boston. There a granite yard and gypsum storehouse near Wales's Wharf attracted William's artistic eye and hand when he was a lad of ten. All the Rimmer children had musical and artistic tastes, and in spite of their poverty, their home life was refined and gentle. At fourteen, William helped the household with his earnings as draftsman and sign-painter; at fifteen, he carved in gypsum a creditable figurine called "Despair," suggested by his father's history. During the next six years he worked at typesetting, soap-making, decorative sign-painting, and lithography. He painted a huge picture, impressive but ugly, of Cromwell at Marston Moor, and taking a studio in School Street, produced religious paintings for the Endicott Street Catholic Church, and other chapels. He worked furiously on an eight-foot canvas, "After the Death of Abel," and, financed by a friend who lost sixty dollars in the venture, exhibited it at an entrance fee of twenty-five cents.

After his marriage in 1840 to Mary Hazard Peabody, a New Bedford Quakeress, he began a tour of painting portraits, through the towns of Randolph and Brockton, Mass., charging from five to fifty dollars apiece. At Brockton he found a friend in Dr. A. W. Kingman, with whom he studied medicine, receiving a degree some years later. He practised dissecting and disclosed a real genius as anatomist. During his ten years in the vicinity of Brockton, when he was unable to support his family by painting or by medicine, he toiled at shoemaking. He also played the organ in the Catholic Church at Randolph and taught music to the children of the parish. Whatever time he could snatch was given to art; he continued painting pictures for Catholic churches, and cut in marble, directly from the block, a head of his little daughter, three years old.

In 1855, he moved to Chelsea, Mass., where he practised medicine, and thence went to East Milton, in the granite district. Too proud to push himself as a physician, he turned to granite cutting to eke out his income. While here he painted a "Hagar and Ishmael" and a "Massacre of the Innocents." He also made in granite an interesting head of his wife. A meeting with Stephen H. Perkins, who advised him to become an artist, resulted in his carving in four weeks, directly from granite, a head called "St. Stephen," exhibited at Williams and Everett's, and noticed in the *Boston Evening Journal* of Dec. 10, 1860. Perkins then advanced him $100, to begin in clay a life-sized statue, "The Falling Gladiator," which was completed within a few weeks, under very adverse conditions. In 1862 Perkins showed casts of these two works in London, Paris, and Florence. In Paris critics gave the "Gladiator" the treatment accorded fifteen years later to Rodin's "Age of Bronze": they called it a cast from life. Rimmer had made it wholly from his anatomical knowledge, with no model but himself. In Boston, his sculpture brought him a reputation, but little income. He was invited to teach art anatomy, at first privately (1861), later at Lowell Institute (1863). His inspiring personality, his profound knowledge of his subject, and his felicity in swift sketching on a blackboard made his lectures popular. For two years he was head of a successful private art school. In 1864, he received a commission for a nine-foot granite statue of Alexander Hamilton. He used no models and worked too rapidly; the result, placed on Commonwealth Avenue, disappointed expectations, but Rimmer was strangely indifferent to the fact. His genius was for the nude, not for the draped figure; original and self-centered, he was arrogant and uncompromising; moreover, he was always overworked. From 1861 to 1865, besides giving lectures and lessons, and publishing his *Elements of Design* (1864), he created three nude statues, over life size: "Chaldean Shepherd," "Endymion," and "Osiris." For the "Osiris," his favorite work, completed in a week, he had a nude model for a few hours only. This statue he furnished with a choice of two heads, a man's and a hawk's.

The years from 1866 to 1870, the happiest of his life, were spent in New York, as director and chief instructor in the School of Design for Women, Cooper Institute, at a salary (after the first year) of $4000. He worked prodigiously at a comprehensive plan, with excellent results, better appreciated by a French commissioner in his report to his government than by most Americans (Armand-Dumaresq, *post*), but differences of opinion arose, and he resigned. Talented and indefatigable though he was, he was unable to work with a group. The painter William Morris Hunt [*q.v.*] admired his genius, and invited his collaboration in mural painting for the New York State Capitol at Albany, but after an initial attempt, the project failed. In 1870 Rimmer resumed his work in Boston. His fame increased; he lectured at Worcester, gave an address at Yale, and delivered thirty-six lectures at Providence, R. I. (1871–73), which were reported in full in the *Providence Daily Journal*. In 1875–76 he gave a course at the Massachusetts Normal Art School. In 1877, through the interest of a Boston lady, he published his impressive *Art Anatomy*, with reproductions from nearly 900 pencil drawings illustrating every phase of the subject. From that time until shortly before his death, he was a valued instructor in anatomy at the school of the Boston Museum of Fine Arts.

Rimmer was a man of extraordinary gifts, too widely lavished. In many ways he was far ahead of his time. Twentieth-century modernists in art have hailed his principles as to direct carving and the restricted use of the living model. He worked at a driving speed, without preliminary sketches; in clay he did not build up the figure but cut it from a mass. In his painting as in his sculpture he worked with speed and intensity. He "had no wish to be influenced by anything around him" (Bartlett, *Rimmer*); his colors were harsh, his figures antique. His work was very uneven in quality, the best of it possessing power rather than charm. Artists, physicians, students, and laymen profited by his lectures, and John La Farge the painter and Daniel Chester French the sculptor were gladly his pupils.

[T. H. Bartlett, *The Art Life of William Rimmer, Sculptor, Painter, and Physician* (1882), a full and painstaking biography, well illustrated; T. H. Bartlett, in *Am. Art Rev.*, Sept.–Oct. 1880; Lorado Taft, *The Hist. of Am. Sculpture* (1903); *Boston Museum of Fine Arts Bulletin*, 1880, covering exhibition of sculpture, oil paintings, and drawings by Rimmer; Suzanne LaFollette, *Art in America* (1929); *Boston Transcript*, Aug. 21, 1879; C. E. Armand-Dumaresq, *Rapport sur une Mission dans l'Amérique du Nord* (1872).]
A.—e. A.

RINDGE, FREDERICK HASTINGS (Dec. 21, 1857–Aug. 29, 1905), philanthropist, collector, was the son of Samuel Baker and Clarissa (Harrington) Rindge of Cambridge, Mass., where he was born. Five brothers and sisters all died in childhood. His father, a shipping merchant and banker, was able to afford him ample opportunities for study and social life. He entered Harvard, but because of precarious health spent most of his senior year in Florida; he was granted his degree in 1890 as of the class of 1879. After a winter in Colorado, New Mexico, and California, in 1881 he entered a Boston commission house. Finding the northern climate injurious, however, he went to Los Angeles in 1882 and passed much of his time during the following years in California. In 1890 he purchased a ranch of 13,000 acres near Santa Monica, in the mountain canyon of Rancho Topango Malibu, where he built a beautiful mansion and raised fruit, cattle, and angora goats. In 1895 he named his home "Laudamus Farm." Becoming deeply interested in aboriginal life on the Pacific coast, he made a collection of implements used by native races; these are now in the Peabody Museum, Harvard University. Another of his avocations was numismatics, and his collection of over 5800 coins is in the Museum of Fine Arts in Boston.

In 1887, when he was twenty-nine years old, he inherited $3,000,000 from his father. After long consultations with Col. Thomas Wentworth Higginson [*q.v.*] and Mayor William E. Russell, he gave to Cambridge, Mass., funds for a public library, with 141,000 square feet of land; a school for manual training, a branch of instruction in which he was greatly interested; and a city hall. These he called his "didactic public buildings," possibly because they bear long moralizing inscriptions, cut in the walls and gilded. Rindge's religious tendencies were marked and he wrote a number of books giving expression to his beliefs and feelings—all privately printed —among which were *Can You Read Your Title Clear to a Mansion in the Sky?* (1889), and *The Best Way* (1902). He built Methodist churches in Cambridge and Santa Monica to foster the spread of his own faith. Sunday schools in the South and the Young Men's Christian Association movement shared in his generosity. In 1888 he gave Lowell, or Cat, Island, comprising fifteen acres, to the Children's Island Sanitarium at Salem, Mass. He also made donations to the

American University, Washington, D. C., and to the University of Southern California, Los Angeles.

In business his mind worked along constructive lines, and he fostered companies dealing with electricity, oil, artesian wells, navigation, and insurance. The Middle River Navigation & Canal Company and the Rindge Navigation & Canal Company, two concerns in which he was largely interested, reclaimed about 25,000 acres of bottom lands near Stockton, Cal. The Artesian Water Company, which he also controlled, carried on a real estate and colonization project in the state of Sinaloa, Mexico, covering a million acres of choice lands. He was proud of his New England origin, and belonged to many patriotic societies. Until the destruction of his home by fire two years before his death, he continued to live on his ranch. Thereafter he resided at Santa Monica, and later at Los Angeles. His summers were spent at Marblehead, Mass. On May 17, 1887, he was married at Trenton, Mich., to Rhoda May Knight, and they had three children. He died suddenly at Yreka, Siskiyou County, Cal., where he had gone on a business trip.

[*Harvard Coll.; Class of 1879, Fiftieth Anniversary* (1929); A. R. Willard, "The Rindge Gifts to Cambridge," in *New England Mag.*, Feb. 1891; *New Eng. Hist. and Geneal. Reg.*, Apr. 1906, supplement; *Boston Transcript*, Aug. 30, 1905.]   C. K. B.

RINEHART, WILLIAM HENRY (Sept. 13, 1825–Oct. 28, 1874), sculptor, was born on a farm near Union Bridge, Md., the fifth of the eight sons of Israel and Mary (Snader) Rinehart. His father was the grandson of Ulrich Rinehart (1704–1787), who emigrated from the Palatinate to Philadelphia in 1733 and established himself as a printer in Germantown. Later he settled in Chester County, Pa., on a three-thousand-acre farm, and opened the first woolen mill in that region. The next two generations were notable for the number of clergymen as well as farmers in the family, and for the generally influential position the members held in their communities. David Rinehart, a son of Ulrich's second wife, and the sculptor's grandfather, moved to Frederick County, Md., where his branch of the family established themselves as farmers. David's second son, Israel, married Mary Snader, who was of English and German ancestry. Tradition shows Israel Rinehart to have been a man of stern character, who yet was held in wide respect among his neighbors, and to have attained a high degree of prosperity in the garden section of the state where he lived. His opposition to the artistic career of his son was overcome only after the son had failed as a

farmer. Mary Rinehart, on the contrary, seems to have had the sensibility, if not the artistic gifts, of her son. In the light of her tasks as mother of a large family, the nurture of William's genius, we are told, was "her only offering on the altar of what might have been." Of medium height, graceful, gentle, and poetic, with soft, waving auburn hair, she was adored by her son. After her death he sent for his early clay bust of her, which had first revealed to his family his artistic ability, and "the last cap she wore," that of the Dunkards. He then made the bust, now in the Peabody Institute, Baltimore, but until his death in his studio in Rome.

His childhood included schooling at "Quaker Hill" near Union Bridge, at that time a log school, at "Priestland," near Linwood, and finally at Calvert College, New Windsor, scholastically a high school. In all three environments stories are told of his robust love of companionship and of his lack of scholastic aptitudes. From early years he had aided in the farm work, and when schooling failed to bring results he was put at teaming by his father, being sent to Baltimore each week with the produce of the Rinehart and neighboring farms. These trips ceased when his father found him "wasting his time" modeling a bust of his mother, while the horses were resting with their plough under a nearby tree. Thereupon a position was secured for him as the helper of a stone-worker who was building walls in the neighborhood. When the work proved too heavy for the boy's strength, the first piece of good fortune fell to his lot. A marble quarry was opened on the Rinehart farm, and the boy was set to polishing and lettering blocks for tombstones, window and door sills, for sale through the neighborhood, thereby gaining, as Lorado Taft observes, wider scope for the development of his talent than was usual for farm boys. At twenty-one he became an apprentice to Baughman & Bevan, the largest stone-cutters in Baltimore. In two years he was foreman, with a studio of his own, and was soon allowed to accept private commissions. Tradition records how at this time he repaired a mantel in the home of W. T. Walters with such freedom that the interest of this leading merchant and art connoisseur was aroused. Meanwhile he was supplementing his practical training with art courses in the night school of the Maryland Institute, where he received a gold medal in 1851 for a copy in stone of Teniers' "Smokers." The earliest publicly exhibited works of which the record remains (1853) were a bust of the Rev. Dr. John G. Morris and a reclining figure, "Faith."

While considerable disagreement in detail

arises to annoy the biographer at this point, it seems evident that with the patronage of Walters and other local philanthropists, he set out for Italy in 1855. Presumably, this first European period was centered in Florence, where he maintained himself as stone-cutter, returning with four marble bas-reliefs in 1857. After a vain attempt to start the practice of his profession in a city where no models were available and where only a few cosmopolitan citizens patronized sculptors, he left Baltimore for Rome in 1858, and kept his studio there for the rest of his life. Walters remained his chief patron throughout his career. The caryatid figures for the clock in the House of Representatives, Washington, represent the occasional commission he received during his short stay in America. The period of eight years which followed his establishment in Rome as a professional sculptor was a busy one. He first completed the bronze doors for the Capitol at Washington left unfinished by Thomas Crawford, at the request of the latter's widow. Then followed a series of "ideal" subjects of Indian, medieval and classic inspiration, "The Sleeping Children" (a funereal group for the Sisson family lot in Greenmount Cemetery, Baltimore), and "Love Reconciled with Death" for the Walters lot, also in Greenmount. The Walters family were in Paris for some years during this period, and Rinehart spent several short vacations with them. The death of Walters' wife occasioned the last-named commission. A short visit to America in 1866 saw the award of the Taney commission, and the completion of a bust of Walters.

Another period of intensive work in Rome followed, lasting for six years and marked by many orders for portrait busts, a profitable but wearisome occupation for one who was eager to do imaginative work. "Latona and Her Children," in the Metropolitan Museum in New York, the Taney, and "Clytie," perhaps his masterpiece, were brought back with him in 1872. The first and third of these works were in marble, the second in bronze. The Taney was unveiled with elaborate ceremonies at Annapolis, Md., before the State House in the same year, while subsequently a replica was presented to Baltimore by Walters and placed in Washington Square. The "Clytie" is owned by the Peabody Institute, the gift of J. W. McCoy, and is to be seen in the reading room. The Rinehart of this mature period is described by his niece as being of medium height, of compact build, with a fine head covered with brown curly hair. The bright and cheerful disposition of the boy had remained. He was a warm friend and radiated enthusiasm.

Elihu Vedder, the painter, knew him in both Florence and Rome and tells of his effervescent spirits, subdued only when his art was involved. He also speaks of his habit of underrating himself, his sensitiveness in regard to his early struggles, and of his premonition of an early death. "No one ever quarreled with Rinehart," Vedder adds, "he belongs to the Roman period and formed one of its best features."

After a short stay in Baltimore, where he was established once more in a studio, followed by a trip to California, he was off again to Rome. The remaining six years of his life were marked by the attempt to fulfill more commissions than could be done without undue strain. Busts were dispatched to America as fast as he could cut them, as well as portrait figure compositions and funereal groups, and ideal figures. Perhaps the finest of these last is the "Endymion," which was cut in marble for W. W. Corcoran of Washington, and a bronze replica of which was subsequently placed over the sculptor's own grave in Greenmount Cemetery, Baltimore, by his executors. In 1874 overwork and an unwise decision to stay in Rome during the summer in order to catch up with his commissions led to an attack of Roman fever, complicated by congestion of the lungs, and resulted in his death on Oct. 28. Funeral services were held in the Protestant Cemetery at Monte Testaccio, attended by the entire artist colony, and again in Baltimore upon the arrival of the body, Jan. 2, 1875. Contemporary opinion of the sculptor's work is reflected in an obituary notice in the *Boston Pilot,* a paper usually partial to the works of W. W. Story, where we read: "In his art no American of the present day could compete with him. Inspired by the true spirit of Greek art he conveyed his inspirations into his work and even the very jealous class to which he belonged acknowledged him as first among them." Rinehart's will appointed W. T. Walters and B. F. Newcomer executors and directed that the residue of his estate be used for the advancement of art. He never married. Among his patrons not already indicated should be mentioned the Garrett, Newcomer, and Riggs families in Baltimore.

The style of Rinehart's best work is neo-classic, modified by a sensitiveness and refinement which marks it off from the classicism of his older colleagues on the one hand as much as it does from the growing realism of his younger contemporaries on the other. The comparison of Powers' "Greek Slave" and Palmer's "White Captive" with the "Clytie" will make the point clear. Saint-Gaudens knew him when he was at work on the "Latona." Homer Saint-Gaudens in his life of his father notes that he mentions Rinehart alone of all the classicists whom he met in his student days in Rome. The younger sculptor remarked the dignity and breadth and power of the composition of "Latona," qualities not usual in the work of a classicist. One of the many newcomers befriended by Rinehart, Saint-Gaudens was with him when he died and wrote feelingly of his departure to his chief American patron, L. H. Willard. Lorado Taft says that in his day "he was doing the most beautiful sculpture that any American had yet produced in Italy" (*post*, p. 179). In the field of portraiture, the massive seated figure of Chief Justice Taney remains one of America's most successful public monuments. In funereal art the "Endymion" in bronze wears well, unless one would exclude even restrained sentiment from such works. Among his ideal figures, the "Clytie," the "Leander" in the Riggs collection, and the "Woman of Samaria" in the Walters collection promise to survive the changing tastes of the critics, marked as they are by a fragile beauty which brings the story of classicism in American sculpture to a close expressed in a wistful poetry of form.

Under the skilful management of the executors the residue of Rinehart's estate increased until it approximated one hundred thousand dollars in 1891. It was then turned over to a Rinehart Fund Committee of the trustees of the Peabody Institute, Baltimore. A Rinehart School of Sculpture was established at the Maryland Institute, scholarships to Paris and Rome were inaugurated, and in general the fund was made available for whatever seemed likely to advance the interests of sculpture and sculptors. Centers for the examination of Rinehart's works are the Peabody Institute, Baltimore, where most of the casts and several originals are preserved, the Metropolitan Museum of Art in New York, and the Corcoran Gallery of Art in Washington. The Peabody Institute also possesses interesting compositions sent over by the successive Rinehart Scholars during their student years.

[Manuscript sources include: Mrs. Jos. B. Meredith, "Ulrich Rinehart and Family"; Mrs. Daniel Rinehart, "Life of Wm. H. Rinehart"; and W. S. Rusk, "Wm. Henry Rinehart, Sculptor" (to be published). Printed sources include: A. McB. Rinehart, article in the *Baltimore American*, Jan. 21, 1900; Lorado Taft, *The Hist. of Am. Sculpture* (1925); Elihu Vedder, *The Digressions of V.* (1910); *The Reminiscences of Augustus Saint-Gaudens* (2 vols., 1913), ed. by Homer Saint-Gaudens; the *Sun* (Baltimore), Oct. 30, 1874, Jan. 4, 1875.]
W. S. R.

RINGGOLD, CADWALADER (Aug. 20, 1802–Apr. 29, 1867), naval officer, was born at "Fountain Rock," his father's estate in Washington County, Md., the son of Samuel Ringgold, a prominent Democrat and congressman, and his first wife, Maria, the daughter of John Cadwalader [*q.v.*]. He was descended from Thomas Ringgold, who settled in Kent County, Md., in 1650. He was appointed midshipman on Mar. 4, 1819, made lieutenant in 1828, and commander in 1849. His notable service in this period included command of the schooner *Weasel* against West Indian pirates; cruises in the *Vandalia* to the Pacific, 1828–32, and in the *Adams* to the Mediterranean, 1834–35; and command of the *Porpoise* in the Wilkes Exploring Expedition, 1838–42. Under Wilkes he cruised along the antarctic continent, participated in a skirmish with Fiji islanders on Aug. 18, 1840, made surveys along the west coast of America, and returned via the East Indies. In 1849 and 1850 he engaged in further surveys on the California coast, and published in 1851 *A Series of Charts, with Sailing Directions . . . to the Bay of San Francisco,* which reached a fifth edition the following year, and *Correspondence to Accompany Maps and Charts of California.* He subsequently commanded the North Pacific surveying and exploring expedition, which left Norfolk in June 1853, charted numerous Pacific shoals and islands, and reached China in March 1854. He delayed there to protect foreigners during revolutionary disturbances, and suffered a severe attack of intermittent fever which greatly weakened him physically and mentally. Commodore Matthew Calbraith Perry [*q.v.*], returning to Canton from Japan in July, ordered a medical survey, and on its pronouncement that he was insane put the expedition under Commander John Rodgers and sent him home on Sept. 4 in the *Susquehanna.* Ringgold, who had considerably recovered in the meantime, resented Perry's action bitterly, and his resentment increased when he was placed on the reserved list on Sept. 13, 1855, by a board of which Perry was a member. A medical survey upon his return had declared him fully recovered, and in 1857, after a review of his case, he was made captain on the active list with his promotion to date from Apr. 2, 1856.

After working in Washington on charts of his expedition, which remained unpublished (*U. S. Navy Department, Report of the Secretary for 1860,* pp. 18, 48), he commanded in the Civil War the sail-frigate *Sabine,* which left Norfolk on Sept. 24, 1861, for blockade duty off Georgetown, S. C. During the gale which scattered Du Pont's squadron approaching Port Royal on Nov. 2, Ringgold, displaying expert seamanship, rescued a marine battalion from the disabled steamer *Governor,* saving all but seven of the 400 men aboard. He was to have joined Du Pont for the Port Royal attack on Nov. 9, but, owing to delayed orders, he arrived too late, and this, with the fact that Du Pont was also on the board of 1855, probably explains the latter's slight acknowledgment of his services. After returning to New York in December he sailed on Mar. 12, 1862, in search of the U. S. S. *Vermont,* adrift rudderless between New York and Bermuda, and, again exhibiting creditable seamanship, located her on Mar. 29 off Bermuda, and provided supplies and assistance which enabled her to proceed unaccompanied. For his first rescue he received commendatory resolutions from the New York aldermen and the legislature of Maryland, and for both exploits a vote of thanks from Congress, though the departmental attitude is reflected in Secretary Welles's comment that it was secured by "intrigue" (*The Diary of Gideon Welles,* 1911, vol. I, p. 534). He was made commodore in July 1862, and in October, still in the *Sabine,* he sailed to the vicinity of the Cape Verdes in search for the *Alabama,* where he remained till June 1863. Save for brief coastal cruises this was his last wartime employment until his retirement for age on Aug. 20, 1864. Two years later he was made rear admiral, retired. He was unmarried. He died of apoplexy in New York City, and was buried in Greenmount Cemetery, Baltimore, Md.

[G. A. Hanson, *Old Kent: The Eastern Shore of Md.* (1876); three vols. of manuscript material on the North Pacific Exploring Expedition in the Navy Dept. Library; *Memorial of Commander Cadwalader Ringgold . . . to the Cong. of the U. S.* (1856); *Defence of Commander Cadwalader Ringgold Before the Court of Inquiry No. 2, Convened at Washington City* (1857); A. W. Habersham, *My Last Cruise* (1857); *War of the Rebellion: Official Records* (*Navy*), 1 ser., I, 346 ff., and XII, 236 ff.; *Army and Navy Jour.,* May 4, 1867; *N. Y. Times,* Apr. 30, 1867.]   A. W.

RINGLING, CHARLES (Dec. 2, 1863–Dec. 3, 1926), circus proprietor, was the son of August Frederick Rüngeling, an immigrant to the United States at the age of twenty-one, and Marie Salome (Juliar). An ancestor of the family named Richelin, a Huguenot refugee from France, settled, in the seventeenth century, in Hanover, Germany, where the name gradually became metamorphosed into Rüngeling. August F. Rüngeling's sons, the showmen, still further altered it for euphony's sake to Ringling. Charles Ringling was born in McGregor, Iowa, and was one of seven brothers. Of these, August G. (1854–1907) and Henry (1869–1918) seem never to have had much to do with the circus business. The father, a harness maker, removed with his family to Baraboo, Wis., when Charles was a child. A few years later, in 1882, five of the brothers, Otto (1858–1911), Albert C. (1852–1916), Alfred T. (1861–1919), Charles, and John (the only surviving brother in 1934), began giving amateurish little concerts, first in their own and then in neighboring towns. Two could dance, two could play musical instruments (Charles was a fiddler), and one sang. They at first called their troupe the Classic and Comic Concert Company, and later the Ringling Brothers Classic and Comic Concert Company. But with the circus business as their ultimate goal, they trained themselves in other accomplishments, Albert becoming a capable juggler and John a clown. The first full season of their company left them with $300 net profit, or $60 for each of the five, and it is said that they invested all the money in evening suits and top hats. In 1884 they organized their first little circus, which traveled by wagon, a trained horse and a dancing bear being the only animal performers or exhibits. They had the veteran showman "Yankee" Robinson, as partner, but he died before the first season was over. For several years their progress was slow. It was not until 1888 that they acquired an elephant; but from that time on their business grew rapidly. In 1890 they first used railway cars. Their success is said to have been due in no small degree to the genius of Charles Ringling.

By 1900 they had one of the largest shows on the road, and began absorbing other circuses, beginning with John Robinson's. In 1904 they acquired a half-interest in the Forepaugh-Sells show, and, two years later, complete control. In 1907, after the death of James A. Bailey [*q.v.*], they bought the Barnum & Bailey aggregation for $410,000, and could truthfully claim to possess the world's greatest circus. Their winter quarters which had, up to that time, remained at their home town, Baraboo, were now removed to the old Barnum quarters at Bridgeport, Conn. But a spacious theatre, a hospital and other civic improvements given by them remained as memorials to them in Baraboo. They had established winter homes in Sarasota, Fla., after attaining prosperity, and their coming brought that little town many benefits. Charles organized the Charles Ringling Company, which had much to do with the enlargement and beautification of the municipality—building Ringling Boulevard and a civic center around it as well as a large winter resort hotel. He organized and was president of the Ringling Bank and Trust Company, and was a prominent factor in the realty development of Florida's west coast. But the circus was his first love, and each year he spent most of the time from spring until autumn in traveling with it. He died at Sarasota of cerebral hemorrhage. He was survived by his wife, Edith Conway of Baraboo, and a son and daughter, the former a prominent grand-opera baritone singer.

[The files of the *Baraboo News*, later the *News-Republic*, are the principal source of information. Its obituary of Charles Ringling, including a sketch of the family, appeared on Dec. 4, 1926. Obituaries also appeared in *N. Y. Times*, *Chicago Daily Tribune*, Dec. 4, 1926, and in other newspapers. A "magazine" distributed to patrons of the circus *c.* 1905–10 contained a sketch of the Ringling brothers' career. See also Harry E. Cole, ed., *A Standard History of Sauk County, Wis.* (2 vols., 1918); *Life Story of the Ringling Brothers* (1900), pub. by their authority; E. C. May, *The Circus from Rome to Ringling* (1932).]

A. F. H.

RIORDAN, PATRICK WILLIAM (Aug. 27, 1841–Dec. 27, 1914), Roman Catholic prelate, was born at Chatham, New Brunswick, Canada, from which place, in 1848, his parents, Mathew, a ship carpenter, and Mary (Dunn) Riordan, recent immigrants from Ireland, removed to Chicago. Here the boy prepared for college at the academy of St. Mary's of the Lake, later entering Notre Dame University, from which he was graduated in 1858. A pious youth with a vocation for the priesthood, he was sent by his bishop to Saint Sulpice in Paris for a few months, then to the North American College in Rome as one of the original class, and finally to Louvain, where he did the major part of his work for the doctorate in theology (1864) but was not awarded the degree until the occasion of the jubilee of the University, and then *causa honoris*. Ordained a priest by Cardinal Stercks at Mechlin, June 10, 1865, he was given an assignment to teach canon law and theology at the Seminary of St. Mary's of the Lake, where he remained until 1868, when he was transferred to pastorates at Woodstock and Joliet, Ill. After three years of parochial work, he was made rector of St. James's Church in Chicago, in which position he demonstrated marked ability as a preacher, a tactful administrator, and, following the great fire, as a successful collector for diocesan rehabilitation. Known as a Roman student, he was named by Pope Leo XIII as coadjutor *cum jure successionis* to the aged Archbishop Alemany [*q.v.*] of San Francisco, with the title of Archbishop of Cabesa. Consecrated by Archbishop Feehan [*q.v.*] of Chicago, Sept. 16, 1883 (*Monitor*, Sept. 26), he had hardly reached the Pacific coast when Alemany resigned and retired to his native Valencia in Spain.

The archdiocese developed rapidly under Archbishop Riordan's fostering care: St. Mary's Cathedral was erected along with over forty churches; St. Patrick's Seminary at Menlo Park was established; several hospitals, orphanages, homes for the aged, industrial schools, and a deaf-mute asylum were founded; and the number of priests and communicants about doubled. National parishes were organized and the old Spanish traditions were emphasized, though the Archbishop himself was not especially concerned with the old Spanish civilization. A number of religious orders were invited into the diocese. Riordan inaugurated the parochial school system; fostered the Christian Brothers' College of St. Mary at Oakland and a normal school at San Jose; and assigned the purse given him on his silver jubilee to build Newman Hall at the University of California, an indication of his solicitude for Catholic students in secular institutions. He inaugurated the movement which led to the constitutional amendment (1900) exempting churches from taxation; as a delegate (1902) before the International Arbitration Court at The Hague, with the firm support of President Roosevelt and Secretary John Hay, he contributed largely to the settlement of the Pious Fund claims against Mexico. His diocese was in a most prosperous condition when in 1906 the San Francisco earthquake and fire damaged church properties to the extent of several million dollars. Aided by contributions of churches throughout the country, he headed Catholic relief work and commenced a rebuilding campaign. A prudent and far-seeing business man, Riordan placed the Church in California upon sound foundations and left his diocese free from all serious monetary obligations.

[Some authorities state that Riordan was born in Ireland, but in a deposition made in connection with the Pious Fund case he gave his birthplace as New Brunswick, Canada. For source material see *Most Rev. P. W. Riordan* (1914); *Foreign Relations of U. S.*, 1902, *U. S. vs. Mexico, in the Matter of the Pious Fund of the Californias* (1903); *Records Am. Catholic Hist. Soc.*, Mar. 1915; *Am. Catholic Who's Who* (1911); *Who's Who in America*, 1914–15; *Catholic Encyc.*, XIII, 441; *Jour. Am.-Irish Hist. Soc.*, XIV (1915), 347–49; *Leader* and *Monitor* (Catholic papers, San Francisco), for Jan. 1915; *San Francisco Chronicle*, Dec. 28–31, 1914; information as to certain facts from the Rt. Rev. J. J. Cantwell.]

R. J. P.

RIPLEY, EDWARD HASTINGS (Nov. 11, 1839–Sept. 14, 1915), soldier and financier, was born at Center Rutland, Vt., the son of William Young and Zulma DeLacy (Thomas) Ripley. His father, a descendant of William Ripley who came to Hingham, Mass., from England in 1638, was a banker and pioneer in the development of marble quarries in Vermont. Julia Caroline Ripley Dorr [*q.v.*] was his sister. In 1861 Edward was a junior in Union College, Schenectady, N. Y. He remained in college until May 1862 when he enlisted in the army, afterwards receiving the A.B. degree. He was immediately engaged in recruiting a company for the 9th Vermont Volunteers. The regiment was sent to Winchester, Va., and was a part of the force which surrendered to "Stonewall" Jackson at Harpers Ferry, W. Va., in September 1862, being interned in parole camp at Chicago until an exchange was effected in January 1863. Ripley's conduct had marked him for promotion, and in March, although he was the youngest captain, he was appointed major.

The regiment was now sent to join the troops defending Suffolk, Va. In May Ripley was promoted to the rank of lieutenant-colonel and in the following month, colonel. During this period of irksome service, marked by minor operations and much sickness and hardship, his energy and attention to the details of training were unflagging, and his regiment acquired distinction for superior discipline and efficiency. In recognition of these services he was brevetted brigadier-general of volunteers on Aug. 1, 1864. In September he joined the XVIII Corps in front of Richmond, Va., and, in command of a brigade of Heckman's division, participated in the attack on Chaffin's Farm on Sept. 29–30. His brigade shared in the capture of Fort Harrison, but was repulsed in front of Fort Gilmer, Va., an action in which Ripley was wounded. In Butler's demonstration north of the James River on Oct. 26–27, Ripley led his brigade in an unsuccessful attack on Longstreet's position near Fair Oaks. In March 1865, the command of the 1st Brigade, 3rd Division, XXIV Corps, devolved upon him, and when Lee's army evacuated Richmond, Ripley's brigade was the first Federal infantry to enter the city. He found it in flames, the people in terror, the pillaging mob in control, but acted with such energy that before the next sunrise the fire was extinguished and order restored. He remained on this duty until the restoration of civil authority, securing the safety of the city and winning the approbation of the citizens.

After the war Ripley became prominent as a financier and business executive in Rutland, Vt. He was founder and director of the United States and Brazil Steamship Line, and carried on profitably the shipment of horses to Argentina. Other business ventures included the operation of two Rutland banks, the building of the Raritan River Railroad and the Holland House, New York City. He also served as a representative from Rutland County in the state legislature. On May 23, 1878, he married Amelia

Dyckman Van Doren who, with their two daughters, survived him when he died at Rutland after an illness of three weeks.

[H. W. Ripley, *Geneal. of a Part of the Ripley Family* (1867); A. V. Honeyman, *The Van Doorn Family* (1909); F. B. Heitman, *Hist. Reg. and Dict. of the U. S. Army* (1903); G. G. Benedict, *Vt. in the Civil War*, vol. II (1888); *Revised Roster of Vt. Volunteers, 1861–66* (1892); *Cat. of the Officers and Alumni of Union College* (1884); *Rutland Daily Herald*, Sept. 15, 1915.]   T. F. M.

RIPLEY, EDWARD PAYSON (Oct. 30, 1845–Feb. 4, 1920), railroad president, was the son of Charles P. and Anne Robinson (Payson) Ripley. He was born at Dorchester, Mass., and attended the local high school. Except for a few preliminary years spent in the dry-goods business, his entire career was devoted to railroad service. His first position was that of contracting agent at Boston for the Star Union Line. From October 1870 to 1872, he was clerk to the general eastern agent of the Chicago, Burlington & Quincy Railroad; and from the latter date to 1875 he was New England agent of the same company. He then became general eastern agent, and on June 15, 1878, he was made general freight agent. In 1887 he was appointed traffic manager, and in the following year general manager of the Burlington. In August 1890, Ripley left this road to become third vice-president of the Chicago, Milwaukee & St. Paul Railway. On Jan. 1, 1896, he became president of the Atchison, Topeka & Santa Fé Railway. This position he held until Jan. 1, 1920, when he was named chairman of the board of directors. His death followed a month later, at Santa Barbara, Cal., where he maintained a winter home.

Ripley was already well and favorably known during the years which he spent with the Burlington and with the St. Paul. His reputation mainly rests, however, upon the skill, integrity, and energy which he displayed in the management of the Santa Fé after he became its president. The road had just emerged from a receivership preceded by a period of mismanagement that has never been excused or explained. A considerable portion of the system was in poor condition, equipment was inadequate, and during the first six months of 1896 the company earned only $141,720 above its fixed charges. Twenty-one years later, when the federal government temporarily took the system over for war purposes and Ripley's term of service was nearly done, the lines of the Santa Fé had been repaired and its mileage increased from 6,435 to 11,291 miles; the equipment in service had been enlarged from 962 locomotives and 28,360 cars to 2,069 locomotives and 74,252 cars; and the annual surplus had risen to $7,057,000. The best energies of Ripley's life went into the transformation which these figures represent.

Among his larger transactions for the Santa Fé during his administration was the sale of its interest in the St. Louis & San Francisco Railway, and the exchange of the company's Sonora branch for the line of the Southern Pacific reaching from Mojave to the Colorado River. Time has shown the wisdom of both decisions. Extensions of the system up to 1919 included the construction of the Belen cutoff, affording a through line from Kansas City across Oklahoma and the Panhandle; the addition of a route across Texas, linking the Gulf, Colorado & Santa Fé with the western portions of the Santa Fé system; and the purchase of the San Joaquin Valley Railroad, making possible access to San Francisco Bay. Even more important were the improvements in plant, methods, and internal organization for which Ripley was responsible. These included reductions in grades and curves, building new terminals, and the like; but special attention was also paid to such matters as the handling of stores, and to the relations between the railroad and its employees. Ripley had a fixed policy of promoting only from the ranks of his own organization whenever possible; he established a pension and insurance system, a shop-bonus plan, and an excellent apprentice system. Such methods helped to build up an unusually loyal and efficient organization.

Ripley's active life covered the entire period from the beginning of federal regulation of railways in the United States to the close of federal railroad operation after the World War. In view of his training, it is not surprising that he was skeptical of the wisdom of government control, especially during his early years. He could not see what the public had done for the railways that entitled it to so large a voice in their affairs. He maintained that railroads should be treated either as private or as public, that they should either be left free to manage their own affairs or be protected against outside attack, as the post-office is. Yet he was one of a very few railroad presidents who were willing to accede to President Roosevelt's demand in 1905 that the power to fix a maximum rate be conferred upon the Interstate Commerce Commission (as done in the Hepburn Act, 1906). Ripley did not take this position publicly, because he yielded to the opinion of his friends, but he argued for it in the conferences in which the railroads reached their decision to refuse the proposal of Roosevelt.

Among Ripley's personal characteristics were quickness of decision, willingness to delegate authority, aggressiveness, and skill in selecting men. Before his death he had become one of the railroad men whose influence reached beyond the limits of their own system, and who spoke, after a fashion, for the railways as a whole in matters in which their interests were involved. He was active in carrying through the project for the World's Columbian Exposition at Chicago in 1893, serving as a director and on the committees of ways and means and transportation. He was for many years trustee of the town of Riverside, Ill., and served as its president. On Oct. 4, 1871, he married Frances E. Harding, of Dorchester, Mass., and by her had four children.

[*Railway Age*, Feb. 13, 1920; *Railway Review*, Feb. 7, 1920; *N. Y. Times*, Feb. 5, 1920; *Outlook*, Feb. 18, 1920, p. 270; files of *Santa Fé Employes' Mag.*; *Who's Who in America*, 1918–19.]   S. D.

RIPLEY, ELEAZAR WHEELOCK (Apr. 15, 1782–Mar. 2, 1839), soldier, was born in Hanover, N. H., the son of Sylvanus and Abigail (Wheelock) Ripley. His father was graduated with the first class at Dartmouth College, became professor of theology there, and died in 1787. His mother was the daughter of Eleazar Wheelock [*q.v.*], the founder of the college. He graduated at Dartmouth in 1800, and, after studying law in the offices of relatives, was admitted to practice. He was active in politics as a "Democratic Republican," and from 1807 to 1809 was a member of the legislature of Massachusetts, of which Maine was still a part. In 1811 he was married to Love Allen, the daughter of Thomas Allen of Pittsfield, Mass. They had two children. Entering the army when war was declared between the United States and Great Britain, he was commissioned lieutenant-colonel to rank from Mar. 12, 1812, and, since no colonel had as yet been designated, was assigned to the command of the newly organized 21st Infantry of the regular army, after 1815 a part of the present 5th Infantry which claims its history and battle honors. Until the spring of 1813 he was engaged in organizing and drilling his regiment and was promoted to its colonelcy on Mar. 12, 1813. He saw his first fighting at the attack on York, now Toronto, in April 1813. He was present at the action at Fort George on May 27, and was in Wilkinson's abortive invasion of Canada that summer. On Apr. 15, 1814, he was appointed brigadier-general and, commanding a brigade in Gen. Brown's army in the Niagara campaign, fought at Fort Erie, Chippewa, and Lundy's Lane, until he was severely wounded on Sept. 17. From the first he disapproved of the campaign, and there was a good deal of unseemly wrangling between him and the commanding general. Once in action, he fought his troops with courage and determination, but Brown frequently criticised his slowness and at Lundy's Lane held him directly responsible for the abandonment of the captured British guns and for the failure to keep possession of the battle-field, from which the enemy had retired. Ripley asked for a court of inquiry, which finally convened in 1815 but was dissolved by President Madison before it had taken much testimony, on the ground that Congress, by voting Ripley its thanks and a gold medal, had sufficiently vindicated his character.

In 1820 he resigned from the army, practised law at New Orleans, and later removed to West Feliciana, La., where he passed the remainder of his life. Some years after the death of his first wife he was married to Mrs. Smith, a widow of West Feliciana. He was a member of the Louisiana Senate in 1832. Elected to the federal Congress, he served from Mar. 4, 1835, until his death. As a soldier, Ripley was a good disciplinarian and a stubborn fighter. Gen. Jacob Brown in his diary expressed the opinion that "he dreaded responsibility more than danger; in a word, that he had a greater share of physical than moral courage" (Ingersoll, *post*, p. 105; Cruikshank, *post*, p. 86). In politics he was an ardent Jackson democrat; he was opposed to nullification and to the bank and was in favor of the annexation of Texas.

[Nicholas Baylies, *Eleazer Wheelock Ripley* (1890); C. J. Ingersoll, *Hist. Sketch of the Second War between the U. S. and Great Britain* (2 vols., 1845-49); E. A. Cruikshank, *Documents Relating to the Invasion of the Niagara Peninsula* (1920); G. T. Chapman, *Sketches of the Alumni of Dartmouth College* (1867); F. B. Heitman, *Hist. Register and Dict. of the U. S. Army* (2 vols., 1903).]   T. M. S.

RIPLEY, EZRA (May 1, 1751–Sept. 21, 1841), Unitarian clergyman, a native of Woodstock, Conn., was the fifth of the nineteen children of Noah and Lydia (Kent) Ripley and a descendant of William Ripley who settled in Hingham, Mass., in 1638. The family moved to Barre, Mass., in 1762, and Ezra's boyhood was spent in hard farm labor. At sixteen he began to prepare for Harvard College, where he graduated in 1776. After teaching for a time at Plymouth and spending a year in the study of theology with the Rev. Jason Haven at Dedham, he was ordained and installed pastor of the First Church in Concord, Mass., on Nov. 7, 1778. He took up his abode in the Old Manse, married Mrs. Phebe (Bliss) Emerson, the widow of his predecessor, the Rev. William Emerson, and be

came the father of two sons and one daughter and the step-grandfather of Ralph Waldo Emerson [*q.v.*]. His pastorate continued for sixty-three years and he was the only minister in the town of Concord for about half a century. He declared that he had never accepted the Calvinistic and Trinitarian doctrines in whose atmosphere he was reared, and that on reaching manhood he had definitely rejected them, finding himself in line with the rising tide of Unitarianism in eastern Massachusetts. He adhered to the doctrines of grace, however, and always remained a fervent evangelical. He held his people with a strong hand and was greatly revered and respected by the entire community. His rare pastoral instincts enabled him to be a counselor and friend to all ages and classes. His activities continued till near the end of his life, and he preached his last sermon on the day after his ninetieth birthday.

He was a leader in all social and civic activities, was always a member of the school committee, and in 1784 drew up the constitution of the Concord Library. He was deeply interested in the Revolutionary history of the town and when the Battle Monument was erected in 1836, gave the land on which it stands and the avenue leading to it. His *History of the Fight at Concord* (1827) is of considerable interest and value. His publications were chiefly sermons, however, one of which, his *Half Century Discourse Delivered Nov. 16, 1828*, contains much that is of historical and biographical interest. He was an early advocate of peace and a pioneer in the cause of temperance, signing the total abstinence pledge against the advice of his physician and organizing what was perhaps the first temperance society in the country.

Ripley had a strong will and was born to govern, but he was always courteous, exceedingly charitable, and much given to hospitality. He was a picturesque figure, invariably wearing till the end of his days the costume of his early manhood. He was below the medium height, but so great was his dignity that his shortness was hardly noticeable. His portrait still hangs in the First Parish Meeting House at Concord.

[H. W. Ripley, *Geneal. of a Part of the Ripley Family* (1867); W. B. Sprague, *Annals Am. Pulpit*, vol. VIII (1865); S. A. Eliot, *Heralds of a Liberal Faith*, (1910), vol. I; William Ware, *Am. Unitarian Biog.*, vol. I (1850); Barzillai Frost and Convers Francis, *Two Sermons on the Death of Rev. Ezra Ripley* (1841); *Concord, Mass., Births, Marriages, and Deaths, 1635-1850* (n.d.); H. R. Hudson, "Concord Books," *Harper's New Mo. Mag.*, June 1875, containing silhouette of Ripley; *Christian Register*, Oct. 9, 16, 1841; *Christian Examiner*, Jan. 1842; *Boston Daily Advertiser*, Sept. 22, 1841.]   F. T. P.

RIPLEY, GEORGE (Oct. 3, 1802–July 4, 1880), editor, reformer, literary critic, was born in Greenfield, Mass., the youngest but one of ten children of Jerome and Sarah (Franklin) Ripley, and a descendant of William Ripley who settled in Hingham, Mass., in 1638. He gave early promise of editorial capacity in his boyhood desire to "make a dictionary." The dictionary finally became an actuality in an encyclopedia, but meanwhile George Ripley had experienced an active career in the midst of the social, religious, and political ferment of the generation following his graduation at the head of his class at Harvard in 1823. The next year the keen-eyed youth, teaching mathematics at Harvard for a livelihood, enrolled in the Harvard Divinity School. Graduating in 1826, and being ordained to the ministry on the eighth of November of that year, he became minister of the newly organized Purchase Street Church, Unitarian, in Boston. His fifteen-year ministry opened auspiciously, and within a few months, in August 1827, he married Sophia Willard Dana, daughter of Francis Dana and niece of Richard H. Dana, Sr. During the next ten years he was studying German theology, Herder, Kant, and especially Schleiermacher. For a short period he edited the *Christian Register,* and during the decade between 1830 and 1840 he wrote ten articles for the *Christian Examiner,* including the remarkable blast against conservatism contained in his review of Martineau's *Rationale of Religious Enquiry* (November 1836), a review which stirred Professor Andrews Norton, of the Harvard Divinity School, to answer the "leaning toward infidelity."

Ripley dropped the controversy and, with F. H. Hedge, began editing the *Specimens of Foreign Standard Literature,* a series of translations of Cousin, Jouffroy, Schleiermacher, and DeWette, which were of profound influence on New England intellectual life and which introduced many of the Transcendentalists to the great documents of their philosophy. The first two volumes appeared in 1838 and the series continued, with translations contributed by J. S. Dwight, W. H. Channing, James F. Clarke, Margaret Fuller, and others, until fourteen volumes had been issued. The Unitarian controversy resumed in 1839 when Andrews Norton answered Emerson's Divinity School address by an address of his own called "The Latest Form of Infidelity." Ripley, recognizing in this address an attack on his own *Discourses on the Philosophy of Religion* (1836) as well as upon Emerson's address of 1838, replied in a series of letters gathered in 1840 into a book entitled *Letters on the Latest Form of Infidelity,* and in 1841 he withdrew from the Unitarian ministry.

The next decade saw the practical application of his theories. Four years before, Sept. 19, 1836, the first meeting of the "Transcendental Club" had been held in his home, and during the four years the group, Emerson, Ripley, Hedge, Clarke, A. B. Alcott, O. A. Brownson, and after 1837 Theodore Parker, Margaret Fuller, and Elizabeth Peabody, had planned various projects to bring into practice the theories they were discussing. The founding of a magazine, the *Dial,* in 1840 was the first definite act of the club, which was never an organized club in the accepted sense of the term. Ripley aided Miss Fuller in editing this quarterly, contributed two articles, "Orestes A. Brownson" and a "Letter to a Theological Student," besides numerous unsigned and still unassigned reviews, and then relinquished this editorial activity for the more arduous task of organizing the Brook-Farm colony. He and Mrs. Ripley were indefatigable in fostering this experiment in the practical application of what he and William Ellery Channing considered the New Testament social order. Urged by Theodore Parker, Ripley assumed charge of the enterprise and on Apr. 1, 1841, he and about twenty others, including his wife and sister and later two members of the Transcendental Club, Hawthorne and Dwight, occupied a West-Roxbury farm nine miles from Boston, and in high hopes began what was called "Mr. Ripley's community," but which had the official name of "The Brook Farm Institute of Agriculture and Education" and which throughout its history had George Ripley for its president. The story of the Brook Farm Community is a story of heroism. Its members, seeking a balance between manual labor and intellectual pursuits, met and counterbalanced the communism of property by an extreme individualism of temperament.

Ripley had no idea of experimenting with the regimentation involved in socialism and when, in January 1844, he, with Minot Pratt, the other leader of the group, and Charles A. Dana, signed the new constitution which made Brook Farm a Fourierite Phalanx as Albert Brisbane's *Social Destiny of Man* (1840) had described the phalanxes, he did it with a feeling of compromise and expediency. Practically, the life at Brook Farm changed little with the change of charter. The brave group, shifting in personnel from year to year, kept doggedly on with an experiment which had much of sacrifice and much of pleasure in it. The individuals had a happy life together, but the community did not prosper. Ripley taught and farmed and lectured and wrote; after June 1845 he edited the magazine published by the association, the *Harbinger,* successor to the *Dial* and a Fourierite journal. The company, under his inspiration, indulged in the "plain living and high thinking" which was the Transcendental ideal. It was not until March 1846, when fire destroyed the Phalanstery or main building, that fears began to assert themselves at Brook Farm; and even so the community continued through the summer, the members deserting one after another until finally, in August 1847, Ripley's dream and his small fortune alike had dissolved; and, taking the *Harbinger,* a harbinger of poverty for him, to New York, he moved to Flatbush, Long Island, where Mrs. Ripley taught school; and he, in a bare room in Greeley's *Tribune* building, pursued his editorial labors on the *Harbinger,* which continued until Feb. 10, 1849. Debts, which it took more than a score of years to pay, and the affection of his Brook-Farm associates were his reward, those and the consciousness of having made history, for, "it was George Ripley, and Ripley alone, who truly originated Brook Farm, and his should be the honor through all time. And a very high honor it will be sooner or later" (W. H. Channing's letter to J. H. Noyes, Jan. 13, 1870).

For two years the Ripleys struggled in poverty until, Feb. 10, 1849, the *Harbinger* appeared for the last time. Almost immediately Ripley succeeded Margaret Fuller as literary critic of the *New York Tribune.* The beginning was modest financially, five dollars a week at first, then ten dollars a week, and twenty-five dollars a week only after three years. But the critical acumen of the man is not to be measured by the early salary; he seemed to know by instinct what was important, and first in America judged the importance of Hawthorne's *Scarlet Letter* and Darwin's *Origin of Species.* In his thirty-one years as critic on the paper hardly an important American book escaped his intelligent estimate. In 1850 he was one of the founders of *Harper's New Monthly Magazine* and for years edited its literary department. His value to the *Tribune* began to be recognized and paid for, and other income began to relieve the burden of debt and poverty inherited from Brook Farm. *A Handbook of Literature and the Fine Arts* (1852), prepared by Ripley and his friend Bayard Taylor, was a successful venture; and, having at last achieved the boyhood ambition to "make a dictionary," he set about at once with Charles A. Dana, managing editor of the *Tribune* and later

owner of the New York *Sun,* producing a *New American Cyclopædia* in sixteen volumes, the first of which appeared in 1858 and the last in 1863. Two editions of the work sold more than three million copies; and Ripley, after having done the bulk of the editing, had his labors rewarded (Grant Overton, *Portrait of a Publisher,* 1925, p. 45).

"Of a little more than middle height" and "endowed with that soberly habited plumpness," with a "large, benevolent head, thickly fringed with hair of a gray russet tinge, curling closely inward," and wearing a thick, straight beard, George Ripley settled down to a comfortable old age ("George Ripley and the Brook Farm Association," *Living Age,* December 1860, p. 571). His first wife had died in 1861 and, having been a Catholic since 1849, was buried from the old Purchase Street meeting house, at the time of her death a Catholic church, to which he had brought her a bride thirty-four years before. Work on the *Cyclopædia* absorbed his time and helped him to weather the blow. His second marriage was to Mrs. Louisa A. Schlossberger, a young German widow thirty years younger than Ripley. Hesitating to marry one but half his age, he first proposed to adopt her as his daughter; but, this being impracticable, he married her in the autumn of 1865. The marriage brought him out of his seclusion and into the social world; he went for the first time to Europe; his career as a public man began; his world enlarged. In 1869–70 he went again to Europe, where, in London, he came into contact with James Martineau, John Bright, Tyndall, Huxley, Carlyle, and Herbert Spencer. He was unanimously elected president of the Tribune Association after Greeley's death in 1872 and unanimously reëlected each year thereafter. The reformer whom Carlyle described as "a Socinian minister who left his pulpit in order to reform the world by cultivating onions" and who, in the words of his biographer, Frothingham, was "the prophet of a better dispensation, the critic of codes and institutions, the devotee of ideas," did not lose his hopefulness; but, tempering his just reviews with gentleness, whether as social reformer, as editor and critic, or as encyclopedist, Ripley seems to have had but one end in view, the uplifting and enlightening of whatever part of mankind came within his influence.

[O. B. Frothingham, *George Ripley* (1882), American Men of Letters Series, is eulogistic but presents many of Ripley's letters. See also: *In Memoriam, George Ripley, LL.D.,* New York Tribune, Extra No. 63, July 1880; H. W. Ripley, *Geneal. of a Part of the Ripley Family* (1867); J. T. Codman, *Brook Farm, Hist. and Personal Memoirs* (1894), which presents the best material on Ripley's leadership at Brook Farm;

Lindsay Swift, *Brook Farm, Its Members, Scholars, and Visitors* (1900); and the chapter on "The Ripleys" in G. W. Cooke, *An Hist. and Biog. Introduction to Accompany the Dial* (2 vols., 1902).]

R. W. A.

RIPLEY, JAMES WOLFE (Dec. 10, 1794–Mar. 15, 1870), soldier, the son of Ralph and Eunice (Huntington) Ripley, was born in Windham County, Conn. He was a descendant of William Ripley who came to Hingham, Mass., from England in 1638. He received his elementary education in the county schools and in 1813 was appointed a cadet to the United States Military Academy. Under the pressure of wartime demands he was graduated on June 1, 1814, commissioned second lieutenant of artillery, and ordered to duty at Sacketts Harbor, N. Y. After the war he served in garrisons until 1817 when he joined General Jackson on the Escambia River in Florida and served for two years under that intrepid fighter in the Seminole Indian war and the subsequent invasion of Florida. During this time he was promoted to the rank of first lieutenant. Following several years of garrison and recruiting duty, he was detailed in 1823 as assistant commissioner under James Gadsden [*q.v.*] to run the boundaries of the Indian reservations of Florida. He was commended by his chief and William Pope Duval [*q.v.*], governor of the territory, for his excellent work on this detail.

After eight more years of garrison and recruiting duty, he was ordered to Charleston Harbor in 1832 when South Carolina threatened nullification of the federal tariff act. His work there was highly praised by General Winfield Scott in command at Charleston, who wrote to the Secretary of War, "Captain Ripley has no superior in the middle ranks of the Army, . . . in general intelligence, zeal, or good conduct" (Cullum, *post*, p. 120). Having transferred to the ordnance corps, Ripley was assigned to command the arsenal at Kennebec, Me., in 1833, where he remained for eight years and received his promotion to major. From 1841 to 1854 he commanded the armory at Springfield, Mass. Through his efforts this institution was rebuilt and transformed into a more modern arms production plant. For meritorious services here during the Mexican War he was brevetted lieutenant-colonel. In 1854 he was transferred to command the arsenal at Watertown, Mass., and in the same year was promoted to the rank of lieutenant-colonel. The next year he went to California as chief-of-ordnance of the Pacific department and in 1857 was made inspector of arsenals.

At the outbreak of the Civil War he was on a special mission in the Orient. He hurried home and on Apr. 23, 1861, was appointed chief-of-ordnance of the army with the rank of colonel and the following August was promoted to brigadier-general. He devoted himself with energy if not always with the best judgment to the task of supplying the army with arms and ammunition. In the large disbursements which this involved he continually fought favoritism, fraud and political influence, maintaining throughout unquestioned personal integrity. He was retired on Sept. 15, 1863, but continued to serve as inspector of armaments until 1869. He was brevetted major-general in 1865 for long and faithful service. This venerable officer had the distinction of having served his country continuously for over fifty-five years and in four wars. On Aug. 11, 1824, he married Sarah Denny who, with three of their nine children, survived him. He died at Hartford, Conn., and was buried in Springfield Cemetery.

[H. W. Ripley, *Geneal. of a Part of the Ripley Family* (1867); C. C. Denny, *Geneal. of the Denny Family* (1886); G. W. Cullum, *Biog. Reg. . . . U. S. Mil. Acad.* (1891); *Annual Reunion, Asso. of Grads., U. S. Mil. Acad.*, 1870; F. B. Heitman, *Hist. Reg. and Dict. of the U. S. Army* (1903); F. A. Shannon, *The Organization and Administration of the Union Army* (2 vols., 1928); *Cong. Globe*; 37 Cong., 2 Sess.; *Hartford Daily Courant*, Mar. 17, 1870.]

S. J. H.

RIPLEY, ROSWELL SABINE (Mar. 14, 1823–Mar. 29, 1887), soldier, was a native of Worthington, Franklin County, Ohio, and the son of Christopher Ripley, a captain in the War of 1812, and Julia (Caulkins) Ripley. His first American ancestor was William Ripley who settled in Hingham, Mass., in 1638. An uncle, Gen. James W. Ripley [*q.v.*], probably inspired him to choose a military career. In 1839 he entered the United States Military Academy on an appointment from New York, and was graduated in 1843. He was brevetted second lieutenant and assigned to the 3rd Artillery. From 1843 to 1846 he served at Fort McHenry, Md., Fort Johnston, N. C., the Augusta Arsenal, Ga., and as assistant professor of mathematics at West Point. He was with the Coast Survey from Jan. 24 to May 19, 1846, in the meantime, Mar. 26, being commissioned second lieutenant, 2nd Artillery. He served in the Mexican War with distinction, first under General Taylor and later on General Pillow's staff. He participated in most of the battles from Monterey to the city of Mexico, was commissioned first lieutenant, Mar. 3, 1847, and brevetted captain, Apr. 18, for gallantry at Cerro Gordo, and major, Sept. 13, for meritorious conduct at Chapultepec. In 1848–49 he was on leave, engaged in writing a history, *The War with Mexico* (2 vols., 1849). He saw service in the hostilities against the Seminoles in Florida, and was later stationed at Fort McHenry, Md., Fort Monroe, Va., and Fort Moultrie, S. C. On Mar. 2, 1853, he resigned from the army. He was married at Charleston, Dec. 22, 1852, to Alicia, daughter of John and Mary (Burroughs) Middleton and widow of William A. Sparks.

After his retirement from the army he engaged in business, but did not lose his interest in military matters; serving as an officer in the state militia. In 1860 he was appointed a major of ordnance and after the evacuation of Fort Moultrie by Major Anderson, was promoted lieutenant-colonel. He commanded and reconditioned Moultrie and, after its fall, Fort Sumter. Promotion was slow, and he was about to resign when a group of leading Charleston citizens urged him to remain for the sake of the city. In August he was made a brigadier-general and placed in command of South Carolina. Gen. John C. Pemberton [q.v.] replaced him in 1862 and soon afterwards, on account of a fundamental difference of opinion as to the defense of Charleston, in which Ripley, as subsequent events proved, was correct, the latter asked to be relieved. He was now on bad terms with General Beauregard and other superiors, and Adjutant-General Cooper, in October 1861, had suggested replacing him, but had been over-ruled by President Davis. At first, General Lee, who was familiar with Ripley's excellent work, declined to relieve him, but later placed him in command of a brigade. He was severely wounded at Antietam but was soon back in service. Upon the request of Beauregard and Governor Pickens, he was immediately sent to Charleston and placed in command of the first artillery district. He was soon again involved in serious quarrels with his superiors and subordinates. In June 1863 Beauregard offered to send him to General Johnston, if Johnston would apply for his transfer, saying of him in a letter: "One of the best, General R. S. Ripley, is at present on bad terms with my chief of staff ... and ... is not satisfied with my system and rule ... an excellent officer in the field ... could be of much use to you" (*Official Records,* 1 ser. XXIV, pt. 3, 969). Ripley retained his command, always, however, a storm center. In November 1864 the residents of Charleston protested against his removal as did Governor Bonham (*Ibid.,* 1 ser. XXXV, pt. 2, pp. 646–47). Growing increasingly discontented with what he regarded as the neglect of the state, on Christmas Day, 1864, Ripley wrote Governor Magrath a letter, bitterly criticizing the Confederate government and offering to resign and take a command with state troops to resist Sherman; he also

suggested the enlistment of slaves. After the fall of Charleston he was ordered to the army of the West and joined Johnston the day of the battle of Bentonville. He was at once ordered back to South Carolina, where he was stationed when the war ended.

Subsequently, he went to England and engaged in a manufacturing venture in London, which soon failed. He resided in Charleston thereafter, but spent most of his time in New York, where he died of apoplexy. Outside of the army, Ripley was widely popular, particularly in Charleston. Timrod wrote a poem in his honor (*Poems of Henry Timrod,* 1899, pp. 148–50). He had a wide reputation as a raconteur, and his reminiscences of the bombardment of Fort Sumter appeared in the New York *World* in 1885. He also published *Correspondence Relating to Fortification of Morris Island* (1878), a pamphlet.

[H. W. Ripley, *Geneal. of a Part of the Ripley Family* (1867); G. W. Cullum, *Biog Reg. Officers and Grads. U. S. Mil. Acad.* (1891), vol. II; *Eighteenth Ann. Reunion, Asso. Grads. U. S. Mil. Acad.,* 1887; E. M. Seabrook, *Address Delivered at the Unveiling of the Ripley Monument ... Apr. 3, 1894* (1894); *News and Courier* (Charleston), Mar. 30, Apr. 1, 2, 4, 1887; the *World* (N. Y.), Mar. 30, 1887.]   J. G. deR. H.

RISING, JOHAN CLASSON (1617–April 1672), Swedish colonial governor, was born in Risingé parish, Östergötland, Sweden, the son of the local pastor, Clas Botvidi. After completing the course in the Linköping Gymnasium, he matriculated in 1635 at the University of Upsala and took his doctor's degree there in 1640. While at Upsala he was influenced profoundly by the historian and legal scholar, Johannes Loccenius, and found a friend and patron in Magnus Gabriel de la Gardie, the rector of the University. For the next eleven years he was engaged chiefly in study and travel. As tutor (1646–48) to the young Count Clas Åkesson Tott he made a tour of northern Sweden and visited England and France. He had a passion for the study of trade and commerce, and the ambition of his life, never relinquished, was to formulate the policies and describe the methods by which Sweden would become a great commercial power. He was the first Swede to publish writings of any importance in political economy. A warm admirer of the Dutch, he made several visits to Holland and was at one time a student at the University of Leyden. By 1651 he was recognized as an expert in his subject and was appointed secretary of the newly established Commercial College or governmental department of commerce. The College had jurisdiction over the colony of New Sweden, and when the authorities could no longer ignore the petitions of Gov. Johan Björnsson Printz [*q.v.*] for relief, Rising was appointed to succeed him. He resigned his post at the Commercial College in October 1653; was knighted by Queen Christina and received various grants; and sailed from Gothenburg Feb. 2, 1654, on the *Örn.* A long and adventurous voyage brought him to Fort Elfsborg, on the Delaware, May 20, 1654.

Rising was director (governor) of New Sweden for a little less than fifteen months. He got along well with his subjects and with the Indians and worked intelligently to advance the agricultural and commercial activities of the colony. On the first day after his arrival, however, he made a fatal blunder. In 1651 Pieter Stuyvesant [*q.v.*] had established Fort Casimir at what is now New Castle, Del., and Printz, diplomat as well as soldier, let it alone, realizing that if the Dutch could be played against the English he would be the gainer. Rising, with a new broom's zeal for a clean sweep, and with no eye for the remoter complications, took the fort and renamed it Fort Trefaldighet. Stuyvesant bided his time. He seized the Swedish supply ship, the *Gyllene Haj,* when it put in at New Amsterdam, and in August 1655 he appeared in the Delaware with three ships and an overwhelming force of men. In the two weeks' campaign that ensued, Stuyvesant did not lose a man, and the Swedes lost only one, a deserter shot while fleeing. On Aug. 15 Fort Christina capitulated, the Swedes receiving easy terms, and with the loss of the colony Rising returned home by way of England and Holland. His journals and reports are the chief source of information about New Sweden during his governorship.

For a few years he was in the Swedish customs service, being stationed at Elbing in East Prussia. He published two works, *Itt Uthtogh om Kiöp-Handelen aller Commercien* (1669) and *Een Landbook* (1671), and worked heroically to complete a comprehensive treatise on political economy. He had no regular source of income, was miserably poor, and died in a garret over a tailor's shop. He was unmarried.

[Amandus Johnson, *The Swedish Settlements on the Delaware, 1638–64* (2 vols., 1911), "Dir. Johan Rising's Report to the Commercial Coll., June 14, 1655," *Ger.-Am. Annals,* n.s., VIII (1910), 87–93, and *Johan Classon Rising, the Last Gov. of New Sweden* (1915); A. C. Myers, ed., *Narratives of Early Pa., West N. J., and Del., 1630–1707* (1912).]   G. H. G.

RITCHIE, ALEXANDER HAY (Jan. 14, 1822–Sept. 19, 1895), engraver and painter, was born in Glasgow, Scotland, and studied drawing in Edinburgh, under Sir William Allan, R.A., a distinguished historical painter. He came to the United States in 1841, worked for a short time in Canada, and then settled in New York. About 1847 he established himself as a general engraver in New York City, and was soon enjoying a profitable business and employing assistants, although it is said that he put the finishing touches upon every plate produced in his shop. Especially able were his engravings of portraits in mezzotint, some of them reproducing his own paintings. He painted in oils and exhibited at the National Academy, making his first appearance there in 1848. Among his paintings were "Mercy Knocking at the Gate" (1860), "Fitting Out Moses for the Fair" (1862), and "The Death of Lincoln"; while among his best-known portraits are those of Dr. James McCosh, president of Princeton College, and Professors H. M. Alexander and Charles Hodge of the Princeton faculty.

He engraved "The Death of Lincoln," "Washington and His Generals," and "Mercy Knocking at the Gate," after his own paintings; "Contemplation," after the original by Seymour J. Guy; "Lady Washington's Reception" (otherwise known as "The Republican Court"), by Daniel Huntington, a very elaborate composition containing no less than sixty portraits; also several of Felix O. C. Darley's historical pictures—"The First Blow for Liberty," depicting the battle at the Concord bridge (1858), "The Last Words of Captain Nathan Hale" (1858), "Washington Entering New York," and "On the March to the Sea." His skill and facility in reproductive work were generally recognized, and he was as much at home in mezzotint and etching as in line engraving. Occasionally he yielded to the need for rapid production and adopted the expedients to which engravers of portraits were occasionally driven, such as scraping out the head on a plate and substituting another; thus his full-length portrait of Abraham Lincoln was originally that of Calhoun (Weitenkampf, *post,* p. 55). Some very ambitious undertakings in the line of portrait groups were confided to Ritchie, for example, "The Class of 1863" (at Yale College), with no less than forty-eight members; and the "Authors of the United States" (1866), after the original by Thomas Hicks. This last-mentioned plate portrays Irving, Bryant, Cooper, Poe, and the New England writers, in stiff poses, gazing into vacancy with intense earnestness. Ritchie spent his last days in Connecticut, dying in New Haven at the age of seventy-three.

[D. M. Stauffer, *Am. Engravers upon Copper and Steel* (1907), vol. I; Frank Weitenkampf, *Am. Graphic Art* (rev. ed., 1924); C. E. Clement and Laurence Hutton, *Artists of the Nineteenth Century* (1880); *Critic,* Sept. 28, 1895; N. Y. *Evening Post,* Sept. 21, 1895.]

W. H. D.

RITCHIE, ANNA CORA [See MOWATT, ANNA CORA OGDEN, 1819–1870].

RITCHIE, THOMAS (Nov. 5, 1778–July 3, 1854), journalist and politician, was born in Tappahannock, Essex County, Va. His father, Archibald Ritchie—a Scotch immigrant, the community's chief business man, and an effective if tardy supporter of the American Revolution—died early in the life of Thomas. The latter's mother, Mary (Roane) Ritchie, unsuccessfully set him to reading, first law under his cousin, Spencer Roane [*q.v.*], and then medicine in Philadelphia. Disgusted with both subjects and believing in universal education, he turned enthusiastically and successfully to teaching in Fredericksburg, simultaneously reading widely in the classics of economics and politics; and when his health failed under the double strain he set up a small bookstore in Richmond (1803).

Then opportunity came. The Republican newspaper in Richmond had ceased publication; Judge Roane wanted another, and President Jefferson would help with federal printing. Accordingly, with eloquent professions of unbounded zeal for independent and honorable service through a new form of public education, Ritchie brought out the *Enquirer,* May 9, 1804. The paper was a complete success. For forty-one years he continued it (later as the *Richmond Enquirer*), thrice a week with occasional "extras" after 1806, himself writing the ringing editorials, culling the news intelligently and doing most of the reporting, keeping it morally clean and free from abusive language, sometimes helped and sometimes hindered by partners but always dominating it, making it a power in the land. Probably no other editor of his time was equally successful in holding in the bonds of friendship a varied host of men, and in securing for his paper discussions of the greatest public questions by men whose opinions carried the weight of authority.

Already a successful man, on Feb. 11, 1807, he married Isabella, daughter of Dr. William Foushee, a progressive Richmonder and "war hawk." They had twelve children. On July 1, 1807, he was secretary of a Richmond mass-meeting, which the *Enquirer* had promoted, in protest against British outrages, and soon was marching to Norfolk with the Republican Blues; later he served briefly in the War of 1812. In 1814 the legislature elected him state printer, a lucrative position which he deemed only reasonable compensation for the *Enquirer's* services

and which he continued to hold by legislative favor for twenty-five years, with the exception of a short interval in 1834.

Men were now talking of the "Richmond Junto," which included Ritchie and his Essex cousins, Spencer Roane and Dr. John Brockenbrough of the Virginia State Bank. Combining the complementary functions of editor and political manager, Ritchie was secretary of the Republican (Democratic) central committee, while the *Enquirer* was becoming the "Democratic Bible." Believing democratic reform in representation and suffrage necessary and right, he ardently favored the state constitutional convention of 1829; and he edited and published its *Debates* with care and pride. He favored public schools, also, and extensive state internal improvements. Thenceforth western Virginia backed him consistently. In national politics Ritchie's influence rested first on an alliance with Van Buren, whom he sincerely liked and in whose interest he published another Richmond paper, the *Crisis,* in 1840. This combination, he thought, preserved the Virginia "principles of '98, '99" against the corrupting influence of Henry Clay (whom he had detested since 1825) and the divisive tactics of John C. Calhoun, whose nullification and Southern-party policies he frankly opposed; but, far from subservient, he urged his own ideas on banking, denounced abolitionists even while urging gradual emancipation, and in 1844 supported Polk for president because ever since the Missouri Compromise (which he had opposed) he had deemed annexation of Texas a necessity for the South.

From 1845 to 1851, with considerable reluctance, he conducted in Washington the *Union,* a national administration organ established at Polk's request. But, though he greatly aided the compromise measures of 1850, the public would no longer be taught by him. And Richmond had lost its most conspicuous figure—a tall, lean, quick-moving man, with brilliant eyes and striking profile, always clinging to the old low shoes and silk stockings, secretary of all the public meetings, toastmaster of the dinners, leader of the dances, welcomer of distinguished guests, the state's "Father Ritchie," his intimates' "Tom Ritchie." The *Enquirer* was firmly established and continued to be powerful even though his sons, one of whom fought a famous duel with John H. Pleasants [*q.v.*], the editor of the rival *Richmond Whig,* lacked his journalistic ability. His last years were divided between Washington and "Brandon," the home of a married daughter on the James, where he indulged an old fondness for gardens, poetry, and children. Though he held no public office, his funeral in Washington was attended by the nation's great.

[C. H. Ambler, *Thomas Ritchie: A Study in Virginia Politics* (1913); R. W. Hughes, *Editors of the Past* (1897); *The John P. Branch Hist. Papers of Randolph-Macon Coll.* (1902, 1911, 1915), which contain a biographical sketch by C. T. Thrift and family letters; Frederic Hudson, *Journalism in the United States* (1873); the *Enquirer*, the *Crisis*, and the *Richmond Compiler*, a commercial newspaper edited by Ritchie for several years around 1830, in Va. State Lib.; letters in various collections, especially in the Van Buren MSS. and Jackson MSS., Lib. of Cong.; suggestions from Frank W. Scott, who has made a special study of MS. materials; obituary in *Daily Richmond Enquirer*, July 6, 1854.]

C. C. P.

RITNER, JOSEPH (Mar. 25, 1780–Oct. 16, 1869), governor of Pennsylvania, was born in Berks County, Pa., the son of a German emigrant and ardent Revolutionary patriot, Michael Ritner. Six months' schooling and instruction in weaving constituted his formal education, but he taught himself English from books and after his marriage to Susan Alter in 1802 explored her brother's library of German treatises. His annual wage at farm labor rose from $80 to $120; and then he sought the Washington County frontier, where he developed a prosperous farm. In the War of 1812 he was a private. In his home community he became supervisor of roads, in building which he introduced the plow, and he participated in numerous Democratic caucuses. His thrifty habit of hauling freight and driving stock to Philadelphia in slack seasons made this stout countryman, with his massive head, strong face, and broad chest, a familiar sight along main-traveled roads; and his extensive family connections made him favorably known in ten German counties. During service to the Assembly, 1821–26, the speakership came to him twice, 1825 and 1826, unanimously the second time.

Aversion to secret societies made him the anti-Masonic gubernatorial candidate four times, 1829, 1832, 1835, 1838. His modest initial vote increased in 1832 with National Republican support, in spite of Democratic broadsides averring that this "Deist" propagated the principles of Paine's *Age of Reason* and that "a respectable and well-known citizen saw Joseph Ritner on the Sabbath Morning, keep tally, while others were amusing themselves playing ball, in his meadow!" (*Joseph Ritner a Deist*, in Political Broadside Collection of the Historical Society of Pennsylvania). The split in 1835 among the Democrats over Jackson and the schools gave him his one term as governor, just when Pennsylvania was exceptionally upset. The ill-assorted coalition of Whigs and anti-Masons behind his election was at one on nothing but opposition to Jacksonianism. Warfare over bank deposits and the antiquated constitution, financial panic, canal and railroad lobbying, anti-abolitionist rioting, and the fanatic genius of Thaddeus Stevens, together taxed Ritner beyond his ingenuity. The hostile press incessantly abused his administration. Even nature opposed him, with a flood on the Juniata engulfing forty miles of costly canal construction, just when he was solicitous over canal appropriations. Yet he achieved something in the democratic movement. He obtained a large increase in the permanent school appropriation and the number of common schools. Into a "schoolhouse-fund" he directed the $500,000 received from the federal government, to prevent the sacrifice of instruction to equipment. But he lost his campaign for a separate office of state school superintendent and for an "immediate and efficient means . . . for the preparation of common school teachers" (Wickersham, *post*, p. 346). More independent than most contemporary executives of northern states, he denounced the gag law, practised and preached temperance, and investigated the new "manufacture of iron with mineral coal." He opposed Jackson's bank policy on economic as well as political grounds, impatiently awaiting the safe resumption of specie payments, and finding the event, as he wrote Biddle, "to me, personally, truly gratifying" (Aug. 1, 1838, Etting Collection of the Historical Society of Pennsylvania). His real integrity of purpose was obscured by inability to limit canal appropriations, to prevent the chartering of banks wholesale, and to stop dictation to the state by "private companies and sectional jealousies." He long distrusted Stevens and tried vainly to break his hold on the anti-Masonic party, but finally he named him canal commissioner and manager of his 1838 campaign. His party lost that virulent contest and brought upon him the "Buckshot War" and much loss of dignity.

Nevertheless, as ex-governor, prestige returned. Whigs chose him to cast an electoral vote for Harrison in 1840, Taylor nominated him for director of the Mint in 1849, Republicans sent him in Pennsylvania's delegation to the Frémont convention in 1856, and the Civil War found him serving as an enthusiastic, though elderly, inspector of the educational institutions so near his heart.

[Letters of Ritner, Stevens, and Biddle, and Political Broadsides of 1832, Hist. Soc. of Pa.; Gubernatorial Papers, Educational Building, Harrisburg; *Life of Joseph Ritner, Farmer of Washington County* (1835); *Lives of D. R. Porter and Joseph Ritner* (1838); *Report of Proceedings in Relation to the Gov. Jos. Ritner Monument* (n.d.); W. C. Armor, *Lives of*

the Governors (1872); Commemorative Biographical Record of Washington County (1893); E. W. Biddle, Gov. Joseph Ritner (1919); L. G. and M. J. Walsh, Hist. . . . of Education in Pa. (1930); J. P. Wickersham, Hist. of Education in Pa. (1886); H. R. Mueller, The Whig Party in Pa. (1922); S. W. McCall, Thaddeus Stevens (1899).]
J. P. N.

RITTENHOUSE, DAVID (Apr. 8, 1732–June 26, 1796), instrument maker, astronomer, and mathematician, was born at Paper Mill Run near Germantown, Pa., in a house yet standing in Fairmount Park, Philadelphia, the great-grandson of William Rittenhouse [q.v.], and the third of the ten children of Matthias and Elizabeth (Williams) Rittenhouse. His mother, a Welsh Quakeress, possessed a vigorous and comprehensive mind poorly educated. His father farmed in Norriton about twenty miles from Philadelphia. The boy evidenced extraordinary mathematical and mechanical ability, stimulated at the age of twelve by a chest of books and tools inherited from his maternal uncle. Little schooling was available, but he worked and studied assiduously and at nineteen opened an instrument shop on his father's farm, chiefly for clock-making. Here he is said to have mastered an English translation of Isaac Newton's *Principia,* and he acquired a sound knowledge of physical science at the expense of a lifelong injury to his health. Thomas Barton, an Episcopal clergyman, graduate of the University of Dublin, who later married David's sister Esther, taught in the neighborhood, assisted in procuring scientific works, and introduced him in Philadelphia.

Limited by his environment, he developed an extraordinary ability of supplying his own needs, acquiring great proficiency in observational, practical, and theoretical astronomy and in instrument making. He was interested in optics and the construction of a telescope in 1756. Rush's eulogy (*post,* p. 9) credits him with the independent discovery of fluxions at this time, but evidence is lacking. His first public service was a boundary survey for Penn in 1763–64 to settle a dispute with Lord Baltimore. So accurate was the work that it was accepted by Mason and Dixon. In 1767 he designed his celebrated orrery. A description of the orrery, acquired by Princeton but now lost, occupies first place in the first volume of the *Transactions of the American Philosophical Society* (*post,* pp. 1–3). A second orrery is a cherished possession of the University of Pennsylvania, loaned to the Franklin Institute. This instrument represents motions of bodies of the solar system and illustrates solar and lunar eclipses and other phenomena "for a period of 5000 years, either forward or backward" (*Ibid.,* p. 2). Much of

his contemporary fame was due to it. Jefferson wrote: "He has not indeed made a world; but he has by imitation approached nearer its maker than any man who has lived from the creation to this day" (*Notes on the State of Virginia,* 1782, p. 120). He experimented on the compressibility of water, solved the problem of Archimedes, and about this time invented a metallic thermometer later credited to Abraham Louis Brequet. His "Easy Method of Deducing the True Time of the Sun's Passing the Meridian" in 1770 (*Transactions, post,* I, 47–49) was incorporated by Von Zach with favorable comment in the *Tabulae Motuum Solis* (1792). His observations and orbital determination of Lexell's comet in 1770 found John Winthrop, 1714–79 [q.v.], in error.

In 1768 his calculations on the transit of Venus that was to occur in 1769 were presented to the American Philosophical Society. Committees were appointed and three observing sites selected, the state house square, the Rittenhouse farm, and Cape Henlopen. For the event Rittenhouse built an observatory and constructed equipment including a transit telescope, now considered the first telescope made in America, an equal-altitude instrument, and an excellent clock (*Transactions, post,* I, 4–81). The accuracy of the Norriton observations, due to his skill assisted by William Smith, 1727–1803 [q.v.] and John Lukens, was attested by Nevil Maskelyne and by Simon Newcomb. Newcomb wrote that "his observations of the celebrated transit of Venus in 1769 have every appearance of being among the best that were made" (*North American Review,* January 1876, p. 95). Combination with Greenwich results by a method improved by Rittenhouse gave 8".805 for the solar parallax, in striking agreement with the modern value 8".803. Rittenhouse also reported an "effect of the atmosphere of Venus" (*Transactions, post,* I, pp. 27–28); Robert Grant, however, credits its discovery to Schroeter the following century (*History of Physical Astronomy,* 1852, p. 235).

In 1770 he removed to Philadelphia. Including work at his observatory there, he also observed transits of Mercury, eclipses and transits of Jupiter's satellites, solar and lunar eclipses, variable stars, the new planet Uranus, and comets, including one discovered by himself in 1793 and reported to the American Philosophical Society (*Transactions, post,* III, 261). Regarding work in Philadelphia one week after the British evacuation, S. A. Mitchell says "The first eclipse of the sun to be carefully observed in the British colonies of America was that of June 24, 1778, which was watched by the astronomer, David

Rittenhouse of Philadelphia" (*Eclipses of the Sun,* 1923, p. 128). To adjust instruments in the meridian, when buildings prevented a distant mark, he invented the collimating telescope in 1785, a useful contribution to practical astronomy that was duly credited. The same year he introduced spider threads in the eyepiece of his instruments; but according to Troughton this was first done by Fontana (*Monatliche Correspondenz,* August 1800, p. 215). Rittenhouse subjected problems and theories "to the test of experiment." In this way he verified his explanation of the apparent conversion of intaglios into cameos in 1779, before Brewster's observations. To solve a problem involving the "inflexion" of light he made a plane transmission grating in 1786, anticipating Fraunhofer in their construction and use (T. D. Cope, "The Rittenhouse Diffraction Grating," *Journal of the Franklin Institute,* July 1932, p. 99). Newton had previously used "scratches made in polished plates of glass," but Rittenhouse measured grating intervals and deviations of several orders of spectra. He experimented on magnetism and electricity, and he measured the barometric effect on a pendulum clock rate and the expansion of wood by heat. He made a compensating pendulum, contrived one that beat faster in a dense medium than in a rare, and constructed a wooden hygrometer.

In mathematics he solved the problem "of finding the sum of the several powers of the sines" in 1792 to demonstrate "a very elegant theorem for determining the times of vibration of a pendulum:" His solution was by demonstration to the second power, by infinite series to the sixth and by the "law of continuation" for higher powers (*Transactions, post,* III, 155–56). It corresponds with the formulae for the definite integral $\int_0^{\frac{\pi}{2}} \sin^n x \, dx$. His "Method of Raising the Common Logarithm of any Number," in 1795, limited to ordinary arithmetical operations including division, evolution, and compound fractions, was "true to the ninth place" (*Ibid.,* IV, 69–71). His paper, "To Determine the True Place of a Planet, in an Elliptical Orbit" in 1796, gave a series in eccentricity and mean anomaly, carefully considered for convergency and an alternate expansion to use when expedient (*Ibid.,* pp. 21–26).

He was frequently engaged on boundary surveys and commissions involving Pennsylvania, Delaware, Maryland, Virginia, New York, New Jersey, and Massachusetts—over half the British colonies in America. Many settlements were based on his field work with instruments of his own construction. He also conducted canal and river surveys. Commissions and offices were thrust upon him, some petty, some important. He served committees to test specimens of flint glass, to tend rain gauges, to inspect the first steam-engine in the United States, and to visit Fitch's steamboat. He had charge of the state-house clock and the apparatus of the College of Philadelphia and of the library of the American Philosophical Society. He delivered the annual oration of that society on astronomy in 1775 (*An Oration Delivered Feb. 24, 1775, before the American Philosophical Society,* 1775). Plans for a public observatory with Rittenhouse at the head were before the legislature and received encouragement from Lord North and Maskelyne, the royal astronomer, but war intervened. Rittenhouse responded to the war as engineer of the Committee of Safety in 1775. To obtain lead for bullets he substituted iron for lead clockweights throughout Philadelphia. He supervised the casting of cannon and manufacture of saltpeter, selected a site for a powder-mill and a magazine for military stores, experimented on rifling cannon and musket balls, devised chain protection for the harbor, and became vice-president of the Committee of Safety in 1776 and president of the Council of Safety in 1777. He was a member of the General Assembly and the state constitutional convention in 1776, trustee of the loan fund, member of the board of war, and state treasurer. He was professor of astronomy in the University of Pennsylvania and served on its board of trustees. Franklin consulted him to explain the micrometer scales on his telescope; and electrical apparatus remains that was used by both. He made and repaired instruments for Washington, and he presented spectacles and a reading glass. For Jefferson he standardized the foot by pendulum measurements in a project to establish a decimal system of weights and measures. He served on the commission to organize the United States bank and was appointed first director of the Mint by Washington, Apr. 14, 1792, accepted on the solicitation of Jefferson and Hamilton, and served until June 1795. He contributed many articles to the American Philosophical Society, served as curator, librarian, secretary, and vice-president, and was on many important committees. At Franklin's death he was elected president of the society, Jan. 7, 1791, and by reëlection continued until death. The highest of his many honors was his selection as a foreign member of the Royal Society of London in 1795.

On Feb. 20, 1766, he married the daughter of

a neighboring farmer, Eleanor Colston, a Quakeress who died in 1770. They had two daughters. Two years later he married Hannah Jacobs who ably assisted him in the loan office and state treasury. Their one daughter died in infancy. He was described as tall, slender and erect, quick and active. He was painted by Peale and by Trumbull; a marble bust was made by Ceracchi and a bronze medal by Barber, engraver of the Mint. His character was irreproachable, possessing good nature and universal good will. His weakness, if any, was due to extreme modesty. His constitution was frail yet possessed great endurance under stress. On June 22, 1796, he suffered an attack of cholera, and his nephew, a physician, was summoned. Four days later his last words were (Barton, *post*, p. 444), "You have made the way to God easier."

[Papers, letters, manuscripts, and instruments exhibited at the Rittenhouse bicentenary celebration; papers in Lib. of Cong.; *Trans. Am. Philosophical Soc.*, vols. I–IV (1771–99); Wm. Barton, *Memoirs of the Life of David Rittenhouse* (1813); Benjamin Rush, *A Eulogium . . . to . . . David Rittenhouse* (1796); James Renwick, "David Rittenhouse," *The Library of Am. Biog.*, ed. by Jared Sparks, 1 ser., vol. VII (1837); D. K. Cassel, *A Genea-Biog. Hist. of the Rittenhouse Family*, vol. I (1893); M. J. Babb, "David Rittenhouse," *Pa. Mag. of Hist.*, July 1932; James Stokley, "The Rittenhouse Exhibition," *Ibid.*]   W. C. R.

RITTENHOUSE, WILLIAM (1644–Feb. 17, 1708), Mennonite minister, pioneer paper manufacturer, was born in Mülheim-am-Ruhr, in Rhenish Prussia, opposite the town of Broich. His name is variously spelled Rittenhausen, Rüddinghuysen, and, by William Penn, Rittinghausen. He was the son of George Rittenhausen and Maria (Hagerhoffs), and some genealogists have claimed that he was descended from a kinsman of the Hapsburg emperors (Cassel, *post;* A. P. Rittenhouse, *post*). Authentic but less ambitious records show that William Rittenhouse himself was a Mennonite minister of Broich in the Rhineland. Sometime in the latter part of the seventeenth century, he removed with his family to Arnhem, in the Netherlands, where with a brother he carried on a paper-making business. His family consisted of two sons—Klaas (1666–1734), later called Nicholas or Claus, and Gerhard (1674–1742/43), later called Garret—and a daughter, Elizabeth. There are no records of his wife. From Arnhem Rittenhouse and his children moved to Amsterdam. On June 23, 1678, he became a Dutch citizen, and the document recording his naturalization refers to him as a paper maker (Cassel, p. 51). From Amsterdam the family emigrated to America in 1688. They settled in Germantown, Pa., which had been founded five years before by thirteen families, who were mostly weavers by trade and Mennonite in religion. William Rittenhouse was chosen to be their first minister, and in 1703, he was elected bishop of the first Mennonite church in America by the authority of four ministers of the Hamburg congregation in Germany. Since none of the ministers who had elected him was able to come to America to install him as bishop, he refused to exercise the functions of that office, but he continued as minister and gave the land on which the first Mennonite church was built.

Shortly after settling in Germantown, Rittenhouse formed a company for the purpose of building a paper mill. The partners included Robert Turner, Thomas Tresse, and William Bradford, 1663–1752 [*q.v.*], one of the first printers in the colonies. The company leased twenty acres of land in Roxborough Township from Samuel Carpenter for 999 years. Here on Paper Mill Run, near the Wissahickon Creek, the first paper mill to be erected in the colonies was built in 1690. When Bradford moved to New York in 1693, he leased his one-quarter share in the mill to William Rittenhouse and his son Klaas for ten years, and sold it to them outright in 1704. By purchasing the holdings of the other partners, Rittenhouse and his son became sole proprietors by 1705/06. The water-mark of the Rittenhouse paper was a clover leaf, with the letters "WR" and the word "Pensilvania." In the early years of the mill almost the whole output was taken by Bradford.

The original mill was destroyed by flood either in 1700 or in 1701, during William Penn's second visit to America, and Penn recommended that "such persons as should be disposed to lend them aid . . . give the sufferers relief and encouragement in their needful and commendable employment" (Cassel, p. 57). The mill was rebuilt a little farther down the stream in 1702, and after the death of the elder Rittenhouse at Germantown, in 1708, the business was carried on by his son Klaas, who also became a minister. The latter married Wilhelmina Dewees.

[D. K. Cassel, *A Genea-Biog. Hist. of the Rittenhouse Family and All its Branches in America* (1893); A. P. Rittenhouse, "The Pedigree and History of the Rittenhouse Family" (MS., 1924), and H. G. Jones, "Historical Sketch of the Rittenhouse Paper Mill" (MS.), in library of the Hist. Soc. of Pa., Phila.; N. B. Grubb, *The Mennonite Church of Germantown* (1906); S. W. Pennypacker, *The Settlement of Germantown, Pa.; and the Beginning of German Emigration to North America* (1899); H. S. Bender, in *Mennonite Quart. Rev.*, Jan. 1933, Apr. 1934.]   M. P. S.

RITTER, FRÉDÉRIC LOUIS (June 22, 1834–July 6, 1891), composer, author of works on musical history, and professor at Vassar, was born in Strasbourg, Alsace, and was descended from a Spanish family named Caballero. He showed musical talent at an early age, and after studying with Hans Schletterer and Franz Hauser, and with his cousin, J. G. Kastner, in Paris, he became professor of music at the Protestant Seminary of Fénéstrange in Lorraine in 1852. Four years later he accompanied his parents to America. He established himself in Cincinnati and founded there the Cecilia Society (choral) and the Philharmonic Orchestra. Though the city at the time of Ritter's advent boasted several German male choruses and a sacred choral organization, the best patronized musical entertainments were the concerts of the negro minstrel troupes. With the two societies he had founded Ritter gave programs of the best classic music and promoted musical appreciation in his section of the Middle West. In 1861 he left Cincinnati to settle in New York, where he was very active during the period after the Civil War, and he played his part in the intensive development of interest in music that marked the time. He was the conductor of the Sacred Harmonic Society and the "Arion" male chorus society, and directed a series of seven annual concerts for the latter group. In 1867 he became professor of music at Vassar College and retained the position until his death.

After he went to Vassar, Ritter devoted his time to his academic work and to writing. His *History of Music* (2 vols., 1870–74) was followed by *Music in England* (1883), *Music in America* (1883), a *Manual of Musical History* (1886), and some works of practical pedagogy, including *Musical Dictation* (2 vols., 1887–89) and *Practical Harmony* (1888). In collaboration with the Rev. J. Ryland Kendrick, he compiled *Laudamus: A Hymnal* (1877). He also contributed English, French, and German articles to musical journals. His *Music in America,* the most interesting of his works, at the time of its publication was especially valuable in calling attention to a neglected subject. Its author was in various ways unfitted to treat his subject sympathetically and with the necessary breadth of viewpoint, and many of his conclusions are open to question, but the work was distinctly useful. His compositions included three symphonies, a symphonic poem, "Stella," a concert-overture, "Othello," concertos for piano and for 'cello, and a fantasia for bass-clarinet with orchestra, as well as some chamber-music—a string quartet, three piano quartets, and trios. They were all played in their day by orchestras and chamber-music organizations in New York, Brooklyn, and Boston. He also composed an organ fantasia and fugue, choral settings for the fourth, twenty-third, forty-sixth, and ninety-fifth Psalms, and more than a hundred songs. His wife, Frances (Raymond) Ritter (1840–1890), was known as an authoress and translator. Her writings include *Woman as a Musician: An Art-Historical Study* (1876), *Some Famous Songs: An Art-Historical Sketch* (1878), and a volume of poetry, *Songs and Ballads* (1887). She also made good translations of Ehlert's *Letters on Music, to a Lady* (1870), and of Schumann's *Music and Musicians* (1877). Gifted with a fine mezzo-soprano voice, she gave a successful series of historical song recitals in New York during the winter of 1869–70, in which she introduced a number of *lieder* and folksongs.

[See *Grove's Dict. of Music and Musicians*, 3rd ed., vol. IV (1928), and the *Am. Supp.*, vol. VI (1930); *Vassar Miscellany*, Oct. 1891; *N. Y. Times*, *N. Y. Tribune*, July 7, 1891.]   F. H. M.

RIVERA, LUIS JOSE MUNOZ [See MUNOZ-RIVERA, LUIS JOSE, 1859–1916].

RIVERS, WILLIAM JAMES (July 17, 1822–June 22, 1909), teacher and writer, was born in Charleston, S. C., the son of John David and Eliza Frances (Ridgewood) Rivers. He received his preparatory education there and was graduated in 1841 from the South Carolina College. He then returned to Charleston and established a private school, which he conducted with marked success, until he was elected in 1856 professor of Greek literature in South Carolina College. When this institution was reopened in 1865 as the University of South Carolina, he became professor of ancient languages and literature. In the summer of 1873 he resigned to accept the presidency of Washington College at Chestertown, Md., where he served until 1887. An excellent scholar and an enthusiastic and earnest teacher, he won the love and admiration of his students, to whom he was known as "Hoi Potamoi."

Besides his interest in classical studies, he was a careful student of the history of his native state. He was one of the founders, in 1855, and was the first corresponding secretary of the South Carolina Historical Society. His first contribution to the history of South Carolina was a small volume published in 1850 at Charleston, *Topics in the History of South Carolina.* Six years later he published his most important historical work, *A Sketch of the History of South Carolina to the Close of the Proprietary Government by the Revolution of 1719. With an Appendix Containing Many Valuable Records Hitherto Unpublished.* This work was prepared from abstracts of the papers in the Public Record Office in London, from the manuscript journals of the Commons House or Council, and from the few printed sources available. It has not been superseded. The volume entitled *A Chapter in the Early History of South Carolina*, published in 1874, appeared as a supplement to the book of 1856. Among his contributions to periodicals are three articles in *Russell's Magazine* on certain events in the history of the state, based on documents not used before. "Introduction of Printing into South Carolina" in September 1858, an article not signed but attributed to him by Salley (*post*, p. 4), "Attack on Charleston by the French and Spaniards in 1706," in the issue of August 1859, which he had had copied from the Public Record Office in London, and "The Carolina Regiment in the Expedition against St. Augustine in 1740," in the issue of September 1859. He also compiled the "Roll of Honor," a manuscript record of the soldiers of South Carolina who were killed or died in the Civil War, "the best piece of work done before or since" on these records (Salley, *post*, p. 6). In Justin Winsor's *Narrative and Critical History of America* he wrote the chapter on "The Carolinas" (vol. V, 1887). *Addresses and Other Occasional Pieces* was issued in 1893, when he had taken up his residence in Baltimore, where he remained with his family till his death. He was survived by five children. His wife Maria (Bancroft) Rivers died in 1901.

[A. A. Salley, *William J. Rivers* (1906); M. La-Borde, *Hist. of the S. C. College* (1859); E. L. Green, *A Hist. of the Univ. of S. C.* (1916); *Baltimore American*, June 24, 1909; *News and Courier* (Charleston), June 24, 1909.]   E. L. G.

RIVES, GEORGE LOCKHART (May 1, 1849–Aug. 18, 1917), lawyer and historian, born in New York City, blended in ancestry, character, and achievement the spirit of North and South in American life and letters. His father, Francis Robert Rives, was the son of William Cabell Rives [*q.v.*] of Virginia, a United States senator and minister to France. His mother, Matilda (Barclay), was the grand-daughter of Thomas Barclay [*q.v.*], British consul general at New York. After graduation from Columbia College in 1868 and from Trinity College, Cambridge, in 1872, Rives studied law at Columbia (LL.B. 1873), and in 1874 was admitted to the New York bar. In his early thirties he revealed a talent for organization and administration that brought him a succession of calls to public service in varying capacities. As a member from 1882 of the board of trustees of Columbia College, and as chairman of that body from 1903

to 1916, he had a significant share in the conversion of the institution into a university. As a trustee of the Astor Library, 1883–88, and of the Lenox Library, 1893–95, he was influential in their consolidation to form the New York Public Library, of which he was a trustee from 1895 and president from 1914. As assistant secretary of state of the United States from 1887 to 1889 he performed signal service in regulating the consular system and the business methods of the department. Chosen counsel for the first Rapid Transit Commission of New York City and a member of that body from 1896 to 1902, he handled with ability and success the intricate questions that arose in connection with the building of subways. The same distinction of effort and accomplishment marked his duties as president in 1900 of the commission appointed to revise the charter of Greater New York. From 1902 to 1904, as corporation counsel for that city, he undertook the task of redistributing and coördinating the legal services of the several boroughs.

As president of the board of governors of the New York Hospital and member of the Municipal Art Commission, of a committee to pass upon the qualifications of candidates for admission to the bar, and of numerous groups in charge of civic ceremonies and the affairs of charitable agencies, he evinced a like devotion to the welfare of the community.

Amid his many public functions, he found time for the composition of several volumes and a large number of articles on literature, history, biography and law. Foremost among his publications are: *An Essay on the Authorship of the First, Second and Third Parts of Henry the Sixth; Commonly Attributed to Shakespeare* (Cambridge and London, 1874), for which he was awarded the Harness Prize; *Selections from the Correspondence of Thomas Barclay* (1894); *The United States and Mexico, 1821–1848* (2 vols., 1913). Based upon authorities available in print and upon manuscript sources in Mexico, London, and Washington, the last-named work was the first comprehensive account of the subject, revealing its author as a scholar capable of applying the erudition acquired in other realms of thought to the narration and interpretation of historical events. It won for him admission to the American Academy of Arts and Letters.

Personally, Rives was a man whom in its finest sense the word "aristocrat" was altogether befitting. Distinguished in appearance, punctilious in deportment, he disliked publicity as he despised vulgarity. A Jeffersonian Democrat in political principles, he never was a candidate for office, centering his public interests in civic reform. By inclination and training a counsellor, rather than an orator or pleader, he exemplified in the spoken and written word a brevity and directness indicative of candor and sincerity no less than of wealth of knowledge and breadth of culture worthy of his heritage. He was twice married: on May 21, 1873, to Caroline Morris Kean, who died Mar. 29, 1887; and on Mar. 20, 1889, to Sara (Whiting) Belmont. From these marriages two sons and one daughter were born. He died at Newport, R. I.

[*Columbia Alumni News*, Sept. 28, 1917; *Columbia Univ. Quart.*, Sept. 1917; *N. Y. Times*, Aug. 19, 21, 23, 1917; S. H. Olin, "Memorial of George L. Rives," in *Asso. of the Bar of the City of N. Y., Year Book*, 1918, also pub. separately the same year; *Bull. N. Y. Pub. Lib.*, Sept. 1917; W. M. Sloane, *Commemorative Tribute to George Lockhart Rives* (Am. Acad. of Arts and Letters, 1922); *Who's Who in America*, 1916–17; Alexander Brown, *The Cabells and Their Kin* (1895).]
W. R. S—d.

RIVES, JOHN COOK (May 24, 1795–Apr. 10, 1864), journalist, was probably the son of George Rives of Franklin County, Va. At eleven years of age he went to Kentucky to live with his uncle, Samuel Casey. There he received a good frontier education before he went to Edwardsville, Ill., to work as a clerk in a branch of the Bank of the United States. About 1824 he became cashier in a bank in Shawneetown. Meantime he read law and was admitted to the bar, but he never practised. For three years he worked in the office of the *United States' Telegraph*, where he won the esteem of Duff Green who recommended him to Jackson in 1829 as a devoted Democrat entitled to his confidence and friendship. He was soon appointed to a clerkship in the fourth auditor's office and served there until on Apr. 11, 1832, he became an employee of Francis Preston Blair [*q.v.*] of the Washington *Daily Globe*. In 1833 he became a partner of Blair and the financial manager of the *Globe*. With the exception of a farm that he created out of lands known as "the Bladensburg races," everything he touched made profits. Upon the dissolution of the Blair-Rives partnership in the *Globe* in 1849 Rives received over $100,000 for his share. He maintained an expensive country estate with several slaves for the benefit of his children, whom he wanted to rear on a farm. He had the respect and confidence of the Democratic presidents from Jackson to Buchanan. He remained steadfastly an orthodox Democrat and spent his money freely for the party during presidential campaigns. Blair loved Rives so much that he entrusted his investments to him, and he is said to have asked for a dissolution of the firm of Blair and Rives to avoid any embarrassment to Rives, when Blair followed Van Buren into the Free-Soil party. Rives was one of the most philanthropic citizens of Washington, D. C., during his successful business career. In one year he gave over $17,000 to widows and orphans. As an editor he wrote in a facetious, forceful, and graphic style. He filled the editorial columns of the *Globe,* when Blair felt indisposed to write. Blair attacked the powerful political enemies in a vitriolic fashion, while Rives in his short editorials damned the recalcitrant small fry of his party with faint praise. He often produced fake defenses purposely to ruin the disloyal Democratic politicians.

His great contribution was the *Congressional Globe.* His was the idea of reporting the congressional debates impartially. For thirty years from Dec. 2, 1833, to Apr. 10, 1864, he published them, and his son Franklin continued the work until the beginning of the *Congressional Record* in 1873 by act of Congress. In 1842 he became a partner of Peter Force [*q.v.*] in publishing the documentary sources of the American Revolution. He was a loyal Union man, opposed to slavery in principle, but he denied the right of the national government to force the abolition of slavery. He agreed with Clay on internal improvements and foreign affairs. His big rugged body and deep voice were remembered by those who once met him. He was six feet five inches high and weighed normally two hundred and forty pounds. At the age of thirty-eight he married Mary, one of his bindery girls. She died in 1859, the mother of seven children. By will the *Globe* was left to two of the sons, Franklin and Jefferson, over $50,000 in bonds were divided among his other five children, and his farm was left to his family with the specification that it should revert to the government if his descendants refused to live on it

[Blair Papers in possession of Gist Blair, Washington, D. C.; Blair-Rives Papers, Lib. of Cong.; Records in Supreme Court Bldg., Washington, D. C. Records in Congressional Cemetery; Rives vault in Congressional Cemetery; W. B. Bryan, *A History of the National Capital* (1916), vol. I; Frederic Hudson, *Journalism in the United States from 1690 to 1872* (1873); R. R. Wilson, *Washington the Capital City* (2 vols., 1901); J. R. Childs, *Reliques of the Rives* (1929); *Daily Globe* (Washington), June 23, 1856.]
W. E. S.

RIVES, WILLIAM CABELL (May 4, 1793– Apr. 25, 1868), political leader in Virginia and minister to France, was the son of Robert and Margaret Jordan (Cabell) Rives. Robert Rives served as a private at the battle of Yorktown and at the close of the Revolution entered commercial pursuits. In 1790 he married the daughter of Col. William Cabell [q.v.] of "Union Hill," Amherst County, Va. The young couple resided with the wife's family while the husband was building his own home at "Warminster," also in Amherst County. In 1791 the Rives family took up residence at the new estate, but their third child, William Cabell, was born at "Union Hill." He was educated at Hampden-Sidney College and the College of William and Mary, being graduated from the latter in 1809. During the next few years he studied law and politics under Thomas Jefferson. In 1814 he acted as aide to Gen. John H. Cocke who was then commanding troops on the Chickahominy (A. C. Gordon, *William FitzHugh Gordon*, 1909, pp. 81–82); and in 1816 he represented Nelson County (formed from Amherst) in the constitutional convention held at Staunton. His apprenticeship in politics was served from 1817 to 1821 as representative of Nelson County in the House of Delegates.

It was during this period, on Mar. 24, 1819, that he was married to Judith Page Walker, of Albemarle County, the daughter of Francis Walker and grand-daughter of Dr. Thomas Walker [q.v.]. The seat of the Walker family at "Castle Hill" near Charlottesville soon became the home of the young Rives family also, and as Mrs. Rives became heir to the property, it remained their home as long as they both lived. In 1822 Rives was sent to represent Albemarle County in the House of Delegates, and in 1823 he was elected to the federal House of Representatives. In this position he remained until 1829. These were the years during which the Jackson movement was organized and carried to national success, and Rives became an important member of the Ritchie group of politicians who bore the banner of Democracy in Virginia. So acceptable were his services that President Jackson sent him to France in 1829 as minister of the United States. It was he who handled the negotiations leading to the conclusion of the famous indemnity treaty with that country in 1831; and so amicable were his relations with the French court, that Queen Amélie stood godmother to his eldest daughter at christening and conferred her own name upon the child.

Returning to the United States, Rives was elected to the United States Senate in 1832. It was only after he had declared his principles to be "anti-bank, anti-tariff and anti-nullification" that the opposition in the Virginia legislature subsided and the election was carried through with few dissenting votes (H. H. Simms, *The Rise of the Whigs in Virginia*,

1929, p. 64). But issues were not so easily settled, and in 1834 the Assembly passed resolutions instructing the Virginia senators to take a stand against Jackson's removal of the federal deposits from the Bank of the United States. Since Rives approved of the removal, he resigned his seat rather than obey instructions. Before the Baltimore convention of 1835, he was a strong candidate for the vice-presidential nomination, but New York deserted him and Richard M. Johnson became the running mate of Van Buren (C. H. Ambler, *Thomas Ritchie*, 1913, pp. 170–71). The next year John Tyler resigned his seat in the Senate when instructed to support Benton's expunging resolution, and Rives was elected to replace him. Up to this time Rives had supported all the principal measures of the Jackson administration, but he expressed dissatisfaction with the specie circular and came out squarely against Van Buren's subtreasury system. His followers in Virginia, calling themselves "Conservatives," insisted that the federal monies should be deposited in the state banks (*Ibid.*, pp. 193–97). They acted as a separate political group. Rives's term in the Senate expired in 1839 and he became a candidate to succeed himself, opposed by John Tyler the regular Whig candidate, and John Y. Mason, the regular Democrat. Many of the Whigs now deserted Tyler and threw their support to Rives, but a few of them refused to do so, and no election was effected either that year or the next. During the struggle it was revealed that Henry Clay was supporting the move to draw Rives into the Whig fold, and he even made a proposition to Tyler to secure his nomination for the vice-presidency in 1840 if he would withdraw from the senatorial race and acquiesce in the election of Rives. It appears that Tyler did not give assent to this bargain, but it nevertheless happened that he was nominated for the vice-presidency in 1840, and Rives was elected to the Senate in 1841 (L. G. Tyler, *Letters and Times of the Tylers*, vol. I, 1884, pp. 587–93). In 1840 Rives backed Harrison for the presidency, but in 1841 he stood with Tyler in his struggle with Clay on the bank question (Henry A. Wise, *Seven Decades of the Union*, 1872, p. 187), and he did not become a full-fledged Whig until 1844, when he supported Clay (J. W. Bell, *Memoirs of Governor William Smith of Virginia*, 1891, pp. 19–21).

In 1845 his term in the Senate expired and he retired to private life for several years beginning during this period his voluminous work on the life of James Madison. From 1849 until 1853 he served again as minister to France, and it is said that the horrible effects of civil war which he witnessed at that time helped to set his mind upon peace when the crisis came between the sections of his own country a few years later. In 1861 he was a member of the peace convention which met in Washington at the instance of Virginia. During the same year he was a member of the Virginia convention to decide upon the course which the state should take in the crisis. He published an address opposing secession as unjustifiable under the circumstances, but declaring that Virginia would join the Southern group if the federal government should attempt to coerce the seceded states. This platform was adopted by the convention. After Virginia had seceded, Rives sat as a member of the Confederate Provisional Congress at Montgomery, and later as a member of the first regular Congress of the Confederacy, but his health gave way and he resigned in 1862. He died at "Castle Hill" and is interred in the private burying plot of that estate.

In addition to his political activities, Rives had a wide range of intellectual interests. He published a *Discourse ... on the Ethics of Christianity* (1855) and a *Discourse on the Character and Services of John Hampden* (1855), but his principal literary work is the *History of the Life and Times of James Madison* (3 vols., 1859–68), which ends with the year 1797. It was taken in considerable detail from the documents, was written with dignity and sound scholarship, and remains the classic treatment of the subject. He venerated the ideals of the "Fathers" and strove constantly to follow in their footsteps.

["William Cabell Rives, A Biography," by R. S. Wingfield, in *Richmond Coll. Hist. Papers*, vol. I (1915), no. 1, gives a brief survey of his life. There is additional personal material in Alexander Brown, *The Cabells and Their Kin* (1895), pp. 407–14. The notice in the *Biog. Directory of the Am. Congress* (1928), gives the date of his birth as May 4, 1792, but the dates of birth, marriage, and death as given above were verified from family records by the Princess Troubetzkoy of "Castle Hill," his grand-daughter. There is an obituary in the *Richmond Whig*, Apr. 28, 1868.]   T. P. A.

RIVINGTON, JAMES (1724–July 4, 1802), bookseller, printer, journalist, born in London, was the sixth son of Charles Rivington (1688–1742), a native of Chesterfield in Derbyshire, founder of the London publishing house of Rivington, and his wife, Eleanor Pease, of Newcastle-on-Tyne. James and his brother John (1720–92) continued their father's business in St. Paul's Churchyard till March 1756, when James formed a partnership with James Fletcher, Jr., in the same neighborhood. This firm reaped ten thousand pounds profit from the publication of Smollett's *History of England,* and otherwise

prospered. Success was Rivington's undoing. He neglected his affairs, played the races at Newmarket, and otherwise endangered his fortune in high living. Though a supposed bankrupt, he paid his creditors in full and had capital left over for himself. But this experience induced him to remove to America in 1760, where he opened a bookstore in Market Street, Philadelphia, and on Sept. 25 of that year he also "opened a Store at the House of the late Doctor Ascough, in Hanover Square," New York (Parker's *Post-Boy,* Oct. 2, 1760), and offered to supply "all public libraries" as well as individuals with imported books from England (*Post-Boy,* Nov. 10). He was the "only London book-seller in America" and the principal importer of English books. In 1761 he had as a partner Samuel Brown, son-in-law of Henry De Foreest, the first native printer of New York. They sold general merchandise as well as books. In 1763 they "opened a very elegant Picture Gallery, exhibiting the finest Collection of Pictures that ever were seen in America," to be sold "exceedingly cheap" (*Post-Boy,* June 2).

Rivington extended his chain of stores to King Street in Boston, in 1762, conducting this place in partnership with William Miller, a Scotchman, until the latter's death in 1765 (Fleet's *Boston Evening Post,* Feb. 18, 1765). It was about this time that Rivington confined his business interests to New York. But in June 1766 he was resident at Annapolis, as the proprietor of "The Maryland Lottery," a land scheme for which he issued 8,000 tickets (*Post-Boy,* Feb. 27, June 19, 1766). He became again a bankrupt, but soon recovered, and in 1767 the firm was J. Rivington & Company. In November 1768 Rivington moved his shop from Hanover Square to the lower end of Wall Street. At this time he published the poetical works of Charles Churchill, for which he had 2,200 advance subscriptions (Gaine's *New-York Mercury,* Nov. 21, 1768). He was admitted a freeman of the city of New York in January 1769.

Rivington married twice: first, on Sept. 14, 1752, Elizabeth, a daughter of Thomas Minshull of Charlton Hall, Manchester, by whom he had one child that died in infancy; and second, in March 1769, Elizabeth Van Horne, a lady of good connections, by whom he had two sons and a daughter. She died much lamented on July 18, 1795 (New York *Daily Advertiser,* July 21, 1795). It was as the result of his second union that he steadied himself and expanded his influence and business. In 1773 he added a printery, where he printed for himself and others. On Mar. 18, 1773, he announced his chief project, a newspaper, in a preliminary issue, gratis, which was followed on Apr. 22 with the first regular issue of *Rivington's New-York Gazetteer; or the Connecticut, New Jersey, Hudson's River, and Quebec Weekly Advertiser*. This newspaper was a departure in American journalism. In its purpose it catered to every human interest, and Isaiah Thomas (*post*, II, p. 123) said "few men, perhaps, were better qualified . . . to publish a newspaper," and "no newspaper in the colonies was better printed, or was more copiously furnished with foreign intelligence." In tabular matter, ornament borders, cuts, alignment, registration, and other typographical niceties it excelled. He announced his editorial policy as "never to admit any Performance, calculated to injure Virtue, Religion or other public Happiness, to wound a Neighbour's Reputation, or to raise a Blush in the face of Virgin Innocence." Furthermore, he proposed to print both sides of a question, which he did in the tea-act controversy, and he printed all the tracts in the bitter Westchester Farmer tract war, in which Alexander Hamilton made his political début. When the newspaper was little more than a year old its circulation was 3,600 copies, and was, as he says, "constantly distributed thro' every colony of North-America, most of the English, French, Spanish, Dutch, and Danish West India islands, the principal cities and towns of Great Britain, France, Ireland, and the Mediterranean" (*Gazeteer*, Oct. 13, 1774).

Rivington's open policy became offensive to the Sons of Liberty, of whom Isaac Sears was the New York leader. He had not spared Sears in their warfare of words. Several Whig meetings condemned Rivington's policy, and in 1775 the popular resentment reached a climax. On Nov. 27 of that year, a party of the Sons of Liberty from Connecticut attacked and ruined his printing plant, notwithstanding he had, after a previous arrest, signed the "General Association" of the Whigs. He left New York for London in the ship *Sansom* in January 1776 and after more than a year abroad returned with a new printing plant and appointment as the King's printer in New York. He resumed publication of his newspaper on Oct. 4, 1777, with a decidedly altered policy and in the Loyalist interest. He continued it, with varying names, to Number 758, Dec. 31, 1783. From May 1778 through July 1783, Rivington managed with the other printers of newspapers in New York to establish a mutual daily gazette, first for five and then for six days a week, an arrangement that produced virtually the first daily newspaper in America.

After the British evacuation in 1783, Rivington was allowed to continue in the United States, it is believed on account of his apologies and, as alleged, because of secret aid given to Washington's spies during the British occupancy, but his existence was worse than exile. He was obliged a few weeks later to discontinue his printery and was also given a violent beating by Nicholas Cruger in reprisal. In the spring of 1797 Rivington was in a debtor's prison for the debts of others. He held the British sympathy till the end, and Sir Guy Carleton, the last of the British commanders at New York, gave his sons, John and James, who had seen no active service, the benefit of half pay for life through commissions in the British army in 1783. The father gave up printing, but continued some years as a New York bookseller and stationer. He failed again, and died poor, after an illness of a few days, on Independence Day, 1802. Rivington Street in the city was named for him. Thomas estimated him as "possessed of good talents," having "polite manners," and being "well informed." To his gentlemanly qualities "he added benevolence, vivacity," and "punctuality in his business." In his better days he is said to have dressed gaudily and well. His fine face is preserved in Gilbert Stuart's portrait in the New York Historical Society.

[The newspapers of Rivington and his contemporaries are primary sources. Other principal accounts, more or less reliable, are: Henry Curwen, *A Hist. of Booksellers* (n.d.), containing a chapter on the Rivingtons, reprinted with revisions and a genealogy by Septimus Rivington in *The Publishing House of Rivington* (1894), and expanded with additions as *The Publishing Family of Rivington* (1919); H. R. Plomer and others, *A Dict. of the Printers and Booksellers . . . 1726 to 1775* (1932); Isaiah Thomas, *The Hist. of Printing in America* (2 vols., 1874); C. R. Hildeburn, *Sketches of Printers and Printing in Colonial N. Y.* (1895), and the *N. Y. Herald*, July 7, 1802. A complete record of his newspaper is given by C. S. Brigham, in *Proc. Am. Antiquarian Soc.*, n.s. vol. XXVII (1917). A. M. Lee in *Editor & Publisher*, Mar. 10, 1934, clarifies his leadership in New York journalism. G. W. P. Custis in *Recollections and Private Memoirs of Washington* (1860), ed. by J. B. Lossing, reveals Rivington's spy work for Washington, but this is modified by Morton Pennypacker's unpublished account furnished to the author from the former's "Gen. Washington's Spies on Long Island and in New York." J. W. Francis has a personal description of Rivington in *Old New York* (1858), p. 119. The best file of his newspaper is in the N. Y. Hist. Soc.]   V. H. P.

RIX, JULIAN WALBRIDGE (Dec. 30, 1850–Nov. 24, 1903), landscape painter, etcher, was born at Peacham, Vt., the son of Alfred and Maria Chastina (Walbridge) Rix, and a descendant of Thomas Rix who settled in Salem, Mass., before 1649. Early in life Julian went West. He obtained employment in San Francisco as an errand boy for a paint store, and soon began to decorate the walls with drawings. His parents evidently refused to aid him, for in his will he referred to a time when "my own relatives and family did not put forth a helping hand to me" (Rix, *post*, p. 94). Thus, instead of attending an art school, he became a sign and decorative painter. He loved outdoor life and especially admired the beauty of the California coast; it was quite natural, therefore, for him to turn his artistic talent to landscape painting. He began his career in 1875 with black and white sketches of local scenery, and though he later did water colors and oil paintings with equal skill, he continued to work also in black and white, making etchings until the time of his death. In 1888, after he had gained recognition in the West, he was induced by William Ryle, a Paterson visitor in San Francisco, to try his luck in the East. Accordingly, Rix opened a studio, first in Paterson, N. J., then in New York City, and soon began to attract attention by his excellent work. Some of his most notable landscapes were painted in his summer studio on the Ryle estate at North Caldwell, N. J.

Rix's earlier etchings and paintings were on subjects found in California, and among these is his well-known "Golden Gate." Later he chose subjects from New Jersey and other parts of the East, notably Maine. Like Jules Tavernier, whose work must have influenced his own, he loved to paint deep shadows, gray skies, and shady trees. He tried to put what he called "feeling" and atmosphere into his work (*International Studio*, April 1901, p. 149), destroying many of his earlier pictures because he felt that they lacked the proper atmospheric effect. He also made a number of fine etchings to illustrate articles on California for *Harper's Magazine* (see issue for October 1889) and *Harper's Weekly*. Among his notable paintings may be mentioned: "Pompton Plains, New Jersey" (1898), in the Corcoran Gallery of Art, Washington; "Noon-Day," a fine study of the effect of sunlight on trees and a winding country lane; "Sunset, California Coast"; "High Tide, Coast of Maine"; "The Woodland Spring, Mike Marr's Camp, Moosehead, Maine"; and "St. John's Harbor" (1903). His work is to be found in private collections in Baltimore, New York, Paterson, and Rochester.

Rix is described by intimate friends as exceptionally good-natured, a Bohemian, and something of a raconteur. He liked to travel, going back and forth between New York and San Francisco quite frequently. He never married. He died in New York City and was buried in the Ryle plot in Cedar Lawn Cemetery, Paterson, N. J. In his will (Rix, *post*, p. 93), he requested that Thomas B. Clarke, art connoisseur, examine all his paintings and "destroy any which, in his judgment, is not worthy of my name."

[G. S. Rix, *Hist. and Geneal. of the Rix Family* (1906); *International Studio*, Apr. 1901; *N. Y. Herald*, Nov. 25, 1903; *Morning Call* (Paterson, N. J.), Nov. 24, 1903; *Newark Evening News*, Nov. 29, 1903; *N. Y. Times*, Nov. 25, 1903; date of birth from tombstone; certain information from intimate friends.]

J. E. F.

ROACH, JOHN (Dec. 25, 1813–Jan. 10, 1887), shipbuilder, was born at Mitchelstown, County Cork, Ireland, the son of Patrick and Abigail (Meany) Roche. At the age of sixteen he came to the United States. When he was naturalized, Nov. 8, 1842, the clerk of the court spelled his name Roach, and since the mistake was not corrected he bore that name thereafter. He settled in Howell, N. J., and learned the trade of an iron moulder at the Howell Iron Works operated by James P. Allaire [*q.v.*]. In 1840, he took a part of his savings, which had been placed in the hands of his employer, and went to Illinois, where he made the first payment on a farm near the site of the present Peoria. Soon afterward his employer failed, and Roach lost his land. Returning to New York, in association with other mechanics he purchased a small iron works in New York City of which within a few years he became the sole owner. In 1856, he bought the land which his foundry occupied and added to his plant, but shortly afterward the shops were wrecked by a boiler explosion. Roach now found himself practically penniless, but his ability and integrity enabled him to borrow capital, and his business was resumed. In 1860 he obtained the contract for constructing an iron drawbridge over the Harlem River in New York City and thereafter he prospered so that by the end of the Civil War his foundry and engine works was one of the best equipped in the United States.

Among the first to recognize the importance of the shift from wooden to iron vessels and its possible effects upon the American merchant marine, he sent a representative to England to make a careful study of the methods of iron shipbuilding on the Clyde. In 1868, he began to carry out plans for the development of an iron shipbuilding industry in the United States, purchasing a number of small marine-engine plants in and near New York City, and consolidating them with the Morgan Iron Works, which he had purchased from G. W. Quintard [*q.v.*]. Three years later he transferred his headquarters to Chester, Pa., acquiring the ship yard of Reany, Son & Archbold. Here he engaged in iron shipbuilding on a large scale. Among the iron vessels he built for the foreign service were the *City* of *Peking* and the *City of Tokio,* built in 1874 for the Pacific Mail Steamship Company, up to that time the largest steamers constructed in the United States. He was of great service to the federal government in the development of new types of marine engines, being among the first to recognize the superiority of compound engines for marine work. He was authorized by the Navy Department, as an experiment, to install the first of such engines built in the United States in the *Tennessee.* The success of this effort demonstrated the value of this improvement and Roach was given contracts to install compound engines in other naval vessels. The first ships constructed by him for the government were the sloops-of-war *Alert* and *Huron,* launched in 1874. He next built the sectional dry-dock at Pensacola, Fla., and then, in 1876, received the contracts for the monitors *Miantonomoh* and *Puritan.* In 1883, the construction of the dispatch boat *Dolphin* and the cruisers *Atlanta, Boston,* and *Chicago* was begun. When the *Dolphin* was completed the vessel was accepted by the Naval Advisory Board but for political reasons the secretary of the navy refused to accept their decision and cancelled the contract for the three cruisers (*House Report 2166,* 51 Cong., 1 Sess.). Fearing that this action might possibly result in embarrassment to his bondsmen and creditors, and because of his own failing health, he decided to close his works, and accordingly made an assignment on July 18, 1885, though he was perfectly solvent. The matter was later adjusted, but he never again took an active part in the business.

While not the first to build iron vessels in the United States, Roach launched 126 such vessels from his yard between 1872 and 1886 (Duffield, *post*), and deserves the title of "father of iron shipbuilding in America" which has often been accorded him. He was active in awakening public opinion in favor of an American merchant marine and became perhaps the most influential and most highly respected authority on this subject in the country. In 1836, he married Emeline Johnson and they had nine children, of whom five survived their father. He died in New York City.

[H. B. Grose, *John Roach* (n.d.); U. G. Duffield, *Souvenir of Roach's Shipyard, . . . Chester, Pa.* (1895); L. M. Williamson, *Prominent and Progressive Pennsylvanians of the Nineteenth Century* (1898), vol. I; Henry Hall, *America's Successful Men of Affairs,* vol. I (1895); J. H. Martin, *Chester (and Its Vicinity), Delaware County, in Pa.* (1877); J. M. Swank, *Intro. to a Hist. of Ironmaking and Coal Mining in Pa.* (1878); Henry Hall, "Ship-Building Industry in the U. S.," in *Census Reports, 10th Census,* vol. VIII (1884), being *House Misc. Doc. 42,* pt. 8, 47 Cong., 2 Sess.; *N. Y. Times* and *Public Ledger* (Phila.), Jan.

11, 1887; family records in possession of Wm. M. Roche, Chester, Pa.]
J. H. F.

ROANE, ARCHIBALD (1759–Jan. 4, 1819), second governor of Tennessee, was born in Derry township, Lancaster (now Dauphin) County, Pa., the son of Andrew and Margaret (Walker) Roane. His father, a weaver, who had emigrated from Ireland in 1739, died when the lad was but eight years of age, and his death was followed shortly by that of his wife. Left thus an orphan, the child became the ward of his uncle, John Roane, a Presbyterian clergyman, who gave him a careful education (Margaret C. Pilcher, *Historical Sketches of the Campbell, Pilcher and Kindred Families,* 1911, pp. 121–22). Having studied law, young Archibald, under what inspiration we do not know, turned his face toward the frontier country of the Southwest where lawyers were in great demand. For a time he made his home at Liberty Hall, Rockbridge County, Va., where the Presbyterians maintained an academy. It was possibly here that he met Anne Campbell, daughter to David and Mary Hamilton Campbell of Virginia, who became his wife. In any event, it is clear that he became associated with some of the leading men of the Southwest on his first arrival in that region. In 1787, along with another budding lawyer of the frontier, Andrew Jackson, he signed a petition wherein the people of western North Carolina asked that state to grant them independence (Walter Clark, ed., *The State Records of North Carolina,* vol. XXII, 1907, p. 708). The following year he and Jackson were simultaneously granted permission to practise their profession before the court of Washington County, then in North Carolina, now in East Tennessee (John Allison, *Dropped Stitches in Tennessee History,* 1897, p. 4). When in 1790 Tennessee became a territory of the United States, Roane became attorney-general for the district of Hamilton, while Jackson occupied the same position in Mero district. When the territory became a state in 1796, Roane was a member of the convention which framed her constitution, and immediately thereafter he was placed upon the bench of the superior court of errors and appeals. In 1801 he was elected governor (James Phelan, *History of Tennessee,* 1888, pp. 186, 200, 242).

His term of office proved most dramatic. John Sevier, who had preceded him as governor, ran against Andrew Jackson, now a judge of the superior court, for the major-generalship of militia. The vote was tied and Roane, as governor, decided the contest in favor of Jackson. In connection with this election, charges of corruption were brought against Sevier by Roane and Jackson, and bitter enmities were engendered. In 1803 Sevier ran against Roane for the governorship and defeated him. This vindication by the people has generally been accepted as adequate acquittal of Sevier, but the evidence is strongly in favor of the case which Roane and Jackson made against the popular hero. The whole incident, however, seems to have been merely a matter of politics for all concerned. The state was divided into two factions, one adhering to Sevier, the other following Senator William Blount who had been governor of the territory. Jackson and Roane were of the Blount faction, and when Sevier came back into office in 1803, Roane retired to private life for a number of years. In 1811, with the Blount faction back in power under the leadership of Willie Blount, Roane became a circuit judge, and in 1815 he was once again placed upon the bench of the superior court. He died in 1819.

Roane was a man of good education, reflective habits of mind, and quiet demeanor. While endowed with a commanding physique, he was not marked by the crude virility, the military glamor, nor the ardent temperament which characterized the figures of most of the western heroes (W. H. Egle, *Pennsylvania Genealogies: Scotch-Irish and German*, 1886, p. 541). Sound intellect and good connections accomplished for him what very different qualities accomplished for others.

[Roane's connection with the Jackson-Sevier embroglio has been widely noticed, but other phases of his career have been left in comparative obscurity. The best brief account of him is in J. W. Caldwell, *Sketches of the Bench and Bar of Tenn.* (1898), pp. 19–21. His political career is discussed in T. P. Abernethy, *From Frontier to Plantation in Tenn.* (1932), ch. X. There is an obituary in the *Nashville Whig*, Jan. 16, 1819. The monument erected in 1918 at Pleasant Forest Graveyard, Campbell Sta., Knox County, Tenn., bears the dates 1759–1819.]   T. P. A.

ROANE, JOHN SELDEN (Jan. 8, 1817–Apr. 8, 1867), planter, lawyer, public official, soldier, was born in Wilson County, Tenn., the son of Hugh and Hannah (Calhoun) Roane. He was descended from Rev. Andrew Roane (or Rowan), who moved from Lanarkshire to Ulster, Ireland, in 1561, through Andrew Roane, who settled in Pennsylvania shortly before the middle of the eighteenth century. Descendants moved from there to North Carolina, following the Scotch-Irish drift southward. When the settlement of the "state of Franklin" began, Hugh Roane took his family into that region, and there John Selden Roane grew up. He attended Cumberland College, Princeton, Ky., and followed an elder brother to Arkansas, settling at Pine

Bluff. In 1842, when he was twenty-five, he moved to Van Buren, and two years later was sent to the legislature and elected speaker. At the outbreak of the Mexican War he volunteered and was mustered in as lieutenant-colonel of Archibald Yell's regiment. At the battle of Buena Vista, where Colonel Yell was killed, the regiment became disordered but Roane took command, restored order, and contributed to the victory. Later he fought a bloodless duel with Albert Pike [q.v.] because of Pike's criticism of his conduct in this battle. After the war he settled again at Pine Bluff and engaged in planting.

Elected governor Apr. 19, 1849, at a special election held to fill the vacancy caused by the resignation of Gov. T. S. Drew because of the low salary, he served until 1852, when he was succeeded by Elias Nelson Conway [q.v.]. His administration came during a critical period in national politics and he warmly espoused the Southern side of the controversy (Message to the legislature, Nov. 5, 1850, *Journal of the House of Representatives for the Eighth Session*, 1851, pp. 37 ff.). In state affairs he favored a geological survey, recognition and settlement of the debt growing out of the failure of the state banks, use of the lands granted by Congress for internal improvements to promote railroad building, and education. Naturally he indorsed Memphis as the starting point of the proposed Pacific railroad. He utterly condemned the legislative policy of 1848 for dividing the proceeds of the internal improvement lands among the counties and advised a state system of roads; this advice was finally adopted in 1927. He held that there could be "no higher or more holy obligation resting upon the law-making power, than the encouragement of Education," but said that the common-school system of New England was unsuited to a frontier community and condemned the distribution of the proceeds of the seminary funds among the counties, advising instead the establishment of seminaries in different parts of the state (*Ibid.*, pp. 31–33).

In 1861 he opposed secession, but on the outbreak of war volunteered and was commissioned brigadier-general Mar. 20, 1862. For a brief period he was in chief command of Arkansas, but was soon superseded by Gen. T. C. Hindman [q.v.], to whom he rendered valuable assistance in the battle of Prairie Grove. He continued in the service in Arkansas, Louisiana, and Texas until the end of the war and then retired to his home at Pine Bluff. On July 5, 1855, he married Mary K. Smith, who bore him three daughters and one son. He died at the age of fifty, and was buried in Oakland Cemetery, Little Rock.

[Fay Hempstead, *Hist. Rev. of Ark.* (1911), vol. I; D. T. Herndon, *Centennial Hist. of Ark.* (1922), vol. I; D. Y. Thomas, *Ark. in War and Reconstruction* (1926); C. A. Evans, *Confed. Mil. Hist.* (1899), vol. X; F. W. Allsopp, *Albert Pike: A Biog.* (1928); *War of the Rebellion: Official Records* (Army); *Daily Ark. Gazette* (Little Rock), Apr. 10, 1867; genealogical information from M. L. Bell, a grandson.]

D. Y. T.

ROANE, SPENCER (Apr. 4, 1762–Sept. 4, 1822), jurist and political writer, was born in Essex County, Va., about fifty miles northeast of Richmond. His parents were of good stock, widely connected and locally important: his mother was the daughter of Col. Spencer Ball, though apparently not Judith Ball, as sometimes stated (*William and Mary College Quarterly*, Apr. 1910, p. 265); and his father, William Roane (the son of William Roane, who came to America in 1741, one of four sterling Scotch immigrant brothers), was a burgess and a Revolutionary volunteer. From Scotch tutors at home and academic courses at the College of William and Mary, where he was active in the Phi Beta Kappa Society, Spencer Roane gained a broadened outlook and an abiding liking for good literature. Simultaneously, devotion to personal liberty and hostility to special privileges were being fixed in his mind as first principles of good government by his father's admiring talk of Patrick Henry and the reading of current political writings, especially George Mason's Declaration of Rights and Jefferson's bill for establishing religious freedom, which he later often called "sublime." The lectures of George Wythe [*q.v.*], some instruction in Philadelphia, and much reading at home, especially of Coke, fitted him for the bar, to which he was admitted in 1782. While in the House of Delegates (1783, 1784) he roomed with Richard Henry Lee, served on committees with John Marshall and Patrick Henry, and voted rather independently though oftenest with Henry. Elected by the legislature to the Council of State at twenty-two, he was for two years an advisor to Governor Henry, whose eldest daughter, Anne, he married Sept. 7, 1786, with Henry's warm approval and promise of financial assistance. He preferred amendment of the Articles of Confederation to the proposed federal Constitution and as "A Plain Dealer" attacked Governor Edmund Randolph for wavering in the matter (P. L. Ford, *Essays on the Constitution*, 1892, p. 387); but when the Constitution had been ratified and clarified by amendment he strongly supported it.

After two sessions in the state Senate, in 1788 and 1789, he became in 1789 a judge of the General Court. Having tried cases for five years, in all parts of the state and before an able bar, he was elected by the legislature in 1794, at thirty-two, to the supreme court of appeals, whose other members were elderly and distinguished men. Of his twenty-seven years' service here the report of competent observers and scholars is: that he read widely; that he attacked each case eagerly and penetratingly and, insisting upon individual judgment and responsibility, wrote clear and vigorous opinions on most of them; that his opinions were generally sound, strongest in constitutional law, inclining (though not unfairly) to the side of liberty rather than property, mindful of precedent and the law as a science but also keenly alert to the public policies of his own progressive age. In 1793 he had upheld the right of the General Court to declare void an unconstitutional act of the legislature (*Kamper* vs. *Hawkins, 1 Virginia Cases,* 20); he supported the legislature's right to deprive the clergy of their glebes notwithstanding his belief in the political value of religion (*Turpin* vs. *Lockett, 6 Call,* 113); he approved the manumission of slaves according to "the policy of the country" (*Pleasants* vs. *Pleasants, 2 Call,* 344). Though his warm temper and the energy of his character sometimes brought discord into the court, he was admitted to be (certainly after the death of Pendleton in 1803) its ablest member and the stoutest defender of its independence against legislative imposition as well as the federal Supreme Court's assertion of superiority.

Simultaneously, Roane was becoming politically important. A strict constructionist, like most of Henry's old following, he had damned the Alien and Sedition Acts and supported positively the Virginia Resolutions of 1798 and Report of 1799. He felt that the latter contained "the renewed sense of the people of Virginia" (4 *Munford,* 29), and regarded Jefferson's election as a ratification of their doctrines. Though Federalist tactics prevented his becoming federal chief justice, as Jefferson desired (*American Historical Review,* July 1907, p. 776), he founded the Richmond *Enquirer* (1804) and with its editor, his cousin Thomas Ritchie [*q.v.*], and President Brockenbrough of the Virginia State Bank (the "Essex Junto"), supported Madison and union in 1808 and Madison and war in 1812. Support of the Union against foreign powers, however, by no means implied acceptance of internal consolidation—especially when it came through the devices, which he regarded as insidious and usurping, of the federal Supreme Court under John Marshall. In the Fairfax case (4 *Munford,* 3) his court flatly refused (1815) to execute the federal court's order. Less dramatic but more important because he led a reaction now becoming nation-wide (Charles Warren, *The Supreme Court in United States History*, 1922, vol. II, ch. 13) were his articles signed "Amphictyon," "Hampden," and "Algernon Sidney" in the *Enquirer* of May and June 1819, and May 1821 (reprinted in *Branch Historical Papers, post*, 1905, 1906). Being opinion-building in intent, these articles were lengthy and not without extreme and sometimes abusive language. As any one but "a deplorable idiot" could see, he said, "there is no earthly difference between an *unlimited* grant of power and a grant limited in its terms, but accompanied with *unlimited* means of carrying it into execution" (*Ibid.*, June 1905, p. 80). The federal Supreme Court, being not "master" but "subordinate agent," should be corrected by the sovereign people through the interposition of the states— though, of course, only on occasions "deeply and essentially affecting the vital principles of their political system" (*Ibid.*, p. 60). Heartily approved by many Republican leaders, including Jefferson, these articles estranged certain others; they frightened without converting John Marshall; they led to fruitless legislative resolutions seeking constitutional amendment; they reinvigorated the extreme state-rights theory. Though some have deemed Roane a disunionist and a father of secession, he himself described his position as "entirely federal"; he had in mind, no doubt, a Union of dignified and powerful states, each able to protect individual freedom and initiative against mere numbers or wealth.

Roane maintained at "Spring Garden" in Hanover County a good-sized estate which he supervised with interest and practical intelligence; here he lived after moving from Essex about 1802 until he went to Richmond, where about 1815 he built a substantial residence close by John Marshall's. Continually interested in the details of state government, he has sometimes been pictured as a state boss. None, however, has accused him of seeking personal profit therefrom; and undue interference awaits printed proof. After his first wife's death in 1799 he married Elizabeth Hoskins but without any lessening of affectionate and practical interest in his nine living children by the former, one of whom, William H. Roane, he rejoiced to see seated in Congress. Keen-minded and self-possessed to the end, he died at the Virginia Warm Springs of a "lingering indisposition" from which he had long suffered.

[*The John P. Branch Hist. Papers of Randolph-Macon College*, June 1904, June 1905, June 1906, especially June 1905, containing a biographical sketch by E. J. Smith and some of Roane's newspaper articles and private letters; *Va. Law Register*, Nov. 1896, containing a youthful portrait and a useful sketch by T. R. B. Wright based partly on the *Richmond Enquirer*, Sept. 13, 17, 1822; W. W. Henry, *Patrick Henry* (1891), vol. II, especially the autobiographical material in Roane's recollections of Henry; W. E. Dodd, "Chief Justice Marshall and Virginia," in *Am. Hist. Review*, July 1907; D. J. Mays, *Sketch of Judge Spencer Roane* (1929) reprinted from *Proc. of the Va. State Bar Asso.*, Aug. 1928, vol. XL; A. J. Beveridge, *The Life of John Marshall* (4 vols., 1916–19), *passim*, a most unfriendly interpretation.]   C.C.P.

ROARK, RURIC NEVEL (May 19, 1859–Apr. 14, 1909), educator, was born at Greenville, Muhlenberg County, Ky., the son of Martin Jefferson and Nancy (Davis) Roark, substantial citizens, descendants of old settlers in western Kentucky. His father as a young man taught school in Muhlenberg County; he served as a captain in the 11th Kentucky Infantry (Federal) during the Civil War and was wounded at Shiloh. Roark's early education was obtained in the public schools of Greenville and the Greenville Academy. Inspired with an eagerness for knowledge and a desire to teach, he then attended the National Normal School (now Lebanon University), Lebanon, Ohio, from which he received the degree of B.S. in 1881. In the same year he married Mary Creegan, one of his teachers and his senior by a few years. He was immediately employed as a member of the faculty, and held this position for four years, during which time he obtained his master's degree. In 1885 he returned to his native state and until 1889 was principal of Glasgow Normal School, Glasgow, Ky. He then accepted the deanship of the normal or teacher training department of the State College of Kentucky at Lexington, forerunner of the State University of Kentucky. Despite meager appropriations from the state and prejudice against a normal department in the college, he soon commanded the respect and confidence of his co-workers by his scholarship, tact, and efficiency. He continued his personal study and research in the field of education and in 1905–06 was an honorary fellow of Clark University.

In company with other educators, he sponsored a movement for the establishment of separate teacher-training institutions in Kentucky which resulted in the creation of two state normal schools in 1906. Of one of these, Eastern Kentucky State Normal School, now Eastern State Teachers' College, at Richmond, he was elected the first president, which position he held until his death, in a Cincinnati hospital, in 1909. Ruric N. Roark Hall at the Eastern Kentucky State Normal School was named in his honor. After his death, his widow, who had encouraged and aided him in his useful and busy life, was made acting president of the school for about a year and was later appointed dean of women, in which capacity she served several years. Both Roark and his wife were buried in the cemetery at Richmond, Ky. They were survived by two sons and one daughter.

Roark's pleasing personality, coupled with his knowledge and initiative, placed him in the forefront in every progressive educational movement in Kentucky. He was in great demand as an institute instructor and lecturer, being called into other states even as far north as Wisconsin. He was the author of three textbooks on education —*Psychology in Education* (1895), *Method in Education* (1899), and *Economy in Education* (1905)—and of numerous tracts and pamphlets on various phases of pedagogy and kindred topics.

[*Who's Who in America*, 1908–09; O. A. Rothert, *A Hist. of Muhlenberg County* (1913); E. P. Johnson, *A Hist. of Ky. and Kentuckians* (1912), vol. I; *Biennial Report of the Supt. of Public Instruction of Ky., 1907–09* (1909); Barksdale Hammett, *Hist. of Educ. in Ky.* (1914); information from Prof. McHenry Rhoads, Univ. of Ky., and Hon. James W. Cammack, Sr., Owenton, Ky.] J. V. C.

ROBB, JAMES (Apr. 2, 1814–July 30, 1881), banker and railroad president, was born at Brownsville, Fayette County, Pa. His mother was a Meetkerk. His father was drowned in the Monongahela River when James was about five years old, and at the age of thirteen, the boy left home and walked twenty-two miles through snow at Morgantown, Va. (now in W. Va.), to seek his fortune. Employed in a bank at Morgantown, he became its cashier at the age of twenty-one, with a salary of $800 per year. He removed to New Orleans three years later, and was a resident of that city for more than two decades, becoming active in the establishment of banking and commercial houses or agencies in New Orleans, St. Louis, Philadelphia, New York, San Francisco, and Liverpool. In New Orleans he set up a private bank, the Bank of James Robb. According to an autobiographical statement (*post*), he made six visits to Europe and fifteen to Cuba. In 1842 he became president of the New Orleans Gas Light & Banking Company, and two years later he headed a newly established gas light company of Havana, Cuba, with the capital, as he observed, divided equally between himself and the queen mother of Spain. He sold out this Havana interest in 1854, however, and thereafter was chiefly interested in railroads.

He was prominent in New Orleans commercial and railway conventions of the early fifties and was president of one of them. He was very much interested in projecting rail connections from New Orleans northward, and in 1852 became

president of the New Orleans, Jackson & Great Northern Railroad. In 1859 he changed his residence to Chicago, becoming receiver for the St. Louis, Alton & Chicago Railway Company and, upon its reorganization in 1862 as the Chicago & Alton, its president until 1864. He removed to New York in that year, was for a short time head of the Atlantic & Great Western Railroad, and a little later, president for about a year of the Dubuque & Sioux Railway Company. In the autumn of 1865 he returned to New Orleans to establish the Louisiana National Bank, which started operation with capital of $1,000,000. He withdrew from the presidency of this bank in 1869 and retired from business two years later, with a fortune diminished but ample for his wants. In 1873 he removed to "Hampden Place," at Cheviot, Ohio (now part of Cincinnati), which he had purchased for his mother in 1844, and there spent the remaining years of his life, taking an interest in the industrial expositions of Cincinnati. "His marriage, which occurred in New Orleans, proved in later years an unhappy one, and he lived alone for years before his death" (*New Orleans Daily Picayune*, July 31, 1881).

During the period of his residence in New Orleans he was a member for one session of the state Senate and also saw service as a member of the city council. He owned a fine house on Washington Avenue and was an art collector of prominence, owning canvases by Rubens, David, Salvator Rosa, and others. Sixty-seven of his pictures were offered for sale in 1859 but part of his collection was retained to be handed down in the family.

[A great-grandson, J. Hampden Robb, of Beverly, Mass., possesses a full-length portrait of James Robb by Sully. The *Cincinnati Commercial*, July 31, 1881, and the *New Orleans Daily Picayune*, Aug. 4, 1881, contain an autobiographical statement. See also J. S. Kendall, *Hist. of New Orleans* (1922), vol. II; Henry Rightor, *Standard Hist. of New Orleans, La.* (1900).] H. C. H.

ROBBINS, CHANDLER (Feb. 14, 1810– Sept. 11, 1882), Unitarian clergyman, was the son of Peter Gilman and Abba (Dowse) Robbins. At the time of his birth, his father, a physician, was practising in Lynn, Mass.; later he removed to Roxbury. Chandler's grandfather and his great-grandfather had been Congregational ministers, however; the former, Chandler (1738– 1799), was long pastor of the First Church, Plymouth, and the latter, Philemon (1707– 1781), was for almost fifty years pastor at Branford, Conn. Their original forebear in America was Richard Robbins who settled in Charlestown, Mass., some time before 1640, and later moved to Cambridge. Young Robbins received his early instruction from clergymen and in private schools. In 1825 he entered Harvard College, from which he graduated in 1829, having shown especial excellence in writing and public speaking. His course in the Harvard Divinity School, interrupted by a year of teaching in the Boston Latin School, was completed in 1833, and in October of that year he was called to succeed Ralph Waldo Emerson as pastor of the Second Church, Boston. He was ordained Dec. 4, 1833, and eight days later married Mary Eliza, daughter of Samuel Frothingham of Boston. He remained in charge of the Second Church, which passed through numerous vicissitudes, for forty-one years, during which he preached in five successive church edifices and in four temporary places of worship.

In addition to his pastoral work, he took an active part in denominational affairs—more particularly in his earlier years—and was prominent in the philanthropic activities and intellectual life of Boston. From January 1837 to April 1839 he was editor of the *Christian Register,* and during these years was one of the executive committee of the American Unitarian Association. He served as chaplain of the Massachusetts Senate in 1834, and as chaplain of the Massachusetts House of Representatives in 1845. He was an officer in several charitable organizations, and in 1869 one of the founders of the Children's Hospital, serving on its board of managers until his death. He became a member of the Massachusetts Historical Society in December 1845, was a member of its standing committee from 1854 to 1857, its recording secretary from 1857 to 1864, and its corresponding secretary from 1864 to 1877. He contributed to its *Proceedings,* and delivered one of the lectures given by some of its members before the Lowell Institute on "The Early History of Massachusetts." It was published in 1869, under the title: *The Regicides Sheltered in New England.* He edited *The Works of Henry Ware, Jr., D.D.* (4 vols., 1846–47), was chairman of the committee that published "The Mather Papers" (*Massachusetts Historical Society Collections,* 4 ser., vol. VII, 1865), and wrote *A History of the Second Church, or Old North, in Boston* (1852). Some thirty of his sermons and addresses were published and he issued *Hymn Book for Christian Worship* (1854), and *A Liturgy for the Use of a Christian Church* (1854). Among his own hymns is "Lo, the day of rest declineth," which came into general use. He was a member of the American Antiquarian Society, and of the American Academy of Arts and Sciences. A sharp

blow over his right eye in 1870 resulted finally in almost total loss of sight. "I cannot read or write," he said in 1877, "cannot see a flower or tree or the sweet faces of my infant boys. But I have no right to complain, and do not complain. I have seen many beautiful things—the faces of friends most beautiful of all—during my life journey. And their pictures are safely stored in the memory" (*Proceedings of the Massachusetts Historical Society, post,* p. 413). His first wife died in 1870, leaving a son and six daughters. In June 1874 he married Mrs. Sarah Ripley (Fiske) Willard, by whom he had three sons. He died at his summer home in Weston, Mass.

[*Proc. Mass. Hist. Soc.,* vol. XX (1884); S. A. Eliot, *Heralds of a Liberal Faith,* vol. III (1910); A. P. Peabody, *Harvard Reminiscences* (1888), pp. 187 ff.; for geneal., L. R. Paige, *Hist. of Cambridge, Mass.* (1877), pp. 641–42; *Boston Transcript,* Sept. 11, 1882; *Christian Register,* Sept. 21, 1882.]   H. E. S.

ROBBINS, THOMAS (Aug. 11, 1777–Sept. 13, 1856), Congregational clergyman, antiquarian, was born in Norfolk, Conn., grandson of the Rev. Philemon Robbins, for nearly fifty years pastor at Branford, and ninth child of the Rev. Ammi Ruhamah and Elizabeth (LeBaron) Robbins. His father, in addition to his pastoral duties, prepared boys for college, and Thomas received his English and classical training from him. He entered Yale in 1792, but in his senior year transferred to Williams College, chartered in 1793, of which his father was trustee, with the understanding that he should nevertheless receive his degree in course from Yale. Accordingly, he was graduated from both institutions in 1796. During the next two years he taught in Sheffield, Mass., and Torringford, Conn., at the same time studying theology under several New England divines. On Sept. 25, 1798, he was licensed to preach by the Litchfield North Association of Congregational Ministers. After supplying the church in Marlboro, Conn., for a few months, he made a missionary tour into Vermont. He taught an academy in Danbury, Conn., in 1800, preaching as opportunity offered in the neighborhood, and in 1801–02 made a missionary journey into the newly settled districts of New York. In May 1803 the Missionary Society of Connecticut appointed him missionary to the Western Reserve, Ohio, and in June he was ordained at Norfolk, Conn. After more than two years of strenuous service he returned to Norfolk broken in health. From 1809 to 1827 he was pastor in what is now South Windsor, Conn.; then, after supplying various churches, was installed in Stratford, Conn., Feb. 3, 1830, but remained there only until Sept. 15, 1831. His last pastorate (1832–44), during the first four years of which he was colleague of his uncle, Lazarus LeBaron, was in the town now called Mattapoisett, Plymouth County, Mass. He was one of the original members of the Massachusetts board of education and served theron until he left Mattapoisett; from 1842 to 1853 he was one of the corporation of Williams College.

Throughout all his ministerial vicissitudes, Robbins fostered a keen interest in history and research. While in Danbury he delivered and published *An Oration Occasioned by the Death of General George Washington* (1800), which went through several editions; also *A Century Sermon . . . January 1, A.D. 1801,* which reviewed the most remarkable events of the eighteenth century. He contributed articles to the press and beginning in 1811 wrote for the *Connecticut Evangelical Magazine* a series of biographical articles, published in 1815 under the title, *An Historical View of the First Planters of New England.* He also edited a number of works, among them the first American edition, 1820, of Cotton Mather's *Magnalia Christi Americana.* In connection with his historical researches he began to collect books and pamphlets. In 1809 he found that he had 130 of these, and resolved to add at least 100 a year from that time on; by 1830 the number had increased to 1600 or more. This library was known to contain much that was rare and valuable, and various institutions coveted ultimate possession of it. Finally, in June 1844, the Connecticut Historical Society, which Robbins had helped to found in 1825 and which had been revived under the leadership of his friend Henry Barnard [*q.v.*], invited Robbins to place his library in the Society building at Hartford, and become librarian of the organization, at an annual salary of $300. Two years later ownership of the library passed to the Society, which settled a life annuity of $600 on Robbins. He served as librarian until 1854, when he retired because of age. He had never married and died at the home of a niece in Colebrook, Conn., but was buried in Hartford near the library which had been his life work. His journal, *Diary of Thomas Robbins, D.D., 1796–1854,* edited by Increase N. Tarbox, was published in two volumes, in 1886–87.

[F. B. Dexter, *Biog. Sketches Grads. Yale Univ.,* vol. V. (1911); *Memorial Biogs. of the New England Hist. Geneal. Soc.,* vol. III (1883); W. DeL. Love, *Reverend Thomas Robbins* 1906); Henry Barnard in *Am. Jour. of Educ.,* Mar. 1857.]   W. G. L.

ROBERDEAU, DANIEL (1727–Jan. 5, 1795), merchant, Revolutionary patriot, only son of Isaac and Mary (Cunyngham) Roberdeau, was born on the island of St. Christopher, British West Indies. His father, a French-Huguenot, fled from La Rochelle, France, to St. Christopher on the revocation of the Edict of Nantes, and is spoken of as "a gentleman of family and fortune." Mary Cunyngham was the daughter of a wealthy planter and a descendant of the Earl of Glencairn of Scotland. Following the death of Isaac Roberdeau in Daniel's childhood, the family removed to Philadelphia. There Daniel continued his education, which he had begun in England, with the aim of preparing himself for a mercantile career. Until the beginning of the Revolution he was a successful merchant, engaged largely in the West Indies trade.

His political career began as a warden of Philadelphia, and from 1756 to 1761 he sat in the provincial assembly. An uncompromising patriot throughout the Revolutionary period, from the time of the non-importation agreements he was almost invariably the choice of the public for chairman of mass meetings held in the State House yard. Merchants and politicians respected his judgment on public matters and the Loyalist press acknowledged his immense hold on the people. As a member of the Pennsylvania committee of safety he labored indefatigably to improve the defenses of the colony. As an agitator for independence and a new state government and as chairman of the Philadelphia mass meeting on May 20, 1776, he was an important factor in uniting the popular group in the city with the back country, thus paving the way for a new constitution. He interested himself financially in fitting out privateers which were successful in capturing valuable prizes. When bullets were needed for the army he volunteered in Congress to establish a lead mine at his own expense in western Pennsylvania (1778) and built Fort Roberdeau to protect the mine. He also served with the Pennsylvania Associators, first as colonel of the 2nd Battalion, and later as brigadier-general of the 53 Battalions, to which post he was elected on July 4, 1776, and in which capacity he participated in the New Jersey campaign of 1776.

Beginning Feb. 5, 1777, Roberdeau sat in Congress for two years. While in that body he served on the important committee of foreign affairs, and with his wide knowledge of business matters rendered valuable assistance in reorganizing the clothier general's, the commissary, and the treasury departments. A foe of inefficiency and dishonesty, he strenuously advocated both in Congress and in his state the strictest economy, adequate provisions for the army, and measures to prevent a depreciated currency, characteristically declaring that "these will be more effectual than an army with Banners" (Oct. 14, 1777; *Pennsylvania Archives,* 1 ser., V, 671). In an inflammatory speech at a public meeting at which he presided in 1779 he contended that the prices of the necessaries of life would have to be reduced forcibly to keep monopolizers from grinding down the people with their high prices. After spending a year traveling in Europe (1783–84), he moved to Alexandria, Va., and subsequently to Winchester, Va., where he died. He was a man of large frame, great vitality, and persistent initiative. Always interested in projects of philanthropy, he was for twelve years a manager of the Pennsylvania Hospital. On Oct. 3, 1761, he married Mary, daughter of the Rev. David Bostwick, Presbyterian minister of New York. She died at Lancaster in the winter of 1777 while nursing him through a serious illness. On Dec. 2, 1778, he married Jane, daughter of James Milligan of Philadelphia; she died in 1785. His eldest son, Isaac [*q.v.*], was an engineer of note.

[Roberdeau Buchanan, *Geneal. of the Roberdeau Family Including a Biog. of Gen. Daniel Roberdeau* (1876); *Pa. Archives,* 1 ser. V–VIII (1852), 2 ser. I (1852); *Pa. Col. Records,* vols. X–XIII (1852–53); and *Pa. Mag. of Hist. and Biog.,* vols. III (1879), IX (1885), XXII (1898); information from William Patten, Esq., New York.]   J. H. P—g.

ROBERDEAU, ISAAC (Sept. 11, 1763–Jan. 15, 1829), civil and military engineer, the eldest of nine children of Daniel Roberdeau [*q.v.*] and his first wife, Mary Bostwick, was born in Philadelphia, Pa. After an early education in Philadelphia he visited the West Indies with his father in 1783 and then went to London to study engineering, returning to the United States in 1787. His French ancestry, as well as his technical ability, commended him to the notice of Pierre Charles L'Enfant [*q.v.*] when the topographical force was assembled to lay out the new city of Washington. Roberdeau was employed there in 1791 and 1792, gaining much experience and some notoriety. He was put in charge of the party of workmen who, under L'Enfant's orders, destroyed the masonry of the uncompleted Carroll house (see sketch of Daniel Carroll)—an action which was a principal cause of President Washington's dismissal of L'Enfant. He was also involved in other difficulties with the commissioners resulting from a conflict between their views and L'Enfant's, but through no fault of his own. He loyally carried out the orders of his temperamental chief, as he was bound to do so long as he retained his employment. After L'Enfant's dismissal at Washington, Roberdeau worked with him at Paterson, N. J., when the former was creating a new industrial city under the direction of Alexander Hamilton. On Nov. 7, 1792, he married the grand-daughter of Samuel Blair and William Shippen [*qq.v.*], and immediately afterward took up the practice of his profession in his native state, where he remained for the next twenty years.

His most important work was the beginning of a canal to connect the Schuylkill and the Susquehanna rivers, completed many years later. His real ambition was for service in the army, but he was unable to secure appointment until the war with Great Britain broke out and Congress made provision for a force of topographical engineers. He was appointed a major in the new organization on Apr. 29, 1813, and assigned to duty at Fort Mifflin, near Philadelphia. He was employed on fortification work at various places during the war, and was discharged through the abolition of his corps on June 15, 1815. The War Department, however, was unwilling to dispense with the topographical engineers, and pending legislation Roberdeau was "provisionally retained" as a civilian and charged with the survey of the northern boundary, which he carried westward as far as Sault Sainte Marie. He was reinstated to his former rank in the army on May 2, 1816, and stationed at West Point, the headquarters of his corps, until 1818, when the topographical bureau was moved to Washington with Roberdeau as its chief. He spent the rest of his life in the capital, a prominent figure in society "as well known here then as the President" (Buchanan, *post,* p. 122). He entertained many notable guests at his home in Georgetown, among them, Lafayette. Roberdeau was given brevet rank as lieutenant-colonel in 1823. He was tall and of a distinguished military bearing, resembling the Duke of Wellington so strongly that he was mistaken for him when traveling in England. He was the author of *Observations on the Survey of the Seacoast of the United States* (1827), of "Mathematics and Treatise on Canals" (Manuscripts Division, Library of Congress), and of *An Oration Upon the Death of General Washington,* delivered at Trenton, N. J., on Feb. 22, 1800, and published the same year. His manuscript memorandum on the family's ancestry is in the possession of the Historical Society of Pennsylvania, which also has a miniature portrait of him and some of the family silver. He and his wife had three daughters.

[Roberdeau Buchanan, *Geneal. of the Roberdeau Family* (1876), the best source of information, written by a close friend and relative; *The Memoirs of Gen. Joseph Gardner Swift* (1890); E. S. Kite, *L'Enfant and Washington* (1929); and *Daily Natl. Intelligencer* (Wash., D. C.), Jan. 16, 1829.]   T. M. S.

VOLUME VIII, PART 2
ROBERT - SEWARD

(VOLUME XVI OF THE ORIGINAL EDITION)

CROSS REFERENCES FROM THIS VOL-
UME ARE MADE TO THE VOLUME
NUMBERS OF THE ORIGINAL EDITION.

CONTRIBUTORS
VOLUME VIII, PART 2

Wilbur Cortez Abbott	W. C. A.
Thomas P. Abernethy	T. P. A.
Adeline Adams	A. A.
James Truslow Adams	J. T. A.
Nelson F. Adkins	N. F. A.
Cyrus Adler	C. A.
Robert Greenhalgh Albion	R. G. A.
William F. Albright	W. F. A.
Carroll S. Alden	C. S. A.
Gardner W. Allen	G. W. A.
Joseph Sweetman Ames	J. S. A.
Gertrude L. Annan	G. L. A.
John Archer	J. A.
John Clark Archer	J. C. A.
Preston A. Barba	P. A. B.
Thomas S. Barclay	T. S. B.
John H. Barnhart	J. H. B—t.
Adriaan J. Barnouw	A. J. B.
Harold K. Barrows	H. K. B.
George A. Barton	G. A. B.
Ernest Sutherland Bates	E. S. B.
G. Philip Bauer	G. P. B.
Marcus Benjamin	M. B.
C. C. Benson	C. C. B.
Elbert J. Benton	E. J. B.
Theodore C. Blegen	T. C. B.
Willard Grosvenor Bleyer	W. G. B.
Louise Pearson Blodget	L. P. B.
Lansing B. Bloom	L. B. B.
George Verne Blue	G. V. B.
Louis H. Bolander	L. H. B.
Robert W. Bolwell	R. W. B.
Sarah G. Bowerman	S. G. B.
Julian P. Boyd	J. P. B.
Jessica Hill Bridenbaugh	J. H. B—h.
John E. Briggs	J. E. B.
Paul Brockett	P. B.
Margaret Louise Brown	M. L. B.
Solon J. Buck	S. J. B.
George K. Burgess	G. K. B.
Huntington Cairns	H. C.
William B. Cairns	W. B. C.
Leon Campbell	L. C.
Samuel McCrea Cavert	S. M. C.
F. Stanton Cawley	F. S. C.
Zechariah Chafee, Jr.	Z. C., Jr.
Wayland J. Chase	W. J. C.
Samuel Harden Church	S. H. C.
Charles E. Clark	C. E. C.
Eliot Clark	E. C.
Hubert Lyman Clark	H. L. C.
Jane Clark	J. C.
Robert C. Clark	R. C. C.
Robert Glass Cleland	R. G. C.
Frederick W. Coburn	F. W. C.
Joseph B. Code	J. B. C.
Fannie L. Gwinner Cole	F. L. G. C.
Guy N. Collins	G. N. C.
Royal Cortissoz	R. C.
E. Merton Coulter	E. M. C.
Isaac J. Cox	I. J. C.
Katharine Elizabeth Crane	K. E. C.
Avery O. Craven	A. O. C.
Frederic R. Crownfield	F. R. C.
Merle E. Curti	M. E. C.
Carl C. Cutler	C. C. C.
Edward E. Dale	E. E. D.
Norman H. Dawes	N. H. D.
Clive Day	C. D.
Richard E. Day	R. E. D.
William H. S. Demarest	W. H. S. D.
Herman J. Deutsch	H. J. D.
Irving Dilliard	I. D.
Charles Wright Dodge	C. W. D.
Elizabeth Donnan	E. D.
Randolph C. Downes	R. C. D.
William Howe Downes	W. H. D.
Carl S. Driver	C. S. D.
Stella M. Drumm	S. M. D.
W. E. Burghardt Du Bois	W. E. B. D-B
Edward A. Duddy	E. A. D.
Raymond S. Dugan	R. S. D.
Edward Dwight Eaton	E. D. E.
Edwin Francis Edgett	E. F. E.
Everett E. Edwards	E. E. E.
L. Ethan Ellis	L. E. E.
Milton Ellis	M. E.
William M. Emery	W. M. E.
Carl Engel	C. E.
Charles R. Erdman, Jr.	C. R. E., Jr.
Paul D. Evans	P. D. E.
Walter G. Everett	W. G. E.
John O. Evjen	J. O. E.
Charles Fairman	C. F.
John I. Falconer	J. I. F.
Paul Patton Faris	P. P. F.
Hallie Farmer	H. F—r.
James Waldo Fawcett	J. W. F.

Contributors

HARRIET FAXON	H. Fa—n.	ROBERT L. JONES	R. L. J.
FELIX FELLNER	F. F.	RUFUS M. JONES	R. M. J.
VERGILIUS FERM	V. F.	PHILIP D. JORDAN	P. D. J.
JOHN T. FLYNN	J. T. F.	JAMES R. JOY	J. R. J.
ARTHUR FOOTE	A. F.	PAUL KAUFMAN	P. K.
HENRY THATCHER FOWLER	H. T. F.	HERBERT ANTHONY KELLAR	H. A. K.
JOHN H. FREDERICK	J. H. F.	KATHARINE AMEND KELLOCK	K. A. K.
EDNA TUTT FREDERIKSON	E. T. F.	LOUISE PHELPS KELLOGG	L. P. K.
HERBERT FRIEDMANN	H. Fr—n.	REMINGTON KELLOGG	R. K.
CHARLES B. GALBREATH	C. B. G—h.	RAYNER W. KELSEY	R. W. K.
ESSON M. GALE	E. M. G.	WARNICK J. KERNAN	W. J. K.
WILLIAM A. GANOE	W. A. G.	JOHN KIERAN	J. K.
HAZEL SHIELDS GARRISON	H. S. G.	MAX J. KOHLER	M. J. K.
WINFRED ERNEST GARRISON	W. E. G.	JOHN A. KOLMER	J. A. K—r.
SYLVESTER GATES	S. G—s.	JOHN A. KROUT	J. A. K—t.
WINFIELD R. GAYLORD	W. R. G.	ERNEST A. KUBLER	E. A. K.
GEORGE HARVEY GENZMER	G. H. G.	LEONARD W. LABAREE	L. W. L.
W. J. GHENT	W. J. G.	ARTHUR B. LAMB	A. B. L.
M. B. GIFFEN	M. B. G.	WILLIAM G. LAND	W. G. L.
LAWRENCE H. GIPSON	L. H. G.	WINTHROP D. LANE	W. D. L.
COLIN B. GOODYKOONTZ	C. B. G—z.	WILLIAM CHAUNCY LANGDON	W. C. L.
ARMISTEAD CHURCHILL GORDON, JR	A. C. G., Jr.	JOHN H. LATANÉ	J. H. L.
DOROTHY GRAFLY	D. G—y.	KENNETH S. LATOURETTE	K. S. L.
CHARLES GRAVES	C. G.	HENRY LEFFERT	H. L.
DOROTHY GREENWALD	D. G—d.	MAX LERNER	M. L.
FREDERICK GRILL	F. G.	CHARLES LEE LEWIS	C. L. L.
SIDNEY GUNN	S. G—n.	ANNA LANE LINGELBACH	A. L. L.
EDWIN H. HALL	E. H. H.	JOHN STOCKTON LITTELL II	J. S. L.
THOMAS B. HALL	T. B. H.	CHARLES SUMNER LOBINGIER	C. S. L.
J. G. DER. HAMILTON	J. G. deR. H.	MILDRED E. LOMBARD	M. E. L.
TALBOT FAULKNER HAMLIN	T. F. H.	ELLA LONN	E. L.
J. W. HAMMOND	J. W. H.	EARNEST W. LUNDEEN	E. W. L.
WILLIAM A. HAMMOND	W. A. H.	WILLIAM T. LYLE	W. T. L.
LEWIS HANKE	L. H.	CHARLES H. LYTTLE	C. H. L.
ELIZABETH DEERING HANSCOM	E. D. H.	ALEXANDER MCADIE	A. M.
JOSEPH MILLS HANSON	J. M. H.	PHILIP B. MCDONALD	P. B. M.
EDWARD ROCHIE HARDY, JR.	E. R. H., Jr.	W. J. MCGLOTHLIN	W. J. M.
ALVIN F. HARLOW	A. F. H.	SETH SHEPARD MCKAY	S. S. M.
MARGARET HARWOOD	M. H.	KATHERINE MCNAMARA	K. M.
EINAR I. HAUGEN	E. I. H.	T. F. MCNEILL	T. F. M.
EARL L. W. HECK	E. L. W. H.	JAMES C. MALIN	J. C. M.
SAMUEL J. HEIDNER	S. J. H.	LOUIS L. MANN	L. L. M.
ELIZABETH WILTBANK HEILMAN	E. W. H.	WILLIAM W. MANROSS	W. W. M.
GRANVILLE HICKS	G. H.	H. A. MARMER	H. A. M.
JOHN DONALD HICKS	J. D. H.	FREDERICK H. MARTENS	F. H. M.
WILLIAM J. HINKE	W. J. H.	DANIEL GREGORY MASON	D. G. M.
WILLIAM H. HOBBS	W. H. H.	WILLIAM R. MAXON	W. R. M.
OLIVER W. HOLMES	O. W. H.	ROBERT DOUTHAT MEADE	R. D. M.
W. STULL HOLT	W. S. H.	DONALD H. MENZEL	D. H. M.
WALTER HOUGH	W. H.	NEWTON D. MERENESS	N. D. M.
JOHN TASKER HOWARD	J. T. H.	ROBERT L. MERIWETHER	R. L. M.
LELAND OSSIAN HOWARD	L. O. H.	GEORGE P. MERRILL	G. P. M.
M. A. DEWOLFE HOWE	M. A. DeW. H.	FRANK J. METCALF	F. J. M.
JOHN G. JACK	J. G. J.	HERMAN H. B. MEYER	H. H. B. M.
JOSEPH JACKSON	J. J.	GEORGE L. MEYLAN	G. L. M.
T. CARY JOHNSON, JR.	T. C. J., Jr.	BROADUS MITCHELL	B. M.
HOWARD MUMFORD JONES	H. M. J.	STEWART MITCHELL	S. M.
		WALTER MITCHELL, JR.	W. M., Jr.

Contributors

Carl W. Mitman	C. W. M.	Marvin B. Rosenberry	M. B. R.
Conrad Henry Moehlman	C. H. M.	William Sener Rusk	W. S. R.
Frank Monaghan	F. M.	William L. Russell	W. L. R.
Edward Caldwell Moore	E. C. M—e.	George H. Ryden	G. H. R.
Richard B. Morris	R. B. M.	Bernard Sachs	B. S.
Edmund C. Mower	E. C. M—r.	Lazare Saminsky	L. S.
George Fulmer Mull	G. F. M.	Verne Lockwood Samson	V. L. S.
Carl Murchison	C. M.	David J. Saposs	D. J. S.
J. Florence Murray	J. F. M.	Wallace S. Sayre	W. S. S.
William Allan Neilson	W. A. N.	Joseph Schafer	J. S.
Lowry Nelson	L. N.	Israel Schapiro	I. S.
Lyman C. Newell	L. C. N.	Herbert W. Schneider	H. W. S.
A. R. Newsome	A. R. N.	Frank W. Scott	F. W. S—t.
Jeannette P. Nichols	J. P. N.	James Lee Sellers	J. L. S.
Robert Hastings Nichols	R. H. N.	Robert Francis Seybolt	R. F. S.
Herman C. Nixon	H. C. N.	William Bristol Shaw	W. B. S.
John Scholte Nollen	J. S. N.	Augustus H. Shearer	A. H. S.
Fillmore Norfleet	F. N.	Richard H. Shryock	R. H. S—k
George A. Orrok	G. A. O.	Eleanor M. Sickels	E. M. S.
Robert B. Osgood	R. B. O.	Wilbur H. Siebert	W. H. S—t.
Francis R. Packard	F. R. P.	Francis Butler Simkins	F. B. S—s.
Victor H. Paltsits	V. H. P.	Frederic W. Simonds	F. W. S—s.
Stanley M. Pargellis	S. M. P.	Mary B. Slade	M. B. S.
Henry Bamford Parkes	H. B. P.	David Eugene Smith	D. E. S.
Clarence Paschall	C. P.	Edward Conrad Smith	E. C. S.
Charles O. Paullin	C. O. P.	Marion Parris Smith	M. P. S.
Frederic Logan Paxson	F. L. P.	William E. Smith	W. E. S.
C. C. Pearson	C. C. P.	Herbert Solow	H. S.
John B. Peddle	J. B. P.	James P. C. Southall	J. P. C. S.
James H. Peeling	J. H. P.	Charles L. Souvay	C. L. S.
Dexter Perkins	D. P.	E. Wilder Spaulding	E. W. S.
Ralph Barton Perry	R. B. P.	Oliver L. Spaulding, Jr.	O. L. S., Jr.
Benjamin H. Pershing	B. H. P.	C. P. Stacey	C. P. S.
Frederick T. Persons	F. T. P.	Harris Elwood Starr	H. E. S.
James M. Phalen	J. M. P—n.	Bertha Monica Stearns	B. M. S.
Paul Chrisler Phillips	P. C. P.	Francis Borgia Steck	F. B. S—k.
Charles S. Plumb	C. S. P—b.	Wendell H. Stephenson	W. H. S—n.
David deSola Pool	D. deS. P.	Helen R. Steward	H. R. S.
John M. Poor	J. M. P—r.	Tracy E. Strevey	T. E. S.
Dorothy B. Porter	D. B. P.	William Strunk, Jr.	W. S., Jr.
Kenneth Wiggins Porter	K. W. P.	R. H. Sudds	R. H. S—s.
Charles Shirley Potts	C. S. P—s.	William W. Sweet	W. W. S.
Alden L. Powell	A. L. P.	William A. Taylor	W. A. T.
Richard J. Purcell	R. J. P.	David Y. Thomas	D. Y. T.
James Watt Raine	J. W. R.	Milton Halsey Thomas	M. H. T.
Belle Rankin	B. R.	C. Mildred Thompson	C. M. T.
Albert G. Rau	A. G. R.	Ernest Trice Thompson	E. T. T.
P. O. Ray	P. O. R.	Frederic L. Thompson	F. L. T.
Philip M. Rhinelander	P. M. R.	Charles J. Tilden	C. J. T.
Charles Dudley Rhodes	C. D. R.	Edward Larocque Tinker	E. L. T.
Leon B. Richardson	L. B. R.	James A. Tobey	J. A. T.
Burr Arthur Robinson	B. A. R.	Francis A. Tondorf	F. A. T.
Henry Morton Robinson	H. M. R.	Charles C. Torrey	C. C. T.
William A. Robinson	W. A. R.	Rexford G. Tugwell	R. G. T.
William M. Robinson, Jr.	W. M. R., Jr.	George B. Utley	G. B. U.
Octavia F. Rogan	O. F. R.	Clarence H. Vance	C. H. V.
Allen Rogers	A. R.	Edward M. Van Cleve	E. M. V-C.
Lois K. M. Rosenberry	L. K. M. R.	Henry R. Viets	H. R. V.

Contributors

DICTIONARY OF
AMERICAN BIOGRAPHY

Robert — Seward

ROBERT, CHRISTOPHER RHINE-LANDER (Mar. 23, 1802–Oct. 27, 1878), merchant and philanthropist, son of Daniel and Mary Tangier (Smith) Robert, was born near Brook Haven, Suffolk County, Long Island, on the estate of his father, a physician educated at Columbia College and at Edinburgh University. His great-grandfather, also Daniel Robert, was a Huguenot of La Rochelle who reached New York in 1686. Becoming a New York shipping clerk at the age of fifteen, Christopher five years later entered business on his own account, first in New Orleans and later in Galena, Ill. In 1830 he returned to New York and married Anna Maria, daughter of William Shaw of that city. Establishing in 1835 the firm of Robert & Williams, importers of sugar, cotton, and tea, he had made a considerable fortune by 1862, when the partnership was dissolved. Active in many other business enterprises, he was from 1858 to 1863 president of the Delaware, Lackawanna & Western Railroad Company. Always deeply religious, he served for nearly thirty years as superintendent of the Sunday school and elder of the Laight Street Presbyterian Church and supported financially a German congregation on Rivington Street. His appeal to the Home Missionary Society in 1828 led to the establishment in Galena of the first church in Northern Illinois. Henceforth Robert was closely connected with this society, a member of its executive committee after 1838, and treasurer from 1855 to 1870. To its work, to Beloit and Hamilton colleges, and to Auburn Theological Seminary he made substantial anonymous gifts. At the close of the Civil War he bought from the government its hospital buildings at Lookout Mountain, Tennessee, and established there in 1866 a college

for the "poor whites" of the South, but local opposition to its Yankee origin led him soon to abandon the experiment.

While visiting Constantinople during the Crimean War he became acquainted with the educational work which Cyrus Hamlin [q.v.] was doing under the American Board of Commissioners for Foreign Missions. After the war he became interested in the scheme of James H. and William B. Dwight for founding a purely secular college at Constantinople but he believed that little financial support could be obtained in the United States without a definitely Christian basis. When this plan fell through, he offered in 1859 the task of establishing an institution in accordance with his own ideas to Hamlin. The latter accepted the offer and on Sept. 16, 1863, opened at Bebek, a suburb of Constantinople, Robert College, adopting this name despite repeated objections from the founder. In the following year the state of New York granted a charter providing for an American board of trustees, whose dominating personality was Robert. Eventually Hamlin secured a magnificent site above Rumeli Hissar on the Bosphorus and supervised the construction of a building. In 1870 when the new quarters were occupied, Robert visited the college, which had over a hundred students. On this visit as on another in 1875 he investigated in detail every phase of the work, giving freely both advice and criticism, and obtained an intimate understanding of the situation. When campaigns for endowment by Hamlin and his successor, George Washburn [q.v.], proved unsuccessful, practically the whole burden of supporting the institution fell upon Robert, who covered the yearly deficit of $10,000 or more until his death in Paris while seeking to mend his broken health by European travel. One-fifth of his estate was left to the college, raising the amount of his gifts to at least $600,000. A cultured and unassuming gentleman of unusual ability and most decided character, Robert cherished such democratic austerity that he refused a decoration offered by the Ottoman government. The college which he founded has trained many of the builders of the Balkan and Near Eastern nations and remains one of the finest monuments of American philanthropy.

[See: Cuyler Reynolds, *Geneal. and Family Hist. of Southern N. Y. and the Hudson River Valley*, vol. I (1914) ; Geo. Washburn, *Fifty Years in Constantinople* (1911) ; Cyrus Hamlin, *My Life and Times* (1893) ; F. A. Virkus, *The Compendium of Am. Geneal.*, vol. IV (1930) ; *Home Missionary*, Dec. 1878 ; *N. Y. Herald*, Oct. 31, 1878 ; *N. Y. Observer*, Nov. 7, 1878 ; information as to certain facts supplied by Arthur Remington Robert, London, England.]   W. L. W., Jr.

ROBERTS, BENJAMIN STONE (Nov. 18, 1810–Jan. 29, 1875), soldier, engineer, inventor, was born at Manchester, Vt., of Welsh ancestry, the son of Gen. Martin and Betsey (Stone) Roberts. His grandfather was Gen. Christopher Roberts, of the colonial wars. After a common-school preparation, he was graduated from the United States Military Academy with the class of 1835, fifty-third in a class of fifty-five. He joined the 1st Dragoons as a lieutenant, and after frontier service in Iowa and Kansas, resigned in the year 1839 to become chief engineer of the Champlain & Ogdensburg Railroad. He became geologist of the state of New York in the year 1841, and the following year was an assistant to George Washington Whistler [*q.v.*] in the construction of a railway in Russia from St. Petersburg to Moscow. When he returned to the United States he studied law and began to practise in Des Moines, Iowa, in 1843. He served as lieutenant-colonel of the state militia from 1844 to 1846. At the outbreak of the Mexican War, he was reappointed a first lieutenant with the Mounted Rifles, and was promoted captain in February 1847. He participated in the battles of General Scott's campaign and was brevetted major on Sept. 13, 1847, for gallantry in leading a storming party at the taking of Chapultepec (Smith, *post*, p. 164). On Nov. 24, 1847, he was brevetted lieutenant-colonel for gallantry in action against Mexican guerrillas near Matamoras, and when he returned to the United States, he received a sword of honor from the state of Iowa.

During the following decade, he served at various parts of the frontier, and was promoted to the rank of major, 3rd Cavalry, on May 13, 1861, commanding the southern military district of New Mexico under General Canby, and partici-

pating in engagements at Fort Craig, Albuquerque, Valverde, and Peralta. For gallant and meritorious service at Valverde, he was brevetted colonel on Feb. 21, 1862. He was promoted brigadier-general of volunteers the following June, and as a member of General Pope's staff, was engaged in the battles of Cedar Mountain, Rappahannock Station, Sulphur Springs, and Second Manassas (Ropes, *post*, p. 20 ff.). For gallant services in this campaign he was brevetted brigadier-general and major-general on Mar. 13, 1865. In the fall of 1862, he was detached to lead an expedition against hostile Chippewa Indians in Minnesota, but was recalled to Washington in 1863 to command a unit in the defenses of that city. In the summer of 1864, he was placed in command of the 1st Division, XIX Corps, in Louisiana, and until January 1865, was chief of cavalry, Department of the Gulf. During the remainder of the year he commanded the district and the cavalry division of West Tennessee, and after discharge from the volunteer service on Jan. 15. 1866, was promoted to the rank of lieutenant-colonel, 3rd Cavalry. He served in New Mexico during 1867 and 1868, and was an instructor in military science at Yale College from 1868 to 1870.

He was retired from active service on Dec. 16, 1870, and entered upon the practice of law and the prosecution of claims before the government in Washington. While so engaged, he organized a stock company to finance the manufacture of a breech-loading rifle of his own invention, and although he succeeded in negotiating a European contract, the venture was not successful. He died of pleuro-pneumonia at Washington, D. C., in the sixty-fourth year of his age. He was survived by his wife, Elizabeth, daughter of Anson and Laura (Pierpont) Sperry, of Plattsburg, N. Y., to whom he was married on Sept. 18, 1835. They had three children. Among his writings are, *Description of Newly Patented Solid Shot and Shells for Use in Rifled Ordnance* (1864), and *Lieut.-General U. S. Grant* (1869), an address delivered at Yale College.

[R. B. Moffat, *Pierrepont Geneal.* (privately printed, 1913) ; F. B. Heitman, *Hist. Register and Dict. of the U. S. Army* (1903) ; J. H. Smith, *The War With Mexico* (1919) vol. II ; *Battles and Leaders of the Civil War*, vol. II (1887) ; J. C. Ropes, *The Army Under Pope* (1881) ; *Annual Reunion, Asso. of Grads., U. S. Mil. Acad.*, 1875.]   C. D. R.

ROBERTS, BENJAMIN TITUS (July 25, 1823–Feb. 27, 1893), clergyman, one of the organizers of the Free Methodist Church, was born in Gowanda, Cattaraugus County, N. Y., the son of Titus and Sally (Ellis) Roberts. He was a descendant of William Roberts of East Hartford, Conn., whose father (Robards), husband of Catharine Leete, or Leeke, emigrated to New England about the middle of the seventeenth century. As a boy Benjamin showed more than ordinary mental alertness, won renown in the spelling matches of the countryside, and revealed a genius for mathematics. At the age of sixteen he was teaching school. In 1842 he entered a law office in Little Falls, N. Y., but returned to his home town two years later to continue his legal training in an office there. About this time he experienced conversion and a call to the ministry. After a few months' preparation in Lima Seminary, he entered the sophomore class of Wesleyan University, Middletown, Conn., in 1845, and graduated in 1848. That same year he was admitted to the Genesee Conference of the Methodist Episcopal Church on trial, and on May 3, 1849, he married Ellen Lois Stowe, by whom he had seven children. He was ordained deacon, Sept. 29, 1850; and elder, Sept. 12, 1852. Until the fall of 1858 he was pastor of various churches in Western New York.

Roberts was one of a group of preachers in the Genesee Conference who laid much stress on the doctrine of Christian perfection, or sanctification, and whose piety was fervid and aggressive. They felt that the Conference as a whole had flagrantly departed from the precepts and practices of early Methodism, and condemned especially violation of the Discipline rules regarding plain churches with free seats and the wearing of adornments; the compromising attitude of the Church toward slavery; and membership of Christians in secret societies. They also contended that the Conference was virtually controlled by a band of secret-society men. A conflict arose, carried on in part through pamphlets and religious periodicals, which resulted in disciplinary measures being taken by the Conference against some of the reformers. On specifications based on an article entitled "New School Methodism," published in the *Northern Independent* of Aurora, N. Y., in 1857, Roberts was charged with unchristian and unmoral conduct. At the annual meeting of the Conference, 1857, he was tried, found guilty, and reprimanded. At the Conference of the following year, because of the republishing and circulation of his article—with which he claimed to have had nothing to do—he was expelled. Against both decisions he appealed to the General Conference, but without avail.

A result of this disturbance was the organization at Pekin, N. Y., in August 1860, of the Free

Methodist Church, of which Roberts was elected the first general superintendent, an office which he held until his death, thirty-three years later. During this period he served the interests of the growing denomination vigorously and in manifold ways. In January 1860 he established the *Earnest Christian,* which he published and edited for the remainder of his life; from 1886 to 1890 he was also editor of the *Free Methodist.* He took the leading part in the founding of Chili Seminary (A. M. Chesbrough Seminary) at North Chili, N. Y., in 1866, and served for a time as its principal. In the midst of his varied duties, which entailed much travel, he found time to write several books, among them: *Fishers of Men or, Practical Hints to Those Who Would Win Souls* (1878); *Why Another Sect* (1879); *First Lessons in Money* (1886), called forth by the prevailing discussion of the silver question; and *Ordaining Women* (1891), in which he advocated on Scriptural grounds the right of women to be admitted to the ministry. His death occurred at Cattaraugus, N. Y., in his seventieth year.

[*Alumni Records of Wesleyan Univ., Middletown, Conn.* (1911); B. H. Roberts, *Benjamin Titus Roberts* (1900); W. T. Hogue, *Hist. of the Free Meth. Ch. of North America* (2 vols., 1915); Elias Bowen, *Hist. of the Origin of the Free Meth. Ch.* (1871); F. W. Conable, *Hist. of the Genesee Ann. Conference of M. E. Ch.* (1876); *Buffalo Courier,* Mar. 1, 1893; information from a son, Benjamin T. Roberts.] H. E. S.

ROBERTS, BRIGHAM HENRY (Mar. 13, 1857–Sept. 27, 1933), Mormon leader, was born in Warrington, Lancashire, England, the son of Benjamin Roberts, a blacksmith, and Ann Everington Roberts. Before his birth the family had joined the Mormon Church. To this new faith his mother was passionately devoted, and in 1862 she left her husband in England and made the trip to Utah, taking with her the two youngest children. Brigham Henry and an elder sister were left with fellow religionists until the mother could send for them. In 1866 the son joined his mother who was living in Bountiful, a few miles north of Salt Lake City. He worked on farms and in mines, and in his early teens attended school for the first time in his life, in Davis County. At seventeen he was apprenticed to a blacksmith. In 1877 he entered the University of Deseret (now the University of Utah) and completed his course in 1878 as valedictorian of his class. He then taught school and also worked at his trade. His talents as an orator and debater were early recognized by the Mormon Church authorities who, in 1880, called him on a mission to the Middle Western and Southern states. He returned in 1882 but went on a sec-

and mission in 1883, when he became mission president. In 1886 he was transferred to the British Mission where he remained for two years and was engaged primarily in the task of editing the *Millennial Star,* a church periodical. In 1888, upon his return from England, he was made one of the First Council of Seventy. He was president of the Eastern States Mission from April 1922 to April 1927. In politics he affiliated himself with the Democratic party in 1890 and was active in the campaigns of 1892 and 1894. In the latter year he was elected a member of the Utah constitutional convention which framed the organic law of the state. In 1898 he was elected to Congress, but the House of Representatives, by action taken on Jan. 25, 1900, refused him a seat on account of his being a polygamist. He was the father of fifteen children, seven by his first wife, Louisa Smith, whom he married in 1878, and eight by his second wife, Celia Dibble, whom he married about 1885. There were no children by his third wife, Margaret Shipp.

Roberts served as chaplain on the staff of Governor Bamberger in 1917 and later as chaplain of the 145th Field Artillery. He was at Camp Kearney in California and with the regiment in France from August 1918 to January 1919. After the war he was chairman of the Mormon Battalion Monument Committee which raised two hundred thousand dollars for the Monument which now adorns the grounds of the Utah State Capitol. His chief work was in the field of historical and ecclesiastical writing. When the conflict between his people and the outside world was at its height, he brought his power of oratory and writing to bear in behalf of his people, by whom he was loved and revered as the great "Defender of the Faith." Upwards of thirty volumes and numerous pamphlets came from his pen. From 1890 to 1896 he was with the *Salt Lake Tribune,* first as associate editor and later as editor-in-chief. The crowning effort of his life in the field of historical writing was the publication, in 1930, the centennial year of the Mormon Church, of *A Comprehensive History of the Church of Jesus Christ of Latter Day Saints, Century I,* in six volumes. It represents a revision of the series of articles which he published in the *Americana* from June 1909 to July 1915. Among his other publications are: *The Life of John Taylor* (1892); *Outlines of Ecclesiastical History* (1893); *New Witnesses for God* (3 vols., 1895); *The Missouri Persecutions* (1900); *The Rise and Fall of Nauvoo* (1900); *Mormonism: The Relation of the Church to Christian Sects* (1908); *The Seventy's Course*

in Theology (5 vols., 1907–12); *The Mormon Battalion* (1919); *Why Mormonism* (1919); and *Rasha—the Jew* (1932). Roberts was a man of striking physical appearance, about six feet in height, with a well-proportioned frame, a somewhat massive head adorned in his later years by a shock of white hair. In spite of the fact that he was largely self-educated, he possessed perhaps the most sophisticated mind among his ecclesiastical contemporaries. This often resulted in his being in intellectual conflict with them. He was able to see the history of his people with the perspective of one viewing it in terms of the entire sweep of history.

[The sketch is based largely upon a manuscript autobiography of Roberts in the possession of Ben Roberts, Salt Lake City. For printed sources see: *Latter-Day Saint Biog. Encyc.,* vol. I (1901); *Cong. Record,* 56 Cong., 1 Sess., pp. 47–49, 1072–1104, 1123–49, 1175–1217, App. pp. 23, 25, 40; *Deseret News,* Sept. 28, 1933; *Salt Lake Tribune,* Sept. 28, 29, 1933.] L. N.

ROBERTS, EDMUND (June 29, 1784–June 12, 1836), merchant and special diplomatic agent of the United States in the Far East, was born at Portsmouth, N. H., to Captain Edmund and Sarah Griffiths Roberts. His father died when Edmund was a small child; his mother when he was sixteen, leaving him to the care of his bachelor uncle, Capt. Joshua Roberts, a merchant then at Buenos Aires. After eight years of commercial apprenticeship and travel, he succeeded upon his uncle's death to a substantial business. Returning to Portsmouth he was married in September 1808 to Catharine Langdon, daughter of a distinguished Portsmouth family. The Berlin and Milan decrees injured his mercantile business. French and Spanish privateers caused him heavy losses, and although he eventually recovered small amounts from the French government, he remained in straitened circumstances until his death. In 1823 he was appointed American consul at Demerara, British Guiana, but apparently did not serve. Four years later he borrowed money, chartered the brig *Mary Ann,* and sailed to Zanzibar. There he encountered costly delays and a vexatious government monopoly of trade. He protested vigorously to the ruler of Zanzibar, the Sultan of Muscat, formed an intimate acquaintance with that potentate, visited Bombay, and returned home to urge upon his kinsman through marriage, Senator Levi Woodbury of New Hampshire, a mission to the Far East to negotiate a number of commercial treaties. Roberts also urged that American naval vessels be sent occasionally to the Indian Ocean. John Shellaber, American consul at Batavia, was advocating a similar mission and hoping to receive the appointment. But through the influence of

Woodbury, who had become Jackson's secretary of the navy, Roberts was appointed on Jan. 26, 1832, special agent of the United States to negotiate treaties with Muscat, Siam, and Cochin China. On Oct. 28, 1832, he was authorized to negotiate also with Japan if practicable, and was instructed to investigate the operations of the British East India Company. His mission, however, was to be secret, and he was given as "ostensible employment" the position of clerk to the commander of the United States sloop *Peacock* at $1500 a year.

Roberts went first to Cochin China, but disagreeing with the authorities upon questions of etiquette, sailed for Bankok where on Mar. 20, 1833, he concluded a treaty of amity and commerce with Siam. The treaty freed American trade with Siam from governmental monopoly and from all export and import duties. The *Peacock* then sailed to Muscat where Roberts signed on Sept. 21, 1833, a treaty of amity and commerce with the Sultan. This treaty granted the American consul extraterritorial powers, fixed duties at five per cent., and contained a most-favored-nation clause. Although he had received further instructions to proceed to Japan, he thought it unwise and returned to Portsmouth, arriving in April 1834. In March of the following year Secretary of State Forsyth instructed him to proceed to Muscat and Siam to exchange the ratifications of the treaties he had negotiated and to attempt to negotiate commercial treaties with Cochin China and Japan. After successful visits to Muscat and Siam, he contracted a disease which caused his death at Macao on June 12, 1836. His treaties with Muscat and Siam were proclaimed June 24, 1837.

[The Edmund Roberts Papers at the Lib. of Cong. contain letters, journals, copies of diplomatic correspondence, and prepared biographical material. The archives of the Department of State contain numerous dispatches from and some instructions to Roberts. See W. M. Malloy, *Treaties, Conventions, International Acts, Protocols* (2 vols., 1910) or 8 *U. S. Statutes at Large* for the treaties of 1833 with Siam and Muscat. Edmund Roberts, *Embassy to the Eastern Courts of Cochin-China, Siam and Muscat; in the U. S. Sloop of war Peacock* (1837) suffered from official censorship. The story of the last voyage is contained in W. S. W. Ruschenberger, *A Voyage around the World: Including an Embassy to Muscat and Siam* (1838). See also: Tyler Dennett, *Americans in Eastern Asia* (1922) and H. M. Wriston, *Executive Agents in Am. Foreign Relations* (1929).]   E. W. S.

ROBERTS, ELIZABETH WENTWORTH (June 10, 1871–Mar. 12, 1927), painter, was born at Philadelphia, Pa., the daughter of well-to-do parents, G. Theodore and Sarah (Green) Roberts. They spent their summers in New Hampshire where Elizabeth, known to her friends as "Elsie," early revealed talent for outdoor sketching. She was given the best masters —Elizabeth Bonsall and Henry R. Poore in Philadelphia, and Tony Robert-Fleury, Jules Lefebvre, and Luc-Olivier Merson in Paris— and in 1889 she was awarded the Mary Smith Prize of the Pennsylvania Academy of the Fine Arts. At the Paris Salon, 1892, she received honorable mention. From Paris her studies extended into Italy where she gave special attention to Botticelli and other masters of religious art. She returned to the United States after six years' study and for a short time she had a studio in New York. During a summer at the Emerson house, Concord, Mass., while she was engaged in making a series of paintings of the historic and literary landmarks of the neighborhood, she formed friendships and associations that induced her to establish an all-year residence at Concord. Her services to American art and her assistance to other artists were even more remarkable than her own professional achievement, highly creditable though the latter was. She devoted much of her large income to forwarding the exhibitions of the Concord Art Association which under her management were of metropolitan quality. Sedulously following the seasonal exhibitions of the principal cities, she secured for the annual summer show at Concord many of the finest paintings and sculptures, and she offered generous prizes and bought many works of art for the association's permanent collection. The catalogues of these exhibitions, which Miss Roberts wrote, were models of biographical completeness and accuracy. She served also as president of the Concord Antiquarian Society.

While engaged in these and other activities Miss Roberts painted proficiently and with fervor: at first religious paintings, some of them mural decorations for the Church of St. Asaph, Bala, Pa. (described by Downes, *post*); many sketchy seascapes, made at Cape Ann and elsewhere, exquisite in tone, refined in color; and occasionally a larger, more ambitious conversation piece, such as her full-size portrait of such veterans of the Civil War as survived at Concord after the World War. The last-named work, now owned by the town of Concord, was favorably criticized by John Singer Sargent (see Coburn, *post*). During the World War Miss Roberts organized in New York and Boston several exhibitions of her "Figures on the Sand" which were sold for the benefit of the war sufferers in France. "Painted in a thin, rapidly wrought medium, her pictures of the broad and shining expanse of sand beach showing the North Shore, with the agile, buoyant, active figures of children at play or wading or swimming or digging against the splendid background of the blue ocean, are brilliant and luminous in the extreme, and notable for their expression of atmospheric spaciousness. The bigness and freedom of these scenes lend them a joyous and stimulating charm which is unique." Physically frail, emotionally subject to periods of deep melancholy, Miss Roberts was following her useful and outwardly pleasant career when she shocked her many friends by taking her life at her Concord home. She left to the Concord Art Association its building which shortly after her death housed a memorial exhibition of her works.

[Sources include: W. H. Downes, "Miss Roberts's Religious Paintings," *New Eng. Mag.*, July 1901, and "Figures on the Sand," *Boston Transcript*, Mar. 25, 1919; F. W. Coburn, "Civil War Piece at Concord," *Sunday Herald* (Boston), July 6, 1924; "Sand Pictures by Elizabeth W. Roberts," *Am. Art News*, Mar. 9, 1918; *Boston Transcript*, Mar. 12, 1927; *Lowell Courier-Citizen*, Mar. 17, 1927; information from associates of Miss Roberts, and personal recollections.]

F. W. C.

ROBERTS, ELLIS HENRY (Sept. 30, 1827–Jan. 8, 1918), congressman, financier, was born in Utica, N. Y., then a village, his parents, Watkin and Gwen (Williams) Roberts, having emigrated from North Wales some ten years previously. His father died when Ellis was four years of age, and the boy was early thrown on his own resources. He learned the printer's trade, and with his own earnings pursued his education at Whitestown Seminary and Yale College, where he graduated in 1850. Returning to Utica, he became identified with the *Oneida Morning Herald,* a daily newspaper of which his brother was one of the owners. This journal, later known as the *Utica Morning Herald,* he continued to serve in an editorial capacity, save for an interim of a few months, until the year 1890.

In politics he was a Republican; in 1866 he was elected to the state legislature, where he served one term, and in 1870 he was elected to Congress; he was returned in 1872, but defeated in 1874 by Scott Lord in the Democrat landslide of that year. In his early political life he was a supporter of Roscoe Conkling [q.v.], taking an active part, when a member of the New York legislature, in Conkling's first election as United States senator, but very shortly thereafter there was a breach in their friendly relations which was never healed. Roberts became the leader of the local faction of the Republican party known as the "Half-Breeds," opposed to Conkling and his "Stalwart" supporters, and in 1884 the diminished Republican vote in Oneida County, where the two leaders had their residence, was sufficient to account for the small plurality

by which the electoral vote of New York was lost to the Republican presidential candidate.

In 1889 Roberts was appointed assistant treasurer of the United States by President Benjamin Harrison, in which office he served until 1893, when he became president of the Franklin National Bank of New York. In 1897, he was appointed treasurer of the United States by President McKinley, continuing in that office until 1905. After his retirement he returned to Utica, where he died in 1918 at the advanced age of ninety years.

Roberts early acquired distinction as a writer and speaker, and during his service in Congress gained recognition as one versed in questions of finance. He took a prominent part in the discussion and enactment of legislation for the resumption of specie payments, the refunding of the national debt, the redemption of bonds, and the reduction of war debts, as well as at all times advocating a policy of protection. In his first term he was accorded the unusual honor of an appointment upon the ways and means committee. He was also a member of a sub-committee which investigated the collection of customs, with a report which prompted several resignations and helped to bring about the repeal of the moiety laws. In 1884 he delivered a course of lectures at Cornell University which formed the basis of a volume entitled *Government Revenue: Especially the American System; an Argument against the Fallacies of Free Trade* (1884; 4th ed., 1888). He also wrote *New York: The Planting and the Growth of the Empire State* (2 vols., 1887), in the American Commonwealths Series. In June 1851 he married Elizabeth Morris, but they were without children.

[M. M. Bagg, *Memorial Hist. of Utica* (1892); H. J. Cookinham, *Hist. of Oneida County, N. Y.* (1912), vol. I, esp. pp. 289–92; D. E. Wager, *Our County and Its People . . . Oneida County, N. Y.* (1896); J. G. Blaine, *Twenty Years in Congress*, vol. II (1886); *Obit. Record Grads. Yale Univ.*, 1918 (1919); D. S. Alexander, *A Pol. Hist. of the State of N. Y.*, III (1909), 169–70, 388; *N. Y. Times*, Jan. 9, 1918; files of *Utica Daily Press* and *Utica Observer-Dispatch*.]

W. J. K.

ROBERTS, GEORGE BROOKE (Jan. 15, 1833–Jan. 30, 1897), railroad executive, was born on his father's farm, "Pencoed," near Bala, Montgomery County, Pa., the son of Isaac Warner and Rosalinda Evans (Brooke) Roberts. He received his early education in the schools near his home and then attended the Rensselaer Polytechnic Institute at Troy, N. Y., where he was graduated in 1849. Two years later he entered the service of the Pennsylvania Railroad as a rodman on the mountain division. In 1852, he became assistant engineer on the Sunbury &

Erie Railroad, forerunner of the Philadelphia & Erie, and for the next ten years he was in the employ of various railroad companies engaged in construction work. In 1862, he became assistant to the president of the Pennsylvania Railroad, J. Edgar Thomson [q.v.], being in full charge of the building of the company's lines. He served also as a director after May 3, 1869, and in that year was promoted to the fourth, soon afterward to the second, vice-presidency. In 1874, when Thomas A. Scott [q.v.] became president of the company, Roberts succeeded him in the position of first vice-president. He now assisted the president in all business pertaining to leased or controlled roads and had charge of all engineering matters relating to the construction, extension, and improvement of the company's lines, as well as a general supervision of its accounts. On June 1, 1880, he was elected president of the Pennsylvania Railroad Company to succeed Scott, and served in that capacity until his death. During his administration much additional trackage and a number of new feeder lines were constructed, equipment and terminals were improved, grades were reduced, and many grade crossings eliminated. A number of roads west of Pittsburgh were leased and reorganized as part of the Pennsylvania system; the Philadelphia, Wilmington & Baltimore Railroad was taken over to afford a connection with the South; and the company's financial position was improved until its credit standing was unequaled in the country at the time.

Roberts frequently served as chairman of the board of presidents of the Trunk Line Association, in which position he did much to solve the problems growing out of the incessant competition then existing between rival railway interests. He was always ready to aid any movement looking to the bettering of the condition of the company's employees and in this connection encouraged the formation and development of the railroad departments of the Young Men's Christian Association. He was a devout Episcopalian and a liberal giver to charitable and public objects, serving as a director of the Free Public Library of Philadelphia and vice-president of the Fairmount Park Art Association. He was twice married: in 1868 to Sarah Lapsley Brinton, and in 1874 to Miriam P. Williams. He died on his family's farm near Bala, Pa., survived by two daughters and four sons.

[Minute on the Death of George B. Roberts, Adopted by the Board of Directors of the Pa. R. R. Company (1897); official biog. of G. B. Roberts (MS.), in possession of the Pa. R. R. Company, Phila.; W. B. Wilson, Hist. of the Pa. R. R. Company (1899), vol. II, and Hist. of the Pa. R. R. Dept. of the Y. M. C. A. of Phila. (1911); H. W. Schotter, The Growth and Development of the Pa. R. R. Company (1927); A. K. McClure, Old Time Notes of Pa. (1905), vol. I; Railroad Gazette, Feb. 5, 1897; Pub. Ledger (Phila.), Feb. 1, 1897; name of mother from Roberts' sons, G. B. Roberts and T. W. Roberts.]   J. H. F.

ROBERTS, HOWARD (Apr. 9, 1843–Apr. 18, 1900), sculptor, the son of Edward Roberts, merchant, and Mary Elizabeth Reford, was born in Philadelphia, Pa., the last of a family of nine children. He was descended from ancestors who emigrated from North Wales and settled in Merion, Pa., in 1683. His grandfather, Algernon Roberts, was an officer in the Pennsylvania militia in the Revolution, while earlier members of the family were prominent in affairs of the provincial government. Howard Roberts attended the Classical Institute of the Rev. John W. Faires in Philadelphia and began to study art under J. A. Bailly at the Pennsylvania Academy of the Fine Arts. At the age of twenty-three he entered the École des Beaux-Arts in Paris, working under Dumont and Gumery. After completing his European studies he returned to America in 1871 and established a studio in Philadelphia where in the following year he modeled his first important work, a statuette of Hester and Pearl based upon Hawthorne's Scarlet Letter. Exhibited at the Pennsylvania Academy, it attracted considerable attention and won for its sculptor membership in the Academy itself. Roberts had joined the Sketch Club in 1861 and served that organization variously through succeeding years as treasurer, vice-president, and president.

In Paris again from 1873 to 1876 Roberts produced "La Première Pose" (now in the Philadelphia Museum of Art), which won him at the Philadelphia Centennial Exhibition of 1876 one of the three medals accorded work by American sculptors. His "Hypatia" (now at the Pennsylvania Academy) and "Lot's Wife" were considered bold compositions in their day. At the time of the Centennial, when his popularity was at its height, his work was said to have "technical qualities the highest, perhaps, of any among the American statuary" (Illustrated Catalogue of the Masterpieces of the International Exhibition, 1876). As the result of a competition for the life-size statue of Robert Fulton for the Rotunda of the National Capitol, Washington, D. C., Roberts won a national reputation, having been selected from among thirty leading sculptors. The statue was erected in 1883. Always active in art and intellectual circles, Roberts became a member of the Penn Club in which he was associated with men of art, science, and literature, and his name appears as a member of the Club's board of management when a charter was granted in 1889. In addition to statues and statuettes of literary or classical flavor, Roberts produced many portrait busts. An ideal head, "Eleanor," acquired by Henry C. Gibson for his collection, has passed through bequest to the Pennsylvania Academy of the Fine Arts. Roberts was married, on June 1, 1876, to Helen Pauline Lewis. In 1900, with his wife and son, he went to Paris expecting to remain three years, but his career was abruptly terminated by his sudden death.

[Sources include: C. J. Cohen, *The Penn Club* (1924); C. E. Clement and Laurence Hutton, *Artists of the Nineteenth Century* (1885); Lorado Taft, *The Hist. of Am. Sculpture* (1924); *Am. Art Annual*, 1900–01; *Who's Who in America*, 1899–1900; J. W. Jordan, *Colonial and Revolutionary Families of Pa.*, vol. I (1911); *Pub. Ledger* (Phila.), Apr. 19, 1900; Roberts family papers in the possession of the Pa. Hist. Soc.]

D. G—y.

ROBERTS, ISSACHAR JACOB (Feb. 17, 1802–Dec. 28, 1871), missionary to China, began his picturesque existence in Sumner County, Tenn. When he was about nineteen years old he was converted, and later pursued his studies at the Furman Theological Institution, South Carolina. On Apr. 27, 1827, he was ordained at Shelbyville, Tenn. Subsequently, he organized the Roberts Fund and China Mission Society on the basis of property which he owned in Mississippi, reputedly worth $30,000, and in 1836 sailed for China under this fund, arriving there the following year. He began his missionary labors at Macao, working as a saddler and preaching to a colony of lepers, which connection ostracized him from his fellow missionaries. Finding his income insufficient, in 1841 he joined the Baptist Mission and following the organization of the Southern Baptist Convention transferred to the latter (Jan. 1, 1846); in 1852 he finally reverted to a completely independent status. He helped open the Baptist Mission at Hong Kong in 1842, laboring first at the village of Chek-chu—partly among British troops (*Baptist Missionary Magazine*, June 1843)—and the next year at Victoria (Hong Kong). In 1844 he moved to Canton, where he leased a lot and built a chapel. The plundering of his house by a mob in 1847 formed the basis of a long-standing claim against the Chinese government (*Senate Executive Document No. 30*, 36 Cong., 1 Sess., pp. 105–06); subsequently, January 1849, an attack was made on his life, which resulted in an appeal to the American consul for "official interposition" and protection (China Despatches, MSS., Department of State, Jan. 27, 1849).

About 1847 Roberts gave instruction for two months to an inquirer named Hung, who afterward, as the Tien Wang ("Heavenly King"),

became leader of the pseudo-Christian Taiping Rebellion. In 1853 he addressed from his capital at Nanking a letter to Roberts asking him to come and instruct the people. The zealous missionary felt "constrained to go" and, disregarding the strong disapproval of the project on the part of the American Commissioner, he turned up in Shanghai with two rebel princes (L. S. Foster, *Fifty Years in China*, 1909, pp. 80–81) and made a futile attempt to reach Nanking. He contented himself for the time being with fulsome and egotistical writings on the revolution and on his own unique connection with its leader (see *Spirit of Missions*, May 1854; *Putnam's Magazine*, October 1856). On Oct. 13, 1860, he finally reached Nanking, where he was assistant to the chief minister of state, a former "convert" named Hung Jin and denoted the Kan Wang ("Shield King"). Roberts wore yellow robes and a crown, and became minister of foreign affairs. On Jan. 13, 1862, he accused the Kan Wang of murdering his servant and the dignified mandarin retaliated by dousing his astonished assistant with the dregs of a cup of tea. Roberts, fearing for his life, fled to Shanghai, where he published a letter giving his version of the incident and asserting furthermore that the Tien Wang was mad and his movement hopeless (*North China Herald*, Feb. 8, 1862, quoted in Henri Cordier, *Histoire des Relations de la Chine avec les Puissances Occidentales*, vol. I, 1901, p. 209). In 1866 Roberts returned to the United States, whither his wife and two children had preceded him in 1855. He had gone back to marry her in 1849, a former wife, to whom he was married Jan. 4, 1830, having died in 1831. Roberts died of leprosy at Upper Alton, Ill. He was strikingly uncouth and had marked eccentricities. On one occasion he ignored a dying missionary with the remark, "Let the dead bury their dead, but I must preach the gospel." His writings, however, reveal religious sincerity.

[G. W. Hervey, *The Story of Baptist Missions* (1884); K. S. Latourette, *The Hist. of Early Relations between the U. S. and China* (1917); Alexander Wylie, *Memorials of Protestant Missionaries to the Chinese* (1867); E. F. Merriam, *A Hist. of Am. Baptist Missions* (1900); W. A. P. Martin, *A Cycle of Cathay* (1896); Tyler Dennett, *Americans in Eastern Asia* (1922); Lindesay Brine, *The Taeping Rebellion in China* (1862); *The Missionary Jubilee* (1865).]

J. S. L.

ROBERTS, JOB (Mar. 23, 1756–Aug. 20, 1851), pioneer agriculturist, was born at "Woodlawn Farm," Whitpain, near Gwynedd, Pa. He was the third son and ninth child of John Roberts and Jane Hank, and a great-grandson of Robert Cadwalader who emigrated from Wales some time prior to 1698. Cadwalader's children adopted the surname Robert, which was later again changed to Roberts. According to tradition, the family joined the Society of Friends shortly after their arrival, for Roberts' grandfather married according to the order of the Friends in 1706, and for generations his descendants have been members of Gwynedd Meeting. Job Roberts married first Mary Naylor, on May 22, 1781, by whom he had two daughters. His second wife, to whom he was married on Oct. 12, 1820, was Sarah (Williams) Thomas, daughter of Joseph Williams. For his achievements in better farming, crop experiment, and improved farm machinery, "Squire Job Roberts" deserves to be remembered. His interest in scientific agriculture is said to have been inspired by the Philadelphia Society for Promoting Agriculture which was founded in 1785. He experimented with fertilizers, the use of lime, plaster, and various barnyard manures, and in the deep ploughing of land. In 1804 he published the results of experiments in *The Pennsylvania Farmer,* a practical book, simply written, full of interesting material, and still valuable. He records intensive methods of cultivation which resulted in bumper wheat crops of sixty bushels to the acre.

His experiments with plaster of Paris and with gypsum as fertilizers began in 1785. In 1792 he built an improved harrow and devised a new roller. In 1797 he attached a water-wheel to a dairy churn making it possible to produce with it 150 pounds of butter a week. In 1815 he invented a machine for planting corn at even distances in hills. By soaking the grains of Indian corn in water before planting, to bring about quick germination, he advanced the growing season, and it is recorded that he rarely produced less than eighty bushels to an acre. He introduced into Pennsylvania Merino sheep; and he was interested, as were the other scientific farmers of his age, in cultivating the mulberry for silk culture. He substituted green fodder for his cattle in place of grazing, and built a barn "which was enormously large, according to usual standards, but which he soon had full of crops." Despite the obvious utility of his experiments and activities, his neighbors and chroniclers seem to have been most impressed by the fact that in 1780 "he built himself a carriage, the first to be seen in the county, in which for the next twenty-five years, he drove himself to Gwynedd Meeting." In 1791 Governor Mifflin appointed Roberts justice of the peace. Beyond that he would accept no public office, though he devoted much of his time to public trusts and to private charity, and he was "habitually consulted by his neighbors in matters of difficulty, whether in political, personal or rural affairs" (Tyson, *post,* p. 10).

[See: J. R. Tyson, *Address Delivered Before the Montgomery County Agric. Soc.* (1856); H. M. Jenkins, *Hist. Colls. Relating to Gwynedd* (1897); *Germantown Telegraph,* Dec. 17, 1856.]   M. P. S.

ROBERTS, JONATHAN (Aug. 16, 1771– July 21, 1854), congressman and senator from Pennsylvania, was born near Norristown, Pa., the son of Jonathan and Anna (Thomas) Roberts and the descendant of John Roberts, a Welsh Friend who emigrated to Pennsylvania in William Penn's time. On that portion of his original plantation known as "Swamp Vrass," in Upper Merion Township, Montgomery County, his great-grand-son passed his childhood. The boy received private tutoring, learned farming, and acquired a fondness for books under the guidance of his mother, who taught him to appreciate the ancient Stoics. After apprenticeship to a wheelwright, he returned to farming, and he and his brother reported, "in seven years we could command seven thousand dollars, and had greatly increased our stock and improved our land" (Auge, *post,* p. 73). Nurtured upon the excitements of the whiskey and house tax rebellions and breathing naturally the atmosphere of violent partisanship characteristic of that period, he equipped himself carefully for polemical politics and joined the Republicans in wresting control of Montgomery County from the Federalists. He helped to make up the majority of two in the lower house of the Assembly, 1799–1800, confronting the Senate Federalist majority of one. His next activity was in the state Senate, 1807–11, from which he was carried, along with other "war hawks," into the federal Congress, 1811 to 1814. There he confidently faced a war with the traditional enemy, "I repose safely in the maxim, 'Never to despair of the Republic.'" While the vote for war with Great Britain was pending, he prevented delay through indefinite adjournment by cannily proposing to suspend members' pay while adjourned, and at a crucial moment he called for the previous question (*Annals of Congress,* 12 Cong., 1 Sess., cols. 1337–38, 1340). This stand, perforce, severed his religious connections with the Friends; but political connections grew apace. His close relations with Madison were revealed in his controversial letters defending the administration in the *Aurora.* As a committeeman on ways and means he guarded the national pursestrings and took the rôle of floor defender of the secretary of the treasury, Albert

Gallatin, against Cheves, Calhoun, and Lowndes. At Gallatin's instance he visited Governor Snyder to urge veto of a Pennsylvania bank bill. Meanwhile, he had married in 1813 Eliza Hite Bushby of Washington. They had nine children. Soon, in February 1814, factional warfare deprived Michael Leib [q.v.] of his seat in the Senate, and the Pennsylvania legislature placed Roberts in it. There he marvelled at the peaceful years ensuing, "I never knew a time so politically tranquil. . . . There is nothing indicative of that acrimony we have long been accustomed to" (Roberts to Monroe, June 9, Aug. 22, 1818, in possession of Historical Society of Pennsylvania). But Roberts' existence speedily became normal, for from his cordial disapproval of Jackson's Florida foray sprang a lifelong antipathy between them. The Maine-Missouri question also brought conflict, for Roberts stoutly defended a plan of his own to prevent the introduction of any more slaves into Missouri (*Annals of Congress,* 16 Cong., 1 Sess., cols. 85–86, 116–17, 119–28, 335–46).

After leaving the Senate in 1821, he endeavored to diminish Jackson's presidential chances, being "very decided" (*Life of Gallatin, post,* p. 588) that the Democracy needed Gallatin as a candidate in 1824 and serving in the Pennsylvania House, 1823–26, to stem the tide of Jacksonianism. The economic advancement of his own state he also held dear, advocating internal improvements, serving on the canal commission, and attending pioneer tariff conventions. After membership upon Biddle's bank board in 1836 he naturally gravitated into the Whig camp, supporting Clay, and he nominated Tyler for vice-president at the Harrisburg convention in 1839. Characteristically, when made collector of the port of Philadelphia he balked over the spoils system, and the president removed him in 1842. With this bold engagement the active political warfare of this sturdy Roman was concluded. He died on his farm in Montgomery County.

[Manuscript memoirs willed to his grandson, Jonathan Roberts of Atlantic City; letters to Madison, Monroe, and Gallatin in Lib. of Hist. Soc. Pa., and Lib. of Cong.; Moses Auge, *Lives of the Eminent Dead* (1879); Henry Adams, *Hist. of the U. S.,* vol. VII (1891) and *The Life of Albert Gallatin* (1872); H. R. Mueller, *The Whig Party in Pa.* (1922); *Hist. Sketches. A Collection of Papers Prepared for the Hist. Soc. of Montgomery County, Pa.,* vol. III, IV (1905–10); *Letters and Other Writings of James Madison* (1865), vol. III.]

J. P. N.

ROBERTS, JOSEPH JENKINS (Mar. 15, 1809–Feb. 24, 1876), first president of Liberia, West Africa, was born of free, colored parents at Petersburg, Va., having seven-eighths or more of white blood. He married at an early age in Virginia but lost his wife, and in 1829 he migrated to Liberia with his widowed mother and younger brothers and there became a merchant. The governor of the colony at that time, Thomas H. Buchanan, a white appointee of the American Colonization Society, was having trouble with the natives, who were not reconciled to the invasion of the American freedmen. During the fighting with the Dey and Golah tribes, Roberts became one of Buchanan's most efficient leaders. Owing to his energetic work, most of the more threatening natives were reduced to submission. He then made every effort to make friends with the natives, and, after Buchanan died, he was appointed in January 1842 the first colored man to become governor of Liberia, at that time, however, comprising only the northern part of what is now its best territory. Although the colony of Maryland was not formally a part of Liberia until 1857, its governor, John Russwurm [q.v.], gave Roberts full cooperation. The necessity of organizing the country, pacifying the natives, and repelling the illicit slave traders, called for larger revenues than Roberts or Russwurm had. Accordingly, they decided to lay import duties on goods brought to Liberia. This precipitated grave international difficulties, for Liberia was not a sovereign country, nor was it, on the other hand, a recognized colony of the United States. The British approached the United States on the subject but received a non-committal answer. Since positive action seemed to be necessary, Roberts, after strengthening his treaties with the native tribes, visited the United States in 1844 in the hope of adjusting the matter. At such a difficult time, when the question of the annexation of Texas was forcing the slavery question to the front, the American government avoided taking any strong ground in defense of Liberia, and the American Colonization Society gave up all claims upon the colony.

He returned, continued his purchase of lands from the chiefs, and in 1847 called a conference at which the new republic of Liberia was proclaimed. He was elected as the first president, and, reëlected in 1849, 1851, and 1853, he served his country carefully and wisely. As soon as the new nation was proclaimed, he hurried to England. His unexpected success there was due largely to his own character and finesse. He was a man of intelligence and poise, slight and handsome, with olive skin and crisp hair. He was an excellent conversationalist and had the manners of a gentleman. His second wife, Jane (Waring) Roberts, to whom he was married in Monrovia in 1836, was a woman of education and spoke excellent French. In Europe he received unusual attention. He signed a commercial treaty in 1849 with Great Britain, which recognized Liberia as an independent nation and gave Englishmen freedom of domicile. Before he left England, ten thousand dollars was raised by his English friends and given to him to buy the territory between Liberia and Sierra Leone, where the slave trade was flourishing. Later he visited France and Belgium, where he was received by Leopold I, and also Holland and Prussia. In 1852 he again visited France, where he was received by the prince president, afterward Napoleon III. These visits were largely instrumental in obtaining speedy recognition of Liberia. After finishing his term he continued to be active in the interests of Liberia, even to the extent of taking the field against rebellious natives. In 1856 he was elected first president of the new College of Liberia and continued in that office until his death. He visited Europe again in 1854 and 1862, and on his return from the last trip he was appointed Belgian consul in Liberia. In 1869 he visited the United States, where he addressed the annual meeting of the African Colonization Society at Washington on *African Colonization* (1869). When there arose in Liberia the financial difficulties with regard to a British loan (see sketch of Edward James Roye) Liberia came near to revolution. At the age of 63 and already broken in health by his long service, he was again elected to the presidency in 1871. Reëlected, he served until January 1876 and died at Monrovia in February.

[H. H. Johnston, *Liberia* (1906), vol. I; B. G. Brawley, *A Social Hist. of the Am. Negro* (1921); "A Visit to Monrovia," *African Repository*, Jan. 1876; "Obituary," *Ibid.*, Apr. 1876; *Sixtieth Ann. Report of the Am. Colonization Soc.* (1877), p. 6; date of death from *African Repository* and *Report of the Am. Colonization Soc.*]   W. E. B. D–B.

ROBERTS, MARSHALL OWEN (Mar. 22, 1814–Sept. 11, 1880), capitalist, was apparently the son of Owen Roberts, a Welsh physician who settled in New York City about 1800 and died when Marshall was a child. The latter is said to have worked for a grocer, a saddler, and a ship chandler. By 1834 he was a ship chandler himself. He engaged in Hudson River navigation and is said to have been among the original promoters of the Erie and the Lackawanna railroads: of the former he was a director. Although he was financially successful almost from the beginning of his independent career, a search of the records reveals no basis for the story that President Harrison appointed him naval agent in charge of contracts at New York and that

heavy naval contracts in the Mexican War were the basis of his fortune.

In 1847 Roberts came into prominence through connection with government subsidy of mail steamships. With George Law [*q.v.*] and others as joint trustees, he took over the contract just awarded to Albert G. Sloo. This contract granted $290,000 annually for ten years for fortnightly service from New York to New Orleans, touching at Havana, where a branch line was run to the Isthmus of Panama to connect with the Pacific Mail Steamship Company of William Henry Aspinwall [*q.v.*]. Their first ship sailed late in 1848, just at the start of the gold rush, an unforeseen piece of luck which tremendously increased business. In 1851, they started direct lines from New York and New Orleans to Aspinwall on the Isthmus, in addition to the stipulated Havana run, receiving no added subsidy. Meanwhile in 1850 Roberts and his associates organized the United States Mail Steamship Company (incorporated Apr. 6, 1850), to which they assigned their interests in the Sloo contract. In 1854 Roberts, who had been New York agent, succeeded Law as president and two years later, in a suit in equity brought by Sloo (3 *Blatchford, Circuit Court Reports,* 459) he in particular was charged with unscrupulous manipulation of "the business controlled by the trustees" in favor of the United States Mail Steamship Company. Sloo was granted an injunction which somewhat hampered Roberts' operations. By this time the gold rush had waned and the competition of Cornelius Vanderbilt [*q.v.*] had materially reduced profits; in 1858 when the contract expired, Roberts estimated that the company had lost two millions. He then made a brazen attempt to recover this loss from the government on the flimsy ground that there had been no added subsidy for the extra direct service to Aspinwall. Intensive lobbying finally produced an act of Congress referring Roberts' case to the Court of Claims, which rejected his claim (6 *Court of Claims Reports,* 84), but in 1875 Roberts and an associate received $1,031,000 through a Supreme Court decision (*Roberts* vs. *U. S.*, 92 *U. S.*, 41, and 11 *Court of Claims*, 774).

Roberts' chartering and selling of steamships during the Civil War forms an interesting chapter in the history of profiteering. He made nearly three millions from a half dozen steamers picked up for a song. The $12,500 he received for sending the *Star of the West* to relieve Fort Sumter was a mere bagatelle. It is said that he sold the *Union* as a transport for $100,000 and she sank almost at once. He bought the *Empire City* at auction from his old company for

$12,000 and the army alone paid him at least $900,000 in addition to what he received from naval charters. The *Illinois* brought some $414,000 in charters and then, early in 1865, was purchased at Lincoln's order for $400,000. This price was set by a board headed by Roberts' friend Moses Taylor, though army officers thought her worth only half that price. Congress investigated these dealings in 1866 and 1878 but nothing happened. Roberts made several generous gestures during the war with gifts and bond purchases, and, as his obituary remarked, "his patriotism stood him in good stead" (*New York Herald,* Sept. 12, 1880).

His political career may partially explain this success. He was rated with A. T. Stewart as one of the leading Republican contributors. An anti-Seward Whig and then a Republican, he was defeated for Congress in 1852 and was a delegate to the first Republican National Convention in 1856. In 1865, he lost the New York mayoralty to J. T. Hoffman [*q.v.*] by a narrow margin. In 1868, he was a presidential elector and helped finance the senatorial election of R. E. Fenton [*q.v.*], but Fenton's backing failed to secure for Roberts the nomination for governor in 1870. Just before the exposure of the "Tweed ring," Roberts, John Jacob Astor, Moses Taylor, and three others certified that its financial affairs were "administered in a correct and faithful manner" (Lynch, *post*, p. 347).

Roberts continued active in shipping, running a line to Havana, planning Nicaragua service, and keeping alive the Mexican charter for a Tehuantepec railroad. He was for many years president of the North River Bank. In 1854, he had been one of a group of five to finance Field's first cable venture. He had an art collection appraised at half a million in his mansion at 107 Fifth Avenue. He worshipped for years at the Broadway Tabernacle; finally at Calvary Church. The first of his three wives was a Miss C. D. Amerman of New York City; the second, Caroline D. Smith of Hartford, whom he married in 1847; she was an organizer of the Young Women's Christian Association, and died in 1874. His third wife was Susan Lawrence Endicott, daughter of John Endicott of New York City. Roberts died at Saratoga Springs at the age of sixty-six.

[Gustavus Myers, *Hist. of the Great Am. Fortunes* (1910); D. T. Lynch, *"Boss" Tweed* (1927); D. S. Alexander, *A Pol. Hist. of the State of N. Y.,* vol. III (1909); E. H. Mott, *Between the Ocean and the Lakes: The Story of Erie* (1899); for the U. S. Mail S. S. Company, *Sen. Report 440,* 34 Cong., 3 Sess., *Sen. Report 326,* 35 Cong., 1 Sess., *House Report 648,* 36 Cong., 1 Sess., pp. 797, 809, 823–29, *Sen. Report 292,* 36 Cong., 2 Sess., *House Report 49,* 37 Cong., 3 Sess., pp. 94–96; for Civil War charters and sales, *House Report 49,* 37 Cong., 3 Sess., p. 95; *House Ex. Doc. 65,* 39 Cong., 2 Sess.; *House Ex. Doc. 337,* 40 Cong., 2 Sess.; *House Ex. Doc. 92,* 45 Cong., 2 Sess.; *Official Records of the Union and Confederate Navies,* 1 ser. IV, 245, VII, 158–64.]   R. G. A.

ROBERTS, NATHAN S. (July 28, 1776–Nov. 24, 1852), civil engineer, was born in Piles Grove, N. J., the son of Abraham Roberts, a native of New Hampshire whose Puritan forefathers, emigrating from England in 1640, had settled in Auburn, Mass. During his minority Nathan helped to support his parents and younger brothers. When he became of age he purchased a hundred acres of land in Vermont, where he began the cutting of timber, but he returned to New Jersey and taught school at Plainfield during the winter. In 1804, he moved to Oneida County, N. Y., where he acquired some land. He taught school at Oriskany until 1806, when he was appointed principal of the academy at Whitesboro. Here, on Nov. 4, 1816, he married Lavinia, daughter of Ansel White and grand-daughter of Judge Hugh White, pioneer settler of the region; in the same year he purchased a farm in Lenox, Madison County, which was his home during the remainder of his life.

In July 1816 he became an assistant to Benjamin Wright of Rome, engineer in charge of the building of the middle section of the Erie Canal, in making a survey of the route. From that time until 1822 he was engaged in exploratory surveys and location work on the section of the canal between Rome and Rochester, including the drafting of plans for locks between Clyde and Rochester. From 1822 until its completion in 1825, he was in charge of the construction of the western section of the canal, from Lockport to Buffalo. He drafted the plan which was adopted and superintended the construction of five pairs of locks at Lockport to overcome the barrier formed by a sixty-foot rocky ridge—a more elaborate scheme of locks than had ever been constructed in America.

Upon the completion of the Erie Canal, he became a consulting engineer for the Chesapeake & Delaware Canal and in 1826, for the state of New York, made a survey and reported on a route for a ship canal around Niagara Falls. Then followed service as chief engineer of the western end of the Pennsylvania State Canal, that part between Pittsburgh and Kiskimenetas. During a visit home he made an investigation and report for the New York State Canal Board on the practicability of supplying the summit level of the projected Chenango Canal with water. In association with James Geddes [*q.v.*] he reviewed the estimates of the line of the Chesapeake & Ohio Canal for the secretary of war and subsequently examined the country between Johnstown and Franktown for a possible route for a railroad or portage over the mountains to connect the eastern and western sections of the Pennsylvania State Canal. From December 1828, as a member of the board of engineers of the Chesapeake & Ohio Canal Company, he was engaged for some two years in the revision and location of extensions of that canal, building the section between Point of Rocks and Harpers Ferry, and during the same period was associated with Jonathan Knight [q.v.] in preliminary work in the same territory for the Baltimore & Ohio Railroad. Having made a reputation as a canal engineer, he was appointed by the federal government to take charge of surveys for a ship canal around Muscle Shoals in the Tennessee River, Alabama. In the spring of 1835, in association with John B. Jervis [q.v.] and Holmes Hutchinson, he made a series of examinations and surveys for the New York State Canal Board to estimate the expense of enlarging the Erie Canal, and in 1839, as chief engineer, began the enlargement of the canal between Rochester and Buffalo. In 1841, while still thus engaged and about to complete his last great task, the Rochester Aqueduct, he was removed from office for political reasons, by the new Whig administration. Since through his profession he had attained sufficient means to make him financially independent, he now retired to his farm in Madison County, where he spent his remaining years.

[Practically the only biography is that in C. B. Stuart, *Lives and Works of Civil and Military Engineers* (1871), although scattered references occur in material on the Erie Canal and the other works with which Roberts was connected. Since Roberts had a son named Nathan Smith Roberts, it seems probable that Smith was the father's middle name. See A. S. Kellogg, *White Geneal.* (1860).]   B. A. R.

ROBERTS, ORAN MILO (July 1815–May 19, 1898), lawyer, jurist, soldier, statesman, was born in Laurens District, S. C., the son of Obe Roberts, of Welsh ancestry, and Margaret Ewing. From South Carolina his father removed with his family to Ashville, in the mountain region of northern Alabama, where he died when Oran was but ten years of age. Soon thereafter the widow moved to a small farm on which her son labored until he was sixteen. At that age he announced that he was going to college, a resolve that he was enabled to carry into execution with the financial assistance of his brother-in-law, Robert Bourland, a blacksmith, and with the tutoring of Ralph P. Lowe [q.v.], afterward a member of the supreme court of Iowa, who prepared him to enter the university. In 1836, at the age of twenty-one, he graduated from the University of Alabama. He at once began the study of law with Judge Ptolemy Harris, whose children he tutored to defray his expenses. Later he read law in the office of William P. Chilton, who was subsequently a member of the supreme court of Alabama. He was admitted to the bar on Sept. 22, 1837, and for four years practised law, first in Talladega and later in Ashville, Ala. During this time he served one term in the legislature to which he was elected when but twenty-three years of age. In 1841 he answered the call of the new West and moved to Texas and took up the practice of law at San Augustine, near the eastern border of the infant republic. Although this little city then had one of the strongest bars in the country, young Roberts rose rapidly and was soon riding an extensive circuit of eastern Texas counties along with the district judge and the lawyers of established practice. On Feb. 6, 1844, a little more than two years after his arrival in Texas, President Houston appointed him district attorney. Two years later he was appointed district judge by J. Pinkney Henderson, the first governor of Texas. This position he held until 1851. On Feb. 1, 1857, he was elected associate justice of the supreme court of Texas to fill the vacancy caused by the death of Judge A. S. Lipscomb.

In spite of his position on the bench, he took an active part in the slavery controversy and was elected by acclamation president of the convention that met in Austin in January 1861 and submitted the secession ordinance to a vote of the people. Late in 1861 he resigned from the court and early in 1862 he raised a regiment, the 11th Texas Infantry, and became its colonel. For two years he served in the army with distinction, but upon the death of Chief Justice Royall T. Wheeler, Roberts, while still with his command in Louisiana, was elected chief justice in 1864. This office he held until the collapse of the Confederate cause in 1865. He was chairman of the judiciary committee in the constitutional convention of 1866. In August of that year he was elected to the United States Senate but was not allowed to take his seat. During the next eight years he practised his profession at Tyler, and at Gilmer, where for a time he conducted a law school.

After the Democratic party returned to power in Texas in 1873, Roberts in January 1874 was appointed chief justice of the supreme court. His opinions show a capacity for research and a power of analysis that mark him as one of the greatest judges the state of Texas has ever had. In *Hancock* vs. *Butler* (21 *Tex.*, 804) he introduced into the jurisprudence of Texas the rule in Shelley's Case and explained its intricacies; while in *Chambers* vs. *Fisk* (22 *Tex.*, 504) he discussed the action of trespass to try title to land and gave a comprehensive history of the land law of Texas from early Spanish days. In *McCoy* vs. *The State* (25 *Tex.*, 33) he gave an exhaustive treatment of "malice aforethought" in murder, while an equally thorough treatment of assault is to be found in *McKay* vs. *The State* (44 *Tex.*, 43). In *Houston Tap and Brazoria Railway Company* vs. *Randolph* (24 *Tex.*, 317) and in his dissenting opinion in *Kuechler* vs. *Wright* (40 *Tex.*, 600, 647) he strongly argued that, in a government divided into separate and coördinate departments, no court could have jurisdiction to issue a writ of *mandamus* to the head of any executive department to compel the performance of an official duty, but in this opinion the majority of the court refused to follow him, and their view was incorporated into the constitution of 1876.

In 1878, while still chief justice, Roberts was elected governor, and in 1880 he was reëlected. As governor he adopted as his motto "Pay as you go," and as a result the financial condition of the state was greatly improved. The outstanding achievement of his administration was the establishment of the University of Texas, which opened its doors in the fall of 1883. Upon his retirement from the governor's office, in 1883, he was elected professor of law in the University. He resigned this position in 1893 and died in Austin on May 19, 1898. In December 1837, shortly after having been admitted to the bar, he had married Frances W. Edwards, daughter of Maj. Peter Edwards, of Ashville, Ala. They lived together until her death in 1883 and reared a family of six children, a seventh having died in infancy. In December 1887 he was married at Tyler to Catherine E. Border, widow of one of his earliest friends in Texas, Col. John P. Border, who had fought in the battle of San Jacinto and had been a colonel in the Confederate army. In spite of his arduous duties as a public officer and a teacher of law, the "Old Alcalde," as Roberts was affectionately called, found time to do some literary work. In 1881, while serving as governor, he published *A Description of Texas, Its Advantages and Resources*, a booklet of 133 pages. In 1890 he published *The Elements of Texas Pleading*, and two years later *Our Federal Relations, from a Southern View of Them*. In 1898, there appeared from his pen the political history of Texas down to 1895, published as the first 325 pages of Volume II of D. G. Wooten's *Comprehensive History of*

Texas. He also contributed chapters on Texas to Clement A. Evans' *Confederate Military History* (vol. XI, 1899).

[See: L. E. Daniell, *Types of Successful Men of Tex.* (1890); J. D. Lynch, *The Bench and Bar of Tex.* (1885); D. G. Wooten, "The Life and Services of Oran Milo Roberts," *Quart. of the Tex. State Hist. Asso.*, July 1898; 92 *Tex. Reports*, v–xii; *Biog. Encyc. of Tex.* (1880); W. S. Speer and J. H. Brown, *The Encyc. of the New West* (1881); H. S. Thrall, *A Pictorial Hist. of Tex.* (1879); *Daily Express* (San Antonio, Tex.), May 20, 1898. Roberts' opinions are to be found in 19–27 and 40–49 *Tex. Reports*.]

C. S. P—s.

ROBERTS, ROBERT RICHFORD (Aug. 2, 1778–Mar. 26, 1843), bishop of the Methodist Episcopal Church for nearly twenty-seven years, was born in Frederick County, Md. His father, Robert Morgan Roberts, of Welsh descent, was a farmer of small means and a Revolutionary soldier; his mother, Mary, daughter of Thomas and Esther Richford, was probably of Irish ancestry. Robert was one of thirteen children and the third of that name, two others to whom it was given having died when young. He was taught the rudiments of reading, writing, and arithmetic and instructed in the catechism of the Church of England, of which his father was a stanch adherent. In 1785 the family moved to Ligonier Valley, Westmoreland County, Pa., undeveloped country where frontier conditions prevailed. Although he was but seven years old, Robert's schooling was now practically ended; his time was occupied in helping clear the land for cultivation. Methodist preachers entered the neighborhood, and yielding to their influence in spite of his father's Episcopalian prejudices, Robert was converted and joined a Methodist society. In the spring of 1796, with several companions, he made an exploratory expedition into the Shenango district, now Mercer County, Pa., and the following year with two of his brothers took up land there. For some five years he was a frontiersman, living in a log cabin, clearing land, planting crops, fishing, hunting, and selling furs. In January 1799 he married Elizabeth, daughter of Thomas and Hannah Oldham of York County, Pa.

From the time of his conversion he was regarded by his Methodist associates as suited for the ministry. Although without education, he had a good mind, was sincerely religious, and possessed the qualities of character that command confidence. The Shenango settlement grew and a Methodist society was formed there, Roberts becoming class leader. He was urged to become a preacher but natural diffidence and a feeling of unpreparedness held him back. In 1802, however, he applied for a license, which was granted, and the same year he was admitted on trial to the Baltimore Conference. On Apr. 28, 1804, he was ordained deacon by Bishop Asbury, and on Mar. 20, 1806, elder. The first years of his ministry were spent on long and hard circuits in Pennsylvania, Maryland, and Virginia. He received little salary, was very poor, and, unlike most of the itinerant preachers, was encumbered by a wife. In the hope of adding to his means of support he built a mill on land he owned in Erie County. This took him from his calling and caused some grumbling. One person, zealous for the interests of the kingdom of God, harshly declared that "it would be well for the people if his (Roberts') wife were dead and the mill swept down the river" (Elliott, *post*, p. 131). His Conference reproved him in 1808 for neglecting his appointments. That same year he started for the General Conference to be held in Baltimore with only a dollar in his pocket, and biscuits, cheese, and oats in his saddle-bags. During the session he preached to the Methodists of Baltimore with such acceptance that on their request Bishop Asbury stationed him there. Later he was appointed to Fell's Point (1810), Alexandria (1811), Georgetown (1812), and Philadelphia (1813–14). In 1815 he became presiding elder of the Schuylkill district. Owing to the death of Bishop Asbury and the illness of Bishop McKendree, it was necessary to elect a presiding officer at the Philadelphia Conference of 1816, and Roberts was chosen. He filled the chair with such dignity and displayed such well-balanced judgment that he became the nominee of the Northern Conferences for bishop. The Westerners were surprised and delighted to have one of their "fellow backwoodsmen" put forward, and at the General Conference of 1816 he was elected.

For more than a quarter of a century he performed the arduous duties of his office, involving thousands of miles of travel to all sections of the country. Of more than average height and of heavy frame, he was physically fitted for strenuous activity, and his frontier training stood him in good stead. During the last year of his life he visited six different states and four Indian territories, on horseback and in carriage, stage, and steamboat covering 5,484 miles. He was a simple, direct, and effective speaker, and a dignified, imperturbable, and judicious administrator. "It was his peculiar temperament," says a contemporary, "to pursue with steady and untiring perseverance whatever he undertook, without even the appearance of zeal, or any movement that would create the least noise, or attract the gaze of public attention to his course. He was

always silent, except when compelled to speak; he was in the rear and shade, except when thrust out into observation . . ." (Elliott, pp. 256–57). In some respects he remained a backwoodsman. His first episcopal residence was his old cabin in Shenango; in 1819 he moved to Lawrence County, Ind., where he had as a home another rough cabin, built in part by himself. Here he died, and his body was buried in a cornfield on his own farm. Soon, however, it was removed to the grounds of Indiana Asbury University (now De Pauw), Greencastle, Ind.

[Chas. Elliott, *The Life of the Rev. Robert R. Roberts* (1844); *Minutes of the Ann. Conferences of the M. E. Ch., for the Years 1842–1843* (1843); *Ladies' Repository*, Apr. 1844; T. L. Flood and J. W. Hamilton, *Lives of Meth. Bishops* (1882); Abel Stevens, *Hist. of the M. E. Ch. in the U. S. A.*, vol. IV (1867).]

H. E. S.

ROBERTS, SOLOMON WHITE (Aug. 3, 1811–Mar. 22, 1882), civil engineer, was born in Philadelphia, Pa., the son of Charles and Hannah (White) Roberts. His father taught in one of the Friends' schools of that city and there the boy received his early education. When about sixteen years old he left school and was employed by his uncle, Josiah White, manager of the Lehigh Coal & Navigation Company's works at Mauch Chunk, Pa., as an assistant in the building of the first tramway constructed in Pennsylvania, opened for use in the spring of 1827. Shortly afterward he became rodman with a party of engineers of this same company and was subsequently assistant engineer on a section of the Lehigh Canal being built near Mauch Chunk. Here he was associated with William Milnor Roberts [*q.v.*], who was later his colleague on the Allegheny Portage Railroad. Upon completion of the Lehigh Canal in the autumn of 1829, he entered the service of the state of Pennsylvania in connection with its canal construction on the Conemaugh River, and was stationed at Blairsville, Pa., as assistant to Sylvester Welch, the principal engineer, until the work was completed in the spring of 1831. He then became a principal assistant engineer on the Portage Railroad over the Alleghanies, another section of the Pennsylvania public works, and led the exploring and locating party upon the western half of the line. Later he designed and supervised the construction of a masonry viaduct to carry the railroad over the Conemaugh River at Horse Shoe Bend. After the completion of the Portage Railroad he remained as its resident engineer and superintendent of transportation until 1836, when he resigned and went to England to procure and superintend the manufacture of iron rails for the Philadelphia & Reading and other railroads. During the two years which he spent in this way he formed a friendship with George Crane, a Welshman who had obtained a patent from the British government for the application of the hot-blast to the smelting of iron ore with anthracite coal. It was through Roberts' explanation of Crane's process to his uncle, Josiah White, and to the Franklin Institute of Pennsylvania, that the first successful anthracite furnace in the Lehigh Valley was built, at Catasauqua, Pa., in 1839–40, by the Lehigh Crane Iron Company. From 1838 to 1841, Roberts was the chief engineer of the Catawissa Railroad. In 1842 he became president of the Philadelphia, Germantown & Norristown Railroad Company and in 1843, president of the Schuylkill Navigation Company, holding this office until 1845. In 1847 he took an active part in securing the charter of the Pennsylvania Railroad Company and that same year was elected to the state House of Representatives, where he served during the session of 1848. During this session much important railroad legislation was passed and his experience in railroad matters enabled him to take a leading part in shaping it. In 1848 he became the chief engineer of the Ohio & Pennsylvania Railroad then being constructed from Pittsburgh to the Ohio state line and was responsible for the location of the line as far as Crestline, Ohio; he selected both the sites and the names of the towns of Crestline and Alliance. He planned the railroad bridge across the Allegheny River at Pittsburgh, connecting the Ohio & Pennsylvania Railroad with the Pennsylvania Railroad. As the various sections of the Ohio & Pennsylvania were opened he became the general superintendent and remained in charge of the road until 1856, when he resigned and returned to Philadelphia to accept the position of chief engineer and general superintendent of the North Pennsylvania Railroad, which was completed to Bethlehem, Pa., in 1857. He retained this position until 1879, when he retired. He was a member of a number of learned societies and contributed several papers to the *Transactions* of the American Philosophical Society and to scientific journals. He also wrote "Reminiscences of the First Railroad Over the Allegheny Mountain" (*Pennsylvania Magazine of History and Biography,* vol. II, no. 4, 1878; separately printed, 1879) and a published address, *The Destiny of Pittsburgh and the Duty of Her Young Men* (1850). He was married to Anna Smith Rickey. He died while on a visit to Atlantic City, N. J.

[W. B. Wilson, *Hist. of the Pa. Railroad Company* (1899), vol. I; J. M. Swank, *Introduction to a Hist. of Ironmaking and Coal Mining in Pa.* (1878) and *Hist. of the Manufacture of Iron in All Ages* (1884); *Biog.* *Encyc. of Pa.* (1874); *Railroad Gazette,* Mar. 31, 1882; *Public Ledger* (Phila.), Mar. 24, 1882.]   J. H. F.

ROBERTS, THEODORE (Oct. 8, 1861–Dec. 14, 1928), actor, was born in San Francisco, the son of Martin R. and Mary E. (Newlin) Roberts, and was educated in the public schools there and at the California Military Academy in Oakland. With the exception of two and a half years at sea, a part of the time as captain of a schooner trading along the Pacific coast, he was uninterruptedly on the stage, acting many rôles, especially those to which he was individually suited because of his large stature, his heavy voice, and his imperious manner. He made his first appearance at the Baldwin Theatre in San Francisco, May 1, 1880, as Baradas to James O'Neill's Richelieu; but he soon found, as he said later, that he was "too big to support an American tragedian," meaning that his size, even if not his acting, would be to the disadvantage of the star by turning the eyes of the audience too often in his own direction. One of his earliest traveling engagements was in *Our Bachelors,* in support of Stuart Robson and William H. Crane, with whom he made his first New York appearance in 1881. After his return to the stage following his sea adventure, he acted for several seasons in support of Fanny Davenport, playing leading parts in her repertory; later he was with Mrs. Leslie Carter as Colonel Fulton Thorpe in *The Heart of Maryland,* as Colonel Sapt in *Rupert of Hentzau,* and as Henry Canby in Augustus Thomas' *Arizona,* in which he gave an extremely realistic portraiture of a typical stage ranchman, a part he played in 1902 at the Adelphi Theatre in London. Other stars whom he supported were Lawrence Barrett, James K. Hackett, and Bertha Kalich. When he appeared in New York as Tabywana in *The Squaw Man,* he equipped himself for the accurate interpretation of the Indian manner and nature by engaging a Ute Indian as coach; this, however, was not his début as an Indian, for twelve years before he had acted Scar Brow in *The Girl I Left Behind Me.* For a number of years thereafter he acted many rôles in a varied assortment of plays, the last that of Buck Kamman, the sheriff in *Believe Me, Xantippe,* in 1913. His final years as an actor, after a brief experience on the vaudeville stage, were spent in California in the making of motion pictures, his attitude towards that modern development of his profession being expressed in his remark (*New York Herald Tribune, post*) that he "looked upon the industry as a retiring place for broken-down actors." He died in Los Angeles while he was in the midst of preparations for the making of a new film.

His stalwart and heavily built figure, his long, straight features, his ruddy complexion and dark blue eyes especially adapted him to the impersonation of Indians, frontiersmen, sheriffs, and other primitive and robustious types conspicuous in the characteristically American plays that have long been popular in the United States. His first wife was Clyde O'Brien, known on the stage as Clyde Harron, whom he married in San Francisco in 1890 and later divorced; his second wife, according to an interview in the *New York Herald Tribune* (*post*), was Florence Smythe.

[*Who's Who in America,* 1918–19; John Parker, *Who's Who in the Theatre,* 1925; *N. Y. Dramatic Mirror,* Jan. 11, 1911; *N. Y. Herald Tribune,* Jan. 3, 1926; obit. notice in *Boston Transcript,* Dec. 15, 1928.]

E. F. E.

ROBERTS, WILLIAM CHARLES (Sept. 23, 1832–Nov. 27, 1903), Presbyterian clergyman, educator, was born at Galltmai, near Aberystwyth, Wales, the son of Charles Cross and Magdalene (Evans) Roberts. His father was a well-educated farmer. During William's seventeenth year financial reverses brought the family to America while the cholera epidemic of 1849 was raging at New York. Within a week after landing both parents and two of the children died of the disease. Left the eldest of six orphans, William in a few months began work for a leather manufacturer at Elizabeth, N. J. The ambition to become a professional man which had led him to Evans Academy in Aberystwyth soon took him, however, to the school of the Rev. David H. Pierson, and in 1852 he entered the College of New Jersey as a sophomore. After graduation with honors in 1855, he read law and served as private tutor, but during the winters studied in Princeton Theological Seminary, from which he was graduated in 1858. On Oct. 13 of that year he was ordained by the Presbytery of Newcastle, and six days later was married to Mary Louise Fuller.

His initial pastorate was at the First Presbyterian Church, Wilmington, Del., where he remained until 1862. The next two years he served the First Church, Columbus, Ohio. In December 1864 he became the colleague of his former pastor, Dr. David Magie, at the Second Church, Elizabeth, N. J., and, on the latter's death the following May, his successor. When the city's growth required the organization of another church, Westminster was formed with one hundred members—all except seven from Second Church—with Roberts as pastor. The congregation grew rapidly, and in time erected one of the most costly edifices in New Jersey. He was sent to Great Britain in 1877 as a delegate to the Council of Presbyterian Churches, an honor twice repeated in later years. In 1889 he was moderator of the General Assembly.

Although Roberts held these notable pastorates, his most marked contribution was to Christian education. While at Wilmington he served Lafayette College as a trustee (1859–62); during his pastorate at Columbus, he was a member of a committee that prepared the way for the founding of the College of Wooster; he was a trustee of the College of New Jersey (1866–86); and he declined the presidency of Rutgers College in 1882. In that year he became secretary of the denomination's Board of Home Missions, holding the position until 1886 and again from 1893 to 1898. During the intervening seven years he was president of Lake Forest College, Ill. Under his leadership, the faculty was augmented, new departments were created, and funds amounting to about $1,000,000 were raised. The number of students increased to more than 1,500. His last five years were spent as president of Centre College, Danville, Ky., during which period, in 1901, Centre College and Central University at Richmond, Ky., united to form the Central University of Kentucky. His death occurred at Danville two years after the union.

A versatile man, Roberts attained appreciable success in education, as a preacher and pastor, as an executive, and as a writer. He published numerous religious pamphlets in both English and Welsh, and several books, of which *Great Preachers of Wales* (1865) and *New Testament Conversions* attracted most attention.

[H. E. Dosker, *In Memoriam* (1908); *The Biog. Encyc. of N. J. of the Nineteenth Century* (1877); *Gen. Cat. of Princeton Univ., 1746–1906* (1908); *Princeton Theological Sem. Biog. Cat.* (1909); *Necrological Report . . . Alumni Asso. of Princeton Theological Seminary* (1904); *The Presbyterian,* Dec. 2, 1903; *Who's Who in America,* 1903–05; *Evening Post* (Louisville, Ky.), Nov. 28, 1903.]

P. P. F.

ROBERTS, WILLIAM HENRY (Jan. 31, 1844–June 26, 1920), clergyman, leader in the Presbyterian Church, was born at Holyhead, Wales, the son of the Rev. William Roberts and Catherine (Parry). His father came to the United States in 1855, and for thirty years was a famous preacher in the Welsh Presbyterian Church. From him, in New York City, William Henry received much of his schooling, and then entered New York Free Academy (now the College of the City of New York), graduating in 1863. After four years as a statistician in the Treasury Department at Washington, he was assistant librarian in the Library of Congress from 1867 to 1872. During the later part of this time he carried on study in Princeton Theological Seminary, where he graduated in 1873. He was ordained by the Presbytery of Elizabeth on Dec.

5, 1873, and until 1877 was pastor of the Presbyterian Church at Cranford, N. J. During the next nine years he was librarian of Princeton Seminary. He was elected permanent clerk of the General Assembly of the Presbyterian Church in 1880, and in 1884, its stated clerk. From 1886 to 1893 he was professor of practical theology in Lane Theological Seminary, also having charge for two years of the Second Presbyterian Church of Cincinnati. To devote himself to the office of stated clerk he removed in 1893 to Philadelphia, thenceforth his home. From 1894 to 1899 he preached in the Second Presbyterian Church of Trenton, N. J. Intensely occupied with administration, he kept his enthusiasm for preaching, especially for evangelism. In Philadelphia he was a leader in social reforms and charities.

As stated clerk of the General Assembly for thirty-six years Roberts displayed an encyclopedic knowledge of the history, doctrine, law, and work of the Presbyterian Church, and a convinced devotion to Presbyterianism which would allow superiority to no other Christian organization. He managed the general organization of the Church with the ardor which marked his preaching. To keep pace with its rapid growth, he introduced improvements in administrative methods and records. Through the contacts with all of the church's activities—missionary, educational and philanthropic—which his office gave him, he exerted a wide and strong influence. Especially learned in church law, he edited *Supplement to the Presbyterian Digest, 1898–1906* (1907) and a revision of the *Manual of Law and Usage* (1913), and wrote *Laws Relative to Religious Corporations* (1896). In sessions of the General Assembly he displayed unequaled grasp of details, accomplished parliamentary skill, and a dynamic personality. His services won him unanimous election as moderator in 1907.

He was an inveterate foe of everything narrow and provincial in church life, and a tireless worker for larger fellowships. For forty-two years he was American secretary of the Alliance of Reformed Churches Holding the Presbyterian System and was president of the Council of the Alliance at Glasgow in 1896. As chairman of the commission on church cooperation and union of the General Assembly he did much to bring his church closer to others. For unity among Presbyterians he strove especially, and the unions of the Cumberland Presbyterian Church and the Welsh Presbyterian Church with the Presbyterian Church in the United States of America were largely due to him. In his personal capacity and then as a representative of his church he presided over the long negotiations which issued

in the formation of the Federal Council of the Churches of Christ in America in 1908; and he was always foremost in its leadership. He zealously promoted the work preparatory to the World Conference on Faith and Order (Lausanne) which was done before the World War and was a member of a deputation representing the American churches which in 1914 visited the non-Anglican churches of the British Isles to secure their participation in the Conference.

Besides his legal works, he published *A History of the Presbyterian Church* (1888), *The Presbyterian System* (1895), *A Concise History of the Presbyterian Church in the U. S. A.* (1917), and numerous articles and addresses. He also edited the *Minutes of the General Assembly* from 1884 to 1919. He was married on June 11, 1867, to Sarah Esther McLean, of Washington, and left two sons and two daughters.

[*Princeton Theol. Sem. Biog. Cat.* (1909); *Necrological Report . . . Alumni Asso. of Princeton Theol. Sem.* (1921); J. R. Stevenson, "Churchmanship of William Henry Roberts," *Princeton Theol. Rev.*, Oct. 1920; *Minutes Gen. Assembly, passim*; *Who's Who in America,* 1920–21; *Public Ledger* (Phila.), June 27, 1920.]
R. H. N.

ROBERTS, WILLIAM MILNOR (Feb. 12, 1810–July 14, 1881), civil engineer, was born in Philadelphia, Pa., the son of Thomas Pascal and Mary Louise (Baker) Roberts. He was of Welsh Quaker descent, his family having come to America with William Penn. Roberts was educated in a Friends' school in Philadelphia, then took a special course in mathematics for two terms, after which he studied architectural drafting under John Haviland [*q.v.*]. Completing his education at the age of fifteen, he joined the engineering corps under Sylvester Welch which was engaged in the construction of the Union Canal of Pennsylvania from the Schuylkill at Reading to the Susquehanna a little below Harrisburg. In 1826 he was a rodman in the preliminary survey for the construction of a macadam road across the Alleghany Mountains in Pennsylvania to connect the canal system on the eastern with that on the western slope, and in the following year he began work as an assistant in the survey and construction of the Lehigh Canal between Mauch Chunk and Philadelphia. He helped in the improvement of the inclined planes at Mauch Chunk and took part in the construction and operation of the coal railroad connected therewith. Four years later, in 1831, he was appointed senior assistant engineer under Welch for the survey of the proposed Allegheny Portage Railroad. William Milnor Roberts was in charge of the location of the eastern part of the line, from the headwaters of the

Conemaugh over the summit and down to Holli-daysburg, and subsequently superintended the construction of eight of the ten inclined planes. Upon the completion of this work in 1834 he served as general manager of the road until January 1835, when he became chief engineer of the Lancaster & Harrisburg Railroad.

Roberts was now only twenty-five years old, but he had had ten years' experience in canal and railway transportation, possessed much mechanical ability, and had developed a special aptitude for design. He remained with the Lancaster & Harrisburg from 1835 to 1837, assuming, in addition, the position of chief engineer of the Cumberland Valley, and completed the construction of both roads. One of his greatest engineering feats at this time was the construction at Harrisburg in 1837 of a two-level lattice-truss bridge across the Susquehanna River, carrying a double-track railroad above and a double carriage-way and footpaths below. Continuing in the capacity of consulting engineer for the railroads, he was given charge, 1838–40, of the extensions of the Pennsylvania state canals, particularly in the western part of the state. For the next eight years he was engaged chiefly in canal construction, enlarging the Welland Canal in Canada, directing the enlargement of the Erie Canal of Pennsylvania, and acting as chief engineer of the Sandy & Beaver Canal in Ohio. In 1849 he returned to railroad work, building the Bellefontaine & Indiana, the Allegheny Valley, the Atlantic & Mississippi, and the Iron Mountain railroads, and serving as chairman of a commission appointed by the legislature to consider the reconstruction of the Allegheny Portage Railroad. During this period the battle of railroad gauges was being waged, some railroads favoring a 6′ and others a 4′ 8½″ width. Roberts strongly advocated the latter gauge and succeeded in bringing about its adoption as the standard. In 1855–57 he was engaged in the construction of a number of Middle-Western railroads, and late in the latter year went to Brazil, where he obtained the contract to build the Dom Pedro Segundo Railroad. This difficult undertaking involved considerable tunneling and required eight years' time to complete.

Roberts returned to the United States in 1866, was almost immediately appointed on the commission to propose improvements of the Mississippi River at Keokuk, Iowa, and was also made United States engineer in charge of the improvement of navigation of the Ohio River. Taking leave of absence in 1868 from this position, he served as associate chief engineer in the construction of the Eads Bridge across the Mississippi at St. Louis. Late in 1869 he was appointed chief engineer of the Northern Pacific Railroad and continued in that position for a decade, during which time he also served as a member of the Mississippi River Jetty Commission by appointment of President Grant. In 1879 he accepted the appointment of chief engineer of all public works in Brazil, and for the remaining two and a half years of his life was occupied with the examination of rivers, harbors, and waterworks there.

Roberts was vice-president (1873–78) and president (1878) of the American Society of Civil Engineers. His writings, published principally in its *Transactions,* were usually descriptions of actual observations and expressions of opinion as to the application of experience to new engineering problems. He rarely developed mathematical theories, for he was opposed to the too free use of theoretical formulae. He was married twice: in June 1837 to Annie Gibson of Pennsylvania, who died in 1857; and in November 1868 to Adeline Beelen of Pittsburgh, who with three children and six children of his first wife survived him. He died of typhus fever at Soledade, Brazil, and was buried in Philadelphia.

[John Bogart, "William Milnor Roberts," in *Trans. Am. Soc. Civil Engineers,* vol. XXXVI (1897); Frederick Fraley, obituary notice of Roberts, in *Proc. Am. Philosophical Soc.,* vol. XX (1883); S. W. Roberts, "Reminiscences . . . ," *Pa. Mag. of Hist. and Biog.,* vol. II, no. 4 (1878); *N. Y. Tribune,* July 22, 1881.]

C. W. M.

ROBERTS, WILLIAM RANDALL (Feb. 6, 1830–Aug. 9, 1897), politician, Fenian leader, congressman, was born at Mitchelstown, County Cork, Ireland. His parents are said to have been Randall and Mary (Bishop) Roberts. After receiving a limited schooling, he emigrated to New York in 1849. He worked as a dry-goods clerk until 1857, when he set up in the same business on his own account, only to be ruined in the panic of that year. He succeeded in reëstablishing himself, however, and his store on the Bowery later became so popular that in 1869 he was able to retire with the reputation of being a millionaire.

During the Civil War he became prominent in the Irish societies of New York. In 1865 he was president of the Knights of St. Patrick. In 1863 he joined the Fenian Brotherhood, becoming president of its senate when the latter was organized in October 1865. He was a leader in the agitation against the president of the Brotherhood, John O'Mahony [*q.v.*]; and when in December an open quarrel occurred, the senate deposed O'Mahony and elected Roberts in his stead. O'Mahony and his followers continued their attempts to foment revolution in Ireland, while Roberts, on the other hand, with Gen. T. W. Sweeny [q.v.] as his "secretary of war," set in motion plans for invading Canada. They hurried the project on because of their desire to appear the party of action, and in the first week of June 1866, concentrated several thousand men at various points along the border. Except for a temporary success obtained by John O'Neill [q.v.], however, the scheme was a complete fiasco. The United States government, which so far had offered no opposition to the Fenian plans, now interfered; President Johnson issued a proclamation, and on June 7 Roberts and other leaders were arrested on charges of breech of the neutrality laws. Roberts, refusing to give bail, was soon released, and the government chose to *nolle prosequi* the charges before the congressional elections that autumn. In June 1867, Roberts went to Paris to meet representatives of the Brotherhood in the British Isles, to arrange for cooperation between their organization and his own; but the agreement then made does not seem to have been effectively implemented. At the end of 1867 he resigned from the presidency of the Brotherhood, believing mistakenly that his resignation would be followed by a reunion of his group with that formerly headed by O'Mahony.

His Fenian record was a useful foundation for a political career in New York City; and in 1870 he was elected as a Democratic representative to the Forty-second Congress, and reëlected in 1872. He did not stand for reëlection in 1874. Among the causes which he particularly supported in the House were the protection of American citizens abroad (with special reference to the Fenians imprisoned in Canada) and opposition to repressive measures in the South. He made more than one vehement attack on British policy. In 1878 and 1879 he was a member of the New York board of aldermen, and president of the board in the former year. In the Democratic rout of 1879, running on the Tammany ticket, he failed of election for sheriff. Although he had been a faithful Tammany man, he was one of the group that seceded from Tammany Hall in 1881 to form the New York County Democracy. For supporting Grover Cleveland in his state and national campaigns, he was rewarded by appointment in 1885 as United States minister to Chile (1885–89). His tenure of the post was uneventful, and before its end he suffered a paralytic stroke, May 18, 1888. He was brought back to the United States in 1889, and lived eight years longer without recovering his mental and physical health. He died at Bellevue

Hospital, New York, in greatly reduced circumstances, survived by his wife, from whom he had been separated for some years, and by one son. Though he had once been a popular figure in New York politics, his reputation does not seem to have outlived his good health, and his death attracted little attention.

[John Rutherford, *The Secret Hist. of the Fenian Conspiracy* (2 vols., 1877); M. P. Breen, *Thirty Years of New York Politics* (1899); C. P. Stacey, "Fenianism and the Rise of National Feeling in Canada" (*Canadian Hist. Rev.*, Sept. 1931); *Papers Relating to the Foreign Relations of the U. S., 1888* (1889), pt. 1; *Biog. Dir. Am. Cong.* (1928); *Trow's New York City Directory,* 1869–70, 1879–80; *Irish American* (N. Y.), Jan. 13, Mar. 31 (portrait), 1866; *N. Y. Herald,* June 7, 8, 1866, Apr. 1, 1885; *Indianapolis News,* Aug. 12, 1897; *N. Y. Times,* Aug. 13, 1897; *Irish World* (N. Y.), Aug. 21, 1897.]
C. P. S.

ROBERTSON, ALICE MARY (Jan. 2, 1854–July 1, 1931), representative in Congress from Oklahoma, educator and social worker, was born at Tullahassee Mission, Indian Territory, the daughter of William Schenck [q.v.] and Ann Eliza (Worcester) Robertson. Her mother was the daughter of the noted missionary to the Cherokees, the Rev. Samuel A. Worcester [q.v.], and both parents gave the greater part of their lives to missionary work among the Creeks. When the Civil War broke out the Robertsons left the Indian Territory. Alice attended school in Wisconsin and at Highland, Kan., but returned with her parents to Tullahassee in 1866. For the next five years she received no formal schooling but studied under the direction of her father. In 1871 she entered Elmira College, New York, where she remained until 1873. Compelled to leave before graduating in order to provide for the education of her sister, she received from the college the honorary degree of A. M. in 1886. From 1873 to 1880 she was clerk in the Office of Indian Affairs at Washington and for the following two years she was secretary to Captain Pratt of Carlisle Indian School, but the death of her father and the failing health of her mother caused her to return to Indian Territory in 1882. Here she taught in an Indian school at Okmulgee and collected funds to erect the Creek school called Nuyaka Mission. In 1885 she was placed in charge of a Presbyterian school for girls at Muskogee. This later became Henry Kendall College and was eventually removed to Tulsa and became the University of Tulsa.

For nearly fifteen years Miss Robertson held various positions in Henry Kendall College. Her services to soldiers during the Spanish-American War brought her honorary membership in the organization of the Spanish American War Veterans. In 1900 she was made superintendent of Creek schools in Indian Territory and in 1905 was appointed postmaster of Muskogee by President Roosevelt. She held this position until 1913. For the next seven years she lived at her country place near Muskogee and operated it as "Sawokla Dairy Farm," at the same time operating "Sawokla Cafeteria" in Muskogee. During the World War she provided food and hot coffee for the soldiers who passed through Muskogee. Others joined her in this work and she became head of the canteen service of the city which fed thousands of soldiers. At her cafeteria, where no soldier was permitted to pay for a meal, she fed hundreds more. Her work attracted so much attention that in 1920 she was elected to Congress on the Republican ticket from the second Oklahoma district. When her term expired in 1923 she entered the Veterans' Hospital at Muskogee and for two years served as a welfare worker. Later she went to Washington as correspondent for the Muskogee *News*. Returning to Oklahoma she was employed by the Oklahoma Historical Society for two or three years to do research work, but age and ill health at last forced her to retire from active employment. The University of Oklahoma has named one of its largest dormitories for women, Robertson Hall, in her honor.

[Most of Alice Robertson's papers are in the manuscript collections of the University of Tulsa. Others consisting mostly of personal letters are in the possession of her sister, Mrs. Augusta R. Moore of Haskell, Okla. For printed sources see especially Grant Foreman, "The Lady from Okla.," *Independent*, Mar. 26, 1921 ; *Who's Who in America*, 1930–31 ; *Biog. Dir. Am. Cong.* (1928) ; S. A. Worcester, *The Descendants of Rev. Wm. Worcester* (1914) ; *Muskogee Daily Phœnix*, Nov. 19, 1922; July 2, 1931.]   E. E. D.

ROBERTSON, ARCHIBALD (May 8, 1765–Dec. 6, 1835), miniaturist, the eldest son of William Robertson and Jean Ross, was born at Monymusk, Scotland. The father was an architect who removed to Aberdeen when Archibald was a child. Here, at King's College, the latter received his education, although apparently he was not graduated. In 1782 he went to Edinburgh to study the art of painting, having as associates Henry Raeburn, Walter Weir, and George Watson. After a few years he returned to Aberdeen for the benefit of his health, and in 1786 went to London, where he sought introductions to Benjamin West [q.v.] and Sir Joshua Reynolds. The latter was then the president of the Royal Academy, and told Robertson the steps necessary to enter that school. After a period of study there, Robertson again returned to Aberdeen where he became a successful painter of portraits of all sizes, including miniatures,

and of devices for jewelry. He also conducted a drawing academy until 1791, when he was invited by Dr. John Kemp [q.v.] of Columbia College (through Dr. Gordon of King's College, Aberdeen) to come to America. The Earl of Buchan, upon hearing of his intended departure, commissioned him to paint a portrait of George Washington. This he did in Philadelphia, then the capital of the United States, a few months after his arrival. He was received with much cordiality by Washington and his family, and while with them painted miniatures of both the President and Mrs. Washington. In 1792 Robertson sent for his brother, Alexander, still abroad studying art, and together they opened the Columbian Academy of Painting at 89 William St., New York. Four years later they settled at 79 Liberty St., and here Archibald continued his painting until 1828. Alexander conducted a drawing academy at various addresses in the city. Another brother, Andrew, was a very successful artist in London. A collection of his paintings is in the South Kensington Museum, London.

In addition to his work in portraiture, Robertson executed a number of water-color views of New York City. He had drawings and miniatures in the first, and later, exhibitions of the American Academy of Fine Arts (from 1816 on), and is listed as an Academician in 1817 when his brother, Alexander, was secretary. In that year he exhibited in the Academy his well-known cabinet portrait of Washington, painted in water-color on marble, and now, together with a number of his family miniatures, in the possession of the New York Historical Society. From 1817 to 1833 he served as a director of the Academy, and, with another artist, recommended the establishment of schools in that institution, but this proposal was defeated by the president through his influence with the board of directors, and the Academy became merely a society for the exhibition of pictures. Robertson wrote a "Treatise on Miniature Painting" which he sent to his brother Andrew at Aberdeen. This valuable work is printed in the *Letters and Papers of Andrew Robertson, A.M., Born 1777, Died 1845*, edited by Emily Robertson and published in London in 1895. He also edited a treatise for the use of his pupils, published under the title, *Elements of the Graphic Arts* (1802). At the opening of the Erie Canal in 1825 Robertson was placed in charge of the department of the fine arts in connection with the celebration, designing the badge used and the medal struck upon that occasion. His report is printed in Cadwallader D. Colden's *Memoir . . . at the*

Celebration of the Completion of the New York Canals (1825).

Robertson was a gentleman and a scholar. His literary pursuits included the study of several languages; as an amateur architect he made several designs for buildings; and he also recorded that he had an acquaintance with the construction of ships. In 1794 he married Eliza Abramse, daughter of Jacob Abramse, Jr., and Rachel Walker, his wife; to them were born ten children, six sons and four daughters. Mrs. Robertson was also an artist, judging by her pen-and-ink sketches of Shakespearian subjects in the possession of the family. The latter years of Robertson's life, when he was nearly blind, were spent in retirement.

[William Dunlap, *A Hist. of the Rise and Progress of the Arts of Design in the U. S.* (1834; rev. ed., 3 vols., 1918, ed. by F. W. Bayley and C. E. Goodspeed); I. N. Phelps Stokes, *The Iconography of Manhattan Island* (6 vols., 1915–28), esp. vols. I, III, V, VI; *N. Y. Hist. Soc. Quart. Bull.*, Apr. 1929; New York City directories; catalogues of the American Academy of Fine Arts; article by Edith Robertson Cleveland, a great-grand-daughter, in *Century Mag.*, May 1890; *N. Y. Geneal. and Biog. Record*, Apr. 1920.]

A. J. W.

ROBERTSON, ASHLEY HERMAN (Dec. 14, 1867–July 13, 1930), naval officer, the son of Alsephus Turner Robertson and Rebecca (Mitchell) Robertson, was born at Ashmore, Ill. He was graduated from the United States Naval Academy in 1888, and commissioned ensign in 1890. During the Spanish-American War he served in the gunboat *Castine* of the North Atlantic Fleet. In 1905 he was made executive officer of the monitor *Terror,* and in 1906 engineer officer of the battle-ship *Tennessee.* Two years later he became executive officer of the same ship, and was transferred to the navy yard at Puget Sound in 1909, being raised to the grade of commander the same year. After completing his tour of duty here in 1913, he commanded successively the cruisers *Charleston* and *Denver.* He was raised to the grade of captain on July 1, 1914, and took command in the same year of the battle-ship *California.* In 1915 he was made commander of the battle-ship *Colorado* and was then assigned to the *San Diego,* retaining that command until July 1, 1916, when he was sent to the Naval War College at Newport, R. I.

When the United States entered the World War in 1917, he was chief of the first naval district with headquarters at Boston. In July of that year he was placed in command of the transport *Mount Vernon,* formerly the German liner *Kronprinzessin Cecilie,* which had been taken over by the United States for naval transport

service. After a short period of liaison work with the army in the spring of 1918, he was given command of the battle-ship *New Mexico,* the first electric-drive battle-ship in the American navy. The year following the war he was made chief-of-staff at the Naval War College. In 1918 he was commissioned rear admiral and, from 1920 to 1922, commanded the destroyer force in the Atlantic Fleet. He was made assistant to the chief of naval operations in 1922 and served in this position until May 1923. He was then ordered to duty as commandant of the eleventh naval district and naval operating base with headquarters at San Diego, Cal. In 1926 he was given command of the Scouting Fleet for two years, with the rank of vice admiral, and was then ordered back to his former duty at San Diego.

In his forty-two years of active service he became one of the most notable figures of the American sea force, having commanded some of the best fighting units in the service, as well as having risen to the highest rank in the power of the navy to bestow. At his death he was third in rank by reason of seniority in his grade. For his services during the war he was awarded the Navy Cross and the Distinguished Service Medal. In 1908 he married Mrs. Juliette Winston Graham Bixby, who survived him at his death in San Diego. He was buried at Arlington National Cemetery, Washington, D. C.

[*Who's Who in America*, 1930–31; W. H. Perrin, A. A. Graham, D. M. Blair, *The Hist. of Coles County, Ill.* (1879); U. S. Navy Dept. Registers; *U. S. Navy Dept., Record of Medals of Honor Issued to Officers and Men of U. S. Navy* (1924); H. R. Stringer, ed., *The Navy Book of Distinguished Service* (1921); *Army and Navy Jour.,* and *Army and Navy Register,* July 19, 1930; *N. Y. Times,* July 14, 1930.]

L. H. B.

ROBERTSON, GEORGE (Nov. 18, 1790–May 16, 1874), congressman from Kentucky, jurist, author, was born near Harrodsburg, in Mercer County, Ky., the son of Alexander and Margaret (Robinson) Robertson who had moved to the Kentucky region from old Virginia in 1779. He was the grandson of James Robertson who, with his father of the same name, emigrated from the north of Ireland about 1737 and settled in western Virginia. After receiving an elementary education in his community, the boy was sent to Joshua Fry's school five miles from Danville, where he was taught Latin, French, and geography. He then studied at Transylvania University for about a year before going to Lancaster to enter the Rev. Samuel Finley's classical school. In this school he studied for about four months and taught for the following six months. Deciding to study law, he went to Frankfort to begin under Martin D. Hardin [*q.v.*], but, changing his mind, he returned to Lancaster to complete his course. In September 1809 he received his license to practise, and the following Nov. 28, he married Eleanor Bainbridge and began housekeeping in the small two-room house in which John Boyle [*q.v.*], Samuel McKee, his brother-in-law, and later Robert P. Letcher [*q.v.*] also set up housekeeping and from which each was first elected to the federal Congress. Elected to the Fifteenth Congress and two years later returned to the Sixteenth he served from 1817 until his resignation in 1821. He declined a third term. In Congress he developed a reputation as an able debater and fearless leader, connecting his name with at least three important questions. He introduced and helped push through the bill organizing the territory of Arkansas, and in the debate that followed he opposed the restrictions the antislavery members attempted to fasten upon the region; he initiated the legislation, passed in 1820, changing the land system, whereby the minimum acreage that could be bought was reduced to eighty and the price to $1.25 an acre; and he took a prominent part in opposing the attempt made to force the president to recognize the revolted South American countries, in spite of the facts that Clay was strongly advocating it and that Robertson was a Whig and had never before supported an administration measure.

He returned to Kentucky to pursue his own desires, resolutely refusing to be enticed away by high position either at home or abroad. Among the honors he pushed aside were the attorney-generalship of Kentucky, the governorship of the Territory of Arkansas, and a ministership to each of the countries of Colombia and Peru. Instead he served in the lower house of the Kentucky legislature, from 1822 to 1826 for Garrard County and in 1848 and 1851 to 1853 for Fayette County, and during the years 1823, 1825, 1826, and 1851 to 1853 he was the speaker. He took especial interest in the development of a common-school system of education for the state, and in 1823, as chairman of a committee on education, he made a detailed report to the legislature. In 1828 he accepted the appointment by Gov. Thomas Metcalfe of the secretaryship of state, but he soon relinquished it for a more important and congenial position. Back in the early twenties, when attempts had been made to legislate people out of their property, he had been a leader in the anti-relief party organized to combat the money heresies. In the old-court and the new-court troubles that fol-

lowed, he introduced a powerful protest in the legislature against banishing the old court. By 1828 the contest had been largely settled, and he was appointed to the court of appeals. The next year he was elevated to the chief justiceship, where he remained until 1843, when he resigned from the court. In 1834 he agreed to become a lecturer in the law school of Transylvania University, and this position he held for twenty-three years. He opposed emancipation as a cure for slavery; but when the Civil War came, he supported the Union. With the passing of time, in common with many other loyal Kentuckians, he became increasingly impatient with the military régime that was settled down upon the state. By 1864 many Kentuckians, having reached the limits of their patience, sent out, on the day of the election of a judge to the court of appeals, the name of Robertson in opposition to the military candidate. He was elected. He held his judgeship until 1870 when he became again the chief justice. The next year he was stricken with paralysis, and he became almost totally blind. He resigned on Sept. 5, 1871. Three years later he died in Lexington, where he had long made his home. His reputation as a jurist was high; he was an able orator, and he was a writer of some note. The state created a new county to be named for him. Among his writings are, *Scrap Book on Law and Politics, Men and Times* (1855), made up of various addresses, lectures before his law classes, formal papers, and reports; *An Address Delivered at Camp Madison, on the Fourth of July, 1843* (1843), and *An Outline of the Life of George Robertson, Written by Himself, with an Introduction and Appendix by his Son* (1876).

[Autobiography, *ante*; Lewis and R. H. Collins, *Hist. of Ky.* (2 vols., 1874); *Annals of Cong.*, 15 Cong., 2 Sess., cols. 1235, 1272, 1273, 16 Cong., 1 Sess., col. 1866–87, 2 Sess., cols. 1043–55; *Biog. Encyc. of Ky.* (1878); *Biog. Cyc. of the Commonwealth of Ky.* (1896); *Daily Lexington Press*, May 17, 19, 1874.]

E. M. C.

ROBERTSON, JAMES (b. 1740), Royalist, printer and journalist, learned the printing trade from his father in Edinburgh, Scotland, and came to Boston with some of his countrymen before 1766. He worked as a journeyman with Mein & Fleming, who like himself were Royalists. His younger brother, Alexander (1742–1784), also trained as a printer at home, joined James at New York in a partnership on Beaver Street near the residence of General Gage, where, on May 8, 1769, they began the *New-York Chronicle,* a small quarto newspaper, which did not last a year; but it printed a number of distinctive articles, with diagrams, by members of the King's College faculty, on the theory of comets and the transit of Venus. They removed to Albany, where, subsidized by Sir William Johnson, they began a printery, and on Nov. 25, 1771, issued the first newspaper printed in the province outside of New York City. This newspaper, the *Albany Gazette,* continued until after Aug. 3, 1772, the last issue traced. The firm continued to do public printing in Albany as late as June 1776. Thomas (*post,* I, p. 313) says their press and types were left with a friend, who buried them on his farm outside of Albany, and that they were used in 1782 by Albany's second printing house.

In the same period the Robertsons formed a partnership with John Trumbull of Norwich, Conn., as general printers and publishers of the *Norwich Packet and the Connecticut, Massachusetts, New-Hampshire, & Rhode-Island Weekly Advertiser,* established on Oct. 7, 1773. Partnership with Trumbull was dissolved the beginning of May 1776, when Trumbull announced his adherence to the Whig interests. On May 29 of this year James's wife, Amy, died at Norwich, which seems to prove that James was active there while Alexander carried on simultaneously joint interests at Albany. These brothers, both Royalists, removed to New York City after the British captured the city in September 1776. James began there, at Queen Street, on Jan. 16, 1777, the *Royal American Gazette.* From this time until the end of July 1783 the journal was published by him, or with his brother, or by Alexander alone, or, as from Jan. 1, 1782, until the partnership was dissolved on Aug. 5, 1783, by the Robertsons in partnership with Nathaniel Mills and John Hicks.

James Robertson had followed the British army to Philadelphia in February 1778 and opened a printing office on Front Street, between Chestnut and Walnut Streets, establishing the *Royal Pennsylvania Gazette,* a semi-weekly, on Mar. 3, which was suspended with Number 25, May 26, 1778. The two last issues printed descriptive accounts of the Meschianza entertainment given in honor of General Sir William Howe. James Robertson returned to New York when the British evacuated Philadelphia in June 1778 and opened a new business at 857 Hanover Square. With Donald Macdonald and Alexander Cameron, fellow countrymen whom he had known in Philadelphia, he went to Charleston, S. C., and began, at 20 Broad Street, in the spring of 1780, the *Royal South Carolina Gazette.* In time he became the sole proprietor, and carried on till the issue of Sept. 12, 1782,

and then suspended publication. After the British evacuation of New York the Robertsons removed to Shelburne, Nova Scotia, where, on King Street, they revived the *Royal American Gazette* for several years, continuing the volume and series numbering from New York. Alexander suffered illness, being "deprived of the use of his limbs, and incapacitated for labor," dying at Roseway, a point near Shelburne, in 1784. He was "intelligent, well educated, and possessed some abilities as a writer" (Thomas, *post,* I, p. 193). James continued the newspaper in Nova Scotia for some time thereafter and eventually returned to his native city of Edinburgh, engaging in the printing business until 1810, or later. According to Thomas he "was a worthy man and a very good printer."

[The major sources are the various newspapers printed by the Robertsons and their partners. These are very rare, and information of fragmentary files is given by C. S. Brigham in "Bibliog. of Am. Newspapers," in *Proc. Am. Antiquarian Soc.,* n.s. XXIII (1913), XXVII (1917), XXXII (1923), XXIV (1925). Contemporary and therefore useful secondary information is in Isaiah Thomas's *Hist. of Printing in America* (2nd ed., 1874), vols. I and II; also "Additions" of Wm. McCulloch, in *Proc. Am. Antiquarian Soc.,* n.s. XXXI (1922), p. 201; of less account, because full of errors, is C. R. Hildeburn's *Sketches of Printers and Printing in Colonial N. Y.* (1895), pp. 98–104.]

V. H. P.

ROBERTSON, JAMES (June 28, 1742–Sept. 1, 1814), pioneer, the eldest son of John and Mary (Gower) Robertson, was born in Brunswick County, Va. In his youth his parents removed to Wake County, N. C. There on Oct. 20, 1768, he married Charlotte Reeves, the daughter of George Reeves, who became the mother of his eleven children. In 1770 with a party of hunters he visited the lands on the Holston in search of a place for a home. He located a claim and planted a crop near other settlers on the Watauga. In the autumn he returned to Wake County and removed his family to the West in 1771. He became a member of the court created by the Watauga Association and one of the agents for the settlers in treating with the Indians for the lease under which their land was held before 1775. He participated in Lord Dunmore's War at the battle of Point Pleasant in 1774.

When in 1775 Richard Henderson [*q.v.*] made his purchase of Kentucky lands from the Indians, Robertson was present and probably exerted influence on the negotiations. He signed the petition of the Wataugans for incorporation into North Carolina in 1776. He acted as agent to the Cherokee for North Carolina and Virginia during these early years and for a time lived among them, but in 1777 he accompanied the Virginia troops on an expedition against them. He also conducted the defense of the Watauga fort in 1777, holding the rank of captain. In 1778 the North Carolina Assembly instructed him as agent to reside permanently among the Cherokee, but he resigned the following year. During the latter year he carried a warning to the Wataugans of a Chickamauga attack. In 1779 he headed an exploring party that contemplated a settlement at French Lick, a trading post on the Cumberland, on land purchased by the Transylvania Company. He returned to Watauga to lead a group of settlers who, on Jan. 1, 1780, arrived on the Cumberland at the present site of Nashville. They, with others who came in April, adopted the Cumberland Compact as a basis of government, and he served as presiding officer of the court set up. In 1781 he made an alliance with the Chickasaw Indians in order to avert danger of their further attacks. He was elected colonel of the militia for the region and exhibited a firm and wise leadership during the early, critical years on the Cumberland. He had received a meager education from his wife, and he took an interest in providing educational facilities in the settlement. When the North Carolina Assembly chartered Davidson Academy, later the University of Nashville, in 1785, he became a trustee. In 1785 he represented his county in the North Carolina Assembly. When difficulties in the western settlements led the frontiersmen to believe that the states were indifferent to their interests, he, with others, played an active though obscure part in the Spanish Conspiracy from 1786 to 1789 (see Whitaker, *post*). In 1787 he again sat in the North Carolina Assembly. During the same year, he led the Coldwater expedition against the Indians.

When William Blount organized the territorial government southwest of the Ohio, he nominated Robertson as one of the brigadier-generals, a position from which he resigned in 1794 after ordering the Nickajack campaign. He also aided Blount in negotiating the Holston treaty in 1791. He represented Davidson County in the constitutional convention of Tennessee in 1796. In 1798 he entered the Tennessee Senate in place of Thomas Hardeman, who had resigned. During that year Governor Sevier appointed him to represent Tennessee at the first treaty of Tellico between the United States and the Cherokee. In 1807 he acted with Return J. Meigs in negotiating another treaty with the Cherokee. During the later years of his life, he served as Indian agent to the Chickasaw and resided for some time at the agency

at Chickasaw Bluffs. There he died. In 1825 his remains were removed to Nashville and reinterred in the old city cemetery. He was one of the few really influential frontier leaders in Tennessee. Although he did not aspire to official position, he assumed county and state offices when urged by the settlers, who had confidence in his ability. His influence was personal rather than political, and men of all groups sought his counsel. His fairness, wisdom, and firmness brought him his greatest success as a mediator between the settlers and the Indians. Although he associated himself with land companies, he did not attempt speculation on an extensive scale. According to his grand-daughter's description, he was of medium height, heavy but not fat, and his manner quiet and business-like. As a typical pioneer, he remained the leader in the Cumberland settlements until his death.

[Correspondence of James Robertson, Lib. George Peabody College for Teachers, Nashville; MSS. and documents, Tenn. State Archives; MSS., Lib. of the State of Tenn.; MSS., Tenn. Hist. Soc.; Draper Coll. of MSS., Wis. Hist. Soc., Madison, Wis.; "Correspondence of Gen. James Robertson," *Am. Hist. Mag.* (Nashville), Jan. 1896–July 1900; L. R. H. Brown, "The Family of Gen. James Robertson," *Ibid.*, Jan. 1896; "Letters of James Robertson and Daniel Smith," ed. by A. P. Whitaker, *Miss. Valley Hist. Rev.*, Dec. 1925; *The State Records of N. C.*, vols. XII, XIII, XVIII, XX, XXIV (1895–1905); A. W. Putnam, *Hist. of Middle Tenn. or the Life and Times of Gen. James Robertson* (1859); John Haywood, *The Civil and Pol. Hist. of the State of Tenn.* (1823); J. G. M. Ramsey, *Annals of Tenn.*, with index by J. T. Fain (1926); Archibald Henderson, *The Conquest of the Old Southwest* (1920); T. E. Matthews, *General James Robertson* (1934).]
C. S. D.

ROBERTSON, JEROME BONAPARTE (Mar. 14, 1815–Jan. 7, 1891), physician, soldier, Texas official, the fourth and youngest son of Cornelius and Clarissa (Hill) Robertson, was born in Woodford County, Ky. His parents had moved to Kentucky from Maryland in 1808. In 1819 they lost their property and in the same year the father died, leaving his widow and five small children penniless. The boys were apprenticed to neighboring tradesmen, and at the age of twelve Jerome Bonaparte was serving a hatter of Union County. Upon the death of his master, three years later, he was transferred to a man in St. Louis with whom he remained till he was seventeen, when, through his industry and frugality, he was able to buy release from the last three years of his contract. During his apprenticeship he had only three months of schooling, but a physician of St. Louis, Dr. M. W. Harris, who was attracted by the lad's fine characteristics, gave him informal instruction in both literary subjects and medicine. In 1832 Dr. Harris moved to Owensboro, Ky., and young Robertson went with him as pupil and office assistant. In 1835 he graduated in medicine from Transylvania University. He returned to Owensboro to practise his profession, but he was interested in the reports of the Revolution in Texas and raised a company of volunteers. When they arrived in Texas in May 1836, the battle of San Jacinto had been fought, and Texan independence was already assured, but the company joined the Texan army and remained with it until it was mustered out in June 1837.

Robertson then began the practice of medicine at Washington on the Brazos. On May 4, 1838, he married Mary Elizabeth Cummins, a daughter of Moses Cummins. Three children were born of this marriage, and in 1845 the family moved to Independence for school advantages. There Robertson practised medicine for thirty-four years and was the beloved physician for a large part of Washington County. From 1838 to 1844 he participated in as many as two yearly campaigns against the Indians and won a reputation throughout Texas as an Indian fighter. He also took an active part in the campaigns against Vasquez and Wohl. Besides his military service he held many minor civil offices in Washington County, ranging from coroner to state senator. He was a member of the convention that passed the ordinance of secession in 1861, and was one of the first in Texas to raise a company for service in the Civil War. He entered the Confederate army as a captain in the 5th Texas Infantry, Hood's brigade, but was advanced step by step until he became, in 1862, a brigadier-general and succeeded General Hood in command. During the war, Robertson fought in more than forty battles and was severely wounded three times. After the war he returned to his practice at Independence, but upon the death of his wife in 1868 he gave up active practice, and in 1874 became superintendent of the state Bureau of Immigration. In 1879 he moved from Independence to Waco, and in that same year he married Mrs. Harriet (Hendly) Hook. During the last ten years of his life he was an active promoter of railroad building in West Texas, in which section he is still remembered as a benefactor.

[Sources include: C. A. Evans, *Confed. Mil. Hist.* (1899), vol. XI; Sid S. Johnson, *Texans Who Wore the Gray* (1907); H. S. Thrall, *A Pictorial Hist. of Tex.* (1879); *Biog. Encyc. of Tex.* (1880); W. S. Speer and J. H. Brown, *The Encyc. of the New West* (1881); Comptroller Military Service Records, Nos. 873, 1409, Tex. State Lib.; information as to certain facts from Robertson's grandson, Judge Felix D. Robertson, and from his grand-daughter, Mrs. Julia R. Cleveland.]
                                            A. W—s.

ROBERTSON, JOHN (Apr. 13, 1787–July 5, 1873), congressman, jurist, author, was born at

"Belfield," below Petersburg, Va., of stock descended from the Princess Pocahontas, son of William and Elizabeth (Bolling) Robertson, and brother of Wyndham and Thomas Bolling Robertson [*qq.v.*]. After graduating from the College of William and Mary, he studied law, was admitted to the bar, and commenced practice in Richmond, whither his parents had removed about 1803. He married Anne, daughter of John A. Trent of Cumberland County. His personal charm combined with his industry, his ingenuity and ability of intellect, and his high sense of honor to win him rapid distinction; he served three terms, 1816–19, in the legislature; and in 1823 was made attorney-general of the state, filling this office conscientiously and well for eleven years. A "doctrinal Democrat of the Jefferson school," he was too independent to be a thrall to party and in 1834 was elected as a Whig to succeed Andrew Stevenson in Congress. Reëlected to the Twenty-fourth and Twenty-fifth congresses, he made himself known as a stinging and aggressive debater, a stickler for the Constitution, and an uncompromising critic of Jacksonian policy. His candor and veneration for truth gained him a reputation for eccentricity, for he is said never to have cloaked a thought. On Mar. 18, 1841, he was appointed judge of the twenty-first Virginia judicial circuit, to administer the chancery side of the superior court of law and chancery. Upon the reorganization of the judiciary ten years later, he became judge of the circuit court of Richmond and Henrico. Over both courts he presided with a dignity approaching severity, but with recognized impartiality and discernment. As the break between North and South threatened, Robertson, although a stern exponent of the inviolability of his state's domestic system, so earnestly deprecated violent measures that in January 1861 he was chosen commissioner from Virginia to urge forbearance upon the seceding states, pending the proposed peace convention. His overtures failing and Virginia having subsequently seceded, Governor Letcher commissioned him to invite Robert E. Lee, Joseph E. Johnston, and other Virginians holding federal military or naval appointments, to transfer to the service of their state. A similar interview with his former college-mate, Winfield Scott, proved unsuccessful. His public career ended with his duties in the Virginia Senate, 1861–62 and 1862–63, but he continued an active supporter of the Confederacy, giving his Richmond home as a soldiers' hospital, and dying an unreconstructed and "unrepentant rebel."

Besides occasional speeches, he published at widely separated intervals four volumes, three of them deriving largely from pride in and love for his family and his state, and too local, too definitely dated to have enduring appeal save to antiquarian or genealogist. These were a translation of Robert Bolling's memoirs of the Bolling family from the French (published in 1868 under the title: *A Memoir . . . of the Bolling Family in England and Virginia*); a metrical romance, *Virginia, or the Fatal Patent* (1825), dealing with the separation of the colony from the British crown; and, shortly before his death at Mount Athos in Campbell County, a miscellany, *Opuscula* (1870), which, while primarily concerned with Virginian affairs, looses numerous satirical barbs at New England intolerance and guile. More significant artistically was *Riego, or the Spanish Martyr* (1850), based on the revolution in Spain in 1820. A conventionally romantic five-act tragedy, in correct if undistinguished verse, it was superior to the average American play of its time and proved fairly popular in print, although Robertson was destined to be disappointed in his hope that Boucicault would produce it.

[Wyndham Robertson, *Pocahontas . . . and Her Descendants* (1887); E. G. Swem and J. W. Williams, *Reg. of Gen. Assembly of Va.* (1918); *Jour. of the Senate of the Commonwealth of Va. . . . Extra Sess.,* 1861; *Richmond Enquirer* and *Daily Dispatch* (Richmond), July 8, 1873.]   A. C. G., Jr.

ROBERTSON, MORGAN ANDREW (Sept. 30, 1861–Mar. 24, 1915), author, was born at Oswego, N. Y., the son of Andrew and Ruth Amelia (Glassford) Robertson. His father was a ship-captain on the Great Lakes. After a public-school education, Morgan went to sea in the merchant service, 1877–86, attaining the rank of first mate. He then gave up seafaring, and went to New York, where he studied the jeweler's trade at Cooper Union and opened a small shop, specializing in diamond setting. On May 27, 1894, he married Alice M. Doyle, daughter of William and Anna (Ross) Doyle of New York. Two years later, impaired eyesight forced him to give up his business and he was soon financially embarrassed. The reading of a sea story by Kipling now determined him to capitalize his own sea experiences and he spent a night writing an 8000-word story on the backs of circulars he had been hired to distribute. For this story, "The Destruction of the Unfit," finally accepted by a magazine, he received twenty-five dollars. The following year he wrote some twenty stories, the cream of his work, thus earning about a thousand dollars. The wolf was often just outside the door, and when his frail wife was ill, he did both the cooking and the washing. For one story an editor traded a bicycle, Rob-

ertson's choice of the merchandise advertised in the magazine. Writing steadily, however, he produced more than two hundred stories, which appeared in leading American magazines and in English periodicals.

After the publication of a collection of his stories in book form he was paid more for his work and in time enjoyed a fairly comfortable income, although he never earned as much as $5000 a year. He was never a spendthrift, he declared ("Gathering No Moss," *post,* p. 28), but he was improvident and a poor business man and was never entirely free from financial worries. His education being limited, he found writing painfully tedious, and eventually his ideas grew scarce. Threatened with a nervous breakdown and fearing insanity, he voluntarily entered the psychopathic ward of Bellevue Hospital. A psychologist whom he later consulted turned his mind to invention, and he undertook, after visiting a submarine, to solve the problem of the periscope; this he accomplished practically, but he could not patent his device because a fantastic description embodying the same principle had previously appeared in a French magazine. Returning to his writing, he found, as he said, that "my punch was gone" ("Gathering No Moss," p. 32); his work gradually declined in sales value, and he became practically penniless. A few months before his death, of heart disease, in an Atlantic City hotel, he was given financial relief by the publication of a special edition of his works, sponsored by friends. He had no children, but was survived by his wife, a brother, and a sister.

Robertson's published books include: *A Tale of a Halo* (1894), an unusual allegorical poem; *Spun-Yarn: Sea Stories* (1898), *"Where Angels Fear to Tread" and Other Tales of the Sea* (1899), *Shipmates* (1901), *Down to the Sea* (1905), and *Land-Ho!* (1905), all collections of short stories; *Futility* (1898), a short novel; *Masters of Men: A Romance of the New Navy* (1901); and *Sinful Peck* (1903), another full-length novel. His stories deal with sailing ships, steam vessels, and the long, steel men-of-war. They treat of mutiny and bloody fights, shipwreck and rescue, brutality, shanghaiing, courage and wild daring, telepathy, hypnotism, dual personality, and extraordinary inventions. "His stories are *bully,*" wrote Booth Tarkington, "his sea is foamy, and his men have hair on their chests" (*McClure's Magazine,* October 1915, p. 90). He gave life and reality to his characters, the most famous being Finnegan, a sort of Mulvaney of the sea, but he was more concerned with the reality of adventurous action than the psychological aspects of the sailor like Conrad, who wrote to Robertson (*Ibid.*): "Indeed, my dear sir, you are a first rate seaman—one can see that with half-an-eye."

[Bibliography by Merle Johnson in *Publishers' Weekly*, Mar. 15, 1930; obituaries in *Truth Seeker*, Apr. 3, 1915, *Bookman*, May 1915, *N. Y. Times*, Mar. 25, 1915, and *Daily Press* (Atlantic City, N. J.), Mar. 26, 1915; "Gathering No Moss: An Autobiography," *Saturday Evening Post*, Mar. 28, 1914; *Morgan Robertson, the Man* (1915); *Who's Who in America*, 1914–15; James MacArthur, "Books and Bookmen," *Harper's Weekly*, Apr. 29, 1905; *Reedy's Mirror*, July 16, 1915.]   C. L. L.

ROBERTSON, THOMAS BOLLING (Feb. 27, 1779–Oct. 5, 1828), third governor of the state of Louisiana, was born near Petersburg, Va., the son of William and Elizabeth (Bolling) Robertson. He was an elder brother of John Robertson [*q.v.*], the Virginia jurist and congressman, and of Wyndham Robertson [*q.v.*], who was governor of Virginia. For a time he attended the College of William and Mary. In 1806 he was admitted to the bar and began the practice of law at Petersburg, but he soon removed to the territory of Orleans where he became territorial attorney-general. In 1807 President Jefferson appointed him secretary of the territory with the power of succession to the governorship in case of a vacancy. When the territory was admitted to the Union under the name of Louisiana in 1812, he was elected as the first representative to Congress from the new state, and he was three times reëlected. While visiting France during his congressional career he wrote a series of letters which appeared in the *Richmond Enquirer* (Sept. 30–Dec. 23, 1815) and were also published in book form as *Events in Paris* (Philadelphia, 1816).

Robertson resigned from Congress in April 1818, but ill health, of which he complained after his removal to Louisiana, did not long keep him out of politics. In 1820 he was elected governor of Louisiana, and he went about his new duties with somewhat fiery manifestations of republicanism, expressing sympathy in messages and pronouncements for the Greeks and Latin Americans in their struggles for independence and advocating the abolition of imprisonment for debt. He opposed the relinquishment by the United States of the claim to Texas in the treaty acquiring Florida, complained of the neglect of Louisiana coast defenses, and criticized the national land policy in Louisiana as interfering with land improvement and progress. His administration was marked by legislation for the benefit of parish schools and for highway improvement, especially on the Louisiana link of the road connecting New Orleans with Nash-

ville, Tenn. Licenses were granted to six gambling houses for payment of $5000 fees for the benefit of Charity Hospital, New Orleans, and the College of Orleans. In 1824 Robertson resigned the governorship to accept from President Monroe the appointment to the United States district judgeship for Louisiana, and he resigned the judgeship in 1828, a few months before his death at White Sulphur Springs, Va. He was married to Lelia Skipwith, daughter of a political friend, Fulwar Skipwith, governor of West Florida. According to descriptions, he was tall and handsome. He was capable of using strong denunciatory language, and his comparatively short life was crowded with public activity and office-holding, to which he applied himself with energy and conviction.

[References include: Alcée Fortier, *Louisiana*, vol. II (1909) and *Hist. of La.*, vol. III (1904), with a portrait; Catherine B. Dillon, manuscript on Robertson in Howard Memorial Lib., New Orleans (published in part in the *New Orleans States*, Mar. 1, 1931); Wyndham Robertson, *Pocahontas . . . and Her Descendants* (1887); Mrs. Eugene Soniat du Fossat, *Biog. Sketches of Louisiana's Governors* (1885). The date of Robertson's birth is variously given. The date in this sketch is that given in the *Biog. Dir. Am. Cong.* (1928).]   H. C. N.

ROBERTSON, WILLIAM HENRY (Oct. 10, 1823–Dec. 6, 1898), politician, son of Henry and Huldah (Fanton) Robertson, was born at Bedford, Westchester County, N. Y. He was educated in the district schools and the academy of his native town. At the age of seventeen he began his political career by making speeches for Harrison and Tyler in the campaign of 1840. His first public office was superintendent of schools of Bedford, followed by four terms as a supervisor of Westchester County. He spent his leisure in studying law and was admitted to the bar in 1847. His practice, though continued throughout the remainder of his life, was constantly interrupted by office-holding and by party activities. After two terms in the New York Assembly and a term in the Senate, he served as county judge of Westchester County, 1855–67. In addition to his duties on the bench he was county draft commissioner during the Civil War, county leader of the Republican party organization, and a frequent participant in political conventions, national, state, and local. He was sometimes credited with having made possible Andrew Johnson's nomination to the vice-presidency in 1864. In 1866 he was elected to Congress but after a single term he declined a renomination. In 1871 he was again elected to the state Senate and by reëlection served continuously for ten years.

In 1872 it was generally thought that Robertson would receive the Republican nomination for governor, but at the last minute the convention was stampeded into choosing another candidate. Robertson believed that Senator Conkling, the state Republican leader, was responsible for his disappointment, and his attitude toward the state organization, always rather independent, changed into open hostility. In 1876 and in 1879 he was a candidate for the gubernatorial nomination against men whom Conkling was known to favor. In 1880 he opposed the efforts of Conkling and other "Stalwarts" to obtain a third nomination for Grant and organized a strong minority group of delegates who announced that they would not obey the instructions of the state convention. The "Stalwarts" then planned to introduce the unit rule into the national convention and thus force the whole delegation to vote for Grant. But Robertson's group, reinforced by independent delegates from other states, prevented the adoption of the rule. After a prolonged deadlock Garfield was nominated. The new president in recognition of Robertson's part in making his nomination possible considered inviting him into his cabinet, but instead sent his nomination to the Senate for the collectorship of the port of New York. The nomination provoked the most noteworthy of all the controversies over the right of senators to dictate appointment from their states. Conkling and Platt, the senators from New York, did everything in their power to prevent its confirmation. When it became evident that a majority of the Senate would uphold the President, both resigned and sought reëlection as a vote of confidence from the legislature of New York. Robertson led the opposition to their candidacies and both were defeated. After the expiration of his term as collector in 1885 Robertson again returned to the state Senate in 1887. His last active participation in politics was in the state Republican convention of 1896. He died at Katonah, N. Y., survived by his wife, Mary (Ballard) Robertson, whom he had married in 1865.

[*Biog. Dir. of the State of N. Y.* (1900); *Biog. Dir. Am. Cong.* (1928); DeA. S. Alexander, *A Pol. Hist. of the State of N. Y.,* vol. III (1909); *The Autobiog. of Thos. Collier Platt* (1910); Royal Cortissoz, *The Life of Whitelaw Reid* (1921), vol. II; T. C. Smith, *The Life and Letters of Jas. A. Garfield* (1925), vol. II; *N. Y. Tribune,* Mar. 24, 25, 1881, Mar. 20, Dec. 7, 1898; *Sun* (N. Y.), Dec. 7, 1898.]   E. C. S.

ROBERTSON, WILLIAM JOSEPH (Dec. 30, 1817–May 27, 1898), lawyer, was born in Culpeper County, Va., the son of John and Sarah (Brand) Robertson. His father, an emigrant from Glasgow, Scotland, had settled in Albemarle County in 1791 and had opened there a school for boys which he subsequently removed to Culpeper County. He died in 1818, but his son was given the best education then available in the Virginia piedmont. At the age of nine the boy was sent to the school of John Lewis of Llangollen in Spotsylvania County and in 1834 he entered the academic schools of the University of Virginia. During the course of his third session there, he left the University, taught school for two years, and then returned for the study of law. He was graduated from the law school in 1842 and began practice at Louisa Court House, but in a short time he moved to Charlottesville where he resided for the remainder of his life. In 1852 he was elected attorney for the commonwealth for the county of Albemarle. It was while he held this office that he conducted the prosecution of John Singleton Mosby [*q.v.*], then a student at the University, in such a way as to secure both Mosby's conviction and his respect and lifelong friendship. From 1853 to 1859 he served on the board of visitors of the University. He also served as the attorney of the University and in 1854 finally forced the administrator of President Madison's estate to surrender books bequeathed to its library.

In 1859 he was elected by popular vote to the bench of the supreme court of appeals of Virginia. In 1865 Virginia became Military District No. 1, and the judges of its supreme court were removed by order of the major-general commanding. During the six years, 1859–65, that Robertson was on the bench there was not a great deal of litigation before the court and Robertson himself delivered the opinion of the court in only twelve cases. He had had an average of six months for the preparation of each opinion. It was as a practising attorney rather than as a judge that he made his mark. When the courts were reopened after the war he began anew the practice of law. His professional reputation and income grew steadily. He became the great "corporation lawyer" of post-bellum Virginia, and for his time and section a rich man. He was made general counsel of the Chesapeake & Ohio Railroad Company and also of the Norfolk & Western Railroad. The Samuel Miller Will Case (27 *Grattan,* 110) and that of *Gilbert* vs. *Railroad Company* (33 *Grattan,* 586) were two of his conspicuous successes in the Virginia courts. The Arlington cases (*United States* vs. *Lee* and *Kaufman* vs. *Lee,* 106 *U. S.,* 196) were perhaps his greatest victories before the United States Supreme Court. In July 1888 he was elected the first president of the Virginia State Bar Association. He died in Charlottesville, May 27, 1898. He was twice married: first, on

Aug. 16, 1842, to Hannah, daughter of Gen. William F. Gordon [q.v.] of Albemarle, who died in 1861, and on July 16, 1863, to Alice, daughter of Gen. Edward Watts and widow of Dr. G. W. Morris of South Carolina. He had nine children by his first marriage and five by his second marriage.

[See: C. M. Blackford, "Wm. J. Robertson," *Report of the . . . Va. State Bar Asso.*, 1898; A. C. Gordon, "Wm. Jos. Robertson," in *Great Am. Lawyers*, vol. VII (1909), ed. by W. D. Lewis, reprinted in Gordon's *Virginian Portraits* (1924); J. S. Patton, "Mosby the Ranger as a College Student," in the Baltimore *Sun*, Jan. 15, 1911; the *Times* (Richmond, Va.), May 28, 1898.]

T. C. J., Jr.

ROBERTSON, WILLIAM SCHENCK (Jan. 11, 1820–June 26, 1881), pioneer educator among the Indians, was born at Huntington, Long Island, the son of the Rev. Samuel and Dorcas (Platt) Robertson. He was graduated from Union College, Schenectady, N. Y., in 1842 and began the study of medicine but, after completing about two-thirds of the course, gave it up to become a teacher. He taught for a few years in various academies in the state of New York and after uniting with the Presbyterian Church at Northport, Long Island, offered his services to the Presbyterian board for foreign missions. Requesting to be assigned to work among the Indians, he was given the position of principal teacher at the new manual labor boarding school among the Creeks later known as Tullahassee Mission in Indian Territory. He reached Tullahassee in the summer of 1849 to find the building still unfinished. On Jan. 1, 1850, however, he opened a day school, and two months later thirty boarding students were received. This number was increased to the full quota of eighty, when school opened in the autumn. On Apr. 15, 1850, he was married to Ann Eliza Worcester, the eldest child of the Rev. Samuel A. Worcester [q.v.] who had for some years been in charge of the Cherokee mission at Park Hill. One of their daughters was Alice Mary Robertson [q.v.]. For more than ten years Robertson continued, without interruption, his work at Tullahassee. With the able help of his wife he published in the Creek language a first and a second reader, which were widely distributed. When the Civil War broke out the school was closed by the southern wing of the Creeks, who had obtained control of the tribal government. With his family he went north and spent the winter of 1861–62 at his father's home at Winneconne, Wis. For the next two years he taught in Illinois, the first year at Mattoon and the second at Centralia.

In 1864 the Presbyterian mission board placed him in charge of the orphan institute at Highland, Kan., where he remained for two years. He was ordained a minister by the presbytery of Highland early in November 1866 and was then sent by the mission board to reopen Tullahassee, since the Creeks had earnestly requested that he be returned to them. To stimulate interest in education he obtained a small printing press and with the aid of his son and daughter published and distributed for four years a small newspaper in the Creek language called *Our Monthly*. In 1876 he was for a month in charge of the Indian educational exhibit at the Philadelphia Centennial Exhibition. He was also for years interested in the work of the Indian international fair held annually at Muskogee. During the later years of his life he began the translation of the New Testament into the Creek language, based on the earlier work of Robert M. Loughbridge [q.v.], and issued in parts between 1875 and 1886. After his death the complete edition, *Pu Pucase Momet Pu Hesayecv Cesus Klist in Testament Mucvsat*, was finished by his wife and published in 1887.

[Letters in the Alice Robertson Papers, University of Tulsa, Okla., in files of Indian Office, Washington, D. C., and among the missionary letters in the Lib. of Andover Theological Seminary; MSS., including a brief sketch of his life written by his widow, in possession of Okla. Hist. Soc.; J. B. Thoburn and M. H. Wright, *Okla.* (1929), vol. I; A. H. Abel, *The Indian as Slaveholder and Secessionist* (1915); J. H. Beadle, *The Undeveloped West* (1873), pp. 380–86; J. D. Benedict, *Muskogee and Northeastern Okla.* (1922), vol. I.]

E. E. D.

ROBERTSON, WYNDHAM (Jan. 26, 1803–Feb. 11, 1888), twentieth governor of Virginia, was born near Richmond and lived during the greater part of his active life in that city. He was the brother of John and Thomas Bolling Robertson [qq.v.] and grandson of William Robertson who emigrated from Scotland in the early eighteenth century and settled in Bristol Parish near the present Petersburg, Va. His father, William Robertson, was a native of Bristol Parish and served it in the capacity of vestryman, warden, and deputy from 1779 to 1789. He was also a member of the Council of Virginia and its secretary for many years. He married Elizabeth Bolling, and Wyndham was their seventh child. The boy was educated in Richmond and at the College of William and Mary. He studied law for several years and was admitted to the Richmond bar in 1824. In 1830 and again in 1833 he was elected to the Executive Council of Virginia and during this period took an active part in the development of internal improvements within the state, especially in connection with the organization of the James River and Kanawha Company, the object of which was to connect Richmond and Lynchburg by canal. In 1836 he became senior member of the Council and as such succeeded to the governorship, when Taze-well resigned the office in that year. Being a Whig in politics, he was succeeded after one year by David Campbell, a Democrat. From 1838 to 1841 he served as a member of the House of Delegates. In the latter year on account of his health he retired to the country, where he engaged in agricultural pursuits to the exclusion of all public business. In 1858 he returned to Richmond and from 1859 to 1865 served continuously in the House of Delegates. After John Brown's raid he became captain of a company of home guards organized in Richmond. During the crisis of 1861 he opposed secession and was author of the resolution adopted by the legislature declaring against separation but warning the North that Virginia would join the South in case coercion were attempted against those states that had already seceded. During 1863 and 1864 he strenuously opposed in the legislature a movement designed to fix the prices of food by law. After the war he removed to the home of his wife, Mary T. (Smith) Robertson of Abingdon, Va., and resided there until the end of his life. During these latter years he took no active part in public affairs but devoted his time to literary pursuits, publishing in 1887 his most important work, *Pocahontas, alias Matooka, and her Descendants through her Marriage . . . with John Rolfe*. This was his last effort, for he died the next year.

[Wyndham Robertson MSS. in the Lawson McGhee Library, Knoxville, Tenn.; R. A. Brock, *Virginia and Virginians* (1888), Vol. I, pp. 171–75; M. V. Smith, *Virginia, . . . A History of the Executives* (1893); W. A. Christian, *Richmond* (1912), pp. 116, 119, 129; E. G. Swem and J. W. Williams, *A Register of the Gen. Assembly of Va.* (1918); *Richmond Whig*, Feb. 15, 1888.]   T. P. A.

ROBESON, GEORGE MAXWELL (Mar. 16, 1829–Sept. 27, 1897), attorney-general of New Jersey, secretary of the navy, was born at Oxford Furnace, Warren County, N. J., the son of William Penn and Ann (Maxwell) Robeson. He was descended from Andrew Robeson, of Scotland, who emigrated to America in 1676. His father was an iron manufacturer. Immediately after graduating with honors from the College of New Jersey (Princeton) in 1847, Robeson began the study of the law in the offices of Chief Justice Hornblower in Newark. He was admitted to the bar in 1850, practised law in Jersey City, and was licensed as a counselor in 1854. In 1859 he was appointed by Governor Newell prosecutor of Camden County, a political move which occasioned much criticism, because Robeson was not at the time a resident of Camden. During the Civil War he was appointed a brigadier-general by Governor Olden and took an active part in the organization of the state troops, commanding the camp of volunteers at Woodbury, N. J. In January 1867 he was appointed attorney-general of New Jersey by Governor Ward. Following the resignation of A. E. Borie as secretary of the navy, Robeson was appointed by President Grant to fill the vacancy in the cabinet. It was reported at the time that the appointment was made on the recommendation of Borie (*Nation*, July 1, 1869). Robeson held office from June 25, 1869, until Mar. 12, 1877. His administration of the Navy Department was so severely criticized by the newspapers, which charged him with extravagance and favoritism, that a congressional investigation was instituted (*House Miscellaneous Document 170*, 44 Cong., 1 Sess., and *House Reports 788* and *789*, 44 Cong., 1 Sess.), but no definite action resulted. In 1871 Robeson was instrumental in securing the federal appropriation for the ill-fated North Polar Expedition of Capt. C. F. Hall, who, before his death in northern Greenland, named Robeson Channel in recognition of the services of the Secretary of the Navy (C. F. Hall, *Narrative of the North Polar Expedition*, 1876, ed. by C. H. Davis).

In January 1877 Robeson was the Republican candidate for United States senator from New Jersey, but he lost the election by one vote in the legislature, where he was suspected of trying to buy the vote of a Democratic member (Sackett, *post*, p. 134). In March 1877 he retired from the cabinet and returned to Camden, where he resumed his law practice. In 1878 he was elected to Congress from the first New Jersey district, being reëlected in 1880. Although a newcomer, he was one of the leaders in the House and was said to be "as strong in parliamentary debate as he was known to be in argument at the bar" (J. G. Blaine, *Twenty Years of Congress*, II, 1886, 638). He was again an unsuccessful senatorial candidate in 1881 and following his defeat in the congressional elections of 1882 devoted himself to the practice of law, at first in Camden and later in Trenton where he died. His striking personal traits and his size made him a favorite with cartoonists. *Puck* had a cartoon featuring him almost every week and it has been said that he was the most caricatured man of his day. In 1872 he married Mary Isabelle (Ogston) Aulick, a widow with a son, Richard Aulick. They had one daughter.

[*Proc. N. J. Hist. Soc.*, 3 ser. II (1897), 195–96; W. E. Sackett, *Modern Battles of Trenton*, vol. I (1895); *A History of Trenton*, II, 620–21, pub. by the Trenton Hist. Soc. (1929); Geo. R. Prowell, *The Hist. of Camden County* (1886); S. S. Robeson and

C. F. Stroud, *An Hist. and Geneal. Account of Andrew Robeson* (1916) ; *Daily State Gazette* (Trenton), Sept. 28, 1897.]

C. R. E., Jr.

ROBIDOU, ANTOINE (Sept. 24, 1794–Aug. 29, 1860), trapper, trader, was born in St. Louis, Mo., the son of Joseph and Catherine (Rollet) Robidou and the brother of Joseph (1783–1868), François (1788–1856), Louis (1796–c. 1862), and Michel (b. 1798) Robidou, all of them noted frontiersmen. Signatures of both Joseph and François show that the name was spelled without the terminal *x* used by the present generation of the family. "The first fur trader out of old Taos," Antoine has been called, and unless a prior claim can be proved for Ewing Young or William Wolfskill the distinction stands ; he may have reached Taos as early as 1822. On what was probably his second expedition he set out with a small party, Sept. 20, 1824, from Fort Atkinson, north of the present Omaha ; and the *Missouri Intelligencer* (Franklin, Mo.) of Apr. 19, 1825, mentions him as having been encountered in the previous fall on the "Green River (probably the Colorado of the West)" at some point in the present Utah. In 1828 Robidou married Carmel Benavides, of a prominent New Mexican family, and established a home either in Taos or Santa Fé. It was probably in the same year that he built a trading post on the Gunnison in what is now Colorado; about 1832 he established another post, Fort Robidou or Fort Uinta, in the Uinta Valley, northeastern Utah, that became a famous rendezvous for trappers, and for the next ten or eleven years he seems to have spent most of his time between these two posts and his New Mexican home. He probably revisited the Missouri region in the winter of 1840–41, since there is general agreement that he was the "Roubideaux" who set in motion the first emigrant wagon train to the Pacific by telling John Bidwell [*q.v.*] wonderful stories about California. John Charles Frémont [*q.v.*], who was at the Uinta post on June 3–5, 1844, writes that it was attacked by Utes during Robidou's absence and that all its inmates were killed. Robidou may have returned to the mountains in 1841 or 1842 ; in 1845 he abandoned them and moved with his wife and adopted daughter to St. Joseph, Mo., laid out by his brother Joseph two years before, July 1843. But his western adventures were not yet over, for in the spring of 1846 he engaged with Gen. S. W. Kearny [*q.v.*] as interpreter for the New Mexican expedition, accompanied the detachment later sent to California, and was desperately wounded at the battle of San Pascual, Dec. 6, 1846. In 1847, partly recovered, he returned once more to St.

Joseph. He is said to have become blind in 1852, and on May 23 of that year Congress voted him a small pension. He died in St. Joseph. Robidou was of slight figure—"a thin man," writes Lieutenant Emory (*post*, p. 111)—and his portrait reveals a handsome, refined, and intelligent face. Well known over the whole frontier and highly regarded, he was one of the most energetic, daring, and adventurous of all the trader-trappers.

[See J. J. Hill, "Antoine Robidoux," *Touring Topics* (Los Angeles), Dec. 1928 ; W. H. Emory, *Notes of a Mil. Reconnaissance, from Fort Leavenworth in Mo. to San Diego in Cal.* (1848) ; J. C. Luttig, *Jour. of a Fur-Trading Expedition on the Upper Missouri, 1812–1813* (1920), ed. by S. M. Drumm ; E. L. Sabin, *Kit Carson Days* (1914) ; H. M. Chittenden, *The Am. Fur Trade of the Far West*, vol. II (1902) ; C. L. Camp, ed., "The Chronicles of George C. Yount," *Cal. Hist. Soc. Quart.*, Apr. 1923. Voluminous data concerning the Robidou family, some of it unreliable, will be found in C. L. Rutt, *The Daily News' Hist. of Buchanan County and St. Joseph, Mo.* (n.d.), and O. M. Robidoux, *Memorial to the Robidoux Brothers* (1924).]

W. J. G.

ROBINS, HENRY EPHRAIM (Sept. 30, 1827–Apr. 23, 1917), Baptist clergyman, educator, son of Gurdon and Julia (Savage) Robins, was born at Hartford, Conn. Descended from old New England stock, he numbered among his ancestors Peter Bulkeley of Concord, Mass., and Charles Chauncy, second president of Harvard College. His grandfather, Ephraim Robins, broke with the Standing Order, becoming a Baptist lay-preacher. In Gurdon Robins' home, with Ephraim Robins as prime mover, there was drawn up a petition on behalf of the Baptists which was influential in securing the inclusion of an article upon religious freedom in the new constitution adopted by Connecticut in 1818. The father of Henry E. Robins abandoned a business career to become editor of the *Christian Secretary,* the organ of Connecticut Baptists ; he was later a Baptist minister, and finally a publisher and retailer of books.

After attending Fairmount Theological Seminary and graduating from the Newton Theological Institution in 1861, Henry E. Robins was ordained a Baptist minister, at Hartford, Dec. 6, 1861. For twelve years he continued in the pastorate, efficiently serving the Central Baptist Church of Newport, R. I. (January 1862–May 1867), first as associate and then as full pastor, and the First Baptist Church of Rochester, N. Y. (1867–73). In Rochester an addition to the church building, costing in excess of $53,000, was erected to be used for educational and social purposes, and the Memorial Mission of the church was developed until it became in 1871 the Lake Avenue Baptist Church. From 1873 to 1882, Robins was president of Colby University (now Colby College), Waterville, Me. Finding it with fifty students, he left it with an enrollment of 157. During his administration, through the bequest of Gardner Colby [*q.v.*] and other gifts, over $120,000 was added to its resources. His arduous and intense labors for the college impaired his health to the extent of making a leave of absence and at last a reluctant resignation unavoidable. Returning to Rochester, he was appointed professor of Christian ethics in the Rochester Theological Seminary (now the Colgate-Rochester Divinity School). Although he delivered only a few lectures, he held this professorship nominally until 1903. During the next decade and a half, he engaged in literary work. His minor writings include *Qualifications for Baptism* (circa 1867); *Harmony of Ethics with Theology* (1891); *The Christian Idea of Education as Distinguished from the Secular Idea of Education* (1895); *Faith Rational* (no date). His one major work was a comprehensive survey, of nearly 500 pages, *The Ethics of the Christian Life* (1904).

Robins was a preacher of exceptional excellence, a minister of spiritual fervor, sympathetic with young people, lovable yet of great strength of will, mature in his convictions, familiar with the educational problems of his denomination. A firm believer in the theory that right thinking precedes right living, he was alert, energetic, magnetic, and possessed unusual business and executive ability. Recognized throughout the East as a Baptist leader, he held the office of president of the New York State Baptist Convention in 1873 and of the Maine State Baptist Convention in 1879 and 1880. He was married thrice: first, Aug. 11, 1864, to Martha J. Bird of Hartford, Conn., who died in 1867; second, Sept. 4, 1872, to Margaret Richardson of Rochester, N. Y., who died the following year; and third, Aug. 7, 1876, to Cornelia Ewell Nott of Boston, who died in 1888. He died at the home of a daughter in Greenfield, Mass., survived by her and by a son.

[*Who's Who in America*, 1916–17; H. S. Burrage, *Hist. of the Baptists in Me.* (1904); *Gen. Cat. Colgate-Rochester Divinity School* (1930); *The Newton Theol. Inst. Gen. Cat.* (1899); *N. Y. Baptist Union for Ministerial Educ., Ann. Report*, 1883, 1903; *Springfield Republican*, Apr. 24, 1917; records of Central Bapt. Ch., Newport, R. I., First Bapt. Ch., Rochester, N. Y., and Newport Hist. Soc.; unpub. hist. of the Robins family prepared by Henry E. Robins and genealogy traced by a nephew, Henry B. Robins.]   C. H. M.

ROBINSON, ALBERT ALONZO (Oct. 21, 1844–Nov. 7, 1918), civil engineer, railway builder and operator, younger brother of Stillman Williams Robinson [*q.v.*], was born in South Reading, Vt., the son of Ebenezer and Adeline (Williams) Robinson. He was descended from William Robinson, one of the early settlers of Newton, Mass. His father, a country school-teacher, farmer, and carpenter of unusual mechanical ability—a talent which later appeared in his son—died in 1848. In 1853 his mother married Albert Childs and the family moved to the West. After graduating from the academy at Milton, Wis., Albert entered the University of Michigan, from which he received the degrees of B.S. and C.E. in 1869 and that of M.S. in 1871. Outside of school hours he worked on a farm or as a clerk in stores, and while a student at the University of Michigan he spent about five months of each year as assistant engineer with the United States Lake Survey.

His active career in railroad construction and administration began in May 1869, when he joined the engineering corps of the St. Joseph & Denver City Railroad. He continued with this road in various positions from axeman to assistant engineer until Apr. 1, 1871, when he went to the Atchison, Topeka & Santa Fé as assistant engineer in charge of location and construction. He was with the Santa Fé road for twenty-two years, eventually becoming second vice-president and general manager. When he became connected with the road it was scarcely a hundred miles long; when he left, it had grown to a system of over 9,000 miles, more than half of which, as chief engineer, Robinson had built. He was personally in charge of the party which early in 1878 occupied Raton Pass a few hours ahead of the force sent out by the rival Denver & Rio Grande, thus capturing for the Santa Fé the only practicable gateway into northern New Mexico; and he designed and constructed the "switchback" by means of which, before the completion of the tunnel, the first Santa Fé locomotive crossed the summit of the Pass and entered that region. The tremendous expansion of the Santa Fé system during his term of service was due in no small measure to his engineering skill and keen judgment, particularly in the selection of men.

In 1893 he became president of the Mexico Central Railway Company, Ltd., with headquarters in Boston, Mass., which position he held until Dec. 1, 1906, when he retired because of age and ill health. He proved himself an able administrator as well as a great engineer. On Dec. 9, 1869, he was married to Julia Caroline Burdick of Edgerton, Wis., who died Aug. 3, 1881; on Sept. 3, 1885, he married Ellen Frances (Burdick) Williams, sister of his first wife, who with a daughter by his first marriage survived him.

[G. A. Davis, *Hist. of Reading, Windsor County, Vt.*, vol. II (1903); G. D. Bradley, *The Story of the Santa Fe* (1920), dedicated to Robinson; J. B. Robinson, *A Hist. Sketch of the Robinson Family of the Line of Ebenezer Robinson* (1903); J. M. Meade in *Trans., Am. Soc. of Civil Engineers*, vol. LXXXIII (1921); *Topeka State Jour.*, Nov. 7, 1918; *Who's Who in America*, 1916–17.]
         B. A. R.

ROBINSON, BEVERLEY (Jan. 11, 1722 o.s.–Apr. 9, 1792), Loyalist, was born in Middlesex County, Va., from a family active in the life of the colony. He was the brother of John Robinson [*q.v.*] and the sixth son of Catherine (Beverley) and John Robinson who was president of the Council and, at the time of his death in 1749, acting governor. In 1746 Beverley Robinson raised a company for the expedition intended against Canada and was ordered with it to New York. There on July 7, 1748, he had the good fortune to marry the daughter of Frederick Philipse, Susanna, sister of Mary the wife of Roger Morris [*q.v.*]. Susanna was heiress to part of the vast estates on the Hudson. By trading ventures and capable management of the estate, he increased his wife's fortune until he was one of New York's wealthiest landowners. During the French and Indian War, he was one of the commissaries and paymasters of the New York troops and after its conclusion served the colony in various capacities.

Retirement on his estate in Dutchess County was interrupted by the Revolution. Although he objected to some of the measures of the British ministry, he tried "from the very earliest period of the Rebellion to stop its progress" (Robinson memorial, Dec. 11, 1783). He refused to take the oath of allegiance to the state on Feb. 20, 1777, and was obliged to fly to the British in New York City. Offering his services to the army, he raised the Loyal American Regiment, of which he was made colonel, and was later also colonel and director of the loyal Guides and Pioneers. According to Sir Henry Clinton, Robinson "distinguished himself upon several occasions, particularly at the storming of fort Montgomery," Oct. 6, 1777 (Robinson's memorial and "Evidence," Dec. 16, 1785, *post*). His chief services, however, were not in the field. He was constantly employed on various boards and committees. His inclination, though, was toward the secret service, for which his knowledge of the country, his wide acquaintance, and a certain shrewdness in his nature admirably fitted him. He furnished information as to the terrain, roads, and disposition of the people; he directed spies and messengers; and he was active in cases of defection from the American side. He was eager to have Vermont join the British and sent the first invitation to Ethan Allen [*q.v.*]. He also sounded out General Putnam. There is no sound basis for the supposition that it was he who urged Benedict Arnold to change colors. He knew of the treasonable correspondence, though, and offered himself to Sir Henry Clinton for the rôle afterwards played by Major André. He was conspicuous, too, in the attempts to arrange a meeting between the conspirators. He accompanied André up the Hudson to his fateful interview with Arnold and, when André was captured, wrote Washington, who had been his friend before the Revolution, urging the prisoner's release (*Sparks, post,* pp. 533–34).

With his wife and eldest son he was banished by New York state in October 1779, and their property was confiscated. At the conclusion of the war, however, when, in reduced circumstances, he was faced with the necessity of leaving his native land, he could still write: ". . . was it to do over again I should take the same part" (Robinson to Clinton, Aug. 8, 1782). He was recommended to the British government by every officer he had served under, especially by Sir Henry Clinton who wrote, "It is impossible to speak too highly of him" (Robinson's memorial and "Evidence," *post*), and Parliament voted him a partial compensation for his losses. He died in England, where he lived after the Revolution, and his body was buried in St. James' Church at Bath. His wife and seven children survived him, and all of his five sons, four of whom served the British during the Revolution, achieved in later life a measure of distinction.

[See Robinson's Revolutionary correspondence in Sir Henry Clinton Papers, William L. Clements Lib., Univ. of Mich.; the American Loyalists Transcripts, N. Y. Pub. Lib., contain autobiographical material, including memorials cited, and estimates ("Evidence") by Sir Henry Clinton and others, vol. 43, 203–282; *Mag. of Hist.*, July 1909, pp. 47–48; *The Writings of George Washington*, vol. VII (1835), app. vii, ed. by Jared Sparks; compare literary style, etc. of Robinson to Ethan Allen, Mar. 30, 1780, and Feb. 2, 1781, in John Pell, *Ethan Allen* (1929), with letter supposedly written by Robinson to Arnold, in Winthrop Sargent, *The Life and Career of Major André* (1861), pp. 447–49; see also *Parish Register of Christ Church, Middlesex Co., Va.*, 1653–1812 (1897); Great Britain, Hist. MSS. Commission, *Report on American MSS. in the Royal Institution* (4 vols. 1904–09); *Calendar of Hist. MSS. . . . in the Office of the Secy. of State, Albany* (2 vols. 1868); *Memorial History of the City of N. Y.* (1892), II, ed. by J. G. Wilson; *Gentleman's Mag.*, Oct. 1749, p. 476, May 1792, p. 479; inscriptions from tombstone, Bath, and memorial tablet, Thornbury, Bristol, England; of the secondary sources, all with inaccuracies, the best is Lorenzo Sabine, *Biog. Sketches of Loyalists of the Am. Rev.* (1864), vol. II.]   J. C.

ROBINSON, CHARLES (July 21, 1818– Aug. 17, 1894), pioneer, first governor of the state of Kansas, was born at Hardwick, Mass., the son of Jonathan and Huldah (Woodward) Robinson. He grew up in an abolition atmosphere, attended a private school in his native town, and was then sent to Hadley and Amherst academies. He entered Amherst College but was forced to withdraw after a year and a half because of weak eyes. Subsequently he studied medicine under Dr. Amos Twitchell at Keene, N. H., and attended medical lectures at Pittsfield, Mass., and Woodstock, Vt. In 1843 he was married to Sarah Adams of Brookfield, and in the same year he began to practise his profession at Belchertown, Mass. Two years later he and Josiah G. Holland [q.v.] opened a hospital at Springfield. After his wife's death in 1846 he joined a brother at Fitchburg and there continued the practice of medicine. In 1849 he accompanied a party of about forty Bostonians to California. After two weeks at mining on Bear Creek he formed a partnership and established a restaurant at Sacramento. In the contest between land speculators and settlers he was chosen president of the squatters' association. In an armed collision with town officials he received a wound thought to be fatal. He was arrested and placed on a prison ship, where he unexpectedly recovered. After miners and squatters had elected him to the legislature, he was admitted to bail and soon became co-editor of the *Settlers' and Miners' Tribune* at Sacramento. In the state Assembly he was antislavery and supported Frémont for the federal Senate. Eventually a *nolle prosequi* was entered on charges of assault, conspiracy, and murder. He returned to Massachusetts by way of Panama in 1851, and on Oct. 30 of that year he was married to Sara Tappan Doolittle Lawrence, a young woman of good birth and education, daughter of Myron Lawrence of Belchertown, Mass. She shared his interests and ambitions and was an important factor in helping him throughout his life. Her *Kansas: its Interior and Exterior Life* (1856) is a history of the Kansas struggle with a Free-State bias. For two years Robinson edited the *Fitchburg News* and practised medicine.

In 1854 Eli Thayer appointed him Kansas resident agent of the New England Emigrant Aid Company. He was well qualified for the position since his California adventure had given him a glimpse of Kansas and had introduced him to the contentious life of the frontier. In July 1854 the company sent him to the territory to arrange for its settlement. He had noted the beauty and fertility of the Kansas valley in 1849, so he explored the Missouri to Fort Leavenworth while a companion followed the Kansas to Fort Riley. He then went to St. Louis to meet the first body of New England emigrants and continued to conduct a second to the terri-

tory, which arrived at Kansas City in September. The two groups united at the present site of Lawrence and began the settlement of that town. In the spring of 1855 he conducted another party to the territory, which arrived in time to participate in the election of a legislature on Mar. 30. Although there was illegal voting on both sides, proslavery candidates won a large majority of the seats. Three days after the election he wrote to Thayer for the loan of 200 Sharps rifles and two field pieces. At the first Fourth of July celebration at Lawrence he breathed defiance as he recommended, "Let us repudiate all laws enacted by foreign legislative bodies" (*Kansas Conflict, post,* p. 152). During the summer and fall of 1855 he attended numerous conferences held to unite antislavery factions in the territory. At the Lawrence convention of Aug. 14, he was appointed chairman of a Free-State executive committee of twenty-three, but a month later it was superseded by a smaller body headed by James H. Lane [q.v.]. A Free-State party was organized at Big Springs in September, and a constitutional convention was called to meet at Topeka on Oct. 23. He was a delegate and led the radical wing of the party that opposed discrimination against free negroes, but without success. Largely through his influence, however, the convention refused to indorse the principle of popular sovereignty, urged by Lane and the administration faction.

When proslavery Missourians gathered on Wakarusa River in December and threatened to destroy Lawrence, he was appointed commander-in-chief. His cautious policy probably averted bloodshed for the belligerent Lane wished to take the offensive. The timely arrival of Gov. Wilson Shannon ended the controversy, and both sides disbanded their forces. Yet the Wakarusa War was significant for it gave Lane the leadership of the radicals. On Jan. 15, 1856, the Free-State party elected officers under the Topeka constitution, and Robinson was chosen governor. A legislature was organized at Topeka on Mar. 4, and he delivered an inaugural address. He was soon indicted by a proslavery grand jury for treason and usurpation of office. While on his way east in May to obtain aid for Kansas he was arrested near Lexington, Mo. After four months of imprisonment at Lecompton he was released on bail, but the charges remained until the following year. In the fall of 1856 he resigned the governorship and went east; but the Free-State legislature did not act upon his resignation, and he withdrew it when he returned. He and Lane advised participation in the October election of 1857 for members of a territorial legislature. That policy was adopted, the Free-State party captured control of the territorial government, and the Topeka movement came to an end. In 1859 the Republican party supplanted the Free-State organization, and a new constitution was framed at Wyandotte.

Robinson was nominated for governor and elected over the Democratic candidate, Samuel Medary, but of course he did not take office until the state was admitted in 1861. He was sworn in as governor on Feb. 9, and summoned the legislature to meet Mar. 26. His message to the Assembly was able and comprehensive, and he evinced sound statesmanship in inaugurating the forms and functions of a new state government. Nevertheless, his administration of two years was beset with difficulties. Before he had been in office a year an abortive attempt was made to displace him. An election was held, but the canvassing board refused to count the votes, and the state supreme court held it illegal. Early in 1862 articles of impeachment were preferred against the auditor, secretary of state, and the governor because of alleged irregularities in the sale of state bonds. The first two were found guilty and removed from office, but Robinson was acquitted almost unanimously. Nevertheless, the bond transactions hurt him politically. In raising and officering state troops for the Civil War he and Lane worked at cross purposes. Lane had the confidence of Lincoln and Stanton, controlled Kansas patronage, and even usurped a part of the governor's prerogative.

After the expiration of his term of office, he remained a great deal in retirement at his country home of "Oakridge" a few miles from Lawrence, although he engaged in politics sporadically. Always an independent, he joined the Liberal Republican movement. He was elected to the state Senate in 1874 and again in 1876. A decade later he was defeated for Congress on the Democratic ticket, and in 1890 he was an unsuccessful candidate for governor on a fusion ticket composed of Greenbackers, Populists, and Democrats. Throughout his Kansas career he was a promoter of education. As a member of the state Senate he obtained the passage of a comprehensive law regulating the public school system. From 1864 to 1874 and again from 1893 to 1894 he was a regent of the University of Kansas. As superintendent of Haskell Institute, 1887–89, he adopted a policy of industrialization, under which the school began to flourish. He was president of the Kansas State Historical Society from 1879 to 1880 and in 1892 published *The Kansas Conflict.* Cautious and calculative, logical and shrewd, judicious and argumentative, his greatest service to Kansas was that he gave the Topeka movement equilibrium and was the brake and balance wheel of the Free-State party. He was never very popular, but his common sense and business acumen gave great weight to his judgment, and his decisions were usually sound.

["Webb Scrap Book," 17 vols., a collection of newspaper clippings, 1854–56, 1859, in the Kan. State Hist. Lib.; *The Kansas Conflict* and *Kansas: its . . . Life, ante*; F. W. Blackmar, *The Life of Charles Robinson* (1902), and "A Chapter in the Life of Charles Robinson, the First Governor of Kansas," *Am. Hist. Asso. Report . . . 1894* (1896); Eli Thayer, *A Hist. of the Kansas Crusade* (1889); *Kan. Hist. Colls.,* vol. XIII (1915); D. W. Wilder's *Annals of Kansas* (new ed., 1886).]
                                    W. H. S—n.

ROBINSON, CHARLES MULFORD (Apr. 30, 1869–Dec. 30, 1917), city planner, author, and journalist, was born at Ramapo, Rockland County, N. Y., the son of Arthur and Jane Howell (Porter) Robinson, who soon moved to Rochester, N. Y. He attended school there and in 1891 received the degree of A.B. from the University of Rochester. After college and between trips abroad he became an associate editor of the Rochester *Post-Express,* 1891–1902; in 1904 he was employed in an editorial capacity by the *Public Ledger* (Philadelphia), and in 1907 by the *Municipal Journal* (New York). He was also a regular contributing editor to the *Survey,* the *Architectural Record,* the *National Municipal Review,* and the *Boston Transcript.* His career as a city planner began with a series of three articles on municipal improvement contributed to the *Atlantic Monthly* in 1899, which aroused such interest that *Harper's Magazine* asked for a similar series on civic improvement abroad. The abundant material gathered in preparation for the articles was used later in a book that, strangely enough in view of its later success, went begging for a publisher and was finally brought out at the author's expense under the title of *The Improvement of Towns and Cities; or The Practical Basis of Civic Æsthetics* (1901). This was followed in 1903 by *Modern Civic Art; or The City Made Beautiful,* and in 1908 by *The Call of the City,* a collection of essays and verse. In 1911, largely as the result of a year at Harvard as a guest of the University, he published *The Width and Arrangement of Streets; A Study in Town Planning,* which five years later he rewrote as *City Planning: With Special Reference to the Planning of Streets and Lots.*

His work was not limited to writing, however. Early in his career he served as acting secretary of the American Park and Outdoor Art Association, made up largely of landscape architects, park commissioners and superintendents, and a few public-spirited citizens; and in 1904 he was influential in forming the American Civic Association at St. Louis, a union of the American Park Association and a federation of civic improvement societies in the Middle West. For a while he acted as secretary but soon retired from the position in order to devote more time to his increasingly active practice.

His work as a consultant began when Buffalo, N. Y., through its recently formed Society for Beautifying Buffalo, asked him to make a report (published in 1902) upon local conditions. Later he was consulted by many other cities, among them Detroit, Denver, Omaha, Los Angeles, Oakland, Cal., Cedar Rapids, Iowa, and Columbus, Ohio; his recommendations for all of these and for many towns, large and small, have been embodied in published reports. In the Detroit project Robinson was associated with Frederick Law Olmsted, Jr.; in Omaha with George B. Ford and E. P. Goodrich; and in Columbus with Austin W. Lord, Albert Kelsey, Charles N. Lowrie, and H. A. McNeil. In 1915 he associated himself professionally with William Pitkin, Jr., a landscape architect of Rochester, N. Y. In 1913 he accepted and held until his death the Chair of Civic Design established at the University of Illinois, the first of its kind in any American university although the subject had been taught for years at Harvard. Robinson's approach to city planning was primarily an æsthetic one and his rôle—for he was virtually without technical training—that of publicist and teacher rather than technical designer. It was to the lasting advantage of the profession in which he so ably pioneered that its cause was sponsored by a man of such broad vision, rare initiative, and good judgment. He died after a brief illness on Sunday, Dec. 30, 1917, at Albany, N. Y., survived by his widow, Eliza Ten Eyck Pruyn of Albany, whom he had married in 1896. After his death appeared *The City Sleeps* (1920), a volume of his verse and essays compiled and edited by Mrs. Robinson. His professional library, comprising books, reports, periodicals and original studies, maps, and plans, was given by his widow to Harvard University as a memorial collection.

[*Who's Who in America*, 1916–17; *Landscape Architecture*, July 1919, reprint with portrait and bibliography from *Trans. Am. Soc. Landscape Architects*, 1909–21, pp. 93–99; *Revista Municipal* (Havana), Mar. 1908, bibliography and notes on life and work corrected by Robinson; *Nat. Municipal Rev.*, Mar. 1918; *Municipal Jour.* (N. Y.), Jan. 5, 1918; *Albany Evening Jour.*, Dec. 31, 1917.]   K. M.

ROBINSON, CHARLES SEYMOUR (Mar. 31, 1829–Feb. 1, 1899), Presbyterian clergyman, hymnologist, editor, was born in Bennington, Vt., son of Henry and Martha Prime (Haynes) Robinson. The family was related to John Robinson, pastor of the Pilgrims in Leyden, and included honored founders of Bennington and the state. Charles prepared for college at Union Academy, East Bennington, and graduated at Williams in 1849. After teaching for two years he spent a year at Union Seminary, New York, and graduated in 1855 at Princeton Seminary. He was ordained Apr. 19, 1855, as pastor of the Park Presbyterian Church, Troy, N. Y. Freshness of thought and personal charm gave marked attractiveness to his ministry. He was married in 1858 to Harriet Reed Church of Troy, who died in 1896. In 1860 he was called to the First Presbyterian Church of Brooklyn, N. Y.

From boyhood Robinson had been passionately fond of music; he played the flute and would walk miles to hear a good band; as pastor he was deeply interested in promoting a higher type of congregational singing. To this end, during his pastorate in Brooklyn he entered upon the studies in hymnology which were his absorbing avocation for thirty years and greatly extended his influence and usefulness. His first venture in the preparation of hymnals was *Hymns of the Church,* published in 1862. This was followed in 1865 by *Songs for the Sanctuary,* which met with wide acceptance especially in Presbyterian and Congregational churches; over half a million copies of it were issued.

In 1868 he resigned his charge at Brooklyn and became pastor of the American Chapel in Paris, which under his leadership united the work of several Christian bodies and became the "American Church in Paris." Obliged to leave that city when it was besieged by the German army in 1870, he returned to New York and was called to the pastorate of the Eleventh (later Madison Avenue) Presbyterian Church, where he gave devoted service for seventeen years. In 1875 he published *Psalms and Hymns,* which became the official hymnal of the Southern Presbyterian Church, and in 1878, *Selection of Spiritual Songs,* which showed the influence of the modern English hymn and tune writers. This influence was much more marked in *Laudes Domini* (1884), characterized in Julian's *Dictionary of Hymnology* (London, 1915) as "a book of great excellence," which came into extensive use; *New Laudes Domini* appeared in 1892. Regarding all this work in hymnology as his special contribution to the life of the churches, Robinson would not use his large royalties from his hymnals for himself or his family, but devoted them to the building fund of his church and other benefactions.

The breaking of his health under continuous overstrain led him to resign his pastorate, and he turned to literary work, still doing much preaching. He had edited the *Illustrated Christian Weekly* in 1876–77; he now conducted *Every Thursday*, a periodical of his own (March 1890–April 1891). Besides the hymnals already mentioned he had edited some fifteen minor collections and had written several volumes mainly of an expository character. He now published *Sabbath Evening Sermons* (1887), *The Pharaohs of the Bondage and the Exodus* (1887), *Simon Peter, His Early Life and Times* (1889), *Simon Peter, His Later Life and Labours* (1894), and *Annotations upon Popular Hymns* (1893). Notwithstanding his rapidly failing strength, he undertook a brief pastorate (1891) with the Thirteenth Street Presbyterian Church, and another (1892–98) with the New York Presbyterian Church on 128th Street. He died in New York and was buried in Bennington.

[Obituary and editorial, *N. Y. Evangelist*, Feb. 9, 1899; *N. Y. Tribune*, Feb. 2, 1899; John Julian, *A Dictionary of Hymnology* (1915); letters from Mary Robinson Gaylord.]   E. D. E.

ROBINSON, CHRISTOPHER (May 15, 1806–Oct. 3, 1889), lawyer, diplomatist, was born in Providence, R. I., the son of Benjamin Robinson and his wife, Ann (Pitts). He was sent to a private school and thence to Brown University, where he was graduated in 1825. His personal inclinations were toward a career in which success would depend upon powers of speech: in education, religion, or the law. He chose the last, retaining a practical interest in the other two throughout his life. After his graduation he engaged for a time in academy teaching, and then read law under Senator Albert C. Greene. He was admitted to the bar in 1833, and made his appearance in public life the same year as Fourth-of-July orator in Woonsocket, where he had settled. A Universalist, he preached for the Universalist society before the completion of their meeting-house in 1839. In 1847 he was prominent, though unsuccessful, in an effort to link Woonsocket to Boston by a railroad. He was thrice married: to Mary Tillinghast, by whom he had one child who died; to Mary Jencks, who had no issue; and to Louisa Aldrich, to whom four children were born.

Robinson did not enter politics until after the death of his third wife, in 1853. His political ambitions were rewarded when he was made attorney-general of Rhode Island, 1854–55. He was elected to the Thirty-sixth Congress (1859–61), where he voted for John Sherman for speaker and was a member of the Judiciary Committee and of the select committee of thirty-three on the "state of the Union." His sentiments were strongly anti-slavery and pro-Union. He was not returned in the election of 1860, but on June 8, 1861, was appointed minister to Peru by President Lincoln. This was an important, even critical, post, for diplomatic relations had been suspended in November 1860 by President Buchanan, and there were many partisans of the Confederacy in Lima. Robinson presented his credentials Jan. 11, 1862, and with patient persistence and unruffled temper urged upon dilatory and changing ministries the settlement of the claims of American citizens. He yielded to the Peruvian contention that the two most controversial cases should be submitted to arbitration (which was never effected, since the King of the Belgians declined to act as arbitrator), but he obtained the satisfactory settlement of the other claims by means of a mixed commission. He also won Peruvian sentiment over to the Federal government, turning to his advantage Peru's fears of European aggression, of which he offered Mexico as an example. When these fears were realized in 1864 by Spain's seizure of the Chincha Islands, he exerted himself to assure Peru of the active sympathy of the United States.

Robinson's mission was terminated in a peculiar manner. In July 1865 he received an instruction from the Department of State that his resignation had been accepted. He replied that any document purporting to be his resignation was a forgery, but that he was ready to retire. The investigation which followed involved the secretary of the legation, who was recalled. A new minister arrived in November, and Robinson's last important official act was to assemble the diplomatic corps at the legation (he was acting without instructions), where it was resolved to recognize a revolutionary government which had just overthrown the old. Robinson left Peru on Dec. 21, and returned to private life in Woonsocket, Jan. 16, 1866. He lived quietly and in comfortable circumstances there until his death at the age of eighty-three.

[E. Richardson, *Hist. of Woonsocket* (1876); Woonsocket and other Rhode Island newspapers, esp. obituary notice in *Providence Daily Journal*, Oct. 5, 1889, and note in Brown Univ. Necrology, *Ibid.*, June 18, 1890; Robinson's dispatches in the archives of the State Dept.; and Woonsocket tax records.] G. V. B.

ROBINSON, CONWAY (Sept. 15, 1805–Jan. 30, 1884), lawyer and author, the son of John and Agnes Conway (Moncure) Robinson and brother of Moncure Robinson [*q.v.*], was born in Richmond, Va. He was descended from John Robinson who is recorded as owning land in New Charles Parish in 1653. He was not related to John Robinson, the colonial treasurer, nor to Christopher Robinson, the president of the council. His father put in a long life as a law clerk. From 1787 to 1812 he was assistant or principal clerk in one or more of the local courts, and from 1827 to his death in 1850 he was clerk to the state circuit court in Richmond. He was presumably well qualified for his task as compiler of *A Collection of . . . Forms . . . used in the . . . Courts of Law in Virginia* (1809). Conway Robinson attended the school of a Mr. Terrill until he was thirteen years old. At that age he began to follow in his father's footsteps. He became the assistant of Thomas C. Howard, clerk of two of Richmond's local courts, and after six years of the latter's teaching he became clerk of a local court. In 1827 he was admitted to the bar. In the following year he was made clerk of the general court. He had already (1826) issued a new edition of his father's *Forms.* Resigning his clerkship in July 1831 to engage in practice, he became a successful attorney and in January 1839 was admitted to the bar of the United States Supreme Court. In the conduct of his cases he made both reputation and money, but from the first he devoted a part of his time and energy to legal and historical scholarship. In 1831 he assisted in founding the Virginia Historical and Philosophical Society. He prepared for it several studies, some of which were published in *An Account of Discoveries in the West until 1519, and of Voyages to and along the Atlantic Coast of North America, from 1520 to 1573* (1848). In 1832 he published Volume I of his *Practice in the Courts of Law and Equity in Virginia,* followed by Volume II in 1835, and Volume III in 1839. This work is still spoken of with respect and affection by Virginia lawyers of the old school. It was as a "black letter lawyer" that Conway Robinson attained eminence, and his accurate, scrupulous scholarship and luminous style never appear to better advantage than in his "Old Practice."

In 1836 he became president of the struggling Richmond, Fredericksburg & Potomac Railroad Company. By November 1838 he had established it so firmly that in spite of the unanimous request of the stockholders that he continue at its head he felt free to resign. In 1842 he became official reporter of the court of appeals and issued two volumes of *Virginia Reports.* As a preface to the first of these volumes he inserted a sketch of the development of the judicial system of the state. In 1846 he and John Mercer Patton [*q.v.*] were chosen by the legislature to revise the civil code, and in 1847, the criminal code of Virginia. In 1852 he was elected to the legislature to assist in adapting these codes to the new constitution, adopted by the state in 1851. In 1854 he published the first volume of his *Practice in Courts of Justice in England and the United States,* the seventh and last volume of which appeared in 1874. Because of the superior libraries in the national capital, he moved his residence to the District of Columbia in 1858. At the time of his removal from Virginia he had appeared as counsel before the Virginia court of appeals in 137 cases, and before the United States Supreme Court in five of the fourteen cases brought before that court from Virginia since 1839. He disapproved of secession, but three of his sons served the Confederacy and two of them died for it. After 1866 he resumed his practice before the Virginia court of appeals and continued to practise before that court until 1878 and before the United States Supreme Court until his death. In 1882 he published the first volume of his *History of the High Court of Chancery and Other Institutions of England.* This volume was an exhaustive exposition of English constitutional development to the death of Henry VIII. Work on the second volume was cut short by Robinson's death at the home of his brother in Philadelphia on Jan. 30, 1884. He had married, on July 14, 1836, Mary Susan Selden Leigh, daughter of Benjamin Watkins Leigh [*q.v.*] of Virginia, who with five children survived him.

[John Selden, "Conway Robinson," *Va. Law Reg.,* Jan. 1896; A. H. Sands, "Conway Robinson," *Va. Law Jour.,* May 1884; H. E. Hayden, *Va. Geneals.* (1891); the *State* (Richmond), Feb. 1, 1884.]   T. C. J., Jr.

ROBINSON, EDWARD (Apr. 10, 1794–Jan. 27, 1863), philologist, geographer, and professor of Biblical literature, was the son of Rev. William Robinson by his fourth wife, Elisabeth (Norton). His earliest American ancestor was William Robinson who was in Dorchester, Mass., as early as 1637. Edward was born in Southington, Conn., where his father was pastor for forty-one years and also a shrewd and successful farmer. The boy attended the common schools of the vicinity and for a time was a student in the family of a neighboring pastor. At the age of sixteen he was apprenticed to a Southington merchant who put him in charge of the drug department of his store. Robinson was eager for further education, however, and in a couple of years was allowed to go to Hamilton College, Clinton, N. Y., where an uncle, Seth Norton, was a professor. After graduating in 1816, he studied law for a year in Hudson, N. Y., and the next year was tutor in mathematics and Greek at Hamilton. On Sept. 3, 1818, he married Eliza Kirkland, daughter of Samuel Kirkland [q.v.], missionary to the Oneidas. After her death, the following July, he remained on a farm she had owned, where he combined agricultural pursuits with study.

In 1821, he went to Andover, Mass., in order to see through the press certain portions of the *Iliad* which he had edited with a Latin introduction and notes—*Iliadis Libri Novem Priores Librique XVIII et XXII* (1822). At Andover he came under the influence of the distinguished Hebraist, Moses Stuart [q.v.], professor in the Theological Seminary, who persuaded him to devote himself to Hebrew studies. On Oct. 1, 1822, he was licensed to preach by the Hartford South Association and the following year he became instructor in Hebrew at the Seminary, continuing in this capacity until 1826. During this period he assisted Stuart in preparing *A Greek Grammar of the New Testament* (1825), a translation from the German of G. B. Winer, and himself made and published in 1825 a translation of Wahl's *Clavis Philologica Novi Testamenti*. The year 1826, in which he went to Germany to study, was a turning point in his career, since he then came into direct contact with German scholarship and methods at a time when scholarly research, in the modern sense of the term, was quite unknown in America. For four years he pursued studies at Göttingen, Halle, and Berlin, making a great impression by his ability, and becoming the personal friend of the philologists Gesenius and Rödiger, the theologian Tholuck, the historian Neander, and especially of the great geographer Ritter, whose influence on him was to be decisive. In 1828 he married Therese Albertine Louise, the brilliant daughter of Ludwig Heinrich von Jakob, professor of philosophy at Halle [see Therese A. L. von Jakob Robinson].

After his return to America, Robinson was appointed professor extraordinary of Biblical literature at Andover, a post which he combined with that of librarian. In 1831 he founded the *American Biblical Repository*, of which he was editor for four years and to which he contributed much of the material; later, 1843, he founded the *Bibliotheca Sacra*, which the next year was taken over by Edwards A. Park and Bela B. Edwards [qq.v.] of Andover. Subject to attacks of epilepsy, he was forced by ill health to resign his professorship in 1833. Removing to Boston, he continued his work, however, publishing several books and numerous papers. The most important of these were *A Hebrew and English Lexicon of the Old Testament* ... (1836), a translation of Gesenius' work with additions and alterations; and *A Greek and English Lexicon of the New Testament* (1836). In 1837 he was invited to the chair of Biblical literature at Union Theological Seminary, New York City, and at the same time given leave of absence in order to visit the Holy Land. From March to July 1838 he traveled in Sinai, Palestine, and southern Syria, with the aid of an American missionary, Eli Smith [q.v.]. Robinson himself emphasizes the invaluable assistance given him by Smith, whose command of Arabic and knowledge of the people formed a perfect complement to his own historical and philological training. It is difficult to overestimate the value of their joint achievement. For the first time a trained scholar, possessed of a sound critical method in historical and topographical research, explored Palestine, paying the most careful attention to cartography, to the correct Arabic form of place-names (*sine qua non*), and to the vestiges of antiquity. It is not surprising that the publication of his great work, *Biblical Researches in Palestine, Mount Sinai and Arabia Petraea* (3 vols., London, 1841), and the simultaneous appearance of a German translation, at once established his reputation as one of the foremost geographers and Biblical scholars of his time. The lapse of three generations has placed him even higher in the history of scholarship, for it is now recognized that his work marks an epoch in the development of historical geography and related fields. In 1852 he visited Palestine again, for a shorter period, and in 1856 brought out the results of this reconnaissance in a second edition of his work, with a supplementary volume, *Later Biblical Researches in Palestine and the Adjacent Regions*. Three years later he published a *Memoir of the Rev. William Robinson* (1859), with a genealogy of his family. Unhappily, his health began to interfere seriously with his activities, and he was at last stricken with an incurable disease of the eyes. He died in New York City after a short illness.

[H. B. Smith and R. D. Hitchcock, *The Life, Writings, and Character of Edward Robinson* (1863); Robinson's *Memoir of the Rev. William Robinson* (1859); H. R. Timlow, *Ecclesiastical and Other Sketches of Southington, Conn.* (1875); G. L. Prentiss, *The Union Theological Sem. in the City of N. Y.* (1889); *N. Y. Tribune,* Jan. 29, 1863.]   W. F. A.

ROBINSON, EDWARD (Nov. 1, 1858–Apr. 18, 1931), director of the Metropolitan Museum of Art, only son of Edwin Augustus and Ellen (Coburn) Robinson, was born in Boston, Mass. He attended the Boston Latin School and graduated from Harvard in 1879. In 1881 he married Elizabeth H. Gould, of Boston, and a son was born in 1882. After five years spent in study in Europe, including fifteen months in Greece and three semesters at the University of Berlin, he returned to Boston in 1885 and became curator of classical antiquities at the Museum of Fine Arts. He was elected its director in 1902, holding this position until 1905, when he went to New York as assistant director and curator of classical art at the Metropolitan Museum of Art. In 1910 he was elected director, remaining in office during his lifetime. He was the third to hold the chief administrative position, and the first of American parentage.

Robinson's administration was notable. His first care was the assembling of a scientific staff and the organizing of departments with a competent curator at the head of each. His own chosen field was classical archaeology, and he set the same high standard for the classical department of the Metropolitan Museum that had made the collection in the Boston Museum outstanding, but he was equally interested in the development of other departments, which all came under the influence of his sound judgment and unerring taste. Several new wings were built to house the rapidly growing collections, many of which, coming as gifts or bequests, presented special problems in their exhibition and care. At the same time the increased use of the Museum by the public made necessary constant cooperation in the way of publications, lectures, and temporary exhibitions. A new stage of Museum development was reached with the establishment, in 1925, of a branch museum, The Cloisters, and the series of symphony concerts given each winter after 1919. In spite of all these activities, which made so great a demand on the time of the Director, he found it possible to serve on the boards of several other institutions. He was a member of the Council of the Archaeological Institute of America and president of its New York society; a member of the managing committee of the American School of Classical Studies in Athens; a trustee of the American Academy in Rome; a member of the Executive Committee of the American Society for the Excavation of Sardis; a director of the American Federation of Arts; a trustee of the Museum of the City of New York, and a member of the Commission for the Excavation of the Agora of Athens. He was also a fellow of the American Academy of Arts and Sciences; a

member of the German Archaeological Institute; a corresponding member of the American Institute of Architects; a member of the Architectural League of New York; a member of the Commission des Musées royaux des Beaux Arts de Belgique, and of many other learned societies.

While in Boston Robinson served for eight years as secretary of the art commission of the city of Boston. He selected and arranged the collection of casts of classical and renaissance sculpture in the Slater Memorial Museum at Norwich, Conn., and also formed the collection of casts in the Metropolitan Museum. In 1893–94 and from 1898 to 1902 he was lecturer in classical archaeology at Harvard University. His catalogues of Greek and Roman casts and Greek, Etruscan, and Roman vases in the Boston Museum, as well as scholarly publications in the annual reports, were of value to scholars and students alike. After taking up work in New York, his administrative duties restricted his writing to short articles, appearing chiefly in the *Bulletin* of the Metropolitan Museum. In recognition of his long and varied service to the world of art numerous degrees and foreign orders were conferred upon him.

[See Harvard College, Class of 1879, *Ninth Report* (1929); *Who's Who in America*, 1930–31; and the *Bulletin* of the Metropolitan Museum of Art, May 1931. New York newspapers, as well as other papers and periodicals, published obituary articles and editorials at the time of Robinson's death.] H. Fa—n.

ROBINSON, EDWARD MOTT (Jan. 8, 1800–June 14, 1865), merchant, son of James and Mary (Attmore) Robinson, was born in Philadelphia, where his father had married and engaged in mercantile business. He was taken to South Kingstown, R. I., to which his ancestor, Rowland Robinson a Quaker, emigrated from England, late in the seventeenth century. He was the great-grandson of William Robinson, a large landed proprietor and deputy governor of Rhode Island in the middle of the eighteenth century. After his academic education had been completed, at the age of twenty-one he began business in Wakefield, South Kingstown, with his elder brother. They first engaged in cotton and woolen manufacturing, subsequently carrying on a commission business in sperm oil in Providence, R. I. Some time after 1830 he removed to New Bedford, Mass., where he soon entered the firm of Isaac Howland, Junior, & Company, whaling merchants. On Dec. 29, 1833, he was married in New Bedford to Abby Slocum Howland, the daughter of Gideon Howland and grand-daughter of Isaac Howland, his partners in the whaling firm. The young partner was forceful, energetic, and far-sighted, and through his shrewd management helped make the house of Howland one of the wealthiest and most prominent in the golden days of the whaling industry. For nearly thirty years he was a leading figure in New Bedford. His firm owned more than thirty vessels, administered successfully the details of equipment and personnel, and exerted a wide influence on the community and the industry. He served as president of the Bedford Commercial Bank. Entering politics, he was elected to the city government, though failing in an ambition to reach the mayor's chair. A man who had known him wrote in 1918 that "he was not personally popular" (Emery, *post,* p. iv), but an anonymous writer of 1851 characterized him as "affable and colloquial . . . with the soubriquet of 'Black Hawk,' to which he answers with good nature. In business matters he is strictly honorable, but he does not claim to be anything more" (*Rich Men, post,* p. 190).

After the death of his wife in 1860 and the outbreak of the Civil War with its adverse consequences to the whale fisheries, he removed to New York, where he joined the firm of William T. Coleman & Company, in which he became a large owner. They were proprietors of a line of California packets, at one time being in control of more than seventy vessels. He also added to his wealth by successful operations in Wall Street. Tall and distinguished, he was always well-dressed, though many stories were told of his personal economies. He once refused an imported cigar, remarking that he was satisfied with cheap ones and was fearful of a cultivated taste, which he could not afford. At his death in New York he left a fortune somewhat in excess of $5,000,000, the bulk of which, after a bequest of $10,000 to the town of South Kingstown and small legacies to friends, he bequeathed, mostly in trust, to his then unmarried daughter, who, as Hetty Howland (Robinson) Green [*q.v.*] subsequently became known as "the richest woman in the world." He refused to name her as his executor, believing women could not take care of money and little dreaming she would expand his wealth twenty-fold.

[W. M. Emery, *The Howland Heirs* (1919); Abner Forbes and J. W. Greene, *Rich Men of Massachusetts* (1851); T. R. Hazard, *Recollections of Olden Times* (1879); *Providence Daily Journal,* Apr. 7, 1873.]
W. M. E.

ROBINSON, EDWARD VAN DYKE (Dec. 20, 1867–Dec. 10, 1915), economist, was born at Bloomington, Ill., the son of Charles Stanley and Wilhelmina (von Schwanenflügel) Robinson. He graduated from the University of Michigan (A.B., 1890, A.M., 1891) and received his doctorate at Leipzig in 1895. Prior to study in Europe he had been superintendent of schools at Schoolcraft, Mich., and on his return to America he reëntered secondary school work, becoming principal of high schools in Muskegon, Mich., Rock Island, Ill., and in St. Paul. During this period he was at different times special lecturer on economics and politics at Augustana College at Rock Island, and acting professor at Albion College, Albion, Mich. He had taught physiography and commercial geography in the summer school of the University of Minnesota, and in 1907 was appointed professor of economics in this institution. Two years later he revisited Europe, as delegate of his university to the Darwin Centennial Celebration, at Cambridge, England, and to the five hundredth anniversary celebration of the University of Leipzig. He was a student of wide interests—geography, economic history, taxation, transportation, governmental administration, education. His inquiries in remote fields and periods were matched by others of immediate importance to Minnesota. He worked closely with the Minnesota Tax Commission, as director of its department of research and statistics, and for its report, 1912, prepared the studies of the cost of the state's government, and of railroad taxation in Minnesota. The University published his elaborate account of *Early Economic Conditions and the Development of Agriculture in Minnesota* (1915). Scientific journals were carrying articles from his pen which showed his skill in less utilitarian investigations, such as into the division of governmental power in ancient Greece.

Robinson's high school teaching had yielded a textbook on commercial geography in 1910, which, many times reprinted, influenced the teaching of this subject. He was opposed to the rigidity which characterized the curriculum and system of promotion of pupils in the public schools and was among the earliest to advocate the junior high school as a means of reform. In 1915, following a year of study abroad, he was elected to a professorship in economics in Columbia University, his responsibility being chiefly for the undergraduate department. For this work he was fitted not only by his competent scholarship (particularly evident in his "War and Economics in History and in Theory," in the *Political Science Quarterly,* December 1900), but by his knowledge of pedagogy and his pronounced turn for educational administration. He had barely entered upon his new duties, however, when he died of an attack of heart disease. He was survived by his wife, Clare (Howard) Robinson, whom he had married at Muskegon, Mich., on June 30, 1897, and by a daughter.

Robinson was a man of fine presence, good judgment, sincerity, and much personal magnetism. He put students under obligation by his generous devotion of time to their individual problems.

[*Minneapolis Morning Tribune*, Dec. 11, 1915; *Minn. Alumni Weekly*, Dec. 20, 1915; *Who's Who in America*, 1914–15; *N. Y. Times*, Dec. 11, 1915.]   B. M.

ROBINSON, EZEKIEL GILMAN (Mar. 23, 1815–June 13, 1894), Baptist clergyman, educator, for seventeen years president of Brown University, was born on the ancestral farm in South Attleboro, Mass., the youngest of the four children of Ezekiel and Cynthia (Slack) Robinson. His early boyhood was spent at his birthplace and in that portion of Pawtucket which was then in the state of Massachusetts. He attended various schools, which in general, he states, did him more harm than good, and was poorly prepared for college at two academies, one in New Hampton, N. H., and the other in Pawtucket. He graduated from Brown University in 1838, having, as he says, "drifted aimlessly into college and drifted aimlessly through it, waking up only during the last year to see what I might and ought to have done" (*An Autobiography, post*, p. 18). He seems also to have drifted into the ministry. Judging him to be a promising candidate, the Baptist Church in Pawtucket of which he was a member licensed him to preach before he had finished his college course. After his graduation, for six months or more he represented the American Tract Society among the churches of Hartford County, Conn., with notable success. He then did some graduate work at Brown, occasionally preaching with acceptance to his hearers and encouragement to himself. He was thus led to enter Newton Theological Institution, from which he graduated in 1842.

His first pastorate was at the Cumberland Street Baptist Church, Norfolk, Va., where he was ordained in November 1842. Here he remained until the autumn of 1845, serving on leave of absence (1843–44) as chaplain of the University of Virginia, where he preached each Sunday and lectured once a week. During this period he was married, Feb. 21, 1844, to Harriet Richards Parker, daughter of Caleb Parker of Roxbury, Mass. From October 1845 to September 1846 he was pastor of the Old Cambridge Baptist Church, Cambridge, Mass. Leaving here in the interest of his wife's health, he became professor of Biblical interpretation in the Western Baptist Theological Institute, recently established at Covington, Ky. With the virtual breaking up of that school in 1848 over the question of slavery, he accepted the pastorate of the

Ninth Street Baptist Church, Cincinnati. Early in 1853 he resigned to become professor of Biblical theology at the Rochester Theological Seminary, Rochester, N. Y.

In spite of the somewhat fortuitous character of his early career, Robinson later revealed a vigorous will, intense application, and a bold, keen, acquisitive intellect. Preëminently a thinker, and endowed with no little oratorical ability, he took high rank among preachers of the scholarly type. "Tall, erect, broad-shouldered, with an intellectual cast of countenance made venerable by the hoary locks which even in the prime of manhood were prematurely gray," he was a man whose "words gained weight from his physical stature and his dignified demeanor" (*Memorial Address, post*, p. 5). He had an unconquerable dislike for pastoral duties, however, and felt that teaching was his proper vocation. This feeling was justified by his success at Rochester. Fearlessly devoted to the truth, scornful of superficiality and sham, relentlessly logical, intensely virile, he captivated the students and inspired them with something of his own spirit. Theologically he was unchained, rationalistic, and in advance of his times. The substance of his lectures at Rochester is contained in his *Christian Theology* (1894). Among his other published works are a translation of Neander's *Planting and Training of the Christian Church* (1865); *Lectures on Preaching* (1883), delivered in 1882 at Yale; *Principles and Practice of Morality* (1888, 1891, 1896); *Christian Evidences* (1895); *Christian Character, Baccalaureate Sermons* (1896); and numerous articles, some of them in the *Christian Review* of which from 1859 to 1864 he was the editor.

From 1860 until 1872 he served as president of Rochester Theological Seminary, and in the latter year succeeded Alexis Caswell [*q.v.*] as president of Brown University. He at once perceived the defects and needs of the institution and with all the force of his inflexible will inaugurated improvements. A little lacking in patience and tact, and brusque in manners, he sometimes made his lot unnecessarily difficult. A certain sternness and a rigorous attitude in the matter of discipline prevented him from commanding the affection of the students. In spite of these defects, after seventeen years of leadership he left the college far richer in equipment and much further advanced in educational policy. Resigning in March 1889 at the age of seventy-four, he continued active for the remainder of his life, preaching, lecturing, and from the fall of 1892 serving as professor of ethics and apologetics at the University of Chicago. His death occurred in a Boston hospital and he was buried in Rochester.

[*Ezekiel Gilman Robinson, An Autobiog.* (1896), ed. by E. H. Johnson; T. D. Anderson, *Memorial Address on Ezekiel Gilman Robinson* (1895); W. C. Bronson, *The Hist. of Brown Univ.* (1914); *Providence Jour.,* June 14, 1894.]   H. E. S.

ROBINSON, FREDERICK BYRON (Apr. 11, 1855–Mar. 23, 1910), anatomist and surgeon, was born on a farm near Hollandale, Iowa County, Wis., where his parents, William and Mary Robinson, English immigrants, had settled in 1845. After elementary instruction in the log school house of Hollandale he attended Mineral Point Seminary and later worked his way through the University of Wisconsin, where he obtained the degree of B.S. in 1878. He taught school to finance his course through Rush Medical College, Chicago, receiving his medical degree in 1882. He practised medicine at Grand Rapids, Wis., for six years broken by study trips to Heidelberg, Berlin, Vienna, London, and Birmingham. A course under Lawson Tait at Birmingham had a lasting influence upon his career. In 1889 he moved to Toledo, Ohio, where he was made professor of anatomy and clinical surgery in the Toledo Medical College. Two years later he took up his residence in Chicago and was appointed professor of gynecology in the Chicago Post-Graduate Medical School. Later, he was professor of gynecology and abdominal surgery successively at the Illinois Medical School and the Chicago College of Medicine and Surgery. For many years he served on the staff of the Woman's Hospital and of the Mary Thompson Hospital. In 1894 he married Dr. Lucy Waite, head surgeon of the Mary Thompson Hospital, and they were thereafter associated in hospital and office work.

Though always a busy practitioner of surgery, his chief claim to distinction rests upon his researches and writings in the field of anatomy. For years he frequented the morgue of the Cook County Hospital, where he made a study of the material which came for autopsy. He confined his studies to the abdomen and pelvis and their contents. Most notable were his investigations upon the physiological anatomy of the peritoneum, but they included the anatomy and pathology of the ureters, the seminal vesicles, the biliary and pancreatic ducts, and the abdominal sympathetic nervous system. Of particular interest to the practising surgeon were his investigations upon the pathology of the psoas muscle and its relation to appendicitis. His untiring industry and enthusiasm brought to him an astonishing wealth of material. Equally no-

table is the quantity of his literary output. He is credited with having written over five hundred articles, in addition to several large volumes devoted to surgery and anatomy. His books include *Experimental Intestinal Surgery* (1889), *Practical Intestinal Surgery* (2 vols., 1891), *Landmarks in Gynecology* (2 vols., 1894), *The Peritoneum—Histology and Physiology* (1897), and *Abdominal and Pelvic Brain* (1906). Another of his important achievements was a life-size chart illustrating the sympathetic nervous system. Many of his articles are but slight variations of the same theme. As might be expected, their literary quality suffered much from this overproduction. His writings are marked by poor arrangement and faulty diction and are seriously marred by a bizarre technical terminology. That his investigations were in the main sound is evidenced by their frequent citation in the standard works on anatomy. His name is carried by several anatomical eponyms. Personally he was short and heavy-set, an intense person with tireless nervous energy, egotistical, and intolerant of criticism or of the opinions of others. He had developed highly the "gentle art of making enemies." The glaring faults of his literary style and his unattractive personality doubtless account in some measure for the fact that his books never had the backing of a leading publisher, that his articles seldom appeared in the more substantial journals, and that he never achieved the highest recognition as a teacher.

[Lucy Waite, *In Memoriam: Byron Robinson* (1910); *Am. Medic. Compend.* (Toledo), Jan. 1907; *Am. Jour. of Clinical Medicine*, July 1910, Apr. 1922; *Medic. Standard* (Chicago), Sept. 1910; *Who's Who in America*, 1908–09, where he is listed as Byron Robinson; H. A. Kelly and W. L. Burrage, *Am. Medic. Biogs.* (1920), where he is listed as Fred Byron Robinson.]   J. M. P—n.

ROBINSON, HARRIET JANE HANSON (Feb. 8, 1825–Dec. 22, 1911), woman's suffrage leader, was born in Boston, of old New England stock, the daughter of William and Harriet (Browne) Hanson. When about eight years old she moved with her widowed mother and three brothers to Lowell "where they lived for some years on one of the manufacturing 'corporations'" (*Loom and Spindle, post,* p. 160). Here she received her early education, and then became an operative in a Lowell mill. As one of Lowell's literary mill girls she wrote for *The Lowell Offering,* and was on intimate terms with its editors. She also contributed to the "annuals" and newspapers of the time, and it was through such contributions to the *Lowell Courier* that she met the journalist and reformer, William Stevens Robinson [*q.v.*] whom, on Nov.

30, 1848, she married; they had two daughters and two sons. Throughout his lifetime, she loyally and enthusiastically supported her husband's activities in the anti-slavery crusade and other reform movements.

Her own particular interest, however, was in the advancement of women, and, following Robinson's death in 1876, she wrote and spoke freely in their behalf. She was the first woman to appear before the Select Committee on Woman Suffrage in Congress, and she advocated the cause of suffrage before the legislature of Massachusetts. In 1888 she served as a member of the International Council of Women which met in Washington. She was keenly interested in the women's club movement, assisting in the formation of the General Federation of Women's Clubs in 1890, and serving as a member of its first advisory board. In association with Julia Ward Howe [q.v.] and others she helped to organize the New England Women's Club. She was also one of the first members of the Wintergreen Club of Boston.

Her earliest book was *"Warrington" Pen-Portraits* (1877), a memoir of her husband with selections from his writings. This was followed by *Massachusetts in the Woman Suffrage Movement: A General, Political, Legal and Legislative History from 1774 to 1881* (1881, 1883); *Captain Mary Miller* (1887), a suffrage drama; *The New Pandora* (1889), a classical drama and "the heart-and-brain product of one who grew up as a working-girl"; *Early Factory Labor in New England* (1883, 1889); and *Loom and Spindle, or Life Among the Early Mill Girls* (1898). The closing years of her life were spent in Malden, Mass., where she died in her eighty-seventh year.

[Lucy Larcom, in *Loom and Spindle* (1898); E. C. Stanton, S. B. Anthony, and M. J. Gage, *Hist. of Woman Suffrage* (4 vols., 1881–1902); *Who's Who in America*, 1910–11; *Boston Transcript*, Dec. 22, 1911.]

W. R. W.

ROBINSON, HENRY CORNELIUS (Aug. 28, 1832–Feb. 14, 1900), lawyer and legislator, was the son of David Franklin and Anne (Seymour) Robinson of Hartford and a descendant of Thomas Robinson who settled at Guilford, Conn., in 1664. After preparation at the Hartford Grammar School and at the Hartford Public High School, he was sent in 1849 to Yale where he achieved both social and scholastic success. After graduation in 1853 he studied law with his brother Lucius F. Robinson and with Judge William Lucius Storrs [q.v.], and on Aug. 17, 1855, he was admitted to the bar at Hartford. In 1858 he became his brother's partner, and from 1861 to 1888, when he was joined by his eldest son, he continued the firm alone. On Aug. 28, 1862, he married Eliza Niles Trumbull, daughter of John F. Trumbull of Stonington, thus joining the heritage of two of Connecticut's oldest families. His legal practice became outstanding, for he not only secured a large private clientele, but as a corporation counsel he came to represent the largest interests in the state. He was an ardent supporter of the Republican party from its foundation and in 1866 was appointed by Governor Hawley as fish commissioner. Since his college days he had been interested in the fisheries problem, an important one on the Connecticut River, and with this opportunity to put his theories into practice he demonstrated that it was possible to hatch shad artificially. Unfortunately his proposals for conservation were soon brought to an end by a change in administration.

In 1872 Robinson was elected mayor of Hartford. His two-year term showed him to be an able and popular administrator, and in 1876 he was nominated by acclamation as candidate for governor, but he was defeated. In 1879 he was elected a member of the lower house of the legislature. As chairman of the judiciary committee he championed measures of judicial reform and in a strenuous campaign carried them through. Yet he was a liberal rather than a reformer, for he tempered his natural desire for progress with his conservative point of view. In 1880 he was a member of the Republican National Convention at Chicago and drafted a considerable portion of the platform. In 1888 he was active in securing Harrison's election and was offered the appointment as minister to Spain. He declined the honor, for he was at that time at the height of his professional career. He was counsel for many large enterprises, among them the Connecticut Fire Insurance Company and the firm of Pratt & Whitney. He was also a director of the New York, New Haven & Hartford Railroad, and as its counsel successfully opposed in 1889 the building of a parallel line between New Haven and New York by the Housatonic and "Air-Line" interests. Shortly afterward he was offered its presidency, but again felt that he could not leave his extensive legal practice. In the years 1891–93 he headed the counsel for the Republican party in the dispute which grew out of the contest for the governorship.

In addition to his work as lawyer and legislator Robinson was one of the leading laymen of the Congregational denomination. For fifty years he was a member of the South Church in Hartford, and active in the social and religious enterprises of the community. "In times of theological controversy he warmly espoused, but in a truly conservative spirit, the side of liberty and progress" (*Yale Class of 1853 Report*, 1903). At the height of the Andover religious disputes he set forward a legal argument for a liberal interpretation of creeds. Throughout his life he was in demand as an orator on public occasions. Two of his addresses were published. Other writings, on legal and religious subjects, appeared in the *Yale Law Journal* and the *New Englander and Yale Review*. Robinson suffered injuries in a fall which cut short a life of ceaseless activity, and for some time before his death he was confined to his home. He died in Hartford on Feb. 14, 1900, survived by three sons and two daughters.

[See especially the published reports of the Yale class of 1853: 1856, 1859, 1893, 1903, the last of which contains a list of Robinson's writings. Other sources include: Dwight Loomis and J. G. Calhoun, *The Judicial and Civil Hist. of Conn.* (1895); *Obit. Record of Grads. of Yale Univ. . . . June 1900*; *The Robinson Family Geneal. and Hist. Asso.* (1902); the *Hartford Courant*, Feb. 15, 1900.]   W. G. L.

ROBINSON, JOHN (Feb. 3, 1704–May 11, 1766), speaker of the House of Burgesses and treasurer of Virginia, was the grandson of Christopher Robinson who emigrated from England to Virginia in the seventeenth century, the son of John and Catherine (Beverley) Robinson, and the brother of Beverley Robinson [*q.v.*]. His father was a man of considerable consequence in the colony, having inherited the estate of an uncle, John Robinson, the Bishop of London, and having held, for a short time, the office of president of the Council. The son was educated at the College of William and Mary and in 1736 became a member of the House of Burgesses from the county of King and Queen. Two years later he became speaker of the House and treasurer of the colony, both of which offices he held until his death. His administration, however, ended in disaster to himself. In 1765 panic bore down upon Virginia, and the treasury found it difficult to redeem certain notes which it had previously issued and which now fell due. An investigation into the financial situation was ordered by the House of Burgesses under the leadership of Richard Henry Lee. The following year Robinson died, and a report showed that his accounts were short by more than one hundred thousand pounds. It appeared that he had been induced not to destroy notes the treasury had redeemed, as required by law, but to reissue them. For these treasury notes he had received the personal notes of the borrowers. The executors of his estate proposed that they make good the deficit out of his property, but the Revolu-

tion came on before the transaction was completed. In 1765 and 1767 efforts were made to establish a public loan office on the basis of capital to be borrowed in England, but both attempts were defeated by the Council (Eckenrode, *post*, pp. 15–17). It has been charged that the first of these attempts was an effort on the part of Robinson to transfer his loans to the public account, but there is no direct evidence to substantiate the accusation. While the treasurer was guilty of a breach of trust, it is not clear that he was guilty of a design to defraud the public. Proceedings were never instituted against the borrowers, whose notes Robinson had taken, nor were their names ever published. Some reform was accomplished, however, in that Robert Carter Nicholas, who had had a part in the exposure of the scandal, was now made treasurer, and Peyton Randolph became speaker of the House (Charles Campbell, *History of the Colony and Ancient Dominion of Virginia*, 1860, pp. 544–48).

John Robinson was typical of the colonial aristocracy of Virginia. He belonged to a distinguished family, was wealthy, suave, and popular. His home was at "Mount Pleasant" on the Mattapony in King and Queen County. He was married three times, first to Mary Storey, then to Lucy Moore, and last to Susanna Chiswell, the daughter of Col. John Chiswell of Williamsburg. For more than a quarter of a century he was, after the governor, the most powerful man in the province, but his fall ruined his house, and Virginia has made every effort to forget him.

[Fully documented account of Robinson's defalcation in *Jour. of the House of Burgesses of Virginia*, 1766–1769, ed. by J. P. Kennedy (1906), pp. x–xxvi; M. V. Smith, *Va., . . . a Hist. of the Executives* (1893); L. G. Tyler, *Encyc. of Va. Biog.* (1915), vol. I; *Va. Mag. of Hist. and Biog.*, Apr. 1897, Apr. 1902, Apr. 1908, Oct. 1909; H. J. Eckenrode, *The Revolution in Va.* (1916).]   T. P. A.

ROBINSON, JOHN CLEVELAND (Apr. 10, 1817–Feb. 18, 1897), soldier, born at Binghamton, N. Y., the son of Dr. Tracy and Sarah (Cleveland) Robinson, was a descendant of the Rev. John Robinson, pastor of the Pilgrims in Leyden. His early schooling was under tutors and at Oxford Academy, Oxford, N. Y. He entered the United States Military Academy in June 1835 and left in March 1838 to study law. The following year he became a second lieutenant of the 5th Infantry. During the Mexican War he was regimental and brigade quartermaster, and saw action at the battles of Palo Alto, Resaca de la Palma, and at the siege of Monterey. After the war he continued in the army, becoming captain in 1850. Between the two wars which were the high spots of his career, he was engaged in various services in the expanding West, with the exception of one period of campaigning against the Seminole Indians in Florida in 1856–57. Of his service in Utah in 1857–58, he wrote clearly and engagingly, expressing the opinion that the large expedition directed against the Mormons was a part of a plot to denude the eastern states of troops, so that "the dissolution of the Union" might be the easier (J. C. Robinson, "The Utah Expedition," *Magazine of American History*, April 1884, p. 340).

Robinson was in command of Fort McHenry when the 6th Massachusetts Infantry was attacked in the streets of Baltimore, Md., on Apr. 19, 1861. Although commanding only sixty men, threats and cajoling on the part of city officials failed to move him. He turned the guns towards the city, secretly revictualled the fort, and made such an excellent show of resistance that the rioters decided it was best not to attack at that time. He was elected colonel of the 1st Michigan Volunteers while on a recruiting trip in the West in September 1861. On Apr. 28, 1862, he was appointed brigadier-general of volunteers and assumed command of the 1st Brigade of Kearney's division of the III Corps, Army of the Potomac. He served with distinction throughout the Peninsular campaign, and later commanded the 2nd Division in the I and V Corps. His military career in the Civil War was full of honors. He was brevetted for actions at Gettysburg and for gallant conduct in the battle of the Wilderness. He served continuously with the Army of the Potomac until Spotsylvania, where he was wounded in the left knee while leading his command and suffered amputation of the leg. Upon his recovery, he was given command of military districts in New York. In June 1864 he was brevetted major-general, and in March 1865, by special appointment of the president, he became military commander and commissioner of the Bureau of Freedmen in North Carolina, with the rank of brigadier-general bestowed for bravery at Spotsylvania. He was commander of the Department of the South in 1867, and in 1868 was commander of the Department of the Lakes. He was retired with the rank of major-general on May 6, 1869.

After his retirement Robinson was lieutenant-governor of New York from 1872 to 1874, and thereafter was prominent in the activities of veterans' organizations. He was commander-in-chief of the G. A. R., 1877–78, and president of the Society of the Army of the Potomac in 1887. On the one-hundredth anniversary of his birth,

a statue was dedicated to him at Gettysburg, at the place where, with two brigades, he held at bay five brigades of the enemy for four hours and materially aided the Union victory. Three years before his death he was awarded the Congressional Medal of Honor for "most distinguished gallantry" at Laurel Hill, Va. He spent the latter years of his life in Binghamton, being totally blind from the year 1893 as a result of his old wound. On May 15, 1842, he married Sarah Maria Pease, in Green Bay, Wis. From this marriage, seven children were born.

[*N. Y. State Monuments Commission. In Memoriam, Abner Doubleday . . . and John Cleveland Robinson* (1918); E. J. and H. G. Cleveland, *The Geneal. of the Cleveland and Cleaveland Families* (1899), vol. II; C. E. Robinson, *Robinson Geneal.* (1926), vol. I; *Army and Navy Register*, Feb. 20, 27, 1897; *N. Y. Times*, Feb. 19, 1897.]

D. Y.

ROBINSON, JOHN MITCHELL (Dec. 6, 1827–Jan. 14, 1896), jurist, was a descendant of English Protestants who settled in Sussex County, Del., about 1700. His grandfather, Ralph, and his father, Peter, were Delaware farmers; his mother, Sarah Mitchell, was the daughter of John Mitchell, a merchant of Milford, Del. John Mitchell Robinson, the second son of this marriage, was born on his father's farm in Tuckahoe Neck, Caroline County, Md. His father died while John was very young and his mother moved to Denton, Md., where he was educated in the public schools. When he was sixteen years old he entered Dickinson College where he graduated in 1847. He at once began the study of law with William M. Meredith of the Philadelphia bar, but shortly afterward he returned to Centreville and continued his studies in the offices of Judge Richard B. Carmichael and of Madison Brown. He was admitted to the bar in November 1849 and immediately established himself in practice in Centreville.

In January 1851 Robinson was appointed deputy attorney-general for Queen Anne's and Kent counties. In November of that year a new constitution went into effect under the provisions of which he was elected state's attorney for Queen Anne's County. He held this office for four years (1851–55). While still in his thirties, Robinson had built up a lucrative trial practice which he hesitated to relinquish, but during the unsettled war days he was approached by a committee of citizens who persuaded him that his place was on the bench. His election in November 1864, as judge of a new circuit, which comprised Kent and Queen Anne's counties, was the turning point in his life and for the following twenty-nine years he was continuously on the bench. He was elected in 1867 to the court of appeals, the highest court in Maryland, and in 1882 he was reëlected. In 1884 he was a candidate for the Democratic nomination for the United States Senate; his defeat, which he always attributed to the activities of Senator Arthur Pue Gorman [q.v.], the party boss in Maryland, is one of the dramatic incidents in the political history of the state. Robinson was appointed chief judge of the court of appeals on May 1, 1893, and retained the office until his death. During his years on the bench he delivered over four hundred opinions which have had a considerable influence on the development of the jurisprudence of the state. It had been the custom for the judges in writing opinions to give the reasons for their conclusions at length but Robinson anticipated the modern style, emphasizing the conclusions and treating summarily the arguments and authorities. His most important decisions were concerned with the validity of a tax imposed upon the gross receipts of railroad companies, in which his views prevailed over those of Judge Richard Henry Alvey, one of the state's ablest judges (*The State of Maryland* vs. *The Northern Central Railway Company*, 44 Md., 131, 1876; *The State of Maryland* vs. *The Philadelphia, Wilmington & Baltimore Railroad Company*, 45 Md., 361, 1876; *State* vs. *Baltimore & Ohio Railroad Company*, 48 Md., 49, 1878). Robinson had, on Nov. 19, 1857, married Marianna Stoughton Emory, daughter of Arthur Emory of "Poplar Grove," Queen Anne's County; they had five daughters and one son. He died suddenly in Annapolis and was buried at "Waverly," their country home on the Chester River.

[Sources include: *Report of the Seventeenth Ann. Meeting of the Md. State Bar Asso.* (1912); C. T. Bond, *The Court of Appeals of Md.: A Hist.* (1928); 82 *Md. Reports*, xix–xxvii; *Baltimore American*, Jan. 15, 1896; *Baltimore News*, Jan. 17, 1896; information as to certain facts from Ralph Robinson, Esq., Baltimore, Md. Robinson's opinions appear in 26–82 *Md. Reports*.]
H. C.

ROBINSON, MONCURE (Feb. 2, 1802–Nov. 10, 1891), civil engineer, was born at Richmond, Va., the eldest son of John Robinson, a merchant, and Agnes Conway (Moncure) Robinson, and a descendant of John Robinson who emigrated to Virginia from England and died in New Charles Parish in 1688. Conway Robinson [q.v.] was his younger brother. As a child Moncure attended Gerardine Academy where he received a grounding in the French language which later proved useful; in 1816–17 he was a student at the College of William and Mary. His father intended him to be a lawyer, but the boy's taste for adventure led him into another career.

In 1818 the Board of Public Works of Virginia authorized a topographic survey and connected line of levels from Richmond to the Ohio River, and young Robinson applied for a position on the corps of surveyors. This was refused on account of his youth, but he was permitted to accompany the party as a volunteer, without compensation. On this trip he made accurate notes of the coal deposits in the region that is now West Virginia. In 1819 he undertook a second trip of reconnaissance toward Pittsburgh for the purpose of locating and examining his father's wild lands. Two years later, having reached maturity, he was employed in the location of an extension of the James River Canal in Virginia. That same year he made a professional visit to the Erie Canal, then in process of construction. This inspection changed his opinion as to the relative advantages of canals and railroads, and from this time forward his interest was mainly in railroad building. For some three years, 1825–28, he was in Europe, attending lectures in mathematics and science in France, and studying public works in France, England, Wales, and the Low Countries.

After his return, he was called upon in 1828 by the canal commissioners of Pennsylvania to make surveys for the Pottsville and Danville railway in the interest of the development of the anthracite coal fields, and was also appointed to make surveys for the Allegheny Portage Railroad. During the next three years he was engaged in railroad construction in Virginia, building the Petersburg and Roanoke and the Richmond and Petersburg lines. For the latter railroad he constructed a bridge over the James River which attracted attention both at home and abroad (see Michel Chevalier, *Histoire et Description des Voies de Communication aux États-Unis et des Travaux d'Art qu'en Dépendent*, 1841, pp. 567, 571–76). This bridge was 2,844 feet long, with a grade line sixty feet above the water. There were nineteen spans of lengths varying from 140 to 153 feet. The superstructure was latticed.

In 1834 Robinson began his *chef-d'œuvre*, the Philadelphia & Reading Railroad, which involved the construction of a 1,932-foot tunnel at Phoenixville and a stone bridge of four spans, each seventy-two feet long. In connection with the building of this road he formulated three fundamental rules for determining grades and curvatures. In 1836 he went to England in its interest and succeeded in procuring large investments for its completion to Pottsville. The locomotive *Gowan and Marx* was built in Philadelphia from Robinson's plans and named for his English banker friends. So noteworthy were Robinson's achievements as an engineer of railroads that in 1840 the Czar of Russia made advances toward the procuring of his services as engineer in charge of the system of railroads which was then being planned for the Russian empire. Robinson gave valuable counsel to the Czar's emissaries, but declined to serve. In 1839 he made a reconnaissance for a railroad from Brunswick on the Georgia coast to the Gulf of Mexico. By appointment of the secretary of the navy in 1842 he served with Commodores Shubrick and David Conner [q.v.] on the commission which recommended Wallabout Bay as the site for the drydock to be constructed in New York Harbor.

He retired from professional activity in 1847, making his home in Philadelphia, and for more than forty years devoted his attention to his personal investments. He died in 1891. On Feb. 2, 1835, he had married Charlotte Randolph Taylor, daughter of Bennett Taylor, a member of the Richmond bar. They had five sons and five daughters, of whom all but two daughters survived their father. As an engineer Robinson belonged to the old school. As were the other engineers of his day, with the exception of those from West Point, he was untrained in the technique of the profession. These men worked out their technique in the school of experience, and for that reason their lives were characterized by a peculiar initiative and resourcefulness. By extensive travel and inspection Robinson equipped himself for those positions of responsibility which he occupied in rapid succession. He was elected to membership in the American Philosophical Society (1833) and by his professional brethren of a younger generation was awarded one of the highest honors within their power to bestow, that of honorary membership in the American Society of Civil Engineers.

[Robinson's reports of 1829 and 1831 in regard to the Allegheny Portage R. R. were printed, with an editorial note, in *Trans. Am. Soc. Civil Engineers*, vol. XV (1886). For biographical material see R. B. Osborne, *Professional Biog. of Moncure Robinson, Civil Engineer* (1889); *Proc. Am. Soc. Civil Engineers*, vol. XVIII (1892); *Proc. Engineers' Club of Phila.*, vol. X (1892); *Illustrated American*, Dec. 5, 1891; H. E. Hayden, *Va. Geneals.* (1891); *Phila. Press*, Nov. 11, 1891; *N. Y. Tribune*, Nov. 11, 1891.]			W. T. L.

ROBINSON, MOSES (Mar. 26, 1742–May 26, 1813), soldier, jurist, statesman, was a dominant figure in the early history of Vermont. He was born in Hardwick, Mass., the son of Samuel and Mercy (Lennard, or Leonard) Robinson and a descendant of William Robinson, an early settler in Newton. In 1761 his father helped

to found the town of Bennington, Vt., and in the next few years was prominent in the pioneer life of the future state. He died in 1767 while on a mission to England in behalf of the settlers on the New Hampshire Grants. Moses Robinson played a varied and distinguished rôle in the establishment of the republic, later the state, of Vermont. He was one of the outstanding leaders in the resistance interposed by the inhabitants of the New Hampshire Grants to the authority of New York. With the outbreak of the Revolutionary War he threw himself into the conflict, serving as a colonel of militia. He was a member of the Vermont Council of Safety and took part in the measures resorted to by that body, in 1777, to secure aid from Massachusetts, New Hampshire, and Connecticut against impending invasion by the British. In January 1777 he sat in the convention which declared the independence of Vermont, under the name of New Connecticut, and he was elected a member of the Governor's Council by the first General Assembly under the constitution adopted the same year. With Ethan Allen and three others he was chosen, in 1779, to appear before Congress as a representative of Vermont empowered to enter into articles of union and confederation with the United States; and later, in 1782, he served on a committee authorized to agree upon terms for the admission of Vermont into the Union. The main obstacle to such admission was the long-pending boundary dispute with New York, and he took a prominent part in its adjustment. He also served as a member of the third Council of Censors, charged with supervision over the state constitution, and over the legislative and executive departments of the state government.

Although Robinson was not a lawyer by profession he was elected the first chief justice of the supreme court of Vermont—at first called the superior court—in 1778, holding that office, except for one year when he failed of election, until 1789, when he was elected governor of Vermont by the General Assembly. Twice thereafter, in 1797 and 1798, he was a candidate for the same office. In January 1791 he was a member of the convention which ratified the Constitution of the United States, and later in the same month he was elected United States senator from Vermont, sharing with Stephen R. Bradley [q.v.] the honor of being the first senator from the newly admitted state. He served in the Senate until he resigned in 1796. His most conspicuous activity in that body was his determined opposition to the Jay treaty of 1794—an opposition he continued in his state after the ratification of the treaty, in support of the movement to defeat the appropriation by Congress of the funds necessary to carry it into effect. He performed his last public service in 1802 when he represented the town of Bennington in the General Assembly. Robinson was twice married. His first wife was Mary Fay, by whom he had six sons. His second wife was Susana Howe.

[See: A. M. Hemenway, ed., *The Vt. Hist. Gazetteer*, vol. I (1868); W. H. Crockett, *Vermont*, vol. II (1921) and vol. V (1923); J. G. Ullery, *Men of Vt.* (1894); J. B. Robinson, *A Hist. Sketch of the Robinson Family of the Line of Ebenezer Robinson* (1903); *The Robinson Family Geneal. and Hist. Asso.*, 1 ser. (1902), 2 ser. (1904); Manning Leonard, *Memorial: Geneal., Hist., and Biog., of Solomon Leonard* (1896); Leonard Deming, *Cat. of the Principal Officers of Vt.* (1851).]   E. C. M—r.

ROBINSON, ROWLAND EVANS (May 14, 1833–Oct. 15, 1900), author, was born in Ferrisburg, Addison County, Vt., on the farm cleared by his paternal grandfather in 1796. The youngest of the four children of Rowland Thomas and Rachael (Gilpin) Robinson and a descendant of Rowland Robinson, who settled at Narragansett, R. I., about 1675, he was of English stock and a birthright Quaker; in his boyhood the dress, speech, and manners of the primitive Friends were natural to him, and the ways of the "world's people" strange. He attended the country schools and the Ferrisburg Academy but was by his own account an unwilling pupil. He formed his literary taste by repeated readings of the poems and novels of Sir Walter Scott and became familiar with every aspect of the life of the fields and woods. Technically he was a farmer for the greater part of his life, but although he did not neglect his farm he was interested primarily in other things. From his mother he inherited a propensity for drawing, and the butter-tubs that he sent to market were often adorned with home-made political cartoons. On coming of age he went to New York, hoping to learn something of drawing while working in a draftsman's shop, but he soon returned home disappointed. In 1866 he went again to New York, made illustrations on wood of rural scenes for the periodicals of Orange Judd and Frank Leslie [*qq.v.*], did fashion-plate and catalogue work, and sold a cartoon occasionally to a comic paper, but working at night on rush orders injured his eyes, and in 1873 he returned once more to his native farm, this time to stay. Meanwhile, in 1870, he had married Anna Stevens of East Montpelier, who with their two daughters and son survived him.

His literary work began in 1877. At his wife's suggestion he wrote an article on "Fox-Hunting in New England" and sent it to *Scribner's Monthly*, which published it in January 1878 after inquiring about the identity and qualifications of the unknown author. He was on the staff of *Forest and Stream* for a number of years and was later a contributor to the *Atlantic Monthly* and other magazines. As an illustrator he was never distinguished, and when his sight began to fail in 1887 he turned altogether to literature. Even after he became totally blind in 1893 he was able to write by using a grooved board to guide his pencil. His wife revised his manuscripts and copied them on the typewriter. His publications were: *Forest and Stream Fables* (1886); *Uncle Lisha's Shop: Life in a Corner of Yankee-land* (1887; Centennial edition, Rutland, 1933); *Sam Lovel's Camps: Uncle Lisha's Friends under Bark and Canvas* (1889); *Vermont: A Study of Independence* (1892, American Commonwealths Series); *Danvis Folks* (1894); *In New England Fields and Woods* (1896); *Uncle Lisha's Outing* (1897); *A Hero of Ticonderoga* (1898); *In the Green Wood* (1899); *A Danvis Pioneer* (1900; republished with *Uncle Lisha's Shop*, 1933); *Sam Lovel's Boy* (1901); *Hunting without a Gun, and Other Papers* (1905); *Out of Bondage, and Other Stories* (1905); and *Silver Fields, and Other Sketches of a Farmer-Sportsman* (1921). His style is simple, graceful, and apparently effortless, and he wrote only on themes that he knew intimately and loved. His work is permeated by an old man's memories of his youth and by a blind man's memories of the beauty of the visible world. He was rather a humorist and essayist than a novelist; a master in depicting manners and easily recognized types of character, he shunned, or touched only lightly, the graver aspects of personality and experience. He recorded the dialect of rural Vermonters and of English-speaking French-Canadians with minute attention to detail. His best volumes are secure of their place as Vermont classics. For the last eighteen months of his life he was bedridden with an inoperable cancer, but he bore his afflictions serenely and cheerfully. He died in the room in which he had been born.

[H. L. Bailey, "The Chronicler of 'Danvis Folks,'" *New Eng. Mag.*, Dec. 1900; Mrs. M. F. Allen, "In Memoriam: Rowland E. Robinson," *Vermonter*, Dec. 1900; J. C. R. Dorr, "Rowland Robinson," *Atlantic Monthly*, Jan. 1901; Rowland E. Robinson, "Recollections of a Quaker Boy," *Ibid.*, July 1901; biog. preface to *Hunting without a Gun* (1905); Genevra Cook, sketch in *Vermonters* (1931), ed. by W. H. Crockett; T. R. Hazard, *Recollections of Olden Times: Rowland Robinson of Narragansett* (1879); *Burlington Free Press and Times*, Oct. 16, 1900.]   G. H. G.

ROBINSON, SOLON (Oct. 21, 1803–Nov. 3, 1880), pioneer, agriculturist, author, was born at Tolland, Conn., the fourth child of Jacob and Salinda (Ladd) Robinson and a descendant of the Rev. John Robinson, pastor of the Pilgrims at Leyden. An orphan at the age of ten, a carpenter's apprentice at fourteen, and a Yankee pedler at eighteen, he made his way alone in the world. In 1828 he had become a cashier for a theatre in Cincinnati, and in October of that year married Mariah Evans of Bucks County, Pa.

Two years later, at Madison, Ind., the young man was writing for the local press and interested in the promotion of an urban land site near North Vernon. In the fall of 1834, because of a dearth of buyers, he disposed of most of his land and traveled to northern Indiana. Here, in the wilderness, he opened a general store and soon built up a large trade with the Potawatomi Indians and incoming settlers. The Indians gave him the name of "Wyonett Tshmokeman," sometimes translated "Chief Big Knife." To preserve his own holdings and those of others, in the area then known as Robinson's Prairie, he formed a Squatters' Union in 1836 for protection against speculators and made it possible for some five hundred members to secure their land at government prices. Henceforth, by popular acclaim, he was known as the "King of the Squatters." After Lake County was organized in 1837, he served at various times as county clerk, justice of the peace, register of claims, and postmaster. At the county seat, Crown Point, on the first printing press in the region he published intermittently a small news sheet. Active in politics, he took a prominent part in the Log Cabin Convention at LaFayette in 1840. In 1847 he delivered a detailed address, later published under the title, *History of Lake County*.

As early as 1837 Robinson began to contribute articles on various aspects of the frontier to the Albany *Cultivator* and other agricultural periodicals. The simple, homely, and often humorous style of these essays, signed "Solon Robinson of Indiana," reflected the personality of the author, and they soon won a large following. His enthusiasm and spirit carried conviction. Before 1840, in company with James Mercer Garnett, Henry L. Ellsworth [*qq.v.*], and others, he advocated the formation of a national agricultural society (*Cultivator*, May 1838) and in 1841 presided at a preliminary meeting held for that purpose in Washington (*Ibid.*, October 1841). The society had hoped to establish a national agricultural school and journal, but failure to receive an anticipated bequest made by James Smithson to the United States defeated this plan and was largely responsible for the premature dissolution of the organization. How-

ever, these activities paved the way for the formation of the United States Agricultural Society in 1852 by Robinson and others. This in turn played an influential rôle in the establishment of the Department of Agriculture ten years later.

Robinson's descriptions of rural life observed on his journey to and from Washington in 1841 were the first of his discerning travel sketches. During the next decade he made a number of tours, covering practically every state in the Union, and regularly reported his observations in the *Cultivator, Prairie Farmer,* and *American Agriculturist,* from which they were reprinted in the *Southern Cultivator* and other periodicals. These travel sketches today form an invaluable historical record of rural society of that period (see especially *American Agriculturist,* 1849–51). In 1852 at New York City he published a periodical called *The Plow,* and the following year became agricultural editor of the *New York Tribune.* His editorial work, combined with visits to various parts of the country, was largely responsible for the widespread circulation of the weekly edition of the *Tribune* and the subsequent national influence of that publication. At Westchester, N. Y., Robinson conducted an experimental farm which provided the basis for many of his articles.

Illness in 1868—he suffered nearly all his life with tubercular tendencies—forced him to retire to Florida. Residing at Jacksonville, he published the *Florida Republican,* wrote for the *New York Tribune,* and carried on other literary work. He was the author of novels, short stories, and poetry, in addition to his travel sketches and agricultural articles. Among his books were *The Will; A Tale of the Lake of the Red Cedars and Shabbona* (1841); *Guano, a Treatise of Practical Information for Farmers* (1852); *Hot Corn: Life Scenes in New York, Tales of Slum Life* (1854), of which 50,000 copies were sold in six months; *Facts for Farmers: Also for the Family Circle* (1864, and subsequent editions); *Me-won-i-toc, A Tale of Frontier Life and Indian Character* (1867); and *How to Live; Saving and Wasting; or Domestic Economy Illustrated by the Life of Two Families of Opposite Character, including the Story of a Dime a Day* (1873). After the death of his first wife, by whom he had five children, he married, June 30, 1872, Mary Johnson of Barton, Vt. He died at Jacksonville in November 1880.

[Robinson's own writings, and files of the periodicals mentioned above; *Robinson Geneal.: Descendants of the Rev. John Robinson* (1926); *Counties of Porter and Lake, Ind.* (1882); J. C. Derby, *Fifty Years among Authors, Books, and Publishers* (1884); T. H. Ball,

Encyc. of Geneal. and Biog. of Lake County, Ind. (1904) ; G. S. Cottman, Centennial Hist. and Handbook of Ind. (1915) ; Susan B. Eppes, Through Some Eventful Years (1926) ; N. Y. Tribune, Nov. 5, 1880 ; Lake County Star (Crown Point, Ind.), Sept. 15, 1916 ; Gary Evening Post (Gary, Ind.), Aug. 27, 1918, Aug. 27, 1921 ; MSS. and other historical material relating to Solon Robinson in the possession of the writer.]

H. A. K.

ROBINSON, STILLMAN WILLIAMS

(Mar. 6, 1838–Oct. 31, 1910), engineer, educator, inventor, author, son of Ebenezer and Adeline (Williams) Robinson, was born on his father's farm near South Reading, Vt. He was descended from William Robinson, one of the early settlers of Newton, Mass. After attending the district school of his native town, he was bound out to a farmer, but his desire for more education and his interest in mechanics and mathematics caused him to give up farm work in 1855 to learn a trade as a means of acquiring money for his education. He served a four-year apprenticeship as a machinist, studied in his spare time, and in January 1861 entered the University of Michigan. He paid his expenses by working at his trade, attaining considerable proficiency as an instrument maker and during his college course devising a machine for graduating thermometers.

For three years after his graduation (C.E.) in 1863 he was an assistant engineer in the federal survey of the Great Lakes, then returned to the University of Michigan (1866–70), first as assistant and then as assistant professor in the department of mining engineering and geodesy. Called to the Illinois Industrial University (now the University of Illinois) in 1870, he there established a department of mechanical engineering which was one of the first in the United States. Eight years later he was made dean of the college of engineering, but resigned almost at once to accept the professorship of physics and mechanical engineering at Ohio State University. Here he continued until his resignation and retirement from academic life in 1895. Robinson was a pioneer in the field of experimental instruction in engineering education, and as early as 1870 ideas now accepted as fundamental in this field had become settled convictions with him. He was instrumental in organizing in 1890 an association of teachers of mechanical engineering which in 1893 became the Society for the Promotion of Engineering Education. He retained until his death an interest in Ohio State University, establishing a fellowship in the department of mechanical engineering and contributing from time to time to its equipment.

In the course of his career Robinson secured over forty patents, all of which were based upon scientific research and mathematical investigation. A group of eight or ten were concerned with shoe manufacture, the most profitable being the flattened and threaded shoe-sole fastening (Patent No. 265,149, Sept. 26, 1882). The development through a number of years of this device and the many machines which he contrived to manufacture it and to drive the fastening rapidly and automatically through the sole illustrates Robinson's ability to utilize his profound knowledge of mechanics in the solution of difficult practical problems. The variety of his inventions was unusual and they were all profitable to him. Others which he patented were a clock escapement, a steam rock drill, valve gearing for steam engines, an improvement in the telephone, a metal piling and substructure, a gauge for measuring the flow of natural gas, an automatic air-brake mechanism, and a right-angled shaft coupling for transmitting power. Throughout his career he was called in as a consultant in a variety of industrial and professional undertakings. Thus he was inspector of railways and bridges for the railroad commission of Ohio (1880–84), consulting engineer for the Lick telescope and mountings (1887), and consulting engineer (1887–90) for the Atchison, Topeka & Santa Fé Railroad, of which his brother, Albert Alonzo Robinson [q.v.], was second vice-president and general manager. He was the author of a number of important technical books and contributed many papers to technical journals. His report as a result of his inspection of the railways and bridges of Ohio includes what is probably some of his best scientific work; it was published by D. Van Nostrand under the title Railroad Economics in 1882. His Principles of Mechanism, first published in 1896, is still widely used as a college textbook, and his Practical Treatise on the Teeth of Wheels, with the Theory and the Use of Robinson's Odontograph (1876) is still in wide circulation. Among his other publications were Strength of Wrought-Iron Bridge Members (1882), and A Treatise on the Compound Engine (1884) written in collaboration with John Turnbull. He was a member of numerous engineering societies and a fellow of the American Association for the Advancement of Science. Twice married—first on Dec. 29, 1863, to Mary Elizabeth Holden, and after her death, on Apr. 12, 1888, to Mary Haines of Ada, Ohio, he was survived by his second wife and three daughters by his first marriage. He died in Columbus, at the age of seventy-two.

[J. B. Robinson, A Hist. Sketch of the Robinson Family of the Line of Ebenezer Robinson (1903) ; Stillman Williams Robinson : a Memorial (Ohio State Univ., 1912) ; Who's Who in America, 1910–11 ; Trans. Am.

Robinson Robinson

Soc. Mechanical Engineers, vol. XXXII (1911); Ohio State Journal (Columbus), Nov. 1, 1910.] C. W. M.

ROBINSON, STUART (Nov. 14, 1814–Oct. 5, 1881), Presbyterian clergyman, editor, was born in Strabane, County Tyrone, Ireland, the fourth son of James and Martha (Porter) Robinson, both of Scotch-Irish descent. The father, for a time successful as a linen merchant, lost his property and emigrated to America in 1816, settling first in New York City, and later in or near Martinsburg, then in the state of Virginia. His mother died when Stuart was about twelve years of age, and the boy was put out to work on the farm of some German Presbyterians, Troutman by name, who, seeing his promise, took him to the Rev. James M. Brown, their pastor. Brown trained and educated him as if he had been his own son; he attended the clergyman's private school and the academy at Romney, and then entered Amherst College. Graduating in 1836, he studied during the following year at Union Theological Seminary, Virginia. After teaching in an academy at Charleston (1838–39), he spent a year at Princeton Seminary.

He was licensed by Greenbrier Presbytery Apr. 10, 1841, and ordained Oct. 8, 1842. The same day he was installed pastor of the church at Kanawha-Salines (now Malden, W. Va.), from which he was released May 8, 1847. He served the Presbyterian Church at Frankfort, Ky., from June 18, 1847, to Sept. 2, 1852, and the Fayette Street Church (Independent) in Baltimore for nearly one year, at the end of which time he organized the Central Presbyterian Church of that city, continuing as its pastor until Oct. 27, 1856. In this year the General Assembly transferred him to Danville Theological Seminary, Kentucky, to fill the chair of church government and pastoral theology. On Apr. 27, 1858, he became pastor of the Second Presbyterian Church of Louisville, Ky., which position he retained until June 16, 1881. In addition to his pastoral work he did much teaching. While at Kanawha-Salines he conducted a school; at Frankfort he carried on a flourishing seminary for girls, and for a time in Louisville he taught a boy's school. In September 1841 he married Mary Elizabeth Brigham, eldest daughter of Col. William Brigham, a native of Massachusetts; they had eight children, five of whom died in early childhood.

Robinson also entered the field of religious journalism. In collaboration with Thomas E. Peck [q.v.] he published in Baltimore (January 1855–November 1856) the *Presbyterial Critic and Monthly Review*, a controversial journal which sought to maintain the pure traditions of Presbyterianism. In Louisville he bought the *Presbyterian Herald*, changed its name to *True Presbyterian*, and became its aggressive editor. He contended especially for the "spirituality of the church," insisting that the church should deal only with spiritual matters and take no stand on the political issues dividing the nation. His zeal brought him into sharp conflict with other Presbyterians in Kentucky, especially Dr. Robert J. Breckinridge [q.v.], a former colleague in Danville Seminary. During the Civil War he was suspected of disloyalty and, facing active persecution, in July 1862 sought refuge in Toronto, Canada. Here he preached, lectured, and wrote; aided Southern refugees; and refuted a slanderous charge of conspiracy to infect the Federal armies with yellow fever. His paper was suppressed by the military authorities in 1864. Returning to Louisville in April 1866, he resumed the editorial direction of the publication, which had been continued with the same policy under the title *Free Christian Commonwealth*.

He was a commissioner to the General Assembly of 1866 at St. Louis, which refused to seat him and his colleagues from Louisville Presbytery because of a "Declaration and Testimony" signed by members of this Presbytery protesting against the political deliverances of the Assembly since the beginning of the war. It was mainly through Robinson's efforts that the main part of the Synod of Kentucky, excluded finally from the Northern Assembly, was induced to unite with the General Assembly of the Southern Presbyterian Church in 1869. He was elected moderator of the Assembly that year by acclamation. Through his influence the Southern Church (Presbyterian Church in the United States) in 1875 became a constituent member of the Alliance of Presbyterian and Reformed Churches throughout the World. Among his publications were: *The Church of God, an Essential Element of the Gospel* (1858); *Slavery as Recognized in the Mosaic Civil Law* (1865); *Discourses of Redemption* (1868); *The Infamous Perjuries of the 'Bureau of Military Justice' Exposed* (1865), a letter to Hon. Mr. Emmons. He died of cancer of the stomach, having been active in religious and civic affairs almost to the end.

[Robinson's scrapbook, in Presbyterian Hist. Foundation, Montreat, N. C.; J. M. Saunders, Memorial upon the Life of Rev. Stuart Robinson (1883); T. E. Peck, in Southern Presbyterian Rev., Apr. 1882, and in Miscellanies, vol. I (1895); H. A. White, Southern Presbyterian Leaders (1911); Alfred Nevin, Encyc. of the Presbyterian Church in the U. S. of America (1884); Presbyterian Visitor, May 1909; Courier-Jour. (Louisville), Oct. 6, 1881.] E. T. T.

ROBINSON, THEODORE (June 3, 1852–
Apr. 2, 1896), artist, was born in Irasburg, Vt.,
the son of Elijah and Ellen (Brown) Robinson,
both originally of Jamaica, Vt. In 1855 the father, a minister, moved west with his family,
settling at Barry, Ill., and later at Milwaukee,
Wis.; because of ill-health, he resigned from the
ministry and started a clothing store at Evansville, Wis. Encouraged by his mother, at the
age of eighteen Robinson went from the Evansville Seminary to Chicago to study art; then,
having acquired a certain proficiency in making
"likenesses," he returned to Evansville, and devoted himself to crayon portraits which he enlarged from photographs. At this period he seems
also to have studied music and was for several
years organist in the church at Evansville of
which his father at one time had been pastor.
Always of a frail constitution, from childhood
he had suffered from asthma and was advised by
the local doctor to go to Denver for his health.
Strengthened by his western experience, he
came to New York in 1874 to continue his studies
at the school of the National Academy of Design. During the short interim in which the
Academy schools were discontinued, Robinson
and a number of his fellow students, as a means
of continuing their instruction, organized the
Art Students' League of New York, the name
of which he suggested. Going to Paris in 1877
he studied first in the atelier of Carolus-Duran
and later under Jean-Léon Gérôme. Here he
not only acquired a thorough academic training
but made many friends who were later to be
famous—John Singer Sargent, Robert Louis
Stevenson, Will Low, Carroll Beckwith, J. Alden
Weir, and others. On returning to the United
States, he was made a member in 1881 of the
newly organized Society of American Artists,
receiving the Webb Prize for landscape in 1890
and the Shaw Prize for figure in 1892. After a
short term as art instructor in a private school,
he became an assistant of John La Farge [q.v.]
in carrying out the mural decorations for the
Vanderbilt house in New York. The following
year he accepted a position in the firm of Prentice Treadwell of Boston, where he remained
three years, thus being enabled to save enough
money to allow him to follow his more individual
purposes. Accordingly he returned to Paris in
1884, a decisive period in his career, for he came
under the influence of the French impressionists
and went to Giverney, where Monet had established himself a few years before. From then
on, until his final return to America in 1892,
he divided his time between the two countries,
and many of his most noteworthy canvases

were painted at Giverney. After 1889 he moved
from studio to studio in New York in search of
one that suited his frugal habits and inclination,
finally escaping from what he called "the tyranny
of modern conveniences" to a studio in East
Fourteenth Street formerly occupied by his
friend J. Alden Weir. His health had been
gradually declining and he was often compelled
to lay aside his brush, but he was always un-
complaining. For a short time he was not seen
by his intimates. He died alone, Apr. 2, 1896.

Robinson combined a determined will and an
indefatigable energy with a frail body. Will Low,
his devoted friend and artistic executor, gives a
vivid description of him: "Frail, with a husky
asthmatic voice and a laugh that shook his meagre
sides, and yet hardly made itself heard, timid
and reticent, saying little, yet blessed with as
keen a sense of humor as any one I have ever
known" (*post*, p. 66). Sociable and spirited in
manner, Robinson nevertheless lived much alone
and he never married. From an early age he
had accustomed himself to the utmost frugality
and by means of it maintained a true independence. Although he had had simply the elements
of early education, his receptive interest enabled
him to acquire a varied culture, and his sensitive nature made him an excellent critic. He
contributed to the *Century*, September 1892, an
essay on Claude Monet; a posthumous poem,
"A Normandy Pastoral," published in *Scribner's*
for June 1897, shows his literary interest.

Robinson's position in the impressionist movement in America was an important one, rather
like that of William Morris Hunt in relation to
the Barbizon school. He was both a pioneer of
the new realism and an apostle, led by the principles of the impressionists to Monet and by
Monet to nature itself. Painting directly from
nature, avoiding any preconceived idea of what
a picture ought to be, he saw his subject under
the transient effects of light and in the surroundings of his everyday environment. In consequence, his pictures convey a sense of intimacy
that comes only from first-hand observation. His
mood is pensive and serene, or joyous; his pictures full of delicate neutral hues—violet, with
cool greens and vivacious touches of gold—and
beautiful, closely related harmonies of color. His
technique is sensitive and reserved, yet direct
and emphatic; and his style is characterized by
integrity and sincerity, the true stamp of his
own nature. Once considered radical, his pictures today seem highly refined and naturalistic.
Robinson maintains, however, a definite and
unique place in American painting and, with
John Twachtman, J. Alden Weir, and Childe

Hassam, must be considered one of the outstanding painters of the impressionist movement in America.

[Eliot Clark in *Art in America,* Oct. 1918, and *Scribner's,* Dec. 1921; Birge Harrison, "With Stevenson at Grez," *Century,* Dec. 1916; W. H. Low, *A Chronicle of Friendships, 1873–1900* (1908); *N. Y. Times,* Apr. 4, 1896; F. F. Sherman, "Theodore Robinson" (in press, 1934).]   E. C.

ROBINSON, THERESE ALBERTINE LOUISE VON JAKOB (Jan. 26, 1797–Apr. 13, 1870), author, translator philologist, was born in Halle, Prussian Saxony, the daughter of Ludwig Heinrich von Jakob, professor of philosophy at the University of Halle. In 1807 the latter accepted a call by the University of Kharkov to help in the revision of the Russian code of criminal laws in St. Petersburg, and took his small daughter with him. Residence in a foreign land in the midst of the social and political changes wrought by the Napoleonic wars developed in the young girl a rich inner life which yearned for expression. She listened to the peasant songs in the markets and was moved to undertake serious study of the Slavic languages and history. In 1816 she returned to Halle with her father, and endeavored to master the classical languages as well as Anglo-Saxon, Scandinavian, English, French, and Spanish. She translated and published, in 1821, Walter Scott's *Old Mortality* and *The Black Dwarf,* under the name Ernst Berthold, for the pen-name, Talvj, which she coined from the initials of her full name, was not used before 1825. The works of Jacob Grimm directed her interest toward Serbian popular poetry, and in 1825–26 three editions of her *Volkslieder der Serben* were published. The preparation of this work brought her into intimate contact with Goethe, who expressed a deep appreciation for her work (J. P. Eckermann, *Gespräche Mit Goethe,* Jena, 1908, vol. I, p. 165).

On Aug. 7, 1828, at the beginning of a very promising literary career in Europe, she was married to Edward Robinson [*q.v.*], of Southington, Conn., and came to Andover, Mass., with him two years later. In 1833 they established their home in Boston, each exhibiting a keen interest in the work of the other. Therese Robinson, as she came to be known, began to study the customs and poetry of the Indians and early life in the American colonies. In 1834 she translated into German John Pickering's *Essay on . . . the Indian Languages of North America* (1820), and added very valuable philological notes, many of them original. Her first literary work in English, *Historical View of the Slavic Language,* published in 1834, appeared first in

the *Biblical Repository* for April and July of that year. Several essays on the popular poetry of the Teutonic and Slavic nations were published in the *North American Review,* April, July, and October 1836; these appeared four years later together with other material as: *Versuch einer Geschichtlichen Charakteristik der Volkslieder germanischer Nationen,* and included a survey of the popular songs outside of Europe, largely the poetry of the Indians. The publication of this work was followed by *Die Unächtheit der Lieder Ossians und des Mcpherson'schen Ossians insbesondere* (Leipzig, 1840), a treatise which settled for many years the dispute among scholars about the genuineness of Mcpherson's *Ossian.*

In 1837 she went to Europe and moved in the literary circles of Hamburg, Leipzig, and Dresden. She returned to the United States in 1840, and opened her home in New York to such literary figures as George Bancroft, William Cullen Bryant, and James Bayard Taylor [*qq.v.*]. A visit by Friedrich von Raumer, the historian, led to the publication of *Aus der Geschichte der ersten Ansiedlungen in den Vereinigten Staaten (Captain John Smith)* in 1845, followed two years later by her *Geschichte der Colonisation von Neu-England.* Her training in the observation of cultural habits and traditions gave to this work a sociological emphasis which has made it a valuable source book for American history, although the heavy German style did not add to its popularity among her contemporaries. Many of her articles were accepted by leading European or American magazines, among them, *Putnam's Monthly Magazine,* the *North American Review,* the *Atlantic Monthly, Westermann's Monatshefte,* and Raumer's *Historisches Taschenbuch.* Her best known novels are *Heloise,* published in 1850, and *Die Auswanderer,* 1852. *Heloise* was published in America three times in one year and *Die Auswanderer* found its way to the American reader as *The Exiles* or *Woodhill* (1853). Although her novels lacked "a wide appeal, they possess a depth and truth in the portrayal of characters and situations which should insure for them a lasting existence in literature" (Voigt, *post,* p. 125). In her scientific work she followed the ideas of Herder, Goethe, and Grimm, emphasizing the cultural more than the philological aspect. In her esthetic work she was spurred by the idea of drawing closer together the nations to which she belonged, and was guided in all her undertakings by an impartial and scholarly attitude. After the death of her husband in 1863, she returned to Hamburg where she spent the rest of her life. She was survived by two children.

[Talvj's manuscripts and letters were destroyed by fire. The best source of information is J. C. Voigt, *The Life and Works of Mrs. Therese Robinson (Talvj)*, a doctoral thesis, University of Ill., 1913, and also published in the *Jahrb. der Deutsch-Amerikanischen Historischen Gesellschaft von Ill.*, vol. XIII (1914). See also, G. P. Körner, *Das Deutsche Element in den Vereinigten Staaten* (1884); H. R. Timlow, *Ecclesiastical and Other Sketches of Southington, Conn.* (1875); *Allgemeine Deutsche Biog.*]   E. A. K.

ROBINSON, WILLIAM (Nov. 22, 1840–Jan. 2, 1921), inventor, engineer, was born in Coal Island, County Tyrone, Ulster, Ireland, the son of Scotch-Irish and English parents. When he was four years old the family emigrated to the United States, settling in Brooklyn, N. Y. Here William received his early schooling and prepared for college. He graduated from Wesleyan University, Middletown, Conn., in 1865 and during the school term following was principal of the high school in Ansonia, Conn. Part of the year 1866 he spent in the Pennsylvania oil fields, but in 1867 resumed teaching, serving as principal of Spring Valley Academy, New York, for two years. In 1869 he returned to western Pennsylvania and for three years was engaged in the oil business, making his headquarters in St. Petersburg, Clarion County.

Meanwhile his attention had been given for some time to the development of an automatic signal system as a means of preventing accidents of various kinds on railroads. Choosing electricity as the active agent, he had devised what is now known as a "wire" or "open circuit" system of signalling, and in 1869 he constructed an elaborate model illustrating a road-crossing gong signal operated by trains approaching in either direction. He exhibited his model at the American Institute Fair in New York in 1870, and the same year installed a practical automatic block signal of this character on a section of the Philadelphia & Erie Railroad at Kinzua, Pa. It worked perfectly, but Robinson, dissatisfied with its inherent limitations, immediately undertook to correct them and after much study devised the closed track circuit system of automatic electric signalling which he patented both in the United States and France, his United States patent being No. 130,661, dated Aug. 20, 1872. This invention is conceded to be the basis of every block signalling system used on the railroads of the world today, and "perhaps no single invention in the history of the development of railway transportation has contributed more toward safety and dispatch in that field than the track circuit" (*Third Annual Report of the Block Signal and Train Control Board to the Interstate Commerce Commission, Nov. 22, 1910*, 1911, p. 177). After receiving his patents and exhibit-

ing his signal at the State Fair in Erie, Pa., Robinson made his first installation of the system on the Philadelphia & Erie Railroad at Kinzua and Irvine, Pa. In 1873 he organized the Robinson Electric Railway Signal Company in St. Petersburg, Pa., and as president and general manager made a number of installations on railroads in Pennsylvania and Maryland. In 1875 he transferred his headquarters to Boston, Mass., and in the course of the next six years installed his signalling system on many railroads of New England. In 1878, having received by this time nine signal patents, he reorganized his company as the Union Electric Signal Company, but in 1881 sold his entire holdings to George Westinghouse [*q.v.*], who reorganized the concern as the Union Switch & Signal Company.

After two years of foreign travel, Robinson settled in Brooklyn, N. Y., where he resided for the balance of his life, practising electrical engineering and continuing to exercise his inventive talent. He devised the bond wire system of connecting adjacent rails electrically which has made modern electric railroading possible; he developed the use of fiber for insulated rail joints; he invented the wireless electric railway signal system; he patented the radial car truck now extensively used on electric railways, and made some important improvements in steam turbines. He also invented a bicycle coaster-brake and roller-bearing skates. He never married, but had nine nieces and nephews. In 1906 he published *History of Automatic Electric and Electrically Controlled Fluid Pressure Signal Systems for Railroads* and the following year, at the age of sixty-seven, completed a post-graduate course in electrical and mechanical engineering at Boston University and received the degree of Ph.D. He was a fellow of the American Institute of Electrical Engineers and an honorary member of the American Railway Association. He died in his eighty-first year and was buried in Brooklyn, N. Y.

[*Alumni Record of Wesleyan Univ.* (1911); *The Invention of the Track Circuit: The Hist. of Dr. Wm. Robinson's Invention* (1922), pub. by the Signal Section of the Am. Railway Asso.; *Brooklyn Daily Eagle*, Jan. 4, 1921; *N. Y. Times*, Jan. 5, 1921; *Railway Age*, Jan. 7, 1921; Patent Office records.]   C. W. M.

ROBINSON, WILLIAM CALLYHAN (July 26, 1834–Nov. 6, 1911), legal educator and author, was born at Norwich, Conn., the son of John A. and Mary (Callyhan) Robinson. He was educated in the public schools of his native town, at Wesleyan University, Middletown, Conn., and Dartmouth College, whence he graduated in 1854. Entering the General Theological Seminary in New York City, he prepared for the priesthood of the Episcopal Church to which he was ordained on Feb. 9, 1859 (*Protestant Episcopal Quarterly Review,* April 1859, p. 307). He had been reared in the Methodist Episcopal Church, and his adherence to Anglicanism proved but the half-way house in a profound change of religious conviction. That he was of a speculative turn is evident from his *Clavis Rerum* (printed anonymously at Norwich in 1883), which probably represented the results of a long period of reflection and internal conflict and in which he sought to reconcile the fundamentals of orthodoxy with the new ideas of science, then just becoming popularly known. Boldly, for that day, he declared therein that "the law of life is a law of evolution"; but he also asserted that he was "permanently committed to no theory or hypothesis." Whatever the process, it led him eventually to adopt the Roman Catholic viewpoint and, after a few years in the Episcopal ministry, as missionary at Pittston, Pa., and rector at Scranton, where he came into contact with some of the Paulist Fathers, he left that fold for the former. Undoubtedly he would have entered the Catholic priesthood but for the bar of marriage. That necessitated a complete change of vocation and he chose the law.

Entering upon the study of his new profession in 1862, he was admitted to the bar of Luzerne County, Pa., two years later and began practice at New Haven, Conn., in 1865. For a time he served on the city and common pleas courts of New Haven County, and in 1874 sat in the Connecticut House of Representatives. Meanwhile the Yale Law School had reached a crisis in its history and Robinson was one of three selected in 1869 to take charge of it. In 1872 he became a full professor there teaching elementary, criminal, and real property law, and pleading, to undergraduates, and patent and Canon law to graduate students. In 1875 he published *Notes on Elementary Law,* expanded into a book in 1882, with a larger edition in 1910. The work met a longfelt want by reason of the growing disuse of Blackstone's *Commentaries* and because the "case method" of instruction had not yet come into general use. From 1884 to 1886 he was chairman of the Connecticut Tax Commission, and its *Report,* signed by Robinson and eight others, was published in 1886. In 1890 he published a three-volume work, *The Law of Patents for Useful Inventions.* His *Forensic Oratory* followed in 1893.

Robinson remained at Yale for twenty-seven years; but the establishment of the Catholic University of Washington called for an eminent non-clerical jurist to head its Law Department. Robinson was chosen, accepted the position in 1896, and remained in it for the rest of his life. He not only gave direction to the new school but found ampler opportunity to continue his legal literary work. His *Elements of American Jurisprudence* appeared in 1900 and his edition of Andrew Horne's *Mirrour of Justices* in 1903, both representing a high order of workmanship and the latter affording a real contribution to the source books of early English law. Robinson died in 1911 in his seventy-eighth year. On July 2, 1857, Robinson married Anna E. Haviland of New York City. After her death he was married, on Mar. 31, 1891, to Ultima Marie Smith of New Haven. There were five children by the first marriage and four by the second.

[See: *Who's Who in America,* 1910–11; obituary notice in the *Yale Law Jour.,* Jan. 1912; Leonard M. Daggett, "The Yale Law School," *Green Bag,* June 1889; *Cath. World,* Dec. 1911; *Washington Post,* Nov. 7, 1911.]   C. S. L.

ROBINSON, WILLIAM ERIGENA (May 6, 1814–Jan. 23, 1892), journalist and politician, son of Thomas and Mary (Sloss) Robinson, was born at Unagh, County Tyrone, Ireland. He received his early education in the village schools of Tubermore and Lipan, entered the classical school, Cookstown, at the age of twelve, and the Royal Academical Institution in Belfast in 1832. Enfeebled by typhus fever, he retired to his father's farm; there he remained until he emigrated to the United States in 1836. Arriving in New York City in August of that year, he resumed his classical studies and entered Yale College in 1837. Poverty forced him to seek employment; while a junior in college he made over a hundred speeches in the successful presidential campaign of William H. Harrison. He also contributed poetry and prose to Horace Greeley's *Log Cabin.* He founded the *Yale Banner* and established a chapter of the Psi Upsilon Fraternity at Yale. During his college days he contributed much of the original matter in the *New Haven Daily Herald.* Following his graduation in 1841, he studied at the Yale Law School (1842–43).

In the political campaign of 1844 he spoke extensively for Henry Clay and became connected with the *New York Tribune.* To this paper he contributed, under the signature of "Richelieu," the Washington dispatches from 1844 until 1848, with the exception of a brief period in 1846 when he was editor of the *Buffalo Daily Express.* He was active in Irish circles during the famine of 1847 and was an ardent supporter of the Young Ireland Rebellion of

1848. He collaborated in the foundation of *The People* (1849), a short-lived publication devoted to European politics. From 1850 to 1853 he was editor of the *Newark Daily Mercury* and, until 1853, weigher in the New York custom house. When these occupations failed him he turned to the law and was admitted to the New York bar in 1854. He occasionally dabbled in politics, running for office independently and unsuccessfully. In 1859 he visited Ireland and toured the Continent. He was appointed in 1862 by President Lincoln as assessor of internal revenue for the Third District of New York (Brooklyn); he served in this capacity until 1867, resigning to take his seat in Congress, to which he had been elected on the Democratic ticket. As a member of Congress he was chiefly responsible for the bill establishing the right to expatriation (*Congressional Globe,* 40 Cong., 1 Sess., p. 791; 3 Sess., Appendix, p. 258). He was a member of the editorial board of the *Irish World* during 1871; during the following year he published the *Shamrock,* a Brooklyn weekly newspaper. He was returned to Congress in 1880 and 1882. His wife, the former Helen Augusta Dougherty, whom he had married in 1853, died in 1875; they had four daughters and two sons.

Robinson's tall, bent figure and his shaggy white hair were a familiar sight in New York City, where he enjoyed a reputation for his extensive acquaintance with men in public life and for his intense hatred of England. He was a political changeling: originally a Whig, he became a Republican and later a Democrat. When he could find no place on any regular ticket he ran independently. He was a prodigious egotist, a ready wit, and an animated and bombastic public speaker. His eloquence was chiefly effective before Irish patriotic societies, to which he presented many times during a half century a speech on Saint Patrick and the Irish that he had originally given at New Haven in 1842. The declining years of his life were spent in collecting materials for a treatise on the "Origin and Source of the American People," intended to demonstrate the superiority and preponderance of the Irish in American life.

[*Semi-centennial Hist. and Biog. Record of the Class of 1841 in Yale Univ.* (1892); *Obit. Record Grads. Yale Univ., 1890–1900* (1900); class records in Yale Univ. Library; *The Tenth Gen. Cat. of the Psi Upsilon Fraternity* (1888); *World* (N. Y.), Jan. 24, 1892; *N. Y. Tribune,* Jan. 24, 1892; *Irish World and Am. Industrial Liberator* (N. Y.), Jan. 30, 1892; *Brooklyn Eagle,* Jan. 24, 1892.]   F. M.

ROBINSON, WILLIAM STEVENS (Dec. 7, 1818–Mar. 11, 1876), journalist, was born in Concord, Mass., the sixth and last child of William and Martha (Cogswell) Robinson, and a descendant of Jonathan Robinson of Exeter, N. H., who died in 1675. After attending the town school, he learned the printer's trade and in 1837 joined his brother in the office of the *Norfolk Advertiser* of Dedham, a strong temperance paper. In 1839 he became editor of the *Yeoman's Gazette,* later *The Republican,* of Concord, a Whig paper, and as an ardent Whig he attended, as delegate, the Whig Convention in Baltimore in 1840. Two years later he became assistant editor of the *Lowell Courier and Journal,* acting for a time as its Washington correspondent. In 1845 he went to Manchester, N. H., to edit *The American,* but soon returned to the *Lowell Courier,* in which connection his strong anti-slavery views began to attract marked attention among the radicals of Massachusetts. His vigorous condemnation of slavery and caustic comments on Massachusetts politics and politicians finally cost him his position, and in 1848 he removed to Boston to succeed Charles Francis Adams [*q.v.*] as editor of the *Boston Daily Whig,* later the *Boston Daily Republican,* which he conducted through the presidential campaign of 1848. The same year he served as secretary of the Free-Soil Convention which met in Worcester. Again, however, his vigorous opinions on slavery and Massachusetts politics cost him his position, and he returned to Lowell to start the *Lowell American,* which he conducted for nearly four years, becoming recognized as one of the most radical of Massachusetts anti-slavery journalists. In 1852, and again in 1853, he was elected to the Massachusetts legislature, and in the latter year served as clerk of the constitutional convention. Following the failure of the *Lowell American* in 1854, he joined the editorial staffs of *The Commonwealth* and the *Boston Telegraph* and violently opposed the rising tide of Know-Nothingism in Massachusetts. In 1856 his "Warrington" letters on Massachusetts politics and politicians began to appear in the *Springfield Republican* and at once attracted state-wide attention because of their thorough knowledge of Massachusetts politics and their frank personal comment on the public men of the state. Similar letters over the pen name "Gilbert" were contributed to the *New York Tribune,* on which paper Robinson was offered an editorial berth in 1859 which, feeling that his best work could be done in Massachusetts, he refused.

The friend of Charles Sumner, John A. Andrew, Henry Wilson, John G. Whittier, and other Massachusetts radicals, he was early associated with the fortunes of the Republican party in the state, and in 1861, on the eve of the Civil War, he aided in editing *The Tocsin*, a campaign paper "published by an association of Republicans who are in earnest, and who will be heard" (*"Warrington" Pen-Portraits, post*, p. 94). In 1862 he was chosen as clerk of the Massachusetts House of Representatives, a position which he held for eleven years, during which he became known as the "Warwick" of Massachusetts politics. In 1863 he was made secretary of the Republican state committee, which important office he occupied until 1868, writing many of the addresses and memorials of the committee during these critical years of war and reconstruction. The strength of Robinson's political power in Massachusetts was most evident, perhaps, in 1871 and 1872 when he successfully led the opposition against Benjamin F. Butler [*q.v.*] in the latter's efforts to gain the governorship of Massachusetts. It was due to Butler's machinations, he believed, that he finally lost his clerkship in 1873. He then served for a short time on the staff of the *Boston Journal*, but in 1874 increasing ill health caused him to make a European trip, following which he returned to complete and publish *Warrington's Manual* (1875), a handbook of parliamentary law. He died the following year at his home in Malden, Mass.

Robinson is described as "a lymphatic, shut-in man, smiling only around the mouth, which is carefully covered with hair to hide the smile; short, thick-set, with his head . . . set . . . directly on his shoulders; high forehead; slightly bald; thin hair; ruddy of face; . . . the keenest political writer in America, and the best political writer since 'Junius'" (quoted in *"Warrington" Pen-Portraits*, p. 128). On Nov. 30, 1848, he married Harriet Jane Hanson [see Harriet Jane Hanson Robinson], one of the literary mill girls of Lowell and for many years a leader in the woman suffrage movement in Massachusetts, a cause in which Robinson himself took much interest. They had four children, of whom three survived their father.

[Memoir in *"Warrington" Pen-Portraits* (1877), ed. by Harriet J. H. Robinson; *New England Hist. and Geneal. Reg.*, Oct. 1885, July 1890; *Springfield Republican*, Mar. 13, 1876.]   W. R. W.

ROBOT, ISIDORE (July 18, 1837–Feb. 15, 1887), Catholic missionary and prelate, was born at Tharoiseau in Burgundy, France, of a patriarchal family which maintained the traditions of faith and piety. He was threatened with consumption while in school and in the seminary, but at the age of twenty he entered the austere

Benedictine Preachers of the Monastery of Pierre-Qui-Vire, in the diocese of Sens, under the founder, the Venerable Mary John Baptist Muard (1808–54), whose life by Abbé Brullée he later translated and published (1882). Here he completed his theological studies and was ordained to the priesthood in December 1862. After several years in the monastery, he volunteered for the American missions on the invitation of Archbishop Napoleon Joseph Perché of New Orleans and arrived in New Orleans in 1871. Four years later he founded a monastery of the Benedictine Congregation Casinese of the Primitive Observance at Sacred Heart, Okla.

The Benedictines became the first resident priests in Indian Territory, and under the indomitable Robot, who lacked no courage for the arduous and dangerous labors on the frontier, they founded the first Catholic mission among the Potawatomi Indians. Stations were soon established for the Choctaws at Atoka, MacAllister, and Caddo, while the Jesuits were assigned to the Osages. In 1876 Indian Territory was made a prefecture-apostolic under Dom Isidore, and a year later his monastery was elevated to an abbey by Pius IX. As prefect apostolic, Robot labored ten years, laying the foundations of Catholicity in the region, building a college for boys at Sacred Heart, establishing Indian agricultural and missionary schools, founding an academy for girls, and conducting annual visitations on horseback to the isolated mission stations and scattered settlers. In 1884 he took a prominent part in the deliberations in the Third Plenary Council of Baltimore where he pleaded the cause of the Indian missions. A year later he was in Europe seeking recruits and further financial aid for the construction of stations and schools in the villages along the Missouri Pacific Railroad. In 1886 he resigned his duties to his successor, Ignatius Jean, O.S.B., and retired to Dallas, Tex., where he died. His remains were interred in the monastic cemetery at his Sacred Heart Abbey.

[*Cath. Encyc.*, XI (1911), 233; *Sadliers' Directory* (1888), p. 35; *N. Y. Freeman's Jour.*, Feb. 10, 1877, Nov. 16, 1878; materials from Robot's associates, Bernard Murphy, O.S.B., and Father Leo, O.S.B.]
R. J. P.

ROBSON, STUART (Mar. 4, 1836–Apr. 29, 1903), actor, was a comedian whose humorous appeal depended largely upon an odd voice and a quaint personality that underwent but little change during his many years of popularity. He was born in Annapolis, Md., the son of a lawyer named Charles Stuart, his own name being Henry Robson Stuart. When he was about twelve years of age, the family moved to Baltimore. After a brief schooling and employment as a page in the Capitol at Washington until he was about sixteen, he ventured on the stage, and with his name on the program as S. Robson acted the part of Horace Courtney in *Uncle Tom's Cabin as It Is,* a play written as a counterblast to *Uncle Tom's Cabin,* at the Baltimore Museum. Thereafter he was on the stage continuously for fifty-one years and acted over seven hundred characters, by far the greater number of them in the first half of that period. After some ten years with stock companies in Baltimore, Washington, Troy, Cincinnati, Richmond, St. Louis, and other cities, and in touring companies on the western circuit, he became a comedian at Laura Keene's Theatre in New York in the season of 1862–63, making his début there on Sept. 15, 1862, as Bob in *Old Heads and Young Hearts.* For three seasons following he was a member of Mrs. John Drew's stock company at the Arch Street Theatre in Philadelphia, and for three seasons more with the stock company at Selwyn's (afterwards the Globe) Theatre in Boston. His first appearance at the Union Square Theatre in New York was made on Oct. 1, 1873, as Simon Carmichel in *The Geneva Cross,* and his success there as Hector in Dion Boucicault's *Led Astray* led to his going with Charles R. Thorne, Jr., to London, to play the same part at the Gayety Theatre. He was Picard in *The Two Orphans* during its long run at the Union Square, Suter in *The Wicked World,* Gaston in *Camille,* Jean Ruse in *Love's Sacrifice,* and Moulinet in *Rose Michel.*

An attempt to star in 1876 in *Two Men of Sandy Bar,* for which he paid Bret Harte $6,000, was a failure. His association with William H. Crane [*q.v.*] which began early in 1877 at the Park Theatre in New York and continued for twelve years, is the most notable episode in his career, and indeed in the careers of both actors. After acting most successfully in *Our Boarding House* for a few months, they formed a congenial partnership, and on Sept. 3, 1877, began their first joint starring tour. A contemporary critic said of Robson acting in *Our Boarding House:* "He was Gillypod last night in the same sense that he was Colonel Starbottle a few months ago. In other words, he assumed the clothing and the wig of Gillypod and thus presented Mr. Robson in a new disguise. He was as funny as he has been before, and as he will be to the end of the chapter" (*Evening Post,* New York, Jan. 30, 1877). Their repertory through successive seasons ranged from such trivialities as *Our Bachelors, The Two Cherubs, Champagne and Oysters,* and *D. A. M.,* to *Twelfth*

Night, She Stoops to Conquer, A Comedy of Errors, with the stars as the two Dromios, and *The Merry Wives of Windsor,* which gave Crane, in his own words, "a fine chance as Falstaff, but . . . Robson as Slender no chance at all" (*Footprints and Echoes,* 1927, p. 113). Of this performance Crane writes: "Robson and I were totally unlike, both as to face and figure. It was necessary for him to use a good deal of padding and to increase his height, while I had the difficult task of imitating his voice, manner and peculiar laugh" (*Ibid.,* p. 103). After two seasons in *The Henrietta,* written especially for them by Bronson Howard and produced Sept. 26, 1887, they gave their last performance together at the Star Theatre in New York on May 11, 1889. Thereafter for a time Robson continued to play in *The Henrietta;* then he revived *She Stoops to Conquer, A Comedy of Errors,* and the more modern English comedy of *Married Life,* and produced a number of new plays, among them *An Arrant Knave, Mrs. Ponderbury's Past, The Jucklins, Oliver Goldsmith, The Meddler,* and *Is Marriage a Failure?* He died suddenly of heart disease in New York City, in the midst of a starring tour. His first wife, whom he married in 1858, was the daughter of the Rev. Henry Johnson of Baltimore; in 1891, a year after her death, he married May Waldron, a member of his company, who, with their son and a daughter by his first wife, survived him.

[L. C. Strang, *Famous Actors of the Day in America* (1900); C. M. Skinner in *Famous American Actors of Today* (1896); J. B. Clapp and E. F. Edgett, *Players of the Present,* Pt. III (1901); *N. Y. Clipper,* Mar. 15, 1884; *N. Y. Dramatic Mirror,* Feb. 1, 1896, July 16, 1898; interview in *N. Y. Times,* Aug. 25, 1901; obit. notices in *N. Y. Times, Boston Transcript,* Apr. 30, 1903, and *N. Y. Dramatic Mirror,* May 9, 1903.]

E. F. E.

ROCHAMBEAU, JEAN BAPTISTE DONATIEN DE VIMEUR, Comte de (July 1, 1725–May 10, 1807), the commander of the French army in America during the War of the Revolution, was born at Vendôme, France, of an ancient and honorable family, the third son of Joseph Charles de Vimeur, Comte de Rochambeau, and his wife, Marie Claire Thérèse Bégon. He was sent to the Collège de Vendôme in 1730, and received under Père Houbigant an excellent training in history, literature, mathematics, and the physical sciences. Being a puny lad and a younger son he was designated for the priesthood. The Bishop of Blois, a friend of the family, snatched the youth from the dangerous heresies of Jansenism at Vendôme and placed him in a Jesuit school at Blois. He was about to receive the tonsure when his elder brother died, and he returned to the Hôtel de Rochambeau to continue his studies. There, and at Paris, he came in contact with authors and scholars and so became acquainted with some of the advanced thought of the century. At the outbreak of the War of the Austrian Succession he secured a commission as junior officer of cavalry in the regiment of Saint-Simon. He was given command of a troop of horse in July 1743 and three years later became aide-de-camp to the Duc d'Orléans. Shortly afterwards he was employed in the siege of Namur under the Comte de Clermont. Rochambeau returned to the army in 1747 as colonel on Clermont's staff, was severely wounded at the battle of Lawfeld, and served gallantly in the battle of Maestricht in 1748.

He married Jeanne Thérèse Tellez d'Acosta, daughter of a wealthy merchant, in December 1749, and retired to Vendômois. He disliked the intrigue and pomp of Versailles and found the life of a provincial country gentleman most congenial. This leisurely existence was interrupted by garrison duties at Verdun, Metz, and Besançon. In 1756 he participated in the brilliant campaign against Minorca and in the capture of Port Mahon from the English. He distinguished himself at Crefeld in June 1758 and during the following March he was placed in command of a regiment of infantry of Auvergne. His skilful maneuvering and personal bravery saved the French from a surprise attack and a disaster at Clostercamp in October 1760. Early in 1761 he was made a brigadier-general and was called to the post of inspector of cavalry. In this latter position he introduced a number of tactical improvements and displayed his unusual solicitude for the welfare of the soldiers—and for discipline. He was appointed governor of Villefranche-en-Roussillon in 1776.

France allied herself with the American insurgents early in 1778. D'Estaing's attempts to cooperate with the Americans in that year had been futile and unfortunate, but the following year the French were persuaded, chiefly by Lafayette, that a military and naval force ought to be sent to the assistance of the Americans: the momentous decision was finally made in February 1780. Lafayette had hoped to secure the command of this expeditionary army, but he cheerfully acquiesced in the appointment of Rochambeau and embarked for America to inform Washington of the imminent aid from France. Elaborate preparations were made for the expedition. Rochambeau's administrative skill and his unceasing application did something to counteract the characteristic inefficiency of the French war department, but nothing could prevail against the ineptitude of the naval department and the refusal of the Spanish to cooperate. In April 1780 some 7,600 soldiers had assembled at Brest ready to embark for America, but there were accommodations for only 5,500. After several tedious delays the fleet of ten ships of war and thirty convoys sailed from Brest on May 1. Admiral Ternay, with caution and ability, brought his fleet across the Atlantic and anchored off Rhode Island on July 11. The following day Rochambeau wrote to Washington that he had arrived full of "submission" and "zeal" and that the king's orders placed him and his army at the disposal of Washington (Washington Papers, Library of Congress). The admirable conduct of the French soldiers, together with the tact, courtesy, and charm of the officers, removed many old American prejudices against the French and prepared the way for effective cooperation and mutual good-will.

Rochambeau's position as commander of the French forces was complicated by the interference of Lafayette. In his impetuous zeal Lafayette, in August 1780, urged Rochambeau to cast off his lethargy and attack New York. But the French commander still awaited the remainder of his troops from France and was unwilling to attempt such a dangerous project unless the French had command of the sea. He rebuked Lafayette, but added a delicate touch: "it is always the old father Rochambeau who talks to his dear son whom he loves . . ." (Doniol, *post*, IV, 380). Washington felt that there might be difficulties in giving Lafayette too active a part in the dealings between himself and Rochambeau and accordingly arranged a conference with the French commander at Hartford on Sept. 21. Washington was inclined to favor an attack against New York, but when he observed that the opinion of the French generals was unfavorable he tactfully abandoned the project. However, Washington, Rochambeau, and Ternay joined in a request to the French government for more men and money; they declared that an attack against New York would be desirable only if the allies had a superiority at sea. Rochambeau and the French army then went into winter-quarters in Rhode Island.

Early in May 1781, the Comte de Barras arrived at Boston with the Vicomte de Rochambeau, who brought his father the unwelcome news that there was no second division of French troops to be expected. But he brought news that the French king had consented to a new subsidy of six million *livres tournois* and that the Comte de Grasse, in command of a powerful fleet, had sailed to the West Indies and would later cooperate with Washington and Rochambeau. A second conference between Washington and Rochambeau was held at Wethersfield, Conn., on May 21. Washington still favored the attempt against New York, but Rochambeau urged that operations against Cornwallis in Virginia be undertaken in conjunction with the fleet under De Grasse. This insistence upon the Virginia campaign was the work of La Luzerne, the French minister to the United States (Jusserand, *post*, pp. 61–63). It was agreed at Wethersfield that the movement against New York was perhaps the only practicable one, because of the great difficulties in transporting the troops to Virginia. The French fleet was to remain at Newport, but the army was to join the American forces on the Hudson. On June 10 the French broke camp at Newport and on July 5 the two armies were united at White Plains, N. Y. The combined Franco-American forces now numbered some 10,000. There were several skirmishes with the British, but Washington did not wish to hazard a general engagement. The strategy of the Franco-Americans was to depend upon the destination of De Grasse. On Aug. 14 news arrived that the French fleet was sailing for the Chesapeake. Washington, urged by Rochambeau, now prepared to march southward against Cornwallis who was being harassed by Lafayette in Virginia. If the British lost control of the sea and if Clinton at New York did not attempt to succor the British forces in Virginia, the fate of Cornwallis was sealed.

On Aug. 19 Washington and Rochambeau began their long march southward; William Heath [*q.v.*], with about 3,000 men, was left before New York to deceive the British. By Aug. 26 the rest of the army had gained the west side of the Hudson and they marched directly southward, still feinting an attack against New York. On the 29th they turned their backs on New York and marched rapidly towards Philadelphia. The American treasury was so bare that Rochambeau lent 20,000 hard dollars to enable Washington to pay his troops a month's salary. The speed with which both armies traveled and the skill with which two fleets and two armies formed a perfect union were both extraordinary. De Grasse anchored his fleet in the roadstead of Chesapeake Bay late in August and within several days disembarked 4,000 soldiers, who joined the army of Lafayette. The English fleet under Graves were repulsed in an attack against De Grasse on Sept. 5, and four days later the arrival of Barras with

the French fleet from Newport gave the French forces such an advantage that Graves withdrew to New York. Barras had been induced to assist De Grasse only after repeated urgings by Rochambeau and Washington. Lafayette resisted the temptation to attack Cornwallis and wrote Washington and Rochambeau to make all haste to Yorktown, where the British were now encamped.

On Sept. 14 Washington and Rochambeau joined Lafayette and Saint-Simon at Williamsburg, Va. After a conference with De Grasse plans for the siege were drawn up: preparations were expedited by the fear that De Grasse would soon withdraw his fleet to the West Indies. There were skirmishes and bombardments by the siege guns, but casualties were small on both sides. Seventeen days after the siege was formally begun Cornwallis sent a flag of truce to consider terms of surrender. Rochambeau and Barras signed the articles of capitulation for the French. On Oct. 19 the surrender took place. The British wished to surrender themselves to the French, but Rochambeau discreetly held to a strict observance of the proprieties.

Following the surrender of Cornwallis, De Grasse sailed for the West Indies, Washington returned to the Hudson and Rochambeau and the French army went into winter quarters near Williamsburg. The Virginians thought the war was over and did not look kindly upon the presence of an army. But the French soldiers were kept under extraordinarily good discipline by Rochambeau and his staff. The French commander had requested his recall in June 1781, because his health had long been poor, and there was not much glory to be gathered in America. Fortunately for his fame he did not receive the message granting him permission to return until Dec. 6, 1781. After making a short tour in Virginia he finally embarked for France on Jan. 11, 1783. In one of his several last conferences with Washington the American commander spoke enthusiastically of a Canadian expedition, but Rochambeau knew that Vergennes did not favor any such campaign and politely declined. Rochambeau was suitably fêted before his long-delayed departure for France.

Upon his return to France there was no great public celebration for him, since Lafayette monopolized the public attention, but the king declared that he owed the peace to Rochambeau. Early in 1784 he was made commander of an important military district, with headquarters at Calais. He was an active member of the Society of the Cincinnati. Rochambeau participated in the second Assembly of Notables. In 1789 he was made commander of the important district of Alsace; poor health caused his retirement in December of that year. In September 1790 he was placed in charge of the northern military department and was created a marshal of France in December 1791. During the Terror he was arrested, imprisoned, and was about to be guillotined when Robespierre's death stopped the wholesale carnage. Rochambeau was honored by Napoleon and made a member of the Legion of Honor before his death at his château in 1807. He is buried at Thoré.

[Comte de Rochambeau, *Mémoires militaires, historiques et politiques* (2 vols., Paris, 1809); *Memoirs* (extracts translated by M. W. E. Wright, Paris, 1838); J. E. Weelen, *Rochambeau* (Paris, 1934); D. R. Keim, *Rochambeau. A Commemoration by the Congress of the U. S. A....* (Washington, 1907); J. J. Jusserand, *With Americans of Past and Present Days* (1916); J. B. Perkins, *France in the American Revolution* (1911); Henri Doniol, *Histoire de la participation de la France à l'établissement des États-Unis ...* (5 vols., Paris, 1886–1899). Weelen has written the only satisfactory biography, but has failed to use the large collection of Rochambeau MSS. in the Lib. of Cong.; this collection was partly used by Jusserand. Doniol prints almost three hundred pages of Rochambeau documents from French archives. The materials listed in the bibliography of the Lafayette article should also be consulted for Rochambeau in America.] F. M.

ROCHE, JAMES JEFFREY (May 31, 1847– Apr. 3, 1908), journalist and poet, son of Edward and Mary Margaret (Doyle) Roche, was born at Mountmellick, Queen's County, Ireland, from which place his parents emigrated to Charlottetown, Prince Edward Island. Here his father taught mathematics, conducted a school, and became provincial librarian. James was educated by his father and at St. Dunstan's College. In 1866 he went to Boston, where he made friends easily in Irish circles and succeeded in a business way. In 1883, he became assistant editor of the Boston *Pilot*, which had long been the leading Irish Catholic journal in the United States. Seven years later he succeeded John Boyle O'Reilly [*q.v.*] as editor and as the idol of a Catholic intellectual group in Boston. A man of humor and generous social qualities, he became a leader in the St. Botolph and Papyrus Clubs, where the sons of old New England enjoyed his romances and cherished his friendship. While not a violent Irish partisan, he was, however, an intense nationalist, keenly concerned with the uplifting of the Irish in America. In 1904, he welcomed an appointment as consul at Genoa from the hands of President Theodore Roosevelt as a relief from business worries and from a severe climate which made his delicate health more precarious. His life was prolonged for four years but the end came at Berne in the Alps where he was then consul.

He was twice married: first, to Mary Halloran, who died in 1885; and second, in 1904, to Mrs. Elizabeth Vaughan Okie; the latter, a son and a daughter survived him. He was buried in Holyhood Cemetery, Brookline, Mass.

He contributed much to the *Pilot* and to other periodicals, including the *Atlantic, Century,* and *Harpers,* and was the author of a stirring novel of adventure, *The Story of the Filibusters* (1891), translated into Spanish (1908), and reissued as *By-Ways of War: the Story of the Filibusters* (1901), which Richard Harding Davis described as a classic. He published a *Life of John Boyle O'Reilly* (1891) and contributed an introduction to Henry B. Carpenter's *A Poet's Last Songs* (1891), and a biographical and critical introduction to *The Collected Writings of Samuel Lover* (10 vols., 1901–13). He edited Thackeray's *The Mahogany Tree* (1887), and with Justin McCarthy, Lady Gregory, Maurice Francis Egan, and Douglas Hyde, he collaborated in preparing *Irish Literature* (10 vols., 1904). In his *Songs and Satires* (1886), *Her Majesty the King; a Romance of the Harem* (1898), *Ballads of Blue Water and Other Poems* (1895), *The V-a-s-e and Other Bric-à-Brac* (1900), and *The Sorrows of Sap'ed* (1904), Roche displayed a delicate touch, sweetness of voice, humorous satire, and ringing patriotism as a balladist.

[*James Jeffrey Roche: A Memorial and Appreciation* (1908); *Jour. Am. Irish Hist. Soc.,* vol. VIII (1909); J. B. Cullen, *The Story of the Irish in Boston* (1889); *Who's Who in America,* 1908–09; C. McGuire, *Catholic Builders of the Nation,* IV (1923), 175; *Boston Transcript,* Apr. 3, May 3, 1908; *Boston Globe,* Apr. 4, 1908.] R. J. P.

ROCHESTER, NATHANIEL (Feb. 21, 1752–May 17, 1831), merchant and founder of Rochester, N. Y., was born in Westmoreland County, Va., the son of John and Hester (Thrift) Rochester and the grandson of Nicholas Rochester who emigrated from England to Westmoreland County at the end of the seventeenth century. His father died when the boy was only four years old, and his mother, marrying again, took the family to Granville County, N. C. The young Nathaniel must have received but a limited education, and there is no reference to schooling in his modest autobiography (*post,* pp. 305–14). At the age of sixteen he was employed in a country store in Hillsboro, N. C., and was taken into partnership in 1773. He was a member of the revolutionary committee of safety for Orange County in 1775 and of the two provincial conventions of 1775 and 1776. He saw brief active service as a major of militia, receiving the surrender of a part of the

British force defeated at Moore's Creek in February 1776. On Apr. 22, 1776, he was appointed lieutenant-colonel of the North Carolina troops. He also acted as deputy-commissary general of military stores and clothing. In 1777 he was appointed a commissioner to establish and superintend an arms manufactory at Hillsboro, and he served in the Assembly the same year. For reasons not entirely clear, perhaps from lack of health, he gave up the pursuit of arms, and in 1778 he went into business with Col. Thomas Hart, first at Hillsboro and a little later at Hagerstown, Md. The two partners rented a gristmill and established nail and rope factories. In 1792 the partnership was dissolved. While in Hagerstown, Rochester served one term in the legislature but refused reëlection because of disgust "with the intrigue and management among the members" (autobiography, *post*, p. 311). In 1807 he became president of the Hagerstown bank, a modest establishment housed for seven years in his own dwelling.

Associated with him in his bank were Charles Carroll and William Fitzhugh. Carroll and Fitzhugh's brother, Peregrine Fitzhugh, had visited western New York in 1799. It was through these men that Rochester became interested in western New York, which was then opening up to settlement. Visiting the Genesee country in 1800, he bought a small amount of land there, especially a tract at Dansville, covering the water-power sites along the Canaseraga. In 1803, with his friends, he purchased the one-hundred-acre tract at the so-called Upper Falls of the Genesee for the large price of $17.50 an acre. The tract was not laid out, however, till some time later, and sales of land did not begin till November 1811. In the meantime he decided to close out his business at Hagerstown and remove to the Genesee country. He settled first at Dansville with his wife, Sophia (Beatty) Rochester, whom he had married in 1788, and nine children, and there established three mills and a wool-carding shop. From Dansville he removed to Bloomfield and in 1818 to Rochester, a village of some 700 persons and called from 1817 to 1822 by the name of Rochesterville. In 1821 he took an active part in obtaining the creation of the county of Monroe, in which Rochester is situated, and became clerk of the county when it was set up. In 1824 he organized a bank at Rochester. He was then a man of over seventy years; yet he took an active interest in the campaign of 1828, strongly supporting the claims of John Quincy Adams to the presidency. He was steadily weakening, and his last years were not marked by any further participation in public affairs. In appearance he was tall, and rather spare, with distinctly attractive features. Notwithstanding the fact that his manners were somewhat austere, and his temper was strong, it is clear that he commanded a high degree of respect in the community in which he settled.

[*N. C. Colonial Records,* esp. vol. X (1890); *N. C. State Records,* esp. vols. XI, XII (1895); a number of accounts of his life in the *Rochester Hist. Soc. Publication Fund Series,* vol. III (1924), including autobiography, excerpts from correspondence, and a bibliography; Henry O'Reilly, *Sketches of Rochester* (1838), pp. 407–415.]   D. P.

ROCK, JOHN (Aug. 19, 1836–Aug. 9, 1904), nurseryman, was born in Lauter, Hesse-Darmstadt, Germany, the son of Heinrich and Elisabeth Roch. As a youth he left home secretly and emigrated to America, where he changed his name to Rock. He first resided in New York, employed as a florist and later as a nurseryman. At the outbreak of the Civil War he joined the Union forces, enlisting with the 5th New York Regiment, Duryée's Zouaves. He was in many engagements, was made a sergeant, and remained in the army until the end of the war. In 1866 he moved to California and was one of the pioneer nurserymen of that state. His first nursery was at Santa Clara. Later he opened the Rock Nurseries on the Milpitas Road and in 1884 established the California Nursery Company at Niles. This nursery, which became a great storehouse of horticultural material, played a most important part in California horticulture. It was here that he assembled the large collection of grape varieties from all parts of the world that provided the material from which phylloxera-resistant stocks were developed. He also introduced many fig varieties into California and was the first to call the attention of American investigators to the fig collection of the London Royal Horticulture Society. When in 1894 the United States Department of Agriculture imported this collection it was placed in Rock's hands for propagation and all of the sixty-six varieties were successfully established. Among the other plants that he introduced into California were the pistacia, black Spanish mulberry, rose-colored seedless Sultana grape, Moorpark apricot, Cork oak, Oriental plane tree, Cedar of Lebanon, Deodara cedar, Damson and Mirabelle plums, thin-shelled almonds, and Italian chestnut. In a tribute to Rock it has been said of him: "Intensely in love with his work, it is no wonder that he spent thousands of dollars in exploiting new and little known fruits and plants, many of which proved worthless; nor that, on the other hand, his untiring zeal in the development of California horticulture has been the direct means of introducing a larger number of varieties of fruits and plants into this State than any other one man" (Kruckeberg, *post*, p. 5). Personally Rock was modest and retiring, a man of few words. It would seem that his influence on California horticulture, generally recognized by his contemporaries and successors, was due as much to his personality as to his material contributions.

[Sources include: H. W. Kruckeberg, "John Rock, A Tribute," *Trans. and Proc. of the Second Ann. Meeting of the Cal. Asso. of Nurserymen* (1913); E. J. Wickson, "Cal. Nurserymen of Second and Third Decade," *Trans. and Proc. of the Seventh Annual Meeting of the Cal. Asso. of Nurserymen* (1917); L. H. Bailey, *The Standard Cyc. of Horticulture*, III (1915), 1593; *San Francisco Examiner*, Aug. 11, 1904. Information for this sketch was supplied by Dr. Gustavus Eisen, one of Rock's associates, W. V. Eberly, and by members of the family.]   G. N. C.

ROCKEFELLER, WILLIAM (May 31, 1841–June 24, 1922), industrialist and financier, born in Richford, Tioga County, N. Y., was the third child of William Avery and Eliza (Davison) Rockefeller and the younger brother of John D. Rockefeller. The family apparently originated in Germany, the original American ancestor, Johann Peter Rockefeller, and his son Peter, coming to America from Sagendorf, Germany, about 1722 and settling in Somerville, N. J. William's father departed from the long ancestral vocation of farming to become an itinerant peddler of patent medicines. He moved his family about a great deal, to Moravia in Cayuga County and, in 1850, to Owego, the county seat of Tioga, where, after some instruction in a small village school, William, with his more famous brother, John D., attended Owego Academy. In 1853 the roving father moved his family again to Strongsville, Ohio; then, in a year, to Parma, a neighboring district, and in 1857 to Cleveland, where the family settled definitely. There, after attending the public schools, William, when about sixteen years of age, began his business career as a bookkeeper for a small miller in Cleveland. After a year he went into the produce business in which his brother was already laying the first foundation stones of his vast fortunes and, when but twenty-one years of age, set up in business for himself under the firm name of Hughes and Rockefeller, commission merchants.

Meantime, petroleum had been found by Edwin L. Drake [*q.v.*] in Venango County, Pa., an event which changed the whole course of business in Cleveland. John D. Rockefeller became interested, like most Cleveland business men, and ventured into the refining industry with Samuel Andrews, as Rockefeller and An-

drews. This firm was the progenitor of the Standard Oil Company. When the oil industry, which then consisted largely of refining and selling kerosene for illuminating purposes, gave signs of becoming a great export business, John D. Rockefeller invited his younger brother to join his firm to take charge of its export selling functions in New York. A new firm, William Rockefeller & Company, was formed in 1867, which was in reality only a subsidiary of Rockefeller and Andrews. Its habitat was New York City to which place William went that year to remain throughout his life. He built up the great export business and this firm became in time the Standard Oil Company of New York, of which William Rockefeller was president until 1911. On May 25, 1864, he married Almira Geraldine Goodsell, to which union were born six children, four sons and two daughters.

With his brother he played a leading rôle in the troublous battles between the refiners' combinations and the crude oil producers in 1872 and the years following. He was active in bringing the Eastern refiners, who had opposed the young Standard Oil group—men like Henry H. Rogers, Charles Pratt, Alfred C. Bedford, and others—into the Standard Oil mergers which combined most of the able leaders of the industry against the horde of small refiners and producers. When the first trust agreement was made, William was a member of the trust until its dissolution in 1890 by the Ohio courts. Later he played an important rôle in that extensive series of combinations and absorptions in which the Standard Oil Company of New Jersey, acting as a holding company, gathered under its wing the vast organization of refineries, pipe lines, oil fields, ship lines, and related manufacturing industries which the Supreme Court of the United States dissolved as a violation of the Sherman Anti-Trust Law in 1911.

While John D. Rockefeller's supreme talent was for organization, William blossomed first as an able salesman and commercial diplomat and later as a financier and promoter of extraordinary ability. Unlike his famous brother, who disliked speculation and all sorts of adventures in securities, William formed one of the group made up chiefly of himself, Henry H. Rogers, and James Stillman [*qq.v.*] of the National City Bank, and which came to be known as the "Standard Oil Gang." They carried on numerous adventurous and audacious promotions in Wall Street, chief of which was the Amalgamated Copper deal which led Thomas W. Lawson to write his sensational denunciation under the title, *Frenzied Finance* (1905). The years

1898 to 1912 were the golden years of the promoters. William Rockefeller and Rogers went heavily into numerous corporate fields. Rockefeller became a director in countless corporations. They centered their attention finally on railroad and gas companies. Occupying strategic positions because of the Standard's control over artificial gas fields and petroleum, which was coming into use for making gas, they got control of the Consolidated Gas Company of New York and the United Gas Improvement Company in Philadelphia, which was a forerunner of the modern holding company form of organization applied to utilities.

After 1911 and the dissolution of the Standard Oil Trust, William, like his brother and other leaders of the great corporation, withdrew from an active part in the management of the industry. He devoted himself chiefly to his investments and those railroad properties, like the Chicago, Milwaukee & St. Paul Railroad, in which he held a dominant position. He differed in many characteristics from his brother. He was a jovial man who loved good living. He had but small piety, though he occasionally made contributions to the Baptist Church. He had little interest in philanthropy and such gifts as he made he was very secretive about. In his later years he retired to the beautiful estate, "Rockwood Hall," adjoining his brother's at Tarrytown, N. Y., and there died of pneumonia June 24, 1922, at the age of eighty-one. He left a fortune variously estimated at between $150,-000,000 and $200,000,000, a large part of it in Standard Oil securities, but many score millions in widely diversified corporation bonds and shares. There were no charitable bequests, the whole fortune being left to his four surviving children.

[H. O. Rockefeller, ed., *The Transactions of the Rockefeller Family Asso.* . . . (3 vols., 1910, 1915, 1926); E. M. Avery. *A Hist. of Cleveland and Its Environs* (1918), vol. III; Ida M. Tarbell, *The Hist. of the Standard Oil Co.* (2 vols., 1904); J. T. Flynn, *God's Gold, The Story of Rockefeller and His Times* (1932); *Who's Who in America,* 1922–23; obituary in *N. Y. Times,* June 25, 1922.]   J.T.F.

ROCKHILL, WILLIAM WOODVILLE (April 1854–Dec. 8, 1914), Orientalist and diplomat, was born in Philadelphia, Pa., the son of Thomas Cadwallader and Dorothy Anna (Woodville) Rockhill. After graduating from the École Spéciale Militaire de St. Cyr, France, in 1873, he served three years as lieutenant in the French army in Algeria. Throughout a career of thirty years he combined a profound interest in Far-Eastern studies with the professional duties of a diplomat. His first assignments involved appointments to Peking as second secretary of the American legation from Apr. 9, 1884, as secretary of the legation from July 1, 1885, and as chargé d'affaires at Seoul, from Dec. 11, 1886, to Apr. 3, 1887, at a time when China, Russia, and Japan were each centered on gaining control of Korea. While at Peking Rockhill had viewed his appointment as an opportunity to continue Tibetan studies commenced at Paris. He had already published (1884) a translation into French of the *Prâtimoksha Sutra* (*Le traité d'émancipation*) and *The Life of the Buddha* (1884). Upon his temporary withdrawal from the diplomatic service on July 5, 1888, he engaged himself to the Smithsonian Institution, under whose auspices he made two scientific expeditions to Mongolia and Tibet (1888–89 and 1891–92). His journeys, directed into eastern and southern Tibet, regions difficult to traverse but rich for geographical and ethnographical observations, produced a variety of valuable reports and works on the then secluded and little-known country. His researches in later years included the pre-modern relations of China with the Western world by the routes along the coasts of India and overland through Turkestan. While at St. Petersburg, he edited and translated with Professor Friedrich Hirth of Columbia University the *Chu-fan-Chï* (1912) of Chau Ju-kua, Imperial trade commissioner at Amoy, on Chinese and Arab trade in the twelfth and thirteenth centuries. His researches on the relations and trade of China with the Eastern Archipelago and the coasts of the Indian Ocean during the fourteenth and fifteenth centuries continued until his death. His interest in East Asiatic bibliography was expressed in gifts of over 6,000 volumes of rare Chinese works to the Chinese Division of the Library of Congress. The Library acquired from him also a 1733 edition of the Tibetan *Kanjur*.

Rockhill's public services still remain to be fully recognized. Secretary of State John Hay associated him with Henry White as one of the two best American diplomats of the time (W. R. Thayer, *Life and Letters of John Hay,* 1908, II, 244). He had returned to the service of the Department of State, Apr. 14, 1893, as chief clerk, and was made third assistant secretary of state a year later. Until 1899 he served in various capacities, as delegate to the International Congress of Geography, London, in 1895, as assistant secretary of state from Feb. 14, 1896, until May 10, 1897, as minister and consul-general to Greece, Roumania, and Servia from July 8, 1897, to May 19, 1899, when he resigned to accept an appointment as director of the International Bureau of the American Republics, a position said to have been secured for him in order that the Department of State might still have the benefit of his advice on diplomatic matters in Asia. His hand is clearly evident in the policy of John Hay throughout the Boxer insurrection in China, and the subsequent settlements. Just prior to the international cataclysm of 1900, Hay had announced his open-door doctrine as applicable to China, employing almost the precise words of a lengthy memorandum of Rockhill under date of Aug. 28, 1899. In July 1900, Hay dispatched Rockhill to China as special agent of the United States to perform, in the ensuing negotiations, his most notable diplomatic services. It was Rockhill's rôle to adhere to the formula, announced in Hay's circular note to the powers of July 3, 1900, of regarding the Boxer disturbance as a state of anarchy, not of war against the Chinese Empire. The American phase of the negotiations thus facilitated the mitigation of the penalties imposed upon the Chinese people in the protocol of Sept. 7, 1901. The eventual determination of the monetary indemnity ($333,-000,000) was doubtless less than it would have been but for the good offices of the United States. The subsequent proposal for the remission of one half of the unexpended balance of the American portion of the indemnity for the education of Chinese was a part of the general benevolent policy advocated by Rockhill for the strengthening of China.

Rockhill's subsequent public career included his resumption of duty as director of the International Bureau of American Republics on Oct. 24, 1901, his resignation on Mar. 7, 1905, enabling him to return to China as American minister, a congenial post which he held until appointed ambassador to Russia, May 17, 1909. His diplomatic career terminated as ambassador to Turkey (Apr. 24, 1911, until the autumn of 1913). In 1914 he revisited China, including a journey to Mongolia, under the auspices of the American Asiatic Association. In the same year he accepted an appointment as personal advisor to the President of China, Yuan Shih-k'ai, whose acquaintance as the representative of China he had first made in Korea in 1886. While returning to China for this purpose, Rockhill died at Honolulu. He had married twice. His first wife was Caroline Adams of Philadelphia, whom he had married on Dec. 14, 1876. In April 1900 he was married to Edith Howell Perkins of Litchfield, Conn. Two daughters survived him. His principal published works, aside from those already mentioned, comprised: "Tibet, . . . from Chinese Sources" *Journal of the Royal Asiatic*

Society, January, April 1891; *Udânavarga, the Northern Buddhist Version of Dhammapada* (1883); *The Land of the Lamas* (1891); *Diary of a Journey in Mongolia and Tibet in 1891 and 1892* (1894); *Notes on the Ethnology of Tibet* (1895); *The Journey of William of Rubruck* (1900); *Report of William W. Rockhill, late Commissioner to China* (1901); *China's Intercourse with Korea from the XVth Century to 1895* (1905), *Conventions and Treaties with or concerning China and Korea* (1904), supplemented by another volume in 1908; and monographs appearing in *T'oung Pao* (Paris) and other journals.

[Rockhill's papers, now in private hands, have not yet been published. The *Registers* of the Department of State contain data of his official career. Other sources include: Henri Cordier, tribute in *T'oung Pao,* Mar. 1915, supplemented by an article and bibliography of Rockhill's writings by Berthold Laufer, *Ibid.,* May 1915; A. E. Hippisley, memoir in *Jour. Royal Asiatic Soc.,* Apr. 1915; F. E. Hinckley, memoir in *Jour. North-China Branch Royal Asiatic Soc.,* vol. XLVI (1915); E. F. Egan, in *Jour. Am. Asiatic Asso.,* Jan. 1915; Tyler Dennett, *Americans in Eastern Asia* (1922); A. L. P. Dennis, *Adventures in Am. Diplomacy* (1928); *Who's Who in America,* 1912–13; *Papers Relating to the Foreign Relations of the U. S.,* 1901, App.; *N. Y. Times,* Dec. 9, 1914. Every Rockhill letter in the Hay papers has disappeared.]   E. M. G.

ROCKNE, KNUTE KENNETH (Mar. 4, 1888–Mar. 31, 1931), football coach, the son of Lars Knutson and Martha (Gjermo) Rockne, was born in Voss, Norway. He was the second child and the only son in a family of five children. His father, a stationary engineer with a taste for invention, came to the United States in October 1891 to prepare a carriage of his contrivance for exhibition at the Columbian Exposition in Chicago. The family followed eighteen months later and Knute grew up in Chicago where he attended Brentano Grammar School and the Northwest Division High School. Before he finished high school, however, he was dropped for cutting classes. He washed windows in Chicago, worked on a ferry-boat, harvested in Wisconsin, and was for four years a mail dispatcher in the Chicago Post Office. He saved enough money to begin a delayed college career and entered the University of Notre Dame, Ind., in 1910 and was graduated with the degree of B.S., with distinction, in 1914, having specialized in chemistry.

In college he was an all around athlete and a good scholar. He was editor of the college literary annual in his senior year and in 1913 was captain of the Notre Dame team which astonished the intercollegiate football world by defeating the strong Army team at West Point by brilliant use of the forward pass. Football critics agree that the work of Charles Dorais and Rockne in that game opened the eyes of the football coaches of the country to the possibilities of the "open game." After graduation, Rockne became a chemistry instructor at Notre Dame and assistant football coach. Upon the retirement of Jesse Harper in 1918 he became head football coach and from that year he developed football teams of remarkable excellence. During the thirteen years of his coaching, Notre Dame won 105 games, lost twelve, and tied five. He was an advocate of intersectional football and the Notre Dame team traveled all over the country, meeting strong opponents in the East, the West, and the South. Rockne's colorful and highly trained teams became favorites with the non-college public and attracted huge crowds. Over 110,000 spectators witnessed the game between Notre Dame and the University of Southern California on Nov. 16, 1929. Five of the Rockne-coached Notre Dame teams were undefeated and several were acclaimed unofficial national champions. The so-called "Rockne System" featured speed and deception and provided a place for the lighter and faster man on the football field. Though Rockne originated little in football strategy, he brought the forward pass, the shift, the spinner plays, and the flexing-end play to a high type of perfection. Through the success and popularity of his teams, he became a figure of national prominence and a powerful influence in the development of the game. His players went out in great numbers to be football coaches at colleges all over the country, carrying with them the splendid technique and infectious enthusiasm of their famous coach.

Medium in size, muscular, bronzed, and prematurely bald, he was a man of energy, with a keen mind, a ready tongue, and a rollicking sense of humor. He became noted as an after-dinner speaker, and met many demands for radio talks, moving pictures, and syndicated articles on football. He conducted summer schools for football coaches, managed a tour of Europe, and was for a brief time a partner in a brokerage firm in South Bend, Ind. His contact with the Studebaker Corporation as sales promotion manager began in May 1928 and continued until his death. Partly as a result of his many activities he suffered a serious breakdown in 1929 but was well on the road to complete recovery when, on Mar. 31, 1931, he met death in an airplane crash on the plains of southeastern Kansas. He is buried at Notre Dame, Ind. He was married on July 15, 1914, to Bonnie Gwendoline Skiles, who, with their four children, survived him. He became a Roman Catholic in 1925.

[*Who's Who in America*, 1930–31; Bonnie Skiles Rockne, ed., *The Autobiog. of Knute K. Rockne* (1931); Warren Brown, *Rockne* (1931); Robert Harron, *Rockne, Idol of Am. Football* (1931); McCready Huston, *Salesman from the Sidelines, being the Business Career of Knute K. Rockne* (1932); D. W. Lovelace, *Rockne of Notre Dame* (1931); Harry A. Stuhldreher, *Knute Rockne* (1931); *N. Y. Times*, Apr. 1, 1931.]

J.K.

ROCKWELL, ALPHONSO DAVID (May 18, 1840–Apr. 12, 1933), pioneer in electrotherapeutics, was born in New Canaan, Conn., the son of David S. and Betty (Comstock) Rockwell. He was educated at the New Canaan Seminary conducted by his father and at Kenyon College at Gambier, Ohio. His father had purchased a farm near Milan, Ohio, and here he returned after graduation to teach a rural school and begin the study of medicine with a local practitioner. In the spring of 1862 he served a three-months' enlistment in the 85th Ohio Infantry, guarding Confederate prisoners at Camp Chase at Columbus. He spent a year in the medical department of the University of Michigan and a second at the Bellevue Hospital Medical School in New York where he received his medical degree in 1864. He immediately took the examination for the army medical service, was appointed an assistant surgeon, and was assigned to the 6th Ohio Cavalry in Gregg's division of Sheridan's cavalry corps. Joining his regiment at Warrenton, Va., he participated in the campaign which began at the Wilderness and ended with the investment of Richmond, and was with Sheridan's cavalry when it blocked the Confederate retreat at Appomattox. In the meantime he had been promoted to the office of surgeon with the grade of major. Discharged with his regiment in August 1865, he settled in New York City for practice.

In 1866 Rockwell became associated with George M. Beard [*q.v.*] in the investigation of the therapeutic applications of electricity, an association which later developed into a business partnership. At this time electricity was not used to any extent by physicians in the United States, and very little elsewhere. They issued a series of articles in the *Medical Record* (1866–67, 1867–68), published in book form in 1867 under the title, *The Medical Use of Electricity,* which created wide interest. In these articles emphasis was placed upon general electrization with its constitutional tonic effects. In 1871 he published with Beard their larger work: *A Practical Treatise on the Medical and Surgical Uses of Electricity,* which went through eleven editions and was introduced into Germany by a translation by Professor Väter of the University of Prague. In this exhaustive work they described and illustrated in detail the modus operandi of general electrization which they had been the first to give systematic investigation, and directed attention to the growing importance of "central galvanization," especially galvanization of the sympathetic system. Numerous carefully prepared case reports gave added value to the book. Individually or in collaboration with Beard, Rockwell produced a flow of articles for the literature of neurology and electro-therapeutics. Their association was terminated in 1876 by an estrangement, which was later healed. In 1884 Rockwell edited a volume on *Sexual Neurasthenia* from the posthumous manuscript of Beard and in 1888 he brought out a second edition of Beard's *Practical Treatise on Nervous Exhaustion.* He edited an American edition of Sir William Atkin's *Complete Handbook of Treatment* (1887) and wrote the chapter on electrotherapeutics for H. A. Hare's *System of Practical Therapeutics* (1891). In 1920 he published *Rambling Recollections: An Autobiography.* He was appointed professor of electro-therapeutics at the New York Postgraduate Medical School in 1886, holding the position for four years. Owing to his admitted limitations as a public speaker, he was extremely modest concerning his success as an instructor. He was neurologist and electrotherapeutist to the Flushing Hospital and served on the medical staffs of the Woman's Hospital and Demilt Dispensary in New York. He was a member and one-time president of the American Electro-Therapeutic Association.

When the New York state law was enacted changing the method of legal execution from hanging to the electric chair, Rockwell was chosen by the commissioner of prisons as one of a committee of three to advise the state as to the best method of carrying out the provisions of the law. Not only did he advise upon the apparatus and its application, but he gave testimony for the state in defense of the new law and was a witness of some of the earliest electro-executions in the state. He retired from active professional work some years before his death. He was married on Oct. 7, 1868, in New York, to Susannah Landon of that city. It is to be said of Rockwell and his associate, Beard, that they wrested electro-therapeutics from the grasp of charlatanry, gave it respectability, and placed it upon a scientific basis.

[In addition to Rockwell's autobiography see: *New Eng. Medic. Monthly* (Sandy Hook, Conn.), Apr. 1884; *Jour. Am. Medic. Asso.,* May 20, 1933; R. F. Stone, *Eminent Am. Physicians and Surgeons* (1898); *Who's Who in Am. Medicine,* 1925; *N. Y. Times,* Apr. 13, 1933. By a curious error, an obituary notice of Rock-well appeared in the *Jour. Am. Medic. Asso.* at the time of his wife's death in 1925.]   J. M. P—n.

ROCKWELL, KIFFIN YATES (Sept. 20, 1892–Sept. 23, 1916), soldier and aviator in the World War, one of the original members of the Escadrille Lafayette, was born in Newport, Tenn., the son of James Chester and Loula (Ayres) Rockwell. He was a descendant of William Rockwell who in 1630 came to America and settled in Dorchester, Mass., later removing to Windsor, Conn.; his great-grandfather, Chester, born in Middletown, Conn., married a Southern girl and went to South Carolina, where he bought a plantation near Whiteville; both his grandfathers served in the Confederate army. His father died when Kiffin was barely a year old. The boy spent several months each year on the plantation of his maternal grandfather in South Carolina, where he early learned to hunt and fish, became an excellent horseman, and, stirred by stories of the chivalry displayed in the Civil War, made up his mind to be a soldier. When he was fourteen the family moved to Asheville, N. C., and after attending the high school there, in 1908 he entered the Virginia Military Institute. The following year, believing he was more likely to see action in the navy than in the army, he secured an appointment to the United States Naval Academy. Soon, however, persuaded that wartime service on either sea or land was but a remote possibility, he resigned the appointment and entered Washington and Lee University, where an older brother, Paul, was a student. The impulse to roam strong within him, in 1912 he journeyed to the Pacific Coast, and for a time ran an advertising agency in San Francisco. In January 1914 he joined his brother in Atlanta.

The outbreak of the World War that same year brought him his opportunity. On Aug. 3, in a letter to the French consul at New Orleans, he offered his services to France. Not waiting for a reply, he hastened to New York and with his brother Paul sailed for Europe and enlisted in the Foreign Legion. After a brief training he went to the front as a private in the Second Foreign Regiment. During the winter he saw hard and dangerous service in the trenches, the squad to which he belonged, composed of the tallest men in his battalion, being assigned the most exacting and unpleasant tasks. Rockwell proved himself a born soldier, doing more work and guard duty than any one else, and displaying exceptional physical stamina and morale. Transferred to the First Foreign Regiment in March 1915, he took part in the fierce battle of May 9, when the Legion stormed La Targette, and was shot through the thigh. After hospitalization and convalescence he returned to his regiment, but in September was permitted to transfer to aviation. Having received his training as a pilot, in April 1916 he became one of the Escadrille Lafayette.

Rockwell's letters, published after his death, reveal the motives that led him to enter the war. "You would not wish my life to be a failure in my own mind . . .," he wrote his mother. "If I should be killed in this war I will at least die as a man should and would not consider myself a complete failure" (*Letters, post,* p. 7). "I pay my part for Lafayette and Rochambeau," he said, and was happy in the consciousness that he was adventuring "for a greater cause than most people do—the cause of all humanity" (*Ibid.,* p. 57). As an aviator he showed great courage, endurance, and good judgment. Whenever possible he was in the air, and where he was no enemy passed. He was the first of the Escadrille, May 18, 1916, to bring down a plane. On May 24, he was wounded in the face by an explosive bullet that hit his windshield, but in a couple of days was active again. During July and August he fought more than seventy combats. On Sept. 23, flying at 12,000 feet, he attacked a German plane below him, and received an explosive bullet through his breast, his plane crashing to the ground near Thann, Alsace. He was buried, as he had requested in the event of his death, where he fell. The Médaille Militaire and the Croix de Guerre with four palms and one star had already been conferred upon him, and after his death he was awarded the Cross of Chevalier of the Legion of Honor. He had also been proposed for promotion from the grade of sergeant to that of second lieutenant.

[*War Letters of Kiffin Yates Rockwell* (1925), with memoir by P. A. Rockwell; *The Story of the Lafayette Escadrille* (1921), translated by Walter Duranty from the French of Georges Thenault; Laurence La Tourette Driggs, *Heroes of Aviation* (1918); P. A. Rockwell, *Am. Fighters in the Foreign Legion* (1930) and *Three Centuries of the Rockwell Family* (1930).]

H. E. S.

RODDEY, PHILIP DALE (1820–Aug. 1897), Confederate soldier, merchant, was born at Moulton, Ala., the son of Sarah Roddey. His parentage is obscure and his early schooling was fragmentary. After working several years in Moulton as a tailor, he served a term of three years as sheriff, and was subsequently engaged in steam-boating on the Tennessee River. He married Margaret A. McGaughey of Lawrence County, Ala., and from this union four children were born. At the outbreak of the Civil War he formed a troop of cavalry and was elected cap-

tain. Like Nathan Bedford Forrest [*q.v.*], with whom he was later associated, Roddey had an almost uncanny *flair* for cavalry command, considering the totally unmilitary nature of his training. His troop was used for mounted scouting and such was its reputation that it formed Bragg's personal escort at the battle of Shiloh. Roddey received high commendation from Bragg for actions during this battle, and was given a squadron and sent on semi-independent missions. In December 1862 he was commissioned colonel, and organized and commanded the 4th Alabama Cavalry. In this capacity he was destined to spend more than three years defending the banks of the Tennessee River. Usually dispatched on independent or semi-independent missions, his quick-riding, disappearing habits made the Confederate cavalry the despair of the North during the first two years of the war. In August, still operating under Bragg, he executed a successful raid towards Corinth, Miss., that drew high praise from his superiors and netted 123 prisoners. In the winter of 1862–63 he repulsed a Federal expedition from Corinth into northern Alabama.

As circumstances demanded, he acted under the command of Joseph Wheeler [*q.v.*] or Forrest, but never got very far away from northern Alabama. He was called "the Swamp Fox of the Tennessee Valley." In the early spring of 1863 he operated in Mississippi, and was so successful in actions at Tuscumbia, Ala., and Columbia, Tenn., that he was commissioned brigadier-general and given a composite brigade. He operated in close connection with Forrest, sometimes raiding for himself, and was often left along the Tennessee River to protect flanks and communications while Forrest's cavalry harried far into northern territory. He made a successful raid against Rosecrans, and prevented Dodge and his men from joining the Federal forces, while Forrest annihilated Streit's forces in a brilliant campaign. He was active both in the Atlanta campaign and in Hood's campaign in Tennessee, and the force under his command became a composite division which he maneuvered with particular distinction at the battle of Iuka. In Forrest's last desperate attempts to stem the Federal invasions in the spring of 1865, Roddey's command was indispensable. Here parrying, there withdrawing, continually fighting against greatly superior forces and resources, he was finally pushed back to Selma, Ala., where with Forrest, Armstrong, and Adams, he made a last stand on Apr. 1, 1865. Although his own lines were not penetrated, the situation was untenable and he escaped with

Forrest by swimming the river under cover of darkness. Following Forrest's decision to discontinue the struggle after General Johnston surrendered, he took the oath of allegiance and was paroled in May 1865. He engaged in the commission business in New York after the war, and died while on a business trip to London.

[M. J. Wright, *General Officers of the Confed. Army* (1911); *War of the Rebellion: Official Records (Army),* see general index; *Confed. Mil. Hist.* (1899), vol. VII; T. M. Owen, *Hist. of Ala. and Dict. of Ala. Biog.* (1921), vol. IV; B. F. Riley, *Makers and Romance of Ala. Hist.* (1915); Willis Brewer, *Alabama: Her Hist., Resources, War Record, and Public Men* (1872); J. D. Cox, *The March to the Sea* (1882); E. W. Sheppard, *Bedford Forrest* (1930); J. W. DuBose, *Gen. Jos. Wheeler and the Army of Tenn.* (1912).]   D. Y.

RODENBOUGH, THEOPHILUS FRANCIS (Nov. 5, 1838–Dec. 19, 1912), soldier and author, was born at Easton, Pa., the son of Charles and Emily (Cauffman) Rodenbough. His family on both sides were of pioneer, pre-Revolutionary stock, his paternal ancestor, Heinrich Rodenbough, having come from the Palatinate to settle in Hunterdon County, N. J., in 1738. His early schooling was in private schools and under tutors and he attended Lafayette College in 1854. Upon the outbreak of the Civil War he was appointed by President Lincoln second lieutenant of the 2nd Dragoons, later the 2nd Cavalry. He served in staff capacities at the Cavalry School of Practice at Carlisle, Pa., in 1861 and 1862. In 1863 and 1864 he saw combat service with his regiment in all actions of the Army of the Potomac during that period. He was promoted to the rank of captain in July 1862, and was captured in the second Manassas campaign. He was soon exchanged, however, and took part in Stoneman's raid. At Beverly Ford, Va., in June 1863, he was slightly wounded and had two horses shot under him. He commanded his regiment in all the cavalry engagements of the Gettysburg campaign. His conduct was noticeable in the engagements before Richmond in 1864. He was severely wounded and lost his right arm while leading a charge at Winchester, Va., on Sept. 19, 1864. He was brevetted major for this action, lieutenant-colonel for gallant and meritorious conduct at Todd's Tavern, and brigadier-general for gallantry at Cold Harbor.

Following the war, he was commissioned colonel, United States Army, and by special direction of the president was given command of the 18th Pennsylvania Cavalry and District of Clarksburg, W. Va., with the rank of brigadier-general. He was mustered out of the Volunteer Service in October of that year and upon the reorganization of the army was appointed major

of the 42nd Infantry. He served at Fort Leavenworth, Kan., and Madison Barracks, N. Y., until he was retired with the rank of colonel on Dec. 15, 1870. After retirement, he was deputy governor of the Soldiers' Home in Washington, D. C., for two years. He was further distinguished by being awarded the Congressional Medal of Honor for gallantry at Trevilian Station, Va., in 1864. During the latter part of his life, Rodenbough wrote extensively. In 1873 he published: *From Everglade to Cañon with the Second Dragoons,* a full and interesting history of the 2nd Cavalry; *Afghanistan and the Anglo-Russian Dispute* (1885); *Uncle Sam's Medal of Honor* (1886); and a genealogical work, *Autumn Leaves from Family Trees* (1892). He also contributed articles to numerous periodicals. He acted for a time as general eastern agent for the Pullman Company after 1872, was associate editor of the *Army and Navy Journal,* 1876–77, corresponding secretary of the Society of the Army of the Potomac, 1878, secretary and editor for the *Army and Navy Journal,* 1878–90, secretary of the Military Service Institute from 1878 to 1891 and from 1902 until his death, and chief of the Bureau of Elections, New York City, from 1890 to 1901. His wife, Elinor Frances Foster, to whom he had been married on Sept. 1, 1868, survived him at his death in New York City.

[For genealogical material see Rodenbough's *Autumn Leaves from Family Trees,* and for verification of his military record *From Everglade to Cañon.* See also, *Who's Who in America,* 1912–13; the *Army and Navy Jour.,* Dec. 21, 1912; and the *N. Y. Times,* Dec. 20, 1912.]   D. Y.

RODES, ROBERT EMMETT (Mar. 29, 1829–Sept. 19, 1864), Confederate soldier, was born at Lynchburg, Va., the son of Gen. David Rodes, Virginia State Militia, and Martha (Yancey) Rodes. His ancestors had been established in Virginia in the seventeenth century. He entered the Virginia Military Institute in 1845, was graduated with distinction in 1848, and was appointed an assistant professor. He aspired to a professorship in 1850, but Thomas Jonathan Jackson [*q.v.*] was chosen instead, and Rodes resigned in 1851 to adopt the profession of civil engineering in which he had acquired some experience. He became chief engineer of the N. E. and S. W. Alabama Railroad in 1858. Late in 1860 he was elected professor of civil engineering and applied mechanics in the Virginia Military Institute, but the Civil War began before he could assume his chair.

He volunteered at the first clash of arms, and in May 1861 became colonel of the 5th Alabama Infantry. In the Manassas campaign his military ability attracted notice, and he was commissioned brigadier-general the following October. He commanded a brigade with conspicuous gallantry at the battle of Fair Oaks, Va., in which he was badly wounded. He resumed his command to take part in the battle of Gaines's Mill before his wound was healed and a long illness followed. He rejoined his brigade in the fall of 1862 and distinguished himself by prolonged and stubborn resistance to McClellan's passage of South Mountain on Sept. 14. Three days later, at Antietam, he shared the desperate fighting at the "Bloody Lane." Upon the transfer of Daniel Harvey Hill [q.v.] to North Carolina in January 1863, Rodes was given command of Hill's division. On May 2, Rodes, with "Stonewall" Jackson riding at his side, led the van of the flank march at Chancellorsville, and with his division launched the surprise attack against the rear of the Union army which gave Lee the victory on that field. Jackson, mortally wounded, asked promotion for the man whose hopes he had thwarted twelve years before. Five days later Rodes was appointed major-general.

In June his division led the advance into Pennsylvania and at Gettysburg, on July 1, he delivered a decisive attack in a critical moment and drove the Union forces back through the town. General Lee complimented him on the battlefield for this action and on the retreat Rodes's division formed the rear-guard. In the battle of the Wilderness on May 5, 1864, Rodes made the counter-attack south of the Plank Road which stopped Warren's victorious advance. At Spotsylvania he directed the defense of the salient, and by his coolness and skill prevented penetration of Lee's position. His division was sent to the Shenandoah Valley in June as a part of Early's command, and participated in the battle of Monocacy and the raid on Washington. On July 18, Rodes defeated a Federal force at Castleman's Ferry, Va., and helped to defeat Crook at Kernstown six days later. Sheridan, taking advantage of a temporary dispersion of Early's army, attacked Winchester on Sept. 19, 1864. Rodes arrived as the Confederate line was breaking, and launched a charge before which Sheridan's attack recoiled. Rodes fell mortally wounded and died on the battlefield, but his timely action saved the army from annihilation. He was known as a fighting general and as a battle leader he had few superiors in either army. On Sept. 10, 1857, he was married to Virginia Hortense Woodruff, at Tuscaloosa, Ala. She and their two children survived him.

[S. R. Patterson, *A Short Hist. and Geneal. of the English Family Rodes* (1929); sketch by Maj. Green Peyton in C. D. Walker, *Memorial, Va. Mil. Institute* (1875); J. C. Wise, *The Mil. Hist. of the Va. Mil. Institute* (1915); J. B. Gordon, *Reminiscences of the Civil War* (1904); G. E. Pond, *The Shenandoah Valley in 1864* (1883); *Battles and Leaders of the Civil War* (4 vols., 1887–88); *War of the Rebellion: Official Records (Army)*, 1 ser., vols. II, V, X, XVII, and XXV. part 1.]
T. F. M.

RODGERS, CHRISTOPHER RAYMOND PERRY (Nov. 14, 1819–Jan. 8, 1892), naval officer, was born at Brooklyn, N. Y., the son of George Washington Rodgers, 1787–1832 [q.v.], and Ann Maria (Perry) Rodgers. On Oct. 5, 1833, he was appointed a midshipman from New London, Conn. After a brief period at the New York naval school he went to sea in the *Brandywine* of the Pacific Squadron. A brief term of duty at the New York navy yard, 1836–37, was followed by a cruise on the *Fairfield* of the Brazil Squadron. In the Seminole War, 1839–42, he served on board the *Flirt, Wave,* and *Phoenix,* commanding the last-named vessel. He was promoted passed midshipman from July 8, 1839, and lieutenant from Sept. 4, 1844. From 1842 to 1843 he was with the *Saratoga* of the African Squadron, and from 1843 to 1845 with the *Cumberland* of the Mediterranean Squadron, serving on both ships as acting master. After a year with the Coast Survey, he participated in the Mexican War and was present at the reduction of Vera Cruz and the capture of Tabasco and Túxpan. Returning to the Coast Survey, he remained there more than three years, then transferring to the *Congress* of the Brazil Squadron. In 1852–53 he was with the *Constitution,* flagship of the African Squadron; in 1856–58, with the Coast Survey; and in 1858–59, with the *Wabash* of the Mediterranean Squadron. His next duty was performed at the Naval Academy where he served as commandant of midshipmen from 1860 to 1861. He drew sharp distinctions between the four classes and made of the first or senior class a quasi-aristocracy. This action left a mark on the school that has never been effaced (Benjamin, *post,* p. 219). At the outbreak of the Civil War he took an active part in removing the Academy to Newport, R. I., and tried to arouse the disaffected midshipmen from the South to a loyalty to the Union.

On Sept. 19, 1861, he was detached from the Academy and ordered to take command of the *Wabash* of the fleet of Admiral Du Pont. In the battle of Port Royal his vessel served as the flagship. He was promoted to the rank of commander from Nov. 15. He was employed in reducing the coast towns of Georgia and Florida early in 1862 and received himself the surrender of St. Augustine. He cooperated with the army in the bombardment of Fort Pulaski, going into the trenches and participating in the surrender. In August he was made fleet captain of the South Atlantic Blockading Squadron, and served on board the flagship *New Ironsides* during the battle of Charleston, Apr. 7, 1863. In a report of the battle Du Pont referred to the "invaluable assistance" rendered by Rodgers and declared that for "over eighteen months in this war this officer has been afloat with me, and, in my opinion, no language could overstate his services to his country, to this fleet, and to myself as its commander in chief" (*Official Records, post,* XIV, 8). On July 6 he was relieved from duty with the squadron. In the following October he was ordered to the *Iroquois* and until the end of the war cruised in European, South American, and East Indian waters, searching for the *Shenandoah* and other Confederate privateers. At Saint-Nazaire and Bordeaux, he went ashore in civilian clothes and inspected some ships being built by the French for the Confederates.

Rodgers was promoted captain from July 25, 1866, commodore from Aug. 28, 1870, and rear admiral from June 14, 1874. After three years at the Norfolk navy yard, he commanded the *Franklin* of the European Squadron, 1868–70, being detached therefrom for special duty in Europe. From 1871 to 1874 he was chief of the Bureau of Yards and Docks, and for part of this period acting chief of the Bureau of Equipment. From 1874 to 1878 he served as superintendent of the Naval Academy, the first in that office to have had preliminary service there as an officer. He cherished high ideals, and attempted to institute reforms, but with only a measure of success. He established elective courses in advanced studies, enforced the rules against hazing, elaborated the punishment for misdemeanors, and prohibited smoking. His unfriendly critics accused him of trying to make a "galaxy of Sidneys and Bayards" out of a collection of school boys of divers origins (Benjamin, *post,* p. 302).

He performed his last active service as commander in chief of the Pacific Squadron from 1878 to 1880. After a few months as superintendent of the Academy he was retired from Nov. 14. In 1875–78 and 1882–83, he served as president of the United States Naval Institute, and in 1884 as president of the International Meridian Conference. He contributed an article entitled "Dupont's Attack at Charleston," to *Battles and Leaders of the Civil War* (1887–88). He died in Washington and was buried at Annapolis, beside his wife Jane (Slidell) Rodgers, to whom he had been married on July 7, 1845. Of the five children born to them, two entered the navy and rose to the rank of rear

admiral. Rodgers was of distinguished appearance, and was devoutly religious, being a member of the Episcopalian church.

[Record of Officers, Bur. of Navigation, 1832–93; *Navy Register,* 1834–81; *War of the Rebellion: Official Records (Navy),* 1 ser., vols, III, XII–XIV; Park Benjamin, *The U. S. Naval Acad.* (1900); obit. in *Evening Star* (Wash., D. C.), Jan. 9, 1892.]   C. O. P.

RODGERS, GEORGE WASHINGTON (Feb. 22, 1787–May 21, 1832), naval officer, was born in Cecil County, Md., on the Susquehanna River, opposite Havre de Grace, the youngest of the eight children of John and Elizabeth (Reynolds) Rodgers. On Apr. 2, 1804, he entered the navy as a midshipman, a warrant having been procured for him by his brother, John Rodgers, 1773–1838 [*q.v.*]. In 1804–06 he cruised in the Mediterranean on board the *President.* Returning home in the *Essex,* he was again sent to the Mediterranean within a few months. In January 1809, he was ordered to the *Vixen* as sailing master and a month or two later to the *United States* as acting lieutenant. He was promoted lieutenant from Apr. 24, 1810. In the following year he joined the *Wasp* and was serving on board her at the outbreak of the War of 1812. He participated in the successful engagement of that vessel with the *Frolic,* and was commended by his commodore in the official account of the victory. When both vessels were captured later by a superior force, he was made prisoner, taken to Bermuda, and sent thence in a cartel to New York. Congress recognized his services in the engagement with the *Frolic* by voting him a silver medal; and his native state rewarded him by giving him a sword. From Dec. 20, 1812, to Apr. 25, 1814, he was attached to the *Macedonian,* kept in port at New London, Conn., because of the British blockade. When the war came to an end he was serving on board the *Mohawk* at Sacketts Harbor, N. Y.

On Mar. 10, 1815, Rodgers was ordered to command the *Fire Fly,* one of the smaller vessels assembled at New York by Commodore Stephen Decatur for service in the American war with Algiers. Soon after sailing she encountered a heavy gale, sprang her masts, and was compelled to return to port. She joined the Mediterranean Squadron at Cartagena, Spain, too late to take part in the war with Algiers.

Promoted master commandant from Apr. 27, 1816, Rodgers served as commander of the *Peacock* of the Mediterranean Squadron from 1816 until 1819. In the latter year he was ordered to the New York navy yard where he remained until 1825, part of the time acting as commandant. He was promoted captain from Mar. 3,

1825. For several years he was relatively inactive, waiting orders or serving on the Naval Board of Examiners. On Nov. 26, 1831, he was chosen to command the Brazil Squadron, with the *Warren* as his flagship. The seizure of American sealing vessels at the Falkland Islands and the political disturbances on the mainland made his duties somewhat arduous. Arriving at Rio de Janeiro on Mar. 13, 1832, he proceeded to Montevideo, and thence to Buenos Aires, where, after a brief illness, he died of visceral inflammation, endemic to South American ports. His full habit of body and close confinement on shipboard made him an easy prey to the disease. He was buried in the Protestant cemetery at Buenos Aires. In 1850 his remains were disinterred, conveyed to New York on board the U. S. S. *Lexington,* and reinterred at New London, Conn., where he had made his home. He had been married on July 5, 1815, to Ann Maria Perry, a daughter of Christopher Raymond Perry, and a sister of Oliver Hazard and Matthew Calbraith Perry [*qq.v.*]. Two of his sons, George Washington Rodgers, and Christopher Raymond Perry Rodgers [*qq.v.*], distinguished themselves in the navy. A third son, Alexander P. Rodgers, was killed in 1847 at the storming of Chapultepec, Mexico. Several of his grandsons reached the highest naval rank.

[Record of Officers, Bur. of Navigation, 1804–40; Navy Dept. Archives, Letters to Officers, Ships of War, 1831–34, Captains' Letters, Mar.–May 1832; *Navy Register,* 1815–32; C. O. Paullin, *Commodore John Rodgers* (1910); Niles' *Weekly Register,* Nov. 28, Dec. 5, 1812.]   C. O. P.

RODGERS, GEORGE WASHINGTON (Oct. 30, 1822–Aug. 17, 1863), naval officer, was born in Brooklyn, N. Y., the son of George Washington Rodgers [*q.v.*], and Ann Maria (Perry) Rodgers. He entered the navy as midshipman on Apr. 30, 1836, and saw his first sea service in the West Indies on board the *Boston* and *Constellation.* From 1839 to 1841 he served on the *Brandywine* in the Mediterranean. Soon after returning home he entered the Philadelphia naval school, and was promoted to the rank of passed midshipman from July 1, 1842. In 1844–45 he was with the *Saratoga* of the African Squadron. In the Mexican War he served in the Gulf of Mexico, first on board the *Colonel Harney* and later the *John Adams.* During 1848–50 he was with the Coast Survey, part of the time as acting master of the steamer *Bibb.* His first sea duty after his promotion to a lieutenancy on June 4, 1850, was with the *Germantown* of the Home and African Squadrons. After shore duty at the New York naval rendezvous from 1853 to 1856, he sought more active service, and

was ordered to the *Falmouth* of the Brazil Squadron. Detached from her in 1859, he was engaged in ordnance duties for more than a year at the New York navy yard. In September 1860 he took command of the *Constitution,* the school ship at the Naval Academy. Early in the war he conveyed the midshipmen to Newport, R. I., where the Academy had been moved and saved the *Constitution* from falling into the hands of some secessionists who had resolved that she should be the first captured ship of war to fly the Confederate flag. For a brief period at the Boston navy yard he instructed officers in ordnance duty and received the commendation of the commandant for his efficiency, zeal and ability.

On Sept. 22, 1861, he succeeded his brother, Christopher Raymond Perry Rodgers [*q.v.*], as commandant of midshipmen. Desiring more active duty, he was placed in command of the *Tioga* of the James River Flotilla on May 16, 1862. With the West India Squadron she was later engaged in searching for Confederate commerce destroyers. Rodgers was promoted commander from July 16, 1862. His first command in his new rank was the *Catskill,* one of the ships of the fleet of Admiral Du Pont off the South Atlantic coast. He arrived on the station on Mar. 5, 1863, in time to take part in the attack on Charleston a month later, and gave a good account of himself, approaching within six hundred yards of Fort Sumter. On July 19 Rear Admiral Dahlgren appointed him chief of staff. When Dahlgren attacked Charleston again on Aug. 17, Rodgers resumed command of the *Catskill,* since that station offered greater opportunity for service. He placed his vessel within a very short distance of the enemy, having resolved that no other commander should be nearer. At the beginning of hostilities a heavy shot struck the pilot house and Rodgers was killed instantly. Dahlgren described him as "brave, intelligent, and highly capable, devoted to his duty and to the flag under which he passed his life" (*Official Records, post,* XIV, 453). Unworldly and devoutly religious, Rodgers was a man of gentle manners and shy, retiring nature. On Aug. 21, 1842, he was married to Kate Margaret Lane. He left no children.

[Record of Officers, Bur. of Navigation, 1832–63; *Navy Register,* 1837–63; *War of the Rebellion: Official Records* (Navy), 1 ser., vols. I, VI, VII, XIII, XIV; C. B. Perry, *The Perrys of R. I.* (1913); *Portrait Monthly,* Nov. 1863; *Army and Navy Jour.,* Aug. 29, 1863; *Daily Natl. Intelligencer* (Wash., D. C.), Aug. 25, 1863.]   C. O. P.

RODGERS, JOHN (Aug. 5, 1727–May 7, 1811), Presbyterian clergyman, was born in Boston, Mass., the son of Thomas and Elizabeth (Baxter) Rodgers, who six years before had emigrated to that city from Londonderry, Ireland. In 1728 the family moved to Philadelphia. During George Whitefield's visit there in 1739, young Rodgers held a lantern for him as he spoke to a crowd of people from the courthouse steps. So absorbed in the speaker's words did the boy become that he dropped the lantern. Whitefield's effect on Rodgers was lasting and finally led to his entering the ministry and being a stanch supporter of New Side views. His education was received, first, under a Mr. Stevenson, an Irishman who had established a grammar school in Philadelphia; next, at the school in Neshaminy, Pa., conducted by Rev. John Roan; and finally, under Rev. Samuel Blair [q.v.], at Fagg's Manor, Chester County, with whom he began the study of theology. On Oct. 14, 1747, he was licensed by the Presbytery of New Castle.

His first assignment was to accompany Rev. Samuel Davies [q.v.] to Virginia and assist him in evangelistic work. When, however, he presented himself to the general court at Williamsburg to qualify for a license to preach in the dominion, the court refused to consider his credentials, and he crossed over to Somerset County, Md., where he labored during the summer of 1748. In the autumn he accepted a call to St. George's, New Castle County, Del., where on Mar. 16, 1749, he was ordained and installed. His sixteen years' service here was marked by extraordinary success. He was a zealous pastor and preached with moving effect. His church, though more than once enlarged, was invariably filled, including aisles, doors, and windows. In 1765 he was elected a trustee of the College of New Jersey, to the duties of which office he gave faithful attention for more than twenty years. His wife, Elizabeth, daughter of Peter Bayard of Cecil County, Md., whom he married Sept. 19, 1752, died in January 1763, having borne him four children, and on Aug. 15, 1764, he married Mary (Antrobus) Grant, widow of William Grant, a Philadelphia merchant; by this marriage he had one child.

His pastorate in St. George's was followed by one in New York, covering a period of forty-five years (1765–1810). Here his congregation so increased that it was soon necessary to build a second church, the congregation utilizing both, but remaining one ecclesiastical body. He was an active member of the convention created in 1766 by non-episcopal churches to oppose an American episcopate. Driven from New York during the Revolution, he resided chiefly in Connecticut towns and ministered to several churches. From April to November 1776, however, he was chaplain in General Heath's brigade, and in April 1777 was elected chaplain of the Convention of the State of New York, later serving the Council of Safety in the same capacity. After the war he gathered his congregation together and restored its places of worship, which had been partly destroyed by the British. When the first legislature of the state convened he was its chaplain. He was a member of the committee that revised the standards of the Presbyterian Church in 1788 and was moderator of the first General Assembly under the new arrangement, held in Philadelphia the following year. When the legislature in 1784 created the Board of Regents of the University of the State of New York, he was chosen vice-chancellor and served till his death.

Among the leaders of Presbyterianism during the late colonial period and the early days of the republic, Rodgers exerted a calm, wise influence. He was a friend of Gilbert Tennent, Samuel Finley, and Alexander MacWhorter [qq.v.], and also of John Witherspoon [q.v.], whose funeral sermon he preached. On the recommendation of Franklin, prompted by George Whitefield, the University of Edinburgh conferred upon him in 1768 the degree of D.D. His prudence and practical wisdom were widely recognized; Washington consulted him on several occasions during the Revolution. In him evangelistic zeal and tolerance were united in a rather rare degree. He refused to denounce the errors of others, saying, "let us out-preach them, out-pray them, and out-live them, and we need not fear" (Miller, post, p. 329). As he walked the streets, a middle-sized, thick-set person, grave and sedate, always punctiliously dressed, and wearing a large white wig, he was the personification of clerical solidity and dignity. Several of his sermons survive in published form. His death occurred in New York in his eighty-fourth year.

[A Report of the Commissioners of the City of Boston Containing Boston Births, 1700–1800 (1894); Samuel Miller, Memoirs of the Rev. John Rodgers, D.D. (1813); W. B. Sprague, Annals Am. Pulpit, vol. III (1858); Richard Webster, A Hist. of the Presbyt. Ch. in America (1857); S. D. Alexander, The Presbytery of N. Y., 1738 to 1888 (n.d.); N. Y. Evening Post, May 8, 10, 1811.]   H. E. S.

RODGERS, JOHN (1773–Aug. 1, 1838), naval officer, was born on a farm two miles from Lower Susquehanna Ferry (now Havre de Grace), Md., the son of Col. John and Elizabeth (Reynolds) Rodgers. The father, founder of one of the most noted of American naval families, was born in Scotland, and came to America from Glasgow and settled in Harford County, Md., about 1760. He was an officer of the Maryland militia during the Revolution. The mother was the daughter of a Presbyterian clergyman of Delaware. John was one of the first of eight children. He acquired the rudiments of an education at the village school and through his reading of books about the sea received an impress that determined his career. At an early age his father bound him out as an apprentice to a Baltimore shipmaster trading with French and West Indian ports. He was a first mate before he was eighteen, and, after two years of service in that grade was made master of the ship *Jane,* sailing out of Baltimore for European ports.

After spending eleven years in the merchant service, Rodgers found in the naval war with France an opportunity for a wider career. On Mar. 8, 1798, President Adams appointed him second lieutenant on board the *Constellation* under Thomas Truxtun [*q.v.*], then fitting for sea at Baltimore, and when the first lieutenant resigned soon afterwards Rodgers succeeded him, becoming executive officer of the ship. He participated in the capture of the frigate *Insurgente,* and received with the other officers of the *Constellation* the thanks of the secretary of the navy and the president. In further recognition of his services he was promoted captain on Mar. 5, 1799, the first lieutenant in the navy under the Constitution to be advanced to this rank. After a cruise in command of the *Insurgente,* he was transferred to the *Maryland* and again sailed in the West Indies, part of the time as the senior officer on the Surinam station. At the close of the war he had the honor to be selected to convey John Dawson, the bearer of the new French-American treaty, to France.

Under the peace establishment of 1801 it was for a time uncertain whether Rodgers should be retained in the navy. In the fall of that year he returned to the merchant service and sailed for Santo Domingo as master of the *Nelly,* with a cargo of American products. Since the islanders were at war with France the cruise was not without stirring incidents. On the night of the burning of Cape Français, Rodgers was on shore leading a band of friendly negroes in their work of rescue and succor. The American consul, Tobias Lear [*q.v.*], bore witness that the young captain saved many lives and much property from destruction. Later he was arrested and imprisoned by the French general, LeClerc, who confiscated his property and finally ordered him under penalty to leave the island. He took passage on the *Pomona* and arrived at Baltimore in May 1802.

He was recalled to the navy, and, with the exception of a brief visit to America, was in the Mediterranean from the fall of 1802 until the summer of 1806. He participated in the wars with the Barbary corsairs, playing a part exceeded in importance by that of no other naval officer. As senior officer under Commodores Morris and Barron he served as their chief of staff and as commander of the blockading fleet off Tripoli. Two of the largest cruisers of the Tripolitan navy and several smaller craft surrendered to him. President Jefferson in a message to Congress referred to his services in most complimentary terms. He was commander in chief of the squadron three times, the first time at the age of thirty, the office entitling him to the designation of "commodore." In the negotiations for a treaty with Morocco he shared the honors with Commodore Preble, during the peace negotiations with Tripoli he commanded the squadron, and in an expedition to Tunis, he was the most prominent figure and the commanding officer.

As a result of a war-scare growing out of the affair of the *Chesapeake* and *Leopard,* he was placed in command of the New York flotilla and naval station in July 1807. This was the most important office at the disposal of the navy department, and in the following year the duty of enforcing the Embargo in the waters between the Delaware and the Passamaquoddy Bay fell to him. When President Madison decided to follow a more active naval policy in 1810, Rodgers received orders to command the "northern division of ships for the protection of the American coast," with the frigate *President,* 44 guns, as his flagship (Paullin, *post,* p. 210). Cruising under these orders, on May 16, 1811, he engaged off Cape Henry the British naval sloop *Little Belt,* 20 guns, for some fifteen minutes and inflicted on her a loss of thirteen men killed and nineteen wounded. His conduct was cordially approved by the secretary of the navy and the president and he was hailed and toasted as a popular hero. His request for a court of inquiry was at first refused by the federal government but it was later granted when it appeared that there were discrepancies between his account of the fight and that of the British captain. The court considered the details of the fight at great length and made a report confirming Rodgers' account in every essential particular.

In the War of 1812 Rodgers was the ranking officer in active service. Three days after the declaration of war he went to sea with a fleet of five vessels and two days later sighted the British frigate *Belvidera.* A long chase ensued and in a running fight the *Belvidera* escaped after a small loss on both sides. A gun of the *President* burst, fracturing one leg of the commodore, who, supported by his men, continued to direct the fight. The cruise was extended as far eastward as the coast of Spain and ended at Boston after the capture of eight merchantmen. Rodgers made three additional cruises, and during one captured the British schooner *High Flyer*. While his services were not as brilliant as those of some of his juniors in rank who fought the famous sea duels of the war, they were with a few exceptions the more useful. He understood best the principles of naval strategy (A. T. Mahan, *From Sail to Steam*, 1906, 1907, pp. 5–6). In the spring of 1814 Rodgers was placed in command of the Delaware flotilla and the *Guerrière*, then under construction at Philadelphia. When the British made their expedition against Washington he was ordered to the capital with a detachment of sailors and marines, and arrived in time to harass the enemy's squadron in its retreat down the Potomac. When Baltimore was threatened later he came to its defense with his detachment, part of which manned a small fleet in the Patapsco River and the rest some land batteries on Hampstead Hill.

In February 1815, Rodgers was chosen by President Madison to head the newly created Board of Navy Commissioners, authorized by Congress to administer the naval material. The commissioners ranked next to the members of the cabinet in the administrative hierarchy of Washington, and were always chosen from the most distinguished officers of the navy. In 1821 Rodgers became the senior officer of the navy, and in 1823 he served for a time as secretary of the navy *ad interim*. His service in Washington was interrupted in 1825–27 by a tour of duty in the Mediterranean, where once again he commanded the American Squadron, this time with the 74-gun ship *North Carolina* as his flagship. This duty, which proved to be his last sea service, was marked by an interview with the Turkish minister of marine respecting a treaty with Turkey, by a visit to the capital of the Greek revolutionists, and by an improvement in the discipline of the squadron.

On May 1, 1837, Rodgers resigned his commissionership, owing to declining health, partly the result of an attack of cholera. He died at the Naval Asylum in Philadelphia and is buried in the Congressional Cemetery, Washington, D. C. On Oct. 21, 1806, he had been married to Minerva Denison at Sion Hill, Md. She was a descendant of Capt. George Denison, called the "Miles Standish of Connecticut." After 1815,

they made their home in Washington, D. C. Their last residence, an historic one in the annals of the capital, was built on the site of the present Belasco Theatre. They had eleven children, one of the sons, John Rodgers [*q.v.*], reaching the rank of rear admiral. Many of their descendants entered the army or the navy. A daughter, Louisa, married Montgomery Cunningham Meigs [*q.v.*]. Rodgers was of middle height, solid, compact, well-proportioned. He was grave in demeanor, rather bluff, independent and a stickler for the forms of his profession.

[This sketch has been prepared from C. O. Paullin, *Commodore John Rodgers* (1910), in which is a bibliography of sources, pp. 405–10. A naval order, announcing Rodgers' death, was published in *Poulson's Am. Daily Advertiser* (Phila., Pa.), Aug. 3, 1838.]

C. O. P.

RODGERS, JOHN (Aug. 8, 1812–May 5, 1882), naval officer, was born at Sion Hill near Havre de Grace, Md., the fourth child of John Rodgers [*q.v.*] and Minerva (Denison) Rodgers. On Apr. 18, 1828, he was appointed midshipman and saw his first active service on board the *Constellation* and the *Concord* in the Mediterranean. On his return he entered the Norfolk naval school preliminary to an examination for passed midshipman, to which he was promoted in 1834. After a year at the University of Virginia where he was engaged in general study, he was ordered to the Coast Survey and then to the *Dolphin* of the Brazil Squadron. At the end of three years of duty with that squadron, he was employed in surveying the coast of Florida and in cooperating with the army in the Seminole War, first as commander of the *Wave* and later of the *Jefferson*. He was promoted lieutenant from Jan. 28, 1840. From 1842 to 1844 he commanded the *Boxer* of the Home Squadron. In the latter year he was sent to Pittsburgh, Pa., to aid in the construction of the steamer *Alleghany*. He spent the next three years on the coast of Africa and in the Mediterranean. On his return in 1849 he was three years with the Coast Survey, part of the time in command of surveying vessels.

On Oct. 12, 1852, he was ordered to duty in connection with the North Pacific Exploring and Surveying Expedition, which lasted, with a few brief interruptions, until the Civil War. He was second in rank, commanding the *John Hancock*, but succeeded Cadwalader Ringgold [*q.v.*] in command of the expedition in the summer of 1854. At the Liu-Kiu Islands he landed a detachment and forced the natives to guarantee the performance of their obligations under their treaty with the United States. After surveying the Liu-Kius, Ladrones, and other islands, the coast of Japan, and the sea of Okhotsk, he sailed into the Arctic Ocean where he explored unknown regions and obtained information that corrected the Admiralty charts. He next surveyed the Hawaiian and Society islands. In 1856, he returned to the United States and was placed in charge of an office in Washington engaged in preparing for publication the results of the expedition. The reports, however, were never published. During his absence he had been promoted commander from Sept. 14, 1855.

On May 16, 1861, Rodgers was ordered to special duty under General McClellan at Cincinnati, Ohio, where he purchased and fitted out three small steamers, the nucleus of the Mississippi Flotilla. On Oct. 17 he was appointed to command the *Flag* of the squadron of Admiral Du Pont. At the battle of Port Royal he acted as aide to Du Pont, who showed his appreciation of his services by allowing him to hoist the "first American flag on the rebellious soil of South Carolina" (*Official Records, post,* XII, 265). Later he commanded a small fleet of gunboats on the Savannah River. On Apr. 21, 1862, he was ordered to command the *Galena,* the flagship of a small fleet operating on the James River. At Drewry's Bluff he encountered obstructions in the river and an action lasting three hours took place, the brunt of which was borne by the *Galena* at close range, with a loss of twenty-four men. He was promoted to the rank of captain from July 16 and in November was transferred from the *Galena* to the *Weehawken,* one of the new monitors. In the attack on Fort Sumter on Apr. 7, 1863, the *Weehawken* headed the line of ships and for two hours received the concentrated fire of the Confederate batteries, being struck fifty-three times. On June 17 in Wassaw Sound, Ga., she encountered the *Atlanta,* reputed to be the strongest of the Confederate ironclads, and received her surrender after an engagement of fifteen minutes. In recognition of Rodgers' services President Lincoln recommended to Congress that he be thanked for his exhibition of "eminent skill and gallantry" in the fight with the *Atlanta,* and for his "zeal, bravery, and general good conduct" shown on other occasions (*Official Records, post,* XIV, 184). Congress complied with the President's recommendation, promoting him to the rank of commodore from the date of the battle. In July he was ordered to command the *Canonicus* and in November was transferred to the *Dictator,* in which he saw his last active service in the war.

In September 1865, Rodgers was placed in command of a small fleet, with the *Vanderbilt* as his flagship, and proceeded with it to the Pacific.

On his arrival at Valparaiso early in the following year he found a Spanish squadron threatening to bombard the city. He proposed to join with the English, French, Prussians, and Italians in an armed intervention, but when they declined he refused to act alone. He did what he could, however, to protect peacefully American and neutral interests. He was commandant of the Boston navy yard from 1866 to 1869. He commanded the Asiatic Squadron as a rear admiral, 1870–72, his promotion to that rank being dated Dec. 31, 1869. In 1871 he conveyed to Korea, on board the flagship *Colorado,* Frederick Ferdinand Low [*q.v.*], the American minister to China, who was authorized to negotiate a treaty with the Koreans. After anchoring his fleet of five vessels in the Salée or Han River he sent up the river a surveying party, which was attacked by the Koreans and suffered a loss of two men wounded. Rodgers landed a detachment which destroyed five forts, killed two hundred and forty Koreans, and captured about 500 pieces of artillery, with a loss of three men killed and ten wounded. No treaty was concluded.

Rodgers was president of the Naval Examining and Retiring boards, 1872–73; commandant of the Mare Island navy yard, 1873–77; superintendent of the Naval Observatory, 1877–82; and chairman of the Light-House Board, 1878–82. He secured for the observatory its present site and made certain its reconstruction on more ample lines. In the last years of his life his eminence led to his selection as president of the United States Naval Institute, of the Transit of Venus Commission, of the First Naval Advisory Board, from which dates the new navy, and of the *Jeannette* Relief Board.

Until the approach of his last illness, Rodgers preserved a remarkable vigor of mind and body, never losing his faculty for initiative. Independent and straightforward, he was open to argument in preliminary discussion, but was persistent and tenacious in action. He was a charter member of the National Academy of Sciences. At the time of his death in Washington, D. C., he was the senior rear admiral on the active list. On Nov. 27, 1857, he was married to Ann Elizabeth Hodge of Washington, D. C., by whom he had three children.

[Record of Officers, Bur. of Navigation, 1825–88; *War of the Rebellion: Official Records* (*Navy*), 1 ser., vols. VII, VIII, XII, XIV, XXII; Asaph Hall, "Biog. Memoir of John Rodgers," *Nat. Acad. of Sci., Biog. Memoirs,* vol. VI (1909); J. R. Soley, "Rear-Admiral John Rodgers," *Proc. of the U. S. Naval Institute,* vol. VIII, no. 2, 1882; *Ann. Report of the Sec. of the Navy* (1871); Wilhelm Heine, *Die Expedition in die Seen von China, Japan und Ochotsk* (1858); *The Am. Ann. Encyc. and Register, 1866,* vol. VI (1867); *Evening Star* (Wash., D. C.), May 6, 1882.]   C. O. P.

RODGERS, JOHN (Jan. 15, 1881–Aug. 27, 1926), naval officer, aviator, son of Rear Admiral John Augustus and Elizabeth (Chambers) Rodgers, was born in Washington, D. C., although the Rodgers' home was at Havre de Grace, Md. He was of a family long distinguished in the annals of the United States Navy, being a great-grandson of John Rodgers [1773–1838, *q.v.*], who was one of the first of the name to attain renown as an American naval officer. Sarah (Perry) Rodgers, daughter of Matthew C. Perry [*q.v.*], was his grandmother. John attended the Lawrenceville School, Lawrenceville, N. J., served on the *Columbia* during the Spanish-American War, and in 1899 entered the Naval Academy, from which he graduated in 1903. During the ensuing years he was promoted through the various grades and was made commander, Nov. 4, 1920. Becoming interested in aviation, he attended the Wright Flying School, Dayton, Ohio, and was the second naval officer to be licensed as an aviator. During the World War he was in the submarine service and on North Sea mine barrage duty. Returning later to aviation, from 1922 to 1925 he was commander of the Naval Air Station, Pearl Harbor, Hawaii. In the latter part of 1925, the resourcefulness and heroism he displayed as commander of the San Francisco-Hawaiian flight brought him wide acclaim. On Aug. 31, two navy seaplanes took off from near San Francisco. One of these was forced down after covering about 300 miles. The second, which contained Commander Rodgers and four others, was obliged to descend on Sept. 1, when 400 miles from its destination, because of lack of fuel. For nine days it was tossed about on the deep, its occupants never losing courage. They subsisted on the scanty emergency rations which they had with them, and on sea water which Rodgers distilled in a still given him by his mother. From the fabric of a wing he also fashioned a sail. On Sept. 10 they sighted Kauai and were picked up by a submarine when about fifteen miles from that island. The following day Rodgers wrote a concise and vivid account of the adventure, which was published in United States papers. In recognition of his sterling qualities as an aviator and his ability as a seaman and navigator, he was appointed assistant chief of the Bureau of Naval Aeronautics. Office work at Washington was not suited to his taste or temperament, however, and on Aug. 16, 1926, he was placed in command of a new scouting seaplane squadron, created for experimental purposes, at San Diego, Cal. Eleven days later he started in a land plane from the Naval Air Station, Washington, for Philadelphia, where he was to inspect some new planes at the aircraft factory of the Navy Yard. When nearing the city, his plane fell from a comparatively low height into the shallow water of the Delaware, and Rodgers was pinioned in the cockpit. After an hour of intense suffering he was released and taken to the Naval Hospital, where he died. At the time of his death he was listed for promotion to captain. His wife, from whom he was divorced in 1924, was Ethel Greiner Rodgers.

[*N.Y.Times,* Sept. 11, 12, 1925, Aug. 28, 1926; *Washington Post* and *Evening Star* (Washington), Aug. 28, 1926; *Army and Navy Register,* Sept. 4, 1926.] H. E. S.

RODMAN, ISAAC PEACE (Aug. 18, 1822–Sept. 30, 1862), legislator, Union soldier, was born at South Kingstown, R. I., the eldest of sixteen children of Samuel Rodman and his first wife, Mary Peckham, both of pre-Revolutionary ancestry. His father, a prosperous merchant, was a descendant of Thomas Rodman, a Quaker physician, who settled in Newport, R. I., in 1675. Rodman received a common-school education, and at an early age entered business as an associate of his father. For several years he was president of the town council of South Kingstown and director of the Wakefield Bank. He entered state politics, serving in both branches of the legislature. On June 17, 1847, he was married to Sally Lyman Arnold, the daughter of Gov. Lemuel N. Arnold. They had seven children.

When the Civil War was imminent, Rodman, true to his religious training, was strongly on the side of peace, but when war was declared, he was a member of the state Senate and strongly supported the government, giving proof of his loyalty by accepting a captaincy in the 2nd Rhode Island Infantry on June 6, 1861. For his gallantry at the first battle of Bull Run he was later commissioned lieutenant-colonel. He was assigned to command the 4th Rhode Island Volunteers and was commissioned colonel on Oct. 30. He spent the winter of 1861–62 at Alexandria, Va., training his regiment. In the early spring of 1862 Rodman joined Burnside in North Carolina, his regiment being in General Parke's 3rd Brigade, and took a distinguished part in the capture of Roanoke Island on Feb. 8, 1862. At this battle his troops being the only ones wearing blue overcoats, were mistaken by the enemy for regulars, and consequently received the heaviest fire. Rodman himself believed this to be his hottest engagement. At the battle of New Bern on Mar. 14, at his own suggestion, he was permitted to charge a weak point in the enemy trenches with the bayonet. His regiment pierced the defenses, captured cannon and colors, and turned the tide of battle. Burnside gave him full credit for his perspicacity and bravery, and for this and his gallantry at the capture of Fort Macon in April he was advanced to the rank of brigadier-general on Apr. 28, 1862.

Rodman's campaigning in the swamps of North Carolina undermined his health, and, ill with typhoid, he was sent home to South Kingstown to recuperate until August. Still weak from fever, he joined Reno's IX Corps for the Maryland Campaign at Frederick and was given the 4th Division. On the morning of Sept. 13 he was ordered to support Pleasanton's cavalry reconnaissance in the mountains, but missed the road and supported other forces. The following day he took active part in the battle of South Mountain and advanced across a ford against heavy hostile fire towards Sharpsburg. At the battle of Antietam on Sept. 17, he was wounded in the chest while leading his troops and died twelve days later. His body was moved to Providence, R. I., where it lay in state in the Old State House, and he was buried at South Kingstown.

[C. H. Jones, *Geneal. of the Rodman Family* (1886); W. W. Rodman, *Notes on Rodman Geneal.* (1887); *War of the Rebellion: Official Records (Army)*, 1 ser., vol. XIX; *Ann. Report of the Adj.-Gen. of the State of R. I.*, 1865, vol. I (1893); Frederick Phisterer, *Statistical Record of the Armies of the U. S.*, (1907), supp. vol. to *Campaigns of the Civil War*; J. R. Bartlett, *Memoirs of R. I. Officers* (1867); *Representative Men and Old Families of R. I.* (1908), vol. II; J. D. Cox, *Reminiscences of the Civil War* (1900), vol. I; *Boston Daily Advertiser,* Oct. 6, 1862.]   D. Y.

RODMAN, THOMAS JACKSON (July 30, 1815–June 7, 1871), soldier, inventor, was born on a farm near Salem, Ind. His father, James Rodman, was a descendant of Thomas Rodman, a Quaker physician, who came to Newport, R. I., from Barbados in 1675. His mother was Elizabeth (Burton) Rodman of Virginia. Although his early educational advantages were quite limited, he entered the United States Military Academy in 1837 and was graduated four years later, seventh in a class of fifty-two members. He was commissioned in the ordnance department, and was promoted through all grades to the rank of captain in 1855, and lieutenant-colonel in 1867. From the first, he demonstrated marked gifts as an inventor, with a decided bent towards mechanics and the details of practical shop construction—his earlier service having been spent with government arsenals at the Alleghany Arsenal, Pittsburgh, Pa., Richmond, Va., and Baton Rouge, La. During the Mexican War, he served as ordnance officer at Camargo and Point Isabel.

After studying closely the heavy ordnance devised by George Bomford [*q.v.*] and used by Americans in the War of 1812, and the improvements in manufacture developed by Henri Joseph Paixhans of the French army and Dahlgren of the American navy, Rodman conceived the original idea of casting guns upon a hollow core, cooling the inner surface by a flow of water so that each successive layer of metal was compressed by the shrinkage of outer layers. He received little or no encouragement from the ordnance department, which rejected the offer of his invention and refused him an opportunity to develop his ideas, so the manufacture of ordnance under Rodman's patented processes was begun by private enterprise. The results demonstrated a marked increase in strength and endurance for heavy ordnance and much greater resistance to gas erosion in the bore.

About the same time, his experiments resulted in the successful manufacture of so-called mammoth and perforated-cake or prismatic gunpowder, both types being used by him in the testing of his large-bore cannon. A detailed description of his work is contained in his admirable book, *Reports of Experiments on the Properties of Metals for Cannon, and the Qualities of Cannon Powder,* published in 1861. His inventions were finally approved and adopted by the government in 1859, about fourteen years after their conception, and his methods were promptly utilized by the governments of Russia, Great Britain, and Prussia. Rodman was placed in command of the arsenal at Watertown, Mass., and during the Civil War, supervised the casting of twelve-inch, fifteen-inch, and twenty-inch smooth-bores, and of twelve-inch rifled guns. He applied his methods to the casting of projectiles, and greatly increased the capacity of his plant for making field and sea-coast artillery carriages. His guns were mounted by Captain Ericsson in the newly constructed monitors of the navy and many military authorities of the period held that Rodman's inventions had a pronounced deterrent effect in staying foreign intervention during a critical period of the Civil War. His personal application and his interest in the success of his labors were so constant at this time that he suffered a severe illness as a result in the summer of 1864, recovering only with difficulty. In 1865, he was honored with the brevets of lieutenant-colonel, colonel, and brigadier-general, for faithful, meritorious, and distinguished services in the ordnance department.

At the close of the war he was transferred to the command of Rock Island Arsenal in Illinois, where, with characteristic energy, he perfected elaborate plans for the construction on a large scale of a combined armory and arsenal. Adequate Congressional appropriations were secured and the work was started when Rodman's health, already impaired, broke down under the strain of responsibility, and he died at his post after a prolonged illness. He was survived by his widow, Martha Ann (Black) Rodman, daughter of a Presbyterian clergyman of Pittsburgh, Pa., to whom he had been married in 1843, and by five sons and two daughters.

[Information from Mrs. Florence Rodman Butler, of Honolulu; W. W. Rodman, *Notes on the Rodman Family* (1887); G. W. Cullum, *Biog. Reg. . . . U. S. Mil. Acad.* (1891); *Army and Navy Jour.*, June 17, Aug. 5, 1871; *Orders from the Ordnance Office, War Dept., Series 1871*; *N. Y. Herald*, June 8, 1871.]   C. D. R.

RODNEY, CÆSAR (Oct. 7, 1728–June 26, 1784), statesman, was the eldest child of Cæsar Rodney, the son of William Rodeney [*sic*] who emigrated to America about 1681, and of Elizabeth (Crawford) Rodeney, daughter of the Rev. Thomas Crawford, the first missionary sent to Dover, Del., and its environs by the Society for the Propagation of the Gospel in Foreign Parts. Born on his father's farm near Dover, Cæsar Rodney was reared in a cultured home and probably secured most of his education from his parents. When his father died in 1745, he was placed under the guardianship of Nicholas Ridgely, prothonotary and clerk of the peace of Kent County. He entered public life in 1755 when he was commissioned as high sheriff of Kent County. Reappointed to this office the two following years, he subsequently served his county as register of wills, recorder of deeds, clerk of the orphans' court, clerk of the peace, and justice of the peace. In 1769, he was appointed co-trustee with John Vining of the Kent County Loan Office and sole trustee from 1775 until his death. Appointed third justice of the supreme court for the Three Lower Counties in 1769, he was commissioned second justice of the same court in 1773.

In 1758 Rodney was elected for the first time as delegate from Kent County to the colonial legislature at New Castle. From 1761 to 1776, with the exception of the assembly of 1771, he served continuously as a member of the legislature and was elected speaker in 1769, 1773, 1774, and 1775, holding that post until the end of the colonial régime in 1776. In 1765 he was elected by the House of Assembly as the representative of Kent County in the Stamp Act Congress and together with Thomas McKean [*q.v.*] took an active part in the work of that body. When the Assembly adopted several resolutions condemning the Townshend Act in October 1768, Rod-

ney, McKean, and George Read [*q.v.*] were designated a committee of correspondence and instructed to draw up an address to the king. Following the passage by Parliament of the Boston Port Bill in the spring of 1774, Rodney, as speaker of the Assembly and upon express requests from mass meetings held in the three counties in June and July, took the extra-legal step of calling the Assembly for a special session (the prerogative of the proprietary governor) to meet in New Castle on Aug. 1, 1774. This body appointed Rodney, McKean, and Read to attend the First Continental Congress.

After meeting Rodney for the first time at the Congress, John Adams wrote in his diary for Sept. 3, "Cæsar Rodney is the oddest looking man in the world; he is tall, thin and slender as a reed, pale; his face is not bigger than a large apple, yet there is sense and fire, spirit, wit, and humor in his countenance" (*The Works of John Adams,* vol. II, 1850, p. 364). The colonial assembly, at a regular session held in March 1775, approved the acts of the irregular meeting of the previous August and the report prepared by the three delegates to the First Continental Congress, and reëlected them to the Second Continental Congress scheduled to meet in May. Meanwhile, Rodney was elected colonel of the so-called "Upper"' regiment of Kent County militia and in the following September, was elected brigadier-general of the militia of Kent County and of the western battalion of Sussex County. He presided as speaker over the regular session of the assembly in October 1775 and together with McKean and Read was again returned to Congress. In June 1776 he presided over the session of the colonial assembly at New Castle which passed a resolution supplanting the authority of the crown in the government of the Three Lower Counties and which issued new instructions to Rodney and his two colleagues from Delaware, authorizing them to cooperate with the other colonies.

On June 22 Rodney hurried to Sussex County to investigate a threatened Loyalist uprising there and had just returned to his home in Kent County when he received an "express" from his colleague, McKean, urging his immediate return to Philadelphia to vote on Richard Henry Lee's resolution for independence. He rode eighty miles on horseback, arriving in the late afternoon of July 2, 1776, in time to cast Delaware's vote for independence—his vote and McKean's overriding the negative vote of Read, the more conservative member of the delegation. He likewise voted with McKean for the adoption of the Declaration of Independence. On

July 22 he was back in New Castle presiding over the last session of the colonial assembly which he had summoned for the purpose of fixing a date for the assembling of a state constitutional convention and of arranging for the election of delegates. The conservatives of Kent County defeated him as delegate to the convention and, when the new state constitution went into effect, he also failed of election to the first state legislature and was not returned by that body in the autumn as a delegate to the Congress. This demonstration of ingratitude on the part of his contemporaries did not affect Rodney's patriotic fervor for he now turned to military affairs again, and in November 1776 was made chairman of the Kent County branch of the council of safety. When the American cause seemed at its lowest ebb in December, Rodney was busily engaged in recruiting men in his county and sending them forward to join the main army. In January 1777, after Washington had taken up his winter-quarters at Morristown, he was placed in command of the post at Trenton for a few weeks of active service. He was in command of the Delaware militia with the rank of brigadier-general when the British invaded the state in September, but only succeeded in harassing the enemy's outposts. A few days later the acting president of the state, Thomas McKean, commissioned Rodney as major-general of the Delaware militia.

Rodney's political star rose again in 1777. In the spring the legislature elected him as judge of the admiralty and in December as member to the Continental Congress. In the spring of 1778 it also elected him president of the state for a term of three years to succeed John McKinly [q.v.] who had been captured by the British when they temporarily occupied Wilmington. He served as Delaware's war executive seven months beyond the full term until November 1781. It fell to his lot during this critical period to furnish Delaware's quota of Continental troops, and to arm and clothe them as well as to raise Delaware's quota of provisions and money. For about ten years Rodney had suffered from a serious cancerous growth on his face and when he relinquished the duties of president, he immediately went to Philadelphia to obtain medical and surgical relief. The malady, however, had made too great an inroad upon his physical constitution and although he returned to Dover in a hopeful mood after several months of treatment, he constantly lost strength until his death. In the fall of 1783, he was elected once more to office, this time as member of the upper house of the legislature. This body honored him

with the speakership, but before the legislative year had expired Rodney was dead.

His main interests, aside from political affairs, had been those of a land owner. He died a comparatively wealthy man, and, since he never married, most of his real estate was bequeathed to his nephew, Cæsar Augustus, son of his brother, Thomas Rodney [qq.v.]. His remains lay buried on his farm, "Poplar Grove," for over a century when, in 1888, they were removed to the Christ Episcopal Churchyard in Dover. Although he did not enjoy the legal training of his three immediate collaborators, Thomas McKean, George Read, and John Dickinson [q.v.], Cæsar Rodney was a man of clear perception and understanding, of high courage, and of effective application.

[The principal primary material is to be found in the public archives of the State of Del. at Dover, Kent County Records at Dover, Hist. Soc. of Del. at Wilmington, Lib. of Cong., Geneal. Soc. of Pa., N. Y. Public Lib., and in the private collections of the Hon. Richard S. Rodney, New Castle, Del., Frank H. Stewart, Woodbury, N. J., John Stuart Groves, Wilmington, Del., and others. The principal printed material will be found in G. H. Ryden, ed., *Letters to and From Cæsar Rodney, 1756–1784* (1933); *Jour. of the Continental Cong., 1774–1789* (1904–); E. C. Burnett, ed., *Letters of Members of the Continental Cong.* (1921–); *Minutes of the Council of Del. State, 1776–1792* (1887); Hezekiah Niles, *Principles and Acts of the Revolution in America* (1822); *Del. Archives,* vols. I, II, III (1911, 1912, 1919); W. T. Read, *Life and Correspondence of George Read of Delaware* (1870); C. J. Stillé, *Life and Times of John Dickinson, Memoirs of the Hist. Soc. of Pa.,* vol. XIII (1891); Reprints of the *Votes and Proceed. of the House of Rep. of the Government of the Counties of New Castle, Kent, and Sussex, 1762,* reprinted 1930; *1765 to 1770 inclusive,* reprinted 1931.]   G. H. R.

RODNEY, CÆSAR AUGUSTUS (Jan. 4, 1772–June 10, 1824), lawyer, statesman, and diplomat, was born in Dover, Del., the son of Thomas Rodney [q.v.] and Elizabeth (Fisher) Rodney. He was the nephew of Cæsar Rodney [q.v.], who, having never married, took a particular interest in the boy and not only assisted in his education but bequeathed to him most of his real estate. After living for two years in Philadelphia, and then again in Dover, the family settled in 1780 in Wilmington, Del., where for upwards of two years Thomas Rodney was engaged in the flour exporting business. In 1786 Cæsar Augustus matriculated at the University of Pennsylvania. Upon his graduation in 1789 he commenced the study of law under Joseph B. McKean [q.v.] in Philadelphia. He was admitted to the bar in 1793 and began practice in Wilmington and New Castle. In 1796 he entered the Delaware House of Representatives as a member from New Castle County and continued a member of that body until the year 1802. A stanch supporter of Jefferson, he was prevailed upon to run for Congress in that year against the Federalist candidate, James A. Bayard [*q.v.*]. With Jefferson's backing, he succeeded in defeating Bayard and served as a member of the House of Representatives for two years. During this term he proved himself a firm supporter of the administration relative to the Louisiana Purchase treaty and of the Twelfth Amendment to the Federal Constitution.

In January 1804 Rodney was chosen one of the House managers to conduct the impeachment proceedings against John Pickering, judge of the United States district court for New Hampshire, and in December of the same year he was appointed one of the House managers to conduct the impeachment proceedings against Justice Samuel Chase. On Jan. 20, 1807, he became Jefferson's attorney-general, continuing in this post in Madison's administration as well until he resigned on Dec. 5, 1811. In the War of 1812 he served actively in the defense of his state. Commissioned on Apr. 7, 1813, as captain of the 2nd Company of artillery attached to the 1st Brigade of the militia, he was promoted major of a battalion of artillery after the close of the war on Mar. 15, 1815. In the meantime, he had been elected a member of the state Senate and served in the sessions beginning Jan. 3, 1815, Jan. 2, 1816, and Nov. 11, 1816. In 1817 he was appointed by President Monroe a member of a special commission to South America for the purpose of ascertaining the political status of newly established republics in that continent. His fellow commissioners were Theodorick Bland and John Graham. Proceeding directly to Buenos Aires, the commission remained there from February 1818 until the last of April. Rodney and Graham then returned to the United States while Bland proceeded to Chile. Reports by the commissioners were transmitted to Congress on Nov. 17, 1818 (*House Document 2, 15 Cong., 2 Sess.*).

As a result of his vigorous stand in opposition to the extension of slavery into the territories, Rodney was elected to Congress in 1820. He took his seat in December 1821 but in the following January he was elected by the Delaware legislature to fill a vacancy in the Senate. He resigned from the House on Jan. 24, 1822, and qualified as a member of the Senate the same day. A year later he resigned to accept an appointment by Monroe as the first United States minister plenipotentiary to the Argentine Republic. He arrived in Buenos Aires on Nov. 14, 1823, a few days before the President promulgated the Monroe Doctrine. The appointment was very acceptable to the Argentinians but Rodney's ca-

reer as a minister proved to be a short one. Falling dangerously ill on Nov. 23, he recovered sufficiently to speak at a public dinner held in his honor on May 27, 1824, but died, following a relapse, on June 10. His remains were interred in the English churchyard in Buenos Aires. When not in the public service of the United States, Rodney maintained with his large family a lovely home in Wilmington, Del., named "Cool Spring." His wife was Susan Hunn, daughter of Captain John Hunn of Philadelphia. By her he had fifteen children, ten daughters and five sons.

[Sources include: W. T. Read, *Biog. Sketch of Cæsar Augustus Rodney* (1853) ; *Del. Archives*, vols. IV and V (1916) ; W. R. Manning, *Diplomatic Correspondence of the U. S. Concerning the Independence of the Latin-American Nations* (1925), vol. I, published by the Carnegie Endowment for International Peace; *Biog. Dir. Am. Cong.* (1928) ; J. B. Moore, *A Digest of Internat. Law* (1906), vol. I ; *Letters to and from Cæsar Rodney, 1756–84* (1933), ed. by George H. Ryden ; *Governors' Reg.: State of Del.*, vol. I (1926) ; J. T. Scharf, *Hist. of Del.* (1888), vol. I ; J. M. McCarter and B. F. Jackson, *Hist. and Biog. Encyc. of Del.* (1882) ; Henry C. Conrad, *Hist. of the State of Del.*, vol. III (1908).]

G. H. R.

RODNEY, THOMAS (June 4, 1744–Jan. 2, 1811), farmer, soldier, and jurist, was the eighth and youngest child of Cæsar Rodney, the elder, and Elizabeth (Crawford) Rodney. He was born on his father's farm in St. Jones Neck, Kent County, Del. When Thomas was about a year old his father died and his mother married Thomas Wilson. The task of educating the son fell to her and she early inculcated in the boy a taste for reading. Three years before he attained his majority, Thomas left his childhood home to live with his brother, Cæsar Rodney [*q.v.*], in order to assist him in the management of his farms, and in 1764 removed with him to Dover to assist him there in his official duties as a county officer. With the exception of two years spent in Philadelphia (1772–74) as a shop-keeper and two years in Wilmington, Del. (1781–83) in a business partnership for the exporting of flour, he was engaged principally in farming, both as a manager of Cæsar's lands, when the latter was absent in Philadelphia on public business, and as a landowner himself. In 1770 he was appointed a justice of the peace in Kent County and in 1774 was reappointed to that position. Elected in 1775 as a member for Kent County of the colonial Assembly of the Government of the Three Lower Counties of New Castle, Kent, and Sussex, he participated in the legislative steps taken to transform the colonial government into the state government of Delaware in the summer of 1776.

In 1775, shortly after the Battle of Bunker Hill, Thomas Rodney organized a volunteer militia force and in the same year was elected a member of the Council of Safety and of the Committee of Observation for Kent County. When in the autumn and early winter of 1776 Washington's army was retreating across New Jersey, Rodney, in command as captain of a company of Kent County militia, joined the division of General Cadwalader at Bristol, Pa., at Christmas time, and led his men in the second battle of Trenton on Jan. 2 and in the battle of Princeton the following day. Later in the same year (1777), when General Howe's army invaded northern Delaware on its way from the Head of Elk to Philadelphia, Thomas Rodney acted as adjutant to his brother Cæsar who was then in command of the Delaware militia encamped near the British posts in New Castle County.

From 1778 to 1785 Thomas Rodney served his state as judge of the admiralty court, and between the years 1781 and 1788 he was elected by the General Assembly five times to membership in the Confederation Congress. Elected twice to membership in the lower house of the General Assembly (1786 and 1787), he was chosen speaker of that body in October 1787, but after serving for a few days he asked to be relieved. Appointed associate justice of the supreme court of Delaware in December 1802, he held this post until August 1803, when he resigned to accept an appointment by President Jefferson as United States judge for Mississippi Territory. He remained in this position until his death at Natchez in 1811. Rodney was married, Apr. 8, 1771, to Elizabeth Fisher, daughter of Jabez Maud Fisher of Philadelphia. Two of their children attained maturity, one of whom was Cæsar Augustus Rodney [q.v.].

[The principal public depositaries of Thomas Rodney manuscripts are the Delaware Public Archives, Hist. Soc. of Del.; the Geneal. Soc. of Pa., and the Lib. of Cong. For printed material see: "Diary of Capt. Thos. Rodney, 1776–77," *Papers of the Hist. Soc. of Del.*, vol. VII (1888); Simon Gratz, "Thos. Rodney," *Pa. Mag. of Hist. and Biog.*, Jan. 1919–Oct. 1920; *Letters to and from Cæsar Rodney* (1933), ed. by George H. Ryden; *Letters of Members of the Continental Cong.*, vols. I–VII (1921–34), ed. by E. C. Burnett; *Del. Archives*, vols. II and III (1912–19).]
G. H. R.

ROE, EDWARD PAYSON (Mar. 7, 1838– July 19, 1888), author, was born in what is now New Windsor, Orange County, N. Y., fourth of the six children of Peter and Susan (Williams) Roe. His father was a New York merchant who, having saved a competence, retired to the country to spend the last forty years of his life; he was enough of an abolitionist to convoy at least one fugitive negro across the ice-bound Hudson

in mid-winter. Roe's mother, who died in 1859, was for as long as he could remember her an invalid; to her literary taste, nourished largely on the Bible and "Paradise Lost," her son attributed his own gift for writing. He attended Burr and Burton Seminary in Manchester, Vt., and entered Williams College with the class of 1863, but developed a dangerous case of eye strain and on the advice of President Mark Hopkins pursued a special two years' course. Then for another year he studied at the Auburn Theological Seminary. Having been ordained at Somers, N. Y., in the summer of 1862 by the North River Presbytery, he served as chaplain of the 2nd (Harris' Light) New York Cavalry and later of the hospital at Fortress Monroe, Va., until the close of the Civil War, and was pastor of the Highland Falls, N. Y., Presbyterian Church, 1866–74. During the war he was married, Nov. 24, 1863, to Anna Paulina Sands of New York City, who with five children survived him.

The Chicago fire of 1871 turned the country clergyman into the most popular American novelist of the period. Drawn by a curiosity so powerful that he could neither resist it nor approve it, he visited the city while the embers were still smoldering, wandered about the ruins for several days, and returned home with the germ of a novel in his head. His *Barriers Burned Away* was published as a magazine serial and also in book form in 1872, and became immediately and lastingly popular. With proper caution Roe composed a second novel, *Opening a Chestnut Burr* (1874), to determine whether the amazing sale of the first was an accident or the product of a dependable formula. Satisfied on that point, he resigned his charge in 1874, bought an estate at Cornwall on the Hudson, and devoted himself to authorship. His seventeen novels were all best-sellers and continued in demand long after their first publication. The great favorites, besides the first two, were: *Near to Nature's Heart* (1876); *A Knight of the Nineteenth Century* (1877); *Without a Home* (1881); *He Fell in Love with His Wife* (1886); and *The Earth Trembled* (1887). His income from his books and magazine work was about $15,000 a year. He worked methodically, took pains with his style, and, despite the unremitting efforts of Lyman Abbott, Julian Hawthorne, and other friends to flatter him into the illusion that he was the equal of Thackeray, always had a fairly accurate notion of his literary status. He was one of several clerical novelists who, combining entertainment with moral purpose, helped to dispel the lingering American prejudice against the novel. His work, however, did not rise above the popular level.

The adulation that was lavished on him as a writer he deserved as a man. In all the relations of life he was kindly, helpful, and decent. Characteristic of him was his behavior in 1882 when his brother, whose notes he had indorsed, defaulted. Roe was forced into bankruptcy and had to sell his copyrights at auction, but he accepted his responsibilities without complaint and ultimately paid his brother's creditors in full. His avocation was horticulture and the growing of small fruits. For a number of years he did a thriving business as a nurseryman. Five books —*Play and Profit in My Garden* (1873; new ed., 1886), *A Manual on the Culture of Small Fruits* (brochure, 1876), *Success with Small Fruits* (1880), *Nature's Serial Story* (1885), and *The Home Acre* (1889)—were his literary harvests from this field. He was fond of hospitality, using every means he could devise to keep his guest-room occupied. For several years he was host to the Authors' Club of New York on an annual junket to Cornwall. He died, practically without warning, of a heart attack, after reading aloud to his family from one of Hawthorne's novels.

[E. P. Roe, "My First Novel," *Cosmopolitan,* July 1887, and "'A Native Author Called Roe,'" *Lippincott's Mag.,* Oct. 1888; Roe's letters to Edgar Alexander Mearns, Div. of MSS., Lib. of Cong.; *Report of the Class of 1861 Williams College* (1887); Mary A. Roe, *E. P. Roe: Reminiscences of His Life* (1899); *Critic,* July 28, Aug. 4, 1888; *Publishers' Weekly,* July 28, 1888; E. D. Walker, "Edward P. Roe," *Cosmopolitan,* Sept. 1888; *N. Y. Daily Tribune,* July 21, 1888; names of parents from Prof. Wm. J. Hinke of Auburn Theol. Sem.; for a terse, exact description of Roe's novelistic formula see Carl Van Doren, *The Am. Novel* (1921), p. 122.]   G. H. G.

ROE, FRANCIS ASBURY (Oct. 4, 1823– Dec. 28, 1901), naval officer, was a descendant in the sixth generation of David Roe, who settled in Flushing, Long Island, in the latter part of the seventeenth century. His great-grandfather, Benjamin Roe, fought in the French and Indian War, his grandfather, John Roe, in the Revolution, and his father, Isaac Roe, in the War of 1812. His mother, Hannah Drake, was said to be a direct descendant of Sir Francis Drake. Born in Elmira, N. Y., he had his schooling in Elmira Academy. He was appointed an acting midshipman in 1841, cruised on the coast of Brazil and the southeast coast of Africa, and then joined in the suppression of the slave-trade on the west coast of Africa. He was later ordered to the *Boston* and was to have joined the squadron of Commodore O. H. Perry at Vera Cruz, but was prevented from taking an active part in the Mexican War by the ground-

ing and loss of that vessel. A year of instruction at the newly established Naval Academy followed. In October 1849, he was dismissed from the service by a sentence of court martial for the disobedience of an illegal order, but was reappointed a passed midshipman and given his former place on the navy list the following year. In 1854, as executive officer of the *Porpoise,* he had an engagement with thirteen pirate junks at Koulan Bay, China, destroying six and dispersing the others.

In the Civil War he was ordered as executive officer to the *Pensacola,* fitting out at Washington, and after the defeat of the Union army at Bull Run he occupied Fort Ellsworth near Alexandria, Va., with 500 seamen for the defense of Washington. Later he made a perilous run down the Potomac, past nine miles of Confederate batteries, on his way south to join Farragut's fleet. In the attack on New Orleans, the *Pensacola* steamed past the forts below the city, her position being in the van of the fleet, immediately after the gunboat *Cayuga,* which led the Union forces. For his capable handling of the ship, Roe was especially commended by Captain Morris in his report. Promoted to the rank of lieutenant commander, he was given command of the gunboat *Katahdin,* in the fleet that was to keep the Mississippi open from New Orleans to Port Hudson—a task that involved constant fighting. In September 1863, he took command of the double-ended paddle-wheel steamer *Sassacus,* and while engaged in the blockade of Wilmington, N. C., destroyed two blockade-runners, the *Wild Dayrell* and the *Nutfield.* On May 5, 1864, when the Union "paste-board fleet" in Albemarle Sound was ineffectually engaging the heavy Confederate ironclad *Albemarle,* the *Sassacus* captured the gunboat *Bombshell,* and then attacked the *Albemarle* and drove her bronze beak into the casemate of her enemy. In this courageous but unequal combat, the *Sassacus* was disabled by a shell that exploded her boiler. She fought on, however, until the *Albemarle* withdrew up the Roanoke River. For this action Roe received a letter of commendation from the secretary of the navy and was advanced five numbers in rank. In 1867 he was ordered to command the Mexican division of the Gulf Squadron. In the *Tacony* at Vera Cruz he rendered important service at the time when Maximilian was executed and the Mexican imperial government was changed to republican. For his skilful handling of affairs he was given a commendatory letter by the secretary of the navy and was presented to President Johnson at a cabinet meeting. Various assignments followed, the last being that of governor of the Naval Asylum for Retired Seamen at Philadelphia. In 1884 he was promoted to the rank of rear admiral, and in October of the next year was placed on the retired list. He was married in September 1849, to Eliza J. Snyder. In 1865 he wrote a book that received considerable recognition on *Naval Duties and Discipline*. After retirement he made his home in Washington, D. C., and took an active part in the patriotic societies of which he was a member. He occasionally wrote articles for magazines, the most important being a description of the actions of Farragut's fleet in the capture of New Orleans in *Self Culture*, January 1899.

[*Who's Who in America*, 1901–02; Marcus Benjamin, "Francis Asbury Roe," *Memorial Papers of the Soc. of Colonial Wars, District of Columbia, no. 4, 1903*; C. A. Torrey, *David Roe of Flushing, L. I., and Some of His Descendants* (1926); *War of the Rebellion: Official Records (Navy)*, 1 ser., vols. III, IV, IX, X, XVIII, XIX, XXVI; personal papers and journals in the possession of a relative; *Washington (D. C.) Post*, Dec. 29, 1901.]   C. S. A.

ROE, GILBERT ERNSTEIN (Feb. 7, 1865–Dec. 22, 1929), lawyer, author, was born in the town of Oregon, Dane County, Wis., the son of John and Jane (McKeeby) Roe. Of English and Scotch descent, he was educated at the University of Wisconsin and graduated from the law school in 1890. He immediately entered the law firm of Robert M. LaFollette, with whom he was intimately associated for thirty-five years. It was in this association that Roe, as the trusted political and legal adviser of LaFollette, found the opportunity for his most significant activities in public affairs. Particularly in connection with direct primary, and with railroad and insurance legislation was his political and legal skill of value in effectuating the LaFollette program. He led the successful contest in the Republican State Convention of 1898 for a platform declaration favorable to the direct primary, and his advice was influential in the subsequent political and legislative development of the proposal. In the drafting of the railroad and insurance statutes he was equally valuable, returning several times from New York City, whence he had removed in 1899, to aid in the solution of some difficult problem.

After several years spent in establishing a law practice in New York City, from 1905 to 1910 in partnership with William F. McCombs, Roe became prominent in the movement to apply in New York state the major ideas of the Wisconsin plan. He was a member of the commission appointed by Gov. William Sulzer to draft a direct primary law; he was active in behalf of workmen's compensation legislation and,

when the New York court of appeals declared the original law unconstitutional in 1911, he drafted the new and improved law. His devotion to the liberal tenets of the Progressive movement led him to defend those who opposed the war activities of the government and who were prosecuted for violation of the espionage acts. He was *amicus curiae* in the appeal of the Debs case to the United States Supreme Court; he won all his jury cases which involved charges of disloyalty; he successfully contested exclusion of several anti-war newspapers from the mails; and he was counsel to the five Socialist New York assemblymen who were deprived of their seats for their war attitudes. As counsel to the Teachers' Union in New York he was influential in the repeal of the Lusk laws. In the unsuccessful proceedings to expel LaFollette from the Senate in December 1918 for alleged seditious activities, he was counsel to the Senator (*Senate Report 614*, 65 Cong., 3 Sess.).

During 1922–23, as counsel to the Senate committee on manufactures, of which LaFollette was chairman, Roe made an investigation of the oil industry which laid the basis for the Teapot Dome and other investigations of the Harding administration (*Senate Report 1263*, 67 Cong., 4 Sess.). He was throughout his life a critic of the judicial process. His *Selected Opinions of Luther S. Dixon and Edward G. Ryan, Late Chief Justices of the Supreme Court of Wisconsin* (1907) expressed his opposition to the conservative tendencies of the law. In *Our Judicial Oligarchy* (1912) he developed the thesis that the courts had usurped authority in their review of legislative acts, and elaborated, through a careful analysis of judicial decisions, his charge that judges were disposed to preserve property rights at an excessive cost to society. His pronounced ideas on this subject were the mainspring for LaFollette's proposal in 1912 and in 1924 that the courts be curbed in their power to nullify the decisions of the law-making agencies. Roe died in New York City in the winter of 1929. He had married, on Nov. 12, 1899, Gwyneth King, who with three children survived him.

[A considerable portion of the Roe papers are in the LaFollette collection, Wis. State Hist. Soc.; the remainder are in the possession of Mrs. Gilbert E. Roe, New York City. See also: A. O. Barton, *LaFollette's Winning of Wis.* (1922); R. M. LaFollette, *LaFollette's Autobiog.* (1913); *Who's Who in America*, 1928–29; *N. Y. Times*, Dec. 23, 1929.]   W. S. S.

ROEBLING, JOHN AUGUSTUS (June 12, 1806–July 22, 1869), engineer, bridge builder, and manufacturer, was born in Mühlhausen, Thuringia, Germany, the youngest son of Christoph Polycarpus Roebling and his wife, Friederike Dorothea (Mueller). The family traced its history in a direct line to Nicholaus Roebling, or Rebeling, who was born in Tennstedt in 1560. He appears to have been a man of substance and a city official. Christoph, the father of John Augustus, is noted in the records of Mühlhausen as a tobacco manufacturer.

For the time and place, John's education was unusually good. He attended the Mühlhausen public schools and the city Gymnasium, and was also tutored privately to qualify him for entrance to the Royal Polytechnic Institute in Berlin. For his opportunity to study there he was chiefly indebted to his mother, whose determined self-denial and thrift had made it possible, because the family circumstances were far from affluent. In the Institute his course included architecture and engineering, bridge construction, hydraulics, languages, and philosophy. He was a pupil of the great Hegel, and there is a tradition in the Roebling family that he was the philosopher's favorite disciple. At the age of twenty he was granted the degree of civil engineer, and for three years thereafter worked for the Prussian government on road building in Westphalia. His keenest interest was in bridge construction, especially that of suspension bridges. He made a special study of a chain suspension bridge at Bamberg, in Bavaria, and subsequently presented his observations of the structure as a thesis for his state examination.

Roebling showed already that originality and inventiveness which was later to carry him so far in the field of long-span bridge construction. He was eager to develop his ideas but found himself hampered by red tape and official inertia. It is not surprising therefore that his thoughts turned to America, whither so many of his countrymen were looking. With his brother he planned carefully the contemplated step and read as widely as he could on opportunities in the United States. He seems to have decided that the best field to enter would be agriculture, and it was with the intention of buying farm land in the new country that he left Germany. His strong feeling against slavery, considered by many essential to agricultural progress, turned him definitely against the South and in favor of the North. With his brother Karl he left Mühlhausen for Bremen in the spring of 1831 and a little later sailed for Philadelphia on the bark *August Eduard,* intending to find and purchase a tract of land for some of their countrymen. They reached Philadelphia on Aug. 6, and after a few weeks in that city, left for Pitts-

burgh, traveling mainly by the Pennsylvania Canal, and crossing the mountains by means of the inclined planes of the Allegheny Portage Railroad. Roebling kept a journal of the trip which was printed in 1832 and a century later, translated from the original German by Edward Underwood, was published under the title, *Diary of My Journey from Muehlhausen in Thuringia via Bremen to the United States of North America in the Year 1831, Written for My Friends* (1931). The brothers bought seven thousand acres of land in Butler County, about twenty-five miles from Pittsburgh, and settled it, in company with the little group of thrifty German colonists with whom they were associated. The small town or hamlet was first known as Germania and afterwards as Saxonburg. The colonists kept in touch with their friends and relatives in Germany, persuading a number of them also to emigrate and join the community in Butler County. Among these later emigrants was Ernst Herting, who came to Saxonburg from Mühlhausen in 1834. In May 1836 John Roebling married Johanna, Herting's eldest daughter.

Roebling was not a successful farmer. This cannot be charged, however, entirely to his lack of experience, for the colonists certainly chose anything but prime agricultural land when they settled on the western slope of the Alleghanies. It was not many years before he felt a yearning to get back to the professional work for which he had been so well trained. The year after his marriage (1837) he went to Harrisburg and applied for employment by the state as an engineer. In this year he became a naturalized citizen of the United States. He spent several months on the state canal projects, mainly in building dams and locks on Beaver River, then joined a surveying party which was laying out a railway over the mountains.

At this time the canal era was about at its height, and the Allegheny Portage Railroad was an important link between the eastern and western sections of the Pennsylvania Canal. Roebling was evidently impressed by the long reaches of steeply inclined railway, up and down which the canal boats were moved in specially constructed wheeled cradles, and by the clumsy and expensive cables used for hauling the cars up and down the slopes. These hawsers, generally about three inches in diameter, made of Kentucky hemp, were subjected to severe usage which necessitated frequent replacement. Roebling conceived the idea of substituting for these hempen cables ropes of twisted wire which would give far greater strength and longer life, with the added advantage of smaller diameter and consequently greater ease in handling. He made a number of experiments and had the usual difficulty of the pioneer in convincing the Pennsylvania board of public works that the idea was of value. These obstacles were finally overcome, however, and in 1841 he manufactured the first wire rope made in America in a small factory in Saxonburg equipped with machinery of his own design and fabrication. Additional uses for the new wire rope were found and although the demand for the product for canal use waned with the diminishing importance of the canals, rope for rigging vessels, for tow lines, and for dredges was increasingly demanded. Roebling wrote an article describing his product which was published in the *American Railroad Journal* of November 1843. In 1848 or 1849 he moved his factory to Trenton, N. J.

While becoming a manufacturer he also continued his interest in bridge building and designed a number of notable structures. In 1844–45 he built a wooden aqueduct for the Pennsylvania Canal, comprising seven spans of 162 feet each, carried on two continuous wire cables each seven inches in diameter. The design was without precedent in America although it made use of some of the principles of the chain suspension bridge at Bamberg, Bavaria, which Roebling had studied in his youth. In 1846 he completed his first suspension bridge, built to carry a highway over the Monongahela River at Pittsburgh. This bridge comprised eight spans of 188 feet each, supported by two 4½-inch cables which were constructed on the bank of the river and hoisted into place from flatboats. Roebling described it in an article in the *American Railroad Journal,* June 13, 1846. The structure was in use for thirty-five years. In the years 1848–50, Roebling constructed four suspension aqueducts for the Delaware & Hudson Canal.

In spite of his early interest in canals and canal operation, he readily foresaw that the faster and surer agency of the railway must absorb the greater part of the service heretofore given by the canals. In 1847 he read a paper before the Pittsburgh Board of Trade in which he strongly advocated a railroad through Pennsylvania. Early in 1850, four years before Cyrus W. Field [*q.v.*] became actively interested in such a project, Roebling wrote to the *Journal of Commerce,* expressing his conviction that a transatlantic telegraph was perfectly feasible. He gave detailed estimates of the cost, which he believed should not exceed $1,300,000.

The list of Roebling's works in the field of important bridge construction is a long one. In many ways the most striking structure was the pioneer railroad suspension bridge which he built at Niagara Falls in the years 1851–55. In addition to the natural obstacles to be overcome, there was a cholera epidemic at the bridge site in 1854. The bridge was opened in March 1855, and stood for many years, a monument to the ingenuity and resourcefulness of its builder. It was described by him in a memoir included in *Public Works of Recent Construction Both British and American* (London, 1856). In 1856 Roebling's plans for a bridge over the Ohio River, between Cincinnati and Covington, Ky., were accepted and work was begun, but the undertaking was interrupted by the Civil War and not completed until 1867. In 1858–60 the bridge over the Alleghany River at Pittsburgh was built, in which work Roebling and his son Washington A. Roebling [*q.v.*] were associated. Roebling's hatred of the institution of slavery had continued unabated and he vigorously supported the Union cause, encouraging his son Washington to offer his services to the Federal army.

In June 1857, Roebling had written a letter to Abram S. Hewitt [*q.v.*], of New York, suggesting the possibility of a bridge over the East River between lower Manhattan and Brooklyn which would not interfere with navigation, but it was ten years later before the project finally assumed shape and a charter for the construction of the work was granted. Roebling was appointed chief engineer, and plans for the bridge were perfected by him and received the approval of the commission early in 1869. The surveys had been made and work was about to begin when he suffered the accident—at first believed not to be serious—which cost his life. On June 28, 1869, he was making certain observations at the bridge site, from a point of vantage on a cluster of piles at the Fulton Ferry slip on the Brooklyn side. A ferry-boat entering the slip pushed back the piling on which he was standing, catching his foot and crushing several of his toes. He was taken at once to his son's home in Brooklyn, and the injured toes were amputated. Although he was in considerable pain, there was every expectation that with his vigorous physique he would soon be about again, but tetanus set in, and he died on Thursday, July 22, less than six weeks after his sixty-third birthday.

Roebling at his death was a rich man for his time. He had accumulated his wealth by means of mental and physical energy of a high order and relentless personal industry. In addition to his professional activity and the management of his factory he was a prolific writer for technical and scientific periodicals, and at the time of his death a book by him, *Long and Short Span Railway Bridges* (1869), was in press. His one recreation appears to have been music, and he usually found opportunity for practising the flute and the piano. He was jealous of his time, never wasted it himself, and would not allow others to do so. Punctual to the minute himself, if an associate was five minutes late in keeping an appointment, Roebling would postpone the conference. When he established the wire-rope factory in Saxonburg in 1841 and began the manufacture of a product up to that time unknown in America, he founded an industrial dynasty. The John A. Roebling's Sons Company of Trenton has developed without a break from the little ropewalk in Saxonburg, and at no time has it been out of the control of the Roebling family—sons, grandsons, and great-grandsons of the founder. John Augustus Roebling and his wife Johanna had nine children, of whom four sons and three daughters were living at the time of their father's death in 1869. The youngest daughter, Josephine, became the wife of the pianist Charles H. Jarvis [*q.v.*]. Johanna (Herting) Roebling died Nov. 22, 1864, and Roebling married, second, Lucia W. Cooper, whom he survived five years.

[Hamilton Schuyler, *The Roeblings—A Century of Engineers, Bridge-Builders and Industrialists* (1931), is a standard work, with many quotations from diaries, letters and other original sources. See also "John Augustus Roebling," *Trans. Am. Soc. of Civil Engineers,* vol. XCVIII (1933); C. B. Stuart, *Lives and Works of Civil and Military Engineers of America* (1871); *John A. Roebling: An Account of the Ceremonies at the Unveiling of a Monument to His Memory* (1908); J. K. Mumford, *Outspinning the Spider: The Story of Wire and Wire Rope* (1921); *N. Y. Daily Tribune,* July 23, 1869.]   **C. J. T.**

ROEBLING, WASHINGTON AUGUSTUS (May 26, 1837–July 21, 1926), civil engineer, industrialist, was born in Saxonburg, Butler County, Pa., eldest of the nine children of John Augustus Roebling [*q.v.*] and Johanna (Herting) Roebling. His father was the leader of a group of German colonists who settled Saxonburg in 1831. Washington spent his boyhood in that town under stern paternal discipline, sharing the privations and limitations of pioneer life until his thirteenth year. At that time the family moved to Trenton, N. J., where John A. Roebling established a new factory for the production of wire rope.

Washington all his life used English and German with equal facility. As a little child he had a tutor; he now entered the Trenton Academy, and after four years of preparation, matriculated at Rensselaer Polytechnic Institute, Troy, N. Y.,

then the leading school of professional engineering in the country. The Rensselaer curriculum of the day he described as "that terrible treadmill of forcing an avalanche of figures and facts into young brains not qualified to assimilate them as yet" (Schuyler, *post,* p. 173); his class numbered sixty-five on entering but only twelve were graduated three years later. Immediately after receiving his degree as civil engineer, young Roebling started to work in his father's wire-rope mill, in which he had already had some experience, and apparently for considerable periods of time he was in charge during his father's prolonged absences. After a year in the mill he joined his father at Pittsburgh to assist in building the Alleghany River Bridge, and remained on that job until its completion in the summer of 1860, when he returned to Trenton. On Apr. 16, 1861, four days after the attack on Fort Sumter, he enlisted as a private in the National Guard of New Jersey, in June joined the 83rd New York Infantry, and in January 1862 became a second lieutenant in the 6th New York Battery, from which he was discharged in April 1864 to accept a commission as major of volunteers. On Dec. 2, 1864, he was brevetted lieutenant-colonel for gallant service before Richmond and on Mar. 13, 1865, he was brevetted colonel of volunteers, "for gallant and meritorious service during the War." His duties were mainly those of an engineer officer and included a considerable amount of bridge building, notably the construction of suspension bridges across the Rappahannock and Shenandoah rivers. He served on the staff of Gen. Irvin McDowell and later on that of Gen. John Pope [*qq.v.*]. He took part in the campaign which ended in the second battle of Bull Run and was also at Antietam and South Mountain. At one time, after Chancellorsville, it was his daily task to ascend in a captive balloon to observe and report on Confederate movements. He was on the staff of Gen. Gouverneur K. Warren [*q.v.*] at the battle of Gettysburg and throughout the fierce campaign around Richmond.

The war over, he returned to his profession of civil engineering. For two years (1865–67) he assisted his father in completing the bridge between Cincinnati and Covington, Ky. He then spent a year abroad conferring with the leading engineers in England, France, and Germany and studying especially the principles and practice of caisson foundations, with a view to helping his father in the newly projected Brooklyn Bridge, of which the elder Roebling had been appointed chief engineer. Immediately on his return from Europe, he entered his father's office as principal assistant and prepared the detailed plans and specifications for the great bridge. The elder Roebling died just as the field work was beginning and his son succeeded him as chief engineer.

For the next three years Roebling's work was continuous and unusually severe. The Brooklyn Bridge project was unprecedented in many ways and the details of procedure needed constant watching and direction. The foundations of the great towers were built by the caisson method, under compressed air, and the chief engineer spent long hours in the damp high-pressure of the caisson chambers. Caisson disease, the dreaded "bends," attacked the laborers; at that time little was known of methods of treatment and much had to be learned by costly experience. One afternoon in the spring of 1872, Roebling was taken almost unconscious from the caisson on the New York side, but in a few days he was back on the work. By the end of the year, however, his health had been seriously and permanently affected, and he did not visit the bridge site again. From that time until the bridge was finished in 1883, except for six months abroad in a vain attempt to regain his health, he directed the work from his house in Brooklyn, too sick to leave it. Such a record, a decade of exacting work, is a rare tribute to the man's mental alertness, minute knowledge of technical detail, and gift for effective organization. During much of this time he maintained an active part in conducting the business of the John A. Roebling's Sons Company, of which he became president upon its incorporation in 1876.

Shortly after the bridge was completed and opened to traffic, he moved with his wife to Troy, N. Y., where they lived from 1884 to 1888 while their son, John A. Roebling II, was a student at Rensselaer Polytechnic Institute. They then removed to Trenton and established a permanent home. Owing to his seriously impaired health, Roebling took no further active part in professional engineering work, although for a short time, at the age of eighty-three, after the death of his nephew, Karl G. Roebling, he resumed the presidency of the Roebling company, and during his brief administration took and filled the contract for the Bear Mountain Bridge over the Hudson. For the most part, however, he lived quietly in Trenton, read widely, and indulged his hobby of collecting rare minerals, of which he had some fifteen thousand specimens. His remarkable collection is now in the Smithsonian Institution in Washington. In 1924 he wrote a paper on the early history of Saxonburg for the Butler County Historical Society.

Washington Augustus Roebling was twice married. His first wife, whom he married Jan. 18, 1865, was Emily Warren, of Cold Spring, N. Y., daughter of Sylvanus Warren and sister of Major-General G. K. Warren on whose staff Roebling served during the Civil War. By her he had one son, born in Mühlhausen, Germany, the birthplace of his ancestors. Mrs. Roebling died Feb. 28, 1903, and five years later, Apr. 21, 1908, Roebling married Mrs. Cornelia Witsell Farrow, of Charleston, S. C. He died at his home in Trenton a few weeks after his eighty-ninth birthday.

[Hamilton Schuyler, *The Roeblings* (1931), the standard work, contains many additional references, including an extensive list of works relating to the Brooklyn Bridge. See also *Who's Who in America*, 1918–19; Wm. C. Conant and Montgomery Schuyler, *The Brooklyn Bridge . . . With an Account of the Opening Exercises* (1883), reprinting articles first pub. in *Harper's Mag.*, May 1883, and *Harper's Weekly*, May 26, 1883; E. F. Farrington, *Concise Description of the East River Bridge . . . Lectures Delivered at the Cooper Union* (1881); *N. Y. Times*, July 22, 1926.]

C. J. T.

ROEDING, GEORGE CHRISTIAN (Feb. 4, 1868–July 23, 1928), horticulturist and nurseryman, was born in San Francisco, Cal., of German parentage. His father, Frederick Christian Roeding (Dec. 31, 1824–July 18, 1910), was a native of Hamburg who went to Chile in 1846 and thence, in 1849, to California. He engaged briefly in mining but soon became a successful banker. In 1867 he married Marianna Lazarus, who had emigrated from Germany the year before. George Christian was the eldest of their five children. Shortly after his birth, his father, with some compatriots, bought 80,000 acres of land in the San Joaquin Valley; subsequently, some 1200 acres of this tract, given by the elder Roeding to the Southern Pacific Railroad, became a part of the city of Fresno. George's early years were spent mostly in San Francisco, where he graduated from the Boys' High School in 1885, but his summer vacations were passed on a farm in Contra Costa County. His interests in plants dated from childhood and is said to have been aroused by botanizing trips taken with Dr. H. H. Behr. In 1886 he began work with the three-year-old Fancher Creek Nurseries at that time owned by his father and Dr. Gustavus Eisen. He soon became manager and eventually owner of these nurseries, to which were added others in various parts of the state. In 1910 he was president of the Pacific Coast Association of Nurserymen and in 1911 organized the California Association of Nurserymen, of which he was an active member until his death. He was an ardent advocate of plant quarantine and of a protective tariff on agricultural products.

Roeding has been called the father of Smyrna-fig culture in California, and undoubtedly his greatest single contribution to American horticulture was the part he took in establishing that industry. Figs had been grown in 'California since the time of the early missionaries but none of these early introductions were equal in quality to figs of the Smyrna type. In 1887 Roeding's father imported fig cuttings from Smyrna with the hope of producing a fig to compete with the imported fruit. These first plantings were augmented until the Roedings had some sixty acres planted to Smyrna figs. The trees prospered, but they matured no fruit. The father became discouraged and retired from the enterprise, but the son persisted, in the face of many disappointments and great expense, until the problem was solved.

The chief difficulty that had to be surmounted was caprification, or the fertilization of the female flowers through the agency of a small wasp. This age-old process was thought by most European botanists to be unnecessary, and the practice of hanging male capri figs containing the Blastophaga wasp in the fruit-bearing trees was considered a superstition, but when the Smyrna figs introduced into America failed to produce fruit, attention was directed to the absence of the fig insects. Roeding was captivated by the idea of the intricate cooperation of plant and insect whereby the wasp, mistaking the edible female figs for the capri figs in which she wishes to lay her eggs, is entrapped and dies without posterity, but not before she has distributed pollen to the female flowers of the fig, thus enabling them to develop for the use of man and providing for future generations of fig trees. Roeding was the first to demonstrate that when pollinated the Smyrna fig would mature. This he did by introducing pollen through the opening at the tip of the fig. He cooperated with the Department of Agriculture in introducing the Blastophaga wasp, and it was in his trees that the insects were liberated and became established. In 1901 he visited Smyrna to study the fig industry and in 1903 he published *The Smyrna Fig at Home and Abroad,* an account of his trip and description of Smyrna fig culture in California. He was the author also of *The Fruit Growers' Guide* (1919), a practical treatise on fruit growing. He married, Dec. 15, 1897, Elizabeth Evelyn Thorne, whose father was one of the pioneers of Fresno County. They had three daughters and one son. Roeding died by his own hand after about a year spent in a sanitarium following a nervous breakdown from overwork.

[In addition to Roeding's *The Smyrna Fig at Home and Abroad,* see H. W. Kruckeberg, *George Christian Roeding, a Tribute* (1930) ; *Trans. and Proc. of the Cal. Asso. of Nurserymen,* 1911–28 ; L. H. Bailey, The *Standard Cyc. of Horticulture,* III (1915), 1593; *Sacramento Union,* July 25, 1928.]   G. N. C.

ROEMER, KARL FERDINAND (Jan. 5, 1818–Dec. 14, 1891), German geologist, better known simply as Ferdinand Roemer, was born in Hildesheim, Hanover. His father, Friedrich Roemer, councilor of the high court of justice (*Obergerichtsrath*), was of Prussian descent, a native of Magdeburg; his mother, Charlotte Lüntzel, a daughter of the last of the independent burgomasters of Hildesheim. Roemer's early education was along classical lines, but during his Gymnasium days he became deeply interested in natural sciences, especially geology. Family influence, however, induced him to undertake the study of law at Göttingen (1836–39) where, on the side, he listened with much satisfaction to the lectures on geology by Dr. Hausmann. In 1840, having abandoned the law, he matriculated as a student of science at the University of Berlin. Here he attended the lectures of Heinrich and Gustav Rose, Weiss, von Dechen, and other celebrated professors. On May 10, 1842, he was awarded the doctor's degree and soon thereafter began his contributions to the *Neues Jahrbuch für Mineralogie, Geologie und Palæontologie* which were continued at frequent intervals for forty-five years.

In the spring of 1845, with funds provided by the Society for the Protection of German Emigrants in Texas and the Berlin Academy of Science, and with the approval of Alexander von Humboldt, Roemer sailed for America. His special mission was to study the condition of the colonists in Texas and to report upon the natural resources of the country. Of his many publications those resulting from this trip are of the greatest interest to Americans. Omitting letters and briefer articles, they are: *Texas-Mit besonderer Rücksicht auf deutsche Auswanderung und die physischen Verhältnisse des Landes nach eigener Beobachtung geschildert* (Bonn, 1849), *Die Kreidbildungen von Texas und ihre organischen Einschlüsse* (Bonn, 1852), and *Die silurische Fauna des westlichen Tennessee* (1860). The first work treats of a great variety of subjects, personal, descriptive, and scientific, and is accompanied with the first geological map of the state printed in color; the second, a quarto volume, deals with the physiography and geology of the state in general, but particularly with the Cretaceous formations, followed by a description of fossils illustrated by eleven beautifully executed plates. This work, still a useful reference, has given Roemer a permanent place among the geologists of Texas. Long after his return to Germany he prepared and published the third work—a monograph on the Silurian fossils of western Tennessee.

In 1848 Roemer became privat-docent in mineralogy and paleontology at Bonn. Later, in 1855, he accepted a call to Breslau where, in addition to his professorship in geology and paleontology, he undertook the directorship of the mineralogical cabinet which under his fostering care became one of the finest in Germany. His success as a teacher was notable and his reward ample, for under his guidance there were given to the scientific world many distinguished scholars. He traveled extensively. It has been said that he visited every country in Europe and some of them several times. The bibliography of his publications lists more than three-hundred and fifty titles. Important among his works is his *Geologie von Oberschlesien* (3 vols., with maps and plates, 1870). In recognition of his unusual ability as a researcher, he was the recipient of many honors from both the state and learned societies. In 1885 he was awarded the Murchison Medal by the Geological Society of London. Aside from his scientific attainments Roemer was well versed in the classics. He possessed great aptitude in acquiring foreign languages, a gift of no little importance in prosecuting his studies outside of Germany. In the spring of 1869 he married Katharina Schäfer with whom he lived happily for twenty-three years. He died, without issue, in Breslau.

[W. Dames, memoir and bibliography of Roemer's writings in *Neues Jahrbuch für Mineralogie, Geologie und Palæontologie*, vol. I (1892), Supp.; Carl Hintze, "Karl Ferdinand Roemer," *Allgemeine Deutsche Biographie*, LIII (1907), 451–58; Frederic W. Simonds, "Dr. Ferdinand von Roemer, the Father of the Geology of Tex.," with a bibliography, *Am. Geologist*, Mar. 1902, reprinted, without the bibliography, in the *Geol. Mag.* (London), Sept. 1902.]   F. W. S—s.

ROGERS, CLARA KATHLEEN BARNETT (Jan. 14, 1844–Mar. 8, 1931), singer, author, composer, was born in Cheltenham, England. Her father, John Barnett, a composer, was the son of Bernhard Beer, a Prussian watch-maker, who had settled in Bedford and had changed his name to Barnett. Clara Kathleen, growing up in a musical household, studied with her parents until 1856. She then went to the Leipzig Conservatory where she studied piano with Moscheles and Plaidy, theory with Papperitz and Richter, ensemble with David and Rietz, and singing with Goetze. After further study in Berlin, and with San Giovanni

and Bruni in Milan, she made her début in Turin in 1863 as Isabella in Meyerbeer's *Roberto il Diavolo* under her stage-name, "Clara Doria." Later she sang in Genoa, Leghorn, Florence, and Naples, in *Lucia di Lammermoor, Maria di Rohan,* in which she sang the title rôle, *Maria Padilla, La Sonnambula, La Vestale, Rigoletto.* Leaving Italy she went to London where she was prominent on the concert stage for five years. In 1871 she came to America with the Parepa-Rosa Opera Company, of which Tom Karl was the tenor. She made her début on Oct. 4, 1871, at the New York Academy of Music in *The Bohemian Girl*, and subsequently sang Donna Elvira in *Don Giovanni*, the Countess in *The Marriage of Figaro*, and other soprano rôles. She appeared in New York, Boston, and Philadelphia, and in 1872-73 sang with the Maretzek company.

Leaving the operatic stage, she went to Boston as the solo soprano of Trinity Church, and there, on Apr. 24, 1878, she was married to a Boston lawyer, Henry Munroe Rogers. She continued active as a concert singer, teacher, composer, and author, and in 1902 became professor of singing at the New England Conservatory of Music. Her compositions include a number of albums of songs, some piano pieces, and a sonata for violin and piano. She also wrote a number of educational books on her art: *The Philosophy of Singing* (1893), *Dreaming True* (1899), *My Voice and I* (1910), *English Diction, in Song and Speech* (1912), *Your Voice and You* (1925) and *Clearcut Speech in Song* (1927). As an opera singer Clara Kathleen Rogers seems to have fallen short of the first rank, and there is probably much truth in Carlo Rosa's remark to her: "If you only had two more notes in your voice you would be one of the great artists of the world" (*Memories, post*, p. 395). She died in Boston at the age of eighty-seven.

[The main sources of information are the autobiographical *Memories of a Musical Career* (1919), and *The Story of Two Lives: Home, Friends, and Travels. Sequence to "Memories of a Musical Career"* (1932). See also: *Who's Who in America*, 1930–31; *Musical America*, Mar. 25, 1931; *Boston Herald*, Mar. 9, 1931. There are biographies of John Barnett and Robert Lindley in the *Dict. Nat. Biog.*]   F. H. M.

ROGERS, EDWARD STANIFORD (June 28, 1826–Mar. 29, 1899), horticulturist, was born in the family homestead on Essex Street, in Salem, Mass., a descendant of Rev. John Rogers, who was president of Harvard College in 1682-84; his parents were Nathaniel Leverett Rogers, an old-time Salem merchant, and Harriet Wait, his wife. Edward was educated in Master Ira Cheever's school, made several sea voyages in his father's ships as clerk and super-cargo, and then entered the counting room of his father's firm, where he was employed until its dissolution. After his father's death in 1858, he continued to live in the family home with his brother and his mother. In the half-acre garden extending from the house on Essex Street to Federal Street he indulged his taste for horticulture and conducted his experiments in grape hybridization. The garden was quite large for a city lot, although, according to the horticulturist Marshall P. Wilder, it was "150 years old; a cold, matted soil, filled with old apple, and pear trees, currant bushes, flax, and everything mingled in together. It is in a close, hived up place in the city of Salem, and it is a wonder that he [Rogers] ever had a bunch of grapes to show" (*Proceedings of the Ninth Session of the American Pomological Society*, 1862, p. 148). The suggestion which incited his experiments in hybridizing came from an article by Dr. Lindley of the University of London, printed in the London *Horticulturist* and reprinted in Downing's *Horticulturist* for September 1847. This article, "Remarks on Hybridizing Plants," was a general discussion of the results of plant-breeding practices so far as they were then known. In the summer of 1851, Rogers crossed one of the native American grapes, *Vitis labrusca,* by two representatives of *Vitis vinifera,* or European wine grape. The seeds obtained were sown, and from these came forty-five seedlings which finally fruited. These, known as the Rogers Hybrids, were unique in that the standard of quality was very high in each of them, and their weaknesses were also equally distributed. Only one of them, Rogers' No. 15, which was named Agawam, is still in cultivation, but it remains one of the more popular home varieties of grapes. Rogers gained practically no profit from his grapes, since he gave them away freely, especially his better seedlings. His chief claim to remembrance lies not in the varieties which he produced but rather in the impetus his results gave to grape growing in America; never before or since has grape growing in the United States received the attention given it during the decade following the introduction of the Rogers Hybrids.

By temperament, Edward Rogers was quiet and retiring. When he left the counting room, for fifteen years he withdrew almost wholly from the public eye and devoted himself to his garden. While he possessed some literary ability and was an extensive reader, he could rarely be drawn into discussion except among those intimate friends who were wont to "drop in"

at his long, low greenhouse in the garden or at his office, extemporized in the old colonial barn at the rear of the house. After the death of their mother in 1882, the two brothers moved to another house in Salem, and some years later, after his brother died, Edward Rogers bought a place in Peabody, Mass., where he continued his grape-breeding experiments. None of his later seedlings ever showed promise equal to the original forty-five, however, and none was ever introduced. An accident which resulted in permanent lameness kept him from much physical labor during his last years and probably in some measure hastened his death. He never married and was the last survivor of his family.

[G. B. Brackett, in L. H. Bailey, *The Standard Cyc. of Horticulture,* III (1915), 1593; U. P. Hedrick, *The Grapes of New York* (1908), containing a portrait of Rogers as the frontispiece; obituary in Salem *Evening News,* Mar. 30, 1899, which contains several errors; *Boston Transcript,* Mar. 30, 1899; *Gardening* and *Am. Gardening,* both Apr. 15, 1899; *New-Eng. Hist. and Geneal. Reg.,* Jan. 1859; abundant references in the horticultural literature of the day.]

R. H. S—s.

ROGERS, HARRIET BURBANK (Apr. 12, 1834–Dec. 12, 1919), pioneer oral teacher of the deaf, was born in North Billerica, Mass., the daughter of Calvin and Ann (Faulkner) Rogers. An older sister was a teacher of Laura Bridgman [*q.v.*]. Harriet was educated in the public schools of Billerica and for six years in the academy at Westford, Mass., where she was associated with John D. Long, later governor. In November 1864 she consented to undertake the instruction of a little deaf child. The manual method—using finger spelling and signs—was at that time universally used in the schools for the deaf in the United States. She knew that in Germany deaf children were taught to speak and to read speech from the lips, but she knew nothing of the method employed. She obtained the consent of the parents of her pupil to attempt to teach the child to speak. Encouraged by her success with this pupil, in June 1866 she opened a small private school for deaf children in Chelmsford, with her first pupil as one of these. She and one assistant took the entire care of these children both in and out of school hours. At the end of a year the little school numbered eight pupils.

On Oct. 1, 1867, she assumed the principalship of the new Clarke Institution for Deaf Mutes, now The Clarke School for the Deaf, which was to be opened in Northampton, Mass., being established by the endowment of John Clarke of that city. This was the first school for teaching deaf children under the oral method in the United States. Its establishment was obtained through the influence of Gardiner Green Hubbard [q.v.], whose own little daughter, later the wife of Alexander Graham Bell [q.v.], had been taught orally by a private teacher under her mother's direction. Schools for the deaf in the country violently opposed this new dream of "visionary enthusiasts," but from the first she quietly and unobtrusively carried on her work. Her teachers were inexperienced but eager to follow suggestions and try experiments. Soon after the school at Northampton was opened, Alexander Graham Bell was for some months a member of the staff of Clarke School. His marvelous knowledge of phonetics and his personal magnetism were a strong influence in the further development of the methods of the school. At this time Miss Rogers spent a year in Europe, mostly in Germany, studying the methods employed in teaching the deaf there, and returned to continue more enthusiastically the work she had so well begun. In 1884 failure of health obliged her to go to Colorado. In 1886 her resignation was accepted by the official board of the school. She later returned to North Billerica but was never able to resume the burden of teaching. She adapted herself to the situation and became active in supervising the village kindergarten and in various other concerns. The work she had begun has continued to broaden and strengthen. Today schools for the deaf throughout the country to an increasing extent employ the oral method she introduced, and the number of schools using this method exclusively steadily increases.

[Harriet B. Rogers, "Reminiscences of Early Days of Speech Teaching," in *Clarke School and Its Graduates* (1918); C. A. Yale, *Years of Building* (1931); A. G. Bell, *The Growth of Oral Method in America* (1917?); *Deaf-Mute Education in Mass., Report of the Joint Committee of the Legislature* (1867); *Institution for Deaf-Mutes, Annual Report,* 1868–84; personal acquaintance.]   C. A. Y.

ROGERS, HENRY DARWIN (Aug. 1, 1808–May 29, 1866), geologist, educator, third of the four sons of Patrick Kerr and Hannah (Blythe) Rogers, was born in Philadelphia. Of his three brothers, William [q.v.] also became a geologist and James and Robert [qq.v.], chemists. Henry received much of his early education from his father. After conducting a school in Windsor, Md., for a time, in company with his brother William, in 1828 he accepted a position as lecturer in chemistry in the Maryland Institute, Baltimore. Two years later he was appointed professor of chemistry and natural philosophy in Dickinson College, Carlisle, Pa. Becoming disgusted with the narrow bigotry of the trustees, he soon resigned, however, and for

a brief period was employed on a railway survey in New England. An interest in socialism led him in 1832 to accompany Robert Dale Owen [q.v.] to London, with no more definite plans than "to be useful." Fortunately, he soon became associated with friends who introduced him to the Geological Society of London, where he met De la Beche, Lyell, and others, and quickly became converted to a more strenuous calling.

Returning to the United States in 1833, he gave lectures on geology at the Franklin Institute in Philadelphia, and in 1835 was appointed to the chair of geology and mineralogy in the University of Pennsylvania. This same year he was also made director of the geological survey of New Jersey, and in 1836 he accepted a like position with the newly organized geological survey of Pennsylvania. The work of the New Jersey survey was practically finished in 1838, and the final report issued in 1840; that of Pennsylvania came to an untimely end in 1842 through lack of appropriations by the state legislature. Rogers was unwilling, however, to leave the work in its unfinished condition and continued it at his own expense until he was able in 1847 to present his final report, though through legislative indifference it was not printed until 1858. In the meantime, he moved to Boston, where the final revision was prepared, funds being supplied by legislative action in 1851–55. Finding that the work of publication could be carried out more satisfactorily by an Edinburgh firm than in the United States, he went to that city in 1855, and while there was appointed Regius Professor of Natural History in the University of Glasgow, a position he held until his death. This appointment marked the beginning of the Glasgow University school of geology, though as to his success as a teacher, expressed opinions are divided.

Of his geological work in New Jersey, little need be said, since but a brief time was devoted to it. The work of the Pennsylvania survey cannot be passed over so lightly, however, since it is upon this and what grew out of it that his fame as a geologist largely rests, as well as that of his brother William, with whom he worked in hearty cooperation. His report was beyond question the most important document on the geology of America that had appeared up to that time, with the possible exception of the final reports of the New York survey. In it the two brothers advanced noteworthy ideas, previously announced to the Association of American Geologists and Naturalists (see *Proceedings and Transactions, 1840–42,* 1843) regarding the structures of the Appalachian Mountains. These mountains, they showed, were not as had been commonly supposed, uplifted by an intrusion of molten material, but consisted of a series of parallel ridges characterized by predominant southeastern dips, and that they were true folds in the strata, in some cases so sharp and abrupt that the northwestern limb was bent back under the southwestern, or inverted. This view has been proved to be essentially correct. Their ideas as to the cause of the folding—that the flexures "are the result of an outward, billowy movement proceeding from beneath"—have not, however, stood the test of time, indeed were never generally accepted; nor were those they put forward on the subject of glaciation. An objection raised by Rogers to the use of geographical names for the geological systems led him to adopt a wholly fanciful and, as it proved, impractical, scheme in which he represented the Paleozoic time as a geological day and subdivided it according to successive stages, as *primal, auroral, matinal, levant,* and so forth.

Rogers' health, never of the best, began failing soon after he went to Edinburgh, causing him to spend much time in the south of England and on the Riviera. In the fall of 1865, he returned to America, but in April 1866 went back to his University work at Glasgow, only to be taken seriously ill and die on May 29 following. He is described as dignified, quiet, and unassuming, even shy, but admired by all who knew him intimately. As a lecturer, he displayed varied knowledge and no little skill and grace of expression. In March 1854 he was married in Boston to Eliza S. Lincoln, a half-sister of the wife of his brother William; they had one child, a daughter.

[*Life and Letters of William Barton Rogers* (2 vols., 1896), ed. by his wife; J. W. Gregory, *Henry Darwin Rogers: An Address to the Glasgow Univ. Geological Soc.* (1916), with bibliography; G. P. Merrill, *Contributions to a Hist. of Am. State Geological and Natural Hist. Surveys* (1920) and *The First One Hundred Years of Am. Geology* (1924); M. L. Ames, *Life and Letters of Peter and Susan Lesley* (1909), II, 511; *Proc. Am. Acad. Arts and Sci.,* vol. VII (1868); William Sabine, in *Proc. Royal Soc. of London,* vol. XVI (1868); *Am. Jour. Sci.,* July 1866; *Popular Sci. Mo.,* Dec. 1896.]   G. P. M.

ROGERS, HENRY HUTTLESTON (Jan. 29, 1840–May 19, 1909), capitalist, was the son of Rowland and Mary Eldridge (Huttleston) Rogers, both of early New England ancestry. His middle name is often given as Huddleston, which appears to have been the earlier form in the family; to this spelling his son and namesake returned. He was born at Mattapoisett, Mass., but was brought up at Fairhaven, near by, where in boyhood he carried newspapers and delivered groceries. He later served for a time as a railroad brakeman and baggageman. He was twenty-one when the newly discovered oil fields in Pennsylvania drew fortune seekers to that region. Rogers and a friend, Charles P. Ellis, went together to the Oil City district, each having about $600 in savings. They presently built a small refinery at a cost of $1,800, borrowing the additional funds necessary. On a visit to his home town in 1862, Rogers was married to Abbie Palmer Gifford. In Pennsylvania he met several men destined to become leaders in the oil industry, among them Charles Pratt [*q.v.*], who in 1866 asked Rogers to become associated with him in his refinery business in Brooklyn. There Rogers devised the machinery by which naphtha was first successfully separated from the crude oil—an epochal invention for the industry (*Current Literature,* July 1909). A patent (No. 120,-539) was granted on Oct. 31, 1871.

When the Rockefellers organized the Standard Oil Company in 1874, they took over the Pratt business and with it Rogers, now recognized as both an expert oil man and an able executive with a genius for organization. He was made chairman of the manufacturing committee of the new corporation, a little later a trustee, and before 1890 he was vice-president. He conceived the idea of long pipe lines for transporting oil, and organized the National Transit Company, the first corporation with such an object. This was his favorite promotion, and he remained president of the company long after the actual technical management of the oil business itself had been given over by him to others so that he and William Rockefeller [*q.v.*] might devote their time to the operation of the huge financial machine known to Wall Street as "Standard Oil." Either personally or in behalf of this trust, Rogers was interested in several businesses other than oil—gas, copper, steel, banking, and railroads. In 1884 with associates he formed the Consolidated Gas Company, and thereafter for several years he was instrumental in gaining control of great city plants, fighting terrific battles with rivals for some of them, as in the case of Boston. Almost the whole story of his gas interests was one of warfare, as was his connection with copper. During the '90's, when he was virtually the directing head of Standard Oil, he became interested in Anaconda and other copper properties. In 1899 he formed the first $75,000,000 section of the gigantic trust, Amalgamated Copper, which was the subject of such acrid criticism then and for years afterward. In the building of this great trust, some of the most ruthless strokes in modern business history were dealt—the $38,000,000 "watering" of the stock of the first corporation, its subsequent manipulation, the seizure of the copper property of the Butte & Boston Consolidated Mining Company, the using it as a weapon against the Boston & Montana Consolidated Copper and Silver Mining Company, the guerrilla warfare against certain private interests, the wrecking of the Globe Bank of Boston. Standard Oil's interest in steel properties led to Rogers' becoming one of the directors of the United States Steel Corporation when it was organized in 1901. He was long the transportation magnate of Staten Island, being the principal owner of its railroads, traction lines, and ferries. He was a director of the Santa Fé, St. Paul, Lackawanna, Union Pacific, and several other railroads. He was a close associate of E. H. Harriman [q.v.] in the latter's extensive railroad operations, and when Harriman became interested in the insurance business, Rogers, who had long been a trustee of the Mutual Life, was drawn with him into the scandal and governmental investigation of 1905, but as usual emerged almost unruffled. He sustained his worst tactical defeat, however, in an ouster suit brought by the State of Missouri in 1905, in which he, at first defiant, was forced to testify and admit the Standard's secret ownership of certain subsidiary oil companies (218 *Missouri Reports*, 1; 116 *Southwestern Reporter*, 902; see also 224 *United States*, 270). His last great individual enterprise was the building of the remarkable, low-grade Virginian Railway from the West Virginia coal fields to Norfolk. It was an achievement unique in business annals for one man to build a $40,000,000 railroad on his own resources and credit, and that, too, partly in a time of financial stress, the panic of 1907. But the strain of doing it proved fatal to him. He was at his desk on May 18, 1909, but the next morning, in New York City, suddenly died of an apoplectic stroke. His first wife had died May 21, 1894, leaving four children. He afterward married Emelle (or Emelie) Augusta Randel, the divorced wife of Lucius Hart, who, together with a son and three daughters, survived him.

Rogers was a tall, handsome man of distinguished presence and a curious duality of nature. In business he was known as a man of cold steel; away from business he was democratic, a faithful friend, a wit and raconteur. Even the bitterest of his enemies testified to the almost hypnotic charm of his presence when he chose to exercise it. To the end of his life some of the humblest of the citizens of his boyhood home remained his

intimate friends and called him "Hen." His summer home was there, and there at week-ends he found his happiest relaxation. He paved Fairhaven's streets, he gave it a town hall, grammar and high school buildings, a handsome public library, a Masonic lodge building, a costly Unitarian church and parsonage. There he founded the Atlas Tack Company, the largest concern of its kind in America. His fondness for Mark Twain's writings led to an acquaintance with the humorist, and finding the latter in difficulties because of the failure of his publishers, Rogers practically took charge of his affairs and remained his business manager and counselor until death.

[*Who's Who in America*, 1908–09; obituaries in all New York evening and morning papers, May 19, 20, 1909; N. Y. *World*, Mar. 12, Sept. 5, 1907; all New York newspapers of Jan. 6–8, 1906, when the Missouri suit against Standard Oil was being tried; *Harper's Weekly*, May 29, 1909; *Nation* (N. Y.), May 27, 1909; *Current Literature*, July 1909; *World's Work*, May 1905; Thomas W. Lawson, *Frenzied Finance* (1905), the most violent of all the criticisms of Rogers; Ida M. Tarbell, *The Hist. of the Standard Oil Company* (2 vols., 1904); R. I. Warshow, *The Story of Wall Street* (1929); *Dedication of the Memorial Monument to Henry Huttleston Rogers, Jan. 29, 1912. Town Hall Fairhaven, Mass.* (n.d.); George Huddleston, comp., *Huddleston Family Tables* (1933); information in regard to the spelling of his middle name from his son, Col. Henry H. Rogers.]   A.F.H.

ROGERS, HENRY J. (Mar. 10, 1811–Aug. 20, 1879), a pioneer in the development of telegraphic communication and an inventor, was born in Baltimore, Md., the son of Col. John H. Rogers. He was educated in St. Mary's College, Baltimore, and immediately applied himself to the art of telegraphy and signaling, which from his early youth had appealed to him strongly. He was engaged in developing a system of marine signals with flags when he was attracted to the work of Samuel F. B. Morse [q.v.] and his electro-magnetic telegraph. As a result, about 1843, he obtained employment with Morse in the construction of the demonstration telegraph line between Baltimore and Washington, sponsored by the federal government, and when this line was opened for public business under the direction of the Post Office Department, he was appointed telegraph operator at Baltimore. When the government refused to buy Morse's invention at his stipulated price of $100,000 and the privately owned Magnetic Telegraph Company was organized, May 15, 1845, Rogers was a subscriber to the new company and one of the incorporators. In 1848 he joined the North American Telegraph Company, which used the telegraph invented by Alexander Bain. Its line extended from New York to Washington but the system failed to work properly until Rogers introduced certain modifications. He continued with the company as superintendent until 1852 when, as a result of the successful infringement suit brought by the Morse interests, it was absorbed by the Morse company. Rogers then became superintendent of the House Printing Telegraph Company, organized about 1852, and operating between New York and Washington. In 1855 he severed his connections with it, in order to devote his time to perfecting his marine signaling system, which he had patented on Sept. 27, 1844. He succeeded in having the system adopted by the United States Navy, but failed, after making two trips to Europe, to secure its adoption by any foreign power.

At the outbreak of the Civil War, he was called to Washington and rendered important service in the establishment of field telegraph lines, particularly for the Army of the Potomac. He served also as secretary of the Potomac flotilla and as a navigation officer at the Washington Navy Yard. While in Washington, May 17, 1864, he patented his semaphore telegraph system. At the close of the war he became superintendent of the Bankers' and Brokers' Telegraph Line between New York and Washington, but eighteen months later relinquished this position in order to accept a similar one with the Southern and Atlantic Telegraph Line. He continued in this capacity, with headquarters in New York, until 1873, when he retired to his home in Baltimore. There he engaged in writing a history of the telegraph, but his death prevented the completion of the work. In addition to his two signaling systems, he devised a code of flare signals for use at night and a system of insulation for telegraph lines patented on Dec. 3, 1872. He was married to a Miss McGlennan of Baltimore, and at the time of his death in that city was survived by his widow and four sons.

[J. D. Reid, *The Telegraph in America*, 1879; *Shaffner's Telegraph Companion*, Jan. 1855; S. I. Prime, *The Life of Samuel F. B. Morse, LL.D.* (1875); E. L. Morse, ed., *Samuel F. B. Morse: His Letters and Jours.* (1914); *Baltimore American and Commercial Advertiser* and *Sun* (Baltimore), Aug. 21, 1879; Patent Office records.]

C. W. M.

ROGERS, HENRY WADE (Oct. 10, 1853– Aug. 16, 1926), educator and jurist, was born in Holland Patent, N. Y. He was adopted at an early age by an uncle for whom he was named, Henry W. Rogers of Buffalo, N. Y., later of Ann Arbor, Mich. From the University of Michigan Rogers received the degrees of B.A. in 1874 and M.A. in 1877. Admitted to the bar in the latter year, he practised law for a short time in Minnesota and then in New Jersey. In 1882 he became Tappan Professor of Law at the University of Michigan and in 1886, dean of its law department. His administration was vigorous and successful, and at the time of his retirement this law school was the largest in point of numbers in the United States. His administrative skill so impressed the trustees of Northwestern University, Evanston, Ill., that he was chosen president of that institution in 1890.

At Northwestern, Rogers united a loosely joined federation of schools under separate boards of trustees into an organized whole. He urged the creation of a scientific department and effected the introduction of courses in political science and government. He secured funds for the erection of needed new buildings, including the Orrington Lunt Library. During his administration, the net resources of the University increased more than a hundred per cent., and the enrollment of students was nearly doubled. At times he was forced to work against some opposition, to which he was sensitive, but he surmounted all obstacles and left the University upon a sound basis.

In 1900, feeling that he had accomplished what he could for the institution, he tendered his resignation and immediately went to the Yale School of Law as a lecturer. Here he served until 1921: from 1901 to 1921 as a professor, and from 1903 to 1916 as dean. He continued to teach for eight years after his appointment in 1913 as judge of the federal circuit court of appeals sitting in New York City. His judicial career was terminated only by his death, although he was then planning to retire from the bench to become the first research professor in the newly created Institute of Research in Law at the University of Michigan.

Several commentators upon his career have expressed the view that Rogers' greatest work was done as dean of the Yale School of Law. His administration was marked by the adoption of the case method of legal instruction, and the college-degree requirement for admission, and by the restriction of the faculty to full-time teachers. These steps, initially advocated by the younger group of his faculty, were whole-heartedly and skilfully supported by Rogers so that they were ultimately accepted without friction by a group of older faculty members at first strongly opposed to the changes. Among these men was Simeon Eben Baldwin [q.v.], who for more than fifty years had been the guiding force of the faculty. Rogers later nominated Baldwin for the governorship of Connecticut (1910) and for the presidency (1912), and Baldwin recommended Rogers to President Wilson for appointment to the federal bench. To successive groups of Yale men Rogers was a striking, even a portentous, figure, because his classroom methods reduced the most strong-minded of his students to a state somewhat akin to panic. Except as he occasionally employed a touch of sarcasm, his manner was all mildness and his personal contacts were most friendly, yet his skilful, merciless, and persistent cross-examination caused his students to work harder for him, probably, than for any other instructor. When he was appointed judge he had had little legal and no judicial experience, but he at once showed himself a competent, though possibly not great or original, jurist. His written opinions evinced much labor and learning. Besides the law, his chief interests were the Democratic party and the Methodist Episcopal Church. He acted as delegate and chairman at various Democratic conventions, he was president of the Association of American Law Schools in 1906, chairman of the American Bar Association's committee (later council) on legal education and admission to the bar from 1906 to 1920, member of the National Conference of Commissioners on Uniform State Laws in 1910, and chairman of the World's Congress on Jurisprudence and Law Reform of the Chicago exposition of 1893. He was president of the General Laymen's Association of the Methodist Episcopal Church after 1920, chairman of the judiciary committee in the General Conferences from 1908 to 1920, member of the committee on Organic Union of the Methodist Episcopal Church with the Methodist Episcopal Church South from 1916 to 1920, chairman of the committee on international relations of the Federal Council of Churches, 1908, and trustee of the Church Peace Union of the Carnegie Foundation after 1913. He was the author of several legal treatises, including *Illinois Citations* (1881) and *The Law of Expert Testimony* (1883, 1891); associate editor of *Johnson's Universal Cyclopædia* (8 vols., 1893-97); contributor to the tenth edition of the *Encyclopædia Britannica* (1902), to the *American Supplement* (1897); and author of the article on *Injunctions* in the *Cyclopedia of Law and Procedure* (vol. XXII, 1906); as well as author of many articles in popular magazines and law reviews.

Rogers was married on June 22, 1876, to Emma Ferdon Winner of Pennington, N. J., who survived him. He died at his summer home at Pennington, near Trenton, in his seventy-third year.

[B. A. Hinsdale, *Hist. of the Univ. of Mich.* (1906); A. H. Wilde, *Northwestern Univ., A Hist.* (1905), vol. I; *Yale Shingle* (Law School Annual), 1903-11; *Reports to the President of Yale Univ.,* 1926-27; *New Haven Journal-Courier* and *N. Y. Times,* Aug. 17,

1926; *In Memory of Henry Wade Rogers,* memorial booklet, privately printed, containing the funeral address of Aug. 19, 1926, addresses at a memorial service of Nov. 21, 1926, a sketch, and tributes; *N. Y. Law Journal,* Mar. 23, 1928; *Who's Who in America,* 1925-26; *Asso. of the Bar of the City of N. Y., Year Book,* 1927.]   C. E. C.

ROGERS, ISAIAH (Aug. 17, 1800–Apr. 13, 1869), architect, was born in Marshfield, Mass., the son of Isaac and Hannah (Ford) Rogers. His father, a shipbuilder, was descended from John Rogers, an early settler of Marshfield. Isaiah was educated in the local schools. His family wished him to be a farmer, but at the age of sixteen, much against their will, he left for Boston, where he apprenticed himself to a carpenter named Shaw. When his apprenticeship was over, he went South and spent the years 1820 and 1821 in Mobile, Ala. While there he won a competition for the first Mobile Theatre, a barn-like, undistinguished building, finished in 1824. In 1822 he returned to Boston and entered the office of Solomon Willard [*q.v.*], the eminent architect, sculptor, and master mason. Willard later supplied granite for many of Rogers' buildings; in 1842 they took a five-year lease together on one of the Quincy quarries; and as a mark of his affection for the older man Rogers named his son after him.

Rogers' name first occurs in the Boston directory in 1826, and it was probably about this time that he started his own architectural practice. His first large commission was the Tremont Hotel in Boston, the first example of the luxurious, elaborately planned American hotel with extensive plumbing. Its corner stone was laid July 4, 1828, and it was opened in 1829. Probably as a result of his success in this building, Rogers was chosen architect of the new Astor House in New York, where he lived from 1834 to 1842. The Astor House was somewhat similar in general style to the Tremont, but, much larger, it carried luxury and complicated mechanical equipment to a still higher level. Its corner stone was laid July 4, 1834, and it was opened in 1836. His other New York work included the Bank of America (Wall and William Streets), 1835, the façade of which was later reconstructed as the entrance to Pine Lodge Park, Methuen, Mass.; the very similar Merchants' Bank; the Lafayette Place Reformed Dutch Church, 1836; the Astor Place Opera House, later altered into the Mercantile Library and called Clinton Hall, 1847; and especially the Merchants' Exchange, 1836-42. This lavish building, which was unprecedented at that time, in that it cost over a million dollars, had a great interior rotunda and a magnificent Ionic colonnade which Philip Hone called "worthy . . . of Palladio or Michelangelo" (diary note of July 12, 1842, *The Diary of Philip Hone*, 1927, edited by Allan Nevins, II, 611). It has since been incorporated in the present National City Bank. At about the same time Rogers designed the graceful and original Boston Merchants' Exchange.

Rogers was the father of the modern hotel. It was in his work that the combination of lavish public rooms, numerous bedrooms (some in suites), and elaborate mechanical equipment was first made. The list of his hotels includes the Bangor House, Bangor, Me.; the Exchange Hotel, Richmond, Va., 1841, an exquisite design; the Battle House, Mobile; the Charleston Hotel, Charleston, S. C., with its superb Corinthian frontispiece; the magnificent second St. Charles Hotel at New Orleans, *c.* 1851; the second Galt House, Louisville, Ky., *c.* 1865; the enormous Maxwell House, Nashville, Tenn., begun in 1859, during the Civil War used for barracks, and not finally opened till 1869; and the famous Burnet House in Cincinnati, opened in 1850, which the *Illustrated London News* called the best hotel in the world (Williamson, *post*, p. 100).

It was probably to superintend the building of the Burnet House that Rogers moved to Cincinnati, where he lived thereafter. In that city he designed, among other work, St. John's Protestant Episcopal Church, a Romanesque building; the Longview Insane Asylum, with an interesting plan; and considerable alterations to the Ohio State Capitol. In 1855 he designed the Egyptian Judah Touro memorial gate to the Jewish cemetery in Newport, R. I. He was associated at various times with Henry Whitestone, with his son Solomon Willard Rogers, and with A. B. Mullett. He was something of an inventor, and between 1841 and 1863 patented three improvements in iron bridge design and a burglar-proof safe. From 1862 to 1865 (and nominally till 1868, the dates are confused and contradictory) he was supervising architect of the Treasury Department in Washington, being the first formal incumbent of this position. During his administration little important work was done, because of the Civil War, but he completed the west side of the Treasury Building, following the original design of Robert Mills [*q.v.*].

Once the ideas of the Greek Revival are accepted, Rogers can be appreciated as one of the greatest of the designers of his time. The austerity of the Tremont and Astor House exteriors, the recessed vestibule and superb rotunda of the New York Merchants' Exchange, the interest-ing diagonal towers of St. John's Church, Cincinnati, all show an imaginative mind, an appreciation of true classic dignity, and a thoroughly trained taste. Unlike many of his contemporaries, he succeeded in keeping his classicism alive during his later life, refusing to accept the ugliness of contemporary fashion.

Rogers was married at twenty-three to Emily W. Tobey, of Portland, Me.; they had at least two children. Rogers was for years subject to acute heart attacks, and died as the result of one at the age of sixty-eight.

[A photograph of Rogers and many illustrations of his work appear in Montgomery Schuyler, "The Old 'Greek Revival,'" pt. 4, in the *Am. Architect*, May 3, 1911; later research has rendered doubtful some of the attributions in this otherwise valuable article. See also W. H. Eliot, *A Description of Tremont House, with Architectural Illustrations* (1830); *Ann. Reports of the Commissioner of Patents*, 1841, 1856, 1865; W. W. Wheildon, *Memoir of Solomon Willard* (1865); *The Biog. Encyc. of Ohio* (1876); J. H. Drummond, *John Rogers of Marshfield and Some of His Descendants* (1898); I. N. P. Stokes, *The Iconography of Manhattan Island* (6 vols., 1915–26); Jefferson Williamson, *The Am. Hotel, an Anecdotal Hist.* (1930); J. M. Howells, *Lost Examples of Colonial Architecture* (1931); R. H. Thayer, *Hist., Organization and Functions of the Office of Supervising Architect of the Treasury Dept.* (1886); Darrell H. Smith, *The Office of the Supervising Architect of the Treasury* (1923); *Cincinnati Daily Gazette*, Apr. 15, 1869.]　　　　　　T. F. H.

ROGERS, JAMES BLYTHE (Feb. 11, 1802–June 15, 1852), chemist, educator, was born in Philadelphia, the son of Patrick Kerr and Hannah (Blythe) Rogers. The father was himself a physician, chemist, and teacher of note. Born in Ireland in 1776, he was employed in a counting-house in Dublin when the Irish rebellion of 1798 broke out, and, having written newspaper articles inimical to the government, he found it advisable to emigrate to the United States. He settled in Philadelphia; married in 1801 Hannah, daughter of James Blythe, a native of Glasgow and a Londonderry publisher; received the degree of M.D. from the University of Pennsylvania in 1802; practised in Philadelphia and Baltimore; and in 1819 succeeded Dr. Robert Hare [*q.v.*] as professor of natural philosophy and chemistry at the College of William and Mary, which position he held until his death in 1828.

James was the eldest of four brothers, the others being William Barton, Henry Darwin, and Robert Empie [*qq.v.*], all of whom became distinguished scientists. Their tastes were similar, they worked much together, and formed, it has been said, a "family group scarcely to be excelled for native powers and acquirements, in the history of science, in this or any age or country" (F. A. Walker, in *National Academy of Sciences, Biographical Memoirs*, vol. III, 1895, p.

3). James received his early education from his father and in the Baltimore schools, studied at the College of William and Mary (1820–21), and in 1822 received the degree of M.D. from the University of Maryland. After several years' experience, he found the practice of medicine distasteful. From boyhood he had been keenly interested in chemistry and had become proficient in delicate and complicated analysis. Accordingly, when the Baltimore firm of Tyson & Ellicott offered him the superintendency of its chemical works in 1827, he accepted the position. While engaged in his duties there he was appointed professor of chemistry in Washington Medical College, Baltimore. About 1829 he and his brother Henry became lecturers at the Maryland Institute, where until recently William Rogers had also served. During the latter part of his stay in Baltimore, he made investigations, with George W. Andrews and William R. Fisher, which resulted in an interesting contribution to forensic chemistry—"Minutes of an Analysis of Soup Containing Arsenic," published in the *Journal of the Philadelphia College of Pharmacy* (July 1834). He also carried on experiments with James Green, an instrument maker, which likewise produced valuable results, recorded in "Experiments with the Elementary Voltaic Battery" (*American Journal of Science and Arts,* April 1835). In 1835 he was called to the professorship of chemistry in the medical department of Cincinnati College. He had married in 1830 Rachel Smith of Harford County, Md.

Rogers remained in Cincinnati until 1839, declining in the meantime the position of melter and refiner in the branch mint at New Orleans. In 1837 he became associated with his brother William in the work of the Virginia Survey. In 1840 he took up his residence in Philadelphia and assisted his brother Henry, who was directing the Pennsylvania geological survey. He succeeded John K. Mitchell in 1841 as professor of chemistry in the Medical Institute of Philadelphia, and in 1844 was elected to a similar position in the Franklin Institute. He was made a member of the American Philosophical Society in 1846, and the following year succeeded Robert Hare, whom his father had succeeded at William and Mary twenty-eight years before, as professor of chemistry in the University of Pennsylvania.

With Robert Empie Rogers he published in 1846 *A Text Book on Chemistry,* and also an important article, "On the Alleged Insolubility of Copper in Hydrochloric Acid . . ." (*American Journal of Science and Arts,* November 1848). Much of his work was so bound up with that of his brothers that it is impossible to designate and

evaluate it. As a clear and interesting lecturer on scientific subjects he had few superiors in his day. Always of delicate constitution, he died of albuminuria in his fifty-first year, survived by his wife, two sons, and a daughter. His brother Robert succeeded him as professor of chemistry at the University of Pennsylvania.

[Joseph Carson, *A Memoir of the Life and Character of James B. Rogers, M.D.* (1852), and *A Hist. of the Medic. Department of the Univ. of Pa.* (1869); E. F. Smith, *James Blythe Rogers* (1927); W. S. W. Ruschenberger, "A Sketch of the Life of Robert E. Rogers, M.D., LL.D., with Biog. Notices of His Father and Brothers" in *Proc. Am. Philosophical Soc.,* vol. XXIII, 1886; *Life and Letters of William Barton Rogers* (2 vols., 1896), ed. by his wife; H. A. Kelly and W. L. Burrage, *Am. Medic. Biogs.* (1920).]   H. E. S.

ROGERS, JAMES HARRIS (July 13, 1856–Dec. 12, 1929), inventor, the son of James Webb and Cornelia (Harris) Rogers, was born in Franklin, Tenn. His father was a clergyman and chaplain during the Civil War on the staff of Gen. Leonidas Polk [*q.v.*]. James's earliest education was received from private tutors. In 1866 his father, having given up the ministry, took the family to Europe, and for a year young Rogers studied in St. Charles College, London. From his earliest boyhood he was intensely interested in the science of electricity and through study and experimentation soon acquired a knowledge of the subject remarkable for one so young.

Beginning his research work while living in France in 1867, he continued it in New York, where the family took up residence in 1868, and later in Peekskill, N. Y. Here, in cooperation with an older brother, he perfected a system of printing telegraph patented Aug. 20, 1872. Rogers continued his experimental work in New York for the succeeding five years, devising a number of interesting improvements in multiplex telegraphy. In 1877, when twenty-one years old, he went to Washington, D. C., where, upon the recommendation of Joseph Henry [*q.v.*], secretary of the Smithsonian Institution, he was appointed chief electrician of the United States Capitol. He carried on this work for the next six years, at the same time pursuing his electrical researches, one of the most interesting results of which was the invention of a system of secret telephony, for which Rogers received United States patents granted Dec. 20, 1881 (No. 251,292) and Jan. 10, 1882 (No. 252,257). Upon resigning his position at the Capitol in 1882, he devoted his full time to research in Washington, eventually, 1895, establishing a laboratory at Hyattsville, Md., where he lived until his death. In the course of these years he was granted some fifty patents for inventions relating to telephony, telegraphy, electric lighting, high frequency currents, and the transmitting of sounds through metal pipes. Probably the most interesting and valuable of these inventions was his system of printing telegraphy, for which he was granted patents between 1887 and 1894, and his underground and subsea radio transmission system, for which he received patents between 1917 and 1921. His printing telegraph system was in many respects a forerunner of the modern method in that a key operator was eliminated and messages were written on a typewriter. By the use of the principle of visual synchronism messages were transmitted at what was then phenomenal speed—approximately two hundred words a minute. About 1908 Rogers turned his attention to wireless telegraphy and to the possibility of transmission through the earth and sea. After undertaking a bit of experimental work at that time, he turned to other things until 1916, when he resumed his investigations and made such progress that with his underground antenna he could pick up messages from across the ocean. Although his discoveries had not yet been patented, in 1917 he offered them to the government. His offer was accepted and patents were issued to him later. Thereafter, until his death, he continued his researches in this same field, considerably interrupted, however, by litigation instituted to defend his patent rights. Among other recognitions of his work, he was awarded the Inventor's Medal of the Maryland Academy of Sciences. He never married.

[*Who's Who in America*, 1926–27; *Electrical Engineer*, Feb. 13, 1895, p. 149; *Scientific American*, Dec. 28, 1889; *Evening Star* (Washington), Dec. 12, 1929; *Washington Post*, Dec. 13, 1929; *Sun* (Baltimore), Dec. 13, 1929; information from relatives; Patent Office records.]

C. W. M.

ROGERS, JOHN (Dec. 1, 1648–Oct. 17, 1721), founder of the Rogerenes, was born in Milford, Conn., the son of Elizabeth (Rowland) and James Rogers who emigrated probably from England, settled at New London, Conn., about 1660, and became one of the richest merchants and landowners in Connecticut. The son was converted by the Seventh-Day Baptists of Newport, R. I., in 1674; he converted his father and brothers to the same creed, and elders from Rhode Island baptized them and admitted them into the Newport church. Having started to study the Bible independently, he gradually developed novel opinions, in which the Rhode Island Baptists could not follow him. Though still accepting the Calvinist doctrine of a new birth, he opposed salaried clergy, the use of meeting houses, formal prayers, and all connection between church and state. He freed his slaves and advocated non-resistance; and he refused to use medicine, believing that diseases should be cured by prayer and anointing with oil. He afterward abandoned the Seventh-Day Sabbath, holding religious services on Sunday but declaring labor on that day to be lawful. Rogerene services were held on the family farm at Great Neck in New London. He toured New England to propagate his doctrines but made few converts outside his own family. He wrote thirteen pamphlets in defense of his opinions, of which *The Book of the Revelation of Jesus Christ* (1720) is perhaps the most important. They are filled with involved theological arguments and do not show any great eloquence or learning. His methods of asserting his opinions were often lacking in tact and good taste; but the courage and firmness with which he endured half a century of persecution cannot be praised too highly. If his character had not been consistently blackened by orthodox historians, he would be remembered as a pioneer of religious freedom.

The state and ecclesiastical authorities, notably Gurdon Saltonstall [*q.v.*], were bitterly hostile to the new sect. The Rogerenes were repeatedly fined for non-attendance at meeting, laboring on the Sabbath, refusing payment of the minister's rates, non-attendance at military training, and entertaining Quakers. Rogers was imprisoned seven times, his various sentences totaling fifteen years; he was whipped twice, on the second occasion receiving seventy-six stripes on a charge of blasphemy. The Rogerenes retaliated by marching into the meeting house in New London during service and making public protests. They seem to have had the sympathy of their neighbors; Rogers was elected to various official positions in the town, juries acquitted him whenever possible, and the government had difficulty in finding officers who would enforce payment of fines. In 1670 he had married Elizabeth, the daughter of Matthew Griswold of Lyme. While under religious conviction he told her of some sexual misdemeanor he had committed before marriage. After his conversion she returned with their two children to her own family, who in 1676 persuaded the General Court to give her a divorce, alleging as sufficient reason what Rogers had confessed to her and accusing him of the most revolting vices. In 1699 Rogers took as a second wife a maid-servant, Mary Ransford, refusing to have any legal ceremony performed. The marriage was unhappy, and there were lawsuits between Mary Ransford and the Rogers family. In 1703 the county court imprisoned her for having a child without being legally married; she was rescued and sent to Block Island, where in 1710 with Rogers' approval she married Robert Jones. In 1714, after unsuccessful attempts to recover his divorced wife Elizabeth, Rogers married Mrs. Sarah Cole, a Quaker widow of Oyster Bay. In 1721 he caught smallpox in Boston and died after his return to New London. He was succeeded as leader of the Rogerenes by John Rogers, Jr., his son by Elizabeth (Griswold) Rogers, who had been brought up by his mother but had at the age of fourteen voluntarily returned to his father. The sect became extinct during the nineteenth century.

[See J. R. Bolles and A. B. Williams, *The Rogerenes* (1904); J. S. Rogers, *James Rogers of New London, Ct., and His Descendants* (1902); F. M. Caulkins, *History of New London* (1852); for the slanders on Rogers' moral character see a letter from William Leete to John Winthrop, Jr., *Mass. Hist. Soc. Colls.*, 4 Ser., Vol. VII (1865), p. 582; these slanders were repeated by most of the older historians of New England.]

H. B. P.

ROGERS, JOHN (Oct. 30, 1829–July 26, 1904), sculptor, was born at Salem, Mass., the son of John Rogers and the grandson of Daniel Denison Rogers, both merchants of Boston. He was descended from the Rev. Nathaniel Rogers who settled at Ipswich, Mass., in 1636, through the latter's son John, who was president of Harvard College in 1682–84. His mother, Sarah Ellen Derby, was the daughter of John Derby, a Salem merchant. His early education was obtained in the Boston public schools and was followed by a period as clerk in a local dry-goods store. After trouble with his eyes had put an end to the study of engineering, he spent some eight years in the occupation of machinist. Part of this time he lived in Manchester, N. H., where his statue of Lincoln was later erected, and part, after a trip to Spain in the search of health, in the Middle West. Eventually he had charge of a railroad repair shop in Hannibal, Mo. From the time he had seen a Boston craftsman moulding clay, he had spent many leisure hours with that pliant medium, and had exhibited at various New Hampshire fairs. Toward the end of 1858 he even went to Europe for a visit to Paris and a few months' training in the Roman studio of the English sculptor, Spence. Finding himself without an interest in the neo-classicism of that environment, however, he returned to America. He had learned little, perhaps, except the way to reproduce clay groups in plaster form, and he determined to continue in his original calling. He was in the city surveyor's office in Chicago when opportunity arrived with unmistakable steps. For a local charity fair in the interest of the United States Sanitary Commission, he exhibited "Checkers up at the Farm." The interest aroused was so great that he went to New York at the end of 1859 with the "Slave Auction." Although it was a sensational success in the stormy days of *Uncle Tom's Cabin* and Abolition oratory, Rogers yet had to have it peddled from door to door, so hesitant were the art dealers of the city to risk antagonizing their Southern patrons. For several years his situation in New York was financially precarious, but before the war had ended he was prospering.

From the Paris Exposition of 1867, where several bronze figures were shown, and the Centennial Exhibition at Philadelphia in 1876, where he had twenty-nine groups on view, to the World's Fair at Chicago, in 1893, marked by his seated Lincoln, and the award of a gold medal, Rogers was the recipient of critical as well as popular acclaim. He was a member of the National Academy after 1863, and of the National Sculpture Society. The "Rogers groups" may be conveniently divided into three classes. There are the Civil War groups, historically important, and containing some of Rogers' best portraits—the Lincoln in the "Council of War" is said by the Lincoln family to be the best likeness ever made. Then there are the literary and dramatic groups, marked by the spacing of a theatrical performance, and including the series for which Joseph Jefferson posed in his character of Rip Van Winkle, and the miniature scenes from Shakespeare. Perhaps a certain naïve tenderness is the chief charm of these fragile compositions. Then there are the *genre* groups, which include many of his most popular works. He perhaps never surpassed the "Checkers up at the Farm," but the "Charity Patient," with the drapery suggestive of a Tanagra figurine, the "Coming to the Parson," with the cat and dog motif poking gentle fun at the absorbed young lovers, and "Fetching the Doctor," where something of the movement and mass of monumental sculpture is caught, reveal the facility of this folk-artist. Occasional groups or figures were cast in bronze. There are also the equestrian statue of General Reynolds, at the City Hall, Philadelphia, and the seated Lincoln at Manchester to show his skill in work of heroic size. The horse of the former monument is especially notable. But it is not by forcing Rogers into competition with craftsmen of other types that one can best appreciate his work. His was not a monumental style. Nor was it primarily a style of exquisite grace, as the miniature proportions he preferred might lead one to suppose. It was rather the direct embodiment of what he saw, and knew, and thought about his environment. Such abstract elements of plastic beauty as occur are incidental.

Rogers married in 1865 Harriet Moore Francis, of New York City, the daughter of Charles Stephen Francis [q.v.]. They had five sons and two daughters. By 1877 he had established a home in New Canaan, Conn., where he spent his time when he was absent from his New York studio, long at 14 West Twelfth Street. After 1893 a nervous affection in his hands forced him to give up his work as sculptor. He died in New Canaan, July 26, 1904, and was buried in the Lakeview Cemetery. He has been described as a person of very gentle, but determined character, about whom friends of equal simplicity and sincerity liked to gather. His theory of plastic art seems to have been that the telling of a story should be the first consideration in creative work, emotion, whether pathos or humor, being a natural accompaniment. Opposing as he did the belief then current that the nude was the basis of plastic beauty, he held that it had no place in the art of a time in which the nude body was not habitually seen. The total number of his groups is uncertain. One writer gives eighty-seven as a fair estimate, though as yet no complete series has been collected. With the "gelatine mould" and bronze "master cast" as means of reproducing groups accurately and cheaply, the sculptor was able to sell over 100,000 copies during his lifetime. The prices asked in a catalogue published in 1876 vary from five to fifty dollars. The majority of the groups were made of red plaster around a metal frame; they were then dipped in gray paint, and averaged upward to twenty inches high. For the repair of the groups when the surface paint cracked, bottles of "refinishing color" were sold by the master craftsman. He patented the designs, sold pedestals and garden urns as accessories, and freely advertised his products.

In the galleries of the New York Historical Society and of the Essex Institute, Salem, the largest collections of Rogers groups are available to the public. The Metropolitan Museum, New York, and the Brooklyn Museum own a number of bronze "master casts." The cycle of criticism of Rogers' work seems now complete. Delighted wonder attended the exhibition of his early work, but in the nineties the tone of the critics was patronizing, a note which had not altogether disappeared when Taft wrote his *History of American Sculpture* in 1903. More recently, both those who value native sincerity in art, and those who are coming to agree that the

anecdote is a legitimate phase of plastic beauty, have encouraged a new appreciation of America's sculptor laureate in the age of horse-hair covered furniture, involved bric-a-brac, and festooned draperies.

[J. J. Jarves, *The Art Idea* (1864); H. T. Tuckerman, *Book of the Artists* (1867); Lorado Taft, *The Hist. of Am. Sculpture* (1903); Suzanne LaFollette, *Art in America* (1929); W. P. Eaton, "Catching up to John Rogers," *Am. Mag. of Art*, Sept. 1920; W. O. Partridge, "John Rogers, the People's Sculptor," *New Eng. Mag.*, Feb. 1896; *Descriptive Cat. . . . of Group Statuettes from the Studio of Mr. John Rogers* (1895); Mabel Beard, "Up from the Junk Pile," *N. Y. Herald Tribune*, Nov. 22, 1931; "America Discovers a Neglected Folk Art of Its Own," *N. Y. Times*, Nov. 8, 1931; *Who's Who in America*, 1903–05; *N. Y. Times*, July 27, 1904; information as to certain facts supplied by the sculptor's daughter, Miss K. R. Rogers.]
W. S. R.

ROGERS, JOHN ALMANZA ROWLEY (Nov. 12, 1828–July 22, 1906), Congregational clergyman, educator, was born in Cromwell, Conn., the son of John C. and Elizabeth (Hamlin) Rogers. He attended Williams Academy, Stockbridge, Mass., until his parents moved to Ohio, and then entered Oberlin College. After receiving the degree of A.B. in 1851, he prepared for the ministry in Oberlin Theological Seminary, supporting himself by teaching in Oberlin Academy and, during the long vacations, in New York City. He graduated in 1855 and the following year married Elizabeth Lewis Embree of Philadelphia, a Quaker girl.

On his wedding trip he was asked to take a group of orphans to Roseville, Ill. After preaching in the Congregational church of that town, he was invited to become its pastor and was there ordained. He remained in Roseville for about two years, and then, hearing that a friend had given up missionary work in Kentucky because of hardship and danger, he felt impelled to go there himself. The spirit and ideals of anti-slavery Oberlin had made a deep impression upon him, and he felt that nothing could help Kentucky so much as a similar Christian college. A few years before, John Gregg Fee [q.v.] had established an anti-slavery church in what came to be known as Berea, Madison County, Ky., and in 1855 had opened a school. Rogers chose this place for his labors and in April 1858 moved to Berea with the indorsement and financial support of the American Missionary Association. Here he and his wife began teaching fifteen pupils in a room the sides and roof of which were of split clapboards. Rogers made desks, maps, and charts, and introduced such startling innovations as music, pictures, and lectures. The school proved popular, and before the close of the term its enrollment had greatly increased. The following term two additional teachers were employed. Rogers was one of the little group which drew up a constitution for a college, completed and signed in July 1859, a stipulation of which was that the college should be "under an influence strictly Christian, and, as such, opposed to sectarianism, slaveholding, caste, and every other wrong institution or practice." John Brown's raid on Harpers Ferry inflamed the whole South and in December 1859 Rogers and ten others were ordered by an armed mob to leave the state. They appealed to Governor Magoffin, who answered that he could not protect them. They then left the state, but continued to make payments on land they had bought for the site of the college.

After serving for a time as traveling secretary of the American Missionary Association, in New York and New England, Rogers became pastor of the Presbyterian church in Decatur, Ohio, with the understanding that he might leave at a month's notice and return to Kentucky. In 1865 the exiles went back to Berea and reopened the school. Rogers conducted it and was also associated with Fee in the pastorate of the church. A college charter was obtained and the institution grew rapidly. Rogers was instrumental, in 1868, in having the trustees call Edward H. Fairchild, then head of the preparatory department at Oberlin, to the presidency, but remained as professor of Greek until 1878, and served as trustee up to the time of his death. After resigning his professorship, he was pastor of a church in Shawano, Wis., for five years. He then retired to Hartford, Conn. His death occurred at the home of a daughter-in-law in Woodstock, Ill. John Raphael Rogers [q.v.] was his son.

[J. A. R. Rogers, *Birth of Berea College* (1903); *Berea College* (1883); *Oberlin College: The Alumni Cat. of 1926* (1927); *Berea Quart.*, Oct. 1926; *Chicago Tribune* and *Courier-Jour.* (Louisville), July 24, 1906.]
J. W. R.

ROGERS, JOHN IGNATIUS (May 27, 1843–Mar. 13, 1910, lawyer, was born in Philadelphia, the son of Matthew and Catharine (Dimond) Rogers, who had emigrated from County Kerry, Ireland (Campbell, *post*, p. 514). He attended the public schools of his native city and graduated from the Central High School. Later, he studied law and in 1865 was admitted to the bar. Specializing in corporation and real-estate law, he was selected to administer the legal affairs of the Building Association League. In this connection he was largely instrumental in formulating and securing the approval of state laws dealing with the incorporation, and relief from certain taxation, of state building associations. In the year 1869 he was elected to the state House of Representatives, but was later defeated for the state Senate. Politically an ardent Democrat, in 1881 he was one of the founders of the Democratic Committee of Thirty-one which cooperated with the Committee of One-Hundred in electing a mayor of Philadelphia. In the year following, he declined nomination for the office of register of wills.

From his youth he took an active interest in state military affairs, enlisting as a private in the Philadelphia City Troop in 1873 and seeing active service in the serious Pittsburgh labor riots of the year 1877. As poet of this celebrated local organization, he prepared and read an original ode at the troop's centennial celebration, Nov. 17, 1874. In 1883 he was appointed by Governor Pattison colonel and judge-advocate general of the National Guard of Pennsylvania; and in 1887 and 1891 was reappointed to this office by succeeding governors. He was active in organizing the bureau of military justice and in securing adoption by the legislature of a revised military code (Act of Apr. 13, 1887). At the time of his resignation, Oct. 6, 1893, he was considered the foremost authority on military law in the state of Pennsylvania.

For many years Rogers was connected with professional baseball, and in 1882, became the principal stockholder and directing head of the Philadelphia National Baseball Club. As counsel for the club, he secured many legal decisions affecting to this day the status of baseball players. Noted as an eloquent speaker as well as a facile writer, he was in much demand as an orator at banquets and public gatherings. He was one of the founders of the Catholic Club of Philadelphia, and an active member of the Friendly Sons of St. Patrick, the Historical Society of Pennsylvania, and other local organizations. While on a business and pleasure trip in the West, he died suddenly from heart disease at Denver, Colo. He was survived by his widow, Elizabeth (Henkles) Rogers, of Germantown, to whom he was married June 20, 1876, and four sons and a daughter.

[L. M. Williamson and others, *Prominent and Progressive Pennsylvanians of the Nineteenth Century* (1898), vol. II; *A Biog. Album of Prominent Pennsylvanians* (1889), vol. II; J. H. Campbell, *Hist. of the Friendly Sons of St. Patrick* (1892); *Who's Who in Pa.*, 1904; *Public Ledger* (Phila.) and *North American* (Phila.), Mar. 14, 1910; *Phila. Inquirer*, Mar. 20, 1910.]
C. D. R.

ROGERS, JOHN RANKIN (Sept. 4, 1838–Dec. 26, 1901), governor of Washington, son of John and Margaret Ann (Greene) Rogers, was born at Brunswick, Me. His mother was a descendant of John Greene who settled in Rhode Island in 1637. At an early age John Rankin went to Boston to learn the druggist's trade, and from 1856 to 1861 he practised it in Mississippi, managing stores at Jackson and Terry. Opposed to the secession movement, he moved to Cumberland County, Ill., where he taught school and farmed until 1870. He then returned to Maine and for about five years was again engaged in the drug business. Removing to Kansas in 1876, he devoted himself to agriculture and helped organize the Farmer's Alliance. As a Greenback Republican he secured some local offices in Harvey County. His career as a publicist began in 1887 when he established and edited the *Kansas Commoner*.

In 1890 Rogers went to the state of Washington and established himself at Puyallup, Pierce County, where he dealt in real estate and conducted a mercantile business. His first and outstanding literary work, *The Irrepressible Conflict; or, An American System of Money* (1892), attracted wide attention. The following year he published a novel, *The Graftons; or Looking Forward*, reprinted in 1898 as *Looking Forward*. It had appeared originally in the *Kansas Commoner* in 1889 and is a typical newspaper serial for a populist organ. In 1894 he was elected to the lower house of the legislature and in the session of 1895 he introduced bills to redistribute the burden of taxation so as to relieve the small property holder, to improve conditions for workers in coal mines, and to broaden the scope of public education. The last-named measure, the only one of the three which passed, was the unique "Barefoot Schoolboy Law," which provided a maximum state tax of four mills to subsidize the county schools to the extent of at least six dollars for each child of school age.

A coalition of Populists, Silver Republicans, and Democrats elected him governor in 1896. His executive program, decidedly Populist, emphasized restraint in expenditures and more centralized administration for the various state institutions. After a hard struggle he defeated the plan to construct a state capitol building at a cost of $822,951 and negotiated instead the purchase of the Thurston County court house. Additional tax levies on the basis of his "Barefoot School Boy" principles and the furnishing of school textbooks by the state, free or at cost, were among his urgent recommendations to the legislature. The latter scheme, adopted in part, was not successful. When a pernicious lobby fought his measures for the control of railroads and rates he retaliated by calling public attention to its operations. Himself an indefatigable party worker, he was suspicious of orthodox machine politics. Amounting almost to an obsession was his belief in the sanctity of public opinion; no measures, even those in the interest of salutary reforms, would endure, he believed, without a decided mandate from a substantial majority of the people. That the people appreciated this confidence was revealed in the state elections of 1900, when he was reëlected governor by a substantial vote though all the rest of the offices went to orthodox Republicans.

He was in some respects a striking figure, slender, over six feet tall, with bold features set off by a large drooping mustache. His deep voice carried well; his speeches, marked by wide reading and an especial acquaintance with history, were forceful but a little heavy and tedious. On Mar. 17, 1861, he married Sarah L. Greene, of Illinois, by whom he had three sons and two daughters. He died at Olympia from an attack of lobar pneumonia.

[*"Washington," in *Appletons' Ann. Cyc.*, 1896–1901; obituary, *Ibid.*, 1901, p. 464; *Steel and Searle's Legislative Souvenir Manual*, 1895–96; G. S. Greene and L. B. Clarke, *The Greenes of R. I.* (1903); *Spokesman-Review* (Spokane), Dec. 27, 1901, Jan. 2, 1902; *Seattle Daily Times*, Dec. 27, 1901.]   H. J. D.

ROGERS, JOHN RAPHAEL (Dec. 11, 1856–Feb. 18, 1934), inventor, son of the Rev. John Almanza Rowley Rogers [*q.v.*] and Elizabeth Lewis (Embree), was born in Roseville, Ill. His father was connected with Berea College, Kentucky, in its early days, and after spending three years as a student there, John went to Oberlin College, from which he was graduated with the degree of A.B. in 1875. He then began teaching in the public schools of Michigan and later accepted a position in Berea College. From 1877 to 1881 he was superintendent of schools at Lorain, Ohio. For the next two years he was engaged in railroad engineering work in Iowa and Michigan, at the end of which time he returned to Lorain to teach, remaining there until 1888. Meanwhile, he had become interested in mechanical type setting, having, as early as 1881, begun experiments with the view of finding a way to space the lines of type, that is, to "justify" them, mechanically. He worked steadily on this problem in his spare time for seven years, and on Sept. 4, 1888, obtained a patent (No. 389,108) for a machine making stereotype matrices. Thereupon, he gave up his teaching position in Lorain, moved to Cleveland, Ohio, and organized the Rogers Typograph Company to manufacture this machine. Two years later, however, his Typograph came into competition with the Mergenthaler Linotype, and through a suit brought against Rogers' company, the

Mergenthaler company obtained an injunction upon the production of a slug. Prior to this, Rogers had devised a form of double-wedge space band and applied for a patent. This invention brought him into a three-cornered interference suit with Ottmar Mergenthaler [q.v.] and another inventor, Jacobs W. Schuckers, who had filed applications for patents involving similar principles about the same time. The wedge-spacing mechanism was essential to each inventor's machine, and Rogers bought Schuckers' application. After some years of litigation, credit for the broad principle of the double-wedge was awarded to Schuckers and the right to utilize it became the property of the Rogers Typograph Company. Since the Linotype also required the double-wedge space band, the Mergenthaler company finally bought all the assets of the Rogers company, and in July 1895 the two were consolidated. Rogers then entered the employ of the Mergenthaler Linotype Company in Brooklyn, N. Y., as consulting engineer and chief of its experimental department, in which capacity he served for the remainder of his life.

Rogers must be given much credit for broadening the scope and increasing the usefulness of Mergenthaler's original one-letter Linotype. He considered thousands of ideas submitted by machinists and operators and developed and refined those that were worth while, making them commercially profitable. In the course of his many years he patented between 400 and 500 devices in the field of composing machines. He was one of the few inventors whose ability yielded due financial reward, and this he used largely for the education of young people. He was for many years a member of the board of directors of the American Missionary Association and a trustee of Oberlin College and of Berea College. He was married twice: first, on Dec. 25, 1878, to Clara Ardelia Saxton of Oberlin, who died in 1932; second, to Mrs. Marion Rood Pratt of Cleveland, Ohio, who with two adopted daughters survived him. He died in Brooklyn, N. Y., and was buried in Berea, Ky.

[*Who's Who in America*, 1930–31; *Printing Equipment Engineer*, Mar. 1934; *N. Y. Times*, Feb. 19, 1934; *Oberlin Alumni Mag.*, Dec. 1924; *Necrological Record of Oberlin Alumni* (1934); Patent Office records; information from the Mergenthaler Linotype Company.]   C. W. M.

ROGERS, MOSES (c. 1779–Oct. 15, 1821), early steamboat captain, was born in New London, Conn., the eldest of seven children of Amos and Sarah (Phillips) Rogers. The family, which included among its members many mariners and fishermen, traced its American ancestry to James Rogers who was living in New London

as early as 1660. Moses learned to manage a sailboat in boyhood and by 1800 was in command of a sailing vessel on Long Island Sound. On Feb. 18, 1804, he married Adelia Smith, by whom he had three sons and two daughters. He became greatly interested in steamboat experiments, especially those of John Stevens [q.v.], in some of which he may have had a part. It is frequently stated that he commanded Fulton's *Clermont,* but no original record has come to light which proves this assertion. In any event, he could have commanded it for only a few trips in the fall of 1807 before he was selected by John and Robert L. Stevens [q.v.] to command their steamer, the *Phoenix.* The monopoly of Hudson steam navigation granted to the Fulton-Livingston interests made it necessary to send the *Phoenix,* in 1809, by Sandy Hook and Cape May to the Delaware River for service, and Rogers was captain on this, the earliest ocean voyage of a steam vessel. He continued as captain while the *Phoenix* plied between Philadelphia and Bordentown, N. J., the first steamer on the Delaware and the western link of a stagecoach-steamboat route from New York to Philadelphia. In 1815 he commanded the *Eagle* on the first voyage made by steamer from New York to Baltimore, and later he became part owner of a bi-weekly line between these ports. He also took out patents in 1814 and 1815 for a horse-power ferry-boat which was adopted on several ferry-lines in New York harbor and evidently used in other places.

In 1818, seeing the future *Savannah* under construction in New York, Rogers persuaded Scarborough & Isaacs, a Savannah shipping firm, to purchase it, fit it with engines, and experiment in the use of steam on the ocean. Rogers superintended the building of the engines, paddle wheels, and accompanying machinery. The paddle wheels he constructed so that they could be quickly taken from the water and placed on board in case it was desired to use only sail, an innovation dictated by his experience on the maiden trip of the *Phoenix* when the paddle wheels were badly damaged by storm. After having made the journey from New York to Savannah, Rogers left the latter city on May 22, 1819, for Liverpool. With him on this voyage, as navigator, went Stevens Rogers (Feb. 13, 1789–Nov. 30, 1882), also of New London, designer of the *Savannah's* rigging, who had been associated with him in the *Phoenix* and the *Eagle* and later became his brother-in-law. This first voyage of a steamship across the Atlantic can scarcely be called the first crossing of the ocean by steam, since the passage consumed twenty-nine days and eleven hours, of which time sails were used for twenty-six days and three hours. The voyage was continued to Stockholm and St. Petersburg, where the *Savannah* was visited by many of the nobility, including the Prince of Sweden and the Emperor of Russia. On the stormy voyage home sails were used until the ship was in the Savannah River. The owners were forced to sell the *Savannah,* and Rogers formed new connections with a company about to operate steamers on the Great Peedee River between Georgetown and Cheraw, S. C. He superintended the construction of the *Peedee* in 1820, and while in command of it the following year was stricken with malarial fever. He died and was buried in Georgetown. Though his *Savannah* undertaking did not bear immediate fruit in promoting transatlantic steamship service, Rogers deserves credit for mechanical ingenuity and courageous seamanship.

[The best source of information is J. E. Watkins, "The Log of the Savannah," in *Ann. Report of the Board of Regents of the Smithsonian Institution . . . 1890* (1891), based on the original logbook, preserved in that institution, and on contemporary newspaper references; obituary notice reprinted from the *Georgetown Intelligencer* shows 1821 rather than 1822 to be the correct date of Rogers' death. See also J. S. Rogers, *James Rogers of New London, Ct., and His Descendants* (1902), and A. D. Turnbull, *John Stevens, An Am. Record* (1928).]   O. W. H.

ROGERS, RANDOLPH (July 6, 1825–Jan. 15, 1892), sculptor of the "Columbus doors" of the Capitol at Washington, was born at Waterloo, N. Y., the son of John and Sara (McCarthy) Rogers. The father was a carpenter from the neighborhood of Syracuse, who in successive stages was moving west. He eventually settled in Ann Arbor, Mich., where the future sculptor lived from his eighth to his eighteenth year, a period marked by some education in the common schools and by some clerical experience in a general store. For the next five years he worked in the wholesale dry-goods store of John Stewart in New York City. Long an amateur in the various artistic media, he had been paid ten dollars for a wood engraving of a log cabin and flags by an Ann Arbor paper, and had thereby supplied the party emblem for Harrison's campaign in 1840; now he attracted the attention of his employers by his modeling of the children of one of them, Lycurgus Edgerton, and by a bust of Lord Byron. As a result Stewart and Edgerton lent their clerk the funds for a period of study in Italy. From 1848 to 1851 he worked at the Academy of St. Mark in Florence under Lorenzo Bartolini, celebrated as a neo-classicist of ability. With the proceeds of the sale of an ideal bust called "Night" and a kneeling figure, "Ruth,"

made at the close of the period, he repaid his benefactors their loans to him and for the following two years was established in a studio of his own in Rome, modeling his most popular figure, "Nydia," Bulwer-Lytton's blind girl of Pompeii, prior to his return to America in 1853. The commission for a statue of John Adams for Mt. Auburn Cemetery in Cambridge, and for the bronze doors to face the corridor leading from Statuary Hall to the new House wing of the Capitol at Washington fell to his lot at this time. In 1855 he was again in his studio in Rome, where he centered his activities for the rest of his life, save for occasional professional trips to America. A short visit in the fall of 1857 was marked by his marriage to Rosa Gibson of Richmond, Va., who became the mother of his nine children.

In 1861 the "Isaac" was modeled, and the Washington Monument in Richmond, left incomplete by Thomas Crawford, was finished with two historical figures, and six allegorical figures in place of the eagles originally planned. The Colt funereal monument in Hartford, Conn., "The Angel of the Resurrection," followed in 1862. During the winter of 1863, which he passed in Cincinnati, he received the commission for the first of his military monuments, "The Soldier of the Line." An amazing number of orders for portrait busts, nineteen in the winter of 1866 alone, as well as for medallions, bas-reliefs, and other private commissions, kept him busy until his great opportunity came in 1867 with the order for colossal soldiers' and sailors' monuments for Providence and for Detroit. These were masses of granite, fifty feet in height, decorated with bronze figures and reliefs. Toward the close of his active career came the soldiers' monument at Worcester, Mass., the seated Lincoln in Fairmount Park, Philadelphia, and the Seward in Madison Square, New York City. His last ideal works were the "Lost Pleiad," which has vied in popularity with the "Nydia" of his early days, the "Genius of Connecticut" for the state capitol at Hartford, and the "Last Arrow," an equestrian Indian group. After 1882 the sculptor had to give up his work because of paralysis. Between 1886 and 1888 he forwarded most of the casts representing his life work to the Museum of Art and Architecture of the University of Michigan at Ann Arbor. He died in Rome, Jan. 15, 1892, and, having become a member of the Roman Catholic Church in his later years, was buried with his wife in San Lorenzo Cemetery, the grave marked by his finest funereal monument, representing a freed soul rising with lightness, dignity, and grace.

Randolph Rogers is described as having been

a large, powerful man of great vigor and of unsparing industry. He was of distinguished appearance, with the massive forehead, the strong features, and the long beard of the patriarch—an indispensable member of the American colony in Rome. He has been depicted as a convivial friend and amateur actor, the companion of Greenough and Crawford, entertaining in his studio Hawthorne one day and royalty the next, going his whole-souled, generous way in a somewhat heroic fashion. In 1873 he was chosen professor of sculpture at the Academy of St. Luke in Rome, and a councilor of the Academy in 1875. He was decorated with the order of Cavaliere della Corona D'Italia in 1884. His "Ruth" and "Nydia" attracted much attention at the Centennial Exhibition in Philadelphia in 1876, and as recently as 1931 the exhibition of a bust of his wife in the art museum of Grand Rapids occasioned appreciative comment in the local press.

The University of Michigan is the center for any present-day study of Rogers' work. The set of original casts there is nearly complete, although the models of the "Columbus doors" are duplicates. Rogers' style is that of the neo-classic period, his subject matter is narrative in character, his modeling approaches realism. Of his popular successes, the "Nydia" is at the Chicago Art Institute, the "Lost Pleiad" at the art museum in San Francisco, and the "Ruth" in the Metropolitan Museum in New York. The doors at Washington are now placed at the main entrance of the rotunda, and wear well as narrative rather than as decorative or creative art. They follow in general the designs Ghiberti used for his second pair of doors on the Baptistry at Florence. With borders marked by mouldings, trophies, and niches, eight panels and a culminating lunette tell the story of Columbus' adventures clearly and dramatically. But perhaps Rogers at his best is represented by the "Michigan," a heroic figure on the top of the Detroit monument, or by the heroic negro figure of "Emancipation" on the same monument.

[Sources include: A manuscript biography of Rogers by his wife; J. J. Jarves, *The Art Idea* (1864); H. T. Tuckerman, *Book of the Artists* (1867); Nathaniel Hawthorne, Preface to *The Marble Faun* (1860); Lorado Taft, *The Hist. of Am. Sculpture* (1903); M. L. D'Ooge, *Cat. of the Gallery of Art . . . in the Univ. of Mich.* (n.d.); C. E. Fairman, *Art and Artists of the Capitol* (1927); *N. Y. Times*, Jan. 16, 1892.]
                                                    W. S. R.

ROGERS, ROBERT (Nov. 7, 1731 o.s.–May 18, 1795), colonial ranger, was born in the frontier village of Methuen, Mass., the son of James and Mary Rogers. As he grew to manhood on his father's farm near Rumford, now Concord, N. H., he developed a remarkable physique, early

devoted himself to hunting, Indian trading, and exploring the northern wilderness, and became a typical roving frontiersman. In January 1755 he was discovering his exceptional talents as a recruiting officer in raising men for William Shirley's expedition to Nova Scotia, when, to escape prosecution on the charge of counterfeiting New Hampshire currency, he entered the New Hampshire regiment, and he soon became a captain on William Johnson's Crown Point expedition. His boldness in procuring intelligence by scouting enemy forces and positions and by capturing prisoners commended him to Johnson, and he remained in the services of the colonies during the winter. In March 1756 Shirley appointed him captain of an independent company of rangers, paid from British contingent funds, and in 1758 Abercromby promoted him to be major of nine such companies, the scouting arm of the British army. Valuable though these companies were, their independence and lack of discipline diminished their usefulness. Rogers himself sometimes preferred spectacular and hazardous exploits to a more reasoned course. Nevertheless, he made scores of raids in winter and summer and participated in several bloody engagements, enlivened with such dashing courage, incredible hardihood, and humorous pranks, that he became famous alike in England and the colonies, the most romantic figure of the war. He was with Loudon at Halifax in 1757, with Abercromby at Ticonderoga in 1758, with Amherst at Crown Point in 1759, when he destroyed the Saint Francis Indians in a daring raid, and again in 1760 in the final campaign about Montreal. Later that year he was sent west as far as Detroit and Shawneetown to receive the surrender of all French posts ("Journal of Robert Rogers . . . on His Expedition for Receiving the Capitulation of Western French Posts," *Bulletin of the N. Y. Public Library*, April 1933).

During the next fifteen years he proved himself incapable of coping with the problems of peace and civilization. He saddled himself with debts, amounting in time to £13,000. He failed to utilize opportunities in Portsmouth opened by his marriage on June 30, 1761, with Elizabeth Browne, the daughter of the Rev. Arthur Browne. In 1761 he served as captain of an independent company against the Cherokee in South Carolina, where the governor and council recommended him as superintendent of southern Indians; in 1763, as captain of a New York independent company, he accompanied Dalyell's force to Detroit and aided in the defense of that post against Pontiac. The want of principle displayed by his illicit trading with Indians and his incapacity for administration kept him from receiving further employment in America, and in 1765 he sailed for England to solicit preferment. There he published his *Journals* and *A Concise Account of North America,* both in 1765, and a crude play, *Ponteach: or the Savages of America. A Tragedy,* anonymously in 1766, one of the first dramas written by a native New Englander. He was lionized in the public prints. Though his proposal to lead an expedition to discover the Northwest Passage was refused, he was successful in gaining appointment to the command of the fort at Michilimackinac.

For two years, with his wife, he lived in that desolate post. There he commissioned Jonathan Carver [*q.v.*] to undertake the exploratory journey into the present Minnesota and seems to have been the first person to use in writing or in print the word Ouragon (Oregon). Disregarding his implicit instructions from Johnson and Gage, he tried to administer his territory, and especially the Indian trade, in his own interests, and schemed for a separate civil and military establishment. He was finally arrested on a charge of treasonable dealings with the French but acquitted for want of evidence. The journal he kept from Sept. 21, 1766, to July 3, 1767, was printed by William L. Clements in the *Proceedings of the American Antiquarian Society* (Oct. 1918). In England again in 1769, after vain efforts to gain reimbursement or employment, he brought unsuccessful suit against Gage for assault and imprisonment and was finally thrown into a debtor's prison, from which his brother James rescued him by assuming his chief debts. In 1774—so he later asserted—he served under the Dey of Algiers. He returned to America in 1775 and for a time courted both the Americans and British. Washington suspected his motives and in 1776 imprisoned him as a spy. Escaping to the British, he raised the Queen's American rangers but was utterly defeated in a skirmish near White Plains and deprived of his command. Thereafter he was employed in recruiting, but the same dishonesty and dissipation that had wrecked his other ventures rendered him useless for this service. In 1778 the New Hampshire legislature granted his wife's petition for divorce, and she continued to have the custody of their only child. In 1780 he fled to England to escape condemnation. Fifteen years later, still receiving half-pay, he died in a cheap London lodging-house and was buried at St. Mary, Newington.

[Manuscript copy of Rogers' journal of the march from Montreal to Detroit, 1760–61, is in the Canadian archives; among the Treasury Solicitor Papers in the Public Record Office in London is a copy of his court-martial, in connection with his King's Bench action against General Gage; additional manuscript material can be found in the Amherst Papers in the Public Record Office, in the Loudoun Papers in the Huntington Lib., San Marino, Cal., and in the Gage and British Headquarters Papers in the William L. Clements Lib., Ann Arbor, Mich.; see also biog. sketch by Allan Nevins in *Ponteach* (Caxton club ed. 1914); M. M. Quaife, "Robert Rogers," *Burton Hist. Coll. Leaflet,* Sept. 1928; Arthur Pound, *Native Stock* (1931); T. C. Elliott, "Jonathan Carver's Source for the Name Oregon," *Quart. of Ore. Hist. Soc.,* Mar. 1922, esp. p. 66; birth date from *Vital Records of Methuen, Mass.* (1909) and verification with the manuscript records.]

S. M. P.

ROGERS, ROBERT EMPIE (Mar. 29, 1813–Sept. 6, 1884), chemist, educator, son of Dr. Patrick Kerr and Hannah (Blythe) Rogers, was born in Baltimore, Md. His middle name was of his own choosing, adopted in his youth out of regard for the Rev. Adam Empie, president of the College of William and Mary (1827–36). Robert was the youngest of the celebrated Rogers brothers, scientists, the other three being James Blythe, William Barton, and Henry Darwin [*qq.v.*]. He received his early education from his father, who in 1819 became professor of natural philosophy and chemistry at William and Mary; after the father's death in 1828, he was taken in charge by his brothers James and William. His first work was in the field of engineering, and in 1831–32 he was connected with railroad surveying parties in New England. He then entered the University of Pennsylvania and graduated with the degree of M.D. in 1836, his thesis, *Experiments upon the Blood* (1836), showing that at this early age he possessed rare manipulative skill and the spirit of a true investigator.

He did not become a practising physician, however. While at the University he had spent much time in the chemical laboratory of Robert Hare [*q.v.*], and he now became chemist to the first Pennsylvania geological survey, of which his brother Henry was the head. Much of his work was routine, although he and Martin H. Boyé [*q.v.*] made an independent analysis of limestones. In 1842 he became professor of general and applied chemistry in the University of Virginia, a position involving the kind of work best suited to his tastes and ability—teaching and investigating. His teaching was characterized by dexterity in experiment and lucidity in exposition; moreover, he was sincerely interested in the everyday life of his students, and in turn was beloved by them. His investigations during this period were mostly done in conjunction with his brother William. Together they devised a new process for preparing chlorine (still commonly used), improved processes for making formic acid and aldehyde, and perfected a method of determining the carbon in graphite. They studied the volatility of potassium and sodium carbonates, the decomposition of rocks by meteoric water, and the absorption of carbon dioxide by liquids, the last named investigation being a helpful contribution to the analysis of mineral waters. At about this time, in collaboration with his brother James, he studied the alleged insolubility of copper in hydrochloric acid, and also published *A Text Book on Chemistry* (1846), a compact work compiled from contemporary books by English authors.

James died in 1852 and Robert succeeded him as professor of chemistry in the medical school of the University of Pennsylvania, becoming dean four years later. In 1855 he edited *Physiological Chemistry,* a translation by G. E. Day of Karl Gotthelf Lehmann's work. In the succeeding years he engaged in expert chemical work and for a time during the Civil War performed numerous duties as assistant surgeon in the West Philadelphia military hospital. In this institution he lost his right hand while showing a laundress how to use an ironing machine. He speedily learned to write with his left hand, however, and to use with remarkable skill what remained of his right arm. On Feb. 21, 1863, occurred the death of his wife, Fanny Montgomery, daughter of Joseph S. Lewis of Philadelphia, whom he had married Mar. 13, 1843. On Apr. 30, 1866, he married Delia Saunders. His interest in applied chemistry led him to make a study of petroleum, and through unfortunate speculations in 1864 in connection with the Humboldt Oil Company he sustained a considerable financial loss. Because of his knowledge of precious metals and their ores he was appointed in 1872 to investigate the waste of silver in the Philadelphia mint; soon afterward he made helpful suggestions about refining which were adopted with profit. In 1875 he prepared the plans for the equipment of the refinery of the mint in San Francisco; and that same year, under instructions of the Director of the Mint, he investigated the Virginia and California mines in Nevada, for the purpose of estimating their probable total yield of gold and silver. In 1877 he resigned his position at the University of Pennsylvania to accept the professorship of medical chemistry and toxicology in Jefferson Medical College, Philadelphia, which position he held until just before his death. He was a member of many scientific organizations and served them in various official capacities. In 1840 he shared in the organization of the Association of American Geologists and Naturalists (later the American Association for the Advancement of Science);

he was also an original member of the National Academy of Sciences.

[W. S. W. Ruschenberger, "A Sketch of the Life of Robert E. Rogers with Biog. Notices of His Father and Brothers," in *Proc. Am. Philosophical Soc.,* vol. XXIII (1886); E. F. Smith, in *Biog. Memoirs, National Acad. Sci.,* vol. V (1905), which includes bibliog., and *Chemistry in America* (1914), which includes bibliog.; *Jour. of Chemical Educ.,* Apr. 1932; H. A. Kelly and W. L. Burrage, *Am. Medic. Biogs.* (1920); *Life and Letters of William Barton Rogers* (1896); *Phila. Press,* Sept. 7, 1884.] L. C. N.

ROGERS, ROBERT WILLIAM (Feb. 14, 1864–Dec. 12, 1930), Orientalist, was born in Philadelphia, the son of Dr. Samuel and Mary (Osborne) Rogers. Irish and Welsh strains mingled in his ancestry, but the Irish, of which he was most proud, dominated. He was educated at the Central High School in Philadelphia and at the University of Pennsylvania, where he graduated in 1886 with the degree of bachelor of arts; in 1887 he received the same degree from Johns Hopkins University. His interest in Oriental studies was awakened when he was in his fifteenth year. While reading John Stuart Blackie's *On Self-Culture, Intellectual, Physical, and Moral* (1874), he came across the statement that the Book of Job in the Old Testament was the greatest book in all literature. He determined, therefore, to read it for himself. Finding in it much he could not understand, he acquired the commentary on Job in Lange's series. Since it contained many Hebrew words, he sought the help of a neighboring Lutheran minister and began the study of Hebrew. This study he continued while at college, adding, at Johns Hopkins University, the study of Assyrian under Prof. Paul Haupt [*q.v.*]. When in 1887 Prof. J. Rendel Harris left Hopkins for Haverford College, Rogers followed him thither as instructor in Greek and Hebrew. Continuing his Oriental studies, he received from Haverford the degree of doctor of philosophy in 1890. As a boy he had been brought up in the Protestant Episcopal Church, but later allied himself with the Methodist Episcopal, and in 1890 he was admitted on trial to the Philadelphia Conference; in 1894 he was ordained elder. From 1890 to 1892 he was professor of English Bible and Semitic history in Dickinson College, Carlisle, Pa. In 1893 he was called to the professorship of Hebrew and Old Testament exegesis in Drew Theological Seminary, Madison, N. J., a position which he filled until 1929. He was an instructor at the summer sessions of Columbia University from 1915 to 1921. In 1919 he was made professor of ancient Oriental literature in Princeton University, on the Paton Foundation, which position he held conjointly with his professorship in Drew until 1929. On June 3, 1891, he married Ida Virginia Ziegler of Philadelphia, who with two children survived him.

Throughout his life Rogers was an ardent student of Assyriology, Hebrew, and the Old Testament and made his contributions to knowledge in these fields. He spent many of his summers at Oxford and other European centers prosecuting his researches in their libraries. In addition to numerous articles, he was the author of *Outlines of the History of Early Babylonia* (1895); *A History of Babylonia and Assyria* (2 vols., 1900; 6th ed., rewritten, 1915); *The Religion of Babylonia and Assyria* (1908); *Cuneiform Parallels to the Old Testament* (1912); *The Recovery of the Ancient Orient* (1912); *The History and Literature of the Hebrew People* (2 vols., 1917), comprising a manual for teachers and a textbook for students; *Great Characters of the Old Testament* (1920); *A Book of Old Testament Lessons* (2 vols., 1921), a lectionary; *A History of Ancient Persia* (1929). Rogers' work, while intelligent and accurate, was that of an interpreter rather than a discoverer of new material or one who blazes new paths. His *History of Babylonia and Assyria* was, when published, not only the most competent history of these nations in any language but so interestingly written that it found many enthusiastic readers beyond the circle professionally concerned with the subject. As a lecturer, he was often in demand in various parts of the United States, and at one time visited Japan and China, in both of which countries he delivered courses of lectures to continually increasing audiences. He had the gift of making the ancient world live again until his listeners shared with him something of the thrill which he found in the story of ancient life. Although he fully accepted the modern critical view of the Old Testament, he possessed such tact and consideration for the normal growth of his students that he escaped the ecclesiastical censure visited by his Church upon some of its other Old Testament scholars.

His contributions to scholarship were rewarded by recognition from many institutions. In addition to the degree from Haverford College, he received that of Ph.D. from the University of Leipzig in 1895; and numerous honorary degrees. He was a member of Oriental and archeological societies, both American and foreign, and towards the close of his life was elected a member of the American Philosophical Society. In 1929, owing to physical infirmities, he resigned both his professorships and retired to a farm near Chadds Ford, Pa., which he named

"Omagh Farm." Here he was living at the time of his death.

[*Who's Who in America*, 1930–31; *Methodist Who's Who*, 1915; *Methodist Rev.*, May–June, 1931; *Christian Advocate*, May 2, 16, 1929, and Dec. 25, 1930; *N. Y. Times*, Dec. 13, 1930.]   G. A. B.

ROGERS, STEPHEN (January 1826–May 23, 1878), surgeon, was born at Tyre, N. Y. His father, a farmer of very limited means, could give his son few opportunities for study and until the age of seventeen Stephen was employed on the farm, educating himself meanwhile by extensive reading. Later, by working in a store and hiring himself out as a farm laborer, he saved enough money to obtain a scanty education in nearby schools. He read freely in the library of a local physician, spent some time in hospitals in New York, and heavily in debt, accepted an appointment as surgeon to the Panama Railroad, then being built (1849–55). Five years of arduous work in the tropics seriously impaired his health, but he recovered after a prolonged convalescence in Havana, Cuba. During this period he became thoroughly acquainted with Spanish and his knowledge of this language, combined with his professional skill, secured for him a post as surgeon to the Southern Railroad of Chile, with headquarters in Santiago. While there, in 1857, he married the daughter of Samuel F. Haveland. The degree of M.D. had been granted to him by the New York Medical College in 1856, before he went to Chile.

Returning to New York in 1865, he practised surgery in that city and made several contributions to medical jurisprudence while connected with the coroner's office. These were contained in papers read before the Medico-Legal Society of New York, a society in which he took a great interest, serving as president in 1871. His most important medical contribution was a paper on ruptured extra-uterine pregnancy (*Transactions of the American Medical Association*, vol. XVIII, 1867). In it he not only gave a careful description of the signs and symptoms of this condition but also advocated immediate surgical treatment. This paper was enlarged and published as a monograph, *Extra-uterine Foetation and Gestation, and the Early Signs Which Characterize It* (1867). Other papers include an early report on excision of the scapula (*American Journal of the Medical Sciences*, October 1868), which was reprinted separately that same year; on the use of quinine in treating tropical malaria (*Transactions of the Medical Society of the State of New York*, 1862); and a timely protest against the hypodermic use of the same drug (*New York Medical Journal*, September

1874), also printed separately. In 1875, his health again somewhat impaired, he was appointed United States commissioner to the International Exhibition of Chile. While there, he resumed his practice as a surgeon in Santiago, but died three years later while on a visit to Valparaiso.

Dignified in manner and military in bearing, Rogers was much beloved by his associates. He was a scholarly, able surgeon, esteemed in both Chile and New York. Honorary degrees were conferred upon him by the University of Havana (1857) and the University of Chile (1857) and he held membership in the New York Academy of Medicine and the Obstetrical Society of Berlin, Germany. For a short period he was professor of physiological and microscopic anatomy in the New York Medical College.

[William Shrady, in *Bull. Medico-Legal Soc. of N. Y.*, Dec. 1878; *Boletín de la Esposición Internacional de Chile en 1875* (1875), pp. 466 ff.; *Am. Gynecology*, Sept. 1903, p. 266; H. A. Kelly and W. L. Burrage, *Am. Medic. Biogs.* (1920).]   H. R. V.

ROGERS, THOMAS (Mar. 16, 1792–Apr. 19, 1856), inventor, locomotive builder, son of John and Mary (Larrabee) Rogers, was born on his father's farm in Groton, Conn. He was descended from James Rogers who was in New London, Conn., as early as 1660, and was a great-great-grandson of John Rogers, 1648–1721 [*q.v.*], founder of a sect known as the Rogerenes. At the age of sixteen, after receiving a common-school education, Thomas became a carpenter's apprentice and then learned blacksmithing from an uncle. When twenty years old he left home and settled in Paterson, N. J., just at the beginning of the War of 1812. After serving throughout that struggle, he returned to Paterson and soon found employment in a shop that made wooden looms. He also learned pattern making and in the course of four years saved some money with which, in 1819, he purchased the manufacturing rights for a newly imported power loom. He and John Clark then organized the firm of Clark & Rogers and began the manufacture of the new loom, undertaking, also, the spinning of cotton. The business was immediately successful; a second partner, Abraham Godwin, was taken into the company in 1820; the plant was enlarged in 1822; and nine years later Rogers withdrew with $38,000 as his share of the profits.

With this capital he began the construction of a new textile machine manufacturing plant in Paterson, which he called the "Jefferson Works." Upon its completion in 1832 he organized the Rogers, Ketchum & Grosvenor Machine Works and, with Rogers as president, the company began operations. During the first year, in addition to textile machinery the company began making railroad car wheels and boxes and other railroad castings. These were of such good quality that Rogers was soon approached by the leaders in railroad enterprises with the urgent request that he engage in the construction of locomotives. After three years he acceded to these requests and late in 1836 publicly announced in the *American Railroad Journal* (Dec. 24) that his company "was prepared to receive orders for locomotives and tenders." In the meantime, the company had constructed additional buildings and also had imported from England machine tools of all kinds. Rogers, furthermore, had made a close study of the "McNeill," the first locomotive on the Paterson & Hudson River Railroad, imported from England in 1833, and from this had prepared his first design. Immediately following its announcement, the company began the construction of a locomotive intended for the New Jersey Railroad & Transportation Company. The task was an extremely trying one for Rogers, but after many months the locomotive was completed and on Oct. 6, 1837, made a successful trial trip. It was immediately purchased by the newly organized Mad River & Lake Erie Railroad, given the name "Sandusky," and shipped to Ohio, although not a foot of track had been laid. Since it was the first locomotive west of the Alleghany Mountains, its gauge was made the standard for Ohio. In this locomotive the driving wheels were made with cast-iron centers and hollow spokes, and the crank and connecting rod were counterbalanced by adding sufficient extra weight to the section of the wheels opposite the crank. For these improvements Rogers was responsible; he did not patent them, but in order to insure their being public property, he filed specifications in the patent office on July 12, 1837. Three additional locomotives similar to the "Sandusky," each with a single pair of driving wheels, were completed by Rogers, Ketchum & Grosvenor by the middle of 1838. In 1839 Rogers designed and built a new type of locomotive, and, in 1842, produced the "Stockbridge," with cylinders outside of the frame. Two years later, he produced the type of locomotive which was subsequently adopted generally throughout the United States. This had two pairs of coupled driving wheels and was remarkable in that it was the first example of the use of equalizing beams between the driving wheels and front swiveling truck. Always progressive, Rogers took the lead in adopting improvements that others regarded with distrust. Thus to him belongs the credit of introducing the shifting link valve motion on locomotives in the United States; he was the first, also, in 1850, to apply the wagon top boiler. In his twenty years of locomotive building, as in his earlier manufacturing work, he was extremely successful and was actively connected with his company to the day of his death. A skilful workman himself, he always insisted on first-class work being maintained in his shops. Accordingly, the Rogers locomotives had a high reputation for efficiency, safety, and durability, and were used in all parts of the United States, in Cuba, and in South-American countries as well. Rogers married Marie Small of Paterson, N. J., and at the time of his death in New York City he was survived by five children.

[J. S. Rogers, *James Rogers of New London, Ct., and His Descendants* (1902), which is in error as to date of death; J. L. Bishop, *A Hist. of Am. Manufactures* (3rd ed., 1868), vol. III; C. A. Shriner, *Paterson, N. J.* (1890); Angus Sinclair, *Development of the Locomotive Engine* (1907); M. S. Forney, *Locomotives and Locomotive Building . . . Origin and Growth of the Rogers Locomotive and Machine Works, Paterson, N. J.* (1886); *Am. Railroad Jour.*, Dec. 24, 1836; death notice, *N. Y. Times*, Apr. 21, 1856.]   C. W. M.

ROGERS, WILLIAM ALLEN (May 23, 1854–Oct. 20, 1931), cartoonist, son of William Allen and Elizabeth (Smith) Rogers, was born at Springfield, Ohio. An early aptitude for drawing won him a position with a farm-implement company, making fancy scrolls on plows and mowing machines. At fourteen he was selling cartoons to a group of Middle-Western newspapers, and thus became the first American cartoonist to be syndicated. In 1873 he joined the staff of the original *Daily Graphic* in New York City, served on this paper till 1877, and then commenced a long association with *Harper's Weekly*. At that time newspaper photography was impracticable, and all illustration was the work of an artist who actually sketched the event as it was happening. It was customary, in making a sketch of an inauguration or a parade, to visit the scene somewhat in advance, make a careful drawing of the setting, and fill in the principal figures later. Naturally, the artist had to work rapidly. In making a death-bed sketch of President Garfield, Rogers had only a few moments in which to absorb and record the scene. On the back of a paper bag he indicated the outline of the dying president, the attendant doctors and relatives, then elaborated these from photographs. The original drawing is with many others, now in the permanent collection of the New York Public Library.

Rogers' career as a political cartoonist began on Oct. 2, 1880. Thomas Nast happened to be absent from Harper's office, and Rogers leapt into the breach by making a pungent cartoon on the Garfield-Hancock campaign, depicting the moribund Democratic party receiving a transfusion of blood from the "stalwart" general. With that cartoon Rogers laid the cornerstone of his reputation, and for the next forty years his pictorial commentary on political events and the news of the day—woman's suffrage, vivisection, silver, Zeppelins, Wall Street, cold storage, Tammany Hall—appeared in *Harper's Weekly, Harper's Monthly Magazine, Life, Puck,* and the *New York Herald.*

In these cartoons Rogers gave a direct and simplified "pictorializing of opinion," which could be easily apprehended by the commonest intelligence. Caricaturist he was not; there is no trace of distortion in the lineaments or physique of his characters. Both his line and his viewpoint, while far from saccharine, lack the savagery of Nast and Daumier, and one has the feeling that Rogers was essentially a well-tempered, healthy, and sympathetic human being. Only during the World War did he lose his balance. In 1914 James Gordon Bennett sent his editors a cable from Europe saying, "Tell Rogers there is only one issue in this war. It is the issue between civilization and savagery" (*A World Worth While,* p. 256). Rogers responded with a series of war cartoons, afterward published in a volume entitled *America's Black and White Book: One Hundred Pictured Reasons Why We are at War* (1917), in which he brutally and often hysterically assailed Germany's leaders and war ideals. So powerful and effective were these cartoons, however, that the French government awarded Rogers membership in the Legion of Honor at the close of the war.

If Rogers had not gained fame as a political cartoonist he would still be affectionately remembered as an illustrator of children's books. As a boy, Booth Tarkington was of the opinion that the illustrator of *Toby Tyler* "must be a pretty fine man." The stories of James Otis and Kirk Munroe were enriched by Rogers' gentle, humorous drawings as they appeared serially in *Harper's Young People* and later in book form. Between 1920 and 1922 Rogers was director of the Illustrators' School for Disabled Soldiers, financed by the Federal Board for Vocational Education. Thereafter he was on the staff of the *Washington Post,* and also found time to write his memoirs, *A World Worth While* (1922)—an autobiography that reveals his essential belief in the goodness of life and humanity. His other published works include:

Danny's Partner (1923), *The Miracle Mine* (1925), and *The Lost Caravan* (1927). On Oct. 20, 1931, Rogers succumbed to a heart malady after a brief illness in his home at Washington, D. C. He had married, on Apr. 10, 1879, Sarah Butler of Springfield, Ohio. A son and a daughter survived him.

[In addition to Rogers' autobiography, see Frank Weitenkampf, "Wm. Allen Rogers in 'A World Worth While,'" *Bull. of the N. Y. Pub. Lib.,* Mar. 1933; *Who's Who in America,* 1928–29; *N. Y. Times,* Oct. 21, 1931; Mar. 10, 1933.]

H. M. R.

ROGERS, WILLIAM AUGUSTUS (Nov. 13, 1832–Mar. 1, 1898), mathematician, astronomer, and physicist, was born at Waterford, Conn., the only son in a family of three children. His parents, David Potter Rogers and Mary Anna (Rogers) were both descended from James Rogers, who was in New London, Conn., as early as 1660. David Rogers was for a time master of a fishing vessel, but later became interested in farming. His son William prepared for college at De Ruyter and at Alfred Academy, N. Y., taught school for a short time at New Market, N. J., and in 1854 entered Brown University, where he received the degree of M.A. in 1857. He was at once appointed tutor and instructor in mathematics in Alfred Academy, in 1859 became professor of mathematics at Alfred University, and the following year was made professor of industrial mechanics there. Here he remained for the succeeding decade, with three absences on leave: to pursue advanced mechanics at Yale, to study practical astronomy under Professor Bond at Harvard Observatory, and to serve in the navy for fourteen months toward the close of the Civil War. In 1865, he built and equipped an astronomical observatory at Alfred University, erecting, among other instruments, an up-to-date nine-inch equatorial refractor.

In 1870 he accepted an assistantship at Harvard Observatory under Joseph Winlock and was placed in charge of the newly erected eight-inch meridian circle. His chief work was the observation of the catalogued stars between 50 degrees and 55 degrees north declination, as a part of the general scheme of the Astronomische Gesellschaft to secure the most accurate positions of all the brighter stars in the sky. In 1877, when Edward C. Pickering [*q.v.*] assumed the directorship of the Observatory, Rogers was made assistant professor of astronomy. He held this position, directing the work of a large corps of assistants, until 1886, when he resigned to become professor of physics and astronomy at Colby University. So valuable were his services in the work of the star catalogue that he was prevailed upon to continue its supervision until its completion in 1896.

His work with the meridian circle, requiring the greatest precision, led him to seek still greater refinement in apparatus than was then available. He became proficient in the etching of lines on glass for reticles, and in the making of more accurate screws and the determination of their errors. In 1879 he was sent by the American Academy of Arts and Sciences to Europe to obtain copies of the imperial yard and of the French meter. During his twelve years at Colby, he organized a physical laboratory which was a model for accurate measurements and the determination of physical constants. His resignation as professor there was accepted by the trustees to take effect Apr. 1, 1898, in order that he might assume the directorship of the new physical laboratory at Alfred University, the erection and the equipment of which he had planned and directed during the previous year, but his death in March 1898 frustrated this plan.

Rogers was a man of genial disposition, unassuming and modest, but courageous in his convictions. His industry and perseverance were illimitable, and he considered no task too great where accuracy was required. Like his parents and grandparents he was devoutly religious, and belonged to that class of Baptists who strictly observe the sabbath beginning at sunset on Friday. He maintained an active interest in civic matters, and greatly enjoyed sports. During his final illness, when it was impossible for him to go to the lecture room or laboratory, he met his classes in his home. In 1857 he married Rebecca Jane Titsworth of Shiloh, N. H., who assisted him in connection with the reduction and publication of his numerous astronomical observations. Three sons were born to them. His many scientific papers appeared in ten volumes of the Harvard *Annals,* and in numerous publications of the several academies of which he was a member. His researches on the value of the yard and meter, and changes therein, are among the most important ever made. He was closely associated with Albert A. Michelson and Edward W. Morley [*qq.v.*] in the application of optical methods to the determination of minute changes in length, and he undertook researches in meteorology for the special purpose of learning more about the coefficient of expansion as applied to metal objects and thermometers. He was an honorary fellow of the Royal Society of London, a fellow of the Royal Microscopical Society and of the American Association for the Advancement of Science, member of the American Microscopical Society (president 1887), of the American Academy of Arts and Sciences, and of the National Academy of Sciences.

[W. L. Stevens, in *Science*, Apr. 1, 1898; E. W. Morley in *Nat. Acad. Sci. Biog. Memoirs*, vol. IV (1902); S. I. Bailey, *The Hist. and Work of Harvard Observatory* (1931); J. S. Rogers, *James Rogers of New London, Ct., and His Descendants* (1902); *Bangor Daily Whig and Courier*, Mar. 2, 1898.] L. C.

ROGERS, WILLIAM BARTON (Dec. 7, 1804–May 30, 1882), geologist and educator, son of Patrick Kerr and Hannah (Blythe) Rogers, was born in Philadelphia, Pa. He was the second of four brothers, all of whom became distinguished scientists, the other three being James Blythe, Henry Darwin, and Robert Empie [*qq.v.*]. William was educated under the tutelage of his father, in the public schools of Baltimore, and at the College of William and Mary, where his father became professor of natural philosophy and chemistry in 1819. For a time, with his brother Henry, he conducted a school at Windsor, Md., and in 1827 became a lecturer at the Maryland Institute. While connected with this institution, he presented to the governors, at their request, a plan for a proposed high school. On the death of the father in 1828, William succeeded to his professorship, but in 1835 was called to the chair of natural philosophy in the University of Virginia. This same year he was also commissioned state geologist in the newly organized survey of the state.

In 1848, becoming dissatisfied with his position at the University for various reasons, and "longing for an atmosphere of more stimulating power," he resigned, but was induced to reconsider and remain five years longer. He then removed to Boston. Some years before, he and his brother Henry had formulated provisional plans for a polytechnic school. Under the stimulus of the Boston atmosphere and with the opportunities for the establishment of such a school in the rapidly improving Back Bay district before him, Rogers so successfully advocated the project that in 1861 the legislature passed an act incorporating the Massachusetts Institute of Technology. The following year he was elected its first president. This position he held until 1870, when ill health caused his resignation. In 1878, with improved health, he again became president, continuing as such until 1881, when he resigned but remained as professor emeritus of geology and physics. He died on May 30 of the following year as he was beginning the delivery of diplomas to the graduating class.

Rogers' early predilection was toward chemistry and physics with particular reference to their industrial application. One of his earliest publications had to do with the greensand marls of Virginia and their fertilizing value (see *Farmers' Register*, August and November 1834, May 1835). As state geologist of Virginia, with a small group of assistants, one of whom was his brother Henry, he entered upon his duties in 1835, continuing as such until by legislative enactment the geological survey was abolished in 1842. Annual reports were submitted, but no provision made for a final report, and but for the energetic action of Maj. Jed Hotchkiss in bringing them together and publishing them with a map in 1884 under the caption *A Reprint of Annual Reports and Other Papers on the Geology of the Virginias,* the results would have been largely lost. Rogers' chief claim to recognition as a scientist rests not, however, on his career as state geologist, but rather on his joint work with his brother Henry on the structure of the Appalachian chain. At the time of his removal to Boston, he was working largely on physical problems and in 1861 was appointed by Governor Andrew state inspector of gas meters, a position he accepted with reluctance after having recommended another, but in which he rendered important service in the way of improved standards of measurement.

He was a man of broad views, a true philosophic spirit, and an all-round scientist. His greatest achievements, however, were in connection with the establishment and administration of the Massachusetts Institute of Technology. He possessed oratorical powers of a high order, a voice of commanding quality, and had a rare gift of diction and poetic expression. In personal appearance he was distinguished and impressive. He was a member of many scientific organizations: was chairman of the Association of American Geologists and Naturalists in 1845 and 1847; corresponding secretary of the American Academy of Arts and Sciences from 1863 to 1869; and an original member of the National Academy of Sciences, which he served as president from 1878 to 1882. On June 20, 1849, he was married to Emma Savage of Boston; they had no children.

[*Life and Letters of William Barton Rogers* (2 vols, 1896), ed. by his wife, which contains bibliog. of his writings; W. S. W. Ruschenberger, "A Sketch of the Life of Robert E. Rogers, with Biog. Notices of His Father and Brothers," in *Proc. Am. Philosophical Soc.*, vol. XXIII (1886); *Proc. Am. Acad. of Arts and Sci.*, vol. XVIII (1883); *Proc. Am. Asso. for the Advancement of Sci.*, vol. XLVIII (1899); *In Memory of William Barton Rogers* (Soc. of Arts, Mass. Inst. of Tech., 1882); F. A. Walker, in *Nat. Acad. Sci., Biog. Memoirs*, vol. III (1895); *Popular Sci. Monthly*, Sept. 1876; *Phila. Press*, May 31, 1882.] G. P. M.

ROGERS, WILLIAM CROWNINSHIELD (July 26, 1823–July 2, 1888), clipper-ship captain, was born at Salem, Mass., the eldest son of

Richard Saltonstall and Sarah (Crowninshield) Rogers. Through his father he was descended from Rev. John Rogers, president of Harvard College in 1682–84; through his mother he was a grandson of Jacob Crowninshield [q.v.]. He attended the Salem Latin School and in 1839 entered Harvard College. In the spring of his junior year he left, apparently because of a weakness which had developed in his lungs, and went to sea as supercargo. He made several voyages, principally to the East Indies, in ships of N. L. Rogers & Brother, of which firm his father was a member. Thereafter, for several years, he commanded the *Thomas Perkins,* one of the "lucky ships" of Salem, and was one of few successful masters who had never served as seaman or subordinate officer on a vessel. In this ship he made a passage during 1849 from New York to San Francisco in 126 days, a remarkable feat for a full-built ship of that type. Leaving the *Perkins,* he took command in 1851 of the new clipper ship *Witchcraft,* of 1310 tons, one of the largest and handsomest clippers then afloat. Sailing from New York, Apr. 4, 1851, he ran to San Francisco in 103 days, net sailing time, the shortest passage but one that had been made up to that time. He was dismasted and compelled to put into Rio de Janeiro for repairs, making the run from that port to San Francisco in 62 days, a record which is believed to be still unbeaten. At the outbreak of the Civil War, Rogers enlisted and was assigned to the command of the clipper barque *Wm. G. Anderson,* with the rank of volunteer lieutenant. On Apr. 12, 1862, he was placed in command of the U. S. S. *Huntsville.* On Feb. 11, 1864, he was attached to the Eastern Gulf Squadron, in command of the U. S. S. *Iuka.* He was promoted to volunteer lieutenant-commander, Oct. 24, 1864. From June 15, 1865, to July 16, 1866, when he resigned from the service, he was engaged in shore duty.

With the death of his father, Rogers was left financially independent. He had retired from business before the war, because of his health, and did not thereafter engage in it actively, although he was a silent partner in the Boston branch of the London banking house of J. S. Morgan & Company and continued to be interested in a number of enterprises. He was instrumental in bringing about the consolidation of several small lines to form the Eastern Railroad Company, in which matter he acted as co-trustee with W. B. Bacon and Willard P. Phillips. In 1865 he received the degree of A.B. from Harvard. On July 6, 1871, he married Mary Ingersoll Bowditch. His only child, William Bowditch Rogers, was born on the Island of Madeira, Sept. 14, 1874. His wife died at Funchal twelve days later. Rogers died of pleurisy in London on the 2nd day of July, 1888.

[Sources include: *Bull. of the Essex Inst.,* vol. XXI (1889); *Salem Gazette* and *Boston Evening Transcript,* July 3, 1888; *Salem Reg.,* July 5, 1888; *New-Eng. Hist. and Geneal. Reg.,* July 1851, Jan. 1859; *War of the Rebellion: Official Records* (Navy), ser. 1 and 2; A. H. Clark, *The Clipper Ship Era* (1910); G. G. Putnam, *Salem Vessels and Their Voyages* (1930); and marine columns of the *N. Y. Herald.*]   C. C. C.

ROHÉ, GEORGE HENRY (Jan. 26, 1851–Feb. 6, 1899), medical educator and psychiatrist, was born in Baltimore, Md., the son of John and Mary (Fuchs) Rohé, both immigrants from Bohemia. He was educated in the Baltimore public schools, began the study of medicine under the preceptorship of Dr. A. F. Erich, and graduated M.D. at the University of Maryland in 1873. He then studied and practised dermatology in Boston under Dr. Edward Wigglesworth, 1840–1896 [q.v.], served as assistant physician to the Boston Dispensary for Skin Diseases in 1876, and the following year returned to Baltimore to become assistant to his former preceptor, now professor of gynecology in the College of Physicians and Surgeons, where Rohé also served as lecturer on skin diseases. He entered the United States Signal Service in 1878, but three years later, settled once more in Baltimore, became professor of obstetrics in the College of Physicians and Surgeons, with which institution he was connected, in one capacity or another, until 1890. During this period he was editor of the *Medical Chronicle* (1882–85), associate editor of the *Independent Practitioner* (1882) and the *Annual of Universal Medical Science* (1890), author of *A Text Book of Hygiene* (1885) and *Practical Notes on the Treatment of Skin Diseases* (2 vols., 1885–86), and co-author with G. A. Liebig of *Practical Electricity in Medicine and Surgery* (1890).

In 1890 he was appointed health commissioner of Baltimore and proved a capable executive, but resigned the following year to become superintendent of the Maryland State Asylum for the Insane, at Catonsville. Four years later, when a new state asylum was erected at Sykesville, he was put in charge, and in the new institution made a departure from previous practice by putting no locks or fastenings on either windows or doors. Dr. A. L. Gihon, who inspected this asylum, reported: "Here then the problem has been solved, so far as human intelligence can do it, of the humane treatment of those unfortunates, whose minds have gone adaft" ("A Modern Madhouse," *Philadelphia Medical Journal,* Nov. 5, 1898, p. 976). Rohé was in advance of his time in his decided opinions with regard to the indeterminate penal sentence. He is quoted as saying, "A prisoner who shows no evidence that he will cease to be a menace to the community should certainly remain where he can do no mischief; and, on the other hand, there is no common sense in continuing to confine one who has experienced an honest change of heart" (*Journal of the Alumni Association of the College of Physicians and Surgeons, Baltimore,* April 1901, p. 7). He was quite convinced that "if the State were to spend more money on modern insane asylums, less money need be spent on jails and penitentiaries" (*Ibid.*). He pointed out in several papers the connection between mental and pelvic diseases and advocated surgical treatment for the relief of certain forms of insanity in women. He was noted among his medical colleagues for his supreme confidence in himself, and there was literally almost no position or duty which he did not consider himself competent to undertake. He was president of the American Association of Obstetricians and Gynecologists and of the Medical and Chirurgical Faculty of Maryland in 1893–94, and of the American Public Health Association, 1898–99. He was attending a meeting of the National Prison Congress at New Orleans, of which he was a prominent member, when death came to him suddenly, Feb. 6, 1899, from heart disease. He had known the danger of his condition for more than a year, but had refused to curtail his activities. He was survived by his wife, Mary Laudemann (Coffin) Rohé, whom he had married Jan. 18, 1890, and by their only child, a daughter.

[E. F. Cordell, *The Medic. Annals of Md.* (1903); *Jour. Alumni Asso., Coll. of Physicians and Surgeons, Baltimore,* Apr. 1899, Apr. 1901; H. A. Kelly and W. L. Burrage, *Am. Medic. Biogs.* (1920); *Md. Medic. Jour.,* Feb. 11, 1899; *Pub. Health Papers and Reports,* vol. XXV (1900); *Am. Jour. of Insanity,* Apr. 1899; *Buffalo Medic. Jour.,* Mar. 1899; H. M. Hurd and others, *The Institutional Care of the Insane in the U. S. and Canada,* vol. IV (1917); *Trans. Am. Asso. Obstetricians and Gynecologists,* vol. XI (1899); *Who's Who in America,* 1899; *Sun* (Balto.), Feb. 7, 1899.]
J.J.W.

ROLETTE, JEAN JOSEPH (Sept. 23, 1781–Dec. 1, 1842), pioneer fur trader on the Wisconsin and Upper Mississippi, was Canadian born, his grandfather having emigrated from Normandy about the middle of the eighteenth century. His father, Jean Joseph Rolette, and his mother, Angélique (Lortie), destined him, their eldest son, for the priesthood, and sent him to the Jesuit college at Quebec. Young Joseph, however, preferred a fur-trading career and in 1805 left for the West, spending one year opposite Detroit, in British territory. In 1806 he formed a partnership with a Scotchman, Murdoch Cameron, for trade at Prairie du Chien and on the Upper Mississippi, then entirely within the British sphere of influence. Lieut. Zebulon M. Pike [*q.v.*], sent in 1805 to recover this region for the United States, found Rolette on the Upper Mississippi, and later dined with him at Prairie du Chien. Rolette married in 1807 Marguerite Dubois, ward of Julien Dubuque, and by her had three daughters. During the War of 1812, like all his fellow traders, he served the British cause. He participated in the capture of Mackinac in 1812 and was in the British force that recaptured Prairie du Chien in 1814. After the latter expedition he was sent to Mackinac to announce the victory.

Following the American reoccupation of Prairie du Chien, Rolette was distrusted by the officers at Fort Crawford and for one winter was imprisoned on an island in the Mississippi. He was pardoned by Calhoun, when secretary of war, and became a citizen of the United States in 1823. Three years previously he had accepted the agency for the American Fur Company under Astor. He was a most successful trader. The Indians called him *Zica* (the pheasant) because he traveled so rapidly, and also *Ah-kay-zaup-ee-tah* (five more) because of his demands when trading. Many stories are told of his humor, vivacity, and good temper. By the *voyageurs* he was known as "King" Rolette, and when appointed (in 1830) chief justice for Crawford County he aided in keeping good order among the French-Canadians of Prairie du Chien. Nevertheless he had a reputation among the chief traders of this region for sharp practice, and his dealings were watched with suspicion. Astor trusted him, and at one time Rolette took his family to visit Astor in New York. His first wife died in 1817, and two years later he married Jane Fisher, a very young girl. He was reputed to be wealthy, but after his death there was much difficulty in settling his estate. He was survived by two daughters and a son, together with his widow, who later became the wife of his former clerk, H. L. Dousman.

[*Wis. Hist. Soc. Colls.,* esp. IX (1882), 293, 465, X (1888), 479; Joseph Tassé, *Les Canadiens de l'Ouest* (Montreal, 1878), I, 143–211; Juliette Magill Kinzie, *Wau-bun* (ed. of 1930); Elizabeth Fisher Baird's narratives in *Wis. Hist. Soc. Colls.,* XIV (1898), 55, and XV (1900), 219; MSS., including Rolette's will and papers relating to the administration of his estate, in Wis. Hist. Lib., Madison.]
L.P.K.

ROLFE, JOHN (1585–1622), colonist, was the son of John and Dorothea (Mason) Rolfe and was christened on May 6, 1585, at Heacham, in Norfolk, England. He was married, probably in 1608, and in June 1609 sailed for Virginia with his wife in the *Sea Adventure.* The vessel was wrecked on the Bermudas, and the voyagers were stranded many months. While there a daughter was born to him but soon died. The company built two pinnaces and in them escaped to Virginia, where his wife died. In 1612 he began experimenting with the native tobacco, which was unpalatable to Europeans. His methods of cultivation proved so successful that he produced a leaf as "pleasant, sweet, and strong" as any "under the sunne" (Hamor, *post,* p. 34). Immediately the staple of Virginia became tobacco, whose influence in shaping the economic, social, and even religious life of the colony can hardly be exaggerated. When in 1613 Pocahontas [*q.v.*] was brought captive to Jamestown, he fell in love with her and, having obtained the consent of Thomas Dale and of Powhatan [*qq.v.*], married her in April 1614. This union brought peace with the Indians for eight years, during which time the English established themselves firmly. In 1616 Rolfe took his wife to England, where she died leaving one son. While in England he wrote a description of Virginia for the King and Sir Robert Rich (no. 208, Duke of Manchester's Manuscripts in Public Record Office, London; *Southern Literary Messenger,* June 1839). He returned to Virginia in May 1617. He was secretary and recorder of the colony from June 1614 to 1619; and in 1621 he was appointed to the Council of State. His third wife was Jane, the daughter of William Pierce, or Pyers. In 1622 Bermuda Hundred, where Rolfe had his home, was wiped out in an Indian massacre, and here he seems to have met his death. His wife and daughter survived.

In the planting of England's first permanent settlement in America his part was vital, since failure might have resulted had it not been, on the one hand, for the peace that followed his marriage with Pocahontas and, on the other, the prosperity resulting from his experiments with tobacco.

[Ralph Hamor, *A True Discourse of the Present State of Va.* (1615; facsimile reprint 1860); Alexander Brown, *The Genesis of the United States* (2 vols., 1890); John Smith, *The Generall Historie of Va.* (1624); William Strachey, *The Hist. of Travaile into Virginia Britannia* (1849).]   T. J. W.

ROLFE, WILLIAM JAMES (Dec. 10, 1827– July 7, 1910), teacher, philologist, was born in Newburyport, Mass., the eldest child of John and Lydia Davis (Moulton) Rolfe and eighth in descent from Henry Rolfe, who, with his wife and son, emigrated from England in 1635 and settled in Newbury. His father was a hatter. Rolfe spent an active, happy boyhood in Haverhill and Lowell, graduated from the Lowell High School, learned proof-reading from the editor of the *Lowell Daily Courier,* spent a year in the counting-room of a cotton-mill, and attended Amherst College for three years as a member of the class of 1849. During the long winter vacations he taught country schools to defray his expenses. He greatly enjoyed his years at Amherst, but in 1848 he departed, feeling that it would be a waste of time to stay longer. He always cherished a strong affection for his college and received honorary degrees from it in 1865 and 1887.

After serving a short apprenticeship at Kirkwood Academy in Maryland, he was for twenty years a schoolmaster in his native state: first as principal and sole teacher in Day's Academy, Wrentham (1848–52)—a strenuous but educative experience—and afterward as principal or master of the Dorchester High School (1852–57), the Lawrence High School (1857–61), the Salem High School (1861–62), and the Cambridge High School (1862–68). What made his work significant was his introduction into the school curriculum of regular instruction in English literature. He had felt keenly the lack of such instruction in his own youth and found a sympathetic response among his pupils. For several years he did not realize that he was the pioneer of a sweeping reform in American secondary education. His work, however, came early to the attention of Cornelius Conway Felton and Francis James Child [*qq.v.*] and won their approbation, and in 1859 Harvard College conferred on him the honorary degree of A.M. In 1868 Rolfe retired from regular teaching and made the first of his many voyages to Europe. For the rest of his long life, he continued to live in Cambridge, devoting himself to various literary activities, but chiefly to the preparation of school books. He taught in the summer sessions of several universities, was president of the Martha's Vineyard Summer Institute (1882–88) and of the Emerson College of Oratory, Boston (1903–08). Until well advanced in years he was an enthusiastic traveler and tramper. In particular, he had an intimate and affectionate knowledge of every trail and summit in the White Mountains.

Thanks to methodical habits of work and to the care with which he guarded his not too robust health, he accomplished an astonishing amount of work. He had the passion for accuracy and thoroughness of a born textual critic, but because these qualities were expended on the editing of school books Rolfe has not received quite the recognition that he deserves. He was appreciated, however, by Child and H.

H. Furness [*q.v.*] in the United States and by Tennyson, Browning, Furnivall, and Halliwell-Phillipps in England. In 1907 he reckoned that he had written or edited 144 volumes in addition to his voluminous contributions to newspapers and periodicals. His first venture was *A Handbook of Latin Poetry* (1866), edited in collaboration with J. H. Hanson. This was followed by a series of science textbooks done in collaboration with J. A. Gillet and by the *Satchel Guide for the Vacation Tourist in Europe* (1872), which underwent annual revisions for many years. From 1869 to 1893 he was co-editor with J. R. Nichols [*q.v.*] of the *Boston Journal of Chemistry* and its successor, *Popular Science News*. He produced a long series of school editions of various English classics: *The Complete Works of Alfred, Lord Tennyson* (12 vols., 1895–98) and the "Cambridge edition" of *The Poetic and Dramatic Works of Alfred, Lord Tennyson* (1898); *The Poetical Works of Sir Walter Scott* (1888), based on a thorough, and much needed, collation of the original editions; and two school editions, each in forty volumes, of Shakespeare (1871–84 and 1903–06). No other editions of Shakespeare have been so widely used in the United States, and the originality, pithiness, and sound scholarship of his annotations have been often praised. A true child of his time, Rolfe idolized Shakespeare and expurgated what he wrote. His innumerable notes on Shakespeare, published for the most part in the *Critic,* the *Literary World,* and the *Nation,* are always exact and pointed. He also published *A Life of William Shakespeare* (1904). The original manuscript of this work was stolen, and Rolfe rewrote it completely.

He was married July 30, 1856, to Eliza Jane Carew, of Dorchester, who had been one of his pupils. She died Mar. 19, 1900. Their three sons outlived him. Rolfe died at the home of a son on Martha's Vineyard and was buried in Newburyport. Sound of mind and happily occupied to the end, he seems not to have anticipated death at the age of eighty-two. The last of his characteristic letters to the *Nation* was published June 30, 1910; the last to the New York *Evening Post* appeared on July 7, the day of his death.

[*A Bibliog. of William James Rolfe* (Cambridge Pub. Lib., 1907); *Emerson Coll. Mag.,* Rolfe Memorial Number, Nov. 1910, including Rolfe's autobiography; W. J. Rolfe and Edward Hitchcock, *Amherst Coll.: The Class of 1849* (1899); *Obituary Record of Grads. of Amherst Coll. for the Academic Year Ending June 28, 1911* (1911); *Amherst Coll.: Biog. Record . . . 1821–1921* (1927); F. W. Stearns, "Two Amherst Philologists," *Amherst Grads. Quart.,* Jan. 1912; *Who's Who in America,* 1899–1911; *Nation* (N. Y.), July 14, 1910; *Boston Transcript* (obituary and editorial), July 8, 1910.]   G. H. G.

ROLLINS, ALICE MARLAND WEL-LINGTON (June 12, 1847–Dec. 5, 1897), author, daughter of Ambrose and Lucy Jane (Kent) Wellington, was born in Boston. Her father, a descendant of colonial New Englanders, was a graduate of Harvard College and a lawyer; her mother was the daughter of Col. William Kent, a member of the New Hampshire legislature. Alice was taught at home by her father until she was fourteen, when she was sent to the Everett School in Boston and later to Lasell Seminary. A year abroad completed her formal education. She taught for several years, then, in 1876, married Daniel M. Rollins, of New York City, then connected with the firm of Henry Foster & Company, merchants trading with Brazil. Because of her husband's business relations, she traveled much in South America and Europe, and for a time lived in Brazil.

She began writing shortly after her school days were over. She was long a reviewer for the *Critic,* and contributed to almost all the leading periodicals of the day, including those for children and young people. Her first published book was *My Welcome Beyond and Other Poems* (1877), followed in 1878 by another volume of verse, *The Ring of Amethyst.* She next wrote several books for children, among them, *The Story of a Ranch* (1885), *All Sorts of Children* (1886), and *The Three Tetons: A Story of the Yellowstone* (1887). Her novel, *Uncle Tom's Tenement* (1888), based on New York tenement life, was an outgrowth of her essays on the subject and was credited with some reform influence. In 1889 she published another volume of verse, *From Snow to Sunshine.* In *From Palm to Glacier . . .* (1892) she related her experiences in Brazil, Bermuda, and Alaska. Two later volumes, *Aphorisms for the Year* (1894) and *Unfamiliar Quotations* (1895) are compilations. Her more mature poetic work is represented by *The Story of Azron* (1895), while *Little Page Fern and Other Verses* (1895) and *The Finding of the Gentian* (1895) are respectively books of verse and stories for children. Her verse is without especial distinction of idea or phrase, introspective, sad without being morbid, and often inspired by love of nature. Her prose is smooth, well phrased, and shows some humor and good description. Of all her books, *Uncle Tom's Tenement* probably received most attention from reviewers and was most read. During her long final illness she was writing a series of stories, of which those completed were published in the *Ladies' Home Journal* (1897–98). Shortly before her death she penned her last poem, *"Vita Benefica,"* which was published in the *Century Magazine* (February 1898). During her later years she lived at Lawrence Park, Bronxville, N. Y., where she died. She was very active there in social and club life. One son survived her.

[F. E. Willard and M. A. Livermore, *American Women* (1897) ; *Critic*, Dec. 11, 1897 ; *Literary World*, Dec. 11, 1897 ; *Ladies' Home Jour.*, Mar. 1898 ; *N. Y. Tribune*, Dec. 6, 1897.]   S. G. B.

ROLLINS, EDWARD HENRY (Oct. 3, 1824–July 31, 1889), politician, legislator, railroad financier, was born at Rollinsford, N. H., eldest of the six children of Daniel and Mary (Plumer) Rollins. On both sides of the family he was of good colonial stock, his father being a descendant of James Rawlins who came to New England in 1632, and settled at Ipswich, Mass. Edward spent his youth on his father's farm and once declared that no one knew better "the sorrows of hill-farm husbandry than I did until my twenty-first year." His early education was scanty, and while he began preparation for Dartmouth, lack of means obliged him to relinquish his ambition for a college education. He was an omnivorous reader, however, and overcame many of his early handicaps, writing and speaking with facility and vigor. After leaving home he spent several years as clerk in a Concord drug store, school-teacher, and employee of a wholesale drug firm in Boston. In 1847 he bought a drug business in Concord, N. H., with which he was associated until 1861. On Feb. 13, 1849, he married Ellen Elizabeth West.

His business prospered, his store became a rendezvous for local politicians and party workers, and the proprietor, an anti-slavery Whig, was soon a rising politician. He was a state committeeman for the Whig party in its moribund years, 1850–53, and passed via the Know-Nothing route into the new Republican organization. He was elected to the lower house of the legislature in 1855 and became speaker a year later. He performed important services in the merger of Know-Nothings, Free Soilers, Whigs, and anti-slavery Democrats into a coherent and enthusiastic party. The even balance of party strength and the fact that New Hampshire elections came in the spring made the state a pivotal one in national affairs and the work of Rollins attracted much attention. He was chairman of the Republican state committee from 1856 to 1861, resigning in the latter year because of his election to Congress.

He served three consecutive terms in the House and proved himself a conscientious committeeman, a stalwart supporter of war measures, and an indefatigable worker for the inter-

ests of his state and constituents. After the expiration of his third term he was again elected chairman of the state committee, serving from 1868 to 1872, and exercising a great influence on campaigns and policies when no longer a member. A textbook on party methods and practices could be written from his experiences in keeping New Hampshire in the Republican column. A profound believer in Republican principles, opposed to conciliation with the South, a conservative with scant tolerance for reform in any guise, but personally honest and fearless, he was distinctly a product of the era. He was a skilful manager of caucuses and conventions, an adept distributor of patronage and spoils, but emerged unsmirched from the political scandals of the period.

In 1869, through the influence of Oakes Ames [*q.v.*], a personal friend, he became assistant treasurer of the Union Pacific Railroad and secretary of its board of directors ; two years later he was promoted to the post of treasurer. He had no connection with the Crédit Mobilier organization but his relationship to the railroad company caused increasing opposition to his candidacy for the United States Senate, and after his election for the term 1877–83 he deemed it advisable to sever it. In the Senate he followed much the same course he had pursued earlier in the House. His failure to secure a reëlection, due to the popularity of the doctrine of rotation which he had done much to foster and to the increasing restiveness of other leaders under the dominance of the Rollins machine, was a severe disappointment and led to his gradual retirement from active politics.

On his return to Concord he became increasingly active in New Hampshire business affairs, heading the banking firm of E. H. Rollins & Sons. From 1886 to 1889 he was president of the Boston, Concord & Montreal Railroad. A paralytic stroke from which he never recovered was probably the result of severe work over a long period of years. He retained an interest in farming, was a breeder of choice live stock, and did much for the agricultural improvement of the state. He died at Isles of Shoals, N. H., survived by four children, one of them being Frank West Rollins [*q.v.*].

[J. O. Lyford, *Life of Edward H. Rollins* (1906), based on Rollins' correspondence and other papers ; J. R. Rollins, *Records of Families of the Name Rawlins or Rollins, in the U. S.* (1874) ; *Biog. Dir. Am. Cong.* (1928) ; *Granite Monthly*, Sept. 1877 ; *Concord Evening Monitor*, Aug. 2, 1889 ; *Independent Statesman* (Concord), Aug. 1, 8, 1889.]   W. A. R.

ROLLINS, FRANK WEST (Feb. 24, 1860–Oct. 27, 1915), banker and politician, was the fourth of the five children of Edward Henry [*q.v.*] and Ellen (West) Rollins. He was born in Concord, N. H., and like his father was devoted throughout his life to the upbuilding of the interests of his native state. Having received his early education in the Concord public schools and under private tuition, he was a student in the Massachusetts Institute of Technology from 1877 to 1880. He then studied law at Harvard (1880–81) and in a Concord office, was admitted to the New Hampshire bar in 1882, but having little taste for the profession, soon entered the investment banking business of E. H. Rollins & Sons. On Dec. 6, 1882, he married Katharine W. Pecker of Concord.

He was notably successful in business, and a public-spirited citizen, serving on numerous administrative boards and directorates, charitable and educational. In 1894 he was elected for a term in the New Hampshire Senate, serving as president of that body. Four years later he was elected governor of the state, holding office from 1899 to 1901. In his inaugural message he anticipated later policies by urging a comprehensive system of good roads and a thorough study of highway construction in relation to development of the economic and scenic resources of the state. He was an efficient but unspectacular executive, although on Apr. 6, 1899, his Fast Day proclamation stirred a local tempest by calling attention to the decadence of the churches in rural New Hampshire and implying the decadence of rural New England in general.

In 1898, at a gathering of natives of New Hampshire in Boston, he in:tiated a movement which subsequently spread throughout the country—that of "Old Home Week." He regarded himself as the father of this characteristically American institution and several of his addresses on the subject were subsequently collected and published. A more important activity, which he furthered while governor, and also as a private citizen, was conservation. Deeply interested in forestry, he gave generously of time and money to preserve existing forests in the White Mountains and to develop interest in reforestation in the state at large. As in the matter of highways, subsequent developments owed much to his initial efforts.

He had numerous literary interests, accumulated a valuable library, contributed articles and stories to local journals, and published several novels and collections of stories; *The Lady of the Violets* (1897) was probably his best-known work. While his literary efforts enjoyed some temporary popularity, they were minor incidents in his career. He died in Boston, survived by his wife and one son.

[J. R. Rollins, *Records of Families of the Name Rawlins or Rollins, in the U. S.* (1874) ; C. R. Corning, "Governor Rollins," *Granite Monthly*, Sept. 1899; *Who's Who in America*, 1914–15 ; *Daily Patriot* (Concord), Oct. 28, 1915 ; *Boston Transcript*, Oct. 28, 1915.]

W. A. R.

ROLLINS, JAMES SIDNEY (Apr. 19, 1812–Jan. 9, 1888), congressman, was born at Richmond, Ky., the son of Anthony Wayne Rollins, a native of Pennsylvania and prominent physician, and Sallie (Rodes) Rollins. His grandfather, Henry Rollins, was a native of Ireland. James Sidney attended Richmond Academy, spent two years at Washington College, and graduated in 1830 with highest honors from the Indiana University. Rejoining his family in Columbia, Mo., he read law for a time in the offices of Abiel Leonard, then served in the Black Hawk War. In 1834 he completed his legal education at Transylvania University. He developed a large practice, but the routine and delay of the law irked him, and as early as 1836 he turned to public affairs. By inheritance and by conviction a Whig, he edited the *Columbia Patriot* and in 1838 was elected to the legislature from a strongly Whig county. As a legislator he achieved marked distinction in the decade 1838–48. His lifelong interests were education and public improvements. He sponsored in 1839 legislation which gave form and substance to the state university, while his effective and eloquent leadership of the cause of higher education resulted in public grants and in private donations which secured the location of the institution at Columbia. Through successive sessions he urged upon politically hostile and indifferent colleagues the desirability of internal improvements, of wider educational opportunities, and of social legislation. He was an ardent supporter of Clay, and by 1848 he had become the recognized leader of the Missouri Whigs, the minority party in the state. As candidate for governor in 1848 he secured the largest vote ever cast for a Whig. He echoed no popular slogans and had no effective political organization, but his eloquence and presentation of issues attracted many followers.

After several years of successful practice, Rollins returned in 1854 to the legislature, when the issue of slavery in the territories was a threat to the maintenance and integrity of his party. Although a slave-owner, he believed and maintained that it was the right and duty of Congress to prohibit slavery in the territories. He was again a candidate for governor in 1857, receiving the support of former Whigs, Native Americans, and many Benton Democrats (*Weekly Jefferson Inquirer*, May 2, 1857). His defeat by

230 votes ended a brilliant but futile party leadership of twelve years. As the crisis of 1860 approached, he supported the Bell-Everett ticket and became a candidate for Congress. As a border-state moderate in a slave-owning constituency he was willing fully to recognize the complaints of the South but refused to sanction secession. Both he and John B. Henderson, his opponent, emphatically disavowed any anti-slavery sentiment, and Rollins won. He was reëlected easily in 1862, as a Conservative-Unionist. Primarily concerned with preserving the Union, with or without slavery, he had the confidence of Lincoln and gave the government loyal and courageous support. He opposed confiscation, the Emancipation Proclamation, military government, and had grave doubt of the compensated emancipation plan for loyal slave-owners in Missouri. "I am for the Constitution and the Union as our fathers made them—I want no change" (*Congressional Globe*, Appendix, 37 Cong., 3 Sess., p. 106). By 1865, however, he realized that slavery must be abolished, and he supported the resolution submitting the Thirteenth Amendment. Singularly free from the intolerance and fanaticism of some border-state politicians, he opposed the proscriptive and punitive spirit and measures both in Missouri and in the nation.

In 1866 a crisis in the affairs of the University induced Rollins to reënter the legislature where he remained until 1872. The institution was in a dismal plight. The Republican majority was hostile toward it; the resources were almost exhausted, and public opinion generally indifferent. He met the difficult situation with tact and enthusiasm, and, by judicious concessions, was instrumental in securing the enactment of five significant statutes, 1867–72, relating to the University and to the newly created College of Agriculture. By these measures the institution was placed upon a solid and permanent foundation. Opposed to radical Republicanism, he aided in the restoration of the state Democracy in 1867–68, although he was never in complete accord with the Democratic party. His conciliatory policy, wisely dictated in behalf of educational legislation, was unpopular with many. With Carl Schurz and B. Gratz Brown he was a leader in the Liberal Republican movement. His lifelong ambition to be governor was finally frustrated in 1872 when the former Confederate element defeated him in the Democratic state convention. He retired from active politics in that year. Of tall and commanding presence, with resonant voice and facile rhetoric, he captivated his audiences and was easily one of the

first citizens of the state for half a century. He died after a lingering illness, survived by his wife, Mary E. Hickman, whom he had married on June 6, 1837, and by seven of their eleven children.

[Sources include: W. B. Smith, *Jas. Sidney Rollins Memoir* (1891), containing selections from his speeches and letters; *Hist. of Boone County, Mo.* (1882); W. E. Smith, *The Francis Preston Blair Family in Politics* (2 vols., 1933); *Mo. Republican*, Jan. 10, 1888; Rollins Papers in the possession of Rollins' son, C. B. Rollins, Columbia, Mo.]   T. S. B.

ROLLINSON, WILLIAM (Apr. 15, 1762–Sept. 21, 1842), engraver, was born in Dudley, Worcester, England, eldest son of Robert and Mary (Hill) Rollinson. On May 10, 1782, he was married, in Birmingham, to Mary Johnson, ten years his senior, and on Nov. 29, 1788, he saiłed for America. During the voyage he improvised tools and engraved ornaments and monograms on jewelry for officers and passengers. He wrote in his diary, "By when I arrive in America it will bring my hand in and I shall be capable of turning cypher cutter in general to the United States" (Reid and Rollinson, *post*, p. 13). Arriving in New York Feb. 15, 1789, he soon was employed in ornamenting silver buttons for the coat worn by Washington at his inauguration. Other similar work followed, and in about a year he returned to England to bring over his wife and child.

In the American spirit of turning one's hand to anything, he soon began, with no experience, to engrave on copper, and chose for his first effort the subject then most popular with engravers—a portrait of George Washington. For *The Self-Interpreting Bible* (1792), edited by the Rev. John Brown, he engraved seven plates, pronounced "crude" by Stauffer (*post*), who adds that he improved rapidly. About 1796 he changed from line to stipple engraving, doing work for magazines, as also an engraving of Archibald Robertson's portrait of Alexander Hamilton (1804). He engraved bookplates, maps, and certificates. A noted plate is the aquatint view of New York from Long Island (1801) from a drawing by John Wood. Though he "had no knowledge of . . . processes used by those brought up to the profession," he "had perseverance and ingenuity to surmount all difficulties" (Dunlap, *post*, I, 188). He naturally turned to banknote engraving, developing a method of ruling lines by machine to prevent counterfeiting. Engaging W. S. Leney [*q.v.*] to engrave his vignettes in order to improve the artistic element of his products, he took his place among those who perfected methods of banknote engraving, specially cultivated in the United States by many capable engravers.

Tall, and of great bodily strength, Rollinson was "easy going, bright and jovial" (Brand, *post,* p. 4). He was a Mason, a volunteer fireman, a member of the Society of Mechanics and Tradesmen, and a lieutenant of artillery. Three of his grandsons entered the ministry: William Rollinson Whittingham [*q.v.*], Episcopal bishop of Maryland, Richard Whittingham, and William Rollinson.

[Rollinson's diary of his voyage to America is in the possession of his great-grandson, Charles Rollinson. A portrait by F. S. Agate, mentioned by Dunlap, has not been found, but the late D. M. Stauffer possessed a silhouette of him. Two portraits were reproduced with an article by R. W. Reid in the *Masonic Outlook,* Feb. 1931. See also D. M. Stauffer, *Am. Engravers upon Copper and Steel* (2 vols., 1907); R. W. Reid and Charles Rollinson, *William Rollinson, Engraver* (privately printed, 1931); Mantle Fielding, *Am. Engravers upon Copper and Steel* (1917); W. F. Brand, *Wm. Rollinson Whittingham, Fourth Bishop of Md.* (2 vols., 1883); Wm. Dunlap, *A Hist. of the Rise and Progress of the Arts of Design in the U. S.* (3 vols., 1918), ed. by F. W. Bayley and C. E. Goodspeed; *Evening Post* (N. Y.), Sept. 22, 1842.]   F. W.

ROLSHOVEN, JULIUS (Oct. 28, 1858–Dec. 7, 1930), painter, was born at Detroit, Mich., the son of Frederick and Maria Theresa Hubertina (Hellings) Rolshoven. As a youth he had training in art at Cooper Union and the Plessman Academy, New York. In 1878 he registered at the Düsseldorf, Germany, Academy as a pupil of Hugo Crola. A year later he was studying at Munich under Professor Ludwig Loefftz. There, with other young Americans, he came under the spell of the technique and teaching of Frank Duveneck [*q.v.*]. He was of the group of "Duveneck Boys," which included John W. Alexander, John H. Twachtman, Ross Turner, J. Frank Currier, and Harper Pennington, who painted at Florence, Italy. Of his character it has been said: "Rolshoven, too, was endowed by nature with the artistic temperament, making it especially difficult for him to adapt himself to routine work" (Norbert Heermann, *Frank Duveneck,* 1918, p. 46). In 1882 he became a pupil of Tony Robert-Fleury and Adolphe William Bouguereau in Paris. He exhibited his landscape and genre paintings at the Salon and the Société Nationale des Beaux-Arts, Paris; the Munich Secession; Chelsea Art Club, London, and other exhibitions. In 1890 he established at Paris life classes which drew an international attendance, and from 1896 to 1902 he continued in London.

Rolshoven was married first in 1887, at Florence, to Anna Eliza Chickering. She died in 1897, and in 1915 he was married to Harriette Haynes Blazo. Throughout his long residence in Europe he kept up his contacts with Detroit where his mother lived into her ninety-third year. In 1912 an exhibition of some eighty of his paintings from North Africa made a favorable impression on the Detroit public. Many American collectors acquired his paintings, and he was represented in his life-time in the Detroit Institute of Arts by "The Refectory of San Damiano, Assisi"; in the Cincinnati Art Museum, by "Chiogga Fishing Girl" and "Church of St. Francis at Assisi"; by canvases in the museums of Brooklyn, Baltimore, Minneapolis, and Santa Fé.

During a visit to the West in 1914 he became impressed by the landscape and Indians of New Mexico, and during the disturbed war years he was a member of the artist colony at Taos. An exhibition of his New Mexican pictures was held at Detroit in 1923. In 1924 he was awarded the Richard S. Greenough memorial prize of the Newport, R. I., Art Association. After the war he gave residential addresses in three cities, Detroit, Paris, and Florence. He held membership, as an associate, in the National Academy of Design and in the National Arts Club, New York; the Secession, Munich; the Society of Arts and Letters, Paris; the Foreign Arts Club and the Bene Merensa Società di Belle Arti, Florence; the International Fine Arts Congress; the Taos Society of Artists, and the Detroit Fine Arts Society. The extensive list of organizations of which he was a member revealed something of Rolshoven's personality. He was an internationalist, believing that the American artist should associate with the artists of other countries, should experience no inferiority complex in such association, and should demand from the American public at least as generous treatment as that accorded to the foreign artist.

Rolshoven died in New York City while on his way to the bedside of his mother in Detroit, who outlived him by about four hours. A memorial exhibition of his works was held at the Detroit Institute of Arts. He had received during his career such honors as the second medal of the Paris Exposition, 1889; honorable mention, Paris, 1900; a bronze medal, Pan-American Exposition, Buffalo, 1901; silver medal, St. Louis Exposition, 1904; and medals from seasonal exhibitions of Munich, Berlin, Brussels, Florence, and Chicago. His self-portrait is in the gallery of artist portraits at the Uffizi, Florence.

[See: *Bull. of the Detroit Inst. of Arts,* Apr. 1931; *Biog. Sketches of Am. Artists* (1924); pub. by the Mich. State Lib.; *Am. Art Annual,* 1931; *Art News,* Dec. 13, 1930; *Who's Who in America,* 1920–21, 1928–29; *N. Y. Times,* Dec. 8, 1930; information from F. W. Robinson, Asst. Curator, Cincinnati Art Museum.] F. W. C.

RÖLVAAG, OLE EDVART (Apr. 22, 1876–Nov. 5, 1931), author and educator, was born on the island of Dönna, Helgeland, Norway, the son of Peder Jakobsen and Ellerine Johanna (Olson) Rölvaag. He attended school between the ages of seven and fourteen and read diligently in the local library. After some years of fishing—the traditional occupation of his people—he decided to emigrate and, forfeiting the command of a beautiful boat, secured a ticket from an uncle in South Dakota. He landed in New York in August 1896, worked three years as a farm hand, and then entered Augustana College, a Norwegian Lutheran preparatory school in Canton, S. Dak. After four years at St. Olaf College, Northfield, Minn., he was graduated with honors in 1905. After a year of graduate study at the University of Oslo, Norway, he was appointed professor of Norwegian at St. Olaf College, and in 1916 became head of the department. In the summer of 1926 he suffered a complete breakdown, caused by heart disease, from which he only partially recovered. On Dec. 31, 1926, he was created by King Haakon of Norway a knight of the Order of St. Olaf. He taught again during the first semester of 1927–28, during the second semester was a guest of the Norwegian government at the Ibsen centennial, and returned to teaching in 1928–29. On Aug. 31, 1931, he resigned, intending to devote himself entirely to literary pursuits, but he died at his home in Northfield early in November of that same year. He married Jennie Marie Berdahl of Garretson, S. Dak., on July 9, 1908. Of his four children only two survived him.

Rölvaag's childhood in Norway left a deep imprint on his literary work. This land of contrasts, with its dark winter and its midnight sun, stimulated his imagination and gave him his passionate love of the sea. His later reading added an intense cultural patriotism which determined much of his activity. He deplored the tendency of Norwegians in America to drift away from their racial culture, and sought to stem it by determined propaganda. During the World War he was stung into activity by the "Americanizers," and between 1918 and 1922 published three Norse readers and a collection of essays, *Omkring Fædrearven* ("Concerning our Heritage"). From its founding in 1925 he was secretary of the Norwegian-American Historical Association.

He wrote his first novel as a senior in college, an idyllic (and unpublished) effort entitled *"Nils og Astri, eller Brudstykker av norsk-amerikansk Folkeliv"* (". . . Fragments of Norwegian-American Popular Life"). In 1912 appeared *Amerika-Breve* ("Letters from America"), professing to be letters written to father and brother in Norway by one P. A. Smevik and collected by Paal Mörck. This essentially autobiographical novel, like all his earlier books published in Minneapolis, was an attempt to reveal the gradual accommodation of the immigrant to his new surroundings. In 1914 appeared the more ambitious *Paa glemte Veie* ("On Forgotten Paths"), still under the pseudonym Paal Mörck. The war years left their deposit of bitterness in *To Tullinger* ("Two Simpletons"), 1920, which has been translated and amplified in English as *Pure Gold* (1930). Another novel appeared in 1921, *Længselens Baat,* published in English as *The Boat of Longing* (1933). It was inspired by Rölvaag's grief over the distressing death of his youngest child, and embodied more of the tremendous scenery of Norway and of his own lyric magnificence than any of his other books. Its purpose was to depict the tragic effect of American city life on the soul of a sensitive immigrant.

Rölvaag's earlier works were first issued in Minneapolis. National and world-wide fame came to him with the series begun by *I de Dage* ("In Those Days"), published in Norway in 1924, and *Riket grundlægges* ("The Kingdom is Founded"), 1925, both translated in 1927 with the aid of Lincoln Colcord and published in America under the title, *Giants in the Earth.* The scene is South Dakota of the seventies. In the persons of Per Hansa and Beret Holm, Rölvaag embodied the glory and the tragedy of the immigrant pioneer. The book's success both in Norway and America was instantaneous and phenomenal. American critics were unanimous in acclaiming the integrity of Rölvaag's art and the validity of his interpretation of the frontier. *The Nation* (July 13, 1927, p. 41) called it "the fullest, finest, and most powerful novel that has been written about pioneer life in America." Vernon Parrington and Carl Sandburg gave it high commendation, the former praising Rölvaag's work for its "creative realism and brooding imagination." Within a few years of the book's publication in English it was translated into Swedish, Finnish, Dutch, German, and Hungarian. Two sequels followed: in 1928, *Peder Seier* (English version, *Peder Victorious,* 1929), and in 1931 *Den signede Dag* ("The Blessed Day"), translated in the same year as *Their Fathers' God.* These were well received, although their concern with the less impressive problems of the second generation in the land deprived them of the epic sweep of *Giants in the Earth.*

Artistically Rölvaag found his models among the classic novelists of Norway, especially Jonas Lie, with later impulses from Knut Hamsun and Sigrid Undset. He fused in his work the scrupulous truth of detail demanded by modern realism with an essentially optimistic view of life.

[*Who's Who in America,* 1930–31; Lincoln Colcord, Introduction to *Giants in the Earth* (1927) and "Rölvaag the Fisherman Shook His Fist at Fate," *Am. Mag.,* Mar. 1928; Kristine Haugen, "Glimt fra Rolvaags Liv," *Decorah-Posten* (Decorah, Iowa), Dec. 8, 1931; obituaries in *Northfield News,* Nov. 13, 1931, *N. Y. Times,* Nov. 6, 1931, and *Publishers' Weekly,* Nov. 14, 1931; P. H. Boynton, "O. E. Rölvaag and the Conquest of the Pioneer," *English Journal,* Sept. 1929; Jörgen Bukdahl, *"Riget grundlægges,"* in *Det skjulte Norge* (Copenhagen, 1926); Henry Commager, "The Literature of the Pioneer West," *Minn. Hist.,* Dec. 1927; Einar I. Haugen, "O. E. Rölvaag: Norwegian American," *Studies and Records* (Norw.-Am. Hist. Asso.), vol. VII (1933); Addison Hibbard, "Analysis of O. E. Rölvaag's *Pure Gold,"* *Creative Reading: Discussions in Current Lit.* (Cambridge, Mass.), Feb. 15, 1930; J. E. Olson, "Rölvaag's Novels of Norwegian Pioneer Life in the Dakotas," *Scandinavian Studies and Notes,* 1927; Vernon Parrington, editor's introduction to *Giants in the Earth* (Harper's Modern Classics, 1929), reprinted in Parrington's *Main Currents in Am. Thought,* vol. III (1930); Georg Strandvold, "Rolvaags Præriesaga," *Decorah-Posten,* Dec. 11, 1931–Jan. 29, 1932; Aagot D. Hoidahl, "Norwegian-American Fiction since 1880," *Studies and Records* (Norw.-Am. Hist. Asso.), vol. V (1930); partial bibliog. of Rölvaag's writing in *Giants* (Parrington ed.), pp. 467–68.]
E. I. H.

ROMAN, ANDRÉ BIENVENU (Mar. 5, 1795–Jan. 28, 1866), governor of Louisiana, was born in St. Landry Parish, the son of Jacques Étienne and Marie Louise (Patin) Roman and the grandson of Jacques Roman who emigrated to Louisiana from Grenoble, France, before 1741. He was early taken to St. James Parish, where his father established a sugar plantation. After graduating from St. Mary's College at Baltimore in 1815, he was married in 1816 to Aimée Françoise Parent and established himself on a plantation in St. James Parish. They had five children. His public life began in 1818 with his election to the Louisiana House of Representatives, where he retained his seat, often without opposition, for many years, during four of which he served as speaker. This service was interrupted in 1826 for two years, while he acted as parish judge. This office he resigned, however, to return to the lower house, where he was again discharging the duties of speaker when he was elected governor. His two gubernatorial terms, with the four years' interval required by law, embraced the period from 1831 to 1843, a period of disaster when the state was scourged by epidemics and flood. Under the governor's insistence a board of public works and a fund for internal improvements was created by law. Under this act many of the water courses were cleared of their obstructions and numerous improvements accomplished. The board effected also the incorporation of the New Orleans drainage company. Roman accepted the presidency of that company after his retirement from office and held it long enough to render important service to the city in planning a system of drainage to relieve it of the immense swamp lying behind it. Since Roman headed the list of private subscribers who sponsored the opening of Jefferson College in St. James Parish, and since he obtained its incorporation in 1831, he may justly be regarded as the founder of that institution. The construction of the state penitentiary at Baton Rouge, based on modern ideals of prison management, was due to him, and the incorporation in 1834 of the New Orleans chamber of commerce won his hearty indorsement. His natural solicitude for the planting interests prompted the formation of a state agricultural society, of which he later became the zealous president. An experimental farm was created in St. James Parish, but, as adequate support was not forthcoming, both the farm and society ceased to exist. His suggestions and exertions, continued through both terms, gave the first practical impetus to the establishment of public common schools in the state. Equally important on the negative side was his courageous use and threat of use of the veto power against plunging the state into debt by unsound railroad legislation, an action that brought upon him general and severe condemnation. His historical interest led him to obtain a small appropriation for the copying of manuscripts in the Paris archives on the colonial history of the state. His second term was notable for financial derangements, during which he insisted on Louisiana paying her bonds. In spite of his effort to retire quietly to his plantation after his second term, he was recalled to public life for special services. In 1845 and 1852 he was called to state constitutional conventions; in 1848 he was sent to Europe as agent for two banks to obtain extension of time for payment of interest and renewal of the bonds.

A Whig in politics, moderate in his attitude toward the abolition movement, he opposed disunion strenuously; but as a delegate to the state secession convention of 1861 he yielded to the majority. He even accepted appointment from the Confederate provisional government on the commission created to confer with the United States for peaceable separation. Although he was too old to enter military service, he remained faithful to the Confederacy, refusing to protect his property by the oath of allegiance after the occupation of the state by federal troops. At the close of the war, about six weeks before his death, destitute and despondent, he accepted from Governor Wells a petty office, recorder of deeds and mortgages in New Orleans. The qualities of good judgment and unflinching firmness could scarcely be denied him, and he has been conceded to be one of Louisiana's ablest governors.

[Mrs. Eugene Soniat-du-Fossat, *Biog. Sketches of La. Governors* (1885); Arthur Meynier, *Louisiana Biographies* (1882); J. F. Condon, "Annals of Louisiana," App. to F. X. Martin, *The Hist. of La.* (1882); Alcée Fortier, *A Hist. of La.* (1904), vols. III, IV; C. E. A. Gayarré, *Hist. of La.,* vol. IV (1886); W. H. Sparks, *The Memories of Fifty Years* (1870); "A. B. Roman of Louisiana, Agriculturist," *De Bow's Southern and Western Review,* Oct. 1851; S. C. Arthur and G. C. H. de Kernion, *Old Families of La.* (1931); *New Orleans Times* and *New Orleans Bee,* Jan. 29, 1866, *Daily True Delta* (New Orleans), Jan. 30, 1866.]

E. L.

ROMANS, BERNARD (*c.* 1720–*c.* 1784), civil engineer, naturalist, cartographer, author, and captain of artillery, was born in the Netherlands about 1720. He studied engineering in England and about 1757 was sent to North America by the British government on professional work. In 1766 he was appointed deputy surveyor of Georgia, but went to East Florida to survey Lord Egmont's estates on Amelia Island and the St. John's River, and was thus enabled to make observations in the northern part of the peninsula. In January 1767, he petitioned for a grant of land in the province; in that year and the next he took up lands at Savannah and on the Ogeechee River, and in 1769 he acquired a tract on Nassau River in Florida, and subsequently extended his investigations to the middle and western parts of the peninsula. In 1769–70 Romans was appointed principal deputy surveyor for the Southern District by the surveyor general, William Gerard De Brahm [*q.v.*], at a salary of £30 a year; but since De Brahm was suspended by Gov. James Grant in October 1770, Romans failed to receive his salary and brought suit. Nevertheless, he went on a voyage of nearly a year's duration at his own expense, selling his Florida land in 1771. He thus completed his exploration of the Florida and Bahama banks and the west coast as far as Pensacola. There he was employed by Gov. Peter Chester and John Stuart [*q.v.*], superintendent of Indian affairs, to assist in the survey of West Florida and to prepare maps. Finding that Romans understood botany, Chester obtained permission from England to pay him £50 or £60 a year to make botanical discoveries, and the surveyor thus became the king's botanist in the province. Having voyaged as far as New Orleans, he sailed for Charlestown in February

1773, to resume employment under Stuart in South Carolina. His vessel capsized on the journey, and, after his arrival at his destination, for some reason Stuart declined his service.

Romans thereupon proceeded to New York to get subscribers for a book he planned to write on the Floridas. In the following August he was elected a member of the Marine Society of that city and attended a meeting of the American Philosophical Society in Philadelphia, before which he described two Florida plants, previously unknown, presented a paper on an improvement in the mariner's compass, and exhibited a navigation chart for the Florida waters. In January 1774 he was made a member of the society; he was then in Boston seeing about the engraving of his maps and endeavoring to obtain more subscribers for his book. Meanwhile he had found time to contribute an article on indigo to the *Royal American Magazine* (January 1774). On Mar. 9 he met the Rev. Ezra Stiles [*q.v.*] in Newport, R. I., with whom he later talked at length about Indians, Stiles recording in his diary that "Capt. Romans" had traveled among all the tribes "from Labradore to Panama" (*The Literary Diary of Ezra Stiles,* 1901, I, 524–25). At the end of March the busy author was in New York, when he wrote an article on the cultivation of madder for the *Royal American Magazine* (April 1774).

Settling shortly afterward in Hartford, Romans was appointed in April 1775 a member of the Connecticut committee to take possession of Ticonderoga and its outposts. He disagreed with the other leaders about the mode of attack, went on to Fort George, then in the custody of an invalided officer and one assistant, and on May 12 seized it single-handed. He behaved "very genteel and civil" toward his prisoner, permitting him to go to Connecticut. After accepting employment with the New York committee of safety to construct fortifications on the Hudson near West Point, he gave allegiance to the provincial congress on Sept. 18. He complained of his difficulties while building Fort Constitution, opposite West Point (Sept. 30, 1775–Feb. 9, 1776), and criticized the committee's plan. Although signing himself "Colonel," he failed to receive his commission from the provincial congress, resented the countermanding of his orders, and refused to serve as "an overseer" instead of as "sole director" of his plan. By direction of the Continental Congress he was paid up to Feb. 9, 1776.

Returning to Philadelphia, Romans was commissioned in February 1776 captain of a company of Pennsylvania artillery for service in

Canada. In November, Gen. Horatio Gates deputed him to inspect the works at Fort Anne and Skenesboro. Later he retired to Wethersfield, Conn., where he married Elizabeth Whiting, Jan. 28, 1779. His son Hubertus was born on Oct. 23 of that year. About July 1780, Romans was ordered to South Carolina to join the southern army. His vessel was captured and conducted to Montego Bay, Jamaica, where he was kept prisoner. At the end of the Revolution he was put on board ship for some port of the United States, having with him a large sum of money. He is said to have died at sea. His widow tried unsuccessfully to obtain a pension, and died in New York, May 12, 1848, at the age of eighty-nine years.

Romans' most noted book is *A Concise Natural History of East and West Florida,* of which vol. I was published in New York in 1775, and issued in a second edition in 1776. A second volume was projected but never published. The appendix to the *History,* containing contributions from De Brahm and other navigators, was published in 1789 as *The Complete Pilot for the Gulf Passage,* and reprinted in 1794 as *A New and Enlarged Book of Sailing Directions,* and again in 1797 with a slight change in title. The first volume of Romans' *Annals of the Troubles in the Netherlands* appeared at Hartford in 1778, and the second volume at the same place in 1782. These he compiled and translated "from the most Approved Historians." His printed maps include plans of Pensacola Harbor, Mobile Bar, and Tampa Bay, printed in the Appendix to the *Concise Natural History;* "A Map of the Whole Navigation, Showing Lieut. Cook's Tracks," in John Hawkesworth's *A New Voyage Round the World* (vol. I, 1774) ; *Part of the Province of East Florida* (1774), reprinted in the *Concise Natural History; A Map of the Seat of Civil War in America* (1775), showing Boston and the neighboring region; "A General Map of the Southern British Colonies in America," in *The American Military Pocket Atlas* (1776) ; *A Chorographical Map of the Northern Department of North America* and *A Chorographical Map of the Country Round Philadelphia,* both advertised for sale in 1778.

[W. H. Siebert, *Loyalists in East Florida, 1774–85* (1929), vol. II ; P. L. Phillips, *Notes on the Life and Work of Bernard Romans* (1924) ; A. D. Candler, *The Colonial Records of the State of Ga.,* vol. X (1907) ; Secretary of State's Letter Book A . . . Florida MSS. (MSS. Div., Lib. of Cong.), pp. 176–77, 190–91, 224; *Jours. of the Provincial Cong.,* State of N. Y., vols. I, II (1842) ; *Conn. Hist. Soc. Colls.,* vol. I (1860) ; *Am. Archives,* 4 ser. II–VI (1839–46), 5 ser. I (1848) ; *Pa. Archives,* 5 ser. III (1906) ; *New-Eng. Hist. and Geneal. Reg.,* Apr. 1866, p. 124; *N. Y. Daily Tribune,* May 13, 1848.]

W. H. S—t.

ROMAYNE, NICHOLAS (September 1756– July 21, 1817), physician, was the eldest son of John Romeyn, a New York silversmith, and his wife Juliana McCarty. His brother Jeremiah and several of his close relatives were Dutch Reformed clergymen (W. B. Sprague, *Annals of the American Pulpit,* vol. IX, 1869). Nicholas, who altered the spelling of his name, received his early education at the Hackensack Academy under Peter Wilson [*q.v.*] and entered the medical school of King's College, New York, in 1774. He secured the M.D. degree at Edinburgh in 1780, writing a thesis on the formation of pus, *De Generatione Puris* (Edinburgh, 1780), and continued his education for a time on the Continent. Returning to America, he settled first in Philadelphia, then after the evacuation, in New York, where he married Susan, daughter of Isaac Van Dam, merchant, of the Island of St. Eustatia (*Collections of the New York Historical Society,* Publication Fund Series, vol. XXXVII, 1905, p. 389).

He was one of the original board of regents of the University of the State of New York from 1784 to 1787, and when the trustees of Columbia College were independently chartered in 1787, he was made an original member of this board, resigning in 1793. In 1785 he was elected professor of the practice of physic in the revived Medical School of Columbia College, holding the title until 1787, and in 1791–92 he was lecturer in chemistry, anatomy, and the practice of physic; but this faculty having performed but small service, Romayne was mainly occupied from 1787 in the instruction of private classes. Being a man of learning and wide culture, he attracted many students, and in time he had a medical school of his own. In 1791 he addressed the regents of the University, asking their protection and direction for the school, and shortly afterward he and six associates, young physicians, addressed a second memorial describing their proposed plans for instruction. The regents were favorably disposed, and granted a charter to Sir James Jay [*q.v.*], Romayne, and others as the College of Physicians and Surgeons. The Columbia trustees made immediate objection, representing that they were engaged in establishing a medical department according to their charter, and the Romayne proposal was suspended. Romayne then approached the trustees of Queen's (now Rutgers) College at New Brunswick, N. J., for a degree-conferring arrangement, and was able to secure degrees from that institution for some of his students in 1792 and 1793. The Queen's affair, however, placed him under the ban of his profession in New York, and he went to Europe for further study and observation. Here he was made a licentiate of the Royal College of Physicians in London and a fellow of the Royal College of Physicians in Edinburgh.

Romayne's next appearance was as a speculator in Western lands, implicated in the Blount conspiracy of 1797. The scheme having failed, Romayne, conceiving that his countrymen looked upon him with suspicion, left the country (C. R. King, *post*, III, p. 258). In 1806, "by a sudden and singular change of sentiment," he was called from his retirement and honored by election as first president of the medical society of the city and county of New York (Hosack, *post*, p. 92). In 1807 the College of Physicians and Surgeons, dormant since 1791, was revived and Romayne was made president and trustee, and in 1808 professor of the institutes of medicine; during 1807-08, in the absence of a professor, he gave lectures in anatomy. He made the *Address Delivered at the Commencement of the Lectures* in the school, published in New York in 1808. It was not long, however, before difficulties arose. In 1811 he and several of the professors resigned, and Romayne was back at Queen's College for degree-granting connections. Some of the more distinguished members of the faculty had stood by him, and again in 1812 Queen's established a faculty of medicine and appointed these men to professorships, making Romayne professor of the institutes of medicine and forensic medicine. The school was carried on, as before, in quarters in New York City. Twenty-one students, including Joseph Rodman Drake [*q.v.*], received the Queen's degree, but in 1816 the school was closed. Dr. Hosack said "it fell in its own weakness" (*post*, p. 34). Romayne died in New York the next year at the age of sixty-one. Samuel Latham Mitchill is quoted as having said of him: "His superior attainments in literature and medicine elevated him with high notions, and filled him with contemptuous notions of some who had been less fortunate in education than himself" (Hosack, *post*, pp. 90-91).

[Sources include: David Hosack, *An Inaugural Discourse, Delivered at the Opening of Rutgers Medic. Coll. . . . N. Y.* (1826); *A Communication from the Regents of the Univ., Transmitting a Report of a Committee of the Regents . . . Appointed to Visit the Coll. of Physicians and Surgeons* (1826); manuscript minutes of the Trustees of Columbia and the Coll. of Physicians and Surgeons; J. G. Curtis, "The Genesis of the Coll. of Physicians and Surgeons," *Columbia Univ. Quart.*, Supp. to Dec. 1907; J. C. Dalton, *Hist. of the Coll. of Physicians and Surgeons* (1888); John Shrady, *The Coll. of Physicians and Surgeons* (n.d.); James Thacher, *Amer. Medic. Biog.* (1828), II, 25-29; W. H. S. Demarest, *A Hist. of Rutgers Coll.* (1924); Rutgers College, *Cat. of the Officers and Alumni* (1916); C. R.

King, *The Life and Correspondence of Rufus King*, II (1895), III (1896). Although Romayne's death date is usually given as July 20, 1817, the *N. Y. Columbian* of July 21, 1817, says he "died this morning at 10 o'clock."]

M. H. T.

ROMBRO, JACOB (Oct. 10, 1858–Nov. 28, 1922), editor, author, labor leader, best known under his pen name, Philip Krantz, was born in Zuphran, Province of Wilna (then a part of the Russian Empire), although some biographers give Khodaki, Podolia, as his birthplace. His parents were Baruch Rombro and Bella Rosa (Uger). When he was fourteen years old, he entered the Rabbinical Seminary in Zhitomir, Volhynia, but a year later the Seminary closed its doors, and he then attended the Realschule in Krementchug, graduating in 1879. The next two years he spent at the Technological Institute at St. Petersburg. While still a student at the Realschule he became interested in the Revolutionary movement which was fermenting in Russian educational institutions, and was sentenced to be imprisoned for a year in Charkov for political propaganda, and to remain under the supervision of the police. After the assassination of Alexander II in 1881 he was compelled to leave the country, on account of his alleged affiliations with the conspirators Grinevetzki, Zheliabov, Sophia Perovskaya, and others. He settled in Paris, where he continued his studies at the Sorbonne. Here he commenced his prolific literary career with a lengthy treatise on Spinoza in *Razsviet*, and wrote continuously for other Russian magazines, including *Russki Evrey, Woskhod, Kievskaya Zarya,* an association which he maintained even later in London and New York. Here, too, began his propagandist activity for the ideals of Social Democracy among the Jewish working classes, and he was among the founders of a Jewish *Arbeiter Verein* which during its existence was an active center of Socialism for the many emigrants from Czarist Russia, consisting mainly of workers and students.

In 1883 Rombro went to London where he was asked by Morris Winchevsky [*q.v.*] to contribute to his Yiddish weekly socialist journal *Der Polischer Yidel.* Speaking of Winchevsky's request to write for his paper a description of the riots against the Jews in Russia, Rombro said (Wiener, *post*, p. 223): "It was a hard job for me, and it took me a long time to do it. I never thought of writing in the Jewish Jargon, but fate ordered otherwise, and, contrary to all my aspirations, I am now nothing more than a poor Jargon journalist." His evil plight was his people's gain, however, since for the remainder of his life he devoted his many talents to their enlightenment, his medium being Yiddish. Within two years he had mastered that language to such a degree that he was able to accept the editorship of the newly founded *Arbeiter Freund,* a socialist monthly. In 1888 he helped to found a Jewish Social-Democratic group, at whose request he supplied a Yiddish translation (London, 1889) of Lassalle's *Das Arbeiter-Programm.* The following year he was chosen by the Jewish workers of London as delegate to the first International Socialist Congress in Paris.

In 1890 he came to the United States, having been invited to act as editor of a new Social-Democratic weekly, the *Arbeiter Zeitung,* his associates being Abraham Cahan, Louis Miller, and M. Zametkin. In addition to editorials and articles on socialism, he furnished numerous translations of popular fiction. As the first socialist paper in Yiddish, the *Arbeiter Zeitung* had a marked influence both on the development of the Jewish labor movement and the Yiddish press in the United States. Rombro's editorship continued for several years after the paper, under the name *Abend-Blatt,* had been converted into a daily in 1894 and had become the official organ of the Socialist-Labor party. In 1892 Rombro was also appointed editor of the newly established *Zukunft,* a Yiddish monthly devoted to socialism, belles-lettres, and popular science. Either as editor or contributor, he was associated with practically every Jewish socialist periodical published in America during his lifetime, and at the time of his death was on the staff of the *Jewish Daily Forward* in New York City.

Rombro played an important part in the development of socialist ideas among the Jewish working classes, but he was far from being a blind partisan. He treated events of general interest without bias. During the last twenty years of his life he took no active part in the socialist movement, but his pen was always at its service. He was much more the teacher of social and political progress than the agitator, believed in evolution rather than revolution, advocated peaceful arbitration rather than the use of force, and died an avowed opponent of the Bolshevist régime. His wide erudition and mastery of many languages helped him in his rôle as interpreter to the Jewish masses of Western sociology, science, history, and culture, and aided him in his endeavor to adjust the newly arrived immigrants from Eastern Europe to American institutions and practices. His writings are characterized by great earnestness and a flowing style. Among his Yiddish books, some of which went into several editions, were a history of Socialism, a history of the French Revolution, a history of civilization, and a popular astronomy, as well as a method for the study of English, a "History of All America: . . . of all the countries in the New World," and a series of biographies which appeared in book form, of Aristotle, Bar Kokhba, Josephus Flavius, Mohammed, Don Isaac Abravanel, Baruch Spinoza, Shabbethai Zebi, Lessing and Mendelssohn, the Rothschilds, and Meyerbeer. He married Eva Gordon; his death occurred in New York City.

[Zalmen Reisen, *Lexicon fun der Yiddisher Literatur,* vol. III (Wilna, 1929); Leo Wiener, *The Hist. of Yiddish Literature in the Nineteenth Century* (1899); Morris Winchevsky, "Reminiscences," being vol. X of his collected Yiddish works (New York, 1927); *Am. Jewish Year Book,* 1904–05; *N. Y. Times,* Nov. 29, 1922.]
                                                            I. S.

ROMEIKE, HENRY (Nov. 19, 1855–June 3, 1903), originator of press clipping service, was born in Riga, Russia. He was of mixed German and Lithuanian stock, the son of Albert and Henriette (Szabries) Romeike. After a fragmentary common-school education in Memel, East Prussia, he was apprenticed to the dry-goods trade at the age of thirteen, but two years later ran away and went to Berlin. There he worked in dry-goods shops for about ten years, but he did not like the business, and finally gave it up and drifted about Europe two or three years, looking for something congenial. During a conversation over a newspaper with a chance acquaintance on a park bench in Paris in 1883, he was struck by the idea that persons of prominence might like to be supplied in a comprehensive way with clippings of newspaper articles regarding themselves. Romeike was almost entirely without funds, and he therefore had great difficulty in getting copies of newspapers sufficient to launch his business. He introduced it by making personal calls on the individuals he wished to serve, leaving small batches of clippings with each. He found that the suggestion pleased many of them, and his business slowly developed. But after about a year in Paris, he decided that the English read more newspapers than the French, and removed to London, though he continued to serve his French customers. Here he took in a partner named Curtice. His clipping bureau was the first in England, and it found many clients there, eventually acquiring patronage even among the nobility and royalty. But reports of advancement in America and the prosperity of its daily newspapers again made him restive, and in 1885 he sent Samuel Leavitt to the United States to make a survey. Leavitt reported that there was more newspaper reading done there than in England, and under Romeike's direction, he established a clipping bureau in New York. Romeike sold his interest in his London business to his partner Curtice and came to New York. In America, even more than in the other countries, he seemed to have filled a long-felt want, and his business, after a slow and modest start, presently brought him emolument and even a measure of fame. Politicians, persons of social prominence, actors, writers, and musicians quickly took to the new idea, and professional and even business men followed them. Romeike was credited with having made America more self-conscious. His novel business brought about the coining of a new slang verb; an article or a book compiled from press clippings was said to be "romeiked." His service was extended to many foreign countries, and not a few titled personages were among his patrons. Romeike was married in London, Sept. 26, 1884, to Jane Sarah Mary Ganther; on July 12, 1892, he was married in New York to Suzanna Dayes. There were two children by the latter union, but the marriage was annulled in 1902. Romeike died about a year later, at the early age of forty-eight.

[Sources include: *Who's Who in America*, 1901–02; obituaries in all New York newspapers, June 4, 1903; *Baltimore Herald*, June 6, 1903; *Utica* (N. Y.) *Observer*, June 8, 1903; *Collier's Weekly*, June 20, 1903. A scrap-book of letters and clippings in the possession of Romeike's brother, Albert Romeike, of New York, was also consulted.]　　　　　　　　　　　A. F. H.

RONDTHALER, EDWARD (July 24, 1842–Jan. 31, 1931), bishop of the Moravian Church, was born at Schoeneck near Nazareth, Pa., the great-grandson of Emanuel Rondthaler who had been a Moravian pastor in Sarepta, Russia, emigrated, and then became pastor at York, Pa. The boy's father was Edward Rondthaler, also a Moravian pastor. His mother was Sarah Elizabeth (Rice) Rondthaler of Bethlehem, Pa. In early childhood his parents were sent in succession to take charge of the churches at Graceham, Md., and at Philadelphia, and his elementary education was acquired in private schools in the latter city. In 1853 he was sent to Nazareth Hall for five years and then entered the Moravian College and Theological Seminary, at Bethlehem, Pa., of which his father had been president at the time of his death in 1855. Edward received his bachelor's degree in divinity in 1862. For a year after graduation he studied theology and philosophy at the University of Erlangen, Bavaria, and returned to America in 1864 to become a teacher at Nazareth Hall. In 1865 he was ordained a deacon and given his first charge at Brooklyn, N. Y., where a burned

church edifice had very nearly extinguished the life of a small congregation. He was married on Oct. 1, 1867, to Mary E. Jacobson of Bethlehem, who with a son survived him. In six years his sympathetic and forceful attitude had reunited the congregation and rebuilt the church, and when he left Brooklyn in 1873 he was considered one of the most promising young men in the Moravian group. He remained in Philadelphia for four years and was then called to Salem, N. C., to the pastorate of the mother congregation of the southern province, where for the rest of his long life he devoted himself to the revival of the physical and spiritual forces that had been sadly weakened by the Civil War and the later Reconstruction. From 1884 to 1888 he was the head of the Salem Academy and, after that, president of the provincial governing board for thirty-five years. During this time he continued his increasingly arduous duties as pastor of what he called the "Home Church." Through his administrative genius a group of half a dozen disunited and struggling churches was changed into a closely knit federation of four times the number of members, practically dominating the life, both social and spiritual, of the Wachovia region. On Apr. 12, 1891, he was consecrated a bishop, the ceremony being conducted by three bishops, Van Vleck, Levering, and Bachman.

His strength lay in his ability to control and to inspire those who came into contact with him. His devotion to spiritual ideals and his uncanny ability to sense the potentialities of an economic situation were combined with an infinite tact and patience. He used these gifts at a critical time in the development of Winston-Salem to reorganize and direct social forces that otherwise might have worked themselves out in futile cross-purposes. Moreover, he possessed a magnificent voice of great range and power, which enlarged his audience and widened his circle of influence. When Winston-Salem, the largest industrial city in North Carolina, had grown out of the little village of Salem, his directing share in the unusual development of the community was recognized at a great civic assembly, at which with the presentation of a loving cup he was proclaimed the "first citizen." Yet what he prized above all social honors was scholarship; and when he had passed the usual span of life he still laid aside knotty administrative problems to find rest in the plays of Aristophanes or in the solution of problems in calculus. In 1928 he published *The Memorabilia of Fifty Years*, a series of papers he had issued at the close of each year, in which he discussed local and international affairs from 1877 to 1927. After his death there was published an *Appendix to the Memorabilia of Fifty Years* (1931).

[Biog. in *Appendix to the Memorabilia, ante*; *Winston-Salem Journal*, Feb. 1, 1931; *Twin City Sentinel* (Winston-Salem), Feb. 1, 1931; *Moravian*, Feb. 4, 1931.]   A. G. R.

ROOD, OGDEN NICHOLAS (Feb. 3, 1831–Nov. 12, 1902), physicist, son of Rev. Anson Rood and Alida Gouverneur (Ogden), was born in Danbury, Conn., and died in New York City. His father was a Congregational clergyman whose ancestors, of Scottish origin, had settled in Massachusetts in early colonial days; and his mother, daughter of Uzal Ogden [*q.v.*] and a descendant of John Ogden who was one of the founders of Elizabeth, N. J., belonged to an aristocratic family of New York. Young Rood entered Yale College at seventeen years of age, but soon afterwards transferred to the College of New Jersey (Princeton), where he graduated in 1852. Already he had begun to show a predilection for experimental science; and during the next two years, except for several months at the University of Virginia, he pursued a postgraduate course in the new Sheffield Scientific School at Yale. From 1854 to 1858 he was in Germany studying physics and chemistry at Berlin and Munich under Liebig, Magnus, and Dove, and at the same time devoting much of his leisure to the cultivation of painting and music, for both of which he had talent. In Munich he married Mathilde Prunner.

Returning to the United States with his bride in 1858, he accepted the post of professor of chemistry in a small denominational college at Troy, N. Y. Here, despite an uncongenial environment and scant facilities, he threw himself into his new work with enthusiasm and during the five or six years he was at Troy contributed a series of notable papers to the *American Journal of Science*. These studies included investigations of the polarization of light produced by the passage of light through a block of glass that had been strained in the process of annealing, the after-images that are perceived by looking at a bright surface through the open sectors of a revolving disk and the connection between the sensation of color and the persistence of vision, stereoscopic phenomena, especially stereoscopic lustre (which he had begun to study in Germany under Dove), photography and the duration of electric sparks, and spectrometry. He was one of the first to adapt the microscope to photography and to take binocular pictures with that instrument.

In 1864 he was made professor of physics in Columbia College, New York City, and here spent the rest of his life, becoming identified with the institution as one of its leading spirits and soon being recognized as one of the foremost scientific investigators of his day. He had little taste for the complicated problems of mathematical physics; on the other hand he had a positive genius for experimenting and a consummate ingenuity in the use of simple contrivances for obtaining results of the highest precision and value. "He delighted in the *tour de force* required to push the sensibility of an apparatus to its limit or in the invention of some novel device for determining the hitherto unmeasurable. At one time he devised a means for determining details which the microscope failed to reveal; at another he modified and defined Bunsen's photometric device so as to greatly enhance its sensitiveness. Where Wheatstone measured intervals of time not greater than a millionth of a second, he carried the determination to times as much smaller relatively as a quarter of a minute is smaller than an hour" (Nichols, *post*, p. 468). While Rood was always keenly interested in optics, especially in physiological optics, there is scarcely any part of the physics of his generation that he did not touch and enrich by his work. He was continually improving old methods and devising new ones. His modification of the Sprengel airpump enabled him to produce and measure high vacua far in excess of any that had been obtained before. An exceedingly important experimental device which he developed is the flicker photometer by which the brightness of light of different colors can be compared; this instrument has become indispensable in heterochromatic photometry. Towards the end of his life Rood investigated with characteristic curiosity and ingenuity the properties of the X-rays discovered by Röntgen in 1895. During these latter years also he devised a remarkable method of measuring prodigiously great electrical resistances.

In 1879 he published a notable book entitled *Modern Chromatics with Applications to Art and Industry*, which was translated into French, German, and Italian and soon after republished in England. It contains the mature conclusions and results of the author's numerous contributions to the physics of the color sensations and has become almost a classic in its field. For "lucidity and simplicity of treatment" and for the admirable style in which it is written it deserves to be ranked with Helmholtz's popular scientific lectures or with Tyndall's *Heat* (1863) and *Sound* (1867). The difficult subject of color and color-mixing is treated from both the standpoint of the physicist and that of the artist, and it is this rare combination that lends the book so much charm and gives it so much authority.

Rood has been described as "striking in appearance and in manners, possessing and possibly affecting certain peculiarities, working behind locked doors, sometimes living with his family and sometimes not, in part a recluse, although not averse to congenial company or an evening at the Century Club" (*Popular Science Monthly,* January 1903). In 1865, soon after the foundation of the National Academy of Sciences, he was elected a member of that body. He was an honorary member of the American Water Colour Society and at the annual meetings his paintings were frequently on exhibition. He was a vice-president of the American Association for the Advancement of Science.

[*Columbia Univ. Quart.,* Dec. 1902; *Am. Jour. Sci.,* Jan. 1903; *Science,* Dec. 5, 1902; *Physical Rev.,* May 1903; E. L. Nichols in *Nat. Acad. Sci. Biog. Memoirs,* vol. VI (1909), bibliog.; F. P. Keppel, *Columbia* (1914); *Who's Who in America,* 1901–02; W. O. Wheeler, *The Ogden Family in America* (1907); *N. Y. Times,* Nov. 13, 1902.] J. P. C. S.

ROOSA, DANIEL BENNETT ST. JOHN (Apr. 4, 1838–Mar. 8, 1908), physician, son of Charles Baker Roosa and Amelie Elmer (Foster) of Bethel, N. Y., was of sturdy Colonial descent, his four great-grandfathers (Duryea, Foster, Heard, and Roosa) having served in the Continental Army. All four names appear in the early history of New York State. As a boy he attended the lower schools in his native village and later the academies of Monticello, N. Y., and Honesdale, Pa. His freshman year at Yale, 1856, was marred by ill health, and he was forced to give up his college course. The following year, however, with characteristic perseverance, he entered the Medical Department of the University of the City of New York (now New York University), from which he was graduated M.D. in 1860. His first appointment was as assistant house surgeon of the New York Hospital, but he left it shortly, after the outbreak of the Civil War, to become assistant surgeon to the 5th New York Volunteers. He served for three months at this time and reënlisted in 1863 for the last part of the war. Between 1861 and 1863 he studied abroad in the ophthalmological clinics of Berlin and Vienna. In 1863 he was appointed professor of diseases of the eye and ear in the University of the City of New York and at the close of the Civil War assumed his duties, serving in this capacity until 1874, and thereafter until 1882, as professor of ophthalmology. For several years he was also professor of diseases of the eye and ear at the University of Vermont.

A man of large vision, Roosa was one of the first to conceive the idea of organizing a medical school for post-graduate work. He was responsible for the founding in 1883 of the New York Post-Graduate Medical School, to which, as president, he devoted the last twenty-five years of his life. This institution is his monument. He possessed a strong and inspiring personality; his militant, pioneer spirit was tempered with sympathy and calm judgment. In his determined struggle to make legally equal homeopaths, osteopaths, and others who had passed the State Regents' medical examinations, he displayed courage, enthusiasm, and steadfastness of purpose. His oratorical skill made him a prominent figure in promoting legislation in regard to many other matters affecting the interests of the medical profession, such as the transfer of chronic insane from county asylums to state institutions, measures for the prevention of blindness, and the raising of standards of academic requirements for medical students. He was one of the founders of the American Otological Society, and its president 1874–76; president of the International Otological Congress in 1876 in New York City, of the Medical Society of the State of New York in 1879, of the New York Academy of Medicine in 1893–94; and vice-president of the International Congress of Ophthalmology at Edinburgh in 1894. His most important publications include: *A Vest-Pocket Medical Lexicon* (1872); *A Practical Treatise on Diseases of the Ear* (1873), long used as a standard textbook; *A Doctor's Suggestion to the Community* (1880); *Determination of the Necessity for Wearing Glasses* (1887); *The Old Hospital and Other Papers* (1889); *A Clinical Manual of Diseases of the Eye* (1894); *Defective Eyesight* (1899), a large number of short articles, and two valuable translations: *The Diseases of the Ear* (1864), from the German of A. F. von Tröltsch, and, in collaboration with Charles E. Hackley, *Treatise on the Diseases of the Eye* (1868), from the German of Carl Stellwag von Carion.

Roosa was twice married, first to Mary Hoyt Blake, who died in 1878, and later, July 8, 1879, to Sarah Elizabeth (Haughwout) Howe, widow of Col. Francis E. Howe. There were no children. Roosa died very suddenly and painlessly of heart complications in Bright's disease, having been vigorous and active until almost the very moment of his death. He was survived by his second wife.

[*Who's Who in America,* 1908–09; *Who's Who in N. Y.,* 1907; H. A. Kelly and W. L. Burrage, *Am. Medic. Biogs.* (1920); *N. Y. Geneal. and Biog. Record,* Oct. 1902; D. W. Howe, *Howe Geneals.* (1929); *Gen.*

Alumni Cat., N. Y. Univ., Medic. Alumni (1908); T. J. Harris, "Early History of the American Otological Society," *Annals of Otology, Rhinology, and Laryngology,* June 1926; *Contributions to the Science of Medicine and Surgery by the Faculty . . . N. Y. Post-Graduate Medic. School* (1908); *Post-Graduate,* Apr. 1908; *N. Y. Tribune,* Mar. 9, 1908.]   G. L. A.

ROOSEVELT, HILBORNE LEWIS (Dec. 21, 1849–Dec. 30, 1886), organ builder and inventor, a first cousin of Theodore Roosevelt [*q.v.*] and the son of Silas Weir and Mary (West) Roosevelt, was born in New York City. His grandfather, Cornelius Van Schaack Roosevelt, had been a prominent merchant and philanthropist, and a founder and director of the Chemical National Bank. In Hilborne Roosevelt's youth the dividing line between the gentleman and "mechanic" was strictly drawn, and his interest in the details of organ building was frowned upon by his family; nevertheless, in opposition to their wishes he entered the shop of Hall & Labagh, New York City, and later made several trips to Europe to study organ construction there. He became a pioneer in the development of the electric organ and in the application of new electrical devices to organ manufacture, and in April 1869 he took out the first patent for an electric organ action (No. 88,909). In 1872 he opened his own factory on Eighteenth Street, New York City, and by 1881 his success as an organ builder necessitated the removal of the business to larger quarters. He added factories in Philadelphia and Baltimore, and constructed some of the largest church organs then known in the United States, among them those of the Garden City (L. I.) Cathedral, and of Grace Church and Trinity Church in New York City. The organ he constructed for the main building of the Philadelphia Centennial Exhibition in 1876, later acquired by the Massachusetts Charitable Mechanic Association, attracted much attention, as it combined the best points of European voicing with some effects never before produced ("The Roosevelt Centennial Organ Scheme," *Roosevelt Organ Journal,* July 1876). It is said to have been the first electric-action organ built in America.

Roosevelt did not confine his attention solely to organ building. Widely known among the creative electricians of his day, he was largely interested in the Bell Telephone Company, and invented several telephone devices, including the automatic switch-hook, on which he received royalties for a number of years. On Feb. 1, 1883, he married Kate, daughter of William Watson Shippen, of Hoboken, N. J. After his untimely death at the age of thirty-seven, his organ business was continued by his brother, Frank H. Roosevelt, until 1893, when the stock and patents were sold to the Farrand & Votey Company of Detroit. In Hilborne Roosevelt the creative rather than the commercial impulse predominated. He was primarily an inventor, and he spent thousands of dollars in electrical experiments and in developing the principle of the electric valve. To him the initial impetus of all subsequent improvement in American organ building is largely due.

[H. C. Lahee, *The Organ and Its Masters* (1902); Alfred Dolge, *Pianos and Their Makers,* vol. I (1911); *Hilborne L. Roosevelt, Manufacturer of Church, Chapel and Chamber Organs* (1883); C. B. Whittelsey, *The Roosevelt Geneal., 1649–1902* (1902); *N. Y. Tribune,* Dec. 31, 1886.]   F. H. M.

ROOSEVELT, NICHOLAS J. (Dec. 27, 1767–July 30, 1854), inventor, engineer, was born in New York City, the youngest child of Jacobus and Annetje (Bogard) Roosevelt. His father, a shopkeeper in New York, had been admitted as a freeman of that city on Feb. 22, 1748, and was a private in the New York colonial troops. Nicholas was educated in New York and developed a great love for mechanics. As early as 1782, when he was living on the farm of Joseph Oosterhaudt, near Esopus, N. Y., he built a model boat, propelled by paddle wheels over the sides. The wheels were turned by hickory and whalebone springs which unwound a cord wrapped around the wheel axles.

After the evacuation of New York by the British, Roosevelt returned there to pursue his mechanical interests. In 1793 he became a director of the New Jersey Copper Mine Association, organized to rework the abandoned Schuyler copper mine, an enterprise which was given up eighteen months later. Meanwhile he had become much interested in steam engines and their manufacture and succeeded in inducing his associates to purchase some land on Second River, now Belleville, N. J., and erect a metal foundry and shop. Following the completion of these works, called Soho after the establishment of Boulton and Watt in England, Roosevelt's associates retired and left him to carry on the enterprise alone. Sanguine and ambitious, he at first had some success, building engines for various purposes, including those for the Philadelphia water works. He also contracted to erect a rolling mill and supply the federal government with copper drawn and rolled for six 74-gun ships which were to be built. After he had gone to great expense to complete this contract, a change in federal administration caused the abandonment of ship construction and a consequent great financial loss to Roosevelt. About 1797 he entered into an agreement with Robert R. Livingston and John

Stevens [*qq.v.*] to build a steamboat on joint account, the engines for which were to be constructed at his foundry. The work of building this experimental boat was slow and tedious and it was not until the middle of 1798 that steam was applied to the machinery. At first the boat was not successful, but on a trial trip, Oct. 21, 1798, after improvements had been made, the *Polacca,* as it was named, attained a speed equivalent to three miles an hour in still water. During the construction of this vessel Roosevelt tried to induce Livingston to use paddle wheels over the sides, but Livingston would have nothing to do with such a plan. In 1801 Livingston was appointed United States minister to France and the whole undertaking was dropped.

By this time Roosevelt's business was in such chaotic condition that he was compelled to abandon his works entirely. In 1809, however, he became associated with Robert Fulton [*q.v.*] in the introduction of steamboats on Western rivers, and in 1811 built at Pittsburgh the steamboat *New Orleans.* In this he descended the Ohio and Mississippi rivers from Pittsburgh to New Orleans in fourteen days. In the belief that he was entitled to a patent for use of vertical paddle wheels, he now applied for such a patent which was granted him on Dec. 1, 1814. The following January he applied to the New Jersey legislature for protection as the inventor of such paddle wheels, but the legislature decided, primarily because of the objections of Fulton and Livingston, that "it was inexpedient to make any special provision in connection with the matter in controversy before the body" (Latrobe, *post,* p. 31), and there the matter rested. Roosevelt soon retired from active work and resided for the remainder of his life with his family in Skaneateles, Onondaga County, N. Y. He married Lydia Latrobe, daughter of the elder Benjamin Henry Latrobe [*q.v.*] of Baltimore, Md., Nov. 15, 1808, by whom he had nine children, six of whom died in their early youth.

[C. B. Whittelsey, *The Roosevelt Geneal. 1649–1902* (1902); J. H. B. Latrobe, *A Lost Chapter in the Hist. of the Steamboat* (1871); William Nelson, "Josiah Hornblower and the First Steam Engine in America," in *Proc. of the N. J. Hist. Soc.,* 2 ser. VII (1883); G. H. Preble, *A Chronological Hist. of the Origin and Development of Steam Navigation* (1883); Patent Office records.]   C. W. M.

ROOSEVELT, ROBERT BARNWELL (Aug. 7, 1829–June 14, 1906), political reformer, writer, pioneer in conservation, was born in New York City, the fourth son of Cornelius Van Schaack and Margaret (Barnhill) Roosevelt. Christened Robert Barnhill, he later adopted Barnwell as his middle name. His father was a wealthy banker and merchant, a descendant of Claes Martenszen van Rosenvelt who was an early settler of New Amsterdam. His mother was a member of a prominent family of Quaker merchants of Philadelphia. In his early youth Roosevelt showed a diversity of interests that characterized him throughout his life. He was fond of hunting, yachting, and other forms of outdoor sport, and showed a precocious interest in politics and in English composition. After receiving an excellent preparatory education he studied law and was admitted to the bar on attaining his majority. In 1850 he married Elizabeth Ellis of New York who bore him two sons and two daughters, and during most of his life he resided on East Twentieth St., next door to his brother Theodore, the father of President Theodore Roosevelt.

He quickly attained a prominent position at the bar, at the same time giving much attention to writing and to public affairs. During his more than twenty years of practice he was counsel in an unusual number of cases in which the public interest was involved. At the beginning of the Civil War he identified himself with the group of Democrats who strongly supported the Union cause, and was a founder of the Loyal National League and of the Union League Club, both important propagandist organizations. In 1864 he became secretary of the Citizens' Association and represented it in proceedings before courts and legislative committees. One of his prosecutions resulted in abolishing the offices of the incompetent health wardens and in establishing a model board of health. He was also instrumental in creating a paid fire department. He later became associated with Charles G. Halpine [*q.v.*] in the editorship of the *New York Citizen,* the official organ of the association, and by his editorials helped to arouse the city against the "Tweed ring." He was one of the organizers of the famous Committee of Seventy which overthrew the ring, assuming the special task of leading the opposition among independent Democrats. In 1872 he had practically the sole responsibility for managing the successful mayoralty campaign of the reform ticket. He elected to the Forty-second Congress (1871–73) and signalized his brief service by exposing a corrupt ring operating in the District of Columbia.

Roosevelt's early writings dealt with hunting, fishing and outdoor life—fields that were then almost wholly unexploited. His first three books, *Game Fish of the Northern States of America, and British Provinces* (1862), *Superior Fishing* (1865), and *The Game Birds of the Coasts and*

Lakes of the Northern States of America (1866), had an important influence in creating the cult of the hunter-naturalist. Foreseeing the eventual destruction of all game and fish unless measures for conservation were undertaken, he assiduously promoted the work of state and international sportsmen's associations. In 1867 he secured from the New York legislature the passage of a law, widely copied in other states, creating the state fishery commission. As chairman or member of that body for twenty years he supervised the introduction and perfecting of artificial methods of propagating fish and the protection of streams against indiscriminate dumping of sewage and mill wastes. His later writings were: *Five Acres Too Much* (1869), and *Progressive Petticoats* (1874), both of which were satires; *Love and Luck* (1886), a novel; *Fish Hatching, Fish Catching* (joint author with Seth Green, 1879), *Florida and the Game Water-Birds of the Atlantic Coast and the Lakes of the United States* (1884); and a memorial edition (1869) of the *Poetical Works of Charles G. Halpine* (*Miles O'Reilly*).

In 1872 Roosevelt received a large inheritance and retired from the bar to become a director of several railroad and industrial companies and to supervise widely dispersed investments. He was a commissioner of the Brooklyn bridge, 1879–81; a member of the Board of Aldermen, 1882, devoting his attention chiefly to securing the passage of a pure-food ordinance; minister to the Netherlands, 1888–89; chairman of a relief committee during the Spanish-American War; and a member of committees formed to aid the Boers. After the death of his wife in 1887 he married Mrs. Marion T. (O'Shea) Fortescue, on Aug. 18, 1888. During his later years he was the leader of various Democratic reform associations which carried on an unequal contest with Tammany Hall. He wanted to be mayor of New York, but his uncompromising zeal for reform deprived him of the support of Tammany and his thoroughgoing support of Democratic policies prevented his indorsement by the Republicans. In the presidency of his nephew, Theodore Roosevelt [*q.v.*], whose party allegiance he disapproved, he lived to see the frequent expression of the principles of conservation and of political reform which seem to have been the dominant interests of his life. He died at Sayville, L. I.

[The most complete sketch of Roosevelt is in the second number of the *New Amsterdam Year Book, 1898*. Briefer accounts are in C. B. Whittlesey, *The Roosevelt Genealogy, 1649–1902* (1902); *Who's Who in America*, 1906–07; *Biog. Directory of the Am. Cong., 1774–1927* (1928); M. A. Hamm, *Famous Families of N. Y.* (1901), vol. II; *N. Y. Herald*, June 15, 1906.

The Roosevelt House in New York City has a collection of his scrapbooks, letters, and other materials, including his Political Black Book.]   E. C. S.

ROOSEVELT, THEODORE (Oct. 27, 1858–Jan. 6, 1919), twenty-sixth president of the United States, was born at No. 28 East 20th St., New York City, the son of Theodore and Martha (Bulloch) Roosevelt. Of the four children, Anna was older, and Elliott and Corinne were younger than he. In his *Autobiography* he stated that his ancestor, Klaes Martensen van Roosevelt, came from Holland to New Amsterdam as a "settler" about 1644; in various genealogies the name appears as Claes Martenszen van Rosenvelt and the date as 1649 (Whittlesey, Clemens, Johnson, *post*). Thereafter, six generations of Roosevelts before his own were identified with Manhattan, and the more recent of them were well-to-do. Robert Barnwell Roosevelt [*q.v.*] was his uncle. His mother, the daughter of James Stephens Bulloch of Roswell, Ga., and a descendant of Archibald Bulloch [*q.v.*], first president of the Provincial Congress of Georgia, was of the aristocracy of the Old South. His parents maintained in their brownstone residence a home of dignity, culture, and restraint; they were established in, though not highly valuing, the society of New York. Handicapped in childhood by asthma, and always by defective eyesight, Theodore rebuilt his body from sheer determination, teaching himself to ride, shoot, and box, though his early interests were more in natural history than sport. His parents gave him tutors and travel as a child and sent him to Harvard. He made Phi Beta Kappa there, but was not thrilled by academic opportunity, and was graduated in 1880, lacking a career but free to choose one.

Law, which he undertook to read, failed to interest him; so he turned to the history of the United States, beginning, with the publication in 1882 of *The Naval War of 1812; or, the History of the United States Navy During the Last War with Great Britain,* a literary and historical career of which he never tired. A freelance historian, he later dreaded the possibility that he might be forced to enlist among "these small men who do most of the historic teaching in the colleges" (Bishop, *post*, II, 140). Chance, however, saved him from this fate, for a local Republican boss needed an eminently respectable candidate for the 21st Assembly district. Roosevelt was sent to Albany for three sessions, 1882–84, and won acceptance as a leader on his merit. Here his freedom served him well. Irritating to his seniors, he was attractive to reporters in search of news. He attacked misbehavior as he chose, saw to it that the newspapers had his side of every story, and supported with zest laws for the relief of workingmen and for the better government of New York City. His associates saw him as "a light-footed, agile, nervous yet prompt boy, with light-brown, slightly curling hair, blue eyes and an eyeglass, and ready to rise and speak with a clear, sharp, boyish voice" (*Frank Leslie's Illustrated Newspaper,* May 10, 1884, p. 183).

His father had died in 1878. Beginning late in 1883, Roosevelt risked more than $50,000 of his patrimony in ranch lands in Dakota Territory, which he retained until 1887 (Hermann Hagedorn, *Roosevelt in the Bad Lands,* 1921). He lost most of his investment, but gained far more in access to the open air, in valuable experience in the ways of men and cattle, and in solace after the death of his young wife. On Oct. 27, 1880, he had married Alice Hathaway Lee, daughter of George C. Lee of Chestnut Hill, Mass. She died on Feb. 14, 1884, shortly after the birth of their daughter Alice Lee (later Mrs. Nicholas Longworth), and only a few hours after the death of Roosevelt's own mother. These tragic events darkened the year of his last fight in the legislature at Albany and his earnest effort to block the nomination of James G. Blaine for the presidency. Still under twenty-six, he won place as delegate at large to the Chicago Republican National Convention, where he stood by George F. Edmunds [*q.v.*] until the end. The ranch occupied his summer. He was discouraged by the nomination of Blaine and Logan, but came east at last to engage in what was described as a "most remarkable performance in the crow-eating line" (New York *World,* Oct. 19, 1884). He supported the ticket and always despised the Mugwumps. In quick succession he wrote *Hunting Trips of a Ranchman* (1885); *Thomas Hart Benton* (1886); *Gouverneur Morris* (1888); *Ranch Life and the Hunting-Trail* (1888); *Essays on Practical Politics* (1888); and the first two volumes of *The Winning of the West* (1889). He returned to practical politics in 1886, when he entered a thankless contest to run against Abram S. Hewitt and Henry George for mayor of New York. After finishing third in this election he hastened to London where, on Dec. 2, 1886, he was married to Edith Kermit Carow, in St. George's Church, Hanover Square (S. L. Gwynn, *The Letters and Friendships of Sir Cecil Spring Rice,* 1929, vol. I, p. 48). In 1888 he supported a winning presidential ticket and stood in line for a minor reward in national politics.

Harrison made him a civil-service commissioner in May 1889, and Roosevelt was soon convinced that the spoilsmen were alarmed at his arrival in Washington. There was some reason to fear that civil-service reform had died a-borning, for politicians tried to evade the specific requirements of the Pendleton Act of 1883. The commissioners were inconspicuous until Roosevelt brought a glare of happy publicity into his petty office. For six years he lived in and learned his Washington. The Roosevelts kept simple but open house on a side street, the Adams-Hay circle accepted them, Lodge and Spring Rice were in and out. The mysteries of high policy and "backstage" intrigue were open before their eyes. Already set to the notion that in ethics lay the cure of politics, Roosevelt wrote and spoke as a lay evangelist, and applied great energy to the task of keeping out the crooks and protecting the competent. This philosophy remained with him for life (*American Ideals and Other Essays, Social and Political,* 1897). The personal conflicts that were its consequence made good news stories in which he was generally as right as he always looked (*The Strenuous Life; Essays and Addresses,* 1900).

The municipal election of 1894 brought him back to New York the following year, still with no fixed career, but with *The Wilderness Hunter* (1893) added to his list, and *The Winning of the West* (vols. III, IV, 1894-96) nearly done. Writing at the same time and following in the tracks of Frederick J. Turner [*q.v.*], he missed the point that Turner raised in *The Significance of the Frontier in American History* (published separately in 1894), and remained of the school of Francis Parkman, ever interested in heroic events and literary narrative. As president of the American Historical Association in 1912, he expounded his theory at length (*History as Literature, and Other Essays,* 1913). In New York a reform mayor, William L. Strong, organized a non-political administration in 1895. Roosevelt took the presidency of the board of police commissioners, and for two years learned to command men. He was doubtless overzealous and accomplished relatively little, but, with Jacob A. Riis [*q.v.*] as his Boswell (J. A. Riis, *Theodore Roosevelt, the Citizen,* 1904), he penetrated the lowest levels of slum life, observed an unholy alliance of graft, politics, and crime, and again by his ability to turn his daily routine into pungent news brought public attention to a focus on the cesspool.

He envied the career of his friend Henry Cabot Lodge, while Lodge was more than willing to assist him into one. There was chance of this after the election of McKinley in 1896, but it took laborious wire-pulling before McKinley could be persuaded to offer Roosevelt a place as assistant secretary of the navy. Roosevelt took this gladly, for it brought him back to Washington and to official society. In the Navy Department, with an easy-going chief, John D. Long [*q.v.*], he was as jingo as Lodge, and hoped with Leonard Wood [*q.v.*] that war would come out of Cuba. He burned the naval appropriations in target practice, and showed the ambitious Dewey how to let politics aid merit (*Autobiography of George Dewey, Admiral of the Navy,* 1913, pp. 167–68). On an afternoon (Feb. 25, 1898) when Secretary Long was out of town he, as acting secretary, cabled Dewey in the event of war to "see that the Spanish squadron does not leave the Asiatic coast, and then offensive operations in Philippine Islands" (*Ibid.*, p. 179). Roosevelt, resigning on May 6, turned to active service in the field. Wood and he organized the first volunteer cavalry regiment, procured its equipment, and secured its inclusion in the expeditionary force mobilizing at Tampa. The Rough Riders, dismounted of necessity, fulfilled his expectations. In the fighting before Santiago they took Kettle Hill (July 1, 1898); and when Wood was promoted to higher rank Roosevelt became their colonel. Richard Harding Davis [*q.v.*] chronicled their glory, as did Roosevelt himself in *The Rough Riders* (1899). For the rest of his life he attended reunions of his men, found them jobs, and occasionally kept them out of jail. With no army career to risk, Roosevelt took a lead in the "round robin" of July, directing public attention to the precarious situation of the troops in the tropics, because of health and sanitary conditions. This insubordination caused acute irritation in the War Department; but most of the army was evacuated in August for hospitalization at Montauk Point, and he, now "Teddy" to everybody in spite of his intense dislike of the nickname, came home an authentic hero of the war. His sudden popularity, and his expansive grin beneath his spectacles and army hat, upset the plans of Thomas Collier Platt [*q.v.*] for the approaching campaign. Platt yielded gracefully to his nomination for the governorship. Roosevelt took his escort of Rough Riders up and down the state and was elected over Augustus Van Wyck by a small majority. He was inaugurated in January 1899.

He would have been less than human if he had not now suspected that even higher place might come within his reach. He advanced practical reform as much as seemed possible without breaking with Platt, the most important contribution, in his own opinion, being a tax on corporation franchises. The abundant testimony (displayed in the libel suit of William Barnes in 1915) leaves it still uncertain whether he or Platt was boss; but there is no doubt that after two years of Roosevelt in Albany, Platt was ready for his promotion to any office outside the state. Roosevelt feared that he would be side-tracked as vice-president, but it suited Platt to encourage the boom; and the fact that Roosevelt was unacceptable to McKinley and Hanna was good reason for his indorsement by Quay. He was soon torn between his judgment that the vice-presidency was destructive of a future, and his desire to prove that he could not be kept off the ticket. He was nominated at Philadelphia in June 1900, with no negative voice but his own, and with McKinley prudently keeping hands off. His canvass matched that of Bryan in vivacity, making it possible for McKinley to remain at home in both dignity and safety. But when elected Roosevelt despaired of the future, talked of reading law under Justice White (Thayer, *post,* p. 153), and looked with reluctance to the tame life of president of the Senate. Just before his forty-third birthday, through the assassination of William McKinley, he became twenty-sixth president of the United States.

He took his oath of office in Buffalo, Sept. 14, 1901, pledging himself "to continue, absolutely unbroken, the policy of President McKinley for the peace, the prosperity, and the honor of our beloved country"; and suspecting that there were many who feared for the office in the hands of "this crazy man" (Thomas Beer, *Hanna,* 1929, p. 236). Since the basic pledges of the Republican party had been fulfilled, and since McKinley had given no more than a suggestion of a future course, this pledge was less informing than comforting to timid minds. Roosevelt might well have followed his urge as a reformer, exercising his great skill as an administrator, without breaking with the business statesmen. Yet there were new philosophies abroad, calling for more than an ethical approach to government. A younger generation of political leaders, among whom Robert M. LaFollette [*q.v.*] was best known, were leading crusades for fair play and governmental control, and were using the ideas of Populism which were now becoming respectable since there was no danger that the People's party would establish them. Roosevelt disliked the technical detail now at the bottom of reform, but there was a chance for a flexible president to place himself at the head of a national movement for the reorganization of the American pattern. For his first term he kept McKinley's advisers in his cabinet, and announced no change in doctrine. Yet from the moment that he moved his family into the White House, with Alice and the five younger children—Theodore, Kermit, Ethel, Archibald, and Quentin—there was a new virility in the Executive Mansion and a new technique in the office of the president.

Quick administration was one of the changes. Roosevelt trusted his subordinates and cleared his desk, thus saving time to play where his predecessors felt forced to labor over bundles of official papers. He played beyond the speed of his secretarial advisers and soon surrounded himself with a group of agile companions—the "tennis cabinet"—for hikes, or rides, or games. Toward the end of his presidency, when the army complained of an order to keep physically fit, he rode (Jan. 13, 1909) one hundred miles over rough Virginia roads to shame it. From his playmates of the open he obtained a view of the workings of the government that was obscured by red tape from their superiors. At his hospitable table he sampled with insatiable curiosity the wit of the procession of visitors to Washington, meeting prize-fighter or royalty with equal ease. There was new dignity and formality in White House life, after the residence of several simpler predecessors; the paragraphers smiled at the cockades and livery on the White House coachmen. Decisions flowed from his desk, more often right than wrong, but always swiftly. Washington, under his eye and hand, turned into a world capital, with new monumental beauty and fresh, if somewhat disturbing, importance. There were changes in the diplomatic corps as Europe realized this fact. The French appreciated his tastes, and sent him Jusserand, who could both talk and tramp with him. The British fumbled after the death of Pauncefote, but in 1907 found him James Bryce, a mountain climber whose knowledge of American life was nearly as encyclopedic as his own. The Foreign Office also allowed Cecil Spring Rice, who was an honorary member of the Roosevelt household, to slip in and out of Washington and to maintain a revealing contact with the Roosevelt mind. The Germans, after Von Holleben, gave him his old friend Speck von Sternburg, with whom he had been intimate in Washington as a young man. Through these experiences, Roosevelt sat, mobile and watchful, rarely holding to a lesser advantage at the cost of a greater one, and bringing informed opportunism to a new level of national dignity.

He took over the presidency in the midst of readjustments caused by the war with Spain.

Hay had nearly completed a new isthmian canal treaty with Great Britain, allowing the United States a free hand. This superseded both the old Clayton-Bulwer Treaty (1850) and Hay's own first agreement with Lord Pauncefote, which the Senate had wrecked in 1900. Roosevelt, then governor, had opposed it; but he approved the new treaty, signed Nov. 13, 1901, and the Senate gave assent within a month. In the following June, Congress, by passing the Spooner Act, approved the Panama route for the canal, if an agreement could be made in "a reasonable time" with Colombia; otherwise, the canal was to be built in Nicaragua. Under Roosevelt's immediate direction the Hay-Herran Treaty was soon negotiated; it was ratified by the United States Senate on Mar. 17, 1903, but on Aug. 2 was rejected by Colombia. The Colombians objected to certain limitations upon their sovereignty and sought more money, though it would appear that they expected this to come out of the payment of $40,000,000 from the United States to the New Panama Canal Company rather than from the Treasury itself. Roosevelt, enraged at the "inefficient bandits," apparently did not consider turning to Nicaragua, and regretted that in his official position he could not stir up secession in Panama. Representatives of the New Panama Canal Company, who had long been active propagandists for the Panama route, did the necessary stirring. Roosevelt was prepared to interpret an old treaty of 1846 with New Granada (now Colombia) as warranting the preservation of peace on the isthmus by the United States, even against Colombia when trying to put down insurrection. Panama seceded Nov. 3, 1903, received prompt recognition from the United States, and within the month negotiated in its own name the treaty that Colombia had rejected. "I took the canal zone and let Congress debate, and while the debate goes on the canal does also," said Roosevelt later, on one of the many occasions when he felt prodded to defend the summary action (*New York Times*, Mar. 24, 1911). He guided every step in the construction of the canal (J. B. and Farnham Bishop, *Goethals, Genius of the Panama Canal*, 1930). On Apr. 20, 1921, in the administration of Harding, the Senate ratified a treaty with Colombia, whereby $25,000,000 was paid that aggrieved republic though without the formal apology that Wilson had favored. (On the entire affair, see Bishop, I, chs. XXIV, XXV, XXXV; Hill, *post*, ch. III; Pringle, *post*, pp. 301–38, and the references cited there.)

Panama was only one among Roosevelt's problems. China was in disorder; and so near to

China lay the Philippines that the safety of the islands was involved. Hay continued to press discreetly for the extension of the doctrine of the "Open Door." The Latin-American republics were troubled by the consequences of economic penetration and their own recklessness, and, in the United States, capital was for the first time showing serious desire for the profits to be obtained in the exploitation of backward economic nations. In 1902 there was European intervention in Venezuela that bore on both the Monroe Doctrine and canal strategy. Roosevelt had announced that the Monroe Doctrine did not guarantee the Latin republics immunity from punishment after misbehavior, but it was no accident that Dewey was in Caribbean waters at the end of 1902 when intervention began with a "pacific blockade." Later, Roosevelt remembered an informal verbal "ultimatum" to Von Holleben which has not been corroborated (Hill, pp. 123–25; Bishop, I, 222–24). The Venezuelan claims were compromised or submitted to arbitration, and the blockade was lifted, but the dilemma remained. Should the Monroe Doctrine be abandoned, or should the United States permit the doctrine to protect defaulters and assume, itself, their liabilities? When in 1904 the Dominican Republic was threatened with intervention Roosevelt persuaded it to invite him to set up a financial receivership, with an American comptroller to collect and disburse its revenues. The Roosevelt corollary to the Monroe Doctrine, now advanced, asserted the interest of the United States in so guiding the affairs of weaker neighbors that they might avoid clashes likely otherwise to involve the Monroe Doctrine. Roosevelt's Dominican convention, submitted in February 1905, lacked Senate confirmation for two years (until February 1907) but his comptroller began work at once. The Senate resented but could not block his action.

He settled the old Alaskan boundary dispute on his own terms, by an adjudication under a convention signed on Jan. 24, 1903; and he recognized no American limits to American interests, but took a hand with Germany and France at Algeciras (S. B. Fay, *The Origins of the World War*, 1930, vol. I, 185, 189, 191). His cautious and friendly pressure upon Russia and Japan resulted in the Peace of Portsmouth, Sept. 5, 1905 (Dennett, *post*). Behind this diplomatic play the defenses of the United States were being modernized. Roosevelt had no confidence in arbitration as a substitute for preparedness. Elihu Root, as secretary of war, continued the army reforms of the McKinley ad-

ministration, set up a general staff (1903), and returned to law in New York. The navy, new for the war with Spain, became newer each year until it could assemble a battle fleet of sixteen units. It was most likely to be tested in the Orient. Japan was sensitive, feeling its new strength, and finding the position of Orientals in the United States humiliating to them and at the same time unacceptable to American labor interests and Pacific Coast opinion. San Francisco, in 1906, engaged in discussions over the proper status of adult Japanese in attendance with American children in the lower grades of the schools, until Roosevelt was drawn into the discussion because of Japanese protest. Openly he soothed Japan, procured a "gentlemen's agreement" to prevent the emigration of Japanese laborers, and exercised coercive pressure on the San Francisco schoolboard; privately he was uneasy lest Japan might have overt action in mind. Against this background, and because no one yet knew how effective any fleet could be in long-range operations, he sent the whole fleet to the Pacific, and then around the world, on a practice cruise. He asked no permission for the demonstration, and left Congress no option but to pay the bills. The tour was a triumph of accurate administration. The fleet kept to its schedule, was greeted with enthusiastic hospitality in Japan, and, on Feb. 22, 1909, was welcomed back at the Capes of the Chesapeake, whence Roosevelt had dispatched it Dec. 16, 1907. "Speak softly," he liked to say, "and carry a big stick, you will go far" (Roosevelt to Henry L. Sprague, Jan. 26, 1900, Pringle, p. 214).

But the embarrassments due to too big a stick, or to one too often displayed, were visible in Latin America where recent events seemed to set a pattern of North American aggression inconsistent with the altruistic promise of the Monroe Doctrine. South American jurists insisted that their own courts ought to be final over aliens, and Drago of Argentina had recently added a protest against the forcible collection of debts. These matters were scheduled for debate by the third Pan-American conference to be held at Rio de Janeiro in July–August 1906, and were likely to want a hearing at The Hague in 1907. To explain away the illusion of a North American menace, Root, now secretary of state after the death of Hay, was sent on tour among the southern neighbors.

Roosevelt's freedom of action in foreign affairs was in sharp contrast to presidential limitations at home, where the industrial revolution was remaking American society. He had need of such a technique as would recognize the existence of Congress, of the courts, and of a public opinion faster than which it was hazardous to go. This technique he never found. He threw aside obstacles until, by their mere accumulation, they jammed his progress. Always a boxer, he clung to his maxim: "Don't hit at all if it is honorably possible to avoid hitting; but *never* hit soft" (Bishop, II, 437). He knew that the best defence is to hit one's adversary first; but this sometimes made it hard for his friends to work with him, and embittered his enemies more than was necessary. He maintained that no utterance purporting to be from him was true unless he authorized as well as uttered it. He contradicted many who tried to interpret him; and from denial passed easily to the lie direct. The cartoonists recalled the biblical story of Ananias and devised a club to which none was eligible until he had been called a liar by Theodore Roosevelt. As the membership grew, it included some who were merely indiscreet or inconvenient. E. H. Harriman and the Bellamy Storers, Alton B. Parker, "Ben" Tillman and William E. Chandler, Delavan Smith, George Harvey, Thomas Collier Platt, William J. Long, Poultney Bigelow were added to the list of the Ananias Club, until unseemly altercation became a jest rather than a discredit. Yet behind these costly quarrels lay the fact that Roosevelt was trying to dominate a government of checks and balances in which the coordinate branches were as constitutional as was the President himself. No President since Thomas Jefferson had ranged his mind over so broad a field. None since Andrew Jackson had been so certain that he had a special mandate.

The domestic wrangle grew steadily more acrimonious, with the direction of Roosevelt swerving cautiously towards the left. Republicans of the school of McKinley sensed this, and feared and fought him. Radical aspirants tried to steal his glory. The fight involved a new hypothesis of the control of industrial society in order to save individual economic freedom. Through the four Congresses of his presidency the Republican party controlled the federal government. There was no effective Democratic opposition. But the key positions were held by conservative leaders, who were more apt to distrust Roosevelt's applications of the "square deal" than to cooperate with him. Joseph G. Cannon [*q.v.*], speaker in the last three of his Congresses, was "stand-pat" and unashamed. Nelson W. Aldrich [*q.v.*], and his elderly and seasoned coadjutors in the Senate, made no pretense of favoring a new theory of government.

Furthermore, Roosevelt's relations with those who saw with him were hindered by the roughness of his technique.

Though president by accident, Roosevelt assumed headship of the Republican party in 1901. Before he moved into the White House he was in contact with Booker T. Washington [*q.v.*] on the problem of negro appointments; and shortly thereafter he slipped into the political error of inviting the negro educator to a meal in the White House (Oct. 16, 1901). This undermined his effort to break the Solid South by annoying the white South. He annoyed the negroes by summary dismissal of negro soldiers after the Brownsville, Tex., riot (Aug. 13–14, 1906), which also brought the fiery Foraker upon his trail (J. B. Foraker, *Notes of a Busy Life,* 1916, vol. II). But he kept to his task; occasional negroes received federal appointment, while he held the Southern white Republicans as well, so that the votes of their delegations to national conventions in 1904 and 1908 were at his disposal. He had greater difficulty with Senator Marcus A. Hanna [*q.v.*], who was chairman of the Republican National Committee and understood both business men and organized labor. In 1903 Roosevelt took from the Ohio convention an indorsement of himself over Hanna's undisguised opposition, on the ground of impropriety. But Hanna was ill; he died in 1904, leaving to conservative Republicans no possible leader. His supporters were ready for peace, and Roosevelt was willing to pay something for an undivided front in a campaign in which he hoped for election in his own right. His fear of missing this was far greater than any of the obstacles. Nominated at Chicago without opposition, he put the national committee in its place, appointing a member of his cabinet, George B. Cortelyou, as chairman. The canvass against Judge Alton B. Parker [*q.v.*], choice of the anti-Bryan Democrats, was without clear issue. The easy victory gained, Roosevelt issued on election night, Nov. 8, 1904, a disclaimer of a third term for himself, holding to the merit of the two-term tradition and conceding that for its purpose his fractional term constituted a first term. He later regretted the pledge, but it gave him freedom.

Among the specific domestic problems that confronted him in both terms, the tariff was a vexatious embarrassment. From the liberal western Republicans came the "Iowa idea" that the tariff made life too easy for the trusts and needed to be revised. This was anathema to protectionists, and though Roosevelt approved it the time never seemed ripe for action. The sharp fight that delayed his Cuban reciprocity bill

(Dec. 17, 1903) indicated the risk that would be run in a general revision. As his second term ended, this revision was indicated as the first thankless task for his successor.

The trusts, however, were fair game. The Republican party had no official policy respecting them, while there was enthusiastic public approval for every exposure of their bad behavior. The "muck-rakers" were raging, but Roosevelt had preceded them, demanding at Pittsburgh, July 4, 1902, that trusts be subjected to public control in the public interest. His speeches were popular in both parties, revealing a cleavage that cut across party lines. They had political value in covering the threatened tariff defection in the West, where Speaker David B. Henderson (Sept. 16, 1902) declined even to submit his record to his Iowa district, and left politics. Through Attorney-General Philander C. Knox [q.v.], Roosevelt attacked the Northern Securities Company as a conspiracy in restraint of trade, and on Mar. 14, 1904, procured its dissolution by the Supreme Court (Northern Securities Company vs. the United States, 193 United States, 197), so that he was a "trust-buster" in time for the campaign. He urged, and Congress added to the cabinet in 1903, a secretary of commerce and labor, whose bureau of corporations was to be the eye of the government in matters of business. The Elkins Law (Feb. 19, 1903) forbade one form of vicious favoritism, the rebate of freight rates. The expedition act (Feb. 11, 1903) gave the government power to hasten to trial its prosecutions under the interstate commerce and anti-trust acts. But there was more enthusiasm than certainty in trust control. Most efforts were based on resentment rather than understanding, and politicians were impatient of the scientific harness with which economists were likely to hamper their freedom of action. The guides to sound decisions lagged behind the desire for correction. But in 1906 the interstate commerce act was strengthened; while the unpopularity of business, increased by the "muck-rakers," made possible sweeping laws for the protection of the consumer of food and drugs. So violently did the orgy of exposure and denunciation proceed that when David Graham Phillips [q.v.] launched his series on "The Treason of the Senate" in Hearst's Cosmopolitan Magazine, March 1906, Roosevelt himself tried to call a halt. First in the privacy of the Gridiron Club, Mar. 17, 1906, then publicly, Apr. 14, 1906, he spoke to the text of "The Man with the Muck Rake," and emphasized the need for constructive law. The "muck-rake" period gradually died out, but he

was left unpopular with business and the party stalwarts. A financial reverse in Wall Street in 1907, caused by gross speculation, was termed the Roosevelt panic, and he was described as an enemy of business and of his class. But he was on his way to another extension of government control, this time over natural resources.

More than most presidents, Roosevelt knew the West. In 1902 he approved the Newlands Act for a reclamation service, and the conviction grew on him that the national endowment had been squandered. To call attention to the problem, and to the inadequacy of existing law, he made enlargements of the forest reserves, withdrawing land from entry whether suitable for forests or not when he had reason to think that a useful resource lay within its area. He named a public lands commission in 1903, drafting civilian experts who knew the land, and placing at their service the clerical staff of the government ("Report of the Public Lands Commission," 1905, 58 Cong., 3 Sess., Senate Document No. 189). There was a similar inland waterways commission in 1907 ("Preliminary Report," 60 Cong., 1 Sess., Senate Document No. 325). On May 13, 1908, he assembled at the White House a conference of governors of most of the states, and elder statesmen of every persuasion, to discuss the inclusive theme of natural resources; and in June he named a conservation commission with Gifford Pinchot at its head. The report of this body in three volumes (60 Cong., 2 Sess., Senate Document No. 676) roused resentment because of its intrusion upon a field of action that Congress had left untouched. Congress forbade its wide circulation as a public document and rebuked Roosevelt by prohibiting further use of public funds upon any investigation not authorized in advance by law. Roosevelt avowed in retort that he was free to do as he pleased in that "twilight zone" lying between the prohibitions of the law and duties required by specific enactments. His presidency ended in open defiance on the part of Congress, which restricted the secret-service appropriations lest they be used to trail congressmen.

Blocked though Roosevelt was, the "Roosevelt policies" gained repute, and the question of a third term died hard. His decision to sponsor actively the candidacy of his secretary of war, William Howard Taft [q.v.], seems to have been due to his desire to quiet suspicions of his own intentions. By the use of traditional methods, which four years later Roosevelt condemned, the nomination of Taft was effected. Roosevelt was happy in the hope that his administrative team would be held together. He had in both terms escaped the ineptitudes of a cabinet made for politics. His official family had worked well in harness. Taft, after his election in 1908, preferred to select his own cabinet, and Roosevelt left office somewhat disappointed, it may be, but still cordial.

The activities of the presidency, many as they were, could not keep Roosevelt busy. He had continued to write. He had traveled much, breaking a precedent when he left the country to visit the canal in 1906; and breaking it still more by reading Milton and Tacitus in odd moments. His letters were voluminous, and his talk was incessant. His enemies called him "quack," "demagogue," and "liar"; and even "drunkard" until he quieted this by a libel action at Marquette, Mich., in 1913. But his intimates loved him with an unreasoning devotion (L. F. Abbott, ed., *The Letters of Archie Butt,* 1924; *Taft and Roosevelt. The Intimate Letters of Archie Butt, Military Aide,* 2 vols., 1930). To the ordinary voter he had become the prophet of the "square deal."

Out of office in 1909, he had to find work. His comfortable estate (probated at under a million) yielded less income than he required. He took a post with the *Outlook* as contributing editor, sold literary work to the *Metropolitan Magazine* and the *Kansas City Star,* and received generous royalties from the publishers of his books, describing himself as "an elderly literary man of pronounced domestic tastes." But before taking up letters as an ex-President he arranged a hunt (*African Game Trails: An Account of the African Wanderings of an American Hunter-Naturalist,* 1910). There were only occasional echoes from the jungle while he was buried in it; but on his emergence at Khartum, Mar. 14, 1910, there began a progress of unexpected sparkle. He discussed intimate problems of colonial government with a pungency that made men gasp (*African and European Addresses,* 1910); visited the Kaiser to tell him that he alone among European sovereigns could carry his ward in New York; rebuked the Vatican and snubbed its critics; lectured formally at the Sorbonne, at Oxford, and at Christiania in return for his Nobel Prize; counted the birds in New Forest with Sir Edward Grey; and represented the United States at the funeral of Edward VII, where he had the time of his life. On June 18, 1910, he returned home to a triumphant reception (*New York Times,* June 19, 1910).

Already he had learned of the growing breach between the conservative and insurgent groups in the Republican party, and tales told on Taft were reaching him. He said that all he wanted

was privacy, but it was not in his nature to abstain from political activity. He soon entered the unsuccessful fight for a direct primary law in New York and made it clear that in state affairs he would support the progressives (*New York Times,* June 30, Aug. 17, 1930). In the late summer he began a speaking tour in the West. On Aug. 31, at Ossawatomie, Kan., he declared that "property shall be the servant and not the master," and that the Constitution if too rigid to conform to the needs of life must be amended (*New York Tribune,* Sept. 1, 1910; Roosevelt, *The New Nationalism,* 1910). In the autumn he did more speaking, and asserted his leadership in New York, where he was elected temporary chairman of the Republican state convention and brought about the nomination of Henry L. Stimson for the governorship, though he was unable to bring about his election in November. His meetings with Taft had been unsatisfactory (Pringle, pp. 536, 538). By the summer or early autumn of 1911 the unhappy estrangement of the two friends had become complete. Roosevelt might have forced the nomination of LaFollette, the most conspicuous member of the progressive group that was seeking to block the renomination of Taft in 1912, but did not believe that LaFollette could command the movement and allowed himself to be persuaded that the "Roosevelt policies" were lost unless he reëntered politics. His reëntry was staged to follow an appeal from seven Republican governors (Howland, *post,* pp. 212–13); he declared to a reporter that his hat was in the ring (*New York Times,* Feb. 23, 1912) and on Feb. 25 released his acceptance of the memorial (*Ibid.,* Feb. 26, 1912). Taking the aggressive by advocating direct primaries instead of conventions, he rolled up majorities wherever he could enter primary contests and demonstrated that he was the choice of the Republican rank and file. By his advocacy of the initiative, referendum, and recall, however, he had alienated the conservative leaders, among them his old friend Henry Cabot Lodge; and the administration controlled the party machinery, as it had four years before. Elihu Root steered the convention that seated Taft delegates in disputed cases and renominated him. In vain Roosevelt shouted "naked theft!" His delegation became the nucleus of the Progressive party which met Aug. 5, 1912, to nominate him for president and Gov. Hiram Johnson of California for vice-president on a platform that embraced most of the programs of liberal reform. He led Taft in November, but only succeeded in opening the breach through which Woodrow Wilson marched to victory as minority president. (For the entire campaign and its controversies, see Pringle, pp. 525–71, and references.)

Shot by a fanatic in Milwaukee, Oct. 14, Roosevelt recovered in time to finish his canvass, but the days of his youth were gone. In 1914 he tried one more major expedition, and one too many. Visiting the republics of La Plata he plunged into the blank spaces of the map (*Through the Brazilian Wilderness*, 1914), where he found the "River of Doubt," but whence he narrowly escaped with his life. He never recovered from the tropical infections, and was already blind in one eye, the consequence of a boxing accident while in the White House. He returned to his desk (*A Book-Lover's Holidays in the Open*, 1916) to watch the world at war. Roosevelt was a neutral until his old suspicions of Germany were revived, his sympathies with the Allies aroused, and he had persuaded himself that had he been president he would have stopped the war. The diplomatic course of President Wilson was generally offensive to him. Army officers told him stories, he supported the National Security League, and with tongue and pen sought to arouse the country (*America and the World War*, 1915; *Fear God and Take Your Own Part*, 1916; *The Foes of Our Own Household*, 1917). He was convinced that the Progressive party was dead and in 1916 he had a moment of hope that the Republican breach might be healed behind him, again a candidate. Between Hughes and Wilson he had to support Hughes, though each time he spoke he alienated the German vote which Hughes must gain to win.

When war came at last, his four sons were soon at the front while he besieged the War Department and overcame aversion to besiege the White House for permission to raise a volunteer division and to command one of its brigades. Despite the incumbrances of age, accident, disease, and the lack of professional military training, he found no justice in the refusal to accept his service. Bitter, he stayed at home to talk and write (*The Great Adventure; Present-Day Studies in American Nationalism*, 1918), until in January 1918, he rushed to Washington "to tell the truth and speed up the war." It may be that the way was being paved for his return as the presidential candidate of a united party in 1920. But, on Jan. 6, 1919, he died peacefully in his sleep. His career had personalized the American recognition of a changing world. His flaws were on the surface and undisguised; his human values were timeless.

[His official biography, J. B. Bishop, *Theodore Roosevelt and His Time Shown in His Own Letters* (2 vols.,

1920), was begun under his direction and is in fact largely autobiographical; it supplements *Theodore Roosevelt: An Autobiography* (1913). All of his writings, cited above, are highly personal, and his earlier biographers found it easier to accept his estimate of himself than to reconstruct events from the evidence of working documents. His books, articles, journalistic releases, speeches, letters, and state papers are so numerous as to have defied complete collection; but selections from his works began to be assembled as early as *Sagamore Ed.* (15 vols., 1900); and *Executive Ed.* (14 vols., 1901); among subsequent but incomplete collections are *Elkhorn Ed.* (28 vols., 1906–1920), and *National Ed.* (20 vols., 1926) in which the Roosevelt Memorial Asso., Hermann Hagedorn, ed., cooperated with the publishers. This association maintains an invaluable collection of Rooseveltiana at the Roosevelt Birthplace in New York City. His letter files he deposited in the Lib. of Cong., subject to reasonable restrictions that have permitted their examination to 1909. J. H. Wheelock, *A Bibliography of Theodore Roosevelt* (1920), is reasonably complete to its date. Tyler Dennett, *Roosevelt and The Russo-Japanese War* (1925); A. L. P. Dennis, *Adventures in Am. Diplomacy, 1896–1906* (1928); and H. C. Hill, *Roosevelt and The Caribbean* (1927), have made careful use of his papers in correcting part of the record. H. F. Pringle, *Theodore Roosevelt; A Biography* (1931), is a thoroughly judicious work with an excellent bibliography. W. F. McCaleb, *Theodore Roosevelt* (1931), has used the manuscripts but is inaccurate and shows bias. Roosevelt's presidency was lived under the observation of J. F. Rhodes, who covered it inadequately in *The McKinley and Roosevelt Administrations, 1897–1909* (1922); and under the admiring gaze of Mark Sullivan, *Our Times* (vols. II–V, 1927–33). Among the genealogies are W. M. Clemens, *The Ancestry of Theodore Roosevelt; A Genealogical Record from 1649* (1914); F. M. Smith, *Roosevelt Arms and Family History* (1909); C. B. Whittlesey, *The Roosevelt Genealogy, 1649–1902* (1902); A. P. Johnson, *Franklin D. Roosevelt's Colonial Ancestors* (1933).

The biographies that appeared during his life are little more than compilations of the growing newspaper legend, tinctured often with uncritical hero-worship: T. W. Handford, *Theodore Roosevelt, the Pride of the Rough Riders, an Ideal American* (1897); Murat Halstead, *The Life of Theodore Roosevelt* (1902); R. C. V. Meyers, *Theodore Roosevelt, Patriot and Statesman* (1901); F. E. Leupp, *The Man Roosevelt, A Portrait Sketch* (1904); J. A. Riis, *Theodore Roosevelt the Citizen* (1904); James Morgan, *Theodore Roosevelt, the Boy and the Man* (1907); Sydney Brooks, *Theodore Roosevelt* (1910); Max Kullnick, *From Rough Rider to President* (1911); C. G. Washburn, *Theodore Roosevelt; the Logic of his Career* (1916). A more useful group of works followed his death: L. F. Abbott, *Impressions of Theodore Roosevelt* (1919); H. C. Lodge, *Theodore Roosevelt* (1919); W. D. Lewis, *The Life of Theodore Roosevelt* (1919); W. R. Thayer, *Theodore Roosevelt, An Intimate Biography* (1919); J. B. Bishop, ed., *Theodore Roosevelt's Letters to His Children* (1919); W. A. White, *Political Adventures of Theodore and Me* (1920); H. J. Howland, *Theodore Roosevelt and his Times; A Chronicle of the Progressive Movement* (1921); Corinne R. Robinson, *My Brother, Theodore Roosevelt* (1921); Anna R. Cowles, ed., *Letters from Theodore Roosevelt to Anna Roosevelt Cowles 1870–1918* (1924); *Selections from the Correspondence of Theodore Roosevelt and Henry Cabot Lodge* (2 vols., 1925); Earle Looker, *The White House Gang* (1929), *Colonel Roosevelt, Private Citizen* (1932); L. D. Einstein, *Roosevelt, his Mind in Action* (1930); Owen Wister, *Roosevelt, The Story of a Friendship, 1880–1919* (1930). Among the journalists who enjoyed his friendship and recorded his *dicta* are: A. W. Dunn, *Gridiron Nights* (1915); J. J. Leary, *Talks with T. R.* (1920); H. H. Kohlsaat, *From McKinley to Harding; Personal Recollections of our Presidents* (1923); O. K. Davis, *Released for Publication; Some Inside Political History of Theodore Roosevelt and his Times, 1898–1918* (1925) ; C. W. Thompson, *Presidents I've Known and Two Near Presidents* (1929). An interesting collection of cartoons is Raymond Gros, ed., *T. R. in Cartoon* (1910).]   F. L. P.

ROOT, AMOS IVES (Dec. 9, 1839–Apr. 30, 1923), apiarist, was born on a farm near Medina, Ohio, the son of Samuel Homer and Louisa (Hart) Root and a descendant of John Roote who settled at Farmington, Conn., in 1640. His early days were spent on the farm and in the local schools, with two winter terms in an academy at Wellsville, Columbiana County. A nervous and sickly boy, he decided to follow some other occupation than farming. He entered the employ of a local jeweler and at the age of twenty-one started a watch-repair shop of his own which soon expanded into a jewelry manufacturing business.

One day in August 1865 a stray swarm of bees passing through the air attracted his attention, and from that time on he was a student and breeder of the bee. In 1869 he began the manufacture and sale of beekeepers' supplies, later abandoning his jewelry business, after seventeen years, to give his entire attention to the bee industry. He perhaps did more than any other man in America to commercialize beekeeping. By 1876 he had twenty men working on bees and bee supplies. Later the work of the A. I. Root Company required a force of a hundred or more employees. Root himself, primarily a business man, did very little scientific work, but he popularized the results of the scientific work of C. C. Miller and Lorenzo L. Langstroth [*q.v.*], introducing the Langstroth method throughout the world. He built and perfected the first comb foundation machine and the first simple hive without porticos, and was the first to put out comb honey section boxes holding a pound of honey. In January 1873 he began the publication of a monthly periodical, *Gleanings in Bee Culture,* which he edited till 1890. From 1865 to 1887 he wrote profusely on the general subject of bees, *ABC of Bee Culture* (1877; subsequent revisions under slightly altered title) being perhaps his best-known book. In the late eighties his health broke down and he found it necessary to spend a large amount of time out of doors. He established a vegetable garden of about ten acres, experimented with new plants, and was one of those responsible for the introduction of the Grand Rapids lettuce. He was author or co-author of several books on such subjects as strawberry, potato, and tomato culture, and from his press at Medina issued other volumes on agricultural subjects, for some of which he supplied editorial additions. Ability to write, business tact, and above all a restless energy and intensity of spirit characterized him. Brought up in a God-fearing family, he drifted in his early manhood into the skepticism of Ingersoll and Tom Paine, but in the seventies was converted, returned to his Congregational allegiance, and almost immediately took up Sunday-school work. In 1875, he started the "Our Home" page in *Gleanings in Bee Culture,* in response to his burning desire to help human beings live better and happier lives. He was one of the founders of the Anti-Saloon League. To foreign missionaries he sent *Gleanings in Bee Culture* free of charge. For a long time he offered to send a bee smoker to any reader who would quit the use of tobacco. In 1909 he began a crusade in his paper against whiskey advertisements in newspapers. During much of his early life he was in poor health, but about 1895, having established a successful business, he began to allow himself more leisure and thus regained his health and with it the quiet spirit which marked his later life. He married Susan Hall on Sept. 30, 1861, and for many years his son was associated with him in business.

[Paper read by A. R. Webber before the school children of Medina on the day of the funeral of A. I. Root (MS. in the possession of E. R. Root) ; Root's autobiography, *Gleanings in Bee Culture,* July 1923–Oct. 1928 ; E. R. Root, "A Son's Memories of A. I. Root," *Ibid.,* June 1923 ; *Ohio State Journal* (Columbus), May 1, 1923 ; *Who's Who in America,* 1922–23 ; J. P. Root, *Root Geneal. Records* (1870) ; correspondence with E. R. Root and personal interviews with apiarists and horticulturists in Ohio.]   J. I. F.

ROOT, ELISHA KING (May 10, 1808–Aug. 31, 1865), mechanic, inventor, was the son of Darius and Dorcas (Sikes) Root and a descendant of Thomas Root who settled in Hartford, Conn., in 1637. Born on his father's farm at Ludlow, Mass., he received a common-school education and then became a machinist's apprentice. Upon completing his apprenticeship, he worked at his trade in various shops in Ware and Chicopee Falls, Mass., and in 1832, when twenty-four years old, went to Collinsville, Conn., to work for the Collins Company, manufacturers of axes. He began there as a lathe hand in the repair shop but because of his unusual and mechanical aptitude very soon became foreman. He remained with this company for seventeen years, the last four as superintendent, and during this time, through his inventions and improvements in axe-manufacturing machinery and methods, he converted the Collins establishment from a primitive shop into a modern factory, thereby enabling the company to increase its business greatly and attain virtual control of the American axe market.

In 1849 Root was offered positions by four

different manufacturers, and accepted the superintendency of the newly established Colt Armory at Hartford, Conn., at a very large salary. He then removed with his family to Hartford and in the course of the next five years designed and built the Colt Armory as well as most of the machinery for it. In this plant the principle of interchangeable parts was adopted and automatic or semi-automatic machinery was substituted for most of the handwork. Even before the armory was completed in 1855, Root had devised and patented much of the automatic machinery, one of the most ingenious of his devices being a drop hammer, patented Aug. 16, 1853. In addition, he devised machines for boring and rifling gunbarrels, for stock-turning, for splining, and for making cartridges, and worked out the whole system of jigs, fixtures, tools, and gauges. It is said that many of the machines devised by Root are still running, and are on a par in accuracy and economy of production with those produced today (1934). Every process in the Colt Armory showed his influence. It is said that his drop-hammer inventions of 1853 and 1858 put the art of die-forging on its present basis; his form of drop hammer remained in vogue until the present board drop was developed. Besides his inventions bearing on the manufacture of firearms, Root patented a cam pump (1856), designed especially for use in raising water from the Connecticut River to a reservoir from which the workmen's village built up around the armory was supplied.

Upon the death of Colt [*q.v.*] in 1862, Root became president of the armory and continued in this capacity until his death in 1865, receiving, it is said, the highest salary paid in the state of Connecticut. He was one of the ablest mechanics New England ever produced and the success of both the Collins and Colt companies was in a large measure due to him. Furthermore, many of the most famous of America's later tool builders received their mechanical training under his supervision. "The credit for the revolver belongs to Colt; for the way they [the revolvers] were made, mainly to Root" (Roe, *post*, p. 169). Root married, first, Charlotte R. Chapin of Springfield, Mass., on Oct. 16, 1832; after her death, he married Matilda Colt of Hartford, Oct. 7, 1845. At the time of his death in Hartford he was survived by his widow and four children, one of whom was a son by his first wife.

[J. P. Root, *Root Geneal. Records, 1600–1870* (1870); J. L. Bishop, *A Hist. of Am. Manufactures,* vol. II (1864); J. W. Roe, *English and American Tool Builders* (1916); *Hartford Daily Courant,* Sept. 2, 1865; Patent Office records.]   C. W. M.

ROOT, ERASTUS (Mar. 16, 1773–Dec. 24, 1846), lawyer and politician, was born at Hebron, Conn., the son of William and Zeruiah (Baldwin) Root. His paternal ancestor, Thomas Root, emigrated to America about 1637 and was one of the first settlers of Hartford, Conn. Erastus graduated from Dartmouth College in 1793, taught for a while, published in 1796 *An Introduction to Arithmetic for the use of Common Schools* (reputed to be the first to use the decimal system in coinage), and then read law with Sylvester Gilbert of Hebron. He began practice at Delhi, N. Y., but soon went into politics. Between 1798 and 1844 he served several terms in the state Assembly and Senate, and presided over the latter body as lieutenant-governor of the state in 1823 and 1824. In 1821 he represented Delaware County at the state constitutional convention, where he was a leader in the movement to broaden the suffrage and democratize the state government. In 1824 he brought suit against Charles King and Johnston Verplanck, editors of the *New York American,* for libel, because they had printed an article stating that he had appeared before the Senate in an intoxicated state during his term as lieutenant governor (*New York American,* Aug. 25, 1824). The basis of the case was political and was probably attributable to Root's blocking the passage of an electoral law. The controversy was bitter, and after Root had won a verdict in the circuit court the case was carried to the court of errors, where the first judgment was affirmed (4 *Wendell,* 113, 1829).

In the twenties Root had been a leader in the anti-Clintonian wing of the Democratic party. In 1830 he hoped for the Democratic nomination for the governorship but failed to receive it. He was offered the nomination by the Working Men's party but declined it. While in the legislature, he debated frequently, but showed special interest in certain reforms such as the abolition of capital punishment and negro slavery. He was a representative in Congress from New York during the years 1803–05, 1809–11, 1815–17, and 1831–33. Having become dissatisfied with his party in 1830, he refused to support Jackson in 1832 and later became an avowed Whig. In Congress he showed an interest in most subjects, but was always on the alert to protect the interests of his state. According to a contemporary historian, "though a little uncouth in his manner, and rough, and . . . sometimes rude in his expressions, his wit was keen and his sarcasms severe and biting. He seized with great force and effect upon . . . those points most likely to make an impression on the popular ear . . . and his attacks upon his opponents were severe almost to ferocity. . . . He had much parliamentary tact, and although . . . reckless in his expressions . . . and though irregular in his habits, of highly cultivated intellect" (Hammond, *post,* I, 372). He was one of the chief figures of his day in the political history of the state and was rated among the most able politicians of the time. He was married, on Oct. 4, 1806, to Elizabeth Stockton of Walton, N. Y., by whom he had five children. He died suddenly in New York City, in December 1846, while on his way to Washington.

[See: G. T. Chapman, *Sketches of the Alumni of Dartmouth Coll.* (1867); J. D. Hammond, *The Hist. of Pol. Parties in . . . N. Y.* (2 vols., 1842); C. Z. Lincoln, *The Const. Hist. of N. Y.* (1906), vol. I; D. S. Alexander, *A Pol. Hist. of the State of N. Y.* (vols. I and II (1906); D. R. Fox, *The Decline of Aristocracy in the Politics of N. Y.* (1919); *N. Y. American,* June 17, 19, 20, 1826; David Murray, *Delaware County, N. Y.* (1898); *Biog. Dir. Am. Cong.* (1928); J. P. Root, *Root Geneal. Records* (1870); *N. Y. Herald,* Dec. 25, 1846.]   M. L. B.

ROOT, FRANK ALBERT (July 3, 1837–June 20, 1926), newspaper publisher, author, was born in Binghamton, N. Y., the son of Albert Berthoud and Marinda (Boyden) Root. He served an apprenticeship in a printer's shop at Wellsboro, Pa., and in 1853 set out as a journeyman. Four years later, Apr. 21, 1857, he arrived in Kansas Territory, with which region he was thereafter chiefly identified. Between 1857 and 1861 he worked successively on the *Herald of Freedom* (Lawrence), the *Chindowan* (Quindaro), the *Weekly Highlander* (Highland), and the *Champion* (Atchison).

Between 1861 and 1863 he was assistant postmaster at Atchison, then became express messenger and later local mail agent at Latham Station, Colorado Territory, and after that, mail agent on the Denver division of the Overland Stage Line. On Oct. 21, 1864, at Atchison, Kan., he married Emma Clark, daughter of John Hawkins and Margaret (Allen) Clark. He was associated with F. G. Adams in publishing the *Free Press* (Atchison), 1865–68, and after the *Free Press* was consolidated with the *Champion,* was associated with John A. Martin [*q.v.*] until 1869. He was owner or part owner successively after 1869 of the *Telegraph* (Waterville), the *Courier* (Seneca), the *Express* (Holton), and the *Times* (North Topeka), and at the last two places held the office of postmaster. He established the *Review-Express* at Gunnison, Col., and conducted it from 1880 to 1886, then returned to Topeka, Kan., where he published the *Mail* (North Topeka) from 1886 to 1893.

Root traveled extensively, in addition to frequent changes from one paper to another, thus acquiring a quantity of first-hand information on the West. He possessed a natural talent for descriptive writing, and wherever he went recorded carefully his observations in diaries or in voluminous letters to newspapers. He thus accumulated data which later served him in his most distinctive achievement. After retiring from active publishing in 1893 he devoted his time largely to gathering additional information from participants in the making of the West, and from other sources, and embodied much of this material in an authentic book, *The Overland Stage to California* (privately printed, Topeka, 1901), published in association with William E. Connelley.

[F. W. Blackmar, *Kansas* (1912), II, 606; *Topeka Daily Capital* and *Topeka Daily State Journal,* both June 21, 1926; *Who's Who in America,* 1920–21; *Trans. Kan. State Hist. Soc.,* vols. I–II (1881); Root Papers, the property of George Allen Root, deposited with the Kansas State Historical Soc., Topeka, Kan., including diaries, scrapbook of newspaper letters, clippings, autobiographical sketch, letters containing information on the overland stage and kindred subjects, and a manuscript (unfinished) of a volume of memoirs.]   J. C. M.

ROOT, FREDERIC WOODMAN (June 13, 1846–Nov. 8, 1916), teacher, composer, organist, and conductor, was born in Boston, Mass., the eldest of eight children of George Frederick [*q.v.*] and Mary Olive (Woodman) Root. Both parents, of English descent, came from several generations of New England ancestors, and both were musicians. Frederic began the study of piano with his father at the age of five and at thirteen he was placed under Benjamin Colman Blodgett, one of the most distinguished organists and educators of his time. He also began the study of voice with his father, and when he subsequently went to New York for further training, he studied piano with William Mason and Robert Goldbeck, organ with James Flint and E. A. Bowman, and voice with Carlo Bassini. In 1858 his father became a partner in the music house of Root & Cady in Chicago and in 1859 removed his family there. Frederic continued his education in the new home and when still quite young he began assisting his father in various ways—conducting choruses at "conventions" and especially at the "normal institutes" so characteristic of this period. The proficiency of the enthusiastic young musician was further recognized when, in 1864, he was made editor and arranger for the publications of Root & Cady.

In 1863 Root became organist of the Third Presbyterian Church of Chicago and in 1865 of the Swedenborgian Church, where (except for two years in Europe) he remained until 1884. In 1869–70 he was abroad for further study and travel, devoting much of his time to the study of voice under Vannuccini in Florence, Italy. Hitherto his main interest was centered on instrumental music (piano and organ), but during his sojourn abroad he turned his attention to voice production, in which field he later became a most successful teacher and brought out many important singers. When the firm of Root & Cady went out of existence at the time of the Chicago fire, he devoted considerable time to composition and to writing for musical magazines, especially the *Song Messenger,* which he edited for many years. He was in great demand as a lecturer and became one of the pioneers in shaping the musical taste of the early women's clubs. From 1884 to 1886 he was choral director of the First Baptist Church, but he returned to the Swedenborgian church as organist until 1890. He was the first director of the Mendelssohn Club (1879–85) and in 1885 served as music critic of the *Chicago Herald.* In 1889 he organized and conducted a festival chorus of four hundred voices in a series of concerts given by Gilmore's Band and in 1893, during the Columbian Exposition in Chicago, he directed the chorus in connection with the Folklore Congress. In 1895 he resumed his organ work and was successively organist at the Auditorium and at the First Church of Christ, Scientist. He was a member and president (1904–05) of the Chicago Literary Club, a charter member of the Cliff Dwellers, and member of other social organizations. He died in Chicago in 1916. He had married, Apr. 30, 1874, Fanny, daughter of Samuel Sherwood Smith of Cincinnati, who, together with a daughter and two sons, survived him. Among his most important books are *The Technic and Art of Singing, The Polychrome Lessons in Voice Culture, Introductory Lessons in Voice-Culture,* and numerous collections of exercises, studies, and songs. His compositions are limited largely to church music and songs. Of these the best undoubtedly are the following sacred songs: "Love Never Faileth" and settings of four poems by Mary Baker Eddy—"O'er waiting harp-strings of the mind," "Blest Christmas morn," "Saw ye my Saviour" and "Shepherd, show me how to go."

[*Who's Who in America,* 1916–17; *Internat. Who's Who in Music* (1918); *Grove's Dict. of Music and Musicians, Am. Supp.* (ed. 1928); *Etude,* Jan. 1917; *Chicago Evening Post,* Nov. 8, 1916; information as to certain facts from members of the family.]

F. L. G. C.

ROOT, GEORGE FREDERICK (Aug. 30, 1820–Aug. 6, 1895), music educator, composer, was born in Sheffield, Mass., the son of Frederick Ferdinand and Sarah (Flint) Root, and a descendant of John Roote who was one of the first settlers of Farmington, Conn. When George was six the family moved to North Reading, Mass. In 1838 he went to Boston for study with the choirmaster and organist, A. N. Johnson, and soon he became his instructor's assistant in teaching, and also his assistant as organist at the Winter Street and Park Street churches. While in Boston he met Lowell Mason and helped him in his work at the Boston Academy of Music. In 1844 he moved to New York to become singing teacher at Abbott's school for young ladies, and organist of the Mercer Street Presbyterian Church. He was soon invited to teach also at the Rutgers Female Institute, as well as at Miss Haines's school for young ladies, the Union Theological Seminary, and the New York State Institution for the Blind. In August 1845 he married Mary Olive Woodman, an accomplished singer, sister of J. G. Woodman, an organist and composer.

In the autumn of 1850 Root went abroad, where he remained until the following summer, studying in Paris with two singing teachers, Giulio Alary and Jacques Potharst. Following his return to America he established in 1853 the New York Normal Institute, in association with William Bradbury, "to afford thorough musical instruction, and especially to qualify teachers of music" (advertisement in *Dwight's Journal of Music,* Jan. 22, 1853). The principal teachers at the first session were Lowell Mason, Root, Bradbury, and Thomas Hastings; the assistants were Root's brother-in-law, J. C. Woodman, and John Zundel, organist of Brooklyn's Plymouth Church. Root's success in training teachers led him to follow Mason's example in holding "musical conventions," gatherings of teachers in various parts of the country, who came from different towns in their districts to learn the latest methods of class instruction in singing. For many years this was one of Root's principal activities, and in many ways it was his most important contribution to the musical development of America. In 1859 he moved to Chicago, for he had already taken a financial interest in a music store (the firm of Root & Cady) which his younger brother, E. T. Root, had founded the year before. The fire of 1871 ruined the firm, and its book-catalogue, plates, and copyrights were sold to the John Church Company of Cincinnati, with whom Root maintained connections in Chicago under the firm of George F. Root & Sons. He continued his normal courses, principally in the summer months, when teachers were on vacation. Some of his classes were held in the building of the University of Chicago. In 1886 he took another trip abroad and spent most of his time during a several months' visit in England, observing the English tonic-sol-fa methods.

Root's career as a composer was more spectacular than his work as teacher, even though his most permanent cultural contribution was made through his "normals" and his teachers' conventions. His first composing was undertaken to provide a musical playlet for the pupils in his classes. To this end he wrote "The Flower Queen" in 1851, for which the verses were supplied by Fanny Crosby, then one of his pupils at the New York Institute for the Blind. The cantata was soon published, and much to the composer's surprise, met with a ready sale. Impressed with the success of Stephen Foster's songs, and newly aware of his own facile gift for melody, Root tried writing songs of his own, in similar vein. Under the pen name of "Wurzel" he published "Hazel Dell," and "Rosalie, the Prairie Flower." Later, as he became further involved in musical education for the people, he dropped his *nom de plume* and did not hesitate to associate himself with a style of music that was frankly popular. In the years between 1853 and 1855 he composed "The Shining Shore," an evangelical hymn that has been the best known of his sacred songs. His first Civil War song, "The First Gun is Fired," was unsuccessful, but his second venture, "The Battle Cry of Freedom," composed within a few hours after he had read Lincoln's proclamation calling for troops, was sung throughout the North. "Tramp, Tramp, Tramp, the Boys are Marching" was almost equally popular. He also composed sentimental songs relating to incidents in the war, such lyrics as "Just Before the Battle, Mother," and "The Vacant Chair." His compositions number more than two hundred individual songs, and he compiled more than seventy song collections, musical entertainments for schools, and educational works on music. His work as a composer belongs to a past generation, yet it exerted a powerful influence in its time.

[Root published an autobiography in 1891 under the title: *The Story of a Musical Life*. See also: W. S. B. Mathews, *A Hundred Years of Music in America* (1889); F. J. Metcalf, *Am. Writers and Compilers of Sacred Music* (1925); J. T. Howard, *Our Am. Music* (1930); G. P. Upton, *Musical Memories* (1908); *Grove's Dict. of Music and Musicians, Am. Supp.* (ed. 1928); J. P. Root, *Root Geneal. Records, 1600–1870* (1870); *Chicago Daily Tribune*, Aug. 8, 1895.]

J. T. H.

ROOT, JESSE (Dec. 28, 1736 o.s.–Mar. 29, 1822), jurist and member of the Continental Congress, was born at Coventry, Conn., the eighth and youngest child of Ebenezer and Sarah (Strong) Root and the descendant of Thomas Roote or Root who emigrated from England about 1637 and settled in Hartford. The boy was educated in the common school of Coventry and, showing himself able and industrious, continued to college. In 1756 he graduated from Princeton University, then known as the College of New Jersey. On May 18, 1758, he was married to Mary Banks of Newark, N. J. They had nine children. He had returned to Connecticut to study theology with the Rev. Samuel Lockwood of Andover and was licensed to preach by the Hartford south association on Mar. 29, 1757. On account of the death of his brother in 1758 and of the illness of his father, who died in 1760, he did not long continue his ministerial work. Furthermore, he was not at all sure that he was fitted for it, and when at the time of the settlement of his father's estate Judge Trumbull suggested that he might make a good lawyer, he found that others, notably Judge Eliphalet Dyer of Windham, agreed with the suggestion. Thus in February 1763 he was admitted to the bar at Windham but chose Hartford in which to practise.

For the next thirty-four years he was continually in the public service and soon found opportunity to defend the colonies with both tongue and pen as a member of the Council of Safety. On Dec. 30, 1776, he received a captain's commission from Governor Trumbull and three days later set out for the army at Peekskill with a company of volunteers he had raised in Hartford. He soon rose in rank to be lieutenant-colonel and then adjutant-general. In December 1778 he presented his credentials in the Continental Congress and sat in that body until the end of 1782. From 1780 to 1789 he was a member of the state Council, the upper house of the legislature under the old constitution, and was for a time its chairman. In 1789 he was appointed assistant judge of the superior court and in 1798 succeeded to the duties of chief justice. In the same year he published *Reports of Cases Adjudged in the Superior Court and Supreme Court of Errors . . . 1789 to . . . 1793* and added a second volume in 1802. In 1807 he returned to private life, believing that men of high office should in the public interest retire while at the height of their powers. For two years, 1807 and 1808, however, he was a member of the legislature, and in 1808 a presidential elector. Likewise in 1818 he was a member of the convention to frame the new state constitution; yet he esteemed it no less an honor to hold the office of school visitor in his own town of Coventry and filled it punctiliously to the last days of his life. He had nine children, all born in Coventry, a wealth of friends, and was beloved and respected for his charity and public works. In stature he was tall, with an easy yet dignified manner. He was characteristically punctual in all business and presided on the bench with both firmness and complaisance. He died at his home in Coventry after a brief illness and lies buried there in the Nathan Hale Memorial Cemetery.

[*Christian Spectator*, July 1824; J. P. Root, *Root Geneal. Records* (1870); J. H. Trumbull, *The Memorial Hist. of Hartford County, Conn.* (1886), vol. I; *Connecticut* (1904), vols. II, III, ed. by Forrest Morgan; *General Cat. of Princeton Univ.* (1908); F. B. Heitman, *Hist. Register and Dictionary of the U. S. Army* (1903), vol. I; *Jour. of the Continental Cong.*, vols. XII, XXIV (1908–22); Thomas Day, *Reports of Cases . . . in the Supreme Court of Errors . . . Conn.*, vol. I (1817), p. xxxii; *Conn. Courant* (Hartford), Apr. 2, 1822.]   W. G. L.

ROOT, JOHN WELLBORN (Jan. 10, 1850–Jan. 15, 1891), architect, was born in Lumpkin, Ga., the son of Sidney and Mary (Clark) Root. His father, a descendant of Thomas Root or Roote, one of the first settlers of Hartford, Conn., was a native of Vermont. As a lad, despite an eager wish to become an architect, he had been apprenticed to a jeweler. In his twenties he left the North and settled in Georgia, opened a dry goods store in Lumpkin, and married the daughter of Judge James and Permelia (Wellborn) Clark. The Clarks were a brilliant family, not without eccentricity. Judge Clark wrote voluminously, and carefully destroyed what he had written. An uncle of Mary Clark Root, John Wellborn, for whom the architect was named, was well-to-do and at one time a member of Congress; in middle life he suddenly gave all his wealth to the church and devoted himself to preaching to the poor.

John Wellborn Root's talents showed early. He was a precocious musician as well as a draftsman, and is said to have made recognizable portraits at the age of seven. In the house in Atlanta to which the family moved during his boyhood he had a special studio room. When the Civil War began, Sidney Root invested all his spare capital in blockade runners and made a fortune trading with England. After the capture of Atlanta, John was sent to Liverpool where his father had many friends. He was put in school at Claremont, nearby, and in June 1866 matriculated at Oxford. He also continued to study music, especially the organ. Soon after the close of the war, however, the Roots settled in New York, where the father lost his fortune almost as swiftly as he had made it, and John entered the University of the City of New York as a sophomore in the civil engineering department. He graduated in 1869 at the head of his class and was Commencement orator. Since the family fortunes were by this time insufficient to allow him to be sent to Paris, he entered the architectural office of James Renwick the younger [*q.v.*], where he stayed for a year without pay; then he got a job in the office of J. B. Snook, the designer of the old Grand Central Station. In 1871, Peter B. Wight [*q.v.*], who had seen some of Root's drawings in New York, invited him to Chicago to become head draftsman for the firm of Carter, Drake & Wight.

Here in 1872–73 Root met another young draftsman, Daniel H. Burnham [*q.v.*], and an instant sympathy developed between the two. In July 1873 they went into partnership. The panic of that year almost at once wiped out their first prospect, a new suburb, and for a while their progress was difficult. They could only give part time to the partnership, spending the rest in other offices earning their office rent; at one time Root helped out by serving as organist in the First Presbyterian Church. Late in 1874 their first big job, the house for John B. Sherman, came to the office through a real estate friend of Root's, and after 1875 their rise was rapid and the firm of Burnham & Root became well known. Burnham was the job-getter and developed the primary plan idea, while Root designed the exteriors—sometimes following rough sketches of his partner's, often developing the whole himself. His engineering training stood him in good stead; although he was never a brilliant mathematician, he had the creative engineering mind. Thus, in order to save space in the cellar of the ten-story Montauk Building he devised the system of grillage foundations, by which the weights on piers are spread over sufficient area by means of steel rails (he later used rolled beams) set criss-cross and embodied in concrete—a method more economical than the cut stone foundations formerly used. This method has since become standard practice except where loads are extraordinarily heavy.

Root's design was in many ways epoch-making. Though—like most of the work of his period, even that of the rebel, Louis Sullivan [*q.v.*] —it was superficially based on the Romanesque of H. H. Richardson [*q.v.*], it was all essentially personal and, as far as Root could make it, modern, honest, and structurally true. His business buildings showed a continually growing grasp of the fundamentals: the verticality, the uniformity, the composition of the whole became ever more important, the dressing of Romanesque detail less and less so. The climax was the Monadnock building. Its simplicity was the result of a suggestion by Burnham, but the superb working out of that simplicity, the beauty of proportion, the masterly handling of the simple base and the slight outcurving of the cornice, were all Root's and these created a building that more than a generation later still seems modern.

The cooperation between Burnham and Root was superb. Each, in his way, idolized the other, and to Burnham's freely expressed admiration for his partner's talents is due in no small measure their success. Moreover, Root himself was exceedingly popular. He loved playing the piano, chiefly extemporizing, and his playing was widely appreciated; it was much more than a mere amateur's talent. Next to music, his chief recreation was sailing. He was witty and something of a Bohemian; as an amateur actor he was widely sought; and this personal popularity helped his professional reputation. He was one of the founders of the Western Association of Architects, and was instrumental later in its merging with the American Institute of Architects, of which he was secretary at the time of his death. When Chicago was finally settled upon as the location for the World's Columbian Exposition, it was natural that Root, as the foremost Chicago architect, should be appointed consulting architect (August 1890); on Sept. 4, 1890, at his request, this appointment was changed to include his partner. While to the latter belongs the credit for the formation of the board of architects and the generalship of the whole; to Root must go much of the credit for the final choice of a lakeside site and the settlement of the basic plan. The World's Fair activity was the climax of his life. It was after a dinner to the architects that he caught a cold which rapidly developed into the pneumonia from which he died.

John Root married Mary Louise Walker in 1880; already a victim of tuberculosis, she died six weeks after the wedding. On Dec. 12, 1882, he married Dora Louise Monroe. They had three children, two daughters and a son who became an architect. Root was co-author with Russell Sturgis, Bruce Price, Donald G. Mitchell, and others, of *Homes in City and Country* (published in 1893, after his death), to which he contributed "The City House in the West."

[Harriet Monroe, *John Wellborn Root* (1896), with many illustrations of his architectural work, and many quotations from his writings and lectures; Theodore Starrett, "John Wellborn Root," *Architecture and Building*, Nov. 1912; Montgomery Schuyler, *Am. Architecture* (1892); J. P. Root, *Root Geneal. Records* (1870); Charles Moore, *Daniel H. Burnham* (2 vols., 1921); *Chicago Daily Tribune*, Jan. 16, 1891; information from Harriet Monroe.]   T.F.H.

ROOT, JOSEPH POMEROY (Apr. 23, 1826–July 20, 1885), physician, diplomatist, son of John and Lucy (Reynolds) Root, was born in Greenwich, Mass. His father was descended from John Roote who settled in Farmington, Conn., about 1640. After his early schooling was completed, he attended the Berkshire Medical College, Pittsfield, Mass., graduating in 1850. The following year he moved to New Hartford, Conn., and in September married Frances Evaline Alden, by whom he had five sons. He joined the practice of politics to that of medicine, and was elected as a Whig to the Connecticut legislature in 1855. Moved by his social and political convictions to throw himself into the anti-slavery movement, he joined a company of emigrants (the Beecher Bible and Rifle colony) starting for Kansas in March 1856. He settled at Wyandotte, and at once began an active part in the affairs of the distracted territory. He was chairman of the Free-State Executive Committee, and in August 1857 was elected to the Kansas Senate under the Topeka constitution. He was one of the pioneer corps who located the public road from Topeka to Nebraska City, and he was sent East as an agent to obtain arms and aid for the free-soilers.

He contributed editorially to the Wyandotte papers, the *Register* (1857) and the *Gazette* (1858). In December 1859 he was elected lieutenant-governor of the new state on the Republican ticket. In 1861 he was chosen one of the officers of the first annual meeting of the Kansas State Temperance Society. During the Civil War he was surgeon of the 2nd Kansas Cavalry (as it was finally designated) and was medical director of the Army of the Frontier. In 1866 he presided over the Republican state convention. On Sept. 15, 1870, President Grant appointed him minister to Chile, an act which recognized his services and at the same time eliminated him from active participation in state politics. He presented his credentials on Dec. 2, 1870, and since diplomatic duties were not pressing, he gave much time to a general interest in Chilean affairs. He traveled extensively. Once he crossed the Andes into Argentina and reported the trip to the Department of State in the form of a treatise on the cause of earthquakes. Later he accompanied the minister of foreign affairs to southern Chile to investigate the Indians. Improvements in transportation fascinated him; he was enthusiastically in favor of an intercontinental railroad, he urged subsidies by the United States to West-Coast steamship lines, and he undertook on his own account to have Chile establish a system of towboats in the Straits of Magellan.

Root won great popularity with the Chileans for his efforts during a frightful smallpox epidemic in 1872. He served on the Santiago Board of Health and contributed his services to hospitals and private patients, laboring to improve the sanitary treatment of the disease. In recognition of his work a street in Santiago, the "Calle de Root," was named for him. He was recalled in June 1873 to make a place for Cornelius Logan [q.v.]. In 1874 he was elected a vice-president of the Temperance Convention which forced the Republican convention to adopt an anti-liquor plank. Governor St. John appointed him surgeon-general of Kansas. In 1876 he published *Catechism of Money,* advocating greenbackism; in this same year he was named a member of the Chilean Centennial Commission. In 1884 he was a delegate to the Republican National Convention. Except for two years (1877–79) when he was on the staff of a sanitarium at Clifton Springs, N. Y., he lived at Wyandotte until his death. He took a lively interest in the Kansas Historical Society and contributed several manuscript writings to its archives, among them a memoir of his experiences in Kansas in 1856.

[*Topeka Capital,* July 22, 1885; *Weekly Commonwealth* (Topeka), July 23, 1885; *The U. S. Biog. Dir., Kan. Vol.* (1879); J. P. Root, *Root Geneal. Records* (1870); H. C. Evans, *Chile and Its Relations with the U. S.* (1927), p. 96, where Root's given name appears incorrectly as Thomas; *Trans. Kan. State Hist. Soc., 1901–02* (1902); D. W. Wilder, *The Annals of Kan.* (1886); *Papers Rel. to the For. Relations of the U. S., 1871–73;* Root's dispatches (3 vols.) in the Archives of the Dept. of State.]   G. V. B.

ROPES, JAMES HARDY (Sept. 3, 1866– Jan. 7, 1933), theologian, New Testament scholar, was born in Salem, Mass., the son of William Ladd Ropes, librarian of Andover Theological Seminary, and Harriet Lawrence (Peirson) Ropes. Graduating from Phillips Academy, Andover, in 1885, with first honors in classics, and from Harvard College in 1889, *summa cum laude,* he spent a year under the United States Geological Survey in New England and the West. In 1893 he graduated from Andover Theological Seminary, receiving the foreign fellowship. He then spent two years in Germany in study of the New Testament and of early church history at the universities of Kiel, Halle, and Berlin, traveling also in England, Russia, and Italy. He was instructor in New Testament criticism and interpretation in the Harvard Divinity School, 1895–1901; assistant professor, 1898–1903; Bussey Professor, 1903– 10, succeeding in this chair Prof. Joseph Henry Thayer [q.v.]. From 1910 he held the Hollis Professorship of Divinity. He was ordained a minister of the Congregational Church in 1901. On Nov. 23, 1897, he married Alice, daughter of

Edward Jackson Lowell of Boston, by whom he had a daughter and a son.

In 1910 he suggested a combination of the institutions of learning in and about Boston to give the public the benefit of selected college courses. He was chairman of the joint committee which carried out this plan, and in charge of university extension from 1910 to 1922. He was a member of the corporation of Radcliffe College, 1905– 12, and of the corporation of Simmons College; a trustee from 1899 of Phillips Academy, Andover, and of Andover Theological Seminary (until the separate incorporation of the latter in 1907); and president of the board of trustees of the Academy from 1929 until his death. During his connection with this institution he effected a reorganization of the school, which was termed a masterpiece, showing real genius, and putting him in the forefront of those interested in the betterment of secondary education. He was of greatest service to the Harvard Divinity School and to Andover Seminary at the time of the removal of the latter to Cambridge in 1908. The schools entered into closer affiliation in 1922, but were separated by a decree of the supreme court in 1926, Andover Seminary removing, in 1931, to Newton. He was a fellow of the American Academy of Arts and Sciences, a member of the American Oriental Society, of the Society of Biblical Literature and Exegesis, and of the Archæological Institute of America. From 1921 he was editor of the *Harvard Theological Review.*

Besides many articles in professional journals, he published *Die Sprüche Jesu die in den Kanonischen Evangelien nicht überliefert sind* (1896); *The Apostolic Age in the Light of Modern Criticism* (1906); *A Critical and Exegetical Commentary on the Epistle of Saint James* (1916); *The Text of Acts* (1926); *The Singular Problem of the Epistle to the Galatians* (1929). The qualities essential to the interpreter of the New Testament were preëminent in Ropes, thoroughness, perspective, solidity of judgment, restraint of imagination, and religious insight. His colleages, whether in the theological school or in the faculty of arts and sciences, knew his absolute sincerity and selflessness. His work on the *Review* was characterized by punctilious care in the supervision of every smallest detail, whether of form or substance. The appreciation in which under his leadership it came to be held at home and abroad was extraordinary. His *Text of Acts,* awarded the British Academy's medal for Biblical studies, is the most comprehensive survey of all the manuscripts extant, with the object of finding out by a comparison of progressive variations the most probable text from which those known to us have been derived. His scholarship, the prescience of his mind, and the perfection of his self-discipline make this book the model of a critical edition.

[*Who's Who in America,* 1932–33; *Class of 1889, Harvard Coll. . . . Seventh Report* (1914) and *Eighth Report* (1919); *Harvard Theological Rev.,* Jan. 1933; *Harvard Univ. Gazette,* Apr. 1, 1933; *Boston Transcript,* Jan. 9, 1933; personal acquaintance.]

E. C. M—e.

ROPES, JOHN CODMAN (Apr. 28, 1836– Oct. 28, 1899), military historian, was born in St. Petersburg, Russia, the son of William and Mary Anne (Codman) Ropes. His father, a merchant and ship-owner of Salem, had gone to Russia a few years before to establish a branch house. In 1837 the family removed to London for a similar purpose and in 1842 returned to Boston. The boy began preparation for college at Chauncy Hall School but in 1850, on account of a spinal trouble resulting from an injury in infancy, had to leave school for treatment. A year later he was able to resume his studies under a private tutor, William W. Goodwin [*q.v.*], and in 1853 he entered Harvard College, where he graduated in 1857. He then entered the Harvard Law School, graduated in 1861, and entered upon the practice of law in Boston. With John C. Gray [*q.v.*] he edited the *United States Law Review* from 1866 to 1869. From boyhood he had been intensely interested in military affairs, and hence it was a keen disappointment to him that his physical disability prevented his entering the army at the opening of the Civil War. Being unable to do this, he followed the course of operations with close and intelligent observation. He often visited the army in the field, living in camp with his friends, generally with the 20th Massachusetts Infantry, the regiment of his brother Henry, who was killed at Gettysburg. Much of his Civil War correspondence is contained in *War Letters, 1862–1865 of John Chipman Gray . . . and John Codman Ropes* (1927).

After the war he turned his taste for historical study to military subjects and in 1876 was a founder of the Military Historical Society of Massachusetts. Among his writings on the Civil War, the most important were *The Army under Pope* (1881) in the Campaigns of the Civil War Series and his *Story of the Civil War* (2 vols. 1894–98). At his death, the latter was completed only to include the campaigns of 1862. Later his friend William R. Livermore wrote and published an additional volume (1913). Even before he went to college he had read much

on Napoleon, for whose military genius he always had a great admiration. This study he always continued, and he wrote extensively upon the Napoleonic campaigns. Of these writings, perhaps the most important are *The First Napoleon* (1885) and *The Campaign of Waterloo* (1892) with *An Atlas of the Campaign* (1893). His style was clear and lively; he habitually took the view of the higher commanders and discussed operations in terms of corps and divisions, rarely going into the tactical details of smaller units. In his work on the Civil War, in spite of his strong Northern sympathy, he presented the Southern views with fairness. His judgments of commanders and their plans were positive, but he generally presented the evidence on both sides, giving the reader a basis for disagreement. His writings were based upon careful study of the best sources of information and enjoy a high reputation.

His interest in military affairs was by no means an indication of a militaristic turn of mind. Quite the contrary, he was unqualifiedly opposed to war, theoretically; he believed that the Spanish-American War could have been avoided, and in the controversies resulting from it he was definitely an anti-imperialist. Yet he accepted war as a fact and considered it useful to trace its intellectual element and the logical processes of its conduct. He was an active member of Trinity Church in Boston, where he served for many years as a vestryman. He was a student of theology and planned, had he lived, to write a series of essays on theological subjects. Personally, he was much loved and admired by his large circle of friends. His spinal trouble caused a slight deformity, but this was not particularly noticeable and did not prevent ordinary physical activity. He continued always in the practice of law, gradually withdrawing, however, from court work to office practice; he visited his office even on the last day of his life. He was never married.

[*A Memoir of the Life of John Codman Ropes* (1901) with sketches and addresses by numerous associates; personal information from Mrs. Albert T. Leatherbee of West Roxbury, librarian of the Military Historical Society of Massachusetts; *Daily Evening Transcript* (Boston), Oct. 29, 1899.]

O. L. S., Jr.

ROPES, JOSEPH (Dec. 15, 1770–Sept. 29, 1850), privateersman and merchant, was born in Salem, Mass., the son of David Ropes, a noted privateersman of the Revolution who was killed in battle in 1781, and Ruth Hathorne, a kinswoman of Nathaniel Bowditch and Nathaniel Hawthorne. While still a boy he ran away to sea and made a voyage to the West Indies. His pay was four dollars a month at first, but the life suited him and he rose steadily from cabin boy to shipmaster. In 1794 he commanded the ship *Recovery* and in 1797 the ship *John*. He made many voyages to China, the East Indies, Arabia, and the Isle of France. In 1809 he took command of the *America,* of 473 tons, 114 feet long, with 30 feet breadth of beam, a large vessel in those days and one of the fastest ships of her time. She made a voyage to the Mediterranean and was the first American merchantman to visit Constantinople. Ropes remained here ten months and was received by the Sultan, who wished to negotiate through him a commercial treaty with the United States.

When the War of 1812 broke out the *America* was converted into a privateer. Her upper deck was removed, her sides fortified with oak, and her yards and royalmasts lengthened. She carried 20 guns and 150 men. Ropes commanded her on her first cruise and sailed from Salem Sept. 7, 1812. He cruised in the chops of the English Channel. He was a strict disciplinarian and quelled a mutiny on board the ship. Although he fell in with no war vessels and fought no battles, he captured six prizes during the cruise valued at $158,000. When the *America* returned to Salem about the end of the year Ropes gave up his command and retired permanently from a seafaring life. Why he did so in war-time, at the end of a successful cruise, is not known. He was, however, chosen captain of a company of Sea Fencibles—an artillery force for coast defense. After the war he settled down into the life of a useful and public-spirited citizen. He served as selectman of the town and for several terms in the state legislature. He was director of a bank and of an insurance company, and one of the founders of the East India Marine Society. He had married, Feb. 3, 1801, Sarah, daughter of Zachariah Burchmore, another Salem privateersman. They had two daughters.

[*Hist. Colls. of the Essex Inst.,* vols. IV (1862), VII (1865), and XXXVII (1901); E. S. Maclay, *A Hist. of Am. Privateers* (1899); *Salem Reg.,* Oct. 3, 1850.]
                                        G. W. A.

RORER, DAVID (May 12, 1806–July 7, 1884), lawyer, legal writer, was the son of Abraham Rorer who lived on a farm in Pittsylvania County, Va. On the foundation of a country-school education, he studied law in the office of Nathaniel H. Claiborne [*q.v.*] and was admitted to the Virginia bar before he was twenty years old. Accompanied by a slave, he set out on horseback in the fall of 1826 for Little Rock, Ark. In 1827 he married Martha (Daniel) Martin, by whom he had two sons and two daughters. On

the western frontier he practised law, superintended the construction of a military highway, investigated the condition of the Indians, and dabbled in politics, eventually becoming prosecuting attorney. In the autumn of 1835 he resigned that office, went to St. Louis, and thence in the following spring to the pioneer settlement of Burlington on the west bank of the Mississippi River in Michigan Territory. At Burlington he made his home during the remainder of his life. There his first wife died in 1838, and in the following year he married Delia Maria Viele; two daughters by this marriage survived him. Within the first three years of his residence in Burlington, that town became successively the capital of Wisconsin Territory and of the Territory of Iowa. Rorer plotted the town, drafted the charter and some of the ordinances, contributed most generously toward the erection of a church, suggested the sobriquet "Hawkeyes" for the inhabitants of Iowa, participated in a convention to petition Congress for the creation of Iowa Territory, and ran as an independent Democrat for the office of delegate to Congress. As a consequence of the bitter partisanship of that candidacy he engaged in a street fight and fatally shot a newspaper editor who abused him (J. C. Parish, *Robert Lucas,* 1907, p. 181). That was the end of his political career, for which he had little talent or inclination.

For approximately four decades Rorer was one of the most active members of the Iowa bar. Colleagues and rivals knew him as a thorough scholar, a vigorous advocate, and a close reasoner who could on occasion be eloquent without oratorical vacuity. Though reared as a slave owner, he early perceived the evils of negro bondage and manumitted his own slaves. He was associated with three notable fugitive slave cases. In the first trial before the Iowa territorial supreme court in 1839, his argument that Iowa was free territory according to the Ordinance of 1787 and the Missouri Compromise convinced the court that prohibition of slavery in a territory annihilated slave property, and Ralph, by living in Iowa with the consent of his master, had become free (*Iowa Reports,* 1 *Morris,* 1)—a judgment contrary to the Dred Scott decision seventeen years later. In behalf of a Missouri slave owner, however, he won a verdict in 1850 for the recovery of several fugitive slaves "harbored and concealed" among the Quakers near Salem, Iowa (*Ruel Daggs* vs. *Elihu Frazier et al.*). Although Iowa was free soil, he maintained that the state was bound to respect federal law. Five years later he defended an alleged fugitive slave named Dick and won his release by lack of identification. During the Civil War he was energetic in support of the Union and advocated immediate emancipation as a salutary and effective measure.

Beginning in 1853, Rorer was continuously employed for the next quarter of a century as a railroad attorney, as solicitor, first, of the Burlington & Missouri River Railroad Company, which he had helped to organize in 1852, and in the same capacity after its consolidation with the Chicago, Burlington & Quincy, Dec. 31, 1872. As a result of his extensive experience in railroad litigation and to gratify his taste for research, he wrote three exhaustive works: *A Treatise on the Law of Judicial and Execution Sales* (1873), *American Inter-state Law* (1879), and *A Treatise on the Law of Railways* (2 vols., 1884). The scope and detail of these works indicate the author's grasp and accuracy; the publication of second editions of the first two is evidence of their popularity and usefulness to the legal profession.

[E. H. Stiles, in his *Recollections and Sketches of Notable Lawyers and Public Men of Early Iowa* (1916), and in *Annals of Iowa*, July 1907; accounts of the fugitive slave cases, *Ibid.*, July 1899, Apr. 1903; A. M. Antrobus, *Hist. of Des Moines County, Iowa* (1915), I, 399; *Biog. Rev. of Des Moines County, Iowa* (1905); *Weekly Hawkeye* (Burlington), July 10, 1884.]

J. E. B.

ROSA, EDWARD BENNETT (Oct. 4, 1861–May 17, 1921), physicist, was born in Rogersville, N. Y., the son of Edward D. and Sarah Gilmore (Rowland) Rosa. His father was a descendant of Albert Heymans Roosa who came from Holland and settled near Newburgh, N. Y., in 1660. Edward graduated from Wesleyan University, Middletown, Conn., at the head of the class of 1886, and after two years of teaching pursued advanced studies at the Johns Hopkins University, from which he received the doctorate of philosophy in 1891. There, under the direction of H. A. Rowland [*q.v.*], he began the work on electrical measurements which later gave him world-wide recognition. Son of a Methodist minister, he was endowed with a strict moral sense and a confidence in his own judgment which never wavered. Training in banking and bookkeeping strengthened the sense of exactitude which found expression in his later activities in scientific and public affairs.

In 1891 he returned to Wesleyan as associate professor of physics, and from 1892 to 1903 he held a professorship there. He was notably successful as instructor and administrator, but also continued his investigative work. Jointly with Professor Wilbur O. Atwater [*q.v.*], he devised apparatus and made measurements which showed that the physical law of conservation of energy

applied to animal processes as it does to inanimate ones, and thus gave a scientific basis for study of problems of nutrition.

In 1902, on leave of absence from Wesleyan, he took charge of the electrical work of the National Bureau of Standards, which had been established in 1901. All his energies thereafter were directed to the development of that institution. In fact, he became a martyr to its welfare, in the trying period of readjustment after the World War, for he died suddenly at his desk in 1921, as a direct result of over-exertion in preparing data regarding the status of personnel in the Bureau of Standards and other scientific organizations of the government.

Rosa's first decade of service in the Bureau was devoted to the establishment of precise electrical units and standards and the building up of a staff capable of carrying on the specialized work in electrical measurements which he developed, while the second decade was marked by an intensive practical application of these facilities, including work on many military problems which arose during the war. His fundamental work on electrical measurements included precise determination of the value of the ampere as measured by the mechanical forces exerted between coils carrying current, and a determination of the relation between electrical units derived from magnetic effects and those derived from electrostatic forces. Both of these were done with the collaboration of N. Ernest Dorsey. From the latter relation between units, it is possible to predict the velocity of light, and it has been found that the electrical measurements of Rosa and Dorsey gave a result nearer the true value than had been obtained up to that time by direct measurements on light itself. Rosa also took a leading part in the researches and the negotiations which led to the establishment of the present international system of electrical units, being secretary of the International Committee on Electrical Units and Standards which had jurisdiction over this work.

His later activities included studies of many engineering problems arising in the operation and the regulation of public-utility services. He urged effectively the principle of solving such problems by scientific study carried on jointly by the utilities and regulatory authorities, with consequent agreement on just and reasonable rules and practices. One outgrowth of this method of cooperative action was the enlargement and reorganization of the American Engineering Standards Committee, which has since become the American Standards Association. His final work was an analysis of federal governmental expenditures, showing the immense costs of war and of preparation for war, in contrast with small expenditures for productive functions of the government. The widespread publication of these analyses played a great part in promoting intelligent discussion of government finances, and in developing public support for the limitation of armaments which was begun at the Washington Conference of 1921.

Rosa's writings were largely detailed technical studies, appearing in appropriate periodicals and in the publications of the Bureau of Standards. The more important among them were the following: "A New Respiration Calorimeter and Experiments on the Conservation of Energy in the Human Body" (*Physical Review*, September, October 1899), with W. O. Atwater; "A New Determination of the Ratio of the Electromagnetic to the Electrostatic Unit of Electricity" (*Bureau of Standards Bulletin*, vol. III, 1907, pp. 433–604), with N. E. Dorsey; "Formulas and Tables for the Calculation of Mutual and Self-Inductance" (*Ibid.*, vol. VIII, 1911, pp. 1–237), with F. W. Grover; "A Determination of the International Ampere in Absolute Measure" (*Ibid.*, pp. 269–393), with N. E. Dorsey and J. M. Miller; "The Silver Voltameter" (*Ibid.*, vol. IX, 1912–13, pp. 151–207, 209–282, 493–551, and vol. X, 1914, pp. 475, 536), with G. W. Vinal and A. S. McDaniel; and "Expenditures and Revenues of the Federal Government" (*Annals of the American Academy of Political and Social Science*, May 1921). Rosa was married on Mar. 22, 1894, to Mary, daughter of William W. Evans of Harrisburg, Pa.; they had no children.

[F. W. Nicolson, *Alumni Record of Wesleyan Univ., Middletown, Conn.* (1931); *Who's Who in America, 1920–21*; *Science*, June 24, 1921; *N. Y. Times*, May 18, 1921; family records; official records, Bureau of Standards; personal acquaintance.]   G. K. B.

ROSATI, JOSEPH (Jan. 12, 1789–Sept. 25, 1843), Roman Catholic prelate, was born at Sora in the Kingdom of Naples. Early in life he was destined for the Church, and on May 30, 1801, received clerical tonsure. His classical studies were completed in 1807 in the Diocesan Seminary, and on June 23 of that year he entered the Congregation of the Mission in Rome. He took his vows Apr. 1, 1808, and in the fall commenced his theological studies under Father Andrew James Felix Bartholomew de Andreis [*q.v.*]. On Feb. 10, 1811, during the last year of his course, he was raised to the priesthood. After four years in home mission work through the Papal States, he received a note from De Andreis asking him whether he would join the Louisiana Mission recently organized

at the instance of Bishop Du Bourg [*q.v.*]. He replied emphatically in the affirmative, and with six companions embarked, Oct. 21, 1815, for Marseilles, whence they later sailed for America. They reached Baltimore July 26, 1816, and Bardstown, Ky., Dec. 4 following. Here, at St. Thomas' Seminary, Rosati began in earnest to learn English while helping the local clergy minister to their scattered flocks. In November 1817 he succeeded De Andreis, who had gone to Missouri, as professor of theology in the Seminary, serving in this capacity until, with the Louisiana band, he started for "the Barrens" (Perryville, Mo.) in the following year. They reached their destination on Oct. 1, 1818, and almost at once opened St. Mary's Seminary in temporary quarters.

This institution of classical and theological learning, the first of its kind west of the Mississippi and the nursery of many pioneer Catholic missionaries in the Middle West, may be said to be, under the fostering care of Bishop Du Bourg, Rosati's own creation. He it was who devised the plan of the institution and superintended its construction, while teaching the most important courses and acting as pastor to the Catholics of the surrounding country. Upon him likewise devolved, after the death of De Andreis, Oct. 15, 1820, the superiorship of his Congregation in America. On Nov. 26, 1822, scarcely nine months after the completion of the seminary building, he received the pontifical brief appointing him Bishop of Tenagra and vicar apostolic of Mississippi and Alabama. His representations to Rome (he sent back the brief) and Du Bourg's plea that the creation of the new vicariate was a premature and ill-advised step, resulted only in having the title changed: on July 14, 1823, Pius VII appointed Rosati coadjutor to the Bishop of Louisiana, and forbade him further resistance. Accordingly, he received episcopal consecration at Donaldsonville, La., Mar. 25, 1824, and for two years continued his multitudinous functions at "the Barrens," while caring for the interests of the Catholics in Upper Louisiana. On Nov. 4, 1826, he was notified of Du Bourg's resignation and the division of Louisiana into two dioceses, New Orleans and St. Louis, both of which he was to administer for a time. Pope Leo XII desired him to accept the See of New Orleans, but he himself wished to remain in St. Louis; finally on Mar. 20, 1827, the matter was settled according to his wishes, although he continued to administer Lower Louisiana until the consecration (June 24, 1830) of Rev. Leo De Neckere, Bishop of New Orleans. During these four years Rosati could scarcely do more than attend to the routine work; nevertheless, this period saw the establishment of the Ladies of the Sacred Heart in St. Louis (1827); the building of St. Mary's College at "the Barrens" (1827); the opening of the St. Louis Hospital (Nov. 26, 1828) by the Sisters of Charity from Emmitsburg, Md.; and the erection of St. Louis College by the Jesuits (1829).

In the fall of 1830 Rosati settled in St. Louis and for ten years labored strenuously in the vast territory under his spiritual care. Among the many churches he erected, the cathedral of St. Louis (built 1831–34) remains as a lasting monument of these strenuous days of religious growth. On Apr. 27, 1840, he left St. Louis to attend the provincial Council of Baltimore, and thence proceeded to Rome. Sent as Apostolic Delegate to negotiate an arrangement between the Haytian Republic and the Holy See, he stopped at Philadelphia on his way to consecrate Peter Richard Kenrick [q.v.], whose appointment as his coadjutor he had obtained in Rome. His difficult and laborious mission resulted in the draft of an agreement with which he returned to Rome. Since he had won the favor of the authorities of Port-au-Prince, he was sent to Hayti once more by the Pope to complete the work. While on his way thither, he was seized by illness in Paris, and advised to return to Rome, where he died.

[Rosati MSS. (17 vols.) in archives of Kenrick Seminary, Webster Groves, Mo.; "Vita di Monsig. Giuseppe Rosati" (MS.), archives of the Congregation of the Mission, Collegio Leoniano, Rome; "Necrologia di Monsig. Rosati," in *Diario di Roma*, Nov. 7, 11, 1843; "Necrologia di Monsig. Giuseppe Rosati," in *Annali delle Scienze Religiose*, vol. XVIII, fasc. lii (1844); R. H. Clarke, *Lives of the Deceased Bishops of the Cath. Church in the U. S.* (1872); J. G. Shea, *The Hierarchy of the Cath. Church in the U. S.* (1886); J. E. Rothensteiner, *Hist. of the Archdiocese of St. Louis* (1928), vol. I; *Life of the Very Rev. Felix De Andreis . . . Chiefly from Sketches by the Rt. Rev. Joseph Rosati* (1900); F. G. Holweck, "The Arkansas Mission under Rosati," *St. Louis Cath. Hist. Rev.*, July–Oct. 1919; *Cath. Expositor and Lit. Mag.*, Dec. 1843.]
C. L. S.

ROSE, AQUILA (c. 1695–1723), poet, was born and educated in England. Misfortune of some kind induced him to enlist as a common sailor, and, after visiting various cities on the Mediterranean, he chanced to come to Philadelphia and remained there, being too ill for further duty aboard ship. The date of his arrival is unknown but must have been sometime before Gov. William Keith's visit to the Indians at Conestoga (July 1717), which he commemorated in verse. While convalescing he made friends, James Logan, 1674–1751 [q.v.], among them, and a place was found for him as compositor in the printing office of Andrew Bradford

[q.v.]. He married Maria ——, and was esteemed for his amiable disposition and accomplishments. When he petitioned the Assembly for the right to operate a ferry on the Schuylkill, the corporation of Philadelphia objected to granting the ferry franchise to a private party, but an amicable arrangement was made. The corporation established the ferry and leased it to Rose for twenty-one years, stipulating that he improve the approaches and erect a house and boatsheds. In 1722 he was made clerk of the Assembly. The next year, while retrieving a boat washed from its moorings in a freshet, he took a chill, became desperately ill, and died. The day of his death was given by Samuel Keimer [q.v.] in his *Elegy on the Much Lamented Death of the Ingenious and Well-Beloved Aquila Rose* (1723) as the 24th of Fourth Month (*i.e.*, June) and by Elias Bockett, in *A Poem to the Memory of Aquila Rose* (London, printed for the author, 1723–24), as the 22nd of August. The latter date has the support of Rose's son Joseph, who was apprenticed to Benjamin Franklin in 1730 and in 1740 published *Poems on Several Occasions, By Aquila Rose: To Which Are Prefixed, Some Other Pieces Writ to Him, and to His Memory after His Decease.* The small, neatly printed octavo contains two translations from the *De Tristibus* of Ovid (Bk. I, Elegies ii and iii); lines to Richard Hill [q.v.]; the aforementioned poem, "To his Excellency Sir William Keith, Bart. on his Journey to Conestogoe, and Treaty with the Indians there"; three carriers' addresses for New Year's Day, 1720, 1721, and 1722; seven other short pieces in couplets or quatrains, and several addressed to him or to his memory, including a reprint, with a separate title-page, of Bockett's elegy. Rose's poems are the work of a cultured amateur, the best versifier in English that Philadelphia could show before the younger Thomas Godfrey [q.v.]. His own estimate of their worth may be inferred from the fact that, with good opportunity to publish his work, he refrained from doing so.

[The Library of Congress and the Hist. Soc. of Pa. have each a copy of the *Poems on Several Occasions*. See also the headnote to the reprint of Keimer's *Elegy* in Samuel Hazard's *Reg. of Pa.*, Nov. 1828; J. F. Fisher, "Some Account of the Early Poets and Poetry of Pa.," *Memoirs of the Hist. Soc. of Pa.*, vol. II, pt. 2 (1830); J. T. Scharf and Thompson Westcott, *Hist. of Phila.*, vol. I (1884); F. H. Williams, "Pa. Poets of the Provincial Period," *Pa. Mag. of Hist. and Biog.*, Apr. 1893; M. K. Jackson, *Outlines of the Lit. Hist. of Colonial Pa.* (1906).]
G. H. G.

ROSE, CHAUNCEY (Dec. 24, 1794–Aug. 13, 1877), railroad builder, financier, and philanthropist, was born at Wethersfield, Conn., and died at Terre Haute, Ind. He was the grandson of John Rose who emigrated from Scottish Highlands early in the eighteenth century, and the son of John and Mary (Warner) Rose. His education was brief and limited to that furnished by the common schools of his native village. In 1817 he visited Indiana, Illinois, Missouri, Kentucky, Tennessee, and Alabama, looking for a place to establish himself. Favorably impressed with Terre Haute and its people he returned there in April 1818, but the following year went to Rosedale, where he built and operated a grist and saw mill. In 1825 he moved back to Terre Haute and immediately became active in the affairs of this pioneer village as a merchant, farmer, and contractor. His native energy combined with thrift, forethought, and upright business methods brought him a deserved prosperity and considerable wealth.

Rose was greatly interested in securing railroad facilities for Terre Haute. A road had been projected from Richmond, Ind., to Springfield, Ill., but in spite of many difficulties, he succeeded in diverting it to Terre Haute. It is an evidence of his strong-willed and self-reliant character that he also successfully fought an attempt to get a land grant from the government to build the road and, largely by his own efforts, financed the building operations by private subscription. The Terre Haute & Richmond Railroad (later the Terre Haute & Indianapolis) was organized in 1847 with Rose as its first president. This office he resigned in 1853 after the portion of the road lying between Terre Haute and Indianapolis was built and in running order. His efforts and his money were important factors in bringing other railroads to, or through, Terre Haute. Among these were the Evansville & Crawfordsville Railroad, which was completed between Evansville and Terre Haute in 1853; an extension of the Crawfordsville branch, which later became known as the Logansport Division of the Terre Haute & Indianapolis; and an extension of the Evansville road to Danville and Chicago, known as the Evansville, Terre Haute & Chicago Railroad. It was only on account of advancing years that he took no active part in the completion of the St. Louis, Vandalia & Terre Haute Railroad in 1870, although the preliminary surveys had been made under his direction.

Rose gave way the greater part of his fortune to philanthropic causes, the most of it during his lifetime. Among the objects of his generosity were the Indiana State Normal School and Wabash College; he also helped many young women who wished to attend the Normal School,

his annual outlay for this purpose often exceeding $5,000. His largest gifts in Terre Haute were to the Providence Hospital, the Rose Ladies Aid Society, the Rose Dispensary, the Chauncey Rose School (formerly the Rose Orphan Home), and the Rose Polytechnic Institute. This last institution was one in which he was greatly interested towards the close of his life, the more so, perhaps, because he had felt the need of trained engineers in various industrial enterprises. The school was incorporated in September 1874 as the Terre Haute School of Industrial Science and the name was changed later, over his protest, to the Rose Polytechnic Institute. In March 1883, it was formally opened under the presidency of Charles O. Thompson [q.v.]. Rose made gifts to the school during his lifetime and left it a specific bequest in his will. It was also made the residuary legatee of the Rose estate. He was unmarried and outlived a sister and six brothers, none of whom left any children.

[*Rose Polytechnic Institute Memorial Volume* (1909); *Saturday Evening Mail* (Terre Haute), Aug. 18, 1877; H. W. Beckwith, *Hist. of Vigo and Parke Counties* (1880); *A Biog. Hist. of Eminent and Self-Made Men of the State of Ind.* (1880), vol. II; Blackford Condit, *The Hist. of Early Terre Haute from 1816 to 1840* (1900); C. C. Oakey, *Greater Terre Haute and Vigo County* (1908), vol. I; *Terre Haute Gazette*, Dec. 16, 1899; Loren Hassam, *A Hist. Sketch of Terre Haute, Ind.* (1873); W. H. Smith, *The Hist. of the State of Ind.* (1903), vol. I; *Indianapolis Sentinel*, Aug. 16, 1877.]   J.B.P.

ROSE, EDWARD (fl. 1811–1834), guide, was the son of a white trader among the Cherokee. His mother was a half-breed Cherokee, negro woman. Irving says he was once a Mississippi River pirate (*Astoria, post*, chap. xxiv). He may have gone up the Missouri with the party led by Manuel Lisa [q.v.] in 1807 or with the Missouri Fur Company's expedition in 1809. He had been living among the Crows for two or three years when Wilson Price Hunt [q.v.] engaged him at the Arikara village in June 1811 as hunter, guide, and interpreter, but, becoming suspicious, paid him off at a Crow village near Big Horn Mountain on Sept. 2. In May 1812 Rose joined Lisa's expedition to the upper Missouri.

In 1823 Joshua Pilcher [q.v.] called Rose "a celebrated outlaw who left this country in chains some ten years ago" (Chittenden, *post*, II, 685). For whatever reason, he apparently returned to the Crows and remained with them until his popularity aroused factional jealousy. He then lived among the Arikara for several years. In 1823 he became interpreter to William H. Ashley [q.v.] of the Rocky Mountain Fur Company, whom he vainly cautioned against the Arikara just before the defeat of June 2. The Arikara called a warning to Rose before opening fire. When Col. Henry Leavenworth [*q.v.*] arrived to punish the hostiles Rose was made an ensign and on Aug. 11 was the only man willing to visit the village after the bombardment. Leavenworth called him "a brave and enterprising man" (Robinson, *post*, p. 225). In 1825 he was interpreter to Gen. Henry Atkinson [*q.v.*] on his treaty-making expedition up the Missouri and at a conference with the Crows quelled a dangerous brawl with his rifle-butt. Late in 1832 Zenas Leonard [*q.v.*] with his party encountered Rose in a Crow village at the mouth of Stinking River, where he ranked as a chief, had four wives, and helped recover some stolen horses. In November 1834 the "old negro" performed his most famous exploit in leading the storm of a Blackfoot fortification, himself killing five (Leonard, *post*, pp. 264–67; *Rocky Mountains*, *post*, chap. xxii; Parkman, *post*, chap. x; Bonner, *post*, chap. xiv, but see also *James Clyman, American Frontiersman*, 1928, ed. by C. L. Camp). Rose's death apparently occurred before 1837. According to one account he and some companions blew themselves up with a keg of gunpowder near Fort Cass, while beset by Arikara. Chittenden, however, states that Rose's grave is "on the banks of the Missouri nearly opposite to the mouth of Milk river" (*post*, II, 688; see also *Rocky Mountains*, chap. xxii). Chittenden remarks that while Rose "bore a bad reputation," everything definitely known of him is entirely creditable (*post*, II, 685). He was powerfully built, taciturn and moody, nicknamed, from a scar, *Nez Coupé*. Of surpassing courage and sagacity, he was also renowned as buffalo-stalker and interpreter. Irving admits that he not only strengthened the Crows against the Blackfeet but also established a tradition of friendship for the whites.

[Overland journals, Astor Papers, Baker Lib., Boston; H. M. Chittenden, *The Am. Fur Trade of the Far West* (1902), vols. I, II; Washington Irving, *Astoria* (1836), esp. chap. xxiv and *The Rocky Mountains* (1837), later ed. as *The Adventures of Capt. Bonneville*; *Leonard's Narrative*; *Adventures of Zenas Leonard* (1904), ed. by W. T. Wagner; "Official Correspondence pertaining to the Leavenworth Expedition of 1823," ed. by Doane Robinson, *S. D. Hist. Soc. Colls.*, vol. I (1902); J. C. Luttig, *Journ. of a Fur-Trading Expedition to the Upper Missouri* (1920), ed. by S. M. Drumm; T. D. Bonner, *The Life and Adventures of James P. Beckwourth* (1856); D. H. Coyner, *The Lost Trappers* (1847) of doubtful authenticity; Francis Parkman, *The California and Oregon Trail* (1849), chap. x.]   K. W. P.

ROSE, ERNESTINE LOUISE SIISMONDI POTOWSKI (Jan. 13, 1810–Aug. 4, 1892), reformer, was born in Piotrkow, Russian Poland, of Jewish parentage. Her father was a rabbi, strict in religious observances to the point of asceticism; but she, precocious and independent-minded, revolted early against orthodox Judaism. When Ernestine was sixteen her mother died, and soon afterward the daughter left home. For some years she traveled on the continent, spending considerable time in Prussia and France and interesting herself in the cause of the oppressed wherever she went. In 1832 she was in England, where she met Elizabeth Fry, Robert Dale Owen, and other congenial spirits. In 1835 she presided at the organization in England of the Association of All Classes of All Nations, which made no discrimination regarding sex, religion, race, party, or condition. At about this time she married William E. Rose, an English gentile of wealth and culture who sympathized with her views; and, coming to the United States to live, in 1836 they made their home in New York City.

Her alien race, nationality, and the deistic views she now professed roused considerable feeling against her; but this merely increased her already extensive sympathies and stimulated her zeal for the cause of all humanity, and she threw herself heartily into the various reform movements of the country. Paying her own expenses, she traveled through the eastern states and as far west as Michigan, lecturing to large audiences on religion, free schools, the science of government, abolition, and woman's rights. During the Civil War she worked with the Women's National Loyal League. Her special interest seems to have been in obtaining justice for women, and for this she worked untiringly. During the eleven years of campaigning for the married women's property bill in New York State, 1837–48, she petitioned the legislature almost annually, and five times she addressed it on the subject of the measure. Beginning in 1850, for nineteen years she attended practically every New York state and national convention relating to woman's rights; and she played an important part in many of them. As a public speaker she was pointed, logical, and impassioned (for examples see *Speech of Mrs. Rose . . . at the Anniversary Paine Celebration, 1850,* and *An Address on Woman's Rights, Delivered before the People's Sunday Meeting in Cochituate Hall . . . Oct. 19, 1851,* 1851). In a time when it was easy to be led off by fanatical 'ologies and 'isms, her remarkably keen mind picked out the fundamentals and helped her colleagues to maintain a steady course. In 1869 she and her husband returned to England, where she spent most of her remaining years working, as much as broken health permitted, for the causes that she loved. She died at Brighton.

[E. C. Stanton, S. B. Anthony, and M. J. Gage, *Hist. of Woman Suffrage,* esp. vols. I, III (1881–87) ; I. H. Harper, *The Life and Work of Susan B. Anthony* (3 vols., 1898–1908) ; Henry Lewis, "Ernestine Rose, First Jewish Advocate of Women's Rights," *Forward* (N. Y.), June 19, 1927 ; *Woman's Jour.,* Aug. 13, 1892 ; *Times* (London), Aug. 6, 1892 ; private information ; death date from *Times, ante.*]   M. W. W.

ROSE, JOHN CARTER (Apr. 27, 1861–Mar. 26, 1927), jurist, reformer, author, was born in Baltimore, Md., the son of Mary Elizabeth Hall and John Rose and a descendant of Robert Rose who left Ipswich, England, in 1634 and settled at Wethersfield, Conn. He received his early education in the primary schools of Baltimore and attended the Baltimore City College from 1873 to 1876. He began the study of law in the office of his cousin, Thomas W. Hall, a Baltimore lawyer, and in 1882, when he was twenty-one, he graduated from the law school of the University of Maryland. On Oct. 19, 1886, he married Grace Harvey Beatson, the daughter of George Harvey Beatson of Baltimore. During his first years at the bar Rose wrote editorials for the Baltimore *Sun* on public questions. Early in his career he aligned himself with a reform group who were working to eliminate the political abuses prevailing throughout the state, and for ten years he served as counsel to the Reform League, of which he was a charter member. Largely through his efforts many of the aims of this organization, such as the adoption of the Australian ballot, were realized, and upon the passage of a new election law in 1896, he became counsel to the Supervisors of Election of Baltimore City. In 1890 he acted as supervisor of the census for Maryland.

Rose's prominence as a reformer resulted in his appointment by President McKinley as district attorney (May 1898), an office which he held through successive administrations until his elevation to the district judgeship by President Taft on Apr. 4, 1910. He had built up a lucrative practice and the acceptance of the latter office, which he had neither sought nor desired, entailed financial sacrifices. He possessed unusual arithmetical ability and an almost infallible memory, and his grasp of the fundamental principles of the law, coupled with an extensive knowledge of economics, political science, and history, made him an unusually able member of the federal judiciary. During the twelve years that he held the office of district judge he was never reversed in a criminal case and seldom in a civil action. He delivered many notable opinions, including *United States* vs. *Curry* (201 *Fed.,* 371), which resulted in an

amendment of an act of Congress because of his criticism of its basic unfairness, and *The Virginia* (264 *Fed.,* 986), a landmark in admiralty law. He enjoyed the confidence and respect of the members of the United States Supreme Court, and it was at the request of one of the justices that he undertook, in the last year of his life, a revision of his *Elementary Treatise on the Jurisdiction and Procedure of the Federal Courts* which was first published in 1915. Rose also enjoyed the friendship of Roosevelt and, as a member of the "tennis cabinet," was frequently consulted concerning public papers. His wit, and the speed with which he grasped the essential elements of a case, made his courtroom a disciplinary chamber, where circumlocution and long arguments were banned, where he was feared, sometimes disliked, but always respected. It is to his credit that he maintained his poise and sense of proportion during the war hysteria of 1917–18 and during the supposed "Red" menace that immediately followed. In December 1922, he was promoted by President Harding to the United States circuit court of appeals for the fourth circuit. In 1925 Rose was elected president of the Maryland State Bar Association. He died of heart trouble in his sixty-sixth year at Atlantic City and was buried in Baltimore. Three of his four children survived him.

[*John Carter Rose Memorial Proc.* (1928) ; *Report of the Thirty-Second Ann. Meeting of the Md. State Bar Asso.* (1927) ; E. F. Cordell, *Univ. of Md., 1807–1907* (1907), vol. II ; *Who's Who in America,* 1926–27 ; the *Sun* (Baltimore), Mar. 26, 27, 28, 1927 ; information as to certain facts from Douglas H. Rose, II, and Morris A. Soper ; personal acquaintance.]   H. C.

ROSE, JOSEPH NELSON (Jan. 11, 1862– May 4, 1928), botanist, was born on a farm near Liberty, Union County, Ind., the son of George W. Rose and Rebecca Jane (Corrington). The Rose family came originally from Monmouth County, N. J., to southern Indiana. George W. Rose was born and brought up near Fairfield, Ind. He was drafted for service during the latter part of the Civil War, and was sent to camp at Vicksburg, Miss., where he died, leaving two infant sons. The Corrington family, of English origin, settled in New Jersey before the American Revolution. Joseph Corrington removed to Cincinnati, Ohio, in 1792, and his grandson Joseph Corrington was the maternal grandfather of Joseph Nelson Rose.

The latter received his early education in the common schools of Union County and was graduated from the Liberty High School in 1880. In the fall of that year he entered the preparatory department of Wabash College and in 1881 the college proper, from which he was graduated with the degree of A.B. in 1885. He at once re-entered Wabash as its first post-graduate student, receiving the degree of A.M. in 1887 and that of Ph.D. in 1889. During the last two years he acted as assistant in botany to Prof. John M. Coulter [*q.v.*], whose influence undoubtedly inspired his future career. On Aug. 8, 1888, he married Lou Beatrice Sims, of Delphi, Ind., the daughter of Joseph Allen Sims, originally of Culpeper, Va., and Susanna (Hawkins) Sims. He was the father of five children, four of whom, with their mother, survived him.

In August 1888 Rose accepted a position as assistant botanist in the United States Department of Agriculture, Washington, D. C., under Dr. George Vasey. His studies thus far had been upon fungi, pines, the flora of Indiana, and the *Umbelliferae* of North America, the last a difficult family of phanerogams upon which he published monographically, both then and later, for the most part jointly with Coulter. It fell to Rose's lot to report upon the rich botanical collections brought out of Mexico by Edward Palmer, and for the next twenty years his numerous published papers related primarily to the flora of that country. They include a series entitled "Studies of Mexican and Central American Plants," published in *Contributions from the United States National Herbarium* (1897–1911). These consist largely of synoptical studies and revisions in many families of flowering plants, increasing attention being given to several groups of succulents, especially *Agave* and the families *Crassulaceae* and *Amaryllidaceae*. Meanwhile, in 1896, the National Herbarium had been returned by the Department of Agriculture to the United States National Museum, under the custody of the Smithsonian Institution, and Rose was transferred to the Museum as assistant curator. During the next fifteen years he made nine trips of botanical exploration to Mexico, visiting nearly every state in the Republic and collecting many thousands of specimens, hundreds of which represented species new to science. Besides herbarium material large series of living plants of *Cacti* and *Crassulaceae* (live-forevers) were forwarded to Washington for greenhouse cultivation, marking the beginning of important living collections which later were to form the basis of monographic studies. His first paper on *Crassulaceae*, published jointly with Dr. N. L. Britton in 1903, contained descriptions of many new species. This was followed two years later by a joint systematic treatment of the entire family as represented in North America. Subsequently, up to 1927, he published many other papers upon the

American members of this group, on which he was the acknowledged authority.

Rose's studies of the *Cactaceae* found expression similarly. His special interest in this family appears to have developed principally through field-work in the mountains of Mexico. His first paper appeared in 1907 and during the next two years about a dozen more were published, several of them written in collaboration with Britton. In 1912 Rose was furloughed from his position as associate curator in the Museum (to which he had been promoted in 1905) to accept appointment as research associate of the Carnegie Institution of Washington for the purpose of preparing, in collaboration with Britton, a monographic treatment of the *Cactaceae* of the world. Setting about this task with characteristic patience, quiet enthusiasm, and thoroughness, he visited Europe at once, to study historic museum material and to acquaint himself with the species cultivated in all the important gardens. In 1913 he collected in the West Indies. Between 1914 and 1918 he made four trips of exploration, covering a large part of South America and assembling an extraordinarily rich collection of herbarium material and of living plants. The final results of this extended investigation are contained in a beautifully illustrated monograph of four volumes by Britton and Rose entitled *The Cactaceae* (1919–23). This is an exceedingly important treatise, not only because it presents a well-considered new classification of this difficult family, but also because it has been influential in bringing into present general favor a fascinating and intricate group of plants which are almost exclusively American.

In 1923 Rose returned to the National Herbarium as associate curator, and besides continuing his studies of succulents undertook, again jointly with Britton, a revision of the North American leguminous plants of the families *Mimosaceae* and *Caesalpiniaceae*, the results of which have mostly appeared since his death. His published work includes nearly 200 titles, among them many important papers written in association with no fewer than twelve botanists. This spirit of cooperation was an outstanding well-recognized characteristic—a reflection of his invariable tolerance, helpfulness, and remarkably even temperament, and a judicial attitude which though deliberately critical was always friendly and unbiased. Despite rapidly failing strength he continued steadily at work to the very day of his death. His name and work are fittingly commemorated in four genera of plants named in his honor.

[William Trelease, "Joseph Nelson Rose, 1862–1928," *Science*, LXVII, 598–99 (June 15, 1928); Alwin Berger, "Joseph Nelson Rose," *Zeitschrift für Sukkulentenkunde*, III, 281–83 (July 1928); J. J. Verbeek Wolthuys, "In Memoriam, Dr. Joseph Nelson Rose," *Succulenta*, X, 125–27 (July 1928); H. Wegener, "Dr. Joseph Nelson Rose," *Desert*, I, 105 (Jan. 1930); *Who's Who in America*, 1928–29; *Evening Star* (Washington, D. C.), May 5, 1928.]   W.R.M.

ROSE, URIAH MILTON (Mar. 5, 1834–Aug. 12, 1913), jurist, was born at Bradfordsville, Marion County, Ky., the son of Dr. Joseph and Nancy (Simpson) Rose. At the age of five he was studying Latin and his father gave him the best educational advantages available up to the time of his own death in 1849. The small estate which Dr. Rose had accumulated now went into the hands of an administrator, and Uriah had to shift for himself. Fortunately R. H. Roundtree, an able and kindly lawyer, took an interest in him and found a place for him as deputy county clerk. He studied law at night and saw it administered at first hand daily by some of the most celebrated lawyers and jurists of the state. In September 1853 he graduated in law at Transylvania University and on Oct. 25 following married Margaret T. Gibbs. He set out in December of the same year for Batesville, Ark., where he formed a law partnership with William E. Gibbs, a brother-in-law, hoping to recover his lost health riding the circuits. First he had to master the highly technical common-law pleading then in vogue in Arkansas, but his graceful courtesy and refinement of manner disarmed the rough-and-tumble lawyers of the frontier, and he was soon able to meet the best lawyers of the state on terms of equality. In 1860 Governor Conway appointed him chancellor in Pulaski County. He hesitated to accept the post, but did so on the advice of friends and held the office until the Federals captured the state capital. He had opposed secession, but at the outbreak of war cast in his lot with the state and remained loyal to it to the end. In the fall of 1865 he moved to Little Rock and formed a partnership with George C. Watkins, formerly chief justice of Arkansas. After the death of Judge Watkins in 1867, Rose's name stood first in that of the leading law firm of the state. In this year he published *Digest of the Arkansas Reports* (1867), covering the first twenty volumes of reports. In 1874 he went to Washington to lay before President Grant the claims of Elisha Baxter [*q.v.*] in the Brooks-Baxter war over the governorship.

In 1872 Rose began a series of travels which took him all over Europe, the West Indies, Mexico, and Hawaii. He was a good linguist, reading German and speaking French fluently. He collected a library of some eight thousand volumes in different languages and was familiar with most of it. He exercised a powerful influence over the Arkansas bar, leading it toward sobriety and higher moral standards, and adding dignity to the profession. He was frequently in demand for addresses at bar association meetings and as an after-dinner speaker. A happy success on such an occasion when he proposed a toast in honor of President Theodore Roosevelt at the time of the latter's visit to Little Rock led to his appointment as delegate to the Second Peace Conference at The Hague in 1907. In 1891 he published *The Constitution of the State of Arkansas*, with notes; his occasional addresses were collected and published after his death as *Addresses of Uriah M. Rose* (1914). He served as president of the Arkansas Bar Association, 1899–1900, and of the American Bar Association, 1901–02. After his death his statue was placed by the state in the Statuary Hall of the National Capitol, an honor accorded to few private citizens. He died in his eightieth year, survived by his widow and eight of their ten children.

[Memoir by G. B. Rose in *Addresses of U. M. Rose* (1914); W. E. Hemingway, *In Memoriam: U. M. Rose* (n.d.); Fay Hempstead, *Hist. Rev. of Ark.* (1911), vol. I; J. M. Moore, in *Proc. . . . Bar Asso. of Ark.*, 1914; *Case and Comment*, Nov. 1913, Jan. 1914; *Ark. Gazette* (Little Rock), Aug. 12, 1913.]   D.Y.T.

ROSE, WALTER MALINS (Nov. 25, 1872–Feb. 12, 1908), legal annotator and digester, was born in Toronto, Canada, the son of Henry J. Rose. The family moved to Ontario, Cal., where Walter attended Chaffey College. In 1895 he received the degree of A.B. from Stanford University and the following year graduated from the law school of Cornell University, winning also the Boardman thesis prize. In September 1896 he was admitted to the California bar and entered into practice with Robert Hayne in San Francisco. Three years later he was admitted to practice before the United States Supreme Court, but owing to ill health, he was forced to relinquish his practice and moved to Arizona. Between 1899 and 1901 he published a twelve-volume work, with an additional index volume, entitled *Notes on the United States Reports*, treating cases reported from 2 *Dallas* to 172 *U. S.* The work purported to show "the present value as authority of the cases therein reported as disclosed by all subsequent citations in all the courts of last resort, both Federal and state." Clearly it was an ambitious undertaking for one so recently called to the bar. His classification of material followed a chronological arrangement, in outline, of points of law determined in Supreme Court decisions, with subsequent citing cases listed. The citations of each annotated case were arranged under the respective points of law involved, and by a further classification, cases affirming a principle were treated separately from those qualifying or denying it. Both the conception and the method were new and afforded a distinct departure in the field of legal authorship. In 1917 a revised edition of the work was published by Charles L. Thompson.

Rose's next undertaking was an application of the new method to the case law of a single state. In a five-volume work, *Notes on Texas Reports,* published in 1902, he presented a "chronological series of annotations of the decisions of the Supreme Court and the various civil and criminal appellate courts of Texas, showing their present value as authority as disclosed by all the subsequent citations" thereof. A posthumous edition was published in 1910 and there have been later supplements. In 1903 he published a three-volume *Digest of the United States Reports from the Beginning to the October Term, 1902*—a task for which his previous labors had especially fitted him. This was followed in 1907 by his *Code of Federal Procedure,* in three volumes, based upon Robert Desty's manual relating to the same subject but with material rearranged "along more modern and satisfactory lines." His "Code" provisions were taken from the Constitution, acts of Congress, court rules, and decisions, all topically arranged. He also published monographs on leading cases.

About 1906 he moved to Los Angeles and established himself in active practice. He served as counsel for various corporations and in the relatively brief interval before his death was unusually successful. He died suddenly, at the age of thirty-five, after an operation for appendicitis. His wife was Mary (Holt) Rose, of Holt, Ky., whom he had married on Oct. 19, 1899. She, with a son, survived him.

[*Who's Who in America,* 1908–09; *Cornell Alumni News,* Feb. 19, 1908; *Stanford Alumnus,* Mar. 1908; *Times* (Los Angeles), Feb. 13, 1908.]   C. S. L.

ROSECRANS, SYLVESTER HORTON (Feb. 5, 1827–Oct. 21, 1878), Roman Catholic prelate, was born in Homer, Ohio, son of Crandall Rosecrans, a native of Wilkes-Barre, Pa., and Jemima (Hopkins) Rosecrans. On his father's side he was descended from Harmon Rosenkrans who emigrated from Norway to New Amsterdam about 1657; his mother was a descendant of Stephen Hopkins [*q.v.*] of Rhode Island, a signer of the Declaration of Independence. In 1845, while a student in Kenyon College, Sylvester, influenced by the conversion of

his brother William Starke Rosecrans [*q.v.*] to Catholicism and the instructions of Rev. J. B. Lamy [*q.v.*], also entered the Catholic Church. He then transferred from Kenyon to St. John's College, Fordham, N. Y., from which he was graduated a year later. After studying theology at Mount St. Mary's Seminary of the West (Cincinnati) and at the Propaganda in Rome, where he was awarded a doctorate in divinity, he was ordained a priest on July 16, 1852. As a curate at St. Thomas' Church and at the cathedral in Cincinnati, as a teacher and finally rector of the collegiate department of the archdiocesan seminary, and as associate-editor with Father Edward Purcell of the *Catholic Telegraph,* Father Rosecrans won local renown and the favor of Archbishop Purcell [*q.v.*], at whose suggestion he was named titular bishop of Pompeiopolis and coadjutor of Cincinnati by Pope Pius IX. Although consecrated by Purcell, Mar. 25, 1862, he humbly continued to teach for two years and published a small volume, *The Divinity of Christ* (1866). As the brother of General Rosecrans he attracted wide attention during the Civil War, and seconded the bold patriotism of his ordinary, for which he was severely criticized by the antiwar editor of the powerful *New York Freeman's Journal.* A man of spirit, he showed courage in 1865 when he was wounded by burglars on his refusal to surrender a church collection.

In 1867 he was given the pastorate of St. Patrick's Church, Columbus, in preparation for his elevation to the new see of Columbus (Mar. 3, 1868). During his tenure of ten years, there was a marked growth in the diocese because of the heavy Irish and German immigration. In addition to about forty churches, he built St. Joseph's Cathedral; established the *Catholic Columbian* in 1875, to which he himself was a regular contributor; fostered religious confraternities, especially much-needed temperance societies; instituted St. Aloysius Seminary (1871); and, through the various religious communities which he encouraged to enter the diocese, promoted a number of convents, monasteries, and orphanages. Beloved by the bishops of the province, Rosecrans was a scrupulously orthodox, dependable, and unambitious ecclesiastic, rigorous with himself, lenient with his priests, and honored by his people irrespective of their racial antecedents.

[Allen Rosenkrans, *The Rosenkrans Family in Europe and America* (1900); R. H. Clarke, *Lives of the Deceased Bishops of the Catholic Church in the U. S.,* vol. III (1888); J. G. Shea, *The Hierarchy of the Catholic Church in the U. S.* (1886); G. F. Houck, *The Church in Northern Ohio and in the Diocese of Cleveland* (1887); J. H. Lamott, *Hist. of the Archdiocese of Cincinnati* (1921); *Catholic Encyc.,* XIII, 192; M. J.

Kelly and J. M. Kirwin, *Hist. of Mount St. Mary's Seminary of the West* (1894) ; L. W. Mulhane, "Maj.-Gen. William Starke Rosecrans," in *Records of the Am. Catholic Hist. Soc.*, Sept. 1924 ; *Cleveland Leader,* Oct. 22, 1878.]   R. J. P.

ROSECRANS, WILLIAM STARKE (Sept. 6, 1819–Mar. 11, 1898), soldier, was born in Kingston township, Delaware County, Ohio, the eldest son of Crandall and Jemima (Hopkins) Rosecrans. He was a descendant, in the sixth generation, of Harmon Hendrick Rosenkrans, who came to America about 1657. The family had been represented in Ohio since about 1809. His great-grandfather had served as a captain in the Revolutionary War, and his father with the same rank in the War of 1812. His mother was a descendant of Stephen Hopkins [*q.v.*], one of the signers of the Declaration of Independence. He received his preparatory education in the public schools, entered the United States Military Academy in 1838 and was graduated in 1842. He was commissioned brevet second lieutenant of engineers and his first duty was on the fortifications of Hampton Roads, Va. In 1843, after having been promoted second lieutenant, he was brought back to West Point, where he served four years as assistant professor in the departments of engineering and of natural and experimental philosophy. On Aug. 24, 1843, he was married to Ann Eliza, the only daughter of Judge Adrian Hegeman of New York City. For the next ten years he was assigned to various posts in New England, and became a first lieutenant, but resigned his commission on Apr. 1, 1854. He began civil life as an engineer and architect in Cincinnati, Ohio, where he remained for a year, and then was engaged in coal mining and river navigation in western Virginia. He returned to Cincinnati in 1857 as head of an oil refining company.

On Apr. 19, 1861, he became a volunteer aide-de-camp to General McClellan, then commanding in Ohio. He was made colonel and chief engineer of the department of Ohio, and also appointed colonel of the 23rd Ohio Volunteer Infantry in June, but almost immediately was commissioned brigadier-general in the regular army. In McClellan's campaign in western Virginia he commanded a brigade, and won the battle of Rich Mountain in July, one of the first battles of the Civil War. He succeeded McClellan as commanding general of the department of the Ohio, and later as chief of the new department of western Virginia, he continued the operations which ended, late in the fall, in the complete expulsion of the Confederate forces, and the formation of the state of West Virginia. In May 1862, he commanded the left wing of Pope's Army of the Mississippi which formed a part of Halleck's command in a movement upon Corinth, the important railway junction of northern Mississippi. In June, when Pope was called east, Rosecrans succeeded him in command. His reduced force constituted the left wing of the army in the region of Corinth, now under the command of Grant, who had succeeded Halleck. Early in September the Confederate general, Price, moved up and occupied Iuka, on the Memphis and Charleston Railway twenty miles southeast of Corinth. General Van Dorn, cooperating with him, was at Holly Springs, fifty miles southwest, and Grant planned to concentrate upon Price before the two Confederate forces could effect a junction. Rosecrans attacked Price, but failed to cut off his retreat to the south, and returned to Corinth. Price and Van Dorn joined forces and attacked his entrenched position there on Oct. 3, 1862. The battle was hotly contested, and losses were heavy on both sides. The advantage was with the Confederates on the first day, but on the second they were decisively defeated and driven back to Holly Springs. Rosecrans followed, but was unable to bring the enemy to battle again. He was now promoted major-general of volunteers and ordered to relieve Buell in Kentucky, his command finally being reorganized as the Army of the Cumberland, with three army corps.

After the battle of Perryville in Kentucky, the Confederate forces under General Bragg had fallen back into Tennessee and were concentrating at Murfreesboro. Rosecrans joined Buell's army on Nov. 2, and, after reorganizing the army, advanced to Nashville where he remained for a month, accumulating supplies to provide against probable interruption of communications. Late in December he moved out against Bragg, and the two armies met on Stone River, just west of the town, on Dec. 29. Both moved to the attack two days later, each army advancing the left wing. Bragg gained the first success and rolled up the Federal right, but Rosecrans, by great exertion, established a new line which held against all attacks. Fighting continued for the next two days, and on Jan. 3, 1863, Bragg retreated to Shelbyville, twenty-five miles south. Here the armies faced each other for six months, undertaking only minor operations.

On June 23 Rosecrans began an advance, and in nine days very skilfully maneuvered Bragg out of his positions at Shelbyville and Tullahoma, and back into Chattanooga. For some time Rosecrans had felt that he had been hampered in developing the efficiency of his command by the headquarters in Washington. During the six months of waiting at Murfreesboro there arose an unfortunate controversy between Rosecrans, Halleck, and Stanton over Halleck's offering a major-generalship either to Grant or to Rosecrans depending upon which of the two first won an important victory. A testy and untactful letter to headquarters, referring to this auctioning-off of military honors, brought Rosecrans into decided disfavor in Washington. Now, as after the battle of Murfreesboro, Halleck constantly pressed Rosecrans to advance, and as before, Rosecrans steadily declined to move until he considered the time ripe. At last, on Aug. 16, he came forward, made a feint up the Tennessee River above Chattanooga, then crossed in force below that place and maneuvered Bragg out of it. Rosecrans followed him, his lines greatly extended, but Bragg, having been reinforced, turned to face him and defeated him badly in the hard-fought and bloody battle of Chickamauga on Sept. 19 and 20, 1863. Rosecrans had to fall back to Chattanooga where he was besieged. The disaster at Chickamauga was brought about on the field by an officer who executed to the letter an order from Rosecrans which was obviously in error and which opened up a wide gap in the Federal line.

The army was in a most desperate situation and all the resources of the North were turned to its relief. Strong reinforcements which Rosecrans had previously requested were now put in motion toward Chattanooga and Grant was placed in command of all the western armies. The error at Chickamauga cost Rosecrans his command. He was relieved on Oct. 19, and was assigned to command the department of the Missouri. In December 1864, he was sent to Cincinnati, Ohio, to await orders, and remained on this status or on leave until Mar. 28, 1867, when he resigned his commission in the regular army. On Mar. 13, 1865, he received the brevet rank of major-general for his services at Murfreesboro. Rosecrans was generally regarded as an able commander and has been called the "greatest strategist of the war . . ." (Cist, post, p. 235). He accomplished an incredible amount of work, and in campaign seemed to be able to do without sleep. He had a hot temper, which he was not always able to control, and was often hasty and indiscreet in speech. He especially resented interference from above with his plans, and seemed to persist the more obstinately in his own decisions. These characteristics brought him into conflict with his superiors, as in the Tullahoma and Chickamauga campaigns, and ultimately led to his relief. He was, however, well liked in the army and was affectionately called "Old Rosy" by the soldiers.

In 1868 and 1869 he was minister to Mexico. He returned to Ohio, declined the Democratic nomination for governor, and soon afterward went west to engage in mining operations first in Mexico and later in California. From 1881 to 1885 he was a representative in Congress from California, and became chairman of the committee on military affairs. By special act of Congress he was commissioned a brigadier-general on the retired list of the regular army, Mar. 2, 1889. Upon leaving Congress he was appointed register of the treasury and served until 1893. He then returned to California and took up his residence on his ranch at Redondo, near Los Angeles, where he remained until his death. He took an active interest in civic affairs and was particularly energetic in trying to induce Americans to invest in Mexico. He was buried at Rosedale Cemetery, Los Angeles, but was reinterred in 1902 with much ceremony at Arlington National Cemetery, Washington, D. C., the president being the principal speaker on the occasion. He was survived by three of his eight children. While at West Point he had been converted to the Roman Catholic church and converted his brother, Sylvester Horton Rosecrans [q.v.], to that faith.

[Allen Rosenkrans, *The Rosenkrans Family in Europe and America* (1900); Timothy Hopkins, *John Hopkins . . . and Some of his Descendants* (1932); G. W. Cullum, *Biog. Reg. . . . Officers and Grads., U. S. Mil. Acad.* (1891); *Biog. Dir. Am. Cong.* (1928); L. W. Mulhane, "Major-Gen. Wm. Starke Rosecrans," *Records of the Am. Catholic Hist. Soc.*, Sept. 1924; Joseph Taggart, *Biog. Sketches of the Eminent Am. Patriots* (1907); H. M. Cist, *The Army of the Cumberland, in Campaigns of the Civil War*, vol. VII (1882); *War of the Rebellion: Official Records (Army)*, *passim*; San Francisco *Bulletin*, Mar. 11, 1898.]

O. L. S., Jr.

ROSELIUS, CHRISTIAN (Aug. 10, 1803–Sept. 5, 1873), lawyer, son of Johann Conrad and Anna Marie (Wacker) Roselius, was born near the German city of Bremen. He was baptized Johann Christian, but in later life did not use his first name. His parents were poor, and at the age of sixteen he went without money to Bremen, where four years later, by the sale of future services, he secured passage to New Orleans on the Dutch brig *Jupiter*. He served an apprenticeship as a printer in his adopted city and in 1825 started a magazine, *The Halcyon*, which was destined to a short existence. By hard study he sought to overcome his deficiencies of education, adding a speaking command of French and English to his native German and acquiring proficiency in Latin. Beginning the study of law in the office of Auguste D'Avezac [q.v.] in company with Alexander Dimitry [q.v.], he developed a passion for French civil law and its ancient background and thus acquired an important legal equipment for Louisiana practice. He married the directress of a school for girls and himself resorted to teaching while struggling for a beginning at law. He was admitted to the bar in 1828 and was engaged in the active practice of law with little interruption during the rest of his life. He attained the front rank of the Louisiana bar, ranking with Pierre Soulé and Edward Livingston.

In 1840 he was elected to the state legislature, and the following year was named state attorney general for a two-year term. He served as a member of the state constitutional convention in 1845. He was an important participant in drawing and subsequently executing the will of John McDonogh [q.v.], the wealthy benefactor whose name has become closely associated with the New Orleans public schools. In the pursuit of his profession he acquired a competence but tended to reduce it by a generous munificence. He was ready with hand and purse to help the unfortunate, including kinsmen whom he aided on one of his visits to his native country. A Whig in politics, he opposed secession as a member of the state convention that voted such a step on the eve of the Civil War. In 1863 he declined appointment to the highest judicial office in the reconstructed state government, expressing a refusal to serve on a court subject to military interference. He was a member of the board of administrators of the University of Louisiana (later to become Tulane University) at New Orleans, 1847–55; professor of civil law in the University, 1850–73; and dean of the law department, 1865–72. He took great interest in his law teaching, preparing written lectures on the status of civil law in Louisiana that were marked for clarity and methodical organization; his name is closely connected with the development of this law school.

Of ordinary height, Roselius was rather spare and angular and had a physical appearance that suggested a greater age than was his. He was more forceful than attractive as a public speaker. His private library was rich in Shakespeare and the Latin classics, which he read constantly. He owned a spacious home in Carrollton, a suburb of New Orleans in his day, and his hospitality was enjoyed by not a few distinguished visitors to the city. He died at New Orleans, and his funeral was held at a Lutheran church on St. Charles Avenue with interment in the old St. Louis cemetery. Of his three children, one daughter survived him.

[*Berühmte Deutsche Vorkämpfer für Fortschritt, Freiheit und Friede in Nord-Amerika* (Cleveland, 1888); *Sketches of Life and Character in Louisiana* (1847) by a member of the New Orleans bar (J. S. Whitaker); *Green Bag*, Mar. 1890; *New Orleans Daily Picayune*, Sept. 6, 1873; *New Orleans States*, Dec. 10, 1922 (devoted chiefly to the Roselius home in the Carrollton suburb); names of parents from Bremen records through the courtesy of Dr. R. L. Jaeger, German consul at New Orleans.]   H. C. N.

ROSENBERG, ABRAHAM HAYYIM (Oct. 17, 1838–Aug. 5, 1925), author, Biblical scholar, was born in Karlin (Pinsk), Russia, the son of Uzziel Yaffa Rosenberg and Leah Lieberman. His father, a Hebrew scholar, tutored him in Hebrew and the Talmud, his acquaintance with secular studies beginning only at the age of twenty-two, after he had already lost his first wife and was the father of four children. He entered the Rabbinical Seminary in Zhitomir, and after his graduation served as district Rabbi in Pinsk from 1872 to 1881. Here he married his second wife, Clara Bercinsky. In 1881 he accepted the post of district Rabbi in Nikolayev, and was also instructor of Jewish history and religion at the classical gymnasium in the same city. He was exposed to petty police persecution on account of his liberal views, and moved from the city in 1888, accepting a Rabbinical post in Poltava. Still further subjected to police hostility, he quit the country and emigrated to the United States in 1891.

He started his literary career by writing articles in the field of Jewish learning and sketches of Jewish life which were published in the Russian magazines, *Russkiy Evrey, Voskhod, Razsviet, Evreiskia Zapiski,* and in the Hebrew journals, *Ha-melitz, Ha-karmel, Ha-eshkol.* He was also the author of a Jewish history in Russian. His chief field of study, however, was the Bible. While still in Russia he had conceived the idea of publishing a Hebrew cyclopedia of Biblical literature, containing an historical and geographical description of the persons, places, and other subjects mentioned in the Old Testament. He was able to publish this *magnum opus,* to which he devoted his life, only many years later in America. Settling down in the ghetto of New York City he deliberately chose to maintain himself with the aid of a small printing press in a basement, his main concern being the printing of his cyclopedia. Indeed, the first two volumes were set up by himself, appearing in 1898 and 1899. The whole work, consisting of ten volumes, entitled *Ozar ha-shemoth,* was published by a group of admirers two years before his death, and won wide recognition, definitely establishing Rosenberg's reputation as a Biblical scholar.

Apart from his chief interest, Rosenberg devoted time to other branches of both Hebrew and Yiddish literature. In 1891 he was editor of the Hebrew weekly *Ha-ibri,* published by Kathriel Sarasohn, an editor of the Hebrew literary monthly *Ner ha-maarabi* in 1895. He also contributed numerous articles to *Ha-leom, Ha-pisgah, Ha-yom, Ha-modia le-hodashim* and other Hebrew periodicals. He began to write Yiddish after coming to the United States, and contributed popular historical articles to the Yiddish press and longer works published in installments. These include a history of ritual murder cases and a discussion of agriculture among Jews in times of the prophets and the Talmud. Several books in Yiddish, including a life of the patriarch Abraham and an account of the expulsion of the Jews from Spain, *Gerush Spanien,* came from his pen. His most ambitious undertaking in Yiddish was the translation and adaptation of Johann Gustav Vogt's *Weltgeschichte* in twelve volumes, to which he added much new material and an additional section devoted to Jewish history and literature and published in 1918.

[Hutchins Hapgood, *The Spirit of the Ghetto* (1902); Salomon Wininger, *Grosse Jüdische National-Biographie,* vol. V; Zalmen Reisen, *Lexicon fun der Yiddisher Literatur,* vol. IV (1929); *Am. Hebrew,* Aug. 14, 1925; M. Tausner, in *Hadoar,* a Hebrew weekly published in New York City, Aug. 14, 1925.]

I. S.

ROSENBERG, HENRY (June 22, 1824–May 12, 1893), merchant, banker, philanthropist, christened Heinrich, was born in the mountain village of Bilten, Canton Glarus, Switzerland, the second child of Johan Rudolf Rosenberger, shoemaker, and Waldburg (Blum) Rosenberger. He was early apprenticed as a fabric printer and was later transferred to a store in Glarus, where he met his employer's son, John Hessly. Failing to obtain a desired clerkship, in 1843 he emigrated to the seaport village of Galveston in the Republic of Texas, where this son employed him in his little dry-goods store at eight dollars a month. Three years later Rosenberg bought out his employer.

The story of Rosenberg's life is closely connected with the history of Galveston's development. He participated in directing capacities in nearly every enterprise that contributed to its expansion. By 1859 he owned the largest retail dry-goods store in Texas. In 1874 he organized the Galveston Bank & Trust Company, of which from 1882 he was sole owner until his death. He was also actively interested in the First National Bank, the Galveston City Railway Company, the Gulf, Colorado & Santa Fé Rail-

way Company, serving as its president from 1874 to 1877, and the Galveston Wharf Company. He served as president of the Board of Harbor Improvements (1869–73) and as alderman (1871–72, 1885–87). Childless, he took a great interest in child welfare, and in 1886 gave to the city the Rosenberg School; for many years, also, he was connected with the directorate of the Galveston Orphans' Home. He was a vestryman of Trinity Episcopal Church, and in 1882 contributed about half the cost of Eaton Chapel. He also renovated the little church in Bilten in which he had been christened and confirmed. From Apr. 13, 1866, to Sept. 6, 1869, he was vice-consul for Switzerland, and from the latter date to his death, consul. On June 11, 1851, he married Letitia Cooper of Galveston, a native of Virginia, who died in 1888; on Nov. 13, 1889, he married Mary Ragan Macgill of Hagerstown, Md., who had been practically an adopted daughter. He had no children. He is described as a ruddy-faced gentleman of benevolent countenance, with short beard, short, rotund figure, always well but unostentatiously dressed, cane in hand, and flower in lapel.

His will placed him at the head of Texas philanthropists up to that time. He made provision for the maintenance of an orphanage in Bilten, but more than sixty-two percent of his estate, valued at something over one million one hundred thousand dollars, he turned back in bequests to Galveston. Among these were buildings for the Island City Protestant and Israelitish Orphans' Home, and for Grace Episcopal Church; sites and buildings for the Letitia Rosenberg Woman's Home and for the Young Men's Christian Association—the first such building in Texas; a charity fund for the German Lutheran Church; seventeen drinking fountains for men and beasts. A foreigner from a liberty-loving country seeking freedom and a livelihood in the seven-year-old Republic of Texas, where he doubtless heard heroic stories of the Texas Revolution, he also left $50,000 for a Texas Heroes' Monument, which was designed by Louis Amateis [*q.v.*]. A residuary legacy provided for the endowment of a free public library. The residuary assets promised to be about $400,000; but through the excellent management of Maj. A. J. Walker, executor, the assets at his death in 1904 had almost doubled, and the Rosenberg Library opened in that year, by far the wealthiest library in the state. Under the judicious policies of the directors, the assets had increased by 1930 to nearly a million dollars, and the book collection to about 85,000 volumes. Rosenberg was buried in Loudon Park Cemetery, Baltimore, Md. In

1906 a bronze statue of him, executed by Louis Amateis, was placed by the citizens of Galveston in front of the library.

[*Henry Rosenberg, 1824–1893* (1918), pub. by the Rosenberg Lib.; J. H. Brown, *Indian Wars and Pioneers of Tex.* (n.d.); scrapbook of clippings chiefly from the *Galveston News* and *Galveston Tribune*, 1871–1904, and manuscripts and other data collected by Frank C. Patten, librarian, for the Rosenberg Library.]

O. F. R.

ROSENBLATT, JOSEPH (May 9, 1882–June 19, 1933), cantor, concert artist, was born in a small South Russian town, Biélaya Tzerkov (White Church), near Kiev, capital of the Ukraine, the tenth child of Raphael Shalom and Chäyé Sarah (Prylutzky) Rosenblatt. His father was a synagogue precentor of some ability. At eight years of age Joseph was already touring Central Europe, officiating as boy-cantor in synagogues of Germany and Austria and giving sacred concerts. His chief protector, Dr. Bloch, editor of the Vienna *Wochenschrift,* was extremely active in fostering and glorifying this wonder-boy. At fourteen, Rosenblatt began to compose, and in 1900, when he was eighteen, he received his first appointment, that of cantor of the Munkácz synagogue in Hungary. Soon after, in competition with forty others, he won the coveted position of chief cantor in Pressburg, a major Austrian city. In 1906 he became the chief cantor at the largest Hamburg synagogue, one of the most prominent positions in the Jewish cantorate, but even this success did not stop his ardent studies in music.

His fame brought him at last, in May 1912, an invitation to officiate at the Ohab Tzedek Congregation of New York and he then emigrated to America, destined soon to become one of the most beloved singers of the country of his adoption. Possessing a nature of rare kindliness and generosity, he was easily persuaded to tour the United States in 1916 for the benefit of sufferers in the World War. His first great triumph took place on May 19, 1918, however, when a concert of classical, secular, and synagogal music at Carnegie Hall, New York, brought him enthusiastic acclaim from the public and the press. He immediately received lucrative and flattering offers from the Chicago Opera Company and other operatic organizations; but his strong Orthodox convictions, as well as a noble conception of his duties to Levitical functions and the worldly behavior appropriate to the same, made him firmly refuse all offers of operatic appearance. A Jewish paper to which he had given financial support failed in 1926, involving him in a heavy indebtedness. He then resigned his position as cantor that he might earn money on the concert stage to meet his obligations. In 1923 he gave brilliant concerts in almost every European country. In 1928 he again gave concerts in Europe, and in 1929, in South America. Finally, in March 1933 he was able to realize his life-dream, that of visiting and concertizing in Palestine. His career was cut short, however, by his death, in Jerusalem, after a short illness, when he was at the height of his artistic power and fame. He was buried on the Mount of Olives, twenty thousand people attending his funeral. His wife, Taube (Kaufman) Rosenblatt, member of a prominent family of Brzesko, Austria, whom he married in 1900, and eight children survived him.

Rosenblatt left a number of compositions, among them a choral setting for Psalm CXIII, dedicated to President Harding; an effective synagogal *Uvnucho Yomar* for cantor and choir; and a collection of his own cantorial recitatives, published in Hamburg and New York. Of these synagogal songs the most interesting is *"Elohai neshomo"* (My Lord, the soul, you have given me) and *"K'gavno."* They have a modal freshness and a spiritual charm that come from the true Hebrew melodic instinct and the fineness of the composer's soul. As a singer, he was famous for the ease, flexibility, power, and brilliance of his tenor voice. He was endowed with a natural vocal virtuosity, faultless pitch, and a *falsetto* that was world-known.

[*Musical America,* June 22, 1918, July 1933; *Am.-Jewish Chronicle,* May 24, 1918; *Musical Courier,* June 24, 1933; *N. Y. Times,* June 19, 1933.]

L. S.

ROSENFELD, MORRIS (Dec. 28, 1862–June 22, 1923), poet, was born in Bokscha, Suwalki, at that time part of Russian Poland, the son of Ephraim Leib Rosenfeld and his wife, Rachel Wilchinsky. His ancestors for several generations had been fishermen; his father a military tailor. He received at home the education allotted to Jewish boys of humble family, and studied Hebrew and the Talmud. When his father moved to Warsaw later, he acquired some knowledge of Polish and German. At the age of eighteen he was married to Bella Guttenberg, and with the birth of his first child began a bitter struggle for a livelihood. In 1882 he went to London and learned the tailoring trade. After a short stay in England he proceeded to Amsterdam, Holland, where he tried his hand at diamond-grinding. In 1886 he emigrated to the United States, where he remained until his death.

For fourteen wretched years he eked out a miserable existence as a presser and tailor in the sweatshops of New York City, and their squalor and oppression are well reflected in his plaintive muse. But earlier in London he had already composed melodious threnodies which touched the hearts of his readers, themselves the toilers and oppressed. At the end of a long day with the needle he would take up the pen, and sing the sorrows and woes of the underdog. Two years after his arrival in New York City he printed his first collection of folk and revolutionary songs, *Die Glocke*; another collection, *Die Blumenkette,* appeared in 1890; and, in 1917, *Dos Liderbuch.* He also made occasional contributions to the Yiddish press, but Yiddish journalism was then in so precarious a state financially that he was unable to live from his pen and continued to work in the sweatshop. Here he would probably have remained had it not been for Leo Wiener of Harvard University, who was drawn by the unusual talent displayed in *Dos Liderbuch.* Wiener at once introduced him to the outer world in 1898 by publishing his *Songs from the Ghetto,* containing some of Rosenfeld's poems with a prose translation, glossary and introduction. This booklet aroused a great interest in the poet both in America and abroad, and he was enabled to devote himself entirely to literature. He became editor and contributor to several Yiddish papers; wrote poetry and prose sketches; gave readings at Harvard and the University of Chicago, at Wellesley and Radcliffe colleges, and in many cities in Europe.

Morris Rosenfeld stands out as the most original poet in Yiddish literature. His fiery talents express themselves in many fields but his genius is at its highest in his depiction of the sad fate of the poor and oppressed. Himself one of the submerged tenth, he was the mouthpiece of the victims of a dehumanized society. Dramatic action and lyric indignation are welded into one in his poems, among which "My Boy," "Whither," "Despair," "Songs of Labor" or "Sephirah," "On the Bosom of the Ocean," "The Jewish May," "The Candle Seller," are already considered classics. Wiener characterizes the poet in these terms: "It was left for a Russian Jew at the end of the nineteenth century to see and paint hell in colors not attempted by any one since the days of Dante; Dante spoke of the hell in the after-life, while Rosenfeld sings of the hell on earth, the hell that he has not only visited, but that he lived through . . ." (Wiener, *post,* 130). Rosenfeld lived to see his poems translated into many languages: English, German, Hebrew, Russian, Roumanian, Polish, Bohemian, Hungarian, and many of his songs were set to music. Adolf von Sonnenthal, the great Viennese actor, included Rosenfeld's poems in his program of dramatic recitals.

During the last few years of his life his health was seriously impaired and he lived a lonely existence. He was stricken with paralysis and died soon after his sixtieth birthday. His funeral was attended by thousands of the working class and he was buried in the plot of the Workingmen's Circle at Mount Carmel Cemetery, New York City. His wife and children survived him.

[Leo Wiener, *The Hist. of Yiddish Literature in the Nineteenth Century* (1899); foreword by Alex. Harkavy, *The Works of Morris Rosenfeld* (3 vols., 1908); M. Pines, *Di Geschichte fun der Yiddisher Literatur* (1911), vol. II; Zalmen Reisen, *Lexicon fun der Yiddisher Literatur,* vol. IV (1929); *N. Y. Times,* June 22, 25, 1923.]   I. S.

ROSENTHAL, HERMAN (Oct. 6, 1843– Jan. 27, 1917), author, librarian, was born in Friedrichstadt, province of Courland, then part of Russia, a son of Moritz Rosenthal and Pauline Birkhahn. He was educated at the district school in Bausk and the progymnasium in Jakobstadt, both in Courland. He soon acquired a phenomenal command of Hebrew, German, and Russian, and was equally at home in the literature of all three languages. At the age of sixteen he commenced writing poetry of his own and translating into German the poems of famous Russian poets. In 1870 he published a collection of poems, *Gedichte,* while he was employed in a printing establishment in Krementchug, Russia. During this period he was also a contributor to *Hameliz* and other Hebrew periodicals, and in 1872 he published a humorous story, *Die wunderliche Kur.* Four years later he assisted in founding a Russian daily, *Zarya,* in Kiev. He served in the Russian Red Cross during the Russo-Turkish war and received the society's medal for distinguished services.

Soon after his arrival in the United States in 1881 Rosenthal began to carry out a long-cherished plan to found agricultural colonies for Russian Jews who had been compelled to emigrate to the United States due to the repressions of the Czarist régime, and, along with Michael Heilprin [*q.v.*], became one of the pioneers of Jewish colonization in the United States. While still in Russia he had been deeply interested in the promotion of culture among the Jews, and in the United States he desired to further these efforts along economic lines. He succeeded in founding the first agricultural colony of Russian Jews in Louisiana in December 1881. Soon afterward he organized another in South Dakota, and in 1891 took a prominent part in the administration of a settlement in Woodbine, N. J. He also identified himself with other movements and societies for the furtherance of liberty and enlightenment, but his chief services were enlisted on behalf of his co-religionists. As German poet, English essayist, Hebrew and Russian scholar, he used all four languages to fight for his ideals, to ease the burden of the oppressed, and to shed light upon the history and achievements of the Jews in Russia and Poland. In 1887 and 1888 Rosenthal was in the book trade, but gave up business to become chief statistician for the Edison Electric Company. At the request of James Jerome Hill [q.v.], he went to Japan, China, and Korea, 1892–93, to investigate economic conditions and trade in the interests of the Great Northern Railway. In 1894 he was appointed chief of the discharging department of the Immigration Bureau at Ellis Island. In 1898 he accepted the post of chief of the Slavonic division at the New York Public Library, which he held until his death.

Rosenthal was a contributor to the *Staatszeitung* and the *Outlook* in New York, and to other periodicals. Together with Abraham Hayyim Rosenberg [q.v.], he edited a Hebrew monthly, *Ha-modia le-hodashim*, from 1900 to 1902. In 1900 he became a member of the editorial board of the *Jewish Encyclopedia* as chief of the Russian department, and his historical knowledge, his brilliant style, and linguistic proficiency were of high value to this great enterprise. He rendered into German verse the book Ecclesiastes, *Worte des Sammlers* (1885); Song of Songs, *Lied der Lieder* (1893); was the author of *Spätherbstnebel, Poems* (1906); *Report on Japan, China and Corea* (1893); *A List of Russian, other Slavonic and Baltic Periodicals in the New York Public Library* (1916); and translated into English Hugo Ganz' *The Land of Riddles* (1904), and the *Memoirs of a Russian Governor, Prince Serge Dmitriyevich Urussov* (1908). In June 1864 he was married to Anna Rosenthal of Vilna. Their two sons survived him.

[*Who's Who in America*, 1916–17; *The Jewish Encyc.*, vol. X; *Library Jour.*, Feb. 1917; *Am. Hebrew*, Feb. 2, 1917; J. D. Eisenstein, *Ozar zikhronothai* (1929); *N. Y. Times*, Jan. 31, 1917.]   I. S.

ROSENTHAL, MAX (Nov. 23, 1833–Aug. 8, 1918), lithographer and mezzotint engraver, was born in Turck, near the city of Lodz, in what then was Russian Poland. He was the youngest of six children of Wolf and Rebecca Rosenthal. His father was a chemist and glass manufacturer, his mother a talented amateur sculptor, and his eldest brother, David, an artist, who is said to have surreptitiously painted altar pieces for churches near his home. When he was twelve, young Rosenthal was sent to Paris to study art and escape conscription in the Imperial Russian Army, which recognized the Jewish rule of regarding a boy as of age at thirteen. In Paris he was apprenticed to Martin Thurwanger, a lithographer, and in 1849 was brought by Thurwanger to the United States, where color lithography was struggling in the darkness of ignorance. Though his master remained only eighteen months, Rosenthal decided to stay with his elder brother, Louis, who was living in Philadelphia. He studied in the school of the Pennsylvania Academy of the Fine Arts and afterwards worked for a time in the establishment of Napoleon Sarony in New York. When Louis Rosenthal started his own business about 1850, Max returned to Philadelphia to work for him and subsequently entered into partnership with him, working chiefly in chromolithography, then a comparatively new field. Within a short time Max Rosenthal produced the illustrations for C. W. Webber's *The Hunter-Naturalist* (1851) and in the same year made some color lithographs for H. L. Stephens' *The Comic Natural History of the Human Race* (1851). For Matthias W. Baldwin, the locomotive builder, he produced large color lithographs of some of his locomotives. His large view of the interior of Masonic Hall, Philadelphia, published in 1854, attracted great attention as a remarkable example of pen lithography and the largest piece of chromolithography produced in the United States up to that time. During the first years of the Civil War, Rosenthal followed the Army of the Potomac, making sketches of the camps which he published in lithographic reproductions. About 1870 he began to make a series of lithographic portraits for such collectors as Dr. Thomas Addis Emmet and David McN. Stauffer of New York, and E. Coppee Mitchell and Ferdinand J. Dreer of Pennsylvania; these, about two hundred in all, were copies of portraits of distinguished Americans of whom no engraved portraits existed. About 1882 he began to etch, and before he retired from that field had produced about a hundred and fifty portraits of eminent American and British officers of the Revolutionary period. It was not until 1892, however, that he began the really important work of his artistic life. In that year he began experiments in mezzotint engraving and, having mastered it, devoted most of his remaining years to the production of important mezzotint engravings. He won so conspicuous a place among American engravers in this field that his reputation is likely to rest upon these achievements, though he turned to painting toward the end of his career. The majority of his mezzotint plates were portraits.

usually of eminent American statesmen, generals, and jurists. In 1859 Rosenthal had been married in Philadelphia to Caroline Rosenthal, who, though of the same name, was not related to him; their son Albert became a portrait painter.

[Who's Who in America, 1918–19; Who's Who in Pa. (1904); D. McN. Stauffer, Am. Engravers Upon Copper and Steel, vol. I (1907); The Print Connoisseur, Sept. 1921; List of Portraits, Lithographs, Etchings, Mezzotints by Max Rosenthal and Albert Rosenthal (1923); Harry T. Peters, America on Stone (1931); obit. notice in Public Ledger (Phila.), Aug. 9, 1918.]

J. J.

ROSENTHAL, TOBY EDWARD (Mar. 15, 1848–Dec. 23, 1917), genre and portrait painter, born in New Haven, Conn., was the son of Jacob and Ernestine (Germanus) Rosenthal. The family moved to New York in 1857 and to San Francisco in 1861, where Toby began the study of drawing and painting under Henri Bacon and Fortunato Arriola. In 1865 he was sent to Munich, where he continued his art education at the Bavarian Royal Academy for some seven years under Alexander Straehuber, Karl Raupp, and Carl von Piloty. He took a studio in Munich and exhibited there frequently, taught classes in painting and design, became a trustee of the Kunstgenossenschaft, and in all respects was thoroughly imbued with the methods and ideals of the Munich school. In 1880 he married Sophie Ansbacher of Nürnberg. He made occasional visits to the United States and from time to time sent pictures to the American exhibitions.

One of the earliest of his figure pieces to elicit more than casual attention from the public was his "Sebastian Bach and his Family at their Morning Devotions" (1870), purchased by the Leipzig museum. "Elaine," exhibited in Boston, New York, and Philadelphia in 1875 and 1876 and subsequently acquired by the Art Institute of Chicago, aroused still greater interest; for this work the artist was awarded a medal at the Centennial Exhibition of 1876 in Philadelphia, where his "Young Monk" was also shown. One of the critics characterized "Elaine" as "a good loud translation of our household Tennyson into the dialect of Munich" (quoted in Isham, post, p. 378), and another writer could not find in it any trace of "a lofty or subtle insight for beauty personal to the artist" (Ibid.). Still another commentator (Art Journal, vol. I, 1875, p. 126) considered that "the wisdom of choosing so sad a subject" was doubtful. Nevertheless, in 1876 the picture was a strong popular favorite, for Rosenthal's vein of sentimentality appealed to a very large element of the pub-lic. His "Vacant Chair," which was sold for $650 in New York in 1909; his "Trial of the Escaped Nun, Constance de Beverley" (1883), a motive taken from Sir Walter Scott's Marmion; his "Dancing during the Empire," and a number of similar compositions were received with pronounced approbation both in Germany and America. He was given a medal at one of the international exhibitions held in Munich, and he received the cross of the Bavarian Order of St. Michael. Isham commends his workmanship but points out that, while he had mastered the Munich technique thoroughly, he had also accepted the mental and emotional viewpoint of the school, so that one will not find in his works a trace of anything distinctly American. He died in Munich in the seventieth year of his age.

[Am. Art News, Jan. 5, 1918; Boston Transcript, Dec. 29, 1917; Am. Art Annual, 1918; Samuel Isham, The Hist. of Am. Painting, 1905; Zeitschrift für Bildende Kunst, vol. XIX (1884), p. 263; Who's Who in America, 1910–11; obituary in Berliner Tageblatt und Handels-Zeitung, Dec. 24, 1917.]

W. H. D.

ROSENWALD, JULIUS (Aug. 12, 1862–Jan. 6, 1932), merchant and philanthropist, was the son of Samuel and Augusta (Hammerslough) Rosenwald. He was born in Springfield, Ill., almost directly across the street from the house where Abraham Lincoln lived, and he was undoubtedly influenced by the strong Lincoln tradition. He was educated in the public schools of Springfield, and in 1879 began his business career with Hammerslough Brothers, wholesale clothiers of New York City, remaining with that concern until 1885. He then became president of Rosenwald & Weil, a Chicago clothing firm, continuing in that capacity until 1906. From 1895 to 1910 he was vice-president and treasurer of Sears, Roebuck & Company; from 1910 to 1925, president; and until his death, chairman of the board of directors. On Apr. 8, 1890, he married Augusta Nusbaum of Chicago, who died May 23, 1929; to this union were born five children—two sons and three daughters. On Jan. 8, 1930, he married Adelaide (Rau) Goodkind, mother of the wife of his eldest son.

Rosenwald built up a great establishment through seeing the possibilities of the mail-order business, appreciating his own limitations, and surrounding himself with experts. He will be remembered, however, as a philanthropist and humanitarian. He attended the religious services of Chicago Sinai Congregation, of which he was vice-president, regularly; and he freely confessed that he derived his social vision and social passion from that source. His good works covered a wide range. He was one of the leaders and pioneers who brought about the Federation of Jewish Charities in Chicago in 1923. As a member of the American Jewish Committee, he helped to protect the Jew against unjust discrimination. Feeling that the Jewish problem in Russia must be worked out in Russia itself, he contributed six million dollars to further a plan for the colonization of Jews in that country. Through his far-sightedness, the Hebrew Union College of Cincinnati, and the Jewish Theological Seminary of America, in New York City, were put on a firm financial footing, though not endowed. In helping the former, he paid a tribute to Isaac M. Wise [q.v.]; in assisting the latter, he memorialized a warm friend, Louis Marshall [q.v.]. Though never a Zionist and not sympathetic with any form of Jewish nationalism, he gave to the Hebrew University of Jerusalem and to other cultural agencies in Palestine, and aided in the relief of the unfortunate of that country. He believed that Jews are a people and not a nation; he interpreted Judaism in terms of service to humanity.

His philanthropies transcended the prejudices of race, creed, country, and nationality. The most of his gifts were made through the Julius Rosenwald Fund, which he created in 1917. Its chartered purpose was the "well-being of mankind." In 1929 its capital amounted to $30,000,000, and his will provided that principal as well as interest should be spent within twenty-five years after his death. He helped to establish colleges in Assyria and Constantinople. Immediately after the World War, he fed the hungry children of Germany; later, he established a dental clinic in Berlin. His contributions to work for the advancement of the negro were doubtless the outstanding feature of his philanthropy. Feeling that it was wrong to give without causing others to give, and especially without insisting that those who were to be helped make an effort in their own behalf, he contributed part of the total cost (about $3,850,000) of twenty-five negro Young Men's Christian Association, and three negro Young Women's Christian Association buildings in twenty-five cities with approximately 2,000,000 negro population. Like Booker T. Washington, he felt that the salvation of the negro lay in education. He also contributed $3,660,000 toward the total cost of $23,200,000 for 4,500 negro public schools in the South; 339 of these were built in 1929.

As a citizen of Chicago, Rosenwald was socially minded and gifted with civic vision. He was one of the founders of the Municipal Voters League. As a member of the Committee of Fifteen, he was fearlessly active in banishing the "red light district." The Public Efficiency Bureau found him among the most conscientious in trying to minimize graft and corruption. During the race riots in Chicago he served valiantly to restore peace and good will. He was an ardent champion of the Chicago Planning Commission, and president of the Jewish Charities of Chicago. He gave to the city, in 1929, an industrial museum, to be known as the Museum of Science and Industry founded by Julius Rosenwald. His gifts to the University of Chicago amounted to almost five million dollars, but money was the least part of his contribution to this institution, for he later gave his thought, his vision, his energy, and his enthusiasm during more than twenty years of service on its board of trustees.

Rosenwald had no sympathy with jingoism and chauvinism, he abhorred war, but both in war and in peace he served his country. In 1916 President Wilson appointed him a member of the Advisory Commission of the Council of National Defense and chairman of the committee on supplies. At the request of the secretary of war, he went on a special mission to France in 1918, and was a member of the Second National Industrial Conference in 1919. His Americanism was manifest in his abounding faith in the common man; he believed that the common sense of the common man was uncommonly good. He loved maxims, some of which he created; others, many of which motivated him, he appropriated. He did not believe in endowments, feeling that endowments for specific purposes intended for a blessing, may, and frequently have, become a curse. He sought to influence foundations not to tie up great sums in perpetuity. His articles, "Principles of Public Giving" and "The Trend Away from Perpetuities" (*Atlantic Monthly,* May 1929, December 1930) created history in the realm of philanthropy. In season and out of season, he would say: "I believe that large gifts should not be restricted to narrowly specified objects, and that under no circumstances should funds be held in perpetuity. . . . I have confidence in future generations and in their ability to meet their own needs wisely and generously" (*Ibid.,* May 1929, p. 606). He died in Chicago, survived by his wife and all his children.

[B. C. Forbes, *Men Who Are Making America* (1917); Edwin Wildman, *Famous Leaders of Industry,* 2 ser. (1921); *Who's Who in American Jewry,* 1928; *Who's Who in America,* 1930–31; L. L. Mann, *Julius Rosenwald, A Memorial Tribute* (1932); *Jour. of Negro Hist.,* Apr. 1932; Graham Taylor, in *Survey,* Feb. 1, 1932; *N. Y. Times,* Jan. 7, 8, 1932.] L. L. M.

ROSEWATER, EDWARD (Jan. 28, 1841–Aug. 30, 1906), Nebraska journalist and politician, was born in the village of Bukowan,

Bohemia. His parents, Herman and Rosalia (Kohn) Rosenwasser, were of German Jewish descent, but were Bohemian rather than German in sentiment. Edward went to school in Prague until he was thirteen, learned German of a tutor, and in 1854 came with his parents and their eight other children to the United States. The Rosenwassers settled in Cleveland, changed their name to Rosewater, and were speedily absorbed into the main currents of American life.

The boy Edward found work, first as a store clerk, later as a book-keeper, and after 1858 as a telegrapher. When the Civil War broke out he was stationed in the South, where he remained until 1862. He then entered the United States military telegraph corps, and served with Frémont in West Virginia, with Pope during his disastrous Virginia campaign of 1862, and with the War Department at Washington. In 1863, he yielded to the persuasions of Edward Creighton [q.v.] and accepted a position with the Pacific Telegraph Company at Omaha, Nebr. Through his connection with this company, and later with other western telegraph lines, Rosewater learned much about the sources of news. He established a news bureau to contribute items from the Rocky Mountain area, and became an agent of the Associated Press.

With this background, his transition to the newspaper world was easy. After a brief connection with the *Omaha Daily Tribune*, he made his real début into newspaper work with the establishment of the *Omaha Daily Bee* in 1871. That year, as a member of the Nebraska legislature, he had advocated the creation of a school board for the city of Omaha. Such a measure passed the legislature, but had to be submitted to the voters of the city for their approval. To insure ratification of the project at the polls, Rosewater established the *Bee,* a sort of tabloid newspaper "not much larger than a full-page theater program," as a medium for his arguments. The *Bee* was at first distributed without cost, but its spicy editorials and its well-chosen telegraphic news won such hearty support that when the campaign for a better school system was won the *Bee* lived on. Enlarged to the usual newspaper size and offered to subscribers as an afternoon daily, it outstripped its local competitors and soon became one of the outstanding newspapers in the United States. Rosewater was always among the first to adopt the latest improved methods of publication, he maintained unabated his keen sense of news values, and he fought valiantly through his editorials for the rights of the common man. Had the *Bee* been less vigorous in its denunciation of railway

abuses, probably Rosewater would have won in 1901 the seat in the United States Senate that he coveted.

Rosewater was a loyal citizen of Omaha and contributed in many ways to the material advancement of that city. The *Bee* building, an eight-story fire-proof structure erected in 1887–88, was long regarded as one of the architectural triumphs of the West. The Trans-Mississippi Exposition, held at Omaha in 1898, was originally projected by Rosewater, and he, more than any other man, was responsible for its conspicuous success. He was married on Nov. 13, 1864, to Leah, daughter of Loeb and Ella Colman, of Cleveland, Ohio, by whom he had five children. Shortly before his death he handed over to his two sons, Victor and Charles, the active management of the *Bee*. He died suddenly, in August 1906, without having shown previously any signs of failing health.

[*Omaha Daily Bee,* Sept. 1, 2, 1906; J. S. Morton, Albert Watkins, and G. L. Miller, *Illus. Hist. of Nebr.,* I (1905), 744–46, using material furnished by Rosewater himself; A. C. Edmunds, *Pen Sketches of Nebraskans* (1871); *Who's Who in America,* 1903–05; additional information from Victor Rosewater, Esq., of Philadelphia.]   J. D. H.

ROSS, ABEL HASTINGS (Apr. 28, 1831–May 13, 1893), Congregational clergyman, was born in Winchendon, Mass., the seventh of the nine children of Phineas and Betsey (Marshall) Ross. The family lived at different times on farms in Winchendon, Gardner, and Ashburnham, and the boy's life was one of poverty and hard labor. Lacking financial backing, he gained his education by his own indomitable persistence. After some study at Winchendon Academy, he entered the preparatory department of Oberlin in 1851 and the college in 1853, graduating from the latter in 1857. Returning to New England, he continued his studies at Andover Theological Seminary, from which he was graduated in 1860. Ordained in the Congregational Church at Boylston, Mass., on Oct. 17, 1861, he served as pastor there until 1866, being absent for several months during the Civil War in the service of the Christian Commission. His other pastorates were at the First Church, Springfield, Ohio, 1866–73; Plymouth Church, Columbus, Ohio, 1873–75; and Port Huron, Mich., 1876–93, where he died. From 1871 to 1891 he was lecturer on church polity at Oberlin Theological Seminary and from 1882 to 1886, Southworth Lecturer on Congregationalism at the Andover Theological Seminary.

Ross was an authority on the history and polity of the Congregational denomination and one of its best known and most influential leaders. He early realized the imperfections of the denominational organization and the loss of power resulting therefrom, and he labored for a generation to correct them. "There can be no doubt," it has been said regarding his service to Congregationalism, "that our churches owe more to him than to almost any other man of his generation for their growing sense of a common life and of the need and the possibility of a more perfect union in their fellowship and their activities" (W. H. Ryder, in *Andover Theological Seminary Necrology,* 1892–93, p. 90). He was a strong advocate of an ecumenical Congregational council which should be advisory in its nature but destitute of authority, and like the local and national councils of the denomination, should not infringe on the independency of the churches. His views on this subject set forth in his article "An Ecumenical Council of the Congregational Churches" (*Congregational Quarterly,* April 1874) bore fruit in the International Congregational Council in London in 1891, in the proceedings of which he had a prominent part. He was a constant contributor on social, denominational, and religious subjects to the reviews and quarterlies, and was the author of twenty-three books and pamphlets. His *Church-Kingdom* (1887), comprising his Southworth Lectures at Andover, is of permanent value, and his *Pocket Manual of Congregationalism* (1889) ranks as one of the best treatises on the polity of that order. Other publications of his worthy of mention are *The Ohio Manual; Statement of the Historical, Doctrinal and Ecclesiastical Position of the Congregational Churches* (1877); *The Church of God; a Catechism* (1881); *Sermons for Children* (1887); *Immanuel Catechism for Infant Classes* (1893). His literary work was marked by clearness of definition and lucidity of statement and when on controversial ground he was fair and good tempered. His simple and sincere manner and kindly spirit gained him a wide circle of friends. On Oct. 15, 1860, he married Mary Maria Gilman, an Oberlin classmate, who survived him.

[*Congregational Year Book,* 1894; *Congregationalist,* May 18, 1893; *Advance,* May 18, 1893; *Detroit Tribune,* May 15, 1893; information from the secretary of Oberlin College and several of Ross's friends.]
F. T. P.

ROSS, ALEXANDER (May 9, 1783–Oct. 23, 1856), fur trader, explorer, author, was born in Nairnshire, Scotland, the son of Alexander Ross, a farmer. He received a good education and on his emigration to Canada in 1804 obtained employment as a schoolteacher. At Montreal, in May 1810, he met Wilson Price Hunt [*q.v.*], with whom he engaged as a clerk of Astor's Pacific Fur Company and in September sailed from New York on the *Tonquin.* He aided in the building of Fort Astoria, and later of Fort Okanogan, of which he was several times in charge. In 1813 he married an Indian woman, an Okinagan, by whom he had several children and to whom he remained devotedly attached. In 1814, following the sale of Astoria, he joined the North West Company and in 1816 was second in command at Fort George. He was a member of the expedition that in July 1818 founded Fort Nez Percés, popularly known as Fort Walla Walla, where he remained in charge for more than five years. For a time after the absorption of the North West Company by the Hudson's Bay Company he continued at his post. In the fall of 1823 he resigned and started east but was persuaded to lead an expedition into the Snake River country. Leaving Flathead House, at the present Eddy, Mont., on Feb. 10, 1824, he penetrated the present Idaho as far as the mouth of Boise River, unexpectedly encountering six American trappers, led by Jedediah S. Smith [*q.v.*]. By November he was back at his starting place. In the spring of 1825, with his wife and children, he again started east but halted at the Red River colony, where he was to reside for the remainder of his life. On the site of the present Winnipeg he received a grant of 100 acres of land. He was appointed the colony's first sheriff and retained the post for many years. His *Adventures of the First Settlers on the Oregon or Columbia River* was published in London in 1849. Six years later came *The Fur Hunters of the Far West* in two volumes and in 1856 *The Red River Settlement.* Many years after his death a few of his letters were published by George Bryce in *Transactions of the Historical and Scientific Society of Manitoba* (No. 63, 1903) and his journal of the Snake Country expedition in 1824 was edited by T. C. Elliott in the *Quarterly of the Oregon Historical Society* (December 1913). He died in "Colony Gardens," now a part of Winnipeg. His widow, familiarly known in her later days as "Granny Ross," survived him by thirty years.

Ross was a man of exceptional abilities and was greatly esteemed by all who knew him, white and red alike. For the first fourteen years of the white man's occupation of Oregon he was an energetic and influential participant in the activities of the region, and for the history of a considerable part of the period he remains almost the sole first-hand authority. The captious criticism of his writings in Bancroft (*post,* esp. I, 579 and II, 238) has been generally disregarded by later students.

[Autobiog. material in own writings, esp. letters edited by Bryce, *ante; H. J. Morgan, Bibliotheca Canadensis* (1867); H. H. Bancroft, *Hist. of the Northwest Coast* (2 vols., 1884); H. M. Chittenden, *The Am. Fur Trade of the Far West* (1902), vols. I, III; H. W. Scott, *Hist. of the Oregon Country* (1924), vols. I–III, comp. by L. M. Scott; *Canadian Mag.*, June 1917; *Queen's Quarterly*, July 1903.]   W. J. G.

ROSS, ALEXANDER COFFMAN (May 31, 1812–Feb. 26, 1883), song writer and jeweler, was born in Zanesville, Ohio, one of twelve children of Elijah and Mary (Coffman) Ross. Elijah Ross, who like his wife had been born in Pennsylvania, settled in Zanestown, afterwards Zanesville, in 1804. He was a gunsmith and during the War of 1812 was ordered to remain at home to repair guns, swords, and military accoutrements. The son became familiar at an early age with the repair and manufacture of guns in the little shop kept by his father, soon learned to handle tools, and at seventeen was apprenticed to a jeweler of the town. After completing his knowledge of his trade in New York, he returned to Zanesville and on Apr. 2, 1838, married Caroline Granger, by whom he had three children. He died in Zanesville. As a boy he had supplemented the elementary education he received at home by reading as widely as possible, especially on scientific subjects; and although he was a jeweler by trade until his retirement in 1863, he never lost his early interests. An amateur photographer, he took in 1839 what he believed to be the first daguerreotype taken in the United States west of New York; he afterwards made improvements in his process and took good daguerreotype portraits as early as 1843. He was a lover of music as well; in New York he had been a member of an orchestra led by Ureli C. Hill [*q.v.*] and later was influential in bringing many musical troupes to Zanesville. He also had a fondness for the circus and was quick to pick up the popular songs that in those days were sung by the clowns.

It was his interest in both popular songs and politics that brought him his chief distinction. In the presidential campaign of 1840, which has been popularly known as the "Log Cabin and Hard Cider Campaign" but was preëminently also the campaign of music and song, he took an active part. For a Zanesville club, organized in enthusiastic support of Harrison and Tyler, Ross wrote to the tune of "Little Pigs" the famous "Tippecanoe and Tyler, Too," contriving the chorus in church, it is said, while the sermon was being given. Soon afterward, at a great Whig meeting in Lafayette Hall, New York, at which he was present, the chairman called for some one to sing a song before the speaking began. Ross volunteered and, answering the questions of the crowd as to his identity with "I am a Buckeye, from the Buckeye state," sang his song, the chorus of which was as follows:

For Tippecanoe and Tyler, too—Tippecanoe and Tyler too;
And with them we'll beat little Van, Van, Van,
Van is a used-up man;
And with them we'll beat little Van.

It was followed by a storm of cheers, encored over and over again, and almost overnight became throughout the country the most popular song of the campaign.

[C. B. Galbreath, in *Ohio Archaeological and Hist. Quart.*, Jan. 1905; J. N. Granger, *Launcelot Granger of Newbury, Mass., and Suffield, Conn.: A Geneal. Hist.* (1893); *Cincinnati Enquirer*, Feb. 26, 1883; letters from the Ross family.]   C. B. G—h.

ROSS, ARAMINTA [See TUBMAN, HARRIET, *c.* 1821–1913].

ROSS, BETSY (Jan. 1, 1752–Jan. 30, 1836), legendary maker of the first stars-and-stripes, was born in Philadelphia, the eighth of the seventeen children of Samuel and Rebecca (James) Griscom, and a great-grand-daughter of Andrew Griscom, a carpenter, who emigrated from England to West Jersey in 1680 and later moved to Philadelphia. The building business that he established was continued by Betsy's father. She is supposed to have attended the Friends' school in South Fourth Street and early evinced an aptitude for fine needlework. She also evinced considerable independence of mind, for on Nov. 4, 1773, she eloped to Gloucester, N. J., with John Ross, son of the Rev. Æneas Ross of New Castle, Del., and was there married to him. The next May the Society of Friends disowned her, with evident reluctance, for marrying out of meeting. For a number of years she attended Christ Church and later, with her third husband, became a loyal member of the Society of Free Quakers.

Ross opened an upholsterer's shop on Arch Street, on the site of what is now No. 233, and the young couple lived on the premises. On Jan. 21, 1776, Ross, then a soldier in the militia, was killed by an explosion of gunpowder on a wharf that he was patrolling. Throughout the uncertain years that followed Mrs. Ross continued to carry on the business. The well-known story of her making the first stars-and-stripes at the behest of Washington, Robert Morris, and George Ross, is based on a family tradition that was first made public by her grandson, William Canby, in a paper that he was permitted to read before the Historical Society of Pennsylvania in March 1870. That making flags was a part of her business is attested by the minutes of the Pennsylvania State Navy Board, which, on May 29, 1777, ordered the payment to her of £14/12/2 for "making ships' colours, etc." (*Pennsylvania Archives*, 2 ser., vol. II, 1874, p. 164), but other documentary evidence has not been found. The stars-and-stripes was adopted as the national flag June 14, 1777, by a resolution of the Continental Congress (*Journals of the Continental Congress, 1774–89*, vol. VIII, 1907, p. 464). Whatever her connection with the flag, it could hardly have been as important or romantic as her descendants supposed. On June 15, 1777, at Old Swedes' Church, Wicaco, she married Capt. Joseph Ashburn, by whom she had two daughters. The brigantine *Patty,* of which he was first mate, was captured at sea by the British. Ashburn died Mar. 3, 1782, in the Old Mill Prison, Plymouth, England. Word of his death was brought to his widow by his fellow prisoner, John Claypoole, who had been a life-long friend of them both. Betsy and he were married May 8, 1783. They had five daughters. Claypoole died Aug. 3, 1817, and Betsy spent the last years of her long life in the home of one of her daughters. Her remains now rest in Mount Moriah Cemetery.

[E. S. Parry, *Betsy Ross, Quaker Rebel* (1930); Lloyd Balderston, *The Evolution of the Am. Flag* (1909), from materials collected by Geo. Canby; G. H. Preble, *Hist. of the Flag of the U. S.* (2nd rev. ed., 1880); Byron McCandless, "The Story of the Am. Flag," *Nat. Geographic*, Oct. 1917; Morton Pennypacker, "Capt. John Hulbert and His Flag of 1775," *N. Y. Hist.*, Oct. 1933; A. J. Wall, "The Flag with an Eagle in the Canton," *N. Y. Hist. Soc. Quart. Bull.*, Oct. 1933; Joseph Jackson, "Arch Street's Place in the Annals of Old Phila.," *Public Ledger* (Phila.), Nov. 30, 1913; J. W. Jordan, *Colonial Families of Phila.*, II (1911), 1250–51; R. I. Graff, *Geneal. of the Claypoole Family of Phila.* (1893), pp. 68–76; *N. Y. Times*, May 28, 1933; *Evening Star* (Washington), June 14, 1933.]   G. H. G.

ROSS, EDMUND GIBSON (Dec. 7, 1826–May 8, 1907), journalist, United States senator, was born at Ashland, Ohio, the son of Sylvester F. and Cynthia (Rice) Ross. When he was about ten years old he was apprenticed to a printer at Huron, and, after learning the trade, he traveled for some years as a journeyman printer. In 1848 he married, at Sandusky, Fanny M. Lathrop, the daughter of Rodney Lathrop of New York. He lived for a time at Janesville, Wis., and for four years at Milwaukee, where he was foreman of the job printing office of the *Sentinel*. Although born a Democrat, Ross, in his own words, was "baptized in politics in the old Abolition party of 1844." Joining the Republican party in 1856, with the spirit of a crusader he led a colony of free-state settlers, heavily armed, to Kansas, driving an oxteam all the way. Here he began a period of great activity against the pro-slavery party. In 1857 he and his brother bought the Topeka *Kansas Tribune,* and two years later

founded the *Kansas State Record* (Topeka), which they sold in 1862. He was a member of the Wyandotte Constitutional Convention of 1859 from Wabaunsee. In 1862 he enlisted in the 11th Kansas Regiment and later recruited a company and became its captain. A brave and dashing soldier, he was promoted to major in 1864, and served on the Missouri border until the war ended. In 1865 he became editor of the Lawrence *Tribune.*

The following year he was appointed to the United States Senate to succeed James H. Lane [*q.v.*], who, mentally deranged, partly because of criticism of his support of President Johnson, had committed suicide. Interestingly enough, Ross was one of his critics. The appointment was popular and in 1867 the legislature elected him to fill out the term. He entered the Senate an intense Radical and an earnest opponent of Johnson. He voted for all the radical measures of reconstruction, including the tenure-of-office act, of which, however, he was quite doubtful. When Johnson removed Stanton in January 1868, Ross voted for the Senate resolution declaring the act illegal. After the President's impeachment, however, he was insistent that Johnson should have a fair trial and voted on many questions with the known opponents of conviction, notably in connection with the admission of evidence for the defense. The rumor spread among the Radicals that Ross was "shaky," and he was continually importuned by them, flooded with letters and telegrams from Kansas. At this time he rather favored conviction, but the character of the pressure upon him made him doubtful. In answer to a telegram of instruction from Kansas, he replied: "I have taken an oath to do impartial justice . . . and trust I shall have the courage and the honesty to vote according to the dictates of my judgment and for the highest good of the country" (*Scribner's, post,* p. 521). His final conclusion to vote against conviction for lack of evidence, was reached in face of the belief that he would thereby secure his own political destruction. He said later: "I almost literally looked down into my own grave. Friends, position, fortune, everything that makes life desirable to an ambitious man, were about to be swept away by the breath of my mouth, perhaps forever" (*Ibid.,* p. 524). The burst of bitter denunciation which followed the first vote fell most heavily on Ross. He was a "poltroon and traitor," it was said; "littleness had borne its legitimate fruit"; "Kansas repudiates you as she does all perjurers and skunks," were the words of a telegram from his home state (Dewitt, *post,* p. 545). Charges of corruption were made and every species of pressure known to politicians was exerted. Ross "bore the ordeal with the fortitude of a stoic and the inscrutability of a sphinx" (*Ibid.*, p. 574), and again voted "not guilty." Immediately thereafter he demanded an investigation of the charges against him, but none was ever made. Several times, however, he defended his position in the Senate (*Congressional Globe*, 40 Cong., 2 Sess., pp. 2598–99, 4513–17). During the remainder of his term, which ended in 1871, he was an independent. He favored the absolute repeal of the tenure-of-office act, and supported the Fifteenth Amendment although he believed that Congress had power to grant negro suffrage.

At the conclusion of his term he returned to Kansas and published a weekly newspaper at Coffeyville. In November 1879 he began to edit the Lawrence *Standard* and in February of the following year bought the Leavenworth *Press* and merged the two. He left the Republican party in 1872, partly because of its treatment of him, but also because of his dislike of the protective system and the character of Grant's administration. For the rest of his life he was a Democrat, although he violently opposed Bryan and free silver. In 1876 he was a Democratic candidate for elector and in 1880 for governor, but was badly beaten. Two years later he moved to New Mexico and became again a journeyman printer. Cleveland appointed him governor of the territory in May 1885, and he filled the position for four stormy years of struggle with what he asserted was a corrupt ring, antagonizing Democrats as well as the Republican legislature. In 1893 he was an unsuccessful candidate for reappointment. He spent the rest of his life in Albuquerque. Shortly before his death a messenger brought him greetings from the governor and legislature of Kansas, expressing appreciation of his conduct in the impeachment trial. He was utterly fearless, honest, and of good ability, but lacked tact, was brusque and headstrong, and, in the words of an opponent, "rejoiced in opposition." Two sons and three daughters survived him.

[Information concerning Ross himself appears in his *Hist. of the Impeachment of Andrew Johnson* (1896) and in articles by him in *Forum*, July 1895, and *Scribner's Mag.*, Apr. 1882. See also D. M. Dewitt, *Impeachment and Trial of Andrew Johnson* (1903); D. W. Wilder, *The Annals of Kan.* (1886); *Trans. Kan. State Hist. Soc.*, vols. I, II (1881); R. E. Twitchell, *The Leading Facts of New Mexican Hist.*, II (1912), 496–502; *Albuquerque Morning Jour.*, May 9, 10, 1907.]
J. G. deR. H.

ROSS, ERSKINE MAYO (June 30, 1845–Dec. 10, 1928), federal judge, son of William Buckner Ross and Elizabeth Mayo (Thom), was born in Belpré, Culpeper County, Va., the fourth of five children. On his father's side his ancestry was English, and on his mother's, Scotch. As a boy he attended the Virginia Military Institute, and while enrolled as a cadet there participated in various engagements in the Civil War. He graduated in 1865, and on Sept. 11 of that year, together with Otis Allen Glazebrook and Alfred Marshall, organized the Alpha Tau Omega college fraternity in Richmond, Va. Projected as a national organization, it was the first such fraternity to be formed after the Civil War (W. R. Baird, *Baird's Manual, American College Fraternities*, 12th ed., 1930). The thirty-first congress of the fraternity, held in Los Angeles in 1929, was known as the Ross Memorial Congress.

In 1868 Ross began the practice of law in Los Angeles. He soon obtained a commanding position in the legal profession of Southern California, in 1879 was elected justice of the state supreme court for the short term, and in 1882 was reëlected for the full term of twelve years. He resigned this position in 1886 to engage in private practice as a partner of Stephen M. White [*q.v.*], but within a year was appointed by President Cleveland to the federal district court of the southern district of California, and in 1895 advanced to the United States circuit court. This latter position he held until his resignation thirty years later, when he was nearly eighty years of age. His service on the federal bench is thus one of the longest on record (see letter from President Coolidge at the time of his retirement, *Los Angeles Times*, Dec. 11, 1928).

Ross's decisions were recognized for their clarity, impartiality, and fearlessness, and were seldom reversed by the higher courts. On Sept. 5, 1893, in the case of Chum Shang Yuen, a Chinese laborer resident in California, who had failed to register in accordance with the provisions of the so-called Geary Act of May 5, 1892, Ross upheld the validity of this act, and ordered the deportation of the defendant (57 *Fed. Reporter*, 588). The decision led to a bitter quarrel between the Judge and Richard Olney [*q.v.*], attorney general of the United States, who was opposed to the enforcement of this particular section of the act, but in California the decision was exceedingly popular. On July 22, 1895, Judge Ross declared the so-called Wright Irrigation law unconstitutional under the "due process" clause, thereby invalidating some millions of dollars worth of bonds, and throwing the water laws of California into great confusion (68 *Fed. Reporter*, 948). His decision confirming the title of Leland Stanford Junior University to its endowment made possible the continuation of that great educational institution (69 *Fed.*, 25; 161 *U. S.*, 412). Of greater significance both from a legal and a social point of view was his decision, at the time of the Pullman strike in 1894, in the case of W. H. Clune and three associates, that a concerted action of a number of individuals to prevent the transportation of trains with Pullman cars was an unlawful conspiracy punishable as such, and in contempt of the Court's order against interference with the transportation of mail and interstate commerce (62 *Fed. Reporter*, 834). In his charge to the Grand Jury in connection with this case he stated that "no man has a legal or moral right while continuing in the employment of another to refuse to do the work he is employed and engaged to do" (p. 835).

Ross was a charter member of the California Club, one of the five founders of the city of Glendale, and a horticulturist of note. The suburb of Glendale known as Rossmoyne perpetuates his name. On May 7, 1874, he married Ynez Hannah Bettis; one son was born of this marriage. After the death of his first wife, he married, June 1, 1909, Ida Hancock, widow of Henry Hancock of Los Angeles; she died in 1913. Ross died in Los Angeles, leaving by his will nearly a quarter of a million dollars to various philanthropic and educational institutions, including $100,000 as a prize foundation to the American Bar Association.

[J. C. Bates, *Hist. of the Bench and Bar of Cal.* (1912); Willoughby Rodman, *Hist. of the Bench and Bar of Southern Cal.* (1909); O. T. Schuck, *Hist. of the Bench and Bar of Cal.* (1901); *An Illustrated Hist. of Los Angeles County, Cal.* (1889); *Am. Bar Asso. Jour.*, Feb. 1929; *Los Angeles Times*, Mar. 17, 1925, Dec. 11, 1928; scrapbook deposited by Judge Ross shortly before his death with the librarian of the Los Angeles County Law Library.]   R. G. C.

ROSS, GEORGE (May 10, 1730–July 14, 1779), jurist, signer of the Declaration of Independence, eldest son of the Rev. George Ross and his second wife, Catherine Van Gezel, was born at New Castle, Del. His father, a graduate of the University of Edinburgh, prepared for the Presbyterian ministry, but, deciding during his studies that this Church was too censorious and hypocritical, he took orders in the Church of England, came to America as a missionary, and for many years served as rector of Immanuel Church, New Castle. George received a classical education and studied law with his step-brother, John, of Philadelphia. Following his admittance to the bar in 1750, he established himself at Lancaster, Pa., his ability as a lawyer soon winning him an extensive practice. One of his first clients was a beautiful and accomplished lady of Scotch-Irish descent, Anne Lawler, whom he married Aug. 17, 1751, and by whom he had two sons and a daughter.

Excepting for twelve years' service as prosecutor for the Crown in Cumberland County, his political career began with his election to the provincial Assembly in 1768. During his seven years in that body he gained a reputation for his deep interest in Indian problems and for his championship of the Assembly in disputes with the governor. His growing political influence secured his election to the Provincial Conference at Philadelphia in July 1774, and to the First Continental Congress in the same year, though at this time he was generally recognized as a Tory. The following year, however, witnessed his conversion to the ranks of the Whigs, and as a member of the Assembly, of the Pennsylvania committee of safety, and of the Second Continental Congress to November 1775, he was one of the most untiring workers for the patriot cause in Pennsylvania. During this period he also saw brief service as a colonel of associators, and in 1776 assisted in negotiating a treaty to pacify the Indians of northwestern Pennsylvania. He was vice-president of the Pennsylvania constitutional convention of 1776, aided in drawing up the declaration of rights, and otherwise played a conspicuous part in the convention's deliberations. On July 20, 1776, the convention elected him to Congress, but illness compelled his withdrawal in January 1777. For several years after its inauguration he was a firm friend of the new state government, but in 1779, like many of his lawyer brethren, he began to feel that the evils of the times demanded constitutional revision.

On Mar. 1, 1779, he was commissioned judge of the admiralty court of Pennsylvania, although he had been serving in that capacity earlier, and as such had sat in the famous case of the sloop *Active*. Though his sympathies were with the plaintiff, Gideon Olmsted [q.v.], the jury found the Connecticut captors entitled to only one fourth of the prize and Ross held that he was bound by law to confirm this verdict. When the committee on appeals of Congress reversed his judgment he defied that body and declared he would submit to no usurpation of the power of his court. In an elaborate vindication of his action he contended that the court of appeals had authority to set aside the decree of a judge in a question of law, but there its power ended; that under Pennsylvania's law the verdict of the jury was conclusive upon the facts without an appeal (*U. S.* vs. *Judge Peters*, 5 *Cranch*, 115 at p. 120). In the midst of the controversy between Congress and the state of Pennsylvania, which dragged on for more than thirty years, Ross died suddenly, in Philadelphia, from a violent attack of the gout. Noted for his genial manner and good humor, he loved conviviality, and on his death bed complacently remarked that he was going on a long journey to a cool place—"there were most excellent wines there"—and he should fare deliciously.

[*Hist. Papers and Addresses of the Lancaster County Hist. Soc.*, vol. I (1897); H. P. Read, *Rossiana* (1908); *Pa. Archives*, 1 ser. VI, VII (1853), 2 ser. III (1875); *Minutes of the Provincial Council of Pa.*, vols. X–XII (1852–53); *Pa. Mag. of Hist. and Biog.*, IV (1880), 230, 257–58; vol. XVI (1893), pp. 385–98; *Pa. Evening Post* (Phila.), July 16, 1779.] J. H. P.

ROSS, JAMES (July 12, 1762–Nov. 27, 1847), lawyer, United States senator, son of Joseph and Jane (Graham) Ross, was born near Delta, York County, Pa. His grandfather, Hugh Ross, of Scotch ancestry, came to America from northern Ireland about 1723. James studied the classics at Slate Ridge Presbyterian Church school and at an academy in Pequea, Pa. At the age of eighteen he was induced by the Rev. John McMillan, a close friend of the Ross family, to go to western Pennsylvania, where he taught Latin and Greek in McMillan's academy near Canonsburg (now Washington and Jefferson College, Washington, Pa.). He had originally intended to enter the ministry, but while he was at Canonsburg, Hugh Henry Brackenridge [*q.v.*], a Pittsburgh lawyer, persuaded him to take up law, and in 1782 encouraged him to continue his studies at Philadelphia. He returned to Washington County in 1784 and was admitted to the bar. Specializing in land cases, he soon acquired a large practice, and in 1795 moved to Pittsburgh. He was attorney for President Washington's estates in western Pennsylvania and numbered among his clients prominent and wealthy business men.

His first connection with state politics was as a member of the Pennsylvania constitutional convention in 1789–90. A member of the committee that drafted the new frame of government, he was a stanch Federalist and attracted attention by his zealous advocacy of a clause for religious liberty similar to that in the federal Constitution. During the Whiskey Insurrection (1794) he used his influence to restrain popular fury against the federal government. President Washington appointed him one of the federal commissioners to treat with the insurgents and his efforts were in a large measure responsible for the amicable settlement of the uprising, and the saving his friend Brackenridge from prosecution for treason. In 1794 the Pennsylvania legislature elected him to the United States Senate in place of Albert Gallatin [*q.v.*],

who was disqualified on account of the residence requirement. Reëlected in 1797, he served until 1803, and in 1799 was president *pro tempore* of the Senate. A firm believer in Hamiltonian ideas and policies, he worked diligently, though unsuccessfully, in 1800, to keep Pennsylvania in the Federalist ranks and to insure a national victory for his party by urging the passage of an act under which the legality of electoral votes for president and vice-president would have been decided by a grand committee composed of the chief justice and six members from each house of Congress. Under the Republican administration he defended Federalist legislation against Jeffersonian attacks, notably the excise law and the Judiciary Act of 1801, asserting that the repeal of the latter would erect Congress into "a complete tyranny" and render the judiciary totally subservient to Congress (*Annals of Congress*, 7 Cong., 1 Sess., p. 166). A series of resolutions introduced by him on Feb. 16, 1803, following Spain's withdrawal of the right of deposit at New Orleans and designed to embarrass the administration and provoke war with Spain, demanded the immediate seizure of the mouth of the Mississippi River, the fortification of its banks, and then negotiations for navigation advantages. In 1799, 1802, and 1808 he was Federalist candidate for governor of Pennsylvania, but the high tide of Jeffersonianism, his liberal religious views, and his refusal to canvass the state conspired in each instance to defeat him. From 1816 to 1833 he was president of the Pittsburgh select council, but otherwise he was not active in politics after 1808, his law practice and land speculations, which proved highly profitable, engaging his attention. He was distinguished for his polished manner, his legal learning, and his forensic ability, and displayed an independence of judgment which sometimes cost him political preferment. His wife, whom he married on Jan. 13, 1791, was Ann, daughter of George Woods, of Bedford, Pa. He died at Allegheny City, now a part of Pittsburgh, survived by one son.

[J. I. Brownson, *The Life and Times of Senator James Ross* (1910); Boyd Crumrine, *Hist. of Washington County, Pa.* (1882); Thomas Mellon, "Reminiscences of the Hon. James Ross," in *Western Pa. Hist. Mag.*, July 1920; *Annals of Congress*, 1794–1803; *Pa. Mag. of Hist. and Biog.*, XIII (1889), 4; *Biog. Dir. Am. Cong.* (1928); *Daily Morning Post* (Pittsburgh), Nov. 30, 1847.] J. H. P.

ROSS, JOHN (Oct. 3, 1790–Aug. 1, 1866), Cherokee chief, was born near Lookout Mountain, Tenn., the son of David and Mary (McDonald) Ross. His Indian name was Cooweescoowe or Kooweskowe. His father was a

Scotchman of Loyalist sympathies who had settled among the Cherokee at the close of the American Revolution, and his mother was also Scotch but of one-fourth Cherokee blood. He was taught at home by a private tutor and later attended the Kingston academy in Tennessee. In 1809 he was sent by the United States Indian agent on a mission to the western Cherokee, who had removed to what was then the wilderness region of Arkansas. During the War of 1812 he served as adjutant of a Cherokee regiment in the army of Andrew Jackson and fought in the battle of Horseshoe Bend against the Creeks. In 1817 he became a member of the national council of the Cherokee, and, made president of that body in 1819, he served until 1826. He helped draft the Cherokee constitution of 1827 and in that year was elected assistant chief. In 1828 he was elected principal chief of the eastern Cherokee and held this position until 1839. Many times he was in Washington with a Cherokee delegation to oppose removal. He became the leader of the Cherokee party opposed to westward removal, and, in spite of Major Ridge [q.v.] and the treaty party, he resisted the efforts of the federal government to force them to leave their fertile lands. After all his efforts had failed, in 1838–39 he led his people to their new home in what is now Oklahoma and helped make the constitution of 1839, uniting the eastern and the western Cherokee under one government. Chosen chief of this united Cherokee Nation in 1839, he held office until his death, though his right to it was disputed by the Southern wing of Cherokee and by the government of the United States for a time during the period of the Civil War. At the outbreak of the Civil War he sought to keep the Cherokee neutral but in October 1861 signed a treaty of alliance with the Confederacy, which was repudiated in 1863.

He was married in 1813 to a full blood Cherokee woman called Quatie, who died at Little Rock, Ark., in 1839 on the way to Indian Territory. In 1845 he was married to Mary Bryan Stapler of Wilmington, Del., a white woman of the Quaker faith who was many years his junior. She died in 1865. He was of aristocratic training and manner. His home near Park Hill resembled the "mansion houses" of the Old South and was surrounded by fields cultivated by his numerous slaves. When Northern troops invaded Indian Territory in 1862, he went to Philadelphia, which he continued to make his home. He died in Washington, D. C., where he had gone to assist in making the Cherokee treaty of 1866. He has had many violent critics as well as many warm defenders. That he had great ability as a statesman and diplomat cannot be questioned, and the fact that he was for nearly forty years the head of his nation is evidence that he possessed the confidence of a majority of his people.

[Papers in files of Office of Indian Affairs, Washington, D. C., and in possession of Univ. of Okla., the Okla. Hist. Soc., and various members of Ross family in Okla.; John Howard Payne MSS. in Newbury Lib., Chicago; A. H. Abel, *The Slaveholding Indians* (3 vols., 1915–25); R. C. Eaton, *John Ross and the Cherokee Indians* (1921); F. H. Hodge, *Handbook of Am. Indians*, pt. II (1910); Emmet Starr, *Hist. of the Cherokee Indians* (1921).]   E. E. D.

ROSS, LAWRENCE SULLIVAN (Sept. 27, 1838–Jan. 3, 1898), Confederate soldier, governor of Texas, was born at Bentonsport, Iowa. His father, Capt. Shapley P. Ross, and his mother, Catherine (Fulkerson) Ross of Virginia, moved to Texas about 1839, where Captain Ross was Indian agent. Young Ross was graduated from Wesleyan University, Florence, Ala., in 1859. He spent his vacations in service against the Comanche Indians on the Texas frontier, and was once dangerously wounded. In 1859 Governor Houston made him captain of a company of rangers employed to guard the border and to crush the Comanches. In one engagement he rescued a white woman, Cynthia Ann Parker, who had been captured at Parker's Fort in 1836 and who later became the mother of Quanah [q.v.]. Ross killed Chief Peta Nocona in a hand-to-hand combat. Gen. Winfield Scott then offered him a commission in the United States Army and Governor Houston made him an aide-de-camp with the rank of colonel. He entered the Confederate service as a private, was made major of the 6th Texas Cavalry in September 1861, and was promoted to the rank of colonel in May 1862. As a result of his skill in covering the retreat of General Van Dorn from Corinth, Miss., he was made a brigadier-general on Feb. 5, 1864. He returned, penniless, to his home in 1865 at the age of twenty-seven, with a long record of 135 military engagements behind him and facing the prospect of earning a livelihood on the Texas frontier. He engaged in farming with marked success in the Brazos bottom and soon bought a plantation, where he reared and educated his children.

He served two arduous years as sheriff of McLennan County, having been elected in 1873 when lawlessness in Texas was at its height. As a member of the state constitutional convention of 1875, he advocated a policy of retrenchment but urged long terms and adequate salaries for judges. As a state senator from 1881 to 1885, he supported the policies of Governors Oran Milo Roberts and John Ireland, 1827–1896 [*qq.v.*], for economy in government, improvement in elementary and higher education, and a stricter enforcement of the laws. During the two terms Ross served as governor, 1887–1891, Texas enjoyed unusual peace, progress, and prosperity. He led and advised the legislature in passing laws which prohibited dealing in cotton futures, enlarged the powers of the land commissioner, and closed the sale of public lands to corporations. A beginning was made in the regulation of railroads and in the fight for the railroad commission which was established during the administration of his successor. He was the first governor to occupy offices in the new capitol building.

Ross served as president of the Agricultural and Mechanical College of Texas at College Station from 1891 until his death. Governor Culberson offered him an appointment as railroad commissioner in 1895, and he accepted, but the news of his contemplated withdrawal from the college aroused such great opposition from friends and patrons that he reconsidered and declined the new office. His death resulted from an illness contracted from exposure while enjoying his favorite sport, fox hunting, on the Trinity River. He was buried in Waco and his funeral was attended by a crowd estimated at thirteen thousand people. He was married at Waco in 1859 to Elizabeth Tinsley. His widow and six children survived him. In his public life he made no pretense of being an effective speaker, but was endeared to Texans because of his common sense, patriotism, and inflexible honesty.

[Sinclair Moreland, ed., *Governors' Messages, Exec. Series, Archives and Hist. Dept., Tex. State Lib. Coll.* (1916) ; D. G. Wooten, *A Comprehensive Hist. of Tex.* (1898), vol. II ; *House* and *Senate Jour.*, 1881–91 ; S. S. McKay, *Debates in the Texas Constitutional Convention of 1875* (1930) ; *Confed. Mil. Hist.* (1899), vol. XI ; F. M. Clarke, "A Chapter in the Hist. of Young Territory," *Quart. of Tex. State Hist. Asso.*, July 1905 ; Elizabeth Brooks, *Prominent Women of Tex.* (1896), p. 67 ; *Houston Daily Post*, Jan. 4, 1898 ; *Dallas Morning News*, Jan. 6, 1898.]   S. S. M.

ROSS, MARTIN (Nov. 27, 1762–1827), Baptist clergyman, was born in Martin County, N. C., third of the ten children of William Ross, a Scotchman from Virginia. His childhood and youth were probably those of the normal farmer's son. Entering the Revolution as a boy, he served until its close. In January 1782 he joined the neighboring Baptist Flat Swamp Church. The next year he married Deborah (Clayton) Moore, widow of James Moore, and in 1806, Mary Harvey, widow of Miles Harvey, each of

whom bore him children. Licensed to preach in 1784, he was pastor of Skewarkey, Martin County (1787–96), Yoppim, Chowan County (1796–1806) and Bethel, near Hertford on the road to Edenton (1806–27). Francis Asbury in 1804 found him "much thought of," left him "in great affection," visited him again in 1806 (*The Journal of the Rev. Francis Asbury*, 1821, III, 132, 189). Cool and competent Thomas Meredith (*post*) declared him "dignified," "chaste and instructive in his conversation," in all private relations "amiable and exemplary," a "mild and humane master," "a useful citizen," of a hospitality "plain but cordial and substantial," in his ministerial character combining "those qualities which were useful, rather than dazzling."

Without discouraging or undervaluing the remarkable emotional revivals of his day, Ross emphasized the formation of churches and the discipline of members, and in 1826 wrote the circular letter of the Chowan Association on discipline. While the lowly and illiterate were asserting themselves in loud and lengthy "sermons" and even sensible men were contending against pay for preachers, he openly deplored his early lack of formal education, read and reflected much, gave useful advice publicly to other preachers, and boldly argued on grounds of professional usefulness as well as Scripture that preachers ought to "live of the gospel" (circular letters, Kehukee Association, 1791, Chowan Association, 1809). Finding the Baptists of the Kehukee Association out of line with "that missionary spirit which the great God is so wonderfully reviving amongst the different denominations of good men in various parts of the world" (Hassell, *post*, p. 721), he promoted a famous meeting at Cashie Meeting-house (near Windsor) in June 1805, where the pioneering "Philanthropic Missionary Society" was formed. Three years later he was working for a "Meeting of General Correspondence," composed of delegates from the Kehukee and its daughter associations. His proposal (modified the next year to conform to the Virginia manner) led to a joint meeting of all North Carolina Associations each year from 1811 to 1820, with missions apparently the main interest. In 1826 he began working for a North Carolina Baptist State Convention, which he apparently intended should foster ministerial education as well as missions. Though ill health and domestic affliction blocked him in this endeavor, in 1830, under the immediate leadership of Thomas Meredith, his neighbor, friend, and successor at Bethel, the Convention was constituted. This powerful organization today recognizes him as its father.

[N. C. Chowan Baptist Association, *Minutes*, especially 1828, containing Thomas Meredith, "Memoir of Elder Martin Ross"; C. B. and Sylvester Hassell, *Hist. of the Church of God* (copr. 1886), which largely follows Lemuel Burkitt and Jesse Read, *A Concise Hist. of the Kehukee Baptist Asso.* (1803) and Joseph Biggs, *Concise Hist. of the Kehukee Baptist Asso.* (1834); J. D. Hufham, "The Baptists in N. C.," in *N. C. Baptist Hist. Papers*, July 1898; N. C. Baptist State Convention, *The Growth of One Hundred Years* (1930); G. W. Paschal, *Hist. of N. C. Baptists* (1930), vol. I.]

C. C. P.

ROSSER, THOMAS LAFAYETTE (Oct. 15, 1836–Mar. 29, 1910), soldier and engineer, was born on his father's farm in Campbell County, Va., the eldest son of John and Martha Melvina (Johnson) Rosser. When the boy was thirteen, John Rosser, experiencing reverses, emigrated to the sparsely settled Sabine River country in Texas. Here Thomas, working with his father and a few slaves in developing the frontier plantation, grew up; a stalwart youth, six feet, two inches tall, endowed with extraordinary strength and endurance. By rigid economies his parents sent him, at sixteen, to a school at Mount Enterprise, Tex. On July 1, 1856, he entered West Point, becoming a member of the five-year class that was graduated in May 1861 without him for, at the outbreak of the Civil War, he resigned. George A. Custer [*q.v.*], who entered in 1857, was an intimate friend.

Hastening South, Rosser was assigned to the Washington Artillery as first lieutenant, serving creditably at first Manassas. Promoted captain, he was severely wounded in May 1862 on the Peninsula. On his return to duty, General Stuart obtained his commission as colonel of cavalry, giving him the 5th Virginia Regiment, which he commanded brilliantly for fifteen months. Leading the van when Pope's headquarters were captured at Catlett's Station, distinguishing himself at second Manassas, South Mountain, and in many cavalry engagements, he abundantly demonstrated the abilities which caused Stuart to pronounce him "a fine artillerist as well as bold Cavalier" (*Official Records, 1* ser., vol. XII, pt. 2, p. 737).

On May 28, 1863, he married Betty Barbara Winston, of Hanover Court-House, and in September, following the Gettysburg campaign, was promoted brigadier-general. Assuming command of the noted Laurel Brigade at Buckland Mills in October, he roundly defeated Custer, who thenceforth became his perennial rival. Rosser contributed decisively to the Confederate victory at Trevilian (June 11, 1864), and in October went to the Shenandoah Valley to command Early's cavalry. Largely outnumbered, he suffered defeat by Custer at Woodstock (Oct. 8). But though beaten again at Cedar Creek (Oct. 18), he kept his troops keen by independent operations, and was promoted major-general on Nov. 1, 1864. In December he raided New Creek, W. Va., taking 700 prisoners, 3,000 horses and cattle, and destroying the railroad shops at Piedmont. The following month, with 300 picked men, he crossed the snow-covered mountains and surprised and captured two entire regiments at Beverly, W. Va. After Pickett's defeat at Five Forks (Apr. 1, 1865), Rosser's division held the Southside Railroad open during the following night, and behaved with desperate valor throughout the subsequent retreat, twice successfully attacking pursuing Union cavalry and taking many prisoners. At Appomattox Rosser charged through the Union lines with two cavalry divisions and escaped to Lynchburg, thus avoiding surrender with Lee's army. He was captured, however (May 2), near Hanover Court-House.

Hard-pressed after the war to support his family, in 1871 Rosser found employment with the Lake Superior & Mississippi Railroad and in 1872 with the Northern Pacific. By ability and energy he soon became chief engineer of the latter, superintending construction to Livingston, Mont. In the Indian country his friendship was renewed with Custer, whose troops often guarded Rosser's surveyors. After a period as chief engineer of the Canadian Pacific (1881–86), Rosser, having acquired a competence, in 1886 purchased a fine property, "Rugby," near Charlottesville and became a gentleman farmer. Commissioned brigadier-general, United States Army, by President McKinley in 1898, he commanded a brigade of Northern volunteers at Chickamauga throughout the Spanish-American war. In 1905 he was appointed postmaster at Charlottesville, and was filling this office when he died. Two daughters and a son survived him. Rosser was a gifted cavalry leader of the audacious American school. Many of his operations deserve attentive study, while his courage and resolution throughout a stormy life compel enduring admiration.

[J. M. Hanson, "Thomas Lafayette Rosser," in *Cavalry Journal*, Mar.–Apr. 1934; W. N. McDonald, *A Hist. of the Laurel Brigade* (1907); H. B. McClellan, *The Life and Campaigns of Major-General J. E. B. Stuart* (1885); J. W. Thomason, Jr., *Jeb Stuart* (1930); C. A. Evans, ed., *Confed. Mil. Hist.*, III (1899), pp. 658–60; E. L. Wells, *Hampton and His Cavalry in '64* (1899); *War of the Rebellion, Official Records (Army)*, 1 ser., esp. vol. XLIII, pts. 1, 2, and vol. XLVI, pt. 1; Frederick Whittaker, *A Complete Life of Gen. George A. Custer* (1876); letters to the author from Thomas L. Rosser, Jr., Malcolm E. Rosser, and from officials of the Northern Pacific and Canadian Pacific Railroads; obituaries in *Confederate Veteran*, Aug. 1910; *Times Dispatch* (Richmond), Mar. 30, 1910.]

J. M. H.

ROSSITER, THOMAS PRICHARD (Sept. 29, 1818–May 17, 1871), historical and portrait painter, born in New Haven, Conn., was the son of Harry Caldwell and Charlotte (Beers) Rossiter and a descendant of Edward Rossiter, who came to America in 1630 and settled in Connecticut. He began the study of drawing and painting in New Haven under Nathaniel Jocelyn, and by the time he was twenty had taken a studio and begun the painting of portraits. In 1840 he sailed for Europe in company with A. B. Durand, J. F. Kensett, and J. W. Casilear. After studying six months in London and traveling through England and Scotland, he spent a year with Kensett in Paris, where he studied in a life class made copies in the Louvre. In the fall of 1841 he went with Thomas Cole by way of Switzerland to Rome; there he took a studio in the Via Felice and passed five consecutive winters studying in the museums and painting, his summers being given to travel in Italy, Germany, and Switzerland. After his return to America in 1846, he settled in New York, where, on Oct. 15, 1851, he married Anna Ehrick Parmly, and the same year, with Kensett and Louis Lang, moved into a new studio in Broadway which had been planned and built especially for them. In the spring of 1853, he again set forth on extended travels abroad and in December took a studio in Paris, where he stayed almost three years. He exhibited in the Salon of 1855 and received a gold medal. He had previously (1849) been elected to the National Academy of Design.

In the summer of 1856 he returned to New York and was kept busy painting portraits until October 1857, when he began several large historical compositions, notably his well-known "Washington and Lafayette at Mount Vernon, 1776," also called "Palmy Days," which was bequeathed to the Metropolitan Museum, New York, in 1905. This large painting, finished in 1859, depicts Washington in a dark blue coat and knee-breeches, standing on the veranda of his house in conversation with Lafayette. Mrs. Washington and Nellie Custis are seated at a table, with a little girl beside them; on the lawn is a boy with a colored nurse and two dogs. In the distance, beyond a line of trees, is the Potomac. The landscape part of the work was done by Louis R. Mignot [*q.v.*]. In 1860 Rossiter left the city and moved to Cold Spring, N. Y., a beautifully situated village on the east bank of the Hudson, where he lived in a house that he designed and constructed for his professional purposes. There he made another historical picture entitled "The Prince of Wales and President Buchanan with Other Dignitaries at the Tomb of Washington, 1860," now in the National Gallery of Art, Washington. The painter's other contributions to Washingtoniana are "Washington in his Library at Mount Vernon" and "Washington's First Cabinet." He devoted much time towards the end of his life to a series of pictures of the life of Jesus. In earlier years he had made a number of large biblical illustrations, such as "The Return of the Dove to the Ark," "The Jews in Captivity," "The Parting of Ruth, Orpha and Naomi," and "Rebecca at the Well," the last being in the Corcoran Gallery of Art, Washington. He died suddenly in 1871 at his home on the Hudson, leaving three children.

[H. T. Tuckerman, *Book of the Artists* (1867); H. W. French, *Art and Artists in Conn.* (1879); Samuel Isham, *The Hist. of Am. Painting* (1905); *The Metropolitan Museum of Art: Cat. of Paintings* (1926); *The Nat. Gallery of Art: Cat. of Colls.* (1922); *Cat. of Paintings in the Corcoran Gallery of Art* (1908); *Bull. of the Metropolitan Museum of Art*, Nov. 1905, p. 10; death notice in *N. Y. Daily Tribune*, May 19, 1871.]

W. H. D.

ROSSITER, WILLIAM SIDNEY (Sept. 9, 1861–Jan. 23, 1929), statistician, publisher, was born at Westfield, Mass., the only child of Samuel E. Chadwick and Margaret Harvey (Rossiter). When the boy was five years old his parents were divorced, the mother being given custody of the child, and four years later his name was changed to that of his mother's father. His mother soon removed to Washington where she lived for many years with two unmarried sisters. The influence of a family friend, Julius H. Seelye, drew Sidney to Amherst College in 1880. After graduating (1884) he entered the business office of the *New York Tribune* and continued for sixteen years in newspaper work or publishing.

In 1900 he was given charge of printing and publishing for the Census Bureau, his duties being those of a liaison officer between the Bureau and the Government Printing Office. The appointment proved a turning point in his life. His new duties brought him into intimate contact with a group of statisticians who were interpreting the population statistics of the Census of 1900; this experience gave him what was virtually post-graduate training in economics and statistics; he wrote the reports on printing and publishing for the censuses of manufactures of 1900 and 1905, and in time the human significance of population statistics became perhaps his main intellectual interest. His lack of formal statistical training proved no handicap, for it emboldened him to go beyond the actual meaning of his figures. William Rush Merriam [q.v.], the director of the Census, leaned heavily on him, and Merriam's successor, Simon Newton Dexter North [q.v.], made him his chief clerk and acting director. Rossiter's management of the Census printing and his magazine articles on the subject led to his appointment in 1908 by President Theodore Roosevelt to investigate the increasing cost of government printing. His report (*House Document 974*, 60 Cong., 1 Sess.), besides contributing to the resignation of the Public Printer, made constructive recommendations which have influenced the subsequent administration of the Government Printing Office.

While superintending the publication of the names of heads of families recorded at the census of 1790, he prepared *A Century of Population Growth from the First Census of the United States to the Twelfth, 1790–1900* (Department of Commerce and Labor, Bureau of the Census, 1909), which contained an estimate of the proportion of English, Scotch, Irish, German, Dutch, and French blood in the population of the United States, based upon classification of families according to the stock indicated by the last name. Although he failed to allow adequately for the effects of translating or transforming foreign into English names and so overstated the proportion of English blood, he presented in this study an approximate solution of a problem previously thought insoluble, and his estimate in improved form is now used in determining immigrant quotas from European countries to the United States.

When Director North resigned, in 1909, as the result of a departmental controversy, Rossiter resigned also, and for some years thereafter divided his time between the drygoods business of R. H. Stearns & Company in Boston and the Rumford Press of Concord, N. H. The latter enterprise throve under his management until it absorbed all his energies. During the twenty years of his connection with it as treasurer, vice-president, and president, its employees increased ten-fold, the value of its capital twenty-fold, and the quality of its publication was equal to the best. In 1918 he persuaded the secretary of commerce to invite the American Statistical Association and the American Economic Association to cooperate with the director of the Census by appointing a joint advisory committee. Rossiter became its chairman and retained that post until his death. He had long

made his summer home in Vermont, first at Greensboro and later at Morgan, and in 1911 he printed "Vermont: an Historical and Statistical Study of the Progress of the State" in the *Publications of the American Statistical Association*. This had been planned as a state document and prepared with the cooperation of the federal Census Office. It was followed by several less technical articles and addresses, all contributing to the organization of state councils and the New England Council, which aimed to deal constructively with social and economic problems in that group of states. He was chairman of the New Hampshire Council and an active member of the New England Council. In 1922 he was president of the American Statistical Association and in this same year published *Increase of Population in the United States, 1910–1920* (Census Monograph No. 1). He was a loyal member of his college class, attended forty-eight of the annual reunions held for fifty years after graduation, and prepared and published the annual class record. On Oct. 21, 1891, he married Nellie C. Budd of New York; they had one child, a daughter. He died in Concord, N. H.

[Memorial volume containing Rossiter's published articles, placed by his class in the Amherst College Library; *Amherst Coll. Biog. Record* (1927); *Class of Eighty-four of Amherst Coll.: The Class Book* (1894); *Who's Who in America*, 1928–29; *N. Y. Herald Tribune*, Jan. 24, 1929; *Concord Daily Monitor* (Concord, N. H.), Jan. 24, 1929; personal acquaintance.]

W. F. W.

ROTCH, ABBOTT LAWRENCE (Jan. 6, 1861–Apr. 7, 1912), meteorologist, brother of Arthur Rotch [q.v.], was born and died in Boston, Mass. His father, Benjamin Smith Rotch, was a great-grandson of William Rotch [q.v.], the noted Nantucket merchant; his mother, Annie Bigelow (Lawrence), was a daughter of Abbott Lawrence [q.v.] of Boston, founder of the Lawrence Scientific School at Harvard. Rotch was therefore born to the possession of ample means and into a tradition of public service. He received his preliminary education from tutors and in private schools, then entered the Massachusetts Institute of Technology. Before his graduation in 1884 he conceived and carried into execution plans for the erection of an observatory on the summit of Great Blue Hill, ten miles south of Boston, for the study of weather phenomena. His purpose was to establish an institution free from official control, where investigation might be independent of prescribed duties and requirements. The building was completed by the close of 1884, and observations were begun Feb. 1, 1885. Rotch maintained the observatory at his own expense until his death in 1912, when he bequeathed it, with an endowment of $50,000, to Harvard University.

The study of cloud heights, directions, and velocities as carried on at Blue Hill is one of the best of American contributions to knowledge of the clouds. Rotch suggested the use of daily maps at local Weather Bureau stations, and defrayed the expenses connected with the issue of the first such map, at the Boston weather station in May 1886. An extensive traveler and an expert mountain climber, he visited and studied the equipment of nearly all European high-level observatories. He made the ascent of Mont Blanc six times, reaching the famous Vallot cabin five times and the summit thrice. He made two balloon ascensions from Paris, Nov. 12 and 14, 1889, in which modern instruments were used. On July 4, 1910, he took part in the International Balloon Ascensions at Strassburg.

He was much interested in the development of aeronautics, was one of the founders of the Aero Club of America, and also a prime mover and president of the Aero Club of New England and the Harvard Aeronautical Society. He was a firm believer in the ultimate success of flight through the air at a time when such belief was regarded as fantastic. He was a friend of Professor Samuel P. Langley [q.v.] and of the Wright brothers. These and others interested in aviation were welcomed spectators of the kite flights at Blue Hill in the late nineties. He was the pioneer in the United States in exploring the free air. In 1894 at Blue Hill he first used a kite to lift recording instruments; he was the first to obtain meteorological data by means of kites flown from the deck of a moving steamer (1901), by sounding balloons made the first observations in the United States at heights of five to ten miles (1904), and was the first to make trigonometric measurements of the flight of pilot balloons (1909). It was in large measure the success of his exploration of the free air that led Léon Teisserenc de Bort to found a private observatory for the study of dynamic meteorology at Trappes, near Paris, and, indirectly, led to the founding of the aeronautical observatory near Berlin under Richard Assmann. The important discovery by Teisserenc de Bort of the isothermal region, beginning about twelve kilometers above sea level in temperate latitudes, later named the stratosphere, may thus be considered in part a result of Rotch's work.

With Teisserenc de Bort in 1905 he cooperated in fitting out an expedition to explore the atmosphere over the tropical and temperate parts of the Atlantic Ocean, thus securing data which later were of great service in discussions of the best routes for transatlantic flying. With Andrew Henry Palmer he prepared and published *Charts of the Atmosphere for Aeronauts and Aviators* (1911), a first attempt at mapping the conditions of the upper air. He wrote two books, *Sounding the Ocean of Air* (1900) and *The Conquest of the Air* (1909), and contributed many papers to scientific periodicals; the bibliography of his publications comprises 183 titles. For more than a decade (May 1884–April 1895) he was associate editor of the *American Meteorological Journal*. He also edited the Blue Hill observations which after 1887 were regularly published in the *Annals of the Astronomical Observatory of Harvard College*.

Rotch was personally known to the leading meteorologists of Europe, for he made it a point to attend all meetings of the International Meteorological Committee, and on many occasions was the sole representative of the United States. His work was known and appreciated abroad more than at home. He was exceedingly modest, preferring to remain unnoticed, but always encouraging others and giving his assistants fullest credit. From 1888 to 1891 and from 1902 to 1906 he held the title of assistant in meteorology at Harvard, and in 1906 he became the first professor of meteorology there, in both these capacities serving without salary. For many years he was a trustee of the Massachusetts Institute of Technology and from 1899 was librarian of the American Academy of Arts and Sciences. Just before his death he was chosen as exchange professor for 1913 at the Sorbonne.

Rotch married, Nov. 22, 1893, Margaret Randolph Anderson of Savannah, Ga., a descendant of Thomas Jefferson. He was survived by his wife, two daughters, and a son.

[R. M. Lawrence, *The Descendants of Maj. Samuel Lawrence* (1904); Alexander McAdie, *The Founder of the Blue Hill Observatory* (1914); memoirs by R. DeC. Ward, in *Proc. Am. Acad. Arts and Sci.*, vol. XLVIII (1913), *Harvard Graduates' Mag.*, June 1912, and *Science*, May 24, 1912; Frank Waldo, "The Blue Hill Meteorological Observatory," *Pop. Sci. Mo.*, July 1901; *Quart. Jour. Royal Meteorological Society*, vol. XXXVIII (1912); *Who's Who in America*, 1912–13; *Technology Review*, May 1912; *Nature* (London), Apr. 25, 1912; *Boston Transcript*, Apr. 8, 1912.]
A.M.

ROTCH, ARTHUR (May 13, 1850–Aug. 15, 1894), architect, was born in Boston, the son of Benjamin Smith and Annie Bigelow (Lawrence) Rotch and brother of Abbott Lawrence Rotch [q.v.]. He was a grandson of Abbott Lawrence [q.v.] and a great-great-grandson of William Rotch [q.v.] of Nantucket. His immigrant ancestor on his father's side was an earlier William Rotch, who was in Salem before 1692 and went to Provincetown, Mass., in 1719, and whose son Joseph, moving to Dartmouth, on Buzzard's Bay, in 1765 to become a whaler, was one of the founders of the town of New Bedford. Arthur was educated at Mr. Dixwell's school in Boston and then at Harvard, from which he was graduated in 1871. He had long been interested in architecture, and in the fall entered the school of architecture of the Massachusetts Institute of Technology, where he remained two years, leaving to go to Paris and enter the École des Beaux Arts. In Europe he spent a leisurely period of almost seven years, traveling and studying not only architecture but painting—water color and decorative—as well. During this time he is said to have had charge of part of the restoration and redecoration of the château of Chenonceaux. Shortly after his return to Boston, he formed, in 1880, a partnership with George T. Tilden. Rotch and Tilden's work, which was principally domestic and ecclesiastical, comprised large houses in Boston, Washington, Bar Harbor, and Lenox, and the Churches of the Messiah and the Ascension in Boston, and of the Holy Spirit in Mattapan, Mass. It also included the art museum at Wellesley College, the Rindge Manual Training School at Cambridge, the gymnasium of Phillips Exeter Academy at Exeter, N. H., and public libraries at Bridgewater and Groton, Mass., and Eastport, Me. Rotch married, Nov. 16, 1892, Lisette de Wolf Colt, with whom he took an extended trip abroad. He had been for some time troubled with severe rheumatism, and the European trip did not help him; a trip south in the winter of 1893–94 was equally fruitless. He died the following summer at his summer home in Beverly, Mass.

Rotch is important for reasons far more significant than his own architectural work, which is often tentative and inconclusive. It is true that it is frequently more polished, more advanced than other work of the time, which was still trying vainly to follow the creative genius of H. H. Richardson [q.v.] and achieving for the most part only a pallidly picturesque incoherence; Ventfort Hall, at Lenox, is notably good Jacobean for the early nineties, and the Mattapan church, in the mid-eighties, remarkable in its attempt to achieve both academic polish and simple, direct picturesqueness. But Rotch's most important contribution was to the taste of his time and to architectural education. A man of large means, he stinted neither time nor money in aiding his beloved profession. He

was a trustee of the Boston Museum of Fine Arts (incidentally, an accomplished water colorist and a frequent exhibitor both in Boston and New York), and he was influential in the founding of the Rotch Traveling Scholarship endowed by his father in 1884 to enable draftsmen or architects under thirty who have worked two years in a Massachusetts office to have two years of study abroad. Moreover, he furnished the architectural library of Massachusetts Institute of Technology, and when the Harvard School of Architecture was founded in 1893 he financed its entire first year at his own expense. On his death he left $25,000 to the Boston Museum of Fine Arts and $40,000 to the school of architecture of the Massachusetts Institute of Technology.

[Daniel Ricketson, *The Hist. of New Bedford, Bristol County, Mass.* (1858); Z. W. Pease, "Arnold's Garden," in *Old Dartmouth Hist. Sketches,* No. 48 (1919), and Julia W. Rodman, "Samuel and Elizabeth Rodman, Their Forebears and Associates," *Ibid.,* No. 54 (1926); C. H. Jones, *Geneal. of the Rodman Family, 1620 to 1886* (1886); *Vital Records of New Bedford, Mass.* (2 vols., 1932); *Vital Records of Nantucket, Mass.,* vol. II (1926); C. E. Banks, *The Hist. of Martha's Vineyard,* vol. III (1925); *Am. Architect,* May 5, 1920; *Mass. Inst. of Technology, Ann. Report of the President and Treasurer* for 1892 and 1895; *Eleventh Report of the Class of 1871 of Harvard Coll.* (1921); obituaries in *Am. Architect and Building News,* Aug. 18, 1894, and *Boston Transcript,* Aug. 16, 1894.]
T.F.H.

ROTCH, THOMAS MORGAN (Dec. 9, 1849–Mar. 9, 1914), pediatrician, first cousin of Arthur and Abbott Lawrence Rotch [qq.v.], was born in Philadelphia, the son of Rodman and Helen (Morgan) Rotch. His father came of a New Bedford family, being a great-grandson of William Rotch [q.v.]; his mother was a collateral descendant of John Morgan [q.v.], the founder of the University of Pennsylvania medical school. Rotch was graduated by Harvard College in 1870 and by the Harvard Medical School in 1874. During the last year of his medical course he served, as was customary at the time, as house officer at the Massachusetts General Hospital. On June 4, 1874, he married Helen, daughter of his uncle, William J. Rotch of New Bedford. His internship was followed by two years of study abroad, particularly in Berlin, Vienna, and Heidelberg; he returned to Boston in 1876, a well-educated physician.

Rotch began at once the practice of pediatrics, a "specialty" unknown before his time; no other physician in the United States had yet attempted to limit his practice to patients in the first two years of life. Entering boldly into a field where the death rate was highest, he established in 1881 and became medical director of the West-End Nursery and Infants' Hospital, the first hospital in the United States to admit only patients with-in so restricted an age limit. As early as 1878 he began teaching pediatrics at the Harvard Medical School. The faculty of that institution were soon impressed by the value of his studies and in 1888 a chair of Diseases of Children was founded with Rotch as the incumbent. He was made a full professor in 1893; his title was changed to professor of pediatrics ten years later, and he held the latter position until his death. His book, *Pediatrics: the Hygiene and Medical Treatment of Children*, one of the first to be written on that branch of medicine, was published in 1896.

Rotch realized, early in his career, that the high death rate of infants was largely due to bad nutrition. He soon devised a "percentage" meth-od of artificial feeding (*Archives of Pediatrics*, August 1887) based on a careful estimation of the caloric value of milk. Varying the formula of cow's milk to meet the requirements of the infant and compounding a product free from impurities, he placed the feeding of infants upon a scientific basis. Later he used the Röntgen ray as a means of studying the bone development of growing children, and in 1910 published *Living Anatomy and Pathology: the Diagnosis of Diseases in Early Life by the Roentgen Method*. He was a member of many medical asso-ciations, and served as president of the American Pediatrics Society in 1891. His work was recog-nized abroad and in 1902 he addressed the Brit-ish Medical Association on American methods in the modification of milk for infants (*British Medical Journal*, Sept. 6, 1902). His paper led to the establishment of a milk laboratory in Lon-don, and in 1903 Rotch was appointed consulting physician to an infants' hospital in that city.

Rotch's only child, a son, died in 1902, shortly after graduating from Harvard College, and on Apr. 18, 1903, in consideration of the gift of a fund raised by the father's friends to provide a new building, the name of the West-End Nursery and Infants' Hospital was changed to Thomas Morgan Rotch, Jr., Memorial Hospital for In-fants. The new building, erected on the grounds of the Harvard Medical School, was completed in the year of Rotch's death.

[J. C. Warren, in *Harvard Graduates' Mag.*, June 1914; *Tenth Report of the Class of 1870 of Harvard College* (1920); *Boston Medic. and Surgic Jour.*, Apr. 9, 1914; L. E. Holt, in *Archives of Pediatrics*, 31: 161, 1914; Abraham Jacobi, in *Trans. Am. Pediatrics Soc.*, vol. XXVI (1914); *Twenty-first Ann. Report of the West-End Nursery and Infants' Hospital, Now Thomas Morgan Rotch, Jr., Memorial Hospital for In-fants, Jan. 1903–Jan. 1904* (1904); *Boston Herald*, Mar. 10, 11, 1914; *Boston Transcript*, Mar. 10, 1914.]

H. R. V.

ROTCH, WILLIAM (Dec. 4, 1734 o.s.–May 16, 1828), whaling merchant, was born in Nan-tucket, Mass., the son of Joseph and Love (Macy) Rotch. He was the grandson of Wil-liam Rotch who was in Salem, Mass., before 1692. On Oct. 31, 1754, he married Elizabeth Barney, the daughter of Benjamin Barney of Nantucket. With his father he amassed wealth in the whale fishery, continuing at Nantucket after the elder man had removed to New Bed-ford, Mass. Although he suffered a loss of $60,-000 by the Revolution, his abhorrence of war led him on one occasion to cast a large consignment of bayonets into the sea. British depredations afloat and ashore during hostilities threatened the very existence of the island town, until a committee led by Rotch obtained promises of future safety from the King's officers at New-port and New York, a procedure that brought about the impeachment of the delegation by the Massachusetts authorities for high treason, al-though they were not convicted. In 1783 Rotch's ship *Bedford* entered the Thames flying the American flag, probably the first display of "the rebellious stripes of America" in any British port.

When, after the Revolution, the American whale fishery was virtually ruined through the heavy duty imposed on sperm oil by Great Brit-ain, he attempted to establish an enterprise in England. He had fruitless interviews to that end in 1785 with Pitt and Lord Hawkesbury, who refused concessions yet relented after the Quaker merchant had succeeded in founding a prosperous business in Dunkirk, France. When certain civil and religious questions affecting the Friends required decision by the French Na-tional Assembly Rotch's earnest plea before that body, where he persisted in wearing his hat, drew a friendly reply from Mirabeau. The subsequent Reign of Terror drove him back to America in 1794. When he was eighty he wrote a brief rec-ord of his experiences in these eventful years, *Memorandum Written by William Rotch* (1916 and in *New-England Historical and Genealogi-cal Register*, July 1877–Oct. 1878). Meantime his son, William Rotch, Jr., had removed to New Bedford, where he engaged in maritime and other commercial ventures of an extensive char-acter, and thither the father repaired to live in retirement but to contribute from his ripe ex-perience an impetus to the whaling industry, in which New Bedford long stood preëminent. The Rotch ships had been known the world over. Their owner had made numerous friends among prominent merchants and men in public life in this country and abroad. To his imposing "Man-sion House" came a stream of distinguished guests, including the Duc de la Rochefoucauld. A friend of the colored race, the wealthy merchant did not hesitate to dine with a negro ship captain. He was an influential factor in the Yearly Meeting of Friends and became a loyal patron of the Friends school in Providence, R. I., in later years the Moses Brown School. Tall and dignified, attired in Quaker garb, he commanded the profound respect of his townsmen, who admired his generosity and his liberal views.

[Autobiographical sketch, *ante;* manuscript copies of letters in Mass. Hist. Soc.; *Vital Records of Nantucket, Mass.,* vols. II, IV, V (1926–28); Augustine Jones, *William Rotch of Nantucket* (1901); Daniel Ricketson, *The Hist. of New Bedford, Mass.* (1858); R. W. Kelsey, *Centennial Hist. of Moses Brown School* (1919); C. E. Banks, The Hist. of Martha's Vineyard, vol. III (1925); birthdate from statement of birthdate in *Vital Records, ante,* vol. II, as 10th mo., 4th day, 1734.] W. M. E.

ROTHERMEL, PETER FREDERICK (July 8, 1817–Aug. 15, 1895), artist, the last American painter in the art tradition of the Peales, Sully, and Inman, was born in Nescopeck, Luzerne County, Pa., the son of Peter Rothermel, a native of northwestern Pennsylvania and a descendant of early settlers. Young Rothermel received a common school education, supplemented, at the insistence of his father, by the study of surveying, but at twenty years of age, following his own inclination, went to Philadelphia and became a sign painter. A few years later, through the influence of a friend, James McMurtrie, he began the study of drawing under John R. Smith, but before the end of his first quarter of tuition, enrolled in the classes of the Pennsylvania Academy of the Fine Arts. He studied subsequently under Bass Otis [*q.v.*], the teacher of Inman.

For a time the young painter worked at portraits, but his first success came with the painting of "De Soto Discovering the Mississippi," which was purchased by the Art Union. Edward Carey, a patron, advised him to go abroad, but Rothermel refused to leave his old mother, and argued his conviction that all Americans went to Europe too early. In 1847 he became a director of the Pennsylvania Academy of the Fine Arts, and as chairman of its committee on education endeavored to raise the standard of its schools, urging the purchase of casts from Greek and Roman sculpture for use in the antique class, the opening of the library of the Academy to artists and students, and the inauguration of school prizes and public lectures on art. He was also active in the promotion of the Artists' Fund Society.

In 1855 Rothermel resigned his post, and the following year set out for Europe, traveling at his own expense, although James L. Claghorn, art connoisseur and later president of the Academy, urged upon him a list of fifty patrons for whom he might paint pictures. In London Rothermel made sketches of the actor, Edwin Forrest [*q.v.*], to be used in his painting, "King Lear," then journeyed through Belgium, up the Rhine, and across the Alps to Florence and Genoa. For two years he resided in Rome, completing "King Lear" and "St. Agnes," the latter bought by Count Conchilef. His "Virtuoso" went to St. Petersburg; a preliminary study for "King Lear," his "Rubens and Van Dyck," and his "Fountain Gen-net-z-zano" were bought by members of the Russian nobility. By way of Venice and Munich, Rothermel traveled back to Paris, where he exhibited in the Salon of 1859. Shortly afterward he returned to America.

His most ambitious canvas, "The Battle of Gettysburg," was begun only after three years of preliminary research and sifting of the conflicting stories told by participants in the battle; the actual painting required a year and a half, and the picture was completed in 1871. It represented Pickett's charge on the afternoon of the third day. This heroic work, exhibited at Chicago, was rescued from the great fire by a young artist who carried it to Pittsburgh. For some time it hung in Memorial Hall, Philadelphia; it was exhibited in London in the eighties, and was finally installed in the Hall of Trophies in the Capitol at Harrisburg, for which it had been ordered by the Pennsylvania legislature. Rothermel's work was colorful, though inclined to the photographic, and his compositions were filled with well-handled figure groups. He contributed to the major exhibitions of his day, including the Centennial Exhibition at Philadelphia in 1876. Many of his paintings, including "Paul at Ephesus," "The State House on the Day of the Battle of Germantown," "Desdemona," and "The Bather," are to be found at the Pennsylvania Academy of the Fine Arts.

He married Caroline, the daughter of John Goodhart of Philadelphia, and had three children. In 1877 he removed from Philadelphia to his country home, "Grassmere," near Linfield, Montgomery County, Pa., where he died eighteen years later.

[*Public Ledger* (Phila.), Aug. 16, 1895; *N. Y. Tribune,* Aug. 16, 1895; H. T. Tuckerman, *Book of the Artists* (ed. of 1882); C. E. Clement and Laurence Hutton, *Artists of the Nineteenth Century and Their Works,* vol. II (1879); J. D. Champlin and C. C. Perkins, *Cyc. of Painters and Paintings,* vol. IV (1887); *Catalogue of the Permanent Collection . . . Pa. Acad. of the Fine Arts* (1902); J. W. Jordan, *Encyc. of Pa. Biog.,* vol. VI (1916); Mantle Fielding, *Dict. of Am. Painters, Sculptors, and Engravers* (1926).] D. G—y.

ROTHROCK, JOSEPH TRIMBLE (Apr. 9, 1839–June 2, 1922), physician, botanist, forester, was born in McVeytown, Mifflin County, Pa., the son of Dr. Abraham and Phoebe Brinton (Trimble) Rothrock and a descendant of Abraham Rothrock who emigrated from the Palatinate to Berks County, Pa., early in the eighteenth century. Prepared in the village school, Freeland Seminary (now Ursinus College), and Academia, a preparatory school in Juniata County, Joseph entered the Lawrence Scientific School at Harvard in 1860. Meanwhile a period spent for the sake of his health as axeman on the Philadelphia & Erie Railroad had given him a keen interest in botany and forestry, and through the kindly interest of William Darlington [q.v.], a distant kinsman, he was accepted by Asa Gray [q.v.] as a special student and assistant. At the outbreak of the Civil War he enlisted in the 131st Pennsylvania Infantry, and on July 1, 1863, was commissioned captain, 20th Pennsylvania Cavalry. He fought at Antietam and Fredericksburg, where he was wounded. Honorably discharged, June 6, 1864, he returned to Harvard, and received his degree of B.S. in July.

The following winter he spent at the medical school of the University of Pennsylvania, but in 1865–66, under appointment from the Smithsonian Institution, he accompanied the exploring expedition to British Columbia and Alaska headed by Robert Kennicott [q.v.] and Maj. Frank Pope. His plant collections were lost in the Fraser River, but his "Sketch of the Flora of Alaska" was published in the *Report* of the Smithsonian Institution for 1867. He received the degree of M.D. from the University of Pennsylvania in that year and immediately became professor of botany at the Pennsylvania State Agricultural College. In 1869 he moved to Wilkes-Barre, where he established a medical practice and was instrumental in founding the Wilkes-Barre Hospital, but hard work again undermined his health, and in 1873 he became botanist and surgeon to the government survey in Colorado, New Mexico, and California, under Lieut. G. N. Wheeler. His report (*United States Geographical Surveys West of the 100th Meridian*, vol. VI, 1878), enumerated and described 1,168 species belonging to 637 genera, representing 104 natural orders of plants. The plant genus *Rothrockia* and at least six species perpetuate his fame as a botanist.

After a year as principal of a young ladies' academy in Wilkes-Barre, he accepted a post at the University of Pennsylvania, where he was professor of botany from 1877 to 1904. In 1877, he was appointed Michaux lecturer on forestry

by the American Philosophical Society. In 1880, he spent nine months as a student at the University of Strassburg. Deeply impressed by the German forest-conservation policies, he came home dedicated to the task of arousing public opinion to the need of protecting the forests. He was one of the founders of the Pennsylvania Forestry Association and its president in 1886. In 1893, Governor Pattison appointed him to a commission to study the forests of Pennsylvania; and he was the author of its report. Following the submission of this document to the legislature in March 1895 the division of forestry in the state department of agriculture was created, with Rothrock as its first commissioner, and when in 1901 a separate department of forestry was created, he was again the first commissioner. This post he held until 1904, and remained on the advisory board after his retirement. He inaugurated the policy of purchasing lands at the head waters of rivers for flood control, established tree nurseries to facilitate reforesting on both private and public lands, organized the fire wardens, and founded the State Forest School at Mount Alto to train workers in the forest service.

Some of Rothrock's other interests are suggested by his book, *Vacation Cruising in Chesapeake and Delaware Bays* (1884). In 1880 he cruised to the Bahamas and the West Indies in his yacht *White Cap,* collecting valuable scientific material for the University. As early as 1876, he began to take delicate boys to the woods for camp life, and in time founded the School of Physical Culture in Luzerne County, Pa. In 1902, he opened an informal camp for tubercular patients on the State Forest Reserve near Mount Alto; it proved successful and in 1907 was put under the newly created state department of health. He married, May 27, 1868, Martha E. May, daughter of Addison and Elizabeth Shafer May, and they had five children. His associates describe him as a man small in stature, abounding in energy, and with great charm of manner. He wrote of himself in an autobiographical sketch, "I am an Episcopalian, and politically a Republican when my conscience will endure it" (Kelly, *post*, p. 213). He died at his home in West Chester, Pa., survived by two sons and a daughter.

[*Biog. and Portrait Cyc. of Chester County, Pa.* (1893); autobiog. material in address by Rothrock, *Bull. Chester County Hist. Soc.,* Sept. 27, 1913; "Exercises in Appreciation of Dr. Joseph Trimble Rothrock," *Ibid.,* Mar. 19, 1914; *A Tribute to Dr. Joseph Trimble Rothrock, by His Friends* (1923); H. A. Kelly, *Some Am. Medic. Botanists* (1914); J. W. Harshberger, *The Botanists of Phila. and Their Work*

(1899); *Who's Who in America*, 1922–23; *Public Ledger* (Phila.), June 3, 1922.] M. P. S.

ROTHWELL, RICHARD PENNEFA-THER (May 1, 1836–Apr. 17, 1901), mining engineer, editor, was born at Oxford, Ontario, son of the Rev. John Rothwell. The father was a native of County Meath, Ireland, where the family (probably originally Scottish) held large estates under a grant from William and Mary. He graduated from Trinity College, Dublin; became a clergyman of the established church; married Elizabeth Garnett of Athearn Castle; and emigrated to Canada. Richard entered Trinity College, Toronto, but after a year there transferred to the Rensselaer Polytechnic Institute at Troy, N. Y., and was graduated as a civil engineer in 1858. He then went to Paris and entered the Imperial (now National) School of Mines, where, two and a half years later, he received the degree of engineer of mines. After pursuing specialized courses at the mining academy in Freiberg, Saxony, he entered the employ of W. T. Henley, a manufacturer of wire rope and telegraph cable in North Woolwich, England, where he showed ability and firmness of character. In connection with the wire business he was in France for a time examining some copper deposits. Declining an offer to be assistant superintendent at the wire works in England because he did not wish to give up mining engineering, he returned to Canada and examined iron-ore lands for the English owners of the Bessemer-steel rights.

In 1864, at the age of twenty-eight, he came to the United States and opened an office as engineer at Wilkes-Barre, taking up work also at the near-by towns of Eckley and Drifton, the latter of which he surveyed and laid out. Much of his work was for the anthracite operators, but he also designed for the Hazard Manufacturing Company what was then the largest wire-rope-making plant in the world. The machinery showed ingenuity and novelty in invention, and remained in operation for many years. At his suggestion the first underground locomotives in the anthracite mines were adopted in 1869, near Mauch Chunk, Pa., by the Lehigh Coal & Navigation Company. Some of the maps which he made after topographical surveys in several states between Massachusetts and the Gulf were accepted by national and state geological surveys. On the subject of ventilation and fires in coal mines he wrote a number of articles for the *American Journal of Mining* (later *Engineering and Mining Journal*). These were based on his experience in connection with mine explosions, disasters, in which he had displayed personal courage and leadership, on one occasion being overcome by gas while leading a rescue party.

In 1871 Rothwell joined with Eckley B. Coxe [q.v.], Martin Coryell, and Rossiter W. Raymond [q.v.] in founding the American Institute of Mining Engineers. Perhaps the conception came from him; at all events he was chairman at the preliminary meetings in Wilkes-Barre. Despite his modesty he held at various times high office in the Institute, being president in 1882. He also contributed many technical papers to its published *Transactions*. His practice as a consulting engineer grew so rapidly that in 1873 he moved his office to New York and made long trips from there. The next year he joined Raymond as editor of the *Engineering and Mining Journal* and later took over its ownership from Raymond. For many years these two able and courageous editors maintained a high standard of technical journalism; their paper became the leading organ of the mining engineering profession and led the way to free publicity for technical improvements. They had a friendly disagreement over the question of the coinage of silver which led to Raymond's withdrawal as editor in 1890; thereafter he was a special contributor. Rothwell's somewhat positive views on silver were published in a book, *Universal Bimetallism, and an International Monetary Clearing-House* . . . (1893), which incidentally cost his paper some subscribers. As head of the Scientific Publishing Company, of New York, which pioneered in the exchange of technical information, he began issuing in 1893 a voluminous annual compilation called *The Mineral Industry; its Statistics, Technology and Trade*. This book set an example in liberalizing the publicity policy of the mining industry and in 1898 won its author the gold medal of the Société d'Encouragement pour l'Industrie Nationale de France. Rothwell's greatest service to the engineering profession was his intelligent and persistent emphasis on the need of American industrial corporations publishing their technical experience. A short time before his death he became president of the United Correspondence Schools of New York.

Among his inventions and improvements in American engineering practice were his wire-rope machine and its accessories, a cylindrical roaster for ores, a pressure-filter, a method of mining soft ore, coal-breakers for reducing anthracite, and methods of chlorinating gold ores. He was a member of many technical and professional societies, both in America and Europe. On May 29, 1862, he married Bertha Hillebrand of Baden, Germany; she and their daughter survived him. Shortly before his death Rothwell established, partly from money left by a business associate, Sophia Brauenlich, the Sophia Fund. The object of this Fund is the care of friendless girls under six years of age and the securing of their adoption by suitable persons.

[R. W. Raymond, in *Trans. Am. Inst. of Mining Engineers,* vol. XXXI (1901), with bibliog. of Rothwell's publications; *Engineering and Mining Jour.,* Apr. 20, 1901; *Biog. Record Officers and Grads. Rensselaer Polytechnic Inst.* (1887); *Bulletin de la Société d'Encouragement pour l'Industrie Nationale de France,* July 1898; *Who's Who in America,* 1899–1900; *N. Y. Times* and *N. Y. Tribune,* Apr. 18, 1901; dates of birth and marriage verified by office of the Sophia Fund.]

P. B. M.

ROULSTONE, GEORGE (Oct. 8, 1767–1804), the first printer in Tennessee, was born in Boston and probably learned his trade there. While still in his nonage he launched the *Salem Chronicle and Essex Advertiser,* which ran from March till August 1786. He is next heard from three years later, in Fayetteville, N. C., where he was employed on the *Gazette,* later the *North Carolina Chronicle.* When William Blount [*q.v.*] became governor of the Territory of the United States South of the Ohio, he foresaw the advantage of a newspaper favorable to himself and persuaded Roulstone to accompany him across the mountains to the new country. Since Knoxville, which was to be the territorial capital, was as yet hardly more than a name, Roulstone set up his press temporarily at Hawkins Court House (Rogersville) and issued there, Nov. 5, 1791, the first number of the *Knoxville Gazette.* It was a three-column, four-page sheet, published fortnightly, but because of the difficulty of obtaining paper and other supplies in the wilderness it was subject to variations in format and date of issue. Paine's *Rights of Man* was run as a serial in the early numbers. The first issue printed at Knoxville appeared Oct. 10, 1792. Roulstone was a man of more than ordinary capacity and judgment, and his paper made friends for himself and for Blount. Except during 1798, or a part of that year, he continued to publish the *Gazette* until his death early in 1804. As the territorial printer he produced the volume of *Acts and Ordinances of the Governor and Judges of the Territory of the United States South of the River Ohio* (1793); two volumes (1794–95) of the acts passed at the first and second sessions of the Territorial Assembly, and the journals of the legislature. After the admission of Tennessee as a state he continued as public printer until his death. Other issues of his press, known only from advertisements in the *Gazette* are: *A Sermon on Psalmody, Preached at Salem Church at the*

Opening of the Presbytery of Abingdon, October 12, 1786, by Hezekiah Balch, A.M., Pastor of Mt. Bethel Church, Greenville (1794); *The Sermon Given at Knoxville, February 25, 1794, in the Presence of the Governor William Blount and Assembly of the Territory South of the Ohio, by Samuel Carrick, A.M., Pastor of the Church in Knoxville* (1794); and *Toplady's Translation of Zanchius on Predestination* (1795). His most important production was the *Laws of the State of Tennessee* (1803). Roulstone was clerk of the Legislative Council, one of the five commissioners of the city of Knoxville, and postmaster of the town. To facilitate the delivery of his paper he also maintained a private post. He was a trustee of Blount College (later the University of Tennessee), of which Samuel Carrick [*q.v.*] was the first head. His widow, a daughter of Devereaux Gilliam of Nashville, was public printer for a few years after his death, and married William Moore, public printer in 1808, who continued the *Gazette.*

[See J. G. M. Ramsey, *The Annals of Tenn.* (1853; 1926); Wm. Rule, ed., *Standard Hist. of Knoxville, Tenn.* (1900); D. C. McMurtrie, *Pioneer Printing in Tenn.* (Springfield, Ill., 1931; reprinted from *Nat. Printer Journalist,* Nov. 1931); *Proc. Am. Antiquarian Soc.,* n.s., XXVIII (1918), 299, XXXV (1925), 87–89. A file of the early issues of the *Knoxville Gazette* is in the library of the Tenn. Hist. Soc.]

G. H. G.

ROUND, WILLIAM MARSHALL FITTS (Mar. 26, 1845–Jan. 2, 1906), journalist and prison reformer, was born at Pawtucket, R. I., the son of a Baptist minister, Daniel Round, and his wife, Elizabeth Ann Fitts. He attended the public schools and studied for a while at the Harvard Medical School, but ill health prevented his graduation. Brown University in 1892 bestowed upon him the honorary degree of master of arts. Shortly after his attendance at Harvard he entered upon journalistic work, being connected at different times with the *Boston Daily News,* the New York *Independent,* the *Golden Rule* (Boston), and other papers. In 1872 he was appointed United States commissioner to the world's fair to be held in Vienna the following year, and there had charge of the New England department. Five years later (1877) he married Ellen Miner Thomas, grand-daughter of Hon. Charles Miner [*q.v.*] of Wilkes-Barre, Pa.

Interested in plans for social betterment, Round was chosen in 1881 a member of the executive committee of the Prison Association of New York, and in 1882 became its corresponding secretary. Among the purposes of this body were the amelioration of conditions of prisoners, improvement in government and discipline of prisons (county, municipal and state), and assistance to released prisoners; it also possessed legal powers of inspection of county jails and prisons. Round threw himself into the work with persistence and vigor. His are among the most relentless and illuminating descriptions that have been written of the overcrowding, idleness, filth, and political corruption of county jails; and improvement followed his efforts. At the same time he gave strong support to movements for the indeterminate sentence, the development of systems of parole, establishment of suitable prison industries, and mitigation of severe physical punishments in penal institutions. He even advocated curtailment or abolition of the almost universal county jail—a proposal which not till later took the form, in a few states, of state farms for misdemeanants. In 1883 he assisted in the reorganization of the National Prison Association, the name of which was changed in 1908 to American Prison Association; for a few years he was its secretary.

In 1887 he was called by Frederick G. Burnham as advisor in connection with a plan for establishing a farm school for unmanageable boys, and was subsequently the virtual director of the Burnham Industrial Farm at Canaan, N. Y., for several years. He introduced the cottage housing system, and what was then called the "mill" system by which, through good conduct, extra privileges might be earned. In part, his ideas were drawn from the system established by Wichern at the Rauhe Haus near Hamburg and from that of F. A. Demetz at Mettray, France. Among the employees at Canaan, Round founded the non-sectarian Order of St. Christopher, as a training order for workers in public institutions. After leaving the Burnham Industrial Farm he lived for a while at College Point, Long Island, and there had charge of a small orphan asylum. Because of failing health he resigned his position as secretary of the Prison Association of New York in 1900.

Earlier in his life, under the pen name of Rev. Peter Pennot, Round had published several novels, among which were: Achsah: a New England Life Study (1876), Torn and Mended, a Christmas Story (copyright 1877); Child Marian Abroad (1878); Hal, the Story of a Clodhopper (1880); and Rosecroft, a Story of Common Places and Common People (1881). In the latter part of his life his work was in Boston, and there in 1903 he was associated with Edward Everett Hale [q.v.] in the publication of the Lend a Hand Record. His work was done in the pioneer days of the effort to reach a scientific approach to the problems of delinquent conduct, but many of his ideas have stood the test of later

social and psychological analysis. He died at Acushnet, Mass., survived by his wife; there were no children.

[Annual reports of the Prison Association of N. Y., 1882–1900, and especially the memorial notice in Prison Asso. of N. Y., Sixty-first Ann. Report, 1905–06; Who's Who in America, 1906–07; Hist. Cat. Brown Univ. (1905); N. R. Nichols, Round-Rounds Geneal., Descendants of John Round of Swansea, Mass. (1929); N. Y. Daily Tribune, Jan. 17, 1892; Boston Transcript and N. Y. Tribune, Jan. 6, 1906; names of parents from records of Brown Univ.]   W. D. L.

ROUQUETTE, ADRIEN EMMANUEL
(Feb. 13, 1813–July 15, 1887), priest and poet, was born in New Orleans, a younger brother of François Dominique Rouquette [q.v.], and the son of Dominique and Louise (Cousin) Rouquette. When he was five, his father died, and when he was eight, he was sent to the Collège d'Orléans, but he frequently ran away to live with the Choctaw Indians in the back parishes. Later, to overcome his truancy and to perfect his neglected English, his mother sent him to Transylvania University in Kentucky. After her death, when he was sixteen, his guardian shipped him off to Paris, where he matriculated at the Collège Royal, but later went to the Collège Royal at Nantes, and finally graduated (1833) from the College of Rennes in Brittany.

He had always been moody, introspective, vacillating, a romantic dreamer and psychologically maladjusted, and upon his return to Louisiana he soon drifted back into a life with the Indians on Bayou Lacombe. Tradition says he fell in love with a beautiful Indian maiden, Oushola (the bird singer), and that grief over her sudden demise so prostrated him that he left the country. At any rate, he went back to Paris and began to study law. Fantastically unfitted for so practical a profession, he soon neglected his studies and divided his time between student dissipations and the courts, where he listened enthralled to the oratory of the great French avocats. At last, when overcome by homesickness and dissatisfaction with his futile mode of living, he was so impressed by the Lenten lectures of an eloquent ecclesiast, Father de Ravignan, that he collected a small library on church history and returned to New Orleans in 1836, intending to study. Soon, however, he left the city and went back to the Indians in St. Tammany Parish.

He continued to lead this rudderless life, writing occasional poetry for his own amusement, until, encouraged by the success in France of a small volume of verse by his brother Dominique, he sailed for Paris and published Les Savanes (1841), a collection of his own poems. It was enthusiastically received by French poets and critics, Brizeux, Barthélemy, Deschamps, and even Sainte-Beuve; while in England Thomas Moore hailed him as "the Lamartine of America." Despite this praise, he returned to New Orleans again, only to find it as hard as ever to adjust himself to his surroundings. In this restless mood he was easily persuaded by Abbé Perché that the church could afford him a refuge from his *"mal de siècle."* He began his studies with avidity and in 1846 took holy orders. Almost immediately he sprang into fame as an orator by reason of the eloquent sermons he preached in the St. Louis Cathedral of New Orleans, but his new duties complicated his life and he longed for solitude, pouring out his desire in a rambling, mystical book, *La Thébaïde en Amérique, ou Apologie de la Vie solitaire et contemplative* (1852). He had previously published in English, *Wild Flowers: Sacred Poetry* (1848).

During the late 1850's he preached a series of anti-slavery sermons which made him many powerful enemies. This was the last straw which made unbearable the burden of adjusting himself to life in a city, so he asked permission to devote himself to ministering to the Indians. He joined the Choctaws, whose entire confidence he won, and was christened by them "Chahta-Ima" (Choctaw-like). In time he built several small, crude wooden chapels in St. Tammany Parish. He still gave a great deal of time to writing, continued to contribute to *Le Propagateur Catholique*, and in 1860 brought out a long volume of mystical verse, *L'Antoniade, ou la Solitude avec Dieu*, in which he contended that all the accomplishments of genius were born of poverty and solitude.

During the Civil War the Indians took refuge in the deepest swamps and the Abbé kept them alive by bringing them food and quinine, through the Northern lines, in pirogues. Some years later, inspired by Châteaubriand, he published *La Nouvelle Atala* (1879), an account of the spiritual adventures of a preposterously idealized Indian maiden. Toward the end of his life he viciously attacked George W. Cable [*q.v.*], who had aroused the intense resentment of the Creoles by his books. Rouquette called his diatribe *Critical Dialogue between Aboo and Caboo* (1880), signed it with the pseudonym "E. Junius," and included a "poem" in the Creole dialect making charges against Cable that were both untrue and vulgar. It was a sign of his declining powers; in 1885, while at work upon a dictionary of the Choctaw language, he lost his reason and was taken to the Hôtel-Dieu in New Orleans, where

he died—the last of the "Black robe" fathers— on July 15, 1887.

[E. L. Tinker, *Les Écrits de Langue Française en Louisiane au XIXe Siècle* (1932), with comprehensive bibliog.; J. A. Reinecke, "Les Frères Rouquette," *Comptes Rendus de l'Athénée Louisianais*, Jan., Apr., July 1920; J. W. Davidson, *The Living Writers of the South* (1869); Susan B. Elder, *Life of Abbé Adrien Rouquette* (1913), not very reliable; C. P. Dimitry, "The Rouquette Family," *New Orleans Times-Democrat*, Nov. 20, 1892, condensed in *Old Families of Louisiana* (1931), ed. by S. C. Arthur and G. C. H. de Kernion, A. N. De Menil, *The Literature of the La. Territory* (1904); *N. Y. Freeman's Jour.*, Aug. 6, 1887; *New Orleans Times-Democrat*, July 16, 1887.]
E. L. T.

ROUQUETTE, FRANÇOIS DOMINIQUE (Jan. 2, 1810–May 1890), poet, was born at his parents' summer place on Bayou Lacombe, Louisiana. His father, Dominique, was a native of France, from near Bordeaux, who came to New Orleans about 1800, set himself up as a wine merchant, and married a Creole, Louise Cousin. Young Dominique played so much with the Choctaw children in the nearby Indian camps that he learned their language at an early age and could shoot a bow and arrow with the best of them; and as soon as his brother Adrien [*q.v.*] was old enough to walk he took him along on these excursions. At the age of seven the elder boy was sent to the Collège d'Orléans, where he stayed for five years and exhibited the lack of emotional control that is so often considered a peculiarity of poets. Then, at twelve, he crossed the ocean alone and matriculated at the Royal College of Nantes in Brittany.

In due course he graduated and in 1828 returned to New Orleans, but his relatives persuaded him to go to Philadelphia to study law in the office of William Rawle [*q.v.*], then the leader of the Pennsylvania bar. A dreamer and unconquerably indolent, he soon tired of this profession and went back to Bayou Lacombe to divide his days between idly wandering with the aborigines and writing occasional verse. He was forever falling in love, and then going to France to get over it. In 1839, during one of these visits, he published in Paris a thin volume of poems in praise of life among the Indians, which he called *Meschacébéennes*, the ancient name of Mississippi. Châteaubriand had created a vogue for this type of literature, and Rouquette's little book was an immediate success. Hugo, Béranger, Barthélemy, as well as lesser critics, praised it enthusiastically and predicted a future for its author.

He returned to New Orleans in the same year, and in 1846, married Laura Verret. He had wasted most of his patrimony on his gay trips to Paris and so, to make a living, began to write poems and articles for *L'Abeille* and *Le Propagateur Catholique,* and in time opened a boys' school in New Orleans. When this venture ceased to pay in 1849 he took his family to Fort Smith, Ark., and opened another school; but the citizens of that frontier town were more interested in having their sons learn how to fight Indians and ride wild horses than in having them taught to read and write. Rouquette was soon forced to convert the school into a grocery store, but he was so impractical that this too failed, and he went back to New Orleans in 1851. Meanwhile (1850), he had published a translation, *The Arkansas,* by J. B. Bossu, Rouquette's only work in English. In 1852 he opened still another school at Bonfouca, in St. Tammany Parish, where he made his older pupils teach the younger ones while he went away for two or three days at a time to smoke, read, and write poetry under the oaks of Matassa. This was his last attempt to support his family; his wife soon died of consumption, and his two sons were turned over to his nephew, Cyprien Dufour, to be reared.

In 1856 Rouquette published a second collection of poems under the title, *Fleurs d'Amérique.* The French critics received it as enthusiastically as they had the *Meschacébéennes.* Émile Deschamps wrote: "Your *Fleurs d'Amérique* have all the grace, all the perfume, all the freshness of their living models"; and most flattering letters arrived from Méry and from Eugène Guinot of *Le Pays.* For the rest of his life Dominique drifted without bag or baggage from the house of one relative to that of another, repaying hospitality with poems for birthdays, baptisms, and weddings, which he sang at the feasts. When he was older he wandered the streets of his city, in broken shoes and wrinkled, patched clothes, always with a blanket around his shoulders, a palm-leaf fan in one hand and a stick in the other. Sitting on someone's doorstep, he scribbled poetry on a piece of brown manilla paper and then found some friend to buttonhole on the corner, to whom to recite with flashing eyes the lines he had just finished. His many women relatives would walk blocks rather than meet him on the street, for he always insisted upon enveloping them in the folds of his musty old blanket as he kissed them and asked solicitously after the health of each member of their families. He never failed to present them with a grimy little caramel wrapped in yellow straw paper, a supply of which he carried in his pocket together with loose tobacco and his very rank pipe. Had he lived in the days of the troubadours when poets had patrons, he would have had fame and

riches; but born too late, he died in penury, even though his verses had been much praised by some of the best critics in France. On May 10, 1890, he was buried under the grass of Bonfouca.

[E. L. Tinker, *Les Écrits de Langue Française en Louisiane au XIXe Siècle* (1932); Alcée Fortier, in *Comptes Rendus de l'Athénée Louisianais,* July 1890; J. A. Reinecke, "Les Frères Rouquette," *Ibid.,* Jan., Apr., July, 1920; C. P. Dimitry, "The Rouquette Family," *New Orleans Times-Democrat,* Nov. 20, 1892; E. A. Alderman and J. C. Harris, *Lib. of Southern Lit.,* vol. X (1909); Charles Testut, *Portraits Littéraires* (1850); "Dominique Rouquette," *L'Avant-Coureur* (St. Charles Parish), Dec. 17, 1859, printing the letters from the French critics, Méry, Eugène Guinot, and Émile Deschamps; congratulating Rouquette on his *Fleurs d'Amérique.*]   E. L. T.

ROUSSEAU, HARRY HARWOOD (Apr. 19, 1870–July 24, 1930), engineer and naval officer, was born at Troy, N. Y., the son of William White and Jeanette (Parker) Rousseau. After graduating as valedictorian from the Troy High School he entered Rensselaer Polytechnic Institute and completed the civil engineering course in 1891. During the next seven years he engaged in structural engineering work in Albany, in Brooklyn, and with the Pittsburgh Bridge Company. In October 1898, he entered the civil engineer corps of the navy as lieutenant, serving in the Bureau of Yards and Docks, 1899–1903, and subsequently at the Mare Island Navy Yard, California. Being personally known by Secretary of the Navy Metcalf, a Californian, and by President Roosevelt, under whom he had occasionally served as aide, he was appointed chief of the Bureau of Yards and Docks in January 1907, with the temporary rank of rear admiral.

That same year the President made him a member of the new Isthmian Canal Commission headed by Lieut.-Col. George W. Goethals [*q.v.*]. On this commission he served until it went out of existence in 1914, after 1908 being in charge of the second division of the chief engineer's office with the title of assistant to the chief engineer. In this capacity he had special supervision of the "design and construction of canal terminals, including dry-docks, ship repair shops, piers, coaling plants, fuel oil plants, breakwaters, and floating cranes." Goethals, with whom he worked in perfect harmony, placed a high value upon his technical training, experience, and administrative ability, and considered him, together with Col. Harry F. Hodges [*q.v.*], one of his "indispensable" subordinates. The Navy Department "desired his return to duty at Washington, and on one occasion the Secretary of the Navy especially requested . . . his relief from duty on the Isthmus in order that the Navy Department might avail itself of his services" (J.

B. Bishop, *The Panama Gateway,* 1913, p. 182), but he remained at Panama until the terminal works were completed in 1916, within the estimated cost and time. Congress by special act, Mar. 4, 1915, authorized his advancement from lieutenant commander to rear admiral.

After his return from Panama he was a member of the commission on navy yards and naval stations, 1916–20, that made a study of the coasts of the United States with a view to locating naval and aviation bases. Goethals also secured his services for the Shipping Board, during the World War, and he was assistant general manager and head of the shipyard plants division of the Emergency Fleet Corporation from 1917 to 1919, with many additional naval duties as project manager in charge of expenditure of naval funds for improvements in shipyards, member of the government Munitions Board, and a member of the Port Facilities Commission. He was awarded the Navy Cross for "exceptionally meritorious service in a duty of great responsibility."

While acting on many important naval and other government boards, his chief post-war duty was as government receiver, 1924–27, during litigation over Naval Petroleum Reserve No. 1 (the Elk Hills suit), and subsequently as director of naval petroleum and oil shale reserves until his death. In this later period he was also chief coordinator of the budget, administering, under the director of the budget, all federal coordinating agencies, a duty which required great application and labor and is thought to have broken his strength. His death occurred on the steamship *Cristobal* en route to Panama for an inspection of the Panama Railway, of which he had been a director since 1907. His funeral services were held in St. Thomas' Episcopal Church, Washington, of which he was a vestryman, and he was buried in Arlington National Cemetery. During his canal service he published two articles on engineering work there: *The Isthmian Canal* (Government Printing Office, 1909), a paper presented at the twentieth annual session of the Trans-Mississippi Commercial Congress, and "Terminal Works, Dry docks, and Wharves of the Panama Canal" (*Transactions of the International Engineering Congress,* 1915, vol. I, pt. 2, pp. 371–432). He was married at Panama in 1908 to Gladys Fargo Squiers, daughter of Herbert G. Squiers, United States minister to Panama, and was survived by his widow and three sons. Of undoubted engineering ability, Rousseau has been characterized personally as a man of reserved yet kindly nature, keen sense of humor, and unusual social charm.

[F. T. Chambers, "Harry Harwood Rousseau," *Trans. Am. Soc. Civil Engineers,* vol. XCV (1931); J. B. and F. Bishop, *Goethals, Genius of the Panama Canal* (1930); *Who's Who in America,* 1930–31; *N. Y. Times,* July 25, 27, 1930.]   A. W—t.

ROUSSEAU, LOVELL HARRISON (Aug. 4, 1818–Jan. 7, 1869), soldier, congressman from Kentucky, was born near Stanford, Lincoln County, Ky., of inconspicuous parentage. His father, who had removed to Kentucky from Virginia, died in 1833 and left a large family with scanty resources. The boy managed to attend the common schools for a short time, but soon he was forced to the pounding of rock in the construction of the turnpike from Lexington to Lancaster. On becoming of age he settled in Louisville, where he took up the study of law, and, proceeding feverishly without the aid of a teacher for fourteen hours a day, he acquired a great deal of information but undermined his health. In 1840 he moved across the Ohio into Indiana and settled in Bloomfield, where he was admitted to the bar the next February. He served as a Whig in the state House of Representatives during 1844 and 1845. On the outbreak of the Mexican War he became a captain in the 2nd Indiana Infantry. He participated in the battle of Buena Vista and was mentioned for gallantry in the engagement. On June 23, 1847, he was honorably mustered out, and four days after his return he was elected to the state Senate. However in 1849, a year before his term of office had expired, he returned to Louisville. His constituency refused to let him resign, so theoretically he still served Indiana.

In Louisville he established a reputation as an able criminal lawyer. In 1855 he helped to quell the riot that broke out there, incident to the Know-Nothing movement. Five years later he was actively back in politics with a seat in the Kentucky Senate. So vigorous was his opposition to secession that he resigned from the Senate in 1861 and began to raise troops for the Union. To keep from violating the neutrality Kentucky had announced, he set up his training camp across the river from Louisville, in Indiana, and called it Camp Jo Holt. His efforts were largely responsible for saving the state for the Union. On Sept. 9, he became colonel of the 3rd Kentucky Infantry, and on Oct. 1 he was promoted to be brigadier-general of volunteers. He played a prominent part at the battle of Shiloh and later at Perryville so distinguished himself that he was promoted to be major-general of volunteers on Oct. 8, 1862. He fought in the Chickamauga engagement and also in the battle of Nashville. He took part in many minor activities in Alabama, Mississippi, and western Tennessee. He was an excellent soldier, handsome in appearance, and beloved by his men. In January 1865 the Radical element in Kentucky supported him for the federal Senate, and he was barely defeated by James Guthrie. A few months later he was elected to the federal House of Representatives by a majority of almost a thousand votes. Shortly before the meeting of Congress he resigned from the army, on Nov. 30, 1865. Forsaking his radicalism, within less than a month he was in the thick of the Reconstruction debates, boldly opposing the Freedmen's Bureau Bill and other legislation and policies that appeared to him extreme. As he listened to the vindictive speeches of his fellow members of Congress who had fought only with their tongues during the war, he lost his temper, and at times his better judgment, and made bitter comments. Josiah B. Grinnell, of Iowa, replied in a tone which greatly enraged him, and, upon the former's delay in offering an apology, in the corridors of the Capitol he beat the Iowan in the face with a cane. The House, urged on by Thaddeus Stevens, reprimanded Rousseau, whereupon he resigned his seat on July 21, 1866, and stood for reëlection (*Address of Hon. Lovell H. Rousseau to his Constituents*, 1866). His Kentucky constituency returned him, and he served until Mar. 3, 1867. The same month he reëntered the army and was made a brigadier-general with the brevet rank of major-general in the regular army and was soon dispatched to Alaska to receive that territory from the Russians. The next year he was summoned to Washington to testify in the Johnson impeachment proceedings. He arrived too late, and on expressing a desire not to be returned to Alaska he was put in charge of the department of Louisiana. He died in New Orleans the following year and was buried in the Arlington National Cemetery.

[*Am. Annual Cyc. . . . 1869* (1870); Lewis and R. H. Collins, *Hist. of Ky.* (2 vols., 1874); *Biog. Cyc. of . . . Ky.* (1896); F. B. Heitman, *Hist. Register and Directory of the U. S. Army* (1903), vol. I; *Ky. Statesman* (Lexington), Jan. 14, 1869.]   E. M. C.

ROWAN, JOHN (July 12, 1773–July 13, 1843), jurist, congressman and senator from Kentucky, was born near York, Pa., the son of William and Eliza (Cooper) Rowan. His father, having lost his modest fortune during the Revolution, removed to Kentucky about 1783 and settled at Louisville. Soon thereafter he removed to a site on the Green River, now called Calhoun, where he remained only for a short time before finally settling in Bardstown. There John received his formal education in the celebrated school of James Priestley [*q.v.*], before going on to Lexington to study law. He received his license in 1795 and, beginning the practice of his profession immediately, he became in time an able criminal lawyer and a celebrated orator. In 1799 he represented Nelson County in the constitutional convention that drew up Kentucky's second constitution, and five years later he became secretary of state under Gov. Christopher Greenup [*q.v.*]. In 1806, he was elected to Congress as a Republican from his old home, in spite of the fact that he was now living in Frankfort, in another district. When Aaron Burr sought his assistance in the court procedure in Frankfort in 1806, he refused on the ground that he was a congressman elect. The next year, when he entered the Tenth Congress, he moved a set of resolutions to bring about an investigation of the alleged Spanish intrigues of Harry Innes [*q.v.*], a federal judge in Kentucky. Rowan was made chairman of the committee of investigation but was unable to find evidence sufficient to warrant impeachment proceedings. From 1813 to 1817 he represented Nelson County in the Kentucky House, and in 1822 and 1824 he represented Jefferson County. In 1819 he was appointed to the court of appeals, the highest state court, but a year on the bench convinced him that the work of a judge was too confining, so he resigned in 1821. By this time his sympathy with the relief party had led him into a disagreement with the extreme conservatism that characterized the court. In 1823–24 he led the fight against the old court, though in the end it turned out to be futile. The state always reposed great confidence in his ability and integrity. In 1820 the legislature appointed him with John J. Crittenden [*q.v.*] to adjust the troublesome boundary dispute with Tennessee; and three years later it gave him and Henry Clay the task of protecting the state's interests in the complicated dispute with Virginia over the occupying claimants laws. In 1839 the United States made use of his services by appointing him on the commission set up to adjust the claims against Mexico. In the meantime, in 1824, the legislature had elected him to the federal Senate for the term from 1825 to 1831. While in this position he took a prominent part in its deliberations, directing his efforts especially toward amending the federal judiciary system and abolishing imprisonment for debt. He also took part in the Webster-Hayne debate.

His ability as an orator obtained for him the commission from the legislature to make the commemorative address on the battle of Tippecanoe, and his interest in history brought about in 1838 his election to the presidency of the newly formed Kentucky Historical Society, a position he held until his death. In further recognition, a new county was created and named for him. He died in Louisville, where he had made his home part of the time, but he was buried in the family cemetery near his Bardstown home, the famous "Federal Hill" of today, the home in which he entertained Lafayette and many other celebrated people, and where tradition erroneously holds that Stephen Collins Foster wrote "My Old Kentucky Home." He married Annie, the daughter of William Lytle, federal surveyor-general and large landholder in Ohio, and the aunt of William Haines Lytle [q.v.]. They had eight children.

[Lewis and R. H. Collins, *Hist. of Ky.* (2 vols. 1874); W. E. Connelley and E. Coulter, *Hist. of Ky.* (1922), vols. I, II; *Biog. Encyc. of Ky.* (1878); *Biog. Cyc. of the Commonwealth of Ky.* (1896).]

E. M. C.

ROWAN, STEPHEN CLEGG (Dec. 25, 1808–Mar. 31, 1890), naval officer, was born near Dublin, Ireland, of Protestant parents, and was named for his maternal grandfather. His father's name was John Rowan. Having been severely burned at an open fire in a Wexford hotel, where the family stopped en route to America, Stephen was left with his grandparents, and was ten years old when he joined his parents, brother, and sisters at Piqua, Ohio. He was appointed a midshipman in February 1826, while studying at Oxford, Ohio, and made his first cruise on the *Vincennes,* 1826–30. This sloop was the first American man-of-war to circumnavigate the globe. After two years at New York on a revenue-cutter, he spent four years in West Indies waters as passed midshipman and master on the schooner *Shark* and the sloop *Vandalia.* The *Vandalia* received news of the Dade massacre, at Pensacola, hurriedly provisioned the ship for three months, and sailed for Florida to cooperate in the Seminole War. Rowan subsequently commanded dangerous boat expeditions on the Withlacoochee River, in Charlotte Harbor, and on Miakka River.

He was promoted to the rank of lieutenant in 1837 and the following year was ordered to the coast survey. He served from 1841 to 1844 in the *Delaware* on the Brazil and Mediterranean stations, and in July 1845 became executive officer of the *Cyane* on the Pacific Station. News of imminent war with Mexico reached the squadron at Mazatlán, and the *Cyane,* under Capt. S. F. Du Pont, proceeded to Monterey where it cooperated with Commodore Sloat in the capture of the city on July 7, 1846. Rowan was ordered to build earthworks, blockhouse, and stockade, a task which would have presented unlimited difficulties for many a seaman, but which he accomplished quickly and effectively. He was then ordered to take a detachment of marines and seamen and occupy San Diego where the *Cyane* blockaded the port until provisions were exhausted. She later sailed for San Francisco and then returned to San Diego, where Rowan, commanding a battalion of seamen and marines, joined the army under Stockton and Kearney. He fought in the battles, Rio San Gabriel and the Mesa, and helped to retake Los Angeles. Later at Mazatlán, he led a boat expedition to San José to relieve Lieutenant Heywood's detachment, besieged by Mexicans and nearly starved. During the ten years following the Mexican War, he served two tours of duty as ordnance inspector at the New York navy yard, commanded the supply-ship *Relief,* and the receiving-ship *North Carolina.* He was made commander on Sept. 14, 1855.

At the beginning of the Civil War, he was in command of the steam-sloop *Pawnee,* which supplied the chief defense of Washington during Lincoln's inauguration, and cooperated in the unsuccessful attempts to relieve Fort Sumter, and to burn the Norfolk navy yard. In May 1861 he directed against the batteries at Aquia Creek the first shot fired from a naval vessel in the war. The *Pawnee* joined Stringham's squadron in August and helped to capture two forts and about 600 men at Hatteras Inlet. Rowan's most distinguished service was rendered on Feb. 8, 1862, when, commanding a flotilla of nondescript vessels in the North Carolina sounds, he cooperated with General Burnside in the capture of Roanoke Island and destruction of a Confederate gunboat. The next day he made a dashing attack at Cobb's Point on the Pasquotank River, destroyed the fort and captured or routed the Confederate squadron, and took both Elizabeth City and Edenton. He assisted the army, on Mar. 14, to capture New Bern, taking seven small forts mounting thirty-four guns. He was promoted to the rank of captain on July 16, 1862, and the same day, as a reward for his gallantry, was made a commodore. He next commanded the *New Ironsides,* South Atlantic Blockading Squadron, and was under fire fourteen times in Charleston harbor from July 18 to Sept. 8, 1863, being struck 164 times. In August 1864, he was detached to command for two months all naval forces in North Carolina sounds and he was then placed on waiting orders. On July 25, 1866, he was promoted to rear admiral.

He was in command of the Norfolk navy yard, 1866–67, Asiatic Squadron, 1867–70; and the New York navy yard, 1872–76; governor of the Naval Asylum at Philadelphia in 1881, superintendent of the Naval Observatory in 1882, and president of various important naval boards. He was commissioned vice admiral on Aug. 15, 1870, and retired in 1889. He died at the Ebbitt House, Washington, D. C., and was buried in Oak Hill Cemetery, Georgetown, beside his wife, Mary (Stark) Rowan, born in Norfolk, Va., whom he had survived about fifteen years. Their only child who lived was Maj. Hamilton Rowan of the United States Army. The elder Rowan published his recollections of the Mexican War in the *Proceedings of the United States Naval Institute,* volume XIV, 1888.

[Letter of Mar. 20, 1931, from Capt. Stephen Clegg Rowan, U. S. Navy, a grandson; autobiographic memoranda and official papers, Naval Records and Library, Navy Dept.; *War of the Rebellion: Official Records (Navy),* 1 ser., vol. VII; L. R. Hamersly, *The Records of Living Officers of the U. S. Navy and Marine Corps* (4th ed., 1890); S. C. Ayres, *Sketch of the Life and Services of Vice Admiral S. C. Rowan* (1910); J. T. Headley, *Farragut and Our Naval Commanders* (1867); *Evening Star* (Washington, D. C.), Mar. 31, 1890.]   C.L.L.

ROWELL, GEORGE PRESBURY (July 4, 1838–Aug. 28, 1908), advertising agent, publisher, was born at Concord, Essex County, Vt., the son of Samuel and Caroline E. (Page) Rowell, and a descendant of Thomas Rowell, a seventeenth-century emigrant from England. When he was thirteen, his family settled on a farm near Lancaster, N. H., where he was entered in Lancaster Academy. During the winters of 1854–56 he taught school and "boarded round." In 1856 he secured a job in a Boston store, but lost it in the panic of 1857, and returned to teaching. The next year he started collecting bills for the *Boston Post.* Soon he began to sell advertising space in the paper, and was earning $14.00 per week when, on Sept. 1, 1862, at Lancaster, he married Sarah Burnside Eastman.

Rowell's first independent enterprise was the introduction in Boston of a scheme of theatre program advertising which he had noted in New York. The success of this plan encouraged him in 1865 to launch an advertising agency with his friend Horace Dodd. Net profits for the first year were five times the capital of $2,000 which the partners had invested in equal shares. Their success was due to Rowell's novel list system whereby columns of space, engaged from country weeklies by the year, were retailed to advertisers at $100 for a one-inch advertisement inserted four times in 100 papers. He soon sold out the Boston office to Dodd and set up the new firm of George P. Rowell & Company in New York, Apr. 1, 1867. Since the "list system" was by that time widely imitated, he credited the immediate success of his new venture more largely to his unique reputation for prompt payment to publishers and his assumption of responsibility for collecting from advertisers. He placed large quantities of patent medicine and lottery advertising, and at one time originated and unsuccessfully advertised Ripans Tabules, which, though advocated for various ills, were a dry form of a common household remedy—rhubarb and soda—sold at a fabulous price. In later years, however, his views changed, and he extolled "Truth in Advertising" campaigns. In 1869 *George P. Rowell and Company's American Newspaper Directory* first appeared, listing geographically and by class 5,411 United States publications and 367 periodicals in Canada. The second edition, in 1870, was considerably more ambitious, including brief histories of over fifty well-known advertisers, and an "American Newspaper Rate-Book," but the following year the simpler form was resumed and continued with slight variations until the final edition in 1908, when it was absorbed by *N. W. Ayer & Son's American Newspaper Annual.* The most significant result of its publication was the deflation of false circulation figures formerly customary among publishers.

In 1871 Rowell decided to take four months of vacation every year, and did so almost invariably the rest of his life. He had sold a quarter interest in the business to Charles Nelson Kent, a boyhood friend who proved an able partner. At the Centennial Exhibition in Philadelphia, 1876, he erected for public use a building to house the eight thousand or more newspapers donated regularly by their publishers during the period of the fair. In 1880 he bought "Prospect Farm" near Lancaster, N. H., and for six years seldom visited his office. His activities during this time included an unsuccessful campaign for the state legislature, the founding of the Percy Summer Club as a fish and game preserve, and a money-losing experience as the owner-editor of the village newspaper.

At Boston in 1866 Rowell and Dodd had started a house organ called the *Advertiser's Gazette* which was continued in New York until sold in 1878 to an unsuccessful publisher who had soon discontinued it. On July 15, 1888, Rowell began the publication of *Printers' Ink,* a journal for the advertising trade. Though soon imitated by many other publications, it remained a leading periodical in its field, and representative of the best long-time interests of advertising. It fought with the Post Office Department in the interest of equitable rates for advertisers and publishers, advocated better ethics among advertisers and agencies, and successfully promoted in 1911 the statute against misleading advertising which was later adopted by a number of states.

In the autumn of 1890 Rowell was divorced by his first wife, by whom he had had one daughter, and on Jan. 27, 1891, he married Mrs. Jeannette (Rigney) Hallock, daughter of Thomas Rigney of New York City. He sold his business to his employees in 1892, was forced to resume control some years later to avert bankruptcy, and sold out finally in 1905. In that year he wrote his reminiscences in a series of fifty-two informal papers, published weekly in *Printers' Ink,* and later in book form under the title, *Forty Years an Advertising Agent* (1906). His health broke during a trip to Switzerland and Egypt in the winter of 1907–08, and in August following, at Poland Springs, Me., he died.

[G. P. Rowell, *Forty Years an Advertising Agent* (1906) ; Roland Rowell, *Biog. Sketch of Samuel Rowell and Notices of Some of His Descendants* (1898) ; *Who's Who in America,* 1903–05 ; *Daily Patriot* (Concord, N. H.), Aug. 29, 1908 ; *Printers' Ink,* Sept. 2, 1908 ; information as to certain facts from Rowell's daughter, Persis Eastman Martin.]   W. M., Jr.

ROWLAND, HENRY AUGUSTUS (Nov. 27, 1848–Apr. 16, 1901), physicist, son of the Rev. Henry A. Rowland and his wife, Harriet (Heyer), was born in Honesdale, Pa. His father, grandfather, and great-grandfather were all clergymen and graduates of Yale; his mother was descended from a New York family. The boy was sent to Phillips Academy, Andover, to be prepared for Yale College, but evinced so much greater interest in natural science than in literature and kindred subjects that he was permitted to enter the Rensselaer Polytechnic Institute at Troy, N. Y., instead. He was graduated with the degree of civil engineer in 1870. During the next two years he did some field work and taught natural science at Wooster University, Ohio; but in the spring of 1872 he returned to Rensselaer as instructor in physics, becoming assistant professor in 1874. In 1875 he was chosen by President Daniel Coit Gilman [*q.v.*] to become the first professor of physics in the new Johns Hopkins University. After a year in Europe, spent partly in purchasing apparatus and investigating laboratories and partly in the laboratory of Von Helmholtz at Berlin pursuing certain researches of his own which he had long had in mind, he assumed his academic duties in Baltimore.

In Rowland were combined to a marked degree the scientist's grasp of fundamental principles, the engineer's understanding of practical mechanics, mathematical aptitude, and manual dexterity. His greater contributions to experimental physics were of three kinds: those which involved distinctly original concepts, those concerned with the accurate measurement of certain physical constants, and those in which his engineering talent was most conspicuous. His first important investigation, carried on at Troy, was inspired by Faraday's researches and especially by his concept of magnetic lines of force. Rowland put the physical concept into mathematical language, deducing the consequences of his own theory and testing them by actual experiment. The resulting paper, "On Magnetic Permeability, and the Maximum of Magnetism of Iron, Steel, and Nickel," he sent to Clerk Maxwell in England, who had it published in the *Philosophical Magazine* of August 1873. This investigation provided the basis for subsequent study of both permanent and induced magnetization and the starting point for all calculations for the design of dynamos and transformers. A second important experiment grew out of a question which had occurred to Rowland in his student days, before he was familiar with Faraday or other writers on electrical theory; namely, whether a moving charged conductor would have an effect upon a magnet similar to that of an electric current. By direct experiment in the laboratory of Von Helmholtz during his winter in Berlin, 1875–76, he answered this question in the affirmative (*"Bericht betreffend Versuche über die elektromagnetische Wirkung elektrischer Convection," Monatsberichte der Berliner Akademie,* Mar. 16, 1876). This experiment is of very great significance in connection with the modern theory of electrons.

Another notable contribution resulted from his interest in the study of the spectrum of the sun and the spectra of the elements. Dissatisfied with the cumbersome apparatus necessitated by the gratings of Fraunhofer and Lewis Morris Rutherfurd [*q.v.*], which were made on plane surfaces, he combined the principle of the grating with that of the concave mirror, eventually producing gratings ruled on concave surfaces and thus obviating many of the experimental difficulties inherent in the use of plane gratings. He was always interested in the mechanism of electric currents, as is shown by many of his early experiments, and it was in the course of testing some of his deductions as to the nature of a current that Dr. E. H. Hall was led to the discovery of what is called the "Hall Effect" ("Preliminary Notes on Mr. Hall's Recent Discovery," *American Journal of Mathematics,* 1879). The cause of terrestrial magnetism was anothe problem which attracted Rowland from early youth; he persistently believed that terrestrial magnetism is in some way connected with the rotation of the earth, and one of his last experiments was an attempt to discover whether a piece of matter in rapid rotation would give rise to a difference of potential.

In the field of measurements, he obtained values that are still accepted for the mechanical equivalent of heat (this he considered one of his principal achievements), the ohm, the ratio of the electric units and the wave-lengths of various spectra. When he first went to Johns Hopkins, he insisted upon the establishment and equipment of an adequate workshop in which the apparatus for original research could be produced, and not the least of his contributions to his science were the machines he himself devised. To produce gratings for spectrum analysis more accurate than any previously known, he designed a ruling machine with a screw from which, by a process he devised, errors and irregularities had been virtually eliminated; this was the fundamental part of the machine, but the other details were also finished with a skill almost inspired. His ability to foresee difficulties and guard against them was conspicuously evident in the design of this machine. As a young man, in the early seventies he made for himself a small direct-current dynamo with an original system of automatic regulation, and the existence of this machine was one reason why, in the decades that followed, certain fundamental patents on dynamos could not be secured in the United States. Consulted in regard to the installation of the electrical equipment at the Niagara Falls Power Plant, he became interested in the theory of alternating currents, and after months spent in working out the mathematical formulæ involved, felt himself fully equipped to undertake the design of almost any machine involving the use of such currents. He designed many types of measuring instruments, several of which were adopted for commercial use. He also devised a successful printing telegraph.

Rowland's teaching was less by precept than by example. Passionately interested in his own research, he paid little attention to most of the students in his laboratories, and was a severe critic of those who attracted his notice, though his ardor in itself was a stimulating influence to the talented. He was co-author with J. S. Ames of a textbook, *Elements of Physics* (1900). Outside the University, he found great pleasure in nature, and made hobbies of photography, fishing, sailing, and fox-hunting. He

was a useful citizen, fearless when public questions were involved. As a man, he was remembered by associates as "the embodiment of unselfishness, high ideals, patience and enthusiasm." On June 4, 1890, he married Henrietta Troup Harrison of Baltimore, who with two sons and one daughter survived him. He died in April 1901, after an illness of many months.

[*The Physical Papers of Henry Augustus Rowland* (1902) contains a biog. memoir by T. C. Mendenhall which is printed also in *Nat. Acad. Sci. Biog. Memoirs,* vol. V (1905). See also J. S. Ames, "Henry Augustus Rowland," *Johns Hopkins Alumni Mag.,* Jan. 1916; *Who's Who in America,* 1899–1900; H. B. Nason, *Biog. Record Officers and Grads. Rensselaer Polytechnic Inst.* (1887); *Science,* May 3, 1901; *Nature,* May 2, 1901; the *Sun* (Baltimore), Apr. 17, 1901.]
J. S. A.

ROWLAND, HENRY COTTRELL (May 12, 1874–June 6, 1933), physician, author and traveler, was born in New York City, the son of George and Maria Townsend (Durfee) Rowland. He was a descendant of Henry Rowland, who settled in Fairfield, Conn., in the seventeenth century, and of Thomas Durfee, who settled in Portsmouth, R. I., about 1660. After attending private schools in New York City and Stamford, Conn., and studying for one year at Williams College, he went to Yale and graduated from the Yale School of Medicine in 1898. After graduation he enlisted in the navy as an able seaman on the United States auxiliary cruiser, *Yankee,* and participated in the bombardment of Santiago; the next year he transferred to the army medical service as acting assistant surgeon on a hospital ship, made two voyages to the Philippine Islands, and took part in the insular campaign of 1898–1900. From 1900 to 1905 he practised surgery in New York City. In 1903 he published his first book, *Sea Scamps: Three Adventurers of the East,* a collection of eight short stories. These were followed in 1904 by a novel, *To Windward,* an entertaining, though crudely written story whose action was laid on board ship and in the wards of a city hospital. From that time on, for nearly thirty years, he was a prolific writer of articles, short stories, and novels of mystery and seagoing adventure. On June 22, 1910, he married Mary Fulton Parkinson, in London. When the outbreak of the World War found them living in Vermenton, France, Rowland offered his services to the Allies; for two years he was physician to the war sufferers at Vermenton and Accolay, and during 1916 director of the local military auxiliary hospital at Accolay. The next year he carried on publicity and propaganda for the Allies in the United States, and in 1918 acted as an accredited special agent of the intelligence department of the United States Navy and as war correspondent for *Collier's Weekly*. After the war he established his home in Washington, D. C., and resumed his practice of writing in the winter and traveling in the summer. He died in Washington, survived by his wife and two children.

Rowland's unquenchable zest for adventure shaped both his stories and his life. In 1905 he sailed as a surgeon aboard the *Endymion* in a transatlantic yacht race, went ashore for a few days, found France to his liking, and began a sojourn there that lasted fourteen years. In 1907 he and two friends crossed the English Channel in a motor boat, cruised inland across Europe through rivers and canals from the mouth of the Seine to the Black Sea, and were wrecked in a violent storm off the Bosporus (*Across Europe in a Motor Boat*, 1908). In 1924, with a friend, he sailed to Central and South American ports on a five-thousand-mile cruise in a ketch of his own design and construction, writing several serial stories while on board. These travels and his profession furnished him with the literary materials he most prized. He had a lively, vigorous style, and he acquired great skill in shaping and weaving incidents into plot, though he regarded the study of technique as belonging to the later years when the search for physical adventure becomes impossible (*Woman's Home Companion*, August 1925, p. 112). For Rowland, however, no quiet years in which to achieve a finished technique intervened between adventurous living and death.

[D. H. Hurd, *Hist. of Fairfield County, Conn.* (1881); W. F. Reed, *The Descendants of Thos. Durfee of Portsmouth, R. I.* (2 vols., 1902–05); *Obit. Record Grads. Yale Univ.*, 1933; obituaries in *N. Y. Times*, June 7, 1933, in *Washington (D. C.) Post*, June 7, 1933, and editorial and obituary in *Evening Star* (Washington, D. C.), June 6, 1933; *Who's Who in America*, 1932–33; *Bookman*, Oct. 1912.]   V. L. S.

ROWLAND, THOMAS FITCH (Mar. 15, 1831–Dec. 13, 1907), inventor, manufacturer, was born in New Haven, Conn., the son of George and Ruth Caroline (Attwater) Rowland. His first Rowland ancestor in this country is said to have been Henry, who was in Fairfield, Conn., as early as 1649; he was also a lineal descendant of Thomas Fitch [*q.v.*], a colonial governor of Connecticut. Thomas received his early education in New Haven and at the age of thirteen entered his father's grist mill as the miller's boy. Upon the construction of the New York & New Haven Railroad through New Haven a few years later, the grist mill was demolished and Rowland entered the employment of the railroad, becoming the first apprentice in the machine shop. While in this service he fired the third passenger train that was sent over the railroad from New Haven to New York. In 1850 he gave up this work to accept an appointment as second assistant engineer of the steamboat *Connecticut*, plying between Hartford and New York; but when control of the company owning this vessel changed hands in 1852 and all of the employees were discharged, he obtained a job with the Allaire Works of New York, an old established engine-building concern. A year or two later Rowland left this company and in the succeeding six or eight years was variously employed about New York in the designing and construction of steamboat machinery.

In 1859, in association with Samuel Sneden, a prominent builder of wooden vessels, he established a business at Greenpoint, L. I., for the construction of wooden and iron steamships and for structural iron works. The first contract the new firm obtained was with the Croton aqueduct department for a wrought-iron water-pipe, 7½ feet in diameter and a quarter of a mile long. It was to be located on top of the high bridge over the Harlem River for the purpose of carrying water from the aqueduct to the new reservoir in Central Park. This work, requiring 450 tons of wrought-iron plate and 400 tons of castings, was successfully carried out. The partnership was severed in 1860 and Rowland thereafter continued business alone under the name of "The Continental Works." At the outbreak of the Civil War he began the manufacture of gun carriages and mortar beds for the navy department and fitted out most of the steamers purchased from the merchant service, which vessels took part in the capture of Port Royal and were known as the "Porter Mortar Fleet." In 1861 Rowland contracted with John Ericsson [*q.v.*] for the building of an iron-clad floating battery, afterwards known as the original *Monitor*. Upon its completion he built the monitors *Montauk*, *Catskill*, and *Passaic*, the double-turreted monitor *Onondaga*, and the light-draft gunboats *Cohoes* and *Muscoota*. In the 1870's he built a number of ferryboats for the Union Ferry Company, New York, and constructed steamboats for Cuban waters. He also began the design and manufacture of steam engines and boilers especially adapted for use in the oil industry, and was engaged in designing and constructing gas-manufacturing plants in various parts of the country. For many years he experimented in the art of iron and steel welding and about 1887 designed the process and apparatus used by his company in the manufacture of the Fox corrugated and Morison suspension furnaces widely used for many years in the internal furnace type of boiler. At the same time he incorporated his business as the "Continental Iron Works," and served as the president until his death. He married, in 1855, Mary Elizabeth Bradley of New Haven, Conn., and was survived by three sons. He died in New York City.

[J. L. Bishop, *A Hist. of Am. Manufactures* (1868), vol. III; *Trans. Am. Soc. of Mech. Engineers,* vol. XXIX (1908); *Trans. Am. Soc. of Civil Engineers,* vol. LXII (1909); *N. Y. Tribune,* Dec. 14, 1907; Patent Office records.]   C. W. M.

ROWLANDS, WILLIAM (Oct. 10, 1807–Oct. 27, 1866), clergyman and editor, was born in London, the eldest of the four children of Thomas and Mary (Jones) Rowlands. Both parents were natives of central Wales. After the death of his father, a thrifty milk dealer, in 1814, and of his mother five years later, William, the only surviving child, was cared for by relatives in Wales. If his formal education ended after four years of study at Ystradmeurig and Llangeitho, he had by then gained command of both English and Welsh. From 1824 to 1829 he taught school at Merthyr Tidfil and Pontypool, meanwhile preaching occasionally in Calvinistic Methodist chapels. He was not ordained, however, until 1832. Having come into a small inheritance, he gave up teaching in 1829 and bought a printing establishment, where, among other things, he issued a monthly Sunday-school paper of which he was editor. He married on Aug. 25, 1829, Ann Jacob of Cardiff, whose substantial dowry and his own sanguine temperament led him to overexpand his business activities. By the autumn of 1833 he was bankrupt. Misfortune crowded upon him; the church forbade his preaching; in September 1834 he lost his wife, and, eighteen months later, his only child. His reinstatement in the ministry was but partial solace for all his troubles. He was obliged to begin his life anew and America seemed to offer the fairest future.

Rowlands arrived in New York in the summer of 1836. Not yet thirty, vigorous and energetic, he was conscious of his ability both as preacher and as editor. At once he began preaching to the Welsh community in New York City. Here and in Oneida County, N. Y., he ministered for the rest of his life save for a two-year pastorate at Scranton, Pa. (1856–58). Less eloquent than some of his colleagues, he gained an abiding reputation among the Welsh-Americans for the clarity, the vigor, and the deep sincerity of his preaching. In his pastoral work he was equally successful, for his quick sympathy and ready understanding won him the confidence and affection of his parishioners. His greatest influence, however, was exerted through the religious press. In 1836 no Welsh newspaper or periodicals existed in America. Believing there was need for a religious publication among his countrymen, in January 1838 he issued the first number of *Y Cyfaill* ("The Friend"), a monthly periodical which survived until December 1933. Rowlands' intention to make his paper independent in both religion and politics proved impossible. Soon the Congregationalists and the Baptists founded religious periodicals of their own and *Y Cyfaill* then became the accepted organ of the Calvinistic Methodists. A Democrat who joined the Republicans only in 1861, Rowlands rigorously excluded partisan politics from his paper. Though opposed to slavery, he refused to support abolition, which Robert Everett [*q.v.*] was urging in *Y Cenhadwr.* He condemned the liquor trade roundly and continuously. Though *Y Cyfaill* in Rowlands' lifetime never reached a circulation of two thousand, its influence was deep and widespread. Through it he shaped the thinking of a large proportion of the Welsh-Americans.

Even his active work as pastor and editor did not exhaust his energies. Besides numerous pamphlets, including a short history of his denomination in America, he published a volume of sermons: *Dammeg y Mab Afradlon* (1860). He became a life member of the American Tract Society (1851) and a life director of the American Bible Society (1852). On May 17, 1838, he married Catherine Parry of Remsen, N. Y. By her he had thirteen children, of whom only five survived their father. His indefatigable activity continued almost unabated until his death in Utica.

[Howell Powell, *Cofiant—William Rowlands* (Utica, 1873); biog. material scattered through the first thirty volumes of *Y Cyfaill; R.* D. Thomas, *Hanes Cymry America* (Utica, 1872); *Utica Daily Observer,* Oct. 27, 1866.]   P. D. E.

ROWLANDSON, MARY WHITE (*c.* 1635–*c.* 1678), Indian captive and author, was born about 1635, probably in England, the daughter of John White, wealthiest of the original proprietors of Lancaster, Mass. About 1656 she married Joseph Rowlandson, the first minister of Lancaster, to whom she bore four children. For twenty years following her marriage, she led the hard, uneventful life of a frontier housewife; but on Feb. 10, 1675/76, during King Philip's War, the Indians attacked Lancaster, burnt the village, and carried away captive Mrs. Rowlandson and her three surviving children, of whom the youngest died from exposure shortly after. For eleven weeks, while the Indians wandered about in north central Massachusetts and southern New Hampshire in an effort to avoid the colonial forces, she remained a captive. She suffered, as the Indians did, from lack of food, but the prospective ransom and her skill in making shirts and knitting stockings apparently won her comparatively good treatment. On May 2, 1676, after considerable diplomatic bargaining in which the blusterings of the government probably counted for less than the influence of John Hoar (Shurtleff, *post,* and H. S. Nourse, *The Hoar Family in America,* 1899), she was returned to her friends for a payment of twenty pounds; soon afterward her two children were released. In 1677 the family moved to Wethersfield, Conn., where Mr. Rowlandson had been called as minister. After his death in 1678, the town voted his widow an "allowance of £30 per year so long as she remains a widow among us" (Stiles and Adams, *post,* p. 328). The town records fail to show how long the allowance was paid or the date of Mrs. Rowlandson's death.

The *Soveraignty & Goodness of God, Together with the Faithfulness of His Promises Displayed; Being a Narrative of the Captivity and Restauration of Mrs. Mary Rowlandson* was first published in Cambridge in 1682. Designed by the author "to be to her a memorandum of Gods dealings with her" and *"to declare the Works of the Lord,"* this was one of the most widely-read pieces of seventeenth-century prose. A London edition under a slightly different title appeared within a few months; apparently two second editions came out the same year in Cambridge, and some thirty editions and reprints have been issued since then. No first edition is known. Historians have praised the *Narrative* for its picture of Indian life (J. G. Palfrey, *History of New England,* vol. III, 1864, p. 183) and for "its pure, idiomatic and sinewy English" (M. C. Tyler, *A History of American Literature,* vol. II, 1878, p. 139); it illustrates as well the contempt felt by the colonists for the Indians and admirably fulfills its author's intentions, for Mary Rowlandson in even the darkest hours of her captivity was able to strangle the doubts of God's mercy that assailed her, to assert repeatedly her utter and submissive confidence in God, and finally to believe "as *David* did, *It is good for me that I have been afflicted"* (*Narrative,* p. 73).

[See C. H. Lincoln, ed., *Narratives of the Indian Wars,* 1675–1699 (1913); the excellent ed. of H. S. Nourse and J. E. Thayer, *The Narrative of the Captivity and Restoration of Mrs. Mary Rowlandson* (1903; reprinted in 1930 without bibliog.), a facsimile of a second ed. of 1682; Jos. Willard, ed., *Narrative of the Captivity and Removes of Mrs. Mary Rowland-*son (1828). See also A. L. White, *Geneal. of the Descendants of John White* (2 vols., 1900); H. S. Nourse, "Mrs. Mary Rowlandson's Removes," in *Proc. Am. Antiq. Soc.,* n.s., vol. XII (1899), *The Early Records of Lancaster* (1884), and *Lancastria,* vol. I (1900); S. G. Drake, *The Old Indian Chronicle* (1867) and *Biog. and Hist. of the Indians of N. America* (7th ed., 1837); N. B. Shurtleff, ed., *Records of the Gov. and Company of the Mass. Bay,* vol. V (1854); H. R. Stiles and S. W. Adams, *The Hist. of Ancient Wethersfield* (1904), vol. I.]

L. H.

ROWSE, SAMUEL WORCESTER (Jan. 29, 1822–May 24, 1901), painter, illustrator, and lithographer, was born at Bath, Me., one of six children of Edward and Mercy (Blake) Rowse. The family, its name more usually spelled Rouse, is genealogically interesting, coming down from Capt. Augustus Rouse of the *Dunkirk* (concerning whose settlement in Boston see H. W. Foote, *Annals of King's Chapel,* vol. I, 1882, p. 233). Samuel was baptized June 23, 1822 (Records of the Winter Street Congregational Church, Bath). The family a little later moved to Augusta, where after common schooling young Rowse was apprenticed to a local engraver. This occupation brought him to Boston, where he learned lithography, probably in the shop of Tappan and Bradford (Peters, *post*). In the work of his early years in Boston there have been identified a portrait of Richard Fletcher, justice of the supreme court of Massachusetts, and several minor pieces delineated for Tappan and Bradford. Among his illustrations were those for Louise Chandler Moulton's *This, That, and the Other* (edition of 1856). A reticent, reserved man, who never married, Rowse had a brief stage experience, appearing in *King Richard III* at Boston. Convinced that his talent did not lie in that direction, he resumed the making of delicate, well-characterized crayon drawings through which he gained a national and international reputation. Among his familiar portraits are those of James Russell Lowell, Ralph Waldo Emerson, and Nathaniel Hawthorne. His studio for many years was in the old Studio Building, Tremont Street, where his closest friend and professional associate was Eastman Johnson [*q.v.*]. In 1872 Rowse visited England, where he became acquainted with John Ruskin, of whom he later said, "He wanted me to hold the brush while he painted" (Peters, *post*). Having moved to New York in 1880, Rowse made his home at Morristown, N. J., where he died after amassing a considerable estate. He was an occasional exhibitor in his later years, but his celebrity among collectors rests upon his early portraits.

[A MS. on the Maine Rouses, prepared by W. J. Rouse, M.D., was owned in 1931 by Miss Mary Pelham Hill, of Topsham, Me. Other sources are Bath, Me., Church Records, 1795–1829, compiled by Mary P. Hill and deposited in MS. at the New England Hist.

Geneal. Soc., Boston; H. T. Peters, *America on Stone* (1931); C. E. Clement and Laurence Hutton, *Artists of the Nineteenth Century* (1884); Theodore Bolton, *Early Am. Portrait Draughtsmen in Crayons* (1923); E. W. Emerson, *The Early Years of the Saturday Club, 1855–1870* (1918); *N. Y. Tribune*, May 26, 1901.]

F. W. C.

ROWSON, SUSANNA HASWELL (*c.* 1762–Mar. 2, 1824), novelist, actress, educator, was born in Portsmouth, England, of a family which produced several British and American naval officers and at least two other authors, her cousin Anthony Haswell [*q.v.*] and her brother, Lieut. Robert Haswell (F. W. Howay, *Washington Historical Quarterly*, April 1933). Her mother, Susanna Musgrave (or Musgrove), died giving birth to her daughter. When the child was about five, her father, Lieut. William Haswell, who was stationed in Massachusetts and had remarried there, returned to England for her; and the clearest recollection of her childhood was that of the stormy passage, ending in shipwreck, vividly narrated in her novel *Rebecca*. Her girlhood was happily spent at her father's home in Nantasket, where at ten she surprised their summer neighbor, James Otis, by her familiarity with Spenser, Shakespeare, and Homer and Virgil in Pope's and Dryden's translations. In 1775 her father's estate was confiscated and his family interned at Hingham and later Abington, until he was exchanged in 1778 and they all returned to England. In 1786, encouraged by the success of Fanny Burney and Harriet and Sophia Lee, she published her first novel, *Victoria*, dedicated to the Duchess of Devonshire and favorably noticed (January 1787) by the *Critical Review* and the *Monthly Review*. Later in the year, she married William Rowson, then in the hardware business in London and trumpeter in the Royal Horse Guards, a personable young man and a fair musician but of no great stability of character. Her next few works, *The Inquisitor or Invisible Rambler* (1788), *Poems on Various Subjects* (1788), and *Mary, or the Test of Honour* (1789), added little to her reputation. But early in 1791 (Vail, *post*) she produced the novel, *Charlotte, a Tale of Truth*, which was to make her famous. Supposedly based on an actual amour of her kinsman, Col. John Montrésor [*q.v.*], this book, sentimental and didactic, yet unusually unified and direct for her and treating a situation of universal appeal with genuine pathos, captivated the American fancy when reprinted in Philadelphia in 1794 and became the chief American "best-seller" before *Uncle Tom's Cabin*, passing through more than 160 editions before 1905. *Mentoria, or the Young Lady's Friend*, a collection of didactic

tales and essays, came later in 1791, followed by *Rebecca, or the Fille de Chambre* (1792), largely autobiographical and second-best among her novels despite its disorderly plot. In 1792 William Rowson failed, and the family turned for support to the stage, in which Mrs. Rowson had already shown her interest by the versified critique, *A Trip to Parnassus* (1788). In the winter season of 1792–93 the Rowsons played in Edinburgh and other cities but were stranded when Thomas Wignell [*q.v.*], recruiting in England for his company at the New Chestnut Street Theatre, Philadelphia, met and engaged them. From the end of 1793 to 1796 they acted, mostly in minor parts, in Philadelphia, Baltimore, and Annapolis. For the Philadelphia company, Mrs. Rowson wrote *Slaves in Algiers*, acted June 30, 1794, and the musical farce *The Volunteers*, Jan. 21, 1795, and adapted Massinger's *The Bondman* as *The Female Patriot*, June 19, 1795. (For bibliographical details, see Vail, *post*.) Her appeal to contemporary interest and to American patriotic sentiment (shown in these plays and in her verse address, "The Standard of Liberty," recited at Baltimore, Oct. 29, 1795) aroused her fellow-countryman, William Cobbett [*q.v.*], to a coarse satire, *A Kick for a Bite* (1795), that led her to allude to him in the preface to *Trials of the Human Heart,* published later in the same year, as "a kind of loathsome reptile." In 1796 the Rowsons went to the Federal Street Theatre, Boston, for which Mrs. Rowson wrote a comedy, *Americans in England* (1796), first presented on Apr. 19, 1797, and later assigned to John Hodgkinson [*q.v.*], who performed it as *The Columbian Daughter, or Americans in England*.

In the spring of 1797 she left the stage to devote the rest of her life to conducting a select school for young ladies in or near Boston. In this career she was notably successful, furnishing her pupils with musical training under competent foreign instructors and infusing them with her own fine qualities of character. She did not relinquish her interest in letters, serving from 1802 to 1805 as editor of the *Boston Weekly Magazine*, to which she contributed in serial form her novel "Sincerity" (separately published as *Sarah, the Exemplary Wife* in 1813), poems, and the greater part of an essay series, "The Gossip." After 1805 she continued to write for the magazine's successor, *The Boston Magazine*, for *The Monthly Anthology and Boston Review*, and J. T. Buckingham's *New England Galaxy*. A collection of her poems and songs—more than thirty of the latter were separately published between 1794 and 1824—was issued as *Miscellaneous Poems* (1804). *Reuben and Rachel*, a very poorly organized historical novel tracing the fortune of certain descendants of Christopher Columbus through three centuries and numerous countries, appeared in 1798. Another novel, left in manuscript at her death and printed in 1828 as *Charlotte's Daughter, or The Three Orphans,* is a sequel to *Charlotte Temple,* in which Lucy, Charlotte's illegitimate daughter, narrowly escapes an incestuous marriage with her half-brother, a theme perhaps suggested by William Hill Brown's *The Power of Sympathy* (1789) and *Ira and Isabella* (1807). More than thirty editions, mostly under the title *Lucy Temple,* were issued. Most of her later publications, however, were textbooks or monitory works for young women.

Herself childless, Mrs. Rowson devoted a mother's care successively to her husband's younger sister, Charlotte; to his illegitimate son, William; and to at least one adopted daughter. In her later life, while her husband held a government clerkship, she was able to contribute to many philanthropic enterprises, serving as president of the Boston Fatherless and Widows Society. She died in her house in Hollis Street, Boston, Mar. 2, 1824. William Rowson survived her and remarried, dying at Boston in 1842.

[See esp. R. W. G. Vail, *Susanna Haswell Rowson, the Author of Charlotte Temple: A Bibliographical Study* (1933), an invaluable bibliog., and Elias Nason, *A Memoir of Mrs. Susanna Rowson* (1870), based in part on a memoir by her friend Samuel L. Knapp, printed in the preface to *Charlotte's Daughter* (1828). An obit. notice appeared in the *Evening Gazette,* Mar. 6, 1824. Other sources of value are J. T. Buckingham, *Personal Memoirs and Recollections of Editorial Life* (1852), vol. I, pp. 83–85; Eliza S. Bowne, *A Girl's Life Eighty Years Ago* (1887); Wm. Cobbett, *A Kick for a Bite* (1795); F. W. Halsey, ed., intro. to *Charlotte Temple* (1905); and John Spargo, *Anthony Haswell, Printer-Patriot-Ballader* (1925), which gives the best account of the Haswell family.]   M. E.

ROYALL, ANNE NEWPORT (June 11, 1769–Oct. 1, 1854), traveler, author, was born in Maryland. Her father, William Newport, may have been an illegitimate son of one of the Calverts (see letter of Lord Baltimore to Governor Sharpe from London 1767, Porter, *post,* p. 19), and all that is known of her mother is that she had relatives in Virginia named Anderson. After a wandering childhood, spent chiefly in frontier Pennsylvania, Anne returned to Virginia and entered in menial capacity the household of William Royall, scholar, gentleman farmer, Revolutionary veteran, and ardent Mason. Royall became interested in his dependent, undertook her education, and in 1797 was married to her. At his death, sixteen years later, he left her the bulk of his property, but after ten years of litigation, spent by her chiefly in the South, his

other heirs succeeded in breaking the will, leaving her penniless at the age of fifty-four. During the illness and poverty she suffered in the following months she was assisted by friendly Masons and, in her disappointing struggle for a government pension as wife of a Revolutionary officer, by no less an advocate than John Quincy Adams.

In 1824 she started out to earn her living by traveling over the United States and publishing accounts of her journeys. She was an ardent pro-Mason and anti-Evangelical, for which she suffered both adulation and assault. Her attitude against the Presbyterians led to her trial and conviction in Washington in 1829 on the trumped-up, obsolete charge of being a common scold. After this unpleasant experience she found it difficult to travel, so, aided by her life-long friend, Mrs. Sarah Stack, she embarked on the proprietorship and editorship of a small, independent newspaper in Washington. Her two papers, *Paul Pry* (Dec. 3, 1831–Nov. 19, 1836) and *The Huntress* (Dec. 2, 1836–July 24, 1854) ran in succession from 1831 to a few months before her death. She was a vigorous editor, noted for her ability to uncover graft in any department of government. She advocated the veto of the United States Bank charter, Sunday mail transportation, non-partisan tariff regulations, no nullification, sound money, tolerance for Roman Catholics, no union of church and state, territorial expansion, internal improvements, liberal appropriations for scientific research, and state rights in the matter of slavery. She attained a kind of unenviable fame throughout the country, many enemies, a few stanch friends. In 1848 her pension was at last awarded, but after various fees were paid it proved to be only a trifle. In her last years she was often miserably poor. She died at her home on B Street, now part of the grounds of the Library of Congress and was buried in the Congressional Cemetery.

Between 1826 and 1831 she published ten volumes of travels, of which the first, *Sketches of History, Life and Manners in the United States, by a Traveller* (1826) is probably in all respects the best. It was followed by *The Black Book, or a Continuation of Travels in the United States* (3 vols., 1828–29), *Mrs. Royall's Pennsylvania* (2 vols., 1829); *Mrs. Royall's Southern Tour* (3 vols., 1830–31), and *Letters from Alabama* (1830). All bear the faults of hasty execution and reveal the gaps in the author's early education, which her later wide reading never filled. She was given to personalities of doubtful taste, and the violent expression of both her sympathies and antipathies is often tiresome. Withal, she was a tireless traveler, a shrewd observer, a careful verifier of facts, and a strictly honest writer. Her own vigorous, aggressive personality pervades her work; she is always readable and nearly always reliable. There is scarcely a city or town of any importance in the United States of 1826–30 that her keen observant pen did not sketch. Her "pen portraits" include nearly 2,000 of the great and near-great of her day. She was the author of a novel, *The Tennessean* (1827), which in plot, execution, and characters is one of the worst ever written in America. She tried her hand at drama with a play, *The Cabinet, or Large Parties in Washington,* the text of which has disappeared, but which was given one performance at the Masonic Hall in Washington. Her works deserve to survive as valuable sources for the study of the social history of the United States. In her journalism as well she was always vigorous and straightforward, but often amateurish and ungrammatical. She was grossly personal, given to tirades against her opponents, and long praises of her benefactors. She was steadfastly loyal to her cause, or to anyone who befriended her. Her kindness to "fallen women" in an age without charity and her devastating generosity in her brief periods of prosperity show the violence of her likes and dislikes, and her sincere consistency in both. At once pathetic and admirable, the Miss Flite of the Capitol, with tongue and eyes that were a terror to any dishonest congressman, "Godless Anne Royall," yet with more true charity about her than the "saints" against whom she railed, she is a figure to be included in some lesser national gallery.

[S. H. Porter, *The Life and Times of Anne Royall* (1909), and in *Columbia Hist. Soc. Records,* vol. X (1907); Heber Blankenhorn, "The Grandma of the Muckrakers," *American Mercury,* Sept. 1927; R. L. Wright, *Forgotten Ladies* (1928); *Evening Star* (Washington), Oct. 2, 1854.]　　　　J. H. B—h.

ROYCE, JOSIAH (Nov. 20, 1855–Sept. 14, 1916), philosopher and teacher, was the youngest child and only son of Josiah and Sarah Eleanor (Bayliss) Royce, who crossed the continent to California in the "gold rush" of 1849. Both parents were English by birth, the father having been born in Ridlington, Rutlandshire, in 1812, and the mother in Stratford-on-Avon in 1819. The father emigrated to Canada, the mother to the United States, both in childhood; and they met and were married at the latter's home in Rochester, N. Y. In 1848 they moved to eastern Iowa, the point of departure for their journey to California, which began on Apr. 30 of the following year. The little family, now including Mary, a child of two years of age, met with the adventures and risks characteristic of this great migration. They reached Council Bluffs on June 4, and Salt Lake City on Aug. 20. They lost their way in the Carson desert, and were forced to retrace their steps for many miles to the Humboldt Sink, but eventually, in a state of exhaustion, reached the Carson River at the foot of the Sierras on Oct. 12. Here they met a rescuing party of the United States Government Relief Company, abandoned their wagon and proceeded on muleback, camping in the open, and crossing the divide just in time to escape the first heavy snowfall of winter. They finally reached Weaverville, Cal., on Oct. 24, approximately six months from their date of departure. After a brief sojourn here and at Sacramento the family passed three years in San Francisco, where they arrived Jan. 1, 1850. After unsuccessful ventures in store-keeping and merchandising in the vicinity of Sacramento, a more permanent settlement was made in Grass Valley, Nevada County, a relatively populous and pleasant mining town in the foot-hills of the Sierras. A second daughter, Harriet, had been born in San Francisco, and a third, Ruth, during their subsequent wanderings. The fourth child and only son, Josiah, was born in Grass Valley on Nov. 20, 1855.

The record of this Odyssey was preserved in the diary of the mother, Sarah Eleanor Royce. She was a remarkable woman, combining a profound and vital spirituality with intellectual interests and attainments. Through many years of hardship and uncertain family fortunes, in an environment which tended to reduce life to elementals, she clung firmly to her faith and ideals and did what she could to preserve the standards of life to which she was accustomed. The young Josiah was indebted to his mother not only for his inheritance but also for his early education, religious and secular. Finding no adequate school in Grass Valley, she organized one and taught it herself, in her own house. When Josiah reached the age of eleven, however, the family returned to San Francisco, where he entered the Lincoln Grammar School, and in 1869, the Boys' High School. Here he was most fortunate both in his associates and in his teachers. A number of his classmates afterwards distinguished themselves in their several professions, among them Albert A. Michelson [*q.v.*], the celebrated physicist. The principal, Theodore Bradley, and many of his staff, were men of marked individuality; the spirit of the school was stimulating, its methods and curriculum were progressive. The young Royce, already an omnivorous reader, spent many of his out-of-school hours in the Mercantile Library. The extremely modest circumstances of his family life combined with his personal traits to limit his social contacts with his contemporaries, but even at this early age he showed remarkable intellectual gifts, especially in the field of mathematics, where he soon outstripped his teachers. After some further preparatory instruction in Oakland, he matriculated at the recently established University of California in Berkeley in the fall of 1871.

The influence of the California environment upon the growing boy was intellectual and moral rather than physical. For bodily activities, except walking, he had neither capacity nor taste. His mother and his three sisters protected him from any lessons which he might otherwise have learned from physical hardship. Nor did he acquire the pioneer's readiness and self-sufficiency in dealing with his fellows. In social situations he was timid, sensitive, and conscious of himself (to quote his own reminiscence) as "redheaded, freckled, countrified, quaint." At an early age he formed the habit of thoughtful solitude. But the influence of California was nevertheless deeply imprinted on his soul. His interest in its romance, and his memory of early experience, bore fruit in two books: *California . . . A Study of American Character* (1886), in the American Commonwealth Series; and his only novel, entitled *The Feud of Oakfield Creek* (1887). He judged himself to be a "born non-conformist," and California ripened this tendency. The majestic scenery with which he was surrounded in boyhood and youth encouraged the cosmic sweep of his imagination, and filled him with awe. In 1879, referring to his intention of dealing with problems of life, he said he would deal with them independently and reverently—"independently, because I am a Californian, as little bound to follow mere tradition as I am liable to find an audience by preaching in this wilderness; reverently, because I am thinking and writing face to face with a mighty and lovely Nature, by the side of whose greatness I am but as a worm" (*Fugitive Essays*, p. 7).

But while his genius and his circumstances combined to render him detached and shy, nevertheless (or perhaps for this very reason), he felt a wistful need of social relations; and the belief that a man's fullest development can be found only in the life of the "community" became the central article of his creed and a major topic in his philosophizing. The lack of an established social order in a pioneer community was calculated to call attention to the need of it. To California, also, Royce owed his profound Americanism. He never acquired the cosmopolitanism of eastern scholars, and his philosophical

development consists essentially in the interaction of his instinctive (and incorrigible) Protestantism and moral individualism with the pantheistic and esthetic doctrines which he acquired from his German teachers, Lotze, Schelling, Schopenhauer, Fichte, and Hegel.

The University of California of Royce's student days provided no instruction in philosophy, but Joseph LeConte, geologist and pioneer Darwinian, and Edward Rowland Sill [*qq.v.*], poet and essayist, were his beloved teachers. They supplied him with nourishing philosophical pabulum in the name of science and literature. At the same time, like other eager American youths of his generation, he read Herbert Spencer and John Stuart Mill for himself. But with his lively intellectual interest, his feeling for literature, and his exceptional memory, his education was mainly a voyage of discovery in which he himself supplied both the motive power and the guiding hand. He had discovered *Faust* and other literary classics in his high-school days, and had read widely in history. His graduation thesis on the theology of the *Promethus Bound* of Aeschylus (*California University Bulletin*, June 1875) illustrated the characteristically philosophical method of his studies, whatever their subject matter. It was to the friendly interest excited by the high quality of this thesis that the young scholar owed the opportunity of studying in Europe after receiving his bachelor's degree in 1875. He spent the next year mainly at Göttingen and Leipzig, where through the lectures of Lotze, Wundt, and Windelband, and through his studies of Kant, Schopenhauer, and others, his thought received a spiritualistic-idealistic impress which it never lost. In 1876 Daniel Coit Gilman, who had been the president of the University of California during Royce's undergraduate days, invited him to be one of the first twenty fellows appointed at the new Johns Hopkins University. Here he received the degree of Ph.D. in 1878, with a dissertation (read and approved by President Noah Porter of Yale) entitled, "Of the Interdependence of the Principles of Knowledge," and on the basis of examinations set by Prof. George S. Morris of the University of Michigan.

Royce's fellowship at the Johns Hopkins had been in literature, the field of his examinations for the doctorate had been the history of philosophy, together with German literature in the eighteenth and nineteenth centuries, and he began his teaching career as an instructor in English at the University of California, where he spent the next four years. This literary emphasis of his early studies and teaching colored his writings, his first literary ventures including critical essays on Schiller, Shelley, George Eliot, and Browning (republished posthumously in *Fugitive Essays*, 1920). But it was the philosophy of his authors which most deeply interested him. His permanent attraction to Schelling and others of the German Romantic movement was due to their union of philosophy and literature. In his teaching of rhetoric he found an opportunity of introducing logic, and of preparing a *Primer of Logical Analysis for the Use of Composition Students* (1881). He had long since found his vocation in philosophy, and he schooled himself in its technicalities by continuous reading and thinking. In an entry of his diary for July 25, 1880, he remarked: "The use of writing a diary is that every day vies with its neighbors in saying something for itself. A day like this that has nothing to say, is ashamed." He counted that day lost that did not see some step forward in his soul's progress toward speculative truth. His reading during this California period embraced a reëxamination of Kant and Hegel, together with a study of contemporary writers such as William James, Charles S. Peirce, Shadworth Hodgson, and the psychologists Wundt and Bain. He improved his knowledge of mathematics. He wrote copiously on philosophical subjects and provisionally draughted a systematic treatise to be called "Outlines of Critical Philosophy," or "The Work of Thought." In an article on "Mind and Reality," which appeared in *Mind* in January 1882, he announced his adhesion to the philosophical school of post-Kantian idealism and sketched several of his most characteristic doctrines.

In proportion as Royce grew in philosophical attainment he felt his isolation. At California he had no philosophical students to teach, and no philosophical colleagues to confirm his intellectual faith and criticize his ideas. In the summer of 1877 he had visited William James in Cambridge, and at a crucial moment had received encouragement to undertake the doubtful venture of philosophy. He heard James's lectures at the Johns Hopkins during the following winter, and he corresponded with him when he went to California. For the next thirty years the affectionate friendship of these two men conspicuously illustrated the philosopher's favorite theme of unity in difference. James began in 1880 to look for an opportunity for Royce in the East. Finally his own leave of absence for the year 1882–83 provided the opportunity of calling Royce to Harvard as his substitute. The probable absence of George Herbert Palmer in the following year made it possible that the appointment would be extended for two years. There was little prospect of permanence. But Royce took the risk, and with his wife, Katharine Head Royce, whom he had married on Oct. 2, 1880, and their eldest son, then an infant, he crossed the continent to Cambridge in the summer of 1882. At Harvard Royce remained during the balance of his days. He began his teaching with some misgivings, doubting his ability to enter into sufficiently "close relations" with his students. He soon earned however, the good opinion of his students, his colleagues, and of President Eliot. He was appointed to an assistant professorship in 1885, to a professorship in 1892, and finally, upon the retirement of George Herbert Palmer in 1914, to the Alford Professorship of Natural Religion, Moral Philosophy and Civil Polity.

During the earlier years of his career Royce's development was greatly influenced by his association with James. As James's substitute in 1882–83 he was obliged to teach psychology, even "advanced psychology." He also taught psychology at the Massachusetts Institute of Technology (in addition to his Harvard work), conducted experiments (on invention) in the Harvard psychological laboratory, took part actively in the work of the American Branch of the Society for Psychical Research, and in 1903 published his *Outlines of Psychology*. But the influence of his colleague and friend was much more central than this. In July 1879 James had published in *Mind* an article entitled "The Sentiment of Rationality," in which he undertook to analyze the motives which induce men to reason, construing thought as an expression of will and emotion. Royce, influenced by Fichte, Schopenhauer, and the Romanticists, found himself on common ground. He conceived his essay on "Mind and Reality" to be a sequel to James's "Sentiment of Rationality," and thought of James and himself as collaborators in inaugurating a new method of philosophizing, of which the cardinal principle should be the essentially active and creative character of the knowing mind. This partnership did not last long. It soon became clear that whatever they might say, James and Royce meant very different things. When James spoke of a "sentiment" of rationality or a "will" to believe, he referred to natural minds. To Royce, on the other hand, consciousness was a universal principle, governed by its own inward dialectical necessities. As early as 1883 he wrote down in his diary a criterion of truth which in slightly different terms he often reaffirmed. A given statement is true, he said, when "the contradictory of this statement would involve this statement itself." The mind thinks what, if it is to think at all, it cannot avoid thinking without contradicting itself. It is under this dialectical compulsion that the mind escapes the scepticism of the passing moment, and the relativities of a merely human experience—all of which is widely removed from James both in matter and in doctrine. For Royce the mind is absolutely compelled to affirm the being of an Absolute; for James the mind is doubtfully inclined to believe in a world of change and chance, where God is only one of many. On this issue they fought for decades, exchanging first words and letters, then articles, and finally books. The feud was inherited by their pupils. Royce the protagonist of monism, or the essential and necessary oneness of things, and James the friend of pluralism, or of manyness and differences, have became symbolic of long-lived and good-humored philosophical controversy. But though the breach was wide the affinities and connections were never wholly forgotten. Towards the close of their careers Royce was still building bridges such as "The Eternal and the Practical," or "absolute pragmatism," and inviting James to cross over; while James, though he still rejected monism, made it clear that the only monism that really tempted him was that morally "richer and thicker" variety provided by his colleague Royce.

The first of Royce's major philosophical works was *The Religious Aspect of Philosophy,* published in 1885, and summing up the philosophical tendencies and influences of his early years. He turns to religious problems because, as he tells us, these first "drove the author to philosophy." Having ceased long since to be connected with any "visible religious body," he does not pride himself on the fact (like the fox who lost his tail), but proposes to set forth a religious view of the world which, though it does not imply, is nevertheless consistent with, a more positive creed. The method of the book is a variant of the method of doubt, and the argument falls into two main parts. The first part is an appeal to the thinker to play the nobler part and "postulate" what is not given in experience. Common sense postulates an external world, science postulates the simplicity and orderliness of nature, hence why should religion not postulate that goodness at the heart of things which "satisfies the highest moral needs"? But in the second part of the argument the author supports postulate by proof. Doubt itself implies the possibility of error. What, then, is error, and what are its conditions? Error attaches only to judgments, and judgments refer to objects. They are erroneous only provided they are in some sense inadequate or inap-

propriate to their own objects, that is, to objects which they themselves select and consciously identify. The object referred to must be given, and the judgment entertained must be recognized as, relatively to that object, erroneous. But most human cognitive situations are incomplete, because their objects are not given. This is the case, for example, with one man's knowledge of another's mind, or with his knowledge of past and future. Since even in these cases his judgments are either true or false, there must be a more comprehensive knowing, embracing this man's judgment, but transcending his temporal and other limitations so as to embrace the missing objects. This universal knower, affirmer of all judgments, experiencer of all objects, and thus uniquely qualified to bring judgments and their objects together, is the famous "Absolute." Although this is only one of many ways of arriving at such a conclusion, it is Royce's most original contribution to its proofs. The general metaphysical implications are evident. They are idealistic, since all reality is essentially the act, idea, or experience of a mind; they are monistic, since there is one such mind to which all others are related as parts to whole, and which stands not only as the ultimate being of metaphysics, but as the object of worship and the standard of value.

In the next of Royce's constructive treatises these moral and religious implications assume a crucial importance. In 1895 he delivered before the Philosophical Union of the University of California an address on "The Conception of God." This was afterward published (1897) together with discussions of Royce's address by G. H. Howison, Joseph LeConte, and S. E. Mezes. To this volume Royce also contributed a supplementary essay on "The Absolute and the Individual," which contained a critical comparison of the Thomist and Scotist doctrines of the principle of individualism. Howison, expounding his so-called "personal idealism," attacked the monistic trend of Royce's thought as failing to provide for the autonomy of the moral individual, thus appealing to Royce against himself. For despite his argument for an all-enveloping mind, here reiterated and strengthened, Royce was not prepared to abandon, or even to disparage, the human prerogatives of freedom and responsibility. And yet how shall these prerogatives be reconciled with a metaphysical Absolute? In *The Conception of God* the author attempted to meet the difficulty by insisting that the principle of individuation is choice or preference, that the Absolute is an individual consisting ultimately in a sheer act of will, and that this Absolute Will is parcelled out among human beings, each of which wills independently within its own province.

At the same time that Royce was thus restating, amplifying, and applying his characteristic metaphysical doctrines he found time to give numerous public lectures, and to renew his literary interests. From these activities there resulted, in 1892, the most brilliantly written and the most widely read of his works, *The Spirit of Modern Philosophy* (see also his *Lectures on Modern Idealism* published posthumously in 1919). This book is, on the one hand, a work of historical narrative and exposition, distinguished by its imaginative sympathy, its playful humor, and by paragraphs of sustained eloquence. The author's beloved Romanticists, together with Kant, Hegel, and Schopenhauer, are treated with peculiar tenderness and insight. But the book serves also, on the other hand, to make clear Royce's own historical orientation; in particular, his view of the limits of science. By subordinating the "world of description" to the "world of appreciation," he argues the inadequacy of the new positivistic and evolutionary school, in which he, like all English and American students of his day, was widely read.

In 1899 and 1900 Royce delivered the Gifford Lectures at the University of Aberdeen, and these lectures in their published form, under the name of *The World and the Individual* (1900, 1901), constitute the most important of his systematic works. In the first volume the author pays his respects to rival philosophical tendencies, mysticism, realism, and "critical rationalism," the last serving as a sort of blanket designation for diverse forms of empiricism and materialism. Against all of these doctrines, affirming as they do that being is above or beyond experience, or a mere possibility of experience, Royce argues an unqualified idealism, according to which reality belongs exclusively to the conscious life of an all-enveloping mind. The constructive portion of the book gives to this characteristic doctrine a new and significant development. In *The Religious Aspect of Philosophy* Royce had used the term "thought" to designate the processes of the Absolute, while in *The Conception of God,* the emphasis had been shifted to "will." In the present book the term "purpose" plays a mediating rôle. Thought is essentially purposive. The key to its nature is found in the double meaning of ideas. An idea's "internal meaning" consists of the universals or ideal possibilities which constitute *what* is judged; its "external meaning" consists in the particular object to which it refers, and which constitutes

that which is judged *about.* This object, while it lies beyond the idea, is embraced within mind as the experience to which the idea points as its own "fulfilment." The second volume of *The World and the Individual* is devoted to cosmological and practical applications. The author introduces the interesting speculation that the so-called unconscious parts of nature belong to minds whose "time-rate is slower or faster than those which our consciousness is adapted to read or to appreciate" (*Ibid.,* II, 240). The practical applications pursue the general line of thought already adopted in *The Conception of God.* The reality of the human individual must somehow be reconciled with the doctrine of the Absolute. This can be done, the author believes, by making the Absolute *consist* of human or other finite individuals; which it embraces, supplements, and completes, but does not supersede. Each finite individual makes his unique and indispensable contribution to the whole. But if this notion is to be adhered to consistently, it is evident that Royce is confronted by the ancient "problem of evil" in an aggravated form. Pain and sin, like everything else, make their contributions: what, then, becomes of the pity or remorse which condemns them? Royce's answer, the inevitable and universal answer of pantheism in its last line of defense, is that the supreme value of the world lies in moral conflict, struggle, and overcoming; and that what in the limited, finite view is reprobated, is in the higher view accepted as affording the necessary resistance to the moral will.

After 1900 Royce's interests developed in opposite but complementary directions—toward a more technical and specialized treatment of logic, and toward a more popular treatment of moral, social, and religious problems. Both of these tendencies reacted upon his central philosophical doctrines. Royce was one of the first Americans after Charles S. Peirce [*q.v.*] to enter the field of symbolic logic and the philosophical foundations of mathematics. He wrote a number of technical papers on these subjects and on the allied subject of scientific method, the most important being the "Principles of Logic," contributed to the *Encyclopædia of the Philosophical Sciences* in 1913 (original German edition in 1912); and "The Relations of the Principles of Logic to the Foundations of Geometry," published in the *Transactions of the American Mathematical Society,* vol. VI (1905). The effect of his logical and mathematical studies was to give additional emphasis and a more vigorous formulation to his favorite principle of non-contradiction, and to provide him with an interpretation of infinity. The difficulty of infinity was inherent in his system. Reality is a "self-representative" system, like the ideally perfect map which must contain itself. Every fact of experience is the fulfilment of a purpose; but this fulfilment is itself a fact which fulfils another purpose, and so on, *ad infinitum*. Such an endlessly repetitive process was regarded by F. H. Bradley and others as a vicious regress, which must somehow be escaped. To Royce, however, it signified the fact that reality is infinite, and infinite neither in the bad sense, nor in the edifying sense, but in the sense of modern mathematics. In the "Supplementary Essay," appended to the first volume of *The World and The Individual*, he gave a masterly exposition and philosophical interpretation of the views of Cantor, Bolzano, and others, who had defied infinity as a multitude or series having parts which may be placed in one-to-one correspondence with the whole; as, for example, the odd numbers may be placed in one-to-one correspondence with the positive integers.

Royce had always applied his philosophy to the concrete moral issues of his day (see his *Race Questions, Provincialism, and Other American Problems,* 1908). A series of public lectures on ethics, given before various audiences and finally in 1907 before the Lowell Institute in Boston, were published in 1908 as *The Philosophy of Loyalty.* The book had a wide appeal. Its central thesis is the salvation of the individual through loyalty to a cause. To escape a conflict of loyalties, the maxim of loyalty to one's own cause is supplemented by the maxim of "loyalty to loyalty," by which the loyal individual will indirectly support the whole realm of causes. A fuller development of the same ideas appeared in a set of lectures delivered at Manchester College, Oxford, and published under the name of *The Problem of Christianity* (2 vols., 1913). These lectures contained Royce's final interpretation of that Christian faith which in the person of his mother had been so powerful an influence in his childhood, and contained at the same time his most thorough treatment of the subject of religion (see also *The Sources of Religious Insight,* 1912). He selected as the three central Christian ideas, the Pauline Church, the "lost" state of the natural man, and atonement. These ideas he interpreted in terms of the "community," as being the supreme object of the individual's loyalty, by estrangement from which man is lost, and by whose spirit and service he is restored.

The effect of these ethical and religious studies, embracing in addition to major works numerous special essays and addresses, was to bring the metaphysical Absolute into nearer relation to man. The Absolute assumes the form of a personified "Beloved Community," to which the individual man was bound by a sort of patriotic fervor, or blend of self-sacrifice and self-aggrandizement. But even the more technical aspects of Royce's metaphysics were modified by the new emphasis. From Peirce he borrowed the notion that there is a kind of object, namely a sign, which cannot as such be either perceived or conceived but must, if it is to be apprehended at all, be "interpreted." Whereas perception and conception are "dyadic" relations (involving only two terms, subject and object), interpretations are triadic, involving a sign, an interpreter, and a second mind to which the interpretation is communicated. Thus, Royce argues, interpretation involved a *community* of two or more minds. Already, in his *Studies of Good and Evil* (1898), he had emphasized the dependence of self-consciousness on social relations; and in the second volume of *The World and the Individual* had adopted the view that nature is a social product, or a construction dictated by the exigences of stable and cooperative human intercourse. In *The Problem of Christianity* this view receives confirmation and restatement. As from the beginning of Royce's whole development, knowledge is creative of being; but knowledge is now construed as a social affair —a community of interpretation.

The moral issues of the World War stirred Royce profoundly, and won him to a vigorous public support of the cause of the Allies. At a mass-meeting held in Tremont Temple, Boston, on Jan. 30, 1916, he electrified a great audience by the daring, candor, and solemnity of his address. His humanity was shocked by the cruelty and waste of war and he devoted much thought and ingenuity to the problem of its prevention. The obvious depth and sincerity of his feeling, and his moral courage embodied in physical gentleness, won him a new and reverent regard during his last days. For he had begun to fail from 1912, and the emotional strain of the war years told heavily upon him. He died on Sept. 14, 1916, leaving a widow and his two younger sons, Edward and Stephen. Immediately after his death his addresses on war and peace were published under the title of *The Hope of the Great Community* (1916), a title admirably summarizing both his deepest and his latest interests.

After the death of James, Royce had become the most influential American philosopher of his day. For twenty-five years he was the leading exponent in America of that post-Kantian idealism which at the close of the nineteenth century numbered more adherents among students of philosophy than any rival tendency. Within this idealistic school he represented the voluntaristic wing. His method, it is true, was rationalistic. He believed it possible to *prove* ultimate truths, and had a growing fondness for the technical apparatus of logic. But the truth which he proved was a voluntaristic truth. He proclaimed the priority of action to passivity, of appreciation to description, of interpretation to perception and conception, of purpose and choice to necessity, and of moral to intellectual or even esthetic categories. He stands, therefore, closer to Fichte than to any other of the immediate followers of Kant; and belongs with Rickert, Windelband, and Münsterberg among Fichte's later followers. Such a classification does not, however, do him justice. He was distinguished from German neo-Fichteans not only by his profound metaphysical passion, but also by the English and American strains in his inheritance. With all of his *a priori* metaphysics, he was also something of a British empiricist; and with all his doctrinal monism and pantheism, he was profoundly American in his individualism and moral dualism. A mere doctrinal classification of Royce is inadequate, furthermore, because he was so much more than a doctrine. He was a man of rich experience and varied talents, with an exceptional understanding of music, and a vivid appreciation of literature. He was a scholar and a teacher. His historical scholarship was of that breadth and depth which is attainable only by men happily endowed with extraordinary memories. He was a teacher who both respected and did honor to his vocation. Through his voluminous writings and numerous public lectures he was a teacher of the general public, the more acceptable because his teachings provided a positive support for moral and religious conviction. His success as a teacher in the stricter sense was proportional to the seriousness and alertness of his students. Of the limitations of the average undergraduate mind he was not sufficiently aware, and his lectures were too discursive to be easily followed. With smaller groups of advanced students, and especially with his seminary, frequently attended by younger colleagues from scientific and other departments of the University, he was a truly great teacher. His learning gave him inexhaustible resources of allusion and comparison; his dialectical skill made him invincible in discussion; his sympathy and humor enabled him to interpret, amplify, and

confirm the poorest efforts of his younger associates. His peculiar genius lay in finding some grain of significance in the feeblest thinking, and some basis of agreement with his most remorseless critics.

His defects as a thinker and writer flowed mainly from one source, namely, a tendency to prolixity. He had a prodigious capacity for work, was a wide reader, and a voluminous writer. There was, apparently, some connection between his prodigality of effort and the quality of the product. In 1883 he remarked in his diary, "As usual I spin out the business a trifle too long." He lacked dexterity, intellectually as well as physically. His processes of mind were powerful, massive, but laborious. As a colleague expressed it: "He needed considerable sea-room." His style sometimes reached great heights of eloquence, but was never wholly free from a certain grandiose quality. Similarly, his thinking was marked by profusion and sheer power, rather than by refinement, pointedness, or focal illumination. He carried big guns but they were too big to hit the center of a small target.

Royce was an original and unique individual. His body was of medium stature, round and youthful in appearance, and with slight muscular development. His great dome-like head and Socratic features gave him an appearance which, without physical attractiveness, served none the less as a medium of spiritual beauty. He was faithful, brave, generous, and above all unworldly and high-minded, as became the philosopher that he was in person as well as by profession.

[Brief accounts by Royce himself of his parentage and early life are to be found in his *California* (1886), pp. 240–46, and in his *The Hope of the Great Community* (1916), pp. 122–36. The narrative of his mother, Sarah Royce, based on her diary of 1849, has been edited by R. H. Gabriel and published under the title, *A Frontier Lady: Recollections of the Gold Rush and Early California* (1932). The author has also had access to Royce's own diaries; to the unpublished correspondence between Royce and William James; and to the recollections of his wife and sister. A bibliography of Royce's published works and of articles on his philosophy by Benjamin Rand, is in the *Philosophical Review*, May 1916; and of his unpublished works, by Jacob Loewenberg, *Ibid.*, Sept. 1917. The following expositions and criticisms of Royce's philosophy are especially recommended: "Papers in Honor of Josiah Royce on his Sixtieth Birthday," *Philosophical Review*, May 1916; Jacob Loewenberg, editor's introduction to *Fugitive Essays, by Josiah Royce* (1920); Gabriel Marcel, "La Métaphysique de Josiah Royce," *Revue de Métaphysique et de Morale*, May–June, July–Aug. 1918; Jan.–Feb., Mar.–Apr. 1919; M. J. Aronson, *La Philosophie Morale de Josiah Royce* (1927); George Santayana, *Character and Opinion in the United States* (1920), ch. iv. For more personal materials, see G. H. Palmer, in *Harvard Graduates' Mag.*, Dec. 1916.]
R. B. P.

ROYE, EDWARD JAMES (Feb. 3, 1815–Feb. 12, 1872), fifth president of Liberia, was born in Newark, Ohio. His father, John Roye, who had been born in Kentucky, was thrifty and on his death in 1829 left his son some personal property and land. The boy was educated in the public schools of Ohio. He taught school a few years in Chillicothe. He then started in business as a sheep-trader and shop-keeper and lived in various parts of the Middle West. On the death of his mother in 1840, he began to consider the possibility of emigrating to some foreign country in order to escape American prejudice. He first chose Haiti and began to study French at Oberlin, but he finally changed his mind and went to Liberia.

He arrived there with a stock of goods in 1846. His energy soon made him the leading merchant in the country; he exported African products to England and to the United States and was rated in 1870 as the richest man in Liberia. In 1849 he was speaker of the House of Representatives, and he served as chief justice from 1865 to 1868. Three times he was candidate for the presidency, was finally elected, and in January 1871 was inaugurated president. He immediately announced a progressive policy. He wished to undertake a complete financial reconstruction, some measures for general education, and an improved system of roads (*Inaugural Address of President Edward James Roye,* 1870). For these purposes Liberia needed capital, and he began to negotiate for a loan from Great Britain. He went to England in 1870 to settle a boundary dispute and conducted negotiations for the loan. Unfortunately, he made the initial mistake of yielding too much to Lord Granville, agreeing to a rectification of the boundary that practically gave back to England land Liberia had formerly bought. He returned to Liberia before finishing the matter of the loan but left negotiations in the hands of two Liberians and a white man, David Chinery, who was consul for Liberia in London. A loan for $500,000 was finally negotiated on very severe terms, carrying interest at seven per cent. and issued at thirty per cent. below par with three years' interest deducted. He hastily agreed to the terms without consulting the legislature and ordered certain goods to be charged against the loan. As a final result, Liberia actually received something like $89,515 cash, while her bonds were issued for at least $400,000. The result of all these negotiations caused great resentment in Liberia against him. He was also accused of embezzling some of the money and foolishly made matters worse by seeking to extend the two-year term of the presidency by edict. Public indignation was excited to fury, and the people, rising in insurrection, overpowered him and his friends, seized his house, and imprisoned him with one of his sons. In October 1871 he was deposed from his office, an executive committee was appointed to carry on the government until a new president was elected and Joseph J. Roberts [*q.v.*] was recalled from retirement. He was then summoned to trial before the supreme court but escaped during the night, either because of carelessness or connivance, and tried to reach an English steamer in the harbor. He was drowned in the attempt to ride the breakers in a native canoe.

[*African Repository,* Apr. 1870, July, Aug. 1872; *Fifty-fifth Annual Report of the Am. Colonization Soc. . . . 1872* (1872); H. H. Johnston, *Liberia* (1906), vol. I; T. H. B. Walker, *Hist. of Liberia* (copr. 1921).]

W. E. B. D–B.

ROYSTER, JAMES FINCH (June 26, 1880–Mar. 21, 1930), philologist, university administrator, was born at Raleigh, N. C., the second son of Wisconsin Illinois and Mary Wills (Finch) Royster. Prepared at the Raleigh academy, in 1897 he entered Wake Forest College, where the enthusiasm of Benjamin Sledd awoke a continuing interest in linguistic and literary studies. Grounding himself on Latin and Greek, the young student displayed an increasing ability in Germanic philology, particularly Old English and Middle English. He was graduated from Wake Forest in 1900. He entered the graduate school of the University of Chicago, where he was strongly influenced by John M. Manly. After eighteen months at the University of Berlin, 1902–03, he became an instructor in English at the University of Colorado, 1904–05, where he met his future wife, Carrie Belle Lake, to whom he was married on June 17, 1908. An assistant in English at the University of Chicago in 1906–07, he won his doctorate in 1907, his dissertation, an edition of an unpublished *Middle English Treatise on the Ten Commandments* (1911) being characteristically workmanlike. He was immediately called to the University of North Carolina, where he served as associate professor of English, and where his two children were born. Linguistic articles marked by commonsense methods, editorial work on *Studies in Philology,* and the fostering of graduate study increased his reputation; and in 1914 the University of Texas called him as professor of English with a view to modernizing its literary curriculum. Although his research interests were linguistic, he battled what he regarded as philological antiquarianism in the name of modern letters, but, feeling that academic conservatism was too strongly entrenched to be routed, he welcomed a recall to the University of North Carolina in 1921 as Kenan professor of English philology. At Chapel Hill he was in his element, a member of perhaps the most brilliant group of literary scholars in the South including Edwin Greenlaw, then dean of the graduate school, and Thornton Shirley Graves. As dean of the college of liberal arts, 1922–25, he steadily labored for a humane and vigorous curriculum. Upon the translation of Greenlaw to The John Hopkins University in 1925, he was appropriately made his successor as dean of the graduate school, with the task of maintaining and extending the brilliant work of his predecessor in fostering university research work. Under the Greenlaw-Royster régime Chapel Hill became notable as the flourishing center of graduate study. His devotion to the institution led to over-work, and the death of his beloved wife in 1928 shook a personality already suffering from strain. Appointed to the directorship of the American University Union in London, he left to take up his duties in the summer of 1929, broke down in mental health after reaching England, and returned to die at Richmond, Va., from self-inflicted burns.

Inevitably his writing suffered from his administrative labors; an occasional article on Chaucerian or similar problems was all he could find time for. He left behind him no body of writing fully representative of his great powers. Besides various textbooks characteristic articles are "Old English Causative Verbs" (*Studies in Philology,* July 1922) and the revolutionary "I'll Not Trust the Printed Word—" (*Ibid.,* July 1917). His best platform was the classroom.

[Personal recollections; family letters; *Who's Who in America,* 1928–29, *Studies in Philology,* July 1930, October 1931, p. v; *New York Times,* Mar. 22, 1930.]

H. M. J.

RUBLEE, HORACE (Aug. 19, 1829–Oct. 19, 1896), editor and diplomat, was born in Berkshire, Franklin County, Vt., the son of Alvah and Martha (Kent) Rublee. Attracted by reports of rich farming land in the Middle West, his father journeyed to Wisconsin in 1839 and settled at Sheboygan, where his family joined him the following year. The boy's early education was obtained in the district schools of Vermont and Wisconsin. Lacking the rugged physique necessary for his father's occupations, lumbering and farming, he taught school near his home until, at the age of twenty, he decided to go to college. In 1850 he entered the University of Wisconsin, then in its first year as a prepara-

tory school, housed in one small building, with a faculty of one teacher. While attending the university he supported himself by setting type on one of the Madison newspapers, but his constitution was not equal to the strain of study and work, and he was compelled to withdraw from college on account of poor health. Returning to his home in Sheboygan, he again taught in a district school. He began his newspaper work by reporting the sessions of the state legislature during 1852 and 1853 for the *Wisconsin Argus,* a Democratic weekly paper that published a daily edition while the legislature was in session. In the spring of 1853, during the temporary absence of its editor, Rublee became editorial writer on the *Wisconsin State Journal,* a Madison daily, established the previous year by David Atwood [*q.v.*]. The following year Rublee bought a half-interest in the paper, which he retained until he went abroad in the diplomatic service fifteen years later.

His political activities began with the movement against the extension of slavery that led to the birth of the Republican party. At the first state convention of that party, held in Madison on July 13, 1854, Rublee was one of the secretaries. During 1856–57 he was state librarian. In 1856 or 1857 he married Kate Hopkins of Washington County, N. Y., one of whose brothers, James C. Hopkins [*q.v.*], became United States judge for the western district of Wisconsin. From 1859 to 1869, Rublee served as chairman of the Wisconsin Republican state committee, and in 1868 was a delegate to the Republican National Convention that nominated General Grant for the presidency.

President Grant appointed him minister to Switzerland in 1869, a post that he held for seven years. Studious in his tastes, he acquired a considerable knowledge of the German language and literature during his residence in Switzerland. After resigning his diplomatic position, he returned to Wisconsin in 1877 and again became chairman of the Republican state committee. When the Republican state convention adopted a weak plank on "Greenbackism," Rublee, as chairman of the state committee with the support of some of the other Republican leaders, issued an address to the Republican voters demanding the resumption of specie payments. He carried the Republicans to victory on this issue.

During 1877 he contributed articles to the *Evening Wisconsin,* the leading Republican evening newspaper in Milwaukee. He went to Boston in 1879 to act as temporary editor of the *Daily Advertiser,* but, although urged to remain in journalism in the East, soon decided to return to Wisconsin. In 1881 he organized a company to purchase the *Daily Milwaukee News,* a Democratic morning paper. With Rublee, a stanch Republican, as editor, its name was changed to the *Republican and News.* The following year the company bought the *Milwaukee Sentinel,* then the oldest as well as the most important morning paper in the state. It was in his connection with the *Sentinel,* from 1883 until he died in 1896, that Rublee won distinction as editor and editorial writer. He made it more than a party organ; it was the leading newspaper of the commonwealth, and his editorials were quoted by other newspapers both within and without the state. At his death he was survived by two sons.

[A. M. Thomson, *A Political Hist. of Wis.* (1902); *The Columbian Biog. Dict. . . . Wis. Vol.* (1895); H. P. Myrick, in *Proc. Wis. Press Asso.,* 1897; *Papers Relating to the Foreign Relations of the U. S.,* 1870–76; *Milwaukee Sentinel* and *Milwaukee Jour.,* Oct. 19, 1896.]
                 W. G. B.

RUDGE, WILLIAM EDWIN (Nov. 23, 1876–June 12, 1931), printer and publisher, was born in Brooklyn, N. Y., son of William Edwin and Lavina (Knapp) Rudge. He attended the public school and at twelve or thirteen entered his father's printing office at Nassau and Liberty streets, New York, where he learned his trade, meanwhile taking a three-year course in engineering at Cooper Union. His father soon suggested that the boy take over three presses in the plant and work for himself. This was the beginning of "The Printing House of William Edwin Rudge." In 1895, the plant was moved to 83 Murray St., where an electric motor was substituted for foot-power on the presses. The father became ill in 1900, and the son succeeded to the business. A fire at the Murray Street shop in 1905 necessitated another removal, to 218 William St. In 1921, the plant was moved to Mount Vernon, N. Y., which for some time had been Rudge's place of residence. Here, in a picturesque rural setting, a one-story, graystone building, once used for glass manufacture, was gradually remodeled and furnished with equipment capable of doing high quality work.

Before 1912, Rudge had done general commercial printing. About that time he became associated with the group of typographers, designers, collectors, and others who founded the American Institute of Graphic Arts. He became sensitive to art, design, and quality, and set for himself the ideal of producing books and printed matter in the most beautiful form. For design of books he secured the services of such men as Frederic W. Goudy, Bruce Rogers,

Frederic Warde, and W. A. Dwiggins. At his press in Mount Vernon he assembled a library on the graphic arts, consisting of histories and source books, together with examples of fine printing from the best presses.

Rudge produced many works of outstanding merit, notably, Joseph Pennell's *Adventures of an Illustrator* (1925), Mary Vaux Walcott's *North American Wild Flowers* (5 vols., 1925), with faithful reproductions of water color sketches, produced by the "Smithsonian Process," a method perfected by Rudge, consisting of four-color printing on all-rag, uncoated paper; Robert Bridges' *The Testament of Beauty* (1929); the *Private Papers of James Boswell* (1928), edited by Geoffrey Scott and Frederick Pottle; books by Hervey Allen, Ford Madox Ford, Cass Gilbert, Christopher Morley, Arthur Symons, and wood-engraving by Timothy Cole. He was constantly critical of his own work and always experimenting with new methods and processes in the hope of achieving finer results. "Expense, profit, all the limitations of the ordinary printer, have been brushed aside by the largeness of imagination which touched everything he did" (*Saturday Review of Literature,* July 25, 1931, p. 15). He received many medals and awards; his work ranks with that of the foremost American printers and is highly regarded by fellow craftsmen of all countries. He was a member of the advisory board at New York University for the course given by the American Institute of Graphic Arts, and an officer of many organizations connected with the graphic arts. In 1925, Herbert Hoover, then secretary of commerce, appointed him to represent the printing industry at the International Exposition of Modern Decorative and Industrial Art in Paris. He made friends easily and kept them. He displayed a keen interest in his employees, with the result that several young men who began with him became designers of national reputation. On Apr. 18, 1906, he married Lillie May Gould of Mount Vernon, N. Y. His two sons followed their father as printers.

[*American Printer,* June 5, 1920; *N. Y. Evening Post,* Jan. 4, 1923; *San Francisco Printer,* Dec. 1930; *Typothetae Bulletin,* July 1, 1931; *Bookbinding Magazine,* July 1931, p. 41; *Inland Printer,* July 1931; "The First Reader," *N. Y. World Telegram,* June 16, 1931; *Publishers' Weekly,* June 20, 1931; *Sat. Rev. of Lit.,* July 25, 1931; *News-Letter* (American Institute of Graphic Arts, July 1931); *Chicago Evening Post,* Sept. 25, 1931; *N. Y. Times,* June 13, 1931; *Who's Who in America,* 1930–31.] J. A.

RUFFIN, EDMUND (Jan. 5, 1794–June 18, 1865), agriculturist and publisher, was born in Prince George County, Va., the son of George and Jane (Lucas) Ruffin. He was educated at home until his sixteenth year when he entered the College of William and Mary for a brief and unprofitable period ending in his suspension for neglect of classroom work. He served as a private in the War of 1812, but saw no active fighting, and, after six months of drill and camp duty at Norfolk, returned home to marry, in 1813, Susan Travis of Williamsburg and assume charge of the Coggin's Point farm which the recent death of his father had left to him. Here he began the agricultural experiments which were to bring him fame and to restore his section to prosperity.

Agriculture in Virginia at this time was at low ebb. The continual planting of a single crop on the same lands, and the use of bad methods in plowing and planting had depleted the soils, ruined the planters, and sent thousands of emigrants from the state. With little knowledge, either practical or theoretical, Ruffin set to work to discover the fundamental trouble and to find a remedy. After early failures, he observed that sorrel and pine always grew on poor lands and that calcareous earths were absent. Adopting a suggestion from Sir Humphrey Davy's *Elements of Agricultural Chemistry* (1815), he began experimenting with marl in various quantities upon his fields. Favorable results led to the conclusion that soils, once fertile but reduced by harmful cultivation, had become "acid" and had, thereby, lost their power to retain manures. This condition he now believed could be corrected by the application of calcareous earths (marl) and that a fertility equal to or greater than the original could then be acquired by the use of fertilizers, crop rotation, drainage, and good plowing. The experiences of the next few years were to prove the practical correctness of his conclusions.

In October 1818, Ruffin presented his theories and results before the Prince George Agricultural Society and three years later printed them in enlarged form in the *American Farmer* (Dec. 28, 1821, vol. III, 313–24). By 1832, they had grown into a volume of 242 pages, published under the title, *An Essay on Calcareous Manures*. This work ran through five editions and grew to nearly five hundred pages. Still further to advance the cause of agriculture, Ruffin began, in June 1833, the publication of an agricultural journal, the *Farmer's Register*. It appeared monthly, first from "Shellbanks" and then from Petersburg. The editor, himself, wrote nearly half of the articles offered but he also reprinted the best articles from foreign sources and presented the ideas and experiences of the most enterprising local planters. For ten

years this journal rendered invaluable service to the whole South and then failed because of the editor's activities for banking reform, especially the publication of another periodical, the *Bank Reformer* (Sept. 4, 1841–Feb. 5, 1842).

Ruffin early took a hand in the organization of agricultural societies. He was one of the founders of the Prince George society and one of the leaders in the move to associate local societies for the purpose of opposing protective tariffs. In 1841 he was appointed a member of the first Virginia State Board of Agriculture and served as its first corresponding secretary. In 1842 he became agricultural surveyor of South Carolina, publishing after a year's work the excellent *Report of the Commencement and Progress of the Agricultural Survey of South Carolina* (1843), which became a landmark in the agricultural history of the state. When the Virginia State Agricultural Society was organized in 1845 he was elected as its president but declined to serve under the impression that his work had not been sufficiently appreciated in his native state. He accepted this honor, however, in 1852 and two years later became commissioner for the society in an effort to put it on firm financial foundations and enlarge its usefulness. His work toward the establishment of experimental farms and agricultural education was particularly notable.

In 1843 Ruffin moved to a new estate, "Marlbourne," in Hanover County, where he made his home until retirement in 1855. He wrote and spoke much on agricultural improvement in these years for newspapers, farm journals, and agricultural societies. His *Address on the Opposite Results of Exhausting and Fertilizing Systems of Agriculture* (1853), given before the South Carolina Institute, and his *Premium Essay on Agricultural Education* (1853), presented to the Southern Central Agricultural Association, were of high merit. In 1855 he gathered together a number of articles and issued them in book form under the title, *Essays and Notes on Agriculture*. His *Notes on the Cane-brake Lands* (of Alabama) were published in 1860, and his *Agricultural, Geological and Descriptive Sketches of Lower North Carolina, and the Similar Adjacent Lands* in 1861.

Ruffin was always interested in politics. He served for three years in the Senate of Virginia (1823–26) but resigned in disgust at the methods employed by politicians. He early became a Whig but drifted over into the Democratic ranks as the struggle over slavery and state rights developed. He was from the first an ardent defender of slavery and was one of the first secessionists in Virginia. He wrote much for the Richmond and Charleston newspapers, *DeBow's Review,* and the *Southern Literary Messenger.* His views on slavery were brought together in four pamphlets: *Address to the Virginia State Agricultural Society on the Effects of Domestic Slavery on the Manners, Habits, and Welfare of the Agricultural Population of the Southern States, and the Slavery of Class to Class in the Northern States* (1853), reprinted in part as an appendix to the second pamphlet, *The Political Economy of Slavery* (n.d., probably 1858); *African Colonization Unveiled* (n.d.), printed also in instalments under varying titles in *De Bow's Review* for April, July, September, October, November 1859 and November 1860; and *Slavery and Free Labor Described and Compared* (n.d.), printed also in the *Southern Planter,* December 1859–January 1860. In 1860 he published a book entitled *Anticipations of the Future,* designed to show the necessity of secession and the glories of an independent South.

An advocate of direct trade with Europe, he attended three Southern commercial conventions and served as chairman of the Virginia delegation at the one held in Montgomery, Ala., in 1858. He originated the League of United Southerners, and secured and presented one of John Brown's pikes to the governor of each Southern state. He was invited to sit in three seceding conventions and as a volunteer with the Palmetto Guard of Charleston was permitted to fire the first shot from Morris Island against Fort Sumter (Craven, *post,* pp. 217, 270). He was with his company as a "temporary" private at the first Battle of Manassas (Bull Run) and fired the shot that blocked the bridge over Cub Run. He spent the war period wandering about from one of his plantations to another as "Yankee" invasions necessitated but returned to Charleston from time to time to "aid" in her defense. With the collapse of the Confederacy, he ended his own life at "Redmoor" in Amelia County on June 18, 1865, and was buried in the family graveyard at "Marlbourne." Three of his eleven children survived him.

[H. G. Ellis, "Edmund Ruffin: His Life and Times," in *John P. Branch Hist. Papers of Randolph-Macon Coll.,* June 1910, vol. III, 99–123; W. P. Cutler, "A Pioneer in Agricultural Science," in *Yearbook of U. S. Dept. Agriculture, 1895* (1896), pp. 493–502; *DeBow's Review,* Oct. 1851, pp. 431–36; E. G. Swem, *An Analysis of Ruffin's Farmer's Register with a Bibliography of Edmund Ruffin (Bulletin of Va. State Lib.,* XI, July–Oct. 1918); A. O. Craven, *Edmund Ruffin, Southerner* (1932); MS. Diary of Ruffin, 1856–65 (14 vols.) in Lib. of Cong.; obituary in *Richmond Times,* June 20, 1865.]   A.O.C.

RUFFIN, THOMAS (Nov. 17, 1787–Jan. 15, 1870), jurist, the eldest child of Sterling and Alice (Roane) Ruffin of Essex County, Va., was born at "Newington," King and Queen County, Va. Prepared for college at Warrenton, N. C., he entered the junior class of the College of New Jersey, and, graduating in 1805, immediately began the study of law under David Robertson, a learned Scotch lawyer in Petersburg. In 1807 he followed his father to North Carolina and continued his studies under Archibald D. Murphey [*q.v.*]. Admitted to the bar in 1808, he settled in Hillsboro, where on Dec. 9, 1809, he married Anne, the daughter of William Kirkland.

He rose rapidly at the bar, and in 1813, 1815, and 1816, as an ardent Jeffersonian Republican, he represented the borough of Hillsboro in the House of Commons, serving as speaker in 1816. He never held a purely political office again, although he was a Crawford candidate for elector in 1824. At the close of his legislative term he was elected superior court judge, but resigned two years later and returned to practice in order to make good a security debt. He habitually attended two courts a week for forty-three weeks in the year—a herculean task in the day of bad roads; was reporter of the supreme court for a short time (1820–21); and by 1825 was at the head of the profession in the state. In that year he returned to the bench, but in 1828 he again resigned, this time to become president of the state bank, which had become heavily involved. A year later the bank was safe, and he was elected associate justice of the supreme court, becoming chief justice in 1833. He resigned in 1852 and retired to his farm in Alamance County, where he had made his home for many years. In 1858, by almost unanimous election of the legislature, he was called back to the supreme court, but served for only one year. He represented North Carolina at the peace conference in 1861, as an ardent supporter of the Union, and sought in every way to secure the adoption of a compromise that would preserve it. He returned to North Carolina still denying any constitutional right of secession, but eager for a revolutionary separation from the North. Without being a candidate, he was elected to the secession convention, where he voted for the Badger ordinance of revolution; offered a compromise between that and outright secession; and, both failing, voted for the ordinance of secession, and thereafter spared no effort in support of the war. In 1866 he opposed, on constitutional grounds, the right of the "Johnson" convention to submit a new constitution and was largely responsible for its rejection. Bitterly opposed to congressional reconstruction, he was no less opposed to the use of violence to undo it, and the

Ku Klux movement excited in his mind only horror. His last years were spent in Hillsboro where he died.

It is as a judge that Ruffin is chiefly known and remembered, and in the quarter-century of his service he established a reputation extending wherever English law is known. Constantly cited as an authority in American state and federal courts, he was quoted as well at Westminster (J. M. Vanfleet, *The Law of Collateral Attack*, 1892, Section 634; *Steel* vs. *Dixon*, 17 *Chancery Division*, 825). In constitutional law, authorities rank him with Marshall and Lemuel Shaw [*qq.v.*] as a pioneer. In common law and equity he was equally noted—a rare combination. His opinions, 1460 in number, embrace almost every topic of civil and criminal law. They are noted for their breadth of view, fullness of discussion, force of reasoning, strength and simplicity of language, lack of citation of authority, and the almost inevitable character of their conclusions. Though respecting precedent, he was not hampered by it in administering justice. He was responsible for two important departures in equity from English precedents: one, the rejection of the doctrine of part performance as a basis for decreeing the specific execution of a verbal contract for sale of land; the other, the discarding of the doctrine of vendor's lien upon land sold upon credit. In *Hoke* vs. *Henderson* (15 *N. C.*, 1) the first case of its kind in the United States, he held, contrary to the doctrine later adopted by the federal courts and those of every other state, that the holder of an office had an estate in it of which he could not be divested except by the abolition of the office. This remained the rule in North Carolina until 1903, when it was reversed (134 *N. C.*, 131). In *Raleigh and Gaston R. R. Co.* vs. *Davis* (19 *N. C.*, 451) he laid down the doctrine, then new, that the legislature had the power to provide for condemnation of a right of way for railroad purposes without the owner's being entitled to jury trial for assessment of damage. His opinion in *State* vs. *Mann* (13 *N. C.*, 263) illustrates his relentless logic as applied to slavery. As executive officer of the court he greatly improved its procedure and that of the courts below.

Ruffin was also an agriculturist of some note, operating profitably two plantations many miles apart. Like his kinsman, Edmund Ruffin [*q.v.*] of Virginia, he believed in scientific agriculture and kept abreast of every new development. For six years (1854–60) the active president of the state agricultural society, he exerted a powerful influence in extending agricultural knowledge. He rose to eminence by unremitting labor rather than by brilliance of mind. In appearance and manner he was austere and seemingly cold, but in reality his was a fiery nature in severe restraint. Of dominating will, he was inclined to be dictatorial, and he disliked opposition. His whole outlook on life was serious, but he had a genial human side, as the number of his devoted friends gave evidence. He was deeply religious, a devoted member of the Episcopal Church, and several times a delegate to its General Convention. Actively interested in the University of North Carolina, he was a trustee from 1813 to 1831 and again from 1842 to 1868, when reconstruction terminated the old board's existence. Thirteen of his fourteen children survived him.

[*The Papers of Thomas Ruffin* (4 vols., 1918–20), ed. by J. G. deR. Hamilton; W. A. Graham, *Life and Character of the Hon. Thomas Ruffin* (1871); Walter Clark, "Thomas Ruffin," in *Great Am. Lawyers*, vol. IV (1908), ed. by W. D. Lewis; Francis Nash, "Chief Justice Thomas Ruffin," *Charlotte Daily Observer*, Mar. 19, 1905; S. A. Ashe, *Biog. Hist. of N. C.*, vol. V (1906); 13–43, 51, 57 *N. C. Reports*; *Daily Standard* (Raleigh), Jan. 18, 1870.]   J. G. deR. H.

RUFFNER, HENRY (Jan. 16, 1790–Dec. 17, 1861), Presbyterian clergyman, educator, author, was born in Shenandoah County, Va., son of David and Ann (Brumbach) Ruffner. Having come to the Valley in 1739, the Ruffners—a German-Swiss people, big-bodied and heavy-fisted—moved on in 1796 to the wild Kanawha country, where, also, they bought land, started manufacturing, and helped build schools and churches. Prepared at Dr. McElhenney's Academy near by, Henry, in 1813, graduated from Washington College, Lexington, Va. After a year of theology and a year of travel he was licensed to preach and returned for mission work in the Kanawha country. On Mar. 31, 1819, he married Sarah, daughter of Capt. William Lyle, a farmer living near Lexington.

For thirty years thereafter he was identified with Washington College, first as teacher (thrice acting as president), and then (1836–48) as president and teacher. Under him the school took on the characteristics of a modern college, especially architecturally, though competition with the new Virginia Military Academy kept its numbers small. Meantime, his unusual energy was finding other outlets. From 1819 to 1831 he preached regularly at the Timber Ridge Church. At the educational convention in Lexington in 1842 he was the moving spirit and submitted "'the most valuable document on general education issued in Virginia since the early days of Thomas Jefferson, viz., an elaborate plan for the organization of an entire educational system of public instruction'" (Ambler, *post*, p. 277, quoting the United States

Commissioner of Education). From 1840 to 1847 he was preparing "The Early History of Washington College" (*Washington and Lee Historical Papers,* vol. I, 1890), in which appear his views on "the general management of literary institutions and the subject of liberal education." Out of a debate in the Franklin Literary Society of Lexington on the advisability of dividing Virginia into two states at the Blue Ridge, grew his *Address to the People of West Virginia . . . Showing that Slavery is Injurious to the Public Welfare, and that it May be Gradually Abolished, Without Detriment to the Rights and Interests of Slaveholders, by a Slaveholder of West Virginia* (1847). In it he argued for confinement of slavery to the region east of the Blue Ridge and its gradual abolition there on broad grounds of public policy. This "Ruffner Pamphlet" became important politically, especially in 1859.

With the reluctant consent of the trustees, Ruffner left Washington College in 1848 for the Kanawha mountains. There he hoped to recover fortune and health at farming and mining; but after a few years he returned to preaching, this time in what is now Malden, W. Va. Meanwhile, as "literary recreations," he had written and published "Judith Bensaddi," a romance which appeared in revised form in the *Southern Literary Messenger,* July 1839, with the statement that the first version had been published in a Philadelphia periodical ten years before; two Calvinistic treatises, *A Discourse on the Duration of Future Punishment* (1823) and *Against Universalism* (1833); and *The Fathers of the Desert* (2 vols., 1850). As an exponent of its energy and hard sense and of its views on slavery and education, ante-bellum western Virginia had no better representative than Henry Ruffner. Two of his four children survived him, one of whom was William Henry Ruffner [q.v.].

[William Henry Ruffner, "Hist. of Washington Coll., now Washington and Lee University," in *Washington and Lee Hist. Papers,* nos. 5, 6 (1895, 1904), a continuation of Henry Ruffner's *Early Hist. of Washington Coll.;* C. H. Ambler, *Sectionalism in Va.* (1910); *Southern Lit. Messenger,* Dec. 1838, Jan.–Apr. 1839, containing his "Cincinnati Address" and his "Notes on a Tour from Va. to Tenn. . . . 1838."]   C. C. P.

RUFFNER, WILLIAM HENRY (Feb. 11, 1824–Nov. 24, 1908), Presbyterian clergyman, educator, was born in Lexington, Va., son of Henry [q.v.] and Sarah (Lyle) Ruffner. His boyhood was spent on his father's farm near Lexington and in Washington College, from which he graduated in 1842 and to which he returned for the degree of M.A. in 1845 after a year as manager of his father's salt work in the

Kanawha country. From 1845 to 1846 he studied at Union Theological Seminary, then located at Hampden-Sidney, Va., and from 1846 to 1847, at Princeton Theological Seminary. After traveling as colporteur and preaching to country churches in the Valley, he spent two leisurely years as chaplain of the University of Virginia (1849–51). During this time he planned a series of discourses by Presbyterian ministers on the evidences of Christianity, which were published (Bruce, *History of the University of Virginia,* vol. III, 1921, p. 136), and studied moral philosophy under William Holmes McGuffey [q.v.], who, Ruffner said later, "resolved my intellectual forces into common sense." On Sept. 3, 1850, he married Harriet Ann Gray, by whom he had four children. He was ordained, Jan. 14, 1852, by the Presbytery of Philadelphia, and became pastor of the Seventh (Tabernacle) Presbyterian Church of Philadelphia.

Despite marked success in this work, a chronic throat trouble compelled his resignation in 1853. For sixteen years thereafter he was principally a successful farmer, first in Rockingham County and then at "Tribrook," near Lexington, preaching only occasionally. From 1865 to 1876, he served Washington College as trustee. Sharing Henry Ruffner's reasoned anti-slavery views, he opposed both abolition and secession; but after Lincoln's call for troops in 1861 he heartily supported the Southern cause. During Reconstruction his attitude, while entirely self-respecting, was conciliatory and constructive. Though in 1866 he deemed a state system of general public education impracticable, in 1867 he openly advocated state provision for the education of negroes. A state system of public schools having been made mandatory by the constitution, in 1869 he energetically sought from the Conservative majority in the legislature election as state superintendent, receiving convincing support from his friends and neighbors, notably Gen. Robert E. Lee. He was elected on Mar. 2, 1870.

Quickly and with but little assistance Ruffner drew the school law—which became a model for other Southern states—and secured its enactment. For twelve years thereafter he gave unremitting attention to the details of administration, believing that "there is more in the right execution of any plan than in the plan itself." Quite as important were his eleven annual *Reports* and his miscellaneous writings, through which he built up a philosophy of public education that prevailed over the strong individualistic beliefs and the antipathy to education of the negroes at the expense of the whites. Especial commendation has been given his solution to the problem of the relation of church and state in the educational field, which has been described as "co-operation without alliance" (Sadie Bell, *The Church, the State, and Education in Virginia,* 1930, chapters x, xi). For these services he has frequently been called the "Horace Mann of the South." In the clash between the bondholders and the schools over state revenues Ruffner was a moderate Readjuster; but when the Readjusters became radical, he adhered to the Conservatives. Consequently, he was not reëlected superintendent either by the former in 1882 or by the latter in 1886. Meantime as *ex officio* trustee of the new Agricultural and Mechanical College he had drawn up a plan for the institution, earnestly recommending emphasis upon advanced technical training. He was first president of the State Female Normal School, at Farmville, which he had helped to secure and which he endeavored to organize along practical lines, serving from 1884 to 1887. Thereafter, his unusual energy and versatility found outlet for ten years principally in making extensive physical surveys for large corporations. Among his published reports in this field were *A Physical Survey Extending from Atlanta, Georgia . . . to the Mississippi River* (1883), in collaboration with J. L. Campbell; *Report on the Landed Property of the Buena Vista Company* (1889); and *A Report on Washington Territory* (1889). He also edited his father's "Early History of Washington College" and continued it down to 1848 (*Washington and Lee Historical Papers,* no. 5, 1895; no. 6, 1904). To all his work Ruffner brought a strong mind, a progressive disposition, good judgment, and absolute honesty. Characteristically, when his superintendency took him into politics, he had sought and obtained his demission from the ministry. He died in Asheville, N. C.

[Ruffner Papers in Hist. Foundation of the Presbyt. and Reformed Churches, Montreat, N. C.; O. K. Lyle, *Lyle Family* (1912); *Va. Jour. of Educ.,* Jan. 1909; E. L. Fox, "William Henry Ruffner and the Rise of the Public Free School System of Va.," in *The John P. Branch Hist. Papers of Randolph-Macon Coll.,* June 1910; C. C. Pearson, "William Henry Ruffner: Reconstruction Statesman of Va.," in *South Atlantic Quart.,* Jan., Apr. 1921 and *Readjuster Movement in Va.* (1917); *Asheville Gazette,* Nov. 25, 1908.]

C. C. P.

RUGER, THOMAS HOWARD (Apr. 2, 1833–June 3, 1907), soldier, was born in Lima, Livingston County, N. Y., the son of Thomas Jefferson Ruger and Maria (Hutchins) Ruger. His father, an Episcopal minister, moved to Janesville, Wis., when the lad was thirteen years of age. The latter received academic schooling in preparation for the United States Military Academy and entered in his seventeenth year.

As a cadet he was reticent and retiring, unusually diligent and careful of speech, and, though without college training, was graduated number three in the class of 1854. Within a year he resigned his commission in the corps of engineers to practise law at Janesville.

Upon the outbreak of the Civil War, he was commissioned lieutenant-colonel of the 3rd Wisconsin Infantry, and became colonel a few months later. He participated creditably in the Maryland and Shenandoah operations of 1861–62, and distinguished himself at the battle of Antietam. He was promoted to the rank of brigadier-general of volunteers on Nov. 29, 1862, and ably commanded a brigade in the Army of the Potomac throughout the Rappahannock and Pennsylvania campaigns of 1862–63. At Gettysburg, where he succeeded to the command of a division, his brilliant service won him the brevet of brigadier-general, United States Army. On Aug. 15, 1863, he was ordered to New York City to suppress draft riots. In the following October he was transferred to a brigade in the West, and took part in all of Sherman's operations. He commanded a division in the Tennessee campaign against Hood, and in the subsequent operations in North Carolina from February to June 1865. He was brevetted major-general of volunteers for his services at the battle of Franklin, Tenn., on Nov. 30, 1864.

Following the war, he commanded the department of North Carolina for a year, and served as provisional governor of the state of Georgia from January to July 1868. He had been appointed colonel of the 33rd Infantry, Regular Army, on July 28, 1866, and was transferred to the 18th Infantry in 1869. During the years 1871–76, he served as superintendent of the United States Military Academy, where he maintained a high standard of scholarship and discipline. Until the year 1878 he commanded the department of the South, and until 1885, the district of Montana—taking command during the latter year of the important infantry and cavalry school at Fort Leavenworth, Kan. He became a brigadier-general on Mar. 19, 1886, and a major-general on Feb. 8, 1895. He commanded various military departments during this period and successfully conducted an expedition against hostile Indians in the Northwest. He also suppressed serious railway riots in Sacramento and San Francisco, Cal. He was retired from active military service by operation of law on Apr. 2, 1897, and spent two years traveling with his family on the continent of Europe. Upon his return, he made his home in Stamford, Conn., and lived the rest of his life very quietly in the enjoyment of his books and his garden. He was survived by his wife, Helen Lydia Moore, to whom he had been married in 1857, and their two daughters.

[*Who's Who in America,* 1906–07; G. W. Cullum, *Biog. Reg. . . . Officers and Grads., U. S. Mil. Acad.* (1891); O. O. Howard, biographical sketch in *Ann. Reunion, Asso. of Grads., U. S. Mil. Acad., 1908* (1908); J. D. Cox, *The March to the Sea* (1906), and *Atlanta* (1909), vols. IX and X in *Campaigns of the Civil War; N. Y. Times,* June 4, 1907.]   C. D. R.

RUGGLES, SAMUEL BULKLEY (Apr. 11, 1800–Aug. 28, 1881), lawyer, descended from John Ruggles who settled in Roxbury, Mass., in 1635, was born in New Milford, Conn., the son of Philo and Ellen (Bulkley) Ruggles. His father, a lawyer, removed to Poughkeepsie, N. Y., in 1804. The boy gave evidence of precocity, and by private tutoring was prepared for college at the age of twelve. He was admitted to the sophomore class at Yale and graduated in 1814. He then passed several years at Poughkeepsie, studying in his father's law office, and finally, after admission to the bar in 1821, began practice in New York City. He was successful in his profession, but long before he had reached his fortieth year he had retired from active practice to devote his time to public interests.

As early as 1831, when little thought had been given in New York to the providing of breathing spaces in city blocks, Ruggles was working out a plan by which a subdivision could be developed with a small park as its central feature, to be held in perpetuity by the surrounding lot-owners. He had bought land (lying between Third and Fourth Avenues, Twentieth and Twenty-second streets) as farm acreage, and through a costly process of leveling and filling converted it into a desirable residential district. He realized little profit from his investment, but in Gramercy Park the community had a permanent object-lesson in the beauty and value of small parks, which became the more impressive as the city was closely built around it in the course of years. In 1931 the centenary of the park was observed, with tributes to its founder (see editorial, *New York Times,* May 16, 1931). Ruggles was also active in promoting the creation of Union Square, one of the earliest of the city's public parks. Later he was one of the Croton Aqueduct commissioners. His election to the lower house of the state legislature in 1838 and his selection as chairman of the Ways and Means Committee gave his zeal for public service a wider scope. His *Report upon the Finances and Internal Improvements of the State of New York* (1838) was epoch-making in New York's canal policy. Ruggles was one of the few men after the time of DeWitt Clinton [*q.v.*] to make a

sincere, broadly conceived effort to formulate a canal policy for the future. As canal commissioner 1839–58 and president of the commission from 1840, he carried far beyond the state boundaries his inquiries into traffic conditions and the products then needing the Erie Canal for transport to the seaboard (see his *Report . . . in Respect to the Enlargement of the Canals for National Purposes,* 1863).

His familiarity with the transportation problems of the day made it natural that he should have a part, with James Gore King [*q.v.*] and other New Yorkers, in the building of the New York & Erie Railroad. He continued his statistical studies over a long period, publishing many pamphlets on economic themes. His chief public service in later years was rendered as delegate of the United States to the International Statistical Congress at Berlin in 1863 and at The Hague in 1869 (see his report, *Internationality and International Congresses,* 1869), and to the International Monetary Conference at Paris in 1867. His reports on the last-named conference were published under the titles, *International Coinage* (1867) and *International Coinage: Supplemental Report* (1870). On the complicated issue of bimetallism he was far more at home than were most of his countrymen. He had been interested in banking since 1839, when he had helped to found the Bank of Commerce.

In one other field Ruggles was for years distinctly in advance of his times. While he was serving as trustee of Columbia College (1836–81) the opposition of some of his colleagues, in 1854, to the election of Oliver Wolcott Gibbs [*q.v.*] to the chair of chemistry because of his Unitarianism, called out from Ruggles a ringing protest, *The Duty of Columbia College to the Community* (1854). The conflict seems to have set clearly within his vision the development of the college into a university. From that ideal he never wavered and in 1880, while he was still a trustee, he took part in the erection of the School of Political Science, headed by Dr. John W. Burgess, in the conviction that the University had at last arrived. Ruggles was married, May 15, 1822, to Mary Rosalie Rathbone, who died in 1878. They had two sons and a daughter. Ruggles died at Fire Ireland, N. Y., as the result of a paralytic stroke.

[Samuel Orcutt, *Hist. of the Towns of New Milford and Bridgewater, Conn.* (1882); Charles King, *Progress of the City of N. Y. during the Last Fifty Years* (1852); J. B. Pine, *The Story of Gramercy Park, 1831–1921* (1921); *Portrait Gallery of the Chamber of Commerce of the State of N. Y.* (1890), comp. by George Wilson; J. W. Burgess, *Reminiscences of an American Scholar* (1934); H. S. Ruggles, *The Ruggles Family* (1917), vol. II; F. B. Dexter, *Biog. Sketches*

Grads. Yale Coll., vol. VI (1912), which gives year of birth as 1799; *N. Y. Times,* Aug. 29, 1881; data supplied by John Ruggles Strong, a grandson of Ruggles.]

W. B. S.

RUGGLES, TIMOTHY (Oct. 20, 1711–Aug. 4, 1795), soldier, judge, and Loyalist, son of Rev. Timothy and Mary (White) Ruggles, was born in Rochester, Mass. The founder of his family in America was Thomas, who settled in Roxbury in 1637; his descendants were substantial men and office holders. Young Timothy graduated from Harvard in 1732. Because of his combative energy and bluff wit he seemed ill-suited to the ministry, and became an advocate practising at Rochester and representing that town in the General Court in 1736. In that year he moved to Sandwich, where he married Bathsheba (Bourne) Newcomb, a rich widow, and became proprietor of a tavern. He was a leading lawyer in Barnstable and adjacent counties, and for eight years between 1739 and 1752 was in the legislature.

About 1753 he moved to Hardwick, in Worcester County, where in 1686 his family had acquired a large tract of land. Here he lived in elegant style, keeping a well-stocked stable, hounds, and a deer park, though in his personal habits, especially in eating and drinking, he was most temperate. He was a justice of the peace and member of the legislature almost continually until 1770, and in 1762 serving as speaker. Commissioned colonel in 1755 of one of the Massachusetts regiments which served under Sir William Johnson, he took part in the hard-fought battle of Lake George, contributing to the defeat of Baron Dieskau, fought subsequently in the campaigns of 1756 and 1757, and in 1758 was commissioned a brigadier-general under Lord Amherst and shared in the invasion of Canada. In 1760 he left the service, receiving substantial grants from King and province. In the meantime, 1757, he had been appointed judge of common pleas for Worcester County, and in 1762 he became chief justice, an office he held down to the Revolution.

Ruggles' personality was distinctive and forceful. Young John Adams, who later came to detest his politics, made this diary entry in 1759: "Ruggles's grandeur consists in the quickness of his apprehension, steadiness of his attention, the boldness and strength of his thoughts and expressions, his strict honor, conscious superiority, contempt of meanness, &c. People approach him with dread and terror" (*The Works of John Adams,* vol. II, 1850, p. 67). He was very tall, dark, bold of countenance, given to no silly talk; his speech was blunt, often witty, sometimes profane. He was known as "the Brigadier," and became the subject of many ancedotes, not all authentic. In Mercy Otis Warren's dramatic piece, *The Group,* he figures as Brigadier Hateall. Ruggles was not of the Otis faction; when the people of Boston almost unanimously elected James Otis [*q.v.*] to the General Court, Ruggles prophesied that "out of this election will arise a d—d faction, which will shake this province to its foundations" (*Ibid.,* vol. X, 1856, p. 248).

As the movement toward revolution began to develop, Ruggles lost popularity and influence. At the Stamp Act Congress of 1765 he was elected president over Otis by a single vote, but Otis dominated the scene. Ruggles would not sign the petitions drawn up, alleging scruples of conscience. Thomas McKean [*q.v.*] of Pennsylvania reflected on Ruggles' sincerity, and the Brigadier replied with what McKean interpreted as a challenge, but no duel was fought. Returning to Boston, Ruggles was censured by the legislature and was not allowed to place his reply in its journal. He remained a strong supporter of Gov. Thomas Hutchinson [*q.v.*], threatening, it is said, to put in jail every man who signed the non-importation agreement of 1774. In that year he was made a member of the Council by the King's *mandamus,* but seems not to have taken the oath of office (Stark, *post,* p. 136). At this time a Committee of Correspondence was formed at Hardwick, and Ruggles was obliged to take refuge in Boston. There in December 1774 he strove to form an association of Loyalists pledged not to "acknowledge or submit to the pretended authority of any Congress, Committees of Correspondence, or any other unconstitutional assemblies of men" (Sabine, *post,* II, 244).

In November 1775 General Howe appointed Ruggles to command three companies of volunteers, to be called the Loyal American Associators (Jared Sparks, *The Writings of George Washington,* vol. III, 1834, p. 162, note), but it is doubtful if Ruggles ever fought in the field against the American army, although it appears that he was present for a short time with the British on Long Island. His name was fourth on the list of those banished from Massachusetts by the Act of 1778; his estates were confiscated, and in 1783 he moved to Nova Scotia, where he received a large grant in the wilderness. To the clearing of this tract he devoted the remainder of his life. He died on his estate at Wilmot, and was buried in the church near by. His three sons followed him into exile, but his four daughters remained in the States. One, Bathsheba, wife of Joshua Spooner, caused her husband to be murdered in 1778; apparently insane, she was convicted and hanged, July 2, 1778, after a most sensational trial.

[Lorenzo Sabine, *Biog. Sketches of Loyalists of the Am. Rev.* (1884), vol. II; J. H. Stark, *The Loyalists of Mass.* (1910); E. A. Jones, *The Loyalists of Mass.* (1930); H. S. Ruggles, *Gen. Timothy Ruggles* (1895); *Am. Quart. Reg.*, May 1841, p. 406; C. C. Baldwin, in *Worcester Mag. and Hist. Jour.*, May 1826; W. T. Davis, *Hist. of the Judiciary of Mass.* (1900); D. H. Hurd, *Hist. of Worcester County, Mass.* (1889), I, xviii ff.; L. R. Paige, *Hist. of Hardwick, Mass.* (1883) and *An Address at the Centennial Celebration in Hardwick, Mass.* (1838); Herbert Parker, *Courts and Lawyers of New England* (1931), vol. I.]   C. F.

RUMFORD, BENJAMIN THOMPSON, COUNT [See THOMPSON, BENJAMIN, 1753–1814].

RUMSEY, CHARLES CARY (Aug. 29, 1879–Sept. 21, 1922), sculptor, poloist, was born in Buffalo, N. Y., the son of Laurence Dana and Jennie (Cary) Rumsey. A maternal uncle, Seward Cary, had a local reputation as a sculptor, but Charles's father achieved prosperity in tanning and railroads. The boy's preliminary education was received at the Nichols School, Buffalo. He early began to develop what later became his two major interests—indicated by his exhibition of a sculptured figure at thirteen and by his friendship with Devereux Milburn, the poloist. Between 1893 and 1895 Rumsey resided in Paris and received instruction from Paul Bartlett [*q.v.*]. Later he entered Harvard University, from which he graduated in 1902, having in the meantime continued his training in sculpture at Boston under Bela Lyon Pratt [*q.v.*]. Between 1902 and 1906 he was again in Paris. During this period, while he was enrolled at the Julian and Colarossi academies, Emmanuel Frémiet became his chief advisor. In 1906 he returned to America and from this time until his death, resulting from an automobile accident, he practised his profession in New York and vicinity. His wife, Mary Harriman, the daughter of Edward H. Harriman, whom he had married May 26, 1910, and three children survived him.

Always enthusiastically interested in amateur athletics and at one time the amateur boxing champion of France, for years he devoted his leisure time to polo. From 1913 he was a member of every United States polo team to compete in international cup matches, and in 1921 was classed as an eight-goal man, only two below the highest rating in the modern game. At the time of his death he was competing in the preliminaries for the international matches of that year. During the World War he attained the rank of captain of cavalry.

Rumsey's most certain fame as a sculptor rests on his bronzes depicting polo ponies and their riders. In this particular field he unconsciously achieved masterpieces. His patrons for such figures included H. P. Whitney, August Belmont, Thomas Hitchcock, Jr., and J. E. Madden. For the last named he modeled "Nancy Hanks," set up in the equine cemetery at Lexington, Ky. In the other phases of his sculpture Rumsey's work is marked by the zeal of the experimenter and the ability to find inspiration from outstanding sculptors of animals, especially, perhaps, from Barye and even Myron. Notable among his monumental works is the equestrian "Pizarro," awarded a medal at the Panama-Pacific International Exposition in 1915, and later given by the sculptor's widow to the city of Lima, Peru, where Pizarro's bones are deposited (*New York Times*, Dec. 8, 1934). Other heroic figures include the "Dying Indian" given to the Brooklyn Museum, the "Centaur," the "Bull," and "Victory." The last of these marks the war memorial erected in Brooklyn for Brownsville and vicinity, from which district Rumsey enlisted. As examples of his decorative and experimental works may be mentioned the "Buffalo Hunt," a frieze designed to decorate the end of the Manhattan Bridge, the frieze for three sides of the stadium in Rice Memorial Playground, Pelham Park, N. Y., and, in colored cement, the "Pagan," the central figure in the courtyard of his studio at Wheatley Hills, Long Island. Commissions for fountain figures were receiving attention from the sculptor at the time of his death.

An important exhibit of Rumsey's works was held in 1917 at the Sculptor's Gallery in New York City, when the critical public had its first opportunity to form an opinion of his growing facility. Five years after his death, the Société Nationale des Beaux-Arts held a retrospective exhibition in Paris, at which some ninety-four examples of his compositions in bronze and colored cement were shown. In 1930 Rumsey was included in the exhibition of works by current American sculptors at the Brooklyn Museum. To his friends his vitality and versatility were constant sources of amazement. His supple vigor and recklessness as rider added to his personal charms. As a sculptor he infused his own love of life and movement into his compositions, attaining a rhythm and dynamic power which gave them individuality in spite of the evident influences of Rodin, Bourdelle, and Maillol.

[*Harvard Coll. Class of 1902 . . . Sixth Report, June 1922* (1922); *N. Y. Times*, Apr. 15, 1917 (mag. section), Sept. 22, 1922; *Boston Transcript*, Dec. 19, 1914; *N. Y. Evening Post*, Saturday Mag., Apr. 21, 1917; *Exposition Rétrospective de l'Oeuvre de Charles Cary Rumsey, 1879–1922 . . . Société nationale des Beaux-Arts Exposition* (Paris, 1927); W. H. Fox, "Two Important Works by American Sculptors," in *Brooklyn Museum Quart.*, July 1930; Arsène Alexandre, "Charles Cary Rumsey," in *La Renaissance de l'Art Français*, June 1927; *Public Ledger* (Phila.), Nov. 5, 1922 (mag. section); *Who's Who in America*, 1922–23.]

W. S. R.

RUMSEY, JAMES (March 1743–Dec. 20, 1792), inventor, son of Edward and Anna (Cowman) Rumsey, was born on his father's farm at Bohemia Manor, Cecil County, Md. Information regarding the first forty years of his life is scanty. He had an elementary schooling, learned blacksmithing, and is said to have served in the Revolutionary War. He was living in Baltimore in 1780 and two years later, in partnership with a friend, began operating a grist mill at Sleepy Creek, Md. This enterprise lasted less than a year, however, because Rumsey paid no attention to the business and spent his time dreaming of "impossible things." In 1783 he went to Bath, now Berkeley Springs, W. Va., and, with another friend, opened a general store and engaged in the building trade as well, for Bath even then was popular as a health resort. He was busy with these concerns throughout 1783 and 1784 and had the honor of building a house and stables for General Washington on his lands at Bath.

Meanwhile, he had been working in secret on a mechanically propelled boat, at the same time endeavoring to interest capital in his undertaking. While he failed to secure any money, the House of Delegates of the Virginia Assembly in June 1784, by resolution, indicated a sympathetic interest in his boat plans; Washington, after seeing a model of Rumsey's craft, gave him a kindly worded certificate in September; in November, the Virginia legislature granted him the exclusive rights to build his special boats and navigate the waters of the state with them; and two months later, the Maryland legislature granted him a similar privilege. In gaining these advantages, however, Rumsey had neglected his family and business, and by the summer of 1785 he was in bad repute and much in debt. Accordingly, he was glad to accept a position as superintendent of construction of canals for the Potomac Navigation Company, of which General Washington was president. He held it for only a year, however, giving it up because he was dissatisfied with the "pay and emoluments" allowed him (Washington, *Diaries, post*, III, 85).

He now became engrossed in perfecting a steamboat. It is said that he had considered the use of steam power for a boat as early as 1783, but it was not until the winter of 1785 that he actually began to experiment with a steam engine. He worked in secret on his plans throughout 1786 and 1787, but because of the publicity which John Fitch [*q.v.*] was getting in Philadelphia with his project, Rumsey was urged by Washington and others to come out in the open and demonstrate his plans. This he did on Dec. 3, 1787, and again on Dec. 11, exhibiting on the Potomac River, near Shepherdstown, W. Va., a boat propelled by streams of water forced out through the stern, a steam engine being employed to operate the force pump. Having no money to proceed with his experiment and being unable to secure any locally, Rumsey went to Philadelphia in the spring of 1788 and presented his case to the American Philosophical Society, whereupon, on May 9, a number of the members formed the "Rumseian Society," to promote Rumsey's several projects. These included, in addition to his steamboat, an improved steam boiler; an improvement in a saw mill; an improvement in a grist mill; and a plan for raising water by means of a steam engine. Because Fitch held the public's interest in America, the Society immediately sent Rumsey to England to patent his improvements and to interest English capital. He soon secured English patents on his boiler and steamboat, and through his friends, similar patents were granted him by the United States in 1791. For over four years he labored abroad to perfect his second steamboat but throughout that time had the most disheartening experiences, due mostly to the lack of money. Even the Rumseian Society failed him. By the winter of 1792, however, the completion of the *Columbia Maid*, so christened by Rumsey, was in sight; but just a few months before it was finished Rumsey died in London, at the age of forty-nine. His friends in England buried him in St. Margaret's churchyard, near Westminster, but the grave is unmarked.

Rumsey published two pamphlets in 1788 bearing on his steamboat work: *A Plan Wherein the Power of Steam is Fully Shewn* . . . and *A Short Treatise on the Application of Steam*. Rumsey was married twice, his second wife having been Mary Morrow. At the time of his death he was survived by his widow and three children, one a daughter by his first wife.

[Letters of Rumsey are in the MSS. Division of the Library of Congress; papers in the suit of *McMechen vs. Rumsey*, brought against the Rumsey estate, are in the Va. State Library, and letters from these are printed in *William and Mary Quart.*, Jan.-July 1916. See also *House Report No. 324*, 27 Cong., 2 Sess., and *No. 403*, 29 Cong., 1 Sess.; Ella May Turner, *James Rumsey* (1930); J. L. Bishop, *A Hist. of Am. Manufactures*, vol. I (1861); G. M. Beltzhoover, *James Rumsey* (1900); J. C. Fitzpatrick, *The Diaries of George Washington* (1925), vols. II, III; U. S. Nat. Museum records; Patent Office records.]

C. W. M.

RUMSEY, WILLIAM (Oct. 18, 1841–Jan. 16, 1903), jurist and author of legal works, was born at Bath, N. Y., a son of David and Jane (Brown) Rumsey. He attended schools in Steuben County, N. Y., and then entered Williams College in the class of 1861. He was awarded his degree, though in April of his senior year he left college to become a first lieutenant on the staff of his uncle, Gen. Robert B. Van Valkenburgh of the New York militia. In October he was appointed adjutant of the 1st New York Light Artillery. Promoted to captain and then major, he served on the staff of Gen. William W. Averell [q.v.]. He was twice wounded—at Fair Oaks and at Moorfield—and was brevetted lieutenant-colonel, Mar. 13, 1865, for gallantry in action. He wished to remain in the army after the war, but his father persuaded him instead to travel in the Orient and recuperate from a severe attack of inflammatory rheumatism which had resulted from wounds and exposure. While abroad he was for a time secretary to General Van Valkenburgh, who was then the American minister to Japan.

Early in 1868 he returned to America and began studying law in his father's office. Before the close of the year he was admitted to the bar. Favorable reputation came rapidly. When his father became a justice of the state supreme court, in 1873, William succeeded to his extensive practice; and in 1880, when his father retired from the bench, he was elected to the vacant justiceship, which he held continuously for twenty-one years. He was nominated by the Republicans for judge of the court of appeals in 1888, and was narrowly defeated. After 1895 he sat on the appellate division of the supreme court (first and fourth departments) until 1901, when he resigned to engage in private practice in New York City. Besides his duties on the bench, he aided in formulating the code of civil procedure and the proposed code of evidence, from which experience grew his three-volume work, *The Practice in Actions and Special Proceedings in the Courts of Record in the State of New York* (1887–90). It immediately became the recognized standard on the subject. A second edition under the title, *The Practice in Civil Actions in the Courts of Record in the State of New York under the Code of Civil Procedure,* appeared in 1902–04. It was rendered valueless, however, by the civil practice act of 1920 which repealed the code on which the work was based.

Rumsey was deeply read in legal history. He possessed a phenomenal memory which enabled him to recall accurately the minute details of the development of legal principles. With such an equipment he was able to do his work without drudgery and in an amazingly short time. In general he was conservative; but he did not hesitate to develop—as in the case of *Roberson* vs. *Folding Box Company* (64 *App. Div.,* 30), which sustained a new common-law "right of privacy"—significant extensions of the law, which followed logically from principles already established. On Feb. 1, 1877, he married Ella Moore of Brooklyn, N. Y. He was survived by his widow, two daughters, and a son.

["Proc. in the Appellate Division of the Supreme Court, Fourth Department," 76 *App. Div. Reports,* 631–35; Edward Patterson, in *Asso. of the Bar of the City of N. Y., Annual Report,* 1904; F. B. Heitman, *Hist. Reg. and Dict. U. S. Army* (1903), vol. I; *Who's Who in America,* 1901–02, incorrect in some details; *N. Y. Herald* and *N. Y. Tribune,* Jan. 17, 1903; information as to certain facts from members of Rumsey's family and from his partner, John S. Sheppard.]

E. C. S.

RUNCIE, CONSTANCE FAUNT LE ROY (Jan. 15, 1836–May 17, 1911), composer, pianist, was born in Indianapolis, Ind., the daughter of Robert Henry Faunt Le Roy, a Virginian in the service of the United States Coast Survey as astronomer, and Jane Dale (Owen) Faunt Le Roy, daughter of Robert Owen [see *Dictionary of National Biography*] and sister of David and Robert Dale Owen [qq.v.]. Constance seems to have inherited musical gifts from both her parents; her father was an amateur composer and her mother, from whom she received her first music lessons, a finished performer on the piano and the harp. After a childhood spent in New Harmony, Ind., a village purchased from the Rappists by her grandfather, she was taken in 1852 to Stuttgart, Germany, for five years' training in piano and composition. On Apr. 9, 1861, she married the Rev. James Runcie, an Episcopal clergyman who had officiated at intervals in the little church in New Harmony, where the family had settled once more on returning to the United States. After her marriage she went with her husband to his rectorship in Madison, Ind., and in 1871 to St. Joseph, Mo., where she lived until her death, surviving her husband, who died in 1889, by almost a quarter century. In 1897 an accident deprived her of her hearing. She died in Winnetka, Ill., survived by her two sons and two daughters.

Her music is seldom heard today; but she was well known in her time, and her life and her music were characteristic of the period and environment in which she lived. According to tradition, no musical composition that she submitted to a publisher was rejected. It is said (*Musical America, post*) that William Mason [q.v.], the pianist, once remarked to the composer, "I thought when hearing your music it was that of a man. It is both virile and dramatic." Among her songs the most widely used were "I've Wandered Far Away," "Invocation to Love," "Das Vöglein Singt," and "Take My Soul, O Lord." Besides much published music, she left the manuscript of a romantic opera, *The Prince of Asturia*. She also tried her skill as a writer, published *Poems, Dramatic and Lyric* (1888), and completed two unpublished novels. In addition to her musical activities, she is credited with being the founder of one of the first regularly organized women's clubs in the United States, the Minerva Society, formed in New Harmony, Sept. 13, 1859. The quaint Rappite house in which the club was first organized later became the property of the Indiana Federation of Women's Clubs. In St. Joseph she founded a literary and musical club that still continues and bears her name, the Runcie Club.

[Faunt Le Roy sometimes appears as Fauntleroy. Information about Mrs. Runcie's life has been supplied by her daughter, Elinor Dale Runcie. Printed sources are Stella Reid Crothers in *Musical America*, Aug 21, 1909; A. H. Estabrook, "The Family History of Robert Owen," *Ind. Mag. of Hist.*, Mar. 1923; W. S. B. Mathews, *A Hundred Years of Music in America* (1889); E. E. Hipsher, *American Opera and Its Composers* (1927); *Who's Who in America*, 1910–11; obituary in *N. Y. Times*, May 18, 1911.] J.T.H.

RUNKLE, JOHN DANIEL (Oct. 11, 1822–July 8, 1902), mathematician, educational administrator, son of Daniel and Sarah (Gordon) Runkle, was born at Root, Montgomery County, N. Y., and spent his early life on a farm. Although handicapped at this time in his efforts to secure an education, he persevered, and at the age of twenty-five was able to enter the newly established Lawrence Scientific School at Harvard. In the Harvard catalogue of 1848–49 his name stands alone as "student in mathematics." He was a member of the first graduating class of the Lawrence Scientific School, receiving the two degrees of S.B. and M.A. simultaneously in 1851; after his graduation he sent two of his four younger brothers to Harvard. In 1852 he contributed papers to the *Astronomical Journal* on the elements of Thetis and Psyche (June 26, July 24, 1852). In 1856 his *New Tables for Determining the Values of the Coefficients in the Perturbative Function of Planetary Motion*, were published in the Smithsonian Contributions to Knowledge, and other tables followed in 1857. In 1858 he began the publication of the *Mathematical Monthly*, but the time was not yet ripe for such a journal and only three volumes appeared (October 1858–September 1861). In 1849 he had begun a connection with the *Nautical Almanac*, a relationship which continued in one form or another for thirty-five years. Benjamin Peirce [*q.v.*] thought so highly of him in

his early relations with this publication that in the preface of his *System of Analytic Mechanics* (1855) he said that Runkle had been influential in causing him to publish the work.

In 1862 Runkle married Catharine Robbins Bird. In that same year the Massachusetts Institute of Technology was founded and he became its first secretary. He was professor of mathematics from 1865 to 1868 and from 1880 to 1902, when he was made professor emeritus. In 1868, when illness incapacitated President William Barton Rogers [*q.v.*], Runkle became acting president, and from 1870 to 1878 he was president. In 1871 he conducted an expedition of students to Colorado and Utah for the purpose of observing mines and the processes of mining. In 1872 he established the Lowell School of Practical Design. After resigning his presidency of the Massachusetts Institute of Technology, he spent two years in Europe; during this time he investigated technological schools, and upon his return presented his findings in three papers: "Technical and Industrial Education Abroad" (*Massachusetts Institute of Technology; Abstract of the Proceedings of the Society of Arts*, 1881); "The Manual Element in Education" (*Forty-fifth Annual Report of the Massachusetts Board of Education, 1880–81*, 1882); and "Report of Committee on Industrial Education," in *Fifty-fourth Annual Meeting of the American Institute of Instruction . . . 1883* (1884). His *Manual Element in Education* (1882) was reprinted separately. He also wrote a textbook, *The Elements of Plane Analytic Geometry* (1888), and a report published under the auspices of the Massachusetts Institute of Technology on *The Russian System of Shop-Work Instruction for Engineers and Machinists* (1876).

[*Proc. Washington Acad. of Sci.*, vol. V (1903); *Proc. Am. Acad. Arts and Sci.*, vol. XXXVIII (1903); *Technology Rev.*, July 1902, Apr. 1925 (portr.); *Quinquennial Catalogue of Harvard Univ.* (1925); *Who's Who in America*, 1901–02; *Boston Transcript*, July 10, 1902.] D. E. S.

RUPP, ISRAEL DANIEL (July 10, 1803–May 31, 1878), historian, translator, was born in East Pennsboro (now Hampden) Township, Cumberland County, Pa., the fourth of the fourteen children of George and Christina (Boeshor) Rupp, and was a grandson of Johann Jonas Rupp, a native of Reihen, near Sinsheim, Baden, who emigrated to Pennsylvania in 1751 and in 1772 bought the land on which Israel Daniel was born. He was baptized in the Reformed faith by the Rev. John Winebrenner [*q.v.*] and got his first taste of book-learning from a pious German schoolmaster, Peter Blaeser. He learned English a few years later; Dutch he picked up from his maternal grandfather; and from a Rev. Mr. Vorhoof he acquired the rudiments of French and Latin. Altogether he learned to read eight or nine languages. A German biography of Franklin first awoke his interest in history, which, fed by strong family feeling and love for his native soil, became the preoccupation of his life. In August 1823 he was prostrated by a severe illness, and on his recovery his father allowed him to leave the farm and map out a career for himself. He studied for a while with his physician, Asa Herring, and in 1825 opened a subscription school first at Silver Spring and then at Mechanicsburg. On July 19, 1827, he married Caroline Aristide, daughter of a French physician. They had five daughters and three sons and lived to celebrate their golden wedding.

It was in the year of his marriage that he formed his plan for a great history of Pennsylvania and began his long quest for materials. For some twenty of the next thirty-three years he was a schoolmaster, and according to tradition a very good one, in Cumberland, Dauphin, Lebanon, and Lancaster counties, and perhaps elsewhere; but whenever teaching was not sufficiently peripatetic for his purposes he took to the road in other capacities. At one time he was an itinerant book-seller, and at various times he was an insurance agent. He was a delegate to political conventions, electioneered for John Quincy Adams throughout the German counties in 1828, and, after his hero's defeat, took to the stump in behalf of James Brown's magnificently complicated "American system of syntax"— probably with even less success. Later he went about the state with Josiah Holbrook [q.v.] organizing county, township, and family lyceums. In 1830 he wandered as far west as Cincinnati and there published his *Geschichte der Märtyrer, nach dem ausführlichen Original des Ehrw. Johann Fox und anderer kurz gefasst, besonders für den gemeinen deutschen Mann in den Ver. Staaten von Nord-America aus dem Englischen übersetzt* (new ed., 1832), the first of the eleven works, several of great bulk, that he translated from English into German or from German and Dutch into English. (For a complete list see Seidensticker, *post*.) The next year saw him ensconced as postmaster at Rupp's, Pleasant Township, Marion County, Ohio, but in 1832 he was back in his native state. He edited the Carlisle *Herald* in 1833 and the *Practical Farmer* in 1837. At Harrisburg, whither he was frequently drawn by the state library and archives, he not only taught school but reported the doings of the Senate for the newspapers and wrote speeches for members of both houses of the legislature.

All the while he lost no opportunity to consult books, documents, and public records of all kinds, and he was a constant practitioner of the genial art of pumping information out of magistrates, parsons, and old inhabitants with long memories. His affability and his willingness to receive as well as to impart information made him welcome everywhere.

His *History of Lancaster County* (1844) was the first of six volumes devoted to the history of twenty-three counties of the state. His other historical works were an *Early History of Western Pennsylvania* (1846), *A Collection of Thirty Thousand Names of German . . . Immigrants in Pennsylvania . . . 1727 to 1776* (1856; rev. ed., 1876; a new ed. in prep. by W. J. Hinke), and *A Brief Biographic Memorial of Joh. Jonas Rupp* (1875). His textbooks were *The Lyceum Spelling-Book* (1836), *The Geographical Catechism of Pennsylvania and the Western States* (1836), and *The Farmer's Complete Farrier* (1843; 1847). He edited *The Practical Farmer* (Mechanicsburg, 1837) and *He Pasa Ekklesia: An Original History of the Religious Denominations at Present Existing in the United States* (1844). Even during his lifetime his publications became rare and were much sought after. He laid an enduring foundation for the study of Pennsylvania local history and made the subject popular. Though his books are written in a rough, homespun style, are sometimes poorly arranged, and are peppered with some of the most fantastic of typographical errors, they are generally accurate, show much acumen in separating fact from fancy, and preserve a vast quantity of information that would otherwise have been lost or left all but inaccessible in widely scattered archives. Among his unpublished writings is a diary kept with conscientious care for half a century. In April 1860 he removed to Philadelphia, where he spent the rest of his life. With his simple tastes, industrious habits, and rugged health, he was able by his writing to keep his family in decent comfort and to find much leisure for historical studies. In 1866 he visited Colorado, which he described in delightful letters to the *Reformed Church Messenger*. A week before his death he suffered an apoplectic stroke.

[W. H. Egle, "Our Hist. Writers: I. Daniel Rupp," *Hist. Mag.*, Feb. 1871, and obit. notice, *New Eng. Hist. & Geneal. Reg.*, Jan. 1879; Oswald Seidensticker, "Memoir of Israel Daniel Rupp, the Historian," *Pa. Mag.*, Jan. 1891.]   G. H. G.

RUPP, WILLIAM (Apr. 17, 1839–Apr. 3, 1904), clergyman, theological professor, editor, was born in Lowhill Township, Lehigh County, Pa., son of Solomon and Maria (Frey) Rupp, and eldest of eight children. He was of German ancestry, a lineal descendant of George and Ursula (von Peterholtz) Rupp who came from Alsace about 1750 and settled in Lehigh County. His father was a carpenter and a farmer. Industry, thrift, and domestic piety were the characteristics of the community in which his boyhood was passed. His formal education was begun in the Allentown Seminary. In 1862 he graduated with highest honors from Franklin and Marshall College, and in 1864, from the Theological Seminary of the (German) Reformed Church, then located at Mercersburg, Pa. Since he was only fifteen years old when his father died, his education must have been largely of his own choosing and direction, and significant entries in his diary show that he suffered many privations for the sake of it. He was married on Nov. 16, 1865, to Emma A. Hambright, daughter of Adam F. Hambright of Lancaster, Pa. Eleven children were born to them.

On Feb. 6, 1865, he was ordained to the ministry by the Lebanon Classis of the Reformed Church, and for the next twenty-eight years he served in the active pastorate with comparatively small rural congregations for his field of labor. Thus he had the leisure he craved for further study, some of the subjects he pursued being Hebrew, Greek, and French; Homer, Shakespeare, and Goethe; ancient philosophy and patristic literature; botany and geology. In recommending his practice to his fellow ministers he naively added: "And some degree of such study [the physical and moral laws of the universe] is even required to teach men how to leave such subjects wisely alone" (*An Inaugural Service: Rev. William Rupp, D.D.*, 1894, p. 79). He preached in both English and German, but preaching in the popular sense was not his forte; nevertheless it was through his sermons and in greater degree through his articles in the church periodicals that he became known as a thinker and writer of great force and influence. Thus he was unwittingly qualifying for his election to the chair of practical theology in the theological school of his denomination at Lancaster, Pa.

He entered upon the duties of his office Jan. 1, 1894. The theme upon which he rang the changes throughout his inaugural address was expressed in these words of his own underscoring: *"And the ministry which presents Christ in His full adaptation to the spiritual needs of men at any place or time will be the ministry for the times"* (*An Inaugural Service*, p. 36). He accepted the Christological principle as fundamental to all right thinking in speculative theology and put his faith in it, also, as the determin-

ing factor in practical theology. He contended against traditionalism for a more rational faith —biblical, scientific, liberal—but kept free from what he called the "common rationalism of popular protestantism." His courses in sociology and ethics were regarded as a contribution of great value to the philosophy and practice of the Christian life. His most important writings will be found in the pages of the *Reformed Church Review,* for which he wrote his first article in 1871, later becoming associate editor (1893), and finally, sole editor (1897). Much of his writing was thought-provoking; some of it stirred up a wholesome intellectual strife. He rendered a noteworthy service to his Church in a critical period of controversy and left his impress upon the trend of contemporary theological thought.

[*Franklin and Marshall College Obit. Record,* June 1904; H. H. Rupp, "Excerpts from the Diaries of Wm. Rupp," in *Bull. of the Theological Sem. of the Reformed Church,* Oct. 1930; *An Inaugural Service* (Phila. 1894); files of *Reformed Church Rev.,* 1871–75, 1883–1904; *Reformed Church Messenger,* Apr. 14, 1904.]

G. F. M.

RUSH, BENJAMIN (Dec. 24, 1745 o.s.–Apr. 19, 1813), physician, patriot, humanitarian, was born on a plantation near Philadelphia, in the agricultural community of Byberry, the fourth of the seven children of John and Susanna (Hall) Harvey Rush. He was descended from John Rush, a yeoman from Oxfordshire, who came to Byberry in 1683. His father, a gunsmith and farmer, died when Benjamin was but five years old. At eight he was sent to school with an uncle by marriage, Samuel Finley [*q.v.*], and then to the College of New Jersey (now Princeton), where he received the A.B. degree in 1760. Upon returning to Philadelphia Rush first thought of studying law, but changed his mind in favor of medicine. He was a student under Dr. John Redman from 1761 to 1766 and, in addition to this apprenticeship, attended the first lectures of Dr. William Shippen and Dr. John Morgan in the College of Philadelphia.

During these years he displayed an interest in public affairs, was swayed by Whitefield's preaching, and aroused to youthful patriotism by the Stamp Act controversy; but revivals and politics were forgotten in the zest of professional adventure. On Dr. Redman's advice, he sailed in 1766 to complete his medical education at the University of Edinburgh. There he sat under such masters as Monro, *Secundus,* Joseph Black, and John Gregory, and became the friend and disciple of the great William Cullen. He also found time in the society of fellow students to doubt and debate all things, and so became some-

thing of a republican and a philosopher as well
as a physician. He received his doctor's degree
in June 1768, and immediately went to London
for further training in St. Thomas's Hospital.
In London he was on friendly terms with Benjamin Franklin, in whose society he learned,
among many things, the art of being agreeable.

After a short visit to Paris, Rush returned
to Philadelphia in 1769, and at once began to
practise medicine. Although he claimed to be
without influential friends, he had already arranged an appointment as professor of chemistry in the College of Philadelphia, the first such
chair established in the colonies. While holding
it Rush published the first American text in that
subject, *A Syllabus of a Course of Lectures on
Chemistry* (1770, reissued 1773). His practice
grew, at first largely among the poor; but within five years he had a very fair income. Rush
attracted attention by his unusual ability and
training, and also as the practitioner of a new
"system." Instead of that of the famous Dr. Hermann Boerhaave, he preached the system of his
master, Cullen, with such a scorn for the "old
school" that he alienated many of his colleagues.
He began writing almost at once, and in 1772
published anonymously one of the first American works on personal hygiene, *Sermons to Gentlemen upon Temperance and Exercise* (London, 1772).

Meanwhile he had become a member of the
American Philosophical Society and cultivated
other than purely professional interests. In
1773 he published *An Address to the Inhabitants
of the British Settlements in America, upon
Slave-keeping,* and in 1774 helped to organize
the Pennsylvania Society for Promoting the
Abolition of Slavery. Maintaining his interest
in the quarrel between the colonies and the
mother country, he wrote articles for the local
press, and associated with such patriot leaders
as Thomas Paine, John Adams, and Thomas
Jefferson. When war began he offered his services in the patriot cause. While waiting for action, he was married, on Jan. 11, 1776, to Julia
Stockton, eldest daughter of Richard Stockton
of Princeton. In June he was elected to the
Provincial Conference, in which he was a leader
in declaring for independence, and a month later
was made a member of the Continental Congress. He thus became a signer of the Declaration of Independence.

In April 1777 he was appointed surgeon-general of the armies of the Middle Department.
Finding the medical service in a deplorable condition he protested to General Washington, accusing Dr. Shippen, the director general, of mal-

administration. Washington referred the matter to Congress, which decided in favor of Shippen, and Rush resigned in consequence. Washington's defeats near Philadelphia, in addition
to his own personal experiences, now led Rush
to question the general's ability; and caused him
to be associated indirectly with the Conway
Cabal (Rush Manuscripts, XXIX, 136, Ridgway Library). He finally wrote an anonymous
letter to Governor Patrick Henry of Virginia,
urging that Washington be replaced by Gates
or Conway. Henry forwarded this to Washington, who recognized Rush's excellent hand and
accused him of personal disloyalty. (Rush's letter, dated Yorktown, Jan. 12, 1778, is printed in
John Marshall, *The Life of Washington,* 2 ed.,
1832, vol. I, note 12, pp. 29, 30.)

This affair ended Rush's military career, and
he returned to his practice in Philadelphia. In
the new University of the State of Pennsylvania,
opened in 1778, he began to deliver lectures in
1780. In 1783, he became a member of the staff
of the Pennsylvania Hospital and served in that
capacity for the rest of his life. Here he saw
something of the needs of the sick and the poor,
and this aroused again his interest in social reform. Stirred, moreover, by the idealism of the
Revolution, he now became a sponsor of the various ameliorative movements which were to re-
mould America in the ensuing century. He established the first free dispensary in the country
(1786), became president of the Pennsylvania
Society for Promoting the Abolition of Slavery
(1803), condemned public and capital punishments, and demanded real "penitentiaries" by
way of prison reform. His advocacy of temperance was so effective that he has been formally
recognized as the "instaurator" of the American
temperance movement. His republican enthusiasm led him to favor an improved education
for girls, a comprehensive system of schools
culminating in a national university, and a theory of education which gave greater freedom to
children and encouraged their training in science and utilitarian subjects rather than in
the traditional disciplines. Practising what he
preached, he persuaded the Presbyterians to
found Dickinson College (1783), and served as
one of its trustees. Most of his essays on social
reform appeared in magazines of Philadelphia,
and were later collected and published in 1798
under the title of *Essays, Literary, Moral and
Philosophical.* While these were extravagantly
praised by contemporaries as masterpieces of
prose, they have long since been subjected to a
similarly extreme neglect by American readers.

For a brief period in 1787, Rush once more

resorted to the newspapers in the cause of nationalism, this time to urge the acceptance of the new federal Constitution. As a result he was elected to the Pennsylvania ratifying convention, in which he and James Wilson led the successful movement for adoption. In 1789 these two men inaugurated a campaign which secured for the state a more liberal and effective constitution—the last achievement of Rush's political career. His only direct reward was a later appointment by President Adams as treasurer of the United States Mint (1797–1813). After 1789 Rush devoted himself primarily to his profession. The College of Philadelphia, now reestablished, was merged in 1791 with the University of the State of Pennsylvania to form the University of Pennsylvania. Since the medical faculties of both schools were retained, there was some shifting of academic chairs. Rush had succeeded, upon the death of Dr. Morgan in 1789, to the chair of theory and practice in the college; in January 1792 he became professor of the institutes of medicine and clinical practice in the new university, and in 1796 succeeded Dr. Adam Kuhn as professor of theory and practice as well. In addition to the university connection, he was associated with those who organized the Philadelphia College of Physicians in 1787, although he resigned from this body in the course of the first yellow-fever controversy.

Three aspects of Rush's medical work deserve attention: his "system" of theory and practice; his specific contributions to medical science; and his influence as a teacher. He had inherited from Cullen a complicated nosology, a distrust of natural healing powers, and a corresponding confidence in the use of special remedies for each species of disease. He probably also acquired from Cullen, as well as from the general medical philosophy of the day, the view that all theory should be organized, on rational principles, into a "system" that would make practice simple and intelligent (William Cullen, *First Lines of the Practice of Physic*, 1796, pp. 9–52). Cullen had urged that each generation formulate new systems, in order to keep pace with advancing scientific knowledge; and during the eighties two of his ablest pupils, John Brown of Edinburgh and Rush, began to take him at his word. It happened that Cullen's pathology had emphasized the rôle of the nervous system and nervous energy, rather than the old conceptions concerning the humors and solids. Exaggerating this point, Brown concluded that all diseases were due either to an excess or to a lack of nervous stimulation, and thus indicated either "depleting" or stimulating remedies (John Brown, *The Ele-*

ments of Medicine, 1788, *passim*). This view soon had a wide following in Europe, and Rush in America was so impressed that he decided to carry "Brunonianism" one step further to its logical conclusion. It is impossible to describe his system briefly without over-simplification, but the essential principle was the reduction of Brown's two types of disease to one. All diseases, he decided, were due to one "proximate" cause, a state of excessive excitability or spasm in the blood vessels, and hence in most cases called for the one treatment of "depletion" through bleeding and purging. Thus, as he himself declared, there was after all but one disease and one type of treatment (Manuscript Lectures on the Practice of Physic, 1796, I, Lecture No. 31, University of Pennsylvania Library). This conception was so simple, and so completely the antithesis of the nosology in which he had been trained, that it came to hold for his speculative mind all the fascination of an ultimate panacea. It was, literally, too good to be true, but he confidently proclaimed it when the initial volume of his *Medical Inquiries and Observations* was published in 1789.

The system was soon pronounced fanciful by various critics, who also declared that its author's fondness for depletion led him to dangerous extremes in practice. He seems to have averaged about ten ounces in ordinary bleedings, but often took more, and was actually willing to remove as much as four-fifths of all the blood in the body (*Medical Inquiries and Observations,* 3 ed., 1809, vol. IV, 353). Rush scorned the first criticism on the ground that reasoning and deduction were essentials in scientific method, and claimed that his treatment succeeded in practice. The real test of this claim seemed to have come in the epidemic of yellow fever which descended upon Philadelphia in 1793. Rush worked with desperation and devotion for three months, while several thousand of his fellow citizens, including members of his own household, died of the "yellow monster." His treatment, he declared, was practically always effective when employed promptly. But the only supporting data he offered were aggressive and dogmatic assertions as to his diagnoses and cures. He wrote a justly famous account of the epidemic as a whole, but failed to keep an exact record of his own cases. In a word, while correct in his view that hypotheses have their place in medicine, he was largely blind to his obligation to check them against the facts. Vital statistics of a sort were already available but he did not use them. The way was thus open for a lay critic, William Cobbett, to point out the correlation between the increasing employment of Rush's treatment and the increasing mortality rate—the more bleeding, the more deaths! The doctor's system, Cobbett observed, is "one of the great discoveries . . . which have contributed to the depopulation of the earth" (*The Rush-Light*, New York, Feb. 28, 1800, p. 49). The pamphleteer's motives were not above suspicion, and Rush's treatment was not the only variable involved; yet it was indeed impossible to reconcile his claims with the stark fact of the mortality tables. He was not guilty of deliberate misrepresentation, but rather the victim of a certain credulity about diagnoses and cures which characterized much of his work.

The epidemic had several immediate effects, so far as Rush was concerned. His view that its "remote" cause was unsanitary conditions antagonized many citizens, and particularly those doctors who ascribed the disease to importation and contagion. Both this issue and that relating to treatments, were taken into the newspapers, and Rush again found himself the center of controversy. Nevertheless, his published accounts of the epidemic, and of those which followed it, won for him recognition by several European governments and learned societies. The chief essay is *An Account of the Bilious Remitting Yellow Fever, as it Appeared in the City of Philadelphia, in the Year 1793* (1794).

It has been remarked that Rush was an observant man, but not a good observer. His shortcomings as a systematic observer have been noted; it remains to point out that he was indeed an observant man in special fields of medicine. There is reason to believe that he was the pioneer worker in experimental physiology in the United States. He was the first American to write on *cholera infantum,* and the first to recognize focal infection in the teeth. He was probably the first to advocate the study of veterinary medicine. His repudiation of current nosology was valuable, in that he strove to reduce the confusion of treatments associated therewith—he favored purging the *materia medica* as well as his patients. Most notable were his contributions to psychiatry, made while working with the insane at the Pennsylvania Hospital, where he inculcated a scientific and fairly humane attitude toward this class of patients. His famous work, *Medical Inquiries and Observations upon the Diseases of the Mind* (1812) shows some appreciation of what would today be known as mental healing and even of psycho-analysis. He was, finally, the first medical man in the country to achieve a general literary reputation.

Rush, therefore, was probably the best-known American physician of his day, though his reputation as a scientist was exaggerated because of his popularity as a teacher. He was hated by his enemies, but there is overwhelming evidence that he was admired by his students to a degree rare in the history of any of the professions. His classes grew ever larger, and his fame spread throughout the country, especially in the South and West. His son James declared that while before 1790 Rush's classes numbered from sixteen to forty-five annually, by 1812 he had had 2872 in his medical classes, and, including private students, 3000 in his lifetime (cited by Goodman, *post,* pp. 132, 162). No wonder he contributed, more than any other one man, to the establishment of Philadelphia as the leading American center of medical training during the first half of the nineteenth century.

Rush was well and active until a few days before his death on Apr. 19, 1813. He was buried in Christ's Church graveyard in Philadelphia and here his wife was buried thirty-five years later. Of his thirteen children six sons, among them James and Richard Rush [*qq.v.*], and three daughters survived him. He died a professing Christian, but without strict denominational attachments. He was at various times a member of the Episcopalian and the Presbyterian churches, accepted the Universalists' view of salvation, and has been claimed by the Unitarians. In fact his education so broadened his mind as to destroy any spirit of denominationalism, without weakening a generally pious outlook which was the result of early training. His piety, however, was complacent and inconsistent at times; and his occasional use of theological arguments in medical reasoning was a survival of medievalism in method entirely foreign to his abler contemporaries. The truth is that Rush had an able and versatile, but not a fundamentally critical mind.

[The majority of Rush's manuscripts are in the Ridgway Branch of the Philadelphia Lib. Co.; others are in the Pa. Hist. Soc., the Univ. of Pa., the Philadelphia Coll. of Physicians, the Girard Estate, the N. Y. Academy of Medicine, the N. Y. Hist. Soc., the Lib. of Cong., and in the private possession of Mr. Lynford Biddle of Chestnut Hill, Philadelphia. Important printed sources are: E. C. Burnett, ed., *Letters of Members of the Continental Cong.,* vols. I–III (1921–1926), containing selections from his diary and correspondence; *A Memorial Containing Travels through Life or Sundry Incidents in the Life of Dr. Benjamin Rush. . . . Written by Himself* (1905); H. G. Good, *Benjamin Rush and His Services to Am. Education* (1918); sketches in various collections of American medical biography, of which the most detailed is that by Samuel Jackson in S. D. Gross, ed., *Lives of Eminent Am. Physicians and Surgeons of the Nineteenth Century* (1861), pp. 2–85; and the most reliable, that by Francis Packard, in H. A. Kelly and W. L. Burrage, eds., *Diction-*

ary of *Am. Medical Biography* (1928); the favorable essay of David Ramsay, *An Eulogium upon Benjamin Rush, M.D.* (1813); the critical essay by Victor Robinson, "The Myth of Benjamin Rush," *Medical Life*, Sept. 1929, vol. XXXVI, pp. 445–48. A list of Rush's publications and a general bibliography are in Good, pp. 259–75; and an almost complete list is in the *Index Catalogue of the Lib. of the Surgeon-General's Office, U.S.A.*, XII (1891), pp. 398–400. N. G. Goodman, *Benjamin Rush, Physician and Citizen, 1746–1813* (1934), the latest and most complete study, is well documented and contains an excellent bibliography. A death notice appeared in *Poulson's American Daily Advertiser*, Apr. 21, 1813.]   R. H. S—k.

RUSH, JAMES (Mar. 15, 1786–May 26, 1869), physician and psychologist, was born in Philadelphia, seventh of the thirteen children of Dr. Benjamin Rush [*q.v.*] and his wife, Julia (Stockton), and brother of Richard Rush [*q.v.*]. He graduated from the College of New Jersey (Princeton) in 1805, and was granted the degree of M.D. at the University of Pennsylvania in 1809. He then followed his father's example by continuing his medical training at Edinburgh, where he was as much influenced by current philosophical thought as by strictly professional interests. Upon returning to Philadelphia in 1811, he began to practise medicine, and gave some private lectures, though, contrary to certain statements regarding him, he never held a regular chair. Personally attractive and of some means, he gave considerable time to social life, and on Oct. 19, 1819, married Phoebe Anne Ridgway, daughter of Jacob Ridgway, a wealthy Philadelphia merchant. She eventually inherited an estate of more than a million dollars and became something of a leader in local society, though tradition has it that, having come from "north of Market Street," she always experienced some opposition in her social aspirations.

Rush gradually gave up his practice and came to devote himself largely to social and scientific interests. In 1827 he published in Philadelphia *The Philosophy of the Human Voice,* in which a medical approach to the subject was followed by a detailed treatise on elocution. Although unattractive to the modern reader, this work achieved popularity in an age of declamation, and went through six editions by 1867. In 1834 he published *Hamlet, a Dramatic Prelude, in Five Acts.* During his younger years, he had worked occasionally on psychological studies, only to abandon them in middle age; but the death of his wife on Oct. 23, 1857, led him to retire from social life and to return to his earlier interests. He finally published his *magnum opus,* a two-volume *Brief Outline of an Analysis of the Human Intellect* (1865), which proved to be a learned and rather original work, but one that was verbose and almost unreadable. It is of some

interest, however, in that it expressed a relatively early American concern with the development of psychology as an objective science. "The mind," he observed, "has been and still is regarded as the working of a *spiritual something* in the brain, and therefore not to be investigated, as a physical function of the senses and the brain conjoined. This appears to be the principal cause why the problem of the mind has not been finally solved, on the clear and assignable data of observation and experiment: for who has ever experimented upon Spirit? And certainly Thinking and Wrangling, in the metaphysical way of demonstration, have never been able to show . . . any thing within, or round about it" (vol. II, p. 475). This general point of view he claimed to have held since the beginning of the century.

Rush really represented that mid-stage in the modernization of a science in which one theorizes about avoiding theory and establishing facts; and he was apparently unaware that the final stage, that of systematic inductive procedures, was already being attained by the German psycho-physicists of the time. Rush died, a childless, embittered recluse, in his old home on Chestnut Street in 1869; his last book, *Rhymes of Contrast on Wisdom and Folly* (1869), expresses ironic condemnation of the younger generation and all its wicked works. He left his estate to the Library Company of Philadelphia, to establish the Ridgway Branch of that institution, stipulating that every ten years during the half-century following his death, the Library Company should publish an edition of 500 copies of each of his books, to be sold at cost (*Provisions of the Last Will and Testament of Dr. James Rush, relating to the Library Company of Philadelphia,* 1869). He added, furthermore (*Ibid.,* p. 27), "Let it not keep cushioned seats for time-wasting and lounging readers, nor places for everyday novels, mind-tainting reviews, controversial politics, scribblings of poetry and prose, biographies of unknown names, nor for those teachers of disjointed thinking, the daily newspapers."

[*Provisions,* cited above; *A Memorial . . . of Dr. Benjamin Rush . . . Written by Himself* (1905); MSS. in the Ridgway Branch, Library Co. of Phila.; *Public Ledger* (Phila.), May 28, 1869.]   R. H. S—k.

RUSH, RICHARD (Aug. 29, 1780–July 30, 1859), lawyer, diplomat, and statesman, was born at Philadelphia, Pa., the second son and third child of the celebrated physician, Benjamin Rush [*q.v.*], and Julia (Stockton) Rush. The boy grew up in a cultivated household, and at the age of fourteen was ready for entrance into the College of New Jersey (now Princeton), from which his father and his maternal grandfather had graduated. In college he was the youngest member of his class, and, while not a distinguished student, showed great interest and ability in debating. After finishing his course he studied law in the office of William Lewis, a well-known legal luminary of Philadelphia, and was admitted to the bar in December 1800. His early years of practice were not particularly brilliant, but during them Rush met many interesting persons who came to his father's house, and read widely in law, history, government, and literature. His reputation as a speaker began to be established when in 1807 he made an eloquent speech on the sinking of the *Chesapeake* at a public meeting in the State House yard in Philadelphia. In 1808 he defended William Duane, the editor of the *Aurora,* against the charge of libel for an attack upon Gov. Thomas McKean of Pennsylvania, and thus made his first important political contacts. He refused, however, to be a candidate for Congress at this time.

In January 1811, he was appointed attorney-general of Pennsylvania, the beginning of nearly twenty years of uninterrupted office-holding. An ardent Republican, he warmly opposed the renewal of the charter of the Bank of the United States, and in November, having attracted the favorable attention of President Madison, to whom he long remained devoted, he became comptroller of the treasury. On July 4, 1812, the administration put him forward to defend the war with Great Britain in an address at Washington. Rush's temperament, in general, was not belligerent, and the cool and objective character of his mind was ill-suited to whipping up the war-spirit. The speech is almost apologetic in tone, far too argumentative to be a great war speech, but it seemed to be well received, and encouraged him to more political pronouncements, which helped to make him better known. In February 1814, he was offered the choice of the offices of secretary of the treasury, or of attorney-general, and chose the latter. In this post he was charged with the duty of editing the *Laws of the United States* from 1789 to 1815 (5 vols., 1815), which he performed in authoritative fashion. On the inauguration of Monroe, Rush was made secretary of state, pending the return of John Quincy Adams from Europe to assume that office. In this capacity, he negotiated the famous Rush-Bagot convention (Apr. 28, 1817), establishing a limitation of naval armaments on the Great Lakes, one of the earliest treaties of this kind in the history of the United States. On Oct. 31, 1817, he was appointed minister to Great Britain.

Rush was undoubtedly amongst the most efficient and amongst the best liked of American ministers to the Court of St. James's. A man of high breeding, emphatically a gentleman, he moved with ease in the British society of the period, and his genuine regard for the British people, coupled with wide intellectual interests and a tact that was almost unfailing, gave him a wide measure of success. He was confronted with a great variety of difficult problems at the very outset, a number of important disputes with Great Britain left over by the War of 1812 not having yet been liquidated. These included the fisheries question, the matter of compensation for the slaves carried off by the British in the war, and the troublesome problem of the northwestern boundary. The convention of Oct. 20, 1818, did not really settle all of these, only the question of the slaves being put in the way of a final solution. But Rush negotiated a treaty of joint occupation of Oregon which served as a basis of understanding for nearly thirty years, and he secured important concessions on the fisheries problem. In 1819 he dealt with great wisdom with the issue raised by Andrew Jackson's recent invasion of Florida, and the execution of two British subjects, Ambrister and Arbuthnot. British public opinion was exceedingly inflamed, and Lord Castlereagh, the foreign secretary, afterwards told the minister that war might have been brought about if he had but lifted a finger (*Memoranda of a Residence at the Court of London,* 1845, p. 152). In his conversations with Castlereagh, Rush set forward the American point of view with remarkable candor, and yet without offense. His description of his interview with Castlereagh on this occasion may be regarded as a model of diplomatic manners.

Rush played an important rôle in the diplomatic negotiations which led up to the enunciation of the Monroe Doctrine. In the summer of 1823, French troops had invaded Spain, and George Canning, the British foreign secretary, had received certain intimations from Sir Charles Stuart, the British minister in Paris, with regard to a projected congress on the affairs of South America. Suspecting that such a congress might pave the way for the re-conquest of the Spanish colonies, Canning asked if it might not be possible for Rush to join him in a joint prohibition of such action. Rush had, of course, no instructions. After carefully pondering the matter, he decided that he could not accept the proposal, barring British recognition of the independence of the colonies. When Canning stated his inability to act on this basis, Rush, despite new and pressing overtures from Canning, refused to commit himself. The dispatches which he wrote in August and September 1823 were an important factor in persuading James Monroe and John Quincy Adams to take the strong stand which they assumed in the memorable message of Dec. 2. The message was not well received in England. In particular, that part of it (directed against Russia in the northwest, and not concerned with the Spanish colonies) which forbade new colonization by European powers in the American hemisphere, was most unacceptable to Canning. Rush had to do what he could to defend it, and, acting under instructions, he brought it forward in the new discussions on the northwest question which took place in 1824. He did not, however, succeed in persuading the British commissioners to acquiesce in it.

In the course of his long stay in England, Rush examined many different aspects of British institutions. He made a special study of the British navy, and it was his desire, when John Quincy Adams became president in 1825, that he might become secretary of the navy in the new administration. At Adams' insistence however, he accepted the office of secretary of the treasury, and discharged the duties of this post with extraordinary fidelity, never having been absent from office a single day in the course of four years, except for one week's illness. In this period of his life he was a protectionist, though of a rather mild type. He was no doubt partly influenced by the opinion of his state, and also apparently by the infant industry argument. He desired, however, to institute a warehouse and drawback system, not unlike that which existed in Great Britain. He played no prominent part in connection with the tariff of abominations in 1828, but does not seem to have been hostile to that measure. In 1828 he accepted a place on the ticket with John Quincy Adams, as a candidate for vice-president, but went down to crushing defeat with the rise of the Jacksonian Democracy. At this period came one of Rush's rare lapses from the urbanity which was characteristic of him. On his appointment to the Treasury, he had been the object of a slashing attack by John Randolph, who stigmatized his appointment as the worst since Caligula had made his horse a consul (Powhatan Bouldin, *Home Reminiscences of John Randolph, of Roanoke,* 1878, p. 317). Rush was stung by this, and other attacks, into publishing under the pen name of Julius an attack upon Randolph, splenetic in the extreme. He declared his willingness to avow his authorship, and accept a challenge to a duel, if Randolph cared to take the pains to look into the matter (Julius, *John Randolph, Abroad and at Home,* 1828, p. 13).

For some years after 1828 Rush was in private life. In 1829 he was sent abroad by the towns of Georgetown and Alexandria and the city of Washington to negotiate a loan of one and a half million dollars for the Chesapeake & Ohio Canal. Received with considerable coolness in Great Britain, despite his many personal friendships there, he finally succeeded in getting very favorable terms from the Dutch bank of the Crommelins. His efforts were not as gratefully received as he thought they should have been by those who sent him. In the Anti-Masonic agitation Rush took a prominent part, and he was the first choice of the new political group for the presidency. He declined to run, however. The struggle over the Bank in 1832 brought him back into the Democratic party. He sympathized strongly with President Jackson on this issue. In 1835, together with Gen. Benjamin Chew Howard of Baltimore, he was commissioned to settle a boundary dispute between the states of Ohio and Michigan, which threatened to result in an appeal to force. He succeeded in preventing an armed clash, though not in settling the question. In the summer of 1836 he sailed for England to secure the Smithson bequest to the United States. James Smithson, an Englishman, had died without issue, and had left the whole of his estate, on the death of a nephew, to the United States. The estate had become tied up in the chancery court, however, and it required much time and patience to liquidate the matter. Rush conducted his mission with efficiency and patience, and made use of his stay in Great Britain to resume many old connections, and to make new ones (*Occasional Productions, Political, Diplomatic, and Miscellaneous,* 1860, pp. 219–57). He was also extremely successful in disposing on very favorable terms of the British securities which composed the Smithson estate, and, in August 1838, brought back to this country in English gold coin the sum of upwards of £104,000, which was used to establish the Smithsonian Institution. He always retained a great interest in this establishment, of which he was elected a regent, a post which he held to his death (Cyrus Adler, "The Relation of Richard Rush to the Smithsonian Institution" in *Smithsonian Miscellaneous Collections,* vol. LII, 1910, pp. 235–51).

The next public service to which this interesting man was called (Mar. 3, 1847) was that of minister to France, in the administration of President Polk. From 1838 to 1847 he had lived quietly on his estate outside of Philadelphia, but though now sixty-seven years old, he cheerfully accepted political office once more. He arrived in France in the closing days of the July monarchy, and was a witness to the stirring events of the February revolution, which he described with much skill (*Occasional Productions*, pp. 355–82). After a brief period of reflection, he decided to recognize the republic then set up, without waiting for instructions from Washington, and despite the reserve of all the other members of the diplomatic corps. He followed with obvious mistrust the course of the red republican revolt of July, but seems to have witnessed without extravagant regret the election of Louis Napoleon as president in December 1848. He was recalled with the entry of the Whigs into power in 1849.

This was Rush's last political office. He lived for ten years more, and still entertained an interest in public affairs. He approved the compromise measures of 1850, but was, in general, sympathetic with the attitude of the Democratic party towards slavery. He much feared the dissolution of the Union, censured the extravagance of the anti-slavery agitation, and voted for Buchanan in 1856. He died in Philadelphia on July 30, 1859. He had married Catherine E. Murray on Aug. 29, 1809; of their ten children, three sons and two daughters survived him.

Of the men of the second rank who played a rôle in politics in the Middle Period, Richard Rush is decidedly one of the most attractive. He no doubt betrays a certain conventionality of mind, in the general character of his political thought, but he was by no means unwilling to accept personal responsibility, or to act on his own initiative when the occasion required. He had singularly few enemies; indeed, outside of the feud with the acid Randolph, and one youthful political altercation in Pennsylvania, his life was remarkably free from personal controversy. Laborious to a degree, of judicious mind, of wide intellectual interests, and of engaging manners, he played worthily every rôle to which he was called. A certain fastidiousness may have had something to do with the limited character of his political success, as compared with that of other men decidedly his inferiors in capacity. In appearance he was distinctly impressive. He had remarkable eyes, a broad and high forehead, and an air of scholarship that was decidedly attractive. His writings are not literary masterpieces, but they are usually interesting, and reveal a keen observer of men and things. The most important are his *Memoranda of a Residence at the Court of London*, the first edition of which (1833) covered only two years, a second edition (1845) comprising the rest of his mission; and *Occasional Productions, Political, Diplomatic and Miscellaneous*, published by his executors in 1860.

[In addition to the works mentioned in the text, see an excellent account of Rush's career down to 1840, in the *U. S. Mag. and Democratic Rev.*, Apr. 1840, pp. 301–25. C. K. Webster, *The Foreign Policy of Castlereagh, 1815–1822* (1925); Dexter Perkins, *The Monroe Doctrine, 1823–1826* (1927); W. C. Ford, "John Quincy Adams and the Monroe Doctrine," in *Am. Hist. Rev.*, July 1902; J. M. Callahan, "Agreement of 1817. Reduction of Naval Forces upon the Great Lakes," in *Ann. Report of the Am. Hist. Asso. for the Year 1895* (1896); Beckles Willson, *America's Ambassadors to England, 1785–1928* (1928), and *America's Ambassadors to France, 1777–1927* (1928); *A Memorial . . . of Dr. Benjamin Rush . . . Written by Himself* (1905); *Am. State Papers. Foreign Relations*, vols. IV, V (1834, 1858); obituaries in *Daily National Intelligencer* (Washington), *Public Ledger* (Philadelphia), Aug. 2, 1859; Trescott Papers, Lib. of Cong.; his diplomatic dispatches in the State Department.]   D. P.

RUSH, WILLIAM (July 4, 1756–Jan. 17, 1833), the first native American sculptor, was of direct descent in the fourth generation from John Rush, who had commanded a troop of horse in Cromwell's army, and came to Pennsylvania in 1683. William, born in Philadelphia, was the son of a ship-builder, Joseph Rush, coroner of the city from 1780 to 1785, and Rebecca (Lincoln) Rush, of the same family as Abraham Lincoln; his father was a first cousin of Dr. Benjamin Rush [*q.v.*]. The boy was early apprenticed to Edward Cutbush, from London, England, a wood-carver, whom within three years Rush surpassed in creating the figures which were then much in demand for the prows of ships. He is said to have served in the Revolution, and on Dec. 14, 1780, he married Martha Wallace of Philadelphia. Intelligent, industrious, and gifted, at once artist and craftsman, he established for himself a thriving business. His laurel-crowned "America" adorned the prow of the United States frigate *America*. For the frigates *Constellation* and *United States* he carved figures representing respectively "Nature" and the "Genius of the United States." It is recorded that London wood-carvers enthusiastically copied his "Indian Trader," on the ship *William Penn*, and that Hindus reverenced his "River God," on the ship *Ganges*. In "Suggestions of William Rush to Naval Constructor Joshua Humphreys, for designs for figureheads for naval vessels," dated Apr. 30, 1795 (*Pennsylvania Magazine of History and Biography*, April 1907), are mentioned various emblems dear to Rush: the cardinal virtues, the flaming torch, the Goddess of Liberty supported by Law and Justice, "the American Eagle Darting upon and Destroying the Vitals of Tyranny, with the shackels of Despotism."

Rush's once famous figureheads have now vanished, except for the well-known life-size statue of Washington, now in Independence Hall, Philadelphia, intended originally as the figurehead for a ship to be named *Washington*. Many of his other carvings remain, however. Among these are the naïve figures of "Comedy" and "Tragedy" loaned to the Pennsylvania Museum of Art; and several important works preserved at Fairmount Park, Philadelphia. These last include "Wisdom" and "Justice," colossal figures made to crown a triumphal arch in front of Independence Hall in honor of Lafayette's visit in 1824, and now in the assembly room of the Fairmount water works. At Fairmount, also, is a bronze replica of Rush's most notable work, the "Spirit of the Schuylkill," the first public fountain figure erected in the United States. The original wood carving was placed in Centre Square, now Penn Square, to commemorate the founding of the Philadelphia water system. Critics of opposing camps agree as to the grace, refinement, and good proportion of this female figure in symbolic rippling drapery, girdled with sedge and holding up a bittern spouting water. This work is often called the "Nymph with Bittern," and (mistakenly) "Leda and the Swan." A belle of the day "consented to pose" for the sculptor—an episode later celebrated in a painting by Thomas Eakins [*q.v.*]. Similar in conception to the "Spirit of the Schuylkill," but more commonplace in design and execution, are the two carvings in wood of reclining draped figures, now placed outside the Fairmount water-works buildings, and entitled respectively "Schuylkill Enchained," and "Schuylkill Released." A life-size group in wood, "Liberty Crowning the Bust of Washington," was exhibited at the Metropolitan Museum, New York, in 1927. From internal evidence, according to the Museum authorities, it may safely be attributed to Rush. He worked in clay as well as in wood and greatly regretted that he had not time to try marble. It is said that when orders pressed, he would stand over an apprentice, directing him where to cut, Rush's belief being that, whatever material is used, the artist must clearly visualize within it the form he wills to release, and that the rest of the work is merely mechanical. He studied nature carefully, as his work shows.

The Pennsylvania Academy owns a plaster cast of his symbolic self-portrait, carved in pine, his shoulders shaped in the semblance of a rough log, with a pine branch over it. Despite a touch of the grotesque in the vigorous treatment, it presents a noble, kindly head, in harmony with the few facts known of him as a public-spirited citizen. After initial attempts (1789–91), the painter Charles Willson Peale [*q.v.*] and a small group of others including Rush were finally able in 1805 to found the Pennsylvania Academy of the Fine Arts, the earliest organization of the kind in the United States, Rush serving as one of the directors from that time until his death. He was also an influential member of the city council for a period stated as "more than a quarter of a century" (Taft, *post*, p. 23). In 1812 he exhibited at the Academy a group of his later works, of which Dunlap lists busts of Linnæus, William Bartram, and the Rev. Henry Muhlenberg, together with figures of "Exhortation," "Praise," and "a Cherubim." To this number others have added two busts of William Penn, a self-portrait, busts of Voltaire, Franklin, Rousseau, and Lafayette, and figures of "Architecture," "Agriculture," and "Christ on the Cross." Other titles of works by Rush are "Winter," "Commerce," "Peace," and "War."

[J. T. Scharf and Thompson Westcott, *Hist. of Phila.* (1884), vol. III; *Pa. Mag. of Hist. and Biog.*, July 1907; *A Memorial . . . Incidents in the Life of Dr. Benjamin Rush . . . as well as a Short Hist. of the Rush Family in Pa.* (privately printed, 1905); C. H. Hart, *Browere's Life Masks of Great Americans* (1899); J. M. Beck, in *Fairmount Park Art Asso.: 50th Anniversary* (1922); Wilfred Jordan, in *Art and Archaeology*, June 1921; William Dunlap, *Hist. of the Rise and Progress of the Arts of Design in the U. S.* (Goodspeed ed., 1918), inaccurate in some details; Lorado Taft, *The Hist. of Am. Sculpture* (1904), Suzanne LaFollette, *Art in America* (1929); C. R. Post, *A Hist. of European and Am. Sculpture* (1921); F. D. Whittemore, *George Washington in Sculpture* (1933).]
         A. A.

RUSK, JEREMIAH McCLAIN (June 17, 1830–Nov. 21, 1893), congressman, governor of Wisconsin, secretary of agriculture, was born on a farm in Morgan County, Ohio, the son of Daniel Rusk and Jane Faulkner, both natives of Pennsylvania and children of Scotch-Irish immigrants to Maryland. Both his grandfathers had fought in the Revolution shortly after their arrival in America. Jeremiah's common-school education was meager. At the age of sixteen, after the death of his father, he managed his mother's farm; later he drove a stage and became a railway construction foreman. In 1853 he removed to Wisconsin, settling in Viroqua, Vernon County, as tavern keeper. To this business he soon added the ownership of a stage line and a good farm, and in time the part ownership of a bank. His extraordinary activity, sound practical judgment, and personal popularity made his numerous business enterprises uncommonly successful.

Equal or greater success waited on his political ambitions. In 1855 he was elected sheriff of his county, and two years later, coroner. In 1861, he was elected to the state Assembly, resigning in 1862 to become major in the 25th Wisconsin Infantry, a regiment he had recruited. He rose in rank from major to lieutenant-colonel, won distinction for his soldierly conduct at "The Crossing," in the battle of Salkehatchie River, February 1865 (*War of the Rebellion: Official Records, Army*, 1 ser. XLVII, pt. 1, p. 387), and at the close of the war was brevetted colonel and brigadier-general. After his return to Wisconsin, he was elected state bank controller in 1865 and reëlected in 1867. In 1871 he went to Congress as successor to C. C. Washburn, and served for three terms.

He declined diplomatic appointment in 1881, but was that year elected governor of Wisconsin. He set a record for length of service as governor of his state: he was elected three times and one of his terms was extended by statute, so that he was in office seven years. During this period he made his deepest impression upon the people of the state, earning the title of affection: "Uncle Jerry." His governorship, strong in every respect, was marked by two highly dramatic episodes—the feeding of 1700 desperate railway workers left stranded without pay by a bankrupt railway company, and the quelling of the industrial strike riots in Milwaukee in May 1886. In the first case Rusk enforced the remedy, "bread, not bayonets." In the second, after his repeated warnings that violence and property destruction would not be tolerated, he gave the order to fire, which put an end to the rioting. His most characteristic remark, known to millions, was uttered in connection with that grim incident: "I seen my duty and I done it."

His devotion to duty was acclaimed so universally as to make him appear to many an available candidate for the presidential nomination in 1888. In consequence, when Harrison upon his inauguration found himself with a new office to fill in the secretaryship of agriculture, he called Rusk to that position, afterwards saying of him: "He not only filled the measure of the man I wanted, but enlarged it" (Casson, *post*, p. 2). Rusk's service was noteworthy for at least two achievements: he secured the inspection of all American meat exports, with the consequent eradication of cattle and swine diseases complained of by importing countries, and thus prepared the way for the removal of European restrictions on such imports; and he at once popularized the new department's activities and policies by engaging the interest of the newspapers.

After Mar. 4, 1893, he retired to his farm, where he died eight months later.

Jerry Rusk was a character to inspire legend. Tall (six feet, three inches), broad, and well set up, he was physically fit for any emergency. His democratic ways, cheery manner, spontaneous humor, and great good sense, coupled with his loyalty and dependableness, endeared him not only to business and political associates, but to the people of Wisconsin generally. Though practically uneducated and never a reader, he was a clear, straightforward, logical thinker and writer on every day business and administrative subjects. His was fundamentally the active, not the reflective type of mind. In politics he was a strict party conformist, and a conciliator of factional differences.

On Apr. 5, 1849, in Ohio, Rusk married Mary Martin, by whom he had three children. She died in January 1856, and in December of that year, at Viroqua, he married Elizabeth M. Johnson, by whom he had two children.

[Henry Casson, *Uncle Jerry* (1895), the only general biography, is diffuse and eulogistic, but presents the main facts of Rusk's life. It contains an introduction written by Benjamin Harrison, also speeches on Rusk by John C. Spooner. An attack in violent language on Rusk as secretary of agriculture was printed anonymously at Lincoln, Nebr., Aug. 1, 1892. Volumes of pamphlets and newspaper clippings by and about Rusk are in the Wis. State Hist. Library. Rusk's letters are in the Keyes, Fairchild, and LaFollette collections, in the same institution, and Mary E. Rusk, a daughter, has deposited there such papers as were left in the Viroqua home. A brief notice appears in *Biog. Dir. Am. Cong.* (1928) and an obituary in the *Madison Democrat*, Nov. 22, 1893.]   J. S.

RUSK, THOMAS JEFFERSON (Dec. 5, 1803–July 29, 1857), soldier, chief justice of Texas, and senator, was born in Pendleton District, S. C., the son of John and Mary (Sterritt) Rusk. His father, a stonemason, had emigrated from Ireland in 1791 and settled on land belonging to John C. Calhoun. His mother taught him to read the Bible and other literature, and Calhoun furnished him law books, allowed him to use his office, and obtained him a position in the office of William Gresham, clerk of the district court. Rusk studied in this office and worked in a grocery store until 1825, when he removed to Clarksville, Ga., and began the practice of law. There he remained for ten years, was unusually prosperous in his profession, was married in 1827 to Mary F. Cleveland, the daughter of John Cleveland, and became the partner of his father-in-law in the mercantile business. He invested heavily in a gold-mining company, the managers of which embezzled its funds and fled to Texas. He was financially ruined and pursued them to Nacogdoches only to find that they had squandered the funds. Well pleased with the new country, he decided to settle there and engage in farming and stock-raising. He became interested in the quarrel with Mexico, was elected captain of a company of troops, and joined Austin at San Antonio. He was soon made colonel and was authorized to raise men, arms, and food in East Texas.

In the convention of 1836 he took an active part, signed the declaration of independence for Texas, aided in the drafting and adoption of the constitution of the republic, and was elected on Mar. 16 secretary of war in the provisional government. When the convention adjourned, the situation looked gloomy for the Texas cause. It is claimed that President Burnet sent him to influence Houston to stop the retreat toward Nacogdoches and to fight Santa Anna, and that he succeeded in this delicate mission (but see Samuel Houston sketch). At San Jacinto Rusk fought bravely and led successful charges after Houston was wounded. He took command of the Texas army after the battle and served several months, was made secretary of war in Houston's cabinet, but soon resigned to enter the practice of law at Nacogdoches. As a member of the House of Representatives in the Second Congress of the republic he took a leading part in the enactment of laws concerning the courts. He was elected major-general of militia and after the adjournment of Congress cleared East Texas of hostile Indian tribes by October 1839. This aggressive policy was contrary to the wishes of President Houston but met the full approval of his successor, M. B. Lamar. Congress had elected Rusk chief justice of the supreme court in 1838, and he presided over its first session from January to June 1840.

After four years of service to the Republic of Texas, usually without pay, he returned to Nacogdoches to resume the practice of law; but threats of a Mexican invasion of Texas had created a demand for a counter-invasion of Mexico, and in 1843, over the veto of President Houston, he was made major-general to lead the campaign. Houston, desiring an armistice, withheld his commission for five months and hampered the proposed expedition in other ways. Rusk finally resigned in disgust. He favored the annexation of Texas to the United States and was president of the Texas convention that confirmed annexation and formulated the constitution of 1845.

He was elected to the Senate of the United States in 1846, 1851, and 1857. There he and Houston worked harmoniously for the interests of Texas. He was seldom absent from his post and was considered the working member of the Texas delegation. He enjoyed the renewed friendship with Calhoun, but this intimacy served to handicap him in his relations with President Polk. He declined a commission as major-general but as a senator gave full support to the administration in the war with Mexico. He worked consistently for the improvement of the mail and transportation service. He was a leader in the long fight for government support of a Southern Pacific railroad. He fought steadfastly for the Rio Grande boundary as opposed to the Nueces River and voted finally for the present arrangement as provided in the compromises of 1850. He sponsored the final settlement of the debt of Texas in 1854. He favored the Kansas-Nebraska bill, and he denounced the principles and methods of the Know-Nothing group at every opportunity. He served for several terms as chairman of the committee on post offices and post roads and in March 1857 was elected president *pro tempore* of the Senate. He was the choice of many delegates as nominee for president in the Democratic convention of 1856 but was unwilling to have his name entered. He is said to have declined an offer to enter Buchanan's cabinet as postmaster-general. He was a man of large and impressive figure, with deep-set, dark eyes. His good judgment, unfailing courtesy and tact made him one of the popular men in the federal Senate. He was a forceful speaker but not an orator, and his most effective work was done in committees. His fondness for home life and retirement caused him to resign several important offices and to decline to seek several others. He had seven children, two of whom died in infancy. His devotion to his family, including his brother David, many years his junior, attracted the notice of Houston and other contemporaries. His wife died of tuberculosis in 1856. Her loss brought him a despondency, which resulted in his suicide the following year at his home in Nacogdoches.

[*Texas Almanac* (Galveston), 1857–61 ; D. G. Wooten, *A Comprehensive History of Texas* (2 vols., 1898) ; S. H. Dixon and L. W. Kemp, *The Heroes of San Jacinto* (1932) ; Marquis James, *The Raven* (1929) ; J. D. Lynch, *The Bench and Bar of Texas* (1885) ; R. W. Stayton, "Thomas J. Rusk," *Texas Law Review*, Oct. 1925 ; E. C. Barker, "The San Jacinto Campaign," *Quart. of the Texas Hist. Asso.*, Apr. 1901 ; L. F. Blount, "A Brief Study of Thomas J. Rusk, 1835–1856," *Southwestern Hist. Quart.*, Jan., Apr. 1931 ; H. S. Thrall, *A Pictorial Hist. of Texas* (5th ed., 1879) ; S. S. McKay, "Texas and the Southern Pacific Railroad, 1848–1860," *Ibid.*, July 1931 ; C. B. Sterrett, "The Life of Thomas J. Rusk," manuscript thesis in Univ. of Texas Lib.]   S. S. M.

RUSS, JOHN DENNISON (Sept. 1, 1801– Mar. 1, 1881), a pioneer teacher of the blind in the United States, physician, penologist, was born in Essex, Mass., the son of Dr. Parker and Elizabeth (Cogswell) Russ. His earliest American ancestor was Henry Rust who came to Hingham, Mass., some time between 1633 and 1635. John's father was the first of his line to adopt the name Russ. Graduated in arts from Yale College in 1823, the son chose his father's profession and in 1825 received from Yale the degree of M.D. After a year spent in European hospitals, he entered upon the practice of his profession in New York City. In 1827, however, the young physician, fired with a desire to aid the Greek patriots in their struggle for independence, sailed for Greece in charge of a shipload of food sent by American sympathizers. For nearly three years he remained there as distributor of food and organizer of hospitals. In this work he was closely associated with that other philanthropic physician, Samuel G. Howe [q.v.], later, in Boston, to become devoted as was Russ in New York to the interests of the blind. Russ returned to New York in 1830 and resumed the practice of his profession. On his way back he had married, in England, a widow, Eliza Phipps Jenkins, whose children he adopted, giving them his name. His wife died in 1860, having borne him no children, and in 1872 he married Elsie Birdsell, who survived him.

In 1830–31 New York City was visited by epidemics of cholera and of ophthalmia and Russ was drawn into public hospital work. Thus his attention was directed to the prevalence of blindness due to ophthalmia among children and he was moved to seek means for their education. He joined with another physician, Samuel Akerly, and a well-known Friend, Samuel Wood, in establishing a school under the name of the New York Institution for the Blind, which was opened Mar. 15, 1832, with three pupils; Russ himself served as teacher. Soon the enrollment increased, the accomplishments of the pupils were exhibited, a house was procured for the school, and the board of managers appointed Russ superintendent. His enthusiasm and ardor, along with innate intelligence and remarkable sensing of the needs of the blind, gave the institution immediate success. With only meager assistance, he taught a growing number of pupils, busying himself, also, with the invention of devices for use in their work, and managing the business affairs of the school until his retirement in the spring of 1835.

Practising his profession all the while, Russ next rendered humanitarian service in connection with prison reform. One of the organizers in 1843 of the Prison Association of New York,

he became its secretary and from 1845 to 1853 served in this capacity and as investigator of conditions in the city and state prisons. His reports were comprehensive in character and had considerable effect. In 1851 he was one of the corporators of the New York Juvenile Asylum (now the Children's Village of Dobbs Ferry) and became its first executive. He served as superintendent from 1853 to 1858. An instinct for discovering fields of service and generously giving himself in them was further shown in his professional contacts. It is reported that as a physician Russ answered every call of distress but payment for attendance he never exacted, the patient making return therefor or not according to his own conscience and ability.

After his retirement from active public work in 1858, he again turned his attention to the needs of the blind. He invented a phonetic alphabet, but since it proved unwieldy, he atttempted again, as he had done thirty years before, to improve the Braille system of writing and reading by embossed points. Through almost a decade he studied this subject and sought to promulgate his findings, with seemingly no encouragement or evidence of interest on the part of educators of the blind. About this time, however, the superintendent of the New York Institution, William B. Wait [q.v.], was carrying on similar studies, without any apparent connection with the experiments of Russ, and he was able to promulgate the so-called New York Point System, a variant of the embossed dot system of Louis Braille. The last years of Russ's life were spent in retirement on an estate which he purchased and developed at Pompton, N. J., and there he died. His body lies in the family tomb at Essex, Mass.

[Robert Crowell, *Hist. of the Town of Essex* (1868); A. D. Rust, *Record of the Rust Family* (1891); L. E. Richards, ed., *Letters and Journals of Samuel Gridley Howe* (2 vols., 1906, 1909); *Obit. Record Grads. Yale Coll.*, 1881; H. A. Kelly and W. L. Burrage, *Am. Medic. Biogs.* (1920); *N. Y. Tribune*, Mar. 3, 1881; records of the N. Y. Institution for the Blind; reports of the Prison Asso. of N. Y.; *In Memoriam, John Dennison Russ* (n.d.); letters of John D. Russ in the possession of the family.]   E. M. V–C.

RUSSELL, BENJAMIN (Sept. 13, 1761–Jan. 4, 1845), journalist, was born at Boston, Mass., eldest son of John Russell, a mason. While yet attending the public school, he frequented the printing office of Isaiah Thomas [q.v.] and learned to set type. On Apr. 19, 1775, with several schoolmates he followed a detachment of troops to Cambridge and because of sudden developments in the preparations for war was unable to return home; after spending three months in doing errands for officers quartered in the

Harvard Yard and in acting as clerk for a company of Connecticut troops, he encountered his father, received a thrashing, and next day was taken to Worcester and apprenticed to Isaiah Thomas, who had recently removed the *Massachusetts Spy* there from Boston. At the time of the Declaration of Independence, he impulsively enlisted in the army but, being not yet sixteen years old, was released; in 1780, however, Thomas was drafted and employed Russell as his substitute. He joined the army at West Point, was a member of the guard at the execution of Major John André, but served in no engagement. At the end of his six months' enlistment he returned to continue his apprenticeship, from which Thomas reluctantly relieved him in 1781 when he reached his twentieth year, and he became a full-fledged journeyman. Equipped with two years' experience as journeyman, some familiarity with writing (gained mainly by making surreptitious contributions to the *Spy*), and a young wife to whom he had been married two months, he decided in November 1783 to set up a newspaper in Boston, but difficulty in obtaining equipment delayed until Mar. 24, 1784, the publication of the first number of *The Massachusetts Centinel and the Republican Journal*, to be issued twice a week by William Warden and Benjamin Russell. At the end of the second year, Russell became sole owner and editor and so continued until 1828, when he retired from journalism. The title was soon shortened to the *Massachusetts Centinel* and in 1790 changed to the *Columbian Centinel.*

Russell soon proved his ability as a journalist, not only by energetic news gathering, vigorous writing, ingenious typography, and novel incipient cartoons, but by associating himself and his paper with mechanics and merchants and by taking an active part in politics. Thus he soon became an important citizen, and his paper the most enterprising and influential in Massachusetts. With him as voluntary contributors were associated such men as Fisher Ames, John Lowell, George Cabot, Stephen Higginson, and Timothy Pickering [*qq.v.*]. Though the first number of the *Centinel* bore the motto "Uninfluenced by party, we aim only to be just," Russell was naturally a thoroughgoing Federalist. He denounced Shays's rebellion and all disorder, was strongly nationalistic, and vigorously urged ratification of the Constitution. He joyously acclaimed the adherence of each state, was leader among the Boston mechanics who influenced the Massachusetts convention in favor of ratification, and in the next issue after that event uttered a column of ecstatic verse. He gave the administrations of Washington and Adams unqualified support and, as the Federalist party took shape, made the *Centinel* its leading organ in New England. The proceedings of the first session of Congress he printed gratis, though later when funds were available Washington asked for and paid the cost. During the French Revolution and the Napoleonic Wars no other American paper was so noted for its "foreign intelligence" and the accurate details of the movements of forces and operations in Europe. It was said that Russell had the map of all the seats of conflict in his head and could trace and define every league of ground traversed by Bonaparte from the Battle of Marengo to Waterloo. To "Major Ben's" office Louis Philippe and Talleyrand, during their residence in Boston, regularly went for news, and the former gave Russell an atlas of which the editor made constant use. Russell thought the election of Jefferson a national calamity; no act of his administration or Madison's won the approval of the *Centinel,* and during this period of verbal violence no paper was more vituperative in denouncing the Republicans and all their works. He reluctantly supported De Witt Clinton [*q.v.*] against Madison and bitterly opposed the War of 1812. But the influence of Russell and his paper in national politics declined with the Federalist party, and it was still further weakened when the editor took a leading part with old political enemies in honoring Monroe on his visit to Boston in 1817. If he thus destroyed his influence, however, he gained renown by coining the phrase, "era of good feelings." He is also among those who have been credited with the invention of the word *gerrymander* (Buckingham, *post,* p. 91).

As a citizen, Russell was public-spirited and generous. Though associated with the well-to-do, he was always proud of being a mechanic; he was president of a printers' mutual protective society and in 1795 founded the Massachusetts Charitable Mechanic Association, of which he was president from 1808 to 1817. He held many public offices, especially after his retirement from journalism. For several years he was president of the Boston board of health, successively member of the school committee, member of the Common Council, and alderman. From 1805 until 1821 and 1828 until 1835, he was a member of the Massachusetts House of Representatives; he was twice elected senator from Suffolk County (1822 and 1825) and ended his political career as a member of the Executive Council in 1836 and 1837. He was married on Sept. 21, 1783, to Esther Rice of Worcester, Mass., daughter of Lemuel and Abigail Rice. After her death, he married Guest Campbell, a widow, in 1803. He had two sons and a daughter.

[The fullest account of Russell's life, with a portrait, is in J. T. Buckingham, *Specimens of Newspaper Literature* (1850), vol. II. See also Frederic Hudson, *Journalism in the United States from 1690 to 1872* (1873); D. A. Goddard, *Newspapers and Newspaper Writers in New England, 1787–1815* (1880); Francis Baylies, *Eulogy on the Hon. Benj. Russell* (1845); C. A. Cummings, "The Press and Literature of the Last Hundred Years," in Justin Winsor, *Memorial Hist. of Boston*, vol. III (1881); Joel Munsell, *The Typographical Miscellany* (1850); Isaiah Thomas, *The Hist. of Printing in America* (2 vols., 1874); A. H. Ward, *A Geneal. Hist. of the Rice Family* (1858). Brief obit. notices are to be found in the *Boston Daily Atlas*, Jan. 6, 1845; and *Boston Daily Advertiser*, Jan. 7, 1845.]   F. W. S—t.

RUSSELL, CHARLES TAZE (Feb. 16, 1852–Oct. 31, 1916), religious leader, generally known as "Pastor Russell," was born at Pittsburgh, Pa., the son of Joseph L. and Eliza (Birney) Russell, both of Scotch-Irish descent. His education was confined to that offered in the common schools, supplemented by some work with private tutors. Received at an early age into the Congregational church of which his parents were ardent members, he revolted against the doctrine of eternal punishment and after several years' study of the Bible became convinced that there was no scriptural authority for it. Meanwhile he was supporting himself by selling shirts. In 1872 he believed himself to have discovered through his studies that the second coming of Jesus would be in invisible form in the autumn of 1874. These conclusions he embodied in a booklet, *The Object and Manner of Our Lord's Return,* which obtained wide circulation. In 1878 he became pastor of an independent church in Pittsburgh, and in the following year he began to publish a magazine, *The Watch Tower and Herald of Christ's Presence,* which was issued later as *Zion's Watch Tower* and still later under its original title. Appearing semi-monthly, with no advertisements, and devoted entirely to religious topics, it ultimately obtained an Anglo-American circulation of 45,000 copies, besides being translated into fifteen foreign languages. In 1881 Russell published his most important work, *Food for Thinking Christians,* reissued in 1886 as *Millennial Dawn,* vol. I, with the subtitle, "The Plan of the Ages," later incorporated in a six-volume series of Studies of the Scriptures. It attained a circulation of over five and a half million copies. All of Russell's publications after 1884, embracing numerous pamphlets in addition to Studies of the Scriptures, were issued by the Watch Tower Bible and Tract Society organized in that year.

Gradually he began to establish branch church-es throughout the United States and later in Canada, England, and Europe, until there were more than 1200 congregations of which he was regarded as the pastor. In 1909 his wife, Maria Frances Ackley, whom he had married in 1879, brought suit for divorce, alleging immoral conduct on Russell's part with female members of the church. The divorce was granted and though appealed five times by Russell was always sustained. This unpleasantness led to the transfer of his headquarters to Brooklyn, N. Y., where in the same year he bought the old Bethel Chapel under the Brooklyn Bridge. This soon became too crowded for his following, and he moved to more expansive quarters uptown, establishing the "Brooklyn Tabernacle." In 1910 he traveled to Palestine, where his speeches exerted some influence on the nascent Zionist movement. The next year he was in further trouble, owing to the sale in his church (at sixty dollars a bushel) of so-called "Miracle Wheat" alleged to possess new and very marvellous agricultural properties; exposed by the *Brooklyn Daily Eagle,* he sued the paper for $100,000 damages in October 1911 but lost the case. In the midst of these difficulties he sailed away for a trip around the world, during which he devoted some time to a study of missionary work in the Orient. On his return, he was given a great ovation in the Hippodrome by thousands of New York Jews. The scandals connected with his name do not seem to have materially lessened his influence. During all the later years of his life, aside from special trips, he averaged annually over thirty thousand miles of travel in visiting his various pastorates, including that of the "London Tabernacle," one of the strongest centers of Russellism. He died suddenly from heart failure on a train in Texas, his last words being, "Please wrap me in a Roman toga" (*Watch Tower,* Dec. 1, 1916, p. 365) —a request fulfilled so far as possible by means of an improvised toga made out of Pullman sheets. The essence of his teaching lay in the doctrine that the world since 1874 has lived in the "Millennial Age" or "Day of Jehovah," to be marked shortly by an international revolution of the working classes reducing society to chaos, after which will occur the resurrection of the dead, a last judgment occupying a thousand years, and finally the establishment of the messianic kingdom on earth.

[See *Watch Tower,* June 1, 1916, for Russell's account of the development of his theology; *Ibid.,* Dec. 1, 1916, for a biog. sketch, reprinted in the 1924 ed. of *The Plan of the Ages*; obituaries in the *N. Y. Times* and *N. Y. Tribune,* Nov. 1, 1916; files of the *Brooklyn Daily Eagle,* Sept., Oct., 1911, esp. Sept. 23, Oct. 19; M. S. Czatt, *The International Bible Students: Jehovah's Witnesses* (1933).]   E. S. B.

RUSSELL, CHARLES WELLS (Mar. 16, 1856–Apr. 5, 1927), lawyer, diplomat, government official, was born at Wheeling in what is now West Virginia, the son of Charles Wells and Margaret Wilson (Moore) Russell. He attended Georgetown University (Washington, D. C.) from 1870 to 1873 and received the degree of LL.B. there in 1883 and that of LL.M. in 1884. Meanwhile, on Feb. 19, 1879, he married Lucy Floyd Mosby, sister of Col. John S. Mosby [*q.v.*]. There were three children, two of whom predeceased him. After the death of his first wife he married, on Oct. 1, 1885, her sister, Lelia James Mosby. The following year he was appointed to a position in the federal Department of Justice and was given charge of many of the French spoliation cases. From 1893 to 1895 he was the legal adviser of the joint commission of Congress, headed by A. M. Dockery, appointed to investigate the status of the laws organizing the federal executive departments; he then engaged in general practice in Washington. In the winter of 1897–98 he investigated conditions in Cuba for the Washington authorities, assisted the Evacuation Commission in Porto Rico, and successfully resisted, before the United States–Spanish Treaty Claims Commission, claims arising out of the destruction of the battleship *Maine*.

Reëntering the Department of Justice in 1902 as special assistant to the attorney general, he was detailed to investigate the French Panama Canal Company's title, which was accepted pursuant to his recommendation, and he later arranged the details of transfer, visiting Paris twice in the course of the proceedings. His next important assignment was to defend an action against the American commander at Havana, Gen. John R. Brooke [*q.v.*], brought by the Countess O'Reilly to enforce her slaughter-house monopoly there (*O'Reilly de Camara* vs. *Brooke*, 209 *U. S.*, 45). Successful in this, he continued in charge of insular matters for the Department until 1905, when he became assistant attorney general, serving until 1910. It was during this latter period that he was detailed to investigate and prosecute peonage in the South. He prepared a report on the subject in which he recommended: "That an incessant fight be made against peonage in every district in which it is to be found; . . . that Federal supervision of the interstate labor-supplying business of places like New York, Philadelphia, Pittsburg, and Chicago be provided for by law;" and that "the definition of legal peonage be made broad enough to include the holding of persons in servitude, whether in liquidation of an indebtedness 'or otherwise'" (*Report of Hon. Charles W. Rus-*

sell, Assistant Attorney General, Relative to Peonage Matters . . . Oct. 10, 1907, 1908). His prevailing argument on demurrer in the cases at Muskogee, Okla., involving allotments of the five civilized tribes, was considered of sufficient importance to be published by the Government Printing Office (*Suits at Muscogee . . . Argument on Demurrer by Charles W. Russell, Assistant Attorney General, 1909*).

On Dec. 21, 1909, Russell was appointed envoy extraordinary and minister plenipotentiary from the United States to Persia. During his four years of service there, the crisis resulting from the invasion of Persian sovereignty by certain European powers became acute, and the Persian government approached that of the United States, through the Persian legation at Washington, with a request for assistance in obtaining the services of American financial experts. As a result, W. Morgan Shuster, of Washington, D. C., went to Persia as treasurer general, with four other Americans, and served from May to December 1911. Russell met the party on its arrival and was in close touch therewith during the whole of the tense period which followed. Persian rights were for the time protected and it is probably due to the experience of the Medjlis (national elective assembly) during that period and the support given by the Americans, that Persia was able to maintain her integrity until after the World War, when a new era dawned.

While in Persia, Russell published *The Secret Place and Other Poems* (Washington, 1911) and *Iranian Rest and Other Lyrics* (Teheran, 1912). Toward the close of his mission, which ended in September 1914, he was designated as the President's representative at the Shah Amed's coronation ceremonies. After his return to the United States, Russell edited *The Memoirs of Colonel John S. Mosby* (1917). The narrative is in the first person as if by Mosby himself; but there are notes and an introduction by Russell. He also published *Poems* (1921), apparently a complete collection of his verse. He died at his home in Washington, D. C.

[*Reg. of the Dept. of State, Sept. 20, 1911* (1911); *Who's Who in America, 1926–27*; W. M. Shuster, *The Strangling of Persia* (1912); *Evening Star* (Washington, D. C.), Apr. 7, 1927.]   C. S. L.

RUSSELL, DAVID ALLEN (Dec. 10, 1820–Sept. 19, 1864), soldier, the son of David Abel and Alida (Lansing) Russell, was born in Salem, N. Y. His father was a congressman from New York from 1835 to 1841. David was appointed a cadet to the United States Military Academy in 1841 and was graduated in 1845, number thirty-eight in a class of forty-one members. He was commissioned brevet second lieutenant in the 1st Infantry and assigned to duty at Fort Scott, Kan., being promoted to the rank of second lieutenant on Sept. 21, 1846. During the Mexican War he served in General Scott's army, participated in the battle of Cerro Gordo and minor engagements, and was brevetted first lieutenant for meritorious conduct. After the Mexican War he served in garrisons and on frontier duty in Oregon and Washington where he was engaged in hostilities with the Yakima Indians in 1855 and 1856. He was promoted to first lieutenant on Jan. 1, 1848, and to the rank of captain on June 22, 1854.

At the beginning of the Civil War he served in the defenses of Washington, D. C. As colonel of the 7th Massachusetts Volunteers he commanded with distinction in the Peninsular and Maryland campaigns during the summer and autumn of 1862. He became a brigadier-general of volunteers in November 1862 and was assigned to the command of a brigade in the VI Corps in the Army of the Potomac, participating in the battle of Fredericksburg in December, and in the battle of Gettysburg in July 1863. At Rappahannock Station, Va., on Nov. 7, 1863, he led his brigade in a gallant charge against Confederate intrenchments which resulted in the capture of a large number of prisoners, some artillery, and eight battle flags. In recognition of his heroic services on this occasion, he was designated by General Meade to go to Washington and present the captured battle flags to the secretary of war. He had also to recover from a wound which he had received in the charge. He resumed command of his brigade in January 1864 and continued in that capacity until May, when he was assigned to the command of a division.

He fought in all the battles of Grant's Virginia campaign of 1864 from the Wilderness to Petersburg. Early in July 1864, his division accompanied the VI Corps in a hurried move to repel Early's raid on Washington and afterwards joined Sheridan's army in the Shenandoah Valley. At Winchester on Sept. 19, 1864, while leading one of his brigades at a critical moment of the battle, he received a wound in the breast. He concealed the wound from his men, and remained in the saddle, urging them forward, until, a little later in the day, he was killed by a fragment of shell which passed through his heart. For his gallant and meritorious conduct he was four times given brevet grades in the regular army, the last being that of major-general at Winchester. General Wright, in command of the VI Corps, wrote in his official report that Russell

was "an officer whose merits were not measured by his rank, whose zeal never outran his discretion, whose abilities were never unequal to the occasion, a man tenderly just to his friends and heartily generous to his foes" (*War of the Rebellion: Official Records, Army*, 1 ser., XLIII, part I, 151).

[G. W. Cullum, *Biog. Reg. . . . Officers and Grads., U. S. Mil. Acad.* (1891); *Dedication of the N. Y. Auxiliary State Monument on the Battlefield of Gettysburg* (1926); N. V. Hutchinson, *Hist. of the Seventh Vol. Infantry* (1890); *Battles and Leaders of the Civil War* (1887–88), vols. III, IV; records of the Pension Bureau and Adj.-General's office, Washington, D. C.; *Albany* (N. Y.) *Evening Jour.*, Sept. 26, 1864.]

S. J. H.

RUSSELL, IRWIN (June 3, 1853–Dec. 23, 1879), poet, was the son of Dr. William McNab Russell, a native of Ohio but of Virginian extraction. While still young, Dr. Russell had established his practice in Port Gibson, Miss., and there had married Elizabeth Allen, a native New Yorker of New England extraction, who had taught for several years in the Port Gibson Female College. Irwin was born in Port Gibson, but his family soon moved to St. Louis, whence, however, they returned to Port Gibson at the outbreak of the Civil War. Irwin, though always of frail physique, had early displayed precocity. At four he could read, and at six he could understand Milton's poetry. Food was scarce during the Civil War, and the growing boy was certainly undernourished. At the end of the war the family returned to St. Louis, where they remained till 1869, when Irwin graduated with credit from St. Louis University. He then went to Port Gibson to study law in the office of Judge L. N. Baldwin. By special act of the legislature of Mississippi he was admitted to the bar at the age of nineteen. Meanwhile he had several times run away from his studies—once to New Orleans, and once to Texas with his chum Austin Wharton. While on these trips he lived in sailors' boarding houses and frequented Mississippi steamboats, with many of whose captains he was on terms of intimacy. He thus acquired an unusual penetration into human character and motives, but also a fondness for strong drink, which remained one of his besetting weaknesses. In 1877 he became Judge Baldwin's assistant. He had always been more interested in literature than in the law, however, and had already produced considerable verse. His first poem, "A Chinese Tale," a juvenile effort on the origin of foot-binding, appeared in 1869. "Ships from the Sea" received a great deal of attention locally when it was published in the *Port Gibson Standard* of Oct. 13, 1871. One of the first of Russell's poems in negro dialect, "Uncle Cap

Interviewed," appeared in January 1876 in the "Bric-à-Brac" department of *Scribner's Monthly*. Many of his poems appeared in *St. Nicholas, Appleton's Journal, Popular Science Monthly, Puck,* and other periodicals. Much of his work was published anonymously or under various pen names. He was one of the first to recognize the literary possibilities offered by the negro, and his mastery of negro dialect and character was acknowledged by such connoisseurs as Joel Chandler Harris and Thomas Nelson Page.

In 1878 an epidemic of yellow fever reached Port Gibson. Immediately there was an exodus from the town, but out of sixteen hundred people, between six and seven hundred remained. Dr. Russell stayed to tend the sick, and his son became his assistant. For several months they toiled night and day to alleviate the suffering. The girl Russell is said to have loved, Dora Donald, died in the epidemic. In the latter part of December, Russell went to New York, where he was welcomed by such literary notables as Henry Cuyler Bunner, Richard Watson Gilder, and Robert Underwood Johnson, but despite the interesting book shops of the city and the literary life there, he did not find New York conducive to writing. In May 1879 his father died as a result of the exertions he had made during the epidemic, and there ensued a period of deep despair for the poet. In August, sick and practically penniless, he reached New Orleans, having worked his way down as a fireman. He soon secured a connection with the *New Orleans Times,* but the hardships he had undergone proved too much for his physique, and without appealing for aid from his friends or his family, he died in a cheap boarding house on Dec. 23. With a premonition of death, not ten days before, he had published in the *New Orleans Times* his melancholy poem, "The Cemetery." He is chiefly significant historically as a pioneer in the use of negro dialect for literary purposes, but his was an authentic poetic voice even if a minor one.

[Russell's one volume of verse, *Poems by Irwin Russell,* was compiled and published posthumously in 1888 with a preface by Joel Chandler Harris. It was added to and republished in 1917, under the title, *Christmas-Night in the Quarters and Other Poems,* with a good sketch of the author by Maurice Garland Fulton. Articles by A. A. Kern in the *Tex. Rev.,* Oct. 1916 and by C. C. Marble, in the *Critic,* Oct. 27 and Nov. 3, 1888, are illuminating. See also W. M. Baskervill, *Southern Writers: Biog. and Crit. Studies* (1897), vol. I; M. W. Musgrove, "Memories of Irwin Russell," *Daily Picayune* (New Orleans), Sunday, June 2, 1907; *New Orleans Times,* Dec. 24, 1879.]   H. L.

RUSSELL, ISRAEL COOK (Dec. 10, 1852–May 1, 1906), geologist, was born of New England ancestry at Garrattsville, N. Y., the son of Barnabas and Louisa Sherman (Cook) Russell.

He spent the first twelve years of his life near his birthplace and then went with his parents to Plainfield, N. J. He was educated in the schools of Clinton, N. Y., the Hasbrook Institute at Jersey City, the University of the City of New York, where he received the degree of B.S. and C.E. in 1872, and the School of Mines at Columbia College. On completing his university training Russell went as photographer of the United States Transit of Venus Expedition to New Zealand and Kerguelen Island, an experience that opened to him the field of physiography, afterwards the subject of much of his study. In 1878, after two years as assistant professor of geology in the School of Mines at Columbia, he joined the Wheeler survey for geological exploration in New Mexico under the direction of John J. Stevenson [*q.v.*], and the following year traveled in Europe.

In 1880 he was appointed to the newly established United States Geological Survey and assigned to the Great Basin division under G. K. Gilbert [*q.v.*], later one of the most distinguished of American geologists. After a year as assistant to Gilbert, he was given independent work investigating the Quaternary history of a series of desert basins in northern Nevada and adjacent parts of California and Oregon. His four years' study of these areas saw the light in a massive monograph published by the government under the title *Geological History of Lake Lahontan of Northwestern Nevada* (1885), which remains a classic of the science. Transferred in 1885 to the Southern Appalachian province, he labored diligently on the difficult problem of the structure of an area of much-metamorphosed rocks. In 1888 he began an extensive correlation of the Triassic formation of the United States, an undertaking which, being interrupted, resulted in the publication of a correlation of the Atlantic provinces only, "Correlation Papers: The Newark System," in the *United States Geological Survey Bulletin No. 85* (1892). In 1889 he began a series of expeditions to Alaska. On the first of these, made for the United States Coast and Geodetic Survey, he studied the northern section of the eastern boundary; and during two succeeding summers, under the joint auspices of the United States Geological Survey and the National Geographic Society, he explored the glaciers and the slopes of Mount Saint Elias, making two attempts, the second of which very nearly succeeded, to conquer the summit of the mountain. (See "An Expedition to Mount Saint Elias" in the *National Geographic Magazine,* May 1891, and "Second Expedition to Mount Saint Elias in 1891" in the *Thirteenth Annual*

Report of the United States Geological Survey,
1893, pt. 2.)

When in 1892 he became professor of geology
at the University of Michigan, he continued to
devote his summer vacations to exploration,
mainly in the northwestern United States and in
northern Michigan. In addition to numerous
technical reports he wrote five popular volumes
described as "Reading Lessons for Students of
Geography and Geology." The first of these,
Lakes of North America, appeared in 1895; later
came *Glaciers* (1897), *Volcanoes* (1897), and
Rivers of North America (1898), and finally a
general geographic study entitled *North America* (1904). He was recognized as an authority
in the geography of North America, particularly
Alaska and the northwestern states and territories, and as a geologist of high repute in the
field of dynamical geology, especially glaciology.
He served as vice-president of the American
Association for the Advancement of Science
(Section E), as president of the Michigan Academy of Science, and as president of the Geological Society of America. Russell was married on
Nov. 27, 1886, to Julia Augusta Olmsted, of
Cambridge, Mass., by whom he had three daugh-
ters and a son. He died of pneumonia in Ann
Arbor, Mich.

[See Bailey Willis in *Bull. of the Geological Soc. of
America,* vol. XVIII (1907), which gives a complete
bibliog. of Russell's publications; W. P. Lombard and
M. L. D'Ooge in *Science,* Oct. 5, 1906; G. K. Gilbert
in *Jour. of Geology,* Nov.-Dec. 1906; C. A. Davis in
Ninth Report of Mich. Acad. of Sci., 1907; W. H.
Hobbs in *Michigan Technic,* Feb. 1907; *Who's Who in
America,* 1906–07; obituary in *Detroit Free Press,* May
2, 1906.]   W. H. H.

RUSSELL, JOHN HENRY (July 4, 1827–
Apr. 1, 1897), naval officer, was born at Frederick, Md., the son of Robert Grier Russell and
Susan Hood (Worthington) Russell. He entered the navy as midshipman in 1841, made one
cruise in the Pacific, was then attached to the
sloop *St. Mary's* in the Gulf of Mexico, and participated in the capture of Corpus Christi and
in the blockade of Vera Cruz. Commissioned
passed midshipman on Aug. 10, 1847, he entered
the United States Naval Academy that autumn
and was graduated in 1848. In 1853 he was assigned to the North Pacific Exploring Expedition under Cadwalader Ringgold [*q.v.*] serving as acting lieutenant and navigator in the
sloop *Vincennes.* When the expedition reached
China, Russell, under Robert Milligan McLane
[*q.v.*], the American commissioner, was present at an interview with the Chinese imperial
commissioner. After two years spent in Arctic
and North Pacific waters, Russell returned to
San Francisco. He was commissioned master

on Sept. 14, 1855, and lieutenant the following
day.

At the outbreak of the Civil War he was on
ordnance duty at the Washington navy yard.
He was immediately sent to the Norfolk yard to
assist in saving the Union vessels there from
capture by the Confederates, and had command
of the last boat to leave the yard on Apr. 21, 1861.
He was then assigned to the frigate *Colorado.*
On the night of Sept. 13, 1861, he commanded a
boat expedition of a hundred sailors and marines
to destroy the privateer *Judah* at Pensacola.
Though she was protected by shore batteries
and a force of a thousand men, Russell approached boldly in the night and, after a severe
hand-to-hand fight in the early morning, succeeded in burning her to the water's edge. Admiral Porter called it "the most gallant cutting-
out affair that occurred during the war" (Porter, *post,* p. 51). Gideon Welles extended him
the special recognition of the navy department,
and President Lincoln thanked him personally.
The Maryland legislature also gave him a vote
of thanks.

He was then given command of the steamer
Kennebec in Farragut's squadron. In the celebrated passage of the forts below New Orleans,
the *Kennebec,* being slow and near the end of
the line, failed to pass the forts and withdrew
from action, but Russell was present at the surrender of both forts and received the garrison
of Fort Jackson on board his ship. He participated in all the operations of Farragut's squadron up the Mississippi to Vicksburg. Commissioned lieutenant commander on July 16, 1862,
he commanded the *Kennebec* in the blockade of
Mobile and the *Pontiac* in the South Atlantic
Blockading Squadron. In 1864 he was sent to
the Pacific Coast where he commanded the
Cyane until the end of the war. In September
1869 he won distinction for rescuing during a
great storm in the Gulf of California the passengers and crew of the steamer *Continental.*
After the war he rose successively through the
grades to the rank of rear admiral on Mar. 4,
1886. He retired voluntarily in August 1886,
after forty-five years of active service. He married Cornelia Pierpont Treadway in 1864 and
had three children. He was a capable officer and
seaman, as well as a man of unflinching courage;
his spectacular exploits won him the confidence
and esteem of his superiors and paved the way
for subsequent promotions.

[Family information from a son; *War of the Rebellion: Official Records (Navy),* 1 ser., vols. III–V, VI,
XVI, XVIII–XX; *Senate Exec. Doc. No. 22,* 35 Cong.,
2 Sess., p. 340; L. R. Hamersly, *The Records of
Living Officers of the U. S. Navy and Marine Corps*
(4th ed., 1890); D. D. Porter, *The Naval Hist. of the*

Civil War (1886); *Jour. of the Proc. of the House of Delegates* (Md.), Dec. 1861 (1861); *Army and Navy Jour.,* Apr. 3, 1897; *Evening Star* (Washington, D. C.), Apr. 2, 1897.]

L. H. B.

RUSSELL, JONATHAN (Feb. 27, 1771–Feb. 17, 1832), orator and diplomat, son of Jonathan and Abigail (Russell) Russell, was born at Providence, R. I.; on his father's side he was a descendant of John Russell who was in Charlestown, Mass., as early as 1640. He was graduated in 1791, with highest honors, from Rhode Island College (later Brown University) and studied law, practising it little but becoming a moderately successful merchant. On July 4, 1800, in the Baptist Meeting House in Providence, he delivered an oration which seems to have coincided with the opinions of the political revolution of that year; it was published and went through more than twenty editions. In 1810, having become prominent as a leader of the Jeffersonian party, he was appointed chargé d'affaires at Paris by Madison, and by appointment of July 27, 1811, filled the same office in London. From January 1814 to October 1818 he served as United States minister to Sweden and Norway, at Stockholm.

In 1814, Russell joined John Quincy Adams, James A. Bayard, Henry Clay, and Albert Gallatin [qq.v.] at Ghent, to engage in the negotiation of the treaty of peace with Great Britain; in the course of the negotiations he alone voted with Clay against Gallatin's proposal to concede the free navigation of the Mississippi in exchange for express recognition of the right to the Northeastern fisheries. After four years in Sweden, he was recalled by Monroe, and returned to America by way of Germany and Italy. Of this tour he kept an interesting journal, which was printed a century later in the *Proceedings of the Massachusetts Historical Society* (vol. LI, 1918). In 1819 he settled at Mendon, and in the following year was elected to the General Court in May, to the constitutional convention at Boston in October, and to the United States House of Representatives in November. Here he served one term (1821–23).

In 1822 he had a controversy with John Quincy Adams, who believed that Russell, as the tool of Clay, was seeking to destroy Adams' reputation in the West by pointing him out as one of the majority of the Ghent commissioners who had been ready to trade free navigation of the Mississippi for the restoration of the Northeastern fisheries. Russell published what purported to be a copy of his letter of Feb. 11, 1815, to Secretary Monroe, setting forth his dissent from the majority; Adams secured the original letter from President Monroe, accused Russell of treachery, and published *The Duplicate Letters, the Fisheries and the Mississippi: Documents Relating to the Transactions at the Negotiation of Ghent* (1822), calling attention to the differences in phrasing between Russell's "copy" and the original. Although he later found sufficient reason to forgive Clay, he wrote of Russell more than a year after the latter's death, "He is gone to his account, and is sufficiently punished in this world for his perfidy" (Adams, *Memoirs, post,* IX, 3). For many years, to "Jonathan Russell" an opponent was current political slang in New England for overwhelming him in a dispute. This controversy with Adams is supposed to have been the cause of Russell's retirement from public life, although as late as March 1829, "a broken down man" as the result of "two or three paralytic shocks," he was said to have been expecting a foreign post from Jackson (*Ibid.,* VIII, 111).

Russell was married on Apr. 3, 1794, to Sylvia Ammidon of Mendon, Mass., by whom he had four children, and on Apr. 2, 1817, to Lydia Smith, who also bore him four children. She was the daughter of Barney Smith, Boston merchant and owner of the Hutchinson house on Milton Hill, and in 1829, after the death of Smith, the Russells moved from Mendon into that house. Here, after several years of broken health, Russell died. His remains were ultimately buried in Forest Hills.

[The Russell Papers are in the Library of Brown Univ., Providence, R. I. See also "Journal of Jonathan Russell, 1818–1819," *Proc. Mass. Hist. Soc.,* LI (1918), 369–498, with miniature by Dumont, and engraving by Bance; "Letters to Jonathan Russell," *Ibid.,* XLVII (1914), 293–310, and LIV (1922), 76–80; *Memoirs of John Quincy Adams* (12 vols., 1874–77); J. G. Metcalf, *Annals of the Town of Mendon* (1880); A. K. Teele, *The Hist. of Milton, Mass., 1640–1887* (n.d.); *Hist. Cat. Brown Univ.* (1914); *Biog. Dir. Am. Cong.* (1928); J. R. Bartlett, *Geneal. of ... the Russell Family* ... *Descendants of John Russell of Woburn* (1879); *Boston Daily Advertiser and Patriot,* Feb. 20, 1832. Negatives of photographs of a bust of Jonathan Russell, by Trentanove, made in Rome in 1819, are in the Mass. Hist. Soc.]

S. M.

RUSSELL, JOSEPH (Oct. 8, 1719 o.s.–Oct. 16, 1804), merchant, ship-owner, was born in the township of Dartmouth, Mass., the son of Joseph and Mary (Tucker) Russell. His great-grandfather, John Russell, is counted as his first American ancestor, although tradition has it that John Russell was the son of Ralph Russell of Pontypool, Monmouthshire, who emigrated to New England and is said to have established the first iron works in America at Raynham, Mass., in 1652. The part of Dartmouth in which Joseph Russell was born has since become the city of New Bedford, and the village out of which the city grew originated on his farm. In 1760 he sold an acre of land to one John Loudon, who was by trade a caulker and probably supported himself by work on Russell's vessels. Other workers followed Loudon in purchasing lots and building dwellings on them, and in 1765 Joseph Rotch [q.v.], attracted by the deep water and other advantages for shipping, bought ten acres for business and dwelling houses. The resulting village was called Bedford (later New Bedford) because the family name of the English dukes of that title was Russell, and Joseph Russell was nicknamed "the Duke" as a consequence.

Russell was also prominent in the development of the whaling industry. Capturing whales by posting lookouts on shore and sending boats after those seen was practised early in Southampton, L. I., and from there spread to New England settlements, though operations conducted from shore were gradually paralleled and finally supplanted by deep-sea whaling, in which vessels that constantly grew in size and made increasingly long voyages served as a base. As early as 1755 Russell owned ships that made whaling voyages or traded with the West Indies; he kept a store for the sale of imported goods, and he was a pioneer in the manufacture of spermaceti candles, paying a Captain Chaffee, who had been in the business in Lisbon, the then very large salary of £100 a year to superintend the process. In the Revolution (in which his sentiments are indicated by his naming one of his vessels No Duty on Tea) he not only lost his capital through the cessation of American maritime commerce but had most of his ships and buildings burned by the British when they raided New Bedford in 1778. After the Revolution, however, he rapidly recovered. His prominence and initiative are shown by his engaging George Claghorn, the builder of the frigate Constitution, to construct a ship for him of the extraordinary burden, for that day, of 175 tons; it was this vessel, the Rebecca, that in 1791–93 made the first whaling voyage around Cape Horn to the Pacific hunting grounds.

He was a Quaker and strict in adhering to Quaker practices, but he did not lack independence. Though he refused to allow his famous ship Rebecca to be launched with a figure-head, he had also refused in 1772 the demand of his sect that he free his two negro slaves. Of slender build and medium height, he nevertheless was physically equal to the rough life of his period and gave many evidences of his endurance and resourcefulness. In 1744 he married Judith Howland, who was also of an old Dartmouth Quaker family. They had five sons and six

daughters, several of the sons being partners in their father's business and prominent citizens of New Bedford.

[Daniel Ricketson, The Hist. of New Bedford, Bristol County, Mass. (1858); L. B. Ellis, Hist. of New Bedford and Its Vicinity, 1602–1892 (1892); B. B. Russell, The Descendants of John Russell of Dartmouth, Mass. (1904), reprinted from New England Hist. and Geneal. Reg., Oct. 1904, Jan. 1905.]

S. G—n.

RUSSELL, LILLIAN (Dec. 4, 1861–June 6, 1922), comic opera prima donna, internationally famous beauty, was the daughter of Charles E. and Cynthia (Howland) Leonard and was named Helen Louise. Her father was a newspaper and book publisher, and her mother an ardent and well-known feminist. The future toast of Broadway, one of five daughters, was born in Clinton, Iowa. In 1865 the family removed to Chicago, where "Nellie" was educated at the Convent of the Sacred Heart and at Park Institute, a finishing school. Ambitious to become an opera singer, she studied singing in New York under Leopold Damrosch [q.v.], and in 1879 made her first stage appearance in the chorus of Edward E. Rice's Pinafore company. The following year saw her real début. Tony Pastor [q.v.] had heard her sing at a friend's house, and offered her seventy-five dollars a week to appear at his Bowery variety theater. She first appeared there on Nov. 22, 1880, billed as "Lillian Russell, the English Ballad Singer," and made a favorable impression with her clear young soprano voice and vivacious personality. The stage name then chosen was retained for the remainder of her professional career.

After further study, both vocal and dramatic, and a California tour as the lead in Babes in the Wood, she returned to New York to achieve her first real success as D'Jemma in Edwin Audran's The Great Mogul: or, the Snake Charmer, which opened on Oct. 29, 1881. She played in a series of successful comic operas, including Gilbert and Sullivan's Patience and The Sorcerer, and by the spring of 1883 was receiving $150 a week with the McCaull Opera Company. In 1880 she had married Harry Braham, conductor of Rice's Pinafore orchestra, but separated from him shortly thereafter. In June 1883, she eloped to London with Edward Solomon, an English Jew who wrote comic operas. At the time she was playing in The Princess of Trebizonde, and her departure was entirely unexpected. Braham then divorced her in New York, and she and Solomon were married in Hoboken on May 10, 1884. There was one child of this marriage, a daughter. Subsequently it developed that Solomon had never been legally separated from his first wife. Lillian Russell left him in 1886, and later brought suit in New York for an annulment, which was granted on Nov. 16, 1893. Her attorney was the notorious Abe Hummel.

She made her London début at the Gaiety Theatre, on July 16, 1883, playing in *Virginia and Paul,* by Solomon. From the time of her return to the United States in 1884, the popularity of "airy, fairy Lillian" mounted rapidly. Beauty of face and figure and an excellent natural voice —not highly trained, nor adapted to grand opera —were her chief assets. An unfailing *flair* for publicity added to her box-office appeal. She kept herself constantly in the public eye—in one season she signed five contracts and broke four of them; in another, she sought a permanent injunction restraining any manager from requiring her to appear in silk tights. Probably the most difficult parts she sang were Fiorella in Offenbach's *The Brigands* (1889), and the title rôle in the same composer's *The Grand Duchess* (1890). She specialized in the type of comic opera in which only the soprano lead was of importance, and in which practically no dramatic ability was required.

On Jan. 21, 1894, Lillian Russell was married, in Hoboken, to John Haley Augustin Chatterton, known on the stage as Signor Perugini and then playing as her leading man in *The Princess Nicotine.* In May of the same year both announced that they would never live together again, and on Oct. 23, 1898, Perugini finally obtained a divorce. The next year a new phase of Lillian Russell's career began. She joined the burlesque company of Weber and Fields, and played with them for several seasons in such offerings as *Fiddle-dee-dee* and *Whoop-dee-doo.* She left the company only when it was broken up by a quarrel between Weber and Fields. After an appearance as Lady Teazle in a musical version of *The School for Scandal* in 1904–05, and a brief interlude in vaudeville, she tried straight comedy. Her first venture in this field, *Barbara's Millions,* which reached Broadway on Oct. 8, 1906, was a complete failure. Said a critic the next day: "Singers, as a rule, are incompetent to act. Miss Russell furnishes no exception to the rule" (*New York Tribune,* Oct. 9, 1906, p. 7). Later she appeared in *Wildfire,* a melodrama of the race-track, which was a tremendous success, first on the road and then in New York. In 1912 she joined the Weber and Fields Jubilee Company to appear in *Hokey-Pokey.* At the end of its run she was married in Pittsburgh, on June 12, to Alexander Pollock Moore, publisher of the *Pittsburgh Leader* and, after her death, ambassador to Spain. Her professional career, except for occasional vaudeville engagements, was ended.

The last ten years of her life saw such varied activities as the writing of beauty articles for the woman's page of the *Chicago Herald* and the *Chicago Daily Tribune,* and Liberty Loan and Red Cross work during the World War years. In 1920 she took the stump for Warren G. Harding, who sent her abroad in 1922 on a special mission to investigate immigration problems. She submitted a report favoring future restriction and temporary suspension of immigration. Her death in Pittsburgh was due to complications following a fall on shipboard while returning to the United States.

[The material about Lillian Russell is confined chiefly to periodicals of the period of her popularity. The Robinson Locke Dramatic Collection in the N. Y. Pub. Lib. contains 6 vols. of clippings devoted to her. Her own "Reminiscences" appeared in *Cosmopolitan,* Feb.– Sept., 1922. Two useful articles are in the *Literary Digest,* Apr. 22 and June 24, 1922. Material for this sketch has been drawn also from *Who's Who in America,* 1922–23, the files of the *N. Y. Tribune,* 1880–1906, esp. issues of June 8, 1883, Apr. 2, Sept. 24, Oct. 1, 1886, Feb. 10, 1891, Aug. 30, Nov. 15, 17, 1893, Jan. 20, 22, May 16, 1894, May 21, 1897, June 24, July 1, Oct. 23, 1898, Oct. 9, 1906, and from obituaries in the *N. Y. Herald,* June 6, 1922, *N. Y. Times,* June 6, 1922, *World* (N. Y.), June 7, 1922, and *Times* (London), June 7, 1922.]   L. P. B.

RUSSELL, Mother MARY BAPTIST (Apr. 18, 1829–Aug. 6, 1898), founder of the Sisters of Mercy in California, was born in Newry, Ireland, and baptized Katherine. She was the daughter of Margaret Mullan by her second husband, Arthur Russell, a sea-captain in the Norway trade who on his marriage had turned to the less hazardous occupation of brewer. Margaret Mullan reared six children by a first husband, John Hamill, a wealthy Belfast merchant, of whom two became distinguished nuns; another, a South American patriot; and still another, a royal judge in Roscommon. Of the Russells there were also six, of whom Sarah and Elizabeth became nuns; Charles a member of Parliament, an attorney general of England, Lord Chief justice, and finally Baron Russell of Killowen; and Matthew, a Jesuit litterateur. Left fatherless, they were carefully trained by a spiritual mother and an uncle, Dr. Charles William Russell [see *Dictionary of National Biography*], later president of royal Maynooth, who took his guardianship most seriously. Katherine, her mother's first freeborn child after the enactment of Catholic emancipation, was educated in schools of Killowen and Belfast and inured to hardship as a volunteer nurse in the famine and cholera days, when in 1848 she joined the Institute of Mercy at Kinsale. Having attracted attention as a student and a nurse, she made her final vows of profession,

Aug. 2, 1851, and took the name in religion of Sister Mary Baptist. In 1854 she was named superior of a colony of eight selected nuns and novices who enlisted for the archdiocese of San Francisco at the solicitation of Rev. Hugh Patrick Gallagher [q.v.]. Fortunately, Gallagher's party, which included Levi S. Ives [q.v.] and a number of Presentation nuns, missed the ill-fated *Arctic* and sailed from Queenstown on the *Canada* (Sept. 23, 1854), for New York. Thence they journeyed via Panama to the straggling town of San Francisco, where they arrived on Dec. 8, 1854—in time to suffer from Know-Nothing abuse.

With the assistance of Archbishop Alemany, Mother M. Baptist established a convent and school. Within a year, she was given charge of the county hospital where cholera victims were isolated. With their Irish experience, these nurses were most successful in combatting the disease. Hostility to the nuns ended in gratitude. Two years later, she bought the building and christened it St. Mary's Hospital; it became one of the largest institutions of its kind in the country. In the course of time, as superior (1854–67; 1870–76) and as guiding counselor to other superiors, she established orphanages for boys and girls, a Magdalen Asylum, a home for destitute aged, a retreat house for the community, a branch house at Sacramento (1857), a convent school and orphanage at Grass Valley (1863), St. Peter's and St. Brendan's schools in San Francisco, St. Anthony's school in Oakland, and St. Hilary's Sanitarium in Marin County (1897). She took charge of the smallpox hospital in the epidemic of 1868, fed hundreds of unemployed in the hard years of 1893 and 1894, and furnished nurses at the Presidio during the Spanish-American War. Her devotion and disinterested spirit of boundless charity won people of all classes. In 1878 she made a journey to Ireland for novices. She had the loyal devotion of the growing Irish colony in California and when, worn out by a life of labor, obedience to rule, and soliciting campaigns for her charities, she died, the *San Francisco Chronicle* (Aug. 10, 1898) declared that "no dead sovereign ever had a prouder burial than Mother Mary Russell, whose life of self-denial and good works has crowned her in a city's memory."

[Matthew Russell, *The Three Sisters of Lord Russell of Killowen* (1912), reprints his *Life of Mother Mary Baptist Russell* (1901); Mother Austin Carroll, *Leaves from the Annals of the Sisters of Mercy* (n.d.); C. G. Herbermann, ed., *Diary of a Visit to the U. S. A. in the Year 1883 by Charles Lord Russell of Killowen* (1910); *San Francisco Chronicle*, Aug. 7, 10, 1898, and *San Francisco Examiner*, Aug. 7, 8, 10, 1898.]

R. J. P.

RUSSELL, OSBORNE (June 12, 1814–*c.* 1865), trapper, Oregon and California pioneer, and author, was born probably in Hallowell, Me. Of his parents nothing is recorded. Though he had little schooling, his studious and observant turn of mind gave him in time a practical education. At sixteen he ran away to sea but at New York, with the remainder of the crew, deserted his vessel; he then engaged with a fur company operating in Wisconsin and Minnesota, where he remained for nearly three years. At Independence, Mo., in April 1834 he joined Nathaniel J. Wyeth [q.v.] in his second expedition for the mountains, took part in the building of Fort Hall, Idaho, which was begun in July, and later served as a trapper and hunter. For the next six or seven years, part of the time under James Bridger [q.v.] and at other times with two or three companions or alone, he trapped over a wide region, experiencing rather more than his share of desperate adventures. In 1842 he went to Oregon with Dr. Elijah White's emigrant party, reaching the falls of the Willamette in September. He took an active part in political affairs; on May 14, 1844, he was chosen one of the three executive committeemen of the Provisional Government, and in the following year he was a candidate for governor, but toward the close of the campaign apparently threw his influence to George Abernethy [q.v.], who was elected. In 1848, hearing of the gold discoveries in California, he started for the placers and in September arrived in Hangtown (which his *Journal of a Trapper* calls Gallowstown), later Placerville. For a time he panned gold; later with a partner, Gilliam, he kept a provision store and boarding house, and still later operated two trading vessels between Sacramento and Portland. When his partner absconded with all the firm's money and one of the vessels, he was financially ruined, and he spent the remainder of his life in trying to pay off his creditors. He died in the county hospital at Placerville.

Through all his wanderings in the beaver country he kept a journal. At some time between 1843 and 1848 he sent it to New York for publication, but it did not appear until 1914 at Boise, Idaho, under the title, *Journal of a Trapper Or Nine Years in the Rocky Mountains, 1834–1843.* As a precise and intimate first-hand account of the daily life of the trapper explorer the book has no equal. Russell is characterized by Burnett, who knew him well, as a man of education, refined feelings, and virtuous habits, and as one who "always remained true to his principles." Burnett gives him the title of judge, a distinction apparently won by the part he took in a vigilance court at Placerville, which sentenced three murderers to be hanged.

[Publisher's note in 1921 ed. of *Jour. of a Trapper*; P. H. Burnett, *Recollections and Opinions of an Old Pioneer* (1880), pp. 161–62; incidental references in H. H. Bancroft, *Hist. of Oregon* (1886); C. H. Carey, *Hist. of Oregon* (1922), and H. W. Scott, *Hist. of the Oregon Country* (6 vols., 1924).]   W. J. G.

RUSSELL, SOL SMITH (June 15, 1848–Apr. 28, 1902), actor, was born in Brunswick, Mo., the son of Charles Elmer Russell, keeper of a small country store, who had been at one time an itinerant physician and preacher, and of Louisa Mathews, daughter of Edwin Mathews, a teacher of music in Cincinnati, Ohio. He was named for the actor, Sol Smith [q.v.], who was his uncle by marriage. During his boyhood and youth, he lived with his parents in St. Louis, Mo., and Jacksonville, Ill., but soon after the outbreak of the Civil War he ran away from home and remained with a Union regiment for several months as a drummer boy, not being allowed to enlist because of his youth and the absence of formal parental consent. His departure from home, however, was the beginning of a long professional career on the stage. Joining a company at the Defiance Theatre in Cairo, Ill., he made slow advancement from small beginnings; he often appeared in a variety of parts in one evening, besides singing between the acts and drumming in the orchestra.

This opening engagement struck the keynote of his career. He could turn his mind, his hands, his agile body to almost anything that would amuse an audience. Soon afterwards he was acting and singing his songs in stock companies and on tours through the Middle West; he joined the Peak family of bell ringers, and in 1868 the Berger family, giving character bits and songs, and proving so popular with the Bergers that they were later advertised as the "Berger Family and Sol Smith Russell Concert Troupe." After a season in 1867 with the stock company at the Chestnut Street Theatre in Philadelphia, he spent three seasons touring in his own monologue entertainment. His first New York engagement was at Lina Edwin's Theatre in 1871; and after a season of twenty-six weeks at the Olympic Theatre, nineteen weeks at the Howard Athenaeum in Boston, and various other engagements, he joined Augustin Daly's company at the Fifth Avenue Theatre in New York, making his debut there on Aug. 25, 1874, as Mr. Peabody in *What Could She Do, or Jealousy,* a version of Emile Augier's *Gabrielle.* The theatre records show that he appeared in three other characters that season, Trip in *The School for Scandal,* the present Mrs. Peters in *Moorcroft,*

or the Double Wedding, by Bronson Howard, and Colander in *Masks or Faces,* written by Tom Taylor and Charles Reade and later the basis for Reade's novel, *Peg Woffington.* He made his first starring appearance in 1880 in *Edgewood Folks,* a comedy *pasticcio* designed by J. E. Brown with the assistance of William Seymour especially to fit him, in which he sang a number of songs and made ten changes of costume. After a season in 1884–85 as leading comedian at the Boston Museum, he continued starring without further interruption in a succession of comedies of homely life, his rôles inspired by and invested with his own quaint personality. They included *Felix McKusick,* by J. E. Brown; *Pa,* by C. W. Walters; *Bewitched* and *Peaceful Valley,* by E. E. Kidder; *The Tale of a Coat,* rewritten to order for him by Dion Boucicault, and a dire failure; *April Weather,* by E. E. Kidder; and *A Bachelor's Romance,* by Martha Morton. Once in a while he escaped from these characters to act in his own inimitable and characteristic manner, such old-time stage favorites as Dr. Pangloss in *The Heir-at-Law,* and Bob Acres in *The Rivals*; and during the season of 1897–98 he made an especial feature of a triple bill consisting of *Mr. Valentine's Christmas, The Taming of the Shrew,* and *The Spitfire.* He was an intimate friend of James Whitcomb Riley, whose poems he recited with humor and pathos. He made his last appearance on the stage in Chicago, Jan. 7, 1901, in the title rôle of *The Hon. John Grigsby,* a comedy by Charles Klein. After a lingering illness with locomotor ataxia, he died in Washington, having acquired a considerable fortune through hard work and thrift. Tall and slight in appearance, deliberate in action, he had a dry, crackling comedy manner that was irresistible in its appeal to an audience. His first wife was Louise Berger; after her death he married Alice M. Adams (daughter of William T. Adams [q.v.], known to boy readers as Oliver Optic), who with their two children survived him.

[E. A. Dithmar, *Memories of Daly's Theatres* (1897); *Famous Am. Actors of Today* (1896), ed. by F. E. McKay and C. E. L. Wingate; J. B. Clapp and E. F. Edgett, *Players of the Present* (1901), pt. III; *Illustrated American,* June 17, 1893; *Boston Transcript,* June 29, 1895; *St. Louis Republic,* Mar. 12, 1899; *N. Y. Dramatic Mirror,* Nov. 20, 1897; obit. notices in *Phil. Record, Boston Herald, Boston Jour.* and *Boston Globe,* Apr. 29, 1902, and *N. Y. Dramatic Mirror,* May 3, 1902; letter by William Seymour in *Boston Herald,* July 1, 1923; *Who's Who in America,* 1899–1900.]
                                                    E. F. E.

RUSSELL, WILLIAM (Apr. 28, 1798–Aug. 16, 1873), educator, was born in Glasgow, Scotland, the son of Alexander and Janet (Jamieson) Russell. After a period of preparatory study in a local grammar school, he matriculated in 1811 at the University of Glasgow. He did not receive a degree upon completing his studies, because he could not afford the journey to Oxford or Cambridge, which alone had the privilege of granting degrees at that time. He had decided to devote his life to teaching, but before he was able to establish himself in his native city, a pulmonary ailment made it necessary for him to seek a warmer climate. Accordingly, he sailed for Georgia early in 1817. He seems to have improved here sufficiently to take employment as a tutor in the home of Judge John McPherson Berrien of Savannah. Later in the year he revisited Glasgow, and was convinced that the Scottish climate was too severe for his health.

Returning to Savannah in 1818, he conducted a private school for about two years in connection with the Chatham Academy. In 1821 he was appointed principal of the Academy and on Aug. 22, married one of the teachers, Ursula Wood, daughter of the Rev. Luke and Ann (Pease) Wood of Somers, Conn. It is probable that his wife influenced him to remove, in 1822, to New Haven, where they conducted a school in the New Township Academy building. In 1825 he became headmaster of the Hopkins Grammar School; he also gave private lessons in elocution and oratory to students at Yale College. Suffering a recurrence of his ailment, he resigned and moved to Boston, where, for five years, he gave instruction in elocution in several schools and to students attending Harvard College. In 1826 he became first editor of the *American Journal of Education*, carrying on his editorial work at night. During this period he gave many lectures on educational topics before teachers' institutes, reading circles, and lyceums, and took an active part in the discussions of the Transcendentalists in Boston and neighboring towns. Late in 1830 he removed to Philadelphia, with Amos Bronson Alcott [q.v.], and the following year established a school for girls in connection with the academy at Germantown. He organized the first teachers' association in Philadelphia (1831) and founded a *Journal of Education* there a year later. In 1833 he withdrew from the Germantown academy and established a school for girls in Philadelphia, where he remained until 1838. Returning then to Boston, he again taught elocution and later, in partnership with James E. Murdoch [q.v.], opened a school of speech. From 1842 to 1844, he resided in Andover, teaching elocution and oratory at Phillips Academy, the theological seminary, and Abbot Academy. He also lectured at the Theological Institute, East Windsor, Conn., a con-

nection which he maintained for about twenty years. Although he removed to Medford, Mass., in 1846, he did not sever his affiliations with these various institutions; in fact, he lectured periodically at others as well, among them Brown University, Union Theological Seminary, and Princeton.

In 1849, he founded the Merrimack Normal Institute, at Merrimack, N. H., a private normal school which he conducted successfully until 1852. The year following he taught in the normal school at Providence, R. I. In response to an invitation from the town of Lancaster, Mass., he opened the New England Normal Institute there on May 11, 1853, but because of failing health, closed it in 1855. During the two years of its existence, it became an important center of Pestalozzianism in the United States. He resided in Lancaster until his death, devoting his later years to lecturing and writing for various teachers' journals. He was one of the organizers of the American Institute of Instruction, and did much to further its important work.

Russell was a voluminous writer. His publications include: *A Grammar of Composition* (1823), *Suggestions on Education* (1823), *Manual of Mutual Instruction* (1826), *Lessons in Enunciation* (1830), *Rudiments of Gesture* (1830), *Exercises in Elocution* (1841), *The American Elocutionist* (1844), *Orthophony, or the Cultivation of the Voice* (1845), *Elements of Musical Articulation* (1845), *Pulpit Elocution* (1846), *Harper's New York Class Book* (1847), *Primary Reader* (1847), *Exercises on Words* (1856), *Teaching a Profession* (1858).

[*Papers Read at a Reunion of McGaw Normal Institute, Aug. 19, 1885 . . . a Memorial of the Life, Work, and Character of Professor William Russell* (Manchester, N. H., 1885) ; A. P. Marvin, *Hist. of the Town of Lancaster, Mass.* (1879) ; *Am. Jour. of Educ.,* Mar. 1857 ; W. S. Monroe, *Hist. of the Pestalozzian Movement in the U. S.* (1907) ; Charles Northend, *The Annals of the Am. Institute of Instruction . . . 1830–1883* (1884) ; W. I. Addison, *The Matriculation Albums of the Univ. of Glasgow from 1728 to 1858* (1913), p. 259 ; *Boston Transcript,* Aug. 18, 1873.]
R.F.S.

RUSSELL, WILLIAM EUSTIS (Jan. 6, 1857–July 16, 1896), governor of Massachusetts, was born at Cambridge, the ninth child and fourth son of Charles Theodore and Sarah Elizabeth (Ballister) Russell. He was descended from William Russell who settled in Cambridge in 1645. Having received his early education in the public schools, he entered Harvard College, from which he was graduated in 1877. His career in college was distinguished by the fact that he campaigned for Tilden, although his classmates, or their fathers, were overwhelmingly Republican. He led his class at Boston University Law School, where, in 1879, he received the first *summa cum laude* degree ever given there. He was admitted to the bar in April 1880.

Having begun the practice of law with his father, an old Democrat and a former mayor of Cambridge, Russell easily drifted into politics. At twenty-four, he was elected to the common council without his knowledge, defeating the regular nominee by one vote in a "sticker" campaign. In 1882 and 1883 he was elected to the board of aldermen. Four times (1884–87) he was chosen mayor on a non-partisan ticket, enforcing during his incumbency the "pay-as-you-go" policy in municipal finances. Cambridge voted for local prohibition while he was mayor, and although opposed to this policy, Russell strenuously enforced the decision of the electorate. A street-car strike added to his difficulties. In 1886 he declined the Democratic nomination to Congress from the fifth district.

When only thirty-one, he received the first of his five Democratic nominations for governor. Defeated in 1888 and 1889, he was elected in 1890, 1891, and 1892. His terms were notable, not so much for what he performed, as for what he prevented; for during all three years his hands were tied by a Republican legislature and council. All his vetoes were sustained, however, although he vainly urged personal responsibility as against commission government. Remaining startlingly youthful in appearance, Russell won friends and adherents by his tact, adaptability, memory for names and faces, and peculiar charm of manner. To these qualities were added firmness in decision, extraordinary energy in the search for facts, and a directness of statement that appealed to the most varied types of audiences. Though devoid of the usual arts of the political orator, he was adept in politics and a dangerous opponent on the stump. He was a tireless and intelligent foe of protection, with the unusual power of making a tariff speech interesting. He was the first governor to campaign through the small towns and to stay over night in the annual state troop encampments.

Although in 1894 he had retired from politics to the practice of law, his remarkable victories in a Republican state, his forcible defense of Cleveland in the *Forum* for May of that year, his addresses, and especially his speech at "Monticello," Apr. 13, 1896, with its courageous opposition to free silver and its call to duty to the Democratic party, had given him national prominence and caused him to be talked of widely for the presidency. In June 1896, at the personal request of Cleveland, he accepted election as a delegate to the Democratic National Convention at Chicago, where, with William C. Whitney and other leading gold Democrats, he conducted a vigorous, though unsuccessful fight against free silver.

Returning to Cambridge exhausted with the struggle and the heat, he set out, July 13, for B. F. Dutton's fishing camp at St. Adelaide, on the Little Pabos, in the Province of Quebec. The morning after his arrival he was found dead in his cabin, with a book by his side. Rumors that he died from sleeping medicine were utterly without foundation. President Cleveland attended his funeral at Cambridge. On June 3, 1885, at Cambridge, Russell had married Margaret Manning Swan, by whom he had three children.

[*Speeches and Addresses of William E. Russell* (1894), ed. by C. T. Russell with introduction by T. W. Higginson; C. C. Everett, *Memoir of the Hon. William Eustis Russell* (1898), also found in *Pubs. of the Colonial Soc. of Mass.*, vol. V (1902); C. E. Norton, *The Public Life and Services of William E. Russell* (1896), reprinted in *Harvard Grads. Mag.*, Dec. 1896; *Harvard Coll. Class of 1877, Seventh Ann. Report*, June 1917; *Boston Daily Advertiser*, July 17, 1896; information from Francis Peabody, and P. P. Chase; information and suggestions from Charles Warren, formerly private secretary and law partner of Russell.]   S. M.

RUSSELL, WILLIAM HENRY (Oct. 9, 1802–Oct. 13, 1873), politician, California pioneer, was born in Nicholas County, Ky., the son of Robert Spottswood and Deborah (Allen) Russell and grandson of Gen. William Russell. He practised law in his native county and in 1830 represented it in the legislature; about this time he married Zanette Freeland of Baltimore. He early came to the attention of Henry Clay, who befriended him, and it is said that for a time he was Clay's secretary. In 1831 he emigrated to Callaway County, Mo., and in the following year served in the Black Hawk War; in 1841 he was appointed United States marshal of the District of Missouri, which included the Indian Country. He had by this time acquired the courtesy title of "colonel." His term ended in 1845, and in May 1846, near Independence, Mo., he joined a wagon-train of California emigrants, among whom was Edwin Bryant, later the author of *What I Saw in California* (1848), in which Russell figures. He was elected captain of the company but near Fort Laramie was displaced. With Bryant and seven others he continued the journey on muleback by way of Fort Bridger to the site of the future Salt Lake City and then across the Great Salt Desert, the first to follow Frémont's track of the year before. Arriving at Sutter's Fort on Sept. 1, and proceeding to Yerba Buena and Monterey, Russell joined Frémont's California Battalion with the rank of major and was one of the peace commissioners who framed the treaty of Cahuenga, Jan. 13, 1847. Frémont [*q.v.*] a few days later appointed him secretary of state. On the downfall of the Frémont administration in March, Russell left for the east by way of Santa Fé, reaching the Missouri settlements in July and thence going to Washington; he was one of Frémont's principal witnesses in the court-martial, which began in November. In 1849 he returned to California and practised law at San José and elsewhere until at least 1854. Later he went east again and in 1861 was appointed consul at Trinidad, Cuba. By 1865 he was back in the United States, and two years later sought vainly to get the post of consul-general at Havana. He died in Washington and was buried in Oak Hill Cemetery.

Russell appears as "Col. R——" in one passage in Parkman's *The California and Oregon Trail* (1849, ch. x) and in many passages in other Western books of the time. He was a large man, expansive in manner, boastful and bombastic in speech. His egotism sometimes made him the sport of his companions. In a story often told about him, he is said to have mistaken the chorus of "tu-whoo's" from a flock of owls for a challenge of "Who are you?" and to have thundered back, "Col. William H. Russell, of Kentucky—a bosom friend of Henry Clay!" Ever after he was known as "Owl" Russell. He was, however, a man of many substantial and endearing qualities, and was widely popular. He is sometimes confused with William Hepburn Russell [*q.v.*], the founder of the Pony Express.

[Anna Russell des Cognets, *William Russell and His Descendants* (1884); W. H. Davis, *Seventy-Five Years in California* (1929); H. H. Bancroft, *Hist. of California*, vol. V (1886); L. H. Garrard, *Wah-To-Yah and the Taos Trail* (1850), chs. XXIII–XXV: *Appletons' Ann. Cyc.*, 1873; *Daily Nat. Republican* (Washington, D. C.), Oct. 14, 1873; information from Ludie J. Kinkead and Mrs. Jouett T. Cannon, Frankfort, Ky.]

W. J. G.

RUSSELL, WILLIAM HEPBURN (Jan. 31, 1812–Sept. 10, 1872), freighter and founder of the Pony Express, was born in Burlington, Vt., the son of William Eaton and Myrtilla (Hepburn) Russell, and grandson of Benjamin and Betsy (Eaton) Russell. His father, a soldier in the War of 1812, died in 1814; some years afterward the widow married a Colonel Bangs, with whom she moved to Missouri. Beginning work as a clerk at sixteen, Russell in time became a merchant and for a period was a partner in a bank at Richmond, Mo. On June 9, 1835, at Lexington, Mo., he married Harriett Elliott Warder, daughter of the Rev. John Warder. By the late forties he was engaged in freighting on government contracts and on Dec. 28, 1854, he joined Alexander Majors [*q.v.*] and W. B. Waddell in a partnership, with its operating center at Leav-

enworth, which four years later became the firm of Russell, Majors & Waddell. From the first, the business grew rapidly; in 1857 it underwent a vast expansion when the contract was obtained for supplying the army ordered to Utah. In May 1859 Russell and John S. Jones, as an independent venture, started a stage line from Leavenworth to Denver, but it was taken over by the firm within a year; in February 1860 the Central Overland California and Pike's Peak Express Company was chartered, with Russell as president, and first-class coaches began running through to California. Though Northern sentiment demanded that the bulk of the Pacific mail should be carried over the central route, Southern dominance in Washington had in 1857–58 dictated the giving of the contract to the Butterfield Company, operating from Memphis, Tenn. Determined to prove that the use of the central route was not impracticable, Russell persuaded the reluctant Majors to join him in the operation of a Pony Express; on Apr. 3, 1860, with all preparations made, riders set out simultaneously from Sacramento and a point opposite St. Joseph, and relays of dauntless men and swift horses speeded the mail across the western half of the continent in the incredible time of ten days. Russell, now perhaps the most talked-of man in the United States, was hailed as the "Napoleon of the West."

His period of glory, however, was a brief one. Going to Washington to obtain funds for his ruinously expensive venture, he became involved in the greatest financial scandal of the time. The government was bankrupt and could not fulfil its obligations; John B. Floyd [*q.v.*], the secretary of war, when pressed for payment, availed himself of the services of Godard Bailey, a clerk in the Interior Department, who abstracted $870,000 in bonds from the Indian Trust Fund and turned them over to Russell, substituting for them acceptances given by Floyd to Russell. When the transaction became known in mid-December, both the House of Representatives and the District of Columbia grand jury took action. At the end of December Floyd resigned. On Jan. 30, 1861, Floyd, Russell, and Bailey were indicted; Russell, who on Jan. 18 had made a statement before a select committee of the House, protested his innocence, and in March the criminal court, evidently with the intent of leaving the matter to Congress, dismissed the last of the three indictments. The Civil War came on, and the case was swallowed up in the rush of preparation for the conflict, though for many years thereafter it was to reappear in litigation. On Apr. 26, Russell was succeeded as president of the stagecoach company by Bela M. Hughes. With the completion of the overland telegraph, on Oct. 24 the Pony Express came to an end; on Mar. 21, 1862, the company was disposed of at public sale to Ben Holladay [*q.v.*], and some time later Russell transferred his interest in the freighting business to Majors. Each of the partners lost a fortune. Russell attempted a new start in New York City, where he seems to have engaged in several speculative enterprises. In the summer of 1872, while in Washington, he fell ill and was taken to the home of a son, a banker of Palmyra, Mo., where shortly afterward he died, survived by his wife and five children.

[B. M. Little, *Brief Sketch of the Nat. Old Trails Road* (Lexington, Mo., 1928); L. R. Hafen, *The Overland Mail* (1926); *Collectors Club Philatelist*, Jan., Apr. 1929; W. E. Connelley, *A Standard Hist. of Kansas and Kansans* (5 vols., 1918); *Cong. Globe*, 36 Cong., 2 Sess., pp. 874 ff.; obit. notice in *St. Louis Daily Globe*, Sept. 14, 1872; information from Floyd C. Shoemaker, Columbia, Mo., Frank H. Sosey, Palmyra, Mo., and Mrs. W. J. Boyer, Wilmington, Del.]   W. J. G.

RUSSWURM, JOHN BROWN (Oct. 1, 1799–June 17, 1851), first superintendent of public schools in Liberia and governor of the Colony of Maryland, was born at Port Antonio, Jamaica. He was the son of a white American and a colored woman. When his father left the island, he put the boy in school in Canada. The father afterward married a white woman in Maine, who learned of the existence of the boy, then called John Brown. She insisted that he join the family and assume his father's name. After the death of the father and her remarriage, she still cared carefully for the boy. He was sent to school in Maine and eventually entered Bowdoin College, where he graduated in 1826. He was reported by his classmates to have been a young man of sound intelligence, a great reader with a special fondness for history and politics (Cleaveland, *post*, p. 354). He was probably the first person of acknowledged African descent to finish an American college course. He settled in New York City, where in 1827 he established one of the first colored papers in the United States, *Freedom's Journal*. His paper espoused the abolitionists' cause and opposed emigration to Africa; but after a time he changed his mind and said: "We consider it mere waste of words to talk of ever enjoying citizenship in this country" (*African Repository*, Dec. 1851, p. 357).

Thereupon, he emigrated to Liberia in 1829 to become superintendent of public schools and to carry on trade. From 1830 to 1834 he acted as colonial secretary, editing and publishing at the same time the *Liberia Herald*. In 1836 he was appointed governor of the Maryland Colony at Cape Palmas, a position he held until his death in 1851. The Maryland Colony was established under the auspices of the Maryland State Colonization Society. The territory there was obtained through James Hall, a friend and schoolmate of Russwurm. The president of the society bore the testimony as to how well Russwurm discharged his difficult duty in averting the perils of the surrounding savage tribes, in quieting the controversies of civilized and angry white men, and resisting unreasonable popular clamor among the colonists (Cleaveland, *post*, pp. 353–54). Although the Maryland Colony was distinct from Liberia, Russwurm worked in careful collaboration with Joseph J. Roberts [*q.v.*] of Liberia and was instrumental in the final union of the two colonies. Even before an actual union, they acted together in foreign affairs and established a common customs tariff. Russwurm encouraged agriculture and trade, built a stone jail that could also be used as a fort, took a census in 1843, and established a court with presiding justices. He married a daughter of Lieutenant-Governor McGill of Monrovia and at his death in 1851 left four children.

[*African Repository*, esp. July 1846, Nov., Dec. 1851; Nehemiah Cleaveland and A. S. Packard, *Hist. of Bowdoin College* (1882); *General Cat. of Bowdoin College* (1912); Archibald Alexander, *A Hist. of Colonization on the Western Coast of Africa* (1846); H. H. Johnston, *Liberia* (1906), vol. I; W. E. B. Du Bois, "The College-bred Negro," *Atlanta Univ. Pubs.*, no. 5 (1900).]   W. E. B. D–B.

RUST, RICHARD SUTTON (Sept. 12, 1815–Dec. 22, 1906), Methodist Episcopal clergyman, educator, was born in Ipswich, Mass., the son of Nathaniel Rust, Jr., and his second wife, Mary (Sutton) Kimball. He was descended from Henry Rust who emigrated from England and settled in Hingham, Mass., as early as 1635. Richard's father, a cordwainer and dealer in boots and shoes, died when the boy was but six years old; his mother, when he was nine. He tried working on an uncle's farm, then cabinetmaking, but, eager for an education, he bought back a part of his time of apprenticeship and entered Phillips Academy, Andover, Mass. Expelled with several students who refused to resign from an anti-slavery society, he became a student at Canaan, N. H., in an academy which admitted negroes. When local opposition closed this, he went to Wilbraham Academy, Wilbraham, Mass., and from there to Wesleyan University, Middletown, Conn., from which he received the degree of A.B. in 1841. While a student he earned money by giving anti-slavery lectures. He was received into the New England Conference of the Methodist Episcopal Church on trial in 1844, and ordained elder in 1846. During a pastorate in Worcester, Mass., he founded and edited *The American Pulpit* (1845–48), a collection of sermons including a few of his own. Transferred to the New Hampshire Conference in 1846, he became principal of the New Hampshire Conference Seminary (now Tilton School) and state school commissioner. He made some improvements in the school system, but soon returned to preaching. In 1841 he married Sarah A. Hubbard; after her death he married, in 1875, Elizabeth A. Lownes.

Rust's early concern for the negro became his dominating interest. Transferred to the Cincinnati Conference in 1859, he was made president of Wilberforce University, a school for negroes, serving until it was sold to the African Methodist Episcopal Church in 1863. For the next two years he was president of Wesleyan Female College, Cincinnati. He shared the intense local interest in the early Contraband Relief Association, later the Western Freedmen's Aid Commission, of which he became corresponding secretary in 1865. When, finally, the many relief societies were united into the American Freedman's Union Commission, Rust became a member of the western branch of the executive committee. He soon grew dissatisfied with the work of this large, undenominational body, however, for he was sectarian in his interests, violently prejudiced against the "Romanists," and insisted that the mission of the teacher sent to the South was to evangelize as well as educate. He therefore helped to organize the Freedmen's Aid Society of the Methodist Episcopal Church, at Cincinnati, in 1866, served as its general field agent for two years, and then as corresponding secretary for over twenty years. He vigorously directed and helped in the work of securing funds, overseeing schools in operation and suggesting improvements, selecting sites for new schools, planning buildings, and keeping the needs of the society constantly before the laity. One of these schools, Rust University at Holly Springs, Miss., was renamed for him. It was estimated in 1882 that the teachers sent out from these institutions had taught more than three-fourths of a million children. When, in 1892, he finally retired, he was still alert, impressive though grizzled in appearance, and forceful in address. He died in Cincinnati in his ninety-second year. His publications include: *Freedom's Gifts: or Sentiments of the Free* (1840), a compilation, including two contributions of his own; *Method of Introducing Religion into Common Schools* (n.d.); and *The Freedmen's Aid Society of the Methodist Episcopal Church* (1880); he also edited and con-

tributed to *Isaac W. Wiley, Late Bishop of the M. E. Church, a Monograph* (1885).

[J. M. Buckley, *A Hist. of Methodists in the U. S.* (1896); A. D. Rust, *Record of the Rust Family Embracing the Descendants of Henry Rust* (privately printed, 1891); Matthew Simpson, ed., *Cyc. of Methodism* (5th ed., 1882); *The Biog. Encyc. of Ohio of the Nineteenth Century* (1876); *Ann. Cat., Rust Univ.*, 1889–90; *Wiley Coll. Announcements, 1924–25; Alumni Record of Wesleyan Univ., Middletown, Conn.* (1921); *Am. Freedman*, Apr. 1866.]   H. R. S.

RUTER, MARTIN (Apr. 3, 1785–May 16, 1838), Methodist clergyman, educator, and missionary to Texas, son of Job and Sarah Ruter, was born in Charlton, Mass., but at the age of eight went with his parents to central Vermont, where he lived in the towns of Bradford and Corinth. Here he came under fervid Methodist influence; his father's house was a stopping place for itinerant ministers, and for a time Martin boarded in the home of Margaret (Appleton) Peckett, who had been a housekeeper for John Wesley. When he was fifteen years old he delivered an exhortation to a throng of people at a quarterly meeting which so impressed the presiding elder, John Broadhead, that he took the boy with him as an assistant on the circuit. The next year, in spite of his youth, Ruter was admitted to the New York Conference on trial. He was ordained deacon in 1803, and elder in 1805, becoming that year a member of the New England Conference. In the meantime he had labored with noticeable success on circuits in New Hampshire and Massachusetts and had had a year of missionary service in Montreal, Canada. Until 1816, when he was stationed at Philadelphia, his ministry was to churches in New England. During this period he came to be held in increasingly high esteem for both his spiritual and intellectual qualities, and rose to a place among the leaders of the denomination, being sent to the General Conference for the first time as early as 1808.

After 1818, when he was put in charge of the Wesleyan Academy, New Market, N. H., the establishment of which by the New England Conference he had fostered, his major work until almost the end of his life was that of furthering the educational interests of the denomination. He stayed at New Market two years and was then chosen by the General Conference of 1820 to open the western branch of the Book Concern at Cincinnati. Following eight years' successful management of this enterprise, he was appointed first president of Augusta College, Augusta, Ky. The desire to be directly engaged in the work of evangelization was ever uppermost with him, and in 1832 he resigned to undertake a pastorate in Pittsburgh, but two years later was persuaded to accept the presidency of Allegheny College, which had recently come under Methodist control. A preacher at fifteen, he himself had had little schooling, but by persistent private study he had become a broadly, if not a deeply, learned man. He had a good command of the French language, acquired when he was in Montreal; he was well versed in the classics; his knowledge of Hebrew, Chaldaic, and Syriac was such that he was called to the professorship of Oriental languages at Cincinnati College in 1821, and in 1824 he published *An Easy Entrance into the Sacred Language: Being a Concise Hebrew Grammar, Without Points.* He had an aptitude for mathematics, published *The Juvenile Arithmetick and Scholar's Guide; Wherein Theory and Practice Are Combined* (1827), and taught astronomy. In addition he prepared a primer, a speller, and a small treatise on the conjugation of French regular verbs. He published a church history in 1832, based on the works of George Gregory, a second edition of which appeared in 1834 under the title *A Concise History of the Christian Church,* long used as a textbook in Methodist Conferences. As early as 1820 Transylvania University conferred upon him the degree of D.D., said to have been the first awarded to an American Methodist. The incident created a furor in Methodist circles, since a degree after one's name was considered an adornment comparable with gold and costly apparel. His reputation for both learning and goodness gave prestige to the institutions with which he was connected; he proved himself an able administrator and set high educational ideals.

The crowning work of his life was brief but potent in effect. Always apostolic in zeal, he resigned the presidency of Allegheny in June 1837 to superintend missionary work in Texas. In less than a year, having labored indefatigably and laid a foundation "which, had there been no other service of his lifetime to his church, would have assured him a permanent place as a maker of Methodism in America" (Smith, *Martin Ruter, post,* pp. 103–04), he died of typhoid pneumonia, a martyr to his devotion. He was buried in Washington, Tex., on the banks of the Brazos; later his body was moved to Navasota, where in 1901 a shaft of Vermont granite was erected as a memorial. His second wife, Ruth Young of Concord, N. H., whom he married in April 1809, and seven children survived him; his first wife, Sybil Robertson of Chesterfield, N. H., to whom he was married in June 1805, died in 1808.

[*Vital Records of Charlton, Mass.* (1905); *Minutes of the Ann. Conferences of the M. E. Ch. 1829–39* (1840); T. O. Summers, *Biog. Sketches of Eminent Itinerant Ministers* (1858); W. B. Sprague, *Annals Am.*

Pulpit, vol. VII (1859); E. A. Smith, *Allegheny—A Century of Education* (1916) and *Martin Ruter* (1915); Macum Phelan, *A Hist. of Early Methodism in Texas* (1924); P. N. Garber, *The Romance of Am. Methodism* (1931).]

H. E. S.

RUTGERS, HENRY (Oct. 7, 1745–Feb. 17, 1830), Revolutionary officer, landed magnate, and philanthropist, the son of Hendrick and Catharine (de Peyster) Rutgers, was the last descendant in his direct line of the Dutch immigrant, Rutger Jacobsen Van Schoenderwoert, who came to Fort Orange in 1636, and who rose to affluence by investing the profits of prosperous breweries in merchandise and Manhattan real estate. Coming to manhood during the pre-revolutionary period of opposition to Great Britain, he joined his clan in supporting the Sons of Liberty, formidable agitators who met at the Rutgers farm. His formal education was completed on graduation from King's College with the class of 1766. Relieved from the necessity of an active business career, he devoted his mature life to caring for his property, a considerable tract in what was to become New York's lower East Side around Chatham Square, and performing the duties of the public-spirited citizen. These activities were prefaced by an interlude of soldiering in the Revolution, during which he was mentioned as a captain at the battle of White Plains. Military interests continued until 1795 when he resigned the command of the 1st Regiment of New York militia (manuscript letter of Mar. 3, 1795, to Gov. DeWitt Clinton in the Rutgers University Library).

His interests were manifold, ranging from local and state politics to the patronage of numerous educational and religious projects. He was a member of the state assembly in 1784 and in 1800 was again a successful candidate for that body as a member of the group formed by Aaron Burr for use in building his own and the Jeffersonian fortunes. His continued interest in local politics was evidenced by his prominence in raising a fund of $28,000 for the construction of the first Great Wigwam of Tammany Hall in 1811.

Many educational institutions felt the benefit of his advice and support. He gave the land for the second free school, established for the city's poor, and frequently met deficits out of his own pocket. He succeeded Governor Clinton as president of the Free School Society in 1828 and served until his death. He was a regent of the University of the State of New York from 1802 to 1826, a trustee of Princeton University from 1804 to 1817, and of Queen's College from 1816 to 1821. Four years later Queen's College petitioned the New Jersey legislature for a change of name. This move was simultaneous with the election of Philip Milledoler [q.v.], pastor and personal friend of Rutgers, as president, and the name of Milledoler's erstwhile elder, now an octogenarian, was given to the struggling institution. So far his donations had not been considerable, and the honor was probably conferred in a combined desire to compliment a prominent member of the Dutch Reformed Church (he was then president of its Board of Corporation) and to share in the benefactions of one whose generosity had been proverbial and might, through gift or bequest, become perennial. The last hope was not largely realized, as his known gifts thereafter consisted of $200 for the purchase of a bell and $5,000 in cash.

He added to lifelong devoutness a rather high catholicity and generosity in matters religious. When he broke up the Rutgers farm, called the "Bouwery," into long-time leaseholds, he offered several lots for the building of churches, including in his tender the Baptists and Presbyterians as well as his own Dutch Reformed. He was at various times an elder in the First Presbyterian Church and in the Market Street Dutch Reformed Church, for which last he gave the site. The Rutgers Street Presbyterian Church, opened in 1798, was also built on land which he gave. In spite of continued disbursements, so great that at his death it was asserted that "it may be questioned, whether any one individual in our country has given so much in the whole amount, to objects of general charity," he died worth the very respectable sum of $907,949. Gilbert Stuart's portrait of Washington hung in the Rutgers mansion for many years.

[E. H. Crosby, "The Rutgers Family of N. Y.," *N. Y. Geneal. and Biog. Record*, Apr. 1886; Frederick Brückbauer, *The Kirk on Rutgers Farm* (1919); W. H. S. Demarest, *A Hist. of Rutgers College, 1766–1924* (1924); Wm. McMurray, *A Sermon Occasioned by the Death of Col. Henry Rutgers* (1830); I. N. P. Stokes, *The Iconography of Manhattan Island*, vol. III (1918); *N. Y. Daily Advertiser*, Feb. 18, 1830.]   L. E. E.

RUTHERFURD, LEWIS MORRIS (Nov. 25, 1816–May 30, 1892), astrophysicist, was born at Morrisania, N. Y. He was the son of Robert Walter and Sabina (Morris) Rutherfurd and a great-grandson of Lewis Morris, 1726–1798 [q.v.], signer of the Declaration of Independence and Maj. Walter Rutherfurd, a British army officer who served in the French and Indian War, and married Catherine, daughter of James Alexander [q.v.]. Rutherfurd entered Williams College in the sophomore class at the age of fifteen. While an undergraduate he assisted in the preparation of lecture experiments in chemistry and physics. After graduation he studied law under

William H. Seward and was admitted to the bar in 1837. On July 22, 1841, he married Margaret Stuyvesant Chanler, by whom he had seven children. He gave up his law practice in 1849 and for the next seven years, largely on account of his wife's health, resided in France, Germany, and Italy. He had already been in the habit of devoting much of his leisure time to the study of chemistry, mechanics, and astronomy, and while in Florence he profited greatly from an intimacy with Amici, who was experimenting on the achromatism of microscope objectives.

On his return to New York in 1856, Rutherfurd built a small observatory in his garden on Second Avenue at Eleventh Street and fitted up a study and machine shop in the house. Here he started his pioneer work in astronomical photography and spectroscopy. His first photographs of the moon were secured in 1858 at about the same time that the experiments of De la Rue were meeting with success. Impatient with the unsatisfactory results obtained in photographing with a visual telescope, he devised a combination of lenses which would convert the instrument into a photographic telescope. This he tried out with reasonable success, in 1860, at a solar eclipse in Labrador. His first scientific paper, dated July 28, 1862 (*American Journal of Science*, September 1862), confirmed Clark's discovery of the companion of Sirius and gave a series of measures of position.

The laboratory experimentation of Kirchhoff and Bunsen in spectroscopy was attracting great attention. Turning his attention to this field, Rutherfurd followed up the observational work of Fraunhofer and succeeded in observing the general characteristics of the spectra of the sun, moon, and a number of stars. In his paper, dated Dec. 4, 1862 (*Ibid.*, January 1863) he attempted, for the first time, a classification of stellar spectra, which agrees essentially with that published later by Secchi. During this investigation he realized that the spectroscope could be used to determine the color curve of a telescope objective and, using this discovery to test his work as it progressed, he succeeded, in 1864, in finishing an objective, $11\frac{1}{4}$ inches in diameter, designed solely for photography. A 13-inch telescope which could be converted from a visual to a photographic instrument by the addition of a third lens was finished in 1868. With these instruments he made many fine photographs of the sun and moon.

Realizing the value and convenience of obtaining a photographic record of the relative positions of stars, Rutherfurd inaugurated a long program of photographing numerous star fields.

The measurement of the plates was carried out on an engine which he devised and built. In the first design the micrometer wire was carried entirely across the plate by a very long screw. Later, however, a glass scale was added, making it necessary to use the screw for measuring short distances only, and thus greatly reducing the errors inherent in the screw. Troubled by the possibility that the photographic film might not stay fixed in position and thus vitiate the measures, Rutherfurd experimented and found that treatment with dilute albumen secured this necessary condition (*Ibid.*, December 1872). He is to be credited with overcoming the mechanical difficulties of making an efficient spectroscope of hollow prisms filled with liquid maintained at uniform density. It was with a spectroscope of this type that he secured a photograph of the solar spectrum showing many new lines. He also devised the now well-known method of connecting the prisms so that they all automatically come to the angle of least deviation. During 1870 he built an engine with which he succeeded in ruling interference gratings, which was superior to all others down to the time of Henry A. Rowland [*q.v.*]. Rutherfurd was a trustee of Columbia College for more than twenty-five years and took a leading part in establishing the department of geodesy and practical astronomy in 1881. In 1883 he made an unconditional gift to the college of his entire observatory equipment, following this gift in 1890 with that of all his negatives and twenty folio volumes of plate measures. The work of measurement and reduction was later carried on by John K. Rees [*q.v.*] and Harold Jacoby.

[Livingston Rutherfurd, *Family Records and Events, Compiled Principally from the Original Memorials in the Rutherfurd Collection* (1894); B. A. Gould, in *Nat. Acad. Sci. Biog. Memoirs*, vol. III (1895); J. K. Rees, in *Contributions from the Observatory of Columbia Univ.*, no. 1 (1906); J. K. Rees and others, *Lewis Morris Rutherfurd: A Brief Account of His Life and Work; Discussion of Some of His Stellar Photographs* (2 vols., 1898-1906); *Astronomy and Astrophysics*, Oct. 1892; *Mo. Notices of the Royal Astronomical Soc.*, vol. LIII (1893); *Astronomical Jour.*, June 13, 1892; *N. Y. Times*, June 1, 1892.]   R. S. D.

RUTLEDGE, EDWARD (Nov. 23, 1749–Jan. 23, 1800), signer of the Declaration of Independence, governor of South Carolina, was born in Charlestown (now Charleston) or in Christ Church Parish across the bay, being the seventh and youngest child of Dr. John and Sarah (Hext) Rutledge, and the brother of John Rutledge [*q.v.*]. He was admitted in 1767 to the Middle Temple and called to the English bar in 1772. He returned home in January 1773, and a few months later represented the printer, Thomas

Powell, in the noted *habeas corpus* proceedings before Assistant Justice Rawlins Lowndes [*q.v.*]. His public life began when he was elected in July 1774 to the First Continental Congress. Aggressive but not radical, he bent his efforts toward procuring a bill of rights and a plan of permanent relief, and supported so vigorously the stand of his brother John that he brought upon himself one of the choicest compliments distributed by John Adams who called him "a perfect Bob-o-Lincoln—a swallow, a sparrow, . . . jejune, inane and puerile" (*Works*, vol. II, 1850, p. 401). Despite his youth and the lack of the eloquence and finish in his speeches that he later acquired, his winning personality and soundness of thought brought him growing esteem. He was elected to the first and second provincial congresses of 1775 and 1776, and in the same years to the Continental Congress, where, after the departure of his brother and of Christopher Gadsden [*q.v.*], he was the leader of the South Carolina delegation. Restrained more by the opinion of his constituents than by his own, he staved off action on the resolution for independence for nearly a month. On July 2, however, the South Carolina delegation voted for it under his influence. Rutledge felt that confederation should have been achieved before independence, but opposed building a strong government, and in August repudiated the proposed plan as dangerous, fearing especially the "low Cunning, and those levelling Principles" of the New England States (letter to John Jay, June 29, 1776, Burnett, *post*, I, 518).

In November 1776 he returned home to take part in the defense of the state and to look after his private affairs. The state gained a captain of artillery but lost a delegate in Congress whose service in the critical years to come would have been of the greatest value. In 1778 he was elected to the state House of Representatives from Charlestown, and by that body in 1779 to Congress, but did not reach Philadelphia. He was in the fight at Beaufort in February 1779, and was captured at the fall of Charlestown. From September 1780 to July 1781 he was one of the St. Augustine "exiles," but was exchanged in time to take his seat in the legislature in January 1782. He drew up the bill proposing the confiscation of the properties of Loyalists, and favored the measure as necessary to finance the state, but used his influence to moderate its effect.

The years following the Revolution brought honors in public life and success in law practice to the genial and charming gentleman. He added to his property and obligations by investing in plantations in partnership with his brother-in-law, Charles Cotesworth Pinckney [*q.v.*]

From 1782 to 1796 he represented Charleston in the House of Representatives as well as in the state conventions of 1788 and 1790. His efficient work brought him an increasing burden, especially in matters of finance, until in the session of 1792 he was chairman of nineteen committees. He was stiffly conservative and rarely conceded anything to the democratic elements in the state. An influential Federalist, he was presidential elector in 1788, 1792, and 1796, voting in the last-named year for Thomas Pinckney and Jefferson. In 1796 and 1798 he was elected from Charleston to the state Senate, and in the latter year became governor. At the time of his election, however, his health was broken. He performed his duties with care but in great physical distress, and died in Charleston nearly a year before the end of his term. He was twice married, first, on Mar. 1, 1774, to Henrietta, the daughter of Henry Middleton [q.v.], by whom he had three children. She died on Apr. 22, 1792, and on Oct. 28, he married Mary (Shubrick) Eveleigh.

[David Ramsay, *The Hist. of S. C.* (1809), vol. II; J. B. O'Neall, *Biog. Sketches of the Bench and Bar of S. C.* (1859), vol. II; John Sanderson, *Biog. of the Signers* ... vol. III (1823); A. S. Salley, Jr., *Delegates to the Cont. Cong. from S. C.* (1927); M. L. Webber, "Dr. John Rutledge and His Descendants," *S. C. Hist. and Geneal. Mag.*, Jan. 1930; see also *Ibid.*, Apr. 1911, pp. 49–50, Jan. 1916, pp. 4–6, 11–13, Jan. 1926, pp. 2–9, July 1926, pp. 153–55; E. C. Burnett, *Letters of Members of Cont. Cong.*, I, II, IV (1921, 1923, 1928); *Jour. of Cont. Cong.*, IV–VI (1906); John Drayton, *Memoirs of the Am. Rev.* (1821), vol. I, pp. 131–41, 167–76; *Correspondence of Mr. Ralph Izard of S. C.* (one vol., 1844); U. B. Phillips, "The S. C. Federalists," *Am. Hist. Rev.*, July 1909; Register of Mesne Conveyance, Charleston, K7, 293; Inventories, D, 1800–1810, 19, Will Book C, 640–42, Charleston courthouse; manuscript journals of S. C. House and Senate; *Charleston City Gazette*, Jan. 25, 1800.]   R. L. M.

RUTLEDGE, JOHN (Sept. 1739–July 18, 1800), statesman and jurist, the eldest son of Dr. John and Sarah (Hext) Rutledge, and a brother of Edward Rutledge [q.v.], was born in Charlestown (now Charleston), S. C., or in Christ Church Parish nearby, when his mother was just turned fifteen years of age. John received his early education from his father, who died in 1750, from the Anglican minister of Christ Church, and from a tutor of the classics in Charlestown. After studying in the Middle Temple he was called to the English bar in February 1760, and returned to an immediate and brilliant success in Charlestown. In 1761 he was elected to the Commons House from Christ Church Parish and represented it in the provincial bodies until the Revolution placed him in the governor's chair. In this compact and vigorous assembly, with its traditions of rule by the planters and their allies, and of legislative dominance under imperial supervision, his political philosophy was matured, and it changed but little thereafter.

In 1762 the twenty-three year old lawyer, as chairman of a committee, presented a powerful indictment of the action of Governor Boone in the noted dispute over the election of Christopher Gadsden [q.v.]. In the Stamp Act Congress of 1765 he was chairman of the committee which wrote the memorial and petition to the House of Lords. In the heated discussions of July 1774 he proved acceptable to the cautious merchants as well as to the aggressive planters, and was sent to the First Continental Congress. There he based his arguments solely on English constitutional precedent, of which he was the foremost exponent in the province, and, like Joseph Galloway [q.v.], was bent on maintaining self-government without breaking up the empire. With the rest of the South Carolina delegation he wished a complete embargo, but the northern delegates wanted a boycott only on trade with Great Britain, thus leaving their income practically untouched, while destroying that of South Carolina. Rutledge led the successful fight to except rice from the boycott list, and this achievement, with his attitude toward colonial rights, carried him a long step toward the political leadership of South Carolina. He was reëlected to the Second Continental Congress and his efforts for the establishment of regular governments in the colonies culminated in the advice of Congress to South Carolina Nov. 4, to take such action if it should seem necessary. The next day he set out for Charlestown, keenly ambitious to play a part in the coming reorganization. He was elected to the Council of Safety, and during December and January became second in influence only to the president, Henry Laurens [q.v.]. He was one of the large committee which wrote the South Carolina constitution of 1776, and when the Provincial Congress, by its adoption of that instrument, became the General Assembly he was elected president. The following December he was reëlected for the regular term of two years.

The trust of the troubled commonwealth in the young lawyer was due in part to the completeness of his identification with the opinions and interests of its rulers; in part to his political training and abilities; in part to certain personal qualities: his courage, tact—although he was intolerant when aroused—his unremitting industry, and his intensity of conviction and purpose. The new government passed through its first tests with fine success. The British attempt upon Charlestown was repulsed in June and the Cherokees were subdued in July, and for more than two years the state suffered no invasion and enjoyed some prosperity. Meanwhile, a liberal movement in the state gained momentum, and found expression in March 1778 in a revision of the constitution which substituted a senate elected by the people for the legislative council, the creature of the House, and disestablished the Anglican Church. Profoundly distrusting democracy, Rutledge protested against even so short a step toward it, vetoed the new constitution, and resigned. His rival, the more liberal though cautious Rawlins Lowndes [q.v.], was elected to fill out his term, and the constitution was reënacted. But when the state faced invasion in January 1779, Rutledge was elected governor and took the field in a desperate effort to supply Lincoln and Moultrie with men. The organized power of the state was exhausted, however, and Congress was unable, even unwilling, to send adequate forces to protect the outlying states. When the British commander in May slipped behind Lincoln in a dash upon Charlestown, the governor proposed a parley, and after a conference with the Privy Council made an offer of neutrality. Rutledge's purposes in the affair are obscure, and the whole matter is involved in contradictions (see McCrady, post, 1775–1780, pp. 360–81). Immediate danger passed because of a dispute over terms and the approach of Lincoln, but in March 1780 Charlestown was besieged by land and sea in overwhelming force. The Assembly adjourned to meet no more for two years, after hastily granting the governor and "such of his council as he could conveniently consult, a power to do everything necessary for the public good, except the taking away the life of a citizen without a legal trial" (Ramsay, Revolution of South Carolina, post, II, 47–48). A month before the fall of the city, Rutledge slipped out and strove to gather militia for its relief, but in May it was surrendered with practically all of the Continental troops and the militia and civil leaders of the state as well.

The destruction of Gates's army at Camden in August seemed to most people merely confirmation of the conviction that the war in South Carolina was over, but Governor Rutledge retired to the North Carolina border towns and did not for a moment despair. Realizing that without regular troops the British could not be driven out of South Carolina, he laid siege to Washington and Congress by letter and in person. He pinned great hopes upon General Greene, but at the same time encouraged Thomas Sumter, Francis Marion [qq.v.], and other militia officers who had escaped the physical and moral débâcle of Charlestown and Camden, to wage detached and intermittent warfare, in order to wear down the British and to bring into the field men who would not enter the regular service. Accordingly, a new set of military leaders appeared in the state, and were rapidly promoted as they showed enterprise and ability. In August 1781 he was back in South Carolina and by a well planned coup impressed a large quantity of indigo which he sold at Philadelphia for sadly needed army supplies. At the same time he set about a skilful restoration of civil government, working to a large extent through the militia officers. A proclamation suspending the use of currency and forbidding suits for debt was followed on Sept. 27 by an offer of pardon, with a long list of exceptions, to those who had joined the British, on condition that they appear in thirty days for six months' militia service. Finally, on Nov. 20, he issued a call for election of members of a legislature to meet in January.

The Assembly thanked the governor in glowing terms for his service, though a more significant tribute was the prompt enactment of each of his recommendations, including a confiscation proposition which probably prevented even harsher measures. He laid down the office in which the constitution forbade him to succeed himself on Jan. 29, and a few days later took his seat in the ranks of the House as a member for St. Andrew's Parish. He had already been elected to Congress, however, and attended from May 1782 to September 1783. The next year he began his judicial career with his election to the chancery court of the state, and from 1784 to 1790 sat in the House of Representatives. His votes were conservative but not illiberal.

With Charles Cotesworth Pinckney, Charles Pinckney, and Pierce Butler [qq.v.], he was elected to the Federal Convention of 1787, and became chairman of the committee of detail. His speeches and motions reflected the needs of his hard-pressed state and of the planters in the somewhat isolated lower South, or were designed to win concessions necessary for ratification. He fought for wealth as part of the basis of representation, for assumption of state debts, against restrictions on the slave trade, and—unchanged in his attachment to legislative supremacy—for election of the president by Congress, and of Congress by the legislatures. The first electoral vote of South Carolina was cast for Washington and Rutledge, and the latter was appointed senior associate justice of the Supreme Court. He accepted the appointment but delayed taking his seat, and later resigned to accept the office of chief justice of the state, to which he was elected in February 1791. On June 12, 1795, he wrote

Washington indicating his wish to be appointed chief justice of the Supreme Court in place of John Jay who was about to resign. Washington wrote at once offering the place. At the same time the text of Jay's treaty was published with its discriminations against the southern states and France and in favor of Great Britain. On each score it ran counter to Rutledge's deepest feeling, and in a public meeting in St. Michael's Church in Charleston, he outdid the other leaders of the city in the bitterness of his attack. As a result his nomination was rejected by the Senate in December. In the interim Rutledge had held one term of the Supreme Court but the intermittent insanity, of which he had occasionally shown signs since the death of his wife in 1792, definitely ended his public career. He was survived by eight of the ten children borne him by Elizabeth, the daughter of Frederick Grimké, whom he married on May 1, 1763.

The most gifted and devoted leader of the ruling group of eighteenth-century South Carolina, John Rutledge embodied, perhaps, more perfectly than any other man, the ideas of his class.

[For general accounts, see Edward McCrady, *The Hist. of S. C. in the Rev., 1775–1780* (1901), *1780–1783* (1902); Henry Flanders, *The Lives . . . of the Chief Justices*, 1 ser. (1855); manuscript paper by St. J. R. Childs. For his early life, see *S. C. Hist. and Geneal. Mag.*, Jan. 1930; Flanders, pp. 433–42; David Ramsay, *The Hist. of S. C.* (1809), vol. II, pp. 510–11; E. A. Jones, *Am. Members of the Inns of Court* (1924). For his public life, 1761–76, see manuscript journals of the Commons House; *Jour. of Cont. Cong.*, vols. I, III (1904, 1905); E. C. Burnett, *Letters of Members of Cont. Cong.*, vol. I (1921); John Drayton, *Memoirs of the Am. Rev.* (1821), vol. I, pp. 131–41, 166–79; *Colls. of the S. C. Hist. Soc.*, vol. III (1859). For his career as president and governor, see A. S. Salley, Jr., *Jour. Gen. Assembly*, Mar.–Apr. 1776 (1906), Sept.–Oct. 1776 (1909), 1782 (1916); William Moultrie, *Memoirs of the Am. Rev.* (1802), vol. I, pp. 192–218, vol. II, pp. 407–14; David Ramsay, *The Hist. of the Rev. of S. C.* (1785), vol. I, pp. 132–38, vol. II. pp. 45–48; *Hist. of S. C.*, vol. I, pp. 469–70; R. W. Gibbes, *Doc. Hist. of the Am. Rev.*, 1776–1782 (1857), pp. 129–32, 223, 1781 and 1782 (1853), pp. 32, 130–35, 162, 175–78, 182, 184–85, 191; *The State Records of N. C.*, XIV (1896), pp. 805, 819–22, XV (1898), p. 368; *S. C. Hist. and Geneal. Mag.*, Oct., 1916, Jan., Apr., July 1917, Jan. 1926; McCrady, *The Hist. of S. C. in the Rev., 1780–1783*, p. 511. For the period 1782–1800, see Burnett, *Letters*, VI (1933); manuscript journal of House of Reps. of S. C.; Flanders, pp. 509–600, 621–42; Max Farrand, *The Records of the Federal Convention* (3 vols., 1911); Charles Warren, *The Supreme Court in U. S. Hist.* (rev. ed. 1932), vol. I.] R. L. M.

RYAN, ABRAM JOSEPH (Feb. 5, 1838–Apr. 22, 1886), Catholic priest, poet of the Confederacy, was the son of Matthew and Mary (Coughlin) Ryan, who emigrated from Clonmell, Ireland, to Norfolk, Va., some time between 1828 and 1838. From there they soon moved to Hagerstown, Md., where Abram was born. While claims to his birthplace have been put forth in behalf of Norfolk and also in behalf of Rathkeale and Limerick, Ireland, and while various dates have been given for his birth, the baptismal record in Hagerstown, the Vincentian records at Germantown, Pa., and a letter of Feb. 21, 1859, in which he notes his age as twenty-one years, all indicate that he was born at Hagerstown on Feb. 5, 1838. Seeking their fortunes in the West, the Ryans settled in St. Louis, Mo., where a daughter, Ellenor (d. 1856), entered the community of the Sisters of St. Joseph of Carondelet as Sister Mary Herman. Abram attended the Christian Brothers' school and studied theology at Niagara University, Niagara Falls, N. Y., under the Vincentian Fathers, whose novitiate in Germantown, Pa., he entered in 1854. Two years later, Nov. 1, 1856, he took his solemn vows. After completing his work in theology, he taught at Niagara University and at the diocesan seminary at Cape Girardeau, Mo., until, on Sept. 1, 1862, he joined the Confederate service as a free-lance chaplain.

An impulsive, mystic person of deep spiritual sense and humanitarian interests, Father Ryan shrived the dying on the battlefield and carried the wounded to safety, through the years of "victory and defeat until the Conquered Banner was furled at Appomattox." At Gratiot prison in New Orleans, when the chaplain fled and no other minister would accept the assignment, it was Ryan who appeared and ministered to the smallpox victims. Of himself he had no thought; and of death he had no fear. Touched by a Celtic melancholy, after a favorite younger brother was killed in his gray uniform, Ryan wrote "In Memory of My Brother" and "In Memoriam." When the war was over, he wrote the beautiful, pathetic verses of "The Conquered Banner" to the measures of a Gregorian hymn (see *Freeman's Journal*, New York, May 19, 1866), and the "Sword of Robert E. Lee," which were long sung in households and schools of the Southland. These were followed by "The Lost Cause," "Gather the Sacred Dust," "March of the Deathless Dead," and similar lyrics. He thus became the recognized poet of the Confederacy, described by Robert Taylor of Tennessee in his lecture on "The Blue and Gray" as "the Tom Moore of Dixie, whose spirit shall keep watch over the Stars and Bars until the morning of the Resurrection."

After the war, Father Ryan lived for a time near Beauvoir, Miss., in terms of friendly intimacy with the family of Jefferson Davis. Irreconcilable and unreconstructed until the North joined in relief work during the cholera plague in the South in 1878, he finally sang forgiveness in the poem "Reunited." For a time, he edited the ephemeral *Pacificator* in Augusta, Ga., where he was stationed as a curate at St. Patrick's Church, and later, *The Banner of the South,* in which he was apparently assisted by John Quinn, an Irish schoolmaster. Ill health compelled him to discontinue the paper five years later, though as a pastor in New Orleans he again edited a Catholic weekly, *The Star.* He was constantly on the move and served in his priestly capacity at Biloxi, Miss., Nashville, Knoxville, and Clarksville, Tenn., Macon, Ga., and finally at Mobile, Ala., where he was pastor of St. Mary's Church (1870–83). He made frequent lecture tours through the United States, and into Canada and Mexico, at times for the relief of Southern orphans and widows or of the victims of recurrent plagues. His audiences were as greatly interested in seeing him as in hearing him; he is described as somewhat stooped, with black hair reaching to his shoulders, pensive, sad, unworldly. His poems, collected and published in 1879 (*Father Ryan's Poems*), passed through several editions, and selections were included in various anthologies. They were followed by a scarcely known but beautifully written book of devotions, *A Crown for Our Queen* (1882). Going to the Franciscan monastery in Louisville for religious quiet, he died there, leaving an incomplete manuscript on the life of Christ. His remains were interred in Mobile, where a monument has been erected by the children of the South through a dime collection which the *Mobile Register* promoted.

[C. W. Hubner, *Representative Southern Poets* (1906); M. L. Rutherford, *The South in Hist. and Lit.* (1906); *Proc. of the Ceremony of Unveiling of the Monument Erected . . . to the Memory of the Rev. Father Abram J. Ryan* (1913); *Records Am. Catholic Hist. Soc.,* Mar. 1928; *Irish Mo.* (Dublin), Dec. 1891; *Commonweal,* Sept. 18, 1929; *America,* Dec. 3, 1927; *Cath. World,* Jan. 1928; *Lit. Digest,* May 31, 1913; *Southern Bivouac,* Aug. 1886; *Courier-Jour.* (Louisville, Ky.), Apr. 23, 1886; *Daily Register* (Mobile, Ala.), Apr. 23, 1886.]   R. J. P.

RYAN, ARTHUR CLAYTON (Dec. 28, 1879–June 22, 1927), missionary, was born on a farm at Grandview, Louisa County, Iowa, eldest of the eight children of Charles Hammond and Nettie (Lockwood) Ryan. After preparation at the Wilton (Iowa) Academy he entered Grinnell College. While a student there, he married, Dec. 24, 1907, Edith, daughter of Henry and Sarah (Hubbard) Hoover of Muscatine. Later he attended Oberlin College, returning to Grinnell in 1909 to receive the degree of A.B. He graduated from Oberlin Theological Seminary in 1911; during his final year there he was appointed as a missionary by the American Board of Commissioners for Foreign Missions.

On May 11, 1911, at Oberlin, he was ordained to the Congregational ministry, and in September set sail for Turkey. On his arrival he was stationed at Talas, near Cæsaraea. He spent the following year in language study and in travel through Central and Southern Anatolia, familiarizing himself with the country and the general work of the mission. When the missionaries at Constantinople were overwhelmed with relief work among both Moslem and Christian refugees who had fled to the neighborhood of the capital as a result of campaigns and changes in boundaries during the Italo-Turkish and Balkan wars, he was transferred to that station, September 1912. Assigned to relief work, he acted during 1913 and 1914 as agent of the American and British Red Cross societies in their attempt to rehabilitate devastated Thrace. His great energy and ability led to his appointment as secretary of the Constantinople chapter of the American Red Cross, a position which he held until the end of the Dardanelles campaign, while simultaneously engaged in mission activities. In March 1916 he left for the United States by way of Switzerland, and immediately after his arrival threw himself with characteristic vigor into the work of raising funds for the Near East Relief. With headquarters in Chicago, he not only campaigned for this organization, but also aided in the home promotion work of the American Board. In August 1919 he returned to Constantinople and was occupied with the delicate task of reclaiming mission property seized by the Turkish government during the war when, in October 1920, he was appointed secretary of the Levant agency of the American Bible Society. Though his office was in Constantinople, he spent most of the next four years in travel throughout Eastern Europe and Nearer Asia, studying the problems connected with translating, publishing, and distributing the Scriptures.

While on a year's furlough in the United States in 1924, he was called to the Society's headquarters in New York to fill temporarily the vacant office of general secretary. So deeply did his ability, thoroughness, and capacity for work impress the board of managers that they chose him unanimously to hold the position permanently. For two years he was engaged in the most intense activity, for he had administrative charge not only of the central organization but also of publicity and the task of interesting individuals, churches, and other bodies in supporting the Society's work. Traveling extensively through the country, he made frequent and effective addresses both on the activities of the organization and on his own experiences abroad.

In promoting the expanding program of the Society he proved himself both a good administrator and a most capable manager of campaigns for contributions. While apparently in the prime of life and abounding in vigor, he fell ill of pneumonia and died at his home in Scarsdale, N. Y., after only two days of sickness, survived by his wife and two children.

[*Missionary Herald*, Sept. 1927; *Bible Society Record*, vol. LXXII, p. 84; *N. Y. Times*, June 24, 1927; *Congreg. Year Book, 1927* (1928); records of the Am. Board of Commissioners for Foreign Missions, Boston; information furnished by Mrs. A. C. Ryan and Charles H. Ryan.]   W. L. W., Jr.

RYAN, EDWARD GEORGE (Nov. 13, 1810– Oct. 19, 1880), jurist, one of the most colorful and striking figures in the history of the bar of Wisconsin, was born at "New Castle House," near the village of Enfield, in the county of Meath, Ireland, the son of Edward and Abby (Keogh) Ryan. He was educated at Clongowes Wood College, where he spent seven years. In 1830, after having studied law for two years, he emigrated to the United States and completed his preparation for the bar in the city of New York, supporting himself meantime by teaching. He was admitted to the bar on May 13, 1836, and in the same year went to Chicago. In 1842, he was married to Marv, the eldest daughter of Hugh Graham, who died in 1847; and in 1850, to Caroline Willard Pierce of Newburyport, Mass. He removed to Racine, Wis., in 1842, and in December 1848, to Milwaukee. While living in Racine, he was elected a delegate to the first constitutional convention, held in 1846, and took a prominent part in the deliberations of that body. His great abilities quick'y won for him a place among the leaders of the bar. He was a law partner of James G. Jenkins and Matthew H. Carpenter [*qq.v.*], and appeared upon one side or the other in nearly every important case down to the time he went upon the bench.

Upon the resignation of Chief Justice Luther S. Dixon [*q.v.*], Governor Taylor, on June 17, 1874, appointed Ryan to succeed him. While his surpassing abilities as advocate and lawyer were well known and everywhere recognized, grave doubts were expressed as to the propriety of the appointment because of his violent and uncertain temper. A contemporary, William F. Vilas [*q.v.*], said: "His passion burned, when lighted, like a flaming volcano, shaking him with fearful violence, and belching the hot lava of his wrath on everything and everybody which stood in opposition" (50 *Wis.*, 31). This trait was the great defect of his character and undoubtedly limited his usefulness as a lawyer and citizen, although it did not mar his work as a judge. He wrote the

opinion for the court in many important cases, two of which deserve special mention—*Attorney General* vs. *The Railroads* (35 *Wis.*, 425) and *State ex rel. Drake* vs. *Doyle* (40 *Wis.*, 175). The first involved the power of the state legislature to regulate the rates to be charged by railway companies. The question was then comparatively new and the issues at stake were very important. The court's opinion lays down principles of law which have been followed from that time forward. The second case mentioned involved the right of a state to prescribe the conditions upon which foreign corporations might transact business in the state. This opinion is also a landmark in constitutional law. Though he was a brilliant advocate and profound lawyer and had won the highest laurels in the forum, his work as a justice of the supreme court placed him in the first rank of jurists and furnishes his principal claim to fame.

Judge Ryan was a profound scholar and classicist and had an intimate knowledge of contemporary literature. As a writer his style was clear and lucid, and possessed unusual force; his logic was faultless. His *Address Delivered Before the Law Class of the University of Wisconsin* (1873) is a legal and literary classic, and is probably more often referred to and quoted than any other similar production. He was of a deeply religious nature. Born and reared in the Roman Catholic faith, he subsequently became a member of the Episcopal Church. Among his papers was found a prayer, apparently much used by him, which in simple beauty and pathos compares favorably with many to be found in books of devotion. He moved to Madison while a member of the supreme court, and died in that city, survived by three sons.

["Death of Mr. Chief Justice Ryan," 50 *Wis.*, 23; J. W. Hinton, *Memorial Address on Edward G. Ryan, Late Chief Justice of Wis.* (1880), pamphlet in Wis. State Lib.; J. R. Berryman, *Hist. of the Bench and Bar of Wis.* (1898); P. M. Reed, *The Bench and Bar of Wis.* (1882); J. B. Winslow, "Edward George Ryan," in W. D. Lewis, *Great Am. Lawyers* (1909), vol VI; G. E. Roe, *Selected Opinions of Luther S. Dixon and Edward G. Ryan* (1907); *Milwaukee Daily Sentinel*, Oct. 20, 1880.]   M. B. R.

RYAN, JOHN DENNIS (Oct. 10, 1864–Feb. 11, 1933), capitalist, copper miner, was born in Hancock, Mich., the son of John C. and Joanna Ryan. His father was a mining expert and prospector, a pioneer in the Lake Superior copper district, but the son for a number of years showed little interest in mining. Nor did he accept the college education which his parents offered him. At seventeen he went to work in a general store owned by an uncle in one of the Michigan copper towns, and for the next eight years was a clerk.

At twenty-five he went to Colorado, and obtained work as a traveling salesman of lubricating oils. A part of his territory was in Montana, and there he met and sold oils to Marcus Daly [q.v.], the copper magnate, who more than once offered him a position. But Ryan, so far satisfied with his job, refused. Not until he married an old playmate, Nettie Gardner of Hancock, Mich., in 1896, did ambition begin to stir within him. He was then thirty-two and earning $200 a month. He now began buying stock in Daly's bank and trust company in Montana, and in the course of several years became an important factor in its affairs.

Around the turn of the century, the Montana copper busines was in a turmoil. The Amalgamated Copper Company had been organized by H. H. Rogers and the Rockefellers, and had taken over the Daly-Haggin-Tevis holdings in the Anaconda properties, being opposed by William A. Clark and later by Frederick Augustus Heinze [q.v.]. The rival factions waged political as well as litigious and physical warfare. Rogers asked Ryan to take charge of affairs in Montana for the Amalgamated. Ryan made so many friends among the voters that Heinze's faction sustained a serious political defeat, and Heinze was forced to sell out to the Amalgamated in 1906. When Rogers died in 1909, Ryan was elected his successor as president of Amalgamated. He dissolved the corporation, turning it back again into the Anaconda Copper Mining Company. The great expansion in the use of copper, especially for electrical purposes, was now in full swing, and under Ryan's direction Anaconda became one of the greatest industrial enterprises in existence. At his death it was the world's largest producer of copper and fabricator of copper products, and its assets were said to be more than $700,000,000. The company, with its great buying power, was able to take over, often at low prices, and to put on a paying basis, valuable properities in Mexico and South America, including the Chile Copper Company, which owned one of the largest known bodies of copper ore. In 1922 the American Brass Company, America's largest consumer of copper ore, was also absorbed. Ryan organized the Montana Power Company, and sold it several years later to a subsidiary of the Electric Bond and Share Company for more than $82,000,000. While at the head of his company he brought about the first important use on the North American continent of hydro-electric power for railroads— namely, in the electrification of the Chicago, Milwaukee & St. Paul Railway through the Rocky Mountains. His power company also supplied most of the current for domestic use in Montana and for nearly all the mines of the state. In 1926 he was accused by the Interstate Commerce Commission of making contracts with the Chicago, Milwaukee & St. Paul (of which he was a director) so advantageous to his copper company that they aided in bringing about the insolvency of the road.

The World War had greatly increased the use of copper, and the Anaconda's profits had mounted enormously. Ryan resigned its presidency in 1917, however, in order to serve as a member of the war council of the American Red Cross. Shortly afterward, he became director of the Bureau of Aircraft Production (May 1918), assistant secretary of war (August 1918), and chairman of the Aircraft Board, his particular task being the stimulation of lagging aircraft production. Under his direction, $1,000,000,000 was spent in aviation. Following charges that not one fighting plane of American manufacture reached the front, Ryan, before a congressional investigating committee after the armistice, vigorously defended his administration. On Nov. 21, 1918, he had resigned his government post. He was then elected chairman of the board of directors of the Anaconda Company, which place he held until his death. He was also president of the United Metals Selling Company, and chairman of the boards of the Andes Copper Mining Company, the Chile Copper Company, and the Chile Exploration Company. He was a director in several banks and corporations. For his church activities and benefactions, Pope Pius XI made him a Knight of St. Gregory the Great in 1923. He died in New York City. His only surviving child was a son, John Carlos Ryan.

[Literary Digest, Mar. 21, 1914, p. 605; May 23, 1914, pp. 1247–48; "Investigation of Chicago, Milwaukee & St. Paul Railway Co.," 131 Interstate Commerce Commission Reports, 615–72; War Expenditures. Hearings before Sub-Committee No. 1 (Aviation) of the Select Committee on Expenditures in the War Department. House of Representatives, Sixty-sixth Congress . . . Serial 2 (3 vols., 1919–20); Who's Who in America, 1932–33; obituaries in N. Y. World-Telegram, N. Y. Evening Post, Feb. 11, 1933; N. Y. Times, N. Y. Herald-Tribune, Feb. 12, 1933.]
A. F. H.

RYAN, PATRICK JOHN (Feb. 20, 1831– Feb. 11, 1911), Catholic prelate, son of Jeremiah and Mary (Toohey) Ryan, was born in Thurles, Ireland, where he attended the Christian Brothers' school before going to Naughton's School in Rathmines, Dublin. As a schoolboy, he presented an address to Daniel O'Connell, a prisoner in Richmond Bridewell, and won the latter's approval as a youthful orator of promise. In 1852 he was graduated as a deacon from St. Patrick's College, Carlow, and emigrated to St. Louis,

Mo., where he completed his theological training and was ordained a priest, Sept. 8, 1853. As a curate at the cathedral, rector of the church of St. John the Evangelist, builder of the Church of the Annunciation, spiritual adviser of Confederate prisoners, of whom he was said to have converted several hundred, and as a preacher of exceptional power, Father Ryan won popular favor and the good will of Bishop Peter R. Kenrick [q.v.]. In 1866 he accompanied the latter as theologian to the Second Plenary Council of Baltimore, where he was selected as one of the official preachers. In 1868 he was invited by Pius IX to preach the English Lenten sermons. During Kenrick's absence at the Vatican Council, Ryan and Henry Muehlsiepen as vicar generals administered the diocese. On the nomination of the American bishops at the Council, he was named coadjutor bishop of St. Louis with the titular see of Tricomia (1870), but was not consecrated by Kenrick until Apr. 14, 1872.

As a coadjutor, he was exceedingly active, especially since Archbishop Kenrick, said to be somewhat annoyed by the promulgation of papal infallibility, rarely officiated in public for several years. Preaching and lecturing on all occasions, Ryan, described as the Chrysostom of the West, became recognized as one of the greatest preachers in the Church and one of the leading orators in the country. He was a tall, well-built, powerful figure with a leonine head crowned with auburn hair. He had a resonant but mellow voice, a sense of humor, striking ability as a raconteur, and was sane and tolerant in his utterances. In 1871 he addressed the legislature of Missouri on "Arts and Sciences"; in 1877 he gave a series of lectures in St. Louis, published in 1878 under the title *What Catholics do not Believe,* which had wide circulation; he was invited by Cardinal McCloskey to preach at the dedication of St. Patrick's Cathedral in New York (1879). Invited to Rome in 1883 in preparation for the Third Plenary Council of Baltimore, he returned in 1884 as titular archbishop of Salamis. At the Council, he was an active figure and preached the opening sermon. On June 8, 1884, he was transferred to the metropolitan see of Philadelphia, the second largest in the United States (see *St. Louis Globe-Democrat,* Aug. 18, 1884).

Again, it was as an orator and preacher that he gained renown—at the funerals of Archbishops Corrigan, Hennessy, and Kenrick, at the foundation of the Irish Church in Rome, at the centennial celebration of the Church in Baltimore, at the Republican National Convention of 1900, at the McKinley memorial service in Philadelphia,

and at numerous other ecclesiastical and civil functions. In 1896 he arbitrated a riotous streetcar strike. On behalf of President Cleveland, he presented a copy of the Constitution of the United States to Pope Leo XIII; President Theodore Roosevelt appointed him to the Board of Indian Commissioners because of his interest in the Indians and his connection with various Catholic Indian missionary enterprises. As the spiritual leader of a third of the population of Philadelphia, he was potent in public affairs and commanded the respect of all classes in the community. He did not hesitate, however, to speak boldly when Catholic interests were at stake. Because of his reputation in Rome, priests of his careful training were elevated to bishoprics. He was uncompromising in urging pastors to build parochial schools; he cooperated in the foundation of the Roman Catholic High School endowed by Thomas Cahill, of the Central Catholic High School for Girls, and of an Industrial Home at Eddington, donated by the Drexels (1886). The establishment of the Protectory for Homeless Boys near Morristown (1896) he regarded as his crowning work. With the assistance of various communities of nuns, he fostered a number of other charitable institutions. During his régime, churches increased from 127 to 297, including two negro churches and about eighty racial churches for Poles, Slovaks, Lithuanians, Greeks, and Italians. He was simple and unusually democratic in his manner of living; approachable, though somewhat condescending in manner; emotional, but not contentious. A cultured man rather than a learned scholar, he was deeply interested in the local Catholic colleges, acted as editor-in-chief of the *American Catholic Quarterly Review* from 1890 to his death, published several lectures, and was honored with degrees by a number of institutions.

[R. F. Crowley, *The Episcopal Silver Jubilee of the Most Rev. P. J. Ryan* (1897); *Am. Catholic Who's Who,* 1911; *Who's Who in America,* 1910–11; J. L. J. Kirlin, *Life of the Mt. Rev. P. J. Ryan* (1903); *Catholicity in Phila.* (1909); *Cath. Encyc.,* XIII, 282; John Rothensteiner, *Hist. of the Archdiocese of St. Louis* (1928); F. J. Zwierlein, *The Life and Letters of Bishop McQuaid* (1925–27); files of Ryan's diocesan *Cath. Standard and Times,* esp. Feb. 1911; *Records of the Am. Catholic Hist. Soc.* from 1884, esp. Mar. 1911; *N. Y. Freeman's Jour.,* Aug. 20, 1887; *Am. Cath. Quart. Rev.,* Jan. 1896, Oct. 1903, Apr. 1911; *Rev. of Reviews,* Oct. 1900; *Harper's Weekly,* Sept. 8, 1906; *Outlook,* Feb. 25, 1911; *Catholic World,* Mar., Apr., 1911; *America,* Feb. 18, 1911; *Phila. Inquirer* and *Public Ledger* (Phila.), Feb. 11–18, 1911; information from associates.]   R. J. P.

RYAN, STEPHEN VINCENT (Jan. 1, 1825–Apr. 10, 1896), Catholic prelate, son of Martin and Catherine (McCarthy) Ryan, recent immigrants from County Clare, Ireland, was born near Almonte, Lanark County, Ont., where some selected Irish peasants had been settled as an experiment in British colonization. Discouraged over agriculture in the cold North, the family in 1828 found its way to Pottsville, Pa., where Stephen received his early training and experienced a vocation for the priesthood. He entered St. Charles Borromeo Seminary in Philadelphia, but on joining the Congregation of the Mission (Lazarists, Vincentians) in 1844 he was enrolled at St. Mary's Seminary at the Barrens, Mo., where he completed his theological studies and on June 24, 1849, was ordained a priest by Archbishop Peter R. Kenrick [q.v.] of St. Louis. An instructor at St. Mary's Seminary from 1849 to 1851, and later a professor and rector of the Lazarist College of St. Vincent at Cape Girardeau, Mo., in 1857 at a general synod in Paris he was elected visitor general of his order in America. In addition to managing its churches and seminaries for years, he established in 1867 a new motherhouse and novitiate of the order at Germantown, Pa., and St. John's College in Brooklyn. On the death of his fellow Vincentian, Bishop John Timon [q.v.] of Buffalo, he was elevated, against his will, to that see by Pope Pius IX and consecrated on Nov. 8, 1868. (See *New York Freeman's Journal*, Nov. 21, 1868.) As bishop, he found himself in continual disagreement with Bishop Bernard McQuaid [q.v.] of Rochester. There were not only diocesan boundary disputes (which were not settled by Rome to the satisfaction of McQuaid until Ryan's death) but marked differences over matters of policy. As a liberal who was in harmony with Archbishop John Ireland [q.v.], he disagreed with the rigorous McQuaid on the school question, on the affair of Edward McGlynn [q.v.], on the candidacy of Sylvester Malone [q.v.] for a regency of the University of New York, and on episcopal "autocracy" in handling priests out of joint with the administration. Indeed, he supported Fathers Louis A. Lambert [q.v.] and James M. Early against McQuaid, who winced under the criticism of the independent *Catholic Union and Times,* a diocesan paper founded by Ryan in 1872 as the *Catholic Union* of Buffalo and merged in 1881 with the *Catholic Times* of Rochester as the *Catholic Union and Times.* He was sufficiently interested in Catholic education to publish a sound pastoral on the eve of his *ad limina* visit to Rome (*New York Freeman's Journal,* Sept. 14, 1878), to improve vastly Our Lady of Angels Seminary at Niagara, to promote secondary schools, and to build a number of parochial schools. In other ways, too, he developed his diocese and saw its population and its priesthood

double during his régime. A controversialist of considerable ability, he published *Claims of a Protestant Episcopal Bishop to Apostolic Succession and Valid Orders Disproved* (1880) as a result of a controversy with Bishop A. C. Coxe [q.v.] of Western New York, and a substantial article on *Early Lazarist Missions and Missionaries* (1887).

[Patrick Cronin, *Memorial of the Life and Labors of Rt. Rev. Stephen Vincent Ryan* (1896); files of *Cath. Union and Times,* esp. Apr. 1896; ann. official Cath. directories; J. N. Larned, *A Hist. of Buffalo* (1911); F. J. Zwierlein, *The Life and Letters of Bishop Mc-Quaid* (3 vols., 1925–27); *Buffalo Courier,* Apr. 10, 1896.]   R. J. P.

RYAN, THOMAS FORTUNE (Oct. 17, 1851–Nov. 23, 1928), financier and promoter, was born on a small farm in Lovingston, Nelson County, Va., of southern Irish stock. According to an obituary notice (Baltimore *Sun,* Nov. 24, 1928), his father was George Ryan and his mother's maiden name was Fortune. His early life followed the accepted pattern of the American success story. He was left orphaned and penniless at fourteen, and at seventeen made his way to Baltimore. The lanky, angular country boy walked the streets for days until he was finally hired as an errand boy in the dry-goods commission house of John S. Barry. In 1872, at the age of twenty-one, Ryan went to New York, where he started as a messenger, or "pad-shover," in a Wall Street brokerage firm. Soon, largely with the financial aid of Barry, whose daughter, Ida M., he married on Nov. 25, 1873, he became a partner in a firm of his own, Lee, Ryan and Warren; and in 1874 he purchased a seat on the Stock Exchange. For a decade he carried on his brokerage work with skill and silence. He became a Tammany man, a contributor to Tammany funds, and a member of the general committee of the Hall. He was at thirty-three a slender, long-legged, long-armed young man, over six feet in height, fashionably dressed, with a knack for making the right contacts.

His opportunity for carving out a real fortune came with the struggle for street-railway franchises in New York City. In 1883 he organized the New York Cable Railroad, a paper organization which entered a three-cornered fight with Jacob Sharp and William C. Whitney [q.v.] for the control of the Broadway surface franchise from Union Square to the Battery. Sharp won, by distributing a half million in cash to the "boodle aldermen." Ryan and Whitney stood ready to parcel out three quarters of a million in bribes, but only half was in cash and the rest in stock Ryan's next step was to persuade Whitney and Peter A. B. Widener [q.v.], in December

1884, to pool their resources and continue the fight for the franchise. Ryan was in direct charge of operations, pushing legal suits against Sharp, and inaugurating a state legislative investigation. Sharp, seeing that all was lost, sold his stock to the Ryan syndicate, but the matter had gone too far to be hushed up. The legislature annulled the franchise; Sharp was sentenced to four years' imprisonment for bribery but died, uttering incoherent accusations, before appeal could be taken. The syndicate, after a two-year court fight waged through Elihu Root, succeeded in having the annulment declared unconstitutional, and bid in the franchise and the property of Sharp's railroad for $25,000. Using this as their basis they extended their properties until by 1900 the Metropolitan Street Railway Company (incorporated in 1893) controlled practically every line in the city. The methods used in this process have served as a model in public-utility promotion. The Metropolitan Traction Company, which was organized (1886), in Ryan's own words, as a "great tin box" to hold the securities of the various companies of the syndicate, is considered to have been the first holding company in the United States. Franchises were acquired through political influence; small lines were bought up, their stock was watered, and then exchanged at absurdly inflated valuations for the stock of the Metropolitan; other roads were leased at excessive rentals, the members of the syndicate securing large sums for negotiating the leases and meanwhile buying into the stock of the leased road, whose dividends were guaranteed through the fixed rentals; when new lines had to be constructed or old lines overhauled the work was done at fantastic costs by companies under the control of the syndicate members; the Metropolitan securities were boosted in value by artificially maintained dividends, and when in 1899 the stock had been pushed to $269 the insiders unloaded on an enthusiastic public. In 1902, when disaster to the roads was impending, Ryan persuaded Jacob H. Schiff, of Kuhn, Loeb & Company, to join him in a reorganization, the Metropolitan Securities Company.

In 1905 Ryan found himself threatened by the competition of the new subway system, which August Belmont had been shrewd enough to finance. Ryan first sought to persuade and then determined to frighten Belmont into merging his enormously profitable Interborough Rapid Transit Company with the Metropolitan. When Belmont attempted to extend his subway franchises, Ryan bid for the franchise himself, offering to give transfers that would be good on his surface lines as well, thereby achieving a "unified" city transportation system. He took care to accelerate public enthusiasm for his proposal by the efforts of Lemuel E. Quigg [q.v.], one of the most skilful, and one of the earliest, publicity agents. Belmont finally surrendered in 1905, and the two systems were consolidated and further overcapitalized in a new $200,000,000 corporation. Ryan invested his financial methods with an air of respectability by calling in, as the president of the new Interborough-Metropolitan Company, Theodore P. Shonts, a member of Roosevelt's Panama Canal Commission. In 1906 Ryan retired from his traction interests, leaving behind him doom and collapse. The Metropolitan went into receivership in 1907. In 1908 Frederick W. Whitridge, the receiver for the Third Avenue System, estimated that of a thirty-five million dollar Ryan bond issue fifteen million could not be accounted for at all, and the other twenty million had been spent recklessly on padded construction contracts and in the distribution of political plums. Soon the remaining Ryan traction companies went into bankruptcy. Robert M. LaFollette stated on the floor of the Senate, Mar. 19, 1908, that "the Metropolitan Interborough Traction Company cleaned up, at the lowest estimate, $100,000,000 by methods which should have committed many of the participants to the penitentiary" (Congressional Record, 60 Cong., 1 Sess., p. 3568). Ryan was always the financial executive, and even before Whitney died in 1904 he had become the controlling person in the syndicate, which became known as the "Ryan crowd." Whitney called him "the most adroit, suave and noiseless man" that American finance had known, and had prophesied in 1901 that if he lived Ryan would become one of the wealthiest men in the country. In 1905, before he withdrew from the Metropolitan, his fortune was at a low estimate in excess of $50,000,000, and his power extended over resources in banking, public utilities, and industrial enterprises totalling over a billion dollars.

Early in the nineties he and Whitney organized the American Tobacco Company with a capitalization of twenty-five million dollars. In 1898 it was recapitalized at over seventy million; in 1904, after several mergers, it was again recapitalized at a total, including bonds, of over $250,000,000. Through a series of mergers it secured virtually complete monopolistic control of the industry, and on May 29, 1911, it was ordered dissolved by the federal government (United States vs. American Tobacco Company, 221 United States Reports, 106). Since the Ryan-Whitney syndicate was never completely trusted by the Wall Street banking houses it was essential, at a relatively early date, to secure control of some banks. In 1898 Ryan and Whitney gained control of the State Trust Company, which was closely tied up with the American Surety Company. Its board of directors was changed and it was used as a source of loans as well as a bank of deposit for the Metropolitan. In 1900 one of the stockholders petitioned for an investigation, charging gross violations of the banking laws. One investigation was ended as soon as it was begun; another, by the state superintendent of banks, Frederick S. Kilburn, resulted in a report, on which no action was taken. The New York *World*, however, obtained and published a copy of the Kilburn report (Mar. 12, 1900). It implicated Ryan, Root, and others in the syndicate in attempts to use the funds of the trust and surety companies to cover up and facilitate the operations of the Metropolitan. Particular instances of loans, such as that for $100,000 to the lobbyist Louis F. Payn, seemed to indicate that they were intended as concealed payments. There was a great scandal, and a bill was finally pushed through the state legislature amalgamating the State Trust Company with the Morton Trust Company, another Ryan venture; when the Morton Trust was in 1910 merged with the Guaranty Trust Company, Ryan took a prominent part in the latter. In 1903 Ryan organized the National Bank of Commerce. In the same year he gained control of the Seaboard Air Line Railroad, after ruthlessly breaking John Skelton Williams [*q.v.*], who had originally organized it.

In 1904 Ryan secured control of the Washington Life Insurance Company. In 1905 he astounded the financial world by buying James Hazen Hyde's controlling block of shares in the Equitable Life Assurance Society. Ryan acquired stock that was normally worth $7,500,-000 for $2,500,000, despite the fact that Harriman was willing to pay twice that sum. Harriman never forgave Ryan, and the incident was the beginning of a feud between them. Harriman "did not think that Ryan was a suitable man to have control of the Equitable, with its $400,000,-000 of assets" (George Kennan, *E. H. Harriman*, 1922, vol. I, 413). Ryan's own statement of his motives in buying the stock ran in terms of a desire to save it from a receivership (*North American Review*, August 1913, pp. 163–64). The Armstrong legislative committee, investigating the insurance business in 1905, elicited from John Tatlock, Ryan's president of the Washington Life Insurance Company, the information that during 1905 Ryan invested several millions of its assets in the stock of his other properties, and had placed its deposits in his own banks. In

the outcry that was raised when he bought the Hyde stock Ryan moved adroitly to place the voting power of the stock for five years in the hands of three trustees, including former President Cleveland. He placed Paul Morton [*q.v.*], formerly of Theodore Roosevelt's cabinet, in the chairmanship of the company.

Perhaps the most glamorous of Ryan's ventures were his enterprises in the Congo. King Leopold of Belgium invited him to head a syndicate to reorganize financially and develop industrially his African properties. After a series of conferences between the two the Société Internationale Forestière et Minière du Congo ("Forminière") was organized, Ryan receiving for the promotion one-quarter of the stock. The original objective was rubber, but nothing much came of that, due to cheaper production costs in other fields. But diamond, gold, and copper mines were developed. Ryan said in an interview in June 1910, "I sleep like a baby. I don't remember ever having been in better health or spirits. . . . I am interested not only in the industrial development of the Congo but also in its social and moral conditions" (*Collier's*, Dec. 30, 1911, p. 22). In America his influence was considered in certain quarters far from moral. William Jennings Bryan and the silver Democrats attributed the nomination of Judge Alton B. Parker for the presidency in 1904 largely to Ryan's influence. In the 1912 convention of the Democratic party, to which Ryan was a delegate from Virginia, Bryan attacked Ryan and Belmont for coming "with their paid attorneys" to "seek secret counsel with the managers of this party," and accused them of attempting to control the nominations (*Proceedings*, p. 131). He introduced and forced through a resolution by which the convention declared itself "opposed to the nomination of any candidate for president who is the representative of or under obligation to" Ryan, Belmont, or Morgan (*Ibid.*, p. 129).

After 1910 Ryan increasingly retired from the active management of his far-flung enterprises. His home was at 858 Fifth Avenue in New York City; a third of the block had been turned into a private garden containing expensive statuary. His collection of Limoges enamels was one of the finest in the world, and he had a magnificent collection of tapestries, bronzes, and other art objects. His first wife died on Oct. 17, 1917; she had borne him five sons, of whom three survived him. On Oct. 29, 1917, he was married to Mary Townsend (Nicoll) Lord Cuyler, a widow and the sister of De Lancey Nicoll [*q.v.*]. Ryan's benefactions and those of his first wife to the Catholic church were very extensive, amounting in all to about twenty million dollars. His estate, when he died, was estimated to be over two hundred million dollars.

[For Ryan's street railway activities and banking ventures, see B. J. Hendrick, "Great American Fortunes and Their Making. Street-Railway Financiers," in *McClure's Mag.*, Nov., Dec. 1907, Jan. 1908; B. J. Hendrick, *The Age of Big Business* (1919), ch. V; C. E. Russell, "Where Did You Get it, Gentlemen?" in *Everybody's Mag.*, Aug.–Dec. 1907, Jan., Mar. 1908; A. H. Lewis, in *Cosmopolitan*, July 1908, pp. 141–52; *State of N. Y. Public Service Commission, First District. Investigation of Interborough Metropolitan Co.* (5 vols., 1908); H. J. Carman, *The Street Surface Railway Franchises of N. Y. City* (1919); W. N. Amory, *The Truth about Metropolitan* (2 ed., 1906); Garrett Garet, "How Failure Pays," in *Collier's*, Dec. 30, 1911. For the American Tobacco Co., see H. R. Seager and C. A. Gulick, *Trust and Corporation Problems* (1929); *Report of the Commissioner of Corporations on the Tobacco Industry*, vol. I (1909), vol. II (1911). For Ryan's activities in insurance, see *State of N. Y. Assembly Document No. 41. Report of the Joint Committee . . . Appointed to Investigate the Affairs of Life Insurance Companies* (1906); and *Testimony Taken before the Joint Committee . . .* (1905), vols. V, VI; as well as Ryan, "Why I Bought the Equitable," *North American Review*, Aug. 1913. For the Congo, see I. F. Marcosson, *An African Adventure* (1921), pp. 225–35; for the episode in the Democratic National Convention of 1912, see *Official Report of the Proceedings* (1912), pp. 129–138. For personal details, see *Who's Who in America*, 1928–29; obituaries in *N. Y. Times*, and *Sun* (Baltimore), Nov. 24, 1928.]

M. L.

RYAN, WALTER D'ARCY (Apr. 17, 1870–Mar. 14, 1934), illuminating engineer, was born at Kentville, Nova Scotia, the son of James William and Josephine (Rasuse) Ryan. He was educated at Kentville Academy, Professor Currey's School and St. Mary's College at Halifax, Memramcook College at Memramcook, N. B., and the Royal School of Cavalry at Quebec. In 1892 he became a student engineer at Lynn, Mass., in the shops of the Thomson-Houston Electric Company, which that year was merged with other organizations into the General Electric Company. After varied and intensive experience he became a commercial engineer and investigated the use of power for operating metal-cutting and wood-working machinery.

In the late nineties he determined to specialize in electric illumination, and upon his representations the General Electric Company, on Jan. 1, 1899, established at Lynn an illuminating engineering laboratory. Five years later Ryan was formally appointed illuminating engineer, the first person in the electrical profession to be so designated. Under his direction electric illumination was developed into both a science and an art. The scientific side embraced a photometric and spectro-photometric studies of lighting units and efficiencies and methods of light distribution. Globes and reflectors were developed by scientific procedure and various instruments were introduced for making light measurements. Both arc and incandescent searchlights benefited from these laboratory studies. The artistic aspect of electric illumination, greatly facilitated by the appearance, about 1913, of high capacity incandescent lamps, found expression in spectacular applications of light, with contrasting shadow effects, in combination with color. The first disclosure to the public of these artistic possibilities occurred in 1915, during the Panama-Pacific International Exposition at San Francisco. There Ryan departed from prevailing conventional practices by illuminating the façades of the buildings from concealed sources—from which procedure arose the art of floodlighting of public buildings, business structures, monuments and statuary. He had previously supervised the lighting of the expositions at Buffalo in 1901 and St. Louis in 1904, and subsequently carried out many other spectacular lighting displays, notably the lighting of the Brazilian Centennial Exposition in 1922 at Rio de Janeiro and of "A Century of Progress" in 1933 at Chicago.

From 1909 until his death in 1934, Ryan's headquarters and those of the Illuminating Engineering Laboratory were at the main works of the General Electric Company in Schenectady. Between 1920 and 1930 he introduced the revolutionizing conception of high-intensity street lighting. He was constantly engaged in educational work in his chosen field, and from 1917 until his death was lecturer in illuminating engineering at Rensselaer Polytechnic Institute. Among the more significant of his published papers were *Light and Illuminating Engineering* (General Electric Company, 1903); "Luminous and Flame Arcs versus Open and Enclosed Carbon Arcs for Street Illumination" (*Proceedings of the National Electric Light Association*, vol. I, 1910); "Illumination of the Panama-Pacific Exposition" (*Scientific American Supplement*, June 12, 1915); "Building Exterior, Exposition and Pageant Lighting" (*Illuminating Engineering Practice*, University of Pennsylvania lectures, 1917); "Illumination of the Panama-Pacific International Exposition" (*Proceedings of the American Institute of Electrical Engineers*, vol. XXXVI, 1917); "Lighting the Exposition" (*Architectural Forum*, July 1933). He was actuated in his work by the precision of the engineer combined with the imagination of the artist. Both were sustained by an intense energy, a contagious enthusiasm, and great affability of disposition. These qualities made him a leader of men in all the technical associations of his profession, particularly in the Illuminating Engineering Society, of which, in 1906, he was one of the founders. On June 13, 1932 he was appointed a consulting engineer of the General Electric Company. He died at his home in Schenectady, survived by his wife, Katharine (Haskins), a son, and three daughters.

[French Strother in *World's Work,* July 1915; A. A. Willoughby, in *American City,* Mar. 1915; *Scientific American,* Feb. 20, 1915; F. M. Todd, *The Story of the Exposition* (1921), II, 343; obituary in *N. Y. Times,* Mar. 15, 1934; records of the General Electric Company, Schenectady, N. Y.; personal acquaintance.]

J. W. H.

RYBNER, MARTIN CORNELIUS (Oct. 26, 1853–Jan. 21, 1929), composer, pianist, teacher, the son of Johan William Rybner and Charlotte (Gosch), was born in Copenhagen, Denmark. He was educated at the University of Copenhagen and studied music at the Royal Conservatory, where his teachers included Niels Wilhelm Gade and J. P. Hartmann in composition, Tofte and Ferdinand David in violin, Neupert, Reinecke, Von Bülow, Rubinstein, and Liszt in piano. After his débuts in Copenhagen and in Leipzig as a concert violinist and a concert pianist, he made successful tours in Scandinavia, Germany, France, England, and Italy, earning merited recognition. He was awarded several decorations and was appointed court pianist to the King of Denmark and the Grand Duke of Hesse. He established himself in Baden-Baden, as the director of its choral society, in 1875. In 1886 he was appointed director of the College of Music and the Philharmonic Society of Karlsruhe, in Baden, and, in addition to these responsibilities, in 1902 became Felix Mottl's assistant conductor at the Karlsruhe Opera, where in 1903 he conducted the first performances in Germany of Massenet's oratorio *Marie Madeleine* and Klose's "Grand Mass." The following year, when Edward MacDowell [*q.v.*] resigned the professorship of music at Columbia University, Rybner was called as his successor and held the position, in which he won the friendship and esteem of his pupils, until 1919, when he resigned it to devote his time to composition and recital work. After 1924 he also taught composition at the New York College of Music.

As a composer his output comprised a number of meritorious works, including a three-act ballet, "Prince Ador" (Karlsruhe, 1903), a symphonic poem, *Friede, Kampf und Sieg,* a Fest-Ouverture in C major, two marches for orchestra, a piano trio, a violin concerto in G minor, and a festival cantata for solo, chorus, and orchestra. In addition he wrote mixed choruses, songs and duets, violin and 'cello pieces, and some excellent Wagner concert-transcriptions for piano, including "Siegmund's Love Song," "Wotan's Farewell and Fire Music," "Siegfried's

Funeral March," and the *"Liebestod"* from *Tristan und Isolde.* He was also the author of a pedagogic work, *Phases of Piano Study,* and an appreciation, "Niels Wilhelm Gade: On the Centenary of His Birth" (*Musical Quarterly,* January 1917). His wife was Claudine Pezel de Corval; their daughter, Dagmar de Corval Rybner, became an accomplished pianist, after 1912 being active in New York as a solo artist and in duet with her father until his death.

[*Who's Who in America,* 1928–29; *Musical America,* Feb. 2, 1929; *Musical Courier,* Jan. 24, 1929; *Sun* (N. Y.), Jan. 22, 1929.]

F. H. M.

RYDBERG, PER AXEL (July 6, 1860–July 25, 1931), botanist, was born in Odh, Vestergötland, Sweden, the son of Adolf Fredrik and Thekla Elfrida (Otterstrom) Rydberg. Graduating from the royal gymnasium at Skara in 1881, he left Sweden for the United States the following year. At this time he planned to become a mining engineer, but a serious accident suffered in an iron mine in Michigan soon put an end to this ambition, and he turned to teaching as a profession. For six years, 1884–90, he taught mathematics at Luther Academy, Wahoo, Nebr., meanwhile entering the state university, where he graduated in 1891 and where he renewed his boyhood interest in botany. For the next four years he was actively engaged in the work of the botanical survey of Nebraska and spent the summers in botanical exploration in Nebraska and South Dakota for the United States Department of Agriculture, teaching at Luther Academy in the winter. His first two important botanical works, the *Rosales* (part of the projected "Flora of Nebraska") and the *Flora of the Sand Hills of Nebraska,* appeared in 1895. In the same year he received his master's degree from the University of Nebraska, spent the summer in Montana under the auspices of the United States Department of Agriculture, and then went to New York, where he registered as a graduate student at Columbia University. While at Columbia he was a professor at Upsala Institute in Brooklyn (which later became Upsala College, first at Kenilworth, then at East Orange, N. J.) and continued his summer fieldwork in Montana. In 1898 he received from Columbia University the degree of Ph.D., his dissertation being *A Monograph of the North American Potentilleae,* a large quarto volume. In 1899 he became a member of the scientific staff of the newly organized New York Botanical Garden, and it was to the work of this institution that he devoted the remaining thirty-two years of his life, studying plants in the herbarium and publishing the results of his studies. His field trips, though few, extended from New York to North Carolina and California; he revisited Sweden only once, in 1901. A member of various scientific societies, he was not particularly active in any of them except the Torrey Botanical Club of New York City; it was in publications of the Torrey Club that nearly two-thirds of his papers first appeared, the remainder being mostly in publications of the New York Botanical Garden. The total number of his contributions to botanical science exceeds one hundred and sixty. His most important books are *Catalogue of the Flora of Montana and the Yellowstone National Park* (1900), *Flora of Colorado* (1906), *Flora of the Rocky Mountains* (1917; second edition, 1922), and the posthumously published *Flora of the Prairies and Plains* (1932). In the course of his studies on the flowering plants of North America, he described as new at least a hundred genera and seventeen hundred species. How many of these will stand the test of time, must long remain uncertain. His work was done in such a painstaking and conscientious manner, however, that later generations of botanists may reasonably be expected to appreciate it even more than his contemporaries. In his lifetime two genera (Rydbergia and Rydbergiella) and various species were dedicated to him.

On Nov. 11, 1903, he married the daughter of one of his cousins, Alfrida Amanda Rydberg, who with their son and two of their three daughters survived him. His health failed gradually for several months before his death, which occurred in New York, but he continued work on the proofs of his last book until the day before the end. Throughout his life in America he was active in Lutheran affairs, at first in churches of the Augustana Synod, later in a church of the Missouri Synod.

[*Who's Who in America*, 1930–31; *Am. Men of Sci.* (1927), ed. by J. M. and Jacques Cattell; *Jour. of N. Y. Botanical Garden*, Oct. 1931; obituary in *N. Y. Times*, July 26, 1931; personal acquaintance.]   J. H. B—t.

RYDER, ALBERT PINKHAM (Mar. 19, 1847–Mar. 28, 1917), painter, was born in New Bedford, Mass., one of four sons of Elizabeth (Cobb) Ryder and Alexander Gage Ryder, custom-house officer and coal dealer. His father was a native of Yarmouth, Mass., and a descendant of Samuel Rider, first known in America about 1638. The boy studied in the Middle Street grammar school in New Bedford and in his teens, having been given a box of colors and brushes, set out to experiment in picture making, early discovering the futility of the attempt to rival nature. When the family moved to New York City about 1868, he began the serious study

of art under William E. Marshall [*q.v.*], painter and engraver, pupil of Thomas Couture; in 1871 he entered the antique class of the National Academy of Design and there two years later exhibited a picture, "Clearing Away," the first of a long series of contributions to the Academy's annual exhibitions. From 1878 to 1887 he also sent regular contributions to the exhibitions of the Society of American Artists, of which he was a member, omitting only one exhibition. Although he was made an Academician in 1906, surprisingly small attention was paid to his early work. It was Daniel Cottier, the picture dealer, who first discovered its unusual distinction and beauty and found a market for it, Sir William Van Horne and Thomas B. Clarke being among the earliest patrons (Sherman, *post*, p. 18).

Since Ryder's life was as simple as it was uneventful, even a very small income was sufficient for his needs. The artist, he thought, needs but a roof, a crust of bread, and his easel; "all the rest God gives him in abundance" (quoted in Sherman, p. 21). He himself was so unsophisticated that he once kept a check for a large sum in a cupboard for several months and marveled at the financial knowledge of the friend who told him how to use it; he gave away some of his best pictures (one of them to a blacksmith), would share his last dollar with a beggar, and in other ways manifested the unworldliness that is one of the traditional traits of genius. His Fifteenth Street studio—an attic where for years he lived, worked, ate, and slept in perfect contentment—was encumbered with dusty furniture, packing boxes, frames, trunks, heaps of old magazines and papers, unwashed dishes, tin pails, oil cans, milk bottles, teacups, and empty cereal packages. Yet from this dust and disorder came strange and fascinating visions that are of the rarest achievements of poetic painting. He never married and, though he had many friends among artists and amateurs of art, lived almost like a recluse, occupied with painting, music, and poetry (which he sometimes tried, not altogether successfully, to write). In 1893 he went abroad with Cottier and Olin Warner [*q.v.*], the sculptor, but he was apparently not much interested in the old masters and travel did not appeal to his taste. He preferred long solitary walks in the park, occasional visits to Cape Cod, where he could make studies of moonlight on water, and for the rest, undisturbed seclusion in his own familiar, untidy studio in Fifteenth Street. His vivid though fragmentary record of his esthetic experiences in youth and maturity, "Paragraphs from the Studio of a Recluse," published in *The Broadway Magazine*, September 1905, makes it clear that his mode of living was due not at all to misanthropy but to deep absorption in his work and to a conviction that the artist must sacrifice everything but his own integrity. Brooding for years over a tiny picture, never wholly satisfied with what he had done, he worked with the utmost patience and care, often hampered, too, by an affection of the eyes, the result of poisoning from vaccination in childhood. Commenting both on his slowness and on his inability to achieve satisfaction, he once wrote to a friend: "Have you ever seen an inch worm crawl up a leaf or twig, and there clinging to the very end, revolve in the air, feeling for something to reach something? That's like me. I am trying to find something out there beyond the place on which I have a footing." (See Sherman, p. 28.) His most productive years and his best work came between 1873 and 1898. After that his inspiration seemed to wane somewhat, and the dull tone of much of the later work is in marked contrast with the rich, enamel-like quality of his earlier painting. In 1915, after a serious illness that obliged him to spend several months in a hospital, he went to stay with friends at Elmhurst, L. I., and there spent his last years in seclusion, leaving many paintings unfinished at his death.

In accordance with precedent, the death of the artist was followed by a memorable outburst of cordial appreciation. So rare is imaginative work of a high order in modern painting, so strong the appetite for ideal as opposed to realistic art that he was proclaimed as one of the elect who see nature *en beau,* not as literalists see it but with "richer enthralments." He has been likened at times to George Fuller [*q.v.*] and Matthew Maris, and particularly to Adolphe Monticelli and William Blake, "whose faults are manifest to the most casual and obtuse critic, but whose fascination is felt only by the peculiarly receptive" (Isham, *post,* p. 394). Certainly, a cold analysis of its qualities cannot do justice to a charm that is amenable to no rigid academic formula, overleaps the barriers of pictorial conventions, and is wholly spontaneous and original. In his seventy years Ryder produced hardly more than a hundred and fifty pictures, but not one was perfunctory. Although his small marines, structurally and technically, represent him at his best (Sherman, p. 51), he painted not only marines and pastoral landscapes and an occasional still life (some of these with great fidelity to reality) but symbolic and "literary" pictures as well. It is worth noting that such subjects as "Macbeth and the Witches," "Ophelia," "Jonah and the Whale," "The Race Track" (sometimes called "Death on a Pale Horse"), though they offer plentiful opportunity for melodrama or sentimentality, under his treatment are marked instead by genuine poetic feeling, delicate or powerful but never insincere. This is due in part to the intensity of his vision and in part to the firmness of the design. For, though content with a mere blur of white to represent a girl's dress and neglectful of craftsmanship in other ways, he was a master of design. A boat lying firmly beached beneath a rock in the moonlight not only conveys an inexplicable emotion but forms part of a satisfying pattern. "The Flying Dutchman," which Isham calls "a swirl of delicately matched old ivory and violet grays," is at the same time a symbol of the vastness and portentousness of the sea and a richly beautiful arabesque. Unfortunately, all of Ryder's work has suffered with the years from the cracking and dulling of the pigment. His technical methods, painstakingly slow as he was, were those of a man indifferent to the permanence of his work, as he was indifferent to mere skill and to a literal reproduction of nature.

A year after his death a noteworthy memorial exhibition of his work was opened at the Metropolitan Museum of Art, New York. American museums throughout the country contain his paintings in permanent collections. In the Museum of the Brooklyn Institute are no less than nine examples; the Metropolitan Museum has his "Toilers of the Sea," "The Curfew Hour," "The Bridge," and "Smugglers' Cove." The Albright Art Gallery, Buffalo, is fortunate in the possession of his "Temple of the Mind," formerly in the Clarke collection. Others may be seen in the Phillips Memorial Gallery and the National Gallery of Art, Washington, where there is a fine "Moonlight at Sea."

[The best source is F. F. Sherman, *Albert Pinkham Ryder* (1920); F. N. Price, *Ryder (1847–1917) A Study of Appreciation* (1932), gives a vivid impression of Ryder but is wholly uncritical. See also *The Rider Family of Yarmouth* (1913), no. 66 in Lib. of Cape Cod Hist. and Geneal.; *Who's Who in America,* 1916–17; obituary in *N. Y. Times,* Mar. 29, 1917; Lewis Mumford, *The Brown Decades* (1931); Suzanne La Follette, *Art in America* (1929). Among mag. articles the most useful are those by Henry Eckford, in *Century,* June 1890; Duncan Phillips, in *Am. Mag. of Art,* Aug. 1916; Marsden Hartley, in *Seven Arts,* May 1917; R. E. Fry, in *Burlington,* Apr. 1908; Anon., *Art Amateur,* July 1884; H. E. Schnakenberg, in *The Arts,* Nov. 1924; Elliott Daingerfield, in *Scribner's,* Mar. 1918; J. L. French, in *Broadway,* Sept. 1905; W. de S. Beck, in *International Studio,* Apr. 1920; Walter Pach, in *Scribner's,* Jan. 1911; F. J. Mather, Jr., in *Nation,* Apr. 12, 1917. Important items are the Metropolitan Museum Cat., *Loan Exhibition of the Works of Albert P. Ryder* (1918), and D. M. Cheney's reminiscences in *New Bedford Standard,* June 10, 1917. See also Samuel Isham, *The Hist. of Am. Painting* (1907); C. H. Caffin, *The Story of Am. Painting* (1907); Leo Stein, in *New Republic,* Apr. 27, 1918; *Cat. of the Thos. B. Clarke Coll.* (1899); *Cat. of Am. Paintings Belonging to Wm.*

T. Evans (1900) ; W. H. Downes and F. T. Robinson, in *New England Mag.*, Apr. 1896; *Lit. Digest,* June 7, 1930, and newspaper articles far too numerous to mention, many of them of unusual interest.] W. H. D.

RYERSON, MARTIN ANTOINE (Oct. 26, 1856–Aug. 11, 1932), capitalist, philanthropist, art collector, was descended from Dutch ancestors who came to America about 1646. His father, Martin Ryerson, born near Paterson, N. J., went to Michigan at sixteen, where he worked for Indian traders at Grand Rapids and Muskegon and laid the foundation of a substantial fortune by purchasing large timber tracts near Muskegon. As his third wife he married Mary A. Campau of Grand Rapids and there young Martin was born. In childhood he accompanied his parents to Chicago, where an office of the lumber company had been opened in 1851. He attended the Chicago public schools until he was twelve, when his parents placed him in a boarding school in Paris. He remained in school abroad for seven years, going to Geneva when the Franco-Prussian War broke out. On his return to the United States he entered the Harvard Law School, where he was graduated in 1878.

He began practice with the Chicago law firm of Dexter, Herrick & Allen, but a severe illness and his father's urging soon persuaded him to forsake the confinement of a law office for the lumber business. He took charge of the Chicago office and on his father's death in 1887 assumed control of the business of Martin Ryerson & Company. He was also a director of the Elgin National Watch Company and of leading Chicago banks, and a trustee of the O. S. A. Sprague Memorial Institute from its beginning. In the early nineties he retired from active business with a fortune sufficient to allow him to devote most of his time and money thenceforth to the Art Institute, the Field Museum, and the University of Chicago.

His connection with the Art Institute began when he became governing member in 1887. He served as trustee from 1890 until his death, as vice-president, 1902–25, and president, 1925–26, and was then made honorary president. He was a serious student of art, and with Charles L. Hutchinson [*q.v.*], president until his death in 1924, formulated the policies of the Institute, maintained its standards of acquisitions, and fostered its educational departments. He built and endowed its Ryerson Library for the study of art, and by his will bequeathed it his fine collections, previously loaned—not only of paintings, but of prints, textiles, tapestries, porcelains, and furniture—together with a considerable endowment. He was one of the incorporators of the Field Museum of Natural History, a trustee from its organization in 1893, and first vice-president from 1894 until his death; to it he gave freely and generously of his fortune both during his lifetime and in his will. He was a member of the original board of trustees of the University of Chicago selected in 1890; in 1892 he became president of the board and served in that capacity until his voluntary retirement in 1922. He was made an honorary trustee in 1931. Here again, the record is eloquent of his sound judgment, his insight into educational policies, his zeal for promoting the artistic and material interests of the young institution. Together with his friend Charles L. Hutchinson, who served as treasurer, he established artistic standards and architectural ideals which influenced the design of the University buildings and the plan of its quadrangles, while under his chairmanship the University grew from a modest beginning to a corporation whose assets exceeded $50,000,000. His gift of Ryerson Physical Laboratory in memory of his father was supplemented by funds for equipment and research to assist the work of Albert A. Michelson [*q.v.*] and his colleagues, and by his will, after the death of his widow the University was to share with the Art Institute and the Field Museum the sum of approximately six million dollars. Notable among his many other gifts were those of a park (the farm on which he was born) and a public library to his birthplace, Grand Rapids, Mich.

Ryerson was married, Oct. 26, 1881, to Caroline Hutchinson, daughter of Charles and Emily (Smith) Hutchinson, formerly of Gloversville, N. Y. There were no children.

[*Mich. Pioneer and Hist. Soc. Colls.,* vol. I (1877), XIII (1889); *Bull. Art. Inst. of Chicago,* Sept.–Oct. 1932, Jan 1933; *Field Museum News,* Dec. 1932; *Univ. Record* (Univ. of Chicago), Oct. 1932; A. W. Ryerson and A. L. Holman, *The Ryerson Geneal.* (1916); *Who's Who in America,* 1932–33; T. W. Goodspeed, *A Hist. of the Univ. of Chicago, 1891–1916* (1916); *Chicago Tribune,* Aug. 12, 23, 1932; *N. Y. Times,* Aug. 12, 1932.]   E. A. D.

RYLAND, ROBERT (Mar. 14, 1805–Apr. 23, 1899), Baptist clergyman, educator, was the son of Josiah and Catharine (Peachey) Ryland of "Farmington," King and Queen County, Va. From 1820 to 1823 he was a student at Humanity Hall Academy, conducted by Peter Nelson in Hanover County, and in 1826 he was graduated from Columbian College, Washington, D. C. Entering the Baptist ministry, he accepted a call to the Second Baptist Church in Lynchburg, Va. When, in 1832, the Baptists established at Richmond the Virginia Baptist Seminary to educate young men for the ministry, he was placed in charge. No detail of direction was too minute for his watchful care. He recruited likely students as he drove through the state, combining the mission of preacher and teacher. When the Seminary was chartered as Richmond College in 1840, he was made president and continued to direct its affairs with fidelity to two principles he had adopted—to keep the college out of debt and to make no educational claims that he was not able to substantiate. When the Civil War interrupted its logical development, the faculty, student body, buildings, and endowment attested his successful and constructive leadership.

In addition to his college work, he labored among the negroes of Richmond, serving as pastor of the First African Church from 1841 to 1865, during which time nearly four thousand members were added to the church roll. The catechism he wrote for his unlettered members required only two answers, "yes" or "no," with a passage of scripture to be memorized to support the answer. Many of the leaders of the negroes in Richmond in the early decades of their struggle up from slavery had been taught their standards in life by him and gratefully acknowledged their indebtedness. When the war was over, he resigned in the belief that the church would prefer a preacher of the negro race, an arrangement not hitherto permitted under Virginia law.

Before the war, in an address published under the title *The American Union* (1857), he had advised against the defense of slavery as right in the abstract, though he saw in the institution a means used by God to teach the negroes the Christian religion. He favored colonization in Africa, was opposed to disunion, counseled compromise on the part of the South, and recommended abstinence from all agitation on the subject of the "peculiar institution." He supported the Confederacy, however; devoted his time and resources to the care of wounded soldiers; invested his own savings in the Confederate cause, and advised the investment of the endowment funds of Richmond College in Confederate bonds. In 1866, feeling that younger minds should direct the affairs of a college to serve the new generation, he resigned the presidency of Richmond College. Subsequently, he accepted a position to teach in the National Theological School for negro preachers in Richmond, and was connected, also, with the Richmond Female Institute, a Baptist school for girls. In 1868 he moved to Kentucky to become president of the Shelbyville Female College, served a similar institution at Lexington (1871–78), and another at New Castle (1878–81). He spent succeeding years with a daughter in Lexington, and in 1893, when nearly ninety years old, became chaplain of Southwest

Virginia Institute, at Bristol, acting in that capacity for four years.

His published books and pamphlets include *Baptism for the Remission of Sins* (1836); *A Scripture Catechism for the Instruction of Children and Servants* (1848); *Lectures on the Apocalypse* (1857); *The Virginia Baptist Educational Society: The Society—The Seminary—The College* (1891); and "A Sketch of the Life of the Late Rev. Robert Baylor Semple," in the *Virginia Baptist Preacher* (Richmond), April 1852. His first wife, whom he married in 1830, was Josephine, daughter of Thomas Norvell of Richmond; she died in 1846, and he later married Betty Presley Thornton, daughter of Anthony and Ann Thornton of Caroline County. There were four children by the first marriage and three by the second.

[Papers and letters of Ryland are in the possession of the Va. Baptist Hist. Soc., Univ. of Richmond; his *Va. Baptist Educ. Soc.: the Soc.: the Sem.—the Coll.*, with intro. by C. H. Ryland, gives an account of his services as president of Richmond Coll.; see also, H. A. Tupper, *The First Century of the First Baptist Church of Richmond, Va.* (1880); G. B. Taylor, *Va. Baptist Ministers* (4 ser., 1913); M. C. A. Cabell, *Sketches and Recollections of Lynchburg* (1858); *Times* (Richmond), Apr. 25, 1899; G. B. Taylor, *Life and Times of James B. Taylor* (copr. 1872).]   M. H. W.

RYNNING, OLE (Apr. 4, 1809–September 1838), immigrant leader and author, was born at Ringsaker, Norway, the son of the Rev. Jens Rynning and his wife, Severine Cathrine Steen. His father, then curate at Ringsaker, later minister at Snaasen, was noted for his writings on scientific subjects. Ole was tutored privately for matriculation at the national university in Christiania, where he studied from 1830 to 1833. He then opened a private school at Snaasen and soon became interested in the economic conditions of Norwegian farmers and laborers. The Gordian knot of their difficulties could be cut, he believed, by emigration, and in 1837 he set out for America as the leader of a group of eighty-four emigrants who sailed from Bergen for New York on Apr. 7, aboard the bark *Ægir*. Celebrating the Norwegian national holiday in mid-ocean, these country people of western Norway voiced, in an emigrant song that Rynning wrote for them, the pull of destiny westward and sounded an undertone of affection for the viking North.

The *Ægir* reached New York, on June 9, and a week later the immigrants started for Illinois. From Chicago, Rynning and three companions made their way to the Beaver Creek region in Iroquois County, where they selected a settlement site to which about fifty of the immigrants came later. The low land of the vicinity, dry in the late summer, was flooded the next spring; ultimately the colony was devastated by malaria; and in 1840, the last of the Norwegian pioneers of 1837 departed from it. Meanwhile, Rynning had written a work that became known throughout Norway as the "America Book." He had gone away on a trip to explore the surrounding country-side and had been caught in a blinding blizzard. When he was found both his feet were frozen and lacerated. While confined to his bed he wrote *A True Account of America for the Information and Help of Peasant and Commoner,* reading each chapter aloud to his neighbors and inviting their criticisms. He met misfortune with simple courage and rose above local circumstance to take a broad view of the American scene. He completed his book in February 1838, and the next spring, Ansten Nattestad, a member of the colony, journeyed back to Norway by way of New Orleans, taking the manuscript with him. It was published at Christiania late in the year and created a sensation among the common folk of Norway. No book like it had appeared in that country before. Compact and informative, "the work of a keen observer," as Prof. Edward Channing has said, it is one of the most interesting of all immigrant guide-books (*A History of the United States,* V, 1921, p. 469). A second edition appeared in 1839, and for many years the book stimulated Norwegian emigration. "Many who were scarcely able to read," said one immigrant, "began in earnest to practice in the 'America-book'" (*Billed-Magazin,* Apr. 17, 1869).

In thirteen concise chapters Rynning discussed such topics as the climate, soil, and products of America; the cost of provisions and of land; the American government; the religious situation; the problem of language and of education; the fortunes of the earlier settlers from Norway; and the prospects for immigrants. He disposed of many absurd rumors about America with quiet common sense and gave much shrewd advice. He praised the ideas of general freedom and equality, but denounced the slavery system and predicted that the United States ultimately would witness a separation of the North and South or violent civil disputes. A fourteenth chapter, in which he criticized the Norwegian state church, was excised by a state-church dean who, unluckily, read the proof.

Rynning regained the use of his feet, but in September 1838 he fell victim to the epidemic then scourging the Beaver Creek colony and died. Only one of his neighbors was well at the time; he chopped down an oak and from it hewed a crude coffin; in this, Rynning's body was placed and buried in an unmarked grave on the

prairie. Of this captain of people in dispersion, Nattestad, who knew him well, said, "When sickness and suffering visited the colonists, he was always ready to comfort the sorrowing and to aid those in distress so far as it lay in his power. Nothing could shake his belief that America would become a place of refuge for the masses of people in Europe who toiled under the burdens of poverty" (*Billed-Magazin,* Feb. 20, 1869).

[Rynning's *Sandfærdig Beretning om Amerika* was reprinted by R. B. Anderson under the title *Student Ole Rynnings Amerikabog* (1896); the original and an English translation are given in T. C. Blegen, ed., *Ole Rynning's True Account of America* (Norwegian-Am. Hist. Asso., *Travel and Description Series,* vol. I, 1926). The original text of Rynning's emigrant song is presented, with an English translation, by Blegen and Martin B. Ruud in *Norwegian-American Studies and Records,* vol. VIII (1934). For further information see Anderson, *The First Chapter of Norwegian Immigration 1821–1840* (1895); Blegen, *Norwegian Migration to America, 1825–1860* (1931); Knud Langeland, *Nordmændene i Amerika* (1888); B. J. Muus, *Jens Rynnings Æt* (1894); articles on Jens and Ole Rynning in J. B. Halvorsen, *Norsk Forfatter-Lexikon 1814–1880,* vol. IV (1896); Ole K. Nattestad, *Beskrivelse over en Reise til Nordamerica* (Drammen, 1839), translated by Anderson in *Wis. Mag. of Hist.,* Dec. 1917; and Svein Nilssen's reports of interviews with Ansten and Ole K. Nattestad in *Billed-Magazin* (Madison, Wis.), vol. I, Feb. 13 and 20, 1869.]   T. C. B.

SABIN, CHARLES HAMILTON (Aug. 24, 1868–Oct. 10, 1933), banker, was born at Williamstown, Mass., a son of Thomas and Cordelia (Eldridge) Sabin. Growing up on a farm, he obtained his schooling chiefly at the Greylock Institute in South Williamstown, from which he was graduated at the age of seventeen. He first found employment in a flour store in Albany, N. Y., but by the time he was twenty-one he held a clerkship in the National Commercial Bank of Albany, which he left for a subordinate position in the Park Bank. After seven years with the Park Bank, he was made cashier in 1898 of the Albany City National Bank. To that institution he brought so much new business—the deposits were doubled in four years—that he again attracted the attention of the directors of the National Commercial Bank, who elected him vice-president in 1902. During the panic year of 1907, when the position had rather an uncertain future, he was called to the presidency of the National Copper Bank of New York City and held it for three years, until a merger with the Mechanics and Metals National Bank was accomplished. At that time he took a vice-presidency in the Guaranty Trust Company, then in a period of rapid expansion, and in 1915 was promoted to the presidency. Under his direction the Guaranty Trust Company took a leading part both during and after the World War in enlisting the interest of American capital in financial and economic conditions abroad, publishing a series of pamphlets on the subject. In the foreword to *The Solvency of the Allies*, Sabin wrote in 1919: "This is a time when all thought of profits should be forgotten and the simple necessities of the situation faced. Our first and single duty now is to help restore the world to normal conditions." In 1921 he gave up the presidency to become chairman of the board, and with the exception of a part of one year he held that position until his death. He also held directorships in various corporations. His distinction lies in the fact that he was a "career man," who owed little to circumstances and almost everything to his own adaptability and energy, and that he represented the New York bankers in dealing with the tremendous and imperfectly undertsood problems of international finance that followed the war. Although, like other individual bankers, he was overshadowed by his institution, it was he who held the helm through the stormy years 1915–21.

In New York in the later years of his life he devoted much time and thought to the advancement of the Boys' Club on the East Side founded by E. H. Harriman. A polo enthusiast and a devotee of golf, he engaged actively in outdoor sports to the last. He died of cerebral hemorrhage at his Long Island country home in the Shinnecock Hills. He had been married first on Dec. 29, 1897, to Mabel Whitney of Albany, from whom he was divorced in 1915; and second, on Dec. 28, 1916, to a daughter of Paul Morton [*q.v.*], Pauline (Morton) Smith, who took a prominent part in the campaign for the repeal of the Eighteenth Amendment. His second wife, with a son by his former marriage, survived him.

[*Who's Who in America*, 1932–33; *N. Y. Times*, Dec. 29, 1916, and Oct. 12, 1933; *N. Y. Herald Tribune*, Oct. 12, 1933; brief article and portrait in *Bankers Mag.*, Oct. 1921.]   W. B. S.

SABIN, JOSEPH (Dec. 6? 1821–June 5, 1881), bibliographer and bibliophile, was born probably at Braunston, Northamptonshire, England. He was educated in the schools of his native village and of Oxford but never attended the university. At fourteen he was apprenticed to Charles Richards, a prominent book dealer of Oxford, to learn the bookbinding trade. He had been at the bookbinder's bench only a few months, when his employer realized that he would be far more valuable in the salesroom. After three years as assistant salesman, he became general manager and had charge of the buying of books. He was always ready to place his rapidly accumulating knowledge of books at the disposal of customers and, in spite of a somewhat brusque manner and a decided impatience with pretentious mediocrity, he won and held the respect of his patrons, who learned to trust his judgment implicitly. While serving as apprentice he became interested in the temperance question and all his life was ready to write and speak in advocacy of the cause. During the last year of his apprenticeship, which ended in 1842, he became acquainted with the family of Mr. Winterborn, an architect and builder of Oxford, with one of whose sons he formed a partnership to carry on the business of a bookseller and auctioneer, and to one of whose daughters he was married in 1844. In 1844 he published anonymously his first regular book, *The Thirty-nine Articles of the Church of England, with Scripture Proof and References.*

In 1848 he sold his business and sailed on the ship *West Point*, with his wife and two sons, for New York City. From New York he soon removed to Philadelphia, where he obtained employment with George S. Appleton. He settled his family on a farm he purchased on Chestnut Hill, since 1854 within the corporate limits of the city. While with Appleton he introduced half binding in calf and morocco, then unknown in America. In 1850 he was employed by Cooley & Kesse, book auctioneers at 191 Broadway, and later by their successors, Lyman & Rawdon. He devoted much time to the preparation of sales and auction catalogues, of which he issued about 150 during his life. His first important catalogue, for the collection of Samuel Farmar Jarvis, was issued in 1851. That year he was engaged by the rival firm of Bangs, Brother & Company, with whom he remained five years, cataloguing among other collections the extensive library of Americana brought together by E. B. Corwin. The sale of this library drew attention to Americana and started Sabin on his life work, *Dictionary of Books Relating to America, from its Discovery to the Present Time* (14 vols., 1868–84), known as well by the fly-leaf title, "Bibliotheca Americana." In 1856 he opened a second-hand book store on Canal Street, New York, but after a year he returned to Philadelphia and at No. 27 South Sixth St. developed a good business with the South, where an active group of collectors was then to be found. The breaking out of the Civil War brought this business to an abrupt close. In 1861 with H. A. Jennings he opened an auction room on Fourth Street in New York. Probably in 1865 he retired and devoted himself to the handling of rare books and prints, at No. 84 Nassau St., working steadily on his "Bibliotheca Americana," for which he issued a prospectus on Dec. 5, 1866. He also was interested in publishing *Sabin & Sons' American Bibliopolist* and the *Sabin's Reprints.* He became known, not only in this country but in Europe, as an expert in all matters relating to books and prints. In twenty years he made thirty trips to Europe in quest of rare books and managed to attend all the more important sales of this period.

In 1879 he determined to give all his time to the *Dictionary* and gave up the business, which was, however, carried on under the firm name of J. Sabin's Son. His "Bibliotheca Americana" occupied most of his active hours during the last years of his life, exhausted all his spare funds, and left him a poor man. He undertook to give with accuracy the title of every book and pamphlet, in every language, relating in any way to America. The entries are arranged alphabetically by author, and, in addition to a complete bibliographical description, some idea is given of the character of the work as related to America. The work was begun in 1856, but the first part of volume I was not published until 1867 (issued in parts; vol. I dated 1868). Twelve volumes had been published when he died.

[Since Sabin's death the *Dictionary of Books Relating to America* has been continued, vols. XV–XX (1885–92) ed. by Wilberforce Eames and since then by R. W. G. Vail; the largest collection of Sabin's catalogues is in the N. Y. Public Lib. and the next in Lib. of Cong.; S. A. Allibone, *A Critical Dictionary of Eng. Lit.*, vol. II (1870); *Publishers' Weekly*, June 11, 1881; *N. Y. Times, N. Y. Tribune, World* (N. Y.), and *Commercial Advertiser* (N.Y.), for June 6, 1881.]

H. H. B. M.

SABINE, LORENZO (July 28, 1803–Apr. 14, 1877), historian, was born in Lisbon, N. H., spent twenty years in Eastport, Me., and died in Boston Highlands, Mass. His mother was Ann (or Harriet) Clark, the daughter of John Clark. His father was Elijah R. Sabin, as the name was then spelled, a Methodist clergyman and in 1811 chaplain of the House of Representatives of Massachusetts. He was the descendant of William Sabin who was in Rehoboth, Mass., as early as 1643. When Lorenzo was fifteen years of age his father died in Savannah, Ga., where he had gone because of illness; and from that time the boy provided his own livelihood and whatever education he received, and occasionally he aided his five younger brothers and sisters. For a time he was apprenticed to Lincoln & Edmonds, Boston publishers, but the poverty of the family sent him forth in 1821 to seek his fortune on "the eastern frontier of the union." In Eastport, Me., which had been incorporated in the limits of the United States, he obtained a small clerkship, and there after a short time he set up trade on his own account. Within a year he was bankrupt, but, undiscouraged by his fail-

ure, after a second period of clerking and of keeping the books of the Passamaquoddy Bank, he again ventured an independent business. Of his activities during the years that followed he later wrote that he "built and owned vessels, fitted out fishermen, and was a petty dealer in codfish and molasses" (*Proc. Mass. Hist. Soc., post.* p. 378). This life he pursued for fifteen years, combining with it a variety of activities. In 1834 and 1835 he was a member of the Maine House of Representatives. He was also deputy commissioner of customs, and for a short time edited the *Eastport Sentinel*. About 1848 he removed to Framingham, Mass.

In his local community he was known as an indefatigable reader and, as a young man, he was the prime source of vitality in a forum that achieved some small fame. His keen curiosity about all aspects of his occupation, his unremitting study, and his persistent efforts to formulate his ideas acceptably laid the foundation for his later historical publications. The proximity of Eastport to the Canadian border had brought him into contact with the descendants of many of the American Loyalists, and the interest thus roused resulted in his most valuable historical work, *The American Loyalists or Biographical Sketches of Adherents to the British Crown in the War of the Revolution* (1847), a work that drew upon many family records and recollections as well as on more easily accessible public material. The second and enlarged edition of the study in two volumes, *Biographical Sketches of Loyalists* (1864), is still in frequent use. In 1847 he also contributed a *Life of Commodore Edward Preble* to Jared Sparks's Library of American Biography Series. One of his early ambitions had been to obtain a place in the pages of the *North American Review* and this he seems first to have achieved by an article on "The Whale Fishery" in January 1834. Another article on "American Forest Trees" appeared in April 1837. His business had given him an abundant knowledge not only of Maine forests but also of the fisheries of the northeast coast, which he incorporated in articles for that journal between 1843 and 1846. Of these perhaps the most important were on "Fisheries" (July 1843), "Our Commercial History and Policy" (October 1843), and the "American Fisheries" (April 1846). Other articles in the same magazine were "The Forest Lands of Maine" (April 1844), "Simcoe's Military Journal" (October 1844), "British Colonial Politics" (January 1845), and "Life and Works of John Adams" (July 1857). Some of these articles may have attracted the attention of the administration to him for, in

1852, he was called to Washington, and for a year worked, under the direction of the department of the treasury, on problems connected with the fisheries. The result of this work appeared as *Report on the Principal Fisheries of the American Seas* (1853).

Elected as a Whig to complete the congressional term of Benjamin Thompson, he served in the federal House of Representatives from Dec. 13, 1852, to Mar. 3, 1853. In 1857 he became secretary of the Boston board of trade, a position he held for ten years. The annual reports of the board during his term constitute a genuine contribution to the history of the period. He also published *Notes on Duels and Duelling . . . with a Preliminary Historical Essay* (1855), several addresses for special occasions, and numerous articles. His historical work is characterized by his industrious research, a love for the past, and great interest in the personal aspects of historical problems. Of him the *Boston Evening Transcript* wrote: "Probably no man living has so accurate and general a knowledge of the individual history of the period of the Revolution as Mr. Sabine has acquired" (quoted in *New England Historical & Genealogical Register*, April 1860, pp. 179–80). Little is recorded of his family life. We know only that he was three times married: on Nov. 20, 1825, to Matilda F. Green, on July 13, 1829, to Abby R. D. Deering, and on Sept. 17, 1837, to Elizabeth M. Deering. Of his five children but one survived him.

[E. E. Hale, "Memoir of the Hon. Lorenzo Sabine," *Proc. Mass. Hist. Soc.*, vol. XVII (1880); *New Eng. Hist. and Gen. Reg.*, Oct. 1878; *Daily Evening Transcript* (Boston), Apr. 16, 1877.]   E. D.

SABINE, WALLACE CLEMENT WARE (June 13, 1868–Jan. 10, 1919), physicist, was born in Richwood, Ohio. He was the son of Hylas and Anna (Ware) Sabine and a descendant of William Sabine or Sabin who was settled in Rehoboth, Mass., in 1643. According to family tradition, each of his four names represented one of the four racial strains that were joined in him: Scotch, Dutch, English, and French. His English forebears were Quakers and his French forebears probably Huguenots, and, though he subscribed to no religious creed, his moral qualities were such as one might expect from such a lineage.

He was graduated A.B. from Ohio State University in 1886, having been a student of Thomas Corwin Mendenhall [*q.v.*], and the same year enrolled as a graduate student in mathematics and physics at Harvard. Here he received the degree of A.M. in 1888, the next year was made an assistant in physics, and rose through the various grades thereafter to a professorship in 1905. He never became a candidate for the doctorate, although he possessed remarkable aptitude for research requiring a high degree of experimental skill. His published papers were remarkably few and remarkably significant. Giving most of his time and strength to teaching rather than to research, he was apparently content for some years to remain obscure himself while setting his pupils in the way of distinguished achievement. In 1895, however, upon the completion of the Fogg Art Museum, designed by Richard Morris Hunt [*q.v.*], its auditorium proved to be "monumental in its acoustic badness," and Sabine was designated by President Eliot to remedy the defect. As a result of the interest thus aroused and the consequent experimentation, "so far as the properties of auditoriums are concerned, Sabine in less than twenty years brought architectural acoustics from the empirical state, in which success with any new structure was a happy accident and failure was a misfortune often made ridiculous by such attempted remedies as the stringing of wires in the overhead space, to the status of a reasoned science and a precise art" (Hall, *post.* p. 12).

After the death of Professor Nathaniel Southgate Shaler [*q.v.*] in 1906, Sabine was made dean of the Lawrence Scientific School, and in 1908 of the Harvard Graduate School of Applied Science, which was initiated under his influence. After about seven years this school disappeared in a merger between Harvard and the Massachusetts Institute of Technology for applied science teaching, an arrangement which Sabine approved. In the spring of 1917 he gave a course of lectures on architectural acoustics at the Sorbonne and soon afterward devoted himself, without official status but very effectively, to a study of aerial warfare and the promotion of a better understanding between England, France, and Italy as to the means and methods of such warfare. Returning to America in the fall of 1917, he placed the experience and knowledge he had thus gained at the service of the government, and from that time until the end of the World War he, though still as a civilian, held an important office in the military air service, being "the final authority to select from the samples sent from overseas" instruments to be reproduced in the United States. He divided his time between this service and teaching at Harvard, going back and forth weekly between Cambridge and Washington, though his health had been seriously broken since the fall of 1916. He survived the war, but died soon after its close.

Sabine married, Aug. 22, 1900. Dr. Jane

Downes Kelly, a physician of established reputation who continued in practice after marriage. Two daughters were born to them. After his death his most significant writings were brought together in a volume with the title *Collected Papers on Acoustics* (1922), published by the Harvard University Press.

[E. H. Hall in *Memoirs Nat. Acad. Sci.*, vol. XXI (1927), with bibliography of Sabine's fifteen published papers; W. D. Orcutt, *Wallace Clement Sabine: A Study in Achievement* (1933); *Who's Who in America*, 1918–19; *Boston Transcript*, Jan. 10, 1919.]

E. H. H.

SACAGAWEA (*c.* 1787–Dec. 20, 1812), interpreter of the Lewis and Clark expedition, was born in a Shoshone village of which her father was the chief, probably in the neighborhood of Lemhi, Idaho. In the fall of 1800 she was captured with several others at the Three Forks of the Missouri by a war party of Hidatsas. Taken to the Hidatsa village at the mouth of Knife River, she and another girl were later sold to Toussaint Charbonneau, a Canadian living with the tribe, who married, according to Indian rites, both of them. In the winter of 1804–05, when Meriwether Lewis and William Clark [*qq.v.*] were at Fort Mandan, Charbonneau was engaged as an interpreter to the expedition, with the understanding that Sacagawea was to accompany him. On Feb. 11, 1805, at the fort, she gave birth to her first child, a boy. Less than two months later, on Apr. 7, the expedition set forth; and Sacagawea, with her infant strapped to her back, went with it, sharing all the hardships and privations of the journey. Her services were inestimable; without the aid she obtained from the Shoshones it is hardly possible that the expedition could have proceeded beyond the headwaters of the Salmon. On the return the Charbonneaus remained with the Hidatsas. Clark had become deeply attached to the boy, John Baptist, whom he nicknamed "Pomp" and for whom doubtless he named Pompey's Pillar (originally Tower) on the Yellowstone; and he offered to take the lad, when weaned, to educate as his own child. A few years later, probably in the fall of 1809, Sacagawea, with her husband and child, arrived in St. Louis. Under Clark's patronage Charbonneau tried farming for a time, but the venture was unsuccessful. Leaving the boy with Clark, the Charbonneaus took passage with the expedition led by Manuel Lisa [*q.v.*] that left St. Louis in April 1811, and returned to the Hidatsas. In August 1812, with an infant daughter, Lizette, they rejoined Lisa at his new post, Fort Manuel, on the Missouri near the present boundary of the two Dakotas. On Dec. 20, 1812, John C. Luttig, Lisa's clerk, entered on his journal the record: "this Evening the Wife of Charbonneau a Snake Squaw, died of a putrid fever she was a good and the best Women in the fort, aged abt 25 years she left a fine infant girl" (Luttig, *post*, p. 106). She was buried in the grounds of the fort, and her infant was taken to St. Louis and placed under the guardianship of Clark.

No other American woman has been honored with so many memorials as Sacagawea. A river, a peak, and a mountain pass in Montana bear her name; a bronze statue of her was exhibited at the St. Louis exposition of 1904; there is another bronze statue in Portland, Ore.; a statue at the capitol in Bismark, N. Dak.; a boulder with bronze tablet at Three Forks, Mont.; a monument at Armstead, Mont.; a public fountain at Lewiston, Idaho, and a cement shaft at the grave assumed to be hers on the Shoshone reservation. Her character and services have evoked many tributes. Though Lewis mentions her in one instance (July 29, 1805) somewhat disdainfully, Clark gives many evidences of a deep regard for the woman whom he whimsically nicknamed "Janey." To Brackenridge (*post*), a fellow-voyager on the expedition of 1811, she was "a good creature, of a mild and gentle disposition, greatly attached to the whites, whose manners and dress she tries to imitate," and she has been described as a "modest, womanly, unselfish, patient, enduring little Shoshone squaw" who "proved time and again the inspiration, the genius of the occasion" (Wheeler, *post*, vol. I, p. 124).

Though the Luttig entry has been generally accepted as the authentic death record of Sacagawea, the matter is still warmly controverted. The theory has been advanced that Sacagawea returned to her people, among whom she lived until she was nearly one hundred years old, and that she is identical with the woman known as "Bazil's mother," interred Apr. 9, 1884, in the Shoshone burial grounds (Hebard, *post*). This theory has been reflected in a bill before Congress and in an effort to compel a decision from the Commissioner of Indian Affairs. The controversy also includes a lively disputation over the heroine's name.

[The spelling of Sacagawea's name in this article follows the precedent of Lewis, Clark, and Ordway. See *Original Jours. of the Lewis and Clark Expedition* (7 vols., 1904–05), ed. by R. G. Thwaites; J. C. Luttig, *Jour. of a Fur-Trading Expedition . . . 1812–1813* (1920), ed. by Stella M. Drumm; H. M. Brackenridge in *Early Western Travels*, vol. VI (1904), ed. by R. G. Thwaites; O. D. Wheeler, *The Trail of Lewis and Clark* (2 vols., 1904); Doane Robinson, in *S. Dak. Hist. Colls.*, XII (1924), 71–84; Grace R. Hebard, in *Jour. Am. Hist.*, Sept. 1907, and *Sacajawea, a Guide and Interpreter of the Lewis and Clark Expedition* (1933); manuscript articles by Dr. Chas. A. Eastman and J. E. Rees.]

W. J. G.

SACCO, NICOLA (Apr. 22, 1891–Aug. 23, 1927) and Bartolomeo Vanzetti (June 11, 1888–Aug. 23, 1927), principals in the Sacco-Vanzetti case, were both natives of Italy. Sacco, who was christened Ferdinando but took the name of an elder brother when the latter died, was born at Torre Maggiore, province of Foggia, in Southern Italy. His father, Michele Sacco, was a substantial owner of vineyards and olive orchards. In April 1908 he emigrated to the United States, where in 1912 he was married; he had a son and a daughter. With the exception of an absence in Mexico (1917–18) to avoid the draft, Sacco at the time of his arrest in 1920 had been for eleven years employed as a skilled edger in a shoe factory at Milford, Mass., where he was known as a steady workman absorbed in his family, his work, and his garden. During his residence in Massachusetts Sacco first became interested in Socialism and later, like Vanzetti, came under the influence of Luigi Galleani, a philosophical anarchist of the school of Blake and Tolstoy. Vanzetti, whose parents, Battista and Giovanna Vanzetti, were of well-to-do farming stock, was born at Villafalletto, province of Cuneo, Piedmont, and, following his mother's death, emigrated to New York in June 1908. Of a reflective temperament and a roving disposition, he never married and sampled a variety of employments in different parts of the country before 1915, when he settled in Plymouth, Mass. There he remained, save for a visit to Mexico in 1917–18 to avoid the draft, and was at the time of his arrest in 1920 engaged as a fish peddler.

In the winter of 1919–20 a wave of anti-radicalism swept the United States. In Massachusetts several members of the Galleani group were deported or imprisoned and the press was full of the machinations of the "Reds." At the height of this campaign, on Apr. 15, 1920, the paymaster and guard of a shoe factory were shot dead in the main street of South Braintree, Mass., and robbed of some $16,000. The shots were fired by two men of foreign appearance who were immediately driven away in a car by their accomplices. It was with this brutal crime that Sacco and Vanzetti, arrested on May 5, were charged. Their joint trial began on May 31, 1921, at Dedham, before Judge Webster Thayer. No money had been traced to the defendants nor was there any evidence that either of them had ever been in possession of the car in which the murderers made their escape. The prosecution relied on two main points: (1) evidence of eye-witnesses identifying the defendants as participants in the crime; (2) the fact that on arrest the defendants made to the police false statements as to their movements and circumstances, from which a guilty consciousness of murder might be inferred. The defence sought to meet the first of these points by the evidence of the defendants themselves and of numerous other witnesses placing them elsewhere at the time of the crime. To the second it replied that the nervousness and admitted falsehoods of the defendants were explained by their consciousness, not of murder, but of radicalism and their fear of sharing the fate of some of their fellow radicals. At the time of their arrest they were actually obtaining a car in order to dispose of incriminating Socialist literature in their possession. On July 14, both defendants were found guilty of murder in the first degree.

After the trial, applications for a re-hearing were made to Judge Thayer, partly on the ground of fresh evidence, partly on the ground that the question of radicalism, unavoidably introduced by the defence, had been improperly capitalized by the prosecution and the presiding judge. It was claimed that the district attorney's cross examination, ostensibly directed to disprove, was really calculated to emphasize and exploit the defendants' evasion of military service and their unpopular opinions for the double purpose of prejudicing them in the eyes of the jury or, if they were acquitted, of providing the federal agents with materials for a deportation order against them. These motions were all denied and the supreme court of Massachusetts, whose power of review is limited to questions of law, refused to intervene. Meanwhile, the spontaneous confession in 1925 of a condemned criminal named Madeiros (or Medeiros) exonerating the defendants had led to the discovery (1926) of much corroborative detail pointing to the theory that the murder was the work of a gang of professional bandits from Providence, R. I. Sacco and Vanzetti were now defended by a prominent and conservative Boston lawyer, William G. Thompson, whose courageous, powerful, and disinterested presentation of their case aroused doubts of their guilt in many minds. Meetings of protest took place all over the world and such famous names as Mazaryk, Einstein, Anatole France, and Romain Rolland were associated with petitions for the men's release. In Massachusetts, however, opinion remained predominantly hostile. To the native New England element Sacco and Vanzetti were aliens and agitators; to the Catholics they were renegades in religion. Both elements were united to resent outside intervention with local institutions, and to citizens the vindication of those institutions appeared of greater importance than the guilt or innocence of the accused. Nevertheless, so insistent was the demand for an impartial review that on June 1, 1927, Gov. Alvan T. Fuller of Massachusetts announced the appointment of an advisory committee to report to him on the fairness of the trial and the justification for the conviction. (The death sentence had been imposed on Apr. 9, 1927.) The members of this committee were President A. Lawrence Lowell of Harvard University, President Samuel W. Stratton of the Massachusetts Institute of Technology, and a former probate judge, Robert Grant.

On Aug. 3 the Governor, who had meanwhile conducted his own inquiry, announced that both he and the advisory committee were unanimous in finding the trial fair and the defendants guilty. But the committee's report, published a few days later (*New York Times*, Aug. 7, 1927), was at once the object of serious and detailed criticism, particularly in regard to its treatment of the charge of prejudice against Judge Thayer. The defence unsuccessfully attempted to persuade the federal courts to intervene and demonstrations in favor of the defendants continued both at home and abroad. As the day fixed for the executions drew nearer, Boston was placed under something resembling martial law and on Sunday, Aug. 21, 1927, over 150 persons were arrested for picketing near the State House. After midnight of Aug. 22, that is, in the first hours of Aug. 23, both defendants were electrocuted.

During his long imprisonment Vanzetti had devoted himself to reading and improving his command of English; and a number of his letters written during this period have been published. Unless they can be thought to have been deliberately concocted for the purpose, these letters may be thought to provide some psychological confirmation of the material evidence against his having committed a murder for profit. For they display him as a man of considerable native intelligence striving after education and as an idealist with an unexpected vein of realistic humor. Throughout his imprisonment he was supported by the belief, eloquently expressed in a passage from his statement on receiving sentence, that he was promoting the cause he had at heart: "Now we are not a failure. . . . Never in our full life could we hope to do such work for tolerance, for joostice, for man's understanding of man as now we do by an accident. Our words—our lives—our pains—nothing! The taking of our lives—lives of a good shoemaker and a poor fish-peddler—all! That last moment be-

longs to us—that agony is our triumph" (Ehrmann, *post,* p. 245).

An opinion as to the guilt of Sacco and Vanzetti must depend on the consideration of a mass of detail which it is impossible to summarize in this article. Communists came to value the case as a proof of their thesis that no "Capitalist" society can afford justice to its opponents in the class war. Others, not subscribing to this general proposition, felt grave misgivings in the particular instance.

[*The Sacco-Vanzetti Case* (5 vols., 1928–29), a transcript of the record; *The Letters of Sacco and Vanzetti* (1928), ed. by Marion Frankfurter and Gardner Jackson; Fernand Collin, *L'affaire Sacco et Vanzetti* (Louvain, 1927); Eugene Lyons, *The Life and Death of Sacco and Vanzetti* (1927); Felix Frankfurter, *The Case of Sacco and Vanzetti* (1927); O. K. Fraenkel, *The Sacco-Vanzetti Case* (1931); H. B. Ehrmann, *The Untried Case* (1933).]   S. G—s.

SACHS, JULIUS (July 6, 1849–Feb. 2, 1934), educator, was born at Baltimore, Md., the son of Joseph and Sophia (Baer) Sachs. He took the degrees of A.B. and A.M. at Columbia in 1867 and 1871. After studying in Germany at the universities of Würzburg, Berlin, Göttingen, and Rostock from 1867 to 1871, he returned to America with the degree of Ph.D. from Rostock. In 1871, in a deliberate attempt to raise the standard of secondary education in the United States, he established a preparatory school in New York City, the Sachs Collegiate Institute School of Boys, of which he remained the head for more than thirty years. In spite of his youth, he was unusually well-equipped for such a venture and the moment a singularly propitious one, for colleges and universities, having raised their own standards, had begun to make demands that few private and no public schools of the time could properly meet. The Sachs Collegiate Institute had a widespread influence on American educational standards and methods. It was not only a model school for boys but also a training school for teachers under wise and considerate leadership. There was no paltering with educational nostrums, no attempt merely to interest a student, but a sincere belief that the only durable satisfaction for the student is proportional to his own thoughtful labor.

Sachs's own scholarly investigations were not made impossible by his other activities. His "Observations on Plato's Cratylus" (*Transactions of the American Philological Association,* 1878) was the first of a long series of learned articles, the most notable being "Observations on Lucian" (*Ibid.,* 1880), "Notes on Homeric Zoology" (*Ibid.,* 1886), and "Echoes of Greek Epic Poetry in Vase Paintings" (a lecture delivered before the New York Society of the Archaeological Institute of America, Mar. 6, 1893). He also contributed many articles on educational subjects to the *Educational Review* from 1905 to 1918. In 1912 he published a very complete study, *The American Secondary School and Some of Its Problems*.

Sachs was a man of fine appearance, great vigor of mind and body, and exceptional intellectual equipment. His career seems almost consciously to have been shaped on that of Hermann Sauppe of Göttingen, under whose influence he had come in 1869 and whom he described as "a master of his craft, ready to share his resources as a practical teacher and an investigator with the young aspirants, a veritable professor of the teaching method" (Sachs, "Reminiscences of German University Days," article prepared for *Teachers College Record,* March 1917, printed separately, but not published in that issue). Throughout the years his leadership as a teacher and scholar was clearly recognized by his election to head the Schoolmasters' Association of New York, 1889, the American Philological Association, 1890–91, the Headmasters' Association of the United States, 1899, and the New York Society of the Archaeological Institute of America, 1900–03. In 1902 he was invited to join the faculty of Teachers College in Columbia University as professor of secondary education, an opportunity greatly to extend his influence. His success in this work until his retirement in 1917 is amply attested by numbers of mature students and especially by very sincere tributes at the time of his death from President Nicholas Murray Butler, Dean Frederick J. E. Woodbridge, and others. On June 23, 1874, he married Rosa Goldman of New York, with whom, at their fiftieth wedding anniversary, he established at Columbia the Julius and Rosa Sachs Endowment Fund, designed to promote scholarship in the field of secondary education. They had a daughter, and a son who became a surgeon.

[*Cat. of the Sachs Collegiate Inst. School of Boys* (1906); *Teachers Coll. Record,* Mar. 1934; "In Memoriam: Memorial Services for Dr. Julius Sachs, Held in Milbank Chapel, Teachers College, Columbia University ... May 15, 1934" (MS.); *Who's Who in America,* 1932–33; *N. Y. Times,* Feb. 3, 1934; personal acquaintance.]   F. L. T.

SACHS, THEODORE BERNARD (May 2, 1868–Apr. 2, 1916), physician, was born of Jewish parents, Bernard and Sophia Sachs, at Dinaberg, Russia. His father, a well-to-do merchant, gave him a good education in the Kherson High School and the University of Odessa, from which he was graduated in law in 1891. He then emigrated to America and settled in Chicago, where he became a sewing-machine operator for a clothing manufacturing firm and thus supported himself while he attended the College of Physicians and Surgeons (later affiliated with the University of Illinois). He graduated in 1895 and, after two years as intern and house physician at Michael Reese Hospital, established his office in the Jewish quarter of Chicago's west side. From the first he had an especial interest in tuberculosis. In 1900 he established in the Jewish Aid Dispensary the first clinic in Chicago devoted exclusively to patients suffering from pulmonary tuberculosis, and awoke a storm of protest by denouncing the neglect of tuberculous patients at the county institutions at Dunning and Oak Forest. In 1905 he was attending physician to a camp for tuberculous patients at Glencoe, the first of its kind in the state; later there were established a camp at Dunning and the Edward Sanitarium at Naperville, where he was director and examining physician from its foundation to his death. He was in the forefront of the campaign successfully waged in 1909 for the establishment of the Chicago Municipal Tuberculosis Sanitarium, begun in 1911 and completed in 1915. As secretary of the first board of directors and later its head, he exercised much influence upon the plans of the buildings and upon the organization of its services. A corrupt city government, however, made efficient administration impossible and brought accusations of inefficiency and dishonesty against the board of directors. Sachs submitted his resignation on Mar. 20, 1916, and two weeks later committed suicide by morphine poisoning at the Edward Sanitarium, leaving a letter addressed to the people of Chicago that called for an inquiry into the affairs of the sanitarium and protested against its exploitation by politicians. A report of the finance committee of the Chicago city council later exonerated the sanitarium board of charges of any misuse of public funds. In the midst of his municipal work Sachs was director and president of the Chicago Tuberculosis Institute, secretary of the United Hebrew Charities, and attending physician to several hospitals. In 1915–16 he was president of the National Association for the Study and Prevention of Tuberculosis. The most notable of his few articles are *Tuberculosis in the Jewish District of Chicago* (1904), *Children of Tuberculous Parents* (1908), and *The Examination of Employees for Tuberculosis* (1912). He was greatly assisted in his investigations and writings by his wife, Lena Louise Wilson of Chicago, whom he married Jan. 4, 1900.

Sachs had exalted ideas of professional responsibility and of citizenship, an unusual capacity for initiative and for organization, and an untiring industry that made him ruthless in the prosecution of inefficiency. Yet he was an oppressively serious person, with an habitual expression of sadness. He was usually preoccupied, overwrought and nervous, and frequently highly irritable; furthermore, though lavish in sacrifice of his personal interest and with total disregard of pecuniary gain, he loved honors, which he sought and earned. It was probably on account of these personal qualities that, in spite of his ability and sincerity, he never achieved the support of the medical profession of Chicago but always met either apathetic unconcern or secret opposition.

[*Alumni Record, Univ. of Ill.* (1921) ; *Proc. Inst. of Medicine of Chicago, 1916–17* vol. I (1917); S. A. Knopf, *A Hist. of the Natl. Tuberculosis Assoc.* (1922); *Medic. Times* (N. Y.), June 1916; *Jour. of the Outdoor Life,* May 1916; *Ill. Medic. Jour.,* Apr. 1916; H. A. Kelly and W. L. Burrage, *Am. Medic. Biographies* (1920) ; obituary in *Chicago Daily Tribune,* Apr. 3, 1916.]   J. M. P—n.

SACHSE, JULIUS FRIEDRICH (Nov. 22, 1842–Nov. 14, 1919), antiquary, author, the son of Johann Heinrich Friedrich and Julianna Wilhelmina (Bühler) Sachse, was born, lived, and died in Philadelphia. His father, a pupil of Thorwaldsen's, was an artist and designer in bronze and other metals. After attending the old Lutheran Academy, Sachse became a haberdasher and maker of men's shirts. He received several medals for work of his manufacture which he exhibited at fairs in Vienna, Paris, and Philadelphia. On May 15, 1864, he married Emma Caroline Lange, who with their five children survived him. About 1890 he retired from business in order to devote himself to research, writing, and photography. He joined numerous historical societies and was one of the founders, in 1891, of the Pennsylvania-German Society, of which he was treasurer 1891–1913, president 1913–14, and a member of the executive committee until his death. To its *Proceedings* he contributed eleven monographs and translations. He was one of the editors of the *American Journal of Photography* and in 1913 was made librarian and curator of the Grand Lodge of the Free and Accepted Masons of Pennsylvania. As the latter post gave him access to a large amount of historical material, he produced a number of books and articles on Masonry in Pennsylvania, of which the one of most general interest is *Benjamin Franklin as a Freemason* (1906). He was employed as a photographer by the *Ladies' Home Journal* and by the publishers of various illustrated books; perhaps his most beautiful work in this field was a series of studies, made in his own hothouse, of

the development of the night-blooming Cereus. His various books, which he always issued privately, were lavishly embellished with photographs, zincographic facsimiles, and pen-and-ink drawings, which he made with much skill; and he was more than generous in providing illustrations for his friends' publications. The subject to which by temperament he was most strongly attracted, and which he made peculiarly his own, was the history of the Seventh Day Baptists of Ephrata and of their predecessors, the band of millenarians, led by Johannes Kelpius [*q.v.*], who settled on the Wissahickon near Germantown in 1694. In its pursuit he made a number of trips to Europe and unearthed, there and in Pennsylvania, an astonishing quantity of books, pamphlets, papers, documents, and other relics more or less relevant to the subject. This collection he later gave to the Seventh Day Baptist Historical Society. The chief literary products of this investigation were *The German Pietists of Provincial Pennsylvania 1694–1708* (1895), *The German Sectarians of Pennsylvania 1708–1800* (2 vols., 1899), *The Music of the Ephrata Cloister* (1903), and *Justus Falckner, Mystic and Scholar* (1903). He also published various articles on certain ramifications of the subject and translations of some of his important sources. The chief merits of his historical work were his unflagging enthusiasm and his faculty for discovering materials. In spirit he was hardly an historian at all but a romantic discoverer of the past. As a scholar he was almost wholly self-trained. In form and substance his works leave much to seek, but they have done more than the writings of anyone else to awaken interest in Pennsylvania German history. Much of his influence was due to his engaging personal qualities. He was in bad health for some four months before his death, although active until the very end.

[C. F. Randolph, "Julius Friedrich Sachse, Litt. D.," *Sabbath Recorder,* Mar. 15, 1920 ; *Who's Who in America,* 1920–21 ; *Public Ledger* (Phila.), Nov. 16, 1919 ; H. M. M. Richards, obituary, *Proc. Pa.-German Soc.,* vol. XXXI (1925) ; portrait, *Ibid.,* vol. XXV (1917) ; letter from his daughter, Miss Emma Florence Sachse, June 27, 1932.]   G. H. G.

SACKETT, HENRY WOODWARD (Aug. 31, 1853–Dec. 9, 1929), lawyer, was born at Enfield, near Ithaca, N. Y. The son of Solon Philo Sackett, a physician, and his wife, Lovedy K. Woodward, he was descended from Simon Sackett who came from England to New England in 1631. Henry attended the Ithaca Academy and Cornell University, where he graduated in 1875. After teaching for one year, he began the study of law in New York and at the same time, for the *New York Tribune,* wrote special reports of cases in process of adjudication before the court of appeals and the state supreme court. He was admitted to the bar in 1877 and shortly thereafter became associated with Cornelius A. Runkle, whom he later succeeded as counsel for the *Tribune,* a position he continued to hold with this paper and its successor, the *New York Herald Tribune,* until his death. In 1888 he formed a law partnership with Charles Gibson Bennett, which in later years became the well-known firm of Sackett, Chapman, Brown & Cross, corporation lawyers and attorneys for estates.

In the course of his service as counsel for the *Tribune,* Sackett became a leading authority on the law of libel. During the last years of his life he was special lecturer on that subject in the School of Journalism of Columbia University. As a defender of the freedom of the press he exerted a substantial influence. In 1914 the crucial cases of *Burdick* vs. *U. S.* and *Curtin* vs. *U. S.* (236 *U. S.,* 79, 96) came, on appeal, before the United States Supreme Court. George Burdick, city editor of the *Tribune,* and W. L. Curtin, a reporter on the same newspaper, had each been fined $500 for contempt of court in refusing to divulge confidential information involving prominent persons in a smuggling case. In an effort to induce them to testify, President Wilson offered pardons to both men, but the pardons, tendered in the Grand Jury room, were rejected. Sackett delivered the closing argument before the Supreme Court, which handed down a decision in favor of his clients. He argued that the exercise of the presidential pardoning power in the present case would "tend to destroy some of the most essential safeguards of free government. It would pervert the grand jury . . . and would tend to destroy to a dangerous degree the separation of powers between the executive and the judicial branches of the government and in practical effect would arm the executive with summary powers which ought to be possessed only by the judicial branch." (236 *U. S.,* 81–82.)

In 1897 Governor Black appointed him to his staff with the rank of colonel. Thereafter he was commonly known by his military title. For thirty years he was a trustee of Cornell University. By his will he made the University his beneficiary to the extent of eleven-twelfths of his residuary estate. He had long been interested in the extraordinary scenic beauties of the Cornell campus, particularly in what he conceived to be their spiritual influence on the observer's mind. In 1927 he gave to the University $200,000 for the conservation of these natural and picturesque values and for making them comfortably acces-

sible to students and the general public. He was trustee and vice-president of the American Scenic and Historic Preservation Society, commissioner for Fire Island State Park, president of the Andrew H. Green ("father of greater New York") Memorial Association, and president of the Empire State Society of Sons of the American Revolution. He was married on Nov. 17, 1886, to Elizabeth Titus who died in 1926. They had no children.

[C. H. Weygant, *The Sacketts of America* (1907); *N. Y. Herald Tribune,* Dec. 10 and editorial, Dec. 11, 1929; *Cornellian Council Bulletin,* Jan. 1930; *Who's Who in America,* 1928–29; *N. Y. Times,* Dec. 10 and 20, 1929.]   W. A. H.

SADLIER, DENIS (1817–Feb. 4, 1885), Catholic book publisher, was born in the shadow of the Rock of Cashel in County Tipperary, Ireland. His father, James, died in Liverpool en route to America but his mother courageously continued the journey, arriving in New York with her family in January 1830. For two years Denis and his brother James attended St. Peter's School in Barclay Street. They then entered the book-binding shop of Arthur & Company, and in 1836 established a similar concern of their own in Carmine Street under the name of D. & J. Sadlier & Company. They soon entered the publishing field, bringing out in 1837 an edition of Alban Butler's *Lives of the Saints* and in 1838 a quarto Bible. As the business grew rapidly, they continually moved to larger quarters until finally, in 1860, they located in Barclay Street, with a branch in Montreal. As job printers, contrivers of designs for churches, publishers of Bibles, prayer books, school texts, and a Household Library of 164 titles, and as compilers of the official, annual *Sadlier's Catholic Directory* (1864–96), the firm of Sadlier became a national Catholic institution. It also published from June 1857 to December 1881 the *New York Tablet,* which attracted numerous writers of distinction. In 1869, on the death of James, who had supervised the publication department, Denis carried on the business alone. He passed through the panic of 1873 unscathed, but in 1879, under the pressure of financial troubles, he assigned all properties, including the dower of his wife, Julia Browne, whom he had married in 1841, as a pledge to his creditors; by 1884, however, the business was readjusted and continued for several years.

In 1850 Sadlier established a residence in the anti-Catholic neighborhood of Harlem, where he became popular enough to be chosen a public school trustee, then a most unusual honor for a Catholic citizen. A passionate, intense man of marked business integrity and of liberal charities, a stout Democrat with no ambition for political office, a trustee of Manhattan College, and a self-trained reader of good books, he won recognition in both the business and the social life of New York. In 1864 he moved to Wilton, Westchester County, where he died. At the obsequies in St. Patrick's Cathedral, Monsignor Quinn declared that it was Sadlier's "chief object in life to preserve the Catholics of America from the temptation to peruse such [bad] literature by giving them attractive Catholic books," and added, "There is hardly a Catholic book which does not bear the well-known imprint of the name which has become a household word throughout the length and breadth of the English speaking Catholic world."

[*Sadlier's Cath. Directory*, 1886; *N. Y. Freeman's Jour.*, Sept. 15, 1877, Feb. 14, 1885; the *Sun* (N. Y.), Feb. 5, 6, 1885; information as to certain facts from Anna T. Sadlier (1854–1932) of Ottawa, Canada.]

R. J. P.

SADLIER, MARY ANNE MADDEN (Dec. 31, 1820–Apr. 5, 1903), author, was born at Cootehill, County Cavan, Ireland. After the death of her father, Francis Madden, a prosperous merchant, she emigrated, in 1844, to Montreal. Here, in November 1846, she married James Sadlier, manager of the local branch of the New York publishing house of D. & J. Sadlier, by whom she had six children. In 1860 she removed to New York, where her husband died in 1869.

A voluminous writer of short stories, essays, and translations for *La Belle Assemblée* (London), the *New York Tablet*, the *New York Freeman's Journal*, the *Boston Pilot*, D'Arcy McGee's *The American Celt*, and *The Literary Garland*, she became a favorite among Catholic readers. In all, she wrote about sixty novels dealing with Irish historical episodes and with the social, religious, and educational problems of the Irish in America. To the latter she strongly recommended pride of background, reconciliation with the customs of the New World, Americanization without secularization, and compromise between the old folks and their American-born children. Thus she performed a real service beyond mere entertainment, and as social studies some of her books retain a pronounced value.

Among her best-known works were *The Blakes and the Flanagans* (1855, 1858), translated into German by J. P. Bachem as *Alt-Irland und Amerika* (1857), dealing with the school question; *Willie Burke* (c. 1856); *The Fate of Father Sheehy* (1863), a story of Tipperary; *Con O'Regan* (1864, 1885), a tale of emigrant life in America; *Aunt Honor's Keepsake* (1866), which stressed the need of saving the Irish orphans for

the old faith; *Bessy Conway* (c. 1865), based on the problems of Irish immigrant girls; *Eleanor Preston* (c. 1865); *Alice Riordan* (1851); *Confessions of an Apostate* (1868); *Maureen Dhu* (1870), a picturesque story of the Claddagh in Galway; *New Lights; or, Life in Galway* (1855, 1885); *MacCarthy More* (1868, 1885); *The Red Hand of Ulster* (1850), a stirring tale of the rising of the Northern Earls against Elizabeth; *The Confederate Chieftains* (1860, 1895), a story of the rebellion of 1641, which went through several editions; *Purgatory: Doctrinal, Historical and Poetical* (1886), a compilation dedicated to her son, Francis Xavier, who died a Jesuit in 1885; *Catechism of Sacred History and Doctrine* (1864), in which she collaborated with Mother Angela [*q.v.*]; and *Stories of the Promises* (1895), in collaboration with her daughter Anna Teresa Sadlier (1854–1932), an author of numerous short stories and books. She edited the *Poems of D'Arcy McGee* in 1869, and in 1885 she published *Life of the Blessed Virgin, Mother of God*, translated from the French of Matthieu Orsini, in a volume which also contained her translation of Francis de Ligny's life of Jesus Christ. In 1895 she was awarded the Laetare Medal by Notre Dame University as an outstanding lay contributor to the general work of the Church, and in 1902 she received a special blessing from Pope Leo XIII in recognition of her illustrious services for the Catholic Church. The closing years of her life she lived in Montreal with her children.

[*Catholic Encyc.*, XIII, 323; *The Messenger*, May 1903; *Gazette* (Montreal), Apr. 6, 1903; W. S. Wallace, *Dict. of Canadian Biog.* (1926); *A Round Table of Representative Am. Catholic Novelists* (1897); list of pubs. under Sadlier's advertisements in *Sadlier's Cath. Directory*, 1865 ff., from which approximate dates of publication can be determined; especially, information from the late Miss Anna T. Sadlier of Ottawa, Canada.]

R. J. P.

SADTLER, JOHN PHILIP BENJAMIN (Dec. 25, 1823–Apr. 28, 1901), Lutheran clergyman, college president, was born in Baltimore, the son of Philip Benjamin and Catharine Sadtler. His father, a German by birth, was a goldsmith and an amateur of optics. Sadtler graduated from Pennsylvania College (later Gettysburg College) in 1842, stayed on at Gettysburg as a student in the theological seminary under Samuel Simon Schmucker [*q.v.*], and was licensed by the Maryland Synod in 1844. By his marriage Oct. 9, 1845, to Schmucker's daughter, Caroline Elizabeth, he became a member of one of the most influential of Lutheran ministerial families. He was pastor of churches in and near Pine Grove, Schuylkill County, Pa., 1845–49; at

Shippensburg, 1849–53; of St. Peter's, Middletown, 1853–56; and of St. John's, Easton, where he succeeded Charles Frederick Schaeffer [q.v.], 1856–62. In the latter year, seeking a somewhat milder climate for the sake of his wife's health, he accepted the principalship of a girls' school at Lutherville, Md., a suburb of Baltimore. The school and the village where it was located owed their existence to the enterprise of John Gottlieb Morris [q.v.]. Sadtler was a good teacher and administrator, and by conducting Lutherville Seminary prosperously through the Civil War years and the hard times that followed he gained the reputation of a financial wizard. He declined the presidency of Pennsylvania College, of which he was a trustee 1862–77, but was induced a few years later to succeed Frederick Augustus Muhlenberg [q.v.] as the second president of Muhlenberg College at Allentown, Pa. He took charge Jan. 1, 1877, and with his formal inauguration later in the year the college became the property of the Lutheran Ministerium of Pennsylvania. Its future was still dim. The students, drawn mostly from humble Pennsylvania-German homes, were not always the most likely candidates for a higher education; the teachers were some of them men of genuine ability, but they were hampered by insufficient books and apparatus, long hours, and the necessity of giving instruction in two or more departments; the institution was heavily in debt and had little ready money. Sadtler, however, was devoted to the college and was confident of its growth, and he was the kind of man who inspires the devotion and confidence of others. During his administration the debt was reduced, endowment funds were received, students increased slightly in number, and the work of the college improved measurably. In 1885 he was crippled permanently by a fall on the ice, and, fearing that he could no longer fulfill all the duties of his position, he retired at the end of the year. Theodore Lorenzo Seip [q.v.] was his successor. For the rest of his life Sadtler made his home in Baltimore. He contributed articles to the *Evangelical Review* and the *Workman,* was president of the Society for the History of the Germans in Maryland, and was as active as his health would permit in the work of the church. He died while on a visit to Atlantic City. He was survived by his wife, two daughters, and seven sons (the *Sun, post*), one of them Samuel Philip Sadtler [q.v.], the chemist.

[Biog. sketch by G. T. Ettinger in S. E. Ochsenford, *Muhlenberg Coll.* (1892); the *Sun* (Baltimore), Apr. 20, May 2, 1901; obituary in *Fifteenth Ann. Report of the Soc. for the Hist. of the Germans in Md.,* 1900–01; A. R. Wentz, *Hist. of the Gettysburg Theol. Sem.* (1926).]

G. H. G.

SADTLER, SAMUEL PHILIP (July 18, 1847–Dec. 20, 1923), teacher, chemist, author, was born in Pinegrove, Schuylkill County, Pa., the son of J. P. Benjamin Sadtler [q.v.] and Caroline Elizabeth (Schmucker). Both his father and his maternal grandfather, Samuel Simon Schmucker [q.v.], were Lutheran ministers. His early education was obtained at Easton, Pa., and he graduated from the Easton High School in 1862. The same year he entered Pennsylvania (now Gettysburg) College, Gettysburg, where he was graduated in 1867, his course having been interrupted in 1863 by the battle of Gettysburg. During his senior year his attention was turned from classical studies toward the study of science, which he determined to choose for his life work. In the fall of 1867, therefore, he went to the newly established Lehigh University, where for a year he studied chemistry, physics, and mineralogy, and in the fall of 1868 he became a student at Harvard, pursuing advanced work under Wolcott Gibbs [q.v.], one of the most distinguished chemists in America. In January 1870 he received the degree of S.B. from Harvard and a month later sailed for Germany to complete his chemical education.

After spending one year at the University of Göttingen he was granted the degree of Ph.D. and returned to America to accept the professorship of chemistry and physics at Pennsylvania College, which he held from 1871 to 1874. In the latter year he was called to the professorship of general and organic chemistry in the University of Pennsylvania, and in 1878 became professor of chemistry at the Philadelphia College of Pharmacy. These chairs he held concurrently until 1891, when he relinquished that at the University of Pennsylvania to open an office as consulting chemical expert. He continued as professor at the College of Pharmacy, however, until 1916, when he was made professor emeritus. Associated with him in his consulting office, which he maintained until his death, was his son, Samuel S. Sadtler. As expert he prepared chemical testimony in at least fifty cases of important patent litigation.

In 1877 Sadtler published *Chemical Experimentation: Being a Hand-Book of Lecture Experiments in Inorganic Chemistry . . . for the Use of Lecturers and Teachers.* For many years, from 1883 until his death, he was chemical editor of *The Dispensatory of the United States.* In 1891 he published the first edition of his *Hand-Book of Industrial Organic Chemistry,* which went through several editions and was translated into German and Russian. In 1892, with Prof. Henry Trimble, he brought out the first

edition of *A Text-Book of Chemistry Intended
for . . . Pharmaceutical and Medical Students*
(parts I and II), better known in the enlarged
edition of 1895. The third edition (1900) appeared under the names of Sadtler and Dr.
Virgil Coblentz, and the sixth edition (1927)
was entitled, *Pharmaceutical and Medical Chemistry*. Sadtler was an active member of the
Committee on Revision of the *United States
Pharmacopœia*. He contributed many articles to
chemical journals and delivered many addresses
on chemical and other technical subjects. He
was a founder and the first president (1908–09)
of the American Institute of Chemical Engineers
and was a member of the American Philosophical
Society, the American Association for the Advancement of Science, the Franklin Institute,
and many other professional and scientific bodies. An active layman in the Lutheran Church,
he was president of the General Council Board
of Publication in 1906, and from 1919 to his
death was president of the Board of Publication
of the United Lutheran Church. He married
Mary Julia Bridges of Baltimore on Dec. 17,
1872, and was the father of two sons and two
daughters.

[*The Alumni Record of Gettysburg Coll.* (1932) ; *The
First Century of the Phila. Coll. of Pharmacy* (1922) ;
Who's Who in America, 1922–23 ; *Am. Jour. Pharmacy*,
July 1916 ; *Industrial and Engineering Chemistry*, Feb.
1924 ; *Lutheran*, Dec. 27, Jan. 3, 1924 ; *Pub. Ledger*
(Phila.), Dec. 21, 1923 ; information from family.]
                                                A. R.

SAENDERL, SIMON (Sept. 30, 1800–Feb.
22, 1879), Catholic priest and missionary, first
superior of the Redemptorists in the United
States, was a native of Malgerzdorf, Lower Bavaria. He was ordained in 1825 and entered in
1829 the order of the Redemptorists. In the latter
year the Rev. Frederick Rese [*q.v.*], then vicar
general at Cincinnati, visited Vienna and persuaded the Redemptorists to send missionaries
supported by the Leopoldine Foundation to his
diocese. Father Saenderl, as superior, with two
other priests and three lay brothers left Vienna
in 1832 and arrived at Cincinnati on July 17. In
the autumn of 1832 he was sent to Green Bay,
Wis., where he dedicated a church on Nov. 1 and
for a year ministered to the French inhabitants
and to the Menominee Indians, with whom he
had considerable success. The plan had been to
establish a Redemptorist center at Green Bay
but, finding economic conditions unfavorable,
the Redemptorists left there, Saenderl going as
missionary to the Ottawa Indians at Arbre
Croche, Mich., where he studied Indian languages and worked on a dictionary. He officiated
at this mission from 1833 to 1835, and again

from 1836 to 1839. In the interim, with the new
superior, Joseph Prost, he again visited Green
Bay, walking for nine miles over the ice in order
to reach there. His desire for a community life
led him to leave Arbre Croche; his superior,
however, sent him in 1841 to Rochester, N. Y.,
to minister to the German Catholics, and after
two years there he was at Pittsburgh for a few
months. After 1843 he became involved in strife
with his superiors concerning a murderer, whom
he attended to the scaffold (*United States Catholic Magazine*, March 1844, pp. 195–98). He
finally left for Toronto, where he had a small
mission, and later ministered at Monroe, Mich.,
and several neighboring towns. Becoming involved in new controversies, however, he was in
1848 suspended from the order. In 1852, after
visits to the Holy Land and Austria, he joined
the Trappist order, professed on Easter, 1853,
and was made master of German novices. After
joining the Trappists he shut himself from the
world in their convent at Gethsemane, Ky.,
where he passed his remaining years. He was a
quiet, simple man, and, though inclined to controversy, was of a saintly personal character, and
devoted to his mission work. On coming to
America he was too inexperienced for his responsibilities in establishing the order in a new
country but is important for his position as the
first superior.

[Rev. J. F. Byrne, "The Redemptorists in America,"
in *Records Am. Cath. Hist. Soc.*, June 1930–Mar. 1932 ;
Rev. Theodore Roemer, "The Leopoldine Foundation
and the Church in the U. S. (1829–1839)," in *U. S.
Cath. Hist. Soc. Monograph Series*, vol. XIII (1933) ;
A. I. Rezek, *Hist. of the Diocese of S. Ste. Marie and
Marquette* (2 vols., 1906–07) ; *Berichte der Leopoldine
Stiftung* (50 annual issues, 1831–80), of which an
English translation, not yet published, is being made
by Father P. L. Johnson, St. Francis. Wis.] L. P. K.

SAFFORD, JAMES MERRILL (Aug. 13,
1822–July 3, 1907), geologist and educator, the
son of Henry and Patience (Van Horne) Safford, was born in Zanesville, Ohio. His immediate ancestors were from New England, descendants of Thomas Safford who emigrated
from England to America in 1630 and in 1641
settled at Ipswich, Mass. James passed his youth
and received his early training in Zanesville. He
was graduated from the Ohio University at
Athens, receiving the degree of A.B. in 1844,
and then took a special course at Yale. While
here, in 1847, he was called to the professorship
of chemistry and the natural sciences at Cumberland University, Lebanon, Tenn., where he remained until 1872. He then became professor of
chemistry in the medical school of the University
of Nashville, retaining this professorship when,
two years later, the school was combined with

the medical department of Vanderbilt University. In 1875 he was also chosen professor of geology and natural history at Vanderbilt, a position he continued to hold until he retired as professor emeritus in 1900. His teaching is said to have been characterized by simplicity, clearness, and thoroughness. He was eminently practical and avoided all unessential technicalities and doubtful hypotheses. The students all liked him.

In 1854 he was made state geologist of Tennessee, serving in that capacity by successive reappointments until 1860, when the office was abolished. Under an act of 1871 he was again appointed and served until 1900. As a geologist he was eminently successful, particularly when the time and the conditions are considered. There were no good maps; much of the state was still a wilderness; travel was by foot or on horseback over none too good dirt roads. In 1856 he published his first report, *A Geological Reconnoissance of the State of Tennessee,* following it in 1869 with his *Geology of Tennessee,* a volume of 550 pages with a geological map and seven plates. In securing the data for this book, he is said to have had no instruments except a compass and a pocket level; over much of the area surveyed he was obliged to travel on foot, covering some 11,000 miles in this manner: yet "for compactness and clearness, this work is not excelled, perhaps not equalled, by any other official report published in this country" (Stevenson, *post,* p. 524). The enterprise was carried on, also, under financial conditions that would have been ridiculous had they not been pitiful. By the act of 1854 his salary was fixed at $1,500 a year, payable quarterly with no allowance for expenses or assistance. The act of 1871, under which he was appointed for his second period of service as state geologist, stipulated that that official should receive $300 a year, but for a part of the time the legislature failed to make the necessary appropriation. In 1874 Safford was co-editor with J. B. Killebrew of an *Introduction to the Resources of Tennessee,* and in 1884 he contributed to the *Reports of the Tenth Census* (vol. V) a discussion of the physical geography and agricultural features of the state.

He is described as "a man among men, everywhere commanding respect by his common sense, his integrity, and his manly recognition of others" (*Stevenson,* p. 524). That he was not more widely known among his collaborators was due to his geographic isolation and inability to attend the society meetings of his fellow workers. Further than this, he shrank from public speaking and debates and disliked controversy. He preferred putting his views on paper and letting

them be taken at their face value. He was married in 1859 to Catherine K. (Howard) Owen, and passed his later days with a daughter in Dallas, Tex., where he died.

[S. M. Culbertson, *The Ohio Valley Saffords* (1932); E. S. Safford, "The Saffords in America, June 1923" (MS. in Lib. of Cong.); J. J. Stevenson, in *Bull. Geol. Soc. of America,* Jan. 30, 1909; J. T. McGill in *Trans. Tenn. Acad. Sci.,* vol. II (1917); *Who's Who in America,* 1906–07; *Nashville Banner,* July 4, 1907.]

G. P. M.

SAFFORD, TRUMAN HENRY (Jan. 6, 1836–June 13, 1901), astronomer, mathematician, and teacher, eldest of eight children of Truman Hopson and Louisa (Parker) Safford, was born at Royalton, Vt. He was descended from Thomas Safford who became a freeman of the Massachusetts Bay Colony in 1630; his great-grandfather, John Safford, born at Preston, Conn., in 1729, was among the original grantees of Royalton (1781); his grandfather, Nathan, is said to have carried the town's assessment list in his head. Both parents were well qualified to direct his development. His father, a farmer, took a lively interest in public affairs while his mother before marriage had been a teacher. Delicate health prevented his regular attendance at school, but his father's library offered opportunities to his liking. At two years he knew his letters and at six he showed extraordinary skill and speed in lengthy mental and written computations. Stimulated by a visit to Dartmouth College, he computed an almanac for 1846 for Bradford, Vt., and for 1847 he computed almanacs for Bradford, Cincinnati, Philadelphia, and Boston. At this period skeptics subjected him to severe mental tests: one examination lasting three hours was discontinued only when, after multiplying mentally 365,365,365,365,365,365 by itself in about one minute, he confessed that he was tired. How his results were obtained he never completely disclosed, but his processes showed gain by practice and loss by neglect. Though urged to do so, his parents always refused to employ his talents for their own financial profit.

In 1847 President Everett and Professor Benjamin Peirce [*q.v.*] of Harvard became interested in him, and the family moved to Cambridge, Mass., where after fitting for college he graduated from Harvard with honor in 1854. For twelve years thereafter he was a member of the staff of Harvard Observatory and after the death of Professor George P. Bond [*q.v.*] was acting director for about a year. Volumes IV and V of the *Annals* were completed and published under his supervision. In 1866 he became professor of astronomy at the old University of

Chicago and director of the Dearborn Observatory, but the Chicago fire of 1871 put an end to public support of this observatory and for the five years following he was occupied with astronomical work connected with United States geographical surveys.

In 1876 he became Field Memorial Professor of Astronomy at Williams College, and this position he held until his death. He took part at various times in teaching physics and mathematics and also acted as librarian. With the Repsold circle of the Field Memorial Observatory, established in 1882, he made the observations for *The Williams College Catalogue of North Polar Stars* (1888). His astronomical interests lay mainly in the fields of the older astronomy and his many papers on orbits, ephemerides, positions of stars, proper motions, methods of reduction, instrumental and personal corrections to observations, the proper motion of Sirius before and after discovery of its companion, etc., appeared in the *Astronomical Journal*, the *Sidereal Messenger*, the *Proceedings of the American Academy of Arts and Sciences*, and other scientific journals of the United States, England, and Germany. He also published *Mathematical Teaching and Its Modern Methods* (1887), *The Development of Astronomy in the United States* (1888), an address at the fiftieth anniversary of the observatory at Williams College; and a paper on "The Psychology of the Personal Equation" (*Science*, Nov. 26, 1897).

He married at Cambridge, Mass., Mar. 8, 1860, Elizabeth Marshall Bradbury, and to them were born six children. Five of these, with their mother, survived him. He suffered a paralytic stroke some years before his death, which occurred at the home of a son in Newark, N. J.

[E. M. W. Lovejoy, *Hist. of Royalton, Vt.* (1911); M. D. Gilman, *The Bibliog. of Vt.* (1897); *Williams Alumni Rev.*, June 1926; *Littell's Living Age*, Jan. 8, 1848; *Ladies' Repository*, Apr. 1849; *Science*, July 5, 1901; *Observatory*, Aug. 1901; *Mo. Notices of the Royal Astron. Soc.*, vol. LXII (1902); *Proc. Am. Acad. Arts and Sci.*, vol. XXXVII (1902); S. I. Bailey, *The Hist. and Work of Harvard Observatory* (1931); *N. Y. Times*, June 14, 1901.]   J. M. P—r.

SAFFORD, WILLIAM EDWIN (Dec. 14, 1859–Jan. 10, 1926), botanist, ethnologist, and philologist, was descended from Thomas Safford, who emigrated from England in 1630, and was in Ipswich, Mass., by 1641. Later ancestors lived in Vermont, but his grandfather, Eliel Todd Safford, married Ann Tyler Harrison, of Prince William County, Va., and died at Parkersburg, Va. (now W. Va.), in 1840. The latter's son, William Harrison Safford (Feb. 19, 1821–Apr. 20, 1903), born in Parkersburg, married Anna Marie Pocahontas Creel, daughter of Dr. David Creel of Wood County, Va. (now W. Va.), and moved to Ohio in 1848, settling in Chillicothe. He was a distinguished jurist and the author of *The Blennerhasset Papers* (1861). William Edwin Safford, born in Chillicothe, was the fifth of ten children. From his home surroundings, and notably through the influence of his mother, Safford grew up with a strong interest in natural history, and from his association with German children in school early acquired an idiomatic knowledge of that language which led later to his special linguistic studies. His enthusiasm for the natural sciences was further fired by the requirement of reading aloud, as a youth of sixteen, the writings of Darwin and Huxley to his vigorous-minded grandfather Creel, who died at the age of ninety-two.

In 1876 Safford entered the United States Naval Academy, and on completing the four-year course was assigned in the autumn of 1880 to the *Powhatan*. A cruise to Panama next spring afforded him a first view of the tropics. On the return voyage he chanced to meet Alexander Agassiz at Key West, and, adopting willingly enough that famous scientist's advice, resolved to fit himself for scientific collecting on future cruises. He was later detailed to post-graduate studies in botany and zoölogy at Yale (1883–85) and in marine zoölogy at Harvard (1885). There followed a voyage around Cape Horn and a long cruise in the southern Pacific, during which Safford's botanical and ethnological bent found full play, and then a detail of two years as instructor in modern languages at the Naval Academy. In 1890 he was detached from duty and appointed commissioner to Peru and Bolivia (1891–92) for the World's Columbian Exposition, his researches in South America centering in ethnology. He returned to the navy in 1893 and saw service in the Spanish-American War, after which there followed immediately a colorful year as vice-governor of newly acquired Guam. He resigned from the navy in August 1902, when ranking as lieutenant, to accept appointment as assistant botanist in the United States Department of Agriculture, and was promoted in 1915 to economic botanist, a position which he held up to the time of his death. From George Washington University he received the degree Ph.D. in 1920. He was married, Sept. 14, 1904, to Clare, daughter of Chief Justice Decius S. Wade, of Montana, and was survived by his wife, a son, and a daughter.

Safford's life in the navy, though uncongenial in some ways, gave him an exceptional opportunity of observing man and nature in strange places. An omnivorous student of the history of exploration, he gained a first-hand knowledge of South Sea peoples that was matched by his knowledge of ancient American cultures. The period from 1902 onward, when for the first time he was really free to write, proved one of great productiveness. His remarkable breadth of interest is well shown in a series of articles published in the *Plant World* (Sept. 1902–Dec. 1904), brought together in book form under the title, *A Year on the Island of Guam* (1904, later republished); in *The Chamorro Language of Guam* (n.d., preface 1909), reprinted from the *American Anthropologist* (1903–05); and especially in a volume entitled, *The Useful Plants of the Island of Guam* (*Contributions from the United States National Herbarium*, vol. IX, 1905), which is classic. The last is virtually a handbook of the island, but its usefulness is by no means restricted to Guam, since it contains detailed information regarding many widely distributed plants and plant products of the Pacific region. It at once established Safford's reputation as an ethnobotanist. There now followed at frequent intervals many important ethnobotanical papers, of which only a few may be mentioned: "An Aztec Narcotic, *Lophophora Williamsii*" (*Journal of Heredity*, vol. VI, 1915, pp. 291–311); "*Lignum Nephriticum*" (*Annual Report of the Smithsonian Institution . . . 1915*); "Food Plants and Textiles of Ancient America" (*Proceedings of the Second Pan-American Scientific Congress*, 1917, vol. I); "Narcotic Plants and Stimulants of the Ancient Americans" (*Annual Report . . . of the Smithsonian Institution . . . 1916*); "Daturas of the Old World and New" (*Ibid., 1920*); "Foods Discovered with America" (*Scientific Monthly*, Aug. 1925), "Peyote, the Narcotic Mescal Button of the Indians" (*Journal of the American Medical Association*, Oct. 15, 1921); and "The Potato of Romance and of Reality" (*Journal of Heredity*, 1925, vol. XVI). It was Safford's special facility with Nahuatl and other ancient American tongues and with Polynesian dialects which contributed so largely to the value of this work.

At the same time Safford was publishing systematic papers on certain groups of tropical American plants, for example, the genus *Dahlia*, the cactus family, the bull-horn acacias and their ant inhabitants, and an important long series upon the family *Annonaceae*, besides dictionary work, notes of exploration and travel, biographical sketches, and numerous botanical articles for Bailey's *Standard Cyclopedia of Horticulture* (6 vols., 1914–17). The taxonomic papers are noteworthy, especially those upon *Annonaceae*, but in Safford's complete bibliography of about 100 titles it is those subjects of ethnobotanical scope in which his genius found full expression. To the art of masterly exposition he brought a wealth of observed fact and of deep and varied erudition derived from almost innumerable historical sources. The complicated story of the potato was his last published paper. On Mar. 17, 1924, he was stricken with paralysis, but partially recovered and continued at work almost to the day of his death, which resulted from pneumonia with attendant heart complications.

Safford was intensely dynamic, with a genius for friendship, "one who loved nature profoundly but humanity not less" (Smith, *post*). He was witty and jovial, keenly inquisitive of all things, trained to acute perception that amounted almost to intuition, and extremely fluent in self-expression. Of his generation there were few better deserving of that old term of distinction—naturalist.

[W. C. Barnes, "William E. Safford," in *Science*, new ser., vol. LXIII, Apr. 23, 1926; D. C. Peattie, "Dr. William Safford," in *Am. Botanist*, vol. XXXII, Apr. 1926; T. H. Kearney, "William Edwin Safford," and E. F. Smith, "William Edwin Safford, the Man," *Jour. of Heredity*, vol. XVII, Oct. 1926; *The Official Record, U. S. Dept. of Agriculture*, vol. V, no. 3, p. 4, Jan. 20, 1926; editorial in *Evening Star* (Washington), Jan. 11, 1926; *Who's Who in America*, 1926–27; S. M. Culbertson, *The Ohio Valley Saffords* (1932); E. S. Safford, compiler, "The Saffords in America, June 1923" (typed MS., Lib. Cong.); records of Navy Dept.; personal recollections and family sources.]

W. R. M.

SAGE, BERNARD JANIN (Feb. 5, 1821–Sept. 2, 1902), lawyer, author, was born near New Haven, Conn., of New England parentage. Through his mother, *née* Lewis, he was connected with the Louisiana family which furnished Gov. Francis T. Nicholls [*q.v.*] to the latter state. Despite an early ambition to become a sailor, Bernard accepted a school training and studied law. In early manhood he entered the law office of Thomas H. Lewis in New Orleans, and in time became the owner of a sugar plantation. His marriage was said to have been prevented by the death of his fiancée and he remained a bachelor. He loved music, was somewhat pedantic, and was given to puns. He received praise for financial encouragement to young men seeking an education.

Sage was a Whig in ante-bellum politics and in 1860 supported the Bell-Everett ticket, but after the outbreak of the Civil War he served the Confederacy. He was a master in the Confederate navy, with special duties of an executive or secret nature, and was sent abroad by President Davis on special missions. After the fall of the Confederacy, he made a documentary and interpretative study in Europe of the treaty of

1783 recognizing the independence of the United States. This study, supporting the state-rights view of the origin of the Union, he expected to use in his capacity of counsel for the defense in the projected trial of Jefferson Davis. The results of the study were published in book form under the pseudonym "P. C. Centz, Barrister," the name being an adaptation, with initials, of "Plain Common Sense." The first edition appeared in London in 1865 under the title *Davis and Lee,* and the book was subsequently issued in America with the title changed to *The Republic of Republics* (4th ed., 1881). Upon its first appearance, it was referred to in the Southern press as a brilliant work by a British lawyer. It presented the argument that Davis and Lee, who were taught the doctrine of state rights at West Point, could not be considered traitors for being loyal to their respective states in the war. Sage maintained that primary allegiance was to the state, that the Union and the Constitution were formed of and by the states, and that secession, as well as the subsequent conquest of the South by the North, was a legitimate act or step under international law involving no violation of national law. Thus Davis could be defended, against any charge of treason, on the grounds of history and international law without an implication of protest as to the outcome of the war.

For a few years after the war Sage was a resident of Washington, D. C., but he spent the last thirteen years of his life in New Orleans. In 1890 he contributed the chapter on Louisiana to *Why the Solid South,* edited by Hilary A. Herbert. As the result of financial reverses he lost his plantation and became dependent, in his last days, upon the kindness of friends. He died of apoplexy in New Orleans and was buried in the Nicholls cemetery lot at Thibodaux, La.

[*Daily Picayune* (New Orleans), Sept. 3, 1902; *Times-Democrat* (New Orleans), Sept. 3, 1902; A. B. Booth, *Records of La. Confed. Soldiers and La. Confed. Commands* (1920), vol. III, bk. 2, p. 432; *The Republic of Republics* (4th ed., 1881); information from Frank Nicholls, Thibodaux, La.]   H. C. N.

SAGE, HENRY WILLIAMS (Jan. 31, 1814–Sept. 18, 1897), merchant, lumber manufacturer, and philanthropist, was born in Middletown, Conn., a descendant of David Sage who emigrated from Wales, and settled in Middletown about 1652. Henry's father was Charles Sage, who was shipwrecked on the Florida coast in 1838 and killed by Indians; his mother, Sally (Williams) Sage. Most of his youth was spent in Bristol, Conn., until 1827, when the family moved to Ithaca, N. Y. This removal thwarted his early ambition to enter Yale College. He still cherished the hope of a professional career,

however, and for a time studied medicine with Dr. Austin Church of Ithaca; but circumstances conspired to make him a business man. Ill health interrupted his medical studies, and in 1832 he found it expedient to enter the employ of his uncles, who, under the firm name of Williams & Brothers, were merchants and owners of transportation lines over the waterways of central New York. He revealed abilities of a high order, and in five years became proprietor of the business. Soon he was one of the substantial and influential men of the region and in 1847 was elected on the Whig ticket to the legislature.

Appreciating the demand for lumber that the rapid development of the country would create, he undertook to supply it on an extensive scale. Buying in 1854 a large tract of timber land around Lake Simcoe, Canada, he manufactured it there, and soon after, with John McGraw, began to draw upon the Michigan forests, his manufacturing establishment being at Winona. In 1857 he moved to Brooklyn, where he was intimately associated with Henry Ward Beecher in the affairs of Plymouth Church. Returning to Ithaca in 1880, he made that city his home until his death seventeen years later.

Sturdy in frame, with a full beard, clean-shaven upper lip, firm mouth, and shrewd eyes, Sage was in appearance the typical successful business man of the Victorian era. Deprived of a college education, he found time for private study, and was especially interested in religion, psychology, and philosophy. The furtherance of education became, moreover, in his later years, one of his chief concerns, and, since he was a friend of Ezra Cornell [*q.v.*], Cornell University was the principal object of his thought and benefactions. In 1870 he was elected to the board of trustees and in 1875 succeeded Cornell as chairman, serving until his death. In 1870 he offered to erect a college for women, and although there was opposition to making the university a coeducational institution, his offer was accepted and Sage College, a woman's dormitory, with lecture rooms and other equipment, was opened in 1874. He exerted his influence against the sale of the national lands held by the college, at a time when the trustees were sorely tempted to dispose of them, thereby "saving the future of the university . . . and making it possible for it to become one of the representative universities of the land" (Hewitt, *post*, p. 430). He furnished the funds for the erection of a chapel, dedicated in June 1875, established the Sage School of Philosophy at a cost of more than a quarter of a million of dollars, gave $560,000 to the library and its endowment, made a substantial gift to the museum of archeology, and otherwise contributed to the financial needs of the institution. No less valuable was the business sagacity which he exercised in the administrative work of the university during more than twenty-five years of its early history. His benefactions were not confined wholly to Cornell, but schools, libraries, and churches, in various parts of the country, were aided by him. In 1871 he founded the Lyman Beecher Lectures on Preaching at the Yale Divinity School. His wife was Susan Elizabeth (Linn) Sage, who died in 1885. Both are buried in the apse of Sage Chapel at Cornell.

[*Geneal. Record of the Descendants of David Sage* (1878) ; W. T. Hewitt, *Cornell Univ., a Hist.* (1905); *Memorial Exercises in Honor of Henry Williams Sage* (1898) ; *Cornell Era*, Sept. 25, 1897 ; *Albany Jour.*, Sept. 18, 1897; *Brooklyn Eagle* and *N. Y. Tribune*, Sept. 19, 1897.]   H. E. S.

SAGE, MARGARET OLIVIA SLOCUM

(Sept. 8, 1828–Nov. 4, 1918), philanthropist, was born in Syracuse, N. Y., the daughter of Joseph and Margaret Pierson (Jermain) Slocum. She was the descendant of Anthony Slocombe or Slocum, an English Quaker who emigrated to Massachusetts before 1637. Her father was a well-to-do merchant, a state assemblyman, and agent of the government to introduce American agricultural implements and methods into Russia. After studying in local schools until she was eighteen, she attended Mrs. Emma Willard's school, the Troy Female Seminary, now Russell Sage College, from which she graduated in 1847. Later, because of the financial reverses of her father, she taught at Chestnut Street Seminary, later Ogontz School, of Philadelphia for two years and thereafter from time to time as her health permitted. She spent her vacations at the Jermain estate near Troy, where she was especially welcome for her enlivening social qualities. In 1869 she became the second wife of Russell Sage [*q.v.*], who laid the foundation for his financial success in Watervliet and Troy. They had no children. During her married life she was a devoted wife; she lived the conventional existence of a well-to-do church member. In the *North American Review* of November 1905 she published an article "Opportunities and Responsibilities of Leisured Women," which reflects many of her religious and social ideas. She grasped many contemporary ideas: she believed in woman's suffrage, in practical education such as manual training schools for the children of wage-earners, in specialization in education for the self-supporting woman. She identified herself with every community in which she lived, and, especially after the inheritance of her husband's fortune made it possible, she gave liberally and discriminatingly to each of those communities. She died in New York City.

Upon her husband's death in 1906 she inherited by his will practically the whole of his fortune, something more than $63,000,000, and at once she began to distribute this money. The wide range of the objects of her charity is indicative of the character and variety of her interests. She was especially interested in the Woman's Hospital of New York, in the New York Exchange for Woman's Work, and in home and foreign missions. She gave the money to found the Russell Sage Institute of Pathology in connection with the city hospital of New York on Blackwell's Island, as well as to support the American Seamen's Friend Society, Home for the Friendless, Mount Sinai Hospital, and various relief, social, and educational agencies. She made substantial donations to the Y. W. C. A., to naval and railway Y. M. C. A. building projects, and to the international Y. M. C. A. She also bought 70,000 acres on Marsh Island in Louisiana for a bird refuge and made large bequests to the Botanical and Zoölogical Gardens, the American Natural History Museum, and the Metropolitan Museum. The enumeration in her will of eighteen colleges, the Northfield Seminary, the Northfield Training School, Tuskeegee Normal and Industrial Institute, the Idaho Industrial Institute, bespeak her interest in education. She made an initial gift of $250,000.00 to Emma Willard School for practical arts, which was supplemented until it totalled $1,000,000 and resulted in the founding of Russell Sage College in 1918.

Perhaps her greatest distinction was her gift of $10,000,000 to the Russell Sage Foundation for the improvement of social and living conditions in the United States. Established in April 1907, it was empowered by a liberal charter to use any means that should seem expedient to its members or trustees. Although Robert De Forest, her attorney and the president of the Charity Organization Society of New York City, advised her wisely in regard to this endowment, nevertheless it must be remembered that she was a woman of vigorous opinion and always acted from firm conviction. Desirous of helping the unfortunate, she was convinced that the wisest aid was to provide for the less fortunate a good environment, protect them from the unscrupulous, and give them opportunity for self-support and individual responsibility. The Sage Foundation, at that time heralded as the largest single gift to philanthropy in the history of the world, received a third of all her gifts and bequests.

[*Emma Willard and Her Pupils* (copr. 1898) ; C. E. Slocum, *Hist. of the Slocums*, vol. II (1908) ; Henry Whittemore, *Hist. of the Sage and Slocum Families* (1908) ; *Survey*, Nov. 9, 23, 1918, Apr. 3, 1909; *World's Work*, Nov. 1906; *Bird Lore*, Feb. 19, 1915; *N. Y. Times*, Nov. 4, 5, 7, 14, 1918 ; *Troy Record*, Nov. 14, 1918.]
E.E.W.

SAGE, RUSSELL (Aug. 4, 1816–July 22, 1906), congressman and financier, came of pioneer New England stock, being a descendant of David Sage who was living in Middletown, Conn., as early as 1652. His father, Elisha Sage, veteran of the War of 1812, his mother, Prudence (Risley) Sage, and five children were emigrating by ox train from Connecticut towards Michigan when Russell was born, in the covered wagon, in Verona township, Oneida County, N. Y. Observing that the land was good, Elisha Sage settled in Oneida County, and there Russell grew to the age of twelve, working on the farm and getting a few bits of primary schooling. In 1828 he went to work in his brother Henry's store in Troy, N. Y. Notwithstanding his long hours, he attended a night school, paying a dollar and a half of his monthly salary of four dollars to learn arithmetic and bookkeeping; meanwhile, he also studied markets and read newspapers omnivorously. Before he reached manhood he began to do trading on his own account and at twenty-one, with the capital thus acquired, he bought out the store of his brother Elisha Montague, and a year or so later resold it at a profit. He then (with a partner) started a wholesale grocery business in Troy. The firm had its own sailing vessels on the Hudson—and traded in other things than groceries—Vermont and Canadian horses, for example, fresh and cured meats, and grain.

In 1845 Sage was elected alderman of Troy and later treasurer of Rensselaer County. In 1848 he was a delegate to the National Whig Convention. He was nominated for congressman in 1850 and defeated, but ran again successfully in 1852. He was reëlected representative in 1854, but retired at the end of that term. In Congress he advocated the Homestead Law and free soil for Kansas, but his most noteworthy act was a resolution asking that the government take over the old mansion, "Mount Vernon," and make it a permanent memorial to Washington (*Congressional Globe*, 33 Cong., 1 Sess., pp. 52–54; Dec. 15, 1853). This was one of the first moves toward its restoration and preservation.

Leaving Congress in 1856, Sage continued to build up his fortune, adding banking to his other activities. A chance meeting with Jay Gould [*q.v.*] in a railroad station was a momentous incident in his life, for it led to a close association and to Sage's interest in railroad affairs. He had already loaned some money to the La Crosse Railroad, a small line in Wisconsin, and was compelled to advance more to save the first loans. The road was eventually expanded into the Chicago, Milwaukee & St. Paul system, in which promotion Sage made large profits. He was for years a director and vice-president of the corporation. By 1863 he was giving most of his attention to stocks and finance, and he decided to move to New York. His first wife, Maria Winne of Troy, whom he had married in 1841, died in 1867, and on Nov. 24, 1869, he married again, in Troy, his second wife being Margaret Olivia (Slocum) Sage [*q.v.*], who outlived him.

Sage is credited with being the originator of "puts and calls" in the stock market about 1872. His fortune was greatly increased by advances in the value of securities under the skilful manipulation of his ally, Jay Gould. The methods used in their campaign to gain control of the New York elevated lines in 1881 were bitterly criticized by the press and business men. Cyrus W. Field [*q.v.*], whom they had taken in with them to court public confidence, was eventually ruined, but Gould and Sage came through unscathed and with the desired control. Sage was one of the shrewdest and most conservative of all great financiers. Though at times a large operator, he was never a plunger. He preferred small, sure profits or those which resulted from manipulation, and his occasional speculative purchase was usually based on very canny foresight. He was caught short only once in his life, in the little Wall Street panic of 1884, when he lost fully $7,000,000. He was, at one time or another, stockholder and director of many railroad corporations. He was actively concerned in the organization of the Atlantic & Pacific Telegraph Company, and in its consolidation with the Western Union.

During the last quarter century of his life he was best known as a money lender. At one time he is said to have had $27,000,000 out on call loans. He might have from five to eight millions in cash bank deposits in the morning, and loan nearly all of it before the day was over. His frugality was proverbial; he loved to chaffer, even over the price of an apple, and there was no epicureanism in him. He preferred comfort rather than elegance; plain food and cheap clothing satisfied him as well as the richest. His homes on Fifth Avenue and Long Island were comfortably furnished, however; he indulged himself in a love of good horses, and did not question his wife's expenditures. His philanthropies, such as the education of more than forty Indian children and the presentation of a dormitory to Troy Female Seminary, were popularly credited to Mrs. Sage's prompting. In 1891 Sage was seriously injured in his office by a bomb exploded by one Henry W. Norcross, who had first demanded $1,200,000. Norcross and a clerk were killed, but Sage, despite his years, fully recovered. He died at his home on Long Island at the age of ninety, and his fortune at that time was estimated at $70,000,000.

[Among many newspaper references to Sage, see obituaries in all New York newspapers of July 23, 1906; *N. Y. Times,* Dec. 27, 1881, Dec. 5, 1891, Jan. 11, 1899; *World* (N. Y.), Apr. 27, July 10, 1902; *N. Y. Daily News,* Jan. 30, 1904; R. I. Warshow, *Jay Gould; the Story of a Fortune* (1928); Henry Clews, *Twenty-eight Years in Wall Street* (1887); *Who's Who in America,* 1906–07; Henry Whittemore, *Hist. of the Sage and Slocum Families* (1908); *Bench and Bar,* Sept. 1906; *N. Y. Geneal. and Biog. Record,* Oct. 1906.]
A. F. H.

ST. ANGE DE BELLERIVE, LOUIS (*c.* Oct. 1698–Dec. 27, 1774), soldier, commandant of St. Louis, and acting governor of Upper Louisiana, was born in Montreal, Canada, son of Robert Groston de St. Ange and Marguerite Crevier de Bellerive, and baptized Oct. 16, 1698. The family was of the nobility, and possibly the name St. Ange was taken from the district in Canada known as *la côte de St. Ange.* The father, who seems to have come from the province of Champagne in France, went to Canada in 1687 as a sergeant and married there in 1692. Having been sent with his father to the Missouri, in 1724 Louis went in command of one detachment with Étienne Venyard, Sieur de Bourgmont [*q.v.*], on an expedition westward for the purpose of making an alliance with the Padouka Indians. That accomplished, they returned to Fort Orleans on the Missouri. St. Ange was later stationed at a new fort established near the mouth of the Kansas River and in 1736 was appointed to succeed Jean Baptiste Bissot, Sieur de Vincennes [*q.v.*], on the Wabash River with the rank of captain. Remaining at this post for twenty-eight years, he took part in the French resistance to the English, who were crowding out the French in the Ohio Valley; and in 1764, when the treaty of Paris had ended the conflict, he conducted the evacuation of Fort Chartres as successor to Neyon de Villiers, the commandant. He retained this command for about fifteen months, until the English commander, Capt. Thomas Stirling, came to take possession on Oct. 10, 1765. A few weeks later, with his few soldiers and most of the white inhabitants, St. Ange moved across the Mississippi River to St. Louis.

At this time the territory west of the river had been transferred from France to Spain in the secret treaty of San Ildefonso, but it was incumbent upon France to govern the country until Spain should take possession. This portion of what was called the Illinois Country was never surrendered to the English and continued under the command of St. Ange until 1770, when Don Pedro Piernas arrived as the Spanish authority. St. Ange then took service as a captain in the Spanish army, but he was now advanced in years and remained in St. Louis until his death. During this time his wise counsel was much sought not only by the people, who depended on him as their friend and able intermediary with the Spanish authorities, but by the Spanish lieutenant-governor as well. He died a bachelor at the home of Madame Marie Thérèse (Bourgeois) Chouteau, where he had lived for some time.

[Cyprien Tanguay, *Dictionnaire Généalogique des Familles Canadiennes,* vol. IV (1887); W. B. Douglas, "The Sieurs de St. Ange," *Ill. State Hist. Soc. Pubs.,* no. 14 (1910); *Wis. Hist. Soc. Colls.,* vol. XVII (1906); Baron Marc de Villiers du Terrage, *La Découverte du Missouri et l'Histoire du Fort d'Orléans* (1925) and *Les Dernières Années de la Louisiana Française* (1904); Pierre Margry, ed., *Découvertes et Établissements des Français dans l'Ouest,* vol. VI (1886); J. P. Dunn, "Docs. Relating to French Settlements on the Wabash," *Ind. Hist. Soc. Pubs.,* vol. II (1895); C. W. Alvord, "The Critical Period 1763–1765," *Ill. State Hist. Lib. Colls.,* vol. X (1915); will of St. Ange, MS. in possession of *Mo. Hist. Soc.,* printed in F. L. Billon, *Annals of St. Louis* (1886), pp. 125–27.] S. M. D.

ST. CLAIR, ARTHUR (Mar. 23, 1736 o.s.– Aug. 31, 1818), soldier, governor of Northwest Territory, was born in Thurso, Caithness County, Scotland. He is often erroneously said to have been the son of Margaret Balfour (Wedderburn) and James St. Clair, an officer in the French army, and the grandson of the Baron of Rosslyn. He was probably the son of William Sinclair, a merchant, and the great-grandson of James Sinclair, second Laird of Assery. His mother may have been Elizabeth (Balfour) Sinclair (John Henderson, *Caithness Family Hist.,* 1884, p. 335; L. A. Morrison, *The Hist. of the Sinclair Family,* 1896, p. 43). It is said that he enjoyed the advantages of an incomplete term at the University of Edinburgh and an unsuccessful apprenticeship under William Hunter, the celebrated anatomist of London. In 1757 he became an ensign in the British army and served with Amherst in Canada. On May 15, 1760, he married Phoebe Bayard, of Boston, a niece of Gov. James Bowdoin [*q.v.*]. They had seven children. He resigned from the army in 1762 with the commission of lieutenant, and, later, with a legacy of £14,000 from the Bowdoin estate and his own military service claims he purchased an estate of some 4,000 acres in the Ligonier valley of western Pennsylvania. As the largest resident property owner in Pennsylvania west of the mountains, he was placed in an anomalous position, when Governor Penn in 1771 made him the agent of colonial government in this frontier country. As justice of the county court of Westmoreland County after its formation in 1773, he was obliged to extend the form but not the substance of government into the Pittsburgh area, at the same time that John Connolly, captain of the militia and after 1774 justice of the district of western Augusta County, Va., sought to extend the substance as well as the form of Virginian control over the same region. St. Clair was unsuccessful before the superior military force and greater popular appeal of the Virginians, who rebuilt and garrisoned the fort abandoned by the British in 1772 and prepared for the surveying and occupation of the Kentucky country. Supported by the fur traders, he refused to cooperate in these and other actions offensive to the Shawnee Indians and thus probably relieved Pennsylvania of the vengeance of that tribe in Dunmore's War of 1774. He favored rewarding the Delaware Indians for their neutrality in the face of frontier insults but acquiesced in the refusal of Penn and the legislature to establish and garrison a satisfactory trading post at the Delaware town of Kittanning.

As the Revolutionary War came on, he was made a member of the Committee of Safety of Westmoreland County, but he was powerless to extend Pennsylvania control over the Pittsburgh area, as the Virginia committee sent John Neville [q.v.] to occupy the fort and as Virginia's commissioners undertook most of the financial burdens and diplomatic manipulation at the treaty of Pittsburgh in 1775, by which the outstanding issues of Dunmore's War were settled and a Loyalist-Indian uprising prevented. At this treaty he occupied the minor position of secretary to the relatively insignificant commissioners of the Continental Congress. In 1775 he was sent as colonel to take part in the retreat of the American army from Canada. In the winter of 1776–77, as brigadier-general, he was with Washington in the campaign and the battles of Trenton and Princeton. In the spring of 1777, as major-general, he was ordered to the defense of Fort Ticonderoga, which was popularly considered as impregnable. His evacuation of the post, probably as the result of factors beyond his control, filled the public mind with such dismay that he was recalled by Congress from service in the field. Although he was completely exonerated by a court martial in September 1778 (*Proceedings of a General Court Martial . . . for the Trial of*

Major General St. Clair, Aug. 25, 1778, 1778, and reprinted in *New York Historical Society Collections,* vol. XIII, 1881), he was not, for the rest of the war, placed in a position to render conspicuous service.

On his return to civil life he entered Pennsylvania politics as an anti-constitutionalist. As a member of the council of censors in 1783, he unsuccessfully opposed the constitution of 1776, and he wrote the majority report recommending a new constitutional convention in order to abolish the unicameral legislature and other radical features. Elected state delegate to the Continental Congress he served from Nov. 2, 1785, to Nov. 28, 1787, and was president in 1787. With the creation of the Northwest Territory in 1787, he was appointed governor and served until 1802. As administrator of Indian affairs he was obliged to defend the treaties made with the tribes in 1784 and 1785, which deprived them of much land north of the Ohio, and which the Indians claimed had been forced upon them by fraud and military compulsion. They insisted upon a treaty to make the Ohio River the boundary and to be drawn up at a grand council in which all the tribes were fairly represented. At the treaty of Fort Harmar in 1789, however, he met only part of the Indians concerned, permitted those present to weaken their strength by quarreling among themselves, and finally manipulated the tribes into an apparent acceptance of the earlier and much hated treaties. The resulting dissatisfaction led into a war in which he, as major-general and commander of the federal army, was surprised and overwhelmingly defeated on Nov. 4, 1791, on a branch of the Wabash about a day's march from the site of Fort Wayne. The defeat was administered by a confederated Indian army with the Miami, Little Turtle [q.v.], which was inferior in numbers to the American army.

St. Clair was under positive and unalterable orders to erect a chain of military posts from Fort Washington, near the mouth of the Miami, to the rapids of the Maumee in the heart of the country of the then powerful Miami confederacy. Few military enterprises have been more poorly planned and executed. He was originally directed to set out from Fort Washington in July, but he did not do so until September. The result was that the frosts destroyed the grass, which was the only source of food for the horses and cattle. The delay was caused in part by the prolongation of the peace mission of Thomas Proctor, until the final and unsuccessful outcome of which St. Clair was obliged to postpone all offensive movements. Blundering in the quartermaster's department resulted in the failure to provide adequate supplies and arms. The morale of the army, two-thirds of which was militia and from which many had deserted, was also undermined by the fact that during their six months' service they received their monthly pay of three dollars but once, by short rations, and by the rigorous and non-military services required of them by St. Clair. St. Clair himself was not so experienced in frontier and Indian warfare as was his second in command, Gen. Richard Butler [q.v.], though he seems to have been more able. He declined to accept Butler's opinions and advice on certain technical matters, and the resulting estrangement continued throughout the campaign. At no time during the expedition did St. Clair have sufficient knowledge of the numbers and location of the Indians opposing him. The disaster was most humiliating, and, although he was exonerated from blame by Washington and by a committee of the House of Representatives, he resigned from the army and devoted himself to his duties as governor of the Northwest Territory. His ambitions for advancement in Federalist politics were, of course, checked.

In governing the frontiersmen of the Northwest Territory, he sought to enforce the spirit and the letter of the highly centralized and undemocratic Ordinance of 1787. With an overbearing manner and a paternal zeal too uncomplimentary to his frontier citizens, he objected to much proposed legislation that was aimed to decentralize the functions and control of local institutions. He objected to statehood as premature and sought to gerrymander the territory into smaller territories so as to postpone statehood indefinitely. The result was a movement by the local Jeffersonians in 1801 to remove him from office, and, at the same time, to create the state of Ohio. They were successful in the latter but failed in the former, until St. Clair at the constitutional convention of 1802 denounced as a nullity the Ohio enabling act of Congress. He was thereupon removed from office by Jefferson. He retired to his home, the "Hermitage," near Ligonier, Pa., where he developed his estate and built an iron furnace to manufacture stoves and castings. Owing to generous lending of money, signing notes for friends, and the failure of the Republican Congress to reimburse him for moneys advanced for government use while he was the Federalist governor of the Northwest Territory, he lost the whole of his fortune. In 1812 he published in defense of himself, *A Narrative of the Manner in which the Campaign against the Indians in . . . [1791] was conducted under the command of Major General St. Clair, together with . . . the Reports of the Committees appointed to*

inquire into the causes of the failure thereof. His later years were spent in poverty and political oblivion, and he died in the log cabin that was his home on Chestnut Ridge.

[St. Clair Papers in Ohio State Lib., Columbus, Ohio; some papers in Lib. of Cong.; papers of proceedings of the treaty of Fort Harmar, Draper Coll., Frontier Wars MSS., vol. XXIII, pp. 75–143, State Hist. Soc. of Wis., Madison; *Territorial Papers of the U. S.*, vols. II, III, "The Territory Northwest of the River Ohio" (1934), ed. by C. E. Carter; *Pa. Archives*, 1 ser. vol. IV (1853); *American State Papers: Military Affairs*, vol. I (1832); *Military Jour. of Maj. Ebenezer Denny* (1859); W. H. Smith, *The St. Clair Papers* (2 vols., 1882); Ellis Beals, "Arthur St. Clair, Western Pennsylvania's Leading Citizen," *Western Pa. Hist. Mag.*, Apr., July 1929; R. C. Downes, "The Statehood Contest in Ohio," *Miss. Valley Hist. Rev.*, Sept. 1931 and *Frontier Ohio*, Ohio Arch. and Hist. Soc. Series, vol. II (in proof 1934); birthdate from statement of the contents of register of baptisms in Thurso (Henderson, ante), and dependent on validity of above statement of parentage.]   R. C. D.

ST. DENIS (DENYS), LOUIS JUCHEREAU de

ST. DENIS (DENYS), LOUIS JUCHEREAU de (Sept. 17, 1676–June 11, 1744), French explorer, colonizer, commandant, was born in Canada at Beauport, Que., of which his father Nicolas was seigneur; his mother was Marie-Thérèse Giffard. After a Canadian boyhood he joined at the age of twenty-two the expedition of Pierre le Moyne, Sieur d'Iberville [q.v.], when he founded Louisiana, and in 1700 accompanied Jean Baptiste le Moyne, Sieur de Bienville [q.v.], on a trip of exploration to the Red River of Louisiana. Somewhat later (1702–05) he was in charge of a post on the lower Mississippi, while the capital of the colony was at Biloxi. He engaged in several expeditions into the Indian country and in 1710 again mounted Red River to the country of the Natchitoches Indians, where he traded with these and neighboring tribes in what is now Texas. In 1711 a Spanish missionary in that region wrote to the French officer at Mobile offering opportunities to trade with the Texas Indians. In 1713 Cadillac, then governor, sent St. Denis to open a route across Texas and begin the Indian trade. Once more ascending Red River to the Natchitoches, he founded a post there and crossed to the Rio Grande but was detained by the Spaniards at the presidio of San Juan Bautista until orders could come from Mexico. During his detention he wooed the commandant's grand-daughter, Mañuela Sánchez Ramón, and Feb. 17, 1716, they were married— a romantic incident unduly magnified by Gayarré (*post*) and older historians of Louisiana. Meanwhile he had been sent to Mexico, where he was kept in prison until he persuaded the authorities to allow him to accompany as guide a Spanish expedition which in 1716 was sent to found missions in the region north of Mexico. Because of this service he has been accused of bad faith or double dealing; apparently at that time he attempted to be all things to all men, Spanish as well as French. Returning to Mobile and reporting his success to Cadillac, he was furnished with new goods and in 1717 went back via Natchitoches to San Juan, where his goods were seized. Going to Mexico city to protest, he was a second time imprisoned but finally escaped on Sept. 5, 1718, arriving at Natchitoches early the next year. His escapades and smuggling enterprises created an international incident when the king of France asked his agent at Madrid to find out secretly what Spain meant to do with this adventurer; but as the two nations were at peace no further attempt was made to restrain his trading incursions. He arrived at Natchitoches from Mobile in 1719; there his wife joined him, and there he spent the remainder of his life, a thorn in the side of the Spanish in Mexico. When the news of his death reached Mexico city the governor of that time exclaimed in effect, "St. Denis is dead, thank God! Now we can breathe easier."

An incident of his later years was the repulsion in 1731 of an attack by the rebellious Natchez Indians upon Fort St. Jean at Natchitoches, which he commanded. Four years later the fort was moved to the site of the present Natchitoches, where, "fortified by all the sacraments of the church," St. Denis was buried within the walls of the old church building, his Spanish wife beside him. He had great influence with the Indians of Texas and Louisiana, for he spoke their languages and they trusted him; and he maintained for a quarter of a century an outpost for France on the Spanish border which was useful in commercial and diplomatic affairs.

[G. P. Garrison, *Texas* (1903), first correctly outlined St. Denis's history after its gross exaggeration by Charles Gayarré, *Hist. of La.*, vol. I (1854). See also Cyprien Tanguay, *Dictionnaire Généalogique des Familles Canadiennes*, vol. I (1871); L. G. Bugbee, "The Real Saint-Denis," *Texas Hist. Assoc. Quart.*, Apr. 1898; Charmion C. Shelby, "St. Denis's Second Expedition to the Rio Grande 1716–1719," *Southwestern Hist. Quart.*, Jan. 1924; C. E. Castañeda, "Silent Years in Tex. Hist.," *Ibid.*, Oct. 1934; H. E. Bolton, *Tex. in the Middle Eighteenth Century* (1915); S. C. Arthur and G. C. H. de Kernion, *Old Families of La.* (1931); C. W. Hackett, ed., *Pichado's Treatise on Limits of La. and Tex.*, vol. I (1931).]   L.P.K.

SAINT-GAUDENS, AUGUSTUS (Mar. 1, 1848–Aug. 3, 1907), sculptor, owed his salience in American art to a dual significance in his work. It was rooted primarily in intrinsic gifts and then in the influence which he exercised upon his contemporaries. He was a recognized *chef d'école*, long leading and accelerating the movement liberating sculpture in the United States

from an arid convention. There had been distinguished men before him and one of them, whom he came to know in his young manhood, J. Q. A. Ward [*q.v.*], an artist of very high abilities, had already pointed the way promising escape from a thin academic hypothesis. But it was left to Saint-Gaudens to effect the essential modernization of a school, to gather up the elements of progress and illustrate their potency through large and varied achievement.

He was wont to say that "no one ever succeeded in art unless born with an uncontrollable instinct toward it," and he had such an instinct. How he came into possession of it is a mystery. He sprang from a family of French shoemakers, settled in the little town of Aspet, some fifty miles from Toulouse. Bernard Paul Ernest Saint-Gaudens, his father, was taught the trade in an elder brother's factory at Carcassonne. He seems to have been of a roving disposition for he is presently found in London and subsequently, for full seven years, in Dublin. It was in Dublin that he married Mary McGuinness, who was native Irish, and there, in a house on Charlemount Street, Augustus was born. Two elder brothers died young, but later there were younger ones. Within six months of his birth the family had taken ship for the United States, landing in Boston. Shortly afterwards they were established in New York, where Bernard Saint-Gaudens was for years to flourish as a maker of shoes. It was in the workroom that Augustus, making pen drawings of the shoemakers, first disclosed his "uncontrollable instinct." His father was wholly sympathetic. Augustus tells how, when he was thirteen and had finished his modest schooling, he was informed that it was time to go to work and asked what he would like to do. "I don't care," he said, "but I should like it if I could do something which would help me to be an artist" (*Reminiscences*, I, 38). Promptly Bernard apprenticed him to one Avet, a pioneer stone-cameo cutter and a hard taskmaster. Later he was employed by Jules Le Brethon, a shell-cameo cutter. This experience at the lathe was doubly valuable for it not only nurtured his artistic aptitude but gave him a craft with which he was to eke out a livelihood while engaged in the struggle of a young and unknown sculptor.

He describes himself as "a terrific worker" at this time, cameo cutting all day and studying drawing at Cooper Union at night. There followed a period of drawing from the nude at the National Academy of Design. He developed rapidly in his work and had, besides, sublime confidence in himself. He was only nineteen when the wise and kind Bernard asked him if he wouldn't like to see the Paris Exposition, that of 1867. He sailed in February, with his passage paid and a hundred dollars in his pocket, launched upon a strenuous career. The first necessity was a means of self-support. His skill as a cameo cutter won it for him at once, with Lupi, an Italian in the Rue des Trois Frères. He could not as readily obtain entrance into the École des Beaux-Arts. That required a paper from the American Legation, which turned up nine months after his application for it had been made. While waiting he frequented a small school in the Rue de l'École de Médecine. "Here," he says, "I modeled my first figures from the nude, and laid an excellent foundation for the future" (*Ibid.,* I, 69). When at last he was accepted at the Beaux-Arts he chose the *atelier* of Jouffroy. He confesses that he was not a brilliant pupil and did not shine in the competitions. But Jouffroy grounded him well and the whole atmosphere of this period of pupilage stimulated the talent stirring within him without fixing it in any mould, the master's or that of any one else. The antique interested him and helped him but could not land him in a formula. Already he was sympathetic also to the naturalistic elements in the Renaissance and when, at the time of the Franco-Prussian War, he left for Rome, he continued, even under the tremendous pressure of that city's august tradition, to be his own man. Rome enchanted him, as it was to do all his life long. "It was as if a door had been thrown wide open to the eternal beauty of the classical" (*Ibid.,* I, 104). Yet it is significant that he began in Rome not with an Apollo or a Venus but with a Hiawatha.

At this point it is well to pause upon some consideration of Saint-Gaudens as a man. He had been a lively boy and from his youth up he was the same energetic and resilient type, sensitive, gay, full of humor, incurably independent, and avid of experience. Born when he was, divers great personalities and events came to touch his imagination. He could recall seeing Rachel act and hearing Brignoli sing. He could recollect the repercussions of the Civil War and one of the vividest pictures in his memory was of himself as a lad falling into line at the City Hall to see the body of Lincoln lying in state. His first period in Paris, as has been noted, was terminated by the War of 1870, and in Rome he watched the famous entry of Victor Emmanuel II. The sensations of life crowded in upon him and fertilized his mind and character. Through it all he worked like a demon. There never was a more industrious artist, one readier to tackle arduous tasks and to see them through in the highest spirits. In

the *atelier Jouffroy* he used to electrify, and possibly amuse, his comrades by singing the Marseillaise (*Ibid.,* I, 78) and often at his work he was wont to sing. He drew upon unusual stores of resolution and perseverance. The story of Saint-Gaudens is not by any means one of swift growth and facile triumph but, on the contrary, one of persistent effort and hard-won success.

Some of his severest tests were to come in Rome, where he was dogged by illness and economic difficulties. There, to be sure, the dealer Rossi paid him well for the cameo cutting which was ever in reserve as a crutch, but when the "Hiawatha" was about ready to be cast in plaster he lacked the money to have the work done. But it was in Rome, too, that fortune began to smile. There he had the first of the friendly encounters which were frequently to smooth his path. Montgomery Gibbs appeared upon the scene, to make the casting of the "Hiawatha" possible, and to order portraits of his two daughters in return (*Ibid.,* I, 113). Through the Gibbs family also there came about commissions for copies of the busts of Demosthenes and Cicero, for William M. Evarts, and the opportunity to make a bust of that eminent personage. He attacked the Evarts problem in New York, on the occasion of a visit home, but it was not long before he was in Europe again, to meet in Rome Augusta F. Homer, who on June 4, 1877, at Roxbury (now part of Boston), Mass., was to become his wife. The Evarts bust suggests the strain that was to run like a leading motive throughout the sculptor's career, the strain of portraiture. But side by side with it, subordinated to it only by fate and not by choice, ran his interest in imaginative design. The "Hiawatha," in marble, now at Saratoga, offers one early testimony to this. The "Silence," a figure in the Masonic Temple in New York, offers another. In Rome also he made a study for a slave holding the young Augustus on the top of a column, setting a laurel crown upon his brow. Saint-Gaudens was ever to have his dreams, his vein of poetic feeling. From his boyhood he remembered climbing a hill on Staten Island, to find that there were other hills farther away, the source of his "first feeling of the ever-mysterious beyond." When for a time Europe was left behind him and he was settled in a prosaic studio in New York he would "turn on the water at the little wash-basin, let it run continuously with a gentle tinkle, and thus recall the sound of the fountain in the garden at Rome" (*Ibid.,* I, 157). Only a poet could have done that. In the life he now began to organize at home the artist above all others whose influence he recognized, whose friendship was most important to him, was

John La Farge [*q.v.*]. But the making of portraits was to prove a portentous factor.

Two full-length statues fell to his lot, the "Admiral Farragut" for Madison Square in New York and the "Captain Randall" for Sailors' Snug Harbor, Staten Island. To keep replenished the poetic fire in him there was also the large relief, "Adoration of the Cross by Angels" which John La Farge got for him to do, in association with certain paintings of his own, in the chancel of St. Thomas's Church, in New York (burnt in 1905). Of the relief La Farge said, "there is a breath of Italy in it" (*Ibid.*, I, 201), by which he must have meant its grace, its tenderness. Quite other traits were requisite in the "Farragut," the first production in which Saint-Gaudens was authoritatively to affirm his ability and leadership. He needed now force, directness, insight into the springs of character, and the power to express character in monumental design. Richer in these things than perhaps he himself knew, he leapt into something like fame. The "Farragut," exhibited in the plaster at Paris in 1880 and unveiled in 1881, when Saint-Gaudens was in his early thirties, was to prove a landmark in his life and in the history of American sculpture; in the former because it decisively disclosed his mastery, and in the latter because it did so much to further what might be called the humanization of a national art. Gone was the old convention. Some trace of idealism, it is true, remained, in the symbolical figures depicted in relief on the pedestal. But the surmounting admiral, set four-square as though upon his quarter-deck, challenged all the formulas of the academy. He was placed realistically before the world, a living embodiment, and, moreover, the whole design struck a new and vital note. Here was racy characterization joined to original composition, a public memorial with the stamp of creative art upon it. It was the better because Saint-Gaudens had the collaboration of Stanford White [*q.v.*] in the pedestal. This was a happy augury. The two were thenceforth to be similarly allied upon numerous occasions, White's genius for a pedestal being akin to his friend's genius for a statue. They worked together in extraordinary harmony. But what is peculiarly prefigured in the "Farragut" is Saint-Gaudens' function as interpreter of major figures in American life, especially those of the Civil War. It is impossible, of course, to traverse in detail the conception and development of each project in this field, interesting as it would be to describe, for example, the long struggles from which the "Farragut" emerged and the slow, infinitely painstaking way in which, at home or abroad, Saint-Gaudens worked out his many problems. But treating the subject at large emphasis may justly first be placed upon the historical content of the sculptor's work.

Curiously, it did not rest, at the outset, upon exhaustive research. He was not, until he had reached his prime, a great reader. One hears little in the *Reminiscences* of the sources of his inspiration for portraiture. But some subtly clairvoyant quality seems to have served him well. One feels it in "The Puritan" (1885), which began with some thought of a particular personality (Deacon Samuel Chapin) but ended as the embodiment of a type. One feels it far more in those commemorative figures for which Saint-Gaudens could find authentic documentation. Thus it is in the standing "Lincoln" in Lincoln Park, Chicago, which came within six years of the "Farragut," and the seated "Lincoln" for the Chicago Lake Front, which dates from 1907. Thus it is likewise with the equestrian "General John A. Logan" (1897), at Chicago, and the "Shaw Memorial" opposite the State House, Boston, which, long delayed, was unveiled in the same year. Thus finally it is with the equestrian "Sherman," of 1903, in Fifth Avenue Plaza, New York. These works are nothing if not eloquently expressive of the different individualities portrayed. If they are beautiful as monuments they are also intensely human as records. Allusion has been made to the sculptor's clairvoyance in these matters, his dependence upon some mysterious *flair* for the secrets of personality. The time came when he went more deliberately into the subject. His son assigns this time to the early nineties, the period immediately following the Stevenson relief (1887) and the Sherman bust (1888). Both men profoundly stirred Saint-Gaudens and spurred in him "a desire to comprehend the mental significance of the man before him," so that afterwards he would begin a portrait "by reading all possible biographies of the subject, or, if the person he planned to model was alive, keeping him in a constant state of conversation" (Homer Saint-Gaudens, in *Reminiscences*, I, 388–89). He would spare no pains to build his portrait from within and this, as it happened, was at one with his habit of work, which was slow, even hesitant, subject not only to his own criticism but to that which he asked of his friends, ever anxious as he was to get at "the last word" of truth. On the other hand, the hypothesis of a piercing, half-unconscious, imaginative penetration to the heart of a problem, directing and governing all his other resources, still holds. His statues carry conviction because they are spiritually "of the centre," based on a spontaneous, inner understanding of what he was doing. That he was himself possibly aware of this is dimly suggested by one of his axioms: "Conceive an idea. Then stick to it. Those who hang on are the only ones who amount to anything" (*Ibid.*, II, 19). He hung on. With the saying just quoted there may well be bracketed another: "After all, it's the way the thing's done that makes it right or wrong, that's about the only creed I have in art" (*Ibid.*, I, 344).

The way in which the thing was done meant, with Saint-Gaudens, a singular union of delicacy and strength. Perhaps the best introduction to a study of his technique is to be had through consideration of the portraits in low relief which he began to model as far back as the seventies, the "Rodman Gilder" (1879), the "Bastien-Lepage" (1880), the "Homer Saint-Gaudens" (1882). That passion for the classical which so stirred him on his first sojourn in Rome and which never really left him, was transmuted into something very suave yet free and bold, something akin to the realism of the Renaissance masters. His early medallions, so exquisitely touched, so tender in the modulation of surfaces, are also vitalized portraits, as declarative of personality as the figures which he was later to do in the round. The outstanding example is the "Bastien-Lepage" and its great merit, it should be remarked, lies not alone in its truth and subtle modeling but in the feeling for design which pervades it. The placing of the head and shoulders within the rectangle, the disposition of the painter's palette and brushes, to say nothing of the hands themselves, point to a trait constant in Saint-Gaudens, his solicitude for simple—and charming—composition. It embraced also, of course, the matter of lettering which always went with the subject, though this might amount to nothing more than the name of the sitter, the date, and the artist's signature. The inscription was made part and parcel of the whole. In the Paris studio in which the big "Stevenson" for Saint Giles' Cathedral, Edinburgh, was carried to completion (1887–1902) a friend sat with the sculptor and watched an assistant working over the letters under criticism and instructions that might, in their minute concern, have been evoked over the handling of the figure itself. It has been told that the 1052 letters composing this inscription were modeled twelve times over. Sometimes the medallions were more or less elaborately conceived, as in the case of "The Children of Jacob H. Schiff," with its dog and the gracefully decorative festoons flung from one pilaster to another, but as a rule Saint-Gaudens reduced his design to the sparest elements. The simplicity of unity belongs also to the reliefs which he executed on a large scale,

such as the "Shaw Memorial" and the "Dr. James McCosh" (1889).

Portraiture, it is obvious from the foregoing, incessantly engaged him, yet more attention should be given to Saint-Gaudens as an imaginative artist in the broadest sense than he commonly receives. The lure of that "ever mysterious beyond" was with him all his life. It was surely not a predilection for bald prose that moved him in his early manhood to make the "Hiawatha" and the "Silence," and those productions of his immaturity foreshadow the gusts of purely creative invention which were repeatedly to visit him. In one of his letters from Paris, written in 1898, there is a passage warmly tinctured by this recurrent emotion. "I have been having a desire lately to do a nude," he says, "suggested by a man in the street; a working-man coming home from work carrying his child (who had rushed out to meet him) astride his shoulders. I want to make a Venus carrying a winged figure of Love on her shoulders in some such fashion, and the little God of Felicity and Misery shooting his bow" (*Ibid.*, II, 192–93). There were so many portraits to do that it would seem as if all his dreams of sailing off into the blue were bound to be frustrated. As a matter of fact he had more than one opportunity to turn his thoughts into idealistic paths. There was the relief of the "Adoration of the Cross," for St. Thomas's. There were the angels for the Morgan tomb at Hartford, Conn.—which by coincidence were also lost by fire (1882). The angelic figure haunted Saint-Gaudens and left a distinct mark upon his art. He divined it with great feeling in the lovely figures for the Morgan tomb and again in the celebrated "Amor Caritas" (1887) which represents him in the Luxembourg. The truly spiritual visage and the slender uplifted arms in that bronze are illustrative of his gift for etherealized beauty. The drapery shows his technical skill also, that and his command over line and over light and shade. Even a condensed survey of his imaginative works must take account, further, of the nude "Diana" modeled in 1892 for the tower of Madison Square Garden in New York, and of the symbolical groups for the Boston Public Library which were left unfinished at his death. One of the last things upon which he worked was the head for the Christ forming part of the Phillips Brooks monument in Boston. Of all this idealistic work of his it is to be said that it is touched with nobility. There is nothing in it that is earth-bound, that is sensuous, that partakes of the super-sophistication so often encountered in modern sculpture. Saint-Gaudens was puzzled when he tried to philosophize life but some indefinable groping toward the light brought him to a state of mind in which he saw things with a certain loftiness. "In one of my blue fits the other day," he once wrote, "I felt the end of all things, and, reasoning from one thing to the other and about the hopelessness of trying to fathom what it all means, I reached this; we know nothing (of course), but a deep conviction came over me like a flash that at the bottom of it all, whatever it is, the mystery must be beneficent; it does not seem as if the bottom of all were something malevolent. And the thought was a great comfort" (*Ibid.*, II, 120). Once he said to his friend Dr. Henry Shiff that "beauty must mean at least some goodness" (*Ibid.*, II, 203).

He was a meditative man, with whom reverie had a curiously grave undertone and it is characteristic that, despite his natural gayety, his imaginative work has a marked seriousness about it. There is no gross strain in the "Diana," only a spare, refined elegance. Nowhere is his art purer, more elevated, than in the "Adams Monument" (1891), in Rock Creek Cemetery, Washington, his one essay in the grand style. The bronze figure, seated in its heavy drapery on granite, against granite, has taxed the ingenuity of observers eager to find a title for it and to identify the artist's symbolical purpose. Some have sought to invest it with the meaning of Eastern philosophy, of Buddha. Others have attached to it a Christian symbolism. Henry Adams, who commissioned the monument for his wife's grave, was inclined to call it "The Peace of God." Saint-Gaudens himself, pressed for an explanation, suggested "The Mystery of the Hereafter," adding that his idea was to express something "beyond pain, and beyond joy" (*Ibid.*, I, 362–63). The bronze remains enigmatic. This silent form, muffled as in unearthly garments, is "a mysterious, sphinx-like presence, strange and massive with something of terror, but more of solemn dignity and beauty, in its broad simple lines" (Cortissoz, *Augustus Saint-Gaudens*, p. 30). Simplicity! It is the keynote to the sculptor's art, the most durable of the elements which he drank in when Rome opened for him the door to "the eternal beauty of the classical." In the "Adams Monument" he "conceives an idea" in its quiddity and never wavers from his central inspiration but, like your genuine poet, he leaves something that defies analysis in his work. He swathes his figure in a robe itself free from teasing details and in arranging its folds, in carrying them to a hood-like formation around the head and arm, he attains to an effect of heroic majesty. It is impossible to avoid superlatives in touching upon

this monument. The truth is that nothing quite like it for tragic power has been put forth in American or European sculpture in recent times. The French Dubois, for whom Saint-Gaudens had unmeasured admiration, might have given it a more antique accent. His countryman, Rodin, might have made it more palpitant, more romantic. But neither of them could have produced so poetically the atmosphere of the "ever mysterious beyond," and neither of them could have left it more impressively stamped with the distinction of style. Saint-Gaudens did many fine things. The standing "Lincoln" at Chicago, for example, is a masterpiece of characterization and of plastic design. The "Sherman," in New York, is one of the few great equestrian monuments of modern times, if not the greatest of them all. But for creative energy and originality, for spiritual force and for the sure fusion of dramatic purpose with technical authority and breadth, the "Adams Monument" is Saint-Gaudens' best bid for immortality.

That bid was established primarily upon an imaginative conception but the technical authority just mentioned had much to do with it and with the ever-widening scope of the sculptor's influence. A distinguished French critic, Paul Leroi, once exclaimed over what he called the beautiful integrity of Saint-Gaudens' work. "It is work well done," he said. "It is true; it is sincere; . . . he has never made any sacrifices to réclame" (*Ibid.*, p. 24). His contemporaries in the United States were quick to recognize this and his example reacted upon the whole body of American sculpture. Explaining in his *Reminiscences* why the "Shaw Memorial" had taken him an unconscionable time to complete, he says: "My own delay I excuse on the ground that a sculptor's work endures for so long that it is next to a crime for him to neglect to do everything that lies in his power to execute a result that will not be a disgrace. There is something extraordinarily irritating, when it is not ludicrous, in a bad statue" (*Reminiscences*, II, 78–79).

He not only endeavored to improve existing conditions by making good statues but in divers other ways did what he could to keep American art on the side of the angels. An old Parisian comrade of his, Bion, once called him a "righter of wrongs." It was an apt designation. A sketch of his life would be incomplete without some reference to the share he took in the general development of artistic matters. In 1877, when he was but twenty-nine, he plunged with avidity into the controversy between the older and the younger generations in the National Academy of Design that then came to a head, and he acted as one of the founders of the Society of American Artists. This organization crystallized the newer ideas arising from contact with Paris, it assembled under a liberal program many of the finest talents thrown up in American art, and Saint-Gaudens was a constructive leader in its campaign. He was all for progress and the world well lost. As time went on he steadily participated in the various projects looking to advance. He taught, devotedly, at the Art Students' League (c. 1888–97). He took promising young artists into his studio, as helpers, always admonishing them "to develop technique and then to hide it." When the Chicago Exposition of 1893 was toward he went on with Richard Morris Hunt and Charles F. McKim to confer with Daniel H. Burnham [qq.v.], who wanted him to supervise the entire sculptural aspect of the fabric. He could not do this but in an advisory capacity he watched over the modeling of the "Columbus" before the Administration Building by Mary Lawrence (later Mrs. Tonetti) and it was on his suggestion that Daniel Chester French made the stately "Liberty" in the lagoon and that Frederick W. MacMonnies did his famous fountain. The satisfaction that he had in this work by Mac-Monnies, who had begun professional life in his studio, was like Saint-Gaudens in its generosity. He was wonderfully appreciative of his juniors when he felt that they were on the right track. One of them, a total stranger to him, had on a certain occasion just put a fine relief into place. Saint-Gaudens on seeing it promptly ferreted out the young man's address and drove to it, post haste, in a cab. "I am Mr. Saint-Gaudens," he said to the astonished sculptor who opened the door, "and I've come down to tell you what I think of the beautiful work you have done" (Cortissoz, *Augustus Saint-Gaudens,* pp. 73–74).

When Charles F. McKim was founding the American Academy in Rome Saint-Gaudens labored to promote its interests, even bringing himself to what was, for him, the agonizing point of making speeches in support of them. It is pertinent to borrow some sentences from one of these, as throwing light upon his point of view: "In the repeated attacks that are made on the Roman Academy and on the École des Beaux Arts and in the incessant cry for greater freedom in the development of the artistic mind, there is a certain amount of truth. But in such reaction the pendulum swings too far and the real question is lost sight of. There is a middle ground on which to stand. It seems to be rarely realized that the very men who are shown as examples against the

schools were, if not actually brought up in the School of Rome, all men of thorough academic training. Only after such training does the mind become sufficiently mature and the individual personality so developed as to be able to indulge in unqualified freedom and liberty of expression" (*Reminiscences,* II, 262). In such ideas he may be said to have stated his artistic testament. He knew that the "divine fire," as he recognized it in sculptors so varied as Houdon, Rude, and Dubois, in such painters as Baudry and Puvis de Chavannes, was indispensable. But so, he believed, was rigorous training, the technical power without which the divine fire glows in vain. When Dubois died and a friend wrote to Saint-Gaudens expressing his sympathy, the sculptor replied: "I agree with what you say about Dubois. I agree with both hands and all my heart. He . . . has had more to do with keeping a high standard among those who believe, as you say, in 'thorough discipline' than any other man in a century at least" (*Ibid.,* II, 49–50). Thorough discipline was his own watchword. If the long list of the works with which he enriched American sculpture embraces so many affirmations of beauty it testifies also to his devoted craftsmanship.

His struggles toward achievement were arduous to the point of exhaustion. "People think a sculptor has an easy life in a studio," he said to a friend as in his workshop they threaded a maze of clay models, plaster casts, scaffolds and ladders in which assistants were at work. "It's hard labor, in a factory" (Cortissoz, *Augustus Saint-Gaudens,* p. 78). Yet the strain of constant effort was lightened in many ways. The work was itself a joy, accompanied by song. It involved inspiring contacts with men like La Farge, White, Henry Adams, Stevenson, John Hay, Sherman, William Dean Howells, John Sargent, Bastien-Lepage, indeed a veritable host of distinguished friends. He had delightful relations with Theodore Roosevelt over what the President called his "pet crime," the reformation of the United States coinage. In 1905 they put their heads together with the result that Saint-Gaudens made his memorable designs for the twenty-dollar gold piece and other coins. It is interesting to observe that he was, according to his wont, endlessly thoroughgoing in the enterprise, seeking to reconcile the practical issues involved with his dream of reviving something of the spirit of the ancient Greek coins and that of the Renaissance medals. There is a peculiarly felicitous touch in the circumstance that, after having erected here and there monuments in memory of heroes in American history he should have rounded out his career with work destined for widespread circulation amongst his fellow countrymen.

The full stream of his activities had flowed through many channels and scenes. His work had been done variously in Rome, in Paris, in New York, involving travels too frequent and too complicated for the tale of them to be set forth in anything less than an exhaustive biography. But one aspect of the subject of the sculptor's locale is of an importance requiring special comment. This was his discovery, in 1885, of the place in Cornish, N. H., which was thenceforth to be his headquarters, a sanctuary to which it was always good to return. "Aspet," as he called it, out of ancestral memories, he gradually formed into a beautiful estate, embellishing the old house that he had found there, erecting studios, and slipping into a life serener than that which he knew in the city or abroad. He knew misfortune at "Aspet." Fire, which had destroyed the relief at St. Thomas's and the angels for the Morgan tomb, destroyed also one of the Cornish studios, in 1904, and some of his most cherished possessions were lost—the drawing he had made of his mother, the portraits of himself by Bastien-Lepage, John Sargent, and Kenyon Cox, with innumerable precious papers, including his letters from Robert Louis Stevenson. The ruined "Parnell" for Dublin and the seated "Lincoln" could be done over again but these other things could only be mourned. He bore the disaster with courage. High courage, in fact, was in his blood. "Life is a battle, bitter or friendly, but nevertheless a battle," he wrote, "and to my mind a wholesome one" (*Reminiscences*, I, 292). He fought it unflinchingly. A friend who knew him well met him in Paris when he had received the first intimations of the illness that was ultimately to prove fatal. He was worried and confessed it but in his demeanor there were only cheerfulness and a kind of sweet resolution. He faced the end with a brave heart. Shortly before it came, in his retreat at Cornish, he watched the sunset behind Ascutney Mountain. "It's very beautiful," he murmured, "but I want to go farther away" (*Reminiscenes*, II, 359).

He went away at fifty-nine, in the full tide of his creative powers, the studios teeming with activity. Though the fight for health had fatigued him, recovery would have found him, in technical grasp and in imaginative fervor, well abreast of his task. In that event the groups for the Boston Public Library, to name only one of his last commissions, would have undoubtedly ranked high in his *œuvre*. Yet he could have legitimately rested upon his laurels for he had

put forth an imposing series of statues and reliefs, erecting in them a standard to which the sculptors of the United States could gratefully repair. They have persistently recognized him as their chief and early and late he was the recipient of honors testifying to their confidence. While he was still a young aspirant in Europe he was appointed to the jury for the American exhibition in the Paris exposition of 1878 and this was prophetic of the distinctions to be bestowed upon him. His fellow artists loved to pay him tribute and tokens of appreciation flowed in from other sources. Princeton, Harvard, and Yale all conferred degrees upon him. As it was at home so it was abroad. The Luxembourg acquired the "Amor Caritas," and he was allied with the Legion of Honor as a matter of course. In Paris he was hailed as a master, having extraordinary success in the Salon, where, in 1900, he received the Grand Prix. In London he was elected to the Royal Academy. In his own country, where so many notable productions keep his name and fame alive, there is also a special monument to his genius. "Aspet" was handed over to a board of trustees by his widow and his son Homer and as the Augustus Saint-Gaudens Memorial, crowded with replicas of the works in bronze and plaster, it annually draws thousands of visitors. These pilgrims can thus study at full length the sculptor's purely artistic traits. All that is missing is the handsome *gaillard* charm of the man, the blithe spirit, the puissant driving force, the rich quality and *élan* of one of the most endearing personalities ever known to American art.

[The canonical source of information is *The Reminiscenes of Augustus Saint-Gaudens* (2 vols., 1913) edited and amplified by his son, Homer Saint-Gaudens. There is a comprehensive bibliography in *Index of Twentieth Century Artists*, May 1934. Other publications include: Royal Cortissoz, *Augustus Saint-Gaudens* (1907), and *The Painter's Craft* (1930), pp. 403–12; Kenyon Cox, *Old Masters and New: Essays in Art Criticism* (1905), and *Artist and Public and other Essays and Art Subjects* (1914); C. L. Hind, *Augustus Saint-Gaudens* (1908), special extra number of *The International Studio*; C. R. Post, *A Hist. of European and Am. Sculpture*, vol. II (1921), pp. 240–43; Lorado Taft, *The Hist. of Am. Sculpture* (1924); Adeline Adams, *The Spirit of Am. Sculpture* (1929); W. H. Law, *A Chronicle of Friendship, 1873–1900* (1908), pp. 215–26, 273–75, 387–95, 401–02, 477–86, 499–506; Maitland Armstrong, *Day Before Yesterday: Reminiscences of a Varied Life* (1920); Louis Réau, *L'Art Français aux États-Unis* (1926), pp. 177–81; C. H. Caffin, *Am. Masters of Sculpture* (1903); obituary in *N. Y. Times*, Aug. 4, 1907.]   R. C.

ST. JOHN, ISAAC MUNROE

(Nov. 19, 1827–Apr. 7, 1880), commissary-general of the Confederate States Army, and engineer, the eldest child of Isaac Richards and Abigail Richardson (Munroe) St. John, was born in Augusta,

Ga., where his father was then in business. He was a descendant of Matthias St. John who came to Dorchester, Mass., before 1632. A few years after the child's birth the family removed to New York City. He entered Yale in 1841 and was graduated in 1845, the youngest member of his class. He began the study of law in New York City but gave up these studies to become assistant editor of the *Baltimore Patriot,* Baltimore, Md. In 1848, he gave up journalism to become a civil engineer. Until 1855 he was on the engineering staff of the Baltimore & Ohio R. R., and then moved to Georgia, where, for five years, he was in charge of construction divisions of the Blue Ridge R. R.

When the Civil War began, St. John was in South Carolina, and he at once entered the Confederate service as a private of the Fort Hill guards of that state. He was soon transferred, however, to Magruder's army of the peninsula for engineering duty, became chief engineer of that army, and, in February 1862, was commissioned captain of engineers. The energy and ability which he displayed in Magruder's army attracted the attention of the Confederate war department, and he was promoted to major on Apr. 18, 1862, and assigned to duty in Richmond as chief of the nitre and mining bureau. He efficiently performed the difficult task of supplying the Confederacy, which was blockaded on all sides, with nitre for the manufacture of gunpowder, and with metals for the construction of implements of war. His accomplishments were recognized by his successive promotions to lieutenant-colonel and colonel. Near the end of the war, when the problem of feeding the Confederate armies had become acute, St. John was selected to direct this important activity. On Feb. 16, 1865, he was appointed commissary-general with the rank of brigadier-general, and at once organized an efficient system for collecting and storing supplies and for forwarding them to the armies. He continued on this duty after the evacuation of Richmond and until the final collapse of the Confederacy. An article on the "Resources of the Confederacy" appeared under his name in the *Southern Historical Society Papers,* March 1877.

After the war he returned to his profession of civil engineering. From 1866 to 1869 he was chief engineer of the Louisville, Cincinnati, & Lexington R. R. and then for the next two years he was city engineer of Louisville, Ky. He made the first topographical map of Louisville and planned the first complete sewerage system of that city. In 1871 he declined reëlection as city engineer and became consulting engineer of the

Chesapeake & Ohio R. R. In 1873 he was chief engineer of the Elizabeth, Lexington & Big Sandy R. R. He died suddenly of apoplexy while in residence at the "Greenbrier," White Sulphur Springs, W. Va. His wife was Ella J. Carrington, the daughter of Col. J. L. Carrington of Richmond, Va. They were married on Feb. 28, 1865, and had six children.

[O. St. John Alexander, *The St. John Geneal.* (1907); *Obit. Record of Grads. of Yale College,* June 1880; M. J. Wright, *Gen. Officers of the Confed. Army* (1911); *Memorandum Relative to the Gen. Officers . . . of the Confed. States, Sen. Doc. 244,* 60 Cong., 1 Sess. (1908); Special Orders of the Adjutant and Inspector General's Office, Confed. States, Lib. of Hist. Section, Army War College; *Courier-Jour.* (Louisville, Ky.), Apr. 10, 1880.]   S. J. H.

ST. JOHN, JOHN PIERCE (Feb. 25, 1833–Aug. 31, 1916), governor of Kansas, prohibitionist, the son of Samuel and Sophia (Snell) St. John, was descended from Matthias St. John who was made a freeman in Dorchester, Mass., in 1634. Born in Brookville, Franklin County, Ind., he lived on a farm, acquired a scanty education, and learned to hate liquor when his father became a victim of alcoholic drink. When he was twelve he began to earn a living for himself, and during the next fourteen years he worked at various occupations, made an unfortunate marriage with Mary Jane Brewer at the age of nineteen, and participated in the gold rush to California. He was admitted to the bar at Charleston, Ill., and at the same place, Mar. 28, 1861, was married to Susan J. Parker, his first wife having secured a divorce. After the Civil War, during which he won the rank of lieutenant-colonel in the 143rd Illinois Regiment, he practised law for a time at Independence, Mo., but in 1869 removed to Olathe, Kan.

He made his first appearance in public life as a Republican member of the Kansas Senate of 1873–74, where he worked for strict liquor regulation. The woman's crusade, the temperance movement started by Francis Murphy [*q.v.*], and the rise of anti-liquor organizations in Kansas produced the moment when a temperance candidate could profit most from his principles, and St. John was elected governor in 1878. At that time he was forty-six years old. He was slightly above medium height, well proportioned and vigorous physically, with deep-set, piercing eyes, dark hair, and a rather thin face festooned with a long and drooping but carefully kept moustache. The outstanding event of his first administration (1879–81) was the submission to the electorate of a constitutional amendment prohibiting the manufacture and sale of intoxicating liquor for beverage purposes. By reason of his oratorical ability and his prestige as governor, he became the leader in the fight for the amendment. In the election of 1880 it was adopted, and he was re-elected. Credit for the adoption of the first constitutional prohibitory amendment in history has ordinarily been assigned more to him than to any other person. His second term was chiefly occupied with a moderately successful attempt to enforce prohibition. In 1882 he made a fight for a third term, but was defeated, owing mainly to objection to the third term, a reaction against prohibition, credence given to an unsubstantiated charge that he favored railroad corporations, and the jealousy of a number of influential politicians who secretly combined against him. His principle of prohibition, however, was sustained in the election of local officials and the state legislature.

By 1882 St. John had become a character of national significance, largely through his connection with the adoption of constitutional prohibition in Kansas. After his defeat for a third term—the first Republican gubernatorial defeat in Kansas—he was practically expelled from his party, and devoted himself to lecturing on prohibition. In 1884 he accepted the nomination of the National Prohibition Party for president and drew fifteen times as many votes as any candidate of this party had ever received before. His campaign was centered in New York, in the hope of securing the balance of power in this pivotal state. Grover Cleveland carried the state by a plurality of 1,149 votes; if the Republicans had carried New York, the electoral vote would have stood 218 for Blaine and 183 for Cleveland. St. John received 25,016 votes in New York, and both major parties agreed that his vote was drawn almost exclusively from Republican ranks. For this reason, although any one of a number of factors might have been influential in producing the result in this state, St. John at the time was held responsible for the election of the first Democratic president since the Civil War, and the abuse and vilification heaped upon him by the Republicans knew no bounds. He was the only third party candidate between 1860 and 1912 who could plausibly be credited with turning an election.

In 1896 he broke with the Prohibition party, and from this time was a free lance in politics. His temperance lectures were less in demand, and he turned to mine speculation and real estate, but he was never successful in financial ventures. During his last years he again became popular as a prohibition speaker, and found himself restored to public favor in Kansas. He died at Olathe, survived by one son, a daughter having died in 1903.

[Senate and House Journals of the State of Kan., 1873–74, 1879–83; Correspondence of the Governors of Kan., 1879–83 (MS.), Kan. State Hist. Soc., Topeka; St. John's scrapbooks (13 vols.), in the possession of Miss May Parker, Olathe, Kan.; *Hist. of the State of Kan.* (1883), ed. by W. G. Cutler; D. W. Wilder, *The Annals of Kan.* (1886); Orline St. John Alexander. *The St. John Geneal.* (1907); *Who's Who in America*, 1914–15; *Emporia Gazette*, Sept. 1, 1916; Edna Tutt Frederikson, "John P. St. John, the Father of Constitutional Prohibition," doctoral dissertation (1931), Univ. of Kan.]   E. T. F.

ST. LUSSON, SIMON FRANÇOIS DAUMONT, Sieur de (d. 1674), French soldier and explorer, went to Canada in 1663 with the Commissioner Gaudais-Dupont. The next year he received a grant of land and thereafter acted as agent for the intendant Jean Talon. In 1668 he asked permission to return to France, probably with Talon, and came back with him to New France in 1670. In his second term of service (1670–73) Talon made extensive plans for enlarging New France and for exploring the interior of the continent of North America. Consequently, when news reached him in the year of his return of the discovery of copper on Lake Superior and of new alliances with the tribes around the upper Great Lakes, he determined to send an expedition, headed by St. Lusson, to take formal possession of this distant territory for the king of France and explore for mines near Lake Superior. It was October 1670 before the flotilla got under way. This was late for an expedition to so distant a destination, and St. Lusson was forced to camp with his men on the north shore of Lake Huron, spending the winter in hunting excursions. Early in the spring he sent Nicolas Perrot [q.v.] to Green Bay to summon the chiefs of the tribes there to the ceremony, while he himself proceeded to Sault Ste. Marie, where there was a Jesuit mission. On June 14 the pageant of annexation took place. Aided by the Jesuit missionaries, St. Lusson marched in state from the mission house and, in the presence of representatives from fourteen different tribes, performed a feudal ceremony of taking possession in the name of Louis XIV of all land "discovered and to be discovered." With the chanting of Latin hymns, the raising of a cross and the arms of France, and an oration to the Indians, the ceremony was concluded. He later advanced into the Lake Superior region but found no mines.

After his return to Quebec he served in Acadia and then went to France, where at Dieppe in May 1672 he sold a ship for Talon and sent gifts to the king of a young moose, a fox, and wild geese from Canada. Probably he went back the next year to Canada, where a son was christened in June 1673. Since his wife, Marguerite Bérin, remarried in 1675, it is supposed that he died in

1674. His fame rests on the great ceremony of annexation in 1671.

[See Louise P. Kellogg, ed., *Early Narratives of the Northwest* (1917) and *The French Régime in Wis. and the Northwest* (1925). The text of St. Lusson's official report is in *Wis. Hist. Colls.*, vol. XI (1888), reprinted from E. B. O'Callaghan, *Docs. Relative to the Colonial Hist. of the State of N. Y.*, vol. IX (1855), where Talon's report also appears, and in Pierre Margry, *Découvertes et Établissements des Français dans l'Ouest*, vol. I (1876), pp. 92–99. Perrot's account is in E. H. Blair, *Indian Tribes of the Great Lakes and Upper Miss. Region* (1911), vol. I. The account of the Jesuits is in R. G. Thwaites, ed., *The Jesuit Relations and Allied Docs.*, vol. LV (1899). See also Benjamin Sulte, "Les Français dans l'Ouest en 1671," *Proc. and Trans. Royal Soc. of Canada*, 3 ser., vol. XII (1919); *Le Bulletin des Recherches Historiques*, May 1931.]

L. P. K.

SAINT-MÉMIN, CHARLES BALTHAZAR JULIEN FEVRET de (Mar. 12, 1770– June 23, 1852), artist and engraver, was born in Dijon, France, the son of Bénigne Charles Fevret de Saint-Mémin and Victoire Marie de Motmans, a Creole from Santo Domingo. Privately educated in Dijon until he was fourteen, he entered the École Militaire in Paris, graduated in 1785, and in 1788 became an ensign in the French guards with the intention of following a military career. The French Revolution, however, obliged the family to flee to Switzerland. In 1793 he and his father left Switzerland for the West Indies to prevent the sequestration of Madame de Saint-Mémin's estate in Santo Domingo, but in New York they learned of the negro rebellion and went no farther. In need of money, they first started a vegetable garden, and when this venture failed Saint-Mémin turned to account his artistic ability, formerly a mere pastime.

His first American work (done in 1796) was a panoramic pencil sketch of New York, which he afterwards engraved and colored, getting his knowledge of the engraver's art from an encyclopedia. After executing several other landscapes, he turned to the more lucrative branch of portraiture. With a physionotrace, invented in 1786 by Gilles-Louis Chrétien, he secured an exact profile of the sitter on red paper (which later faded to a soft pink) and then drew in the features, hair, and clothing with black and white crayon. Afterwards, by means of a pantograph, he reduced the large profile to the size of a miniature about two inches in diameter and recorded it directly on a copper plate with graver and roulette. Both machine and tools he made himself, using the instructions of an encyclopedia and his own ingenuity. After a short partnership with an engraver named Valdenuit, he continued to work alone in New York until 1798, when he moved first to Burlington, N. J., where his

mother and younger sister had established a girls' school, and later to Philadelphia. From 1804 to 1809 he lived successively in Baltimore, Annapolis, Washington, Richmond, Va., and Charleston, S. C. The following year he returned to France. Coming back to New York in 1812, he gave up engraving because of his impaired eyesight and painted portraits and landscapes in oils. Two years later, with his mother and sister, he returned to France, where from 1817 until his death he served as director of the museum at Dijon.

Nothing is known of Saint-Mémin's portraits in oils. Of his water colors there exist three portraits of women, owned by the Maryland Historical Society, and five profile portraits of Osage Indians probably done in Washington in 1804 (Lockwood, *post*). Most of the crayon portraits are in private collections. The eight hundred and more profile engravings include portraits of practically all distinguished Americans of the first part of the nineteenth century, as well as a portrait of Washington that is said to be the last one done from life. Saint-Mémin himself made the two identical groups of these in American collections, writing the name of the subject and the date of the engraving on each print. One of these (privately owned) was photographed and published with biographical data pertaining to the subject of each profile in *The St.-Mémin Collection of Portraits . . . To Which Are Prefixed a Memoir of M. de St. Mémin* (1862). The other collection is in the Corcoran Gallery of Art, Washington, together with some small engravings of public buildings executed for a proposed asylum for French refugees on the Susquehanna River, several silhouettes, and a line map entitled "Plan of the Siege of Savannah."

[Philippe Guignard, *Notice Historique Sur la Vie et les Travaux de M. Fevret de Saint-Mémin* (1853); J. H. Morgan, "The Work of M. Fevret de Saint-Mémin," in *Brooklyn Museum Quart.*, Jan. 1918; Frederick Houston, "Collecting the Portraits of St. Mémin," *House and Garden*, Nov. 1924; Alice Van Leer Carrick, "Saint-Mémin and His Profiles," *House Beautiful*, Nov. 1928, reprinted in *Shades of Our Ancestors* (1928); L. V. Lockwood, "The St. Mémin Indian Portraits," *N. Y. Hist. Soc. Quart. Bull.*, Apr. 1928; Theodore Bolton, *Early Am. Portrait Draughtsmen in Crayons* (1923), inaccurate in some details; critical study and hist. of the landscapes in I. N. P. Stokes, *The Iconography of Manhattan Island* (6 vols., 1915–28).]

F. N.

SAINT–MÉRY, MOREAU de [See MOREAU DE SAINT-MÉRY, MÉDÉRIC-LOUIS-ELIE, 1750– 1819].

ST. VRAIN, CERAN DE HAULT DE LASSUS de (May 5, 1802–Oct. 28, 1870), Santa Fé trader, pioneer merchant, soldier, was born at Spanish Lake, near St. Louis, Mo., the son of Marie Felicité Chauvet (Dubreuil) and Jacques Marcellin Ceran DeHault DeLassus de St. Vrain, an officer in the French navy who had come to America and settled near Ste. Genevieve, Mo., in 1793–94. At an early age the son embarked in the fur trade. He was in Taos, N. Mex., on Mar. 21, 1825, having just finished a troublesome journey of five months to that place. About this time he dissolved partnership with François Guerin, with whom he had conducted an expedition to the southwest outfitted by Bernard Pratte & Company of St. Louis. On Aug. 29, 1826, Gov. Antonio Narbona of New Mexico issued a passport at Santa Fé to St. Vrain and William S. Williams [q.v.] to the state of Sonora for private trade. At this time St. Vrain, in partnership with Paul Baillio since the previous June, was engaged in equipping trappers. He sold his interest to Sylvestre Pratte in the fall of 1826 and worked for Pratte as his clerk until the latter's death, Sept. 1, 1828. About Jan. 1, 1831, he formed a partnership with Charles Bent [q.v.], under the name of Bent, St. Vrain, & Company, which lasted until Bent's assassination and was surpassed in importance only by the American Fur Company.

Like most of the Santa Fé traders, he became a citizen of Mexico. In 1844, for valuable services in maintaining the peace on the Mexican frontier, he and Cornelio Vigil received a land grant from the Mexican government comprising four million acres in the fertile valleys of the Huerfano, Apishapa, Purgatoire, and other tributaries. The title to this land was confirmed by the United States government after Vigil's death, application for confirmation being made by St. Vrain as manager of Vigil's estate and probably as surviving partner. At the time of the Taos anti-American revolt during the Mexican War, he was the organizer and captain of a company of volunteers. When the Apaches and Utes made war on the ranches and villages, 1854–55, he was appointed lieutenant-colonel of volunteers. In June 1861 he was appointed colonel of the first New Mexico cavalry, but he resigned on October 12, 1861, "on account of age" and was succeeded by Kit Carson.

He had married Luisa Branch of Mora, N. Mex., and had two sons and a daughter. He was a large powerful man, whose sturdiness of character, courage, and honesty made a deep impression on the southwest. In books written by western visitors he is described as a polite gentleman and an amiable fellow traveler and is pictured as an outstanding figure. When he died at Mora, his funeral was attended by officers from Fort Union and more than two thousand other persons.

[Information from St. Vrain's daughter; Baptismal Reg., Old Cathedral, St. Louis; W. B. Douglas, "Geneal. of family of De Lassus and St. Vrain" (MS.), and Bent and St. Vrain Collection (MSS.), in Mo. Hist. Soc.; T. M. Marshall, "St. Vrain's Expedition to the Gila in 1826," *Southwestern Hist. Quart.*, Jan. 1916; Annie H. Abel, *The Official Correspondence of James S. Calhoun While Indian Agent at Santa Fé* (1915); Benj. M. Read, *Illustrated Hist. of N. Mex.* (1912); R. E. Twitchell, *The Leading Facts of New Mexican Hist.*, vol. II (1912); Le Baron B. Prince, *A Concise Hist. of N. Mex.* (1912), and *Hist. of the Ark. Valley, Colo.* (1881); Louis Houck, *A Hist. of Mo.* (1908), vol. I; F. L. Billon, *Annals of St. Louis* (1886); L. H. Garrard, *Wah-To-Yah and the Taos Trail* (1850); *Mo. Republican* (St. Louis), Nov. 17, 1870.]   S. M. D.

SAJOUS, CHARLES EUCHARISTE DE MÉDICIS (Dec. 13, 1852–Apr. 27, 1929), physician, was born at sea while his parents, Count Charles Roustan de Médicis-Jodoigne of Florence, Italy, and his wife, Marie Pierette (Cort), were traveling to France. When he was two years old his father died; eight years later his mother married Charles Sajous, and the youth assumed the surname of his stepfather. He began his medical studies at the University of California, but finished them at Jefferson Medical College, Philadelphia, from which he graduated in 1878. After serving a term as resident physician at the Howard Hospital in Philadelphia, he began practising laryngology in that city. From 1880 to 1882 he was professor of anatomy and physiology in the Wagner Free Institute of Science, and from 1881 to 1890, clinical lecturer on laryngology in Jefferson Medical College. In 1891, having become greatly interested in the new field of endocrinology, he went abroad to study the subject in the European clinics. He remained in France and Germany for several years engaged in this pursuit and throughout the rest of his life the study of the physiology and therapeutics of the ductless glands chiefly absorbed his energies. In 1897–98, after his return to America, he was professor of laryngology and dean of the faculty of the Medico-Chirurgical College of Philadelphia. From 1909 to 1922 he held the chair of therapeutics in the medical college of Temple University. Here he had an opportunity to expound his views on endocrinology which was further extended when in 1921 he was appointed professor of applied endocrinology in the Post Graduate School of the University of Pennsylvania. This position he held until his death.

Sajous was a voluminous writer and an indefatigable editor. In 1885 he published *Hay Fever and Its Successful Treatment by Superficial Organic Alteration of the Nasal Mucous Membrane*, and in the same year, *Lectures on the Diseases of the Nose and Throat*. From 1888 to 1896 he undertook editorial charge of the *Annual of the*

Universal Medical Sciences, published by the F. A. Davis Company of Philadelphia, and during the nine years of its existence not only edited but contributed innumerable articles to the forty-five volumes of this work. In 1898 he assumed the editorship of a somewhat similar project published by the same firm, at first called the *Annual and Analytical Cyclopædia of Practical Medicine* and later, *Sajous's Analytic Cyclopædia of Practical Medicine,* of which ten editions, in from six to nine volumes each, were issued before his death. He was the author of *The Internal Secretions and the Principles of Medicine* (2 vols., 1903–07), in which he reviewed all the available literature on endocrinology and set forth his own views on the subject. This book also went through a number of editions, but it is marred by the uncritical enthusiasm with which its author indorsed the views of many writers whose statements were not based upon exact scientific observation. From 1911 to 1919 he was managing editor of the *New York Medical Journal.* He was the first president of the Association for the Study of the Internal Secretions, a member of the American College of Physicians, the American Therapeutic Society, and the American Philosophical Society, and a fellow of the College of Physicians of Philadelphia. In 1926 he published *The Strength of Religion as Shown by Science.* He married, Jan. 30, 1884, Emma Christine Bergner of Philadelphia. Their only child, Louis Theodore de Médicis Sajous, graduated in medicine at the University of Pennsylvania in 1909 and was closely associated with his father in his studies in endocrinology. He died Jan. 16, 1929, and three months later his father died, from cardio-renal disease, at his home in Philadelphia.

[Victor Robinson, in *Medic. Life,* Jan. 1925, with full bibliog. to that date; *N. Y. Medic. Jour.,* Dec. 9, 1911; *Medic. Jour. and Record,* May 15, 1929; *Jour. Am. Medic. Asso.,* May 4, 1929; J. M. Anders, in *Trans. Coll. of Physicians of Phila.,* 3 ser. LII (1930); *Pa. Medic. Jour.,* June 1929; *Who's Who in America,* 1928–29, inaccurate in the spelling of names; *Pub. Ledger* (Phila.), Apr. 28, 1929; personal acquaintance.]
F. R. P.

SALISBURY, ALBERT (Jan. 24, 1843–June 2, 1911), educator, eldest of six children of Oliver and Emily (Cravath) Salisbury, both of New England stock, was born in Lima, Rock County, Wis. His father was a farmer, sheep-raiser, and nursery-man, and the son served an apprenticeship in all these callings. His mother, a teacher before her marriage, supplemented effectively the instruction he gained in the little district school. At eighteen he began attendance at Milton Academy, continuing till he enlisted in December 1863 as private in the 13th Wisconsin

Infantry. He saw service in the Army of the Cumberland, and for three months after the ending of the Civil War, in Texas. For a time after his return to Wisconsin he was farmer, nursery-man, and teacher in a rural school. Then, as was to have been expected of a man who had taken his Latin textbooks with him when he went to the war, he continued his studies. Milton Academy had now become Milton College, and here he was graduated A.B. in 1870. In that same year he became principal of the Brodhead, Wis., high school, and three years later, instructor of history and the first conductor of teachers' institutes for the state normal school at Whitewater, Wis. Through his service for nine years in the latter capacity he was largely instrumental in shaping in Wisconsin that form of training teachers in service.

In 1882 he resigned his Whitewater positions and began work for the American Missionary Association as superintendent of schools for the freedmen of the South and the Indians of the West, but in 1885 returned to the Whitewater Normal School as its president, in which office he remained until his death. He was a man of commanding presence and both from the chapel platform and through conference with individuals exerted a strong influence on the lives of his students. A vigorous force in community and state, he urged the establishment of a state institution for the feeble minded and the improving of the rural schools. As chairman of committees of the Wisconsin Teachers' Association which had espoused both these causes, he investigated conditions, reported them by voice and pen, and agitated vigorously and persistently for reform of the prevailing ills. After several failures, he was instrumental in securing, in 1895, the establishment of a state institution for the feeble minded. In the fall of 1900 he was one of those who participated by invitation in the "Teachers' Visit to Europe" under the auspices of the National Civic Federation. After his return in the spring of 1909 he rendered a report to the National Education Association on teacher training in Great Britain. As author and editor his chief works were: *Historical Sketch of Normal Instruction in Wisconsin, 1846-76* (1876); *Orthoepy and Phonology* (1879); *The Duty of the State to the Feeble-Minded* (1890); *Historical Sketches of the First Quarter-Century of the State Normal School at Whitewater* (1893); *The Rural School Problem* (1897); *Theory of Teaching and Elementary Psychology* (1905); *School Management: a Textbook for County Training Schools and Normal Schools* (1911). He was an active member and for long one of the trustees of the

Congregational Church of Whitewater. He was twice married: on Nov. 20, 1866 to Abba A. Maxson who died in 1881, and in 1883 to Agnes Hosford, who, with three children of his first marriage, survived him.

[*Bull. of the State Normal School, Whitewater, Wis.,* Jan. 1912; *Who's Who in America,* 1910–11; *Whitewater Register,* June 9, 1911; *Milwaukee Free Press,* Feb. 19, 1905; *Milwaukee Sentinel,* June 3, 1911; typewritten autobiographical sketch in possession of Salisbury's widow (Whitewater, Wis.).]   W. J. C.

SALISBURY, EDWARD ELBRIDGE (Apr. 6, 1814–Feb. 5, 1901), Orientalist and teacher, was born in Boston, Mass. His father, Josiah, was of English ancestry, of a noted family; his mother, Abby (Breese) Salisbury, was of Huguenot descent. His early education was given him by his father, who, having been connected with the mercantile business of the family, then for a time a clergyman in Boston, had retired to private life. Fitted for college at the Boston Latin School, he went to Yale, where his brother-in-law, Theodore Dwight Woolsey [*q.v.*], became professor of Greek in 1831. After graduating, in 1832, he spent several years in advanced study in New Haven, paying especial attention to Hebrew and the cognate languages. In 1836 he married his cousin, Abigail Salisbury Phillips, daughter of Edward Phillips of Boston, and with her proceeded to Europe, where for nearly four years he studied Oriental languages, especially Arabic with De Sacy and Garcin de Tassy in Paris, and Sanskrit with Bopp in Berlin. On his return to America in 1841 he was appointed professor of Arabic and Sanskrit at Yale; but before assuming the duties of the office he spent the year 1842–43 in Europe, studying chiefly Sanskrit in Bonn and Paris.

When he began his work at Yale, in 1843, he was the only scholar of his kind in America, and he at once began to supply what was greatly needed. It was given to him to open the wide field of Oriental studies in this country, to arouse interest in great literatures and in chapters of history hitherto little known, and to prepare the way for scientific research in the two chief domains which his chair included. In the early years of the American Oriental Society (founded in 1842) he was one of its main pillars. He contributed to its first volume, and provided at his own expense fonts of Oriental type. "For some ten years he was virtually the Society, doing its work and paying its bills. He gave it standing and credit in the world of scholars" (*In Memoriam, post,* p. 6). In the *Journal* of the Society he published papers dealing with Arabic, Sanskrit, Persian cuneiform, Assyrian, and Phoenician, as well as an able essay on the genuineness of the Nestorian monument of Singan-fu. He was in constant correspondence with American missionaries in the East, who provided him with valuable material.

In 1854 he relinquished the professorship of Sanskrit to his former pupil, William Dwight Whitney [*q.v.*], retaining, however, the chair of Arabic until 1856. It was after the latter date that he did his principal work on research and publication. The following papers, printed in the *Journal of the American Oriental Society,* deserve especial mention: "Contributions from Original Sources to Our Knowledge of the Science of Muslim Tradition" (1859; vol. VII); "Materials for the History of the Muhammadan Doctrine of Predestination and Free Will" (1863; vol. VIII); "The Book of Sulaimân's First Ripe Fruit, Disclosing the Mysteries of the Nusairian Religion" (1864; vol. VIII). While his tastes were chiefly literary and historical, nevertheless his philological attainments were of a very high order. His knowledge of the Arabic language was thorough and accurate, and he was well acquainted with the literature which up to that time had been made available. In his later years he gave much time to studies in the fields of art and history. His eyesight failing, he devoted himself to genealogical research, with the skilful assistance of his second wife, Evelyn McCurdy Salisbury, daughter of Judge Charles J. McCurdy of Lyme, Conn.; his first wife had died in 1869. First published were his *Family-Memorials* ... (2 vols., 1885); then the *Family-Histories and Genealogies* ... (5 vols., 1892), dealing with his wife's family.

Salisbury's public-spirited benefactions were many. To Yale University he gave large sums for buildings, books, and collections; also (thirty years before his death) his own very valuable library, containing a large part of De Sacy's library and collection of Arabic manuscripts. It was only through funds contributed by him that Yale was enabled to secure for its faculty Professors William Dwight Whitney and James Dwight Dana [*q.v.*]. He was elected a member of the Société Asiatique in 1838, a corresponding member of the Imperial Academy of Sciences and Belles Lettres, Constantinople, in 1855, and a corresponding member of the Deutsche Morgenländische Gesellschaft in 1859.

[*Obit. Record Grads. Yale Univ.,* 1901; *New Eng. Hist. and Geneal. Reg.,* Oct. 1901; E. W. Hopkins, "Memorial Address in Honor of Professor Salisbury" (presented Feb. 16, 1901, at Yale Univ.), pub. in his *India Old and New* (1901), reprinted in abstract, "In Memoriam," in the *Jour. Am. Oriental Soc.,* vol. XXII, pt. I (1901); E. M. Salisbury, in *Family-Histories and Geneals.* (1895); *Biog. Memoranda Respecting All Who Ever Were Members of the Class of 1832 in Yale*

Coll. (1880), ed. by E. E. Salisbury; Salisbury's "Jour. of Travels in Europe," MS., in the Yale Lib.] C. C. T.

SALISBURY, JAMES HENRY (Oct. 13, 1823–Aug. 23, 1905), physician, was born at Scott, N. Y., the son of Nathan and Lucretia (Babcock) Salisbury, both of English colonial ancestry. After attending Homer Academy near his birthplace, he received the degree of bachelor of natural science from Rensselaer Institute of Troy, N. Y., in 1846, his medical degree from Albany Medical College in 1850, and the degree of M.A. from Union College in 1852. Appointed assistant chemist of the New York state geological survey at Albany in 1846, he became chief chemist in 1849. In 1851–52 he also lectured on elementary and applied chemistry at the state normal school. During this period he wrote *Anatomy and Histology of Plants* (1848) and *History and Chemical Investigations of Maize* (1849), the latter a voluminous pamphlet issued by the state agricultural society.

Although he later settled at Newark, Ohio, for practice, his chief interest was still in research. In addition to *Ancient Earth and Rock-Writing* (1863), a book on the mound builders written in collaboration with his brother, C. B. Salisbury, and such books as *An Account of Some Experiments and Observations on the Influence of Poisons and Medicinal Agents upon Plants* (1854), *Some Experiments on Poisoning with Vegetable Alkaloids* (1862), *Experiments Connected with the Discovery of Cholesterin and Seroline* (1863), and *Histology and Anatomy of the Spleen* (1866), his early work included the analysis of various fruits and vegetables and, in the field of phytopathology, a book on *Blight in Apple, Pear, and Quince Trees and Decay of their Fruit* (1863). Influenced by his work in plant pathology he conceived the idea that human disease was also largely due to fungus infestation. In 1862 he wrote an article (*American Journal of the Medical Sciences*, July 1862) attributing measles in the army camps to fungi found on straw, and a second (*Ibid.*, October 1862) on experimental inoculation with straw fungi for prevention of the disease. Later he identified certain "algoid vegetations" as the causative agents in malaria, syphilis, gonorrhea, variola, vaccinia, and typhoid fever, and reported these investigations in detail in *New Algoid Vegetations* (1868) and *Microscopic Examinations of Blood* (1868). Similarly, in *Original Investigations in Diphtheria and Scarlet Fever* (1882), he affirmed that the two diseases were nearly related and that both were due to what he called "mucor malignans," a fungus he found in the blood and excretions of patients. It is evi-

dent that he was groping vaguely about in the dawn of the germ theory of disease, near to the solution of some of its problems but always falling short of realization. By the time germ causation was well established, his interests were elsewhere and he shared none of the honors. He was then advocating the preponderant influence of food and drink in the production of disease, including in his list abnormal growths and mental alienation. He wrote two books in support of this idea, *Brief Statement of the So-Called "Salisbury Plans" of Treating by Alimentation* (1887) and *Relation of Alimentation and Disease* (1888). Meanwhile he had assisted in the organization of the Charity Hospital Medical School in Cleveland, where from 1864 to 1866 he was professor of physiology, histology, and pathology. From about 1880 he lived in New York City. He died suddenly from a cerebral hemorrhage at his summer home in Dobbs Ferry, N. Y. He had been married on June 26, 1860, to Clara Brasee of Lancaster, Ohio, daughter of John T. Brasee. A final estimate of his work marks him as an able microscopist and a painstaking investigator; his articles, which received serious consideration when published, are scholarly and well illustrated with charts. Of all his researches those in medicine are the least useful, although a little later he might have achieved world fame through them.

[*Who's Who in America*, 1903–05; anonymous, *Sketch of Life of James H. Salisbury* (1884), with portrait; *Albany Medic. Annals*, Nov. 1905, pp. 777–79; H. A. Kelly and W. L. Burrage, *Am. Medic. Biogs.* (1920); obituary in *N. Y. Tribune*, Aug. 24, 1905.]

J. M. P—n.

SALISBURY, ROLLIN D. (Aug. 17, 1858–Aug. 15, 1922), geologist and educator, was born at Spring Prairie, Walworth County, Wis., the son of Daniel and Lucinda (Bryant) Salisbury. He attended the public schools, graduating from the state normal school at Whitewater in 1877, and after a year of teaching entered Beloit College, where Thomas Chrowder Chamberlin [*q.v.*] was professor of geology. Soon after his graduation in 1881 he became Chamberlin's assistant in his work for the United States Geological Survey, thus beginning a quasi-official connection which lasted until 1910. In 1882, when Chamberlin resigned from Beloit, Salisbury replaced him, attaining the rank of professor in 1884. Here—except for the year 1887–88 which he spent in study abroad, especially at Heidelberg—he continued until 1891, when he became professor of geology at the University of Wisconsin. The following year he accompanied Chamberlin to the new University of Chicago, as professor of geographic geology, and there spent the rest of his life. He was head of the department of geography from 1892 to 1919, and from then until he died Chamberlin's successor as head of the department of geology. In addition, he was dean of the University Colleges, 1894–96, and dean of the Ogden Graduate School of Science from 1899 until his death. He was closely associated with Chamberlin in the management of the *Journal of Geology* from its foundation in 1893, and for the last four years of his life was the responsible editor.

As a teacher Salisbury took high rank. His master, Chamberlin, said that his "greatest service to science lay in his singular success in stimulating and training young talent, not only for the teaching of science but for research." As dean of the Ogden School he came in touch with thousands of young minds to whom he imparted "effective impulses toward sound scholarship and the higher life" (Chamberlin, *post*, p. 481). It has been stated that at one time fully a third of the state geologists of the country had been his pupils. He required a great deal of his students and was harshly critical of failure, but eagerly spent himself to further the development of those in whom he saw promise. He was a lucid writer, and for ease of comprehension, even by those who were not geologists, had few equals.

Salisbury limited his geological researches chiefly to glacial and Pleistocene deposits, and in his field became a leading authority. During his year at European universities in 1887–88 he studied particularly the glacial deposits of the North German lowlands, and he subsequently made an extended trip through South America. For the purpose of studying glacial action at close hand, he took part in the Peary Relief Expedition of 1895. From 1891 to 1915 he was geologist in charge of the Pleistocene division of the Geological Survey of New Jersey, and in 1919 he was appointed a member of the board of commissioners in charge of the Illinois Survey. His most notable contributions in his special field were "Preliminary Paper on the Driftless Area of the Upper Mississippi Valley" (*Sixth Annual Report of the United States Geological Survey . . . 1884–'85,* 1885), in which he collaborated with Chamberlin, and his articles on "Surface Geology of New Jersey" in the *Geological Survey of New Jersey: Annual Reports of the State Geologist.* With Chamberlin he was also the author of *Geology* (3 vols., 1904–06), in the American Science Series.

Salisbury was a man of exceptional presence, straightforward, unpretentious, possessing culture, refinement, and marked conversational ability. Though a lover of children and family life,

he never married. From his college days he was regarded almost as a son by the Chamberlins and for years looked upon their house as his real home. He was stricken with coronary thrombosis on May 31, 1922, and died in the following August.

[The "D." in Salisbury's signature was merely a letter, standing for no name (Keyes, *post*, p. 97). Sources include *Who's Who in America,* 1922–23; E. S. Ames, in *Univ. Record* (Univ. of Chicago), Oct. 1922; Charles Keyes in *Pan-American Geologist,* Sept. 1922; T. C. Chamberlin, in *Jour. of Geol.,* Aug.-Sept. 1922; H. D. Densmore, in *Wis. Mag. of Hist.,* Sept., Dec. 1931; *N. Y. Times,* Aug. 17, 1922; *Chicago Herald and Examiner,* Aug. 16, 17, 1922; personal acquaintance.] G. P. M.

SALM-SALM, AGNES ELISABETH WINONA LECLERCQ JOY, Princess (Dec. 25, 1840–Dec. 21, 1912), whose part in the Mexican adventure of Emperor Maximilian made her internationally conspicuous, was born on a farm in Franklin County, Vt., or possibly in Philipsburg, Que., where part of her girlhood was spent. The daughter of William and Julia (Willard) Joy and the grand-daughter of Micah Joy, a Revolutionary soldier, she was descended from Thomas Joy [*q.v.*]. Her adventurous spirit, which found vent in escapades which lived long in local tradition, took her to Washington early in the Civil War, where, under the name of Agnes Leclercq, she was married, Aug. 20, 1862, to a German soldier of fortune, Felix Constantin Alexander Johann Nepomuk, Prince Salm-Salm (1828–1870), a colonel on Gen. Louis Blenker's staff. Her energy and cleverness secured for him the colonelcy of the 8th New York Infantry, and later of the 68th. Accompanying her husband, she became a notable figure in camp, field, and hospital—the toast of the officers and the talk of the men. Her husband was brevetted brigadier-general of volunteers at the close of the war, and was appointed military governor of Atlanta.

Upon being mustered out, he embarked in February 1866 for Mexico, where the Austrian archduke, Maximilian, was struggling to maintain himself as emperor in the face of the forces headed by President Juarez. Salm-Salm became Maximilian's chief aide, and his wife followed him to Mexico and shared all his anxieties. When Querétaro fell by treason and Maximilian and his suite were captured and threatened with summary execution, she braved all obstacles and dangers to go to their rescue. When intercession failed, she plotted the Emperor's escape, offering his keeper large bribes of money or anything else within her gift; failing, she clasped the knees of President Juarez, praying for mercy, but without success. Before his execution Maximilian decorated her with the Grand Cordon of the Order of San Carlos, and later his brother, the Austrian emperor, pensioned her. Salm-Salm next became a major in the Prussian Guards, and in the ensuing war with France was killed (1870). The Princess, experienced in army relief work in America, obtained from General von Steinmetz permission to accompany his staff on horseback and to carry on a relief work in camps and field hospitals like that since developed under the Red Cross. Generals von Goeben and Fransecky thanked her personally and in the name of the army for her services; she received the Prussian Medal of Honor and was recommended for the Iron Cross, a decoration reserved for men. The Empress Augusta gave her an onyx brooch.

Left a widow at thirty, after a decade of breathless activity, she went to Rome to consult Pope Pius IX with regard to entering a convent, but he told her that she had no vocation to be a nun, and she eventually settled down to the routine of German social life, residing first at Bonn and later at Karlsruhe. In 1875, at Stuttgart, she published *Zehn Jahre aus Meinem Leben,* three volumes covering her decade of war service. It was published in English as *Ten Years of My Life* (2 vols., London, 1876; Detroit and New York, 1877). In 1876 she married the secretary of the British legation at Berlin, Charles Heneage, from whom she later separated. She revisited America in 1899, bringing the flags of the Prince Salm-Salm's regiments and being warmly greeted by Carl Schurz and other wartime friends; in 1899–1900 she came again, seeking funds for an ambulance corps for the Boers. Twelve years later she died at Karlsruhe. Her appeal to Juarez is the subject of a historical painting by Manuel Ocaranza (1873), owned formely by Gen. Mariano Ruiz, Mexico City. She also figures in the drama *Juarez and Maximilian* by Franz V. Werfel, produced in Vienna, Berlin, and New York (1925–26), and in several novels.

[*Ten Years of My Life* (1876), mentioned above; Prince Felix Salm-Salm, *My Diary in Mexico in 1867* (2 vols., London, 1868); German edition (3 vols., Stuttgart, 1868), repr. 1928 as *Maximilian von Mexico . . . Blätter aus dem Tagebuch des Prinzen Felix zu Salm-Salm,* ed. by Otto Hellinghaus; J. R. Joy, *Thomas Joy and His Descendants* (1900), with portrait; *Almanach de Gotha,* 1894 and later issues; Sara Y. Stevenson, *Maximilian in Mexico* (1899); Eagon Cæsar, Count Corti, *Maximilian and Charlotte of Mexico* (2 vols., 1928); J. L. Blasio, *Maximilian, Emperor of Mexico, Memoirs of His Private Secretary* (1934), ed. by R. H. Murray; *Metropolitan,* Aug. 1899; *N. Y. Times,* Dec. 22, 1912.]

J. R. J.

SALMON, DANIEL ELMER (July 23, 1850–Aug. 30, 1914), veterinarian, was born at Mount Olive, N. J., the son of Daniel Landon and Eleanor (Flock) Salmon. After a prepara-

tory education in the public schools of Mount Olive and in Chester Institute nearby, he entered Cornell University in 1868 with the first freshman class and became interested in the veterinary department. Graduating in 1872 with the degree of bachelor of veterinary science, after a course which included six months at the Alfort Veterinary School in Paris, he married Mary Thompson Corning of Ithaca, N. Y., and settled in Newark, N. J., for the practice of veterinary medicine. In 1876 he received the degree of doctor of veterinary medicine from Cornell. In 1875, on account of impaired health, he had moved to Asheville, N. C. Two years later he delivered a course of lectures on veterinary medicine at the University of Georgia, and in the same year he began special study of the disease of swine. After sharing in a campaign carried on by the state of New York in 1879 for the eradication of contagious pleuro-pneumonia of cattle, he accepted an appointment with the United States Department of Agriculture to investigate diseases of domestic animals in the southern states, with special reference to Texas fever. Early in 1883 he was asked to organize in the Bureau of Agriculture a veterinary division, which in the following year became the Bureau of Animal Industry. He was made chief of the bureau and held the post until a controversy with the department head caused his resignation in December 1905.

The period of his incumbency marks an epoch of notable achievement. His early contacts with contagious pleuro-pneumonia and Texas fever led him to concentrate the attention of the bureau upon them, with the result that these two serious menaces to the cattle industry were soon under complete control. Other investigations concerned the cause and prevention of fowl cholera, contagious diseases of swine, and nodular disease of sheep. In his earlier career Salmon had been a skilful laboratory technician, but the exactions of administrative duties early took him away from the details of research. In addition to a genius for the selection of assistants, he had great administrative ability and professional vision. As head of the bureau he directed its policies and planned the work of his assistants and found time to write nearly one hundred articles, either alone or in collaboration with others, which collectively cover the whole field of veterinary research of the period. In the field of public health administration he was responsible for the inauguration of a nation-wide system of meat inspection, for a quarantine system for imported live stock, and for the inspection of exported cattle and the ships carrying them. In 1906 he accepted an invitation from the government of Uruguay to organize the veterinary department of the University of Montevideo and remained there five years. Returning to the United States, he took up the manufacture of veterinary biological products. In 1913 he assumed the management of a laboratory for the production of serum for the prevention of hog cholera in Butte, Mont. He died there of pneumonia and was buried in Rock Creek Cemetery in Washington. After the death of his first wife he married on Nov. 15, 1904, Agnes Christina Dewhurst of New York. He had been president of the American Public Health Association and of the American Veterinary Medical Association and was a member of many foreign and American scientific societies.

[For a list of Salmon's publications, see C. W. Stiles and Albert Hassall, *Index-Catalogue of Medic. and Veterinary Zoology* (36 nos., 1902–12). See also *Who's Who in America,* 1914–15; D. E. Salmon, *The U. S. Bureau of Animal Industry . . . 1884–1900* (1901); *Cornell Veterinarian,* Oct. 1914; *Am. Veterinary Rev.,* Oct. 1914; H. A. Kelly and W. L. Burrage, eds., *Am. Medic. Biogs.* (1920); *Evening Star* (Washington, D. C.), Sept. 3, 1914]   J. M. P—n.

SALMON, LUCY MAYNARD (July 27, 1853–Feb. 14, 1927), educator, historian, was born in Fulton, N. Y. Her parents, George and Maria Clara (Maynard) Salmon, were both natives of Massachusetts. She attended Falley Seminary in Fulton and had a year of preparation at the Ann Arbor (Mich.) high school before she entered the University of Michigan, from which she received the A.B. degree in 1876. After five years spent in McGregor, Iowa, where she was principal of the high school, she returned to the University of Michigan for graduate work in history. There she studied under Charles Kendall Adams and took the A.M. degree in 1883. Her thesis, the "History of the Appointing Power of the President," was published in the first volume of the *Papers of the American Historical Association* (1886). For three years then she taught history at the Indiana state normal school and returned to graduate study, this time to Bryn Mawr College. As fellow in history, 1886–87, she worked under Woodrow Wilson, then in his second year of teaching at Bryn Mawr. In 1887 she went to Vassar College, first as associate professor, and two years later as professor of history, and made that the center of her life work. She was still in active teaching at the time of her death.

While she wrote and published a number of books and articles, it was as teacher that her greatest influence was felt. The present day theory of making the student the chief agent in his own instruction was the cardinal principle of her teaching, and from this she never wavered.

The project method, dear to the progressive school in recent time, was years ago made notable by her use of the special topic in her own history classes. Under her teaching the library was the laboratory of the student of history. She made it her special concern to see that the college library was well equipped with original sources for research. In the field of history teaching her influence spread far beyond her own class-room. She was a member of the committee of seven of the American Historical Association, 1896–99, whose report *The Study of History in Schools* (1899), formed the standard guide for the teaching of history in secondary schools for the next generation. She was founder and the first president of the Association of History Teachers of the Middle States and Maryland, 1903–04. She was an active life member of the American Historical Association and served, 1915–19, as the first woman elected to its executive council. In the field of historical scholarship her most significant influence was in her fresh view of what constitutes historical material. To her the matter from which history is to be written was not primarily the consciously significant document, the Constitution of the United States or Magna Carta, but the daily newspaper, a railway time-table, the place name of a region, something of ordinary observation on Main Street or in the back yard. She was profoundly interested in the material of every-day living as significant for interpretation of the past. Her volume, *Domestic Service* (1897) was written as an examination of the common sphere of the household for the elucidation of historical and economic forces. The study of the newspaper as historical material was the most extensive of her published work. The two companion volumes, *The Newspaper and the Historian* and *The Newspaper and Authority,* both published in 1923, are undoubtedly the works by which her quality as historical scholar will be measured. She took active part in the civic life of Poughkeepsie and consistently impressed upon her students the ideals of good citizenship, whether the civic unit be the college campus or the home town or the nation. No one who knew her could fail to recall her continuous and consistent devotion to peace. Even in wartime she remained quietly and steadily loyal to this principle. In 1926, the year before her death, her former students and other friends established at Vassar the "Lucy Maynard Salmon Fund for Research," and under this fund the first publication was her posthumous volume, *Why is History Rewritten?* (1929). Another posthumous volume, *Historical Material,* was published in 1933.

[*Who's Who in America*, 1926–27; *Vassar Miscellany News*, Feb. 19, 1927; *New York Times*, Feb. 15, 1927; *Am. Hist. Rev.*, Apr. 1927; *Addresses at the Memorial Service for Lucy Maynard Salmon, Held at Vassar College*, Mar. 6, 1927 (1927); *Proc. of the Assn. of Hist. Teachers of the Middle States and Maryland*, No. 25 (1927), No. 31 (1933) with an appreciative notice and a portrait; MS. bibliography in Vassar College Library; personal association over a long period of years.]   C. M. T.

SALMON, THOMAS WILLIAM (Jan. 6, 1876–Aug. 13, 1927), physician, psychiatrist, pioneer in mental hygiene, was born in Lansingburg, Rensselaer County, N. Y. His father, Thomas Henry, a physician, and his mother, Annie (Frost), were natives of England. Salmon's formal education was obtained in the village schools and academy. Graduating from the Albany Medical College in 1899 with the degree of M.D., he spent a year in private practice, at Brewster, N. Y., and served temporarily at the Willard, N. Y., state hospital for mental disorders. During an epidemic of diphtheria in that institution he made with W. L. Russell one of the earliest studies of human carriers, the results of which were printed in the report of the state commission in lunacy (October 1904), and published separately the following year (*Report of an Epidemic of Diphtheria in the Willard State Hospital*).

In 1903 he entered the United States Public Health Service. As a result of a medical trip on a revenue cutter, he proposed and drew plans for a hospital ship for fishermen at sea, which was afterwards provided (see *Modern Hospital*, June 1914). In 1905 he was assigned to the immigration service at Ellis Island, New York Harbor. There, for six years, during one of which (1911) he was on leave of absence as chief medical examiner for the New York state commission in lunacy, his interest and efforts were directed to measures for preventing an influx of the mentally unfit from foreign countries, and for dealing adequately with the problem of mental disorders in the immigrant population. His work at Ellis Island, his writings, and his representations at Washington contributed much to what is best in the present laws, regulations, and methods relating to this problem. In 1912 he made for the National Committee for Mental Hygiene an extremely productive survey of the treatment of mental disorders throughout the country. He was appointed medical director of this committee in 1915 and became the leading spirit and guide in a widespread movement for improvement in the treatment and prevention of mental disorders. He was one of the founders and a member of the first editorial board of the magazine *Mental Hygiene*. The excellent statistical studies of the insane and feeble-minded, which are now conducted by the federal Bureau of Census, were established under his initiative and guidance.

During the World War he mobilized the psychiatric resources of the country, and enabled the United States Army to adopt remarkably effective measures for preventing the admission of recruits who were nervously and mentally unfit and for dealing with mental disorders and disabilities among the soldiers. He was awarded the distinguished service medal, and retired to the reserve corps with the rank of brigadier-general. He then directed his attention to the mentally disabled ex-service men, and the superior hospital and out-patient service provided for their care was in great measure due to his capable, indefatigable efforts.

In 1921, he resigned his position with the National Committee to become professor of psychiatry at Columbia University and a consulting psychiatrist. At Columbia he reorganized his department and added greatly to its teaching and research resources by securing from the state the establishment, at the medical college, of a psychiatric institute and hospital. Salmon was an interesting and convincing speaker and made many addresses. He published numerous articles in current journals; edited, with Norman Fenton, the section on "Neuropsychiatry," in volume X (1929) of *The United States Army in the World War*, and wrote the chapter on immigration in W. A. White and S. E. Jelliffe, *Modern Treatment of Nervous and Mental Diseases* (1913), and the chapter on mental hygiene in M. J. Rosenau, *Preventive Medicine and Hygiene* (1913). In 1899 he married Helen Potter Ashley; four boys and two girls were born to them. He died by accidental drowning.

[*Who's Who in America*, 1926–27; *Mental Hygiene*, Oct. 1927; bibliog. of ninety titles, *Ibid.*, Jan. 1928; *N. Y. Times*, Aug. 15–19, 1927; personal acquaintance.]   W. L. R.

SALOMON, HAYM (*c.* 1740–Jan. 6, 1785), merchant, banker, Revolutionary financier, was born at Lissa, Poland, of Jewish-Portuguese ancestry. In his youth he traveled widely, acquired an excellent knowledge of foreign languages, and, returning to Poland about the age of thirty, became an ardent advocate of Polish independence. In 1772 he fled to England and thence to New York, where he opened a brokerage and commission merchant's business. His previous association with the cause of liberty in his native country drew him naturally to the side of the American Whigs and later to the movement for American independence. During the British occupation of New York his activities led to his arrest as a spy (Sept. 22, 1776) and consequent imprisonment. The British, however, put him to use as an interpreter and assigned him to the Hessian general, Heister, who placed him in the commissary department. There he made use of his increased freedom to induce Hessian soldiers to resign or to desert. Paroled after a brief imprisonment, he resumed his business as merchant and continued to act as an under-cover desertion agent among the Hessians. On Jan. 2, 1777, he married Rachel, daughter of Moses B. Franks, an influential Jewish merchant.

In August 1778 Salomon was again arrested, charged with being an accomplice in a plot to burn the King's fleet and to destroy British warehouses around New York. He was confined in the dreaded prison, the Provost, and condemned to death, but on Aug. 11, by turning to advantage a string of golden guineas which he had concealed on himself, he bribed his jailer and escaped to the American lines, leaving his family behind in the city. Fourteen days later found him in Philadelphia addressing a memorial to Congress setting forth his services to the cause and asking for some employment, but to no avail. With the assistance of friends he thereupon opened an office as dealer in bills of exchange and other securities. The business prospered, and within the next few years he became a leading broker in the city and one of the largest depositors in the Bank of North America, to which he was a subscriber. He was paymaster-general for the French forces in America and most of the war subsidies of France and Holland passed through his hands. As almost sole broker for the office of finance in the sale of bills of exchange he contributed much to maintain the bankrupt government's credit. The diary of Robert Morris shows no less than seventy-five transactions with Salomon between August 1781 and April 1784. Original checks and vouchers presented before a later committee of Congress show that he advanced in specie to the superintendent of finance at various times a total of $211,678. In addition he held government obligations of various sorts amounting to $353,729.33, six promissory notes to the amount of $92,600, making an aggregate indebtedness against the government of $658,007.43, as shown by his papers and later recognized by committees in Congress. To calculate the full extent of Salomon's financial assistance there should be added to the above figures advances of more than $20,000 to pay the salaries of men holding government posts in order to keep them in the service, and untold additional advances during the war to army officers,

to foreign agents, and for the outfitting of soldiers (*Senate Report No. 93*, 38 Cong., 1 Sess., June 24, 1864). These liberal advances in specie and equally liberal investments in Revolutionary paper furnish a singularly outstanding example of unselfish devotion to the American cause, particularly when it is remembered that the family was left practically penniless at his death.

Following the war Salomon suffered heavy financial reverses. His plans to return to New York in 1785 as a factor, broker, and auctioneer were interrupted by his sudden death, undoubtedly hastened by an impaired constitution owing to his imprisonment by the British. In the settlement of his estate all assets, including Revolutionary securities, were given a value of $44,732 against an indebtedness of $45,292. Repeated efforts were made by the heirs to secure a settlement of the Salomon claim from the government. Although the case was considered by Congress at least ten times between 1848 and 1926 and a Senate committee in 1864 recognized the claim as one of "undeniable merit," all such efforts proved unsuccessful.

[Most helpful in reconstructing the story of Salomon, which had dropped from sight for many years, is *Senate Doc. No. 178*, 69 Cong., 2 Sess., Dec. 20, 1926, containing the committee report of June 24, 1864, a sketch by Salomon's son, Haym M., a biographical sketch by H. B. Adams, and an invaluable bibliography by J. H. Hollander. Much of the same material is in *Pubs. of the Am. Jewish Hist. Soc.*, No. 2 (1894). Major instances of congressional consideration of the family claim may be found in the following: *House Report No. 504*, 30 Cong., 1 Sess. (1848) ; *Senate Report No. 219*, 30 Cong., 1 Sess. (1848) ; *Senate Report No. 177*, 31 Cong., 1 Sess. (1850) ; *Senate Report No. 127*, 36 Cong., 1 Sess. (1860) ; *Senate Report No. 65*, 37 Cong., 2 Sess. (1862) ; and *Senate Report No. 93*, 39 Cong., 1 Sess. (1864). Salomon's story has been the subject of a novel, H. S. Baron, *Haym Salomon, Immigrant and Financier of the American Revolution* (1929). C. E. Russell, *Haym Salomon and the Revolution* (1930), gives all the entries concerning the subject to be found in Robert Morris's unpublished diary. See also M. C. Peters, *Haym Salomon, The Financier of the Revolution* (1911), and *The Jews Who Stood by Washington* (1915) ; Isaac Markens, *The Hebrews in America* (1888) ; Simon Wolf, "Are Republics Ungrateful?," *Reform Advocate*, Feb. 20, 1892 ; article by Herbert Friedenwald, in *The Jewish Encyclopedia* (1925), vol. X ; *Pa. Journal and Weekly Advertiser* (Philadelphia), Jan. 8, 1785.]   J.H.P.

SALTER, WILLIAM (Nov. 17, 1821–Aug. 15, 1910), Congregational clergyman, author, and historiographer, was born in Brooklyn, N. Y., the son of William Frost Salter, owner of the ship *Mary and Harriet*, upon which William played as a youth, and of Mary (Ewen) Salter who had come to New York with her husband from Portsmouth, N. H. He was a descendant of John Salter, mariner, who emigrated from England about 1680 and settled in Rye, N. H.

In 1840 he graduated from the University of the City of New York and then entered the Union Theological Seminary, but at the end of two years transferred to Andover, where he was graduated in 1843. Stirred by the need of religious and educational facilities on the frontier, he, with ten other Andover graduates, went to the Territory of Iowa under the auspices of the Home Missionary Society. The Iowa Band, as this group came to be known, proceeding by train, boat, and wagon, arrived at a point on the eastern bank of the Mississippi, opposite Burlington, on Oct. 24, 1843. Soon thereafter Salter preached his first sermon at Keosauqua, in a little room over the blacksmith shop, and on Nov. 5, 1843, was ordained at Denmark. Becoming missionary pastor in Maquoketa, he served there during a part of the years 1844–46, frequently riding a circuit and preaching whenever he could gather a few persons. In April 1846 he became pastor of the First Congregational Church of Burlington, and continued as such until his death sixty-four years later.

In the critical years previous to the Civil War he conducted an underground railway station for the assistance of runaway slaves. During the conflict he served as army chaplain in the Christian Commission and ministered to Union and Confederate wounded in several hospitals. Returning to Burlington at the close of the war, he resumed his parish work and writing. During his long pastorate, he was in intimate touch with many of the prominent Iowa pioneers, and his published works include a number of biographical sketches among which are: *Sermon with Reference to the Death of James G. Edwards* (1851); *Augustus C. Dodge* (1887); and *James Clarke, Third Territorial Governor* (1888). During the period of the Civil War he published *Our National Sins and Impending Calamities* (1861) and *The Great Rebellion in the Light of Christianity* (1864). In the religious field he wrote: *On Some Objections to the Old Testament—Their Origin and Explanation* (1853); *The Progress of Religion in Iowa for Twenty-five Years* (1858); *Studies in Matthew* (1880); *The Christian Idealism of R. W. Emerson* (1886); *Cooperative Christianity* (1888). His major works are: *The Life of James W. Grimes* (1876); *Iowa: The First Free State in the Louisiana Purchase* (1905); and *Sixty Years and Other Discourses* (copr. 1907). He was married on Aug. 25, 1846, to Mary Ann Mackintire of Charlestown, Mass.

[W. T. Salter, *John Salter, Mariner* (1900); J. L. Hill, *Rev. William Salter, D.D., 1821–1910* (n.d.), reprinted with bibliog. added from *Annals of Iowa*, Jan. 1911; Ephraim Adams, *The Iowa Band* (1870); P. D.

Jordan, "The Discovery of William Salter's Almanac-Diary," *Annals of Iowa*, Oct. 1930, and "The Life and Works of James Gardiner Edwards," in *Jour. of the Ill. State Hist. Soc.*, Oct. 1930; *Who's Who in America*, 1908–09; *Register and Leader* (Des Moines), Aug. 16, 1910; diary, covering the period 1843–1851, marriage book, containing a list, with dates, of all marriages performed, 1843–1910; and Civil War diaries, containing his experiences as chaplain, in private hands.]   P. D. J.

SALTER, WILLIAM MACKINTIRE (Jan. 30, 1853–July 18, 1931), Ethical Culture lecturer, philosopher, author, was the son of Rev. William [*q.v.*] and Mary Ann (Mackintire) Salter, of Burlington, Iowa. His early religious and educational training was stimulated by his Congregational father who put the boy to the study of Latin at the age of ten and introduced him to Greek two years later. When he was fourteen, he entered Knox College, Galesburg, Ill., where he became skeptical with respect to orthodox religion. This skepticism expressed itself in his graduating oration in 1871, "Is Orthodoxy in Theology Necessary for the Christian?"; which led some Knox trustees to question, but not deny, the right of the candidate to the degree of bachelor of arts. He entered the theological department of Yale College in the fall of 1871, where he searched theology and sacred writings for a justification of orthodoxy, but gradually, he relates, "one article after another of my former faith became wrapped in uncertainty." In 1873 he left Yale for the Harvard Divinity School, thinking that "I might at least hold on to enough to be a Unitarian minister if I could not be an Orthodox one." During the summers of 1872–73 he preached at Somesville, Me., and from Aug. 16, 1874, to July 4, 1875, in the Unitarian Church at Wayland, Mass. While in the latter place he attempted to formulate his own creed in a series of sermons beginning with "Man's Need of Religion," but found, after re-entering Harvard in 1875, that "solid grounds for distinctive Christian faith in any form had slipped away." He was granted the degree of bachelor of divinity in 1876 and appointed Parker Fellow of Harvard at the University of Göttingen.

While in Germany he turned his attention from the Christian fathers to the pagan philosophers, studying Plato, Aristotle, and others, not alone for themselves, but with the thought of tracing pagan influence on the development of Christian doctrine. His health failed, however, and he returned to the United States, where he herded sheep in Colorado from February 1878 to October 1879. While tending his flocks he prepared a pamphlet, *On a Foundation for Religion* (1879), based upon the "enthusiasm of humanity" which John Robert Seeley's *Ecce Homo*, a volume much beloved by him, described. In 1879 he met Felix Adler and heard him describe a new type of religious movement which laid stress on human service and not upon theological arguments and explanations. During 1881–82 he was a student at Columbia University. In 1881 he affiliated himself with Dr. Adler's ethical culture movement and later wrote: "I moved slowly—perhaps I always do, I have to weigh and ponder—but at last I had no choice: I joined the pioneer with heart and soul, and count myself blessed that for twenty-five years, in whatever limited and fragmentary way, I responded to his high example" (autobiographical sketch, MS., 1926). His rise in the movement was rapid; from 1883 to 1892 and again from 1897 to 1907 he was lecturer for the Chicago society, and from 1892 to 1897 for the Philadelphia society. He was a special lecturer on Nietzsche at the University of Chicago from 1909 to 1913.

On July 19, 1913, he sailed for Europe and, after traveling in Italy and the Austrian Tyrol, settled down in Munich to begin work on his book, *Nietzsche the Thinker* (1917). Interrupted by the World War, he returned to the United States to study, lecture, and write at "Hilltop," his home on Silver Lake, N. H. He completed his book, upon which his fame as a scholar rests, contributed articles on Nietzsche and the World War to magazines, and in the winter of 1920–21 lectured on Nietzsche at Johns Hopkins University. Although gentle and lovable, Salter possessed great moral strength. He pleaded for a fair trial for the bombers of the Chicago Haymarket riots when public opinion was against him, and he remained unswervingly pro-German and anti-British during the World War. In addition to about eighty printed lectures, he published: *Die Religion der Moral* (Leipzig, 1885), *Moralische Reden* (Leipzig, 1889), *Ethical Religion* (1889), *First Steps in Philosophy* (1892), *Anarchy or Government* (1895), *Walt Whitman* (1899), and *Burgess's Political Philosophy as Indicated in His Recent "The Sanctity of Law"* (1929). On Dec. 2, 1885, he was married to Mary S. Gibbens, of Cambridge, Mass.; a daughter by this marriage died and they adopted a boy.

[Material for this sketch was taken from MSS. in private hands; the lib. of the Ethical Culture Soc. of N. Y. contains Salter's Ethical Culture MSS., and the lib. of Knox Coll., his Nietzsche and World War material. See *Proc. and Addresses of the Am. Philosophical Asso.*, vol. V (1931); *Who's Who in America*, 1930–31; *Standard*, Nov. 1931; *N. Y. Times*, July 19, 1931.]
P. D. J.

SALTONSTALL, DUDLEY (Sept. 8, 1738–1796), naval officer, was born at New London, Conn., the fifth of fourteen children of Gen. Gurdon Saltonstall and Rebecca (Winthrop) Saltonstall. He was a direct descendant of Richard Saltonstall and the grandson of Gurdon Saltonstall [*qq.v.*]. In 1765 Dudley was married to Frances, the daughter of Dr. Joshua Babcock, of Westerly, R. I., and they had seven children.

Saltonstall took to the sea early in life, was a privateersman in the French and Indian War, and commanded merchant vessels before the Revolution. At an early period of this contest he commanded the fort at New London and in the fall of 1775, when the first Continental fleet was assembled, he was given command of the ship *Alfred*, flagship of Commodore Esek Hopkins [*q.v.*]. John Paul Jones was first lieutenant. Early in 1776 this fleet cruised to the Bahamas and captured the island of New Providence. Upon the return voyage the fleet took two small prizes off Block Island, and later engaged the British frigate *Glasgow*, but failed to capture her. For allowing her to escape and for other reasons Hopkins was eventually dismissed from the navy, but Saltonstall was exonerated and, on Oct. 10, 1776, was appointed fourth on the list of captains. In 1777 he was ordered to command the new frigate *Trumbull*, but she did not get to sea for two years. However, in some manner unexplained, he sailed in another ship of the same name and reported the capture of two British transports.

Saltonstall is best remembered for his connection with the disastrous Penobscot expedition of 1779. The British having taken possession of Bagaduce, now Castine, in Penobscot Bay, the State of Massachusetts fitted out an expedition for its recapture. The force comprised a fleet of nineteen naval vessels and privateers carrying more than 200 guns and 2,000 men, commanded by Saltonstall in the Continental frigate *Warren*, of 32 guns, with about twenty transports conveying the troops under Gen. Solomon Lovell. The militia contingent which Lovell had been able to recruit within the short time allowed him consisted of less than 1,000 men. The expedition arrived in Penobscot Bay on July 25. Three British sloops of war, mounting altogether 56 guns, lay in Bagaduce harbor and would readily have surrendered to the American force. Saltonstall, however, did nothing; the urging of his officers could not move him. The army made a successful landing but could not take the fort without the assistance of the navy, which could only be rendered from an anchorage in the harbor. There followed nearly three weeks of delay and aimless discussion, waiting for reinforcements which could not possibly have arrived in time. Then, on Aug. 13, a British fleet appeared in the bay. The troops were hastily reëmbarked on the transports and the whole American fleet fled ignominiously up the river. Two of the ships were taken by the British; all the others were destroyed to prevent capture. Saltonstall was dismissed from the navy. Later in the war he was successful in privateering and afterwards returned to the merchant service. He died of yellow fever at Mole St. Nicolas, Haiti, the exact day and month being unknown.

[Leverett Saltonstall, *Ancestry and Descendants of Sir Richard Saltonstall* (1897); F. M. Caulkins, *Hist. of New London, Conn.* (1860), pp. 509, 531; G. W. Allen, *A Naval Hist. of the Am. Rev.* (2 vols., 1913), and authorities there cited; note furnished by L. F. Middlebrook, Esq., of Hartford, Conn.]   G. W. A.

SALTONSTALL, GURDON (Mar. 27, 1666 o. s.–Sept. 20, 1724 o. s.), clergyman, colonial governor, was born in Haverhill, Mass., the eldest son of Nathaniel and Elizabeth (Ward) Saltonstall, the grandson of Richard Saltonstall [*q.v.*], and the great-grandson of Nathaniel Ward [*q.v.*]. His father also was a Massachusetts magistrate. He graduated from Harvard College in 1684 and was ordained minister of the church at New London, Conn., in 1691. Through his orthodoxy, learning, and unusual eloquence he soon rose to a position of prominence among the clergy of the colony; because of his practical wisdom he became the confidant and advisor of his leading parishioner, Fitz-John Winthrop, later the governor. Only two years after his ordination the Assembly asked him to go to England with Winthrop to represent the colony in a dispute over the New York governor's claim to command the Connecticut militia. Flattering though the invitation was, he declined to go. During Winthrop's governorship, 1698–1707, both he and the Assembly relied more and more upon Saltonstall's help in drafting state papers and in adjusting disputes within the colony and with its neighbors. Upon Winthrop's death the Assembly, at a special meeting called for Dec. 17, 1707, o. s., asked Saltonstall to leave the pulpit and assume the governorship. Such a step was unprecedented, even in Puritan New England, and it has few parallels in all American history. At the time, the deputy governor, Robert Treat [*q.v.*], was eighty-five, and none of the magistrates had so fully the public confidence as had the New London minister. His patrician ancestry, his dignity of bearing, which amounted almost to pompousness, his wealth and orthodoxy were just the attributes

that eighteenth-century Connecticut expected and demanded of its governors. Yet Saltonstall had not advanced to leadership through the regular apprenticeship of the magistracy as law and custom demanded, and his choice as acting governor of the tradition-bound colony was an outstanding tribute to his abilities—and perhaps to his political management. When he accepted the call, the Assembly amended the law to permit his election by the freemen in the following May even though he had not previously been nominated a magistrate. These proceedings of the Assembly met the approval of the voters, and he was annually reëlected until his death.

As governor, he faced the usual problems of his times: warfare with the French and Indians, boundary disputes with neighboring colonies, the defence of the colony's charter from threatened cancellation in England. In these and similar crises the governor's adroit management fully justified the confidence placed in him. It is not altogether a coincidence, however, that the most lasting decisions reached during the administration of this learned divine had to do with church government and higher education. In the solution of these problems his influence was felt long after his death. One of the first acts of the Assembly after his election was to call upon the churches of the colony to appoint delegates to a synod at Saybrook, which was to draw up a system of ecclesiastical discipline. The result of this meeting was the Saybrook platform of 1708, which, with its indorsement of the Savoy Confession and its provision for consociations of churches and associations of ministers, set the course for Connecticut Congregationalism for generations to come. Under the governor's leadership the Assembly approved the platform, and he had it printed in 1710 at the New London press he had recently caused to be established (*A Confession of Faith . . . by Delegation at Say-Brook*). Even before his translation to the governorship, he had been interested in the founding of a college in Connecticut. Though never a trustee, he was one of the ministerial leaders in the movement that led to the chartering of the Collegiate School in 1701. As governor he actively protected the institution, soon named Yale College, from the factional jealousies and Anglican defections that endangered its early career. During the controversy over the location of the college, he used the great influence of his office to support the majority trustees in their decision to settle permanently at New Haven. His attitude so angered the ministerial leaders of the Hartford faction, Timothy Woodbridge and Thomas Buckingham, that they obtained their own election to the Assembly in 1719 in a strenuous effort to bring about his defeat for reëlection. The unedifying spectacle of two clergymen entering the political arena for the purpose of driving another minister from the highest public office of the colony ended with the complete victory of the governor. In 1722 his firm but temperate leadership was again invoked when the conversion to Anglicanism of Timothy Cutler, Samuel Johnson [qq.v.], and others intimately associated with the college threatened the very foundations of conservative Puritanism upon which it had been built.

In his religious and political views Saltonstall was thoroughly conservative, and some of the bolder spirits of the colony showed restlessness under the restraining influence of his administration. His years in office were marked by a number of personal and factional attacks. But he successfully overrode all opponents, and at his death, which came suddenly through apoplexy, was sincerely mourned throughout New England. Cotton Mather outdid himself in eulogy, likening his old friend to a *"Silver Basket* of a comely Body, carrying in it the *Golden Apples* of a well-furnished and well-disposed Soul," and adding "We will not call him a *Star,* but even a *Constellation* of the most fulgid Endowments" (Sibley, *post*, pp. 283–84, from Mather, *post*). Saltonstall was married three times: to Jerusha, the daughter of James Richards of Hartford, to Elizabeth, the daughter of William Rosewell of Branford, and to Mary, the daughter of William Whittingham and the widow of William Clarke of Boston. His third wife and seven of his ten children survived him. A contemporary portrait by an unknown artist, presented to Yale by his son, hangs in the Gallery of Fine Arts in New Haven.

[*The Public Recs. . . . of Conn.,* IV–VI (1868–72); Eliphalet Adams, *Discourse on the Death of the Hon. Gurdon Saltonstall* (1724); Cotton Mather, *Decus ac Tutamen. A Brief Essay . . . in Commemoration of . . . Gurdon Saltonstall* (1724); F. B. Dexter, *Doc. Hist. of Yale Univ.* (1916); Benjamin Trumbull, *A Complete Hist. of Conn.* (1797); F. M. Caulkins, *Hist. of New London, Conn.* (rev. ed. 1895); Leverett Saltonstall, *Ancestry and Descendants of Sir Richard Saltonstall* (1897); J. L. Sibley, *Biog. Sketches of Grads. of Harvard Univ.,* vol. III (1885); Edwin Oviatt, *The Beginnings of Yale* (1916); Williston Walker, *The Creeds and Platforms of Congregationalism* (1893).]
L. W. L.

SALTONSTALL, RICHARD (*c.* 1610–Apr. 29, 1694), Massachusetts colonist, born at Woodsome, Almondbury, Yorkshire, England, and baptized Oct. 1, 1610, was the eldest son of Sir Richard Saltonstall and Grace, daughter of Robert Kaye. His father, the nephew of Sir Richard, Lord Mayor of London, was an original patentee and Assistant of the Massachusetts Bay Company. Richard, Jr., was admitted fellow commoner at Emmanuel College, Cambridge, in 1627 and, in 1630, accompanied his father to Massachusetts Bay, where they established the settlement of Watertown. After being admitted freeman, May 18, 1631, young Saltonstall returned to England, studied law, and on July 4, 1633, married Muriel, daughter of Brampton Gurdon of Suffolk. With their first child, the Saltonstalls returned to New England in 1635 and settled in Ipswich.

Richard was prominent in local affairs as an important property holder, proprietor of the only gristmill in town, and deputy, 1635–37. After the removal of John Winthrop, Jr., Saltonstall's name appeared first on all town petitions and the townspeople referred to him as the "Worshipful Mr. Saltonstall." His residence in Ipswich was interrupted by three sojourns in England (1649–63; 1672–80; and 1686–94), during which he was appointed in 1650, a commissioner of a High Court of Justice to repress the enemies of the Commonwealth, and, in 1654, a trustee for settling sequestrated estates in Scotland (C. H. Firth and R. S. Rait, *Acts and Ordinances of the Interregnum,* 1911, II, 362, 885). Saltonstall undertook these journeys to England for the sake of his wife's health and, also, to oversee the family property which, contrary to the usual practice of the New England colonists, was retained.

In colony affairs he occupied important offices, serving as an Assistant, 1637–49, 1664, and 1680–82. As a magistrate he kept court at Ipswich, Newbury, and Piscataqua. In military affairs he served as a sergeant-major in Colonel Endicott's regiment, and he was an alternate commissioner of the New England Confederacy in 1644 and substitute agent of the Colony to England in 1660. He was one of that liberal Ipswich group, which included Bellingham, Simon Bradstreet, and Nathaniel Ward [q.v.], whose members were able, by virtue of their piety and devotion, to defy successfully arbitrary methods in government. In a manuscript, no longer extant, Saltonstall condemned the proposed Life Council as sinful and contrary to the charter, which condemnation caused trouble for the author. In 1643 the Ipswich group remonstrated with Governor Winthrop with respect to his policy of extending aid to Charles de LaTour in his quarrel with his rival D'Aulnay, Acadian official, and hinted at the neutrality of Ipswich in the event of hostilities. Saltonstall petitioned the Confederacy, in 1645, against unneutral aid to LaTour as impolitic and dishonorable (John

Winthrop, *The History of New England,* 1853, ed. by James Savage, II, 464–67). His advanced views are also indicated by his formal protest, in 1645, against the slave trade and by his opposition to the course taken by the authorities against Dr. Robert Child, Samuel Maverick [*q.v.*], and others who had petitioned for exemption from the prevailing ecclesiastical restrictions. Governor Winthrop found it difficult to cope with an opponent of unquestioned religious orthodoxy and assured social position.

To the regicides, Whalley and Goffe, Saltonstall gave fifty pounds in 1672 and to Harvard College over four hundred and fifty pounds (*Publications of the Colonial Society of Massachusetts,* vol. XV, 1925, "Harvard College Records," pt. I, p. 214). As a Harvard overseer he recommended, in 1671–72, an unnamed candidate for the then vacant presidency. He died at Hulme, Lancaster, England, survived by four children. His grandson, Gurdon [*q.v.*], became governor of Connecticut.

[Henry Bond, *Geneals. of the Families and Descendants of the Early Settlers of Watertown, Mass.* (1855); "Early Inhabitants of Ipswich, Mass.," in Abraham Hammatt, *The Hammatt Papers,* nos. 1–7 (1880–99); N. B. Shurtleff, *Records of the Governor and Company of the Mass. Bay* (5 vols., 1853–54); *New Eng. Hist. and Geneal. Reg.,* Apr. 1879, p. 228; Leverett Saltonstall, *Ancestry and Descendants of Sir Richard Saltonstall* (1897); John and J. A. Venn, *Alumni Cantabrigienses,* vol. IV (1926); T. F. Waters, *Ipswich in the Mass. Bay Colony,* vol. I (1905); John Noble, *Records of the Court of Assistants of the Colony of the Mass. Bay* (3 vols., 1901–28).]

N. H. D.

SALTUS, EDGAR EVERTSON (Oct. 8, 1855–July 31, 1921), novelist, essayist, poet, was the son of Francis Henry Saltus and Eliza Howe (Evertson). His great-grandfather, Solomon Saltus, came to New York City from Bermuda in the late eighteenth century and became a successful merchant; on his mother's side he was descended from an old Dutch family. He attended St. Paul's School, Concord, N. H., and entered Yale College with the class of 1876, leaving after one year and returning for a brief time with the class of 1877. He spent three or four years abroad, studying in Paris, Heidelberg, and Munich. In 1880 he received the degree of LL.B. from Columbia College, but he never practised law.

After his marriage to Helen Sturgis Read in November 1883, he turned to authorship, publishing in 1884 a slight but interesting biography of Balzac. While in Germany he had studied under Eduard von Hartmann, and in 1885 he paid tribute to Hartmann's influence in *The Philosophy of Disenchantment,* an account of Schopenhauer and his school. This led to *The*

Anatomy of Negation (1886), a study of antitheistic philosophies from the early Asiatic cults to contemporary positivism and atheism. In 1887 his first novel, *Mr. Incoul's Misadventure,* appeared, and by the end of 1894 he had written more than a half dozen others. During this period he also issued a collection of essays and sonnets, *Love and Lore* (1890), made translations from the French, and published an account of the Roman emperors, *Imperial Purple* (1892).

With the exception of *Mary Magdalen* (1891), an historical novel of the time of Christ, Saltus' early fiction dealt with New York society. Adopting an involved and epigrammatic style, he sought to cloak with glamor the melodramatic stories he unfolded, and by writing of murders, suicides, and adulteries, to illustrate the philosophy of disenchantment he had preached. His best work of this period is not in his novels, but in *Imperial Purple,* which, however lacking in historical accuracy, displays all the virtues of his style: his unusual vocabulary, his bizarre and sometimes genuinely epigrammatic mode of expression, and his skill in innuendo.

Between 1894 and 1903 he published little under his own name. In the late nineties he was employed by P. F. Collier & Son. For this firm (see Honce, *post*) he probably compiled *The Lovers of the World* (n.d.) and *The Great Battles of All Nations* (2 vols., 1899); for it he wrote supplementary chapters for the Nations of the World Series. Divorced from his first wife, he married, on Oct. 8, 1895, Elsie Welsh Smith, from whom he soon after separated. There was one daughter by this marriage. In 1903, with the publication of a collection of short stories, *Purple and Fine Women,* he returned to fiction, writing four novels in the next decade. He also wrote *Historia Amoris* (1906) and a history of religions, *The Lords of the Ghostland; a History of the Ideal* (1907). On Aug. 16, 1911, he married Marie Giles, subsequently his biographer. In his later years, despite ill health, he wrote two novels and various shorter pieces, and in *The Imperial Orgy* (1920) sought to do for Russia what, in *Imperial Purple,* he had done for Rome. Throughout his life he spent much of his time abroad. He was converted by his third wife to theosophy, a doctrine that made itself felt in all his later work.

From the first Saltus set himself against the main currents in American literature. His early novels, denounced as shocking by the moralists, were justly criticized by the more discriminating for weakness in characterization and sensationalism in style. Merely because he was a rebel, he attracted the attention of a small and somewhat esoteric group, counting among his admirers James Huneker and Elbert Hubbard. In his later years, and after his death, such critics as Carl Van Vechten and Gorham Munson attempted, with some immediate success, to awaken an interest in his work. The revival they initiated was, however, of brief duration, for it soon became apparent that the stylistic virtues these critics praised were vitiated by Saltus' inability to distinguish between the original and the merely bizarre. His importance, it became clear, was chiefly historical, that of a rebellious and exotic writer who, in his own time, did something to broaden the range of American literature, but without achieving any significance in his own right.

[Marie Saltus, *Edgar Saltus the Man* (1925) has little material on the early years, and is in general unsatisfactory. It may be supplemented by Ethel Saltus Ludington, *Ludington-Saltus Records* (1925); *Yale Seventy-Seven: Their Lives and Letters* (*circa* 1892); O. J. Bannard and E. P. Howe, *Biog. Record of the Class of 1876, Yale College* (1911); J. G. Huneker, *Steeplejack* (1920), vol. II; *Who's Who in America*, 1920–21. For critical estimates see Ramsay Colles, in *Westminster Rev.*, Oct. 1904; Carl Van Vechten, *The Merry-Go Round* (1918); G. B. Munson, "The Limbo of American Literature," in *Broom*, June 1922. For bibliography see Van Vechten, *op. cit.; Publishers' Weekly*, June 23, 1923; bibliog. by Charles Honce in Saltus' *The Uplands of Dream* (1925).]   G.H.

SAMPSON, MARTIN WRIGHT (Sept. 7, 1866–Aug. 22, 1930), professor of English, a descendant of Alexander Sampson, who came to Boston from England early in the eighteenth century, was born in Cincinnati, Ohio, the son of William S. Sampson, a manufacturer, whose father had settled there about 1830, and of Virginia Ada (Wright) Sampson. Before his graduation, in 1888, from the University of Cincinnati, where his literary and scholarly tastes were encouraged by James Morgan Hart [q.v.], he spent a year in study at the University of Munich. In 1890 he received the degree of M.A. from Cincinnati. Meanwhile he had begun the work as teacher of English which, with intervals of study and travel abroad, occupied the remainder of his life: first at the University of Iowa (1889–91), then at Stanford (1892–93), then at Indiana (1893–1906), and finally at Cornell University (1908–30).

His favorite subjects were the English romantic poets, the modern novel, the Elizabethan drama, and the history of the drama. As teacher he had the twofold object of imparting to his students his own keen appreciation and of developing in them as well the scholarly instinct which, not content with mere enjoyment, insists upon full knowledge and understanding. His lectures were informal, and his lifelong interest

in other arts than literature furnished him with happy illustrations of the principles of poetry and drama. While at Indiana University, by insisting that no pupil should be graduated who could not write clear and correct English, he raised the standard of English in the high schools of the state. He also founded the university's first dramatic club. At Cornell he gave afternoon readings before the students of engineering, who dropped in from their shops and laboratories bringing their pipes with them. Entertaining them at first with stories by popular authors and with humorous verse, often of his own composition, he gradually introduced more substantial fare, and soon had them listening with genuine interest to Milton and Plato. He encouraged the literary aspirations of the undergraduate by founding the Manuscript Club, a group of students who met at his house on Saturday evenings to read aloud their original stories, poems, and plays. In 1909 he established the Frances Sampson Fine Arts Prize, awarded annually for evidence of appreciation. In 1917 he organized the Cornell unit of the American Ambulance Field Service, the first to reach the front under the American flag. He edited *Camion Letters from American College Men, Volunteer Drivers of the American Field Service in France, 1917* (1918) and just before his death, which resulted from an automobile accident, he completed the editing of *Military Records of Cornell University in the World War* (1930).

Sampson published a textbook, *Written and Oral Composition* (1907), in collaboration with E. O. Holland, and edited a number of works of English and American literature, among them *The Lyric and Dramatic Poems of John Milton* (1901), Webster's *The White Devil and the Duchess of Malfy* (1904), *The Two Gentlemen of Verona* (1912), Middleton's plays (1915), and Henry James's *Daisy Miller* (1927) and *The Ambassadors* (1930). His introductory essays are urbane in style and illuminating as criticism. A collection of tales written originally for his own children, *The Good Giant* (1928), met with public favor. His attitude toward academic problems was entertainingly presented in a one-act satire, *The Soul of a Professor* (published in *Cornell University Plays*, 1932). A volume of his poems, *Voices of the Forest*, was published posthumously in 1933.

He married in 1892 Frances Van Rensselaer Gardiner, who died in 1909. In 1910 he married Julia Dauchy Pattison, by whom he had four children.

[*Who's Who in America*, 1914–15, 1930–31; *Letters of Edward Dowden* (1914); Dowden, Richard Garnett, and W. M. Rossetti, *Letters About Shelley* (1917), ed.

by R. S. Garnett, pp. *232, 233*; *N. Y. Times*, Aug. 24, 1930; *Cornell Alumni News*, Sept. 18, 1930, Mar. 29, 1932; personal acquaintance.]   W. S., Jr.

SAMPSON, WILLIAM (January 1764–Dec. 28, 1836), lawyer, Irish patriot, son of Rev. Arthur and Anne (Wilson) Sampson, was born at Londonderry into the privileged caste of Ireland, and was brought up under influences favorable to England. He is said to have attended the University of Dublin, and in 1790 studied law at Lincoln's Inn, London. He was admitted to the Irish bar and obtained a good practice. Experience and observation then brought him—very late, as he afterward regretfully wrote—into the movement for political reform. He contributed articles and poems to nationalist newspapers, defended state prisoners, took the oath of the United Irishmen in open court, and in December 1796 presided over a meeting at Belfast which was called treasonable. After the outbreak of war he collected information regarding the atrocities of the government troops. These activities and the false report that he held a major-general's commission in the French army led to his arrest and continued imprisonment without a trial. He was offered his release on condition that he would submit to official examination and then go into exile in some country at peace with England; and in order to save the life of a friend he accepted the offer. Admission to the United States being denied by Adams' administration, he was sent to Portugal in 1799, and by that country to France. He remained there six years and then spent nearly a year in Hamburg. In 1806, he appeared in London with a passport from the British minister to Hamburg. He was at once arrested and sent at the expense of the British government to New York. His family arrived four years later.

In America Sampson won prominence in the practice of law, the reporting of cases, and propagandist writing. He was admitted to the bar almost immediately after his arrival, and while practising turned his knowledge of stenography to account by publishing a dozen or more verbatim reports of cases which had attracted popular attention. As a lawyer, he achieved high rank chiefly through his eloquence and his vigorous advocacy of personal rights. In one of the first American cases involving organized labor he defended the journeymen cordwainers who were accused of conspiring to raise their wages by means of a closed shop; and, though the decision went against them, his argument clearly stated the principle on which the closed shop has since been justified (William Sampson, reporter, *Trial of the Journeymen Cordwainers*, 1810). In 1813

he successfully interposed as *amicus curiae* to prevent a Catholic priest's being required to disclose secrets imparted to him in confession. To his report of the case, entitled *The Catholic Question in America* (1813), he appended a treatise on the doctrine of penance. Though himself a Protestant, he helped to prosecute Orangemen who had attacked Catholic Irishmen in Greenwich Village, N. Y., in 1824, and he defended Irishmen charged with rioting in Philadelphia in 1831. During the years 1825–30 he resided in Georgetown, D. C., and appeared in several cases before the Supreme Court of the United States.

In 1807 he published *Memoirs of William Sampson* in the form of a series of letters to a friend. Ostensibly an account of his experiences in the Irish rebellion, the volume was really a scathing denunciation of the whole British policy toward Ireland. It was favorably received in America; a second edition, revised and enlarged, was published at Leesburg, Va., in 1817; and a third edition, less complete, at London in 1832.

Sampson best deserves to be remembered as the chief exponent of the early movement to codify the common law. In 1823 he delivered an address before the New York Historical Society (*An Anniversary Discourse . . . Dec. 6, 1823*, 1824) which contained a violent and radical attack on certain barbarities in the common law, and a recommendation that the American people discard its undesirable features and preserve the best by codification. In the controversy that followed, Sampson, by correspondence, brought his proposal to the favorable consideration of jurists and political leaders in many parts of the country. His work was moderately successful during his lifetime and influenced the leaders of the following generation. Among his other writings was a *History of Ireland* (2 vols., 1833), being a continuation of W. C. Taylor's *History of the Civil Wars of Ireland* (2 vols., 1831). He married Grace Clarke in 1790 and had three children; he died in New York City, survived by his widow and a daughter.

[*Dict. of Nat. Biog.*; R. R. Madden, *The United Irishmen*, 2 ser. II (1843), 335–88; introduction to the London edition of Sampson's *Memoirs*; C. C. Beale, *William Sampson, Lawyer and Stenographer* (1907), repr. from *Proc. N. Y. State Stenographers' Asso.*, 1906; E. J. McGuire, "William Sampson," *Jour. Am. Irish Hist. Soc.*, Oct. 1916; L. B. Sampson, *The Sampson Family* (1914); *N. Y. American*, Dec. 29, 1836. Most accounts give the day of Sampson's birth as Jan. 17, but Madden's copy of his tombstone inscription gives Jan. 27.]   E. C. S.

SAMPSON, WILLIAM THOMAS (Feb. 9, 1840–May 6, 1902), naval officer, was born at Palmyra, N. Y., the eldest of seven children of James and Hannah (Walker) Sampson. His great-grandparents had come to America from northern Ireland. With an excellent record in the Palmyra schools, he gained an appointment to the United States Naval Academy, and was graduated first in the class of 1861. After duty earlier in the Civil War as instructor at the Naval Academy at Newport, he joined the monitor *Patapsco* in 1864, as executive officer, and was on her turret when she was blown up while removing mines in Charleston harbor, Jan. 15, 1865, with a loss of sixty lives. He was made lieutenant in 1862, and lieutenant commander in 1866, while serving in the *Colorado* of the European Squadron. Admiral Dewey, his shipmate in the *Colorado,* speaks of Sampson as possessing "a most brilliant mind and the qualities of a practical and efficient officer on board ship," and as being one of the handsomest men he had ever seen (*Autobiography of George Dewey,* 1913, p. 139).

He was at the Naval Academy from 1868 to 1871, and after service on the European station returned to Annapolis as head of the physics department, 1874–78. Not a great reader of general literature or a man of wide interests, he developed in these years of study and teaching an outstanding proficiency in the scientific side of his profession, especially in physics, chemistry, metallurgy, and astronomy. Characteristic of the man and his methods were his academy lectures, delivered quietly but with great clearness, and with such painstaking attention to detail that in his illustrative experiments a former student could "not recall a single failure" (I. N. Hollis, "Rear-Admiral Sampson," *World's Work,* Nov. 1901, p. 1421). After commanding the *Swatara* in the Orient, 1879–82, he was stationed at the Naval Observatory, and in 1884 was a delegate to the International Meridian Conference. He commanded the Newport Torpedo Station from 1884 to 1886 and was also a member of an inter-service board on coast defenses, the naval aspects of which he treated in an article in the *Proceedings of the United States Naval Institute,* April 1889. From 1886 to 1890 he was superintendent of the Naval Academy. After two years in command of the *San Francisco,* he became superintendent of the naval gun foundry at Washington and later chief of the ordnance bureau, 1893–97. During his tenure of this office he was credited with making great advances in guns, explosives, and gunnery practice (Long, *post,* p. 227).

In June 1897 he joined the North Atlantic Squadron in command of the battleship *Iowa.* He was president of the board of inquiry on the *Maine* disaster, and was selected to command the squadron on the eve of the war with Spain, when the health of Admiral Montgomery Sicard [*q.v.*] was judged unequal to the task. This appointment over a dozen capable senior officers gave signal recognition of his high service reputation. Though the Spanish opposition was not such as to try his leadership to the utmost, he met with notable success the constant tests of judgment and severe mental and physical stress of the extended tropical campaign. In deference to departmental orders not to endanger his ships against shore defenses before meeting the Spanish fleet, he gave up his early design of an attack on Havana, and, at the declaration of war on Apr. 21, 1898, left Key West with twenty-six vessels to establish a blockade of the north coast of Cuba. In the later stages of the war, especially, a general supervision of fleet movements was maintained by the departmental strategy board in which Mahan had a guiding hand. Still, much was necessarily left to the command at sea, and it is high tribute to Sampson that the only move criticised later by Mahan was the cruise eastward to Puerto Rico and bombardment of San Juan on May 12, which left Havana open, with the destination of the approaching Spanish squadron as yet unknown.

Upon receiving news of Cervera's arrival at Martinique, also on May 12, Sampson hastened westward, and was joined at Key West by the Flying Squadron from Norfolk, under the command of Winfield Scott Schley [*q.v.*]. This force, now operating under Sampson's orders, was dispatched on May 19 to blockade Cienfuegos, chief southern port of Cuba, where it was expected Cervera would next appear. There was some constraint in the arrangement by which Schley, though two numbers senior to Sampson, was placed under him, and this was increased by Schley's delay in moving eastward from Cienfuegos to Santiago upon receiving news of Cervera's arrival there on May 19, and his still further delay in establishing a close blockade of that port. To the department's anxious query as to when and for how long he could himself blockade Santiago, Sampson replied that he could go at once and blockade indefinitely. He joined Schley at Santiago on June 1, and the combined forces took up their month-long vigil off the port, with ships in close semicircle around the narrow entrance and searchlights at night playing directly upon it. In this blockade Sampson's genius for patient and painstaking organization found full play. His health was not of the strongest, and from the time of the *Maine* inquiry he had been under a heavy burden, his duties including at this time supervision of the whole

Cuban blockade, cooperation with the army, direction of minor operations, and control of over a hundred vessels in his total force. Undoubtedly towards the end he suffered some slackening of physical and mental powers.

On the morning of July 3, Sampson in his flagship, the *New York,* had gone about seven miles eastward for a conference with General Shafter. He had signaled, "Disregard movements of flagship," but had not turned over the command to the next in rank, Schley; he was in sight of the squadron, and probably within signal range of the nearer units. When the suspense was ended by the coming out of Cervera's squadron at 9:35 A. M., the *New York* hastened back toward the battle, but though under fire from the entrance forts and in position to control later operations, she did not actually fire on any of the larger enemy ships. Schley, meantime, in the fast cruiser *Brooklyn,* was conspicuous in the action, and the early newspaper dispatches gave him chief credit for the victory. Sampson's first message— "The fleet under my command offers the nation as a Fourth of July present the whole of Cervera's fleet" (*Annual Report of the Navy Department,* 1898, *post,* p. 505) was ridiculed. Popular opinion made Schley the hero, though the department and the service in general strongly supported Sampson. Politics also entered into the long and bitter controversy which ensued, and the provisional promotions of Aug. 10, 1898, advancing Sampson eight numbers and Schley six, were not confirmed by the Senate. Both became permanent rear admirals by the Personnel Act of 1899, but Sampson, with manifest injustice, never received special recognition for his excellent work throughout the war. Actually, the question of command in the battle was not vital, since no squadron orders of consequence were issued. In his final decision in the matter, President Roosevelt stated that "technically Sampson commanded," but that his real credit rested "upon the excellence of the blockade: upon the preparedness of the squadron . . . and the standing orders in accordance with which they instantly moved to the attack" (Long, *post,* II, 208). Sampson published an article on the Atlantic fleet in the Spanish-American War in the *Century Magazine,* April 1899.

The hostility of the press correspondents was unquestionably due largely to Sampson's austere, uningratiating manner. He was reticent by nature, and gave an initial impression of coldness. With subordinates he was uniformly courteous, and he won their devotion, but he was not quick to praise. For a time after the Santiago victory it was planned to send a force under Sampson to

the Spanish coast, but the plan was abandoned and after the close of hostilities he brought his fleet on Aug. 20 to New York. From September to December 1898, he was in Cuba with the Puerto Rico Evacuation Commission, and subsequently continued in command of the Atlantic fleet until October 1899. Thereafter until his death he was in charge of the Boston navy yard. His death from paresis occurred in Washington, D. C., and he was buried in the National Cemetery at Arlington. He was married in 1863 to Margaret Sexton Aldrich of Palmyra, and in 1882 to Elizabeth Susan Burling of Rochester, N. Y. By his first marriage he had four daughters, and by his second, two sons.

[*Who's Who in America,* 1901–02; L. B. Sampson, *The Sampson Family* (1914); L. R. Hamersly, *The Records of Living Officers of the U. S. Navy and Marine Corps* (6th ed., 1898), *Biog. Sketches of Distinguished Officers of the Army and Navy* (1905); W. A. M. Goode, *With Sampson Through the War* (1899); E. S. Maclay, *A Hist. of the U. S. Navy* (1902), vol. III; J. D. Long, *The New Am. Navy* (2 vols., 1903); *Ann. Report of the Navy Dept., 1898, Append.* to the *Chief of Bur. of Navigation* (1898); articles on Sampson by Sec. of Navy J. D. Long and Admiral A. T. Mahan, *Fortnightly Review,* Aug. 1902; speeches by Mahan and others at the unveiling of the Sampson Memorial Window, Naval Academy, *Proc. U. S. Naval Institute,* Mar. 1909; *Washington* (D. C.) *Post,* May 7, 1902. For additional material, see the bibliography for the article on Schley.]   A. W—t.

SAMUELS, EDWARD AUGUSTUS (July 4, 1836–May 27, 1908), ornithologist, nature lover, and sportsman, the son of Emanuel and Abigail Samuels, was born in Boston and resided throughout his life in eastern Massachusetts. His father was interested in outdoor life and encouraged him in his studies in natural history, but his schooling was limited to that provided by the city. Early in life he began writing for the press and in 1860 he became assistant to the secretary of the Massachusetts State Board of Agriculture, in which capacity he served for twenty years. His duties allowed him ample time for other pursuits and in 1870 his musical tastes led him to begin the publication of music, which he continued until about 1890. His spare hours, however, were devoted to the promotion of the study of birds and to work for the protection of fish and game. His election as president of the Massachusetts Fish and Game Protective Association in 1885, a position which he held for seven years, was one in which he took the greatest pride. Under his leadership the association increased greatly in numbers and influence, and became an important force in improving the state laws and in developing public sentiment in support of them.

While not a scientist in the modern sense of the word, Samuels was a good observer and keenly interested in the habits of animals, especially birds. He felt the lack of any popular book on the birds of Massachusetts, and having a taste for writing, and excellent judgment in selecting what was well written, he published a number of papers in the *Reports* of the State Board of Agriculture intended to meet this need. Meanwhile he undertook the preparation of a volume entitled *Ornithology and Oology of New England,* the first edition of which appeared in 1867. It met with immediate success, and the legislature made a special appropriation to purchase a thousand copies for public libraries throughout the state. New editions were soon called for and in 1870 the fifth edition was issued, under the title *The Birds of New England,* by which the work is most widely known. The technical matter for this very popular and useful book was taken from the publications of Spencer F. Baird [*q.v.*], and there are liberal quotations from Audubon, Wilson, and Nuttall, as well as from the letters of less-known naturalists. But the matter is so well chosen that it probably meets the needs of the reader better than any attempt at original writing could have done. There is no doubt that Samuels' *Birds of New England* did more to stimulate bird study and to increase the public interest in birds in New England than any other publication of the last half of the nineteenth century. Of his subsequent publications, none met with comparable success, but his *With Fly-Rod and Camera* (1890) was very well received and did much to develop and stimulate the love of outdoor life which is now so general. It was perhaps the first publication to suggest the "hunting with a camera," instead of a gun, which has been so marked a feature of twentieth-century field work. Among his associates, Samuels was regarded as one of the best-informed men on all subjects pertaining to the natural history of the New England states. He was approachable and eager to help any one who showed an interest in that field and many a student owes him a debt for help freely and cheerfully given.

He married Susan B. Caldwell, a school-teacher and author of stories for young people, while his sister Adelaide was also a writer of no little reputation. After 1890, his eyesight began to fail and in his later years, he was blind. His affliction was increased by paralysis, which completely prevented his actual writing, but he nevertheless, by dictation, continued his contributions to *Forest and Stream* and similar publications. He died at the home of his daughter, Mrs. John A. Barton, in Fitchburg, Mass.

[*Who's Who in America,* 1908–09; *Boston Transcript,* May 28, 1908; *Forest and Stream,* June 13, 1908; *Auk,* July 1908.]   H. L. C.

SAMUELS, SAMUEL (Mar. 14, 1823–May 18, 1908), mariner, has been called the greatest of American transatlantic packet commanders. He was born in Philadelphia and at eleven, after a disagreement with his step-mother, ran away to become a cabin boy on a coasting schooner. This was the beginning of a lively series of maritime adventures later recounted in his memoirs, *From the Forecastle to the Cabin* (1887). He was shipwrecked on the Florida coast; was sentenced to be flogged while serving on a revenue cutter at Mobile; was shanghaied aboard a Baltimore cotton ship for Liverpool; was chased by West Indian pirates; served on the Texas frigate *Houston;* sailed around the world, fighting cannibals in the Pacific; became an officer at seventeen; and married a girl who was a passenger on a trip from New Orleans to New York. At twenty-one, already a father, he was given the command of a ship bound for the Mediterranean. There he declined a proffered post of admiral in the Turkish navy and rescued from a Constantinople harem a Swedish lady who had been enslaved in Egypt. He survived attacks of banditti near Pisa, pirates near Leghorn, and cholera at Hamburg, and was rescued when washed overboard off the Cape of Good Hope. For three years he commanded Schuchardt & Gebhard's packet *Angelique* between New York and Amsterdam.

His chief fame came from his seventy-eight fast voyages between New York and Liverpool as commander of the packet *Dreadnought.* Built under his supervision at Newburyport, Mass., by a group of New York merchants for their Red Cross Line, this vessel was ready for sea in February 1854. Samuels says of her, "She was never passed in anything over a four-knot breeze. She was what might be termed a semi-clipper, and possessed the merit of being able to bear driving as long as her sails and spars would stand. By the sailors she was nicknamed the 'Wild boat of the Atlantic,' while others called her the 'Flying Dutchman'" (*Forecastle to Cabin,* p. 250). Samuels was a great driver, keeping full sail on his heavily sparred ship long after most others were under reefed topsails. He drove her night and day and always used the short northern passage in spite of the extra danger from gales and ice. He was a firm disciplinarian and left a graphic account of overcoming a particularly tough crew of Liverpool "packet rats" who had sworn to throw him overboard (*Ibid.,* pp. 267–91). He established a packet speed record in

324

1859, reaching Liverpool in thirteen days and eight hours from New York, but the latest research discredits the story of a run from New York to Queenstown the following year in nine days and seventeen hours (Paine, *post,* p. xvi). Samuels maintained a remarkable regularity of fast voyages between 1854 and 1862, his first eight averaging twenty-four and a half days. Because of the combination of speed and safety, the *Dreadnought's* staterooms were booked a year in advance and she commanded freight rates midway between those of the steamships and the regular sailing packets, her owners offering to refund freight charges if delivery were not made on time.

During the Civil War, Samuels commanded the *John Rice* in 1863, was general superintendent of the Quartermaster's Department at New York in 1864, and commanded the *G. B. McClellan* at the taking of Fort Fisher in 1865. In 1866, he was captain of the steamship *Fulton,* the last of the American liners to Havre, and in December won the first transatlantic yacht race, driving James Gordon Bennett's *Henrietta* from "Sandy Hook to the Needles" just ahead of the *Fleetwing* and *Vesta.* In 1870, in the *Dauntless,* he was beaten by the British yacht *Cambria* in a race from Head of Kinsale to Sandy Hook and in 1887, the *Coronet* beat him in the old *Dauntless.* By that time he had long been ashore, in various business capacities. His Samana Bay Company in 1872 hoped to exploit a concession in Santo Domingo, which, however, was revoked in 1874. He organized the Rousseau Electric Signal Company and the United States Steam Heating & Power Company, served as general superintendent of the Pacific Mail Steamship Company, and in his last years was president of the Marine Journal Company. He died at his home in Brooklyn.

[The chief source for Samuels' career through 1862 is his *From the Forecastle to the Cabin* (1887), reprinted, with a critical foreword, by R. D. Paine in 1924. See also "Capt. Samuel Samuels of the Dreadnought," illustrated, in *Outing Mag.,* Dec. 1905; F. B. C. Bradlee, "The Dreadnought of Newburyport," *Essex Inst. Hist. Colls.,* vol. LVI (1920); A. H. Clark, *The Clipper Ship Era* (1910); O. T. Howe and F. C. Matthews, *Am. Clipper Ships,* vol. I (1926); C. C. Cutler, *Greyhounds of the Sea* (1930); J. H. Morrison, *Hist. of N. Y. Ship Yards* (copr. 1909); J. D. J. Kelley, *American Yachts* (1884); R. F. Coffin, *The America's Cup* (1885); *Who's Who in America,* 1906–07; *N. Y. Herald,* Apr. 1, 1905, May 19, 1908.]   R. G. A.

SANBORN, EDWIN DAVID (May 14, 1808–Dec. 29, 1885), educator, was born at Gilmanton, N. H., the son of David Edwin and Hannah (Hook) Sanborn, and a descendant of John Sanborn (or Samborne), who came from England to Boston in 1632 and later settled in Hampton, N. H. He attended Gilmanton Academy and was graduated from Dartmouth College in 1832. After a period of teaching and the study of law, he entered Andover Theological Seminary in 1834, but in the next year was summoned back to Dartmouth as a tutor. Soon he became professor of Latin and Greek, and in 1837, professor of Latin. In 1859 he assumed a similar chair in Washington University, St. Louis, but returned to Dartmouth in 1863 as professor of oratory and belles-lettres. In 1880 he was appointed to the newly established Winkley Professorship of Anglo-Saxon and English Literature, resigning two years later because of ill health. Sanborn was a voluminous contributor to the periodical press, and was in much demand throughout the state as a speaker on a great variety of occasions. Many of his addresses were printed in pamphlet form. He assisted Fletcher Webster in editing the correspondence of the latter's father, Daniel Webster, and in 1875 he published a *History of New Hampshire.* Twice he was a member of the state legislature, and in 1850 of the constitutional convention.

It was as a teacher of the old school, however, that he showed his greatest strength. His reading was remarkably wide, his memory prodigious, and his power of interesting and inspiring students equaled by that of few teachers of his day. His opinions were pronounced and he was ready at all times to set them forth; he was bluff, abrupt, and downright, saying what was on his mind with little regard for the feelings of others. Eager, brimful of learning, quick at repartee, for more than forty years he inspired generations of undergraduates with some measure of his own vigor and enthusiasm. The students were amused at his peculiarities, but they were drawn to him by the contagion of his personality and held him in sincere admiration. The term "Bully," applied to him in his earlier days, became, in later years, a mark of real affection. He is an example of the college teacher at his best in the days before productive scholarship, in the technical sense, became a requirement of the professor. The Sanborn English House, erected at Dartmouth in 1929 by the use of part of a bequest by his son, Edwin Webster Sanborn, perpetuates his name, and, in its purpose and application, his ideals. In 1837 he was married to Mary Ann, daughter of Ezekiel Webster of Boscawen, N. H., and niece of Daniel Webster: she died in 1864, and in 1868 he married Mrs. Sarah Fenton Clark of Detroit. By his first wife he had four children, one of whom was Katherine Abbott Sanborn [*q.v.*], lecturer and author. He died in New York City.

[See V. C. Sanborn, *Geneal. of the Family of Samborne or Sanborn in England and America* (1899); J. K. Lord, *A Hist. of Dartmouth Coll.* (1913); L. B. Richardson, *Hist. of Dartmouth Coll.* (1932); *N. Y. Daily Tribune*, Dec. 30, 1885. Much of Sanborn's correspondence is preserved in the lib. of Dartmouth Coll.]

L. B. R.

SANBORN, FRANKLIN BENJAMIN

(Dec. 15, 1831–Feb. 24, 1917), author, journalist, philanthropist, was born on his ancestral farm in Hampton Falls., N. H., the fifth of the seven children of Aaron and Lydia (Leavitt) Sanborn, and the sixth in descent from John Sanborn, who settled in Hampton in 1640. His father was a farmer and, when his son was born, clerk of the town. The boy's intellectual development was stimulated by his love for Ariana Walker, daughter of James Walker of Peterborough. With her encouragement he completed his preparatory schooling at Phillips Exeter Academy and entered Harvard College as a sophomore in 1852. He enjoyed his college life, but from his teachers he derived far less than from Theodore Parker, whose preaching he attended regularly, and from Ralph Waldo Emerson, on whom he first ventured to call in 1853. On Aug. 23, 1854, he was married to Ariana Walker, who was on her deathbed and succumbed eight days later. Sanborn graduated from Harvard in 1855 and removed to Concord, Mass., where at Emerson's suggestion he had already opened a school.

It was a happy move, for Concord was his spiritual home. Less original than the elder literary men of the village, he was their fellow in vigor and independence of mind and in breadth of interests, and he had a practical sagacity and knowledge of the world that some of them lacked. He was soon in the thick of the abolition movement. As secretary of the Massachusetts Free Soil Association he went on a tour of inspection in the West in the summer of 1856 and, although he did not actually enter Kansas Territory, brought back with him an enduring interest in the problems of that region. The next January he met John Brown in Boston, was captivated by the man, and became his New England agent. He was apprised of Brown's intentions at Harpers Ferry, did what he could to dissuade him, but, when dissuasion proved futile, aided him. Later, he refused to leave Massachusetts to testify before a committee of the United States Senate, grounding his refusal on an appeal to the doctrine of state rights, and on Feb. 16, 1860, the Senate ordered his arrest. Sanborn retreated twice to Quebec but returned on the advice of his friends. The sergeant-at-arms of the Senate delegated the power to arrest him to one Carleton of

Boston, who with four assistants apprehended him at Concord on Apr. 3, 1860. He was released at once on a writ of *habeas corpus* issued by Judge E. R. Hoar; a *posse comitatus* chased the arresting party out of town; and the next day the state supreme court, by a decision written by Chief Justice Shaw, ordered Sanborn's discharge.

To newspaper work, philanthropy, and literature he devoted the greater part of his long life. On Aug. 16, 1862, he married his cousin, Louisa Augusta Leavitt, by whom he had three sons. He succeeded Moncure Daniel Conway [*q.v.*] as editor of the *Boston Commonwealth* (1863–67) and was a resident editor of the *Springfield Republican* (1868–72). He had been a correspondent of the *Republican* since 1856 and remained on its staff until 1914. As a newspaper man he was noted for his blistering criticism of various Massachusetts politicians. In 1863 Gov. John Albion Andrew [*q.v.*] appointed him secretary of the state board of charities. This office was the first of its kind in the United States, and Sanborn made it important and influential. He instituted a system of inspection and report for state charities that has been widely copied, made himself an expert on the care of the insane, and drafted many bills that were enacted into law. He retired as secretary in 1868 but remained on the board and was its chairman from 1874 to 1876; from 1879 to 1888 he was state inspector of charities. He was a founder and officer of the American Social Science Association, the National Prison Association, the National Conference of Charities, the Clarke School for the Deaf, and the Massachusetts Infant Asylum, and for all of them he worked hard and effectively. He lectured at Cornell University, Smith College, and Wellesley College, and joined with William Torrey Harris [*q.v.*] in establishing the Concord School of Philosophy. He knew intimately all the men and women who made Concord famous, was their sympathetic, helpful friend while they lived and their loyal, intelligent editor and biographer after their death. His publications include: *Henry D. Thoreau* (1882); *The Life and Letters of John Brown* (1885), a fourth edition of which was issued under the title *John Brown, Liberator of Kansas and Martyr of Virginia* (1910); *Dr. S. G. Howe, the Philanthropist* (1891); *A. Bronson Alcott: His Life and Philosophy* (2 vols., 1893), with W. T. Harris; *Memoirs of Pliny Earle, M.D.* (1898); *The Personality of Thoreau* (1901); *Ralph Waldo Emerson* (1901); *The Personality of Emerson* (1903); *New Hampshire* (1904); *New Hampshire Biography and Autobiography* (1905); *Michael*

Anagnos (1907); *Bronson Alcott at Alcott House, England, and Fruitlands, New England* (1908); *Hawthorne and His Friends* (1908); *Recollections of Seventy Years* (2 vols., 1909); and *The Life of Henry David Thoreau* (1917). He published many magazine articles and did much editorial work on the literary remains of his friends. In some conservative circles his reputation as a subversive thinker lingered even into the twentieth century. He made two extensive visits to Europe and in his latter years enjoyed his membership in the Massachusetts Historical Society. Retaining his faculties to the end, he never lost his passion for liberty and justice or his admiration for the great men whom he had known in his prime. He died at his son's home in Plainfield, N. J., and was buried in Concord.

[Sanborn's writings contain much biog. material, especially his *Recollections of Seventy Years* (2 vols., 1909) and "An Unpublished Concord Jour.," ed. by G. S. Hellman, *Century Mag.*, Apr. 1922. See also: V. C. Sanborn, *Geneal. of the Family of Samborne or Sanborn* (1899), and "Franklin Benjamin Sanborn, A.B.," *New England Hist. and Geneal. Reg.*, Oct. 1917, and *Kan. State Hist. Soc. Colls.*, vol. XIV (1918); Lindsay Swift, "Franklin Benjamin Sanborn," *Proc. Mass. Hist. Soc.*, vol. L (1917); Ed. Stanwood, memoir, *Ibid.*, vol. LI (1918); *The Report of the Secretary of the Class of 1855 of Harvard Coll., July 1855 to July 1865* (1865); *Apocrypha Concerning the Class of 1855 of Harvard Coll. and Their Deeds and Misdeeds during the Fifteen years between July, 1865, and July, 1880* (1880); *Springfield Republican*, Feb. 25, 27, 1917; Alexander Johnson, "An Appreciation of Franklin B. Sanborn," *Survey*, Mar. 10, 1917; W. E. Connelley, "Personal Reminiscences of F. B. Sanborn," *Kan. State Hist. Soc. Colls.*, vol. XIV (1918); H. D. Carew, "Franklin B. Sanborn, an Appreciation," *Granite Mo.*, Nov. 1922.]
G. H. G.

SANBORN, KATHERINE ABBOTT (July 11, 1839–July 9, 1917), author, teacher, and lecturer, was born in Hanover, N. H., the eldest daughter of Edwin David Sanborn [*q.v.*] and Mary Ann (Webster) Sanborn and the descendant of John Samborne, an English emigrant who settled in Hampton, N. H., about 1640. She was usually called Kate and most of her writing appeared under that name. Her mother was the daughter of Ezekiel Webster, the gifted brother of Daniel Webster, and of this relationship she was always proudly conscious. Her father, professor of Latin, gave more than forty years of service to Dartmouth College, interrupted by four years of teaching at Washington University in St. Louis. The family and community life in which she grew up was intellectually invigorating and socially stimulating. Books and lectures abounded, distinguished writers and scholars were frequent guests, and there was an unfailing supply of young men to entertain a lively girl.

She was taught by her father and his colleagues along the lines of the college curriculum, and she studied music in Andover, Mass., and elocution in Boston. Her chief education, however, was from reading and conversation; and in her writing she always retained much of the casual, anecdotal manner of the ready talker. She was almost inevitably a writer and teacher, beginning to publish at the age of eleven and opening a school in her father's house before she was twenty. From 1859 to 1863, during her father's years in St. Louis, she taught girls in Mary Institute, connected with Washington University. Later she taught elocution at Packer Collegiate Institute in Brooklyn, where she formed a close friendship with Anne Charlotte Lynch Botta [*q.v.*]. Her wit and wide knowledge of books attracted many to the "talks" on current literature that she gave first in Mrs. Botta's drawing room and later in various clubs and schools. In this line of lecturing she was among the pioneers, and likewise she was among the early organizers of women's clubs. She was always avid for novel experiences and susceptible to new influences. She wrote constantly for periodicals, and her *flair* for journalism was shown even in the titles of her lectures and publications, such as "Hunting Indians with a Taxicab," "Are Women Witty?" The gifts of quick association and retentive memory made her an excellent raconteur and determined her interest in anthologies and quotation calendars, of which she edited many. For three years, from 1880 to 1883, she taught English literature at Smith College. Although a stimulating and suggestive teacher, she had not the sound scholarship and intellectual patience necessary for real college work. On leaving Smith she made an extended lecture tour in the West and extended her travels to Alaska.

A break in health sent her to the country and she settled in Metcalf, Mass., for the remainder of her life. The records of her experiences *Adopting an Abandoned Farm* (1891) and *Abandoning an Adopted Farm* (1894) are delightfully humorous and may be counted as among the early contributions to "back to the land" writings. Lightly as she wrote them, the experiences were not all easy or remunerative, and the wise may read many a warning and much sage advice under the flow of wit. This is true also of her *A Truthful Woman in Southern California* (1893). Her last serious work, *Memories and Anecdotes* (1915), written too late to show her qualities at their best, abounds in clever turns and apt quotations and exhibits many of her chief characteristics, her redundancy, her lack of continuity, her wide and delighted reading, her love of people, and her unfailing zest in life. "Refreshing" was the word chosen by her friend,

Edna Dean Proctor, as most applicable to her. "A stout, buxom, red-headed woman, with hair all a-flying" a country neighbor is quoted as saying of Kate Sanborn. She was a purely New England product, with Yankee versatility and adaptability, and she went "all a-flying" down many new paths that later and soberer feet have worn to smoothness and even to monotony.

[*Memories and Anecdotes, ante*; E. W. Sanborn, *Kate Sanborn* (1918); V. C. Sanborn, *Geneal. of the Family of Samborne or Sanborn* (1899), esp. p. 429; *New York Times*, July 10, 1917; *Daily Evening Transcript* (Boston), July 9, 1917.]   E. D. H.

SANBORN, WALTER HENRY (Oct. 19, 1845–May 10, 1928), judge, descended from William Sanborn who came to Boston from England in 1632, was born at Epsom, N. H., the son of Henry Frederick and Eunice (Davis) Sanborn. He attended the local district school and academy, taught in the country districts after he was fifteen, and graduated from Dartmouth College as class valedictorian in 1867. For three years following he was principal of the high school at Milford, N. H., then went to St. Paul, Minn., and studied law in the office of his uncle, Gen. John B. Sanborn. He was admitted to the bar Jan. 28, 1871, and joined his uncle in a partnership which lasted more than a score of years. On Nov. 10, 1874, he married Emily F. Bruce of Milford, N. H.; two sons and two daughters were born of this marriage.

While his professional interests were always paramount with him, he also found time for other duties. From 1878 to 1880 and again from 1885 to 1892 he served in the St. Paul City Council; during the latter period he also had office in state and county bar associations. He had entered the Masonic order, becoming interested especially in the Knights Templars, and in 1889 was their Grand Commander for Minnesota.

In 1891 Sanborn was selected by President Harrison as one of three judges of the newly created circuit court of appeals for the eighth circuit. His commission was dated Mar. 17, 1892, and he exercised it for the remainder of his life—more than a generation. On June 4, 1903, he became presiding judge of the circuit. Notable administrative work which he did in his judicial capacity included conducting receiverships of the Union Pacific Railway (1893–98), the Chicago and Great Western (1908–09), the St. Louis & San Francisco (1913–14), and the Denver & Rio Grande (1918–19). The best exemplification of his work, however, is found in his opinions, and the bar of the circuit soon learned that it had in him a master builder of the law. Among the earliest of his significant opin-

ions was that in the Omaha Bridge Cases in 1892 (51 *Fed. Reporter*, 309), when he upheld the right of the Rock Island Railway to use the Union Pacific bridge across the Missouri. In *U. S.* vs. *Trans-Missouri Freight Association* (58 *Fed. Reporter*, 58), 1893, he held the Sherman Anti-trust law inapplicable to an agreement between competing railways to maintain freight rates recommended as reasonable by a committee of their own choosing. His ruling was reversed by a vote of five to four in the Supreme Court (166 *U. S.*, 343), but he was able to say that a majority of the judges (including those of his own court) who had passed on the case were of his view, and a decade later (1903), in *Whitwell* vs. *Continental Tobacco Company* (125 *Fed. Reporter*, 454), he maintained a somewhat similar position, holding the same act inapplicable to a corporation and its employee with an arrangement for special rates on its products to purchasers who refrained from handling those of its competitors. The large number of personal injury cases which came to his court enabled him to specialize in that field. His discussion (*Chicago, St. Paul, Minneapolis, and Omaha Railway Company* vs. *Elliot*, 55 *Fed. Reporter*, 949) of what constitutes the proximate cause of an injury is probably unexcelled in judicial opinions in English; masterly expositions of the "fellow servant doctrine" are found in *City of Minneapolis* vs. *Lundin* (58 *Fed. Reporter*, 525), *What Cheer Coal Co.* vs. *Johnson* (56 *Fed. Reporter*, 810), and *Gowen* vs. *Harley* (56 *Fed. Reporter*, 973), all rendered in 1893. An important precedent on contributory negligence is found in *Union Pacific Railway Company* vs. *Jarvi* (53 *Fed. Reporter*, 65), 1892; the employer's duty to warn minor employees of latent dangers, in *Bohn Manufacturing Company* vs. *Erickson* (55 *Fed. Reporter*, 943). He held the Federal power of naturalization exclusive, and his opinion in *City of Minneapolis* vs. *Reum* (56 *Fed. Reporter*, 576), 1893, is a valuable contribution to the literature of that subject. With a strong intellect, highly trained, deep learning gathered by long and exhaustive study, and a clear and incisive style of expression developed by extensive judicial service he has had few superiors on the American bench. In 1927 the Bar Association of St. Louis gave him a testimonial dinner in celebration of his service of thirty-five years.

[C. E. Flandrau, *Encyc. of Biog. of Minn.* (1900), vol. I; H. J. Boswell, *Am. Blue Book: Attorneys of Minn.* (1923); *Walter Henry Sanborn: A Testimonial Vol.* (Bar Asso. of St. Louis, 1927); *Who's Who in America*, 1926–27; J. B. Sanborn, *Sanborn Family in the U. S.* (1887); *St. Paul Dispatch*, May 10, 1928.]
                    C. S. L.

SANDEMAN, ROBERT (Apr. 29, 1718–Apr. 2, 1771), promoter in the American colonies of a religious sect which came to be known as the Sandemanians, was born at Perth, in Scotland, the eldest son of David and Margaret (Ramsay) Sandeman. His father was a merchant, and from 1736 until 1744 Robert was a linen manufacturer in partnership with his brother William. As a young man, probably while at the University of Edinburgh, he came under the influence of John Glas [see *Dictionary of National Biography*], whose daughter Catherine he married in 1737. She died in 1746. He became an elder in the Glassite churches in 1744 and served successively at Perth, Dundee, Edinburgh, and London. The Glassites, or Sandemanians as they were later called in England and America, originated in 1728 as a protest against the established Church of Scotland and formed an independent body, rejecting the Covenant, asserting the independence of church and state, preaching the doctrine that faith is mere intellectual assent, and practising many of the primitive Christian rites. The chief article of their belief was that "the bare Work of Jesus Christ without a Deed or Thought on the Part of Man is sufficient to present the chief of Sinners spotless before God" (Sandeman's epitaph, Edes, *post*, p. 112). Sandeman became widely known by his controversial writings, particularly *Letters on Theron and Aspasio Addressed to the Author*, published in Edinburgh in 1757, a criticism of James Hervey's *Dialogues*. In 1760 he organized the London congregation of the sect.

Perceiving the interest aroused in America by his writings and being in correspondence with Ebenezer White, pastor at Danbury, Conn., and others of the New England clergy, he sailed for America on Aug. 10, 1764, accompanied by James Cargill. At Providence, R. I., he was joined by Andrew Oliphant. He and his associates preached in many towns of New England and within a few years organized congregations at Boston, Portsmouth, N. H., Taunton, Mass., Newtown and Danbury, Conn. In 1764, at Boston, he published *Some Thoughts on Christianity*. By 1767 he had made his home at Danbury, which became the chief stronghold of the sect in America and where remnants of the congregation existed until about 1900.

Sandeman and his followers were vigorously opposed by the leading New England ministers for their defense of "the voluntary principle." They were especially suspect for their rejection of the Covenant of Grace and of the doctrine of justification by faith as an act of regeneration. Sandeman taught that "every one who obtains a just notion of the person and work of Christ . . . is justified and finds peace with God simply by that notion" (Letter II, *Epistolary Correspondence, post*). Samuel Langdon [*q.v.*] said of the Sandemanians that they were of "a very malevolent Spirit and high Enthusiasm very much like that of the hottest New Lights, however frigid Sandeman's notions may seem to his readers" (Letter to Ezra Stiles, Sept. 7, 1766, *Literary Diary, post*, II, 171). In 1770 Sandeman was brought before the judge at Danbury and fined £40 for remaining in town four weeks after being warned to depart as an undesirable transient. At the hearing he pleaded that the law was not intended "against harmless strangers but against persons of ungoverned and dishonest conversations" (Walker, *post*, p. 154), and the sentence was never executed. Several of his disciples, however, were ordered out of New Haven in 1777 for the expression of Loyalist views.

Ezra Stiles described Sandeman as "of a middling Stature, dark Complexion, a good Eye, uses accurate Language, but not eloquent in utterance, has not a melodious voice, his expressions governed by Sentiment, his dialect Scotch, not graceful in his Air and Address, yet has something which deforces attention, and this is chiefly by the Sentiments he infuses or excites in his Auditory—generally grave and decent, and not a noisy speaker" (Walker, p. 151). He died at Danbury.

[*An Epistolary Correspondence between S. P. and R. S.* (1760), correspondence between Samuel Pike and Robert Sandeman, begun in 1758; Sandeman's *Discourses on Passages of Scripture with Essays and Letters . . . with Biog. Sketch of the Author* (Dundee, 1857); Samuel Langdon, *An Impartial Examination of Mr. Robert Sandeman's Letters on Theron and Aspasio* (Portsmouth, N. H., 1765); Walter Wilson, *The Hist. and Antiquities of Dissenting Churches*, III (1810), 274–75; Andrew Fuller, *Strictures on Sandemanianism* (New York, 1812); H. H. Edes, "The Places of Worship of the Sandemanians in Boston," *Col. Soc. Mass. Pub.*, vol. VI (1904); Williston Walker, "The Sandemanians of New England," *Ann. Report Am. Hist. Asso., 1901* (1902), vol. I; J. G. Sandeman, *The Sandeman Geneal.* (1895); F. B. Dexter, *The Literary Diary of Ezra Stiles* (3 vols., 1901).]   H. W. S.

SANDERS, BILLINGTON McCARTER (Dec. 2, 1789–Mar. 12, 1854), Baptist minister, educator, the eldest son of Ephraim and Nancy Sanders, was born in Columbia County, Ga. Early left an orphan, he was reared in a friendly and pious home. He prepared for college in Kiokee, or McNeil's, Seminary, and entered Franklin College, Athens, Ga., about 1806, but in 1808 transferred to South Carolina College, Columbia, S. C., where he graduated in 1809. After teaching for two years in Columbia County Academy, Ga., he was a succesful farmer for about twenty years. In 1817 he served in the lower House of the state legislature, but declined to be a candidate for reëlection. He joined Kiokee Baptist Church in January 1810, being baptized by Abraham Marshall. Some years later, feeling called to preach, he was licensed by Union Church, Warren County, Ga., and on Jan. 5, 1825, was ordained. He continued to farm, but now devoted much time to itinerant preaching and pastoral work. At different times he was pastor of Williams Creek, Pine Grove, Union, Powelton, Shiloh, Greensboro, Penfield, Sugar Creek, Griffin, and other Georgia Baptist churches. Tall and slender, with a tendency to tuberculosis, he was energetic and punctual, with a strong, clear, practical mind, sound judgment, and great moral earnestness. He was neither a great scholar nor a very eloquent preacher, but his practical, pungent sermons were so effective that he was much sought after by the churches of Georgia.

Recognition of his character, business ability, energy, and influence as a preacher led to his selection as first principal of Mercer Institute on its establishment at Penfield in 1832. He continued as head of the institution until 1839 when it was made Mercer University. During this formative period he was financial agent, teacher, and general administrative head of the institution, and has been justly called the real founder of Mercer University, of which for its first few months he served as president. After his resignation (see *Valedictory Address . . . Dec. 16, 1839,* 1840) he was for several years secretary and treasurer of the board of trustees, and remained a member of that body until his death.

Perhaps his chief title to fame is his service to Mercer University, but he occupied other important positions in the Baptist denomination in Georgia and in the public life of his state. He was moderator of the Georgia Association for nine years and clerk for a number of years, was for six years president of the Baptist State Convention and for many years chairman of its executive committee. He edited the *Christian Index* for a year, was a frequent delegate to the Triennial and the Southern Baptist Convention. On Mar. 17, 1812, he married Martha Lamar, by whom he had nine children. After her death in 1822 he married, Feb. 25, 1824, Cynthia Holliday, by whom he had thirteen children. Two children of the first marriage and eight of the second survived their father, who died at Penfield after a long illness. He was one of the most important of the Baptist preachers and educators of Georgia during the first half of the nineteenth century.

[C. D. Mallary, *Living and Dying unto the Lord: A Discourse in Commemoration of Elder Billington M. Sanders* (1854), which is the authority for year of death, sometimes erroneously stated as 1852; W. B. Sprague, *Annals Am. Pulpit,* vol. VI (1860); B. D. Ragsdale, *Story of Ga. Baptists* (1932); S. G. Hillyer, *Reminiscences of Ga. Baptists* (1902); J. H. Campbell, *Ga. Baptists, Hist. and Biog.* (1874); Wm. Cathcart, *The Bapt. Encyc.* (1881); *Hist. of the Bapt. Denomination in Ga., with Biog. Compend.* (1881); minutes of Ga. Association and Baptist State Convention.]

W. J. M.

SANDERS, CHARLES WALTON (Mar. 24, 1805–July 5, 1889), educator, was born at Newport, N. Y., one of ten children of Jacob and Lydia (Martin) Sanders, and a direct descendant of John Sanders, who came to Salem, Mass., from Wiltshire, England, in 1630. His father was a farmer in modest circumstances, but was desirous of educating his children, and at the age of four Charles was sent to a local school where he acquired as much knowledge as his teacher could impart. When he was nine his father moved to Homer, Cortland County, N. Y., where the son finished his slender country-school education. He became a licensed teacher in 1821, and at the age of twenty-four was elected inspector of common schools, serving for several years. He taught seventeen years in the schools of Homer and Cortland County. In 1837 or 1838, meaning to capitalize the experience and observation resulting from his years of country-school teaching, he moved from the back-country to the metropolis, and plunged into the writing and compilation of spellers and readers for elementary schools. The next twenty-five years saw an amazing succession of more than forty titles of primers, spellers, a series of six graded readers, grammars, speakers, charts, and cards for teaching children, school singing-books, all bearing the name of the author on the cover, title-page, and every left page throughout every volume. An advantageous association with the leading educational publisher of the day, combined with the solid merits of the books, brought such popularity that 13,000,000 Sanders' readers were reported sold between 1838 and 1860, and the author at one time received about $30,000 yearly in royalties.

In preparing his textbooks, he had in mind certain definite aims, to the achievement of which he brought industry, originality, and the instincts of a born teacher, sharpened by years of experience with under-privileged country children. Previous to his time, reading-books had been composed of selections from the masters of English literature, often pedantic, and in most cases beyond the easy comprehension of children. Characteristics which contributed to the worth and popularity of the Sanders' readers were:

careful grading, pictures, moral and ethical tone; the simplicity and interest, as well as literary merit, of the contents; emphasis on articulation and inflection in teaching reading and in class exercises. Much of the matter in the first, second, and third readers was Sanders' own. By putting a few songs with music at the end of each reader, he has shared credit for introducing singing into the public schools. In his public school music interests he was associated with William Batchelder Bradbury [q.v.]. He maintained close touch with his constituency for many years by spending three months annually in visiting and lecturing before schools and teachers' meetings, and in giving entertaining illustrative readings. He was present at the organization of the New York State Teachers' Association, in 1845. He was interested in the early temperance movement, and was a steadfast Republican until Cleveland claimed his vote in 1884. On Aug. 2, 1842, he was married to Elizabeth Barker, the daughter of John and Anna Barton Barker, of White Plains, N. Y., and had three children. He died in New York City.

[W. R. Cutter, *Geneal. and Family Hist. of Central N. Y.* (1912), vol. III; C. W. Sanders, *Geneal. of the Cortland County, N. Y., Branch of the Sanders Family* (1908); S. A. Allibone, *A Critical Dictionary of English Literature,* vol. II (1870); *State of N. Y., Dept. of Public Instruction, 37th Annual Report, 1891* (1891); *N. Y. Times,* July 6, 1889.]   J. I. W.

SANDERS, DANIEL CLARKE (May 3, 1768–Oct. 18, 1850), preacher and educator, was born at Sturbridge, Mass., the fourth child and only son of Michael and Azubah (Clarke) Sanders. After the death of his father in 1773, his mother married Capt. Ebenezer Fisher of Needham, where the boy was prepared for college under the direction of Rev. Samuel West. He entered Harvard, graduating in 1788. Burdened with the formidable debt of one hundred dollars, he immediately took employment "keeping a common school in Watertown." Soon afterward he became preceptor of the grammar school in Cambridge. Here he studied theology under the guidance of Rev. Thomas Prentiss of Medfield. Licensed by the Dedham Association in 1790, he preached as a candidate and as a supply in various pulpits in Massachusetts, New Hampshire, and Vermont. In 1794 he was ordained as pastor in Vergennes, Vt., where two years earlier he had married Nancy, daughter of Dr. Jabez Fitch. In 1799 he accepted a call to preach in Burlington, where he also kept a private school until the organization of the University of Vermont. He was made a trustee of that embryo institution in January 1800, and in October became its first president.

His duties while directing the new university during its first fourteen years were varied and onerous. He managed its lands and finances, supervised in part the erection of its first building, and for some years carried the entire burden of instruction, continuing meantime his pastoral duties until 1807. Though students increased from four the first year to over fifty in 1813, the university was in financial trouble. Hostilities on Lake Champlain during the second war with Great Britain disrupted its activities. In the spring of 1814 the trustees suspended instruction, leased the university building to the government for use as barracks, and dismissed all salaried officers, including the president. Sanders at this time was almost overwhelmed with misfortunes: his book, *A History of the Indian Wars with the First Settlers of the United States, Particularly in New England,* published anonymously at Montpelier in 1812, had aroused bitter criticism because of its strictures on colonial bigotry and cruelty to the natives (see *Historical Magazine,* February 1858); his wife was a victim of occasional attacks of insanity; five of his eight children had recently died in an epidemic. Now he was without employment and with few resources save a claim on the University for arrears of salary.

After preaching for a time in New York City he reluctantly accepted a call (May 1815) to become pastor of the First Congregational Church of Medfield, Mass., where his parents and grandparents had been born and where he had preached his first sermon. During the fourteen years of his pastorate here he gained a wide reputation as a thoughtful and eloquent speaker. A moderate man, averse to theological controversies, he attempted unsuccessfully to guide his church through that stormy period. After the stricter Calvinists had seceded, he found it impossible to stay with the thorough-paced Unitarians and resigned his pastorate in the spring of 1829, though he continued to reside in Medfield until his death.

The last phase of his career was devoted to occasional preaching and to public life. He was a delegate to the state constitutional convention of 1820–21; represented the Medfield district in the Massachusetts House, 1833–36; and during the same years was one of the selectmen of his town, where later he held other minor positions. His last years he spent caring for his invalid wife, whose death in 1850 he survived by only two months. He published a number of sermons, one of which, *A Sermon, Preached in Medfield . . . Near the 166th Anniversary of the Incorporation of the Town* (1817), was the first historical sketch of Medfield.

[W. S. Tilden, *Hist. of the Town of Medfield, Mass.* (1887); *Vital Records of Sturbridge, Mass., to the Year 1850* (1906); A. M. Hemenway, *The Vt. Hist. Gazetteer*, vol. I (1868); *Vt. Alumni Weekly*, Oct. 10, 1923; J. A. Savage, *First Congreg. Church*, reprint from *Medfield, Mass.: Proc. at the Celebration of the 250th Anniversary of the Incorporation of the Town* (1902); copy in Univ. of Vt. Library of an autobiography and journal (MSS.) of Sanders.]   P. D. E.

SANDERS, DANIEL JACKSON (Feb. 15, 1847–Mar. 6, 1907), Presbyterian clergyman, educator, editor, the son of William and Laura Sanders, was born in slavery near Winnsboro, S. C., on the plantation of Thomas Hall, a Methodist preacher. His owner permitted him to learn the letters of the alphabet, and before he became free he had learned to spell and to read. At the age of nine years he was given his first instruction in the shoemaker's trade; he served as an apprentice for five years, making such remarkable progress that at the end of three years his master was able to collect pay for his services. In 1866 he left his master's home and set out for Chester, S. C., taking with him only a small shoemaker's kit. As he worked he secured tutelage from a Mr. W. B. Knox, and in 1869 and 1870 attended Brainerd Institute, at Chester, where he proved so apt a pupil that after two years of study he was made a tutor in the school. By 1871 he was prepared to enter Western Theological Seminary at Allegheny, Pa., where in 1874 he graduated with honors. He then became pastor of the Chestnut Street Presbyterian Church in Wilmington, N. C. Here he assembled the colored Presbyterians, who until then had been worshipping in the galleries of the churches of their former owners, into the northern Presbyterian Church (Presbyterian Church in the United States of America).

Because of his religious attitude, his forensic power, and sound logic, Sanders soon became a leader in the educational world. He was elected principal of the public schools in Chester, S. C., and in 1875, principal of the city schools in Wilmington, N. C. This position he resigned shortly in order to go abroad to raise money for the work of the Board of Missions for Freedmen. He spent over a year in Scotland and England and raised a large sum of money for the Board. In addition, he raised $6,000 as an endowment for an African scholarship fund to prepare men at Biddle University, a Presbyterian institution at Charlotte, N. C., for mission work in Africa. Upon his return from Europe he resumed his pastorate.

Feeling that the church needed an organ of publicity, he began on Jan. 1, 1879, the publication of the *Africo-American Presbyterian*, which had a wide influence in building up the Presbyterian cause among the colored people. This publication he edited until his death. On Sept. 16, 1880, he married Fannie Price, and of this union nine children were born. In 1891, he was elected president of Biddle University, of which he had been a trustee for fourteen years. He was its first colored president. His unusual executive ability and untiring interest in the expansion of the university enabled it to make rapid advancement. As a teacher of theology and church government he was well liked by his students, who called him "Zeus." He continued as president of Biddle (which later became Johnson C. Smith University) until his death.

Sanders was the first colored moderator of both the Yadkin and Cape Fear presbyteries, he served as a stated clerk in the Atlantic and Yadkin presbyteries and the Catawba Synod, and three times was delegate to meetings of the Alliance of Reformed Churches Holding the Presbyterian System—at Toronto, Liverpool, and Washington. He was many times a member of the General Assembly, where his voice was heard and given recognition. With an extremely simple philosophy of life to guide him he commended himself each day to God and did his best in each day's work. He died at the age of sixty.

[*Johnson C. Smith Univ. Alumni Jour.*, D. J. Sanders Edition, Apr. 1928; *Africo-American Presbyterian*, Mar. 15, May 3, 1888; *Minutes of the Gen. Assembly of the Presbyt. Ch. in the U. S. A.*, 1870–1907; *Who's Who in America*, 1906–07; *Charlotte Daily Observer*, Mar. 7, 1907; information as to certain facts from Mrs. D. J. Sanders and a son, Brooks Sanders.]   D. B. P.

SANDERS, ELIZABETH ELKINS (Aug. 12, 1762–Feb. 19, 1851), author and reformer, was the daughter of Thomas and Elizabeth (White) Elkins. She was born in Salem, Mass., and spent her entire life there, living to be called "our most delightful old lady" by a writer on Salem life (Silsbee, *post*, p. 95). Friends and relatives united to praise her powers of mind and her magnanimous spirit. On Apr. 28, 1782, she married Thomas Sanders, who after a period spent in the counting-room of her relative, Elias Hasket Derby [*q.v.*], East India merchant, became one of the most successful business men in Salem. In a handsome house on Chestnut Street she reared her two sons and three daughters, dispensed hospitality, and devoted her leisure to wide reading. The elder son, Charles, is remembered at Harvard University as the donor of Sanders Theatre.

Mrs. Sanders took an active part in all movements for bettering the condition of the unfortunate or the oppressed. She gave liberally of her wealth, and frequently contributed to local papers articles approving prison reform, measures for reclaiming delinquents, and greater educational opportunities for the poor. She lent her aid also to the health reformers, and protested against doctors who were too liberal in their use of drugs. Her most ardent championship, however, was reserved for the cause of the American Indians, whom she regarded as "the dethroned monarchs of the land." In 1828 she published, anonymously, *Conversations Principally on the Aborigines of North America,* a little volume in the form of talks between a mother and her children, setting forth her views on the lack of justice and humanity with which the Creeks had been treated by General Jackson. Influenced by the writings of Charlevoix and of William Bartram [*qq.v.*], she argued that the simplicity of primitive races was especially favorable to the development of lofty sentiments, and urged more considerate treatment of all Indians. The following year, in a somewhat similar volume entitled *The First Settlers of New-England,* she dealt with the conquest of other tribes. In this book she elaborated her statements concerning the unchristian conduct of the usurpers toward the natives, and contended that while wrongs at home remained unredressed it was absurd to expend vast sums to maintain missions in foreign lands.

This disapproval of foreign missions found further expression in magazine articles, later published in pamphlet form as *A Tract on Missions* (1844), *The Second Part of the Tract on Missions* (1845), and *Remarks on the "Tour Around Hawaii," by the Missionaries, Messrs. Ellis, Thurston, Bishop, and Goodrich, in 1823* (1848). Mrs. Sanders insisted in these works that missionaries to heathen lands accomplished no good results. As a stanch Unitarian she was especially indignant with those who carried "the appalling dogmas of Calvinism" to virtuous and happy Polynesians. She praised Melville's *Typee* (1846) for revealing the "scandalous and wicked transactions" of missionaries in the Sandwich Islands, and defended it against critics who wished to suppress the book. Besides her controversial works she published one other volume, *Reviews of a Part of Prescott's 'History of Ferdinand and Isabella,' and of Campbell's 'Lectures on Poetry'* (1841).

[M. C. D. Silsbee, *A Half Century in Salem* (1887); *Vital Records of Salem,* vols. I (1916), III (1924); *Ancestry and Descendants of Sir Richard Saltonstall of New England* (1897); *Salem Gazette,* Feb. 21, 1851; information from family.]   B. M. S.

SANDERS, FRANK KNIGHT (June 5, 1861–Feb. 20, 1933), Biblical scholar, author, was born at Batticotta, Jaffna, Ceylon, son of the Rev. Marshall Danforth and Georgianna (Knight) Sanders. He was of old New England ancestry running back to Robert Sanders, a resident of Rhode Island in 1736; to Richard Knight, who came from England in 1635; and to Roger Williams and Chad Brown of early Rhode Island fame. He prepared for college in the academy at Lakeville, Conn., and in the preparatory department of Ripon College, Ripon, Wis., from which institution he was graduated with the degree of A.B. in 1882.

After his graduation he went out as an instructor to Jaffna College, of which his father was the first principal, although he died before the teaching work of the college was actually begun. Returning to the United States, Sanders entered the Yale Divinity School, in 1886, where he came under the vital instruction of William Rainey Harper [*q.v.*], a contact which proved determinative in Sanders' career, leading him to graduate work in Semitic languages and Biblical studies. In 1889 he received the degree of Ph.D. For the next sixteen years he was a member of Yale faculties, serving as instructor in Semitic languages, as Harper's successor in the Woolsey chair of Biblical literature in Yale College (1891–1901), and as dean of the Divinity School and professor of Biblical history and archæology (1901–05). On Jan. 6, 1902, he was ordained, in New Haven, to the Congregational ministry.

Sanders' administrative gifts were such that he was inevitably called to fill executive positions. From 1905 to 1908 he was secretary of the Congregational Sunday-School and Publishing Society, with headquarters in Boston; from 1908 to 1914 he served as president of Washburn College, Topeka, Kan.; from 1914 to 1927 he was in New York as director of missionary preparation for the Foreign Missions Conference of North America. Throughout his entire career, however, from his days as student assistant with Dr. Harper to the last weeks of life, he maintained personal teaching relations through the conduct of correspondence courses. For years, too, he conducted "The Senior Bible Class" department in the *Sunday School Times* and frequently served as special lecturer in important schools and colleges. He was a voluminous writer. Of his published books his *History of the Hebrews,* first issued in 1914 and revised and enlarged as late as 1928, had the widest circulation. Among his other works are *The Student's Life of Christ* (copr. 1906), *Historical Notes on the Life of Christ* (copr. 1907); *The Program of Christianity* (1919), *Old Testament Prophecy* (1921), *Old Testament History* (1922). With various associates he was co-editor or co-author of some forty volumes. He understood the art of multiplying efficiency through collaboration, but never used the services of another without giving recognition; to him an associate, however young and unknown, was a "colleague." In writing and lecturing, he had rare ability to make Biblical characters and events living and vital without transgressing the limits of sound historical criticism.

He entered whole-heartedly into the life of the Church and various religious societies. There was never an interruption in his active interest in the Young Men's Christian Association; at Jaffna he founded the first college association in the East and in later years in America served on state committees and the national council. When the nation-wide Religious Education Association was founded in 1903, he was chosen its first president. As chairman of the Commission on Inter-Church Relations which consummated the union of Congregational and Christian Churches in 1931 ("the first union of two denominations in the United States in which there had been no previous historic relationship") he made a contribution to American church history. He was a member of the Society of Biblical Literature and Exegesis, the American Oriental Society, the Archaeological Institute of America, and the American Academy of Political and Social Sciences. A man of intense vitality, tall, of muscular build, his black hair and moustache only just graying at seventy-one, he worked always at high speed, getting the heart of an important new volume in an evening's rapid, selective reading, and formulating notes for a well-ordered lecture with similar rapidity. He was a rare companion in time of leisure, a stimulating fellow-worker, a mediator of the newer Biblical scholarship and the old faith. On June 27, 1888, he was married to Edith Blackman of Whitewater, Wis., who with two sons and a daughter survived him. He died at his home in Rockport, Mass.

[Letters, family documents, and personal acquaintance; *Who's Who in America*, 1932–33; *Boston Herald, Boston Transcript*, Feb. 21, 1933; *N. Y. Herald Tribune*, Feb. 22, 1933; *Ripon Alumnus*, Mar. 1933; *Congregationalist*, Mar. 2, 9, 1933; *Yale Univ. Obit. Record*, 1933; *Congregational Year Book*, 1933.]
H. T. F.

SANDERS, GEORGE NICHOLAS (Feb. 27, 1812–Aug. 12, 1873), promoter, revolutionist, Confederate agent, was born in Lexington, Ky., the son of Lewis Sanders, who was locally noted as a breeder of fine horses, and of Ann (Nicholas) Sanders, daughter of Col. George Nicholas [*q.v.*]. As a youth, he was associated with his father as a trader in stock. In November 1843, at Ghent, Ky., he engineered a political meeting which authorized him to correspond with presidential candidates on their attitude towards the annexation of Texas. About 1845 he went to New York City where he engaged in political wire-pulling and financial promoting, furthering his ends, in political conventions and the lobbies of hotels, legislatures, and Congress, by fair means and foul. His numerous enemies insisted that as agent of the Hudson's Bay Company he had reaped questionable rewards when he adjusted its claims in the Oregon country, but he was nevertheless in perpetual debt. His correspondence with Stephen A. Douglas indicates that he was a go-between for Eastern capitalists who were speculating in Chicago real estate. As the agent of George Law [*q.v.*], he made a deal whereby Law took over forty thousand antiquated muskets from the war department to sell to the French revolutionists of 1848, but Sanders arrived in Paris too late to conclude the sale.

Committed by conviction as well as by financial interest to the revolutionary cause in Europe, he became, in the early fifties, the leader of a movement known as "Young America" (M. E. Curti, in *American Historical Review*, October 1926). He contended that a crusade for European republicanism would divert attention from sectional controversies, open European markets to American surplus, and fulfil the American mission of furthering the cause of democracy and freedom throughout the world. Seizing on Stephen A. Douglas as the most likely Democratic politician to sponsor such a policy, Sanders in 1851 acquired the *United States Magazine and Democratic Review* (thereafter simply the *Democratic Review*), and in a series of vindictive articles beginning in January 1852 excoriated the political rivals of Douglas, erratically championed the program of "Young America," and greatly added to the number of his enemies.

In 1853 he received a recess appointment to the London consulship. He went over before the appointment was confirmed and his house became the headquarters of Kossuth, Garibaldi, Herzen, Ledru-Rollin, Mazzini, and other exiles. He engaged in wild dreams and bizarre plots, promising the revolutionaries American financial support, sending their secret communications to the Continent in the dispatch bags of the American embassy, and writing fulminating letters to London newspapers advocating the assassination of Napoleon III. He also influenced Buchanan and Soulé in issuing the Ostend Manifesto (J. B. Castleman, *Active Service*, 1917, p. 135; A. A. Ettinger, *The Mission to Spain of Pierre Soulé*,

1932). As a result of his reckless activities and of bitter attacks at home, the Senate refused to confirm his appointment. Victor Hugo, Garibaldi, and Mazzini wrote him affectionate letters and regretted the blow to European liberalism which his departure meant. In 1857 he was given a recess appointment as navy agent at New York, which was confirmed.

During the Civil War, Sanders played an audacious rôle as a Confederate agent in Europe and Canada. His grandiose imagination led him to plot various schemes to outwit the Federal blockade. He was also a member of the Niagara Peace Conference in 1864, to which he came disguised as a Welsh miner (E. C. Kirkland, *The Peacemakers of 1864,* 1927, pp. 71–72). Although he probably had no connection with the assassination of Lincoln, President Johnson, on May 2, 1865, offered $25,000 for his arrest (D. M. DeWitt, *The Assassination of Abraham Lincoln,* 1909, p. 101).

Sanders spent much of the later part of his helter-skelter life in Europe. During the siege of Paris he was deep in the counsels of the radicals, and his enthusiastic friends gave him a great popular ovation at the Hôtel de Ville. Half idealist, half charlatan, impulsive and prodigal, he had the talent of making and keeping warm friends and bitter enemies. He was a large-framed, powerful man with radiant blue eyes, dishevelled hair, and unkempt appearance. After a courtship conducted by correspondence, he married, a week after their first meeting, Anna Reid, editor of a weekly literary paper in New York. Her unusual accomplishments added much to the lavish entertainments for which her husband was noted.

[M. E. Curti, "George N. Sanders, Patriot of the Fifties," *So. Atlantic Quart.,* Jan. 1928; sketch by a friend, W. M. Corry, in *The Biog. Encyc. of Ky.* (1878); *The Political Corresp. of the Late Hon. George N. Sanders* (1914); G. F. Milton, *The Eve of Conflict* (1934); *N. Y. Times,* Aug. 13, 1873; copies of letters from Sanders to Douglas, through the courtesy of G. F. Milton. A collection of Sanders MSS. is in the possession of Dudley Holland, Greenwich, Conn.]
M. E. C.

SANDERS, JAMES HARVEY (Oct. 9, 1832–Dec. 22, 1899), agricultural journalist, was born in Union County, Ohio, of colonial Virginia ancestry. He received a common-school education and some academy training in Ohio, and in 1852 accompanied his family to southeast Iowa, settling on farm property near Talleyrand, Keokuk County. Notwithstanding his incomplete education, he added school teaching to his work on the farm. Having married Martha Rodgers of Ohio, he moved to Sigourney, the county seat, where he engaged for a time in banking and pro-

moting a new railway. Becoming interested in journalism, however, he purchased the *Sigourney News* in 1863 and thus began a notable career as a publisher and editor.

In May 1869, he began publishing the *Western Stock Journal,* the first periodical devoted to animal husbandry. The following year the *National Livestock Journal* was established at Chicago, and in November 1870 the two consolidated, with Sanders as associate editor though he continued to reside in Iowa. In the financial crisis of 1873 he lost all his savings, and for a year thereafter served as editor of the *Spirit of the Times,* a New York journal mainly interested in promoting the trotting horse and the race track. After a year in the East he went to Chicago, where he and S. G. Brabrook purchased the *National Livestock Journal,* Sanders becoming its editor in January 1876. In his hands this monthly periodical was extremely successful. His son, Alvin H., born in 1860, gave him valuable assistance after 1876. In October 1881, he disposed of his interests in the *National Livestock Journal* and in December began the publication, at Chicago, of the *Breeders' Gazette,* a weekly, thus launching on its career the most important livestock journal of its day. He had a keen conception of what was necessary in a high-class livestock journal to secure the support of intelligent stockmen. In 1888 he accepted a commission from the United States Department of Agriculture to go to Europe and investigate the health of herds from which cattle were being exported to America. He gave up the editorial cares of the *Breeders' Gazette* to his son in 1888, thus terminating his active service in journalism, although his name appeared as joint editor of the periodical until 1891.

Sanders was a great lover of farm animals, especially the horse. In 1868 he purchased in Ohio the noted Percheron stallion, Victor Hugo, and later the imported horses Dieppe, Diligence, and Tempest, paying $3,000 for Dieppe and $2,500 for Diligence. He was the author of the *Norman Stud Book* (1876), the first book of its kind devoted to French draft horses in America; a second edition was entitled the *Percheron-Norman Stud Book.* When in France in 1883, he rendered valuable assistance to French horsemen by establishing the *Percheron Stud Book* (*Hippique Percheronne Français*). He was a great student of heredity and his library contained the works of noted scientists in this field. In 1881 he published in cooperation with Kentucky breeders, a register of pedigrees, the *Breeders' Trotting Stud Book.* In 1885 he brought out *Horse-Breeding,* and in 1887, *The Breeds of Livestock and the Principles of Heredity,* both of which circulated extensively at home and abroad. Sanders died at his own hand (*Commercial Appeal,* Memphis, Dec. 23, 1899) in Memphis, Tenn.

[*Breeders' Gazette,* Dec. 27, 1899; A. H. Sanders, *At the Sign of the Stock Yard Inn* (1915); A. H. Sanders and Wayne Dinsmore, *A Hist. of the Percheron Horse* (1917); W. E. Ogilvie, *Pioneer Agricultural Journalists: James Harvey Sanders* (1927); *A Biog. Cat. of the Portrait Gallery of the Saddle and Sirloin Club* (1920), pp. 68–70; *Commercial Appeal* (Memphis), Dec. 23, 1899.]   C. S. P—b.

SANDERS, THOMAS (Aug. 18, 1839–Aug. 7, 1911), telephone financier, was born in South Danvers, Mass., then part of Salem, of a family settled in Salem and Gloucester since the seventeenth century. His father was George Thomas Sanders and his mother, Mary Ann (Brown). He was educated in the common schools. Keenly interested in fine animals, he rode horseback all his life, and very early went into the business of breeding horses on a farm near East Brookfield, Vt. In 1870 he sold this farm, taking a smaller place near by at Williamstown, and moved to Haverhill, Mass. There he established a successful leather business and continued also his interest in horses. He acquired a beautiful estate in Haverhill, which he called "Birchbrow," where he and his family kept open house to their friends during the rest of his life.

Sanders married Susan Bradley Howe of Haverhill on June 6, 1866. The eldest of their eight children, George, was born deaf, and it was while seeking the best possible means of education for this boy that Sanders was introduced by Miss Sarah Fuller, principal of the School for the Deaf in Boston, to the young instructor in Visible Speech, or lip-reading, Alexander Graham Bell [*q.v.*]. In the fall of 1873 Sanders engaged Bell to teach his son, and for several years thereafter Bell lived with the child and his grandmother in Salem, going often to Boston for his other work. In Mrs. Sanders' house Bell conducted experiments that led up to the invention of the telephone, in connection with these experiments giving little George manual training coördinated with his regular lessons. Deeply grateful for the extraordinary results of Bell's teaching, though skeptical of the practical value of his scheme of "talking by telegraph," Sanders undertook to give the inventor whatever money he needed for his experiments.

Sanders advanced the money required during the period of experiment and early organization of the telephone enterprise, putting more than $110,000 into it before he got a dollar back, but by an agreement signed Feb. 27, 1875, with Bell and Gardiner Greene Hubbard [*q.v.*], who contributed executive ability and business acumen to the combination, he received an equal share in the ownership of Bell's inventions. When the Bell Telephone Company was formed with Hubbard as trustee in July 1877, Sanders was made treasurer. When his own resources gave out, he enlisted the financial support of George L. Bradley and others, thus bringing about in 1878 the formation of the New England Telephone Company, of which Sanders was treasurer and then president. Soon he and Bradley enlisted the support of the Forbes interests and secured the union of the telephone organizations in 1879 into the National Bell Telephone Company, with William H. Forbes as president. Sanders continued as a director of the Telephone Company until his death.

Meantime, he was actively interested in a silver and antimony mine in New Brunswick, and he also invested $250,000 in a silver mine at Ouray, Colo., but the repeal of the silver-purchase clause of the Sherman Act in 1893 caused him severe losses. At Haverhill and also in Vermont he continued his interest in fine breeding. He did a great deal in the development of the Morgan horse, Merino sheep, and Jersey cattle. He was the organizer of the Vermont Livestock Company, a regular exhibitor at the Vermont State Fair, a member of the Essex Agricultural Society, and a life member of the New England Agricultural Society, and was active in all these organizations. It was while driving up to his Vermont farm that he was suddenly taken ill and died of a heart attack in Derry, N. H., at the age of seventy-two.

[Thomas Sanders, "The Early Days of the Telephone" (MS.), address before the Fortnightly Club of Haverhill, Mar. 23, 1903; W. C. Langdon, "The Early Corporate Development of the Telephone," *Bell Telephone Quart.,* July 1923, and "Two Founders of the Bell System," *Ibid.,* Oct. 1923; D. W. Howe, *Howe Geneals. . . . James of Ipswich* (1929); *Boston Transcript,* Aug. 8, 1911, which contains a number of errors; Thomas Sanders Collection, Am. Telephone Hist. Library, N. Y. City; information from the family, esp. George T. and Charles Bradley Sanders.]   W.C.L.

SANDERS, WILBUR FISK (May 2, 1834–July 7, 1905), pioneer lawyer, senator, was born at Leon, Cattaraugus County, N. Y., the son of Ira Sanders, a farmer from Rhode Island, and Freedom (Edgerton) Sanders, of Connecticut. Wilbur attended public school and an academy at Phelps, N. Y., taught school for a while, and in 1854 went to Akron, Ohio, where he continued teaching while studying law with his uncle, Sidney Edgerton [*q.v.*]. In 1856 he was admitted to the bar and into partnership with his uncle. On Oct. 27, 1858, he married Harriet P. Fenn; to this union five children were born. With the outbreak of the Civil War in 1861 Sanders enlisted in the Federal army, and in October was commissioned first lieutenant, 64th Ohio Infantry. In 1862 he became acting assistant adjutant general on the staff of Gen. J. W. Forsyth but his health failed, and in August he resigned.

The next spring he accompanied Sidney Edgerton, who had been appointed territorial chief justice, to Bannack, in what was then eastern Idaho. In this mining camp, which was soon to become the first capital of Montana, he began the practice of law. The country was terrorized by "road agents" who held up stages and wagon trains and killed with reckless freedom, and when a particularly atrocious murder in December 1863 aroused some miners to arrest the murderers, Sanders was the only lawyer who dared undertake the prosecution. Despite threats by friends of the accused, he secured the conviction and speedy execution of the criminals. He was subsequently one of the organizers of the Vigilantes, who cleared the country of outlaws.

He was a leader in the movement to form a separate territory from eastern Idaho, and after the organization of the territory of Montana in 1864, in a region peopled largely by Irish and Southern Democrats he promoted the Republican party and bitterly opposed the policies of the territorial secretary, Thomas Francis Meagher [q.v.], who was also acting governor. He was Republican candidate for delegate to Congress in 1864, 1867, 1880, and 1886, and each time was defeated. He was a delegate to the Republican National Convention in 1868, 1872, 1876, and 1884, and from 1873 through 1879 he sat in the territorial legislature. When Montana was admitted as a state in 1889, the legislature elected Sanders one of the first United States senators, and he drew the short term (Jan. 1, 1890–Mar. 3, 1893). The election was contested, but Sanders and the other Republican candidate were seated by the Senate. Here he urged legislation allowing citizens the right to cut timber from the public domain and sought federal money for irrigation projects, to make the Missouri River navigable to Great Falls, and for various state purposes. His vagueness on the question of silver doubtless lost him support in Montana, and at the end of his term the Republican legislature did not reëlect him.

In spite of his political activities Sanders was an eminent lawyer. His practice extended to all sorts of cases, from the Davis will case, involving millions of dollars, to a fight against an attempt of labor unions to boycott Chinese, and another against the city of Helena for persecuting the Salvation Army. He was founder and for many years president of the Historical So-

ciety of Montana, organized the Montana Bar Association, and was active in many other such organizations. His power of sarcasm and ridicule aroused dread in his opponents. He spoke bitterly against the rising Populists and in the Republican state convention of 1896 savagely attacked the free-silver stand of the majority. In one of his last speeches he criticized the technical rulings of the supreme court in language so violent that newspapers did not dare print his address. Yet people said that in his later years his tongue was not so sharp, and his courage, honesty, personal generosity, and kindness were widely extolled at the time of his death by friends and life-long opponents.

[*Biog. Dir. Am. Cong.* (1928); *Progressive Men of the State of Mont.* (n.d.); *Contribs. to Hist. Soc. of Mont.*, vols. I–VIII (1876–1917); A. K. McClure, *Three Thousand Miles Through the Rocky Mountains* (1869); Granville Stuart, *Forty Years on the Frontier* (1925), vol. II; *Montana Daily Record* (Helena), July 7, 8, 12, Oct. 6, 1905; *Boston Herald*, July 8, 1905; *Billings Gazette*, Sept. 29, 1896; T. J. Dimsdale, *The Vigilantes of Montana* (1866); N. P. Langford, *Vigilante Days and Ways* (1890), vol. II; *Who's Who in America*, 1903–05; *Report of the . . . Am. Bar Asso.*, 1905; Tom Stout, *Montana* (1921), vol. III; *Proc. Mont. Bar Asso., 1903–14* (n.d.).]   P. C. P.

SANDERSON, JOHN (1783–Apr. 5, 1844), author and teacher, was born near Carlisle, Pa. His father, William Sanderson, was a farmer who served as a soldier in the American army throughout the Revolution. His mother, Agnes McClellan (Buchanan) Sanderson, is said to have been descended from the Douglas family of Scotland. Since schools in the country districts were few and inadequate at that time, John was educated by private tutoring. In 1806 he went to Philadelphia to study law, but soon became a teacher and assistant principal in the Clermont Academy. He married Sophie, the daughter of John T. Carré, the head of the school, with whom for a number of years he was associated in teaching. He became distinguished for his mastery of the classics and later of the English language and of French literature.

Sanderson developed a gift for writing and became a popular contributor to several publications of his day, especially the *Aurora*, the *Portfolio*, and the *Knickerbocker*. After the retirement of William Duane [q.v.] he seems to have been for some months the editor of the *Aurora*. There is no question that he bought an interest in the paper from Duane in 1822 which he sold to Richard Penn Smith the following year (receipt from Sanderson to Smith, July 15, 1823, Historical Society of Pennsylvania). Meanwhile, in 1820, with his brother, Joseph M. Sanderson, he published the first two volumes of the *Biography of the Signers to the Declaration of*

Independence that was later completed in seven additional volumes (1823–27) by Robert Waln, Jr., and others. He was an ardent champion of classical training at a time when the public schools afforded no opportunity for the study of Greek or Latin, and in an able pamphlet he insisted that the ancient languages should not be excluded from the curriculum of Girard College (*Roberjot's Remarks on Mr. Biddle's Discourse,* n.d.).

His health declining, he gave up teaching for a time. In 1835 he went abroad and spent nearly a year in Paris, where he was well received in literary circles. During this period he wrote a series of articles later brought together and published as *Sketches of Paris: in Familiar Letters to His Friends; by an American Gentleman in Paris* (1838). Marked as it was by vivid descriptions of personalities and events, a keen sense of humor, and kindly understanding, this work was widely read. It was published in London with the title, *The American in Paris* (2 vols., 1838), and was translated into French by Jules Janin and published in Paris in 1843. A rather brief stay in England furnished material for "The American in London," a part of which appeared in the *Knickerbocker*.

In the autumn of 1836 Sanderson returned to America. The educational system of Pennsylvania had been recently assured of state aid, and its public schools were expanding under the impetus of intelligent interest and support. The Central High School of Philadelphia was opened in 1838, Dr. Alexander Dallas Bache [*q.v.*], the great-grandson of Benjamin Franklin, became its first principal the following year, and in September 1840 Sanderson, who had been Bache's teacher, became professor of Greek and Latin and assisted in the department of English and belles-lettres. His culture and experience, a certain originality of approach, together with unusual charm of personality, made him an inspiring teacher, and in this position he continued until his death.

[J. T. Scharf and Thompson Westcott, *Hist. of Phila.* (1884), vol. II ; Henry Simpson, *The Lives of Eminent Philadelphians* (1859) ; F. S. Edmonds, *Hist. of the Central High School of Phila.* (1902) ; R. W. Griswold, *The Prose Writers of America* (1847) ; obituary by J. L. Hart, in *Proc. Am. Phil. Soc.*, Apr.–June 1844 ; editorial in the *U. S. Gazette* and obituary in *Public Ledger* (Phila.), Apr. 6, 1844 ; family records.]

A. L. L.

SANDERSON, ROBERT (1608–Oct. 7, 1693), silversmith, was born in England and emigrated to America as a young man. He and his wife, Lydia, were among the first settlers in Hampton, N. H., in 1638. The following year he became a landholder and a freeman of Water-

town, Mass., and in this village his first child was born. In 1642, after the death of his first wife he married Mary, the widow of John Cross, of Middlesex County, Mass. She lived until 1681 and bore Sanderson four children. His third wife, Elizabeth, and three sons of his second marriage, all silversmiths, survived him.

Although his fame as a silversmith has suffered because of his association with John Hull [*q.v.*], whose many sided activities made his name better known, Sanderson deserves a place in the front rank of the New England silversmiths (Bigelow, *post,* p. 110). Having learned and practised his trade in England before coming to America, he was undoubtedly sought out for instruction by those who aspired to his craft. He was probably Hull's first teacher, through whom the principles of his art descended to Jeremiah Dummer, 1645–1718, John Coney, and the two Reveres [*qq.v.*]. For the splendid tradition of the New England masters in exquisite workmanship and in a fine feeling for form and line, Sanderson, with his surviving work as evidence, must claim some credit. His mark consisted of his initials in crude capitals, surmounted by a rose or sun in outline, or by a sun in full splendor.

In 1652 John Hull was appointed to establish a mint in the colonies. He immediately chose Sanderson as his partner and the two men worked together for many years. The workshop was doubtless often left in the hands of Sanderson because of Hull's many public activities, trading and land interests. The following year Sanderson moved to Boston where he lived the rest of his life. He became a deacon of the old First Church in 1668.

[Benjamin Worcester, *The Sanderson Homes at Piety Corner* (1899) ; Henry Bond, *Geneal. of the Families . . . of the Early Settlers of Watertown, Mass.* (2nd ed., 1860) ; *Pubs. of the Colonial Soc. of Mass.,* vol. VII (1905) ; *Historic Homes and Places and Geneal. . . . Middlesex County, Mass.* (1908) ; *The Diaries of John Hull, Trans. and Colls. of the Am. Antiquarian Soc.,* vol. III (1857) ; F. H. Bigelow, *Hist. Silver of the Colonies and Its Makers* (1917) ; Hollis French, *The Walpole Soc., A List of Early Am. Silversmiths* (1917) ; S. S. Crosby, *The Early Coins of America* (1875) ; *New-England Hist. and Geneal. Register,* Jan. 1898.]

K. A. K.

SANDERSON, SIBYL (Dec. 7, 1865–May 16, 1903), dramatic soprano, was born in Sacramento, Cal., the daughter of Silas W. Sanderson, a jurist who was at one time justice of the supreme court of California, and later chief counselor of the Union Pacific R. R. Sibyl Sanderson was educated in the public schools of San Francisco, and after her father's death was taken with her three sisters to Paris by her mother. In January 1886 she entered the Paris Conservatory, where she studied under Massenet, Sbriglia and Marchesi. It is said also that she had some lessons from Jean de Reszké. Two years later, under an assumed name, she made her operatic début at The Hague in Massenet's *Manon*. Massenet was so much impressed with her voice that he wrote *Esclarmonde* for her, and in this opera she made her Paris début at the Opéra Comique in 1889. Following this engagement she sang at the Théâtre de la Monnaie in Brussels and was the leading prima donna for two seasons. A few years later Massenet composed *Thaïs* for her, and the work was presented at the Paris Grand-Opéra in 1894. Enthusiastic in his praise, Massenet called her an "ideal" Manon and an "unforgettable" Thaïs (*Mes Souvenirs*, p. 178). Meanwhile, in 1893, Sanderson had created the title rôle of Saint-Saëns' *Phryné*. In spite of her tremendous popularity in Paris, and in other foreign cities—Brussels, St. Petersburg, Moscow—she was received coldly in London and never found favor in America. She sang for two seasons at the Metropolitan Opera House in New York under the régime of Maurice Grau [*q.v.*]—first in 1895, and again in 1901. It is said that "her voice was pure and sweet, but small, and cold; as an actress she was completely lacking in emotional warmth; but her personal beauty and charm of manner were extraordinary" (*Baker's Biographical Dictionary*, p. 811). Her first American failure may be attributed to the fact that she was suffering from a cold during her visit. Her chief rôles during her American engagements were Manon, Michaela, and Juliette.

Her domestic affairs gained her as much publicity as her singing. After a long engagement she was married, on Dec. 1, 1897, to a wealthy Cuban planter, Antonio Terry, following his divorce from his first wife. She suffered a stroke of paralysis soon after her marriage and lived quietly at her husband's château at Chenonceaux, France, until his death in 1899. A daughter was born to them but she died shortly after birth. From 1899 until her death frequent rumors were circulated about her possible marriage to others. The summer of 1903 had been set as the time for her marriage to Count Paul Tolstoi, a cousin of the Russian novelist. Her friendship with Massenet also caused comment. It was common gossip in Paris that "Massenet composed *Le Jongleur* to answer the flings of the boulevardiers that his inspiration required the spur of Sibyl Sanderson's charms" (Krehbiel, *post*, p. 124). She died of pneumonia in Paris at the age of thirty-eight, and her body was cremated at the Cemetery of Père la Chaise.

[*Who's Who in America*. 1901–02; *Grove's Dict. of Music and Musicians, Am. Suppl.* (1930); *Baker's Biog.*

Dict. of Musicians (3rd ed., 1919); J. M. Green, *Musical Biog.* (1908), vol. II; H. C. Lahee, *Famous Singers of To-day and Yesterday* (1898); Jules Massenet, *Mes Souvenirs* (1912); *Musical Courier*, May 20, 1903; Henri de Curzon, obituary in *Le Guide Musical*, May 31, June 7, 1903; *N. Y. Times*, May 17, 1903; *Record-Union* (Sacramento, Cal.), May 17, 1903; H. E. Krehbiel, *More Chapters of Opera* (1919).]   J.T.H.

SANDHAM, HENRY (May 24, 1842–June 21, 1910), painter and illustrator, was born in Montreal, Canada, the son of John Sandham, a house-decorator, and Elizabeth (Tait) Sandham, both British subjects. He was educated in the public schools of Montreal, and became assistant in William Notman's photographic studio, where he was eventually promoted to a partnership. His success in retouching portraits led him to make experiments in painting which were measurably encouraging. He then tried his hand at landscapes, making sketches along the St. Lawrence. His work was seen by John A. Fraser, later art editor of the *Century*, who did much towards helping him. On May 23, 1865, he married Agnes Fraser, daughter of John Fraser, a Canadian journalist; four of their six children died before reaching maturity. Within a few years he had attained some reputation in Canada as portrait painter and landscapist; in 1879 (Morris, *post*, p. 22) he was one of the few artists chosen to form the Royal Canadian Academy of Arts; and about that time Princess Louise selected his "Beacon Light, St. John Harbor" for the National Gallery collection at Ottawa.

After a visit to England and France in 1880 he went to Boston, where he became a successful illustrator. He made drawings for a number of books, including Edgar Allan Poe's *Lenore* (1886), F. J. Stimson's *King Noanett: A Story of Old Virginia and the Massachusetts Bay* (1896), and Helen Hunt Jackson's *Ramona* (1900). He also illustrated the last-named author's *Glimpses of California and the Missions* (1902), going to California for the purpose. In 1909 he illustrated A. R. H. Moncrieff's *Adventures in America*. Among the drawings he made for the *Century* were those which accompanied George Kennan's papers on Siberia, in 1888–89. He contributed illustrations to other periodicals, designed bookplates and Easter cards, and wrote and illustrated a paper on Haiti for *Harper's New Monthly Magazine*, August 1899. A volume published about 1920, *Pictures of Canadian History* (n.d.), contains a number of his drawings.

Sandham's first large historical picture, "The Dawn of Liberty," delineating the fight on Lexington Common in 1775, now hangs in the town hall of Lexington. It was first shown at the Boston Art Club, of which Sandham was vice-president. Subsequent essays in historical painting comprise his "Founding in Maryland," exhibited at the World's Columbian Exposition, Chicago, 1893, showing Calvert and his colonists taking formal possession of the grant in the name of Lord Baltimore, and a very large composition called "The March of Time," twelve by twenty-one feet, containing forty-six life-size figures, many of them portraits of veterans of the Civil War, shown marching across Boston Common during a reunion of the Grand Army of the Republic in 1889. This work was exhibited at the Boston Art Club in 1890, with some ninety other pictures by Sandham, and was later acquired by the National Gallery of Art in Washington.

In 1901 Sandham left Boston and went to London, where he lived until his death nine years later. He was buried at Kensal Green. He had exhibited at the Royal Academy and the Paris Salon and had received medals in London, Philadelphia, Boston, and Lisbon. A memorial exhibition of his works was held at the Imperial Institute, London, in June 1911.

[F. T. Robinson, *Living New England Artists* (1888); Will Jenkins, "A Canadian Artist in the Azores," *Internat. Studio,* Jan. 1903; *Am. Art Annual,* vol. X (1913); *Boston Transcript,* June 23, 1910; E. M. Morris, *Art in Canada* (n.d., c. 1911); cat. of sale coll., Leonard's Gallery, Boston, Jan. 1901; cat. of exhibition at Toronto, Ont., Mar. 1898; cat. of exhibition at Boston Art Club, 1890; cat. of memorial exhibition, London, 1911; W. S. Wallace, *The Dict. of Canadian Biog.* (1926); *Who Was Who, 1897–1916* (London, 1920); *Dict. Nat. Biog., Second Supp.* (1912).]   W. H. D.

SANDLER, JACOB KOPPEL (Aug. 6, 1856–Feb. 23, 1931), composer, son of Isaac Moses and Bathsheba (Ostrowsky) Sandler, was born in Bialozerkove, Russia. He studied Hebrew and sang in the choir of his local synagogue, ruining his voice by singing soprano parts after adolescence. His musical training was limited to learning how to read, write, and harmonize a melody. When he was seventeen, friends carried him off to Kiev to enter him in the conservatory, but his parents brought him back and married him to a bride of fifteen, Rebecca Sherman. Thereafter, he earned a meager living as the leader of an itinerant synagogue choir. When his six growing children lacked educational opportunities in the Pale of Settlement of Czarist Russia, and his parents had emigrated to America, he followed them, landing in New York in February 1888.

An unworldly idealist without competitive spirit, always yielding to life with self-critical humor, he could scarcely provide for his family, which joined him a year later. After brief periods as an unsatisfactory operator in a shirt factory, and as an even more unsatisfactory pedler of goods sold on the instalment plan, he found employment in his favorite pursuit, that of directing a synagogue choir. The precarious living this work afforded he eked out as chorus director in a Yiddish theater of New York's Ghetto, receiving a salary of from eight to ten dollars a week when the play was successful. Sandler wrote the required irrelevant songs and choruses for such worthily forgotten pieces as *The Princess Oath,* and *Die B'ne Moishe.* When the latter drama proved an expensive failure, M. Horowitz Halevi undertook to write another to be entitled "Brocha, or the Jewish King of Poland." He asked Sandler for the incidental music, including a lament by a girl who was being crucified. That same night Sandler wrote several numbers, and in the early hours of the morning turned to his Hebrew Bible for inspiration for the lament. He found it in the first words of Psalm XXII, *"Eili, Eili, lama azavtani"*—"My God, my God, why hast Thou forsaken me?" Halevi's play was produced in April 1896 at the Windsor Theater in the Bowery, and Sandler's inspired *"Eili, Eili,"* gave it the phenomenal run of three months. Then the play was forgotten, and the song led an obscure half life in the Ghetto of New York.

Later Sandler drifted away from the uncongenial commercialism of the theater, and, after supplementing his uncertain earnings as a synagogue musician by serving as salesman or messenger, he spent the last eleven years of his life in a minor but secure position in the office of the *New York Times.* Meanwhile, his *"Eili, Eili,"* virtually forgotten in America, had been carried back to Russia, the land of its spiritual origin. In 1909, M. Shalit, a pupil of Rimsky-Korsakoff, arranged it for publication by the St. Petersburg Society for Jewish Folk Music. In this form it was brought back to the United States by Kurt Schindler as a Jewish folk melody, and was first sung by Jacob Medvedieff on Dec. 26, 1915, and later by Sophie Braslau at the Metropolitan Opera House. One of Sandler's daughters who was in the audience gave her father the exciting news of the resurrection of his song after almost twenty years of oblivion. Then began a contest, waged not by the unassuming Sandler but by others, to prove him the composer of this *soi-disant* folk song. What Sandler himself craved was not the fortune in royalties that had been paid to publishers by singers, violinists, and phonograph companies, but the credit of authorship of the sublime lament. A lawsuit to establish his copyright proved unsuccessful, but in the last years of his life concert programs gave him credit for the song. Few, however, knew Jacob Koppel Sandler, who died as he had lived, humbly, obscurely, leaving the poetry and beauty of his soul imperishably enshrined therein.

[*N. Y. Times*, Mar. 1, 1931; Meyer Beer (Joseph Kotchock), in *Am. Jewish News*, Mar. 21, 1919; J. G. Huneker, in *N. Y. Times*, May 4, 1919; B. A. Bergman, in *Jewish Tribune*, Aug. 19, 1921; Grenville Vernon, in *Musical Observer*, Jan. 1922.]   D. deS. P.

SANDS, BENJAMIN FRANKLIN (Feb. 11, 1812–June 30, 1883), naval officer, was born in Baltimore of an old Maryland family, the son of Benjamin Norris and Rebecca (Hook) Sands. In his infancy the family moved to Louisville, Ky., where he lived until he was sixteen. After a year's schooling in Washington, under the care of his uncle, Maj. J. H. Hook, he entered the navy as midshipman Apr. 1, 1828. He had a Brazilian cruise in the *Vandalia,* 1828–31, followed by a year in the West Indies in the *St. Louis* and then by several months' study at Norfolk, with promotion to passed midshipman, June 14, 1834. During the next seven years he was employed in coast survey work, chiefly in New Jersey, spending his winters in Washington and summers in field expeditions. In these he was frequently accompanied by his wife Henrietta Maria, sister of Gen. William H. French [*q.v.*], whom he married in Washington, Nov. 15, 1836. He was promoted to lieutenant in 1840. A Mediterranean cruise in the *Columbia,* 1842–44, preceded three years in the Bureau of Charts and Instruments at the Naval Observatory. As executive of the *Washington* during the last summer of the Mexican War, he participated in operations at Laguna and Tabasco, and thereafter became executive of the *Porpoise,* African Squadron, which he commanded on the homeward voyage, January to April 1850. During the next eight years he was again on survey and hydrographic duty, commanding the steamer *Walker* in the Gulf of Mexico. His scientific bent appears in the invention of a deep-sea sounding apparatus and other devices useful in this work. He was made commander in 1855, and was chief of the Bureau of Construction from 1858 to 1861.

In February 1861 he conveyed secret instructions to the ships at Pensacola, Fla., and in April went with the expedition sent to evacuate the Norfolk, Va., navy yard, where he had charge of the party that fired the ships and ship-houses. After a year on the Pacific coast in the survey steamer *Active*—a remote assignment probably due to the department's early suspicion of officers from border states—he was made captain in July 1862, returned east in October, and served as senior officer on the Cape Fear River and Wilmington blockade till late in 1864, first in the *Dacotah* and after December 1863 in the fast side-wheeler *Fort Jackson.* In his autobiography, *From Reefer to Rear Admiral* (copyright 1899), Sands says that during this duty he never fully undressed or enjoyed a whole night's sleep, the strain telling severely on his health. His division captured some thirty steamers and twenty-three sailing vessels. There were engagements with shore defenses and a raid, Apr. 21, 1864, on salt works near Wilmington which netted a hundred and sixty prisoners. Sands also claims to have originated the idea of an additional outer line of blockaders. In October 1864, preparatory to operations against Fort Fisher, his ship was attached to the second division under Capt. Joseph Lanman [*q.v.*], but Sands understood he was still in charge of the blockade and disputed vainly the award of $14,000 prize money to Lanman. His ship was in both attacks on Fort Fisher, Dec. 24–25, 1864, and Jan. 13–15, 1865. Afterward, until July 1865, he commanded the second division, West Gulf Squadron. The surrender of the last Confederate troops occurred on his ship, June 2, and on June 5 he hoisted the flag at Galveston, Tex.

Made commodore in 1866 and rear admiral in 1871, he had charge of the Naval Observatory from 1867 to 1874. His maintenance of hearty cooperation between officer and civilian personnel did much to assure continued control of the observatory by the navy, and his experience and interest stimulated its progressive development. The "Great Equatorial," then the largest refracting telescope in the world, was added to the equipment, and expeditions were organized to observe the eclipses of Aug. 7, 1869, and Dec. 22, 1870, the reports of which appeared under Sands's name. After his retirement on July 11, 1871, he lived in Washington, D. C., where he died. His funeral was in St. Matthew's Catholic Church and his interment in Mount Olivet Cemetery. He had three daughters and five sons, the three eldest sons serving in the navy during the Civil War.

[The chief source is Sands's autobiography. See also *War of the Rebellion: Official Records* (Navy), esp. vols. VIII, X, XI; L. R. Hamersly, *Records of Living Officers of the U. S. Navy and Marine Corps* (ed. 1890); obituaries in *Evening Star* (Washington), July 2, 1883, and *Army and Navy Jour.*, July 7, 1883. Information on the family has been supplied by a grandson, W. F. Sands, Washington, D. C.]

A. W—t.

SANDS, COMFORT (Feb. 26, 1748–Sept. 22, 1834), merchant, Revolutionary patriot, was born on the Cowneck, now Sands' Point, Long Island, N. Y., fifth of the eight children of John and Elizabeth (Cornell) Sands. He was descended from James Sands who emigrated from England to Plymouth, followed Anne Hutchinson to Westchester County and Rhode Island,

and in 1661 settled on Block Island. After a good elementary schooling, Comfort started at twelve as a clerk at Cowneck, went to New York City as a clerk for his brother, and in May 1769 opened a store of his own in Peck Slip. He prospered rapidly in the West Indian business and within six years was credited with a considerable fortune. He identified himself prominently with the Revolutionary movement in New York from the outset. In 1765 he was in the group that seized and burned ten bales of stamped paper from a brig. He participated in the non-importation agreements and served on most of the important committees. He was a member of several of the provincial congresses and state assemblies, and he sat in the New York constitutional convention. In 1776, as a member of the Committee of Public Safety, he sent three vessels to the West Indies for supplies. Unlike some other merchants, such as Thomas Buchanan and Lewis Pintard [qq.v.], he did not remain in New York City during the British occupation. In 1776 he and his family barely escaped capture, when the redcoats destroyed the fine new home he was building near New Rochelle. For the next seven years, he was steadily on the move, sometimes in or near Philadelphia, at other times at Poughkeepsie, and other places in upstate New York. This absence did not prevent him from serving steadily as auditor-general of New York, province and state, from 1776 to 1782. His functions included the analysis of claims against the state, and he did not hesitate to deduct a private account from the amount paid a state creditor, "Stop 7/6 for a pr. Shoes he Owes me for" (Knight, post, p. 135). In 1778 he served on a commission at New Haven to regulate the price of labor and commodities for the army, and at the close of the war he was, with two others, in charge of the exchange of state and federal securities.

His fortunes, somewhat disturbed by the Revolution, were soon restored. He and his brother Joshua formed a partnership for foreign trade and also purchased, at the sales of confiscated Loyalist property, an extensive tract in Brooklyn. In 1784 he was, with Alexander Hamilton, one of the founders and directors of New York's first bank, the Bank of New York. He was president of the Chamber of Commerce from 1794 to 1798. The Anglo-French wars stimulated his commerce to such an extent that his bank deposits between 1795 and 1797, it is said, amounted to $3,443,873. The wars were not an unmixed blessing, however, and so many of his ships were seized by the French and British that in June 1801 he was declared a bankrupt, but the final

settlement left a surplus of $118,000. He later retired to a country estate in New Jersey. He was described as "tall, of a clear florid complexion and prominent features; in character he was firm, open and unsuspecting, generous to friends, relatives and dependents, and liberal of his time and property in all matters pertaining to the public good" (Wilson, post, p. 198). On June 3, 1769, he was married to Sarah Dodge and, after her death, he was married on Dec. 5, 1797, to Cornelia Lott who survived him. He had eighteen children: ten sons and five daughters by the first marriage, and one son, Robert Charles Sands [q.v.], and two daughters by the second. The census of 1800 showed that he owned one slave. He died in Hoboken, N. J.

[Temple Prime, *Descent of Comfort Sands* (1886); George Wilson, *Portrait Gallery of the Chamber of Commerce of the State of N. Y.* (1890); *Catalogue of Portraits in the Chamber of Commerce of the State of N. Y.* (1924); E. C. Knight, *N. Y. in the Revolution as Colony and State, Supplement* (1901); L. C. Hatch, *The Administration of the Amer. Rev. Army* (1904); J. A. Scoville (pseud. Walter Barrett on title page), *Old Merchants of N. Y.*, 3 ser. (1865); *N. Y. Geneal. and Biog. Record*, July 1915, Jan. 1924.]   R. G. A.

SANDS, DAVID (Oct. 4, 1745–June 4, 1818), Quaker preacher, abolitionist, was born at Cowneck, Long Island, N. Y., the son of Nathaniel and Mercy Sands, who were members of the Presbyterian Church. When David was fourteen the family moved to Cornwall on the Hudson, at that time a sparsely settled farming community. He possessed a keen mind and seized every opportunity to promote his education, often studying by firelight in the evening. At about twenty years of age, with his father's help, he started a mercantile business in Cornwall, which took him frequently to New York City. Meantime he had come under the influence of itinerant Quaker preachers and members of the Quaker Society in Cornwall and in New York City. In his twenty-first year he became a member of the Society of Friends, joining the meeting at Nine Partners, N. Y. He was married in 1771 to Clementine Hallock of Nine Partners, and they settled for life in Cornwall. He began to give religious messages in Quaker meetings in 1772 and quickly revealed a rare gift for public speaking. He was officially recorded a minister in the Society of Friends in 1775 and immediately began what proved to be a life-long itinerant service.

The most effective contribution he made was on his second journey through the New England colonies. The first preparatory journey was in 1775–76. This was followed in 1777 by extensive services in the New England sections, where there were settled Quaker meetings, followed by a journey into pioneer sections of what is now the state of Maine. Much of his pioneer **work** was in the regions bordering on the Kennebec River, two years after Benedict Arnold's famous expedition. During the years 1777–79 Sands traveled on horseback four successive times through the Kennebec settlements, often cutting the paths for his horse to travel in. He left behind in these regions a long line of Quaker meetings, whose establishment was mainly due to his labors, and he is historically the founder of Quakerism in central Maine. His numerous visits to New England likewise led to an expansion of Quakerism in Massachusetts and New Hampshire. He paid a fifth visit to the Kennebec Valley in 1795 continuing through the settlements in northern and eastern Maine and sailing from Halifax for England. The years from 1795 to 1805 were spent in itinerant ministry in Europe. He visited during these ten years many groups of Quakers in Great Britain and Ireland and on the Continent. He was permitted to have an interview with King George III and was received with much kindness and friendly feeling. He was in Ireland in the agonizing period during the "Great Rebellion." His travels in Germany and France were also extensive and were marked by profound religious influence. He represented in the later part of the eighteenth century a strong reaction against Quietism and in the direction of an evangelical awakening. There was an evangelical note in his preaching that was at that time new in Quaker circles. With this religious intensity was joined a strong human sympathy for slaves and a passion for the overthrowing of the system of slavery. In his old age he made a final journey through New England and the provinces of Ontario and Quebec. He died in his own home.

[*Journal of the Life and Gospel Labours of David Sands* (1848); *The Annual Monitor for 1819* (1819); *Quaker Biographies*, ser. 2, vol. I (n.d.); R. M. Jones, *The Society of Friends in Kennebec County* (1892), *The Quakers in the American Colonies* (1911), and *The Later Period of Quakerism* (1921).]   R. M. J.

SANDS, JOSHUA RATOON (May 13, 1795–Oct. 2, 1883), naval officer, was born in Brooklyn, N. Y., son of Ann (Ayscough) and Joshua Sands, collector of the port of New York and twice United States representative, and nephew of Comfort Sands [*q.v.*]. Entering the navy in June 1812, he saw active service on Lake Ontario in the engagement with the *Royal George* off Kingston, Nov. 9, 1812, the attack on Toronto in April following, and the capture of Fort George in May. During the rest of the war he was in the *General Pike*, in a shore battery, and then in the *Superior*. Promoted to lieutenant

in 1818 after three years in the Mediterranean, he fought two duels—the first at Valparaiso, Oct. 7, 1823, with Lieut. T. S. Hamersley, which caused injury to neither participant but led to Sands's court martial and long confinement in his ship; the second at Rio, Aug. 20, 1830, in which Sands, then executive of the *Vandalia*, killed his opponent, Surgeon H. Bassett, but was completely exonerated. (See B. F. Sands, *From Reefer to Rear Admiral*, 1899.) Through the Mexican War he commanded the small steamer *Vixen*, participating in operations at Alvarado, Tabasco, Laguna, and elsewhere, and served as governor at Laguna until the investment of Vera Cruz, where with other vessels the *Vixen* carried a reconnaissance close under the fortress. After the capture of Tampico and Tuxpan, he returned home in 1847 in the *St. Mary's*. In 1851 he commanded the *St. Lawrence*, carrying American exhibits to the London world's fair. In 1857 in the *Susquehanna* he assisted in Atlantic cable-laying operations and later lay several months at Grey Town, Nicaragua, where on Dec. 24, 1857, he captured a remnant of the filibusters of William Walker [*q.v.*]. In August his ship, ravaged by yellow fever, landed over a hundred patients in New York. In 1859–61 he commanded the Brazil station in the *Congress*.

Promoted to captain in 1854, he was retired in this grade in December 1861, but was made commodore (retired) in 1862 and rear admiral in 1866. He was lighthouse inspector on the lower Great Lakes, 1862–66, and port admiral at Norfolk, Va., 1869–72. Thereafter he lived chiefly in Baltimore, Md., where he died at the home of his daughter. His funeral was at St. Ann's Episcopal Church, Brooklyn, and his burial in Greenwood Cemetery. He was married first in 1826 to Mary, daughter of John Stevens of Hoboken, N. J., who died in 1828; second in 1830 to her younger sister Henrietta, who died in 1847; and third to Ellen Ann Crook of Baltimore, described as a handsome girl of nineteen. He had a son John (1840–1914) by his second wife, and a son and two daughters by his third. Admiral A. T. Mahan [*q.v.*], once a young aide on his staff, pictures him interestingly in *From Sail to Steam* (1907) as of slight frame, handsome and active, with a reputation for high courage, "not of particular distinction" but with the salt savor of the old navy.

[Temple Prime, *Descent of Comfort Sands* (1886); records of St. Ann's Church, Brooklyn, N. Y.; death notice in *The Sun* (Baltimore), Oct. 3, 1883, and obituaries in *Evening Star* (Baltimore), Oct. 3, 1883, and *Army and Navy Jour.*, Oct. 6, 1883; C. O. Paullin, "Dueling in the Old Navy," *Proc. U. S. Naval Inst.*, vol. XXXV (1909); record of court martial, *Am. State Papers* (*Naval Affairs*) (1860), vol. II, pp. 487–605;

T. H. S. Hamersly, *Gen. Reg. U. S. Navy . . . 1782 to 1882* (1882); L. R. Hamersly, *Records of Living Officers U. S. Navy and Marine Corps* (eds. 1870, 1878).]
             A. W—t.

SANDS, ROBERT CHARLES (May 11, 1799–Dec. 16, 1832), author and journalist, was born in New York City, the son of Cornelia (Lott) and Comfort Sands [*q.v.*]. It was probably from his mother that he inherited his love of learning. At seven he began the study of Latin and became so proficient in the classical languages that in October 1812, he was admitted to the sophomore class of Columbia College, where he distinguished himself both in the classics and in other branches of learning. At Columbia he made the acquaintance of James Eastburn, and their friendship became in time one of the most intimate in early Knickerbocker literature, rivaled only by the more picturesque friendship of Joseph Rodman Drake and Fitz-Greene Halleck. In college they established in succession two short-lived literary periodicals. As New York at this period offered little financial opportunity to a young man with literary ambitions, Sands in 1815 began the study of law. During the next four years his legal studies were both arduous and extensive, but he found time to form with Eastburn and two other friends an association known as the "Literary Confederacy." In addition to writing and circulating a manuscript periodical called the "Aeronaut," the members of this organization, in its social life so typical of early literary New York, contributed to the *New-York Daily Advertiser* in 1817 a series of essays called "The Neologist" and in 1819 to the *Commercial Advertiser* another called "The Amphilogist." In 1817 Sands published *The Bridal of Vaumond*, a metrical romance in the manner of Scott dedicated to Washington Irving, which was attacked for its immaturity by the *Analectic Magazine*, February 1818. With Eastburn he had begun another poem, *Yamoyden*, based on the life of the Indian chief, Philip. Before it was finished, Eastburn died, and Sands edited and completed it as a memorial to his friend, publishing it in 1820.

In the same year he was admitted to the bar but after a few years withdrew to devote himself to literature. In 1821 the "Literary Confederacy" began to publish a periodical called *St. Tammany's Magazine*, its contents consisting largely of literary parody and burlesque. In 1824 Sands became for a short period editor of the *Atlantic Magazine;* and when in 1825 the magazine merged with the *New York Review*, under the editorship of William Cullen Bryant [*q.v.*], he was engaged as an assistant. In May 1826 the magazine was discontinued. In 1827 he joined the editorial staff of the *New-York Commercial Advertiser*, a position he held until his death. In the meantime other literary schemes had also occupied his attention. His study of the Spanish language and history resulted in a biographical sketch of Hernando Cortés, which was translated into Spanish and prefixed to an edition of Cortés' letters published under the title *Historia de Méjico* (1828). In the same year he joined with Bryant and Gulian C. Verplanck in the publication of an annual called *The Talisman*, to which he contributed some of his best work. In 1830 he edited the *Life and Correspondence of John Paul Jones*, and in 1832 he contributed to the *Tales of Glauber-Spa* his best short story, "Boyuca." In the midst of his literary labors his life was suddenly cut short by an apoplectic stroke. He was unmarried and lived during the latter part of his life at the family home in Hoboken, where he died. He mingled freely in New York society, where "his warmth and kindness of disposition," writes his friend Verplanck (*post*), "attracted and strongly attached to him many intimate friends, whom he loved with an unwavering constancy and affection." His reputation as a poet must rest primarily on his contributions to *Yamoyden* and "The Dream of the Princess Papantzin," published in *The Talisman* (1829). The former, modelled on Scott, is as a whole diffuse and unsymmetrical; yet it contains detached passages fraught with genuine feeling that bear some claim to poetry. Historically, it is important for its early use of the American Indian. "The Dream of the Princess Papantzin," a blank verse poem founded on a Mexican legend, is on the whole inferior to the best portions of *Yamoyden*. Much of the prose is in a satirical or mock-heroic vein, with here and there a Rabelaisian touch typical of early Knickerbocker literature. His best serious work in prose is undoubtedly "Boyuca," a by-product of his Spanish-American studies.

[*The Writings of Robert C. Sands in Prose and Verse* (2 vols., 1834) contains an excellent biog. sketch by G. C. Verplanck. Other biog. articles may be found in *N. Y. Mirror*, Dec. 29, 1832; *Knickerbocker*, Jan. 1833, Mar. 1834. For geneal. material, see Temple Prime, *Descent of Comfort Sands* (1886). Reviews of *Yamoyden* may be found in *Lit. and Sci. Repository*, Jan. 1821; *N.-Y. Jour. and Belles-Lettres Repository*, Dec. 1820; *North Am. Rev.*, Apr. 1821; *American* (N. Y.), Dec. 11, 1820; *Lit. Gazette*, Jan. 27, 1821; Nathan Drake, *Evenings in Autumn* (1822), vol. I. For obituaries see *N.-Y. American*, Dec. 17, 1832; *N.-Y. Daily Advertiser*, Dec. 18, 1832; *N. Y. Commercial Advertiser*, Dec. 17, 1832. Much reliable manuscript material is preserved in the N. Y. Hist. Soc.]   N. F. A.

SANDYS, GEORGE (Mar. 2, 1577/78–Mar. 4, 1643/44), colonist and poet, was born at Bishopsthorpe, near York, seventh and youngest son of Edwin Sandys, archbishop of York, and his wife Cicely, daughter of Sir Thomas Wilford; Sir Edwin Sandys was his brother. Save that he had three noble godparents, that he entered St. Mary Hall, Oxford, Dec. 5, 1589 (he appears to have taken no degree), and that he was admitted to the Middle Temple Oct. 23, 1596, little is known of his youth or early manhood. In 1610 he left England on an extended foreign tour, visiting France, Italy, Turkey, Egypt, and Palestine; and after returning home published *A Relation of a Iourney Begun An: Dom: 1610* (1615), an authoritative account of his travels which proved popular and influential. Early interested in colonial enterprise, he was a shareholder in the Virginia Company under its third charter (1611) and in the Bermudas Company, disposing of his shares in the latter organization in 1619, after an unsuccessful effort to obtain the governorship of the islands. In April 1621, however, upon Southampton's recommendation, he was appointed treasurer of the Virginia colony, and that autumn accompanied Governor Wyatt (who had married his niece, Margaret Sandys) to Jamestown, remaining in Virginia until 1628 or later.

His duties as treasurer consisted not only in accounting to the Company in England for all quitrents and other annual revenues, "but also in carrying out that body's directions for promoting the cultivation of . . . the 'staple commodities'" (P. A. Bruce, *Institutional History of Virginia*, 1910, II, 602). He was, however, no book-suffocated scholar or clerk: besides his cultural accomplishments he possessed initiative, an observant practicality, and exceptional industry. He commanded a punitive force against the Tappahannock Indians; he offered to lead an expedition in search of a route to the South Sea; he built the first water-mill in America; he sponsored iron manufacture, engaged in the making of glass, and after the massacre of 1622, devoted considerable effort to reviving silk culture and grape culture; and he is credited with having introduced ship-building into the colony. He was made a member of the council, September 1624, and was reappointed in 1626 and 1628. He managed successfully the 1500 acres with which his office was endowed and acquired other property, about which he sometimes quarreled with the colonial council. Best remembered of all his achievements, however, was his *Ovid's Metamorphosis Englished by G. S.* (1626) in verse, the first five books of which he had translated and seemingly had published before sailing for Virginia. A second complete edition, handsomely printed and illustrated, was issued in 1632, and

included a translation of Book I of Virgil's *Æneid*.

A member of the commission for the better plantation of Virginia, 1631, and having "spent the ripest of his years in the public employment" (*Calendar of State Papers, post,* p. 138) there, he applied for the secretaryship of the Crown's special commission "to govern the plantations"; his petition failing, he settled permanently in England, and was shortly made a gentleman of the privy chamber to King Charles. At court he became intimate with Lucius Cary, second viscount Falkland, and subsequently spent part of his time at Carswell, home of Sir Francis Wenman (who had married the poet's niece, Anne Sandys), where he could associate easily with the circle which gathered about Falkland at Great Tew, Oxfordshire. His closing years, however, were passed mainly at Boxley Abbey, near Maidstone, Kent, the residence of his niece Margaret, widow of Francis Wyatt, whither he "retired himself for his poetry and contemplations." In 1636 he published, under special license from the King, the first of his celebrated poetic renditions of the scriptures, *A Paraphrase vpon the Psalmes of David and vpon the Hymnes Dispersed throughout the Old and New Testaments,* to a second augmented edition of which (1638) Sidney Godolphin, Carew, Waller, and others contributed commendatory verses while Henry Lawes added music. Favorably as this volume impressed individual poets and churchmen—it was one of the three books which comforted Charles I during his imprisonment at Carisbrooke—Sandys' *Psalmes* were not generally adopted in divine service, doubtless, as Richard Baxter observed, in consequence of their not being "fitted to the usual tunes" (*Poetical Fragments,* 4th ed., 1821, p. v). Meanwhile, he had not lost interest in, or connection with, Virginia, and during the 1630's, as a result of his friendly relations with the King, he acted as an unofficial London representative of the colonial liberal party. In 1640, when the Virginia Assembly sought the restoration of their ancient charter rights, Sandys was appointed agent of the colony in England. Instead of presenting the Assembly's petition to the King, Sandys proffered it to Parliament, which renewed the original charter. Perturbed by this action, Charles supplanted Governor Wyatt with the royalist Sir Francis Berkeley, who forthwith convened a new assembly at Jamestown. Under Berkeley's domination this body protested against the renewal of the charters, assuring the King— as most histories erroneously assume to be the truth—that Sandys in presenting the former petition to the Commons "had mistook his instructions" (Alexander Brown, *English Politics in Early Virginia History,* 1901, pp. 96–105). Except for the publication of *Christs Passion* (1640), translated from the Latin of Grotius, and *A Paraphrase vpon the Song of Solomon* (1641), his last years were uneventful. He died, presumably unmarried, at Boxley Abbey and was buried in Boxley Church, the register of which with understandable pride designates him *"Poetarum Anglorum sui saeculi facile princeps."* By numerous of his distinguished associates he had long been esteemed no less for his unfailing nobility of character, his modesty, gentle disposition, and piety, than for his indubitable poetic talents.

The first man in America to devote himself seriously to literature and scholarship, Sandys, hampered as he was by distraction, hardship, and danger, with his *Ovid* nevertheless succeeded in accomplishing a work of real magnitude, acclaimed by his contemporaries, and passing through eight editions before the close of the century. The infrequency of his original compositions may account for a subsequently diminished interest in his writings, but his decasyllabic couplets show a deftness, a metrical freedom and variety, that had no little share in developing the capacity of heroic verse; his style is direct and prevailingly simple, often vigorous, picturesque, and eloquent. Speaking of his later versification, which is smoother and more harmonious than that of the *Ovid,* Joseph Warton observed that Sandys did more to polish and tune the English language by his *Paraphrases* than either Denham or Waller had done; Dryden, who objected that Ovid's poetry is evaporated in Sandys' hands from a too close adherence to the original, elsewhere paid tribute to "the ingenious and learned Sandys, the best versifier of the former age"; and Pope, who liked the *Ovid* "extremely," declared that "English poetry owes much of its present beauty" to Sandys' translations.

[Richard Hooper, *The Poetical Works of George Sandys* (2 vols., 1872); A. W. Ward and A. R. Waller, *The Cambridge Hist. of English Lit.,* vol. VII (1911); Alexander Brown, *The Genesis of the U. S.* (2 vols., 1890), and *The First Republic in America* (1898); Thomas Fuller, *The Hist. of the Worthies of England* (1840), ed. by P. A. Nuttall, III, 434; W. N. Sainsbury, *Calendar of State Papers, Colonial Ser., 1574–1660* (1860).] A. C. G., Jr.

SANFORD, EDMUND CLARK (Nov. 10, 1859–Nov. 22, 1924), psychologist and college president, was born in Oakland, Cal., the son of Jennie (Clark) and Edmund Philo Sanford. His father was a descendant of Thomas Sanford, an early emigrant from England whose name appears on a bridge built at Milford, Conn., as a memorial to those who founded the town in 1639;

his mother was born in Farmington, Conn., where five generations had preceded hers. Young Sanford was trained as a clerk in his father's drug store, the only one in Oakland, and had his early education in the public schools of Oakland. He received the degree of A.B. from the University of California in 1883 and went to Oahu College, Honolulu, where for two years he taught the classics, mathematics, and ancient history. In 1885 he entered the Johns Hopkins University as a graduate student in psychology and received the degree of Ph.D. in 1888. After a year, 1888–89, as instructor in psychology at Johns Hopkins, he went to Clark University. Made assistant professor of psychology in 1892 and professor of experimental and comparative psychology in 1900, he resigned in 1909 to become the second president of Clark College. In 1920, after the resignation of President Granville Stanley Hall [*q.v.*] of Clark University, he left the presidency of Clark College to become professor of psychology and education in Clark University, a position he held at his death. On Dec. 28, 1901, he married Florence Bartling, of Oakland, who died Dec. 1, 1922. They had no children.

Before the days of Hugo Münsterberg and Edward Bradford Titchener [*qq.v.*], Sanford ranked easily as one of the best three experimental psychologists in the United States. In 1902 he was president of the American Psychological Association, but his relative importance diminished rapidly during his years of administrative work as president of Clark College. On the *American Journal of Psychology* he served as acting editor, 1888–89; associate editor, 1895–1920, and cooperating editor, 1920–24. During his connection with Clark University, he supervised the writing of twenty-four Ph.D. theses. The seventy-seven titles of his own bibliography include poems, songs, essays, addresses, and humorous speculations as well as scientific articles. The latter are remarkably excellent in quality but few in number. His one book, *A Course in Experimental Psychology* (2 vols., 1894–98), was first published in six installments in the *American Journal of Psychology* between April 1891 and April 1896 and concerned itself entirely with the field of sensation, though it comprised only half of what the writer planned eventually to include. As the only laboratory manual in English for a time, it gained wide use in academic circles. Titchener and other equally competent fellow psychologists comment on his artistic skill in the investigation of minor problems. Ill throughout most of his life, he lacked the necessary vigor and enthusiasm for sustained research on fundamental problems. It is possible, too, that he was overwhelmed by the dominating personality of Stanley Hall, with whom he worked for many years, and that he avoided the basic problems in which Hall delighted. Sanford is described as a man of unfailing courtesy and gentleness, with great poise of personality and an unusual ability to make lasting friendships.

[L. N. Wilson, ed., "Edmund Clark Sanford, Nov. 10, 1859–Dec. 22, 1924," *Clark Univ. Lib. Pubs.*, no. 1 (1925), with bibliog.; W. H. Burnham, *Pedagogical Seminary and Jour. of Genetic Psych.*, Mar. 1925; E. B. Titchener, *Am. Jour. Psych.*, Apr. 1925; C. E. Sanford, *Thomas Sanford* (2 vols., 1911); *Who's Who in America*, 1924–25; *Boston Post*, Nov. 23, 1924.]

C. M.

SANFORD, EDWARD TERRY (July 23, 1865–Mar. 8, 1930), jurist, was born at Knoxville, Tenn., the son of Edward Jackson Sanford, who had moved there from Connecticut in 1852, and Emma (Chavannes) Sanford, of Swiss descent. On his father's side he was descended from Thomas Sanford who was in Dorchester, Mass., as early as 1634, and later settled at Milford, Conn. Sanford was graduated B.A. and Ph.B., 1883, at the University of Tennessee, received the degrees of B.A., 1885, and M.A., 1889, at Harvard, and that of LL.B., 1889, at the Harvard Law School. He then traveled in Europe for more than a year. Meanwhile, in 1888, he had been admitted to the Tennessee bar and on his return to America he began practice with a Knoxville law firm. On Jan. 6, 1891, he married Lutie Mallory Woodruff, who bore him two daughters, one of whom predeceased him. From 1897 to 1923 he was a trustee of the University of Tennessee, and from 1909 until his death, of the George Peabody College for Teachers. He was a man of unusual culture, with a deep appreciation of music, literature, and the fine arts, and, in the words of one of his colleagues, "was born to charm" (285 *U. S.*, xlviii). His first important official position was that of assistant attorney general of the United States, to which he was appointed by President Theodore Roosevelt in 1907. After he had served about a year in that capacity, he was appointed judge of the United States district court for the middle and eastern districts of Tennessee, where he served until President Harding nominated him as justice of the Supreme Court on Jan. 24, 1923, to succeed Justice Pitney. After confirmation he took the oath on Feb. 5 and his seat on the bench on Feb. 19.

As a district judge, Sanford seemed "sometimes . . . to be slow in coming to a decision" (285 *U. S.*, xlvi). As a justice of the Supreme Court he delivered the opinion of the Court in only 130 cases during his seven years' service,

but some of the cases in which he wrote opinions were of more than average importance. As a district judge he had frequent occasion to administer the Federal Bankruptcy Act, and two of his seven opinions on the Supreme Court enumerated by the Chief Justice as outstanding construed that act: *Meek* vs. *Banking Co.*, 268 *U. S.*, 426 (1925) and *Taylor* vs. *Voss*, 271 *U. S.*, 176 (1926). He wrote the opinion, dissented from by Justices Holmes and Brandeis, in *Gitlow* vs. *New York*, 268 *U. S.*, 652 (1925), upholding a conviction for publishing a Communist Manifesto; and also that in *Whitney* vs. *California*, 274 *U. S.*, 357 (1927), in which all concurred, affirming a conviction for "criminal syndicalism" by reason of membership in the Communist Party. On the other hand, in *Fiske* vs. *Kansas*, 274 *U. S.*, 380 (1927), he wrote the opinion reversing such a conviction where the organization to which the accused belonged was not shown to have advocated unlawful measures; and he dissented from the majority in *U. S.* vs. *Schwimmer*, 279 *U. S.*, 644 (1929), denying citizenship to a pacifist. In *Liberty Warehouse Co.* vs. *Grannis*, 273 *U. S.*, 70 (1927), he wrote the opinion holding that a federal court could not render a "declaratory judgment"—a declaration of rights in an *ex parte* controversy—though such a proceeding was authorized by a state law passed at the active urge of many eminent lawyers. Probably his most important opinion was in what is known as the "Pocket Veto" case, 279 *U. S.*, 655 (1929), holding inoperative a bill passed by Congress and referred, less than ten days before its adjournment, to the President who neither signed nor returned it. This disposed of a question open for a hundred and forty years.

[*Proc. of the Bar and Officers of the Supreme Court of the U. S. in Memory of Edward Terry Sanford* (1931), found also in 285 *U. S. Reports*; *Who's Who in America*, 1928–29; J. A. Fowler, in *Am. Bar Asso. Jour.*, Apr. 1931; C. E. Sanford, *Thomas Sanford* (2 vols., 1911); *Class of 1885, Harvard Coll., Secretary's Report No. VII* (1910) and *No. IX* (1925); *N. Y. Times*, Mar. 9, 1930.]

C. S. L.

SANFORD, ELIAS BENJAMIN (June 6, 1843–July 3, 1932), Congregational clergyman, was of Puritan ancestry, a descendant of Thomas Sanford who was in Dorchester, Mass., as early as 1634 and later settled in Milford, Conn. The son of Rev. Isaac Sanford, a Methodist minister, and Lovisa Ann (Weeks) Sanford, he was born at Westbrook, Conn. Prepared for college chiefly at the Goshen (Conn.) Academy, he entered Wesleyan University in 1860, receiving the degree of A.B. in 1865. He was licensed as a Methodist preacher and received into the New York East Conference in 1865, the year of his graduation, and began his ministry as pastor of the Methodist Church in Thomaston, Conn. In 1867, he transferred to the Congregational body, becoming pastor of the First Church of Cornwall, Conn. While there, he married (Oct. 10, 1870) Martha Sanford of Thomaston, a distant relative. Becoming interested in religious journalism, he assumed in 1873 the associate editorship of a new publication, *Church Union,* launched in the interest of Christian unity, but soon left it to become editor of the *Alliance,* of Baltimore, Md., a short-lived publication. In 1882, he took charge of the *Golden Rule,* of Boston, forerunner of the *Christian Endeavor World.* After occupying this editorial post for a few months, he was forced by serious illness to give up all work for a time, after which he returned to the pastorate, becoming minister of the Congregational church in Westbrook, Conn., his native town, where he remained until 1894.

In 1895, Sanford was chosen secretary of a new organization known as the Open and Institutional Church League, designed to promote a more adequate church program, especially in social service, and interchurch cooperation in carrying it out. Five years later, when increasing interest in church cooperation had led to the organization of the National Federation of Churches and Christian Workers, he became its general secretary. This organization, despite its name, had no official relation with the denominations, but it paved the way for an official federation. In 1905 a Conference on Interchurch Federation was held in Carnegie Hall, New York, as a result of which, under the organizing genius of Sanford, the constitution for the Federal Council of the Churches of Christ in America was formulated. Owing chiefly to Sanford's persistent and persuasive urging, the constitution had been ratified by the group of interested denominations by 1908, in which year the Council came into formal existence. At the outset, Sanford was elected its corresponding secretary, a position which he held until 1913, when failing health forced him to resign. He was then elected honorary secretary, in which office he continued until his death in 1932. The intervening years he spent in retirement at Middlefield, Conn.

During this period of retirement from active labors, Sanford wrote the history of the formative period of the church federation movement, under the title, *Origin and History of the Federal Council of the Churches of Christ in America* (1916), and also *A History of the Reformation* (1917). He had previously published *A History of Connecticut* (1887), *A Concise Cyclopedia of Religious Knowledge* (1890), and *Church Federation—Inter-Church Conference* on Federation . . . *1905* (copyright 1906), of which he was editor.

[The first chapter of Sanford's *Origin and Hist. of the Fed. Council of the Churches of Christ in America* is largely autobiographical. See also C. E. Sanford, *Thomas Sanford* (2 vols., 1911); F. W. Nicolson, *Alumni Record of Wesleyan Univ.* (1931); *Hartford Courant,* July 4, 1932; unpub. correspondence in the files of the Fed. Council of the Churches of Christ in America.]

S. M. C.

SANFORD, HENRY SHELTON (June 15, 1823–May 21, 1891), diplomatist, founder of Sanford, Fla., was born at Woodbury, Conn. A descendant of Thomas Sanford who was in Dorchester, Mass., as early as 1634 and later settled in Milford, Conn., he was the only son of Nehemiah Curtis and Nancy Bateman (Shelton) Sanford. From his father, a manufacturer, he inherited an ample fortune. He attended Washington (later Trinity) College, Hartford, for two years, but was obliged by ill health to abandon his formal studies in 1841. Six years later he began his diplomatic apprenticeship as an attaché at St. Petersburg. In 1848 he went to Frankfort as acting secretary of legation, and the following year to Paris as secretary of legation, a post which he held until early in 1854, acting as chargé d'affaires in 1853. In connection with this service he published *The Different Systems of Penal Codes in Europe; also a Report on the Administrative Changes in France* (1854). He resigned after the arrival of the new minister, John Young Mason [*q.v.*], when the latter discarded the plain civilian dress prescribed by Secretary Marcy.

In 1861 Sanford was appointed minister resident to Belgium, where he served for eight years, enjoying cordial relations with the court, discharging special duties in the purchase of military supplies, and observing the activities of Confederate agents. On May 20 and July 20, 1863, at Brussels, he signed on behalf of the United States the Scheldt Treaties relating to import duties and to the capitalization of the Scheldt dues. In 1868 he signed a naturalization convention with Belgium, a consular convention, and an additional article, concerning trademarks, to the commercial treaty of July 17, 1858. On Sept. 21, 1864, in Paris, he married Gertrude E. du Puy of Philadelphia, by whom he had seven children.

After his return to the United States in 1870 he bought a large tract of land on the St. John's River in Florida, establishing himself in a commodious house on a plantation which he called "Belair," and setting out extensive orange groves. Three miles from "Belair" he built a sawmill and a store, the beginnings of the town of Sanford. The place was at first regarded as a "Yankee nest" and there was some local bitterness against Sanford's early attempt to bring in negro laborers, whereupon he established a colony of Swedish immigrants at New Upsala, near by. In 1880, interesting British capital, he formed a company to promote the development of the Sanford region; he was also concerned in the building of the South Florida Railroad.

Shortly after the creation, in 1876, of the International Association for the Exploration and Civilization of Central Africa, under the leadership of Leopold II, King of the Belgians, Sanford was appointed a member of its executive committee. It was through his exertions as the Association's representative that on Apr. 22, 1884, the United States recognized the flag of the Association "as that of a friendly government." This was the earliest form of recognition, and King Leopold was much gratified. He had already, in 1878, made Sanford a grand officer of the Order of Leopold. At the Conference of Berlin (1884–85), Sanford sat as associate delegate of the United States with John A. Kasson [q.v.], American minister to Germany, and with Kasson he signed the General Act of the Conference, establishing the status of the Congo Free State. In 1890 Sanford discharged his last diplomatic service and participated for the last time in the affairs of Africa, when, on July 2, at Brussels, he signed with Edwin H. Terrell, minister to Belgium, the General Act between the United States and other powers for the repression of the slave trade and the restriction of commerce in firearms and liquor in Africa. He died in the following year, at Healing Springs, Va. The title "General," by which he was commonly known, was derived from the fact that the state of Minnesota had enrolled him as a major-general in its militia during the Civil War, in recognition of his gift of a pair of field pieces to the 1st Minnesota Volunteers.

[C. E. Sanford, *Thomas Sanford* (2 vols., 1911); *Some Account of Belair* (1889); *Am. Jour. of Internat. Law,* vol. III (1909), Supp., "Official Docs."; D. C. Boulger, *The Reign of Leopold II* (1925), vol. I; R. S. Thomson, *Fondation de l'État independent du Congo* (1933); J. S. Reeves, "The International Beginnings of the Congo Free State," *Johns Hopkins Univ. Studies in Hist. and Pol. Sci.,* 12 ser. (1894); *Papers Relating to Foreign Affairs*; archives of the Department of State; W. W. Folwell, *A Hist. of Minn.,* II (1924), 87; information from the Registrar of Trinity College; obituary in *N. Y. Tribune,* May 23, 1891.] M. B. G.

SANFORD, NATHAN (Nov. 5, 1777–Oct. 17, 1838), legislator and jurist, was descended from Robert Sanford, an early settler of Hartford, Conn., through his son Ezekiel, who was one of the first settlers of eastern Long Island. The son of Thomas Sanford and his wife Phebe (Baker?), widow of Theophilus Howell, Nathan

was born at Bridgehampton, L. I. He received his early education at Clinton Academy, Easthampton, and at Yale, although he did not graduate. In New York City he studied law in the office of the elder Samuel Jones, and was admitted to the bar in 1799. In 1802 he became a leader of the Tammany faction of the Jeffersonian Republican party and during the next twenty-nine years was almost continuously in public office. He was United States commissioner of bankruptcy in 1802, and from 1803 to 1815 held the lucrative post of United States attorney for the district of New York, from which he was thought to have derived $100,000 annually in fees (*The Diary of Philip Hone,* 1927, ed. by Allan Nevins, II, 526). He was a member of the assembly in 1808–09 and 1811, being speaker in 1811 until forced to retire on account of illness, was state senator, 1812–15, and United States senator, 1815–21. Though a candidate for reëlection to the Senate he was thrust aside by his party in favor of Van Buren (Hammond, *post,* I, 561). As a member of the state constitutional convention of 1821 he introduced and promoted the adoption of the resolution which abolished property qualifications for the suffrage. On the retirement of James Kent [q.v.], Aug. 1, 1823, he became chancellor and served until Jan. 24, 1826. He was an unsuccessful candidate for vice-president in 1824, and two years later once more became United States senator, serving from Jan. 31, 1826, to Mar. 3, 1831.

As chancellor, Sanford's opinions were characterized by clarity, good sense, and the absence of attempts to parade his legal learning. In his eleven years in the Senate he took little part in the debates on great questions, confining his attention to administrative problems and to measures for improving the organization of the government. He urged the creation of a department of the interior and the expansion of the attorney-general's office into a department of justice. He advocated the vigorous policy of collecting the French spoliation claims afterward followed by Jackson. In 1830 he presented a report on the currency (*Register of Debates in Congress,* vol. VII, App., pp. cxxxi–cxxxvii) which was the basis of subsequent legislation. He proposed constitutional amendments to require the choice of presidential electors by districts and to allow the president to remove judges with the consent of two-thirds of each house of Congress.

Besides his interests in law and public affairs he was a student of foreign languages and delighted in reading the Latin poets. He was married three times—on May 9, 1801, to Eliza Van Horne of New York, who died in 1811; on Apr.

14, 1813, to Mary Isaacs of New Haven; and subsequently to Mary Buchanan of Baltimore, each of whom bore him one or more children. He died, at Flushing, L. I., from a pulmonary affection of long standing, having carried on an active existence, to the wonder of physicians, for a quarter of a century after he had lost the use of one lung.

[B. F. Thompson, *Hist. of Long Island* (3rd ed., 1918), vol. IV; J. T. Adams, *Hist. of the Town of Southampton* (1918); D. S. Alexander, *A Pol. Hist. of the State of N. Y.*, vol. I (1906); *Legal and Judicial Hist. of N. Y.* (3 vols., 1911), ed. by Alden Chester; J. D. Hammond, *The Hist. of Pol. Parties in the State of N. Y.*, vols. I, II (1842); *Biog. Dir. Am. Cong.* (1928); C. E. Sanford, *Thomas Sanford* (1911), II, 1339; death notice in *N. Y. American*, Oct. 18, 1838.]
E. C. S.

SANGER, CHARLES ROBERT (Aug. 31, 1860–Feb. 25, 1912), chemist, was born in Boston, the son of George Partridge Sanger [*q.v.*] and Elizabeth Sherburne (Thompson) Sanger. His great-grandfather, Zedekiah Sanger, was minister at Duxbury and South Bridgewater; his grandfather, Ralph Sanger, minister of Dover; and his father, a judge of the court of common pleas and United States district attorney for Massachusetts. His mother came of a family of Portsmouth, N. H., sea captains.

Early in Sanger's boyhood his father moved to Cambridge, and he was fitted for college at the high school there. Entering Harvard College in 1877, he displayed much interest in chemistry, was prominent in student activities, and was elected permanent class secretary in his senior year. Graduated in 1881, he spent the next year in research work with Prof. Henry Barker Hill [*q.v.*] at Harvard, and the succeeding year in similar work at the universities of Munich and Bonn. He then returned to Harvard to continue his researches with Professor Hill and was granted the degree of doctor of philosophy in 1884. He remained at Harvard as an assistant until 1886, when he was appointed professor of chemistry at the United States Naval Academy, Annapolis. In 1892 he was made Eliot Professor of Chemistry at Washington University, St. Louis. He was called back to Harvard in 1899 as assistant professor of chemistry, to give the course on qualitative analysis previously given by Professor Hill. Later, he also initiated a course on industrial chemistry. Upon the death of Hill in 1903, Sanger was promoted to a full professorship and appointed director of the chemical laboratory.

In his work with Hill, Sanger made notable contributions to the chemistry of pyromucic acid and its derivatives. His most important investigations, however, were concerned with the de-
tection of arsenic in the tissues and excreta of persons exposed to arsenic-containing wallpaper. He improved the well-known Berzelius-Marsh test for arsenic and was able to demonstrate a marked correlation between the degree of exposure to such wallpaper, the amount of arsenic in the excreta, and the intensity of the morbid symptoms. In cases where arsenic was present in wallpapers but where the formation of dust was precluded by a covering of paint or other paper, he was able, nevertheless, to demonstrate the absorption of arsenic by persons exposed to such wallpapers, and thus to confirm the conclusion of Gosio that in some way a gaseous effluvium containing arsenic was given off from them. Later, he improved the Gutzeit method for the detection of arsenic and antimony until it surpassed in delicacy even the above mentioned Berzelius-Marsh method. (For papers dealing with this subject, see *Proceedings of the American Academy of Arts and Sciences*, vol. XXVI, 1891; XXIX, 1894; XLIII, 1908.) His last researches were concerned with the preparation and properties of pyrosulphuryl chloride and chlorosulphonic acid, the action of sulphur trioxide on silicon tetrachloride, and the detection of fluorine.

Sanger was quiet, scholarly, and methodical, and phenomenally accurate and careful in all his observations and deductions. He was vice-president of the Northeastern Section of the American Chemical Society in 1902–03. He was also a Fellow of the American Academy of Arts and Sciences and was editor of its *Proceedings* in 1909–10. On Dec. 21, 1886, he was married to Almira Starkweather Horswell, who died Jan. 6, 1905, leaving three children. On May 2, 1910, he married Eleanor Whitney Davis. He died at Cambridge, Mass.

[*Proc. Am. Acad. Arts and Sciences*, vol. XLVIII (1913); *Harvard Coll., Class of 1881, Fiftieth Anniversary* (1931); *Harvard Grads. Mag.*, June 1912; *Who's Who in America*, 1912–13; *Boston Transcript*, Feb. 26, 1912.]
A. B. L.

SANGER, GEORGE PARTRIDGE (Nov. 27, 1819–July 3, 1890), lawyer and editor, son of the Rev. Ralph and Charlotte (Kingman) Sanger, was born at Dover, Mass., where his father was a minister for more than half a century. He was descended from Richard Sanger, who settled as a blacksmith in Sudbury, Mass., in 1646. George received his preliminary education under his father and at Bridgewater Academy, taught in country school, and in 1836 entered Harvard College. He was graduated A.B. in 1840 and for two years had charge of a private school at Portsmouth, N. H. In 1842 he became a proctor at Harvard and enrolled in the law school, and the following year was appointed tutor in Latin. He received the degree of LL.B. in 1844, and upon his admission to the bar in 1846 severed his connection with Harvard (except as a Latin examiner) and entered into a law partnership with Stephen H. Phillips of Salem. Later, for some time, he lived in Charlestown. On Sept. 15, 1846, he married Elizabeth Sherburne Thompson of Portsmouth, N. H., who bore him five sons, one of whom was Charles Robert Sanger [q.v.].

From 1848 to 1861 Sanger edited *The American Almanac and Repository of Useful Knowledge,* and from May 1851 to March 1855, the *Monthly Law Reporter.* From 1849 to 1853 he was assistant United States attorney and in 1853–54 was state's attorney for the Suffolk district, with residence in Boston. In 1853–54 he was also captain of the Ancient and Honorable Artillery Company, having previously served as captain of the Charlestown Guards. Appointed judge of common pleas by Governor Washburn in 1854, he served in that capacity until the court was abolished in 1859. During this service, in conjunction with George Minot, he edited the eleventh volume of the *Statutes at Large of the United States of America,* covering the period from 1855 to 1859. Beginning with the twelfth volume (1859–63), he took over the sole editorship of the series, which he held until the completion of the seventeenth volume (1871–73), after which the Department of State assumed exclusive charge of the publication. Meanwhile, in 1859, with Judge William A. Richardson [q.v.], he was designated by the state legislature to revise and edit *The General Statutes of the Commonwealth of Massachusetts* (1860), and after the appearance of the revision of that year, with Richardson supervised the publication of annual supplements down to 1881. He also revised and consolidated the municipal laws and the Boston ordinances, in collaboration with John G. Locke. In 1873 he was elected to the lower branch of the General Court and later in the same year President Grant appointed him United States attorney for Massachusetts. This office he held until after Cleveland became president, retiring in 1886 and resuming practice in Boston. In addition to his public duties, he was the first president of the John Hancock Mutual Life Insurance Company, organized in 1863. His career, if not spectacular, was creditable and marked by unusual industry and satisfactory service.

[J. C. Rand, *One of a Thousand* (1890); Abner Morse, *The Geneal. of the Descendants of Several Ancient Puritans,* I (1857), 129; *Green Bag,* Aug. 1890; *Boston Daily Advertiser,* July 4, 1890.]   C. S. L.

SANGSTER, MARGARET ELIZABETH MUNSON (Feb. 22, 1838–June 4, 1912), author, editor, daughter of John and Margaret (Chisholm) Munson, was born at New Rochelle, N. Y. Her father, a Wesleyan Methodist, was born in England in 1786; her mother was of Scotch Covenanter parentage. The austere atmosphere of the Munson home was due to the serious mother, twenty years her husband's junior, for John Munson was of a cheerful, spontaneous temperament. When Margaret was three, the family removed to New York. Under her mother's instruction, she became able to read at the age of four almost any book, and at six she recited at Miss Halstead's private school Pitt's speech on the Stamp Act. John Munson's restlessness and real-estate changes caused the family to remove to Paterson, N. J., when Margaret was eight. There she attended Passaic Seminary, a Baptist institution, and became much interested in foreign missions. The only other school in which she was a pupil was that of Monsieur Paul Abadie in Brooklyn, N. Y., where she studied Latin, Greek, and French, and secured a diploma. In 1854 her father died and her mother's brother, David Chisholm, came to live with the family and assumed its responsibilities.

Having filled many blank books with verse and essays, about 1855 Margaret wrote *Little Janey,* the story of a child's life, which was purchased for forty dollars and printed by the Presbyterian Board of Publication. The Board then gave her a commission for a hundred juvenile stories related to assigned pictures. In an effort to earn more money she "wasted" time studying music and painting and teaching embroidery to children. These activities were abandoned when, in October 1858, she was married to George Sangster, a native of Scotland, whom she had met at a Sunday school convention at which he was one of the speakers. He was a widower with two little girls, to whom Margaret became devoted. Though her mother's expertness and her own lack of aptitude had kept her from learning the domestic arts, she soon became a "not unsuccessful housekeeper" (*Autobiography, post,* p. 162). In 1859 a son, her only child, was born. During the Civil War George Sangster became an officer in the Union army and after the war the family settled at Norfolk, Va., where, in spite of existing bitterness between Northerners and Southerners, they made many warm friends. In 1870 they removed to Brooklyn, N. Y., and in 1871 George Sangster died.

In Norfolk Mrs. Sangster had contributed prose and verse to the *Christian Intelligencer, Sunday-School Times, Independent,* and *Hearth and Home.* Faced with the necessity of earning a living, she naturally turned to writing. The editor of *Hearth and Home,* George Cary Eggleston [*q.v.*], engaged her to write a series of articles, and a year later put her in charge of the children's page, formerly conducted by Mary Elizabeth Mapes Dodge [*q.v.*]. Shortly after, she became assistant editor. Within the next three years she was thrice offered the position of dean in women's educational institutions, but preferred to continue in journalism. Questions that came to her office made her feel that she had a "mission to girlhood" and prompted her to write letters and short essays addressed to girls and young women which were published in various magazines. When *Hearth and Home* ceased publication, Dec. 25, 1875, other editorial positions were offered her. She edited the family page of the *Christian Intelligencer,* was literary adviser for Harper & Brothers, postmistress of *Harper's Young People,* and finally editor of *Harper's Bazar* (1889–99). She was also a contributor to the *Christian Herald,* the *Ladies' Home Journal,* and the *Woman's Home Companion.* Though she wrote several novels, most of her volumes of prose and verse are compilations from her magazine articles. Among the best of her works are *Poems of the Household* (1882), *Little Knights and Ladies* (1895), *Home Life Made Beautiful in Story, Song, Sketch, and Picture* (1897), *Cheerful To-days and Trustful To-morrows* (1899), *Winsome Womanhood* (1900), *Lyrics of Love, of Hearth and Home, and Field and Garden* (1901), *Janet Ward, a Daughter of the Manse* (1902), *Eleanor Lee* (1903), *Good Manners for All Occasions* (1904), *What Shall a Young Girl Read?* (1905), *Fairest Girlhood* (1906), *Ideal Home Life* (1910), *Eastover Parish* (1912), *My Garden of Hearts* (1913), a collection of stories and essays issued posthumously. In 1909 she published *An Autobiography: From My Youth Up; Personal Reminiscences.* The tone of all her writings is cheerful, practical, rather sentimental, and very religious. Her prose is clear and direct, her poetry simple and full of fancies which appeal to children. She said of her method that she never waited for inspiration but was a "day-laborer." During her later years she lived at Glen Ridge, and at Maplewood, N. J., where she died. She had been blind for several years but continued her writing with the aid of secretaries. The *Christian Herald* for June 5, 1912, the day after her death, carried her "Home Chats," and the issue of June 12, an article, "Choosing a Partner for Life" and a poem by her, "The End of the Day."

[In addition to Margaret E. Sangster's *Autobiog.,* see *Who's Who in America,* 1912–13; F. E. Willard and M. A. Livermore, *A Woman of the Century* (1893); *N. Y. Times,* June 5, 1912; "A Voice That is Still," in *Christian Herald,* June 19, 1912.]   S. G. B.

SANKEY, IRA DAVID (Aug. 28, 1840–Aug. 13, 1908), singing evangelist, son of David and Mary Sankey, was born in Edinburg, Lawrence County, Pa. In a family the members of which were musically inclined he early acquired ability to read music and familiarity with sacred songs and tunes. In 1857 his father was made president of a bank in Newcastle, Pa., in which Ira, after attending the high school, became a clerk. Joining the local Methodist church, he was soon chosen choir leader and superintendent of the Sunday School. Upon the outbreak of the Civil War he served a term of enlistment in the Union army and then returned to Newcastle to be assistant to his father, who had been appointed collector of internal revenue. On Sept. 9, 1863, he married a member of his choir, Fanny V. Edwards, daughter of Hon. John Edwards. Singing had now become one of his chief interests, and his services were frequently utilized at Sunday School conventions and political gatherings in his section of the country. In 1870 he was a delegate to the international convention of the Young Men's Christian Association at Indianapolis. Here his singing attracted the attention of Dwight L. Moody [*q.v.*], who persuaded him to join him in the religious work he was then carrying on in Chicago. He assisted Moody in the remarkable series of meetings held in England, Scotland, and Ireland from 1873 to 1875, and in the years that followed he contributed in no small degree to the success of Moody's evangelistic campaigns in the United States and abroad, the names of the two becoming inseparably associated.

Sankey had had little training in the art of singing, nor was his voice—a strong baritone of moderate compass—at all exceptional; nevertheless, he could move vast audiences profoundly. Generally accompanying himself on a small reed organ, he sang simply but with careful enunciation and much feeling and expression. He had a dramatic sense that enabled him to choose the song best fitted to the occasion, and frequently he prefaced it with words that added to its effect. Although his chief work was to sing the Gospel, he could also make moving verbal appeals and was successful in dealing with individuals in inquiry meetings. Nothing in his personal appearance was of assistance to him. He was bulky in figure, weighing over 220 pounds, his face was adorned with long side-whiskers, and he was somewhat unctuous in manner; yet his audiences, forgetting all this, were captivated by the sweetness and compelling emotion of his singing. Published collections of the songs used in the Moody and Sankey meetings gained almost world-wide popularity. The first of these, *Sacred Songs and Solos*, was published in England in 1873. This was followed by *Gospel Hymns* (nos. 1–6, 1875–91) and other collections. They were compilations from various sources; Sankey wrote comparatively few, though he supplied the music for more; and in the editing he was assisted by others. The successors of the camp-meeting spirituals, they are characterized by a contagious melody, pathetic or ringing, a frequence of march or dance rhythm, and the use of solo effects, climactic catchwords, and the chorus (L. F. Benson, *The Hymnody of the Christian Church*, 1927, pp. 266–67). Neither Moody nor Sankey profited from the immense sale of the hymn books. The royalties, turned over to a board of trustees, went chiefly to the support of the Northfield School which Moody established. In 1906 Sankey published *My Life and the Story of the Gospel Hymns*. His last years were spent in blindness at his home in Brooklyn, N. Y. He was survived by his wife and two sons.

[In addition to references above, see W. R. Moody, *D. L. Moody* (1930); Gamaliel Bradford, *D. L. Moody: a Worker in Souls* (1927); *Who's Who in America*, 1908–09; John Julian, *A Dict. of Hymnology* (1891); *Harper's Weekly*, Aug. 29, 1908; *Outlook*, Aug. 22, 1908; *Current Literature*, Oct. 1908; *N. Y. Times* and *N. Y. Herald*, Aug. 15, 1908; *Brooklyn Eagle*, Aug. 14, 1908.]
H. E. S.

SAPPINGTON, JOHN (May 15, 1776–Sept. 7, 1856), physician, son of Dr. Mark Brown and Rebecca (Boyce) Sappington, was born in Maryland, but when he was a schoolboy his family moved to Nashville, Tenn. He studied medicine under his father and for a time practised with him at Nashville, later moving to Franklin, Tenn., where he practised alone. On Nov. 22, 1804, he married Jane Breathitt, daughter of Gov. John Breathitt of Kentucky. He rode on horseback from his home in Tennessee to Philadelphia, where he attended for one term (1814–15) a course of medical lectures at the University of Pennsylvania. In 1817 he went to Missouri, locating in Howard County. After practising there for two years he moved across the Missouri River to Saline County, where he established his permanent residence, "Fox Castle," near Arrow Rock.

Sappington's life may be said to have been devoted to the cause of quinine. In the early development of the Southern and Western states,

malaria was so prevalent that it was one of the greatest obstacles with which the early settlers had to contend. Soon after quinine (isolated from Peruvian Bark in 1820) became available in the United States, Sappington recognized its specific nature in the treatment of malaria, and strongly advocated its use without recourse to bleeding, vomiting, and purging which, as late as 1850, such a prominent member of the medical profession as Daniel Drake thought necessary. Unable to change the erroneous opinions of his fellow practitioners and realizing the urgent need of making quinine available to people in the intensely malarious districts, he began in 1832 the wholesale distribution of Dr. John Sappington's Anti-Fever Pills. Over one million boxes of these were distributed through the Western and Southern states. He also wrote and published *Theory and Treatment of Fevers* (1844), perhaps the first medical treatise written west of the Mississippi. In it he gave in detail his method of preparing his quinine-containing pills and advocated quinine, properly used, as the only thing necessary to cure malaria. Although living in a frontier community far removed from the seats of medical learning, Sappington's views regarding the treatment of fevers was more in accord with modern medical practice than were those of his more favored contemporaries. Among his friends he numbered Andrew Jackson, Thomas Hart Benton, and Nathaniel Beverly Tucker.

[Sappington manuscript collection in the State Hist. Soc. of Mo.; T. B. Hall, "John Sappington," *Mo. Hist. Rev.*, January 1930; H. L. Conard, *Encyc. of the Hist. of Mo.* (1901), vol. V; Univ. of Pa. records; W. B. Napton, *Past and Present of Saline County, Mo.* (1910); Daniel Drake, *A Systematic Treatise . . . on the Principal Diseases of the Interior Valley of North America* (1854); Robert J. Terry, "Dr. John Sappington, Pioneer in the Use of Quinine in the Miss. Valley," *Proc. of the Celebration of the Three Hundredth Anniversary of the First Recognized Use of Cinchona* (St. Louis, 1931), pp. 165–80.]
T. B. H.

SARGENT, AARON AUGUSTUS (Oct. 28, 1827–Aug. 14, 1887), United States senator, was born in Newburyport, Mass., son of Aaron Peaslee and Elizabeth (Stanwood) Flanders Sargent. He was a descendant of William Sargent who was in Ipswich, Mass., as early as 1633. After attending the common schools, he was apprenticed to a cabinet maker for a short time, and then learned the printer's trade. This he followed for several months in Philadelphia in 1847, and then moved to Washington, where he became secretary to a member of Congress.

In December 1849 he went to California, and for a time found employment in the freight-carrying business between San Francisco and Stockton. In 1850 he was on the Sacramento

Placer Times, but soon moved to Nevada City, Cal., and became a compositor on the *Daily Journal.* Returning to San Francisco, he was compositor on the *Placer Times and Transcript* and the *Alta California,* but soon went back to Nevada City, and not long after bought the *Daily Journal.* As editor and manager, he conducted this paper as a Whig organ, studying law in his spare time. In 1854 he was admitted to the bar. He was nominated for the California assembly by the new American Party in 1852, and from that time he seems to have been dominated by a consuming political ambition which quite subordinated his career as a lawyer. He was active in the organization of the Republican party in California, and for some years was a member of the party's state executive committee.

In 1855–56 he served as district attorney for Nevada County, and in 1857 was the unsuccessful Republican candidate for the attorney-generalship. In 1860 he was a delegate to the Republican National Convention, and was elected representative in Congress, serving from 1861 to 1863. As a member of the select committee on a Pacific railroad, he displayed energy and ability in procuring the enactment of the first Pacific railroad bill to pass Congress. Of this measure he and Theodore D. Judah [*q.v.*], chief engineer of the Central Pacific Railroad, were the authors. At the end of his term, Sargent unsuccessfully sought his party's nomination for the governorship, and then resumed the practice of law. In 1867, he was an unsuccessful candidate for the United States Senate, and in 1868 and 1870 was reëlected to the House of Representatives. After a bitter campaign, he succeeded, in 1872, in supplanting Cornelius Cole as United States senator. In the Senate, Sargent was a member of the committees on naval affairs, mines and mining, and appropriations. He successfully opposed the nomination by President Grant of Caleb Cushing [*q.v.*] to be chief justice of the Supreme Court because of statements contained in a letter from Cushing to Jefferson Davis. At the close of his senatorial term in 1879, Sargent again returned to his law practice. In 1882 President Arthur appointed him minister to Germany, but owing to his outspoken criticism of Germany's unfriendly discrimination against American pork, he became *persona non grata* to the German government and resigned in April 1884. President Arthur immediately offered him the ministry to Russia, but this he declined. Returning to California, he soon became the Republican candidate for election to the Senate. The legislature chosen in 1884 appears to have contained a majority of Sargent supporters, and the public

generally assumed that he would be reëlected with little opposition. The Republican legislative caucus, however, unexpectedly nominated Leland Stanford [*q.v.*], and he was elected. Stanford and Sargent had been close friends and this apparent treachery came as a blow from which the latter never recovered. He died in San Francisco and was buried in Laurel Hill Cemetery. On Mar. 14, 1852, he was married to Ellen Clark; his widow, a son, and two daughters survived him.

Sargent was a man of strong and forceful personality, aggressive in political contests, untiring and persevering in pursuit of his ends. He was a good German scholar, well read on all political topics, and an able debater. He spoke with great rapidity; as a contemporary expressed it, "his volubility was manifest both in tongue and pen" (*Memoirs of Cornelius Cole, post,* p. 235). Closely identified with the militant Pacific railroad interests, he became a masterful machine politician, "placing or displacing men according to the will of a syndicate."

[E. E. Sargent, *Sargent Record* (1899); *Vital Records of Newburyport, Mass.* (1911), I, 342; *San Francisco Chronicle,* Aug. 15, 1887; *San Francisco Evening Bull.,* Aug. 15, 16, 1887; *Biog. Dir. Am. Cong.* (1928); H. H. Bancroft, *Hist. of Cal.* (1890), VII, 291–92, 548–49; *Memoirs of Cornelius Cole, Ex-Senator of the U. S. from Cal.* (1908); C. C. Phillips, *Cornelius Cole* (1917), pp. 262–64; E. C. Kemble, *A Hist. of Cal. Newspapers* (1927).]
P. O. R.

SARGENT, CHARLES SPRAGUE (Apr. 24, 1841–Mar. 22, 1927), arboriculturist, was born in Boston, Mass., the son of Ignatius and Henrietta (Gray) Sargent. His father was a well-known merchant in trade with the East Indies, a descendant of William Sargent who was in Gloucester, Mass., in 1678. Educated in private schools and at Harvard University, from which he graduated in 1862, Charles enlisted on the northern side in the Civil War in 1863, rising through successive grades to the rank of major of volunteers, and was honorably mustered out of the army in 1865. After three years of European travel he married Mary Allen Robeson on Nov. 26, 1873. They had two sons and three daughters, one of whom married Guy Lowell [*q.v.*]. For a time he was occupied with the development of his garden, one of the best in the vicinity of Boston, and with the study of botany. In this he had the advantage of close association with Asa Gray [*q.v.*], by whose friendship his work was undoubtedly influenced. In 1872 he became director of the Harvard Botanic Garden in Cambridge. He was professor of horticulture at Harvard in 1872–73 and professor of aboriculture from 1879 until his death.

In 1873 he was appointed director of the newly created Arnold Arboretum. Though for a time he also held the directorship of the Botanic Garden, in 1879 he gave it up to devote all his energies to the Arboretum and to work relating to trees and forests. The plans for the Arboretum, worked out in cooperation with Frederick Law Olmsted [q.v.], involved much opposition and long delays in preparation; it was not until the spring of 1886 that the first trees were planted in their permanent groupings. Until his death the development and enlargement of the living collections of the Arboretum was Sargent's chief consideration, although with this was coordinated important research work on ligneous plants, particularly those composing a part of the North American flora. These studies resulted most notably in *The Silva of North America* (1891–1902), fourteen folio volumes with illustrations of every species of tree then known north of Mexico. Before this his appointment as special agent of the Tenth Census (1880) enabled him to explore forested regions throughout the United States and led to collaboration with many of the best field botanists in the country. The results were published in Volume IX of the Tenth Census, *Report on the Forests of North America* (1884), the first complete synopsis of the trees of North America and a splendid foundation for the future work on the *Silva*. This appointment also furnished the opportunity to bring together the Jesup collection of woods of North America, established by Morris K. Jesup [q.v.] and now a part of the exhibits in the American Museum of Natural History in New York, described in Sargent's *The Woods of the United States* (1885).

As a member of the Northern Pacific Transcontinental Survey in 1882–83, he was impressed with the desirability of establishing national parks in the western mountains and took an active part in the effort to secure them. He likewise helped in 1884 to establish a conservation policy in the Adirondack forests of New York. His journeys undertaken for the study of trees included a visit to Japan in 1892, a trip around the world in 1903, and travel in South America in the winter of 1905–06. From 1888 to 1897 he published and edited *Garden and Forest*, a weekly magazine that helped to awaken an interest in arboriculture and forestry in the United States. His own writings include *Forest Flora of Japan* (1894), *Manual of the Trees of North America* (1905), and many articles. He also edited the three volumes of *Plantae Wilsonianae* (1913–17), a description of plants collected by Ernest Henry Wilson [q.v.]. He never engaged in class work or gave public lectures, preferring to do his share of educational work through writing, but he inspired many by his wise counsels and did much to clarify problems in dendrology and landscape gardening.

[No extended biog. of Sargent has yet been written, but there is an excellent account of his life and work, with bibliog. and portrait, in *Jour. of Arnold Arboretum*, Apr. 1927. See also E. W. and C. S. Sargent, *Epes Sargent of Gloucester and His Descendants* (1923); *Who's Who in America*, 1926–27; S. E. Morison, ed., *The Development of Harvard Univ.* (1930); *Class Report: Class of 'Sixty-Two, Harvard Univ., Fiftieth Anniversary* (1912); *Harvard Grads.' Mag.*, June 1927; *Nat. Acad. Sci. Biog. Memoirs*, vol. XII (1929), with bibliog.; *Am. Forestry*, Nov. 1921; obituary in *Boston Transcript*, Mar. 23, 1927.] J.G.J.

SARGENT, DUDLEY ALLEN (Sept. 28, 1849–July 21, 1924), director of physical culture, physician, was born in Belfast, Me., the son of Caroline (Rogers) and Benjamin Sargent, a ship-carpenter and spar maker who died in 1856. The visit of an itinerant circus in Belfast when he was fifteen and later a gymnastic exhibition by students from Bowdoin College seem to have determined his career. Endowed with unusual strength and agility, he was soon the leader of a group of high-school boys who practised assiduously to master gymnastic and acrobatic feats and attained sufficient skill to give exhibitions in Belfast and neighboring towns. He himself won an engagement with a circus as a result of mastering the exceedingly difficult feat of sitting in a rocking chair balanced on a swinging trapeze. In 1869 he became director of the gymnasium at Bowdoin College. Two years later, though he retained his position as director, he was admitted as a freshman. In 1872 he spent three months of the winter term at Yale College, introducing his plan of physical training, and until his graduation from Bowdoin in 1875 he continued to divide his time between the two institutions. In 1875 he became instructor in gymnastics in Yale College and a student in the Yale Medical School, from which he obtained the degree of M.D. in 1878. The same year, he opened his Hygienic Institute and School of Physical Culture, a private gymnasium in New York, and only a year later he was appointed assistant professor of physical training and director of the Hemenway Gymnasium at Harvard.

During the forty years in which he held the position he exerted a greater influence on the development of physical training in American colleges and schools than any other man. Since he early recognized that the introduction of physical training in colleges and schools was dependent upon an adequate supply of trained teachers, he organized in Cambridge in 1881 the

Sanatory Gymnasium, which became the Sargent School for Physical Education. In 1887 he organized courses in physical training in the Harvard University summer school, which were given under his direction until 1919. He worked unceasingly in the interest of wholesome and nation-wide physical training, and against excesses in athletics, the abuse of military drill in schools, and other unwise measures. He was active in the organization of the American Association for the Advancement of Physical Education (later the American Physical Education Association) and the Society of Directors of Physical Education in Colleges. He served as president of the first in 1890, 1892–94, and 1899–1901, and of the second in 1899. In 1882 he published *A Handbook of Developing Exercises*; in 1887, *Anthropometric Apparatus, with Directions for Measuring and Testing the Principal Physical Characteristics of the Human Body* and an article in *Scribner's Magazine* for July 1887, "The Physical Proportions of the Typical Man." In 1893 he exhibited life-size statues of typical American students at the Columbian Exposition in Chicago. *Health, Strength and Power* appeared in 1904, and in 1906 twelve of his papers and essays were published under the title *Physical Education*. In 1927 appeared *Dudley Allen Sargent: an Autobiography*, edited by L. W. Sargent. He was a man of strong convictions, very loyal to those who shared his views but often intolerant toward those who opposed him. An indefatigable worker, he devoted all his time to professional interests even at the expense of social and family responsibilities. His wife, Ella Fraser Ledyard of Brooklyn, N. Y., whom he had married on Apr. 7, 1881, left him about 1898, and he lived alone during the last twenty-five years of his life. He retired from Harvard at seventy but continued to teach in his normal school until his death. He was survived by his wife and a son.

[*Who's Who in America,* 1924–25; F. E. Leonard, *A Guide to the Hist. of Physical Ed.* (1923); R. T. McKenzie, ed., *Hist. of Physical Ed.* (1927); L. C. Hatch, *Hist. of Bowdoin Coll.* (1927); *Obit. Record Grads. Yale Univ.* (1925); *Jour. Am. Medic. Assoc.,* Aug. 16, 1924; *Boston Transcript,* July 21, 1924; long personal acquaintance.]
G. L. M.

SARGENT, EPES (Sept. 27, 1813–Dec. 30, 1880), journalist, poet, dramatist, advocate of spiritualism, and indefatigable literary worker, was of the sixth generation of his family in America, a descendant of William Sargent who received a grant of land in Gloucester, Mass., in 1678. He numbered among his other early ancestors Gov. John Winthrop and Gov. Joseph Dudley [*qq.v.*]. The poet was the son of Epes

Sargent, a Gloucester ship-master, and his second wife, Hannah Dane Coffin, also of Gloucester. In 1818 the father removed from his native town to Roxbury and began a not wholly successful career as a Boston merchant, after which he returned to the sea. The son entered the Boston Latin School in 1823 and was graduated in 1829 (information from the Headmaster, Public Latin School, Boston, 1931). His course was interrupted for some months while he accompanied his father on a voyage to Russia, and the *Literary Journal,* published in 1829 by students of the Latin School, contained extracts from his letters from St. Petersburg. There is a persistent, but unverifiable, tradition that he attended Harvard College for a short time and contributed to the *Collegian,* on which his elder brother, John Osborne Sargent [*q.v.*], had been a collaborator with Oliver Wendell Holmes and others.

In the early thirties he joined the editorial staff of the *Boston Daily Advertiser,* and later that of the *Boston Daily Atlas.* For some time he was Washington correspondent of the *Atlas,* and thus formed many political acquaintances, particularly among the Whigs. A later result of this experience was his *Life and Public Services of Henry Clay* (1842, and subsequent revisions). After leaving the *Atlas* he devoted himself to miscellaneous literary work. His first plays—*The Bride of Genoa* (written 1836; published 1837) and *Velasco* (written 1837; published 1839) were both produced at the Tremont Theatre, Boston. The last-named tragedy, written for Miss Ellen Tree, was, so far as acting possibilities were concerned, the most successful of his dramatic attempts, and won some slight vogue on the English as well as on the American stage. From about 1839 to 1847 Sargent was engaged in various ventures in New York. He worked with Morris on the *New York Mirror,* with Park Benjamin on the *New World,* founded and conducted for a few months *Sargent's New Monthly Magazine* (January–June 1843), and edited *The Modern Standard Drama* (7 vols., beginning in 1846). In 1847 he returned to Boston and until 1853 was editor of the *Boston Transcript.* On May 10, 1848, he married Elizabeth W. Weld of Roxbury.

Throughout his active career Epes Sargent was a contributor to many magazines and other periodicals; a frequent author of occasional verse, particularly for theatrical occasions; and at times a lecturer. S. G. Goodrich [*q.v.*] in his *Recollections* (1856, II, 275) mentions him as one of those who assisted in the preparation of the Peter Parley books, and later as a writer of verse for the *Token.* His best volume of verse was *Songs of the Sea with other Poems* (1847; 2nd ed. 1849), based largely on experiences during a voyage to Cuba. Some of the sonnets in this collection have merit, but the only piece now remembered is the song, "A Life on the Ocean Wave." Another collection of poems appeared in 1858, and a narrative in verse, *The Woman who Dared,* in 1870. Among his works of fiction were *Fleetwood, or the Stain of Birth* (1845), and *Peculiar, a Tale of the Great Transition* (1864). More miscellaneous are *American Adventure by Land and Sea* (1841); *Arctic Adventure by Sea and Land* (1857, 1860). Plays, besides the two already named, were a comedy, *Change Makes Change,* and a tragedy, *The Priestess* (privately printed, 1854). Sargent edited the works of several English poets, among them Hood, Rogers, Campbell, Gray, and Goldsmith; two miscellanies, *The Emerald* (1866) and *The Sapphire* (1867); and *Harper's Cyclopædia of British and American Poetry,* published posthumously in 1881. He compiled a series of school speakers, one of school readers, and other works for schools. It was the success of these that for a time made his name almost universally known in America. The works mentioned, both original and edited, are but a few of those that bear his name. Large as was the bulk of his literary work, a great part of it was completed before he had passed his early fifties. In the later years of his life he was interested in Spiritualism, devoted much of his waning energy to the exposition of his new faith, and did relatively less of other writing. He was in correspondence with the leading students of Spiritualism at home and in Europe, and wrote, besides many articles for periodicals, *Planchette, or the Despair of Science* (1869), *The Proof Palpable of Immortality* (1875), and *The Scientific Basis of Spiritualism* (1880). His attitude toward the subject and the development of his ideas may be inferred from a comparison between the title of the last of these three works and the subtitle of the first.

Sargent was in poor health during his later years, suffering from a complication of ailments, especially bronchial; but his death resulted from a cancer of the mouth, which was distressingly painful and impaired his power of utterance. While never ranked as great in any department of literature or scholarship he was a writer of taste and sound ideals whose work met the needs of his time, and he was deservedly respected in his day. A contemporary wrote: "A dapper, elegant little man he was, neatly attired, swinging a thin, polished back [black?] bamboo cane, and seeming the embodiment of cheer"—a descrip-

tion not inconsistent with the somewhat less patronizing portrayal given by Poe in his *Literati.*

[Most published sketches are full of misstatements. Sargent left no direct descendants; and his career has sometimes been confused with those of other members of his family. The purely genealogical information in E. W. and C. S. Sargent, *Epes Sargent of Gloucester and His Descendants* (1923) is probably accurate, but the biographical sketch is an untrustworthy compilation; this volume also contains "A List of Publications of the Descendants of Epes Sargent," comp. by Julia M. Johnson. See, further, *The Complete Works of Edgar Allan Poe* (1908), ed. by N. H. Dole, IX, 36–38; E. A. and G. L. Duyckinck, *Cyc. of Am. Lit.* (1875), II, 569–71; *Boston Transcript,* Dec. 31, 1880.]

W. B. C.

SARGENT, FITZWILLIAM (Jan. 17, 1820–Apr. 25, 1889), physician, was born in Gloucester, Mass. His father, Winthrop, was descendant of William Sargent, who came to Gloucester from England before 1678, many of whose descendants distinguished themselves in the civil and military affairs of the colonies and some in literary or artistic paths. His mother, Emily Haskell, was a descendant of William Haskell, who came to New England about 1637. Winthrop Sargent succeeded his father in the management of large shipping interests belonging to his family, but the business failed in 1829, and in the following year he removed to Philadelphia, where he engaged in the commission business. He returned to Massachusetts in 1843, but in 1862 went back to Pennsylvania and lived at Morgan's Corner (now Radnor), near Philadelphia, until his death in 1874.

FitzWilliam Sargent studied at Jefferson College, Canonsburg, Pa., from which he received the degree of B.A., in 1837. Sometime later he entered the medical department of the University of Pennsylvania, from which he graduated in 1843. In the last year of his medical course he served as resident physician in the Wills Eye Hospital of Philadelphia. After graduating, he served two years as resident physician in the Pennsylvania Hospital and then entered on general practice in Philadelphia, paying particular attention to ophthalmology. In 1849 he was elected one of the attending physicians to the Wills Hospital, changing his position to attending surgeon in 1852. He resigned from the Hospital in 1857. He was elected a Fellow of the College of Physicians of Philadelphia in 1852. In 1848 he edited an American edition of *The Principles and Practice of Modern Surgery,* by Robert Druitt, and wrote a little book, *On Bandaging and Other Operations of Minor Surgery,* which went through several editions, being also translated into Japanese and published at Osaka in 1874. It was illustrated by the author. In

1852 he edited the American edition of James Miller's *The Principles of Surgery*, of which a second edition was published in 1856. He also contributed several articles to the *American Journal of the Medical Sciences*. On June 27, 1850, he married Mary Newbold Singer, a daughter of John and Mary (Newbold) Singer. Thereafter he lived principally in Europe. His wife was an accomplished musician and also had considerable talent in drawing and painting. She is said to have had much to do with the cultivation of the artistic genius of their son John Singer Sargent [*q.v.*], born while his parents were living in Italy in 1856. In 1887 while living in Florence, Italy, FitzWilliam Sargent suffered an apoplectic stroke, and in the spring of 1888 the family moved to Calcot, near Reading, England. The following winter was passed in Bournemouth, where Sargent died.

[E. W. and C. S. Sargent, *Epes Sargent of Gloucester and His Descendants* (1923); E. E. Charteris, *John Sargent* (1927); W. C. Posey and S. H. Brown, *The Wills Hospital of Phila.* (1931); H. A. Kelly and W. L. Burrage, *Am. Medic. Biogs.* (1920).]   F. R. P.

SARGENT, FRANK PIERCE (Nov. 18, 1854–Sept. 4, 1908), labor leader and federal official, was born at East Orange, Vt., and died at Washington, D. C. His parents were Charles Edwin and Mary C. (Kinney) Sargent and he was a descendant of William Sargent who was living in Ipswich, Mass., as early as 1633. His early education was received in the common schools, and for one year he attended Northfield Academy, Northfield, Mass. In his teens he worked on a farm and in the mills at Montpelier, Vt., and Manchester, N. H.

In 1878 he went to Arizona for his health, enlisted there in the United States Cavalry, and was active in the Geronimo campaign against the Apache Indians. Honorably discharged in 1880, he went to work for the Southern Pacific Railroad as an engine wiper at Tucson, Ariz. Within three months he became a locomotive fireman, and joined the Brotherhood of Locomotive Firemen, his initiation taking place Oct. 20, 1881, in one of the coal bins in the railroad yards. From 1883 to 1894 he lived in Terre Haute, Ind., and from 1894 to 1902 in Peoria, Ill. He was a delegate to the national convention of the Brotherhood of Locomotive Firemen at Terre Haute in September 1882, and at the Denver convention in 1883 he was elected vice grand master. In 1885, at the Philadelphia convention, he was elected grand master of the order, which office he held until 1902. He was prominent in the Chicago, Burlington & Quincy strike in 1888, and the American Railway Union strike against the Great Northern Railroad in 1894, and became known as a forceful leader for the firemen, while his moderation and reasonable methods in dealing with employers gained their confidence.

In 1898 he was appointed by President McKinley on the Industrial Commission, from which he resigned. He declined appointment in 1900 as director of the Bureau of Engraving and Printing. On May 7, 1902, he was nominated by President Roosevelt as commissioner general of immigration, and the nomination was confirmed the following day. In this office he was instrumental in the initiation of methods which aimed at the prevention of fraud against intending immigrants, and at the exclusion of undesirable and criminal elements. He also gave especial attention to the prevention of the smuggling of Chinese across the Mexican and Canadian borders. He was hindered, however, in carrying out what he conceived to be the policy of American labor, by the opposition of powerful diplomatic, industrial and political forces, which brought influence to bear upon those in higher authority. After the Chicago and New York anarchistic riots he made a special study of the changing character of the immigration into the United States and called attention to the fact that its sources were no longer so largely among the Germanic races of Northern Europe, but were then, to a great extent, in southern and southeastern Europe and Asia Minor. His reports included recommendations for amendments in the immigration laws to meet the changing conditions, and the delays in securing these were a cause of deep disappointment to him. Later developments more than justified his wisdom, and compelled the adoption of policies more in line with his thought. His writings include: "The Need of Closer Inspection and Greater Restriction of Immigrants" (*Century Magazine*, January 1904); and "Problems of Immigration" (*Annals of the American Academy of Political and Social Science*, July 1904). He had the confidence and friendship of Samuel Gompers [*q.v.*], and had a part in the conferences of Gompers and John Mitchell [*q.v.*] with President Theodore Roosevelt in 1902 which led up to the appointment of the federal commission for the settlement of the great anthracite coal strike. He was also a member of the group chosen to represent the interests of labor in the National Civic Federation. He was a man of large stature and commanding personality, and his winning manner and keen executive ability gained and held for him the loyalty of those associated with him. He was married on Oct. 17, 1881, to

Georgia M. McCullough of Saugus, Mass., who with an adopted daughter survived him.

[E. E. Sargent, *Sargent Record, William Sargent of Ipswich* (1899); *Brotherhood of Locomotive Firemen and Enginemen's Mag.*, Oct. 1908; Samuel Gompers, *Seventy Years of Life and Labor* (2 vols., 1925); A. P. Kellogg, "The National Conference on Immigration," in *Charities and the Commons*, Dec. 16, 1905; *Who's Who in America*, 1908–09; *Evening Star* (Washington, D. C.), Sept. 4, 1908; *N. Y. Times*, Sept. 5, 1908.]

W. R. G.

SARGENT, FREDERICK (Nov. 11, 1859– July 26, 1919), engineer, specialist in the design and construction of electrical generating stations, was born at Liskeard, Cornwall, England, on the farm of his parents, Daniel and Jane (Yates) Sargent. He early developed a taste for mechanics and became an apprentice in the famous engineering works of John Elder & Company on the Clyde, near Glasgow. While serving his apprenticeship, he attended night classes at Anderson's College, Glasgow. In 1880 he came to the United States and found employment designing marine steam engines in the shipbuilding yards on the Atlantic Coast. The following year he was designer for the Sioux City (Iowa) Engine Company and in 1882 went to Milwaukee to join the engineering staff of E. P. Allis & Company. He soon became acquainted with the Western Edison Light Company of Chicago and in 1884 went to work for them; on the organization of the Chicago Edison Company in 1887 he became its consulting engineer, holding this connection with the Edison Company and its successor, the Commonwealth Edison Company, until his death. To the duties of this post he added, in 1889, those of chief engineer of the Edison United Manufacturing Company, with headquarters in New York, and on the reorganization of this concern as the Edison General Electric Company he became its assistant chief engineer. In August 1890 he returned to Chicago to establish himself as a consulting electrical and mechanical engineer, and in 1891 formed the firm of Sargent & Lundy. He was consulting engineer for the World's Columbian Exposition in 1891 and 1892, and his firm after that period was continuously engaged in the design and construction of central generating stations for important companies in various parts of the United States and even in England and in South America. During the World War, he was consulting engineer for the government in connection with the Edgewood Arsenal and other projects.

While his early training had been in the design and construction of reciprocating engines, Sargent was among the first to recognize the great advantages of the steam turbine, and his purchase of the first large turbine for the Fisk Street Station, Chicago, began a new epoch in central station design. He saw the advantages in the use of high pressures and temperatures, took the lead in the introduction of pressures of 400 and 600 pounds, and had recommended the employment of 1200-pound pressures, which were introduced after his death. His mechanical mind indicated the economical and satisfactory solution of serious construction troubles in installations where large fluctuations in the condensing water levels existed.

Sargent had an active mind and a broad outlook; his thinking was always simple, direct, and practical. His designs were usually in advance of the times, but his experimenting was held in restraint by sound practical common sense. A genius in the design and operation of steam electric generating stations, he left his imprint indelibly on the central-station industry of his generation. He was awarded a medal by the World's Columbian Exposition and was a member of the jury of awards for power engineering at the St. Louis exposition of 1904. He was a member of the American Society of Mechanical Engineers, the American Institute of Electrical Engineers, the Western Society of Engineers, and other organizations. He married at Sioux City, Iowa, in 1885, Laura S. Sleep, daughter of William H. Sleep, a manufacturer, of Plymouth, England. His wife, with two sons and a daughter, survived him. He died at his home in Glencoe, Ill.

[*Trans. Am. Soc. Mech. Engineers*, vol. XLI (1919); T. C. Martin and S. L. Coles, *The Story of Electricity*, vol. II (1922); *Who's Who in America*, 1918–19; A. N. Marquis, *The Book of Chicagoans*, 1917; *Power*, Aug. 5, 1919; *Electrical World*, Aug. 2, 1919; *N. Y. Times*, July 27, 1919.]

G. A. O.

SARGENT, GEORGE HENRY (May 5, 1867–Jan. 14, 1931), journalist, bibliographer, was born, lived during many years of his life, and died in the old family farmhouse in Warner, N. H. He was the son of Walter and Addie C. (Morrill) Sargent, being descended on the paternal side from William Sargent, who emigrated from England and was in Ipswich, Mass., as early as 1633. George Henry was educated in the schools of his native town, and, giving up his original intention of entering college, went West in 1887 and began his life work in journalism as a reporter on the *St. Paul Daily Pioneer Press*, of which paper he was city editor from 1890 to 1895. In the latter year he returned East, and joined the staff of the *Boston Evening Transcript*, continuing his connection with that newspaper uninterruptedly throughout the rest of his life, as reporter, writer of special articles, and for over twenty-seven years as the writer of "The Bibliographer" department, every issue of which was from his own hand. In 1914, as the result of an illness which made it inadvisable for him to continue to live and work in the city, he left Boston, and thereafter made his home on his ancestral farm. He carried on his literary work there by correspondence, and through occasional visits to Boston, New York, Philadelphia, New Haven (where he delivered lectures on his special subject), and other cities, maintaining contact with book collectors and dealers. In 1889 he was married to Carrie Florence Dietz of Iowa City, Iowa, and it was largely due to her care that he was enabled to go on with his work through fifteen years of semi-invalidism.

He had many other interests in addition to those of journalism and bibliography, being active in the political affairs of his town and state, and directing the work of the New Hampshire farm where he lived. In face and stature he was the typical and gaunt New England Yankee. His friends and acquaintances were many, and everybody interested in bibliography, not only in the United States but also in England, looked upon him as a leading authority. He was an assiduous worker, and during the years of his labors upon "The Bibliographer" department of the *Boston Transcript,* he never failed to have his articles—usually totaling two columns every Wednesday—ready on time. He died early on a Wednesday morning, and the last installment of his work, mailed a day or two previously, appeared in the *Transcript* that evening. He was, moreover, not merely a looker-on and a casual writer in the field of bibliography, his own collection of books being extensive and valuable. Among his published works, in addition to a number in pamphlet form, were *The French Revolution and Napoleon in Literature and Caricature* (1906), *Amy Lowell, a Mosaic* (1926), *The Writings of A. Edward Newton, a Bibliography* (1927), and *A Busted Bibliophile and His Books* (1928).

[*Who's Who in America,* 1930–31; E. E. Sargent, *Sargent Record, William Sargent of Ipswich* (1899); Karl Schriftgiesser, "George Sargent, 1867–1931," in *The Bookman,* Mar. 1931; *Boston Transcript,* Jan. 14, 1931; *Publishers' Weekly,* Oct. 27, 1923, and Jan. 31, 1931; introduction to *The Fine Lib. of the Late George H. Sargent, Sold . . . at Unrestricted Auction Sale . . . Dec. 19th 1931* (1931); personal acquaintance.]
E. F. E.

SARGENT, HENRY (*c.* November 1770–Feb. 21, 1845), painter, military man, was born at Gloucester, Mass., and baptized on Nov. 25, 1770. Son of Daniel and Mary (Turner) Sargent and brother of Lucius Manlius Sargent [*q.v.*], he was a great-grandson of William Sargent who received a grant of land at Gloucester in 1678. His father was a prosperous and public-spirited merchant. Henry was sent as a young boy to Dummer Academy, South Byfield, and then, the family having moved to Boston, he continued his studies under local teachers. After a period in the counting house of Thomas Handasyd Perkins [*q.v.*], he continued his commercial apprenticeship with his father, but suddenly, as he was attaining his majority, without having previously shown special partiality for the arts of design, he determined to become an artist. An elder brother's efforts in this direction seem to have stimulated him, and his mother encouraged him. John Trumbull [*q.v.*], who visited Boston in 1790, saw some of his work and found it promising.

In 1793 Sargent went to London, where he studied with Benjamin West and had courteous treatment from John Singleton Copley [*qq.v.*]. A letter of Sargent's dated Mar. 27, 1795 (Addison, *post,* p. 279), shows that he found living in London expensive and the painter's profession much depressed. He returned to Boston in 1799, still strongly conscious of "the apathy then existing towards the arts" (Dunlap, *post,* II, 192). Accordingly, in that same year he took a commission in the national army then being raised under command of Alexander Hamilton. This service was brief, but it gave Sargent a taste for military life which motivated his long connection with the Massachusetts militia. In or shortly after 1799 he joined the Boston Light Infantry, which had been organized the year before and of which his brother, Daniel Sargent, was captain. Records of the adjutant-general's office in the Massachusetts State House show that Henry Sargent became first lieutenant of this company Oct. 1, 1804, and captain, Mar. 31, 1807. Of the tall, thin, Yankee build, he was a handsome officer and an efficient drill master. During the War of 1812 his company aided in the fortification of Fort Strong, and on May 31, 1815, he was appointed aide-de-camp to the governor, with the rank of colonel. In 1812, 1815, 1816, and 1817 he was a member of the state Senate.

In the course of the following decade, growing deafness caused him gradually to withdraw from public services and to devote himself entirely to his painting and to mechanical inventions, in which latter field he achieved no great celebrity. His painting was that of a diligent and gifted artist whose talent fell short of genius. His portraits were less masterful than those of his fellow townsman, Gilbert Stuart [*q.v.*], with whom he was personally intimate. Like Copley, whom he somewhat resembled as a painter, Sargent enjoyed intensive elaboration of textures and accessories. He had capacity for doing canvases that required sustained effort. The well-known

"Landing of the Pilgrims," at Pilgrim Hall, Plymouth, attributed to him, is not representative of his best work. Far better are the two conversation pieces, "The Tea Party" and "The Dinner Party," owned by the Museum of Fine Arts, Boston. These have something of the exquisiteness of the so-called Little Dutchmen and they give fascinating glimpses of social life in Boston homes of the early nineteenth century. An altar painting, "The Christ Crucified," which Sargent made for the Church of the Holy Cross, Boston, won contemporary favor. The full-length portrait of Peter Faneuil, in Faneuil Hall, if by Sargent, to whom it is ascribed, must be a copy after John Smibert (see note in Dunlap, *post*, II, 196). Sargent's self-portrait is at the Boston Museum; his likenesses of Jeremy Belknap, D.D., and John Clarke, D.D., both friends of his parents, are at the Massachusetts Historical Society. Continuing to paint at intervals down into old age, he was elected in 1840 an honorary member of the National Academy of Design and in 1845, president of the newly organized Artists' Association of Boston. He had married, Apr. 2, 1807, Hannah, daughter of Samuel and Isabella (Pratt) Welles, of Boston, and they had two daughters who died in infancy and two sons, one of whom was Henry Winthrop Sargent [*q.v.*].

[Wm. Dunlap, *A Hist. of the Rise and Progress of the Arts of Design in the U. S.* (3 vols., 1918), ed. by F. W. Bayley and C. E. Goodspeed; L. M. Sargent, *Dealings with the Dead* (1856), II, 538; H. T. Tuckerman, *Book of the Artists* (1867); C. E. Mann, *The Sargent Family and the Old Sargent Homes* (1919); E. W. and C. S. Sargent, *Epes Sargent of Gloucester and His Descendants* (1923); Albert Welles, *Hist. of the Welles Family* (1876); Julia deW. Addison, in *Art in America*, Oct. 1929; *Museum of Fine Arts, Boston, Cat. of Paintings* (1921).]   F. W. C.

SARGENT, HENRY WINTHROP (Nov. 26, 1810–Nov. 11, 1882), horticulturist and landscape gardener, was born in Boston, the first child of Hannah (Welles) and Henry Sargent [*q.v.*]. Educated at the Boston Latin School and at Harvard College, where he was graduated in the class of 1830 with a creditable record, he first studied law in the office of Samuel Hubbard in Boston but never engaged in the practice of this profession. He next became a partner in the banking house of Gracie and Sargent, New York agents of his uncle, Samuel Welles, a Paris banker. On Jan. 10, 1839, he married Caroline Olmsted, daughter of Maria (Wyckoff) and Francis Olmsted of New York, who survived him. There were three children of this marriage, two of whom predeceased their father. In 1841 Sargent retired and removed to "Wodenethe," an estate of about twenty acres on a plateau overlooking the Hudson just above Fishkill Landing

(now Beacon), N. Y., which soon became famous for its distant views and its vistas cut through the native forest to the Hudson and the mountains, and for its extensive plantation of coniferous trees. In planning it, the owner was without doubt assisted and inspired by his friend and neighbor, Andrew Jackson Downing [*q.v.*], the foremost American landscape gardener of the day.

In 1847–49 he travelled with his family in Europe and the Levant, primarily to gather plants and to study the design of parks and country places. As a result he later published a comprehensive garden guide entitled *Skeleton Tours* (1870), which included the British Isles, the Scandinavian peninsula, Russia, Poland, and Spain. He was a frequent contributor to horticultural papers, especially to the *Horticulturist*, and in 1873 with Charles Downing [*q.v.*] he wrote a supplement to Andrew Downing's *Cottage Residences* (1842). But his most important literary contribution is his supplement to the sixth (1859) and subsequent editions of Downing's *A Treatise on the Theory and Practice of Landscape Gardening* (1841). In this he gave an account of the newer deciduous and evergreen plants and told in considerable detail of the development of his own "Wodenethe" and of the estate of his relative, Horatio Hollis Hunnewell [*q.v.*], at Wellesley, Mass. A second supplement, added in the edition of 1875, gives a brief account of trees and shrubs introduced since 1859. In a period which marks the beginning of the professional practice of landscape architecture in America, this book and its supplement exerted a great influence on popular taste. Sargent's influence may also be seen more directly in the horticultural interests of his kinsmen, H. H. Hunnewell and Charles Sprague Sargent [*q.v.*].

[Emma W. and C. S. Sargent, *Epes Sargent of Gloucester and His Descendants* (1923); *1830, Harvard Univ. Memoirs* (1886); L. H. Bailey, ed., *Standard Cyc. of Horticulture*, vol. III (1915); J. H. Sheppard, *Reminiscences of Lucius Manlius Sargent* (1871); Albert Welles, *History of the Welles Family in England and Normandy, with . . . Some of the Descendants in the U. S.* (1876); obituary in *Gardener's Monthly and Horticulturist*, Dec. 1882; *N. Y. Tribune*, Nov. 11, 1882.]   K. M.

SARGENT, JAMES (Dec. 5, 1824–Jan. 12, 1910), inventor, was the son of William and Hannah (Allen, Allan, or Allyn) Sargent and was born on his father's farm at Chester, Vt., where until he was eighteen he helped in the farm work and obtained something of an education in the district schools. At that time, because of his intense interest in machinery, he went to work in a woolen mill and soon became an expert in the care of machines. A year or so later he became foreman of a woolen mill at Ashuelot, N. H., where he remained until 1848. Meanwhile he became interested in daguerreotyping, mastered the art, outfitted himself, and from 1848 to 1852 was occupied with marked success as a traveling daguerreotyper. During this period he perfected an apple parer he had invented and in 1852 went to Shelburne Falls, Mass., where in partnership with a man named Foster he began manufacturing and selling this device. After five years he became associated with the Yale and Greenleaf Lock Company as a traveling salesman. Making a careful study of lock mechanisms, he soon was able to pick any lock by means of a special micrometer of his own invention that detected variations in the combination wheels. When he became so expert that he could pick even the lock he sold, he experimented in secret to produce a combination lock he could not pick. About 1863 he succeeded and offered the invention to his employer. When the offer was rejected, he resigned his position and in 1869 formed the partnership of Sargent and Greenleaf in Rochester, N. Y., to manufacture the new device. It proved immediately successful. By the use of a powerful magnet within the lock mechanism, other parts of the lock were held sufficiently under control so that not even the micrometer could detect the relative positions of the unlocking devices.

Sargent's business grew rapidly in the succeeding years, especially when he proved that the locks of the United States Treasury were unsafe and obtained the federal business for his company. To improve his invention he substituted a simple mechanical device for the permanent magnet in his combination lock and perfected his first time lock about 1873, the first of which he personally installed in May 1874 on the door of the iron safe of the First National Bank, Morrison, Ill., where it gave satisfactory service for forty years. Until his retirement some years before his death, he not only directed the affairs of his extensive lock business but invented and manufactured such devices as railway semaphore signals, automatic fire alarms, smoke consumers, and glass-lined steel tanks. In his later years he was closely associated with the Pfaudler Vacuum Fermentation Company of Rochester, N. Y., manufacturers of enameled steel tanks, and did experimental work for the Gordon Railway Signal Company; he was also president of the Waterloo Gold Mining Company of California. On Apr. 29, 1847, he married Angeline Morse Foster in Winchester, N. H., and at the time of his death was survived by an adopted daughter.

[A. A. Hopkins, *The Lure of the Lock* (1928) ; *Who's Who in America,* 1908–09; data from Sargent and Greenleaf, Inc., and the Pfaudler Company, Rochester, N. Y.; obituary in *Democrat and Chronicle* (Rochester), Jan. 13, 1910; Patent Office records.]

C. W. M.

SARGENT, JOHN OSBORNE (Sept. 20, 1811–Dec. 28, 1891), lawyer, journalist, author, was born in Gloucester, Mass., the second child and eldest son of Epes and Hannah Dane (Coffin) Sargent, his mother being the second of his father's three wives, and he one of a total of twelve children by the different marriages. Both his father and his mother were of families long established in New England, and he enjoyed the best social and educational advantages. After attending the Boston Latin School, he entered Harvard College, where he distinguished himself for scholarship and took a prominent part in conducting the *Collegian,* an undergraduate publication. Upon his graduation in 1830 he studied law in Boston and was admitted to the bar in January 1834; but a letter he wrote to the *Boston Daily Atlas,* a Whig newspaper, so impressed the editor that he was engaged to write its political editorials. This led him into politics, and in 1836 and 1837 he was elected to the lower house of the Massachusetts legislature. Offered an associate editorship by the *Courier and Enquirer* of New York in 1838, he left Boston to help conduct it till after the election of Harrison to the presidency. He was now in a position of political influence, but the death of the president changed this, and in 1841 he returned to the practice of law in New York. The candidacy of Taylor brought him back into political journalism, however, for he conducted a publication supporting his candidacy and later went to Washington as joint editor of the *Republic,* the official organ of the administration. Because of a disagreement with the cabinet he withdrew, but on the accession of Fillmore he rejoined the paper and helped to conduct it, refusing appointment as minister to China to do so.

Though in 1853 he resumed the practice of law in New York, he devoted much time to literary interests. He had already assisted in editing the *New England Magazine* for January and February 1835, and he had published *A Lecture on the Late Improvements in Steam Navigation* (1844) and articles on other practical subjects. He now turned towards belles-lettres, rather as a translator than a creator. After 1861 for about twelve years he spent most of his time in Europe publishing a translation of *The Last Knight* (1871) from the German of A. A. von Auersperg, several pamphlets on the legal decision in Minot's case, and *Chapters for the Times*

(1884), anti-Blaine campaign literature. For the most part, however, he devoted himself to translating Horace, on which he expended endless pains. Very little of this was published during his life, most of it appearing in *Horatian Echoes* (1893), for which Oliver Wendell Holmes wrote an introduction. Much of what he wrote apart from this is untraceable because of its journalistic character, and some of his substantial work appeared under the name of his brother Epes [*q.v.*]. More significant even than his important legal documents and influential political arguments was his interest in Horace. He not only translated the urbane Roman's words but realized his ideal of life to a notable extent, investing his own mode of living both with the Horatian spirit and with the amenities and refinements of a later age.

On Jan. 17, 1854, he married Georgiana, daughter of Benjamin Welles of Boston, by whom he had one daughter. He was influential in making the Board of Overseers of Harvard University include persons from outside Massachusetts, and in 1880 he was elected as the second member from outside the state. From 1886–87 on, he offered a prize of one hundred dollars for the best translation from Horace by a Harvard or Radcliffe student, an award made permanent by his daughter in 1892.

[See Emma W. and C. S. Sargent, *Epes Sargent of Gloucester and His Descendants* (1923), biog. sketch and bibliog.; editorial on Sargent's journalistic career, *Boston Herald*, Dec. 30, 1891; Eugene Field on his poetic activities, *Chicago Daily News*, Jan. 12, 1892; biog. sketch in *Horatian Echoes* (1893); obituary in *Boston Transcript*, Dec. 29, 1891. A journal of Sargent's and some correspondence are in the Widener Lib., Harvard Univ.]
S. G—n.

SARGENT, JOHN SINGER (Jan. 12, 1856–Apr. 15, 1925), portrait, genre, and mural painter, was born in Florence, Italy. He was the son of Dr. FitzWilliam Sargent [*q.v.*], a native of Gloucester, Mass., who attained prominence as a physician in Philadelphia, and of Mary Newbold (Singer) Sargent of the latter city. On the paternal side the family came of English Puritan stock from Devonshire. His mother's ancestry is traced back to Caspar Singer, who came from Alsace-Lorraine to America about 1730, and to the Newbolds, who were from Yorkshire. In 1854 FitzWilliam Sargent was persuaded by his wife, a woman of means and culture, and an excellent musician, to give up his practice and go to Italy. Thus it fell out that John Sargent was born in the Casa Arretini, on the Lung' Arno, near the Ponte Vecchio. His parents wandered from place to place during his childhood. Four daughters were born to them, two of whom died, leaving to John two younger

sisters, Emily and Violet, who eventually survived him; a younger brother died in 1869.

His father saw John as a future admiral in the United States navy, but this plan was thwarted by the boy's manifest bent, which was sagely abetted by his mother. His first crude essays in drawing were made under her supervision. He received some elementary lessons at the Academy of Fine Arts in Florence, where he got a prize. He made sketches in the Boboli Gardens and in the suburbs. Wherever he went he made careful drawings from nature. At Nice (1862), in the Pyrenees (1865), in Spain (1868), in Rome (1869), at Dresden and in Switzerland (1872), his pencil was never idle. Finally, in the summer of 1874, the family moved to Paris, and his career as a painter was definitively decided upon. He began work in the École des Beaux-Arts, taking courses in anatomy, perspective, and decorative design. In October, at the age of eighteen, he entered the atelier of Carolus Duran. Among the things that he acquired there was a facile and fluent technique quite suited to his temperament, an extraordinary dexterity in seizing instantaneous effects. He was not only the cleverest student in the class; he soon bid fair to outstrip his accomplished master. This precocious virtuosity was not altogether pleasing to Carolus, and a time came when there was a certain coolness between master and pupil. Nevertheless, Sargent always recognized his debt to the teaching of Carolus Duran. Velasquez was held up as the beau ideal, the model, to whom all the young men were advised to look for guidance; and that alone might be regarded as a vital item of artistic faith and practice.

Sargent was twenty years old when he made his first visit to the United States (1876), in company with his mother and his sister Emily. His Americanism has been the subject of much debate; those who knew him best testified to his lifelong loyalty to the country of his fathers. Returning to France in the autumn, he painted his "Gitana," now in the Metropolitan Museum, and the "Rehearsal of the Pasdeloup Orchestra at the Cirque d'Hiver" (Boston Art Museum). In 1877 he sent his first picture to the Salon, a portrait of Miss Watts. He passed the summer at Cancale, at a country house near Lyons, and in Switzerland. In 1878 his "En Route pour la Pêche" (Corcoran Gallery) was shown at the Salon. It was painted at Cancale, where he made several other sketches. To the same year is referred an early portrait, that of Mrs. H. F. Hadden, whose sister posed for the full-length figure called "The Lady with the Rose," exhibited at the Salon of 1881. In the fall of 1878 he spent several weeks at Capri, painting with his usual zest. In 1879 his portrait of Carolus Duran appeared; also the portrait of Robert de Civrieux and his dog (Boston Art Museum), "Luxembourg Gardens at Twilight" (Minneapolis Institute of Art), and a replica of the latter work which went into the great collection of John G. Johnson at Philadelphia. He made his second trip to Spain in 1879, and in January 1880 paid his first visit to Morocco. This expedition brought forth the "Fumée d'Ambre-Gris" which Henry James so much admired. The Spanish journey resulted in the production of "El Jaleo," one of the masterpieces of his early period, now in Fenway Court, Boston; several pictures of the Alhambra; a group of fine copies after Velasquez; and the beautiful "Spanish Courtyard" of the McCagg collection.

The life story of a painter so prolific and indefatigable tends to reduce itself to a long descriptive catalogue of his works. Sargent seldom rested; his so-called vacations became sketching-tours. He was blessed with a fine physique, and felt little need of husbanding his strength. Following the Spanish and Moroccan sojourn of 1880 and a visit to Venice, came a period of pleasant activity to which belong the portraits of the Boit children (Boston Art Museum), the Misses Vickers, and Mrs. Henry White, and the thrice-famous "Madame Gautreau" (Metropolitan Museum), around which centered a veritable tempest of unaccountable abuse when it was first exhibited in Paris. The few sane critics were powerless to offset the storm of disparagement. Sargent was astonished and hurt. The outcry was in fact much ado about nothing. The portrait, painted at "Les Chênes," Paramé, not far from St. Malo, was entirely serious and devoid of malice; it depicted the lady in a costume of her own choosing. The episode is generally supposed to have had something to do with Sargent's departure from Paris for London; however this may have been, he decided upon London as his domicile. So far as press criticism was concerned, he was but turning from Scylla to Charybdis. The *Athenaeum* (June 21, 1884, p. 798) called the portrait of Mrs. White hard, metallic, raw in color, and tasteless. In a plebiscite organized by the *Pall Mall Gazette* in 1886 the popular vote declared by a large majority that "The Misses Vickers" was the worst picture in the Academy exhibition; while the *Spectator* (May 1, 1886, p. 581) pronounced it shallow, pretentious, and untrue. In the aristocratic circles of London, however, the exotic style and brilliance of Sargent's portraits, offer-

ing such a novel contrast to the prosaic academic manner of the British painters of the time, soon brought him all the patrons he could desire, and his vogue steadily increased.

He was twenty-eight when, in 1885, he established himself in the Tite Street studio which was to become the scene of his greatest triumphs. The first of these came from the picture called "Carnation, Lily, Lily, Rose," painted at Broadway, Worcestershire, 1884–86, and exhibited at the Royal Academy in 1887. It is now in the Tate Gallery. It depicts two pretty children working in a flower garden in the twilight. The charm of this composition was felt by every one. It became a universal favorite. It was the first of a long series of pictures of children in which the artist revealed the most tender and lovable side of his nature. He did not usually wear his heart upon his sleeve, but when he was happily inspired by a thoroughly congenial subject he did work of remarkable delicacy and pure beauty. The Davis and Meyer groups, the portraits of the Boit children, Beatrice Goelet, the Hon. Laura Lister, and Homer Saint-Gaudens are to be especially remarked as pages of unsurpassed artistry, picturing with sympathy and understanding that exquisite thing, youth, in all its freshness and purity.

In 1887 Sargent was called to the United States to paint some portraits, among them those of Mrs. H. G. Marquand, Mrs. Charles E. Inches, and Mrs. John L. Gardner. The first exhibition of his works ever held was opened at the St. Botolph Club, Boston, in December 1887. It contained several of the above-mentioned portraits, which had been painted in Frederic P. Vinton's studio; "El Jaleo" (bought by T. Jefferson Coolidge); the large square picture of the Boit children; and a few small figure pieces. The picture of the Boit children, dating from 1882, had been seen in the Salon of 1883 under the title of "Portraits d'Enfants," and it was later shown in the Paris Exposition of 1900. In 1919 it was given to the Boston Art Museum by the daughters of Edward D. Boit in memory of their father, an artist-friend of Sargent's. It is one of the important works of his early period, and one of his best. From the Boston sojourn of 1887–88 dates the pronounced American appreciation which was to Sargent a source of so much satisfaction throughout his career. This was the first of a long series of visits to Boston. That city became his American headquarters; several important exhibitions of his works were held there; a great group of his watercolors was acquired by the Museum of Fine Arts; and all his mural decorations were made for the Public Library, the Art Museum, and the Widener Library of Harvard University.

In the spring of 1889 his father died. In the summer the artist, who was never married, took, with his mother and sisters, Fladbury Rectory, near Pershore, Worcestershire, for three months, and there they entertained a number of guests— Edwin A. Abbey, Alfred Parsons, Alden Weir, M. and Mme. Paul Helleu, Flora Priestley, and Violet Paget (Vernon Lee). Sargent painted a portrait of Miss Priestley which was exhibited at the New English Art Club in 1896 and drew an elaborate and fervent critique from the fastidious George Moore (Downes, *post,* pp. 176–77). He also painted a picture of Helleu sketching on the banks of the Avon while his wife reclined on the ground and leaned against his shoulder (Brooklyn Museum). The portrait of Ellen Terry as Lady Macbeth (now in the Tate Gallery), which was exhibited that year, was pronounced "the picture of the year"; it was also called the "best-hated picture of the year."

The next trip to America occurred in 1890. New York, Philadelphia, and Boston were visited in turn. Sargent painted his celebrated picture of Carmencita, the Spanish dancer, now in the Luxembourg. By many judges it is considered his masterpiece. He made the likenesses of three famous American actors, Edwin Booth, Joseph Jefferson, Lawrence Barrett. In Boston he painted a dozen portraits, the most important being the fine full-length group, "Mother and Child" (Mrs. Edward L. Davis and her small son), exhibited at the National Academy of Design in 1890 and afterwards in many other places. In the spring, in New York, Sargent was one of the ushers at the wedding of his close friend Abbey. The trustees of the Boston Public Library commissioned Sargent and Abbey to paint the mural decorations for two of the rooms of the library just then completed. From this time forth a large part of Sargent's time and energy was given to this mural work. He was already tired of so much portrait painting and welcomed the change. He decided to adopt as the subject of his decoration the development of religious thought from paganism through Judaism to Christianity. In 1891 preliminary work was begun in a huge studio built by Abbey for this purpose in Fairford, Gloucestershire. Sargent had been in Egypt and Greece, getting firsthand data about the pagan deities. The first part of his work (a lunette, frieze, and a section of the ceiling) was completed in 1894 and installed in 1895; and he went to Boston to see to the emplacement. While there, as usual, he painted several portraits. His full-length picture of Ada

Rehan was first seen in 1895; to the same year belong his "Coventry Patmore" (National Portrait Gallery, London) and his stylistic "W. Graham Robertson." The outstanding work of 1897 was the portrait group of Mrs. Carl Meyer and her children; but the culminating event was the appearance in 1898, 1901, and 1902 of the Wertheimer family portraits (Tate Gallery, London). It would be difficult to exaggerate the sensation caused by this prodigious series of works. In them he reached the climax of his life as a portraitist. The record of his achievements would not be complete without at least a mention of his large portrait groups of "Lady Elcho, Mrs. Tennant and Mrs. Adeane" (1900), "The Misses Hunter" (1902), "The Ladies Alexandra, Mary and Theo Acheson" (1902), and the "Four Doctors" (1906) belonging to the Johns Hopkins University.

Sargent was made a Royal Academician in 1897. His diploma picture, "A Venetian Interior" (1900), is characterized by all of the finest qualities of his art. The room depicted is the grand sala of the Palazzo Barbaro, and the four figures in it are those of the Curtis family of Boston. In 1899 the Copley Hall Sargent loan exhibition in Boston was opened—the most comprehensive showing of his work held during his lifetime. It contained 110 of his pictures. In 1903 the Boston Art Museum sponsored another loan exhibition of twenty portraits, for the most part of Boston and Philadelphia people. His visits to Boston now increasing in frequency and duration, he established a studio in the Pope Building, Columbus Avenue, which he occupied at intervals during the ensuing twenty years. In this time he crossed and recrossed the Atlantic almost every year; these voyages gave him the only real rest periods he allowed himself to take. He found time to make many summer and autumn trips to Italy, Spain, Switzerland, Majorca, Corfu, and other places, but he was always sketching busily. The fateful summer of 1914 found him in the Dolomites, where he continued to paint serenely for a long time after the war had begun. Early in 1916 he came again to America for the purpose of installing the last of the Boston Public Library decorations. That summer he went off on a sketching expedition to the Canadian Rockies and the Glacier National Park. The beautiful landscape, "Lake O'Hara" (Fogg Art Museum, Harvard University), and a group of watercolors were the principal fruits of this tour. Returning to Boston, he worked hard on the scaffoldings in the library until the Christmas holidays, when the completed decorations were at last unveiled to the public gaze. At about the same time another exhibition of his easel paintings was in progress at the Boston Art Museum; and in 1917 his Rocky Mountain pictures were displayed in a loan exhibition at the Copley Gallery in aid of the American Ambulance Hospital at Paris.

Having completed the library decorations, the artist now undertook to decorate the rotunda of the Art Museum. In the midst of the preparatory studies for this commission, the British Government invited him to go to the front in northern France and to record his impressions of the war for the Imperial War Museum in London. He proceeded at once to the British General Headquarters in June 1918. Thence he went to Bavincourt, to Arras, and to various places in the war zone. He saw very little that was paintable; was taken with influenza and spent a wretched week in a casualty clearing station, under canvas, surrounded by wounded soldiers; and went back to England in October. His picture "Gassed"—a pathetic scene which he actually witnessed—was exhibited in the Royal Academy of 1919. Soon after the close of the war he was commissioned to paint for the National Portrait Gallery, London, a large portrait group of twenty-two members of the British General Staff.

The Sargent exhibition of 1924 in New York, assembled by himself, contained seventy-two works. The press reviews served to prove that a hostile bloc was forming, recruited mostly from the ranks of the modernists. Public opinion was sharply divided, but the opposition was aggressive. In July Sargent left for London to carry to completion the mural paintings for the Boston Art Museum and to execute two or three portrait commissions. His death, which occurred in London in April, was due to heart failure. The funeral, Apr. 18, was private, the burial being at Brookwood, Surrey. Imposing memorial services were held in Westminster Abbey, Apr. 24. Memorial exhibitions were held at the Royal Academy, London, the Metropolitan Museum, New York, and the Boston Art Museum. Honorary degrees were conferred on Sargent by the Universities of Oxford, Cambridge, Harvard, Yale, and Pennsylvania. The list of his medals, prizes, and orders would fill a whole page. He declined a knighthood offered by the premier in 1907, saying that he was an American citizen. In 1918 he was asked to be a candidate for the office of president of the Royal Academy, but he did not choose to run. At the post-mortem sale of his pictures and sketches in 1925, at Christie's, London, 237 items brought a total of about $850,000.

As a portrait painter Sargent may be ranked beneath such masters as Titian, Holbein, Velasquez, Rembrandt, and Hals, but he will be rated as the equal of the best British eighteenth-century painters, Reynolds and Gainsborough. The vitality of his personages insures the future fame of the artist. As a painter of genre he is original, piquant, objective, and often has great charm of style. His interiors in Italy and Spain —the "Venetian Interior," the "Spanish Courtyard," the "Hospital at Granada," the "Breakfast in the Loggia" (Freer Gallery)—are delightful, personal, and full of flavor. In landscape he was not so preëminent, though the "Lake O'Hara" is a handsome canvas, and some of his Alpine subjects have excellent points. His water colors, of which there are large groups in the museums of Brooklyn, Boston, New York, and Worcester, are truly superb for their spontaneity, freedom, luminosity, and limpid style. He was doubtless the most masterful water colorist of his time, with the single exception of Winslow Homer.

As to his mural paintings, there is much to be said pro and con. He daringly violated the accepted canons which place a ban on relief and perspective, and as a consequence his walls do not have the plane surface and vertical aspect demanded by sound architectonic principles. In this respect it cannot be said that his Boston Public Library work, his *magnum opus,* compares favorably with Puvis de Chavannes' mural paintings which adorn the same building. Again, Sargent's want of flatness of modeling is in some sort matched by the overwhelming complexity and superabundant quantity of images and symbols. In a word, he is not simple enough. His redundancy is an esthetic sin. On the other hand, it must be allowed that his splendor of effect, however obtained, is most impressive. It is magnificent, if it is not war. Perhaps it is permissible for a man of great talent to disregard the rules of the game, to flout conventions. Sargent's mental attitude towards his subject is singularly objective; he records, he does not judge; one might call him an unbiased historian, viewing the religious faiths of Pagan, Jew, and Christian, from the outside, without preference and without conviction, simply as a great spectacle. There are those who assert that his Christian symbolism betokens sincere religious feeling, but it would be difficult to establish this contention. His fertility of invention is undeniable. Old ideas are used freely, but they are invested with new forms. They are combined and related with ability and ingenuity. The ancient traditions and doctrines are presented with a new accent. Richness and pictorial effectiveness are not wanting; the intellectual and esthetic grasp is firm. If the work has little of the impassioned conviction and ingenuous sentiment of the age of faith, this is hardly to be imputed to the artist as a serious fault; he was of his own time, and he was true to himself; one can but accept gratefully what he had to give.

Sargent was modest, generous, and absolutely sincere. Adulation and flattery were distasteful to him. He underrated his own ability and at times made fun of his own paintings. He was not avaricious, and cared little for luxuries. He was an accomplished linguist and a musician of talent, but found his chief pleasure in his work.

[Evan Charteris, *John Sargent* (1927); W. H. Downes, *John S. Sargent, His Life and Work* (1925); *The Work of John S. Sargent, R.A.* (1903); introductory note by Alice Meynell; Nathaniel Pousette-Dart, compiler, *John Singer Sargent* (1924); A. L. Baldry, in *Studio*, Feb. 15, Mar. 15, 1900; R. V. S. Berry, in *Art and Archaeology*, Sept. 1924; Christian Brinton, *Modern Artists* (1908); F. W. Coburn, in *Am. Mag. of Art*, Feb. 1917, Jan. 1923; Royal Cortissoz, *Art and Common Sense* (1913), and article in *Scribner's Mag.*, Mar. 1924; Samuel Isham, *The Hist. of Am. Painting* (1905); Henry James, *Picture and Text* (1893); Arthur Layard, in *Die Kunst*, vol. XVII, 1907–08; Robert Ross, in *Art Journal*, Jan. 1911; William Starkweather, in *Mentor*, Oct. 1924; Walter Tittle, in *Illustrated London News*, Apr. 25, 1925; J. C. Van Dyke, *Am. Painting and Its Tradition* (1919); Forbes Watson, in *The Arts*, Mar. 1924; E. W. and C. S. Sargent, *Epes Sargent of Gloucester and His Descendants* (1923); *Boston Evening Transcript*, Apr. 15, 24, 1925.]   W. H. D.

SARGENT, LUCIUS MANLIUS (June 25, 1786–June 2, 1867), author, antiquary, temperance advocate, was born in Boston, the youngest of seven children of Daniel and Mary (Turner) Sargent, and brother of Henry Sargent [*q.v.*]. His father was a merchant dealing in fishermen's supplies who had moved from Gloucester to Boston and profited so much by his industry, prudence, and popularity that he occupied what was for those days a conspicuously expensive mansion, although his character was notable for thrift and dread of ostentation. Lucius Manlius attended a number of elementary and secondary schools, including Phillips Exeter Academy, from which he passed to Harvard in 1804. He did not complete his course there, for a pamphlet published by him in 1807, *No. 1 of the New Milk Cheese,* pours furious scorn on an official of the college with whom he had had a dispute about the quality of the food at the commons table. He studied law after leaving college and was admitted to the bar on Feb. 19, 1811, but he never practised to any extent, for he inherited a competence and greatly increased it by conservative speculation. He turned to literature as an avocation, publishing *The Culex of Virgil; with a Translation into English Verse* and a collection

of Latin riddles in 1807 and *Hubert and Ellen,* a volume of poems, in 1812. At the Boston peace celebration on Feb. 22, 1815, an ode of his, "Wreaths for the Chieftain," was sung. On Apr. 3, 1816, he married Mary Binney of Philadelphia, by whom he had three children, one of whom attained the brevet rank of brigadier-general in the Civil War. After the death of his first wife in 1824, he married Sarah Cutler Dunn, July 14, 1825.

He wrote constantly for the newspapers and became well known for his literary interests, but he found a more popular subject in temperance reform, which he took up with characteristic assertiveness. From 1830 till the approach of the Civil War he spoke and wrote on this theme so frequently and vigorously that he became one of the most uncompromising and conspicuous leaders in the crusade against liquor. He wrote *The Temperance Tales* (2 vols., 1848), stories of a tract-like nature bearing such titles as "My Mother's Gold Ring," "I Am Afraid There Is A God," "Groggy Harbor," "An Irish Heart," and others to the number of twenty-one, first published in separate issues between 1833 and 1843. These were widely distributed by religious and temperance societies as well as by Sargent himself.

He also achieved prominence as an antiquary. In 1848 he began a series of weekly articles in the *Boston Evening Transcript* entitled "Dealings with the Dead" (published in book form in 1856), which in spite of their name did not lack light touches. Under such pseudonyms as Sigma, Amgis, Saveall, and others, he wrote for numerous other publications, and he aroused considerable interest by attacking the coolie trade of the British in India (*Evening Transcript,* Apr. 16–Oct. 3, 1856) and by assailing Macaulay for statements derogatory to William Penn (*Dealings with the Dead,* I, pp. 231–69). Though he showed enthusiasm for the past, his efforts were generally directed towards blasting something offensive to him out of existence. At seventy-five he published *The Ballad of the Abolition Blunder-buss* (1861), which abuses Emerson and others for their anti-slavery views as violently as his *Temperance Tales* do the saloon-keeper. Even one of his obituaries refers to him as a man of "harsh prejudices," though it acknowledges the urbanity of his manners in ordinary intercourse and the warmth of his attachment to his kindred and friends. In 1842 Harvard conferred the degree of A.M. on him, thereby recognizing his public services and condoning his undergraduate contumacy, for the violence of which he often expressed regret. He was preeminently a good hater, but he was a conspicuous man in his day and helped to develop a sentiment in favor of prohibition, besides making rather valuable contributions to local history.

[Emma W. and C. S. Sargent, *Epes Sargent of Gloucester and His Descendants* (1923); J. H. Sheppard, *Reminiscences of Lucius Manlius Sargent* (1871); *New England Hist. and Geneal. Reg.*, July 1871; obituaries in *Boston Post* and *Boston Daily Advertiser*, June 4, 1867.]   S. G—n.

SARGENT, NATHAN (May 5, 1794–Feb. 2, 1875), journalist, was born in Putney, Vt., the son of Samuel and Mary (Washburn) Sargent, and seventh in a family of eleven children. He was a descendant of William Sargent, who emigrated from Northampton, England, to Charlestown, Mass., in 1638, and settled in that part of the town which in 1649 was set off as Malden. After receiving an academic education in his native town, Nathan studied law with Judge Phineas White of Putney; later, he studied in the office of Stephen Ross, Troy, N. Y., teaching school at the same time. Admitted to the bar in 1818, he immediately moved to Cahawba, Ala., where he practised law and served for some time as judge of the county and probate courts. On Feb. 14, 1821, he married Rosina (Hodgkinson) Lewis, who became the mother of his four children, three of whom died in infancy. In 1826, because of ill health, he moved to Buffalo, N. Y. About 1830 he gave up his profession of law and established in Philadelphia, Pa., the *Commercial Herald,* a Whig newspaper, which he edited for some years. This venture did not pay financially, however, and he became a successful correspondent of the *United States Gazette,* Philadelphia. His first letter, signed "Oliver Oldschool," under which name he became widely known, appeared in that publication on Jan. 3, 1842.

He was an ardent Whig and later a devoted Republican. In an age of letter writers, he wrote from Washington, D. C., where he went to live in the forties, witty, vivid, sarcastic, but gentlemanly reports of the proceedings in Congress and of events at the Capital. His articles were published in many newspapers throughout the North. A kindly nature and unusual ability as a correspondent gained for him a national reputation. He was honest, faithful to his party, and infrequently very partisan. He accepted the American system and reviewed Tyler's veto message on the tariff in 1842 with pain and indignation. He believed it was suicidal for the Whigs to adopt Tyler in 1840. Congress, he said, was the supreme organism in our free government, not the Jacksonian type of executive. Congress should never strike its flag and legislate at the foot of the throne. His pungent articles were introduced in newspapers as editorials during the forties and his editorial quarrels with the leading Democratic editors were greatly enjoyed by the Whigs. He delighted in poking fun at the Democrats to provoke merriment in their opponents. His description of John C. Calhoun as a debater in Congress is illustrative of his poignant style and manner of describing public characters. "Mr. Calhoun," he wrote (Aug. 8, 1842), "utters his sentences with surprising rapidity and great indistinctness, pausing long between each; his voice is sharp, unmusical and unmodulated, he seems, therefore, to throw his sentences out by jerks, and to stop as if he had run plump against a post or period. Every sentence appears to be an embodiment of a maxim, principle, or axiom . . . and his whole speech a string of these connected, if at all, by very distant ties . . . of reasoning; hence he is one of the most difficult speakers to report." The task which he considered most important was to interpret public opinion for his readers. Abraham Lincoln had no warmer supporter than Oliver Oldschool, who considered him the successor of Henry Clay. His party maxim was *Fas est ab hoste doceri* (It is right to learn from the enemy).

He served as sergeant-at-arms of the House of Representatives (1847–51), as register-general of the United States Land Office (1851–53), as commissioner of customs (1861–71), and for years as the president of the Washington reform school. Among his publications were *Brief Outline of the Life of Henry Clay* (1844), reissued under slightly varying titles, and *Some Public Men and Events* (2 vols., 1875). He was survived by his widow and one daughter.

[*New England Hist. and Geneal. Reg.*, July 1875; J. S. and Aaron Sargent, *Sargent Geneal.* (1895); *National Republican* (Washington), Feb. 3, 1875; A. M. Hemenway, *Vt. Hist. Gazetteer*, vol. V (1891), pt. 2, pp. 246–48.]   W. E. S.

SARGENT, WINTHROP (May 1, 1753–Jan. 3, 1820), soldier, territorial administrator, was born at Gloucester, Mass., the son of Winthrop and Judith (Sanders) Sargent. His ancestor, William, had emigrated from England and received a grant of land in Gloucester in 1678. Winthrop graduated from Harvard College in 1771 and at the outbreak of the Revolution enlisted in the Continental Army, earning by meritorious service the brevet rank of major. In 1786 he was surveyor on the Seven Ranges in Ohio and that same year he attended the meeting in Boston at which the Ohio Company was organized. The next year he was elected secretary of this organization, and during the summer rendered valuable assistance to Manasseh Cutler in the purchase of the land which the company proposed to settle. He reached Marietta in July 1788, and took an active part in the planting of the new colony.

On Oct. 7, 1787, he was designated by Congress as secretary of the Territory Northwest of the River Ohio. During the frequent and prolonged absences of Gov. Arthur St. Clair [q.v.], Sargent assumed the executive responsibilities with the same disinterested devotion to public duty that he always manifested. Recent research has cleared him of the criticism formerly made of his course in the organization of Wayne County (Detroit) in 1796. He was St. Clair's adjutant-general in the expedition of 1791 against the Indians and in the defeat at Fort Recovery, Nov. 4, 1791, he was twice wounded. After this defeat, as acting governor he organized the militia to repel anticipated Indian attacks. On Feb. 9, 1789, he married Rowena Tupper, who died in 1790, shortly after the birth of an infant son who did not long survive.

In 1798 Sargent resigned his secretaryship to become the first governor of Mississippi Territory. His Federalism, impartial enforcement of law, and unfortunate connection with one of the factions in the territory led to such criticism that President Jefferson refused to reappoint him in 1801, and he retired to the plantation of his second wife, formerly Mary (McIntosh) Williams, whom he had married Oct. 24, 1798. He died in 1820, on a north-bound steamboat near New Orleans. Two sons survived him.

Sargent's numerous papers reveal the varied intellectual interests which led to his membership in the American Philosophical Society, the American Academy of Arts and Sciences, and the Massachusetts Historical Society. He contributed to the *Memoirs* of the American Academy "List of Forest and Other Trees Northwest of the River Ohio" (vol. II, pt. I, 1793), "Meteorological Observations" (vol. III, pt. I, 1809), and "An Account of Several Shocks of an Earthquake" (vol. III, pt. 2, 1815); and in 1796 published *Papers Relative to Certain American Antiquities,* later reprinted in the *Transactions of the American Philosophical Society* (vol. IV, 1799). As a public servant he was conscientious, energetic, and patriotic in the discharge of responsibilities placed on him, although his Federalism and his New England training made him unpopular amid the democracy of the frontier and involved him in many unpleasant controversies. His contribution to the West of his day was that of one who modestly aids in the laying of foundations.

[Sargent Papers in Mass. Hist. Soc., Boston, and Ohio State Archaeol. and Hist. Soc., Columbus; *Diary of Col. Winthrop Sargent during the Campaign of* *MDCCXCI* (1851), repr. in *Ohio Archæol. and Hist. Quart.,* July 1924; with extracts from Jour. of 1793–95; *The Records of the Original Proc. of the Ohio Company* (2 vols., 1917), ed. by A. B. Hulbert; *The Miss. Terr. Arch., 1798–1803* (1905), ed. by Dunbar Rowland; *The St. Clair Papers* (2 vols., 1882), ed. by W. H. Smith; *Am. State Papers, Misc.,* I (1834), 233–41; *Papers in Relation to the Official Conduct of Gov. Sargent* (1801), and *Political Intolerance . . . Exemplified in a Recent Removal from Office* (1801), attacks on Jefferson for removing Sargent; Dunbar Rowland, *Hist. of Miss.* (2 vols., 1925); Winthrop Sargent, *Early Sargents of New England* (1922); E. W. and C. S. Sargent, *Epes Sargent of Gloucester and His Descendants* (1923); B. H. Pershing, "Winthrop Sargent," in *Ohio Archæol. and Hist. Quart.,* Oct. 1926, and "Winthrop Sargent: A Builder of the Old Northwest," dissertation (1927), Univ. of Chicago.]

B. H. P.

SARGENT, WINTHROP (Sept. 23, 1825–May 18, 1870), author, grandson of Winthrop Sargent [q.v.] and son of George Washington and Margaret (Percy) Sargent, was born in Philadelphia, Pa., where he received his early education. He graduated from the University of Pennsylvania in 1845 and received a law degree at Harvard two years later. He began the practice of law in Boston, but he enjoyed an income large enough to make him independent of his profession and he was more interested in the history of the American Revolution than in his legal career. On April 22, 1851, he married Sarah Ellery Gray of Boston and soon after his marriage established himself in Philadelphia, where he remained until the outbreak of the Civil War. Shortly after his return to Philadelphia in 1851 he became interested in the military history of the French and Indian War and edited for the Historical Society of Pennsylvania *The History of an Expedition against Fort Du Quesne, in 1755; under Major-General Edward Braddock. . . .* This work, published in 1855, was based upon manuscript sources and edited with a skill not then common in American historiography; it remained for many years the standard work on the Braddock expedition. In 1860 he published an edition of *The Loyal Verses of Joseph Stansbury and Doctor Jonathan Odell, Relating to the American Revolution,* characterized by moderate and very fair-minded notes. At about the same time he ended his labors on Major André, whom he sought to rehabilitate, by the publication of the *Life and Career of Major John André* (1861). Sargent's view was extreme in favor of André. In spite of a florid treatment and other literary defects, his book was long regarded as the definitive work upon the subject.

During the Civil War he lived in Mississippi, where, at Natchez, his father was brutally murdered in 1864. At the close of the war he moved to New York City and began the practice of law, but he was depressed by the death of his father and his own poor health. He soon gave up the law to seek rest in Europe. He died of consumption in Paris in 1870, survived by one son.

[Emma W. and C. S. Sargent, *Epes Sargent of Gloucester and His Descendants* (1923), brief biog. sketch and complete bibliog.; private information from James W. Winter of Paris; obituary in *N. Y. Times*, May 19, 1870.]   F. M.

SARPY, PETER A. (Nov. 3, 1805–Jan. 4, 1865), fur trader, was probably the first white resident of Nebraska. He was born at St. Louis of French parentage, the second son of Gregoire Berald and Palagie (L'Abadie) Sarpy. His father was a merchant and fur trader. Peter was favored with the best educational and social opportunities in St. Louis. His father died in 1824, and his elder brother, John B. Sarpy, was employed in the firm of Berthold & Chouteau, the promoters of the Missouri Fur Company, and later associated with the American Fur Company. At an early age, probably 1823, Peter was employed as clerk of John P. Cabanné, the agent for the Missouri and American Fur companies at Council Bluffs. He was put in charge of the post established at Bellevue on the west bank of the Mississippi. For Cabanné he executed the arrest of the Leclerc party, 1832, and this is one explanation of his military title. He was unusually successful in dealing with the Indians. Nicomi, his Indian wife, the daughter of an Iowa chief, was a strong ally, but her generosity cost him large quantities of supplies.

As a licensed fur trader at the fork of the Missouri and Platte rivers he commanded a post of strategic importance. Situated on the edge of the Indian reservation he carried on a large business with both the natives and the whites. Frémont, returning in 1842, employed Sarpy to build a ship for him and sold his overland equipment at Sarpy's post. Brigham Young on his first expedition sought the trader's assistance, and the latter, after offering supplies and ferrying the party over the river, negotiated with the Indians for a friendly passage and escorted the Mormon leader beyond the point of greatest danger. Sarpy had a significant part in the negotiation of the land session treaties with the Omaha and Oto Indians in 1854. The next year two regiments of Nebraska volunteers were raised for defense against the Indians, and he was made quartermaster of the brigade. To carry the immigrants and travelers he established ferries over the Missouri, the Elkhorn, and Loup rivers. He introduced a steam ferry service between St. Mary, Iowa, and Bellevue, Nebr. He also established a post store at St. Mary chiefly for supplying the white travelers and settlers, and he founded the St. Mary *Gazette*. He participated in the laying out of the towns of Bellevue and Decatur, Nebr. In 1862 he removed to Plattsmouth, Nebr., where he lived until his death. He was buried in St. Louis. He left no descendants, and his estate, except an annuity for Nicomi during her lifetime, went to relatives in St. Louis. He was a colorful leader, short of stature with a handsome face and piercing dark eyes, a man of prompt action, unfailing courage, and vivid emotions. The Indians called him "White Chief."

[Date of birth from statement of the record in Baptism Register Diocesan Chancery Office, St. Louis, given in a paper on Sarpy before the Nebraska Historical Society in 1921 by the Rev. M. A. Shine, now in possession of Nebraska Historical Society; J. S. Morton, *Illustrated History of Nebraska*, vol. I (1905); H. M. Chittenden, *The American Fur Trade of the Far West* (1902), vol. I; J. C. Frémont, *Report of the Exploring Expedition to the Rocky Mountains* (1845); *Nebr. State Hist. Soc. Proc. and Colls.*, 2 ser., vols. I, II, V (1894–1902); *Nebr. State Hist. Soc. Pubs.*, vol. XX (1922); *Omaha Daily Herald*, Dec. 8, 1874; *Papillion Times* (Hist. ed.), June 18, 1931.]   J. L. S.

SARTAIN, EMILY (Mar. 17, 1841–June 18, 1927), painter, engraver, educator, was born in Philadelphia, the daughter of John Sartain [*q.v.*] and Susannah Longmate (Swaine) Sartain. Her great-grandfather, Barak Longmate, and her grandfather, John Swaine, were both noted English engravers. Samuel and William Sartain [*qq.v.*] were her brothers. Reared in a family devoted to art and literature, Emily's talent developed early and as a girl she accompanied her father on trips to Europe and studied in great art centers. She learned mezzotint engraving from her father and worked with him on portraits and prints, becoming the only woman mezzotint engraver of her day on either side of the Atlantic. After an intensive year of study abroad, she returned to America to attain success in book-portrait work and the engraving of large framing prints. Subsequent study from 1864 to 1870 under Christian Schussele [*q.v.*], at the Pennsylvania Academy of the Fine Arts, four years more in the studio of the French painter, Evariste Luminais, in Paris, and two winters in the galleries of Italy, completed her education in the handling of colors. In 1875 a three-quarter-length portrait of Mlle. Del Sarte was accepted by the Paris Salon together with a genre picture "La Pièce de Conviction" which, under the title of "The Reproof," was awarded a medal the following year at the Centennial Exhibition in Philadelphia. The artist now divided her time between portrait-painting and engraving. In 1881 and again in 1883 she was awarded the Mary Smith prize at the Pennsylvania Academy of the Fine Arts for the best work shown by a woman artist. From

1881 to 1883 she was art editor of *Our Continent,* an illustrated journal published in Philadelphia, and of the de luxe edition of *New England Bygones* by Ella H. Rollins, published in 1883.

In 1886 she accepted the invitation of the board of directors of the School of Design for Women to become principal of the institution, thus beginning her career as an educator. She was made a director of the Philadelphia public schools in 1890, but pressure of work forced her to resign two years later. Her preoccupation with educational work was detrimental to her own personal career as an artist, although she still executed a few oil portraits, and finished two large etchings for New York publishers. For the Columbian Exposition in Chicago in 1893, she acted as chairman of the committee of women artists who decorated the women's room of the Pennsylvania State Building with murals and paintings. She was also the first woman ever appointed to the bureau of judges for an international exposition —a distinction which, however, barred her from awards in Chicago. In 1899 she was invited to London to speak before the International Council of Women on opportunities offered women of America in applied design. The following year she was appointed official delegate to represent the United States in Paris at the International Congress of Instruction in Drawing, rendering a similar service in Berne, Switzerland, in 1904. An exhibit at the Pan-American Exposition at Buffalo in 1901 brought her an honorable mention for oil portraits, and her various services in the interest of art and education brought a long list of medals, certificates and diplomas, including one from the London Society of Literature, Science and Art.

Until the outbreak of the World War she spent the summer months studying in Europe. She was an accomplished linguist in French, Italian, German, and Spanish. After thirty-three years as principal of the School of Design for Women she resigned active work, becoming principal emeritus. During the many years of her public life she had been interested in local as well as in international cultural movements and sponsored the organization of many art and literary clubs in Philadelphia. After her retirement she spent two years in California, then went to Europe, where she established residence in Paris. In 1927 she returned to Philadelphia where she died of acute heart trouble. She is buried in Monument Cemetery.

[A short account of the life of Emily Sartain by her niece, Harriet Sartain, Dean of the School of Design for Women, deposited at Strawberry Manshion in Philadelphia; C. E. Clement, Laurence Hutton, *Artists of the Nineteenth Century* (1907), vol. II; J. D. Champlain, ed., *Cyclop. of Painters and Paintings,* vol. IV (1887); Mantle Fielding, *Dict. of Am. Painters, Sculptors and Engravers* (1926); *Who's Who in America,* 1926–27; *Public Ledger* (Philadelphia), June 19, 1927.]
D. G—y.]

SARTAIN, JOHN (Oct. 24, 1808–Oct. 25, 1897), engraver, publisher, was born in London, the son of John Sartain and Ann (Burgess) Sartain. The father died when John was eight years of age, and four years later the lad, in an effort to help support the family, entered upon his first job with an Italian pyrotechnist and scene artist, who made him "powder monkey" and assistant to the head scene-painter in the "department of steam, smoke and fire" at Charles Kemble's Theatre and at Vauxhall Gardens (*Reminiscences, post,* p. 52). Soon a relative set him the task of tending turnpike, but he was rescued from this occupation by a bequest from his grandmother. He decided then to become an engraver and apprenticed himself for seven years in 1823 to John Swaine to learn heraldry and letter engraving. He practised drawing in his spare time and his talent attracted the attention of William Young Ottley, who was writing an historical sketch of the early Florentine school of painters. Ottley gained Swaine's permission to have the apprentice execute eighteen plates and work up fourteen left previously unfinished. Through this work, published in 1826, Sartain was introduced to the art of the masters and met such distinguished men as Sir Thomas Lawrence and Thomas Sully. When Sartain returned to his apprenticeship, he accepted occasional commissions for engravings, dividing the profits with Swaine. One of these plates, sold to Eliakim Littell [q.v.] in 1830, was engraved in mezzotint for Sartain's instructor in miniature, Henry Richter, after that artist's picture "The Tight Shoe."

He was married to Susannah Longmate Swaine, daughter of his employer, on Jan. 11, 1830, and six months later sailed with his bride to America. He secured a letter of introduction to John Vaughn and through him held an exhibition at the Franklin Institute. His first important commission was from Thomas Sully who had him engrave his portrait of Bishop White. Commissions followed from the painters, Jacob Eicholtz and John Neagle [qq.v.], and from the Penn Society. He also executed plates for the *Gentleman's Magazine,* the *Casket,* and *Godey's Lady's Magazine.* In 1841 he became associated with *Graham's Magazine,* and through that medium introduced pictorial illustration as a distinctive feature of American periodicals. His prompt success necessitated the turning out of one plate every two weeks in addition to other work which, in 1847, included the owning and editing of a quarto-volume entitled *The American Gallery of Art*. In 1843 Sartain entered upon an ill-starred venture as proprietor of *Campbell's Foreign Semi-Monthly Magazine*. He also had a financial interest in the *Eclectic Museum,* but neither was profitable. After Graham's failure in 1848, however, he joined with William Sloanaker in purchasing for $5,000 the *Union Magazine* and creating under the name, *Sartain's Union Magazine of Literature and Art,* a publication of rare cultural value. The first issue appeared in January 1849. The noted men and women writers of the day, including Longfellow, John Howard Payne, Lucy Larcom, Harriet Martineau and Edgar Allan Poe, whose poem, "The Bells," Sartain was the first to publish, contributed to *Sartain's Magazine*. The venture was, however, a monetary failure, and Sartain spent the next seven and a half years paying off its debts.

When his magazine was discontinued in 1852, the engraver turned to general work, his output of plates being estimated at 1500. He made engravings and vignettes for early banknotes and indulged his versatility further in oil-painting, watercolor, and miniature. In 1855 he attended the international exposition in Paris, being entrusted in 1862 with a second mission to deliver diplomas of honorary membership in the Pennsylvania Academy of the Fine Arts to European notables. Sartain was made chief of the bureau of art for the Centennial Exhibition in Philadelphia in 1875, and was honored by four Italian societies of letters and the arts. In 1886, as chief of the American art department, he began collecting pictures to exhibit at a London exposition. In 1885 he received the Star of Merit (Laureat) of the rajah of Calcutta and in 1892 was made Commander of the Royal Order of Melusine by the princess of Jerusalem, Cyprus, and Armenia. About this time, also, he was made a Freeman of London. For fourteen years he was vice-president of the Philadelphia School of Design for Women, with which his daughter Emily Sartain [*q.v.*] was closely associated. He was a prominent Freemason, a member of the Artists Fund Society (president in 1844) and of the Society of St. George. Sartain's additional skill as an able architectural designer was responsible for the unique arrangement of galleries and rooms at the Pennsylvania Academy of the Fine Arts, of which he was a director and Academician for twenty-three years, and for the design of the monuments to Washington and Lafayette at Monument Cemetery in Philadelphia.

The first important mezzotint produced in the United States was executed by Sartain shortly after his arrival from England. It was after Neagle's painting, "Old Age." His "Christ Rejected" after Benjamin West, and "The Iron-Worker and King Solomon" after Christian Schüssele, are among the largest and finest ever executed in America (see Clement and Hutton, *post*, p. 235). Sartain had eight children of whom three, Samuel, William and Emily [*qq.v.*], were all distinguished. When he died in Philadelphia, Sartain had completed his autobiographical volume *Reminiscences of a Very Old Man*, published in 1899. He is buried in Monument Cemetery.

[John Sartain, *Reminiscences of a Very Old Man* (1899), *Annals of the Sartain Tribe* (privately printed, 1886), Mantle Fielding, *Dict. of Am. Painters, Sculptors and Engravers* (1926); *Bryan's Dict. of Painters and Engravers,* vol. V (1905); C. E. Clement, Laurence Hutton, *Artists of the Nineteenth Century* (1907), vol. II; *A Biog. Album of Prominent Pennsylvanians,* vol. II (1889); *Public Ledger* (Philadelphia), Oct. 26, 1897, Mar. 15, 1908.]   D. G—y.

SARTAIN, SAMUEL (Oct. 8, 1830–Dec. 20, 1906), engraver, the eldest child of John Sartain [*q.v.*] and Susannah Longmate (Swaine) Sartain, was born in Philadelphia, a few months after his parents had come to America. Before the boy was seventeen years of age he won fame among artists by engraving Harlow's portrait of Benjamin West. He had studied the art under his father, and at the Pennsylvania Academy of the Fine Arts. About 1851 he established his own business in Philadelphia, working for various publishers. He was commissioned by the Art Union of Philadelphia in 1854 to engrave the painting "Clear the Track" by Christian Schüssele [*q.v.*], and won for this work a silver medal from the Franklin Institute. Many of his best plates were engraved after works by Peale, Sully, and Neagle. He excelled especially in mezzotint and line engravings, and his skill was sought for illustrating biographical works with portrait-engravings. One of his most important engravings, a portrait of Alexander Johnston Cassatt [*q.v.*], was completed a year before Sartain's death. He also engraved many plates of biblical subjects popular during the period of the Civil War. From these plates enormous editions were printed and sold. In some instances sales were so great that the original plate was worn beyond repair and a duplicate plate had to be substituted to satisfy the demand. Among the most popular were: "Christ Blessing Little Children," after Eastlake; "One of the Chosen," after Guy; "Christ Stilling the Tempest," after Hamilton; and "The Song of the Angels," after Moran. Sartain's patience and technical dexterity were evidenced in his mechanical engraving of the Lord's Prayer on a silver dollar.

An active interest in various phases of scientific research led the artist to establish contact with the Franklin Institute, of which he was manager for thirty years and treasurer for the last fifteen years of his life. He was also an expert amateur photographer, and for many years was vice-president of the Photographic Society of Philadelphia. He was married to Harriet Amelia Judd of Waterbury, Conn., on Dec. 11, 1854. She became one of the leading pioneer women physicians of the country, combining domestic and professional life until her retirement from active work in 1889. They had three children, one of whom died young. Sartain died in Philadelphia.

[Information from the family; *Who's Who in America*, 1903–05; John Sartain, *Annals of the Sartain Tribe* (privately printed, 1886); *Philadelphia and Popular Philadelphians* (1891); Mantle Fielding, *Dict. of Am. Painters, Sculptors and Engravers* (1926); *Public Ledger* (Philadelphia), Dec. 21, 1906.]   D. G—y.

SARTAIN, WILLIAM (Nov. 21, 1843–Oct. 25, 1924), painter, was the third son of John Sartain [*q.v.*] and Susannah Longmate (Swaine) Sartain. He was born in Philadelphia, Pa., and received his academic training in the public high school of that city. His early leaning toward art was encouraged by his father, under whom the boy studied drawing and engraving until he entered the classes in the Pennsylvania Academy of the Fine Arts in 1867. In 1864 he produced a plate titled "Young America Crushing Rebellion and Sedition," and in 1866, "Little Samuel," a plate after a painting by James Sant. Although well on the road to success as an etcher of portraits and mezzotints, young Sartain turned definitely to painting at the age of twenty-four and worked for a year under Christian Schussele [*q.v.*].

He went abroad in 1868 to continue his study at the École Nationale Supérieure des Beaux Arts in Paris and under Léon Bonnat, and remained in Europe for eight years. He sketched in Spain, England, Holland, Belgium, Germany, and Italy, spending several winters in Seville and Rome, and the year 1874 in Algiers. He collected a valuable note-book of material from which, in later years, he could develop landscapes and figure compositions. While in Italy and Algiers he painted such subjects as "View in the Street in Algiers," "Arab Cemetery," "Tombs of the Saints at Bouzareah," and made studies of Italian types. It was in 1874 that he completed his "Narcissus," a canvas now owned by Smith College, Northampton, Mass. His first success came when he exhibited some of his work in London in 1875 and was "hung on the line," an honor infrequently bestowed upon foreigners. This recognition encouraged him to make his début in an exhibition at the National Academy of Design in New York City in 1876. With his reputation already established, he returned to the United States the next year and settled in New York. Using the sketch material from his European note-book, he produced "Nubian Scheik" in 1879–80, and "A Chapter of the Koran" in 1883.

In 1879 he began a parallel career as teacher when he was put in charge of all the life classes of the Art Students' League at Cooper Union. He also taught for some years at the Philadelphia School of Design for Women of which his father was vice-president and his sister Emily Sartain [*q.v.*] was principal. By 1880 he was well established in New York, and was in that year elected an Associate National Academician. The following year he received a silver medal in an exhibition in Boston, and in 1884 held a special exhibition of his own at the Williams and Everett's gallery in that city, being warmly received by the critics. In 1887 he won honorable mention in Philadelphia; at the Pan-American Exposition in Buffalo in 1901 he won a bronze medal; and at the Charleston Exposition of 1902 he was granted a silver medal.

Sartain's special interest and talent lay in landscape-painting, and such canvases as "The Valley" (1902) and "The Passing Shower" (1903) illustrate his gift for portraying wide expanses of earth and sky with the simple devices of mass composition and a limited use of color. In 1910 he sent some of his work to the international exposition at Buenos Aires, winning a silver medal and the honor of purchase by the Argentine government. His "Nubian Scheik" was also purchased by the French government for its collection in the Luxembourg. Sartain is further represented in various public and private collections in the United States, including that of the Corcoran Gallery in Washington, D. C., and the Metropolitan Museum in New York City. He was active in American art affairs from the moment he returned to his native land, being a founder of the Society of American Artists, and, later in his life, president of the New York Art Club. He was also an occasional contributor on art subjects to magazines.

Thirty years before his death actually occurred, it was reported that he had died. One of the leading art dealers on Fifth Avenue gave credence to the rumor and enhanced the value of Sartain's pictures by trying to corner the market. Sartain, however, was quietly painting in a New England village. He was never married.

[Information from the family; *Who's Who in America*, 1924–25; Arthur Hoeber, "William Sartain, Painter," *New England Mag.*, Mar. 1903; J. D. Champlain,

ed., *Cyclop. of Painters and Painting*, vol. IV (1887);
Mantle Fielding, *Dict. of Am. Painters, Sculptors and
Engravers* (1926); *Bryan's Dict. of Painters and En-
gravers*, vol. V (1905); *Art World*, May 1917; *N. Y.
Times*, Oct. 26, 1924.]   D. G—y.

SARTWELL, HENRY PARKER (Apr. 18,
1792–Nov. 15, 1867), physician, botanist, was
born at Pittsfield, Mass., of Scotch ancestry, the
son of Eleanor (Crofut) and Levi Sartwell, a
mechanic. Of vigorous physique and adventurous
spirit, he early left home and went to Utica, N. Y.,
where he began to study medicine under the tutelage of a local physician. He finished work with
his preceptor and was granted a license to practise medicine by the Oneida County Medical Society on Sept. 7, 1811. With a horse, saddle, and
bridle, purchased on credit, he started for New
Hartford, N. Y., where he soon had a good practice, owing largely to his agreeable personality
and his successful treatment of his first patients.
In riding about the country on professional business, he found an opportunity to cultivate a boyhood interest in natural history and began to
collect various specimens, at this period chiefly
minerals. His collection, which became quite extensive, was later acquired by the Penn Yan
Academy. During the War of 1812, he served as
surgeon in the United States army and at the end
of the war settled in Springville, N. Y. He removed thence to Bethel (later Gorham), continuing his practice, and there began the study
of botany which later made him widely known.
In April 1832 he removed to Penn Yan, N. Y.,
where he lived and practised his profession until
his death. He is said to have been married four
times.

A highly respected member of the medical profession in New York and for a time president of
the Yates County Medical Society, he was also
widely known locally for his knowledge of geology, mineralogy, and natural history, and he
contributed liberally to *Catalogue of Plants
Found in Oneida County and Vicinity* (1865) by
John Alsop Paine [*q.v.*]. At one time he made
a considerable collection of insects, which was
later destroyed by fire, while his meteorological
observations were so completely and carefully
prepared that they are now on reference at the
Smithsonian Institution. He was also an expert horticulturist. His extensive and thorough
knowledge of the subjects he pursued places him
unquestionably in the front rank of early American naturalists. The branch he chiefly cultivated, however, was botany. He became acquainted, largely by correspondence, with the
leading botanists of his time, both American and
European, and often sent them specimens and
even quite large collections of plants. The genus

Sartwellia was named for him, and he was regarded as a capable, reliable, and energetic collector. His own most valuable work is *Carices
Americae Septentrionalis Exsiccatae*, of which
two volumes were published, 1848–50; the third
he was engaged on at the time of his death. His
herbarium, the work of nearly a half century,
consists of about eight thousand specimens, many
gathered by exchange with botanists in all parts
of the world. It now forms part of the collection
of Hamilton College, Clinton, N. Y., which conferred upon him the honorary degree of Ph.D.
in 1864.

[*Yates County Chronicle*, Nov. 21, 1867, Nov. 4,
1868, and Oct. 28, 1869; *Amer. Jour. Sci. and Arts*,
Jan. 1868; *Ann. Report of . . . Smithsonian Inst.*,
1871; *Am. Ann. Cyc.*, 1867; H. A. Kelly and W. L.
Burrage, *Am. Medic. Biogs.* (1920); C. S. Sargent, ed.,
The Sci. Papers of Asa Gray (1889), vol. II; *Buffalo
Commercial Advertiser*, Nov. 18, 1867.]   C. W. D.

SASLAVSKY, ALEXANDER (Feb. 8, 1876–
Aug. 2, 1924), violinist and conductor, was born
at Kharkov, Russia, the son of Michael and
Anna (Gantz) Saslavsky. He was trained as a
violinist by Gorski in Kharkov, and later by
Jakob Gruen in Vienna. In 1893 he was graduated from the Vienna Conservatory of Music.
During the same year he made a concert tour of
Canada, and then went to New York City, where
he became one of the first violins of the New
York Symphony Society. He was a member of
this organization for twenty-five years, and in
1903 he became concert-master and assistant
conductor under Walter Damrosch. On one occasion in 1911 he took the orchestra to Spokane,
Wash., for a five weeks' engagement and conducted two concerts daily. In 1904 Saslavsky
was one of the organizers of the Russian Symphony Orchestra, and for four years acted as its
concert-master, until he resigned because of the
conflict with his duties as concert-master of the
New York Symphony Society. He settled in Los
Angeles, Cal., in 1918 and the following year became concert-master of the newly formed Philharmonic Orchestra of that city. He remained in
California until his death in San Francisco.

During his entire career Saslavsky was important as a teacher, and for his work in introducing chamber music to a larger public. In
1906 and 1907 he organized two string quartets.
He spent his summers in the Northwest, giving
chamber-music concerts in Denver, Colo., and
other cities. He often appeared as a soloist, both
in recital and playing concertos with orchestra.
He introduced many new works in his programs,
and as soloist with the Russian Symphony Orchestra he gave New York and other American
cities first hearings of such compositions as

Mlynarski's violin concerto, a romance and caprice by Rubinstein, and the newly discovered violin *Concerto in C* by Haydn. A contemporary spoke of Saslavsky as an "artist who has worked unceasingly in the interests of true art and artistic ideals . . . a remarkable violinist, possessed of all the necessary attributes a player should possess—a fine, big tone, faultless intonation, complete mastery of the bow, a genuinely artistic sense of interpretation—and, above all, a thorough musician in everything he undertakes . . ." (Saenger, *post*, p. 1270). On June 18, 1906, he was married to C. Izolee Todd of Boston, Mass.

[Material regarding Saslavsky is meager. There is a brief account in *Grove's Dict. of Music and Musicians*, vol. IV (1928) and the *Am. Supp.* (1930), in *Who's Who in America*, 1924–25, and in *Baker's Biog. Dict. of Musicians* (3rd ed., 1919). See also Gustav Saenger, "Alexander Saslavsky, Soloist—Concertmaster—Conductor," *Musical Observer*, Apr. 1913; an obit. article by Alfred Metzger, *Pacific Coast Musical Rev.*, Aug. 11, 1924; and *San Francisco Chronicle*, Aug. 3, 1924.]
J. T. H.

SASSACUS (*c.* 1560–June 1637), chief sachem of the Pequots in 1633, was born probably near Groton, Conn., the son of Wopigwooit, whom he succeeded to leadership in the tribe. About the time of his accession the tribal power declined as a result of war with the Dutch and the defection of the Mohegan chieftain, Uncas [*q.v.*]. Relations with the English settlers, too, were strained; but a treaty of submission staved off a breach with them until the fall of 1636, when an expedition sent from Massachusetts to enforce the terms of the agreement precipitated hostilities. Sassacus tried without success to bring the Narragansetts into league with him, urging that unless a stand were made the white men would soon overrun the whole country. During the ensuing winter and spring his followers made frequent raids upon the Connecticut settlements. Finally, in May 1637, the new colony determined to end the irregular warfare by a vigorous offensive. John Mason [*q.v.*], with a small force, made a sudden attack upon the savage stronghold situated on the Mystic River and, according to his own estimate, slaughtered nearly 700 Indian men, women, and children (Orr, *post,* pp. 21–29). The stroke was decisive. The bands separated and were soon either subjugated or exterminated while Sassacus, himself, fleeing westward, was assassinated by the Mohawks.

[Charles Orr, *Hist. of the Pequot War* (1897); "Letters of Roger Williams," ed. by J. R. Bartlett, *Narragansett Club Publications*, 1 ser., vol. VI (1874); J. W. De Forest, *Hist. of the Indians of Connecticut* (1851); *Bradford's Hist. of Plymouth Plantation* (1908), ed. by W. T. Davis; John Winthrop, *The Hist. of New England*, vol. I (1825), ed. by James Savage; F. W. Hodge, *Handbook of Am. Indians,* pt. II (1910).]
G. P. B.

SATTERLEE, HENRY YATES (Jan. 11, 1843–Feb. 22. 1908), Episcopal clergyman, first bishop of the diocese of Washington, was born in New York City, the second of eight children. The Satterlees were an old English county family of Suffolk and Devonshire. Benedict, the founder of the American line, emigrated to New London, Conn., in 1685. Edward, Henry's grandfather, settled in Albany; his son, another Edward, the bishop's father, a well educated and cultivated man, had marked artistic and literary tastes. His wife, Jane Yates, came of ancestry noted for public service. Her grandfather, Christopher Yates, served on General Schuyler's staff in the Revolution. One of his sons, Joseph Christopher [*q.v.*], was governor of New York from 1823 to 1825. Another, Henry, the bishop's grandfather, served as state senator and as mayor of Schenectady, N. Y. To his mother the bishop chiefly owed his spiritual sensitiveness and strong convictions.

His young boyhood was passed in Albany, but in 1856 the family moved to New York, where he attended the Columbia Grammar School, and, in 1863, received the degree of B.A. from Columbia College. After a serious inclination to a military career, he decided on the ministry, and was prepared at the General Theological Seminary in New York. Ordained deacon on Nov. 21, 1865, he was appointed assistant minister in Zion Parish, Wappinger Falls, the following September. On June 30, 1866, he was married to Jane Lawrence Churchill of New York, and on Jan. 11, 1867, he was ordained priest. Eight years later, he succeeded to the rectorship of the parish. At Wappinger Falls were born his two children.

In 1882 he accepted the rectorship of Calvary Parish, New York City. He rapidly became a power in the community and in the counsels of the Church, giving early proof of that capacity for leadership which marked his later years. Twice he declined elections to the episcopate, in Ohio (1887) and in Michigan (1889). In 1895, he issued the most important of his several books: *A Creedless Gospel and the Gospel Creed*. In it he endeavored to show that Christianity is not a mere human aspiration, but a dramatic self-revealing of God, in the person of Jesus Christ, not only in past history, but in present experience. This creed was the center of his faith and the source of his spiritual power. A few years later he published *New Testament Churchmanship and the Principles upon Which It Was Founded* (1899).

In 1896, he was elected bishop of the newly formed diocese of Washington. His parochial ministry of twenty years, almost equally divided between a country town and the metropolis, had brought him into close touch with every stratum of American life. This experience proved an admirable equipment for his new work. In organizing his diocese, he kept in mind the potential influence which the Episcopal Church in Washington, if fully equipped and wisely led, might wield in the nation's spiritual life. This ideal led to his vision of a national cathedral, fully furnished for its mission by the beauty and majesty of its architecture and the appeal of its spiritual ministrations. He threw himself into the cathedral project with dynamic faith and courage. Yet he was no visionary; practical wisdom marked each step. At his death, no stone of the great building of his dreams was in its place save the foundation stone: but every development of Washington Cathedral, material and spiritual alike, has been in line with his far-seeing plans.

President Theodore Roosevelt, who came into close contact with the bishop, wrote of him: "To an unusual degree, he combined spiritual-mindedness with the purpose to do efficient, practical work and I do not think any one came in contact with him without becoming conscious of a certain elevation of thought and temper, and the power of inspiring others" (Brent, *post*, p. 117). His body now lies beneath the altar of the Bethlehem Chapel, which forms the crypt of the choir and apse of the cathedral and was built in his memory by loving friends.

[C. H. Brent, *A Master Builder; Being the Life and Letters of Henry Yates Satterlee* (1916); *Who's Who in America*, 1908–09; *Living Church*, Feb. 29, 1908; *Churchman*, Feb. 29, 1908; *Evening Star* (Washington), Feb. 22, 1908.]   P. M. R.

SATTERLEE, RICHARD SHERWOOD (Dec. 6, 1798–Nov. 10, 1880), army surgeon, was born in Fairfield, Herkimer County, N. Y., the son of Major William Satterlee, an officer of Connecticut troops in the Revolutionary army, and Hannah (Sherwood) Satterlee. His native town was the seat of Fairfield Academy, with a medical college and faculty which in his day ranked with the best in the country. It is probable that he obtained his education here, though he did not obtain a medical degree. He was licensed to practise in 1818 and moved to Seneca County, N. Y., and shortly thereafter to Detroit, Mich., where, on Feb. 25, 1822, he entered the United States army as an assistant surgeon. In this city in June 1827, he was married to Mary S. Hunt. His early years in the army were spent in routine duty in frontier posts of the Middle West. During the Seminole War in Florida he served with the brigade of Col. Zachary Taylor who gave him an official commendation for his care of the wounded at the battle of Okeechobee on Dec. 25, 1837. During the Mexican War he landed with the army which took Vera Cruz after a siege, and in the advance to Mexico city he acted as senior surgeon of Worth's division of regulars. He directed the medical service of that division at the battles of Cerro Gordo, Churubusco, Molino del Rey, and Chapultepec and, on July 5, 1847, forwarded to the war department a detailed report upon the health of the army.

After the occupation of Mexico city he was appointed medical director upon the staff of General Scott, and in that capacity was charged with the establishment of a general hospital to care for the bulk of the army casualties. He had been advanced to the grade of major in 1832, and in 1853 was appointed medical purveyor. In this capacity he served through the Civil War. So satisfactory was his service that he was brevetted lieutenant-colonel and brigadier-general. The accompanying citation commended him "for diligent care and attention in procuring proper army supplies as Medical Purveyor and for economy and fidelity in the disbursement of large sums of money" (Hamersly, *post*, p. 741). General Scott gave active support to his candidacy for surgeon-general when a change was made in 1862, but William Alexander Hammond [*q.v.*] was given the place. As a result of a reorganization of the medical department of the army in 1866 he was appointed chief medical purveyor with the grade of lieutenant-colonel. He was in charge of the medical supply depot in New York City until his retirement from active service in 1869.

[A. C. Wildey, *Geneal. of the Descendants of Wm. Chesebrough* (1903); biog. sketch by Albert Allemann, in H. A. Kelly, W. L. Burrage, *Am. Med. Biog.* (1920); W. B. Atkinson, *The Physicians and Surgeons of the U. S.* (1878); R. F. Stone, *Biog. of Eminent Am. Physicians and Surgeons* (1898); H. E. Brown, *The Med. Dept. of the U. S. Army* (1873); T. H. S. Hamersly, *Complete . . . Army Reg. of the U. S., 1779–1879* (1880); *Army and Navy Jour.*, Nov. 13, 20, 1880; *N. Y. Times*, Nov. 11, 1880.]   J. M. P—n.

SAUGANASH (c. 1780–Sept. 28, 1841), Indian sub-chief, was born in Canada. His name is often spelled Sagaunash, and he is also known as "Englishman" or Billy Caldwell. His father was said to be William Caldwell, an Irish officer in the British service, and his mother was a Potawatomi. He was trained by Roman Catholic priests at Detroit, and, in addition to the several Indian dialects that he spoke, he acquired fluency in both French and English. From about 1807 he was closely associated with Tecumseh [*q.v.*] for some six years as an interpreter and perhaps as a secretary. He opposed the government of the United States and the frontier settlers, but there seems good authority for believing that he used his influence against the perpetration of atrocities. He arrived at Fort Dearborn the day after the massacre of Aug. 15, 1812, and it is certain that he was the means of saving several lives. He was probably at the Battle of the Thames on Oct. 5, 1813, when Tecumseh was killed, and thereafter may have remained for some years in Canada. Under the British government he had the title of "captain of the Indian Department," which he is known to have used in signing documents as late as 1816. About 1820 he made his residence at the present Chicago and avowed his allegiance to the United States. In 1826 he was appointed a justice of the peace. With two other negotiators, he rendered valuable aid to the settlers and the government in 1827 by keeping the Winnebago chief, Big Foot, at peace. In 1828, at a point a few miles north of the mouth of the Chicago River, the government built for him a house, probably the first frame structure erected in the Chicago region. He again exerted his influence for peace in 1832 by dissuading Indians from joining Black Hawk's band. By successive treaties culminating in the one of 1833, at Chicago, the Potawatomi ceded virtually all of their lands east of the Mississippi, and in the summer of 1836 they began their long migration to Western Iowa. Sauganash accompanied them. He died in the vicinity of the present Council Bluffs. Sauganash was more than six feet tall. By reason of his height, his powerful frame, and his erect bearing he was sometimes called the "Straight Tree." He was a man of exceptional intelligence and ability, and he was highly regarded by his white neighbors. Upon his tribesmen he urged the acceptance of the white man's mode of life and was especially interested in the education of the Indian youth. He had but one wife, the sister of the Potawatomi chief, Yellow Hand, and but one child, a son who died before reaching manhood.

[*Handbook of Am. Indians*, ed. by F. W. Hodge, pt. II (1910); C. A. Burley, *Sauganash* (copr. 1920); Mrs. John H. Kinzie, *Wau-Bun, the Early Day in the Northwest*, esp. pp. 186, 253 (1930), ed. by L. P. Kellogg.] W. J. G.

SAUGRAIN DE VIGNI, ANTOINE FRANÇOIS (Feb. 17, 1763–c. May 19, 1820), naturalist, physician, scientist, philosopher, was born in Paris, France, son of Antoine and Marie (Brunet) Saugrain, the de Vigni in his name, after a Paris custom, merely indicating the place where he was nursed as an infant. His ancestors were librarians, booksellers, and publishers. He was educated in physics, chemistry, and mineral-

ogy. While still a very young man, he went into the service of the king of Spain, and in 1785 and again in 1786 he was in Mexico for the purpose of examining mines and mineral productions. In 1787 in the company of two friends, M. Raquet and M. Picque, he sailed for the United States, remained for a while in Philadelphia, where he enjoyed the intimate friendship of Benjamin Franklin, and in the spring of 1788 traveled westward in the hope of finding a suitable spot for a French settlement. In an attack by Indians opposite the Big Miami, Picque and Raquet were killed, and Saugrain was wounded and taken captive. Escaping, he reached Louisville, Ky., Mar. 29, 1788, but suffered the loss of part of one foot from an infected frost-bite. In April 1790, after a visit to France, he returned with a party of French immigrants, destined for the settlement of Gallipolis, Ohio. After six years in that settlement and some time in Lexington, Ky., and Portage des Sioux, Mo., he reached St. Louis in 1800 and settled there. At St. Louis he was appointed post surgeon by the Spanish lieutenant-governor, Delassus. After the American occupation he was appointed army surgeon by Jefferson and served from June 17, 1805, until he resigned in 1811. When the Lewis and Clark expedition was being fitted out in St. Louis, he supplied gratuitously a medicine chest, thermometers, barometers, and matches.

Besides having the distinction of being the only practising physician in St. Louis when Upper Louisiana was transferred to the United States, he was known far and wide for his chemical laboratories. He made and sold ink, thermometers, phosphoric lights for hunters, barometers, and matches of glass tubes containing phosphorus; he conducted experiments in electricity and had an electric battery. He was also famed for treatment of smallpox by inoculation; in 1809 he introduced the first smallpox vaccine virus brought to St. Louis and publicly offered to vaccinate, free of charge, all indigent persons, paupers, and Indians. Although very small of stature, he was a hero in combat with the Indians. He was high-spirited and full of fire, but at the same time a man of rare good nature. He was married in Kanawha County, Va., Mar. 20, 1793, to Genevieve Rosalie Michau, born in Paris, July 23, 1776. Many of the descendants of their six children became prominent in St. Louis in later years.

[Saugrain died during the night of May 18–19, 1820; see *St. Louis Enquirer, Mo. Gazette* (St. Louis), May 24, 1820. See also "Généalogie de la Famille Saugrain, par Claude M. Saugrain en 1810, Continué par Antoine P. Saugrain en 1865" (chart); Saugrain MS., Mo. Hist. Soc.; H. M. Brackenridge, *Recollections of Persons and Places in the West* (1868, rev. ed.); *The Rec-*

ord of the Celebration of the Two Hundredth Anniversary of the Birth of Benjamin Franklin (6 vols., 1906–08), vols. IV and V, Am. Philos. Soc.; W. V. Byars, A Memoir of the Life and Work of Dr. Antoine François Saugrain, the First Scientist of the Miss. Valley (n.d.); N. P. Dandridge, Antoine François Saugrain (de Vigni) (1904), reprinted in Ohio Archaeological and Hist. Quart., Apr. 1906; E. F. Bliss, "Dr. Saugrain's Note-Books, 1788," Proc. Am. Antiquarian Soc., n.s., vol. XIX (1909) and "Dr. Saugrain's Relation of his Voyage down the Ohio River . . . in 1788," Ibid., n.s., vol. XI (1898); E. S. Meany, Wash. Hist. Quart., Oct. 1931.]   S. M. D.

SAULSBURY, ELI (Dec. 29, 1817–Mar. 22, 1893), United States senator, brother of Gove and Willard Saulsbury [qq.v.] and son of William and Margaret (Smith) Saulsbury, like his brothers was born in Kent County, Del. He attended the local schools and in 1839, having joined the Methodist Church the year previous, entered Dickinson College at Carlisle, Pa., where he pursued a special course. He seems to have lived on the ancestral farm for a considerable time thereafter. In 1853 he became a member of the state legislature from his native county. Meanwhile, however, he had been studying law both at home and in the office of his brother Willard at Georgetown, Del., and in 1857 was admitted to the bar and commenced practice at Dover. With Willard he was elected delegate to the National Democratic Convention at Chicago in 1864. In 1871, on the expiration of Willard's term in the United States Senate, and of Gove's as governor, Eli, with Willard's help, defeated Gove and was elected United States senator. In spite of their rivalry for office, the three brothers were in practical accord in their political views, which were those of the northern Democrats generally. Eli's first important speech in the Senate (Jan. 30, 1872) was in favor of the removal of political disabilities of former Confederates and against the Civil Rights bill. On Apr. 22, 1874, he spoke against recognition of the Louisiana state ("carpet bag") government and in favor of white supremacy. He served on several committees, rendering his most conspicuous service on the Committee on Privileges and Elections, which passed on the large number of contests from the southern states. He opposed the eight-hour law in 1876 and the contract-labor law in 1885. He supported the anti-polygamy bill in 1882 with evident reluctance and sought to make its penal provisions prospective only. He did not vote on the civil service reform bill in 1882 but in 1888 advocated the selection of civil service employees according to their political affiliations. He opposed the bill to restrict Chinese immigration in 1888 on the ground that it would violate existing treaties, and he was the author of a resolution to inquire into conditions in Samoa. He favored an international coinage in 1888 and presented many petitions for legislation prohibiting the liquor traffic, but opposed the Blair Educational Bill in 1884 and the international copyright bill in 1888. He was a working senator, and few important measures escaped his participation.

Reëlected twice, Saulsbury, as he neared the end of his third term, encountered an opponent in the person of James L. Wolcott, a former student of law in his office. After bitter strife between their followers, the Wolcott faction prevailed in the Kent County caucuses and, by invoking the unit rule in the county convention, nominated a legislative ticket pledged exclusively to their leader, thus eliminating Saulsbury from the contest. A large number of his followers "bolted" the party ticket, however, to elect the Republican nominees, and that party thereby for the first time secured a senator from Delaware. After the expiration of his term, Mar. 3, 1889, Saulsbury returned to his home in Dover, where he died. He never married.

[Biog. Dir. Am. Cong. (1928); J. T. Scharf, Hist. of Del. (1888), vol. I; H. C. Conrad, Hist. of the State of Del. (3 vols., 1908); W. A. Powell, A Hist. of Del (1928); Every Evening and Wilmington Daily Commercial, Mar. 22, 1893.]   C. S. L.

SAULSBURY, GOVE (May 29, 1815–July 31, 1881), physician, governor of Delaware, was the eldest of three brothers who attained political distinction in that state in the middle nineteenth century. They were of Welsh descent, sons of William Saulsbury of Mispillion Hundred, sheriff of Kent County, Del., and his wife, Margaret Smith. Gove, born on the ancestral acres, attended free schools of the vicinity, then Delaware College at Newark. After a period of teaching country schools, he entered the medical college of the University of Pennsylvania, where he was graduated M.D. in 1842, having written a thesis on rheumatism. He at once entered upon the practice of his profession at Dover. In 1843 he joined the Methodist Episcopal Church and eventually became active in its affairs. He was president of the board of trustees of Wilmington Conference Academy and just before his death had been chosen delegate to the Ecumenical Council of Methodism in London, September 1881. On Nov. 1, 1848, he married Rosina Jane Smith of Snow Hill, Md., by whom he had five children, only one of whom survived him.

Saulsbury was a delegate to the National Democratic Convention in 1856, and in 1862 was elected to the Delaware Senate, where he took a prominent part in the sessions of 1863 and 1864. He supported in the latter year a joint resolution to inquire into the enlistment of negroes within the state, and later presented a committee report severely arraigning the Republican governor, William Cannon [*q.v.*], for his policy in furnishing Federal troops. Soon becoming the recognized Democratic leader, Saulsbury was elected speaker of the Senate at the opening of the session of 1865, upon the death of Governor Cannon, Mar. 1, became acting governor, and in the following year was elected governor by a majority of 1312. He served for nearly six years, longer than any other governor of Delaware. During his public service he opposed successively each of the amendments to the Federal Constitution growing out of the Civil War, and each was rejected by the Delaware legislature, in part, no doubt, because of his urgent messages. In 1869 he characterized the reconstruction measures enacted by Congress as "the most flagrant usurpation of power" and in his last message (1871) he referred to the Fifteenth Amendment as having been "adopted by fraud and coercion."

His term as governor expired less than two months before that of his brother Willard [*q.v.*] as United States senator, and the two, as well as the third brother, Eli [*q.v.*], became candidates for the senatorship. Gove held, throughout, his following of fourteen, rising on the third ballot to fifteen, but Eli, on the fourth ballot, with Willard's support, received sixteen votes and was elected, Jan. 17, 1871, on the day of Gove's retirement from the governorship. Gove Saulsbury seems never to have held public office thereafter, although he was a delegate to the National Democratic Convention in 1876 and again in 1880.

[J. T. Scharf, *Hist. of Del.* (1888), vol. I; J. M. McCarter and B. F. Jackson, *Hist. and Biog. Encyc. of Del.* (1882); W. A. Powell, *A Hist. of Del.* (1928); H. C. Conrad, *Hist. of the State of Del.* (3 vols., 1908); *Every Evening and Wilmington Daily Commercial,* Aug. 1, 1881.]   C. S. L.

SAULSBURY, WILLARD (June 2, 1820– Apr. 6, 1892), United States senator, chancellor of Delaware, brother of Gove and Eli Saulsbury [*qq.v.*] and son of William and Margaret (Smith) Saulsbury, was born in Mispillion Hundred, Kent County, Del. He attended local schools, Delaware College at Newark, and Dickinson College, Carlisle, Pa., then studied law under James L. Bartol, later chief justice of Maryland, and Martin W. Bates, later United States senator. Admitted to the bar in 1845, he opened an office at Georgetown, Del., entered politics, and soon acquired a local reputation as an orator. On May 11, 1850, he married Annie Milby Ponder. A daughter and two sons were born of this marriage; one son, John P., became secretary of state of Delaware, and the other, Willard

[*q.v.*], a United States senator. In the year of his marriage Saulsbury was appointed attorney-general of Delaware. His five years of service (1850–55) gave him state-wide acquaintance and reputation, and in 1856 he was chosen a delegate to the National Democratic Convention at Cincinnati which nominated James Buchanan for the presidency. Two years later he was elected to the United States Senate, entering that body in 1859, on the eve of the Civil War. On Apr. 2, 1860, he defended slavery in an elaborate speech (*Congressional Globe,* 36 Cong., 1 Sess., pp. 1480–88). On Dec. 5 following he declared, apropos of the President's message, that Delaware "having been the first to adopt the Constitution, will be the last to do any act or countenance any act calculated to lead to the separation of the states" (*Ibid.,* 36 Cong., 2 Sess., p. 14); he later supported the resolutions of J. J. Crittenden [*q.v.*] "for taking the sense of the people" on proposals which would virtually have restored the compromises of 1820 and 1850. He was exceedingly critical of arrests in Delaware for alleged disloyalty to the Union and he opposed interference by military and naval forces in elections and the suspension of the writ of *habeas corpus.* On Jan. 29, 1862, he spoke against the resolution to expel Senator Bright of Indiana for alleged treason and on Feb. 7, 1863, he proposed a referendum on compensated emancipation in Missouri. In the following year he was a delegate to the National Democratic Convention at Chicago and in the ensuing winter he was reëlected to the Senate. During his service there he was a member of the committees on commerce, mines and mining, patents, and pensions. A candidate for reëlection in 1871, he was opposed by his brothers Gove and Eli, and threw his support to the latter. Two years later, in November 1873, he was appointed by his brother-in-law, Governor Ponder, chancellor of the state, and he held that position for the remainder of his life. His opinions are published in 6 *Delaware Chancery Reports* (edited by his son Willard) and seem amply fortified by authority, the cases being generally well briefed. Especially notable is his opinion in *Green* vs. *Saulsbury* in the appendix to the volume, wherein he defined the jurisdiction of the Orphans' Court and traced its history from its establishment in 1683 at Philadelphia, when "the three lower counties" were a part of Pennsylvania. The bar in each of the counties adopted commendatory resolutions at the time of his death.

[The best account of Saulsbury's life is found in Appendix C to 6 *Del. Chancery Reports,* and was evidently written by his son Willard. See also *Biog. Dir. Am. Cong.* (1928); J. T. Scharf, *Hist. of Del.* (1888);

H. C. Conrad, *Hist. of the State of Del.* (3 vols., 1908);
W. A. Powell, *A Hist. of Del.* (1928); *Every Evening
and Wilmington Daily Commercial,* Apr. 6, 1892.]
C. S. L.

SAULSBURY, WILLARD (Apr. 17, 1861–
Feb. 20, 1927), senator, was born at Georgetown, Del., the son of Willard Saulsbury [*q.v.*]
and Annie Milby (Ponder) Saulsbury. After
attending private schools and the University of
Virginia (1877–79), he studied for the bar in his
father's office and was admitted in October 1882.
He became associated in the practice of law with
Victor DuPont of Wilmington, with whom he
continued in partnership until the latter's death
in 1888. On Dec. 5, 1893, he married May Du-
Pont, the daughter of his former partner. During his last years he was the head of the firm of
Saulsbury, Morris & Rodney, with offices in both
Wilmington and Washington, D. C. His business achievements included the consolidation of
the Wilmington traction companies and the organization of the Equitable Trust Company of
which he was long a director, as he was likewise
of the Union National Bank.

Scion of a family which had produced several
prominent Democratic leaders, he became active
in the councils of that party. He was chairman
of the county committee from 1892 to 1900, state
committeeman for a score of years and chairman
from 1900 to 1906, and from 1908 to 1920 national committeeman from Delaware. He was a
delegate to four national conventions between
1896 and 1920; in 1896 he was chairman of the
delegation and in 1904, a member of the committee on resolutions. At the convention of 1924 the
Delaware delegation presented his name as a
candidate for the presidency. From 1899 to 1913
he was his party's nominee for the United States
Senate, regularly receiving the entire Democratic vote in the legislature, but not until the
last-named year was he successful, and then only
after a desperate struggle. He was the last Delaware senator elected by the legislature.

In the Senate he soon became known as a leading supporter of President Wilson. He was assigned to the committee on foreign relations, and
became chairman of the committee on the Pacific Islands and Porto Rico. During the recess
of Congress in 1915 he visited the Far East,
reaching China while the twenty-one Japanese
demands were being pressed upon China and acquiring much first-hand knowledge of the situation. He also gave special attention to the needs
of the United States Court for China, and endeavored to strengthen its position in the international community. At the opening of the session of 1916 he was elected president *pro tempore*
of the Senate, a rare honor for so new a member,

and continued as such for the balance of his term.
He was nominated for reëlection to the Senate
in 1918, but the tide had already turned against
the Wilson administration and Saulsbury, as one
of its leading exponents, was defeated, though by
a narrow margin.

After the expiration of his term he resumed
the practice of law. When the Washington Conference on the Limitation of Armaments was in
process of incubation, he was invited by President Harding, with whom his personal relations
in the Senate had been most friendly, to serve on
the Advisory Committee. In 1923 he was a member of the Pan-American Conference at Santiago
de Chile. His last four years were passed quietly; he died at Wilmington, and was buried at
Dover in the churchyard of Christ Church (Episcopal), to which he belonged. He was a man of
polished manners, excellent address, and winsome
qualities. His long experience in practical politics taught him the art of handling men and,
had his lot fallen in an earlier era when his party
was stronger in his native state, he might well
have served for a long period in the Senate and
have become one of the leading statesmen of his
time.

[J. T. Scharf, *Hist. of Del.* (1888), II, 607; *Biog.
Dir. Am. Cong.* (1928); H. C. Conrad, *Hist. of the
State of Del.* (1908), III, 1048; *Who's Who in Amer-
ica, 1926–27*; *N. Y. Times,* Feb. 21, 1927; *Wilmington
Morning News,* Feb. 21, 1927; personal acquaintance.]
C. S. L.

SAUNDERS, ALVIN (July 12, 1817–Nov. 1,
1899), territorial governor of Nebraska, United
States senator, was born ten miles south of Flemingsburg, Ky. His father, Gunnell Saunders, a
native of Virginia, married Mary Mauzy, likewise a Virginian. When Alvin was about twelve
years old the family removed to Springfield, Ill.
Here Alvin attended district school two months
each winter. At nineteen he went west, working
on a farm at Mount Pleasant, Iowa, for a short
time, and then becoming clerk in a dry-goods
store. Realizing the importance of further education, he prevailed on one of the qualified citizens to establish a night school and became a
faithful attendant. In 1839 he was appointed
postmaster of Mount Pleasant, but seven years
later was superseded by an appointee of President Polk's. In 1846 he was the youngest delegate to the convention that framed the constitution under which Iowa was admitted to the
Union. He was elected to the Iowa Senate in
1854 and reëlected in 1858. The first Republican
state convention, at Iowa City, Feb. 22, 1856,
found him one of the participants. He was chairman of the Iowa delegation in 1860 to the national convention that nominated Lincoln and

was active during the campaign in behalf of Lincoln, with whom he had previously formed an acquaintance.

On Mar. 26, 1861, Lincoln appointed Saunders governor of Nebraska territory. He assumed office May 15 and three days later issued a proclamation calling for volunteers. In his first official message to the legislature he advocated a transcontinental railway; as one of the Commissioners for the Union Pacific, he delivered the principal address at the ground-breaking ceremonies, Dec. 2, 1863. In January 1861 he urged the legislature to ask Congress to pass a homestead law, an action taken by Congress May 20, 1862. In 1865 he intimated he would not seek another term, but the legislature, disregarding party affiliations, adopted a resolution sent to the President asking his reappointment. Saunders went to Washington and on Apr. 14, 1865, called upon the President. The signing of his commission was probably Lincoln's last official act. Saunders continued as territorial governor until March 1867, when Nebraska became a state.

In 1868 Saunders was a delegate to the Republican National Convention. The following year he was appointed by the governor as one of the board of regents for the control of the old capitol grounds in Omaha for school purposes, serving as president of the board until it was superseded by the board of education, of which, in 1874, he was a member. In 1877 he was elected United States senator from Nebraska, serving until 1883. Among his special interests in Congress were Indian affairs and the development of inland waterways. He was also interested in numerous business and semi-public enterprises in Omaha. He founded the State Bank of Nebraska in Omaha and served for several years as its president, and assisted in establishing the street railway system and the gas works. He lost heavily during the financial difficulties of 1875, but met all his indebtedness and in time again accumulated a competence. One of the organizers of the Omaha Real Estate Exchange in 1886, he was its first president. He actively promoted the Trans-Mississippi and International Exposition in 1898, and was the resident vice-president. A member of the church of the Disciples of Christ, he was an incorporator and a zealous promoter of Nebraska Christian University (later Cotner University and after 1919 Cotner College), at Bethany Heights, a suburb of Lincoln. He was married in Washington, D. C., Mar. 11, 1856, to Marthena Survillar Barlow of Greencastle, Ind. A son and a daughter were born to them; the latter married the only son of President Benjamin Harrison. Saunders died in his home in Omaha at the age of eighty-two and was buried in Forest Lawn Cemetery.

[J. S. Morton, *Illus. Hist. of Nebr.*, I (1905), 550–52, with portr.; J. W. Savage and J. T. Bell, *Hist. of the City of Omaha* (1894); *Biog. Dir. Am. Cong.* (1928); *Omaha Daily Bee*, Nov. 2, 1899; L. A. Moomaw, *Hist. of Cotner Univ.* (1916); T. W. Tipton, "Forty Years of Nebraska," *Nebr. State Hist. Soc. Colls.*, 2 ser. IV (1902).]   E. W. L.

SAUNDERS, FREDERICK (Aug. 14, 1807–Dec. 12, 1902), librarian, author, pioneer in work for international copyright, was born in London, England, the son of W. Saunders of the publishing firm of Saunders & Otley. He married Mary Ann Farr of London, Sept. 18, 1833, and for several years during his early manhood worked in his father's office. In 1837 he came to America, primarily to arrange for the publication of Bulwer Lytton's novel, *Rienzi*, but secondarily to launch a movement for an international copyright agreement that would prevent the reprinting of the works of English authors in America without remuneration to the writers. The first man to lay the matter before Congress, he made three separate appeals, one of them backed by a petition signed by fifty-six leading British authors that was carried to Washington by Charles Dickens and placed in the hands of Henry Clay. With the support of all writers in both countries, Saunders was at first confident of success. But, though he succeeded in making thoughtful Americans ashamed of the situation, he was ahead of his time, and two generations passed before the seed he planted and never ceased to nurture, bore fruit. He did not even succeed in getting a valid copyright on *Rienzi*; it was "pirated" by several publishers, and he said that his firm lost £7,000 on the venture. Notwithstanding his ill-success in this matter, he remained in the United States as a member of the staff of the New York *Evening Post* in the days when William Cullen Bryant, John Bigelow, and Parke Godwin were its luminaries. Meanwhile, he had begun publishing books, mostly collections of original essays or compilations. *Memories of the Great Metropolis* (1852); *Salad for the Solitary* (1853), which had a large sale and continued to be read for decades afterward; *Salad for the Social* (1856); *Pearls of Thought* (1858); *Mosaics* (1859); *Festival of Song* (1866); *About Woman, Love and Marriage* (1868); *Evenings with the Sacred Poets* (1869), treating of hymnology from ancient to modern times, and *Pastime Papers* (1885) were his principal works. He edited *Our National Centennial Jubilee* (1877) and, with Henry T. Tuckerman, *Homes of American Authors* (1853). His friend Washington Irving [*q.v.*], who had suggested the founding of the Astor library, was influential in securing for him in 1859 the position of assistant librarian. In 1876 he became librarian and remained at that post for twenty years, meanwhile continuing to write for literary periodicals. He had a part in the negotiations that led to the consolidation in 1895 of the Astor library, the Lenox library, and the Tilden Trust into the great New York Public Library. In 1896, at the age of eighty-nine, he retired by his own request but continued to serve as a trustee of the library until his death. He lived to see the New York Circulating Library, with eleven branches, combined with the other units in 1901. His "Recollections of a Retired Librarian" appeared in the *Critic,* Apr. 17, 1897.

[*Who's Who in America,* 1901–02; obituaries in *Evening Post* (N. Y.), Dec. 13, 1902; *N. Y. Times,* Dec. 14, 1902; scrap album on the Astor library compiled by Saunders, now in N. Y. Pub. Lib.; "A Book-lover's Memories," *N. Y. Times,* July 18, 1895; *Lib. Jour.,* Nov. 1896, Jan. 1903; *Publishers' Weekly,* Dec. 20, 1902.]   A. F. H.

SAUNDERS, PRINCE (d. Feb. 1839), negro reformer and author, was the son of Cuff and Phyllis Saunders. He was born either in Lebanon, Conn., or in Thetford, Vt. In Thetford he spent part, at least, of his boyhood and owned property in 1805. He was baptized on July 25, 1784, at Lebanon, Conn. He taught a colored school at Colchester, Conn., was a student in Moor's Charity School at Dartmouth College in 1807 and 1808 under the patronage of Judge Oramel Hinckley of Thetford, formerly of Lebanon, and in November 1808 was recommended by President John Wheelock of Dartmouth as a teacher in Boston. There he taught a school for colored children, and through his influence Abiel Smith, a merchant, left a legacy for the work. He enjoyed the friendship of such men as William Ellery Channing (1780–1842) and William S. Shaw [*qq.v.*], and he founded the "Belles Lettres Society" for young white men and was active in its administration. While in Boston he became engaged to the daughter of Paul Cuffe [*q.v.*], but the engagement was later broken. He was sent from Boston to England by friends as delegate of the Masonic lodge of Africans and probably for other reasons, as he had letters from prominent Americans. He at once stepped into English society, mingling with the nobility, meeting the King, and making the acquaintance of Wilberforce, who was at the time interesting himself in behalf of Hayti and the emperor, Christophe, and had been commissioned by Christophe to send teachers to Hayti.

Saunders was sent with others. He was entrusted with the task of organizing a school system on the English Lancastrian plan and was to aid in changing the religion of Hayti from Catholic to Protestant. In the process he was intimately connected with the family life of Christophe. In 1816 he introduced vaccination into Hayti under the direction of Wilberforce and personally vaccinated Christophe's children. He was sent back to England as messenger or envoy by Christophe, probably more than once, and memoirs of the period indicate that this honor added to his social prestige. While in England he published his first volume, *Haytian Papers* (1816), being a translation of laws of Hayti and the Code Henri with his own comments. The frontispiece is a striking engraving of Saunders, which was said by a contemporary to be a "perfect likeness." It shows a face of pronounced African characteristics with the air of a man of the world. In 1818 an American edition of this book was published in Boston by Bingham & Company, without the portrait. He apparently overstepped his authority in London, considering himself more of an ambassador than messenger, and was recalled by Christophe. We find him next in Philadelphia, then a center of activity and culture of the free colored people of America. There he served as lay reader for several months in the African church, later called the African Episcopal Church of St. Thomas and published *An Address . . . before the Pennsylvania Augustine Society* (1818) and *A Memoir . . . to the American Convention for promoting the Abolition of Slavery* (1818). He was a gifted man especially in the use of language. His manners were cultivated, and the stories of his life in England show him to have had a shrewd wit. That he enjoyed the attentions showered upon him is evident. The overthrow and suicide of Christophe in 1820 gave Saunders an opportunity to go back to Hayti under Boyer, and at his death he is spoken of as attorney general. He died at Port-au-Prince, Hayti.

[Dartmouth College Archives; William Bentley Fowle MSS., in possession of Mass. Hist. Soc., Boston; Schomberg Colls., N. Y. Pub. Lib.; records of Lebanon, Conn., and Thetford, Vt.; *Amer. Almanac . . . 1840* (1839), ed. by J. E. Worcester, p. 298; Vernon Loggins, *The Negro Author* (1931); Wm. Douglass, *Annals of St. Thomas' Church* (1862); O. D. Hine, *Early Lebanon* (1880), p. 40; *Emancipator,* July 4, 1839; spelling of name varies, on title page of *Haytian Papers* (ante) spelled Sanders and under portrait (*Ibid.*) spelled Saunders.]   M. B. S.

SAUNDERS, ROMULUS MITCHELL (Mar. 3, 1791–Apr. 21, 1867), congressman, diplomat, was born in Caswell County, N. C., the son of William and Hannah (Mitchell) Saunders. His mother died soon after his birth and the family moved to Sumner County, Tenn.

Romulus was sent back to North Carolina to be educated and, prepared for college at Caswell and Hyco academies, entered the University of North Carolina in 1809 and was a student there for two years. Returning to Tennessee, he studied law under Hugh L. White and was licensed in 1812. He then went back to his native state and settled in Milton. On Dec. 22, 1812, he married Rebecca Peine Carter, who died after having borne him three sons and two daughters; on May 26, 1823, he married Anna Heyes Johnson, the daughter of William Johnson [q.v.], associate justice of the Supreme Court of the United States, by whom he had two sons and four daughters.

Saunders entered public life in 1815 as a member of the North Carolina House of Commons. In 1816 he was a member of the state Senate but returned to the House in 1818 and served until 1821, being speaker in 1819 and 1820. Elected to Congress, he served three terms (1821-27). In 1820 and 1824 he supported William H. Crawford [q.v.] for president and voted for him when the election was thrown into the House of Representatives. In 1828 he was elected attorney general of North Carolina, occupying that office until 1831. In 1834 he was appointed a member of the commission on the French Spoliation claims, in connection with which he acquired considerable reputation. Elected a judge of the superior court in 1835, he resigned in 1840 to accept the Democratic nomination for governor. With his opponent, John M. Morehead [q.v.], Saunders engaged in the first statewide canvass, and although he proved himself the abler campaigner, he lost the election. The next year he was again elected to Congress and served two terms (1841-45). Here he proved himself an active partisan and won from John Quincy Adams the following characterization: "There is not a more cankered or venomous reptile in the country" (Memoirs of John Quincy Adams, 1876, XI, 197). In 1842 he was an unsuccessful candidate for the United States Senate. He was a delegate to the Democratic national convention of 1844 and moved the adoption of the two-thirds rule which defeated Van Buren and became a permanent part of Democratic nominating machinery.

On Feb. 25, 1846, President Polk appointed him minister to Spain and gave him a special commission to negotiate for the purchase of Cuba for $100,000,000. Saunders did not bring up the matter at once, the Amistad case and a prolonged discussion of Spanish debts to American citizens making the time inappropriate. He spent most of 1847 in Paris, leaving Thomas C. Reynolds, the

secretary, in charge of the legation. A quarrel arose between them in which Saunders appears clearly in the wrong but which led to the dismissal of Reynolds. In July 1848 Saunders broached the Cuban matter and in December received a curt refusal to discuss the question (House Executive Document 121, 32 Cong., 1 Sess., p. 57). He resigned May 1, 1849, and returned to Raleigh, which had been his residence since 1831. From 1850 to 1854 he represented Wake County in the House of Commons. In 1852 he was again unsuccessfully a candidate for the United States Senate, but was elected superior court judge, remaining on the bench until 1867. He was a member of the North Carolina code commission of 1852-54, and from 1819 to 1864 served as a trustee of the University of North Carolina. He had excellent abilities but lacked balance. His partisanship and his ceaseless quest for public office made enemies for him, but he always retained a large measure of popularity.

[S. A. Ashe, Biog. Hist. of N. C., vol. III (1905); J. H. Wheeler, Hist. Sketches of N. C. (1851), and Reminiscences and Memoirs of N. C. (1884); Alumni Hist. of the Univ. of N. C. (2nd ed., 1924), ed. by D. L. Grant; Biog. Dir. Am. Cong. (1928); The Works of James Buchanan (12 vols., 1908-11), ed. by J. B. Moore; Tri-Weekly Standard (Raleigh, N. C.), Apr. 25, 1867; N. C. Legislative Jours.; Cong. Globe; Instructions to Ministers, Spain, vol. XIV and Dispatches, Spain, vol. XXXV (MSS., State Dept. Archives).]

J. G. deR. H.

SAUNDERS, WILLIAM (Dec. 7, 1822– Sept. 11, 1900), horticulturist, landscape gardener, was born at St. Andrews, Scotland. He came of a family of gardeners and received a thorough practical training in the art, together with a course in horticulture, at the University of Edinburgh. In 1848, shortly after his marriage in England to Martha Mildwaters, he removed to America, settling at first in New Haven, Conn. Here he began a series of contributions that continued for nearly forty years to the leading horticultural periodicals of the time, Hovey's Magazine of Horticulture, the Horticulturist, the Farmer and Gardener, Philadelphia Florist and others. In 1854 he formed a partnership with Thomas Meehan [q.v.] in Philadelphia for the practice of landscape gardening. He designed the Clifton Park estate of Johns Hopkins and the Ross Winans place in Baltimore; Rose Hill Cemetery, Chicago, and a number of cemeteries and private estates.

In 1862 he was appointed superintendent of the experimental gardens of the newly created Department of Agriculture. He designed the grounds of the Department at Washington and had charge of their development until his death in 1900. In 1863 he designed the national cemetery at Gettysburg and in 1865, at the suggestion of General Grant, selected the site and designed the grounds of the Lincoln monument at Springfield, Ill. In addition to establishing conservatories and greenhouses for the study of plants economically important, he assembled for the Department of Agriculture and established on the Mall an extensive collection of trees and shrubs regarded as adapted to the conditions of the middle Atlantic tidewater. From about 1870 until the realignment of the Mall in 1931 this was considered the most comprehensive arboretum in North America south of the Arnold Arboretum near Boston. As a member of the parking commission, an advisory body created in 1871, he helped to develop the system of street tree planting used in the District of Columbia. He organized and directed the exhibits of the Department of Agriculture at the Centennial Exhibition in Philadelphia in 1876, the New Orleans exposition of 1884, and the Paris exposition of 1889. He was also a pioneer in the introduction of foreign plants. As early as 1866 he introduced the Australian *eucalyptus globulus* into California. In 1870 he imported from Russia and later distributed through the northern states scions of some three hundred varieties of Russian apples, one of which, Yellow Transparent, became a widely planted summer apple. From Japan he introduced the hardy trifoliate orange, the dominant understock for the Satsuma group of oranges, and in 1871 from Bahia, Brazil, the Washington Navel orange, which promptly became the leading commercial variety in California and gave strong impetus to the development of the citrus industry in the southwest.

Furthermore, he sensed the needs and desires of rural people and as early as 1855 outlined an organization for mutual help. One of the seven organizers of the order of Patrons of Husbandry, he wrote its constitution and preamble in 1867, and served as master of the national organization for the first six years. He wrote widely on general horticulture. His published papers include some three thousand titles, among them the first bulletin of the Department of Agriculture (1862), a report on the objects and aims of the United States propagating garden, with a catalogue of the plant material available for distribution.

[*Yearbook U. S. Dept. of Agriculture,* 1900, pp. 625–30, and other Dept. of Agriculture pubs.; L. H. Bailey, ed., *Standard Cyc. of Horticulture,* vol. III (1915); T. C. Atkeson, *Semi-Centennial Hist. of the Patrons of Husbandry* (1916); *Evening Star* (Washington, D. C.), Sept. 11, 1900; manuscript jour. and list of Saunders' important published papers and existing unpublished MSS. in lib. of Dept. of Agriculture, Washington, D. C.; personal acquaintance.]   W. A. T.

SAUNDERS, WILLIAM LAURENCE (July 30, 1835–Apr. 2, 1891), editor, historian, was born in Raleigh, N. C. His father was the Rev. Joseph Hubbard Saunders and his mother, Laura, daughter of Dr. Simmons J. Baker of Halifax County, N. C. Prepared for college at the Raleigh Academy, Saunders entered the University of North Carolina in 1850 and was graduated in 1854. He returned to study law under Judge William H. Battle [*q.v.*], was licensed in 1856, and received the degree of LL.B. in 1858. He began practice in Salisbury, N. C., where he also edited the *Salisbury Banner,* but in 1861 he volunteered for military service and during the war rose from the rank of private to that of colonel, at Appomattox being in command of the 46th North Carolina Regiment. He was twice wounded, both times seriously, and always thereafter suffered greatly from the results.

At the close of the war he settled in Florida. He had married, Feb. 3, 1864, Florida Cotten, daughter of John W. Cotten of Edgecombe County, N. C. She died in July 1865, and Saunders soon returned to North Carolina, settling at Chapel Hill, where he watched the course of Reconstruction with passionate interest. When conditions seemed no longer bearable, he assumed direction of the activities of the "Invisible Empire," or Ku Klux Klan, although he was never a regular member of it and was bound by no oath. He began to write regularly for the newspapers, and from 1872 to 1876 was one of the editors of the *Wilmington Journal.* In 1870 he was elected chief clerk of the Senate and held the place until 1874. During this period he was summoned to appear in Washington before the congressional committee which was investigating the Ku Klux activities. His friends urged him to leave the country but he refused and appeared in Washington, where he declined to answer any questions bearing in any way upon the Ku Klux and quietly defied the committee to punish him. He was badgered and threatened for several days without losing his calm poise, and was then released.

In 1876 he moved to Raleigh and with Peter M. Hale established the *Observer,* which he edited with great ability for three years, retiring then on account of ill health. In the same year he became secretary of state and retained that post until his death. During this period he was one of the most influential leaders in the Democratic party. He gave sound advice, planned campaigns, and edited the party handbooks. He played a large part in the reopening of the University of North Carolina, which had been closed by Reconstruction since 1870, and was a trustee from 1875 until his death and for most of that time secretary of the board of trustees. Saunders' greatest achievement, however, was his part in the publication of *The Colonial Records of North Carolina* (10 vols., 1886–90). His influence with Gov. T. J. Jarvis [*q.v.*] made the work possible, and he himself gave to the task of editing and publication eleven years of his life. Apart from the high value of these ten volumes in themselves, their influence in the state and elsewhere in stimulating historical research and the preservation of historical material has been very great.

Saunders was possessed of a keen, alert mind and excellent judgment. Modest, self-effacing, and unselfish, he had a deep passion for service. Quiet and retiring always, he was nevertheless widely popular. He died in his fifty-sixth year.

[S. A. Ashe, *Biog. Hist. of N. C.*, vol. IV (1906); A. M. Waddell, *The Life and Character of William L. Saunders* (1892), also pub. in the *News and Observer* (Raleigh), June 1, 1892; *Alumni Hist. of the Univ. of N. C.* (2nd ed., 1924), ed. by D. L. Grant; *House Report No. 22*, 42 Cong., 2 Sess., pt. 2, pp. 354–62; *Trinity Archive*, June 1896; obituary article in *News and Observer* (Raleigh), Apr. 2, 1891.]   J. G. deR. H.

SAUNDERS, WILLIAM LAWRENCE (Nov. 1, 1856–June 25, 1931), engineer, inventor, was born in Columbus, Ga., the son of the Rev. William Trebell and Eliza (Morton) Saunders. After graduating from the University of Pennsylvania in 1876 with the degree of B.S., he engaged in newspaper work in Philadelphia for two years but gave this up to become an engineer with the National Storage Company, Communipaw, N. J., in the construction of docks. This work involved considerable subaqueous rock excavation for which no satisfactory rock drilling equipment was available. In the course of his four years' work, however, Saunders developed a compressed-air drilling apparatus for submarine use, patented Jan. 9, 1883, which has been in general use in subaqueous work such as that in the Baku oil fields of Russia. Shortly after this, he joined the engineering staff of the Ingersoll-Sergeant Drill Company in Jersey City and had much to do with the development of the rock drill in its diversified forms. Patents granted to him between 1883 and 1898 dealt with the radialaxe system of coal mining, the apparatus for Ingersoll track and bore channelers and gadders for quarrying stone, and the pumping of liquids by compressed air. He was successively engineer, secretary, and vice-president of his company. On its reorganization as the Ingersoll-Rand Company in 1905, he became president and ultimately chairman of the board, an office he held at the time of his death.

Besides being a director in a number of business enterprises he was a government director and department chairman of the Federal Reserve Board of New York and a member of the district committee on capital issues, Federal Reserve Board. Under President Woodrow Wilson he served as a member of the New Jersey harbor commission, the New Jersey board of commerce and navigation, and as chairman of the United States naval consulting board. He was also a member of the advisory committee of the Federal Trade Commission and chairman of the industrial training committee of the National Civic Federation. He was twice mayor of North Plainfield, N. J., his residence for upwards of thirty years, and had long been prominent in New Jersey politics; he served as a member of the New Jersey State Committee, as Wilson's personal representative from New Jersey on the national campaign committee in 1916, and as a delegate to the Democratic National Convention in 1924. In December 1926, through the American Society for the Control of Cancer, he offered a prize of $50,000 for the discovery of the nature of human cancer and an equal amount for the discovery of a positive cure, but after two years, convinced of the futility of the search, he withdrew his offer. He also founded the medal awarded annually by the American Institute of Mining and Metallurgical Engineers in recognition of achievements in mining methods. Throughout his career he maintained his membership in such engineering societies as the American Institute of Mining and Metallurgical Engineers, of which he was president in 1915, and the United Engineering Society, of which he was president, trustee, and a member of the finance committee. He wrote on both engineering and political subjects, and was editor of *Compressed Air Magazine*. In 1903 he edited *Compressed Air Information*; in 1911 with R. T. Dana he published *Rock Drilling*, and in 1912 with G. H. Gilbert and L. I. Wightman *The Subways and Tunnels of New York*. Among his political articles were "Business and Politics and the Anti-Trust Laws," "Right and Strength in Equal Suffrage," and "Government Regulation of Commerce as Affecting Foreign Trade" (*New York Times*, post). He married Bertha Louise Gaston on August 4, 1886. At the time of his sudden death in Teneriffe, Canary Islands, while on a world tour, he was survived by two daughters.

[*Who's Who in America*, 1926–27; *Cassier's Mag.*, June 1907; *Mech. Engineering*, Aug. 1931; *Compressed Air Mag.*, Aug. 1931; *Engineering-News Record*, July 2, 1931; *Mining and Metallurgy*, Aug. 1931; obituary in *N. Y. Times*, June 26, 1931; Patent Office records.]   C. W. M.

SAUR, CHRISTOPHER [See SOWER, CHRISTOPHER].

SAVAGE, EDWARD (Nov. 26, 1761–July 6, 1817), painter, engraver, was born at Princeton, Mass., the second child of Seth and Lydia (Craige) Savage and a grandson of Edward Savage, of Huguenot descent, who emigrated from Ireland to Massachusetts in 1696. The younger Edward, according to a family tradition which is probably true, learned the goldsmith's trade, and thus probably received some practice in engraving. He was evidently intimate with Paul Revere (*Christian Science Monitor*, June 16, 1924). By 1789 he had attained such proficiency as a painter that he was commissioned by the president of Harvard College to paint a portrait of Washington. The latter recorded in his diary, Dec. 21, 1789: "Sat from ten to one o'clock for a Mr. Savage, to draw my Portrait for the University of Cambridge, in the State of Massachusetts." The picture was delivered at Cambridge probably in August 1790, the artist having in the meantime, while he was in New York, made for John Adams another Washington portrait—not, as has been asserted, a replica of the first one (Hart, *post*, p. 7).

Savage went in 1791 to London, where he is said to have had instruction from Benjamin West and where he engraved several plates in mezzotint and stipple. His journeying seems to have extended to Italy. Returning to the United States, he married at Boston, Oct. 13, 1794, Sarah Seaver, who survived him. His older brother John had become a successful merchant in Philadelphia and thither the young artist went in search of opportunities. In 1795 he exhibited at Philadelphia a panorama depicting London and Westminster in a circle. Leaving Philadelphia about 1801, he joined with Daniel Bowen in opening the New York Museum, exhibiting works of art and curiosities. These were later reassembled at Boston in the Columbian Museum, which, with most of its treasures, was burned in 1803, reërected and again burned in 1807, only to be re-inaugurated and continued until 1825 when it was absorbed by the New England Museum.

Savage's ability as a painter and engraver was disparaged by William Dunlap [*q.v.*] in an account (*post*) the inaccuracies of which have since been corrected (Hart, and Bayley and Goodspeed, *post*). The portraits of George and Martha Washington, now owned by the Boston Museum of Fine Arts, are certainly creditable paintings, and such mezzotints as Savage made after his own portraits in oil of Gen. Anthony Wayne, Dr. Benjamin Rush, and Thomas Jefferson, to say nothing of his familiar stippled plates of "Liberty" and "The Washington Fam-

ily," even though they do not evidence supreme technique, do not merit Dunlap's characterization of them as "wretched pictures."

Savage's name is not found in the Philadelphia directory after 1801. His fifth child was born at New York, Mar. 31, 1802; his sixth child, Aug. 22, 1805, at Princeton, Mass., where a seventh and an eighth also were born. Here Savage ended his days. Like many artists of his era, he gave much attention to mechanics and invention. He was a partner from 1809 onward in the Poignaud and Plant Cotton Factory at the nearby town of Lancaster (Blake, *post*, p. 296). Savage himself was effectively portrayed in profile by Saint-Mémin [*q.v.*] and in full face by himself. The self-portrait is in the Worcester Art Museum, where his engraved work is best preserved. In October 1921 the Massachusetts Historical Society, Boston, received from Miss Catharine Colvin of Lake Forest, Ill., who had them from Charles Henry Savage, grandson of the artist, an extensive collection of his miniature portraits, engravings, and other family souvenirs. To the Chicago Art Institute Miss Colvin had previously given an original Savage portrait of Washington, recorded (*Transcript, post*) as painted in 1793, though the artist in that year was in England.

[*A Descriptive Catalogue of an Exhibition of Early Engraving in America* (Mus. of Fine Arts, Boston, 1904); C. H. Hart, *Edward Savage, Painter and Engraver* (1905); Wm. Dunlap, *Hist. of the Rise and Progress of the Arts of Design in the U. S.* (1834); rev. ed., by F. W. Bayley and C. E. Goodspeed, 3 vols., 1918); Frank Weitenkampf, *Am. Graphic Art* (1912); F. E. Blake, *Hist. of the Town of Princeton, . . . Mass.* (1915), vol. I; *Boston Transcript*, Oct. 14, 1921.]

F. W. C.

SAVAGE, HENRY WILSON (Mar. 21, 1859–Nov. 29, 1927), real-estate operator and theatrical producer, was born at New Durham, N. H., the son of Capt. M. Henry and Betsey T. (Woodhouse) Savage. He received the degree of A.B. at Harvard in 1880 and entered the real-estate business in Boston, in which he prospered for more than fifteen years. The turning point in his career came soon after he built the Castle Square Theatre in Boston in 1894. He had no thought at the time of any connection with the stage as a business, the theatre being merely a realty investment. For a while, however, it did not prosper, and during the winter of 1895 the manager of a German company which was playing light operas there stole away on a boat for Europe, leaving his company stranded. The actors sought aid from Savage, and he decided to take over the company himself.

Shortly afterwards he organized his own company to give light opera in English at moderate prices. Thus began the Castle Square Opera Company, one of the most famous organizations of its kind that the American stage has known. It became a school for light opera stars, and whether in Boston or touring the country, as it did from coast to coast, it was everywhere exceedingly popular. It presented not only light opera, but began giving the more tuneful of the grand operas, such as *The Bohemian Girl, Maritana, Martha, Faust, Romeo and Juliet,* and *Der Freischutz,* all in English. Next, Savage daringly ventured upon *Tannhäuser, Lohengrin,* and *Die Meistersinger* in English. By this time the Castle Square Company had become virtually a double organization, one section for grand opera, the other for the lighter pieces. In 1900 Savage's office was in New York; he had taken over the Studebaker Theatre in Chicago, and his operetta troupe was disintegrating into various organizations for the production of newly written musical comedies. Several of these, such as *Tarantella* (1899), *King Dodo* (1900), *The Sultan of Sulu* (1902), and *The Prince of Pilsen* (1903), were first seen at the Studebaker. Meanwhile, from New York and Boston, he was launching *The Yankee Consul* (1903), *Peggy from Paris* (1903), *Woodland* (1904) and others. He also brought out George Ade's highly successful spoken comedies, *The County Chairman* (1903) and *The College Widow* (1904).

For a quarter of a century he was one of America's most successful producers, and with the most varied repertoire, embracing comedy both sung and spoken, grand opera, and an occasional serious drama. The Henry Savage Grand Opera Company continued for several years after 1900, most of the time playing at a top price of one dollar. He did not have the greatest of opera stars, but his company was well balanced, had good voices, and won high praise from critics. Some famous American singers, such as Grace Van Studdiford, Maude Lillian Berri, and Maude Lambert, were graduates from it. One of its singers became a star in Paris, and another in the Russian Royal Opera. In 1904 it gave Wagner's *Parsifal* for the first time in English, and received high acclaim. In 1906 it gave Puccini's *Madame Butterfly* its first American production, also in English; and in 1911 the same composer's *The Girl of the Golden West*. One of the cleverest strokes of Savage's career was his capture of the American rights to Franz Lehar's operetta, *The Merry Widow,* which he first presented in America in 1907, and which scored the most enormous success in light-opera history. It ran in New York and elsewhere for several

years; women's hats and toilet articles were named in its honor, and its lilting waltz songs were played and whistled in every hamlet on the continent, as well as all over the world. In 1921 Savage staged a beautiful revival of this play, with stars in all the principal rôles. Another of his remarkable productions was that of *Everywoman,* a modern imitation of the medieval morality plays, first presented in 1910, and on tours for several years thereafter. He also introduced the Hungarian dramatist Ferenc Molnar to American audiences, presenting his play, *The Devil,* in 1908 with George Arliss in the leading rôle. Some others of his productions were *Madame X, Along Came Ruth, Easy Dawson, The Sho-Gun, Excuse Me, Tom Jones, The Galloper, Cornered, The Little Damozel, Shavings, Mary Jane's Pa, Miss Patsy, Pom-Pom, Have a Heart, Little Boy Blue, The Love Cure, Sari, Head Over Heels, Lady Billy,* and *The Clinging Vine.* His list is notable for wholesomeness and high quality. His last production was *Lass o' Laughter* in 1925. On Oct. 24, 1889, Savage married Alice Louise Batcheler of Boston, and two children survived him. He was long a director of the National Association of Theatrical Producing Managers, and was its president from 1907 to 1909.

[*Who's Who in America,* 1926–27; *Who's Who in Music and Drama,* 1914; *N. Y. Times,* Nov. 30, Dec. 2, 1927; *World* (N. Y.), Nov. 30, 1927; *N. Y. Herald-Tribune,* Nov. 30, 1927; *Boston Transcript,* Nov. 29, 1927; "Grand Opera in English," in *The Theatre,* Feb. 1904; *Robinson Locke Dramatic Collection,* N. Y. Public Lib.; *The New Yorker,* Dec. 10, 1927.] A. F. H.

SAVAGE, JAMES (July 13, 1784–Mar. 8, 1873), antiquary, was born in Boston, one of the eleven children of Habijah and Elizabeth (Tudor) Savage. His father was a merchant descended from Thomas Savage who emigrated from England to Boston about 1635. He was educated at Derby Academy at Hingham, Mass., Washington Academy at Machias, Me., and Harvard College, where he graduated in 1803. He made a voyage to the West Indies in 1805, after which he studied law in the offices of Isaac Parker [*q.v.*] and others till he was admitted to the bar in 1807. He prepared for the press and compiled an index for the *Charters and General Laws of the Colony and Province of Massachusetts Bay,* published by the state in 1814. In 1816, when the third volume of John Winthrop's history of New England was found in manuscript, he was entrusted by the Massachusetts Historical Society with the duty of copying and annotating it. He decided to edit the whole work instead of the new volume only, and his edition, *The History of New England from 1630 to 1649,* appeared in two volumes in 1825–26. Another, with additions and corrections, was issued by him in 1853. This was an important piece of antiquarian scholarship, and he did much other miscellaneous writing and editing, for he was very industrious. He is perhaps best known for his *Genealogical Dictionary of the First Settlers of New England, Showing Three Generations of Those Who Came before May, 1692, on the basis of Farmer's Register.* This work, involving enormous labor, occupied him seventeen years, and was published in four volumes between 1860 and 1862. It is a standard work for the American genealogist.

He happened to see a plan of a London savings bank, and he at once took up the project of providing something similar for Boston. His energy and persistence overcame apathy and opposition, and in 1816 the Massachusetts legislature incorporated the Provident Institution for Savings, one of the first savings banks incorporated in the United States and perhaps the first in the world to be established by the act of a public law-making body. In 1818 he was active in contending that the law made mandatory the provision of elementary schools, and, when a town meeting adopted his view in spite of opposition, he served six years on the body charged with the duty of putting the new schools in operation. From 1811 to 1862 he held a great variety of offices imposing responsibility and labor. He was several times elected to the lower house and to the Senate of the Massachusetts legislature, in addition to service in the Executive Council and as delegate to the Massachusetts constitutional convention in 1820. He also served in the common council, board of aldermen, and school committee of Boston; and he was for fifteen years a member of the board of overseers of Harvard University. He was one of the founders of the Boston Athenaeum, was long active in and for a time president of the Massachusetts Historical Society, and was connected with many other organizations or institutions of a public or semi-public character. In all of these he exerted influence and enjoyed respect, for, though given to rather extreme opinions and violent expression of them, this did not obscure the value of his services. In April 1823 he married Elizabeth Otis (Stillman) Lincoln, the widow of James Otis Lincoln of Hingham, Mass., and the daughter of George Stillman, of Machias, Me. They had one son and three daughters. Savage died in Boston.

[*Letters of James Savage to his Family* (1906); Charles Deane, *Brief Memoir of James Savage, Prepared for the . . . Amer. Acad. of Arts and Sciences* (1874); *Tribute of the Mass. Hist. Soc. to the Memory of . . . James Savage* (1873); J. S. Loring, *The Hundred Boston Orators* (1852), pp. 353–60; *One Hundred*

Years of Savings Bank Service; a Brief Account of Provident Institution for Savings (1916); *New England Hist. and Geneal. Register,* Jan. 1847; *Boston Morning Journ.,* Mar. 8, 1873.]   S. G—n.

SAVAGE, JOHN (Dec. 13, 1828–Oct. 9, 1888), journalist, was born in Dublin, Ireland, where he attended the art school of the Royal Dublin Society, winning the silver medal of the society in 1847. He became infatuated with the "Young Ireland" movement and, when the government closed the art school because of student agitation, he became active in plotting against the authorities. In April 1848 he and J. De C. Young issued an inflammatory publication, the *Patriot,* which was promptly suppressed. Two months later he promoted the *Irish Tribune,* issued by the "Students' Club" to further the old views of Mitchel toward Irish independence. Late in July he fled from Dublin, assisted in the abortive insurrection of September, and then sought refuge in the United States. He arrived in New York City on Nov. 7, 1848. There he met William Erigena Robinson [*q.v.*], who presented him to Horace Greeley [*q.v.*]; within a week Savage was installed as a proof-reader on the *New York Tribune.* Beginning in January 1854 he was the literary editor of the *Citizen,* a newspaper founded by John Mitchel [*q.v.*], which continued publication for one year. He married Louise Gouverneur, a daughter of Captain Samuel Chester Reid [*q.v.*] in August 1854 and for the next three years was hard pressed to earn a living by free-lance journalism. He published in 1856 his *'98 and '48: the Modern Revolutionary History and Literature of Ireland.*

In 1857 he went to Washington and there became the leading editorial writer on the *States,* the organ of Stephen A. Douglas. In Washington he wrote a mediocre tragedy, *Sybil,* produced in various cities in 1858 and published in 1865. *Our Living Representative Men* was a feeble potboiler published in 1860 to take advantage of the imminent presidential campaign; it contained hasty sketches of those men prominently mentioned for the presidential succession in 1861. One of these sketches was elaborated and published in 1866 as *The Life and Public Services of Andrew Johnson.* At the outbreak of the Civil War he was urged to remove the *States,* of which he had become part owner, into one of the southern states. He refused and is said to have joined the 69th Regiment under General Corcoran and to have served with it throughout the war. His most important contribution to the Union cause, however, was a number of tuneful verses designed to inspirit the northern forces. The most successful of these, "The Starry Flag" (later published in a collection of verse by Savage entitled *Faith and Fancy,* 1864), was written on board the United States transport *Marion* during May 1861 as she sailed up the Potomac through the masked batteries of the enemy.

In the spring of 1864 he visited Cuba and in June of that year accepted a position as leading editorial writer on the *New Orleans Times,* remaining until March 1867. It was then that the news of the Fenian movement reached America. Savage's old revolutionary enthusiasm flared up; he offered his services to the cause and came to New York City, where he wrote and lectured on behalf of the Irish. His prominence resulted in his becoming in 1867 the chief executive of the Fenian Brotherhood in America. In this capacity he toured the United States, organizing Irish societies and collecting funds for the Fenian cause; especially successful was his visit to California in 1870. In 1868 he wrote *Fenian Heroes and Martyrs,* which had been preceded by *Poems* (1867). In 1869 he was proposed by President Johnson as United States consul at Leeds, but a Senate committee reported adversely and the matter was tabled. In his declining years he was popular as a lecturer before Catholic colleges and fraternal organizations. Several years before his death he moved to Scranton, Pa. It was at his summer home at Laurelside, near Spragueville, Pa., that he died in 1888, survived by his wife and an adopted daughter.

[*Dict. of Nat. Biog.* (1921–22 ed.); D. J. O'Donoghue, *The Poets of Ireland* (1912); *The Irish Cause on the Pacific: John Savage in Cal.* (1870); obituaries in *N. Y. Tribune, N. Y. Times,* Oct. 11, 1888; information from Hugh O'Reilly and Miles Bryan of New York City.]   F. M.

SAVAGE, MINOT JUDSON (June 10, 1841–May 22, 1918), Unitarian clergyman, author, and lecturer, was born in Norridgewock, Me., the fourth son of James Lambert and Anne Swett (Stinson) Savage, and a descendant of James Savage who came from England to Boston in 1715. Amid circumstances of severe poverty and labor, Minot began attending district school at four years of age. His boyhood was marked by physical infirmity, intermittent schooling, and religious excitement, the last being due to the interest of his parents in Methodist class meetings (though his father was by conviction a Free-Will Baptist) and revivalism. At the age of thirteen, after six weeks of "horror and fear of hell," he joined the church. After finishing high school, he taught in Newark, Del., and Norridgewock, Me., then entered Bangor Theological Seminary, graduating in June 1864. He was at once ordained to the Congregational ministry and on Aug. 29 of the same year married, in Harvard, Mass., Ella Augusta Dodge, sailing with

her in September, via Panama, as a missionary to San Mateo, Cal. He soon transferred his work to Grass Valley, where his ability in preaching, writing, and lecturing began to attract notice. Returning to the East to assist his parents, in 1867 he was settled over the Congregational Church, Framingham, Mass.

In 1869 he removed to Missouri, where he became pastor of the First Congregational Church of Hannibal. Here he soon developed the largest body of that faith in the state. In the meantime, however, he became conscious of growing heterodoxy of belief. A study of church history, Biblical criticism, science, and evolution made it impossible for him longer to hold the old theories. After a severe mental struggle and in spite of the willingness of prominent Congregational churches in Chicago and Indiana to call him, in September 1873 he became minister of the Third Unitarian Church of Chicago. After a year of most acceptable work there, he went to the pulpit of the Church of the Unity, Boston, where he entered on the most influential and productive period of his ministry.

The circle of his hearers, though always large, was not so numerous as that of the readers of his sermons, published for thirty years in tract form and periodically collected in books, of which *The Religion of Evolution* (1876) is perhaps the most distinctive and historically significant. While not the first American theologian to discern and to define the influence of the Darwinian hypothesis on religion, Savage was the first American preacher to attain such prominence and popularity as to bring the issue squarely and clearly to the attention of the Protestant world, especially its clergy. His insistent message was that a frank acceptance of the new world view necessitated by the theory of evolution in science, social philosophy, and religious culture, enhanced and illuminated the true values of Christian faith and ethics rather than destroyed them; though, of course, obsolete and non-essential points suffered by being disclosed as such. His persuasive and eloquent presentation of evolutionist propositions and corollaries, as well as those of Biblical criticism and comparative religion, performed an invaluable service in negotiating understanding and sympathy between Protestantism and science. This service was performed not only by pulpit work but by a prolific output of books, and by lectures and addresses in America and England.

In September 1896 he became minister of the Church of the Messiah, New York City (now the Community Church), where the crowded congregations and sermonic publicity of the Boston period were repeated. To the advocacy of evolutionist optimism and of humanitarian reform, Savage now added that of spiritualistic faith in personal survival after death (see his *Life Beyond Death,* 1899; *Can Telepathy Explain?* 1902). The strenuousness of his exertions brought on Mencken's disease, in spite of which he preached the conference sermon for the International Congress of Religious Liberals, Geneva, 1905. In 1906 failing health necessitated his retirement from the active ministry and the succeeding twelve years of his life were spent in rest, travel, and publication. He died in Boston and his ashes are buried in Mount Auburn Cemetery, Cambridge. Three of his children survived him, a fourth, Philip Henry Savage [*q.v.*], having died in 1899.

As a preacher, he spoke without manuscript, fluently and impressively. His diction was simple but apt, his presentation lucid and logical. He usually addressed the understanding of his hearers rather than the sentiments, yet his own feelings of faith, compassion, reverence, and hope were deep and strong, and occasionally took command of his thought with moving effect. His faith involved such conceptions as the goodness of life, the friendliness of the universe, the significance of man as epitome and culmination of the cosmic processes; and the competence of man, by virtue of his growing intelligence and ethical impulses to adjust himself successfully to cosmic "laws." Conserving the traditional values of Christian piety, trust in Providence, love to an immanent God and love to man, faith in immortality, consecrated exertion against evil in self and society, he added a powerful optimistic emphasis upon human progress.

Typical of his published works, in addition to those previously cited, are *The Morals of Evolution* (1880), *The Evolution of Christianity* (1892), *Social Problems* (1886), *Beliefs about the Bible* (1883), *The Passing and the Permanent in Religion* (1901), *Poems* (1882), and *Hymns* (1898). Several of his hymns have come into general use. To *My Creed* (1887) he affixed a brief spiritual autobiography.

[*Who's Who in America,* 1918–19; *Christian Reg.,* May 30, 1918; *Unity* (Chicago), June 6, 1918; *Boston Transcript,* May 22, 1918; *Springfield Republican,* May 24, 1918; information from a son, the Rev. Maxwell Savage.]   C. H. L.

SAVAGE, PHILIP HENRY (Feb. 11, 1868–June 4, 1899), poet, was born in North Brookfield, Mass., second of the four children of the Rev. Minot Judson Savage [*q.v.*] and Ella Augusta (Dodge) Savage. His early associations, clerical and literary, offered little support to the skeptical vigor of his mind and the pagan ampli-

tude of his senses and emotions. The rugged beauty of New England nature, however, meant much to him from the start.

After a few years in the English High School at Boston, and before going to college, he tried traveling salesmanship, oddly mingling, in his letters home, news of the shoe business with descriptions of sunsets and red-winged blackbirds. He entered Harvard College at twenty-one (an age when most men are leaving it), and was graduated with the class of 1893. After that he tried a year of the study of divinity, and another of free-lance poetry writing, before settling at last, in 1895–96, to systematic technical study of his chosen art while serving as instructor in the English department at Harvard. He had himself a keen and painful sense of the difficulty he found in orienting himself to his work. As late as 1895, less than four years from his death, and after the publication of his first book, *First Poems and Fragments* (1895), he wrote a friend: "I see other men in full career, ... their power of expression running even with their conception, —while I labor and fail. The paltry inspiration that is in some of the *First Poems* does not comfort me. Where are power and beauty? Where, indeed, are simple purity and grace?" (Mason, *post,* p. xxx.) None the less he was slowly finding himself. Already from college he had written his sister Gertrude: "What is true and beautiful is absolute; and what is stupendous and gorgeous and impressive and wonderful is inferior to it" (*Ibid.*). Already he was consciously forming that noble, pure, and exacting taste which is his most distinctive trait, and which gives his best work its incomparably delicate beauty. In one of his note-books he thus truly analyzed himself: "Master of a little beauty which, because it is born and bearer of the divine essence, I will cherish at the expense of most of the concerns of life" (Mason, *post,* p. xxvi). The whole of his short life, outwardly uneventful, was a search for the frail but perfect beauty he was destined to express. In that laborious search he slowly disentangled himself from one after another of the customary interests, the inherited ideas, the traditional beliefs and conventional ways of expression that were not strictly his own.

His last few years were passed as secretary to the librarian of the Boston Public Library. Their most important event was the publication of his *Poems* in 1898. Fine as was the quality of that slender volume, containing a few lyrics possibly as perfect as any in English, the quantity of his best work still remained small when he was stricken with appendicitis and died at the Massachusetts General Hospital in Boston, at the age of thirty-one.

His life was necessarily one rather of high promise than of full achievement. Yet it was long enough to carry him from the instinctive youthful imitation of conventional models to the intellectual independence of the poems "God, thou art good, but not to me" and "What hard, bright Spirit sits beyond the stars?," to the mellow humanity of "A Wreath of Buds and Lavender," and to the poignant simplicity of the verses which may be taken as his epitaph:

> "Brother, Time is a thing how slight!
> Day lifts and falls, and it is night.
> Rome stands an hour, and the green leaf
> Buds into being bright and brief.
> For us, God has at least in store
> One shining moment, less or more.
> Seize, then, what mellow sun we may,
> To light us in the darker day."

[*The Poems of Philip Henry Savage* (1901), ed. by Daniel Gregory Mason, reprints the two volumes published during Savage's lifetime and offers a biographical and critical Introduction. See also *Who's Who in America*, 1899; *Harvard College: Record of the Class of 1893* (1899); *Christian Reg.*, June 8, 1899; *Boston Transcript*, June 5, 1899.]   D. G. M.

SAVAGE, THOMAS STAUGHTON (June 7, 1804–Dec. 29, 1880), Protestant Episcopal clergyman, physician, missionary, naturalist, was born in upper Middletown (now Cromwell), Conn., son of Josiah and Mary (Roberts) Savage, and a descendant of John Savage who was made a freeman of Middletown in 1654. Although named Thomas Jefferson by his parents, upon beginning his theological studies he dropped the latter name because he believed Jefferson was an infidel, and substituted that of Staughton. His father, who had served as a youth in the Revolutionary army, was a ship-owner, largely interested in the West Indian trade, in which he made a considerable fortune; he was part owner of the celebrated brig *Commerce* of Hartford, wrecked in 1815 on the coast of the Sahara. Thomas' mother was the daughter of Dr. Aaron Roberts, a surgeon in the Revolution. Although of Congregationalist ancestry, young Savage joined the Protestant Episcopal Church while a student at Yale College, from which he was graduated in 1825. Entering the Yale Medical School in 1830, he received the degree of M.D. in 1833. Following his graduation, he undertook an extensive journey, traveling west to Cincinnati, south to New Orleans, and northward along the Atlantic Coast. He then entered the Theological Seminary in Virginia, at Alexandria, from which he graduated; and on Oct. 23, 1836, was ordained priest.

As the first missionary sent to Africa under the auspices of the Protestant Episcopal Church,

Savage arrived at Cape Palmas, Liberia, on Dec. 25, 1836, and established a mission on Mount Vaughan. The next year he visited native villages along the Cavally River, Monrovia, and the "slave factories" at Gallinas River. Serious ill health forced him to return to America, in 1838, where he married Susan Metcalf at Fredericksburg, Va. With his wife he sailed again for Africa and arrived at Cape Palmas on Jan 23, 1839. His wife died in Liberia three months later. In 1840 he took an easterly voyage as far as Akkra, stopping at many points along the Slave, Ivory, and Gold coasts. On June 2, 1842, he married Maria Chapin of Newbury, Vt., who also died the same year from effects of the Liberian climate. Again, in June 1843, Savage was obliged to return home for rest and recuperation. After a year's absence, he sailed a third time for Africa on May 18, 1844, accompanied by four missionaries, including Elizabeth Rutherford of Providence, R. I., whom he married at Cape Palmas on Dec. 18, 1844. In January 1845 they were transferred to the newly opened station at Fishtown, Liberia, remaining there two years. Savage finally resigned from his missionary work, on account of ill health, in December 1846, but did not sail from Cape Palmas until Mar. 3, 1847.

On the way he was detained in the Gaboon River and spent the month of April at the house of Rev. J. L. Wilson, a Presbyterian missionary. Here he saw the skull of a large ape which he recognized as different from the chimpanzee. Seeking further evidence, he obtained, through chiefs of the Mpongwe tribe, four skulls and other bones of this animal which proved to be the largest of the great apes, the gorilla, previously unknown. Upon his arrival in America, he made this anthropoid known to science, publishing "Notice of the External Characters and Habits of *Troglodytes gorilla,* a New Species of Orang from the Gaboon River" (*Boston Journal of Natural History,* December 1847). Almost equally important was his paper on the chimpanzee, "Observations on the External Characters and Habits of *Troglodytes niger*" (*Ibid.,* April 1843, January 1844) in which he made the earliest step toward the scientific understanding of this animal's behavior, a subject that has now become almost a special branch of psychology. Hardly less interesting are his "Observations on the Species of *Termitidae* of West Africa, Described by Smeathman as *Termes bellicosus* and by Linnaeus as *Termes fatalis*" (*Proceedings of the Academy of Natural Sciences of Philadelphia,* vol. IV, 1850) and "The Driver Ants cf Western Africa" (*Ibid.*).

For three years following his return to America, Savage served parishes in Mississippi and Alabama. From 1851 to 1861, and from 1865 to 1867, he lived at Pass Christian, Miss. Removing North in 1868, he was appointed associate secretary of the Episcopal Board of Missions, and from 1869 until his death, he was rector of the Church of the Ascension in Rhinecliff, New York.

[C. C. Adams, *Middletown Upper House . . . 1650 to 1800* (1908); W. A. R. Goodwin, *Hist. of the Theological Sem. in Va.* (2 vols., 1923–24); E. F. Henning, *Hist. of the African Mission of the Protestant Episcopal Church in the U. S.* (1850); *Obit. Record Grads. Yale Coll.*, 1881; *Cat. of Scientific Papers (1800–1863) . . . Pub. by the Royal Soc. of London*, vol. V (1871); *Spirit of Missions*, vol. I (1836) to vol. XVI (1851); *The Churchman*, Jan. 15, 1881; information from family.]

R. K.

SAVERY, WILLIAM (1721–May 1787), cabinet maker, was almost unknown until more than a century and a quarter after his death, although his son William Savery [*q.v.*] had attained distinction before he died, and it is difficult to find the simplest facts about his birth and early life. While he was married, according to the records of the Society of Friends, to Mary Peters, the daughter of Reese Peters, in Philadelphia on Apr. 19, 1746, the records of the Monthly Meeting of that city make no mention of his entrance either into the Society of Friends or of his membership in that Meeting. He is believed to have gone to Philadelphia about 1740, and he is known to have served as assessor of the central wards of that city in 1754 and to have been an agent and collector of taxes for the guardians of the poor of Philadelphia in 1767. The records of the Monthly Meeting show him to have been the father of eleven children, and that he was buried May 28, 1787, when his age was recorded as 65 years. His will, which is dated 9 mo, 8, 1783, was probated Sept. 3, 1787, and in this document he describes himself as "joiner and chair maker." In the Francis White's Philadelphia Directory (1785) he is described as "chair maker."

The discovery of a little printed business label, containing his name and address, attached to a fine specimen of furniture, which is now in the Manor House at Van Cortlandt Park in New York, marked the beginning of his modern fame as a craftsman. In the Palmer Collection of the Metropolitan Museum of Art of New York there are no fewer than three highboys, two lowboys, two, possibly four, tables, and a secretary-desk. These specimens are so extraordinary in the artistic character of their workmanship, that their maker was alluded to as "one of our greatest colonial cabinet-makers" (Halsey, *post*, p. 251).

His shop in Philadelphia, according to his label, was "at the sign of the chair, a little below the Market, in Second Street, Philadelphia" (*Ibid.*), which location, through deeds, has been identified with the present property, No. 17 South Second St. That he did a prosperous business is shown by various documents, which record that in 1766 he received £52 a year as a rental of one house, and that in 1780 he paid taxes on a property valuation of $46,000. While nothing is known of his education or training in his craft, his designs reveal his indebtedness to those early books of design, published in the eighteenth century in England, such as the several volumes by Thomas Chippendale and by Robert Manwaring. The examples of his work in the Palmer Collection prove him to have been an artist. He is supposed to have been self-educated in his trade, but, while undoubtedly owing an obligation to books of design, including those of Batty Langley, he was sufficiently an artist to naturalize and interpret them in an original manner. There is considerable carving in his mahogany pieces, but for the great part his furniture has simple and pure lines, making for dignity and richness. His work, probably with the work of others also, has caused the Philadelphia furniture of the colonial period, especially from 1760 to 1775, to be highly regarded by experts, as "exhibiting the greatest degree of elaboration and ornateness found in American furniture" (Nutting, *post*, p. 452). Skilled artist, as he undoubtedly was, he did not feel it beneath his dignity to repair chairs, and do other odd jobs pertaining to joinery; and it is said that there still is in existence in his handwriting, a bill for sixteen shillings, charged for making a chicken-coop (Hornor, *post*, p. 16). Regarding himself as primarily a chair maker, he excelled in the manufacture of this article of furniture. Some of his chairs, which have been identified, are of great beauty and simplicity, all of them showing an English tendency, but with the added Savery touch that gives them an independent character.

[Records of the Philadelphia Monthly Meeting in the collection of the Penn. Hist. Soc.; A. W. Savary, *A Geneal. and Biog. Record of the Savery Families* (1893); A. H. Savery and F. R. Taylor, *Geneal. and Brief Biog. of the Savery Family of Philadelphia* (1911); F. R. Taylor, *Life of William Savery of Philadelphia, 1750–1804* (1925); R. T. H. Halsey, "William Savery the Colonial Cabinet Maker and his Furniture," *Bulletin of the Metropolitan Museum*, Dec. 1918; W. M. Hornor, Jr., "William Savery, Chair-maker and Joiner," *Bulletin of the Pa. Museum*, Feb. 1928; Wallace Nutting, *Furniture Treasury*, vol. III (1933).]

J. J.

SAVERY, WILLIAM (Sept. 14, 1750 o. s.– June 19, 1804), Quaker preacher, was born at Philadelphia, Pa., the son of William [*q.v.*] and

Mary (Peters) Savery. His mother was of Welsh extraction and his father of French Huguenot. The latter was a cabinet maker of Philadelphia, the producer of some notable pieces of colonial furniture. The younger William served seven years as a tanner's apprentice near Philadelphia, during which time he met Sarah Evans who, on Nov. 19, 1778, became his wife. As a master tanner he operated his own tanneries in Philadelphia and apparently prospered in the business, although at times his absence from home on religious journeys left the burden of affairs on others.

On two rather notable occasions he was present, with other Friends, during treaty negotiations with the Indians. One such occasion was the fruitless attempt, in 1793 near Detroit, to make peace with the western Indians; another, more successful in its outcome, was the council of 1794 with the Six Nations at Canandaigua, N. Y. The report of Savery and his companions concerning the latter occasion led the Friends of Philadelphia into an extensive missionary work among the Seneca Indians.

Aside from his journeys to the Indian country, Savery traveled much "in the ministry" at home and abroad. He visited Quaker centers in various parts of the United States, preaching frequently to large audiences. From 1796 to 1798 he was absent from home, in company with a few other Friends, on a religious pilgrimage to Europe. He visited many of the German states, and preached to the Germans in their own language, apparently with considerable effect. In Holland and France the travelers also found Friends and held meetings with them and with others. In Paris Savery and one of his companions, David Sands, met Thomas Paine, who was born a Friend, but who proved to be not at all amenable to the religious admonitions of his Quaker visitors. Savery also toured Ireland twice in the years 1797–98. The power of his preaching was best exemplified in his meetings in England, where he felt especially called to address those who were not Friends. His fame became so great there that he often spoke to audiences of hundreds and even of a thousand or more people. The buildings were at times crowded to suffocation so that persons in the audience fainted and had to be carried out; yet his hearers would remain quietly through a discourse lasting from one to two hours and were frequently melted to tears by his appeal. The outstanding event of his ministry was the conversion of Elizabeth Gurney (later Fry), whose subsequent ministry to prisoners and influence on prison reform are well known. At the time of Savery's visit to England

she was a rather giddy young girl, very vain and stylish for a Quakeress; but, as she herself testified: "He has caused me to feel a little religion. I have *felt* there is a *God*. I loved the man as if almost he were sent from heaven" (Taylor, *post*, p. 430). She continued under the influence of Savery while he remained in England, and received an impression that changed the whole current of her life.

The preacher who exhibited this remarkable power was a man of average height and of good figure, although somewhat inclined to corpulency. His hearers frequently spoke of his melodious voice, and an English newspaper, the *Bath Chronicle,* after referring to his "good sense, fluency, and even eloquence," added: "He is a man of prepossessing appearance and address, mild and persuasive in his language and manners, and unusually liberal in all his sentiments" (Taylor, p. 424). The most eventful years of his life were past when, in 1798, he ended his work in Europe and returned to Philadelphia. In his home city he carried on his former business, rendered great service in some of the yellow fever scourges of those years, and pursued his religious activities until his death, apparently from dropsy, at the age of fifty-four years.

[The chief secondary authority is F. R. Taylor, *Life of William Savery* (1925); the chief manuscript source is Savery's journal in the possession (1931) of F. R. Taylor, Cheltenham, Pa.; some manuscript and much printed material are at Friends' Lib., Euston Road, London; in the printed version of the journal, *A Jour. of the Life, Travels, and Religious Labors of William Savery* (1837 and later eds.) the reader must allow for large editorial liberties; there are many editions of Savery's sermons, as set down in shorthand at the time of delivery; also *Some Remarks . . .* (1797) by Savery, disapproving the practice of thus reproducing Quaker sermons, which were delivered *ex tempore*; see also, Joseph Smith, *A Descriptive Cat. of Friends' Books* (1867), II, 538–39; A. W. Savary, *A Geneal. and Biog. Record of the Savery Families* (1893); *Poulson's American Daily Advertiser*, June 20, 1804.]   R. W. K.

SAWYER, LEICESTER AMBROSE (July 28, 1807–Dec. 29, 1898), clergyman, Biblical scholar, was born in Pinckney, Lewis County, N. Y., the son of Jonathan and Lucy (Harper) Sawyer. His father was a wagon maker and a soldier of the War of 1812, who died in the service. Leicester was prepared for college privately and graduated as valedictorian of his class at Hamilton College, Clinton, N. Y., in 1828. After a year spent in teaching at Clinton and Philadelphia, he entered Princeton Theological Seminary, from which he was graduated in 1831. He was licensed by the Presbytery of Watertown that same year and on Feb. 23, 1832, was ordained.

After serving several churches in Massachusetts and New York, he became, June 1835, pastor of the North (now United) Congregational Church, New Haven, Conn. Although his pastorate there was attended by marked success, he resigned at the close of two years on account of delicate health and assumed charge of the recently formed Park Street (now Dwight Place) Church in the same city. Retiring from the latter position in 1840, he became president of Central College, Columbus, Ohio. From 1843 to 1854 he was successively stated supply or pastor of Presbyterian churches at Central College and Monroeville, Ohio, and Sacketts Harbor, N. Y. From 1854 to 1859 he was pastor of the Congregational Church at Westmoreland, N. Y., at the end of which time, on account of changes in his theological views, he obtained a letter of retirement from his denomination with the standing of an independent Christian minister. After serving as pastor of the Second (South) Unitarian Church of Hingham, Mass., for the year 1859–60, he retired to Whitesboro, Oneida County, N. Y., where he spent the remainder of his life. From 1868 to 1883 he was night editor of the *Utica Morning Herald,* preparing also for that paper a weekly column headed "Religious Intelligence."

Sawyer was an accomplished classical scholar and a competent and conscientious student of the Bible, in the original languages of which he was well versed. He was one of the earliest American scholars to apply to the study of the Scriptures those literary and historical methods which were later known as the "higher criticism." He translated practically the entire Bible, the work, which appeared in sections at various times, being both a translation and an analytical study. He had the satisfaction of knowing that some of his interpretations which were much criticized at the time were supported by the Revision Committee of 1881. His most noteworthy work in the Old Testament field was that on the Prophets, in which he set forth the then revolutionary conclusion that they contained no reference to Jesus as the Messiah. He published two translations of the New Testament, and in his critical studies reached the conclusion that Jesus was merely a social reformer and that the only genuine portions of the New Testament were five epistles of Paul. The second of these translations, issued in 1891, had a rearrangement of the books, putting what Sawyer regarded as the genuine epistles first and the Gospels last, and an accompanying treatise devoted to an explanation and a defense of this arrangement.

The following are his more important works: *Baptism by Affusion and Sprinkling* (1838);

The Children of Believers Entitled to Baptism (1838) ; *A Critical Exposition of Mental Philosophy* (1839) ; *The New Testament Translated from the Original Greek* (1858) ; *The Holy Bible Translated and Arranged, with Notes* (3 vols., 1860–62) ; *Daniel, with Its Apocryphal Additions Translated and Arranged* (1864) ; *The New Testament Translated from the Original Greek* (1891). Sawyer was a well-equipped scholar and an earnest seeker after truth. Although he dealt with matters that were highly controversial, he never sought controversy nor attacked those who disagreed with him. On Sept. 26, 1832, he married Pamelia Bert Bosworth of Smithville, N. Y., who died in 1881. Seven of their ten children survived their parents.

[*Hamilton Lit. Mag.,* Mar. 1899; *Necrological Report ... Princeton Theological Sem.,* 1899; *Utica Morning Herald,* Dec. 30, 1898; information from a former colleague on the *Utica Morning Herald.*]   F. T. P.

SAWYER, LEMUEL (1777–Jan. 9, 1852), congressman, author, was the youngest of the nine children of Lemuel and Mary (Taylor) Sawyer of Camden County, N. C. Bereft in early life of both parents, he attended local country schools and Flatbush Academy on Long Island, 1793–96. During residence of more than a year in Philadelphia with his brother-in-law, Dempsey Burges, a member of Congress, he devoted irregular study to mathematics and developed habits of extravagance and fondness for gay society which beset him throughout life. Returning to Camden County in 1797, he was both unhappy and unsuccessful in the management of his farm. He early manifested a strong interest in politics, reading, and literary production. In 1799 he attended the University of North Carolina, then studied law for three years—chiefly as an avenue to politics—and achieved local fame as an attorney. He represented Camden County in the House of Commons in 1800. Before casting his vote as Republican presidential elector for Jefferson and Clinton in 1804, he delivered a partisan address in which he hailed Jefferson's election in 1801 as "a greater subject for joy and congratulation than the capture of Cornwallis" (*Raleigh Register and North Carolina State Gazette,* Dec. 17, 1804) ; and the sitting legislature elected him a member of the Council of State.

Sawyer's stanch Republicanism, attractive personality, and prominent family connection resulted in 1806 in his election to Congress, of which he was a member for sixteen years (1807–13, 1817–23, and 1825–29). He retained popular support despite excessive absence from his seat and infrequent contacts with his constituency due to chronic invalidism. During the first interruption in his congressional career, he sold

his farm, resided in Norfolk, Va., and was part
owner and business agent of a store in his native
county; during the second, he wrote *Blackbeard,
A Comedy, in Four Acts; Founded on Fact*
(Washington, 1824), which was staged in New
York in 1833. In Congress, Sawyer was a consistent supporter of the administrations of Jefferson, Madison, and Monroe. He opposed a naval
establishment, advocated rigid economy, and
supported the Embargo, though the distress of
the lumber trade in his district prompted him to
offer, on Nov. 15, 1808, a resolution designed to
open trade with the West Indies. In 1810, convinced of the ineffectiveness of non-intercourse
and in opposition to Nathaniel Macon [*q.v.*], he
urged more vigorous resistance to England. After war began, he proposed, Dec. 16, 1812, a
striking increase in the navy. Retaining after
the war his belief in economy and strict construction of the Constitution, he opposed the federal
policy of internal improvements as unconstitutional and inexpedient, but on Dec. 16, 1825,
proposed the use of a war vessel for the exploration of the polar regions of North America,
declaring in a widely noticed address that "the
time has come when this nation should likewise
enter into this glorious career of discovery and
human improvement" (*Register of Debates in
Congress,* 19 Cong., 1 Sess., p. 814). He voted
against the tariff act of 1828. From 1824 he was
a Jackson Democrat.

Sawyer was married three times: in August
1810 to Mary Snowden of Camden County, who
died in 1812; on Dec. 24, 1820, to Camilla Wertz
of Washington, D. C., who died Jan. 27, 1826;
and in 1828, to a well-to-do widow, Mrs. Diana
(Rapalye) Fisher of Brooklyn, N. Y. Several
children by his first two wives died in infancy.
After a brief unhappy residence in North Carolina following his retirement from Congress in
1829, Sawyer moved to Brooklyn where he employed much of his leisure in study and writing.
He wrote a second drama, *The Wreck of Honor,
a Tragedy, in Five Acts* (1826?); a work of fiction, *Printz Hall; A Record of New Sweden* (2
vols., 1839); *A Biography of John Randolph of
Roanoke, with a Selection from His Speeches*
(1844); and *Auto-biography of Lemuel Sawyer*
(1844). Extravagance, questionable conduct,
and business incapacity dissipated the money obtained from his third marriage, and his latter
years were spent in ill health, unemployment,
penury, and unhappiness. From 1850 until his
death he held a minor departmental clerkship in
Washington, where he died. He was buried in
the family burying ground, Lambs Ferry, Camden County, N. C.

[See *Biog. Dir. Am. Cong.* (1928); *Jour. of the House of Commons* (N. C.), 1800, 1804; *Raleigh Reg. and N.-C. State Gazette,* Dec. 2, 1805; *Raleigh Reg. and N.-C. Gazette,* Jan. 12, 1821, Nov. 25, 1828; "Pasquo-tank Births, Marriages, Deaths, Flesh Marks, and Brands, 1691–1797," in the N. C. Hist. Commission; J. H. Wheeler, *Reminiscences and Memoirs of N. C. and Eminent North Carolinians* (1884); A. H. Quinn, *A Hist. of the Am. Drama from the Beginning To the Civil War* (1923). Although contemporary newspapers give the name of Sawyer's second wife as Wurtz, evi-dence from records and manuscript sources indicates that the correct spelling was Wertz.]   A. R. N.

SAWYER, LORENZO (May 23, 1820–Sept.
7, 1891), California pioneer and jurist, was born
in Leray, Jefferson County, N. Y., the oldest
child of Jesse and Elizabeth (Goodell) Sawyer.
His first American ancestor was Thomas Sawyer, who emigrated from England to Massachusetts about 1636, settling in Rowley and in 1647
moving to Lancaster. His early life was spent
upon his father's farm, and in attending the district school and Black River Institute at Watertown, N. Y. From Pennsylvania, whither his
parents had moved, he went to Ohio and finished
his schooling. For a time he taught Latin and
mathematics at Central College, Ohio, and then
studied law in Columbus with Gustavus Swan
and with Noah H. Swayne [*q.v.*], afterwards a
justice of the United States Supreme Court. In
1846 he was admitted to the Ohio bar, but soon
went to Chicago and passed a year in the law
office of James A. McDougall, then attorney-
general of Illinois and afterwards a United
States senator from California. Moving to Wisconsin, he formed a law-partnership with Lieut.-
Gov. J. E. Holmes.

In 1850 he crossed the plains with a company
of young men from Wisconsin. Arriving in
California, he first worked in the mines in El
Dorado County, but soon entered upon the practice of law, first in Nevada City, then in Sacramento, and for a few months in 1851 in San
Francisco, subsequently returning to Nevada
City. In the autumn of 1853 he moved permanently to San Francisco, and the next year became city attorney. In his private practice he
was retained in important cases involving alienation of homestead, mining, and water rights. In
1861 he was in Washington, seeking appointment as chief justice of Colorado Territory, but
friends persuaded him to return to California,
where he began a long career on the bench the
following year, when Governor Stanford appointed him judge of the district court of the twelfth
judicial district. In 1863 he was elected to the
state supreme court and for two years (1868–
70) was its chief justice. On Dec. 8, 1869, President Grant nominated him as United States circuit judge for the ninth circuit, and on Jan. 10,

1870, the nomination was confirmed. At the time of Sawyer's death in San Francisco in 1891, he was serving as presiding judge of the newly created circuit court of appeals for the ninth circuit. As a judge, he was called upon to decide important questions relating to the settlement and preservation of land titles. His best-known decision, however, was the *habeas corpus* case in 1889 (*In re Neagle, 14 Sawyer's Reports, 9th Circuit,* 232), afterwards affirmed by the Supreme Court (135 *U. S.,* 1).

In politics Sawyer was first a Whig, then a member of the American Party, but throughout most of his life a Republican. As the first president of the board of trustees of Leland Stanford, Junior, University he delivered an address (1887) at the laying of the University's corner stone in Palo Alto. Though not a man of brilliancy or genius, he was richly endowed with common sense, and was temperate, regular, and rigidly correct in all his habits. No success came to him without hard work. He investigated cases with the greatest patience, and was ready to hear the uttermost word that could be offered in behalf of any cause. Stern and inflexible in his public acts and relations, he was of great gentleness, kindness, and simplicity in his private life. On Mar. 10, 1857, he married Jennie M. Aldrich. She died in 1876, leaving two sons and a daughter.

[H. H. Bancroft, *Chronicles of the Builders of the Commonwealth* (vol. II, 1892); O. T. Shuck, *Bench and Bar in Cal.* (1889); Alonzo Phelps, *Contemporary Biog. of California's Representative Men* (1881); *San Francisco Chronicle,* Sept. 8, 1891; *Evening Bull.* (San Francisco), Sept. 8, 1891; *Green Bag,* Oct. 1891; L. S. B. Sawyer, *Reports of Cases Decided in the Circuit and District Courts of the U. S. for the Ninth Circuit,* 1873–1891; 24–38 *Cal. Reports.*]   P. O. R.

SAWYER, PHILETUS (Sept. 22, 1816–Mar. 29, 1900), lumberman and senator, accumulated a large fortune out of the pine lands of northeastern Wisconsin, directed the course of the Republican party in his state for fifteen years, and died a rugged and popular exponent of individualism in business. He was born at Whiting, near Rutland, Vt., but passed his youth at Crown Point, N. Y., to which place his parents, Ephraim and Mary (Potts) Sawyer, took him in infancy. He acquired the rudiments of letters in a few terms of country schools, learned the whole technique of the lumberman in the pineries, and married, in 1841, Melvina M. Hadley, the daughter of a neighbor. Six years later he took his family westward to the vicinity of Oshkosh, Wis., where his home and seat of operations remained until his death. He was a member of the Wisconsin assembly in 1857 and 1861, was twice mayor of

Oshkosh, and attached himself to various Masonic orders. His family mansion, built in the panic year, 1857, became a place of hospitality state-wide in extent; and his fortune, considerable before the Civil War, expanded with the war-time demand for lumber. As his industry evolved from the sawmill and rough-lumber stage to the planing mill and finished woodwork, he amassed profits that he invested in the local banks and the railroads of Wisconsin.

In 1864 he was elected to Congress, thus accomplishing the "redemption" of the fifth Wisconsin district from "the hands of the false Democracy" (*Wisconsin State Journal,* Sept. 16, 1864). With "great energy and practical business talent" he held his seat against only nominal opposition through five terms. He made few speeches but was an able committeeman. Withdrawing from Congress in 1875, he gave his attention again to his business, but did not cease to work in politics with the "Republican regency of Milwaukee." In 1881 he took his seat in the United States Senate, where he remained for twelve years, contributing to the reputation of the Senate as a millionaires' club (*Sunday Sentinel, Milwaukee,* Apr. 6, 1890). In 1885 he received as junior colleague the able young railroad lawyer, John C. Spooner [*q.v.*], who became as effective on the floor as Sawyer was in the committee room. With a family physician to assist him, Sawyer set up an informal pension office that secured passage for many private pension bills. His leadership in Wisconsin politics was impregnable until, in 1890, the party was wrecked by the revulsion against the Bennett law, and the Democrats took possession of the state. Sawyer was replaced by a Democrat in 1893, after he had been compelled by the Democratic administration to make good on the bonds of sundry Republican state treasurers who had, while in office, failed to account for interest received on public deposits. He had also been drawn into significant controversy with the young ex-congressman, Robert M. LaFollette [*q.v.*], who charged him with an attempt at bribery in connection with the treasury interest cases. His explanation of the transaction (*Milwaukee Sentinel,* Oct. 29, 30, 1891) was incapable of either authentication or disproof, but it provided the text for a campaign against boss rule and corruption waged by LaFollette with ultimate success. Sawyer retired to semi-privacy as the "grand old man of Oshkosh," but his hand remained powerful when, after the Democratic interlude, his friends regained power in the state. In his last years the attacks upon him were softened by his reputation for honesty, generosity, and success. He died in Oshkosh, survived by two of his five children.

[The newspapers made Sawyer a legend before he was eighty; see *Daily Northwestern* (Oshkosh), Sept. 19, 1896; *Milwaukee Sentinel*, Mar. 30, 1900. There is a friendly sketch in P. V. Lawson, *Hist. Winnebago County, Wis.* (1908), vol. II. A memorial volume, Horatio Gates, *The Sawyer-Jewell Lineage* (1902), traces his irrepressible vigor to Cerdic the Saxon and King Alfred.]   F. L. P.

SAWYER, SYLVANUS (Apr. 15, 1822–Oct. 13, 1895), inventor, was the son of John Sawyer and was born on his father's farm at Templeton, Mass. From his father, who was a lumberman and mill operator as well as a farmer, he evidently inherited the mechanical ingenuity that he manifested from boyhood. He was never in good health, however, and after obtaining a grade school education he was sent to Augusta, Me., in 1839 to work in the gunsmith shop of his brother-in-law. Poor health soon forced him to relinquish this work and return to his home at Templeton but not before he had gained sufficient knowledge of the gunsmith's art to enable him to repair and make parts for firearms for his friends and neighbors. He also made several inventions, including a small railroad car to be operated by foot power. About 1844 he went to Boston, where he found employment for a short time in a coppersmith's shop. He then spent a year with a manufacturer of locks and house trimmings but was again compelled to return to Templeton because of his health. He had gained a local reputation as a mechanical genius, however, and in the winter of 1845–46 was asked for his advice in the devising of tools to prepare rattan for chair caning and other purposes. After work lasting a year or more on a machine to reduce the eighteen hand operations required to prepare rattan, he felt the need of more experience and obtained employment in the machine shops of Otis Tufts in Boston. In 1849, once more in Templeton, he constructed models of experimental machines and applied for a patent, granted on Nov. 13, 1849, on "machinery for splitting and dressing rattan." When practically applied the device was not satisfactory, but after two years of further experiment he secured a second patent on "machinery for cutting rattan," June 24, 1851. Following this the American Rattan Company was organized and a factory established at Fitchburg, Mass., with Sawyer as superintendent. He continued with the improvement of his rattan machinery and secured additional patents in 1854 and 1855. In 1855, when his company was consolidated with a business rival, he relinquished active connection with it to devote his attention entirely to invention. As early as 1853 he had invented certain improvements in rifled cannon and projectiles (first patented on Nov. 13, 1855), and between 1857 and 1858 he and his brother attempted to demonstrate the practicability of their rifled cannon and projectiles, but nothing came of it. For the succeeding twenty years he continued with a variety of inventions that yielded several patents: dividers and calipers, patented in 1867; a steam generator, 1868; and a shoe-sole machine, 1876. In 1876 he attempted to establish a watch factory in Fitchburg but was compelled by prevailing financial conditions to abandon the enterprise and to turn his attention to the manufacture of watchmakers' tools, particularly a centering lathe, on which he obtained a patent July 10, 1882. In the last few years of his life he gave up all active business and devoted his efforts to horticulture, having a deep interest in progressive farming. He never married. He died in Fitchburg, Mass.

[D. H. Hurd, *Hist. of Worcester County, Mass.* (1889), vol. I; correspondence with Fitchburg Hist. Soc.; Patent Office records; *Boston Transcript*, Oct. 14, 1895.]   C. W. M.

SAWYER, THOMAS JEFFERSON (Jan. 9, 1804–July 24, 1899), Universalist clergyman, editor, and educator, was born in Reading, Vt., one of the ten children of Benjamin and Sally (York) Sawyer. He was a descendant of Thomas Sawyer of Lincolnshire, England, who emigrated to America not later than 1639, and died in Lancaster, Mass., in 1706. Young Sawyer's early life was that of most country boys in his day—six months' labor on the farm and six months' schooling annually. During the year 1822 he lived with the Universalist minister of the town, Samuel C. Loveland, and studied under his direction. He then taught district schools, earning thereby enough money to attend Chester Academy at two different periods, where he completed his preparation for Middlebury College. Entering that institution in 1825, he graduated in 1829 and the same year was ordained to the Universalist ministry at the General Convention, meeting at Winchester, N. H. In April 1830 he became pastor of the Grand Street Universalist Society, recently organized in New York City, which soon afterward established itself in a church edifice on Orchard Street. The following year, Sept. 21, he married Caroline Mehitable (d. 1894), daughter of Jesse and Anna (Kenrick) Fisher of Newton, Mass. She was a woman of considerable literary talent, whose publications include, besides much prose and verse in periodicals, *The Juvenile Library* (4 vols., 1845), and *The Rose of Sharon* (1850–58), an annual;

she also edited from 1861 to 1864 the *Ladies' Repository*, a Universalist monthly. Seven children were born to her.

When Sawyer went to New York, organized Universalism had almost ceased to exist there. For the next fifteen years he was a potent force in its upbuilding. Horace Greeley, who became one of his parishioners in 1831, later said of him that he "was not a brilliant preacher, and never became such; but he possessed qualities more essential to a clergyman than dazzling eloquence —sound judgment, solid learning, immovable integrity, and profound devotion to his Master's cause" (*New York Tribune*, quoted by Eddy, *Life*, p. 252). He was aggressive in the promulgation of Universalist doctrines and quick to take up cudgels in their defense, engaging in numerous public controversies with members of other denominations. The substance of some of these appeared in printed form: for example, *Letters to the Rev. Stephen Remington in Review of His Lectures on Universalism* (1839) and *Review of Rev. E. F. Hatfield's "Universalism as It Is"* (1841). In the interest of the denomination he started and edited, with Philo Price, the *Christian Messenger* (Oct. 29. 1831–Oct. 24, 1835). In November 1835 this was merged with other papers and the *Universalist Union* established, of which Sawyer was an editor for some years.

In 1845 he became principal of Clinton Liberal Institute. A Universalist theological school, for which in General Conventions and elsewhere he had long pleaded, was soon established in Clinton and Sawyer conducted it in connection with his principalship of the Institute. It ceased to exist when he left Clinton, in 1852, but when the Canton Theological School, the beginning of St. Lawrence University, was founded in 1856, he was made first president of the board of trustees, a position he soon resigned. A pioneer advocate of educational institutions under Universalist control, he called the convention held in New York, May 1847, which resulted in the founding of Tufts College. Elected its first president in 1852, he would not accept the position because the trustees could not guarantee him the $2,500 salary for which he asked. From December 1853 to April 1861 he was again pastor of the Orchard Street Church, New York, declining in the meantime the presidency of Lombard University and of St. Lawrence University. Once more he appears in the rôle of an aggressive controversialist, publishing *A Discussion of the Doctrine of Universal Salvation* (1854), a debate with the Rev. Isaac Westcott, a Baptist, in the Broadway Tabernacle; and *Who Is Our God?*

the Son or the Father? (1859), a reply to Henry Ward Beecher. From January 1863 to the end of 1865 he was editor of the *Christian Ambassador*. After relinquishing this position he lived on a farm he had acquired at Star Landing, Woodbridge, N. J., until 1869, when he was called to the Packard professorship of theology at Tufts Divinity School. In 1892 he became professor *emeritus*, having been dean for the ten years preceding, but remained comparatively active until his death in his ninety-sixth year. Among his publications not already mentioned are: *Memoir of Rev. Stephen R. Smith* (1852); *The Damnation of the Heathen, and the American Board* (1888); and *Endless Punishment in the Very Words of Its Advocates* (1891).

[Richard Eddy, *The Life of Thomas J. Sawyer, S.T.D., LL.D., and of Caroline M. Sawyer* (1900), and *Universalism in America*, vol. II (1894); *Cat. of the Officers and Students of Middlebury Coll., 1800 to 1900* (1901); *Hist. of Tufts Coll.* (1896), ed. by A. B. Start; *Universalist Leader*, July 29, 1899; *Boston Herald*, Jan. 10, 1897, July 25, 1899.]   H. E. S.

SAWYER, WALTER HOWARD (May 21, 1867–Dec. 21, 1923), engineer, son of John Marshall and Mary (James) Sawyer, was born at Middletown, Conn. Thrown upon his own resources in his youth, he worked his way through school and graduated from Bromfield Academy at Harvard, Mass. Later, he studied engineering in the office of Shedd & Sawyer of Boston and in the evening schools of that city. Between 1885 and 1902 he made preliminary surveys for the New York & Boston Rapid Transit Railroad and for a sewerage system at Newburyport, Mass.; was resident engineer of the hydro-electric development on the Androscoggin River at Rumford Falls, Me., one of the early larger developments of its kind in New England; and was engaged in other hydraulic and sanitary projects in various parts of New England— including a sewer system for Lisbon, Me., hydraulic developments at Hookset, N. H., and Lewiston, Me.—and in work connected with water-rights cases.

In 1902 he was appointed agent and engineer for the Union Water Power Company of Lewiston, Me., with responsible charge of the large water power development at Lewiston and the operation of the extensive storage system of the Androscoggin River, consisting of the Rangeley Lakes system and totalling about thirty billion cubic feet of capacity. He held this position for the remainder of his life, and through it, and through an active consulting practice as well, he exerted a forceful and important influence on the industrial development of Maine. In 1909 he planned and carried out the Aziscohos Reservoir development in the headwaters of the Androscoggin River, the first project of its kind in New England where coöperative use of stored water upon a large scale was involved. This development was possible because of a concentration of head using this storage, totalling some 425 feet, in the hands of four large utility and paper companies; but it required long negotiations and untiring energy to consummate. The reservoir added about ten billion cubic feet of storage to the Androscoggin River system and made it one of the best power streams of the country. In carrying out the project Sawyer invented an adjustable log sluice of novel design and displayed much ingenuity and good judgment in its construction.

He gave much time to research—maintaining a laboratory for this purpose at Lewiston, and devised a method of measurement of water by electro-chemical means, and a method of sewage treatment. He was a pioneer in developing methods of studying the operation of storage reservoirs and was the author of a monograph on ice expansion. He was active in the civic affairs of his home city, Auburn, Me., serving as alderman and upon several commissions; he also formed the Auburn Sewerage District and had a complete sewerage system planned for the city. During the World War he was an active member of the Maine Public Safety Committee and a member of the Federal Milk Commission of New England. He served as president of the Maine Society of Civil Engineers and was prominent in other national and state organizations of this kind. On Apr. 23, 1900, he married Helen F. Hayes of Wellesley, Mass., and he was survived by one daughter. His death occurred in Auburn after a long illness.

[*Trans. Am. Soc. Civil Engineers,* vol. LXXXVIII (1925); *Jour. Boston Soc. Civil Engineers,* Oct. 1924; *Lewiston Evening Jour.,* Dec. 22, 1923.]   H. K. B.

SAXE, JOHN GODFREY (June 2, 1816–Mar. 31, 1887), poet, was born in Highgate, Franklin County, Vt., the second of the four sons of Peter and Elizabeth (Jewett) Saxe. He was of German stock on his father's side and of English on his mother's. His father was a storekeeper, mill-owner, and local politician. Saxe entered Wesleyan University in 1835 but transferred the next year to Middlebury College and graduated thence in 1839. He then read law at Lockport, N. Y., and St. Albans, Vt.; was married Sept. 9, 1841, to Sophia Newell Sollace, sister of one of his college classmates; was admitted to the bar in 1843; served as superintendent of common schools in Chittenden County, 1847–48, and as state's attorney for the county, 1850–

51; owned and edited a weekly paper, the *Burlington Sentinel,* 1850–56; and ran for governor on the Democratic ticket against Hiland Hall in 1859 and against Erastus Fairbanks in 1860. His law practice was never extensive, and he regarded his political activities as a joke. His real interests were, in a modest way, literary. He early gained a Vermont reputation as a wit, punster, and after-dinner poet, and the humorous poems that he contributed to the *Knickerbocker* prepared the way for his volumes of verse. These were: *Progress: A Satirical Poem* (1846); *Humorous and Satirical Poems* (1850); *The Money-King and Other Poems* (1860); *The Fly-ing Dutchman; or, The Wrath of Herr Vonstoppelnoze* (1862); *Clever Stories of Many Nations Rendered in Rhyme* (1865); *The Masquerade and Other Poems* (1866); *Fables and Legends of Many Countries Rendered in Rhyme* (1872); and *Leisure-Day Rhymes* (1875). With true literary tact he dedicated his first volume to Oliver Wendell Holmes and his last to Frederick Locker-Lampson. He contributed to the leading magazines, and several poems were also issued separately. The first of many editions of his collected work was published in 1850, and *Selections from the Poems of John Godfrey Saxe* in 1905. For many years he was one of the most widely read and frequently quoted of American poets. Holmes, Hood, and Praed are his models, but his tone is more popular, and he is inferior to them in originality, polish, and delicacy of sentiment. Less a poet than a humorist using verse as his medium, he owed much of his vogue to his mediocrity.

After selling the *Burlington Sentinel* in 1856, he was sufficiently prosperous and firmly established to depend for his income on his writings and lectures. He made his home in Albany, N. Y., from 1860 to 1872 and then removed to Brooklyn. He was six feet two inches tall, erect in carriage, his kindly face framed in flowing black hair and beard. A wit and humorist in public, in private he was meditative, home-loving, and subject to periods of dejection. He liked to travel, spent twenty-three successive seasons at Saratoga Springs, and visited Europe with his wife in 1867. Five of his six children lived to maturity, but in 1874 his youngest daughter died of tuberculosis; the next year he was severely injured in a railway wreck and his brain was permanently affected; and in the course of the next six years his wife, his two remaining daughters, his eldest son, and his daughter-in-law died, leaving only his son Charles to survive him. Enveloped in hopeless, ever-deepening melancholia, he spent his last years in almost complete seclusion in his son's house in Albany. He died of a heart attack in his seventy-first year.

[*Hist. of Franklin and Grand Isle Counties, Vt.* (1891), L. C. Aldrich, ed.; J. G. Saxe, *Geneal. of the Saxe Family* (priv. printed, 1930); F. C. Jewett, *Hist. and Geneal. of the Jewetts of America* (2 vols., 1908); *Cat. of Officers and Students of Middlebury Coll. . . . 1800 to 1900* (1901); R. W. Taft, *John Godfrey Saxe* (priv. printed, 1900); R. H. Stoddard, "John Godfrey Saxe," *Nat. Mag.*, May 1853; E. C. Stedman and others, "John Godfrey Saxe," *Critic*, Apr. 9, 1887; J. G. and M. S. Saxe, "Saxe—the Vt. Poet," *Bookman*, June 1916; A. W. Peach in *Vermonters* (1931), W. H. Crockett, ed.; *N. Y. Tribune, Daily Press and Knickerbocker* (Albany, N. Y.), *Albany Eve. Jour.* (obituary and editorial), Apr. 1, 1887.]   G. H. G.

SAXTON, JOSEPH (Mar. 22, 1799–Oct. 26, 1873), inventor, the son of James and Hannah (Ashbaugh) Saxton, was born in Huntington, Pa. His father was engaged in banking and also was the proprietor of a nail factory. After James had obtained an ordinary education he went to work at the age of twelve in the latter establishment for a short time, and was then apprenticed to a watch-maker for two years. In 1817 he went to Philadelphia in the hope of educating himself. He continued working at his trade in this city for about eleven years, studied engraving on the side, and eventually became associated with Isaiah Lukens, a celebrated machinist. During this time he constructed an astronomical clock with a compensating pendulum and escapement of his own design, and also made the clock for the belfry of Independence Hall. He acquired a wide reputation in Philadelphia for his great ingenuity but, in a desire to enlarge his knowledge, he went to England in 1828 where he soon became connected with the Adelaide Gallery of Practical Science in London and made a name for himself through the construction and exhibition of scientific novelties and apparatus. He met many noted engineers, scientists, and mechanicians, and through these friends was introduced to Michael Faraday and to the meetings of the Royal Society. His association with scientists spurred him to go forward with numerous original experiments. He constructed and exhibited in 1833, before the British Association for the Advancement of Science at Cambridge, a magneto-electric machine which produced a brilliant spark, decomposed water, exhibited an intense light between the charcoal points, and gave a rapid series of heavy shocks. Unfortunately, through his failure at the time to publish a description of this machine, the credit for the invention was given to another. During his residence of nine years in England, Saxton acquired a number of British patents, including a locomotive differential pulley, an apparatus for measuring the velocity of vessels, and a fountain pen.

As early as 1829, he improved the medal-ruling machine so that it was capable of copying without distortion the designs of medals and coins.

He returned to Philadelphia in 1837 to accept the appointment of constructor and curator of the standard weighing apparatus of the United States Mint, having declined the position of director of printing machinery of the Bank of England. During his connection with the mint he designed and constructed the large standard balances used for the verification of the standard weights of the government's assay and coining offices. In 1843 he joined the United States coast survey in Washington, D. C., as superintendent of weights and measures and served in this capacity for the next thirty years. His first work in this new position was the construction of the standard balances, weights, and measures subsequently presented to each state of the Union for insuring uniformity of measures in all parts of the country. He also constructed much of the complex apparatus employed by the Coast Survey, and altered the Survey's dividing engine so that it was completely automatic, driven by a water-turbine of his own design. He also patented an anthracite coal-burning stove, a fusible metal seal, a hydrometer, and an ever-pointed pencil. Saxton was more than a practical mechanical genius but not a profound student of science. According to his biographer, he "possessed more wisdom than learning" (Henry, *post*, p. 314). He was one of the fifty original members of the National Academy of Sciences, and a member of the American Philosophical Society. The Franklin Institute awarded him the John Scott legacy medal in November 1834 for his invention of a reflecting pyrometer. He was married in 1850 to Mary H. Abercrombie of Philadelphia who, with their daughter, survived him.

[Joseph Henry, "Memoir of Joseph Saxton," *Nat'l Acad. of Sciences, Biog. Memoirs*, vol. I (1877); J. R. Eckfeldt and Wm. E. Du Bois, *A Manual of Gold and Silver Coins* (1851); records of the Patent Office; *Evening Star* (Washington, D. C.), Oct. 27, 1873.]
C. W. M.

SAY, BENJAMIN (Aug. 28, 1755–Apr. 23, 1813), physician and philanthropist, born at Philadelphia, Pa., was the son of Thomas Say by his second wife, Rebekah (Atkinson) Budd, widow of Thomas Budd and daughter of Samuel Atkinson. A descendant of a French Huguenot family in England and the son of William, who settled in America towards the close of the seventeenth century, Thomas Say (1709–96) began his business life as a harness maker but later opened an apothecary shop and set up as a physician. Although he administered medicines he also claimed to accomplish cures by means of stroking the afflicted part. He was deeply religious, with mystical tendencies. He had a series of visions, an account of the first of which appears in Benjamin's Say's *A Short Compilation of the Extraordinary Life and Writings of Thomas Say* (1796). But in spite of his mysticism he was a good man of business and a public-spirited citizen. He accumulated a comfortable fortune, was active in civic affairs, and was much interested in bettering the condition of the negroes.

There is no definite information as to where Benjamin Say received his medical education. Although he is said to have graduated from the University of Pennsylvania, there is no record in the official registers. Probably his father was his preceptor; at any rate, he followed his example in conducting an apothecary shop in connection with a medical practice. The ledger preserved in the College of Physicians of Philadelphia shows that his practice was both extensive and lucrative. His lack of a degree did not prevent his becoming one of the first junior fellows of the College of Physicians and as such signing the constitution of the college at its adoption on Jan. 2, 1787. He also served as treasurer of the college from 1791 to 1809. He is said to have published a book on "Spasmodic Affections of the Eye" in 1792, but it is not in the library of the Surgeon-General in Washington, D. C., nor in that of the College of Physicians of Philadelphia. His only other publication was *An Annual Oration Pronounced before the Humane Society of Philadelphia* (1799). He was one of the incorporators of the society and its president in 1799. He was also active in the movement to abolish slavery. In 1799 he was elected to the Senate of Pennsylvania but declined to accept a renomination in 1801; in 1808 he was elected representative in Congress from Pennsylvania but resigned in the following year. He and his father were shareholders in the company formed by John Fitch [q.v.] to exploit his steamboat. He was also much in horticulture and in 1802 was president of a "Company for the Improvement of the Vine." He married Ann, daughter of Benjamin Bonsall and grand-daughter of John Bartram [q.v.], the botanist, on Oct. 1, 1776. By her he had four children, one of whom, Thomas Say [q.v.], became a distinguished naturalist. After her death in 1793, he married on Dec. 22, 1795, Miriam Moore, by whom he had two daughters and a son. When he died, in Philadelphia, he left a large estate to his second wife and the six children who survived him.

[H. B. Weiss and Grace M. Ziegler, *Thomas Say, Early Am. Naturalist* (1931), very detailed treatment of the Say family, with bibliog.; W. S. W. Ruschenberger, *An Account of the Institution and Progress of the Coll. of Physicians of Phila. . . . from Jan. 1787* (1887); *Pa. Mag. Hist. and Biog.*, Apr. 1905; death notice in *Poulson's Am. Daily Advertiser*, Apr. 24, 1813; Benjamin Say's account book, 1785–1803, in Pa. Hist. Soc., and ledger, 1796–1804, in Coll. of Physicians of Phila.]

F. R. P.

SAY, THOMAS (June 27, 1787–Oct. 10, 1834), entomologist, conchologist, called "the father of descriptive entomology in America," was born in Philadelphia, of Quaker ancestry. His father, Dr. Benjamin Say [q.v.], a member of the Society of Friends, was a physician and apothecary, served as a state senator and for two terms as a member of Congress, and at the time of his death was said to be one of the richest men in Philadelphia. His mother was Ann (Bonsall), daughter of Benjamin Bonsall of Kingsessing and grand-daughter of John Bartram [q.v.]. Young Say was educated at the Friends' school at Westtown, a short distance from Philadelphia, but this education was not broad and throughout life he is said to have felt the need of wider training. He then studied pharmacy with his father and started a pharmacy shop with a partner, but the business failed because he too trustfully indorsed the notes of a friend.

As a boy Say had been interested in natural history through his mother's uncle, William Bartram [q.v.]. He was one of the original members of the Philadelphia Academy of Natural Sciences (founded in 1812), although he was not present at the first meeting; and from that date he devoted nearly all his time to the study of natural history. After his business failure he lived in the rooms of the Academy, sleeping on the floor and cooking his own meals, thus subsisting at an expense of seventy-five cents a week. He served briefly with the volunteers in 1814 and was a member of the First City Troop for several years thereafter. His great work, *American Entomology,* was planned and begun in 1816, and a ten-page prospectus was issued the following year. In 1818 he visited Georgia and Florida with several other members of the Academy—George Ord, William Maclure, and Titian R. Peale [qq.v.]—and in 1819 he was appointed as zoölogist to accompany the expedition to the Rocky Mountains under Maj. Stephen H. Long [q.v.], by which large collections were made. He accompanied in the same capacity Long's second expedition, in 1823, which explored the sources of the Minnesota River.

During the next few years he was busily engaged in and out of Philadelphia, where he was made curator of the American Philosophical Society in 1821 and professor of natural history in the University of Pennsylvania in 1822. He held the former post until 1827 and the latter until 1828, although much of the time during these years he was away from the city. In 1824 and 1825, respectively, appeared the first two volumes of his *American Entomology; or Descriptions of the Insects of North America,* and he prepared for the press the first volume (1825) of Charles Bonaparte's *American Ornithology; or the Natural History of Birds Inhabiting the United States.* In 1825, in company with William Maclure, Charles Alexandre Lesueur [*q.v.*], Robert Owen, and others, Say (at the age of thirty-eight) went to Indiana, where Owen had bought the village of New Harmony, intending to found there an ideal community. Like other experiments of the kind, this one soon failed; the founders were involved in lawsuits, which finally were compromised, and Owen returned to Europe. In the meantime, Jan. 4, 1827, Say had married Lucy Way Sistaire, and he maintained his home in New Harmony for the rest of his life. During late 1827 and early 1828 he went to New Orleans and Mexico with Maclure, who was failing in health, and visited Vera Cruz, Jalapa, Mexico City, Tacuba, and Chalco.

In person, Say was six feet tall, and slender; he spoke with a slight lisp. His health had been poor even before he left Philadelphia, owing probably in part to his very frugal diet. In New Harmony he carried the same abstinence to excess. He was very often ill, after his return from Mexico, probably with malaria and surely with obstinate stomach trouble. Nevertheless, he worked on industriously and completed the third volume (1828) of his *American Entomology* as well as the six numbers of his *American Conchology* which were published (1830–34) at New Harmony.

Say's work was almost wholly taxonomic and his writings were almost entirely descriptive. He published practically nothing concerning the habits and life histories of the forms he named and described. That he confined his writing to pure description has been ascribed to his consciousness of his faulty education and to his lack of general reading. His published letters, however, are admirably written, and it is believed that he wrote at least a part of the narrative of Long's expeditions. His descriptive work was excellent, and nearly all his species have been recognized. His collections and library went to the Philadelphia Academy of Natural Sciences after his death, and through neglect, the greater part of his collections was allowed to go to ruin, but Dr. John Lawrence LeConte [*q.v.*], in the Preface to his edition of Say's entomological papers, said: "His descriptions are so clear as to

leave scarcely a doubt as to the objects designated." The excellence of his work was early recognized by European zoölogists, and he was made a foreign member of the Linnean Society of London. His earlier papers were published in the *Journal of the Academy of Natural Sciences of Philadelphia* and later ones in the *Boston Journal of Natural History* and the *Annals of the Lyceum of Natural History of New-York.* Others were issued independently by the author at New Harmony. In 1859 J. L. LeConte edited and published in two volumes *The Complete Writings of Thomas Say on the Entomology of North America,* with a biographical memoir by George Ord. The individual titles cover twenty-nine papers, many of them monographic in character. Since the publication of these two volumes, a few other entomological papers of Say's have been found, mainly in agricultural journals. His work on conchology was summarized in 1858 in a volume edited by W. G. Binney, entitled *The Complete Writings of Thomas Say on the Conchology of the United States,* with seventy-five plates. Most of the figures of shells illustrating Say's work were drawn by Mrs. Say; the drawings of insects in his other works were chiefly by himself. His paleontological writings were reprinted in 1896, by G. D. Harris, in the *Bulletins of American Paleontology* (vol. I, no. 5).

[H. B. Weiss and G. M. Ziegler, *Thomas Say, Early Am. Naturalist* (1931); George Ord, "A Memoir of Thomas Say," read before the Am. Phil. Soc., Dec. 19, 1834, and pub. in Preface to LeConte's edition (1859) of Say's entomological writings; B. H. Coates, *A Biog. Sketch of the Late Thomas Say, Esq.* (Phila. Acad. Nat. Sci., 1835); J. S. Kingsley, "Sketch of Thomas Say," *Pop. Sci., Mo.,* Sept. 1882; W. H. Dall, "Some American Conchologists," *Proc. Biol. Soc. of Washington,* vol. IV (1888); F. M. Webster, "Thomas Say," *Entomological News,* Jan.-Apr. 1895; H. S. Barber, "Thomas Say's Unrecorded Journey in Mexico," *Ibid.,* Jan. 1928; Say's correspondence with J. F. Melsheimer, *Ibid.,* 1891–92; S. H. Scudder, "An Unknown Tract on American Insects by Thomas Say," *Psyche,* Jan. 1899; V. Sterki, "A Few Notes on Say's Early Writings and Species," *Nautilus,* July 1907; G. B. Lockwood, *The New Harmony Movement* (1905); *Am. Jour. Sci.,* Jan. 1835; *Poulson's Am. Daily Advertiser,* Nov. 4, 1834.]

L. O. H.

SAYLES, JOHN (Mar. 9, 1825–May 22, 1897), lawyer and writer of law books, was born at Ithaca, N. Y. His father, Welcome, a successful physician, was a member of a Rhode Island family, the founder of which, John, came from England in 1650. His mother was Harriett Elizabeth Sergeant, of Massachusetts, daughter of a noted Presbyterian clergyman and missionary to the Oneida Indians. John began teaching in New York State at the age of fifteen and later taught in Georgia; between school terms he attended college. In 1845 he was awarded the degree of B.A. by Hamilton College, Clinton, N. Y., and in the same year removed to Texas, settling at Brenham. Here he taught school and read law.

He was admitted to the bar in 1846 and three years later became associated in practice with Col. Barry Gillespie, a distinguished lawyer and planter. A later partnership, under the name of Sayles & Bassett, continued for nearly thirty years and was one of the most successful firms in Texas at that time. In 1853–55, he was a member of the Texas legislature. In addition to his work as a lawyer, he served from 1857 to 1860 as a member of the faculty of the law school of Baylor University, which is believed to have been the first law school established in Texas. He was again connected with the school for several years after it was reorganized in 1867. During the Civil War he attained the rank of brigadier-general of militia and rendered distinguished service under Gen. J. Bankhead Magruder [q.v.]. In 1886 he removed to Abilene, in Western Texas, and with his son, Henry, established the firm of Sayles & Sayles.

Though he was an excellent lawyer, his fame rests on the fact that he was the ablest and most prolific writer of law books that Texas has produced. His first volume, *A Treatise on Practice of the District and Supreme Courts of the State of Texas* (1858), consisting largely of his lectures to the law classes in Baylor University, passed through three editions. A complementary volume, *A Treatise on the Civil Jurisdiction of Justices of the Peace* (1867), ran through four editions, the last entitled *Sayles' Guide for Justices* (1894). Another product of his law teaching was *A Treatise on the Principles of Pleading in Civil Actions in the Courts of Texas* (1872). This work formed the basis of three others—*The Rules of Pleading and Practice in the Courts of Record in the State of Texas* (3rd ed., 1882), in preparing which he was aided by his partner, B. H. Bassett; *Revised Statutes of the State of Texas Relating to Organization, Jurisdiction and Practice of the District and County Courts* (1886), in collaboration with his son, Henry Sayles; and, finally, the work of 1872 rewritten and published as the *Precedents and Rules of Pleading in Civil Actions in the County and District Courts of Texas* (1893). In 1871, he brought out *The Probate Laws of Texas*; and in 1876, *A Manual of the Laws of Business*. In collaboration with his son, Henry, he published *Early Laws of Texas* (3 vols., 1888), and *A Treatise on the Laws of Texas Relating to Real Estate* (2 vols., 1891–92). In 1888 there appeared the fourth volume of what was intended to be a four-volume work on the constitution and statutes of Texas. This volume was the third

edition of his *The Constitutions of the State of Texas,* the first and second editions of which had appeared in 1872 and 1884 respectively. The next volume of the series to appear was *The Annotated Statutes, Civil and Criminal, of the State of Texas . . . Supplement for 1889* (1889); the third, *Sayles' Annotated Civil Statutes of the State of Texas* (2 parts), did not appear until 1897, the year of his death. The projected volume on the criminal statutes was not published. At one time Grand Master of Masons in Texas, Sayles was the author of *The Masonic Jurisprudence of Texas* (1879). In 1849 he was married to Mary Elizabeth, only daughter of his first law partner, Col. Barry Gillespie. He had three sons and three daughters.

[Information from a daughter, Mrs. George C. Harris, and a grandson, John Sayles. See J. D. Lynch, *The Bench and Bar of Tex.* (1885); J. C. Townes, *Law Books and How to Use Them* (copr. 1909), p. 185; *Dallas Morning News,* May 30, 1897.]   C. S. P.—s.

SAYRE, LEWIS ALBERT (Feb. 29, 1820–Sept. 21, 1900), orthopedic surgeon, was born at Bottle Hill (later Madison), N. J., the son of Archibald and Martha (Sayer) Sayre and a descendant of Thomas Sayre, who was in Lynn, Mass., in 1638. From his grandfather Ephraim, a quartermaster in the Revolution, and his father, a wealthy farmer, prominent in local affairs, he inherited an unusual capacity for physical and mental labor. After attending the local academy for a time and Wantage Seminary at Deckertown, he lived with his banker uncle, David A. Sayre, in Lexington, Ky., and is said to have graduated from Transylvania University in 1839. Though he considered entering the ministry, he began to study medicine under the preceptorship of Dr. David Green of New York and was graduated from the College of Physicians and Surgeons in New York in 1842. His graduation thesis on spinal irritation was of such unusual merit that it was published. Early in his career he gave evidence of that critical open-mindedness which throughout his life inspired respect. As a student he wrote, "I made up my mind that if what I was taught agreed with my experience as to what I found, I would adopt it, and otherwise not" (letter to his son, R. H. Sayre). He was prosector to Dr. Willard Parker [q.v.], 1842–52, and built up his own practice in New York. On Jan. 25, 1849, he married Eliza Ann Hall. They had a daughter, and three sons all of whom became surgeons, among them Reginald Hall Sayre [q.v.].

In 1853 he was appointed surgeon to the Bellevue Hospital and in 1859 to the Charity Hospital on Blackwell's Island. He played an important part in the organization of the Bellevue Hospital

Medical College in 1861 and occupied the first chair of orthopedic surgery in America. He was one of the founders of the New York Pathological Society and was active in the affairs of the New York Academy of Medicine and of the American Medical Association, of which he was president in 1880. During 1860–66, at great personal sacrifice, he served as resident physician of the city of New York, holding the office under four mayors. Under his vigorous and persistent attacks the bad sanitary conditions of the time, particularly those in tenements, were greatly bettered. He advocated compulsory vaccination, was the first American health officer to deal with cholera as a contagious disease, and almost the only one who could have said, "The cholera which has arrived within our harbor, and has been so near our shores . . . was anchored in the bay, and detained there" (*Annual Report of the Resident Physician of the City of New York for 1865,* 1866). He was the acknowledged leader of orthopedic surgery in America. He had been the first American to perform a resection of the hip for morbus coxarius (1854), and he developed a treatment of lateral curvature that became known throughout the world as the Sayre method. When in 1871 he visited Europe and gave demonstrations and lectures in several countries, his fame became international. As delegate of the American Medical Association he attended the international medical convention in Philadelphia in 1876 and the meetings of the British Medical Association in 1877. His demonstrations and lectures were followed by more honors; Charles XV of Sweden made him a knight of the Order of Wasa in 1871, and the British association passed grateful resolutions.

His mental energy carried his constructive thought beyond his own anatomical field of the bones and joints and muscles. Scarcely graduated from medical school, he proposed radical methods of drainage of the pleural cavity and collapse of the lung, methods of diagnosis and treatment looked upon as sound by thoracic surgeons of a later day. He wrote on croup (*Transactions of the Medical Society of the State of New York,* 1864), on lead palsy (*Transactions of the American Medical Association,* vol. XX, 1869), and on abscess of the cellular tissues of the peritoneum. His contributions to his own branch of surgery were often original and strikingly successful. His publications include *Report on Morbus Coxarius or Hip Disease* (1860), *A Practical Manual of the Treatment of Club Foot* (1869), *On Anchylosis* (1874), *Report on Fractures* (1874), *On Disease of the Hip-Joint* (1875), *Spinal Disease and Spinal Curvature*

(1877), and *Lectures on Orthopedic Surgery and Diseases of the Joints* (1876), distinguished for its terseness and for the practicality of its illustrations. Though there was something of the zealot about him—in his lectures he exhorted as well as taught—his zeal was tempered by kindness and honesty. Patients attributed qualities almost supernatural to him and depended on the courage that overflowed from his exhaustless source. Yet neither their intense admiration nor the recognition of the medical world harmed him; he remained a brilliant and resourceful surgeon; just in thought and action.

[T. M. Banta, *Sayre Family, Lineage of Thomas Sayre* (1901); H. A. Kelly and W. L. Burrage, *Am. Medic. Biogs.* (1920); *First Decennial Cat. of . . . Officers . . . Bellevue Hospital Medic. Coll. . . . 1871 to 1871* (1873); *New England Medic. Jour.,* June 1884; *Mag. Western Hist.,* Nov. 1889; J. G. Kuhns and R. B. Osgood, "Am. Explorers in Orthopaedic Surgery," *Crippled Child,* Oct. 1931; Sir Arthur Keith, *Menders of the Maimed* (1919); Daniel Van Pelt, *Leslie's Hist. of the Greater New York* (1898), vol. III; *Medic. Record* (N. Y.), Sept. 29, 1900; *Boston Medic. and Surgical Jour.,* Sept. 27, 1900; *British Medic. Jour.,* Dec. 15, 1900; *Lancet* (London), Oct. 27, 1900; *N. Y. Times,* Sept. 22, 1900; information from Reginald H. Sayre.]
R. B. O.

SAYRE, REGINALD HALL (Oct. 18, 1859–May 29, 1929), surgeon, was born in New York City, the son of Lewis Albert Sayre [*q.v.*] and Eliza Ann (Hall) Sayre. From the Churchill and Maury School he entered Columbia College, where he won a scholarship in chemistry and was graduated with high honors in 1881. In college he was editor of the *Columbia Spectator,* a member of his class crew and of the varsity track team, and champion intercollegiate mile-walker. Although he matriculated in law school his elder brother Lewis persuaded him to study medicine, and he entered Bellevue Hospital Medical College, planning later to join his father in the practice of orthopedic surgery. He wisely elected not the surgical but the medical service under such masters as the elder Austin Flint and Edward Gamaliel Janeway [*qq.v.*] and acquired a catholicity of view that he never lost. He received the degree of M.D. in 1884. With his brother Lewis, who died six years later, he became the trusted associate of his father, whose reputation was international and whose huge practice and spacious offices represented almost an institution. Beginning in 1885 as assistant to the chair of surgery at Bellevue Hospital Medical College, he afterwards became lecturer and orthopedic surgeon there, succeeded his father in 1898 as clinical professor of orthopedic surgery, and twelve years later became full professor. A cosmopolitan in medicine, he was sought as consultant to numerous hospitals within and without New York City. For years he was an officer of the New York Academy of Medicine; he was a charter member of the American Orthopaedic Association and its president in 1903–04, a charter member of the American College of Surgeons, and a lieutenant colonel in the World War in charge of orthopedic instruction to medical officers. Though he wrote little after 1910, his earlier medical writings were significant. They included *The Treatment of Rotary Lateral Curvature of the Spine* (1888), *The Necessity for Thorough Examination in Suspected Pott's Disease* (1893), *The Treatment of Neglected Cases of Rotary Lateral Curvature of the Spine* (1893), and *Posture in the Diagnosis of Disease* (1897). He never married.

Personally a conservative, he possessed, like his more explosive father, remarkable latent force. Like his father, too, he had a delicious sense of humor and the power of vigorous, homely expressions. Though his devotion to his work was marked—he often made ward rounds on Sundays and holidays—he found time to become champion pistol shot of America and captain of four Olympic pistol teams. He also had a great love of horses and could drive with a rein gentle enough for a smart team or fearless enough for Troop A cavalry. The combination of skill and boldness displayed in these recreations was equally apparent in his professional work. His teaching was of the clinical rather than the didactic sort. Quick to appreciate the merit of sound new methods of surgery, he introduced many of them into the United States, and his wide experience and large fund of knowledge won him the deep respect of students and of his medical peers. He once deplored overwork because of its being "so easy to acquire a way of being slipshod and slovenly from lack of time," a characteristic attitude on the part of one who was himself an able, careful practitioner of a specialty that required a high order of artistry.

[T. M. Banta, *Sayre Family, Lineage of Thomas Sayre* (1901); *Who's Who in America,* 1928–29; *Medic. Jour. and Record* (N. Y.), July 3, 1929; *Jour. of Bone and Joint Surgery,* July 1929; *Bull. N. Y. Acad. of Medicine,* Aug. 1929; *N. Y. Times,* May 30, 1929; information from Miss Mary H. Sayre, a sister; personal acquaintance.]   R. B. O.

SAYRE, ROBERT HEYSHAM (Oct. 13, 1824–Jan. 5, 1907), civil engineer and railroad official, was born in Columbia County, Pa., the son of William H. and Eliza (Kent) Sayre and a descendant of Thomas Sayre who was in Lynn, Mass., as early as 1638. His father was an official of the Lehigh Coal & Navigation Company. Robert received his early education in the common schools and then studied civil engineering under James Nowlin, a mathematician of considerable reputation. In 1840 he was employed on the enlargement of the Morris Canal, and in the following year joined the engineering corps of his father's company for which, in 1843, he was assigned to make surveys and construct the railroad between the coal mines at Summit Hill and Mauch Chunk on the Lehigh Canal. He also built the switchback railroad and inclined planes into the Panther Creek Valley coal field, exhibiting such ability in this type of work that he was placed in charge of all the railroads and inclined planes of the company and the transportation of coal over them from the mines to Mauch Chunk. At the same time he directed the development of the company's mines and the erection and installation of equipment.

From 1852 until his retirement in 1898, with the exception of three years (1882–85) as president and chief engineer of the South Pennsylvania Railroad, he was in the employ of the Delaware, Lehigh, Schuylkill & Susquehannah Railroad and its successor, the Lehigh Valley system. He held successively the positions of chief engineer, general superintendent, second vice-president, assistant to the president, and vice-president. Convinced by his early experience that the future of the Western Pennsylvania coal region depended upon rail outlets to tidewater, he pushed the construction of the Lehigh Valley Railroad until such an outlet was achieved, building feeder lines from the western coal fields in the period 1852–82, the Easton & Amboy Railroad between 1872 and 1875, and the extensions to Buffalo and Jersey City, 1885–98. He was a pioneer in the introduction of iron bridges to replace wooden structures on the line of the Lehigh Valley Railroad (1857), and in the use of steel rails (1864), the fish-bar track joint, and steel-tired driving wheels and steel fireboxes for locomotives. Few men have had as much influence on the development of a single railroad system as did he.

Besides his railroad interests he was one of the promoters of the Bethlehem Iron Company, of which he became vice-president in 1891, and of the Pioneer Mining and Manufacturing Company of Alabama, and held directorates in a number of other corporations. He was chairman of the board of trustees and of the executive committee of Lehigh University, and to that institution presented a fully equipped astronomical observatory. He was much interested in book collecting and in 1899 built a library addition to his residence at South Bethlehem, Pa., to house some ten thousand volumes. He was married four times: on Apr. 15, 1845, to Mary Evelyn Smith, who died in 1869; on Jan. 12, 1871, to

Mary (Bradford), widow of Richard Brodhead, who died in 1877; on Apr. 15, 1879, to Helen Augusta (Packer), widow of Rollin H. Rathbun; and on May 3, 1882, to Martha Finley Nevin, daughter of the Rev. John W. Nevin [q.v.], of Mercersburg. Nine children were born to the first marriage and three to the fourth. Sayre died at South Bethlehem, Pa., survived by his wife and six children.

[T. M. Banta, Sayre Family (1901); The Biog. Dir. of the Railway Officials of America (1906); M. S. Henry, Hist. of the Lehigh Valley (1860), p. 394, portr.; Who's Who in Pa., 1904; The Biog. Encyc. of Pa. of the Nineteenth Century (1874); Public Ledger (Phila.), Jan. 6, 1907.]   J.H.F.

SAYRE, STEPHEN (June 12, 1736–Sept. 27, 1818), merchant, banker, diplomatic agent, was descended from Thomas Sayre, an early settler of Southampton, L. I. There Stephen was born, tenth and youngest child of John and Hannah (Howell) Sayre. He graduated from the College of New Jersey in 1757 and a few years later went to London, where his handsome person and agreeable manners won him a position in society. His charm, however, concealed an impetuous and rash nature which often involved him in difficulties and which prevented him all his life from any solid accomplishment. He became a member of the mercantile house of Dennys De Berdt [q.v.], at that time colonial agent of Massachusetts, and returned to America for a year, collecting debts for the firm, soliciting commissions, and acting also for Charles Townshend, with whom he was a favorite, in the interests of a land scheme which Townshend hoped to promote in the colony of New York.

In 1770 De Berdt died, leaving his firm in financial difficulties, and Sayre organized the banking house of Stephen Sayre & Barth-Coote-Purdon of Oxford Street. He desired De Berdt's position as colonial agent but his candidacy failed. Unofficially, however, he worked constantly for the cause of the colonies. He had already published a pamphlet, *The Englishman Deceived* (London, 1768), which was reprinted in the colonies and widely circulated. He kept in close touch with prominent men both in America and England and was responsible for the beginning of the correspondence of Arthur Lee and Samuel Adams. In 1774, his name headed the list of signers of a petition from Americans in London protesting against the proposed closing of the port of Boston. Meantime (1773), Sayre and William Lee [q.v.] had served for a year as sheriffs of London, an unusual honor to be accorded to Americans.

Sayre's outspoken partisanship finally involved him with the authorities and in October 1775 he

was arrested and lodged in the Tower, charged with having plotted to seize the King, take possession of the Tower, and overthrow the government. After five days of close confinement he was admitted to bail and subsequently discharged for lack of evidence. He then sued Lord Rochford for assault and false imprisonment. A verdict was found in his favor, but a point of law prevented the award of damages. By the time the suit was settled the banking house had failed, and Sayre went to Paris intending to sail for America. In May 1777, Arthur Lee appointed him secretary of his mission to Berlin, but the two men quarrelled constantly, and when Lee, unsuccessful, returned to Paris, Sayre stayed behind. After some months in Berlin, he went unofficially to Copenhagen to propose commercial relations with the United States and to further the suggested neutral league. Early in 1779, he moved on to Stockholm, apparently posing as an official agent of the United States, but accomplished nothing. He then returned to Paris, where Franklin told him he had nothing to offer in the way of employment and referred him to Congress for payment for his past services. His next venture was into Russia on various private projects.

At the end of the war he returned home, where he met the South American patriot, Francesco Miranda, then on a tour of the United States; henceforth he was a warm advocate of Miranda's plans and in frequent communication with him. Sayre petitioned Congress for payment for his European services, but without result, and he went again to Europe. His wife, Elizabeth (Noel), a London heiress whom he had married Feb. 18, 1775, died in 1789, and he married in Paris, 1790, Elizabeth Dorone, also a woman of wealth. Returning to America in 1793, he bought a large estate in New Jersey and recommenced petitioning Congress. At length, in 1807, an act was passed granting him pay for the time he spent in Berlin as Lee's secretary, but ignoring his claim for payment for services at Copenhagen and Stockholm. He died at "Brandon," the home of his son in Middlesex County, Va.

[W. B. Reed, Life and Correspondence of Joseph Reed (2 vols., 1847); Letters of Dennys De Berdt (1911), appearing also in Col. Soc. Mass. Pubs., vol. XIII (1912); W. B. Reed, The Life of Esther De Berdt (1853); B. F. Stevens, "Facsimiles of MSS. in European Archives" (MSS. Div., Lib. of Cong.); Am. State Papers: Claims (1834); T. M. Banta, Sayre Family (1901), with portr.; J. P. Boyd, The Susquehannah Company Papers, vol. II (1930); W. S. Robertson, The Life of Miranda (2 vols., 1929); death notice in Richmond Enquirer, Dec. 10, 1818.]   M.E.L.

SCAMMELL, ALEXANDER (Mar. 27, 1747–Oct. 6, 1781), Revolutionary soldier, was born in that part of the town of Mendon which is now Milford, Mass., and was baptized there on Mar. 22, 1747 o. s. He was the son of Samuel Leslie and Jane (Libbey) Scammell, both of whom emigrated from Portsmouth, England, to Mendon probably in 1737. His father, a physician of standing and affluence, died in 1753 and in his will provided for the care of his two sons by the Rev. Amariah Frost, pastor of the Congregational Church. Alexander was prepared for Harvard College and graduated there in 1769. With such experience in teaching district school as he had already gained during his college course, he taught first in Kingston and then at Plymouth, Mass. In 1772 he went to Portsmouth, N. H., where, with the help of a cousin in government service, he was employed in surveying and exploring for lands and for royal navy timber. He worked with Samuel Holland in surveying and making maps of the region.

The outbreak of the Revolution found him a tall, attractive young man reading law in the office of John Sullivan [q.v.] at Durham, N. H., and hoping to marry Abigail Bishop of Medford, Mass. In this he was, however, to be disappointed by the exigencies of war and the lady's doubts (letters to her in Ballou, *post*, p. 1006, *Historical Magazine, post, New Hampshire Historical Society Collections*, vol. IX, 1889). He became a brigade major in Sullivan's brigade, served in the siege of Boston and in the expedition to Canada the next year, and as aide-de-camp to Sullivan he participated in the Long Island campaign, during which, on the retreat to New York, he was responsible for a blunder that might have been fatal but for the timely arrival of Washington (H. P. Johnston, "The Campaign of 1776," *Memoirs of The Long Island Historical Society*, vol. III, 1878, p. 222). In October 1776 he became brigade major in the division of Gen. Charles Lee [q.v.] and on Dec. 10, 1776, colonel of the third continental battalion to be raised by the state. In 1777 he was with St. Clair at Ticonderoga and was slightly wounded at Saratoga. On Jan. 5, 1778, he was chosen by Congress to succeed Timothy Pickering [q.v.] as adjutant general of the Continental Army and served until Jan. 1, 1781. In that office it became his duty to arrest his old general, Charles Lee, after the battle of Monmouth and in 1780 to take charge of the execution of Major John André. He enjoyed the confidence of Washington, who at the time of his resignation spoke of him in terms of unqualified approval (*The Writings of George Washington*, vol. VII, 1835, ed. by Jared Sparks, p. 314). He resigned to take command of the 1st New Hampshire Regiment,

and he led a party of Continental light horse until on Sept. 30, 1781, he was captured at Yorktown, while reconnoitering as officer of the day. The circumstances of his death at Williamsburg sixteen days later have occasioned some controversy. It has been charged that after his capture he received the wounds from which he died; but the evidence is unconvincing. Contemporary reports of his death are not agreed in making such a charge, and it is not clear by what channels the report of any eye-witness could have found its way back to the American lines.

[Letters in Lib. of Cong., *Historical Mag.*, Sept. 1870, *Mass. Hist. Soc. Proc.*, vol. LII. (1919), and "Letters and Papers of . . . John Sullivan," ed. by O. G. Hammond, *N. H. Hist. Soc. Colls.*, vol. XIII, XIV (1930–31); Charles Coffin, *The Lives and Services of . . . John Thomas . . . Alexander Scammell* (1845); Adin Ballou, *Hist. of . . . Milford* (1882); *Vital Records of Milford, Mass.* (1917); *Vital Records of Medford, Mass.* (1907); *Provincial Papers . . . of New-Hampshire*, vol. VII (1873); *State Papers of New-Hampshire*, vols. VIII (1874), XIV (1885), XV (1886); *Mass. Hist. Soc. Colls.*, ser. 1, vol. II (1793), IX (1804), ser. 2, vols. III (1815), IV (1816); *Proc. Mass. Hist. Soc.*, ser. 1, vols. I (1879), XIV (1876), XIX (1882), ser. 2, vols. III (1888), VI (1891), whole ser. vols. XLVI (1913), LII (1919); Henry Lee, *Memoirs* (1812), vol. II, p. 333; *Mag. of Amer. Hist.*, Jan. 1881, p. 21; E. S. Stackpole and Lucien Thompson, *Hist. of . . . Durham, N. H.* (1913), vol. I; *Continental Jour. and Weekly Advertiser* (Boston), Nov. 8, 1781; date of birth from own statement on entrance to Harvard College, Harvard Univerity records through the courtesy of Clifford K. Shipton, Mass. Hist. Soc., Boston.]
K. E. C.

SCAMMON, JONATHAN YOUNG

SCAMMON, JONATHAN YOUNG (July 27, 1812–Mar. 17, 1890), lawyer and business man, was born on a farm in Whitefield. Me., the son of Eliakim and Joanna (Young) Scammon. With a farmer's life in prospect, the boy's future was suddenly changed by the loss of two fingers on his left hand. Since he was thus handicapped in the farmer's important business of milking cows, his parents decided to equip him for a profession. He prepared for college and at eighteen entered Waterville (now Colby) College, but left at the end of his first year, probably for lack of means. He studied law in a law office in Hallowell and was admitted to the bar in 1835. Fired by enthusiastic reports of the rapid development of the Mississippi Valley, he started west and, not expecting to settle there, arrived in Chicago in September 1835. Not being greatly impressed with the town, he was preparing to move on when the temporary job of deputy clerk in the circuit court was offered him. He accepted, and Chicago became his home for the remaining fifty-five years of his life. Admitted to the Illinois bar he rapidly won a place of prominence and leadership. Appointed as reporter of the Supreme Court of Illinois in 1839 he compiled four volumes of its reports, *Reports of Cases*

Argued and Determined in the Supreme Court of . . . Illinois (copr. 1840–copr. 1844). Deeply interested in public education, he, probably more than anyone else, was responsible for the establishment of free schools in Chicago. For years he was a member of the board of education and president from 1845 to 1848. One of the city's elementary schools bears his name in recognition of his services. In his early years he was a Whig and later a Republican, being delegate to the Republican National Convention in 1864 and 1872. He served as state senator in 1861.

Throughout his career he was interested in newspaper publishing, in 1844 launching the *Chicago Journal* on its long career, in 1865 helping to found the *Chicago Republican,* which was brought to an end by the fire of 1871, and beginning publication of the *Inter Ocean* in 1872. In the late '40s he became actively interested in banking, insurance, and railroads. He did more than perhaps any other man to obtain better banking laws for Illinois. He established the Marine Bank in Chicago in 1851 and the Mechanics National Bank in 1864, serving as president of each, and he developed the Chicago Fire and Marine Insurance Company, of which also he was president in 1849. He had a prominent part in the development of the Galena and Chicago Union Railroad Company and was instrumental in bringing the Michigan Central Railroad into Chicago. Throughout his long life he continued the practice of law, although, as his career developed, business matters occupied an increasing amount of his time. Robert Todd Lincoln studied law in his office. By the early '50s he had become one of the leading business men of Chicago and a rich man by the standards of wealth of that day. Financial reverses were, however, encountered: temporary in 1857, when, during the panic of that year, his bank failed while he himself was absent in Europe with his family, irreparable in 1874, when the conflagration of 1871, the panic of 1873, and a second devastating fire a year later combined to give him a series of blows from which he never financially recovered. He was instrumental in founding many Chicago societies and charitable institutions, most of which he served as president. Among these were the Chicago Historical Society, the Chicago Academy of Sciences, Hahnemann Medical College, the Hahnemann hospital, the Old Ladies' Home, the old University of Chicago, of which he was one of the most liberal supporters, and the Chicago Astronomical Society, for which he provided funds for a telescope and observatory, which, by contract between the society and the university, was erected on the grounds of the latter. His name is perpetuated in the new University of Chicago by "Scammon Court" in the School of Education quadrangle, made possible by the gift of land by his widow in 1901. In religion he was a Swedenborgian, very zealous and prominent for years in the national activities of the New Jerusalem Church. He was married twice: first in 1837 to Mary Ann Haven Dearborn, of Bath, Me., who died in 1858, and second, in 1867 to Mrs. Maria (Sheldon) Wright, of Delaware County, N. Y. He died in Chicago.

[T. W. Goodspeed, *The University of Chicago Biographical Sketches,* vol. II (1925) ; *Chicago Magazine,* March 1857, reprinted with additions in *Fergus' Hist. Series,* No. 6 (1876) ; H. L. Conrad, "Early Bench and Bar in Chicago," *Mag. of West. Hist.,* Aug. 1890 ; *Chicago Daily News,* Mar. 17, 1890 ; *Chicago Daily Tribune* and *Chicago Times,* Mar. 18, 1890.] G. B. U.

SCANLAN, LAWRENCE (Sept. 29, 1843–May 10, 1915), Roman Catholic prelate, was born in County Tipperary, Ireland, the son of Patrick and Catherine (Ryan) Scanlan. Educated at St. Patrick's College in Thurles and at the missionary seminary of All Hallows, Dublin, he was ordained a priest on June 24, 1868, and adopted by Archbishop Joseph Alemany [*q.v.*] of San Francisco, who had a rapidly increasing Irish flock. For five years he served as a curate of St. Patrick's Church and at St. Mary's Cathedral in San Francisco, as pastor in a wild mining-camp at Pioche, Nev., four hundred miles from a railroad, and at Petaluma, Cal. In 1873 he was sent as missionary to Utah with headquarters at Salt Lake City, whose frame chapel had been temporarily served since 1866 by such frontier priests as Edward Kelly, J. P. Foley, and Patrick Walsh. A stalwart, militant man of over six feet in height and two hundred pounds, he was especially well suited for arduous visitations on horseback through wild mountainous country, for the privations and coarse food of camps and diggings, and for a free, informal association with the hard but generous miners, railroad laborers, and stockmen to whom he became a hero. At Pioche he learned his business, and the denizens of that boom-town, who boycotted him for his sermons on death, hell, and judgment and for his attempts at moral reform, came to know and love him for his integrity, courage, and zeal for the poor and broken-down. Regardless of creed, they aided him in building a church, a lean-to shanty, and a hospital. His fame preceding him, he was welcomed by about ninety Catholics in Ogden and Salt Lake City and several hundred who were scattered over his parish of 85,000 square miles. If one may judge from the sympathetic messages from Mormon leaders on

Scanlan's death, the friendly relations established by Father Pierre-Jean DeSmet [*q.v.*] with Brigham Young were maintained, and Mormon elders frequently loaned him the use of their tabernacles. At first single-handed and then assisted by a small corps of self-sacrificing priests, of whom Denis Kiely became his vicar-general, he labored with astounding activity as vicar-forane, as vicar-apostolic of Utah and a large part of Nevada—consecrated titular bishop of Laranda on June 29, 1887, by Archbishop Patrick W. Riordan [*q.v.*]—and finally as bishop of the newly created see of Salt Lake City, Jan. 30, 1891.

A true pioneer and builder of the church and state, he laid the foundations of practically every parish in the diocese; he erected over thirty churches and suffered numerous disappointments when populous mining towns in which there were good congregations became ghost towns with deserted churches. He established All Hallows College, soon assigned to the Marist Fathers, in Salt Lake City in 1855; founded academies with the assistance of the Holy Cross Sisters at Salt Lake City, Ogden, Park City, and Silver Reef; built St. John's Hospital at Silver Reef in 1878, the large Holy Cross Hospital in Salt Lake City in 1875, St. Ann's Orphanage, and the Mary Judge Memorial Home for aged and injured miners, and erected the elaborate St. Mary Magdalene's Cathedral which was dedicated by Cardinal James Gibbons in 1909. He also took an active interest in state and civic affairs and in western immigration. When the end came through rheumatism and neuritis, he left a well-ordered diocese and secure foundations for the future church. Buried in the crypt of his cathedral with services by Archbishops Alexander Christie and Edward Hanna, he typified the Irish missionary. He had a brother, Daniel, who remained in Cashel and two clerical nephews, one in Manchester and the other in Australia.

[W. R. Harris, *The Cath. Ch. in Utah, Including an Exposition of Cath. Faith by Bishop Scanlan* (1909); L. J. Fries, *One Hundred and Fifty Years of Catholicity in Utah* (1926); ann. Cath. official directories; *Cath. Ency.*, vol. XV (1912), p. 240; *Who's Who in America*, 1914–15; *Deseret Evening News* (Salt Lake City), May 10–14, 1915.]   R. J. P.

SCARBOROUGH, WILLIAM SAUNDERS (Feb. 16, 1852?–Sept. 9, 1926), president of Wilberforce University, was born in Macon, Ga., the son of Jeremiah and Francis Scarborough. Both his parents knew how to read and write. His father had been set free in 1846 by the railway company that employed him, but his mother was a slave. Her son took her status and, as a slave boy, had to acquire the

rudiments of education surreptitiously. A white man, J. C. Thomas, helped educate him. By the time he was ten years old he had not only mastered the three R's but had acquired a knowledge of geography and grammar as well. Being thus qualified to make out passes for its members he was at this early age appointed secretary of one of the most prominent negro societies in Macon. He became a shoemaker's apprentice. The end of the Civil War enabled him to attend a common school, the Lewis High School in Macon, and, for two years, Atlanta University. He then took the regular academic course at Oberlin College from which he was graduated with the degree of A.B. in 1875. While at Oberlin he taught school during vacations at Albany, Ohio, Bloomingburg, Ohio, and other places. After graduation he became a teacher of Latin, Greek, and mathematics at the Lewis High School in Macon, Ga., and then served for a short time as principal of Payne Institute at Cokesburg, S. C.

In 1877 he was appointed a professor in the classical department at Wilberforce University, Wilberforce, Ohio, with which he remained affiliated for almost half a century. In 1879 he was appointed the first postmaster of the village. He was elected president in 1908 and served until 1920. During the remaining years of his life he was engaged in literary pursuits. He made a study of the progress of negro farmers in Virginia for the federal department of agriculture and published some of his results as "Tenancy and Ownership among Negro Farmers in Southampton County, Va.," *U. S. Department of Agriculture, Department Bulletin*, no. 1404 (1916). He had an unusual apitude for languages. Beside his interest in modern tongues he in course of time studied Sanskrit, Zend, Gothic, Lithuanian, and Old Slavonic. In 1882 he was made a member of the American Philological Association, before which he read a paper. He was also a member of the Modern Language Association of America, the American Social Science Association, and the American Spelling Reform Association. He was a communicant of the African Methodist Episcopal Church. He was the author of *First Lessons in Greek* (1881) and the *Birds of Aristophanes* (1886). Among his contributions to periodicals are "Future of the Negro" and "The Educated Negro and Menial Pursuits" in the *Forum* (March 1889, December 1898) and "The Negro Farmer's Progress in Virginia" in *Current History* (December 1926). He also published "The Educated Negro and his Mission" in *The American Negro Academy Occasional Papers*, No. 8 (1903). In 1881 he was married to Sarah C. Bierce, of Danby, N.

Y., a white woman, who also taught in Wilberforce. They had no children.

[W. J. Simmons, *Men of Mark* (1887); *Journ. of
Negro History*, Oct. 1926; *New York Times* for Sept.
12, 1926; *Oberlin College Alumni Cat. of 1926* (1927);
Who's Who in America, 1924–25 gives birth date as
1854.]   H. G. V.

SCARBROUGH, WILLIAM (Feb. 18, 1776–
June 11, 1838), financial backer of the pioneer
transatlantic steamship *Savannah,* was born in
South Carolina, the son of Lucy (Sawyer) and
William Scarbrough. In 1805 he married Julia
Bernard of Wilmington, a belle celebrated for
her wit and beauty. They had at least three children. In the Beaufort district of South Carolina
he owned some 100,000 acres, perhaps inherited, and had 400 slaves working· on his plantations. He was more closely associated, however,
with Savannah, where in 1804 he built a handsome house, now a negro school, and he often
appeared in public with his coach and six. He
engaged in shipping and trade, apparently in
partnership with Robert Isaacs.

The event that raised Scarbrough to more than
local prominence was his support of the first
transatlantic steamship venture. The initiative
came from Moses Rogers [*q.v.*]. Scarbrough
became interested with a score of other Savannah
business men, obtained from the Georgia legislature on Dec. 19, 1818, the incorporation of the
Savannah Steamship Company with a capital
stock of $50,000, and was one of the directors.
Under the supervision of Rogers at New York,
the company purchased and equipped the 350-ton
vessel, which was named the *Savannah* (see
sketch of Daniel Dod). The *Savannah* left New
York on Mar. 28, 1819, and reached Savannah
in eight days and fifteen hours, using the engine
only forty-one and a half hours. The next few
weeks were probably the proudest of Scarbrough's life. President Monroe visited the city
in May, spent several days as Scarbrough's guest,
and was taken on a trip down the Savannah
River on the new ship. On her famous trip, she
sailed from Tybee Light on the Georgia coast on
May 24, 1819, and reached Liverpool on June
20, making the trip in twenty-seven days but
using steam for only eighty hours, on eight different days. Her fuel was exhausted soon after
a revenue cutter chased her, off Cork, thinking
her afire. Leaving Liverpool on July 21, she
arrived at St. Petersburg on Sept. 13, touching
at Baltic ports and using steam two hundred and
thirty-nine hours on eighteen of the days. She
anchored in the Savannah River again on Nov.
30, was sent up to Washington in the hope that
she might be purchased as a warship, but, failing

in that hope, proceeded to New York, where her
engines were removed. She was sold, became a
New York-Savannah sailing packet, and was
wrecked on Long Island in 1822. The importance of her voyage has often been discounted,
particularly by the British, who point out that
she was at best an "auxiliary steamer." The chief
drawback was the lack of space for fuel in addition to sufficient cargo to make her profitable.
The effort was premature; Scarbrough and his
associates lost their investment; and permanent
transatlantic steam service had to wait almost
two decades.

There is little definite information about the
later years of Scarbrough's life. It is said that
he later went bankrupt, but this was occasioned
probably not so much by the *Savannah* as by the
yellow fever epidemic of 1820, as well as the fire
and the storm of that year, all of which dealt
staggering blows to the trade of the little city.
He died in New York City, where the arrival of
the *Sirius* and of the *Great Western* on Apr. 23,
1838, seven weeks before his death, marked the
successful achievement of what he had attempted
earlier.

[J. E. Watkins, "The Log of the Savannah," *Ann.
Report of the Board of Regents of the Smithsonian Institution . . . 1890* (1891); *Ga. Hist. Quart.,* June 1919;
F. D. Lee and J. L. Agnew, *Hist. Record of . . . Savannah*
(1869), pp. 76–77; L. L. Knight, *Georgia's Landmarks,*
vol. II (1914); *Hunt's Merchants' Mag. and Commercial Review,* Oct. 1840, p. 297; W. S. Lindsay, *Hist.
of Merchant Shipping,* vol. IV (1876); J. H. Morrison,
Hist. of N. Y. Ship Yards (1909); copy of Scarbrough
tombstone inscription in Colonial Park, Savannah, confirming spelling of name, through the courtesy of the
Ga. Hist. Soc.]   R. G. A.

SCATTERGOOD, THOMAS (Jan.? 23,
1748–Apr. 24, 1814). Quaker preacher, traveler,
was born in Burlington, N. J., the son of Joseph
and Rebecca Scattergood. His father died in
1754. His mother gave him a solid education,
though it was confined in the narrow limits of
that period. At fourteen he was apprenticed in
Philadelphia for training in mercantile business,
but at nineteen he became a tanner of leather. In
this business he continued successfully throughout the remainder of his life. In 1772 he was
married to Elizabeth, the daughter of David
Bacon of Philadelphia. His wife died after eight
years of married life, leaving one son, and he
was married again in 1783 to Sarah, the daughter of John Hoskins of Burlington, N. J.

As a child he was precociously religious and
extraordinarily sensitive to inward intimations
of duty. He was a conscientious objector to war,
and he had many difficulties to face in Philadelphia during the Revolution and the occupation
of the city by the British army. He was a Quaker by birthright, and in early life he identified

himself by personal conviction with the Society of Friends. When he spoke in public assemblies in his youth, his gift in the ministry was quickly recognized by his elders. He started his lifelong travels as an itinerant minister in 1778, his first journey being undertaken in a visit to the meetings of Maryland and Virginia. On a second visit to the meetings in the southern colonies in company with Samuel Emlen and George Dillwyn, he began to keep the diary, which faithfully records the scenes of his labors and the inner states of his mind. This supplied the material for the "Memoirs of Thomas Scattergood," edited by William and Thomas Evans (*Friends' Library,* vol. VIII, 1844, and separately 1845). The *Memoirs* furnish a somewhat unusual opportunity to study the states of mind and spiritual experiences of an over-sensitive soul, almost morbidly honest in his attempts to tell what was going on within him. He belonged in the intimate circle of the Quaker quietists of the last half of the eighteenth century. They reflected the influence of Molinos, Guyon, and Fenelon, and they, further, had profoundly felt in their youth the personal influence of their older Quaker contemporary, John Woolman. In one of his religious journeys in western Pennsylvania Scattergood appointed seven successive meetings, in which he felt that he had no message "divinely given" to him, and consequently he sat through them all in absolute silence. In spite of his inward quietism his outward life revealed a remarkable dynamic driving power. He was almost continuously engaged in public service at home or abroad. He traveled repeatedly over the colonies, where there were Quaker settlements, even to the most remote frontier regions. From 1794 to 1800 he was engaged in extensive religious services in Great Britain, Ireland, and the Orkney Islands, working much of the time in company with contemporary leading Friends, both of England and America. He is generally credited with having been one of the important inspirations for starting Westtown School and the asylum for the insane now called Friends' Hospital. David Sands [*q.v.*] and Scattergood represent two diverse tendencies in the Quakerism of the period. Sands shows the evangelical tendency and Scattergood the profound quietistic tendency. They often traveled together and worked without any conscious disharmony, but they mark in thought the beginning of an important historical divergence. Scattergood died in Philadelphia.

[*Memoirs, ante*; R. M. Jones and others, *The Quakers in the American Colonies* (1911); R. M. Jones, *The Later Periods of Quakerism* (2 vols., 1921).]

R. M. J.

SCHADLE, JACOB EVANS (June 23, 1849–May 29, 1908), laryngologist, was born on a farm near the village of Rauchtown, Clinton County, Pa. His parents, Michael and Phoebe (Sallade) Schadle, were of Revolutionary ancestry of German origin. Graduating from the Millersburg state normal school in 1868, he taught school at Millersburg for six years and at Mifflinburg for one year. At Mifflinburg he met Jane Ray Miller, daughter of Dr. David H. Miller, whom he married in 1878. In 1876 he began the study of medicine with Dr. John S. Crawford of Williamsport, and in 1881 he received his medical degree from Jefferson Medical College in Philadelphia. After a brief period of practice in the village of Pennsdale, near his birthplace, he settled in Shenandoah in the coal region, where he won the appreciation of the community by the skill and courage with which he handled an epidemic of smallpox. After taking a postgraduate course in diseases of the nose and throat under Dr. Charles Euchariste Sajous [*q.v.*], he moved in 1887 to St. Paul, Minn., in order to devote himself exclusively to this specialty, and in a few years he became the leading practitioner of laryngology in that section of the Northwest. He was appointed clinical instructor in laryngology at the University of Minnesota in 1896 and clinical professor in 1897; later he was made professor of rhinology and laryngology, a position he held for the remainder of his life. A skilful operator, he perfected several ingenious instruments for nose and throat work, including a snare for the removal of growths from the nasopharynx, a lymphatome for eradicating adenoid vegetations, and an automatic syringe for intratracheal injections.

From the beginning of his career he was a contributor to journal literature. Two of his early articles are especially noteworthy. In 1885 he reported the successful treatment of five cases of mushroom poisoning by the use of large doses of atropine (*Medical and Surgical Reporter,* Dec. 19, 1885, pp. 713–15), the first recorded use in amanitin poisoning of a treatment which later was universally adopted. In 1888 he reported some observations upon the secondary and remote effects of cocaine (*Medical Register,* vol. V, 1889, pp. 124–25), in which he called attention for the first time to the afterwards generally recognized deleterious effects of cocaine upon the genital system. His chief interests during his professional career, however, were the investigation of the causes and treatment of hay-fever and asthma and of the effects of post-nasal adenoid growths upon the health and development of children. He developed the theory that hay-fever

was due to acid secretions from catarrhal inflammation of the maxillary sinus and that extension of the process to the lower respiratory
mucous membrane caused asthma. He spent
three extended periods of study at German
medical centers and was otherwise a confirmed
traveler. At the time of his death he had accepted an invitation to present the results of his work
on hay-fever and asthma before the International
Medical Society in Budapest in 1909. Genial
and courteous, with a host of personal friends, he
was a public-spirited man prominent in the social and civic life of St. Paul. He died at St.
Joseph's Hospital in St. Paul of cerebral thrombosis following a short illness.

[G. M. Gould, *The Jefferson Medic. Coll. of Phila.*
(1904), vol. I; R. F. Stone, *Biog. of Eminent Am. Physicians and Surgeons* (1894); *St. Paul Medic. Jour.*,
July 1908; H. A. Kelly and W. L. Burrage, *Am. Medic.
Biogs.* (1920); *St. Paul Pioneer Press*, May 30, 1908.]

J. M. P—n.

SCHAEBERLE, JOHN MARTIN (Jan. 10,
1853–Sept. 19, 1924), astronomer, son of Anton
and C. Catherine (Vögele) Schaeberle, fourth
child of a family of six children, was born in
Württemberg, Germany. The family emigrated
to America in 1854 and settled in Ann Arbor,
Mich., where Schaeberle attended the public
schools until at fifteen he entered a machine shop
in Chicago as an apprentice. During his three
years' apprenticeship he chanced to become interested in astronomy. Fired with enthusiasm,
he ground a small mirror and constructed a reflecting telescope upon the roof of his rooming
house, where he spent many nights observing
the heavens. Convinced that he could make
further progress only by mastering the fundamentals of mathematics, he returned to Ann
Arbor, finished high school, and entered the
University of Michigan, from which he was
graduated in 1876 with a degree in civil engineering. During his student days he pursued
his astronomical interests even more actively
than before. Upon his graduation he became
private assistant to James Craig Watson [*q.v.*],
and in 1878 was appointed assistant in the observatory. Later he became acting assistant professor at Michigan, where he remained until
1888, when he was called to Mount Hamilton,
Cal., as a member of the original staff of the
Lick Observatory. For the first five years he
had charge of the work with the Repsold meridian circle. With the thirty-six-inch refractor he
discovered the faint companion of Procyon, the
"Little Dog Star."

A few months after his arrival at the new institution, the solar eclipse of Jan. 1, 1889, total
in northern California, occurred. With Edward

Singleton Holden and Sherburne Wesley Burnham [*qq.v.*] Schaeberle observed it as a partial
eclipse from the observatory. In December of
the same year with Burnham he observed a total
eclipse at Cayenne, French Guiana, where he
obtained good results in spite of adverse conditions. As a consequence, he became interested
in eclipse problems and formulated a mechanical
theory of the solar corona, which, with some
modifications, won and retained many adherents.
Because study of the corona suffered greatly
from lack of large-scale photographs, he built a
long-focus camera, with plate-holder in a movable carriage mounted on a track. When he first
used it at the eclipse in Chile, April 1893, he
detected a faint comet, which otherwise would
not have been seen because of its proximity to
the sun. In 1896 he headed an expedition to
Japan that was unsuccessful because of clouds.
He was also much interested in problems connected with the reflecting telescope, to the theory
of which he made definite contributions. He
built several reflectors, ranging in size from
eight to twenty-four inches in diameter. The
last of these, which had a focal length of only
three feet, was mounted equatorially and was
used for studies of faint extended nebulae and
of the sun. The small ratio between focal length
and aperture gave such great light-concentrat-
ing power that the image of the sun, when focussed upon a moderately thick piece of strap-
iron, could melt holes in it within five seconds.

When Holden retired from directorship of the
Lick Observatory in 1897, Schaeberle served as
acting director until James Edward Keeler
[*q.v.*] arrived as Holden's successor. At that
time he retired from the Lick Observatory. After a trip around the world he returned to Ann
Arbor, where he continued his studies. Throughout his life he was interested in athletics, being
particularly adept at swimming and skating, and
in music. He never married. He was living in
Ann Arbor at the time of his death, which
came very suddenly. Though apparently in good
health, he was seized with a stroke of apoplexy
while doing some light work on the lawn and
died instantly under the sky he had studied so
diligently.

[*Who's Who in America*, 1924–25; *Am. Men of Sci.*,
J. M. Cattell and D. R. Brimhall, eds. (3rd ed., 1921);
Astronomical Soc. of the Pacific Pubs., Dec. 1924; *N.
Y. Times*, Sept. 20, 1924; *N. Y. Herald Tribune*, Sept.
20, 1924; information from a nephew, E. A. Schaeberle,
Ann Arbor, Mich.]

D. H. M.

SCHAEFFER, CHARLES FREDERICK
(Sept. 3, 1807–Nov. 23, 1879), Lutheran clergyman, was born at Germantown, Pa., the
youngest son of Frederick David [*q.v.*] and

Rosina (Rosenmiller) Schaeffer. He attended Zion's parochial school in Philadelphia, graduated from the University of Pennsylvania in 1827, studied for the ministry with his father and with his brother-in-law, Charles Rudolph Demme [q.v.], was licensed by the Maryland and Virginia Synod in 1829, and was ordained by the West Pennsylvania Synod in 1831. On Aug. 27, 1832, he married Susanna, daughter of John George Schmucker [q.v.], by whom he had a son and four daughters. After a short period as assistant to his brother, Frederick Christian [q.v.], in New York, Schaeffer was pastor at Carlisle, Pa., 1830–34 and at Hagerstown, Md., 1834–40. Meanwhile his growing reputation as a conservative Lutheran theologian brought him a call to the English professorship in the seminary of the Joint Synod of Ohio at Columbus, Ohio, and in May 1840 he entered on his new duties. A gentleman of broad culture and polished manners, he was ill fitted to thrive in that Grobian environment and before long got into serious difficulties with his students, his German colleague, Johann Friedrich Winkler, and several influential ministers. The board of directors demanded his resignation, which took effect in June 1843, and Schaeffer, his health permanently injured by overwork and malaria, withdrew to Lancaster, Ohio, where he served as pastor until December 1845. Subsequently he was pastor at Red Hook, Dutchess County, N. Y., 1845–51 and of St. John's, Easton, Pa., 1851–56. In that year, after William Julius Mann [q.v.] had wisely declined the position, he was elected to the Ministerium of Pennsylvania's German professorship at the Gettysburg Theological Seminary. His accession to the Gettysburg faculty was a challenge to the liberal element in the General Synod and helped to hasten the breach between the General Synod and the Ministerium of Pennsylvania. Of the other professors in the Seminary, the president, Samuel Simon Schmucker [q.v.], was the great leader of liberal Lutheranism and was intent on carrying his cause through to victory; and the other professor, Charles Philip Krauth [q.v.], was a middle-of-the-road man, a lover of peace, who looked with about equal disfavor on his extremist colleagues. For the next eight years, with the winds of doctrine blowing from three directions at once, Gettysburg was a theological Medicine Hat. The storm broke in 1864 when the Ministerium of Pennsylvania left the General Synod and opened a seminary of its own in Philadelphia. Leaving Gettysburg precipitately, Schaeffer became the first professor and chairman of the faculty of the Philadelphia Seminary,

where, with Mann and Charles Porterfield Krauth [q.v.], his congenial colleagues, he taught until a year before his death.

Schaeffer's literary work was of considerable importance to his denomination. His contributions to the *Evangelical Review* and to the *Bibliotheca Sacra* were solid and influential statements of the confessional position; he was the translator of J. F. Kurtz's *Manual of Sacred History* (1855) and of G. V. Lechler and Charles Gerok's *The Acts of the Apostles* (1869), Volume IV in the Schaff-Lange *Commentary on the Holy Scriptures*. His revision (1854) of Philip Frederick Mayer's translation of *Luther's Smaller Catechism* (1816) was edited by C. F. Welden, A. T. Geissenhainer, and B. M. Schmucker and has become part of the life of the Lutheran Church in America. Later attempts to improve it have only served to exhibit its all but complete accuracy and its unsurpassable beauty of language. He also made a skilful revision of the common version of Johann Arndt's *True Christianity* (1868) and composed a commentary on the Gospel according to St. Matthew, devotional rather than critical in purpose, which, condensed by his son-in-law, the Rev. Reuben Hill, was published as Volumes I and II of H. E. Jacobs' *The Lutheran Commentary* (1895). Though a good part of his career was marked by bitter controversy, he was little of a fighter at heart; his uneventful latter years in Philadelphia were, in spite of the affliction of deafness, also his happiest.

[*Memorial of Charles Frederick Schaeffer, D.D.* (1880), with contributions by Adolph Spaeth, C. P. Krauth, W. J. Mann, and B. M. Schmucker and a bibliog. of his writings; *Univ. of Pa. Biog. Cat. of the Matriculates of the Coll. . . . 1749–1893* (1894); L. D. Reed, *The Phila. Sem. Biog. Record, 1864–1923* (1923); A. R. Wentz, *Hist. of the Gettysburg Theol. Sem. . . . 1826–1926* (1926); *Pub. Ledger* (Phila.), Nov. 24, 1879.]

G. H. G.

SCHAEFFER, CHARLES WILLIAM (May 5, 1813–Mar. 15, 1896), Lutheran clergyman, was born at Hagerstown, Md., the only child of the Rev. Frederick Solomon Schaeffer (1790–1815) and his wife, Catherine Elizabeth, whose maiden name was either Cremer or Gräber. His father lived the few years of his ministry at Hagerstown, gave proof of eloquence and power, and died of camp-fever contracted while ministering to soldiers quartered near the town. Charles lived his boyhood and youth in the home of his stepfather, the Rev. Benjamin Keller, at Carlisle and Germantown, Pa., and of his grandfather, Frederick David Schaeffer [q.v.], in Philadelphia. He attended the Germantown Academy, graduated in 1832 from the University of Pennsylvania, studied at the Gettysburg Theological Seminary 1833–35, and was licensed in 1835 and ordained in 1836 by the Ministerium of Pennsylvania. In 1837 he married Elizabeth Ashmead of Germantown, who bore him two sons and two daughters and died in 1892. He was pastor at Barren Hill and Whitemarsh (formerly part of the Germantown parish) 1835–41; of Zion's, Harrisburg, 1841–49; and of St. Michael's, Germantown, 1849–75. All these congregations had been served by his grandfather; his uncle, Frederick Christian Schaeffer [q.v.], had preceded him at Barren Hill and Harrisburg, and his stepfather at Germantown. For one-third of his ministerial career Schaeffer was either president or treasurer of the Ministerium of Pennsylvania, and he was a member of many of its committees. He was president of the General Synod in 1859 and of the General Council in 1868, a trustee of Pennsylvania College 1855–73, of Muhlenberg College 1868–76, of the University of Pennsylvania 1859–96, and an editor of the *Lutheran*, the *Foreign Missionary* and the *Philadelphian*. He was an assistant professor in the Philadelphia Theological Seminary from its opening in 1864, and was made Burkhalter professor of church history and pastoral theology in 1874. Though nominally he retired as professor emeritus in 1894, he continued to lecture twice a week and to preside over faculty meetings until the end; three hours before his death he sent directions to his pupils as to their work for the next day. His influence over the Lutheran Church, especially during the last thirty years of his life, was very great.

He was a man of fine intelligence and gracious spirit, prompt, cheerful, and capable in the discharge of every duty, and utterly free from any taint of affectation or self-seeking. In him the rigors of theological orthodoxy were softened and humanized by the devotional spirit. His literary taste was severe and high-bred; in his translations from the German he was able to reproduce not merely the substance but the spirit of the original. His important translations were the *Halle Reports* (1892), consisting of the first three sections of B. M. Schmucker and W. J. Mann's edition of the *Hallesche Nachrichten* (1886); *The Life of Dr. Martin Luther* (1883) by Wilhelm Wackernagel; a thorough revision of the common English version of K. H. von Bogatzky's *A Golden Treasury* (1858); Hans Sachs' *Wittenberg Nightingale* (1883); and a number of hymns, among them three—"Come, O come, Thou quickening Spirit"; "Father, Son, and Holy Ghost"; "O blessed house, that cheerfully receiveth"—that are included in the *Lutheran Common Hymnal* (1917). He contributed

notable articles to the *Evangelical Review* and the *Lutheran Church Review,* and was the author of *The Early History of the Lutheran Church in America* (1857; 1868), which was very good so far as it went, and *Family Prayer for Morning and Evening and the Festivals of the Church Year* (1861), one of the few devotional books of merit that have been composed by Lutheran writers in America. He lived to a patriarchal age with his powers of mind and memory almost unimpaired and died, suddenly but not unexpectedly, at his home in Germantown.

[*Evangelisches Magazin,* 1815, pp. 63–66, 90–91; H. E. Jacobs, "In Memoriam: Charles William Schaeffer," *Luth. Ch. Rev.,* Oct. 1896; L. D. Reed, *The Phila. Sem. Biog. Record, 1864–1923* (1923); A. R. Wentz, *Hist. of the Gettysburg Theol. Sem. . . . 1826–1926* (1926); *Pub. Ledger* (Phila.), Mar. 16, 1896; private information.]   G. H. G.

SCHAEFFER, DAVID FREDERICK (July 22, 1787–May 5, 1837), Lutheran clergyman, was born at Carlisle, Pa., the eldest son of Frederick David [q.v.] and Rosina (Rosenmiller) Schaeffer. He graduated in 1807 from the University of Pennsylvania, studied theology with his father and with the Philadelphia ministers, J. H. C. Helmuth [q.v.] and J. F. Schmidt, assisted his father for a while at Whitpain, Montgomery County, and was called in 1808 to the Lutheran church at Frederick, Md. In accordance with the practice then prevailing in the Ministerium of Pennsylvania, he was licensed by that body at Lebanon June 17, 1808, his ordination not taking place until 1812. On June 28, 1810, he married Elizabeth, daughter of George and Catharine Krebs of Philadelphia, by whom he had six children.

At this period the survival of the Lutherans as a separate denomination depended largely on their success in effecting the transition from worship exclusively in German to worship in both German and English, and on the formation of an inclusive general organization to foster unity of spirit and to guide the home missionary movement. The brunt of the work fell on a few influential ministers, of whom Schaeffer was one of the most conscientious and enlightened. He was one of the organizers of the Maryland Synod in 1820, and at the same time was one of the most active in the formation of the national body, the General Synod. When the first meeting of the General Synod convened in his own church Oct. 21, 1821, he was elected its secretary; he was secretary again in 1825, 1827, and 1829, and president in 1831 and 1833. He founded the first English Lutheran church paper, the *Lutheran Intelligencer,* and conducted it from

1826 to 1831. Until a theological seminary could be started, he trained candidates for the ministry; besides his brothers, Frederick Solomon and Frederick Christian [q.v.], who owed part of their instruction to him, he was responsible for the linguistic and theological education of fourteen ministers, including two who did him much honor, Emanuel Greenwald and Charles Philip Krauth [qq.v.]. When the Gettysburg Theological Seminary was opened in 1826, Schaeffer delivered the charge to its first professor, Samuel Simon Schmucker [q.v.]; the published address is now of considerable doctrinal interest. Though his influence was thus far from being merely parochial, his great reputation actually rests on his strictly pastoral work. For many years he seems to have been an almost perfect embodiment of the ideals of the Christian ministry, and the visible results of his work at Frederick were extraordinary. In spite of opposition he succeeded in introducing English services, and the congregation grew and prospered. He was a man of commanding presence, marked social gifts, and strong intellect. The last year of his life was made unhappy by the illness and death of his wife, by his own broken health, and by difficulties with the Maryland Synod, which disciplined him on a charge of intemperance. He died unexpectedly at Frederick and was buried there.

[Geo. Diehl, "Hist. of the Luth. Ch. of Frederick, Md.," *Evangelical Rev.*, Apr. 1856; W. B. Sprague, *Annals Am. Pulpit*, vol. IX (1869); J. G. Morris, *Fifty Years in the Luth. Ministry* (1878); *Doc. Hist. Ev. Luth. Ministerium of Pa.... 1748 to 1821* (1898); A. R. Wentz, *Hist. of the Evangelical Luth. Synod of Md.... 1820–1920* (1920).]   G. H. G.

SCHAEFFER, FREDERICK CHRISTIAN (Nov. 12, 1792–Mar. 26, 1831), Lutheran clergyman, was born in Germantown, Pa., the son of Frederick David [q.v.] and Rosina (Rosenmiller) Schaeffer. After attending the Germantown Academy, he studied for the ministry under his father, for whom he acted as vicar at Barren Hill. Though the Ministerium of Pennsylvania withheld a full license from him till he came of age, he was called to Harrisburg in July 1812 and took charge in November. He infused new life into his parish, and in 1814 the town congregation, which had been sharing a log church with the Reformed, began work on Zion Church, a commodious brick building. Almost unique in the experience of Lutheran ministers of that generation was his success in establishing English services alongside the German without incurring opposition and uproar. The prosperity of the Lutheran Church in Harrisburg dates from his pastorate.

In New York, meanwhile, Frederick William Geissenhainer, the successor of John Christopher Kunze [q.v.], had been wrestling with the language problem of the United Congregations, and when he finally resigned in despair he advised them to secure Schaeffer as their pastor. Schaeffer accepted the call thus tendered him and removed to New York in the summer of 1815. At Harrisburg he was succeeded by John George Lochman [q.v.]. Although only in his twenty-third year, he was already a man of note. A handsome presence, a keen and versatile intellect, administrative capacity, and engaging social talents were part of his family heritage. He could preach well in German and with eloquence in English, and through his father's influence he had become thoroughly imbued with the distinctive teachings and spirit of Lutheranism. He resisted the tendency, then very strong in New York, for English-speaking Lutherans to unite with the Episcopal Church; and like his close friend, Samuel Simon Schmucker [q.v.], he was one of the bulwarks of his denomination against the popular rationalism of the time. From 1815 to 1822 he was the sole pastor of the United Congregations. On Dec. 22, 1822, St. Matthew's Church on Walker Street was consecrated for the use of the English portion of the parish, and Geissenhainer was recalled as co-pastor to minister to the Germans. The German majority in the United Congregations grew increasingly hostile in its attitude toward the English, and in 1826 St. Matthew's was sold for debt. Schaeffer then resigned and with Jacob Lorillard, Kunze's son-in-law, organized St. James' Church, of which he was pastor until his death. Only two of his sermons are known to have been published: *"The Blessed Reformation"; A Sermon ... on Occasion of the Solemnization of the Third Centurial Jubilee in Commemoration of the Reformation* (1817) and *An Address Pronounced at the Laying of the Corner Stone of St. Matthew's Church, New York, October 22, 1821* (1822). A volume of *Parables and Parabolic Stories* (1829) has been ascribed to him. His early death, from tuberculosis, was a severe loss to the Lutherans of New York.

[M. L. Stoever, memoir in *Evangelical Rev.*, Oct. 1856; W. B. Sprague, *Annals Am. Pulpit*, vol. IX (1869); J. G. Morris, *Fifty Years in the Luth. Ministry* (1878); A. L. Gräbner, *Geschichte der Lutherischen Kirche in America* (1892); D. M. Gilbert, *Services Commemorative of the 100th Anniversary of Zion Ev. Luth. Ch., Harrisburg, Pa.*, Nov. 10–11, 1895 (1896); Peter Anstadt, *Life and Times of Rev. S. S. Schmucker* (1896); *Doc. Hist. Ev. Luth. Ministerium of Pa.... 1748 to 1821* (1898); *N. Y. American*, Apr. 1, 1831.]   G. H. G.

SCHAEFFER, FREDERICK DAVID (Nov. 15, 1760–Jan. 27, 1836), Lutheran clergyman, was born in Frankfurt-am-Main, the son of Johann Jakob and Susanna Maria Schaeffer, and the nephew of a superintendent of the Lutheran Church. Orphaned by the death of both parents, he was obliged to leave the Gymnasium at Hanau in 1774 and some months later accompanied one of his uncles to Pennsylvania. He became a school teacher in York County, was befriended and prepared for the ministry by the Rev. Jacob Goering, was licensed by the Ministerium of Pennsylvania in 1786, and was ordained in 1788. While pastor at Carlisle, 1786–90, he did missionary work at several points in York and Cumberland counties and in 1788 founded a Lutheran congregation at Harrisburg. His second charge, 1790–1812, was St. Michael's, Germantown, and its affiliated churches. There he preached occasionally in English and published an *Antwort auf eine Vertheidigung der Methodisten* (Germantown, 1806) as a counterblast to the horde of proselytizing evangelists whom the Second Awakening loosed upon the countryside. In 1812 he was called to succeed the late Johann Friedrich Schmidt as the colleague of J. H. C. Helmuth [q.v.] at St. Michael's and Zion's in Philadelphia. After Helmuth's retirement in 1820, Charles Rudolph Demme [q.v.] became his assistant and, before long, his son-in-law. He retired in 1834 and spent the brief remainder of his life with his eldest son at Frederick, Md., where he died and was buried.

In the autumn of 1786 he was married to Rosina, daughter of Lewis Rosenmiller of York County, who died less than a year before him. Of their eight children, the four sons who grew to maturity became Lutheran clergymen: David Frederick, Frederick Christian, Charles Frederick [qq.v.], and Frederick Solomon. The last, dying before his twenty-fifth birthday, left a reputation for eloquence and power and a son, Charles William [q.v.], to carry on the family tradition. The qualities that made Schaeffer one of the most admired and most admirable clergymen of his generation descended without modification to his children and grandchildren.

His eminence was due to solid rather than brilliant parts and to his genius for the pastoral office. A man of devout and holy life, with strong intelligence and perfect tact and gentleness, he was an unending source of comfort and consolation to the sick, the needy, and the bereaved. His sermons were simple and practical, yet did not suffer by comparison with those of Helmuth and Demme, who were famous pulpit orators. He was at his best, probably, in his instruction of children. Despite a somewhat irregular education, he became a scholar. The Hebrew Bible and the Septuagint were his daily reading; he was a close student of the Book of Concord, which he read in the Latin version; and he was saturated with the devotional writings of the Lutheran Church, the spirit of which was manifest in his own character. Music and geography were his pastimes, and in his younger days he was something of a poet.

[*Zum Andenken an die hundertjährige Jubelfeier in der deutschen evangel. luther. Sct. Michaelis-Kirche in Philadelphia* (1843); M. L. Stoever, memoir, *Evangelical Rev.,* Oct. 1854; W. B. Sprague, *Annals Am. Pulpit,* vol. IX (1869); C. S. Albert, *Hist. of the Luth. Ch. of Carlisle, Pa.* (1876); J. G. Morris, *Fifty Years in the Luth. Ministry* (1878); D. M. Gilbert, *Centennial of Zion Ch., Harrisburg, Pa.* (1895); *Doc. Hist. Ev. Luth. Mininisterium of Pa. . . . 1748 to 1821* (1898); death notice in *Poulson's Am. Daily Advertiser,* Feb. 11, 1836.]   G. H. G.

SCHAEFFER, NATHAN CHRIST (Feb. 3, 1849–Mar. 15, 1919), educator and lecturer, was born in Maxatawny Township, near Kutztown, Pa., the son of David and Esther Anna (Christ) Schaeffer and a descendant of George Schaeffer, who settled in Pennsylvania in 1750. His ancestors on both sides were Pennsylvania Germans, respected for their industry, active in promoting the establishment of the normal school at Kutztown, and zealous for the education of their sons. After receiving his early education in a rural school and at Maxatawny Seminary (later the Keystone State Normal School), at sixteen he entered the junior class of Franklin and Marshall College (A.B., 1867); he then studied at the Theological Seminary of the Reformed Church at Mercersburg (later at Lancaster) and served as instructor. In 1873 he went abroad to study for two years at Tübingen, Berlin, and Leipzig. Licensed to preach in 1875, he was ordained in 1876 by the German Reformed Church. Throughout his life he was interested in religious education, in the relations between state, church and education, and in church work and Masonry. He organized the Lehigh Classis of the Reformed Church and was called to the missionary field in Japan but declined to enter it.

On returning from Germany in 1875, he was appointed to teach ancient languages at Franklin and Marshall College; in 1877 he resigned to become principal of the Keystone State Normal School, where he remained sixteen years. He married Anna Ahlum of Applebachsville, Pa., July 8, 1880; they had seven children. In 1893 he became superintendent of public instruction in Pennsylvania and held the position until his death. He also served on the Pennsylvania Commission on Industrial Education, on the commission to frame a new state school code, as secretary of the Dental Council, of the Bureau of Medical Education and Licensure, of the National Council of Education, and as lecturer on pedagogy in the graduate school of the University of Pennsylvania (1900–01). At various times he was president of the National Education Association, of the Pennsylvania State Teachers Association, and the Pennsylvania-German Society. He was a popular professional speaker in Pennsylvania and elsewhere. To his friends he became known as the "Pennsylvania Limited," for he could be relied upon to reach the terminal on schedule time. His addresses, with his official reports, constitute the major part of his literary work. Besides these, however, he wrote *Thinking and Learning to Think* (1900), a sketch of the educational system of Pennsylvania (in H. M. Jenkins, *Pennsylvania Colonial and Federal,* 1903, vol. III), and *Bible Readings for Schools* (1897). Fairly representative of his periodical articles are "The Suppression of the Order of Jesuits in the German Empire" (*Mercersburg Review,* January 1875), "Church and State in Germany" (*Ibid.,* July 1875), and "The Literary Activity of the Romans" (*Ibid.,* July 1876). From 1893 to 1919 he edited the *Pennsylvania School Journal.* By local friends and admirers he was extravagantly acclaimed, compared in some respects to Franklin and Lincoln, even likened to Galahad in the days of Arthur, and credited with responsibility for the enormous expansion that occurred in various phases of Pennsylvania education during his incumbency. By others—though they admitted his likable personal qualities, his scholarship, ability and strength of character—he was seen as an extreme conservative under whom, especially in the later years of his superintendency, the schools had been marking time and in many respects hardly holding their own. It is a matter of common knowledge that the schools of Pennsylvania had fallen to a low position in comparison with others. Schaeffer eschewed fads in religion, morals, and education, carrying the tendency to such an extreme that in the eyes of those alive to the problems of the twentieth century the virtue finally became a vice, but he was a gentleman and a scholar of the old school and as such suited the mind and temper of Pennsylvania at the turn of the century.

[*Who's Who in America,* 1918–19; *Report of Superintendant of Pub. Instruction,* 1919, and other ann. reports, 1894–1919; *The Centennial Hist. of Kutztown, Pa.* (1915); E. M. Rapp, address to Hist. Soc. of Berks County, June 1919, MS.; *Pa. School Jour.,* Mar. 1919; *Pa.-German Soc.,* vol. XXX (1924); *Lancaster New Era,* Mar. 17, 1919; *Pub. Ledger* (Phila.), Mar. 16 and 17, 1919.]   T. W.

SCHAFF, PHILIP (Jan. 1, 1819–Oct. 20, 1893), church historian, was born at Chur, the capital of the Swiss canton of Grisons. His father, Philip Schaf [*sic*], was a carpenter in humble circumstances, who died when the child was but a year old; his mother belonged to a family of farmers at Zizers. As a schoolboy in his native town, Philip showed such promise that friends enabled him to continue his education. When he was fifteen he entered the academy of Kornthal, Württemberg, from which, after eight months, he passed to the Gymnasium at Stuttgart. In 1837 he enrolled at the University of Tübingen, where, by nature warmly pious and somewhat mystical, he was more attracted by the evangelical school of Christian Schmid than by the critical school of Ferdinand Baur, although the latter affected lastingly Schaff's historical point of view. In September 1839 he went to the University of Halle, where Friedrich Tholuck was his teacher and friend, and in the spring of 1840, to the University of Berlin. Here he studied under the man who most influenced him, Johann August Wilhelm Neander. In 1841 he received the degree of licentiate of theology, his thesis being the first of his many publications, *Die Sünde wider den Heiligen Geist* (1841). After traveling as a private tutor in southern Europe, he became in 1842 *privat-docent* in the University of Berlin. He was well on his way to a German professorship, when the call to the United States came which changed the current of his life.

Desiring in its theological seminary at Mercersburg, Pa., as successor to F. A. Rauch [*q.v.*] a German scholar of high standing, the Eastern Synod of the German Reformed Church in 1843 engaged Schaff, on the recommendation of Tholuck, Neander, and others. He was ordained to the ministry of the Reformed Church at Elberfeld, Apr. 12, 1844, and in July arrived in the United States. At Mercersburg the villagers, headed by a band, escorted him to Seminary Hill. The noise his coming awakened was not confined to horns and drums, however. In his ordination sermon, he had spoken in reproachful terms of the moral and religious condition of the German emigrants. His remarks became known in the United States, and near and far he was denounced as a defamer of his countrymen. In his inaugural address, furthermore, printed, in enlarged form, in German, and in English as *The Principle of Protestantism* (1845), he set forth the doctrine of historical development, portraying the Reformation, not as a revolution, nor as a restoration, but as a development out of the good forces in the Catholic Church, a development destined to continue, with the possibility of the ultimate union of Protestantism and Catholicism. The address was vigorously criticized, especially because of its alleged leanings toward Puseyism; the classis of Philadelphia adopted resolutions demanding an investigation by the Synod; but in October 1845 the Synod exonerated Schaff of the charges implied in the resolutions.

For nineteen years he remained at Mercersburg, subject to more or less opposition, which was strengthened by his association with John W. Nevin [q.v.] in the development of the controversy-provoking Mercersburg Theology, to the historical and liturgical aspects of which Schaff made substantial contribution. In 1846 he published *What is Church History? A Vindication of the Idea of Historical Development*, and in 1851, *Geschichte der Apostolischen Kirche* (English translation by E. D. Yeomans, 1853), which gave him high rank as a church historian. In 1857 appeared *A Liturgy, or Order of Christian Worship, for the German Reformed Church*, the work of a committee which Schaff headed. He founded and edited (1846–54) *Der Deutsche Kirchenfreund*, the first theological journal in German issued in the United States. During this Mercersburg period he came to be the mediator between the theology of Germany and American scholarship. German theology, he believed, could bear its full fruit only when incorporated into American activity; therefore he endeavored in manifold ways to unite the two. Among the means employed were the works that he edited which appeared later, among them, *A Commentary on the Holy Scriptures* (25 vols., 1865–80), an American edition of John P. Lange's great commentary; and the *Religious Encyclopædia* (3 vols., 1882–84; 3rd edition, 4 vols., 1891), based on the *Real-Encyklopädie* of Herzog, Plitt, and Hauck. He became thoroughly American in interest, though cosmopolitan in spirit and zeal for world-wide Christian union.

In 1865 he resigned his position at Mercersburg after two years' leave of absence, and thereafter resided in New York. For several years, beginning in 1864, he was secretary of the New York Sabbath Committee, an organization aggressively opposed to the secularization of Sunday which many German-Americans favored. He lectured at various theological schools and in 1870 joined the faculty of Union Theological Seminary, transferring his denominational affiliations to the Presbyterian Church. His ecumenical activities were extensive. He was a strong supporter of the Evangelical Alliance, making numerous trips abroad to attend its coun-

cils, and took prominent part in the organization of the American branch. He was also active in the formation of the Alliance of the Reformed Churches. In the work of revising the English Bible, 1881–85, he rendered valuable service, arranging for the organization of the American Committee, selecting its members, and acting as its president. "He had the spirit and habit of universality. He was ubiquitous in person. You could not travel without meeting him or finding that he had been there.... He was ubiquitous in reputation. In Glasgow or Durham, or in the little village of the Bavarian Alps, as an American, you would be asked 'Do you know Dr. Schaff?' And he was equally ubiquitous in mind" (*Papers of the American Society of Church History*, VI, 30). The list of publications which bear his name as author or editor numbers eighty or more. He was by nature a historian, however, and his work was marked by thoroughness of research, accuracy, candor, clearness of style, irenic spirit, and keen interest in the bearing of the past on contemporary problems. His most ambitious work was his *History of the Christian Church* (5th edition, revised and enlarged, 7 vols., 1882–92), which remains a lasting monument to his scholarship and industry. Among his other important publications were *Bibliotheca Symbolica Ecclesiæ Universalis: the Creeds of Christendom* (1877); *A Companion to the Greek Testament and the English Version* (1883; 7th edition, revised, 1896); and *Theological Propædeutic* (1893). His death, from a second cerebral hemorrhage, occurred in New York, soon after his return from the Parliament of Religions at Chicago, a trip his doctors had forbidden. He was married in December 1845 to Mary Elizabeth Schley of Frederick, Md.

[D. S. Schaff, *The Life of Philip Schaff* (1897), contains bibliog. of Schaff's publications and references to many sources of information. See also J. I. Good, *Hist. of the Reformed Ch. in the U. S. in the Nineteenth Century* (1911); *Gen. Cat. of the Union Theolog. Sem. ... 1836–1918* (1919); *Papers of the Am. Soc. of Ch. Hist.*, vol. VI (1894), vol. VII (1895); *N. Y. Times*, Oct. 21, 1893.]

H. E. S.

SCHAMBERG, JAY FRANK (Nov. 6, 1870– Mar. 30, 1934), dermatologist, was born in Philadelphia, Pa., the son of Gustav and Emma (Frank) Schamberg. He attended the public schools and graduated from the University of Pennsylvania in 1892 with the degree of M.D. After serving an interneship in the university hospital for eighteen months, he spent a year in the post-graduate study of dermatology in Vienna, Berlin, Hamburg, Paris, and London, and then began the practice of medicine in Philadelphia. Shortly thereafter he was appointed lecturer on infectious eruptive fevers in the University of Pennsylvania and in 1900 professor of dermatology in the Philadelphia Polyclinic and College of Graduates in Medicine. When this institution was affiliated with the Graduate School of Medicine of the University of Pennsylvania in 1919, he was appointed professor of dermatology and syphilology, a position he held until the time of his death. In the meantime he also held for brief periods the professorship in dermatology and syphilology in the Temple University school of medicine and the Jefferson Medical College. In 1912 he organized the Dermatological Research Laboratories and during the World War, with Dr. John A. Kolmer and Dr. George W. Raiziss, succeeded in synthesizing arsphenamin and neoarsphenamin at a time when supplies of these compounds for the treatment of syphilis were not available. The funds accruing were set aside for medical research and resulted in the establishment of the Research Institute of Cutaneous Medicine, Philadelphia, of which he was director until the time of his death.

In 1912 he served as a member of the Pennsylvania state vaccination commission; in 1920–21 as president of the American Dermatological Association; in 1931 as president of the Philadelphia County Medical Society, and in 1928–29 as chairman of the section on dermatology and syphilology of the American Medical Association. From 1927 to 1934 he served on the editorial board of *Archives of Dermatology and Syphilology*. He was a corresponding member of the dermatological societies of France, Denmark, and the Argentine Republic. He published over a hundred and fifty articles on skin diseases and syphilis and in 1901 described a progressive pigmentary disease of the skin since known as Schamberg's disease (*British Journal of Dermatology*, January 1901). In 1909 he discovered the cause of "grain itch" in collaboration with Dr. Joseph Goldberger, reported in *Epidemic of an Urticarioid Dermatitis Due to a Small Mite . . . in the Straw of Mattresses* (1909). He was also author of *A Compend of Diseases of the Skin* (1898), which went through many editions. With Dr. William Welch he wrote *Acute Contagious Diseases* (1905), republished in collaboration with Dr. John A. Kolmer in 1928 as a textbook on *Acute Infectious Diseases*. In 1908 he published *Diseases of the Skin and Eruptive Fevers* and in 1932, in collaboration with Dr. Carroll S. Wright, *Treatment of Syphilis*. A man of calm demeanor, whose earnestness and cheerfulness were unchanging, he was gifted with an equal enthusiasm for work and for play, and had to an unusual degree the power of stimulating and inspiring his associates. On Oct. 11, 1905, he married May Ida Bamberger of New York; they had a son and a daughter.

[See *Who's Who in America*, 1932–33; *Pa. Medic. Jour.*, May 1934, p. 671; *Archives of Dermatology and Syphilology*, June 1934; *Jour. Am. Medic. Assoc.*, Apr. 14, 1934; *Pub. Ledger* (Phila.), Mar. 31, 1934. No complete list of Schamberg's writings has as yet (1935) been published.]   J.A.K—r.

SCHARF, JOHN THOMAS (May 1, 1843–Feb. 28, 1898), Confederate soldier, historian, collector of Americana, was born in Baltimore, Md., the son of Thomas G. and Anna Maria (McNulty) Scharf. At the age of sixteen, after an elementary education in St. Peter's parish school and in Calvert Hall, he entered the lumber business of his father, but he soon left it for the more congenial work of fighting for the South in the Civil War. On his second attempt, in July 1861, he succeeded in making his way to Virginia, where he enlisted in the 1st Maryland Artillery. With that unit he went through several campaigns, receiving wounds at Cedar Mountain, at the second battle of Bull Run, and at Chancellorsville. While recovering from the last of these he was commissioned a midshipman in the Confederate navy in 1863. In that branch of the service he participated in some minor engagements, later to be unduly magnified in his history of the Confederate navy, but the lack of activity by the winter of 1864 caused him to resign with the intention of transferring back to the army. Instead he was sent by the war department on a mission to Canada. He had hardly crossed the Potomac into Maryland, when he was captured. The end of the war prevented his trial as a spy, and in September 1865 he was pardoned by President Johnson. On Dec. 2, 1869, he was married to Mary McDougall of Baltimore, who with three children survived him. After another experience in his father's business he practised law for about four years, served on the editorial staffs of three Baltimore papers, the *Baltimore News, Sunday Telegram*, and *Morning Herald*, was elected in 1877 a member of the Maryland House of Delegates, and held the office of commissioner of the land office from 1884 to 1892. An appointment as special inspector of Chinese immigration at the port of New York took him to that city in 1893, and there he remained to practise law four years later when a Republican administration came into power.

During these years he devoted himself constantly to the writing of local history. The results appeared in articles in the Baltimore *Sun*, in magazines, and in many heavy books. They won for him recognition as an authority on Maryland history. Nearly all his writings were devoted to local history, and his books suffer from the inclusion of biographies of living men and other devices to make them sell. The one outstanding exception is the *History of Maryland* (3 vols., 1879), which in spite of his many prejudices is the most comprehensive treatment of the subject and one which historians still consult. While less significant, *The Chronicles of Baltimore* (1874), in which he anticipated McMaster in the use of newspapers as a main source for writing history, and his *History of the Confederate States Navy* (1887) are of value to the student of history. At one time he was preparing to write the authorized biography of Jefferson Davis. His use of some of the material in a newspaper article angered Davis, and, perhaps for that reason, the work was never completed (Dunbar, Rowland, *Jefferson Davis,* 1922, IX, 510, 574, 576). Less known but perhaps more deserving of memory than his writings was his success as a collector of historical materials. In 1891 he presented to the library of The Johns Hopkins University a collection of Americana, which was one of the largest and best that had been assembled up to that time. Notable in it were some 50,000 pamphlets especially on Southern history, the files of fifteen or more Confederate newspapers for all or portions of the Civil War period, 3000 broadsides, a large assortment of the papers of important private citizens, and a mass of official Maryland records (described in the *Johns Hopkins University Circular,* June 1891, pp. 110–13). Most of the purely local records, such as rent rolls and muster rolls, which were probably acquired while he was commissioner of the land office, have since been deposited with the Maryland Historical Society.

[*Sketch of J. Thomas Scharf* (1879), reprinted from *The Biog. Cyc. of Representative Men of Md. and District of Columbia* (1879); biog. sketch in *The Johns Hopkins Circular, ante*; F. B. Culver, "The War Romance of John Thomas Scharf," *Md. Hist. Mag.,* Sept. 1926; *Sun* (Baltimore), Mar. 1, 1898, Dec. 22, 1929; mother's name from family information.]   W. S. H.

SCHAUFFLER, HENRY ALBERT (Sept. 4, 1837–Feb. 15, 1905), Congregationalist clergyman, missionary, was born in Constantinople, the son of William Gottlieb Schauffler [*q.v.*]; his mother was Mary (Reynolds), who introduced education for women into the Turkish Empire. Sent to the United States, Henry entered Williams College, from which he was graduated as salutatorian of his class in 1859. After two years at Andover Theological Seminary and one year at the Harvard Law School he went back to Constantinople, where he was for two years professor of law at Robert College. He was ordained at Constantinople on June 3,

1865, and for the next five years was an American Board missionary in that city. As a missionary to Catholics in Austria, he was stationed at Prague from 1872 to 1874, and from 1874 to 1881 at Brünn, where he found the field difficult and suffered many hardships; his labors, however, had the important result of securing a fair degree of religious freedom in the empire.

Returning to the United States in 1882, he was employed by the Missionary Society of Cleveland, Ohio, to conduct religious work among the 20,000 Bohemians in that city. His abilities won immediate recognition and he became known as the "Apostle to the Slavs." Within a few years one Polish and four Bohemian churches were established through his efforts, and in 1884 he was made superintendent of its Slavic work throughout the country by the Congregational Home Missionary Society. Churches and missions were planted in many centers of Slavic population; a work of great importance was founded in Chicago; and in 1885, a department for the training of Slavic-speaking ministers was established in Oberlin Theological Seminary. Probably his most important achievement, however, was the Schauffler Missionary Training School in Cleveland, founded in 1886 as the "Bible Readers' School" for the training of Slavic women for mission work among their own people. From small beginnings this school has become a flourishing institution and has broadened its scope till its pupils now represent many nationalities.

Schauffler was characterized by great missionary zeal, marked executive ability, and indomitable persistence. He was master of five languages and had considerable acquaintance with several others. His publications consist chiefly of addresses on the Slavic peoples and mission work among them. On Nov. 25, 1862, he was married to Clara Eastham Gray, who died Sept. 3, 1883; and on July 28, 1892, to Clara Hobart, who had been the first teacher in his Cleveland school. Seven children by the first marriage and three by the second survived him.

[H. M. Tenney, *The Schauffler Missionary Training School* (1915); *Congreg. Year Book,* 1906; *Congregationalist,* Feb. 25, 1905; *Home Missionary,* Apr. 1905; H. P. Schauffler, *Henry Albert Schauffler, a Sketch of His Life by His Son* (1910); *Sketches of the Life and Work of Henry Albert Schauffler, D.D.* (1906); *Andover Theological Sem. Necrology,* 1904–05; *Cleveland Plain Dealer,* Feb. 16, 1905.]
                        F. T. P.

SCHAUFFLER, WILLIAM GOTTLIEB (Aug. 22, 1798–Jan. 26, 1883), missionary, the son of Philip Frederick and Caroline Henrietta (Schuckart) Schauffler, was born in Stuttgart, Germany. In 1805 his family settled in Odessa,

Russia, where his early education was gained, partly in a German school; he also received private instruction in music and drawing. At fifteen years of age, he was put to work at his father's trade of turner and maker of musical instruments, but, prompted by an insatiable appetite for learning, he soon mastered Russian, French, and Italian, and studied Latin, Greek, and English.

He came early under the influence of "missions" and was converted by an evangelical Catholic, Ignatius Lindl. Urged to enter missionary service by an agent of the Basle Missionary Institute, named Saltet, he was enlisted for work among Moslems by Joseph Wolff. On Feb. 8, 1826, he sailed with Wolff for Constantinople, where he began the study of Turkish and "Islamic controversy." On May 8 he sailed for Smyrna, to begin his missionary activities. A sudden change of plan, however, carried him to America for further education. Arriving in Boston on Nov. 7, he applied, at the suggestion of officers of the American Board of Commissioners for Foreign Missions, for admission to Andover Theological Seminary. There he spent five years, supported by funds of the institution and his own labors, especially as a cabinet maker. His course of study included Greek and Hebrew, but he added, under his own tuition, Chaldaic, Syriac, Arabic, Persian, Turkish, Rabbinic, Coptic, and Ethiopic. Before his career was over, it is said, he could understand twenty-six languages, use ten with facility, and speak extemporaneously in six. He gained experience in preaching by supplying for several months the pulpit of the Park Street Congregational Church in Boston. On Nov. 14, 1831, he was ordained in this church, and commissioned by the American Board as a missionary to the Jews of Turkey.

He spent some time en route in Paris with masters of Arabic, Persian, and Turkish, and visited Stuttgart, Vienna, and Odessa. Arriving in Constantinople on July 31, 1832, he met with no success there, or in Smyrna, to which place he transferred at the end of the year. He then returned to Constantinople to enter government educational service. On Feb. 26, 1834, he married, in Constantinople, Mary Reynolds of the Smyrna Mission. Thereafter, for several years, he engaged in missionary tours and Bible translation. His first Jewish converts were won in 1835. By 1839 he had completed a new translation of the Old Testament into Hebrew-Spanish (Sephardi), which the American Bible Society began publishing in Vienna under his supervision. By 1842, three thousand copies had

been issued, one of which Schauffler presented in person to the Austrian Emperor. A year later, five thousand copies more were printed.

In 1843 Schauffler received a grant of about $2,200 from the Missionary Society of the Established Church of Scotland for his work among the Jews, and he served for a time as chaplain of the Mission to the German (Ashkenaz) Jews. During 1855–56 Jewish missions were transferred to the Free Church of Scotland, and he devoted himself thereafter to the Armenians and Turks under the Turkey Mission of the American Board. He had, in August 1855, represented Armenian missions at a meeting in Paris of the World's Evangelical Alliance, pleading the cause of religious liberty in Turkey. During 1856–57 he aided in the revision of the Turkish New Testament, and began transcribing the Armeno-Turkish Bible into Turkish. Turkey having been at last "opened" by the Crimean War, he visited America in 1857 (arriving in New York Aug. 20) on behalf of Turkish missions. On his way back he secured funds in Edinburgh with which to pay the cost of an English-Turkish lexicon and other literature. Under the auspices of the American and the British and Foreign Bible societies, he translated the New Testament into Turkish (1866), and did further work on the Turkish Old Testament. In 1874 he and his wife left Turkey, and, after spending three years with their son, Henry Albert [q.v.], in Moravia, they proceeded to New York to live with other sons.

In addition to the work of translation, Schauffler wrote "What Drink Did Our Lord Jesus Christ Use at the Institution of the Eucharist?" (*Biblical Repository and Quarterly Observer*, October 1836), "Resources of the Catholic Church for Carrying on Foreign Missions" (in Elias Loomis' *Memoirs of American Missionaries*, 1833), and *Meditations on the Last Days of Christ* (1837). He received several honorary degrees and was decorated by the King of Prussia.

[*Autobiog. of William G. Schauffler* (1887), ed. by his sons; *Missionary Herald*, Mar. 1883; H. C. Haydn, *Am. Heroes on Mission Fields* (1890); C. C. Creegan and J. A. B. Goodnow, *Great Missionaries of the Church* (1895); *N. Y. Tribune*, Jan. 28, 1883.]

J. C. A.

SCHECHTER, SOLOMON (Dec. 7, 1850– Nov. 15, 1915), Hebraist and author, son of Isaac and Chaya Rachel Schechter, was born in Fokshan (Focsani), Roumania. He received his early education, which was confined exclusively to Hebrew literature, from his father; at ten he went to a Hebrew school at the neighboring town of Piatra and at fourteen to Lemberg, where he studied under a great Talmudist, Rabbi Joseph Saul Nathanson. In 1875 he went to Vienna; there, under the guidance of Isaac Hirsch Weiss and Lector Meir Friedmann, the knowledge he had acquired in the Roumanian schools became methodized. He received the rabbinical diploma in 1879 but never exercised the functions of that office. After studying in Berlin, at the Hochschule für die Wissenchaft des Judenthums and attending lectures at the University of Berlin, he went in 1882 to England, where he began an active scholarly and literary career. Here in 1887 he married Mathilda Roth, a native of Breslau who was then teaching in England; by her he had a son and two daughters. He was a lecturer in Talmud at Jews' College in London when in March 1890 the readership in Talmud and rabbinical literature at Cambridge University fell vacant and he was appointed to the post. Though he probably did not know more than a few words of English until he was thirty-five years of age, he rapidly acquired an amazing knowledge of the language and a style attained by few.

Among his first scholarly publications were a number of Hebrew ethical wills (1885), which he found in the British Museum; Saadya's explanation of the rules of interpretation; and a critical edition of the *Aboth de Rabbi Nathan* (1887), one of the minor tractates of the Babylonian Talmud. He received a traveling scholarship to Italian libraries in 1893 and two years later he was invited to Philadelphia to deliver a course of lectures at the newly inaugurated Gratz College. In 1896 he made a discovery that gave him a world-wide reputation. He identified a fragment of a manuscript as a part of the lost original Hebrew of the oldest book of the Apocrypha, the Wisdom of Ben Sira or Ecclesiasticus. Shortly thereafter he undertook a visit to Cairo to investigate the so-called Genizah, a sort of literary burial place, which it was known existed in Jewish synagogues. For months he worked underground with great hardship, which was detrimental to his health, but he finally brought back to Cambridge some fifty thousand manuscripts and fragments, mostly in Hebrew and Arabic, probably the largest collection of manuscript material ever found by one man. In it he discovered many of the remaining chapters of Ecclesiasticus, published in 1899 as *The Wisdom of Ben Sira, Portions of the Book Ecclesiasticus from Hebrew Manuscripts in the Cairo Genizah Collection.* He gave a series of lectures based upon this on the social life of the Jews in the age of Jesus, the Son of Sira (*Stud-*

ies in Judaism, 2 ser., 1908), which tended to disprove many theories that had been advanced concerning the dates of various books in the Biblical canon.

Besides being reader at Cambridge, he had been appointed a curator of the university library, Goldsmith professor of Hebrew at the University of London, and an examiner at the University of Manchester. Still he was not happy in England. As a lover of freedom he had long been attracted by America; moreover, he wished for a more Jewish atmosphere and field of activity. When in 1901 he was invited to become president of the Jewish Theological Seminary in New York, he accepted, breathed new life into the seminary, collected a new faculty, and within a very short time became the acknowledged leader of Jewish scholarship in America. He founded the United Synagogue of America, was one of the editors of the Bible Translation of the Jewish Publication Society, of the *Jewish Quarterly Review,* and of the first edition (1901) of *The Jewish Encyclopaedia.* After arranging his administrative work he issued a number of publications, some of them based upon the Cairo manuscripts. The first of these (1903) was entitled *Saadyana Geniza Fragments of R. Saadya Gaon,* mostly, though not exclusively, unpublished documents of Saadia Gaon, the great scholar of the ninth century; in 1912 he published a document relating to the conversion of the King of Khazars to Judaism (*Jewish Quarterly Review,* n.s., vol. III, p. 485 ff.). But his most important publication after *The Wisdom of Ben Sira* was a two-volume work, *Documents of Jewish Sectaries* (1910). He stimulated other scholars to search among the manuscripts he had collected, and many chapters of Jewish history and works of Jewish literature are gradually being recovered through this great mass of material, so extensive that it will take many generations to explore. Under the modest title of *Some Aspects of Rabbinic Theology,* he published in 1909 the first approach to a methodical presentation of Jewish theology. He wrote many charming essays, collected under the title *Studies in Judaism,* in three series (1896, 1908, 1924), and *Seminary Addresses and Other Papers* (1915). He also edited the *Midrash Hag-gadol to Genesis* (1902), a collection of ancient homiletic interpretations of the Bible. His papers and articles in journals run into the hundreds. He was very imposing-looking, with a massive leonine head. He had great interest in general affairs, and at the time of the Boer War, to which he was opposed, he did not hesitate to speak his mind even in England. When the

Scheel

World War broke out, his sympathies were with the Allies, and he was impatient because America did not at once support what he considered a righteous cause. Besides a distinguished reputation for knowledge, he had great charm of presentation that earned for him real celebrity.

[*Who's Who in America*, 1914–15; Schechter's Application and Testimonials for the post of Lecturer in Talmudic in the University of Cambridge, 1890, printed but not published; Samuel Schulman, in *Yearbook: Central Conference Am. Rabbis*, vol. XXVI (1916); G. F. Moore, in *Menorah Jour.*, Feb. 1916; F. I. Schechter, *Ibid.*, June 1922; Cyrus Adler, in *Am. Jewish Year Book*, 1916; *Students' Ann.*, vol. III (1916), Jewish Theological Sem.; Alexander Marx, "Solomon Schechter," *Pubs. Am. Jewish Hist. Soc.*, no. 25 (1917), pp. 177–92; Alexander Marx and S. M. Stroock, *Memorial Addresses . . . on . . . the Death of Dr. Solomon Schechter* (1917); Joshua Bloch, *Prof. Solomon Schechter, M.A., Litt.D.* (1915); Louis Ginzberg, in *Students, Scholars, and Saints* (1928); Norman Bentwich, *Solomon Schechter* (1931). C.A.

SCHEEL, FRITZ (Nov. 7, 1852–Mar. 13, 1907), violinist, conductor, was born in Lübeck, Germany, the son and grandson of musical conductors. His mother was a talented amateur musician. Scheel had his first musical training in his native town, piano lessons from F. Burjani, and violin instruction from Gottfried Herrmann. Before he was ten years of age Scheel was able to occupy one of the first violin desks in his father's orchestra and on occasion filled vacancies by playing the horn, trumpet, trombone, and tuba. He also organized and conducted a juvenile orchestra of his own. From 1864 to 1867 he studied the violin under Ferdinand David in Leipzig and in 1869 went to Bremerhaven, first as concert-master at the opera, and then as conductor of concerts. In 1873 he went to Schwerin as solo violinist and director of the court orchestra. After a term at Bremen, he went to Chemnitz in 1882 to succeed Hans Sitt as *Kapellmeister*. Here he directed an orchestra of seventy-two players, as well as the *Sitt Chor Gesangverein*, a chorus of several hundred voices. The orchestra became well known and was invited to travel to various cities in Saxony. In 1890 Scheel moved to Hamburg, where he alternated with Hans von Bülow as conductor of the Abonnement Concerts.

At the time he came to America, in 1893, Scheel was a musician with thorough experience in all branches of the profession. He made his first appearances in New York City, and then organized an orchestra which gave concerts at the Trocadero of the World's Columbian Exposition in Chicago. This enterprise was not successful, however, and Scheel later took an orchestra to San Francisco to play at the concerts of the Midwinter Fair. He was induced to remain in San Francisco, and became the first con-

Schele de Vere

ductor of the San Francisco Symphony Society. In 1899 Scheel went to Philadelphia, where he conducted an orchestra at Woodside Park, a summer resort. His concerts attracted the attention of the managers of the Philadelphia Symphony Society, an amateur organization, and he was elected conductor the same year. In 1901 the Philadelphia Orchestra Association was organized, and Scheel made conductor—a post which he held until his death. From the very beginning he insisted upon highly artistic and classical performances, sturdily resisting the demands of the managers for more "popular" programs. This policy, pursued with the rare skill, courage, and unflagging energy which characterized Scheel, laid the solid foundations upon which his successors have built (see the tribute by Leopold Stokowski, Wister, *post*, p. 85). In addition to his work with the orchestra, Scheel directed two choral organizations, the Orpheus and the Eurydice clubs. These labors proved too great a burden for his strength, and he began to suffer a gradual breakdown about a year before his death. He was survived by his widow, three daughters, and a son.

[F. A. Wister, *Twenty-five Years of the Philadelphia Orchestra* (1925); *Grove's Dict. of Music and Musicians, Am. Supp.* (1930); *Baker's Biog. Dict. of Musicians* (3rd ed., 1919); *Music World*, Jan. 1907; *Musician*, Sept. 1904; *Musical Record and Rev.*, Nov. 1903; *Public Ledger* (Philadelphia), Mar. 14, 1907.] J.T.H.

SCHELE DE VERE, MAXIMILIAN (Nov. 1, 1820–May 12, 1898), philologist, was the son of a Swedish *freiherr*, von Schele, officer in the Prussian army, and a French mother named De Vere. He was born in Wexiö, Sweden, but followed his father in allegiance to Prussia; in appearance and disposition he was characteristically French. As a child he evinced great aptitude for languages, early mastering Slavic, French, and German, and so augmenting his knowledge by study and travel that he had won reputation as a linguist before he reached his majority. His formal education was obtained at the Universities of Bonn, Berlin (Ph.D., 1841), and Greifswald (*Juris Utriusque Doctor*, 1842).

After a year or more in the Prussian diplomatic and military services, in 1843 he emigrated to Boston, where he gave private instruction in languages and studied modern Greek at Harvard. His refined and amiable nature combined with his attainments to win him many distinguished friends, and when, Sept. 23, 1844, he was elected professor of modern languages at the University of Virginia, he was recommended for the chair by Longfellow, Josiah Quincy, and Abbott Lawrence (Bruce, *post*, III, 83). In this capacity, he served the state with distinction and ability until advancing age compelled his resignation, fifty-one years later.

In addition to teaching the French, Spanish, Italian, and German languages and literatures and also the literary and political history of these nations, he deserves remembrance for having inaugurated the systematic study of Anglo-Saxon. Likewise, he offered successful courses in comparative philology, at a period when few American colleges had recognized the value of the comparative method. His classes were extremely popular, the students, under the prevailing elective system, seeking out Professor Schele as well for the courtesy and character of the man as for the interest and enthusiasm with which he presented his subject. His published studies of the genesis and development of the English language were original and in advance of similar effort elsewhere: among his more valuable works were his *Outlines of Comparative Philology* (1853), *Studies in English* (1867), *Americanisms; The English of the New World* (1871). He performed an enormous amount of scholarly labor, his other publications including, besides his work for the *Standard Dictionary* (1893–95) and some graceful addresses, articles for magazines and encyclopedias, historical romances, several volumes of popular science, translations from contemporary European authors (especially Friedrich Spielhagen and Emile Gaboriau), a Spanish and a French grammar and other language texts, and his valuable compilation, *Students of the University of Virginia, a Semi-Centennial Catalogue* (copyright 1878). All that he wrote was characterized by vivacity and smoothness of style, by studious accuracy and catholic culture.

Schele was twice married, each time to a daughter of Judge Alexander Rives of Albemarle County, Va.; first, on July 25, 1849, to Eliza Wydown Rives and, nine years after her death in 1851, on Mar. 21, 1860, to Lucy Brown Rives. A daughter by his first wife died in 1864. His own death occurred in Washington, D. C., whither he had removed after his retirement.

[J. S. Patton, in *Lib. of Southern Lit.*, vol. XI (copr. 1909), ed. by E. A. Alderman and J. C. Harris; D. M. R. Culbreth, *The Univ. of Va.* (1908); W. M. Thornton, in *Alumni Bull. of the Univ. of Va.*, July, Nov. 1894; P. A. Bruce, *Hist. of the Univ. of Va.*, vol. III (1921); J. R. Childs, *Reliques of the Rives* (1929), p. 606; *Washington Post,* May 13, 1898.]   A. C. G., Jr.

SCHELL, AUGUSTUS (Aug. 1, 1812–Mar. 27, 1884), lawyer, politician, business man, was the most prominent of four brothers who became well known in the financial circles of New York City. An elder brother, Richard, a brilliant talker, jovial, open-handed, everywhere welcome, was from 1840 to 1873 one of the most daring operators in Wall Street and also served a term in the state legislature and in the House of Representatives. Two younger brothers, Robert and Edward, became presidents of leading banks. All were born at Rhinebeck, N. Y., the sons of Christian and Elizabeth (Hughes) Schell, and the grandsons of Richard Schell, one of a group from the Rhenish Palatinate that settled in the vicinity of Rhinebeck shortly before the Revolution. Augustus graduated from Union College in 1830, studied a year at the celebrated law school at Litchfield, Conn., and read law under John Armstrong at Rhinebeck and John Slosson in New York City. Shortly after his admission to the bar (1833) he was admitted to the Slosson firm. His father having died early, his mother moved to the city and until her death in 1866 provided her sons with a home. It was late in life (March 1873) that Augustus married Anna, daughter of George S. Fox of New York City, who survived him. No children were born to them.

Schell became an expert in the expanding field of corporation law and gave his legal services more and more to firms in which he and Richard were financially interested. Close friends of "Commodore" Cornelius Vanderbilt, 1794–1877 [q.v.], they backed him in all his interests, particularly in building up the New York Central railroad system and in his fight with Daniel Drew [q.v.] over the Erie. Schell became a director of the New York and Harlem Railroad, 1862; of the Hudson River Railroad, 1864; of the New York Central, 1867; of the Lake Shore and Michigan Southern, 1869; and later of the Chicago and Northwestern, the Union Pacific, and a score of others. He was also a director of several banks and insurance companies and was long vice-president of the Union Trust Company. He was heavily interested in the Western Union Telegraph Company, served many years as chairman of its legal committee, and was senior vice-president at his death. His market operations were heavy. Together with Horace F. Clark and Jay Gould [qq.v.] he engineered the corner in Chicago and Northwestern stock, one of Wall Street's notable post–Civil War episodes. Though Richard's house failed in 1873, Augustus managed to weather the panic and at his death was worth several millions, eventually divided among his nieces and nephews.

As a ward leader and then district leader he rose in the Tammany organization until in 1852 he became chairman of the Tammany general committee. The same year he was Tammany's candidate for governor but at the state convention lost the nomination to Horatio Seymour [*q.v.*]. He was chairman of the Democratic state committee, 1853–55, and an efficient worker for Buchanan in 1856, his efforts being rewarded by appointment to the important post of collector of the port of New York, 1857–61. His political career was halted by the war and reconstruction periods, but he was drawn into a second period of political activity when he was persuaded to head a reorganization of Tammany Hall after the Tweed downfall. Accordingly, he succeeded William Marcy Tweed [*q.v.*] as Grand Sachem in 1872 and held the position until his death. He helped name the Committee of Twenty-one to reconstruct Tammany and again became chairman of the Tammany general committee. In 1872 a second attempt to nominate him for governor was prevented by the clever strategy of Samuel Jones Tilden [*q.v.*]. As chairman of the National Democratic Committee, 1872–76, Schell managed Greeley's presidential campaign and, according to John Kelly [*q.v.*], gave enough toward the campaign chest to make an ordinary man rich for life. He opened the National Democratic Convention at St. Louis in 1876, and though he joined with Kelly in opposing Tilden's nomination, he afterwards supported him liberally. Schell was an unsuccessful candidate for state senator, 1877, and for mayor of New York, 1878, having consented to run for these local offices for the sake of Tammany in crucial elections. He lacked appeal for the average Tammany voter, being something of "an old pump that the boys could never cotton to in a thousand years" (*New York Herald*, Nov. 1, 1877). In his later political activities he was closely allied with Kelly, of whose honesty and good intentions he was firmly convinced. He was interested in many clubs, societies, and institutions of the city. He served nineteen years as chairman of the executive committee of the New York Historical Society and was twice president. His favorite charity was the New York Institution for the Blind, of which he was president from 1866 until his death.

[The chief authority is the *Memoir of the Hon. Augustus Schell* (1885) by Francis Schell, a nephew, which contains in its appendix the memorial notice by Dr. George H. Moore of the N. Y. Hist. Soc. and John Kelly's intimate tribute. See also *U. S. Democratic Rev.*, Dec. 1857; *Encyc. of Contemporary Biog. of N. Y.* (6 vols., 1878–90); D. S. Alexander, *A Pol. Hist. of the State of N. Y.* (3 vols., 1906–09); J. F. McLaughlin, *The Life and Times of John Kelly* (1885); obituaries in *N. Y. Tribune, N. Y. Times*, Mar. 28, 1884.]

O. W. H.

SCHEM, ALEXANDER JACOB (Mar. 16, 1826–May 21, 1881), encyclopedist, editor, statistician, was born at Wiedenbrück, Westphalia, Germany, and was baptized Jacob Balthasar Alexander. He was the son of a vinegar manufacturer, Friedrich Schem, and his wife, Adolphine von Felgenhauer. He attended the Gymnasium at Paderborn (1839–43) and then studied Catholic theology at Bonn (1843–45) and at Tübingen (1845–46). Ordained a priest on Apr. 18, 1849, he officiated for two years as "Kaplan" in Bielefeld.

Finding himself less and less in accord with dogma, he gave up his allegiance to the Roman Catholic Church and emigrated to the United States in 1851. His first position was that of tutor in the home of the publisher, Friedrich Gerhard, whose oldest daughter Schem married in 1853. In the same year he accepted a position as teacher of ancient and modern languages at the Collegiate Institute, Mount Holly, N. J. From 1854 to 1860 he was professor of Hebrew and modern languages at Dickinson College and in 1858 published, in collaboration with George R. Crooks [*q.v.*], *A New Latin-English School-Lexicon*. He resigned his professorship in order to devote himself entirely to literary and journalistic work in New York.

In the pursuance of this work he wrote numerous articles for *The New American Cyclopædia* (1858–63), edited by C. S. Dana and George Ripley. He also published a work on church statistics, *The American Ecclesiastical Year-Book* (1860), which was followed by *The American Ecclesiastical Almanac* (1868) and *The American Ecclesiastical and Educational Almanac* (1869). From 1860 to 1869 he was foreign news editor of the *New York Tribune*, as well as a collaborator in preparing the *Tribune Almanac*, the *National Almanac*, and *The American Year-Book and National Register*. On leaving the *Tribune* in 1869, he became editor-in-chief of the *Deutsch-amerikanisches Conversations-lexikon* (11 vols., 1869–74). He was a contributor to *Johnson's New Universal Cyclopædia*, and in 1877 published, with Henry Kiddle, *The Cyclopædia of Education*. In addition to the above, he wrote a book on the Russo-Turkish war, *The War in the East* (1878), as well as numerous magazine articles. From 1874 until his death he was assistant superintendent of the public schools of New York and for some time an editorial contributor to *The Methodist* and *The Methodist Quarterly Review*.

Schem was a man of extraordinarily wide reading in twelve languages and his home in Hoboken was the resort of many scholars. He believed that the development of learning in nineteenth-century Germany was second only to that of

Athens in the fifth century, and he worked consistently for a better understanding among Americans of German scholarship. All his writings are characterized by deep seriousness, thorough scholarship, broad background. His one larger non-encyclopedic work, *The War in the East,* begins with a long discussion of the events that preceded the war, gives detailed descriptions of all the battles, and sketches the repercussions of the war in various diplomatic chancellories of Europe. It is written in a readable style remarkable for a man who was not writing in his native tongue. Unlike many other German-Americans, Schem identified himself fully with the intellectual currents in the English language, without, however, turning his back entirely on undertakings in his own language, as his editorship of an encyclopedia in German shows. He is described as of stocky build, sociable in his habits, extremely tolerant in his views, and indefatigable in his labors—the last-named characteristic probably being responsible for his death, which occurred in Hoboken, since the death certificate reads as follows: "Primary Disease: Cerebral Hyperasthesia. Secondary Disease: Acute Diabetes. Remarks: The foundation of the whole disease was exhaustive mental labor."

[The most comprehensive sketch of Schem's life is in *Der Deutsche Pionier,* Dec. 1882; a short biog., probably written by himself, is found in *Deutsch-amerikanisches Conversations-lexikon,* IX (1873), 743–44; brief estimates of his lifework are given in Rudolf Cronau, *Drei Jahrhunderte deutschen Lebens in Amerika* (Berlin, 1909), and Georg von Bosse, *Das deutsche Element in den Vereinigten Staaten* (1908), pp. 440–41; the names of Schem's parents are from the record of his baptism, at Wiedenbrück; see also, *Appletons' Ann. Cyc. . . . 1882* (1883); *N. Y. Tribune,* May 24, 1881.]   A.E.Z.

SCHENANDOA [See SKENANDO, *c.* 1706–1816].

SCHENCK, FERDINAND SCHUREMAN (Aug. 6, 1845–Apr. 6, 1925), clergyman of the Reformed Church in America, was born at Plattekill, Ulster County, N. Y., the son of the Rev. Martin Luther Schenck and Abigail Van der Veer. His grandfather, Ferdinand S. Schenck, was a distinguished physician of Somerset County, N. J. Ferdinand was graduated from the College of New Jersey in 1865, and then entered the Albany Law School. Receiving the degree of LL.B. in 1867, he practised for two years, and then, convinced of a call to the ministry, gave up the law and became a student in the New Brunswick Theological Seminary. After his graduation and ordination, by the classis of Paramus, in 1872, he served successively four Reformed churches, all in the state of New York—in Clarkstown, 1872–77, Montgomery, 1877–90, Hudson, 1890–97, and University Heights, New York City, 1897–99.

In 1899 he was appointed by the General Synod of the denomination professor of practical theology in the New Brunswick Seminary. In this office he served for twenty-five years, becoming emeritus professor in 1924. His department of instruction included homiletics, liturgics, pastoral practice, and, in a comprehensive way, sociology, to which he gave enthusiastic attention when it first became an academic subject. Other fields of thought and instruction were also familiar to him and he was lecturer on the literary study of the Bible at New York University (1898–1900), acting professor of philosophy (1904–05), and acting professor of ethics (1907–08) at Rutgers College, and acting professor of homiletics at Princeton Theological Seminary (1909–10). In 1892 he was president of the General Synod of the Reformed Church in America.

Schenck's intellectual interests were wide and varied, as his services of instruction suggest; even science was not outside their range, astronomy being one of his favorite studies. His excellence as a preacher lay in the clearness and directness of his thought, the simplicity and aptness of his language, and in his somewhat informal yet dignified and fluent address. He had a warmth of sympathy and a graciousness of personal contact that made him helpful and beloved as a pastor and left a lasting impression upon his students. He wrote much and was the author of books on various subjects. Among them are *The Ten Commandments in the Nineteenth Century* (1889); *The Bible Reader's Guide* (1896); *The Ten Commandments and the Lord's Prayer* (1902); *Modern Practical Theology* (1903); *The Sociology of the Bible* (1909); *Christian Evidences and Ethics* (1910); *Young People's History of the Christian Church* (1911); *The Oratory and Poetry of the Bible* (1915); *The Apostles' Creed in the Twentieth Century* (1918); *Expository Sermons on the Heidelberg Catechism* (1920); and *A Guide to the Stars* (1922). On Aug. 26, 1874, he married Ellie S. Haring of Nyack, N. Y., by whom he had three daughters and two sons. He died at White Plains, N. Y.

[*Acts and Proc. of the . . . Gen. Synod of the Reformed Church in America,* 1925; E. T. Corwin, *A Manual of the Reformed Church in America* (1922); J. H. Raven, *Biog. Record: New Brunswick Theological Sem.* (1934); *Who's Who in America,* 1924–25; *Christian Intelligencer,* Apr. 15, 1925.]   W. H. S. D.

SCHENCK, JAMES FINDLAY (June 11, 1807–Dec. 21, 1882), naval officer, son of Gen.

William Cortenus Schenck and Elizabeth (Rogers) Schenck and brother of Robert Cumming Schenck [q.v.], was born in Franklin, Ohio. On July 1, 1823, he was appointed to West Point but, becoming deficient in his studies, was turned back and resigned. On Mar. 1, 1825, he was appointed midshipman in the navy, promoted to passed midshipman in 1831, to lieutenant in 1835, and to commander in 1855. He first saw service with the Mosquito Fleet in the West Indies against the pirates and in 1828 commanded the sloop *Surprise,* after which his naval career for several years was uneventful. But in 1845 he was assigned to the frigate *Congress* under Commodore Robert Field Stockton [q.v.] and served with that officer during the occupation and conquest of California. He was present at the capture of Santa Barbara and on Aug. 6, 1846, landed in a launch with twenty men at San Pedro and captured that port. At the head of a company of seamen he marched with Stockton's command on Los Angeles, entering the town on Aug. 13, 1846. As second lieutenant of the *Congress* he participated in the bombardment and capture of Guaymas, and the taking of Mazatlán. From May 1849 until 1852 he was in command of the United States mail steamer *Ohio;* in 1858 he was given command of the receiving ship *North Carolina* at the New York navy yard; and on Mar. 8, 1860, he sailed from San Francisco in command of the *Saginaw* for the East India station. His cruise in far eastern waters was uneventful but for one occurrence; on June 30, 1861, while anchored just outside Quin Hon Harbor, Cochin China, he was fired upon by a fort and returned the fire, silencing the guns. The *Saginaw* was de-commissioned at Hong Kong Jan. 3, 1862, as she proved unseaworthy, and Schenck returned to the United States on the merchantman *Swordfish* with his crew. In April 1862 he was given command of the frigate *St. Lawrence,* East Gulf Blockading Squadron, and on her did blockading duty for one year, when he was relieved. He was listed on the navy register from 1862 to 1864 as commander "Not recommended for promotion by the Advisory Board," but in 1864 he was commissioned commodore, dating from Jan. 2, 1863, skipping the grade of captain. On Oct. 14, 1864, he took command of the steamer *Powhatan* and later of the third division of the North Atlantic Blockading Squadron. In this dual rôle he participated in the two attacks on Fort Fisher. He was commended by Admiral David Dixon Porter [q.v.] for gallant conduct. During the next two years he commanded the naval station at Mound City, Ill. Commissioned rear admiral Sept. 21, 1868, he was retired by law, June 11, 1869.

His earlier years in the service were spent at a time when the navy was in an inactive stage that afforded little opportunity for advancement or active duty, but his Mexican War service showed that he had the qualities of a leader. The outbreak of the Civil War found him well past his youth, and it is probable that the advisory board held up his promotion for that reason. During both attacks on Fort Fisher, in a difficult and responsible position, he handled his division with efficiency and precision, his reports to Admiral Porter showing keen observation and judgment. He married Dorothea Ann Smith on July 27, 1829, and had two sons and two daughters. His life following his retirement was spent at Dayton, Ohio.

[A. D. Schenck, *The Rev. William Schenck, His Ancestry and His Descendants* (1883) ; L. R. Hamersly, *Records Living Officers U. S. Navy* (4th ed., 1890) ; *War of the Rebellion: Official Records (Navy),* 1 Ser., vols. I, VII, XI, XII, XVII ; Navy Reg., 1825–70 ; *U. S. Mil. Acad. Reg.,* 1824 ; unpublished archives, Office of Naval Records ; log of U.S.S. *Saginaw,* MS., Navy Dept.; H. H. Bancroft, *Hist. of Cal.,* vol. V (1886) ; D. D. Porter, *The Naval Hist. of the Civil War* (1886) ; *Diary of Gideon Welles,* vol. II (1911) ; S. J. Bayard, *A Sketch of the Life of Com. Robert F. Stockton* (1856) ; *Cincinnati Commercial, Dayton Daily Democrat, Dayton Daily Jour.,* Dec. 22, 1882.]
L. H. B.

SCHENCK, ROBERT CUMMING (Oct. 4, 1809–Mar. 23, 1890), congressman, soldier, diplomat, was a son of Gen. William Cortenus Schenck and his wife, Elizabeth Rogers. The father, a descendant of Roelof Martense Schenck who came to New Amsterdam probably about 1650, had migrated from New Jersey to Ohio, where he served in the legislature and is said to have founded the town of Franklin. Here Robert was born. His father died in 1821, leaving the boy under the guardianship of Gen. James Findlay [q.v.] of Cincinnati. Robert graduated from Miami University in 1827, remained there three years longer studying and teaching, was subsequently admitted to the bar, and commenced practising law in Dayton. On Aug. 21, 1834, he married Rennelche W. Smith, whose sister was the wife of his brother James Findlay Schenck [q.v.].

Robert Schenck's political career began in 1838 with a fruitless campaign for election to the legislature on the Whig ticket. More successful later, he assumed the leadership of his party in the Ohio House during the terms of 1841–43. In the national House of Representatives, 1843–51, he proved himself a vigorous Whig partisan, and upon the expiration of his fourth term in 1851 he was named by President Fillmore as minister to Brazil. Here he served until October 1853, acting with John S. Pendleton [q.v.], chargé d'affaires of the United States to the Argentine Confederation, in negotiating commercial treaties with Uruguay (1852) and Paraguay (1853), which were never proclaimed, and two treaties with the Argentine Confederation, signed July 10 and 27, 1853. He failed, however, to secure from Brazil a treaty providing for the free navigation of the Amazon.

A strong anti-slavery man, Schenck was one of the first to urge Lincoln's nomination and was an active Republican campaigner in 1860. Appointed brigadier-general of volunteers May 17, 1861, he took part in the first battle of Bull Run, served under Rosecrans and Frémont in West Virginia, and was wounded at Second Bull Run in August 1862, his right wrist being permanently injured. On Aug. 30 he was promoted major-general of volunteers. Eliminated from active fighting, he was assigned in December 1862 to the command in Baltimore, where his measures were not always popular (Richard H. Jackson, *To Robert E.* [sic] *Schenck,* pamphlet, 1867, p. 3). In December of the following year he resigned his commission in order to sit once more in Congress.

In the House he disapproved strongly of Lincoln's moderation as shown in the Hampton Roads Conference (J. F. Rhodes, *History of the United States,* vol. V, 1904, pp. 51–52, note). A master of invective and vituperation, he distinguished himself for the violence of his attack on such "Copperheads" as Fernando Wood, whom he called "a specimen of the snake family" (*No Compromise with Treason; Remarks of Mr. Schenck ... Apr. 11, 1864,* 1864) and for his opposition to President Johnson. He was chairman of the House committee on military affairs and later of the Ways and Means committee. He was an advocate of the contraction of the currency at the end of the war (*Public Credit-Gold Contracts: Speech ... Feb. 22, 1869,* 1869).

Failing of reëlection to Congress in 1870, Schenck turned again to diplomacy. He was appointed, Feb. 10, 1871, a member of the Joint High Commission between the United States and Great Britain and in that capacity signed the Treaty of Washington, May 8, 1871. On Dec. 22 preceding he had been designated to succeed the discredited John Lothrop Motley [*q.v.*] as minister to Great Britain, and he traveled to his post in May 1871. Here he was called upon to conduct much of the routine business arising out of the Treaty of Washington and the arbitration of the *Alabama* claims. In spite of his failure to conclude a consular convention with Great Britain and to persuade Derby to support the United States in its demands on Spain for concessions in its Cuban policy (S. F. Bemis, *The*

American Secretaries of State, vol. VII, 1928, pp. 194–200), his record in London seems creditable, but in February 1876 he resigned under a cloud. He had allowed himself to be made a director of the "Emma" silver mine in Utah which in 1871 used his name in the sale of stock in Great Britain. He was reproved by the Secretary of State at that time, and the failure of the Emma Mine brought his resignation, which Grant reluctantly accepted. The committee on foreign affairs of the House, which investigated the incident, found no cause to impugn Schenck's integrity, but condemned such transactions by American diplomats (*House Report No. 579,* 44 Cong., 1 Sess., 1876). After Schenck's resignation he returned to Washington to practise law, achieved a reputation as an authority on draw poker (he published *Draw Poker* in 1880), and died in that city in 1890. He was survived by three of his six daughters.

[A. D. Schenck, *The Rev. Wm. Schenck, His Ancestry and His Descendants* (1883); Robt. C. Schenck, *U. S. A.* (n.d.), pub. by order of Union Central Com., 3rd Cong. District, Ohio; *In Memoriam, Gen. Robt. C. Schenck* (n.d.), proceedings at memorial service in Dayton; *Biog. Dir. Am. Cong.* (1928); Beckles Wilson, *America's Ambassadors to England* (1928); W. A. Taylor, *Hundred-Year Book and Official Reg. of the State of Ohio* (1891); *Papers Relating to the Foreign Relations of the U. S.,* 1871–76; L. E. Chittenden, *The Emma Mine* (1876); War Dept. records; instructions and dispatches to and from Brazil and Great Britain, in Dept. of State; *Washington Post,* Mar. 24, 1890.]
E. W. S.

SCHERESCHEWSKY, SAMUEL ISAAC JOSEPH (May 6, 1831–Oct. 15, 1906), missionary to China, translator of the Bible into Chinese, bishop of the Protestant Episcopal Church, was born in Tauroggen, Russian Lithuania, the son of Samuel and Rosa (Salvatha) Schereschewsky. His father was of the Ashkenazim and his mother of the Sephardim Jews. Both parents died when he was young and he was reared by a half-brother and his wife, who hoped to see him become a rabbi. He was given a careful Jewish training at home, in his native town, and at the rabbinical schools in Krazi and Zitomir. He then spent some time in the University of Breslau. Becoming convinced by his study of the New and Old Testaments that he should become a Christian, in 1854 he went to the United States, where, in a Baptist church, he was immersed. From 1855 to 1858 he studied in the Western Theological Seminary, a Presbyterian institution at Allegheny, Pa., and then, having joined the Protestant Episcopal Church, he was a student from 1858 to 1859 in the General Theological Seminary, New York City.

Some time before completing his education he had formed the purpose of becoming a missionary and translating the Bible into Chinese. He was ordained deacon in New York in July 1859, and that same year arrived in Shanghai as an appointee of the missionary society of his church. Here, Oct. 28, 1860, he was ordained priest. He had begun the study of Chinese on his way out and continued it in Shanghai, making rapid progress, for he had a natural gift for languages. From 1863 to 1875 he spent most of his time in Peking. While there he joined with another missionary in translating the (Anglican) Book of Common Prayer into Mandarin, the vernacular used by the majority of the Chinese, and with four other missionaries in translating the New Testament into that dialect; the latter translation was published in 1872. He himself translated the entire Old Testament into Mandarin (1865–73), and it was published in 1874. In the meantime, 1868, he had married in Shanghai Susan M. Waring, and in 1875, with his wife and two children, he returned to the United States for an extended furlough. While there he was elected to the Protestant Episcopal bishopric of Shanghai. After much hesitation and once declining, he accepted and on Oct. 3, 1877, was consecrated.

In 1878 he returned to Shanghai and there with funds which he had raised while in the United States bought the Jessfield site and erected the first buildings of a college, St. John's (later St. John's University), which he organized and which became one of the leading institutions of higher education in China. In 1879 he translated the entire Prayer Book into classical Chinese. That year he moved to Wuchang, where, in 1881, weakened by overwork in the attempt to carry the duties of bishop, to conduct the local mission, and to continue his translating, he was suddenly smitten with an illness which left him almost completely paralyzed and with impaired speech, but with quite unimpaired mind. From 1882 to 1886 he was in Geneva, Switzerland, for medical care, and from 1886 to 1895 in the United States. In 1883 he resigned his bishopric and seemed destined to spend the rest of his life in idle invalidism. In 1886, however, he resumed once more his work of translation. He could write painfully by pressing the keys of a typewriter with one finger of one hand. Laboring in this fashion and aided by the devoted care of his wife, in the next few years he wrote out in romanized form a revision of his Mandarin version of the Old Testament and a translation of the entire Bible into what is known as "easy Wenli," a form of the Chinese classical style. In 1895 he returned to Shanghai to have this translation put into Chinese characters and published. Because of its better facilities for printing, he went to

Japan in 1897 and there, in Tokyo, spent the remainder of his days. He was able to see through the press his revision of the Mandarin version—which he had once more revised—and his Wenli version of the Bible, also revised. Both were of excellent quality and were widely used. He also completed a reference Bible in both Mandarin and Wenli, and at the time of his death was at work on a translation of the Apocrypha. In collaboration with another missionary he had also translated the Gospel of Matthew into Mongolian and he had prepared, but never published, a handbook of Mandarin, a grammar and chrestomathy, and a dictionary of the Mongolian tongue. He was humble-minded, large-hearted, of marked intellectual as well as linguistic gifts, and an indefatigable and persistent worker.

[*Spirit of Missions,* June 1877, Apr. 1903, Nov. 1906; *Chinese Recorder,* Mar. 1903, Nov. 1906; annual reports of the American Bible Society, 1897–98, and especially 1907, pp. 152–54; annual reports of the board of managers of the Domestic and Foreign Missionary Society of the Protestant Episcopal Church in the U. S. A.; *Who's Who in America,* 1906–07; *Churchman,* Oct. 20, 1906; *Japan Weekly Mail* (Tokyo), Oct. 20, 1906; information from friends and from a daughter, Miss Caroline Schereschewsky.]   K. S. L.

SCHEVE, EDWARD BENJAMIN (Feb. 13, 1865–June 18, 1924), musician, was born in Herford, Westphalia, Germany, the eldest of six children of Edward and Adelaide (Schöneborn) Scheve. Both parents came from Bonn on the Rhine. The father, a Baptist minister, was for many years director of the Kammerung Mission of West Africa. The mother possessed some poetic ability, and was also musical. At the age of eight, Edward began the study of piano and organ under a local teacher, continued at the Cologne Gymnasium and the Geisenheim Institut, and then went to Berlin, where he entered Theodor Kullak's academy in 1885, and for three years studied piano with A. König, organ with F. Grunicke, and composition with Albert Becker. He also taught in the Academy from 1886 until 1888, when he came to the United States. He settled in Rochester, N. Y., as music teacher and organist at the First Baptist Church, and remained until 1892. In the year 1890 he made a trip to Berlin where he was married on Oct. 9 to Lina Amelia Grosch, a singer. In 1892 he became organist of the First German Baptist Church and director of the German-American Conservatory in Chicago. He remained in Chicago for fourteen years, and gave many organ recitals and concerts of his own compositions. In 1906 he was called to the Grinnell College School of Music, Grinnell, Iowa, as professor of theory and composition and instructor in organ. He remained there until his death, which occurred at Longmont, Colo., while on an extended vacation.

Scheve was deeply religious and his devotion to his religious convictions was completely intertwined with his music. At Rochester, N. Y., where for several months he was organist of the Lake Avenue Baptist Church, he was officially known as the Minister of Music, so earnest was his effort to make the position a real spiritual ministry to those who came to worship. Among his most important compositions are the following: "Symphony in D minor, *Opus* 38"; a piano concerto, *Opus* 20; a violin concerto in E flat, *Opus* 35; an oratorio, 'The Death and Resurrection of Christ, *Opus* 11"; "Festival March" for orchestra, organ and chorus; and an organ sonata in E flat. He also wrote many songs, anthems, and piano pieces.

[Information secured from his widow; *Who's Who in America*, 1924–25; *Who's Who in Music and Drama* (1914); *Am. Supp.* to *Grove's Dict. of Music and Musicians* (1930); obit. notice in *Grinnell Register,* June 23, 1924.]   F. L. G. C.

SCHICKILLEMY [See Shikellamy, d. 1748].

SCHIEREN, CHARLES ADOLPH (Feb. 28, 1842–Mar. 10, 1915), inventor, manufacturer, was the eldest child of John Nikolaus and Wilhelmina (Langenbach) Schieren and was born in Neuss, near Düsseldorf, Germany. His father was a business man and a moving spirit in the political revolution of 1848, the failure of which necessitated his fleeing from Germany with his family. In 1856 he brought them to the United States. Young Schieren was then fourteen years old, but he had received a good common school education in Germany and upon his arrival in the United States engaged with his father in conducting a tobacco store in Brooklyn. In 1864, however, he obtained a position in the leather-belting establishment of Philip F. Passquay, New York City, and by his diligence and industry soon mastered the details of this business, particularly the manufacture of leather belting, so that when his employer died in 1865 he was able to conduct the business alone. When this was sold he continued with the successor until 1868; then with the savings he had accumulated he founded his own leather-belting manufactory in New York. For the succeeding fourteen years he conducted his ever growing business alone; in 1882 he took in a partner and the firm name was changed to Charles A. Schieren & Company but, while there were changes in partnership at various times thereafter, Schieren himself directed the affairs of the business to the day of his death. With the coming of high-speed electric

dynamos and motors in the late 1880's the existing types of leather belting proved unsatisfactory, and Schieren devoted much time and experiment to developing suitable belting. During 1887 and 1888 he secured eight patents for the newer forms of belting and for machines to manufacture them. One of these, a so-called "electric belt," perforated and coated with a composition, was the only belt in its day to withstand the terrific strain of high-speed electrical machinery. Another was a leather link belt composed of small leather links strung on steel pins and ingeniously joined together. These inventions, with one or two minor ones, brought him to the forefront of the leather trade as an authority on belting, a position he held throughout his life.

Schieren was a very public-spirited man and identified himself with several important reform movements in New York. Because of his qualities as a business man he was elected mayor of Brooklyn in 1893 and during his term of two years succeeded in bringing the city out of bankruptcy. The construction of the Williamsburg Bridge was planned during his administration and many parks were laid out, including the Narrows Shore Drive along the harbor. In 1898 he was appointed by President McKinley chairman of the Cuban relief committee and treasurer of the national Red Cross; he was a member of the commerce commission appointed by Governor Black to consider the enlargement of the Erie Canal; he served on the Ambrose Channel commission; and he was a member of the greater New York charter commission appointed by Governor Theodore Roosevelt. He was a founder of the Brooklyn Institute of Arts and Sciences, president of the Brooklyn Academy of Music, founder and vice-president of the Hide & Leather National Bank, and a trustee in a number of banks and insurance companies. In 1865 he married Mary Louise Bramm of Brooklyn and at the time of his death was survived by his widow, who lived but twenty-four hours longer, and four children.

[*Who's Who in America*, 1914–15; *Hide and Leather,* Mar. 13, 1915; *Shoe and Leather Reporter,* Mar. 18, 1915; obituary notices in *Brooklyn Daily Eagle,* Mar. 10, 1915, *N. Y. Times* and *N. Y. Tribune,* Mar. 11, 1915; Patent Office records; correspondence with Charles A. Schieren & Co.]   C. W. M.

SCHIFF, JACOB HENRY (Jan. 10, 1847– Sept. 25, 1920), financier, philanthropist, was born in Frankfurt-am-Main and died in New York City. He was the son of Moses and Clara (Niederhofheim) Schiff, and a member of a family that could trace its line back to 1370, through scholars of distinction and men of affairs. He was educated in the local schools and, in addition to secular and Jewish knowledge, gained a fair acquaintance with French and English. At fourteen he was apprenticed to a business firm. Four years later, with some difficulty, he secured his father's permission to come to America, arriving in New York Aug. 6, 1865. For a short time he was engaged with a brokerage firm in New York, and on Nov. 21, 1866, was licensed as a broker. In 1867 he joined the firm of Budge, Schiff & Company, which was dissolved in 1872.

Schiff meanwhile had become a citizen of the United States, being naturalized in September 1870. Upon the dissolution of his firm, he decided to go back to Germany and in the following year was offered a position as manager of the Hamburg Branch of the London & Hanseatic Bank. This connection did not last long, because Schiff returned to Frankfurt upon the death of his father in that same year, but in 1874 he was invited by Abraham Kuhn, senior partner of Kuhn, Loeb & Company, to return to New York and enter that firm. He accepted this proposal in January 1875, bringing to his new association not only his energy and foresight, but also his connections with Sir Ernest Cassel of London, with Edouard Noetzlin, president of the Banque de Paris et des Pays Bas, and with Robert Fleming, then of Dundee and later of London. Through these connections he was able to place large quantities of American securities on the European market. In 1885, at the age of thirty-eight, he became head of the firm.

Schiff was concerned with the financing of nearly all the important railroads in the East, which were not personally owned by families, especially the Pennsylvania Railroad and the Louisville & Nashville. Probably the most sensational episode in his financial career was the struggle between the Union Pacific Railroad and the Great Northern company for control of the Northern Pacific, in which Schiff was allied with Edward H. Harriman [q.v.] against James J. Hill [q.v.] and J. P. Morgan & Company. This contest, because of the importance of the interest, brought about a panic on the stock market, May 9, 1901, and resulted in the formation later that year of the Northern Securities Company. The legality of this organization was challenged, however, by President Theodore Roosevelt, under the anti-trust laws, and his view was sustained by the Supreme Court of the United States.

Schiff also took a hand in the reorganization of the Baltimore & Ohio Railroad (1896–99) and at various times aided the American Smelting & Refining Company, the Westinghouse Electric Company, and the Western Union Telegraph Company. One of his less fortunate ventures was his share, under the persuasion of Thomas Fortune Ryan and William C. Whitney [qq.v.], in financing a reorganization (1902) of the Metropolitan Street Railway Company of New York. As soon as the Federal Reserve Act was passed he resigned his connection with the National City Bank and other banks. He was largely concerned in the great insurance companies, particularly the Equitable Life Assurance Society, of which he was a director. This connection brought him under investigation by a joint committee of the New York legislature in 1905, but he was acquitted of all knowledge of the alleged unscrupulous practices of some of his associates (*Testimony Taken before the Joint Committee of the Senate and Assembly of the State of New York to Investigate . . . Life Insurance Companies*, 1905, II, 1297–1364; *State of New York, Assembly Document No. 41*, 1906, pp. 120 ff.). He was interested in the development of railroads and other enterprises in Mexico. In 1904, at the time of the Russo-Japanese War, he secured for Japan some $200,000,000, and in recognition of this service was awarded the Order of the Sacred Treasure and later the more distinguished Order of the Rising Sun. In 1911 he supported a Chinese loan, partly as a result of the influence of a young diplomat, Willard Straight, who thought that American capital invested in the Manchurian railways might serve to prevent future wars in the Far East.

Schiff was a strong opponent of the Silver Purchase Act of 1890 and actively supported the gold standard on all occasions. As early as 1902 he recognized that the inelasticity of the currency was a potential danger. He early accepted the right of laborers to combine for their own protection, favored arbitration in labor disputes, earnestly befriended the Henry Street Settlement and municipal charities, and supported the National Child Labor Committee. He was a Republican throughout his career, although he voted for Woodrow Wilson in both his campaigns for the presidency. He had a strong sympathy for the colored people and by his voice, his means, and his personal interest, helped to promote Tuskegee Institute and other negro schools in the South. His civic interests were so well known that in 1904 he was suggested as a Republican candidate for mayor of New York, but declined to be considered. He was a member of the board of education, however, and his advice was sought by reform mayors like William R. Grace and Seth Low. In 1908 he seriously put before the Chamber of Commerce the question of a proper budget for New York City.

Schiff recognized his special obligation to the Jewish people in the matter of charities or, as he preferred to call them, philanthropies. He was always glad to help establish loan funds and, with Robert W. De Forest, was instrumental in the establishment of a National Employment Exchange. He was greatly interested in the work of the Red Cross, in 1910 was appointed by the President as a member of the International Relief Board of the American Red Cross, and served as treasurer of the New York chapter for many years. He was president and a great benefactor of the Montefiore Hospital, to which he probably gave more personal attention than to any other single charitable institution. Out of his interest in the Henry Street Settlement there grew a further interest in district nursing to which he contributed much by his influence and his means. He was greatly interested in the establishment of free libraries in New York. He aided Columbia University, established the Semitic Museum at Harvard, built a students' hall for Barnard College in 1915 in celebration of the fiftieth anniversary of his arrival in New York, created an establishment at Cornell University for the promotion of studies in German culture, and furnished the funds for the establishment of the department of Semitic literature at the New York Public Library and a similar department at the Library of Congress in Washington. In 1909 he created a fund which rendered possible a new translation of the Bible, under Jewish auspices, published in 1917 by the Jewish Publication Society of America, and in 1914 he created another fund which resulted in the publication of the Schiff Library of Jewish Classics, some twenty volumes in number. He was one of the major supporters of the Jewish Theological Seminary of New York, gave very considerable funds to the Hebrew Union College in Cincinnati, and was one of the founders of the American Jewish Committee, organized in 1906 to meet emergencies arising among Jews in other countries. He was active in the work of the American Jewish Joint Distribution Committee to relieve suffering in Europe during the World War, and in the Jewish Welfare Board, which ministered to Jewish soldiers and sailors during the same period. His resentment toward Czaristic Russia because of Russia's treatment of the Jews was so strong that he declined to participate in the Anglo-French Dollar Loan, although it would have brought profit to his firm. He was very active in the various Liberty Loan Committees.

Jacob Schiff was a reader, fond of walking and bicycling, most punctilious in all his affairs, deeply religious in his outlook and habit of mind.

On May 6, 1875, he married Therese Loeb, by whom he had a son and a daughter. The former, Mortimer Leo Schiff (June 5, 1877–June 4, 1931), became a valued member of the firm and its head after the death of his father. He devoted a great part of his time to public philanthropic work and particularly interested himself in the Boy Scouts of America, of which organization he was elected president in May 1931.

[Cyrus Adler, *Jacob H. Schiff: His Life and Letters* (2 vols., 1928); B. J. Hendrick, "Great American Fortunes and Their Making: Street Railway Financiers," *McClure's Magazine*, Nov.–Dec. 1907; *Who's Who in America*, 1920–21; *N. Y. Times*, Sept. 26, 1920.]

C. A.

SCHILLING, HUGO KARL (Mar. 28, 1861–July 1931), philologist, Germanist, was born at Saalfeld in Thuringia, Germany, the son of Ferdinand and Henrietta Schilling. Descended from a family in which liberal culture was a tradition, he enjoyed the advantages of a thorough education. After graduating from the Gymnasium in his native city, at seventeen he entered the University of Leipzig where he devoted himself to Germanistic studies, acquired a thorough knowledge of the older Germanic dialects, and specialized particularly in the field of Old English. Two years in France and Ireland, while they delayed the completion of his university course, laid the foundation for a thorough practical command of French and English. In 1885 he received the degrees of M.A. and Ph.D. at Leipzig. In February 1886 he came to the United States and five years later became an American citizen. After a short period at the Johns Hopkins University he was professor of modern languages at Wittenberg College, Springfield, Ohio, until 1891. On July 14, 1887, he was married to Theresa T. Stitt of Carlisle, Ky., by whom he had two sons and two daughters. In 1891 he went to Harvard University as assistant professor of German, and in 1901 to the University of California as professor of the German language and literature and head of the department of German, a position he held for twenty-eight years.

As one of a group of leaders assembled at California by Benjamin Ide Wheeler [q.v.] to assist him in building up a great university, he had to do the work of a pioneer, to surround himself with competent assistants, to organize the work of his department, to build up library facilities adequate to the needs of graduate students, to establish and maintain worthy standards of scholarship. In addition he found time to give counsel and leadership to the teachers of German in the state and to assist them in establishing secondary instruction on a high level. His broad and accurate knowledge of history and literature, together with an unusual talent for lucid, simple, and direct presentation, made him especially effective in aiding students to an orientation in the whole field of German literature, while his semasiological insight and knowledge of the anthropological sciences made him an unusually stimulating teacher of linguistics. He was editor of *Modern Language Notes,* 1899–1901; a member of the editorial board of Publications in Modern Philology of the University of California, 1909–31; president of the Pacific coast division of the American Philological Association, 1907–08; president of the Modern Language Association of America, 1928, and a member of the Gesellschaft für deutsche Philologie in Berlin and the Goethe-Gesellschaft in Weimar. Among his published writings are: *König Ælfred's Angelsächsische Bearbeitung der Weltgeschichte des Orosius* (Halle, 1886); "Notes on the Finnsaga" (*Modern Language Notes,* June, Nov. 1886); "Das wort sie sollen lassen stahn und kein danck dazu haben" (*Ibid.,* Jan. 1901); "Die Fundationsgüter und Zehnten des Stiftes Gandersheim im elften Jahrhundert" (*Zeitschrift des Harzvereins für Geschichte und Altertumskunde,* vol. XXXIII, pt. 2, 1900, pp. 486–93); "Die vermeintliche Urkunde im Gandersheimer Plenar" (*Historische Vierteljahrschrift,* Jan. 2, 1901); "Altsächsische Namen im Gandersheimer Plenar" (*Beiträge zur Geschichte der deutschen Sprache und Literatur,* vol. XXVI, 1901, pp. 558–60); "The Semasiology of *Schenken* 'Skink'" (*Journal of Germanic Philology,* vol. IV, 1902, no. 4). After he became professor emeritus in 1929 he devoted himself to the preparation of a Goethe dictionary, a work to which he brought the fruits of a lifetime of study and upon which he was engaged at the time of his death. He died as the result of a cerebral hemorrhage that occurred while he was alone in the house.

[*Who's Who in America,* 1930–31; *Univ. of Cal.: In Memoriam* (1931); obituary in *N. Y. Times,* July 26, 1931; death notice in *San Francisco Examiner,* July 28, 1931; personal acquaintance.]

                                    C. P.

SCHINDLER, SOLOMON (Apr. 24, 1842–May 5, 1915), Jewish rabbi, was born at Neisse, Germany, the son of Rabbi Julius L. and Bertha (Algasi) Schindler. At thirteen he entered the Breslau Rabbinical School and also attended the Gymnasium there, graduating in 1862. A tutor in private families until 1868, he then took charge of a small congregation in Westphalia but had to resign from it because of his liberal tendencies. At this he entered the Royal Teachers' Seminary at Büren and graduated in 1870. On June 24, 1868, he had married Henrietta Schutz of Holz-

hausen, who was his life-long companion; of the six children she bore him, three sons and one daughter survived. For a time he and his wife conducted a boarding-school but, the venture proving unsuccessful, in 1871 they set out for America, arriving with three infants and no resources. Although Schindler's radical views on the Bible made him hesitate to enter the rabbinate, he yielded to economic necessity after a few months and became rabbi of Congregation Adath Emuno at Hoboken, N. J., where he remained until called to Boston in 1874 to Temple Adath Israel. Once in the rabbinate, true to his convictions, he expounded his views freely and openly. Though personally modest, he was a vigorous and fearless preacher of intellectual radicalism, whose sermons were not hortative but analytical and didactic. In introducing reform Judaism into New England, he made innovations in the synagogue ritual which led to the resignation of fifteen of his forty Boston congregants, but he soon gained so much popularity that in ten years his congregation gave up its chapel and built an imposing structure to accommodate its increased membership and the growing number of Jewish and Christian auditors who came to hear him. In later life he preached a famous sermon, "Mistakes I Have Made," in which he recanted some of his more radical views on Judaism. From 1888 to 1894 he served as a member of the Boston School Board, having been nominated by all the political parties. After twenty years with his congregation he resigned from the rabbinate, though he maintained an active interest in his congregation, which elected him rabbi emeritus in 1908.

On his retirement he took up social work, in which he showed marked ability both as organizer and as administrator. In 1894 he organized the Federation of Jewish Charities of Boston, the first of its kind in American Jewish charity, and served as its superintendent from 1895 to 1899. From 1899 to 1909, when he retired from active work, he was superintendent of the Leopold Morse Home for Infirm Hebrews at Mattapan, Mass. His publications include *Messianic Expectations and Modern Judaism* (1886), in which he maintained that Jewish hopes had lost their national character; *Dissolving Views in the History of Judaism* (1888); *Israelites in Boston* (copyright 1889); a German translation, *Ein Rückblick* (1889), of Edward Bellamy's *Looking Backward,* and a sequel to it called *Young West* (1894). He tried prematurely to establish a Jewish newspaper in Boston in 1879, 1880, and 1893. A child of the age of evolution and the glorification of science, he applied the theory of evolution to his religion more logically than psychologically. Though intellectually a pessimist, he was emotionally an optimist with the heart of a poet, and the cynical iconoclastic philosophy he preached was tempered by a broad tolerance. A brilliant conversationalist, with a deep sense of humor and great *joie de vivre,* he had a fine capacity for making and retaining friends.

[*Who's Who in America,* 1914–15; *Jewish Encyc.* (ed. 1925), vol. XI, p. 102; *Jewish Year Book,* 1905–06; J. C. Rand, *One of a Thousand* (1890); Ephraim Deinard, *Hakundes* (1890); *Hist. of the Jews of Boston* (1892); *Jewish Advocate* (Boston), Apr. 3, 1908, Apr. 19, 1912, May 7, 1915; *N. Y. Times,* May 6, 1915; *Boston Transcript,* May 6, 1915.]   D. deS. P.

SCHIRMER, GUSTAV (Sept. 19, 1829–Aug. 6, 1893), music publisher, was born at Königsee, Saxony, the son of Ernst Rudolph Schirmer, and his second wife, Wilhelmine (Dünkler) Schirmer, daughter of the burgomaster of Saalfeld. He came from a family of Thuringian piano manufacturers. The musical lexicographer, Ernst Ludwig Gerber (1746–1819, Sondershausen), who knew the family, praised its products, and François Joseph Fétis in his *Biographie Universelle des Musiciens* (edition of 1878, vol. VII, p. 465) mentions a Johann Georg Schirmer, "piano manufacturer" (d. 1790), whose pianos were esteemed in Saxony. With one son by the husband's first marriage and five children by the second, of whom Gustav was the eldest, Schirmer's parents emigrated to New York in 1840 on board the bark *Autoleon,* landing in New York on October 8 after a voyage of forty-six days from Hamburg. Until he was fourteen Gustav attended school, occasionally earning a little money by selling matches. At fifteen he was apprenticed for a short time to a cabinetmaker. After several years of employment in the music business of Scharfenberg & Luis, he entered the employ of Kerksieg & Breusing, music dealers, where his ability and energy gained him rapid advancement to the position of manager of the store, which until 1880 was at 701 Broadway. In 1861 with a fellow employee, Bernard Beer, he acquired the business, the firm being changed to Beer & Schirmer. Five years later he bought out Beer's interest and established the house of "G. Schirmer, music publishers, importers and dealers." He married an American, Mary Fairchild, who survived him with their five daughters and two sons, one of them Rudolph Edward Schirmer [*q.v.*].

Equally strong were his ambition to succeed in business and his devotion to his family. When in 1873 he sent his wife and children abroad to spend two years in Weimar, he religiously wrote each of them one letter every week in his own hand, no matter how burdened with work he was. Being himself an indefatigable worker, he demanded untiring effort from his associates and employees. His ideal was German thoroughness and he patterned his organization after German models. He early developed intensive business relations not only with the large music concerns of Germany but with the leading houses of Paris, Brussels, London, Vienna, and Milan. Furthermore, he entered into personal relations with prominent European composers. Mrs. Schirmer's stay in Weimar led to closer acquaintance with Liszt and the illustrious coterie at the "Altenburg"; a photograph inscribed to her by Richard Wagner with "thanks and friendship" still hangs with many similar tokens in the executive office of the firm; and Schirmer was among the original patrons of Bayreuth, who helped to make possible the realization of Wagner's "Festspielhaus." When the composer Tchaikovsky visited New York in April 1891, on the occasion of the inauguration of Carnegie Hall, he repeatedly made mention in his diary of Schirmer and his family.

Certainly, Schirmer was not a mere plodding tradesman; he had vision and a real love and understanding of music. He played the piano as a relaxation, and in a letter he once cautioned his son Rudolph, who was taking violin lessons, to "play nicely in tune, and always with love and inner fire." But his principles in music as in business were strict, Teutonic, uncompromising. When his children took music lessons in Weimar, he frowned, despite his admiration for Wagner, upon a pot-pourri of *The Flying Dutchman* played by one of them, since no one had ever learned anything by playing musical medleys instead of Czerny's scales, Köhler's exercises, and Heller's études. This sound objection, however, did not prevent the company from selling medleys to anyone who asked for them. When the continuous growth of the business required larger quarters, a four-story building, occupied in 1880, was erected for it at 35 Union Square, and there the business remained until in 1910 it was moved to a seven-story building at 3 East Forty-third St. In 1891 Schirmer housed in a six-story building in West Sixteenth Street his own engraving and printing plant, which developed later into a model factory at Woodside, L. I. Although during the early years of music publishing in America the lack of any copyright convention between the United States and Europe enabled American publishers to engage in a flourishing and profitable business with "reprint editions" of the best European sellers, Schirmer was not content with such easy exploits but gave wholesome encouragement to native talent, in the discovery of which he showed great shrewdness. Self-made, he had in him the fine qualities of an old European tradition to the unfolding of which America gave new and rich opportunity. Thus he had succeeded, by the time of his death at Eisenach, Germany, at the age of only sixty-three, in creating a business and a cultural factor of national importance and international renown.

[Letters and family accounts; *N. Y. American*, Oct. 9, 1840; N. Y. directories; Modeste Tchaikovsky, *The Life and Letters of Peter Ilich Tchaikovsky* (1906), ed. and translated by Rosa Newmarch; obituaries in *Signale für die Musikalische Welt*, Sept. 1893, no. 42; *Metronome*, Sept. 1893; *N. Y. Tribune*, Aug. 8, 1893; identical articles on centenary of Schirmer's birth in *Musical America*, Sept. 1929, and *Musical Courier*, Sept. 14, 1929.]   C. E.

SCHIRMER, RUDOLPH EDWARD (July 22, 1859–Aug. 20, 1919), music publisher, was born in New York City, the son of Mary (Fairchild) and Gustav Schirmer [*q.v.*]. Educated in the New York public schools until 1873, he went with his mother, his younger brother Gustave (1864–1907), and four of his sisters to Weimar, Germany, where he spent two years in private schools and had lessons in violin and piano playing from Helene Stahr, pupil and protégée of Liszt, and daughter of Adolf Stahr (1805–1876), the friend of Liszt and early champion of Wagner. Thus the Schirmer family at Weimar came into contact with the circle of celebrities, literary and musical, that gathered around Liszt; on one occasion the two Schirmer boys took part in a children's concert that was given in honor of Liszt. In 1876 Rudolph entered the College of New Jersey (later Princeton) where he was active in the musical life of the college and was one of the presidents of the glee club. After his graduation in 1880 he attended the law school of Columbia College, was graduated in June 1884, and was admitted to the bar in the same year. For a short time he was affiliated with the law firm of Olcott, Mestre & Gonzalez in New York, but when his brother Gustave in 1885 left their father's music business to marry Grace Tilton of Boston and to found there the Boston Music Company (eminently successful later through the publication of compositions by Ethelbert Nevin and others), he abandoned the law in order to replace his brother in his father's business. In 1886 he married Martha Young Barnes of New York, who bore him one child that died in infancy. When bad health required the father to spend more time in Europe, a reconciliation between him and his son Gustave brought the latter back to the business to join with Rudolph in the man-

agement. After the father's death in 1893, when the business had been reorganized and incorporated, Rudolph became president and his brother Gustave (though retaining the independent control of his Boston business) secretary of G. Schirmer, Inc. After the untimely death of his brilliant brother Gustave in 1907, Rudolph assumed the sole direction of the New York business. With a keen appreciation of high artistic ideals and a relish for musical advance, he fostered many young and promising composers. In 1910 he moved the business to 3 East 43rd St. In 1912 he established a branch in London, which was maintained for a short time only. In 1915 he founded the *Musical Quarterly*. On Mar. 28, 1916, a week after a Nevada divorce from his first wife, he married Ann Swinburne, a talented concert singer and comic opera star, by whom he had a son. His health during the last years of his life having grown extremely precarious, he moved to Santa Barbara, Cal., where he died. He was a director of the New York Oratorio Society and of the New York Symphony Society, and a trustee of the Institute of Musical Art in New York.

[Letters and family accounts; obituaries in *New Music Rev.* and *Musical Quart.*, Oct. 1919; *Musical America*, Aug. 30, 1919; *N. Y. Times*, Aug. 21, Sept. 13, 1919.]   C. E.

SCHLATTER, MICHAEL (July 14, 1716–Oct. 31, 1790), German Reformed clergyman and educator, was born in St. Gall, Switzerland, the son of Paulus Schlatter, a bookkeeper, and of Magdalena (Zollikofer) Schlatter. After attending the gymnasium of his native city, he received theological training under the private tuition of Prof. Casper Wegelin of St. Gall and at the universities of Leyden in Holland and Helmstedt in Germany. On Apr. 10, 1739, he was examined for the ministry and ordained. For a while he was a private tutor in Holland, but in 1744 he became vicar to John Jacob Beyel, *Dekan* of Wigoldingen, Thurgau, Switzerland, and, a year later, Sunday evening preacher in Linsebühl, a suburb of St. Gall. In January 1746 he left St. Gall for Heidelberg, where he met Prof. Johan Caspar Cruciger, one of the leading men of the Reformed church of the Palatinate, who directed his attention to the needs of the Reformed churches of Pennsylvania. As a result, Schlatter offered his services to the Synods of Holland, under whose auspices the missionary work was carried on.

He was commissioned for service in Pennsylvania on May 23, 1746, and arrived at his post in September 1746, beginning at once a strenuous and many-sided missionary activity. His first efforts were directed towards organizing the Reformed churches of Pennsylvania into a synod under the supervision of the Reformed Church of Holland. This task was accomplished in September 1747, when the Coetus of the Reformed congregations of Pennsylvania was called into existence, with four ministers and twenty-eight elders. His next task was to organize the widely-scattered Reformed congregations into regular pastoral charges. He made a series of extensive missionary tours throughout Pennsylvania, Maryland, Virginia, and New Jersey, and found forty-six congregations which he organized into sixteen pastoral charges. There were, however, only four ordained Reformed ministers in the province, so he returned to Holland, in February 1751, in order to secure more pastors. His appeal, printed in Dutch in 1751 and in German in 1752, was so successful that he not only gained the consent of the Holland synods for a larger number of missionaries in Pennsylvania, but was also able to interest the states of Holland and West Friesland in his work, so that they voted a subsidy of fl. 2,000 annually for a period of five years for his work. With this financial backing Schlatter went to Germany where he secured six young men, who accompanied him to Pennsylvania.

After his return, when a growing dissension between the church leaders made congregational work very difficult, he turned his attention to the education of the children of the new settlers. He found few church schools, poorly equipped, and very unsatisfactory teachers. In the interests of this cause he returned once more to Holland in November 1753. In June 1754 the Synods of Holland released him from their employ so that he might accept the position of superintendent of schools in Pennsylvania under an appointment by an English society, which had been formed to carry on this educational work. The project was conducted in Pennsylvania by a body of general trustees, of whom William Smith, 1727–1803 [*q.v.*], was the secretary. In the fall of 1754, six so-called "charity schools" were opened, the number later being increased to nine. But this undertaking failed because the local Germans were antagonized by the political motives of the English society, and Schlatter retired in 1756. He then entered the British army as chaplain. On Mar. 25, 1757, John Campbell Loudoun [*q.v.*] appointed him as one of the chaplains of the Royal American Regiment and he took part in the siege of Halifax, the capture of Louisbourg, and in the expedition to capture Fort Duquesne.

Schlatter returned to Philadelphia in October 1759 and assumed the pastorate of several independent Reformed churches, notably Barren Hill, near Philadelphia. When Henry Bouquet [*q.v.*] organized an expedition to destroy the Indian forts on the banks of the Muskingum in 1764, Schlatter was commissioned as chaplain of the 2nd Pennsylvania Battalion and thus held a chaplain's commission both under the British and the provincial authorities. During the Revolution he was an ardent patriot, and suffered imprisonment and the loss of his property for his sentiments. He died in Philadelphia and was buried on Nov. 4, 1790, in the Reformed Cemetery, which is now part of Franklin Square, in Philadelphia. He was married to Maria Henrica Schleidorn, daughter of Henry Schleidorn of New York City. They had nine children, one son and five daughters surviving their parents.

[Biographia omnium ministrorum Sangallensium, No. 180, manuscript in the city library, St. Gall; Jacob Scherer, Stemmatologia Sangallensis, Vol. P, Geschlecht 109, also manuscript at St. Gall; Bürger Buch der Stadt St. Gallen, 1867; letters and documents in the city archives at St. Gall; letters and documents in the archives of the General Synod of the Reformed Church of Holland, at The Hague; Henry Harbaugh, The Life of Rev. Michael Schlatter (1857); J. I. Good, Hist. of the Reformed Ch. in the U. S. 1725–1792 (1899); J. H. Dubbs, The Reformed Church in Pennsylvania, part X of Proc. of the Pa.-German Soc., vol. XI (1902); W. J. Hinke, "Famous Pennsylvania-Germans, Michael Schlatter," Pa.-German, Oct. 1900; W. J. Hinke, ed., Minutes and Letters of the Coetus of the German Reformed Congregations of Pennsylvania (1903), and "Diary of the Rev. Michael Schlatter," in Jour. of the Presbyt. Hist. Soc., Sept., Dec. 1905.]   W.J.H.

SCHLESINGER, BENJAMIN (Dec. 25, 1876–June 6, 1932), labor leader, was a native of Krakai, province of Kovno, Lithuania, and the son of Nechemiah and Judith Schlesinger. His father's family name is not known to his descendants, since at some time in his life Nechemiah adopted his wife's maiden name, Schlesinger, as his surname. Born into a rabbinical family, he enjoyed a superior intellectual environment and evidently inherited a superior mental equipment. When transplanted from Krakai to Chicago in 1891, however, like most Jewish immigrant youths irrespective of their background, he was forced to resort to manual labor for a living. Accordingly, in common with large numbers of Russian Jews, he became a needle-trades worker, taking up the occupation of sewing-machine operator on cloaks and suits. Many of these superior immigrant youngsters pursued courses of study while plying their trade, thereby attaining a profession; but Schlesinger, from the outset, was caught in the vortex of official responsibilities connected with the labor movement, and his time and energy were absorbed in its service. From the age of seventeen, two years after he landed in America, he was a guiding spirit in the Jewish labor movement, either as a union official in the ladies' garment trades, or as manager of the *Jewish Daily Forward,* the outstanding Jewish socialist and labor organ. Through these positions he played a dominant rôle in shaping the destinies of both the union and the publication in their rise from poverty to affluence and power.

His first office was that of secretary of the Chicago Cloak Makers' Union, and he had not held this a year when he was elected treasurer of the newly formed International Cloak Makers' Union of America. In 1903 he was made president of the International Ladies' Garment Workers' Union, which was founded in 1900, one of its chief objects being to eliminate sweatshops from the needlework trades. Because of factional differences he was defeated in 1904, but was selected as general manager of the New York Cloak Makers' Union. Three years later he became business manager of the *Jewish Daily Forward,* which was then experiencing a serious struggle for existence. In this capacity he served from 1907 to 1912. In the meantime, controversies within the Ladies' Garment Workers' Union created a critical situation and Schlesinger was again chosen, in 1914, to guide its fortunes, remaining its president until he resigned in 1923. Returning to the *Forward* as business manager of its Chicago affairs, he continued with the paper until 1931, when for the third time he was called to head the International Ladies' Garment Workers' Union. He died in a sanitarium in Colorado Springs a few weeks after having been reëlected, almost unanimously, at the 1932 convention. He was survived by his wife, Rae (Schanhouse), two sons, and a daughter.

Schlesinger, like most Jewish labor leaders, was more the intellectual than the histrionic type. In public speeches his style was conversational rather than oratorical. He spoke fluently, directly, and informatively. Because of his ill health, which he attributed to working in sweatshops in his early youth, he displayed an irascibility which accentuated his domineering characteristics. His strength as a labor leader lay in his extraordinary ability as an organizer and administrator. He was also fearless and independent, as was demonstrated when the union under his presidency applied for an injunction against an employers' association that attempted to break a trade agreement in 1921—one of the first instances wherein a union turned the tables on employers. In this action he was opposed by both the conservatives and radicals in the labor movement, since he went counter to a cherished tra-

dition that unions must not resort to the use of injunctions in labor disputes. Since that time, however, many unions have followed the course laid down by the International Ladies' Garment Workers' under Schlesinger's leadership.

[L. L. Lorwin, *The Women's Garment Workers; a Hist. of the International Ladies' Garment Workers' Union* (1924); files of *Justice,* the official organ of the International Ladies' Garment Workers' Union; files of *Convention Proceedings* of the same organization; *N. Y. Times,* June 7–10, 1932; information regarding parents, wife, and place of birth from a son, Emil Schlesinger, Esq., New York City.]   D.J.S.

SCHLEY, WINFIELD SCOTT (Oct. 9, 1839–Oct. 2, 1909), naval officer, was born on his father's farm, "Richfields," Frederick County, Md., the son of John Thomas and Georgianna Virginia (McClure) Schley, descendant of John Thomas Schley of Bavaria, who settled in Frederick County in 1739, and of Scotch-Irish ancestors who came to Baltimore before the Revolution. In his ninth year the family moved to Frederick, where he attended local schools until his appointment to the United States Naval Academy in 1856. His first cruise after graduation was in the *Niagara* which was detailed to bear back to Japan the first representatives of that nation to visit the United States. Returning at the outbreak of the Civil War, the *Niagara* joined the Charleston blockade, and Schley's earliest command was the prize square-rigger *General Parkhill,* which he brought safely into Philadelphia. Subsequently in the *Potomac,* he twice volunteered for hazardous service off Mobile, first with a cutting-out expedition under Fort Morgan, and again, in January 1862, with a boat party to rescue the U.S.S. *Cuyler,* aground and under fire, both incidents showing courage and characteristic eagerness for distinction. He was made lieutenant in July 1862, and was executive of the gunboat *Winona* off Mobile and later on the Mississippi. In March 1863, he temporarily commanded the *Monongahela* in bombardments of Port Hudson, and was then navigator of the *Richmond.*

On Sept. 10, 1863, during leave, he was married to Annie Rebecca Franklin of Annapolis, Md., who bore him three children. He was executive of the *Wateree* in the Pacific from 1864 to 1866, then taught at the Naval Academy, and from 1869 to 1873 was executive of the *Benicia* of the Asiatic Squadron, showing gallantry as adjutant of land forces in a punitive expedition in Korea in June 1871. After another assignment to the Naval Academy as head of the modern languages department, he commanded the *Essex* in the South Atlantic from 1876 to 1879, and was lighthouse inspector at Boston, 1879–83.

Early in 1884 came hazardous duty as commander of an expedition sent into the Arctic to rescue the party under Lieut. A. W. Greely which had set out in 1881. In the *Thetis* and *Bear* Schley pushed vigorously northward, and on June 22 near Cape Sabine saved 'the seven survivors of Greely's party at the very brink of death, and returned safely after 1300 miles of perilous ice navigation. In recognition of his achievement he was made chief of the bureau of equipment and recruiting, where he remained until July 1889. The romantic story of the rescue is told in detail in Schley's and J. R. Soley's book, *The Rescue of Greely* (1885). His national prominence after this expedition was increased by the Valparaiso affair of Oct. 16, 1891, when two sailors from his ship, the *Baltimore,* were killed by a Chilean mob. Schley handled the matter firmly and tactfully, and won much acclaim on his return. He was inspector of the Third Lighthouse District, 1892–95; commander of the *New York* on the Atlantic coast, 1895–97; and then head of the lighthouse board. He was promoted to the rank of commodore in February 1898.

At the opening of the Spanish-American War he was selected to command the Flying Squadron at Hampton Roads, but with the arrangement—always troublesome in military undertakings—that, should his force operate with the Atlantic Squadron in the West Indies, the commander of the latter, William Thomas Sampson [*q.v.*], though two numbers his junior, should have chief command. When Cervera's ships reached Martinique, the Flying Squadron hastened to Key West, and under Sampson's orders was sent on to blockade Cienfuegos, the chief southern port of Cuba. In the Sampson-Schley controversy, into which the navy and the nation were plunged after the war, Schley's conduct during the crucial moments of the ensuing fortnight came under severe criticism. He was scored for delaying at Cienfuegos from May 22 till nightfall of the 24th, despite urgent advices to proceed immediately eastward to the harbor of Santiago, which the Spanish had entered on the 19th; for his slow movement thither; and for his failure thereafter to establish a close blockade. Instead of remaining at Santiago he temporarily turned back, and cabled on May 27, "Department's orders cannot be obeyed . . . am obliged to return to Key West . . . for coal" (Parker, *post,* pp. 129–130). Fortunately, when Sampson reached Santiago on June 1, Schley was still hanging on. His problems were undoubtedly trying, his information less than the navy department's, his every decision suscepti-

ble of defense; yet the final judgment must be that of the Court of Inquiry of 1901, reviewed and approved by President Roosevelt, that his "conduct . . . prior to June 1, 1898, was characterized by vacillation, dilatoriness, and lack of enterprise" (*Record of Proceedings, post,* II, 1830).

A worthy officer, of outstanding record, he wavered under responsibilities of high command. Much of this might have been erased by his creditable work in the battle at Santiago, had it not been for the new issues raised there. During the month-long blockade preceding the battle Sampson's and Schley's forces were joined, with slightly strained relations between first and second in command. At 9:00 on the morning of the action, July 3, Sampson in the *New York* had steamed about seven miles eastward for a conference with General Shafter. At 9:35 the Spanish ships emerged from the harbor and turned westward. Schley's flagship, the *Brooklyn,* westernmost of the blockading line, at first closed eastward toward the enemy, then made her much-debated semicircle outward and away from them—a maneuver defensible tactically, though it forced the *Texas* to back water to avoid collision—and continued the fight on parallel courses westward at greater range, still leading the American column and effectively engaging the Spanish ships until the last survivor, the *Cristobal Colon,* surrendered at 1:15 P.M. Sampson, never beyond sight of his forces, had meanwhile approached rapidly from the rear, and his ship was third to reach the *Colon* about 2:00 P.M. Nevertheless, Schley assumed, then and afterward, that he was in chief command during the battle. Influenced doubtless by his genial approachability and repelled by Sampson's coldness, the press and nation supported him and made him the hero, but the navy department and most of the officers as strongly opposed his claims. The provisional promotions of Aug. 10, advancing Schley six numbers and Sampson eight, thus reversing seniority, were not confirmed by the Senate, though both officers became rear admirals in 1899.

After the return of the fleet to New York on Aug. 20, Schley served on the Puerto Rico Evacuation Commission from September to October 1898; was president of the retirement board in 1899; and commander of the South Atlantic Squadron until shortly before his retirement on Oct. 9, 1901. Meanwhile, the controversy had continued, and an account of Santiago, bitterly hostile to him, published in E. S. Maclay's *History of the Navy* (1901), vol. III, led Schley to request a court of inquiry. Presided over by

438

Admiral Dewey, with Rear Admirals Benham and Ramsay as associates, the court gathered voluminous testimony from Sept. 12 to Dec. 12, 1901. It reached a judgment in general adverse to Schley, though on certain minor points, notably on the question of chief command during the battle (which was not properly before the court), Dewey rendered a minority opinion in his favor. Despite this blow, Schley retained much of his popularity, which he frankly enjoyed, and which he stimulated by his affability, humor, and the bluff, hearty manner of an old-time sailor. After retirement he made his home in Washington, D. C. His death from apoplexy occurred in New York City, and he was buried at Arlington.

[*Who's Who in America*, 1908–09; autobiography, *Forty-five Years Under the Flag* (1904); Park Benjamin, biog. sketch in *Rev. of Revs.* (N. Y.), Sept. 1901; James Parker, *Rear-Admirals Schley, Sampson, and Cervera* (1910); J. D. Long, *The New Am. Navy* (2 vols., 1903); *Record of Proc. of a Court of Inquiry in the Case of Rear-Admiral W. S. Schley* (2 vols., 1902), *House Document No. 485*, 57 Cong., 1 Sess.; "Nauticus," *The Truth About the Schley Case* (n.d.); *Army and Navy Jour.*, Oct. 7, 1911. A few of Schley's personal letters are preserved in the manuscripts division of the Lib. of Cong. See also the bibliog. for the Sampson article.]   A. W—t.

SCHMAUK, THEODORE EMANUEL (May 30, 1860–Mar. 23, 1920), Lutheran clergyman, the son of the Rev. Benjamin William and Wilhelmina Catherine (Hingel) Schmauk, was born at Lancaster, Pa. He was the grandson of Benjamin Friedrich Schmauk, who came from Württemberg, Germany, to the United States with his brother in 1819. He was graduated from the University of Pennsylvania in 1880, and from the Philadelphia Lutheran Theological Seminary in 1883, entering the same year upon a pastorate at Lebanon, Pa., where he served until his death. For the first fifteen years he was assistant to his father, who died in 1898. A man of towering physique, commanding presence, and marked ability as an organizer, Schmauk exerted an influence upon the General Council of the Evangelical Church in America which was perhaps surpassed by no one. He was editor of the three leading periodicals of the Council: the *Lutheran Sunday School Lessons and General Council Graded Series,* from 1896; the *Lutheran Church Review,* from 1895 and the *Lutheran,* the Council's official organ, from 1889. He wrote many practical booklets for Sunday school work, but was less fortunate in his book, *The Negative Criticism and the Old Testament* (1894), which was a more zealous than thorough work. He wrote against T. K. Cheyne and others of the negative critical school, also against James Hastings, the editor of *A Dictionary of the Bible* (5 vols., 1898–

1904), for their choice of liberal scholars to deal with vital subjects.

He was elected president of the General Council in 1903 and as such became the moderator and curator of its fundamental principle—an uncompromising confessionalism. He held many other positions of trust, being president of the trustees of the General Council, since 1907; trustee of Muhlenberg College; member of the church book committee; president of the board of directors of the Philadelphia seminary from 1908, and special lecturer from 1911; chairman of the committee on ways and means which planned the merging of the General Synod, General Council, and Synod of the South into the United Lutheran Church in America in 1918. He claimed that the General Council was the one conservative body in America accepting unreservedly both the "Confessions" and the "history of the church"; and, as such, was ecumenical in outlook and best adapted to weld together the various Lutheran synods—a claim, however, which failed to prevent the Augustana Synod, one-third of the communicants of the General Council, from seceding in 1918. He had but a faint understanding of the liberal cultural and deeply religious background of the people of Scandinavian antecedents. In his discussion about "confessional subscription" with James William Richard [*q.v.*] he showed little appreciation for the superior scholarship of his opponent, regarding his own book, *The Confessional Principle and The Confessions of the Lutheran Church* (1911), as a thorough refutation of Richard's patiently and carefully written volume, *The Confessional History of the Church* (1909).

His attitude toward the Bible was not legalistic; yet he could say that the Bible was inerrant. He opposed ecclesiastical "Unionism," yet assigned the Missouri Synod and the Joint Synod of Ohio to the realm of the closed mind. He maintained that extra-ecclesiastical agencies and organizations have no lawful power. Out of sympathy with the more advanced teaching of J. T. Beck, Karl Heim, and Paul Althaus, the philosophy of his attitude towards contemporary political events was rooted in the *Ständeordnungen* of passive Lutheranism. Schmauk's *magnum opus* is *A History of the Lutheran Church in Pennsylvania,* published in the *Proceedings and Addresses of the Pennsylvania-German Society* (vols. XI, XII, 1902–03) a comprehensive, though not critical, work, following his book *The Early Churches of Lebanon County* (1902). He was a member of the Lebanon County Historical Society and the Pennsylvania German

Society, being president of the latter in 1896. Schmauk died in Philadelphia and was survived by his sister. He was never married.

[Manuscript diary, archives of Philadelphia Luth. Theol. Seminary, Mt. Airy; G. W. Sandt, *Theodore Emanuel Schmauk* (1921); *Who's Who in America*, 1920–21; J. L. Chamberlain, ed., *Univ. of Pa.*, vol. II (1902); *Lutheran*, Apr. 1, 8, 1920; *Allg. Evangel.-Luth. Kirchenzeitung*, July 8, 1910; *Public Ledger* (Philadelphia), Mar. 24, 1920.]　　　　　J. O. E.

SCHMIDT, ARTHUR PAUL (Apr. 1, 1846–May 5, 1921), music publisher, was born at Altona, Germany. He was married on Dec. 24, 1868, to Helene Philippine Suck, many of whose family were musicians; his wife survived him but their one child, a daughter, died before him. After working for ten years as a clerk in the music store of G. D. Russell & Company in Boston, in October 1876 he began a prosperous and valuable career as a publisher and importer of music (chiefly at first as agent of the well-known Litolff edition), with branches later at Leipzig and New York. The publications listed in the catalogue in 1932 reached the number of nearly fifteen thousand. In January 1916 he transferred the business to Henry R. Austin, Harry B. Crosby, and Florence J. Emery as partners in the Arthur P. Schmidt Company.

A chief interest with him from the first was the encouragement of American composers. He often gave new writers their first opportunity and brought to better notice others who were already somewhat known. Most important, he was a pioneer in the publication of works in larger forms (orchestral scores and parts, for example) that had no possibility of being commercially successful. The first score of an important composition of the kind in the United States was the second symphony, "Im Frühling," of John Knowles Paine [*q.v.*], published in 1880 by subscription. For the large number of such works that followed in the form of orchestral and chamber music Schmidt himself was financially responsible, a remarkable undertaking when the cost of publishing such works is considered. Generous in all ways and not satisfied to restrict himself to the commercial and profitable side of the business, he was quite willing to spend money for an ideal. Furthermore, as a German who had come to the United States and found success, he wished (as he sometimes said) to repay the country in some way for his good fortune. This was his practical way of doing it, and his plan was to let no year pass without at least one such publication. In the forty years from 1880 to 1920 he published among others the larger works of such composers as Mrs. H. H. A. Beach, Arthur Bird [*q.v.*], George W. Chadwick, Ar-

thur Foote, Henry Hadley, Edward MacDowell [*q.v.*], and Sigismond Stojowski. The encouragement he thus gave to composers cannot be overestimated; in a period of remarkable development in American music he made a noteworthy contribution.

[*Grove's Dict. of Music and Musicians, Am. Supp.* (ed. 1930); obituaries in *Musical America*, May 14, 1921, and *Boston Transcript*, May 6, 1921; private information.]　　　　　A. F.

SCHMIDT, FRIEDRICH AUGUST (Jan. 3, 1837–May 15, 1928), Lutheran theologian, the son of Martin and Helena (Wirth) Schmidt, was born at Leutenberg, Thuringia, Germany, and came at the age of four with his parents to St. Louis, Mo., where he attended parochial school and Concordia Theological Seminary. He was graduated from the preparatory department of the seminary in 1853 and from the theological in 1857. He was pastor at Eden, N. Y., from 1857 to 1859, and at Baltimore, Md., from 1859 to 1861. For the following eleven years he was professor at Luther College, Decorah, Iowa, and from 1872 to 1876 professor of theology at his alma mater. When the Norwegian Synod established its own school of theology at Madison, Wis., in 1878, Schmidt was transferred to this institution, where he taught till 1886. Due to the acrid controversy about predestination, one-third of the Norwegian Synod started their own theological seminary in 1886 at the St. Olaf school in Northfield, Minn., and, on receiving synodical censure, organized themselves as the Anti-Missourian Brotherhood. Schmidt forthwith became a professor in this school. When the Brotherhood, in 1890, merged to form the United Norwegian Lutheran Church, Schmidt suffered another transfer to Augsburg Seminary in Minneapolis, Minn., where he taught until 1893. Because of friction in the new faculty and new church body, Augsburg Seminary was abandoned and the United Norwegian Lutheran Church founded the Luther Theological Seminary at St. Anthony Park, St. Paul, Minn., where Schmidt was professor of systematic theology from 1893 to 1912, when he resigned.

Schmidt's name figured extensively in the predestination controversy, there being few doctrinal controversies among the Lutherans of German or Norwegian antecedents in the West in which he did not participate. Up to 1878 he was an ardent admirer of the Missouri Synod and its leader, C. F. W. Walther, but when the latter began to press the claim that God elected man to salvation prior to the foundation of the world, independent of any fore-knowledge of faith, Schmidt changed his allegiance. To combat the new "Calvinism" he edited *Altes und Neues.*

1880–85, and *Lutherske Vidnesbyrd*, 1882–90. For these and similar efforts the Evangelical Lutheran Inter-Synodical Conference in 1882 refused to receive him as delegate from the Norwegian Synod. Schmidt knew his Latin tomes and seventeenth-century Lutheranism. In the controversy which engaged him for thirty-five years, his method of attack and defense was, like that of his opponents, scholastic—and antiquated, as if a Kant had never existed. Like them, he failed to recognize the limits of human knowledge about the will-problem and its distribution on various levels of discussion. His opponents regarded him as liberalistic and synergistic, but he was neither. Indeed he was liberal enough to stand for "open questions" in eschatology, to doubt the wisdom of subscribing to the Book of Concord as too theological for the laity, and to distinguish between fundamental and non-fundamental doctrines. But he believed in verbal inspiration and *jure divino* ministry, and regarded ecclesiastical "unionism" as sinful. He was happy that his one-time plan to study in Germany had been shattered because he considered it to be the land of rationalism. Besides the publications already mentioned, he edited the *Lutheran Watchman*, 1866–67, was joint editor of the *Luthersk Kirkeblad*, 1890–95, and *Der Sprechsaal*, 1901–03. He was author of *Naadevalgsstriden*, 1881, *Intuitu fidei*, 1895, and *Sandhed og Frihed*, 1914. Schmidt was a small-statured man, kind, sociable, honest to the core, and versatile. His wife was Caroline Sophia Allwardt, to whom he was married on Dec. 8, 1858. They had eight children, six of whom survived their father.

[*Who's Who in America*, 1920–21; *Who's Who Among Pastors in All the Norwegian Luth. Synods of America* (1928); O. M. Norlie, O. A. Tingelstad, K. T. Jacobson, *Luther Coll. Through Sixty Years* (1922); J. A. Bergh, *Den Norsk Lutherske Kirkes Historie i Amerika* (1914); Luth. Pub. Soc., *The Distinctive Doctrines and Usages . . . of the Evang. Luth. Ch.* (4th ed., 1914); *Luth. Quart.*, Jan. 1906.]   J. O. E.

SCHMUCKER, BEALE MELANCHTHON (Aug. 26, 1827–Oct. 15, 1888), Lutheran clergyman, was born at Gettysburg, Pa., the second of the twelve children of Samuel Simon Schmucker [*q.v.*] by his second wife, Mary Catherine Steenbergen. He graduated from Pennsylvania (later Gettysburg) College in 1844 and from the Gettysburg Theological Seminary in 1847, was licensed by the West Pennsylvania Synod in 1847, and was ordained by the Virginia Synod in 1849. On Mar. 6, 1860, he married Christiana M. Pretz of Allentown, by whom he had two sons. His first charge was Martinsburg and Shepherdstown, Va. (now W. Va.), where he succeeded his friend Charles Porterfield Krauth [*q.v.*] from 1848 to 1851. The winter of 1851–52 he spent in his father's house at Gettysburg, recovering from an affection of the throat. Subsequently he was pastor of St. John's English Lutheran Church, Allentown, 1852–62; of St. John's, Easton, with Philip Pfatteicher as his German colleague, 1862–67; of St. James', Reading, 1867–81; and of the Church of the Transfiguration, Pottstown, from 1881 till his death seven years later. Though exemplary in the fulfillment of his parochial duties, he exercised his greatest influence as a parliamentarian and scholar.

From his father he had inherited his dignity and self-control, his profound piety, his logical habits of thought, and his capacity for severe, sustained intellectual toil, but in their religious temper father and son differed radically. The elder Schmucker was the most gifted and most influential evangelical among the Lutherans of America; the younger, intellectually in closer sympathy with Charles Porterfield Krauth, became one of the leaders of the extreme churchly party which discredited Samuel Simon Schmucker and remoulded almost completely the doctrine and life of the Lutheran Church in America. The breach between father and son never became personal; amid the theological strife of that generation Beale could write of his father with a serenity, tenderness, and understanding profoundly moving; but there was tragedy, however concealed, in their intellectual estrangement.

He was English secretary of the board of directors of the Philadelphia Theological Seminary from 1864 to 1888, secretary of the board of foreign missions of the Ministerium of Pennsylvania and of the General Council of the Evangelical Lutheran Church in America. As a liturgical scholar he had no equal in the United States and few in Europe. His knowledge of the early Lutheran liturgies and of those of the undivided church was profound; he had an intuitive sense for the proprieties of worship; and his literary taste was impeccable. The first-fruit of his work in this field was *A Liturgy for the Use of the Evangelical Lutheran Church* (1860; 1868; 1871), in which he collaborated with A. T. Geissenhainer; it was nominally a translation of the second edition (1855) of the *Liturgie und Kirchenagende* edited by Charles Rudolph Demme [*q.v.*], but was really based on older, more conservative principles and was a finer achievement. With Frederic Mayer Bird [*q.v.*] he edited the *Hymns for the Use of the Evangelical Lutheran Church* (1865; 1868), which was the best American hymnbook that had yet appeared.

His drastic criticism, from the floor of the Ministerium, of the provisional edition (1871) of the *Kirchenbuch* resulted in his addition to the committee engaged on it, and the completed *Kirchenbuch* (1877), like the English liturgies and hymnbooks of the Ministerium and the General Council, bears the stamp of his taste and scholarship. When a joint committee of the General Council, the General Synod, and the United Synod of the South was formed to prepare a Common Service for the use of the three bodies, Schmucker, Edward Traill Horn [*q.v.*], and George U. Wenner constituted the sub-committee that did most of the work. He wrote the preface to the first edition of *The Common Service* (1888) published by the United Synod of the South, and he continued to work on the forms for ministerial acts until the end. His editorial work is incorporated in *The Church Book* (1891) and *The Common Service Book* (1919). No other one man has so influenced the liturgical development of the Lutheran Church in America.

Schmucker was averse to publishing anything under his own name, but late in life he produced a number of historical and biographical studies of importance, and he collaborated with William Julius Mann and Wilhelm Germann on an annotated edition of the *Hallesche Nachrichten* (1886–95). He collected what was probably the best liturgical library in the United States (now at the Philadelphia Theological Seminary). On Oct. 15, 1888, he left his home in Pottstown to take the completed manuscript of *The Church Book* to the publishing house in Philadelphia. He ran to catch his train and died of a heart attack near Phoenixville. The burial service that he had completed two weeks before was used for the first time at his grave.

[Published material on Schmucker includes Adolph Spaeth, *Charles Porterfield Krauth* (2 vols., 1898–1909) and "Memorial of Beale Melanchthon Schmucker," *Luth. Ch. Rev.*, Apr. 1889; H. E. Jacobs, "The Making of the Church Book," *Ibid.*, Oct. 1912; L. D. Reed, "Hist. Sketch of the Common Service," *Ibid.*, Oct. 1917; G. W. Sandt, "Luth. Leaders as I Knew Them: Rev. Beale M. Schmucker, D.D.," *Ibid.*, Jan. 1918; A. R. Wentz, *Hist. of the Gettysburg Theol. Sem.* (1926). The C. P. Krauth and B. M. Schmucker papers are in the library of the Lutheran Theological Seminary, Mount Airy, Phila.]   G. H. G.

SCHMUCKER, JOHN GEORGE (Aug. 18, 1771–Oct. 7, 1854), Lutheran clergyman, was born in Germany at Michelstadt in the Odenwald, the second of the six children of John Christopher Schmucker, and came to Pennsylvania with his parents in 1785. After tarrying a year in Lehigh and another year in Lancaster County, the family settled in the Shenandoah Valley just west of Woodstock, Va. There, in his nineteenth year, Schmucker began his preparation for the ministry under Paul Henkel [*q.v.*], whom he accompanied on one or more trips to the back country. In later years he had tales to tell his children of encounters with Indians and border ruffians and of a narrow escape from drowning in a spring freshet. In 1790 he tramped north to Philadelphia to study for two years under J. H. C. Helmuth [*q.v.*] and J. F. Schmidt. He then became a catechist at Quickel's Church, York County, Pa., under the supervision of the celebrated Jacob Goering, with whom he read Hebrew.

He was licensed in 1793 and ordained in 1800 by the Ministerium of Pennsylvania. From 1794 to 1809 he was pastor of the Lutheran Church at Hagerstown, Md., and its affiliated congregations; he came to Hagerstown a pale, emaciated, diffident youth, whom his parishioners regarded half with wonder and half with pity, but he developed steadily into one of the ablest, most influential ministers of his denomination. After Goering's death he was called to take charge of the congregations in and about York, Pa., and held this post from 1809 to 1836. On May 1, 1814, the York congregation dedicated a new church building, Christ Church, the act of consecration being performed by Friedrich Valentin Melsheimer [*q.v.*]. Schmucker began about 1820 to conduct some of the services at Christ Church in the English language, and in 1829 he received a congenial assistant in the Rev. Jonathan Oswald. A few years later he precipitated a local tempest by advocating temperance; for a while he was so unpopular that he could collect only half his salary. He was president (1820–21) of the Ministerium of Pennsylvania and one of the founders of the General Synod, the Gettysburg Theological Seminary, Pennsylvania (now Gettysburg) College, and the West Pennsylvania Synod, and his services to all these organizations and institutions were important and continued over many years.

Schmucker's published works include *The Prophetic History of the Christian Religion, or Explanation of the Revelation of St. John* (2 vols., 1817–21); *Vornehmste Weissagungen der Heiligen Schrift* (1807); *Die Wächterstimme an Zion's Kinder* (1838); *Reformations-Geschichte zur Jubelfeier der Reformation* (1817); *Schwärmergeist unserer Tage entlarvt zur Warnung erweckter Seelen* (1827); *Lieder-Anhang zum Evangelischen Gesangbuch der General Synode* (1833); and *Erklärung der Offenbarung Johannis* (n.d.). He left in manuscript a huge commentary on the Epistle to the Hebrews and an explanation of Luther's Shorter Catechism, which B. M. Schmucker described as "among the most excellent of its whole class, simple, clear, precise, thoroughly evangelical and distinctly Lutheran in doctrine" ("Luther's Small Catechism: Explanations Prepared for Use in America," *Lutheran Church Review,* July 1886, p. 173).

Schmucker resigned his pastorate at York in 1836 and was succeeded by Augustus Hoffman Lochman. He continued to act as pastor of Quickel's Church, which he served in his youth, until 1852. He was married twice; to Elizabeth Gross of Quickel's, who bore him twelve children and died in 1819; and in 1821 to Anna Hoffman, sister-in-law of John George Lochman [*q.v.*], who bore him seven children and outlived him. The last few years of his life were spent at Williamsburg, Blair County, Pa., where he died. He was buried in front of Christ Church at York. Great as were his services to the Lutheran Church of his generation, his most enduring claim on remembrance is that he was the father of Samuel Simon Schmucker [*q.v.*].

[*Evangelical Rev.,* Jan. 1855; W. B. Sprague, *Annals Am. Pulpit,* vol. IX (1869); J. G. Morris, *Fifty Years in the Luth. Ministry* (1878); Peter Anstadt, *Life and Times of Rev. S. S. Schmucker, D.D.* (1896); *Doc. Hist. Ev. Luth. Min. of Pa. . . . 1748–1821* (1898); B. M. Schmucker, "The Luth. Ch. in York, Pa.," *Luth. Quart.,* Oct. 1888; A. R. Wentz, *Hist. of the Gettysburg Theol. Sem.* (1926).]
G. H. G.

SCHMUCKER, SAMUEL SIMON (Feb. 28, 1799–July 26, 1873), Lutheran clergyman, theologian, educator, was born at Hagerstown, Md., where his mother, Elizabeth (Gross), and his father, the Rev. John George Schmucker [*q.v.*], were shepherding a small Lutheran flock. The atmosphere of the parental home was that of a warm pietism after the pattern of the German school of Spener and Francke, mixed with the rigorous Puritanism which then dominated American Protestantism. The home had contacts, however, with broad interests through the father's active participation in the affairs of organized Lutheranism. While still a youth it was given to the son to help carry forward to success the efforts of his father and a few others in the organization of the General Synod, the first united Lutheran Church in America.

Samuel's formal education consisted of discipleship under his father's theological preceptor, Dr. Justus H. C. Helmuth [*q.v.*], a veteran of the days of the patriarch Henry M. Mühlenberg [*q.v.*], who carried over the confessional strain from that earlier time. In 1819 Schmucker was graduated *gratiae causa* from the University of Pennsylvania, and in 1820, from the Princeton Theological Seminary, where he learned anew to respect puritanical notions and

practices (evidenced in his legalistic view of the Christian Sabbath, in strict observation of certain religious customs, and in a rather rigid sense of decorum), and where he came into a close fellowship with other denominational leaders which gave him a characteristic catholic outlook. All through the years he remained a student, and in his day he was the best-trained man in his church. Licensed in 1820 and ordained a year later, he served his only parish, consisting of five congregations with New Market, Va., as center, for nearly six years. He was three times married: first, Feb. 28, 1821, to Elenora Geiger of Hagerstown, Md., who died July 3, 1823, having borne him one son; second, Oct. 12, 1825, to Mary Catherine Steenbergen of the Shenandoah Valley, Va., who died Feb. 11, 1848, the mother of twelve children; third, Apr. 28, 1849, to Esther M. Wagner of Germantown, Pa. Of his four gifted sons, one, Beale Melanchthon [*q.v.*], became a conspicuous leader in the conservative camp opposing his father's liberal outlook.

Three *pia desideria* (as he called them) gripped him upon leaving Princeton: the translation of some one important work on Lutheran dogmatics, the establishment of a Lutheran theological seminary, and the founding of a college. All three were early realized: his *Biblical Theology of Storr and Flatt, Translated from the German* appeared in two volumes in 1826; in 1825, he was elected first professor in the theological seminary at Gettysburg, opened in 1826, which he helped to found; and the classical school, which he initiated in 1827, became, under a charter granted five years later, Pennsylvania College (now Gettysburg). From 1832 to 1834 Schmucker served as president of the college. His *desideria,* however, were more than realized. He framed model constitutions for congregations and synods; he published in 1834 the first English Lutheran work on systematic theology appearing in this country, *Elements of Popular Theology;* he helped to prepare hymnbooks, liturgical forms, new editions of Luther's catechism containing free interpretations; he took active part in the efforts toward church unity, particularly by his publication in 1838 of the widely discussed *Appeal to the American Churches* (a document antedating the fellowship plan of the present Federal Council of Churches) and by active participation in the organization of the Evangelical Alliance in 1846.

For many years he held the reins of theological leadership in the General Synod. In the 1840's, however, forces began to gather strength which ultimately took the reins from his hands. A huge tide of German immigration swept in and with it was transplanted to American soil a conservative Lutheran theology chained by a full allegiance to the symbolical books and treatises of the sixteenth and seventeenth century German theologians. Cognizant of the rising tide of conservatism, he launched, from about 1845 on, a quiet campaign defending in carefully prepared discourses the type of Lutheranism which he had come to know as consonant with "that liberty of thought which all Protestants must retain." From apologetics he turned to vigorous polemics, dividing the issue squarely between an "American" and an "Old" Lutheranism. The impending explosion came with the publication of the anonymous document called the *Definite Platform, Doctrinal and Disciplinarian, for Evangelical Lutheran District Synods* (1855), prepared by Schmucker, in which the advocates of an American Lutheranism sought to have adopted their confessional position in a recension of the Augsburg Confession as a minimum platform of agreement. The controversy was only aggravated; one by one his followers turned away to follow the new stream. The issuance of the manifesto, he came to believe, was a blunder, and he tried in vain to atone for it, but the time and tide were against him. Heresy charges instituted by the man who came to be his successor were opposed by those who had not in the heat of the controversy lost the perspective of gratitude. When he left his chair in 1864 he could truthfully say to his church and particularly to his some four hundred students that he had not in the main departed from the doctrines taught in the classroom nor from the liberal professorial oath formulated by himself thirty-eight years before.

His some forty-four published works reveal a systematic mind. He generally presented the argument of a theme only after he had carefully marshaled and set forth facts; he sought for intelligent judgment and not for emotional assent. By nature he was even-tempered and irenic; though graciously tolerant of the views of others, he steadfastly and openly defended convictions of his own. He excelled greatly in the virtue of integrity. The paradox of his professional life is a curious one: a savior of his church in the third decade of the nineteenth century, he was looked upon as its betrayer in the fifth and afterward; he set out to make his Church more Lutheran, and that same Church later waved him aside because he was not Lutheran enough.

[A list of the published works and discourses of Schmucker, together with much valuable source material, is given in Vergilius Ferm, *The Crisis in Am. Lutheran Theology* (1927). See also, B. M. Schmucker, "Samuel S. Schmucker," in *The Pa. Coll. Book,* *1832–1882* (1882); Peter Anstadt, *Life and Times of Rev. S. S. Schmucker, D.D.* (1896); A. R. Wentz, *Hist. of the Gettysburg Theological Sem.* (1926), and "The Work of S. S. Schmucker," in *Lutheran Quart.,* Jan. 1927; J. L. Chamberlain, *Universities and Their Sons: Univ. of Pa.,* vol. II (1902); Adolph Spaeth, *Charles Porterfield Krauth* (2 vols., 1898–1909).]

V. F.

SCHNAUFFER, CARL HEINRICH (July 4, 1823–Sept. 4, 1854), poet, soldier, editor, was a German political refugee in America after the Revolution of 1848. He was born in Heimsheim, near Stuttgart, Germany, the son of a dyer, Johann Heinrich Schnauffer, and Karoline (Hasenmaier) Schnauffer. Owing to the early death of his father Schnauffer's schooling was cut short and, after serving an apprenticeship in Grossbottwar, he entered the employ of a Mannheim merchant. His employer recognized his literary ability and gave him the necessary time for study. At this time Schnauffer met two men whose ideals influenced the whole course of his life, Gustav Struve and Friedrich Karl Franz Hecker [qq.v.], revolutionary leaders in Baden and emigrants to America after 1848. In 1846 he entered the university at Heidelberg, where he associated with the liberal student groups, and published his first volume of verse, strongly influenced by Pierre-Jean de Béranger and Ferdinand Freiligrath. In the next year he joined the staff of the liberal *Mannheimer Abendzeitung,* and in 1848 followed Hecker into the field and fought in a number of engagements of the ill-starred uprising of the South-German liberals. He fled to Switzerland, but in 1849 he joined in the renewed fighting, and on June 22 he was taken prisoner at Mannheim and transported to Prussia. He escaped from prison disguised as a locksmith, and once more took refuge in Switzerland where he wrote his *Todtenkränze,* inspired probably by a work of the same title by Christian von Zedlitz. But instead of the Austrian poet's resignation, Schnauffer sounds a ringing call to battle for freedom in the name of those executed by the reactionaries. In April 1850 he was seized by the Swiss government and forced to leave for London along with other revolutionary leaders. In London he met Struve and together they went to the estate of Thomas Fothergill, a friend from Heidelberg days who offered them asylum. He performed manual labor for his keep, among other things training race horses, and also began a five-act drama in the style of Schiller, *Koenig Karl I oder Cromwell und die englische Revolution,* which was privately printed in Baltimore in 1854. Characteristically the play ends with the death of the tyrant and the establishment of the British republic.

In Mannheim he had become engaged to Elise Wilhelmine Moos who had, however, emigrated to Baltimore, Md., with her family in 1847. For several years Schnauffer had no news of her but, in 1850, correspondence was renewed and in May of the following year he joined her in Baltimore where they were married. He identified himself enthusiastically with the "Turner" movement and founded, in October 1851, a German daily, *Baltimore Wecker,* which stood for popular education, freedom, and enlightenment, and opposed the current "Know-Nothingism." Unlike some other "Forty-eighters" Schnauffer never preached economic revolution, but in his lyrics he continually elaborated on the theme that the noble man should at all times be ready to fight and die for freedom. The best works by Schnauffer are poems in the style of Arndt or Herwegh, which expressed the ideals of the "Turner" so well that they became their favorite songs. His collected poems were published in 1879 under the title, *Lieder und Gedichte aus dem Nachlass von Carl Heinrich Schnauffer.* He died at the age of thirty-one from typhoid fever, just before news reached him that one of his lyrics had won the first prize at the "Turner" convention in Philadelphia. His widow continued the *Wecker* in his memory and in his spirit. No English-language paper in Maryland was anti-slavery and on the outburst of the Civil War a mob stormed the *Wecker* office, smashing its windows. At this moment Mrs. Schnauffer, with the smaller of her two children in her arms, stepped out of the building to face the mob and successfully appealed to them to abandon further destruction. Schnauffer was quite short in stature but military in bearing, and he had a personality that inspired enthusiastic devotion in his friends.

[*Jahrbücher der Deutsch-Amerikanischen Turnerei,* Apr. 1891; L. P. Henninghausen, "Reminiscences of the Political Life of the German-Americans in Baltimore during 1850–1860," *Seventh Ann. Report of the Soc. for the Hist. of the Germans in Md.,* 1892–93; J. T. Scharf, *Hist. of Baltimore City* (1881); Baltimore *Sun,* Sept. 5, 1854; reminiscences and unpublished letters furnished by his grandson, John Dickinson.]

A. E. Z.

SCHNEIDER, ALBERT (Apr. 13, 1863– Oct. 27, 1928), bacteriologist, was born in Granville, Ill., the son of John and Elizabeth (Burcky) Schneider. He married Marie Louise Harrington of Minneapolis, Minn., on June 28, 1892; they had one daughter. After taking the degree of M.D. at the College of Physicians and Surgeons, Chicago, Ill., in 1887, he became instructor in botany at the University of Minnesota. In 1894 he took the degree of M.S. at Minnesota; in 1897 he received the degree of Ph.D. at Columbia University and returned to teaching. He was professor of pharmacology and bacteriology at Northwestern University, 1897–1903; of pharmacognosy and bacteriology at the University of California, 1903–19; of pharmacology at the University of Nebraska, 1919–22; and dean of pharmacy at North Pacific College of Oregon, Portland, 1922–28. In addition, he was director of the experiment station of the Spreckels Sugar Company, 1906–07; pharmacognosist, United States Department of Agriculture, 1909–15; and editor of the *Pacific Pharmacist,* 1910–15, through which he attempted to raise the standards of pharmacy as a profession and to secure pure foods and drugs. Apart from his strictly professional work, he was a man of some inventive genius. Apparatus and instruments of his design were to be seen in his laboratory, and he invented a ventilating system for Pullman cars. He was interested in the scientific detection of criminals, wrote several papers on the subject, re-introduced the "lie detector" in 1927, and lectured at the police schools in Berkeley, Cal., and Portland, Ore., at various times.

His writings include books and articles on a wide range of subjects: bacteriology, botany, microscopy, food analysis, lichenology, toxicology, pharmacology, glandular therapy, and criminology. One of his early books was *The Limitations of Learning and Other Science Papers* (1900); later he wrote such technical books as *Pharmaceutical Bacteriology* (1912; 2nd ed. 1920), *Bacteriological Methods in Food and Drugs Laboratories* (1915), *The Microbiology and Microanalysis of Foods* (1920), and *The Microanalysis of Powdered Vegetable Drugs* (2nd ed., 1921). In 1896 he produced *A Compendium of General Botany,* translated from the German of Maximilian Westermaier. The papers he contributed with frequency to scientific journals exhibit great care in preparation. It was his habit to repeat experiments many times in a methodical way in order to satisfy himself that the results were worth publication; he strongly discouraged the type of research work that, as he expressed it, "clutters up" the journals. He was a member of the international jury of awards at the Panama Pacific International Exposition in 1915, one of a committee for the tenth revision of the United States Pharmacopoeia, a member of the American Pharmaceutical Association and of the American Association for the Advancement of Science. He died in Portland, Ore.

[*Who's Who in America,* 1928–29; J. McK. and Jaques Cattell, *Am. Men of Sci.* (ed. 1927); *Jour. Am. Pharmaceutical Assoc.,* Nov. 1928; *Morning Oregonian* (Portland), Oct. 28, 1928.]

F. G.

SCHNEIDER, BENJAMIN (Jan. 18, 1807–
Sept. 14, 1877), missionary in Turkey, was born
at New Hanover, Montgomery County, Pa., the
son of Henry and Mary (Noyce) Schneider.
After preparatory education at academies in Norristown and Reading, Pa., in 1826 he entered
Hamilton College, but at the end of his second
year transferred to Amherst, where he was graduated in 1830. He then attended Andover Theological Seminary, completing his course there
in 1833. On Sept. 15 of the same year he married Eliza Cheyney, daughter of Josiah Abbott
of Framingham, Mass., and on Oct. 2 was
ordained to the ministry of the Presbyterian
Church, at Nottingham, Md. Having been appointed a missionary to Turkey by the American
Board of Commissioners for Foreign Missions,
he sailed from Boston three months later and
reached Smyrna on Jan. 14, 1834. Commissioned
to establish a station at Brusa, he proceeded at
once to his post and commenced the study of modern Greek and Turkish. For the next fifteen
years that city was his headquarters for evangelical work, principally among Greeks and Armenians. Frequent tours on horseback spread
his influence through the surrounding provinces.
So great was the opposition from local Ottoman
officials and priests of the Oriental Christian
Churches, however, that in 1848 the sole tangible
fruit of his labors in preaching and in distributing tracts and Bibles was a Protestant Church
of seven members in Brusa.

In 1849 he was transferred to Aintab in South-
Central Anatolia, and found among the Armenians there a more fertile field for his activities.
The one small Protestant Church in the place
developed during his seventeen years of work
into two entirely self-supporting congregations
with several hundred members, Sunday Schools,
day schools, and a high school. Meanwhile,
Aintab had become one of the largest centers of
missionary work in Turkey, with several missionaries in residence. In Marash, Urfa, Diarbe-
kir, Adana, and many other towns out-stations
had been established and were flourishing under
the care of missionaries or of native pastors who
were given their theological training by Schneider. In 1856 his wife died at Aintab, and while
on a furlough in the United States two years
later he married her sister, Susan Maria. He
returned in 1868 to his former post at Brusa and
spent there four more years under conditions
vastly more favorable to missionary work than
had obtained during his former residence. Ill
health forced him in 1872 to take another furlough of two years at home, and when he went
back to the mission field it was to the less strenu-

ous task of teaching in the theological seminary
at Marsovan (now Merzifon). His strength was
unequal to the work, however, and after one
more year of service he retired. He spent the
last two years of his life in New Britain, Conn.,
and in Boston, where he died.

Among the pioneer missionaries to Turkey
Schneider was preëminently the preacher rather
than the translator or explorer. Though he
wrote or translated books and tracts into modern
Greek and Turkish, his strength was in the
spoken rather than in the written word, and his
sermons were renowned for an almost faultless
mastery of these languages as well as for eloquence and persuasiveness. Strongly Calvinistic
in his theology and preaching, he was nevertheless a man of great tolerance and simple sincerity.

[*Amherst Coll. Biog. Record* (1927); J. K. Greene,
Leavening the Levant (1916); *Missionary Herald,*
Dec. 1877.]   W. L. W., Jr.

SCHNEIDER, GEORGE (Dec. 13, 1823–
Sept. 16, 1905), journalist and banker, was born
in Pirmasens, Rhenish Bavaria, the son of Ludwig and Josephine (Schlick) Schneider. He
obtained his early education at the Latin school
of his native town. Upon reaching his majority
he became engaged in journalism. Keenly interested in public affairs, he denounced the arbitrary government of his native state and in
1848 joined an insurrection against it. Having
eventually to leave the country because of his
political views, he went first to France and
thence to the United States. Arriving in New
York in July 1849, he was attracted by the
glamorous stories of the new West. Within a
few months he had reached St. Louis and founded the *Neue Zeit,* a paper which soon became
conspicuous for its opposition to the extension
of slavery. In 1851 the home of the *Neue Zeit*
was destroyed by fire, and in August of the same
year Schneider became managing editor of the
Illinois Staats-Zeitung, a conservative weekly
paper which he soon transformed into a thriving
daily with a Sunday edition, the first in Chicago. Although more conservative than the *Neue
Zeit,* the *Staats-Zeitung* bitterly opposed the
Douglas program and the repeal of the Missouri Compromise. On Jan. 29, 1854, Schneider
convoked a public meeting, perhaps the first of
its kind in the United States, to draft resolutions against the Nebraska Bill, and on Mar. 16
at a mass meeting of German citizens in which
Schneider was an active participant, Douglas
was branded as "an ambitious and dangerous
demagogue." On Feb. 22, 1856, Schneider was
one of a group of anti-Nebraska editors who

assembled at Decatur, Ill., and issued a call for the first Republican state convention in Illinois, to be held at Bloomington in the following May. At the Bloomington convention, with Lincoln's assistance, he managed to get a plank adopted which was a clear-cut pronouncement against Know-Nothing policies hostile to naturalized citizens, especially Germans, who were antislavery men. He also was chiefly responsible for the adoption of the tenth plank of the Philadelphia platform of 1856 which invited the "affiliation and coöperation of the men of all parties." He actively espoused Lincoln's candidacy for the presidency after his nomination in 1860, and the nation-wide circulation of the *Staats-Zeitung,* one of the most influential German papers in the Northwest, did much to consolidate the great foreign-born vote without which Lincoln would have failed of election (D. V. Smith, *Mississippi Valley Historical Review,* September 1932).

In 1861 he was appointed consul at Elsinore, Denmark, primarily to influence the public opinion of northern Europe in favor of the Union cause. Resigning from this office in 1862, he returned to the United States and in 1863 became collector of internal revenue for the Chicago district, having in the meantime (1862) disposed of his interest in the *Staats-Zeitung.* After four years in the internal revenue service, he became chief executive of the State Savings Institution at Chicago, and in 1871 he was chosen the first president of the newly organized National Bank of Illinois, a position that he held until 1897. Although he was now primarily interested in banking, he continued to be active in public life in Illinois. Declining to accept a diplomatic appointment to Switzerland in 1877, he became the treasurer of the Chicago South Park Board in the following year, serving in this capacity until 1882. As a director of the Chicago Festival Association, he was instrumental in 1885 in bringing excellent musical talent to Chicago. He was intensely interested in the formation of relief societies for German immigrants, and he served for many years as a director of the Illinois Humane Society, which through his efforts in 1879 established a separate department for helpless children. On June 6, 1853, he married Matilda Schloetzer, by whom he had seven children, all daughters. He died in Colorado Springs, Colo.

[*Who's Who in America,* 1903–05; *Trans. Ill. State Hist. Soc.,* no. 35 (1928); *Encyc. of Biog. of Ill.,* vol. I (1892); John Moses and Joseph Kirkland, eds., *Hist. of Chicago* (1895), vols. I, II; Newton Bateman and Paul Selby, eds., *Hist. Encyc. of Ill.* (1900); A. C. Cole, *The Era of the Civil War,* 1848–1870 (1919); "Meeting . . . Commemorative of the Convention of

May 29, 1856," *Trans. McLean County Hist. Soc.,* vol. III (Bloomington, Ill., 1900); *Chicago Daily Tribune,* Sept. 18, 1905; information from Chicago Pub. Lib.]
A. L. P.

SCHNEIDER, THEODORE (Apr. 7, 1703–July 10, 1764), Roman Catholic missionary, was born at Geinsheim in the diocese of Speyer in the Rhenish Palatinate. On the completion of his preparatory schooling at Speyer, he joined the Society of Jesus (Sept. 25, 1721) and made a brilliant record in philosophy and theology. Hoping to be sent to India as a missionary, he studied medicine. Fate and his provincial decreed a quite different future and he became professor of philosophy and polemics at the Jesuit College of Liège and later rector of the Jesuit House of Studies at the University of Heidelberg, the philosophy courses of the University then being in the charge of the Jesuits. In 1738 he was elected Rector Magnificus of the University. Two years later he was ordered by the General of the Society to go to the Pennsylvania missions, where the English Jesuits were finding difficulty in ministering to the Germans and it was feared they were being lost to the Church. After a brief sojourn in London, where he probably joined the English province, Schneider arrived in Philadelphia in 1741 and was assigned temporarily to St. Joseph's Church before going to Goshenhoppen in Berks County on the Philadelphia-Pottstown Road.

After living for a time with a German carpenter, Schneider built a house and chapel with the assistance of his Catholic fellow countrymen and friendly Mennonites. A powerful man, he was fitted for the rough life and arduous travel. A physician in a land where there were few healers of repute, he was welcomed on his journeys by the people regardless of creed. As a former rector of Heidelberg, he was glorified by the Germans, among whom there were some scholarly ministers. His character overcame much prejudice and gained him considerable favor. In his quest for Catholics and in his efforts to revive their faith, he traveled by horse and afoot to Philadelphia, and aided Robert Harding [*q.v.*] in the eastern counties of Pennsylvania and in a large portion of New Jersey, saying Mass in small chapels and in private homes. No man did more for the early Germans. Bishop Carroll described him as "a person of great dexterity in business, consummate prudence and undaunted magnanimity" (quoted in J. G. Shea, *post,* p. 387). He founded a number of chapels, built a large church at Goshenhoppen, established schools, and even taught little children himself. A diligent man, he kept records and, as an economy and a penance, he copied two complete missals of several hundred pages each (one of which is preserved in the archives of Georgetown University). Broken in health by labors and hardships, Father Schneider was awaiting a recall to Germany to recuperate, when he died after a brief illness.

[Lambert Schrott, *Pioneer German Catholics in the Am. Colonies* (1933); *Cath. Univ. Bull.*, Oct. 1907; J. G. Shea, *The Catholic Church in Colonial Days* (1886); Bernhard Duhr, *Deutsche Auslandsehnsucht im Achtzehnten Jahrhundert* (1928).]   R. J. P.

SCHNELLER, GEORGE OTTO (Jan. 14, 1843–Oct. 20, 1895), inventor, manufacturer, was the son of Henry and Elizabeth (Ruckert) Schneller and was born in Nürnberg, Germany. The father was a civil engineer and architect for the German government and directed his son's education, through private schooling and the local technical schools, toward engineering. At the age of seventeen, however, Schneller left his home and emigrated to the United States, landing in New York City. Being an excellent penman and having some knowledge of accountancy, he soon found employment in New York with a commission merchant dealing in brass goods. He became interested in brass manufacture and within a short time, giving up his position in New York, he went to Ansonia, Conn., then the center of the brass industry. There as cashier and accountant he entered the employ of Osborne and Cheesman Company, an influential and notably successful brass manufactory, and in the course of the succeeding eight years advanced rapidly. In 1870, however, he returned to Germany, primarily to visit his home, and there began the study of electrical engineering, as well as other subjects likely to fit him for a manufacturing career. When in 1872 he returned to the United States, he engaged in surveying in Ansonia, made a detailed map of Derby and Ansonia, and as a result of his earlier experience with brass manufacture tried his hand at invention. Between February 1872 and July 1873 he obtained four patents on corset springs. About 1874 he spent two years in a variety of mining ventures in the west but returned to Ansonia and bought a spectacle factory at Shelton, Conn., which he sold within six months. He then turned his attention to the manufacture of brass corset eyelets. In an effort to improve the slow and wasteful methods of insertion then in use, he devoted three or four years to experimentation. In the next few years he secured patents on a die for making eyelets (November 1880), an eyelet machine, and a punch and die for eyelet machines (May 1884), the latter two inventions being designed primarily for insert-

ing eyelets in corsets. Meanwhile in 1882 he bought the Osborne and Cheesman business, reorganized it as the Ansonia O. & C. Company, and began the manufacture of brass goods under his patent rights. Since by his process the amount of waste brass was greatly reduced and the rate of inserting eyelets greatly increased— three hundred dozen corsets could be completed in ten hours—the corset industry of the world was completely revolutionized. Until his death Schneller continued as manager, secretary, and treasurer of his company; he also founded and was treasurer of the Union Fabric Company in Ansonia. With all these activities he found time to continue his inventions, patenting among other things a hook and eye, a bustle, a machine for covering dress stays, a button press, and a button-fastening device. He was active in the building of the electric street railway system between Derby, Ansonia, and Shelton; he also served for a number of years on the board of education of Ansonia and represented that city in the lower house of the state legislature from 1891 to 1893. On May 1, 1873, in Ansonia, he married Clarissa Alling, who with their three children survived him.

[*Commemorative Biog. Record of New Haven County, Conn.* (1902), vol I; *Leading Business Men of New Haven County* (1881); Patent Office records; *New Haven Evening Reg.*, Oct. 21, 1895.]   C. W. M.

SCHNERR, LEANDER (Sept. 27, 1836– Sept. 3, 1920), Roman Catholic cleric, third archabbot of St. Vincent, Latrobe, Pa., was born at Gommersdorf, Baden, Germany, the son of Ernst Schnerr, a Lutheran in faith and a brewmaster by trade, and Barbara Melly, a native of Bamberg, Bavaria, and a Catholic. The day after his birth the child was baptized in the local Catholic church, receiving the names Karl Otto August. A few years later the family emigrated to America and settled in Pittsburgh, Pa., where the father continued to follow his trade. Just before his fourteenth birthday, Karl entered the college at Latrobe, Pa., conducted by the Benedictines of St. Vincent Abbey, and after six years decided to become a member of that Order. He made his solemn vows on Jan. 6, 1857, taking the name Leander in religion. Two years later, Sept. 20, 1859, he was ordained priest by the Rt. Rev. George A. Carrell at Covington, Ky.

Appointed for the missionary field of St. Vincent Abbey, he began as pastor of Stony Hill, N. J., but was soon transferred to the congregations of Augusta and Mullin's Station, Ky. In 1861 Abbot Boniface Wimmer promoted him to priorship and the pastorate of St. Joseph

Church, Chicago, Ill. Here he worked faithfully for ten years, only to see the whole parish plant destroyed in the great fire of 1871. He began to rebuild at once, but before he could finish this task he was sent to St. Mary's, Erie, Pa. Five years later he became pastor of St. Joseph's Church, Johnstown, Pa., and in 1877, after a short administration of St. Bernard Church, Indiana, Pa., assumed charge of St. Mary's Church and priory at Pittsburgh. During the next fifteen years he was prominent in Catholic affairs in that city, especially among the Germans. He practically built a new St. Mary's and in 1884 founded St. Boniface parish. In 1892, after the resignation of the Rt. Rev. Andrew Hintenach, the second archabbot of St. Vincent, Father Leander was elected as his successor.

At his installation on Oct. 5, 1892, the cornerstone of a new abbey church was blessed and during the next twenty-eight years building operations rarely ceased at the archabbey; besides the church, a library, gymnasium, dormitory, various shops, and farm buildings were constructed. At the same time, the Archabbot sought to improve the course of studies. The classical and scientific departments were remodeled to conform to the requirements of the Association of Colleges of the Middle States and Maryland and the philosophical and theological courses were improved to obtain from the Roman authorities the power of granting doctors' degrees in both these branches of learning. Twice he went to Rome in the interest of the whole Order. In 1903 Pius X conferred on him the privilege of the Cappa Magna in church functions and in 1910 he was chosen as a member of the Roman Arcadia. He celebrated the golden jubilees of his profession and ordination in 1907 and 1909. In 1918 he asked the Roman authorities for a coadjutor and the capitulars of the archabbey chose his long-time secretary, Aurelius Stehle, as his successor in office.

Externally, with his stately figure and long flowing beard, Archabbot Leander seemed more a prophet of old than a churchman of the twentieth century. He was not a learned man, but eminently practical and very methodical in his ways. He contributed to the expansion of the Catholic Church and of the Order of St. Benedict in the United States by having St. Bede College, Peru, Ill., raised to an Abbey by Rome in 1910, and by fostering in a special manner the institute of lay-oblates of the Order, an association of men who follow their avocations in life but attach themselves in spiritual matters to a Benedictine monastery.

[Official documents, diary, and letters of the Archabbot, in St. Vincent Archives; *St. Vincent College Journal*, 1892–1920; *Pittsburgh Post*, Sept. 4, 1920.]

F. F.

SCHODDE, GEORGE HENRY (Apr. 15, 1854–Sept. 15, 1917), Lutheran clergyman and educator, the son of George F. and Mary Louise (Tücke) Schodde, was born in Allegheny, Pa. He was graduated in 1872 from the college and in 1874 from the theological department of Capital University, Columbus, Ohio. He pursued his studies further in the universities of Tübingen and Leipzig, receiving in 1877 the degree of Ph.D. from the latter. After returning from Europe he was pastor for one year in Canal Winchester, and for two years in Martins Ferry, both in Ohio. In 1880 he joined the faculty of Capital University as professor of Greek and in 1894 he taught, in addition, New Testament exegesis in the theological seminary of the same institution. His strength as a theologian lay in Biblical text criticism, a field in which he was unusually well informed, though not creative. He abided by the conservative findings of others and, as much as possible, by traditional interpretation without closing the door entirely upon the historical treatment of the text. He regarded the positions of Wellhausen as wholly indefensible; he admired the brilliancy of Harnack, but sought shelter under the rafters of Theodor Zahn. In evaluating creeds, doctrines, and denominations his criterion was orthodox. To him Chemnitz, Hollaz, and Johann Gerhard were "giants of theological thought and research" (Schodde, *The Protestant Church in Germany*, p. 20). He placed the Union Church of Germany, a church that is at least nine-tenths Lutheran, outside the pale of Lutheranism, and assigned the same fate to the Hohenzollerns. He could tolerate a state church, but his ideal was a free church of the Missouri Synod type.

Schodde's attitude was due to a confusion of archaic with historic Lutheranism and to the failure to utilize the research of the Luther-renaissance, well under way in Sweden and Germany at his death. It also caused him to judge the non-Lutheran branches of Protestantism unfairly. They constituted for him, following German theological classification, the Reformed. He called the Lutheran Church a "Bible Church," a distinction which he withheld from the "Reformed," claiming that in the latter it is held that the Spirit in His operations is not bound by certain mediums or instruments, but may and does operate in any way whatsoever (*Ibid.*, p. 14). Schodde was, no doubt, Christocentric in his religion, but his theology was Bibliocentric, historically a loan from some of the

Reformed rather than a heritage from Luther. He was a stranger to the real problems of the new century's theology which were precipitated upon the orthodox by German and Swedish scholars. He admired German theological scholarship, which he found to be "to a great extent evangelical and positive" but not distinctively Lutheran (*Ibid.*, p. 56 ff.).

His booklet, *The Protestant Church in Germany* (1901), is written in a kindly spirit; one other theological book, *Outlines of Biblical Hermeneutics*, was published shortly after his death. He wrote numerous articles and book reviews for church papers and theological magazines, and translated from Ethiopic, *The Book of Enoch* (1882), *The Book of Jubilees* (1888); from German, F. J. Delitzsch, *A Day in Capernaum* (1887), Bernhard Weiss, *The Religion of the New Testament* (1905), and, together with Epiphanius Wilson, *A Commentary on the New Testament* (4 vols., 1906). He was news-editor of the *Lutheran Standard* since 1889; and editor of the *Theological Magazine* since 1897. He also contributed articles to the *Independent, Sunday School Times*, the *Nation, Bible Student and Teacher* and the *Biblical Review*. He was married, on Dec. 22, 1881, to Mary Dorsch, who with one daughter, survived him. At the time of his death no other name on the clerical roll of the Joint Synod of Ohio was better known among the clergy of other Protestant denominations in the United States than that of Schodde.

[*Who's Who in America*, 1916–17; *The New Schaff-Herzog Encyc. of Religious Knowledge*, vol. X (1911); obituary article by Edward Pfeiffer, and an "Appreciation" by the editor, *Luth. Standard*, Sept. 29, 1917; *Ohio State Jour.*, Sept. 17, 1917.]　　J. O. E.

SCHOENHOF, JACOB (1839–Mar. 14, 1903), economist, was born in Oppenheim, Germany, where his father was a school teacher. In 1861 Jacob emigrated to the United States and engaged in the wholesale lace business until 1884, when he retired. In 1867 he married Henrietta Werner.

Schoenhof's business career commenced with the development of large-scale factory industry in the United States, and with his German background he was able to describe the industry of the country as it stood in contrast, in all of its important implications, to the production methods employed in Europe. He was as much struck as had been John Rae, Mathew and Henry C. Carey, Daniel Raymond, and Friedrich List with the desirability of economic capacity as compared with the older objective of wealth in the form of mere physical output. A prosperous country, in his estimation, was one

which has as its principal productive equipment a high standard of living for the working classes, with resulting mental alertness, ingenuity in mechanical invention and business organization, and a high degree of adaptability to changing economic circumstances. His predecessors in this economic school, writing during an earlier stage of American industrial development, had been advocates of a protective tariff, but Schoenhof, seeing the country on the threshold of industrial maturity, was convinced that free trade was essential to her continued advance. The others had written when protection was reluctantly granted, he wrote when protection, ensconced by the Civil War, had begun to work a harmful limitation upon American foreign markets.

President Cleveland's first administration afforded special opportunity for the development and application of Schoenhof's characteristic ideas. Cleveland, at first uninformed on the tariff issue, advocated reduction of duties as the means of breaking up government favoritism and dispelling the surplus which high customs were piling up in the treasury. On Nov. 23, 1885, Schoenhof was appointed United States consul at Tunstall, England, and later, as the confidential agent of Thomas F. Bayard [*q.v.*], Cleveland's secretary of state, he studied industrial conditions in Great Britain, France, and Germany. Bayard was an orthodox Democrat, a believer in economic as well as in political individualism, and a persuasive, if implacable, foe of protection. Schoenhof interpreted his mission broadly, and studied the entire economy of Europe as it bore upon production methods. In most of his works, but particularly in *The Industrial Situation and the Question of Wages* (1885) and in *The Economy of High Wages* (1892) he sought to refute the argument, universally advanced by the protectionists, that killing competition would be offered to American industry by the low-paid labor of Europe were the tariff reduced. He showed, with lavish citation of instances, that high money wages were generally the accompaniment of low unit cost of production, thus forecasting the doctrine later associated with the name of Henry Ford. His wide first-hand observation as traveler and student was supplemented by his own experience as a manufacturer and merchant. The business depressions of 1884 and 1893, coupled with America's industrial proficiency, awoke in him many of the fears which have since been realized by "technological unemployment," and he urged the removal of impediments to trade as the condition of continually mounting output and the only means of insuring economic stability within the country.

While others of the active free trade school of writers dealt principally in theoretical contention, Schoenhof brought to his argument a vast amount of practical documentation, and with boldness and skill made the most of the apparent paradox in his reasoning to the effect that high indirect costs were low direct costs. His *History of Money and Prices* (1896), which owed something to the lesson of the return to specie payments in 1879, was a refutation of the quantity theory of prices that had influenced his earlier work; he concluded that "prices of commodities move in obedience to natural and inherent causes, independent of circulating money quantities," and result from the interplay of a wide variety of economic forces. Besides the works cited above, he wrote *The Destructive Influence of the Tariff Upon Manufacture and Commerce* (1883); *Wages and Trade in Manufacturing Industries in America and in Europe* (1884); *Technical Education in Europe, First Part: Industrial Education in France* (1888); *Influences Bearing on Production* (1888). In 1893 he was appointed assistant appraiser at the port of New York and served as such throughout Cleveland's second administration. He died in New York City.

[*Publishers' Weekly*, Mar. 21, 1903; *N. Y. Times* and *N. Y. Tribune*, Mar. 15, 1903.]   B. M.

SCHOFF, STEPHEN ALONZO (Jan. 16, 1818–May 6, 1904), engraver, was the great-grandson of Jacob Schoff, a German, who settled in New England in 1752. Born in Danville, Vt., third of the eight children of John Chase and Eunice (Nye) Schoff, Stephen removed with his parents, when he was about eight years old, to Bradford on the Merrimack, and subsequently to Newburyport, Mass., the latter place being chosen because of its superior schools. At sixteen he was indentured for five years to Oliver Pelton, a Boston engraver, but after three years, dissatisfied with his progress, he went to Joseph Andrews [*q.v.*] to study. To him, said Schoff, "I owe more than can ever be repaid" (Stauffer, *post*, p. 240). He and Andrews, going to Paris in 1839 or 1840, worked for a while in the studio of Paul Delaroche. On returning to the United States in 1842, Schoff found employment in banknote work, and at the same time, with the aid of A. B. Durand [*q.v.*], who did some work on the plate, he executed his "Caius Marius on the Ruins of Carthage," after the painting by Vanderlyn, for publication by the Apollo Association. This plate, which he seems to have considered his best, was engraved in the regular linear manner of the line-engraver on copper or steel, a manner progressively developed and hardened since the days of Dürer and Goltzius. An interesting and illuminating contrast is offered by Schoff's much later engraving after the "Bathers" of William Morris Hunt [*q.v.*], in which the line is freely and spiritedly varied, broken and twisted to translate the tones, color-values, even brush-marks, of the painting. In this departure from conventions one may find an aim akin to that of the "new school" of American wood engraving of the last quarter of the nineteenth century. Next to this interpretation of Hunt, almost a *tour de force,* there may be set the same engraver's "Bay of New York," after G. L. Brown, of a delicacy that reminds one of the plates by British engravers after Turner for Samuel Rogers' *Italy.*

Throughout much of his long professional life Schoff was kept busy with banknote work, a specialty which gave occupation to many engravers and which had much influence on steel engraving in the United States. Like many engravers of his time, he, too, had to turn his hands to minor jobs in the day's work, jobs which did not bring out the best in a man, weak and conventional conceptions which resulted in inconsequential engraving. But plates such as those of his mentioned above are outstanding, as are his engravings of portraits such as those of William Penn and R. W. Emerson (after S. W. Rowse). He also engraved some of F. O. C. Darley's illustrations, and during the etching vogue of the eighties he reproduced paintings in etching, to which process he brought rich experience.

Schoff was married on Nov. 7, 1843, in Williamsburg, L. I., to Maria Josephine Rosalina Hastings (1824–82), by whom he had five children. He lived at different times in Boston, Washington, New York, Newtonville, Mass., and Brandon, Vt., and died in Norfolk, Conn.

[D. M. Stauffer, *Am. Engravers upon Copper and Steel* (1907), I, 240–41; W. H. Schoff, *The Descendants of Jacob Schoff* (1910); Frank Weitenkampf, *Am. Graphic Art* (2nd ed., 1924); S. R. Koehler's chapter on American etching in *Die Vervielfältigende Kunst der Gegenwart* (Vienna, 1892), pp. 218–19; *Who's Who in America*, 1903–05; *Hartford Courant*, May 7, 1904.]   F. W.

SCHOFIELD, HENRY (Aug. 7, 1866–Aug. 15, 1918), law teacher and legal writer, was born in Dudley, Mass., the son of John and Margaret (Thompson) Schofield. He was educated at Nichols Academy in Dudley and at Harvard College and Law School (A.B. 1887, A.M. and LL.B. 1890). Admitted to the Illinois bar in 1890, he practised for a year in Chicago and then spent a year in Washington as assistant to

Charles H. Aldrich, solicitor general of the United States. Returning to Chicago in 1892, he became associated in practice with Henry M. Bacon. From 1900 to 1902 he was assistant corporation counsel of Chicago. At this time the relations of the city to the local traction systems were giving rise to important questions relating to corporate franchises and the city's powers under its charter. "Constitutional provisions and successive statutory measures raised complex issues calling for great accuracy of research and large understanding of fundamental principles. His [Schofield's] absolute mastery of the whole intricate subject was soon acknowledged" (J. H. Wigmore, Foreword to Schofield's *Essays, post,* p. vi).

On Oct. 23, 1902, he married Marie Therese Stehlin of Chicago, by whom he had four children. Shortly before his marriage he had given up active practice and become professor of law in Northwestern University, lecturing on equity and constitutional law. Regarding his ability to make legal problems interesting, a former student, Prof. Albert Kocourek, writes: "He seemed to make small use of notes or memoranda, but spoke informally, and with the most remarkable ease, clearness, and attraction. He did not make the mistake of taking too much for granted either in the direct or collateral information of his auditors. . . . He never sought in the classroom or elsewhere to make an impression. His object was to make himself understood, and in this he undoubtedly succeeded" (Schofield's *Essays,* p. xii).

By contrast his written style was involved and overcrowded with ideas, but enthusiastically logical. In his investigations of legal problems he sought to reach the right views primarily for his own satisfaction and for his classes, and not at all for publication. Once he had come to what seemed to him a final conclusion about a problem, he lost all interest in its written exposition. If prior to that point his fellow teachers had not succeeded in getting him to put his views in writing, it would then be too late for them to do so. He never wrote a book, but produced a large number of articles and comments on important decisions in legal periodicals. These were collected after his death as *Essays on Constitutional Law and Equity and Other Subjects* (2 vols., 1921).

Because of their difficult style and the absence of systematic treatment, these essays have not had a wide influence, but are valued by legal scholars. Schofield's analysis of significant cases is acute, and his original thinking often demonstrates the fallacy of traditional views. His at-

tention was much directed to constitutional problems which have not been thoroughly discussed by other writers, such as the relations between federal and state courts, and the full faith and credit clause. His essay on "Freedom of the Press in the United States" (*Papers and Proceedings . . . American Sociological Society,* 1914) is a pioneer article of great value and the only satisfactory discussion of the constitutional right of free speech as it existed before the World War.

Many of Schofield's habits conformed to the laymen's notion of a typical professor. He was frequently absent-minded and would become so absorbed in reading that he had to be summoned to a waiting class of students. When interested in an important legal decision he would delve for months into everything bearing upon it in the remotest way, and meanwhile "it would be difficult to get him to talk of anything else because he felt that other things could wait until the matter then on his mind should be settled to his own satisfaction" (Costigan, in *American Law School Review, post,* p. 407). Despite this concentration he had a very real awareness of life and was well informed about many practical affairs. The charm and learning of his conversation were vividly remembered. He invariably selected the topic, often a difficult legal question, and carried on the dialogue on his own terms, delivering with occasional interjections from the listener a luminous essay. Always quiet and unobtrusive, he made no mention of the prolonged illness which cut short his career, but carried on his teaching and writing to the last possible day.

[Albert Kocourek, "Death of Professor Schofield," in *Ill. Law Rev.,* Oct.–Nov 1918, reprinted in large part in Schofield's *Essays;* G. P. Costigan, Jr., "Henry Schofield," in *Northwestern Alumni Jour.,* Nov. 30, 1918, reprinted in *Am. Law School Rev.,* Feb. 1919; *Class of 1887, Harvard Coll., Twenty-fifth Anniversary, 1887–1912* (n.d.); *Harvard Alumni Bull.,* Nov. 28, 1918; *Who's Who in America,* 1916–17; *Chicago Daily Tribune,* Aug. 17, 1918.]   Z. C., Jr.

SCHOFIELD, JOHN McALLISTER (Sept. 29, 1831–Mar. 4, 1906), soldier, was born in Gerry, Chautauqua County, N. Y., the son of James and Caroline (McAllister) Schofield. His father, a Baptist clergyman, was then pastor of a church at Sinclairville, N. Y., but in 1843 he moved to Freeport, Ill., and became a home missionary in Illinois, Iowa, and Missouri. Educated in the local public schools, John spent one summer as a surveyor on public lands in northern Wisconsin and one winter as teacher in a district school. In 1849 he was offered an appointment as cadet at West Point. He graduated in 1853 as No. 7 in his class and, having abandoned his original intention of studying law, accepted his commission as brevet second lieutenant, 2nd Artillery, with station at Fort Moultrie, S. C. Receiving in December his commission as second lieutenant in the 1st Artillery, he joined his battery in Florida, where it was serving in connection with Seminole Indian troubles. Promoted first lieutenant in 1855, he was ordered to West Point as assistant professor of natural and experimental philosophy. In June 1857 he was married to Harriet, daughter of Prof. W. H. C. Bartlett, his chief in the department of philosophy; she died in Washington about 1889, leaving two sons and a daughter. In 1860, without resigning his commission, he left West Point on a year's leave of absence and became professor of physics at Washington University, St. Louis, Mo.

Relinquishing his leave at the opening of the Civil War, he was detailed as mustering officer for the state of Missouri; a few days later he was commissioned major in the 1st Missouri Volunteer Infantry and assisted in organizing that regiment. In June he became chief of staff to Gen. Nathaniel Lyon [q.v.] in his operations in Missouri and served until Lyon's death at the battle of Wilson's Creek, Aug. 10, 1861, when he assumed command of his volunteer regiment and reorganized it as artillery. He was offered a captaincy in the new 11th Infantry of the regular army but declined it and soon afterward was promoted to that grade in his own regiment. In November 1861 he became brigadier-general of volunteers and until the autumn of 1862 held various territorial commands. From October 1862 to April 1863 he commanded the "Army of the Frontier" engaged in field operations in Missouri. He was nominated as major-general of volunteers in November 1863 but, because of the tense political situation in Missouri and the opposition of certain factions, his nomination was not confirmed, and in March he reverted to his rank as brigadier-general. Since this brought him under the command of former juniors, he avoided embarrassments by applying for a new assignment and for a short time commanded a division of the XIV Army Corps in Tennessee. In May, having been appointed major-general, he returned to St. Louis as commander of the Department of the Missouri.

In February 1864 he assumed command of the XXIII Corps and of the Department and Army of the Ohio, with which he took part in Sherman's Atlanta campaign as one of the three army commanders. When Sherman started on his march to the sea, Gen. George Henry Thomas [q.v.] was given command of all troops left in the west and began his concentration at Nash-

ville, Tenn. Schofield, with his own XXIII Corps and part of the IV Corps, covered this concentration against Hood's renewed attempt to invade Tennessee. Gradually retiring upon Nashville, Schofield's force fought the fierce battle of Franklin, which badly shattered Hood's army, and then rejoined Thomas to take part in the battle of Nashville, which definitely put an end to all danger from Hood. For his services in this campaign he was made brigadier-general in the regular army in November 1864 and brevet major-general in March 1865. The XXIII Corps was then moved by rail to Washington and by sea to the mouth of the Cape Fear River, where Schofield assumed command of the newly formed Department of North Carolina, his troops consisting of his own corps and the two divisions of Gen. Albert Howe Terry [q.v.] from Fort Fisher. With this force he first occupied Wilmington, N. C., and then effected a junction with Sherman at Goldsboro, N. C., Mar. 23, his command becoming the center grand division of Sherman's army in the operations against Johnston. He accompanied Sherman at the final meeting with Johnston on Apr. 26, when the terms of surrender were agreed upon, and was designated as commissioner for execution of the details. He remained in command of the Department until the formation of a provisional state government in June.

At the close of the war he was offered command of a force, to be organized under the Mexican republican flag, replacing the fifty thousand men who had been concentrated on the Mexican border with a view to their possible use in connection with the Maximilian affair. Before anything had been done, however, the secretary of state proposed that he go to France, ostensibly on leave but actually as a confidential agent of the State Department to deal with Mexican affairs. He went to France, 1865–66, remaining until it had been decided that the French forces should be recalled from Mexico. Upon his return he was assigned to duty in Virginia, where his command was known as the Department of the Potomac, and later as the First Military District. In the spring of 1868, during the confusion incident to the impeachment of President Johnson, he was made secretary of war, but resigned upon Grant's inauguration. His duties, which had to do both with problems of reconstruction and of army reorganization, were most heavy and perplexing. While he was secretary he took steps toward the organization of a light artillery school at Fort Riley, Kan., later the Mounted Service School and finally the United States Cavalry School. Leaving the War Department, he was promoted major-general and assumed command first of the Department of the Missouri and later of the Division of the Pacific. In 1872 he spent three months in Hawaii, accompanied by a navy officer and by an army engineer, to report upon the military value of the islands to the United States and made recommendations that led to the acquisition of Pearl Harbor as a naval base. From 1876 to 1881 he was superintendent of the United States Military Academy. While he was there he served as president of the board to review the case of Gen. Fitz-John Porter [q.v.], dismissed from the service by sentence of a court martial for misconduct at the battle of Manassas. After a year's leave spent in Europe, he commanded successively the Divisions of the Pacific, of the Missouri, and of the Atlantic. In 1888, upon the death of Sheridan, he became commanding general of the army; promoted to the grade of lieutenant-general in February 1895, he was retired because of age in September. In 1891 he was married for a second time to Georgia Kilbourne of Keokuk, Iowa. His autobiography, *Forty-Six Years in the Army*, was published in 1897. He died in St. Augustine, Fla.

[See G. W. Cullum, *Biog. Reg. Officers and Grads. U. S. Mil. Acad.* (3 ed., 1891), vol. II; *War of the Rebellion: Official Records (Army)*; *Battles and Leaders of the Civil War* (4 vols., 1887–88); J. D. Cox, *The March to the Sea* (1906) and *Atlanta* (1909); obituary in *N. Y. Tribune*, Mar. 5, 1906. For the period after the war, the best source of information is Schofield's autobiography, *Forty-Six Years in the Army* (1897). information has also been supplied by Col. R. M. Schofield of Honolulu, his son.]   O. L. S., Jr.

SCHOFIELD, WILLIAM HENRY (Apr. 6, 1870–June 24, 1920), scholar and author, was born at Brockville, Ontario, son of the Rev. William Henry Schofield and Anna (Parker) Schofield. His father died when the boy was young, and it was left to his mother to guide his early development and form his character and mental habits. She was fortunately admirably fitted for this task. A gifted and precocious student, Schofield received his first academic degree (A.B.) in 1889 from Victoria College, then located at Cobourg. After three years of teaching as master of modern languages at the Collegiate Institute, Hamilton, Ont., he entered the graduate school of Harvard University and received the degree of Ph.D. in 1895.

For the following two years he was in Europe as traveling fellow, studying medieval literature with Gaston Paris at the Collège de France and Old Norse with Sophus Bugge at Christiania. These two great scholars made a deep impression on him, and all the rest of his life he gratefully referred to them as his masters.

In Norway he was something of a phenomenon. He soon acquired a fluent command of the spoken language; young, with an attractive and ingratiating personality, abounding in energy and enthusiasm, he was universally popular in the society of the Norwegian capital, and might have become a social lion, had not conscientious application to his studies held him to his books. His visit to Norway fell in the flowering time of Norwegian literature, the age of Ibsen and Björnson, Lie and Kielland. In later years he was accustomed to enliven his lectures at Harvard with anecdotes of his personal associations with the great men themselves. He made it his mission to correct misconceptions of American civilization current in Scandinavia, particularly after the appearance of Knut Hamsun's witty, temperamental, and one-sided book, *Fra det moderne Amerikas Aandsliv* (1889). A fruit of these efforts was an article on "Amerikas Universiteter" published in the Danish periodical *Tilskueren* (September 1897), which attracted much favorable comment. Interesting testimony of the impression which he made on cultivated Scandinavians is to be found in Georg Brandes's "Dansk og Norsk" (*Samlede Skrifter,* 1905, vol. XV).

In 1897 Schofield returned to America to resume his academic career as instructor in English at Harvard. From 1902 till 1906 he served as assistant professor in the same department, being appointed in the latter year professor of comparative literature, a post he held until his death. In connection with his new department he founded the series of *Harvard Studies in Comparative Literature,* of which he was himself editor. He continued to develop his interest in Scandinavian culture, giving the course in Old Norse instituted some years before by Prof. G. L. Kittredge and adding courses in the Dano-Norwegian language and Dano-Norwegian dramatists considered in their relations to European literature. As president of the American-Scandinavian Foundation for three and one-half years he labored energetically and successfully to promote intellectual cooperation between the United States and the Northern European countries.

Besides numerous articles contributed to American, Danish, French, and German periodicals, he published a series of books in widely various fields of scholarship: *Studies in the Libeaus Desconus* (1895); *The Home of the Eddic Poems* (1899), from the Norwegian of Sophus Bugge; *English Literature, from the Norman Conquest to Chaucer* (1906); *Chivalry in English Literature* (1912); *Mythical Bards and The*

Life of William Wallace (1920), issued in the year of his death. His scholarly contributions are distinguished by originality and independence of thought, careful organization, and an individual charm of style. He set the example corresponding to his precepts, demanding from his students attention to form no less than to substance.

On Sept. 4, 1907, he married Mrs. Mary Lyon Cheney of Boston, who accompanied him on a journey to Iceland and its saga-steads. In 1907–08 he was exchange professor at Berlin; in 1911, lecturer at the Sorbonne and the University of Copenhagen; in 1918, exchange professor at five Western colleges, posts which he filled with great distinction. During the World War he was active as a speaker for the National Security League and chairman of the Committee on International Relations in Education, with headquarters at Washington. He died at Peterboro, N. H., where a beautiful stone church, the gift of his wife, is inseparably associated with his memory.

[*Harvard Univ. Gazette*, May 7, 1921; *Who's Who in America*, 1920–21; D. R. Keys, in *Canadian Mag.*, Aug. 1906; *N. Y. Times*, June 25, 1920; personal acquaintance.]   F. S. C.

SCHOLTE, HENDRIK PETER (Sept. 25, 1805–Aug. 25, 1868), clergyman, pioneer, colonist, was born at Amsterdam, in the Netherlands, the son of Jan Hendrik Scholte, a box manufacturer, and Johanna Dorothea Roelofsz, daughter of an Amsterdam broker. He had excellent schooling, but at sixteen was compelled by his father's death to leave school and take charge of the factory. Left the sole survivor of the family by the death of his mother and brother, he sold the business and resumed his studies in Oct. 1827, at the Amsterdam Athenæum Illustre. Impressed by the atheistic tendencies of the time, especially among students, he decided to prepare for the Christian ministry, and entered the University of Leyden in May 1829. The next year his studies were interrupted by the bloodless "ten days' campaign" against Belgium's claim to independence from the Netherlands, for which service each of the student volunteers received a huge gold medal from a rich and patriotic Dutch lady. In May 1832 he received the degree of doctor of theology; in November he married Sara Maria Brand, daughter of a sugar refiner who had bought packing cases of his father.

Scholte soon became the leading spirit in a group of young clergymen who protested against the secularism of the State Church, seceded from it in 1834 in the name of a purer

Christianity, were persecuted, fined, and imprisoned, and saw their congregations dispersed by police and troops. He edited a periodical, *De Reformatie*, devoted to the dissenting movement, and in this and a series of pamphlets urged emigration as an escape from intolerable ecclesiastical conditions in Holland. An emigration association was formed at Utrecht in 1846, with Scholte as president. In October a preliminary group of thirty sailed to the United States and reported favorably from St. Louis. The main body of emigrants, counting some eight hundred souls, left Holland in April 1847 in four sailing vessels. Scholte's wife having died in 1842, he had later married M. H. E. Krantz. Three daughters of the first marriage and two sons of the second grew to maturity. Scholte and his family traveled by steamer to Boston, whence he proceeded to Albany and Washington to secure information about lands open to settlement. In June 1847 the reunited colonists traveled by rail, canal, and wagon from Baltimore to St. Louis. Scholte and four others then proceeded by boat to Keokuk and by wagon on into Iowa to spy out the land, choosing a location in the newly formed Marion County, near the Des Moines River.

On the day of his arrival at the chosen site (which he named Pella after the place of refuge of the early Christians in Palestine, persecuted by Rome), Scholte immediately contracted with the few settlers in this frontier region for the purchase of all their claims, and entered new lands with the government to a total of 18,000 acres. Upon the arrival of the colonists he promptly had them all declare their intention to become citizens of the United States. Similarly, he insisted on the teaching of English in the school established and encouraged the adoption of American methods and standards. He had the town of Pella platted in September 1847 and was largely instrumental in the location there in 1853 of Central University (later Central College); he gave the grounds, contributed to the funds, and was president of the board of trustees.

The Dominie was personally active in every aspect of the development of the new community. He was gentleman farmer, owner of saw mills and brick and lime kilns, land agent, notary, printer, editor and publisher, broker, banker, express agent, dealer in farm implements, attorney, as well as clergyman; and through all these activities in a rapidly developing community he contrived not to amass a fortune. He built a church at his own expense and preached in it without salary. He took an active interest in politics; he was delegate at large from Iowa to the Chicago convention that nominated Abraham Lincoln, and was recognized as the outstanding representative of the new foreign vote which the supporters of Lincoln had the foresight to cultivate. He died at Pella, Iowa, shortly before his sixty-third birthday.

Scholte's publications after coming to America include *Eene Stem Uit Pella* (Amsterdam, 1848) and *Tweede Stem uit Pella* ('s Bosch, 1848). For some time he was editor of the *Pella Gazette.*

[Anthony Brummelkamp and A. C. van Raalte, *Landverhuizing, of waarom bevorderen wij de Volksverhuizing en wel naar Noord-Amerika en niet naar Java* (1846); John Nollen, *De Afscheiding: Een Gedenkschrift* (1897); Kommer van Stigt, *Geschiedenis van Pella, Iowa, en Omgeving* (Pella, 1897); Cyrenus Cole, "A Bit of Holland in America," *Midland Monthly*, Feb. 1895, and "Pella—A Bit of Holland in America," *Annals of Iowa*, Jan. 1898; Jacob Van der Zee, *The Hollanders of Iowa* (1912); *The Hist. of Marion County, Iowa* (1881), p. 670; W. M. Donnel, *Pioneers of Marion County* (1872).]   J. S. N.

SCHOMER, NAHUM MEIR (Dec. 18, 1849–Nov. 24, 1905), Yiddish novelist and playwright, was born in Nesvizh (Government of Minsk), Russia, a son of Isaac and Hodie Goldberg Shaikewitz. The name Schomer, his *nom de plume,* he afterwards adopted also as a family name, under which his surviving children in the United States are known. He was educated at home and at the famous Talmudic seminary of Volozhin. His orthodox parents intended him for the rabbinate, but his own inclinations led him into other fields. As a youngster he was known as a clever story-teller, with a fertile and inexhaustible imagination which he was to draw on later in his chosen vocation. Marrying at the age of twenty Dinah Bercinsky in Pinsk, he attempted to establish himself there as a merchant. Here he made his literary début in Hebrew journals with stories, historical sketches, and popular scientific articles, but soon relinquished Hebrew in favor of the common vernacular of the Jewish masses, the Yiddish. Shortly after his marriage he became manager of his uncle's business in Wilna, which necessitated some traveling. When he visited Roumania and in Bucharest came in contact with the Yiddish theatre, he resolved to become a dramatic author. Moving to Odessa, he became a theatrical manager and playwright, writing *Lebensbilder,* dramas of current life, the first in this genre to be produced in the Yiddish language. After the Yiddish theatre was closed in Russia by government decree he emigrated in 1889 to New York.

Schomer was an extremely prolific writer. In addition to fifteen novels in Hebrew he was the author of over two hundred in Yiddish, some of which are of bulky proportions; many others appeared in the Yiddish dailies. Over thirty of his plays were produced in Russia and later in the United States. He also experimented in New York as editor and publisher of several magazines. His place in Yiddish literature is that of a pioneer who sensed the need of the masses for a new kind of reading matter to replace the older folk-tales and morality chapbooks. At the time when he began to write, the Jews of the great ghettos in Russia, Lithuania, and Poland were shut up in their communities. Educated Jews, if interested in Jewish culture at all, confined themselves exclusively to Hebrew, while the uneducated masses, if able to read, were restricted solely to Yiddish, in those days considered a mere colloquial jargon. It was to the latter that Schomer addressed himself when he began writing. His novels were partly historical, partly reflections of the Jewish life of his immediate surroundings and of small towns and villages, and to a large extent imitations of the French and German "Schundroman." As his language was simple, near to that spoken by the common people, his novels became so popular that in the span of little more than a decade his readers numbered hundreds of thousands and his name was a household word. With the development of the Yiddish literature and the springing up of more gifted talents, Schomer was the subject of violent attacks by his contemporaries, who accused him of serious literary deficiencies and of a deleterious effect upon the popular taste. But in spite of this harsh criticism he is to be credited with valuable services to Jewish life and literature. He helped to develop the habit of reading among the Yiddish-speaking masses, to mitigate the fanaticism that prevailed in small rural and urban communities, and to introduce to them entirely new conceptions of life.

[Zalmen Reisen, *Lexicon fun der Yiddisher Literatur,* vol. IV (Wilna, 1929), containing a long but admittedly incomplete list of Schomer's works; M. Pines, *Die Geschichte der jüdischdeutschen Literatur* (Leipzig, 1913); Leo Wiener, *The Hist. of Yiddish Lit. in the Nineteenth Century* (1899); Hutchins Hapgood, *The Spirit of the Ghetto* (1902); Leon Kobrin, *Erinerungen fun a Yiddishen Dramaturg* (1925), vol. I; *Am. Hebrew,* Dec. 1, 1905; *N. Y. Times,* Nov. 25, 1905.]   I. S.

SCHOOLCRAFT, HENRY ROWE (Mar. 28, 1793–Dec. 10, 1864), explorer, ethnologist, was born in Albany County, N. Y., the son of Lawrence and Margaret Anne Barbara (Rowe) Schoolcraft and the great-grandson of James Calcraft, as the name was then spelled, who emigrated from England to Albany County, N. Y., in 1727. Henry enjoyed the opportunities of the common school in Hamilton, N. Y., and was able to matriculate in Union College at fifteen. Later he attended Middlebury College. He favored language and natural science, especially geology and mineralogy. His father was a glass maker, and the boy studied this industry and in 1817 started at Utica, N. Y., a book on glass making. He began his explorations with a visit to the mineral regions of southern Missouri and Arkansas in 1817-18, then Indian country. His report, *A View of the Lead Mines of Missouri,* was published in New York in 1819. By this time he was considered a competent geologist, and he was sent on the Cass exploring expedition in 1820 to the upper Mississippi and the Lake Superior copper region. His *Narrative Journal of Travels through the Northwestern Regions of the United States . . . to the Sources of the Mississippi River* appeared in 1821. Later, in 1832, he made another expedition to the sources of the Mississippi, which he described in *Narrative of an Expedition through the Upper Mississippi to Itasca Lake, the Actual Source of the Mississippi* (1834), reissued as *Summary Narrative* in 1855 with an account of the earlier expedition of 1820 and an appendix of official reports and scientific papers. His wide acquaintance with the Indians led to his appointment in 1822 as Indian agent for the tribes of Lake Superior. Thereafter his predilections were for those Algonquian tribes inhabiting the vast forests around the great lake. In 1823 he married a quarter-blood Chippewa girl, who, though educated in Europe, understood and shared much of the primitive Indian culture. She died in 1842.

The importance of the Indian subject was firmly fixed in his mind, and for the remainder of his life he pursued his chosen work in season and out of season. Encouraged by the government, whose need was data on the Indian problem, he was given official promotion as superintendent of Indian affairs for Michigan in 1836 and served in the department until 1841. During this period he negotiated several treaties with the Chippewa, probably most important of which was the treaty of Mar. 28, 1836, whereby the United States obtained title to the northern third of the lower peninsula and the eastern half of the upper peninsula of Michigan. Always active in forwarding the study of Indians, he helped to found the Historical Society of Michigan in 1828 and the Algic Society of Detroit in 1832. In many ways he promoted the study of the ethnology of the Indian, both at home and abroad. His

literary remains are of impressive bulk. They consist of descriptions of his explorations, writings on the manners and customs of the Indians, and tales and legends. Of these perhaps the most important are *Algic Researches* (2 vols., 1839) concerning Indian mental characteristics, *Oneota,* originally issued in eight paper covers (1844-45) describing the Indian history and prospects, *Notes on the Iroquois* (1847), a popular account, and *Personal Memories of . . . Thirty Years with the Indian Tribes* (1851). Most of these works were literary rather than scientific, as is characteristic of the unspecialized anthropological science of the period. Realizing that the scientific material he had collected should be set in order, he projected an Indian encyclopaedia; but this was set aside for the great work on which his reputation as an ethnologist must rest. Subvented by the government, he began in 1851 *Historical and Statistical Information Respecting the History, Condition, and Prospects of the Indian Tribes of the United States* (6 pts., 1851-57). This work, six folio volumes, excellently illustrated with steel engravings from paintings by Seth Eastman, was a collaboration dominated by Schoolcraft. In spite of shortcomings, it contains valuable and indispensable material on the Indians and is a monument to a great American explorer and ethnologist.

Schoolcraft was fluent, interesting, convincing, and made a good public appearance. He traveled much and received many honors. He published nothing after 1857, and it is said that rheumatism and paralysis put an end to his work. He was survived by his wife, Mary (Howard) Schoolcraft of Beaufort District, N. C., to whom he was married in 1847.

["Sketches of the Life of Henry R. Schoolcraft," in *Personal Memories, ante;* G. W. Samson, *Henry R. Schoolcraft* (1864?); J. V. Brower, "The Mississippi River and its Sources," *Minn. Hist. Soc. Colls.,* vol. VII (1893); J. H. Baker, "The Sources of the Mississippi," *Ibid.,* vol. VI (1894); information from the files of the Office of Indian Affairs through the courtesy of Brent Morgan.]   W. H.

SCHÖPF, JOHANN DAVID (Mar. 8, 1752–Sept. 10, 1800), physician, scientist, traveler, was born in Germany at Wunsiedel in the principality of Bayreuth. The son of a well-to-do merchant, he began his education under private tutors, attended the Gymnasium at Hof 1767–70, and studied medicine and the natural sciences at the University of Erlangen 1770–73. Living in the Fichtelgebirge, he had studied mineralogy and metallurgy from his early years, and under Prof. J. C. D. von Schreber he became a serious student of zoölogy and botany. After hearing lectures on forestry at Berlin, he made a trip through Bohemia and Austria to the cities of northern Italy, took his medical degree at Erlangen in 1776, and began practice at Ansbach. The next year, giving up his plans for a voyage to India, he accepted a surgeon's commission in an Ansbach regiment destined for service with the British army in North America and arrived at New York June 4, 1777. His hope of seeing with his own eyes the flora, fauna, and geology of the New World was deferred, however, for six years, while his regiment did duty at New York and on the eastern tip of Long Island, in Rhode Island, and at Philadelphia. Schöpf, meanwhile, learned English well and read everything obtainable about America. At the close of the war he got permission to travel and on July 22, 1783, set out from New York. Accompanying him on the first half of his itinerary was an Englishman, Robert Hare, father of the chemist Robert Hare [q.v.].

They crossed New Jersey to Philadelphia and, after inspecting the Moravian towns of Bethlehem and Nazareth, journeyed through Reading, Lebanon, Carlisle, and Shippensburg to Fort Pitt. They returned through Maryland to Baltimore, Alexandria, Va., and Annapolis, reaching Philadelphia early in November. Schöpf then started south by the so-called "back road," which enabled him to pay a visit, rich for them both in friendship and mutual helpfulness, to G. H. E. Mühlenberg [q.v.] at Lancaster. At Leesburg, Va., the oncoming winter compelled him to change his route; he turned eastward to Fredericksburg and Richmond, continued on to Williamsburg and Yorktown, and then proceeded south through the Carolinas to Charleston, where he took sail for Florida. On Mar. 29, 1784, he embarked at St. Augustine for the Bahamas, and in October of that year he was once more with his friends in Bayreuth.

The fifteen years remaining to him, varied by travel in Italy and Holland, were peaceful, happy, and honorable. In 1795 he was created a Prussian Geheimer Hofrat and made president of the Ansbach Medicinal-collegium, which he continued to preside over when it was united in 1797 with that of Bayreuth. More than any other German of his time he made America his study. Among his articles and monographs are the first systematic work on American geology, *Beyträge zur Mineralogischen Kenntniss des Östlichen Theils von Nordamerika und seiner Gebürge* (Erlangen, 1787); the first paper on American ichthyology; the first on American frogs and turtles; one on the American climate and diseases; and a full American materia medica, *Materia Medica Americana, Potissimum Regni Vegetabilis* (Erlangen, 1787; reprinted in the Lloyd

Library Reproduction Series, Cincinnati, 1903). His last work was an admirable *Historia Testitudinum, Iconibus Illustrata* (Fasc. I–VI, Erlangen, 1792–1801). In all these works he shows himself an able descriptive scientist, but the whole man is seen only in his masterpiece, his *Reise durch einige der mittlern und südlichen vereinigten nordamerikanischen Staaten nach Ost-Florida und den Bahama-Inseln* (2 vols., Erlangen, 1788; American translation by A. J. Morrison, *Travels in the Confederation*, 2 vols., 1911). No aspect of man or nature escaped his eye and pencil. Among travelers in America it would be difficult to find his equal in combined breadth of interests, accuracy of observation and judgment, wit, and serene good temper. Among lesser figures he is one of the best exemplars of the culture of the Enlightenment. His early death resulted from a malady of the throat.

[J. G. Meusel, *Lexikon der vom Jahr 1750 bis 1800 verstorbenen Teutschen Schriftsteller*, vol. XII (Leipzig, 1812), pp. 364–71, with full bibliographical direction; Friedrich Ratzel, article in *Allgemeine Deutsche Biographie*, vol. XXXII (Leipzig, 1891); Hermann Peters, "Johann David Schöpf, Ein deutscher Naturforscher des vorigen Jahrhunderts in Nordamerika," *Pharmaceutische Rundschau* (Milwaukee), July 1895, the best biography; Fred. Hoffman, "Fragmentary Notes from the Reports of Two Early Naturalists on North America," *Pharmaceutical Rev.*, Aug. 1898; A. J. Morrison, "Doctor Johann David Schoepf," *Ger.-Am. Annals*, Sept.-Dec. 1910; J. G. Rosengarten, *The German Soldier in the Wars of the U. S.* (2nd ed., 1890).]
                     G. H. G.

SCHOTT, CHARLES ANTHONY (Aug. 7, 1826–July 31, 1901), geodesist, magnetician, originally called Carl Anton, was born in the south German city of Mannheim, Baden, the eldest of four children of Anton Carl and Anna Maria (Hoffman) Schott. The family belonged to the middle class, the father being a merchant, and was in comfortable circumstances. Schott attended the public schools and lyceum of his native city until he was fourteen and then was sent to the Technische Hochschule at Karlsruhe, where he graduated in 1847 as a civil engineer. He had looked forward to entering the engineering service of the state, but the disturbed political conditions of the time prevented this. In the revolution of 1848 he served for a short time in the liberal ranks but found military life uncongenial. At this time, too, his father met with reverses in business and, being thrown on his own resources, Schott set out for the United States, arriving at New York in August 1848. In December 1848 he became a computer in the Washington office of the United States Coast Survey; the following spring he was assigned to field duty as hydrographic draftsman aboard a survey vessel but a year later was ordered back to the computing division in Washington. In 1853 he became a citizen of the United States, and on Jan. 1, 1854, he married Teresa Gildermeister in Washington.

To a sound training and natural ability, Schott added the qualities of industry and thoroughness. He won early recognition in the coast survey; in 1855 he was made chief of the computing division, and for nearly forty-five years he directed the work of that important division, playing no small part during these formative years in setting and maintaining high scientific standards. Into the computing division came the field data of the survey, which were tabulated, adjusted, correlated, and interpreted. The work involved various technical and scientific aspects of astronomy, geodesy, magnetism, map projections, and tides; to each of these subjects Schott contributed a number of papers that dealt primarily with the correlation and interpretation of observations. His principal contributions were in the fields of geodesy and terrestrial magnetism, both of which were in a relatively early stage of development. In 1898 the French Academy of Sciences awarded him its Wilde Prize with the citation that "the whole of this work furnishes one of the most important contributions in the history of terrestrial magnetism." He also wrote a number of memoirs dealing with meteorology and climatology, especially that of the Arctic regions, which appeared principally in the *Smithsonian Contributions to Knowledge* between 1859 and 1876. In 1869 he was a member of the government party sent to Springfield, Ill., to observe a solar eclipse, and in 1870 he was sent to Catania, Sicily, to observe the solar eclipse of December of that year. His work and attainments received wide recognition and brought him membership in numerous scientific societies, both at home and abroad; in 1872 he was elected to the National Academy of Sciences.

At the beginning of 1900, he was relieved of the administrative duties of chief of the computing division. He now devoted himself to the discussion of the arc measurements in the United States that resulted from the extension triangulation executed up to that time. This necessitated the adjustment of all the triangulation into a single net, a work that involved an enormous amount of computation. In the spring of the following year he fell ill, and in July he died in Washington. His first wife had died in 1862, leaving an only son. On Sept. 28, 1863, at Prairie Home, Ill., he married Bertha Gildermeister, a sister of his deceased wife, by whom he had four children.

[*Science*, Jan. 12, 1900, Aug. 9, 1901; *Bull. Philosophical Soc. of Washington*, Aug. 1905; *Nat. Acad.*

Sci. Biog. Memoirs, vol. VIII (1919); *Evening Star* (Washington, D. C.), Aug. 1901.]   H. A. M.

SCHOULER, JAMES (Mar. 20, 1839–Apr. 16, 1920), lawyer and historian, was born in West Cambridge (now Arlington), Mass. He was the son of William Schouler [*q.v.*], a native of Kilbarchan, Scotland, who was brought to America in early life, and Frances Eliza Warren, who came of colonial Massachusetts stock. In Scotland the name is often spelled Scouler; this conforms to the pronunciation still used by the American family. From Cincinnati, where the family were living at the time, James went to Harvard in 1855. His father's journalistic ventures were never financially successful, and while the son was at Harvard William Schouler returned to Boston in greatly straitened circumstances. Notwithstanding the family misfortunes young Schouler took an active part in college life, became editor of the *Harvard Magazine*, and won prizes in public speaking. He received his bachelor's degree in 1859. After teaching for a year in St. Paul's School, Concord, N. H., he began the study of law in the office of George D. Guild in Boston. At this time, also, he served as private secretary to his father, who had just been appointed adjutant-general of Massachusetts. He was admitted to the bar in 1862, but soon responded to Lincoln's call for volunteers and was commissioned second lieutenant of the 43rd Regiment, Massachusetts Volunteers. He went with his regiment to the coast of North Carolina, where he was detailed on signal service and saw little fighting. A fever which he contracted on his way home from this expedition greatly aggravated a physical defect which had already developed to some extent and which was to influence profoundly the whole future course of his life, that of deafness.

On his return to Boston in 1863 he took up the practice of law. A few years later he won an important case in the Supreme Court of the United States involving war claims against the government (*Hosmer* vs. *The United States, 9 Wall*, 432); this was the beginning of a fairly lucrative practice, much of which was concerned with war claims. In 1869 he opened a branch office in Washington, but as his deafness increased he turned more and more to legal writing. He had begun to contribute articles to the *American Law Review* (July 1867–October 1869), and for a time (1871–73) he published in Washington a legal quarterly, *The United States Jurist*. Treatises on the laws of domestic relations (1870), personal property (2 vols., 1873–76), bailments (1880), executors and administrators (1883), and wills (1887) established his reputation as a legal writer and brought him large royalties. For a number of years he gave annual courses of lectures in the law schools of Boston University (1883–1902) and the National University at Washington (1888–1908). In 1891 he was invited by Herbert B. Adams to give a course of lectures on American history to graduate students at the Johns Hopkins University and this connection continued until 1908; he then retired but established there, and later by his will endowed, a lectureship in history and political science which bears his name.

Schouler had published an article, "Our Diplomacy during the Rebellion," in the *North American Review* in April 1866, and about that time began to think of writing a history of the United States supplementing Bancroft. In 1873 he began serious work, but he was delayed in completing the first volumes by difficulties in finding a publisher. Five of the seven volumes of his *History of the United States of America under the Constitution* (covering altogether the period 1783–1877) appeared between 1880 and 1891, the sixth in 1899, and the seventh in 1913. On this work his reputation as a historian rests. This was the first attempt to cover in a scholarly way the period from the Revolution to the Civil War, although John Bach McMaster [*q.v.*] soon entered the same field. The latter's *History of the People of the United States* (8 vols., 1883–1913) appeared almost contemporaneously. The two works were written from quite different points of view and from different sources. To a large extent they supplement each other. Although Schouler's interpretation was primarily political and constitutional, he did not neglect social and economic forces. Yet such topics as population, agriculture, industry, commerce, education, literature, and religion are dealt with in separate chapters and not closely integrated with political events. He recognized, though to a lesser extent than McMaster, the importance of economic matters, but attempted no economic interpretation of history. As to his methods, Schouler says: "Original records and information are preferable to all others; but secondary sources of knowledge I have largely accepted as a labor-saving means, where I could bring my own accumulated knowledge and habits of verification to bear upon them, so as to judge fairly of their comparative worth" (*Historical Briefs*, p. 42). He was an industrious worker and explored some sources that had not been used before, in particular the manuscript papers of James Monroe and Andrew Johnson, and the recently published *Diary of Gideon Welles*. The first volumes of his *History* made the greatest impression. As he

approached the Civil War, his narrative was colored by his own convictions of the righteousness of the Northern cause. In his last volume he presented an able vindication of Andrew Johnson. His style had certain eccentricities, which were duly criticised by his reviewers, but it had the merit of being cogent and readable. His other historical writings of importance were: *Thomas Jefferson* (1893); *Historical Briefs, with a Biography* (1896); *Constitutional Studies, State and Federal* (1897); *Alexander Hamilton* (1901); *Eighty Years of Union, Being a Short History of the United States, 1783–1865* (1903); *Americans of 1776* (1906); and *Ideals of the Republic* (1908).

Schouler was a man of striking appearance, cordial and kindly in manner, and not lacking in humor. He was always glad to confer with his students, although it was frequently necessary for them to write out the questions or topics on which they sought his advice. Music was his main recreation and he was a constant attendant at symphony concerts, using a mechanical device which enabled him to derive some pleasure from them. On Dec. 14, 1870, he married Emily Fuller Cochran of Boston; the union proved a happy one, although there were no children. She died in 1904 and Schouler spent the remaining years of his life at what had been for many years their summer home at Intervale, N. H.

[Edward Stanwood, "Memoir of James Schouler," *Mass. Hist. Soc. Proceedings*, LIV (1922), 283–88; "Biography," in his own *Historical Briefs* (1896), pp. 169–310; L. E. Ellis, "James Schouler," in *Miss. Valley Hist. Rev.*, Sept. 1929; critical reviews by W. A. Dunning, *Am. Hist. Rev.*, July 1900, and by H. B. Learned, *Ibid.*, April 1917; obituary in *Boston Evening Transcript*, Apr. 17, 1920; notes prepared for the writer by the historian's brother, Rev. William Schouler, of Baltimore.]
            J.H.L.

SCHOULER, WILLIAM (Dec. 31, 1814– Oct. 24, 1872), editor and historian, was born at Kilbarchan, near Glasgow, Scotland, his parents being James and Margaret (Clark) Schouler. The family name was often spelled Scouler in Scotland and was pronounced "Skooler." The senior Schouler, a calico printer, came to the United States in 1816 and after brief residence on Staten Island, N. Y., went to Taunton and Lynn, Mass., and in 1832 engaged in textile manufacture at West Cambridge, Mass., a district later set off as part of the town of Arlington. After a common school education, the son learned his father's trade, but his primary interest was in politics, not calico. As a youth he sent readable contributions on political topics to the *Yeoman's Gazette*, Concord, Mass. He had meantime become a practical cloth printer, and he had married, Oct. 6, 1835, Frances Eliza Warren, daughter of Isaac Warren, by whom he had a daughter and a son, James [*q.v.*].

In 1841, with William Stevens Robinson [*q.v.*] as assistant editor a year later, he undertook to publish and edit the *Lowell Courier,* which had undergone vicissitudes but in their hands became an influential daily newspaper, later known as the *Lowell Courier-Citizen.* In the 1840's it supported the Whig party. After serving in the Massachusetts House of Representatives in 1844, 1845, and 1847, Schouler in 1847 sold his interest at Lowell and became editor-in-chief of the *Boston Daily Atlas.* He again served in the Massachusetts legislature as representative from Boston, 1849–53. Although he had been a stanch supporter of Daniel Webster, he indignantly repudiated his political leadership after the famous speech of Mar. 7, 1850. This change of policy caused so many New England Whigs to brand Schouler as a traitor that he gave up his Boston editorship and in 1853 bought a part ownership in the *Cincinnati Gazette.* This he sold three years later and soon became editor of the *Ohio State Journal* at Columbus. He was a delegate in 1856 to the first Republican National Convention. His political contacts presently brought him an appointment as adjutant-general of Ohio, but in 1858 an offer of the editorship of the *Boston Atlas and Daily Bee* led him to return to Massachusetts. In 1860 he was appointed adjutant-general of the commonwealth, an office he held until at the end of 1866 Gov. Alexander Bullock removed him, apparently on grounds of his hostility to his former Lowell fellow citizen, Gen. Benjamin Franklin Butler (*Boston Morning Journal, post*). This position at the Massachusetts state house gave Schouler an opportunity before and during the Civil War to reveal both his remarkable executive ability and his accurate, painstaking historianship. His *A History of Massachusetts in the Civil War* (2 vols., 1868–71) contains enough that is autobiographical to place its author among the dynamic figures of his era. His annual report of Dec. 31, 1860, included a warning of impending war that stirred Massachusetts toward preparation. In 1862 as adjutant-general, he made a notable inspection of Massachusetts troops beyond the Potomac, and later, through his skilful handling of the situation, a repetition in Boston of the New York draft riots of 1863 was prevented. He won the lasting admiration of Gov. John Albion Andrew [*q.v.*], whose correspondence, much of it unpublished, at the Massachusetts Historical Society contains many references to Schouler's activities and achievements; Andrew's last official act was to express his gratitude to Schouler.

Schouler's home in his last years was at West Roxbury. There he gratified the tastes of a scholarly man, fond of historical studies and the British classics. In 1868 he once more served in the Massachusetts legislature, and during 1870 he contributed to the *Boston Morning Journal* his "Political and Personal Recollections," a valuable source book for students of Massachusetts and American political and military history. In 1872 he was of the Republicans who bolted Grant, and at his death was a candidate for presidential elector on the Greeley ticket.

[See Benjamin and W. R. Cutter, *Hist. of the Town of Arlington, Mass.* (1880) for notes on the Schouler family; F. W. Coburn, *Hist. of Lowell and Its People* (1920), vol. I, for Schouler's editorship of the *Lowell Courier;* complete file of *Lowell Courier* from 1841, believed to be the only one in existence, in Concord, Mass. Pub. Lib.; archives of Adjutant-General's office, Mass. State House, for Civil War activities; James Schouler, *Hist. Briefs* (1896); William Schouler, *A Hist. of Mass. in the Civil War* (2 vols., 1868–71), which contains autobiog. material; obituary in *Boston Morning Jour.,* Oct. 25, 1872.]   F. W. C.

SCHRADIECK, HENRY (Apr. 29, 1846–Mar. 25, 1918), violinist, teacher, conductor, was born in Hamburg, Germany, the son of Heinrich Friedrich Schradieck, and Elizabeth Catharina Johanna (Rutting) Schradieck. He received his first violin lessons from his father, starting on his fourth birthday, and in his sixth year made his first public appearance, playing Beethoven's Sonata in F, *Opus* 17. The distinguished violinist, Teresa Milanollo, heard him play when he was eight years of age, and arranged for his instruction at the Brussels Conservatory, where he studied with Hubert Léonard for four years, winning the second prize in 1857, and the first in 1858. He then studied for two years with Ferdinand David at Leipzig and in 1863 became concert-master of the Bremen Orchestra and violin soloist at Reinthaler's *Privatkonzerte.* He taught violin at the Moscow Conservatory from 1864 to 1868, and lived during this period at Nicholas Rubinstein's home, being closely associated also with Anton Rubinstein, and with Tschaikowsky. He was concert-master of the philharmonic concerts at Hamburg for the following four years and then went to Leipzig, where he became concert-master of the *Gewandhaus* orchestra, leader of the violins at the opera, and professor of violin at the Conservatory succeeding David. In 1882 he was married to J. Alice Bechtel, an American studying in Germany.

The Leipzig years were the most brilliant of Schradieck's career. He was associated with Edvard Grieg, Pablo Sarasate, Joseph Joachim, Carl Reinecke, Salomon Jadassohn, E. F. Richter, Leopold Auer, and Joseph and Henri

Wieniawski, just as he had enjoyed frequent contacts with Brahms in Hamburg. In 1883 he accepted an invitation to become teacher of violin at the Cincinnati College of Music, Cincinnati, Ohio, where he stayed for six years. He also conducted the Cincinnati Symphony Orchestra during the seasons of 1886–87 and 1887–88. In 1889 he returned to Hamburg, where he taught at the Conservatory and played as concert-master in the Philharmonic Society, but he returned to America in 1894 and made his permanant home in Brooklyn, N. Y., where he lived until his death. From 1894 to 1898 he was the principal violin teacher at the National Conservatory of Music in New York. From 1899 he taught at the Combs Broad Street Conservatory in Philadelphia, and from 1912 at the American Institute of Applied Music in New York.

Schradieck's most lasting influence was as a teacher. Among his pupils, abroad and in America, were Maud Powell, Theodore Spiering [qq.v.], Nikolai Sokoloff, Maximilian Pilzer, Felix Weingartner, and Karl Muck. In spite of his international reputation as a performer and as a teacher, Schradieck went into comparative obscurity in his later years. Spiering, his pupil, commented on this after Schradieck's death: "I cannot but feel that Schradieck should never have given up the congenial atmosphere of Leipzig. . . . That a personality like Schradieck's could be brutally forced into semi-obscurity—as was the case during the last ten or more years of his life—demonstrates, to our shame be it said, to what extent the commercializing of art has progressed" (Canadian Journal of Music, post, p. 5). Schradieck's writings were almost entirely of an educational character and made an important contribution to the field of technical training in violin. Besides editing many of the standard works for violin, he was the author of Die Schule der Violintechnik (3 vols., 1899), Tonleiter Studien, or Scale Studies for Violin (1887), Masterpieces for the Violin (8 vols., 1895), and Masterpieces for the Violin and Piano (3 vols., 1895–96).

[Who's Who in America, 1908–09; Internatl. Who's Who in Music (1918); Grove's Dict. of Music and Musicians, Am. Supp. (1930); Baker's Biog. Dict. of Musicians (3rd ed., 1919); W. W. Todd, "Henry Schradieck—An Appreciation," Violinist, Aug. 1916; Theodore Spiering, "Henry Schradieck—A Personal Tribute," Canadian Jour. of Music, May 1918; N. Y. Times, Mar. 27, 1918.]
J. T. H.

SCHRIECK, SISTER LOUISE VAN DER (Nov. 14, 1813–Dec. 3, 1886), American foundress of the Sisters of Notre Dame de Namur, was born at Bergen-op-Zoom, Holland, the tenth of the thirteen children of Joseph and Clara Maria (Weenan) Van der Schrieck, who though ardent Catholics suffered little in person or in fortune during the Napoleonic wars. Baptized Josephine, the child was reared in her native village and in Antwerp where the family moved about 1817, seeking both freedom from the politico-religious system, and enlarged opportunities in the exporting business in which the father and elder sons grew prosperous. She was schooled in a private academy and in the newly established institute of the Sisters of Notre Dame at Namur, a French foundation established at Amiens by Blessed Julie Billiart. Thereafter she continued her educaton under private tutors at home, assisted in the household, and devoted her spare time to religious missionary and social work among the oppressed poor of Antwerp and especially among the apprentice girls in the lace factories. Deeply religious and charitable, she could find little outlet for a life of service and hence with parental consent went to Namur, where in 1837 she entered the novitiate of the Notre Dame nuns. As discipline in her crowded home had been strict, she easily accepted the severe rule of privation, work, and prayer, and was professed as Sister Louise, May 17, 1839.

In the meantime Bishop John Baptist Purcell [q.v.], who had become acquainted with the community while seeking missionaries in Belgium for his frontier diocese, was petitioning the superior of the convent and the bishop of Namur for a colony of teaching nuns for Cincinnati, Ohio. His request was finally granted and on Sept. 3, 1840, eight volunteers, of whom Sister Louise was the youngest, started for America under Sister Louise de Gonzague (d. 1866) as superior and Father Louis Amadeus Rappe, a missionary who later became first bishop of Cleveland, as a protector. Arriving at the wharves of Cincinnati on Oct. 31, the sisters were established in a house on Sycamore Street, the first permanent foundation of the community outside of Belgium. The French Ladies met with favor not only among Catholics who attended their poor school and Sunday schools and boarding academy but among the socially aspiring women of the little packing and commercial town who would learn lace-making and a smattering of French. When in 1845 Sister Louise was named superior the Notre Dame convent had become an accepted institution in the community, and its numbers were increasing through local vocations and enlistments from Belgium. In 1846 Sister Louise assigned some of her German-speaking nuns to the first of the community's growing list of parochial schools, which for a generation could not be adequately staffed by

German religious communities. In 1848 she was appointed superior-provincial with a jurisdiction over all future foundations east of the Rocky Mountains, in which capacity she continued until her death. As a superior, she exacted strict obedience under a firm, benevolent rule; she clung steadfastly to the connection with Namur and to the original rule and purpose of the foundress even at the expense of rigidity and stiffness; and she tactfully managed bishops who vainly sought to make the community in their dioceses independent or diocesan. A capable administrator, she founded twenty-six convents in Washington, D. C., Philadelphia, Pa., and in cities of Ohio and Massachusetts. Her eight hundred nuns engaged in teaching in academies and parochial schools, including an occasional free school for negroes. Only during the Civil War, when she furnished nursing nuns for Fort Denison near Cincinnati, did she turn her full energies from Catholic education. At her death in Cincinnati her pioneer work was generally acclaimed, Archbishop William Henry Elder [q.v.] saying the requiem mass.

[Sister Helen Louise Nugent, *Sister Louise* (1931), an excellent biog. based on community archives in Namur and Cincinnati and on reminiscences of older nuns who served under the first superior, and *Sister Julia* (1928); *Extracts from the Memoirs of Sister Superior Louise* (Cincinnati, n.d.); M. E. Mannix, *Memoirs of Sister Louise . . . with Reminiscences of the Early Days of the Order in the U. S.* (1907); *Cincinnati Enquirer*, Dec. 4, 1886.]   R. J. P.

SCHRIVER, EDMUND (Sept. 16, 1812–Feb. 10, 1899), soldier, son of Daniel and Rebecca (Zinn) Schriver, was born in York, Pa., where he received his early schooling. He entered the United States Military Academy at seventeen; was graduated July 1, 1833, seventeenth in a class of forty-three; performed garrison duty in Tennessee and Alabama during 1833 and part of 1834 as brevet second lieutenant of the 2nd Artillery; and served as assistant instructor in infantry tactics at West Point from March 1834 to November 1835, receiving his regular second lieutenant's commission in July 1834. Excluding a brief interim in 1839 in the Florida War, he served in the office of the adjutant-general from November 1835 until September 1841. He was promoted first lieutenant, November 1836; was brevetted captain, July 1838, serving as assistant adjutant-general; and received his regular captaincy in August 1842. He served in the headquarters of the Department of the East from September 1841 to July 1846, when he resigned from the army to engage in private business. He was treasurer of the Saratoga and Washington railroad, N. Y. (1847–52), of the Saratoga and Schenectady railroad, and of the

Rensselaer and Saratoga railroad (1847–61); he also served for ten years as president of the latter road. He served Gov. Edwin Denison Morgan [q.v.] of New York as aide with the rank of colonel from April to July 1861.

Upon the outbreak of the Civil War, he was commissioned lieutenant-colonel, 11th U. S. Infantry. From July to October 1861 he served at Fort Independence, Mass., and from October 1861 to March 1862 at Perryville, Md.; he was then appointed chief of staff, 1st Corps, Army of the Potomac, and served in that capacity until January 1863 throughout the entire Fredericksburg campaign. In May 1862 he was promoted to the grade of colonel. He participated in the Shenandoah and in the northern Virginia campaigns, fighting at Cedar Mountain, the crossing of the Rappahannock, at Chantilly, and at Manassas in August 1862. He was acting inspector, Army of the Potomac, from January to March 1863 and inspector from then until March 1865. He participated in the battles at Chancellorsville and at Gettysburg, and the subsequent engagements which culminated in the Mine Run expedition of November–December 1863. He was in the Richmond campaign of 1865 from the Rapidan to Petersburg. For conspicuous service in the field, he was brevetted brigadier-general in August 1864 and major-general in March 1865. From March to June 1865 he was on special duty in the office of the secretary of war; he then made an inspection tour of all quartermaster depots and a general inspection of all army posts. Upon returning to Washington in November 1865, he had charge of the inspector's bureau for two periods, 1865–69 and 1871–76. In the intervening period, he was inspector of the United States Military Academy. During 1872–73 he inspected posts in Texas, New Mexico, and Kansas, and from 1876 to 1881 he was inspector-general of the Division of the Pacific. He had a great interest in and devoted considerable time to the affairs of the Freedmen's Bureau. He was retired, Jan. 4, 1881, and then made his home in Washington, D. C. He was buried in Oakwood Cemetery, Troy, N. Y.

[*War of the Rebellion: Official Records (Army)*, esp. 1 ser., XII, pts. 1, 3, XXVII, pt. 3, XXX, pt. 1, XXXVI, pt. 3; G. W. Cullum, *Biog. Reg. Officers and Grads. U. S. Mil. Acad.* (3rd ed., 1891), vol. I; T. H. S. Hamersly, *Complete Regular Army Reg. of U. S.* (1880); records of York County Hist. Soc., York, Pa., and of health departments, Troy, N. Y., and Washington, D. C.; *Army and Navy Reg.*, Feb. 25, 1899; *Evening Star* (Washington), Feb. 11, 1899.]
C. C. B.

SCHROEDER, JOHN FREDERICK (Apr. 8, 1800–Feb. 26, 1857), Episcopal clergyman, author, was born in Baltimore, Md., the son of Henry Schroeder, an immigrant from Hamburg, Germany, and his wife, Mary (Schley) of Frederick, Md. A quiet, precocious child, John had developed a special interest in ancient languages by the time he was eleven. He graduated with highest honors from the College of New Jersey (Princeton) in 1819, then spent a year studying oriental languages under a Philadelphia clergyman. After attending General Theological Seminary for a short time in 1821, he completed his preparation privately, and was ordained deacon by Bishop Kemp of Maryland in 1823 and priest a year later.

He served as rector of St. Michael's parish, Maryland, for a short time, and then (1823) was called as temporary assistant at Trinity Church, New York. His skill as a preacher won him a large following and he was given a permanent appointment within a year. He seems to have inclined toward the Evangelical party of his Church, and this fact probably lessened his favor with the parish authorities, but he retained his position for fifteen years, part of the time having immediate charge of St. Paul's Chapel. In 1829 he was rebuked by Bishop John Henry Hobart [q.v.] for his participation in a short-lived Protestant Episcopal Clerical Association which Hobart suspected of Evangelical tendencies, but Schroeder's relations with his Bishop were generally cordial. When Hobart died in 1830, Schroeder pronounced a eulogy upon him (The Great Man in Israel, 1830) and also wrote a sketch of his life, which was published in a Memorial of Bishop Hobart (1831). He was one of the clergymen who remained at their posts during the cholera epidemics of the early 1830's. In 1838 his wife's health required a visit to Europe, and shortly after his return he became involved in a dispute with the vestry over a question of precedence which led to his resignation in 1839 and, indirectly, to an unsuccessful attempt to separate St. Paul's Chapel from Trinity Parish. He then moved to Flushing, L. I., where he founded a girl's school (St. Ann's Hall), which he continued until his death. In 1846 he moved it to New York, where he became rector of the Church of the Crucifixion, and in 1852 to Brooklyn, where he served as rector of St. Thomas' Church until shortly before his death.

He was a frequent contributor to religious and secular periodicals, edited a collection of Maxims of Washington (1855), and wrote a biography of Washington which was published posthumously (Life and Times of Washington, 2 vols., n.d., 1857–61). He also delivered a number of public lectures, notably a series before the New York Athenæum on oriental literature, one before the New York Horticultural Society, The Intellectual and Moral Resources of Horticulture (1828), and another, A Plea for the Industrious Poor and Strangers in Sickness (1830), at the opening of the New York Dispensary. On May 22, 1825, he married Caroline Maria Boardman, a daughter of Senator Elijah Boardman and Mary Anna (Whiting) Boardman. By her he had eight children, four of whom survived him. In 1849 he published Memoir of the Life and Character of Mrs. Mary Anna Boardman, a rather sentimental biography of his mother-in-law for family distribution. Under different circumstances, Schroeder might have become a distinguished scholar, but his intellectual gifts never seem to have received the discipline necessary to fit them for the fullest usefulness.

[J. G. White, "John Frederick Schroeder," in Memorial Biogs. of the New Eng. Hist. Geneal. Soc., vol. III (1883); Morgan Dix, A Hist. of the Parish of Trinity Church in the City of N. Y., III (1905), 403–05, IV (1906), 197–211; S. H. Turner, Autobiog. (1863), pp. 135–65; J. H. Hobart, A Pastoral Letter ... on the Subject of the Protestant Episcopal Clerical Asso. (1829); Gen. Cat. of Princeton Univ. (1908); Church Journal (N. Y.), Mar. 4, 1857; Church Review, Apr. 1857; N. Y. Tribune, Feb. 27, 1857.]

W. W. M.

SCHROEDER, SEATON (Aug. 17, 1849–Oct. 19, 1922), naval officer, was born in Washington, D. C., the son of Francis and Caroline (Seaton) Schroeder. Since his father was American chargé d'affaires and then minister to Sweden and Norway from 1849 to 1857, he acquired most of his elementary education abroad. He entered the United States Naval Academy in September 1864 and graduated in 1868. By 1872 he had become a lieutenant, but because of the stagnation in the naval service during this period he was retained in this grade for twenty-one years. He first served in the Pacific Fleet in the Saginaw and Pensacola, and from 1869–72 in the Benicia on the Asiatic station. In June 1871 he participated in the expedition of John Rodgers (1812–1882) [q.v.] against the Korean forts on the Salée River. In 1874–75 he served in the Swatara in her voyage round the world with the Transit of Venus expedition. After spending the next three years in hydrographic work in the Mediterranean, in 1879 he secured leave of absence to assist Henry Honeychurch Gorringe [q.v.] in transporting the obelisk in Central Park, New York City, from Egypt to New York, returning to his naval duties the following year. He served for three years as navigator of the Fish Commission steamer Albatross, was transferred to the office of naval intelligence, and in 1888 was assigned to duty in connection with the construction and equipment of the dynamite cruiser *Vesuvius,* which he subsequently commanded until 1893. In 1896 he was made executive officer of the battleship *Massachusetts,* holding the post during the operations off Santiago during the Spanish-American War. For his services during the war he was advanced three numbers in rank "for eminent and conspicuous conduct," and in 1899 he was promoted to the rank of commander. Appointed naval governor of Guam in 1900, he rendered most efficient service on the island, endearing himself to the native population. In 1903, when he was commissioned captain, he was transferred to Washington as chief intelligence officer. During the voyage of the Atlantic Fleet around the world he commanded the *Virginia* from Hampton Roads to San Francisco, where he was commissioned rear admiral in July 1908; during the remainder of the voyage he commanded successively the Fourth and Third Divisions of the fleet. From 1909 to 1911, when he was retired by age, he was commander-in-chief of the Atlantic Fleet. During the World War he was recalled to active duty as hydrographer to the Navy Department. He married Maria C. B. Wainwright, Jan. 16, 1879, and had two sons and three daughters.

An efficient, conscientious officer and a thorough seaman, imbued with a deep love of his profession, he expected scrupulous accuracy and strict attention to duty on the part of his subordinates. Keenly interested in naval development, he collaborated with Lieut. William H. Driggs in perfecting the Driggs-Schroeder gun, 1888–89, and wrote four separate treatises on torpedoes and torpedo boats: *The Development of Modern Torpedo Boats* (1886), *Development of Modern Torpedoes* (1887), *Modern Torpedoes* (1887), and *Modern Torpedo Boats* (1887). He also wrote *The Fall of Maximilian's Empire* (1887) and his autobiography, *A Half Century of Naval Service* (1922), as well as numerous professional articles in American and English naval journals. He collaborated with George M. Totten in writing *Coasts and Ports of the Bay of Biscay* (1876) and with Richard Wainwright in compiling *Arctic Azimuth Tables* (1881).

[See Navy Reg., 1868–1922; L. R. Hamersly, *Records of Living Officers U. S. Navy and Marine Corps* (6th ed., 1898); *Ann. Reports Navy Dept. . . . App. to Report of Chief of Bureau of Navigation* (1898); Lucien Young, *Cat. of Works by Am. Naval Officers* (1888); H. H. Gorringe, *Egyptian Obelisks* (1882); *Army and Navy Jour.,* Oct. 28, 1922; *Army and Navy Reg.,* Oct. 21, 1922; *Who's Who in America,* 1920–21; *Evening Star* (Washington, D. C.), Oct. 20, 1922. For

family material see O. A. Seaton, *The Seaton Family* (1906).]   L. H. B.

SCHUESSELE, CHRISTIAN [See SCHUSSELE, CHRISTIAN, 1826–1879].

SCHULTZE, AUGUSTUS (Feb. 3, 1840–Nov. 12, 1918), Moravian clergyman, educator, author, editor, was the son of J. C. Louis and D. Frederica (Haessler) Schultze and was born at Nowawes, Prussia, a suburb of Potsdam. He received his academic training at Niesky in Silesia and his theological training at Gnadenfeld, where he took his bachelor's degree in divinity in 1861. For one year he taught Latin and Greek at the French Academy, Lausanne, Switzerland, and for eight years he occupied the chair of classics at Niesky, where on Sept. 16, 1869, he was ordained deacon in the Moravian church. In 1870 he was sent to Bethlehem, Pa., to fill the chair of classics in the Moravian College and Theological Seminary. In 1885 he became president of the institution, having meanwhile, Jan. 20, 1882, been ordained presbyter, at Bethlehem, by Bishop Edmund de Schweinitz [*q.v.*]. He served as president until July 1, 1918, and, as president emeritus, he continued his devotion to the classics as professor of Hebrew until his death.

From 1881 to 1893 he was secretary and member of the governing board of the northern diocese of the Moravian Church in America. He was a prolific writer both in German and in English. Many pages of the official papers of the Moravian Church attest the carefulness and clarity of his thinking during thirty years of editorial writing. In 1886 he published "A Brief History of the Widows' Society of Bethlehem" (*Transactions of the Moravian Historical Society,* vol. II, 1886, pp. 51–124); the following year he prepared the annual textbook of devotional readings in the Danish language (*Aarlig Dagbog,* 1888); and in 1890 he brought out *Die Missionsfelde der Erneuerten Brüderkirche.* Meanwhile he had published *A Brief Grammar and Vocabulary of the Eskimo Language of North-Western Alaska* (1889; 2nd ed., 1894), the result of long study and comparison of material submitted by oral evidence, since the language had, up to that time, no written expression. His next work was "The Old Moravian Cemetery of Bethlehem, Pa., 1742–1897" (*Transactions of the Moravian Historical Society,* vol. V, 1899), which, besides carefully locating all burials, gave concise sketches of every life, a truly gigantic task of research. Most of his theological works were published late in his life, the fruit of careful thought. They were *The Books of the Bible Briefly Analyzed* (1889), *The The-*

ology of Peter and Paul (1894), and *Christian Doctrine and Systematic Theology* (1909), the last being the flowering of lectures in dogmatics he had delivered and revised for many years. At the time of his sudden death in Bethlehem, from the effects of a fall, he was engaged in the revision of his Eskimo grammar, enlarged to include a translation of passages from the Bible into that tongue.

Schultze was married twice. His first wife, Julia Reck of Bethlehem, Pa., whom he married Dec. 26, 1871, died in 1874 leaving one son. His second wife, Adelaide E. Peter of Gnadenhutten, Ohio, whom he married July 5, 1876, died Feb. 3, 1918, leaving a son and three daughters.

[Obituary (MS.) in Archives of the Moravian Church, Bethlehem, Pa.; *Who's Who in America,* 1918–19; *Moravian,* Nov. 20, 1918; *Bethlehem Daily Times,* Nov. 13, 1918.]   A. G. R.

SCHURZ, CARL (Mar. 2, 1829–May 14, 1906), minister to Spain, Union soldier, senator from Missouri, and secretary of the interior, was born in the little town of Liblar on the Rhine, near Cologne. He attended the gymnasium at Cologne (1839–46) and became a candidate for the doctorate at the University of Bonn in 1847. His father, Christian Schurz, was first a village schoolmaster and then embarked in business; his mother, Marianne Jüssen, the daughter of a tenant farmer, was a woman of unusual force of character. Both made every sacrifice to help their son to the career of which he dreamed—a professorship of history. Fate in the form of the German revolutionary movement of 1848–49 intervened and altered Schurz's life as it marred or made the lives of many thousands of young Germans who beheld in the United States their ideal of popular government. Of these none was more ardent or more eloquent, and certainly none was more daring, than Schurz. At nineteen he was a leader of the student movement in his university, and was preaching its gospel to the peasants in his neighborhood through the columns of a democratic newspaper, and by word of mouth. His rare gift of oratory he discovered when he suddenly addressed, to great applause, a meeting in the university hall at Bonn to which he came without the slightest intention of speaking.

Profoundly influenced by Prof. Gottfried Kinkel of Bonn, one of the intellectual leaders of the struggle for democratic institutions, Schurz followed him in the abortive revolutionary movement upon Siegburg, on May 11, 1849. Thereafter he became a lieutenant and staff officer of the revolutionary army taking part in the final battles of the united rebel forces of Baden and the Palatinate at Ubstadt and Bruchsal, and those on the line of the Murg River in Baden on June 28–30, 1849. Sent by order into the fortress of Rastatt, just before it was surrendered, he was one of its defenders until the surrender more than three weeks later. Rightly expecting to be shot if captured, Schurz declined to deliver himself up to the conquering Prussians. With two companions he concealed himself for four days, finally escaping through an unused sewer which was their first place of refuge. (See Schurz's account, "The Surrender of Rastatt," *Wisconsin Magazine of History,* Mar. 1929.) They crossed the Rhine and entered French territory, Schurz finally joining the large colony of German refugees in Switzerland.

There he might have stayed indefinitely had it not been for the plight of his beloved teacher, Kinkel, who had been captured, put on trial for his life, and sentenced to life imprisonment. After being treated as a common felon, Kinkel was at length transferred to the prison at Spandau, a fortified town near Berlin. In response to Frau Kinkel's appeals, Schurz undertook the liberation of her husband. Twice, with the aid of a false passport, he reëntered Germany, where he was himself on the proscribed list. The necessary funds were furnished by friends of the Professor. After nine months of preparation and plotting with the complicity of a turnkey, Kinkel was lowered to the street from an unbarred attic window of the prison in the night of Nov. 6–7, 1850. In a waiting carriage Kinkel and Schurz left the city by the Hamburg road, only to alter their course and drive straight to Mecklenburg. They were successfully concealed in Rostock until a tiny schooner conveyed them to England. To this day no single incident of the Revolution is better known in Germany; no other has in it more elements of romantic daring and unselfish personal heroism. Schurz went to Paris in December 1850, but in the summer of 1851 was expelled from France by the police as a dangerous foreigner. He resided in England until after his marriage there to Margarethe (or Margaretha) Meyer, of Hamburg, July 6, 1852. During this period he won the friendship of Mazzini and Kossuth and other great leaders of the democratic movement in Europe. America beckoned him, however. In August he set sail for the United States, following in the footsteps of many of his associates-in-arms of the brief campaign of 1849. He and his wife lived in Philadelphia until 1855.

Before definitely settling, Schurz spent months in traveling through the Eastern and Middle-

Western portion of the United States, and set about acquiring that remarkable mastery of the English language which made it possible for him to make campaign speeches in English within five years after his arrival. In 1856 he purchased a small farm in Watertown, Wis., where an uncle's family had settled. Having espoused the anti-slavery cause with all the ardor and enthusiasm he gave to the revolution of 1849, Schurz was immediately drawn into Republican politics. Speaking in German, he campaigned for Frémont. The next year he was sent as a delegate to the Republican state convention which promptly nominated him for lieutenant-governor although he was not yet a citizen of the United States, a point that did not become pressing because he was defeated by 107 votes despite wide campaigning in both English and German. A year later, the campaign of 1858 found him speaking in Illinois for Abraham Lincoln and against Stephen A. Douglas. From that time on he was in demand for one campaign after another; in April 1859 he aided, by request, Senator Henry Wilson of Massachusetts in his fight against the Know-Nothing movement in that state, delivering one of his most famous speeches, "True Americanism" (*Speeches*, 1865, pp. 51–76), which helped to defeat a proposal to deny the ballot to foreign-born voters in Massachusetts for two years after federal naturalization. Schurz was next put forward for the governorship of Wisconsin; the prize went, however, to another. He was then admitted to the bar and entered into a law partnership, but the anti-slavery cause and politics absorbed most of his time. Chairman of the Wisconsin delegation to the Chicago Republican convention of 1860 which nominated Abraham Lincoln, he and his fellow-delegates voted for Seward until the end. One of the committee which notified Lincoln of his nomination, Schurz spoke for him in Wisconsin, Illinois, Indiana, Ohio, Pennsylvania, and New York with great effectiveness among both natives and foreign-born. His greatest forensic effort—he considered it the greatest success of his oratorical career—was his speech in Cooper Union, Sept. 13, 1860 (*Ibid.*, pp. 162–221), which was devoted to a merciless critique of Stephen A. Douglas and was marked by sarcasm, humor, and his unusual power of clear exposition. It lasted for three hours and was received with the greatest enthusiasm. For all of these services, Lincoln, who had written to him on June 18, 1860, that "to the extent of our limited acquaintance, no man stands nearer my heart than yourself" (*Speeches, Correspondence*, I, 119), appointed Schurz minister to Spain,

although he was in the midst of raising the 1st New York ("Lincoln") Cavalry of which he expected to be colonel.

Arriving at Madrid in July 1861, Schurz devoted himself, like Charles Francis Adams and other American representatives in Europe, to advancing and safeguarding the Union cause abroad, and gave all his leisure time to military campaigns and tactics which he had studied ever since his brief military experience in Germany. Finding, however, that the Northern cause was greatly weakened by the failure of the government to become clearly anti-slavery, and receiving no encouragement in this matter from Secretary Seward, Schurz returned to the United States in January 1862, to put his views before Lincoln. The latter received him kindly, but persisted in his policy of awaiting a more favorable public opinion at home. Schurz then sought to rouse the public for immediate emancipation and to that end delivered an address, previously read and approved by Lincoln, at Cooper Union in March 1862 (*Speeches*, 1865, pp. 240–68), which coincided with the President's request to Congress for authority to cooperate with any state which might adopt gradual emancipation. Schurz resigned as minister in April, was appointed brigadier-general of volunteers, and was given not a brigade, but a division, in Frémont's army on June 10, 1862, thus being placed in command of troops some of whom were veterans of a year's standing.

That Schurz took his military duties seriously, and soon won the respect of his officers and men for his ability and personal courage is beyond question. He was frequently complimented in dispatches, and on one occasion after his troops passed in review with the Army of the Potomac, Lincoln confirmed the press reports that "the division commanded by General Schurz impressed the Presidential party as the best drilled and most soldierly of the troops that passed before them" (Schurz, *Reminiscences*, II, 407). At the second battle of Bull Run, Aug. 30, 1862, the new brigadier of two months' service and his division won high praise in one of the bloodiest and bitterest defeats of the Army of the Potomac, whose final withdrawal they covered. It was, however, the misfortune of this division and the corps to bear the brunt of Jackson's sudden attack at Chancellorsville. Badly placed by the corps commander, Gen. O. O. Howard—despite repeated protests and warnings by Schurz—the division broke and retired in disorder before the overwhelming Confederate onrush, but was finally rallied in part to aid in preventing what threatened to be a complete disaster. For this the XI Corps, and especially its German regiments, was violently abused and charged with cowardice in the press of the entire country. There resulted a long controversy between Schurz and Howard, but the former's efforts to obtain a court of inquiry and justice for his troops failed. Again at Gettysburg, where, because of the killing of General Reynolds and the consequent advancement of General Howard, Schurz took command of the XI Corps, his troops bore the brunt of the Confederate attack upon the right wing. After heavy losses they retired in some disorder through the town to Cemetery Ridge, again in obedience to orders from Howard. Once more there were unwarranted charges that the Germans had failed to stand their ground.

That Schurz was himself not held responsible for the Chancellorsville disaster appears from the fact that on Mar. 14, 1863, he was promoted to major-general. After Gettysburg, the corps was transferred to the western field. Here Schurz again became involved in a controversy, this time with General Hooker. A court of inquiry subsequently found that his conduct had been entirely correct and proper. After Chattanooga the depleted XI and XII Corps were merged into a new XX Corps, and Schurz was appointed to command a corps of instruction at Nashville. Unable to brook the prospect of inaction, Schurz, after some months, asked to be relieved of his command, conferred with Lincoln, and then made many speeches on behalf of the President's reëlection. The end of the war found him chief of staff to Major-General Slocum in Sherman's army. He resigned immediately after the surrender of Lee. Throughout his military service Schurz corresponded irregularly with Lincoln, a most unwise procedure but one welcomed by the President except on one occasion when he found it necessary to rebuke the General, which event, however, did not interrupt their warm friendship (Schurz, *Speeches, Correspondence,* I, 211–13, 219–21). At best it was an anomalous situation; a political campaigner and intimate of the President had been put into a most responsible military command and was known to be in direct relations with the Commander-in-Chief. Had not Schurz displayed real soldierly capacity, and much discretion, the situation might easily have become an impossible one. Instead, he won the regard of Sherman, Hancock, and many others who ranked among the best of the Northern generals.

Before Schurz could decide upon his next course of action, President Johnson asked him to visit the Southern states and to report at length to him upon conditions there. Schurz traveled from July to September 1865, and wrote a lengthy report that has extraordinary historical value to this day, because of its detailed analysis of the situation, its clarity of statement, and its vision (*Speeches, Correspondence,* I, 279–374). Since, however, Schurz thought the extension of the franchise to the colored people should be a condition precedent to the readmission of the Confederate states, his report was unwelcome to Johnson, who neither acknowledged its receipt nor allowed it to be published until Congress demanded it (*Senate Executive Document No. 2,* 39 Cong., 1 Sess.).

With this task accomplished, Schurz accepted an invitation from Horace Greeley to represent the *New York Tribune* as its Washington correspondent, in which capacity he observed the beginning of the struggle between Congress and the President over reconstruction. Resigning in the spring of 1866, Schurz next became editor-in-chief of the Detroit *Post,* then just established by leading Michigan Republicans. Here he remained only a year, when he became joint editor, with Emil Preetorius [*q.v.*], of the St. Louis *Westliche Post,* and one of the proprietors of this German-language daily. This third chapter in his journalistic career was also destined to be a short one. A delegate to the Republican National Convention which met to nominate Grant for the presidency in 1868, Schurz was at once chosen temporary chairman of the convention, and made the keynote address. He drew up the resolution in the platform calling for the removal of disqualifications upon "the late rebels" (*Reminiscences,* III, 284–85). As usual, he made many speeches in the campaign which followed. After a bitter contest between the Radicals and Liberals in the party, he was himself nominated for the United States Senate from Missouri, and duly elected by the legislature (Ross, *post,* p. 29). On Mar. 4, 1869, two days after his fortieth birthday, he took his seat in Washington.

He speedily found himself in the group of anti-Grant senators, joining Sumner in the defeat of Grant's plan to annex Santo Domingo, and opposing at many points the "spoils-loving and domineering partisans" of the President. On Dec. 20, 1869, years before the policy it outlined was adopted, Schurz introduced a bill to create a permanent civil-service merit system (*Congressional Globe,* 41 Cong., 2 Sess., pp. 236–38). William A. Dunning and Frederic Bancroft have written in their addenda to Schurz's unfinished memoirs that his "whole conception of public policy was far above the play of merely personal and party interests"; and that his senatorial career was accordingly one of "exceptional seriousness and dignity" (*Reminiscences,* III, 317–18). He was at his best in his incessant attacks upon public corruption. The news that he would speak at a given hour usually crowded the public galleries. But the high rank he took and held in the Senate, and his national reputation as an orator and a leader, did not assure him reëlection in 1875, for, because of the Republican split, the Democrats had gained control of the Missouri legislature. He was again compelled to turn to journalism and the lecture platform for support.

Schurz, who was disgusted with Grant and distrustful of the Democrats, had probably done more than any other leader to promote the Liberal Republican movement (Ross, pp. 44–50; Schurz, *Speeches, Correspondence,* II, 59–69, 254–60). He was the permanent president of the Cincinnati convention of 1872 that organized the new party and, although profoundly disappointed by the nomination of Horace Greeley and without hope of success, was active in the campaign. His speeches "were naturally against Grant rather than for Greeley" (*Reminiscences,* III, 352). In 1876, to the dismay and anger of many of his Liberal Republican associates, he supported Hayes, being assured that the latter was sound on the money question, would restore the South, and would promote civil-service reform (*Speeches, Correspondence,* III, 249–59; *Reminiscences,* III, 368). On Mar. 4, 1877, Schurz entered the cabinet of Hayes as secretary of the interior. His secretaryship is still remembered because of his enlightened treatment of the Indians (much misunderstood at the time), his installing a merit promotion system in his department, his preservation of the public domain, and the beginning of the development of national parks.

On leaving the cabinet Schurz began his fourth venture into journalism. At the invitation of Henry Villard [*q.v.*], who had just purchased the New York *Evening Post* and the *Nation,* he became head of a triumvirate of remarkable editors comprising besides himself, Edwin L. Godkin and Horace White [*qq.v.*]. The brilliant chapter in journalism which they thus began ended in two and a quarter years, in the fall of 1883, because of differences as to editorial methods and policies between Schurz and Godkin (Nevins, *post,* pp. 455–56). The friendship of the three men remained unbroken; until his death Schurz was a valued counselor of the *Evening Post.* As an editorial writer it was

plain that his style was often more oratorical than journalistic, and lacking in terseness. To both the *Evening Post* and to Schurz, because of his rousing speeches, was attributed to a considerable degree Blaine's loss of New York state in 1884, and the election of Cleveland to the presidency.

Schurz's final venture into journalism began in 1892, when in succession to George William Curtis he for six years contributed the leading editorials to *Harper's Weekly.* Their authorship was at first kept secret, as had been his contribution of many articles to the *Nation,* prior to its amalgamation with the *Evening Post* in 1881, notably some regular letters from Washington in 1872 and 1873. In 1898 his connection with *Harper's Weekly* was ended by his refusal to support the drift toward the war with Spain. When the war came Schurz warmly opposed it, as he did the annexation of the Philippines, declaring that fatal violence was being done the anti-imperialistic, peace-loving ideal of America, free from all entangling foreign alliances. He once wrote that foreign-born citizens were "more jealously patriotic Americans than many natives are," since they watch the progress of the Republic "with triumphant joy at every success of our democratic institutions, and with the keenest sensitiveness to every failure, having the standing of this country before the world constantly in mind" (*Reminiscences,* I, 120). This describes his own attitude toward his adopted country.

The latter years of his life Schurz gave to literary labor, to letters upon public questions, and to occasional public speeches. The latter were as always carefully memorized, were marked by a lofty tone, and, like those delivered in the Senate, were "emphasized by graceful diction, and impressive delivery" (*Reminiscences,* III, 318). An ardent admirer and supporter of Grover Cleveland, except occasionally, as in the matter of the Venezuelan episode of 1895, Schurz championed William J. Bryan in 1900 on the anti-imperialist issue, as he had opposed him on the free-silver question four years earlier. He was for years (1892–1900) president of the National Civil-Service Reform League, and of the Civil Service Reform Association of New York (1893–1906). In every mayoralty election in New York, in which he resided from 1881 on, he made his influence felt in the struggle for good government. Indeed, he held in his last years the unique position of a veteran statesman, a public-spirited citizen, and political philosopher, representing particularly a great group of his fellow-citizens, and battling uninterruptedly for his conception of an America minding its own business, and keeping aloof from foreign aggression and foreign involvements.

Carl Schurz was a man of great personal charm, of commanding presence, despite a very tall and rather lanky figure, of a gay, vivacious, and unusually happy spirit, which was never daunted by his bitter disappointments in the trend of domestic and foreign policy from 1898 on. Devoted to his family, an amateur pianist of talent, blessed with a great sense of humor, together with much playful irony, he took cheerfully those periods of his life when he went counter to public opinion, and willingly paid the price therefor. He remained until his death extraordinarily rich in friends and admirers. His wife died in 1876. Of two sons and two daughters, three survived him; all died without issue. Besides his speeches and unfinished reminiscences (see below), mention should be made of his admirable *Life of Henry Clay* (2 vols., 1887), a notable essay on Lincoln in the *Atlantic Monthly,* June 1891 (also printed separately, 1891 and later), and a pamphlet, *The New South* (1885).

[There are Schurz papers in the Lib. of Cong., and there is a collection of private letters in the Wis. Hist. Soc. Various editions of speeches and writings are: *Speeches of Carl Schurz* (1865); Frederic Bancroft, ed., *Speeches, Correspondence and Pol. Papers of Carl Schurz* (6 vols., 1913); *The Reminiscences of Carl Schurz* (3 vols., 1907–08), containing, in vol. III, "A Sketch of Carl Schurz's Political Career, 1869–1906," by Frederic Bancroft and W. A. Dunning; a German edition, containing letters not in the American, *Lebenserinnerungen* (3 vols., 1906–12); Joseph Schafer, ed. and transl., *Intimate Letters of Carl Schurz, 1841–1869* (*Pubs. of the State Hist. Soc. of Wis., Collections,* Vol. XXX, 1928). Among works about Schurz are: Anton Erkelenz and Fritz Mittelmann, eds., *Carl Schurz, der Deutsche und der Amerikaner* (1929); Otto Dannehl, *Carl Schurz* (1929); C. V. Easum, *The Americanization of Carl Schurz* (1929); Joseph Schafer, *Carl Schurz, Militant Liberal* (1930); C. M. Fuess, *Carl Schurz, Reformer* (1932). See also T. A. Dodge, *The Campaign of Chancellorsville* (1881); E. D. Ross, *The Liberal Republican Movement* (1919); T. S. Barclay, *The Liberal Republican Movement in Mo., 1865–1871* (1926); Allan Nevins, *The Evening Post* (1922); F. M. Stewart, *The National Civil Service Reform League* (1929); obituaries and comment, *Evening Post* (N. Y.), May 14, 1906; *N. Y. Times,* May 15, 1906; *Nation* (N. Y.), May 17, 1906; *Harper's Weekly,* May 26, 1906.]   O. G. V.

SCHUSSELE, CHRISTIAN (Apr. 16, 1826– Aug. 21, 1879), painter, teacher, the son of a baker of good standing, was born in Guebviller, Haut Rhin, Alsace, while that province was French. As a child he spent much time drawing and painting, adorning the walls and doors of his attic at home with copies of pictures seen in the churches of his native village. At the age of fifteen, although entirely self-taught, he was painting portraits of his neighbors. In 1841 he was sent to Strasbourg to enter the art academy,

where he studied the practice of lithography. Two years later he went to Paris, where he worked at first under Paul Delaroche and then with Englemann and Graf. Subsequently he entered the studio of Yvon, painter of battle scenes at Versailles, and was commissioned to make drawings from the pictures at the Versailles gallery for elaborate chromolithographic reproductions. The revolution of 1848, however, put an end to his contract, and turned the young painter's thoughts toward the United States.

While in Paris he had met Cecilia Muringer, the young daughter of an Alsatian lithographer who resided in Philadelphia, and it was to that city Schussele directed his steps upon his arrival in America. He soon married the youthful Cecilia, by whom he had two daughters. In Philadelphia he first worked at chromolithography, supplementing such employment with designing for wood engravers, but his real interest lay in painting. In the spring of 1851 he completed a picture entitled "The Artist's Recreation" which was exhibited at the Pennsylvania Academy of the Fine Arts. A year later came "Clear the Track," a coasting scene, purchased by the president of the Academy. In 1854 this picture was engraved by John Sartain [q.v.] for the Art Union of Philadelphia, thus establishing Schussele's reputation and popularizing his work. Much encouraged, he devoted himself henceforth entirely to his brush. Among his best-known paintings are "Franklin before the Lords in Council" (1856); "Men of Progress" (1857), now in Cooper Institute, N. Y.; "Zeisberger Preaching to the Indians" (c. 1859), painted for the Moravian Society of Bethlehem; "King Solomon and the Iron Worker" (1860), painted for James Harrison, and "Washington at Valley Forge" (1862). Many of Schussele's works were further popularized through Sartain's engravings.

Schussele and his friend Schmolze, who decorated the ceiling of the Philadelphia Academy of Music, were among the first painters to bring to America talent trained in Paris art schools. Schussele was active in local art affairs, a member of the Philadelphia Sketch Club, and for several years president of the Artists' Fund Society. In 1863 he was attacked by scrivener's palsy in the right hand; he completed "Home on Furlough" and "McClellan at Antietam" during that year, but with difficulty. Two years later the disease had so progressed that he found painting painful and sought a cure in Europe. He visited his native place and at Paris underwent an unsuccessful operation. In 1868 he returned to Philadelphia, courageously facing his limitations. Nothing daunted by his physical handicap, he continued to paint, and was unanimously elected to fill the newly established chair of drawing and painting at the Pennsylvania Academy of the Fine Arts, a post which he held until his death. His physical condition made it impossible for him to execute many canvases, but he completed "Queen Esther Denouncing Haman to Ahasuerus" in 1869 and "The Alsatian Fair" in 1870. Despite the palsy that gradually affected his entire body, he continued his teaching almost to the end. He died in the country home of his son-in-law, John Crump, at Merchantville, N. J.

[Sources include: "Philadelphia Art Schools," editorial, in *Public Ledger* (Phila.), Aug. 20, 1879; obituary, *Ibid.,* Aug. 22, 1879; letter (1932) from Schussele's grandniece, Eva Clad; information from Harriet Sartain, Dean, School of Design for Women, Phila.; *Cat. of Loan Exhibition of Hist. Portraits, Pa. Acad. of the Fine Arts, Dec. 1, 1877 to Jan. 15, 1878* (1877); *Descriptive Cat. of the Permanent Colls. of Works of Art* (Pa. Acad. of the Fine Arts, 1897; 1902); *Am. Art Rev.,* Nov. 1879; Frank Weitenkampf, *Am. Graphic Art* (1912). Schussele's name is spelled variously in secondary accounts but according to Miss Harriet Sartain, whose family knew his intimately, he himself used the spelling here given.]   D. G—y.

SCHUTTLER, PETER (Dec. 22, 1812–Jan. 16, 1865), wagon maker, was born in the village of Wachenheim, Grand Duchy of Hesse Darmstadt, Germany. He came to the United States in 1834 and worked first in a wagon shop in Buffalo, N. Y., where he was paid seven dollars a month and his board, and then in Cleveland, Ohio. His inventive skill showed itself in a minor way in his use of a saw instead of an axe for cutting out wagon gearing. Having gathered together a little capital, he went into business for himself but he did not succeed, and after a year or two he moved to Sandusky, Ohio, where he worked at his own bench as a wagon maker for six years. There he married Dorothy Gauch, a native of Prussia, by whom he had three children, a son and a daughter born during the sojourn in Sandusky and another son born in Chicago. Through careful saving he had accumulated from three to four hundred dollars, and with his mind bent on opening a wagon shop he left in 1843 by boat for Chicago. He found no less than thirteen wagon shops already established in the city. Nevertheless, he went to work and made by hand the frames of several wagons, which were ironed on shares by P. W. Gates. He built his own shop and lived in a board shanty behind it. A brief interlude in the brewery business with his father-in-law was marked by failure and left him firmly decided to continue with the wagon business.

With the settlement of the western states, the demand for wagons increased. He hired a blacksmith and helper and ironed his own wagons; later he installed an eight horse-power engine, all work having previously been done by hand; in 1849, with the Gold Rush well under way, he built a new shop of brick, forty feet by seventy and four stories high, and began to manufacture buggies, carriages, and harness, as well as wagons. Though the shop burnt to the ground in 1850, it was immediately rebuilt and he returned to the manufacture of wagons alone. The Schuttler wagon helped to displace the old prairie schooner, prevailingly in use until 1850; it had a capacity of thirty-five hundred pounds and was very strongly made, though it was of comparatively light weight and easy running, and commanded a premium of fifty dollars over other makes. The Mormons were among Schuttler's best customers. During the Civil War he refused to modify the design of his wagon in order to secure army contracts. By 1856 he had forty men at work and was turning out a hundred and thirty-five wagons a week. Up to this time, he himself worked in the plant, directed the work of his men, kept the books, and made the sales. In 1855 he traveled with his elder son, Peter, to Germany and returned to build the finest mansion in Chicago. He died a rich man, leaving the wagon business to Peter. His wife and the three children all survived him. The name of the company remained in the list of Chicago firms for many years; in 1934 it appeared in the Chicago telephone directory as "Peter Schuttler Co., Wagons," but no wagons were manufactured after 1925.

[*Biog. Sketches of the Leading Men of Chicago* (1868); *Chicago and Its Makers* (1929), edited by Paul Gilbert and C. L. Bryson; *Chicago Tribune,* Jan. 17, 1865.]   E. A. D.

SCHUYLER, EUGENE (Feb. 26, 1840–July 16, 1890), diplomat, scholar, was born at Ithaca, N. Y., the son of George Washington Schuyler [*q.v.*] and Matilda (Scribner). Allied by blood or marriage with some of the first families of his state and the son of a man prominent in public affairs, he enjoyed every social, political, and cultural advantage. Graduating from Yale College in 1859, he remained there two years longer doing graduate work in languages and philosophy, and receiving the degree of Ph.D. in 1861. He then studied law at the Columbia Law School, from which he was graduated in 1863, was admitted to the bar, and began practice in New York.

His interest in language study, however, led him in 1865 to apply for a diplomatic post and on July 15, 1867, he was appointed consul at

Moscow, serving in this capacity until the latter part of 1869. During the next nine years he was successively consul at Revel, secretary of legation at Saint Petersburg, and secretary of legation and consul general at Constantinople. In the fall of 1876, while holding the last-named post, he published, before submitting it to the Department of State, a report on Turkish atrocities in Bulgaria which was widely circulated throughout Europe and, later, in America (in J. A. Mac-Gahan, *The Turkish Atrocities in Bulgaria,* London, 1876). It was said that "His report did more to influence England than any other document of the [Russo-Turkish] war" (Memorandum of Jan. 4, 1878, in Notes from Turkish Legation, Department of State), but it invited the criticism that he was subject to Russian influence. His cooperation with the Russian secretary of legation at Constantinople in drafting a plan for an autonomous Bulgaria did not improve his relations with the Porte (Department of State, Notes from Turkish Legation, memorandum of Jan. 4, 1878). The Turkish envoy at Washington protested unofficially in January 1877 and again a year later. Consequently, Schuyler was ordered to report at Washington and was in July 1878 appointed to Birmingham, where he remained only a few months before going to Rome as consul general. He had been married at Paris, in July 1877, to Gertrude Wallace King, daughter of Charles King [*q.v.*], a president of Columbia College.

In June 1880 he became the first American diplomatic representative to Rumania, then a principality, and in July 1882, minister resident and consul general to Greece, Rumania, and Serbia. When Rumania became a kingdom he was instructed to follow the lead of the European powers in recognizing the new government, with which instructions he complied on Apr. 6, 1881. He played a similar rôle in the recognition of the new Serbian government to which he was accredited. Empowered to negotiate treaties with Rumania and Serbia, he conducted negotiations to the satisfaction of the Department, and his commercial treaty with Rumania signed Apr. 11, 1881, and his commercial treaty and consular convention with Serbia, both signed Oct. 14, 1881, were duly ratified by the United States government. The Rumanian treaty, however, did not go into force. After two pleasurable years at Athens, the legation there being abolished in 1884, he returned to the United States to lecture at the Johns Hopkins and Cornell universities and to write. In 1886, however, he went back to Europe and settled at Alassio, where he remained until 1889.

In March of that year he accepted the offer of Secretary of State, Blaine to be assistant secretary of state, but the nomination was withdrawn because of opposition in the Senate committee on foreign relations. He accepted an appointment to Cairo a few weeks later, was taken ill at that post, and died in Italy. In an era of mediocrity in the American foreign service, Schuyler was an outstanding figure.

His literary work was considerable. He edited John A. Porter's *Selections from the Kalevala* (1868) and published *Fathers and Sons* (1867), a translation of Turgeniev's work, and *The Cossacks* (1878), from the Russian of Tolstoi. His *Turkistan: Notes of a Journey in Russian Turkistan, Khokand, Bukhara, and Kuldja* (2 vols., 1876) was critical of Russian administration in the East. His most extensive work was *Peter the Great* (2 vols., 1884), first published in *Scribner's Monthly,* and it was perhaps the frankness of his *American Diplomacy and the Furtherance of Commerce* (1886) which lost him the appointment as assistant secretary of state. He also wrote for the *North American Review, Scribner's Magazine, The Nation,* and other periodicals. From several foreign governments he received decorations.

[*Eugene Schuyler: Selected Essays, with a Memoir by Evelyn Schuyler Schaeffer* (1901); report on conditions in Bulgaria enclosed with dispatch No. 106, Nov. 21, 1876, from the Minister at Constantinople to the Secretary of State (MS., Dept. of State); *Papers Relating to the Foreign Relations of the U. S.,* 1881, 1883; letters, instructions, and dispatches in archives of Dept. of State; *Obit. Record Grads. Yale Univ., 1890–1900* (1900); G. W. Schuyler, *Colonial N. Y.* (2 vols., 1885); *N. Y. Tribune,* July 19, 1890.]　　E. W. S.

SCHUYLER, GEORGE WASHINGTON (Feb. 2, 1810–Feb. 1, 1888), state official, author, was born at Stillwater, N. Y., the son of John H. and Annatje (Fort) Schuyler and a descendant of Philip, a younger son of Philip Pieterse Schuyler, founder of the family in America. In 1811 his father left Saratoga County and purchased a farm several miles west of Ithaca, where George spent his boyhood. Having chosen the ministry for his life's work, he prepared for college and received the bachelor's degree from the University of the City of New York in 1837, but his theological studies, at Union Seminary, were interrupted by his decision to engage in business in order to "extricate a brother from difficulties" (*Colonial New York,* II, 377). He married, on Apr. 18, 1839, Matilda Scribner, daughter of Uriah and Martha Scribner of New York City, a half-sister of Charles Scribner [*q.v.*], and they established a home in Ithaca, where two sons and three daughters were born. Schuyler was highly successful in his mercantile and banking enterprises in Tompkins County. Always active in religious work, he transferred his membership in 1842 from the Presbyterian Church to the Reformed Dutch Church (later Congregational), which he served for many years either as deacon or elder.

In politics Schuyler was a Whig with pronounced anti-slavery sentiments which prompted him to follow William H. Seward into the Republican party. His first political recognition came from the Union Republican convention of 1863 which nominated him for state treasurer. Running on a ticket headed by Chauncey M. Depew [q.v.] as candidate for secretary of state, and pledged to support the Lincoln administration, he was elected and served two years. The convention of 1865 denied him a renomination, but Gov. Reuben E. Fenton [q.v.] appointed him superintendent of the banking department (1866–70) with full responsibility for the banking institutions operating under state charter. Incensed by the reconstruction policies and the political corruption of the Grant régime, Schuyler joined the "reformers" who organized the Liberal Republican movement in 1872. With the support of Democrats and Liberal Republicans he was elected to the state assembly, where he served (1875) as chairman of the committee on banking and participated in the framing of a general savings-bank law. He enthusiastically applauded Gov. Samuel J. Tilden [q.v.] for his exposure of the corrupt "canal ring," and in January 1876 the governor named him auditor of the Canal Department. Here he served until 1880, correcting many of the most notorious abuses and waging a vigorous campaign for the abolition of tolls and the creation of a system of free commercial waterways. He gave generously of his time to the work of Cornell University, serving for twenty years on the board of trustees and acting as treasurer, without compensation, from 1868 to 1874.

Schuyler's interest in the genealogy of his own family drew him into extensive researches in the colonial history of New York, and in 1885 he published Colonial New York: Philip Schuyler and His Family, in two volumes. Although the work was not a comprehensive history of the province, the sketches of the Schuylers were set against the background of seventeenth and eighteenth century New York, which had been carefully, at times brilliantly, reconstructed from manuscript and printed sources. Completed only three years before his death, these volumes stand today as their author's most enduring monument.

[There is a very brief autobiographical sketch in G. W. Schuyler, *Colonial New York* (1885), II, 377. See also D. S. Alexander, *A Pol. Hist. of the State of N. Y.*, vol. III (1909); *First Half-Century Book . . . of the First Church of Christ, Congregational, of Ithaca, N. Y.* (1881); *Cornell Era*, Feb. 4, 1888; *N. Y. Times*, Feb. 2, 1888.]   J. A. K—t.

SCHUYLER, JAMES DIX (May 11, 1848–Sept. 13, 1912), hydraulic and railroad engineer, was born at Ithaca, N. Y., the youngest of nine children of Philip Church and Lucy M. (Dix) Schuyler, and a descendant of Philip, younger brother of Peter Schuyler [q.v.]. His early education was received at Friends College, but for the most part his professional attainments and achievements were the result of his own constant study and reading and of his long and varied experience. He began his engineering career in 1869 as assistant on the location and construction of the Kansas Pacific Railway in Western Kansas and Colorado, and thereafter the West became his home. For six years he continued in railroad work, serving the Denver & Rio Grande Railroad, the North Pacific Coast Railroad in California, and the Stockton & Ione Railroad, of which he was chief engineer.

In 1877 he was made chief assistant state engineer of California and placed in charge of irrigation investigations in Great Central Valley. Resigning this position in 1882, he became chief engineer and general superintendent of the Sinaloa & Durango Railroad in Mexico. Returning to California, he undertook contract work in San Francisco. He built a section of the sea wall on the water front of the city (1884–85); raised the Sweetwater dam (1887–88); and constructed the Hemet dam, at that time the highest masonry dam in western America. In these and other enterprises he showed such skill and ability that thereafter he was a prominent figure in his profession and enjoyed a wide and successful business as consultant, his field of activity including Mexico, British Columbia, Japan, Brazil, and Hawaii. Among the projects with which he was connected were water supply systems for Denver; Ogden, Utah; and Los Angeles. As one of three consulting engineers appointed to report on plans for the Los Angeles aqueduct, fed by the Owens River some 250 miles distant, he made suggestions that ultimately resulted in the avoidance of twenty-five miles of heavy construction, and a saving of several million dollars. He was one of the commission of consulting engineers appointed by President Theodore Roosevelt in 1909 to judge the feasibility of the Gatun Dam and the other structures for the Panama Canal. His paper upon "Recent Practice in Hydraulic-Fill Dam Construction," presented in 1907 before the American Society of Civil Engineers (*Transactions*, LVIII, 1907), received the Thomas Fitch Rowland Prize for the best paper of the year and did much to stimulate the use of this important method of earth dam construction. It is noteworthy that he was twice winner of this prize, his first success having occurred in 1889, when he presented a paper on "The Construction of the Sweetwater Dam" (*Ibid.*, XIX, 1888). He contributed extensively to technical and scientific journals, but his best-known work is his book entitled *Reservoirs for Irrigation, Water-Power, and Domestic Water Supply,* published in 1901, with a second edition in 1908.

Schuyler's most notable work was in connection with dam designing and construction and especially in the development of the use of hydraulic fill dams, in which field he was a pioneer and leading authority. He was a prominent member of the American Society of Civil Engineers, serving as vice-president and director. In July 1889 he was married to Mrs. Mary Ingalls Tuliper of San Diego, Cal., who survived him. He died at Ocean Park, Cal.

[*Engineering News,* Apr. 17, 1913; *Trans. Am. Soc. Civil Engineers,* vol. LXXVI (1913); *Press Reference Lib.: Notables of the Southwest* (1912); *Who's Who in America,* 1912–13.]

H. K. B.

SCHUYLER, LOUISA LEE (Oct. 26, 1837–Oct. 10, 1926), leader in welfare work, was a daughter of George Lee and Eliza (Hamilton) Schuyler of New York, and a great-granddaughter of Gen. Philip John Schuyler and of Alexander Hamilton [*qq.v.*]. Her father, a grandson of General Schuyler, married a cousin who was a grand-daughter of Hamilton and his wife, Elizabeth Schuyler, thus continuing the union of two families distinguished in Revolutionary history. Louisa, her younger sister Georgina, and her brother Philip were reared in a home of unpretentious wealth, described sixty years later in J. H. Choate's autobiography, *The Boyhood and Youth of Joseph Hodges Choate* (1917). The sisters passed many of their girlhood days at the country seat of their grandfather, James Alexander Hamilton [*q.v.*], near Dobbs Ferry, twenty miles up the Hudson. One of the earliest indications of Louisa Schuyler's interest in what has since become known generally as "welfare" work was her appearance at twenty-three as a volunteer teacher for the Children's Aid Society. Within a year the outbreak of the Civil War opened to her, as to thousands of other young Americans, new channels of service and grave responsibilities. She was active from the first in the women's war-relief work organized by Dr. Henry Whitney Bellows [*q.v.*] out of which grew the United States Sanitary Commission, the organization that anticipated

the Red Cross of a later date. In the four years of war she developed marked executive ability and organized information as well as express services but spent her strength so prodigally that almost seven years of rest, largely passed in Europe and Egypt, were required to achieve recuperation.

On her return to New York in 1871 with improved health, she became interested in the care and treatment of dependents committed to poorhouses and other local institutions. A project of her own, the State Charities Aid Association, was formed in 1872 at her father's house with the purpose of promoting visitation and inspection of public institutions by private citizens. In the beginning she had little help but in the course of time the association became an important factor in reforming abuses and in rallying the friends of constructive welfare effort, and similar societies were founded in other states. Within two years, impelled by conditions revealed to the State Charities visitors at Bellevue Hospital in New York City, she appealed successfully for the opening of a nurses' training school at Bellevue, the first in America. In their investigations the association's visitors found nothing more impressive than the plight of dependent insane confined in county poorhouses. The wrongs endured by these unfortunates had been eloquently set forth by Dorothea Lynde Dix [*q.v.*], and some of the extreme abuses had been abolished, but scientific methods of care and treatment could not be had in the average local almshouse of the time. Consequently, Miss Schuyler led a campaign for state care of the insane; in 1890, after many rebuffs, she was at last completely successful and all insane inmates of county poorhouses were by law transferred to commodious, well-administered state hospitals. As a trustee of the Russell Sage Foundation from its formation she became especially interested in work for the prevention of blindness. She was president of the foundation's committee out of which grew in 1915 the National Committee (later Society) for the Prevention of Blindness, an agency which has been the means of recovering vision for countless thousands of American children. The woman whose associates declared that she had "the mind of a lawyer and the will-power of a captain of industry," succeeded as completely in this as in her other humanitarian efforts. Illness overtook her old age, and even while she was engrossed in the task of preserving to others the priceless gift of vision she was herself deprived of its enjoyment. At almost eighty-nine she rounded out a lifetime of distinctively fruitful service.

[See G. W. Schuyler, *Colonial New York: Philip Schuyler and His Family* (2 vols., 1885); L. P. Brockett and Mary C. Vaughan, *Woman's Work in the Civil War* (1867); F. G. Peabody, *Reminiscences of Present-Day Saints* (1927); *Louisa Lee Schuyler, 1837–1926* (n.d.), published by Nat. Committee for the Prevention of Blindness; scattered references in W. R. Stewart, *The Philanthropic Work of Josephine Shaw Lowell* (1911); obituary and editorial, *N. Y. Times,* Oct. 11, 1926. For the story of the renovation of Bellevue Hospital, see Elizabeth C. Hobson, *Recollections of a Happy Life* (1916).]   W. B. S.

SCHUYLER, MARGARITA (1701–August 1782), colonial hostess, was the daughter of Johannes (1668–1747) and Elizabeth (Staats) Schuyler and was baptized Jan. 12, 1701. Her father, the youngest son of Philip Pieterse Schuyler, founder of the family in America, had participated in two expeditions against the French, had been a trusted emissary of Governor Bellomont in his diplomatic contest with the French authorities (1697–1701), and had labored to hold the Iroquois faithful to the English alliance despite French intrigues. As mayor of Albany (1703–06) and member of the board of commissioners of Indian affairs, he realized that New York's evolving policy of neutrality, dictated by the Albany merchants, placed an additional burden of frontier defense on New England, and he strove to assist the New England villages in warding off raids from disaffected eastern tribes. Thus Margarita's childhood was filled with the talk of her elders concerning military expeditions, Indian raids, conferences with the Mohawks and the Onondagas, and strife with the French Canadians. Her knowledge of such subjects was greatly enlarged as a result of her marriage, Dec. 29, 1720, to her cousin, Philip, son of Col. Peter Schuyler [*q.v.*].

The young couple established their home in a large brick house at "The Flatts," on the Hudson just north of Albany. The household routine moved so smoothly under Margarita's expert guidance that she had ample time to make her home the social center of the northern frontier. The Schuylers entertained not only the provincial aristocracy but also British officers and a host of merchants and officials interested in the fur-trade and in Indian relations. Mrs. Schuyler was as well informed as her husband, and many an English official was indebted to her for valuable advice on the traits of neighboring Indian tribes, the difficulties of transportation and the current state of relations with the French. Even after her husband's death in 1758, she continued to make "The Flatts" a sort of military and political headquarters. Having no children of her own, she found pleasure in adopting and educating many of her nephews and nieces and for half a century there was always some rep-

resentative of the younger generation of Schuylers under her tutelage. By these beneficiaries of her generous affection she was greatly beloved. After 1765 she leased a house in Albany where she continued to hold court, but by this time the grace and beauty of her youth were gone. Her guests saw an excessively large woman who "filled a great chair from which she seldom moved. Her aspect was composed, and her manner such as was, at first, more calculated to inspire respect, than conciliate affection" (*Memoirs of an American Lady,* II, 145). Her last years were darkened by the shadows of the American Revolution, for she remained a firm and respected Loyalist to the end. In her will, however, which divided her considerable estate among ten nephews and nieces, she did not discriminate against those members of her family who had supported the colonial cause. She died at Albany in August 1782.

[A. M. Grant, *Memoirs of an American Lady* (2 vols., London, 1808), repr. in 1876 with notes by Joel Munsell, corrected in G. W. Schuyler, *Colonial N. Y.* (2 vols., 1885) and K. S. Baxter, *A Godchild of Washington* (1897); Peter Wraxall, *An Abridgement of the Indian Affairs . . . in the Colony of N. Y.* (1915), ed. by C. H. McIlwaine; E. B. O'Callaghan, *Docs. Rel. to the Col. Hist. of the State of N. Y.,* vols. IV (1854), V, IX (1855).]   J. A. K—t.

SCHUYLER, MONTGOMERY (Aug. 19, 1843–July 16, 1914), journalist, author, was born in Ithaca, N. Y., the son of the Rev. Anthony and Eleanor (Johnson) Schuyler. He was a descendant of Arent Schuyler, fourth son of Philip Pieterse Schuyler, American founder of the family, who came from Holland in 1650, settling at Beverwyck (Albany). Montgomery Schuyler entered Hobart College in 1858, but left without graduating. In 1865 he went to New York City and was soon a member of the brilliant group of young writers gathered about Manton Marble [*q.v.*], then editor of the *World.* He remained on the staff of the *World* until 1883 and then went to the *New York Times,* where he continued until his retirement from active journalism in 1907. Meanwhile, he had been managing editor of *Harper's Weekly* (1885–87) and reader for Harper & Brothers (1887–94). After 1912 he regularly contributed book reviews and articles on literary subjects to the New York *Sun.*

An omnivorous reader and student, Schuyler was able not only to give his editorial and feature writing both dignity and literary grace, but also to illuminate it with an inexhaustible supply of apt quotation and allusion. One series of sketches done for the *Times,* descriptive of an Easterner's impression of the West as seen on the first trip of the "Los Angeles Limited," was enlarged and published in book form as *West-*

ward the Course of Empire (1906). Schuyler also wrote much for the magazines, largely on literature and architecture. Although not a trained architect, he became, after the death of Russell Sturgis [*q.v.*], probably the foremost critic and historian of American architecture. With W. C. Conant, he published *The Brooklyn Bridge* (1883), some of his architectural essays appeared as *American Architecture: Studies* (1892), and a slender volume on *The Woolworth Building* was privately printed in 1913; but most of the material is scattered through the files of periodicals, in particular the *Architectural Record,* of which he was one of the founders (1891). He threw his influence on the side of the Gothic as against the classic tradition; later, he was interested in the skyscraper as an expression of modern American culture.

In the days when the Century Club was a focal center of social and intellectual life in New York, Schuyler was one of the wittiest conversationalists at the Saturday night reunions, where he counted among his intimate friends Homer Martin, John La Farge, Henry Holt, William C. Brownell, F. Hopkinson Smith, and Austin Flint [*qq.v.*]. On his retirement from the *Times* in 1907, he went to live at New Rochelle, where both he and his wife took an active interest in every plan for civic improvement. He had been married, on Sept. 16, 1876, to Katherine Beeckman Livingston, daughter of Robert Dwight and Mary (Armour) Livingston, of New York City, thus becoming allied with two other famous old New York families, the Beeckmans and the Livingstons. His wife was a woman of wit, energy, and talent, who is said to have given up an operatic career to marry him. When she died the shock of the loss seems to have hastened her husband's death, which took place at New Rochelle scarcely more than a week later. They were survived by two sons; a third son died in infancy.

[*Who's Who in America,* 1914–15; *N. Y. Times,* July 8, 17, 1914; *N. Y. Tribune,* July 8, 17, 1914; *Sun* (N. Y.), July 17, 1914; E. R. Smith, "Montgomery Schuyler and the History of American Architecture" (with a bibliog. listing fifty-eight books and articles by Schuyler on architecture), *Architectural Record,* Sept. 1914; G. W. Schuyler, *Colonial N. Y.: Philip Schuyler and His Family* (1885), vol. II; personal recollections of Schuyler's son, Robert Livingston Schuyler.] E. M. S.

SCHUYLER, PETER (Sept. 17, 1657–Feb. 19, 1724), soldier and official of colonial New York, was born at Albany (then Beverwyck), the second son of Philip Pieterse Schuyler, an emigrant from Amsterdam, and his wife, Margarita (Van Slichtenhorst), daughter of the resident director of Rensselaerwyck. Philip Pieterse, whose name first appears in the Albany records on the occasion of his marriage in 1650, was engaged in trade and held the offices of magistrate and captain under both Dutch and English governments. Peter Schuyler may have attended a school founded at Albany in 1650, but his education was derived chiefly from early and prolonged application to public affairs in periods of incessant border warfare. At twenty-seven he was a lieutenant of cavalry in the Albany militia, later he was advanced to the rank of colonel, and when in 1686 Albany received its charter from Gov. Thomas Dongan [*q.v.*], Schuyler became its first mayor, and thus head of the board of Indian commissioners.

Three years later, Jacob Leisler [*q.v.*], who had seized control of New York, ordered the election of new aldermen and a new mayor of Albany, but the citizens refused to recognize his authority and Schuyler continued in office. After the massacre at Schenectady and the destruction of that town by French and Indians, Feb. 9, 1690, he wrote to the governor of Massachusetts appealing for help and asking coöperation in a spring campaign against the French, expressing the conviction that only the conquest of New France would arrest the scourge from which the newer settlements were suffering. In the face of danger and upon the advice of Massachusetts and Connecticut, the men of Albany in March yielded to Leisler's demands, but his commissioners promptly reinstated Schuyler and the other officers. In the following summer Schuyler took part in the unsuccessful coöperative campaign led by Fitz-John Winthrop of Connecticut against Quebec. In October, he was removed as mayor of Albany by order of Leisler, but after the arrival of Governor Sloughter in March 1691 and Leisler's imprisonment Schuyler resumed his duties as if they had never been interrupted.

Schuyler seemed to hold himself responsible for the safety of the pioneer front and always maintained a remarkable influence over the New York Iroquois (by whom he was affectionately called Quidor—their version of Peter), attending numerous conferences with them and visiting their villages to curb the operations of Canadian emissaries as well as to cement the old treaty between the Five Nations and the colony. In 1691 he led a company to Canada, proving in several engagements his superior soldierly qualities, and two years later he routed a party of French near Schenectady. Governor Sloughter made him a judge of common pleas in 1691 and recommended him for the council, and in March 1692, under Governor Fletcher, he was appointed.

Having enjoyed the favor of Fletcher, Schuyler could not win the graces of his successor, Richard Coote [*q.v.*], Earl of Bellomont, who adopted all the quarrels of the preceding ten years in the colony and was jealous, furthermore, of Schuyler's influence in Indian affairs. Nevertheless, in 1698 Bellomont sent him to Frontenac to announce the terms of the Treaty of Ryswick and provide for the return of prisoners of war, and employed him in provisioning the troops. In preparing for the abortive expeditions of 1709 and 1711 against Canada, Schuyler displayed characteristic energy. Between those undertakings he visited the court of Queen Anne, taking with him several Mohawk chiefs, including the famous Hendrick [*q.v.*]. On this occasion, it is said, he declined the dignity of knighthood (G. W. Schuyler, *post*, II, 37; for a disparaging view see E. B. O'Callaghan, *The Documentary History of the State of New York*, 4th ed., vol. III, 1850, pp. 541–42). Schuyler commanded the esteem of Gov. Robert Hunter [*q.v.*]; and, on Hunter's return to England, Schuyler as president of the council was acting governor from July 13, 1719, to Sept. 17, 1720. Some of his appointments alarmed Hunter as indications of a policy of change, and the new governor, William Burnet [*q.v.*], fearing Schuyler as a dangerous leader of opposition, brought about his removal from the council, after nearly fifty years of public service.

Schuyler was married twice: in 1681 or 1682 to Engeltie Van Schaick, by whom he had four children, three of whom died young, and in 1691 to Maria Van Rensselaer, daughter of Jeremiah Van Rensselaer, who also became the mother of four. Margarita, daughter of his first wife, married the nephew of the first Robert Livingston [*q.v.*]; Philip, one of three sons of the second wife, married his cousin Margarita Schuyler [*q.v.*]. Peter Schuyler owned numerous land grants, of which the most extensive was in the Saratoga patent.

[E. B. O'Callaghan, *Docs. Rel. to the Col. Hist. of the State of N. Y.*, vols. III–VII (1853–56), vol. IX (1855); *Calendar of N. Y. Colonial MSS. Indorsed Land Papers* (1864); *Calendar of Council Minutes, 1668–1783* (1902), being *N. Y. State Lib. Bull. 58*: G. W. Schuyler, *Colonial New York* (2 vols., 1885); Wm. Smith, *The Hist. of the Late Province of N. Y.* (1830), vol. I; Peter Wraxall, *An Abridgement of the Indian Affairs . . . in the Colony of N. Y.* (1915), ed. by C. H. McIlwain; H. L. Osgood, *The Am. Colonies in the Eighteenth Century*, vols. I, II (1924).]

R. E. D.

SCHUYLER, PHILIP JOHN (Nov. 11, 1733–Nov. 18, 1804), soldier and statesman, eldest son of Johannes and Cornelia (Van Cortlandt) Schuyler, belonged to the fourth generation of the family which was established in America by Philip Pieterse and Margarita (Van Slichtenhorst) Schuyler. Born at Albany, N. Y., where his father—merchant, alderman and Indian commissioner—died in 1741, Philip was reared in the Dutch tradition by his mother and his aunt, Margarita Schuyler [*q.v.*]. At the age of fifteen he was sent to New Rochelle to complete his formal education under Rev. Peter Stouppe, zealous and eccentric pastor of the French Protestant Church. There he learned to speak French and became so proficient in mathematics that in later years he delighted to solve surveying and engineering problems and to correspond with David Rittenhouse [*q.v.*] on the mathematics of astronomy. The two years at New Rochelle were marred by attacks of rheumatic gout, a hereditary malady which he had occasion to dread throughout his entire life. His study of books was soon supplemented by practical experience drawn from commercial and social contacts. In Albany he moved easily in the circles of the Dutch aristocracy. On his visits to New York he was welcomed by the De Lanceys and the Livingstons, talked politics with William Smith the younger and John Morin Scott [*qq.v.*], attended gay balls and receptions, and enjoyed the acting of the Hallams at the Nassau Street Theatre. However carefree he may have seemed to his associates, he was a purposeful and ambitious young man when he came of age in 1754 and waived his right of primogeniture that his sister and two brothers might share in their father's estate.

He played a minor but not unimportant rôle in the last phase of the struggle between Great Britain and France for North America. In 1755 Gov. James De Lancey [*q.v.*] commissioned him to raise and command a company in Gen. William Johnson's expedition against Crown Point. He participated in the skirmish at Lake George on Sept. 8, 1755, was designated to escort the French prisoners to Albany, took advantage of the brief furlough to marry, Sept. 17, Catherine, talented daughter of John Van Rensselaer of Claverack, and within a few weeks was back at Fort Edward, striving to create a depot of military stores. In the spring of 1756 he was a member of the force under Col. John Bradstreet [*q.v.*] which carried provisions to Oswego and cleared the Oneida portage of enemy raiders, and he became a devoted friend of his superior officer. The following year he resigned his commission, but continued to be interested in the provisioning of the armies, from which he derived a substantial income. He returned to the service in 1758 as a deputy commissary with the rank of major, served under Lord Howe [q.v.] in Abercromby's ill-fated expedition against Ticonderoga, and was with Bradstreet at the capture of Fort Frontenac on Lake Ontario. During the campaigns of 1759–60 he was stationed at Albany, where he collected and forwarded provisions to Amherst's forces. It was valuable experience, for it taught the future general how essential to the success of any army is an efficient service of supply.

In February 1761, Schuyler sailed for England to settle with the War Office the accounts of his friend, Colonel Bradstreet. While there he studied reports of British imports, hoping that his own estates might in the future supply some of the mother country's needs. He was particularly interested in new means of transportation and concluded that English canals could be duplicated in America. He returned to his native province eager for the life of a country gentleman. The final settlement in 1763 of his father's estate, which included one-third of his grandfather's lands, brought him thousands of acres in the Mohawk Valley and along the Hudson, while from his uncle Philip's estate he received additional land in the Saratoga patent and the old Schuyler homestead near West Troy. Saratoga was the favored portion of his heritage. There he cut choice timber from forests of pine and hard woods, developed water-power for his sawmills and gristmills, built the first water-driven flaxmill in the province, maintained a fleet of one schooner and three sloops on the Hudson, and started the products of his plantations and mills on trade routes which terminated in the West Indies or Great Britain. Elected to the Assembly in 1768, he was frankly hostile to ministerial or parliamentary interference with provincial commerce and industry. Although he constantly fought the De Lancey-Colden coalition of royalists, he never sympathized with the radicals among the "Sons of Liberty" or condoned mob violence. Nevertheless, Lieutenant-governor Cadwallader Colden [q.v.] regarded him as a great trouble maker and wrote in 1775 that Schuyler "wish'd to bring this Colony into all the dangerous & extravagant Schemes which Disgrace too many of the Sister Colonies" ("Colden Letter Books," post, II, 399).

Schuyler heartily approved the acts of the First Continental Congress, attended the convention (Apr. 20, 1775) which named New York's delegates to the Second Continental Congress, and accepted membership in the provincial delegation. On June 15 he was appointed one of the four major-generals under Washing-

ton and assigned to command the Northern Department, consisting of New York, in order "to sweeten and to keep up the spirit of that province" (Burnett, post, I, 137). With the half-hearted support of New England he recruited and provisioned an army, strengthened the garrisons at Ticonderoga and Crown Point, enlarged Fort Stanwix, checked the intrigues of Sir John Johnson [q.v.] with restless leaders of the Six Nations, and organized the expedition of 1775–76 against Canada. Ill health compelled him to turn over immediate command of the Canadian forces to Gen. Richard Montgomery [q.v.]. Although his skilful handling of the commissariat was an important factor in Montgomery's success at Montreal, the ultimate failure of the Canadian offensive discredited Schuyler with the New Englanders, many of whom disliked him as a severe disciplinarian and resented his support of New York's claims to the "New Hampshire Grants" (later Vermont).

This mutual antagonism between "Yorker and Yankee," aggravated in 1776 by Schuyler's quarrel with Gen. David Wooster [q.v.] and his controversy with Gen. Horatio Gates [q.v.], partly explains his serious difficulties during the Burgoyne campaign. In March 1777 he was reprimanded by Congress on a flimsy pretext put forward by the New Englanders, and Gates was given an independent command in the Northern Department. Two months later the legislators reversed themselves and recalled Gates (Journals of the Continental Congress, V, 526, VII, 180, 202, 364; Burnett II, 3, 11, 48). Returning to his post, Schuyler found an army "weak in numbers, dispirited, naked, in a manner, destitute of provisions . . . with little ammunition, and not a single piece of cannon" (Jared Sparks, Correspondence of the American Revolution, 1853, I, 394). He was not dismayed, however, and with the exception of his indecision concerning the defense of Ticonderoga, which was terminated by St. Clair's abandonment of the fort, July 6, 1777, he played a difficult game well. His retreat was cleverly designed to impede the British advance and to permit new levies of militia to harass Burgoyne, while his dispatch of Gen. Benedict Arnold [q.v.] to relieve Fort Stanwix wrecked St. Leger's plans. Schuyler did not reap the fruits of his labors, however, for Congress, alarmed by the loss of Ticonderoga, ordered Gates to supersede him, Aug. 4, 1777 (Journals, VIII, 604). There were ugly rumors that the New York general had been both incompetent and disloyal. That Schuyler ever responded to British efforts to win him over is doubtful, but data recently discovered in the

British headquarters papers in the William L. Clements Library may ultimately throw new light on the whole question.

At Schuyler's insistence, and after months of wrangling, Congress preferred charges of incompetence against him. He was acquitted with honor by a court martial in October 1778, and the following spring his resignation from the service was accepted. He remained, however, on the Board of Commissioners for Indian Affairs, advising Washington concerning the Sullivan-Clinton expedition against the Six Nations in 1779 and using his influence in Congress to emphasize the Indian menace along the New York frontier. He participated in the congressional sessions of November-December 1779 and February-April 1780, devoting himself to a report on depreciated currency and the issuance of new bills of credit, which Congress adopted with slight modification (*Journals*, Mar. 13–18, 1780; Burnett, V, 66–67, 71). From Apr. 13 to Aug. 11, 1780, he served as chairman of the committee at Headquarters authorized to assist Washington in reorganizing the staff departments of the army and in devising a scheme of effective cooperation with the French forces.

Schuyler held public office continuously from 1780 to 1798. In the state Senate, which he entered in September 1780, he advocated greater governmental power for both state and nation. He complained that New York had not treated its creditors fairly, suggested the funding of the state debt, urged the legislature to surrender all western land claims to the federal government, and insisted that the states confer upon congressional control of interstate and foreign commerce. His position on the Council of Appointment enabled him to rally the Federalists against the "junto" of George Clinton [q.v.], whose principles were "a state impost, no direct taxation, keep all power in the hands of the legislature, give none to Congress" (H. C. Van Schaack, *Memoirs of the Life of Henry Van Schaack*, 1892, p. 151). Like most of the great landlords in New York, Schuyler supported the movement which culminated in the Philadelphia Convention of 1787. Intimately associated with the career of his son-in-law, Alexander Hamilton [q.v.], he counseled the Federalists in their successful campaign to secure ratification of the Constitution by the Poughkeepsie convention. With Rufus King [q.v.] he represented New York in the first Senate of the United States, and became an aggressive champion of Hamilton's financial program. His holdings of government securities in 1791 probably exceeded $60,000, and Senator William Maclay [q.v.] noted that opposition to the funding of the national debt caused Schuyler's hair to stand "on end as if the Indians had fired at him" (*The Journal of William Maclay*, 1927, p. 228). After the short term he was defeated for reëlection in 1791 by Aaron Burr [q.v.]; his own victory over Burr six years later was an empty honor, for ill health sent him into permanent retirement in January 1798.

From his various estates—in the Saratoga patent, at Cortlandt Manor, along the Mohawk, and in Dutchess County—he received large revenues. If his Saratoga lands may be regarded as typical, he usually rented farms for cash, two pounds per hundred acres annually, on the basis of a twenty-one year lease (Ledger of Rents at Saratoga, 1760–1805, New York Public Library). Although he scorned the unscrupulous land speculator, his own real-estate deals were considerable. Always a stalwart champion of the aristocratic landlords, he also joined the financiers who were becoming interested in banking, manufacturing, and transportation. His own investments included state and federal securities, stock in the Bank of the United States and the Bank of Albany, and shares in the Northern Inland Lock Navigation Company, and the Western Inland Lock Navigation Company. The last two ventures were incorporated under an act of 1792 which he guided through the state legislature. He regarded them as forerunners of a comprehensive canal policy in which he could render service to the state. In the same spirit of benefaction, while a member of the Board of Regents, he promoted a plan for the establishment of Union College at Schenectady and subscribed one hundred pounds toward its endowment.

Physically, Schuyler was a powerful man: tall, erect, and of commanding presence. His portrait by John Trumbull shows a strong countenance dominated by piercing eyes. He was always fashionably dressed, and his conduct seems to have been as conventionally correct as his clothes. His austere manner impressed many as arrogance and added to the list of his enemies, but those who knew him well were his devoted friends and fully appreciated his great service to the American cause in the dark days before Saratoga. Despite his long record in public office, he was seldom happy away from his family, which included three sons and five daughters who survived infancy. The loss of his wife in 1803 hastened his own death a year later. He was buried in the Albany Rural Cemetery, where a tall granite shaft now marks his grave.

[Schuyler Papers in the N. Y. Pub. Lib.; letters in N. Y. State Lib. and Lib. of Cong.; Gates Papers and James Duane Papers in N. Y. Hist. Soc.; B. J. Lossing, *The Life and Times of Philip Schuyler* (2 vols., 1860–73); Bayard Tuckerman, *Life of Gen. Philip Schuyler* (1903); G. W. Schuyler, *Colonial N. Y.* (2 vols., 1885); E. C. Burnett, *Letters of Members of the Continental Cong.* (vols. I–VII, 1921–34); Peter Force, *Am. Archives* (9 vols., 1837–53); *Journals of the Continental Cong.* (1904–); H. P. Johnston, *The Correspondence and Public Papers of John Jay* (4 vols., 1890–93); "The Colden Letter Books," vol. II, being *N. Y. Hist. Soc. Colls.*, vol. X (1878); *Proc. of a Gen. Court Martial .. for the Trial of Maj. Gen. Schuyler, Oct. 1, 1778* (1778); *Public Papers of George Clinton* (10 vols., 1899–1914); E. W. Spaulding, *N. Y. in the Critical Period* (1932).]   J. A. K—t.

SCHWAB, JOHN CHRISTOPHER (Apr. 1, 1865–Jan. 12, 1916), economist and librarian, was born in New York City, the son of Gustav Schwab, a merchant, head of Oelrichs & Company, and Eliza Catherine (von Post) Schwab. On both sides he was descended from German stock; on his mother's, from Henry Melchior Mühlenberg [*q.v.*]. After preparation in private schools he attended Yale College, from which he was graduated with the degree of A.B. in 1886, and continued there as a graduate student for a year, working under William Graham Sumner and Arthur Twining Hadley [*qq.v.*]. He then spent a year in Berlin and a year in Göttingen, studying economics and finance, and received the degree of Ph.D. from the latter institution in 1889. After a year devoted to research in New York, he was made lecturer in political economy at Yale and remained in that institution until his death, being appointed professor of political economy in 1898. His special interest was in public finance. His doctoral thesis, published in German at Göttingen in 1889 and at Jena in 1890, appeared in expanded form under the title *History of the New York Property Tax* (1890) as a publication of the American Economic Association. His most important publication was *The Confederate States of America, 1861–1865: a Financial and Industrial History of the South During the Civil War* (1901). He aimed to base this work on all accessible material, published and unpublished; he examined the archives of the Confederacy and of the Southern states for documents, and utilized files of newspapers of a number of different cities. Thoroughly prepared to interpret the facts he had collected and scrupulously fair in his judgments, he made an important contribution both to national history and to the knowledge of economic behavior under conditions of disordered finance and currency.

Beyond the ordinary services of a professor he was a leader in the reform of the college curriculum by the introduction of new subjects and greater freedom of choice, and showed his practical ability by planning and organizing the elaborate ceremonies, extending over several days and prepared for more than a year in advance, which marked the bicentennial celebration of the college. In recognition of the unusual combination in him of executive ability and scholarship, he was appointed librarian of Yale University, July 1, 1905. Most of his predecessors, distinguished scholars who showed rare judgment in enriching the collection, had not been especially interested in systematizing it and in facilitating its use. Following a much more liberal policy, Schwab extended the hours of use, opened the stacks to qualified students, and devised more effective arrangements for the purchase and distribution of books. In the eleven years during which he served as librarian, the total number of books was greatly increased. He married, Oct. 5, 1893, Edith Aurelia Fisher, daughter of Samuel Sparks Fisher of Cincinnati, by whom he had two children, a daughter and a son. He died in New Haven.

[*Who's Who in America*, 1914–15; Lucy S. White, *Fort Number Eight: The Home of Gustav and Eliza Schwab* (1925); *Obit. Record Grads. Yale Univ.* (1916); *Reports of Librarian of Yale Univ.*, 1905–15; *Yale Alumni Weekly*, Jan. 21, 1916; obituary in *New Haven Evening Reg.*, Jan. 12, 1916; personal acquaintance.]   C. D.

SCHWARZ, EUGENE AMANDUS (Apr. 21, 1844–Oct. 15, 1928), entomologist, was born in Liegnitz, Silesia, the son of Luise (Harnwolf) and Amandus Schwarz, cloth merchant and member of the Common Council of Liegnitz. As a boy, he became acquainted with the elder Gerhardt, a highly skilled entomologist, who taught him the fundamentals of entomology and of the natural sciences. After gymnasium days, he was sent by his parents to the University of Breslau. His main studies were supposed to be philological, but he retained a strong interest in entomology. His first entomological publication appeared in 1869. In 1870 he was with the German army before Paris, in the distributing hospital of the medical corps. After the Franco-Prussian War he returned to the University of Breslau, and in 1872 was a student at the University of Leipzig. During these years he devoted almost his entire attention to entomological studies; finally, fearing to tell his parents that he had neglected to prepare himself for the career they had planned for him, he left Europe without notifying his family and arrived in the United States in December 1872. Bringing with him a letter of recommendation from a famous German entomologist, he was employed by Dr. Hermann August Hagen [*q.v.*] in the Museum of Comparative Zoology at Cambridge. At Cambridge he met Henry Guernsey Hubbard, and the acquaintance ripened into a lifelong friendship. When Hubbard graduated from Harvard, Schwarz went with him to Detroit, Mich., where they founded the Detroit Scientific Association and began the building up of collections. During the winter of 1874–75 they went to Florida together and began a study of the entomological fauna there; in the following year Schwarz repeated the journey. In the summer of 1877 he went with Hubbard on an expedition to the Lake Superior region, where they made a collection of an enormous number of beetles, the basis of their study entitled *The Coleoptera of Michigan* (1879). In 1878 Schwarz went to Colorado to collect *Coleoptera* for John Lawrence LeConte [*q.v.*], but the season had hardly started when he was offered a position in the Department of Agriculture by Charles Valentine Riley [*q.v.*]. This he accepted and spent the following winter investigating the cotton worm from Texas to the Bahamas.

For more than fifty years he remained in the service of the United States government, holding a position with the Bureau of Entomology after March 1881. He was considered to be the most learned coleopterist in America, possibly the most learned in the world. He was, in addition, a general entomologist, whose knowledge of the literature of entomology was stupendous, and one of the best field men in the government service. He was connected with many important investigations, many of which he conducted, and he was the guide and mentor of the younger men who joined the force. In 1898 he was made custodian of the *Coleoptera* in the United States National Museum, and toward the close of his active life in August 1926, when he retired, he was almost completely immersed in museum work. He shunned publicity and would not allow the editors of *Who's Who in America* or of the *American Men of Science* to mention his name. His published bibliography contains almost four hundred titles, mainly relating to *Coleoptera,* but a large field of biological observation. He was one of the founders of the Entomological Society of Washington and in 1916 was made its honorary president for life. He never married.

[*Proc. Entomological Soc. of Washington,* vol. XXX (1928), with portrait, bibliog., and map of Schwarz's expeditions; *Annals Entomological Soc. of America,* Mar. 1929; *Entomological News,* Jan. 1929; *Science,* Nov. 9, 1928; *Evening Star* (Washington, D. C.), Oct. 16, 1928.]   L. O. H.

SCHWATKA, FREDERICK (Sept. 29, 1849–Nov. 2, 1892), explorer, was born at Ga-

lena, Ill., the son of Frederick Schwatka. At the age of ten he was taken by his family to Salem, Ore., where he worked as a printer and attended Willamette University. In 1867 he received an appointment to West Point, from which he graduated in June 1871. Commissioned as second lieutenant in the 3rd Cavalry, he served at various army posts throughout the United States and at the same time studied both medicine and law. He was admitted to the Nebraska bar in 1875 and the following year received a medical degree from the Bellevue Hospital Medical College in New York City.   ,

But it was neither as a lawyer nor as a doctor that he established his reputation. He became interested in exploration, and his adventurous imagination was seized by reports brought from the Arctic regions by Capt. Thomas F. Barry concerning the fate of the famous expedition of Sir John Franklin (see *Dictionary of National Biography*). For thirty years following the loss of this expedition British and American explorers had sought the bodies or the papers of the Franklin party. Schwatka persuaded the American Geographical Society to organize a new search in the Arctic. This expedition, commanded by Schwatka and William Henry Gilder [*q.v.*] of the *New York Herald,* sailed from New York on June 19, 1878, in the *Eothen.* The explorers did not return for more than two years. During their search in King William Land in 1879–1880 they performed the longest sledge journey then on record, being absent from their base of supplies for eleven months and twenty days and traversing 2,819 geographical or 3,251 statute miles. Schwatka's search resolved the last doubts about the fate of the Franklin expedition. He discovered the wreckage of the one untraced ship, located many of the graves of members of the party, gave other mortal remains decent burial, brought back various relics, and established beyond doubt that Franklin's records were lost. "Schwatka's search," described by Gilder in articles in the *Herald,* became a popular phrase, and his discoveries were hailed as a triumph of Arctic exploration. In 1885 he resigned from the army and thereafter devoted himself to expeditions and to writing and lecturing. He explored the course of the Yukon River, described in his *Along Alaska's Great River* (1885) and *Nimrod in the North* (1885); he commanded the Alaskan expedition launched by the *New York Times* in 1886 and published his *The Children of the Cold* (1886); and he later visited northern Mexico and described the Tarahumari Indians of Chihuahua in a volume published posthumously, *In the Land of Cave and Cliff Dweller*

(1893). His amazing and spectacular journeys, much as they appealed to the popular imagination, resulted in no great contributions to scientific knowledge; he did establish the fact, however, that white men could exist and carry on useful scientific work in the Arctic if they conformed to native habits. During the last years of his life he suffered intensely from a stomach complaint which necessitated the use of laudanum. He died in Portland, Ore., of an overdose of this drug.

[G. W. Cullum, *Biog. Reg. . . . Officers and Grads. U. S. Mil. Acad.,* vol. III (1891); *Twenty-Fourth Ann. Reunion . . . Grads. U. S. Mil. Acad.* (1893); Newton Bateman and Paul Selby, *Hist. Encyc. of Ill.* (1900); W. H. Gilder, *Schwatka's Search* (1881); obituaries in *N. Y. Times, N. Y. Tribune,* Nov. 3, 1892; information from Charles Montague of N. Y. City.]   F. M.

SCHWEINITZ, EDMUND ALEXANDER de (Mar. 20, 1825–Dec. 18, 1887), Moravian bishop and historian, the son of Lewis David von Schweinitz [*q.v.*], and Louisa Amelia (Ledoux) de Schweinitz, was born in Bethlehem, Pa. Reared in a vibrating religious atmosphere, all of his education was directed to the end of preparing him for the Moravian ministry. He was enrolled in the parochial school for three years, studied at the preparatory school at Nazareth Hall, Nazareth, Pa., for five years, and then entered the theological seminary at Bethlehem. At the age of nineteen he sailed for Europe, visited a number of Moravian centers, and matriculated at the University of Berlin, where he sat under August Neander and other eminent scholars. In 1846 he returned to America and accepted a teaching post at Nazareth Hall, offering also, during this four-year period, instruction in the theological seminary.

After a brief pastorate at Dover, Ohio, he returned to Europe and at Herrnhut, Saxony, was married in 1850 to Lydia J. de Tschirschky, of a noble Silesian family. Once more in America he was placed in charge of the Moravian Church at Lebanon, Pa., and later was called to Philadelphia to preside over the First Church in that city. In 1855 he added to his duties the professorship of theology in the seminary, the theological students, few in number, taking up their residence in his Philadelphia parsonage. He also became the editor of the *Moravian,* a weekly church paper, which appeared first on Jan. 1, 1856. Up to this period the entire Unitas Fratrum or Moravian Church membership had been under the full control of the General Synod, meeting from time to time at Herrnhut, Saxony. Elected as a delegate from the United States to the Synod in 1851, de Schweinitz exerted himself successfully in bringing about certain fundamental alterations in the principles of church government. As a result, the Synod granted local autonomy to the American province.

During the period of the Civil War de Schweinitz was in charge of the Lititz Church in Pennsylvania, and in 1864 was transferred to Bethlehem, where he remained for sixteen years. In 1867, resigning the editorship of the *Moravian,* he accepted the presidency of the theological seminary—which, after having been shifted from Bethlehem to Nazareth, and from Nazareth to Philadelphia, now was permanently established at Bethlehem—and succeeded in enlisting the financial support of the local churches in its behalf. His elevation to the Episcopate followed three years later, and in 1879 he was elected to the highest office within the Moravian Church when he became president of the General Synod. As a result of this accumulation of executive duties, he was compelled to resign his pastorate of the Bethlehem Church, and in 1885 he also gave up the presidency of the theological seminary to concentrate his attention on the work of the Moravian missionary society.

In 1859 he had published *The Moravian Manual;* in 1861, a work entitled *Systemic Benevolence;* in 1865, *The Moravian Episcopate;* in 1870, the two volumes of *The Life and Times of David Zeisberger,* a work of excellent scholarship and historical value; in 1881, *Some of the Fathers of the Moravian Church;* and in 1885, the first volume of a projected monumental history of the Moravian Church entitled *The History of the Church Known as the Unitas Fratrum.* In 1877 he published *The Financial History of the American Province of the Unitas Fratrum and of its Sustentation Fund,* and in 1887, *The Centennial Anniversary of the Society of the United Brethren for Propagating the Gospel Among the Heathen.* His unceasing labors undermined his health, but he continued his activities as a bishop and author up to the time of his death. He left behind him his unfinished volume on the history of the renewed Unitas Fratrum. His first wife died in 1866, leaving two sons and two daughters. He was married a second time in 1868 to Isabel Allison Boggs and had one child.

[Manuscript records of the Moravian Church in the Bethlehem, Pa., archives; *In Memoriam, Edmund Alexander de Schweinitz, S.T.D. Episcopus Fratrum* (n.d.); J. T. Hamilton, *A Hist. of the Ch Known as the Moravian Ch.* (1900); W. N. Schwarze, *Hist. of the Moravian Coll. and Theol. Seminary, Trans. Moravian Hist. Soc.,* vol. VIII (1909); Augustus Schultze, *Guide to the Old Moravian Cemetery of Bethlehem, Pa., 1742–1910* (1912), also in *Proc. and Addresses, Pa.-German Soc.,* vol. XXI (1912); *Press* (Philadelphia, Pa.), Dec. 19, 1887.]   L. H. G.

SCHWEINITZ, EMIL ALEXANDER de

(Jan. 18, 1866–Feb. 15, 1904), biochemist, was born at Salem, N. C., the son of Bishop Emil Adolphus de Schweinitz and the grandson of Lewis David von Schweinitz [*q.v.*]. His mother was Sophia A. Herman of Salem, N. C. He was christened Emil Adolphus, but in his maturity changed his middle name to Alexander. His father was the administrator of the affairs of the southern province of the Moravian Church and the head of the Salem Academy. The boy's early education was acquired at Nazareth Hall, and the Moravian college at Bethlehem, Pa. Subsequently he entered the University of North Carolina where he received the A.B. degree in 1882 and the Ph.D. in 1885. He then studied at the Universities of Berlin and Göttingen in Germany, receiving from the latter the degree of Ph.D. in chemistry in 1886. He was made assistant in the division of chemistry in the Department of Agriculture in 1888. On Jan. 1, 1890, he was transferred to the Bureau of Animal Industry and placed in charge of the research in biochemistry. A separate division was created for this work in 1894 and de Schweinitz remained its head until his death.

His work was confined to research concerning the metabolic products of disease-producing bacteria, the chemical composition of these bacteria, and the production of means of immunity from them. He took particular interest in devising methods of protection from animal scourges such as hog cholera, tuberculosis, and glanders, and he was the first to record the use of attenuated human tubercle bacilli for the creation of immunity in animals, his scheme being thus in contrast to the bovine *Bacillus-Calmette-Guerin*. His published works consist of a large number of monographs and reports, several of which were prepared in collaboration with Dr. Marion Dorset, and published by his department between 1894 and 1900. *The War with the Microbes* was published in the *Smithsonian Institution Annual Report*, 1896 (1898), but had previously been printed in *Science*, Apr. 9, 1897. His last work done in conjunction with Dr. Dorset appeared in 1905, *The Comparative Virulence of Human and Bovine Tubercle Bacilli*. He represented the United States at the international congress on medicine and hygiene which met in Paris in 1900. In addition to his labors for the government he was dean and professor of chemistry in the medical school of Columbian (now George Washington) University, Washington, D. C. The new buildings and hospital of that institution are, in a real sense, a monument to his arduous labors. His death was caused by uremic poisoning induced by an attack of typhoid fever which he had suffered the preceding summer. He was unmarried and was survived by three sisters.

[*Who's Who in America*, 1903–05; Marion Dorset, "Emil Alexander de Schweinitz," *Proc. of the Washington Acad. of Sciences*, vol. X (1908); *Washington (D. C.) Post*, Feb. 16, 1904.]
       A. G. R.

SCHWEINITZ, LEWIS DAVID von

(Feb. 13, 1780–Feb. 8, 1834), clergyman of the Moravian Church, botanist, and pioneer mycologist of America, was born at Bethlehem, Pa., the eldest son of Baron Hans Christian Alexander von Schweinitz of Leubla, Saxony, who came to America in 1770. He changed the German form of his name, Ludwig David von Schweinitz, to Lewis, and sometimes used Louis von or de Schweinitz. His sons adopted the form de Schweinitz. His mother was Anna Dorothea Elizabeth, daughter of Baron Johannes de Watteville and Henrietta Benigna Justina, daughter of Nicholaus Lewis, Count Zinzendorf [*q.v.*]. At seven years of age he was sent to Nazareth Hall, where, during eleven years he was distinguished for his linguistic abilities, his satiric humor, and for his awakening interest in botany. He accompanied his family to Germany in 1798 and entered the Moravian theological seminary at Niesky, in Silesia, where he distinguished himself in theological studies. He also continued most ardently his investigations in plant life under the inspiring direction of J. B. de Albertini, with whose assistance he published in 1805 his first work, *The Fungi of Lusatia,* a volume of four hundred pages in Latin, containing twelve plates showing seventy-three new species, drawn and engraved by von Schweinitz. He taught at Niesky until 1807 when he began a pastorate of seven years at Gnadenberg. He then served at Gnadau in Saxony until March 1812 when he was appointed general agent of the Moravian Church at Salem, N. C.

In the midst of the troublous days of the Napoleonic breakdown and the War of 1812, he started with his bride Louisa Amelia Ledoux, daughter of a Huguenot family of Stettin, via Denmark for Sweden in order to embark from a neutral country. The travelers were detained for some months at Kiel where his attainments so impressed the authorities that they conferred upon him the degree of Ph.D., *causa honoris.* After thrilling adventures on the privateer-infested Atlantic they reached New York late in the year and at once set out for Salem. In spite of arduous official duties as administrator of the province and as head of the Salem Academy, he nevertheless found time to explore that uncharted botanical area and to keep up a constant correspondence with experts in England, Germany, and France. His next work, *The Fungi of North Carolina,* also in Latin, was published in 1818 at Leipzig, under the editorial care of Dr. D. F. Schwaegrichen. It described over 1,000 species of which 300 were new to science. In 1821 he published, at Raleigh, N. C., a pamphlet describing seventy-six *Hepaticae,* of which nine had been discovered by him, and in the same year submitted to the *American Journal of Science* (published in volume V, 1822), a monograph on the genus *Viola,* naming five new species. He was offered the presidency of the University of North Carolina which he declined because of the pressure of his work (*Popular Science Monthly,* Apr. 1894, p. 837).

In 1821 he became administrator of the northern province of the Moravian Church and removed to Bethlehem, Pa., where he continued his botanical researches and diligently advanced his herbarium. When Thomas Nuttall [*q.v.*] was called to England and unable to continue the description of the plants collected by Thomas Say on the expedition of Stephen Harriman Long [*q.v.*] to the Northwest, von Schweinitz completed the task. The catalogue was published in the second volume of W. H. Keating, *Narrative of An Expedition to the Source of St. Peter's River* (1824). In 1823 he made an analytical table of the genus *Carex* which he presented to the New York Lyceum of Natural History, and which, having been edited by John Torrey, was published under both names in the *Annals* of the society, June and October 1825. The *American Journal of Science* published his "List of the Rarer Plants found near Easton, Penn." in August 1824. During his absence at a meeting of the General Synod in Germany, the *Journal of the Academy of Natural Sciences* of Philadelphia published, volume V, part 1 (1825), his description of a new American species of *Sphacriae.* When he returned to America early in 1826 he devoted his attention to his greatest work, *A Synopsis of North American Fungi,* which he presented, in 1831, to the American Philosophical Society of Philadelphia. It classifies over 3,000 species of 246 genera of which 1,200 species and seven genera were of his own discovery (see *Transactions,* volume IV, new series, 1834).

An unusual pressure of official duties at this time cut off his out of door exercise, and sedentary work undermined his health. A trip to Indiana in the summer of 1831 to establish a church at Hope was temporarily beneficial, but the cold winter of 1833–34 and certain unfortunate exposures cancelled this gain. He died in Beth-

lehem and was buried in the Moravian Cemetery, his widow and four sons surviving him. Edmund Alexander de Schweinitz [*q.v.*] was his son, and Emil Alexander de Schweinitz [*q.v.*], his grandson. Von Schweinitz' collection of plants from all parts of the world, containing 23,000 phanerogams and many thousand cryptogams, was bequeathed to the Academy of Natural Sciences in Philadelphia and is there preserved.

[E. A. de Schweinitz, Hist. of the de Schweinitz Family, manuscript in the archives of the Moravian Church, Bethlehem, Pa.; manuscript journal in the archives at Herrnhut, Saxony; "The Corresp. of Schweinitz and Torrey," edited by C. L. Shear and N. E. Stevens, in *Memoirs of the Torrey Botanical Club,* vol. XVI, no. 3, July 1921; W. R. Johnson, *A Memoir of the Late Lewis David von Schweinitz* (1835); "The Journey of Lewis David von Schweinitz to Goshen . . . in 1831," translated by Adolf Gerber (1927), also published in *Ind. Hist. Soc. Pubs.,* vol. VIII (1930); "Memoirs of Brother Louis David De Schweinitz," *United Brethrens Missionary Intelligencer,* 3rd quart., 1834; *Popular Sci. Monthly,* Apr. 1894; J. H. Martin, *Hist. Sketch of Bethlehem in Pa.* (1872); *Poulson's Am. Daily Advertiser,* Feb. 13, 1834.]
                                                    A. G. R.

SCIDMORE, ELIZA RUHAMAH (Oct. 14, 1856–Nov. 3, 1928), author and traveler, was born in Madison, Wis., the daughter of George Bolles and Eliza Catherine (Sweeney) Scidmore. She was a descendant of Thomas Skidmore (Scudamore), who came to America from Gloucester, England, in 1635 with the company of Gov. John Winthrop, Jr. She was educated in private schools and spent a year, 1873–74, at Oberlin College. She then began writing society letters from Washington to such newspapers as the *New York Times* and the *St. Louis Globe-Democrat.* Graduating from this apprenticeship, she went to Alaska, where she obtained material for newspaper articles which were later incorporated in her first book, *Alaska, Its Southern Coast and the Sitkan Archipelago* (1885). From that time on, she was an inveterate traveler, not only visiting Europe, but also living for many years in the Orient, where she made prolonged stays in Japan, India, China, Java, and the Philippines at a time when "around the world" cruises and guidebooks to the East were still unborn.

She joined the National Geographic Society in 1890, three years after its organization, and during the earlier part of her long membership served as corresponding secretary, associate editor, foreign secretary, and member of the board of managers, the only woman upon whom this honor had ever been bestowed. In 1891 she published *Jinrikisha Days in Japan,* and in 1893, *Appletons' Guide-Book to Alaska and the Northwest Coast.* She served as one of the secretaries to the Oriental Congress held in Rome in 1897 and published her *Java, the Garden of the East* the same year. In 1900 her *China, the Long-Lived Empire* appeared. She was a delegate to the Oriental Congress held in Hamburg in 1902, and the following year brought out her *Winter India*. In 1907 she published *As the Hague Ordains,* for which she was decorated by the Japanese Emperor. In addition to writing she appeared frequently as a lecturer. She was a regular contributor to such publications as the *National Geographic Magazine, Outlook, Century, Asia, World Today,* and *Harper's Weekly.* Her work for the *Geographic* was especially noteworthy because of its illustrations, for she was an accomplished photographer. In an article in the *Century* (Mar. 10, 1910) she relates her long-continued efforts to have Japanese cherry trees planted in Washington, a project which was later carried out by others.

Her writings are noteworthy not only for the material chosen for treatment, but also for their vividness of style. She wrote with the conviction that international friendliness could be promoted by an understanding of the underlying psychology of the customs of peoples alien to her own countrymen. This conviction prevented her books from having the ephemeral quality frequently found in books of travel. Her political articles give evidence of her knowledge of existing conditions and of her penetrating ability to foresee coming political difficulties. Her imaginative faculty enabled her to see the awakening inhabitants of Madura "yawning like alligators." Written in praise of the Japanese treatment of prisoners during the Russo-Japanese War, *As the Hague Ordains* is a delightful book in the memoir style that found favor with readers of belles-lettres. Although known chiefly as a writer, she also merits recognition as an ambassador of good will between America and Japan. In 1925 she settled in Geneva, where she was an ardent advocate of the League of Nations. The Japanese Government requested that her ashes be interred in Yokohama, and the urn containing them was taken there by the Japanese minister to Switzerland.

[E. C. Hawley, *A Geneal. and Biog. Record of the Pioneer Thomas Skidmore* (1911); M. W. Cameron, *The Biog. Encyc. of Am. Women,* vol. I (1924); Oliver Martin, "How the Japanese Cherry Trees Came to Washington," in *Transmitter* (Chesapeake and Potomac Telephone Company), Apr. 1934; *Who's Who in America,* 1920–21; *Woman's Who's Who of America,* 1914–15; *Evening Star* (Washington), Nov. 3, 1928; *N. Y. Times,* Nov. 4, 1928.]   E. W. H.

SCOLLARD, CLINTON (Sept. 18, 1860–Nov. 19, 1932), poet, was born in Clinton, N. Y., the son of James Isaac and Elizabeth (Stephens) Scollard. He received his early education at Clinton Liberal Institute, and graduated from Hamilton College in 1881. He then taught at the Brooklyn Polytechnic Institute until February 1883, when, for his health, he visited Florida, Arizona, and California. A year later he received the degree of A.M. from Hamilton, and in subsequent years he continued his graduate studies at Harvard—where he met Bliss Carman and Frank Dempster Sherman—and at Cambridge, England. While abroad he made the acquaintance of Edmund Gosse, Austin Dobson, and Andrew Lang; and a trip to the Near East left a marked impression on his mind. In 1888 he joined the faculty of Hamilton College as professor of English, continuing as such until 1896; during the year 1911–12 he acted in the same capacity.

Scollard's devotion to literature is marked both by his work as a college professor and by the forty-odd books he published in his lifetime. His first volume, *Pictures in Song* (1884), following a popular trend in American poetry, contained verse chiefly in the miniature forms, those of the French occupying a conspicuous place. A few years later he abandoned this style for the more vigorous "Vagabondia" note made popular by Bliss Carman and Richard Hovey [*q.v.*], but, as with Carman, the spirit of the open road finally yielded to a more mystical view of Nature, which Scollard sought to interpret in its manifold relations to human life. A great admirer of Poe, he found much that was best in life in dreams and visions, but he felt wistfully, too, the Platonic impermanence of our hopes and ideals. If Scollard caught some of Poe's dream-like quality, he retained, however, nothing of his gloom, for his poetry is significant for its courageous optimism.

Scollard's work displays a painstaking care in versification, which he inherited from the late nineteenth century. Seldom carried out of himself by the stress of passion, he seems at times too conscious of the form in which he is working; yet a charming lyricism frequently pervades his work, suggesting a remoteness from the concerns of every-day life. This feeling of escape sought expression in a varied subject matter, often connected with his travels; *Songs of Sunrise Lands* (1892) and *Italy in Arms and Other Poems* (1915) illustrate his absorbing interest in the Orient and in Italy. His return to contemporary American life, however, is evinced in several volumes of lyrics inspired by the World War. Scollard's prose works include a number of romances of Renaissance Italy, a book of nature essays, and a volume of foreign travel sketches.

Scollard was twice married: first, in 1890, to Georgia Brown of Jackson, Mich., by whom he had a daughter; they were divorced in 1924 and that same year he married Jessie B. Rittenhouse, the poet. One of his most intimate friends was Frank Dempster Sherman [*q.v.*], to whom he was drawn by a community of poetic and academic interests; *A Southern Flight* (1905), a volume of verse done in collaboration, was the chief literary product of this friendship. On Sherman's death in 1916, Scollard wrote *Elegy in Autumn* (1917), in which his friend is addressed as "brother in song," and edited *The Poems of Frank Dempster Sherman* (copr. 1917), for which he composed an excellent critical introduction. Scollard was a member of a number of literary associations, including the National Institute of Arts and Letters. He died of heart disease at his home in Kent, Conn.

[The most important source is *The Singing Heart: Selected Lyrics and Other Poems of Clinton Scollard* (1934), ed., with a memoir by Jessie B. Rittenhouse; others are: *Who's Who in America*, 1932–33; *Who's Who in N. Y.*, 1929; *N. Y. Times*, Nov. 20, 1932; *New York Herald Tribune*, Nov. 20, 1932; *Hamilton Coll. Bull.*, Apr. 1933; *Lit. Digest*, Mar. 11, 1933; *Class of '81, Hamilton Coll.: The Record of Forty Years, 1881–1921* (n.d.); J. B. Rittenhouse, *The Younger Am. Poets* (1904); H. W. Cook, *Our Poets of Today* (1923); *Publishers' Weekly*, Nov. 26, 1932; *Clinton Scollard* (n.d.), a pamphlet, with a memorial address by W. P. Shepard and a bibliog. by J. D. Ibbotson; letters from Miss Jessie B. Rittenhouse and J. D. Ibbotson, librarian of Hamilton College. Scollard's papers and MSS. are in the Hamilton College library.]

N. F. A.

SCOTT, AUSTIN (Aug. 10, 1848–Aug. 15, 1922), educator, president of Rutgers College, was born at Maumee, near Toledo, Ohio, the son of Jeremiah Austin and Sarah (Ranney) Scott. He was named Frank Austin, but dropped the first name soon after reaching maturity. Graduated from Yale College with the degree of A.B. in 1869, he spent a year at the University of Michigan, where in 1870 he received the degree of A.M.; and then went abroad and studied at the University of Berlin and the University of Leipzig, receiving the degree of Ph.D. from Leipzig in 1873. His chief interest was history, especially political history, and his ability and learning brought him into important connections even in student days. In Germany, he assisted George Bancroft, at that time minister of the United States to Germany, in preparing his history of the United States. He was also charged with the responsibility of bearing important dispatches from Berlin to Washington.

On his return to the United States he was instructor in German at the University of Michi-

gan from 1873 to 1875, and then, for seven years, an associate in history at Johns Hopkins University, organizing there a seminar of American history. During this period he continued as assistant to Bancroft, assembling and arranging historical material for him. In 1883 he was called to be professor of history, political economy, and constitutional law at Rutgers College. He remained with the college until his death forty years later, becoming at once an important influence in its life. He was an unusual teacher, with abundant learning in his field, fluency of speech, vivacity of manner, and a quick turn of wit. The passing generations of students found him an effectual master of the classroom and acknowledged great indebtedness to his courses and his personality. The subject to which he gave most attention was constitutional law and to his work in this field was due his chief distinction. In time his title became professor of political science.

Austin Scott's eminence and influence as a teacher, his vigorous participation in all faculty activities, and his familiarity with certain administrative questions led to his election as president of Rutgers College in November 1890, and he was inaugurated Feb. 1891. He served with great devotion for fifteen years, during which time the college property and endowment were increased and the educational program enlarged. A gymnasium and a library were erected and the teaching staff was kept at a high level of efficiency. A friendly suit with the state resulted in a clarification of the relations between the state and Rutgers College, the scientific school of which had been made in 1864 the state college for the benefit of agriculture and the mechanic arts. During the entire time of his service as president he continued to some extent the teaching which was always the work most agreeable to him, and in 1906 he resigned the presidency in order to confine himself again to his professorial duties. For sixteen years more he gave valued teaching service to the students and generous administrative support to the succeeding president.

He took an active interest in the civic affairs of New Brunswick. For many years he was president and chief contributor to the Historical Club. In 1912 he was elected mayor of the city on the Democratic ticket and served in that office for three years with advantage to the material and moral welfare of the community. He was an elder in the Second Reformed Church and took an important part in its enterprises; he was also one of the board of superintendents of the New Brunswick Theological Seminary. On Feb.

21, 1882, he married Anna Prentiss Stearns, daughter of Jonathan French Stearns of Newark, N. J. He died at his summer home, Granville Centre, Mass., and was buried there.

[*Memorial Meeting for Austin Scott, Ph.D., LL.D.* (1923); W. H. S. Demarest, *Hist. of Rutgers Coll.* (1924); *Proc. N. J. Hist. Soc.*, vol. VII (1922); *Yale Univ. Obit. Record*, 1923; *Who's Who in America*, 1920–21; *N. Y. Times*, Aug. 17, 1922.] W. H. S. D.

SCOTT, CHARLES (c. 1739–Oct. 22, 1813), soldier, governor of Kentucky, was born in that part of Goochland County, Va., which later became Powhatan County. Scottsville, formerly the county seat of Powhatan, was named in his honor. In his seventeenth year he served as a non-commissioned officer under Washington in the Braddock campaign. At the commencement of the Revolution, he raised the first companies of volunteers from south of James River to enter actual service, and commanded them at Williamsburg, Va., in July 1775. He was appointed lieutenant-colonel of the 2nd Virginia Regiment, Feb. 13, 1776, became colonel of the 5th in May, was transferred to the 3rd in August, and on Apr. 2, 1777, was commissioned brigadier-general in the Continental Army. A great part of the winter of 1777–78 he spent at Valley Forge. He rendered gallant service at Trenton, Germantown, Monmouth, and Stony Point, and in 1780 was captured at Charleston, S. C., remaining on parole thereafter until his exchange near the close of the war. He was brevetted major-general Sept. 30, 1783, and was one of the original members of the Society of the Cincinnati.

By an act of the Virginia legislature in October 1783, Scott was designated one of a deputation of officers of the Continental line to appoint superintendents and surveyors to locate and survey the western lands given by law to the officers and soldiers on the Continental establishment. He removed to Kentucky two years later and settled in that part of Fayette afterwards taken to form the county of Woodford. In 1789 and 1790 he represented Woodford County in the Virginia Assembly. In April 1790 he took part in the fruitless expedition of Gen. Josiah Harmar [q.v.] against the Indians on the Scioto, and in 1791 was a member of the local board of war and commandant of the Kentucky district, with the rank of brigadier-general. Between May 23 and June 4, 1791, with Col. James Wilkinson [q.v.] as second in command, he conducted an expedition against the Indians on the Wabash River, and in the fall, advancing from Cincinnati with a force of Kentuckians, he was with Gen. Arthur St. Clair [q.v.] at the disastrous defeat of Nov. 4, 1791. In 1792 Scott County, created out of Woodford County, was

named for him. On Oct. 24, 1793, with 1,000 mounted Kentuckians, he joined Gen. Anthony Wayne [q.v.] for another projected campaign against the Indians, but the operation was abandoned. In the following summer, however, at the head of about 1,500 mounted Kentucky volunteers, Scott took part with Wayne's army in the battle of the Fallen Timbers (Aug. 20, 1794), which resulted in a decisive victory over the Indians.

Scott had only an elementary English schooling, but in the rugged life of the frontier he gained a fund of practical wisdom which richly reinforced his naturally sound judgment and good sense. He was frank and direct in speech, simple and unaffected in social intercourse. A type of the strong man of the frontier whose military leadership led to leadership in politics, he was chosen presidential elector from Kentucky in 1793, 1801, 1805, and 1809, and in August 1808 was elected governor of the state. He served in that capacity four years. In his public utterances before the War of 1812 he boldly declared the duty of his fellow countrymen in the emergency, and one of his last official acts was to commission Gen. William Henry Harrison [q.v.] of the United States Army a major-general of the Kentucky militia in order to give him unquestioned authority over Kentucky troops participating in the northwestern campaign.

Scott married, Feb. 25, 1762, Frances Sweeney of Cumberland County, Va., by whom he had several children. She died in October 1804, and on July 25, 1807, he married Judith Cary (Bell) Gist, widow of Col. Nathaniel Gist and daughter of Capt. David Bell, formerly of Buckingham County, Va. She survived him, dying in 1833. Scott died at her home, "Canewood," in Clark County, Ky., and on Nov. 8, 1854, his body was reinterred in the State Cemetery, Frankfort.

[F. B. Heitman, *Hist. Reg. and Dict. U. S. Army* (1903); Henry Howe, *Hist. Colls. of Va.* (1846); T. L. Crittenden, in *Obituary Addresses Delivered upon the Occasion of the Re-interment of the Remains of Gen. Charles Scott* (1855); William Littell, *The Statute Law of Ky.* (5 vols., 1809–19), esp. I, 442, 629, II, 140, III, 582; Lewis and R. H. Collins, *Hist. of Ky.* (2 vols., 1874); Thomas Boyd, *Mad Anthony Wayne* (1929); *Ky. Gazette*, Feb. 5, 1791, Jan. 23, 1800, Oct. 26, 1813; *Ky. Reporter*, Nov. 6, 1813; *Va. Mag. of Hist. and Biog.*, Jan. 1925; *Ind. Mag. of Hist.*, Mar. 1925; "Governors Messages and Letters . . . Wm. Henry Harrison," *Ind. Hist. Colls.*, vols. VII, IX (1922); *Reg. Ky. State Hist. Soc.*, Sept. 1903, inaccurate in certain details; court records; acquaintance with members of the family.] S. M. W.

SCOTT, COLIN ALEXANDER (Feb. 11, 1861–Apr. 5, 1925), psychologist, educational reformer, was born in Ottawa, Canada, the son of Isabel Laird (Scott) and the Rev. Robert

Scott. The family later moved to New York City, where the father's work brought them into happy association with Henry Ward Beecher. The son attended the preparatory department of the College of the City of New York in 1876–77 and later Queen's University, Kingston, Ont., where he took the degree of B.A. in 1885. Meanwhile, in 1881, while he was still an undergraduate, he married Helen McColl of Kingston, daughter of the noted Gaelic scholar, by whom he had two daughters and three sons. Although he won honors in chemistry at Queen's University, he was much interested in philosophy and psychology; his graduate study at Clark University (Ph.D., 1896) was in psychology, his doctoral thesis, "Old Age and Death," being published in the *American Journal of Psychology* for October 1896. He taught psychology at the Chicago Normal School, 1897–1901; at Miami University, Oxford, Ohio, 1901–02; at Tufts College, 1910–11; at the Boston Normal School, 1902–10, 1911–15. From 1915 to 1925 he was professor of education at Mount Holyoke College.

His teaching, which was of a radically new kind, found expression in his *Social Education* (1908). He endeavored to foster his conception of socialized teaching in primary and secondary schools as well as in collegiate work, and he had opportunities to carry out his theories in Brookline and in Springfield, Mass., where he was head of the department of records and results in the public schools. But his distaste for the political means necessary to effect important changes in American institutions militated against the practical success of his ideas. His purpose was not only to link the classroom with spontaneous outside interests, with the homes of the pupils, with arts and industries, but also to establish conditions in the classroom that should freely elicit leadership, cooperative undertakings, means of self-government, and sympathetic understanding. The means he employed were various. Perhaps the central one was that later elaborated by others into the "project-method," the "Dalton Plan," and similar widely advertised plans by which self-organized groups voluntarily pursue their own interests during a portion of the school day. Objective tests of progress were employed, such as machines (in some cases of Scott's invention) by which pupils could themselves measure their progress from week to week. His ideas gained impetus through a social education club organized by faculty members of Harvard University, of Massachusetts Institute of Technology, and of Tufts College, together with numerous secondary school teachers,

and by the publication (March 1907–January 1908) of the *Social Education Quarterly*.

Early in his career he found it difficult to decide between painting and teaching as a profession. For a time, 1885–87, he studied in the Ontario Art School, and all his life he painted for pleasure. He exhibited widely in the East, winning high praise for the dramatic vitality, vivid intuition, and joyous quality of his work. At the time of his death he was working on a book on sex and art. As a cultivated scholar rich in kindling ideas he would have graced the presidency of a university, but his detestation of power as such, his self-effacing generosity, and his disinterested liberality led him to choose a life in which his ideas and his art might exert their own influence. He died in Boston.

[*Who's Who in America*, 1924–25; full obituary in *Springfield Daily Republican*, Apr. 7, 1925; brief obituaries in *Boston Transcript*, Apr. 6, 1925, and *Jour. of Education*, Apr. 9, 1925; personal acquaintance.]

J. M. W.

SCOTT, DRED (*c.* 1795–Sept. 17, 1858), slave, was born of slave parents in Southampton County, Va. His early years were spent on the plantation of his master, Capt. Peter Blow, who, in 1827, removed with his family and slaves to St. Louis, Mo. Upon his death in 1831, Scott was assigned to Elizabeth Blow, a daughter. He was purchased two years later by John Emerson, a surgeon in the United States Army, with whom, as a servant, he spent three years in Illinois and two in Wisconsin Territory. He married Harriet, a slave woman purchased by his owner in 1836. Left by Emerson at St. Louis in 1838, he became the body servant of Col. Henry Bainbridge at Jefferson Barracks, and upon Emerson's death, passed to his widow, Irene (Sanford) Emerson. She hired Scott to various families in the city. He was shiftless and unreliable, and therefore frequently unemployed and without means to support his family. He often became a charge upon the bounty of Taylor and H. T. Blow [*q.v.*], the wealthy sons of his former owner, who seemed to feel partially responsible for him. Mrs. Emerson could have emancipated him but did not do so, and left him in St. Louis when she removed to Massachusetts in the middle forties. It seems probable that Scott attempted unsuccessfully to arrange for the purchase of himself and his family (*New York Tribune*, Apr. 10, 1857).

In April 1846, Henry T. Blow instituted and financed suits in the state courts to secure the freedom of Scott and of his family. The contention was that a slave, after sojourning in free territory, was free upon his return to Missouri. The ignorant and illiterate negro comprehended little of its significance, but signed his mark to the petition in the suit. While the case was before the state courts, 1846–52, he remained under the nominal control of the sheriff, being hired out for $5.00 per month until the termination of the suit. After an adverse decision had been delivered by Judge William Scott [*q.v.*] in 1852 (*Scott, a Man of Color*, vs. *Emerson*, 15 *Mo.* 576), it was arranged to take the case to the federal courts, and, for jurisdictional purposes, Dred Scott was transferred by a fictitious sale to his owner's brother, John F. A. Sanford of New York. During the interval when the case was in the federal courts, 1854–57, Scott remained in St. Louis, under practically no restraint, a mere pawn in the game, with no regular employment, running errands and performing janitor service. As a local celebrity, he enjoyed greatly his new and unexpected prominence. The United States Supreme Court in 1857 held that Scott was not free by reason of his removal either to Illinois or to Wisconsin Territory. His status was determined by the courts of Missouri which had decided that he was not free. Not being a citizen of Missouri, within the meaning of the Constitution, he was not entitled, as such, to sue in the federal courts (*Dred Scott* vs. *Sandford*, 19 *Howard*, 393). In May 1857 he was transferred, no doubt by another fictitious sale, to Taylor Blow, who very obviously intended to emancipate him and his family. This action was taken on May 26 of that year (*Missouri Republican*, May 27, 1857). The fact that Mrs. Emerson had meanwhile become the wife of Calvin Clifford Chaffee of Massachusetts, a radical anti-slavery congressman, was the source of much ironical comment and hastened the manumission. Physically unfitted for steady and hard labor, Scott spent the remainder of his life as the good-natured and lazy porter at Barnum's Hotel, St. Louis, where he was an object of interest and curiosity to the guests. He died of tuberculosis, and Henry T. Blow paid his funeral expenses.

[Sources include Blow MSS., in Mo. Hist. Soc., St. Louis; E. W. P. Ewing, *Legal and Historical Status of the Dred Scott Decision* (1909); J. D. Lawson, *Am. State Trials*, vol. XIII (1921); *Proc. . . . Mo. Bar Asso. . . . 1907* (1908), p. 233; E. S. Corwin, "The Dred Scott Decision in the Light of Contemporary Legal Doctrines," *Am. Hist. Rev.*, Oct. 1911, repr., with some verbal changes, in his *The Doctrine of Judicial Review* (1914); Helen T. Catterall, "Some Antecedents of the Dred Scott Case," *Am. Hist. Rev.*, Oct. 1924; F. H. Hodder, "Some Phases of the Dred Scott Case," *Miss. Valley Hist. Rev.*, June 1929; J. M. Turner, "Dred Scott" (manuscript copy, 1882, Mo. Hist. Soc., St. Louis); *Providence Daily Post*, Mar. 17, 1857; *N. Y. Tribune*, Apr. 10, 1857; *Mo. Republican*, May 27, 1857; *Washington Union*, June 2, 1857; *New Hampshire Patriot and State Gazette* (Concord), June 3, 1857; *St. Louis News*, Sept. 20, 1858. In the of-

ficial printed reports of the Dred Scott case the name of the owner, correctly Sanford, is persistently misspelled.]   T. S. B.

SCOTT, FRED NEWTON (Aug. 20, 1860–May 29, 1931), rhetorician, was born in Terre Haute, Ind., the son of Mary (Bannister) and Harvey D. Scott, a lawyer who was a congressman from Indiana in 1855 and for some years a county judge. After taking the degrees of A.B., 1884, A.M., 1888, and Ph.D., 1889, at the University of Michigan, meanwhile serving as library assistant and later as assistant librarian, Scott became an instructor in English and for almost forty years was a member of the university faculty. As head of the department of rhetoric, 1903–21, and of rhetoric and journalism, 1921–27, he exerted a wide influence. He encouraged the establishment of schools of journalism in state colleges, modified the teaching of English composition in colleges through his treatment of the paragraph as the unit of discourse (in *Paragraph-Writing*, 1891, with J. V. Denny), and was a stimulating teacher of graduate students, with the power of suggesting lines of thought often very original. He was president of the Modern Language Association of America, 1907; one of the founders and the first president of the National Council of Teachers of English, 1911–13; president of the North Central Association of Colleges and Secondary Schools, 1913, and of the American Association of Teachers of Journalism, 1917. A member of several British learned societies as well, he had a wide acquaintance and a high reputation among foreign scholars. In 1887 he married Isadore Thompson, daughter of Prof. Bradley M. Thompson of the law school of the University of Michigan, by whom he had a daughter and two sons. A year after her death in 1922, he married Georgia Jackson of New York City, who with his three children survived him. Upon his retirement in 1927 as professor emeritus, he and his wife lived in Tucson, Ariz.; he died in San Diego, Cal.

Although Scott's distinction rests particularly upon his influence as a teacher, his list of more than a hundred publications contains convincing evidence of his scholarly interests and attainments. He edited among other things De Quincey's *Essay on Style, Rhetoric, and Language* (1891) and Herbert Spencer's *The Philosophy of Style* (1892); with C. L. Meader, he translated three plays from the Russian of Leonid Andreyeff, *Plays* (1915), and he wrote numerous essays and technical articles that appeared in magazines ranging from the *Classical Journal* to the *Atlantic Monthly* on subjects that varied from the prosody of Walt Whitman to the psychology of speech. His chief concern was always with matters of style and with the fundamentals of literary effect and appreciation. His most ambitious work, done in collaboration with C. M. Gayley, was *An Introduction to the Methods and Materials of Literary Criticism* (1899), which at the time broke relatively new ground. But his richly suggestive essays on prose rhythms and on his theory of the fundamental distinction between poetry and prose (reprinted in *The Standard of American Speech and Other Papers,* 1926) were perhaps more important. His writing was smooth, polished, urbane, packed with implication. In general he seemed content with indicating fresh approaches to problems of speech and writing, and seldom worked out in fullness even the most promising of his ideas; *The Standard of American Speech* contains ideas enough in brief essay form for many scholarly volumes. Modest and extremely reticent, with a grave courtesy, he was to many of his students an enigmatic figure, whose preference was always for questioning rather than for arriving at fixed conclusions. He was keenly sensitive and easily wounded, but he had a delicate wit and took great pleasure in good talk. He had some reputation as an after-dinner speaker. He was perhaps half the scholar, half the old-style journalist who could write excellent editorials in a style not so far from Addison and sometimes much better for the purpose in hand.

[See Blackford Condit, *The Hist. of Early Terre Haute from 1816 to 1840* (1900) for information on Scott's father; *Univ. of Mich. Cat. of Grads.... 1837–1921* (1923); *The Fred Newton Scott Anniversary Papers* (1929), with portrait and bibliog., ed. by C. D. Thorpe and C. E. Whitmore; *Who's Who in America,* 1930–31; J. L. Brumm, in *Mich. Alumnus,* June 27, 1931; brief obituary in *Language,* Sept. 1931; *N. Y. Times,* May 31, 1931; information from Scott's family and friends.]   D. G—d.

SCOTT, GUSTAVUS (1753–Dec. 25, 1800), lawyer and patriot, was the son of James Scott and Sarah (Brown) Scott. His father had emigrated to America before the middle of the eighteenth century, and was rector of Dettingen Parish, Prince William County, Va., from 1745 until his death in 1782. Gustavus, with his elder brother, John, went to Scotland in 1765, and is said to have studied at King's College, Aberdeen. Two years later he entered Essex Court, Middle Temple, London, where he was engaged in the study of law until 1771, being called to the English bar in November 1772. On his return to America he began to practise law with marked success in Somerset County on the Eastern Shore of Maryland. He became a leader of the liberal party, was elected a delegate to the Maryland Convention, and took his seat in that body on Aug. 7, 1775. He joined the Association of the Freemen of Maryland for resistance to attempts to enforce acts of Parliament by military power, and served as spokesman for the committee of observation relative to military affairs in his county. He served as a member of the constitutional convention of 1776 which drafted the first state constitution of Maryland, and soon after the adoption moved to Dorchester County. In January 1781 he joined in an appeal to the governor of the state for such arms, ammunition, and supplies as would afford more adequate military protection for his county and the entire Eastern Shore.

Dorchester County elected him a member of the Maryland House of Delegates in 1780. He took his seat on Nov. 20, for a term of one year, and served again from December 1783 until January 1785. There is no evidence of active or important service during his first term, but in the second he became one of the more prominent leaders, serving on the committees which drafted the most important bills. He represented Maryland on a joint commission of Maryland and Virginia which submitted a report in response to which Virginia, in 1784, and Maryland, in 1785, chartered the Potomac Navigation Company for the improvement of the Potomac River; this ultimately resulted in the construction of the Chesapeake and Ohio Canal. He participated in the drafting of a bill for the establishment of a state university, and was in favor of granting James Rumsey [q.v.] a monopoly for making and selling steamboats "on a model by him invented" (*Votes and Proceedings, post,* First Session, November 1784, p. 13). The Maryland Assembly, on Dec. 4, 1784, elected Scott a delegate to the Continental Congress for a term of one year, but his health was impaired at this time, and, although his credentials were presented, there is no record of his service in that body. He retired to private life and resumed the practice of law until 1793, when he was appointed chairman of a committee to combat the yellow fever in Baltimore. The following year President Washington appointed Scott to a vacancy in the board of commissioners for the city of Washington and characterized him as "a gentleman eminent in the profession of the Law—a man of character & fortune . . ." (letter to Tobias Lear, Aug. 28, 1794, Washington Papers, Library of Congress). He died at his home "Rock Hill," Washington, D. C., and was buried on his farm in Virginia nine miles distant. He was married to Margaret Hall Caile on Feb. 16.

1777, and they had five sons and four daughters. William Lawrence Scott [*q.v.*] was his grandson.

[*Votes and Proc. of the House of Delegates of the State of Md.*, 1780–85; E. A. Jones, *Am. Members of the Inns of Court* (1924); J. A. Ames, "Genealogies of Four Families of Dorchester County," *Md. Hist. Mag.*, Mar. 1916; Corra Bacon-Foster, "The Story of Kalorama," *Records of the Columbia Hist. Soc.*, vol. XIII (1910), vol. XVII (1914); H. E. Hayden, *Va. Genealogies* (1931); W. B. Bryan, *A Hist. of the Natl. Capitol*, vol. I (1914); *Federal Gazette* (Baltimore, Md.), Dec. 31, 1800.]   N. D. M.

SCOTT, HARVEY WHITEFIELD (Feb. 1, 1838–Aug. 7, 1910), editor, was born on a farm near Groveland, Tazewell County, Ill., the son of Ann (Roelofson) and John Tucker Scott and brother of Abigail Jane Scott Duniway [*q.v.*]. He was a descendant of John Scott who settled in North Carolina shortly before the Revolutionary War. In 1852 he went with his family overland to Oregon. After two years in the lower Willamette Valley he moved with his father to a farm near Shelton in the newly formed territory of Washington, but in September 1856 he returned to Oregon to work on a farm near Oregon City. In December he entered Tualatin Academy, but for lack of funds he was forced to leave school the next April and was unable to continue his education except irregularly until 1859, when he entered Pacific University, Forest Grove, Ore. He graduated in 1863, supporting himself meanwhile by working as a teamster, a woodcutter, and a teacher. After another year of school-teaching he became librarian of the Portland library and studied law in a private office. Though he passed his bar examinations, he never actively practised law. He married Elizabeth Nicklin of Salem, Ore., Oct. 31, 1865, and after her death Margaret McChesney of Latrobe, Pa., June 28, 1876.

In April 1865 he began to write editorials for the Portland *Morning Oregonian*, recognized as the chief spokesman in the state for the Republican party, and a year later Henry Lewis Pittock [*q.v.*], the owner of the paper, made him its editor. He also served as collector of the port of Portland from October 1870 to May 1876, when Senator John Hipple Mitchell [*q.v.*] of Oregon had him removed. According to Scott (*Morning Oregonian*, July 5, 1898), this was because of his refusal longer to contribute financial support to the *Portland Bulletin*, the newspaper organ of Mitchell and Ben Holladay [*q.v.*]. He had left the *Oregonian* in 1872, but in April 1877 he returned as editor and part owner, a connection that lasted until his death. He was never an avowed candidate for an elective office, although in 1903 he made overtures to Republican party leaders for support in the legislative

ballot for United States senator. (For a telegram from Scott to George C. Brownell, see *Oregon Journal*, Feb. 28, 1903, and Lincoln Steffens, "U'Ren, the Lawgiver," *American Magazine*, March 1908, p. 539). He declined a diplomatic appointment to Belgium in 1905 and one to Mexico in 1909. He was president of the Oregon Historical Society, 1898–1901, of the Lewis and Clark Exposition, 1903–04, and a director of the Associated Press 1900–10. He died in Baltimore, Md., of heart failure following a surgical operation; he was survived by his wife, three sons, and a daughter.

He was well equipped for the work of an editor. Persistent reading had given him so thorough an acquaintance with great literary masterpieces that he could quote at will from many, and he read widely in history, economics, religion, theology, and metaphysics as well. He made the *Oregonian* the strongest journal in the Pacific Northwest and brought it national recognition, and he himself came to be numbered among the great editors of the nation, with a style that was, although somewhat dogmatic, forceful and convincing. A thorough-going individualist and conservative, he stood out against all the social and reform movements of his day. He opposed free high schools, state supported schools of higher education, prohibition, woman's suffrage, and the "Oregon System" of direct primary, initiative, referendum, and recall. He was unsympathetic towards the demands of labor and hostile to the socializing tendencies of his time. He conducted a vigorous campaign for "sound money" and fought in turn the Greenback movement and Free Silver. He was a lifelong advocate of "tariff for revenue only" and insisted that his party's policy of protection created monopolies and enriched the few at the expense of the many. On other issues, however, he stood with the conservative wing of his party. After his death his writings were collected by his son and published as *Religion, Theology and Morals* (2 vols., 1917); *History of the Oregon Country* (6 vols., 1924); and *Shakespeare* (1928).

[*Who's Who in America*, 1908–09; articles by Alfred Holman, L. M. Scott, and C. H. Chapman, in *Quart. Ore. Hist. Soc.*, June 1913, the first two being reprinted in H. W. Scott, *Hist. of the Ore. Country* (1924), vol. I; O. C. Leiter, in *Journalism Quart.*, Jan. 1929, an excellent appreciation; obituary and editorial in *Morning Oregonian* (Portland), Aug. 8, 1910.]   R. C. C.

SCOTT, IRVING MURRAY (Dec. 25, 1837–Apr. 28, 1903), ship-builder, was the son of Quaker parents, John and Elizabeth (Leittig) Scott, and was born on his father's farm at Hebron Mills, Baltimore County, Md. Through the grist mill his father ran in connection with his farm, Scott early developed an interest in mechanics. Accordingly, after attending the district school near his home, he took a three-year course at Milton Academy in Baltimore and at the same time began an apprenticeship as machinist. Upon completing this he worked for a time in the shop of Obed Hussey, manufacturer of reaping machinery, and then in 1857, at the age of twenty, entered the steam-engine manufactory of Murray and Hazlehurst in Baltimore. By studying at night in the Baltimore Mechanics' Institute he became proficient in drafting and soon was transferred to the designing department and placed in charge of the construction of stationary engines and fire engines. In 1860 he went to San Francisco to erect an engine purchased from his employers by Peter Donahue; upon completing this he continued to work in Donahue's iron works for two years. After a few months as chief draftsman in the Miners' Foundry and Machine Works in San Francisco, he went back to Donahue as superintendent. In 1865, when Donahue retired, he was taken into the business as a partner, and from that time until his death he was associated with it. During the succeeding ten years he conducted a foundry and iron works, in which the mining machinery for the Comstock mines in Nevada was designed and manufactured. He also designed improved steam engines with a cut-off of his own invention.

In 1880, in a trip around the world, he made an exhaustive study of manufacturing industries, particularly of ship-building in France and England. Soon after his return to the United States in 1882 he and his partners incorporated their business under the name of the Union Iron Works and in 1883 began a ship-building plant covering approximately twenty acres of land; and in 1884 the construction of ships was begun. Two years later Scott secured a contract from the federal government for the construction of the warship *Charleston,* completed in 1889, the first battleship built on the Pacific Coast. In quick succession between 1892 and 1901 followed the *Olympia,* the *San Francisco,* the *Oregon,* the *Wisconsin,* and the *Ohio,* which established Scott's worldwide reputation as a shipbuilder. In 1898 he went to St. Petersburg (later Leningrad) to advise the Russian government in the building of warships. He was intensely interested in all civic affairs of San Francisco and served as president of the Mechanics' Institute of San Francisco, regent of the University of California, and trustee of Stanford University. He was married in 1863 to Laura Harde of Cov-

ington, Ky. (*San Francisco Call, post*); at the time of his death in San Francisco he was survived by his widow and two children.

[*Who's Who in America,* 1901–02; *Trans. Amer. Soc. Mech. Engineers,* vol. XXIV (1903); Alonzo Phelps, *Contemporary Biog. of California's Representative Men* (1881); *San Francisco Call, San Francisco Chronicle,* Apr. 29, 1903.]   C. W. M.

SCOTT, JAMES WILMOT (June 26, 1849–Apr. 14, 1895), journalist, was born in Walworth County, Wis. Both his grandfather and father were newspaper men. His father, David Wilmot Scott, removed to Galena, Ill., shortly after the birth of his son, where he became associated with Charles H. Ray in publishing the *Jeffersonian.* There it was that James Scott became the prize declaimer of the Galena schools and at the age of eleven, upon the outbreak of the Civil War, became a drummer boy engaged in recruiting duty in Illinois. After graduating from the Galena High School, he attended Beloit College two years. Having learned the printer's trade in his father's office, he went to New York soon after his return from college. There he became intensely interested in floriculture, and he contributed short articles to horticultural periodicals. However, his early training asserted itself. He returned to Galena, Ill., and with his father founded the *Industrial Press.*

In 1875, he went to Chicago, where for the remainder of his life he was associated with journalism. In Chicago he first purchased an interest in the *National Hotel Reporter* but at the end of six years withdrew to found a paper of his own. In May 1881 he organized the Chicago Herald Company, in which he later obtained the controlling interest. The growth of the *Chicago Herald* was remarkable, as it was one of the youngest dailies in the western metropolis and a pioneer among two-cent morning papers. Within ten years it had increased from four to twelve pages, and the Herald Company boasted of a fine building equipped with twenty modern presses. The Sunday edition reached a size of forty-eight pages by 1887, featuring new departures in the newspaper field. Although at first supporting the Republican party, in its first year it became independent Democrat, and it supported Cleveland and hard money. The policy of the paper was distinctly conservative, but it consistently advocated a reduction in tariff duties and civil service reform. So successful was the *Chicago Herald* under his management, that he was chosen president of the American Newspaper Publishers' Association, president of the Chicago Press Club for three years, and president of the United Press, an organization for the collection and distribution of news. In connection with the World's Columbian Exposition, he rendered important service in bringing the fair to Chicago. As a member of the committee on arrangements and chairman of the press committee, his was an important voice in the fair. In 1890 plans for the establishment of an evening paper resulted in the appearance of the *Chicago Evening Post*. In 1895 the *Chicago Times* was purchased in order to consolidate it with the *Herald*, but before the plans were completely realized he died suddenly in New York City (see sketch of Herman H. Kohlsaat). Scott was a bluff, big, hearty individual and the soul of fellowship. He was typical of the West in his time and a man of liberal ideas. Through the years he stood firm for civil service reform and was never a violent partisan in politics. In Chicago and the Middle West, he was a power for reform in government and for clean politics. He was married to Carrie Green in 1873. Their one child died in infancy.

[Joseph Kirkland, *The Story of Chicago*, vol. II (1894); John J. Flinn, *The Handbook of Chicago Biog.* (copr. 1893); *Historical Encyc. of Ill.*, ed. by Newton Bateman and Paul Selby (1920); A. T. Andreas, *History of Chicago*, vol. III, 1886; John Moses and Joseph Kirkland, *History of Chicago* (1895), vol. II; *A History of the City of Chicago* (1900); F. W. Scott, "Newspaper Periodicals in Ill.," revised ed. *Ill. State Hist. Lib. Colls.*, vol. VI (1910); *Chicago Daily Tribune, Chicago Record, New York Herald*, Apr. 15, 1895.]   T. E. S.

SCOTT, JOB (Oct. 18, 1751–Nov. 22, 1793), Quaker preacher, was born in Providence, R. I., the son of John and Lydia (Comstock) Scott. He was received as a member of the Society of Friends by his request, apparently about 1771. On June 1, 1780, he married Eunice Anthony, daughter of Daniel and Mary Anthony, who died in 1791 having borne him six children. As early as 1774 he was conducting a school in Providence for Friends' children, and in 1778 he took charge of a school at Smithfield, R. I., established by the local Monthly Meeting of Friends. In 1783 he removed with his family to Glocester, R. I., where he apparently practised medicine for a time in a non-professional way. He had a small library of medical books and was occasionally referred to by contemporaries as a "doctor of physic." Little is known of his activities after his removal to Glocester, however, save those connected with his religious work.

He was one of the outstanding Quaker preachers of his day and traveled widely "in the ministry." In 1784 he went on a preaching pilgrimage to Quaker settlements in Vermont and New York, and in 1786 he spent six months in Pennsylvania and New Jersey. Three years later he started on a visitation of Friends' meetings that

led him along the Atlantic seaboard as far south as Georgia. Of this journey he wrote in his journal: "I was out on this exercising journey a year and about fifteen days, and travelled, by computation, about five thousand three hundred miles" (*Works, post,* I, 353). His last religious journey began when he set sail from Boston in December 1792 for England. Arrived at his destination, he began his usual work of visiting Quaker centers and also of holding meetings among those who were not Friends. He spent some time in Wales and in Bristol and vicinity, returning to London in time for the Friends' Yearly Meeting. Thence he went to Liverpool and took ship to Ireland, where he visited the various Friends' centers and attended the national Half-Year's Meeting at Dublin. Soon after, at Ballitore, he was stricken with smallpox and died at the age of forty-two years.

Historically, the most important thing about Job Scott is his place in the field of religious thought. He was a thoroughgoing mystic and has been called the most outstanding example of quietism in the history of American Quakerism (Jones, *post,* I, 78). His ideal was the utter abasement and death of all his natural powers so that the divine spirit could work through him without hindrance. Even when on special religious journeys he often sat through the meetings "in awful silence," not being sure of the divine promptings to speak. While visiting Friends' meetings in Pennsylvania in 1786 he wrote in his journal: "For twenty days past, I have not dared to open my mouth in one of the public meetings for worship that I have attended; I have been at fifteen" (*Works,* I, 223). Little schooled, he developed various advanced ideas of religion and of Biblical interpretation that anticipated some of the views of Christian modernism. The Scriptures to him were a "very good means of information" but not so important as the inward promptings of the divine spirit (*Ibid.,* I, 44). Christ, in his view, was the eternal spirit of God, once clothed in human flesh, but always, before and since that time, striving to enter into and regenerate human hearts. Thus there is no righteousness imputed nor forgiveness secured to men because of the death of Jesus on the cross. There was precedent for Scott's modernistic views in specific statements of some of the earliest Quaker leaders especially in the doctrine of the Light Within; yet Scott seemed to see with peculiar clarity the ultimate import of the earlier teachings.

During his lifetime his undoubted piety and uprightness apparently shielded him from criticism. After his death, however, doubts of his soundness grew. His own Yearly Meeting (New England) became afraid to publish his works in full. A few years later came the issue between liberalism and orthodoxy that led, among Friends, to the great separation of 1827–28 into the Hicksite and Orthodox branches. Scott's views then became thoroughly suspect among Orthodox Friends, while his writings were published in full under Hicksite auspices—*The Works of that Eminent Minister of the Gospel, Job Scott* (2 vols., 1831), edited by John Comly, the first volume of which contains the most complete printing of Scott's journal. If Friends generally had accepted his emphasis on the spiritual nature of religion they might have escaped the Great Separation, and met the later findings of science and of literary criticism unafraid. Therefore, some students of Quaker history are now looking upon Job Scott not as a heretic but as a prophet.

[H. W. Wilbur, *Job Scott, an Eighteenth Century Friend* (1911); R. M. Jones, *The Later Periods of Quakerism* (2 vols., 1921); *Friends' Miscellany*, Aug. 1834–Mar. 1835; Joseph Smith, *A Descriptive Cat. of Friends' Books* (1867), II, 546–50; manuscript material by and about Scott at Moses Brown School, Providence, R. I.]   R. W. K.

SCOTT, JOHN (*c.* 1630–1696), adventurer, was born, probably at Ashford in Kent, England, and, according to the most probable story, brought to America as a boy by Emmanuel Downing, the father of Sir George Downing, and bound out to Lawrence Southwick of Massachusetts Bay, the husband of Cassandra Southwick, the Quakeress. Thence he went to Long Island, made himself obnoxious to the Dutch, and was imprisoned by them in 1654. On his release he returned to Southampton on Long Island as a blacksmith, "keeping cowes" and trading with the Indians in land, became a freeman, was tax commissioner, married a Deborah Rayner, and visited Narragansett Bay, Boston, and, possibly, Newfoundland. In 1660 he went to England, gained the notice of Thomas Chiffinch, brother of William Chiffinch, and came to the attention of Joseph Williamson, afterward secretary to Sir Henry Bennet who was later Earl of Arlington. He became associated with a group of claimants to the Narragansett lands between Rhode Island and Connecticut known as the Atherton Company, made the acquaintance of one Daniel Gotherson and his wife Dorothea, Quakers, and, through his fancied resemblance to the portraits of her family, the Scotts of Scots Hall in Kent, he gained their confidence. They intrusted to him some £2,000 to invest for them in Long Island land, and their son, whom, upon reaching America, he sold to a New Haven inn-

keeper in 1663. He failed to obtain the grant to large tracts in Long Island which he sought, and the claims of the Atherton Company were thrown out by the Privy Council; but it seems he helped to suggest the seizure of New Amsterdam, and when he returned to Long Island he posed as a representative of the government, on the strength of a document purporting to be a royal grant, though it bore no signature. He was appointed one of three commissioners to negotiate with the Dutch, became "president" of the English settlements on Long Island, declared their independence of Connecticut, and led a futile expedition against Breuckelen. The Dutch recognized his title. Connecticut made him a magistrate but presently arrested him, put him in prison in Hartford, annulled his title, fined him, and put him under bond. Thence he escaped to take some small part in the surrender of New Amsterdam to the English expedition under Richard Nicolls [*q.v.*], whence he returned to his old mode of life at Southampton. It seems that he avenged himself for his failure to gain any advantage from the capture of New Amsterdam by advising that the boundaries of the new province of New York should not include New Jersey.

Accused of dishonest land transactions, of theft, fomenting sedition, and using the pretended royal patent to defraud, he escaped arrest by flight to the West Indies, where he obtained a commission under Lord Willoughby in Sir Tobias Bridge's regiment and saw some service against the French at St. Kitt's in 1665–66. Court-martialed and dismissed for cowardice, he went to England in 1667, renewed his connection with Williamson and Arlington, and, apparently on the strength of a volume he purported to be writing on the coasts and islands of America, which included a description of Guiana, he was made royal geographer. That post he lost, with the favor of Arlington and Williamson, upon Nicoll's return with his story of Scott's behavior and a petition of Mrs. Gotherson to the King. He fled to Holland, where he seems to have had a commission in the Dutch service, and, dismissed for dishonesty, went to Bruges, whence he was driven out for sketching the fortification. Thence he seems to have taken service under the Prince de Condé, going later to Paris, where he set up as a map-maker and geographer. He was throughout, apparently, a spy in the service of various governments. About 1677 he seems to have come into touch with the Duke of Buckingham and presently appeared as a witness in the Popish Plot and against Samuel Pepys, whom he accused of being a Roman Catholic and selling naval secrets to the French. Pepys was arrested but, brought before the Commons, not merely cleared himself but brought such a mass of testimony against Scott as to ruin him. Shortly thereafter Scott killed a man in a drunken quarrel. He was compelled to flee the country, apparently to Norway, and Pepys seized his papers. With the Revolution of 1688 Scott returned to England, was pardoned, and died.

Two hundred years later, as part of the testimony offered in the Venezuelan boundary dispute in 1895, his "Description of Guiana" and his "Relation" brought his name into some prominence. It seems probable from various incidents in his career that he did not write the important parts of these documents but obtained them from their real authors and passed them off as his own, and that conclusion is borne out by examination of the manuscripts.

[The material for this sketch is in "Colonel John Scott" by the present author, published with notes in the *Society of Colonial Wars Publications*, no. 30 (1918), as a separate volume (1918) and is reprinted with additions in his *Conflicts with Oblivion* (1923); its sources are the documents in the Pepys Coll., in Bodleian Lib., Oxford, England, in the Connecticut archives, the records of Southampton, N. Y., and like materials; see also J. C. Pilling, *Bibliog. of the Algonquin Languages* (1891), pp. 397–400; G. D. Scull, *Dorothea Scott* (1883).]   W. C. A.

SCOTT, JOHN MORIN (c. 1730–Sept. 14, 1784), lawyer, Revolutionary leader, was born in New York City, the only child of John Scott, a New York merchant, and a great-grandson of Sir John Scott, baronet, of Ancrum, Roxburghshire, Scotland. His mother was Marian, youngest daughter of Pierre and Marie (Jamain) Morin, Huguenots from La Rochelle. After graduating at Yale College in 1746, Scott studied law in the office of the elder William Smith [*q.v.*], and was admitted to the New York bar in 1752. In law, letters, and politics, early in his career, he definitely aligned himself with the Whig cause. In the celebrated case of *Cunningham* vs. *Forsey* (1764), as counsel for the respondent, he successfully maintained that no appeal in questions of fact lay from the provincial supreme court to the governor in council. In this position he was actively supported by Chief Justice Daniel Horsmanden [*q.v.*], and his stand, an eminently popular one, was subsequently affirmed on appeal (*Acts of the Privy Council . . . Colonial Series, 1745–1766*, 1911, p. 749). He was one of the most active practitioners of the law in the American colonies; his docket for the April term, 1767, of the New York Supreme court of judicature contained 114 cases. At the height of his career he lived in sumptuous style in a handsome rural residence in what is now West Forty-third Street,

between Eighth and Ninth Avenues. John Adams described it in 1774 as "an elegant seat" and the proprietor as "a sensible man, but not very polite," who was reputed to be "one of the readiest speakers upon the continent" (*The Works of John Adams*, 1850, II, 346, 349). Scott also had extensive holdings in the Schoharie Valley and Dutchess County.

He was actively associated with William Livingston and the younger William Smith [*qq.v.*] in literary contributions in behalf of the Whig Presbyterian cause in New York. These appeared in the *Independent Reflector* (1752–53) and in the "Watch Tower" column of the *New York Mercury* (1754–55). His bill for the establishment of King's College upon non-sectarian principles was printed and circulated in 1754 throughout the province. Other contributions of these collaborators include the publication in 1757 of *A Review of the Military Operations in North America . . . 1753–1756*, in defense of Governor Shirley of Massachusetts (reprinted in *Collections of the Massachusetts Historical Society*, 1 ser. VII, 1801), and the series known as the "American Whig" which appeared in the columns of James Parker's *New York Gazette* (1768–69). Scott is known to have been the sole author of the significant essay against the Stamp Act, signed "Freeman," contained in three numbers of John Holt's *New York Gazette* in June 1765, and he was one of the organizers of the New York Sons of Liberty.

He served as alderman of New York City, 1756–61. As a candidate for the Assembly in 1769, indorsed by the Liberty party, he was decisively defeated in a contest marred by charges of bribery and intimidation (I. N. P. Stokes, *The Iconography of Manhattan Island*, vol. IV, 1922, p. 791). On the eve of the Revolution, Scott was listed among the more extreme agitators and was not sent as a delegate to the Continental Congress in 1774. He was a leader of the radical party in the provincial congresses of New York in 1775–77 and of the democratic forces in the constitutional convention of the latter year. The day of the adoption of the constitution he was appointed a member of the committee to prepare a plan for establishing the new government (*Journals of the Provincial Congress . . . of New York*, 1842, I, 892–98), and on its adoption, May 8, he was made a member of the Council of Safety. The week before, he had been elected to the new supreme court but, defeated by John Jay for the chief justiceship, declined to serve (*Ibid.*, I, 910). In the gubernatorial election of the same year Scott ran against George Clinton and Philip Schuyler [*qq.v.*] and polled a number of votes from the middle districts of the state, although the ballots of the southern counties gave the election to Clinton (E. A. Werner, *Civil List of the Colony and State of New York,* 1888, p. 164). In 1778 he was appointed secretary of state, in which office he was succeeded upon his death in 1784 by his son, Lewis Allaire.

Despite the pressure of his political activities, Scott was drawn into the military conflict, participating in the battle of Long Island as a brigadier-general. He later served with General Heath in the lower part of West Chester, but resigned in the spring of 1777 to become state senator, in which position he continued until 1782. He served also as a member of the Continental Congress from 1779 to 1783. As one of the delegates from New York to settle the boundary dispute with Vermont, he opposed the appointment by Congress of a court of commissioners to act in the matter and favored quick action to check the claims of the smaller states (Hiland Hall, *The History of Vermont,* 1868, p. 317; E. C. Burnett, *Letters of Members of the Continental Congress,* vol. V, 1931, pp. 390, 391).

About 1752 Scott married Helena, daughter of Capt. Petrus and Helena (Hoogland) Rutgers, of New York City. A son and a daughter survived him, two sons having died young. Exposure in military service is said to have greatly aggravated a predisposition to acute rheumatism which resulted in his death in early middle age shortly after his return to his native city upon its evacuation by the British.

[Biog. notices appear in F. B. Dexter, *Biog. Sketches Grads. Yale Coll.,* vol. II (1896); Maria S. B. Chance and Mary A. E. Smith, *Scott Family Letters* (1930); *Biog. Dir. Am. Cong.* (1928); B. J. Lossing, *Pictorial Field-Book of the Revolution* (1852), I, 805 n. See also E. B. O'Callaghan, *Docs. Rel. to the Col. Hist of the State of N. Y.,* vol. VII (1856); Thomas Jones, *Hist. of N. Y. during the Rev. War* (2 vols., 1879), ed. by E. F. De Lancey; *Memoirs of the L. I. Hist. Soc.,* vol. III (1878). Many of Scott's law papers are available in the office of the Commissioner of Records, New York City, and, in abundance, in the following boxes: "Supreme Court Pleadings," 1–66; "Supreme Court, Miscellaneous, 1771–1789," 320–631.]

R. B. M.

SCOTT, JOHN PRINDLE (Aug. 16, 1877–Dec. 2, 1932), composer, was born at Norwich, N. Y., the son of Warren L. Scott and Delia (Prindle) Scott. Possessed of a beautiful, clear, baritone voice, he spent four years, from 1896 to 1900, studying in the undergraduate school and conservatory of music at Oberlin College, Oberlin, Ohio. He had the opportunity of singing in the Second Congregational Church choir at Oberlin under the direction of Prof. A. S.

Kimball, teacher of singing at the college, and G. W. Andrews, organist and professor of composition in the conservatory, and was also soloist in the college glee club. In 1914 he furnished a dozen contributions to the book of Oberlin songs, writing for some of them both words and music. After leaving Oberlin he spent two years at Saginaw, Mich., teaching singing and then entered upon a season of public concerts. In his native town he led the church choir and organized the DeKoven male quartet. During the war he was leader of singing in community houses in New York.

Increasing deafness made it necessary for Scott to give up his concerts, and he turned to composition. Among his sacred works were numerous vocal solos and anthems for Christmas and Easter, and also "The Lord is my Shepherd," "Consider the lilies," and "Come ye blessed." He composed the music for the words of A. A. Toms, "O haste the day when wars shall cease." Perhaps the best-known and loved of his secular songs is "The Old Road." Prizes were awarded him for songs written for the state of Nebraska and for Ohio University, Athens, Ohio, and he was presented a very handsome loving-cup by his neighbors in McDonough, N. Y., in appreciation for the "musical sings" which he conducted for a number of years, bringing to them many artists seldom heard in so small a town. Scott was never married. He maintained a summer home at McDonough, called "The Scottage," and during his later years divided his winters between New York City and Washington, D. C. The last concert given in his honor was in Barker Hall, Y. W. C. A., Washington, on the evening of Apr. 11, 1932, when "The Old Road" was rendered by the Chesapeake and Potomac Male Choir. Other pieces of his composition included "Old Bill," "Revelation," "The Dearest Place," "Good Luck, Mr. Fisherman," "Even Song," and "The Trumpet shall sound"—a program which illustrates the versatility of his musical work. With his love for music Scott combined a remarkable sense of humor which made him a delightful companion. He had a magnetic personality, charming social graces, and a deeply spiritual nature which found adequate expression in his sacred compositions.

[Information from the family; *Who's Who in America,* 1932–33; *Internatl. Who's Who in Music* (1918); *Etude,* July 1928; *Evening Star* (Washington, D. C.), Apr. 12, Dec. 3, 1932; *N. Y. Times,* Dec. 3, 1932.]

F. J. M.

SCOTT, LEROY (May 11, 1875–July 21, 1929), author, was born in Fairmount, Ind., the son of Eli J. and Eleanor (Reader) Scott. After graduating from Indiana University in 1897, he worked for a few months on a Louisiana newspaper owned by his brother and then went to Chicago, where he was a reporter for the *Chicago Journal*. In 1900 and 1901 he was assistant editor of the *Woman's Home Companion*. He had developed an interest in settlement work as a result of living at Hull House in Chicago, and in 1902 he became assistant headworker of the University Settlement, New York City. Here he met Miriam Finn, whom he married on June 24, 1904; they had two daughters and a son.

When in 1904 he gave up settlement work to devote himself to writing, he did not give up his interest in social reform. His first novel, *The Walking Delegate* (1905), showed not merely his confidence in organized labor but also his hope for far-reaching social reorganization. In *To Him That Hath* (1907) he revealed the difficulties of a man who has been in prison, and in *Counsel for the Defense* (1912) he described a woman's struggle for economic independence. *The Shears of Destiny* (1910) was concerned with the Russian revolutionary movement and was based on Scott's observations, made during a visit to Russia with his wife in 1905–06. From 1904 to 1912 he wrote frequently for the magazines on such topics as unemployment, life insurance, and strike-breaking. After his return from Russia he contributed several articles to the *Outlook* and to *Everybody's* on conditions in that country, and especially on the activities of the revolutionaries. In short, he is to be numbered among the muck-rakers. He was always moderate in his methods, but a strong social purpose informed what he wrote and is to be observed in his novels as well as his articles. It also found expression in other activities, for he was interested in organizing the Women's Trade Union League, an active worker for child-labor laws, and one of the founders and an executive of the Intercollegiate Socialist Society. When the muck-raking movement declined, he took advantage of another form of popular fiction. In *Partners of the Night* (1916) he dealt with crime and its detection, and the success of the book encouraged him to write a series of stories about the activities of criminals and policemen. These novels were based on an exact knowledge of criminal methods, derived from careful investigation, and all of them indicated the need for changes in the social structure and in the handling of offenders against the law; although the social moral may not have been plain to most of Scott's readers, it was constantly in his mind. His last novel, *The Trail of Glory* (1926), dealt with some of the problems of an amateur tennis

champion. He was drowned at Chateaugay Lake, N. Y. At his best he was a skilful storyteller, but he commonly employed romantic and improbable plots, showed no great insight into character, and had no stylistic distinction. He frankly and successfully competed with writers whose sole aim was to divert their readers; his work is on a higher level than theirs only because of the sincerity and firmness of his social purpose.

[*Who's Who in America*, 1928–29; "Our Own Times," *Reader Mag.*, Sept. 1905; Griffin Mace, "Nine Books of the Month," *Bookman*, May 1912; brief obit. in *Publishers' Weekly*, Aug. 3, 1929; *N. Y. Times*, July 22 and 28, 1929; information from Mrs. Scott.]

G. H.

SCOTT, ORANGE (Feb. 13, 1800–July 31, 1847), anti-slavery leader, was born in Brookfield, Vt., the eldest of the eight children of Lucy (Whitney) and Samuel Scott, a laboring man. The family lived at various places in Vermont and spent six years in Stanstead in Lower Canada. The boy's total schooling was about thirteen months. Beginning to feel religious concern in his twenty-first year, he experienced conversion at a camp-meeting held near Barre, Vt., late in 1820. At this time he was working as a farm laborer, but he was soon giving his Sundays to religious work, assisting the Methodist preacher in charge of the local circuit. His success was such that in November 1821 he gave up farming entirely and began the work of a circuit preacher. In 1822 he was received into the New England Conference on trial and by 1825 was a fully ordained minister in the Methodist Episcopal Church. His advancement was rapid, and within a few years he became, through reading and private study, a most effective speaker. His first important church was in Charlestown, Mass., where he achieved considerable distinction through a public discussion with a Universalist minister. On May 7, 1826, he was married to Amy Fletcher of Lyndon, Vt., who died in April 1835 leaving five children. In 1829, after serving a number of smaller circuits, he was sent to Springfield, Mass., the next year was made presiding elder of that district, and in 1831 was delegate to the General Conference. In 1833 he came in contact for the first time with the anti-slavery movement and was soon an ardent abolitionist. Appointed presiding elder of the Providence district in 1834 he took the leadership in a movement to open the columns of *Zion's Herald*, the Methodist paper in Boston, to a discussion of the slavery issue. This was accomplished, and he became the most active contributor. He also began to deliver public lectures on slavery in the larger New England cities.

When the slavery question came before the General Conference of 1836 at Cincinnati, he made an *Address* (1836) on the subject and was a recognized abolition leader. As a consequence of this abolition activity the bishop refused to reappoint him to the Providence district. After a year's pastorate at Lowell, Mass., he accepted an agency for the American Anti-Slavery Society and spoke throughout New England and New York. In 1838 he published "An Appeal to the Methodist Episcopal Church" in the only number published of the *Wesleyan Anti-Slavery Review*. At the session of the New England Conference in 1838 Bishop Elijah Hedding [*q.v.*] charged Scott with using coarse and disrespectful language, but the charges were not sustained. In 1839 Scott with Jotham Horton undertook the publication of the *American Wesleyan Observer* to plead the abolition cause among Methodists in preparation for the General Conference of 1840. He was a member of that Conference and again led the abolition forces. The radicals however were unable to stem the tide of conservative opinion. He became again the pastor of St. Paul's Church in Lowell, Mass., chosen regardless of episcopal authority. This action led to a bitter fight with the appointing authorities, which was one of the reasons that made Scott consider withdrawal from the Methodist Episcopal Church.

The secession movement rapidly developed under Scott's leadership, ably assisted by Jotham Horton and LaRoy Sunderland. These three leaders withdrew from the Methodist Episcopal Church on Nov. 8, 1841. They began the publication of the *True Wesleyan* on Jan. 7, 1843, to agitate withdrawal of all abolition Methodists to form a new ecclesiastical body, with opposition to slavery as its chief cornerstone. A preliminary convention at Andover, Mass., on Feb. 1, 1843, provided for a general convention at Utica, N. Y., on May 31. Scott was the president of the Utica convention, and there the Wesleyan Methodist Connection of America was formed. In the interests of this new Wesleyan Methodist Church he became the publishing agent in charge of the *True Wesleyan*, and when this business was moved to New York City he took up his residence at Newark, N. J., though his family remained in Newbury, Vt. In 1845 he made an extended tour of the western states that proved disastrous to his health, which had been failing for some time. In 1846 he published his reasons for his withdrawal in a book, *The Grounds of Secession from the M. E. Church: Being an Examination of her Connection with Slavery, and Also of her Form of Government*. A revised and corrected edition was published in 1848. In 1846 he took his family to Newark and attempted to continue his work; but his condition grew rapidly worse, and he died at his home in Newark. He was survived by his widow, Eliza (Dearborn) Scott, whom he had married on Oct. 6, 1835. They had two children.

[The chief sources are his writings, *ante,* and autobiog. in L. C. Matlack, *The Life of Rev. Orange Scott* (1847), which is paged continuously and bound in same vol. with his *Memoir of Rev. Orange Scott* (1848); see also J. N. Norwood, *The Schism in the Methodist Episcopal Church* (1923); L. C. Matlack, *The Hist. of Amer. Slavery and Methodism from 1780 to 1849* (1849).]
W. W. S.

SCOTT, ROBERT KINGSTON (July 8, 1826–Aug. 12, 1900), Union soldier and governor of South Carolina, was born in Armstrong County, Pa., the son of Jane (Hamilton) and John Scott, a farmer. In 1842 the boy went to Stark County, Ohio, to seek educational advantages. In 1850 he went to California, where, for brief periods, he engaged in mining and the practice of his profession. After visiting Mexico and South America he settled in Florida, Henry County, Ohio, probably in 1851, to practise medicine. There he was married to Rebecca J. Lowry and had two children. Aid in the suppression of a cholera epidemic soon gave him considerable local prestige. Profitable investments in real estate enabled him to withdraw gradually from medicine and to engage in merchandising. On the outbreak of the Civil War, Governor Dennison appointed him a major with instructions to organize the 68th Ohio Infantry. In July 1862 he was promoted to the rank of colonel. He received honorable mention for gallantry in action and commanded a brigade in Sherman's march to the sea. On Jan. 12, 1865, he was promoted to the rank of brigadier-general and at the end of the war was brevetted a major-general.

Returning to Ohio after the war, he was recalled into active service almost immediately and made chief of the South Carolina branch of the Freedmen's Bureau with the title of assistant commissioner. He served in that capacity until July 1868. The conservative press of South Carolina praised him for the wise and moderate manner in which he administered the affairs of the bureau. Popularity engendered by his services as the chief dispenser of the charity of the federal government led to his nomination, in March 1868, for governor by the newly formed Union Republican party of South Carolina. He was easily elected. In 1870 he was reëlected by a large majority over Robert B. Carpenter, the candidate of an attempted coalition between Democrats and Republican reformers. As governor from July 1868 to November 1872 Scott was largely responsible for the scandals and disorders that characterized the introduction of Republican rule in South Carolina. His policies led to the increase of the public debt to thrice the amount it had been when he assumed office, and he concealed this fact from responsible investigators. When an attempt was made to impeach him, he stopped the proceedings by bribing the legislature with public funds. He was a leader in conspiracies to defraud the state of money by manipulating printing contracts and the stocks of the Blue Ridge Railroad. Provoking the formation of bands of the Ku-Klux Klan by the unscrupulous tactics through which he obtained reëlection, he professed inability to suppress these organizations and called in the aid of Federal troops. It is probable that Scott would have made a competent governor under normal conditions. His previous record had been creditable and his inaugural address bespoke a desire for conciliation and constructive achievement. That he was not callous to the better interests of the state is attested by his endeavor at times to stem the tide of corruption by the use of the veto. But it would have been impossible for him to make his administration satisfactory to the whites in whose hands ultimately lay the control of the state's destiny. After a half-hearted resistance to the corrupt officials who surrounded him, he conveniently succumbed to their suggestions and personally profited from their acts. He was "subject alike to alcoholic and female allurements," and on one occasion the state officials paid an actress to induce the drunken governor to sign an issue of bonds (E. P. Mitchell, *Memoirs of an Editor*, 1924, p. 326).

On the expiration of his term of office he retired from politics and settled in Columbia as a real estate agent. He declared the experiment of negro suffrage a mistake and in 1876 supported the state Democratic ticket; but on the return of the Democrats to power in 1877 he prudently left South Carolina in the face of possible prosecution and returned to Henry County, Ohio. There he engaged in the real estate development for the rest of his life. On Christmas Day 1880 he killed Walter G. Drury, a young drug clerk, whom he believed responsible for making his young son drunk. On a plea of accidental homicide he was acquitted of the charges that grew out of this act. He died in Henry County.

[*Men of Northwestern Ohio* (1898); L. C. Aldrich, *Hist. of Henry and Fulton Counties, Ohio* (1888); F. B. Heitman, *Hist. Register and Dictionary of the U. S. Army* (1903), vol. I; F. B. Simkins and R. H. Woody, *S. C. during Reconstruction* (1932); *Report of the* *Joint Investigating Committee on Public Frauds . . . Made to the General Assembly of S. C. . . . 1877–78* (1878), esp. pp. 215–21, 271–76, 563, 587–92; *Special Message of . . . Robert K. Scott, Governor . . . in Reply to Charges Made Against Him* (1872); *Charleston Daily News*, Mar. 9, 1868, Aug. 22, 1872; *News and Courier* (Charleston), Dec. 29, 30, 1880; *State* (Columbia, S. C.), Aug. 15, 1900.]   F. B. S—s.

SCOTT, SAMUEL PARSONS (July 8, 1846–May 30, 1929), lawyer, author, Hispanic scholar, was born at Hillsboro, Ohio, the son of William Scott, a lawyer and banker, and his wife, Elizabeth Jane Parsons. He attended the public schools and Miami University, where he graduated B.A. in 1866, studied law, was admitted to the bar in 1868, and practised at Leavenworth, Kan., and later at San Francisco. In 1875, because of his father's failing health, he left his practice and returned to Hillsboro to attend to the extensive property interests which he later inherited. Thenceforth he devoted himself to intellectual pursuits, with business as an avocation. A long sojourn in Spain resulted in a series of articles contributed to *Lippincott's, The Continent,* and *Potter's American Monthly.* In 1886 these papers, collected and revised, with some additional material, were published in book form under the title *Through Spain.* Meanwhile, Scott had begun work on his most ambitious original production, *History of the Moorish Empire in Europe* (3 vols., 1904), in the preface of which he stated that the work "engaged the attention of the author for more than twenty years." His bibliography was extensive, but he neglected to cite authorities for specific points. He was evidently indebted to *A History of the Intellectual Development of Europe* (1863) by John W. Draper [*q.v.*], and was even more favorable in his estimate of Arab culture and influence (Cf. his chap. xiii with Draper's chap. xvi). He held that the Moorish invasion was a deliverance from Visigothic oppression and depicted the Arab régime as the most brilliant period of peninsular history, the Christian hero, *El Cid,* as a cruel and treacherous outlaw, and the Spanish church as a perpetual instrument of enslavement and corruption.

For the remaining quarter century of his life, Scott's chosen task was the translation into English of the chief monuments of the Spanish and the Civil law. He was one of the founders of the Comparative Law Bureau of the American Bar Association and under its auspices published in 1910, with the title of *The Visigothic Code,* his translation from the Latin of the *Forum Judicum (Fuero Juzgo).* He had failed, however, to familiarize himself with the Continental literature of the subject, especially with the later texts; the accuracy of his translation was questioned; and his preface and notes drew adverse criticism from the reviewers; nevertheless, the fact remains that his was the first attempt to put the work into English and it stimulated an interest in the subject. His rendering of *Las Siete Partidas,* the famous medieval code of Spain, appeared posthumously under the same auspices in 1931; but in this instance the Bureau officers had edited the text, the translation had been carefully checked, and an introduction, index, table of contents, and copious bibliography had been prepared by others. Unfortunately, his translations of the Roman legal landmarks, including the *Corpus Juris,* were printed just as he had left them, unedited and unchecked, under the misleading title of *The Civil Law* (17 vols., 1932).

On Oct. 10, 1895, when he was nearly fifty, Scott married Elizabeth Woodbridge Smart of Paint, Ohio. He was by that time deep in his literary labors and the union proved uncongenial. No formal separation took place; but in his will he directed that his wife should receive only a relatively small portion of his estate, allowing a considerable sum for the publication of his remaining manuscripts. This provision was disregarded by his executor, and the works remain unpublished. These include translations of *El Fuero Viejo de Castilla, El Fuero Real, Las Leyes del Estilo, El Ordenamiento de Alcala, Las Leyes Nuevas, El Ordenamiento de las Tafurerias, Las Leyes de Toro, Leyes para los Adelantados Mayores,* and *El Código Penal de España.* In connection with his labors Scott accumulated a large and select library. He died at his home in Hillsboro.

[Scott's *Moorish Empire* was reviewed by F. W. Williams, in *Am. Hist. Rev.,* Jan. 1905; his *Visigothic Code,* by Paul Vinagradoff, in *Law Quart. Rev.,* July 1911, and by Munroe Smith, in *Columbia Law Rev.,* Nov. 1911; *Las Siete Partidas* by A. S. de Bustamante y Sirvén, in *Tulane Law Rev.,* Feb. 1932, by D. E. Grant, in *Columbia Law Rev.,* Apr. 1932, and by A. S. Aiton, in *Am. Bar Asso. Jour.,* May 1932. For biography see C. S. Lobinger, *Ibid.,* Sept. 1929; *Who's Who in America,* 1928–29; *Gen. Cat. Miami Univ.,* 1809–1909 (n.d.); *Cincinnati Enquirer,* May 31, 1929.]

C. S. L.

SCOTT, THOMAS ALEXANDER (Dec. 28, 1823–May 21, 1881), railroad executive, was born at Fort Loudon, Franklin County, Pa., the seventh in a family of eleven children. His father, Thomas Scott, kept a tavern at which the passengers on the stagecoaches stopped for refreshments. His mother, Thomas Scott's second wife, was Rebecca Douglas. The boy attended a country school in the winter months, until at the age of ten he lost his father, and then he worked as a handy man in a general supply store until he was about seventeen, when he went to Columbia, Pa., as a clerk in the office of Maj. James Patton, his brother-in-law, who was collector of tolls on the state system of public roads and canals.

He remained in the employ of the state until 1845, then engaged in private business ventures at Columbia, with an interval in 1847–49 when he was chief clerk in the office of the collector of tolls at Philadelphia. In 1850 he became station agent for the railroad at Duncansville, the point of transfer between the Pennsylvania Railroad and the state canals on the one hand and the Allegheny Portage Railroad over the mountains on the other. In December 1852, when the Pennsylvania Railroad was completed to Pittsburgh, his abilities had so far developed that he was appointed third assistant superintendent in charge of the division starting westward from Altoona, with his office at Pittsburgh. On Jan. 1, 1858, he became general superintendent, and on Mar. 21, 1860, first vice-president of the Pennsylvania Railroad.

In this capacity, as the war clouds thickened early in 1861, Scott advised the President-Elect, who was in Harrisburg as the guest of Governor Curtin, not to go directly to Washington as he had intended, but to return secretly to Philadelphia and proceed thence, with the same secrecy, to the Capital. This plan was adopted, the telegraph wires were disconnected, and Lincoln reached Washington ahead of the time published in the newspapers and by another route. Upon the outbreak of hostilities, Simon Cameron [*q.v.*] of Pennsylvania, then secretary of war, summoned Scott to Washington (Apr. 21, 1861) to operate the Northern Central railroad from Harrisburg to Baltimore for the purpose of transporting men and munitions. Taking with him from the Pennsylvania Railroad service a young telegraph operator named Andrew Carnegie, Scott reported to Cameron. On May 3, 1861, he was commissioned colonel of United States Volunteers; and by an act of Congress of Aug. 3, 1861, he was appointed assistant secretary of war to supervise all government railways and transportation lines. Although he had only advisory power, in the months before his resignation, June 1, 1862, he laid the foundation of a working system. In September 1863 he was called back into the government service and given the temporary appointment of colonel and assistant quartermaster-general on the staff of Major-General Joseph Hooker for the special task of transporting some 13,000 men, with their artillery, wagons, and horses, from Virginia through Nashville to Chattanooga. From time to time throughout the war, Scott was called upon for advice and suggestions regarding the government's use of railroads.

Meanwhile, under the presidency of J. Edgar Thomson [q.v.], with Scott as vice-president, the Pennsylvania Railroad was beginning its period of greatest expansion. In 1862 the company leased the Philadelphia & Erie, which provided a connection between the Atlantic seaboard and the Great Lakes; in 1868–69 control was secured, through lease or stock ownership, of the newly built lines reaching consecutively from Pittsburgh to Cincinnati, Indianapolis, St. Louis, and Chicago; while in 1871 the United Canal and Railroad Companies of New Jersey were leased, extending the line from Philadelphia into New York City. Other leases and purchases opened the railroad's entrance into Baltimore and Washington. The Pennsylvania Company was organized in 1870, with Scott as president, for the purpose of operating and managing all the lines leased and controlled by the Pennsylvania Railroad west of Pittsburgh. In 1871 Scott was instrumental in having the Pennsylvania take a financial interest in the Southern Railway Security Company, which controlled a number of railroad systems built or being constructed south of Richmond, Va. He believed that these roads would prove valuable traffic feeders to the Pennsylvania, but his expectations were not fulfilled and about ten years later the Pennsylvania sold what was left of its investment in the Southern company. In the meantime, the Union Pacific Railroad, which was then the only transcontinental line, had fallen into financial difficulties, and it occurred to Scott that it might be brought into the Pennsylvania's control. On Mar. 8, 1871, he was elected president of that company, succeeding Oliver Ames, 1807–1877 [q.v.], but retained office only until Mar. 6, 1872, eventually selling his holdings to Jay Gould [q.v.]. On June 3, 1874, upon the death of Thomson, Scott succeeded him as president of the Pennsylvania Railroad Company. His task thenceforth was chiefly to consolidate and strengthen the system which had been so greatly expanded. From 1872 to 1880 he was also president of the Texas & Pacific Railway Company.

Scott was a man of striking appearance. He had a keen and quick apprehension, an even temper, inexhaustible patience, and great charm of manner. In spite of his limited schooling he had acquired the habit of wide reading which gave his speech the mark of an educated man. He was married in the fall of 1847 to Anna Margaret Mullison, daughter of Reuben Mullison, of Columbia, Pa. She died in 1855, leaving a

son and a daughter, a second daughter having died in infancy. Ten years later Scott married Anna Dike Riddle, of Pittsburgh. A daughter and two sons, one of whom died in boyhood, were born of this marriage. In 1878 Scott suffered a paralytic stroke, but recovered sufficiently to continue his executive work until June 1, 1880, when he resigned the presidency of the Pennsylvania. He died at his home, "Woodburn," near Darby, Pa., less than a year later.

[The date of birth here given is that appearing in "Thomas A. Scott," biog. address by John P. Green, vice-president of the Pa. RR., formerly Scott's private secretary, and in other memoranda in Pa. RR. archives. Other sources for Scott's career include *Encyc. of Contemporary Biog. of Pa.* (1889), vol. I; J. W. Jordan, *Encyc. of Pa. Biog.*, vol. VII (1916); *Mag. of Western History*, June 1889; W. B. Wilson, *Hist. of the Pa. RR. Company* (1899), vol. II; H. W. Schotter, *The Growth and Development of the Pa. RR. Company* (1927); R. E. Riegel, *The Story of the Western Railroads* (1926); *Am. Hist. Rev.*, July 1917; *N. Y. Tribune*, May 22, 1881; *Phila. Press*, May 21, 25, 1881; *Public Ledger* (Phila.), May 23, 1881.] S. H. C.

SCOTT, THOMAS FIELDING (Mar. 12, 1807–July 14, 1867), Protestant Episcopal clergyman, first missionary bishop of Oregon and Washington Territory, was born in Iredell County, N. C. He was educated at Chapel Hill School, N. C., and at Franklin College (University of Georgia), Athens, graduating from the latter with honors in 1829. Licensed to preach in the Presbyterian Church, he served as a missionary in Hall and Franklin counties and at Columbus, Ga. Subsequently he had more important charges at La Grange and Savannah, Ga., and at Columbia, Tenn. The turning point in his career came about 1842 when he met Bishop James Hervey Otey and Bishop Leonidas Polk. Under the inspiration of these friends he "made thorough study of the Scriptural and historical claims of Episcopacy," came to "the firm and unalterable conclusion that the doctrine was true," and regretfully abandoned Presbyterianism (manuscript biographical sketch, *post*). He was ordained deacon by Bishop Stephen Elliott at St. Paul's Church, Augusta, Ga., Mar. 12, 1843, and priest by Bishop Elliott at Christ Church, Macon, Ga., Feb. 24, 1844. He served successively as rector of St. James' Church, Marietta, Ga., and Trinity Church, Columbus, Ga.

In 1853 he was appointed missionary bishop of the new diocese in the remote Northwest, was consecrated at Christ Church, Savannah, Ga., Jan. 8, 1854, and commenced his work in Oregon in the following April. The district placed in his charge was extensive, conditions of travel were painfully arduous, means of communication were inconstant, money was scarce, and competent assistants almost impossible to secure. For thirteen years, however, in spite of pathetic handicaps, he struggled on, laying the foundations necessary for the achievements of his successor. Several times he was called upon to administer the diocese of California as well. In 1860 he returned East for a few months on business of the church. The unremitting strain of his labors influenced his health, and he fell ill of Panama fever on his way to the General Convention of 1868. He died in New York, and was buried in Trinity Cemetery. In 1830 he had married Evelyn Appleby of Jackson, Ga., by whom he was survived.

Bishop Scott was a man of great energy of mind and wide information. He was gentle in manner and spontaneously generous of spirit, but was capable of forceful and apt expression of his views. As a preacher he was popular in both the South and West. His vision was greater than his opportunity, but he is gratefully remembered for his pioneer endeavors and considered by many an authentic martyr of the American Church.

[W. S. Perry, *The Episcopate in America* (1895); *N. Y. Tribune*, July. 16, 1867; sermons, letters, and biog. sketch by Mrs. Scott in Colburn Collection of autographic and bibliographic material regarding American bishops, archives of Washington Cathedral, Washington, D. C.]
                       J. W. F.

SCOTT, WALTER (Oct. 31, 1796–Apr. 23, 1861), preacher and religious reformer, was born at Moffat, Dumfriesshire, Scotland, the sixth child of John Scott, a music teacher, and Mary (Innes) Scott. He received a good musical education, became a skilled flutist, and was graduated from the University of Edinburgh in 1818. That same year, on invitation of his uncle, George Innes, who had a position in the New York custom house, he emigrated to the United States. For a time he served as tutor in an academy on Long Island. Traveling to Pittsburgh on foot, he arrived there May 7, 1819, and became assistant to George Forrester, who was conducting a private school. Forrester was an immersed Haldanean preacher who had come from Scotland not long before and had organized a church in Pittsburgh. Scott, a Presbyterian, was converted to Forrester's views, was immersed, and joined his church. On Forrester's death by drowning, Scott took over his duties both in connection with the church and with the school. Having read a pamphlet put forth by a Scotch Baptist Church in New York, he resigned his position and went there to learn more about the institution, but was not greatly pleased with what he found. Invited back to Pittsburgh by Nathaniel Richardson as tutor for his son

Robert, he returned to establish a small school and care for the church.

In the winter of 1821–22 he first met Alexander Campbell [*q.v.*] in Pittsburgh and was deeply impressed by his teaching. Scott suggested the name *The Christian Baptist* for the magazine which Campbell began to publish in August 1823, and contributed to the second number an article entitled "On Teaching Christianity," which an editorial note announced as stating "a Divinely authorized plan of teaching the Christian religion." This was followed by three others on the same theme. He became one of the most regular and copious contributors to the periodicals and made Campbell's cause his own. While Campbell thought chiefly of reforming the church, Scott's primary interest was in the conversion of individuals. He continued to conduct his academy in Pittsburgh until 1826, but early in that year moved to Steubenville, Ohio. In August he visited the annual meeting of the Mahoning Baptist Association (of which Campbell was then a member) and preached before it; in 1827, he visited it again and was invited to preach. Although he was neither a member of the Association nor a Baptist, he was chosen as its evangelist. Applying to the process of conversion the principles on which Campbell had based his proposed reformation of the church, Scott developed a remarkably effective technique of evangelism, stressing three points: faith (the belief of testimony regarding the sonship and messiahship of Jesus); repentance (of past sins); baptism (by immersion for remission of sins). Under this preaching over a thousand new members were added in a year to the churches of the Mahoning Association. It was largely through Scott's urgency that the Association was dissolved and the "Reformers" ceased to consider themselves Baptists.

Scott, who had already moved to Canfield, Ohio, soon moved to Cincinnati, where he began the publication of a monthly magazine, the *Evangelist,* and then to Carthage, Ohio, where he lived for thirteen years, traveling and preaching in Ohio, Kentucky, Virginia, and Missouri. For a very short time he was president of Bacon College. In 1844 he returned to Pittsburgh, preached for a church in that city and for one in Allegheny, and published a weekly paper, the *Protestant Unionist.* From 1850 to 1854 he was principal of a female academy at Covington, Ky. From the latter date until his death in 1861 he lived in Mason County, Ky. He was the author of two books: *The Gospel Restored* (1836), and *The Messiahship, or the Great Demonstration* (1859). He was thrice married: on Jan. 3, 1823, to Sarah Whitsett, who died in 1849, having borne him four sons and a daughter; in 1850, to Annie B. Allen, who died in 1854, by whom he had a daughter; and in 1855, to Mrs. Eliza Sandige, who survived him. Scott's significance in the history of the Disciples of Christ is that he established the evangelistic pattern and the form and method of propaganda to which the rapid growth of this group of Christians was largely due.

[William Baxter, *Life of Elder Walter Scott, with Sketches of his Fellow-laborers, William Hayden, Adamson Bentley, John Henry, and Others* (1874); Robert Richardson, *Memoirs of Alexander Campbell* (2 vols., 1868–70); W. E. Garrison, *Religion Follows the Frontier* (1931); the *Christian Baptist*, 1823–29; files of the *Millennial Harbinger*, 1830–61, with obituary notice, May 1861.]   W.E.G.

SCOTT, WILLIAM (June 7, 1804–May 18, 1862), jurist, was born at Warrenton, Fauquier County, Va., of a family resident in the state and province since early colonial days. After his graduation from Fauquier Academy, he studied law with a local attorney and was admitted to the bar in 1825. The next year he removed to Missouri and settled at the then flourishing town of Old Franklin. The choice was not a wise one, for there were many leading lawyers in the locality and, as Scott was hot-tempered and excitable, his experienced opponents found it easy to confuse and irritate him during trials. His industry and knowledge of the law, however, won the respect of the profession and led to his appointment in 1835 as judge of the ninth circuit. The same year he married Elizabeth Dixon, of Jefferson City, by whom he had six children. Living at Union, he traveled on circuit through the large district. As a judge he won immediate recognition. He decided cases soon after hearing the arguments, since there was no opportunity in the pioneer community to examine carefully reports and opinions difficult of access, and he frequently deferred to local conditions and discarded common law doctrines to meet the immediate situation. This frontier judicial pragmatism suited admirably both lawyers and litigants; he was highly regarded for his sense of justice and kind heart.

In August 1841 he was appointed to the supreme bench, an action that was widely indorsed by Democrats and by Whigs alike (*Jeffersonian Republican*, Aug. 28, 1841). He served eighteen years. His opinions, necessarily dealing with a great variety of subjects, were marked by brevity and by conservatism. His legal ability did not equal that of his colleagues, Hamilton Rowan Gamble and William Barclay Napton [*qq.v.*], but he was industrious, just, and competent. He wrote many opinions in cases involving master and slave, including *Emerson* vs. *Harriet* and *Emerson* vs. *Dred Scott* (1848, 11 *Mo.*, 413), and he spoke for the majority in *Scott, a Man of Color* vs. *Emerson* (1852, 15 *Mo.*, 576). In the latter case, he overruled eight Missouri precedents in holding that the laws of other states and territories had no extra-territorial effect in Missouri except as Missouri recognized them, and that a slave who is taken by his master into territory where slavery is prohibited could not, after returning with his master to Missouri, maintain a suit for freedom. He also charged that the free states, in obstructing the return of fugitive slaves, refused to recognize the law of the slave states. The decision assumed, therefore, a political significance. He was an ardent Democrat and during the middle forties became active in the group of radical, pro-slavery opponents of Thomas Hart Benton. He approved the disunionist Jackson Resolutions of 1849 and supported the anti-Benton faction during the bitter party warfare of the fifties. On two occasions, in 1855 and in 1861, he received a significant legislative vote for United States senator. In 1849 Gov. Austin Augustus King [*q.v.*], a Benton Democrat, did not reappoint Scott, but two years later, when the judiciary became elective, he was chosen for a term of six years; in 1857 he was reëlected. He was large and awkward, weighing two hundred and fifty pounds, an ineffective speaker who rarely attempted a public address. Although not an active disunionist, he strongly indorsed the southern attitude in 1860–61 and was in sympathy with the pro-confederate state administration. When he refused to subscribe to the oath of loyalty promulgated by the state convention, his office was declared vacant (*Journal of the Missouri State Convention, 1861*, pp. 10, 16). After his appointment to the supreme court in 1841 he moved to a farm near Jefferson City, where he lived until his death in 1862; in the excitement of the war his passing was scarcely noticed by the bar.

[W. V. N. Bay, *Reminiscences of the Bench and Bar of Mo.* (1878); *The Hist. of the Bench and Bar of Mo.* (1898), ed. by A. J. D. Stewart; H. L. Conard, *Encyc. of the Hist. of Mo.* (1901), vol. V; Helen T. Catterall, "Some Antecedents of the Dred Scott Case," *Am. Hist. Rev.*, Oct. 1924; *Jeffersonian Republican*, Aug. 1841; *Mo. Republican, Daily Mo. Democrat*, May 19, 1862; 7–31 *Mo. Reports*.]   T.S.B.

SCOTT, WILLIAM ANDERSON (Jan. 31, 1813–Jan. 14, 1885), Presbyterian clergyman, educator, and author, was born of Scotch-Irish ancestry in Bedford County, Tenn., the son of Eli and Martha (Anderson) Scott. At the age of fifteen he united with the Cumberland Presbyterian Church. His determination to gain an education led him to employ numerous expedients. Needing books where books were few, on one occasion he entered into an agreement with a neighbor who owned a Greek New Testament to buy the volume for three days' plowing. While toiling among stumps, rocks, and dampness in fulfilling his part of the agreement, he contracted a severe cold which resulted in life-long lameness. Licensed to preach when seventeen, he did missionary work for about a year, then entered Cumberland College at Princeton, Ky., from which he was graduated in 1833. After nine months at Princeton (N. J.) Theological Seminary, he was ordained, May 17, 1835, by the Presbytery of Louisiana and then served as a missionary in Louisiana and Arkansas (1835–36) and as principal of the Female Academy at Winchester, Tenn. (1836–38). For the next two years he had charge of the Hermitage Church, on the Tennessee estate of Andrew Jackson, also serving as president of Nashville Female Seminary; from 1840 to 1842 he supplied a church at Tuscaloosa, Ala.

His pastoral eminence began in 1842 when he commenced a ministry of twelve years at the First Presbyterian Church, New Orleans. While here he became one of the leading clergymen of the city and influential throughout the South and the Southwest. Early in 1854 a group of San Francisco men invited him to that city to organize a church. Arriving there in May, he was instrumental in forming Calvary Church for which a building was erected in the heart of the then semi-lawless city. While pastor here Scott founded and edited the *Pacific Expositor,* a religious publication. With the outbreak of the Civil War in 1861, although his aggressive labors had made Calvary Church "the greatest force for righteousness on the Pacific coast" (Wicher, *post,* p. 129), he found his outspoken Southern sympathies so unacceptable that in October he departed for England. After his return he served the Forty-second Street Church, New York, a congregation of Southern sympathizers, from 1863 to 1870, and then went back to San Francisco, where he organized St. John's Church, which had as a nucleus numerous old Southern families. For many years it was one of the city's strong churches.

Scott's educational work in the West had commenced when in 1856 he helped found City College, San Francisco, an institution which survived for twenty years. The educational center which still (1935) lives to honor his name, however, is San Francisco Theological Seminary, now at San Anselmo. Established in 1871, it at first occupied two rooms of City College. Scott was a director until his death, the first president of the directors, the first elected professor—to the chair of logic and systematic theology—and the first faculty president. Much of the later high standing of the institution is attributed to his early initiative, faithful work, and influence with persons of wealth. The site of the San Anselmo buildings was donated by A. W. Foster, his parishioner and son-in-law. Scott remained actively connected with the seminary, as well as with the St. John's pastorate, until his death, at San Francisco.

He was the author of ten or more religious books which had a considerable circulation throughout the United States. Among the best known were *The Wedge of Gold; or, Achan in El Dorado* (1855), *Trade and Letters* (1856), *The Bible and Politics* (1859), and *The Christ of the Apostles' Creed* (1867). In 1858 he was elected moderator of the Presbyterian General Assembly (Old School). On Jan. 19, 1836, he married Ann Nicholson of Kilkeel, Ireland.

[E. A. Wicher, *The Presbyterian Church in Cal.* (1927); Alfred Nevin, *Encyc. of the Presbyterian Church in the U. S. A.* (1884); *Princeton Theological Sem. Biog. Cat.* (1909); *N. Y. Observer,* Jan. 29, 1885; *Presbyterian Banner,* Jan. 21, 1885; *Herald and Presbyter,* Jan. 28, 1885; *Daily Alta California* (San Francisco), Jan. 15, 1885; information as to certain facts from Scott's grand-daughter, Miss Lou Foster, San Rafael, Cal.]

P. P. F.

SCOTT, WILLIAM LAWRENCE (July 2, 1828–Sept. 19, 1891), railroad and coal magnate, was born in Washington, D. C., the son of Robert James and Mary Ann (Lewis) Scott, and a grandson of Gustavus Scott [*q.v.*]. His father died about 1835; with three other children William was brought up by his mother at Fortress Monroe and attended the academy at Hampden, Va. From 1840 to 1846 he was a page in the House of Representatives, continuing his schooling when Congress was not in session. After learning the coal-forwarding business as a shipping clerk under Charles M. Reed of Erie, Pa., in 1850 he formed a partnership in the same trade with Morrow B. Lowry and a year later became a partner in the coal firm of John Hearn and Company. This marked the beginning of his prosperity. His holdings in coal and iron came to be extensive and important; he manufactured iron in Pennsylvania and Missouri and controlled coal lands in Pennsylvania, Illinois, Iowa, and Missouri, and coal distributing companies in Pennsylvania and the Middle West. The W. L. Scott Company, formed after Hearn's death in 1871, became one of the largest producing and shipping coal firms in the United States.

Well before this time he had reached out to

the allied field of railways. By his marriage, Sept. 19, 1853, to Mary Matilda Tracy of Erie. he had joined himself with a wealthy family prominent in railroading. In 1861 he began operations with the Erie and Pittsburgh Railroad, then not completed; by 1866 he and his associates had completed the road and linked it with the Pittsburgh, Fort Wayne, and Chicago Railway, and shortly afterward he became president of the Erie and Pittsburgh, which bought and closed a canal that competed with it by tapping the Pennsylvania bituminous coal fields. With John F. Tracy, his brother-in-law, president of the Chicago, Rock Island, and Pacific, he promoted the extension of that road from central Iowa to the Missouri River, a work completed in 1869, and he was one of the builders of the first elevated railroad in New York City. He was interested financially in the development of the Canada Southern, Union Pacific, and Canadian Pacific railways, was one of the promoters of the New York, Philadelphia, and Norfolk, and was a stockholder and director of many other roads. His other business interests included banking and real estate. He also acquired farm lands in Erie County and in Virginia, where he bred shorthorn cattle and race horses, but he is said to have been unable to bear defeat and sold out his racing stable a number of times.

Politics, though a side issue with him, was a subject in which he was intensely interested. He was mayor of Erie in 1866 and again in 1871, and his business talent secured for the city the best "waterworks" system known to the times. Three times a delegate to the National Democratic Convention, in 1884 and 1886 he was elected to Congress from a normally Republican district. As a conservative Democrat he supported a low tariff and the gold standard and sponsored the Chinese exclusion bill. He was a warm admirer of Samuel Jones Tilden [q.v.] and a friend of Cleveland. His funeral at Erie was attended by notables in finance and politics, including the governor of the state and President Cleveland. Leaving an estate estimated to be between twenty and thirty millions, he was survived by his wife and two daughters. He was typical of the public-spirited but highly individualistic capitalists of the second half of the nineteenth century: a heavy investor in United States bonds during the darkest days of the Civil War, a citizen charitable and humane to the poor of Erie, but an alleged exploiter of the miners who worked for him and an object of bitter enmity on the part of labor unionists. Coming on the scene at a time when the coal and railroad industries offered great opportunities, he exhibited the tenacity of purpose and the talent for administration that could make effective use of them.

[H. E. Hayden, *Va. Genealogies* (1891); *Pittsburgh Commercial Gazette*, Sept. 21, 1891; *Nelson's Biog. Dict. and Hist. Reference Book of Erie County, Pa.* (1896); *Biog. Directory Am. Cong.* (1928); long biog. sketch in *N. Y. Tribune*, Sept. 21, 1891.] S. J. B.

SCOTT, WINFIELD (June 13, 1786–May 29, 1866), soldier, pacificator, and presidential nominee, was born on the family estate, "Laurel Branch," fourteen miles from Petersburg, Va. His grandfather, James Scott of the clan Buccleuch, having supported the Pretender, escaped to the colonies after the battle of Culloden in 1746. His father, William Scott, a successful farmer who had been a captain in the American Revolution, died when Winfield was in his sixth year, leaving four children, two boys, James and Winfield, and two girls. His mother, Ann Mason, was the daughter of Daniel Mason and the grand-daughter of John Winfield, one of the wealthiest men in the colony (*Memoirs*, I, 3). To her inspiration her son later attributed the continued successes of his long career. Unfortunately she died when he was seventeen. He was already six feet two and of bulky proportions. Two years later he stood six feet five, weighed about 230 pounds, and was physically the strongest man in the neighborhood. He did good scholastic work under the able instruction of James Hargrave and James Ogilvie. It was doubtless fortunate for him that because of legal hindrances he did not inherit the fortune of his grandfather but had to content himself with his modest patrimony. In 1805 he entered the College of William and Mary, but, because of his age and the contention between the student atheists and faculty churchmen, did not remain long. The same year he voluntarily left the institution to study law in the office of David Robinson in Petersburg.

In 1807 he witnessed in Richmond the trial of Aaron Burr. Though impressed by John Marshall, he regretted the outcome (*Ibid.*, I, 16). Following the outrage committed by the *Leopard* on the *Chesapeake*, and immediately after Jefferson's proclamation, he enlisted in the Petersburg troop of cavalry, galloping off with it on July 3. A few weeks later as a lance corporal he was instrumental in capturing a small boat containing two British officers and six men. Later in the year he went to Charleston, S. C., where he hoped to be more quickly admitted to the bar. At the prospect of hostilities, he personally approached President Jefferson in Washington and was tentatively promised a captaincy, but found himself, in March 1808, in Petersburg on the same law circuit as before.

On May 3, the coveted commission of captain of light or flying artillery arrived. Straightway he recruited a company in Petersburg and Richmond and was ordered to Norfolk to be embarked for New Orleans, where he arrived Apr. 1, 1809. The narrowness, unprogressiveness, and inefficiency of many of the army officers of that time decided him to return to the law. But on his way home, when he learned that charges had been preferred against him, he immediately quashed his resignation and went back to face them. It seems that he had stated candidly to another officer that Gen. James Wilkinson [*q.v.*], his department commander, had been as great a traitor as Burr in the testimony given at the trial. Gossip had carried the news to Wilkinson, who set Scott before a court for ungentlemanly conduct and trumped up specifications of fraud. The court suspended Scott from the army for a year because of unofficerlike conduct in making adverse statements against a superior, exonerated him from all suspicion of dishonesty, and recommended a nine-month remittance of the sentence (Mansfield, *post*, p. 28). However, the full year was approved, and Scott began in 1810 his enforced absence at home. Becoming "domesticated" with Benjamin Watkins Leigh [*q.v.*], he improved his liberal education by conversation and reading and his professional education by the study of foreign military works. In the fall of 1811, he set out to join his command with a party of five, traveling by wagons, learning the customs of the Creeks and Choctaws en route, and cutting the first roads through to Baton Rouge. During the winter of 1811–12 he served on Brig.-Gen. Wade Hampton's staff in New Orleans. In the intervals of his peacetime duties he continued to pursue the law, but in February 1812, when he learned that Congress had provided for the addition of 25,000 to the army in prospect of war with Great Britain, he left for Washington with Hampton, to be apprised there that he had been promoted to the rank of lieutenant-colonel. He was immediately ordered to Philadelphia to recruit a regiment, but in September he obtained permission to proceed to Niagara.

He reported to Brig.-Gen. Alexander Smyth at Buffalo Oct. 4, 1812, and came first under fire Oct. 8, at a naval engagement in which some of his troops participated. At the battle of Queenstown Scott begged to accompany the detachment that crossed into Canada, but did not do so on account of his superior rank. However, after Van Rensselaer was wounded, he crossed and was consequently with the heroic group which an overwhelming number of volunteers on the American shore refused to assist. While an unarmed prisoner he was set upon by two stalwart Indians brandishing knives and tomahawks, but was saved by his presence of mind and massive strength, and the timely entrance of a British officer. On Nov. 20, he was paroled and taken to Boston; and in March he was sent to Philadelphia as an adjutant-general with the rank of colonel. Detailed for duty on the northern front, he planned and executed, as Dearborn's adjutant-general, the successful attack on Fort George, where he was wounded when one of the British magazines exploded. In the fall he was placed in command of Fort George, which had carelessly been left defenseless before an aggressive enemy. By supreme efforts, working sometimes twenty out of twenty-four hours, he restored it to strength. Leaving there Oct. 13, he joined Wilkinson's army on the St. Lawrence, commanding a battalion of infantry in Brown's advance guard, defeating the British, and capturing prisoners at the engagement on Uphold's (given by him as Hooppole) Creek. Through the uninterrupted succession of ignominious land defeats of the war, Scott chafed. Almost alone he realized that an exacting apprenticeship of training and knowledge was essential for the prevention of useless sacrifice and the attainment of victory, all the more necessary since soldierly schooling had been held in contempt since the Revolution. President Madison and Secretary Monroe, impressed by his apparent efficiency, sent him to Albany to supervise the preparations for another offensive on the Niagara, promising him a brigadier's commission. However, since affairs temporarily subsided in that quarter, Scott found himself in Albany supervising munitions at the arsenal.

On Mar. 9, 1814, he was made a regular brigadier-general. On Mar. 24 he went to Buffalo, where he played the chief part in training the only American troops who gave a wholly good account of themselves on land during the War of 1812. In the stifling heat of July 4 and 5, it was his brigade that drove the enemy in a running fight for sixteen miles to the Chippewa. Without the aid of Brown, Porter, and Ripley, his 1100 men defeated Riall, who had 1700. It was also his brigade that bore the brunt of the fighting on July 25 at Lundy's Lane, probably as stubbornly and bravely fought a contest as took place on American soil. He had two horses killed under him and was so severely wounded late in the battle that he had to be carried from the field. In this period of military ineffectiveness, it is not difficult to understand how Scott became overnight the idol of the country and a hero abroad. Honors were heaped upon him. He was at once brevetted a major-general. On his journey east and south, invalided, he was stopped by ovations in every town. Congress voted him a medal, as did Virginia, though neither was actually presented until 1825. Gov. Daniel D. Tompkins personally presented him, in 1816, with a sword awarded by New York State. He was elected an honorary member of the Society of the Cincinnati.

Since his wounds prevented him from joining Jackson in New Orleans, Scott made his headquarters in Baltimore, where he became head of a board of inquiry on General Winder in the fiasco of Bladensburg and of another board to write the first standard set of American drill regulations, *Rules and Regulations for the Field Exercise and Manœuvres of Infantry* (1815). In the reduction of the army after peace was declared, when Congress caused the discharge of five officers out of every six, Scott, through the absence or tardiness of his seniors, became virtually the head of a board to make the selections. The difficult task was carried out with sympathy and efficiency. On July 9, 1815, he sailed to Europe, where he met many distinguished personages and studied French military methods. Returning home in 1816, he took up his headquarters in New York City. On Mar. 11, 1817, he married Maria D. Mayo, daughter of John Mayo of Richmond, Va.

During the routine work of a department commander in peace, Scott's vitality vented itself in constructive writing. His "Scheme for Restricting the Use of Ardent Spirits in the United States" (Philadelphia *National Gazette*, Dec. 14, 17, 19, 20, 1821), a plea for light wines and beer to the exclusion of hard liquors, preceded and, according to Scott, led to the formation of the first temperance societies in the country (*Memoirs*, I, 205; Mansfield, *post*, pp. 182–84, 189). In 1818 he began an elaborate set of Military Institutes, which were duly provided for by Congress. He served as the president of boards of tactics in 1815, 1821, 1824, and 1826. In order to gain more knowledge of this subject he traveled again in Europe during 1829. In 1834–35, he alone revised and enlarged the *Infantry-Tactics* (3 vols., 1835) for the army; this work remained the sole standard down to the Civil War, though widely plagiarized before and during that conflict.

In 1828 Scott, who was the logical successor to Jacob Brown as commanding general of the army, was passed over in favor of Alexander Macomb [*q.v.*]. Scott tendered his resignation, which was not accepted, and then protested in vain against being placed under the command of a former junior. For some time there was lack of harmony between the two generals. His chance for active duty came when he set out on July 8, 1832, with about 950 troops to end the Black Hawk War, but on Lake Huron his command was struck by Asiatic cholera. Against the warnings of the doctors he untiringly went among the afflicted. At this time he issued his famous order that any man found intoxicated must dig a grave of his own size and contemplate it with the understanding that he would soon fill it if he persisted in wanton drinking (Ganoe, *post*, pp. 171–72). Because of the cholera, he could not bring up his troops in time for the battle of the Bad Axe. Scarcely recovered from what was felt to be a taint of the plague, he arrived at West Point to find a summons from the Secretary of War. In Washington he was personally commissioned by President Jackson to watch the Nullifiers in South Carolina. Proceeding thence, by his tact, his sagacity in withholding the appearance of military threat, and his kindly dealings with the leaders, he did much to preserve peace in a time of crisis. He was again personally commissioned in 1835 by Jackson to prosecute the war against the Seminoles and Creeks in Florida and the adjacent states. Deprived of everything needful for a campaign, he was unable to make headway beyond the making of vigorous preparations. Jackson had apparently not recovered from the animosity engendered in 1817, when Scott had criticized an order of his as mutinous and had in turn been called a "hectoring bully" (J. S. Bassett, *Correspondence of Andrew Jackson*, II, 1927, pp. 291–92, 325, 338–39, 344; James Parton, *Life of Andrew Jackson*, 1860, II, 371–82). Impatient of Scott's delay, Jackson relieved him later during the Creek campaign, superseded him by Jesup, and placed him before a court of inquiry for not prosecuting the war with vigor. The court not only exonerated him, but praised his "energy, steadiness and ability" (*Proceedings of the Military Court of Inquiry in the Case of Major General Scott . . .*, 1837, being *Senate Document No. 224*, 24 Cong., 2 Sess.). When he returned to the command of the Eastern Division in New York, he was tendered a public dinner and his conduct was applauded.

A great task of pacification came to Scott when, on Jan. 5, 1838, he was commissioned to restore tranquillity on the Canadian border (*Army and Navy Chronicle*, Jan. 18, 1838). The entire military force of the country was then engaged in the South and West. Appearing alone at various points along the northern frontier with unabating rapidity through the long winter, Scott made friends of the leaders on both sides, wrote letters, made speeches, and by the sheer force of his dominant personality was able to prevent another major conflict (*Ibid.*, Feb. 15, 22; Mar. 8, 29, 1838). Scarcely had he finished this exacting commission, when in the spring of 1838 he was entrusted by Van Buren with probably the most difficult ordeal of pacification ever to confront a single individual in the United States. Some 16,000 Cherokees of South Carolina and Tennessee, already enraged at the encroachments and thievery of the whites, were to be dispossessed of their lands and taken beyond the Mississippi. Scott was ordered to conduct them. Changing his psychological approach to satisfy the Indian mood and equation, he ceaselessly went among them, showing them the disaster and fruitlessness of war, mingled with the chiefs, convinced them of his honesty, and finally turned their hatred into complaisance (*Ibid.*, Apr. 12, June 14, Nov. 15, 1838; *Senate Document No. 1*, 25 Cong., 3 Sess., pp. 440 ff.). In addition to leading them westward he had them submit to vaccination without a casualty or a sign of disturbance. He was unable to accompany them all the way because he was called to Washington again by the President to enter upon another great enterprise of pacification. The activities of the "Canadian Patriots" had redoubled, and the Maine boundary disputes were seriously threatening war with Great Britain. Blood had been spilt. Scott hastened east, holding conferences with the governors of Kentucky and Ohio on the way, to find that the country was agog over the brewing strife. Without having lain down during the preceding eighty hours, he presented himself to the Secretary of War. He was immediately turned over to President Van Buren, who gave him full powers to avert the war that then seemed unavoidable. After being instrumental in the passage through Congress of several bills that would aid him in his undertaking, he traveled northward, stopping in Boston long enough to gain the assistance of Gov. Edward Everett. On arriving in Maine, he set out to know personally the members of the legislature and to understand their views. At the same time he initiated correspondence with Lieutenant-Governor Harvey of New Brunswick. Acting energetically and diplomatically through the next weeks, he was able to win over various prominent legislators, to bring about concessions from the British, and finally to induce a meeting of minds that threw the contentions into arbitration between Great Britain and the United States. (For his movements,

see *Army and Navy Chronicle*, Nov. 29, 1838; Dec. 13, 20, 1838; Jan. 3, 10, 1839; Feb. 28, 1839; Mar. 21, 1839; see also H. S. Burrage, *Maine in the Northeastern Boundary Controversy*, 1919, pp. 272–73. Channing wrote: "His exploits in the field, which placed him in the first rank of our soldiers, have been obscured by the purer and more lasting glory of a Pacificator and of a Friend to Mankind" (*The Works of William E. Channing*, 1841, vol. V, 113).

In 1839 Scott's name was mentioned by the Whigs for the presidency, and he felt he was being honestly supported. But his main supporters were merely using him as a mask for their determination to beat Clay, as they did at the Harrisburg convention by nominating Harrison. In June 1841 Scott, on the death of Macomb, was made general-in-chief of the army with headquarters in Washington. His influence upon the service was salutary and profound. During the next five years he was particularly zealous in eradicating cruel punishments and unnecessarily harsh discipline. Although strict in his requirements and rigid as to the niceties of dress and deportment, he was harder on no one than on himself; and he coupled with his apparent inflexibility a personal kindness and sympathy for the individual that made men love and respect him as a leader. He urged and aided officers not only to become well-schooled in their profession, but also to build up their personalities by proper contacts and broad culture. Although he was not a graduate of the United States Military Academy, he manifested an outspoken pride in that institution. It was in this interval of upbuilding in the army that, in connection with a retrenchment bill, an amendment was introduced in Congress to abolish Scott's office, but after John Quincy Adams and C. J. Ingersoll had flayed the proposal with ridicule, it was voted down by a large majority (Mar. 29, 1844, *Congressional Globe*, 28 Cong., 1 Sess., p. 461). In 1842 he was proposed by the Pennsylvania state convention for the presidency. He publicly proclaimed his support of Clay, but there is reason to suppose that he was greatly disappointed at the latter's nomination in 1844.

When war with Mexico approached, Scott, who had seemingly accomplished enough for his country to satisfy the healthiest ambitions, was nearing sixty, but his most hazardous and signal achievement lay before him. As hostilities became evident in 1845, he indorsed Zachary Taylor [*q.v.*] to command the army of occupation at Corpus Christi. Realizing Taylor's limitations, as well as strength, he supplied him with one of the ablest officers in the service, Capt.

W. W. S. Bliss, as his adjutant-general. Despite tactical victories, the fruitlessness of the northern campaign was shortly demonstrated, and Scott desired to take command in person, but he refused to supplant a junior without substantial augmentation of troops. He had, however, worked out a practical strategic plan that would, as he put it, "conquer a peace" (*Congressional Globe*, 29 Cong., 1 Sess., Appendix, pp. 650–51). President Polk, inimical to anything that might advance Scott's political prestige, termed him "visionary" (*Diary,* May 14, 1846). It was at this time that Secretary of War Marcy sent a very peremptory letter to Scott, who was at the time in a restaurant near the War Department. Scott in his reply stated that he had stepped out to take "a hasty plate of soup" (*Memoirs,* II, 385). The Democratic organs, ignoring Scott's labors, later made capital of the phrase to his disparagement. His reputation was at a low ebb, but meanwhile Taylor's successes were bringing the war no nearer a finish. Scott had to be looked to as the only one with a feasible solution. Secretary Marcy, Senator Thomas H. Benton, and others forced Polk to acquiesce. Between the President and Scott there took place a brotherly reconciliation, sincere on Scott's part but formal on Polk's.

On Nov. 23, 1846, Scott was ordered to set out, with full powers, for the scene of hostilities (Smith, *post,* I, 355). He arrived at Camargo to find that Taylor in defiance of his and the President's instructions was not at hand. To this delay were added lack of boats and sailors, and frustrations because of rains and northers. By Mar. 9, 1847, through ceaseless effort, he landed 10,000 men opposite Sacrificios Island below Vera Cruz. It was then that smallpox threatened his command. Against the advice of his senior officers to take the city by assault, he chose to invest it from the rear; the mortalities connected with the capture, Mar. 26, proved to be less than twenty. Immediately fresh obstacles arose. No reënforcements and less than a fourth of his transportation arrived. Yellow fever would be rampant in the city the next month, and the administration was hedging on the fulfillment of his plan. It was felt that Xenophon had been faced with fewer difficulties. Nevertheless, on Apr. 8, Scott pushed forward with a small, poorly equipped force to climb the 8,000-foot mountains toward the distant capital. His advance guard was held up at the stronghold of Cerro Gordo and the command awed into a state of uncertainty; by his arrival morale was restored, an attack organized, and victory secured in the face of inefficiency on the part of some of his senior officers. At once he moved onward to Jalapa where halfway to his goal he was met by sterner obstacles than the enemy. Two companies and seven regiments left him in a body because of the expiration of their enlistments, and the administration had sent neither money nor reënforcements. Although his urgent notes brought ineffective response from the home government and collapse seemed inevitable, he again moved forward, May 6, toward Puebla with not over 4000 privates. Fortunately he did not encounter the expected resistance of 20,000 Mexicans and entered the city with little opposition, but his soldiers had been paid for only two months out of eight and the inhabitants were actively hostile. He secured friendly intercourse with the natives and by vigorous training of the soldiers and incoming recruits increased the efficiency of his command. Then money came and his force was raised to 10,900 effectives. He set off once more on Aug. 5, brushing past barricades until he arrived in the Valley of Mexico. Although Gideon J. Pillow [*q.v.*] by exceeding his instructions brought on the battle of Contreras, Scott's tenacity brought victory. Then promptly he won Churubusco. He has been criticized for not at once assaulting the capital which lay open before him, but analysis shows that he again forsook personal glory in the hope that an armistice would save life and treasure. In this he proved to be mistaken and the bloody battles of Molino del Rey and Chapultepec followed. Although Molino del Rey was perhaps a tactical error, the masterly handling of the assault on Chapultepec and the capture of the city of Mexico fully compensated for it. Scott marched into the capitulated capital Sept. 14, little more than five months after his start from Vera Cruz.

After a miraculous campaign, he entered upon the more difficult task of adjusting a tattered, victorious army to the sane government of occupied territory. So long as his experienced soldiers remained, he had little trouble. His control was so humane and firm that a deputation of Mexicans asked him to be their dictator. Rarely if ever in history was a conquered nation so restored to contentment and order (Smith, II, 323–24). The influx of undisciplined recruits disturbed him, but he managed by redoubled exertions to maintain tranquillity. During this period he sent home, from local revenues, $118,000 to be applied to an army asylum, which afterwards became the Soldiers' Home. The opportunity for the administration to undercut Scott politically came when Pillow sent his own version of Scott's later battles to newspapers in the United States. The account was flattering to Pillow and adverse to the Commander-in-Chief. William Jenkins Worth and Col. James Duncan did much the same thing. When Scott called the officers to account, he was met with defiance and insubordination. He at length preferred charges which he sent to the President, but Polk without further inquiry released the three offenders from arrest, restored one of them to his highest brevet rank, superseded Scott by Butler, and placed the victorious commander before a hand-picked court of inquiry. Justin H. Smith observes that Scott "was a large man, had done a large work and merited large treatment. But there was nothing large about the administration. The confines of mediocrity hemmed it in" (*Ibid.*, II, 188). On Mar. 21, 1848, the court convened in Mexico, but soon adjourned to meet May 29 in Frederick, Md. On Apr. 22, Scott took leave of an army that on the whole loved and trusted him. Robert E. Lee, an engineer on his staff, stated that after performing a task of supreme magnitude he "was turned out as an old horse to die" (Fitzhugh Lee, *General Lee*, 1894, p. 46). Avoiding public honors, Scott stealthily made his way to Elizabeth, N. J., but he was unable to escape the clamor altogether. New York City tendered him a reception and an unprecedented ovation. Congress voted him its second thanks and another gold medal. The charges against him were withdrawn. A resolution to tender him the pay, rank, and emoluments of a lieutenant-general was introduced in Congress, but through political opposition it did not pass until 1855, when he became the first since Washington to hold that office.

In 1852 the Whigs gave him the nomination for the presidency. The campaign was essentially without issues but was marked by exceptionally scurrilous attacks on Scott by newspapers and stump-speakers. Clay and Webster died during the campaign. Other Whig leaders badly advised Scott, whose straight-forwardness was an easy target for the Democrats. He was overwhelmingly defeated by Franklin Pierce [*q.v.*]. It was the last of his entries into the lists for the presidency, although as late as 1860 he retained some hope of being sent to the White House (Coleman, *Crittenden, post*, II, 184–85). After the inauguration of Pierce, on account of differences of opinion on policy with the Secretary of War, Scott again removed his headquarters to New York City. In 1857 he opposed the war against the Mormons as unnecessary and undertaken for profit, but he was overruled. In 1859 he was again called upon to perform the functions of pacificator. Though seventy-three years of age and crippled from a recent fall, he set out Sept. 20 for the extreme Northwest, where controversy over the possession of San Juan Island in Puget Sound had again brought the relations between Great Britain and the United States to the breaking point. After he had mingled with both sides and conducted a judicious correspondence, serious complications were averted.

In October 1860, foreseeing the eventual Civil War, he pleaded with the President to reënforce the southern forts and armories against seizure, but to Buchanan and John B. Floyd his was a voice crying in the wilderness. On Oct. 31, and Dec. 12 he renewed his urgings, but with no better success. In January 1861, he brought back the headquarters of the army to Washington, where at his advanced age he actively oversaw the recruiting and training of the defenders of the capital. He personally commanded Lincoln's bodyguard at the inauguration and put the city in a state of defense. Being a Virginian, he was doggedly besought to join the South, but in spite of natural leanings he stuck to his beliefs and remained with the Union. To Lincoln he accorded all aid in his power. Though he did not approve of George B. McClellan as first choice for command of the Army of the Potomac, he supported him even when the younger man's methods were at least discourteous. Had much of his general plan for the conduct of the Federal forces been heeded, the war would have been curtailed; but since he was too old to mount a horse, he was thought to be too old to give advice. On Oct. 31, 1861, he requested retirement on account of infirmities. The next day Lincoln and the whole cabinet left their offices in a body, repaired to Scott's home, and there the President read an affecting eulogy to the old man. Scott was retired with full pay and allowances the same day. In his first message to Congress Lincoln wrote of Scott: "During his long life the nation has not been unmindful of his merit; yet, in calling to mind how faithfully, ably, and brilliantly he has served his country, from a time far back in our history when few of the now living had been born, and thenceforward continually, I cannot but think we are still his debtors" (Nicolay and Hay, *Abraham Lincoln. Complete Works*, 1894, vol. II, 104). On his journey to New York, Scott was accompanied by the secretaries of war and the treasury. On Nov. 9, 1861, he went abroad, but in Paris upon hearing of the *Trent* affair he immediately returned to America, should his counsel be needed. At West Point he received the Prince of Wales and in 1865 presented to General Grant, one of his subalterns in the Mexican War, a gift with the inscription, "from the oldest to the greatest general" (Wright, *post,* p. 322). When his end was near he was conveyed from New York City to West Point where he died within fifteen days of his eightieth birthday. He was buried in the national cemetery there, some of the most illustrious men of the country attending the funeral. His wife, who died in Rome in 1862, is buried beside him. Of his seven children, two sons and two daughters died early, to his great grief; three married daughters survived him.

Scott had been the associate of every president from Jefferson to Lincoln and the emissary in critical undertakings of most of them. In his public career of nearly half a century he had been a main factor in ending two wars, saving the country from several others, and acquiring a large portion of its territory. Supreme political preferment was doubtless denied him because of conditions and his idiosyncrasies. Called "Fuss and Feathers" because of his punctiliousness in dress and decorum, he often gave the impression of irritability. He possessed a whimsical egotism, was inclined to flourishes of rhetoric, often unfortunate, and was too outspoken in his beliefs for his own advancement. On the other hand, the openness of his generous character led him into acts incomprehensible to calculating natures. He was a scholar, but knew when to discard rules, so that the letter of directions did not shackle him. His initiative and self-reliance never deserted him. He made use of his many talents unsparingly, and the only one of his hazardous undertakings he failed to carry out beyond the most sanguine expectations was that of his own ambition to reach the presidency.

[*Memoirs of Lieut.-General Scott, LL.D. Written by Himself* (2 vols., 1864), rhetorical but still valuable; E. D. Mansfield, *Life and Services of General Winfield Scott* (1852), the best of the campaign biographies; M. J. Wright, *General Scott* (1894); A. M. B. Coleman, *The Life of John J. Crittenden* (2 vols., 1871), containing letters of Scott; Dunbar Rowland, ed., *Jefferson Davis, Constitutionalist,* vols. II, III (1923), containing Scott-Davis correspondence; James Wilkinson, *Memoirs of My Own Times* (3 vols., 1816); M. M. Quaife, ed., *The Diary of James K. Polk* (4 vols., 1910); G. T. Curtis, *Life of James Buchanan* (2 vols., 1883); Harrison Ellery, ed., *The Memoirs of Gen. Joseph Gardner Swift* (1890); W. A. Croffut, ed., *Fifty Years in Camp and Field. Diary of Major-General Ethan Allen Hitchcock, U. S. A.* (1909); correspondence, papers, and documents in Old Files Section, Adjutant-General's Dept., Washington, D. C.; E. A. Cruikshank, *The Documentary Hist. of the Campaign upon the Niagara Frontier* (9 vols., 1896–1908); C. J. Ingersoll, *Hist. Sketch of the Second War between the U. S. . . . and Great Britain,* vols. I, II (1845–49); 2 ser., vols. I, II (1852); B. L. Lossing, *The Pictorial Field-Book of the War of 1812* (1868); J. H. Smith, *The War with Mexico* (2 vols., 1919); L. D. Ingersoll, *A Hist. of the War Dept. of the U. S.* (1879); Emory Upton, *The Military Policy of the U. S.* (1904); W.

A. Ganoe, *The Hist. of the U. S. Army* (1924); obituary in *N. Y. Tribune,* May 30–June 2, 1866; suggestions from Maj. C. W. Elliott, who is preparing a biography of Scott.]   W. A. G.

SCOVEL, HENRY SYLVESTER (July 29, 1869–Feb. 11, 1905), journalist and engineer, better known simply as Sylvester Scovel, was born at Denny Station, Allegheny County, Pa., the son of the Rev. Sylvester Fithian and Caroline (Woodruff) Scovel, and a descendant of Arthur Scovell, who came to Boston about 1660 and settled in Middletown, Conn., in 1670. His father was a Presbyterian minister, son of a president of Hanover College in Indiana, who also became a college president, serving at the University of Wooster, in Wooster, Ohio, from 1883 to 1899. Scovel was educated in the public schools of Pittsburgh and the Michigan Military Academy, from which he was graduated in 1887. For a few months he attended the University of Wooster and spent portions of four years at the University of Michigan, working his way between times as timekeeper in various blast-furnace construction plants. He later worked as an engineer in Tennessee, Kentucky, and Pennsylvania.

Although there is no record of his previous newspaper experience, his aggressiveness as a promoter of several enterprises in Chicago and Cleveland apparently led to his appointment in 1895 as correspondent for the *Pittsburgh Dispatch* and the *New York Herald* to cover the increasingly serious disturbances in Cuba. Here his activities proved so unwelcome to the Spanish authorities that they arrested him in Havana in 1896. By this time he had become a rather conspicuous figure, and after his escape from confinement he was engaged by the New York *World.* During the next two years he made his reputation as one of the most brilliant actors in the drama of the Spanish-American conflict. According to the *World* he did more than any other man to proclaim the wrongs of the Cubans and to arouse the American people against the Spanish régime of oppression. For eleven months he lived with the insurgents, sharing all the hardships and dangers of their guerrilla warfare. With characteristic daring and resourcefulness he ran the Spanish military and police lines twenty times. Finally on Feb. 7, 1897, he was again captured by the Spaniards. This incident created considerable excitement throughout the country; many state legislatures passed resolutions demanding his release, and at the insistence of the Senate the United States government made such strong representations to Spain that he was given his freedom.

After accomplishing his particular mission in Cuba, he was sent by the *World* in 1897 to cover the Turco-Greek conflict, but when the tension between the United States and Spain increased he was recalled and arrived in Cuba just before the *Maine* disaster. When war was declared he was assigned to duty as correspondent for his paper, and he remained with the American forces until the evacuation by Spain in 1899. In this service he was apparently almost as troublesome to his own military authorities as he had been to the Spanish. His zeal for the news led him constantly to disobey army regulations. Official dispatches show that he greatly irritated the American command and that he was summarily threatened with court martial. Boyish in appearance and manner, daring and determined to the point of recklessness, he could not be diplomatic. But, as the files of the *World* show, he "got the story." From 1899 to 1902 he served as consulting engineer to the Cuban customs service of the United States military government of the island. This post he resigned to engage in various commercial promotion projects in Havana, where he died. He was married on Apr. 5, 1897, to Frances Cabanné of St. Louis, Mo.

[*Who's Who in America*, 1903–05, and the obit. article in the N. Y. *World*, Feb. 13, 1905, are the best available general sources. See also F. E. Chadwick, *The Relations of the U. S. and Spain: the Spanish-Am. War* (2 vols., 1911), and *Correspondence Relating to the War with Spain . . . Between the Adjutant-Gen. of the Army and Mil. Commanders* (2 vols., 1902), the latter containing the text of official dispatches concerning Scovel; Walter Millis, *The Martial Spirit* (1931); *Commemorative Biog. Record of Wayne County, Ohio* (1889); H. W. Brainard, *A Survey of the Scovils or Scovills in England and America* (1915); *Pittsburgh Dispatch*, Feb. 13, 1905.]   P. K.

SCOVEL, SYLVESTER [See Scovel, Henry Sylvester, 1869–1905].

SCOVELL, MELVILLE AMASA (Feb. 26, 1855–Aug. 15, 1912), agricultural chemist and educator, the son of Nathan and Hannah (Aller) Scovell, was born at Belvidere, N. J. He was a descendant of John Scovell, who emigrated from England to Connecticut in the seventeenth century. Shortly after his birth, the family moved to Chicago and later to a farm in Champaign County, Ill. After graduation from the local high school in 1871, he entered the Illinois Industrial University (later the University of Illinois), where he specialized in chemistry, becoming student-assistant in his second year, and took three degrees, B.S., 1875; M.S., 1877; Ph.D., 1908. As secretary to John Milton Gregory [*q.v.*] he was influenced by the intellectual atmosphere created by the president of the university. Becoming instructor in chemistry at

Illinois in 1875, he was advanced to a professorship in 1880, a position he held until 1884. On Sept. 8, 1880, he married Nannie D. Davis of Monticello, Ill.

With Henry Adams Weber [*q.v.*] he patented processes for clarifying the juice of sugar-producing plants and for manufacturing glucose, sugar, and syrup from sorghum. He served as secretary of the Illinois Cane Growers' Association in 1880–81, and of the Mississippi Valley Cane Growers' Association during 1881–84. He was superintendent of the Kansas Sugar Works at Sterling, Kan., in 1884, and the following year, as special agent for the United States Department of Agriculture, he managed the diffusion batteries for extracting sugar from sorghum and sugar-cane in Kansas and Louisiana. In 1885 he became the first director of the Kentucky Agricultural Experiment Station. During his twenty-seven years at Lexington he made notable contributions as chemist, agronomist, pure-food exponent, educator, and administrator. As author or joint author he prepared over seventy publications. His first years at Lexington were largely devoted to analyzing and testing fertilizers, the state fertilizer control having been placed with the station; among the accomplishments of Scovell and his associates in this field was a modification of the Kjeldahl method for the determination of nitrogen in nitrates. Later, as a member of the United States Food Standards Commission, he devoted himself to the investigations and educational work that resulted in the enactment of national and state pure-food legislation. He aided in the development of the state department of agriculture at Frankfort, Ky., and his ardent and efficient support of the state fair aroused popular interest in improved agricultural methods and products. His interest in dairying was stimulated by his study of the accuracy and reliability of the Babcock test while he was chairman of the committee on the comparative tests of dairy breeds at the Columbian Exposition in Chicago. In connection with this work he invented a milk-sampling tube. He judged dairy cattle at many fairs and expositions, becoming perhaps the best-known and best-liked judge in America, and the model dairy at his station farm contributed greatly to the public health of the city of Lexington and to the development of dairying in Kentucky. In 1910, in addition to directing the experiment station, he became dean of the agricultural college at the University of Kentucky. In 1911 he visited the Channel Islands as representative of James Ben Ali Haggin [*q.v.*] to purchase cattle for the Elmendorf farm. He was an active member of many professional organizations, including the Association of Official Agricultural Chemists, under whose auspices much of his most effective work was done. Probably his greatest contribution lay in his work as an able administrative officer and as a builder of public sentiment for agricultural education.

[H. W. Brainard, *A Survey of the Scovils or Scovills* (1915); *Who's Who in America*, 1912–13; J. M. and Jaques Cattell, *Am. Men of Sci.* (1910); *Twenty-Fifth Ann. Report . . . Ky. Agricultural Experiment Station*, 1912; *Proc. . . . Soc. for the Promotion of Agricultural Sci.*, vol. XXXIII (1913); U. S. Dept. Agriculture, *Experiment Station Record*, Oct. 1912; *Mech. Engineering and Electrical Engineering Record*, Nov. 1908; *Breeder's Gazette*, Aug. 21, 1912; *Jersey Bull. and Dairy World*, Aug. 21, 1912; *Louisville Times*, Aug. 16, *Courier-Journal* (Louisville), Aug. 16, 18, 1912.]
E. E. E.

SCOVILLE, JOSEPH ALFRED (Jan. 30, 1815–June 25, 1864), journalist and novelist, was born in Woodbury, Conn., the son of Joseph and Caroline (Preston) Scovill and a descendant of John Scovell, who was born in England and died about 1700 at Haddam, Conn. At about twenty-two, Scoville became employed as a merchant in New York; a year later he entered into a short-lived partnership with Lloyd L. Britton. Gradually he now drifted into journalism and politics. In October 1842 we find him writing to his friend John Caldwell Calhoun [*q.v.*] of a "matter of vital importance"—none other than "the control of Tammany Hall" (*American Historical Association Annual Report, 1899, post*, p. 856). Unsuccessful in this ambition, he was nevertheless instrumental in finding a publisher in the North for the *Life of John C. Calhoun* (1843), a campaign biography presumably written by Calhoun himself; and in April 1843 he was made editor of the *Spectator,* a newspaper published in Washington in the interests of Calhoun. Although he failed to please Calhoun's friends, and for this reason remained editor of the paper for only a short time, he continued in the good graces of Calhoun himself, who, probably in the middle or late forties, appointed Scoville his private secretary.

Returning to New York after Calhoun's death in 1850, he became editor of the *New York Picayune,* in part a humorous paper, but about 1852 he resigned to start the *Pick,* a humorous sheet of his own, which he continued to bring out until 1855. Two years later he edited for a brief period the *Evening State Gazette.* It was probably during the fifties that he came under the influence of James Gordon Bennett [*q.v.*], editor of the *New York Herald,* whose sensational journalistic methods profoundly affected him. Scoville's fearless indulgence in personalities and other forms of scandal, together with

his marked Southern sympathies, made him an object of extreme dislike in the North during the war. His novel *Vigor* (1864), republished in England as *Marion* (3 vols., 1864), dealt broadly with the theme of seduction in American bourgeois society. The dedication to Bennett and the introduction of Calhoun as a character suggest the truth of common report that the novel had a significant autobiographical basis. The general antipathy to the story, which by most was called "indecent," although by a few of Scoville's friends "unfortunate," was heightened at this time by the publication in the London *Morning Herald* and *Evening Standard* of Scoville's articles denouncing the Lincoln administration and the prosecution of the war by the North. For the publication of these articles Scoville was brought before Gen. John Adams Dix and warned against any further criticism of the North and its war policies. Another novel, *The Adventures of Clarence Bolton,* has been ascribed to him, but no copy of the work seems to have survived. Of his literary work, *The Old Merchants of New York City* (5 ser., 1863–66?), giving in a rambling, gossipy form the history of the city's commercial life, is perhaps the most important. His customary style was simple and vigorous but, owing to his love of short, detached sentences, his work frequently makes difficult reading. He usually wrote under the pseudonym either of Manhattan or of Walter Barrett. It was during a visit to South Carolina that he met Caroline Schaub, whom he afterwards married. He is said to have acquired financial independence by his literary labors and to have left his wife and daughter well provided for. He died in New York.

[See H. W. Brainard, *A Survey of the Scovils or Scovills in England and America* (1915); William Cothren, *Hist. of Ancient Woodbury, Conn.* (1854–79), vol. I, p. 665, vol. III, p. 80; N. Y. city directories, 1837–64; *N. Y. Leader*, July 2, 1864; *N. Y. Commercial Advertiser*, June 22, 1864; *World* (N. Y.), June 27, 1864; T. L. Nichols, *Forty Years of Am. Life* (1864), vol. II, pp. 221–26; J. A. Scoville, *The Old Merchants of N. Y. City* (1863–66), ser. 2–4, *passim*; Gaillard Hunt, *John C. Calhoun* (1908); W. M. Meigs, *The Life of John Caldwell Calhoun* (1917), vol. II; "Correspondence of John C. Calhoun," in *Am. Hist. Assoc. Ann. Report, 1899* (1900), vol. II; F. L. Mott, *A Hist. of Am. Magazines, 1741–1850* (1930); Goldwin Smith, in *Atlantic Monthly*, Dec. 1864; S. A. Allibone, *A Crit. Dict. of Eng. Lit.* (3 vols., 1858–71). Critical discussions of *Vigor* (*Marion*) may be found in the *Reader* (London), May 21, July 16, Aug. 27, Oct. 22, 1864.]
N. F. A.

SCRANTON, GEORGE WHITFIELD (May 23, 1811–Mar. 24, 1861), iron manufacturer, was born in Madison, Conn., the son of Theophilus and Elizabeth (Warner) Scranton and a descendant of John Scranton who settled in Guilford, Conn., in 1639. His father was the owner of a stage line running from New Haven to Saybrook. He was educated in the common school and at Lee's Academy in his native town. In 1828 he went to live with an uncle at Belvidere, N. J., and obtained work as a teamster; soon afterward he was employed as a clerk in a store there and in a short time was admitted as a partner. In 1835 he married Jane Hiles of Belvidere, sold his interest in the store, and engaged in farming. Four years later, in partnership with his brother Selden, he purchased the lease and stock of an iron furnace at Oxford, N. J., where he met with considerable success. In May 1840 he and his brother, with William Henry, Sanford Grant, P. H. Mattes, and Joseph C. Platt, formed the Lackawanna Iron and Coal Company to acquire an extensive tract of coal-bearing land in the Lackawanna Valley, including the present site of the city of Scranton, Pa., which he founded in the same year. He and his associates conducted experiments in smelting iron with anthracite coal and by January 1842 had developed a successful process. Although they began the manufacture of bar-iron to be converted into nails, they soon planned to build a rolling-mill for the manufacture of railroad iron. Lacking the necessary capital, they contracted to furnish rails to the Buffalo, New York & Erie Railroad at a rate lower than the current one upon the condition that the road advance funds to enable them to proceed with manufacturing. After this start Scranton saw the company develop rapidly into a firmly established and highly lucrative business. In 1846 his first cousin, Joseph Hand Scranton (1813-1872), son of Jonathan Scranton, became general manager of the iron works and in 1858 its president; he also organized the First National Bank of Scranton and was the chief organizer of the Scranton Gas and Water Company.

From 1859 until his death George Scranton served in Congress in the House of Representatives as a Republican. He was not a politician in the ordinary sense, but the nature of his business made him a firm believer in protection for home industries. He was actively interested in the development of transportation facilities in the Lackawanna Valley and projected and constructed the Northumberland division of the Delaware, Lackawanna & Western railroad, of which he was president for several years, as he was of the Cayuga & Susquehanna railroad. He died in Scranton, survived by his wife, two sons, and a daughter. He is described as a man of inexhaustible energy and great moral integrity and is said to have had the faculty of impressing his ideas upon the minds of other

men, qualities that had much to do with his rise from poverty and obscurity to wealth and prominence.

[Erastus Scranton, *A Geneal. Reg. of the Descendants of John Scranton of Guilford, Conn.* (1855); F. L. Hitchcock, *Hist. of Scranton and Its People* (1914), vol. I, with portrait; David Craft, *Hist. of Scranton, Penn.* (1891); *Biog. Directory of the Am. Congress, 1774-1927* (1928); Horace Hollister, *Hist. of the Lackawanna Valley* (2nd ed., 1869); obituary in *Daily Nat. Intelligencer,* Mar. 27, 1861.]   J.H.F.

SCREWS, WILLIAM WALLACE (Feb. 25, 1839–Aug. 7, 1913), editor, was born at Jernigan in Barbour (now Russell) County, Ala., the son of Benjamin and Mourning (Drake) Screws, both of English ancestry. The father, a merchant and a leader of the Whigs in his section of the state, came originally from North Carolina, where the family had lived for several generations; the mother's people came from Massachusetts to North Carolina. William Wallace is said to have been named for the hero of Jane Porter's popular story, *The Scottish Chiefs* (1810). Although he was prepared for college in the schools of Glenville, Ala., and made an excellent record in Latin, Greek, and English literature, he never entered college, for in the panic of 1857 his father failed in business and he had to earn his own living. After working for two years at odd jobs, he went to Montgomery to read law in the office of Thomas H. Watts; though he was not yet of age he was admitted to the bar June 15, 1859. He cast his first vote in 1860 for the Bell-Everett ticket. Although he opposed secession, he enlisted in the army immediately after the secession of Alabama. He saw service with the Montgomery True Blues in Florida and with Hilliard's Legion in Kentucky and in Tennessee, where he took part in the battle of Chickamauga. When Hilliard's Legion was reorganized into the 59th and 60th Regiments, he became first lieutenant of the 59th and took part in the siege of Knoxville. With Gracie's brigade he saw service in the Virginia campaigns of 1864 about Petersburg until he was wounded in the battle of Drewry's Bluff. In 1865, during the evacuation of Richmond, he was captured at Sailor's Creek, taken to Johnson's Island in Lake Erie, and held in prison until June 1865.

He returned to Montgomery to take up the practice of law; during the war, however, he had done some work as a correspondent for the *Montgomery Advertiser,* and he was offered a place on the editorial staff. In a few weeks he was offered a half interest in the paper, with his own time to pay for it; in less than a year he was editor, and presently he was sole owner as well. As editor of the most important Democratic paper in the state, he directed the policies of the party for half a century. Like Henry Watterson and Edwin Lawrence Godkin [*qq.v.*] he was one of the school of personal journalists; he himself shaped the policy of his paper and made the editorial page the center of interest. He was master of a vigorous, simple, and direct style; it is said that he never used a metaphor. Through the *Advertiser* he led the opposition to the reconstruction government in the state. He was relentless in exposing its corruption and tireless in his efforts to destroy it. When the attempt was made to issue bonds for the Alabama and Chattanooga Railroad he opposed it, although his paper was seriously embarrassed at the time and he was offered over fifty thousand dollars to permit the use of its columns for bond issue propaganda. He fought the Farmers' Alliance on the ground that it would inevitably become a political party and divide the white vote of the state. The Alliance boycotted the *Advertiser* and Screws lost heavily, but he never changed his position in the matter. In spite of the fact that he possessed great political influence, he refused political offices throughout his career. During his long life he held only three, and those were insignificant: he was secretary of state in Alabama from 1878 to 1882, he held a position in the Library of Congress during the first Cleveland administration, and he was postmaster of Montgomery, 1893–97. He died suddenly at his summer home at Coosada, Elmore County, Ala., survived by his wife, Emily Frances Holt of Augusta, Ga., whom he had married Apr. 25, 1867, and three sons. Although he was a prolific writer he never published a book; aside from his editorials and newspaper articles he left only an article on the history of Alabama journalism, written for *The Memorial Record of Alabama* (1893, vol. II).

[See esp. *Montgomery Advertiser*, Aug. 8–11, 1913. The Dept. of Hist. and Archives at Montgomery contains some unpublished materials; brief accounts of Screws are to be found in *The Memorial Record of Ala.* (1893), vol. II; B. F. Riley, *Makers and Romance of Ala. Hist.* (n.d.); T. M. Owen, *Hist. of Ala. and Dict. of Ala. Biog.* (1921), vol. IV; *Who's Who in America*, 1912–13.]   H. F—r.

SCRIBNER, CHARLES (Feb. 21, 1821–Aug. 26, 1871), publisher, was born in New York City, the son of Uriah Rogers Scribner and the latter's second wife, Betsey Hawley. He was descended from Benjamin Scrivener, who was in Norwalk, Conn., in 1680; the family name was changed to its present form after 1742. Uriah Scribner was a prosperous merchant and gave his son every educational advantage. Charles Scribner was graduated from the College of New

Jersey (Princeton) in 1840 and studied law but because of bad health gave up practice. In 1846, with Isaac D. Baker as partner, he turned to publishing. The firm of Baker & Scribner made its bow in modest quarters, which formed part of the chapel of the old Brick Meeting House at Park Row and Nassau Street. Baker died and Scribner proceeded to carry on alone, under his own name, in 1850. In 1857 he took in another partner, Charles Welford, organizing the firm of Scribner & Welford to import books, though the publishing continued under his own name. Andrew C. Armstrong was admitted to partnership in 1864, and Edward Seymour in 1869, but the name of the publishing firm remained the same until the death of the founder in 1871, when it became Scribner, Armstrong & Co., the importing firm being Scribner, Welford & Armstrong. It was in 1878 that the final form of Charles Scribner's Sons was established.

The Scribner list, from the outset, was strong in theological and philosophical publications, written by leading authorities, especially those of the Presbyterian Church, such as the Alexanders, Archibald [*q.v.*] and James W., and Presidents Theodore Dwight Woolsey and Noah Porter [*qq.v.*] of Yale. The firm also published the English edition of Johann Peter Lange, *A Commentary on the Holy Scriptures* (25 vols., 1865–80), edited by Philip Schaff [*q.v.*]. Much attention was also given to secular literature. The once widely popular works of Joel T. Headley [*q.v.*], *Napoleon and his Marshals* (1847) and *Washington and His Generals* (1847), bore the Scribner imprint. This also aided the circulation of the works of the internationally known geographer, Arnold Henry Guyot [*q.v.*]. Publications of a more general character included *People I Have Met* (1850), by Nathaniel P. Willis [*q.v.*], a book which greatly heightened the reputation of the house. Mention may be made also of the writings of Donald Grant Mitchell [*q.v.*], better known as "Ik Marvel," *Reveries of a Bachelor* (1850) and *Dream Life* (1851). It was during the last decade of Scribner's life that the firm began to publish reprints and translations of English and European works, of the solid character exemplified by such names as Froude, Mommsen, Ernst Curtius, Friedrich Max Mueller, and Rawlinson. Dean Stanley, Gladstone, and Jowett were later added to the list. The foundations for a liberal tradition were well and truly laid, signifying a quick response to the demands of a more and more exacting reading public. The house grew up while Washington Irving and James Fenimore Cooper were still upon the scene. It reckoned with a generation that appreciated the rising New England group and that welcomed the visits of Dickens and Thackeray. It was committed to a standard of good taste. The elder Scribner established an educational publishing business, but in 1883 the firm sold its school textbook business, maintaining only higher textbooks.

Charles Scribner sponsored a periodical entitled *Hours at Home,* a miscellany edited by the Rev. J. M. Sherwood. It lasted for nearly five years (1865–70) but the fastidious publisher was not quite satisfied. "I want to issue a magazine," he said, "that is handsomely illustrated, beautifully printed, and that shall have as contributors the best authors of the day. I should like to make it different from any now published and to reach also other classes of readers" (Unpublished Papers). He fulfilled his ambition when in November 1870, he brought out the first number of *Scribner's Monthly.* It was launched auspiciously under the editorship of Dr. J. G. Holland, assisted by Richard Watson Gilder [*qq.v.*], but in 1881 was sold to the Century Company and became *The Century Illustrated Monthly Magazine. Scribner's Magazine* was founded in 1887 by the younger Charles Scribner.

Scribner was married, June 13, 1848, to Emma Elizabeth Blair, the daughter of John Insley Blair [*q.v.*] of Blairstown, N. J., a capitalist who was active in railroading and other large business affairs. He died at Luzerne, Switzerland. His sons, John Blair, Charles [*q.v.*], and Arthur Hawley, carried on his work.

[G. W. Schuyler, *Colonial New York* (1885), II, 439–55, for the Scribner genealogy; "Charles Scribner's Sons. The Hist. of a Publishing House, 1846–1894," *Scribner's Mag.*, Dec. 1894; J. C. Derby, *Fifty Years Among Authors, Books and Publishers* (1884); obituaries in *N. Y. Times*, Aug. 28, 1871; *The Trade Circular and Publishers' Bulletin*, Sept. 25, 1871; *Scribner's Monthly*, Oct. 1871.]   R. C.

SCRIBNER, CHARLES (Oct. 18, 1854–Apr. 19, 1930), publisher, was born in New York City, the second son of Charles Scribner [*q.v.*] and his wife, Emma Elizabeth Blair. He began his education in a private school, entered the College of New Jersey (Princeton) in 1871, and was graduated four years later. He went immediately into the publishing house and on the death of his brother, John Blair Scribner, in 1879, became head of the firm, known since 1878 as Charles Scribner's Sons; it was incorporated in 1904. He was succeeded as president in 1928 by his brother, Arthur H. Scribner, but was chairman of the board from that date until his death. During the period of more than fifty years that he remained with the house, he expanded its scope until it became probably the most comprehensive publishing business in the country, and enhanced its prestige.

Inheriting a sound tradition, he brought to its maintenance the acumen of a business man and the discrimination of a man of letters. A portrait of him would, indeed, be incomplete that failed to recognize his peculiarly warm and enlightened literary sympathies. Among the many publications that are significant of his love of books, mention may be made of the beautiful edition of Thomas Shelton's translation, *The History of . . . Don Quixote* (4 vols., 1906–07), illustrated by Daniel Vierge. He cherished a good book and delighted to give it beautiful form. The history of his long administration of the house of Scribner is studded with incidents illustrating his enthusiasm and taste. These were indicative partly of his initiative and partly of the remarkable teamwork developed amongst the men who surrounded him—his younger brother Arthur, his literary adviser, William Crary Brownell [*q.v.*], and the successive editors of *Scribner's Magazine,* Edward L. Burlingame [*q.v.*] and Robert Bridges. Through their concerted efforts the Scribner imprint became a kind of blue ribbon which a host of distinguished authors, native and foreign, were glad to wear.

Charles Scribner took immense pride in his list and was constantly bent upon strengthening it, not being hidebound in his fidelity to tradition but remaining accessible always to the appeal of "new blood." Among American writers of fiction, he published books by Edith Wharton, Thomas Nelson Page, Henry James, Robert Grant, George W. Cable, Richard Harding Davis, John Fox, F. Hopkinson Smith, and, in later days, such new men as Ernest Hemingway and Ring Lardner. In letters at large there may be cited Eugene Field, Henry van Dyke, H. C. Bunner, Brander Matthews, James Huneker, Barrett Wendell, George Santayana, and Theodore Roosevelt. He was the publisher of these authors and he was their friend. As durable ties existed between him and British writers like Robert Louis Stevenson, George Meredith, Rudyard Kipling, J. M. Barrie, and John Galsworthy. His collected editions of them were not simply commercial ventures but labors of love. He was notable, also, for the encouragement he gave young artists and illustrators, many of whom later achieved distinction. The house had its educational books, its subscription department, and that which embraces religious books. In 1881, as a result of his first great decision, *Scribner's Monthly* was sold, to become *The Century Illustrated Monthly Magazine,* under an agreement which restrained the house from entering the periodical field again for five years. *St. Nicholas,* which the firm had published since November 1873, was also sold to the Century Company in 1881. In 1887 was brought out *Scribner's Magazine,* which he had probably anticipated from the beginning. In July 1917 Scribner took over from Forbes & Company the magazine *Architecture.* The subject was close to his sympathies for the house had long been largely interested in the issuance of architectural books. To facilitate and enhance the functioning of all these activities he built in 1908 the Scribner Press, a plant from which much fine printing has flowed. He also developed a notable bookstore that made a specialty of rare books.

From the inception of the plans for the *Dictionary of American Biography,* Charles Scribner was deeply interested in the enterprise. His advice was sought on many occasions. On the choice of the firm as publishers of the *Dictionary,* he and his brother gave themselves whole-heartedly to promotion of the work. There were numerous experiments to secure a format which would be not only attractive in appearance but also of proper dignity and quality for a work which promised to be so distinguished and permanent. As one expression of confidence in the enterprise, they made a generous contribution to assist in the preparation of the manuscript for press.

It is as a wise, generous, and eclectic publisher that Scribner will be remembered, but there were other phases of his activity that demand consideration. His business acumen fitted him to be for years a useful director of the National Park Bank, where he was elected a vice-president in 1926 and served through the period which witnessed the merging of the institution with the Chase National Bank. His judgment served him well, too, as a worker in the interests of his alma mater. When Princeton gave him an honorary degree of Doctor of Letters in 1925, the citation ran: "He stands today as a symbol for whatever is most courteous, honorable and fruitful of good in American endeavor. In his half century since graduation, the head of the house has given every year to labor and love for Princeton. Intimate in her councils, alert in stimulating her literary life, old in wisdom and young in spirit, constant in helping her needs, his unobtrusive, bright and kindly influence is part of all the best we have." The Princeton University Press, an institution organized "not for pecuniary profit," was beautifully housed and thoroughly equipped through his generosity. He had also an ardent enthusiasm for Skidmore College for young women, founded at Saratoga Springs,

N. Y., by the wife of his elder brother. During the last years of his life he was a member of the board of trustees and gave unstintingly of his time and money for the welfare of the college. He was one of the leaders in the fight for international copyright and was present with William Appleton and Robert Underwood Johnson when President Harrison signed the bill of 1891. When the American Publishers' Association was formed in 1900, he was among those who most effectively put their shoulders to the wheel.

His was a rich life and a happy one. He was married to Louise Flagg, the daughter of the Rev. Dr. Jared B. Flagg [*q.v.*], and had two children, a daughter and a son and namesake who, in 1932, became the head of the house. Scribner died at his home in New York.

[*Princeton Alumni Weekly,* May 2, 1930, containing tributes; *Publishers' Weekly,* Apr. 26, 1930; editorials in *N. Y. Times,* Apr. 21, 1930, and *American Mercury,* Aug. 1930; information in regard to the firm from Charles Scribner's Sons; personal acquaintance.]

R. C.

SCRIPPS, EDWARD WYLLIS (June 18, 1854–Mar. 12, 1926), newspaper publisher, was born on a farm near Rushville, Ill., the youngest of the five children of James Mogg Scripps and his third wife, Julia (Osborn) Scripps. He was a half-brother of James Edmund Scripps and Ellen Browning Scripps [*qq.v.*]. He attended a district school near his home and a private school conducted by his half-sister Ellen. At eighteen he began his newspaper work as an office boy on the *Detroit Tribune,* of which his half-brother James was manager. When James in 1873 started the Detroit *Evening News,* the first cheap, popular evening paper in the United States, Edward helped to build up the circulation of the new paper, and became first a member of the news staff and then city editor. In the fall of 1877 he gave up his position to accompany another half-brother, George H. Scripps, on a year's tour of Europe. During his travels he conceived the idea of establishing a paper of his own, and he succeeded in obtaining a promise of about $10,000 from his two half-brothers and his cousin, John Scripps Sweeney, in support of a one-cent evening paper in Cleveland, Ohio. On Nov. 2, 1878, he brought out the first issue of the Cleveland *Penny Press,* its business, editorial and printing offices housed in a four-room shack in an alley. Thus at twenty-four he laid the foundation for an impressive career as owner of a chain of daily papers extending from the Middle West to the Pacific.

Pioneers in establishing cheap evening papers in the Mississippi Valley, in 1880 Edward and his brothers bought the two-cent *Evening Chron-*

icle of St. Louis, and a year or two later a struggling paper in Cincinnati that they named the *Penny Post,* later the *Cincinnati Post.* These two papers with the Detroit *Evening News* and the Cleveland *Penny Press,* constituted the first chain of daily newspapers in the United States. Disagreements with James over the management of the papers led Edward to relinquish control of all the papers except the *Cincinnati Post.* He took Milton Alexander McRae [*q.v.*] into partnership in 1889, and formed the Scripps-McRae League of Newspapers with McRae and George H. Scripps in 1895. Following the decline of the old United Press in the nineties and the rise of the new Associated Press, organized in Chicago in 1892, as the dominant news-disseminating agency in the United States, Scripps felt the need of an independent means of obtaining telegraph news, and in 1897 he organized the Scripps-McRae Press Association to cover the field west of Pittsburgh. In 1904 this organization purchased the Publishers' Press, a similar independent organization that covered the territory east of Pittsburgh. In 1907 the two agencies were combined into the United Press Associations generally known simply as the United Press, the first press association operated in connection with a chain of daily papers. Out of a column of miscellany, which Ellen Scripps prepared for the *Cleveland Press* while she was on the staff of the Detroit *Evening News,* grew the Newspaper Enterprise Association, organized in 1902 by Edward Scripps to supply his papers and others with cartoons, illustrations, and feature articles; this, known as the "NEA," became the first newspaper syndicate connected with a chain of daily papers.

In 1891 Scripps moved to San Diego, Cal., near which he built a villa called "Miramar." Two years later he acquired an interest in the *San Diego Sun,* the first of the Scripps Coast League of newspapers, a chain that later included papers in Seattle, Tacoma, Spokane, Portland, Denver, San Francisco, Los Angeles, Fresno, and Sacramento. To serve these papers with telegraph news, he organized the Scripps Coast Press Association. In 1908 he and McRae retired in favor of Scripps' eldest son, James. The newspapers built up by Scripps were designed, as he used to say, for the "95 per cent.," the common people. Editorially they were independent in politics, sympathetic with union labor, and liberal in their general attitude; in 1912 they supported Theodore Roosevelt for the presidency and in 1924 Robert Marion LaFollette [*qq.v.*]. While retaining a controlling interest in all his papers, Scripps sold stock to members of the editorial and business staffs, and at the time of his death approximately two-fifths of the stock of his papers was in the hands of his employees. With his sister Ellen he endowed the Scripps Institution for Biological Research at La Jolla, Cal. (later the Scripps Institution of Oceanography). In 1920 he established the Science Service, an organization designed to furnish the press with the results of research presented in popular form. He also provided for the Scripps Foundation for population research at Miami University, Oxford, Ohio. He had married on Oct. 5, 1885, Nackie Benson Holtsinger of Westchester, Ohio, by whom he had six children. He died on his yacht in Monrovia Bay, off the coast of Liberia; he was survived by his wife, two daughters, and a son.

[J. E. Scripps, *A Geneal. Hist. of the Scripps Family* (1903); *Who's Who in America,* 1924–25; N. D. Cochran, *E. W. Scripps* (1933); Gilson Gardner, *Lusty Scripps: the Life of E. W. Scripps* (1932); M. A. McRae, *Forty Years in Newspaperdom* (1924); W. E. Ritter, "The Marine Biological Station of San Diego," *Univ. of Cal. Pubs. in Zoology,* Mar. 9, 1912; obit. in *Detroit News,* Mar. 14, 1926.]   W. G. B.

SCRIPPS, ELLEN BROWNING (Oct. 18, 1836–Aug. 3, 1932), newspaper woman and philanthropist, was born in London, England, the daughter of James Mogg Scripps and his second wife, Ellen Mary (Saunders) Scripps. When she was seven or eight, the family came to the United States and settled near Rushville, Ill. She was graduated from Knox College in 1859. For a time she taught school, but after the death of her father in 1873 she turned to newspaper work, in which her brother, James Edmund Scripps, and her half-brother, Edward Wyllis Scripps [*qq.v.*], were already engaged. She went to Detroit, invested her savings in the *Detroit Advertiser and Tribune,* owned by her brother James, and worked as a proof-reader and reporter. When the paper was destroyed by fire, she assisted in launching the Detroit *Evening News.* Her energy and industry, especially in editing for many years a special feature section of miscellany, contributed to the paper's success. In 1878, when her half-brother Edward founded the Cleveland *Penny Press,* she became a stockholder and a regular contributor. Later she invested in the *Cincinnati Post* and other journals in the Scripps-McRae League of Newspapers, which afterwards became the Scripps-Howard chain. More than once she came to Edward Scripps's assistance financially and saved the newspaper chain from failure. She has been called one of the pioneers in modern American journalism.

About 1891 she settled in California, where

she made her home with her brother Edward and his family at their ranch, "Miramar," near San Diego. She invested heavily and profitably in San Diego real estate, and from the fortune she accumulated she gave generously to various enterprises and institutions. She converted the family farm at Rushville, Ill., into the Scripps Memorial Park and later erected a community house upon the site of the farmhouse. She gave liberally to Knox College and to the Bishop School for Girls at La Jolla, Cal., and founded Scripps College at Claremont, Cal. To the city of San Diego she gave a community house and playground, and buildings and equipment for a zoological garden. She provided a lodge and caretakers for the Torrey Pines Park in San Diego and bequeathed to the city as an addition to the park her land holdings of several hundred acres. She and her brother Edward were among the incorporators and were the chief financial supporters of the Marine Biological Association of San Diego, which afterwards, under the name of the Scripps Institution for Biological Research, was moved to La Jolla and transferred to the University of California, becoming in 1925 the Scripps Institution of Oceanography. With her brother she also established at La Jolla the Scripps Memorial Hospital. In 1917 she became a member of the board of directors of the National Recreation Association. In her will she listed bequests and established trust funds totaling more than two million dollars. In spite of her many public benefactions, she succeeded in avoiding publicity and led a very quiet life.

[J. E. Scripps, *A Geneal. Hist. of the Scripps Family* (1903) ; N. D. Cochran, *E. W. Scripps* (1933) ; M. A. McRae, *Forty Years in Newspaperdom* (1924) ; W. E. Ritter, "The Marine Biological Station of San Diego," *Univ. of Cal. Pubs. in Zoology*, Mar. 9, 1912; *Berkeley Daily Gazette*, Aug. 3, 11, 1932; obituary and portrait in *Recreation*, Oct. 1932; *San Diego Union*, Aug. 4, 1932; *N. Y. Times*, Aug. 4, 1932.] P. O. R.

SCRIPPS, JAMES EDMUND (Mar. 19, 1835–May 29, 1906), newspaper publisher, son of James Mogg Scripps and his second wife, Ellen Mary (Saunders) Scripps, was born in London, England. His grandfather had been the publisher in London of the *Sun* and of the *Literary Gazette,* and editor and publisher of the *True Briton* (Cochran, *post*, p. 3). His father, a bookbinder, emigrated to the United States in 1844 and settled on a farm near Rushville, Ill. There James grew up and went to a district school. After attending a Chicago business college, he worked in the city for a time as a bookkeeper. In 1857 he began his newspaper career as a reporter on the *Democratic Press,* published by his cousin, John Locke Scripps, which was merged in 1858 with the *Chicago Daily Tribune.* In 1859 he became commercial editor of the *Detroit Daily Advertiser*; two years later he was part owner of the paper, and in 1862, when it was merged with the *Detroit Tribune,* he retained his interest and was made first business manager and then editor of the combined papers. On Sept. 16, 1862, he was married to Harriet Josephine Messinger of Peru, Vt. His newspaper experience led him to believe that there was an opportunity in Detroit for a small, cheap, but well-written evening paper in which both news and editorial comment should be condensed for busy readers. Accordingly on Aug. 23, 1873, he launched the *Evening News,* a two-cent, four-page daily paper, independent in politics, printed for a time on the press of the *Detroit Free Press.* When, despite the panic of 1873, he decided to set up a printing plant of his own, he obtained additional capital from his brother, George H. Scripps, and his sister, Ellen Browning Scripps [*q.v.*], who also joined the editorial staff. Within a year the little two-cent *Evening News* had secured twice as large a circulation as any of its five-cent rivals. Although Scripps's original intention seems to have been to publish a paper modeled on the *Springfield Republican* and the New York *Evening Post,* the news staff that he employed actually produced a much livelier and more popular little news sheet that appealed to working men and their wives. It was the pioneer among the small, cheap evening papers that developed in the Middle West during the seventies and eighties.

In 1878, with his brother George H. Scripps and their cousin, John Scripps Sweeney, he lent about $10,000 to his half-brother Edward Wyllis Scripps [*q.v.*], who had helped to build up the circulation of the *Evening News* and was now about to start a one-cent evening paper in Cleveland, Ohio. This was the *Penny Press,* later the *Cleveland Press.* Later he joined Edward in establishing two more papers: in 1880 the *Evening Chronicle* in St. Louis, a two-cent paper, which in 1887 became the first penny paper west of the Mississippi River; and a year or two later the Cincinnati *Penny Post,* later the *Cincinnati Post,* in which he had previously invested. These papers in Detroit, Cleveland, St. Louis, and Cincinnati, owned jointly by the three Scripps brothers, with their sister Ellen and their cousin, formed the first chain of daily newspapers in the United States. In 1887 he entered into an agreement with his two brothers concerning the control and management of the papers, and spent two years abroad for his health. After his return his conservatism led to differences, and he ceased to take an active part in the combination. In 1903 he relinquished his holdings in all but the *Evening News,* later called the *Detroit News.* In 1891 he entered the morning newspaper field in Detroit by purchasing the *Detroit Tribune,* which he continued as a morning paper. When the agitation for Free Silver began in the nineties, he espoused the cause of William Jennings Bryan in both his Detroit papers, although personally he had always been a stanch Republican. His advocacy of Free Silver and Bryan in 1896 cost both papers heavily in patronage, and after McKinley's election he returned to the Republican party. In 1902 he was elected to the Michigan state Senate as an advocate of home rule for municipalities.

He was interested in art, architecture, and early printed books, of which he had a large collection. From its inception he served on the commission of the Detroit Museum of Art (later the Detroit Institute of Arts) and contributed to it both money and paintings that he collected on his trips abroad. To the city of Detroit he gave a park that bears his name. He wrote *Five Months Abroad* (1882), *Memorials of the Scripps Family* (1891), *A Genealogical History of the Scripps Family* (1903), and numerous pamphlets. He died in Detroit, survived by his wife, three daughters, and one son.

[J. E. Scripps, *A Geneal. Hist. of the Scripps Family* (1903); *Who's Who in America,* 1906–07; N. D. Cochran, *E. W. Scripps* (1933); Gilson Gardner, *Lusty Scripps: the Life of E. W. Scripps* (1932); L. A. White, *The Detroit News: 1873–1917* (1918); M. A. McRae, *Forty Years in Newspaperdom* (1924); C. M. and M. A. Burton, *Hist. of Wayne County and the City of Detroit, Mich.* (1930), vol. II; obituary in *Detroit News,* May 29, 1906.]   W. G. B.

SCRUGGS, WILLIAM LINDSAY (Sept. 14, 1836–July 18, 1912), diplomat, author, descended from Richard Scruggs who was in Virginia as early as 1665, was the eldest of seven children born to Frederick and Margaret (Kimbrough) Scruggs. His birthplace was his father's plantation, twenty miles above Knoxville, Tenn., on the French Broad River. He attended the grammar school near his home, was further instructed by a private tutor, and finished at Strawberry Plains College in East Tennessee. In 1858 he was principal of the Hamilton Male Academy and on Aug. 3 of that year he married Judith Ann Potts of Stafford County, Va. Removing to Georgia in 1861, he was admitted to the bar, but instead of practising law edited the Columbus *Daily Sun,* 1862–65. He subsequently moved to Atlanta, where from 1870 to 1872 he edited the *Atlanta Daily New Era.*

Politically Scruggs was a Unionist, reflecting the influence of his early environment, and he labored editorially for an intelligent reconstruction of the seceded states. His services were rewarded when he was appointed minister to Colombia, in April 1873. He was arbitrator in a claims case between the British and Colombian governments, settling it satisfactorily to both; he also negotiated a successful settlement of a long-standing maritime case, that of the *Montijo.* Recalled Aug. 16, 1876, when further appropriations for the legation were withheld by Congress, he served as consul at Chin-Kiang, and then at Canton, China, and in 1882 returned to Colombia as minister resident, becoming minister plenipotentiary two years later. Before retiring to private life under Cleveland's administration in December 1885, he succeeded in dissuading the Colombian government from enforcing an increase in customs duties at Panama and Colon.

After Harrison's inauguration, Scruggs returned to the diplomatic service as minister to Venezuela, Mar. 30, 1889, and became deeply interested in the dispute with Great Britain over the British Guiana boundary. After the election of Cleveland, he left his post, Dec. 15, 1892, although he was not formally recalled until Feb. 3, 1893. His espousal of Venezuela's cause won him appointment by that government as its legal adviser and special agent in August 1894. Almost immediately he published an able polemic pamphlet, *British Aggressions in Venezuela; or the Monroe Doctrine on Trial* (1894), and persuaded L. F. Livingston, the congressman from his district in Georgia, to introduce a resolution (Jan. 10, 1895) recommending that both parties to the dispute refer their differences to arbitration. Scruggs pressed his views upon the secretary of state, W. Q. Gresham [*q.v.*], but without complete success, and when the latter fell ill he carried his case directly to President Cleveland. The administration's course was clearly plotted in a dispatch from the new secretary, Richard Olney [*q.v.*], to Ambassador Bayard, July 20, 1895, and confirmed by the President's message to Congress the following December. Scruggs could hardly have asked for more, although it does not appear from the writings of either Olney or Cleveland whether they were moved by his personal pleas or by the considerations of the case itself which he had been instrumental in making an issue. As special agent of Venezuela Scruggs appeared before the Boundary Commission established in 1895, on whose findings the final arbitration (1897–99) was based. His *Brief Concerning the Question of Boundary between Venezuela and British Guiana* was published in 1898.

Scruggs had now finished his public career. Thereafter he wrote extensively, publishing *The Colombian and Venezuelan Republics* (1900; 1905); *Evolution of American Citizenship* (1901); "The Monroe Doctrine; Whence It Came, What It Is, and What It Is Not" (*Southern Law Review*, May 1902), and numerous other articles for historical, economic, and legal reviews. He was a well-read man and a good linguist, especially in Spanish. He bore a striking facial resemblance to Roscoe Conkling, but was tall and slender. His wife, by whom he had one son and four daughters, died in 1897. He survived her fifteen years, dying of apoplexy at his home in Atlanta.

[E. H. S. Dunklin, *Scruggs Geneal.* (1912); *Who's Who in America*, 1910–11; T. D. Jervey, "William Lindsay Scruggs—A Forgotten Diplomat," *South Atlantic Quart.*, July 1928; *Papers Relating to the Foreign Relations of the U. S.*, 1874–76, 1883–85, 1890; *Atlanta Constitution*, July 19, 1912; W. L. Scruggs, *The Colombian and Venezuelan Republics*, mentioned above; Instructions and Dispatches in archives of the Dept. of State.]   G. V. B.

SCRYMSER, JAMES ALEXANDER (July 18, 1839–Apr. 21, 1918), cable and telegraph promoter, capitalist, was a son of James Scrymgeour Scrymser and his wife, Ann Thompson. He was born and grew up in New York City, attending College Hill Academy at Poughkeepsie, N. Y., where he was graduated in 1856. At the outbreak of the Civil War in 1861 he was in his twenty-second year and had made no choice of a profession or calling. With Francis Channing Barlow [*q.v.*], he enlisted as a private in the 12th New York Infantry, one of the units that went to the defense of Washington in the spring of 1861. He was soon commissioned a second lieutenant in the 43rd New York and later received a staff appointment in the division commanded by Gen. William Farrar Smith [*q.v.*]. He served with the VI Corps, winning a captaincy, and later in the XVIII Army Corps, and is said to have been in all the battles of the Army of the Potomac for three years.

Returning to New York after his discharge from military service at the end of the war, he had his attention directed to the need of telegraphic communication between the United States and Cuba. Cyrus Field's final and successful attempt to lay the Atlantic cable was well under way, and submarine cable systems had been projected in many parts of the world. For the International Ocean Telegraph Company, incorporated in 1865, Scrymser undertook almost single-handed to see that 235 miles of cable were

laid from Florida to Cuba and secured sufficient capital to complete the task in 1867. He had from the first been the motive power of the enterprise, and within a few years he became its titular head as well. When, in 1878, Jay Gould acquired the property and annexed it to the Western Union system, Scrymser resigned the presidency and at once turned his attention to the development of telegraph lines in Mexico and Central America. He raised the capital for laying a cable from Galveston, Tex., to Vera Cruz, Mexico, and was the chief executive of the Mexican Cable (later Telegraph) Company after it began to operate in 1881. Within a year new construction enabled the extension of the service to Central and South America, the Central and South American Cable (later Telegraph) Company having been organized in 1879. The company held a fifty-year exclusive concession granted by Porfirio Diaz, president of Mexico, and controlled Mexico's land wires. Its business increased rapidly; by 1893 more than 5,000 miles of cables and land lines had been added to the original "via Galveston" system of 4,600 miles. This addition included a cable from Chorillos, Peru, to Valparaiso, Chile, by way of Iquique, Chile. Land lines connected it with Buenos Aires and Scrymser's company had an exchange agreement with the West Coast of America Telegraph Company (British). The rate, which in 1882 had been seven dollars and a half a word from the United States to Buenos Aires, was reduced to sixty-five cents in 1915. A "via Colon" route from New York to the west coast of South America was completed in 1907, and in 1917 a New York to Brazil line was completed. Scrymser's methods were unobtrusive, direct, and wholly without flourish. Although he was interested in social-welfare efforts and gave much of his time and money to their promotion, his name rarely got into print. In the movement for vacation schools he was active for years. In 1892, When Dr. Charles Henry Parkhurst [*q.v.*] was beginning his crusade in New York against the alliance of the police with protected vice, it was Scrymser who planned the great Cooper Union meeting that brought to the lone clergyman the open and substantial aid of influential elements in the city's population (C. H. Parkhurst, *My Forty Years in New York*, 1923). In 1869 Scrymser was married to Mary C. Prime of New York, who survived him. He died in New York City.

[*Who's Who in America*, 1916–17; obit., *N. Y. Times*, Apr. 22, 1918; *Personal Reminiscences of James A. Scrymser in Times of Peace and War* (priv. printed, 1915); *A Half Century of Cable Service to the Three Americas* (1928).]   W. B. S.

SCUDDER, HORACE ELISHA (Oct. 16, 1838–Jan. 11, 1902), editor and writer, born in Boston, was the youngest boy in a family of six sons and one daughter, children of Charles Scudder, merchant, a deacon of the Union Church of that city, and Sarah Lathrop (Coit) Scudder. The fifth son, Samuel Hubbard Scudder [*q.v.*], became a distinguished entomologist. The Scudders had lived for generations on Cape Cod; the Coit progenitors included Gov. John Winthrop of Massachusetts. In one of Horace E. Scudder's earliest and best books, *Life and Letters of David Coit Scudder, Missionary in Southern India* (1864), a biography of an older brother, the pious and happy influences of his own youth in a household of strict orthodoxy are clearly suggested. After preparatory studies in the Roxbury and Boston Latin schools, he entered Williams College, where he was editor of the *Williams Quarterly* and graduated in 1858. Here he acquired a love for Greek which led to a lifelong habit of reading Homer and other classics—always including the Greek Testament—daily before breakfast. Soon after his graduation he went to New York as a teacher of private pupils and a writer of stories for children—collected under the titles *Seven Little People and Their Friends* (copr. 1862) and *Dream Children* (1864), both published anonymously. The sympathetic understanding of children and the strain of imagination that marked these stories seemed to foreshadow a career in creative writing; instead, he soon found himself, as he put it in later years, "at the desk of a literary workman."

Under the "honorable name" of "Literary Workman," he has been commemorated by T. W. Higginson [*q.v.*]. As a single designation the term applies to the larger portion of Scudder's activities more accurately than any other that could be chosen. His chief work, relating more to books than to magazines, was that of an editor. It began through an early association with Henry O. Houghton [*q.v.*], who in 1864 was combining his established business of printing at the Riverside Press, Cambridge, Mass., with that of publishing, under the firm name of Hurd & Houghton. In this organization Scudder, having returned from New York to Boston, became a reader of manuscripts and general editorial assistant. With an unswerving loyalty to the Riverside Press and to the succession of firms out of which Houghton, Mifflin & Company emerged in 1880, he held this post for the rest of his busy life.

In 1867 the young firm and the young editor launched a juvenile monthly, the *Riverside Magazine for Young People*. Scudder's interest in children here found full expression, not only through his own writings, but in the pains he devoted to the excellent woodcut illustrations and to the securing of such contributors as Hans Christian Andersen, Jacob Abbott, Frank R. Stockton, and Sarah Orne Jewett. Four volumes (1867–70) completed this undertaking. In 1872 he became a member of the firm of Hurd & Houghton, but after three years retired from the partnership in order to apply himself exclusively to editorial duties. In *Henry Oscar Houghton; a Biographical Outline* (1897) he referred (p. 92) to the sentiment for the word "Riverside" entertained by the head of the firm: "'Riverside,' he once said to me, 'is like a diamond which I can hold up before my eye, and turn it this way and that, and let the light fall on it, and see it sparkle.'" For the quality of the light thus described Scudder was largely responsible. The motto, *Tout bien ou rien*, appearing, first in 1885, on the title-pages of innumerable volumes that received his editorial oversight might well have been his own rule. From the planning of books, singly or in series, such as the American Commonwealths and the Riverside Literature series, from the critical reading of manuscripts to preface-writing and index-making, no task was too large or too small to call for the best he had to give.

These labors were largely unseen. While pursuing them he accomplished also the writing of a number of books of his own. Of these the most popular were the eight juvenile "Bodley Books" of travel produced between 1876 and 1884. Among his other books not already mentioned were *The Dwellers in Five-Sisters Court* (1876), a novel; *Stories and Romances* (1880); *Noah Webster* (1882), in the American Men of Letters Series; *Life and Letters of Bayard Taylor* (2 vols., 1884), with Marie Hansen-Taylor; *A History of the United States* (1884), for schools; *Men and Letters* (1887); *George Washington; an Historical Biography* (1890); *Childhood in Literature and Art* (1894); and *James Russell Lowell, a Biography* (2 vols., 1901). His fugitive writing, which was considerable, dealt chiefly with historical, critical, and biographical topics. From 1890 to 1898 he served "the house" of his devotion as editor of the *Atlantic Monthly*.

On Oct. 30, 1873, he married Grace Owen, of Cambridge, who, with one of their twin daughters, survived him. He served the cause of education as a trustee of Williams and Wellesley colleges and of the Episcopal Theological School in Cambridge. In the cause of letters, he rendered notable service as a pioneer in the provision of the best reading for the young, and also through the infinite patience and kindness of his dealings with a host of aspirants to authorship. Of average height and inclined to rotundity, he was noticeable in his later years chiefly for his large bushy beard, which once drew from him the characteristic, whimsical confession to a great curiosity to see what he was like underneath it, if only he dared to cut it off. He died at Cambridge, in the house he had occupied for many years.

[Beyond autobiog. passages in books mentioned, sources include A. V. G. Allen, "Memoir of Horace E. Scudder, Litt. D.," in *Proc. Mass. Hist. Soc.*, 2 ser. XVII (1903), reprinted with slight changes as "Horace E. Scudder; An Appreciation," in *Atlantic Mo.*, Apr. 1903; T. W. Higginson, in *Proc. Am. Acad. of Arts and Sciences*, vol. XXXVII (1902); *Atlantic Mo.*, Mar. 1902; *Who's Who in America*, 1901–02; *Boston Transcript*, Jan. 13, 1902; personal recollections, and information from Scudder's daughter, Mrs. Ingersoll Bowditch.]   M. A. DeW. H.

SCUDDER, JOHN (Sept. 3, 1793–Jan. 13, 1855), missionary to India, a descendant of Thomas Scudder who settled in Salem, Mass., in 1635, and a grandson of Nathaniel Scudder [*q.v.*], was born in Freehold, N. J. His father, Joseph Scudder, was a lawyer, and his mother, Maria Johnston, was a daughter of Col. Philip Johnston of the 1st New Jersey Regiment, who was killed at the battle of Long Island. At the College of New Jersey, where he graduated in 1811, John was known as a young man of integrity and eminent Christian character. The ministry was the profession of his choice but he was deterred from entering it by the stubborn opposition of his father. Graduating from the College of Physicians and Surgeons, New York, in 1813, he began practice in that city, making his home with a family named Waterbury, whose daughter Harriet he married. His success in his profession was immediate and he seemed to be on the way to an extensive and lucrative practice when the chance reading of a tract entitled *The Conversion of the World; or, The Claims of Six Hundred Millions* turned him irresistibly toward the mission field. Accordingly, he accepted an appointment from the American Board of Commissioners for Foreign Missions and sailed from Boston for India, June 8, 1819, as its first medical missionary to that country; his wife, who was in warm sympathy with his purpose, accompanied him. They were stationed at Jaffna, the northern province of Ceylon, where they soon acquired the Tamil language and Mrs. Scudder engaged in school work, while her husband began his life employment of preaching and healing. A member of the Reformed Dutch Church, he was ordained by a council of missionaries, May 15, 1821. A hospital was opened, boarding and day schools were established, and Scudder began the training of native medical students. With him, however, medical work was always subordinate to the great end of evangelization.

In 1836 he was transferred to Madras, where a mission station with a printing press was established. From here as a center he began making extensive tours, often being absent for several months, and once crossing the entire peninsula of India, preaching, healing, and distributing literature. Worn by hardships and the fierce opposition which he encountered, reduced by jungle fever and with one arm paralyzed, he was ordered to America in 1842. His health being greatly benefitted by the voyage, he spent three active years in promoting the cause of missions. Through his influence missionary societies were everywhere organized, and he developed an especial facility in addressing children. While in the United States he attended the ordination of his son, Henry Martyn Scudder, who immediately embarked as a missionary to India. Returning to India in 1846, Scudder resumed work in Madura but in 1849 removed to Madras, where in connection with his son he began an extensive work which he continued till 1854, when because of declining health he made a voyage to South Africa. Being somewhat recovered, he resumed preaching, but died suddenly at Wynberg early in 1855. His son Joseph, who had accompanied him, took his body back to Madras, where it was buried beside that of his wife who had died in November 1849.

Scudder wrote many tracts in the Tamil language, and, after his return from his sojourn in America, many tracts and booklets in English which were issued by the American Tract Society. He had a refined and pleasing address and an intellect of high order. In person he was tall and strong, with an iron will and indomitable courage. On one occasion he lanced a cancer from his own foot without assistance of any kind. He always preached twice a day and often stood in the burning sun for eleven consecutive hours, preaching, and distributing literature. Of his fourteen children, eight sons and two daughters lived to maturity. Seven of the sons became missionaries and one died while in preparation for the work.

[J. B. Waterbury, *Memoir of the Rev. John Scudder, M.D.* (1870); H. H. Holcomb, *Men of Might in India Missions* (1901); pp. 167–89; C. C. Creegan, *Pioneer Missionaries of the Church* (1903), pp. 150–62; Rufus Anderson, *Hist. of the Missions of the A.B.C.F.M. in India* (1874); A. M. Scudder, *A Brief Sketch of the Life and Work of Rev. John Scudder, M.D., His Wife and Descendants* (pamphlet, 1912); P. E. Faure and W. Robertson, *Funeral Addresses . . . on the Occasion of the Interment of the Rev. John Scudder, M.D.*

(1855); letters and extracts from Scudder's journals in the *Panoplist* and its successor, the *Missionary Herald* (1819–1855).]

F. T. P.

SCUDDER, JOHN MILTON (Sept. 8, 1829–Feb. 17, 1894), eclectic physician, was born in Harrison, Hamilton County, Ohio, the son of John Scudder. His father, a cabinet maker by trade, died while his children were still young, and John, to assist his mother, began work in a button factory in the neighboring town of Reading. Later, he returned to Harrison, taking up his father's trade and adding that of painting; still later, he opened a general store. He had the advantages of the village schools and received some further instruction. On Sept. 8, 1849, he married Jane Hannah, of Harrison.

Becoming interested in medicine through Dr. Milton L. Thomas, a local eclectic practitioner, he studied with him and subsequently entered the Eclectic Medical Institute in Cincinnati, graduating in 1856 as valedictorian of his class. In the session following his graduation he was appointed professor of general, special, and pathological anatomy. He began practice in the old section of Cincinnati known as Fulton, and in a short time became one of the busiest and most prosperous physicians of the city. Meanwhile, the fortunes of the Eclectic Medical Institute were at a low ebb, and in 1861 he practically gave up practice to become dean and devote his time and energies to building up the school. In 1858 he had been appointed professor of diseases of women and children; in 1860 he changed to the chair of pathology and principles and practice of medicine; in 1887 he transferred to the chair of hygiene and physical diagnosis, which he occupied for the rest of his life. With the management of the school, he took over the editorship of the moribund *Eclectic Medical Journal,* which he revived and conducted for over thirty years (1861–94). For a short time he edited the *Journal of Health,* a periodical of popular medicine, and also, for a year (1870–71), *The Eclectic,* a literary journal. Immediately upon his taking charge of the school and the *Journal,* they prospered, and from that time to the day of his death, Scudder was the foremost eclectic physician of the country. Aggressive, yet tactful, he was by nature well fitted for leadership; in addition, he was a shrewd business man.

Through the editorial pages of the *Journal* he exercised a continuing influence upon the whole profession of eclectic medicine, and through his writings and his lectures he introduced and established the eclectic doctrine and practice of "specific medication." From the beginning of his teaching career, he continued to produce books which collectively comprised for years the standard textbooks of eclectic medicine. Like his editorials, these books are well written and well arranged. The more important are *Practical Treatise on the Diseases of Women* (1857); *Materia Medica and Therapeutics* (1860); *Eclectic Practice of Medicine* (1864); *Domestic Medicine; or Home Book of Health* (1865), which, under different titles, went through more than twenty editions; *Principles of Medicine* (1867); *Eclectic Practice in Diseases of Children* (1869); *Familiar Treatise on Medicine* (1869); *Specific Medication and Specific Medicines* (1870); *Specific Diagnosis* (1874). An illness in 1891 necessitated the curtailment of much of his activities. He died in his sleep at his winter home in Daytona, Fla. His first wife having died, on Feb. 4, 1861, he married her sister, Mary Hannah. Four sons of this second marriage entered the practice of medicine or dentistry.

[*Bull. of the Lloyd Lib. of Botany, Pharmacy, and Materia Medica* (1912), no. 19; *Eclectic Medic. Jour.* (Cincinnati), Jan. 1895; H. W. Felter, *Hist. of the Eclectic Medic. Inst., Cincinnati, Ohio* (1902); H. A. Kelly and W. L. Burrage, *Am. Medic. Biogs.* (1920); *Cincinnati Times-Star,* Feb. 19, 1894.]

J. M. P—n.

SCUDDER, NATHANIEL (May 10?, 1733–Oct. 16, 1781), soldier, member of the Continental Congress, was descended from Thomas Scudder who emigrated from Wiltshire, England, to Salem, Mass., about 1635. The descendants of Thomas were millers at Huntington, Long Island. Authorities disagree as to whether Nathaniel was born there on Oct. 16, 1733, or near Freehold, N. J., on May 10. At any rate, he was the eldest of the six children of Jacob and Abia (Rowe) Scudder who removed from Huntington and finally settled just southeast of Princeton, N. J., at a place later called Scudder's Mills. He was graduated from the College of New Jersey, now Princeton University, with its fourth class in 1751. He then studied medicine and after a whirlwind romance married, on Mar. 23, 1752, Isabella, the daughter of the wealthy Kenneth Anderson of Monmouth County. They had three sons and two daughters. Nathaniel had a large and apparently lucrative practice at Freehold, Manalapan, and other parts of Monmouth County, and he seems to have endeared himself to all. He took a strong interest in religion, was an elder in the Tennent Church near Freehold, and is said to have worsted Thomas Paine in a religious controversy. He was a trustee of Princeton from 1778 until his death.

As the Revolution approached, he played an active part in public affairs. He was a leader at the Freehold meeting on June 6, 1774, where he drafted resolutions of sympathy for Boston, and soon became a member of the local committee of public safety. He was a delegate to New Jersey's first provincial congress at New Brunswick that year and was speaker of the legislature in 1776. A lieutenant-colonel of the 1st Monmouth County Regiment of militia, he succeeded George Taylor as colonel on Nov. 28, 1776. Some of his property was destroyed during the British occupation at that time, the chief item in his bill of damages being a new colonel's uniform. In 1777 he was elected a delegate to the Continental Congress, where he first appeared on Feb. 9, 1778, and served until just before his second term expired on Dec. 1, 1779. He was frequently absent from the sessions of the Congress, as he was appointed on committees dealing with the quartermaster service, which required personal attention. He was present at the battle of Monmouth, near his own home, during a recess of the Congress. His most important service was writing a letter from Freehold on July 13, 1778, two weeks after that battle, to John Hart, speaker of the New Jersey legislature, urging strongly that the state's delegates to Congress be empowered to ratify and sign the Articles of Confederation (Burnett, *post*, III, p. 326). Some say that he appeared before the hesitant legislature in person. At any rate, his efforts were successful, for the necessary authorization was made on Nov. 20, and the Articles were signed by Scudder and his colleagues on Nov. 26.

After retiring from Congress, he resumed his military duties, assisting David Forman in repelling Loyalist raids. Three days before the Yorktown surrender, when some Loyalist refugees from Sandy Hook tried to land at Black Point, near Shrewsbury, N. J., he was killed. He was buried in the Tennent churchyard on the Monmouth battlefield.

[Sec. of State's Office, Trenton, Manuscript Book 12, p. 479; Book 24, p. 135; records in files for General Alumni Catalogue, Princeton University; Stephen Wickes, *Hist. of Medicine in N. J.* (1879); H. L. Cooley, *Genealogy of Early Settlers of Trenton and Ewing* (1883); *Letters of Members of the Continental Cong.*, vols. II–IV (1923–28), ed. by E. C. Burnett; *N. J. Archives*, 2 ser. vol. I (1901); *Pa. Mag. of Hist. & Biography*, no. III (1879); *A Brief Narrative of the Ravages of the British and Hessians at Princeton* (1906), ed. by V. L. Collins; F. B. Heitman, *Hist. Register of Officers of the Continental Army* (1893); W. S. Stryker, *Official Register of the Officers and Men of N. J. in the Rev. War* (1872), pp. 344, 355.]
R. G. A.

SCUDDER, SAMUEL HUBBARD (Apr. 13, 1837–May 17, 1911), entomologist, was born in Boston and died in Cambridge, Mass. Son of Charles and Sarah Lathrop (Coit) Scudder and brother of Horace Elisha Scudder [*q.v.*], he was of Puritan origin on both sides. His father was a well-to-do hardware and commission merchant. At the age of sixteen Samuel was sent to Williams College. His interest in entomology was aroused during his freshman year by a case of butterflies in the room of a friend, and before the end of his junior year he had decided to devote his life as far as possible to that science. After taking his bachelor's degree at Williams in 1857, he studied in the Lawrence Scientific School under Agassiz, gaining the degree of B.S. in 1862 and the faculty of attention to minute detail that characterized all his later work. He was an assistant to Agassiz until 1864, and then served as custodian of the Boston Society of Natural History until 1870. On June 25, 1867, he married Ethelinda Jane Blatchford. From 1870 to 1879 he held no salaried position, but in the latter year became assistant librarian of Harvard University, resigning in 1882. In 1886 he was appointed a paleontologist in the United States Geological Survey, being charged with the study of fossil insects. Resigning this position in 1892, he thenceforth worked at his home in Cambridge until he was paralyzed, a number of years before his death.

Outside the field of entomology, he published two large and important works: *Catalogue of Scientific Serials of All Countries . . . 1633–1876* (1879) and *Nomenclator Zoologicus* (2 parts, 1882–84), the latter still of enormous value to zoologists a generation later. He was for a long time a member of the Appalachian Club, and wrote many articles for its journal, *Appalachia*. For the Boston Society of Natural History he edited *Entomological Correspondence of Thaddeus William Harris, M.D.* (1869). His true life work, however, dealt with three general topics—American diurnal *Lepidoptera,* the *Orthoptera,* and fossil insects—and here he made striking advances and established himself as one of the great leaders in American entomology. His monumental treatise on butterflies, *The Butterflies of the Eastern United States and Canada, with Special Reference to New England* (3 vols., 1888–89), was the result of thirty years of research in the life histories and affinities of these interesting creatures. While technical in the main, it is filled with popular excursuses treating of a number of extremely interesting subjects relating to New England and its butterflies. His essays on migration, geographical distribution, protective coloration, dimorphism, and other evolutionary aspects attractively opened broad fields of research. He also wrote several smaller and more popular books on butterflies, including

Butterflies: Their Structure, Changes, and Life Histories (1881); *The Life of a Butterfly: A Chapter in Natural History for the General Reader* (1893); *A Brief Guide to the Commoner Butterflies of the Northern United States and Canada* (1893); *Frail Children of the Air: Excursions into the World of Butterflies* (1895); *Every-Day Butterflies* (1899).

He was the greatest American orthopterist of his time, and his work on fossil insects was profound, very extensive and of a pioneer character. The closing years of his productive life were largely devoted to fossil insects and *Orthoptera*. Among his major publications in these fields were: *A Classed and Annotated Bibliography of Fossil Insects* (1890), *The Tertiary Insects of North America* (1891), *Index to the Known Fossil Insects of the World* (1891), *Tertiary Rhynchophorous Coleoptera of the United States* (1894), and *Revision of the American Fossil Cockroaches* (1895), all issued as Bulletins, Monographs, or Reports of the United States Geological Survey; *Revision of the Orthopteran Group Melanopli* (United States National Museum, 1897); and *Alphabetical Index to North American Orthoptera Described in the Eighteenth and Nineteenth Centuries* (Boston Society of Natural History, 1901). Scudder's bibliography comprised 791 scientific titles. His papers were mainly of a descriptive character, but he wrote many popular articles. In the course of his life he named and described 1,884 species, of which 1,144 species and 233 genera are fossil insects, 630 species and 106 genera are recent *Orthoptera,* and the remainder are fossil insects and recent butterflies. He received the Walker prize of the Boston Society of Natural History in 1898. He became a member of the National Academy of Sciences in 1877 and of the American Philosophical Society in 1878. He was an honorary fellow of the Royal Society of Canada and the Entomological Society of London, and foreign associate of the national entomological or zoological societies of The Hague, St. Petersburg, Vienna, Moscow, Madrid, Buenos Aires, and Brussels. He was probably the broadest and most highly cultured American worker in his field in his generation and has been called "the greatest scholar and most charming writer among American entomologists." Personally he was a man of great charm, tall, slender, kindly, and possessed of a keen sense of humor. His final illness, which took the form of creeping paralysis, began in 1896, shortly after the death of his only son.

[A. G. Mayor, in *Memoirs Nat. Acad. Sci.,* vol. XVII (1924); *Science,* Sept. 15, 1911; *Psyche,* Dec. 1911; *Entomological News,* July 1911; *Appalachia,* July 1911; *Canadian Entomologist,* July 1911; *Entomologist's Record* (London), Sept. 15, 1911; *Boston Transcript,* May 17, 1911.]   L.O.H.

SCULL, JOHN (1765–Feb. 8, 1828), pioneer newspaper editor, was born in Reading, Pa., the son of Jasper Scull, of well-to-do Quaker stock. His great-grandfather, Nicholas Scull, emigrated to Philadelphia with his brother John in 1685; his grandfather, Nicholas Scull, II, was the first surveyor-general of the province of Pennsylvania; and his father held offices in Northampton and Berks counties, Pa. His father's sister, Mary Scull, was the mother of Nicholas Biddle, 1750–1778 [*q.v.*]. Opportunities for the son's formal education were doubtless limited, but he evidently acquired a command of good forthright English. In the summer of 1786, young John Scull journeyed over the mountains with his partner, Joseph Hall, to establish in Pittsburgh the first newspaper west of the Alleghenies. Apparently he had been induced to go partly through the persuasions of Hugh Henry Brackenridge [*q.v.*]. Press, types, ink, and paper were brought over the mountains by pack-horse, and the first issue of the Pittsburgh *Gazette* appeared on July 29, 1786. There was no mail-route, and at first the young editor delivered his papers by hand within the village and relied on chance travelers to serve his outlying subscribers. The paper had apparently two chief objects—to attract immigrants to the region, and to support the Federalist party. In the former purpose Scull was aided by Brackenridge's articles praising the western region; but over the latter he and Brackenridge had by 1800 developed bitter antagonism. Before this, however, Scull had published the third volume of Brackenridge's *Modern Chivalry* (1793), the first book, aside from hymn books, almanacs, and the like, to be printed west of the Alleghenies.

Scull's public service to Pittsburgh was considerable aside from his printing. He helped secure a post-route to Pittsburgh and was postmaster from 1789 to 1796; he was president, from 1814 to 1819, of the second bank established in Pittsburgh; he was one of the incorporators of the Western University of Pennsylvania, now the University of Pittsburgh, in 1819; and he was a member of the first council of the borough of Pittsburgh in 1804. During the Whiskey Rebellion, under threat of personal violence, he opened his columns to communications denouncing the excise, but he refrained from editorial indorsement of the insurgents. In 1789 he was married to Mary, the daughter of Col. John Irwin of Westmoreland County, and he had two sons and one daughter. In 1816 he retired from the publication of the *Gazette,* and in 1826 he moved to his farm near the present town of Irwin, Pa., where he died (*Pittsburgh Mercury,* Feb. 19, 1828). His descendants have been prominent in western Pennsylvania, at the bar, in newspaper publication, and in banking.

[Materials on Scull are scattered, fragmentary, and contradictory. The most detailed accounts for family data are in L. B. Thomas, *The Thomas Book* (1896), *Hist. of Bedford and Somerset Counties, Pa.* (1906), vol. III, pp. 16–25, and J. N. Boucher, ed., *Hist. of Westmoreland County, Pa.* (1906), vol. III, pp. 504–508. For the *Gazette,* see R. G. Thwaites, "The Ohio Valley Press before the War of 1812–15," *Proc. of the Am. Antiq. Soc.,* Apr. 1909, n. s., vol. XIX (1909), and the works cited therein. The most complete file of the *Gazette* is in the Carnegie Library of Pittsburgh. Consult also N. B. Craig, *The Hist. of Pittsburgh* (1851), pp. 188–206 (2nd ed. 1917), C. W. Dahlinger, *Pittsburgh, a Sketch of Its Early Social Life* (1916), and J. N. Boucher, ed., *A Century and a Half of Pittsburg and Her People* (1908), vol. II, pp. 79–80, 297, 419, 420.]
S. J. B.

SCULLIN, JOHN (Aug. 17, 1836–May 28, 1920), railroad builder, street-railway operator, manufacturer, was born on a farm near Helena, N. Y., the third of seven children of Nicholas and Mary (Kenney) Scullin, natives of Ireland. He was educated in the country schools and the academy at Potsdam, N. Y. Accustomed to hard work from boyhood, he crossed into Canada at nineteen to serve the Grand Trunk Railway as water-carrier, brakeman, ballast-train conductor, and construction contractor. On Aug. 18, 1863, he married Hannah Perry of Montreal, and that year he went to Minnesota, where he became a construction contractor for the Minneapolis & Cedar Valley Railroad, later part of the Chicago, Milwaukee & St. Paul system. Attracted by reports of gold in Idaho territory, he joined an ox-team party of prospectors, seven of whom were killed by Indians. Leaving the Northwest after several months, he was back in New York by 1865, ready to resume railroad building. Opportunities being more numerous in the West, he settled in Leavenworth, Kan., in 1866 and soon acquired contracts to lay forty miles of the Union Pacific Railroad. In 1868 he built the Missouri Valley railway between Maryville and Savannah, Mo., and the Chicago, Rock Island & Pacific from Leavenworth to Cameron, Mo. In 1869 he undertook his most important railroad construction, that of the major portion of the Missouri-Kansas-Texas system, which began with the section from Emporia, Kan., to Texas and ended with the Missouri division terminating at Moberly in 1874. He also built parts of the Galveston, Harrisburg & San Antonio and the Denison & Southeastern railroads. It was as construction contractor for the Missouri-Kansas-

Texas system that he won one of railroad building's most famous races, the prize being the privilege to build in Indian territory. To defeat his competitors, he laid twenty-six and a half miles of tracks in eleven days, reaching the boundary near Chetopa, Kan., June 6, 1870. A rugged man, he reveled in the railroad camp's rough life.

In 1875 he brought his family from Sedalia, Mo., to St. Louis, where he invested in street railways. In 1883 as president of the Mexican National Construction Company he built the Mexican National railroad from Mexico City to San Luis Potosí and from Acambaro to Morelia. Though he was urged to stay in Mexico, he returned to St. Louis in 1885 to become a street-railway operator. He unified several lines, instituted a system of transfers, and went directly from horse power to electricity while his competitors experimented with cable cars. Selling his interests in 1899, he formed the next year the Scullin-Gallagher Iron and Steel Company, later the Scullin Steel Company, which manufactured large railroad castings and rolling mills and prospered greatly during the World War. He was important in St. Louis banking circles as well as in various railway and transportation companies. In his later life he spent much time on the farm where he had grown up, to which he felt a great attachment. Active in business to the last, he died of uremic poisoning in St. Louis, leaving a son and two daughters, his wife and three sons having predeceased him. He was buried in Calvary Cemetery. Generous in his benefactions, he always stipulated that nothing be said about them. His personal property, not including real estate, was appraised at approximately two and a half million.

[See *The Book of St. Louisans* (1906), ed. by J. W. Leonard; William Hyde and H. L. Conard, *Encyc. of the Hist. of St. Louis* (1899), vol. IV; W. B. Stevens, *Eleven Roads to Success, Charted by St. Louisans Who Have Traveled Them* (1914); Edward King, "The Great South: the New Route to the Gulf," *Scribner's,* July 1873, for an account of the race to Indian territory; *St. Louis Post-Dispatch,* Aug. 22, 1897, and May 29 (obituary), June 3, Aug. 11, 1920. Family information has been supplied by Harry Scullin, a son, of St. Louis.]
I. D.

SEABURY, GEORGE JOHN (Nov. 10, 1844–Feb. 13, 1909), chemist and pharmacist, the son of Michael J. Seabury and Agnes Z. (Calender) Seabury, was born in New York City. His family had been represented in America prior to the Revolution. He received his early education in the public schools of New York City, and then turned to higher studies in chemistry, pharmacy, and medicine. During the Civil War he served in the 12th New York Volunteer Regiment, and was wounded at Gaines's

Mill and Malvern Hill during the Peninsular campaign in 1862. At the close of the war he resumed his professional studies and spent some time in Europe, especially at the Universities of Göttingen and Heidelberg, where he became interested in the discoveries of Sir Joseph Lister in antiseptics and the applications of the germ theory. On his return to the United States, he founded the firm of Seabury and Johnson, pioneers in the manufacture of plasters and surgical dressings, of which he became president and sole owner in 1885.

In 1876 he became a member of the American Pharmaceutical Association and was chairman of the section on commercial interests from 1894 to 1896 and for five terms held a similar relation to the committee on the status of pharmacists in the army, the navy, and the public health and marine hospital service of the United States. He was one of the founders of the New York State Pharmaceutical Association and was president in 1895. He was also a member of the New York College of Pharmacy and a large contributor to its building fund. Always an ardent champion of the cause of the retail druggist in maintaining fair retail prices, he wrote voluminously on that subject, and on many public questions as well. Many of his articles were published collectively in his book *Shall Pharmacists Become Tradesmen* (1899). The most significant of his other literary efforts was *The Constructive and Reconstructive Forces . . . Essential to Maintain American International Supremacy* (1902).

His interest in military affairs continued throughout his life and he was long a member of the famous "Old Guard" of New York City. He did much towards promoting rifle practice in the National Guard and served as honorary secretary and director of the National Rifle Association. He was an active Republican and though importuned to accept office, preferred to remain politically independent. In 1909 he served as a presidential elector for Taft and Sherman. Among the active interests of a very busy life, Seabury included a great enthusiasm for art and music. He died at his home in New York City and was survived by two of his four children. His wife, Ella Green Bensen, to whom he had been married in 1866, preceded him in death.

[Information from the family; *Oil, Paint, and Drug Reporter,* Feb. 22, 1909; *Natl. Druggist,* Mar. 1909; *N. Y. Times,* Feb. 15, 1909.]   M. B.

SEABURY, SAMUEL (Nov. 30, 1729–Feb. 25, 1796), first bishop of the Episcopal Church in America, was born at Groton, Conn., son of the Rev. Samuel Seabury, minister of the Con-

gregational church in North Groton, by his first wife, Abigail (Mumford) Seabury. He was a descendant of John Seabury who emigrated from England to Boston in Massachusetts Bay in 1639, and whose grandson John, married the grand-daughter of John Alden and moved from Duxbury, where his father had settled, to Stonington, Conn., and later, to Groton. Early in 1730 Samuel's father entered the priesthood of the Church of England. He was sent by the Society for the Propagation of the Gospel as a missionary to New London, Conn., and in 1742 was transferred to Hempstead, L. I., to spend the remainder of his life as missionary, physician, and schoolmaster.

Young Samuel entered Yale College in 1744 and received the degree of B.A. in 1748. While studying physic and awaiting the required age for ordination, he served as catechist at Huntington, L. I. He spent the year 1752–53 at the University of Edinburgh, completing his medical training. On Dec. 21, 1753, at Fulham Palace, he was ordained deacon, and two days later, priest. Licensed by the Bishop of London to preach in New Jersey, he was sent by the Society for the Propagation of the Gospel as a missionary to New Brunswick, where he arrived on May 25, 1754. Soon after his return from abroad, he espoused the cause of the Anglicans who were then fighting for control of the proposed King's College, New York, and wrote some of the newspaper articles that appeared in their behalf, thus beginning his career as a controversialist and a pamphleteer, in which he ranked second only to Rev. Thomas B. Chandler [*q.v.*] as a champion of the English Church and government in America. On Oct. 12, 1756, Seabury married Mary Hicks, daughter of Edward Hicks of Staten Island, and the following year, Jan. 12, he was transferred to Jamaica, L. I. When the rector at Westchester, N. Y., resigned, early in 1765, Seabury asked for a transfer to that parish and his request was granted, his induction taking place on Mar. 1, 1767. In addition to his parish duties, he practised medicine and conducted a school. In 1767 the New York City clergy recommended him to Sir William Johnson as the man best fitted to begin a mission at Johnstown, N. Y. They described him as "a Man of great good Sense, of a cheerful Disposition, . . . a good Divine, and an agreeable Preacher, his skill in Medicines also much esteemed" (Vance, *post,* pp. 12-13 note). After much persuasion, he visited Johnstown in 1769, but declined to undertake the work. He served in 1766–67 as secretary of the Convention of New York, composed of Anglican clergy, took an active part in its campaign to secure bishops for America, and in the resulting literary struggle between the Anglicans and the Dissenters. In reply to a series of articles styled "The American Whig," opposing an episcopate, written by William Livingston [q.v.] and others and appearing in James Parker's *New York Gazette* (1768), Seabury, Charles Inglis [q.v.], and others replied with "A Whip for the American Whig," published in Gaine's *New York Gazette and Weekly Mercury* (Apr. 4, 1768–July 10, 1769).

With the beginning of the acts of the British Parliament that finally set off the revolutionary conflagration, Seabury and his colleagues began their major literary struggle to keep the colonies loyal to the Crown. His most important pamphlets were signed A. W. Farmer. With clear, homely, and forceful language and arguments, he endeavored to convince the liberty-seeking Americans that their greatest freedom and good lay in their submitting to, and remaining under, the British government, and in securing the changes they desired through peaceful and orderly appeals to that government. These pamphlets were ably answered by the seventeen-year-old Alexander Hamilton [q.v.], then a student in King's College. Early in 1775, Seabury entered actively into the Loyalists' campaign to prevent the election of committees and delegates to Provincial and Continental congresses and to nullify the measures enacted by those bodies. He and all his colleagues went into hiding, Apr. 29, 1775, to shield themselves from the wrath of the patriots, aroused by the news of Lexington and Concord. He did not remain hidden long; and, on Nov. 22, a troop of Connecticut horsemen, led by Isaac Sears [q.v.], took him prisoner and sent him to New Haven for confinement; on Dec. 23, he was released. The following year, Sept. 1, he entered the British lines on Long Island, and later served as a guide to the army both on the Island and in Westchester County. When the British took possession of New York City, he removed his family thither, and resided there during the war. Myles Cooper and T. B. Chandler [qq.v.], fellow Loyalists who had fled to England, secured for him a gift of fifty pounds, a chaplaincy of a man-of-war, and the degree of D.D. from Oxford. In 1777 he was appointed chaplain of the provincial hospital in New York, and was transferred by the Society for the Propagation of the Gospel as missionary to Staten Island. The year following, he was made chaplain of the King's American Regiment raised by Col. Edmund Fanning [q.v.]. His wife died Oct. 12, 1780.

The Episcopal clergy of Connecticut, on Mar. 25, 1783, chose Jeremiah Leaming [q.v.] and Seabury as suitable candidates for Episcopal consecration to serve the Church in the now independent colonies. Leaming declined the honor and Seabury sailed for England on June 7, to obtain consecration. Since the Anglican authorities believed themselves debarred on legal grounds from performing the rite, he proceeded to Scotland, where on Nov. 14, 1784, he was consecrated by the non-juring Scottish prelates. Embarking for America, Mar. 15, 1785, he reached Newport, R. I., on June 20 and soon sailed for New London, Conn., where he resided as rector of St. James' Church and bishop of Connecticut and Rhode Island until his death. He began at once the revival and reorganization of the churches in his diocese. By Dec. 15, 1785, he had ordained twelve priests from six states, and on July 13, 1792, he reported having traveled more than 6,000 miles, confirmed more than 10,000, and ordained thirty priests and eight deacons. His greatest desires were to see a "valid Episcopacy," free from interference by the laity; and a "strong, complete," and "cordial . . . union in all the churches from uniformity in our worship" (Seabury to William White, Aug. 19, 1785, Nov. 1, 1789, White MSS., New York Historical Society). He stood for unity in essentials and liberty in non-essentials, but had little sympathy for the prevailing liberalizing ideas of his American brethren. His persistent, kindly efforts were eventually successful in uniting the English and Scottish branches into one American Church. As his troubled and fruitful life drew to a close, he felt the cares of his diocese bearing heavily upon him. "To do good to God's Church, and be an humble instrument in His hand to support it, when its destruction seemed near & its enemies rejoiced in the prospect, was what first determined me to do as I have done," he wrote, Oct. 9, 1793 (Hawks MSS., New York Historical Society). During his episcopate, he took no part in politics, and withdrew himself from every study, pursuit, and meditation, "but the sole one of building up the Church of Christ in this country" (letter of Nov. 5, 1794, Hawks MSS.). His labors continued until his death came upon him suddenly, while making parish calls, in his sixty-eighth year. He was survived by three daughters and three sons. His remains were interred in the public burying ground in New London, but now repose beneath the altar of St. James' Church in that city. Two collections of his sermons, *Discourses on Several Subjects* (2 vols., 1793), and *Discourses on Several Important Subjects* (1798), were published.

[Manuscript and transcript colls. of Judge Samuel Seabury, Easthampton, L. I., of the N. Y. Hist. Soc., of the Lib. of Cong., of the Soc. for the Propagation of the Gospel, and of the Public Record Office of Great Britain; W. J. Seabury, *Memoir of Bishop Seabury* (1908); E. E. Beardsley, *Life and Correspondence of the Right Reverend Samuel Seabury* (1881); C. H. Vance, *Letters of a Westchester Farmer by the Rev. Samuel Seabury* (1930), with an introductory essay; F. B. Dexter, *Biog. Sketches Grads. Yale Coll.*, vol. II (1896); W. S. Perry, *The Hist. of the Am. Episcopal Church* (1885), vol. II; *Hist. Mag. of the Protestant Episcopal Church*, Sept. 1934.]   C. H. V.

SEABURY, SAMUEL (June 9, 1801–Oct. 10, 1872), Protestant Episcopal clergyman, was born in New London, Conn., the eldest son of Charles Seabury, then rector of St. James' Church, and the grandson of Bishop Samuel Seabury [*q.v.*]; his mother, Anne (Saltonstall), was a descendant of Richard Saltonstall [*q.v.*]. In 1814 Charles Seabury moved to Setauket, Long Island, as rector of Caroline Church. Because of his poverty he was unable to afford his children a formal higher education. Samuel, however, pursued classical and theological studies while working in New York, and, later, while teaching school in Brooklyn. The influence of Henry U. Onderdonk [*q.v.*], then rector of St. Ann's Brooklyn, confirmed him in the high churchmanship traditional in his family. On Apr. 12, 1826, he was ordained deacon by Bishop John Henry Hobart [*q.v.*] in All Saints' Chuch, New York. After several short engagements he took charge of St. George's, Hallet's Cove (now Astoria), which under him became an organized parish. Here Hobart ordained him to the priesthood on July 7, 1828. Shortly afterwards, he became classical instructor at Muhlenberg's famous school in Flushing. While here he projected a series of textbooks announced in *The Study of the Classics on Christian Principles* (1831).

On Sept. 1, 1833, he became editor of *The Churchman*. Although specially concerned with the diocese of New York, this was the principal weekly of the Episcopal Church. Seabury continued its high-church tradition and maintained an excellent standard of scholarly as well as popular articles. The opening years of his editorship were marked by controversies on minor points of doctrine with his predecessor, William R. Whittingham [*q.v.*], and with the faculty of the General Theological Seminary. From 1835 to 1838 he taught Evidences at the General Seminary. In the latter year the Church of the Annunciation was founded for him.

Loyally supporting Bishop Benjamin T. Onderdonk [*q.v.*], Seabury welcomed the Oxford movement. In 1843 he recommended as examining chaplain and defended as editor the ordination of Arthur Carey, who was attacked for his adherence to Newman's principles. In the fall Carey became his assistant at the Church of the Annunciation, and after the young man's death in April 1844, Seabury delivered a generous tribute to his devotion and pastoral zeal in *The Joy of the Saints* (1844). Seabury continued to support tractarianism and stood by Onderdonk when he was attacked, his policy leading to the foundation of the *Protestant Churchman* in 1846. He was one of the leaders of the high-church party which retained control of the diocesan convention, and in 1848 became a member of the standing committee, to which fell the administration of the headless diocese. In 1850 he barely missed election as provisional bishop.

With the growth of the Church of the Annunciation, he had resigned his editorship in February 1849. In 1853, after the consecration of Bishop Jonathan M. Wainwright [*q.v.*], he refused reëlection to the standing committee. During the next decade his parish enjoyed considerable prosperity. It was conducted on conservative tractarian principles, with daily services. His teachings are illustrated in several sermons preserved from this period and in *The Continuity of the Church of England* (1853). His *American Slavery . . . Justified* (1861) was a not very happy excursion into politics. In 1862 he was elected professor of Biblical Learning at the General Seminary, which, until 1866, being in financial difficulties, gave him a residence, but no salary; he retained his rectorship until 1868, when he surrendered it to his son, William J. Seabury. His work as professor is said to have been conscientious and successful, although he was not primarily a Biblical scholar nor greatly interested in detailed exegesis. His publications of this period include *Mary the Virgin as Commemorated in the Church of Christ* (1868), a defense of the doctrine of her perpetual virginity, and *The Theory and Use of the Church Calendar* (1872).

While Seabury had welcomed and defended the tractarians, his own views remained those of the old high churchmanship of his youth. In the eucharist he stressed the commemorative sacrifice rather than the real presence and devotional habits deduced from that doctrine. Never concerned about ceremonial, he took little part in the "ritualistic" controversy of the later sixties; but in the seminary disputes of 1869–71 he sided with the majority of the faculty against Prof. George F. Seymour [*q.v.*]. Increasing ill health gradually obliged him to give up all but the most essential duties of his position. He died shortly after his return from the summer vacation of 1872. His son, William, edited and published in 1874 some of his father's writings under the title *Discourses Illustrative of the Nature and Work of the Holy Spirit, and Other Papers.* Seabury was married three times: first, May 17, 1829, to Lydia Huntington Bill, by whom he had two daughters; she died on Apr. 16, 1834, and on Nov. 17, 1835, he married Hannah Amelia Jones, by whom he had a son and three daughters; after her death, Sept. 18, 1852, he was married, Oct. 17, 1854, to Mary Anna, daughter of Samuel and Catharine (Schuyler) Jones.

[S. R. Johnson, *A Discourse . . . in Memory of Samuel Seabury* (1873), a brief memoir somewhat inaccurate as to dates; W. S. Perry, *The Hist. of the Am. Episcopal Church* (1885), vol. II; *Hist. Mag. of the Protestant Episcopal Church*, Sept. 1934; *Churchman,* Oct. 19, 26, 1872; *Church Rev.,* July 1885.]

E. R. H., Jr.

SEAGER, HENRY ROGERS (July 21, 1870–Aug. 23, 1930), economist, was born in Lansing, Mich., the son of Schuyler Fiske Seager, a lawyer, and Alice (Berry) Seager. Graduating at the University of Michigan in 1890, he did further work during the succeeding years at the Johns Hopkins University, at the Universities of Halle, Berlin, and Vienna, and at the University of Pennsylvania, where he received the Ph.D. degree in 1894. That year he was appointed instructor in economics in the Wharton School of Finance and Commerce, and in 1896 he was made an assistant professor; in 1902 he became adjunct professor, and in 1905, professor, in Columbia University, where he served till death. On June 5, 1899, he was married to Harriet Henderson of Philadelphia, who died in 1928; their son survived him.

Seager's training as an economist was in English classicism, in the German historical method, and in the peculiar Austrian approach. His published work shows clearly the influence of each. His greatest admiration was for Simon N. Patten [q.v.], with whom he served at the University of Pennsylvania but whose influence on his thought was slight. Seager's mind was orderly and compressive rather than brilliant and generalizing; conservatism was perhaps its distinguishing characteristic. He was solid and patient, slow to conclude, and even slower to write his conclusions. One result of this was that he was less a writing scholar than one who worked with students. Literally hundreds of dissertations passed through his careful hands at Columbia and many generations of students heard his lectures on labor and on corporation problems. Always active in meliorative activities, he assisted materially in the establishment of a system of workmen's compensation in New York; he was a supporter of the *Survey* (formerly *Charities and the Commons*) and for many years a member of its board of directors. During the war he served as secretary of the Shipbuilding Labor Adjustment Board, and, in 1919–20, he was executive secretary of the President's Second Industrial Conference. He was one of the founders and three times president of the American Association for Labor Legislation. He was frequently consulted by philanthropists, legislators, and publicists; he was a member of the editorial board of *The Political Science Quarterly,* and in 1922 was president of the American Economic Association. In all these varied activities he had one purpose: to better social conditions within the framework of *laissez-faire.* He possessed a determined faith that this could be done and worked constantly to show the way. Melioration consisted in making changes here and there, which while not disturbing fundamental arrangements, reduced their burden on less favored individuals. Improvement consisted in legal change, and a large part of his effort was always directed toward reform by legislation.

His most considerable work is *Principles of Economics,* first published under this title in 1913, which grew out of his *Introduction to Economics* (1904 and later editions) and appeared in its final form in 1923. The most important of his other writings are *Trust and Corporation Problems* (1929), with C. A. Gulick, Jr., and the posthumous volume, *Labor and Other Economic Essays* (1931), to which is attached his complete bibliography. Somewhat more than the final half of the *Principles of Economics* is devoted to essays on important problems: banking, the tariff, railroads, trusts, taxation, labor, and social insurance. The theoretical section begins with a consideration of consumption, progresses through value and production, and ends with distribution. There were many books published during this period with much the same outline; but Seager's was characterized by emphasis on all that pertained to human welfare. This led to stress on consumption and on the demand side of the value equilibrium, as well as to extra consideration of monopoly gains. The discussion of distribution was carried out within the framework of the "specific productivity" analysis but with more than usual weight given to such subjective influences as the balancing, in consumers' and producers' minds, of marginal disutilities over against marginal utilities. The conclusions were usually optimistic. Seager believed in progress and believed that, under the going system, it was being achieved. He felt, for instance, that capital goods were multiplying more rapidly than population and that this would tend to raise standards of living. He did not believe, however, that the possibilities of progress which inhere in the system insure automatic betterment. Groups of interested people, with journals and propaganda, need to be vigilant in the public interest. This duty of the good citizen, as Seager saw it, was best exemplified in his own career. He never became aware of a duty that he did not forthwith perform. In his posthumous *Labor and Other Economic Essays* his program is outlined: "The two great objects to be aimed at are: I. To protect wage-earners in the continued enjoyment of standards of living to which they are already accustomed. II. To assist them to attain to higher standards of living" (p. 131). The contingencies which were the principal threats to existing standards were "(1) industrial accidents, (2) illness, (3) invalidity and old age, (4) premature death, (5) unemployment" (*Ibid.*). All these, Seager felt, were legitimate objects of collective action. As for raising standards, this was largely dependent on industrial advance and on better education.

To all persons of Seager's generation the rather sudden rise of a complete alternative system in Russia offered a shock to which adjustment was necessarily slow. Because everything there was so antithetical to the system to which so many theoretical hostages had been given, the immediate impulse was to belittle Soviet accomplishments. Seager was exposed to the full force of the new ideas. Gradually they gained weight in his mind until at last his essential honesty compelled, not acceptance, but exploration. In 1930, with a group of companions, he undertook a journey to the scene of these new economic adventures, in the midst of which he was taken ill. He died in Kiev of pneumonia, Aug. 23, 1930. He was thus lost to the world at the close of an old period and the beginning of a new one. His identification with the economy of the opening decades of the nineteenth century was a fortuitous one, but his progress into the new years cannot be said to have fairly started. He remains an economist of *laissez-faire,* of more than usual significance in foreshadowing the ameliorative program which so soon became a center of interest.

[S. M. Lindsay, in *Columbia Univ. Quart.,* Feb. 1930, pp. 228–431; *Am. Economic Rev.,* Dec. 1930, pp. 794–97; *Pol. Science Quart.,* Mar. 1931, pp. 107–08; "Introduction" by W. C. Mitchell to *Labor and Other Economic Essays* (1931); *Who's Who in Am.,* 1930–31; obituary in *N. Y. Times,* Aug. 24, 1930.]

R. G. T.

SEALSFIELD, CHARLES (Mar. 3, 1793– May 26, 1864), novelist, wrote under this name consistently after 1845. His real name was Karl Anton Postl, and he was born in Poppitz, Moravia, the eldest child of Anton and Juliane (Rabel) Postl. His father was the justice of the village. Destined for service in the church, Karl attended the *Untergymnasium* at Znaim from 1802 to 1807, and in 1808, entered the college of the *Kreuzherrenstift* in Prague, five years later becoming a novice in the monastery. After a few years of monastic life the impetuous and somewhat eccentric young monk, chafing under the Metternich system, sought freedom in flight. All efforts to find him on the part of the police of Prague and Vienna were ineffectual; the fugitive monk, Karl Postl, had vanished forever. In the fall of 1823, however, one Charles Sealsfield appeared in New Orleans. He traveled through the Southern states, through the Mexican province of Texas, and probably also in Mexico, observing with the eye of the artist, the historian, and the ethnographer. In 1824 he came to Kittanning on the Alleghany, near Pittsburgh, where he remained until late in 1825. He returned once more to New Orleans in 1826 and in August sailed thence for Havre.

In 1827 the well-known firm of J. G. Cotta of Stuttgart published the two volumes of *Die Vereinigten Staaten von Nordamerika, nach ihrem Politischen, Religiösen, und Gesellschaftlichen Verhältnisse Betrachtet, by Charles Sidons,* a pseudonym which Sealsfield never used again. In 1828 this work appeared anonymously in English translation in two parts: *The United States as They Are,* and *The Americans as They Are; Described in a Tour through the Valley of the Mississippi. By the Author of Austria as it is.* Before the second part appeared, Sealsfield had already published his vitriolic denouncement of the Metternich régime in *Austria as it is; or Sketches of Continental Courts, By an Eye Witness.* The sale of this book was forbidden in Germany and Austria. In June 1827 Sealsfield returned to America and resided for a time in Philadelphia as correspondent for Cotta's German journals, but he soon returned to his former home at Kittanning, Pa., where he wrote the first of his novels, *Tokeah; or the White Rose,* published in 1828 in two volumes. This novel, which championed the cause of the American Indian, was later rewritten and appeared in German as *Der Legitime und die Republikaner* (3 vols., 1833). In 1828 Sealsfield returned once more to the Southwest and to Mexico, and apparently entered upon various business enterprises. He was active as a journalist from 1829 until 1832, but retired in the latter year to Switzerland where he continued to reside save for return visits to the land of his adoption in 1837, 1850, and 1853.

It was during his sojourn in America that Sealsfield first conceived those plans by which he created a new type of fiction, the ethnographical novel. Instead of concentrating on a single character, he desired to operate with a whole people as his hero. Its social, political and religious life, the clash and conflict of the various cultures and nationalities represented, were all to be depicted. "To transfuse the freshly pulsating blood of the transatlantic Republic into the senile veins of the Old World, to acquaint his countrymen with the spirit of true liberty he considered his sacred duty, a duty which he felt obliged to take upon himself as a mission entrusted to him by a higher power" (see Smolle, *post*, p. 18). The period of Sealsfield's greatest literary activity falls between the years 1834 and 1843. *Der Virey und die Aristokraten; oder Mexiko im Jahre 1812*, in three volumes, appeared in 1834; *Lebensbilder aus der Westlichen Hemisphäre*, five volumes, in 1846; *Morton oder die Grosse Tour*, in 1835; *Die Deutschamerikanischen Wahlverwandtschaften*, four volumes, 1839–40; *Das Cajütenbuch, oder Nationale Charakteristiken*, two volumes, 1841; and *Süden und Norden*, three volumes, 1842–43. All of these novels dealt with the people of the United States and of Mexico. They were widely read and brought fame and fortune to their author, who came to be called the "Great Unknown." Sealsfield continued his anonymity until 1845, when, upon the insistence of his publishers, his complete works were published in fifteen volumes, 1845–47, under the name of Charles Sealsfield. In 1858 he bought a small estate near Solothurn, Switzerland, and spent his remaining years there in great seclusion. He had become a citizen of the United States and insisted upon remaining so during the years of his residence in Europe. Only upon the death of the bachelor recluse of Solothurn, through a provision in his will, was it finally revealed to the world that Charles Sealsfield and the fugitive monk, Karl Postl, were one and the same.

[Franz Brümmer, article in *Allgemeine Deutsche Biog.*, vol. XXXIII (1891); Leo Smolle, *Charles Sealsfield* (Vienna, 1875); A. B. Faust, *Charles Sealsfield* (dissertation, Johns Hopkins University, 1892), and *Charles Sealsfield . . . Der Dichter Beider Hemisphären* (1897); B. A. Uhlendorf, *Charles Sealsfield–Ethnic Elements and National Problems in his Works* (1922); Emil Soffé, *Charles Sealsfield* (Brünn, 1922); Milosch Djordjewitsch, *Charles Sealsfields Auffassung des Amerikanertums und seine literarhistorische Stellung* (Weimar, 1931); *Times* (London), June 6, 1864.]

P. A. B.

SEAMAN, ELIZABETH COCHRANE (May 5, 1867–Jan. 27, 1922), journalist, known as Nellie Bly, was born at Cochran Mills, Armstrong County, Pa. She was educated at home until 1880 when she was sent to school at Indiana, Pa. About 1881 she moved with her family to Pittsburgh, where she began her journalistic career. Having read in the *Pittsburg Dispatch* an article on "What Girls Are Good For," she wrote an angry letter to the editor, who, though he declined to print it, was fascinated by her power of vehement expression. She joined the staff of the *Dispatch,* wrote a series of articles on the conditions of working girls in Pittsburgh, and later became society editor with charge of the drama and art departments. Her pseudonym of Nellie Bly was given her by the managing editor, George A. Madden, who took the name from a popular song of Stephen Collins Foster [*q.v.*]. In 1887, accompanied by her mother, she spent several months in Mexico and produced a series of articles that were published in the *Dispatch*; they were later collected under the title of *Six Months in Mexico* (1888), where she reports that Joaquin Miller [*q.v.*], having met her in Mexico City and learned her story, said, "Little Nell, you are a second Columbus." Returning from Mexico, she found Pittsburgh too limited a field for her abilities and went to New York, where she joined the staff of the *World*. On Sept. 22, 1888, she was asked by the *World* to have herself committed to the insane ward at Blackwell's Island to investigate conditions there. She gained admittance and was declared insane by six doctors; after ten days her release was secured, and her reports resulted in an investigation by the grand jury, though hers was a less successful exposure than that of the Bloomingdale (N. Y.) Asylum made by James Julius Chambers [*q.v.*] in 1872 for the *New York Tribune*. She recounted her experiences in *Ten Days in a Mad-House* (copyright 1887). In 1889 she published *The Mystery of Central Park*, an ephemeral story of little merit that had appeared in the *World*. In the fall of 1889 G. W. Turner conceived the idea of sending her around the world in less than the eighty days of Jules Verne's Phileas Fogg, the exploit for which she is best known. She began her famous tour from New York on Nov. 14 and completed it the following Jan. 25, having circled the world in seventy-two days, six hours, and eleven minutes, with a stop at Amiens, France, to interview Jules Verne. The publication of *Nelly Bly's Book: Around the World in Seventy-two Days* (1890) marked the height of her journalistic career. In 1895 she married Robert

L. Seaman, an aged and wealthy Brooklyn manufacturer. When he died in 1904 she took over the management of his properties, which included the Ironclad Manufacturing Co., makers of enamelled iron ware, and the American Steel Barrel Co. The dishonesty and insubordination of employees, however, brought about protracted litigation from which she emerged successful but impoverished. Once more she turned to newspaper work but her later career was uneventful. She was on the staff of the *New York Journal* when she died in New York City in 1922.

[Nellie Bly's best known exploits are described in her *Ten Days in a Mad-House* (copr. 1887) and *Nelly Bly's Book: Around the World in Seventy-two Days* (1890). See also *A Woman of the Century* (1893), ed. by Frances E. Willard and Mary A. Livermore; *World* (N. Y.), *N. Y. Times, N. Y. Evening Jour., Pittsburg Dispatch,* Jan. 28, 1922.]   F. M.

SEARING, LAURA CATHERINE REDDEN (Feb. 9, 1840–Aug. 10, 1923), poet and journalist, was born in Somerset County, Md., daughter of Wilhelmine (Waller) and Littleton James D. Redden. In her early life, her parents moved to St. Louis, Mo. Until she was about eleven she was unusually healthy; then, after a serious illness, she suddenly became completely deaf and was unable to speak except with great effort and in a sepulchral tone. Her sensitiveness soon led to the development of an impediment in her speech, so that she depended entirely upon writing for conversation except with those who understood the manual alphabet, which she learned while attending the Missouri Institution for Deaf Mutes at St. Louis. She began her literary career in 1859 with editorial work on a religious paper published in St. Louis and with miscellaneous articles and poems contributed to the *St. Louis Republican.* Writing under the pseudonym Howard Glyndon, she expressed such intense patriotism and devotion to the Union cause that her articles were widely copied, and she was sent to Washington as correspondent for the *Republican* during the Civil War. Her first two books were published while she was in the capital: *Notable Men in "the House"* (1862), a series of informal sketches, some by other writers, and *Idyls of Battle* (1864), a volume of war poems. One of the poems, "Belle Missouri," was adopted as the war song of the loyalists of Missouri.

From February 1865 to the close of 1868 she was in Europe, writing articles for the *St. Louis Republican,* the *New York Times,* and the New York *Sun,* and studying languages. Upon her return to New York, she severed her connection with the *Times* but wrote for the *New York Evening Mail* as a staff member and for the *New York Tribune.* Her poems continued to appear in *Harper's Monthly* and *Harper's Weekly,* the *Atlantic Monthly, Putnam's Magazine, Galaxy, Arena,* and the *Alaska-Yukon Magazine.* Her most successful volume of verse, *Sounds from Secret Chambers,* was published in 1873. About 1871 she learned of the new Clarke school for articulation at Northampton, Mass. There, after long patient effort under the guidance of Alexander Graham Bell [*q.v.*], she learned the control of pitch, tone, and enunciation through feeling, so that she could speak freely and naturally. Lip-reading she never mastered, being forced to discontinue study of it under Zerah C. Whipple in Mystic, Conn., where she had gone for her health, seriously impaired now by the double strain of all her study and her literary engagements. In 1876 she was married at Mystic, Conn., to Edward W. Searing, a New York attorney who was a native of Sherwood, N. Y., where they made their home. After 1886 she made her permanent home in Santa Cruz, Cal. For some years before her death she was a semi-invalid, living at the San Mateo home of her only child, writing nothing after 1908, talking little, and seeing but few of her friends. She was buried in Holy Cross Cemetery, San Mateo.

As a poet she retained her memory of sounds and her sense of rhythm, and experimented with many rhymes and meters; contemporary critics commented upon her almost invariable accuracy in both. Of "The Hills of Santa Cruz" in the volume *El Dorado* (1897) her friend Whittier said, "It is fine in conception and felicitous in execution." Religious faith, courage in spite of disillusionment and difficulties, and devotion to a cause, she expressed with a simple sincerity. She had a close familiarity with the Bible and with the great English and American poets. Her newspaper articles dealt in an easy, informal style with people, politics, places, books, and art. In 1921 her daughter published a complete edition of her poems, *Echoes of Other Days.*

[Laura C. R. Searing, *Echoes of Other Days* (1921), with preface by Elsa S. McGinn, contains the best personal information; see also *Who's Who in America,* 1914–15; G. C. Perine, *Poets and Verse Writers of Md.* (n.d.); *Volta Rev.,* Feb. 1923; obituaries in *News* (San Mateo), Aug. 10, 1923; *Bulletin* and *Times* (San Francisco), *San Francisco Chronicle,* Aug. 11, 1923.]
       R. W. B.
       J. F. M.

SEARLE, ARTHUR (Oct. 21, 1837–Oct. 23, 1920), astronomer, was born in London, England, the eldest son of Thomas and Anne (Noble) Searle. His mother, who came from Derby, England, was of English birth and ancestry, but his father, although a partner in a firm of London bankers, was a citizen of the

United States and a descendant of Thomas Dudley, second governor of the colony of Massachusetts Bay. In 1840 Thomas Searle returned to America with his wife and two sons. Within the next two years the parents died, leaving the children to the care of relatives in Brookline, Mass. Searle received his early education in private schools in Brookline and Roxbury and in the Brookline high school; he graduated from Harvard College in 1856, the second scholar in his class. Ancient and modern languages, philosophy, music, mathematics, and the sciences all interested him; his first article, published in the *Harvard Magazine* of April 1855, was on "The Plurality of Worlds," though at that time he had no thought of making astronomy a profession. After his graduation he tried teaching, farming, statistical work, and work in a broker's office; he once joined a project to raise sheep in California, and later he taught English and logic for a term at the University of the Pacific, Santa Clara, Cal.

In 1868 he took a position resigned by his brother as computer and observer at the Harvard Observatory, looking upon it merely as a temporary occupation. To his surprise he found that the work suited him very well, for to his clear, active mind accuracy and precision were second nature. He was appointed assistant in 1869, assistant professor in 1883, Phillips Professor of Astronomy in 1887, and professor emeritus in 1912. After the death of Prof. Joseph Winlock [*q.v.*] in 1875, Searle was acting director of the observatory until Edward Charles Pickering [*q.v.*] became director in 1877. Besides his observatory work he taught astronomy at Radcliffe from 1891 to 1912. He was married Jan. 1, 1873, to Emma Wesselhoeft (d. Dec. 19, 1914), daughter of Dr. Robert Wesselhoeft of Boston and Brattleboro, Vt., by whom he had two daughters. His astronomical work included micrometric and photometric observations of stars, planets, asteroids, and comets, a careful investigation of the zodiacal light and the gegenschein, and the laborious observations and reductions necessary for the Astronomische Gesellschaft catalogue of 8337 stars between 9° 50' and 14° 10' south declination. He collected and published the meteorological observations made at the Harvard Observatory from 1840 to 1888 (*Annals of the Astronomical Observatory of Harvard College,* vol. XIX, pt. 1, 1889), and he wrote a history of the observatory from 1855 to 1876 (*Ibid.,* vol. VIII, 1876). A skilful mathematician, for over forty years he was the chief consultant in the mathematical discussions of all investigations of the observatory. Besides various articles in periodicals, he published *Outlines of Astronomy* (1874).

Although he had a brilliant career as an astronomer he would probably have made an equal success in almost any other field. As a diversion he wrote verse both in Latin and English. He also wrote on mathematical and philosophical subjects; his *Essays I–XXX* (1910) contains a discussion of space and time that is particularly interesting in the light of the theory of relativity. His extremely retiring disposition probably accounts for his not accepting the invitation of Benjamin Apthorp Gould [*q.v.*] in 1869 to go to Córdoba, Argentina, as his assistant. From youth he had not cared for even the ordinary pleasures of society; yet he had warm friends and many acquaintances, and all who knew him well were delighted with his conversational powers and his keen sense of humor. He died in Cambridge, Mass., survived by his daughters.

[See *Who's Who in America, 1920–21*; *Memorial of the Harvard Coll. Class of 1856* (1906); Jeremiah Smith, in *Harvard Grads. Mag.,* Mar. 1921; Margaret Harwood, in *Popular Astronomy,* Aug.–Sept. 1921; E. S. King, in *Proc. Am. Acad. Arts and Sci.,* vol. LVII (1922); S. I. Bailey, *Hist. and Work of Harvard Observatory, 1839 to 1927* (1931); *Boston Transcript,* Oct. 25, 1920. Many of Searle's articles are listed in *Cat. of Sci. Papers, Fourth Ser., 1884–1900,* vol. XVIII (1923), compiled by the Royal Soc. of London.]

M. H.

SEARLE, JAMES (1733–Aug. 7, 1797), merchant and member of the Continental Congress, was born probably in New York City, the youngest child of John and Catherine (Pintard) Searle. His fluent literary style and frequent use of Latin phrases in correspondence suggest that he had received considerable schooling before he went to join his brother John in Madeira, where first as employee and later as a member of John Searle & Company he remained sixteen years. Married in 1762 to Ann (or Nancy) Smith of Waterford, England, he removed soon afterward to Philadelphia, where he acted as agent for his brother while engaging in commercial ventures of his own which brought him prosperity and standing among the merchants of that city. From the beginning of the difficulties with Great Britain, he was actively patriotic, signing the Philadelphia non-importation agreement of 1765 and participating in all later mercantile protests. Returning in November 1775 from a visit to England, he took part in the war preparations, becoming a lieutenant-colonel of Pennsylvania militia, one of the managers of the United States lottery, and, in 1778, a member of the Naval Board. He was constantly a supporter of the attempts of the Continental Congress to raise funds and his wife was a leader among the patriotic ladies of Philadelphia.

In November 1778, Searle was elected to the Continental Congress. He was an active member, serving on many committees, including those on the marine and on commerce and the special committee to investigate foreign affairs and the conduct of the American commissioners abroad. In the faction-ridden Congress he allied himself with the radical Lee-Adams group, seconding James Lovell and Richard Henry Lee [qq.v.] in their hostility to Silas Deane [q.v.] and Beaumarchais. The radicals, trusting him, nominated him for secretary to the embassy to Spain, September 1779, but his name was withdrawn. When Pennsylvania voted to send a special envoy abroad, Searle was appointed, July 1780, as its agent "to such countries or states as you shall Judge most likely to favour your views" to "negotiate with any publick bodies, private companies, or Individuals" (*Pennsylvania Archives*, 4 ser. III, 1900, p. 770), for a loan of £200,000, to be expended largely in Europe for military supplies. Departing immediately for Paris, Searle satisfied himself that Franklin, being the "declared Enemy of private state loans" (Searle to Reed, Feb. 14, 1781, Joseph Reed Papers, *post*) would do nothing to aid him, and, armed with a letter from Reed to John Adams and with introductions to business houses, he proceeded to Amsterdam, where he soon realized that Adams' pessimism about securing money for America was justified. He returned to France, consulted with the Farmers General and the Company of Lyons, but could secure aid only on terms he was unable to meet. Discouraged, he wrote to Joseph Reed that the possibility of borrowing money for a state was even less than for the Continental Congress and that certain men, primarily Deane and Edward Bancroft [q.v.], were doing everything possible to prevent European aid to America. After one more futile journey into Holland, he gladly accepted notice that Pennsylvania had ordered his recall, no discredit for his failure being attached.

Receiving also news that his wife had died (1781) and that much of his fortune had been dissipated through unwise moves made by his partners during the war, he returned to the United States in considerable despondency to face several unprosperous years in New York and New Jersey. John Searle & Company, with thousands of pounds in uncollectable American debts, was badly crippled and Searle's difficulties were increased through his inability to secure full payment from Pennsylvania for his services abroad. In 1787 he expected bankruptcy, but he received in 1788 an appointment as agent for a Madeira firm with a fixed salary and additional commissions, reëstablished himself in Philadelphia, and spent his remaining years in comfort, if not in the wealth of his pre-Revolutionary days. He was married a second time, in 1785, to Isabella West of Monmouth County, N. J., and by this marriage had several children.

[Joseph Reed Papers in N. Y. Hist. Soc.; manuscript collections of the Pa. Hist. Soc.; W. B. Reed, *Life and Correspondence of Joseph Reed* (2 vols., 1847); E. C. Burnett, *Letters of Members of the Continental Cong.*, vols. I–VII (1921–34); *Pa. Archives*, vols. VIII–IX (1853–54); "The Deane Papers," *N. Y. Hist. Soc. Colls.*, Pub. Fund Ser., vols. XXII–XXIII (1890–91); *Pa. Mag. of Hist. and Biog.*, July 1915; Henry Simpson, *The Lives of Eminent Philadelphians* (1859); *Claypoole's Am. Daily Advertiser* (Phila.), Aug. 8, 1797.]

M. E. L.

SEARLE, JOHN PRESTON (Sept. 12, 1854–July 26, 1922), clergyman of the Reformed Church in America, professor of theology, was born at Schuylerville, N. Y., the son of Rev. Samuel Tomb and Cornelia Fonda (Southworth) Searle. He was of a family that furnished the ministry with at least one member in every generation from the coming of Rev. William Searle of Branford, England, to America in 1692. His grandfather, Jeremiah Searle, his grandmother's father, Jacob Tomb, and two of his father's brothers were clergymen. The family tradition and his home life naturally turned John Preston Searle toward the same calling. He was graduated from Rutgers College in 1875 with honors and from the New Brunswick Theological Seminary in 1878. Entering the service of the Reformed (Dutch) Church in America, to which, in New York State, his grandfather had transferred the family connection from the Congregational Church of New England, he was licensed by the Classis of Passaic and ordained by the Classis of New Brunswick. That same year, 1878, he became pastor of the church in Griggstown, N. J., remaining as such for three years. His intellectual gifts and preaching ability were early recognized, and in 1881 he was called to the large and influential First Church of Raritan, Somerville, N. J., where he became greatly honored as a preacher and greatly beloved as a pastor.

His ability and practical interest in affairs soon brought him to the general knowledge of the denomination and its institutions. In 1893 the General Synod chose him professor of didactic and polemic theology, later systematic theology, in the New Brunswick Theological Seminary. He filled this office until his death nearly thirty years later. He was insistent on a sound theology and was well furnished with the learning related to it. As a teacher and as a man he won the confidence and affection of the students and continued to be their helper and adviser after their graduation. Bringing into the life and management of the Seminary his aptness for affairs, he became president of the faculty in 1902, and chairman of the official committee on grounds and buildings, holding these positions with his professorship to the end. He was also an influential member of allied institutions and boards. From 1898 he was one of the trustees of Rutgers College and from 1906 he was secretary of the board. He was a member of the Board of Foreign Missions of the Reformed Church from 1894 and vice-president of it from 1896. In 1917 he was chosen president of the General Synod of the Church. He was one of the founders of the Council of Reformed and Presbyterian Churches and at one time its president.

His publications were chiefly sermons, addresses on special occasions, and contributions to papers and periodicals. He prepared for his students an "Outline Sketch of Theological Encyclopedia" (1907) and was incessantly useful in the drawing up of thorough and important reports for the committees of official bodies to which he belonged. In addition to intellectual clearness he exhibited a singularly spiritual quality in his preaching and conduct of worship, which was made the more appealing by his unusually rich and sympathetic voice. On Dec. 12, 1882, he was married to Susan Bovey, of Cherokee, Iowa, by whom he had four children.

[C. E. E. Corwin, *A Manual of the Reformed Church in America* (1922); *The Acts and Proceedings . . . of the General Synod of the Reformed Church in America, June 1923*; *Biog. Record, Theological Sem. New Brunswick, 1784–1934* (1934); *Who's Who in America, 1922–23*; *N. Y. Times*, July 28, 1922.]   W. H. S. D.

SEARS, BARNAS (Nov. 19, 1802–July 6, 1880), Baptist clergyman, educator, was a descendant of Richard Sears who emigrated from England to Plymouth, Mass., sometime before 1633, later moving to Marblehead, and from there to Yarmouth. The son of Paul and Rachel (Granger) Sears, Barnas was born and grew up on his father's farm at Sandisfield, Berkshire County, Mass., one of ten children. By building stone walls in the summer and teaching in the winter he secured funds for his education, and was able, after a period in the University Grammar School, Providence, to enter the class of 1825 at Brown University. After graduation he spent two years at Newton (Mass.) Theological Institution, and on July 11, 1827, was ordained pastor of the First Baptist Church, Hartford, Conn. A bronchial affection led him to resign in the spring of 1829, and in the fall he became professor of languages in Hamilton (N. Y.)

Literary and Theological Institution (now Colgate University). On July 6, 1830, he married Elizabeth Griggs Corey of Brookline, Mass.; five children were born to them. From 1833 to 1835 he studied in Germany and France, returning to Hamilton to occupy the chair of Biblical theology. In less than a year, however, he was called to Newton Theological Institution to be professor of Christian theology.

He was now fully launched on an educational career, which, marked by considerable variety, was to continue until his death. He taught at Newton from 1836 to 1848, and from 1839 was president of the institution. During this period he was for a time, 1838–41, editor of the *Christian Review*, to which, as well as to the *Bibliotheca Sacra*, he contributed important articles. He also published *A Grammar of the German Language* (1842), based upon C. H. F. Bialloblotzky's eighth English edition of Georg Heinrich Noehden's work; *The Ciceronian: or the Prussian Method of Teaching the Elements of the Latin Language* (1844); and was the principal author of *Classical Studies: Essays on Ancient Literature and Art* (1843), his collaborators being Bela B. Edwards and Cornelius C. Felton [*qq.v.*]. In 1848 he entered the field of public-school education, succeeding Horace Mann [*q.v.*] as secretary of the Massachusetts Board of Education. This position he held for seven years, during which time, not only by his administrative ability but also by his imperturbable temper and genial personality, he won favor for the reforms Mann had initiated and gave them permanence. Called to the presidency of Brown University in 1855, he again succeeded a notable educator, Francis Wayland [*q.v.*]. The administration of President Sears, covering a period of twelve years, though disturbed by conditions incident to the Civil War, was one of peace and quiet, if not notable progress. He brought about modifications in the educational system introduced by Wayland, which in some respects was not working well; the funds of the University were augmented; salaries and scholarships were increased; and a chemical laboratory was built. To his administrative duties were joined those of the professorship of moral philosophy. His personal characteristics made him extremely popular with the students.

In 1867 George Peabody [*q.v.*] established the Peabody Education Fund for the promotion of education in the South. The chairman of the trustees, Robert C. Winthrop [*q.v.*], asked Sears to draw up a statement of his views as to how the Fund should be administered. The outline which he presented so impressed the trustees that they invited him to become general agent. The possibilities of the work appealed to him, and though he was happy in his position at Brown, his old bronchial trouble had returned and he welcomed the chance to live in the South. Accordingly, he accepted the invitation and in September 1867 moved to Staunton, Va. His inauguration of the work for which the Fund was devised was perhaps the most important achievement of his career. The specific recommendations regarding the ends to be sought and the methods to be employed contained in his first report became the stereotyped policy of the trustees. In carrying it out Sears met a difficult and delicate situation with a patience, tact, and wisdom that won confidence and support in the South and ensured success. To the heavy demands of his office he devoted himself vigorously almost up to the time of his death, which occurred at Saratoga, N. Y.; he was buried in Walnut Street Cemetery, Brookline, Mass.

In addition to the publications already mentioned, Sears was the author of *The Life of Luther* (1850) and *Objections to Public Schools Considered* (1875). He also edited (1873) P. M. Roget's *Thesaurus of English Words and Phrases*. He was not an original thinker but his learning was varied and sound; although he was not one to blaze new trails, his dignity and courtesy, his emotional stability, his sagacity and determination, gave him favor with men, and made him an effective administrator.

[S. P. May, *The Descendants of Richard Sares (Sears) of Yarmouth* (1890); Alvah Hovey, *Barnas Sears* (copr. 1902); W. C. Bronson, *The Hist. of Brown Univ.* (1914); J. L. M. Curry, *A Brief Sketch of George Peabody and a Hist. of the Peabody Education Fund Through Thirty Years* (1898); reports of the Mass. Board of Education, 1848–55; *Proceedings of the Trustees of the Peabody Education Fund*, vol. I (1875), vol. II (1881); *Boston Transcript*, July 7, 1880].

H. E. S.

SEARS, EDMUND HAMILTON (Apr. 6, 1810–Jan. 16, 1876), Unitarian clergyman, author, was born in Sandisfield, Berkshire County, Mass., a descendant of Richard Sears who came to Plymouth about 1630, and the son of Joseph and Lucy (Smith) Sears. His father, a landholder and farmer, without education himself, had a marked fondness for books and an instinctive liking for poetry. "My earliest recollections," says the son, "are associated with his reading or rather chanting of poetry. . . . He was a great admirer of Pope's Iliad and would read it by the hour" (Robbins, *post*, pp. 224–25). Hard work and long hours on the farm together with the scarcity of money made education for Edmund a casual and limited affair. He was abnormally shy and timid and all his life shrank

from possibility of criticism. When he was ten he made his first venture in poetry and was only twelve when he wrote and delivered a full-sized discourse "to a full assembly of alder-bushes." At this early age he produced sermons "and lyrics without number." When he was sixteen opportunity came for him to enter Westfield Academy, which he attended for about nine months. In 1831 he entered Union College, Schenectady, N. Y., and by the exercise of rigid economy was able to complete the course, graduating in 1834. His marked literary ability won him an editorial position on the college paper, the *Parthenon,* and a prize for poetry he had written.

After graduating he read law but soon accepted an opportunity to teach in the academy at Brattleboro, Vt. While here he studied theology under the direction of the Rev. Addison Brown and later entered the Harvard Divinity School. Graduating therefrom in 1837, he received an appointment as missionary of the American Unitarian Association and served for the most part at Toledo, Ohio. On his return East he was invited to become minister of the Unitarian Church in Wayland, Mass., where he was ordained on Feb. 20, 1839. On Nov. 7 of that year he married Ellen Bacon of Barnstable, Mass., by whom he had three sons and a daughter. Called to the Unitarian Church in Lancaster, he was installed there Dec. 23, 1840. He was frail in body and seven years later was obliged to relinquish his pastorate, and retire to a small farm in the town of Wayland. Having recovered much of his strength, he yielded to the importunities of his friends in the Wayland Church and again (1848) became their minister, serving in that capacity for seventeen years. In 1866 the church at Weston, Mass., invited him to its pulpit and he accepted. A fall from a tree in 1874 shattered his strength beyond recovery, and he died at his home in Weston some two years later.

Sears was much sought after by larger churches than those he served, but the narrow limits of his physical strength, the exceeding frailty of his voice, and his instinctive bashfulness made him prefer the quieter and more secluded places. Through his writings, however, he reached a large circle. From 1859 to 1871 he served as one of the editors of the *Monthly Religious Magazine*. His writings were marked by a rare mysticism and devotional spirit particularly satisfying to many at that time. Most notable of his books was *The Fourth Gospel, the Heart of Christ* (1872). Though largely forgotten now, it was forceful and important enough in its day to be referred to as "the most unique and precious contribution to Christian literature" (Peabody, *post*, p. 203). His *Regeneration* (1853) and *Athanasia; or Foregleams of Immortality* (1858) were widely read. His interest in family history and genealogy led him to publish in 1857 *Pictures of the Olden Time as Shown in the Fortunes of a Family of Pilgrims*, dealing with his ancestors, and *Genealogies and Biographical Sketches of the Ancestry and Descendants of Richard Sears* (1857). Though his sermons and other prose writings are now quite forgotten, his hymns remain a living force in Christian worship. Two of them at least, "Calm on the listening ear of night" and "It came upon a midnight clear," are among the best known and most beloved in Protestant hymnals.

[*In Memoriam: Edmund Hamilton Sears . . . Ellen Bacon Sears . . . Katharine Sears* (1898); S. A. Eliot, *Heralds of a Liberal Faith* (1910), vol. III; R. C. Winthrop and A. P. Peabody in *Proc. Mass. Hist. Soc.*, vol. XIV (1876); Chandler Robbins, "Memoir of Rev. Edmund Hamilton Sears," *Ibid.*, vol. XVIII (1881); *Unitarian Rev.*, Feb. 1876; *Christian Reg.*, Jan. 22, 29, 1876; *The Hist. of the Church in Weston* (1900); *Boston Daily Advertiser*, Jan. 18, 1876.]   C. G.

SEARS, ISAAC (*c*. July 1, 1730–Oct. 28, 1786), Revolutionary leader, was born at West Brewster, Mass., and christened at Harwich, July 12, 1730. He was a son of Joshua and Mary (Thacher) Sears, and a descendant of Richard Sears who emigrated from England to Plymouth, Mass., about 1630. His father moved to Norwich, Conn., about 1734. At twenty-two Isaac was commanding a sloop trading between New York and Canada; and from then until his death he was nearly always either commander or part owner of a merchantman or a privateer. He married Sarah Drake, and had eleven children.

While commanding privateers during the French and Indian War he won a reputation for bravery which made him a recognized leader among the sailors and petty artisans of the New York waterfront. When the Stamp Act was passed, he became a leader of the resistance in New York City and with John Lamb [*q.v.*] and Joseph Allicocke projected a continental military union of the Sons of Liberty. During the next decade, Sears was at the head of nearly every demonstration of mob violence in New York City, his success as a leader of the populace winning him the appellation "King," and membership on most of the important patriotic committees as well as a seat in the first Provincial Congress. In 1774 he led the Sons of Liberty in returning the first tea ship and dumping the cargo of the second into the river. With Alexander McDougall [*q.v.*], another radical member of the Committee of Fifty-one, he wrote a letter to the Boston Committee of Correspondence, May 15, 1774 (printed in Stokes, *post*, IV, 852–53), proposing a meeting of delegates from the principal towns. While this action was disclaimed by the New York Committee, it was practically ratified by the Committee's letter of May 23, recommending the holding of a general congress.

When arrested for his anti-British activities, Apr. 15, 1775, Sears was rescued at the prison door by his admirers and paraded through the streets like a great hero. Upon the arrival in New York, Apr. 23, 1775, of the news of Lexington and Concord, he and 360 followers put to flight the Loyalist leaders and officials, seized a supply of arms from the arsenal and the keys of the Custom House, and began regular military exercises. Thereafter, although nominally governed by various committees and congresses, until Washington's army arrived the city was virtually under the dictatorship of Sears and his comrades. Late in 1775 he removed to New Haven, but in November led a raid into New York, burning a naval supply ship, threatening to seize the provincial records (removed at once by order of Governor Tryon to the warship in which he had taken refuge), imprisoning the Rev. Samuel Seabury [*q.v.*] and other Westchester Loyalists, and destroying the New York shop of the Loyalist printer James Rivington [*q.v.*]. This raid was condemned by the Revolutionary Committee of New York City, the Provincial Congress, and the New York delegation to the Continental Congress, but public opinion was elated by the raiders' display of patriotic spirit. In January 1776 General Lee commissioned Sears to administer the oath of allegiance to Loyalists on Long Island, to recruit volunteers in Connecticut, and to capture British supplies for the colonial forces.

During 1777–83, Sears resided in Boston, promoting privateering and otherwise endeavoring to aid the American cause. After the war, he resumed his general merchandise business in New York. With Alexander McDougall and Marinus Willett [*q.v.*], he waited upon Rivington, Dec. 31, 1783, and silenced his paper forever. In 1784 and 1786 he was elected to the state Assembly. He was made a trustee and a vestryman (1784–86) of Trinity Church, and in 1784 vice-president of the reorganized Chamber of Commerce of the State of New York. On Feb. 4, 1786, with Samuel Shaw [*q.v.*] and Thomas Randall, he sailed for China to promote a business venture but died of fever at Canton in October, and was buried on French Island, in Canton Harbor.

[Material on Sears is found in the Horatio Gates, Benedict Arnold, William Alexander (Lord Stirling), John Lamb, Alexander McDougall, and F. L. Hawks MSS., in the N. Y. Hist. Soc.; William Smith Papers, N. Y. Pub. Lib.; papers of the Earl of Dartmouth and the Public Record Office, in England. Published authorities include: S. P. May, *The Descendants of Richard Sares (Sears)* (1890); *The Journals of Major Samuel Shaw, with a Life of the Author by Josiah Quincy* (1847); I. N. P. Stokes, *The Iconography of Manhattan Island* (6 vols., 1922–28); I. Q. Leake, *Memoir of the Life and Times of Gen. John Lamb* (1850); C. L. Becker, *Hist. of Pol. Parties in the Province of N. Y. 1760–76* (1909); H. B. Dawson, *The Sons of Liberty in N. Y.* (1859) and *Westchester County, N. Y., during the Am. Rev.* (1886), which appears also in J. T. Scharf, *Hist. of Westchester County, N. Y.* (1886), vol. I; Peter Force, *Am. Archives*, 4 ser. (6 vols., 1837–46); J. A. Stevens, *Biog. Records of the N. Y. Chamber of Commerce* (1867); Thomas Jones, *Hist. of N. Y. during the Revolutionary War* (2 vols., 1879), ed. by E. F. De Lancey. Certain information has been supplied by M. J. Weig, Esq., who is preparing a dissertation (Univ. of Chicago), N. Y. and Mass. Mobs and Mob Leaders in the Prelude to the American Revolution.]

C. H. V.

SEARS, RICHARD WARREN (Dec. 7, 1863–Sept. 28, 1914), merchant, was born in Stewartville, Minn., the son of James Warren and Eliza A. (Benton) Sears, both of English ancestry. His father was a wagon maker who had built up a substantial fortune that he lost in a stock-farm venture when Richard was about fifteen. Two years later, after his father's death, the boy was working in the general offices of the Minneapolis and St. Louis Railway at Minneapolis and supporting his mother and sisters. Believing that he might earn more in a small town, he succeeded in having himself moved to Redwood Falls, Minn., where as station agent he did chores for his board and slept in the loft of the railroad station. He made profits for himself on the side by selling coal and lumber as well as by shipping venison, blueberries, and other commodities purchased from the Indians, and he was started on his way to fortune in 1886 when the town jeweler refused to accept a shipment of watches sent him by the wholesaler. No freight had been paid, and the watches remained in the railway station. Obtaining permission to dispose of them, Sears wrote letters describing his merchandise and offering it for sale at what must have seemed bargain prices. When the supply of watches was exhausted, he had a gratifying profit and a new idea for making money. Buying more watches, he began to advertise in a small way in the St. Paul newspapers; in a few months he abandoned railroading and late in 1886 established himself in the mail-order business in Minneapolis under the name of the R. W. Sears Watch Company.

By the end of a year he was advertising in periodicals of national circulation and had made enough money to move to Chicago, where he did business under the same name. As watches began to come back for adjustment and repair he hired as a watchmaker A. C. Roebuck. In 1889, feeling that he had made enough money to retire, he sold his business for $100,000 and went to Iowa to become a country banker. But banking was not exciting enough for his volatile temper. He was by nature a promoter, forever beset by new ideas (some of them far from practical), always dynamic, the "Barnum of merchandising" in his day. When he sold out in Chicago he had agreed not to go into the same business there for a period of three years; this did not prevent him, however, from returning to Minneapolis, summoning Roebuck, and establishing a mail-order business for the sale of watches and jewelry under the name of A. C. Roebuck & Company, which later became Sears, Roebuck & Company. In 1893 the company was moved to Chicago, where the business increased at a prodigious rate. The catalogue, originally a book of watches that listed some twenty-five items, grew in a few years to a thousand pages. In 1895 when Julius Rosenwald [*q.v.*], a Chicago clothing manufacturer, bought Roebuck's interest in the firm, sales were $500,000; by 1900 they were $11,000,000.

In addition to his duties as president, a position he held until 1909, Sears planned and actually wrote all the advertising, which amounted in 1896 to between fifty and sixty thousand dollars' worth of newspaper space a month. He experimented endlessly in other ways. He sold automobiles by mail, manufacturing a "horseless carriage" for the purpose, and in the early years of the company he started a chain of four or five food stores but this enterprise, like that of the automobile project, took valuable time from the more successful and rapidly growing mail-order business and was dropped. Although Rosenwald supplied the capital demanded by a rapidly growing business and provided the still more valuable administrative ability that could organize the enterprise and keep it functioning smoothly, it was "Dick" Sears's personality that permeated the organization in these early days and his generous spirit for the most part that created the good will which became the most valuable possession of the firm. On June 20, 1895, he had married Anna Lydia Meckstroth of Minneapolis; there were two sons and two daughters, all of whom survived him. After his retirement in 1909 he lived on his farm north of Chicago; he died in Waukesha, Wis.

[*Who's Who in America*, 1914–15; *The Book of Chicagoans* (2nd ed., 1911), vol. II; Robert Littell, "The Great Am. Salesman," *Fortune*, Feb. 1932; obituary in *Chicago Daily Tribune*, Sept. 29, 1914; unpublished material at Sears, Roebuck & Co., Chicago.]

E. A. D.

SEARS, ROBERT (June 28, 1810–Feb. 17, 1892), publisher and compiler, was born at St. John, New Brunswick, a son of Thatcher Sears and his second wife, Abigail (Spurr) Sears, and a descendant of Richard Sares or Sears who was in Plymouth, Mass., in 1633. His father, a furrier and hatter, was a Connecticut Loyalist who had emigrated from the United States to New Brunswick at the close of the Revolution with a group of his compatriots (Lorenzo Sabine, *Biographical Sketches of Loyalists of the American Revolution*, 1864, vol. II, pp. 272–73). The elder Sears died when Robert was nine years old, leaving several other minor children, and Robert's formal schooling was not long continued; he seems to have acquired a fair mastery of English after he entered on an apprenticeship in the printing trade. As soon as he reached his majority he found his way to New York City as a journeyman printer and there succeeded in maintaining himself by his trade, although seriously hampered by the recurring cholera epidemics of that period. In 1832 he married Harriet Howard Martin (d. 1881), by whom he had eight children, and set up a printing and publishing business of his own, but this first attempt was short-lived. However, he had formed an ambition to compile, publish, and market reference books bearing his own imprint, and in due time it came to fruitage. In his thirtieth year he brought out a three-volume work entitled *Pictorial Illustrations of the Bible* (1840–41), which he advertised throughout the United States and of which 25,000 sets were sold, a notable achievement for that date in America. Encouraged by this success the young publisher three years later announced *The Wonders of the World, in Nature, Art, and Mind* (1843), a popular illustrated treatise that was hailed by the *Southern Quarterly Review* of January, 1843, as neither strikingly original nor profound but as sound in structure and tendency. For this, as for his other publications, he employed the best available wood-engravers of the day to supply illustrations. He required so much of this work that he came to have distinction among the publishers of his time as a patron of the engraving art, a distinction possibly due less to the artistic value than to the relatively large number of the cuts that embellished the Sears books.

Sears was credited with at least one merit not generally conceded to the publishers of his day: he could write simple and graceful English.

This is especially to be noted in his *A New and Complete History of the Holy Bible* (1844), the text of which he composed himself (*Southern Quarterly Review*, October 1843). He was also one of the earliest of the New York publishers to make a serious effort to serve the nation as a whole, without regard to sectional differences. He built up a selling organization that seems to have been as efficient in the South and West as in the East. Between 1844 and 1849 he edited and published under various titles a magazine, finally known as the *New Pictorial Family Magazine*, that carried gazetteer material covering every state in the Union, with statistics kept up to date; this appealed with peculiar force to a shifting population eager to learn about new lands opening for settlement in the forties. In 1848 he condensed the gazetteer data and published it separately as *A New and Popular Pictorial Description of the United States*. He published several other digests of knowledge and *The Pictorial History of the American Revolution* (1845). His last important venture was a *Pictorial Bible* (1858) containing more than a thousand engravings. On the outbreak of the Civil War he retired and went to Canada, where he passed the rest of his life, dying at Toronto.

[S. P. May, *The Descendants of Richard Sares (Sears) of Yarmouth, Mass.* (1890); William Hunt, *Am. Biog. Panorama* (1849), with portrait; S. A. Allibone, *A Crit. Dict. of Eng. Lit.*, vol. II (1870); *N. Y. Daily Tribune*, Feb. 19, 21, 1892.]   W. B. S.

SEATON, WILLIAM WINSTON (Jan. 11, 1785–June 16, 1866), journalist, was born at the stately homestead "Chelsea" in King William County, Va., the son of Augustine and Mary (Winston) Seaton. The Seatons, whose forefather, Henry, settled in Gloucester County, Va., in 1690, were of Scottish, and the Winstons of English, ancestry; both were of the Virginia gentry. First trained by tutors, William entered Ogilvie's academy in Richmond, where he acquired a taste for drama, literature, art, and journalism. At eighteen, having already gained a practical knowledge of printing in a Richmond newspaper office, he entered on his journalistic career. After brief service as an assistant editor of the Richmond *Virginia Patriot*, he edited successively the Petersburg *Republican* and the *North Carolina Journal* of Halifax, N. C. In 1809 he moved to Raleigh, N. C., and became associated with the elder Joseph Gales [*q.v.*] of the *Raleigh Register*, a Jeffersonian newspaper; on Mar. 30 of the same year he married Gales's daughter, Sarah Weston Gales. In 1812 he joined his brother-in-law, the younger Joseph Gales [*q.v.*], as associate editor of the *National Intelligencer* of Washington, D. C.

Seaton's policy as an editor of the "Court Paper" for fourteen years became conservative, nationalistic, and free from partisanship. His characteristically short and dignified editorials can hardly be distinguished from those of Gales. His ablest work, however, was done as a reporter of the debates in the Senate while Gales reported the debates of the House. Masters of shorthand, the brothers-in-law were the exclusive reporters of Congress from 1812 to 1829. Upon the authorization of Congress their shorthand reports, with those of the earlier reporters, covering the years from 1789 to 1824, were published by Gales & Seaton (42 vols., 1834–56), as *The Debates and Proceedings in the Congress of the United States,* better known by the half-title, *Annals of Congress.* They also issued the *Register of Debates in Congress,* covering the years 1824–37 (14 vols. in 29, 1825–37), and the monumental series, *American State Papers* (38 vols., 1832–61).

Seaton was sanguine in nature and amused by the bitter attacks made upon him by editors and congressmen of opposite views. He preferred Crawford to Adams for president in 1824, and never accepted the leadership of Jackson, whom he respected as an honest, patriotic citizen but considered a rough frontiersman and an advocate of a low type of democracy. Seaton's personal tastes were aristocratic, although he sympathized with the laboring class, gave freely to the unfortunate, and died a poor man. He was genial, generous, captivatingly courteous, and a good conversationalist; in appearance he was tall, vigorous and handsome. He traveled in America and Europe. Among his friends he counted the leading Southern politicians and planters, and also Daniel Webster. He maintained a farm and a shooting-box in Prince George County to which he could retreat with friends of like tastes and his fine dogs to relax after a strenuous season in Washington. He was skilled in the use of the rod and gun. His witty and charming wife, who translated Spanish documents for him to use in the *National Intelligencer,* was a capable and attractive hostess, maintaining an elegant house to which came men and women of the higher circles of society.

Seaton was a Whig, a Free Mason, and a Unitarian. Much of his time was given to public service. He was an alderman of Washington from 1819 to 1831 and mayor from 1840 to 1850. He served on many committees, made numerous addresses, gave the city a progressive administration, developed the local educational system, led the movement for the Washington Monument, was active in the organization of the Smithsonian Institution and acted as its treasurer from 1846 until his death. He served in the state militia in Virginia, enrolled as a private in the War of 1812, and saw service at Bladensburg. For many years he was an official in the American Colonization Society; he favored gradual emancipation and freed his own slaves, but opposed the Garrison abolitionists and maintained that the national government should not interfere with slavery. Though he was at all times a compromiser on slavery, he was stanchly Unionist. He retired from his editorial work in 1864. His two sons died in 1827 and 1835, respectively; his wife died in 1863, leaving only his daughter, Josephine, to survive him.

[Josephine Seaton, *William Winston Seaton of the "National Intelligencer"* (1871); *Atlantic Monthly,* Oct. 1860, July 1871; Frederic Hudson, *Journalism in the U. S. from 1690 to 1872* (1873); A. C. Clark, "Col. William Winston Seaton and His Mayoralty," *Records of the Columbia Hist. Soc.,* vols. XXIX–XXX (1928); Joseph Henry, "A Sketch of the Services of the Late Hon. W. W. Seaton in Connection with the Smithsonian Institution," *Ann. Report . . . Smithsonian Inst. . . . 1866* (1867), repr. in W. J. Rhees, *The Smithsonian Inst.* (1879); O. A. Seaton, *The Seaton Family* (1906); *Daily Nat. Intelligencer,* June 18, 19, 20, 1866.]

W. E. S.

SEATTLE (*c.* 1786–June 7, 1866), chief of the Dwamish, Suquamish, and allied Indian tribes, was the son of Schweabe, a chief of the Suquamish Indians, and Scholitza, the daughter of a Dwamish chief. It is sometimes, though probably erroneously, said that his baptismal name was Noah Sealth. Born in the neighborhood of the city that now bears his name, he was living there when the first settlers went to the region. He befriended them, signed the treaty of Point Elliott on Jan. 22, 1855, to provide for land cession and agency administration, and remained loyal to the whites during the uprising led by Kamaiakan and Leschi [*qq.v.*]. He became a Roman Catholic and instituted the custom of holding morning and evening services in the tribe, a custom continued after his death. He was unwilling that the rising village of Seattle, Wash., should be named for him, since local Indian belief held that after his death his spirit would be troubled each time human lips spoke the syllables of his name, and in his old age he formed the habit of seeking gifts from the citizens as a kind of tax to recompense himself in advance for this oft-broken sleep of eternity.

[C. B. Bagley, "Chief Seattle and Angeline," *Wash. Hist. Quart.,* Oct. 1931; T. W. Prosch, "Seattle and the Indians of Puget Sound," *Ibid.,* July 1908; Frank Carlson, *Chief Sealth* (1903); L. D. Buchanan, *Souvenir of Chief Seattle and Princess Angeline* (copr. 1909); C. M. Scammon, "Old Seattle, and his Tribe," *Overland Monthly,* Apr. 1870; A. A. Denny, *Pioneer Days on Puget Sound* (1908), ed. by Alice Harriman; Hazard Stevens, *The Life of Isaac Ingalls Stevens*

(1900), vol. I; H. H. Bancroft, *Hist. of Wash.* (1890); *Report of Commissioner of Indian Affairs*, 1854, p. 245; *Ibid.*, 1858, pp. 228, 230; *Ibid.*, 1867, p. 38; *Ibid.*, 1872, p. 295.] K. E. C.

SEAWELL, MOLLY ELLIOT (Oct. 23, 1860–Nov. 15, 1916), author, daughter of John Tyler and Frances (Jackson) Seawell, was born on a plantation in Gloucester County, Va., in a house, "The Shelter," which had been a Revolutionary hospital. Her mother was a native of Baltimore; her father, a nephew of President Tyler, was a lawyer and a student of the classics. Her childhood in the tidewater region of Chesapeake Bay influenced the settings of the novels she was later to write, and an uncle, Joseph Seawell, who lived with the family, contributed to her future literary material by his stories of his seafaring experiences. With occasional intervals at school for instruction in the standard subjects, she was educated in an informal fashion at home, where riding, dancing, and the conduct of a household were given much consideration. At her father's death, she and her mother removed first to Norfolk, Va., then to Washington, D. C., where she spent the remainder of her life.

At Norfolk about 1886 she began to write sketches and stories. After a trip to Europe, which added to her experience and to her material, she became a contributor to several magazines, using pen-names at first but finally overcoming her reticence sufficiently to write under her own name. In Washington she contributed correspondence about politics to New York papers. Her first novel, *Hale-Weston* (1889), written for *Lippincott's Magazine*, was very successful and was translated into German. Her first juvenile story, *Little Jarvis* (1890), a navy tale, won a *Youth's Companion* prize and fixed her prepossession for naval subjects. Later she took *New York Herald* prizes of $3000 and $1000 with *The Sprightly Romance of Marsac* (1896), a novelette, and *John Mainwaring, Financier* (1908), a short story. As she became experienced she developed a number of types of fiction: stories of the American navy, of Virginia before and after the Civil War, of French life in Paris and the provinces, of English historical periods, of Washington society. Some of her best volumes of fiction are *Throckmorton* (1890), *Midshipman Paulding* (1891), *A Virginia Cavalier* (copyright 1896), *The History of the Lady Betty Stair* (1897), *The Lively Adventures of Gavin Hamilton* (1899), *The House of Egremont* (1900), *Papa Bouchard* (1901), *Franczeka* (1902), *The Fortunes of Fifi* (1903), *The Château of Montplaisir* (1906), *The Victory* (1906), *The Secret of Toni* (1907), *The*

Last Duchess of Belgarde (1908), *The Imprisoned Midshipmen* (1908), *The Whirl; a Romance of Washington Society* (1909), *Betty's Virginia Christmas* (1914), *The Diary of a Beauty* (1915). Her *Twelve Naval Captains* (1897) is said to have been used as a textbook in the United States Naval Academy. Certain public questions of her day interested her, and some of them supplied her with subjects for her writing. *Despotism and Democracy* (1903) is a discussion of Washington society and politics; "On the Absence of the Creative Faculty in Women," published in the *Critic*, Nov. 29, 1891, and *The Ladies' Battle* (1911) present her view of woman's suffrage, to which she was opposed. As a writer of fiction she had the ability to create both character and atmosphere. Though sometimes slight, her plots are usually adequate and often full of amusing incidents; her style is sprightly and humorous and, though her popularity has waned, her books are still very readable. For many years her home in Washington was a meeting-place for writers and artists, but after the deaths of her mother and sister and the failure of her own health she led a retired life. She died at her Washington home and was buried in Baltimore, Md.

[Gaillard Hunt, in *Lib. of Southern Lit.*, vol. XI (1909), ed. by E. A. Alderman, J. C. Harris, and C. W. Kent; *Who's Who in America*, 1908–09, 1916–17; Frances E. Willard and Mary A. Livermore, *Am. Women* (1897), vol. II; obituaries in *Evening Star* (Washington), *N. Y. Herald*, Nov. 16, 1916.] S. G. B.

SEBASTIAN, BENJAMIN (*c.* 1745–March 1834), jurist, Spanish agent, was possibly connected with the Sebastians of Fairfax County, Va., and the vicinity. After serving some years as a clergyman (*Virginia Magazine of History and Biography*, October 1933, p. 299), he removed to Kentucky, where a warrant, recorded on Mar. 27, 1784, granted him land as a three-year soldier of the Virginia line, and another warrant, dated Feb. 10, 1785, listed him among those obtaining land in Jefferson County, Ky. He was admitted to the practice of law at Louisville in 1784 and was licensed as attorney on Mar. 6, 1786, by the supreme court of the Kentucky district (*Filson Club Historical Quarterly*, July 1932, p. 262; First Order Book, Filson Club Library). At once he became prominent in law and in politics. A member of the famous "Political Club" at Danville he, like others of its leading members, was suspected of Spanish leanings. In the series of conventions leading up to statehood for Kentucky he espoused prompt separation from Virginia as a step toward obtaining the free navigation of the Mississippi. His attitude, especially in the convention of 1788, led James

Wilkinson [*q.v.*] to recommend him, the following year, for a Spanish pension—a recommendation that drew from the Spanish governor of Louisiana, Esteban Miró [*q.v.*], an offer to bestow substantial land grants upon Sebastian and his companions, should they choose to settle in Louisiana. Nothing came of this colonization project but for other services less openly professed and undertaken in conjunction with Wilkinson, Sebastian hoped to obtain from the Spanish government a substantial pension.

On June 28, 1792, he was appointed one of the judges for the appellate court of the state. This appointment, however, did not prevent him from continuing his correspondence with the Spaniards. Three years afterward both he and George Muter were subjected to a hostile address in both houses of the state legislature because of a decision regarding land titles, but the resolution did not receive a two-thirds majority. In this same year, 1795, the new Spanish governor of Louisiana, Francisco Luis Hector de Carondelet [*q.v.*], renewed overtures to the Kentuckians through Sebastian, now evidently more approachable than General Wilkinson. Through the Spanish intermediary, Thomas Power, Sebastian was induced to confer with Manuel Gayoso de Lemos [*q.v.*], commandant at Natchez, at New Madrid. When some differences arose over the proposed duties on river trade, Sebastian accompanied the Spaniard to New Orleans, in order to settle the question with Carondelet in person. The treaty with Spain providing for the navigation of the Mississippi and a port of deposit rendered unnecessary any private arrangement, and Sebastian thereupon returned to Kentucky. He bore a letter from Carondelet completely justifying his conduct, but this did not forestall considerable speculation among his neighbors concerning this visit. Two years later Power suggested an immediate separation of the western country from the eastern states and the establishment of its independence with Spanish aid. A hundred thousand dollars would be available for the initial expenses and an equal sum, together with warlike equipment, when independence was declared. Those who should lose office because of this service were to receive from the Spanish government a pension equal to the forfeited salary. These proposals, although intended more particularly for Wilkinson, were brought by Sebastian to the attention of his friends, Harry Innes and George Nicholas [*qq.v.*], both of whom seem to have promptly repudiated them. Nevertheless Sebastian went to New Orleans, in 1798, for further conference with Gayoso, who was then governor of Louisiana, and continued to receive his Spanish pension.

In 1804 the payment of this pension proved his undoing. Already suspected by his fellow citizens, the death of the merchant in Natchez through whom one of his vouchers was cashed gave his enemies definite proof of his dealings. At the same time the much discussed visit of Aaron Burr [*q.v.*] caused a revival of the scandals connected with the earlier Spanish conspiracy. The Federalist faction in Kentucky found in Sebastian an easy mark for their virulent attacks, and in November they obtained a petition asking the legislature to investigate his conduct (see sketch of Joseph M. Street). Fearful of the consequences Sebastian resigned at the end of 1806, but the committee continued its work and procured, especially from his associate Innes, testimony that made his guilt certain. The exposure meant elimination from public life. About 1810 he removed to Grayson County and there and in Livingston County purchased extensive tracts of land, built a saw-and-grist-mill and engaged in general merchandise. In 1821 he gave his son Charles power of attorney to represent him. His will was recorded Mar. 17, 1834 (Durrett MSS., *post*). A man of striking presence and of considerable ability, his moral principles were not sufficient to withstand his monetary needs. In a period of uncertain allegiance he followed a course of intrigue that promised to protect personal interest at the expense of state and nation. Thus far he was guilty but, of the dubious group with which he associated, he was the only one to pay full penalty for his guilt.

[Photo-film enlargements from the Papeles de Cuba esp. legajo 2374; Harry Innes Papers, esp. vols. XVIII, XIX, XXIII, in Lib. of Cong.; manuscript material in Filson Club Lib., Louisville, Ky.; Wayne Papers in possession of Pa. Hist. Soc.; Durrett MSS., Univ. of Chicago; Sebastian report, in *Annals of Cong.*, 1 Sess., cols. 2760–90 and *Am. State Papers: Miscellaneous Docs.*, vol. I (1834), pp. 933–35; T. M. Green, *The Spanish Conspiracy* (1891); J. M. Brown, *The Political Beginnings of Kentucky* (1889); Charles Gayarré, *Hist. of La.*, vol. III (1854) with material from the Spanish archives; *Reprints of Littell's Political Transactions*, ed. by Temple Bodley in the *Filson Club Pubs.*, vol. XXXI (1926), esp. introduction; S. F. Bemis, *Pinckney's Treaty* (1926); I. J. Cox, *The West Florida Controversy* (1918); J. A. James, *The Life of George Rogers Clark* (1928); A. P. Whitaker, *The Spanish-American Frontier* (1927) and *The Mississippi Question* (1934); W. R. Jillson, "Old Kentucky Entries and Deeds," *Filson Club Publications*, no. 34 (1926), p. 360, and "Kentucky Land Grants," *Ibid.*, no. 33 (1925), p. 116.]   I. J. C.

SECCOMB, JOHN (Apr. 25, 1708–Oct. 27, 1792), Congregational clergyman, was born at Medford, Mass., son of Peter and Hannah (Willis) Seccomb, and grandson of Richard Seccomb, who settled at Lynn about 1660. He graduated from Harvard in 1728. While at the college he had written poems for the amusement of his friends, and in 1730 when Matthew Abdy, college bedmaker and sweeper, died, Seccomb was inspired to write "Father Abbey's Will," a humorous poem in fifteen six-line stanzas cataloguing the objects which Abdy might have bequeathed to his wife. It was printed in December of that year. He afterwards added "A Letter of Courtship to his virtuous and amiable Widow," twelve stanzas supposed to be written by the sweeper at Yale. These verses had no merit as poetry, but their rhymes and phrasing were neat and amusing. They were published together in Boston in 1731, were dispatched to England by Governor Belcher and printed in 1732 in both the *London Magazine* and the *Gentleman's Magazine,* and were popular among several generations of New Englanders. They were reprinted in the *Massachusetts Magazine* in November 1794, and privately in Cambridge by John L. Sibley in 1854.

Seccomb was ordained minister in the town of Harvard, Mass., on Oct. 10, 1733. In 1739 there was a revival of religion in his congregation, which, stimulated by the Great Awakening which began in New England in 1740, continued for four years. Writing to *The Christian History* (Mar. 17, 1743/44), Seccomb reported that nearly one hundred had been converted, chiefly among the young people; some, he added, had been "so sensibly affected with their Danger that they dare not close their Eyes to sleep lest they should awake in Hell; and would sometimes *arise in the Night* and go to the Windows . . . expecting to hear the Sounding of the Trumpet to summon all Nations to appear before him." Seccomb had been married on Mar. 10, 1737, to Mercy, daughter of the Rev. William Williams of Weston and had had four children. In 1757 she accused him of misconduct; a church council acquitted him of all charges, but, feeling that he could no longer usefully serve as pastor, he asked for a dismission. In 1763 he went as minister to the Congregational church at Chester, Nova Scotia, probably on the invitation of Jonathan Belcher, Jr., lieutenant-governor of the province, whom he had known at college. His income was only twenty pounds a year, and he was compelled to appeal for help in Boston; his difficulties were finally ended by an inheritance, and he stayed at Chester until his death. While there he published three sermons, somewhat pompous in tone and quite undistinguished. Doctrinally, he was an old-fashioned Calvinist.

[H. S. Nourse, *Hist. of the Town of Harvard* (1894); Charles Brooks, *Hist. of Medford* (1855); E. A. and

G. L. Duyckinck, *Cyc. of Am. Literature* (1875), vol. I; *Proc. Mass. Hist. Soc.,* 2 ser. vol. IV (1889).]

H. B. P.

SEDDON, JAMES ALEXANDER (July 13, 1815–Aug. 19, 1880), congressman and Confederate secretary of war, was descended from Thomas Seddon who emigrated from England to Virginia early in the eighteenth century, settled on a large tract of land in Stafford County, near Fredericksburg, and built "Snowden," which was burned during the Civil War by Federal troops. James Alexander Seddon, his great-grandson and the son of Susan Pearson (Alexander) and Thomas Seddon, a banker, was born in Fredericksburg. He graduated from the law school of the University of Virginia in 1835 and began to practise in Richmond, where he was successful and popular. He served in the federal House of Representatives from 1845 to 1847 and again from 1849 to 1851. Peremptorily declining another nomination, he retired to "Sabot Hill," his estate in Goochland County to enjoy the quiet life of a country gentleman and to manage his large property. Though lacking in humor, he was courtly, widely read, and a clever conversationalist. He was known as an ardent follower of Calhoun. In 1845 he was married to Sarah Bruce, the daughter of James Bruce of Halifax, a member of a distinguished Virginia family. She was vivacious and charming, with musical propensities. "Sabot Hill" became a center of hospitality in the happy decade preceding the Civil War. In the peace convention of 1861 he was a member of the committee on resolutions and introduced a minority report (Chittenden, *post,* pp. 47–48) recognizing the right of peaceful secession, and, together with the majority of his delegation, he voted against the compromise proposal of the convention. He was the leader on the floor of the secessionists members and sought assurance from the convention and the delegates of the Republican states that there should, in no event, be war. He was elected to the first Confederate Congress. In November 1862, when George Wythe Randolph [*q.v.*] resigned his position as secretary of war, Jefferson Davis prevailed upon Seddon to assume the important and difficult post. This appointment marked a return to the civilian control so criticized in the case of Judah P. Benjamin. It would have been difficult to obtain for this post a military officer with the requisite ability and energy, combined with deference to Davis. On the whole the choice of Seddon, though much criticized, was a good selection. A politician and man of the world, he brought to his task not only devotion and intellectual capacity but the needed tact and administrative ability. Physically, he was described as gaunt and emaciated, with a sallow and cadaverous look, resembling "an exhumed corpse after a month's interment" (Jones, *post*, I, 380).

He assumed his position in the lull following Antietam and Perryville, when Lee was busy reorganizing his army. A study of the records during this period indicates that Davis largely controlled the conduct of the armies. Yet Seddon had large influence over the president, especially until the summer of 1863, and he continued to hold his confidence. The Confederate military policy was in general too defensive and did not require sufficient coordination of the scattered armies. At times, however, Seddon made decisions that showed sound judgment. Early in 1863 he urged that Joseph E. Johnston take direct command of the western army, and he strove, tactfully but persistently, to make Johnston assume the offensive before Vicksburg. The month before Gettysburg, he wrote Lee a letter heartily concurring in his desire for offensive action. None of the Confederate secretaries of war were more considerate of Lee or worked in closer harmony with him. One of Seddon's blunders was his suggestion that Longstreet be detached for the attack on Suffolk. His chief defect, however, seems to have been his inclination to defer deciding troublesome administrative questions, especially those relating to the commissary and its chief. As a result of his consenting to the removal of Johnston before the fall of Atlanta, Seddon incurred much unpopularity. Early in 1865, when the Confederate situation had become desperate, the Virginia delegation to Congress requested the reorganization of the cabinet. As a consequence, he resigned. Jefferson Davis denounced Congress for what he deemed an unconstitutional interference with his cabinet and wrote a cordial letter to Seddon (Rowland, *post*, VI, 458–61).

Seddon "was completely crushed by the collapse of the Southern Confederacy and considered his life to have been a complete failure" (letter to the writer from his son, Judge James A. Seddon, Jr. of St. Louis). He was imprisoned by the Northern government but was soon released. Retiring to "Sabot Hill," he engaged in agricultural pursuits as far as his health would permit. For many years before his death he was an invalid and suffered from neuralgic pains. He died at "Sabot Hill."

[After Seddon's death it was found that most of his papers had disappeared, presumably destroyed by him; see Edward Pollard, *Life of Jefferson Davis, with a Secret Hist. of the Southern Confederacy* (1869), a critical appraisal; H. J. Eckenrode, *Jefferson Davis*

(1923), a more sympathetic view; L. G. Tyler, *Encyc. of Va. Biog.* (1915), vol. III; W. C. Bruce (a nephew), *Recollections* (copr. 1931); J. B. Jones, *A Rebel War Clerk's Diary* (2 vols., 1866); *Jefferson Davis ... Letters, Papers, and Speeches* (1923), ed. by Dunbar Rowland, vols. V–X; L. E. Chittenden, *A Report of the Debates and Proceedings in the Secret Sessions of the Conference ... 1861* (1864); G. S. Boutwell, *Reminiscences* (1902), vol. I; *War of the Rebellion: Official Records* (Army); *Daily Dispatch* (Richmond), Aug. 20, 1880; *Va. Mag. of Hist.*, Apr. 1904, p. 442; *Wm. and Mary Coll. Quart.*, Oct. 1901, p. 138; suggestions from Douglas S. Freeman, Richmond.]   R. D. M.

SEDELLA, ANTOINE [See Antoine, Père, 1748–1829].

SEDGWICK, ARTHUR GEORGE (Oct. 6, 1844–July 14, 1915), lawyer and journalist, son of Theodore Sedgwick, 1811–1859 [*q.v.*], and Sarah (Ashburner), was born in New York City. He was educated at Harvard, receiving the degree of A.B. in 1864. On completing his undergraduate course he was commissioned as first lieutenant of the 20th Massachusetts Infantry and began a brief and unfortunate military career. He was captured by the Confederates at Deep Bottom, Va., in July 1864 and confined in Libby Prison. While there he suffered a serious illness. He was paroled in September and the following February was discharged from the army on account of physical disability. In March he entered the Harvard Law School, from which he received the degree of LL.B. in 1866. In November 1868 he was admitted to the bar and began practising in the office of Chandler, Shattuck & Thayer in Boston.

On the advice of his brother-in-law, Charles Eliot Norton [*q.v.*], he gave considerable time to writing. Some of his articles were published in the *Nation* before he was twenty-one. In 1868 or 1869 he sent an article every week to that journal. He was also engaged with Oliver Wendell Holmes, Jr., in editing (1870–73) the *American Law Review*. In 1872 he returned to New York to become managing editor of the *Evening Post*, but after a few weeks he resigned because of interference by the business office with his editorial policies. He then became assistant editor of the *Nation*, with which he remained in more or less close association until 1905. From 1881 to 1885 he was also assistant editor of the *Evening Post*. From his first contribution his style impressed the reader as the *Nation's* own. It had much clarity, energy, and personal savor, combined with economy of words. He was at his best in writing short essays on modes and manners, some of which were of more than local and temporary importance.

In 1875 he was admitted to the New York bar and practised for six years. With F. S. Wait he wrote *A Treatise on the Principles and Practice*

Governing the Trial of Title to Land (1882). He edited the fifth, and was co-editor of the seventh, eighth, and ninth, editions of his father's *A Treatise on the Measure of Damages.* In 1896 he published *Elements of Damages,* which, with revisions and additions, was republished in 1909 as *Elements of the Law of Damages.* He delivered a course of legal lectures in 1885–86 at the Lowell Institute in Boston and in 1909 he was Godkin lecturer at Harvard University, speaking in criticism of the working of some traditional principles of democracy in the United States. His lectures were published in 1912 under the title, *The Democratic Mistake.* In his opinion the people of the United States had erred in expecting to obtain responsible government through the election of a great number of officers who served only short terms; the ballot alone would not insure good government. His book was not very favorably received.

Sedgwick married Lucy Tuckerman, Nov. 16, 1882, and had two daughters. After his wife's death in 1904 he spent most of his time at Stockbridge, Mass., keeping an office in New York solely to receive mail. In the summer of 1914 he was injured in an automobile accident from which he never fully recovered. The next spring he had a severe attack of pneumonia. Despondent over his ill health, he took his own life.

[The anniversary number of the *Nation,* July 8, 1915, contains autobiog. material; see also Allan Nevins, *The Evening Post, A Century of Journalism* (copr. 1922); Gustav Pollak, *Fifty Years of Am. Idealism: The N. Y. Nation, 1865–1915* (1915); *Harvard Coll. Class of 1864, Secretary's Report,* no. 6 (1889), no. 8 (1914); *Who's Who in America,* 1914–15; *N. Y. Tribune,* July 15, 1915; *Nation,* July 22, 29, 1915.]   E. C. S.

SEDGWICK, CATHARINE MARIA (Dec. 28, 1789–July 31, 1867), author, was the daughter of Pamela (Dwight) and Theodore Sedgwick, 1746–1813 [*q.v.*], both descendants of seventeenth-century settlers in New England. She was born in Stockbridge, Mass. Throughout her life she was closely identified with this region; her novels dealing with the natural beauty and local customs of the Berkshires are among the first attempts to use American material in fiction. Born into a family of distinction and of modest wealth, she was accustomed to the companionship of books and of cultivated people. She listened to intelligent talk, read widely, and like other girls of her time and class learned to perform all household duties. The district school, with brief periods in boarding schools in Boston and Albany, provided what formal education she had, but she was given private instruction in several languages. When she was in her eighteenth year her mother died, and the following year her father remarried. During the next six years she spent her time largely in Albany with her brother Theodore, 1780–1839 [*q.v.*], or in New York with her sister Mrs. Watson. After her father's death in 1813 she presided over the house in Stockbridge. Later she lived with a much-loved brother in Lenox in the summers and spent her winters in New York with other relatives, who were all deeply devoted to her.

Her literary work grew out of her belief in the importance of the American home. In 1822 she published anonymously her first novel, *A New-England Tale,* frankly designed to "lend a helping hand to some of the humbler and unnoticed virtues" and to set forth humble rustic scenes; two years later came *Redwood,* conventionally romantic in plot but with a background of simple home life. In these pioneer works the American domestic novel had its beginning. A series of novels—*The Travelers* (1825), designed for the entertainment and instruction of young readers, *Hope Leslie* (1827), a story of domestic life among the early settlers in New England, *Clarence; or a Tale of Our Own Times* (1830), and *The Linwoods; or "Sixty Years Since" in America* (1835)—established her as the most popular authoress in the country. Although marked by extravagant and imitative romanticism, they contain realistic presentations of domestic scenes. Harriet Martineau recommended them, with some reservations, in the *Westminster Review* of October 1837 as true pictures of American life, and several were translated into foreign languages. Her *Letters from Abroad to Kindred at Home* (1841) records the pleasant experiences of a sojourn of fifteen months abroad in 1839–40. Besides her longer works, she published two biographical sketches (an account of Lucretia M. Davidson in Sparks's *The Library of American Biography,* 1 ser., vol. VII, 1837, and a *Memoir of John Curtis, a Model Man,* 1858), many short tales, and a number of books designed to be helpful to persons of the less favored classes. Believing that the safety of the republic depended upon the domestic virtues of the people, she tried to render wholesome living and unaffected goodness attractive. Her moral purpose dominates *Home* (1835), *The Poor Rich Man, and the Rich Poor Man* (copyright 1836), *Live and Let Live; or Domestic Service Illustrated* (1837), *Means and Ends; or Self-Training* (1839), *Wilton Harvey* (1845), *Morals of Manners* (1846), *Facts and Fancies for School-Day Reading* (1848), and her last novel, *Married or Single?* (1857), written when she was sixty-eight to contradict the idea that unmarried women were useless.

Her life was outwardly an uneventful one

She took a quietly helpful part in the philanthropic movements of the day but did not ally herself with any radical reform. She was active in the work of the Unitarian Church, to which she turned in 1821 for greater religious freedom, and for many years she gave efficient help to the Women's Prison Association of New York. Her adventures consisted of her good works, her books, and, outstandingly, her friends. Both in New York and in Lenox she attracted the admiration of gifted men and women. Bryant praised her "perfection of high breeding," Hawthorne called her "our most truthful novelist," and Fanny Kemble Butler, the actress, her friend for over thirty years, described her as "one of the most charming, most amiable, and most excellent persons" she had ever known. Foreign visitors sought her out in Lenox, where her home was a center of hospitality, and where as the years passed she devoted herself more and more to her wide correspondence and her gardening. A journey westward as far as the Mississippi gave her great pleasure in 1854, but for the most part during her later life she seldom left New England. She died after a period of invalidism in the West Roxbury home of a niece who had always been to her as a daughter.

[R. De W. Mallary, *Lenox and the Berkshire Highlands* (1902); H. D. Sedgwick, "The Sedgwicks of Berkshire," *Berkshire Hist. and Sci. Soc. Colls.*, vol. III (1900); *Life and Letters of Catharine M. Sedgwick*, ed. by Mary E. Dewey (1871); S. A. Allibone, *A Crit. Dict. of Eng. Lit.*, vol. II (1870); *A Woman of the Century* (1893), ed. by Frances E. Willard and Mary A. Livermore; obituary in *Boston Daily Advertiser*, Aug. 1, 2, 1867; death notice in *Boston Transcript*, July 31, 1867; information from the family.]   B. M. S.

SEDGWICK, JOHN (Sept. 13, 1813–May 9, 1864), soldier, was born at Cornwall Hollow, Conn., the son of Benjamin Sedgwick, farmer and ardent churchman, and Olive (Collins) Sedgwick. The American progenitor of the family was Robert Sedgwick [*q.v.*]. His grandfather, Major John Sedgwick, was an officer in the American War of the Revolution. John Sedgwick, II, was a manly, robust boy, strong-willed, and a leader among his associates. He received his early education in the common schools of Cornwall, with a few months at an academy at Sharon, Conn., and some special instruction at the parsonage of the Rev. William Andrews. For two winters he taught school. Soon afterward he entered the United States Military Academy and was graduated with the class of 1837. He was commissioned in the artillery, and for a decade saw service in the Seminole War, assisted in moving the Cherokee Indians west of the Mississippi, served on the northern frontier during the Canadian border disturbances, and

on various garrison assignments. In 1846 he joined General Taylor's army on the Rio Grande, and saw arduous service until transferred to Scott's army at Vera Cruz, Mexico. He took an active part in all the battles of the Mexican War leading up to the final assault upon the city of Mexico, and for his services at the battles of Churubusco and Chapultepec was brevetted captain and major, respectively. After about eight years of garrison duty, during which he was promoted to the rank of captain, he was honored by appointment as major of the newly organized 1st Regiment of Cavalry. He participated in the Utah Expedition of 1857–58, and in the warfare with the Kiowa and Comanche Indians, 1858–60.

At the outbreak of the Civil War Sedgwick was engaged in constructing the frontier post of Fort Wise, Colo. Quick promotion to the ranks of lieutenant-colonel, colonel, and brigadier-general of United States Volunteers followed, and he received the important assignments of a brigade and a division in the Army of the Potomac. He participated in most of the battles of McClellan's campaign on the Peninsula, including Glendale where he was severely wounded on June 30, 1862. He was promoted major-general of volunteers on July 4, 1862. He took a prominent part in the battle of Antietam, where he was again wounded, in the battle of Chancellorsville, and in the Rappahannock campaign, during which he commanded the V and the VI Corps. Soon afterwards he led his corps in the storming of Marye's Heights at Fredericksburg, Va., and in the battle of Salem Heights on May 3 and 4, 1863. Although not reaching Gettysburg until the second day of the great battle, he entered that contest also and took part in the pursuit of Lee's retiring army. In the subsequent Rapidan campaign he commanded the right wing of the Army of the Potomac with the V and VI Corps, and did brilliant service at the Rappahannock Station in the operations at Mine Run. In the Richmond campaign, still commanding the VI Corps, he was actively engaged in the battle of the Wilderness early in May 1864. A few days later at Spotsylvania, while personally directing the location of artillery, he was shot and killed by a Confederate sharpshooter. A painting of Sedgwick's death, by Julian Scott, hangs in the public library of Plainfield, N. J. He was buried in his native town in Connecticut, where an impressive monument was dedicated to him on May 30, 1892. In 1868, a bronze statue at West Point, and in 1913 an equestrian statue at Gettysburg, were unveiled with appropriate ceremonies. Sedgwick never married. Generous and affable, but withal a strict disciplinarian, this brilliant leader was affectionately known to his soldiers as "Uncle John."

[E. S. Welch, *John Sedgwick, Major-General* (1899); *Corresp. of John Sedgwick* (2 vols., 1902–03); G. W. Cullum, *Biog. Reg.* . . . *U. S. Mil. Acad.* (1891); *The Centennial of the U. S. Mil. Acad.* (1904), vol. II; E. C. Starr, *A Hist. of Cornwall, Conn.* (1926); T. S. Gold, *Hist. Records of the Town of Cornwall* (1904); M. T. McMahon, *Gen. John Sedgwick, Address before the Vt. Officers' Reunion Soc., Nov. 11, 1880* (1880); *Hartford* (Conn.) *Daily Courant*, May 11, 12, 13, 17, 18, 1864.]   C. D. R.

SEDGWICK, ROBERT (*c.* 1613–May 24, 1656), colonist, soldier, son of William Sedgwick and Elizabeth Howe, was baptized at Woburn, Bedfordshire, England, May 6, 1613. "Nurst up in Londons Artillery garden" as a member of the city train bands, he settled in Charlestown in New England in 1636. Because he was "stout and active in all feats of war," he was chosen captain for Charlestown in 1637. To increase the efficiency of the colonial militia by creating a "school of soldiery" for its officers, he helped organize the Military Company of the Massachusetts, and was its captain in 1640, 1645, and 1648. In 1637 he established a "very commodious" brewery, and in 1644 with six others was granted a monopoly of the Indian trade of the colony for twenty-one years. The success of these and other commercial activities enabled him in 1647 to endow Harvard College with a substantial shop in Boston. He served as deputy from Charlestown to the General Court from 1637 to 1644 and again in 1648, and occasionally as assessor of rates, boundary surveyor, arbitrator of petty disputes, and keeper of the peace. The General Court in 1652 recognized his achievements, especially in fortifying Charlestown harbor, by electing him major-general of the colony. Late in 1653 he returned to England and received from Cromwell a commission to lead an expedition against the Dutch of Manhattan Island, who had been troubling the New Haven and Connecticut settlers. He reached Boston with four ships and 200 men in June 1654, raised an additional 700, and would have proceeded against the Dutch even after news came of peace with the Netherlands, had not the New Englanders abandoned the enterprise. Though France and England were nominally friendly, he decided to turn his fleet against the French engaged in trading and fishing on the New England coast, easily captured the Acadian forts of St. John, Port Royal, and Pentagoet on the Penobscot, and garrisoned them. Cromwell showed his approval by giving him charge of twelve ships and 800 men sent to reinforce the joint naval and military expedition of Penn and Venables, operating against the Spanish West Indies. Sedgwick

found the English precariously occupying Jamaica, which they had seized after an ignominious reverse at Hispaniola (Santo Domingo). There had been dissensions between Penn and Venables, who had already gone to England to present their respective cases, leaving their starving and shelterless men dying of dysentery. Sedgwick's efforts to ameliorate the condition of the army were frustrated by its insubordination and general worthlessness. Convinced at length that God did not favor the Western Design, and worried over his inability to carry out his share of the Protector's extensive anti-Spanish program, he died in Jamaica, broken-hearted, on May 24, 1656. His secretary in Jamaica described him as "generally beloved and esteemed by al sorts of people . . . a truly religious man, and of the most innocent conversation I ever accompanied" (Birch, *post*, V, 154–55). Though Sedgwick's widow, Joanna Blake, returned to England and remarried, many of their descendants have been prominent in New England life.

[*Trans. and Colls. Am. Antiq. Soc.*, vol. III (1857); Thomas Birch, *A Coll. of the State Papers of John Thurloe* (1742), vols. II, IV, V; *Calendar of State Papers, Colonial, 1574–1660* (1860); *Calendar of State Papers, Domestic, 1655, 1655–6, 1656–7* (1881–83); *Colls. Mass. Hist. Soc.*, 3 ser. VII (1838), 4 ser. II (1854), 5 ser. I (1871); Edward Johnson, *Wonder Working Providence of Sions Saviour in New England* (1654; ed. by W. F. Poole, 1867); *New-Eng. Hist. and Geneal. Reg.*, Apr. 1888, Oct. 1916; *Col. Soc. of Mass. Pubs.*, vols. III (1900), XV (1925); O. A. Roberts, *Hist. of the Military Company of the Massachusetts Now Called The Ancient and Honorable Artillery Company*, vol. I (1895); N. B. Shurtleff, *Records of the Governor and Company of the Mass. Bay*, vols. I, II (1853), III (1854).]   R. L. J.

SEDGWICK, THEODORE (May 9, 1746– Jan. 24, 1813), legislator and jurist, was born in West Hartford, Conn. His father, Benjamin Sedgwick, who kept a small store, was a great-grandson of Gen. Robert Sedgwick [*q.v.*]. His mother, Ann (Thompson) Sedgwick, came from Wallingford, Conn. In 1748 Benjamin Sedgwick moved to the new township of Cornwall where, when Theodore was ten, he died, leaving little property. Through the sacrifices of his older brother, Theodore entered Yale in 1761, intending to prepare for the ministry. He left before graduating because of infractions of college discipline, but in 1772 received his degree as of 1765. From divinity he soon turned to law, studying under his second cousin, Col. Mark Hopkins, in Great Barrington, Mass. Here he began practice after his admission to the Berkshire County bar in April 1766. Shortly afterward he moved to Sheffield, the next town southward. In 1768 (Mason, *post*, p. 21) he married Eliza, daughter of Jeremiah Mason of Franklin,

Conn., and aunt of Senator Jeremiah Mason [*q.v.*]. She died childless in 1771, of smallpox thought to have been caught from her husband when combing out his hair after he had been discharged from quarantine for the disease. On Apr. 17, 1774, he married Pamela, daughter of Gen. Joseph Dwight of Great Barrington by his second wife, Abigail Williams, who was half-sister of Col. Ephraim Williams [*q.v.*], founder of Williams College, and had been previously married to John Sergeant [*q.v.*], missionary to the Indians. To Sedgwick's second marriage ten children were born, eight of whom attained maturity. Among these were Theodore, 1780–1839, and Catharine Maria [*qq.v.*], while later generations of Judge Sedgwick's descendants included many other persons of distinction in law and literature.

Sedgwick soon became active in the struggle against Great Britain, although as late as May 1776, he was opposed to independence. He was clerk of the county convention called in 1774 to consider resistance to British taxation. Early in 1776 he became military secretary to Gen. John Thomas, whom he accompanied on his invasion of Canada. After Thomas' death on May 30, Sedgwick gave up soldiering—except possibly as a volunteer aid in the Burgoyne campaign—but he performed valuable service in 1776–77 in getting supplies on moderate terms for the northern department of the Continental Army. He served in the legislature as representative in 1780, 1782, 1783, 1787, 1788, and as senator in 1784 and 1785. He was speaker of the House in 1788. Meanwhile he continued practising law and was the leading Massachusetts lawyer west of the Connecticut in 1785, when he established his home in Stockbridge. In his most famous case (1783) he defended a negro slave, Elizabeth Freeman (Mumbet), against the master from whom she had fled. Sedgwick successfully argued that slavery had been abolished in Massachusetts by the Bill of Rights of 1780, which declared all men to be "born free and equal." The liberated negress became nurse of Sedgwick's children and died in his house.

After the recognition of independence Sedgwick became a Federalist and his career was for a time national. He was a member of the Continental Congress, 1785–88. His strenuous activity in suppressing Shays's Rebellion led the insurgents to threaten his life and an unsuccessful attempt was made to attack his house. In the Massachusetts convention of 1788 he was a prominent advocate of ratification of the Federal Constitution. Soon afterward, he was elected to the First Congress by a majority of only seven votes. He continued as representative in the Second, Third, and Fourth congresses. He was a vigorous debater and was chairman of important committees, reported the first fugitive slave law, all bills admitting new states, and some of the first ten constitutional amendments. He led the opposition to Livingston's motion requiring the papers leading up to the Jay treaty (*Annals of Congress,* 4 Cong., 1 sess., p. 514), and thus helped establish the inability of the House to participate in treaty-making. On Hamilton's resignation, Sedgwick declined an offer of the secretaryship of the Treasury. On the resignation of Senator Caleb Strong in June 1796, Sedgwick was elected to the Senate, of which he was president *pro tempore* for a few weeks in 1798. When his term expired in 1799, he returned to the House and was speaker during the Sixth Congress, retiring in March 1801. He was a Federalist of the Adams wing but was an intimate correspondent of all the party leaders.

In 1802 he was appointed for life to the supreme judicial court of Massachusetts, which at once began to show the effect of his personality and ability. Although his decisions did not permanently influence the law, they "were famous in their day for clearness and beauty" (Dexter, *post,* III, 149), and he won the high regard of the bar by introducing a new standard of courteous and cordial treatment from the bench. His hopes of succeeding Chief Justice Dana in 1806 were disappointed by the selection of Theophilus Parsons [*q.v.*].

In 1807 Mrs. Sedgwick died after several attacks of insanity, attributed to her cares and trials during her husband's absence on public duty. In November 1808, much to his children's distaste, he married his third wife, Penelope, daughter of Dr. Charles Russell of Boston and Elizabeth (Vassall) Russell. She survived Sedgwick, having had no children. He died while visiting Boston in 1813, and was buried in the family cemetery at Stockbridge.

Sedgwick was of large size, "with a prepossessing face and a dignified, almost showy manner" (Dexter, p. 149). Aristocratic despite his humble origin, he was rather overbearing to common people and habitually spoke of them as Jacobins and *sans-culottes,* but he kept open house in Stockbridge for rich and poor alike and his relations with his children were delightful. He was a trustee of Williams College from its foundation until his death, and a corporate member of the American Academy of Arts and Sciences.

[The fullest accounts are by H. D. Sedgwick, "The Sedgwicks of Berkshire" (1900), *Berkshire Hist. and Sci. Soc. Colls.*, vol. III; F. B. Dexter, *Biog. Sketches Grads. Yale Coll.*, vol. III (1903), with bibliog.; B. W. Dwight, *The Hist. of the Descendants of John Dwight of Dedham, Mass.* (1874), vol. II; M. E. Dewey, *Life and Letters of Catharine M. Sedgwick* (1871). See also L. H. von Sahler, "Two Distinguished Members of the Sedgwick Family—Robert and Theodore," *N. Y. Geneal. and Biog. Record*, Apr. 1901; T. W. Mason, *Family Record ... Descent from Maj. John Mason* (1909); *Biog. Dir. Am. Cong.* (1928), which is authority for day of birth; *Proc. Mass. Hist. Soc.*, 2 ser. I (1885), and *U. S. Mag. and Democratic Rev.*, Feb. 1840, pp. 129–34, giving information about the negress Mumbet; Theophilus Parsons, *Memoir of Theophilus Parsons* (1859), p. 194; A. B. Hart, *Commonwealth Hist. of Mass.*, vols. III (1929), IV (1930); *Letters from Charles Sedgwick to His Family and Friends* (privately printed, 1870), ed. by C. M. Sedgwick; T. S. Gold, *Hist. Records of the Town of Cornwall* (1904); *Columbian Centinel* (Boston), Jan. 27, 1813. Sedgwick's judicial opinions are in 1–9 *Mass. Reports*.]
Z. C., Jr.

SEDGWICK, THEODORE (December 1780–Nov. 7, 1839), lawyer and writer, was the second child and first son among the ten children born to Judge Theodore Sedgwick [*q.v.*] and his second wife, Pamela (Dwight). He was born in Sheffield, Mass., spent most of his childhood in Stockbridge, graduated from Yale College in 1798, and began the study of law with his distinguished father. The winter of 1800–01 he spent as a student in the office of a New York lawyer (Dewey, *post*, p. 75), and in that year was admitted to the bar. By 1803 he had settled in Albany, where he formed a partnership with Harmanus Bleecker and on Nov. 28, 1808, married Susan Anne Livingston Ridley (*c.* 1789–Jan. 20, 1867), grand-daughter of Gov. William Livingston [*q.v.*] of New Jersey. Much of their time was spent at the family home in Stockbridge where Susan's charm of manner and intellectual accomplishments made her a welcome addition to the cultivated society which centered about the Sedgwicks. To her were born a daughter and a son, the third Theodore Sedgwick [*q.v.*].

In 1821 failing health forced Sedgwick to retire permanently to Stockbridge. Here his sister Catharine Maria [*q.v.*] often spent her summers, and received encouragement in her literary endeavors; here also his wife began in 1829 to write her sentimentally didactic stories for children and young people. Sedgwick himself enjoyed the life of a cultivated gentleman with rural tastes, which are evinced in his collection of essays, *Hints to My Countrymen* (1826). He was president of the Berkshire County Agricultural Society, and his speeches made in this capacity in 1823 and 1830 were justly popular at the time. Here, too, he became a power in the newly organized Democratic party of Massachusetts, a curious apostasy from the ultra-Federal-ist principles of his father. He had his father's great aversion to negro slavery, however, and in February 1831, before the Stockbridge Lyceum, delivered an address, *The Practicability of the Abolition of Slavery*, which was published that same year. Though he had earlier expressed his distrust of party government (*Hints for the People, with Some Thoughts on the Presidential Election*, by Rusticus, 1823), he was several times the unsuccessful Democratic candidate for lieutenant-governor of Massachusetts. He served in the state legislature in 1824, 1825, and 1827. In 1825 he was one of the commissioners on the establishment of institutions for instruction in practical arts and sciences (Report of Commissioners, Jan. 9, 1826), and by his advocacy of state-supervised education identified himself with the movement Horace Mann was soon to direct. He advocated free trade and temperance legislation. In 1827 he introduced into the legislature a bill providing for the construction of the Boston & Albany Railroad at state expense. His long and ardent devotion to this project made him the butt of much ridicule from the less far-seeing, but before his death the stretch from Worcester to Springfield was opened (October 1838). The years 1836–39 saw the publication of his most important work, *Public and Private Economy*, in three volumes, illustrated with his observations during a visit to Europe in 1836. It was probably the outcome of his wish for "a popular work on *American Political Economy*, written expressly for the people" (*Hints to My Countrymen*, p. 35). His brother-in-law, to whom he submitted it for criticism, called it "a fine illustration of the nonsense of teaching science to the common people by stories," yet, though outmoded in doctrine, because of its unusual method it remains interesting reading.

Threatened for some time with apoplexy, Sedgwick looked forward to this end with great courage and cheerfulness. He died from the effects of a stroke suffered at the close of an address to the Democrats of Pittsfield, Mass.

[H. D. Sedgwick, "The Sedgwicks of Berkshire" (1900), *Berkshire Hist. and Sci. Soc. Colls.*, vol. III; M. C. Crawford, *Famous Families of Mass.* (1930), vol. II; *Life and Letters of Catharine M. Sedgwick* (1871), ed. by Mary E. Dewey; A. B. Hart, *Commonwealth Hist. of Mass.*, vol. IV (1930); Basil Hall, *Travels in North America* (1829), vol. I; F. B. Dexter, *Biog. Sketches Grads. Yale Coll.*, vol. V (1911); *U. S. Mag. and Dem. Rev.*, Feb. 1840; B. W. Dwight, *The Hist. of the Descendants of John Dwight of Dedham, Mass.* (1874), vol. II; *Boston Daily Advertiser*, Nov. 11, 1839.]
J. H. B—h.

SEDGWICK, THEODORE (Jan. 27, 1811–Dec. 8, 1859), author, lawyer, and diplomat, was born at Albany, N. Y., the son of Theodore

Sedgwick [q.v.], the second of that name, and of Susan Anne Livingston (Ridley) Sedgwick. Catharine Maria Sedgwick [q.v.] was his aunt. Prepared for college in the public schools of New York City and at Stockbridge, Mass., the family seat, he graduated at Columbia in 1829. He studied law, was admitted to the bar in 1833, and in the same year was appointed attaché at the United States legation in Paris under Edward Livingston [q.v.]. Here he enjoyed a number of stimulating personal contacts, notably with De Tocqueville, the historian, who became his friend and correspondent.

Returning to New York in 1834, Sedgwick began a law practice which in the next sixteen years grew to be very extensive. Ill health, however, made it impossible for him to continue in his profession after 1850, and during 1851–52 he traveled in Italy, Switzerland, France, and England. Upon his return to New York he became president of the newly incorporated Association for the Exhibition of the Industry of all Nations ("Crystal Palace Association"), in which capacity he carried on a voluminous correspondence with eminent men all over the world. After a year, however, the delicate state of his health forced him into retirement, first in New York and then at Stockbridge, where he partially recuperated. In 1857 President Buchanan offered him the post of minister to the Netherlands and later that of assistant secretary of state, both of which offices he declined. In 1858 he was persuaded to accept the position of United States district attorney of the southern district of New York, in which capacity he served until his death in December 1859, at Stockbridge.

Sedgwick was a keen student of legal, judicial, and political problems, and wrote extensively on these subjects. In politics he was, like his father, an advocate of Jeffersonian principles, but some later democratic developments, such as the popular election of judges, "filled him with disgust, and he labored . . . energetically to have the system altered" (*Harper's Weekly*, Dec. 31, 1859). He contributed largely to *Harper's Monthly* and *Harper's Weekly*, and under the pseudonym Veto, to the New York *Evening Post*, then edited by William Cullen Bryant. In the year he was admitted to the bar he published a biography of his great-grandfather, *A Memoir of the Life of William Livingston* (1833), and thereafter books and articles from his pen appeared at frequent intervals: *What is a Monopoly?* (1835); *A Statement of Facts in Relation to the Delays and Arrears of Business in the Court of Chancery of the State of New York* (1838); *Review of the Memoirs of the Life of*

Sir Samuel Romilly (1841); *Constitutional Reform* (1843); *Thoughts on the Proposed Annexation of Texas* (1844); *The American Citizen* (1847), an address at Union College; *Address . . . Delivered before the Columbia College Alumni Association . . . Oct. 27, 1858* (1858). In 1840 he edited *A Collection of the Political Writings of William Leggett,* in two volumes. His most important publication was *A Treatise on the Measure of Damages, or, an Inquiry into the Principles Which Govern the Amount of Compensation Recovered in Suits at Law* (1847; 9th edition, ed. by Arthur George Sedgwick and J. H. Beale, 4 vols., 1912). For some years the only work in English on the subject, this study, in the opinion of a contemporary, was "characterized by a philosophic spirit . . . and by accuracy of detail," and "may well take its place by the side of the more famous works of Chancellor Kent and Mr. Justice Story" (*Solicitors' Journal,* Jan. 14, 1860, p. 183). In 1857 he published another considerable volume, *A Treatise on the Rules Which Govern the Interpretation and Application of Statutory and Constitutional Law,* of which a second edition was issued in 1874, with additional notes by J. N. Pomeroy.

Sedgwick was a man of methodical habits, preserving and carefully labeling all his private correspondence and official documents. He married, Sept. 28, 1835, Sarah Morgan Ashburner, of a Stockbridge family, and was the father of seven children, three of whom died in infancy. His son Arthur George Sedgwick [q.v.] followed his father's profession and a daughter, Susan, married Charles Eliot Norton [q.v.].

[H. D. Sedgwick, "The Sedgwicks of Berkshire" (1900), *Berkshire Hist. and Sci. Soc. Colls.,* vol. III; B. W. Dwight, *The Hist. of the Descendants of John Dwight of Dedham, Mass.* (1874), II, 744–45; Sedgwick's correspondence as president of the Crystal Palace Company, in N. Y. Hist. Soc.; MSS. in the possession of E. L. W. Heck; Horace Greeley, *Art and Industry as Represented in the Exhibition at the Crystal Palace, New York, 1853–4* (1853); *Harper's Weekly,* Dec. 31, 1859; *Solicitors' Journal and Reporter* (London), Jan. 14, 1860; *N. Y. Daily Tribune,* Dec. 10, 1859; *Evening Post* (N. Y.), Dec. 9, 1859.]
E. L. W. H.

SEDGWICK, WILLIAM THOMPSON (Dec. 29, 1855–Jan. 21, 1921), biologist, teacher, and foremost American epidemiologist, was born at West Hartford, Conn. He was the son of William and Anne Louise (Thompson) Barbour Sedgwick and a descendant of Robert Sedgwick [q.v.]. Despite the death of his father when he was eight years of age, Sedgwick attended the Hartford High School and later the Sheffield Scientific School at New Haven, from which he was graduated in 1877. He then entered the Yale Medical School, but the many deficiencies in the teaching of medicine in those days turned him toward pure science. In 1879 he secured a fellowship in biology at the newly established Johns Hopkins University, Baltimore, Md., already distinguished by a faculty of very capable men. Here he came under the influence of a student of Huxley, Henry Newell Martin [q.v.], with whom he served for two years as associate in biology after taking his Ph.D. in 1881. On Dec. 29 of that year, he was married to Mary Katrine Rice of New Haven.

In 1883 Francis Amasa Walker, president of the Massachusetts Institute of Technology, called Sedgwick, whom he remembered as one of his brilliant students at Yale, to be assistant professor of biology. A year later he became associate professor, and in 1891 was appointed professor. For the next thirty years he was head of the department of biology, or biology and public health as it became in 1911, of the Institute. During his career as a teacher, Sedgwick trained hundreds of public-health workers, many of whom are numbered among the leading sanitarians in the United States and abroad. He was also active in public service. In 1888 he was named as consulting biologist to the Massachusetts State Board of Health, a connection which he maintained in some form until his death. When the board was reorganized in 1914 as the State Department of Health he became a member of its Public Health Council. As consulting biologist he conducted many notable investigations on sewage disposal, using the facilities of the Lawrence Experiment Station, which had been established in 1886. In the midst of these studies a severe epidemic of typhoid fever swept down the Merrimac Valley in 1890. Sedgwick and Hiram Francis Mills [q.v.] traced this epidemic to a polluted brook in Chelmsford above the Lowell water supply. Two years later he investigated another epidemic of typhoid fever at Springfield, Mass., and ascertained the cause to be a contaminated milk supply. He was an early advocate of the pasteurization of milk, and he also made a most important contribution to sanitary science by demonstrating how water and sewage could be disinfected by the use of chlorine (Jordan, etc., post, p. 43).

For many years Sedgwick was the foremost American interpreter of sanitary science. In 1902 he published his noteworthy *Principles of Sanitary Science and the Public Health*, a classic work on this subject. He was also author with E. B. Wilson of *General Biology* (1886), with Theodore Hough [q.v.] of *The Human Mechanism* (1906), with H. W. Tyler of *A Short History of Science* (1917), and he edited

the two volumes of the *Life and Letters of William Barton Rogers* (1896). He served as chairman of the administrative board of the school for health officers maintained jointly by the Massachusetts Institute of Technology and Harvard University from 1913 to 1922. He was president of numerous scientific societies, including the Society of American Bacteriologists in 1900, the American Society of Naturalists in 1901, and the American Public Health Association in 1914–15. He was a member of the Advisory Board of the Hygienic Laboratory of the United States Public Health Service and of the International Health Board of the Rockefeller Foundation. In 1920 he was exchange professor at the Universities of Leeds and Cambridge in England, where he represented his country as well as his professional interests so admirably that he was called the United States "ambassador of health" (Tobey, post, p. 244). He died suddenly of heart disease in Boston and was buried at West Hartford, Conn.

[*Who's Who in America*, 1920–21 ; E. O. Jordan, G. C. Whipple, and C.-E. A. Winslow, *A Pioneer of Public Health, William Thompson Sedgwick* (1924) ; *Yale Univ., Obit. Record, 1921* (1921) ; J. A. Tobey, *Riders of the Plagues* (1930) ; G. C. Whipple, "The Public Health Work of Professor Sedgwick," *Science*, Feb. 25, 1921 ; S. C. Prescott, "Life and Work of William Thompson Sedgwick," *Tech. Rev.*, Apr. 1921.]

J. A. T.

SEDLEY, WILLIAM HENRY [See SMITH, WILLIAM HENRY, 1806–1872].

SEE, HORACE (July 17, 1835–Dec. 14, 1909), naval architect, inventor, was born in Philadelphia, Pa., the son of Richard Colhoun See and Margarita (Hilyard) Sellers See. After receiving an early education in private schools, he entered the shops of I. P. Morris & Company in Philadelphia and learned the trade of machinist. A particular interest in ship-building led him to Chester, Pa., where he obtained employment with the firm of Neadie & Levy, shipbuilders. He then worked for the National Armor and Shipbuilding Company at Camden, N. J., and after a number of years in this establishment became superintendent of the George W. Snyder Machine Works in Pottsville, Pa. He returned to the ship-building industry about 1870 when he entered the employment of William Cramp & Sons in Philadelphia. He was promoted to be designer and superintending engineer for that company in 1879, and for ten years continued to design vessels and machinery of greatly improved construction and performance, introducing new methods of work and higher standards, and developing a ship-building plant which could bear comparison with those of Great Britain. During his régime the government contracts for the first vessels of the "New Navy," let under an expansionist program, were received, and he designed the triple expansion engines for six of the cruisers that were built, including the *Yorktown, Bennington, Philadelphia,* and *Vesuvius.*

In 1889 he resigned from William Cramp & Sons to engage in private practice as a marine engineer and architect. He established his office in New York City and at once became consulting engineer for the Newport News Shipbuilding and Dry Dock Company, Newport News, Va. He was also retained by the Southern Pacific Company and by the Pacific Mail Steamship Company as superintending engineer. He served as superintendent for the Cromwell Steamship Company, and was consultant for the Morgan Line. In the course of this work he designed five private yachts, among which were the *Corsair* and *Atalanta*; the steamships *Mariposa, Queen of the Pacific, Caracas* and *Olivette*; the machinery for a number of liners in South American trade; the United States cruisers *Yankee* and *Dixie*; the hospital ship *Solace*; several wrecking launches, and a number of New York police launches. In all of these vessels he introduced many of his inventions, such as a hydro-pneumatic ash ejector and a folding hatch cover. He also invented an automatic siphon fire hydrant, a double furnace water-tube boiler, and introduced a method for producing true crankshafts for multiple-cylinder engines by using his patented cylindrical mandrel for face bearings. In the early part of the Civil War he served as a private in the "Gray Reserves," and in 1862 was a corporal, 7th Regiment, Philadelphia Militia. He was adjutant of the 20th Regiment of the National Guard of Pennsylvania during the riots of 1877, and was later captain of the 1st Pennsylvania Regiment. He was a member of the American Society of Naval Architects and Marine Engineers, of the British Institute of Naval Architects, and of the American Society of Mechanical Engineers, of which he was president in 1888. His wife, Ruth Ross Maffet, of Wilkes-Barre, Pa., to whom he had been married on Feb. 20, 1879, survived him at the time of his sudden death in New York City. He was buried in Philadelphia.

[*Who's Who in America,* 1910–11; *Trans. Am. Soc. Mechanical Engineers,* vol. XXXII (1911); *Jour. Am. Soc. Naval Engineers,* Feb. 1910; *Public Ledger* (Philadelphia), Dec. 16, 1909; Patent Office records.]
C. W. M.

SEED, MILES AINSCOUGH (Feb. 24, 1843–Dec. 4, 1913), manufacturer, was born in Preston, England, the son of Richard and Ann (Ainscough) Seed. He received a public school

education in England, and became vitally interested in photography, then in its infancy. He studied the sciences and continued to do research in physics, astronomy, and chemistry, and to experiment particularly with different processes for making and developing photographic plates. Believing that better opportunities were to be found in America for applying the results of his experiments, he emigrated to the United States in 1865 and settled in St. Louis, Mo., where he obtained a position in the photographic gallery of John Scholton. He soon became chief operator and manager and continued in this work for a number of years, devoting his spare time to further experiments at his home in an effort to simplify the process that he had developed for producing photographic negatives. After several years of persistent effort he perfected a process for the manufacture of a photographic dry plate which appeared so promising a contribution to photography that, with the financial help of friends, he formed the M. A. Seed Dry Plate Company in St. Louis in 1882 and began to manufacture his new product. While the dry plate was a vast improvement over the earlier wet plate, it was so revolutionary a step that for a number of years after he began to manufacture the product Seed found it necessary to travel all over the United States to demonstrate its possibilities and methods of use in order to build up a market.

The introduction of the dry plate fixed the use of chemicals, revolutionized photographic apparatus, and compelled the opticians who manufactured lenses to improve and enlarge the field of their products. By reason of his tenacity he succeeded in overcoming the prejudice of photographers against this new product simply by capitalizing on his personal contacts throughout the country. He remained in close touch with his plant and personally superintended the processing of the plates. In the course of ten years not only did he manufacture dry plates but he also produced celluloid films for negatives, and introduced positive celluloid films, lantern slides, and double-coated non-inhalation plates. His dry plate was the first one sensitive enough to be used for X-ray purposes and for astronomical pictures. As a result, a larger market was opened up to the product of Seed's manufactory and the M. A. Seed Dry Plate Company expanded at a rapid rate. In 1902 he sold the business as well as his formulae to the Eastman Kodak Company, Rochester, N. Y., for the succeeding five years being employed as special advisor to that company. In 1907 he retired and a few years later settled in Pelham, N. Y., where he lived until his death. He was very fond of flowers and gardening, and his homes both in St. Louis and Pelham possessed beautiful gardens in which he cultivated extensive varieties of flowers, ferns, palms, cacti, and water plants. He was also a learned student of the Bible. He was married in 1872 to Martha Krause of St. Louis, and after her death he was married in 1881 to her sister, Lydia. He was survived by his widow and nine children, two being children of his first wife.

[*Willson's Photographic Mag.*, Jan. 1914; *Snap Shots*, published by George Murphy, Inc., Dec. 1913, Jan. 1914; *Bull. of Photography*, Dec. 10, 1913; *N. Y. Times*, Dec. 6, 1913; Natl. Museum correspondence with associates and family.]   C. W. M.

SEEGER, ALAN (June 22, 1888–July 4, 1916), soldier and poet, was born in New York City, the son of Charles Louis and Elsie Simmons (Adams) Seeger, both of New England ancestry. During his early years the family lived on Staten Island, and Alan attended the Staten Island Academy and later the Horace Mann School, New York. In 1900 his father's business took him to Mexico, whither he was accompanied by his family. Returning to the United States when he was fourteen, Alan studied at the Hackley School, Tarrytown, N. Y., and in 1906 entered Harvard College.

Self-centered, extremely individualistic both in garb and in behavior, inviting no intimacy, he at first took little part in the life of the University, finding happiness in solitude and perusing books with the delight of a voyager discovering new countries. He contributed poems to the *Harvard Monthly,* was editor in his senior year, and during the last part of his course mingled more with his fellows. He was turning from intellectual satisfactions to the keener pleasures to be had through the senses, the attainment of which thereafter became his ruling passion (see *Letters and Diary of Alan Seeger,* 1917, pp. 184 ff.). He courted beauty with abandon, not the beauty of form and appearance merely, but the beauty of love and of that which lies in experiencing all that is in the nature of things. After graduating he spent two years in New York, doing little, restless and unhappy; he could not find what he craved, and of American standards and conventions he was contemptuous. In the autumn of 1912 he went to Paris. Here he found congenial surroundings, the beauty that he sought, and the inspiration for his poetry. At the beginning of the World War he enlisted in the Foreign Legion.

His passionate affection for France and especially for Paris was one of the motives which led him to enlist, but it was not the principal one; neither was he much moved by any theory as to the possible moral effect of the war. A fatalist, he believed that war is a law of nature and force the "ultimate arbitrament among humanity, no less than in the rest of the universe." A man fights on the side destiny determines, and "playing a part in the life of nations he is taking part in the largest movement his planet allows him. He thrills with the sense of filling an appointed necessary place in the conflict of hosts . . . and feels . . . a kind of companionship with the stars" (*ante,* p. 38). Eager to experience life in its intense and violent, as well as in its rare and refined forms, Seeger entered the war. "How could I let millions of men know an emotion that I remained ignorant of?" he wrote to a friend (*Ibid.,* p. 186). For almost two years he was in active service, much of the time subjected to the rigorous ordeal of the trenches, individualistic as ever, keeping much to himself, contemptuous of the opinions of others, but full of zest and always a good soldier. After serving on the Aisne he went with his regiment to Champagne, where he took part in the offensive of September 1915. The inactivity of the trenches irked him: he ventured out between the lines by himself on dangerous expeditions; he was eager for the fierce exhilaration of the assault and the glory of victory, or, if fate so decided, the experience of wounds and death. In the battle of the Somme, on July 4, 1916, his great moment came. Going over with the first wave of attack on the village of Belloy-en-Santerre, he was cut down by machine gun fire. He was seen to crawl into a shell hole and the next morning he was found dead. The Croix de Guerre was conferred upon him posthumously and also the Médaille Militaire. Surrounded by the grime and confusion of trench life he produced poems self-revealing and of no little merit, including his widely known "I have a rendezvous with Death," and his "Ode in Memory of the American Volunteers Fallen for France." With his earlier works, these were published in *Poems of Alan Seeger* (1916), with an introduction by William Archer.

[In addition to works cited above, see *Harvard Graduates' Mag.,* Dec. 1916; M. A. De Wolfe Howe, *Memoirs of the Harvard Dead in the War Against Germany,* vol. I (1920); P. A. Rockwell, *Am. Fighters in the Foreign Legion* (1930); *Scribner's,* Jan. 1917; *Outlook,* Mar. 18, 1925; *Century,* Dec. 1926.]   H. E. S.

SEELYE, JULIUS HAWLEY (Sept. 14, 1824–May 12, 1895), clergyman, educator, and publicist, was born at Bethel, Conn., the son of Seth and Abigail (Taylor) Seelye and the brother of L. Clark Seelye [*q.v.*]. He was graduated from Amherst College in 1849 and from the Auburn Theological Seminary in 1852. He then went for a year of philosophical study at the University of Halle. On his return in 1853 he was installed as pastor of the First Dutch Reformed Church in Schenectady, where for five years he discharged his duties with signal success and at the same time pursued his philosophical studies under the direction of Laurens P. Hickok [q.v.]. On Oct. 23, 1854, he was married to Elizabeth Tillman James of Albany. They had four children. In 1858 he accepted the chair of philosophy at Amherst College and began a term of service that was to last, with the exception of one short interval, till his death, thirty-seven years later. On his thirty-fourth birthday he began the work that was to bring him great renown as a philosopher of the intuitive school. A distinguished colleague who knew him well throughout his adult life thus described his philosophic teaching: "Believing the transcendental philosophy as represented by Dr. Hickok to be the truth, the whole truth and nothing but the truth, he carries it with him as a personal presence . . . and breathes it as an element of life and power into all of his classes. At the same time accepting the religion of Christ as a revelation from God for men . . . he holds up that religion as truth without any mixture of error, that life as perfection without any mixture of frailty, and makes his pupils feel that to become Christian philosophers, Christian scholars, Christian ministers, Christian men, is the highest aspiration of which their nature is capable" (Tyler, *post*, p. 435). To him religion and philosophy were inseparable. As a leader of youth he was dignified, well poised, resourceful, strong and benignant. Charles H. Parkhurst [q.v.] said of him: "He quickened us, not his words but he; not his explanations and exposition and demonstrations but he" (*Congregationalist*, May 16, 1895).

He became the acknowledged leader of an able faculty, and when President William Augustus Stearns [q.v.] died in 1876 he became president. The exigencies of the office soon led him to give up most of his class work, but the power of his personality became even more effective throughout the college. His faith in youth, and his understanding, led him to devise the "Amherst plan," a system of student self government, which under his administration proved highly successful at Amherst and profoundly affected the practices in other institutions throughout the country. In other respects also his administration was notable. The pecuniary resources of the college were more than doubled, the physical plant enlarged and im-

proved, and the standard for admission and graduation substantially raised. He was widely recognized as a persuasive and powerful preacher. His tall, broad and stalwart figure, his massive but finely shaped head, and his melodious and resonant voice all contributed no doubt to his success in the pulpit. But more effective yet was his very apparent spiritual quality—the rare but essential union of intellect and emotion —which was set forth not only in his sermons but in his life. That his teaching and example were powerful indeed is clearly evidenced by the large number of leaders in religious circles who acknowledge him as the chief human force in their lives. Further evidence of his persuasiveness is to be found in the record of his visit to India in 1872, where he delivered a series of "Lectures to Educated Hindus," *The Way, the Truth, and the Life* (1873), which aroused much interest among the high-caste natives and were printed and widely circulated at the expense of one of them. In 1887, as chairman of the board of visitors of the Theological Seminary at Andover, he voted for a sentence of "admonition" for all five of the leaders accused of heresy but was outvoted by the other two visitors in the case of Egbert Coffin Smyth [q.v.], who was dismissed. In this trial controversies arose which are still undetermined, but Seelye emerged with a greatly enhanced reputation for magnanimity and liberality.

Throughout his life he was a close student of public affairs. His work as a member of the Massachusetts commission for the revision of the tax laws of the state, combined with local dissatisfaction over party management as well as country-wide criticism of the Republican party, led to his election to Congress on an independent ticket without his conducting any campaign. In Congress, from 1875 to 1877, he generally preferred to act with the Republicans, but he was uniformly opposed to the many proposals whose purpose was to keep alive the animosities of the Civil War. He also acted independently in 1877 by voting against accepting the action of the electoral commission in counting the vote of Louisiana for Hayes. He published many articles on religious and political subjects. He translated Albert Schwegler's *History of Philosophy* (1856), edited and revised L. P. Hickok's *Empirical Psychology* (1882) and also Hickok's *System of Moral Science* (1880), and wrote *Christian Missions* (1875), *Duty* (1891), and *Citizenship* (1894).

[*Amherst Literary Monthly*, June 1895; W. S. Tyler, *Hist. of Amherst College* (1873); *The Andover Defence* (1887); personal acquaintance.]   F. L. T.

SEELYE, LAURENUS CLARK (Sept. 20, 1837–Oct. 12, 1924), college president, was born in Bethel, Conn., the descendant of Robert Seely who was captain of one of the vessels of John Winthrop's fleet, which sailed from England to Salem, Mass., in 1630. His parents, Seth and Abigail (Taylor) Seelye, were both descended from Puritan families that had for some seven generations been thrifty farmers and merchants, and pillars of the Congregational Church. He was the youngest son of a large family and, partly on account of his delicate health, was surrounded in youth by more tenderness and affection than was usual among his undemonstrative kinsfolk. His second brother, Samuel, then minister in Wolcottville (now Torrington), Conn., prepared him for college, and in 1853 he entered Union College at Schenectady, N. Y., graduating in 1857, shortly before he was twenty. While there he lived in the house of his maternal uncle, Laurens P. Hickok [q.v.]. His theological training was begun in the Theological Seminary at Andover, but in his second winter his health was such that he was sent to Europe. He traveled widely through Great Britain, France, Italy, Germany, Switzerland, Spain, Egypt, and Palestine, spending in all nearly three years, and in 1861–62 completing his theological studies in Berlin and Heidelberg. His first and only charge was the North Congregational Church of Springfield, Mass., to which he was inducted in January 1863. Here he ministered for two and a half years with great acceptance. On Nov. 17, 1863, he married Henrietta Chapin of Albany, descended from a Puritan stock similar to his own. In 1865, influenced partly by a return of the bronchial affection that had been the cause of his leaving Andover, he gave up his church to accept the Williston professorship of rhetoric, oratory, and English literature at Amherst College, where his brother Julius Seelye [q.v.] was then professor of philosophy. This position he filled with marked success for eight years, when he resigned to accept, after much hesitation, the presidency of Smith College, which it was proposed to open in the neighboring town of Northampton. Here he found his life work. In 1870 Sophia Smith of Hatfield had left somewhat less than $400,000 to found a college for women, and in the following year it had been chartered by the Massachusetts legislature. But the endowment seemed so inadequate that at first Seelye refused to undertake the responsibility. In 1873, however, he accepted, and from this date his whole energies were devoted to the interests of Smith College. During the two years of deliberation he had matured his ideas of what

such a college should be, and he was ready with a program. The new institution, according to the will of the founder was to "furnish for her own sex means and facilities for education equal to those which are afforded now in our Colleges to young men."

The new president began by insisting on entrance requirements of equal difficulty with those of the New England colleges for men and an equal level of achievement for the degree. There was to be no preparatory school attached, where unprepared candidates might find a haven, for he feared the effect on collegiate standards of such an appendage. The students were to live in small homelike groups, not in one large dormitory such as had been built at Vassar College. Special attention was to be given to art and music. The funds at his disposal for the carrying out of these aims were miserably small; public opinion was far from being unanimous as to their desirability; the local community showed little enthusiasm. But from the time the first class of fourteen entered in September 1875, the institution went forward, carried by Seelye's faith, energy, and practical capacity. After a quarter of a century the number of students was 1133, and the assets had been multiplied by five. Ten years later, when he retired, there were 1635 students, so that it was the largest institution of its kind. The history of Seelye's life from 1873 to 1910 is the history of his college. He did his share as citizen and as church member and was in all ways a leader in his community, but he lived for Smith College. To a remarkable extent he succeeded in realizing his ideals. All the main characteristics he aimed at he built into it, standing always for sound scholarship but putting character and good breeding first. Though in appearance and manner he displayed some of the austerity of his Puritan forebears, his fundamental warmth earned him the affectionate devotion of both students and faculty. The growth of the college in equipment and endowment were due more to the care and skill of his management than to the generosity of outsiders. After his retirement in 1910 till his death, he continued to live in Northampton, taking an interest in church and state, and serving for three years on a commission on the Massachusetts Agricultural College at Amherst. In 1923 he published *The Early History of Smith College,* and in 1925 *Prayers of a College Year* was published posthumously. He was survived by his widow and five children.

[*The Early Hist. of Smith College, ante*; H. C. S. Rhees, *Laurenus Clark Seelye* (1929); Vida Scudder, "Seelye of Smith," *New Republic,* Jan. 14, 1925; *Smith*

College Alumnae Quart., Nov. 1924, May 1925; personal acquaintance.]   W. A. N.

SEEVERS, WILLIAM HENRY (Apr. 8, 1822–Mar. 24, 1895), legislator, jurist, was born on a plantation in Shenandoah County, Va., of pioneering stock. His father, James Seevers, was a soldier in the War of 1812; his mother was Rebecca (Wilkins). William had no more than come of age when he was elected sheriff. At the end of his term he followed his parents, in June 1844, to Mahaska County, Iowa, where he continued the study of law he had begun in Virginia. On Mar. 28, 1846, he was admitted to the bar and opened an office in Oskaloosa, Iowa. He married Caroline M. Lee, Feb. 20, 1849, and made his home in Oskaloosa all the rest of his life.

It was not long before he entered politics. In 1848 he was elected prosecuting attorney of Mahaska County, and served two terms in that capacity. The Whigs nominated him for the office of state auditor in 1850, but he was defeated. Meanwhile, he had developed a reputation for being a capable attorney. In 1852 he was elected judge of the third judicial district of Iowa and occupied that office nearly four years, though he resigned before the end of his term to resume active law practice. Seevers had several able partners at various times, among them his brother-in-law Micajah T. Williams, his cousin George W. Seevers, and Marcellus E. Cutts. His reputation attracted many clients with important cases commanding large fees.

His first conspicuous public achievement was in the state legislature. As a representative in the seventh General Assembly, the first under the constitution of 1857, he served as chairman of the committee to which all bills were referred so that the statutes might be brought into conformity with the organic law. It was an arduous position, involving tremendous responsibility, and the fact that much of the legislation of that session has survived three-quarters of a century is eloquent testimony to his ability. Fourteen years later he was appointed chairman of the commission to codify the statutes of Iowa, and The Code ... of the State of Iowa published in 1873 bears further evidence of his legislative competence. Again in 1876 he was a member of the Iowa House of Representatives.

Before this session of the legislature had ended, Seevers was appointed to fill a vacancy in the Iowa supreme court caused by the resignation of the chief justice. For nearly thirteen years he was a member of that tribunal, in 1876, 1882, and 1887–1888 serving as chief justice. He possessed the rare quality of judicial-mind-edness and was a careful legalist. Indeed, he was so legalistic in his attitude that he lost popular favor, particularly by his decision that a constitutional amendment prohibiting the manufacture and sale of intoxicating liquor had not been legally adopted (Koehler and Lange vs. Hill, 60 Iowa, 543). The resolution adopted by the Eighteenth General Assembly had contained a meaningless phrase which was omitted in the enrolled amendment; the Nineteenth General Assembly had approved the amendment as enrolled and in that form it had been ratified by the people. In the opinion of the supreme court, written by Justice Seevers, the amendment was invalid because it had not passed two successive General Assemblies in the same form, though the meaning was identical. One of the five justices dissented. Chiefly as a result of this decision, Seevers failed to be renominated by the Republicans and retired from the bench at the end of his term in December 1888. Thereafter, until a few weeks before his death, he was active in the legal profession, being engaged in a trial two days before he was stricken with paralysis. Five children survived him.

[Iowa State Register (weekly ed.), Mar. 29, 1895; E. H. Stiles, Recollections and Sketches of Notable Lawyers and Public Men of Early Iowa (1916); Johnson Brigham, Iowa: Its Hist. and Its Foremost Citizens (1915), vols. I, II; Portr. and Biog. Album of Mahaska County, Iowa (1887); Annals of Iowa, 3 ser. II (1895); C. C. Cole and E. C. Ebersole, The Courts and Legal Profession of Iowa (1907), vol. I; information as to certain facts from Seevers' daughter; his opinions, in 43–74 Iowa Reports.]   J. E. B.

SEGHERS, CHARLES JEAN (Dec. 26, 1839–Nov. 28, 1886), Roman Catholic prelate and missionary, was born in Ghent, Belgium, the son of Charles Francis and Pauline Seghers, and as an orphan was reared by uncles who were apparently comfortably situated. Trained at the College of Ste. Barbe at Ghent, at the diocesan seminary, and at the American College at Louvain, he was ordained a priest at Mechlin, May 31, 1863, and enlisted for the Canadian missions at Vancouver under Bishop Modeste Demers of Victoria. From the time of his arrival on Nov. 17, 1863, he entered into his arduous work with marked zeal despite his delicate health, learning the native dialects, living with the Indians, and serving the scattered tribesmen, hunters, and settlers. In 1869 he accompanied Demers to the Vatican Council. When Demers died two years later, he became administrator of the diocese, and in 1873 he was appointed bishop. Consecrated in June 1873 by Archbishop François Norbert Blanchet [q.v.], he visited Europe and more especially his native Belgium in quest of missionaries and financial assistance, for he was intent on bringing Catholicity to Alaska, which knew only a single priest, an Oblate Father.

On his return he busied himself with building chapels, establishing an occasional school, opening mission stations for the Indians (who were acquainted with Christian doctrines through the use of Blanchet's guide or "Catholic Ladder"), and founding St. Joseph's Hospital at Victoria. Not until July 1877 was he able to make his preliminary survey of Alaska. At that time, with Father Mandart, he spent several desperate months of privation at St. Michael, Ulukuk, Nulato, Kaltag, and in various native villages of the Yukon region which knew civilization only through half-breeds and hunter-traders. In 1878 he assigned Father Althoff to establish a mission at Wrangell but could do no more, for he was suddenly named coadjutor to the aged Archbishop Blanchet of Oregon City (Portland), whom he succeeded two years later. His régime was marked only by normal progress and extensive visitations in 1879 and 1882 into the outlying regions of Idaho and of Montana, which at his request was made a vicariate under Bishop John Baptist Brondel [q.v.], who was transferred from Victoria in 1884. While he was in Rome, where he was called in 1883, he made clear his desire to return to British Columbia and to Alaska, on which he had published a widely read account, "The Cross in the North" (*New York Freeman's Journal*, Sept. 21–Nov. 2, 1878, *passim*). On his return, he took part in the Third Plenary Council of Baltimore, in which he spoke on Indian missions, and resigned his archepiscopal see for the episcopal seat at Victoria, to take up his duties in British Columbia and Alaska in 1884, a quite unusual sacrifice. In 1885 he established missions at Juneau and Sitka, Alaska, under Fathers Althoff and Heymen, erected a school and hospital at Juneau, founded two academies for girls, and invited the Jesuits to enter this forbidding mission field. A year later, accompanied by two Jesuits, Paschal Tosti (later prefect-apostolic of Alaska) and Aloysius Robaut, and Frank Fuller, a white attendant, he journeyed over the Chilkoot Pass for the headwaters of the Yukon, where he hoped to establish a mission at Nulato in fulfillment of an earlier promise to the Ten'a tribesmen. Leaving the Jesuits at the mouth of the Stewart River to found a mission among the Stickeen Indians, he continued on with Fuller, who was apparently so affected by fatigue and privation that he developed symptoms of insanity. At Yessetlatoh where they found shelter in an abandoned fishing cabin, Seghers was awakened early in the morning and shot dead by Fuller, who was

brought by the Indian guides to Trader Frederickson and later convicted and sentenced at Sitka to ten years of imprisonment. The remains of the unfortunate missionary were taken to St. Michael and two years later buried in the crypt of his cathedral at Victoria.

[Henry Van Rensselaer, "The Apostle of Alaska," *Am. Cath. Quart. Rev.*, Jan. 1888; R. H. Clarke, *Lives of the Deceased Bishops of the Cath. Ch. in the U. S.*, vol. III (1888), pp. 509–32; Maurice De Baets, *Mgr. Seghers, l'Apôtre de l'Alaska* (Paris, 1896); A. G. Morice, *Hist. of the Cath. Ch. in Western Canada* (1910), vol. II; files of *Cath. Sentinel* (Portland), 1870–86; *N. Y. Freeman's Jour.*, Aug. 6, Sept. 24, 1887; *Cath. Ency.*, vol. I (1907), p. 250, vol. XIII (1912), p. 682; index of *Am. Cath. Hist. Researches*; Sadliers' ann. Cath. directories, esp. that for 1888, p. 35.]

R. J. P.

SEGUIN, EDOUARD (Jan. 20, 1812–Oct. 28, 1880), psychiatrist, was born at Clamecy, France, the son of T. O. Seguin (Kelly and Burrage, *post*) of a family of distinguished physicians. Educated at the College of Auxerre and at the Lycée St. Louis in Paris, he studied medicine and surgery in the medical schools of France and came especially under the influence of Jean Marc Itard and Jean Étienne Esquirol, a famous alienist and one of the pioneers of modern psychiatry. While he was interested in general medicine, he applied himself especially to the study of mental diseases and, at a very early day, to the study of idiots, for whom no scientific treatment had been devised. In 1839 he opened a school for idiots in France that met with the approval of authoritative medical bodies and academies, and was the forerunner of many similar institutions throughout the world. Insisting again and again that the idiot's brain was neither diseased nor abnormal but arrested in its growth, he developed a theory of training that has been universally accepted and a method of physiologic education that has been the foundation of the more successful handling of the imbecile and the idiot. In 1846 he published his chief work, *Traitement Moral, Hygiène et Éducation des Idiots*, which was indorsed by the French Academy and was used as a textbook throughout the world.

Having developed very decided social and political views, he felt uneasy in the revolutionary atmosphere of 1848, and about 1850 he emigrated to the United States. He first lived for some years in Ohio, but he was interested in the work in psychiatry that was going on in a number of different places, among them Syracuse, Mt. Vernon, and New York, where he took an active part in organizing the school for defectives on Randall's Island. In 1861 he received the degree of M.D. from the University of the City of New York (later New York University). In 1866 he published a second book, *Idiocy and Its Treat-*

ment by the Physiological Method, in which he was aided by his son, Edward Constant Seguin [*q.v.*]. This supplied to English and American neurologists and psychiatrists much of the material upon which modern methods of treating mental defectives have been based. There is some doubt as to the relative importance of the kindergarten, the Montessori, and the Seguin methods of training; Seguin himself makes very liberal allusion to the kindergarten methods and acknowledges his indebtedness to all such early masters in his field as Horace Mann, Samuel Gridley Howe, and Hervey Backus Wilbur [*qq.v.*]. In his later years he became much interested in medical thermometry and wrote a number of articles that helped to popularize the use of the clinical thermometer, among them *Family Thermometry* (1873), *The Clinical Thermoscope and Uniformity of Means of Observations* (1875), and *Medical Thermometry and Human Temperature* (1876). He had something of a roving spirit and for that reason failed to establish a great practice anywhere, although he might easily have done so. In 1880 he was married for a second time to Elsie Mead, who for many years after his death conducted a school for the training of defective children. He was a man of many amiable qualities and of remarkable unselfishness. Possessed of a wide general culture, he enjoyed painting and poetry, and is said to have written very good verse.

[Seguin's name appears in the records of New York University as O. Edouard Seguin; on the title-pages of his English books it is usually Edward Seguin. See *Am. Medic. Biogs.* (1920), ed. by H. A. Kelly and W. L. Burrage; Henry Holman, *Seguin and His Physiological Method of Education* (1914); C. L. Dana, in *Annals of Medic. Hist.*, Dec. 1924; obituary in *N. Y. Tribune,* Oct. 29, 1880.]

B. S.

SEGUIN, EDWARD CONSTANT (1843–Feb. 19, 1898), neurologist, was born in Paris, the son of Edouard Seguin [*q.v.*]. At the age of seven he was brought by his father to the United States. In 1864 he was graduated from the College of Physicians and Surgeons in New York. Two years before his graduation he was appointed a medical cadet in the regular army. While the training was irregular, the experiences he gained in those stirring times made amends for the lack of classroom instruction, and they also made of him a thorough American patriot. Shortly after his graduation he was appointed acting assistant surgeon at Little Rock, Ark.; in the spring of 1865 he showed signs of incipient tuberculosis and had himself transferred to New Mexico, where he acted as post surgeon. Returning to New York in 1869, he came under the influence of Dr. William Henry Draper at

the New York Hospital. His earliest interests were in general medicine. In 1866 he published a short paper on the use of the thermometer in clinical medicine, which contained what was probably the first temperature chart on record in the United States (Kelly and Burrage, *post*), and in 1867 two short papers on subcutaneous injections of quinine in malarial fevers, a special form of treatment suggested by Draper. It is of especial interest, inasmuch as this was before the era of asepsis, that he made much of the fact that the hypodermatic needle must be kept clean.

As the son of the elder Seguin, it seems natural that he should have become interested in nervous diseases. He had always insisted upon the importance of a broad general medical training; now, in order to acquire special knowledge of mental and nervous diseases, he went to Paris in 1869 and studied under the great masters of the day, Charles Édouard Brown-Sequard, Jean Martin Charcot, and Louis Antoine Ranvier. Interested in the question of cerebral localization, he contributed much to the recognition of functional and organic nervous diseases, which at that time was making great strides under the influence of Charcot in France, of Leyden and Carl Wilhelm Nothnagel in Germany, and of Hughlings Jackson in England.

On his return to America he became one of the triad of early American neurologists, the other two being Silas Weir Mitchell and William Alexander Hammond [*qq.v.*], both older men of world-wide reputation. From 1868–73 he was lecturer on diseases of the nervous system at the College of Physicians and Surgeons in New York and from 1873–87 clinical professor. He was one of the founders of the American Neurological Association and of the New York Neurological Society and served as president of both. From 1876–78 he was editor of *American Clinical Lectures* and from 1879–84 of *Archives of Medicine*. In 1882 his wife, Margaret Amidon, killed herself and her three small children (*New-York Tribune,* Nov. 1, 1882). Seguin later married again and was in active practice until 1894, when there appeared the first symptoms of the illness that led to his death four years later. Feeling that some of the procedures he had recorded would be of use to medical science, he collected his scientific papers and published them in 1884 as *Opera Minora*. In addition to his excellent contributions to the knowledge of mental and spinal diseases, he may be remembered for his faith in the efficacy of drugs properly administered; he was responsible for a treatment that was often successful when others had failed in which iodides were given in large doses. He was an inspiring teacher and a very careful diagnostician, who took unusual pains to get at all the underlying factors of a case and kept wonderfully accurate and detailed clinical records. Through both his teachings and his practice he had great influence upon the development of neurology in the United States.

[*Am. Medic. Biogs.* (1920), ed. by H. A. Kelly and W. L. Burrage; Bernard Sachs, in *Medic. News*, May 7, 1898; C. L. Dana, in *Annals of Medic. Hist.*, Dec. 1924; *Phila. Medic. Jour.*, Feb. 26, 1898; *N. Y. Tribune*, Feb. 21, 1898; personal association.]   B. S.

SEIDENSTICKER, OSWALD (May 3, 1825–Jan. 10, 1894), philologist, historian, was born in Göttingen, Hanover, the eldest of the five children of Georg Friedrich Seidensticker. His father (Feb. 16, 1797–Dec. 24, 1862) was an influential and highly respected lawyer, a veteran of the Napoleonic wars, in which he had fought on both the French and the Austrian side. As the most prominent of the leaders of the liberal political movement in Hanover, he was arrested for his part in the so-called uprising at Göttingen on Jan. 8, 1831, and after legal proceedings had dragged on for seven years, was finally sentenced to life-imprisonment and remanded to prison at Celle. This family calamity left a deep mark on the character of the son, depriving him of a normally carefree youth and making him reserved, serious, and resolute. While his mother maintained the family by conducting a private school, he attended the Gymnasium and matriculated in 1843 at the University of Göttingen as a student of classical philology. In 1845 his father was released on condition that he emigrate at once, without seeing friends or family, to the United States. He landed at New York, where various German societies welcomed him with banquets, gifts, and speeches. He lived the rest of his life in Philadelphia as a journalist, accountant, and, finally, an official of the customs house. In 1846, as soon as he had taken his doctor's degree at Göttingen with a dissertation *De Oenopida Chio* (1846), Oswald and the other members of the family joined the father in Philadelphia.

Seidensticker studied medicine for two years in Philadelphia but found the work distasteful and turned instead to teaching. He was employed in a private school at Jamaica Plain, Mass., 1849–52, and then conducted schools of his own at Bayridge, near Boston, 1852–55, in Brooklyn, 1855–58, and in Philadelphia, 1858–68. On Dec. 30, 1858, he married Emma Logo of Philadelphia. In 1867 he was appointed instructor in German in the University of Pennsylvania and was advanced next year to the rank

of professor. During his tenure of twenty-five years he never asked for leave and was never absent until five days before his death. To the German work of the University he gave a prestige that it has maintained to the present day.

His interest in the history of the Germans in Pennsylvania was first stimulated by Abraham H. Cassell, the Dunker antiquary and book-collector of Harleysville, Pa. Seidensticker was quick to perceive the significance and wealth of the field and made it the work of his leisure hours. He was the first student of Pennsylvania German history to bring to the subject broad culture, literary power, and a mind thoroughly trained in modern methods of historical investigation. To Heinrich Armin Rattermann's paper, *Der Deutsche Pionier,* he contributed a remarkable series of monographs on various phases of the subject, and in his later years he wrote with equal charm in English for the *Pennsylvania Magazine.* His separate publications consist of: *Geschichte der Deutschen Gesellschaft von Pennsylvanien* (1876); *Die Erste Deutsche Einwanderung in Amerika und die Gründung von Germantown in 1683* (1883); *Bilder aus der Deutsch-pennsylvanischen Geschichte* (1885)— a popularization of his monographs in the *Pionier*; and *The First Century of German Printing in America, 1728–1830* (1893). He also did much writing for newspapers. He was one of the chief supporters of the German Society of Pennsylvania and of the Pennsylvania Historical Society, and was the founder of the Deutsche Pionier-Gesellschaft of Philadelphia. He visited Germany in 1874 and again in 1891. In his latter years he enjoyed to the full the admiration and affection felt for him by many colleagues and friends throughout the United States. He died at his home in Philadelphia after an illness of a few days. His wife and daughter survived him.

[E. R. Schmidt and others, *Dr. Oswald Seidensticker, . . . Ein Lebensbild* (1894); C. F. Huch, "Georg Friedrich Seidensticker," *Ger.-Am. Annals,* Oct. 1904; H. A. Rattermann, "Dr. Oswald Seidensticker und die deutsch-amerikanische Geschichtsforschung," *Deutsch-Amerikanische Geschichtsblätter,* July 1911; *Public Ledger* (Phila.), Jan. 11, 12, 15, 1894.]   G. H. G.

SEIDL, ANTON (May 7, 1850–Mar. 28, 1898), musician, conductor, was born at Pest, Hungary. None of the printed accounts of his life gives the names of his parents, and by some it was supposed that he was the natural son of Franz Liszt (Finck, *My Adventures, post,* p. 200). In 1870 he entered the Leipzig Conservatorium, where he studied music under Ernst Ferdinand Wenzel, Oscar Paul, and Ernst Friedrich Richter; he also matriculated as a student at the university and attended lectures on logic and philosophy. In the same year he returned to Pest, principally for the purpose of studying with Hans Richter, a musician who had been assisting Wagner in preparing the score of *Die Meistersinger*. Upon Richter's recommendation Seidl was engaged by Wagner in 1872 to help him in his work at Bayreuth. He was employed in making the first copy of the *Nibelungen* score, and during the six years he was with Wagner he helped to complete the scores of *Die Götterdämmerung* and *Parsifal*. Wagner came to lean heavily on his assistant, and he entrusted to him many of the details of the first Bayreuth festival in 1876. In 1879 Seidl was appointed conductor at the Leipzig Opera House, where in the season of 1881–82 he conducted the first performances of the *Nibelungen* cycle ever heard in Berlin. The following season he was appointed conductor of the Travelling Wagner Theatre, with which he toured through England and most of Europe. In 1883 he became conductor of the Bremen Opera House. On Feb. 29, 1884, he married Auguste Kraus, a singer who had been associated with the Travelling Wagner Theatre.

A year later he was invited by Edmund C. Stanton, director of the Metropolitan Opera House, to come to New York as conductor of German opera to fill the vacancy caused by the death of Leopold Damrosch [*q.v.*]. He made his début at the Metropolitan conducting a performance of *Lohengrin*, Nov. 23, 1885, and achieved an immediate success. From this time until his death he made his home in New York and in 1891 became a naturalized American citizen. When German opera was temporarily dropped at the Metropolitan in 1891, he became conductor of the Philharmonic Society of New York, succeeding Theodore Thomas [*q.v.*], who had been called to Chicago. He held this position for the seven remaining years of his life, but in 1895–97 he again conducted German opera at the Metropolitan, and in 1897 he visited London and Bayreuth to conduct special performances. During this period of his life he received many invitations from abroad to leave America; he refused them all when a movement was inaugurated in New York to form a permanent Seidl orchestra and to guarantee its expenses. While these plans were materializing he died suddenly of ptomaine poisoning. He was survived by his wife; there were no children. His influence on American musical life was tremendous. He conducted many American premières of Wagner operas (see *Grove's Dictionary, post*, for a complete list), and with his traditions and the years he had spent with Wagner he was able to produce absolutely authentic performances and interpre-

tations. In 1893 he also conducted the American première of the "New World" symphony by Anton Dvořák, who was his intimate friend. Though he had little time for literary work, he acted as editor-in-chief of *The Music of the Modern World* (2 vols., 1895–97), which contained his valuable article "On Conducting," and contributed an important article on "The Development of Music in America" to the *Forum* of May 1892.

[*Anton Seidl, A Memorial by His Friends* (1899), ed. by H. T. Finck, contains the fullest account of Seidl's life. See also *Grove's Dict. of Music and Musicians* (3rd ed., 1928), vol. IV, and *Am. Supp.* (rev. ed., 1930) ; H. T. Finck, *My Adventures in the Golden Age of Music* (1926) ; obituary in *N. Y. Tribune*, Mar. 29, 1898.]   J. T. H.

SEILER, CARL (Apr. 14, 1849–Oct. 11, 1905), laryngologist, was born in Switzerland. Educated abroad, chiefly in Berlin, he studied medicine in Vienna and Heidelberg and then came to the United States with his mother, Emma Seiler, a teacher of singing and a student of voice production. They settled in Philadelphia, where Seiler continued his medical studies at the University of Pennsylvania and received the degree of M.D. in 1871. His thesis, "The Physiology of the Voice," shows the influence of his mother, who in 1858 had studied the action of the larynx in voice production by means of a laryngeal mirror and had written several books on the subject. Immediately after his graduation he devoted himself to laryngology, beginning his work with Dr. Jacob da Silva Solis Cohen [*q.v.*], a distinguished laryngologist, first as a special pupil and later as assistant. In 1876 he married Carrie G. Linn, daughter of Claudius B. Linn of Philadelphia; they had two daughters and a son. From 1877–95 he was instructor and lecturer in laryngology in the University of Pennsylvania and chief of the throat dispensary of the University hospital. He became a fellow of the American Laryngological Association in 1879 and vice-president in 1882. A few years after his resignation from the faculty of the University of Pennsylvania in 1895 he left Philadelphia and lived first in Scranton, later in Reading, Pa., where he died.

He was greatly interested in the microscope and in his earlier years was recorder of the biological and microscopical section of the Academy of Natural Sciences of Philadelphia. In 1881 he published a *Compendium of Microscopical Technology*; the following year he had privately printed a slender quarto volume of photographic reproductions of microscopic histologic preparations. He made a number of contributions to current medical literature, but his only outstanding work was his *Handbook of Diagnosis and*

Treatment of Diseases of the Throat and Nasal Cavities (1879), of which there were several editions under the title *Handbook of the Diagnosis and Treatment of the Throat, Nose, and Naso-Pharynx.* In the fourth and last, published in 1893, he gave the formula of an alkaline, antiseptic wash or spray for the nose that continues to hold its place in the esteem of laryngologists. As this was a great improvement on the previously used Dobell's solution and as Seiler also suggested a method by which the formula could be made up in compressed tablets to be dissolved in water for use, it won immediate popularity, and "Seiler's tablets" for years continued to be sold in great numbers. He was an able surgeon and had great skill in devising special instruments. A man of wide culture and an excellent musician, he was a delightful teacher and a pleasant companion.

[*Am. Medic. Biogs.* (1920), ed. by H. A. Kelly and W. L. Burrage; *Physicians and Surgeons of the U. S.* (1878), ed. by W. B. Atkinson; obituaries in *Jour. Am. Medic. Assoc.*, Oct. 21, 1905, and *Pub. Ledger* (Phila.), Oct. 11, 1905, which give date of death as Oct. 10; personal acquaintance.]   F. R. P.

SEIP, THEODORE LORENZO (June 25, 1842–Nov. 28, 1903), Lutheran clergyman, college president, was born at Easton, Pa., the son of Reuben L. and Sarah A. (Hemsing) Seip. He attended Weaversville Academy, catching from its principal, H. F. Savage, a graduate of Amherst College, a love of Latin and Greek that never left him, and in 1860 he entered Pennsylvania (later Gettysburg) College. During June and July 1863 he was a soldier in the 26th Pennsylvania Volunteers, and for some months of 1864 he was a delegate of the United States Christian Commission in Tennessee and Georgia. Graduating from college in 1864, he became a member of the first class in the Lutheran Theological Seminary in Philadelphia. In the summer of 1865 he was an inspector of the United States Sanitary Commission in Virginia. Toward the close of his seminary course in 1867 he was appointed assistant in the Allentown Collegiate Institute, which was reorganized that summer into Muhlenberg College with Frederick Augustus Muhlenberg [*q.v.*] as its president. Seip was ordained June 16, 1867, by the Ministerium of Pennsylvania but, declining a call to St. John's, Quakertown, he stayed on at the college as principal of its preparatory department. Muhlenberg College became the work of his life. Besides conducting the academy he acted as assistant professor of Greek, 1867–72, and also gave instruction, when necessary, in other subjects. He was professor of Latin, 1872–76, though still giving some instruction in Greek also; was financial

agent of the college from February 1876 till June 1877, collecting some $33,000 sorely needed to pay the debts and current expenses; was professor of Greek and Latin, 1877–80, and Mosser-Keck professor of Greek, 1880–85. During all these years he acted also as secretary of the faculty. On the retirement of John Philip Benjamin Sadtler [*q.v.*] as president at the close of 1885, Seip was elected to his place immediately and unanimously. He had worked loyally and indefatigably under its first two presidents in the long, chill spring of its early growth; his own administration of eighteen years was a period of increasing usefulness and efficiency. The chief problems were still financial, but they were no longer so pressing, and the college was able to assume an honorable place among institutions of its class. Seip's personal qualities made him an almost ideal president of a small college; there was no phase of the work with which he was not familiar, and his urbane, dignified, friendly bearing made friends for him and for Muhlenberg College wherever he was known. He was one of the founders in 1887 of the College Association of Pennsylvania and was president of the Ministerium of Pennsylvania, 1895–98. He was twice married: in 1866 to Emma Elizabeth Shimer of Bath, who died in 1873, leaving him with two sons and a daughter; and in 1877 to Rebecca Keck of Allentown. Music was his favorite recreation. He died at Allentown after a short illness. John August William Haas succeeded him as president of Muhlenberg College.

[*Who's Who in America*, 1903–05; biog. sketch by S. A. Ziegenfuss in S. E. Ochsenford, *Muhlenberg Coll.* (1892); E. S. Breidenbaugh, *The Pa. Coll. Book, 1832–82* (1882); L. D. Reed, *The Phila. Sem. Biog. Record, 1864–1923* (1923); *Pub. Ledger* (Phila.), Nov. 30, 1903.]   G. H. G.

SEISS, JOSEPH AUGUSTUS (Mar. 18, 1823–June 20, 1904), Lutheran clergyman, author, was born on his father's farm near Graceham, Frederick County, Md., of German stock, the eldest of the four sons of John and Eliza (Schuler) Seiss. The family name had originally been Süss. He attended the parochial school; received additional instruction in Latin, history, and the Bible from the pastor, Ambrose Rondthaler; and was confirmed at the age of sixteen in the Moravian Church. Neither his father nor his bishop, however, would allow the boy to study for the ministry. In later life Seiss was never known to take orders from anybody, and his ambition was not to be thwarted now. He left home and, with some assistance from a Lutheran clergyman, Reuben Weiser, betook himself to Gettysburg, Pa., where, for the next two years, he pursued a special course of study in Pennsylvania

College and its affiliated academy. He mastered the Greek Testament and evinced literary ability, but he was compelled to interrupt his studies and teach school for a living. At this juncture the Lutheran Synod of Virginia offered to license him if he would enter upon the work at once, and Seiss, not without misgivings, consented; he was licensed to preach when only nineteen years of age and was ordained two years later.

No other Lutheran clergyman in America has risen to prominence so early. After a year of missionary activity at Mount Sidney and Harrisonburg, Va., he was pastor from 1843 to 1847 at Martinsburg and Shepherdstown, Va. (now W. Va.), from 1847 to 1852 at Cumberland, Md., and from 1852 to 1858 at the Lombard Street Church in Baltimore. In 1843 he married Elizabeth Barnitz, who bore him two sons and three daughters, dying in 1900. His first book, *Popular Lectures on the Epistle to the Hebrews* (1846), was written while his coevals were still theological students, and his reputation as an eloquent preacher was already growing. While in Baltimore he published several other books, carried on a lively, urbane controversy with the Baptist clergyman, Richard Fuller [*q.v.*], and was elected president of the Lutheran Synod of Maryland. In 1858, when St. John's, Philadelphia, the largest English Lutheran congregation in America, sought a worthy successor to Philip Frederick Mayer [*q.v.*], Seiss was its unanimous choice. During his pastorate of sixteen years St. John's prospered despite its location in a decaying neighborhood. In 1864–65, during a period of ill health, he visited Europe and the Near East. Dissatisfied with the location of St. John's, he founded the Church of the Holy Communion at Broad and Arch Streets and was its pastor from 1874 until his death thirty years later.

He was dowered with an astounding capacity for work. One of the founders of the General Council of the Evangelical Lutheran Church in North America, he was its president in 1888 and one of its most active and influential leaders. He was the most admired preacher of his denomination and its most prolific author, his publications extending to more than one hundred separate titles, besides numerous contributions to periodicals. From 1867 to 1879 he was editor of the *Lutheran*. He was president of the board of directors of the Philadelphia Lutheran Theological Seminary from 1865 until his death, managing its affairs with great business acumen and unremitting attention to detail. Henry Eyster Jacobs considered him the chief instrument in establishing the Seminary. He was a close student of liturgics and hymnology. His various

publications in these fields are still useful, and the English *Church Book* of the General Council owes much to him both in substance and form. The same purity of language that made him a master of liturgical form is in evidence in his sermons. He considered the writing of each a work of art and labored to make it perfect. No one else has so influenced the style and content of English Lutheran preaching. His principal volumes of sermons are: *Lectures on the Gospels for the Sundays and Chief Festivals of the Church Year* (2 vols., 1868–72); *Lectures on the Epistles* (2 vols., 1885); *Lectures on the Gospels and Epistles for the Minor Festivals of the Church Year* (1893); *Beacon Lights* (1900); *The Christ and His Church* (1902); and *Recent Sermons* (1904). He was in his day a noted student of eschatology, and his *The Apocalypse: A Series of Special Lectures* (1865) went through many editions and was translated into German and Dutch.

Seiss had the great advantage that he not only worked, but looked, like a great man. He was tall and majestic in his carriage, with a leonine head, a magnificent voice, and equally magnificent manners. A certain arbitrariness in the exercise of his power and a reserve that amounted at times to coldness prevented him from becoming a popular leader. He was more admired and feared than loved, but he was loved. For several months before his death he was confined to his bed; a few weeks before the end he rose to affix his signature, still firm and bold, to the diplomas of the graduating class at the Philadelphia Seminary.

[G. W. Sandt, "Dr. Seiss Has Passed Away," *Lutheran*, June 23, 1904, and "Lutheran Leaders as I Knew Them: J. A. Seiss," *Lutheran Ch. Rev.*, Jan. 1918; G. F. Krotel, "Joseph Augustus Seiss, D.D., LL.D., L.H.D.," *Lutheran*, June 30, 1904; H. E. Jacobs, "Joseph Augustus Seiss," *Ibid.*, July 14, 21, 28, 1904, and "The Making of the Church Book," *Lutheran Ch. Rev.*, Oct. 1912; T. E. Schmauk, "The Death of Dr. Seiss," *Ibid.*, July 1904; J. C. Jensson (Roseland) *Am. Lutheran Biogs.* (1890); L. W. Johnston and F. A. Johnston, *Descendants of My Great-Grandparents* (1924); Adolph Spaeth, *Charles Porterfield Krauth* (1898–1909); E. E. Sibole, *Centennial . . . of Saint John's Church, Phila., 1806–1906* (copr. 1906); J. A. Seiss, *Bibliographica* (privately printed, 1887); *The Alumni Record of Gettysburg Coll., 1832–1932* (1932); L. D. Reed, ed., *The Phila. Sem. Biog. Record, 1864–1923* (1923); *Public Ledger* (Phila.), June 21, 1904.]
G. H. G.

SEIXAS, GERSHOM MENDES (Jan. 15, 1746–July 2, 1816), rabbi, was born in New York City, the son of Isaac Mendez Seixas and Rachel Levy. His father, a native of Lisbon, emigrated to New York in 1730 and established himself in a mercantile business; about 1765 he moved to Newport, R. I., where he resided until his death in 1780. On July 3, 1768, Gershom was chosen as rabbi of Shearith Israel, the Spanish and Portuguese synagogue of New York. His salary was fixed at eighty pounds annually plus a house, firewood, and perquisites. In 1775 he asked for £140 annually and offered to resign if his request were not granted. As a result his salary was raised to that amount, and in 1784 was increased to £200. He contrived on this income to raise two considerable families: by his first wife, Elkaly Cohen, whom he married on Sept. 6, 1775, and who died in 1785, he had four children; by his second, Hannah Manuel, whom he married Nov. 1, 1789, he had eleven.

As rabbi Seixas performed for the Jewish community of New York (and occasionally, somewhat in the manner of a circuit rider, for coreligionists in nearby regions) all the important religious ceremonies. He was for many years the community's chief professor of Hebrew language, literature, and laws. In addition, through a great portion of his fifty-year ministry he was one of the chief spokesmen of American Jewry and recognized as its representative by American society as a whole. His life in New York was interrupted in August 1776, when he quit the city in company with a considerable number of his congregation prior to its investment by the British forces. Most of the evacuating Jews went to Philadelphia, where Seixas joined them after four years in Stratford, Conn., bringing with him the congregation's sacred Scrolls of the Law. In Philadelphia he helped found a new synagogue, Mickve Israel, and served as its rabbi for two years, returning to New York in 1784.

Seixas was, apparently, strictly orthodox in religious principle. The first rabbi to preach sermons in English in an American synagogue, he constantly advocated the new democratic doctrine of full participation by Jews in the life of the state. His Revolutionary patriotism, his appeals (e.g., on the occasion of British-Indian raids on the Northwest Territory in 1813) to his flock to "support the country in its position at all hazards, because . . . it is sufficient for us to know that our rulers are chosen to be Judges on all affairs . . ." (quoted in *Jewish Comment*, Jan. 10, 1902), and the tone of his public prayer for the safety of the state and its rulers illustrate his views of the duty of the Jews in the new democratic régime. On the other hand, he made it plain that the obligation was reciprocal; when the council of censors of Pennsylvania made eligibility to an Assembly seat dependent on recognition of divine origin of the New Testament, Seixas and two other Jews protested formally against an unconstitutional religious test

which was "unjust to the members of a persuasion that had always been attached to the American cause" (Westcott, *post*, p. xxxii). At least two of his sermons were published: *Religious Discourse, Delivered in the Synagogue . . . the 26th November 1789, Agreeable to the Proclamation of the President . . . to be Observed as a Day of Public Thanksgiving* (1789), said to have been one of the first national Thanksgiving sermons preached; and *A Discourse Delivered . . . on the Ninth of May 1798, Observed as a Day of Humiliation* (1798).

Seixas was in fairly frequent communication with Jewish communities and individuals in other parts of the Americas and in Europe. He consulted with the *Beth Din* (Court of Judgment) of the London synagogue on religious problems, helped raise building funds for synagogues in other cities, and supplied David Ottensoser with Americana for his *Geschichte der Jehudim* (Fuerth, 1821). He founded the still extant Hebra Hased Va-Amet, one of New York's earliest charitable organizations and, from 1784 to 1815, when he resigned, served as regent and trustee of Columbia College. Seixas seems to have exchanged pulpits on occasion with other New York clergymen, as, for example, in August 1800, when he addressed the congregation of St. Paul's. He also participated in public "exegetical disquisitions" with prominent Gentile Hebraists. He was buried in the New Bowery cemetery of Shearith Israel Congregation.

[The chief sources for the life of Seixas are manuscript documents in the archives of the Congregation Shearith Israel, N. Y. City, and of the Am. Jewish Hist. Soc.; a considerable number of the latter are printed in its *Publications* of 1896, 1913, 1914, 1920, 1926; see also L. Hühner, "The Patriot Jewish Minister of the Am. Revolution," in *Jewish Comment* (Baltimore), Jan. 10, 1902; Thompson Westcott, *Names of Persons Who Took the Oath of Allegiance to the State of Pa. . . . with a Hist. of the "Test Laws" of Pa.* (1865); *Jewish Encyc.*, vol. XI; Jacob La Motta, *Funeral Address . . . Previous to the Interment . . . of the Rev. Gershom M. Seixas* (1816); Naphtali Phillips, *An Eulogium to the Memory of the Rev. Gershom M. Seixas* (1816); H. S. Morais, *The Jews of Phila.* (1894); *N. Y. Evening Post*, July 2, 1816.]   H. S.

SÉJOUR, VICTOR (June 2, 1817–Sept. 21, 1874), dramatist, was born in New Orleans, La. He was christened Juan Victor Séjour Marcou et Ferrand and was the illegitimate son of François Marcou, a free man of color from Santo Domingo, and Eloisa Phillipe Ferrand, a quadroon of New Orleans. His parents were married afterwards in 1825. François owned and ran a dry-cleaning establishment on Chartres Street in New Orleans and was sufficiently well-off to send his son to the Ste. Barbe Academy conducted by Michel Seligny, an intelligent and well-educated colored man. Victor showed an early interest in literature and when only seventeen read one of his poems in French before a meeting of La Société des Artisans, a social and benevolent association of the Creole mulattoes. Soon after this his family sent him to a college in Paris. When he left it he continued to live in France and made his début as an author with an heroic poem, *Le Retour de Napoléon,* published in 1841. It was so well received that he was welcomed in literary circles and came to know both Alexandre Dumas and Émile Augier, the distinguished French playwright.

His association with Augier turned his attention to the stage, and his first play, *Diégarias* was produced in the Théâtre Français in 1844. It was followed in 1849 by *La Chute de Séjan,* probably an adaptation of Ben Jonson's *Sejanus.* These early dramas of Séjour's were in heroic grandiose verse bristling with pompous, sonorous phrases. Those which followed were more frankly melodramatic. In all, there were twenty-one of his plays produced in Paris; two of them were written in collaboration with Théodore Barrière, and one each with Jules Brésil and Adolphe Jaime, the younger. His greatest successes were *Richard III,* 1852; *Les Noces Vénitiennes,* 1855; *Le Fils de la Nuit,* 1856; *Les Grands Vassaux,* 1859; *Les Fils de Charles Quint,* 1864, and *Les Volontaires de 1814,* 1862, the only work based upon an American theme, that of the brave defenders of New Orleans against the English. All of these were published within a year or two of their production. An insatiable reader of Shakespeare and Victor Hugo, he frankly acknowledged that the greatest source of his inspiration came from them. He had a thorough knowledge of stage direction and was so conscientious a craftsman that he tried to improve his plays until the very last minute, even going so far as to hand little memorandum slips with changes in lines to the actors on first nights as they went on the stage. During the initial performance of *Le Fils de la Nuit,* after the first four acts had been played, he rehearsed during the intermission an entirely new version of the last act. For some time all Paris flocked to his opening nights. The spectacular magnificence of his settings and the sumptuousness of the costumes struck the fancy of the populace which secretly regretted the pageantry and heroics of the first Napoleon, and Séjour's plays became successful in spite of the hollow ring of his pretentious dialogue. Unfortunately, however, popular taste changed, and the grandiose spectacles, which were all he knew how to produce, lost favor. He fell on evil days and was

forced to hawk about from manager to manager his two plays, *Cromwell* and *Le Vampire,* the latter a great fantastic drama. After a heartbreaking experience, for a man who had once had all Paris at his feet, *Le Vampire* was accepted by the Gaîté, but before the play could be produced he was taken to the charity ward of a hospital in Paris, where he died of galloping consumption, the result of the privations he had suffered during his penniless days. He was buried in the cemetery of Père-Lachaise.

[E. L. Tinker, *Les Écrits de Langue Française en Louisiane au XIXe Siècle* (Paris, 1932), with bibliog.; R. L. Desdunes, *Nos Hommes et Notre Histoire* (Montreal, 1911); Pierre Larousse, *Grand Dictionnaire Universel du XIXe Siècle* (17 vols., 1866–90); Gustave Vapereau, *Dictionnaire Universel des Contemporains* (1880); *Lib. of Southern Lit.,* vol. XV (copr. 1910), ed. by L. L. Knight; J. W. Davidson, *The Living Writers of the South* (1869); *Le Gaulois* (Paris), Sept. 22, and *Figaro* (Paris), Sept. 24, 25, 1874; death notice in *Le Soleil* (Paris), Sept. 23, 1874.]   E. L. T.

SELBY, WILLIAM (1739?–December 1798), musician and composer, was probably born in England. Little is known of his early life and the date of his birth must be conjectured from the death notice in the *Columbian Centinel* (Boston) Dec. 12, 1798, which gives his age as fifty-nine. His first appearance in Boston was recorded in a concert advertisement of Oct. 4, 1771, for it was undoubtedly he who was announced as "a gentleman lately arrived from London." O. G. Sonneck (see *Early Concert-Life, post,* p. 262) believed that he was also identical with the William Selby, who, as organist of St. Sepulchre's, played the organ at an anniversary of the Charity School, London, in 1767. By 1772 Selby was acting as organist of King's Chapel in Boston and participating in concerts as an organist and harpsichordist. For a short time in 1774 he played the organ at Trinity Church in Newport, R. I., and in the same city he announced his intention of opening a dancing school. The latter project may or may not have been responsible for his leaving Newport, but in any case he returned to Boston, and by 1777 was again organist at King's Chapel. During the Revolution Selby was forced to seek other fields than music for a livelihood, and in 1780 he kept a small shop, but by October 1782, he is again mentioned as organist at King's Chapel, and once more became active in the musical life of Boston.

Selby was chiefly interested in instrumental music before the war, but he now became engaged in what proved to be his most important contribution to the musical future of Boston, the development of choral singing. He was undoubtedly of great influence in the movement which led to the organization of the Handel and Haydn Society more than fifteen years after his death. While his predecessors had been content with the singing of hymns and anthems, Selby led his singers in the study of cantatas and oratorios as is evidenced particularly by three of the concerts organized and directed by him. The first of these, given on Apr. 30, 1782, advertised a program of "Musica Spiritualis" and contained works by Handel, Arne, and other composers of the period. On Jan. 10, 1786, the Musical Society of Boston (presumably founded by Selby in 1785) offered a concert for the benefit of the prisons. The program consisted of selections from Handel's *Messiah,* an overture by Bach, and works by Selby himself. The third concert, given on Jan. 16, 1887, presented works of Handel, Piccini, and more compositions by Selby. He composed "Ode in Honour of General Washington" which was performed at a concert given for his benefit by the Musical Society on Apr. 27, 1786, and when Washington visited Boston in 1789, the concerts arranged in his honor featured more of Selby's works.

Practically the only compositions by Selby that are extant today are a few songs, some of which are printed in the *Massachusetts Magazine:* "On Musick," April 1789; "The Rural Retreat," October 1789; "Ode for the New Year," January 1790; "The Lovely Lass," July 1790. These songs were later reprinted in the *American Musical Miscellany* (1798), and another, "Ptalæmon to Pastora," appeared in *The Gentlemen and Ladies Town and Country Magazine,* March 1789. Two major works were advertised for subscription in 1782 and 1790, but no record has been found of actual publication: "The New Minstrel," a collection of original compositions, one number to be issued every month, and "Apollo, and the Muse's Musical Compositions," a collection of sacred and secular songs and choruses, as well as instrumental pieces. In addition to these works, the organ and harpsichord concertos which Selby played on concert programs were presumably of his own composition. He was married in Boston on Jan. 7, 1792, to Susannah Parker, who survived him.

[O. G. Sonneck, *Early Concert-Life in America* (1907), and *Bibliog. of Early Secular Am. Music* (1905); J. T. Howard, *Our Am. Music* (1931); *Grove's Dict. of Music and Musicians, Am. Supp.* (1930); *A Vol. of Records . . . containing Boston Marriages* (1903); *Continental Jour.* (Boston), Jan. 13, 1780.]
J. T. H.

SELDEN, GEORGE BALDWIN (Sept. 14, 1846–Jan. 17, 1922), patent attorney, inventor, son of Henry Rogers and Laura Anne (Baldwin) Selden, was born in Clarkson, N. Y. He was of English ancestry, seventh in descent from Thomas Selden who was in Hartford, Conn., in 1639. His father was an able lawyer, lieutenant-governor of New York in 1856 and judge of the court of appeals for two terms in the sixties. After young Selden had attended the local schools and St. Albans (Vt.) Classical Preparatory School, he went to the University of Rochester, 1861–64, his parents having moved to Rochester in 1859, but he did not finish his course. He is said to have enlisted in the 6th New York Cavalry at the beginning of the Civil War. In 1865 he entered Yale College as a classical student. Since he was interested in engineering and technology he found classical studies irksome and therefore welcomed, in a way, a call to go to his father, who had become seriously ill while traveling in Europe. Returning to the United States in 1867, he entered the Sheffield Scientific School for a few months but once more went to Rochester, entered the law offices of his father and uncle, studied law for three years, and in 1871 was admitted to the bar.

Being particularly interested in mechanical subjects, he specialized in patent law, handling the occasional invention and patent litigation cases his father obtained. This was hardly enough, however, to satisfy his interest in technology, and as fast as he could afford it he equipped a shop of his own for experimental work. From his youth he had been interested in mechanical transport on roads, particularly in self-propelled vehicles; he now began a series of investigations on road traction and on the various power agencies. By 1873 he had abandoned steam as the power for a road locomotive, and he began the study of engines using liquid and gaseous fuels. Having a family to support and very little money, he progressed slowly, but in 1875 he had built an engine, which turned out to be unsuccessful, operated by the expanded products of combustion of a mixture of kerosene and laughing-gas. Meanwhile he had engaged in other inventive work, especially in the design of machinery to prepare barrel hoops, and in 1875 he obtained a patent for a machine for shaving half-round hoops; he secured three patents for improvements in 1876 and two more in 1877, all of which he sold at a meager profit. He continued his work on a self-propelled vehicle, especially after 1876, when he came to the conclusion that the type of internal combustion engine best suited to his purpose was one invented by George Brayton in 1872 and 1874 using hydrocarbon liquid fuels. The Brayton engine was a very heavy two-cycle stationary design with an open crankcase. Selden reduced its weight by inclosing the crankcase, increased its power by changing the manner of furnishing fuel to the cylinders, and by 1877 had made a light-weight, high-speed, three-cylinder gasoline compression engine of the Brayton type. He then designed a road-locomotive, virtually an automobile, which combined an engine, running gear, driving wheels, propeller-shaft and clutch, and a carriage body, and on May 8, 1879, applied for a patent. For years he tried without success to secure financial help so that he could build a machine in accordance with his design. Appreciating that he was ahead of his time and acting wholly within his rights, he delayed the issue of a patent to him until Nov. 5, 1895, sixteen years later, when he was granted patent No. 549,160 for a "road engine."

Meanwhile the automobile had made rapid strides, and on Nov. 4, 1899, Selden sold the rights to his patent on a royalty basis to W. C. Whitney of the Columbia Motor Company and Electric Vehicle Company of New Jersey. In 1900 the Electric Vehicle Company successfully brought suit for infringement of the Selden patent against the Winton Motor Carriage Company (104 *Federal Reporter*, 814). As a result nine other automobile makers banded together as the Association of Licensed Automobile Manufacturers and purchased the right to use the Selden patent at a royalty of 1¼ per cent. of the retail price of all automobiles sold. By 1906 Selden was receiving royalties from almost all of the automobile manufacturers in the United States and was able to organize his own company in Rochester, the Selden Motor Vehicle Company. In 1903 he and the Columbia Motor Company instituted an infringement suit against the New York agents of the Ford Motor Company, which had refused to pay royalties. In September 1909, after many delays, the case was argued before the United States circuit court of the southern district of New York, and again the Selden patent was sustained (*Electric Vehicle Company* vs. *C. A. Duerr & Company*, 172 *Federal Reporter*, 923). The Ford Motor Company took an appeal, and on Jan. 11, 1911, a written decision was handed down that Selden had a valid and true patent but that the defendants were not guilty of infringement because they were using the Otto four-cycle type of engine and not the Brayton two-cycle type designated in the patent (*Columbia Motor Car Company* vs. *C. A. Duerr & Company*, 184 *Federal Reporter*, 893). Inasmuch as all manufacturers were using the Otto type of engine this was a far-reaching victory for the automobile industry. Although the patent had but a few

months more to run, Selden's royalties stopped at once. He then turned to his own automobile business, but unfortunately he was a more successful lawyer and inventor than manufacturer and lost heavily in the venture. On Dec. 14, 1871, he had married Clara Drake Woodruff of Rochester, who died in 1903; in April 1909 he married Jean Shipley. At the time of his death in Rochester he was survived by his wife, two sons, and two daughters.

[S. S. Rogers, E. S. Lane, and E. V. D. Selden, *Selden Ancestry* (copr. 1931); *Hist. of the Class of 1868 of Yale Coll.* (1914); J. R. Doolittle, ed., *The Romance of the Automobile Industry* (1916), pp. 15–16, 55–71; L. H. Weeks, *Automobile Biogs.* (copr. 1904); Leroy Scott, "Selden's Explosion Buggy," *Tech. World Mag.*, Sept. 1906; *Motor Age*, Jan. 12, 1911, on the Ford-Selden case; T. F. MacManus and Norman Beasley, *Men, Money and Motors* (1929); U. S. Nat. Museum records; Patent Office records; obituary in *Democrat and Chronicle* (Rochester, N. Y.), Jan. 19, 1922; correspondence with family.]

C. W. M.

SELFRIDGE, THOMAS OLIVER (Feb. 6, 1836–Feb. 4, 1924), naval officer, the son of Rear Admiral Thomas Oliver Selfridge and Louisa Cary (Soley) Selfridge, was born in Charlestown, Mass. His great-great-grandfather, Edward A. Selfridge, had emigrated to Massachusetts from Scotland in the early part of the eighteenth century. He was appointed to the United States Naval Academy from Massachusetts on Oct. 3, 1851, as acting midshipman, and was graduated at the head of his class in 1854. He was promoted successively to the rank of passed midshipman in 1856, master in 1858, and lieutenant in 1860. His first sea duty was on the *Independence* in the South Pacific, from whence, after a short period spent in coast survey work, he was transferred to the *Vincennes* of the African Squadron, to assist in the suppression of the slave trade. He returned to the United States early in 1860, being assigned to the sloop-of-war *Cumberland* the following September. On this ship he was present at the destruction of the Norfolk navy yard in April 1861, and participated in the bombardment and capture of the forts at Hatteras Inlet. In the famous engagement between the *Cumberland* and the iron-clad *Merrimac*, Selfridge was in command of the forward gun-battery, and in this position bore the brunt of the *Merrimac's* raking fire, saving himself only as the *Cumberland* sank with her flag flying. A vivid account of this battle is given by Selfridge in his *Memoirs*, published in 1924. In June 1862 he was assigned to the torpedo boat *Alligator*, the first submarine to be tried out in the Civil War, but this craft proved to be a failure because of her lack of speed and insufficient ventilation. Promoted to the rank of lieutenant commander in July 1862, he was at once sent to the Mississippi Squadron and given command of the gunboat *Cairo,* operating against Vicksburg. This vessel was blown up by a torpedo in December, whereupon he was ordered to the *Conestoga.* During the siege of Vicksburg he commanded a shore battery of naval guns. After the surrender he commanded a flotilla of gunboats with the *Conestoga* as flagship, and succeeded in capturing the Confederate steamers *Louisville* and *Elmira.* When the *Conestoga* was sunk by collision in March 1864 he was ordered to command the *Osage,* and participated in the Red River expedition, supporting General Banks's command. He assisted in the construction of the famous Red River dam, and commanded the entire fleet in the passage of the dam.

When Admiral Porter was transferred to the East, he selected Selfridge to accompany him, giving him command of the gunboat *Huron,* in which he took part in both attacks on Fort Fisher. In the second attack he commanded a landing party of bluejackets and marines in an assault on the fort. He was recommended for a promotion of thirty numbers on the navy list for his conspicuous gallantry during the war, but the recommendation was never acted upon by Congress. In 1869 he was commissioned commander and ordered to conduct a survey of the Isthmus of Darien for an interoceanic canal. He explored all the country south of Panama to the headwaters of the Atrato River in South America and drew up a report which was published in 1874. Four years later he was selected to survey the Amazon and Madeira Rivers, and the following year was invited by Ferdinand de Lesseps to attend a congress on interoceanic canals, meeting in Paris. For his work on the Darien survey he was given the decoration of the Legion of Honor of France, and made an honorary member of the Royal Geographical Society of Belgium. In 1881 he was commissioned captain and given command of the Naval Torpedo Station at Newport, R. I., where he conducted numerous experiments with torpedoes and torpedo-nets. He was court-martialled in 1888 for conducting target practice in Japanese territorial waters, but was acquitted. In 1894 he was commissioned commodore and in 1896 rear admiral. As special representative of the United States he was present at the coronation of Tsar Nicholas II of Russia in 1896. He was married to Ellen F. Shepley in August 1865, and had four sons by this marriage. She died in 1905, and in 1907 he married Gertrude Wildes,

who survived him. After his retirement in 1898, he resided in Washington, D. C.

[*Who's Who in America,* 1922–23; *Memoirs of Thomas O. Selfridge, Jr.* (1924); L. R. Hamersly, *The Records of Living Officers of the U. S. Navy and Marine Corps* (6th ed., 1898); *Argument of Linden Kent . . . in behalf of Capt. T. O. Selfridge, . . . June 8, 1888* (n.d.); Cyril Field, *The Story of the Submarine* (1908); *Army and Navy Jour.,* Feb. 16, 1924; Lucien Young, *Cat. of Works by Am. Naval Authors* (1888); *Evening Star* (Washington, D. C.), Feb. 5, 1924.]

L. H. B.

SELIGMAN, ARTHUR (June 14, 1871–Sept. 25, 1933), merchant, banker, governor of New Mexico, was born at Sante Fé, N. Mex., the oldest of four children of Bernard and Frances (Nusbaum) Seligman. By both parents he was of German-Jewish stock. His father emigrated to Philadelphia from Frankfort-on-the-Main, where he had been employed in the Rothschild banking house. In 1856, however, he followed an older brother, Sigmund, to Santa Fé, and there in 1862 the mercantile house of Seligman & Clever became "Seligman Bros.," a trade name which was to endure for over sixty years. The mother was of a mercantile family in Harrisburg, Pa.

Arthur studied with private tutors, at Swarthmore College Preparatory School (1887), and at the Pierce business college, Philadelphia. Late in 1888 he began his career as a merchant in Santa Fé. On July 4, 1896, he married Frankie E. Harris of Cleveland, Ohio, by whom he had a son and a daughter. From the year of his father's death (1903) to 1926 he was president of Seligman Bros. He early acquired stock in the First National Bank of Santa Fé, and helped to make it the most important banking house between Denver and El Paso. He was long a director and its president from 1924. From boyhood he was keenly interested in the various forms of Indian and Spanish-American handicraft, and all his life he was a collector, especially of Navajo blankets, *santos,* and paintings by Southwestern artists.

He had his first taste of politics as a youth, campaigning with his father. His own political career was notable for the fact that of the many positions of honor and responsibility in which he served from 1888 to 1933 only two were salaried offices. As mayor of Santa Fé (1910–12) he was able and public spirited, and his long and distinguished service to the Democratic party in state and nation was crowned in 1930 by his election as governor of New Mexico, and his reëlection in 1932. Although he always voted the straight ticket, his closest advisers in legislative matters were both conservative and progressive Republicans. During periods of Republican dominance in the state, the healthful and constructive opposition was due in large measure to him. "To many . . . his reliance on men of opposite partisan opinion seemed inconsistent, but results proved it excellent generalship" (*New Mexico Historical Review, post,* p. 311). In an editorial of the *Santa Fe New Mexican,* Sept. 26, 1933, he was characterized as "an able business executive, with tremendous capacity for work; . . . a shrewd, resourceful political manager . . . a man of unruffled temper who took defeat or victory alike calmly; an inveterate politician, who loved the political battle of wits and strategy, and whose poker political face kept the opposition uneasy through many a campaign. . . . He ofttimes exasperated by Fabian tactics and indirection, and played his cards close to the chest." Becoming governor at a time when questions of taxation and revenue made the position a difficult one, he succeeded in keeping expenditures within the state income; he acknowledged to his intimates, however, that taxes would have to be increased to give the people what they wanted. On the other hand, he doubted the wisdom of the vast sums appropriated by the federal government, realizing that the money must eventually come out of the pockets of the tax payers.

Suave, fastidious in dress, aristocratic in taste but democratic in policy, always prominent in social life, he sought and attained a large measure of power through business and political channels. Intensely loyal to his numerous friends and an enemy to be feared, for more than a quarter of a century he had few peers in Democratic circles of the Southwest. The strong position of the Democratic party in New Mexico at the time of his death was largely due to his long, shrewd, and able leadership. He was connected with no church or synagogue; was a life member of the Historical Society of New Mexico; and, from 1920, a member of the Democratic national committee.

[R. E. Twitchell, *Old Santa Fe* (1925); P. A. F. Walter, "Arthur Seligman," in *N. Mex. Hist. Rev.,* Oct. 1933; *Who's Who in America,* 1932–33; *Santa Fe New Mexican,* Sept. 25–28, 1933; personal acquaintance.]
L. B. B.

SELIGMAN, ISAAC NEWTON (July 10, 1855–Sept. 30, 1917), banker and civic leader, born in Staten Island, N. Y., was a son of Joseph Seligman [*q.v.*] and Babette (Steinhardt) Seligman. As a small boy he was tutored by Horatio Alger, Jr.; later he attended Columbia Grammar School and Columbia College, where he was active in the college crew. He graduated with honor in 1876, and became a loyal member of the Alumni Association. His business career began in the New Orleans branch of the international banking house of J. & W. Seligman & Company, which his father had founded. He was transferred to the New York office in 1878, two years before his father died. On the death of his uncle, Jesse Seligman [*q.v.*], in 1894, he became the head of the house. During his membership the firm maintained United States government connections and was particularly interested in the flotation of loans for Venezuela and the financial rehabilitation of that country, and in loans for other countries of Central and South America and the Orient. Under Isaac Seligman's leadership the firm also had charge of the reorganization of several important American railroads, including the Pere Marquette, and of the American Steel & Wire Company and the Cramp Steamship Company. He was very active in municipal political reform movements, particularly in the Citizens' Union (of which he was treasurer for years), interested himself greatly in civil service reform, and was vice-president of the New York Chamber of Commerce and chairman of its committee on taxation. He was one of the founders of the Child Labor Association. For years he served as treasurer of the City and Suburban Homes Company, which became the principal model tenement-house enterprise of the city. He also served as a member of the Committee of Fourteen and later of the Committee of Seven, which sought to remedy the social evil, and was head of the Civic Forum and vice-president of the People's Institute. He was a vice-president of the United Hebrew Charities, an officer of St. John's Guild, and a trustee of Temple Emanu-El. The public became so accustomed to seeing him figure as treasurer of enterprises involving the raising of funds for important civic and charitable purposes that the absence of his name in such connection in any particular instance became a cause for comment. Governor Morton appointed him a trustee of the Manhattan Hospital for the Insane and Governor Theodore Roosevelt reappointed him. He was deeply interested in music, and was a trustee of the New York Symphony Society and of the New York Oratorio Society, and a founder of the Institute of Musical Art. On Nov. 18, 1883, he married Guta Loeb, a daughter of Solomon Loeb of the banking firm of Kuhn, Loeb & Company. Four children were born of this marriage: two daughters who died young and a son and a daughter who survived their father. His death, in New York, resulted from a fractured skull, sustained in a fall from his horse.

[H. S. Mott, in *N. Y. Geneal. and Biog. Record*, Oct. 1918; *Am. Jewish Hist. Soc. Pubs.*, no. 28 (1922); G. S. Hellman, *The Family Reg. of the Descendants of David Seligman* (1913); *Who's Who in America*, 1916-17; *N. Y. Times*, Oct. 1, 1917.]   M. J. K.

SELIGMAN, JESSE (Aug. 11, 1827–Apr. 23, 1894), banker and philanthropist, was born at Baiersdorf, Bavaria, a son of David and Fanny (Steinhardt) Seligman and a younger brother of Joseph Seligman [*q.v.*]. After graduating from the Gymnasium at Erlangen, he joined his brothers in the United States in 1841, spending some years in Alabama with several of them and in 1848, with his brother Henry, moving to Watertown, N. Y. Here they opened a dry-goods store and Jesse became intimate with U. S. Grant, a friendship which was later renewed in California. In 1850, a year after the beginning of the gold rush, Jesse and his brother Leopold went to San Francisco with a supply of merchandise and established what rapidly became a very lucrative business. Jesse Seligman showed his good judgment by selecting as his store the only brick building in the town, with the result that his business was the only one which escaped in the fire of May 1851. He was an active member of the San Francisco Vigilance Committee (see Mary F. Williams, *History of the San Francisco Committee of Vigilance of 1851*, 1921, p. 443) and became a member of the famous San Francisco Committee of Twenty-one, which in 1857 effected the election to both municipal and state offices of candidates pledged to clean and honest government.

In that same year he moved to New York City and became an active member of the importing and clothing firm of which his brother Joseph was the head. He brought a large sum accumulated in California as his contribution to this enterprise and to its successor, the banking firm organized in 1862 under the style of J. & W. Seligman & Company. From the beginning of the banking venture he was an important factor in the main office in New York City, and after the death of Joseph Seligman in 1880, he became head of the firm, continuing in that capacity until he died. During this period the firm became particularly active in flotations of railway securities in the South and Southwest; it also headed the American Syndicate that placed the Panama Canal shares and served as a fiscal agent for the United States government.

Jesse Seligman was a vice-president of the Union League Club of New York for many years, but resigned in 1893 when his son was blackballed because of his race. He was influential in the civic and philanthropic life of New York, and at the time of his death it was said in newspaper obituaries that he had twice declined the Republican nomination for mayor. He served for several decades before his death as president of the Hebrew Benevolent and Orphan Asylum of New York City, and was selected by Baron de Hirsch in 1891 as an original member of the Board of Trustees of the Baron de Hirsch Fund, but his philanthropies were not limited by race or creed. He enjoyed the confidence and esteem of President Grant and several of his successors and their advisers, and was for a generation one of the leading financiers of the country. Seligman married in Munich, Oct. 18, 1854, Henrietta Hellman, who with six of their seven children survived him. He died at Coronado, Cal.

[*In Memoriam: Jesse Seligman* (1894), which includes an autobiographical address giving an interesting account of the family's early experiences in America, delivered at a banquet tendered to him Oct. 1, 1891, to celebrate the fiftieth anniversary of his arrival in America; G. S. Hellman, *The Family Reg. of the Descendants of David Seligman* (1913); *The Jewish Encyc.* (1905), vol. XI; *World* (N. Y.), Apr. 24, 1894.]   M. J. K.

SELIGMAN, JOSEPH (Nov. 22, 1819–Apr. 25, 1880), financier and civic leader, a native of Baiersdorf, Bavaria, was the eldest in the family of eight sons and three daughters born to David and Fanny (Steinhardt) Seligman. He graduated from the Gymnasium of Erlangen and began the study of medicine but, dissatisfied with the lack of opportunities for Jews in Germany, emigrated to the United States in 1837. For some time he was secretary to the Pennsylvania financier Asa Packer [*q.v.*]. As his means permitted, he sent for all seven of his brothers, to whom he bore almost a paternal relationship. William and James arrived in 1839 and engaged in business with him at Lancaster, Pa. Jesse [*q.v.*] came over in 1841, and Henry, Leopold, Abraham, and Isaac soon followed. The elder brothers started a small dry-goods business in Alabama, but in 1848 they moved north, and Joseph, William, and James became clothing merchants in New York City. By 1857 all the brothers had united their capital under Joseph's leadership in a New York clothing and importing firm. They paid for their European purchases with gold bar exported from California under the supervision of Henry Seligman, who had gone to San Francisco during the gold rush and remained there. Joseph's standing in New York City within the next few years was marked by his choice as a vice-president of a huge Union mass meeting in New York City, Apr. 20, 1861, and his election as president of the German Hebrew Orphan Asylum. From a letter of his, Jan. 24, 1862 (MS., Treasury Department, Washington), it appears that the government then owed the Seligmans a million dollars for clothing supplied to the army.

Early in 1862 the clothing firm was transformed into the international banking house of J. & W. Seligman & Company, with its chief office in New York City. Branches were opened soon afterwards in Frankfurt-am-Main, London, Paris, San Francisco, and New Orleans, each in charge of one or more of the brothers, with Joseph as the head of the firm. The Frankfurt branch, Seligman & Stettheimer, organized by Joseph himself in 1862 and left in charge of his brothers Henry and Abraham as resident partners, was able to render particularly valuable service to the Union cause during the Civil War. United States bonds amounting to approximately $200,000,000 were sold in Frankfurt during this trying period, largely through its agency. These sales have been characterized as scarcely less important than the Union victory at Gettysburg (W. E. Dodd, *Robert J. Walker*, 1914), since at that time it was almost impossible to sell a United States bond in English or French markets (Hugh McCulloch, *Men and Measures of Half a Century*, 1888, pp. 183–84). Doubtless in appreciation of its services, on Feb. 28, 1871, the Frankfurt house was appointed fiscal agent of the United States government in connection with the conversion of the 5–20's to new 5% bonds. The New York and London houses were given similar status soon afterwards, and they also acted for years as fiscal agents for the State and Navy departments. The Frankfurt and London houses were members of the Jay Cooke syndicate which entered into the contract of Aug. 11, 1871, with Secretary Boutwell for the conversion of $130,000,000 in 5–20's from 6% to 5% after the effort in the preceding February had failed. Members of the Seligman firm had become intimate with U. S. Grant prior to 1850 and again in California in the decade before the Civil War; after Grant became president, Joseph Seligman was one of his confidential financial advisers, notably at a memorable New York conference on Sept. 21, 1873, in the midst of the panic of that year. President Grant tendered him the post of Secretary of the Treasury, but he declined it for personal reasons.

While the refunding operations of the seventies were under consideration, after the failure of Jay Cooke & Company the Secretary of the Treasury summoned Seligman and other leading financiers to Washington to advise him as to the best method of reducing the government's interest payments and paving the way for the resumption of specie payments. Each financier was requested to prepare separately his proposed plan for immediate submission to the Secretary. The following day, the Secretary announced that he had selected the Seligman firm to execute the plan, and they induced the Rothschilds to join in the undertaking (information furnished by Prof. Edwin R. A. Seligman). The contract of July 28, 1874, with Secretary Bristow, covering a $55,000,000 conversion with an option for $122,000,000 more confirms this story. The firm also figured prominently in five other conversion contracts, 1875–79, and during much of this period Joseph Seligman was recognized as practically the mouthpiece of the Treasury (*John Sherman's Recollections of Forty Years*, 1895, I, 570).

Seligman served for a number of years as a vice-president of the Union League Club of New York. He was an active member of the Committee of Seventy which ousted the "Tweed ring" from control of the city (*New York Times Supplement*, Sept. 5, 1871). He was appointed by Mayor Wickham as one of the five commissioners on rapid transit for New York City and was elected chairman by this commission, which laid out the New York elevated railroad system in its report of Sept. 2, 1875, and organized the Manhattan Railway Company (J. B. Walker, *Fifty Years of Rapid Transit*, 1918, pp. 107 ff.). In 1876 he became one of the chief organizers of the Society for Ethical Culture, with Prof. Felix Adler as its leader, interesting himself particularly in its industrial school. He had served previously, 1873–75, as an active member of the New York Board of Education. He was active in a large number of charitable and financial organizations, and for some years before his sudden death in New Orleans was regarded as the leading Jew in the United States. On Oct. 26, 1848, he had married Babette Steinhardt, who with all their children—four daughters and five sons—survived him.

[Joseph Jacobs in *The Jewish Encyc.* (1905), vol. XI; *In Memoriam: Jesse Seligman* (1894); *Reminiscences of Isaac Seligman of London* (privately printed, 1926); family letters of Joseph Seligman in possession of G. S. Hellman; Isaac Markens, *The Hebrews in America* (1888), pp. 141–42, 174; *N. Y. Times, N. Y. Herald, N. Y. Tribune*, Apr. 27, 1880; *The Family Reg. of the Descendants of David Seligman* (1913), ed. by G. S. Hellman; Georg von Skal, *Hist. of German Immigration to the U. S.* (1908), pp. 61–62.]   M. J. K.

SELIJNS, HENRICUS (1636–1701), Dutch Reformed clergyman, was the son of Jan Selijns Hendrickszoon and Janneken de Marees. He came from a good Amsterdam family which gave several ministers to the Church, received a brief, but apparently thorough, training for the ministry at the University of Leyden, and was the most cultured of all the Dutch preachers who came to New Netherland in the seventeenth century. When the *Deputati ad Res Indicas* of the Amsterdam Classis chose him from among three candidates for the ministry in New Netherland, his knowledge of English, rather uncommon at that time among the Dutch, was one of the qualifications that recommended him. He was ordained Feb. 16, 1660, and reached New Amsterdam on June 11 of that year. He had been promised a salary of 1,200 guilders, but found on arrival that no funds were available. The congregation at Breuckelen (Brooklyn) could not pay more than 300 guilders' worth in grain, to which Governor Stuyvesant offered to add 250 guilders on condition that Selijns preach every Sunday evening in the chapel on his Bouwerie. In a letter to the Amsterdam Classis, dated Oct. 4, 1660 (*Ecclesiastical Records, post*, I, 487–89), Selijns gave an account of his work and the conditions at Breuckelen. The settlement then consisted of thirty-one households, numbering 134 persons, twenty-five of whom were Church members. He started services in a barn, but next winter hoped to erect a church.

Selijns had signed a contract for four years, and in 1664 he returned to Holland and accepted a call to the parish of Waverveen, in the Province of Utrecht. Twice he refused a call to New Netherland, in 1670 after the death of Johannes Megapolensis [*q.v.*] and in 1677 after the death of Johannes Theodorus Polhemius; his salary troubles at Breuckelen had made him wary. In 1681, however, he was prevailed upon to accept a call to New York to fill the vacancy left by the passing of Willem van Nieuwenhuizen. He took the precaution this time of having the conditions drawn up and witnessed before an Amsterdam notary. These guaranteed him a salary of 1,000 guilders, free rent and fuel, a stipend for the Wednesday evening services, and free passage to America for himself and his family. He landed in New York on Aug. 6, 1682, and started preaching immediately. For the sake of the children, "who multiply more rapidly here than anywhere else in the world" (*Ecclesiastical Records*, II, 829), he held a catechetical class on Sunday evenings; three times a year he preached to the people at Bergen, and once a year at Harlem. Labadists from Holland proselytized among his congregation and he had to warn his flock against the "enthusiastic principles" of the Quakers. The rebellion of Jacob Leisler, who was a deacon in the Dutch Reformed Church, brought him further troubles. Since the majority of his elders and deacons

were magistrates and as such opposed to the champion of the common people, he took sides against Leisler, thus antagonizing the members of his congregation who saw in Leisler the leader of a just cause. He was a popular preacher, however, and, to quote from a testimonial signed by Governor Stuyvesant and his fellow elders and deacons in 1670, "left a deep impression among our members by the faithfulness of his ministry, the piety of his life, his peculiar zeal in instructing and catechizing, and his kind and affectionate intercourse" (*Ibid.*, I, 608). A tolerant man in ecclesiastical matters, he allowed the Rev. Mr. Daillé to preach to his French congregation in the Dutch church after Selijns' second service, the English chaplain having the use of it after his morning service. He was on terms of friendship also with the English ministers in Boston, and prefixed a long Latin poem to Cotton Mather's *Magnalia Christi Americana* (1702). Thanks to his persistent efforts, the Dutch Reformed Church, in 1696, obtained the first church charter granted in the colony. The Rev. Gualterus Du Bois was called as his colleague in 1700, and Selijns died in September of the following year (*Ecclesiastical Records*, III, 1484). He had been married twice: first, July 9, 1662, to Machtelt Specht of Utrecht, Holland, who died in 1686, and second, Jan. 10, 1694, to Margaretha de Riemer, widow of Cornelis van Steenwijck.

[*Ecclesiastical Records—State of N. Y.* (7 vols., 1901–16), ed. by E. T. Corwin; E. T. Corwin, *A Manual of the Reformed Church in America* (1902); A. Eekhof, *De Hervormde Kerk in Noord-Amerika* (2 vols., 1913) and article in *Nieuw Nederlandsch Biografisch Woordenboek*, III (1914), 1159–66; H. C. Murphy, *Anthology of New Netherland* (1865), which contains a memoir and a collection of Selijns' poetical effusions—chiefly occasional verse—in the original Dutch and in English translation.]   A.J.B.

SELIKOVITSCH, GOETZEL (May 23, 1863–Nov. 27, 1926), Egyptologist, author, journalist, was born in Rietavas, Russia (now Lithuania), the son of David and Rachel (Zundelewitz) Selikovitsch. As a youngster his brilliant record as a student in Hebrew and the Talmud won him the reputation of a boy prodigy. He attended several Talmudic schools and was tutored privately in the Russian and German languages and in secular subjects. In 1879 he went to Paris, where he studied at the École des Hautes Études, displaying a special aptitude for oriental languages, mastering Egyptian, Ethiopic, Arabic, and Sanskrit and their literatures. He was graduated in 1884 and was attached for a short while to the Bibliothèque Nationale in Paris. In 1885 he was engaged by the British war office as chief interpreter to Lord Wolseley

Selikovitsch   Sellers

for the Arabic and Nubian dialects during the
British expedition to relieve General Gordon
from the Sudanese at Khartum, but was released
from his duties when it was suspected that he
was sympathetic with the natives. Before his
return to France he visited Abyssinia, Morocco,
Algeria, and Asia Minor, familiarizing himself
with the life and customs of the natives and
their tongues. The results of his travels and researches published in French and Hebrew journals gained for him a wide reputation. He came
to the United States in 1887 and lectured on
hieroglyphics and Egyptology at the University
of Pennsylvania and the Franklin Institute in
Philadelphia. He had hoped to follow an academic career, but personal reasons compelled
him to relinquish this idea, and he thereafter
took up Yiddish journalism as a profession. A
journalist of talent and a prolific writer, he
found in the Yiddish press a medium for the exploitation of his versatile personality. For several years he edited Yiddish periodicals in Boston, Chicago, and New York City, and in 1901
he joined the staff of the *Jewish Daily News* in
New York City, with which he was associated
until his death.

Of a restless, adventurous disposition, a true
Parisian Bohemian, Selikovitsch was unable to
concentrate his real powers in any one field. He
was fond of life and of living, possessed a keen
sense of humor, and took a vivid interest in
everything that went on about him. In addition
to scholarly contributions in French and Hebrew, made possible by his extraordinary erudition and phenomenal linguistic knowledge, he
also wrote, in Yiddish, feuilletons, poems and
trivial novels under various pseudonyms. A collection of speeches in Yiddish, Hebrew, and
English, and a series of editorials and articles
and a method for the study of the Arabic language written in Yiddish appeared in book form.
His Yiddish journalism gained for him no worthwhile recognition, with the exception, perhaps,
of his weekly column conducted for a number of
years in the *Jewish Daily News* entitled "Literatur un Lomdos" (literature and learning),
in which he displayed, in the shape of book reviews unusual familiarity with every conceiv-
able subject in several literatures. He wrote a
lucid and arresting style. He was himself not at
all proud of his work in Yiddish, and remarked
in his autobiography that it was dictated purely
by financial considerations. Towards his writings in Hebrew, however, he adopted a different
attitude. These were for him a labor of love
and are of lasting literary value. Of his Hebrew
works which attracted commendation are *Ziure*

Massá (Warsaw, 1910), travel sketches of Africa, and *Torath Buddha* (New York, 1922), an
excellent translation into Hebrew from the Sanskrit of the Tripitaka. His treatises in other languages include *Le Shéol des Hébreux* (1881),
and *The Dawn of Egyptian Civilization* (1887),
published also in the *Journal of the Franklin Institute,* May 1887.

[Autobiographical notes in *Ziure Massá*; *Who's Who
in Am. Jewry,* 1926; Zalmen Reisen, *Lexicon fun der
Yiddisher Literatur,* vol. I (Vilna, 1926); Salomon
Wininger, *Grosse jüdische National-Biographie,* vol.
V.]   I. S.

SELLERS, COLEMAN (Jan. 28, 1827–Dec.
28, 1907), engineer, inventor, was born in Philadelphia, Pa., the youngest son of Coleman and
Sophonisba (Peale) Sellers and a descendant of
Samuel Sellers who received a grant of land in
Pennsylvania in 1682. His father and a number
of paternal ancestors had been engineers; his
maternal grandfather was Charles Willson Peale
[*q.v.*], the portrait painter. During Coleman's
childhood his father died, and after attending
private schools in Philadelphia and completing
the course at Bolmar's academy, West Chester,
Pa., when he was about seventeen, the boy spent
two years on the farm of a kinsman. He then
went to work in the Globe Rolling Mill, Cincinnati, Ohio, operated by his two older brothers.
Here his mechanical ingenuity quickly asserted
itself and under his direction the wiremill belonging to the plant was rebuilt and improved.

From childhood Sellers had been greatly interested in natural philosophy and in the solution of physical problems, and he constantly devoted his spare time to studying and making apparatus in order to demonstrate to himself new
theories as they were announced. Thus while
making wire for the new telegraph lines in the
West, he secured a few batteries and constructed apparatus with which he was able to repeat
the unusual electrical experiments announced
by Michael Faraday. Because of his prompt and
thorough investigation of scientific discoveries
he became the mentor of a group of intellectual
men in Cincinnati and frequently gave lectures,
illustrated by practical experiments, on chemistry, physics, and electricity. At the age of twenty-one he became superintendent of the Globe
Rolling Mill. In 1850–51 he undertook the design and construction of locomotives for the
Panama Railroad and upon the completion of
this contract, took charge of the locomotive
works of James and Jonathan Niles in Cincinnati. Five years later, in 1856, he was induced
by William Sellers [*q.v.*], his second cousin, to
accept the position of chief engineer of William
Sellers & Company in Philadelphia. In this ca-

574

pacity he obtained patents for a variety of inventions, notably the Sellers coupling. He was also much interested in the development of new systems of power transmission. In 1873 he became a partner in the firm.

Failing health led him to resign his position as chief engineer of William Sellers & Company in 1886, but subsequently he was induced to engage in active practice as a consulting engineer. Probably his greatest work in this capacity was in connection with the hydro-electric power development of Niagara Falls. He was consulting engineer of the Cataract Construction Company, a corporation formed to execute this work, and served on the International Niagara Commission which determined the types of turbines and generators and the methods of power transmission finally adopted. Sellers designed the first large dynamos installed in this power plant. Throughout his busy life he continued his interest in physics and telegraphy. In addition he was a microscopist and an expert photographer, devising valuable improvements in both photographic processes and apparatus. From the time of his return to Philadelphia in 1856 he was identified with the Franklin Institute, which he served as vice-president for several years and as president for five consecutive terms. He contributed much to the interest of the Institute's meetings by his lectures, always drawing large audiences. For a number of years after 1886 he was a non-resident professor of engineering practice at Stevens Institute of Technology, Hoboken, N. J., where he delivered lectures at intervals during the school year. He was a member of engineering and scientific societies both in the United States and in Europe, and was a charter member and president of the American Society of Mechanical Engineers. For his scientific attainments he was decorated by King Oscar II of Sweden and Norway with the Order of St. Olaf. Sellers vigorously opposed the movement toward the legal establishment of the metric system (*Transactions of the American Society of Mechanical Engineers*, vol. I, 1880). He was the author of several papers, notably, perhaps, "Electricity as Applied to the Transmission of Energy" (*Proceedings of the American Philosophical Society*, vol. XXXVIII, 1899) and "The Utilization of Niagara's Power," in *The Niagara Book* (1893). He married, Oct. 8, 1851, Cornelia Wells of Cincinnati, who with two sons and a daughter survived him. He died in Philadelphia.

[*Trans. Am. Soc. Mech. Engrs.*, vol. XXIX (1907); *Jour. Franklin Inst.*, Mar. 1908; *Who's Who in America*, 1906–07; *Public Ledger* (Phila.), *Phila. Inquirer*; *Phila. Record*, Dec. 29, 1907; Patent Office records; *Cassiers Mag.*, Aug. 1903; J. W. Jordan, *Encyc. of Pa. Biog.*, vol. XII (1919); J. W. Roe, *Eng. and Am. Tool Builders* (1916).]   C. W. M.

SELLERS, ISAIAH (*c.* 1802–Mar. 6, 1864), pioneer steamboat pilot, was born in Iredell County, N. C., lived and died on the Mississippi, and was buried in St. Louis. Uncertainty clouds the time and circumstances of his removal to the Mississippi Valley. According to Mark Twain's *Life on the Mississippi* Sellers made his inaugural river trip in 1811, "the year the first steamboat disturbed the waters of the Mississippi," but it has also been said that he went west in 1825 "when he was quite a young man" (Darby, *post*, p. 213). His own diary (Gould, *post*, p. 600) shows that he engaged in the commerce of the lower river from 1825 to 1828, shipping first from Florence, Ala., on the *Rambler*, next on the *General Carroll*, and then on the *President*. While he was on the *Carroll* he introduced bell-tapping as the pilot's signal to take soundings, a decided improvement over the shouted commands theretofore employed. Joining the *Jubilee*, he piloted his first steamboat to the upper river, and in 1836 at Pittsburgh he took charge of the palatial *Prairie*, the first boat with a stateroom cabin to visit St. Louis. As pilot of the *J. M. White II*, he made perhaps the most noteworthy of all steamboat runs on the Mississippi. Leaving New Orleans on May 4, 1844, he brought the *White* to St. Louis in the record time of three days, twenty-three hours, nine minutes. This mark stood for a quarter century, and by that time cut-offs had shortened the river's course and refueling from barges in midstream had come into vogue. According to the diary, Sellers introduced in 1857 the signal for meeting steamboats, a distinction freely accorded him by river historians (Hyde and Conard, *post*, p. 1922); although the United States Bureau of Navigation has no records to verify this, it recognizes that rules and signals later approved by Congress "had their source in such men as Isaiah Sellers." While he frequently acted as steamboat master, he preferred the post of pilot, the ninth renewal of his pilot's certificate being issued in St. Louis, Feb. 25, 1862. River disasters were common occurrences, but not once did a Sellers vessel figure in an accident. This remarkable record won him the confidence of business men and caused women passengers to wait for the *Aleck Scott*, long his boat. His years on the Mississippi made him an authority on its habits and changes. No other riverman knew landmarks so well as he, and none could point out more curiosities of nature to admiring passengers. Under the *nom de plume* of Mark

Twain, which Samuel Langhorne Clemens [*q.v.*] later appropriated, he was a contributor to the New Orleans *Daily Picayune* before Clemens took to the pilot's wheel. Indicative of his rank on the river were the honors accorded him when he died of pneumonia at Memphis on a downstream run. When the *Henry von Phul* returned his body to St. Louis, flags on all steamboats along the levee were at halfmast, as they were again seven days later when he was buried in Bellefontaine Cemetery. His wife Amanda had died twenty-one years before. The marble monument he ordered for his grave—a pilot on watch at his wheel—testifies to his high regard for his calling. Tall, dignified, and ruggedly handsome, with hair that in his later years was still "black as an Indian's," he was, wrote the second, if better known, Mark Twain, "the patriarch of the craft."

[S. L. Clemens, *Life on the Mississippi* (1883); E. W. Gould, *Fifty Years on the Mississippi* (1889); J. F. Darby, *Personal Recollections* (1880); William Hyde and H. L. Conard, *Encyc. of the Hist. of St. Louis* (1899), vol. IV; J. T. Scharf, *Hist. of St. Louis City and County* (1883), vol. II; *Daily Evening Gazette* (St. Louis), May 9, 1844; *Daily Mo. Democrat* (St. Louis), Mar. 10, 11, 1864; *Mo. Republican* (St. Louis), Mar. 10, 18, 1864; records of Bellefontaine Cemetery; information from Iredell County, N. C., county court, U. S. Bureau of Navigation, and C. J. Armstrong, Hannibal, Mo.]   I. D.

SELLERS, MATTHEW BACON (Mar. 29, 1869–Apr. 5, 1932), pioneer in aerodynamics, was born in Baltimore, Md., the son of Matthew Bacon and Annie L. (Lewis) Sellers. He was educated under private tutors and at private schools. Just when his interest in the dynamics of the air had its inception is not known, but the studies he undertook at the University of Göttingen in Germany seem to indicate that his interest in the subject came early in life. He spent a year at Évreux, France, and returned to the United States to study at Harvard University where he received the degree of LL.B. in 1892. He later took special courses at the Lawrence Scientific School (Harvard), and the Drexel Institute, Philadelphia. He began his active research work in aerodynamics in 1900, and continued to pursue it throughout his life, even while practising as a patent lawyer and aerodynamic consulting engineer in New York City. President Taft appointed him to the Aerodynamical Laboratory Commission, created in 1912, and in July 1915 President Wilson, on the recommendation of the secretary of the navy, Josephus Daniels, appointed him to serve as one of two representatives of the Aeronautical Society of America on the newly formed Naval Consulting Board. He resigned from the Board in 1918 to become its technical assistant, and re-

signed from that position in 1919 to resume his membership on it. Much of the work done by the Board in connection with aircraft investigation devolved upon him, his independence of thought and critical abilities rendering his assistance of high value. The problems of the helicopter particularly interested him since he felt that the basic idea was probably the oldest of all "heavier-than-air machines."

His theoretical research work led him to build an efficient quadroplane in 1911 for experimental purposes and he demonstrated its possibilities in actual flight. The invention and construction of the lightest aeroplane flying with the least power is attributed to him. He acted as his own pilot and thus was able fully to appreciate the technical difficulties to be encountered. He constructed a wind tunnel for testing propellers and airfoil shapes for discovering their aerodynamic possibilities. Five patents were issued to him: one for aerial apparatus in 1908, for an aeroplane in 1909, for his quadroplane in 1911, and two in 1914 were issued for improvements in steering and running gear on aeroplanes. While technical editor of *Aeronautics* from 1911 he aided others in presenting to the public the results of their work, reviewed books on aeronautics, and carried on a series of answers to questions involving the principles and experimental data of aerodynamics. His most prolific period of publication was from 1909 to 1916. The results of his experimental work appeared in aeronautical periodicals of the day and included his studies of arched surfaces, wings, propellers, wind tunnels, gyroscopic forces, lateral balance, the aerodynamic resistance of solid bodies, and all kindred subjects (see Brockett, *post*).

On June 18, 1918, he was married to Ethel Clark. She and their two sons survived him when he died of a heart attack while recovering from pneumonia at his home, Ardsley-on-Hudson, N. Y.

[Hist. records of the Navy Dept.; records of the Patent Office; *Who's Who in America*, 1930–31; Paul Brockett, *Bibliog. of Aeronautics, Smithsonian Miscellaneous Colls.*, vol. LV (1910), and *Bibliog. of Aeronautics*, 1909–1916, *Natl. Advisory Committee for Aeronautics* (1921); *N. Y. Times*, Apr. 6, 1932.]
                    P. B.

SELLERS, WILLIAM (Sept. 19, 1824–Jan. 24, 1905), machine tool builder, inventor, son of John and Elizabeth (Poole) Sellers, was born in Upper Darby, Pa., on the family estate held under the original patent taken up by Samuel Sellers of Derbyshire, England, in 1682. After being educated in a private school maintained by his father, William at fourteen was apprenticed to his uncle, John Morton Poole of Wilmington,

Del., to learn the machinist's trade. He remained there for seven years, and then took charge of the machine shop of Fairbanks, Bancroft & Company in Providence, R. I. Some three years later he established his own manufactory of machine tools and mill gearing in Philadelphia, where he was soon joined by Edward Bancroft of Providence, with whom he organized the firm of Bancroft & Sellers. In 1853 his younger brother, John Sellers, became a partner, and after Bancroft's death in 1855 the firm name was changed to William Sellers & Company. For fifty years thereafter, until his death, Sellers served as president of this enterprise. From the beginning of his business venture, he departed from the accepted designs of mill machinery and tools. He was among the first to realize that architectural embellishments were a false feature of machine design and was one of the first to make the form of a machine follow the function to be performed. He made his products heavier too, although not unnecessarily so, and from the beginning adhered so closely to the standards he had adopted that fifty years after their original manufacture repair parts could be supplied for his machines.

Beginning in 1857, after Bancroft's death, he brought out a series of inventions, in a variety of fields, for which he was granted some ninety United States patents and many others in foreign countries. These inventions included machine tools of all kinds, steam injectors (which he introduced in the United States when in 1860 he secured the American rights to the patent of Henry Giffard of France), rifling machines, riveters, hydraulic machinery, steam hammers, and turntables. Probably the most original of his machines was the spiral geared planer, patented in 1862. In addition to his original manufacturing enterprises, Sellers in 1868 organized the Edge Moor Iron Company and became its president. This company furnished the iron work for the principal buildings of the Centennial Exhibition in Philadelphia in 1876, and all the structural iron work, except the cables, for the Brooklyn Bridge. He reorganized the William Butcher Steel Works in 1873, renaming it the Midvale Steel Company, and under his management it developed rapidly and became a leader in the production of heavy ordnance.

Sellers was elected a member of the Franklin Institute in 1847 and served as a member of the board of managers from 1857 to 1861 and again from 1864 to 1892, being president of the Institute, 1864–67. While holding this office, he made one of his most significant contributions to industry when he read a paper on "A System of Screw Threads and Nuts" (*Journal of the Franklin Institute*, May 1864), in which he proposed a system of screw threads to supply the need for a generally accepted standard. This paper had a great influence in the United States, and Sellers' system was adopted by the United States government in 1868 and by the Pennsylvania Railroad in 1869, soon thereafter becoming practically universal. It is known today as "the Sellers or United States standard." In 1868 Sellers was elected a member of the board of trustees of the University of Pennsylvania, in which capacity he served continuously thereafter throughout his life. He was a member of the National Academy of Sciences and of the foremost engineering societies of the United States, Great Britain, and France, and at the close of the Paris Exposition in 1889 was made a chevalier of the Legion of Honor. He was the author of "Memoir of James Eads" (*Biographical Memoirs of the National Academy of Sciences*, vol. III, 1895) ; and of "Machinery Manufacturing Interests" in *One Hundred Years of American Commerce* (1895, vol. II), edited by Chauncey M. Depew. Sellers was twice married: first, Apr. 19, 1849, to Mary Ferris of Wilmington, Del., by whom he had a daughter and two sons, one of whom died in infancy; second, Aug. 21, 1873, to Amelia Haasz of Philadelphia, who bore him two sons and a daughter who died young (Jordan, *post*, p. 221). He died in his eighty-first year, survived by his wife and four children.

[*Trans. Am. Soc. Mech. Engrs.*, vol. XXVI (1905); *Jour. Franklin Inst.*, May 1905; J. W. Roe, *English and Am. Tool Builders* (1916) ; J. W. Jordan, *Encyc. of Pa. Biog.*, vol. XII (1919) ; *Who's Who in America*, 1903–05; *Public Ledger* (Phila.), Jan. 25, 1905; Patent Office records.]   C. W. M.

SELLSTEDT, LARS GUSTAF (Apr. 30, 1819–June 4, 1911), painter, was born at Sundsvall, Sweden, a son of Erick and Eva Sellstedt. His paternal grandfather was a prosperous fuller and dyer (Sellstedt, *post*, p. 18) ; his maternal grandfather, a clergyman. Lars was educated at Sundsvall and at Hernösand but, when his father died of consumption in 1828 and his mother remarried, his stepfather treated him with such cruelty as to drive him to seek service at sea. In 1831 he became cabin-boy on a small Swedish trading vessel. Although he spent another winter at school in Sweden, for the most part his life after this was one of hardships and adventures, graphically described in his autobiography, *From Forecastle to Academy: Sailor and Artist* (1904). During a long voyage he learned English from Putnam Coffin, of Salem, Mass. Trying his hand, while voyaging on the South

American west coast, at making some drawings on whales' teeth, he found to his delight that he had artistic ability. He had learned, meantime, by experience that sailors were best treated on American ships, and he had heard that the most agreeable marine service in the world was that on the American Great Lakes. That information brought him in 1842 to Buffalo, which was at first only the headquarters of a young Swedish mariner taking various jobs on lake ships but later became his permanent home. His talent for drawing and painting, remarkable in an untaught sailor, attracted attention. His first commission, to do a lady's portrait, brought him two dollars and, more important, valuable criticism from a local artist. He had useful training as a draftsman while employed one summer on a United States topographical survey of the Lakes, and he finally ventured to take a studio at a hundred dollars a year, then a very high rent. Living on bread and milk, he managed to make his way until sitters began to come at fair prices. In 1849 he spent some months in the West Indies but without much success. On Jan. 19, 1850, he married Louise Lovejoy, with whom he moved to New York, believing Buffalo too small a place for his career. After a short time, however, he was forced to return to Buffalo, and there the young wife succumbed to Asiatic cholera. Sellstedt visited Stockholm in 1853 but once more came back to Buffalo and on June 11, 1856, married Caroline Scott, daughter of William K. Scott of Buffalo, a successful physician. Their home soon became a center of artistic activities.

Sellstedt had grown to be a cultivated, well-read man, deeply religious, active in many good causes. He painted well. His self-portrait, sent to the National Academy of Design in 1872, won commendation from Daniel Huntington [q.v.] and led to his election as an associate; in 1875 he became an Academician. He painted at Buffalo two presidents of the United States: Millard Fillmore, with whom he was intimately acquainted, and Grover Cleveland, whom he first knew as a young lawyer and an enthusiastic angler. Among his other portraits were those of several mayors, hung in the Buffalo city hall. The success of an art exhibition opened at Buffalo in December 1861, which he had helped to arrange, led to the establishment of the Buffalo Fine Arts Academy. Of this he was the principal organizer, and, in 1876–77, the president. In 1875, with his wife, he studied old masters in Europe and made many acquaintances among contemporary painters at Paris and Rome. One of his closest friends in America was the poet

David Gray, under whose encouragement he wrote creditable verse. In 1910 he published *Art in Buffalo*. He was active in the Saturn and Liberal clubs of Buffalo. His long life was saddened by the death of an only son, but it was otherwise in his later years one of notable happiness and of a philosophic calm.

[See esp. L. G. Sellstedt, *From Forecastle to Academy: Sailor and Artist* (1904). See also *Who's Who in America*, 1910–11; H. W. Sprague, in *Pubs. Buffalo Hist. Soc.*, vol. XVII (1913); *Buffalo Express*, June 5, 6, 1911. Information about Sellstedt's family has been supplied by his daughter, Mrs. Eva Sellstedt Potter of Buffalo.]   F. W. C.

SELYNS, HENRICUS [See SELIJNS, HENRICUS, 1636–1701].

SEMMES, ALEXANDER JENKINS (Dec. 17, 1828–Sept. 20, 1898), physician and Roman Catholic priest, was born in Georgetown, D. C., the son of Raphael Semmes of Nanjemoy, Charles County, Md., and Matilda (Jenkins), and a first cousin of Raphael Semmes [q.v.]. Both his grandfathers were officers of Maryland troops in the Revolutionary War. They were descendants of English Catholic gentry who came to Maryland in the following of the Calverts. Alexander received the degree of A.B. in 1850 from Georgetown College. He began the study of medicine in Paris and was given his medical degree in 1851 by the medical department of Columbian College, District of Columbia, after a year's course. For a short time he practised in Washington, and then joined an elder brother, Thomas Jenkins Semmes [q.v.], in New Orleans, where he became resident physician of Charity Hospital.

At the outbreak of the Civil War he was appointed surgeon of the 8th Louisiana Infantry and shortly thereafter was commissioned as surgeon in the Confederate army. He served for two years as brigade surgeon of Hay's Louisiana brigade in Jackson's corps of the Army of Northern Virginia and later was placed in charge of a section of the Jackson Military Hospital in Richmond. In addition to these duties, he was at various times medical inspector of the Department of Northern Virginia, inspector of hospitals, and member of the board for the examination of medical officers. With the close of the war he returned to New Orleans and renewed his connection with Charity Hospital as attending physician; subsequently, he moved to Savannah, Ga., where he became a highly successful practitioner and from 1870 to 1876 was professor of physiology at the Savannah Medical College. He had been married on Oct. 4, 1864, at Savannah, to Sarah Lowndes Berrien, daughter of John MacPherson Berrien [q.v.], attorney general in the cabinet of President Jackson and for many years United States senator from Georgia. She died within a year after their marriage.

At the height of his medical career Semmes applied to the bishop of Savannah for permission to enter the Catholic priesthood. After periods of study at Pio Nono College, near Macon, Ga., and at the Benedictine monastery of St. Vincent at Latrobe, Pa., he was ordained at Macon in 1878. For a short time he was engaged in parish duties and then, 1886, returned to Pio Nono College as its president and lecturer on English and American literature and history. He served thus for five years and was thereafter chaplain of the school and asylum of the Sisters of St. Joseph at Sharon, Ga., with mission duty throughout the state. He continued in this congenial work until a paralytic stroke in 1895 incapacitated him from further active service and he took up his abode with his brother in New Orleans. During his last months he was under the care of the Sisters of Charity at the Hôtel Dieu, where he died.

Father Semmes was a man of uncommon scholarship and his writings for medical and literary periodicals cover a wide range of topics. One of his earliest and most noteworthy articles is *Report on the Medico-Legal Duties of Coroners,* a pamphlet published in Philadelphia in 1857. Other publications include "Poisoning by Strychnia—The Gardiner Case," which appeared in *Stethoscope* (March 1855) and "Reports of Cases of Gunshot Wounds," in the London *Lancet* (June 23, Mar. 5, 1864). Deeply religious from early training, he is described as having been gentle and courteous and yet forceful, a man of ready sympathy and broad charity, qualities which well fitted him for his dual rôle of physician and priest.

[R. T. Semmes, *The Semmes and Allied Families* (1918); *Daily Picayune* (New Orleans), Sept. 21, 1898; W. B. Atkinson, *The Physicians and Surgeons of the U. S.* (1878); R. F. Stone, *Biogs. of Eminent Am. Physicians and Surgeons* (1894); H. A. Kelly and W. L. Burrage, *Am. Medic. Biogs.* (1920).]

J. M. P—n.

SEMMES, RAPHAEL (Sept. 27, 1809–Aug. 30, 1877), naval officer and author, the elder son of Richard Thompson Semmes and his wife Catherine (Middleton), was born in Charles County, Md., of French Catholic ancestry. His grandfather, Benedict Joseph Semmes, was born in Charles County in 1753. Raphael had one brother, Samuel Middleton, a lawyer, named for his maternal grandfather, and a sister who died in infancy. Both parents dying during his early childhood, the boy was brought up in George-

town, D. C., apparently in moderate circumstances by his uncle Raphael, father of Thomas Jenkins and Alexander Jenkins Semmes [*qq.v.*]. Probably owing to the influence of another uncle, Benedict J. Semmes, a Maryland planter prominent in politics, he was appointed by President Adams a midshipman in the United States Navy, Apr. 1, 1826.

His active naval career began on Sept. 8, 1826, when he reported for duty on a sloop-of-war of the Mediterranean Squadron. On Apr. 28, 1832, he completed the three-month course at the Naval School, Norfolk navy yard, and was passed for promotion; but though he stood second in his class it was five years before a vacancy occurred in the commissioned ranks and he was made a lieutenant (Feb. 9, 1837). During this long probationary period he served successively on the sloops *Lexington* and *Erie,* the frigate *Brandywine,* the schooner *Porpoise,* and the frigate *Constellation,* on the Mediterranean, West Indian, South American, and (during the Seminole War) Florida stations. He spent some time on hydrographic surveys and in charge of chronometers. During his considerable leaves of absence he studied and practised law in Maryland and Ohio. In Ohio he fell in love with the daughter of Oliver Marlborough Spencer and Electra (Ogden), Anne Elizabeth Spencer, to whom he was married on May 5, 1837. She and their six children survived him.

From 1837 to the outbreak of the Mexican War Semmes spent most of his time on survey duty on the southern coast and in the Gulf of Mexico on board the brig *Consort* and steamer *Poinsett* (his first command), interspersed with tours of shore duty at the Norfolk and Pensacola navy yards and sea duty on the sloop-of-war *Warren* and the brig *Porpoise.* After a short assignment to the frigate *Cumberland,* he took command (Oct. 23, 1846) of the brig *Somers* on the blockade of the eastern coast of Mexico. On Dec. 8, 1846, while chasing a blockade runner, this unlucky brig (on which the famous mutiny of 1842 had occurred) encountered a sudden tropical squall which knocked her on her beam ends. She sank in ten minutes with the loss of more than half her crew; but a court of inquiry not only exonerated Semmes of blame but also commended him for his seamanship. After the disaster he was detailed as flag-lieutenant to Commodore Conner; he was on shore with the naval artillery at the bombardment of Vera Cruz (March 1847), took part in the expedition against Tuxpan, and accompanied Scott's army to Mexico city on special duty. In addition, he served as a volunteer aide to Major-General

Worth, a divisional commander, who several times cited him for gallantry. In November 1847 he returned to his home at Prospect Hill on the Perdido River, Baldwin County, Ala., near Pensacola, Fla., where he had established his family in 1845.

During the period of peace, until 1861, he was on awaiting-orders status more than half the time, during which he wrote and published his memoirs and practised law. In October 1849 he moved his residence to a point near Mobile in order the better to educate his children. He served as commander of the storeship *Electra* and the schooner *Flirt,* as inspector of clothing and provisions at Pensacola, on sundry court-martial duty, as inspector of the 8th Light House District, and as secretary and as a member of the Light House Board. He became a commander on Sept. 14, 1855, and resigned from the United States service on Feb. 15, 1861.

He proceeded at once to the Confederate capital, where he gave to Congress his views on national defense. He was then dispatched to the North to purchase munitions, ordnance machinery, and ships. He made numerous contracts and succeeded in getting large quantities of percussion caps and powder shipped south before the commencement of hostilities. During his absence he was appointed a commander from Alabama, in the Confederate States Navy, on the first list of nominations confirmed by Congress (Mar. 16). Upon his return to Montgomery (Apr. 4), he was made chief of the Light House Bureau (Treasury Department); but on Apr. 18, 1861, he was relieved and given the first high-seas command in the new navy, the C.S.S. *Sumter,* under orders to "do the enemy's commerce the greatest injury in the shortest time" (quoted by him in *Official Records, Navy,* 1 ser., vol. I, 615). However, the *Sumter* was still only the packet steamer *Havana* lying in her berth at New Orleans, and Semmes had to turn naval constructor and ordnance expert in order to get her rebuilt, equipped, and armed as a man-of-war. With a battery of one eight-inch pivot gun and four thirty-two pounders in broadside, and a crew of 114 officers and men, the *Sumter* put to sea on June 30, 1861, entering upon a game which was to require of Semmes all the courage and audacity, skill and brilliancy, that his varied naval and legal training had developed in him. In every respect he measured up to the requirements, becoming the *beau ideal* of a commerce destroyer, ever outwitting the hostile cruisers sent after him, sensing the lanes and schedules of the enemy's merchantmen, and outarguing those foreign authorities who were disposed to refuse to

him the hospitalities of their ports. The third day at sea, July 3, 1861, off the Isle of Pines, West Indies, Semmes took and burned his first prize, the *Golden Rocket,* of Bangor, Me. After capturing nine other vessels in Caribbean waters, he cruised to Brazil and back to the West Indies, speaking nineteen vessels but finding only two of them to be American; the latter he burned. From this scarcity of Union flags he concluded that, in consequence of the alarm from his operations, the carrying trade of the United States was being rapidly broken up in this quarter; and so he turned across the Atlantic to Gibraltar, making six prizes on the way. Here he was quickly blockaded by the enemy; and, as the *Sumter* was in grave need of extensive repairs to hull and boilers for which no facilities were available, he laid her up (Apr. 13, 1862), discharging her crew and ordering the officers to the Confederacy. The *Sumter* was sold later to a British firm, which returned her to the commercial trade under the name *Gibraltar.* For "gallant and meritorious conduct in capturing and destroying the enemy's commerce on the high seas," Semmes was promoted captain (Aug. 21, 1862) and was voted the thanks of Congress (Sept. 9, 1862); but it was many months before word of these honors reached him.

Semmes's passage homeward was interrupted at Nassau (June 8, 1862) by the receipt of orders to take command of the *Alabama,* or *Enrica* as she had been christened, then nearing completion at Liverpool. In order to observe British neutrality regulations, the *Enrica* took on no warlike equipment in England; but proceeded under the British papers to the Azores, where just outside the maritime jurisdiction of Portugal she received her arms and stores from two consorts, and (Aug. 24, 1862) was transferred to the Confederate government and commissioned as a man-of-war with full ceremony to the tune of "Dixie" and salute guns. The *Alabama* was now officered and armed but had no crew. Semmes addressed the assembled crews, inviting enlistments in the Confederate service, and eighty-two men signed the muster roll. After a short shakedown cruise he set about his old business of destroying the enemy's commerce, commencing at the mid-Atlantic whaling grounds, where he burned ten prizes. Transferring his operations to the American coast, he sailed from Newfoundland Banks to the Caribbean Sea and thence into the Gulf of Mexico. Here he decoyed the U.S.S. *Hatteras* from the blockading squadron off Galveston (Jan. 11, 1863), and sank her in a thirteen-minute running fight. The antagonists were about equally matched. Though the engagement was fought at night, every man of the enemy was rescued by the Confederates and shortly paroled at Jamaica. The *Alabama* remained in the West Indies for a month and then drifted down the shipping lanes to the Brazil coast, where she operated for four months at the great cross roads of trade from the Pacific and Indian Oceans to America and Europe. In all on the American coast forty-four merchantmen had been captured. The bark *Conrad* of Philadelphia, next to the last prize made on this leg of the cruise, was converted into a tender as the bark-of-war *Tuscaloosa,* which in turn captured two merchantmen valued at $310,000. Semmes next sailed for the coast of Africa, arriving at Capetown on Aug. 5, 1863; and then proceeded on an extended cruise across the Indian Ocean through the Straits of Sunda to Singapore (Dec. 21, 1863), thence through the Straits of Malacca into the Bay of Bengal, the Arabian Sea, the Indian Ocean, up the Atlantic Ocean to Cherbourg, France, on June 11, 1864. Since the beginning of the war Semmes had captured a total of eighty-two merchantmen, valued at more than $6,-000,000, defeated and sunk a man-of-war, and had been the star actor in the dramatic and virtual extermination of the United States carrying trade. These successes brought him the epithet of pirate in the North, the admiration of the naval world abroad, and promotion to rear-admiral in the Confederacy (Feb. 10, 1865).

His smart man-of-war, now worn out by twenty-two months continuously at sea, needed general overhauling. While the *Alabama* was awaiting the permission of the Emperor to go into the imperial dockyard, the U.S.S. *Kearsarge* appeared off Cherbourg. By a strange coincidence this vessel happened to have been one of the blockaders of the *Sumter* at Gibraltar, and Semmes determined to fight her despite the disparity in the condition of the two ships. The enemy was lately out of a Holland dockyard, and hull and machinery were in perfect condition. The batteries and crews were about equal. On Sunday, June 19, 1864, with all of Cherbourg and half of Paris gathered on the cliffs to witness mortal combat, the *Alabama* steamed forth to meet the *Kearsarge,* which was in waiting beyond the three-mile line. At 10:57 A.M., the *Alabama* opened fire with her starboard broadside and the *Kearsarge* promptly replied with hers. Each combatant attempted to gain a raking position with the result that they fought in a circle of about one-quarter to one-half mile in diameter. At the beginning of the eighth rotation Semmes perceived that his ship was in a sinking condition and turned out of the circle, setting all sail available in hope of making the French shore. He now opened with his port battery; but the ship filled so rapidly that the fires were soon extinguished, and he hauled down his colors and gave orders to abandon ship. She sank in about fifteen minutes stern first, at 12:24 noon. The *Kearsarge* made tardy efforts to rescue the Confederates, who were picked up mostly by neutral spectators, principally by the English yacht *Deerhound.* Semmes was in the water half an hour before being picked up by a boat from this yacht, which took him to England; there he was kindly received.

After a rest in Switzerland he returned to the Confederacy by way of Mexico. He arrived at Richmond in January 1865, and was assigned as a rear admiral to the command of the James River Squadron, which consisted of three ironclad rams and seven wooden steamers. As his anchorage was flanked by powerful shore batteries, Richmond was amply safe from the enemy's fleet; but when the capital was evacuated by the army Semmes was obliged to burn his own ships and turned his men into a naval brigade, which was surrendered at Greensboro, N. C., as a part of Johnston's army. Upon being paroled (May 1, 1865), he went to his home in Mobile, where he was arrested (Dec. 15, 1865) by order of the Secretary of the Navy, despite the protection which his parole should have afforded him. He was taken prisoner to Washington and held about three months on the absurd charge of having violated the usages of war in escaping from the *Alabama* after her colors had been struck. He was held for trial before a military commission, but after the Supreme Court denied the jurisdiction of these commissions (*Ex parte Milligan,* 71 *U. S.,* 2) he was released by presidential order. Upon his return home he was elected probate judge of Mobile County (May 7, 1866); but was shortly driven out of office by military force under orders from the Secretary of War. In the fall of 1866, he accepted the chair of moral philosophy and English literature at the Louisiana State Seminary, then near Alexandria (now Louisiana State University, Baton Rouge); but was forced out of the professorship by political pressure before the end of the school year. He became editor of the *Memphis Daily Bulletin* and was soon hounded out of this employment. After making some profitable lecture tours, he returned to Mobile and engaged in the practice of law until his death at his home on Point Clear, Mobile Bay. He was buried the next day in the Catholic graveyard, Mobile, with full public honors and mourning.

His chief writings were *Service Afloat and*

Ashore during the Mexican War (1851), of which *The Campaign of General Scott, in the Valley of Mexico* (1852) is an abridgment; and *Memoirs of Service, Afloat, during the War between the States* (1869), later republished under a slightly different title. In addition he lent some of his papers to Saunders, Otley & Company, London, who published them as *The Cruise of the Alabama and the Sumter. From the Private Journals and Other Papers of Commander R. Semmes, C.S.N. and Other Officers* (2 vols., 1864). This work was reprinted in one volume in New York in 1864. It was translated: *Croisières de l'Alabama et du Sumter; livre de bord et journal particulier du Commandant R. Semmes et des autres officiers de son état-major* (Paris, 1864); and *Kruistogten van de Alabama en de Sumter* (Zwolle, 1865).

[Colyer Meriwether, *Raphael Semmes* (1913), with bibliography; R. T. Semmes, *The Semmes and Allied Families* (1918); Anonymous, *The Career of the Alabama (No. 290) from July 29, 1862, to June 19, 1863* (London, 1864), reprinted in *Magazine of History*, extra number, no. 2 (1908), pp. 103–35; Arthur Sinclair, *Two Years on the Alabama* (1895); W. M. Robinson, Jr., "The Alabama-Kearsarge Battle," *Essex Institute Hist. Collections*, Apr., July 1924; J. D. Bulloch, *The Secret Service of the Confederate States in Europe* (2 vols., 1884); *War of the Rebellion: Official Records* (*Navy*) and (*Army*); unpublished records in the Naval library and records in the Old Records Division of the Adjutant General's Office, Washington, D. C.; *Mobile Daily Register*, Aug. 31, 1877; W. L. Fleming, "Raphael Semmes, Professor in Louisiana," in *Daily Picayune* (New Orleans), May 14, 1911.]

W. M. R., Jr.

SEMMES, THOMAS JENKINS (Dec. 16, 1824–June 23, 1899), lawyer, Confederate senator, was born in Georgetown, D. C., the son of Raphael Semmes, a merchant of that place, and Matilda (Jenkins) Semmes. He was a brother of Alexander Jenkins Semmes and a first cousin of Raphael Semmes [*qq.v.*]. He began his formal education at a primary school in Georgetown and was graduated from Georgetown College with high honors in 1842. After one year in the law office of Clement Cox at Georgetown, he entered the Harvard Law School, where he was graduated in January 1845. Admission to the bar in Washington the following March entitled him to begin legal practice, but his removal to New Orleans in December 1850 returned him to the ranks of a student for three months before he had mastered the civil law of Louisiana. Here a partnership with Matthew C. Edwards, a Harvard classmate, was terminated abruptly during the campaign of 1855 as a result of a violent speech by Semmes defending Roman Catholicism against the attacks of the Know-Nothings. Political recognition came to him almost at once and he was sent to the lower house of the legislature in 1856. Appointed by President Buchanan in December 1857 as attorney for the eastern district of Louisiana, he prosecuted Gen. William Walker [*q.v.*] for breach of the United States neutrality laws in leading a filibustering expedition into Nicaragua. The jury disagreed, however, and the case was subsequently *nolle prossed* (*Daily Picayune*, New Orleans, June 3, 1858; W. O. Scroggs, *Filibusters and Financiers*, 1916, p. 369). Semmes resigned the district attorneyship within the year in order to enter and win the campaign for the post of attorney general of Louisiana, in which office he served from 1859 to 1861.

As a member of the Louisiana convention of 1861, he helped to draft the ordinance of secession. In February 1862 he took his seat at Richmond in the Confederate Senate, where he rendered able service until Lee's surrender. At the close of the war he made a hurried visit to Washington and secured a pardon from President Johnson so that upon his return to New Orleans he could resume at once the practice of his profession. His industry and resolution soon enabled him to replace his handsome residence and his law library, both of which had been confiscated.

The most notable part of his career followed the war years. He exerted a guiding influence in the constitutional convention of 1879, where his plea for the payment of the consolidated bonds in full was one of the best speeches made, and in the convention of 1898, as chairman of the judiciary committee; nevertheless it was as an attorney that he chiefly commanded attention. For years his name appeared as counsel in nearly every leading case before the civil courts of Louisiana. In 1873 he accepted appointment to the chair of Civil Law in the University of Louisiana (later Tulane University of Louisiana); pressure of work forced him to resign in 1879, but he subsequently resumed his connection and maintained it until his death. National recognition was accorded him in 1886 when he was elected president of the American Bar Association. Despite his many other responsibilities, he found time to serve for many years as president of the New Orleans School Board.

On Jan. 8, 1850, he married Myra Eulalia Knox, daughter of a Louisiana planter and banker. She, with three sons and two daughters, survived him.

[The accounts of Semmes in the following publications were apparently derived from family sources: E. L. Jewell, *Jewell's Crescent City Illustrated* (1873); *Report of the Twenty-second Ann. Meeting of the Am. Bar Asso.* (1899); R. T. Semmes, *The Semmes and Allied Families* (1918); articles in *Daily Picayune* and *Times-Democrat*, both of New Orleans, June 23, 24

25, 1899. There are no manuscript materials in the possession of the family.]   E. L.

SEMPLE, ELLEN CHURCHILL (Jan. 8, 1863–May 8, 1932), anthropogeographer, was born at Louisville, Ky., the daughter of Andrew Bonner Semple and Emerin (Price) Semple. Her early training was in private schools in Louisville. She entered Vassar at the age of fifteen, and received the B.A. degree with highest honors in 1882, thereafter continuing graduate work in history, her major field of interest. In 1891 and 1892 she went to Germany to study at the University of Leipzig under Friedrich Ratzel, the greatest anthropogeographer of his time. She was Ratzel's first woman student, the only one in a group of about five hundred men. Although not allowed to matriculate, she was permitted to attend lectures by sitting in an adjoining room with the door ajar. She was considered one of Ratzel's most brilliant students and his influence turned her from history to geography as she began the many years of unrelenting study, investigation, and travel that made her a master in her field. Her first publication, "The Influence of the Appalachian Barrier upon Colonial History," appeared in the *Journal of School Geography*, February 1897. This was followed throughout her life by many others in both geographical and historical journals. From 1906 to 1923 she was special lecturer in anthropogeography at the University of Chicago. When the School of Geography was founded at Clark University in 1921, she was the first to be called to the staff and she remained a member until her death. During these times she lectured widely both in the United States and Europe. In 1914 she was awarded the Cullum Geographical Medal by the American Geographical Society in recognition of her work, and in 1921 she was president of the Association of American Geographers, the only woman ever to hold that position.

Her three works, ranking high as to subject matter and presentation, have become indispensable to the students of the field. *American History and Its Geographic Conditions* (1903) at once claimed and held wide attention, but *Influences of Geographic Environment,* published in 1911, with a second edition in 1927, was her *magnum opus.* Originally planned to be a simplified paraphrase or restatement of the principles embodied in Friedrich Ratzel's *Anthropo-Geographie* (see the preface), the author finally resolved her work into a formulation of principles based upon those of Ratzel and interpreted it for the Anglo-American mind. This book is said to "have shaped the whole trend and content of geographic thought in America, and laid the

foundation for the science which has since made such rapid progress" (Atwood, *post,* p. 267). Her last book, *The Geography of the Mediterranean Region* (1931), was heroically completed after she had seen the "end of the Long Trail" (*Vassar Quarterly, post*). It was the result of twenty years of research and field work in the Mediterranean and an exhaustive study of the older literature of the Mediterranean lands. Its historical content is even greater than that of her two earlier works. Her place of leadership among the geographers of her generation will go undisputed. She had indefatigable capacities for research. In the classroom she seemed somewhat hampered, but her contacts with individual students were extraordinarily fruitful. Her travels, always from a scientific interest, took her through most of the northern hemisphere. She died at West Palm Beach, Fla.

[*Who's Who in America,* 1930–31; W. W. Atwood, memorial in *Jour. of Geography,* Sept. 1932; M. T. Bingham, memorial in *Vassar Quart.,* July 1932; "Report on Research Work with Selected Bibliographies of the Faculty of Clark University," July 1, 1932; Clark University *Bull.,* no. 86; *N. Y. Times,* May 9, 1932.]   H. S. G.

SENEY, GEORGE INGRAHAM (May 12, 1826–Apr. 7, 1893), banker and philanthropist, was born at Astoria, N. Y. (later part of the borough of Queens, New York City), the only son of Robert and Jane A. (Ingraham) Seney. His grandfather was Joshua Seney, member of the Continental Congress and of the first Congress under the Constitution, and his grandmother was a daughter of James Nicholson [*q.v.*] of the Revolutionary navy. Robert Seney, a graduate of Columbia College, was a Methodist preacher whose patrimony sufficed to educate George at Wesleyan and New York universities. Graduating at the latter (then the University of the City of New York) in 1846, he was first employed in a Brooklyn bank and later in the Gallatin Bank and the Bank of North America in New York. Becoming paying teller in the Metropolitan Bank in 1853 and within four years cashier, he thereafter retained a place of prominence in New York financial circles for more than a quarter of a century. In the late seventies, at the time of his promotion to the presidency of the bank, he began to take an important part in railroad financing, at first in the construction of the New York, Chicago & St. Louis Railway and later in a project for connecting the Ohio Central Railroad with Kentucky, Tennessee, and Virginia roads in a system to be known as the East Tennessee, Virginia, and Georgia Railroad. In furthering this enterprise Seney, who had built up a reputation as a conservative banker, resorted to "stock-watering" and other reckless methods common in the railroad financiering of that day and thereby incurred the hostile criticism of so astute an observer as Henry Clews (*Twenty-Eight Years in Wall Street*, 1877, pp. 162–67). His rashness brought his own fortunes and those of some of his associates to the brink of ruin. By 1884 several of the affiliated roads were bankrupt, and in May of that year, the month of the Grant-Ward episode in Wall Street, the Metropolitan Bank, seriously involved in the railroad failures through loans, was forced to close its doors. Seney at once resigned the presidency and transferred to the bank property valued at $1,500,000, including his art collection and a costly residence in Brooklyn. The Metropolitan reopened for business but only for a few months. Seney, however, retrieved a large part of his personal estate. The depositors were paid in full.

As a man of wealth he had become known for generous giving, but his philanthropic activities antedated his acquirement of riches. Dr. J. M. Buckley (*Christian Advocate, post*) is authority for the statement that when Seney's yearly income was under $5,000 he gave away one-fifth of it, and this at a period when a growing family must have made heavy demands on his purse. For many years he was a trustee of Wesleyan University, to which he gave more than $500,-000. He gave about $100,000 to Emory University, where he erected the building known by his name and added to the endowment. During the four years prior to the closing of the bank he gave $410,000 for the Methodist Hospital in Brooklyn. The total of his benevolences was estimated at $2,000,000. He was an assiduous collector of paintings and made several gifts to the Metropolitan Museum of Art in New York. After the bank failure his collection was sold for over $200,000, and he later acquired many pictures that brought still higher prices at auction sales. He was aided in his selection of purchases by Samuel Putnam Avery [*q.v.*]. In 1890 he headed the subscription list for the erection of the Washington Memorial Arch. In 1849 he had married Phoebe Moser, of a well-known Brooklyn family; with three sons and six daughters, she survived him at his death from angina pectoris in New York City.

[Comment on the failure of the Metropolitan Bank in *Commercial and Financial Chronicle*, May 17, 1884, and in *Blackwood's Edinburgh Mag.*, July 1884; *Ann. Reports M. E. Hospital in Brooklyn, N. Y.*, 1887–97, with portrait; obituaries in *Christian Advocate* (N. Y.), Apr. 13, 1893; *N. Y. Herald, N. Y. Times, N. Y. Tribune*, Apr. 8, 1893.]   W. B. S.

SENN, NICHOLAS (Oct. 31, 1844–Jan. 2, 1908), surgeon, was born in Buchs, Canton of St. Gall, Switzerland, to John and Magdelena Senn, who emigrated to America about 1852 and settled in the village of Ashford, Wis. After graduating from high school in Fond du Lac in 1864, he taught school and read medicine until 1866, when he entered the Chicago Medical College, from which he was graduated two years later. In 1869 he was married to Amelia S. Muehlhauser of La Crosse, Wis., who with two sons survived him. Following an internship of eighteen months in the Cook County Hospital he settled for practice in Elmore, Wis., but in 1874 he moved to Milwaukee, where he was appointed attending physician to the Milwaukee Hospital. During 1877–78 he studied at the University of Munich, which conferred upon him the degree of M.D. Returning to practice in Milwaukee he was in 1884 appointed professor of surgery at the College of Physicians and Surgeons in Chicago; in 1890 he became professor of surgery and surgical pathology in Rush Medical College, and in the following year he succeeded Charles Theodore Parkes as head of the department of surgery there. Later he became professor of surgery at the Chicago Polyclinic and lecturer on military surgery at the University of Chicago. For nine years he traveled between Milwaukee and Chicago to fill his lecture and clinic engagements, until in 1893 he removed his residence to Chicago. A pioneer in antiseptic surgery, with an unusual knowledge of surgical pathology, he quickly attracted the attention of the profession of the Middle West through his clinics. He was one of the first in this section to systematically pursue experimental surgery upon animals, and he devised one of the earliest mechanical aids for intestinal anastomosis. His experimental work upon abdominal surgery, including gunshot wounds of the intestines, gave him a local preeminence in this field. Though a skilful and daring operator, with a thorough knowledge of anatomy and pathology, he was never able fully to master the technique of surgical asepsis. Furthermore, though he commanded a vast surgical service and a large professional following, he left no group of Senn disciples to perpetuate his traditions. His practice was lucrative, and he was a liberal contributor toward the advancement of medical education. He gave a clinical building to Rush Medical College at a cost of about one hundred thousand dollars; and upon the death of Professor William Baum of the University of Göttingen, he purchased his library of old and rare medical books, the collections of fifty years, and presented it to the Newberry Library of Chicago.

He was a rapid and voluminous writer upon

surgical subjects, military medicine, and travel. His books include *Experimental Surgery* (1889), *Intestinal Surgery* (1889), *Surgical Bacteriology* (1889), *Principles of Surgery* (1890), *Pathology and Surgical Treatment of Tumors* (1895), *War Correspondence* (1899), and *Medico-Surgical Aspects of the Spanish-American War* (1900). His observations upon first aid on the battlefield and the conservative surgery of gunshot wounds are noteworthy. From the beginning of his professional career he had been interested in military medicine. Surgeon general of Wisconsin for a time and later a brigadier-general in the National Guard of Illinois, in 1891 he founded the Association of Military Surgeons of the United States and served as president for the first two years. During the Spanish-American War he saw service in Cuba as chief-surgeon of the VI Army Corps, with the grade of lieutenant-colonel. His pride in his uniform caused considerable amusement to his friends, but his teaching and example had a large influence in stimulating interest throughout the profession in medico-military knowledge. In his later years he traveled much throughout the world. From South America he sent a series of letters to the *Journal of the American Medical Association,* and in 1902 he published the well-illustrated *Around the World via Liberia.* Many of his journal articles were apparently written hurriedly and from memory, and are without lasting value. Physically he was short and heavy set, and quick and impulsive in speech and action. Though kindly and sympathetic by nature, he had a temper easily aroused, and at such times he was a formidable fighter. He was an indefatigable student and worker; even his holidays were filled with exacting activities. In 1907 in South America he suffered an acute dilation of the heart, the result of a mountain ascent of 16,000 feet; he was brought back to Chicago, where he died in St. Joseph's Hospital in a room he had endowed.

[*Who's Who in America,* 1906–07; *Am. Medic. Biogs.* (1920), ed. by H. A. Kelly and W. L. Burrage; F. M. Sperry, *A Group of Distinguished Physicians and Surgeons of Chicago* (1904); I. A. Watson, *Physicians and Surgeons of America* (1896); *Surgery, Gynecology, and Obstetrics,* Feb. 1908; *Mil. Surgeon,* Feb. 1908; *Chicago Daily Tribune,* Jan. 3, 1908; personal information.]   J. M. P—n.

SENNETT, GEORGE BURRITT (July 28, 1840–Mar. 18, 1900), ornithologist, was born in Sinclairville, Chautauqua County, N. Y., the only child of Mary (Burritt) and Pardon Sennett, a prosperous blast-furnace operator. His interest in ornithology apparently did not reveal itself until he was fully grown and well estab-

lished in business. He graduated from Erie Academy, intending to enter Yale, but his eyesight was such that he had to abandon further academic study and he spent the next four years in Europe. In 1865 he began his industrial career as a manufacturer of oil-well machinery at Meadville, Pa.; nearly thirty years later he moved his large works to Youngstown, Ohio, where he died. He served two terms, 1877–81, as mayor of Meadville and did much to make it a sanitary, well-planned city. He married Sarah Essex, by whom he had a daughter.

He did his ornithological work wholly in his spare time. Although he made extensive collections in western Minnesota, where he went in the spring of 1876 on his first ornithological expedition, he never published his results. His most prolonged and important studies dealt with the bird life of the lower Rio Grande region of southern Texas, then virtually a new field for the naturalist. In 1877, having arranged his business affairs so as to have more leisure time, he made a stay of two months along the Rio Grande; in 1878 he made a second trip there, covering a slightly longer period, and in 1882 a third. He published the results of only the first two Texas trips. Although he never went there again, he kept up his interest in the region and dispatched collectors there to gather material for him. It was his intention to study each season's work and publish the results as soon as possible, but his business interests encroached more and more on his time and interfered with his scientific work. His proposed monographic work on the avifauna of the lower Rio Grande he did not live to write; the materials he had gathered over a period of many years, however, were utilized by others (among them Ludlow Griscom and M. S. Crosby, "Birds of the Brownsville Region, Southern Texas," *Auk,* July, October 1925, and January 1926). In 1883 he deposited his splendid collections of birds and mammals in the American Museum of Natural History in New York, where he often worked during the winters from 1883 to 1896. The twenty-nine scientific papers he published are both accurate and reflective. The most important of them are "Notes on the Ornithology of the Lower Rio Grande, Texas, from Observations Made During the Season 1877" (*Bulletin of the United States Geological and Geographical Survey of the Territories,* vol. IV, 1878), "Further Notes on the Ornithology of the Lower Rio Grande of Texas from Observations made During the Spring of 1878" (*Ibid.,* vol. V, 1879), and "Descriptions of a New Species and Two New Subspecies of Birds from Texas" (*Auk,*

January 1888). He described ten forms of birds new to science, and four birds were named in his honor.

[See *Auk*, Jan. 1901; *Ohio State Jour.* (Columbus), Mar. 19, 1900. Many of Sennett's publications are listed in *Cat. of Sci. Papers, Fourth Ser., 1884–1900*, vol. XVIII (1923) of the Royal Society of London.]

H. Fr—n.

SEQUOYAH (1770?–Aug., 1843), inventor of the Cherokee syllabary, was born in the Indian town of Taskigi, Tenn. His father was possibly Nathaniel Gist, a trader who abandoned the mother, a woman of mixed Indian blood, before the birth of the child. During infancy and youth Sequoyah seems to have borne only his Indian name, later taking that of his father, which he understood to be Guess. He grew to manhood wholly ignorant of the English language and but meagerly acquainted with any of the arts and usages of civilization. He was for some years a hunter and fur-trader, but an accident suffered on a hunting trip crippled him for life. He had a natural bent for craftsmanship, which he turned to use in a number of ways, chiefly as a fashioner of the silver ornaments eagerly sought by his people. Increasing contact with the whites caused him to ponder deeply over their "talking leaves"—the written and printed pages by which they communicated ideas—and he resolved to master the secret and apply it to the benefit of his people. It was about 1809 when he began his study, and it was not until 1821, after enduring much ridicule and opposition, that he completed his table of characters for the eighty-five or eighty-six syllables in the Cherokee language. A council of the chief men of the tribe approved his work, with the result that in a short time thousands of his people had learned to read and write. In 1822 he visited the western Cherokees in Arkansas to introduce his syllabary and in the following years made his home with them, re-moving with them in 1828 to Oklahoma. There his invention of an alphabet continued to stimu-late printing of books and a newspaper in Chero-kee and to be important in contributing toward the development of the state. For some years he was active in the political life of his tribe, in which he was highly honored. In 1828, as an envoy, he visited Washington. The Cherokee National Council in 1841 voted him an allow-ance for his invention and two years later al-tered the gift to an annuity of $300, to be con-tinued, in case of his death, to his widow. He had before this time retired from public affairs and had visited many tribes in a search for the elements of a common speech and grammar. Early in 1843 he set out to find a band of Cher-okees who, according to tradition, had removed west of the Mississippi before the Revolution. Somewhere in the southwest, possibly in the state of Tamaulipas, Mex., he fell ill and died.

He was married and had several children. It was with the aid of a six-year-old daughter that in 1821 he gave the first successful test of his invention. He was a man of mild and benignant countenance, with an engaging manner, and his character was upright and devotedly altruistic. He has been sometimes called the ablest intelli-gence produced among the American Indians. His fame is perpetuated in the name of the genus of California giant redwoods and in the statue of him placed by the state of Oklahoma in Stat-uary Hall of the National Capitol.

[J. B. Davis, "The Life and Work of Sequoyah," *Chronicles of Oklahoma*, June 1930; F. W. Hodge, *Handbook of Am. Indians*, pt. II (1910); G. E. Foster, *Sequoyah, the Am. Cadmus and Modern Moses* (1885); K. D. Sweetser, *Book of Indian Braves* (1913); Jas. Mooney, "Myths of the Cherokee," *U. S. Bureau of Am. Ethnology Nineteenth Ann. Report* (1900), pp. 108–27, 147–48; "Statue of Sequoyah," *House Doc.* 240, 68 Cong., 1 Sess. (1917); Emmet Starr, *Hist. of the Cherokee Indians* (1921); S. C. Williams, "Na-thaniel Gist, Father of Sequoyah," *East Tenn. Hist. Soc. Pubs.*, no. 5 (1933); Wm. A. Phillips, "Se-quo-yah," *Harper's Mag.*, Sept. 1870.]

W. J. G.

SERGEANT, HENRY CLARK (Nov. 2, 1834–Jan. 30, 1907), inventor, was born in Rochester, N. Y., said to be the son of Isaac and Ruby (Clark) Sergeant. His parents moved to Ohio when he was young, and after a common school education he went to work in a machine shop. This stimulated his inventive faculties, especially in the direction of special machinery for systematic manufacture. Although he was only eighteen years old, he designed some spe-cial machines for the manufacture of wheel spokes, hubs, and felloes, and obtained contracts for his employer for making such wheel parts in quantity. Two years later he was made a part-ner in a wagon-wheel manufactory but, dislik-ing factory routine, he soon resigned and spent the succeeding six years in a variety of com-mercial pursuits. He began serious inventive work as well and secured his first patent in 1854 for a steam boiler feed. This was followed by a number of others, among them a patent for the invention of a marine engine governor later adopted by the United States navy; four patents on steam boilers and pumps; one on a gas regu-lator in 1862; three for brick machines in 1867; and one for a fluting machine in 1869. During this sixteen-year period he lived in many places; in fact, over the forty-year period between 1854 and 1893 he lived in twenty-six different cities and towns. Gradually working eastward, he came to New York City in 1868 and there es-tablished a machine shop of his own, building a variety of machines and developing many crude ideas brought to him by other inventors. When the business grew he formed the partnership of Sergeant and Cullingworth and took new quarters in a shop owned by José F. de Navarro. To this shop came Simon Ingersoll [*q.v.*] about 1870 to develop his idea of a rock drill. The future of such a machine attracted Sergeant and, while it is not known just how much he contributed to the success of the original Ingersoll drill, at least one patent was issued jointly to the two men. At all events, he induced Navarro to buy out Ingersoll and organize the Ingersoll Rock Drill Company, through which the drill was introduced into rock excavating. Meanwhile he turned his attention to operating the drill by means of compressed air rather than steam and to improving the air compressor; in the course of a few years his improved drills had entirely supplanted the older steam drills. In 1883, however, he sold his interest in his shop and in the Ingersoll Drill Company and went to Colorado to engage in silver mining, but he came back east two years later with an entirely new rock drill, patented in 1884, that had a novel valve motion, and formed the Sergeant Drill Company, with a manufactory in Bridgeport, Conn. Two years later his company and the Ingersoll company joined as the Ingersoll-Sergeant Rock-Drill Company with Sergeant as president, but within a short time he disposed of the bulk of his interests and went abroad to live. After several years he returned, this time as a director in the Ingersoll-Sergeant company, to devote his whole time to invention, and in the succeeding years he perfected among many others his most notable inventions: the "auxiliary" and the "arc" valves; the "tappet" drill; the Sergeant release rotation for rock drills; and the piston inlet valve for air compressors. He had married Caroline Luckhaupt in Columbus, Ohio, on Mar. 19, 1860, and at the time of his death in Westfield, N. J., he was survived by four children.

[*Compressed Air Mag.*, Mar. 1907, June 1910; Patent Office records; obituary in *N. Y. Tribune*, Feb. 1, 1907, *N. Y. Times*, Jan. 31, 1907; correspondence with the Ingersoll-Rand Co.]   C. W. M.

SERGEANT, JOHN (1710–July 27, 1749), missionary to the Housatonic Indians, was the son of Jonathan and Mary Sergeant. His grandfather, Jonathan, had settled in New Haven, Conn., in 1644, and the second Jonathan had been one of the Branford, Conn., congregation which removed to New Jersey some twenty-two years later and founded Newark, in which place John Sergeant was born. Unfitted for farm work or a trade as a result of a scythe-cut on his left hand, he prepared for college and graduated from Yale in the class of 1729. Copies of his Commencement address, *A Valedictorian Oration, by John Sergeant, Delivered at Yale College in the Year 1729*, were printed in 1882 from the manuscript in the possession of Williams College. From 1731 to 1735 he was a tutor at Yale and was "one of the most successful holders of that office in the early history of the College" (Dexter, *post*, p. 395). In addition to his teaching he also pursued studies in theology.

Meanwhile, several clergymen united in an effort to provide Christian instruction for the Indians in what is now Berkshire County, Mass. These Indians were few in number, of good reputation, and occupied two tracts of land—one in the present town of Sheffield, and the other in Stockbridge. To this missionary project the Boston commissioners of the Society for the Propagation of the Gospel in New England gave their support, and the Indians themselves, their consent. Two of the clergymen, having heard that Sergeant had said "he had rather be employ'd as a Missionary to the Natives, if a Door should open for it, than accept a Call any English parish might give him" (Dexter, p. 395), visited him at New Haven in September 1734, and told him the door was open. He readily consented to accept the mission, and later wrote that he would have been ashamed to own himself a Christian had he not been willing to do so, both because of the need of the Indians, and also because the "pains taken by those of the Romish Church, not only in other parts but also in America . . . should methinks excite us to emulation, who at least think we profess Christianity in much greater purity" (Hopkins, *post*, in *Magazine of History*, p. 20). Sergeant spent October and November with the Indians, got them to erect a building between their two settlements to serve as school and church, and returned to New Haven, with two Indian boys, to complete his year at the college, having left Timothy Woodbridge, who was to be his assistant, in charge.

In July 1735 he entered permanently upon his missionary work, and on Aug. 31, was ordained to the Congregational ministry at Deerfield, Mass. Until his death in his thirty-ninth year he lived and worked among the Indians, beloved by them and regarded as their father and best friend. He mastered their language, becoming able to speak it, they said, better than they could themselves, and translated into it some prayers, portions of the Bible, and Watts's shorter catechism. He enjoyed the high regard and cordial support of Gov. Jonathan Belcher [*q.v.*]. In

1736 the General Court secured a tract of land six miles square in what is now Stockbridge that the two settlements of Indians might be united. Later it ordered a meeting house and a school house built there. Sergeant interested himself particularly in the education of the boys and girls, placing some of the former in English homes, and one of his chief ambitions was the establishment of a boarding school in which industrial training should be given to both sexes, a project which was achieved shortly before his death. One of his sermons, *The Causes and Danger of Delusions in the Affairs of Religion Consider'd and Caution'd Against, with Particular Reference to the Temper of the Present Times,* was published in 1743, and the same year, *A Letter from the Rev^d. Mr. Sergeant of Stockbridge to Dr. Colman of Boston; Containing Mr. Sergeant's Proposal of a More Effectual Method for the Education of Indian Children.* On Aug. 16, 1739, he married Abigail, daughter of Col. Ephraim Williams of Stockbridge and half-sister of the founder of Williams College. A son, John, was also a missionary to the Indians, another son was a prominent physician and officer in the Revolution, and a daughter was the grandmother of Mark Hopkins [*q.v.*]. Jonathan Dickinson Sergeant [*q.v.*] was a nephew.

[Samuel Hopkins, *Hist. Memoir Relating to the Housatunnuk Indians* (1753), reprinted in *Mag. of Hist.* (New York, 1911), Extra No. 17; W. B. Sprague, *Annals Am. Pulpit*, vol. I (1857); F. B. Dexter, *Biog. Sketches, Grads. Yale Coll.*, vol. I (1885); E. F. Jones, *Stockbridge, Past and Present* (1854).]   H. E. S.

SERGEANT, JOHN (Dec. 5, 1779–Nov. 23, 1852), lawyer, congressman, was born in Philadelphia, the third child of Jonathan Dickinson Sergeant [*q.v.*] and Margaret (Spencer) Sergeant, and elder brother of Thomas Sergeant [*q.v.*]. He was orphaned at fourteen, and at sixteen, in 1795, was graduated from the College of New Jersey. He then began an apprenticeship in the house of Ellison & Perot, where he learned the rudiments of finance. In March 1797 he entered the law office of Jared Ingersoll [*q.v.*] and on July 17, 1799, was admitted, in Philadelphia, to the practice of law. Within six years, aided by a comfortable fortune, he had established himself, and for the next half-century he was an acknowledged leader of a famous bar.

In 1800 he was appointed by Gov. Thomas McKean [*q.v.*] to be deputy attorney general for Chester County and Philadelphia. Two years later Thomas Jefferson made him commissioner of bankruptcy for Pennsylvania (*Luzerne Federalist,* July 12, 1802). He was elected to the legislature in 1805, and in 1806 declined reëlection as well as an offer of the recordership of Philadelphia (Meredith, *post,* p. 9). Elected to the legislature again in 1807, he served as chairman of the committee on roads and inland navigation, and, though he did not (as claimed, *Ibid.,* p. 9) report the first bill giving direct aid to internal improvements in Pennsylvania, he did demonstrate a deep and lasting interest in transportation and also in banking. At this time, furthermore, he revealed one of his fundamental traits of character as a public man by introducing a bill prohibiting masquerades as dangerous to public morals. Probably his growing law practice among a wealthy clientele and his identification with the vested interests brought about his temporary retirement from politics and, with it, his transition from a McKean-Jefferson Republican to a firm Federalist. Having scholarly tastes, he naturally fell in with the circle of intellectuals led by Joseph Dennie, Nicholas Biddle, and Joseph Hopkinson [*qq.v.*]. His resulting friendship with Biddle lasted until the latter's death and in consequence Sergeant had an influence in the banking affairs of the nation that has never been fully recognized.

He was elected to the Fourteenth Congress to fill the vacancy caused by the death of Jonathan Williams, and served in that body from 1815 to 1823, from 1827 to 1829, and, again, from 1837 to Sept. 15, 1841. He gave entire support to the "American system," despite bitter opposition to a high tariff by the Philadelphia Chamber of Commerce and the mercantile interests of his constituency. The woollen manufacturers of the Middle States, however, wrote him that "the Manufacturing Part of Society . . . observe your zealous regard for their interest" (Sergeant MSS., Historical Society of Pennsylvania, *post,* Jan. 20, 1816). He opposed the Missouri Compromise, favored uniform bankruptcy laws, championed internal improvements, and throughout his terms in Congress was the chief legal and political adviser to the Second Bank of the United States. In 1816, armed with plenary powers and letters of introduction, he was sent by the Bank on a mission to Europe to obtain specie to bolster the banking structure of the country. The skilful diplomacy which this thirty-seven-year-old lawyer used in wresting a signal victory from such lords of the world's financial capital as Baring Brothers and Reid, Irving & Company is a significant index to his abilities. A historian of the Bank, R. H. C. Catterall, criticizes the "pitiably inadequate" amount of specie kept on hand, but does not mention the strategic victory won by Sergeant in the face of great difficulties (*The Second Bank of the United States,* 1903, p. 29); yet Sergeant's successful mission undoubtedly had an ameliorating effect upon the depression of 1819. Besides serving as a director of the Bank and as its adviser, Sergeant fought some of its most notable legal battles before the Supreme Court (Charles Warren, *The Supreme Court in United States History*, 1922, II, 90, 108, and *passim*). He is credited with having had more influence than anyone else in inducing Biddle to apply for a renewal of the Bank's charter (Catterall, pp. 217–18; but *cf.* R. C. McGrane, *The Correspondence of Nicholas Biddle Dealing with National Affairs*, 1919, p. 147). His position on public questions made him an ideal, but unsuccessful, National Republican candidate for vice-president in 1832 (E. M. Carroll, *Origins of the Whig Party*, 1925). In 1834 the Bank sought Sergeant's election to the United States Senate, and, though the attempt failed, it did prevent the election of Richard Rush [*q.v.*], an unfriendly candidate (*Memoirs of John Quincy Adams*, vol. IX, 1876, p. 40).

He was president of the board of canal commissioners of Pennsylvania in 1825–26, and was named a member of the Panama Congress of 1826, though he never proceeded farther than Mexico city on his way to Tacubaya. He was president of the constitutional convention of Pennsylvania in 1837–38 and took the lead in the fight over the judiciary. His stature can be measured by the offices that he declined: these included a seat on the bench of the United States Supreme Court, a cabinet position under Harrison, and the embassy to England under Tyler (H. A. Wise, *Seven Decades of the Union*, 1872, p. 219; H. L. Carson, *The Supreme Court of the United States*, 1891, p. 343; Meredith, *post*, p. 27). His great strength was as a forensic legalist, less eloquent than intellectual, but powerful enough to win such battles as the Girard Will Case (*2 Howard*, 127) over such opponents as Webster. In the famous cases he conducted before the Supreme Court—*Osborn* vs. *United States Bank* (*9 Wheaton*, 738), *Worcester* vs. *Georgia* (*6 Peters*, 515), etc.—he was the advocate of national powers as opposed to state rights, and though he usually defended the strongholds of vested interests, he also fought legal battles for purely humanitarian ends, as in the Cherokee cases (*5 Peters*, 1). He headed several humanitarian and scholarly enterprises in Philadelphia, and his printed lectures were so extensive and well received that his admirers in 1832, possibly as an aid to his campaign of that year, gathered a number of them into a volume, *Select Speeches of John Sergeant of Pennsylvania*, in an effort "to rescue from the precarious tenure of ephemeral publications the reputa-

tion of an eminent man." He was married June 23, 1813, to Margaretta Watmough, by whom he had ten children.

[Sergeant MSS., 5 vols., Conarroe MSS., Etting Papers, and Poinsett Papers in Hist. Soc. of Pa.; Hopkinson MSS. in hands of Hopkinson family, Phila.; Biddle, Sergeant, Clay, and Webster MSS. in Lib. of Cong.; Sergeant MSS. and Canal Board Papers, in Pa. State Lib.; *Biog. Dir. Am. Cong.* (1928); W. M. Meredith, *Eulogium on the Character and Services of the Late John Sergeant* (1853); Horace Binney, *Remarks to the Bar of Phila. on the Occasion of the Deaths of Charles Chauncey and John Sergeant* (1853); S. R. Gammon, *The Presidential Campaign of 1832* (1922); Edward Stanwood, *A Hist. of Presidential Elections* (1884); *Proc. and Debates of the Convention of . . . Pa., to Propose Amendments to the Constitution . . . 1837* (vols. I–XIII, 1837–39); *Pa. Mag. of Hist. and Biog.*, Oct. 1924; *Public Ledger* (Phila.), Nov. 25, 1852.]   J. P. B.

SERGEANT, JONATHAN DICKINSON (1746–Oct. 8, 1793), lawyer, congressman, was born in Newark, N. J., the eldest son of Jonathan and Abigail (Dickinson) Sergeant, and a descendant of Jonathan Sergeant who came to New Haven, Conn., in 1644, and soon moved to Branford. His father was a brother of John Sergeant [*q.v.*], missionary to the Indians; his maternal grandfather was the Rev. Jonathan Dickinson [*q.v.*], first president of the College of New Jersey. His father was treasurer of that institution from 1750 to 1777 and the man under whom he studied law, Richard Stockton, 1764–1828 [*q.v.*], was a trustee. Sergeant was graduated there in 1762, and the following year from the University of Pennsylvania. Like most other young Princetonians, he fell in with the Sons of Liberty and took a prominent part in the Stamp Act controversy.

Six short years, 1774 to 1780, cover the entire official life of Sergeant, yet they were momentous enough to prove that John Adams was correct in speaking of the sociable young lawyer in 1774 as a "cordial friend to American liberty" (*The Works of John Adams*, vol. II, 1850, p. 356). He was clerk of the first Provincial Congress of New Jersey in July 1774; served on the Somerset and Princeton committees of correspondence in 1774 and 1775; was secretary of the second Provincial Congress, and at the meeting in August 1775 was made provincial treasurer, receiving in October the thanks of that body for his services (*Minutes of the Provincial Congress . . . of New Jersey*, 1879, p. 253). In February 1776 he was chosen to represent New Jersey in the Continental Congress, but in June he resigned to accept a seat in the New Jersey Provincial Congress, in which he took the lead in forming a state constitution (C. R. Erdman, *The New Jersey Constitution of 1776*, 1929). Here he learned his first lessons in the art of protecting liberty with laws, directed against the Loyalists, such as he later became expert in enforcing. On Nov. 30, 1776, he was again chosen member of the Continental Congress, serving until September 1777. When Hessians burned his Princeton home on Dec. 25, 1776, he definitely moved his residence to Philadelphia, identifying himself with Pennsylvania politics. He was active in committee work, but as early as February 1777, he wrote that his zeal in the cause had reduced his private affairs to a "melancholy complexion" and offered to resign (Emmet MSS., no. 795, in New York Public Library; *Selections from the Correspondence of the Executive of New Jersey from 1776 to 1786,* 1848, pp. 24–25, 27). He was appointed attorney general of Pennsylvania on July 28, 1777, but not commissioned until Nov. 1, and apparently he engaged in private practice in the interim. His extraordinary procedure in the typical trial of Samuel Rowland Fisher, a Quaker and suspected Loyalist, shows that Sergeant, like most Revolutionary public prosecutors, took rather literally the ancient maxim *inter arma leges silent.* As one of the McKean-Bryan "Constitutionalists," he was made a member of the council of safety because Thomas Wharton thought him a "worthy young man." Here his "honest zeal in noting irregularities of Continental officers" brought him two physical beatings at the hands of army contractors who took advantage of his small person. Arduous labor and small pay did not deter him from conducting a "great . . . number of capital trials" before his resignation, Nov. 20, 1780. He assisted the state in several notable trials, chief of which was the Connecticut-Pennsylvania dispute arbitrated at Trenton in November and December 1782. He declined public office after the Revolution, devoting his attention to law. In June 1787, his twenty-eight-year-old wife, Margaret Spencer, whom he had married Mar. 14, 1775, died, leaving him eight children, two of whom were John and Thomas [qq.v.], and on Dec. 20, 1788, he married Elizabeth, daughter of David Rittenhouse [q.v.], by whom he had two daughters and a son. His defense in 1788 of the Anti-Federalist editor, Eleazar Oswald, indicates that he was still in alignment with the Bryan faction.

Zeal for Republican principles led him to espouse the French Revolution, and during the excitement of the Genet episode, he took a leading part. Years later John Adams said he was informed that "nothing but the yellow fever, which removed Dr. Hutchinson and Jonathan Dickinson Sergeant from this world, could have saved the United States from a fatal revolution of

Government" (*Works,* vol. X, 1856, p. 47). Later John Sergeant sought to clear his father's name of the stigma which he considered Adams thus put upon it. It is true, however, that Sergeant's courageous efforts in behalf of the yellow fever victims brought on his own early death.

[Numerous Sergeant MSS. are in the Revolutionary Papers, XXI to LIX and Post-Revolutionary Papers, I to LIV in the Pa. State Lib.; some MSS. are in the Gratz Coll., Conarroe MSS., IX, 66, 67, 68, and Etting Papers, in the Hist. Soc. of Pa. The only adequate biog. sketch is E. F. Hatfield, "Jonathan Dickinson Sergeant," *Pa. Mag. of Hist. and Biog.,* II (1878), pp. 438–42; see, also, E. C. Burnett, *Letters of Members of the Continental Congress,* vols. I, II (1921–23); and W. C. Ford, *Jours. of the Continental Cong.,* vols. IV–VIII (1906–07); "Jour. of Samuel Rowland Fisher," *Pa. Mag. of Hist. and Biog.,* Apr. 1917; *Pa. Colonial Records; Pa. Archives;* T. J. Rogers, *A New Am. Biog. Dictionary* (2nd ed., 1824); *Memorial Biogs. of the New Eng. Hist. Geneal. Soc.,* IV (1885), 69–75.]
J. P. B.

SERGEANT, THOMAS (Jan. 14, 1782–May 5, 1860), jurist, author of legal works, the son of Jonathan Dickinson Sergeant [q.v.] and Margaret (Spencer), was born in Philadelphia. He graduated second in his class at the College of New Jersey in 1798; then entered the law office of Jared Ingersoll [q.v.]; and was admitted to the Philadelphia bar on June 8, 1802. Shortly afterwards, Thomas McKean [q.v.] appointed him clerk of the mayor's court, indicating that Thomas Sergeant, like his brother John [q.v.], was allied with the McKean-Jefferson Republicans. In 1812 and again in 1813 he was elected to the legislature, but political life attracted him less strongly than the bench, and on Oct. 20, 1814, he accepted a commission as associate judge of the district court of Philadelphia and held this post until 1817.

In the latter year he was appointed secretary of the commonwealth by Gov. William Findlay. During his incumbency he sponsored legislation for, and directed the establishment of, the state law library at Harrisburg. He did not escape the general investigation that was made of Findlay's administration by the legislature. On Dec. 17, 1818, a dissatisfied office seeker in a petition to the legislature charged Sergeant with nepotism and favoritism in the disposal of minor offices. A committee of inquiry was appointed, but reported that the complaints had not been substantiated and asked that the charges be dropped. On July 6, 1819, Sergeant resigned as secretary and the same day was appointed attorney general, which office he held until the administration of Gov. Joseph Hiester [q.v.] began in 1820. Subsequently, he devoted himself to his legal practice and scholarly pursuits until April 1825, when he was appointed solicitor of the district for Philadelphia County. In April 1828 he became postmaster of Philadelphia and served as such throughout Jackson's first administration. His next appointment, Feb. 3, 1834, was that of associate justice of the Pennsylvania supreme court. During the twelve years he occupied this position his decisions, chiefly limited to expounding the equity decisions of the court, were noted for their brevity, clarity, and accuracy: one of his successors stated that he was never reversed in a single instance. Like his brother, he strongly opposed the amendment in the constitutional convention of 1837–38 proposing popular election of judges, and so bitter was his resentment at its inclusion in the state constitution that he resigned his judgeship, Oct. 1, 1846, largely on that account. He was provost of the Law Academy of Philadelphia from 1844 to 1855, trustee of the University of Pennsylvania from 1842 to 1854, president of the Historical Society of Pennsylvania, and a member of the American Philosophical Society.

His greatest achievements were in the field of legal writing. As a young lawyer he contributed articles and poems to periodicals and newspapers; he soon, however, confined himself to legal researches and writings. His first important work was *A Treatise upon the Law of Pennsylvania Relative to the Proceeding by Foreign Attachment* (1811). There followed at various intervals: *Constitutional Law: Being a Collection of Points Arising upon the Constitution and Jurisprudence of the United States, Which Have Been Settled by Judicial Decision and Practice* (1822), of which a second edition under a somewhat different title appeared in 1830; *Reports of Cases Adjudged in the Supreme Court of Pennsylvania, 1814–1829* (17 vols., 1818–29), in collaboration with William Rawle [*q.v.*]; *Sketch of the National Judiciary Powers Exercised in the United States Prior to the Adoption of the Present Federal Constitution* (1824); and *View of the Land Laws of Pennsylvania* (1838). He was one of the editors of *Reports of Cases Argued and Determined in the English Courts of Common Law* (1822–25) and also of *The Law Library* (104 vols., 1833–60). He was married on Sept. 14, 1812, to Sarah Bache, grand-daughter of Benjamin Franklin, by whom he had three sons and a daughter.

[A few of Sergeant's MSS. are in the Gratz Coll., the Coryell Papers, and the McKean Papers, in the possession of the Hist. Soc. of Pa.; there is also in the same repository a volume of newspaper clippings, chiefly obituary notices of Thomas Sergeant. Published sources include *Memorial Biogs. of the New England Hist. Geneal. Soc.*, vol. IV (1885); J. H. Martin, *Martin's Bench and Bar of Phila.* (1883); *Report of the Committee Appointed to Investigate the Official Conduct of Thomas Sergeant, Secretary of the Commonwealth* (1819); *Pennsylvanian* (Phila.), May 7, 1860.]
J. P. B.

SERRA, JUNÍPERO (Nov. 24, 1713–Aug. 28, 1784), Franciscan missionary, was born in Petra, Mallorca, the son of Margarita Ferrer and Antonio Serra. He was baptized Miguel José but took the name Junípero when he finished his probation and made his religious profession in 1731. He entered the Franciscan Order at Palma on Sept. 14, 1730. In St. Francis Friary at Palma he studied philosophy and theology and was ordained priest. Previously honored by the Lullian University of Palma with the degree of Doctor of Theology, he soon gained distinction as professor of philosophy and pulpit orator. A brilliant career in the Church and in the Franciscan Order was awaiting him when in 1749 he obtained permission to join a band of Franciscans destined for the Apostolic College of San Fernando in Mexico city. Here, with Francisco Palóu [*q.v.*] as one of his companions, he arrived on Jan. 1, 1750. His first missionary field was among the Indians of Sierra Gorda, northeast of Querétaro. Nine years later he was recalled and appointed for the San Sabá mission in Texas. When this project failed to materialize, he spent the next years in Mexico city as preacher and confessor. In 1767, when the Franciscans of the College of San Fernando replaced the banished Jesuits in Lower California, he was sent as *presidente* to this new field.

At the instance of the visitor general, José de Gálvez, the authorities of San Fernando agreed to cooperate with the government by founding missions in Upper California, those of the peninsula being entrusted to the Dominican friars. Accordingly five Franciscans with Serra as *presidente* accompanied the military expedition of Gaspar de Portolá [*q.v.*] northward. On July 16, 1769, the San Diego mission was founded, the first of the twenty-one eventually erected on the California coast. During the next fifteen years Serra was the guiding force that resulted in the successful occupation of what is today the state of California. During his presidency nine missions were founded: San Diego, San Carlos, San Antonio, San Gabriel, San Luis Obispo, San Francisco de Assisi, San Juan Capistrano, Santa Clara, and San Buenaventura. In 1773 he went to Mexico but late in the next year returned to California. At the close of 1783, seven months before his death, more than six thousand Indians were recorded as baptized, while more than five thousand had been confirmed. Equally astounding was the material progress under the missions. The live stock totaled nearly 30,000 heads; the annual harvest amounted to about 30,-000 bushels of grain and vegetables; the workshops furnished the necessaries of civilized living. Although Serra suffered from an injury to his leg that had occurred when he first came to Mexico, at regular intervals he held official visitations, traveling on foot from mission to mission and aiding the missionaries by his counsel and encouragement. He died suddenly at the mission of San Carlos, near Monterey. His diary and some letters remain.

He was a man of deep faith and boundless trust in God. Of a keen mind and indomitable will, he mastered the situations that repeatedly threatened Spain's California project, and under his guidance and inspiration Spain's hold on California became secure. In his differences with the military authorities, none could honestly question either his patriotism as a Spaniard or his sincerity and sense of justice as head in spiritual matters and as protector of the rights of the Indians. The missionary friars found in him a sympathetic and congenial confrère, and a solicitous and appreciative superior, while the Indians revered him as a loyal and affectionate friend. Thin and frail in appearance and grave in demeanor, he was wholly absorbed in his missionary labors. Among other memorials are a bronze statue of him in Golden Gate Park, San Francisco, and a granite monument at Monterey. Of the tributes paid to his memory in recent years, the most significant is the statue in the Capitol at Washington, D. C., unveiled on Mar. 1, 1931, as a token of homage to a pioneer missionary who ranks among the foremost in American history.

[Two important works are those of Francisco Palóu, *Noticias de la Nueva California* (4 vols., 1874, ed. by J. T. Doyle), translated and ed. by H. E. Bolton as *Hist. Memoirs of New Cal.* (4 vols., 1926), and *Relación Historica de la Vida y Apostólicas Tareas del Venerable Padre Fray Junípero Serra* (Mexico, 1787), ed. by G. W. James as *Francisco Palóu's Life and Apostolic Labors of the Venerable Father Junípero Serra* (1913). See also Zephyrin Engelhardt, *The Missions and Missionaries of Cal.*, vols. I, II (1908–12), and *Mission San Carlos Borromeo* (1934); H. H. Bancroft, *Hist. of Cal.*, vol. I (1884); Helen Hunt Jackson, *Father Junípero Serra and the Mission Indians of Cal.* (1902); H. I. Priestley, *José de Gálvez* (1916), *Univ. of Cal. Pubs. in Hist.*, vol. V; C. E. Chapman, *The Founding of Spanish Cal.* (1916); D. S. Watson, *The Founding of the First Cal. Missions* (1934), with some hitherto unpublished letters; Agnes Repplier, *Junípero Serra, Pioneer Colonist of Cal.* (1933), a popular biography; material in the archives of the Santa Barbara and San Carlos missions.]   F. B. S—k.

SERRELL, EDWARD WELLMAN (Nov. 5, 1826–Apr. 25, 1906), civil and military engineer, was born in London, England, but was a United States citizen by birthright. His parents were William and Anne (Boorn) Serrell, and he was the tenth of their eleven children. Brought to the United States when he was four and a half years old, he received his early education in the schools of New York City, then took up civil engineering under the direction of his father and elder brother.

From 1845 up to the time of the Civil War, Serrell was engaged in railroad and bridge design and construction. He was successively assistant engineer to the commissioners of the Erie Railroad, and assistant to the chief of the topographical engineers, United States Army. As assistant engineer of the Panama Survey (1848), he accompanied the expedition that located the route between Aspinwall and Panama. Later he had charge of the surveys for the Northern Railroad of New Hampshire, and for a time was engineer of the Central Railroad of New Jersey. He prepared plans and supervised the construction of the suspension bridge across the Niagara River at Lewiston (1850); superintended the construction of the bridge at St. John, N. B.; and planned the bridge over the St. Lawrence at Quebec. Subsequently, he was concerned with the building of the Hoosac Tunnel, the Bristol Bridge over the Avon River in England, which had one of the largest spans of any bridge in that country at the time, and the Union Pacific Railroad.

At the outbreak of the Civil War, he organized and commanded the 1st New York Engineers, with the rank of lieutenant-colonel, but was soon made its colonel. Later he became chief engineer of the X Corps, United States Army, and afterward, chief engineer and chief of staff of the Army of the James. During the siege of Charleston, S. C., he devised and, under fire from the Confederate forces, personally supervised the construction of a battery in a swamp where, it is said, an iron rod would bury itself by its own weight. This battery, dubbed the "Swamp Angel," threw shells into the streets of Charleston, five miles away, and was hailed as a triumph of engineering skill. When he was mustered out, Feb. 13, 1865, he had served in 126 actions, and on Mar. 13, was brevetted brigadier-general. During the war he made many useful inventions, including practical improvements in armor plate, impromptu gun carriages, and the development of electric coast defenses.

Serrell prepared many reports on railroads and canals and served as consulting engineer for numerous corporations, including the American Isthmus Ship Canal Company. He projected an interoceanic canal from San Blas to Pearl Island Harbor, which he claimed could be built at sea level, with no locks, on a straight line less than thirty miles from ocean to ocean, and at comparatively small expense. In 1868 he reported on the location of a suspension bridge to cross the Hudson River from Anthony's Nose, just above Peekskill, on the east, to Fort Clinton, on the west side. His last important engineering work, in the early nineties, was in promoting the construction of a bridge at this location in connection with a railroad from the Pennsylvania coalfields to New England. The enterprise, however, was never carried to completion. Serrell died in New York City. He was married on Apr. 6, 1848, to Jane, daughter of the Rev. Jesse Pound. She died in September 1896 and on Sept. 6, 1900, he married Marion Seaton, daughter of Orville A. Roorbach.

[*Who's Who in America*, 1906–07; P. F. Mottelay and T. Campbell-Copeland, *The Soldier in Our Civil War*, vol. II (1885); report of adjutant general's office, Albany, 1898; F. B. Heitman, *Hist. Reg. and Dict. U. S. Army* (1903); *Engineering News*, May 3, 1906; *Who's Who in N. Y.*, 1905; *N. Y. Times*, Apr. 26, 1906.]   B. A. R.

SERVOSS, THOMAS LOWERY (Oct. 14, 1786–Nov. 30, 1866), merchant, ship-owner, was representative of the Northerners who made threefold profits in the cotton belt by selling Northern goods, sending back cotton in return and also transporting those goods in both directions. He was born in Philadelphia, the son of Jacob and Isabella Servoss. His father was a merchant, trading between Philadelphia and Albany, N. Y. The yellow fever left Thomas an orphan in 1798 and four years later he entered the great Philadelphia counting-house of Daniel W. Coxe who, with forty vessels, carried on a brisk trade with the lower Mississippi. Servoss was married to Elizabeth Courtney at Philadelphia on Oct. 31, 1807. Three years later he started by way of Pittsburgh and the Ohio River to settle at Natchez, Miss., promising his reluctant young wife that as soon as he made money enough, he would return to settle down as a merchant in Philadelphia or New York City. At Natchez, he entered into partnership with one Henry Turner of that place, became one of the most popular residents of the town, and developed a very profitable trade. His particular correspondent in the East was Peter H. Schwenk of New York, a brother-in-law, who sent his manufactures and received cotton in return. Servoss is credited with having sent the shipments of rifles needed for the defense of New Orleans in 1815, but the accounts of that transaction, without naming him particularly, throw little credit on the contractor (See A. S. Colyar, *Life and Times of Andrew Jackson*, 1904, I, 262). Servoss kept his promise to his wife and went to

New York in 1816, but it was too late and she died there on Mar. 3, 1817.

After the death of his wife, Servoss returned to the Mississippi, settled at New Orleans, and engaged in business on a larger scale. He was married in New Orleans to Louisa H., daughter of the prominent John Pintard [*q.v.*] of New York, on Apr. 4, 1824. His business prospered until the "cotton panic" of 1825, when he lost, among other things, 500 bales through the failure of the firm of Jeremiah Thompson [*q.v.*]. He then returned to New York City where he lived until his death. By 1827 he was living on Broome Street, and he later moved to Harlem. His New Orleans friends sent him goods on consignment, and in 1827 he established a regular and very profitable line of sailing packets between New York and New Orleans. He ran this "Louisiana Line" until about 1831, when he sold it to Edward Knight Collins [*q.v.*]. This was one of the most successful of the coastal packet lines, for New Orleans shipped a considerable amount of its cotton, even for ultimate foreign export, to New York. This venture seems to have restored the Servoss fortune. Servoss was a director of the North American Trust & Banking Company, and a trustee of the Chambers Street Bank for Savings. He was active in the American Bible Society, probably through the influence of John Pintard, and he built St. Clements Episcopal Church on Amity Street for his friend, the Rev. Louis Pintard Bayard, who became rector. His appearance in his last years was described as "grand, noble and venerable," with a "towering form, very much resembling that of General Scott" (Scoville, *post*, p. 179). In addition to an infant son who died at Natchez, he had one son by his first marriage and a son and two daughters by his second.

[J. A. Scoville (Walter Barrett, pseud.), *The Old Merchants of N. Y.*, ser. 4 (1866); family papers; *Longworth's N. Y. Directory*, various editions; *Am. Ann. Cyc.*, 1866 (1867), p. 583; *N. Y. Herald*, Dec. 2, 1866.]   R. G. A.

SESSIONS, HENRY HOWARD (June 21, 1847–Mar. 14, 1915), railroad car builder, inventor, was born in Madrid, St. Lawrence County, N. Y., the son of Milton and Rosanna (Beals) Sessions. He was of English ancestry, a descendant of John Sessions, who emigrated to Connecticut in 1768. Henry attended school in his native town until he was fifteen years old, and then, being mechanically inclined, began an apprenticeship in the railroad car and machine shop of the Central Vermont Railroad at Northfield, Vt., of which shop his father was master car builder. Upon completing his apprenticeship he continued as a journeyman car builder under his father until 1870, when he became master car builder of the Rome, Watertown & Ogdensburgh Railroad at Rome, N. Y. After serving in this capacity for eight years, in the hope of bettering himself he went West and at Sioux City, Iowa, became master car builder for the Sioux City & St. Paul Railroad. Early in 1880 he was made master car builder of the International and Great Northern Railroad at St. Paul, Minn., but the following year he went to Texas and during the years 1881–85 held similar positions with the Texas & Pacific Railroad and the St. Louis, Iron Mountain, and Southern railroads, respectively.

Because of his long and varied experience in car construction, in 1885 he was appointed superintendent of the Pullman Company, Pullman, Ill. Two years later he devised several improvements on the railroad car which brought him world-wide recognition. One of these was the bellows projection on the ends of passenger cars which permitted close connection of the cars in a train and provided safe passage from one to another. The original patent for this invention was granted Nov. 15, 1887 (No. 373,098). The following year he improved the "vestibule," as it came to be called, by devising spring equalizers to permit cars to take curves readily (patented May 15, 1888), and on May 14, 1889, he patented the design and manufacture of the fabric bellows coupling that came into common use. A number of other inventions were completed by him in 1891–92, among them a railroad car brake and a car heater. He also designed the standard steel platform for passenger cars. This last contrivance led to his becoming associated with the Standard Coupler Company of New York in 1896 as vice-president and director. In this capacity he continued his work of inventing improvements for railway rolling stock, in the course of which he perfected a street railway air brake, a metallic buffer beam, the friction draft rigging, and the radial buffing and draft rigging for railway cars, the last named being patented Feb. 3, 1903 (No. 719,519) and assigned to the Standard Coupler Company. During this work Sessions maintained his residence in Chicago, where he died. In 1872 he married Nellie L. Maxham of Rome, N. Y.

[F. C. Sessions, *Materials for a Hist. of the Sessions Family* (1890); *Railway Age Gazette*, Mar. 19, 1915; Jos. Husband, *The Story of the Pullman Car* (1917); T. C. Clarke and others, *The Am. Railway* (1889); *N. Y. Times*, Mar. 16, 1915; Patent Office records.]

C. W. M.

SESTINI, BENEDICT (Mar. 20, 1816–Jan. 17, 1890), Roman Catholic priest, mathematician, astronomer, was born at Florence, Italy. He received his earlier education at the Scuola

Pia, near his native town, and so early evinced a mastery of mathematical computation that at the age of eighteen he was appointed assistant to Fr. Inghirami, then the director of the Osservatorio Ximeniano, at Florence. On Oct. 30, 1836, he entered the Society of Jesus at Rome. Three years later he began his philosophical and theological studies at the Roman College and here was privileged to have as professor Fr. Andrea Caraffa, one of the leading mathematicians of his time, who materially encouraged him in the prosecution of the researches of his choice. On the advice of Caraffa he was assigned as assistant astronomer of the Roman Observatory, then under the directorship of Fr. M. DeVico, whose name is identified with one of the periodic comets. During his incumbency at this observatory, which lasted till 1848, Sestini made a special study of star colors and his results were published under the titles *Memoria Sopra i Colori delle Stelle del Catalogo di Baily Osservati* (1845) and *Memoria Seconda Intorno ai Colori delle Stelle . . .* (1847). He was ordained to the priesthood in 1844.

Following the outbreak of the Revolution in Rome in 1848, he emigrated to the United States and became connected with Georgetown University, Washington, D. C., where, at the observatory of the University, he resumed his researches. During the year 1850 he made studies of the sun's surface. Availing himself of a cloudless sky, persisting from Sept. 20 to Nov. 6 of that year, he was able to follow the sun spots, then very pronounced, noting the rate of travel over the surface and the changes in their appearances and, being a skilled draftsman, to commit them to paper. Engravings of the sketches were published in an appendix to *Astronomical Observations Made During the Year 1847 at the National Observatory, Washington*, vol. III (1853). These are rated as among the best studies of the sun's maculae antedating the application of photography to investigations of the skies. In addition to his researches in astronomy, Sestini taught mathematics and natural sciences to the Jesuit seminarians then resident at Georgetown College. In 1852 he published *A Treatise of Analytical Geometry*. This was followed by *A Treatise on Algebra* (1855, 1857). In 1856 there appeared his *Elements of Geometry and Trigonometry* and in 1871, *Manual of Geometrical and Infinitesimal Analysis*. He also wrote *Theoretical Mechanics* (1873), *Principles of Cosmography* (1878), and *Animal Physics* (1874), all of which were privately printed for the use of his scholars. In 1878 he organized an expedition to Denver, Colo., for the observation of the total eclipse of the sun, an account of which was published in the *American Catholic Quarterly Review* (October 1878).

Possessed of no little architectural skill, Sestini is accredited with the planning and the supervision of the construction of Holy Trinity and Saint Aloysius churches, Washington, D. C., and of the Jesuit Seminary at Woodstock, Md. At the last-named institution he frescoed on the ceiling of the college library the solar system of Copernicus. In 1866 he began the publication of the *Messenger of the Sacred Heart,* a periodical which came to have the widest circulation of any Catholic magazine in the United States and possibly in the world. He remained at Georgetown till 1869, except for a year spent at Frederick devoted to studies in ascetic theology, three years at Boston College, and two years at Gonzaga College, Washington, D. C., in which institution he taught higher mathematics. From 1869 to 1885 he gave instruction in astronomy and geology at Woodstock. In the latter year his health became impaired and he was forced to resign the editorship of the *Messenger of the Sacred Heart.* He thereupon entered into retirement at the Jesuit novitiate at Frederick, Md., where, having suffered a severe stroke of paralysis, he died.

[*Woodstock Letters*, XIX, 259, XXX, 99 ; *Messenger of the Sacred Heart,* Mar., May, June, July 1890 ; Carlos Sommervogel, *Bibliothèque de la Compagnie de Jésus,* vol. VII (1896) ; *Washington Post,* Jan. 18, 1890.]   F. A. T.

SETH, JAMES (May 6, 1860–July 24, 1924), philosopher, was born at Edinburgh, Scotland. Both his father, Smith Kinmont Seth, and his mother, Margaret (Little), came of well-to-do country stock. James attended schools in Edinburgh, where his father held a position with the Commercial Bank, and in 1876 entered the University. In 1881 he received the degree of master of arts with first-class honors and the following year he won a Ferguson Scholarship, open to all graduates of the four Scottish Universities. Intending to become a minister, he was for four years a student in the Theological College of the Free Church of Scotland, and was then duly licensed by the Free Church Presbytery of Edinburgh. During his theological course, he spent two semesters at German universities.

His philosophical studies, which he had continued to pursue, determined his career. In 1886 he was called to succeed Dr. Jacob G. Schurman as professor of metaphysics and ethics in Dalhousie College, Halifax, Nova Scotia. After six years there he came to the United States to fill a professorship of philosophy in Brown University, Providence, R. I. In 1891 he had published

Freedom As Ethical Postulate, and during four years spent at Brown he completed *A Study of Ethical Principles,* his most important work, which was published in 1894. In his ethical theory he sought to mediate between Utilitarianism and the Kantian and other rationalistic systems, finding in Personality a conception that unites the truth of both. Not the least merit of the book is its felicitous style, a quality found in all his writings. In 1896 Seth accepted a call from his old friend Dr. Schurman, then president of Cornell University, to the Sage Professorship of Moral Philosophy in that institution. In January of the following year he became co-editor of the *Philosophical Review,* serving in that capacity until November 1902. After the death of his former teacher, Prof. Henry Calderwood, he became the successful candidate for the chair of moral philosophy in the University of Edinburgh, a position which he held from 1898 till the year of his death. At Edinburgh he held the satisfaction of working side by side with his brother, Andrew Seth Pringle-Pattison, who held the chair of logic and metaphysics, once occupied by Sir William Hamilton.

In his *Study of Ethical Principles* Seth had emphasized the ethical meaning of the state. Keenly alive to the moral obligations of citizenship, he devoted increasing thought and effort to social problems. He became interested in methods for the control of the liquor traffic, and was one of four Scottish citizens invited by the Temperance Legislation Board to visit Norway to study the Samlag system, long tested in that country. The results of his observation were given in an article in the *Contemporary Review* (December 1906). He was also keenly interested in the effort of a minority of the Poor Law Commission to secure the repeal of the Poor Law, and gave active support to Sidney and Beatrice Webb in their campaign against this antiquated measure. The deplorable conditions of poverty and degradation which he found existing in quarters of his native city spurred him to promote the foundation of the Edinburgh School of Social Study and Training in connection with the University. The aim of the new school was, in his own words, "by opening the mind of the student to the inter-connections of the several social problems and the subtle action and reaction of causes and effects, to develop in him a scientific understanding of social facts. For," he adds, "we cannot doubt that, here as elsewhere, knowledge is power" (memoir by A. Seth Pringle-Pattison, in *Essays,* p. xxix). His contributions to periodicals were numerous and in 1912 he published *English Philosophers and*

Schools of Philosophy. After his death, his brother Andrew edited *Essays in Ethics and Religion with Other Papers by James Seth* (1926), with memoir and bibliography.

Sensitive and somewhat shy, Seth had a most winning personality, which attracted and held a wide circle of devoted friends. Not the least of his charms was a quaint humor which could, on occasion, assume an ironic edge against all pretense and vulgar self-seeking. It was doubtless as a teacher that he exercised his most important influence. Many hundreds of students both in America and in Scotland will long remember with gratitude his kindly presence and his persuasive initiation into those ethical problems which touch all that is deepest in life and character. He never married.

[In addition to memoir mentioned above, see *Who's Who*, 1924; J. H. Muirhead, "Prof. James Seth," *Nature*, Aug. 23, 1924; *Times* (London), July 26, 1924; *Morning Chronicle* (Halifax), July 26, 1924.]

W. G. E.

SETON, ELIZABETH ANN BAYLEY (Aug. 28, 1774–Jan. 4, 1821), foundress of the American Sisters of Charity, was born in New York City. Her father, Dr. Richard Bayley [*q.v.*], was the first professor of anatomy at King's College and staff surgeon to General Sir Guy Carleton; her mother was Catharine Charlton, daughter of Rev. Richard Charlton, rector of St. Andrew's Episcopal Church, Richmond, Staten Island. She died when her daughter was only three years old, and the entire education of Elizabeth devolved upon the father. Realizing that his child possessed rare moral and intellectual qualities, Dr. Bayley employed unusual methods, which taught her to be unselfish and to think clearly and independently. These traits were further developed by her personal experiences during the days of the American Revolution. Those stirring times schooled the child to alertness and endurance, and fostered that patriotism which all her life was the faithful companion of her religious inspiration.

When not quite twenty, Jan. 25, 1794, she married a wealthy young merchant, William Magee Seton, whose ancestors had figured prominently in Scottish literature and history, and whose father, William, had settled in New York in 1763. To this union were born two sons and three daughters. Domestic cares, however, did not prevent her from being so devoted to the poor that she came to be called "The Protestant Sister of Charity." In 1797, with Isabella Marshall Graham [*q.v.*] and other leading women, she founded the first charitable organization in New York, and probably the first in the United States, the Society for the Relief of Poor Widows

with Small Children. In 1803 she accompanied her husband to Italy in the hope that his health, which had been shattered by worry over the loss of his fortune, would be restored. This hope proved vain, however, for he died at Pisa in December of that year. In Italy she made her first contact with Catholicism, and when she returned to New York she joined the Church of Rome, making her profession of faith in old St. Peter's, Barclay Street, on Mar. 14, 1805. This step estranged her family and friends at a time when she most needed their assistance. After several vain attempts to support herself in New York, in June 1808 she accepted an invitation to open a school for girls in Baltimore. Guided by the Sulpician Fathers at St. Mary's Seminary, she conducted classes in a house on Paca Street, and there, in the spring of 1809, with four companions, formed the community which adopted the name "Sisters of St. Joseph." In the summer they moved to Emmitsburg. They adopted, with some modifications, the rules of the Daughters of Charity of St. Vincent de Paul, and after 1812 were known as the Sisters of Charity of St. Joseph. This first native religious community was destined to number more than ten thousand women and to conduct a nation-wide system of charitable and educational institutions, among them the country's first Catholic orphanage, its first Catholic hospital, and its first maternity hospital. Because Mother Seton had her sisters open in Philadelphia the earliest American parish school, and sent them virtually everywhere to help the bishops in their work of education, she is considered the patroness of the parochial school system in America. Her community may be said to be the index of her character. It ministers to practically every type of educational and social need of the American people, for the glory of God and the good of the country.

As the first superior of the community, Mother Seton braved the hardships of its early days. In spite of the poverty that continually threatened its existence, she somehow formed her sisters into effective teachers and model religious. She herself taught French and music many hours daily, mothered the children of the school and the poor of the neighborhood, wrote thousands of letters, translated French biographies, prepared original meditations, composed exquisite hymns, among them a version of "Jerusalem, My Happy Home," for which she also wrote the music; yet all the while she led a life of recollection. Many of her writings were edited by her grandson, Robert Seton [*q.v.*], and published under the title, *Memoirs, Letters, and Journal of Elizabeth Seton* (2 vols., 1869).

Her extraordinary spiritual discernment made her a power for good when the Church in America was still in its infancy. With the spread of her influence after her death, her reputation for sanctity increased and about 1907 her Cause for canonization was introduced by James Cardinal Gibbons, successor in the see of Baltimore of her nephew, James Roosevelt Bayley [q.v.].

[Archives of St. Joseph Mother House, Emmitsburg, Md.; archives of the Cathedral, Baltimore, Md.; *Memoirs, Letters, and Journal* mentioned above; C. I. White, *Life of Mrs. Eliza A. Seton* (3rd ed., 1879); Hélène Bailly de Barberey, *Elizabeth Seton* (1927), translated and adapted by J. B. Code; J. B. Code, *Great Am. Foundresses* (1929) and *Mother Seton and Her Sisters of Charity* (1930); Robert Seton, *An Old Family, or the Setons of Scotland and America* (1899).]

J.B.C.

SETON, ROBERT (Aug. 28, 1839–Mar. 22, 1927), Roman Catholic prelate, was born in Pisa, Italy. His father was William Seton, a naval officer, son of Mother Elizabeth Ann Seton [q.v.]; his mother, Emily Prime, daughter of Nathaniel Prime, of the historic banking house of Prime, Ward & King. Of noble Scottish and English lineage on his father's side, and connected on his mother's with some of the foremost American families of wealth and social prominence, he possessed a family pride so extravagant at times that it led to eccentricities which made him an enigma even to his coreligionists in America. His childhood was spent at the Seton home, "Cragdon," in Westchester County, N. Y., and at eleven he followed his brother William Seton [q.v.] as a student at Mount St. Mary's College, Emmitsburg, Md., close to the convent of St. Joseph, where his grandmother had founded the American Sisters of Charity. Two years later, he accompanied his parents to southern France, where his mother died at Pau, in 1854. For the next three years he traveled on the Continent, studied at several European institutions, and finally made a short visit to America.

Although the life of a soldier appealed to his romantic nature, he finally decided to become a priest. With this end in view he went to Rome in 1857, where he became a student at the Urban College of the Propaganda until the opening of the North American College in 1859 when he enrolled as its first student. He aroused the interest of Pius IX who in November 1861 had him transferred to the Accademia Ecclesiastica dei Nobili, an institution for the education of nobles studying for the priesthood. Even here, among the scions of the greatest European houses, Seton remained stanchly American, his militant patriotism often getting him into serious difficulties. Once, refusing to attend a reception given by the Roman patriciate for Maxi-

milian and Carlotta, who were about to embark for Mexico on their anti-American Napoleonic venture, he would have been expelled, but for the Pope's intervention. After a brilliant course of studies, first at the Roman College and afterwards at the Roman University, commonly called the Sapienza, he was ordained priest, Apr. 16, 1865. The following year the Pope made him a private chamberlain and one year later named him a prothonotary apostolic, the first American so honored. The same year he received the degree of bachelor of laws and doctor of divinity. In his early twenties he had become the accepted American representative in the ecclesiastical world of Rome.

For some unknown reason, however, he decided against a career that would have led possibly to the cardinalate, and elected to return to America. Here for more than a quarter of a century he led a quietly busy life, first as chaplain to the Sisters of Charity, at St. Elizabeth's Convent, near Madison, N. J., then as pastor of St. Joseph's Church, Jersey City, giving occasional lectures on his great hobby, Christian archeology, at various American colleges and universities. Suddenly in 1902 he returned to Rome, where for twelve years he served as the unofficial link between the Vatican and things and people American. The Rome of the Temporal Sovereignty had disappeared, but he found four of his old classmates cardinals, one a patriarch, two archbishops, two canons of the Vatican, and three others high in ecclesiastical circles. In 1903 he refused the then vacant archbishopric of Chicago, but four months later accepted the mitre in another form when Pius X appointed him titular archbishop of Heliopolis *in partibus infidelium.* The years that followed, the most beautiful of Robert Seton's life, were the years of which Shane Leslie speaks, when the aged archbishop "had become perfect, almost exquisite, in Roman etiquette as well as in pontifical ceremonies" (Introduction to Seton's *Memories of Many Years,* p. 22).

Meanwhile, across the Atlantic he had become almost legendary. In 1914, however, financial reverses had so reduced his patrimony that he reappeared among his countrymen as an impoverished old aristocrat, seeking a home on the eve of a great international conflict. He took up his residence at Emmitsburg, near the tomb of Mother Seton, but a longing for Europe drew him back once more, and he spent three years in France, Spain, and England. When he returned to America he lived at the Convent of St. Elizabeth, cared for by the same sisterhood to which he had given his services as a priest shortly after his ordination. A faithful priest, a distinguished scholar, and a unique personality, he had a career, which in length and strangeness of fortune was without parallel among his countrymen. In 1862 he published *Essays on Various Subjects Chiefly Roman,* and in 1869 he edited many of Mother Seton's writings—*Memoirs, Letters, and Journal of Elizabeth Seton.* Another of his works was a scholarly genealogical study, *An Old Family, or the Setons of Scotland and America* (1899). His own memoirs, *Memories of Many Years,* appeared in 1923. He was also correspondent for the *New York Times,* under the name Fyvie.

[In addition to Seton's own publications, sources of information are archives of St. Joseph Coll., Emmitsburg, Md., of the Coll. of St. Elizabeth, Convent Station, N. J., and of the North Am. Coll., and the Acad. of Noble Ecclesiastics, Rome, Italy; *Catholic News* (N. Y.), Mar. 26, Apr. 2, 1927; *N. Y. Times,* Mar. 23, 1927.]
J. B. C.

SETON, WILLIAM (Jan. 28, 1835–Mar. 15, 1905), author, was born in New York City, the son of William Seton, a lieutenant in the United States navy, and Emily (Prime) Seton. A descendant of William Seton who came to New York in 1763, he was the grandson of Elizabeth Ann Bayley Seton and brother to Monsignor Robert Seton [*qq.v.*], the distinguished Roman Catholic divine. Tracing his ancestry back to the Setons of Parbroath, an ancient Scottish family, he was recognized in Burke's *A Genealogical and Heraldic Dictionary of the Peerage and Baronetage* (1901) as the head of the Parbroath branch of the family. After a brief stay at St. John's College, Fordham, he continued his studies at Mount St. Mary's College, Emmitsburg, Md. Leaving this institution in the early fifties before taking a degree, he studied for a time at the University of Bonn. Upon his return to New York, he entered the law office of T. J. Glover and was admitted to the bar just before the outbreak of the Civil War. He answered the first call for troops, and as captain in the 4th New York Infantry was twice wounded in the battle of Antietam (George Seton, *post,* p. 311). With the advent of peace he devoted himself to literature, giving special attention for some years to the writing of fiction. About 1886, however, while in Europe, he became so absorbed in the study of science that he thereafter gave most of his time to scientific pursuits. He now made annual visits to Paris, where he became acquainted with such authorities as Albert Gaudry and Albert de Lapparent.

Seton began his literary career with the novel *Nat Gregory, or the Old Maid's Secret* (1867). This was succeeded by two historical novels, *Ro-*

mance of the Charter Oak (1871), "a Picture of Colonial Times" in Connecticut, and *The Pride of Lexington* (1873), a story of the American Revolution; later followed by *Rachel's Fate, and Other Tales* (1882) and several other novels. *The Pioneer* (1874), Seton's single excursion into the realm of poetry, which was dedicated to Bryant, deals in a somewhat Wordsworthian manner with a young New Hampshire couple who seek a new home in the wilderness. It is probably, however, as a popularizer of the theory of evolution that Seton did his most effective literary work. Avoiding the ultra-technical, he sought to present clearly to the average man the discoveries of natural science. The simplicity of his handling of scientific subjects is well exemplified in *A Glimpse of Organic Life* (copyright 1897), a work in dialogue form designed primarily for young people but effectively written. Somewhat more technical is his defense of the theory of evolution contributed to the *Catholic World,* November 1897, called "The Hypothesis of Evolution." His interest in science is further reflected in a biographical sketch of Michel-Guillaume Jean de Crèvecœur [*q.v.*] written for the *Magazine of American History,* September 1889. He was also a contributor to a pamphlet entitled *Hear the Other Side* (188–), a plea for freedom of worship among the children committed to the "House of Refuge" on Randall's Island. On Jan. 3, 1884, he married Sarah Redwood Parrish of Philadelphia, a Catholic convert from the Society of Friends, who died in 1895; their only child died in infancy. Toward the close of his life he became well known as a philanthropist. He died in New York and is buried with other members of the family at Mount St. Mary's.

[Monsignor (Robert) Seton, *An Old Family, or the Setons of Scotland and America* (1889), with portrait; George Seton, *A Hist. of the Family of Seton* (1896), vol. I; *Cath. Encyc.* (1912), vol. XIII; *N. Y. Daily Tribune,* Mar. 16, 17, 1905; "Living Cath. Men of Science," *Cath. World,* with portrait, Mar. 1898; *A Supp. to Allibone's Critical Dict. of Eng. Lit. and British and Am. Authors* (1891), ed. by J. F. Kirk; letter from the Rev. B. J. Bradley, president of Mount St. Mary's College.]
N. F. A.

SETTLE, THOMAS (Jan. 23, 1831–Dec. 1, 1888), politician, jurist, was born in Rockingham County, N. C., the fourth child of Thomas and Henrietta (Graves) Settle, and a descendant of Josiah Settle who emigrated from England to North Carolina in the middle of the eighteenth century. His father, a member and speaker of the House of Commons, congressman, and judge of long service, was prominent in state affairs. The younger Thomas graduated from the University of North Carolina in 1850, was private secretary to his brother-in-law, Gov. David S

Reid [*q.v.*], studied law under Judge Richmond M. Pearson [*q.v.*], with whom he was later on the North Carolina supreme bench, was licensed in 1854, and began practice in Rockingham County. About this time, he married Mary, the daughter of Tyre Glenn of Surry County, by whom he had six daughters and three sons.

His father was a Whig, but Settle, in 1852, became a Democrat, and in 1854 began his political career as a member of the House of Commons; he was twice reëlected and during his last term served as speaker. In 1856 he was a Buchanan elector, and in 1860 he supported Douglas. When the cotton states seceded, he opposed similar action by North Carolina. In February 1861 he was chosen a delegate to the convention which the people rejected and about the same time was elected solicitor of the fourth judicial circuit. When the call for troops came, he eagerly volunteered and became a captain in the 3rd North Carolina Regiment. At the close of the year's term of enlistment, however, he did not again volunteer, but resumed the office of solicitor. In 1865 he was a delegate to the "Johnson" convention where, as chairman of the committee on the abolition of slavery and of that on the state debt, he wrote and offered the ordinances abolishing slavery and repudiating the war debt; he also took a prominent part in every question before the convention. In November he was elected to the state Senate and was chosen speaker. In the campaign he had supported William W. Holden [*q.v.*] for governor, and he was, at this period, in hearty accord with President Johnson's policy. At the second session of the convention, however, he gradually identified himself with the group in opposition and favored the ratification of the Fourteenth Amendment. When it was rejected, he championed the congressional policy of reconstruction, participated in the political meeting which organized the radical party in the state, and introduced the resolution which identified it with the Republican party; yet at no time was he possessed by the bitter radicalism which characterized the majority of his party associates.

In April 1868 he was elected associate justice of the supreme court of North Carolina and served until February 1871, when President Grant appointed him minister to Peru. Disliking the position and the climate, early in 1872 he resigned. He was president of the Republican National Convention of 1872 and in the autumn was an unsuccessful candidate for Congress. In December he was reappointed to the supreme court and served until 1876 when he resigned

to accept the Republican nomination for governor. The brilliant campaign carried on by him and his opponent Zebulon B. Vance [*q.v.*] was one which in character and spirit brought honor to both. Settle gave an excellent account of himself but went down in defeat. On Jan. 30, 1877, President Grant appointed him district judge for Florida, and he filled that office until his death.

Settle was a superbly handsome man with a magnetic personality. He was genial, witty, and affectionate in personal intercourse, and courageous and tolerant in his public relationships. His mind was quick and acute, and he was a well-informed and persuasive debater. He was best fitted for the political arena, but made an excellent though in no sense a great judge. He was impartial, humane, and just, and his judicial opinions were terse, concise, and clear.

[W. P. Bynum, Address, in 139 *N. C. Reports*, 649; *Jour. of the Convention of the State of N. C.*, 1865, 1866; 63–65 and 68–75 *N. C. Reports*; Sidney Andrews, *The South Since the War* (1866); J. H. Wheeler, *Reminiscences and Memoirs of N. C. and Eminent North Carolinians* (1884); *Appletons' Ann. Cyc.*, 1888 (1889); *Morning Star* (Wilmington, N. C.), Dec. 2, 4, 1888.]   J. G. deR. H.

SEVERANCE, CAROLINE MARIA SEYMOUR (Jan. 12, 1820–Nov. 10, 1914), founder of woman's clubs, was born in Canandaigua, N. Y., the daughter of Orson and Caroline M. (Clarke) Seymour. Her father was a banker and her home a comfortable one. His death, when she was a child, brought her under the guardianship of an uncle, a strict Presbyterian, whose influence overshadowed that of her Episcopalian mother. She described herself as a serious and supersensitive child, whose life was darkened by her mother's constant grief for her father and tortured by a sense of sin and the threat of eternal punishment which she heard described in the Presbyterian pulpit. When she was fifteen she graduated from the Female Seminary at Geneva, N. Y., valedictorian of her class. On Aug. 27, 1840, she was married, in Auburn, N. Y., to Theodoric C. Severance of Cleveland, a banker; they were the parents of five children. Louis Henry Severance [*q.v.*] was their nephew.

The first years of her married life were spent in Cleveland where she soon became active in public affairs. Having attained some prominence at Woman's Rights conventions, she was invited in 1853 to read a paper before the Mercantile Library Association of Cleveland—the first, according to her own statement, ever presented by a woman before such a society. Her subject was "Humanity; a Definition and a Plea," and she was requested to repeat the reading on several occasions. The Ohio Woman's Rights Association then asked her to prepare a tract on woman's rights for circulation, and she later presented a memorial to the state legislature on behalf of civil equality for women. In 1855 the family moved to Boston and here she soon began to plan what she had long desired, an organization of women associated for mutual benefit and social work. Then came the Civil War when, in the work for the Sanitary Commission and the Freedman's Bureau, women took an important part in great enterprises. When the war was over she took the lead in furthering the desire of some of the women in Boston for a continued association and was instrumental in founding the New England Women's Club. On Feb. 10, 1868, the society was formed and on Mar. 10, 1868, a constitution was adopted. The object of the club was to organize the social force of the women then working alone or in small circles. Men were eligible to membership but the club was to be officered and controlled by women. Mrs. Severance was elected president and held that office until 1871 when she was succeeded by Julia Ward Howe [q.v.]. In 1875 the Severance family moved to Los Angeles, Cal. Her interest in women's organizations did not cease, however, and three years later she founded the Woman's Club of Los Angeles, which existed until 1887. She was also the founder of the Los Angeles Free Kindergarten Association, reorganized in 1891 as the Friday Morning Club, of which she became the first president. Later, the Los Angeles Fellowship Club was formed in her home, as was the Severance Club, an organization of both men and women. She was also instrumental in founding the Ebell Club of Los Angeles. Because of her activity she became known as "the mother of clubs." She wrote papers on a wide variety of topics of public interest, and was a trustee of the public library and of the Unitarian church.

[*Who's Who in America,* 1914–15; J. A. Sprague, *Hist. of the New England Women's Club* (1894); E. G. Ruddy, ed., *The Mother of Clubs* (1906); *Los Angeles Daily Times,* Nov. 11, 1914.]   B. R.

SEVERANCE, FRANK HAYWARD (Nov. 28, 1856–Jan. 26, 1931), author, historian, was born in Manchester, Mass., the son of Lucius Warren and Maria Lucretia (Hayward) Severance. He was directly descended from Richard Warren who came to Plymouth in the Mayflower. The family later was among the earliest settlers in the Champlain Valley but returned to Manchester; when the Civil War ruined Lucius Severance's business, he moved to White-

water, Wis. Severance entered Knox College in 1874 but in 1875 he went to Cornell University, where he partly earned his way by working as a printer during the first two years. During the last two years he was an assistant in microscopic botany and editor of the *Cornell Review* and of the *Cornell Era,* where he published some articles on Cayuga legendry. After receiving the bachelor's degree in 1879, he became a reporter on the *Gazette* at Erie, Pa.; a year later he went to Buffalo as marine editor on the *Buffalo Express.* On Aug. 19, 1885, he married Lena Lillian Hill of Isle Lamotte, Vt., who had been a classmate of his at Cornell. He soon became city editor and in 1886 managing editor of the *Illustrated Sunday Express,* a position he held until 1901, when he was called upon to become secretary of the Buffalo Historical Society. While on the *Express* he reported the funeral of President Garfield and the Johnstown flood of 1889.

It was between 1881 and 1886 that he began assembling information on the Niagara frontier and while he was managing editor of the *Illustrated Sunday Express* that he began to write on the subject. In appreciation of a series of stories on behalf of the Indians of western New York the Seneca Indians adopted him into their tribe, giving him the name of Da-deh'-o-gwat-hah, the carrier of news. He was invited to many of their festivals and to ceremonies of which few whites were permitted to be observers. His writings include *Old Trails on the Niagara Frontier* (1899), *The Story of Joncaire* (1906), *Studies of the Niagara Frontier* (1911), *The Picture Book of Earlier Buffalo* (1912), *Peace Episodes on the Niagara* (1914), and *An Old Frontier of France* (2 vols., 1917). He edited the publications of the Buffalo Historical Society from 1896 to 1930, and in 1904 William Walton's *The Captivity and Sufferings of Benjamin Gilbert and his Family* (1784). He also contributed to historical magazines and encyclopedias. He helped to arouse interest in the early history of western New York and the Great Lakes region not only by writing but by lecturing before historical and learned societies. A trained historian and an editor of marked ability, he served the Buffalo Historical Society as an able guide in its research in regional history, and his work as director of the museum gave the society a position of importance.

His travels included a number of trips to Europe and a tour of the world. Having had a keen interest in natural science from boyhood, he studied the trees of India and Burmah during a winter he spent in those countries; on three occasions he visited Japan, where he found much to interest him in the strangeness and variety of plant growths. He was president of the New York State Historical Association, 1923–25, and served as a member of the fine arts commission of New York state. He was an attendant of Westminster Presbyterian Church in Buffalo. At the time of his death he was survived by his wife, two daughters, and a son.

[*Who's Who in America*, 1930–31; biog. sketch in *Proc. N. Y. State Hist. Assoc.*, vol. XXIII (1925); *N. Y. State Hist. Assoc. Quart. Jour.*, Jan. 1931; *Buffalo Courier Express*, *Buffalo Evening News*, Jan. 27, 1931; *N. Y. Times*, Jan. 28, 1931; additional information from the Severance family.]   A. H. S.

SEVERANCE, LOUIS HENRY (Aug. 1, 1838–June 25, 1913), capitalist and philanthropist, was the younger of the two sons of Solomon Lewis Severance and Mary (Long) Severance. His paternal ancestor, John Severans, who is known to have been living in Ipswich, England, in 1635 and in Boston, Mass., in 1637, was one of the original proprietors of Salisbury, Mass. One of his descendants, Robert Severance, studied medicine with Dr. John Long in Shelburne, Mass., and married the daughter of his patron. Both doctors lived out their time in Shelburne, notable physicians of western Massachusetts. A grandson of Dr. John Long, Dr. David Long, Jr., settled in Cleveland in 1810. Thither, too, the six sons of Dr. Robert Severance, Solomon, Lewis, Theodoric, Cordenio, Erasmus, and John, were attracted a few years later. Solomon Lewis Severance opened a dry goods store, and in 1833 married Mary Long, the only child of Dr. David Long, Jr. Solomon died in 1838, about a month before his son Louis Henry was born. The widowed mother returned with her small family to her father's home, where the boys grew to manhood. Louis Henry Severance attended Cleveland public schools and in his eighteenth year found employment in the Commercial National Bank. Except for 100 days' service with the Union army in 1863, he remained in the banking business until near the end of the Civil War. The oil industry in western Pennsylvania then offered him the opportunity he had been awaiting. In 1864 he went to Titusville, Pa., to engage in the production of oil. Ten years later he returned to Cleveland, drawn into the Standard Oil Company of Ohio. From 1876 until his death, he was a stockholder of that company, and from 1876 until his retirement from active duties in 1894, served as its treasurer. He spent most of the remaining years of his life in New York City, although he died in Cleveland.

Severance's interests and industrial influence were extended through investments in oil, salt, sulphur, and steel. In the nineties, in association with Herman Frasch [*q.v.*], F. B. Squire, and Frank Rockefeller, he formed the Union Sulphur Company, which employed a revolutionary process, invented by Frasch, of dissolving and pumping sulphur from its sources and thereby made the United States a great world producer of sulphur. His chief interest outside of business was in the Presbyterian Church and especially its missions. Hospitals and churches in Japan, Korea, and India stand as monuments to his philanthropy. Severance Hospital and the Severance Medical College at Seoul, Korea, are his benefactions. In 1907–08 he traveled around the world, inspecting missions generally. He was a trustee and generous supporter of Oberlin College, Western Reserve University, and the College of Wooster. After Wooster had been destroyed by fire in 1901, Severance, almost alone, rebuilt the institution on a larger and more attractive scale. He also gave liberally to the Young Men's Christian Association.

Severance was a gentleman of the old school, urbane, conservative in his tastes, critical in his judgments, but always kindly. He was married twice: on Aug. 13, 1862, to Fannie Buckingham Benedict, who died twelve years later, and in 1894 to Florence, daughter of Stephen D. Harkness, a member of the Standard Oil group; she died in 1895. To the first marriage two sons and two daughters were born; a son and two daughters survived their father.

[J. F. Severance, *The Severans Geneal. Hist.* (1893); G. V. Wickham, *The Pioneer Families of Cleveland* (1914), vol. II; E. M. Avery, *A Hist. of Cleveland and Its Environs* (1918), vol. II; *Cleveland Plain Dealer*, June 26, 1913.]   E. J. B.

SEVIER, AMBROSE HUNDLEY (Nov. 4, 1801–Dec. 31, 1848), representative and senator from Arkansas, was born in Greene County, Tenn., the son of John Sevier, the great-grandson of Valentine Sevier who emigrated from England to Baltimore in the middle of the 18th century, and the grand-nephew of John Sevier [*q.v.*]. His mother was probably Susannah (Conway) Sevier, also called Susan and Ann, the sister of James Sevier Conway and Elias Nelson Conway [*qq.v.*]. She divorced her husband, married again in 1812, and died about 1815. The boy received such education as the frontier afforded and studied law with his father. At the age of nineteen he removed to Missouri, and to Arkansas in 1821. There he was soon elected clerk of the territorial House of Representatives, served as a member from 1823 to 1827, and became speaker in 1827. On Aug. 26 of that year he was married to Juliette Johnson, the niece of James and Richard Mentor

Johnson and the sister of Robert Ward Johnson [*qq.v.*], and thereby became a member of the politically powerful Johnson family. They had five children.

Next year Henry W. Conway, the territorial delegate to Congress, was killed in a duel with Robert Crittenden, and Ambrose was elected to succeed him. He had himself already fought a duel, and in Congress he opposed a bill to prohibit dueling in the District of Columbia on the ground that it was a bill to protect members of Congress who had slandered their masters, the people. He kept his seat as delegate from Feb. 13, 1828, to June 15, 1836, when Arkansas was admitted as a state, having taken a prominent part in bringing about that result. As a Democrat he was elected senator and served in that capacity until March 1848. He was tall and handsome, with an irresistible laugh that won him many friends. He was *un bon vivant* and played his part in a banquet in his honor where fifty-eight toasts were drunk (Little Rock *Arkansas Gazette*, Nov. 30, 1830, Nov. 31, 1833; Little Rock *Arkansas Advocate*, Nov. 14, 1832). He worked constantly for his territory and state and obtained numerous favors from Congress, particularly donations of land (Little Rock *Arkansas Gazette*, Jan. 27, Feb. 10, Mar. 14, 1829, Oct. 31, 1832). He was made a member of the committee on Indian affairs and favored the organization of an Indian territory out of the region west of Missouri and Arkansas. He supported Linn's Oregon Bill and declared that the United States should occupy and govern that territory to carry out the Monroe Doctrine. Naturally he supported Polk's Oregon policy, championing even in bellicose language the resolution to give notice of the termination of the treaty of joint occupation (*Congressional Globe*, 27 Cong., 3 Sess., p. 154; 29 Cong., 1 Sess., app. p. 389). He voted to recognize the independence of Texas in 1837, for the treaty of annexation in 1844, and for the second joint resolution, which gave the president the choice of proceeding by treaty or direct annexation; but he took little part in the discussion. He took an active interest in the Mexican War. As chairman of the committee on foreign relations he introduced and pushed through the "3 million dollar bill" appropriating money for peace negotiations (*Congressional Globe*, 29 Cong., 2 Sess., p. 305). When the Trist treaty of peace was amended by the Senate, President Polk, his personal friend, asked Sevier to serve as minister to Mexico to conclude the negotiations. He hesitated but finally resigned, on Mar. 15, 1848, to accept. He was accompanied by Nathan Clifford [*q.v.*].

When the state legislature met in November 1848, Sevier was a candidate for reëlection, but after the legislature had balloted for three days he withdrew. He had been taken ill after his appointment to go to Mexico, had recovered, but was attacked again while in Mexico. From this he never fully recovered, and he died at his home, a large cotton plantation near Little Rock, Ark.

[*The Diary of James E. Polk*, 4 vols. (1910), ed. by M. M. Quaife; John Hallum, *Biog. and Pictorial Hist. of Ark.*, vol. I (1887); Fay Hempstead, *Hist. Rev. of Ark.* (1911); D. T. Herndon, *Centennial Hist. of Ark.* (1922), vol. I; Zella Armstrong, "The Sevier Family," *Notable Southern Families*, vol. IV (1926); *Ark. and its People*, 4 vols. (1930), ed. by D. Y. Thomas; *Biog. Dir. of Am. Cong.* (1928); *Ark. State Democrat* (Little Rock), Jan. 12, 1849; date of birth from inscription on grave in Mt. Holly Cemetery, Little Rock, Ark., quoted in *Ark. Hist. Asso. Pubs.*, vol. II (1908), p. 279.]
D. Y. T.

SEVIER, JOHN (Sept. 23, 1745–Sept. 24, 1815), pioneer, soldier, first governor of the state of Tennessee, was born near the present New Market, Va. When he emigrated from the Shenandoah Valley to the remote frontier region that is now East Tennessee, he was already, at the age of twenty-eight, the father of six or seven children. That was perhaps a sufficient reason for his moving to a country where land was cheap. Given the circumstances of his ancestry and early life, it is no surprise that he turned pioneer. His grandfather had emigrated from France to England, his father, Valentine, from London to Baltimore and thence to the Shenandoah Valley. There Valentine had married Joanna Goade, acquired a farm and a tavern, built up a large trade in furs and rum with Indians and white settlers, and speculated in land. John, the eldest of seven children, soon began to repeat the pattern of his father's life. After receiving a rather haphazard education he married in 1761 a girl of the neighborhood, Sarah Hawkins, moved from place to place, engaged in farming and trading, and laid off town lots at New Market, where he established a tavern and gave the Baptists a site for a church. With this varied training, great courage and personal magnetism, and probably a captain's commission in the militia, he was ready for leadership on a new frontier. The Appalachian Valley system pointed the way southwestward to the Holston River, where he would find in the process of formation a community similar to the one in which he had grown up.

He arrived in the Holston settlements with his family and belongings in December 1773. For the next seventeen years he continued to move down the valley with the advancing frontier. From 1783 to 1790 his home was on the Nolachucky River and after 1790 in or near

Knoxville. From the outset he was one of the acknowledged leaders of the backwoodsmen. It is said that he visited the region in 1771 and 1772 and was made a commissioner of the Watauga Association. He was certainly a member of the local Committee of Safety in 1776, when he signed a petition in that capacity requesting North Carolina to extend its jurisdiction over the Watauga and Holston settlements. When the request was granted, he was elected a representative to the Provincial Congress, which then appointed him lieutenant-colonel of militia. Though an active supporter of the revolutionary cause, he took little part in the fighting until 1780 and seems to have been occupied chiefly with various minor civil offices. It was in 1780, just after the migration of James Robertson to Middle Tennessee had cleared the field of his chief rival, that he rose to preëminence in the Watauga country. In this year he won undying fame among his people by leading two hundred and forty men across the Smokies to the victory of the southern frontiersmen over the British at King's Mountain. Immediately upon his return he set out upon an expedition against the Cherokee that marked the beginning of his career as harrier of the Indians. These events occurred shortly after his marriage on Aug. 14, 1780, to Catherine Sherrill, about seven months after the death of his first wife. In 1781 and 1782 he made three raids against the Indians and in the former year again crossed the mountains with two hundred men to aid Francis Marion against the British.

The "critical period" in American history was certainly a critical period in the life of John Sevier. With the British expelled and the Indians humbled, expansive forces were released along the whole western frontier, and nowhere was the tendency to dispersion more marked than in the settlements on the Holston and Watauga rivers. In most of the symptomatic developments Sevier was deeply concerned. At the close of the Revolution he joined with William Blount [q.v.] and others in a project for the establishment of a colony at Muscle Shoals. While he was thus engaged, a movement for a separate state was set on foot by his neighbors. At first he opposed it, since it might interfere with his Muscle Shoals venture, and he was satisfied with his brigadier-general's commission and other concessions hurriedly offered by North Carolina. Finding the movement irresistible, he put himself at the head of it, was elected governor of the state of Franklin, and tried to convert the new state into an instrument for promoting his Muscle Shoals enterprise. For that and other purposes a military expedition against the Indians was concerted with the state of Georgia. His conduct alienated many of the pioneers, among them doctrinaire liberals who had had quite different plans for the new state. The failure of the Georgians to furnish the expected aid injured his prestige, and the opposition crystallised when a feud broke out between the Sevier and Tipton families. After some skirmishing over the county court records, which may be related to subsequent scandals over land titles, the Sevier faction was defeated in a "battle" in February 1788 which, though there were few casualties, resulted in the virtual extinction of the state of Franklin.

Because he had expressed the spirit of his times with too much vigor, he found himself at the age of forty-three a man with a blasted career. If he had played with land speculation, so had almost every other man in public life in the South and West. If he had scourged the Indians, it was an article of the frontier creed that Indian-baiting was a public service. If he had espoused the Franklin movement, it was only because public opinion had forced him to do so. Yet these things had proved his undoing. In the East, in North Carolina, in his own home country, he was denounced as a reckless disturber of the public peace, and his very life was in danger. In his desperation he took refuge on the extreme frontier with "a lawless banditti," as the governor of North Carolina called his followers. There he sank to the level of a bushwhacker, defied the efforts of Congress to control Indian affairs, and entered into a dubious correspondence with Spanish agents who were seeking to disrupt the Union. Arrested after a brawl in October 1788, he fled to the mountains, when released on bail, and wrote the North Carolina authorities demanding justice and hinting broadly at secession.

A fortunate turn of events in national affairs made possible his rehabilitation, and he was adroit enough to take full advantage of the opportunity. In 1788 North Carolina had failed to ratify the federal constitution, but the successful establishment of the new government made early ratification a certainty. Identifying himself with the rising cause, Sevier came forth as a stanch "federalist,"—indeed, he had always been a friend to the Union when he thought the Union could help the West. Fortunately for him, he had influential friends in the East, among them William Blount, who had long been associated with him in land speculation. There was moreover a general feeling that the recent disturbances on the frontier had been due in part to the blunders of the Confederation and that the new era should begin with a clean slate. The result was that, when Sevier was elected to the North Carolina Senate in 1789, he was fully pardoned, seated, and restored to his position as brigadier-general. As a member of the state convention that met simultaneously, he voted with the majority for the ratification of the federal constitution. When North Carolina completed the cession of its western territory to Congress, Blount was appointed governor, and Sevier was commissioned brigadier-general of militia in 1791. In the meanwhile he had served a brief term in Congress, 1789 to 1791, as the representative of North Carolina's western district before the act of cession was accepted.

The next twenty years of his life, which he spent in Tennessee, were comparatively uneventful. The sharp contrast between their sobriety and the romantic exploits of his earlier years suggests that the Franklin fiasco had cured him of his love of adventure. He took no part in the Genet affair or in the conspiracies of William Blount and Aaron Burr. His last fling in land speculation in the grand manner was a brief connection with the South Carolina Yazoo Company in 1790; and, though while governor of Tennessee he gave some encouragement to the Muscle Shoals enterprise of Zachariah Cox in 1798, he seems to have taken no part in it personally. His last campaign against the Indians was fought in 1793. In 1798–99 he was ready to fight again, but this time under federal authority as brigadier-general in the provisional army. Even politics occupied but little of his time during the territorial period. He was a member of the legislative council in 1794, but he did not sit in the convention that drew up the first constitution of the state of Tennessee in 1796. If his diary is to be trusted, he gave little thought to anything but his plantation, his iron works, his store, his slaves, and his wife and eighteen children. Land speculation he had by no means forgotten, for in 1795 he patented 66,-000 acres of land lying on the Cumberland River; but now it was a purely business transaction. He and his wife moved in polite society, drinking tea at the governor's house, dining out, playing whist, and attending balls. He was a trustee of two colleges, Washington College in Tennessee and Blount College (University of Tennessee), and though not a churchmember, employed a Presbyterian minister to tutor his children and was frequently seen at church with his wife. The leader of "a lawless banditti" had been transformed into a pillar of society.

Most of the remaining years of this Indian fighter were spent in civil employment. Elected the first governor of Tennessee, he served three successive terms, as many as the constitution permitted, from 1796 until 1801, and three more terms from 1803 to 1809. The choice was a natural one, for he was a military hero, still a dashing figure, unaffectedly cordial in his manner, neither cultured nor illiterate, an experienced public officer, and bound by ties of blood and intimate friendship to many families throughout the state. A quarrel with Andrew Jackson, which began about 1796, embittered the rest of his life. Jackson complicated the issue by preferring charges of land frauds that may or may not have been true, but the real source of the difficulty lay in conflicting military ambitions. It was a sign of the changing times that in 1801 the young politician and judge, Jackson, who had never fought a campaign since early youth, was elected major-general of militia over Sevier, the hero of some thirty-five battles and skirmishes. Though the encounter of 1803, in which the affair culminated, was farcical, it left a deep impression upon Sevier, who dreamed that his father appeared to him to assure him that Jackson was "a very wicked base man, and a very improper person for a judge" (Diary, *post*, Dec. 10, 1803).

After his retirement from the governorship, he was elected to the state Senate for one term 1809–11, was then sent to Congress again, and served from 1811 until his death. In the latter body he apparently never took part in debate, though he attended regularly, voted on many important questions, and served on several committees. He usually supported the administration and voted for the declaration of war in 1812, urging that "fire and sword" be carried into the Creek Indian country, where "British emissaries" were no doubt lurking, and that the Floridas be annexed. In 1815 he was appointed a member of the commission to survey the boundary of the Creek cession obtained by Jackson in 1814. He died in Alabama while on this service, and was buried at Fort Decatur on the Tallapoosa River. His remains were later removed to Knoxville, Tenn.

[Sevier Collection in Lib. of State of Tenn., Nashville, some of which already pub. in *East Tenn. Hist. Soc. Pubs.*, no. 1–5 (1929–33); "The Diary of John Sevier," *Tenn. Hist. Mag.*, Oct. 19–April 1920, and in S. G. Heiskell, *Andrew Jackson and Early Tenn. Hist.*, 2nd ed. (2 vols. 1920); C. S. Driver, *John Sevier* (1932); F. M. Turner, *Life of Gen. John Sevier* (1910); S. C. Williams, *Hist. of the Lost State of Franklin* (1924); Zella Armstrong, "The Sevier Family," *Notable Southern Families*, vol. IV (1926); A. P. Whitaker in *Miss. Valley Hist. Rev.*, Sept. 1925, Dec. 1926; A. V. Goodpasture, "Genesis of the Jackson-Sevier Feud," *Am. Hist. Mag.* (Nashville), Apr. 1900.]
A. P. W.

SEWALL, ARTHUR (Nov. 25, 1835–Sept. 5, 1900), shipbuilder, son of William Dunning and Rachel (Trufant) Sewall and brother of Frank Sewall [q.v.], was born at Bath, Me. He was descended from Henry Sewall, who had come from Coventry, England, in 1634 and settled in Newbury, Mass.; his great-grandfather, Dummer Sewall, had moved in 1760 from York, Me., to Georgetown (later Bath), which partly through Sewall influence was to become "the great American shipyard." His father dabbled in railroads and politics and built twenty-nine vessels between 1823 and 1854. After a common school education in Bath, Arthur was sent to Prince Edward Island to become familiar with the cutting of ship timber. He began his active shipbuilding career in 1854 as the American merchant marine reached its zenith. With his elder brother, Edward, he formed the firm of E. & A. Sewall and commenced work in the family yard on the Kennebec. The *Holyhead,* of some 1100 tons, launched in 1855, was the first of his eighty vessels. Upon Edward's death he took a son and a nephew as partners, and the firm in 1879 became A. Sewall & Company. Though English vessels, utilizing iron, steel, and steam, were driving the wooden American sailing vessels out of competition, the Sewalls specialized in the latter type, doing much to keep it alive in the period of decline. They generally retained ownership of the ships they built and at one time owned a fleet of more than twenty-five. Their shipwrights and captains were usually natives of the Kennebec valley. Sewall was given much of the credit for the excellent *esprit de corps* of both groups and for the absence of labor problems; it was said that there was not a single job in his shipyard that he could not perform ably with his own hands. During the Civil War he refused to have his ships take advantage of British registry, and his *Vigilant* was captured on her maiden voyage by the Confederate raider, *Sumter.* In the decade following the war, the Sewalls turned out a number of celebrated ships, including the *Undaunted, Eric the Red, El Capitan, Occidental, Oriental, Continental, Harvester, Reaper, Thrasher,* and *Granger.* Then came a depression without even the usual "ship a year," but in the early nineties they built their "Big Four," the *Rappahannock, Shenandoah, Susquehanna,* and *Roanoke.* Averaging more than 3000 tons, these were the largest and the last of the great American wooden full-rigged ships. The next step was iron. Sewall was interested in Gen. Thomas W. Hyde's Bath Iron Works, organized in 1889, which built the *Machias, Castine,* and *Katahdin*

for the new navy. After visiting England to study the latest methods he began to build steel sailing vessels, and in 1894 the steel *Dirigo* was launched. His last ship, launched a month after his death, was the *William P. Frye,* sunk Jan. 28, 1915, the first American vessel sunk by the Germans in the World War. Unlike Donald McKay [q.v.] and other clipper constructors, Sewall introduced relatively few innovations into naval architecture. His importance comes rather from his large-scale construction of sailing vessels far into the era of steam; during the latter half of the nineteenth century he built, owned, and operated more sailing vessels than anyone else in America.

He was drawn into other fields of business activity more because of his sound common sense and executive ability than because of his wealth. He was at various times president of the Eastern Railroad and of the Central Railroad, and a director of the Boston and Maine Railroad. From 1871 until his death he was president of the Bath National Bank. He was the most prominent of the Maine Democrats, those constant supporters of forlorn hopes in that Republican stronghold, but the only elective offices he ever received were as councilman and alderman in Bath. Since he was an ardent imperialist and a believer in the tariff as a weapon in international trade, his position as a Democrat might have seemed anomalous except for his opposition to the gold standard. He was a delegate to the national conventions in 1876, 1880, and 1888; in the next two campaigns he served on the executive committee of the Democratic national committee, and in 1896 he was nominated for vice-president on the fifth ballot and took an active part in the campaign. In 1859 he had married Emma Duncan Crooker, daughter of a Bath shipbuilder; of their three sons two survived him, one of them Harold Marsh Sewall [q.v.]. His portrait, showing a firm chin and straightforward expression indicates why he could be called "a gentleman who was without fear and without offense" and "the epitome of gallant gentility" (*Lewiston Evening Journal,* Nov. 15, 1924). In 1900 he was stricken with apoplexy at his summer home at Small Point, just below Bath, where he died.

[G. T. Little, ed., *Geneal. and Family Hist. of the State of Me.* (1909), vol. II, pp. 522–24; P. M. Reed, *Hist. of Bath and Environs* (1894); L. C. Hatch, ed., *Maine, A Hist.* (1919), vol. V, with portrait; *Ill. Hist. Souvenir of the City of Bath, Me.* (1899), pp. 311–12, with list of Sewall ships; F. C. Matthews, *Am. Merchant Ships,* 1 ser. (1930); H. V. Poor, *Manual of the Railroads of the U. S.,* esp. for 1885 and 1894; Henry Hall, "Ship-Building Industry in the U. S.," *Reports of Tenth Census* (1884), vol. VIII, p. 71, with list of Sewall ships; obituaries in *Evening Express* (Portland, Me.), *Bath Times*, Sept. 5, and *Daily Eastern Argus* (Portland, Me.), Sept. 6, 1900.]   R. G. A.

SEWALL, FRANK (Sept. 24, 1837–Dec. 7, 1915), Swedenborgian clergyman, was born in Bath, Me., the son of William Dunning and Rachel (Trufant) Sewall, and the brother of Arthur Sewall [*q.v.*]. After graduating from Bowdoin College in 1858, he spent two years in travel in Italy and study at Tübingen in Germany under the great Swedenborg scholar, Johann Friedrich Immanuel Tafel. In 1862 he took the degree of A.M. at Bowdoin. In 1869 he married Thedia Redelia Gilchrist, a sister of William Wallace Gilchrist [*q.v.*]; his wife, with their five daughters, survived him at the time of his death in Washington, D. C. Significant for his later development were his upbringing in a family connected with the New Church in Bath from its earliest days, his early appreciation of nature, music, and art, and his years abroad. Ordained on Aug. 23, 1863, into the ministry of the General Convention of the New Jerusalem in the United States of America (Swedenborgian), he held pastorates in Glendale, Ohio, 1863–70; Urbana, Ohio, 1870–86; Glasgow, Scotland, 1886–87; and Washington, D. C., 1889–1915. To these pastorates he brought not only a keen mind but also a warm human sympathy and insight that endeared him to many who could not appreciate his intellectual gifts. Active in the larger concerns of the Church, he served as president (later called general pastor) of the Ohio Association in 1871 and 1872, and as general pastor of the Maryland Association from 1893 to 1915.

The range of his interests and activities was unusual, but his chief contribution to the life of the New Church was to the development of its forms of worship. The subject had interested him from college days, and his earliest published books were *The Christian Hymnal* (1867) and *A Prayerbook and Hymnal for the Use of the New Church* (1867). He was the chairman and the guiding spirit of the two committees that produced the *Magnificat* (1910), a hymnal, and the *Book of Worship* (1912), authorized by the General Convention in 1912. To them he contributed not only his knowledge but many of his own compositions, both musical and literary. He was also devoted to the cause of New Church education and worked for it throughout his life, especially during his years as president of Urbana (Ohio) University, 1870–86. He looked forward to the day when human society would be so organized as to give expression to Swedenborg's doctrine of love as the ultimate reality of the universe, and he saw that to bring about

such a result and to live in such a world made demands on education which traditional forms were not prepared to meet. In 1896 he published *The Angel of the State; or the Kindergarten in the Education of the Citizen.* Another major interest was philosophy, particularly that of Swedenborg. Products of this interest were *The New Metaphysics* (1888), *Swedenborg and Modern Idealism* (1902), a translation of Swedenborg's *De Anima* under the title of *The Soul, or Rational Psychology* (1887), and the introduction and notes to Emanual F. Goerwitz's translation of Immanuel Kant's *Dreams of a Spirit-Seer* (London, 1900). He was the author of several volumes of sermons, including *The Pillow of Stones* (1876) and *The Hem of His Garment* (1876), and of *The Ethics of Service* (1888), *Reason in Belief* (1906), and *The Pulpit and Modern Thought* (1905). In the field of literature he published *Dante and Swedenborg, with Other Essays on the New Renaissance* (1893), a translation of the *Poems of Giosuè Carducci* (1892), and *The Trophies: Sonnets* (1893), translations from José Maria Heredia.

[Three chapters of a biography by Sewall's daughter, Alice A. S. James, appeared in the *New-Church Rev.*, Jan., July, Apr. 1921. See also G. T. Little, ed., *Geneal. and Family Hist. of the State of Me.* (1909), vol. II; *Who's Who in America*, 1914–15; *Jour. . . . of the Gen. Convention of the New Jerusalem in the U. S. A.*, 1916; *New-Church Messenger*, Jan. 5, 19, May 17, 1916; *New-Church Rev.*, Apr. 1916; *Evening Star* (Washington, D. C.), Dec. 7, 1915.]   F. R. C.

SEWALL, HAROLD MARSH (Jan. 3, 1860–Oct. 28, 1924), diplomat, descended from Henry Sewall who first came to New England in 1634, was born in Bath, Me., the son of Arthur [*q.v.*] and Emma Duncan (Crooker) Sewall and a member of a wealthy shipbuilding family. He graduated A.B. (1882) and LL.B. (1885) at Harvard and through his father's influence as a Democrat, was appointed vice-consul at Liverpool. In 1887, he was appointed consul general at Apia, Samoa. The position was a highly responsible one, for the rivalry of the German, British, and American consuls, frequently supported by cruisers, more than once threatened war. Important decisions had to be made on the spot, for the nearest cable station was at Auckland, New Zealand. On Aug. 24, 1887, shortly after Sewall's arrival, the aggressive German consul Becker, backed by four warships, made a *coup d'état* which nearly gave Germany control of the islands. Becker declared war on the native "king," Malietoa, and set up his rival, Tamatese, with a German as prime minister. Robert Louis Stevenson, who witnessed the events, declared that Sewall was for a while the only one to resist this measure—"standing forth in bold, consistent and sometimes rather captious opposition, stirring up his government at home with clear and forcible dispatches and on the spot grasping at every opportunity to thrust a stick into the German wheels" (Stevenson, *post*, p. 89). Sewall announced his support of Malietoa, steadily protested against Becker's actions, and even released a prisoner personally. His British colleagues, Wilson and then de Coëtlegen, were less active. President Cleveland and Secretary Bayard were less imperialistic than the young consul, however, and enjoined neutrality upon him. To present his views at Washington, Sewall returned on leave late in August 1888, but at a hearing before a Senate sub-committee in January 1889 offended Bayard, who requested his resignation. Sewall was thus absent from Samoa during the naval crisis ended by the hurricane of Mar. 15, 1889. This episode marks his shift to the Republicans, who attached him, as special disbursing agent, to the commission which participated in the Berlin agreement of June 14, 1889, by which the independence of Samoa was recognized. Sewall's firm opposition to Becker had helped to make this solution possible. Under congenial Republican auspices, in 1890, Sewall returned as consul general to Apia, remaining until 1892 and securing the site of the naval station at Pago Pago. With the return of the Republicans to power in 1897 he was appointed minister to Hawaii, and in that capacity received the transfer of the sovereignty of the islands from President Samuel B. Dole [*q.v.*] on Aug. 12, 1898. He remained in Hawaii as special agent of the United States until the establishment of regular territorial government in 1900.

During the remainder of his life he made his home at Bath, Me. One of the wealthiest men in the state, he was noted for his hospitality. On Sept. 14, 1893, he had married Camilla Loyall Ashe of San Francisco, and they had two sons and two daughters. He sat in the Maine House of Representatives in 1897–98 and 1903–07 and in the state Senate 1907–09, was a delegate to his party's national conventions in 1896 and 1916 and in 1900 was the first member of the Republican national committee from Hawaii. He was an unsuccessful candidate for Congress in 1914. He headed the state Committee of Public Safety in 1917 and was on the advisory committee of the Washington Arms Conference. He died in New York, to which place he had gone for a slight operation.

[*Papers Relating to the Foreign Relations of the U. S.,* 1887–92, 1897–98; *Sen. Ex. Doc. 31, 50 Cong.,* 2 Sess., pp. 162–63; R. L. Stevenson, *A Foot-note to History* (1892); G. H. Ryden, *The Foreign Policy of the U. S. in Relation to Samoa* (1933); *Class of 1882, Harvard Coll., Sixth Report* (1907); E. J. Carpenter, *America in Hawaii* (1899); *Who's Who in America,* 1924–25; G. T. Little, *Geneal. and Family Hist. of the State of Me.* (1909), II, 524; *Lewiston Evening Journal,* Oct. 29, 1924; *N. Y. Times,* Oct. 29, 1924.]
R. G. A.

SEWALL, JONATHAN (Aug. 17, 1728–Sept. 26, 1796), lawyer, writer, Loyalist, was the son of Jonathan and Mary (Payne) Sewall, of Boston. The first of his ancestors to come to America was his great-grandfather, Henry Sewall, who emigrated in 1634 and the following year settled in Newbury, Mass., but later returned to England. By 1681 the family was permanently established in Salem, where Jonathan's grandfather, Stephen, died in 1725. Left destitute at an early age by the death of his father, the boy was educated through the charity of friends who had been impressed by his unusual promise. After his graduation from Harvard in 1748, he maintained for a number of years a small Latin school in Salem. This he abandoned in 1756 to read law with Judge Chambers Russell of Lincoln, Mass., and later, with a minimum of legal training, he set up an office in Charlestown. In the pursuit of his profession he frequently came into contact with John Adams and then began the intimacy between the two men which caused Adams to refer to him as the best friend he had in the world (*Works,* II, 302–03). His associates during this period were ardent patriots, with whose sentiments he seems for a time to have been in complete accord. On Jan. 21, 1764 (*Boston Marriages, 1752–1809,* 1903, p. 422), he married Esther Quincy.

On the death in 1760 of his uncle, Stephen Sewall, chief justice of the superior court, the young lawyer undertook the administration of the estate. Finding his uncle's affairs badly involved, he appealed to the General Court for a grant of money with which to satisfy the creditors. The refusal of the Court to grant this petition apparently alienated him from the cause of the patriots. According to Adams, he was especially indignant with James Otis, who had opposed the grant. Friends of the Crown were quick to take advantage of his resentment. By appointing him to a succession of offices they bound him to the royal cause. He was first made solicitor general, then, in 1767, attorney general, and in 1768 judge of the vice-admiralty court of Halifax. On Governor Hutchinson's departure from Massachusetts, Sewall was one of the signers of the barristers' address to him. Close upon this open display of his allegiance to the royal government came a conversation between Sewall and Adams which marked the irreparable rift between the friends. On a Portland hill they discussed the future of America and their own fortunes. Sewall, convinced of the speedy defeat of the colonists, urged Adams to abandon his intention of attending the Philadelphia congress. In reply to his arguments Adams used the memorable words: to "swim or sink, live or die, survive or perish with my country [is] my unalterable determination" (*Works*, IV, 8).

In September 1774 Sewall left his Cambridge home for Boston, from which place he sailed for England early in 1775. His name was included in the act of banishment of 1778 and his property was declared forfeited the next year. For a time he remained in London, one of the group of Loyalists who dined together weekly while they waited for word that the Revolution was crushed and that they might return from their exile. While in London he changed the spelling of his name to Sewell, the form in which he found it recorded at the Herald's office (letter, Mar. 11, 1782, in Massachusetts Historical Society). In 1777 he removed to Bristol where, save for brief excursions, he resided until 1788. In that year he embarked for Halifax, with the hope, as he told John Adams in a brief reunion with him in London, of making provision for his children. This hope he was able to fulfil. His elder son, Jonathan, became chief justice of Lower Canada; the younger, Stephen, became solicitor general. Sewall himself died in St. John, New Brunswick, never having revisited his native land.

Of Sewall's abilities John Adams thought highly: "He possessed a lively wit," Adams wrote, "a pleasing humor, a brilliant imagination, great subtlety of reasoning, and an insinuating eloquence" (*Works*, II, 78). Little record of his legal practice or of the conduct of his offices is available, but in the famous case of *James* vs. *Lechmere,* he gained a decision in favor of the freedom of a slave two years before Lord Mansfield's famous decision in the Somerset case (*Collections of the Massachusetts Historical Society,* 4 ser. IV, 1858, pp. 334-35). Under the names Philanthropos and Long J., he was a frequent and able contributor to the press, though he was not the author of the letters by Massachusettensis, as Adams supposed when he answered those letters in 1774 and 1775. To him was attributed the writing of Gage's proclamations (B. J. Lossing's notes in John Trumbull, *M'Fingal,* edition of 1860, at p. 202). Mercy Otis Warren satirized him in her political drama *The Group* (1775) and John Trumbull

paid his respects to him in *M'Fingal* (1775) with these words:

> "Did not our grave Judge Sewall hit
>   The Summit of news-paper wit?
> Fill'd ev'ry leaf of ev'ry paper
>   Of Mills and Hicks and mother Draper;
> Drew proclamations, works of toil,
>   In true sublime of scarecrow style;
> Wrote farces too, gainst Sons of Freedom
> All for your good and none would read 'em."

[The Mass. Hist. Soc. possesses a manuscript volume of Sewall's letters, parts of which were published in its *Proceedings,* 2 ser. X (1896); for sources, see *The Works of John Adams* (1850–56), especially vols. II, IV; Lorenzo Sabine, *Biog. Sketches of Loyalists of the Am. Revolution* (1864), vol. II; *Jour. and Letters of the Late Samuel Curwen* (1842), ed. by G. A. Ward; J. H. Stark, *The Loyalists of Mass.* (1910); E. A. Jones, *The Loyalists of Mass.* (1930); E. E. Salisbury, *Family Memorials,* vol. I (1885).]   E. D.

SEWALL, JONATHAN MITCHELL (1748–Mar. 29, 1808), lawyer and occasional poet, a grand-nephew of Samuel Sewall [*q.v.*], the diarist, was born in Salem, Mass., where he was baptized on Mar. 27, but spent all his mature life in Portsmouth, N. H. His father, Mitchell Sewall, a graduate of Harvard in 1718 and clerk of the inferior court at Salem, died in October following Jonathan Mitchell's birth. Shortly thereafter the boy was adopted by his bachelor uncle, Stephen Sewall, chief justice of Massachusetts from 1752 until his death in 1760. His mother, Elizabeth (Prince) Sewall, died in 1758. Thus doubly orphaned by the deaths of his parents and guardian, Jonathan Mitchell was left at the age of twelve to make his own way. He is said to have entered Harvard College, but he did not graduate and no trace of him can now be found in the college archives. For a short time he was employed as a clerk in a store; then he studied law in the office of Judge John Pickering, c. 1738–1805 [*q.v.*], of Portsmouth and was duly admitted to the bar. In 1773 he was made register of probate for Grafton County, N. H., presumably to induce him to settle in a thinly populated region which at that time was unprovided with lawyers, but there is no indication that he ever assumed the office. Though his career was interrupted by periods of illness, he rose to be a respected lawyer of Portsmouth with a local reputation for patriotic oratory and occasional poetry. Without ever becoming a candidate for office he took part in politics as a vehement Federalist. After gracing countless public occasions by the display of his talents, he died a bachelor, eminently public-spirited, lettered, and bibulous.

As a poet he first attracted attention by a patriotic ballad called "War and Washington," written at the outbreak of the Revolution and sung by the army in all parts of the country. Thereafter he lost no occasion to act as volunteer laureate of Washington's virtues. When the President visited Portsmouth in 1789, Sewall composed three adulatory odes to be sung at the ceremony of welcome. His *Versification of President Washington's Excellent Farewell-Address* appeared in 1798, and at the commemorative service held in Portsmouth after Washington's death Sewall was chosen to pronounce a eulogy, published in 1800 as *Eulogy on the Late General Washington*. He had previously delivered the first Fourth of July oration at Portsmouth, 1788, and his speeches and odes were in frequent demand at Federalist banquets. His *Miscellaneous Poems*, published at Portsmouth in 1801, consist of patriotic effusions, verse paraphrases of Ossian, epilogues, occasional lyrics, and a few epigrams. They are ephemeral productions. A single couplet from his "Epilogue to Cato" gained wide currency by its use with a slight change as the motto of the *New World* of Park Benjamin, 1809–1864 [*q.v.*], but the most lasting of his compositions are the epitaphs still decipherable on Portsmouth gravestones.

[*Vital Records of Salem, Mass., . . . to 1849*, vols. II (1918), VI (1925); Hamilton Child, *Gazetteer of Grafton County, N. H.* (1886), p. 39; C. W. Brewster, *Rambles about Portsmouth*, vols. I (1859), II (1869); Nathaniel Adams, *Annals of Portsmouth* (1825), p. 318; A. H. Locke, *Portsmouth and Newcastle, N. H., Cemetery Inscriptions* (1907); E. A. and G. L. Duyckinck, *Cyc. of Am. Lit.* (2 vols., 1855); A. M. Payson and Albert Laighton, *The Poets of Portsmouth* (1865), containing reprints of Sewall's poetry; Samuel Kettell, *Specimens of Am. Poetry* (1829), vol. I, pp. 198–200; "Mortuary" from the *Lit. Mirror* (Portsmouth), in the *Port Folio*, June 25, 1808, pp. 415–16.]
G. F. W.

SEWALL, JOSEPH ADDISON (Apr. 20, 1830–Jan. 17, 1917), first president of the University of Colorado, was born in Scarboro, Me., the son of Stephen and Mary Milliken Sewall. His father was a country doctor with a large practice and a small store of worldly goods. The boy was educated in the public schools of Portland and Biddeford, and studied medicine in Boston. He began the practice of medicine in Bangor, Me., but, unable to endure the rigors of the New England climate, in 1854 he moved to Illinois. There he continued his practice and also taught school. The academic year 1859–60 he spent at the Lawrence Scientific School of Harvard University. From 1860 to 1877 he was professor of natural science in the Illinois State Normal University at Normal.

In 1877, on the recommendation of Gov. John L. Routt, he was appointed the first president of the infant University of Colorado. When admitted to the Union in 1876, Colorado was still a frontier state with a population of barely 135,-000; only one high school class had been graduated within its borders. The prospective university possessed but one building, located on a treeless, boulder-strewn hillside overlooking the town of Boulder. Its support was to come from a mill levy which, on the basis of the property valuation in the new state, was expected to bring in $9,000 a year. The institution was opened in September 1877, with two teachers, including the president, two departments (normal and preparatory), and forty-four students; the following year a college department was added. From such humble beginnings Sewall guided the course of the university for the next decade, developing the physical resources, assembling a faculty, and determining the spirit and ideals of the establishment. While fully appreciating the value of the standard classical curriculum of the time, the new president was anxious to give the youth of his frontier state a practical education, hence he stressed also science and the study of history and government as a basis for citizenship. In the midst of great discouragement the foundations were well laid. Although the growth of the University was substantial in the early years, it was not as rapid as some of its supporters desired; the president was blamed, and in 1887 he resigned to become professor of chemistry at the University of Denver, where he also served as dean of the school of pharmacy.

After he retired from teaching in 1899 he acted as chemist for the city of Denver. In addition to proficiency in chemistry, he was a botanist and the author of *A Condensed Botany* (copr. 1872). He was tall and dignified in manner, and a forceful and entertaining public speaker. In his work as teacher and administrator he was assisted by his wife, Ann Edwards (Foss), to whom he was married in Tonica, Ill., on Feb. 11, 1858, and who with four of their six children survived him. In the closing words of his inaugural address, 1877, he declared: "When the University of Colorado shall have an honorable place and name among the institutions of learning of the land, and I shall be sleeping in the shadow of these mountains, or elsewhere, I would ask no prouder eulogy than that some good and true friend should say of me, 'He was in at the birth, he directed its infant steps, and now behold the full grown man.'" In 1914 the University of Colorado recognized his pioneer service in its behalf by conferring on him the degree of doctor of laws.

[*Boulder County News*, for 1877; *Denver Times*, Jan. 18, 1917; *Rocky Mountain News*, Jan. 19, 1917; information from a daughter, Miss Jane Sewall, Boston, Mass., and from Miss Mary Rippon, Boulder, Col.; J. R. Brackett, "Little Journeys in the Year One," in

The Coloradoan, vol. IV (1902), pub. by the class of 1903, and "The Univ. of Colorado; Its Origin and Development," *Civic Quart.*, Jan. 1912.]   C. B. G—z.

SEWALL, MAY ELIZA WRIGHT (May 27, 1844–July 22, 1920), feminist, was born in Milwaukee, Wis., the daughter of Philander Montague and Mary Weeks (Brackett) Wright. A precocious child, she was reading Milton at the age of seven. After studying in the public schools and with her father she taught in Waukesha, Wis., to earn money for a college education. Graduated from Northwestern University in 1866, she taught in Corinth, Miss., Plainville, Mich., and Frankfort, Ind. In Frankfort she married Edwin Thompson, the principal of the school, and with him removed to Indianapolis, where both of them taught in the high school until Mr. Thompson's death, about 1876. On Oct. 30, 1880, she married Theodore Lovett Sewall, a graduate of Harvard who had established a classical school for boys in Indianapolis. Not long after, she established with him the Girls' Classical School; after his death, she was principal for many years.

A feminist from the beginning of her life, she began as soon as she went to Indianapolis to gather groups together to work for public purposes. She was a charter member of many Indianapolis clubs and a founder of the Indiana Association for Promoting Woman's Suffrage. Following the visit of Pundita Ramabai to America, she formed the Ramabai Circle to assist in freeing the women of India from their ancient bondage. One of the first members of the Association of Collegiate Alumnae when it was organized in 1882, she helped in 1883 to organize the Western Association of Collegiate Alumnae, which later joined with the older association. From the outset of her association with these university women she had a vision of a world federation which in 1919 came to completion. From 1883 to 1912 she assisted in suffrage campaigns from Nebraska to Wisconsin and was for many years chairman of the executive committee of the National Suffrage Association. In 1888 she was chairman of the committee which arranged and carried through the first meeting of the National Council of Women in Washington, where she presented a plan for forming an International Council as well; from 1888 to 1899 she held various offices in the National Council. In 1891–92 she traveled abroad to awaken an interest in the World's Congress of Representative Women, at which she presided, held in Chicago in 1893 as a part of the program for the Columbian Exposition. From that time she was a prominent figure in the International Council of Women. She had been a delegate to its meetings in 1889 and in 1899 she became its president, succeeding Lady Aberdeen. She assisted in the formation of fifty women's clubs of various sorts; in 1889, when the Federation of Women's Clubs was formed, she rightly became its first president. In 1894 she edited *The World's Congress of Representative Women*, and in 1915 she published *Women, World War, and Permanent Peace*. Soon after her husband's death in 1895 she became profoundly interested in psychical research. In 1920 she published *Neither Dead nor Sleeping*, an account of her personal experiences.

[H. I. Brackett, *Brackett Geneal.* (1907); *Who's Who in America*, 1916–17; *The Hist. of Woman Suffrage* (6 vols., 1881–1922); Marion Talbot and Lois K. M. Rosenberry, *Hist. of the Am. Assoc. of Univ. Women* (1931); *Proc. Gen. Federation of Women's Clubs, Proc. Nat. Council of Women, Proc. Internat. Council of Women*, 1889–1915, *passim*; *Jour. Assoc. of Collegiate Alumnae*, July, Aug., 1920; obituaries in *Indianapolis News*, July 23, 1920, and *N. Y. Times*, July 24, 1920.]   L. K. M. R.

SEWALL, SAMUEL (Mar. 28, 1652–Jan. 1, 1730), merchant, colonial magistrate, diarist, was the grandson of Henry Sewall, a linen draper of Coventry, England, who acquired a considerable fortune and was several times mayor. In 1634 Samuel's father, Henry, emigrated to New England, where he married Jane, daughter of Stephen and Alice (Archer) Dummer. They soon returned to England, where Samuel, the second of eight children, was born at Bishopstoke. Some months afterward the family moved to Baddesley. There Samuel received his first schooling, going later to the grammar school at Rumsey.

When he was nine years old the family returned to New England and settled in Boston. After further preparation, Samuel entered Harvard College, from which he graduated in 1671. At this time he seems to have been undecided whether he would enter the ministry or embark on a mercantile career. On Nov. 5, 1673, he was chosen resident fellow, or tutor, at Harvard, and was installed on Nov. 26. On Feb. 28, 1675/6 he married the first of his three wives, Hannah, daughter of John Hull [*q.v.*], by whom he had fourteen children.

Made a freeman Apr. 29, 1679 ("Records of the Suffolk County Court," *Publications of the Colonial Society of Massachusetts*, vol. XXX, 1933, p. 1015), he began a long political career. From Oct. 12, 1681, to Sept. 12, 1684, he managed the colony's printing press. He was present at the General Court on Nov. 7, 1683, as deputy from Westfield, Hampden County, and from 1684 to 1686 he was a member of the Council. The twelve months from November 1688 were devoted to a trip to England, during which he spent some time in London and traveled through the provinces, visiting both Cambridge and Oxford. The trip was primarily on private business connected with his mercantile enterprises, but he appeared before the King and Council and gave some assistance to Increase Mather [*q.v.*] in his efforts to recover the Massachusetts charter. Upon his return to Massachusetts, he resumed his position on the Council as one of the officers elected in 1686, and in 1691 he was named a councilor in the new charter which the colony was forced to receive. This post he continued to hold until he declined re-election in 1725.

On June 13, 1692, the governor, Sir William Phips [*q.v.*], appointed him one of the special commissioners of oyer and terminer to try the cases of witchcraft at Salem. The court met during July and August and sentenced nineteen persons to death, the executions taking place Sept. 22, 1692. Sewall was the only one of the judges who ever publicly admitted that he had been in error in this matter. The part he played long preyed on his mind, and for some reason he considered himself as more guilty than any of the other judges. The legislature appointed Jan. 14, 1697, to be a fast day for whatever might have been done amiss in the tragedy, and on that day Sewall stood up in the Old South Church, Boston, while the clergyman, the Rev. Samuel Willard, read a confession of error and guilt which Sewall wished to make for himself thus publicly. On Dec. 6, 1692, he had been appointed a justice of the superior court. He was made a commissioner of the Society for the Propagation of the Gospel in New England in 1699, and shortly afterward became its local secretary and treasurer. He always showed much interest in the Indians and also in the negro slaves, publishing in 1700 a tract entitled *The Selling of Joseph*, one of the earliest appeals in the anti-slavery cause. He believed that the Indians should be set apart on permanent reservations and taught the English language and habits.

Sewall continued to hold various offices until almost the close of his life. In 1701 he was made captain of the Ancient and Honorable Artillery Company. He became judge of probate for Suffolk County in 1715, and chief justice of the superior court of judicature in 1718, which office he held for ten years. He was typical of the provincial judge of his time, without preliminary training in the law and with an unsystematic reading acquaintance with the legal classics ("Diary," *post*, I, 419). Yet he was a competent jurist and of more than average liberality, as evidenced by his modification of the rigorous miscegenation act of 1705 (*Ibid.*, II, 143), his opposition to high-handed interpretations of the treason laws (*Ibid.*, p. 149), and his stand against capital punishment for counterfeiting (*Ibid.*, III, 277).

In the field of authorship he is credited with *Proposals Touching the Accomplishment of Prophesies Humbly Offered* (1713); *A Memorial Relating to the Kennebeck Indians* (1721); and *Phaenomena Quaedam Apocalyptica ad Aspectum Novi Orbis Configurata, or, Some Few Lines Towards a Description of the New Heaven as It Makes to Those Who Stand upon the New Earth* (1697). With Edward Rawson, he wrote *The Revolution in New England Justified* (1691). He also composed many verses which circulated in manuscript form. Chiefly, however, he is remembered for his diary, which was published in three volumes by the Massachusetts Historical Society a century and a half after his death. It covers the period from 1674 to 1729, with a gap of about eight years, 1677–85. There are other American diaries of higher importance from a political point of view, but none in which the journalist's entire world is so vividly reproduced. In it is given an incomparable picture of the mind and life of a Puritan of the transition period. Sewall, as unwittingly portrayed by himself, emerges as mercenary, mercantile, of average mentality, conventional, Puritanically introspective, morbidly fond of dwelling on death, yet playful, affectionate, honorable, strong, and fearless. The rich merchant who could plead for slaves and publicly abase himself for wrongdoing on the bench in the Boston of 1690–1700 was no ordinary man.

Sewall's first wife died Oct. 19, 1717, and on Oct. 29, 1719, he married Abigail, daughter of Jacob Melyen and widow of James Woodmansey and William Tilley. She died on May 26, 1720. Subsequently he courted Madam Katherine Winthrop, with gifts of sermons, gingerbread, and sugar almonds at three shillings a pound (he gave her half a pound); but the lady insisted on his keeping a coach and wearing a wig, which, with a disagreement over a marriage settlement, cooled her suitor's ardor ("Diary," III, 262–75). On Mar. 29, 1722, however, he married Mary Gibbs, daughter of Henry Shrimpton. By his last two wives he had no children. At his death he was buried in the Granary Burying Ground, Boston.

[The "Diary of Samuel Sewall," in 3 vols., was pub. as *Mass. Hist. Soc. Colls.*, 5 ser. V–VII (1878–82); an abridged edition, *Samuel Sewall's Diary*, ed. by Mark Van Doren, was pub. in 1927; Sewall's letter-book, containing mercantile matters chiefly, is printed in *Mass. Hist. Soc. Colls.*, 6 ser., I. II (1886–88); "Letters of Samuel Lee and Samuel Sewall Relating to New England and the Indians," ed. by G. L. Kittredge, appears in *Colonial Soc. of Mass. Pubs.*, vol. XIV (1913). The Judge's son, Joseph Sewall, preached and published a funeral sermon, *The Orphan's Best Legacy* (1730). Other sources include J. L. Sibley, *Biog. Sketches of Grads. of Harvard Univ.*, vol. II (1881); G. E. Ellis, *An Address on the Life and Character of Chief-Justice Samuel Sewall* (1885); Emory Washburn, *Sketches of the Judicial Hist. of Mass. from 1630 to . . . 1775* (1840); N. B. Shurtleff, *Records of the Governor and Company of the Mass. Bay* (1854), vol. V; John Noble, *Records of the Court of Assistants of the Colony of the Mass. Bay*, vol. I (1901); minutes and files of the superior court of judicature, Suffolk County Court House, Boston; R. C. Winthrop, *A Difference of Opinion Concerning the Reasons Why Katherine Winthrop Refused to Marry Chief Justice Sewall* (1885); V. L. Parrington, *Main Currents in Am. Thought*, vol. I (1927).]   J. T. A.

SEWALL, STEPHEN (Apr. 4, 1734–July 23, 1804), Hebraist and classicist, was born in York, Me., the youngest of ten children of Nicholas and Mehitable (Storer) Sewall, and a descendant of Henry Sewall of Newbury, Mass., who arrived at Boston in 1634. The extreme poverty of his father, a tanner, forced him to leave school and to learn the carpenter's trade at which he worked until he acquired the means to prepare himself for Harvard. At college he supported himself by teaching grammar school in Cambridge. Upon his graduation in 1761, he succeeded Judah Monis [*q.v.*] as the instructor in Hebrew at Harvard. During 1762–63 he was also librarian of the college library. On Oct. 2, 1764, he was made the first incumbent of the newly established Hancock professorship of Hebrew and other Oriental languages, and on June 19, 1765, he was publicly installed in this new office, which he held for twenty years. Like other Harvard teachers at that time, he received occasional grants from the General Court of Massachusetts to supplement his insufficient salary.

Trained both in Hebrew and in the classics, he retained his interest in both throughout his active life. Early in his academic career, on Sept. 12, 1763, he submitted to the corporation of Harvard College a plan for the promotion of classical learning in which the most interesting feature is a recommendation to relieve students from compulsory composition of verse and to encourage this sort of exercise only among those who have "a genius and fondness" for it. He himself wrote four odes in Latin, two in Greek, and one in English (numbers 3, 5, 12, 14, 15, 16, 23 in *Pietas et Gratulatio Collegii Cantabrigiensis apud Novanglos*, 1761). His interests included politics and science as well. An early supporter of the Revolution, he represented Cambridge in the General Court as a

Whig in 1777. He was one of the sixty-two original members of the American Academy of Arts and Sciences, and his "Magnetical Observations, Made at Cambridge" appeared in the first volume of *Memoirs of the American Academy of Arts and Sciences* (1785). He is said to have been married twice. On Aug. 9, 1763, he married Rebecca, daughter of Edward Wigglesworth, the first Hollis Professor of Divinity at Harvard; she died in December 1783. Their only child had died in infancy. In September 1785, after having been for nearly three years incapable of performing his duties on account of physical and mental debility, from which there seemed to be no likelihood of his recovery, he was removed from his professorship by the concurring vote of the two governing boards of the college, but, "in consideration of his long and faithful services," he was allowed by them thirty pounds. After about nineteen years of retired life and gradual decay, he died in Cambridge. His published writings include *An Hebrew Grammar Collected Chiefly from Those of Mr. Israel Lyons and the Rev. Richard Grey* (1763), *Nocte Cogitata auctore, anglice scripta, Young, D.D., quae lingua Latii donavit America* (1786), *Carmina Sacra, quae latine graeceque condidit America* (1789), *The Scripture Account of the Schechinah* (1794), and *The Scripture History Relating to the Overthrow of Sodom and Gomorrah* (1796). Lectures on Hebrew and Oriental literature, a lexicon of the Chaldee language in the Old Testament, a Greek and English lexicon, and a discussion of the quantity of Greek vowels exist in manuscript in the library of Harvard College. According to T. M. Harris (*post*), he was considered by his contemporaries the "finest classical scholar and the most learned in Hebrew and oriental languages" that Harvard had produced.

[T. M. Harris, memoir written in 1728, MS. in Harvard Coll. Lib.; Benjamin Peirce, *A Hist. of Harvard Univ.* (1833); Josiah Quincy, *The Hist. of Harvard Univ.* (1840), vol. II; S. A. Eliot, *A Sketch of the Hist. of Harvard Coll.* (1848), pp. 155–57, 173; E. E. Salisbury, *Family-Memorials* (1885); *Essex Inst., Hist. Colls.*, vol. XXV (1888); A. C. Potter and C. K. Bolton, *The Librarians of Harvard Coll.* (1897); S. A. Allibone, *A Crit. Dict. of Eng. Lit.*, vol. II (1870).]   H. A. W.

SEWARD, FREDERICK WILLIAM (July 8, 1830–Apr. 25, 1915), journalist and diplomat, was born at Auburn, N. Y., the son of William Henry [*q.v.*] and Francis (Miller) Seward. In 1849 he graduated from Union College, and then became secretary to his father who had just been elected to the United States Senate. After admisson to the bar, through the influence of his father he became, in 1851, a member of the staff of the Albany *Evening Journal,* conducted by Thurlow Weed [*q.v.*], and served on this paper continuously, most of the time as associate editor, for the next ten years.

With his father's entry into the State Department, Frederick became assistant secretary of state. He had special charge of the consular service, but played a part in the preparation of many diplomatic dispatches. He was present at the signing of the Emancipation Proclamation. In the spring of 1865, when the Secretary was incapacitated by a carriage accident, Frederick became acting secretary of state. In this connection he sent out the notices for the last of Lincoln's cabinet meetings (Apr. 14, 1865), attended the meeting itself, and left an interesting account of what occurred on that day (*Reminiscences,* pp. 254–57). On the same night on which the President was assassinated, one of the conspirators forced his way into William Seward's house. Frederick met him in the hall, and there a tussle ensued in which the younger Seward was seriously hurt, without, however, being able to prevent the would-be murderer reaching his father's bedside and inflicting painful wounds upon him. In 1866 Frederick was sent with Vice-Admiral David D. Porter [*q.v.*] on a diplomatic mission which had in view the leasing or purchasing of the Bay of Samana, in the island of Santo Domingo. The negotiations broke down, temporarily, but some months later a treaty was negotiated in Washington, which, however, was never ratified by the Senate.

With the change of administration in 1869 the two Sewards retired to private life, and Frederick accompanied his father to Mexico. In 1874, two years after his father's death, he was elected to the New York Assembly, and in the subsequent session he introduced two constitutional amendments, providing for a superintendent of public works and a superintendent of prisons; a bill for the construction of an elevated railway (the first of its kind) ; and a measure for the reduction of canal tolls. He was nominated for secretary of state of New York in the fall, but was defeated in the election. With the advent of the Hayes administration, Seward again went to Washington as assistant secretary of state (Mar. 21, 1877–Oct. 31, 1879). In this capacity he laid down the policy pursued by the administration with regard to the recognition of Porfirio Diaz in Mexico, negotiated for the lease of the harbor of Pago-Pago in Samoa, and prepared the presidential proclamation which resulted in the sending of troops to Pittsburgh in connection with the riots of 1877. After retiring from office he took little part in public

life. In 1877 he published *Autobiography of William H. Seward from 1801 to 1834, with a Memoir of His Life and Selections from His Letters, from 1831 to 1846,* reprinted in 1891 as *William H. Seward: An Autobiography,* which he supplemented by *Seward at Washington* (2 vols., 1891), and "Seward's West Indian Cruise" (*Godey's Magazine,* April–November 1894). His *Reminiscences of a War-Time Statesman and Diplomat* (1916) was published after his death. On Nov. 9, 1854, he married Anna M. Wharton of Albany.

[In addition to Seward's own writings, see *Encyc. of Contemporary Biog. of N. Y.* (4 vols., 1878–85); *Outlook,* May 5, 1915; *Who's Who in America,* 1914–15; *Who's Who in New York City and State,* 1907; *N. Y. Times,* Apr. 26, 1915.]   D. P.

SEWARD, GEORGE FREDERICK (Nov. 8, 1840–Nov. 28, 1910), diplomat, was the son of George W. and Tempe (Leddell) Seward of Florida, N. Y. He was educated at Seward Academy, Florida, and at Union College, which he entered in 1857 but from which he withdrew before graduating. On Oct. 24, 1861, his uncle, William H. Seward [*q.v.*], being then secretary of state, he was appointed United States consul at Shanghai, China, an important post, and on Sept. 2, 1863, he became consul general there. During his service at Shanghai he was sent to investigate conditions at the consulate at Bangkok (1868), and on June 27, 1868, was commissioned special diplomatic agent to Korea and empowered to negotiate a commercial and claims convention (*Senate Document 40,* 54 Cong., 2 Sess., p. 8). Feeling, however, that circumstances were not favorable, he never undertook the mission. He was married, Aug. 4, 1870, to Kate Sherman of Marysville, Cal.

After nearly fifteen years of the consular service, he was appointed on Jan. 7, 1876, minister to China to succeed Benjamin P. Avery [*q.v.*]. His services in these positions seem to have met with considerable approval, for he received praise from "Chinese" Gordon and the former American minister, Anson Burlingame, as well as from representatives of the British, French, and Danish governments. Denmark in return for his friendly services in obtaining security for a Danish telegraph system from the Chinese government bestowed on him the Order of the Knights of Danebrog, and France honored him with the Order of the Commander of the Dragon of Annam. In 1866 and 1869 he was president of the North China branch of the Royal Asiatic Society. As minister he supported the American vice consul at Shanghai, O. B. Bradford, who, with considerable British capital, succeeded in building China's pioneer steam railroad at Woosung. In spite of Seward's efforts, the Chinese bought the line soon after its opening in 1876 and destroyed it. Aside from his interest in modernizing China, he worked in harmony with the Chinese government, showing sympathy for its position during the Lew Chew dispute with Japan and urging his own government not to press the Chinese with regard to the question of immigration. California was in arms against the Oriental invaders and Seward was instructed in April 1879 to work towards a new immigration treaty with China. On Mar. 3, 1879, however, a committee of the House of Representatives had recommended that Seward be impeached of "high crimes and misdemeanors while in office." The alleged offenses included irregularities in his accounts as consul general, arbitrary administration, and fraudulent dealings with the Chinese in the Woosung railroad matter. Although steps toward impeachment were taken by the hostile Democratic House in both the Forty-fifth and Forty-sixth congresses (*Congressional Record*, Mar. 3, and June 4, 1879), the prosecution was uncertain of its position and the impeachment was never tried. Nevertheless Seward's usefulness to the State Department was ended and his resignation was requested Dec. 27, 1879. The immigration treaty of 1880 with China toward which he had worked was negotiated by a commission of which his successor, James B. Angell [*q.v.*], was a member.

Seward left Peking on Aug. 16, 1880, and the next year published his best-known volume, *Chinese Immigration in Its Social and Economical Aspects*. He was also the author of *The United States Consulates in China* (1867); *The Treaty With Spain* (1898); *The Russian-Japanese War* (1904); *Insurance is Commerce* (1910); and a series of reports on taxation which he made as chairman of a committee of the Chamber of Commerce of the State of New York. He was connected with numerous business ventures, and in 1887 became vice-president, and, in 1893, president, of the Fidelity and Casualty Company, which office he held at the time of his death. His wife and four children survived him.

[*N. Y. Herald*, Nov. 29, 1910; *Who's Who in America*, 1910-11; Tyler Dennett, *Americans in Eastern Asia* (1922); *Papers Relating to the Foreign Relations of the U. S.*, 1868-1881; *Congressional Record*; *House Report, No. 134* and *No. 141*, 45 Cong., 3 Sess. and manuscript material in the Department of State.]
E. W. S.

SEWARD, THEODORE FRELINGHUYSEN (Jan. 25, 1835-Aug. 30, 1902), musician, humanitarian, author, was born in Florida, N. Y., the son of Israel and Mary (Johnson) Seward. He was a great-grandson of Col. John Seward of the American Revolution. He spent his early boyhood in Florida, N. Y., and received his first education at Seward Institute, founded by his great-uncle, Samuel S. Seward, the father of William Henry Seward [*q.v.*]. Later he went to Boston, where he studied music with Lowell Mason, George Frederick Root, and Thomas Hastings, 1784-1872 [*qq.v.*]. This association and training started him on his career as hymnologist and teacher. He was organist and teacher at New London, Conn., from 1857 to 1859, and in this city was married to Mary Holden Coggeshall on June 12, 1860. He was in Rochester, N. Y., until 1862, when he went to New York City and established headquarters for his editorial and literary work. He taught for a time at Teachers College (later merged with Columbia University), was editor of the *Musical Pioneer* from 1864, of the *Musical Gazette* from 1867, and of the *Tonic Sol-Fa Advocate* from 1881 to 1886 when it was superseded by the *Musical Reform* of which he was editor until 1888. He moved to Orange, N. J., in 1868 and later to his permanent residence in East Orange. From 1870 he was music director of the public schools of East Orange and organist at the North Orange Baptist Church and the Brick Presbyterian Church of East Orange. About 1869 he became interested in the singing of negroes, and was musical director of the second European tour of the Fisk University Jubilee Singers, editing and arranging a collection of *Jubilee Songs* (1872). In helping to preserve the negro spirituals he made his most distinctive contribution.

During his European trip Seward was much impressed with the English Tonic Sol-Fa system, and he became its principal advocate in the United States. He published two treaties on the subject— *The Tonic Sol-Fa Music Reader* (1880), and *A Revolution in Music Teaching* (1888). He edited a number of song and hymn collections, among them *The Temple Choir* (1867), *The Coronation* (1872), and *The Vineyard of Song* (1874). With Lowell Mason he was the author of *The Pestalozzian Music Teacher* (1871). His association with sacred music broadened into a larger concern with religious matters, and the later years of his life were occupied largely with religious writings and the organization of religious societies. In 1891 he instituted the Brotherhood of Christian Unity, in 1897 the Don't Worry Club, and in 1901 the Golden Rule Brotherhood. His published writings in this field include *The School of Life* (1894), *Heaven Every Day* (1896),

Don't Worry (1897), and *How to Get Acquainted with God* (1902). He died at the home of his daughter in East Orange, N. J.

[Material for this article has been obtained largely from members of the Seward family, notably from Dr. F. W. Seward, of Goshen, N. Y.; see also *Grove's Dict. of Music and Musicians, Am. Supp.* (1930); *Who's Who in America*, 1901–02; and *N. Y. Times*, Sept. 1, 1902.]   J. T. H.

SEWARD, WILLIAM HENRY (May 16, 1801–Oct. 10, 1872), statesman, was born in Florida, Orange County, N. Y., the son of Dr. Samuel S. and Mary (Jennings) Seward. After preparatory studies in Florida and the neighboring village of Goshen, he was sent at the age of fifteen to Union College. Graduating in 1820, he began to read law and was admitted to the bar in 1822, establishing himself the next year in Auburn, N. Y., which was to be his home for the rest of his life. Seward's convivial temperament as well as his profession fitted him for politics; the question was with what political group he would affiliate himself. His family had been Democratic-Republicans of the strictest persuasion, but with praiseworthy independence the rising young lawyer chose to ally himself with the opposing elements. In this decision the principal factors, according to his *Autobiography* (p. 54) written nearly fifty years later, were his distrust of the Southern Jeffersonians, and his great interest in internal improvements. At any rate, Seward voted for DeWitt Clinton for governor, and John Quincy Adams for president in 1824, and wrote a good "Address" in support of the former (*Works*, III, 335). The enthusiasm which he then felt for Adams was never dimmed, and undoubtedly had its part in forming his own political ideals as time went on.

The closing years of the 1820's saw the rise of the Anti-Masonic movement in western New York. To this Seward found himself drawn, both by expediency and by conviction. In the deliberations of the new organization, as indeed in previous political discussions, the rising young politician was drawn close to Thurlow Weed [*q.v.*], whose casual acquaintance he had first made in 1824 and with whom he was to maintain one of the most intimate and long-standing friendships in American political annals. It was due to Weed's influence that Seward stood for and was elected in the fall of 1830 to the state Senate. In this body he served for the next four years, as a distinguished member of the minority and later as its leader. He played a prominent part in the debates on Andrew Jackson's bank policy; he sustained the President in his opposition to Nullification; he continued to advocate internal improvements; he supported abolition of imprisonment for debt. Defeated for reëlection in 1833, he was unanimously nominated for governor in 1834. By this time the Whig party had supplanted the Anti-Masons, and it was under the Whig banner that Seward was to fight for the next twenty years. In this first Whig candidacy, however, he was defeated, by William L. Marcy [*q.v.*]. The next few years Seward devoted to the practice of law, and he acquired a modest competence through his success as agent for the Holland Company, in settling disputes with settlers in Chautauqua County (*Autobiography*, p. 328; *Works*, III, 461).

The Whigs carried the New York legislature in the election of 1837 and Seward's political ambitions, which he professed were dead in 1834, rapidly came to life again, with the governorship as their objective. The contest for the nomination lay between him and the dignified Francis Granger [*q.v.*], nearly nine years his senior. Seward professed to be willing to let the convention decide, but an active organization was set on foot, the young voters being particularly active in his favor. Weed, after some hesitation, decided that his protégé should have the nomination, and in a closely contested convention battle Seward was chosen. In the electoral campaign itself, he was compelled for the first time to face the issue of slavery. His attitude in 1838 can hardly be called an advanced one. By the abolitionists he was asked three questions, whether he was in favor of (1) a law granting trial by jury to all fugitives, (2) of abolishing the special qualifications for negro voters, and (3) of repealing a law permitting the importation and detention of slaves in the state of New York for a period of nine months. He answered the first question in the affirmative, but the other two in the negative, declaring that the subjects with which they dealt did not enter "into the political creed" of his party (*Works*, III, 426–32).

The election of 1838 resulted in a victory for Seward, as did that of 1840, though by a reduced plurality. His four years in the governorship reveal the natural ardor and optimism of his temperament, his strong humanitarian sympathies, and also his impulsiveness and tendency to challenge majority opinion. Always warmly convinced of the desirability of internal improvements, Seward courageously urged them upon successive legislatures (see his message of 1840, *Works*, II, 212–55). In the midst of the depression, he refused to acquiesce in the suspension of activities already undertaken, and from first to last boldly defended large expenditures. In this particular case the policy cannot be said to have succeeded. The state's credit was adversely affected, its bonds selling at a discount of twenty per cent. in 1841. When the Democrats regained control of both houses of the legislature in the fall elections, they proceeded to suspend virtually all but the most necessary expenditures, and to levy additional taxes. Seward, however, stoutly insisted that his policy had been wise, and that the obstacles to its accomplishment were merely a blind distrust of the future, on the part of foreign investors and of the American people. His natural impulsiveness, as well as his generosity of feeling, was illustrated also by his attitude on the question of public education in New York City. The schools there, conducted by a private corporation, the Public School Society, had been unacceptable to the rapidly growing Catholic population, and, furthermore, did not attract the children of the immigrant classes. In his message of 1840, after consulting with his old friend, Dr. Eliphalet Nott of Union College, Seward recommended "the establishment of schools in which they (the children of New York) may be instructed by teachers speaking the same language with themselves and professing the same faith" (*Works*, II, 215). This recommendation caused a storm of criticism from the nativist elements in the state, stronger in the Whig than in the Democratic party. Seward was compelled to retreat from the position which he had assumed, though he succeeded in securing the establishment of public schools free from sectarian influence in the city.

On the slavery question Seward took advanced ground during his term of office. He refused to surrender three sailors, who had instigated the flight of a fugitive slave to New York, when the extradition of these men was demanded by the state of Virginia. His act provoked so much irritation in Virginia as to bring about reprisals against New York shipping. But it was typical of his humanitarian spirit, and it won him the ardent support of the growing abolitionist element (for the controversy, 1839–41, see *Works*, II, 449 ff.). No one would maintain, however, that Seward was an uncompromising idealist in the governorship. He dispensed offices on the strict spoils basis, as was the custom of the time; he signed a law requiring registration of voters in New York City under party pressure and very much against his personal convictions; and it may be that other motives than humanitarian interest were operating in the evolution of the policies above described. But he declined to be a candidate for reëlection in 1842, and his letters show that he felt himself at this time to be too far in advance of public opinion to prosper politically.

The years in the governorship depleted Seward's financial resources. During the next seven years he worked assiduously to restore them, at first in his old field, the court of chancery, but, after a little, more and more in patent cases. From time to time he took criminal cases, involving trial before a jury. One of the most striking involved the death sentence on a poor imbecile negro, Freeman, in whose defense Seward made in 1846 one of the most eloquent of his speeches (*Works*, I, 391–475); this he afterwards declared he would have repeated without the alteration of a word. A case which won him still more fame was that in which in a suit for damages he unsuccessfully defended in 1846–47 Van Zandt, an Ohio farmer, who had assisted in the flight of fugitive slaves (*Ibid.*, I, 476 ff.). In these years of private practice Seward was very far from abandoning his interest in politics. He took part in almost every campaign, often outside the borders of the state. He also ardently championed the cause of Irish freedom, gaining the support of the Irish-American voters as a result. The tide was running more and more his way, also, with regard to the question of slavery. By 1848 anti-slavery sentiment had become so strong that it was possible for him to be elected to the United States Senate, many Democrats, as well as all the Whig members of the legislature, voting for him.

When Seward entered the Senate the slavery question had become acute, and the question of its relation to the disposition of the territories just acquired from Mexico was assuming portentous proportions. In the celebrated debate growing out of Henry Clay's famous resolutions of 1850, Seward took his stand firmly against all compromise, and in favor of the unconditional admission of California as a free state. In his well-known speech of Mar. 11 he declared that there was no reason to jumble together a variety of important questions in a single measure, as Clay had wished to do; he boldly asserted that the fugitive-slave law was impossible of enforcement in the North; he wished to abolish, not only the slave trade, as proposed by Clay, but also slavery in the District of Columbia; he was opposed to leaving the territories to organize themselves with or without slavery. In a prescient sentence he declared that the slave system would either be removed "by gradual voluntary effort, and with compensation," within the framework of the Union, or the Union would be dissolved, and civil wars ensue, bringing on violent but complete and immediate emancipation

(*Works*, I, 86 ff.). While thus boldly expressing his views, he disavowed any desire to act by unconstitutional or unlawful means. It was in the speech of Mar. 11, 1850, that he used the famous phrase, "a higher law than the Constitution" (*Ibid.*, II, 74). Partisanship immediately caught up the expression, and sought to make it appear that he advocated action outside of and beyond the great American charter. The context of the speech itself clearly indicates that he was merely declaring that in the discharge of its duties the Senate must take account of moral principle as well as constitutional prescriptions. None the less, when taxed with the phrase, Seward resorted to rather shuffling and unconvincing explanations.

In the years immediately following the compromise measures, the politician in Seward dominated. It may be that he was beginning to nourish presidential ambitions, but it is not necessary to make this assumption to understand his course. He was, after all, still an intense Whig partisan, and he had, in common with Weed, a great interest in party manipulation and party victory. He had favored the candidacy of Zachary Taylor in 1848, precisely because it served to raise so few perplexing questions of principle; and now he worked zealously to secure the nomination of General Winfield Scott in 1852, on much the same grounds. Though he disliked the compromise measures and was by no means convinced of their finality, he nevertheless made no serious effort to prevent the Whigs from indorsing them in the national nominating convention of 1852, and he avoided a vote on the question of repeal of the fugitive-slave law when Sumner brought the matter before the Senate in the session of 1852. In the meantime his place in the Senate gave opportunity for the expression of that ardent nationalism and republicanism which Seward doubtless felt sincerely, and which was highly expedient politically, but which he voiced with such recklessness as to lay him open to the charge of demagogy. He played a leading rôle in the welcome to Kossuth, introducing a resolution of protest against the Russian intervention in Hungary; and he again championed the cause of the Irish.

The elections of 1852 left the Whig party completely routed. The future appeared hardly bright to a rising anti-slavery leader; but soon came the Kansas-Nebraska bill, reopening the whole controversy with regard to slave and free territory. In the debates on this measure, Seward showed greater caution and less forthright courage than in the discussions of 1850. His double rôle of party leader and opponent of slavery, in a measure imposed such a course. However, though he did not take the lead in opposition to the measure, he spoke vigorously and frankly against it, warning the South of the conflict to which he felt it would inevitably give rise. The year 1854 saw not only the rise of the Republican party in the West, but of the Know-Nothing party, principally in the East and South. For Weed and Seward these new organizations created natural embarrassment. Reluctant to abandon the old partisan vessel, they propitiated the anti-Nebraska men by committing the Whigs to a strong anti-slavery platform; by shrewd subterranean work they managed to inter-penetrate the Know-Nothing party and secure Seward's reëlection to the Senate. This latter success was the more remarkable since Know-Nothingism was contrary to the very essence of Seward's political philosophy, and was known to be so. As the Kansas question continued to hold the stage in national politics, the necessity of abandoning the old Whig party, or of merging it in the rising Republican organization, became more and more obvious. The merger was effected in the fall of 1855, and in the campaign of that year Seward signalized the change by speeches of the most forthright character on slavery.

From 1855 to 1860 Seward embodied the growing anti-slavery sentiment of the North as much as any man. That sentiment was grounded on genuine moral convictions; but it was often blindly partisan, and reckless of the crisis which it was rapidly promoting. In the struggle over Kansas in 1856 he took the extreme view, advocating its admission as a free state under the Topeka Constitution (though a fairer solution, perhaps, lay in the Toombs bill, calling for a new election in the territory); in common with other Republicans he denounced the Dred Scott decision as the product of a conspiracy; and on Oct. 25, 1858, he made at Rochester, N. Y., the famous speech in which he declared that the slavery struggle was "an irrepressible conflict" between opposing and enduring forces (*Works*, IV, 292). Yet Seward was not always a firebrand; in 1858, partly perhaps for tactical reasons, he supported the Douglas idea of a decision by popular sovereignty in the territory of Kansas, of course opposing the Lecompton Constitution; and the "irrepressible conflict" speech itself was followed by one in which, perhaps under the influence of the storm of comment which he had aroused, he praised the moderation of the slave-holders, and sought to blame the free Democracy of the North for the events of the last few years. On grounds of political expediency he had been passed over in 1856 in the Republican National Convention for Frémont; and some of his shifts of attitude may be attributed to the fact that he had his eye on the presidential nomination of 1860.

In 1859 Seward went abroad, meeting many celebrities in England and France, and returning to a great reception in New York. In February 1860, he again advocated the admission of Kansas as a free state, and made a speech which may be regarded as an expression of the platform on which he would stand for the Republican nomination (Feb. 29, 1860, *Ibid.*, IV, 619–43). Its general tenor was extremely conciliatory and moderate; with rare exceptions, Seward optimistically believed that Republicanism involved no threat to the unity of the American people. When the Republican National Convention met in Chicago in June 1860, he was undoubtedly the leading candidate, but the hostility of Horace Greeley, the opposition of the Know-Nothings, and Seward's own too widely known radical utterances, conspired to deprive him of the nomination. It was a severe blow, but he bore it with his usual outward equanimity and with very real generosity. He campaigned for the Republican ticket throughout the North, minimizing the Southern threats of secession, and urging the election of Lincoln. In the crisis which followed the election Seward showed characteristic elements of strength and weakness. His invincible optimism inclined him to minimize the dangers that lay ahead; yet, in the face of secession, he employed the language and the method of conciliation. He was also one of the Senate committee of thirteen constituted to consider means of composing the situation; as the spokesman of the section, and at the suggestion of Weed, he proposed on Dec. 24 that Congress guarantee slavery in the slave states, and request the repeal of the personal liberty laws in exchange for the grant of jury trial to fugitive slaves (*Senate Report No. 288*, 36 Cong., 2 Sess., pp. 10, 11, 13). His speech of Jan. 12, 1861, made after three more states had seceded, was admirable in its spirit (*Works*, IV, 651–69). Clearly avowing his loyalty to the Union, he again spoke in the most conciliatory vein, advocating a constitutional convention to settle outstanding difficulties, and even suggesting, in departure from the Republican platform, the admission of the remaining territories as two states without regard to slavery. It is entirely possible that he personally favored the Crittenden Compromise; but the influence of the President-elect was thrown on the other side, and Seward voted against this proposal when it came before the Senate on Mar. 2.

As early as Dec. 8, Seward had been offered the office of secretary of state by Lincoln. He accepted on Dec. 28; and although he was deeply displeased at the selection of Chase and Blair as cabinet colleagues, and even sought to reverse his decision as late as Mar. 2, he yielded to the entreaties of the President. He took office on Mar. 4, no doubt believing that he would be, and deserved to be, the dominant figure in the administration, and the man who could best avert the perils of civil war. In the critical period from Mar. 4 to Apr. 12, 1861 (the date of the firing on Sumter), Seward appears at very far from his best. He still retained the delusion that he might determine the course of the administration; and his famous memorandum, "Some Thoughts for the President's Consideration, Apr. 1, 1861," admits of no apology. In this reckless document he advocated embroiling the United States with most of Europe and waging actual war on Spain and France, as a means of solidifying the Union (Nicolay and Hay, *post,* II, 29). The only concrete grievance on the horizon was the Spanish re-annexation of Santo Domingo, and this had not been officially consummated. A madder or wilder project than Seward's could hardly have been devised. Nor is it possible to imagine anything more arrogant than the last sentence of his memorandum, in which he virtually suggested that the President abdicate his power to the Secretary of State. Seward's course with regard to secession itself is not easy to justify. It is understandable that he entered into negotiations with the Confederate commissioners sent to Washington to demand the surrender of the forts still held by the Union government in the South; but it is not so easy to justify machinations behind the back of the President, by which the reënforcement of Fort Pickens was delayed, and the expedition to Sumter, when it sailed, weakened by the absence of the *Powhatan.* Seward was not even resolutely pacifist; on one occasion he spoke of using force to collect the revenue, and in general he was in favor of holding the Gulf forts, perhaps with a view to a possible war with Spain, though not of holding Sumter. No doubt much to his discomfiture, and with many a wound to his pride, he saw himself overruled and the decisive events which culminated in the opening of the Civil War directed by the chief whose real measure he had not yet taken.

Seward's conduct of the office of secretary of state during the four years of the war deserves high praise. More than any preceding secretary he conducted his diplomatic correspondence with an eye to public opinion at home. It is no chance that the publication of diplomatic dispatches in one or more annual volumes put out by the State Department begins with him (*Papers Relating to the Foreign Relations of the United States*, 2 vols., 1861). He no doubt wrote almost too much for the American public, as compared with those to whom his dispatches were actually directed. But in so doing he did much both to inspirit and to restrain public opinion as occasion demanded. His early dispatches were too blustering in tone, and might have gotten him into serious trouble sometimes had it not been for the wisdom of Lincoln. As time went on, he dropped the truculent tone and expressed the views of the United States with dignity and force. On the occasion of the seizure of Mason and Slidell on board the *Trent*, an act received with something like ecstasy by Northern opinion, he behaved with great coolness in the midst of popular excitement. When the protest of the British government against such action arrived, it was the Secretary, this time somewhat against the opinion of the President, who decided that the protest must be heeded. The dispatch in which he conceded the surrender of the Southern commissioners is a masterpiece (*Works*, V, 295–309). Written with an eye to making palatable an act sure to be violently condemned by the hotheads in the United States, it flattered Northern opinion by its specious reasoning, and made the action appear as in accord with fundamental American traditions.

The possibility of European intervention in the Civil War Seward met, on the whole, with similar adroitness. The optimism of his dispatches, their profound self-confidence, and their array of facts, could hardly fail to make an impression. This tone, maintained through good fortune and bad, and coupled with warning after warning of the dangerous consequences of intervention, was, in general, just what the situation demanded. At times Seward was still a little bumptious, and his habit of publishing many of his dispatches was often irritating, but the general principle was sound. He could depend, too, on the tact and high diplomatic skill of Charles Francis Adams in interpreting his instructions. Seward made skilful use abroad of the question of slavery to check the anti-Northern agitation in France and England. On the Emancipation Proclamation he was at first conservative, because of his fear of its domestic consequences. When it was first discussed in July 1862, he urged Lincoln to postpone action, at least until a Federal victory (Nicolay and Hay, II, 479). But when the preliminary proclamation was issued after Antietam, he used it with great effect in his dispatches to Adams and W. L. Dayton.

The danger of intervention seemed greatest in the fall of 1862 and the winter of 1863. At the end of October, the French government sought to secure joint action with Great Britain and Russia looking to an armistice. The proposal was rejected, and Seward wisely made no protest. But when the French directly proffered mediation early in 1863, Seward responded in one of his most effective dispatches (Feb. 6, 1863, *Senate Executive Document No. 38,* 37 Cong., 3 Sess., p. 11–16).

In his correspondence Seward adroitly defended the broad interpretation of continuous voyage in dispatches that suggest Sir Edward Grey's half a century later, and he protested vigorously against the outfitting of Confederate privateers in British ports. His steady pressure, combined with the skill of Adams, finally led the British government to take due precautions, in the case of the Laird rams, while his protests in the case of the *Alabama* laid the basis for solid pecuniary claims later. Nowhere was Seward more adroit than in his treatment of the French intervention in Mexico, and the establishment of Maximilian on a Mexican throne. From an early period he made the distaste of the United States for the whole project obvious; yet he suavely assumed the rumors of monarchy to be ill-founded as long as he could do so, and until the end of the war never let anything like menace enter into his tone. When the House of Representatives on Apr. 4, 1864, condemned the schemes of Louis Napoleon (*Congressional Globe,* 38 Cong., 1 Sess., p. 1408), Seward penned a masterly dispatch in which he soothed French susceptibilities, explaining that the opinion of the legislative branch of the government did not alter executive policy (Apr. 7, 1864, *Diplomatic Correspondence of the United States,* 1865, vol. III, 356–57). When the Civil War was over, there was much sentiment for vigorous action against the French. Seward handled this delicate situation magnificently. He temporized while he could; the situation of the French grew more and more difficult; and then in dispatches gradually mounting in tone he edged his adversary, Drouyn de L'huys, from one position to another, until he finally secured the promise of the evacuation of Mexico in a fixed period of time. In the latter part of the correspondence Seward fell into his old habit of writing for domestic consumption; and the same may be said of his correspondence with Austria on the same subject; but the total effect of his activity is admirable.

Seward was, in temperament and conviction, an expansionist. During the 1850's this sentiment came in conflict with his anti-slavery views, and led him to oppose such projects as the purchase of Cuba. But when the war was over the strong instinct revived. In 1867 he negotiated the cession of Alaska, and with the aid of Sumner secured the prompt ratification of the treaty by the Senate. He sought to acquire the two most important islands of the Danish West Indies; but this agreement was never ratified. He encouraged overtures from the Dominican Republic looking to incorporation in the United States, again unsuccessfully. In his instructions to the American minister at Honolulu he advocated the annexation of Hawaii. Seward's views were those which a later generation was to accept.

In domestic affairs Seward exercised a constant influence both on the Lincoln and the Johnson administrations. He had a large, indeed it may be said the chief, responsibility for the treatment of political prisoners at the beginning of the war, and contrary to his general temperament he here showed much rigor. He exercised, as has been seen, a positive influence on the policy of the administration with regard to the border states and emancipation. He performed heavy labors as a sort of political liaison officer, and his interest in problems of patronage, while not always wisely exerted, was continuous. In the Johnson administration he was a central figure. He advocated a conciliatory policy towards the South, wrote some of Johnson's most important veto messages, and supported the President in many speeches, making "the swing around the circle" with him in 1866. By doing so he lost both popularity and influence, and he valued both dearly; but whatever the reaction of the moment, the judgment of time has been that he was wiser than his opponents.

The burdens of his last four years at Washington Seward sustained in circumstances that would have daunted a man less tenacious and industrious. He had suffered serious injury in a carriage accident in the spring of 1865, and this had been followed by the brutal attack upon him in his house which was contemporaneous with the assassination of Lincoln; yet he was soon transacting the public business with as much skill and coolness as ever. At the end of his term of office, despite the fact that he was partially crippled, he went around the world, the first important American political figure to do so, and much enjoyed the enthusiasm which his visit evoked. He returned to Auburn in the autumn of 1871, and there increasing paralysis overtook him. He died on Oct. 10, 1872. On Oct. 20, 1824, he had married Frances Miller, the daughter of his law

partner. A woman of liberal sympathies and humanitarian views, she undoubtedly influenced his later career, and especially his attitude toward slavery. They had three sons and two daughters, one of whom died in infancy. Frederick William Seward [q.v.] was closely associated with his father. A nephew, Clarence Armstrong Seward (Oct. 27, 1828–July 24, 1897), who became an orphan in childhood and was brought up in his uncle's family, served for a brief time in 1865 as assistant secretary of state and attained prominence as a corporation lawyer. His cousin, George Frederick Seward [q.v.], another nephew of William H. Seward, was launched upon his diplomatic career under the latter's influence.

In Seward the politician and the statesman are interestingly, and on the whole happily, commingled. It is easy to discover occasions on which he equivocated, as politicians do; it is easy to discover occasions on which he sought the applause of the multitude, not always careful of the consequences. Even in his diplomacy, and strikingly in his early utterances on questions of foreign affairs, this is true. Yet Seward chose his early political creed, it would appear, from conviction; he associated himself with definite policies, and loved to do so; much earlier than most anti-slavery leaders of the political stripe, he adopted that important cause; he often showed real courage in advocating it. He made serious blunders, and might have made more, in estimating the true value of the conflicting forces at the end of 1860 and the beginning of 1861 but his years at the State Department are years of steady growth, and of very creditable achievement, while his rôle in maintaining national morale must not be underestimated. He was the partisan of a wise policy of reconciliation when the war was over. The unswervingly independent mind has its uses in the world; but its possessor is not apt to succeed in politics. It may be fairly argued that Seward combined devotion to principle, and flexibility as to means, in such proportions as to make him most effective.

As a human being, few could have been more lovable. Cheerful, generous, loathing personal controversy, he had a wide range of interests and of sympathies. He read much and widely; he traveled extensively, going to Europe several times, and seeing a great deal of his own country. He was a little vain, and he had his political enemies; he is dwarfed by the master-spirit of his great chief; but, compared with the irascible Stanton, the pompous Sumner, the intriguing Chase, and many others, he looms up as one of the most attractive, as well as most important, figures in a critical period of American history.

[*Autobiography of William H. Seward, from 1801 to 1834, with a Memoir of His Life, and Selections from His Letters, from 1831 to 1846* (1877), ed. by F. W. Seward, the continuation of this by F. W. Seward, *Seward at Washington* (2 vols., 1891); G. E. Baker, ed., *The Works of William H. Seward* (5 vols., 1884); *Life of Thurlow Weed* (2 vols., 1883–84), including his autobiography, ed. by Harriet A. Weed, and a memoir by T. W. Barnes; J. D. Hammond, *The Hist. of Pol. Parties in the State of N. Y.* (3 vols., 1842–48); D. S. Alexander, *A Political Hist. of the State of N. Y.*, vol. II (1906); *Papers Relating to the Foreign Relations of the U. S.* (2 vols., 1861), and *Papers Relating to Foreign Affairs* (14 vols., 1862–66), bound and usually cited as *Diplomatic Correspondence of the U.S.*; Gideon Welles, *Lincoln and Seward* (1874); F. W. Seward, *Reminiscences of a War-Time Statesman and Diplomat* (1916); Olive R. Seward, ed., *William H. Seward's Travels Around the World* (1873); J. G. Nicolay and John Hay, *Abraham Lincoln, Complete Works* (2 vols., 1894); Frederic Bancroft, *The Life of William H. Sew-* ard (2 vols., 1900), which is sympathetic yet critical, and is exceedingly well proportioned; T. K. Lothrop, *William Henry Seward* (1896) and E. E. Hale, Jr., *William H. Seward* (1910), of less importance; an interesting sketch in Gamaliel Bradford, *Union Portraits* (1916); C. F. Adams, *Seward and the Declaration of Paris* (1912); Tyler Dennett, "Seward's Far Eastern Policy," in *Am. Hist. Rev.*, Oct. 1922; studies of Seward's Mexican policy in J. M. Callahan, *Am. Foreign Policy in Mexican Relations* (1932), and Dexter Perkins, *The Monroe Doctrine, 1826–1867* (1933); detailed study of his policy toward Great Britain in E. D. Adams, *Great Britain and the Am. Civil War* (2 vols., 1925); general treatment by H. W. Temple in S. F. Bemis, ed., *The Am. Secretaries of State and Their Diplomacy*, vol. VII (1928); unpublished materials in the possession of Mrs. Thomas G. Spencer, Rochester, N. Y., and W. H. Seward, Auburn, N. Y.; unpublished correspondence in Dept. of State, Washington, D. C.] **D. P.**